THE
CAMBRIDGE BIBLIOGRAPHY
OF
ENGLISH LITERATURE

IN FOUR VOLUMES

VOLUME III

THE
CAMBRIDGE BIBLIOGRAPHY
OF
ENGLISH LITERATURE

Edited by

F. W. BATESON

VOLUME III
1800–1900

CAMBRIDGE
AT THE UNIVERSITY PRESS
1969

PUBLISHED BY
THE SYNDICS OF THE CAMBRIDGE UNIVERSITY PRESS
Bentley House, 200 Euston Road, London, N.W.1
American Branch: 32 East 57th Street, New York, N.Y. 10022

Standard Book Number : 521 04501 0

First published 1940
Reprinted 1955   1966   1969

First Printed in Great Britain at the
University Press, Cambridge
Reprinted by photolithography in Great Britain
by Bookprint Limited, Crawley, Sussex

CONTENTS

VI. THE POLITICAL AND SOCIAL BACKGROUND

2. THE POETRY

I. SURVEYS, CRITICAL STUDIES AND ANTHOLOGIES

II. THE EARLY NINETEENTH-CENTURY POETS

III. MINOR VERSE, 1800–1835

IV. The Mid-Nineteenth Century Poets

V. Minor Verse, 1835–1870

VI. The Later Nineteenth-Century Poets

VII. Minor Verse, 1870–1900

3. PROSE FICTION

V. MINOR FICTION, 1835–1870

VI. THE LATER NINETEENTH-CENTURY NOVELISTS

VII. MINOR FICTION, 1870–1900

4. THE DRAMA

I. GENERAL INTRODUCTION

II. THE EARLY NINETEENTH-CENTURY DRAMA, 1800–1835

III. THE MID-NINETEENTH CENTURY DRAMA

IV. THE LATE NINETEENTH-CENTURY DRAMA

5. CRITICAL AND MISCELLANEOUS PROSE

I. The Early Nineteenth Century Essayists

II. Minor Critics and Essayists, 1800–1835

III. The Mid-Nineteenth Century Essayists

IV. Minor Critics and Essayists, 1835–1870

V. The Late Nineteenth-Century Critics and Miscellaneous Writers

VI. Minor Critics and Essayists, 1870–1900

VII. The Literature of Sport

VIII. Newspapers and Magazines

A. *Technical Development*

B. *The History of Journalism:*

C. *The Daily Papers:*

D. *The Weekly Papers:*

E. *Magazines and Reviews:*

F. *School and University Journalism*

6. PHILOSOPHY, HISTORY, SCIENCE AND OTHER FORMS OF LEARNING

I. PHILOSOPHY

II. HISTORY, BIOGRAPHY AND ARCHAEOLOGY

2

VIII. ENGLISH SCHOLARSHIP

LIST OF CONTRIBUTORS
TO VOLUME III

H. G. A.	H. G. Aldis	C. E. J.	C. E. Jones
J. W. A.	J. W. Adamson	H. K.	H. King
A. T. B.	A. T. Bartholomew	R. W. K.	R. W. King
E. Bl.	E. Blunden	S. V. K.	S. V. Keeling
E. C. B.	E. C. Batho	F. V. L.	Mrs F. V. Livingston
G. A. P. B.	G. A. P. Brown	G. L.	G. Lafourcade
J. G. B.	J. G. Banerjee	S. J. L.	S. J. Looker
G. H. C.	G. H. Cowling	A. N.	A. Nicoll
G. R. C.	G. R. Crone	H. C. N.	H. C. Notcutt
J. P. C.	J. P. Curgenven	E. F. O.	E. F. Oaten
R. D. C.	Miss R. D. Coole	S. L. O.	S. L. Ollard
S. C. C.	Sir S. C. Cockerell	S. O'F.	S. O'Faolain
F. J. H. D.	F. J. H. Darton	F. P.	F. Prescott
H. W. D.	H. W. Donner	G. P.	G. Parsloe
B. I. E.	B. I. Evans	H. G. P.	H. G. Pollard
H. A. E.	H. A. Eaton	H. V. R.	H. V. Routh
P. E.	P. Edgar	T. M. R.	T. M. Raysor
G. E. F.	G. E. Fasnacht	W. R.	W. Reitzel
H. B. G.	H. B. Grimsditch	E. de S.	E. de Selincourt
J. B. G.	J. B. Gregory	J. E. S.	Sir J. E. Sandys
R. G.-H.	R. Gathorne-Hardy	S. N. S.	S. Nowell Smith
C. F. H.	C. F. Harrold	A. H. T.	A. H. Thompson
D. H.	D. Hamer	M. T.	M. Tremaine
F. E. H.	F. E. Hutchinson	W. D. T.	W. D. Templeman
H. H.	H. Higgs	A. S. W.	A. S. Whitfield
P. P. H.	P. P. Howe	G. W.	G. Waterhouse
R. I.	R. Ingpen	T. E. W.	T. E. Welby
A. K. H. J.	A. K. H. Jenkin		

REVISIONS AND SPECIAL CONTRIBUTIONS

R. W. Chapman   M. Sadleir
A. M. Cohn   Miss Dorothy L. Sayers
C. B. Hogan   C. H. Williams
T. H. V. Motter

The compiler's initials will be found at the end of each main section. In sections for which more than one contributor is responsible, each subsection has been initialled. The sections taken over from the *C.H.E.L.* and revised by another hand are signed with the initials both of the original compiler and the reviser, e.g. A. B. C.. *rev.* X. Y. Z. Other revisions are indicated in foot-notes. The uninitialled sections have been contributed by the Editor.

KEY TO ABBREVIATIONS USED

AJPhil.	American Journal of Philology.
Ang.	Anglia.
Ang. Anz.	Anglia Anzeiger.
Ang. Bbl.	Beiblatt zur Anglia.
Archiv	(Herrig's) Archiv für das Studium der neueren Sprachen.
CHEL.	Cambridge History of English Literature.
DNB.	Dictionary of National Biography.
E. & S.	(English Association's) Essays and Studies.
EETS.	Early English Text Society.
EHR.	English Historical Review.
E. Studien	Englische Studien.
E. Studies	English Studies.
GM.	Gentleman's Magazine.
JEGP.	Journal of English and Germanic Philology.
MLN.	Modern Language Notes.
MLR.	Modern Language Review.
MP.	Modern Philology.
N. & Q.	Notes and Queries.
PQ.	Philological Quarterly.
RES.	Review of English Studies.
Sh. Jb.	Shakespeare Jahrbuch.
STS.	Scottish Text Society.
Stud. Phil.	Studies in Philology.
TLS.	(London) Times Literary Supplement.

Italicized abbreviations, e.g. *Miles, Lacy, Cumberland Minor,* are each restricted to particular sections, to the beginnings of which reference should be made for their explanation.

THE NINETEENTH CENTURY
1800–1900

1. INTRODUCTION

I. BIBLIOGRAPHIES, LITERARY HISTORIES AND SPECIAL STUDIES, PROSE-SELECTIONS, AND LITERARY MEMOIRS AND REMINISCENCES

(1) BIBLIOGRAPHIES

[Catalogues of books pbd in the English provinces, including many 19th cent. books, will be found in vol. I, pp. 8–9, where bibliographies of the principal religious bodies are also listed. Other specialized lists will be found under this period's sections on Book Production and Distribution (pp. 70–106 below), The Literature of Sport (pp. 757–79 below), and The Literature of Science (pp. 936–69 below).]

Lowe, R. W. A Bibliographical Account of English Theatrical Literature. 1888.

Griswold, W. M. A Descriptive List of Romantic Novels. 1890.

Hodgkins, L. M. A Guide to the Study of Nineteenth Century Authors. Boston, 1904.

Amherst (later Cecil), A. M. List of English Printed Books on Gardening to 1837. [In A History of Gardening, 1910 (rev. edn).]

Faxon, F. W. Literary Annuals and Gift Books. Boston, 1912.

Baker, E. A. and Packman, J. A Guide to the Best Fiction in English. 1913; 1932 (rev.).

Neild, J. Guide to Historical Novels. 1913.

Woods, G. B. English Poetry and Prose of the Romantic Movement. New York, 1916 (includes a bibliography); New York, 1929 (adds supplementary bibliography).

[Muddiman, J. G.] 'The Times' Tercentenary Handlist of English and Welsh Newspapers, Magazines and Reviews. 1920.

Bibliographies of Modern Authors. London Mercury, III, 1921. [Birrell, Moore, Trench, Doughty, Davidson, Quiller-Couch.]

Danielson, H. Bibliographies of Modern Authors. 1921. [Crackanthorpe, Gissing, Middleton, Symons.]

Barry, F. V. Chronological List of Children's Books from 1700 to 1825. [Appendix B of A Century of Children's Books, 1922.]

Manly, J. M. and Rickert, E. Contemporary British Literature. Bibliographies and Study Outlines. 1922; 1929 (rev.); rev. F. B. Millet, 1935. [Particularly useful for the lists of reviews, etc. for each writer included. Covers most writers of any eminence born after 1850.]

Morgan, B. Q. A Bibliography of German Literature in English Translation. Madison, 1922.

Sadleir, M. Excursions in Victorian Bibliography. 1922. [1st edns of Trollope, Marryat, Disraeli, Wilkie Collins, Reade, Whyte-Melville, Mrs Gaskell.]

Stonehill, C. A. and H. W. Bibliographies of Modern Authors. Ser. 2, 1925. [Davidson, Dowson, Alice Meynell, Pater, Francis Thompson.]

Williams, Judith B. Guide to the Printed Materials for English Social and Economic History, 1750–1850. 2 vols. New York, 1926.

Kennedy, A. G. A Bibliography of Writings on the English Language. Cambridge, U.S.A. 1927.

Sawyer, C. J. and Darton, F. J. H. English Books, 1475–1900. 2 vols. 1927.

Bernbaum, E. Guide through the Romantic Movement. New York, 1930. [Critical bibliographies included.]

Cutter, B. D. and Stiles, V. Modern British Authors, their First Editions. New York, 1930. [Lewis Carroll, Kipling, Moore, Pater, Stevenson, etc.]

Nicoll, A. A History of Early Nineteenth Century Drama, 1800–1850. 2 vols. Cambridge, 1930. [Vol. II, bibliography.]

Muir, P. H., Smith, S. N. and Mitchell, A. Bibliographies of Modern Authors. Ser. 3, 1931.

Parrish, M. L. Victorian Lady Novelists. 1933. [George Eliot, Mrs Gaskell, the Brontës.]

Templeman, W. D., Harrold, C. F., White, H. C. and Faverty, F. E. Victorian Bibliography for 1932. MP. xxx, 1933. [Continued annually.]

Jones, H. M. et al. Syllabus and Bibliography of Victorian Literature. 5 pts, Ann Arbor, 1934–5.

Brussel, I. R. Anglo-American First Editions, 1826–1900. Describing First Editions of English Authors whose Books were published in America before their Publication in England. 1935.

Aubin, R. A. Topographical Poetry in XVIII-Century England. New York, 1936. [Bibliographies (1640–1840), pp. 298–391.]

Ehrsam, T. G. and Deily, R. H. Bibliographies of Twelve Victorian Authors. New York, 1936. [Very full lists of books and articles about: E. B. Browning, FitzGerald, D. G. and C. Rossetti, Clough, Arnold, Tennys , Morris, Stevenson, Swinburne, Hardy, Kipling.]

Graham, W. The Romantic Movement: a Current Selection and Critical Bibliography for 1936. ELH. IV, 1937. [To be continued annually.]

Richards, E. A. Hudibras in the Burlesque
Tradition. New York, 1937. [Has list of
Hudibrastic poems, 1662–1830.]
Batho, E. and Dobrée, B. The Victorians and
After, 1830–1914. 1938. [Vol. IV of Intro-
ductions to English Literature. Critical
bibliography, pp. 147–359.]

(2) LITERARY HISTORIES
(a) General

Cunningham, A. Biographical and Critical
History of the British Literature of the Last
Fifty Years. 1834.
Cleveland, C. D. English Literature of the
Nineteenth Century. Philadelphia, 1852;
Philadelphia, 1869 (rev.). [Many minor
writers; selections.]
Brandes, G. Hovedstrømninger i det 19de
Aarhundredes Litteratur. Vol. IV (Natura-
lismen i England), Copenhagen, 1875; tr.
Eng. (as Main Currents in Nineteenth
Century Literature. Naturalism in England)
1905.
Morley, H. Of English Literature in the Reign
of Victoria. Leipzig, 1881.
Oliphant, M. O. The Literary History of
England in the End of the Eighteenth and
Beginning of the Nineteenth Century. 3 vols.
1882.
—— The Victorian Age of English Literature.
2 vols. 1892. [With F. R. Oliphant.]
Garnett, R. Literature, 1837–1887. [In
T. H. Ward, The Reign of Queen Victoria,
vol. II, 1887.]
Bleibtreu, K. Geschichte der englischen
Litteratur im 19. Jahrhundert. Leipzig,
[1888].
Minto, W. The Literature of the Georgian
Era. Ed. W. Knight, Edinburgh, 1894.
Saintsbury, G. A. History of Nineteenth
Century Literature (1780–1895). 1896.
—— The Later Nineteenth Century. Edin-
burgh, 1907.
Graham, Richard. The Masters of Victorian
Literature, 1837–1897. 1897.
Herford, C. H. The Age of Wordsworth. 1897.
Shorter, C. K. Victorian Literature. Sixty
Years of Books and Bookmen. 1897.
Walker, H. The Age of Tennyson. 1897.
—— The Literature of the Victorian Era.
Cambridge, 1910. [Abbreviated as Outlines
of Victorian Literature, Cambridge, 1913.]
Omond, T. S. The Romantic Triumph.
Edinburgh, 1900.
Vaughan, C. E. The Romantic Revolt.
Edinburgh, 1907.
Kellner, L. Die englische Litteratur im
Zeitalter der Königin Viktoria. Leipzig,
1909; Leipzig, 1921 (rev. as Die englische
Litteratur der neuesten Zeit).

Magnus, L. English Literature in the Nine-
teenth Century. An Essay in Criticism.
1909.
Richter, H. Geschichte der englischer
Romantik. 2 vols. Halle, 1911–6.
Elton, O. A Survey of English Literature
1780–1830. 2 vols. 1912.
—— A Survey of English Literature, 1830–
1880. 2 vols. 1920.
Chesterton, G. K. The Victorian Age in
Literature. 1913.
Hudson, W. H. A Short History of English
Literature in the Nineteenth Century. 1918.
Williamson, C. C. Writers of Three Centuries
1789–1914. 1920. [Includes, in addn to the
major figures, Kingsley, Patmore, Mrs H.
Ward, Mrs Meynell, R. H. Benson, Lionel
Johnson.]
Fehr, B. England im Zeitalter des Indivi-
dualismus (1830–1880). St Gall, 1921.
—— Die englische Litteratur des 19. und 20.
Jahrhunderts. 16 pts, Berlin, 1923–5.
Cazamian, L. Modern Times (1660–1914)
1927. [Vol. II of trn of É. Legouis and L.
Cazamian, Histoire de la Littérature
anglaise, Paris, 1924.]
Wyatt, A. J. and Clay, H. Modern English
Literature, 1798–1919. 1927; 1936 (rev.).
Miller, G. M. English Literature: Victorian
Period. New York, 1933 (rev. edn).

(b) Special Periods and Groups

Douglas, Sir G. The Blackwood Group. [1897.]
[Wilson, Miss Ferrier, Galt, Michael Scott,
Moir, Thomas Hamilton.]
Winchester, C. T. A Group of English
Essayists of the Early Nineteenth Century.
New York, 1910. [Jeffrey, Hazlitt, Lamb,
De Quincey, Wilson, Hunt.]
Brailsford, H. N. Shelley, Godwin, and Their
Circle. [1913.]
Pierce, F. E. Currents and Eddies in the
English Romantic Generation. New Haven,
1918.
Hamilton, Walter. The Aesthetic Movement
in England. 1882.
McCarthy, J. Portraits of the Sixties. 1903.
[Dickens, Thackeray, Carlyle, Tennyson,
the Newmans, Ruskin, Goldwin Smith, etc.]
Russell, G. W. E. Portraits of the Seventies.
1916. [J. McCarthy, Disraeli, Acton,
Labouchere, Liddon, Tennyson, Browning,
'Owen Meredith,' Arnold, etc.]
Vinciguerra, M. Il Preraffaelismo inglese.
Bologna, 1925.
The Eighteen-Seventies. Ed. H. Granville-
Barker, Royal Soc. Lit. 1929. [Novelists,
Women Novelists, Poets, Women Poets,
Houghton, Lang, R. H. Hutton.]

Welby, T. E. The Victorian Romantics, 1850–70. 1929.

Bickley, F. The Pre-Raphaelite Comedy. 1932.

The Eighteen-Sixties. Ed. J. Drinkwater, Royal Soc. Lit. 1932. [Henry Taylor, Clough, Wilkie Collins, Planché-Gilbert, Historians, E. S. Dallas, Whyte-Melville.]

Kennedy, J. M. English Literature, 1880–1905. 1912.

Jackson, Holbrook. The Eighteen-Nineties. A Review of Art and Ideas at the Close of the Nineteenth Century. 1913.

Williams, H. Modern English Writers: 1890–1914. 1918; 1925 (rev.).

Cunliffe, J. W. English Literature during the Last Half-Century. New York, 1919; New York, 1923 (rev.).

—— Leaders of the Victorian Revolution. New York, 1934.

Hutchinson, H. G. Portraits of the Eighties. 1920. [G. W. E. Russell, Huxley, Lubbock, Morris, Swinburne, Meredith, Lang, Gilbert, Wilde, etc.]

Muddiman, B. The Men of the Nineties. 1920.

'Raymond, Ernest' (E. R. Thompson). Portraits of the Nineties. 1921. [Meredith, Spencer, Wilde, J. Morley, Stead, Hardy, J. McCarthy, etc.]

Duthuit, G. Le Rose et le Noir. (De Walter Pater à Oscar Wilde.) Paris, [1923].

Burdett, O. The Beardsley Period. [1925.]

Le Gallienne, R. The Romantic '90s. New York, 1925.

Fehr, B. Englische Prosa von 1880 bis zur Gegenwart. Leipzig, 1927.

The Eighteen-Eighties. Ed. W. de la Mare, Royal Soc. Lit. 1930. [Poets, 'Owen Meredith,' Pater, Minor Fiction, Gilbert, The Coming of Ibsen, Tupper.]

Farmer, A. J. Le Mouvement esthétique et 'décadent' en Angleterre (1873–1900). Paris, 1931.

Wilson, Edmund. Axel's Castle. A Study in the Imaginative Literature of 1870–1930. 1931. [Pater, Yeats, etc.]

Baring, M. The Nineties. [In Lost Lectures, 1932.]

(c) Special Types of Literature

[Excluding poetry (see pp. 156–62 below), fiction (see pp. 364–6) and drama (see pp. 580–5).]

Welsh, Charles. On some of the Books for Children of the Last Century. 1886.

Gausseron, B. H. Les Keepsakes et les Annuaires illustrés de l'Époque romantique. Paris, 1896.

Rickett, A. The Vagabond in Literature. 1906. [Hazlitt, De Quincey, Borrow, Stevenson, Jefferies.]

Fueter, E. Die Geschichte der neueren Historiographie. Berlin, 1911; Munich, 1936 (rev.).

Cairns, W. B. British Criticisms of American Writings, 1783–1815 [–1833]. 2 pts, Madison, 1918–22.

Thayer, W. R. Biography in the Nineteenth Century. North American Rev. ccxi, 1920.

Barry, F. V. A Century of Children's Books. [1922.]

Casford, E. L. The Magazines of the 1890's. Eugene, Oregon, 1929.

Hoevel, E. F. Die soziale Herkunft der neuzeitlichen Dialektliteratur Englands. Leipzig, 1929.

Engel, C. E. La Littérature alpestre en France et en Angleterre au XVIIIᵉ et au XIXᵉ Siècles. Chambéry, 1930.

Darton, F. J. H. From Surtees to Sassoon: some English Contrasts (1838–1928). 1931. [Hunting and war literature.]

—— Children's Books in England. Cambridge, 1932.

Kitchin, G. A Survey of Burlesque and Parody in English. 1931.

James, Philip. Children's Books of Yesterday. 1933.

Law, M. H. The English Familiar Essay in the Early Nineteenth Century. Philadelphia, 1934.

Barnes, H. E. A History of Historical Writing. Norman (Oklahoma), 1937.

Elwood, Anne. Memoirs of the Literary Ladies of England from the Commencement of the Last Century. 2 vols. 1843.

Kavanagh, Julia. English Women of Letters. Vol. ii, Leipzig, 1863. [Maria Edgeworth, Jane Austen, Mrs Opie, Lady Morgan.]

Queens of Literature of the Victorian Era. 1886. [Harriet Martineau, Charlotte Brontë, George Eliot, etc.]

Hamilton, C. J. Women Writers: their Works and Ways. 2 sers. 1892–3. [Edgeworth, Opie, Austen, Morgan, Ferrier, Mitford, Blessington; ser. 2, Hemans, Jameson, Martineau, Landon, Norton, Browning, Gaskell, C. Brontë, Eliot, Procter, etc.]

Mayer, G. T. Women of Letters. 2 vols. 1894. [Vol. ii, Opie, Morgan, Mitford, Shelley, Duff Gordon.]

Bald, M. Women-Writers of the Nineteenth Century. Cambridge, 1923. [Jane Austen, the Brontës, Mrs Gaskell, George Eliot, Mrs Browning, Christina Rossetti.]

Wilson, Mona. These were Muses. 1924. [Lady Morgan, Jane Porter, Frances Trollope, Sara Coleridge, etc.]

(3) SPECIAL STUDIES

(a) *Literary Movements and Ideas*

[Supplementary matter will be found in the sections on the Intellectual Background (pp. 42–70 below), Literary Relations with the Continent (pp. 17–45), and Poetry: General Introduction (pp. 156–62). See also the collections of critical essays listed immediately below (p. 7), and the corresponding sections in the 1660–1800 period (vol. II, pp. 5–8).]

Rushton, W. The Classical and Romantic School of English Literature as represented by Spenser, Dryden, Pope, Scott and Wordsworth. [In Afternoon Lectures on English Literature, 1863.]

Arnold, M. Essays in Criticism. 1865. [The Function of Criticism at the Present Time; The Literary Influence of Academies.]

Courthope, W. J. The Liberal Movement in English Literature. 1885.

Pater, W. Appreciations. 1889. [Style; Postscript (classicism and romanticism).]

Wilson, S. L. The Theology of Modern Literature. Edinburgh, 1899.

Beers, H. A. A History of English Romanticism in the Nineteenth Century. New York, 1901.

Nordby, C. H. The Influence of Old Norse Literature upon English Literature. New York, 1901.

Henley, W. E. Note on Romanticism. [In Views and Reviews. Art, 1902.]

Farley, F. E. Scandinavian Influences on the English Romantic Movement. Boston, 1903.

Watts-Dunton, T. The Renascence of Wonder in Poetry. [In Chambers's Cyclopaedia of English Literature, vol. III, 1903.]

Babbitt, I. The New Laokoon. An Essay on the Confusion of the Arts. Boston, 1910.

—— Rousseau and Romanticism. Boston, 1919. [See, however, review by A. O. Lovejoy, MLN. xxxv, 1920.]

Chapman, E. M. English Literature and Religion, 1800–1900. Boston, 1910.

More, P. E. The Drift of Romanticism. [Shelburne Essays, ser. 8, Boston, 1913.]

Neilson, W. A. The Essentials of Poetry. New York, 1913.

de Meester, M. E. Oriental Influences in the English Literature of the Nineteenth Century. Heidelberg, 1915.

Richardson, G. F. A Neglected Aspect of the English Romantic Revolt. Berkeley, 1915.

Raleigh, Sir W. Romance. Two Lectures. Princeton, 1916.

Quiller-Couch, Sir A. T. On the Terms 'Classic' and 'Romantic.' [In Studies in Literature, ser. 1, Cambridge, 1918.]

Cazamian, L. L'Évolution psychologique et la Littérature en Angleterre (1660-1914). Paris, 1920.

—— Le Romantisme en France et en Angleterre. Études Anglaises, I, 1937.

Egan, R. F. The Genesis of the Theory of 'Art for Art's Sake' in Germany and in England. 2 pts, Northampton (Massachusetts), 1921–4.

Frye, P. H. The Terms Classic and Romantic. [In Romance and Tragedy, Boston, 1922.]

Herford, C. H. Romanticism in the Modern World. E. & S. VIII, 1922.

Inge, W. R. The Victorian Age. Cambridge, 1922. (Rede Lecture.)

Jones, R. F. Some Reflections on the English Romantic Revival. Washington University Stud. IX, 1922.

Tinker, C. B. Nature's Simple Plan. Princeton, 1922.

Cazamian, M. L. Le Roman et les Idées en Angleterre. [I]: L'Influence de la Science (1860–90). II: L'Anti-Intellectualisme et l'Esthétisme (1880–1900). Paris, 1923–35.

Grierson, Sir H. J. C. Classical and Romantic. Cambridge, 1923. [Rptd in The Background of English Literature, 1925.]

Murry, J. M. Adelphi, Sept., Dec. 1923. [Romanticism.]

Barker, F. The Modern Consciousness in English Literature. E. & S. IX, 1924.

Lovejoy, A. O. On the Discrimination of Romanticisms. PMLA. xxxix, 1924.

—— 'Nature' as Aesthetic Norm. MLN. xlii, 1927.

—— Optimism and Romanticism. PMLA. xlii, 1927.

Smith, L. Pearsall. Four Words: Romantic, Originality, Creative, Genius. SPE. 1924. [Rptd in Words and Idioms, 1925.]

Kaufman, P. Defining Romanticism: a Survey and a Program. MLN. xl, 1925.

Ker, W. P. Collected Essays. Ed. C. Whibley, 2 vols. 1925. [Romance; On the Value of the Terms 'Classical' and 'Romantic' as applied to Literature.]

Knickerbocker, W. S. Creative Oxford: its Influence in Victorian Literature. Syracuse, 1925.

Robertson, J. G. The Reconciliation of Classic and Romantic. Cambridge, 1925.

Abercrombie, L. Romanticism. 1926.

Brinton, C. The Political Ideas of the English Romanticists. Oxford, 1926.

Needham, H. A. Le Développement de l'Esthétique sociologique en France et en Angleterre, au 19ième Siècle. Paris, 1926.

Powell, A. E. (Dodds). The Romantic Theory of Poetry. 1926.

Shafer, R. Christianity and Naturalism. New Haven, 1926. [Coleridge, Newman, Huxley, Arnold, Butler, Hardy.]

Hussey, C. The Picturesque. Studies in a Point of View. 1927.

Pierce, F. E. Romanticism and Other Isms. JEGP. xxvi, 1927.

Railo, E. The Haunted Castle. A Study of the Elements of English Romanticism. 1927.

Burgum, E. B. Victorianism. Sewanee Rev. xxxvi, 1928.

Clark, Kenneth. The Gothic Revival. 1928.

Fairchild, H. N. The Noble Savage. A Study in Romantic Naturalism. New York, 1928.
—— The Romantic Quest. New York, 1931.

Blunden, E. Nature in Literature. 1929.

Draper, J. W. The Summa of Romanticism. Colonnade, xiv, 1929.

Huscher, H. Über Eigenart und Ursprung des englischen Naturgefühls. Leipzig, 1929.

Kellett, E. E. The Whirligig of Taste. 1929.

Priestley, J. B. English Humour. 1929.

Rosenblatt, L. L'Idée de l'Art pour l'Art dans la Littérature anglaise pendant la Période victorienne. Paris, 1931.

Yvon, P. Le Gothique et la Renaissance Gothique en Angleterre (1750–1880). Caen, 1931.

Sickells, E. M. The Gloomy Egoist. Moods and Themes of Melancholy from Gray to Keats. New York, 1932.

Strehler, M. Der Dekadenzgedanke im 'Yellow Book' und 'Savoy.' Turbenthal, 1932.

Bruce, H. L. Beneath the Surface, 1800–1815. [In Essays in Criticism. By Members of the Department of English, University of California, ser. 2, Berkeley, 1934.]

Leisering, W. Das Motiv des Einsiedlers in der englischen Literatur des 18. Jahrhunderts und der Hochromantik. Halle, 1935.

Routh, H. V. Money, Morals, and Manners as revealed in Modern Literature. 1935.
—— Towards the Twentieth Century. Essays in the Spiritual History of the Nineteenth. 1937.

Beach, J. W. The Concept of Nature in Nineteenth-Century English Poetry. New York, 1936.

Lucas, F. L. The Decline and Fall of the Romantic Ideal. Cambridge, 1936.

Young, G. M. Victorian England. Oxford, 1936.

Gill, F. C. The Romantic Movement and Methodism. 1937.

Decker, C. R. The Aesthetic Revolt against Naturalism in Victorian Criticism. PMLA. LIII, 1938.

(b) Collections of Essays

[Miscellaneous unconnected studies, mainly rptd from periodicals.]

Hazlitt, W. The Spirit of the Age; or, Contemporary Portraits. 1825. [Bentham, Godwin, Coleridge, Edward Irving, Horne Tooke, Scott, Byron, Southey, Wordsworth, Mackintosh, Malthus, Gifford, Jeffrey, Brougham, Burdett, Eldon, 'Wilberforce, Canning, Campbell, Crabbe, Moore, Hunt, Lamb, Washington Irving.]

Pichot, A. Voyage historique et littéraire en Angleterre et en Écosse. 3 vols. Paris, 1825; tr. Eng. 2 vols. 1825. [Joanna Baillie, Wordsworth, Coleridge, Southey, Moore, Byron, Scott, etc.]

Chorley, H. F. The Authors of England. A Series of Medallion Portraits. 1838; 1861. [Mrs Hemans, Scott, Byron, Southey, Lady Blessington, Coleridge, Lytton, Lady Morgan, Shelley, Moore, Lamb, Miss Mitford, Campbell, Wordsworth.]

Macaulay, T. B. (Baron). Critical and Historical Essays. 3 vols. 1843. [Byron, Southey, Robert Montgomery.]

Horne, R. H. A New Spirit of the Age. 2 vols. 1844; ed. W. Jerrold, 1907 (World's Classics). [Dickens, Barham, Landor, the Howitts, Talfourd, Milnes, H. Coleridge, Sydney Smith, Jerrold, Wordsworth, Hunt, Tennyson, Macaulay, Hood, Hook, the Brownings, Lytton, Mrs Shelley, Robert Montgomery, Carlyle, Taylor, Ainsworth, Marryat, etc.]

Jeffrey, F. (Lord). Contributions to the Edinburgh Review. 4 vols. 1844. [Campbell, Hazlitt, Byron, Scott, Keats, Rogers, Moore, Wordsworth, Mrs Hemans, Miss Edgeworth, Galt, 'Rejected Addresses,' etc.]

Gilfillan, G. A Gallery of Literary Portraits. 3 sers. Edinburgh, 1845–54. [Selection, ed. Sir W. R. Nicoll, 1909 (Everyman's Lib.). Wilson, Dobell, A. Smith, Massey, Hazlitt, Macaulay, Lytton, Carlyle, etc.]

Lester, J. W. Criticisms. 1847; 1848; 1853. [Pollok, Alford, Atherstone, Croly, Coleridge, Heber, Carlyle, Irving, etc.]

Sterling, J. Essays and Tales. Ed. J. C. Hare, 2 vols. 1848. [Vol. i, Coleridge, Napier, Carlyle, Tennyson, etc.]

Powell, T. Pictures of the Living Authors of England. New York, 1849. [Macaulay, Henry Taylor, Horne, Mackay, Lytton, Bailey, Mrs Jameson, Jerrold, Forster, Marston.]

Chasles, P. Études sur la Littérature et les Mœurs de l'Angleterre au XIXᵉ Siècle. Paris, [1850]. [Byron, etc.]

Richardson, D. L. Literary Recreations. 1852. [Lytton, Poetry and Utilitarianism, Jeffrey, Dickens and Thackeray, Byron's Opinion of Pope, Hartley Coleridge, Carlyle, Odds and Ends of Criticism on Some of the British Poets, etc.]

Hannay, J. Satire and Satirists. Six Lectures. 1854. [Byron, Moore, etc.]

Whipple, E. P. Essays and Reviews. 2 vols. Boston, 1856.

Brimley, G. Essays. Ed. W. G. Clark, Cambridge, 1858. [Tennyson, Wordsworth, Patmore, Carlyle, Thackeray, Dickens, Kingsley, etc.]

Hayward, A. Biographical and Critical Essays. 5 vols. 1858–74. [Sydney Smith, Rogers, James Smith, Maria Edgeworth, Canning, etc.]

—— Sketches of Eminent Statesmen and Writers. 2 vols. 1880. [Byron, Tennyson, etc.]

Bayne, P. Essays, Biographical, Critical and Miscellaneous. Edinburgh, 1859. [Tennyson, Mrs Browning, the Brontës, Ruskin, 'Elementary Principles of Criticism.']

—— Lessons from my Masters: Carlyle, Tennyson, and Ruskin. New York, 1879.

Kingsley, C. Miscellanies. 2 vols. 1859. [Vol. I, Tennyson, Alexander Smith, Shelley, Byron, Burns and his School, etc.]

McNicoll, T. Essays on English Literature. 1861. [Pollok, Carlyle, Tendencies of Modern Poetry (= Dobell and Alexander Smith), Gilfillan, Tennyson, 'Christopher North,' Browning, Landor, etc.]

Japp, A. H. Three Great Teachers of our own Time: Carlyle, Tennyson and Ruskin. 1865.

Stirling, J. H. Jerrold, Tennyson and Macaulay: Critical Essays. 1868.

Greg, W. R. Literary and Social Judgments. 1869 (2nd edn). [False Morality of Lady Novelists, Kingsley and Carlyle, etc.]

Friswell, J. H. Modern Men of Letters. 1870. [Lemon, Sala, Lever, Ainsworth, Robertson.]

Hutton, R. H. Essays, Theological and Literary. Vol. II, 1871. [Wordsworth, Shelley, Browning, George Eliot, Clough.]

—— Essays on some of the Modern Guides of English Thought. 1887. [Carlyle, Newman, Arnold, George Eliot, Maurice.]

—— Criticisms on Contemporary Thought and Thinkers. 2 vols. 1894. [Carlyle, Dickens, L. Stephen, Mill, Arnold, Clough, Huxley, Bagehot, Ruskin, Wordsworth, Darwin.]

—— Brief Literary Criticisms. 1906.

Lowell, J. R. My Study Windows. 1871. [Carlyle, Swinburne, etc.]

Morley, J. (Viscount). Critical Miscellanies. 4 vols. 1871–1908. [Byron, Carlyle, Macaulay, Mill, George Eliot, Harriet Martineau, W. R. Greg, etc.]

—— Studies in Literature. 1891. [Wordsworth, Maine, Browning, Macvey Napier, etc.]

Minto, W. Manual of English Prose Literature. Edinburgh, 1872. [De Quincey, Macaulay, Carlyle, etc.]

Buchanan, R. W. Master Spirits. 1873. [Dickens, Tennyson, Browning, William Miller, etc.]

Maginn, W. A Gallery of Illustrious Literary Characters (1830–1838) drawn by Daniel Maclise and accompanied by Notices chiefly by William Maginn. Ed. W. Bates, [1873], 1883 (as The Maclise Portrait-Gallery). [Rptd from Fraser's Mag. 1830–8.]

Milnes, R. M. (Baron Houghton). Monographs, Personal and Social. 1873. [Wiseman, Landor, the Berrys, Sydney Smith, Lady Ashburton, etc.]

Gosse, Sir E. [See pp. 742–4 below.]

Masson, D. Wordsworth, Shelley, Keats, and Other Essays. 1874.

—— Edinburgh Sketches and Memories. 1892. [Scott, Carlyle, C. K. Sharpe, J. H. Burton, John Brown.]

Stephen, Sir L. Hours in a Library. 3 sers. 1874–9. [Scott, De Quincey, Hazlitt, Disraeli, The First Edinburgh Reviewers, Wordsworth, Landor, Macaulay, Charlotte Brontë, Kingsley, etc.]

—— Studies of a Biographer. 4 vols. 1898–1902. [Wordsworth, Scott, Arnold, Jowett, Tennyson, Browning, Ruskin, Bagehot, Huxley, Froude, Southey, Trollope, Stevenson, etc.]

Smith, George B. Poets and Novelists. 1875. [Thackeray, Peacock, Buchanan, E. B. Browning, the Brontës, etc.]

Swinburne, A. C. Essays and Studies. 1875. [Rossetti, Morris, Arnold, Shelley, Byron, Coleridge, etc.]

—— Miscellanies. 1886. [Wordsworth and Byron, Landor, Keats, Tennyson, Emily Brontë, Reade, etc.]

—— Studies in Prose and Poetry. 1894. [Scott, Jowett, Wilkie Collins, Tennyson, Shelley, etc.]

Davey, S. Darwin, Carlyle, and Dickens, with Other Essays. 1876.

Lancaster, H. H. Essays and Reviews. Edinburgh, 1876. [Macaulay, Carlyle, Ruskin, George Eliot, Thackeray, etc.]

Martineau, H. Biographical Sketches, 1852–1875. 1877 (rev. edn). [Mrs Opie, Wilson, Lockhart, Miss Mitford, Charlotte Brontë, Rogers, Croker, De Quincey, Macaulay, Mrs Jameson, Landor, Procter.]

Yates, E. Celebrities at Home. 3 sers. 1877–9. [Tennyson, Disraeli, Carlyle, 'Ouida,' Newman, Miss Braddon, Sala, Milnes, Ruskin, Jowett, Wilkie Collins, Ainsworth, etc.]

Dowden, E. Studies in Literature, 1789–1877. 1878. [Landor, Tennyson, Browning, George Eliot, Wordsworth, Scientific Movement and Literature, etc.]

—— Transcripts and Studies. 1888. [Carlyle, Shelley, Wordsworth, Browning, Victorian Literature, etc.]

Dowden, E. New Studies in Literature. 1895. [Meredith, Bridges, Coleridge, etc.]

Bagehot, W. Literary Studies. Ed. R. H. Hutton, 2 vols. 1879; ed. G. Sampson, 2 vols. 1911 (Everyman's Lib.). [The First Edinburgh Reviewers, H. Coleridge, Shelley, Thackeray, Scott, Dickens, Macaulay, Clough, Crabb Robinson, Wordsworth, Tennyson, Browning, etc.]

Spedding, J. Reviews and Discussions. 1879. [Peacock, Dickens, Tennyson, H. Coleridge, etc.]

Walsh, W. S. Pen Pictures of Modern Authors. New York, 1882.

—— Pen Pictures of Earlier Victorian Authors. New York, 1884.

Skelton, Sir J. Essays in History and Biography. Edinburgh, 1883. [Macaulay, Thackeray, Charlotte Brontë, Disraeli, etc.]

Eliot, George. Essays and Leaves from a Note-Book. Edinburgh, 1884.

—— Early Essays. 1919 (priv. ptd).

Birrell, A. Obiter Dicta. 1885.

—— Res Judicatae. 1892.

—— More Obiter Dicta. 1924.

Montégut, E. Écrivains modernes de l'Angleterre. 3 sers. Paris, 1885–92. [Ser. 1, George Eliot, Charlotte Brontë, 'Guy Livingstone'; ser. 2, Mrs Gaskell, Mrs Browning, Borrow, Tennyson.]

Smith, John Campbell. Writings by the Way. Edinburgh, 1885. [Carlyle, Our Age—its Doings and Drift, Hamilton, Spalding, Moir, etc.]

Dawson, G. Biographical Lectures. 1886. [Pope and Byron, Lamb, Wordsworth, Coleridge, Carlyle, Thackeray, Hood, Cobbett, Cobden.]

Dawson, W. J. Quest and Vision. 1886. [Shelley, Wordsworth, Religious Doubt and Modern Poetry (Arnold, Browning, Tennyson), George Eliot, The Poetry of Despair (Arnold, J. Thomson).]

—— The Makers of Modern Prose. 1899. [Macaulay, Landor, De Quincey, Lamb, Carlyle, Froude, Ruskin, Newman, etc.]

Escott, T. H. S. Politics and Letters. 1886. [Houghton, Hayward, Yates, etc.]

—— Personal Forces of the Period. 1898. [Stubbs, Gore, Lubbock, Meredith, Austin, etc.]

Lang, A. Letters to Dead Authors. 1886.

—— Essays in Little. 1891.

Buchanan, R. W. A Look round Literature. 1887. [Peacock, Dobell, George Eliot, Lewes, Rossetti, etc.]

James, Henry. Partial Portraits. 1888. [Stevenson, George Eliot, Trollope, etc.]

—— Views and Reviews. Boston, 1908.

—— Notes on Novelists. 1914. [Stevenson, The New Novel, The Ring and the Book, etc.]

Salt, H. S. Literary Sketches. 1888. [Shelley, Tennyson, J. Thomson, Godwin, De Quincey, etc.]

Pater, W. Appreciations. 1889. [Wordsworth, Coleridge, Lamb, Rossetti, etc.]

Robertson, J. M. Essays towards a Critical Method. 1889. [Science in Criticism, etc.]

—— Modern Humanists: Sociological Studies of Carlyle, Mill, Emerson, Arnold, Ruskin and Spencer. 1891.

—— New Essays towards a Critical Method. 1897. [Shelley, Keats, Clough, etc.]

—— Criticisms. 2 vols. 1902–3. [Jane Austen, Lang, Ruskin, etc.]

Forster, Joseph. Four Great Teachers: J. Ruskin, T. Carlyle, R. W. Emerson and R. Browning. 1890.

Henley, W. E. Views and Reviews. Literature. 1890. [Dickens, Thackeray, Disraeli, Meredith, Byron, Arnold, George Eliot, Borrow, Tennyson, Landor, Hood, etc.]

Saintsbury, G. Essays in English Literature, 1780–1860. 2 sers. 1890–5. [Hogg, Sydney Smith, Jeffrey, Hazlitt, Moore, Hunt, Peacock, Wilson, De Quincey, Lockhart, Praed, Borrow; ser. 2, Southey, Cobbett, Landor, Hood, Miss Ferrier, Campbell, Hook, Barham, Maginn, 'The Historical Novel,' etc.]

—— Corrected Impressions. 1895. [Thackeray, Tennyson, Carlyle, Swinburne, Macaulay, Browning, Dickens, Arnold, Morris, Ruskin, etc.]

Steuart, J. A. Letters to Living Authors. 1890. [Meredith, Ruskin, Froude, Hardy, Swinburne, Caine, Stevenson, Lang, Black, Buchanan, Blackmore, etc.]

Jacobs, J. George Eliot, Matthew Arnold, Browning, Newman. 1891.

Scherer, E. Essays on English Literature. Tr. (with important Introduction) G. Saintsbury, 1891. [George Eliot, Mill, Wordsworth, Carlyle, Disraeli, etc.]

Woodberry, G. E. Studies in Letters and Life. Boston, 1891.

—— Makers of Literature. New York, 1900. [Shelley, Landor, Browning, Byron, Arnold, Coleridge, etc.]

Watson, Sir W. Excursions in Criticism. 1893. [R. H. Hutton, Saintsbury, Dobson, etc.]

Bridges, R. Overheard in Arcady. 1894. [Meredith, Kipling, Stevenson, Barrie.]

Monkhouse, A. Books and Plays. 1894. [Meredith, Borrow, Stevenson, Henley.]

Harrison, F. Studies in Early Victorian Literature. 1895. [Characteristics of Victorian Literature, Thackeray, Disraeli, Dickens, Trollope, the Brontës, etc.]

—— Tennyson, Ruskin, Mill, and Other Literary Estimates. 1899.

Le Fèvre-Deumier, J. Célébrités anglaises. Paris,1895. ['Christopher North,' 'L. E. L.,' etc.]

Lilly, W. S. Four English Humourists of the Nineteenth Century. 1895. [Dickens, Thackeray, George Eliot, Carlyle.]

Le Gallienne, R. Retrospective Reviews. A Literary Log. 2 vols. 1896. [Rptd reviews —mainly contemporary poets, novelists and essayists.]

—— Attitudes and Avowals. 1910. [Grant Allen, Tennyson, Meredith, Stephen Phillips, Symons, Watson.]

Quiller-Couch, Sir A. T. Adventures in Criticism. 1896. [Reade, H. Kingsley, Kinglake, Calverley, Stevenson, etc.]

—— Studies in Literature. 3 sers. Cambridge, 1918–30. [Meredith, Hardy, Coleridge, Arnold, Swinburne, Reade, etc.]

—— Charles Dickens and Other Victorians. Cambridge, 1925. [Thackeray, The Victorian Background, Disraeli, Mrs Gaskell, Trollope.]

Thomson, James. Biographical and Critical Studies. Ed. B. Dobell, 1896. [Shelley, Wilson, Hogg, Browning, etc.]

Stearns, F. P. Modern English Prose Writers. 1897. [Macaulay, Carlyle, Froude, Scott, Thackeray, Dickens, George Eliot, Müller, Arnold.]

Symons, A. Studies in Two Literatures. 1897. [Jefferies, J. Thomson, Hake, Symonds,etc.]

—— Studies in Prose and Verse. 1904. [De Quincey, Pater, Morris, Buchanan, Yeats, Dobson, Dowson, etc.]

—— Figures of Several Centuries. 1916. [Lamb, Beddoes, Hardy, Patmore, etc.]

—— Dramatis Personae. Indianapolis, 1923; 1925 (rev.). [Emily Brontë, Francis Thompson, etc.]

Traill, H. D. The New Fiction and Other Essays on Literary Subjects. 1897. [The Politics of Literature, Arnold, The Future of Humour, etc.]

Clark, J. S. A Study of English Prose Writers. New York, 1898.

Dixon, W. M. In the Republic of Letters. 1898. [Arnold, Meredith, the De Veres, The Romantic Revival.]

Wilson, P. Leaders in Literature. Edinburgh, 1898. [Carlyle, George Eliot, the Brownings, Arnold, Spencer, Ruskin.]

Adams, Francis. Essays in Modernity. 1899. [Tennyson, Kipling, Swinburne, Some Recent Novels, Shelley, etc.]

Chiarini, G. Studi e Ritratti Letterari. Leghorn, 1900.

Gates, L. E. Studies and Appreciations. New York, 1900. [Tennyson, Charlotte Brontë, The Romantic Movement, Impressionism and Appreciation, etc.]

'Rutherford, Mark' (W. H. White). Pages from a Journal. 1900. [A Visit to Carlyle; Scott; The Morality of Byron's Poetry; Byron, Goethe and Arnold.]

—— Last Pages from a Journal. 1915. [George Eliot as I knew her, William Sewell, Wordsworth, Shelley's Birthplace, Dorothy Wordsworth, Caleb Morris.]

Brownell, W. C. Victorian Prose Masters. New York, 1901. [Thackeray, Carlyle, Arnold, Ruskin, Meredith.]

Collins, J. C. Ephemera Critica; or, Plain Truths about Current Literature. 1901. [Stevenson, De Quincey, Palgrave, Phillips, etc.]

—— Studies in Poetry and Criticism. 1905. [Byron, Watson, Massey, The True Functions of Poetry, etc.]

—— Posthumous Essays. Ed. L. C. Collins, 1912. [Arnold, Browning, Tennyson, etc.]

Murray, Henry. Robert Buchanan, a Critical Appreciation, and Other Essays. 1901. [Swinburne, Ruskin, Kipling, the Brownings, Marie Corelli, etc.]

Paul, H. Men and Letters. 1901. [Arnold, Macaulay, etc.]

—— Stray Leaves. 1906. [George Eliot, Peacock, Lamb, Cory, etc.]

Burton, R. Forces in Fiction and Other Essays. [1902.] [The Historical Romance, The Love Motive in Modern Fiction, Past and Present in Literature, A Note on Modern Criticism, etc.]

'Paston, George' (E. M. Symonds). Little Memoirs of the Nineteenth Century. 1902. [Haydon, Lady Morgan, Lady Hester Stanhope, the Howitts, etc.]

Bryce, J. (Viscount). Studies in Contemporary Biography. 1903. [Disraeli, A. P. Stanley, T. H. Green, Trollope, J. R. Green, Freeman, Sidgwick, Acton, Gladstone, etc.]

Gould, G. M. Biographic Clinics: the Origin of the Ill-Health of De Quincey, Carlyle, Darwin, Huxley and Browning. Philadelphia, 1903. [Vol. II, George Eliot, Lewes, Jane Carlyle, Spencer, etc., 1904.]

Lyttelton, A. T. Modern Poets of Faith, Doubt and Paganism, and Other Essays. 1904. [Tennyson, Browning, The Poetry of Doubt (= Arnold and Clough), Carlyle, George Eliot, Modern Pagan Poetry (= Swinburne and Thomson), etc.]

More, P. E. The Shelburne Essays. 8 sers. New York, 1904—Boston, 1913. [Ser. 2, Hazlitt, Lamb, Kipling, FitzGerald, Crabbe, Meredith; ser. 3, Swinburne, Rossetti, Browning, Byron, Shorthouse; ser. 4, Keats, Lamb; ser. 5, Dickens, Mrs Gaskell, Gissing; ser. 7, Shelley, Wordsworth, Hood, Tennyson, Morris; ser. 8, Newman, Pater, Huxley.]

More, P. E. New Shelburne Essays. Princeton, 1928. [Borrow, Trollope.]

Ainger, A. Lectures and Essays. 2 vols. 1905. [Some Leaders in the Poetic Revival of 1760–1820, The Children's Books of a Hundred Years Ago, etc.]

Nevinson, H. W. Books and Personalities. 1905. [Arnold, Hardy, FitzGerald, Yeats, Lady Gregory, A. E., etc.]

Fyvie, J. Some Literary Eccentrics. 1906. [Landor, Hazlitt, Crabb Robinson, Babbage, Jerrold, etc.]

Lord, W. F. The Mirror of the Century. 1906. [George Eliot, W. E. Norris, Jane Austen, the Brontës, Thackeray, Dickens, Lytton, the Kingsleys, Disraeli, Trollope, Reade.]

Rickett, A. Personal Forces in Modern Literature. 1906. [Newman, Martineau, Huxley, Wordsworth, Keats, Rossetti, Dickens, Hazlitt, De Quincey. Includes Bibliographical Guide and index.]

Elton, O. Modern Studies. 1907. [Tennyson, Swinburne, Meredith, Living Irish Literature, etc.]

Baker, James. Literary and Biographical Studies. 1908. [Macaulay, Blackmore, Coleridge, Southey, Tennyson, etc.]

Ritchie, A. T., Lady. Blackstick Papers. 1908. [Mrs Hemans, Mary and Agnes Berry, 'Jacob Omnium' (M. J. Higgins), Mrs Gaskell.]

Scott-James, R. A. Modernism and Romance. 1908. [Hardy, Stevenson, etc.]

—— The Making of Literature. 1928. [Arnold, Pater, etc.]

Laurent, R. Études anglaises. Paris, 1910. [Pater, Wilde, Pre-Raphaelitism.]

Bailey, J. Poets and Poetry. Oxford, 1911. [Wordsworth, Scott, Keats, Shelley, Swinburne, Pater, FitzGerald, Meredith.]

—— The Continuity of Letters. Oxford, 1923. [The Grand Style, Shelley, Wordsworth, Thackeray, etc.]

Benson, A. C. The Leaves of the Tree. Studies in Biography. 1911. [J. K. Stephen, F. Myers, C. Kingsley, Arnold, etc.]

Jack, A. A. Poetry and Prose. 1911. [Wordsworth, Byron, Arnold, Meredith.]

Figgis, D. Studies and Appreciations. 1912. [Synge, Yeats, Browning, Watson, Trench, Bridges, Meredith, Dickens, Thackeray, Butler.]

Jackson, Holbrook. All Manner of Folk. 1912. [Masters of Nonsense (= Lear), Synge, Carpenter, Jefferies, Morris, Meredith, etc.]

Johnson, Lionel. Post Liminium. Essays and Critical Papers. Ed. T. Whittemore, 1912. [Pater, Borrow, Stevenson, etc.]

—— Reviews and Critical Papers. Ed. R. Shafer, 1921. [Stevenson, Davidson, Morris, Mrs H. Ward, Dobson, Kipling, etc.]

Olivero, F. Saggi di Letteratura inglese. Bari, 1913.

—— Studi sul Romanticismo inglese. Bari, 1914.

Vincent, L. H. Dandies and Men of Letters. Boston, 1913. [Byron, Rogers, Moore, Thomas Hope, Peacock, C. K. Sharpe, Disraeli, Lytton, Crabb Robinson, etc.]

Russell, G. W. E. Selected Essays. 1914. [J. Payn, A. Procter, H. Kingsley, Shorthouse, D. Gray, etc.]

Freeman, J. The Moderns: Essays in Literary Criticism. 1916. [Shaw, Wells, Hardy, Patmore, F. Thompson, Bridges.]

—— English Portraits and Essays. 1924. [Stevenson, Cobbett, Hewlett, Gosse, Patmore.]

Watts-Dunton, T. Old Familiar Faces. 1916. [Borrow, Rossetti, Tennyson, Christina Rossetti, Hake, de Tabley, Morris, F. H. Groome.]

Meynell, A. Hearts of Controversy. 1917. [Dickens, Tennyson, Swinburne, etc.]

Sherman, S. P. On Contemporary Literature. New York, 1917. [George Moore, Synge, Austin, Meredith.]

Chislett, W. The Classical Influence in English Literature in the Nineteenth Century, and Other Essays. Boston, 1918.

Waugh, Arthur. Tradition and Change: Studies in Contemporary Literature. 1919. [Phillips, Lionel Johnson, Symons, Dickens, Swinburne, Butler, Stevenson, etc.]

Clutton-Brock, A. Essays on Books. [1920.] [Dickens, Swinburne, Keats, etc.]

Thorndike, A. H. Literature in a Changing Age. New York, 1920.

Coleridge, Stephen. Letters to my Grandson on the Glory of English Prose. 1922.

Du Bos, C. Approximations. 4 sers. Paris, 1922–30. [Shelley, Browning, Pater, Hardy, etc.]

'Lee, Vernon.' The Handling of Words, and Other Studies in Literary Psychology. 1923. [De Quincey, Landor, Carlyle, Meredith, Kipling, Stevenson, Hardy.]

Williams, S. T. Studies in Victorian Literature. New York, [1923].

Ellis, S. M. Mainly Victorian. 1925. [Whyte-Melville, J. Grant, Smedley, Agnes Strickland, Noel, Kenealy, Dobson, Baring-Gould, Lord A. Douglas, Wratislaw, Mrs Antrobus, etc.]

Ker, W. P. Collected Essays. Ed. C. Whibley, 2 vols. 1925. [Scott, Byron, Keats, Hazlitt, Tennyson, Browning, etc.]

Larbaud, V. Ce Vice impuni, la Lecture. Paris, 1925. [Henley, Patmore, F. Thompson, Wells, Hardy, Bennett, etc.]

Marks, J. Genius and Disaster. New York, 1925. [J. Thomson, Swinburne, F. Thompson, etc.]

Vinciguerra, M. Romantici e Decadenti inglesi. Foligno, 1925. [Carlyle, Wilde, Hardy, Stevenson, Moore, Synge.]

Woolf, V. The Common Reader. 1925. [Jane Austen, George Eliot, Miss Mitford, the Brontës.]

—— The Common Reader. Ser. 2, 1932. [De Quincey, Hazlitt, Gissing, Hardy, etc.]

Fernandez, R. Messages. Paris, 1926. [Newman, Meredith, Pater, etc.]

Newbolt, Sir H. Studies Green and Gray. [1926.] [Shorthouse, Peacock, Scott, Alice Meynell, Barham, etc.]

Baumann, A. A. The Last Victorians. 1927. [Bagehot, Trollope, Jowett, Wyndham, Labouchere, etc.]

Bridges, R. Collected Essays, Papers, etc. 9 vols. Oxford, 1927–35. [Keats, de Tabley, Mary Coleridge, Darley, Kipling, etc.]

Maurois, A. Études anglaises—Dickens, Walpole, Ruskin et Wilde. Paris, 1927.

Ralli, A. Critiques. 1927. [The Brontës, Morris, Hardy, Swinburne, Borrow, Pater, FitzGerald, etc.]

Harper, G. M. Spirit of Delight. New York, [1928]. [Coleridge, the Wordsworths, Hardy, Hudson, Housman, Arnold.]

Weygandt, C. Tuesdays at Ten. Philadelphia, 1928. [L. Johnson, Doughty, Yeats, F. Thompson, Phillips, Dobson, Hudson, etc.]

Bradley, A. C. A Miscellany. 1929. [Tennyson, Jane Austen, Shelley, Coleridge, Keats, Inspiration, etc.]

Ince, R. B. Calverley and some Cambridge Wits of the Nineteenth Century. 1929. [Milnes, Sterling, Kinglake.]

'Kingsmill, Hugh' (H. K. Lunn). After Puritanism, 1850–1900. 1929. [From Shakespeare to Dean Farrar, Samuel Butler, Frank Harris, W. T. Stead.]

Feiling, K. Sketches in Nineteenth Century Biography. 1930. [Croker, Southey and Wordsworth, Coleridge, Newman, Lytton, Bagehot, etc.]

Blunden, E. Votive Tablets. 1931. [Southey, Rejected Addresses, Leigh Hunt, Shelley, Trelawny, Cobbett, Lamb, Hood, Beddoes, H. Coleridge, Darley, etc.]

Chauvet, P. Sept Essais de Littérature anglaise. Paris, 1931. [Thomson, Wilde, Arnold, Tennyson, E. B. Browning.]

Lockhart, J. G. Literary Criticism. Ed. M. C. Hildyard, Oxford, 1931. [Susan Ferrier, Hook, Jeffrey, Tennyson, etc.]

MacCarthy, D. Portraits. 1931. [Blunt, Burton, Clough, Disraeli, Meredith, George Moore, Raleigh, Ruskin, J. K. Stephen, Stevenson, etc.]

—— Criticism. 1932. [Butler, Browning, Patmore, Yeats.]

Partridge, E. Literary Sessions. 1932. [R. E. Landor, Horne, Mrs Clive, etc.]

The Great Victorians. Ed. H. J. and H. Massingham, 1932. [Arnold, the Brontës, Browning, Butler, Dickens, Disraeli, Fitz-Gerald, Hardy, Macaulay, Meredith, Morris, Newman, Pater, Patmore, Rossetti, Ruskin, Stevenson, Swinburne, Thackeray, Tennyson, Trollope, etc.]

Elwin, M. Victorian Wallflowers. 1934. [Wilson, Maginn, Barham, Ainsworth, Forster, Wilkie Collins, Mrs H. Wood, Blackmore, 'Ouida.']

Milner, G. The Threshold of the Victorian Age. 1934. [Includes chs. on Literature, Macaulay, Carlyle, Tennyson and Dickens.]

Clarke, Isabel C. Six Portraits. 1935. [Jane Austen, George Eliot, Mrs Oliphant, John Oliver Hobbes, etc.]

Forster, E. M. Abinger Harvest. 1936. [H. O. Sturgis, Jane Austen, Coleridge, Keats, Wilfrid Blunt.]

From Anne to Victoria. Ed. B. Dobrée, 1937. [Scott, Wordsworth, Coleridge, Keats, Shelley, Byron, etc.]

(c) Miscellaneous Works

Wotton, M. E. Word Portraits of Famous Writers. 1887. [Descriptions of personal appearances of English writers—including sixty-three 19th cent. figures.]

Rawnsley, H. D. Literary Associations of the English Lakes. 2 vols. 1894.

Nicoll, Sir W. R. and Wise, T. J. Literary Anecdotes of the Nineteenth Century. 2 vols. 1895–6.

Spielmann, M. H. The History of 'Punch.' 1895.

Sharp, W. Literary Geography. 1907.

Escott, T. H. S. Club Makers and Club Members. New York, 1914.

Thomas, Edward. A Literary Pilgrim in England. 1917.

Spiller, R. E. The American in England during the First Half-Century of Independence. New York, [1926].

Blunden, E. Leigh Hunt's 'Examiner' Examined, 1805–25, illustrating the Literary History of that Period. [1928.]

Hoevel, E. F. Die soziale Herkunft der neuzeitlichen Dialektliteratur Englands. Leipzig, 1929.

Cruse, A. The Englishman and his Books in the Early Nineteenth Century. [1930.]

—— The Victorians and their Books. 1935.

—— After the Victorians. 1938.

Perugini, M. E. Victorian Days and Ways. 1932.

Abrams, M. H. The Milk of Paradise. The Effect of Opium Visions on the Works of De Quincey, Crabbe, Francis Thompson, and Coleridge. Cambridge, U.S.A. 1934.

Nesbitt, G. L. Benthamite Reviewing: the First Twelve Years of the Westminster Review, 1824–1836. New York, 1934.

Thrall, M. Rebellious Fraser's; Nol Yorke's Magazine in the Days of Maginn, Thackeray, and Carlyle. New York, 1934.

Early Victorian England, 1830–1865. Ed. G. M. Young, 2 vols. Oxford, 1934.

(4) Prose-Selections

[Restricted to non-dramatic prose. For anthologies of 19th cent. verse and drama, see respectively pp. 162–3 and 585 below.]

'Shepard, W.' (W. S. Walsh). Enchiridion of Criticism. The Best Criticisms on the Best Authors of the Nineteenth Century. Philadelphia, 1885.

Mason, E. T. British Letters Illustrative of Character and Social Life. 3 vols. New York, 1888.

Stevenson, E. Early Reviews of Great Writers (1786–1832). [1890.]

Craik, Sir H. English Prose; Selections, with Critical Introductions by Various Writers, and General Introductions to Each Period. Vol. v, 1896.

Haney, J. L. Early Reviews of English Poets: 1757–1885. 1904.

Dawson, W. J. and C. W. The Great English Letter Writers. 2 sers. 1908.

Dickinson, T. H. and Roe, F. W. Nineteenth Century English Prose; Critical Essays. New York, [1908].

Dawson, W. J. and C. E. The Great English Essayists. 1909.

Van Tieghem, P. Le Mouvement romantique (Angleterre—Allemagne—Italie—France): Textes choisis, commentés et annotés. Paris, 1912.

Johnson, R. B. Famous Reviews. 1914. [Reviews of Jane Austen, Tennyson, Charlotte Brontë, Thackeray, George Eliot, Macaulay, Maturin.]

Walker, Mrs H. A Book of Victorian Poetry and Prose. Cambridge, 1915.

Bryan, W. F. and Crane, R. S. The English Familiar Essay; Representative Texts. Boston, [1916].

Woods, G. B. English Poetry and Prose of the Romantic Movement. New York, 1916, 1929 (with supplementary bibliography).

Alden, R. M. Readings in English Prose of the Nineteenth Century. New York, 1917.

—— Critical Essays of the Early Nineteenth Century. New York, 1921.

Rees, B. J. Nineteenth Century Letters. New York, [1919].

Peacock, W. English Prose. 5 vols. 1921–2. (World's Classics.) [Vols. iii–v.]

Jones, Edmund. English Critical Essays of the XIX Century. 1922. (World's Classics.)

Rhys, E. Modern English Essays, 1870 to 1920. 5 vols. 1923. (Everyman's Lib.)

Roe, F. W. Nineteenth Century English Prose; Early Essayists: Lamb, Hazlitt, Hunt, De Quincey, Macaulay. New York, 1923.

Campbell, O. J. and Gingerich, S. F. Critical Essays on Poetry, Drama, and Fiction. Ann Arbor, 1924.

Opdycke, J. B. The Literature of Letters; Famous Literary Letters as Related to Life, to the History of Literature, and to the Art of Composition. Chicago, [1925].

Mordell, A. Notorious Literary Attacks. New York, 1926.

Bell, Mackenzie. Half Hours with Representative Novelists of the Nineteenth Century, Being Passages from their Works with Brief Biographies and Introductions and a Critical Essay. 3 vols. 1927.

Grabo, C. H. Romantic Prose of the Early Nineteenth Century. New York, [1927].

Lieder, P. R., Lovett, R. M., Root, R. K. British Poetry and Prose. A Book of Readings. Part Two: Wordsworth to Yeats. Boston, 1928.

Cofer, B. D. Nineteenth Century Essays, from Coleridge to Pater. New York, 1929.

Craig, H. and Thomas, J. M. English Prose of the Nineteenth Century. New York, 1929.

King, R. W. England from Wordsworth to Dickens. [1929.]

Sampson, G. Nineteenth Century Essays. Cambridge, 1929.

Reed, A. G. English Literature: the Romantic Period. New York, [1929].

Bernbaum, Ernest. Earlier Victorian Period. New York, 1930.

—— Later Victorian Literature. New York, 1930.

—— Anthology of Romanticism and Guide through the Romantic Movement. 5 vols. New York, 1930.

—— The Romantic Period. New York, 1930.

Collins, V. H. From Goldsmith to Landor: Essays and Conversations. 1930.

Foster, F. M. K. and White, Helen C. Victorian Prose. New York, 1930.

Miller, G. M. English Literature: the Victorian Period. New York, 1930.

Reilly, J. J. Masters of Nineteenth Century Prose; a Book of Readings. New York, 1930.

Routh, H. V. England under Victoria. [1930.]

Wellesley, Lady D. The Annual: a Selection from the 'Forget-Me-Nots,' 'Keepsakes,' and Other Annuals of the Nineteenth Century. Introduction by V. Sackville-West. 1930.

Barton, M. and Sitwell, O. Victoriana. A Symposium of Victorian Wisdom. Compiled from many Original Sources. 1931.

Watson, E. H. L. Contemporary Comments: Writers of the Early Nineteenth Century as They Appeared to Each Other. 1931.

Bald, R. C. Literary Friendships in the Age of Wordsworth: an Anthology. Cambridge, 1932.

Boas, G. A 'Punch' Anthology. 1932.

—— Prose of Yesterday: Dickens to Galsworthy. 1937.

Campbell, O. J., Pyre, J. F. A. and Weaver, B. Poetry and Criticism of the Romantic Movement. New York, 1932.

Smith, James H. and Parks, E. W. The Great Critics: an Anthology of Literary Criticism. New York, [1932].

Patterson, R. F. Six Centuries of English Literature. 6 vols. 1933. [Vol. v, Wordsworth to Trollope (introduction by E. Legouis); vol. vi, Meredith to Rupert Brooke (introduction by G. K. Chesterton).]

Withington, R. Essays and Characters: Lamb to Thompson. New York, 1933.

Ffrench, Y. News from the Past, 1805–1877. 1934. Extracts from English newspapers.]

Withington, R. and Van Winkle, C. Eminent British Writers of the Nineteenth Century. Prose. 1934.

Mayer, F. P. Victorian Prose. New York, 1935.

Delafield, E. M. Ladies and Gentlemen in Victorian Fiction. 1937.

Marchant, Sir J. History through 'The Times.' A Collection of Leading Articles on Important Events, 1800–1937. 1937.

Postgate, R. and Vallance, A. Those Foreigners. 1937. [Foreign affairs in English newspapers, 1815–1937.]

Bowyer, J. W. and Brooks, J. L. The Victorian Age: Prose, Poetry and Drama. New York, 1938.

Harrold, C. F. and Templeman, W. D. English Prose of the Victorian Era. New York, 1938.

Macintyre, C. F. and Ewing, M. English Prose of the Romantic Period. 1938.

(5) LITERARY MEMOIRS, REMINISCENCES AND LETTERS

[Restricted to relatively out-of-the-way material. The standard biographies, collections of letters, etc. will be found under the various writers in the appropriate sections below. See also Letters, Diaries and Autobiographies, pp. 149–55 below, and Book Production and Distribution, especially pp. 97–100.]

Hunt, Leigh. Lord Byron and some of his Contemporaries. 1828.

—— Table-Talk. 1851.

Hunt, Leigh. Autobiography. 3 vols. 1850; ed. R. Ingpen, 2 vols. 1903.

Dibdin, T. F. Reminiscences of a Literary Life. 2 vols. 1836. [Index, [1836?].]

Bury, Lady C. Diary Illustrative of the Times of George IV. 1838.

Hood, T. Literary Reminiscences. 1839.

Robberds, J. W. A Memoir of the Life and Writings of William Taylor of Norwich. Containing His Correspondence with Literary Men. 2 vols. 1843.

Foster, John. Life and Correspondence of. Ed. J. E. Ryland, 2 vols. 1848.

Jerdan, W. Autobiography. 4 vols. 1852–3.

Mitford, Mary R. Recollections of a Literary Life. New York, 1852.

Willis, N. P. Pencillings by the Way. New York, 1852 (rev.).

—— Famous Persons and Famous Places. New York, 1854.

Patmore, P. G. My Friends and Acquaintances. 3 vols. 1854.

Thomson, Mrs A. T. ('Grace Wharton'). Recollections of Literary Characters. 2 vols. 1854.

Madden, R. R. Literary Life and Correspondence of the Countess of Blessington. 3 vols. 1855.

Emerson, R. W. English Traits. Boston, 1856.

Balmanno, Mary. Pen and Pencil. New York, 1858.

Redding, C. Fifty Years' Recollections, Literary and Personal. 3 vols. [1858].

—— Literary Reminiscences and Memoirs of Thomas Campbell. 2 vols. 1860.

Leslie, C. R. Autobiographical Recollections. Ed. T. Taylor, Boston, 1860. [Mainly of painting. Coleridge, Lamb, Irving, etc.]

Lady Morgan's Memoirs: Autobiography, Diaries and Correspondence. Ed. W. H. Dixon, 2 vols. 1862.

Berkeley, G. My Life and Recollections. 4 vols. 1864–6.

Hobhouse, J. C. (Baron Broughton). Recollections of a Long Life. 5 vols. 1865 (priv. ptd); 6 vols. 1909–11.

Irving, P. M. The Life and Letters of Washington Irving. 4 vols. New York, 1865–6.

Duncombe, T. H. Thomas Slingsby Duncombe: Life and Correspondence. 2 vols. 1868.

Godwin, P. Out of the Past. New York, 1870.

Hall, S. C. A Book of Memories of Great Men and Women of the Age, from Personal Acquaintance. 1871.

—— Retrospect of a Long Life. 2 vols. 1883.

Meteyard, E. A Group of Englishmen (1795–1815), Being Records of the Younger Wedgwoods and Their Friends. 1871. [Campbell, Coleridge, Godwin, etc.]

Chambers, W. Memoir of Robert Chambers, with Autobiographical Reminiscences of William Chambers. 1872.

Fields, J. T. Yesterdays with Authors. Boston, 1872; Boston, 1900 (enlarged).

Hazlitt, W. C. Anecdotes and Reminiscences of Illustrious Men and Women of Modern Times. 1872.

Pebody, C. Our Great Authors at Work. [1872.]

Chorley, F. Autobiography, Memoir and Letters. Ed. H. G. Hewlett, 2 vols. 1873.

Constable, T. Archibald Constable and His Literary Correspondents. 3 vols. Edinburgh, 1873.

Hall, Spencer. Biographical Sketches of Remarkable People, chiefly from Personal Recollection. 1873.

Paul, C. K. William Godwin, His Friends and Contemporaries. 2 vols. 1876.

—— Biographical Sketches. 1883.

Ticknor, G. Life, Letters and Journals. 2 vols. Boston, 1876.

Bowring, Sir J. Autobiographical Recollections, 1877.

Mackay, C. Forty Years' Recollections of Life, Literature, and Public Affairs. From 1830 to 1870. 2 vols. 1877.

—— Through the Long Day, or, Memorials of a Literary Life during Half a Century. 2 vols. 1887.

Martineau, H. Autobiography. With Memorials by Maria Chapman. 2 vols. Boston, 1877.

Clarke, C. Cowden and M. C. Recollections of Writers. 1878.

Dobell, Sydney. Life and Letters of. 2 vols. 1878.

Hodgson, J. T. Memoir of the Rev. Francis Hodgson, with Letters from Byron and Others. 2 vols. 1878.

Napier, Macvey. Selections from the Correspondence of. 1879. [Macaulay, Mill, Brougham, Carlyle, Jeffrey, etc.]

Frost, Thomas. Forty Years' Recollections: Literary and Political. 1880.

Fitzgerald, P. Recreations of a Literary Man. 1882.

Fox, Caroline. Memories of Old Friends. Ed. H. N. Pym, 2 vols. 1882. [Includes letters of J. S. Mill.]

Payn, J. Some Literary Recollections. 1884.

Stuart, J. M. Reminiscences. 1884.

Yates, E. H. Recollections and Experiences. 2 vols. 1884.

Mason, E. T. Personal Traits of British Authors. 4 vols. New York, 1885.

Whipple, E. P. Recollections of Eminent Men. Boston, 1886.

Francis, J. C. John Francis, Publisher of the Athenaeum: A Literary Chronicle of Half a Century. 2 vols. 1888.

Sandford, Mrs H. Thomas Poole and His Friends. 2 vols. 1888.

Clayden, P. W. Rogers and His Contemporaries. 2 vols. 1889.

Trollope, T. A. What I Remember. 2 vols. New York, 1888–90.

—— Further Reminiscences. 1889.

Reid, T. W. The Life, Letters, and Friendships of Richard Monckton Milnes, First Lord Houghton. 2 vols. 1890.

Smiles, S. A Publisher and His Friends. Memoir and Correspondence of John Murray, with an Account of the House, 1768–1843. 2 vols. 1891.

Masson, D. Edinburgh Sketches and Memories. 1892.

—— Memories of London in the 'Forties. 1908.

—— Memories of Two Cities, Edinburgh and Aberdeen. 1911. [Wilson, Hugh Miller, De Quincey, etc.]

Ritchie, Anne Thackeray, Lady. Records of Tennyson, Ruskin, and Robert and Elizabeth Browning. 1892.

—— Chapters from Some Unwritten Memoirs. New York, 1895.

Scott, W. Bell. Autobiographical Notes. 2 vols. 1892. [Hunt, Lewes, George Eliot, Ruskin.]

Archer-Shee, W. My Contemporaries. 1893.

Bertram, J. Some Memories of Books, Authors, and Events. 1893.

Crosland, Mrs N. Landmarks of a Literary Life. 1893.

Espinasse, F. Literary Recollections and Sketches. 1893.

Vizetelly, H. Glances Back through Seventy Years. 2 vols. 1893.

Fields, Mrs J. T. A Shelf of Old Books. 1894. [Reminiscences of authors.]

Correspondence of Joseph Jekyll with Lady Gertrude Sloane Stanley, 1818–1838. Ed. A. Bourke, 1894.

Saunders, F. Character Studies, with Some Personal Recollections. New York, 1894. [Edward Irving, Mrs Jameson.]

Hogg, J. De Quincey and His Friends; Personal Recollections. 1895.

Sala, G. A. Life and Adventures. 2 vols. New York, 1895.

Skelton, Sir J. The Table-Talk of Shirley. Reminiscences of, and Letters from Froude, Thackeray, Disraeli, Browning, Rossetti, Kingsley, Baynes, Huxley, Tyndall, and Others. 2 vols. Edinburgh, 1895.

Black, Helen C. Pen, Pencil, Baton and Mask: Biographical Sketches. 1896.

Hare, A. J. C. Story of My Life. 4 vols. New York, 1896–1901.

Farrar, F. W. Men I Have Known. [1897.]

Oliphant, M. O. Annals of a Publishing House. William Blackwood and His Sons: Their Magazine and Friends. 3 vols. 1897–8.

Oliphant, M. O. Autobiography and Letters. Ed. Mrs H. Coghill, 1899.

Laughton, Sir J. K. Memoirs of the Life and Correspondence of Henry Reeve. 2 vols. 1898.

[Russell, G. W. E.] Collections and Recollections. 1898.

Festing, G. John Hookham Frere and his Friends. 1899.

McCarthy, J. Reminiscences. 2 vols. 1899.

Palgrave, G. F. Francis Turner Palgrave: his Journals and Memories of his Life. 1899.

Yarnall, E. Wordsworth and the Coleridges, with Other Memories, Literary and Political. 1899.

Clark, J. W. Old Friends at Cambridge and Elsewhere. 1900.

Tinsley, W. Random Recollections of an Old Publisher. 2 vols. 1900.

Champneys, B. Memoirs and Correspondence of Coventry Patmore. 2 vols. 1901.

Kenyon, J. B. Loiterings in Old Fields; Literary Sketches. New York, [1901]. [Tennyson, Morris, Keats, Rossetti, Stevenson.]

Paston, George' (E. M. Symonds). Side-Lights on the Georgian Period. 1902.

—— At John Murray's. Records of a Literary Circle, 1843–1892. Preface by Lord Ernle. 1932.

Jay, H. Robert Buchanan. Some Account of his Life and Literary Friendships. 1903.

B[urne]-J[ones], G. Memorials of Sir Edward Burne-Jones. 2 vols. 1904.

Fifty Years of Fleet Street; Being the Life and Recollections of Sir John R. Robinson. Ed. F. M. Thomas, 1904.

Betham, E. A House of Letters. [1905.] [Coleridge, Lamb, Landor, Southey, Barton, etc.]

Harrison, F. Memories and Thoughts. 1906.

Correspondence of John Whishaw and his Friends, 1813–1840. Ed. Lady Seymour, 1906.

Brown, John. Letters. Ed. J. Brown and D. W. Forrest, 1907. [Includes letters from Ruskin, Thackeray, Hutton, Brooks, etc.]

Layard, G. A Great Punch Editor: Being the Life, Letters, and Diaries of Shirley Brooks. 1907.

Carr, J. C. Some Eminent Victorians. Personal Recollections. 1908. [Tennyson, Browning, Rossetti, etc.]

—— Coasting Bohemia. 1914. [Rossetti, Meredith, Sullivan, Irving, etc.]

Sanders, L. The Holland House Circle. 1908.

Winter, W. Old Friends. New York, 1909. [Dickens, Wilkie Collins.]

Murdoch, W. G. B. Memories of Swinburne: with Other Essays. Edinburgh, 1910.

Clara Novello's Reminiscences. Compiled by Her Daughter, Contessa Valeria Gigliucci, with Memoir by A. D. Coleridge. 1910.

Ellis, S. M. William Harrison Ainsworth and His Friends. 2 vols. 1911.

—— George Meredith: His Life and Friends in relation to His Work. 1920.

Hueffer, F. M. Memories and Impressions. 1911. [Largely of Pre-Raphaelites.]

Williams, O. Life and Letters of John Rickman. 1911. [Lamb, Coleridge, Hunt, Hazlitt, etc.]

Collins, L. C. Life and Memoirs of John Churton Collins. 1912.

Wedmore, Sir F. Memories. [1912.]

Norton, Charles Eliot. Letters. 2 vols. 1913.

Letters of Edward Dowden and His Correspondents. Ed. E. D. and H. M. Dowden, 1914.

Francillon, R. E. Mid-Victorian Memories. 1914. [Lear, Lecky, Stephen, etc.]

Erskine, Mrs S. Anna Jameson: Letters and Friendships (1812–1860). [1915.]

Harris, Frank. Contemporary Portraits. 3 sers. New York, 1915–20.

—— Latest Contemporary Portraits. New York, [1927].

Putnam, G. H. Memories of a Publisher: 1865–1915. New York, 1915.

Whiteing, R. My Harvest. New York, 1915.

Escott, T. H. S. Great Victorians: Memories and Personalities. 1916.

Kernahan, C. In Good Company; Some Personal Recollections of Swinburne, Watts-Dunton, Wilde, etc. 1917.

Ley, J. W. T. The Dickens Circle: a Narrative of the Novelist's Friendships. 1918.

Ward, Mrs H. A Writer's Recollections. 2 vols. 1918. [Browning, Lewes, John Morley, Goldwin Smith.]

Betham-Edwards, M. Mid-Victorian Memories. New York, 1919. [Patmore, George Eliot, etc.]

Mallock, W. H. Memoirs of Life and Literature. 1920.

Aldrich, Mrs T. B. Crowding Memories. Boston, 1920. [Dickens, Wilde.]

Bax, E. B. Reminiscences and Reflections of a Mid and Late Victorian. New York, 1920. [Morris, Sharp, etc.]

Colvin, Sir S. Memories and Notes of Persons and Places 1852–1912. 1921. [Ruskin, Browning, Rossetti, Trelawny, Stevenson, etc.]

Yeats, W. B. Four Years, 1887–91. London Mercury, IV, 1921. [Huxley, Wilde, the Rhymers' Club, etc.]

Ainslie, D. Adventures: Social and Literary. [1922.] [Swinburne, Wilde, Pater, James, etc.]

Ticknor, C. Glimpses of Authors. Boston, 1922. [Anne Thackeray Ritchie, Dickens, Du Maurier, etc.]

Ridge, W. P. A Story Teller; Forty Years in London. [1923.]

—— I Like to Remember. [1925.]

Sichel, W. The Sands of Time: Recollections and Reflections. 1923.

Spencer, W. T. Forty Years in My Bookshop. Ed. T. Moult, 1923. [Meetings with Pater, Gissing, Jefferies, etc.]

Benson, A. C. Memories and Friends. 1924.

Taylor, Una. Guests and Memories. 1924. [Sir H. Taylor, Carlyle, Spedding, Jowett.]

Hill, C. Good Company in Old Westminster and the Temple. [1925.] [Founded on the early recollections of Anne (Rickman) Lefroy.]

Gray, W. F. An Unpublished Literary Correspondence. Cornhill Mag. LXI, 1926. [Includes letters of Wordsworth, Southey, Lamb, Landor, Shelley, Keats, Dickens, from the Watson Collection.]

Dent, H. R. The Memoirs of J. M. Dent, 1849–1926. 1928.

Lucas, E. V. The Colvins and Their Friends. [1928.]

Benson, E. F. As We Were: a Victorian Peep-Show, 1930.

A Victorian Vintage. Being a Selection of the Best Stories from the Diaries of the Right Hon. Sir Mountstuart E. Grant Duff. Ed. A. T. Bassett, 1930.

Masson, Flora. Victorians All. 1931. [Reminiscences of Dickens, Carlyle, Browning, etc.]

Rhys, E. Everyman Remembers. 1931.

Rothenstein, Sir W. Men and Memories; Recollections, 1872–1900. 1931. [Vol. II, (1900–1922), 1932.]

Whyte, F. A Bachelor's London, 1889–1914. 1931.

Newbolt, Sir H. My World as in My Time: Memoirs, 1862–1932. 1932. [Ruskin, Burne-Jones, Morris, etc.]

Roberts, M. Meetings with Some Men of Letters. Queen's Quart. XXXIX, 1932. [Meredith, Hardy, Doyle.]

Tuell, A. K. A Victorian at Bay. Boston, 1932. [Meredith, Christina Rossetti, Mrs Gaskell.]

Pollock, Sir F. Talkers I Have Known. Quarterly Rev. CCLXI, 1933. [Kinglake, Lyall, Maine, Meredith, Huxley, Swinburne, Tennyson.]

Jepson, E. Memories of a Victorian. Vol. I, 1933.

Masson, Rosaline. Poets, Patriots, and Lovers; Sketches and Memories of Famous People. 1933.

Compton-Rickett, A. I Look Back: Memories of Fifty Years. 1933.

Mackenzie, Compton. Literature in my Time. 1933.

Richards, Grant. Memories of a Misspent Youth: 1872–1896. 1933.

—— Memories of Years Spent Mainly in Publishing: 1897–1925. New York, 1934.

A Great Lady's Friendships: Letters to Mary, Marchioness of Salisbury, Countess of Derby, 1862–1890. Ed. Lady Burghclere, 1933. [Includes letters from Bulwer-Lytton, Lord Cowley, etc.]

Sharp, Evelyn. Unfinished Adventure. 1933. [Reminiscences of the Yellow Book Group, etc.]

Gougaud, L. La Société lettrée de Londres observée par un Écrivain français en 1839. Revue d'Histoire ecclésiastique, April 1934.

Milne, J. The Memoirs of a Bookman. 1934. [Tennyson, Rossetti, Meredith, Stevenson, etc.]

Ward, Maisie. The Wilfrid Wards and the Transition. Vol. I, 1934. [Ward's reminiscences of Gladstone, Jowett, Ruskin, Hulton, Newman, etc.]

Knox, E. A. Reminiscences of an Octogenarian: 1847–1934. 1935.

Patmore, D. Portrait of my Family. 1935. [Patmore, Carlyle, Hazlitt, Hunt, Browning, Tennyson.]

W. D. T.

II. LITERARY RELATIONS WITH THE CONTINENT

General Works; France; Germany; Italy; Spain and Portugal; Scandinavia; The Slavonic Countries; Other Countries.

(1) GENERAL WORKS

Arnold, M. Schools and Universities on the Continent. 1868.

Axon, W. A. E. Byron's Influence on European Literature. [In Stray Chapters on Literature, Folk Lore and Archaeology, 1888.]

Baldensperger, F. La grande Communion romantique de 1827: sous le Signe de Walter Scott. Revue de Littérature comparée, Jan.–March 1927.

Beers, H. A. A History of English Romanticism in the Nineteenth Century. New York, 1901.

Betz, L. P. La Littérature comparée. Essai bibliographique. Ed. F. Baldensperger, Strasburg, 1904.

Brandes, G. Naturalismen i England. [In Hovedströmninger i det 19. Aarhundredes Literatur, vol. IV, Copenhagen, 1875; tr. Eng. as Main Currents of Nineteenth Century Literature, 6 vols. 1901–5.]

Brauchli, J. Der englische Schauerroman um 1800. Zurich, 1928.

Buchan, J. Sir Walter Scott. 1932.

Cazamian, L. Quelques Réflexions sur les Problèmes d'influence. Revue germanique, XII, 1921.

Chasles, V. E. P. Vie et Influence de Byron sur son Époque. [In Études sur la Littérature et les Mœurs de l'Angleterre au XIXe Siècle, Paris, 1850.]

Chiarini, G. Lord Byron nella Politica e nella Letteratura della prima Metà del Secolo. Nuova Antologia, XXXIV, 1891.

Cosmopolis. An International Review. 1896–8.

Courthope, W. J. A History of English Poetry, vol. VI, 1910.

Dechamps, J. La Légende de Napoléon et la Littérature comparée. Revue de littérature comparée, IX, 1929.

Elton, O. A Survey of English Literature, 1780–1830. 2 vols. 1912. [Especially vol. I, pp. 23 ff.; vol. II, pp. 405 ff. and notes.]

Foreign Review and Continental Miscellany. 1828–30.

Foreign Quarterly Review. 1827–46.

Frierson, W. C. The English Controversy over Realism in Fiction, 1885–1895. PMLA. XLIII, 1928.

Herford, C. H. The Age of Wordsworth. 1897.

Index Translationum. Paris, 1932– .

Jabram-Desrivaux, L. Thomas Hardy, Européen. Point et Virgule, July 1928.

Jacks, W. Robert Burns in Other Tongues. A Critical Review of the Translations of the Songs and Poems of Robert Burns. Glasgow, 1896.

Kelso, A. P. Matthew Arnold on Continental Life and Literature. 1914.

Kraeger, H. Der byronische Heldentypus. Munich, 1898.

Krug, W. G. Lord Byron als dichterische Gestalt in England, Frankreich, Deutschland und Amerika. Giessen, 1931.

Lecky, W. E. H. History of Rationalism in Europe. 1865.

Loliée, F. A. Short History of Comparative Literature. Tr. Eng. 1906.

Maychrzak, F. Lord Byron als Übersetzer. E. Studien, XXI, XXII, 1895–6.

Merz, J. T. History of European Thought in the Nineteenth Century. 3 vols. 1903.

Omond, T. S. The Romantic Triumph. Edinburgh, 1900.

Pizzo, E. S. T. Coleridge als Kritiker. Ang. XXVIII, 1916.

Reynaud, L. Le Romantisme. Ses Origines anglo-germaniques. Paris, 1926.

Richardson, G. F. A Neglected Aspect of the English Romantic Revolt. Berkeley, 1915.

Richter, H. Geschichte der englischen Romantik. 2 vols. Halle, 1911–6.

Robertson, J. G. The Genesis of Romantic Theory in the Eighteenth Century. Cambridge, 1923.

Rose, W. and Isaacs, J. Contemporary Movements in European Literature. 1928.

Saintsbury, G. History of Criticism. Vol. III, Edinburgh, 1904.

Storoschenko, N. J. Byrons Einfluss auf die europäische Literatur. Iz oblasti literatury, Moscow, 1902.

Storr, V. F. The Development of English Thought in the Nineteenth Century, 1800–1860. 1913.

Van Tieghem, P. Le Mouvement romantique (Angleterre—Allemagne—Italie—France): Textes choisis, commentés et annotés. Paris, 1912.

—— La Littérature comparée. Paris, 1931.

Vaughan, C. E. The Romantic Revolt. Edinburgh, 1900.

—— The Influence of English Poetry upon the Romantic Revival on the Continent. Proc. British Academy, VI, 1913–4.

Weddigen, F. H. O. Lord Byrons Einfluss auf die europäischen Literaturen der Neuzeit. Hanover, 1884.

Williams, O. Is there a European Literature? National Rev. Feb. 1932.

[For the influence of Shakespeare on continental literature in the nineteenth century see vol. I, pp. 599–608 above. For trns of Byron's works into foreign languages see pp. 187–212 below. After Shakespeare and Byron the most popular English authors abroad were Dickens (for trns see pp. 435–55 below), Lytton (pp. 475–8 below), Moore (pp. 184–6 below), Scott (pp. 369–80 below) and Shelley (pp. 212–8 below).]

(2) THE LITERARY RELATIONS OF ENGLAND AND FRANCE

(a) General Works

Angell, J. B. Influence of English Literature upon the French. North American Rev. LXXXVI, 1858.

Archer, W. English Analyses of French Plays. 1879.

Arnold, M. The Popular Education of France, with Notices of that of Holland and Switzerland. 1861.

—— A French Eton; or, Middle Class Education and the State. 1864.

Audra, E. L'Influence de Ruskin en France. Revue des Cours et Conférences, Jan. 1926.

Bain, M. Les Voyageurs français en Écosse (1770–1830) et leurs Curiosités intellectuelles. Paris, 1931.

Bardoux, J. Le Mouvement idéaliste et social dans la Littérature anglaise au XIXe Siècle. John Ruskin. [Paris, 1900.]

Barlow, G. French Plays and English Audiences. Contemporary Rev. Aug. 1893.

Beránek, V. Chateaubriand über die Engländer und Franzosen. Bielitz, 1885.

Beyer, A. Walter Paters Beziehungen zur französischen Literatur und Kultur. Halle, 1931.

Blanc, L. Lettres sur l'Angleterre. Paris, 1865–7.

Blanqui, A. Voyage d'un jeune Français en Angleterre et en Écosse pendant l'Automne. Paris, 1823. [Cf. C.-A. Sainte-Beuve, Le Globe, I, 1825, p. 291.]

Brémond, H. L'Inquiétude religieuse. Ser. 1, Paris, 1919. [Oxford Movement.]

Carré, J. M. Stevenson et la France. [In Mélanges Baldensperger, Paris, 1930.]

Cazamian, L. Le Roman social en Angleterre (1830–1850): Dickens, Disraeli, Mrs Gaskell, Kingsley. 1903.

—— Les Sentiments anglais et l'Entente Cordiale. Revue de l'Enseignement des Langues Vivantes, XXVII, 1910.

Charpentier, J. La Poésie britannique et Baudelaire. Mercure de France, 15 April, 1 May 1921.

Chasles, V. E. P. Études sur la Littérature et les Mœurs de l'Angleterre au XIXe Siècle. Paris, 1850. [See Margaret Phillips, Philarète Chasles, Critique et Historien de la Littérature anglaise, Paris, 1933.]

Chateaubriand, F. R., Vicomte de. Essai sur la Littérature anglaise, Fragment, en Tête de Souvenirs d'Italie, d'Angleterre, et d'Amérique. 1815. [See North American Rev. Oct. 1839, and W. H. Prescott, Chateaubriand's English Literature, in Biographical and Critical Miscellanies, 1845, pp. 215 ff.]

Chefs-d'œuvre des Théâtres étrangers traduits en français. 1822–3.

Curzon, A. de. Les Français en Angleterre sous le Premier Empire. Nouvelle Revue, 15 Dec. 1924, 1 Jan. 1925.

Dechamps, J. Il y a cent Ans. Propos Stendhaliens. Revue des Études Napoléoniennes, XIX, 1922. [England and Napoleon.]

—— Chateaubriand en Angleterre. Paris, 1933.

—— Napoléon en Angleterre. French Quart. x, 1928.

Delattre, F. Swinburne et la France. Revue des Cours et Conférences, Feb. 1926.

Dempsey, M. A Contribution to the Study of the Sources of the Génie du Christianisme. Paris, 1927–8. [Louth, T. Maurice, Milton, Addison, Ossian.]

Draper, F. W. M. The Rise and Fall of the French Romantic Drama, with Special Reference to the Influence of Shakespeare, Scott, and Byron. 1923.

Du Bos, C. Note sur Browning en France. [In Approximations, ser. 2, Paris, 1927.]

Elkington, M. E. Les Relations de Société entre l'Angleterre et la France sous la Restauration (1814–1830). Paris, 1929.

Engel, C. E. Les Influences littéraires anglaises dans l'Œuvre de Verlaine. Revue de Littérature comparée, x, 1930.

Evans, D. O. French Romanticism and British Reviewers. French Quart. IX, 1927.

Faucher, L. Études sur l'Angleterre. Paris, 1845.

Ferguson, W. D. The Influence of Flaubert on George Moore. Philadelphia, 1934.

Forgues, E. Originaux et beaux Esprits de l'Angleterre contemporaine. Paris, 1860.

La France et la Grande-Bretagne: des Rapports littéraires, etc. Revue Européenne, Aug. 1824.

Frierson, W. C. L'Influence du Naturalisme français sur les Romanciers anglais de 1885 à 1900. Paris, [1925].

—— Realism in the Eighteen-Nineties and the Maupassant School in England. French Quart. x, 1928.

Givry, G. de. De l'Influence anglaise sur la Littérature française au XIXe Siècle. The Green Leaf, 15 March 1927.

Gosse, Sir E. French Profiles. 1905. [Includes The Influence of France upon English Poetry.]

—— Lamartine and the English Poets. Browning in France. [Both in More Books on the Table, 1923.]

Hamerton, P. G. French and English. Atlantic Monthly, LVIII, LIX, 1866; 1889.

Hazlitt, W. Notes on a Journey through France and Italy. 1826.

Henley, W. E. Views and Reviews. 1890. [Dumas, Hugo, Rabelais, Banville, Balzac, Labiche, Champfleury.]

Heylli, G. d'. La Comédie française à Londres (1871–1879). Journal de E. Got. Journal de F. Sarcey. Paris, 1880.

Holdsworth, F. Joseph de Maistre et l'Angleterre. Paris, 1936.

Jäckel, H. Der Engländer im Spiegel der französischen Literatur von der Romantik bis zum Weltkrieg. Breslau, 1932.

Jones, E. Les Voyageurs français en Angleterre de 1815 à 1830. Paris, 1930.

Jusserand, J. J. Histoire littéraire du peuple Anglais. 3 vols. 1894–1911.

Lallemand, P. de. Montalembert et ses Relations littéraires avec l'Étranger. Paris, 1928.

Lami, E. Voyage en Angleterre. Paris, 1829–30.

Lang, A. Ballads and Lyrics of Old France. 1872.

Lanson, G. Manuel bibliographique de la Littérature française moderne, 1500–1900. Vol. IV, pp. 949 ff.; 1119 ff.; 1147 ff. Paris, 1913, 1925. [For trns of English writers into French and for literary relations.]

Larat, J. Un Voyageur romantique en Angleterre: Charles Nodier. Anglo-French Rev. Dec. 1920.

Ledru-Rollin, A. P. A. De la Décadence de l'Angleterre. Paris, 1850.

Lehmann, K. Die Auffassung und Gestaltung des Napoleonproblems im englischen Drama. Erlangen, 1931.

Lockwood, H. D. Tools and the Man. A Comparative Study of the French Working-Man and the English Chartists in the Literature of 1830–48. New York, 1927.

Loève-Veimars, F. A. Ballades, Légendes et Chants populaires de l'Angleterre et de l'Écosse. Paris, 1825.

Looten, C. Le Romantisme de Taine. Revue Anglo-Américaine, Feb. 1933.

Maurois, A. Taine et l'Angleterre. Nouvelle Littérature, 2 June 1928.

Michiels, J. A. X. Souvenirs d'Angleterre. Paris, 1844.

Middleton Murry, J. Chronique anglaise. Revue de Genève, VII, VIII, 1923. [French and Russian influence.]

Miller, M. H. Chateaubriand and English Literature. 1929.

Minckwitz, M. J. Einige Beziehungen der englischen Dichterin E. Barrett-Browning zu Frankreich, ins besondere zur französischen Literatur. Zeitschrift für französische Sprache und Literatur, XXVIII, 1906.

Mönch, W. Ch. Nodier und die deutsche und englische Literatur. Berlin, 1931.

Moraud, Marcel. The French Drama in England, 1815–1840. Rice Inst. Pamphlet, April 1928.

—— Le Romantisme français en Angleterre de 1814 à 1848. Paris, 1933.

—— La France de la Restauration d'après les Visiteurs anglais. Paris, 1933.

Mott, L. F. Renan and Matthew Arnold. MLN. XXXIII, 1918.

Murray, K. Taine und die englische Romantik. Munich, 1914.

Needham, H. A. Le Développement de l'Esthétique sociologique en France et en Angleterre au XIXe Siècle. Paris, 1926.

Nolva, R. de. Les Sources anglaises de Leconte de Lisle. Mercure de France, 1 July 1922.

Parigot, H. Le Drame d'Alexandre Dumas. Paris, 1899. [Ch. II.]

Partridge, E. The French Romantics' Knowledge of English Literature, 1820–1848. Paris, 1924.

Pernicious Literature [Zola]. Debate in the House of Commons. With Opinions of the Press. National Vigilance Ass. [1889.]

Phillips, E. M. Sainte-Beuve and the Lake Poets. French Quart. VIII, 1926.

Phillips, E. M. Sainte-Beuve's Criticism of English Poetry. French Quart. IX, 1927.

—— Sainte-Beuve's Criticism of English Prose. French Quart. XIII, 1931.

Pichot, A. Voyage historique et littéraire en Angleterre et en Écosse. 3 vols. Paris, 1825. [Cf. C.-A. Sainte-Beuve, Le Globe, II, 1825, pp. 921, 950, 1027.]

Potez, H. Le Romantisme français et l'Influence anglaise. La Quinzaine, 1 and 16 Oct. 1899.

Qualia, C. B. French Dramatic Sources of Bulwer Lytton's Richelieu. PMLA. XLII, 1927.

Quesnel, L. Le Théâtre anglais contemporain. Revue bleue, no. 25, 1882.

Rathery, J. B. Des Relations sociales et intellectuelles entre la France et l'Angleterre. Paris, 1856.

Renard, G. L'Influence de l'Angleterre sur la France depuis 1830. Nouvelle Revue, XXXV, 1885, pp. 675 ff.

Reul, P. de. Swinburne et la France, Essai de littérature comparée. Brussels, 1904.

Revue anglo-française. Poitiers, 1833–7; 1839–43.

Revue britannique. Paris, 1825– .

Richter, L. Swinburne's Verhältnis zu Frankreich und Italien. Leipzig, 1911.

Roe, F. C. Taine et l'Angleterre. Paris, 1923.

Romer, C. Matthew Arnold and some French Poets [Lamartine, Senancour, Maurice de Guérin, Vigny]. Nineteenth Century, June 1926.

Rudler, G. L'Angleterre et Jeanne d'Arc: de Michelet à Anatole France. French Quart. II, 1920.

Sainte-Beuve, C.-A. Causeries du Lundi. Paris, 1851–62.

Saroléa, C. L'Influence de la Culture française sur la Culture anglaise. Revue française d'Édimbourg, I, 1897.

—— Le Commerce des Idées entre la France et l'Angleterre. Revue de Belgique, 1896–7.

—— Robert Louis Stevenson and France. Edinburgh, 1893.

Schmidt, K. Robert Browning's Verhältnis zu Frankreich. Berlin, 1909.

Sells, I. E. Matthew Arnold and France. The Poet. Cambridge, 1935.

Shepherd, R. H. Bibliography of Swinburne. 1888 (2nd edn.)

Sherard, R. H. Twenty Years in Paris; some Recollections of a Literary Life. 1905.

—— Life of Oscar Wilde. With Bibliography. 1911.

Simond, L. Voyage d'un François en Angleterre. Paris, 1816, 1817.

Smith, Austin. L'Influence des Lakistes sur les Romantiques français. Paris, 1920.

Smith, M. E. Une Anglaise intellectuelle en France sous la Restauration: Mary Clarke. Paris, 1927.

Souriau, M. Introduction à la Préface de Cromwell. Paris, 1897.

Symons, A. Studies in Two Literatures. 1897.

—— The Symbolist Movement in France. 1899; 1908.

Taine, H. Histoire de la Littérature anglaise. Paris, 1863.

Texte, J. Les Relations littéraires de la France avec l'Étranger de 1799 à 1848. [In L. Petit de Julleville, Histoire de la Langue et de la Littérature française des Origines à 1900, vol. VII, Paris, 1899.]

Thomas, J. H. L'Angleterre dans l'Œuvre de Victor Hugo. Paris, 1934.

Tronchon, H. Renan et l'Angleterre. Revue de Littérature comparée, VII, 1927.

Verlaine, P. Notes on England, Myself as a French Master. [London?], 1894.

Ward, W. Newman and Sabatier. Fortnightly Rev. LXXV, 1901.

[The influence of French comedy and farce on English playwrights in the nineteenth century is too vast to receive adequate notice here. The following were among the most successful adapters of French plays to the English stage: D. Boucicault, R. B. Brough, J. Brougham, C. H. Coghlan, J. S. Coyne, S. Grundy, J. M. Morton, T. Taylor. See also pp. 580–628 below.]

(b) Single authors

(i) French

Balzac, Honoré de (1799–1850).
    Balzac in England. Athenaeum, 14 Aug. 1897.
    The Style of Balzac and Thackeray. Dublin University Mag. LXIII, 1864.

Baudelaire, Charles (1821–1867). Les Fleurs du Mal. Paris, 1857, 1861.
    Swinburne, A. C. Poems and Ballads. 3 sers. 1866–89.
    Aubry, J. Baudelaire et Swinburne. Mercure de France, Oct. 1917.
    Delattre, F. Charles Baudelaire et le jeune A. C. Swinburne 1861–1867. [In Mélanges Baldensperger, Paris, 1930.]
    Lafourcade, G. Swinburne and Baudelaire. Revue Anglo-Américaine, II, 1924.
    Symons, A. Charles Baudelaire. 1920.
    Turquet-Milnes, G. The Influence of Baudelaire in France and England. 1913.

Comte, Auguste (1798–1857). Système de Politique positive. Paris, 1822; Paris, 1851–4.
    —— Discours sur l'Ensemble du Positivisme. Paris, 1848.

Comte, Auguste. Cours de Philosophie positive. Paris, 1839–42.
    The Positive Philosophy of Auguste Comte. Tr. Harriet Martineau, 1853.
    The Catechism of Positive Religion. Tr. R. Congreve, 1858.
    Comte's General View of Positivism. Tr. J. H. Bridges, 1865.
    Comte's System of Positive Polity. Tr. J. H. Bridges, E. S. Beesly, R. Congreve, F. Harrison, et al. 1875–7.
    Beesly, E. S. Comte, the Successor of Aristotle and St Paul. 1883.
    —— Comte as a Moral Type. 1885.
    Bridges, J. H. The Unity of Comte's Life and Doctrine—a Reply to J. S. Mill. 1866.
    —— Five Discourses on Positive Religion. 1882.
    —— Essays and Addresses. 1907.
    Faguet, E. Auguste Comte et Stuart Mill. Revue bleue, no. 14, 1899.
    Gaupp, Otto. Auguste Comte und Herbert Spencer. Die Gegenwart, no. 23, 1893.
    Lewes, G. H. Comte's Philosophy of the Positive Sciences. 1853.
    Mill, J. S. Auguste Comte and Positivism. 1865.
    —— Lettres inédites à Auguste Comte, publiées par L. Lévy-Brühl. Paris, 1899.
    Souday, P. La Correspondance de Stuart Mill et d'Auguste Comte. Le Temps, 31 Jan. 1899.
    Whittaker, T. Comte and Mill. 1908.
    Buckle, H. T. History of Civilisation in England. 2 vols. 1857–61.
    Lecky, W. E. H. History of the Rise and Influence of the Spirit of Rationalism in Europe. 1865. [See Mrs Lecky's Memoir of W. E. H. Lecky, 1909.]

Cousin, Victor (1792–1867). Cours de philosophie, Introduction à l'Histoire de la Philosophie. Paris, 1828.
    Introduction to the History of Philosophy. Tr. H. G. Linberg, Boston, 1832.
    Course of the History of Modern Philosophy. Tr. O. W. Wight, Edinburgh, 1852.
    Hamilton, Sir William. The Philosophy of the Unconditioned. Edinburgh Rev. Oct. 1829.

Daudet, Alphonse (1840–1897). Tartarin de Tarascon. Paris, 1872.
    Works. Tr. 1896.
    Delattre, F. Daudet et l'Angleterre. [In Dickens et la France, Paris, 1927.]
    Favreau, A. R. British Criticism of Daudet, 1872–9. PMLA. LII, 1937.
    Le Roux, H. M. Alphonse Daudet à l'Étranger. Revue bleue, 4 April 1885.
    Sherard, R. H. Alphonse Daudet. 1894.

Diderot, Denis (1713–1784).
Carlyle, T. Diderot. Foreign Quarterly Rev. xi, 1833.
Dumas, Alexandre (1803–1870). Le Comte de Monte Cristo. Paris, 1844–5.
The Count of Monte-Cristo. Tr. 1845.
—— Les Trois Mousquetaires. Paris, 1844.
The Three Musketeers. Tr. 1846; tr. W. Robson, 1853. [For other trns see BM. catalogue.]
Roberts, W. Dumas and Sue in England. Nineteenth Century, Nov. 1922.
Schwartz, H. S. The Influence of Dumas on Oscar Wilde. French Rev. vii, 1933.
Dumas, Alexandre, fils (1824–1895).
Archer, W. Dumas and the English Stage. Cosmopolis, Feb. 1896.
Fénelon, François de Salignac de la Mothe (1651–1715). Télémaque. The Hague, 1699.
Lamb, Charles. The Adventures of Ulysses. 1808.
Gaboriau, Émile (1835–1873). L'Affaire Lerouge. Paris, 1866.
—— Monsieur Lecoq. Paris, 1869.
Gaboriau's Sensational Novels. Tr. 1881; 1884 (bis).
Hugo, Victor (1802–1885). Cromwell. Paris, 1827.
Swinburne, A. C. Bothwell. 1874.
—— Notre Dame de Paris. Paris, 1831.
Fitzball, E. Esmeralda; or, the Hunchback of Notre Dame. 1834. [Dramatic adaptation.]
—— Le Roi s'amuse. Paris, 1832.
Taylor, T. The Fool's Revenge. 1869.
—— Ruy Blas. Paris, 1838.
Davidson, J. A Queen's Romance. 1904.
—— Les Châtiments. Brussels, 1852.
Swinburne, A. C. Dirae. 1873.
—— L'Art d'être Grandpère. Paris, 1877.
Swinburne, A. C. A Dark Month. 1882.
Bowley, V. E. A. English Versions of Victor Hugo's Plays. French Quart. x, 1928.
—— Notre-Dame and Les Misérables on the English Stage. French Quart. xi, 1929.
Stevenson, R. L. Victor Hugo's Romances. [In Familiar Studies of Men and Books, 1882.]
Swinburne, A. C. A Study of Victor Hugo. 1886.
Joubert, Joseph (1734–1824). Pensées et Correspondance. Paris, 1842.
Arnold, M. Joubert. [In Essays in Criticism, 1865.]
La Rochefoucauld, François, Duc de (1613–1689). Maximes. Paris, 1665.
Hazlitt, W. Characteristics, in the Manner of Rochefoucauld's Maxims. 1823; 1837.

Marmontel, Jean-François (1723–1799). Contes Moraux. Paris, 1758.
Edgeworth, Maria. Moral Tales. 1801.
Maupassant, Guy de (1850–1893). Une Vie. Paris, 1883.
—— Bel ami. Paris, 1885.
—— La Petite Roque. Paris, 1886.
Crackanthorpe, H. Wreckage. 1893.
Dowson, E. Dilemmas. 1895.
Morrison, A. Tales of Mean Streets. 1894.
Wedmore, Sir F. Renunciations. 1893.
Chassé, C. Maupassant et l'Angleterre. Langues Modernes, July 1926.
Frierson, W. C. Realism in the Eighteen-Nineties and the Maupassant School in England. French Quart. x, 1928.
Rousseau, Jean Jacques (1712–1778). Émile. 1762.
Edgeworth, R. L. Practical Education. 1798.
—— Professional Education. 1809.
Spencer, Herbert. Education, Intellectual, Moral and Physical. 1861.
Schmidt, O. Rousseau und Byron. Ein Beitrag zur vergleichenden Literaturgeschichte des Revolutionszeitalters. Oppeln, 1890.
Sardou, Victorien (1831–1908). Les Pattes de Mouche. Paris, 1860.
Simpson, J. P. A Scrap of Paper. 1861.
—— Dora. 1877.
Stephenson, B. C. and Scott, C. Diplomacy. 1878.
Hart, J. A. Sardou and the Sardou Plays. 1913.
Staël-Holstein, Mme de (1766–1817). De l'Allemagne. Paris, 1810; London, 1813.
Whitford, R. C. Madame de Staël's Literary Reputation in England. Illinois University Stud. 1918.
Sue, Eugène (1804–1857). Les Mystères de Paris. Paris, 1842.
Mysteries of Paris. 1843. [Several trns.]
—— Le Juif errant. Paris, 1844–5.
The Wandering Jew. Tr. 1845; tr. H. D. Miles, 1846; tr. H. L. Williams, 1868.
Roberts, W. Dumas and Sue in England. Nineteenth Century, Nov. 1922.
Verne, Jules (1828–1905). Cinq Semaines en Ballon: Voyages et Découvertes en Afrique par trois Anglais. Paris, 1863.
Five Weeks in a Balloon. Tr. 1870.
—— Vingt Mille Lieues sous les Mers. Paris, 1869.
Twenty Thousand Leagues under the Sea. Tr. 1873.
[For other trns see BM. catalogue and p. 576 below. Verne's popularity in England was only equalled by that of Dumas.]

Vidocq, François Eugène (1775–1857). Mémoires de Vidocq, Chef de la Police de Sûreté. Paris, 1828–9.
   Memoirs of Vidocq. Tr. H. T. R., 1828–9.
Vigny, Alfred de (1797–1863).
   Poems and Romances of Alfred de Vigny. Westminster Rev. xxxi, 1838.
   Lebbin, E. Alfred de Vignys Beziehungen zu England und zu englischer Literatur. Halle, 1936.
Volney, Constantin-François Chassebœuf, Comte (1757–1820). Les Ruines ou Méditations sur les Révolutions des Empires. Paris, 1791.
   Kellner, L. Shelley's Queen Mab and Volney's Les Ruines. E. Studien, xxii, 1896.
Voltaire, François-Marie Arouet de (1694–1778).
   Carlyle, T. Voltaire. Foreign Rev. iii, 1829.
Zola, Émile (1840–1903). L'Assommoir. Paris, 1877.
   The 'Assommoir.' Tr. 1884.
   Reade, C. Drink. 1879. [Dramatic adaptation.]
   —— La Débâcle. Paris, 1891.
   The Downfall. Tr. E. A. Vizetelly, 1892. [Other novels were tr. by E. A. and E. Vizetelly and Count S. C. de Soissons, 1884–92.]
   Maugham, W. S. Liza of Lambeth. 1897.
   Moore, G. Esther Waters. 1894.
   Morrison, A. Tales of Mean Streets. 1894.
   Decker, C. R. Zola's Literary Reputation in England. PMLA. xlix, 1934.
   Ellis, Havelock. Zola: the Man and his Work. The Savoy, no. 1, 1896.
   Jean-Aubry, G. Zola et George Moore. Nouvelles littéraires, 17 Jan. 1925.
   Vizetelly, E. A. Émile Zola, Novelist and Reformer. 1904.

(ii) English

Austen, Jane. Sense and Sensibility. 1811. Tr. Isabelle de Montolieu, Paris, 1815.
—— Pride and Prejudice. 1813. Tr. Paris, 1822.
—— Mansfield Park. 1814. Tr. H. Villemain, Paris, 1816.
—— Emma. 1816. Tr. Paris, 1816.
—— Northanger Abbey. 1818. Tr. Hyacinthe de Ferrières, Paris, 1834.
—— Persuasion. 1818. Tr. Isabelle de Montolieu, Paris, 1821.
Brontë, Charlotte. Jane Eyre. 1847. Tr. Mme Lesbazeilles-Souvestre, Paris, 1854.
—— Shirley. 1849. Tr. C. Romey, Paris, 1859.

Brontë, Charlotte. The Professor. 1857. Tr. H. Loreau, Paris, 1858.
Brontë, Anne. Agnes Grey. Tr. A. Rolet, Paris, 1859.
Browning, Robert.
   Gosse, Sir E. Browning in France. [In More Books on the Table, 1923.]
   Du Bos, C. Note sur Browning en France. [In Approximations, ser. 2, Paris, 1927.]
Browning, Elizabeth Barrett. Sonnets from the Portuguese. 1847.
   Les Sonnets du Portugais. Tr. L. Morel, 1903; tr. F. Henry, 1905.
   Des Guerrois, C. Étude sur Mrs Élisabeth Browning, suivie de ses 44 Sonnets portugais. Paris, 1885.
   Texte, J. Élisabeth Browning et l'Idéalisme contemporain. [In Études de Littérature européenne, Paris, 1898.]
   Mrs Browning in French. Academy, 20 June 1903.
Buckle, Henry Thomas. History of Civilisation in England. 1857–1861.
   Histoire de la Civilisation en Angleterre. Tr. A. Baillot, Paris, 1865.
Burns, Robert.
   Poésies complètes. Tr. L. de Wailly, Paris, 1843. [Selection.] Tr. R. de la Madelaine, Rouen, 1874.
   Demonceaux, L. Poésies imitées de Burns. Paris, 1865.
   Angellier, A. Robert Burns. Paris, 1893.
   Power, W. Burns's French Interpreter [A. Angellier]. [In Cahier Angellier, Paris, 1927. See also W. Jacks, Robert Burns in Other Tongues, Glasgow, 1896.]
Byron, George Gordon, Baron.
   Œuvres complètes de Lord Byron. Tr. Amédée Pichot et Eusèbe de Salle, Paris, 1814–20. [Introduction by Charles Nodier.] Tr. M. Paulin, Paris, 1830–1; tr. B. Laroche, Paris, 1836–7.
   Œuvres [incomplete]. Tr. Orby Hunter and Pascal Ramé, Paris, 1845; tr. 'D. Lesueur' (i.e. Jeanne Loiseau), Paris, 1891–1906.
   Boissy, Marquise de. Byron jugé par les Témoins de sa Vie. Paris, 1868.
   Clark, W. J. Byron und die romantische Poesie in Frankreich. Leipzig, 1901.
   Dargan, E. P. Byron's Fame in France. Virginia Quart. ii, 1926.
   Estève, E. Byron et le Romantisme français. Paris, 1907, 1929.
   —— Le Byronisme de Leconte de Lisle. Revue de Littérature comparée, v, 1925.
   Hugo, V. Lord Byron et ses Rapports avec la Littérature actuelle. Annales romantiques, 1827–8.

Mazure, A. Étude morale sur Lord Byron et sur son Influence à l'égard de la Littérature contemporaine en France. Revue anglo-française, I. Poitiers, 1833.

Muoni, G. La Leggenda del Byron in Francia. [In Poesia notturna pre-romantica, Florence, 1908.]

Pichot, A. Essais sur lord Byron. Paris, 1825.

Ritter, O. Byron und Chateaubriand. Archiv, CIX, 1902.

Vigny, A. de. Œuvres de Lord Byron. Le Conservateur littéraire, III, Paris, 1820.

Weddigen, F. H. O. Lord Byron's Einfluss auf die französische Litteratur. Archiv, LXIX, 1883.

Campbell, Thomas (1777–1844).
Ascher, J. Alfred de Vigny and Thomas Campbell. French Quart. IV, 1922.

Carlyle, Thomas. Sartor Resartus. 1833–4. Tr. E. Barthélemy, Paris, 1899–1904.
—— Critical and Miscellaneous Essays. 1839. Essais choisis de critique et de morale. Tr. E. Barthélemy, Paris, 1907. Nouveaux Essais choisis de Critique et de Morale. Tr. E. Barthélemy, Paris, 1909.
—— The French Revolution. 1837. Histoire de la Révolution française. Tr. E. Regnault, O. Barot and J. Roche, Paris, 1865–7. Les Hommes de la Révolution française. Tr. H. Fauvel, Paris, 1888.
—— On Heroes, Hero-Worship and the Heroic in History. 1841. Les Héros, le culte du Héros, et l'Héroïque dans l'Histoire. Tr. J. Izoulet-Labatières, Paris, 1887.

Taine, H. A. L'Idéalisme anglais, Étude sur Carlyle. Paris, 1864.
Taylor, A. C. Carlyle: sa première Fortune littéraire en France (1825–1865). Paris, 1929.

Crabbe, George.
Roth, G. Sainte-Beuve, Crabbe et le Conte en Vers. French Quart. III, 1921.

Darwin, Charles Robert. On the Origin of Species by means of Natural Selection. 1859. De l'Origine des Espèces. Tr. C. Royer, 1862; tr. J. J. Moulinié, 1873; tr. E. Barbier, 1876.
—— The Descent of Man. 1871. La Descendance de l'Homme. Tr. J. J. Moulinié, 1872; tr. E. Barbier, 1881.

De Quincey, Thomas. Confessions of an English Opium-Eater. 1821. L'Anglais Mangeur d'Opium. Tr. A. de Musset, 1828.

Clapton, G. T. Baudelaire et De Quincey. Paris, 1931.

Lalou, R. De Thomas de Quincey à Baudelaire. Revue germanique, XIV, 1923.
Littlefield, W. Alfred de Musset and the English Opium-Eater. Bookman, July 1902.

Dickens, Charles. Posthumous Papers of the Pickwick Club. 1837–8. Le Club des Pickwickistes. Tr. E. Niboyet. Paris, 1838. Aventures de M. Pickwick. Tr. P. Grolier and P. Lorain, Paris, 1859.
—— Oliver Twist. 1838. Tr. L. Bénard, Paris, 1841; A. Girardin, Paris, 1858.
—— Nicholas Nickleby. 1839. Tr. E. de la Bedollière, Paris, 1839–40.
—— The Old Curiosity Shop. 1840. Le Marchand d'Antiquités. Tr. A. J. B. Defauconpret, Paris, 1841. Le Magasin d'Antiquités. Tr. A. des Essarts, Paris, 1857.

Delattre, F. Dickens et la France. Paris, 1927.
Heussey, R. du P. Dickens à Paris. Le Livre, VII, 1886.
Usanne, O. Charles Dickens en France. Le Livre, X, 1889.

Disraeli, Benjamin (Earl of Beaconsfield). Coningsby, or the New Generation. 1844. La jeune Angleterre. Tr. A. Sobry, Paris, 1846.
—— Sybil, or the Two Nations. 1845. Les deux Nations. Tr. Mme Audley, Paris, 1847; tr. P. Lorain, Paris, 1859.
—— Lothair. 1870. Tr. C. B. Derosne, Paris, 1872.
—— Endymion. 1880. Tr. J. Girardin, Paris, 1881.

'Eliot, George' (i.e. Mary Ann Cross, born Evans). Scenes from Clerical Life. 1858. Scènes de la vie ecclésiastique. Tr. F. d'Albert-Durade, Paris, 1884.
—— Adam Bede. 1859. Tr. F. d'Albert-Durade, Paris, 1861.
—— The Mill on the Floss. 1860. La Famille Tulliver, ou le Moulin sur la Floss. Tr. F. d'Albert-Durade, Paris, 1863.
—— Silas Marner. 1861. Tr. F. d'Albert-Durade, Paris, 1863; tr. M. Maisonrouge, Paris, 1885; tr. A. Malfroy, Paris, 1887; tr. L. Morel, Paris, 1890.
—— Middlemarch. 1872. Tr. M.-J. M., Paris, 1890.
—— Daniel Deronda. 1876. Tr. J. David, Paris, 1881.

Gaskell, Elizabeth Cleghorn. The Sexton's Hero. 1847. Le Héros du Fossoyeur. Tr. E. D. Forgues, Paris, 1867.
—— Cranford. 1853. Tr. L. S. Belloc, Paris, 1856.

Gaskell, Elizabeth Cleghorn. A Dark Night's Work. 1863.
L'Œuvre d'une Nuit. Tr. E. D. Forgues, Paris, 1867.
—— Sylvia's Lovers. 1863.
Les Amoureux de Sylvia. Tr. E. D. Forgues, Paris, 1865.
—— Cousin Phyllis. 1864.
Cousine Phillis. Tr. E. D. Forgues, Paris, 1867.
Hopkins, A. B. Mrs Gaskell in France, 1849–1890. PMLA. LIII, 1938.
Green, John Richard. A Short History of the English People. 1874.
Histoire moderne du Peuple anglais. Tr. Mary Hunt, Paris, 1885.
—— History of the English People. 1877–80. Tr. A. Monod, Paris, 1888.
Hallam, Henry. A View of the State of Europe during the Middle Ages. 1818.
L'Europe au Moyen Age. Tr. A. Borghers and P. Dudouit, Brussels, 1820–2.
—— The Constitutional History of England. 1827.
Histoire constitutionnelle d'Angleterre. Ed. F. P. G. Guizot, Paris, 1832.
Mignet, F. A. M. Hallam. [In Éloges Historiques, Paris, 1839–40.]
Lewis, Matthew Gregory. The Monk. A Romance. 1796.
Le Moine. Tr. Paris, 1801–2.
Baldensperger, F. Le Moine de Lewis dans la Littérature française. Journ. Comparative Lit. III, 1903.
Bulwer-Lytton, E. G. E. L. (Baron Lytton). Pelham. 1828. Tr. J. Cohen, Paris, 1836.
—— Eugene Aram. 1832; tr. J. Cohen, Paris, 1832; tr. A. J. B. Defauconpret, Paris, 1842; tr. M. Frater, Paris, 1873.
—— The Last Days of Pompeii. 1834.
Les derniers Jours de Pompeii. Tr. H. Lucas, Paris, 1859.
—— Rienzi. 1835. Tr. Paris, 1859.
—— The Caxtons. 1850.
La Famille Caxton. Tr. A. Pichot, Paris, 1853; tr. E. Scheffter, Paris, 1857; tr. Mme Bressant, Paris, 1859.
Macaulay, Thomas Babington, Baron.
Œuvres diverses. Tr. A. Pichot, J. and E. D. Forgues, Paris, 1860.
—— Essays. 1843.
Histoire et Critique. Tr. G. Lisse and P. Petroz, Paris, 1860.
Essais politiques et philosophiques. Tr. G. Guizot, Paris, 1862–4.
—— History of England. 1849–61.
Histoire d'Angleterre. Tr. J. de Peyronnet, Paris, 1852–3; tr. E. de Montégut, Paris, 1861.

Maturin, Charles Robert. Melmoth the Wanderer. 1820.
Melmoth, ou l'homme errant. Tr. J. Cohen, Paris, 1821; tr. Mlle Judith, Paris, 1865.
Balzac, H. de. Melmoth réconcilié. Paris, 1836.
Clapton, G. T. Balzac, Baudelaire and Maturin. French Quart. June, Sept. 1930.
Meredith, George.
Mackay, M. E. Meredith et la France. Paris, 1937.
Mill, John Stuart. System of Logic. 1843.
Système de Logique. Tr. L. Peisse, Paris, 1866–7.
—— Principles of Political Economy. 1848.
Principes d'Économie politique. Tr. Dussart and Courcelle-Seneuil, Paris, 1862.
—— August Comte and Positivism. 1865.
August Comte et le Positivisme. Tr. G. Clemenceau, Paris, 1868.
Littré, M. P. E. Auguste Comte et Stuart Mill. Paris, 1866.
Milton, John.
Baker, A. T. Milton and Chateaubriand. French Quart. I, 1919.
Roberts, W. W. Chateaubriand and Milton. MLR. v, 1910.
Telleen, J. M. Milton dans la Littérature française. Paris, 1904.
Moore, Thomas. A Selection of Irish Melodies. 1807–34.
Mélodies irlandaises. Tr. L. S. Belloc, Paris, 1823; tr. T. G. de Mandelsloh, Paris, 1841; tr. H. Jousselin, Paris, 1869.
—— Lalla Rookh. 1817.
Le Paradis et la Péri. Tr. Paris, 1888.
—— The Loves of the Angels. A Poem. 1823.
Les Amours des Anges. Tr. Davesies de Pontès, Paris, 1823; tr. L. Moutardier, Paris, 1830; tr. J. K. Ostrowski, Paris, 1837.
—— The Epicurean. A Tale. 1827.
L'Épicurien. Tr. A. A. Renouard, Paris, 1827; tr. H. Butat, Paris, 1865.
Baldensperger, F. Thomas Moore et Alfred de Vigny. MLR. I, 1906.
Thomas, A. B. Moore en France. Contribution à l'Histoire de la Fortune de ses Œuvres dans la Littérature française, 1819–30. Paris, 1911.
Ruskin, John. Stones of Venice. 1851–3.
Les Pierres de Venise. Tr. M. P. Crémieux, Paris, 1906.
—— Sesame and Lilies. 1865.
Les Lys du Jardin de la Reine. Tr. Paris, 1896.
Mascarel, A. Un Réformateur anglo-saxon. Paris, 1897.

Maurois, A. Proust et Ruskin. E. & S. xvii, 1932.

Milsand, J. L'Esthétique anglaise. Étude sur M. John Ruskin. Paris, 1864.

Murray, J. Marcel Proust et John Ruskin. Mercure de France, 1 July 1926.

Ruskin en Sorbonne. Le Temps, 11 Jan. 1901.

Scott, Sir Walter.

Œuvres. Tr. A. Pichot, Artaud, A. J. B. Defauconpret, etc. Paris, 1820–32.

—— Guy Mannering. 1815. Tr. J. Martin, 1816. Frédéric, D. P. and Victor, H. J. La Sorcière, Mélodrame. Paris, 1821.

—— The Antiquary. 1816.
L'Antiquaire. Tr. Mme de Maraise, Paris, 1817.

—— Old Mortality. 1816.
Les Puritains d'Écosse. Tr. A. J. B. Defauconpret, Paris, 1817.

—— Rob Roy. 1818. Tr. A. J. B. Defauconpret, Paris, 1818.

—— Ivanhoe. 1820.
Castegnier, A. Rébecca. Grand Opéra. 1882.

—— Les Normands. Grand Opéra. 1886. Deschamps, E. and de Wailly, A. F. L. Ivanhoe. Opera, Paris, 1826.

Dargan, E. P. Scott and the French Romanticists. PMLA. xlix, 1934.

Devonshire, J. M. The 'Decline' of Sir Walter Scott in France. French Quart. i, 1919.

Devonshire, M. G. The English Novel in France 1830–1870. 1930.

Garnand, H. J. The Influence of Sir Walter Scott on the Works of Balzac. New York, 1927.

Hallays, A. W. Scott et le Romantisme français. Journal des Débats, 26 July 1898.

Hartland, R. W. Walter Scott et le Roman 'frénétique.' Paris, 1929.

Lacroix, P. Soirées de Walter Scott à Paris. Paris, 1829.

Maigron, L. Le Roman historique à l'Époque romantique: Essai sur l'Influence de W. Scott. Paris, 1898. [See also Quart. Rev. cxc, 1899.]

[Note also the general influence of Scott on historical writers, e.g. Augustin Thierry, Histoire de la Conquête de l'Angleterre, Paris, 1825, and Claude Ignace de Barante, Histoire des ducs de Bourgogne, Paris, 1824–6; see E. Fueter, Geschichte der neueren Historiographie, vol. v, pt iii, Munich, 1911.]

Shelley, Percy Bysshe.
Œuvres poétiques complètes de Shelley. Tr. F. Rabbé, Paris, 1885–7.

Ackermann, R. Shelley in Frankreich und Italien. E. Studien, xvii, 1892. [Review of trns.]

De Nolva, R. Shelley et Lamartine. Nouvelle Revue d'Italie, 25 Nov. 1922.

Sheridan, Richard Brinsley. The School for Scandal. 1777. Tr. Paris, 1788; B. Delille, 1789; P. N. Famin, Paris, 1807; A. H. Chateauneuf, Paris, 1824.

Œuvres dramatiques. Tr. G. Duval, Paris, 1891.

Smith, Adam. Inquiry into the Nature and Causes of the Wealth of Nations. 1776. Recherches sur la Nature et les Causes de la Richesse des Nations. Tr. J. L. Blavet, London, 1778; tr. G. Garnier, Paris, 1802.

Spencer, Herbert. First Principles. 1862. Les premiers Principes. Tr. E. Cazelles, Paris, 1871.

—— Principles of Sociology, 1876–96.
Principes de Sociologie. Tr. E. Cazelles, Paris, 1878–87.

Swinburne, Algernon Charles.
Poèmes et Ballades. Tr. G. Mourey ('avec des Notes par G. de Maupassant'), 1895.

Tennyson, Alfred, Baron. Idylls of the King. 1859–85.
Elaine, Enide, Genièvre, Viviane. Tr. F. Michel, Paris, 1867–9.

—— Enoch Arden. 1864. Tr. X. Marmier, Paris, 1887; tr. R. Courtois, Paris, 1888; tr. E. Duglin, Beauvais, 1889; tr. A. Beljame, Paris, 1892.

Bowden, M. Tennyson in France. Manchester, 1930.

Mallarmé, S. Tennyson vu d'ici. Revue bleue, iii, 1892

Thackeray, William Makepeace. Vanity Fair. 1848.
La Foire aux Vanités. Tr. G. Guiffrey, Paris, 1855.

—— History of Henry Esmond. 1852. Tr. E. Scheffter, Paris, 1856; tr. L. de Wailly, Paris, 1856.

White, Henry Kirke. Remains. 1807.
Sainte-Beuve, C.-A. Poésies de Joseph Delorme. Paris, 1829.

Wordsworth, William.
Ballades et petits Poèmes. Tr. F. Richomme, Paris, 1850.

Texte, J. W. Wordsworth et la Poésie lakiste en France. [In Études de Littérature européenne, Paris, 1898.]

(3) The Literary Relations of England and Germany

(a) General

Althaus, F. Beiträge zur Geschichte der deutschen Colonie in England. Unsere Zeit, N.S. ix, Leipzig, 1873.

Angell, J. B. Influence of the English Literature on the German. North American Rev. LXXXIV, 1857.

The Anti-Jacobin Review and Magazine. [Ed. J. Gifford], 1798–1821.

Arnold, M. Higher Schools and Universities in Germany. 1874.

Baron-Wilson, Mrs. The Life and Correspondence of M. G. Lewis. 1839.

Batt, M. Contributions to the History of English Opinion of German Literature. 1. Gillies and the Foreign Quarterly Review. 2. Gillies and Blackwood's Magazine. MLN. XVII, 1902, XVIII, 1903.

Block, M. The British and Foreign Review, or European Quarterly Journal. Ein Beitrag zur Geschichte der Aufnahme deutscher Literatur in England. Zürich, 1921.

Blumenhagen, K. Sir Walter Scott als Übersetzer. Rostock, 1900.

Bode, W. Die Franzosen und Engländer in Goethes Leben und Urteil. Berlin, 1915.

Boyd, J. Goethe's Knowledge of English Literature. Oxford, 1932.

Bradley, A. C. English Poetry and German Philosophy in the Age of Wordsworth. (Adamson Lecture.) Manchester, 1900. [Rptd in A Miscellany, 1929.]

Brandl, A. Coleridge und die englische Romantik. Berlin, 1886.

Carlyle, T. The State of German Literature. Edinburgh Rev. XLVI, 1827.

—— German Romance. Specimens of its Chief Authors [Fouqué, Goethe, Hoffmann, Musäus, Richter]. 1827.

—— German Playwrights. Foreign Rev. III, 1829.

—— Richter's Review of Mme de Staël's Allemagne. Fraser's Mag. Feb., May 1830.

—— The Nibelungenlied. Westminster Rev. xv, 1831.

—— German Literature of the Fourteenth and Fifteenth Centuries. Foreign Quarterly Rev. VIII, 1831.

—— Lectures on German Literature. 1837.

—— The History of Friedrich II of Prussia, called Frederick the Great. 1858–65.

Conrad, H. George Eliot über die deutsche Literatur. Gegenwart, xv, 1886.

Deutsche Dichtungen in englischen Übersetzungen. Grenzboten, XXVIII, 1869.

Dick, E. Deutschland und die Deutschen bei George Meredith. Germanisch-romanische Monatsschrift, VI, 1914.

Dunn, W. A. T. de Quincey's Relation to German Literature and Philosophy. Strasburg, 1901.

Dunning, W. A. The Political Theories of the German Idealists. Political Science Quart. XXVIII, 1913.

Dunstan, A. C. The German Influence on Coleridge. MLR. XVII, XVIII, 1922–3. [Schiller, Goethe, Herder, Schlegel, Schelling.]

Egan, R. F. The Genesis of the Theory of 'Art for Art's Sake' in Germany and in England. Northampton (Massachusetts), 1921–4.

Eichler, A. John Hookham Frere. Vienna, 1905.

Eimer, M. Byrons Beziehungen zur deutschen Kultur. Ang. XXXVI, 1912.

Eitner, K. Ein Engländer über deutsches Geistesleben im ersten Drittel dieses Jahrhunderts. Weimar, 1871.

'Eliot, George' (Mary Ann Cross, born Evans). Three Months in Weimar. 1855.

Emerson, O. F. Monk Lewis and the Tales of Terror. MLN. XXXVIII, 1923.

Ewen, F. John Gibson Lockhart, Propagandist of German Literature. MLN. XLIX, 1934.

Ferrier, J. F. The Plagiarisms of S. T. Coleridge. Blackwood's Mag. March 1840.

Fischer, W. Die Briefe R. Monckton Milnes an Varnhagen von Ense (1844–1854). Heidelberg, 1922.

Freyl, W. The Influence of 'Gothic' Literature on Sir Walter Scott. Rostock, 1902.

Gillies, R. P. Recollections of Sir Walter Scott. 1837.

—— Memoirs of a Literary Veteran. 1851.

Goede, C. A. G. A Foreigner's Opinion of England. 1802.

Goedeke, K. Grundriss zur Geschichte der deutschen Dichtung. Vols. IV ff. Dresden, 1916 ff. (rev. edn).

Gooch, G. P. Lord Haldane. Contemporary Rev. Oct. 1928.

Handschin, C. H. A Bibliography of English Translations of German Novels. Monatshefte für deutsche Sprache und Pädagogik, IX, 1909.

Haney, J. L. The German Influence on S. T. Coleridge. Philadelphia, 1903.

Harrold, C. F. Carlyle and German Thought: 1819–1834. New Haven, 1934.

Hathaway, L. German Literature of the Mid-Nineteenth Century in England and America as Reflected in the Journals of 1840–1914. Boston, 1935.

Henkel, —. The German Influence on the Poetry of England and America in the Course of the XIXth Century. Eschwege, 1869.

Herzberg, M. J. William Wordsworth and German Literature. PMLA. XL, 1925.

Herzfeld, G. William Taylor von Norwich. Eine Studie über den Einfluss der neueren deutschen Litteratur in England. Halle, 1897.

—— Zur Geschichte der deutschen Literatur in England. Archiv, CX, 1903.

Hohlfeld, A. R. Scott als Übersetzer. Studien zur vergleichenden Litteraturgeschichte, III, 1903.

Holcroft, T. Memoirs. 1816.

Howie, M. D. Achim von Arnim and Scotland. MLR. XVII, 1922.

Jacobsen, A. Kingsleys Beziehungen zu Deutschland. Heidelberg, 1917.

Jaeck, E. G. Madame de Staël and the Spread of German Literature. New York, 1915.

Kellner, L. Carlyle und Goethe. [In Englische Literatur im Zeitalter der Königin Viktoria, Leipzig, 1909, pp. 143–52.]

Koch, J. Sir W. Scotts Beziehungen zu Deutschland. Germanisch-romanische Monatsschrift, xv, 1927.

—— Goethe und Byron. Archiv, LXXXVIII, 1933.

Kornder, T. Der Deutsche im Spiegelbild der englischen Erzählungsliteratur des 19. Jahrhunderts. Erlangen, 1934.

Kräger, H. Carlyles Stellung zur deutschen Sprache und Literatur. Ang. XXII, 1899.

Lees, J. George Meredith's Literary Relations with Germany. MLR. XII, 1917.

Lewis, M. G. Tales of Terror. 1800.

—— Romantic Tales. 1808.

Liddell, M. F. Ferdinand Freiligrath's Debt to English Poets. MLR. XXIII, 1928.

Lotter, K. Carlyle und die deutsche Romantik. Nuremberg, 1932.

Lüdeke, H. Ludwig Tieck und das alte englische Theater. Frankfurt, 1922.

Mackay, R. W. The Tübingen School and its Antecedents. 1863.

Mann, H. Report of an Educational Tour in Germany and Parts of Great Britain and Ireland. 1846.

Morgan, B. Q. A Bibliography of German Literature in English Translation. Madison, 1922.

Morley, E. J. Crabb Robinson in Germany, 1800–1805. Oxford, 1929.

Oxenford, J. and Feiling, C. A. Tales from the German. 1844.

Paulsen, F. Die deutschen Universitäten. Berlin, 1893. Tr. E. D. Perry, New York, 1895; tr. F. Tilly and W. W. Elwang, 1906.

Passow, A. Deutschlands Einfluss auf die englische Literatur. Magazin für Literatur, 1878, pp. 437, 452.

Payne, J. Pestolozzi; Influence of Elementary Education. 1875.

—— Froebel and the Kindergarten. 1876.

—— A Visit to German Schools. 1876.

Perry, T. S. German Influence in English Literature. Atlantic Monthly, Aug. 1877.

Pfeiffer, S. George Eliots Beziehungen zu Deutschland. Heidelberg, 1925.

Pizzo, E. S. T. Coleridge als Kritiker. Ang. XXVII, 1016.

Price, L. M. The Reception of English Literature in Germany. Berkeley, 1932.

Purdie, E. German Influence on the Literary Ballad in England during the Romantic Revival. Publications of English Goethe Soc. N.S. III, 1926.

Rhyn, H. Die Balladendichtung Theodor Fontanes. Berne, 1914.

Richter, H. Die philosophische Weltanschauung von S. T. Coleridge und ihr Verhältnis zur deutschen Philosophie. Ang. XXXII, 1920.

Robinson, H. C. Diary, Reminiscences, and Correspondence. Ed. T. Sadler, 1869.

Schirmer, G. Die Schweiz im Spiegel englischer und amerikanischer Literatur bis 1848. Zurich, 1929.

Scholz, K. Bibliography of English Renditions of Modern German Dramas. German-American Annals, xv, 1917.

Schulze-Gävernitz, G. von. Thomas Carlyles Welt- und Gesellschaftsanschauung. Dresden, 1893.

Schwaninger, C. Die Verdienste der Edinburgh Review um die Verbreitung deutscher Literatur in England, 1802–1829. Zurich, 1921.

Schwarz, F. H. Deutsche Anleihen bei englischen Dramatikern. Jahrbuch des Vereins Schweizerischer Gymnasiallehrer, LIV, 1925.

Seely, Sir J. M. Goethe Reviewed after Sixty Years. 1894.

Shawcross, J. Coleridge's Biographia Literaria. Oxford, 1907.

Shumway, D. B. Thomas Campbell and Germany. [In Schelling Anniversary Papers, New York, 1923.]

Sigmann, L. Die englische Literatur von 1800–1850 im Urteil der zeitgenössischen deutschen Kritik. Heidelberg, 1918.

Spink, G. W. F. Freiligraths Verbannungsjahre in London. Berlin, 1932.

Staël-Holstein, Baroness. Germany. Translated from the French. 1813.

Stephen, Sir L. The Importation of German. [In Studies of a Biographer, vol. II, 1898.]

Stockley, V. German Literature as known in England, 1750–1830. 1929. [Good bibliography.}

Stokoe, F. W. The Appreciation of German Literature in England before 1820. Publications of English Goethe Soc. N.S. III, 1926.

—— German Influence in the English Romantic Period, 1788–1818, with special reference to Scott, Coleridge, Shelley, and Byron. Cambridge, 1926. [Good bibliography.]

Streuli, W. Thomas Carlyle als Vermittler deutscher Literatur und deutschen Geistes. Zurich, 1895.

Taylor, W. Tales of Yore. 1810. [Includes trns of Wieland's Danischmend and Alxinger's Bliomberis.]

—— Historic Survey of German Poetry. 1828–30. [See also Carlyle's review in Edinburgh Rev. March 1831.]

Thackeray, W. M. The FitzBoodle Papers. 1842–3.

Thomas, W. Walter Scott et la Littérature allemande. [In Mélanges H. Lichtenberger, Paris, 1934.]

Thompson, B. German Theatre. 1800–1. [Includes trns of Lessing, Goethe, Schiller and Kotzebue.]

Vaughan, C. E. Carlyle and his German Masters. E. & S. I, 1910.

Vulpius, W. Thackeray in Weimar. Century Mag. LIII, 1897.

Waddington, M. M. The Development of British Thought from 1820 to 1890 with Special Reference to German Influences. Toronto, 1919.

Weber, C. A. Bristols Bedeutung für die englische Romantik und die deutsch-englischen Beziehungen. Halle, 1935.

Weddigen, F. H. O. Vermittler des deutschen Geistes in England und Nordamerika. Archiv, LIX, 1878.

—— F. Freiligrath als Vermittler englischer und französischer Dichtung. Archiv, LXI, 1879.

—— Geschichte der Einwirkungen der deutschen Literatur auf die Literaturen der übrigen europäischen Kulturvölker der Neuzeit. Leipzig, 1882.

Wellek, R. Carlyle and German Romanticism. [In Xenia Pragensia, 1929.]

—— Immanuel Kant in England. Princeton, 1931.

Wenzel, P. Germany and the Germans as seen by English Novelists of the 19th and 20th Centuries. Bielefeld, 1932.

Willoughby, L. A. Dante Gabriel Rossetti and German Literature. 1912.

—— On some German Affinities with the Oxford Movement. MLR. XXIX, 1934.

Winkworth, C. Lyra Germanica. 2 vols. 1855–8.

Zeiger, T. Beiträge zur Geschichte der deutsch-englischen Literaturbeziehungen. Wordsworth, Southey, Shelley. Studien zur vergleichenden Literaturgeschichte, I, 1901.

—— Beiträge zur Geschichte des Einflusses der neueren deutschen Literatur auf die englische. Leipzig, 1901.

Zeydel, E. H. Ludwig Tieck and England. Princeton, 1931.

(b) Single Authors

(i) German

[For more detailed bibliographies of German writers in their relation to England see K. Goedeke, op. cit. For trns see B. Q. Morgan, op. cit.]

Bunsen, Christian Carl Josias (1791–1860). Die Zeichen der Zeit. Leipzig, 1855.
  Signs of the Times. Tr. S. Winkworth, 1856.

—— Gott in der Geschichte. Leipzig, 1857–8.
  God in History. Tr. S. Winkworth, 1868–70.

—— Versuch eines allgemeinen Gesang- und Gebetbuchs. Hamburg, 1833. Tr. Catherine Winkworth, 2 vols. 1855–8. [Lyra Germanica.]

  Rose, H. J. Bunsen, the Critical School and Dr Williams. 1862.
  Savile, B. W. Revelation and Science in respect to Bunsen's Biblical Researches. 1862.
  Williams, R. Bunsen's Biblical Researches. 1860.

Feuerbach, Ludwig (1804–1872). Das Wesen des Christentums. Leipzig, 1841.
  The Essence of Christianity. Tr. George Eliot, 1854.

Fichte, Johann Gottlieb (1762–1814). Sämmtliche Werke Berlin, 1845–6.
  Popular Writings of Fichte, with a Memoir. Tr. W. Smith, 1848–9.

  Adamson, R. Fichte. 1881.
  Morell, J. D. Fichte's Contribution to Moral Philosophy. 1860.

Fouqué, Friedrich Heinrich Karl, Baron de la Motte (1777–1843). Undine. Berlin, 1811. Tr. G. Soane, 1818; tr. T. Tracy, 1841; tr. Sir E. Gosse, 1896.

—— Aslaugas Ritter. Berlin, 1813.
  Aslauga's Knight. Tr. T. Carlyle, 1827.

—— Sintram und seine Gefährten. Berlin, 1814.
  Sintram and his Companions. Tr. J. C. Hare, 1820.

Freytag, Gustav (1816–1895). Soll und Haben. Leipzig, 1854.
  Debtor and Creditor. Tr. W. J. Stewart, 1857; tr. Georgiana Malcolm, 1858.

Froebel, Friedrich Wilhelm August (1782–1852). Die Menschenerziehung. Keilhau, 1826.
  Bowen, H. C. Froebel and Education by Self Activity. 1893.
  Shirreff, Emily A. E. The Kindergarten. 1876.

  Hayward, F. H. The Educational Ideas of Pestalozzi and Fröbel. 1904.

Essays on the Kindergarten: being a Selection of Lectures read before the London Froebel Society. 1881.

Goethe, Johann Wolfgang von (1749–1832).
[For the influence of Goethe in England consult in the first instance: J. M. Carré, Bibliographie de Goethe en Angleterre, Lyons, 1920, and Goethe en Angleterre, Paris, 1920, and the review by A. E. Turner, MLR. xvi, pp. 364–70; also the Publications of the English Goethe Soc. 1886– .]

—— Die Leiden des jungen Werthers. Leipzig, 1774.

Bulwer-Lytton, E. G. E. L. (Baron Lytton). Falkland. 1827.
—— Pelham, or the Adventures of a Gentleman. 1828.

Goldhan, A. H. Über die Einwirkung des Goetheschen Werther und Wilhelm Meister auf die Entwicklung Edward Bulwers. Leipzig, 1895.

Long, O. W. English Translations of Goethe's Werther. JEGP. xiv, 1915.

—— Wilhelm Meisters Lehrjahre. Berlin, 1795–6.

—— Wilhelm Meisters Wanderjahre. Stuttgart, 1829.

William Meister's Apprenticeship. Tr. T. Carlyle, 1824.

Disraeli, Benjamin (Earl of Beaconsfield). Contarini Fleming. 1832.

Howe, Susanne. Wilhelm Meister and his English Kinsmen. New York, 1930.

—— Hermann und Dorothea. Berlin, 1797.

Clough, A. H. The Bothie of Toper-na-Fuosich. 1848.

—— Faust. 2 pts, Tübingen, 1808. Stuttgart, 1833.
[The 'Urfaust or original draft (1770–5) of the First Part was discovered by Professor Erich Schmidt in 1887 in Dresden and pbd by him the same year. There are two trns of the 'Urfaust': (a) by R. McLintock, 1889 (unpublished MS in possession of the compiler); (b) by W. H. van der Smissen, see below. The first thirty-five English trns of Faust are discussed by L. Baumann (see below). See also B. Q. Morgan, Bibliography of German Literature in English Translation, Madison, 1922. The following are the most noteworthy English versions.]

Scenes from the Faust of Goethe. Tr. P. B. Shelley, [1822].

Faust. Pt i. Tr. A. Hayward, 1833. [Prose.]

Faustus, a Dramatic Mystery. Tr. J. Anster. Pt i, 1835. Pt ii, 1864. [Verse. An imitation rather than a trn.]

Faust. Tr. Anna Swanwick. Pt i, 1849. Pt ii, 1878. [Latest edn, with admirable introduction and bibliography by K. Breul, 1928. Verse. A deservedly popular trn.]

Faust. Pt i. Tr. R. McLintock, 1897. [Verse. Very successful reproduction of the original metres.]

Byron, G. G., Baron. Manfred. 1817. [For a detailed bibliography of Byron and Goethe see K. Goedeke, Grundriss zur Geschichte der deutschen Dichtung, vol. iv, pt 2.]

Bailey, P. J. Festus. 1839.

Black, G. A. P. J. Bailey's Debt to Goethe's Faust. MLR. xxviii, 1933.

Gilbert, W. S. Gretchen. 1879.

Phillips, S. and Comyns Carr, J. Faust. Freely adapted. 1908.

Wills, W. G. Faust. 1885.

Baumann, L. Die englischen Übersetzungen von Goethes Faust. Halle, 1907.

Bluhm, H. S. The Reception of Goethe's Faust in England after the Middle of the Nineteenth Century. JEGP. xxxiv, 1935.

Carlyle, T. Faustus. New Edinburgh Rev. ii, 1822.

—— Goethe's Helena. Foreign Rev. i, April 1828.

Courtney, W. L. Faust on the English Stage. Fortnightly Rev. Jan. 1886.

Davidson, T. The Philosophy of Goethe's Faust. Ed. C. M. Bakewell, Boston, 1906.

Hauhart, W. F. The Reception of Goethe's Faust in England in the First Half of the Nineteenth Century. New York, 1909.

Heinemann, W. Goethes Faust in England und Amerika. Bibliographische Zusammenstellung. Berlin, 1886.

McLintock, R. The Five Best English Verse Translations of Faust. Trans. Manchester Goethe Soc. 1894.

Montgomery, M. The First English Version of Faust Part I and 'Dichtung und Wahrheit.' Publications of English Goethe Soc. N.S. iii, 1926.

Nicoll, A. Faust on the English Stage. [In Das Buch des Goethe-Lessing Jahres, Brunswick, 1929.]

Robertson, J. G. Gillies and Goethe. MLR. iv, 1908.

Tait, J. The Literary Influence of Goethe's Faust in England, 1832–52. Trans. Manchester Goethe Soc. 1894.

Waterhouse, G. A Unique Translation of Goethe's 'Faust' [Urfaust]. Discovery, Sept. 1927.

Fiedler, H. G. Goethe's Lyric Poems in English Translation. MLR. xviii, 1923.

Hinz, S. M. Goethe's Lyric Poems in English Translation after 1860. Madison, 1929.

Simmons, L. van T. Goethe's Lyric Poems in English Translation prior to 1860. Madison, 1918.

Alford, R. G. Goethe's Earliest Critics in England. Publications of English Goethe Soc. VII, 1893.

Althaus, F. On the Personal Relations between Goethe and Byron. Publications of English Goethe Soc. II, 1888.

Asher, D. Lord Tennyson and Goethe. Publications of English Goethe Soc. IV, 1890.

Baumgarten, O. Carlyle und Goethe. Lebensfragen, XIII, Tübingen, 1906.

Bernays, M. Beziehungen Goethes zu Walter Scott. Zur neueren Literaturgeschichte, I, Stuttgart, 1895.

Brandl, A. Die Aufnahme von Goethes Jugendwerken in England. Goethe-Jahrbuch, III, 1882.

—— Goethe und Byron. Österreichische Rundschau, I, 1883.

—— Goethes Verhältnis zu Byron. Goethe-Jahrbuch, XX, 1899.

—— Goethe und England. Fortschritte und Forschungen, XXXI, 1932.

Carlyle, T. Goethe. Foreign Rev. II, 1828.

—— Goethe's Works. Foreign Quarterly Rev. X, 1832.

—— The Death of Goethe. New Monthly Mag. XXXIV, 1832.

Correspondence between Goethe and Carlyle. Ed. C. E. Norton, 1887.

Goethes und Carlyles Briefwechsel. Ed. H. Oldenberg, Berlin, 1887; ed. G. Hecht, Dachau, 1914.

Boyesen, H. H. Goethe and Carlyle. [In Essays on German Literature, 1892.]

Carr, M. Goethe in his Connection with English Literature. Publications of English Goethe Soc. IV, 1890.

Carré, J. M. Goethe en Angleterre. Paris, 1920.

Flügel, E. Der Briefwechsel zwischen Goethe und Carlyle. Grenzboten, XLVI, 1887.

Grimm, H. Goethe und Carlyles Briefwechsel. Deutsche Rundschau, IV, 1887.

Henriot, E. Goethe, Carlyle et Thackeray. L'Europe nouvelle, 15 Oct. 1921.

Müller, F. M. Goethe and Carlyle. Contemporary Rev. June 1886.

Heller, O. Goethe and Wordsworth. MLN. XIV, 1899.

Hutton, R. H. Goethe and his Influence. [In Literary Essays, 1888.]

Imelmann, R. Shelleys Alastor und Goethe. Zeitschrift für vergleichende Litteraturgeschichte, XVII, 1909.

Kaufmann, M. Goethe and Modern Thought. Scottish Rev. no. 18, 1891.

Krusemeyer, M. Der Einfluss Goethes auf George Meredith. E. Studien, LIX, 1925.

Lewes, G. H. Life of Goethe. 1855.

Lieder, F. W. C. Goethe in England and America. JEGP. XVI, 1917.

Lovett, R. M. Goethe in English Literature. Open Court, April 1932.

MacIntosh, W. Scott and Goethe: German Influence on the Writings of Sir Walter Scott. Glasgow, 1924.

Mensch, R. A. J. Goethe and Wordsworth. Publications of English Goethe Soc. VII, 1893.

Norman, F. Henry Crabb Robinson and Goethe. Publications of English Goethe Soc. N.S. VI, VII, 1930–1.

—— Goethe und das heutige England. Goethe-Jahrbuch, XVII, 1931.

Orrick, J. B. Matthew Arnold and Goethe. Publications of English Goethe Soc. N.S. IV, 1927.

Oswald, E. Goethe in England and America. Bibliography. Die Neueren Sprachen, VII, 1899–1900; 1909.

Preisinger, H. Matthew Arnold on Goethe Trans. Manchester Goethe Soc. 1894.

Rhyme, O. P. Browning and Goethe. MLN. XLIV, 1929.

Robertson, J. G. Goethe and Byron. Publications of English Goethe Soc. N.S. II, 1925.

—— Goethe und England. Goethe-Jahrbuch, XVIII, 1932.

Roesel, L. K. Die literarischen und persönlichen Beziehungen Sir Walter Scotts zu Goethe. Leipzig, 1902.

Sinzheimer, S. Goethe und Lord Byron. Eine Darstellung der persönlichen und literarischen Verhältnisse mit Berücksichtigung des Faust und Manfred. Munich, 1894.

Strich, F. Goethe und Byron. Die Horen, V, 1929.

Vollrath, W. Goethe und Grossbritannien. Erlangen, 1932.

White, H. C. Matthew Arnold and Goethe. PMLA. XXXVI, 1921.

Grillparzer, Franz (1791–1872). Sappho. Vienna, 1818.

Sappho, a Tragedy. Tr. J. Bramsen, 1820; tr. Ellen Frothingham, Boston, 1876.

—— Das goldene Vliess. Vienna, 1820.

Medea. Tr. F. W. Thurstan and S. A. Wittmann, 1879.

[Trns of Sappho, Der Traum ein Leben, and Weh' dem, der lügt were made by Archer Thompson Gurney before 1858, but never pbd.]
Blankenagel, J. C. Carlyle as a Critic of Grillparzer. PMLA. XLII, 1927.
Grimm, Jakob (1778–1863) and Wilhelm (1786–1859). Kinder- und Hausmärchen. Berlin, 1812–22.
German Popular Stories. Tr. 1823.
Gammer Grethel. Tr. E. Taylor, 1839.
Household Stories. Tr. 1853.
Household Tales. Tr. M. Hunt, 1884.
Grimm's Fairy Tales. [Many edns.]
Lang, A. The Blue Fairy Book, 1889. [Several similar vols.]
Haeckel, Ernst (1834–1919). Die Welträtsel. Bonn, 1899.
The Riddle of the Universe. Tr. J. McCabe, 1900.
Hegel, Georg Wilhelm Friedrich (1770–1831). Phänomenologie des Geistes. Bamberg, 1807.
—— Wissenschaft der Logik. 2 vols. Nuremberg, 1812–6.
—— Enzyklopädie der philosophischen Wissenschaften im Grundriss. Heidelberg, 1817.
—— Grundlinien der Philosophie des Rechts. Berlin, 1821.
The Phenomenology of Mind. Tr. J. B. Baillie, 1910.
The Logic of Hegel. Tr. W. Wallace, 1874.
Hegel's Doctrine of Formal Logic. Tr. H. S. Macran, Oxford, 1912.
Hegel's Logic of World and Idea. Tr. H. S. Macran, 1929.
Hegel's Philosophy of Mind. Tr. W. Wallace, Oxford, 1894.
Hegel's Philosophy of Right. Tr. S. W. Dyde, 1896.
Caird, E. Hegel. 1883.
Caird, J. An Introduction to the Philosophy of Religion. 1880.
Muirhead, J. H. How Hegel came to England. Mind, XXXVI, 1927.
Ritchie, D. G. Darwin and Hegel, with Other Philosophical Studies. 1894.
Stirling, J. H. The Secret of Hegel. 1865.
Wallace, W. Lectures and Essays on Natural Theology and Ethics. 1898.
Heine, Heinrich (1797–1856).
Works. Tr. C. G. Leland, T. Brookshank, and Margaret Armour, 1892–1905.
Poems of Heine, Complete. Tr. E. A. Bowring, 1858.
Poetical Works. Tr. J. Payne, 1911.
Poems and Ballads. Tr. Sir T. Martin, 1878, 1894 (3rd edn).
Poems. Tr. Käthe Freiligrath-Kroeker, 1887.

Lyrics and Ballads. Tr. Frances Hellman, New York, 1892, 1895.
Heine, Heinrich. Das Buch der Lieder. Hamburg, 1827.
Book of Songs. Tr. C. G. Leland, 1864; tr. T. Brooksbank, 1904.
—— Reisebilder. Hamburg, 1826 ff.
Pictures of Travel. Tr. C. G. Leland, Philadelphia, 1855.
Travel Pictures. Tr. F. Storr, 1887.
Pictures of Travel. Tr. R. D. Gillman, 1907.

Arnold, M. Heine. [In Essays in Criticism, 1865.]
Atkins, H. G. Heine. 1929. [Bibliography; especially Heine in English Translation (by Kathleen Kirby).]
[Eliot, George.] German Wit: Heinrich Heine. Westminster Rev. Jan. 1856.
Hayens, K. Heine, Hazlitt and Mrs Jameson. MLR. XVII, 1922.
Katscher, L. Englische Bücher über Heine und Schopenhauer. Magazin, XC, 1876.
Sharp, W. Life of Heinrich Heine. 1888. [Valuable for English trns and criticism.]
Winternitz, M. H. Heine in England. Zeit, no. 178, 1900.
Hoffmann, Ernst Theodore Amadeus (1776–1822). Fantasiestücke in Callots Manier. Bamberg, 1814–5.
—— Nachtstücke. Berlin, 1817.
—— Die Serapionsbrüder. Berlin, 1819–21.
The Golden Pot. Tr. T. Carlyle, 1841.
Hoffmann's Strange Stories. Tr. Boston, 1855.
Weird Tales. Tr. J. T. Bealby, New York, 1885.
Serapion Brethren. Tr. A. Ewing, 1886–92.

Gudde, E. G. E. Th. A. Hoffmann's Reception in England. PMLA. XLI, 1926.
Scott, Sir Walter. E. T. A. Hoffmann. 1827.
Kant, Immanuel (1724–1804). Kritik der reinen Vernunft. Riga, 1781.
—— Kritik der praktischen Vernunft. Riga, 1788.
—— Kritik der Urteilskraft. Berlin, 1790.
Critick of Pure Reason. Tr. F. Haywood, 1838; tr. J. M. D. Meiklejohn, 1856; tr. F. Max Müller, 1881.
Critique of Practical Reason and Other Works on the Theory of Ethics. Tr. T. K. Abbott, 1873, 1909 (6th edn).
Kritik of Judgment. Tr. J. H. Bernard, 1892.
Critique of Aesthetic Judgment. Tr. J. C. Meredith, Oxford, 1911.

Adamson, R. On the Philosophy of Kant. 1879.

[Review of C. Villers, La philosophie de Kant.] Edinburgh Rev. Jan. 1803.

Caird, E. The Critical Philosophy of Immanuel Kant. 1889.

Coleridge, S. T. Biographia Literaria. 1817.

Duncan, G. M. English Translations of Kant's Writings. Kantstudien, II, 1906.

Hamilton, Sir William. The Philosophy of the Unconditioned. Edinburgh Rev. Oct. 1829.

Harrold, C. F. Carlyle's Interpretation of Kant. PQ. Oct. 1928.

Mahaffy, J. P. and Bernard, J. H. Kant's Critical Philosophy for English Readers. 1872.

Schmitt-Wendel, K. Kants Einfluss auf die englische Ethik. Berlin, 1912.

Sidgwick, H. The Philosophy of Kant and Other Lectures and Essays. 1905.

Stirling, J. H. Text Book to Kant. 1881.

Storrs, Margaret. The Relation of Carlyle to Kant and Fichte. Bryn Mawr. 1929.

Wallace, W. Kant. 1882.

Wellek, R. Immanuel Kant in England (1793–1838). Princeton, 1931. [See review in Revue de Littérature comparée, July 1933.]

Winkelmann, E. Coleridge und die Kantische Philosophie. Leipzig, 1933.

Kotzebue, August (1761–1819).

Koeppel, F. Kotzebue in England. E. Studien, XIII, 1891.

Sellier, W. Kotzebue in England. Leipzig, 1901.

Süpfle, T. Kotzebue in Frankreich und England. Zeitschrift für vergleichende Litteraturgeschichte, VI, 1892.

Thompson, L. F. Kotzebue. A Survey of his Progress in France and England. Paris, 1928.

Lessing, Gotthold Ephraim (1729–1781). Laokoon, oder über die Grenzen der Malerei und Poesie. Berlin, 1766.

Laocoön; or, the Limits of Poetry and Painting. Tr. W. Ross, 1836; tr. E. C. Beasley, 1853; tr. Sir R. Phillimore, 1874.

—— Minna von Barnhelm. Berlin, 1767; tr. T. Holcroft, 1805; tr. J. J. Holroyd, Colchester, 1838.

—— Nathan der Weise. Berlin, 1779. Nathan the Wise. Tr. Ellen Frothingham, New York, 1867; tr. R. D. Boylan, 1878; tr. E. K. Corbett, 1883; tr. P. Maxwell, 1895.

Kenwood, S. H. Lessing in England. MLR. IX, 1914.

Todt, W. Lessing in England. Heidelberg, 1912.

Vail, C. C. D. Lessing's Relation to the English Language and Literature. New York, 1936.

Luther, Martin (1483–1546).

Luther's Primary Works. Tr. and ed. H. Wace and C. A. Buchheim, 1896.

Hymns of the Reformation. Tr. H. J. Fry, 1845, 1853.

Table Talk. Tr. W. Hazlitt, 1848.

The Autobiography of Martin Luther. Tr. J. P. Lawson, 1836.

Life of Martin Luther by himself. Arranged by M. Michelet. Tr. W. Hazlitt, 1846.

Mommsen, Theodor (1817–1903). Römische Geschichte. Berlin, 1845–85.

The History of Rome. Tr. W. P. Dickson, 1862–75, 1868–86.

Niebuhr, Barthold Georg (1776–1831). Römische Geschichte. 3 vols. Berlin, 1811–32.

History of Rome. Tr. C. Thirlwall, J. Hare, W. Smith, and L. Schmitz, 1828–44.

Arnold, T. On Niebuhr's History of Rome. Quarterly Rev. XXXII, 1825.

—— History of Rome. 1828–45.

Thirlwall, C. and Hare, J. A Vindication of Niebuhr's History of Rome. Cambridge, 1829.

Nietzsche, Friedrich (1844–1900).

Complete Works. Tr. by several hands; ed. O. Levy, 1909–13.

Ellis, Havelock. Friedrich Nietzsche. The Savoy, nos. 2–4, 1896.

Foerster-Nietzsche, E. Nietzsche in France and England. Open Court, XXXIV, 1920.

Petzold, Gertrud von. John Davidson und sein geistiges Werden unter dem Einfluss Nietzsches. Leipzig, 1928.

—— Nietzsche in englisch-amerikanischer Beurteilung bis zum Ausgang des Weltkrieges. Ang. LIII, 1929.

'Novalis' (i.e. Friedrich Leopold, Freiherr von Hardenberg, 1772–1801). Heinrich von Ofterdingen. Berlin, 1802.

Henry of Ofterdingen. Tr. Cambridge, U.S.A. 1842.

Carlyle, T. Novalis. Foreign Rev. IV, 1829.

Harrold, C. F. Carlyle and Novalis. Stud. Phil. XXVII, 1930.

Richter, Johann Paul Friedrich ('Jean Paul,' 1763–1825).

—— Leben des Quintus Fixlein. Bayreuth, 1796.

Quintus Fixlein. Tr. T. Carlyle, 1864.

—— Blumen-, Frucht- und Dornenstücke, oder Ehestand, Tod und Hochzeit des Armenadvokaten Fr. St. Siebenkäs. Bayreuth, 1796–7.

Flower, Fruit and Thorn Pieces; or the Married Life, Death and Wedding of Firmian Siebenkäs. Tr. E. H. Noel, 1845.

Richter, Johann Paul Friedrich. Levana oder Erziehungslehre. Brunswick, 1807.
Levana, or, the Doctrine of Education. Tr. A. H., 1848.
Brewer, E. V. The Influence of Jean Paul Richter on George Meredith's Conception of the Comic. JEGP. xxix, 1930.
Carlyle, T. Jean Paul Friedrich Richter. Edinburgh Rev. xlvi, 1827.
—— Jean Paul Friedrich Richter again. Foreign Rev. v, 1830.
—— Sartor Resartus. 1833–4.
Christoph, F. Über den Einfluss Jean Paul Fr. Richters auf Thomas de Quincey. Hof, 1899.
Conrad, H. Carlyle und Jean Paul. Gegenwart, xx, 1891.
Geissendoerfer, T. Carlyle and J. P. Richter. JEGP. xxv, 1926.
Pape, H. Jean Paul als Quelle von Carlyles Anschauung und Stil. Rostock, 1904.

Savigny, Friedrich Karl von (1779–1861). Geschichte des römischen Rechts im Mittelalter. Heidelberg, 1815–31.
Maitland, F. W. and Pollock, Sir F. History of English Law before the time of Edward I. 1895.

Scheffel, Joseph Viktor von (1826–1886). Gaudeamus! Stuttgart, 1868.
Gaudeamus! Tr. C. G. Leland, 1872.

Schelling, Friedrich Wilhelm von (1775–1854). System des transzendentalen Idealismus. Tübingen, 1800.
Coleridge, S. T. Biographia Literaria. 1817.

Schiller, Johann Christoph Friedrich von (1759–1805).
Works. Historical and Dramatic. Tr. by various hands, 1846–9, 1897–1903.
Minor Poems. Tr. J. H. Merivale, 1844.
The Poems of Schiller. Tr. E. A. Bowring, 1851.
—— Die Räuber. Stuttgart, 1781.
The Robbers. Tr. H. G. Bohn. [In Works, 1846–9.]
—— Don Carlos. Leipzig, 1787.
Don Carlos. Tr. R. D. Boylan. [In Works, 1846–9.]
—— Wallenstein. Tübingen, 1800.
Wallenstein. Tr. S. T. Coleridge, 1800 (omits 'Lager'); tr. J. A. W. Hunter, 1885; tr. Sir T. Martin ('Lager' only), Blackwood's Mag. Feb. 1892.
—— Maria Stuart. Tübingen, 1801. Tr. J. C. Mellish, 1801.
—— Wilhelm Tell. Stuttgart, 1804.

William Tell. Tr. S, Robinson, 1825; tr. Sir T. Martin (in Works, 1846–9).
J. S. Knowles. William Tell. 1856. [Written 1825.]

Böddeker, K. Über Bulwers Übersetzungen Schiller'scher Gedichte im Vergleich mit den Originalen. Archiv, xlix, 1872.
Carlyle, T. Schiller's Life and Writings. London Mag. viii–ix, 1823–4; 1825 (as The Life of Schiller).
—— Schiller. Fraser's Mag. iii, 1831.
—— Schiller, Goethe, and Madame de Staël, and Goethe's Portrait. Fraser's Mag. v, 1832.
Cooke, M. W. Schiller's Robbers in England. MLR. xi, 1915.
Ewen, F. The Prestige of Schiller in England, 1788–1859. New York, 1932.
Kipka, K. Schillers Maria Stuart im Auslande. Studien zur vergleichenden Literaturgeschichte, v, 1905.
Küchler, F. Carlyle und Schiller. Leipzig, 1902. [See also Ang. xxvi, 1903.]
Machule, P. Coleridges Wallensteinübersetzung. E. Studien, xxxi, 1902.
Meyer, K. J. C. Mellish. Trans. Manchester Goethe Soc. 1894.
Rea, T. Schiller's Dramas and Poems in England. 1906.
Roscher, H. F. G. Die Wallensteinübersetzung von Samuel T. Coleridge. Leipzig, 1905.
Smith, H. Two English Translations of Schiller's Wallenstein. MLR. ix, 1914.
Willoughby, L. A. English Translations and Adaptations of Schiller's Robbers. MLR. xvi, 1921.
—— Schiller's 'Kabale und Liebe' in English Translation. Publications of English Goethe Soc. N.S. i, 1924.

Schlegel, August Wilhelm von (1767–1845). Über dramatische Kunst und Literatur. Heidelberg, 1809–11.
Lectures on Dramatic Art and Literature. Tr. J. Black, 1815.
Helmholtz, A. A. The Indebtedness of S. T. Coleridge to A. W. Schlegel. Madison, 1907.
Herzfeld, G. August Wilhelm Schlegel in seinen Beziehungen zu englischen Dichtern und Kritikern. Archiv, cxxxviii, 1920.
Schnöckelborg, G. August Wilhelm von Schlegels Einfluss auf William Hazlitt als Shakespeare-Kritiker. Münster, 1931.

Schlegel, Friedrich (1772–1829). Philosophische Vorlesungen. Vienna, 1830.
Carlyle, T. Characteristics. Edinburgh Rev. liv, 1831.

Schnitzler, Arthur (1862–1931). Anatol. Berlin, 1893.

    Anatol: a Sequence of Dialogues. Paraphrased by Granville Barker. 1911.

Schopenhauer, Arthur (1788–1860). Die Welt als Wille und Vorstellung. Leipzig, 1818.

    The World as Will and Idea. Tr. R. B. Haldane and J. Kemp, 1883–6.

    Gissing, George. Workers in the Dawn. 1880.

    Steinbach, A. Thomas Hardy und Schopenhauer. [In Anglica, A. Brandl überreicht, vol. ii, Leipzig, 1925.]

    Goodale, R. H. Schopenhauer and Pessimism in XIXth-Century English Literature. PMLA. xlvii, 1932.

Storm, Theodor (1817–1888). Immensee. 1840. Tr. H. Clark, 1863.

Strauss, David Friedrich (1808–1874). Das Leben Jesu. Tübingen, 1835.

    The Life of Jesus. Tr. George Eliot, 1846.

    Das Leben Jesu von Strauss in England und Frankreich. [In Blätter zur Kunde der Litteratur des Auslands, iv, 1839.]

Sudermann, Hermann (1857–1928). Frau Sorge. Berlin, 1886.

    Dame Care. Tr. Bertha Overbeck, New York, 1891.

—— Heimat. Stuttgart, 1892.

    Magda. Tr. C. E. A. Winslow, New York, 1896.

Suttner, Bertha von (1843–1914). Die Waffen nieder! Dresden, 1889.

    Lay down your Arms. Tr. T. Holmes, 1892, 1906.

Tieck, Ludwig (1773–1853). Phantasus. Berlin, 1812–7.

    Tales from the Phantasus. Tr. J. C. Hare, J. A. Froude, et al. 1845.

    Zeydal, E. H. Ludwig Tieck as a Translator of English. PMLA. li, 1936.

Varnhagen von Ense, Karl August (1785–1858). Denkwürdigkeiten und Vermischte Schriften. Mannheim, 1835–46.

    Carlyle, T. Varnhagen von Ense's Memoirs. Westminster Rev. xxxii, 1838.

—— Briefwechsel mit Varnhagen von Ense. Ed. R. Preuss, Berlin, 1892.

Werner, Zacharias (1768–1823).

    Carlyle, T. Life and Writings of Werner. Foreign Rev. i, 1828.

Wyss, J. D. (1743–1818) and Wyss, J. R. (1782–1830). Der Schweizerische Robinson. Zurich, 1812–27. [Many trns in England and America.]

Zschokke, Heinrich (1771–1848). Abällino, der grosse Bandit. Frankfort, 1793 (as novel); 1795 (as play).

    Abaellino, the Great Bandit. Tr. W. Dunlop, New York, 1802.

    The Bravo of Venice. Tr. M. G. Lewis, 1805.

[Among the more popular German writers of the nineteenth century whose works have been widely read in English trn are: Bertha Behrens ('W. Heimburg'), W. Busch (Max und Moritz, 1865), F. W. Carové, Elizabeth, queen of Roumania ('Carmen Sylva'), G. Ebers, Ernst Eckstein, F. Gerstäcker, Ida Hahn-Hahn, F. Hoffmann, H. Hoffmann (Struwelpeter, 1847), A. H. Lafontaine, G. von Moser, Klara Mundt ('Luise Mühlbach'), G. Nieritz, M. Nordau, Ida Pfeiffer, C. von Schmidt, Lola Kirschner ('Ossip Schubin'), K. A. Postl ('Charles Sealsfield'), F. Spielhagen, Johanna Spyri, J. Stinde (Die Familie Buchholz, 1884).]

(ii) English

Brontë, Charlotte. Jane Eyre. 1847. Tr. C. B., Stuttgart, 1870 (2nd edn).

    Birch-Pfeiffer, Charlotte. Die Waise von Lowood. 1855. [Play.]

Buckle, Henry Thomas. History of Civilisation in England. 1857–61.

    Fischer, E. L. Über das Gesetz der Entwicklung auf psychisch-ethischem Gebiete. Würzburg, 1875.

    Ideen aus Buckle: Geschichte der Civilisation. Leipzig, 1868.

Burns, Robert.

    Lieder und Balladen. Tr. H. J. Heintze, Brunswick, 1840; tr. K. Bartsch, Hildburghausen, 1865; tr. A. Laun, Berlin, 1869.

    Lieder. Tr. G. Pertz, Leipzig, 1859; tr. A. Corrodi (into Swiss dialect), Winterthur, 1870.

    Vieruntwintig schöne Lere. Tr. B. Prinz (into Mecklenburg Plattdeutsch), Leipzig, 1869.

    Gedichte. Tr. W. Gerhard, Leipzig, 1840; tr. H. J. Heintze, Leipzig, 1859.

    Ehlers, J. Mikrokosmos. Plattdeutsche Lieder nach Burns. Leipzig, 1877.

    Jacks, W. Robert Burns in Other Tongues. Glasgow, 1896.

    Wihan, S. Franz Stelzhamer und Robert Burns. Euphorion, x, 1903.

Byron, George Gordon, Baron.

    Lord Byrons Sämmtliche Werke. Tr. Frankfort, 1830–1; tr. A. Böttger, Leipzig, 1840; tr. by several hands, Pforzheim, 1842 (2nd edn); tr. O. Gildemeister, Berlin, 1864; tr. A. Seubert, Leipzig, 1874.

    Chamisso, A. von. Lord Byrons letzte Liebe (1827). Chios (1829). [In Gedichte, Leipzig, 1831.]

Müller, W. Lieder der Griechen. Dessau, 1821–4.

Zedlitz, J. C. von. Ritter Haralds Pilgerfahrt. Stuttgart, 1886.

Ackermann, R. Lord Byron. Sein Leben, seine Werke, sein Einfluss auf die deutsche Litteratur. Heidelberg. 1901.

Eimer, M. Byron und Ch. D. Grabbe. Frankfurter Zeitung, 15 Jan. 1903.

Flaischlen, C. Lord Byron in Deutschland. Centralblatt für Bibliothekswesen, VII, VIII, Leipzig, 1890–1.

Holzhausen, P. Lord Byron und seine deutschen Biographen. Beilage zur Allgemeinen Zeitung, nos. 174, 175, 1903.

Melchior, F. Heines Verhältnis zu Lord Byron. Literarhistorische Forschungen, no. 27, 1903.

Ochsenbein, W. Die Aufnahme Lord Byrons in Deutschland und sein Einfluss auf den jungen Heine. Berne, 1905.

Spink, G. W. J. C. von Zedlitz and Byron. MLR. XXVI, 1931.

Wiehr, J. The Relations of Grabbe to Byron. JEGP. VII, 1908.

Wyplel, L. Grillparzer und Byron. Euphorion, IX, X, 1902–3.

Campbell, Thomas. The Pleasures of Hope, with Other Poems. 1799. Tr. K. Lachmann, Hamburg, 1838.

—— Gertrude of Wyoming and other Poems. 1809. Tr. J. Finck, Baden-Baden, 1882.

Carlyle, Thomas. Sartor Resartus; the Life and Opinions of Herr Teufelsdröckh. 1833–4. Tr. T. A. Fischer, Leipzig, 1882; tr. K. Schmidt, Halle, 1900.

—— The French Revolution. 1837.

Die französische Revolution. Tr. P. Feddersen, Leipzig, 1844.

—— Critical and Miscellaneous Essays. 1839. Zerstreute historische Aufsätze. Tr. T. A. Fischer, Leipzig, 1905.

—— On Heroes, Hero-Worship, and the Heroic in History. 1841.

Über Heroen, Heroencultus und das Heroische in der Geschichte. Tr. J. Neuberg, Berlin, 1853.

—— The History of Friedrich II of Prussia, called Frederick the Great. 1858–65.

Geschichte Friedrichs II. Tr. A. Neuberg, Berlin, 1859–69.

Ausgewählte Schriften. Ed. A. Kretschmar, Leipzig, 1855–6.

Sozialpolitische Schriften. Tr. A. Pfannkuche, Göttingen, 1895.

Arbeiten und nicht verzweifeln. Auszüge aus Carlyles Werken. Düsseldorf, 1902.

Darwin, Charles. On the Origin of Species by Means of Natural Selection. 1859.

—— The Descent of Man. 1871.

Die Abstammung des Menschen. Tr. J. V. Carns, Stuttgart, 1871.

Charles Darwins Gesammelte Werke. Tr. J. V. Carns, Stuttgart, 1875–8.

Brace, C. L. Darwinism in Germany. North American Rev. CIX, 1870.

Dickens, Charles.

Boz's Sämmtliche Werke. Tr. C. Kolb et al. Leipzig, 1860–76. Tr. P. Heichen, Naumburg, 1899 (2nd edn).

Die Pickwickier. Tr. H. Roberts, Leipzig, 1837–8.

Oliver Twist. Tr. H. Roberts, Leipzig, 1838.

The German Dickens [W. Raabe]. TLS. 20 July 1922.

Doernenburg, E. and Fehse, N. Raabe und Dickens. Magdeburg, 1921.

Schmidt, J. Bilder aus dem geistigen Leben unserer Zeit. Vols. II, IV, Leipzig, 1870–5.

Freymond, R. Der Einfluss von Charles Dickens auf Gustav Freytag. Prager deutsche Studien, XIX, 1912.

Geist, H. Fritz Reuters literarische Beziehungen zu Charles Dickens. Erfurt, 1913.

Lohre, H. Otto Ludwig und Charles Dickens. Archiv, CXXIV, 1910.

Weizmann, L. Dickens und Daudet in deutscher Übersetzung. Berlin, 1880.

Disraeli, Benjamin. Lothair. 1870. Tr. A. Wünn, Leipzig, 1874.

—— Endymion. 1880. Tr. C. Böttger, Leipzig, 1881.

'Eliot, George' (i.e. Mary Ann Cross, born Evans). Scenes from Clerical Life. 1858. Bilder aus dem kirchlichen Leben Englands. Tr. G. Kuhr, Leipzig, 1885.

—— Adam Bede. 1859. Tr. J. Frese, Berlin, 1860.

—— The Mill on the Floss. 1860.

Die Mühle am Floss. Tr. J. Frese, Berlin, 1861.

—— Middlemarch. 1872. Tr. E. Lehmann, Berlin, 1872.

Green, John Richard. A Short History of the English People. 1874. Tr. E. Kirchner, Berlin, 1899.

Hallam, Henry The Constitutional History of England. 1827.

Geschichte der Verfassung von England. Tr. F. A. Rüder, Leipzig, 1828–9.

Bulwer-Lytton, Edward George Earle Lytton (Baron Lytton). Eugene Aram. 1832.

Eugen Aram mit Bezug auf T. Hood und E. L. Bulwer. Tr. H. A. Ruhe, Bromberg, 1861. [Hood's poem, with extracts from Lytton's novel.]

Bulwer-Lytton, Edward George Earle Lytton (Baron Lytton). The Last Days of Pompeii. 1834.
Die letzten Tage von Pompeii, frei nach E. L. Bulwer von J. A. Pflanz. Tübingen, 1866.
—— The Lady of Lyons. 1838.
Die Herzogin de la Vallière. Tr. G. N. Bärmann, Stuttgart, 1840.
Schmidt, J. Bilder aus dem geistigen Leben unserer Zeit. Vol. I, Leipzig, 1870.
Macaulay, Thomas Babington, Baron. History of England. 1849–61.
Geschichte von England. Tr. W. Beseler, Brunswick, 1863.
Moore, Thomas. A Selection of Irish Melodies. 1807–34.
Erin. Ein Kranz irischer Dichtungen umschlungen mit Moore'schen Liedern. Tr. A. Hinrichsen, Güstrow, 1884 (2nd edn).
—— Poetical Works, collected by himself. 1840–1.
Poetische Werke. Tr. T. Oelckers, Leipzig, 1843 (2nd edn).
—— Lalla Rookh. 1817. Tr. Friedrich de la Motte Fouqué, Vienna, 1825; tr. F. von Pechlin, Frankfort, 1830; tr. — Wollheim, Hamburg, 1846.
Scott, Sir Walter. [For trns see pp. 369–80 below.]
Häring, W. ('Willibald Alexis'). Walladmor. Berlin, 1824.
—— Schloss Avalon. Leipzig, 1827.
Hauff, W. Lichtenstein. Stuttgart, 1826.
Marschner, H. Der Templer und die Jüdin. Dresden, 1829. [Opera.]
Spindler, K. Der Jude. Stuttgart, 1827.
Zschokke, H. Bilder aus der Schweiz. Aarau, 1824–6.
Bachmann, F. W. Some German Imitators of Walter Scott. Chicago, 1933.
Eastman, C. W. Wilhelm Hauff's Lichtenstein [compared with Ivanhoe]. Americana-Germanica, III–IV, 1899–1900.
Klatt, E. Von Scott über Fontane zu Molo. Das Literarische Echo, 1 Feb. 1921.
Kohler, H. F. Walladmor von W. Alexis. Marburg, 1915.
Korff, H. A. Scott und Alexis. Heidelberg, 1907.
Schmidt, J. Bilder aus dem geistigen Leben unserer Zeit. Vol. I, Leipzig, 1870.
Shears, L. A. The Influence of Walter Scott on the Novels of Theodor Fontane. New York, 1922.
Ulrich, P. Gustav Freytags Romantechnik. Beiträge zur deutschen Literaturwissenschaft, III, 1907.
Wenger, K. Historische Romane deutscher Romantiker. Untersuchungen zur

neueren Sprach- und Literaturgeschichte, VII, 1905.
[See also R. Gottschall, Die deutsche Nationallitteratur des 19. Jahrhunderts, vol. IV, Leipzig, 1872.]
Shelley, Percy Bysshe.
Poetische Werke. Tr. J. Seybt, Leipzig, 1844.
Einige Dichtungen. Tr. F. Prössel, Brunswick, 1845.
Ausgewählte Dichtungen. Tr. A. Strodtmann, Hildburghausen, 1866.
Kellner, L. E. Studien, XXII, 1895, pp. 295–8. [Review quoting German trns of Prometheus Unbound.]
Liptzin, S. Shelley in Germany. New York, 1924.
Smith, Adam. Inquiry into the Nature and Causes of the Wealth of Nations. 1776. Tr. — Dörrien and — Garve, Breslau, 1794–6.
Über die Quellen des Volkswohlstandes. Tr. C. W. Asher, Stuttgart, 1861.
Untersuchung über das Wesen und die Ursachen des Volkswohlstandes. Tr. F. Stöpel, Berlin, 1878.
Kühn, E. Der Staatswirtschaftslehrer Chr. Jac. Kraus und seine Beziehungen zu Adam Smith. Berne, 1902.
Spencer, Herbert. First Principles. 1862.
Grundlagen der Philosophie. Tr. B. Vetter, Stuttgart, 1875.
—— The Principles of Sociology. 1876–82.
Die Prinzipien der Soziologie. Tr. B. Vetter, Stuttgart, 1876–7.
Didden, R. A German Appreciation of Herbert Spencer. Westminster Rev. CXLVIII, 1897.
Gaupp, O. Herbert Spencer. Stuttgart, 1897.
Tennyson, Alfred, Baron.
Ausgewählte Dichtungen. Tr. A. Strodtmann, Berlin, 1867; tr. H. A. Feldmann (preface by E. Geibel), Hamburg, 1870; tr. M. Rugard, Elbing, 1872.
—— Idylls of the King. 1859–85.
Königsidyllen. Tr. W. Scholz, Berlin, 1867; tr. H. A. Feldmann, Leipzig, 1871.
—— Enoch Arden. 1864. Tr. R. Schellwien, Quedlinberg, 1867; tr. F. W. Weber, Leipzig, 1869; tr. H. A. Feldmann, Hamburg, 1870; tr. A. Strodtmann, Berlin, 1876; tr. E. Duboc, Hamburg, 1890 (32nd edn).
Meyer, W. Tennysons Jugendgedichte in deutscher Übersetzung. Münster, 1914.
Schmitt, K. Alfred Tennyson in Deutschland. Deutsches Museum, III, 1853.
Wilde, Oscar. The Importance of being Earnest. 1895.
Bunbury. Tr. F. P. Greve, Minden, 1903.

Wilde, Oscar. The Picture of Dorian Gray.
1891. Tr. J. Gaulke, Leipzig, 1901.
  Meyerfeld, M. Oscar Wilde in Deutschland. Das Literarische Echo, 1 Jan. 1903.
  Sherard, R. H. Life of Oscar Wilde.
1911. [Bibliography.]

(4) THE LITERARY RELATIONS OF ENGLAND
AND ITALY

(a) *General*

Arnold, M. England and the Italian Question.
1859.
Bickersteth, G. Introduction to the Poems of
Leopardi. Cambridge, 1923.
Boileau, H. T. Italy in the Post-Victorian
Novel. Philadelphia, 1931.
Bräm, E. M. Die italienische Renaissance in
dem englischen Geistesleben des 19. Jahrhunderts. Zurich, 1932.
Byron, George Gordon, Baron. Childe Harold.
Canto IV. 1818.
Clarke, H. A. Browning's Italy: a Study of
Italian Life and Art in Browning. New
York, 1907.
De Courten, M. L. Shelley e l' Italia. Milan,
1923.
Dupré, H. Un Italien d'Angleterre: le Poète
Peintre D. G. Rossetti. Paris, 1922.
Elkin, F. Walter Savage Landor's Studies of
Italian Life and Literature. Philadelphia,
1934.
Faggi, A. Swinburne Aedo d' Italia. Marzocco,
May 1926.
—— Dante Gabriele Rossetti. Marzocco, 27
May 1928.
Ferretti, L. Carducci e la Letteratura inglese.
Milan, 1927.
Fornelli, G. W. S. Landor e l' Italia. Forlì,
1931.
Fuess, C. M. Lord Byron as a Satirist in
Verse. New York, 1912.
Hogreve, P. Browning and Italian Art and
Artists. Kansas University Bulletin, 1914.
Hunt, L. Stories from the Italian Poets, with
Lives of the Writers. 1846; 1854.
Italian Influence on English Poetry. Edinburgh Rev. Jan. 1896.
King, R. W. Italian Influence on English
Scholarship and Literature during the
Romantic Revival. MLR. xx, xxi, 1925–6.
Koeppel, E. Italienische Einflüsse auf die
englische Literatur. Jahresberichte für
neuere deutsche Literaturgeschichte, I, v,
1892, 1897.
Lüder, A. Lord Byrons Urtheile über Italien
und seine Bewohner, ihre Sprache, Literatur
und Kunst. Dresden, 1893. [See also Ang.
xv, 1903.]
Marchesi, G. Leopardi e la Poesia inglese.
Iride, III, 1899.

Marshall, R. Italy in English Literature
1795–1815. New York, 1934.
Massarani, T. Poeti inglesi nelle Version
italiane. [In Studi di Letteratura e d' Arte
Florence, 1899.]
Olivero, F. Saggi di Letteratura inglese
Bari, 1913.
—— Studi sul Romanticismo inglese. Bari
1914.
—— English Literature in Leopardi's 'Pen
sieri di varia Filosofia.' Turin, 1931.
Pratesi, L. L' Italianità nei Canti di Elisa
betta Barrett Browning. Rocca San Casci
ano, 1928.
Renauld, C. C. A. Swinburne et l'Italie
Nouvelle Revue italienne, 15 Oct. 1920.
Richter, L. Swinburne's Verhältnis zu Frank
reich und Italien. Leipzig, 1911.
Rogers, S. Italy. A Poem. 2 pts, 1822–8.
Roscoe, T. Italian Novelists. 1825. [An
anthology of trns.]
Rossetti, D. G. The Early Italian Poets from
Ciullo d' Alcamo to Dante Alighieri 1100-
1200–1300 in the Original Metres togethe
with Dante's Vita Nuova. 1861; 1874 (rev
as Dante and his Circle: with the Italian
Poets preceding him).
Scalia, S. E. Carducci et la Critique anglo
saxonne. Revue de Littérature comparée
Sept. 1935.
—— Carducci, his Critics and Translators in
England and America, 1881–1932. New
York, 1937.
Segre, C. Relazioni letterarie fra Italia e
Inghilterra. Studi. Florence, 1911.
Swinburne, A. C. A Song of Italy. 1867.
Symonds, J. A. The Renaissance in Italy.
1875–86.
Toynbee, P. The Oxford Dante Society. A
Record of Forty-Four Years. Oxford, 1920
Viglione, F. Ugo Foscolo in Inghilterra.
Catania, 1910.
Waller, R. D. The Rossetti Family. Manchester, 1932.

(b) *Single Authors*

(i) Italian

Alfieri, Vittorio (1749–1803).
  The Tragedies of Vittorio Alfieri. Tr.
C. Lloyd, 1815.
  Byron, George Gordon, Baron. Marino
Faliero. 1821.
  —— The Two Foscari. 1821.
  —— Sardanapalus. 1821.
  Krause, F. Byrons Marino Faliero. Ein
Beitrag zur vergleichenden Literatur-
geschichte. Breslau, 1897.
  Pudbres, Anna. Lord Byron, Admirer
and Imitator of Alfieri. E. Studien, XXXIII,
1903.

Boccaccio, Giovanni (1313–1375). Decamerone. 1348–53.
    Coleridge, S. T. The Garden of Boccaccio. 1828.
    Eliot, G. How Lisa loved the King. 1869.
    Landor, W. S. Pentameron and Pentalogia. 1837.
    Keats, J. Isabella, or the Pot of Basil. 1818.
    Proctor, B. W. Sicilian Story. 1821.
Boiardo, Matteo Maria (1441–1494). Orlando Innamorato. Tr. W. S. Rose, 1823.
Carducci, Giosuè (1835–1907).
    Amram, B. B. Swinburne and Carducci. Yale Rev. v, 1916.
    Carducci in English. TLS. 8 April 1921.
Casti, Giovanni Battista (1721–1803). Gli Animali Parlanti. Paris, 1802.
    The Court and Parliament of Beasts. Tr. W. S. Rose, 1816, 1819.
—— Il Poema Tartaro. Milan, 1803.
    Fuess, C. M. Lord Byron as a Satirist in Verse. 1912.
Dante Alighieri (1265–1321).
    The Inferno of Dante Alighieri. Tr. H. F. Cary, 1805.
    The Vision; or Hell, Purgatory, and Paradise. Tr. H. F. Cary, 1814; tr. I. C. Wright, 1833–40; tr. A. J. Butler, 1880–92.
    Hunt, Leigh. The Story of Rimini. 1816.
    Shelley, Percy Bysshe. The Triumph of Life. 1824.
    Church, R. W. Dante. Christian Remembrancer, xi, 1850.
    Dobelli, A. Dante e Byron. Giornale Dantesco, vi, 1898.
    Farinelli, A. Dante in Ispagna, Francia, Inghilterra, Germania. Turin, 1922.
    Galimberti, Alice. Dante nel Pensiero inglese. Florence, 1921.
    Kraeger, H. Lord Byron und Francesca da Rimini. Archiv, xcviii, 1897.
    Kuhns, O. Dante's Influence on Shelley. MLN. xiii, 1898.
—— Dante's Influence on English Poetry in the XIX Century. MLN. xiv, 1899.
    Monti, G. G. Studi critici. Florence, 1887. [Byron and Dante, Leopardi and Byron.]
    Norton, C. E. Ruskin's Comments on Dante. 1903.
    Scudder, V. D. The Life of the Spirit in the Modern English Poets. Boston, 1895.
    Toynbee, P. Dante in English Literature. 1909.
    Valgimigli, A. Il Culto di Dante in Inghilterra. Giornale Dantesco, vi, 1898.

Goldoni, Carlo (1707–1793).
    Maddalena, E. Goldoni in Inghilterra e in America. Rivista d' Italia, 15 Sept. 1923.
—— Goldoni in inglese. Marzocco, 7 Jan. 1923.
Leopardi, Giacomo (1798–1827). Bologna, 1824; Florence, 1831. Versi.
—— Opere. Florence, 1845.
    The Poems of Leopardi. Tr. F. H. Cliffe, 1893.
—— Operette morali, Pensieri. Milan, 1826–7.
    Essays, Dialogues and Thoughts. Tr. P. Maxwell, 1893; tr. J. Thomson, 1905.
    Essays and Dialogues. Tr. C. Edwardes, 1882.
    Rébora, P. Traduttori e Critici inglesi di Leopardi. Nuova Antologia, 1 June 1920.
    Schanzer, A. Il Leopardi in Inghilterra. Rassegna nazionale, April 1900.
    [See also G. L. Bickersteth, The Poems of Leopardi, Bibliography, Cambridge, 1923.]
Manzoni, Alessandro (1785–1873). I Promessi Sposi. Milan, 1825–6.
    The Betrothed Lovers. Tr. C. Swan, Pisa, 1828.
    The Betrothed. Tr. 1834; tr. 1844.
Petrarca, Francesco (1304–1374).
    Garnett, R. Dante, Petrarch, Camoens. CXXIV Sonnets translated. 1896.
    Rossetti, D. G. The House of Life. 1881.
Pulci, Luigi (1432–1484). Morgante Maggiore. Venice, 1481.
    Canto i. Tr. G. G. Byron, 1822.
    Byron, George Gordon, Baron. Don Juan. 1819–24.
    Frere, J. H. Prospectus and Specimen of an intended National Work intended by William and Robert Whistlecraft. 1817–8.
Redi, Francesco (1626–1698). Bacco in Toscana. Florence, 1685.
    Bacchus in Tuscany. A Dithyrambic Poem. Tr. Leigh Hunt, 1825.
Tasso, Torquato (1544–1595). Gerusalemme liberata. Venice, 1580.
    Jerusalem Delivered. Tr. J. H. Hunt, 1818; tr. J. H. Wiffen, 1824.
—— Aminta. Venice, 1581.
    Amyntas; a Tale of the Woods. Tr. Leigh Hunt, 1820.

(ii) English

Brontë, Charlotte. Jane Eyre. 1847.
    Michély, R. L' Orfanella di Lowood. Naples, 1874.
Byron, George Gordon, Baron.
    Opere complete di Lord Byron. Tr. C. Rusconi, Padua, 1842.
    Opere di Lord Giorgio Byron. Tr. Naples, 1886.

Farinelli, A. Byron e il Byronismo. Bologna, 1924.

Lo Gatto, E. Da Lord Byron ai Poete Slavi. I Libri del Giorno, Sept. 1925.

Monti, G. Giac. Leopardi e Giorgio Byron. [In Studi Critici, Florence, 1887.]

Muoni, G. La Fama del Byron e il Byronismo in Italia. Milan, 1903.

Simhart, M. Lord Byrons Einfluss auf die italienische Literatur. Leipzig, 1909.

'Stendhal' (Henri Beyle). Lord Byron en Italie et en France. Récit d'un Témoin oculaire. Revue de Paris, 1830.

Zacchetti, C. Lord Byron e l' Italia. Palermo, 1920.

Carlyle, Thomas. On Heroes, Hero-Worship and the Heroic in History. 1841.

Gli Eroi. Tr. M. P. Pascolato, Florence, 1847.

Dickens, Charles. A Christmas Carol. 1844.

Una Canzone del Natale in Prosa. Tr. E. de Bendetti, Milan, 1873.

——Oliver Twist. 1838. Tr. G. Basseggio, 1840.

Vigo-Fazio, L. Dickens in Italia. Le Lettere, 1 March 1920.

Green, John Richard. A Short History of the English People. 1874. Tr. F. Santarelli, Florence, 1884.

Keats, John.

Marchesi, G. Leopardi e la Poesia inglese. Iride, III, 1899.

Bulwer-Lytton, E. G. E. L., Baron. The Last Days of Pompeii. 1834.

Peruzzine, G. Ione; Drammo lirico. Milan, [1858?].

—— Rienzi. 1835. Tr. S. M. Maggione, Milan, 1836.

—— The Coming Race. 1871.

La Razza dell' Avvenire. Tr. C. Cazoretti, Milan, 1874.

Macaulay, Thomas Babington, Baron. Essays. 1843.

Saggi biografici e critici. Tr. C. Rovighi, Turin, 1859–66.

Moore, Thomas. A Selection of Irish Melodies. 1807–34.

Melodie irlandesi. Tr. I. Supino, Pisa, 1880.

—— Lalla Rookh. 1817. Tr. G. Camisiani, Milan, 1872; tr. A. Maffei, Milan, 1886.

Il Profeta velato. Tr. G. Flechia, Turin, 1838.

—— The Loves of the Angels. 1823. Tr. Milan, 1882.

—— The Epicurean. 1827. Tr. Milan, 1836.

Rogers, Samuel. Human Life. A Poem. 1819. Tr. N. Paciotti, Turin, 1820.

Scott, Sir Walter. Waverley. 1814. Tr. Pisa, 1823.

—— Ivanhoe. 1820. Tr. Milan, 1869.

Manzoni, A. I Promessi Sposi. Milan, 1825–6.

Marini, G. M. Il Templario. Opera 1868. [Italian and French.]

Agnoli, G. Gli Albori del Romanzo Storico in Italia e i primi Imitatori di Walter Scott. Piacenza, 1906.

Altrocchi, R. Scott, Manzoni, Rovani. MLN. XLI, 1926.

Costa, P. Walter Scott in Italia. Corriere d' Italia, 1 Oct. 1921.

Croce, B. Note sulla Poesia italiana e straniera del Secolo decimo-nono, XXII Walter Scott. Critica, 20 Jan. 1923.

Dotti, M. Derivazioni nei Promessi Sposi di A. Manzoni dai Romanzi di Walter Scott. Pisa, 1900.

D' Ovidio, F. Manzoni e Walter Scott. [In Studi Manzoniani, Caserta, 1928.]

Waille, V. Le Romantisme de Manzoni Algiers, 1890.

Shelley, Percy Bysshe.

Opere poetiche scelte. Tr. G. A., Milan, 1858.

Poesie scelte. Tr. Erasmo di Lustro da Forio, Naples, 1878.

Ackermann, R. Shelley in Frankreich und Italien. E. Studien, XVII, 1892. [Short review of above trns.]

Biagi, G. Gli ultimi Giorni di P. B. Shelley. Florence, 1892.

Bini, B. P. B. Shelley nel Risorgimento italiano. Fiume, 1927.

Chiapelli, Al. Leopardi e Shelley. Marzocco, 17 July 1927.

Chiarini, G. Shelley. [In Ombre e Figure, Rome, 1883.]

Commemorazione di Percy Bysshe Shelley in Roma. Rome, 1893.

Mancini, D. Percy Bysshe Shelley. Città di Castello, 1892.

Raimondi, R. Percy Bysshe Shelley in Italia. Padua, 1920.

Zanella, G. Shelley e G. Leopardi. Nuova Antologia, I, 1881. [Also in Paralleli letterari, Verona, 1885.]

Smith, Adam. Inquiry into the Nature and Causes of the Wealth of Nations. 1776.

Ricerche sopra la Natura e le Cause della Richessa delle Nazioni. Tr. 1851.

Spencer, Herbert. First Principles. 1862.

Allara, G. Studio critico sopra 'I Primi Principii' di E. Spencer. Casale, 1891.

—— The Principles of Sociology. 1876–82.

Principii di Sociologia. Tr. A. Salandra, Biblioteca dell' Economista, III, 1881.

Cesca, G. L' Evoluzionismo di E. Spencer. Verona, 1883.

Tennyson, Alfred, Baron. Idylls of the King. 1859–85.

Idilli, Liriche, Miti e Leggende, Enoch Arden. Tr. C. Faccioli, Verona, 1876.

ennyson, Alfred, Baron. Enoch Arden. 1864. Tr. A. Saggini, Florence, 1885.

5) THE LITERARY RELATIONS OF ENGLAND WITH SPAIN AND PORTUGAL

(a) General

Bejarano, M. M. Vida y Obras de Don J. M. Blanco-White. Madrid, 1921.

Bell, A. Portuguese Literature. Oxford, 1922.

Borrow, George. The Bible in Spain. 1843.

Buceta, E. El Entusiasmo por España en algunos Románticos ingleses. Revista de Filología Española, x, 1923.

—— Relaciones anglo-hispanas: Apuntes preliminares para un Estudio de las traducciones inglesas de Romances en el primer Tercio del Siglo XIX. Madrid, 1930.

Fitzmaurice-Kelly, J. A New History of Spanish Literature. Oxford, 1926.

Ford, J. D. M. English Influence on Spanish Literature in the Early Part of the Nineteenth Century. PMLA. XVI, 1901.

Ford, R. Handbook for Travellers in Spain. 1845.

—— Gatherings from Spain. 1846.

Hespelt, E. H. Shelley and Spain. PMLA. XXXVIII, 1923.

Lockhart, J. G. Ancient Spanish Ballads, Historical and Romantic. 1823.

Morán, C. García. Influencia de los Escritores románticos ingleses en el Romanticismo español. Madrid, 1923.

Peers, E. A. Rivas and Romanticism in Spain. Liverpool, 1923.

—— The Literary Activities of the Spanish 'Emigrados' in England (1814–1834). MLR. XIX, 1924.

—— Minor English Influences on Spanish Romanticism. Revue hispanique, LXII, 1924.

Pelayo, M. Historia de las Ideas estéticas en España. Vol. VIII, Madrid, 1908.

Pfandl, L. Robert Southey und Spanien. Revue Hispanique, XXVIII, 1913.

Piñeyro, E. El Romantismo en España. Paris, 1904.

Southey, R. Letters written during a Short Residence in Spain and Portugal. 1797.

—— Letters from England; by Don Manuel Alvarez Espriella. 1807.

Walter, F. La Littérature portugaise en Angleterre à l'Époque romantique. Paris, 1927.

Zellars, G. G. Influencia de Walter Scott en España. Revista de Filología Española, XVIII, 1931.

(b) Single Authors

(i) Spanish and Portuguese

Calderón de La Barca, Pedro (1600–1681).
Six Dramas of Calderón. Tr. Edward FitzGerald, 1853.

The Mighty Magician and Such Stuff as Dreams are made of. Tr. Edward Fitz-Gerald, 1865.

FitzGerald and Calderón. Academy, 30 May 1903.

Madariaga, S. de. Shelley and Calderón, and other Essays on English and Spanish Poetry. 1920.

Camoens, Luis de (c. 1524–1580). Os Lusiadas. Lisbon, 1572.

The Lusiad of Camoens [Bks I–v]. Tr. E. Quillinan, 1853.

Crónica del Cid. Burgos, 1593.

Chronicle of the Cid. Tr. R. Southey, 1808.

Buceta, E. Opiniones de Southey y Coleridge sobre el 'Poema del Cid.' Revista de Filología Española, IX, 1922.

Montalvo, García Ordoñez de (fl. 1480).
Amadis of Gaul. Tr. R. Southey, 1803; tr. W. S. Rose, 1803.

(ii) English

Buckle, Henry Thomas. History of Civilization in England. 1857–61.
Historia de la Civilización in España. Tr. [extract] F. G. y T., 1861.

Byron, George Gordon, Baron.
Poemas dramáticos de Lord Byron. Tr. Madrid, 1886.
A Peregrinação de Childe Harold. [Portuguese.] Tr. F. J. Pinheiro Guimarães. Lisbon, 1863.
Don Juan, Poema. Tr. F. Villalvra, Madrid, 1876; tr. J. A. R., Barcelona, 1883.
Churchman, P. H. Byron and Espronceda. 1909.
—— The Beginnings of Byronism in Spain. Revue hispanique, XXVI, 1910.
Rycroft, W. S. Espronceda. La Influencia de Byron. Boletín bibliográfico, II, Lima, 1926.

Carlyle, Thomas. Sartor Resartus. 1838. Tr. E. González Blanco, Barcelona, 1905.
—— On Heroes, Hero-worship and the Heroic in History. 1841.
Los Héroes. Tr. J. G. Orbón, Madrid, 1893.

Dickens, Charles. Oliver Twist. 1838.
El Hijo de la Parroquia. Tr. E. L. de Verneuil, Barcelona, 1883.

Gaskell, Elizabeth Cleghorn. Mary Barton. 1848. Tr. E. Quilez, Madrid, 1879.

Lewis, Matthew Gregory. The Monk. 1795.
El Fraile, o Historia del Padre Ambrosio. Tr. 1822.

Macaulay, Thomas Babington, Baron. Essays. 1843.
Estudios críticos. Tr. J. Bender, Madrid, 1880.
Vidas de Políticos ingleses. Tr. J. Bender, Madrid, 1885.

Macpherson, James.
Peers, E. A. The Influence of Ossian in Spain. PQ. III, 1924.
Milton, John.
Peers, E. A. Milton in Spain. Stud. Phil. XXIII, 1926.
Scott, Sir Walter. Waverley. 1814. Tr. Portuguese C. Lopes de Moura, Paris, 1844; tr. A. J. Ramalho e Sousa, Lisbon, 1845.
—— Guy Mannering. 1815. Tr. Portuguese M. A. da Silva, Lisbon, 1842.
—— The Antiquary. 1816.
El Anticuario. Tr. Madrid, 1831; tr. Barcelona, 1834.
—— Old Mortality. 1816.
Os Puritanos da Escossia. Tr. Portuguese C. Lopes de Moura, Paris, 1837.
—— Ivanhoe. 1820. Tr. Portuguese A. J. Ramalho e Sousa, Lisbon, 1838.
Churchman, P. H. and Peers, E. A. A Survey of the Influence of Sir Walter Scott in Spain. Revue hispanique, LV, 1922.
González Palencia, A. Walter Scott y la Censura gubernativa. Revista de la Biblioteca, Archivo y Museo, IV, Madrid, 1927.
Peers, E. A. Studies in the Influence of Sir Walter Scott in Spain. Revue hispanique, LVIII, 1926.
Soldevila, F. Walter Scott y el Renacimento literario en España. Bulletin of Spanish Studies, III, 1926.
Smith, Adam. Inquiry into the Nature and Causes of the Wealth of Nations. 1776.
Investigación de la Naturaleza y Causas de la Riqueza de las Naciones. Tr. J. A. Ortiz, Valladolid, 1794.
Spencer, Herbert. First Principles. 1862.
Los primeros Principios. Tr. Madrid, 1879.
—— Principles of Sociology. 1876–82.
Principios de Sociología. Tr. C. Cazorla, Madrid, 1883.
Tennyson, Alfred, Baron.
Poemas. Tr. D. V. de Arana, Barcelona, 1883.
Young, Edward.
Peers, E. A. The Influence of Young and Gray in Spain. MLR. XXI, 1926.
[For a bibliography of trns into Spanish see Revista de Filología Española, VII, 1920 ff.]

(6) THE LITERARY RELATIONS OF ENGLAND WITH SCANDINAVIA

(a) General

Aas, L. William Archer. Atlantis, II, 1920.
Borrow, George. Romantic Ballads translated from the Danish. 1826.

Burchardt, C. B. Norwegian Life and Literature: English Accounts and Views. Oxford 1920.
Craigie, Sir W. The Northern Element in English Literature. Toronto, 1933.
Farley, F. E. Scandinavian Influences in the English Romantic Movement. Boston 1903.
Gosse, Sir E. Studies in the Literature of Northern Europe. 1879.
Gustafson, A. T. English Influence in Fredrika Bremer. JEGP. XXX, 1933.
Hermansson, H. Sir Joseph Banks and Iceland. Islandica, XVIII, 1928.
Petersens, H.-A. R. P. Gillies, 'Foreign Quarterly Review' och den svenska Litteraturen Samlaren, XIV, 1933.
Powell, F. Y. and Vigfússon, G. Origine Islandicae. Oxford, 1905.
Sverige i England. Göteborg, 1923. [Various contributors.]
Wright, H. G. George Borrow's Translations from the Scandinavian Languages. Edda XVI, 1921.
—— Swedish Literature: its Influence in England. Times, Swedish Supplement 29 May 1923.
—— Southey's Relations with Finland and Scandinavia. MLR. XXVII, 1932.
—— Influence of George Borrow in Norway and Sweden. MLR. XXIX, 1934.

(b) Icelandic Saga.

Grettis Saga. Tr. W. Morris, 1869.
Volsunga Saga. Tr. E. Magnússon and W. Morris, 1870.
Morris, W. The Story of Sigurd the Volsung and the Fall of the Nibelungs. 1876.
McDowell, G. T. The Treatment of the Volsungasaga by William Morris. Scandinavian Stud. and Notes, VII, 1923.
Laxdaela Saga.
Morris, W. The Loves of Gudrun. [In The Earthly Paradise, 1868–70.]
Allen, R. B. Old Icelandic Sources in the English Novel. Philadelphia, 1934.
Herford, C. H. Norse Myth in English Poetry. 1919.
The Saga Library. Ed. E. Magnússon and W. Morris, 1891–5.
Three Northern Love Stories. Tr. E. Magnússon and W. Morris, 1875.

(c) Single Authors

(i) Scandinavian

Andersen, Hans Christian (1805–1875). Eventyr. Copenhagen, 1835–72.
Danish Fairy Tales and Legends. Tr. Caroline Peachey, 1846.

Wonderful Stories for Children. Tr. Mary Howitt, 1846.

Hans Christian Andersen Books. TLS. 5 Feb. 1925.

Asbjörnsen, P. C. and Moe, J. Norske Folke-Eventyr. Christiania, 1843–4.

—— Norske Huldre-Eventyr og Folkesagn. Christiania, 1845–8.

Popular Tales from the Norse. Tr. Sir G. Dasent, 1859.

Bremer, Fredrika (1801–1865).

Works. Tr. Mary Howitt, 1846 (4th edn).

Ibsen, Henrik (1828–1906).

Translations from the Norse. H. Ibsen and P. Dass, by a B.S.S. [i.e. a member of the British Scandinavian Society]. Gloucester, [1879?] (priv. ptd).

Ibsen's Prose Dramas. Tr. W. Archer, 1890–1.

Prose Dramas of Henrik Ibsen. Ed. Sir E. Gosse, 1890.

—— Kejser og Galilœer. Copenhagen, 1873.

The Emperor and the Galilean. Tr. C. Ray, 1876.

—— Samfundets Stötter. Copenhagen, 1877.

Pillars of Society, and Other Plays. Ed. Havelock Ellis, 1888.

—— Et Dukkehjem. Copenhagen, 1879.

Nora. Tr. T. Weber, Copenhagen, 1880; tr. H. F. Lord, 1882.

Jones, H. A. Saints and Sinners. 1884.

—— Judah. 1890.

Ibsen in England. Academy, 23 March 1901.

Archer, W. Ibsen and English Criticism. Fortnightly Rev. XLVI, 1889.

Decker, C. R. Ibsen's Literary Reputation and Victorian Taste. Stud. Phil. XXXII, 1935.

Filon, A. Ibsen à Londres, le Théâtre de Demain. Revue des Deux Mondes, 1 Nov. 1895.

Franc, M. A. Ibsen in England. Boston, 1920.

Gosse, Sir E. Ibsen. 1907.

Shaw, G. B. The Quintessence of Ibsenism. 1892.

Wicksteed, P. H. Four Lectures on Ibsen. 1892 (2nd edn).

Strindberg, August (1849–1912).

Strindberg in England. TLS. 30 Jan. 1930.

Lind-af-Hageby, L. August Strindberg. 1913.

(ii) English

Brontë, Charlotte. Jane Eyre. 1847.

Et Vaisenhuus-barn. Copenhagen, 1859. [A play.]

Burns, Robert.

Sånger och Ballader. Tr. K. H. von Becker and C. R. Mannerheim, Helsingfors, 1854.

Byron, George Gordon, Baron.

Udvalgte dramatiske Digte og Fortællinger af Byron. Tr. E. Lembcke, Copenhagen, 1873–6.

Childe Harold's Pilgrimsfärd. Tr. A. F. Skjöldebrand, Stockholm, 1832.

Junker Harolds Pilgrimsfart. Tr. A. Hansen, Copenhagen, 1880.

Beck, R. Grimer Thomsen—a Pioneer Byron student. JEGP. XXVII, 1928.

—— Gisli Bryngúlfson—an Icelandic Imitator of Childe Harold's Pilgrimage. JEGP. XXVIII, 1929.

Holthausen, F. Skandinavische Byron-Übersetzungen. E. Studien, XXV, 1898.

—— Tegnér und Byron. Archiv, CI, 1899.

Dickens, Charles. Posthumous Papers of the Pickwick Club. 1837.

Pickwick-Klubbens Efterlemnade-Papper. Tr. L. A. Malmgren, Stockholm, 1861.

Udtog af Pikvik-Klubbens efterladte Papirer. Tr. A. Andresen, Copenhagen, 1881–3.

—— Martin Chuzzlewit. 1844. Tr. C. J. Backman, Stockholm, 1871.

Bulwer-Lytton, E. G. E. L. (Baron Lytton).

The Lady of Lyons. 1838.

Lyonesiskan, eller Kärlek och Stolthet. Tr. Stockholm, 1839.

Macaulay, Thomas Babington, Baron. Essays. 1843.

Biografiska Skizzer. Tr. Carlshamn, 1869.

—— History of England. 1849–61.

Englands Historie. Tr. W. Dauditz, Copenhagen, 1852–8.

Moore, Thomas. A Selection of Irish Melodies. 1807–34.

Irländske Melodier och Dikter. Tr. Stockholm, 1825; tr. C. R. Nyblom, Upsala, 1858.

—— Lalla Rookh. 1817. Tr. E. Lembcke, Copenhagen, 1878.

Scott, Sir Walter. The Antiquary. 1816.

Jonathan Oldbuck eller Fornforskaren. Tr. T. Sundler, Stockholm, 1827.

Oldgrandskeren. Tr. Copenhagen, 1856–8.

Tennyson, Alfred, Baron. Idylls of the King. 1859–85.

Idyller om Kong. Tr. A. Munch, Copenhagen, 1876.

—— Enoch Arden. 1864. Tr. A. Munch, Copenhagen, 1866.

(7) The Literary Relations of England with the Slavonic Countries

(a) General

Baring, M. Landmarks in Russian Literature. 1910.

Janecek, B. Bibliography of Czech Literature in English Translation. Bulletin of Bibliography, XVI, 1937.

Jovanović, J. M. Srpsko engleski odnosi. [In Srpski Krijiževni Glasnik, Belgrade, 1931.]

Kozlowski, W. M. Notes sur les Échanges des Idées philosophiques entre l'Angleterre et la Pologne. Revue de Littérature comparée, III, 1923.

Lednicki, W. Mickiewicz and England. Pologne littéraire, 15 April 1929.

Lytton, Edward Robert, Earl of. Serbski Pesme. 1861. [Serbian national songs.]

Mathesius, V. English Studies in Czecho-Slovakia. E. Studies, April 1923.

Morf, G. The Polish heritage of Joseph Conrad. 1930.

Morfill, W. R. Russia. 1890.

—— A History of Russia. 1902.

—— Poland. 1890.

Potter, S. Palacký a anglické písemnictví. Časopis Matice Moravské, LIII, 1929.

Simmons, E. J. Gogol and English Literature. MLR. XXVI, 1931.

—— English Literature in Russia. Harvard Stud. XIII, 1931.

—— English Literature and Culture in Russia (1553–1840). Cambridge, U.S.A. 1935.

Ce que les Écrivains polonais doivent aux Littératures étrangères: Enquête. Pologne littéraire, 1928. [Various contributors.]

Vinogradoff, V. The Evolution of Russian Naturalism. Leningrad, 1929. [In Russian.]

Vočadlo, O. English Influences on Palacky. Slavonic Rev. III, 1925.

—— Anglie a Čechy. Lumir, LVII, 1931. [With bibliography of Anglo-Bohemian relations.]

Williams, A. Russian and British Poets a Hundred Years Ago. TLS. 24 May 1923.

Wright, C. T. H. The Meaning of Russian Literature. Quart. Rev. Jan. 1921.

(b) Single Authors

(i) Russian, etc.

Chekhov, Anton (1860–1904).
Nabokoff, C. Chekhov on the English Stage. Contemporary Rev. June 1926.

Dostoïevski, Fiodor (1822–1881).
Novels. Tr. C. Garnett, 1912.

Lloyd, J. A. T. A Great Russian Realist. 1912.
Mirsky, S. Dostojevski in Frankreich und England. Slavische Rundschau, III, 1931.
Murry, J. M. Fyodor Dostoevsky. 1916.

Gogol, Nikolai (1809–52).
Cournos, J. The First Extensive Studies in English of Gogol and Pushkin. New York Evening Post, Literary Supplement, 12 June 1926.

Sienkiewicz, Henryk (1846–1916). Quo Vadis? Warsaw, 1895. Tr. 1896.

—— Ogniem e mieczem. Warsaw, 1884.
With Fire and Sword. Tr. 1890–5.

Tolstoi, Leo (1828–1910). Разсказы о Севастопольской Оборонѣ. St Petersburg, 1855.
Sebastopol. Tr. (from a French version) F. D. Millet, New York, 1887.
Sevastopol. Tr. Isabel Hapgood, 1889.

—— Война и Миръ. Moscow, 1864–9.
War and Peace. Tr. 1886; tr. N. H. Dole, New York, 1889.

—— Анна Каренина. Moscow, 1873–6.
Anna Karenina. Tr. N. H. Dole, New York, 1886.

—— Крейцерова Соната. Berlin, 1890.
The Kreutzer Sonata. Tr. B. R. Tucker, Boston, 1890; tr. W. M. Thomson, 1896.

Garnett, E. Tolstoi, his Life and Writings. 1914.
Henley, W. E. Tolstoi. [In Views and Reviews, 1890.]
Perris, G. H. Tolstoi: the Grand Mujik. 1898.
Turner, C. E. Count Tolstoi as a Novelist and Thinker. 1888.
Yassukovitch, Antonina. Tolstoi in English, 1878–1929. Bulletin of New York Public Lib. XXXIII, 1929.

Turgeniev, Ivan (1818–1883).
Novels. Tr. Constance Garnett, 1894–9.

Lloyd, J. A. T. Two Russian Reformers; Ivan Turgenev, and Leo Tolstoi. 1910.
Whibley, C. Ivan Turgenev. North American Rev. DXLII, 1902.

(ii) English

Byron, George Gordon, Baron.
Сочиненія Лорда Байрона въ переводахъ Русскихъ Поэтовъ. St Petersburg, 1864–6.
Poezye Lorda Byrona. Warsaw, 1885 ff.

Byrons Don Juan in polnischer Übersetzung. Magazin, LI, 1880.
Harnack, O. Pushkin und Byron. Zeitschrift für vergleichende Literaturgeschichte, I, 1888. [Also in Essays und Studien, Brunswick, 1899.]
Lipnicki, E. Byron im Befreiungskampfe der polnischen Nationalliteratur. Magazin, XLVIII, 1877.
Petrović, I. M. Lord Bajron kod Jugoslovena. Požarevac, 1931.
Spasowicz, W. Байронизмъ у Пушкина и Лермонтова (Pushkin and Lermontov). Vilna, 1911.
Wesselowsky, J. A. Byron. Moscow, 1902.
Zdiechowski, M. Karl Hynek Macha und

Byrons Einfluss auf die tschechische Dichtkunst. Anzeiger der Akademie der Wissenschaften in Krakau, Cracow, 1893.
—— Byron i jego wiek. Studya porównawczoliterackie, Cracow, 1894–7.
Žirmunsky, V. Byron and Pushkin [in Russian]. Leningrad, 1924.
)e Quincey, Thomas. Confessions of an English Opium Eater. 1821. Tr. Russian 1834.
Simmons, E. J. Gogol and English Literature. MLR. Oct. 1931.
)ickens, Charles Dombey and Son. Tr. Russian, St Petersburg, 1847–8.
reen, John Richard. A Short History of the English People. 1874. Tr. Russian P. Nikolaev, Moscow, 1891–2.
acaulay, Thomas Babington, Baron. History of England. 1849–61.
Dějiny Anglické. Tr. Prague, 1862–5.
ilton, John. Paradise Lost. 1667.
Nyegosh, P. P. Lucha Microcosma. Belgrade, 1847.
oore, Thomas. Lalla Rookh. 1817. Tr. Polish, Warsaw, 1826.
oland. National Book Council, 1932.
orter, Jane. Thaddaeus of Warsaw. 1803. [Widely read in Poland in a German trn from about 1810.]
:ott, Sir Walter. The Antiquary. 1816. Tr. Polish, Warsaw, 1828; tr. Russian, St Petersburg, 1845.
Krzyžanowski, J. Z dziejów walterscottyzmu polskiego. Przegl. Współcz, 130, 1933.
Struve, P. Walter Scott and Russia. Slavonic Rev. Jan. 1933.
helley, Percy Bysshe. Works. Tr. Russian, C. Balmont, 1895.
'ennyson, Alfred, Baron. Enoch Arden. 1864. Tr. Serbian Y. Yovanovich; tr. Czechisch P. Sobotka, Prague, 1875.

(8) THE LITERARY RELATIONS OF ENGLAND WITH OTHER EUROPEAN COUNTRIES

(a) The Netherlands

3yron, George Gordon, Baron.
Lennep, J. van. Vertalingen en Navolgingen in Poezy. Amsterdam, 1834.
)ekker, G. Die Invloed van Keats en Shelley in Nederland gedurende die negentiende Eeuw. Amsterdam, 1926.
Dickens, Charles.
Samuel Pickwick en zijne Reisgenooten. Tr. C. M. Mensing, Schiedam, 1868.
De Firma Dombey en Zoon. Tr. C. M. Mensing, Haarlem, 1856–7.
Downs, B. W. Anglo-Dutch Literary Relations, 1867–1900. MLR. XXXI, 1936.
Bulwer-Lytton, E. G. E. L. (Baron Lytton). The Last Days of Pompeii. 1834.

De laetste Dagen en Verwoesting van Pompeja. Tr. C. H. van Boeckel, Ghent, 1846.
Macaulay, Thomas Babington, Baron. Essays. 1843.
Historische en letterkundige Schetsen. Tr. A. Pierson, Haarlem, 1865.
—— History of England. 1849–61.
Geschiedenis van England. Tr. J. C. van Deventer, Amsterdam, 1868.
Moore, Thomas. Lalla Rookh. 1817.
De Vuur aanbidders. Tr. 'T. M.' [J. van Lennep], Amsterdam, 1834.
Pimentel, H. Overzigt van Buckle's Geschiedenis der Beschaving. Hague, 1869–70.
Popma, T. Byron en het Byronisme in de Nederlandsche Letterkunde. Amsterdam, 1928.
Russell, J. A. English Translations of Dutch Novels. Gazette de Hollande, 28 Oct. 1931.
Schults, U. Het Byronianisme in Nederland. Utrecht, 1929.
Scott, Sir Walter. Waverley. 1814. Tr. M. P. Lindo, Delft, 1872.
—— The Antiquary. 1816.
De Oudheidskenner. Tr. Groningen, 1825. Tr. M. P. Lindo, Leyden, 1873.
—— Ivanhoe. 1820. Tr. M. P. Lindo, Delft, 1872.
Vissink, H. Scott and his Influence on Dutch Literature. Zwolle, 1922.
Tennyson, Alfred, Baron. Idylls of the King. 1859–85.
De Konings-Idyllen. Tr. J. H. F. le Comte, Rotterdam, 1893.
—— Enoch Arden. 1864.
Henoch Arden. Tr. S. J. van den Bergh, Hague, 1869; tr. J. L. Werthelm, Amsterdam, 1882.
Worp, J. Engelsche Letterkunde op ons Tooneel. Tydspieghel, Hague, 1887.

(b) Switzerland

Ernst, F. La Tradition médiatrice de la Suisse aux XVIIIe et XIXe Siècles. Revue de Littérature comparée, VI, 1926.
Schirner, G. Die Schweiz im Spiegel englischer und amerikanischer Literatur bis 1848. Zurich, 1929.
Ziehen, E. Philhelvetism. Die neueren Sprachen, no. 4, 1925.

(c) Greece

Byron, George Gordon, Baron.
Τὰ "Απαντα τοῦ Βύρωνος. Athens, 1895.
Jebb, R. C. Byron in Greece. [In Modern Greece, 1880.]
Spender, H. Byron and Greece. 1924.
G. W.

III. THE INTELLECTUAL BACKGROUND

Influences Affecting the Whole Century: Philosophical and Speculative; Humanitarian and Humanistic; Greek and Roman Culture; Inspiration from Northern Epics, the Dark Ages, Mystery and Medievalism; The Cult of the Renaissance; Interest in Modern Europe. *The Period of Spiritual Enthusiasm, Hope and Moral Endeavour.*

The Period of Divided Aims, Disillusionment, Controversy and Social Criticism: Anti-Catholic Reaction and Assertion of 'Higher Criticism'; Philosophical Radicals, Scientific Humanitarians, Constructive Agnostics (uninfluenced by Darwinism); Pre-Darwinian Science, German Christology and Historical Criticism, and their Effect on Moral and Religious Ideas; Criticism of Life and Society in this New and Disturbed Atmosphere of Scientific Enquiry, Biblical Criticism, and the Morals and Manners of Commercial Development and the Theories of the Manchester School.

Mammonism: The 'Economic Man's' Bible; Humanitarian Protests.

Darwinism, New Adjustments to the Responsibilities of Life, the End of an Age: Darwinism and its Immediate Effects; Realism and Naturalism, French Influences; Pessimism, the Reaction from Science and Positivism, Appeal to Humanism; New Spirit of Social and Political Reform, and of Reconciliation between Science and Religion; The Influence of Literary Criticism.

(1) INFLUENCES AFFECTING THE WHOLE CENTURY

(a) *Philosophical and Speculative*

Spinoza, B. de. Tractatus Theologico-Politicus. 'Hamburg' [Amsterdam], 1670. [Complete religious liberty essential to the state.]
—— Tractatus Politicus. [In Opera Posthuma, Amsterdam, 1677. In sympathy with Hobbes, but reserves freedom of thought.]
—— Ethica. [In Opera Posthuma, Amsterdam, 1677. Starts from Descartes to issue in a pantheism congenial to pre-Darwinian monism and post-Darwinian hylozoism.]
—— Tractatus de Deo et Homine ejusque Felicitate, Lineamenta. Ed. E. Boehmer, Halle, 1852.
Wolff, C. F., Baron von. Vernünfftige Gedancken von den Kräfften des menschlichen Verstandes und ihrem richtige Gebrauche. Halle, 1725; tr. Eng. 1770.
Herder, J. G. Journal meiner Reise im Jahr 1769. [In Sämmtliche Werke, vol. IV, Berlin, 1878. Record of his youthful

ideas and dreams of the progress of mankind.]
Herder, J. G. Von deutscher Art und Kunst. Hamburg, 1773. [In collaboration with Goethe and J. Mäser.]
—— Auch eine Philosophie der Geschichte zur Bildung der Menschheit. 1774. [History reveals the scheme of man's advance towards perfection.]
—— Älteste Urkunde des Menschengeschlechts. 2 vols. Riga, 1774–6.
—— Vom Erkennen und Empfinden der menschlichen Seele. Riga, 1778.
—— Ideen zur Philosophie der Geschichte der Menschheit. 4 pts, Riga, 1784–91.
Kant, I. Kritik der Reinen Vernunft. Riga, 1781. [By the co-operation of the metaphysical and the empirical faculties, the spirit can impose itself on experience (*e.g.* art) and gain an inkling of the ultimate reality outside ourselves. Of great importance to the romantic tradition.]
—— Prolegomena zu einer jeden künftigen Metaphysik, die als Wissenschaft wird auftreten können. Riga, 1783. [Popular exposition of elements of Kritik der Reinen Vernunft.]
—— Grundlegung zur Metaphysik der Sitten. Riga, 1785.
—— Recension von Herders Ideen zur Philosophie der Geschichte der Menschheit. Jenaische Literatur-Zeitung, 1785.
—— Kritik der Praktischen Vernunft. Riga, 1788.
—— Kritik der Urtheilskraft. Berlin, 1790.
—— Briefe zu Beförderung der Humanität. Riga, 1793.
—— Die Religion innerhalb der Grenzen der blossen Vernunft. Königsberg, 1793.
Schiller, F. von. Über Anmuth und Würde. Neue Thalia, I, 1792. [Neue Thalia was a periodical edited by Schiller at Leipzig, 1792–3, for the interpretation of literary ideals, especially tragedy, according to Kant's aesthetics.]
—— Briefe über die aesthetische Erziehung des Menschen. Die Horen, I, II, 1795. [What, in itself, is beauty? Die Horen was a periodical edited by Schiller at Tübingen, 1795–7.]
—— Von den nothwendigen Grenzen des Schönen besonders im Vortrag philosophischer Wahrheiten. Die Horen, III, 1795.
—— Über naïve und sentimentalische Dichtung. Die Horen, V, 1796.
Fichte, J. G. Versuch einer Kritik aller Offenbarung. Königsberg, 1792.
—— Grundlage des Naturrechts. Jena, 1796.
—— Erste [Zweite] Einleitung in die Wissenschaftslehre. Philosophisches Journal, V, 1797.

Fichte, J. G. Die Bestimmung des Menschen. Berlin, 1800.

—— Die Wissenschaftslehre in ihrem ganzen Umfange. Berlin, 1810. [This and the two preceding items affirm individualism. The only reality is the ego, which creates its own moral and religious world.]

Schelling, F. W. J. von. Über die Möglichkeit einer Form der Philosophie überhaupt. Tübingen, 1795.

—— Vom Ich als Prinzip der Philosophie oder vom Unbedingten im menschlichen Wissen. Tübingen, 1795. [This and the following items argue that the 'Weltseele' is the only reality, which is reflected in Nature and in our own spiritual activities.]

—— Ideen zu einer Philosophie der Natur. Leipzig, 1793.

—— Von der Weltseele. Hamburg, 1798.

—— System des transcendentalen Idealismus. Tübingen, 1800.

—— Philosophie und Religion. Tübingen, 1804.

—— Über das Verhältniss des Realen und Idealen in der Natur. Hamburg, 1806.

Schleiermacher, F. D. E. Ueber die Religion. Reden an die Gebildeten unter ihren Verächtern. Berlin, 1799.

—— Monologen. Eine Neujahrsgabe. Berlin, 1800.

—— Vertraute Briefe 'über Friedrich Schlegels Lucinde.' Lübeck, 1800.

—— Grundlinien einer Kritik der bisherigen Sittenlehre. Berlin, 1803.

—— Entwurf eines Systems der Sittenlehre. [In Sämmtliche Werke (Zur Philosophie), vol. v, Berlin, 1835.]

Hegel, G. W. F. Phänomenologie des Geistes. Bamberg, 1807. [First exposition of his doctrine that the spirit is not one of many forms of the Absolute, but the Absolute itself, made real in experience through the power of thought. Thus each step in the individual's progress is a moment in the self-development of the Absolute.]

—— Wissenschaft der Logik. Nuremberg, 1812–6.

—— Encyklopädie der philosophischen Wissenschaften. Heidelberg, 1817.

—— Naturrecht und Staatswissenschaft im Grundrisse. Berlin, 1821.

Coleridge, S. T. The Friend. 1812. [Rptd from nos. which appeared 1809–10.]

—— Biographia Literaria. 1817.

—— Principles of the Science of Method. 1818. [Originally A Preliminary Treatise on Method, written as introduction to Encyclopaedia Metropolitana.]

—— Hints toward the Formation of a more Comprehensive Theory of Life. Ed. S. B. Watson, 1848.

Schopenhauer, A. Die Welt als Wille und Vorstellung. Dresden, 1819; 2 vols. Dresden, 1844 (enlarged); tr. Eng. 3 vols. 1883. [Argues that all qualities are mere appearance, except the will, i.e. the tendency of all created things to fulfil and express their inherent nature. In man this urge has been perverted into the will to live, instead of culminating in the will to die.]

De Quincey, T. Letters to a Young Man whose Education has been neglected. v. On the English Notices of Kant. London Mag. July 1823. [Rptd in Collected Writings, ed. D. Masson, vol. x, 1897.]

—— Kant on National Character, in relation to The Sense of the Sublime and Beautiful. A Translation. London Mag. April 1824. [Rptd in Collected Writings, ed. D. Masson, vol. xiv, 1897.]

—— Kant in his Miscellaneous Essays. Blackwood's Mag. Aug. 1830. [Rptd in Collected Writings, ed. D. Masson, vol. viii, 1897.]

—— German Studies and Kant in Particular. Tait's Mag. June 1836. [Original title 'Autobiography of an English Opium Eater Continued. Chap. ii.' Rptd in Collected Writings, ed. D. Masson, vol. viii, 1897.]

Carlyle, T. Sartor Resartus. Fraser's Mag. Nov. 1833–Aug. 1834. [Rptd with preface by R. W. Emerson, Boston, 1836, etc.]

Heine, H. Zur Geschichte der neueren schönen Litteratur in Deutschland. Paris, 1833. [Rptd in Der Salon, vol. ii, Hamburg, 1835.]

—— De l'Allemagne depuis M. Luther. Revue des Deux Mondes, March–Dec. 1834. [Rptd as Die romantische Schule. Hamburg, 1836. These and various other rpts incomplete till the essays appeared in Sämmtliche Werke, vols. v, vi, Hamburg, 1876, as Ueber Deutschland. Tr. Eng. New York, 1882; 1883 (another version). A brilliant and stimulating account of the gradual encroachment of philosophy into the religious kingdom, and of the issue in pantheism and melancholy. See The Autobiography of Mark Rutherford, 1881, chs. 2, 6, 9.]

Emerson, R. W. Journals. 1912. [Pbd 30 years after his death; really the source and often the repository of his best lectures and essays. As a student of Plato, Spinoza, Swedenborg, and the German transcendentalists, who adapted and reinterpreted their metaphysics so as to discover the idea and intention of God in all experience (inaccurately characterised as unitarianism), Emerson's position is most significant. His conception of nature and animal life as leading to an explanation of man should be compared with Darwinism.]

Emerson, R. W. Essays. 2 sers. 1841–4.

Froude, J. A. Spinoza. Westminster Rev. July 1855. [Rptd in Short Studies on Great Subjects, vol. ii, 1867.]

Green, J. H. Spiritual Philosophy. 1865. [Attempts to reduce all Coleridge's lucubrations to a complete philosophy. Task unfinished at death in 1863.]

Arnold, M. A Word more about Spinoza. Macmillan's Mag. Dec. 1863. [Rptd as Spinoza and the Bible in Essays in Criticism, ser. 1, 1865.]

Bosanquet, B. The Introduction to Hegel's Philosophy of Fine Art. 1886.

Bradley, A. C. English Poetry and German Philosophy in the Age of Wordsworth. Adamson Lecture, 1909. [Rptd in A Miscellany, 1929.]

Croce, B. Storia di Europa nel Secolo Decimonono. Bari, 1932.

Elwes, R. H. M. The Chief Works of Spinoza. Translated from the Latin. 1883–4.

Ewh, P. Die Begriffe Pflicht und Tugend in der Sittenlehre Kants und Schleiermachers. Erlangen, 1891.

Fischer, K. Schiller als Philosoph. Frankfurt, 1858.

Green, T. M. Kant: Selections. 1929.

Loewemberg, J. Hegel: Selections. 1929.

Muirhead, J. H. Coleridge as Philosopher. 1930.

Parker, De W. H. Schopenhauer: Selections. 1928.

Perry, B. Emerson Today. Princeton, 1931.

Ribot, T. La Philosophie de Schopenhauer. Paris, 1874.

Routh, H. V. Towards the Twentieth Century. Essays in the Spiritual History of the Nineteenth. 1937.

Schwegler, A. Geschichte der Philosophie in Umriss. Ein Leitfaden zur Übersicht. Stuttgart, 1883 (12th edn, 'ergänzt durch eine Darstellung der Schopenhauer'schen Lehre von R. Koeber'); tr. Eng. Edinburgh, 1867.

Snyder, A. D. Coleridge on Logic and Learning, with Selections from the unpublished Manuscripts. New Haven, 1929.

Stephen, Sir L. The Importation of German. [In Studies of a Biographer, vol. ii, 1898.]

Stirling, J. H. The Secret of Hegel: being the Hegelian System in Origin, Principle, Form and Matter. 2 vols. 1865.

—— Textbook to Kant. The Critique of Pure Reason. Translation, Reproduction, Commentary, Index. With Biographical Sketch. Edinburgh, 1881.

Wild, J. Spinoza Selections. 1930.

Zimmern, H. Schopenhauer. His Life and his Philosophy. 1876.

(b) *Humanitarian and Humanistic*

Rousseau, J.-J. La Nouvelle Héloïse ou Lettres de deux amants. 4 vols. Paris, 1761.

—— Émile ou de l'Éducation. 4 vols. Amsterdam, 1762.

—— Du Contrat Social. Amsterdam, 1762.

—— Confessions. 4 vols. Geneva, 1781–8.

Goethe, J. W. von. Die Leiden des Jungen Werthers. 2 pts, Leipzig, 1774.

—— Wilhelm Meisters Lehrjahre. Ein Roman. 4 vols. Berlin, 1795–6.

—— Wilhelm Meisters Wanderjahre. Oder Die Entsagenden. 2 pts, Stuttgart, 1821–9.

—— Faust. Pt i, Tübingen, 1808. [An 'Urfaust' had been sketched in 1775.]

—— Aus meinem Leben: Dichtung und Wahrheit. 4 pts, Tübingen, 1811–33.

—— Faust. Pt ii, Stuttgart, 1833.

—— Gespräche mit Goethe in den letzten Jahren seiner Leben. 1823–32. Von J. P. Eckermann. 2 pts, Leipzig, 1836; Magdeburg, 1848. [Discusses nearly every topic of interest to the nineteenth century from neo-hellenism and the defects of the romantic school, to man's place in nature, the discovery of electricity, the proposed Panama and Suez canals, and the theory of art which influenced Ruskin, Pater and Wilde. He still believes in a Divine Architect of the Universe.]

Paine, T. Rights of Man. 2 pts, 1791–2.

—— The Age of Reason. 2 pts, 1794–5. [Pt iii, New York, 1807.]

Godwin, W. An Enquiry Concerning Political Justice and its Influence on General Virtue and Happiness. 2 vols. 1793.

—— Things as they are or the Adventures of Caleb Williams. 3 vols. 1794.

Caritat, M. J. A. N. (Marquis de Condorcet). L'Esquisse d'un Tableau Historique des Progrès de l'Esprit Humain. Paris, 1795. [Enthusiastic assertion of the infinite perfectibility of man.]

Richter, J. P. [See p. 55 below.]

Tieck, J. L. Der Gestiefelte Kater; ein Kindermährchen in drey Akten. Aus dem Italienischen. Berlin, 1797.

—— Fantasien über die Kunst, für Freunde der Kunst. Ed. L. Tieck, Hamburg, 1799. [Continuation of W. H. Wackenroder's Herzensergiessungen eines kunstliebenden Klosterbruders, Berlin, 1797.]

—— Leben und Tod der Heiligen Genoveva. Ein Trauerspiel. [In Romantische Dichtungen, vol. ii, Jena, 1800.]

—— Leben und Tod des kleinen Rothkäppchens. Eine Tragoedie. [In Romantische Dichtungen, vol. ii, Jena, 1800.]

—— Kaiser Octavianus. Ein Lustspiel in zwei Theilen. Jena, 1804.

Tieck, J. L. Phantasus. Eine Sammlung von Mährchen, Erzählungen, Schauspielen und Novellen. 3 vols. Berlin, 1812-6. [Earlier romantic stories collected and woven into a continuous narrative.]

Wordsworth, W. Concerning the Relations of Great Britain, Spain and Portugal to each other and to the Common Enemy as affected by the Convention of Cintra. 1809. [Plea for cosmopolitanism.]

De Quincey, T. Jean Paul Richter. London Mag. Dec. 1821. [Rptd in Collected Writings, ed. D. Masson, vol. xi, 1897.]

—— Analects from Richter. London Mag. Feb. 1824. [Rptd in Collected Writings, ed. D. Masson, vol. xi, 1897.]

—— Goethe as Reflected in his Novel of Wilhelm Meister. London Mag. Aug. 1824. [Rptd in Collected Writings, ed. D. Masson, vol. xi, 1897.]

Carlyle, T. Wilhelm Meister's Apprenticeship. 3 vols. Edinburgh, 1824. [Preferred by M. Arnold to the original.]

—— Jean Paul Richter. Edinburgh Rev. no. 91, 1827.

—— State of German Literature. Edinburgh Rev. no. 92, 1827.

—— German Romance. Specimens with Biographical and Critical Notices. 4 vols. Edinburgh, 1827.

—— Life and Writings of Werner. Foreign Rev. no. 1, 1828.

—— Goethe's Helena. Foreign Rev. no. 2, 1828.

—— Goethe. Foreign Rev. no. 3, 1828.

—— German Playwrights. Foreign Rev. no. 6, 1829.

—— Voltaire. Foreign Rev. no. 6, 1829.

—— Novalis. Foreign Rev. no. 7, 1829.

—— Jean Paul Richter Again. Foreign Rev. no. 9, 1830.

—— Death of Goethe. New Monthly Mag. no. 138, 1832.

—— Goethe's Works. Foreign Quarterly Rev. no. 19, 1832.

—— Diderot. Foreign Quarterly Rev. no. 22, 1833.

—— Mirabeau. London and Westminster Rev. no. 8, 1837.

—— On Heroes, Hero-Worship and the Heroic in History. 1841.

Hayward, A. Faust: a Dramatic Poem translated into English Prose. 1833. [Only pt i.]

Brinton, C. The Political Ideas of the English Romanticists. Oxford, 1926.

Calvert, G. H. Coleridge, Shelley, Goethe. Biographical and Aesthetic Studies. 1880.

Carlyle, A Letters of Thomas Carlyle to John Stuart Mill, John Stirling and Robert Browning. 1923.

Courthope, W. J. The Liberal Movement in English Literature. 1885.

Donner, J. O. E. Der Einfluss Wilhelm Meisters auf den Romanen der Romantiker. Berlin, 1893.

Durand, W. Y. De Quincey and Carlyle in their Relation to the Germans. PMLA. xxii, 1907.

Gundolf, F. Romantiker. Berlin, 1932.

Hauhart, W. F. The Reception of Goethe's Faust in England in the First Half of the Nineteenth Century. New York, 1909.

Howe, S. Wilhelm Meister and his English Kinsmen. New York, 1930.

Lehman, B. H. Carlyle's Theory of the Hero. Its Sources, Development, History, and Influence on Carlyle's Work. Durham, North Carolina, 1929.

Paul, C. K. William Godwin. His Friends and Contemporaries. 2 vols. 1876.

Stephen, Sir L. Godwin and Shelley. [In Hours in a Library, vol. iii, 1892.]

Stokoe, F. W. German Influence in the English Romantic Period. Cambridge, 1926.

Vaughan, C. E. Carlyle and his German Masters. E. & S. i, 1910.

Walzel, O. F. Die Romantische Schule. Leipzig, 1920 (4th edn); tr. Eng. New York, 1932.

(c) *Greek and Roman Culture*

Winckelmann, J. J. Gedancken über die Nachahmung der Griechischen Wercke in der Mahlerey und Bildhauer-Kunst. 1755; Dresden, 1756 (enlarged). [Noble simplicity and quiet grandeur of Greek sculpture. Originality displayed not so much in the fundamental idea, as in the interpretation and inferences, and the redirection of art criticism from technique to ideas.]

—— Geschichte der Kunst des Alterthums. Dresden, 1764.

Lessing, G. E. Laokoon: oder über die Grenzen der Malerey und Poesie. Mit beyläufigen Erläuterungen verschiedener Punkte der alten Kunstgeschichte. Pt i, Berlin, 1766. [Enlarged edn containing matter intended for pt ii, Berlin, 1788.]

—— Briefe antiquarischen Inhalts. Berlin, 1768-9.

—— Wie die Alten den Tod gebildet. Berlin, 1769. [Proofs that Death was represented as a beautiful youth with an inverted torch, came as an unexpected revelation of the classical spirit.]

Goethe, J. W. von. Iphigenie auf Tauris. Leipzig, 1787.

—— Die Achilleis. [Epic on Homer's subject and in his manner; only two cantos completed; ptd in Werke, 1808, written 1797.]

Goethe, J. W. von. Die Propyläen. Tübingen, 1798–1800. [Classic art as rediscovered by Winckelmann the only true art. In collaboration with H. Meyer.]

—— Winckelmann und sein Jahrhundert. [In Briefen und Aufsätzen, ed. Goethe, Tübingen, 1805.]

—— Italienische Reise. Aufsätze und Aussprüche über bildende Kunst. Mit Einleitung und Bericht über dessen Kunststudien und Kunstübungen. Ed. C. Schuchardt, Stuttgart, 1862–3. [Compiled from letters, diaries and notes from 1786 onwards.]

Lempriere, J. Bibliotheca Classica; or, a Classical Dictionary, containing a full Account of all the Proper Names mentioned in Antient Authors. Reading, 1788. [One of Keats's favourite books.]

Schiller, F. von. Über naïve und sentimentalische Dichtung. Die Horen, v, 1796. [Naïveté is the essence of the highest poetry, whether primitive or civilised and is to be found at its best among the Greeks.]

—— Gedichte. [In Musenalmanach, Tübingen, 1798. Die Taucher, Der Ring des Polykrates, Die Kraniche des Ibykus, etc.]

Schlegel, F. Ueber das Studium der Griechischen Poesie. [In Die Griechen und Römer, Neustrelitz, 1797.]

—— Geschichte der Poesie der Griechen und Römer. Berlin, 1798.

Hunt, J. H. Leigh. Classic Tales; With Critical Essays on the Merits and Reputation of the Authors. 5 vols. 1807.

—— A Jar of Honey from Mount Hybla. 1848.

Lamb, C. The Adventures of Ulysses. 1808.

Shelley, P. B. The Defense of Poetry. 1821. [Much of Plato and Aristotle.]

Lockhart, J. G. Valerius. A Roman Story. 3 vols. Edinburgh, 1821.

De Quincey, T. Lessing. Blackwood's Mag. Nov. 1826.

—— The Caesars. Blackwood's Mag. Oct. 1832–Aug. 1834. [Rptd in Collected Writings, ed. D. Masson, vol. x, 1897.]

—— A Brief Appraisal of the Greek Literature in its Foremost Pretensions. Tait's Mag. Dec. 1838, June 1839. [Rptd in Collected Writings, ed. D. Masson, vol. x, 1897.]

—— Philosophy of Roman History. Blackwood's Mag. Nov. 1839.

—— Dinner. Real and Reputed. Blackwood's Mag. Dec. 1839. [Rptd as The Casuistry of Roman Meals in Collected Writings, ed. D. Masson, vol. x, 1897.]

—— Theory of Greek Tragedy. Blackwood's Mag. Feb. 1840. [Rptd in Collected Writings, ed. D. Masson, vol. x, 1897.]

De Quincey, T. Homer and the Homeridae Blackwood's Mag. May 1841.

—— Plato's Republic. Blackwood's Mag July 1841.

—— Philosophy of Herodotus. Blackwood's Mag. Jan. 1842.

—— Pagan Oracles. Blackwood's Mag March 1842.

—— Cicero. Blackwood's Mag. July 1842.

Hawker, R. S. Pompei. Oxford, 1827.

Newman, J. H. London Rev. Feb. 1829; ed. A. S. Cook, 1891. [Review of The Theatre of the Greeks, 1827 (2nd edn) Later rptd as Poetry with Reference to Aristotle's Poetics.]

—— Callista: A Sketch of the Third Century. 1856.

—— Literature. A Lecture Read in the School of Philosophy and Letters, November 1858. [In Lectures and Essays on University Subjects, 1859.]

Browning, E. B. Prometheus Bound. 1833.

Lytton, Bulwer. The Last Days of Pompeii. 3 vols. 1834.

—— Athens. Its Rise and Fall. 2 vols. 1837. [Popular but appreciative account of Athenian art, literature, philosophy and manners.]

Talfourd, Sir T. N. Ion. A Tragedy. 1835.

—— The Athenian Captive. A Tragedy. 1838.

—— Early Greek Poetry. The Tragic Poets of Greece. The Lyric Poets of Greece. The Greek Historians. 1850. [In Encyclopaedia Metropolitana, Third Division. History, Biography, Greek Literature, ed. E. Smedley, 1848 ff.]

Becker, W. A. Gallus oder Römische Scenen aus der Zeit Augustus. 3 vols. Leipzig, 1838; tr. Eng. 1844.

—— Charikles. Bilder Altgriechischer Sitten. 2 vols. Leipzig, 1840.

Frere, J. H. The Frogs. 1839.

—— A Metrical Version of the Acharnians, the Knights and the Birds. 1840.

—— Theognis Restitutus. 1842.

Milman, H. H. The History of Christianity to the Abolition of Paganism. 3 vols. 1840.

—— The History of Latin Christianity. 6 vols. 1854.

Blackie, J. S. Lyrical Dramas of Aeschylus. 1850.

Collins, W. W. Antonina; or the Fall of Rome. A Romance of the Fifth Century. 3 vols. 1850.

Froude, J. A. The Homeric Life. Fraser's Mag. July 1851. [Rptd as Homer in Short Studies on Great Subjects, vol. ii, 1867.]

—— Society in Italy. Fraser's Mag. Aug. 1876. [Rptd in Short Studies in Great Subjects, ser. 3, 1877.]

Froude, J. A. Lucian. Fraser's Mag. Oct. 1876. [Rptd in Short Studies in Great Subjects, ser. 3, 1877.]

—— Caesar. A Sketch. 1879.

Kingsley, C. Hypatia, or New Foes with an old Face. Fraser's Mag. Jan.–April 1853; 2 vols. 1853.

—— The Heroes. 1856.

Arnold, M. Poems by Matthew Arnold. 1853. [With Preface in which he explains the omission of Empedocles, on the principles of Aristotle's criticism.]

—— On Translating Homer. 1861.

—— On Translating Homer. Last Words. 1862.

—— Essays in Criticism. Ser. 1, 1865. [Pagan and Mediaeval Religious Sentiment, Marcus Aurelius.]

Landor, W. S. Conversations of Greeks and Romans. 1853.

Mommsen, T. Römische Geschichte. 3 vols. Berlin, 1854–6. [History of all Italy from the earliest immigrations to the end of the Republic. Vast erudition is combined with knowledge of human nature to reinterpret the events and characters of Roman civilisation. By rehabilitating Caesar at the expense of Cicero, he brought a new idea into modern culture.]

Wiseman, N. P. S. Fabiola. A Tale of the Catacombs. 1854.

Swinburne, A. C. Modern Hellenism. Undergraduate Papers (Oxford), Dec. 1857.

Gladstone, W. E. Studies on Homer and the Homeric Age. 3 vols. 1858.

—— Juventus Mundi. 1869.

Newman, F. W. Homeric Translations in Theory and Practice. A Reply to Matthew Arnold. 1861. [All three pamphlets rptd in Essays by Matthew Arnold, Oxford, 1914.]

Spedding, J. Fraser's Mag. June 1861. [Review of Arnold's Homer. Rptd with addns in Reviews and Discussions, 1879. See also Fraser's Mag. June 1862, for a discussion of 6 further trns of Homer.]

Whyte-Melville, G. J. The Gladiators. 3 vols. 1863.

Forsythe, W. Life of M. T. Cicero. 2 vols. 1864.

Munro, H. A. J. Titi Lucreti Cari de Rerum Natura. With a Translation and Notes. 2 vols. Cambridge, 1864.

Grote, G. Plato and the Other Companions of Socrates. 1865.

Conington, J. The Aeneid in Verse. 1866.

Pater, W. H. Winckelmann. Westminster Rev. Jan. 1867. [Rptd in Studies in the History of the Renaissance, 1873.]

—— Marius the Epicurean: his Sensations and Ideas. 2 vols. 1885.

Calverley, C. S. Theocritus Translated into English Verse. 1869.

Jowett, B. The Dialogues of Plato. 4 vols. Oxford, 1871.

—— Thucydides. 2 vols. Oxford, 1881.

Merivale, C. The Contest between Pagan and Christian Society. Christian Evidence Soc. 1872.

Nietzsche, F. W. Die Geburt der Tragödie aus dem Geiste der Musik. Leipzig, 1872. [In subsequent edns Die Geburt der Tragödie oder Hellenismus und Pessimismus. Now recognised to be mistaken. Once of great value as showing how Greek drama could be interpreted in terms of modern art and idealism.][1]

Butcher, S. H. and Lang, A. The Odyssey of Homer done into English Prose. ·1879.

Lang, A. Theocritus, Bion and Moschus rendered into English Prose. 1880.

—— Helen of Troy. 1882.

Lang, A., Leaf, W. and Myers, E. The Iliad of Homer. Done into English Prose. 1883.

Myers, F. W. H. Essays: Classical. 1883.

Campbell, L. Sophocles in English Verse. 1883.

Jebb, R. C. Sophocles with Notes and Translation. Cambridge, 1883–96.

Mackail, J. W. The Aeneid of Vergil, translated into English. 1885.

—— The Eclogues and Georgics of Vergil translated. 1889.

—— Select Epigrams from the Greek Anthology. Edited with a revised Text, Introduction, Translation and Notes. 1890.

—— Latin Literature. 1895.

Butcher, S. H. Some Aspects of the Greek Genius. 1891.

—— Aristotle's Theory of Poetry and Fine Art. 1895.

Farrar, F. W. Darkness and Dawn, or Scenes in the Days of Nero. 1891.

Gissing, G. Veranilda. 1904. [With a preface by F. Harrison.]

Austin, A. The Conversion of Winckelmann. 1897.

Bywater, I. Aristotle on the Art of Poetry with Translation and Commentary. Oxford, 1909.

Collins, J. C. Greek Influence on English Poetry. 1910.

Egger, É. L'Hellénisme en France. 2 vols. Paris, 1869.

Finsler, G. Homer in der Neuzeit, von Dante bis Goethe. Italien, Frankreich, England, Deutschland. Leipzig, 1902.

Lumb, T. W. Authors of Greece. 1924.

Murray, G. What English Poetry may still learn from Greek. Atlantic Monthly, Nov. 1912.

—— The Classical Tradition in Poetry. Oxford, 1927.

Nairn, J. A. Authors of Rome. 1926.

Nitchie, E. Vergil and the English Poets. New York, 1919.

Spindler, R. Robert Browning und die Antike. Leipzig, 1930.

Texte, J. Keats et le Néo-hellénisme dans la Poésie anglaise. [In Études de Littérature Européenne, Paris, 1898.]

Thayer, M. R. The Influence of Horace on the Chief Poets of the Nineteenth Century. New Haven, 1916.

(d) Inspiration from Northern Epics, the Dark Ages, Mystery and Medievalism

Hurd, R. Letters on Chivalry and Romance. 1762.

Percy, T. Reliques of Ancient English Poetry. 3 vols. 1765.

Herder, J. G. (with J. W. von Goethe and J. Möser). Von Deutscher Art und Kunst. Hamburg, 1773. [Triumph of Gothic.]

—— Volkslieder, 2 pts, Leipzig, 1778–9. [Collection of popular songs and ballads of many nations; able trns, entitled 'Stimmen der Völker' by J. Müller, the first editor of Herder's works.]

Bürger, G. A. Lenore. [In Göttinger Musen-almanach, 1774. Suggested by a Low German Volkslied; perhaps the most powerful influence in 'the Rebirth of Wonder.' Tr. W. R. Spencer, 1796.]

—— Der Bruder Graurock und die Pilgerin. Göttinger Musenalmanach, 1778.

Warton, T. The History of English Poetry from the Close of the Eleventh to the Commencement of the Eighteenth Century. 3 vols. 1774–81.

Chatterton, T. Poems supposed to have been written at Bristol by Thomas Rowley. Ed. T. Tyrwhitt, 1777.

Raspe, R. E. Munchhausen. 1785. [Tr. into English and retranslated by G. A. Bürger into German, Göttingen, 1786.]

Scott, Sir W. Apology for Tales of Terror. Kelso, 1799.

—— Minstrelsy of the Scottish Border. Vols. I, II, Kelso, 1802; vol. III, 1803.

—— The Lay of the Last Minstrel. 1805.

—— Marmion. 1808.

—— The Bridal of Triermain. Edinburgh, 1813.

—— Essays on Chivalry and the Drama. Encyclopaedia Britannica, 1814.

—— The Border Antiquities of England and Scotland. 2 vols. 1814–7.

—— Harold the Dauntless. Edinburgh, 1817.

—— Ivanhoe. 3 vols. Edinburgh, 1820.

—— Essays on Romance. Encyclopaedia Britannica, 1822.

—— Quentin Durward. 3 vols. Edinburgh, 1823.

Scott, Sir W. Tales of the Crusades. Edinburgh, 1825.

—— Letters on Demonology and Witchcraft. 1830.

—— Tales of my Landlord. Fourth and last series. 4 vols. 1832.

Godwin, W. Life of Geoffrey Chaucer: including memoirs of John of Gaunt. 2 vols. 1803.

Carey, H. F. The Inferno of Dante Alighieri. With Translation. 1806.

—— The Vision: or Hell, Purgatory and Paradise of Dante. 3 vols. 1814.

—— The Early French Poets. A Series of Notices and Translations. 1846.

Jamieson, R. Popular Ballads and Songs from Traditional Manuscripts and Scarce Editions. 1806.

—— (with H. Weber and Sir W. Scott). Illustrations of Northern Antiquities. 1814.

Thoms, W. J. Early Prose Romances. 3 vols 1827–8.

—— Lays and Legends. 2 vols. 1834.

Carlyle, T. The Nibelungen Lied. Westminster Rev. no. 29, 1831. [Review of Das Nibelungen Lied, übersetzt von Karl Simrock, 2 vols. Berlin, 1827.]

—— German Literature of the Fourteenth and Fifteenth Centuries. Foreign Quarterly Rev. no. 16, 1831. [Review of Reinecke de Fuchs, übersetzt von D. W. Soltau, Lüneburg, 1830 (2nd edn).]

Hugo, V. Notre-Dame de Paris. Paris 1831.

Barham, R. H. The Ingoldsby Legends, or Mirth and Marvels. By Thomas Ingoldsby Esq. 1840.

Daniel, G. Merrie England in the Olden Time 2 vols. 1842.

Jameson, A. B. Sacred and Legendary Art 2 vols. 1848. [Second series: Legends of the Monastic Orders, 1850; Third series Legends of the Madonna as represented in the fine arts, 1852.]

Lytton, Bulwer. Harold, the last of the Saxon Kings. 3 vols. 1848.

Ruskin, J. The Seven Lamps of Architecture 1849. [Expounds the true nature of Gothic as essential to the spiritual welfare of the people.]

—— The Stones of Venice. 1851–3.

—— Mornings in Florence: being Simple Studies of Christian Art, for English Travellers. Orpington, 1875–7.

Reade, C. The Cloister and the Hearth. 4 vols 1861.

Rossetti, D. G. The Early Italian Poetry from Ciullo d' Alcamo to Dante Alighieri 1100–1200–1300 in the Original Metres together with Dante's Vita Nuova. 1861 1874 (rev. edn as Dante and his Circle).

Taine, H. Histoire de la Littérature Anglaise, Paris, 1863. [His theory of the race, the moment and the environment, suggested by Hegel, open to dispute, but his brilliant pictures of the Middle Ages capture the imagination.]

—— La Philosophie d'Art. Paris, 1865–9. [Pt I, ch. 2, § VI.]

Furnivall, F. J. Early English Text Society. [Founded 1864. Ex. Ser. 1867. Chaucer Soc. and Ballad Soc. 1868.]

Gould, S. Baring. A Book of Were-Wolves. 1865.

—— Curious Myths of the Middle Ages. 1866.

—— Grettir the Outlaw. 1889.

—— Urith. 1891.

—— In the Roar of the Sea. 1892.

Kingsley, C. Hereward the Wake. 2 vols. 1866.

Morris, W. Grettis-Saga-translated. 1869.

—— Of the Friendship of Amis and Amile done into English. 1894.

—— The Tale of the Emperor Constans, and of Over Sea, done out of ancient French. 1894.

—— The Tale of Beowulf. 1895. [With A. J. Wyatt.]

—— Old French Romances. 1896.

Magnússon, E. and Morris, W. Volsunga Saga. 1870.

—— Three Northern Love Stories translated from the Icelandic. 1875.

—— The Sagas Library. Vols. I–V, 1891–5.

Froude, J. A. A Bishop of the Twelfth Century. [Review of Magna Vita S. Hugonis Episcopi by J. F. Dimock. In Short Studies on Great Subjects, ser. 2, 1871.]

—— Annals of an English Abbey. [In Short Studies on Great Subjects, ser. 3, 1877.]

—— Life and Times of Thomas Becket. Nineteenth Century, June, July 1877. [Rptd in Short Studies on Great Subjects, ser. 4, 1883.]

Lang, A. Ballads and Lyrics of Old France. 1872.

—— Aucassin and Nicolete. Done into English. 1887.

—— A monk of Fife. Being the Chronicle written by Norman Leslie of Pitcullo, now first done into the English. 1896.

—— The Maid of France. 1908.

Green, J. R. A Short History of the English People. 1874.

Fowke, F. R. The Bayeux Tapestry. With Historic Notes. Arundel Soc. 1878.

Twain, M. The Prince and the Pauper. A Tale for Young People. 1881. [Really a vivid picture of 16th cent. rogues and vagabonds, founded on Awdeley, Harman and Dekker.]

Morley, H. English Writers. 11 vols. 1887–95. [Recast and enlarged from English Writers before Chaucer and From Chaucer to Dunbar, 2 vols. 1864–7.]

Stevenson, R. L. The Black Arrow. 1888.

Doyle, Sir A. C. The White Company. 1891.

Crawford, F. M. Via Crucis. A Romance of the Second Crusade. 1898.

(e) The Cult of the Renaissance

D'Israeli, I. Curiosities of Literature. 2 sers. 1791–1823.

—— Calamities of Authors. 2 vols. 1812–3.

—— Quarrels of Authors. 3 vols. 1814.

Roscoe, W. The Life of Lorenzo de' Medici. 2 vols. Liverpool, 1795.

Lamb, C. Tales from Shakespeare. 2 vols. 1807.

—— Specimens of English Dramatic Poets with notes. 1808.

—— Elia. Essays which have appeared under that signature in the London Magazine. 1823.

—— Last Essays of Elia. 1833.

Coleridge, S. T. Seven Lectures on Shakespeare and Milton. Ed. J. P. Collier, 1856. [Delivered 1811–2.]

Godwin, W. Mandeville. A Tale of the Seventeenth Century in England. 3 vols. Edinburgh, 1817.

Scott, Sir W. Tales of my Landlord: Third Series. 4 vols. Edinburgh, 1819. [The Bride of Lammermoor; Montrose.]

—— The Monastery. 3 vols. Edinburgh, 1820.

—— Kenilworth. 3 vols. Edinburgh, 1821.

—— The Fortunes of Nigel. 4 vols. Edinburgh, 1822.

—— Woodstock; or the Cavalier. 3 vols. Edinburgh, 1826.

Landor, W. S. Imaginary Conversations. 5 vols. 1824–9.

De Quincey, T. Klosterheim or The Masque. Edinburgh, 1832.

Ainsworth, W. H. The Tower of London. 1840.

—— Guy Fawkes. An historical romance. 3 vols. 1841.

—— Old St Paul's: A Tale of the Plague and Fire. 1841.

—— The Lancashire Witches: a Romance of Pendle Forest. 3 vols. 1849.

Hunt, J. H. Leigh. Stories from the Italian Poets, with Lives of the Writers. 2 vols. 1846.

Warburton, B. E. G. Memoirs of Prince Rupert and the Cavaliers. Including their Private Correspondence now first published from the Original Manuscripts. 3 vols. 1849.

Hawthorne, N. The Scarlet Letter. 1850.

Manning, Anne. The Household of Sir Thomas More. 1851.

Kingsley, C. Westward Ho! 3 vols. 1855.

Froude, J. A. A History of England from the Fall of Wolsey to the Defeat of the Spanish Armada. 12 vols. 1856–70.

—— England's Forgotten Worthies. [In Short Studies on Great Subjects, vol. II, 1867.]

—— Times of Erasmus and Luther. Three Lectures delivered at Newcastle. 1867.

—— The Spanish Story of the Armada and Other Essays. 1892.

—— The Life and Letters of Erasmus. Lectures, 1894.

—— English Seamen of the 16th Century. 1895.

Morley, H. Cornelius Agrippa von Nettesheim. 2 vols. 1856.

Masson, D. The Life of John Milton, narrated in connection with the Political, Ecclesiastical and Literary History of his Time. 7 vols. 1859–94.

Burckhardt, J. Die Kultur der Renaissance in Italien. Leipzig, 1860.

Eliot, G. Romola. Cornhill Mag. July 1862–Aug. 1863; 3 vols. 1863.

Taine, H. Histoire de la Littérature Anglaise. Paris, 1863. [Bk II.]

—— La Philosophie d'Art. Paris, 1865–9. [Pt II.]

Blackmore, R. D. Lorna Doone: a Romance of Exmoor. 3 vols. 1869.

Furnivall, F. J. The New Shakespeare Society. [Founded 1873.]

Pater, W. H. Studies in the History of the Renaissance. 1873.

—— Gaston de Latour. 1888.

Pattison, M. Isaac Casaubon, 1559–1614. 1875.

Symonds, J. A. The Renaissance in Italy. 7 vols. 1875–86.

—— Shakespeare's Predecessors in the English Drama. 1884.

—— Life of Ben Jonson. 1886.

Ward, Sir A. W. A History of English Dramatic Literature, To the death of Queen Anne. 2 vols. 1875.

Arber, E. An English Garner. 8 vols. 1877–96.

Shorthouse, J. H. John Inglesant. Birmingham, 1880.

—— Sir Percival. 1886.

Swinburne, A. C. A Study of Shakespeare. 1880.

—— A Study of Ben Jonson. 1889.

—— The Age of Shakespeare. 1908.

Lee, Sir S. A Life of William Shakespeare. 1898.

Lang, A. The Mystery of Marie Stuart. 1901.

—— John Knox and the Reformation. 1905.

(f) Interest in Modern Europe

(i) Modern Italy

Lloyd, C. The Tragedies of Vittorio Alfieri translated. 1815.

Rogers, S. Italy. A Poem. 2 pts, 1822–8.

Dickens, C. Pictures from Italy. 1846.

Grant, J. Adventures of an Aide-de-camp: or, a Campaign in Calabria. 3 vols. 1848.

Browning, E. B. Casa Guidi Windows. A Poem in Two Parts. 1851.

Hawthorne, N. The Marble Fawn. 1860.

Meredith, G. Emilia in England. 3 vols. 1864. [Subsequently entitled Sandra Belloni.]

—— Vittoria. 3 vols. 1867.

Hare, A. J. C. Days near Rome. 2 vols. 1875.

—— Cities of Northern and Central Italy. 3 vols. 1876.

—— Cities of Southern Italy and Sicily. 1883.

—— Venice. 1884.

Butler, S. Alps and Sanctuaries of Piedmont and the Canton of Ticino. [1881.]

Crawford, F. M. A Roman Singer. 2 vols. 1883.

—— Marzio's Crucifix. 2 vols. 1887.

—— The Saracinesca. 3 vols. 1887.

—— Sant' Ilario. 1889.

—— The Children of the King. A Tale of Southern Italy. 1893.

—— Don Orsino. 3 vols. 1892.

—— Corleone. 1896.

Corelli, M. Vendetta. 1886.

Symonds, J. A. Sketches and Studies in Italy and Greece. 3 vols. [1898.]

Schanzer, A. Il Leopardi in Inghilterra. Rassegna nazionale, April 1900.

Gissing, G. By the Ionian Sea. Notes of a Ramble in Southern Italy. 1901.

Wollaston, G. H. The Englishman in Italy. Oxford, 1909.

(ii) Modern France

Croly, G. Paris in 1815. 1817. [See J. Texte, Les Relations littéraires de la France avec l'Étranger, de 1799 à 1840. In Petit de Julleville, Histoire de la Langue et de la Littérature française, vol. VII, Paris, 1899.]

Thackeray, W. M. The Paris Sketch Book by Mr Titmarsh. 2 vols. 1840.

Dickens, C. A Tale of Two Cities. Jan.–Dec. 1859.

Arnold, M. The Popular Education of France with Notices of that of Holland and Switzerland. 1861. [See A. P. Kelso, Matthew Arnold on Continental Life and Literature, 1914.]

—— A French Eton; or, Middle Class Education and the State. 1864.

Arnold, M. Maurice de Guérin, Eugénie de Guérin, Joubert. [In Essays in Criticism, ser. 1, 1865.]
—— Schools and Universities on the Continent. 1868.
—— Obermann. Academy, 9 Oct. 1869. [See also his poems: Obermann (1852); Obermann Once More (1867).]
—— Sainte-Beuve. Academy, 18 Nov. 1869.
—— Amiel. [In Essays in Criticism, ser. 2, 1888.]
Senior, W. N. Correspondence and Conversations with A. de Tocqueville. 2 vols. 1872.
—— Conversations with Thiers, Guizot, and other Distinguished Persons, during the Second Empire. 2 vols. 1878.
—— Conversations with Distinguished Persons during the Second Empire. 1880.
Meredith, G. Beauchamp's Career. 3 vols. 1876. [Especially chs. xxii–xxiv.]
James, H. The American. Boston, 1877.
—— A Little Tour in France. Boston, 1884.
—— The Ambassadors. 1903.
Stevenson, R. L. An Inland Voyage. 1878.
—— Travels with a Donkey in the Cevennes. 1879.
—— The Merry Men and other Tales and Fables. 1887.
—— The Wrecker. 1892. [Chs. i–v.]
—— Tales and Fantasies. 1905.
Swinburne, A. C. A Study of Victor Hugo. 1886.
Hare, A. J. C. Paris. 1887.
Corelli, M. Wormwood, A Drama of Paris. 1890.
Doyle, Sir A. C. Uncle Bernac: a Memory of the Empire. 1896. [Glamour of Napoleon viewed from within his own court.]
—— Rodney Stone. 1896. [Interest in France only by implication, except ch. xii.]
—— The Exploits of Brigadier Gerard. 1896. [Describes humours of the Napoleonic Wars.]
Du Maurier, G. L. P. B. Trilby. 3 vols. 1894.
—— The Martian. 1897.

(iii) Modern Germany

Stäel, G. de. De l'Allemagne. Paris, 1810; 1813.
Howitt, W. The Rural and Domestic Life of Germany with Characteristic Sketches of its Cities, and Scenery, Collected in a General Tour. 1842.
Thackeray, W. M. The Kickleburys on the Rhine. 1851 (2nd edn).
Meredith, G. Farina: a Legend of Cologne. 1857.
—— Harry Richmond. 3 vols. 1871.
—— The Tragic Comedians. A Study in a Well-known Story. 2 vols. 1880.

Arnold, M. Heine. [In Essays in Criticism ser. 1, 1865.]
—— Friendship's Garland. 1871. [Previously ptd in Pall Mall Gazette, July 1866–Nov. 1870. My Countrymen previously ptd in Cornhill Mag. Feb. 1866.]
—— Educational Reform League Special Report on Elementary Education in Germany, Switzerland, and France. 1888.
Hawkins, Sir A. H. ('Antony Hope'). The King's Mirror. 1899.

(2) The Period of Spiritual Enthusiasm, Hope and Moral Endeavour. (At its height, c. 1830–45.)

Butler, J. The Analogy of Religion, natural and revealed, to the Constitution and Course of Nature. 1736. [The evidence of the Bible is confirmed and supplemented by the evidence of nature. It is the counterpart to scripture. The wisdom and beneficence of God is clearly mirrored in this world for those who have eyes to see. This 'analogy' was an immense encouragement and confirmation for believers all through the 19th cent. till Darwinism undermined their confidence.]
Paley, W. Horae Paulinae, or the Truth of the Scripture History of St. Paul evinced. 1790.
—— A View of the Evidences of Christianity. 1794.
—— Natural Theology or Evidences of the Existence and Attributes of the Deity collected from the Appearance of Nature. 1802.
Richter, J. P. F. Die unsichtbare Loge. Eine Biographie. Berlin, 1793. [Nebentitel; Mumien.]
—— Hesperus oder 45 Hundsposttage. Eine Lebensbeschreibung. Berlin, 1795.
—— Leben des Quintus Fixlein. Bayreuth, 1796.
—— Blumen-, Frucht- und Dornenstücke, oder Ehestand, Tod und Hochzeit des Armenadvocaten Fr. St. Siebenkäs. Berlin, 1796–7.
—— Titan. Berlin, 1800–3.
—— Flegeljahre. Eine Biographie. Tübingen, 1804–5.
—— Levana, oder Erziehungslehre. Brunswick, 1807.
Wilberforce, W. Practical View of Christianity. 1797. [Inspired by alarm at the atheism of France; insists on the corruption of human nature, the atonement of the Saviour, the sanctifying influence of the Holy Spirit.]

'Novalis' (*i.e.* F. von Hardenberg). [His writings were pbd in Schlegel-Tiecks Musen-Almanach für das Jahr 1802, Tübingen, 1802. Also in Novalis Schriften, ed. F. Schlegel and L. Tieck, Berlin, 1802, and after. Especially Die Christenheit oder Europa (composed 1799), Hymnen an die Nacht (composed 1800), Heinrich von Ofterdingen (composed 1802).]

Smith, S. Sermons. 2 vols. 1801 (2nd edn with addns). [Especially sermon on Toleration.]

—— Letters on the Subject of the Catholics from Peter Plymley to his Brother Abraham. 1808 (11th edn). [Letters appeared originally in small batches or singly, 1807–8, and hastened catholic emancipation by pouring ridicule on the needless alarm of Protestants.]

Aspland, R. Reflections upon the Liberal Spirit of the Apostles. Harlow, 1805.

—— Causes of the Slow Progress of Christian Truth. 1825.

Talfourd, Sir T. N. An Appeal to the Protestant Dissenters of Great Britain on Behalf of the Catholics. 1813.

Southey, R. The Life of Nelson. 2 vols. 1813.

—— The Life of Wesley; and the Rise and Progress of Methodism. 2 vols. 1820.

Owen, R. A new view of human society, or Essays on the Principle of the Formation of Human Character. 1813.

—— The Book of the New Moral World. 1836.

—— The Revolution in the Mind and Practice of the Human Race. 1849.

Smith, Southwood. Divine Government. 1814.

—— Philosophy of Health. 2 vols. 1835–7. [Human anatomy expounded so as to show the constitution of the mind and its relationship to the body.]

Erskine, T. of Linlathen. An Essay on Faith. 1822. [Inner witness of the heart of more value than creed or text.]

—— The Unconditional Freeness of the Gospel. 1828.

—— The Brazen Serpent. 1831.

—— The Doctrine of Election. 1837.

Ward, R. P. Tremaine; or the Man of Refinement. 1825. [The tired hedonist gradually led by theology, philosophy and love to a nobler view of life's duties.]

Rose, H. J. Discourses on the State of the Protestant Religion in Germany. 1825.

Coleridge, S. T. Aids to Reflection in the forming of a manly character. 1825.

—— Confessions of an Enquiring Spirit. Ed. H. N. Coleridge, 1840. [Dwells on conviction which does not require proof.]

Hare, J. C. and A. W. Guesses at Truth. 1827. [Aphorisms on theology, morals, manners,

literature; Lutheran in spirit, but enlightened by German philosophy.]

Keble, J. The Christian Year. 2 vols. 1827 (anon.).

—— National Apostacy: a sermon. 1833. [The 'Assize-sermon,' which awoke the nation to a sense of the dignity and spiritual influence of the Church, and its power over individual conscience, and so offered a starting point for the tractarian movement.]

Pusey, E. B. Historical Enquiry into the Theology of Germany. 1828. [H. J. Rose answers it in 1829 with 2nd edn of Discourses.]

Martineau, H. Illustrations of Political Economy. 9 vols. 1832–4. [Stories exemplifying the best that was known about the laws of the production of wealth.]

—— Society in America. 3 vols. 1837. [Abolition of slavery, political rights of women.]

—— History of England during the Thirty Years' Peace. 2 vols. 1849–50.

Carlyle, T. Sartor Resartus. Fraser's Mag. Nov. 1833–Aug. 1834. [Rptd with preface by R. W. Emerson, Boston, 1836.]

—— The French Revolution. 3 vols. 1837. [Intended as a last effort, before he relinquished the literary calling, to demonstrate that the Old Testament doctrine of reward and retribution still held true for the modern world.]

—— On Heroes, Hero-Worship and the Heroic in History. 1841. ['He who lives in the inward sphere of things, in the True, Divine and Eternal which exists always, unseen to most, under the Temporary and Trivial.']

—— Life of Sterling. 1851. [Story of a man's search for truth; includes attack on Coleridge's mysticism, pt I, ch. 8.]

Myers, F. H. Catholic Thoughts on the Church of Christ and the Church of England. 2 vols. 1834–41.

Newman, J. H. Tracts for the Times. 6 vols. 1834–41.

—— Sermons preached before the University of Oxford. 1843.

—— An Essay on the Development of Christian Doctrine. 1845. [Though pbd after his conversion, the book, emphasising both the secret appeal to the conscience, and the authoritative tradition of so much piety and erudition, belongs to this period of progress and spiritual reform. See J. B. Mozley, The Theory of Development: A Criticism of Dr Newman's Essay, from The Christian Remembrancer, 1847.]

—— Loss and Gain. The Story of a Convert. 1848. [Obvious touches of autobiography.

The novel pictures a young man intent on convincing his reason before he satisfies his instinctive longing for the Catholic Church. Glimpses of Oxford life unforgettable and suggestive of Arnold's 'regionalism.']

Newman, J. H. The Present Position of Catholics in England. 1851.

—— The Scope and Nature of a University Education. 1852. [Pbd later as The Idea of a University.]

—— Callista: A Sketch of the Third Century. 1856.

Wiseman, N. P. S. Lectures on the Doctrines and Practices of the Catholic Church. 1836.

—— High Church Claims. 1841.

—— Fabiola. A Tale of the Catacombs. 1854.

Howitt, W. Colonization and Christianity. 1838. [Treatment of natives by Europeans condemned. Book led to the establishment of the British India Soc.]

—— Visits to Remarkable Places, Old Halls, Battle-fields and Scenes Illustrative of Striking Passages in English History and Poetry. 2 sers. 1840–2.

Froude, R. H. Remains. 4 vols. 1838–9. [Perhaps the earliest 19th cent. influence towards a more catholic and imaginative conception of religion, culminating in erastianism.]

De Quincey, T. Miracles as Subjects of Testimony. Blackwood's Mag. July 1839. [Rptd in Collected Writings, ed. D. Masson, vol. VIII, 1897. Against Hume. Whether a miracle 'could translate itself upon the wings of testimony from the little theatre of spectators or auditors before whom it had been exhibited to the great theatre of the world and the still greater theatre of posterity.']

—— On Christianity as an Organ of Political Movement. Tait's Edinburgh Mag. April, June 1846. [Rptd in Collected Writings, ed D. Masson, vol. VIII, 1897. In contradistinction to pagan cults, Christianity has inspired the philanthropy of modern reforms.]

Arnold, T. Christian Life. Its Course. Sermons. 1841. [Applied the historical method to biblical study, without relinquishing broad-church orthodoxy. As he hated variance of opinion and wished to fuse Church and State into one spiritual whole, he opposed Newman and the Oxford movement. His influence on his son often acknowledged in M. Arnold's letters to his mother.]

—— Christian Life. Its Hopes. Sermons, 1842.

—— Sermons, chiefly on the Interpretation of Scripture. 1845.

Faber, F. W. Sights and Thoughts in Foreign Churches. 1842.

Lytton, Bulwer. Zanoni. 1842. [Depicts triumph of sympathetic over selfish hate. Love is the power by which the mind grasps the beneficence and harmony of the universe.]

Disraeli, B. Coningsby. 3 vols. 1844.

—— Sybil; or the Two Nations. 3 vols. 1845.

—— Tancred. 3 vols. 1847.

Horne, R. H. A New Spirit of the Age. 2 vols. 1844. [More enthusiasm and sense of progress, if less literary acumen, than in Hazlitt's Spirit of the Age. Alludes to his generation 'who have outgrown our institutions and are obliged to maintain a continual struggle to bring them into something like harmony with our morals and civilization.']

Ward, W. G. The Ideal of a Christian Church. Considered in comparison with Existing Practice. Containing a Defence of Certain Articles in the British Critic in Reply to Remarks on them in Mr. Palmer's Narrative. 1844. [Condemned as injudicious, but certainly idealistic.]

Sewell, W. The Plea of Conscience for Seceding. 1845.

Donaldson, J. W. A Vindication of Protestant Principles by Phileleutherus Anglicanus. 1847. [See De Quincey's review, Tait's Edinburgh Mag. Nov. 1847–Feb. 1848, rptd in Collected Writings, ed. D. Masson, vol. VIII, 1897.]

Harris, F. E. S. From Oxford to Rome. 1847.

Helps, Sir A. Friends in Council. [1847–59.] [Essays and dialogues on morals, manners and social obligations.]

—— Companions of my solitude. [1851.]

Maurice, J. F. D. The Religions of the World. 1847. [All creeds have some truth; early attempt at 'comparative religion.']

—— Theological Essays. 1853. [Kingsley hoped that they would be accepted 'not as a code complete but as a hint towards a new method of thought.']

—— The Doctrine of Sacrifice. 1854.

—— The Epistles of St John: Lectures on Christian Ethics. 1857.

—— The Gospel of the Kingdom of Heaven. 1864.

—— The Conscience, Lectures on Casuistry. 1868.

—— Social Morality. 1869.

Kingsley, C. Yeast, a Problem. Fraser's Mag. July–Dec. 1848; 1851. [Vindication of practical and humanitarian christianity.]

—— Alton Locke, Tailor and Poet. 1850. [Chartism not enough for the betterment of the working classes.]

—— Phaethon: Loose Thoughts for Loose Thinkers. Cambridge, 1852. [Against scepticism.]

Kingsley, C. Two Years Ago. 3 vols. 1857. [Beneficence of Providence.]

Wilberforce, H. W. Reasons for submitting to the Catholic Church: a Farewell Letter. 1851.

Patmore, P. G. My Friends and Acquaintances. 3 vols. 1854.

Robertson, F. W. Sermons preached at Trinity Chapel Brighton. Sers. 1–4, 1855–6; Ser. 5, 1874. [All posthumous. More widely read than Newman. 'It matters little whether fierce Romanism or fierce Protestantism wins the day: but it does matter whether or not in a conflict we lose some precious Christian truth, as well as the very spirit of Christianity.']

Browne, E. G. K. History of the Tractarian Movement. 1856.

Hughes, T. Tom Brown's School Days. 1857 (anon.). [Earnestness in schoolboys.]

Farrar, F. W. Eric; or Little by Little. A Tale of Rosslyn School. Edinburgh, 1858.

—— Saint Winifred's, or The World of School. Edinburgh, 1862.

Braybrooke, E. Some Victorian and Georgian Catholics. 1932.

Church, R. W. The Oxford Movement, Twelve Years 1833–1845. 1891.

Dibdin, Sir L. Establishment in England. 1932.

Froude, J. A. Carlyle. History of the First Forty Years of his Life. 2 vols. 1882.

Gwynn, D. Cardinal Wiseman. 1929.

Hanna, W. Letters of T. Erskine. 2 vols. 1877.

Hutchinson, W. G. The Oxford Movement. 1906.

Hutton, A. W. Cardinal Manning. 1892.

Laski, H. J. The Political Theory of the Oxford Movement. [In The Problem of Sovereignty, New Haven, 1917.]

Reilly, J. J. Newman as a Man of Letters. 1927.

Shuster, G. N. The Catholic Spirit in Modern English Literature. New York, 1922.

Storr, V. F. The Development of English Thought in the Nineteenth Century, 1800–1860. 1913.

Strachey, Lytton. Life of Cardinal Manning. [In Eminent Victorians, 1917.]

Stubbs, C. W. Charles Kingsley and the Christian Social Movement. 1899.

Symonds, J. A. The Catholic Reaction. [In Essays Speculative and Suggestive, 1890.]

Thureau-Dangin, P. La Renaissance catholique en Angleterre au XIXe Siècle. 1899–1906; tr. Eng. 2 vols. 1915.

Tulloch, J. Movements of Religious Thought in Britain during the Nineteenth Century. 1885.

Ward, W. W. G. Ward and the Oxford Movement. 1889.

—— W. G. Ward and the Catholic Revival. 1893.

—— Life of Cardinal Newman. 2 vols. 1912.

Webb, C. C. J. Religious Thought in the Oxford Movement. 1928.

(3) The Period of Divided Aims, Disillusionment, Controversy and Social Criticism. (The nadir, 1850–1870.)

(a) Anti-Catholic Reaction and Assertion of 'Higher Criticism'

Carlyle, T. Oliver Cromwell's Letters and Speeches. With Elucidations. 2 vols. 1845. [With a despairing gesture he turns his back on his own age, to show how manfully they faced the religious and the political problem in the 17th cent.]

Harris, F. E. S. From Oxford to Rome. 1847. [Novel illustrating the fatal error of apostasy to Rome.]

—— Rest in the Church. 1848.

Froude, J. A. The Nemesis of Faith. 1849.

—— The Book of Job. Westminster Rev. Oct. 1853. [Rptd in Short Studies on Great Subjects, vol. i, 1867.]

—— The Dissolution of the Monasteries. Fraser's Mag. Feb. 1857. [Rptd in Short Studies on Great Subjects, vol. ii, 1867.]

—— A Plea for the Free Discussion of Theological Difficulties. Fraser's Mag. Sept. 1863. [Rptd in Short Studies on Great Subjects, vol. i, 1867.]

—— Calvinism: An Address to the Students at St. Andrew's. 1871.

—— The Parable of the Bread Tree. [In Short Studies on Great Subjects, vol. ii, 1867.]

—— A History of England from the Fall of Wolsey to the Defeat of the Spanish Armada. 1856–70. [Unmistakable bias against Newmanism. The history insists on the righteousness of the Reformation and celebrates the great characters which only that movement could produce.]

—— Reminiscences of the High Church Revival. Good Words, 1881. [Rptd as The Oxford Counter-Reformation in Short Studies on Great Subjects, ser. 4, 1883. Generous tribute to Newman's personality and powers, but insistence that the Tractarians ruined Protestantism and forced their generation to choose between agnosticism and Rome.]

Landor, W. S. Popery, British and Foreign. 1851.

Davidson, S. The Text of The Old Testament considered with a Brief Introduction. 1856. [Led to a long controversy and Davidson's resignation from his professorship.]

Bunsen, C. C. J. Hippolytus und seine Zeit. Anfänge und Aussichten des Christenthums und der Menschheit. 2 vols. Leipzig, 1852–3

—— Gott in der Geschichte, oder der Fortschritt des Glaubens an eine sittliche Weltordnung in sechs Büchern. 3 pts, Leipzig, 1857–8.

Groeben, I. von der. Wissenschaft und Bibel mit Beziehung auf Dr Bunsens Hippolytus und auf die Recension dieses Werkes in Dr Hengstenberg's Kirchenzeitung. Stuttgart, 1856.

Trollope, A. Barchester Towers. 3 vols. 1857. [Ch. xx, Dr Arabin's religious crisis.]

Agassiz, L. Essay on Classification. 1858. [Insists on an Intelligent Power as the creator of species.]

Essays and Reviews. 1860. [In an earnest but critical spirit, the contributions put forward a plea for free criticism and do not accept (in Maurice's phrase) 'the full revelation of God in Christ.' Contributors: B. Wilson, B. Jowett, Baden Powell, R. Williams, F. Temple, M. Pattison, C. W. Godwin.]

Colenso, J. W. The Pentateuch and Joshua critically examined. 7 pts, 1862–79.

Savile, B. W. Revelation and Science in respect to Bunsen's Biblical Researches, The Evidence of Christianity and the Mosaic Cosmogony; with an Examination of Certain Statements put forth by the Remaining Authors of Essays and Reviews. 1862.

—— Bishop Colenso's Objections to the Veracity of the Pentateuch. An Examination. 1863.

—— The Truth of the Bible: Evidence from the Mosaic and Other Records of Creation; the Origin and Antiquity of Man; the Science of Scripture. 1870.

Williams, R. Revelation and Science in respect to Bunsen's Biblical Researches. 1862.

Kingsley, C. [Review of Froude's History of England, vols. vii and viii.] Macmillan's Mag. Jan. 1864. ['Truth for its own sake has never been a virtue with the Roman clergy. Father Newman informs us that it need not, and on the whole ought not to be.']

—— What then does Dr Newman mean? A Reply to a Pamphlet lately published by Dr Newman. 1864.

Newman, J. H. Mr. Kingsley and Dr. Newman. A Correspondence on the Question. Whether Dr. Newman teaches that Truth is no virtue? 1864.

Newman, J. H. Apologia pro Vita sua. Being a Reply to a Pamphlet entitled 'What then does Dr. Newman mean?' 1864. [Almost gladiatorial in its thrusts and parries. These personalities omitted and pt vii 'General answer to Mr Kingsley' recast as History of my Religious Opinions, 1865. See W. Ward, Newman's Apologia. The Two Versions of 1864 and 1865. Preceded by Newman's and Kingsley's Pamphlets, 1913.]

Disraeli, B. Lothair. 1870. [Mazzinianism and the intrigues of ultramontanism exposed.]

Liddon, H. P. Thoughts on the Present Church Troubles. 1881.

Renan, E. Souvenirs d'Enfance et de Jeunesse. Paris, 1883.

Ward, Mrs H. Robert Elsmere. 1888. [Against religious sentiment as illumined by Rome or the High Church principle. A scientific background indicated only so far as it will serve this purpose.]

—— Helbeck of Bannisdale. 1898.

—— Eleanore. 1900.

Cox, Sir G. W. The Life of J. W. Colenso, critically examined. 2 vols. 1888.

(b) *Philosophical Radicals, Scientific Humanitarians, Constructive Agnostics (Uninfluenced by Darwinism)*

Locke, J. An Essay concerning Humane Understanding. 1690. [Criticism of innate ideas; inquires how beliefs actually arise in the mind; knowledge depends on impressions received from objects.]

Berkeley, G. Alciphron, or the Minute Philosopher. 1732. [Every fresh piece of knowledge is a fresh act of perception. Influential as an empiricist following on Locke. His idealism is a flash of intuition more than a reasoned system.]

Hume, D. A Treatise of Human Nature: being an Attempt to introduce the Experimental Method of Reasoning into Moral Subjects. 3 vols. 1739–40. [Distrusts abstract reasoning. All science dependent on the science of mankind and must be based on experience and observation.]

—— Philosophical Essays concerning Human Understanding. 1748.

—— An Enquiry concerning the Principles of Morals. 1751.

—— Dialogues concerning Natural Religion. 1779.

Lamettrie, J. de. Œuvres Philosophiques. 1751. [First systematic presentation of materialism. Expelled from France.]

Holbach, P.-H., Baron d'. Le Christianisme dévoilé. Paris, 1756. [Unhappiness of man due to his imagined religion. Morality and conscience are the result of hereditary disposition which modifies the habits and sensations. There is no metaphysics, only determinism, progress, and natural laws.]
—— Théologie portative. Paris, 1768.
—— Système de la Nature. 2 vols. Paris, 1770.
Laplace, P.-S., Marquis de. Mécanique Céleste. Paris, 1799–1825. [Allows no place for God in the scheme of the Heavens, which he subjects to calculation.]
Foster, J. An Essay on the Evils of Popular Ignorance. 1820.
'Beauchamp, P.' (i.e. J. Bentham and G. Grote). The Analysis of the Influence of Natural Religion on the Temporal Happiness of Mankind. 1822. [All religion founded on the fear of an irresponsible power.]
Comte, A. Le Plan des Travaux Nécessaires pour réorganiser la Société. Paris, 1822. [Argues in this and the following books that thought, having passed through a theological and a metaphysical stage, has now reached the positive stage, in which experiences and appearances are recognised to be the limits of human knowledge; and the task of philosophy is to coordinate and interpret all that can be ascertained through science, and apply it to the understanding and bettering of mankind. The most inspiring idea in this system is the conception of the *grand être*, a sort of composite human being, the embodiment of all nations, whose happiness should be the aim of our speculations.]
—— Cours de Philosophie Positive. Paris, 1842.
—— Politique Positive. 1850–7.
Mill, James. Analysis of the Phenomena of the Human Mind. 1829.
Bentham, J. Works. Ed. Sir J. Bowring, 11 vols. 1838–43.
Mill, J. S. A system of Logic, Ratiocinative and Inductive. 2 vols. 1843. [Very significant as demonstrating that truth can be reached not by intuition or consciousness, but only by well-defined, if fallible, processes of thought.]
—— Utilitarianism. 1863. [The happiness of the greater number is the criterion of right and wrong.]
—— Auguste Comte and Positivism. 1865.
Martineau, H. The Positive Philosophy of A. Comte, freely translated and condensed. 1853.

Bain, A. The Senses and the Intellect. 1855.
—— The Emotions and the Wits. 1859.
—— On the Study of Character. 1861.
—— Mental and Moral Science. 1868.
—— Mind and Body. 1873.
Buckle, H. T. History of Civilisation in England. 2 vols. 1857–61. [Historical determinism founded on the study of data; confidence in methodising the movements and developments of man.]
Kingsley, C. The Limits of Exact Science as applied to History. Cambridge, 1860.
Lecky, W. E. H. History of the Rise and Influence of the Spirit of Rationalism in Europe. 2 vols. 1865.
Harrison, F. Social Statics. Translation of Comte's Positive Polity. Vol. II, 1875.
—— The Positivist Library. 1886.
Benn, A. W. The History of English Rationalism in the Nineteenth Century. 2 vols. 1906.
Fouillée, A. Le Mouvement positiviste et la Conception sociologique du Monde. 1896.
Huxley, T. Hume. 1881. (English Men of Letters ser.)
Laird, J. Hume's Philosophy of Human Nature. 1932.
Lévy-Bruhl, L. La Philosophie d'Auguste Comte. Paris, 1900; tr. Eng. 1903.
MacCunn, J. Six Radical Thinkers: Bentham, Mill, Cobden, Carlyle, Mazzini, T. H. Green. 1907.
Morris, C. R. Locke, Berkeley, Hume. 1932. [Critical attitude of Locke, idealism of Berkeley, naturalism of Hume. These philosophers too individualistic and original to be characterised as a school, but the continuity of their thought profoundly influenced Mill, Huxley, Spencer and W. James.]
Neff, E. Carlyle and Mill; Mystic and Utilitarian. New York, 1924.
Pringle-Pattison, A. S. The Philosophical Radicals and other Essays. 1907.
Robertson, J. M. A Short History of Free-Thought. 1915.
Routh, H. V. Money, Morals, and Manners, as Revealed in Modern Literature. 1934.
Taine, H. A. Le Positivisme anglais. Étude sur J. S. Mill. Paris, 1864.
Watson, J. Mill, Comte, Spencer. 1895.

(c) *Pre-Darwinian Science, German Christology and Historical Criticism, and their Effect on Moral and Religious Ideas*

Buffon, G.-L. L., Comte de. Histoire Naturelle. Paris, 1749–88. [Influenced by Descartes and Leibnitz. 'On n'aurait pas tort de supposer que d'un seul être elle [nature] a su tirer avec le temps tous les autres êtres organisés.']

Lessing, E. G. von. Von dem Zwecke Jesu und seiner Jünger. Noch ein Fragment des Wolfenbüttelschen Ungenannten. Brunswick, 1778. [Continues the attempt initiated in Zur Geschichte und Litteratur. Aus den Schätzen der Herzoglichen Bibliothek zu Wolfenbüttel, Brunswick, 1773–81, Beytrag IV, to examine the four gospels by the light of modern knowledge and the methods of historical research.]

Paine, T. The Age of Reason. 3 pts, Paris, 1794–New York, 1807.

Darwin, E. Zoonomia. 1794. [Modifications in animal and plant life due to 'life-force.']

Lamarck, I. G. St H. Histoire Naturelle. Paris, 1795. [Species are interrelated and differentiate through the urge or intelligence inherent in organisms.]

—— Philosophie zoologique. Paris, 1809.

Malthus, T. R. An Essay on the Principle of Population. 1798. [Population controlled by the chances of subsistence. This theory profoundly influenced Darwin, Wallace and Spencer.]

Venturini, K. H. Natürliche Geschichte des grossen Propheten von Nazareth. Copenhagen, 1800–1. [Argues that both Jesus and John were adopted by the sect of the Essenes and trained to appear as spiritual deliverers of the Jews, expressions and embodiments of national aspiration.]

Milman, H. H. History of the Jews. 1829. [Re-examines sacred history in a secular spirit.]

—— History of Christianity. 1840.

—— History of Latin Christianity. 1850–5.

Lyell, C. Principles of Geology. 1830–3. [The earth's surface has been formed, not by the will of any superhuman Being, achieving his purposes by catastrophic change, but by the slow and continuous operation of causes which are still at work. Book had marked influence on men as different as Tennyson and Darwin.]

Owen, R. D. Moral Physiology, or, a Brief and Plain Treatise on the Population Question. New York, 1831.

Knowlton, C. Fruits of Philosophy, or, the Private Companion of Young married People. New York, 1832. [This tract, revived by Mrs A. Besant, restarted controversy on birth control.]

Oken, L. Allgemeine Naturgeschichte. Stuttgart, 1833–42. [Lays foundation for theories of protoplasm and cell-structure.]

Strauss, D. F. Leben Jesu. Tübingen, 1835. [Inspired by Hegel. The Bible narrative is a collection of myths, some of which may happen to be true, but that is immaterial. They are significant because they collectively

express, in the form peculiar to a nation, one of the essential aspirations of the human spirit: the dream of the man-god. Jesus, as known to us through the New Testament, is poetically, not historically, true. The figure represents to what height the soul may rise and is thus a spiritual inspiration, though a theological error.]

Hennell, C. An Inquiry Concerning the Origin of Christianity. 1838. [Hennell retired from a profitable business for two years to complete this work based on Venturini. Analysis in J. W. Cross, George Eliot's Life, ch. II.]

Miller, H. The Old Red Sandstone. 1840.

—— My Schools and Schoolmasters. 1854.

Feuerbach, L. A. Das Wesen des Christenthums. Leipzig, 1841.

Burdach, K. F. Blicke ins Leben. 3 vols. Leipzig, 1842–4. [Phenomena of the spirit collected, observed, classified and studied by the methods of physiology or comparative anatomy, and referred to the same principles. 'Seelenlehre' given the position of 'Organenlehre.']

Chambers, R. Vestiges of the Natural History of Creation. 1844. [Pbd anonymously, the book spread far and wide the doctrine that species are not specially created, but are modified by natural causes. 'Introduced modern science to us under an unexpected aspect, and opened new avenues of thought' (Froude.]

Lewes, G. H. Biographical History of Philosophy. 4 vols. 1845–6.

—— The Life and Works of Goethe. 2 vols. 1855.

—— The Physiology of Common Life. 1859–60.

—— Problems of Life and Mind. 1874–9. [Researches of Carpenter, Laycock, Maudsley brilliantly popularised.]

Eliot, G. The Life of Jesus critically examined. 3 vols. 1846 (anon.). [Trn of Strauss's Leben Jesu.]

—— The Essence of Christianity. Translated by Marion Evans. 1854. [Feuerbach's Wesen des Christenthums.]

Horne, R. H. Judas Iscariot. A Miracle Play. 1848. [Judas believed that Jesus would free himself by a miracle and so precipitate the establishment of his kingdom on earth.]

Bunsen, C. C. J. Die Zeichen der Zeit. Briefe an Freunde über die Gewissensfreiheit und das Recht der Christliche Gemeinde. Leipzig, 1855; tr. Eng. 1856.

De Quincey, T. Judas Iscariot. [In Collected Writings, vol. VII, 1857.]

Mansel, H. L. The Limits of Religious Thought. 1858.

Spencer, H. Essays Scientific, Political and Speculative. 3 vols. 1858–74. [Represent his journalistic labours from 1848 (sub-editorship of the Economist) onwards, and contain the germ of the synthetic Philosophy. N.B. especially: The Development Hypothesis (1852), Progress: its Law and Cause (1856), The Ultimate Laws of Physiology (1857) (introduces the term 'evolution'). It was when revising and arranging all these fragmentary and fugitive essays, that he found them all to fall into place as parts of one scheme. The key to his system was supplied by Helmholtz's The Conservation of Energy (Physical Soc. of Berlin), 1847, and Sir William Grove's The Correlation of Physical Forces, 1846.]

—— A System of Synthetic Philosophy. First Principles. 1862. Principles of Biology. 2 vols. 1864–7. Principles of Psychology. 2 vols. 1870–2. Principles of Sociology. 3 vols. 1876–96. Principles of Ethics. 2 vols. 1879–93.

—— Autobiography. 1904. [Carelessly and egoistically compiled, but nevertheless an absorbing revelation of a scientifically constructive mind.]

Howitt, W. The History of the Supernatural in all Ages and Nations and in all Churches, Christian and Pagan, demonstrating a Universal Faith. 2 vols. 1863.

Renan, E. Vie de Jesus. Paris, 1863. [First treatise of Histoire des Origines du Christianisme, 1863–83; a series designed to establish by the help of science, history and philology the position of the Christian faith among the tendencies of culture. Vie de Jesus is the least penetrating but most picturesque of these researches (not excepting L'Antichrist). The biography rationalises the miraculous elements and represents Jesus as hovering between the claims of his ministry and the all too human attractions of this life in that sunny climate.]

Lubbock, Sir J. (Baron Avebury). Prehistoric Times. 1865.

—— The Origin of Civilisation and the Primitive Condition of Man. 1870.

Seeley, Sir J. R. Ecce Homo. Cambridge, 1865 (anon.). [Accepts the personality of Jesus as an inspired man. Shows how the Kingdom of God was not a mystic or symbolic conception, but a call to a moral and spiritual brotherhood.]

—— Natural Religion. By the Author of 'Ecce Homo.' 1882.

Gould, S. Baring. The Origin and Development of Religious Belief. 1869–70.

—— Some Modern Difficulties. 1875.

—— Mehalah. 1880. [Novel inspired by ethnology.]

Gould, S. Baring. John Herring. 1883. [Novel inspired by ethnology.]

—— The Birth of Jesus. 1885.

—— The Death and Resurrection of Jesus. 1888.

—— Freaks of Fanaticism and Other Strange Events. 1891.

Arnold, M. St. Paul and Protestantism. With an Introduction on Puritanism and the Church of England. 1870. [Carlyle and Froude had lamented the 'petrifaction' of anglicanism in the 'sixties. Arnold tries to give it life in the 'seventies. As the Germans had rationalised by the light of historical criticism, Arnold follows in their steps, and adds the enlightenment of literary criticism. The true message of the Bible is the pursuit of righteousness.]

—— Literature and Dogma. An Essay towards a Better Apprehension of the Bible. 1873.

—— God and the Bible. A Review of Objections to Literature and Dogma. 1875.

—— Last Essays on Church and Religion. 1877.

—— Notebooks, with a Preface by Mrs. Wodehouse. 1902. [Extracts from his reading, containing the germ of nearly all his ideas. Religious sentiment predominates, the need of scope and direction in his life particularly emphasised.]

Stephen, Sir L. Essays on Free-thinking and Plain Speaking. 1873.

—— The Science of Ethics. 1882.

—— An Agnostic's Apology. 1893.

—— The English Utilitarians. 1900.

Besant, A. On the Deity of Jesus of Nazareth. By the Wife of a Beneficed Clergyman. 1873.

—— On the Nature and Existence of God. 1875.

—— My Path of Atheism. 1877.

—— The Christian Creed; or What it is Blasphemy to deny. 1883.

—— Why I dare not believe in God. 1887.

Pattison, M. Memoirs. 1885. [Gradual development of his mind from the interests and intrigues of academic life to the conviction that all religions are 'as efforts of the human spirit to come to an understanding with that Unseen Power whose pressure it feels' (ch. VII).]

Dawson, W. H. Matthew Arnold and his Relation to the Thought of our Time. 1904.

Marvin, F. S. The Century of Hope. Oxford, 1919.

Osborne, H. Whom do Men say that I am? 1932. [Anthology of opinions on Jesus from Newman to D. H. Lawrence.]

Schweitzer, A. Von Reimarus zu Wrede. Eine Geschichte der Leben-Jesu-Forschung. Tübingen, 1906, 1913 (enlarged); tr. Eng. 1910. [A scholarly and critical review of the whole movement towards rationalising the New Testament. 'The Germans have set themselves with all their might to *understand* the Bible, and to learn all that can be known about it,' J. A. Froude.]

Somervell, D. C. English Thought in the Nineteenth Century. 1929.

(d) Criticism of Life and Society in this New and Disturbed Atmosphere of Scientific Enquiry, Biblical Criticism, and the Morals and Manners of Commercial Development and the Theories of the Manchester School

Dickens, C. Oliver Twist. Jan. 1837 Jan. 1838. [Slums, bumbledom.]
—— Nicholas Nickleby. April 1838–Oct. 1839. [Private schools of the old type.]
—— Dealings with the Firm of Dombey and Son Wholesale, Retail and for Exportation. Oct. 1847–April 1848. [Dehumanisation and arrogance of commerce.]
—— The Personal History, Adventures, Experience and Observations of David Copperfield the Younger. May 1849–Nov. 1850.
—— Bleak House. March 1852–Sept. 1853. [The law, 'Cobwebs which may catch small flies, but let wasps and hornets break through.']
– Great Expectations. All the Year Round, Dec. 1860–Aug. 1861. [Convicts; demoralisation of wealth.]

Thackeray, W. M. A Shabby Genteel Story. Fraser's Mag. June–Oct. 1840.
—— The History of Mr. Titmarsh and the Hoggarty Diamond. Fraser's Mag. Sept.–Dec. 1841.
—— The Snobs of England, by one of themselves. Punch, 28 Feb. 1846–27 Feb. 1847.
—— Vanity Fair. Jan 1847–July 1848.
—— The Newcomes. Oct. 1853–Aug. 1855.

Ruskin, J. Modern Painters: their Superiority in the Art of Landscape Painting to all the Ancient Masters proved by Example of the True, the Beautiful, and the Intellectual from the Works of Modern Artists, especially those of J. M. W. Turner. 1843. [Contains indignant protest against Englishmen's insensibility to contemporary art, and denounces 'monetary asceticism, consisting in the refusal of pleasure and knowledge for the sake of money.']
—— Sesame and Lilies. 1865.
—— The Crown of Wild Olive. Three Lectures on Work, Traffic and War. 1866.

Ruskin, J. Fors Clavigera. Letters to the Workmen and Labourers of Great Britain. 9 vols. Orpington, 1871–87.

Carlyle, T. Latter-day Pamphlets. 1850. [Sauerteig and pig philosophy; grotesquely bitter caricature of mammonism and irreligion.]
Froude, J. A. Carlyle: History of his Life in London (1834–81). 2 vols. 1884. [Represents Carlyle writhing under the materialism and religious formalism of his age as well as indigestion and domestic friction.]

Horne, R. H. The Dreamer and the Worker. 1851.

Trollope, A. Barchester Towers. 3 vols. 1857. [Cabals and self-interest of a Cathedral chapter.]
—— Dr. Thorne. 3 vols. 1858. [Financial embarrassments of a landed gentleman; demoralisation of a plebeian millionaire.]
—— Framley Parsonage. 3 vols. 1861. [Extravagances and embarrassments of a country vicar.]
—— The Way we Live Now. 1875. [Satire on idle rich, promoters of companies and parliamentary adventurers.]

Eliot, G. Scenes of Clerical Life. Blackwood's Mag. Jan.–Nov. 1857; 2 vols. Edinburgh, 1858.
—— Adam Bede. 3 vols. Edinburgh, 1859.
—— The Mill on the Floss. 3 vols. Edinburgh, 1860.
—— Silas Marner. Edinburgh, 1861.
—— Middlemarch. 4 vols. Edinburgh, 1871–2.

Mill, J. S. On Liberty. 1859. [A spirited and thoughtful protest against the tyranny of public opinion and the vice of intellectual cowardice. He argues (like Carlyle, Ruskin and Froude) that the English nation has lost its individuality and character, and is powerful only through its numbers and wealth.]
—— Three Essays on Religion. 1873. [Composed in the 'fifties, pbd posthumously to avoid the 'odium theologicum.' He argues that orthodoxy is undermining the character and intellectual honesty of the nation.]

Meredith, G. The Ordeal of Richard Feverel. 1859. [A noble character and promising career poisoned by the aristocratic Englishman's artificial and priggish ideal of conduct.]
—— Emilia in England. 3 vols. 1864. [Afterwards entitled Sandra Belloni. The sentimentalism and affectation of the newly rich.]
—— Beauchamp's Career. 3 vols. 1876. [Radicalism v. the upper classes. Difficulties and disappointments of a high-spirited and disinterested political reformer.]

Meredith, G. Diana of the Crossways. 3 vols. 1885. [Temptations and pitfalls of a gifted woman's career among the intellectuals and the politicians.]

—— One of Our Conquerors. 1891. ['Is it a truth that if we are great owners of money we are so swoln with a force not native to us, as to be precipitated into acts the downright contrary of our tastes?' (ch. XVIII).]

Froude, J. A. A Plea for the Free Discussion of Theological Difficulties. Fraser's Mag. Sept. 1863. [The orthodox have 'a confused sense that theological truth is in some way different from other truth.' Rptd in Short Studies on Great Subjects, vol. I, 1867.]

—— Education. An Address to the Students of St. Andrew's. 1869. [Condemns the modern combination of culture and luxury; advocates emigration.]

—— Calvinism: An Address to the Students at St. Andrew's. 1871. ['We have learnt, as we say, to make the best of both worlds, to take political economy for the rule of our conduct, and to relegate religion into the profession of orthodox doctrines.']

—— England and her Colonies. Fraser's Mag. Jan. 1870. [Demoralisation of town life; need for emigration.]

—— Reciprocal Duties of State and Subject. Fraser's Mag. Mar. 1870. ['Where money is the measure of worth the wrong persons are always uppermost.']

—— The Colonies once more. Fraser's Mag. Sept. 1870. [Public land appropriated by private owners. The masses ought to emigrate, but government discourages the movement as it would raise the price of labour.]

—— Progress. Fraser's Mag. Dec. 1870. ['The accumulation of wealth, with its daily services at the Stock Exchange and the Bourse, with international exhibitions for its religious festivals, and political economy for its gospel, is progress, if it be progress at all, towards the wrong place.']

—— England's War. Fraser's Mag. Feb. 1871. ['We are still able to make ourselves hated; we cannot save ourselves from being despised.']

—— Party Politics. Fraser's Mag. July 1874. [Strong government impossible owing to the short tenures of office, and dissentions within the party.]

Arnold, M. Friendship's Garland. Pall Mall Gazette, July 1866–Nov. 1870; 1871 [Exposes the muddle and purposelessness of British civilisation together with (in My Countrymen) the Englishman's incapacity to enjoy himself.]

—— Culture and Anarchy. Cornhill Mag. July 1867–Aug. 1868; 1869. [Argument

that individualism ('doing what one likes') in foreign policy, internal administration and above all in public worship was hurrying England towards anarchy and that only culture and humanism could save her.]

Spencer, H. The Study of Sociology. 1872. [One of his most readable books. Indicates the prejudices and misunderstandings with which social thinkers have to contend; also the dangers and inconveniences with which democracy is threatened.]

Besant, A. The Law of Population: Its Consequences and its Bearing upon Human Conduct and Morals. 1877. [Recasting of Knowlton's Fruits of Philosophy; see p. 61 above.]

—— Marriage: as It was, as It is, and as It should be. With a Sketch of the Life of Mrs Besant. Ed. A. K. Butts, New York, 1879.

Linton, E. L. The Girl of the Period. 1883.

Nietzsche, F. W. Also Sprach Zarathustra. Ein Buch für Alle und Keinen. 4 pts, Chemnitz, 1883–91. [Insists on the need of nobler and more spiritual motives for living. He exhorts his contemporaries to pursue the ideal of self-realisation, even if it culminates in self-destruction, so that the future may be made free.]

Moore, G. Literature at Nurse, or Circulating Morals. 1885. [Lending libraries.]

Besant, Sir W. The Children of Gibeon. 1886.

Bliss, W. D. P. Socialism. By J. S. Mill. A Collection of his Writings on Socialism, with chapters on Democracy, the Right of Property in Land and the Enfranchisement of Women. New York, 1891.

Cazamian, L. Le Roman Social en Angleterre, 1830–1850. Paris, 1904.

Glasier, J. B. William Morris and the Early Days of the Socialist Movement. 1921.

MacCarthy, J. A Short History of Our Own Times. 1907.

Martin, E. Histoire économique et financière de l'Angleterre (1866–1902). Paris, 1912.

Rose, H. The New Political Economy: the Social Teaching of Carlyle. 1891.

Whitehouse, J. H. The Solitary Warrior. New Letters of Ruskin. 1929. [Reveals Ruskin's disillusionment and depression at the failure of his schemes.]

(4) MAMMONISM

(a) The 'Economic Man's' Bible

Smith, A. The Wealth of Nations. 1776. [All industry and commerce 'led by an invisible hand to promote an end.' So 'enlightened self-interest' is enough guidance for a Christian man of business.]

Malthus, T. R. An Essay on the Principle of Population. 1798. [A reply to Godwin's Inquiry Concerning Political Justice. Population bound by a law of Nature, that is to say of God, to multiply up to the point of starvation. So it was through a divine dispensation that competition should reduce wages to the merest pittance.]

Ricardo, D. Principles of Political Economy and Taxation. 1817. [Law of diminishing returns. Logic of facts compels a vast population to labour in poverty while their proceeds swell the national revenue, and consolidate the power of a small class.]

Senior, N. W. An Outline of the Science of Political Economy. 1836. [Unsocial in spirit. Argues that economists have no more to do with reform than an astronomer with navigation.]

Mill, J. S. Principles of Political Economy, with some of their Applications to Social Philosophy. 1848. [Lucidly restates the principles of the classical school. Tentative leaning towards socialism.]

Cairns, J. E. The Character and Logical Method of Political Economy. 1857. ['Economic science has no more connection than the science of mechanics has with our present system of railways.']

Gray, A. The Development of Economic Doctrine. An Introductory Survey. 1933.

Schumpeter, J. Epochen der Dogmen- und Methodengeschichte. Grundriss der Sozialökonomik. Tübingen, 1925.

(b) Humanitarian Protests

Carlyle, T. Chartism. 1839.
—— Past and Present. 1843. [Perhaps the first attempt by a then fashionable author to bring the real state of England before the notice of the cultured few.]
—— Latter-day Pamphlets. 1850.

Disraeli, B. Sybil; or The Two Nations. 3 vols. 1845. [Graphic descriptions of poverty. Need of statesmanship with ideals.]

Engels, F. Die Lage der arbeitenden Klasse in England in 1844. Leipzig, 1845; tr. Eng. New York, 1886. [A young German socialist spends 21 months in the Midlands to study the enormities of industrialism at their source and centre. His information and bibliography exhaustive; prophesies a revolution.]

Gaskell, E. C. Mary Barton. 2 vols. 1848 (anon.). [Mutual understanding the cure for industrial evils.]

Kingsley, C. Alton Locke: Tailor and Poet. 1849. [Evils of 'sweating'; riots; how a poor man learnt to appreciate the rich.]
—— Yeast. 1851. [How a rich man learnt to appreciate the poor.]

Froude, J. A. Cat's Pilgrimage. 1850. [Clearsighted parable, by the light of the Manchester School, on the egoism of a society founded on competition.]
—— Siding in a Railway Station. Fraser's Mag. Nov. 1879. [Exposure of the inequalities of |society, and of its parasites in high place.]

Thackeray, W. M. The Newcomes. Oct. 1853–Aug. 1855. [Rummun Loll the international swindler, and the Colonel who is bankrupt.]

Dickens, C. Hard Times. Household Words, 1 April–12 Aug. 1854.
—— Little Dorrit. Dec. 1855–July 1857. [Merdle the bank-manager, company promoter, and swindler in high society.]

Marx, K. Zur Kritik der politischen Oekonomie. Berlin, 1859.
—— Das Kapital. Kritik der politischen Oekonomie. 3 vols. Hamburg, 1867–94. [Much of the work incomprehensible. Often refuted by academic economists, but the doctrine of 'surplus value' has had immense influence, and his exposures of oppression and injustice are unforgettable.]

Ruskin, J. Unto this Last. Four Essays on the First Principles of Political Economy. 1862. [Contains his plea for standard wages; his appeal to use wealth for the enjoyment of life; his protest against oppression of the poor; his claim that all work should be an education and pleasure for the workman. The most representative of the innumerable lectures and essays of an art-socialist and the enemy of the Manchester school.]

Reade, C. Put yourself in his Place. 3 vols. 1870. [Characteristically vigorous study of the tyranny of trades-unions; the demoralisation of the labouring class; the self-interest of employers and prejudice of the gentry.]

Lytton, B. The Coming Race. 1871 (anon.).

George, H. Progress and Poverty. 1880. [Maldistribution of wealth, due to the private ownership of land.]

Besant, Sir W. All Sorts and Conditions of Men. 1882. [Study of the dullness and hopelessness of East-End lives.]
—— Children of Gibeon. 1886. [Life and prospects of a seamstress paid by piecework.]
—— Beyond the Dreams of Avarice. 1895. [Clever satire of claimants to an enormous fortune, demoralised by dreaming of wealth which they have not earned, but hope to get.]

Mallock, W. H. Social Equality: A Short Study in a Missing Science. 1882.
—— Landlords and the National Income. 1884.
—— Property and Progress. (An Answer to H. George.) 1884.
—— A Critical Examination of Socialism. 1907.

Gissing, G. Unclassed. 1884. [Unique for the realistic almost tragic spirit in which he describes the tyranny of industrialism over the London proletariat and the fate of paupers bred or educated above their class.]
—— Demos. 1886.
—— Thyrza. 1887.
—— Nether World. 1889.

Bellamy, E. Looking Backward. 1888. [The future communistic state. So well ordered that man has nothing to strive for.]

Morris, W. News from Nowhere. 1891. [The most complete, picturesque and representative of his many protests against the mechanisation of industry and the enslavement of labour by capital. Perhaps the only really inspired vision of socialism.]

Shaw, G. B. Widowers' Houses. 1892.
—— Mrs Warren's Profession. 1895. [Both expose huge incomes derived from tainted sources.]

Frederic, H. The Market Place. 1898-9. [Novel; the best study of the manipulations of the Stock-exchange.]

(5) DARWINISM, NEW ADJUSTMENTS TO THE RESPONSIBILITIES OF LIFE, THE END OF AN AGE

(a) Darwinism and its Immediate Effects

Malthus, T. R. An Essay on the Principle of Population as it affects the Future Improvement of Society. 1798. [The book from which Darwin derived (Oct. 1838) the suggestion which he developed into his theory.]

Darwin, C. R. On the Origin of Species by Means of Natural Selection, or the Preservation of Favoured Races in the Struggle for Life. 1859. [Proved that the development and evolution of species were due to no divine plan, nor universal idea, nor any other metaphysical or spiritual cause, but to the struggle for existence. Neither Mill, Spencer, G. Eliot, or M. Arnold realised the significance of his demonstration.]
—— The Descent of Man, and Selection in relation to Sex. 2 vols. 1871.
—— Formation of Vegetable Mould through the Action of Worms. 1881. [The most

popular of all his works; the revelation of worms as one of man's best friends has produced a profound impression on our sentiment for Nature.]

Huxley, T. H. Man's Place in Nature. 1863. [Huxley first understood that Darwinism meant a revolution in our conception of human destiny. Man is thrown on his own resources in this world, confronting nature like a half-equipped chess-player pitted against a remorseless antagonist (letter to C. Kingsley, 22 May 1863). Our progress depends on acquiring knowledge of the game, and in the courage and judgment which we can muster to make the right moves. Huxley's innumerable essays and addresses were republished in this and the following books.]
—— Lay Sermons, Addresses and Reviews. 1870.
—— Critiques and Addresses. 1873.
—— Science and Culture and Other Essays. 1881.
—— Essays upon some Controverted Questions. 1892.
—— Collected Essays. 9 vols. 1894.
—— Scientific Memoirs. 4 vols. 1898–1901.

Butler, S. Life and Habit. 1873.
—— Evolution Old and New. 1879.
—— Unconscious Memory. 1880.
—— Luck or Cunning. 1886.
—— The Way of All Flesh. 1903. ['The way of all flesh' is the way of heredity.]

Reade, W. The Outcast. 1875. [Hero, become an agnostic through reading Lyell's Principles of Geology, is disowned by his father, but befriended by a doctor, whose house is an amateur laboratory for scientific research.]

Hardy, T. The Return of the Native. 1878. [This and the other novels free from allusions to Darwinism, but full of Darwinian pessimism. His characters are at the mercy of heredity, environment and chance, and the victims of the struggle for life.]
—— The Mayor of Casterbridge. 1886.
—— The Woodlanders. 1887.
—— Tess of the d'Urbervilles. 1891.
—— Jude the Obscure. 1895.

Allen, G. The Colour Sense; its Origin and Development. 1879.
—— The Evolutionist at Large. 1881.
—— Philistia. 1884. [Novel.]
—— Charles Darwin. 1885.
—— Science in Arcady. 1892.
—— The Lower Slopes. 1894. [Poems. Especially: A Ballad of Evolution; The First Idealist; Animalcular Theology; Only an Insect; To Herbert Spencer.]
—— The Woman who Did. 1894. [The Girtonite who relapsed to type.]

Allen, G. The British Barbarians; a Hill-top Novel. 1895. [Reveals a new generation all talking the language of the sciences.]
—— The Evolution of the Idea of God. 1897.
Laing, S. Modern Science and Modern Thought. 1885.
—— Human Origins. 1892.
Oliphant, L. Sympneumata, or Evolutionary Forces now Active in Man. 1885.
—— Scientific Religion. 1888.
Gissing, G. The Emancipated. 1890.
—— Born in Exile. 3 vols. 1892.
Stirling, J. H. Darwinism; Workmen and Works. 1894.
Wells, H. G. The Island of Dr. Moreau. 1896.
—— Tales of Space and Time. 1899.
—— The First Men in the Moon. 1901.
White, A. D. A History of the Warfare of Science with Theology. 1896.
Wallace, A. R. The Wonderful Century, its Successes and its Failures. 1898.
Haeckel, E. Die Welträtsel. Bonn, 1899; tr. Eng. 1900. [The enigmas of existence to be studied and perhaps solved by the accumulation and interpretation of scientific facts, as Darwin had shown. Perhaps the most explicit and uncompromising champion of Darwinism.]
—— Die Lebenswunder. Bonn, 1904; tr. Eng. 1904. [Elaboration of same theme in answer to critics and correspondents.]
Stephen, Sir L. Evolution and Religious Conceptions. [In The 19th Century, 1901.]

Adickes, E. Kant contra Haeckel. Erkenntniss-Theorie gegen naturwissenschaftlichen Dogmatismus. Berlin, 1901.
Cadman, S. P. Charles Darwin and Other English Thinkers, with Reference to their Religious and Ethical Value. 1911.
Ellis, H. Views and Reviews. 2 sers. 1932–4. [Essays of the last fifty years. Illustrates all the period. Anticipates much of the 20th cent.]
Haldane, J. B. S. The Causes of Evolution. 1932.
Judd, J. W. The Coming of Evolution. 1910.
Russell, B. The Scientific Outlook. 1931.
Schmidt, H. Der Kampf um die Welträtsel. Bonn, 1900.
Thomson, Sir J. A. Influence of Darwinism on Thought and Life. [In Science and Civilisation, Oxford, 1926.]
—— The Great Biologists. 1932. [From Aristotle to Pasteur. Discusses Goethe, Müller, Claude-Bernard, Spencer, Huxley, Wallace, Darwin, Mendel, Galton.]
Ward, H. Charles Darwin. The Man and his Warfare. 1928.
Yapp, A. H. Darwin considered mainly as Ethical Thinker, Human Reformer and Pessimist. 1901.

(b) *Realism and Naturalism, French Influences*

Flaubert, G. Madame Bovary. Paris, 1857.
Goncourt, E. and J. de. Sœur Philomène. Paris, 1861. [Many subsequent novels.]
—— Journal des Goncourt. 3 sers. 9 vols. Paris, 1887–95. [Perhaps the best of all examples of the realist's attitude of mind and method of work.]
Reade, C. Griffith Gaunt. 3 vols. 1866. [Tale of instinct, jealousy and passion in realistic circumstances.]
—— A Terrible Temptation. 1871. [Author's methods of documentation; character of a realist.]
Zola, É. Thérèse Raquin. Paris, 1867. [Many following.]
—— La Fortune des Rougon. Paris, 1871. [Préface.]
—— Le Roman Experimental. Paris, 1880.
—— Romanciers Naturalistes. Paris, 1881.
Moore, G. A Modern Lover. 1883. [According to A. Bennett (Fame and Fiction) the first example of English realism.]
—— Piping Hot. 1885. [Trn of Zola's Pot-Bouilli.]
—— Confessions of a Young Man. 1886. [Ch. x, one of the best expositions of the fascination of the new school.]
Voguë, M. de. Roman Russe. Paris, 1886. [Anti-realist.]
'Malet, Lucas' (*i.e.* Mary St Leger Harrison). The Wages of Sin. 1891. [Character of Colthurst the realist painter.]
Gissing, G. Demos. 1886.
—— The Nether World. 3 vols. 1889.
—— New Grub Street. 3 vols. 1891.
—— The Odd Women. 3 vols. 1893.
—— In the Year of Jubilee. 1894.

Bouvier, É. La Bataille Réaliste (1844–57). 1914.
Saintsbury, G. The Later Nineteenth Century. 1904.

(c) *Pessimism, the Reaction from Science and Positivism, Appeal to Humanism*

Peacock, T. L. Gryll Grange. 1860. [Too rapid advance and pretensions of science satirised, especially in the character of Lord Curryfin the apostle of 'panto-pragmatism.']
Cobbe, F. P. Broken Lights: an Enquiry into the Present Condition and Future Prospects of Religious Faith. 1864.
—— Dawning Lights: an Enquiry concerning the Secular Results of the New Reformation. 1868.
—— Darwinism in Morals, and other Essays. 1872.

Cobbe, F. P. The Hopes of the Human Race, Hereafter and Here. 1874.
—— A Faithless World. 1885.
—— The Scientific Spirit of the Age and other Pleas and Discussions. 1888.
—— Life, told by Herself. 1898.
Masson, D. Recent British Philosophy including some comments on Mr. Mill's Answer to Sir W. Hamilton. 1865.
Irons, W. J. An Examination of Mr. Mill's Three Essays on Religion. 1875.
Antichrist. The Jesus Christ of J. S. Mill. 1875.
Leaving us an Example: is it living—and why? An Enquiry suggested by certain Passages in J. S. Mill's 'Essays on Religion.' Paris, 1875.
Bray, C. Christianity viewed in the Light of our Present Knowledge and Moral Sense. 1876.
—— Phases of Opinion and Experience during a Long Life: An Autobiography. 1884.
Is Theism Immoral? An Examination of Mr J. S. Mill's Arguments against Mansel's View of Religion. Swansea, 1877.
Mallock, W. H. The New Republic. 2 vols. 1877. [Platonic dialogue, confronting Darwin, Jowett and Arnold with Ruskin, W. K. Clifford and Pater.]
—— The New Paul and Virginia, or Positivism in an Island. 1878. [A naturalist, wrecked on a desert island with the daughter of an Anglican bishop, starts life anew on positivist ideas.]
—— Is Life Worth Living? An Ethical Study. 187º.
—— Atheism and the Value of Life. 1884.
—— Five Studies in Contemporary Literature. 1884.
—— A Human Document. 1892. [Romantic lovers impregnated with science and philosophy.]
Sully, J. Pessimism. 1877.
Caro, E. M. Le Pessimisme au XIXᵉ Siècle. Paris, 1878.
Romanes, G. J. A Candid Examination of Theism. 1878. [Despairs of religion in the light of science.]
—— The Scientific Evidences of Organic Evolution. 1882.
—— Mental Evolution in Man. 1888.
—— Origin of Human Faculty. 1888.
—— Darwin and after Darwin. An Exposition of the Darwinian Theory and a Discussion of Post-Darwinian Questions. 3 vols. 1892.
—— Thoughts on Religion. Ed. C. Gore. 1895. [His nearest approach to the recovery of religious faith.]
—— Life and Letters. 1896.

Aveling, E. B. The Value of this Earthly Life. 1879. [A reply to Is Life Worth Living?]
Barlow, J. W. The Ultimatum of Pessimism. 1882.
Huysmans, J.-K. A Rebours. Paris, 1884. [Culmination of his earlier realist phase; study of a temperament disorganised by intensive self-culture without ideals.]
—— En Route. Paris, 1895. [First phase of his movement towards mysticism and religion.]
—— Là-bas. Paris, 1897.
—— La Cathédrale. Paris, 1898.
—— L'Oblat. Paris, 1903. [The consummation. His hero finds peace in the Catholic faith.]
Thomson, J. R. Modern Pessimism. 1885.
Williams, C. Modern Pessimism. Its Cause and Cure. Bodmin, 1885.
Harrison, F. The Nature and Reality of Religion. 1885. [Controversy with H. Spencer.]
Hutton, R. H. Essays on some of the Modern Guides of English Thought in Matters of Faith. 1887.
—— Criticism on Contemporary Thought and Thinkers. 1894.
—— Aspects of Religion and Scientific Thought. 1899.
Moore, G. Mere Accident. 1887.
—— Mike Fletcher. 1889.
—— Celibates. 1895.
Corelli, M. Ardath. 1889. [Perhaps the most pronounced of her novels, which are all touched with a certain anti-scientific and almost spiritualistic mysticism. See B. Vyver, Memoirs of Marie Corelli, 1930.]
Bourget, P. Le Disciple. Paris, 1889.
Ritchie, D. G. Darwinism and Politics. 1889.
—— The Principles of State Interference: Four Essays on the Political Philosophy of Mr H. Spencer, J. S. Mill and T. H. Green. 1891.
—— Darwin and Hegel, with other Philosophical Studies. 1893.
Hopps, J. P. Pessimism, Science and God. Spiritual Solutions of Pressing Problems. 1894.
Wenley, R. M. Aspects of Pessimism. Edinburgh, 1894.

(d) New Spirit of Social and Political Reform, and of Reconciliation between Science and Religion

Kingsley, C. Yeast. A Problem. 1851. [Christian spirit directed to social reform.]
Reade, C. Christie Johnson. 1853. [Plea for broadmindedness. Looking at things from three sides.]

Reade, C. It is never too late to mend. 3 vols. 1856. [Prisons. Always looks for the solution of life's problems in action.]

—— Hard Cash. 3 vols. 1863. [Asylums.]

—— Foul Play. 3 vols. 1868. [Ship insurance.]

Spencer, H. Education. Intellectual, Moral and Physical. 1861. [Argues that the best training for a child is that which accords with his inclinations.]

Senior, N. W. Suggestions on Popular Education. 1861.

Arnold, M. The Popular Education of France, with Notices of that of Holland and Switzerland. 1861.

—— A French Eton; or, Middle-Class Education and the State. 1864.

—— Schools and Universities on the Continent. 1868.

—— Higher Schools and Universities in Germany. 1874.

—— Reports on Elementary Schools. 1852–84.

—— Irish Essays and Others. 1882.

—— Educational Reform League Special Report on Elementary Education in Germany, Switzerland and France. 1888.

Mill, J. S. Education: Inaugural Address at St. Andrew's. 1867.

—— On the Subjection of Women. 1869. [While pleading for their political and social rights, he reveals an ideal of home-life based on common interests and intellectual compatibility.]

Farrar, F. W. Essays on a Liberal Education. 1867.

—— The Life of Christ. 2 vols. 1874.

Collins, W. W. Man and Wife. 3 vols. 1870. [Rigours of marriage law; brutality of cult of sport.]

—— The Law and the Lady. 3 vols. 1875. [Laws of marriage; Scotch verdict of non-proven.]

Lytton, B. The Coming Race. 1870. [Picturesque prognostication of the future of science and philosophy applied to life.]

White, C. Ecce Femina. Being an Examination of Arguments in Favour of Female Suffrage by J. S. Mill and Others. 1870.

Swinburne, A. C. Hertha. [In Songs before Sunrise, 1871. The most complete of his many religious avowals.]

Campbell, J. M. Reminiscences and Reflections. 1873.

Picton, J. A. The Mystery of Matter. 1873.

—— The Religion of the Universe. 1904.

Green, J. R. A Short History of the English People. 1874. [A trumpet call to remind Englishmen of the destiny and spirit of their nation.]

Seccombe, J. T. Science, Theism and Revelation, considered in Relation to Mr Mill's

Essays on Nature, Religion and Theism. 1875.

Cox, S. Salvator Mundi. 1877.

Bain, A. Education as a Science. 1878.

Caird, J. Introduction to the Philosophy of Religion. 1880. [Christianity our defence against materialism.]

Hopps, J. P. A Scientific Basis of Belief in a Future Life. 1880.

Besant, Sir W. All Sorts and Conditions of Men. 3 vols. 1882. [Message of self-help and enjoyment to the working classes.]

Morris, W. Hopes and Fears for Art. Five Lectures. 1882.

—— A Dream of John Ball and A King's Lesson. 1888.

—— Signs of Change: Seven Lectures. 1888.

—— News from Nowhere, or an Epoch of Rest; being some Chapters from a Utopian Romance. 1891.

—— Under an Elm-tree; or Thoughts in the Country-side. Aberdeen, 1891.

Carpenter, E. Towards Democracy. 1883.

Drummond, H. Natural Law in the Spiritual World. 1883.

Meredith, G. The Woods of Westermain. [In Poems and Lyrics of the Joy of Earth, 1883. The most thorough of his musings on man's place in Nature.]

Seeley, Sir J. The Expansion of England. 1883.

Mallock, W. H. Atheism and the Value of Life. Five Studies in Contemporary Literature. 1884.

Guyau, M.-J. Esquisse d'une Morale sans Obligation ni Sanction. Paris, 1885.

—— L'Art au Point de Vue Sociologique. Paris, 1889. [Influence on poetry of philosophical and sociological ideas.]

Martineau, J. Types of Ethical Theory. 1885. [Believes in the presence of God but accepts science.]

—— A Study of Religion. 1888.

—— The Seat of Authority in Religion. 1890.

Müller, F. Max. The Science of Thought. 1887.

—— Natural Religion. 1889.

—— Physical Religion. 1891.

—— Anthropological Religion. 1892.

—— Theosophy or Psychological Religion. 1893.

Watson, W. A. Gospels of Yesterday. Drummond, Spencer, Arnold. 1888.

Dowden, E. The Scientific Movement in Literature. [In Studies in Literature, 1889.]

Bruce, A. B. The Kingdom of God. 1889.

—— The Providential Order of the World. 1897.

—— The Moral Order of the World. 1899.

Dale, R. W. The Living Christ and the Four Gospels. 1890.

Tyrrell, G. Nova et vetera: Informal Medita-
tions. 1897.
—— Hard Sayings. 1898.
—— External Religion: its Use and Abuse.
1899.
—— The Faith of the Millions: Essays. 2 sers.
1901.
—— Lex Orandi: or Prayer and Creed. 1903.
—— Lex Credendi: a sequel to Lex Orandi.
1906.
—— Medievalism: a Reply to Cardinal
Mercier. 1908.
—— Christianity at the Cross Roads. 1909.

(e) The Influence of Literary Criticism

Lewes, G. H. English Errors and Abuses of
Criticism. Westminster Rev. xxxviii, 1842.
Planche, G. Mœurs et Devoirs de la Critique.
Revue des deux mondes, 1 May 1856.
Arnold, M. The Function of Criticism at the
Present Time. [In Essays in Criticism,
ser. 1, 1865.]
Dallas, E. S. The Gay Science. 2 vols. 1866.
[Laws under which criticism is produced.
Aims at the fundamental unity of art.]
Purnell, T. Literature and its Professors.
1867.
Bagehot, W. The First Edinburgh Reviewers.
[In Literary Studies, 2 vols. 1879. Charac-
teristics of Horner, Jeffrey, Sidney Smith.]
Caine, Sir T. Hall. Cobwebs of Criticism. 1883.
Lang, A. Manners of Critics. Forum, iv, 1887–8.
Church, A. J. Criticism as a Trade. Nine-
teenth Century, xxvi, 1889. [Reply to W.
Knight (see below).]
Fawcett, E. Should Critics be Gentlemen?
[In Agnosticism, New York, 1889.]
Knight, W. Criticism as a Trade. Nineteenth
Century, xxvi, 1889.
Pellissier, G. Le Mouvement littéraire au
XIXe Siècle. Paris, 1890. [How literature
becomes a document for the study of man-
kind. Discusses Mme de Staël, Villemain,
Nisard, Sainte-Beuve, Taine, Renan.]
Wilde, O. The True Function and Value of
Criticism. Nineteenth Century, xxviii,
1890. [Rptd as The Critic as Artist in
Intentions, 1891.]
Birrell, A. Critics and Authors. New Rev.
vi, 1691.
Buchan, R. The Coming Terror. 1891.
Howells, W. D. Criticism and Fiction. 1891.
Watson, Sir W. Critics and their Craft.
National Rev. xvi, 1891. [Rptd in Ex-
cursions in Criticism, 1893.]
Worsfold, W. B. The Principles of Criticism.
1897.
Trent, W. P. The Authority of Criticism.
New York, 1899.
                                    H. V. R.

IV. BOOK PRODUCTION AND DISTRIBUTION

General Works: Catalogues and Surveys.
Book Production: General Works; Paper
(Bibliographies, History of Production,
Technique and Raw Materials, Qualities and
Trade, Taxation, Directories, Periodicals);
Ink; Manufacture of Type (Typefounding,
Type Design, Stereotyping and Electrotyping);
Printing (General and Literary Works,
Manuals, Business Management, Correct
Composition, Type Composing Machinery,
Presswork, Colour Printing); Graphic Pro-
cesses (General Works, Intaglio Surfaces,
Plane Surfaces, Relief Surfaces); Printing
Style (Aesthetics, Legibility); Private Printing
(General, Particular); Biographies and Studies
of Individual Printers and Presses; Printing
Trade Periodicals; Book Illustration (General
Works, Particular Illustrators); Bookbinding.
Book Distribution: General Works; Copy-
right; Authors' Guides to Publication; The
Practice of Publishing; Works on Particular
Publishers; General Catalogues; Trade
Periodicals; Circulating Libraries; Retail
Bookselling (General Works and the Net
Book Agreement, Particular Firms); The
Antiquarian Book Trade (General Works,
Periodicals, Book Auctions, Particular Firms);
Private Book Collecting; Public Libraries
(The British Museum, Accounts of other
Libraries, The Free Library Movement);
Librarianship.

A. GENERAL WORKS

[In addition to the works listed below, much
information may be found in the general and
special catalogues of the following international
exhibitions: London, 1851, 1862, 1872; Paris,
1855, 1867, 1878, 1889, 1900; Vienna, 1873;
Philadelphia, 1876; Brussels, 1880, 1888,
1897; Amsterdam, 1883; Antwerp, 1886;
Chicago, 1893.]

Katalog der Bibliothek des deutschen
Börsenvereins. 3 vols. Leipzig, 1885–1902.
[Peddie, R. A.] Catalogue of the Technical
Reference Library of the St Bride Founda-
tion. 1919.
Timperley, C. H. A Dictionary of Printers
and Printing. 1839; 1842 (rev. as Encyclo-
paedia of Literary and Typographical
Anecdote).
Hodson, W. H. Booksellers, Publishers and
Stationers' Directory for London and
Country. 1855.
Kelly's Post Office Directory of Stationers,
Printers, Booksellers, Publishers and Paper-
makers of England, Scotland, Wales and
Ireland. 1872; 1876; 1880; 1885; 1889;
1893; 1896; 1900.

Catalogue of the Caxton Celebration Exhibition. Ed. George Bullen, 1877.

Hitchcock, F. H. The Building of a Book. New York, 1906, 1927.

B. BOOK PRODUCTION
(1) GENERAL WORKS

The Sister Arts, or a Concise and Interesting View of the Nature and History of Paper-Making, Printing and Bookbinding. Lewes, 1809. [Attrib. to J. Baxter.]

British Manufacturing Industries. Ed. G. P. Bevan, 1876; 1877; 1892.

Victoria and Albert Museum, South Kensington. Catalogue of Machinery, Models, &c. Pt 2 (Paper Making and Printing Machinery), 1897.

Heath, T. C. How Books are made. 1900.

Leicester Free Public Libraries. Catalogue of the Books on Printing, Bookbinding and Papermaking and Related Industries. Leicester, 1927.

(2) PAPER
(a) Bibliographies

Munsell, J. A Chronology of Paper and Papermaking. Albany, 1857, 1860, 1864, 1870, 1876.

Surface, H. E. Bibliography of the Pulp and Paper Industries. Washington, 1913. [U.S.A. Dept of Agriculture. Forest Service. Bulletin No. 123.]

Paper Makers' Association of Great Britain. Technical Section. Catalogue of the Library. 1934.

(b) History of Production

Koops, M. Historical Account of the Substances which have been used to describe Events and convey Ideas from the Earliest Times. 1800; 1801.

Report from the Select Committee of the House of Commons on M. Koops' Petition. 1801. (55). iii. 127.

Minutes of the Proceedings of the Committee of the House of Lords to whom was referred the Bill for prolonging the term of certain Letters Patent assigned to Henry and Sealy Fourdrinier. 10 Aug. 1807. xiv. 331.

Report from the Select Committee of the House of Commons on Fourdrinier's Patent. 1837. (331). xx. 35. Report on the reconsidered Report. 1837. (405). xx. 91.

Herring, R. A Lecture on the Origin, Manufacture and Importance of Paper. 1853.

—— Paper and Paper Making, Ancient and Modern. 1855; 1856; 1863.

Gamble, J. The Origin of the Machine for Making Endless Paper, and its Introduction into England. Journ. Soc. of Arts, 27 Feb. 1857.

Patent Office. Abridgements of Specifications relating to the Manufacture of Paper, Pasteboard and Papier Mâché. 1858.

—— Abridgements of Specifications [Illustrated Series]. Class 96. Paper, Pasteboard and Papier Mâché, 1855–66. 1904.

Report from the Select Committee of the House of Commons on Paper. Export Duty on Rags. 1861.

Richardson, W. H. On the Manufacture of Paper. [In W. G. Armstrong, The Industrial Resources of the Tyne, Wear and Tees, 2nd edn, 1864.]

Dropisch, B. Der Papiermaschine, ihre geschichtliche Entwicklung und Construction. Brunswick, 1878.

Routledge, T. Minutes of Proc. Institution of Civil Engineers, xcii, 1888, pp. 404–6.

A Brilliant Page in the History of British Papermaking. Mill no. 24. St Neot's. British and Colonial Printer, 13 Sept. 1888.

The Firm of John Dickinson & Co. Ltd. 1896 (priv. ptd).

A History of the Fourdrinier Machines. World's Paper Trade Rev. 1897–8.

Beadle, C. A Short Account of the History of Paper-making. [1897.]

—— The Development of Water Marking in Handmade and Machine-made Papers. Journ. Soc. of Arts, 18 May 1906.

[Didot, A. F.] Le Centenaire de la Machine à Papier continu. Paris, [1900].

Fittica, F. B. Geschichte der Sulfitzellstoff-Fabrikation. Leipzig, 1902.

Maddox, H. A. Paper; its History, Sources and Manufacture. [1916]; [1928]; [1930]; 1933.

Cormack, A. A. 1750–1933. Our Ancient and Honourable Craft. Being an Account of the Rise and Development of Paper-making in Scotland, and at Culter, Aberdeenshire in particular. 1933.

Carter, J. and Pollard, G. An Enquiry into the Nature of Certain Nineteenth Century Pamphlets. 1934. [Ch. iv.]

Clapperton, R. H. Paper; an Historical Account of its making by Hand from the Earliest Times to the Present Day. 1934.

(c) Technique and Raw Materials

Le Normand, L. S. O. Manuel du Fabricant de Papiers. 3 vols. Paris, 1833–4.

Rüst, W. A. Papierfabrikation und die technischen Anwendungen des Papiers. Berlin, 1838.

Müller, L. Die Fabrikation des Papiers. Berlin, 1849, 1855, 1862, 1877.

Saunders, T. H. Illustrations of British Paper Manufacture. 1855.

Bosworth, T. A Few Words on Paper, Flax, Hemp and Plantain Fibre. 1855.

Herring, R. A Letter on the Collection of Rags for the Manufacture of Paper. 1860.

Prouteaux, A. Guide Pratique de la Fabrication du Papier et du Carton. Paris, 1864, [c. 1885]; tr. Eng. Philadelphia, 1866, 1873.

Hofmann, C. A Practical Treatise on the Manufacture of Paper. Philadelphia, 1873.

de la Tréhonnais, F. R. Algerian Esparto Grass for the Manufacture of Paper. 1874.

Routledge, T. Bamboo Considered as a Papermaking Material. 1875.

—— Bamboo and its Treatment. Sunderland, 1879.

The Art of Paper Making: A Guide to the Theory and Practice of the Manufacture of Paper by the Editor of the Paper Mills Directory. 1876 (2nd edn).

Arnot, W. The Technology of the Paper Trade. 1878; rev. J. M. Arnot, British and Colonial Printer, xxviii–xxx, 1891–2.

Dunbar, J. The Practical Paper-Maker. Leith, 1881 (2nd edn); Leith, 1887.

—— Notes on the Manufacture of Wood Pulp and Wood Pulp Papers. Leith, 1894.

Hoyer, E. Das Papier, seine Beschaffenheit und deren Prüfung. Munich, 1882; tr. French, Paris, 1884.

Rattray, J. H. *et al.* Forestry and Forest Products. Edinburgh, 1885.

Wyatt, J. W. The Art of Making Paper by the Machine. [1885.]

Parkinson, R. A Treatise on Paper. Preston, 1886; Clitheroe, 1896.

Davis, C. T. The Manufacture of Paper. Philadelphia, 1886.

Cross, C. F. and Bevan, E. J. A Text-Book of Papermaking. 1888; 1900; 1907; 1916; 1920.

Herzberg, W. Papier-Prüfung. Berlin, 1888; Berlin, 1902; rev. R. Korn and B. Schulze, Berlin, 1932. Tr. Eng. 1892; French, Paris, 1894.

Watt, A. The Art of Paper-Making. 1890; New York, 1908.

Bennett, J. B. Paper-Making Processes and Machinery. Edinburgh, 1892.

Clapperton, G. Practical Paper Making. 1894; 1907; rev. R. H. Clapperton, 1926.

Griffin, R. B. and Little, A. D. The Chemistry of Paper Making. New York, 1894.

U.S.A. Department of State. Vegetable Parchment Paper. Consular Reports, vol. xlvi, Washington, 1894.

Akesson, L., Everling, H. and Fluckiger, M. Lexikon der Papier Industrie. Deutsch-Englisch-Französische. Lucerne, 1895; Lucerne, 1905.

Andés, L. E. Papier-Specialitäten. Vienna, 1896; tr. Eng. (as The Treatment of Paper for Special Purposes) 1907, 1923.

Kirchner, E. Das Papier. 3 vols. Biberach, 1897–1911.

U.S.A. Department of State, Bureau of Foreign Commerce. Paper in Foreign Countries: Uses of Wood Pulp. Special Consular Reports, vol. xix, Washington, 1900.

Henderson, R. Paper Making Machinery. 1900.

MacNaughton, J. Factory Book-Keeping for Paper Mills. 1900; 1902.

Hubner, J. Cantor Lectures on Paper Manufacture. 1903.

Sindall, R. W. Paper Technology. 1906; 1910; 1920 (rev.).

—— The Manufacture of Paper. 1908.

(d) Qualities and Trade

Dusautoy, J. A. The Paper-Maker's Ready Reckoner. Romsey, 1805.

Murray, J. Observations and Experiments of the Bad Composition of Modern Paper. 1823; 1824.

—— Remarks on Modern Paper. Edinburgh, 1829.

The Stationer's Handbook and Guide to the Paper Trade. 1859 (*bis*); 1863; 1868; 1869; 1870; 1871; 1872; 1873; 1874; 1875; 1881; 1893 (17th edn).

Herring, R. A Practical Guide to the Varieties and Relative Values of Paper, illustrated with Samples. 1860.

Piette, L. Manuel de Papeterie. 2 vols. Paris, 1861.

Haines, E. N. The Paper Maker's and Stationer's Calculator. 1862; 1880.

Olmer, G. Du Papier mécanique et de ses Apprets dans les diverses Impressions. Paris, 1882.

Royal Society of Arts. Report of the Committee on the Deterioration of Paper. 1898.

Spicer, A. D. The Paper Trade. 1907.

(e) Taxation

Report from the Committee of the House of Commons on the Booksellers' and Printers' Petition relating to the Duty on Paper. 1802. ii. 89.

Fourteenth Report of the Commissioners of Enquiry into the Excise Establishment. 1835. xxxi. 159.

[McCulloch, J. R.] Observations Illustrative of the Practical Operation and Real Effect of the Duties on Paper. 1836.

Knight, C. The Struggles of a Book against Excessive Taxation. [1850.]

—— The Case of Authors as regards the Paper Duty. 1851.

The Paper Difficulty. Chambers's Journ. Nov. 1854.

Bohn, H. G. The Paper Duty Considered in reference to its Action on the Literature and Trade of Great Britain. 1861 (3 edns).

Petter, G. W. Some Objections to the Repeal of the Paper Duty Considered in reply to Mr H. G. Bohn's Pamphlet. 1860 [1861].

Report from the Select Committee of the House of Commons on Paper. Export Duty on Rags. 1861.

Paper. Cornhill Mag. Nov. 1861.

The Rag Tax. The Paper Makers' Grievance and how to redress it. 1863 (priv. ptd).

The Rag Question in Two Dialogues. 1863 (priv. ptd).

Wrigley, T. The Case of the Paper Makers. [1864.]

Carey, H. C. The Way to outdoe England without fighting her. A Protective Tariff for Paper. Philadelphia, 1865.

[Bruce, H. and Chalmers, D.] Gladstone and the Paper Duties by Two Midlothian Paper Makers. 1885.

Collet, C. D. History of the Taxes on Knowledge. 2 vols. 1899; abridged, 1933.

(f) Directories

A New List of Paper Mills in the United Kingdom. 1859. [By G. T. Mickleburgh?]

The Paper Mills Directory. 1860. [And annually since.]

Craig, J. The Paper Makers' Directory and Diary. [1876.]

Directory of Paper Makers of the United Kingdom. 1876. [And annually since.]

Bryan, C. W. The Paper Mill Directory of the World. Holyoke, Mass. 1883.

Phillips, S. C. Paper Makers' Directory of All Nations. 1884. [And annually since.]

The Paper Trade Directory of Great Britain and the Colonies. 1886. [And annually since.]

Alphabetical List of Paper and Millboard Makers in the United Kingdom. Edinburgh, 1894.

(g) Periodicals

The Paper Trade News. No. 1, 5 Oct. 1860– No. 22, 1 July 1861. [Continued as] The Stationers', Printers', and Bookbinders' Monthly Journal. No. 23, 1 Aug. 1861– No. 27, 1 Dec. 1861. [First weekly, then monthly.]

The Papermakers' Circular. No. 1, 9 Sept. 1861–No. 16, 3 Dec. 1862. [Continued as] The Papermakers' Circular and Rag Price Current. No. 17, 3 Feb. 1863–No. 39, 1 Dec. 1864. [Monthly.]

The Paper Trade Review. No. 1, Nov. 1862– June 1868. [Edinburgh, 1862–5, then London. Monthly.]

The Papermakers' Monthly Journal. No. 1, Jan. 1863–15 March 1932. [Monthly.]

The Paper and Printing Trades Journal. No. 1, Dec. 1872–No. 86, May 1895. [Ed. by A. W. Tuer. Quarterly. Index to Nos. 1–32 by E. R. Pearce, Taunton, 1881.]

The Paper Makers' Circular and Rag Price Current. No. 1, 19 Jan. 1874–No. 433, March 1907. [Weekly, later monthly.]

The Paper Consumers' Circular. No. 1, 22 Feb. 1879–No. 182, 1 Dec. 1882. [Weekly.]

Papermaking. [1881]–1 Nov. 1895 onwards. [In progress. Monthly.]

The Paper Trade Review. New Series. No. 1, 17 Aug. 1883–1 May 1891. [Continued as] World's Paper Trade Review. 8 May 1891 onwards. [In progress; ed. by W. J. Stonhill. Weekly. Before this new series was started 166 nos. had been published from 1879 to 1883 as supplements to The British and Colonial Printer.]

The Paper Record. No. 1, 26 Feb. 1886–Sept. 1895. [Some minor changes of title. Fortnightly at first, then weekly.]

Stationery World and Paper Market. No. 1, 29 Jan. 1892–17 Dec. 1927. [Continued as] Paper Market. 17 Jan. 1927 onwards. [In progress. Monthly.]

The Paper Maker. No. 1, 26 Jan. 1891 onwards. [In progress; ed. by S. C. Phillips. Monthly.]

Amalgamated Society of Paper Makers. First Quarterly Report. Dartford, 1893. [In progress.]

The Paper Exchange News. No. 1, April 1895– June 1896.

Wood Pulp. No. 1, Jan. 1896–9 May 1898. [Continued as] Paper and Pulp. 1 June 1898–1 Jan. 1906. [Incorporated with Papermaking. Fortnightly under first title, then weekly.]

Paper Box and Bag Maker. No. 1, 7 April 1896 onwards. [In progress. Monthly.]

World's Pulp and Paper Industry. No. 1, 21 Sept. 1898–No. 80, 2 May 1900. [Weekly.]

Paper and Printing Bits. No. 1, Oct. 1898– No. 17, April 1900. [Birmingham. Monthly, but irregular.]

(3) INK

Gamble, W. B. Chemistry and Manufacture of Printing Inks. A List of References in the New York Public Library. New York, 1926.

Savage, W. On the Preparation of Printing Ink, both Black and Coloured. 1832.

Haldat, C. N. A. Recherches chimiques sur l'Encre. Nancy, 1852.

De Champour, — and Malepeyre, F. Nouveau Manuel complet de la Fabrication des Encres. Paris, 1856; Paris, 1875.

Underwood, J. The History and Chemistry of Writing, Printing and Copying Inks. [1858.]

Davids, Thaddeus, & Co. The History of Ink. New York, [1860].

[Lorilleux, C.] Notice sur la Fabrication des Encres d'Imprimerie noires et de Couleur. Paris, [1867].

Waldow, A. Kurzer Rathgeber für die Behandlung der Farben. Leipzig, 1868; Leipzig, 1884.

Lehner, S. Die Tinten-Fabrikation. Vienna, 1880, 1885, 1890, 1922. Tr. French, Paris, [1895]; Eng. Philadelphia, 1892, London, 1902 (rev. C. A. Mitchell, 1926).

Andés, L. E. Oel- und Buchdruckfarben. Vienna, 1889; tr. Eng. (as Oil Colours and Printers' Inks) 1903, 1918.

Bannan, J. Modern Ink Making. Inland Printer (Chicago), XVII, pp. 47, 399; XVIII, p. 151, 1896-7.

Jennison, F. H. The Manufacture of Lake Pigments from Artificial Colours. 1900; 1920.

Rubencamp, R. Farbe und Papier im Druckgewerbe. Frankfort, 1900.

Carvalho, D. N. Forty Centuries of Ink. New York, 1904.

Mitchell, C. A. and Hepworth, T. C. Inks, their Composition and Manufacture. 1904.

Seymour, A. Modern Printing Inks. 1910.

Underwood, N. and Sullivan, T. V. The Chemistry and Technology of Printing Inks. 1915.

Burt, F. L. Printing Inks, their History, Composition and Manufacture. Inland Printer (Chicago), Nov. 1919–Feb. 1920.

Wiborg, F. B. Printing Ink. A History. New York, 1926.

Wolf, H. Manufacture of Printing and Lithographic Inks. New York, [1931].

(4) THE MANUFACTURE OF TYPE

(a) Typefounding

Hansard, T. C. Treatises on Printing and Typefounding. Edinburgh, 1841.

Bowers Bros. Proposals for Establishing a Graduated Scale of Sizes for the Bodies of Printing Types. Sheffield, 1841 (3rd edn).

Henze, A. Handbuch der Schriftgiesserei und der verwandten Nebenzweigen. Weimar, 1844.

Johnson, J. R. On Certain Improvements in the Manufacture of Printing Types. Journ. Soc. of Arts, 21 March 1873. [See also Printing Times, April, May 1873.]

Smalian, H. Practisches Handbuch für Buchdrucker im Verkehr mit Schriftgiesserein. Danzig, 1874; Leipzig, 1877.

Gauthier, V. E. Concordance du Point typographique avec la Système Métrique. Nice, 1881 (7th edn).

Reed, T. B. A History of the 'Old English Letter Foundries. 1887.

Fox, W. W. The Printer and the Typefounder: a Modern View of an Ancient Grievance. [1897.]

Figgins, J. Type Founding and Printing during the Nineteenth Century. 1901.

Haddon, W. The Standardisation and Interchangeability of Printing Types. [1902.]

— - Centenary Booklet Descriptive of the Growth of J. Haddon & Co. with Personal Reminiscences. 1914.

Wightman, J. H. A Brief History of Typefounding and the Point System. 1910.

Legros, L. A. and Grant, J. C. Typographical Printing Surfaces; the Technology and Mechanism of their Production. 1916.

McRae, J. F. Two Centuries of Typefounding. Annals of the Letter Foundry established by William Caslon. 1920.

Burdon, C. S. One Hundred Years. To Commemorate the Centenary of Pavyer and Bullen's. 1922.

(b) Type Design

Austin, R. Specimens of Printing Types cast at Austin's Imperial Foundry. 1819. [Preface.]

Vinycomb, J. Origins of the Various Prevailing Forms of Plain and Ornamental Lettering. [1869.]

De Vinne, T. L. Historic Printing Types. A Lecture. Grolier Club, New York, 1886.

—— The Practice of Typography. A Treatise on the Processes of Type Making, the Point System, the Names, Sizes, Styles and Prices of Plain Printing Types. New York, 1900; New York, 1925.

Updike, D. B. Printing Types, their History, Forms and Use. 2 vols. Cambridge, U.S.A. 1922.

Carter, J. and Pollard, G. An Enquiry into the Nature of Certain Nineteenth Century Pamphlets. 1934. [Ch. v.]

Johnson, A. F. Type Designs: their History and Development. 1934.

Berry, W. T. and Johnson, A. F. Catalogue of Specimens of Printing Types by English and Scottish Printers and Founders, 1665–1830. 1935.

Peddie, R. A. Subject Index of Books Published before 1880. Second Series. 1935. [S.v. Type Specimens.]

Gray, Mrs N. Nineteenth Century Ornamented Types and Title-pages. 1938.

(c) Stereotyping and Electrotyping

Camus, A. G. Histoire et Procédés du Polytypage et de la Stéréotypie. Paris, 1801; Paris, 1802.

Wilson, A. Arbitration between the University of Cambridge and A. Wilson. 1806.

—— Stereotype Printing. [1811.]

Brightly, C. Account of the Method of Casting Stereotype. Bungay, 1809.

Hodgson, T. An Essay on the Origin and Progress of Stereotype Printing; including a Description of the Various Processes. Newcastle, 1820.

Le Gentil, J. P. G. (Comte de Paroy). Précis sur la Stéréotypie. Paris, 1822.

Chabert, L. Stéréotypie et Polytypie. Paris, 1829.

Meyer, H. Handbuch der Stereotypie. Brunswick, 1838.

Jordan, C. J. Engraving by Galvanism. Mechanics' Mag. 22 May 1839.

Spencer, T. Instructions for the Multiplication of Works of Art in Metal by Voltaic Electricity. Glasgow, 1840.

Jacobi, M. H. Die Galvanoplastik. Leningrad, 1840.

[Schoenberg, L.] Metallic Engravings in Relief for Letterpress Printing, being a greatly improved Substitute for Wood Engravings called Acrography by the Inventor. 1841.

Smee, A. Elements of Electro-Metallurgy or the Art of Working in Metals by the Galvanic Fluid. 1841; 1843; 1851.

Walker, C. V. Electrotype Manipulation. 1841; 1850; tr. French, Paris, 1843.

Zantedeschi, F. Memorie della Elettrotipia. Venice, 1841.

Knobloch, M. Der Galvanismus in seiner technischen Anwendung seit dem Jahre 1840 oder Galvanoplastik. Erlangen, 1842.

Kobell, F. von. Die Galvanographie. Munich, 1842.

Netto, F. A. W. Anweisung zur Galvanoplastik. Quedlinburg, 1842.

Sampson, T. Electrotint: or the Art of Making Paintings in such Manner that Copperplates and Blocks can be taken from them by means of Voltaic Electricity. 1842.

Palmer, E. Glyphography; or Engraved Drawing for Printing at the Type Press after the manner of Woodcuts. [1843]; [c. 1845].

La Stéréotypie perfectionnée et de son véritable Inventeur [Durouchail]. Paris, 1847.

Dircks, H. Jordantype otherwise called Electrotype: being a Vindication of the Claims of C. J. Jordan as the Inventor of Electro-Metallurgy. 1852.

Dircks, H. Contributions towards a History of Electro-Metallurgy. 1863.

Martin, A. Repertorium der Galvanoplastik und Galvanostegie. 2 vols. Vienna, 1856.

Archimowitz, T. Neues französisches Stereotyp-verfahren. 2 pts, Karlsruhe, 1856–8.

—— Die Papier Stereotypie. Karlsruhe, 1862.

Wood, J. and R. M. Papier Mâché Stereotyping Apparatus. 1860.

Collins, H. G. Electro-Block Printing, especially as applied to enlarging any Printing Surface. Journ. Soc. of Arts, 7 Dec. 1860.

Nicholson, T. Instructions for the Manipulation of the Nicholson Stereotype Apparatus. 1874 (2nd edn).

Wilson, F. J. F. Stereotyping and Electrotyping. [1880]; [1882]; [1898].

Geymet, T. Traité de Galvanoplastie et d'Électrolyse. Paris, 1888.

Bolas, T. Cantor Lectures on Stereotyping. 1890.

Langbein, G. A Complete Treatise on the Electro-Deposition of Metals. Translated into English by W. T. Braunt. New York, 1891; 1920.

Partridge, C. S. Stereotyping. Chicago, 1892.

—— Electrotyping: a Practical Treatise. Chicago, 1899, 1908, 1909.

Pilworth, E. S. Electrotyping in its Relation to the Graphic Arts. New York, 1923.

(5) PRINTING

(a) General and Literary Works

Bigmore, E. C. and Wyman, C. W. H. A Bibliography of Printing. 3 vols. 1880–6.

Bullen, H. L. The Literature of Typography. Inland Printer (Chicago), L–LV, 1913–5.

McCreery, J. The Press: a Poem. 2 pts, Liverpool, 1803–27; 1828.

Timperley, C. H. Songs of the Press and other Poems relative to Printing. 1833; 1845.

Brimmer, G. The Composing Room: A Serio-Comico-Satirico-Poetical Production. 1835.

Savage, W. A Dictionary of the Art of Printing. 1841.

Neuburger, H. Encyklopaedie der Buchdruckerkunst. Leipzig, 1844.

Patent Office. Abridgements of Specifications relating to Printing, 1617–1857. 1859.

—— Abridgements of Specifications relating to Letterpress and Similar Printing, 1858–1866. 1878 (2nd edn).

—— Abridgements of Specifications relating to Letterpress and Similar Printing, 1867–1876. 1878.

—— Abridgements of Specifications [Illustrated Series]. Class 100. Printing, Letterpress and Lithographic, 1855-66. 1904.

Ringwalt, J. L. American Encyclopaedia of Printing. Philadelphia, 1871.

Southward, J. A Dictionary of Typography. 1871; 1875.

—— Progress in Printing and the Graphic Arts during the Victorian Era. 1897.

Waldow, A. Die Buchdruckerkunst in ihren technischen und kaufmannischen Betriebe. 3 vols. Leipzig, 1874–7.

—— Illustrierte Encyklopaedie der graphischen Kunst. Leipzig, 1884.

Wolf, L. Exhibition and Market of Machinery, Implements and Material used by Printers. Official Catalogue. 1880.

—— 2nd Annual Exhibition. 1881.

—— 3rd Printers', Stationers' and Papermakers' Exhibition and Market. 1883.

Faulmann, C. Illustrierte Geschichte der Buchdruckerkunst. Vienna, 1882.

Lorck, C. B. Handbuch der Geschichte der Buchdruckerkunst. 2 vols. Leipzig, 1882–3.

Tuer, A. W. Quads for Authors, Editors and Devils. 1884.

Jacobi, C. T. The Printer's Vocabulary. 1888.

—— Gesta Typographica: or a Medley for Printers and Others. 1897.

The American Dictionary of Printing and Bookmaking. New York, 1894.

Thomson, T. Rhymes and Songs for Printers. Edinburgh, 1897.

Plomer, H. R. A Short History of English Printing. 1900.

Morin, E. Dictionnaire typographique. Lyons, 1903.

Maire, A. La Technique du Livre. Paris, 1908.

The Times. Printing Number. 12 Sept. 1912.

Peddie, R. A. An Outline of the History of Printing to which is added the History of Printing in Colours. 1917.

Arneudo, G. I. Dizionario esegetico, tecnico e storico per le Arte grafiche. 3 vols. Turin, 1917–24.

Thibaudeau, F. La Lettre de l'Imprimerie. 2 vols. Paris, 1921.

(b) Manuals

Wroth, L. C. Corpus Typographicum. A Review of English and American Printers' Manuals. The Dolphin (New York), II, 1935.

Vinçard, B. L'Art du Typographe. Paris, 1806; Paris, 1823.

Stower, C. The Printer's Grammar. 1808.

—— The Compositor's and Pressman's Guide to the Art of Printing. 1808.

Van Winkle, C. S. The Printer's Guide; or an Introduction to the Art of Printing. New York, 1818, 1836.

Johnson, J. Typographia; or the Printer's Instructor. 2 vols. 1824.

Hansard, T. C. Typographia; an Historical Sketch of the Origin and Progress of the Art of Printing: with Practical Directions for Conducting every Department in an Office. 1825.

Partington, C. F. The Printer's Complete Guide. 1825; [1831].

Fournier, H. Traité de la Typographie. Paris, 1825; Brussels, 1826; Tours, 1854 (rev.); Tours, 1870 (rev.). [Introduction only tr. Eng. by C. E. Keymer, Gloucester, 1866.]

Sherman, A. N. The Printer's Manual. New York, 1834.

Hasper, W. Handbuch der Buchdruckerkunst. Carlsruhe, 1835.

Adams, T. F. Typographia; or the Printer's Instructor. Philadelphia, 1837, 1844 (rev.), 1845, 1861.

Timperley, C. H. The Printer's Manual. 1838.

Hansard, T. C. Treatises on Printing and Typefounding. Edinburgh, 1841.

The Printer. 1865; [c. 1880]. [Houlston's Industrial Library, No. 31.]

MacKellar, T. The American Printer; a Manual of Typography. Philadelphia, 1866, 1874, 1879.

Marahrens, A. Vollständiges theoretisch-praktisches Handbuch der Typographie. 2 vols. Leipzig, 1870.

Morton, C. The Cosmopolitan Amateur Printing Office Guide. [1873.]

Gould, J. The Letterpress Printer: A Complete Guide to the Art of Printing. 1876; [1881]; [1888]; [1893]; [1903]; [1927].

Raynor, P. E. Printing for Amateurs: a Practical Guide. [1876.]

Fischer, H. Anleitung zum Accidenzsatz. Leipzig, 1877.

Trueman, H. P. The Eclectic Handbook of Printing. 1880 (2nd edn).

Southward, J. Practical Printing: a Handbook of the Art of Typography. 1882; 1884; 2 vols. 1887; 2 vols. 1892; 2 vols. 1900; 2 vols. 1902; 2 vols. 1921.

—— Modern Printing: a Handbook of the Principles and Practice of Typography and the Auxiliary Arts. 4 vols. 1898–1900; 4 vols. 1904–7; 2 vols. 1912; 2 vols. 1915.

Jacobi, C. T. The Printer's Handbook of Trade Recipes. 1887; 1891; 1905.

—— Printing: a Practical Treatise. 1890; 1893; 1898; 1904; 1908; 1912.

Wilson, F. J. F. and Grey, D. A Practical Treatise upon Modern Printing Machinery and Letterpress Printing. 1888.

Oldfield, A. A Practical Manual of Typography. [1890]; 1898; [1906].

Dumont, J. Vade-mecum du Typographe. Brussels, 1891, 1894, 1906.

Sala, C. Manuale pratico di Tipografia. 2 vols. Milan, 1894.

Fisher, T. The Elements of Letterpress Printing, Composing and Proof Reading. Madras, 1895; Madras, 1906.

(c) Business Management

Rhynd, M. Rhynd's Printers' Guide: being a New and Correct List of Master Printers in London. 1804 (3rd edn).

Magrath, W. The Printer's Assistant to which is added a Correct List of Master Printers in London. 1804.

[Mason, W.] The Printer's Assistant. 1810; 1821 (4th edn).

—— The Printer's Price Book for Job Work in General. 1816; 1820.

Stower, C. The Printer's Price Book. 1814.

Rose, P. and Evans, J. The Printer's Job Price Book. Bristol, 1814; Bristol, 1824.

Cowie, G. Cowie's Printer's Pocket Book and Manual. [c. 1830]; [c. 1835]; [c. 1850].

Day, W. J. A Series of Tables invented and arranged for the Use of the Practical Printer. 1841.

Houghton, T. S. The Printer's Practical Everyday Book. 1841; 1843; 1849; Preston, [1857] (rev.); Preston, [1875] (rev. G. Marshall).

Feeny, R. Master Printer's Price Manual. 1845.

Howitt, F. E. The Country Printer's Job Price Book. [1849] (2nd edn).

Fielding, D. The Typographical Ready Reckoner and Memorandum Book. [1853]; [1858].

Cobbett, T. G. The Master Printer's Handbook of Prices. Birkenhead, 1860.

Ruse, G. and Straker, C. Printing and its Accessories: a Comprehensive Book of Charges for the Guidance of Printers. [c. 1860.]

Crisp, W. F. The Printer's Business Guide. 1866; 1867; 1869; [1873]; [1874]; [1876]; [1881].

[Lawton, F. W.] The Printer's Pocket Companion. Rochdale, [1870].

Ellis, J. B. and Denton, W. The Printer's Calculator and Practical Companion. Leeds, 1876.

Manning, J. The Printer's Vade-mecum and Ready Reference. Aberdeen, 1881.

Ellis, J. B. Hints and Tables for the Printing Office and Paper Warehouse. Leeds, [1887]; Leeds, [c. 1890].

Rowell, G. F. How to Start a Printing Office. 1897.

—— Hints on Estimating. 1897; 1901.

Gotts, J. B. Estimating, Book Keeping, System for Letterpress and Lithographic Printers. 1901; 1906 (3rd edn).

Whitehead, T. L. The Ideal Price List, Estimate Guide, and Cost Book for Commercial Letterpress Printing. Bury, 1901.

Smith, H. L. Printers' Accounts. 1903.

Federation of Master Printers. Profit for Printers; or What is Cost? 1904; 1907; 1909.

Naylor, T. E. How to Start in Business as a Printer. [1905.]

(d) Correct Composition

Stower, C. Typographical Marks used in correcting Proofs. 1805; 1806; 1822.

Graham, J. The Compositor's Text Book; or Instructions in the Elements of the Art of Printing. Glasgow, 1848.

Wilson, J. A Treatise on English Punctuation. Boston, 1850.

F[ord], T. The Compositor's Handbook. 1854.

Wilson, W. The Compositor's Assistant, containing all the Imposition Tables now in use. Exeter, 1855.

Beadnell, H. A Guide to Typography. 2 vols. 1859–61.

Ruse, G. Imposition Simplified. [1860]; 1875.

Goebel, T. Ueber den Satz des Englischen. Leipzig, 1865.

Bidwell, G. H. Printer's New Handbook: a Treatise on the Imposition of Formes. New York, 1866, 1875.

Neill & Co. Guide to Authors in Correcting the Press. Edinburgh, [c. 1870], [c. 1880], 1895, 1897.

Newman, E. The Author's Guide for Printing. 1875.

Gould, J. The Compositor's Guide and Pocket Book. 1878; 1028.

Jowett, H. Hints to Authors; being a Handy Book of Reference in all Matters referring to Printing. 1889 (3rd edn).

Fletcher, W. C. A Simple Guide to the Art of Punctuation for Authors and Printers. Oxford, [c. 1890].

Le Forestier, J. Manuel pratique et bibliographique du Correcteur. Paris, 1890.

Blades, William. How to correct Proofs. 1893.

Hart, H. Rules for Compositors and Readers at the Clarendon Press. Oxford, 1893 (broadside), 1895, 1930 (29th edn).

Mitchell, J. Printers' Blunders; their Causes, Effects and Cure. Edinburgh, 1894.

Teall, F. H. Punctuation; with Chapters on Hyphenisation, Capitalisation, and Spelling. New York, 1898.

—— Proof Reading. A Series of Essays for Readers and their Employers. Chicago, 1899.

De Vinne, T. L. The Practice of Typography. Correct Composition. New York, 1901.

Collins, F. M. Author and Printer: an Attempt to codify the best Typographical Practices of the Present Day. 1905 (*bis*); 1909 (rev. as Authors' and Printers' Dictionary); 1912; 1928; 1933.

Brossard, L. E. Le Correcteur typographe. Tours, 1924.

(e) Type Composing Machinery

Gaubert, E. R. Rénovation de l'Imprimerie. Notice sur le Gérotype, ou Machine à Distribuer et à Composer en Typographie. Paris, 1843.

Bradbury, H. Hattersley's Type Composing Machine. Journ. Soc. of Arts, vii, 1859, p. 451.

Mitchell, W. H. Type-Setting by Machinery. 1863.

Yeaton, C. C. Manual of the Alden Typesetting and Distributing Machine. New York, 1865.

Brown, Orren L. Types; A Description of Brown's Patent Typesetting and Distributing Machine. Boston, 1870.

Mackie, A. Description of Patent Steam Type Composing Machine. 1871.

Fraser, A. On Typesetting Machines with a Description of Fraser's Composing and Distributing Machines. Edinburgh, 1876.

Marchal, J. Rapport sur la Machine à Composer de M. Kastanbein. [Nancy, 1878.]

Barnes, W. C., McCann, J. W. and Duguid, A. A Collation of Facts relative to Fast Typesetting. New York, 1887.

Southward, J. The Thorne Combined Type Setting and Distributing Machine. 1890. [Rptd from Printers' Register, 6 April 1890.]

—— Type Composing Machines of the Past, the Present, and the Future. 1890; Leicester, 1891.

—— The Lanston Monotype Machine. [1897.]

Linotype Co. Ltd. The Linotype Composing Machine. 1891; 1895; [1897].

—— The Linotype: its History, Construction and Operation. [1893] (*bis*).

—— The Solution of a Problem of Four Centuries: the Evolution of the Linotype Composing Machine. [1897.]

Report to the American Newspaper Publishers' Association by the Committee in charge of the Type Composition Machine Tournament held in Chicago, 12–17 Oct. 1891. New Haven, 1892.

Waldow, A. Die Herstellung der Kompositionswalzen und ihre Behandlung. Leipzig, 1894.

Lanston Monotype Machine Co. The Lanston Monotype Machine. Washington, 1896.

An Enquiry into the Claims of the Lanston Monotype Machine. Manchester, 1897.

Steevens, C. W. The Monotype. New Rev. Nov. 1897.

A Revolution in Printing. The Story of the Linotype. Chambers's Journ. Jan. 1897.

Evans, F. The Linotype. Kansas, 1897.

Barclay, E. J. The Linotype Operator's Companion. Cincinnati, 1898.

The Wicks Type Setter. 1898.

The Lanston Monotype Corporation Ltd. The Lanston Monotype Machine. 1901.

Card, H. C. The Lanston Monotype Keyboard. 1902.

Thompson, J. S. The Mechanism of the Linotype. Chicago, 1902, 1905.

—— History of Composing Machines. A Complete Record of the Art of Composing Type by Machinery. Chicago, 1904.

—— The Origin and Development of the Linotype. Inland Printer (Chicago), xxxv, 1905, pp. 665–9.

De Vinne, T. L. The Practice of Typography. Modern Methods of Book Composition. New York, 1904.

Courandy, G. Une Étude sur la Machine à Composer. Brussels, 1904.

Legros, L. A. Type Casting and Composing Machines. 1908.

Giraud, H. Nouveau Manuel complet de Linotypie. Paris, 1909.

Blevins, A. E. The Evolution of Printing and Typesetting Machines. Journ. South African Inst. of Engineers, March-April 1912.

Legros, L. A. and Grant, J. C. Typographical Printing Surfaces: the Technology and Mechanism of their Production. 1916.

Bullen, H. L. On Lynn Boy Benton. Inland Printer (Chicago), Oct. 1922.

Elliott, R. C. The Monotype from Infancy to Maturity. The Monotype Recorder, Feb. 1932.

(f) Presswork

Giroudot, ——. Notice sur les Presses Mécaniques et celles à la Stanhope. Paris, [1835].

Koenig, F. Printing Machines 1810. Patent Specification No. 3321. 1856.

—— Printing Machines 1811. Patent Specification No. 3496. 1856.

Applegath, A. Printing Machines 1822. Patent Specification No. 4640. 1857.

—— Printing Machines 1823. Patent Specification No. 4745. 1857.

—— Printing Machines 1846. Patent Specification No. 11505. 1857.

Read, J. M. Instructions in the Art of Making-Ready Woodcuts. Reading, [c. 1860].

Wittig, C. F. and Fischer, C. F. Die Schnellpresse, ihre Mechanik und Vorrichtung zum Druck aller typographischen Arbeiten. Leipzig, 1861; Leipzig, 1866; Leipzig, 1878.

Eisenmann, A. Die Schnellpresse, ihre Construction, Zusammenstellung und Behandlung. Leipzig, 1865; Leipzig, 1872.

Waldow, A. Die Zurichtung und der Druck von Illustrationen. Leipzig, 1867; Leipzig, 1879.

—— Die Schnellpresse und ihre Behandlung vor und bei dem Drucke. Leipzig, 1872.

—— Hilfsbuch für Maschinenmeister an Buchdruck-Cylinder-Schnellpressen. 3 vols. Leipzig, 1887–92.

Myers, J. A Few Practical Hints to Printers on the Treatment of Rollers. 1871.

Monet, A. L. Le Conducteur de Machines Typographiques. Paris, 1872.

The Walter Press. 1872; 1876 (enlarged).

Rigg, A. On Type Printing Machinery and Suggestions thereon. Journ. Soc. of Arts, 13 Feb. 1874.

Goebel, T. Friederich Koenig und die Erfindung der Schnellpresse. Ein biographisches Denkmal. Brunswick, 1875; Stuttgart, 1883; Stuttgart, 1906 (rev.); tr. French, Paris, 1885.

Gaskill, J. The Printing Machine Manager's Complete Practical Handbook. 1877; [c. 1880]; [1888].

Stevens, C. P. Roller Guide: a Treatise on Rollers and Compositions. Boston, 1877.

Thompson, J. R. Printers' Rollers: How to Treat them. Leeds, 1880.

Wilson, F. J. F. Typographic Printing Machines and Machine Printing. [1880]; [c. 1885]; tr. French, Paris, 1886.

[Wyman, C. W. H.] List of Technical Terms relating to Printing Machinery. 1882.

Noble, F. Difficulties in Machine Printing, and how to overcome them. 1883.

Clowes, E. A. Printing Machinery. Minutes of Proc. Inst. Civil Engineers, LXXXIX, 1887.

Southward, J. The Principles and Progress of Printing Machinery. [1888]; 1890.

Motteroz, C. Essai sur la Mise en train Typographique. Paris, 1891; tr. Eng. Inland Printer (Chicago), Dec. 1891–Jan. 1893.

Patent Office Studies. The British and Colonial Printer, 3 Aug. 1893–12 April 1894.

Powrie, W. Machinery for Book and General Printing. 1899.

Hoe, R. A Short History of the Printing Press and of the Improvements in Printing Machinery from the Time of Gutenberg. New York, 1902.

Thomas, F. W. A Concise Manual of Platen Presswork. Chicago, 1903.

Beschreibung des Modells der Ersten von Friederich Koenig erfundenen Schnellpresse aus dem Jahre 1811. Würzburg, [1908].

Haag, A. Ueber maschinelle Einrichtungen und Arbeitsmethoden im englischen Buchdruckereien. [Vienna, 1910.]

Powell, D. T. The Inking of the Forme. The Imprint, 17 July 1913.

Isaacs, G. A. The Story of the Newspaper Printing Press. 1931.

(g) Colour Printing

[All methods of colour printing involve separate impressions for each colour used, irrespective of the process by which the printing surface has been made. The only exceptions to this are hand colouring of the plate for each impression, Congreve's patent for interlocking blocks separately inked (about 1830), and Stenochromy (about 1875); the last two were never successfully applied to book illustration. This section therefore covers the application of colour to all printing processes including chromolithography. Information on coloured inks is given in some of the books already mentioned p. 73 above; historical works not concerned with technique appear on p. 89 below; and some further details will be found in the biographies of George Baxter and Francis Orpen Morris listed pp. 90–1 below.]

Savage, W. Hints on Decorative Printing. 1822.

The Pictorial Album, or Cabinet of Pictures. 1837. [Preface.]

Netto, F. A. W. Das Geheimniss des Oelbilder-Drucks erfunden vom Maler Liepmann in Berlin. Quedlinburg, 1840.

Rotch, B. Hullmandel's Lithotint Process. Journ. Soc. of Arts, LIV, 1841, pp. 174–5.

Liepmann, J. Der Oelgemalde-Druck erfunden und beschreiben. Berlin, 1842.

Weishaupt, H. Theoretisch-praktische Anleitung zur Chromolithographie. Quedlinburg, 1848.

Digeon, R. H. Cercles Chromatiques de M. E. Chevreul reproduits au moyen de la Chromo-calcographie, Gravure et Impression en Taille-douce combinées. Paris, 1855.

Maxwell, J. Clerk. On the Theory of Compound Colours and the Relation of the Colours of the Spectrum. Philosophical Trans. Royal Soc. CL, 1861, pp. 57–84.

Chevreul, M. E. Des Couleurs et de leurs Applications aux Arts industriels. Paris, 1864.

Ihm, B. A. Die bunten Farben in der Buchdruckerei. Biel, 1865; Biel, 1874.

The Chromolithograph. A Journal of Art, Literature, Decoration, and the Accomplishments. No. 1, 23 Nov. 1867–27 March 1869. [Weekly.]

Zenker, W. Lehrbuch der Photochromie. Berlin, 1868.

du Hauron, L. D. Les Couleurs en Photographie. Paris, 1869.
—— Traité Pratique de Photographie des Couleurs. Paris, 1878.
Watt, P. B. A Few Hints on Colour and Printing in Colours. 1872.
Galton, F. Colour Printing and Cartography. Report of the 42nd Meeting of the British Association, 1872, pp. 198–203.
Simpson, W. A Glance at the History of Chromo-Lithography. The Lithographer, Aug. 1873.
St Victor, P. de. La Photochromie. Paris, 1876.
Weissenbach, H. von. Der xylographische Farbendruck in den verscheiden Phasen. Nuremberg, 1878 (priv. ptd).
Noble, F. The Principles and Practice of Colour Printing. 1881.
Richmond, W. D. Colour and Colour Printing as applied to Lithography. 1882; [c. 1885]; [c. 1890].
Wohlfarth, A. Ueber Farben. Leipzig, 1882 (2nd edn).
Achaintre, A. Étude sur les Impressions en Couleurs. Paris, [1883].
Audsley, G. A. The Art of Chromolithography. 1883.
Waldow, A. Anleitung zum Farbendruck auf der Buchdruckpresse und Maschine. Leipzig, [1883].
Die Heliochromie. Das Problem des Photographierens in natürlichen Farben. Düsseldorf, 1884.
Reich, W. Die Farbenmischung für Druckerein-Steindruck, Buchdruck, Lichtdruck. Berlin, 1887.
Berget, A. Photographie des Couleurs par la Méthode Inférentielle de M. Lippmann. Paris, 1891.
Earhart, J. F. The Color Printer; a Treatise on the Use of Colour in Typographic Printing. Chicago, 1892.
Ives, F. E. Handbook to the Photochromoscope. 1894.
—— The Process of Three-Colour Work. Penrose's Pictorial Annual, VII, 1901, pp. 85–6.
du Hauron, A. D. La Triplice photographique des Couleurs et l'Imprimerie. Paris, 1897.
—— La Photographie des Couleurs et les Découvertes de Louis Ducos du Hauron. Paris, [1899].
Hesse, F. Die Chromolithographie mit besonderer Berücksichtigung der modernen auf photographischer Grundlage basierten Verfahren. Halle [1896]; Halle [1904–6]; tr. French, Paris, 1897.
Hubl, A. F. von. Die Dreifarbenphotographie mit besonderer Berucksichtigung des Dreifarbendrucks und der photographischen Pigmentbilder in natürlichen Farben. Halle, 1897; tr. H. O. Klein, 1904.
Vidal, L. Photographie des Couleurs. Paris, 1897.
—— Traité pratique de Photochromie. Paris, 1903.
Zander, C. G. A Lecture on the Colour Principle of Tri-chromatic Printing. [1899.]
Vaughan, W. E. Autobiographica, with a Gossip of the Art of Printing in Colours. [Brighton], 1900 (priv. ptd).
Soullier, E. Nouveau Traité sur les Impressions modernes en Couleurs. Paris, 1903.
Paton, H. Colour Etching. 1909.
Preissig, V. Zur Technik der farbigen Radierung und des Farberkupferstichs. Leipzig, 1909.
Prideaux, S. T. Aquatint Engraving: A Chapter in the History of Book Illustration. 1909.
Burch, R. M. Colour Printing and Colour Printers. 1910.
Andrews, E. C. Colour and its Application to Printing. Chicago, 1911.
Martin, L. C. Colour and Methods of Colour Reproduction. 1923.
Wall, E. J. The History of Three-Color Photography. Boston, 1925.

(6) Graphic Processes

[Graphic Processes are here divided into four categories according to the nature of the surface from which the impression is taken. Books dealing with impression from relief, plane, and intaglio surfaces are separately listed; while those dealing with more than one kind of surface have been grouped under 'General Works.' No attempt has been made to distinguish between books dealing with the autographic and photographic production of the same kinds of surface.]

(a) General Works

Clark, L. and Brooks, W. Catalogue of the Camera Club Photographic Library. [1894.]
Singer, H. W. and Strang, W. Etching, Engraving, and other Methods of Printing Pictures. 1897.
Levis, H. C. A Descriptive Bibliography of the Most Important Books in the English Language relating to the Art and History of Engraving. 1912. [Supplement and Index, 1913.]
New York Public Library. List of Books on Prints. New York, 1916.
Columbia University. A Catalogue of the Epstean Collection on the History and Science of Photography and its Applications to the Graphic Arts. New York, 1937.

Partington, C. F. The Engraver's Complete Guide. 1825.

Pye, J. Evidence relating to the Art of Engraving taken before the Select Committee on Arts. 1836.

Fielding, T. H. The Art of Engraving. 1841; 1844.

Donlevy, J. The Rise and Progress of the Graphic Arts. New York, 1854.

Kessler, G. Photographie auf Stahl, Kupfer und Stein, zur Anfertigung von Druckplatten für den Kupfer-, Stein- und Buchdruck. Berlin, 1856.

Fromberg, E. Die graphischen oder zeichnenden Kunste der Galvanoplastik. Quedlinburg, 1857.

Sutton, T. A Dictionary of Photography. 1858.

Stannard, W. J. The Art-Exemplar. A Guide to Distinguish one Sort of Print from Another with Pictorial Examples. [c. 1860.]

Poitevin, A. Traité de l'Impression photographique. Paris, 1862; Paris, 1883.

Davenport, S. T. On Prints and their Production. 1869.

Vogel, H. W. Die chemischen Wirkungen des Lichts und die Photographie in ihrer Anwendung in Kunst, Wissenschaft und Industrie. Leipzig, 1874; tr. Eng. 1875.

—— Handbuch der Photographie. 4 vols. Berlin, 1890–7.

Tissandier, G. A History and Handbook of Photography. 1876; 1878.

Wessely, J. E. Anleitung zur Kenntniss und zum Sammeln der Werke des Kunstdruckes. Leipzig, 1876.

Bolas, T. The Application of Photography to the Production of Printing Surfaces. 1878.

—— Cantor Lectures on the Recent Improvements in Photomechanical Printing Methods. 1884.

Hamerton, P. G. The Graphic Arts. 1882.

—— Drawing and Engraving. 1892.

Hodson, J. S. An Historical and Practical Guide to Art Illustration in Connection with Books, Periodicals and General Decoration. 1884.

Pettit, J. S. Modern Reproductive Graphic Processes. New York, 1884.

Wilkinson, W. T. Photo-Engraving on Zinc and Copper, in Line and Half-Tone and Photolithography. 1886; 1887; New York, 1888; 1890; 1894.

—— Photo-Mechanical Processes. A Practical Guide to Photozincography, Photolithography and Collotype. 1892; [1904].

Burbank, W. H. Photographic Printing Methods. New York, 1887.

[Wood, Sir H. T.] Modern Methods of Illustrating Books. 1887; 1898.

Burton, W. K. Practical Guide to Photographic and Photo-mechanical Printing. 1887; 1892.

Harrison, W. J. A History of Photography. Bradford, 1888.

Wall, E. J. The Dictionary of Photography. 1889; rev. F. J. Mortimer, [1933].

Waterhouse, J. Practical Notes on the Preparation of Drawings for Photographic Reproduction, with a Sketch of the Principal Photo-mechanical Printing Processes. 1890.

Werge, J. The Evolution of Photography. 1890.

Boston Museum of Fine Arts. Exhibition Illustrating the Technical Methods of the Reproductive Arts from the XVth Century to the Present Time with Special Reference to the Photo-Mechanical Processes. Boston, 1892. [Introduction by S. R. Koehler.]

Duchochois, P. C. Photographic Reproduction Processes, edited with additional matter by E. J. Watt. 1892.

Harland, J. W. The Printing Arts: an Epitome of Engraving, Lithography, and Printing. 1892.

Eder, J. M. The Grammar of Photo-Engraving. Tr. Eng. New York, 1893; 1895.

Process Work. Penrose's Circular. [1893]–Dec. 1921. [Continued as] Process Work and Electrotyping. Jan. 1922–1929. [Ed. by W. Gamble.]

Blackburn, H. The Art of Illustration. 1894; Edinburgh, 1901 (rev.).

Hinton, A. H. A Handbook of Illustration. [1894.]

—— Practical Pictorial Photography. 2 vols. 1898.

Paton, H. Etching, Drypoint, Mezzotint; the Whole Art of the Painter-Etcher. 1895; 1909 (rev.).

The Photogram. No. 1, Jan. 1895–Dec. 1905. [Continued as] The Process Engraver's Monthly. Jan. 1906 onwards. [Ed. by H. Snowden Ward, C. W. Ward. Monthly. Title varies.]

The Process Work Year Book. Penrose's Annual. Vol. i, 1895–1914. [Continued as] Penrose's Pictorial Annual. 1915 onwards. [In progress. Ed. by W. Gamble, R. B. Fishenden. Bradford. Annual. Title varies.]

Singer, H. W. and Strang, W. Etching, Engraving and other Methods of Printing Pictures. 1897.

Hubl, A. F. von. Die photographischen Reproductionsverfahren. Halle, 1898.

Kirkbride, J. Engraving for Illustration, Historical and Practical Notes. 1903.

Victoria and Albert Museum, South Kensington. Catalogue of the Loan Exhibition of Process Engraving. 1905. [Introduction by J. Waterhouse.]

Baker, W. H. A Dictionary of Engraving. Cleveland, 1908.

Hind, A. M. Short History of Engraving and Etching. 1908; 1910; 1923.

Harrap, C. Textbook of Metalography. Leicester, 1909, 1912.

Clerc, L. P. Les Reproductions photomécaniques monochromes. Paris, 1910.

Garrett, A. E. The Advance of Photography. 1911.

Short, Sir F. Etchings and Engravings. What they are, and what they are not. 1911.

Krueger, O. F. W. Die Illustrationsverfahren. Leipzig, 1914.

Richter, E. H. Prints: a Brief Review of their Technique and History. 1916.

Gamble, W. Photography and its Applications. [1920.]

Horgan, S. H. Photo-Engraving Primer. Boston, 1920.

—— Souvenirs sur l'Histoire des Procédés Photomécaniques. Bulletin Officiel Union Syndicate (Paris), April, July 1932.

Hackleman, C. W. Commercial Engraving and Printing. Indianopolis, 1924.

Ivins, W. M. Photography and the 'Modern' Point of View. Metropolitan Museum Stud. I, 1928, pp. 16–24.

Poortenaar, J. Van Printen en Platten. Amsterdam, 1931; tr. Eng. (as The Technique of Prints) 1933.

Gamble, C. W. Modern Illustration Processes. 1933.

Curwen, H. Processes of Graphic Reproduction. 1934.

(b) Intaglio Surfaces

[Copperplate Engraving; Etching; Aquatint; Photogravure; Heliogravure.]

[Green, J. H.] The Complete Aquatinter. Hartfield, 1801; 1804; 1810.

Landseer, J. Lectures on the Art of Engraving. 1807.

Hassell, J. Chalcographia; or the Art of Multiplying with Perfection Drawings after the manner of Chalk, Blacklead Pencil and Pen and Ink. 1811.

—— Graphic Delineation; a Practical Treatise on the Art of Etching. 1826; 1827.

Eberhard, H. W. Die Anwendung der chemischen Druckart auf Metallplatten. Mainz, 1821.

—— Die Anwendung des Zinks statt der Stein- und Kupferplatten zu den vertieften Zeichnungsarten. Darmstadt, 1822.

Chevreul, M. E. Considérations sur la Reproduction par les Procédés de M. Niepce de Saint-Victor des Images Gravées, Dessinées, ou Imprimées. Paris, 1847.

Alken, H. The Art and Practice of Etching. 1849.

Ashley, A. The Art of Etching on Copper. [1849]; 1851.

Talbot, H. Fox. Photographic Engraving. Journ. Photographic Soc. I, 1853, pp. 42–4, 62–4.

—— Description of Mr Fox Talbot's New Process of Photographic Engraving. Photographic News, I, 1858, pp. 73–5.

Salmon, — and Garnier, —. The Process of Photographic Engraving. Journ. Photographic Soc. II, 1855, pp. 242–4.

Niepce de Saint-Victor, C. M. F. Photographic Researches. Paris, 1855.

—— Traité pratique de Gravure héliographique sur Acier et sur Verre. Paris, 1856.

Lalanne, M. Traité de la Gravure à l'Eau-forte. Paris, 1866; tr. Eng. Boston, 1880; 1884.

[Sawyer, J. R.] The Autotype Process. [1867]; 1871; 1876; 1878.

Shrubsole, W. G. Etching; its Principles and Practice. [1870.]

Hamerton, P. G. The Etcher's Handbook. 1871; 1875.

Scamoni, G. Handbuch der Heliogravure nebst praktischen Wegweiser im Gebiete der bezuglichen Gravirkunst. Leningrad, 1872.

Hannot, A. Gravure sur Cuivre au moyen de la Photographie et de Galvanoplastik. Brussels, 1872.

Tissandier, G. Une Conférence sur l'Héliogravure et ses Applications à la Librairie. Paris, 1874.

—— Histoire de la Gravure typographique. Paris, 1875.

Edwards, E. The Heliotype Process. Boston, 1876.

Husnik, J. Die Heliographie oder eine Anleitung zur Herstellung druckbarer Metalplatten. Vienna, 1878; Vienna, 1888.

Chattock, R. S. Practical Notes on Etching. [c. 1880]; 1883; 1886.

Vidal, L. Traité pratique de Photoglyptie [i.e. Woodburytype]. Paris, 1881; tr. German, Halle, 1897.

—— Le Progrès de la Photogravure. Paris, 1900.

—— Traité pratique de Photogravure. Paris, 1900.

Delaborde, H. La Gravure. Paris, 1882; tr. Eng. (by R. A. M. Stevenson) 1886.

Davanne, L. A. N. Niepce, Inventeur de la Photographie. Paris, 1885.

Leslie, A. F. W. Practical Instructor of Photo-Engraving and Zinc Etching Processes. New York, 1886; New York, 1888.

Roux, V. Manuel de l'Imprimeur héliographe. Paris, 1886.

Fouqué, V. La Vérité sur l'Invention de la Photographie. Paris, 1887.

Short, Sir F. On the Making of Etchings. 1888; 1889; 1893; 1898.

Wilkinson, W. T. Photogravure. 1890; 1895.

Herkomer, Sir H. Etching and Mezzotint. 1892.

Denison, H. A Treatise on Photogravure by the Talbot-Klic Process. 1896.

Huson, T. Photo-Aquatint and Photogravure. [1897.]

Ziegler, W. Die Techniken des Tiefdruckes. Halle, 1901.

Brown, G. E. Ferric and Heliographic Processes. 1907.

Hardie, M. Frederick Goulding, Master Printer of Copper Plates. Stirling, 1910.

Cameron-Swan, D. Pioneers of Photogravure. The Imprint, 17 June 1913.

S[wan], M. E. and K. R. Sir Joseph Wilson Swan. 1929.

(c) Plane Surfaces

[Lithography (Stone, Zinc, Aluminium); Photolithography; Phototype; Collotype. For Chromolithography see p. 79 above.]

[Weitenkampf, F.] Catalogue of an Exhibition Illustrative of the Centenary of Artistic Lithography, 1796–1896. Grolier Club, New York, 1896.

Kampmann, C. Die Literatur der Lithographie. Vienna, 1899.

Senefelder, J. A. A New Method and Process of Performing the Various Branches of the Art of Printing. Patent Specification No. 2518. 1810; [1856.]

—— Vollständiges Lehrbuch der Steindruckerey. 2 pts, Munich, 1818, 1821, 1827; tr. Eng. 1819 and New York, 1911 (as The Invention of Lithography).

Bankes, H. Lithography; or the Art of Making Drawings on Stone for the Purpose of being multiplied by printing. Bath, 1813; 1816.

Engelmann, G. Rapport sur la Lithographie. Paris, [1816].

—— Manuel du Dessinateur lithographe. Paris, 1823; Paris, 1824; Paris, [1830].

—— Traité théoretique et pratique de Lithographie. Mulhouse, [1840].

M[airet], F. Notice sur la Lithographie. Dijon, 1818; Chatillon-sur-Seine, 1824; tr. German, Budapest, 1819.

Raucourt de Charleville, A. Mémoire sur les Expériences lithographiques faites à l'École Royale des Ponts et Chaussées de France. Toulon, 1819; tr. Eng. 1820, 1821, 1832.

P[eignot], G. Essai Historique sur la Lithographie. Paris, 1819.

Ruthven, J. A Short Account of Lithography or the Art of Printing from Stone. Edinburgh, 1820.

Hullmandel, C. The Art of Drawing on Stone. [1824]; 1833; 1835; 1840.

—— On Some Important Improvements in Lithographic Printing. [c. 1825.]

—— On Some Further Improvements in Lithographic Printing. 1829.

Brégeaut, R. L. Manuel complet, théorique et pratique du Dessinateur et de l'Imprimeur lithographe. Paris, 1827.

Phillips, G. F. The Art of Drawing on Stone. 1828.

Croker, T. C The History of Lithography. Foreign Rev. July 1829. [Rev. and rptd separately 1829.]

Tudot, E. Description de tous les Moyens de dessiner sur Pierre. Paris, 1833; Paris, 1834.

Senefelder, K. Lehrbuch der Lithographie. Ratisbon, 1833, 1834.

Pillou, A. C. Instruction sur l'Autographie. Paris, 1833.

Desportes, J. Manuel pratique du Lithographe. Paris, 1834.

Klinkhardt, F. Die anastatische Druckerei. Quedlinburg, 1846.

De la Motte, P. On the Various Applications of Anastatic Printing and Papyrography. 1849.

Cowell, S. H. A Brief Description of the Art of Anastatic Printing. Ipswich, [c. 1851]; Ipswich, 1874.

Stanbury, G. Stanbury's Practical Guide to Lithography. 1851; 1854.

Mason, C. Practical Lithographer. 1852.

Jordan, C. J. A Treatise on Anastatic Printing. 1853.

Salières, P. N. Gravure diaphane. Nouveau Procédé à la Portée de tous les Peintres et de tous les Dessinateurs. Montpelier, 1853.

[Waterlow, A. C.] Every Man his own Printer; or, Lithography made Easy. 1854; 1859.

Aresti, J. Lithozographia; or, Aquatinta Stippled Gradations produced upon Drawings washed or painted on Stone. 1856; 1857.

Schenck, F. Short Treatise on Lithography. 1857.

Scott, A. de C. On Photo-Zincography and other Photographic Processes employed at the Ordnance Survey Office. 1862; 1863.

Berri, D. G. The Art of Lithography. 1864; 1872.

Lemling, J. Die Photoverrotypie. Ludenschied, 1870.

Markl, A. Die neuesten Fortschritte der Phototypie. Prague, 1870.

Sawyer, J. R. Photography in the Printing Press. Photographic Journ. 15 Jan. 1872. [Rptd in The Autotype Process, 5th edn, 1876, 1878.]

The Heliotype Process described and illustrated. [1872.]

Fortier, G. La Photolithographie: son Origine, ses Procédés, ses Applications. Paris, 1876.

Husnik, J. Das Gesammtgebiet des Lichtdrucks. Vienna, 1877; Vienna, 1885.

Doyen, C. Trattati di Litografia, Storico, Teorico, Pratico ed Economico. Turin, 1877.

Richmond, W. D. The Grammar of Lithography. 1878; 1880; [c. 1901] (12th èdn); tr. German, Leipzig, 1880.

Pumphrey, A. Collography for Autographic Printing. Birmingham, 1878.

Vidal, L. Traité pratique de Phototypie ou Impression à l'Encre grasse sur une Couche de Gelatine. Paris, 1879.

Schnauss, J. Der Licht-Druck und die Photolithographie. Dusseldorf, [1879], [1880], [1886]; tr. Eng. 1889, [c. 1895].

Allgeyer, J. Handbuch ueber das Lichtdruck-Verfahren. Leipzig, 1881.

Villon, A. M. Nouveau Manuel complet du Dessinateur et de l'Imprimerie lithographe. 2 vols. Paris, 1891.

Valette, A. Manuel pratique du Lithographe. Lyons, 1891; Lyons, 1894; Paris, 1903.

Voirin, J. Manuel pratique de Phototypie. Paris, 1892; Paris, [1910].

Wilkinson, W. T. Collotype. 1895.

Albert, A. Der Lichtdruck an der Hand- und Schnellpresse sammt allen Nebenarbeiten. Halle, 1898.

Fithian, A. W. Practical Collotype. 1901.

Weilandt, C. Algraphy; or, the Art of Printing from Aluminium Plates. Adapted from the German by J. S. Morriss. [1901.]

Seymour, A. Practical Lithography. 1903.

Cumming, D. Handbook of Lithography. 1904.

Goodman, J. Practical Modern Metalithography. 1914.

(d) Surfaces in Relief

[Wood Engraving; Steel Engraving; Mezzotint; Zincography; Line Blocks; Half Tone. Some works on electrotyping which deal with the conversion of intaglio into relief surfaces are listed, p. 75 above, under Spencer, Jacobi, Schoenberg, Sampson, Palmer, etc.]

Stuart, P. A Method of Engraving and Printing [White on Black]. Patent Specification No. 3307. 1810. [1856.]

Dembour, A. Description d'un nouveau Procédé de Gravure en Relief sur Cuivre, dite Ectypographie Métallique. Metz, 1835; tr. German, Brunswick, 1835.

Jackson, J. [and Chatto, W. A.]. A Treatise on Wood Engraving, Historical and Practical. 1839; rev. H. G. Bohn, 1861.

Laborde, L. de. Gravure en Manière noire [mezzotint]. Paris, 1839.

Tissier, L. Histoire de la Gravure typographique sur Pierre et de la Tissiérographie. Paris, 1843.

Chatto, W. A. The History and Art of Wood Engraving. 1848; 1849.

Michel, V. Specimen des Clichés bitumineux inventés par V. Michel. Paris, 1851.

Gillot, F. Paniconographie de Gillot. Paris, 1852.

Devincenzi, J. Électrographie ou nouvel Art de Graver en Relief sur Métal. Paris, 1856.

Wood Engraving as an Employment for Women. Alexandra Mag. April 1865.

Fitz-Cook, H. On the Graphotype. Journ. Soc. of Arts, 8 Dec. 1865.

Gilks, T. The Art of Wood Engraving. 1866; 1867; 1868; [c. 1885].

Fuller, S. E. A Manual of Instruction in the Art of Wood Engraving. Boston, 1867; New York, 1879.

The Handbook of Graphotype. 1868.

Lewis, J. Printing Surfaces in Relief. The Lithographer, Feb.–June 1871.

Motteroz, C. Essai sur les Gravures chemiques en Relief. Paris, 1871.

Emerson, W. A. Practical Instruction in the Art of Wood Engraving. East Douglas, 1876; Boston, 1881.

Scherer, R. Lehrbuch der Chemigraphie und verwandten Faecher. Vienna, 1877.

Linton, W. J. Some Practical Hints on Wood Engraving. Boston, 1879.

—— Wood Engraving. A Manual of Instruction. 1884.

Marx, G. W. The Art of Drawing and Engraving on Wood. 1881 (2nd edn).

Roux, V. Traité pratique de Zincographie. Paris, 1885; Paris, 1891.

Boeck, J. Zincography: Guide to the Art in connexion with Letterpress Printing. 1886.

Husnik, J. Die Zinkaetzung (Chemigraphie, Zinkotypie). Vienna, 1886.

Geymet, T. Traité de Gravure en Demi-Teinte. Paris, 1888.

Schraubstadter, C. Photo-Engraving. A Practical Treatise on the Production of Printing Blocks by Modern Photographic Methods. St Louis, 1892.

'Verfasser, J.' The Half-Tone Process. Bradford, 1894, 1895, 1896; 1904; 1907; [1912]. Tr. French, Paris, 1895; German, Halle, 1896.

Volkmer, O. Die Photo-Galvanographie zur Herstellung von Kupferdruck- und Buchdruckplatten nebst den noethigen Vor- und Nebenarbeiten. Halle, 1894.

Meisenbach Co. Ltd. Meisenbach Improved Process of Photo-Engraving [half tone]. [1895.]

Swan Electric Engraving Co. Specimens of Reproductions, Press Opinions and some Criticisms. [1895.]

Jenkins, H. Manual of Photo-Engraving. Chicago, 1896, 1902; rev. N. S. Amstutz, Chicago, 1907.

Cronenberg, W. Die Praxis der Autotypie auf amerikanischer Basis. Düsseldorf, 1895; tr. Eng. Bradford, 1896.

Fraipont, G. Les Procédés de Reproduction en Relief. Paris, 1896.

Vidal, L. Die Photoglyphie oder der Wood-bury-Druck. Halle, 1897.

Ives, F. E. British and Colonial Printer, 10, 17 March 1898. [Half-tone process.]

—— Lectures on Photo-process Work. London Technical Education Gazette, Jan. 1899.

Newton, A. J. A Note on Dragon's Blood. Penrose's Pictorial Annual, vi, 1900.

Cox, A. Half-tone Printing. Birmingham, [1903].

Gamble, W. Line Photo-Engraving. 1910.

—— The Beginning of Half-tone. British and Colonial Printer, Dec. 1927; rptd New York, 1928.

Keppel, F. The Golden Age of Engraving. New York, 1910.

D., A. C. A Note on the Art of Mezzotint and Mezzotint Printing in Colours. [1911.]

McCabe, L. R. The Beginnings of Half-tone, from the Note Books of S. H. Horgan. Chicago, [1924].

Horgan, S. H. More about the Beginnings of Half-tone. Chicago, 1925.

Smith, W. J. Photo-Engraving in Relief. 1932.

(7) Printing Style

(a) Aesthetic Considerations

[Works on individual presses and printers are listed pp. 86–8 below.]

Hansard, T. C. Typographia. 1825. [Pp. 609–21.]

Jacobi, C. T. On the Making and Issuing of Books. 1891.

Southward, J. Artistic Printing. 1892.

Morris, W. The Ideal Book. Trans. Bibliog. Soc. i, 1893. [Rptd separately 1908.]

Arts and Crafts Exhibition Society. Arts and Crafts Essays. 1893. [Printing by William Morris and Sir Emery Walker.]

Joyner, G. Fine Printing: its Inception, Development and Practice. 1895.

Ricketts, C. and Pisarro, L. De la Typographie et de l'Harmonie de la Page imprimée. 1898.

Ricketts, C. A Defence of the Revival of Printing. 1899.

De Vinne, T. L. The Practice of Typography. A Treatise on Title Pages. Grolier Club, New York, 1901; New York, 1904.

Sanderson, T. J. Cobden. Ecce Mundus. Industrial Arts and the Book Beautiful. Hammersmith, 1902.

Steele, R. The Revival of Printing. 1912.

Keynes, G. L. William Pickering, Publisher. 1924.

(b) Legibility

Babbage, C. Table of Logarithms. 1827; 1915. [Preface.]

Cattell, J. M. Inertia of Eye and Brain. Brain, viii, 1885, pp. 295–312.

Cohn, H. L. Die Hygiene des Auges in den Schulen. Leipzig, 1883; tr. Eng. (as Hygiene of the Eye in Schools) 1886.

Griffing, H. and Franz, S. I. On the Conditions of Fatigue in Reading. Psychological Rev. (New York), iii, 1896, pp. 513–30.

Javal, E. Physiologie de la Lecture et de l'Écriture. Paris, 1905.

Huey, E. B. The Psychology and Pedagogy of Reading. New York, 1910.

'Typoclastes.' A Plea for Reform of Printing. The Imprint, 17 June 1913.

Pyke, R. L. The Legibility of Print. Medical Research Council. Special Report Ser. No. 110, 1926.

(8) Private Printing

(a) General Works

Martin, J. Bibliographical Catalogue of Privately Printed Books. 1834; 1854 (rev.).

Hume, A. The Learned Societies and Printing Clubs of the United Kingdom. 1847; 1853 (rev.).

Bohn, H. G. Appendix Volume to The Bibliographer's Manual by W. T. Lowndes. 1865.

Quaritch, B. Account of the Great Learned Societies and Associations and of the Chief Printing Clubs of Great Britain and Ireland. Sette of Odde Volumes. Misc. No. 14. 1886.

Morris, W. A Note on his Aims in Founding the Kelmscott Press. Hammersmith, 1898.

Plomer, H. R. Some Private Presses of the Nineteenth Century. Library, i, 1900, pp. 407–28.

Dobell, B. Catalogue of Books Printed for Private Circulation. 1906.

Terry, C. S. A Catalogue of the Publications of Scottish Historical and Kindred Clubs and Societies, 1780–1908. Glasgow, 1909.

Ashbee, C. R. The Private Press. A Study in Idealism. To which is added a Bibliography of the Essex House Press. Broad Campden, 1909.

Steele, R. The Revival of Printing. 1912.

Steeves, H. R. Learned Societies and English Literary Scholarship. New York, 1913.

Tomkinson, G. S. A Select Bibliography of the Principal Modern Presses, Public and Private in Great Britain and Ireland. First Edition Club, 1928.

Williams, H. Book Clubs and Printing Societies of Great Britain and Ireland. First Edition Club, 1929.

Ransom, W. Private Presses and their Books. New York, 1929.

(b) Particular Presses and Societies

Lee Priory Press (Sir Samuel Egerton Brydges, 1812–1822).

Brydges, Sir S. E. The Autobiography, Times, Opinions, and Contemporaries of Sir Egerton Brydges. 2 vols. 1834.

Roxburghe Club (1812 onwards).

[Scott, Sir W.] Quarterly Rev. XLIV, 1831, pp. 447–52.

Haslewood, J. Roxburghe Revels, and other Relative Papers. Ed. J. Maidment, Edinburgh, 1837 (priv. ptd).

Bigham, C. (Baron Mersey). The Roxburghe Club, its History and its Members, 1812–1927. 1928.

Bannatyne Club (1822–1867).

The Bannatyne Club: Lists of Members, Rules and Catalogue. Ed. D. Laing, Edinburgh, 1867.

Abbotsford Club (1833–1866).

The Abbotsford Club. A List of Members; the Rules and a Catalogue of Books. Ed. D. Laing, Edinburgh, 1866.

The Camden Society (1838–1897).

Nichols, J. G. A Descriptive Catalogue of the First Series of the Works of the Camden Society. 1872 (2nd edn).

The Daniel Press (C. H. O. Daniel, 1845–1919).

Madan, F. The Daniel Press: Memorials of C. H. O. Daniel with a Bibliography of the Press. Oxford, 1921. [Addenda and Corrigenda, Oxford, 1922.]

The Kelmscott Press (William Morris, 1891–1898).

Forman, H. Buxton. The Books of William Morris described. 1897.

Morris, W. A Note on his Aims in founding the Kelmscott Press, together with a Short Description of the Press by S. C. Cockerell and an Annotated list of the Books printed thereat. Kelmscott, 1898.

Mackail, J. W. The Life of William Morris. 2 vols. 1899.

Sparling, H. H. The Kelmscott Press and William Morris. 1924.

The Eragny Press (L. and E. Pissarro, 1894–1914).

Moore, T. Sturge. A Brief Account of the Origin of the Eragny Press. 1903.

The Ashendene Press (C. St J. Hornby, 1895 onwards).

A Handlist of the Books printed at the Ashendene Press, 1895–1925. 1925.

The Vale Press (W. L. Hacon and C. Ricketts, 1896–1903).

Ricketts, C. A Bibliography of Books printed between 1896 and 1903 by Hacon and Ricketts. 1904.

The Essex House Press (C. R. Ashbee, 1898–1910).

Ashbee, C. R. The Private Press. A Study in Idealism. To which is added a Bibliography of the Essex House Press. Broad Campden, 1909.

The Doves Press (T. J. Cobden Sanderson and Sir Emery Walker, 1899–1916).

Catalogue Raisonné of the Books printed and published at the Doves Press, 1900–1916. 1916.

Sanderson, T. J. C. Cobden. Cobden Sanderson and the Doves Press. The History of the Press and the Story of its Types. San Francisco, 1929.

(9) PRINTERS AND PRINTING FIRMS

Ballantyne, Hanson & Co. Edinburgh.

Lockhart, J. G. The Life of Sir Walter Scott. 2 vols. Edinburgh, 1837–8.

[Ballantyne, A.] Refutation of the Misstatements and Calumnies contained in Mr Lockhart's Life of Sir Walter Scott respecting the Messrs Ballantyne. Edinburgh, 1838.

[Lockhart, J. G.] The Ballantyne-Humbug Handled. Edinburgh, 1838.

[Ballantyne, A.] Reply to Mr Lockhart's Pamphlet entitled The Ballantyne-Humbug Handled. Edinburgh, 1839.

The History of the Ballantyne Press and its Connexion with Sir Walter Scott. [Edinburgh, 1871.]

[Dobson, W. T. and Carrie, W. L.] The Ballantyne Press and its Founders, 1796–1908. Edinburgh, 1909.

Bemrose & Co., Derby.

Bemrose, H. H. The House of Bemrose, 1826–1926. Derby, 1926.

Thomas Bensley, London. [See William Bulmer.]

William Bulmer, London.

Marrot, H. V. William Bulmer—Thomas Bensley. A Study in Transition. 1930.

Butler and Tanner, Frome.

Rhode, John. A Hundred Years of Printing, 1795–1895. 1927 (priv. ptd).

The Cambridge University Press, Cambridge.

Roberts, S. C. A History of the Cambridge University Press, 1521–1921. Cambridge, 1921.

Cassell & Co., London.

McCoy, M. P. A Visit to a London Printing Office. 1881.

The Catnach Press, Newcastle; London.

Hindley. Charles. The History of the Catnach Press. 1886.

The Co-operative Printing Society, Manchester.

Hall, F. The History of the Co-operative Printing Society, Manchester, 1869–1919. Manchester, 1920.

Edinburgh University Press.

Fleming, L. An Octogenarian Printer's Recollections. Edinburgh, 1893.

Frank Gaskell, Birmingham.

[Gaskell, F.] The Experiences and Maxims of a Practical Printer. [1890.]

King's Printing Office, Edidburgh.

Kinnear, S. Reminiscences of an Aristocratic Edinburgh Printing Office. Edinburgh, 1890.

The Glasgow University Press, Glasgow.

Maclehose, James. The Glasgow University Press, 1638–1931. Glasgow, 1931.

Luke Hansard, London.

Hansard, J. and L. G. Biographical Memoir of Luke Hansard, Many Years Printer to the House of Commons. 1829.

Harrison and Sons, London.

The House of Harrison: being an Account of the Family and Firm of Harrison and Sons, Printers to the King. 1914.

M. Lownds and Son, London.

1855–1905, A Record of Fifty Years' Progress. 1905.

William Morris. [See p. 86 above under Kelmscott Press.]

Neill & Co., Edinburgh.

History of Neill & Co. Ltd. Edinburgh, 1900.

John Nichols, London.

Nichols, J. G. Memoirs of John Nichols. [In Illustrations of the Literary History of the Eighteenth Century, vol. VIII, 1858.]

John Bowyer Nichols, London.

Nichols, J. G. Memoir of the late John Bowyer Nichols. 1864.

John Gough Nichols, London.

Nichols, R. C. Memoir of the late John Gough Nichols. 1874.

Pillans and Wilson, Edinburgh.

A Printing House of Old and New Edinburgh, 1775–1925. Edinburgh, 1925.

Robert Pocock, Gravesend.

Arnold, G. M. Robert Pocock, the Gravesend Historian, Naturalist, Antiquarian, Botanist, and Printer. 1883.

Robert Skeen.

Autobiography of Mr Robert Skeen, Printer. 1876 (priv. ptd).

C. M. Smith.

[Smith, C. M.] The Working Man's Way in the World; being the Autobiography of a Journeyman Printer. 1857.

Spottiswoode & Co., London.

History of Spottiswoode & Co. Ltd. 1739–1909. 1909.

Austen-Leigh, R. A. The Story of a Printing House: being a Short Account of the Strahans and the Spottiswoodes. [1911]; 1912 (rev.).

Charles, Earl Stanhope.

Hart, Horace. Charles, Earl Stanhope and the Oxford University Press. Collectanea, ser. 3, Oxford Hist. Soc. 1896.

A. W. Tuer.

Johnson, A. F. Old Face Types in the Victorian Age. Monotype Recorder, Dec. 1931.

Unwin Brothers.

Unwins. A Century of Progress, being a Record of the Rise and present Position of the Gresham Press, 1826–1926. [1926.]

The Victoria Press (Emily Faithfull), London.

Head, W. W. The Victoria Press: its History and Vindication with an Account of the Movement for the Employment of Females in Printing. 1867.

Waterlow Brothers and Layton, London.

Smalley, G. The Life of Sir Sidney Waterlow, Bart. 1909.

The House of Waterlows of Birchin Lane from 1811 to 1911. [1911.]

Boon, J. Under Six Reigns: being some Account of 114 Years of Progress and Development of the House of Waterlow. 1925.

Wertheimer, Lea and Co.

A Romance of the Printing Trade. [1914.]

C. Whittingham & Co. The Chiswick Press, London.

Warren, Arthur. The Charles Whittinghams, Printers. Grolier Club, New York, 1896.

Plomer, H. R. A Glance at the Whittingham Ledgers. Library, ii, 1901, pp. 147–163.

C. H. Wyman & Sons, London.

Lawrence, A. The Story of Wyman & Sons, Ltd. [1907.]

(10) PRINTING TRADE PERIODICALS

[Although this section contains only periodicals issued in Great Britain, two others must be mentioned for their international importance: Journal für Buchdruckerei, Brunswick, 1834–81; The Inland Printer, Chicago, 1881 onwards.]

Mohr, F. L. Die periodische Fachpresse der Typographie und der verwandten Geschaftszweige. Strasburg, 1879.

The Compositors' Chronicle. No. 1, Sept. 1840–No. 37, Aug. 1843 [–No. 39, Oct. 1843]. [Continued as] The Printer. No. 1, Nov. 1843–No. 19, June 1845. [Monthly.]

The Typographical Gazette. [No. 1, April], No. 2, May 1846–[?]. [Monthly.]

The Typographical Protection Circular. No. 1, Jan. 1849–No. 59, Nov. 1853 [–No. 60, Dec. 1853]. [Continued as] The Typographical Circular. No. 1, Jan. 1854–[No. 54, June, 1858]. [Continued as] The London Press Journal and General Trades Advocate (late the Typographical Circular). [1858]–No. 4, 21 Jan. 1859. [Monthly; ed. by E. S. Mantz.]

The Provincial Typographical Circular. [No. 1, Oct. 1852–No. 297, June 1877. [Continued as] The Typographical Circular. No. 298, July 1877 onwards. [Manchester. Monthly; ed. by Henry Slatter.]

The Scottish Typographical Circular. No. 1, Sept. 1857–No. 568, Dec. 1908. [Continued as] The Scottish Typographical Journal. No. 569, Jan. 1909 onwards. [In progress. Edinburgh, later Glasgow. Monthly; ed. by David Hunter.]

Journal of the Typographic Arts. No. 1, Jan. 1860–No. 29, May 1862. [Monthly.]

Typographic Advertiser. No. 1, June 1862–No. 68, Feb. 1868. [Pbd by J. & R. M. Wood. Monthly.]

The Printers' Register. No. 1, July 1863 onwards. [In progress. Monthly; ed. by W. Dorrington (1863–6), A. J. C. Powell.]

The Printers' Journal and Typographical Magazine. No. 1, 2 Jan. 1865–22 March 1869. [Fortnightly.]

London, Provincial and Colonial Press News. No. 1, 15 Jan. 1866–No. 564, 12 Dec. 1912. [Monthly; ed. by W. Dorrington.]

The Chromolithograph: a Journal of Art Literature, Decoration and the Accomplishments. No. 1, 23 Nov. 1867–27 March 1869. [Weekly.]

The Lithographer. No. 1, July 1870–No. 49, July 1874. [Incorporated with The Printing Times. Monthly; ed. by P. B. Watt.]

The Paper and Printing Trades' Journal. No. 1, Dec. 1872–No. 86, May 1895. [Quarterly; ed. by A. W. Tuer. Index to Nos. 1–32, by E. R. Pearce, Taunton, 1881.]

The Printing Times. No. 1, 1 Jan. 1873–No. 19, July 1874. [Continued as] The Printing Times and Lithographer. 1 Aug. 1874–Dec. 1901. [Fortnightly at first, then monthly; ed. by John Lovell (1873–4), C. W. H. Wyman (1874–83).]

Fleet Street Gazette. A Journeyman's Journal. No. 1, 28 Feb.–No. 7, 23 May 1874. [Fortnightly.]

Hailing's Circular. No. 1, Nov. 1877–No. 24, Autumn 1889. [Cheltenham. Quarterly at first, then irregular.]

The British and Colonial Printer and Stationer and Newspaper Press Record. No. 1, Dec. 1878 onwards. [The subtitle was altered to 'and Paper Trades Review' in 1879. Fortnightly; ed. by W. J. Stonhill.]

Paper and Print. No. 1, 2 Aug. 1879–No. 87, 26 March 1881–[?]. [Weekly; ed. by H. F. Gough.]

The Printing Trades Diary and Desk-Book. 1879–1886. [Annual; ed. by C. W. H. Wyman.]

The Printing Review. No. 1, Jan. 1879–No. 11, Nov. 1879–[?].

The Printers' Friend. No. 1, 8 Nov. 1880–No. 8, 30 June 1883.

The Printers' International Specimen Exchange. 16 vols. 1880–98. [Ed. by A. W. Tuer.]

The Printer: a Quarterly Journal devoted to the interests of printers and printing. No. 1, Nov. 1883–No. 20, Aug. 1888.

The British Printer. [1888 onwards.] [In progress. Leicester.]

The Vigilance Gazette: a Monthly Journal devoted to the interests of the London Society of Compositors. No. 1, May 1888–Feb. 1889. [Continued as] The London Printers' Circular. No. 7, May 1889–No. 11, May 1890.

The English Typographia. Vols. i–ii, 1889–97.

The Printing World. No. 1, 25 Jan. 1891–Sept. 1911.

The Lithographer. No. 1, 15 Sept.–No. 3, 16 Nov. 1891. [Incorporated with The Printing Times.]

The British Lithographer. 1891–5. [Leicester.]

Printing News. No. 1, Aug. 1892–15 June 1894.

The Typographic Chronicle. [No. 1, Jan.]– No. 7, Aug. 1892–[?].

Amalgamated Society of Pressmen. Half Yearly Report. 1892 onwards.

The Printer's Weekly Advertiser. No. 1, 3 June 1893–1 April 1896.

Process Work. Penrose's Circular. [No. 1, 1893]–1929. [Ed. by W. Gamble.]

Amalgamated Society of Printers' Warehousemen. Report of the Committee. 1894 onwards.

The Process Photogram. No. 1, Jan. 1895– Dec. 1905. [Continued as] The Process Engraver's Monthly. Jan. 1906 onwards. [Monthly; ed. by H. Snowden Ward, C. W. Ward. Title varies.]

The Process Work Year Book. Penrose's Annual. Vol. i, 1895–1900. [Continued as] Penrose's Pictorial Annual. 1901 onwards. [In progress; ed. by W. Gamble, R. B. Fishenden. Title varies.]

The British Art Printer. [1895–6.] [Swindon.]

Amateur Printing. No. 1, June 1895–Jan. 1909.

The Printer's Engineer. No. 1, Sept. 1895 onwards.

Print: A Journal for Printinghouse Employés of all grades and departments. No. 1, May– No. 6, Oct. 1896.

The Caxtonian Quarterly. No. 1, Feb. 1898– No. 22, May 1904.

Paper and Printing Bits. No. 1, Oct. 1898– No. 10, April 1900. [Birmingham. Monthly.]

The Printers' Year Book and Diary. 1899–[?].

The Printers' Pocket Guide, Almanack and Diary. 1899–[?]. [Ed. by A. C. Couch.]

(11) BOOK ILLUSTRATION

(a) General Works

Orme, E. An Essay on Transparent Prints and on Transparencies in General. 1807.

[Plowman, J.] An Essay on the Illustration of Books. 1824.

Jackson, J. [and Chatto, W. A.]. A Treatise on Wood Engraving, Historical and Practical. 1839; 1861 (rev. H. G. Bohn).

Hamerton, P. G. Etching and Etchers. 1868; 1876; 1880; Boston, 1883.

Ruskin, J. Ariadne Florentina. 1872; Orpington, 1876; 1907.

Redgrave, S. A Dictionary of Artists of the English School. 1874.

Carr, J. C. Cantor Lectures on Book Illustration, Old and New. 1882.

Woodberry, G. E. A History of Wood Engraving. 1883.

Everitt, G. English Caricaturists and Graphic Humourists of the Nineteenth Century. 1886.

Linton, W. J. The Masters of Wood Engraving. New Haven, 1889.

Crane, Walter. Cantor Lectures on the Decoration and Illustration of Books. 1889.

—— Of the Decorative Illustration of Books. 1896; 1901.

Pennell, J. Pen Drawing and Pen Draughtsmen. 1889; 1894; 1897.

—— Modern Illustration. 1895.

—— English Book Illustration 1860–1870. Royal Soc. of Arts Journ. 3 April 1896.

—— The Illustration of Books. 1896.

Brough, W. S. Book Illustration. Leek, 1891.

Harper, C. G. English Pen Artists of To-Day: Examples of their Work, with some Criticisms and Appreciations. 1892.

—— A Practical Handbook of Drawing for Modern Methods of Reproduction. 1894.

Chapin, W. O. The Masters and Masterpieces of Engraving. New York, 1894.

Green, E. The Beginnings of Lithography. 1894.

—— Bath and Early Lithography. Bath, 1894.

Layard, G. S. Tennyson and his Pre-Raphaelite Illustrators. 1894.

Cundall, J. A Brief History of Wood Engraving. 1895.

Meade, E. Pen Pictures and How to Draw them. 1895.

Vine, C. J. Hints on Drawing for Process Reproduction. 1895.

Wedmore, Sir F. Etching in England. 1895.

White, Gleeson. English Illustration, 1855– 1870. 1897; 1906.

—— Children's Books and their Illustrators. Studio, Winter No. 1897.

Slater, J. H. Engravings and their Value. 1897 (2nd edn).

—— Illustrated Sporting Books. 1899.

Pennell, J. and E. R. Lithography and Lithographers: Some Chapters in the History of the Art. 1898.

Whitman, A. C. The Masters of Mezzotint, the Men and their Work. 1898.

—— Nineteenth-Century Mezzotinters. 2 vols. 1903–4.

Kitton, F. G. Dickens and his Illustrators. 1899.

Doyen, C. Origini e Sviluppo della Litografia durante il Secolo 19. Milan, 1901.

Murdoch, T. The Early History of Lithography in Glasgow. Glasgow, 1902.

Bulloch, J. M. The Art of Extra Illustration. 1903.

Pingrenon, R. Les Livres Ornés et Illustrés en Couleur depuis le XVe Siècle en France et en Angleterre. Paris, 1903.

Sketchley, R. E. D. English Book Illustration of To-Day. Appreciations of Living English Illustrators with Lists of their Books. 1903.

'George Paston' (E. M. Symonds). Old Coloured Books. 1905.

Hardie, M. English Coloured Books. 1906.

Prideaux, S. T. Aquatint Engraving: a Chapter in the History of Book Illustration. 1909.

Salaman, M. C. Old English Colour Prints. 1909.

—— British Book Illustration: Yesterday and To-Day. 1923.

Imeson, W. K. Illustrated Music Titles and their Delineators. 1912.

Nevill, R. H. Old English Sporting Books. 1924.

Robinson, C. N. Old Naval Prints. 1924.

Siltzer, F. The Story of British Sporting Prints. 1925; 1929.

Lewis, C. T. C. The Story of Picture Printing in England in the Nineteenth Century. [1928.]

Reid, Forrest. Illustrators of the Sixties. [1928.]

Ruemann, A. Das illustrierte Buch des XIX. Jahrhunderts in England, Frankreich und Deutschland, 1790–1860. Leipzig, 1930.

Brown, K. S. The Story of Printed Pictures. New York, 1931.

Sleigh, B. Wood Engraving since 1890. 1932.

Balston, T. English Book Illustration, 1880–1900. [In John Carter, New Paths in Book Collecting, 1934, pp. 165–190.]

Thorpe, J. H. English Illustration: the Nineties. 1935.

Tooley, R. V. Some English Books with Coloured Plates. 1935.

(b) Particular Illustrators

Henry Alken (1787–1851).

The Boston Transcript, 20 July 1910.

Sparrow, W. S. Henry Alken. 1927.

Francesco Bartolozzi (1727–1815).

Tuer, A. W. Bartolozzi and his Works. 2 vols. 1881; 1885 (rev.).

Brinton, S. Bartolozzi and his Pupils in England. 1906 (2nd edn).

Bailey, J. T. H. Francesco Bartolozzi: a Biographical Study. 1907.

George Baxter (1804–1867).

Bullock, C. F. Life of George Baxter, Engraver, Artist and Colour Printer. Birmingham, 1901.

Lewis, C. T. C. George Baxter: his Life and Work. 1908.

—— The Picture Printer of the Nineteenth Century: George Baxter. 1911.

Colebrook, F. George Baxter: his Work and Method. 1909.

Clarke, H. G. Baxter Colour Prints: their History and Methods of Production. 1919.

The Baxter Times. A Journal for XIXth Century Print Collectors. Leamington. Vols. I–III, June 1923–Nov. 1925. [Continued as] The Baxter Print Collector and Baxter Times. Leamington. 10 Dec. 1925 onwards.

Aubrey Beardsley (1872–1898).

Symons, A. Aubrey Beardsley. 1898; 1905.

The Early Work of Aubrey Beardsley. 1899; 1912.

The Later Work of Aubrey Beardsley. 1900; 1912.

Ross, R. B. Aubrey Beardsley. 1909.

The Uncollected Work of Aubrey Beardsley. 1925.

Thomas Bewick (1753–1828).

Thomas Bewick. A Memoir written by Himself. 1862; ed. A. Dobson, Newcastle, 1887.

Hugo, T. The Bewick Collector: A Descriptive Catalogue of the Works of Thomas and John Bewick. 1866. [Supplement, 1868.]

Thomson, D. C. The Life and Works of Thomas Bewick. 1882.

Dobson, A. Thomas Bewick and his Pupils. 1884; 1889 (rev.).

Robinson, R. Thomas Bewick: his Life and Times. Newcastle, 1887.

William Blake (1757–1827).

Gilchrist, A. Life of William Blake. 2 vols. 1868; 2 vols. 1880 (enlarged).

Keynes, G. L. Bibliography of William Blake. Grolier Club, 1921.

Thomas Shotter Boys (1803–1874).

Stokes, H. Thomas Shotter Boys. 1925.

Hablot K. Browne (1815–1882)

Kitton, F. G. Phiz (Hablot K. Browne). A Memoir including a Selection from his Correspondence. 1882.

Randolph Caldecott (1846–1886).

Blackburn, H. Randolph Caldecott: a Personal Memoir of his Early Art Career. 1886.

Samuel Cousins (1801–1887).

Pycroft, G. Memoir of Samuel Cousins. Exeter, 1887 (priv. ptd); 1899.

Whitman, A. C. Samuel Cousins. 1904.

Walter Crane (1845–1915).

Konody, P. G. The Art of Walter Crane. 1902.

Crane, Walter An Artist's Reminiscences. 1907.

Massé, G. C. E. Bibliography of the First Editions of Books illustrated by Walter Crane. 1923.

George Cruikshank (1792–1878).

Jerrold, Blanchard. The Life of George Cruikshank. 1882.

Thackeray, W. M. An Essay on the Genius of George Cruikshank. 1884.

Cohn, A. M. George Cruikshank. A Catalogue Raisonné. 1924.

George Dalziel (1815–1902); *Edward Dalziel* (1817–1905).

Dalziel, G. and E. The Brothers Dalziel; a Record of 1840–1890. 1901.

Colebrook, F. Dalziel and the Dalsprites. 1909.

William Dickes (1815–1892).

Docker, A. The Colour Prints of William Dickes. 1924.

Gustav Doré (1833–1883).

Roosevelt, B. Life of Gustav Doré. 1885.

George Du Maurier (1834–1896).

Wood, T. M. George Du Maurier, the Satirist of the Victorians. 1913.

Benjamin Fawcett (1808–1893).

Morris, M. C. F. Benjamin Fawcett, Colour Printer and Engraver. Oxford, 1925.

Sir Luke Fildes (1844–1927).

Thomson, D. C. The Life and Work of Luke Fildes. 1892.

Alfred Henry Forrester (1804–1872).

[Forrester, A. H.] A Bundle of Crowquills dropped by A Crowquill in his Eccentric Flights over the Fields of Literature. 1854.

Harry Furniss (1854–1925).

Furniss, H. The Confessions of a Caricaturist. 2 vols. 1901.

James Gillray (1757–1815).

[Grego, J.] The Works of James Gillray with the History of his Life and Times. Ed. T. Wright, 1873.

Kate Greenaway (1846–1901).

Spielmann, M. H. and Layard, G. S. Kate Greenaway. 1905.

Sir Frank Seymour Haden (1818–1910).

Harrington, H. N. The Engraved Work of Sir Frank Seymour Haden. Liverpool, 1910.

Philip Gilbert Hamerton (1834–1894).

P. G. Hamerton: An Autobiography, 1834–58, and a Memoir by his Wife, 1858–94. 1897.

Arthur Boyd Houghton (1836–1875).

A. B. Houghton: A Selection from his Work in Black and White. 1896.

Charles Keene (1823–1891).

Layard, G. S. The Life and Letters of C. Keene. 1892.

Pennell, J. The Work of Charles Keene. 1897.

Robert Le Blond (1816–1863); *Abraham Le Blond* (1819–1894).

Lewis, C. T. C. The Le Blond Book: a History of the Work of Le Blond & Co. 1920.

John Leech (1817–1864).

Kitton, F. G. John Leech, Artist and Humourist. 1883; 1884 (rev.).

Frith, W. P. John Leech, his Life and Work. 2 vols. 1891.

[Granniss, R. S.] Catalogue of an Exhibition of Works by John Leech. Grolier Club, 1914.

[Slade, B. C.] John Leech on my Shelves. Munich, 1930 (priv. ptd).

William James Linton (1812–1898).

Linton, W. J. Threescore and Ten Years, 1820–1890. New York, 1894; 1895 (as Memoirs).

David Lucas (1802–1881).

[Leggatt, E. E.] Catalogue of the Complete Works of David Lucas. 1903.

Daniel Maclise (1806–1870).

O'Driscoll, W. J. A Memoir of Daniel Maclise. 1871.

John Martin (1789–1854).

Balston, T. John Martin. Library, Jan. 1931.

Phil May (1864–1903).

Thorpe, J. H. Phil May. 1932.

Sir John Everett Millais (1829–1896).

Spielmann, M. H. Millais and his Work. 1898.

Millais, J. G. The Life and Letters of Sir J. E. Millais. 1899; 1905.

Francis Orpen Morris (1810–1893).

Morris, M. C. F. Francis Orpen Morris: A Memoir. 1897.

Samuel Palmer (1805–1881).

Palmer, A. H. The Life and Letters of Samuel Palmer. 1892.

Abraham Raimbach (1776–1843).

Raimbach, M. T. S. Memoirs and Recollections of the Late Abraham Raimbach, Engraver. 1843.

Samuel William Reynolds (1773–1835).

Whitman, A. C. S. W. Reynolds. 1903.

Thomas Rowlandson (1756–1827).

Grego, J. Rowlandson the Caricaturist. 2 vols. 1880.

[Granniss, R. S.] A Catalogue of Books illustrated by Thomas Rowlandson. Grolier Club, 1916.

Frederick Sandys (1829–1904).

Gray, J. M. Frederick Sandys and the Woodcut Designs of Thirty Years Ago. Century Guild Hobby Horse, Dec. 1888.

Reproductions of Woodcuts by F. Sandys, 1860–1866. [1919] (priv. ptd).

Alois Senefelder (1771–1834).

Nagler, G. K. Alois Senefelder und der geistliche Rath Simon Schmid als Rivalen in der Geschichte der Erfindung des mechanischen Steindruckes. Munich, 1862.

Wagner, C. Alois Senefelder, sein Leben und Wirken. Ein Beitrag zur Geschichte der Lithographie. Leipzig, 1914.

Charles Shannon (1863–1937).

Ricketts, Charles. A Catalogue of Mr Shannon's Lithographs. [1909.]

Marcus Stone (1840–1921).

Baldry, A. L. The Life and Work of Marcus Stone. 1896.

Thomas Stothard (1755–1834).

Bray, A. E. Life of Thomas Stothard. 1851.

Coxhead, A. C. Thomas Stothard. 1906.

William Strang (1859–1921).

[Binyon, L.] William Strang. Catalogue of his Etched Work. 1906; 1912.

Sir John Tenniel (1820–1914).

Monkhouse, W. C. The Life and Work of Sir John Tenniel. 1901.

Hugh Thomson (1860–1920).

Spielmann, M. H. and Jerrold, W. Hugh Thomson, his Art, his Letters, his Humour and his Charm. 1931.

Charles Turner (1774–1857).

Whitman, A. C. Charles Turner. 1907.

(12) BOOKBINDING

Grolier Club, New York. List of Books and Articles relating to Bookbinding to be found in the Library. New York, 1907.

Mejer, W. Bibliographie der Buchbinderei-Literatur. Leipzig, 1925.

New Scale of Prices for Bookbinding. 1807. [Broadside.]

Country Scale of Prices for Bookbinding. [1810.]

The Whole Art of Bookbinding. Oswestry, 1811.

The Bookbinders' Price-Book. 1813. [Supplement, 1824.]

The Art of Bookbinding; containing a description of the tools. 1818; tr. German, Leipzig, 1819.

[Martin, G.] The Bookbinder's Complete Instructor. Peterhead, 1823.

Boteler, W. C. Songs for Bookbinders. 1827.

[Cowie, G.] The Bookbinder's Manual. 1829; [c. 1835]; [c. 1838]; [c. 1845] (7th edn).

The Reply of the Journeymen Bookbinders to Remarks on a Memorial addressed to their Employers on the Effects of a Machine introduced to supersede Manual Labour. 1831.

[Hannett, J.] Bibliopegia; or the Art of Bookbinding in all its Branches by J. A. Arnett. 1835; 1836; 1865 (6th edn).

[——] The Bookbinders' School of Design, as applied to the Combination of Tools in the Art of Finishing by J. Arnett. 1837.

The Handbook of Taste in Book-Binding. [c. 1840.]

The Book-Finisher's Friendly Circular. No. 1, Aug. 1845–No. 19, Sept. 1850.

The Bookbinders' Trade Circular. Issued by the London Consolidated Society of Journeymen Bookbinders. No. 1, Oct. 1850–No. 154, 20 Nov. 1877. [Monthly at first, but irregular. Ed. by T. J. Dunning.]

Woolnough, C. W. The Art of Marbling as applied to Book Edges and Paper. 1853; 1881.

Nicholson, J. B. A Manual of the Art of Bookbinding. Philadelphia, 1856, 1882.

Dunning, T. J. Account of the London Consolidated Society of Bookbinders. [In National Association for the Promotion of Social Science, Report, 1860.]

Zaehnsdorf, J. W. The Art of Bookbinding. 1880; 1890; 1903 (6th edn).

Wheatley, H. B. Bookbinding considered as a Fine Art, Mechanical Art, and Manufacture. 1882.

Adam, P. Systematisches Lehr- und Handbuch der Buchbinderei. 2 vols. Dresden, 1883–91.

—— Der Bucheinband. Leipzig, 1890.

—— Practical Bookbinding. 1903.

Crane, W. J. E. Bookbinding for Amateurs. 1885.

The Bookbinder. No. 1, Jan. 1887–No. 36, Dec. 1889. [Continued as] The British Bookmaker. No. 37, Jan. 1890–No. 81, March 1894. [Monthly.]

Bosquet, E. Traité de l'Art du Relieur. Paris, 1890.

Halfer, J. Die Fortschritte der Marmorierkunst. Ein praktisches Handbuch für Buchbinder. Stuttgart, 1891 (2nd edn); tr. Eng. Buffalo, 1893, 1904.

Grolier Club. Commercial Bookbinding: an Historical Sketch. New York, 1894.

Sanderson, T. J. C. Bookbinding: its Processes and Ideals. Fortnightly Rev. Aug. 1894.

Bosquet, L. La Reliure; Études d'un Practicien. Paris, 1894.

Gruel, L. Conférence sur la Reliure et la Dorure de Livres. Paris, 1896.

Cockerell, D. Bookbinding and the Care of Books: a Text Book for Bookbinders and Librarians. 1901.

Royal Society of Arts. Report of the Committee on Leather for Bookbinding. 1901.

Stewart, C. J. Bookbinders' Arbitration Award. 1903.

Prideaux, S. T. Modern Bookbindings: their Design and Decoration. 1906.

Stephen, G. A. Commercial Bookbinding. 1910.

Sadleir, M. The Evolution of Publishers' Binding Styles, 1770–1900. 1930.

—— Yellow Backs. [In New Paths in Book Collecting, ed. J. Carter, 1934, pp. 127–61.]

Carter, J. Binding Variants in English Publishing, 1820–1900. 1932.

—— Publishers' Cloth, 1820–1900. New York, [1935].

C. BOOK DISTRIBUTION

(1) GENERAL WORKS

National Book Council. Books about Books. A Catalogue of the Books contained in the National Book Council Library. 1933; 1935 (rev.).

[Phillips, Samuel.] The Literature of the Rail. 1851.

Rees, Thomas and Britton, John. Reminiscences of Literary London from 1779 to 1853. 1853 (priv. ptd); New York, 1896 (rev.).

Hodson, W. H. Hodson's Booksellers', Publishers' and Stationers' Directory for London and Country. 1855.

Curwen, H. A History of Booksellers, the Old and the New. [1873.]

'The Bookman' Directory of Booksellers, Publishers and Authors. 1893.

Mumby, F. A. The Romance of Bookselling. 1910; 1930 (rev. as Publishing and Bookselling).

Harper, J. H. The House of Harper. New York, 1912.

Shaylor, J. The Fascination of Books. 1912.

Collins, A. S. The Profession of Letters, 1780–1832. 1928.

Cruse, Amy. The Englishman and his Books in the Early XIXth Century. 1930.

—— The Victorians and their Books. 1935.

—— After the Victorians. 1938.

Darton, F. J. H. Children's Books in England. Cambridge, 1932.

(2) COPYRIGHT

Solberg, T. Bibliography of Literary Property. [In R. R. Bowker, Copyright; its Law and its Literature, New York, 1886.]

List of Works on Copyright in the Patent Office Library. 1900.

Montefiori, J. The Law of Copyright. 1802.

Report of the Select Committee [of the House of Commons] on Copyright of Printed Books, and the Delivery of them to the Public Libraries. 1812–3. (292). iv. 999.

—— Minutes of Evidence on the Effect of the Law on Literary Property. 1812–3. (341). iv. 1003. Rptd 1818. (177). ix. 389.

[Duppa, R.] An Address to the Parliament of Great Britain on the Claims of Authors to their own Copyright. 1813 (bis); rptd The Pamphleteer, II, 1813, pp. 169–202.

Report of the Select Committee [of the House of Commons] respecting the Amendment of 54 George III. 1818. (402). ix. 249. Minutes of Evidence. 1818. (280). ix. 257.

Godson, R. A Practical Treatise on the Law of Patents for Inventions and of Copyright. 1823; 1840; 1844. [Supplements: 1832; 1844; 1851.]

Maugham, R. A Treatise on the Laws of Literary Property. 1828.

Report from the Select Committee [of the House of Commons] appointed to inquire into the Laws affecting Dramatic Literature. 1831–2. (679). vii. 2.

Bossange, H. Opinion nouvelle sur la Propriété littéraire. Paris, 1836.

Hood, T. Copyright and Copywrong. Athenaeum, 15, 22, 29 April 1837, 11, 18 June 1842. [Rptd in Works, vols. IV and VI, 1862.]

Blanc, Étienne. Traité de Contrefaçon et de sa Poursuite en Justice. Paris, 1837, 1838, 1855.

Tegg, T. Remarks on the Speech of Sergeant Talfourd. 1837.

Chambers, W. and R. Brief Objections to Mr Talfourd's New Copyright Bill. Edinburgh, 1838.

Mudie, R. The Copyright Question and Mr Sergeant Talfourd's Bill. 1838.

Nicklin, P. H. Remarks on Literary Property. Philadelphia, 1838.

Renouard, A. C. Traité des Droits d'Auteurs. 2 vols. Paris, 1838–9.

Webster, G. Observations on the Law of Copyright in reference to the Bill of Mr Sergeant Talfourd. 1838.

Areopagitica Secunda; or Speech of the Shade of John Milton on Sergeant Talfourd's Copyright Extension Bill. 1838.

A Proposed New Law of Copyright of the highest Importance to Authors in a Letter to T. N. Talfourd. [1838.]

A Few Words on the Copyright Question shewing it to be one of Public Interest, with some Objections to Sergeant Talfourd's Bill. 1839.

Christie, W. D. A Plea for Perpetual Copyright. 1840.

Lieber, F. On International Copyright. New York, 1840.

Lowndes, J. J. An Historical Sketch of the Law of Copyright. 1840; 1842.

Talfourd, T. N. Three Speeches delivered in the House of Commons in favour of a Measure for an Extension of Copyright, to which are added the Petitions in favour of the Bill and Remarks on the Present State of the Copyright Question. 1840.

Balzac, H. de. Notes Remises à MM. les Députés composant la Commission de la Loi sur la Propriété littéraire. [5 March 1841; in Œuvres Complètes, vol. XXII, Paris, 1872.]

Burke, P. A Treatise on the Law of Copyright in Literature. 1842.

—— The Law of International Copyright between England and France. 1852.

—— The Present State of the Law of Copyright with a View to its Amendment. 1863.

The Law of Copyright regarding Authors, Dramatic Writers and Musical Composers as altered by the recent Statute. 1842.

Mathews, C. An Appeal to American Authors and the American Press in behalf of an International Copyright. New York, 1842. [Rptd in The Various Writings of C. Mathews, New York, 1843, pp. 355–70.]

Campbell, J. Considerations and Arguments proving the Inexpediency of an International Copyright Law. New York, 1844.

Muquardt, C. De la Contrefaçon et de son Influence pernicieuse sur la Littérature et la Librairie. Brussels, 1844.

Curtis, G. T. A Treatise of the Law of Copyright in Books. Boston, 1847.

Boosey versus Purday. Assumed Copyright in Foreign Authors. Judgement given in the Court of Exchequer, Westminster Hall 5 June 1849. 1849.

A Brief Statement on the Subject of Assumed Foreign Copyright. 1851.

Bohn, H. G. The Question of Unreciprocated Foreign Copyright. 1851.

Villefort, A. De la Propriété littéraire et artistique au Point de Vue internationale. Paris, 1851.

Mathews, C. J. Lettre de M. Charles Mathews aux Auteurs dramatiques de la France. 1852.

Delalain, A. H. J. Législation de la Propriété littéraire. Paris, 1852 (bis), 1854, 1855 (bis), 1858 (rev.).

—— Nouvelle Législation de la Propriété littéraire. Paris, 1868.

Thackeray, W. M. Mr Brown's Letters. New York, 1853. [Author's Preface.]

Carey, H. C. Letters on International Copyright. Philadelphia, 1853; New York, 1868.

—— The International Copyright Question Considered. Philadelphia, 1872.

Lacan, A. J. B. and Paulmier, C. P. P. Traité de la Législation et de la Jurisprudence des Théâtres. 2 vols. Paris, 1853.

Leverson, M. R. Copyright and Patents; being an Investigation of the Principles of Legal Science applicable to Property in Thought. 1854.

Eisenlohr, C. F. M. Sammlung der Gesetze und internationalen Verträge zum Schutze des literarischen-artistischen Eigenthums in Deutschland, Frankreich und England. Heidelberg, 1856. [Nachtrag, Heidelberg, 1857.]

Laboulaye, E. R. L. Études sur la Propriété littéraire en France et en Angleterre. Paris, 1858.

Compte Rendu des Travaux du Congrès de Bruxelles. Paris, 1858.

Reade, C. The Eighth Commandment. 1860.

—— The Rights and Wrongs of Authors. [In Readiana, 1863, pp. 127–231.]

Law, S. D. Digest of American Cases relating to Patents for Inventions and Copyrights from 1789 to 1862. New York, 1862; New York, 1870 (rev.); New York, 1877 (rev.).

Gastambide, J. A. Histoire et Théorie de la Propriété des Auteurs. Paris, 1862.

Phillips, C. P. The Law of Literature and Art. 1863.

Chappell, F. P. and Shoard, J. A Handy Book of the Law of Copyright. 1863.

Gambart, E. On Piracy of Artistic Copyright. 1863.

Huard, A. Étude comparative des Législations française et étrangères en Matière de la Propriété industrielle, artistique et littéraire. Paris, 1863.

Trollope, A. On the Best Means of Extending and Securing an International Law of Copyright. Trans. Nat. Ass. for Promotion of Social Science, 1867, pp. 119–25.

Le Barrois d'Orgeval, R. La Propriété littéraire en France et à l'Étranger. Paris, 1868.

White, R. G. The American View of the Copyright Question. Broadway Annual (New York), May 1868. [Rptd separately New York, 1880.]

[Helps, Sir Arthur.] International Copyright between England and America. Macmillan's Mag. June 1869.

Copinger, W. A. The Law of Copyright in Works of Literature and Art. 1870; 1881; 1893; 1904 (rev. J. M. Easton); 1915; 1927 (rev. F. E. Skene Jones).

Booth, W. D. Rights of Dramatic Authors at Common Law. New York, 1871.

Hotten, J. C. Literary Copyright. Seven Letters addressed to Earl Stanhope. 1871.

Klostermann, R. Das Urheberrecht und das Verlagsrecht nach deutschen und ausländischen Gesetzen systematisch und vergleichend dargestellt. Berlin, 1871.

Shortt, J. The Law relating to Literature and Art. 1871; 1884.

Memoranda on International and Colonial Copyright. 1872.

Appleton, W. H. Letters on International Copyright. New York, 1872.

Coryton, J. Stageright; a Compendium of the Laws relating to Dramatic Authors. 1873.

Morgan, J. H. The Law of Literature. 2 vols. New York, 1875; 2 vols. 1876.

Dicey, E. The Copyright Question. Fortnightly Rev. 1 Jan. 1876.

Purday, C. H. Copyright: a Sketch of its Rise and Progress. 1877.

Copyright Commission. The Royal Commissions and the Report of the Commissioners. [Evidence and Appendix.] 1878.

[Froude, J. A.] The Copyright Commission. Edinburgh Rev. Oct. 1878.

Levi, L. International Copyright in relation to the U.S.A. and other Foreign States. 1879.

Macfie, R. A. Copyright and Patents for Inventions. Vol. I, Edinburgh, 1879.

M[arston], E. Copyright, National and International from the Point of View of a Publisher. 1879.

Conant, S. S. and Courtney, L. H. International Copyright. Macmillan's Mag. June 1879.

Drone, E. S. A Treatise on the Law of Property in Intellectual Productions in Great Britain and the U.S.A. Boston, 1879.

Putnam, G. H. International Copyright considered in some of its Relations to Ethics and Political Economy. New York, 1879.

—— The Question of Copyright. New York, 1891, 1896.

Harper & Bros. Memorandums on International Copyright. [New York, 1879]; [New York, 1880] (enlarged).

American Publishers and English Authors by Stylus. Baltimore, 1879.

Fliniaux, C. La Propriété industrielle et la Propriété littéraire et artistique en France et à l'Étranger. Tours, 1879.

Pouillet, E. Traité théorique et pratique de la Propriété littéraire et artistique et du Droit de Représentation. Paris, 1879.

Clunet, E. Concordance des Résolutions du Congrès de la Propriété artistique tenu à Paris en 1878. Paris, 1879.

Arnold, M. Copyright. Fortnightly Rev. 1 March 1880. [Rptd in Irish Essays, 1882.]

Collins, W. W. Considerations on the Copyright Question addressed to an American Friend. International Rev. (New York), June 1880. [Rptd separately 1880.]

Jerrold, S. A Handbook of English and Foreign Copyright in Literary and Dramatic Works. 1881.

Longman, C. J. A Publisher's View of International Copyright. Fraser's Mag. March 1881.

Dawson, S. E. Copyright in Books: an Insight into its Origin and the Present State of the Law in Canada. Montreal, 1882.

Scrutton, Sir T. E. The Laws of Copyright. 1883; 1890; 1896; 1903.

Thompson, G. C. Remarks on the Law of Literary Property in Various Countries. 1883.

Lea, H. C. International Copyright. [Philadelphia. 1884.]

Slater, J. H. The Law Relating to Copyright. 1884.

Bowker, R. R. Copyright; its Law and its Literature. New York, 1886.

—— Copyright: its History and its Law. 1912.

Matthews, J. B. Cheap Books and Good Books. New York, 1888.

—— American Authors and British Pirates. New York, 1889.

Association Littéraire Internationale; Son Histoire, 1878–1889. Paris, 1889.

Lyon-Caen, C. and Delalain, P. Lois françaises et étrangères sur la Propriété littéraire. 2 vols. Paris, 1889.

Cutler, E., Smith, T. E. and Weatherly, F. E. The Law of Musical and Dramatic Copyright. 1890.

Lely, T. M. Copyright Law Reform. 1891.

Chamier, D. Law relating to Literary Copyright. 1895.

Chosson, E. La Propriété littéraire. Paris, 1895.

Osterreith, A. Die Geschichte des Urheberrechts in England. Leipzig, 1895.

Cohen, B. A. The Law of Copyright. 1896.

Lancefield, R. T. Notes on Copyright, Domestic and International. Hamilton (Canada), 1896.

Rivière, L. Protection internationale des Œuvres littéraires et artistiques. Paris, 1897.

Report of the Select Committee of the House of Lords on the Copyright Bills [Evidence and Appendix]. 1898. [The same, 1899; the same, 1900.]

Birrell, A. Seven Lectures on the Law and History of Copyright in Books. 1899.

Solberg, T. Copyright Enactments [in U.S.A.] 1783–1900, together with the Presidential Proclamations regarding International Copyright. Washington, 1900.

—— Copyright in Congress, 1789–1904. A Bibliography and Chronological Record. Washington, 1905.

Strong, A. A. The Law of Copyright for Actor and Composer. 1901.

Macgillivray, E. J. Treatise upon the Law of Copyright in the United Kingdom and the Dominions of the Crown and in the U.S.A. 1902; 1906.

Hinkson, H. A. Copyright Law. 1903.

Hamlin, A. S. Copyright Cases: A Summary of Leading American Decisions. New York, 1904.

Recueil des Conventions et Traités concernant la Propriété littéraire. Berne, 1904.

Allen, G. Copyright and Copywrong. The Authentic and the Unauthentic Ruskin. 1907.

Report of the Committee on the Law of Copyright. 1909.

Putnam, G. H. George Pamer Putnam. New York, 1912.

Potu, E. La Convention de Berne. Paris, 1914.

Flower, D. Authors and Copyright in the XIXth Century with Unpublished Letters from Wilkie Collins. Book Collector's Quart. no. 7, July–Sept. 1932.

Pollard, G. Introduction. [In I. R. Brussel, Anglo-American First Editions, 1935.]

(3) AUTHORS' GUIDES TO PUBLICATION

[The following works all profess to instruct an author how to choose and negotiate with a publisher. This function is now fulfilled by the literary agent, who was hardly established as a profession before 1880; and the only work in this list specifically dealing with the literary agent is the collection of testimonials to A. P. Watt ptd in 1893.]

[H., T.] The Perils of Authorship. [c. 1835]; [c. 1840] (4th edn).

—— The Author's Advocate and Young Publishers' Friend; a Sequel to the Perils of Authorship. [c. 1840.]

The· Author's Printing and Publishing Assistant. 1839; 1839; New York, 1839; 1840; [c. 1848] (7th edn). [Attrib. to Frederic Saunders; all English edns pbd by Saunders & Ottley.]

Hints and Directions for Authors in Writing, Printing and Publishing their Works. 1842. [Attrib. to the publisher Edward Bull.]

[Churton, Edward.] The Author's Handbook: A Complete Guide to the Art and System of Publishing on Commission. 1844; 1845 (with addns).

A Description of Publishing Methods and Arrangements. New York, 1855 (4th edn).

The Search for a Publisher, or Counsels to a Young Author. 1855; 1859 (4th edn); 1865; 1870; [1873]; 1881.

[Judd, J. and Glass, A. H.] Counsels to Authors and Hints to Advertisers. 1856; 1857.

Counsels to Authors, Plans of Publishing, and Specimens of Types. 1863.

Comprehensive Guide to Printing and Publishing. 1869; 1877 (10th edn); 1897.

Spon, E. How to Publish a Book. 1872.

[Southward, J.] Authorship and Publication. A Guide in Matters relating to Printing and Publishing. 1882; 1883; 1884.

[Putnam, G. H. and G. P.] Authors and Publishers. A Manual of Suggestions for Beginners in Literature. New York, 1883; New York, 1897 (7th edn), 1900.

Deacon's Composition and Style with a Complete Guide to all Matters connected with Printing and Publishing. Ed. R. D. Blackman, [1885] (5th edn).

Russell, P. The Literary Manual or, A Complete Guide to Authorship. 1886.

The Author's Guide to Printing and Publishing by a Journalist. [1886] (2nd edn).

O'Brien, M. B. A Manual for Authors, Printers and Publishers. 1890.

Sprigge, S. S. Methods of Publishing. 1890; 1891.

The Author. No. 1, 15 May 1890. [In progress. The monthly organ of the Incorporated Society of Authors; ed. by Sir Walter Besant.]

How to Print and Publish a Book. Winchester, 1890.

Jacobi, C. T. On the Making and Issuing of Books. 1891.

—— Some Notes on Books and Printing. 1892; 1902.

Besant, Sir W. The Society of Authors. A Record of its Action from its Foundation. 1893.

—— The Pen and the Book. 1899.

Watt, A. P. Letters Addressed to A. P. Watt by Various Writers. 1893; 1894; 1896.

Eisemann, E. Le Contrat d'Édition et les autres Louages d'Œuvres intellectuelles. Paris, 1894.

Lamb, J. B. Practical Hints on Writing for the Press. 1897.

Wagner, L. How to Publish a Book or an Article. 1898.

Bennett, Arnold. How to Become an Author. 1903; [1908]; 1912.

[Watson, W. L.] The Author's Progress by Adam Lorimer. Edinburgh, 1906.

Booth, W. S. A Practical Guide to Authors in their Relations with Publishers and Printers. Boston, 1907.

(4) THE PRACTICE OF PUBLISHING

[Memoirs of authors have not been included in this list although they contain much relevant material, particularly the auto-biographies of Anthony Trollope, Herbert Spencer, Harriet Martineau, Cyrus Redding, and Edmund Yates, and the biographies of Macaulay by Sir G. O. Trevelyan and of Scott by J. G. Lockhart (as well as his Journal and Correspondence). Works relating to publishers' control of the retail price (the Net Book Agreement and its predecessors) have been listed with those on retail bookselling on p. 102 below.]

Babbage, C. On the Economy of Machinery and Manufactures. 1832.

First Report from the Select Committee on Postage. Minutes of Evidence. 1837–8. xx. 278.

Jerdan, W. Illustrations of the Plan of a National Association for the Encourage-ment and Protection of Authors. 1838.

The Aldine Magazine of Biography, Biblio-graphy, Criticism and the Arts. 1839. [Ed. by William West.]

[Grant, J.] Travels in Town by the Author of Random Recollections of the Lords and Commons. 2 vols. 1839.

Balzac, Honoré de. Code littéraire (May 1840). [Œuvres Complètes, vol. xxii, Paris, 1872.]

James, G. P. R. Some Observations on the Booktrade as connected with Literature in England. Journ. Statistical Soc. of London, Feb. 1843.

[Petheram, J.] Reasons for Establishing an Authors' Publication Society. 1843.

The Present System of Publishing. 1844.

Knight, C. The Old Printer and the Modern Press. 1854.

Spedding, J. Publishers and Authors. 1867.

Ruskin, J. Fors Clavigera. 1871–84. [Letters 6, 11, 16, 53, 57, 62, 89; Notes and Corre-spondence, 10, 14, 15.]

Walker, S. The Road; Leaves from the Sketch Book of a Commercial Traveller. Otley, 1872.

Powell, A. The Law affecting Printers, Pub-lishers, and Newspaper Proprietors. 1887; 1889 (rev.).

The Grievances between Authors and Pub-lishers, being the Report of the Conferences of the Incorporated Society of Authors with Additional Matter and Summary. 1887.

Besant, Sir W. Literary Conferences. 1888.
—— The Society of Authors. A Record of its Action from its Foundation. 1893.
—— Literary Conferences. Contemporary Rev. Jan. 1894.
—— The Pen and the Book. 1899.
—— Autobiography. 1902.

Jessopp, A. A Plea for the Publisher. Con-temporary Rev. March 1890.

Smiles, S. Authors and Publishers. Murray's Mag. Jan., Feb. 1890.

Sprigge, S. S. The Methods of Publishing. 1890; 1891 (rev.).
—— The Society of French Authors. 1890.

The Society of Authors. The Cost of Produc-tion. 1891 (3 edns).

Paul, C. Kegan. The Life and Death of Books. [In Faith and Unfaith, 1891.]

[Heinemann, W.] The Hardships of Pub-lishing. 1893 (priv. ptd).

Jerome, Jerome K. et al. My First Book. 1894.

Buchanan, R. W. Is Barabbas a Necessity? A Discourse on Publishers and Publishing. 1896.

Allen, C. E. Publishers' Accounts; including a Consideration of Copyright and the Valuation of Literary Property. 1897.

Spencer, H. Various Fragments. 1897; 1900 (rev. edn).

International Publishers' Congress. 1899. Report. 1899.
—— 1901. Report. Leipzig, 1902.

[Bennett, Arnold.] The Truth about an Author. 1903; 1914.

Publishers and Publishing a Hundred Years Ago. From Materials collected by Aleck Abrahams, with some Notes by E. Marston. Publishers' Circular, 6, 13 Jan. 1906.

Yard, R. S. The Publisher. Boston, 1913.

Putnam, G. H. Memories of a Publisher, 1865–1895. 1915.

Unwin, S. The Truth about Publishing. 1926; 1929 (3rd edn, rev.).

'On the Road' One Hundred Years Ago. Being an Account of a Journey made [in 1830] by a Traveller of Messrs A. & C. Black's when subscribing the Seventh Edition of the 'Encyclopaedia Britannica.' Ed. James Cannon, Publishers' Circular, 9 Feb.–13 April 1935.

(5) PARTICULAR PUBLISHERS

Rudolph Ackerman (1764–1834).

P[apworth], W[yatt]. N. & Q. 7, 14 Aug. 1869.

Samuel Bagster (1772–1851).

The Centenary of the Bagster Publishing House. 1894.

George Bell (1814–1890).

Bell, Edward. George Bell, Publisher. 1924 (priv. ptd).

Richard Bentley (1794–1871).

Richard Bentley & Son. Reprinted from Le Livre, Oct. 1885 with some Additional Notes. 1886 (priv. ptd).

Sadleir, M. Bentley Standard Novels. The Colophon (New York), April 1932.

Adam Black (1784–1874).

Nicholson, Alexander. Memoirs of Adam Black. Edinburgh, 1885 (*bis*).

John Blackie (1782–1874).

Blackie, W. G. The Origin and Progress of the Firm of Blackie and Son, 1809–1874. 1897.

A Scottish Student in Leipzig, being the Letters of W. G. Blackie, his Father and his Brothers in the years 1839–40. Ed. W. W. Blackie, 1932.

William Blackwood (1776–1834).

Blackwood, John. A Selection from the Obituary Notices. Ed. William Blackwood, Edinburgh, 1880 (priv. ptd).

Oliphant, M. O. Annals of a Publishing House: William Blackwood and his Sons. 2 vols. 1897. [Vol. III, John Blackwood by his Daughter, Mrs Gerald Porter, 1898.]

B., I. C. The Early House of Blackwood. Edinburgh, 1900 (priv. ptd).

Burns and Oates.

'Wilberforce, Wilfrid' (Wilfrid Meynell). The House of Burns and Oates. [1908.]

Cadell and Davies.

The Publishing Firm of Cadell and Davies. Select Correspondence and Accounts, 1793–1836. Ed. T. Besterman, 1938.

Richard Carlile (1790–1843).

Holyoake, G. J. The Life and Character of Richard Carlile. 1848.

Campbell, T. C. The Battle of the Press as told in the Story of the Life of Richard Carlile. 1899.

John Cassell (1817–1865).

Kirton, J. W. John Cassell. 1891.

Pike, G. H. John Cassell. 1894.

James Catnach (1792–1841).

Hindley, C. The Life and Times of James Catnach, Balladmonger. 1878.

William Chambers (1800–1883); *Robert Chambers* (1802–1871).

Chambers, William. Memoir of Robert Chambers with Autobiographic Reminiscences of William Chambers. Edinburgh, 1872; Edinburgh, 1884 (12th edn), 1893 (rev.).

Chambers, William. The Story of a Long and Busy Life. Edinburgh, 1882; Edinburgh, 1884 (13th edn).

Payn, James. Some Literary Recollections. 1886.

Chapman and Hall.

Waugh, Arthur. A Hundred Years of Publishing, being the Story of Chapman and Hall Ltd. 1930.

—— One Man's Road. 1931.

John W. Chapman.

Paul, C. Kegan. Biographical Sketches. 1883.

T. and T. Clark.

The Publishing House of T. and T. Clark. Edinburgh, 1882.

William Cobbett (1763–1833).

[See p. 629 below.]

William Collins, Sons & Co.

William Collins, Sons & Co. The Story of a Great Business, 1820–1909. Glasgow, 1909.

Archibald Constable (1774–1827).

Constable, Thomas. Archibald Constable and his Literary Correspondents. 3 vols. Edinburgh, 1873.

J. M. Dent (1849–1926).

Dent, Hugh R. The Memoirs of J. M. Dent with some Additions by Hugh R. Dent. 1928.

John Francis (1811–1882).

Francis, J. C. John Francis, Publisher of The Athenaeum. 2 vols. 1888.

William Godwin (1756–1836).

Paul, C. Kegan. William Godwin: his Friends and his Contemporaries. 2 vols. 1876.

Charles Griffin & Co.

The Centenary Volume of Charles Griffin and Co., 1820–1920. 1920.

C. Harrison.

Harrison, C. From Office Boy to Publisher: a Record of 43 Years of Work. [1911.]

Hatchard and Co.

Humphreys, A. L. Piccadilly Bookmen: Memorials of the House of Hatchard. 1893.

William Heinemann (1863–1920).

Whyte, Frederic. William Heinemann. A Memoir. 1928.

William Hone (1780–1842).

Hackwood, F. W. William Hone; his Life and Times. 1912.

Jarrold & Co.

The House of Jarrolds, 1823–1923. 1924.

W. and A. K. Johnston.

One Hundred Years of Map Making. The Story of W. and A. K. Johnston. 1925.

Thomas Kelly (1772–1855).

Fell, R. C. Passages from the Private and Official Life of the late Alderman Kelly. 1856.

Charles Knight (1791–1873).

Knight, Charles. Passages of a Working Life. 3 vols. 1864.

Strahan, Alexander. Charles Knight, Publisher. Good Words, Sept. 1867.

Clowes, Alice A. Charles Knight: A Sketch. 1892.

Longmans, Green & Co.

Rees, Thomas. Reminiscences of Literary London from 1779 to 1853 with Additions by John Britton. New York, 1896.

Cox, Harold and Chandler, J. E. The House of Longman, 1724–1924. 1925 (priv. ptd).

Macmillan & Co.

Hughes, Thomas. Memoir of Daniel Macmillan. 1882; 1883.

A Bibliographical Catalogue of Macmillan & Co.'s Publications, 1843–1889. 1891.

Macmillan, George A. Letters of Alexander Macmillan. 1908 (priv. ptd).

Graves, C. L. Life and Letters of Alexander Macmillan. 1910.

Edward Marston (1825–1914).

Marston, Edward. After Work. 1904.

Sir Algernon Methuen (1856–1924).

Sir Algernon Methuen, Bart. A Memoir. 1925.

R. C. Morgan (1827–1908).

Morgan, George E. 'A Veteran in Revival.' R. C. Morgan; his Life and Times. 1909; 1931.

John Murray (I, 1745–1793; II, 1778–1843; III, 1808–1892).

Smiles, Samuel. A Publisher and his Friends [1768–1843]. 2 vols. 1891 (*bis*); 1911 (abridged).

Murray, John [III]. The Origin and History of Murray's Handbooks for Travellers. Murray's Mag. Nov. 1889.

Murray, John [IV]. John Murray III, 1808–1892. 1919.

'Paston, George' (E. M. Symonds). At John Murray's: Records of a Literary Circle, 1843–1892. 1932.

William Nelson (1816–1887).

Wilson, Sir Daniel. William Nelson. A Memoir. Edinburgh, 1889 (priv. ptd).

Sir George Newnes (1851–1910).

Friederichs, Hulda. The Life of Sir George Newnes, Bart. 1911.

James Nisbet (1785–1854).

Wallace, J. A. Lessons from the Life of the late James Nisbet. 1867.

Novello, Ewer & Co.

A Short History of Cheap Music as exemplified in the Records of the House of Novello, Ewer & Co. 1887.

C. Kegan Paul (1828–1902).

Paul, C. Kegan. Memories. 1899.

George Philip.

Philip, George. The Story of the Last Hundred Years, a Geographical Record. 1934.

Sir Richard Phillips (1767–1840).

Memoirs of the Public and Private Life of Sir Richard Phillips. 1808. [Attrib. to Phillips himself.]

GM. Aug. 1840. [Obituary.]

Timbs, John. Recollections of Sir Richard Phillips. [In Walks and Talks about London, 1864.]

William Pickering (1796–1854).

Keynes, G. L. William Pickering, Publisher. 1924.

Sir Isaac Pitman (1813–1897).

Reed, T. A. A Biography of Isaac Pitman. 1890.

Baker, Alfred. The Life of Sir Isaac Pitman. 1908.

The House of Pitman. 1930.

Grant Richards (b. 1872).

Richards, Grant. Memories of a Misspent Youth, 1872–1896. 1932.

—— Author Hunting. 1934.

Rivington & Co.

Rivington, Septimus. The Publishing House of Rivington. 1894.

—— The Publishing Family of Rivington. 1919.

Routledge & Co.

Mumby, F. A. The House of Routledge, 1834–1934. 1934.

Joseph Shaylor (1844–1924).

Shaylor, Joseph. Sixty Years a Bookman. 1923.

Simpkin, Marshall & Co.

Simpkins; Being Some Account of the Origin and Progress of the House of Simpkin, Marshall. 1924.

George Smith (1824–1901).

[Lee, Sir Sidney and Stephen, Sir Leslie.] George Smith; A Memoir. 1902 (priv. ptd).

[Huxley, Leonard.] The House of Smith, Elder. 1923 (priv. ptd).

W. H. Smith (1825–1891).

Maxwell, Herbert. The Life and Times of the Rt. Hon. William Henry Smith. 2 vols. Edinburgh, 1893.

Pocklington, G. R. The Story of W. H. Smith & Son. 1921 (priv. ptd); rev. F. E. K. Foat, 1932 (priv. ptd).

Edward Stanford.

Edward Stanford; with a Note on the History of the Firm, 1852–1901. 1902 (priv. ptd).

Alexander Strahan.

Strahan, Alexander. Twenty Years of a Publisher's Life. The Day of Rest, Jan.-Dec. 1881.

Bernhard Tauchnitz.

Fünfzig Jahre der Verlagshandlung Bernhard Tauchnitz, 1837 bis 1887. Leipzig, 1887.

John Taylor (1781–1864).

Taylor, Olive M. John Taylor. London Mercury, June 1925.

Thomas Tegg (1776–1845).

[Grant, James.] Portraits of Public Characters. Vol. ii, 1841, pp. 24–46.

Memoir of the late Thomas Tegg. Abridged from his Autobiography by permission of his Son William Tegg. 1870 (priv. ptd). [Rptd from City Press, 6 Aug. 1870.]

William Tinsley (1831–1902).

Tinsley, William. Random Recollections of an Old Publisher. 2 vols. 1900.

Downey, Edmund. Twenty Years Ago. 1905.

Nicholas Trubner (1817–1884).

Axon, W. E. A. In Memoriam Nicholas Trubner. Library Chronicle, April 1884.

Henry Vizetelly (1820–1894).

Vizetelly, Henry. Glances Back through Seventy Years. 1893.

Joseph Whitaker (1820–1895).

Publishers' Circular, 18, 25 May 1895.

Effingham Wilson (1783–1868).

In Memoriam Effingham Wilson. 1868 (priv. ptd). [Rptd from City Press, 18 July 1868.]

(6) GENERAL CATALOGUES

[This section lists general catalogues of books in print over a specified period; it does not include catalogues of particular publishers or any limited to particular subjects. Catalogues issued regularly at intervals of less than a year are listed below in the section on Periodicals.]

Growoll, A. and Eames, Wilberforce. Three Centuries of English Book Trade Bibliography. Dibdin Club (New York), 1903.

Pollard, G. General Lists of Books printed in England. Inst. Hist. Research Bulletin, Feb. 1935.

[Bent, W.] The Modern Catalogue of Books (1792–1803). 1803.

—— The New London Catalogue (1800–1805). 1805.

—— The New London Catalogue (1800–1807). 1807.

—— The London Catalogue (1700–1811). 1811.

—— A Modern Catalogue of Books (1811–1812). 1812.

—— The London Catalogue (1800–1814). 1814.

—— A Catalogue of Books (1814–1816). 1816.

—— The Modern London Catalogue (1800–1818). 1818.

—— A Catalogue of Books (1818–1820). 1820.

—— The London Catalogue (1800–1822). 1822.

[Bent, R.] A Catalogue of Books (1822–1824). 1824.

—— The London Catalogue (1800–1827). 1827. [Supplement, 1829.]

—— The London Catalogue (1810–1831). 1831. [Supplement, 1833.]

—— The London Catalogue (1814–1834). 1835. [Supplement, 1837.]

—— The London Catalogue (1814–1839). 1839.

[Low, S.] A Catalogue of Books. 1838–59. [Annually. Incorporated in The English Catalogue.]

—— The British Catalogue. Vol. i (1837–1852). 1853. [Index to the British Catalogue (1837–1857), 1858.]

—— The English Catalogue. 1860 onwards. [Issued annually.]

—— The English Catalogue of Books (1835–1863). 1864. Vol. ii (1863–1872). 1873. Index to vol. ii (1856–1876). 1876. Vol. iii (1872–1880). 1882. Index to vol. iii (1874–1880). 1884. Vol. iv (1881–1889). 1891. Index to vol. iv (1881–1889). 1893. Vol. v (1890–1897). 1898. Vol. vi (1898–1900). 1901.

[Hodgson, T.] Supplement to the London Catalogue (1839–1844). 1844.

[Hodgson, T.] The London Catalogue (1814–1846). 1846. [Bibliotheca Londiniensis: a Classified Index, 1848. Supplement, 1849.]
—— The London Catalogue (1816–1851). 1851. [Classified Index, 1853.]
—— The London Catalogue (1831–55). 1855.
[Whitaker, J.] The Reference Catalogue of Current Literature. 1874 onwards. [Until 1936 this consisted of publishers' catalogues bound together and indexed. Since 1936 it comprises catalogues of *Authors* and *Titles* compiled from publishers' lists.]
Peddie, R. A. and Waddington, Q. The English Catalogue of Books (1801–1836). 1914.

(7) TRADE PERIODICALS

[The following periodicals contain either current lists of books published or comment and correspondence on trade affairs. Some contain both; but no periodicals of literary criticism intended for general circulation have been included.]

The Monthly Literary Advertiser. No. 1, 10 May 1805–10 Dec. 1828. [Continued as] Bent's Literary Advertiser. 10 Jan. 1829–16 June 1860. [Monthly. Incorporated in The Bookseller. Ed. by William Bent (1805–1823), Robert Bent (1823–1842) Thomas Hodgson (1842–1860).]
The Retail Booksellers' and Bookbuyers' Advocate. No. 1, 1 Dec. 1836; No. 2, Jan. 1837; No. 3 [Feb. 1837]. [Probably ed. by Edward J. Portwine.]
The Publishers' Circular. No. 1, 2 Oct. 1837 onwards. [Fortnightly at first, then weekly; ed. by Sampson Low.]
The Intelligencer for Publishers and Booksellers. No. 1, July 1854–No. 7, Jan. 1855. [Monthly.]
The Bookseller. No. 1, Jan. 1858–30 March 1928. [Continued as] Publisher and Bookseller, 6 April 1928–29 Sept. 1933. [Continued as] The Bookseller, 6 Oct. 1933 onwards. [Weekly. Ed. by Edward Tucker, Joseph Whitaker.]
The Stationer. No. 1, 1 May 1859–10 Aug. 1865. [Continued as] The Stationer, Printer, and Fancy Trades Register. 1 Sept. 1865–Feb. 1912.
Index to Current Literature. No. 1, 30 Sept. 1859–No. 8, 31 Dec. 1860. [Quarterly; ed. by Sampson Low.]
The Booksellers' Record. No. 1, 19 Nov.–No. 7, 31 Dec. 1859. [Weekly.]
The Books of the Month. No. 1, April 1861–No. 17, Aug. 1862.
The Literary Gazette. A Monthly Record of Literature. No. 1, 14 Jan.–No. 7, 10 July 1865.
The Bookbuyer's Guide, Being a List of the Principal Books published in the Various

Departments of Literature. No. 1, Dec. 1869–No. 9, March 1872. [Quarterly; ed. by Thomas J. Fenwick from No. 4.]
The Stationer's and Bookseller's Circular. No. 1, 4 March–No. 4, 25 March, 1871. [Weekly.]
The Booksellers' Circular and Bookbuyers' Guide. No. 1, 20 Oct. 1874. [Monthly; ed. by W. E. Goulden.]
The Bookbuyer: A Chronicle of, and Guide to Current Literature. New Series. No. 1, Feb.; No. 2, March 1875.
The Book Circular: A Monthly Record of New Books and New Editions classified according to Subjects. No. 1, 1 Jan.–No. 6, 1 June 1877.
The Stationery Trades Journal. No. 1, 18 March 1880 onwards. [Monthly; ed. by J. Whitaker.]
The Stationery Trade Review. Edinburgh. No. 1, Jan. 1881–Dec. 1887. [Continued at London as] Stationery, Bookselling and Fancy Goods. Vol. I, No. 1, Jan. 1888–Sept. 1897. [Continued as] Morriss's Trade Journal. Oct. 1897–April 1903. [Continued as] The British Empire Paper, Stationery and Printing Trades Journal. Vol. XXIII, No. 5, May 1903–June 1913. [Monthly; ed. by J. S. Morriss from 1888.]
The Stationer and Bookseller. No. 1, 8 May 1883. [Continued as] The Stationers' and Booksellers' Journal. No. 2, 23 June 1883–No. 12, 30 April 1884. [Monthly; incorporated in The Stationery Review.]
Books. A weekly Journal for Those who buy them, sell them, and read them. No. 1, 18 April–No. 3, 4 July 1889.
The Newsagent and Advertisers' Record. No. 1, July 1889–Dec. 1890. [Continued as] The Newsagent and Booksellers' Review. 31 Jan. 1891 onwards. [Weekly.]
The Book World. A Journal for Publishers and Booksellers. No. 1, Aug. 1890–April 1899. [Ed. by 'Boswell.']
The Newsman and Publication Register. No. 1, 25 Oct. 1890–No. 10, 1 Sept. 1891. [Monthly.]
The Stationery World and Fancy Goods Review. No. 1, 29 Jan. 1892 onwards. [Monthly; ed. by S. Phillips.]
The Book Review Index. No. 1, June 1892. [Quarterly.]
The Book and News Trade Gazette. [No. 1, 1893]–1 Jan. 1898–28 Sept. 1907.
Bookselling. No. 1, Jan. 1895–Dec. 1896. [Continued as] Books and Bookselling. Jan.–Dec. 1897. [Monthly; ed. by 'Temple Scott' (J. H. Isaacs).]
New Book List for Bookbuyers, Librarians and Booksellers. No. 1, Sept. 1895–Aug. 1898. [Monthly; ed. by Cedric Chivers and Armistead Cay.]

The Stationers' and Printers' Annual Trade Book of Reference. 1895–1903.

The January Monthly Part of The English Catalogue of Books for 1897. Jan. 1897–Dec. 1900. [Monthly.]

The Booksellers' Review. No. 1, 11 March 1897–27 Jan. 1898.

The Aldine Newsagents' Trade Journal. No. 1, No. 92, Dec. 1897–Dec. 1904. [Monthly.]

(8) CIRCULATING LIBRARIES

Friswell, J. H. Circulating Libraries; Their Contents and their Readers. London Society, Dec. 1871.

George Moore. Literature at Nurse, or, Circulating Morals. 1885.

Preston, William C. Mudie's Library. Good Words, Oct. 1894.

—— W. H. Smith's Library. Good Words, Nov. 1895.

Shaylor, Joseph. Fiction; its Issue and Classification. Publishers' Circular, 14 May 1898. [Rptd in The Fascination of Books, 1912.]

Tinsley, William. Random Recollections of an Old Publisher. 2 vols. 1900.

John and A. Hallam Murray v. Walter and Others. 1908 (priv. ptd).

Society of Bookmen. Report on the Commercial Circulating Libraries. 1928 (priv. ptd).

(9) RETAIL BOOKSELLING

(a) General Works and the Net Book Agreement

The Stationers' Price-Book: Being a Catalogue of Every Article used or vended in that Business. 1800.

Pickering, W. Booksellers' Monopoly: Address to the Trade and to the Public. 1832.

Paternoster Row and the Bookselling Trade. Pinnock's Guide to Knowledge, Aug. 1834.

The Retail Booksellers' and Bookbuyers' Advocate. No. 1, 1 Dec. 1836; No. 2, Jan. 1837; No. 3, [Feb. 1837]. [Ed. by Edward Portwine?]

A Manual of Book-Keeping for Booksellers, Publishers and Stationers. By a Bookseller. 1850.

Chapman, J. W. The Commerce of Literature. Westminster Rev. April 1852. [Rptd as Cheap Books and How to Get Them, 1852; 1852 (rev.).]

A Report of the Proceedings at a Meeting (consisting chiefly of Authors) held 4 May 1852 at the House of Mr John Chapman for the Purpose of Hastening the Removal of the Trade Restrictions on the Commerce of Literature. 1852.

The Opinions of Certain Authors on the Bookselling Question. [Ed. John W. Parker], [1852]. [Additional Letters on the Bookselling Question, 1852.]

[Bigg, J.] The Bookselling System: a Letter to Lord Campbell respecting the late Inquiry into the Regulations of the Booksellers' Association in reference to the Causes which led to its Dissolution. By a Retired Bookseller. 1852.

The Intelligencer for Publishers and Booksellers. No. 1, July 1854–No. 7, Jan. 1855.

Ridge, L. L. Ridge's Scheme for Promoting the Interests of the Country Booksellers and Publishers. Grantham, 1868.

[Wyman, C. W. H.] Wyman's Dictionary of Stationery. [1875]; 1876; 1881.

Prouting, F. J. The Stationer's Guide and Practical Handbook to the Art of Window Dressing. 1881.

Growoll, A. The Profession of Bookselling: a Handbook of Practical Hints for the Apprentice and Bookseller. 2 pts, New York, 1893–5.

Stott, D. The Decay of Bookselling. Nineteenth Century, Dec. 1894.

Heinemann, W. Bookselling. The System adopted in Germany. Taunton, 1895.

Bowes, R. The Friends of Literature. [In Sketches of Some Booksellers of the Time of Dr Johnson by E. Marston, 1902.]

—— Booksellers' Associations, Past and Present. Taunton, 1905.

—— Cambridge Bookshops and Booksellers, 1846–1858. Cambridge, 1912.

The Successful Bookseller. A Complete Guide to Success to all engaged in a Retail Bookselling, Stationery and Fancy Goods Business. 1906.

Net Books Committee. Net Books Question. 1908.

Macmillan, Sir Frederick. The Net Book Agreement, 1899 and the Book War, 1906–1908. 1924.

Gray, G. J. Cambridge Bookselling and the Older Bookshops in the United Kingdom. Cambridge. 1925.

(b) Particular Firms

[Booksellers in alphabetical order.]

J. Brown & Son. The Firm of Three Generations. Glasgow, 1908.

Cowan, S. Humorous Episodes in the Life o a Provincial Bookseller. Birmingham, 1912.

Fitzgerald, J. The Recollections of a Book Collector (1848–58). Liverpool, 1903.

MacAndrew, I. F. Memoir of Isaac Forsyth, Bookseller in Elgin, 1768–1859. 1889.

Humphreys, C. The Life of Charles Humphreys, Bookseller. Told by Himself. [c. 1910.]

H. K. Lewis & Co. Ltd. Lewis's 1844–1931. An Illustrated Account of its Foundation and Development. 1931.

Miller, G. Later Struggles in the Journey of Life. 1833.

Couper, W. J. The Millers of Haddington, Dunbar and Dunfermline. 1912.

The Parkers of Oxford. Oxford, 1914.

Simpson, W. Old Inverness Booksellers. Men and Memories of Byegone Days. Inverness, 1931.

John Smith & Son, Ltd. A Short Note on a Long History, 1751–1925. Glasgow, 1925.

Burdekin, R. Memoirs of the Life and Character of Mr R. Spence of York, Bookseller. York, 1827.

[Thin, J.] Reminiscences of Booksellers and Bookselling in Edinburgh in the Time of William IV. 1905.

[West, W.] Fifty Years' Recollections of an Old Bookseller. Cork, 1835; 1837.

David Wyllie & Sons. A Century of Bookselling, 1814–1914. Aberdeen, 1914.

(10) THE ANTIQUARIAN BOOK TRADE

(a) General

[Dibdin, T. F.] Bibliophobia; Remarks on the Present Languid and Depressed State of Literature and the Book Trade. 1832.

The Directory of Second-hand Booksellers. Ed. Arthur Gyles, Nottingham, 1886; rev. James Clegg, Rochdale, 1888, 1891, 1894, 1899, 1903, etc. [Later continued by A. J. Philip at Gravesend.]

Wheatley, H. B. Prices of Books. 1898.

(b) Periodicals

The Book Exchange, or, Monthly List of Books, Odd Volumes, MSS., wanted to buy, sell, or exchange. No. 1, Sept. 1863–No. 11, July 1864.

The Literary Mart and Book Exchange. No. 1, July 1874–No. 22, March 1876. [Ed. by W. E. Goulden.]

The Clique. Derby. No. 1, June 14, 1890 onwards. [Weekly; ed. by F. E. Murray. Later at London, and twice a week.]

(c) Book Auctions

Sotheby & Co. A List of the Original Catalogues of the Principal Libraries which have been sold by auction [1744–1818] by Mr Sotheby. 1818; 1828 (continued to 1828).

Book Prices Current. 1887. [Annually since; ed. by J. H. Slater. Index, 1887–1896, 1901. Index, 1897–1907, 1909.]

Book Sales of 1895 [–1897/8]. 4 vols. 1896–9. [Ed. by 'Temple Scott' (J. H. Isaacs).]

Hodgson & Co. One Hundred Years of Book Auctions, 1807–1907, being a Brief Record of the Firm of Hodgson's. 1907 (priv. ptd).

List of Catalogues of English Book Sales, 1676–1900, now in the British Museum. 1915.

Hobson, G. D. Notes on the History of Sotheby's. 1917 (priv. ptd).

(d) Particular Firms

Block, A. The Book Collector's Vade Mecum. 1932. [Appendix B (also rptd separately) contains accounts of many antiquarian booksellers active before 1900.]

H. G. Bohn.

Times, 25 Aug. 1884.

Book Monthly, April 1904.

Bertram Dobell.

Bradbury, S. Bertram Dobell; Bookseller and Man of Letters. 1909.

Dobell, P. J. In Memoriam Bertram Dobell, 1842–1914. [1915.]

Ellis.

Smith, George and Benger, Frank. The Oldest London Bookshop. A History of 200 Years. 1928.

Bernard Quaritch.

[Wyman, C. W. H.] B.Q. A Biographical and Bibliographical Fragment. Sette of Odde Volumes, 1880.

Junk, W. [Memoir in] Internationales Addressbuch der Antiquar-Buchhändler. Berlin, 1906.

Thomas Rodd.

GM, June 1849.

Sotheran & Co.

Stonehouse, J. H. Piccadilly Notes. 1934.

Walter T. Spencer.

Spencer, W. T. Forty Years in my Bookshop. Ed. T. Moult, 1923.

B. F. Stevens.

Fenn, G. Manville. Memoir of B. F. Stevens. 1903.

Waverley Book Store, Edinburgh.

Williamson, R. M. Bits from an Old Book Shop. 1904.

(11) PRIVATE BOOK COLLECTING

Dibdin, T. F. Bibliomania; or, Book-Madness, containing some Account of the History, Symptoms, and Cure of the Fatal Disease. 1809; 1811 (enlarged); 1842 (rev.); 1876 (rev.); 4 vols. Bibliophile Soc. (Boston), 1903.

—— The Bibliographical Decameron. 3 vols. 1817.

Dibdin, T. F. A Bibliographical, Antiquarian and Picturesque Tour in France and Germany. 3 vols. 1821; 3 vols. 1829; tr. French, Paris, 1825.

—— The Library Companion; or, the Young Man's Guide and the Old Man's Comfort in the Choice of a Library. 2 vols. 1824.

—— Reminiscences of a Literary Life. 2 vols. 1836.

—— A Bibliographical, Antiquarian and Picturesque Tour in the Northern Counties of England and in Scotland. 3 vols. 1838.

[Beresford, J.] Bibliosophia; or, Book-wisdom, containing some Account of the Pride, Pleasure, and Privileges of that Glorious Vocation, Book-Collecting. 1810.

[Clarke, W.] Repertorium Bibliographicum: or, some Account of the most Celebrated British Libraries. 1819.

Goodhugh, W. The English Gentleman's Library Manual. 1827.

Haslewood, J. Roxburghe Revels and Other Relative Papers. Ed. James Maidment, Edinburgh, 1837 (priv. ptd).

The Book Collector's Handbook. A Modern Library Companion. 1845.

Burton, J. H. The Book Hunter. Edinburgh, 1862, 1863; New York, 1863; Edinburgh, 1882 (with a memoir of the author by K. Burton); ed. J. H. Slater, [1908].

Power, J. A Handy Book about Books. 1870.

Lang, A. The Library. 1881.

—— Books and Bookmen. 1887; 1892.

Slater, J. H. The Library Manual: a Guide to the Formation of a Library and the Value of Rare and Standard Books. [1883]; 1892 (enlarged).

—— Round and About the Bookstalls. 1891.

—— Book Collecting: a Guide for Amateurs. 1892.

—— Early Editions; a Bibliographical Survey of Some Popular Modern Authors. 1894.

—— The Romance of Book Collecting. 1898.

—— How to Collect Books. 1905.

Wheatley, H. B. How to Form a Library. 1886.

Fitzgerald, P. The Book Fancier; or, the Romance of Book Collecting. 1886; 1887.

Ireland, A. The Book-Lover's Enchiridion. 1890.

Quaritch, B. Contributions towards a Dictionary of English Book Collectors. 13 pts, 1892–9.

Roberts, W. The Book Hunter in London. 1895.

—— Rare Books and their Prices. 1896.

Hazlitt, W. C. The Confessions of a Collector. 1897.

—— Memoirs of Book Collecting. 1904.

Fletcher, W. Y. English Book Collectors. 1902.

Jerrold, W. The Autolycus of the Bookstalls. 1902.

de Ricci, S. English Collectors of Books and MSS. Cambridge, 1930.

Carter, J. and Pollard, G. An Enquiry into the Nature of Certain Nineteenth-Century Pamphlets. 1934.

(12) PUBLIC LIBRARIES

(a) The British Museum

Acts and Votes of Parliament relating to the British Museum with the Statutes and Rules relating thereto. 1805; 1828.

Report from the Select Committee on the Condition, Management, and Affairs of the British Museum. [Minutes of Evidence and Appendix] 6 Aug. 1835. [The same, 14 July 1836.]

Edwards, Edward. A Letter to B. Hawes, being Strictures on the Minutes of Evidence taken before the Select Committee on the British Museum. 1836; 1839 (priv. ptd as Remarks on the Minutes).

—— Lives of the Founders of the British Museum with Notices of its Chief Augmentors. 1870.

Millard, J. A Letter containing a Plan for the Better Management of the British Museum. 1836 (priv. ptd).

Panizzi, Sir A. On the Collection of Printed Books at the British Museum, its Increase and Arrangement. [1845] (priv. ptd).

—— On the Supply of Printed Books from the Library to the Reading Room of the British Museum. 1846.

Nicolas, Sir N. H. Animadversions on the Library and Catalogues of the British Museum. 1846.

Report of the Commissioners appointed to inquire into the Constitution and Government of the British Museum. [Minutes of Evidence and Appendix.] 2 vols. 1850.

Cowtan, R. Memoirs of the British Museum. 1872.

—— A Biographical Sketch of Sir Anthony Panizzi. 1873.

Fagan, L. The Life of Sir A. Panizzi, late Principal Librarian of the British Museum. 2 vols. 1880.

Friggeri, E. La Vita, le Opere, e i Tempi di Antonio Panizzi. Belluno, 1897.

Barwick, G. F. The Reading Room of the British Museum. 1929.

Brooks, C. Antonio Panizzi, Scholar and Patriot. Manchester, 1931.

(b) Accounts of Libraries

Hartshorne, C. H. The Book Rarities of the University of Cambridge. 1829.

Edwards, E. Memoirs of Libraries; including a Handbook of Library Economy. 2 vols. 1859.
—— Libraries and Founders of Libraries. 1865.
Macray, W. D. Annals of the Bodleian Library. 1868; Oxford, 1890 (enlarged).
Axon, W. E. A. Handbook of the Public Libraries of Salford and Manchester. Manchester, 1877.
Mason, T. The Public and Private Libraries of Glasgow. Glasgow, 1885 (priv. ptd).
Greenwood, T. Greenwood's Library Year Book. 1897.
—— British Library Year Book. 1900.
Mathews, E. R. N. A Survey of the Bristol Public Libraries. Bristol, 1900.
Hunt, F. W. Libraries of Devonport, Naval, Military, and Civil. Devonport, 1901.
Cowell, P. Liverpool Public Libraries; a History of Fifty Years. Liverpool, 1903.
Rye, R. A. The Libraries of London; a Guide for Students. 1908; 1927 (enlarged).
Savage, E. A. The Story of Libraries and Book Collecting. 1908.

(c) The Free Library Movement

Brougham, H. P. (Baron Brougham). Practical Observations on the Education of the People. 1825.
Edwards, E. A Letter to the Earl of Ellesmere on the Desirability of a Better Provision of Public Libraries in the British Empire, and particularly in the Metropolis. 1848; 1849 (priv. ptd as Remarks on the Paucity of Libraries freely open to the Public).
—— Free Town Libraries, their Formation, Management, and History. 1869.
Report of the Select Committee on Public Libraries. 5 pts, 1849–52.
Hole, J. Essay on Literary and Scientific and Mechanics' Institutions. 1853.
Papworth, J. W. and W. Museums, Libraries and Picture Galleries. 1853.
Reed, Sir Charles. Why Not? A Plea for a Free Public Library and Museum in the City of London. 1855.
Feilde, M. H. On the Advantage of Free Public News Rooms and Lending Libraries. 1858.
De Peyster, J. F. The Moral and Intellectual Influence of Libraries upon Social Progress. 1866.
Phillips, J. H. An Essay on the Advantages of Free Libraries. 1867.
Mullins, J. D. Free Libraries and News Rooms. 1869.
Fowler, J. C. On Public Libraries. 1871.
Chambers, G. F. The Law relating to Public Libraries. 1879.
Hibbert, J. Notes on Free Public Libraries and Museums. Preston, 1881.

Southward, J. Technical Literature in Free Public Libraries. 1883.
Manners, Lady J. Some of the Advantages of easily Accessible Reading and Recreation Rooms and Free Libraries with Remarks on starting and maintaining them. [1885.]
Greenwood, T. Public Libraries: a History of the Movement and a Manual for the Organisation and Management of rate-supported Libraries. [1886]; 1894 (rev.).
—— Sunday Schools and Village Libraries. 1892.
—— Edward Edwards; the chief Pioneer of Municipal Public Libraries. 1902.
Verney, Sir E. Village Libraries. [1897.]
Ogle, J. J. The Free Library; its History and present Condition. 1897.
Mullen, B. H. Salford and the Inauguration of the Public Free Libraries Movement. Salford, 1899.
Morel, E. Essai sur le Développement des Bibliothèques publiques et de la Librairie dans les deux Mondes. 2 vols. Paris, 1908.
—— La Librairie publique. Paris, 1910.
Minto, J. A History of the Library Movement in Great Britain. 1932.

(13) Librarianship

Burton, M. O. and Vosburgh, M. E. A Bibliography of Librarianship. 1934.

(a) Books

Namur, P. Manuel du Bibliothécaire. Brussels, 1834.
Schmidt, J. A. F. Handbuch der Bibliothekwissenschaft, der Litteratur und Bücherkunde. Weimar, 1840.
Jewett, C. C. Smithsonian Report on the Construction of Catalogues of Libraries and their Publication by means of Separate Stereotyped Titles. Washington, 1853 (2nd edn).
de Morgan, A. On the Difficulty of the Correct Description of Books. [Companion to the British Almanack, 1853; ed. Henry Guppy, Library Ass. Record, June 1902; rptd Chicago, 1902.]
Schurtleff, N. B. A Decimal System for the Arrangement and Administration of Libraries. 1856.
Petzholdt, J. Katechismus der Bibliothekenlehre. Leipzig, 1856; Leipzig. 1871 (enlarged); (as Handbuch der Bibliothekslehre, ed. A. Graesel) Leipzig, 1902.
Guild, R. A. The Librarian's Manual. 1858.
Edwards, E. Memoirs of Libraries; together with a Handbook of Library Economy. 2 vols. 1859.
Elliot, J. A Practical Explanation of the Method of Issuing Library Books. 1870.

Dewey, M. A Classification and Subject Index for Cataloguing and Arranging the Books and Pamphlets of a Library. Amherst (Mass.), 1876 (anon.); Boston, 1885 (as Decimal Classification and Relative Index for Arranging, Cataloguing and Indexing Libraries); Boston, 1898; New York, 1919; New York, 1932 (rev. and enlarged).

Transactions and Proceedings of the [First International] Conference of Librarians held in London, 3–5 Oct. 1877. 1878.

Hallett, C. H. Parish Lending Libraries; how to manage and keep them up. 1880.

Wheatley, H. B. How to Catalogue a Library. 1889.

Hoyle, W. E. The Dewey Decimal Classification and the International Catalogue of Science. 1896.

Transactions and Proceedings of the Second International Library Conference held in London 13–16 July 1897. 1898.

Quinn, J. H. Manual of Library Cataloguing. 1899.

Brown, J. D. Manual of Library Economy. 1903.

—— Manual of Practical Bibliography. [1906.]

Roebuck, G. E. and Thorne, W. B. A Primer of Library Practice for Junior Assistants. 1904.

Thorne, W. B. The Library Assistants' Association; an Outline of its Development and Work. [1912.]

Dawe, G. Melvil Dewey, 1851–1931. New York, 1932.

Partridge, R. C. B. The History of the Legal Deposit of Books throughout the British Empire. 1938.

(b) Periodicals

Cannons, H. G. T. Bibliography of Library Economy: a Classified Index to the Professional Periodical Literature. 1910; Chicago, 1927.

Cole, G. W. Index to Bibliographical Papers. Chicago, [1933].

Transactions and Proceedings of the First [–8th] Annual Meeting of the Library Association of the United Kingdom, 1878 [–1885]. 7 vols. 1879–90.

Monthly Notes of the Library Association. 1880–3.

The Library Chronicle. A Journal of Librarianship and Bibliography. Vols. i–v, 1884–8. [Ed. by E. C. Thomas.]

The Library. Vol. i, 1889 onwards. [Quarterly; ed. by J. Y. Macalister.]

The Library Assistants' Association. First Annual Report. 1 July, 1896 [etc.].

The Library Assistant. No. 1, Jan. 1898 onwards.

The Library World. No. 1, July 1898 onwards.

The Library Association Record. No. 1, Jan 1899 onwards. [Monthly; ed. by Henry Guppy, Arundel Esdaile.]

The Library Association Year Book. 1899 onwards. H. G. P

V. EDUCATION

General Works: General Discussions and Suggestions; Historical Works (General Adult Education, Pamphlets, Illustrative Matter); Official Documents.

Educational Establishments: The Universities (General, Admission of Dissenters Individual Universities); Schools, Colleges and Institutes.

Other Aspects: Text Books; Memoirs; Education of Women and Girls; Manuscript Material.

A. GENERAL DISCUSSIONS AND SUGGESTIONS

Acland, A. H. D. and Llewellyn Smith, H Studies in Secondary Education. 1892. [See also Journ. of Education, April 1912.]

Adams, J. Herbartian Psychology Applied to Education. 1897.

—— Exposition and Illustration. 1909.

—— The Evolution of Educational Theory. 1912.

—— Modern Developments in Educational Practice. 1922.

Almond, H. H. Mr Lowe's Educational Theories examined from a Practical Point of View. Edinburgh, 1868.

Amos, A. Four Lectures on the Advantages of a Classical Education as an Auxiliary to a Commercial Education; with a Letter to Whewell. 1846.

Angus, J. Four Lectures on the Advantages of a Classical Education. 1846. [These were two quite distinct essays, written for two prizes offered by Henry Beaufoy. Angus won the first prize; James Pycroft, author of Oxford Memories, 1886, won the second.]

Armstrong, H. E. The Heuristic Method of Teaching or the Art of Making Children Think for Themselves. [In Special Reports on Educational Subjects, vol. ii, 1898.]

—— The Teaching of Scientific Method and Other Papers on Education. 1903.

Arnold, M. Popular Education of France, with Notices of that of Holland and Switzerland. (Report to Newcastle Commission.) 1861.

—— A French Eton, or Middle Class Education and the State. 1864. [See also S. T. Hawtrey, Reminiscences of a French Eton, 1867.]

Arnold, M. Schools and Universities on the Continent. (Report to Schools Inquiry Commission.) 1868.
—— Culture and Anarchy. 1869; ed. J. D. Wilson, Cambridge, 1932.
—— Friendship's Garland. 1871.
—— 'Ecce, convertimur ad Gentes.' Fortnightly Rev. xxv, 1879. [Middle class education.]
—— Higher Schools and Universities in Germany. (Report to Schools Inquiry Commission.) 1882.
—— Special Report on Elementary Education in Germany, Switzerland and France [Cd—4752]. 1886. [See also Quarterly Rev. cxxv, 1868.]
—— Reports on Elementary Schools, 1852–1882. 1889.
—— Thoughts on Education chosen from the Writings of Matthew Arnold. Ed. L. Huxley, 1912.
Arnold, T. Miscellaneous Works. 1845.
—— Sermons. 3 vols. 1850–3.
Arrowsmith, J. P. Art of Instructing the Infant Deaf and Dumb: with Method of Educating Deaf Mutes: by the Abbé de l'Épée. 1819. [See Quarterly Rev. xxvi, 1822, and Edinburgh Rev. cii, 1855.]
Austin, S. Thoughts on Education. 1839. [See Edinburgh Rev. lxx, 1839.]
Babington, T. Practical View of Christian Education in its Early Stages. 1814.
Bain, A. Education as a Science. 1879.
Baines, Sir E. Letters written to the Rt Hon. Lord John Russell. 1846.
—— The Late Struggle for the Freedom of Education. [1846.]
An Alarm to the Nation on the Measure of State Education. 1847.
—— On the Progress and Efficiency of Voluntary Education. 1848.
—— Strictures on the new Government Measure. 1853.
—— National Education. 1856.
—— Our past Educational Improvement. 1857.
—— Voluntary and Religious Education. 1857.
Bamford, R. W. Essays on the Discipline of Children, particularly as regards their Education. 1822.
Barrow, W. An Essay on Education particularly the Merits and Defects of the Discipline and Instruction in our Academies. 2 vols. 1802.
Barwell, L. M. Letters from Hofwyl on the Educational Institutions of De Fellenberg. 1842. [See Edinburgh Rev. lviii, 1833, and Fellenberg below, p. 109.]
Bell, A. An Experiment in Education made at Madras. 1797.
—— An Analysis of the Experiment. 1807 (3rd edn).

Bell, A. Elements of Tuition. Part iii. Ludus Literarius, the Classical and Grammar School. 1815.
—— The Wrongs of Children. 1819, etc.
—— Letters to Sinclair on the Infant School Society at Edinburgh, on the Scholastic Institutions of Scotland, and a Scheme of a Classical School. 1829.
Bernard, Sir T. Of the Education of the Poor. 1809.
—— The New School; an Attempt to illustrate its Principles, Details and Advantages. 1809.
—— The Barrington School. 1812.
Marsh, H. The National Religion the Foundation of National Education. A Sermon. 1811. [Rptd in The Pamphleteer, vol. i, 1813. See Quarterly Rev. vi, 1811 (R. Southey), and Edinburgh Rev. xix, 1811, xxi, 1813.]
—— A Vindication of Dr Bell's System of Education. 1811.
Hollingsworth, N. J. Address to the Public in Recommendation of the Madras System: with a Comparison. 1812.
Southey, R. Origin, Nature and Object of the New System of Education. 1812.
[See also J. Lancaster below, p. 111, T. C. Scott below, p. 113, and Quarterly Rev. vi, 1811, viii, 1812, xix, 1818, xxxix, 1829, and Edinburgh Rev. xix, 1811, xxi, 1813, xxxiii, 1820.]
Bentham, J. Church of Englandism examined: Strictures on the National Society's Schools. 1818. [See Quarterly Rev. xxi, 1819.]
—— Works. Ed. Sir J. Bowring, 11 vols. Edinburgh, 1843. [Papers relative to Codification and Public Instruction (in vol. iv); Chrestomathia (in vol. viii); Memoirs and Correspondence (in vols. x, xi). For J. P. Potter's reply to the Chrestomathic School proposal see p. 113 below.]
Biber, G. E. Christian Education. 1830.
Biggs, W. Lecture upon National Education. Leicester, 1849.
Binney, T. Education. 1847.
Boone, J. S. The Educational Economy of England. Pt i, 1838.
Booth, J. Education and Educational Institutions considered with reference to the Present State of Society. 1846.
—— Examination the Province of the State. 1847.
—— On the Influence of Examination as an Instrument of Education. 1854.
—— On the Female Education of the Industrial Classes. 1855.
—— Systematic Instruction and Periodical Examination. 1857. [See Quarterly Rev. cviii, 1860.]

Bouyer, R. G. A. Comparative View of the two New Systems of Education for the Infant Poor. 1811.

Bowen, H. C. Froebel and Education by Self-activity. 1893.

British and Foreign School Society. Manual of Primary Instruction pursued in the Model Schools. 1834. [See Edinburgh Rev. LVIII, 1833.]

Brougham, H. P. (Baron Brougham and Vaux). Letter to Sir Samuel Romilly. 1818 (9th edn). [The Pamphleteer, vol. XIII.]

—— Speech on the Education of the Poor, June 1820. [The Pamphleteer, vol. XVI; Hansard, vol. II, pp. 49–89. See Edinburgh Rev. XXXV, 1821.]

—— Practical Observations upon the Education of the People addressed to the Working Classes and their Employers. 1825. [See E. W. Grinfield, A Reply to Mr Brougham's 'Practical Observations,' Edinburgh Rev. XLII, 1825; XLV, 1826, and Quarterly Rev. XXXII, 1825.]

—— Inaugural Discourse on being installed Lord Rector of Glasgow University. 1825. [See Edinburgh Rev. XLII, 1825.]

—— Speech in the House of Lords on the Education of the People, 21 May 1835. [Hansard, vol. XXVII, cols. 1293–333.]

'M.A. Queen's College, Oxford.' A Letter to Henry Brougham on the best Method of restoring Decayed Grammar Schools. 1818. [The Pamphleteer, vol. XIII.]

Ireland, J. A Letter to Henry Brougham. 1819. [The Pamphleteer, vol. XIV.]

[See also Edinburgh Rev. XXX, 1818, XXXI, 1819, XXXII, 1819.]

Bruce, H. A. (Baron Aberdare). An Address delivered to the National Association for the Promotion of Social Science. 1866.

Butler, S. Letter to Henry Brougham on certain Clauses in the Education Bills. Shrewsbury, 1820.

Cambridge Essays on Education. Ed. A. C. Benson, Cambridge, 1917.

Cambridge Essays on Adult Education. Ed. R. St J. Parry, Cambridge, 1920.

Clarke, E. H. Sex in Education. Boston, 1875.

Clarke, J. Short Studies in Education in Scotland. 1904.

Classical Education. [See Edinburgh Rev. XXXV, 1821.]

Colquhoun, J. C. The System of National Education in Ireland. 1838. [See Quarterly Rev. LVI, 1836, and Edinburgh Rev. XLIII, 1825, CXXXV, 1872.]

Colquhoun, P. A New and Appropriate System of Education for the Labouring People. 1806.

Combe, G. Lectures on Popular Education. Edinburgh, 1833.

—— Principles of Physiology applied to Physical and Mental Education. 1835.

—— Remarks on National Education. Edinburgh, 1847 (3rd edn).

—— What should Secular Education Embrace? 1847.

—— Education: its Principles and Practice as developed by George Combe: collated and edited by W. Jolly. 1875.

—— Discussions on Education. 1893.

Conington, J. The Academical Study of Latin. 1855. [See Edinburgh Rev. CV, 1857.]

Coulton, G. G. Public Schools and Public Needs: Suggestions for Reform. 1901.

Creasy, C. H. Technical Education in Evening Schools. 1908.

Creighton, M. Thoughts on Education, Sermons and Speeches. 1902; 1906 (abridged).

Crosby Hall Lectures on Education. 1848.

Currie, J. Principles and Practice of Infant-School Education. 1857.

—— Principles and Practice of Common-School Education. [1878] (rev. edn).

Daly, R. Observations upon the State of Education in Ireland. Dublin, 1826.

—— On the Proposed System of Non-Scriptural Education of the Poor in Ireland. 1831. [In collaboration with R. J. McGhie.]

Dawes, R. The Schools, the State, the Church and the Congregation. 1847. [See Kay-Shuttleworth below, p. 111.]

—— Hints on Improved Self-paying National Education. 1847; 1861 (3rd edn). [See Edinburgh Rev. XCV, 1852.]

—— Observations on the Working of the Government Scheme of Education. 1847.

—— Suggestive Hints towards improved Secular Instruction, making it bear on Practical Life. [1849] (3rd edn).

—— Remarks occasioned by the Present Crusade against the Committee of Council on Education. 1850.

—— Schools and other Similar Institutions for the Industrial Classes. 1853.

—— Remarks on the Reorganisation of the Civil Service and its Bearing on Educational Progress. 1854.

—— Teaching of Common Things. 1854.

—— Address to the Huddersfield Mechanics' Institute. [1856.]

—— Mechanics' Institutes and Popular Education. 1856.

—— Manual of Educational Requirements for the Civil Service. With a preface on its Educational Value and Importance. 1856.

—— Effective Primary Instruction the Only Sure Road to Success in Secondary Instruction. 1857.

Garfit, A. Some Points of the Education Question, with Outline of the Progress of Popular Education. 1862.

Gill, J. Introductory Text Book to School Education, Method and School Management. 1863 (9th edn).

—— Systems of Education: a History and Criticism. 1876.

Grant, C. and Hodgson, N. The Case of Co-education. 1913.

Gray, J. Thoughts on Education with Particular Reference to the Grammar School System. 1836.

Gregory, R. Elementary Education: Some Account of its Rise and Progress in England. 1895; 1905 (with an Appendix).

Greig, A. Hints and Suggestions for the Instruction of the Convicts of Millbank: Lectures delivered to the Schoolmasters of that Prison. [1844.]

Grey, Mrs W. (Maria Georgina Shirreff). The Study of Education as a Science. Paper read at the British Association, Belfast. 1874.

Haldane, R. B. (Viscount Haldane). Education and Empire: Addresses on Certain Topics of the Day. 1902.

Hamilton, E. Letters on the Elementary Principles of Education. Bath, 1801.

—— Letters to the Daughter of a Nobleman on the Formation of Principles. 2 vols. 1806.

—— Hints addressed to Patrons and Directors of Schools to shew that the Benefits derived from the New Modes of teaching may be increased by a Partial Adoption of the Plan of Pestalozzi. 1815.

Hamilton, R. W. Institutions of Popular Education. Leeds, 1846.

Hare, J. C. Education, the Necessity of Mankind: Sermon on the Opening of Hurstpierpoint. 1851.

Harrison, F. Politics and Education: an Address. 1887.

Harrison, G. Some Remarks relative to the Present State of Education among the Quakers. 1802.

—— Education surest Means to diminish Crime. 1803.

Hawtrey, M. The Co-education of the Sexes. 1896.

Hawtrey, S. T. A Letter containing an Account of St Mark's School, Windsor. 1859 (3rd edn).

—— A Narrative Essay on a Liberal Education chiefly embodied in an Attempt to give a Liberal Education to Children of the Working Classes. 1868.

Hayward, F. H. The Reform of Moral and Biblical Instruction on the lines of Herbartianism. 1902.

Hayward, F. H. The Meaning of Education as interpreted by Herbart. 1907.

Heberden, W. On Education: a Dialogue after the Manner of Cicero. 1818.

Herbart, J. F. The Science of Education. Translated by H. M. Felkin and E. Felkin. 1892.

—— The Application of Psychology to the Science of Education. Tr. and ed. B. C. Mulliner. Preface by Dorothea Beale. 1898.

—— Letters and Lectures on Education. Translated by H. M. and E. Felkin. 1907. [See also J. Adams, p. 106 and F. H. Hayward above.]

Herford, W. H. The School: Essay towards Humane Education. 1889.

Hill, A. Hints on the Discipline appropriate to Schools. 1855. [See also Hazelwood School, below, p. 132 and G. B. Hill, Life of Sir Rowland Hill, 2 vols. 1880.]

Hill, F. National Education, its Present State and Prospects. 2 vols. 1836.

Hill, F. D. The Children of the State: the Training of Juvenile Paupers. 1868; 1889.

Hinton, J. H. Second Letter to Sir James Graham on the Educational Clauses of the Factories Bill. [1843.]

[Hoare, L.] Hints for the Improvement of Early Education and Nursery Discipline. 1822; 1853.

Hodgson, W. B. Exaggerated Estimates of Reading and Writing as Means of Education. 1868.

—— On the Report of the Commissioners of Public Schools. 1874. [See H. Mann below, p. 111.]

Hook, W. F. On the Means of rendering more Efficient the Education of the People. A Letter to the Bishop of St David's. 1846 (10 edns).

Hoppus, J. Thoughts on Academical Education and Degrees in Arts. 1837.

—— Crisis of Popular Education. 1847.

Horner, L. On the State of Education in Holland [with] Measures to extend and improve Education in Gt. Britain. 1838. [A trn of V. Cousin, De l'Instruction publique en Hollande, with addenda.]

Hull, J. The Philanthropic Repertory. 3 pts, 1835. [Pt I, Hints and Plans relating to Popular Education.]

Huxley, T. H. Science and Education. [Vol. III of Collected Essays, 1893–1894. See Quart. Rev. cxxiii, 1867.]

Infant Schools. Quart. Rev. xxxii, 1825.

Infant Education from Two to Six Years of Age. 1836.

Ingram, R. A. An Essay on Schools of Industry and Religious Instruction. [1808.]

J., W. (i.e. William Johnson, afterwards Cory). Hints for Eton Masters. 1898.

Jardine, G. Outlines of Philosophical Education illustrated. Glasgow, 1818; 1825.

Kay, D. Education and Educators. 1883.

Kay, J. Education of the Poor in England and Europe. 1846.

—— Social Conditions and Education of the People in England and Europe. 2 vols. 1850.

—— The Condition and Education of Poor Children in English and German Towns. 1853.

Kay-Shuttleworth, Sir J. P. The School in its Relation to the State, the Church and the Congregation. 1847. [See Dawes above, p. 108.]

—— Public Education from 1846–52. 1853.

—— Letter to Earl Granville on the Revised Code. 1861.
[See also Kay-Shuttleworth below, p. 139.]

Kingsley, C. Health and Education. 1874.

Lancaster, H. H. Essays and Reviews: Prefatory Notice by B. Jowett. Edinburgh, 1876.

Lancaster, J. Improvements in Education as it respects the Industrious Classes. 1803.

—— Improvement of the Education of the Poor. 1805 (3rd edn).

—— Outlines of a Plan for Educating ten thousand poor children. 1806. [See Edinburgh Rev. xi, 1807.]

—— An Account of the Progress of Joseph Lancaster's Plan. 1809.

—— The British System of Education. 1810.

—— Instructions for Forming a Society for the Education of the Labouring Classes. 1810.

—— Letter to John Foster, Chancellor of the Exchequer for Ireland. N.d.

—— Schools for All. 1812.

Trimmer, S. A Comparative View of the New Plan of Education promulgated by Mr. Joseph Lancaster. 1805. [See Edinburgh Rev. ix, 1806.]

'Eccletus.' A Few Notes relative to Joseph Lancaster's Plan. 1806.

Bowles, John. A Letter addressed to Samuel Whitbread, Esq., M.P., in consequence of the Unqualified Approbation of Mr Lancaster's System of Education, etc. 1807.

Fox, J. A Comparative View of the Plans of Dr Bell and Mr Lancaster. 1808.

—— Scriptural Education the Glory of England, a Defence of the Lancastrian Plan. 1810. [See Edinburgh Rev. xvii, 1810.]

'Liberal, Lady Letitia.' A defence of Joseph Lancaster and the Royal British System. Bath, 1810.

'Pythias.' A Vindication of Mr Lancaster's System. 1812.

[Collyer, N.] Common Sense versus Lancaster. 1812.

Salmon, D. The Practical Parts of Lancaster's 'Improvements' and Bell's Experiment. Cambridge, 1932. [See also A. Bell, above, p. 107 and Pestalozzi, Poole, below, pp. 112–3.]

[See also Edinburgh Rev. ix, 1806, xi, 1807, xvii, 1810, xix, 1811, xxi, 1813, xxxiii, 1820; and Quart. Rev. vi, 1811, viii, 1812, xix, 1818, xxxix, 1829.]

Latham, H. On Examinations as a Means of Selection. Cambridge, 1877. [See also Quart. Rev. cviii, 1860, and Edinburgh Rev. cxxxix, 1874.]

Laurie, S. S. Occasional Addresses on Educational Subjects. 1888.

—— Institutes of Education. Edinburgh, 1892.

—— Training of Teachers and Methods of Instruction. Cambridge, 1902.

L[ord?], E. Discursive Remarks on Modern Education. 1841.

Lowe, R. (Viscount Sherbrooke). Primary and Classical Education. Edinburgh, 1867.

—— Middle Class Education: Endowment or Free-trade? 1868.

Lyschinska, M. J. The Kindergarten Principle: Educational Value and Applications. 1880.

Maclaren, A. System of Physical Education. Oxford, 1869, 1895.

Macleod, N. The Home School. Hints on Home Education. Edinburgh, 1856.

Macnab, H. G. Analysis and Analogy recommended in Education. Paris, 1818. [See also Robert Owen, below, p. 112.]

Magnus, L. et al. National Education: Essays towards a Constructive Policy. 1901.

Magnus, Sir P. Industrial Education. 1888.

—— Educational Aims and Efforts. 1910.

Mann, Horace. Report of an Educational Tour in Germany and Parts of Great Britain and Ireland. Preface by W. B. Hodgson. 1846.

Martineau, H. How to Observe. 1838.

—— Household Education. 1849; 1861; 1867; 1876.

Martineau, J. Essays, Reviews and Addresses. 4 vols. 1890–1.

Marvin, F. S. The Nation at School. Oxford, 1933.

Mason, C. M. S. Home Education. 1886; 1905 (4th edn).

—— Parents and Children. 1897.

—— School Education. 1905.

—— An Essay towards a Philosophy of Education: a Liberal Education for All. [1919]; 1931.

Mason, John. A History of Scottish Experiments in Rural Education. Scottish Council for Research in Education, 1935.

Maurice, J. F. D. The Educational Magazine. 1835, etc.

—— Has the Church or State Power to educate the Nation? 1839.

—— The Christian Socialist. 1851, etc.

—— National Education: A Sermon at St. Mark's College, Chelsea. 1853.

—— The Workman and the Franchise; Chapters from English history on the Representation and Education of the People. 1866.

—— A Few Words on Secular and Denominational Education. 1870.

Maxse, F. A. The Education of the Agricultural Poor. 1868.

—— National Education and its Opponents. 1877.

Mayo, C. Observations on the Establishment and Direction of Infant Schools. 1826.

Mayo, E. Lessons on Objects to Children in the Pestalozzian School at Cheam. 1831 (2nd edn); 1859 (16th edn).

McCombie, W. On Education in its Constituents and Issues. Aberdeen, 1857.

McCrie, J. Autopaedia: Instructions on Personal Education. 1871 (2nd edn).

'A Member of the Church of England.' Thoughts on Popular Education. 1825. [See Edinburgh Rev. XLIII, 1825.]

Mill, J. Education. Ency. Brit. Supplement, 1824.

—— State of the Nation. Westminster Rev. Oct. 1826.

James and John Stuart Mill on Education. Ed. F. A. Cavenagh, Cambridge, 1931.

Mill, J. S. Ethology. [In System of Logic, bk vi, ch. 5, 1843.]

—— Dissertations and Discussions. 4 vols. 1859–75.

—— Inaugural Address, St Andrews University. 1867.

Morley, J., Viscount. The Struggle for National Education. 1873.

—— On the Study of Literature: Address to Students of the University Extension. 1887.

The Museum and English Journal of Education. 5 vols. 1864–9. [Including The Pupil-Teacher.]

Myers, T. Remarks on a Course of Education. 1818.

Newman, J. H. [See below, p. 122.]

Newnham, W. Principles of Physical, Intellectual, Moral and Religious Education. 2 vols. 1827.

Norris, J. P. The Education of our People, Weak Points and Strength. [1869.]

Nunn, T. P. Education, Data and First Principles. 1920; 1930 (rev. edn).

'Outis' (i.e. J. L. Tupper). Hiatus, the Void in Modern Education. 1869.

Owen, Sir H. Letter to the Welsh People. 1843.

Owen, R. A New View of Society, or Essays on the Formation of Human Character. 1813. [See Edinburgh Rev. XXXII, 1819.]

Macnab, H. G. The New Views of Mr Owen impartially examined. 1819. [Bell, Lancaster, Owen.]

Owen, R. D. Outlines of the New System of Education at New Lanark. Glasgow, 1824.

Parsons, B. Education the Birthright of every Human Being. 1845.

Payne, J. The True Foundation of Science Teaching. 1873.

—— The Science and Art of Education. 1874.

—— Pestalozzi: Influence on Elementary Education. 1875.

—— Fröbel and the Kindergarten. 1876.

—— A Visit to German Schools. 1876.

—— Lectures on the Science and Art of Education. 1880.

——Works. Ed. J. F. Payne, 2 vols. 1883.

Pestalozzi, J. H. Address to the British Public to aid a Plan of Preparing Schoolmasters for the People. Yverdun, 1817.

—— Letters on Early Education addressed to J. P. Greaves; with a Memoir of Pestalozzi. 1827; 1850; 1851.

'An Irish Traveller' [C. E. H. Orpen?]. A Biographical Sketch of the Struggles of Pestalozzi to establish his System: compiled and translated from his own Works. Dublin, 1815.

—— A Sketch of Pestalozzi's Intuitive System of Calculation. Dublin, 1815.

—— The Relations and Forms according to Pestalozzi. Dublin, 1817 (anon.).

Krüsi, H. Coup d'Œil on the General Means of Education. Yverdun, 1818.

Pullen, P. H. The Mother's Book exemplifying Pestalozzi's Plan of Awakening the Understanding of Children. 1820.

de Prati, J. The Principles and Practice of Education Illustrative of the Pestalozzian and Chrestomathic Systems. 1829.

Biber, G. E. Pestalozzi and his Plan. 1831.

What is Pestalozzianism? Quart. Educational Mag. II, 1849.

Mayo, C. Pestalozzi and his Principles. 1873.

Russell, J. The Student's Pestalozzi. 1888.

—— Pestalozzi, his Life and Work. 1890; 1900; 1903. [Trn of R. de Guimps, Histoire de Pestalozzi, 1874.]

Hayward, F. H. The Educational Ideas of Pestalozzi. 1904.

Green, J. A. Educational Ideas of Pestalozzi. 1905.

—— Pestalozzi's Educational Writings. 1912.

Brown, S. A Comparative View of the Systems of Pestalozzi and Lancaster. 1925.

[See also R. Dunning, E. Hamilton, E. Mayo, J. Payne above, pp. 110–2 and Edinburgh Rev. XLVII, 1828.]

The Philanthropist. Ed. W. Allen, I, 1811. [Articles on Lancaster, on popular education, etc.]

Phillpots, H. Charge to the Clergy of Exeter, Triennial Visitation. 1839. [The State and religious education.]

Pillans, J. Principles of Elementary Teaching, chiefly in reference to the Parochial Schools of Scotland. Edinburgh, 1828.

—— Three Lectures. 1836.

—— The Rationale of Discipline as exemplified in the High School. Edinburgh, 1852.

—— Contributions to the Cause of Education. 1856.

—— Educational Papers read before the Education Department of the Social Science Association. Edinburgh, 1862. [See also Quart. Rev. XXXIX, 1289.]

Place, F. Improvement of the Working People. 1004.

Playfair, L. Primary Education, Technical Education. Edinburgh, 1870.

Pole, T. Observations on Infant Schools. Bristol, 1823. [See Edinburgh Rev. XXXVIII, 1823.]

Poole, J. The Village School Improved or the New System practically explained. Oxford, 1813 (2nd edn). [Bell and Lancaster.]

Porter, G. R. The Influence of Education shown by Facts in the Criminal Tables for 1845 and 1846. [British Association Report, Statistical Section, Oxford meeting, 1847.]

Potter, J. P. Letter to John Hughes on the System of Education proposed by the Popular Parties, 1828. [In The Pamphleteer, vol. XXIX, 1828. Reply to the Benthamite Chrestomathic School proposal.]

Powell, B. State Education. 1849.

Pycroft, J. Four Lectures on Classical Education as auxiliary to Commercial. 1847.

Quain, R. On Some Defects in General Education; the Hunterian Oration, 1869. 1870.

Quart. Rev. VI, 1811, VIII, 1812, XIX, 1818, XXXII, 1825, XXXIX, 1829, LXI, 1838, LXXVIII, 1846, CX, 1861, CXI, 1862, CXXVIII, 1870, CXXXI, 1871, CXXXV, 1873, CXLVII,

1879, CLXXII, 1891, CLXXXV, 1897 (Education Acts reviewed), CXCIII, 1901. [Chiefly on elementary education.]

Quick, R. H. Essays on Educational Reformers. 1868; 1902.

Raymont, T. The Principles of Education. 1904; 1907; 1919.

—— Education. 1931.

—— A History of the Education of Young Children. 1937.

Religious Instruction in Board Schools. Edinburgh Rev. CLXXX, 1894.

Remarks on Popular Education in reference to the New Code: by One of Practical Experience. Bradford, 1861. [See Quart. Rev. CXI, 1862.]

Robertson, C. Objections to a System of Free Education for the People. N.d.

Rooper, T. G. A Pot of Green Feathers. School and Home Life. 1896.

—— Selected Writings. Ed. R. G. Tatton, 1907.

Ruskin, J. ['Ruskin's references to education are as scattered as voluminous'—too voluminous to be stated here. They will be found arranged under twelve topics in General Index, vol. XXXIX, s.v. 'Education' of Complete Works of John Ruskin, ed. Sir E. T. Cook and A. Wedderburn, 39 vols. 1903–12. See also W. Jolly, Ruskin on Education, 1894.]

Russell, Lord J, (later Earl Russell). National Education: Speech in House of Commons. 4 April 1853. [Another, 6 March 1856.]

Sadler, Sir M. E. Continuation Schools in England and elsewhere: their Place in an Industrial and Commercial State. With a Bibliography. Manchester, 1907.

Scott, R. P. What is Secondary Education? 1899.

Scott, T. C. Address [on] educating the Infant Poor on the Plan of Dr. Bell. 1813.

Secondary Education in Scotland. Edinburgh Rev. CXLIII, 1876.

Conferences on Secondary Education. Edinburgh Rev. CLXXXV, 1897.

Senior, N. W. Suggestions on Popular Education. 1861.

Sewell, E. M. Principles of Education drawn from Nature and Revelation. 2 vols. 1865.

Sewell, W. An Essay on the Cultivation of the Intellect by the Study of the Dead Languages. 1830.

—— A Speech at the Meeting of Friends of National Education at Willis's Rooms, Feb. 7th. 1850.

Shaw, W. Suggestions respecting National Education. Bath, 1801.

Shepherd, W., Joyce, J. and Carpenter, L. Systematic Education, 1815; 1822 (3rd edn).

Sheppard, J. G. Remarks on the Rev. F. Temple's Scheme for the Extension of Middle-class Education. 1857.

Shirreff, E. A. and Grey, M. G. Thoughts on Self-Culture. 2 vols. 1850.

Simons, T. Moral Education the One Thing Needful. 1802.

—— A Sequel to Moral Education. 1805. [Undenominationalism.]

Simpson, J. Necessity of Popular Education as a National Object. Edinburgh, 1834.

—— The Philosophy of Education. Edinburgh, 1836 (2nd edn).

—— The Normal School as it ought to be. Edinburgh, 1850.

Skeats, H. S. Results of Government Education. 1857; 1858.

—— Popular Education in England. 1862.

Skinner, S. Educational Essays: Practical Observations on Instruction, Discipline, Physical Training. 1844.

Smith, Sydney. Works. 2 vols. 1859. [See especially his contributions to Edinburgh Rev.]

Soulsby, L. H. M. Some Thoughts for Mothers and Teachers. 1899.

—— Stray Thoughts on Character. 1900.

Spencer, H. Education, Intellectual, Moral and Physical. 1861, etc.; ed. F. A. Cavenagh, Cambridge, 1932.

Compayré, G. H. Spencer et l'Éducation Scientifique. Paris, [1901].

Sproat, G. M. Education of the Rural Poor. 1870.

Stanley, E. L. (Baron Stanley). Three Letters on Oxford University Reform. 1876.

—— Our National Education. 1890.

Stow, D. The Training System adopted in the Model Schools of the Glasgow Educational Society. Glasgow, 1836; 1853 (9th edn); 1854; 1859. [All in turn 'enlarged.']

—— National Education: the duty of England. Teaching or Training? 1847.

Tate, T. The Philosophy of Education. 1860 (3rd edn).

[Taylor, I.] Home Education. 1838 (2nd edn).

Temple, F. National Education. [In Oxford Essays contributed by Members of the University, 1856.]

—— On Apprenticeship and School. 1858.

—— The Education of the World. [In Essays and Reviews, 1860. See Quart. Rev. CIX, 1861.]

—— Sermons preached in Rugby School Chapel in 1858, 1859, 1860. 3 sers. 1861–71.

—— National Schools. 1870.

—— The True Ideal of the Educator. 1898. [See also Sheppard above.]

Thompson, D'A. W. Day-dreams of a Schoolmaster. Edinburgh, 1864.

—— Wayside Thoughts: Desultory Essays on Education. 1868.

Thomson, A. F. The English School-Room: Thoughts on Private Tuition. 1865.

Thoughts on Advancement of Academical Education in England. 1826. [See Edinburgh Rev. XLIII, 1825. 'London University.']

Thoughts on Education of the Poor and National Schools. [The Pamphleteer, vol. XV, 1820.]

Thring, E. Education and School. 1864.

—— Theory and Practice of Teaching. 1883.

—— Sermons preached at Uppingham School. 2 vols. 1886.

—— Addresses. 1887.

Todhunter, I. The Conflict of Studies and other Essays connected with Education. 1873.

Trimmer, S. The Guardian of Education, a Periodical Work. 5 vols. 1802–6.

—— An Essay on Christian Education. 1812. [See also under Lancaster above, p. 111, A Comparative View.]

Tuckwell, W. Practical Remarks on Teaching Physical Science in Schools. 1865.

Ware, F. Educational Reform the Task of the Board of Education. 1900.

—— Educational Foundations of Trade and Industry. 1901.

Watts, J. On National Education considered as a Question of Political and Financial Economy. 1850.

Welton, J. The Logical Bases of Education. 1899.

—— Educational Theory [s.v. 'Education']. Ency. Brit. 11th edn, vol. VIII, 1910.

—— The Psychology of Education. 1911.

—— What do we mean by Education? 1915.

Weyland, J. A Letter to a Country Gentleman on the Education of the Lower Orders. 1808.

Whately, R. Address to Clergy on Changes in Irish National Education. Dublin, 1853 (2nd edn).

Whewell, W. Thoughts on the Study of Mathematics. Cambridge, 1835. [See Edinburgh Rev. LXII, 1836, LXIII, 1836.]

Wilderspin, S. On the Importance of Educating the Infant Poor. 1824 (2nd edn, 'with considerable additions').

—— Early Discipline illustrated. 1840 (3rd edn).

—— A System for the Education of the Young. 1840. [See Quart. Rev. XXXII, 1825.]

Williamson, J. The Diffusion of Knowledge amongst the Middle Classes. 1835. [See Edinburgh Rev. LXII, 1835.]

Willm, J. The Education of the People. Preliminary Dissertation by J. P. Nicholl. Glasgow, 1847.

Wilson, J. M. Lecture on Mathematical Teaching. Rugby, 1870.

—— Morality in Public Schools. 1882. [Rptd from Journ. of Education, Nov. 1881.]

—— Voluntary Schools and State Education. Manchester, 1894.

—— Education and Popular Control. 1898.

—— The Elementary Education Problem. Manchester, [1898].

—— Education and Crime: a Sermon. 1905.

—— The Day School and Religious Education: a Sermon. 1907.

Wilson, W. System of Infants' Education. 2 vols. 1825 (2nd edn).

—— A Manual of Instruction for Infants' Schools. 1829.

—— Advice to Instructors of Infant Schools. N.d.

[See Quart. Rev. xxxii, 1825.]

Winch, W. H. Educational Problems. 1900.

Wood, J. Account of the Edinburgh Sessional School: With Strictures on Education in General. Edinburgh, 1828.

Woodard, N. A Plea for the Middle Classes. 1848.

Woods, A. Educational Experiments in England. [1920.]

Woods, A. et al. Advance in Co-education. 1919.

Wordsworth, C. Discussions on Public Education. 1844.

—— Diary in France mainly concerning Education and the Church. 1845.

Wordsworth, W. The Excursion. [Bks 8 and 9; with Wordsworth's note in the 1843 edn.]

—— The Prelude [1799–1805]. 1850.

Fotheringham, J. Wordsworth's 'Prelude' as a Study in Education. 1899.

Wyse, Sir T. Education reform, or the Necessity of a National System. Vol. i (all pbd), 1836.

Foster, B. F. Education Reform: a Review of Wyse. New York, 1837.

——Notes on Education Reform in Ireland from the Unpublished Memoirs of Sir Thomas Wyse. Ed. W. M. Wyse, Waterford, 1901.

Yates, J. Thoughts on the Advancement of Academical Education in England. 1826. [See also under Yates, p. 125 below.]

B. HISTORICAL WORKS

(1) GENERAL WORKS

Abbott, A. Education for Industry and Commerce in England. 1933.

Adams, F. History of the Elementary School Contest in England. 1882.

Adamson, J. W. English Education, 1789–1902. Cambridge, 1930.

—— Education. CHEL. vol. xiv, 1916.

Archer, R. L. Secondary Education in the Nineteenth Century. Cambridge, 1921. [Bibliographies.]

Balfour, G. The Educational Systems of Great Britain and Ireland. 1903 (2nd edn).

Barnes, A. S. The Catholic Schools of England. 1926.

Bartley, G. C. T. The Schools for the People: History, Development, etc. 1871.

Beatty, H. M. A Brief History of Education. 1922.

Binns, H. B. et al. A Century of Education, being the Centenary History of the British and Foreign School Society. 1908.

Birchenough, C. History of Elementary Education in England and Wales from 1800. 1914.

Browning, O. Introduction to the History of Educational Theories. 1881; 1905 (6th edn).

—— Aspects of Education: a Study of the History of Pedagogy. Industrial Education Ass. New York, 1887–8.

Christian, G. A. English Education from Within. 1922.

Collet, C. D. History of the Taxes on Knowledge. 2 vols. 1899.

Corcoran, T. State Policy in Irish Education, 1536–1816. Dublin, 1916.

—— Some Lists of Catholic Lay Teachers and their Illegal Schools in the later Penal Times. Dublin, 1932.

Coulton, G. G. A Victorian Schoolmaster, Henry Hart of Sedbergh. 1923.

Craik, Sir H. The State in its Relation to Education. 1883; 1914.

Darton, F. J. H. Bell and the Dragon. Fortnightly Rev. May 1909.

De Montmorency, J. E. G. Progress in Education in England from Early Times. 1904.

Duppa, B. F. Analysis of the State of Education in Manchester. [In Central Society of Education: First Publication, 1837.]

Dybelius, W. England. Tr. Eng. 1930.

Findlay, J. J. The Children of England. 1923.

Gill, J. Systems of Education, a History and Criticism. 1876.

Grant, J. History of the Burgh Schools of Scotland. 1876.

Gregory, R. Elementary Education: its Rise and Progress in England. 1895; 1905 (with appendix).

Halévy, É. La Formation du Radicalisme Philosophique. 3 vols. Paris, 1901–4; tr. Eng. 1928.

Hill, A. Essays upon Educational Subjects read at the Conference. 1857.

Hodgson, G. E. Rationalist English Educators. 1912.
—— A Study in Illumination. 1914. [Wordsworth.]
Holman, H. English National Education. Rise of the Public Elementary Schools. 1898.
Jessop, J. C. Education in Angus, an Historical Survey from Original and Contemporary Sources. 1931. [To 1872.]
Jones, H. B. The Royal Institution: its Founder and First Professors. 1871.
Jourdan, B. A. Essay on Improvements in Education during the 18th and 19th Centuries. 1872.
Kay-Shuttleworth, Sir J. P. Public Education as affected by the Committee of Council from 1846 to 1852: Suggestions as to Future Policy. 1853.
—— Four Periods of Public Education as reviewed in 1832, 1839, 1846, 1862. 1862.
—— Memorandum on the Present State of the Question of Popular Education. 1868. [See also Kay-Shuttleworth above, p. 111.]
Kekewich, Sir G. The Education Department and After. 1920.
Kerr, J. Scottish Education, School and University from Early Times to 1908. 1910.
Leclerc, M. L'Éducation des Classes moyennes et dirigeantes en Angleterre. Paris, 1894.
Leitch, J. Practical Educationists and their Systems of Teaching. Glasgow, 1876.
Maltby, S. E. Manchester and the Movement for National Education, 1800–70. 1918.
Mann, H. Education in Great Britain. 1854.
Martineau, J. Essays and Addresses. 4 vols. 1890. [Vol. i, Thomas Arnold; vol. iv, Academical Education.]
Marvin, F. S. [See above, p. 111.]
Maynooth College. Report of the Commissioners, Irish Education Inquiry. [See Quart. Rev. xxxvii, 1828.]
The Case of Maynooth College; History of the First Establishment, Account of the System and a Review. Dublin, 1836. [See also p. 118 below.]
McCormick, P. J. Survey of the Development of Educational Theory and Practice in Ancient, Mediaeval and Modern Times. 1915.
Minto, J. History of the Public Library Movement. 1932.
Moore, H. K. An Unwritten Chapter in the History of Education, 1811–31. 1904. [See also Quart. Rev. cxxxii, 1872.]
Pestalozzi, J. H.
Pestalozziana. Blackwood's Mag. July 1849. [Experiences at Yverdun of an English boy removed from Westminster School.]
Pestalozzi: the Influence of his Principles and Practice. 1875.

Hayward, F. H. Three Historical Educators: Pestalozzi, Froebel, Herbart. 1905.
Holman, H. Pestalozzi: his Life and Work. 1908.
Green, J. A. Life and Work of Pestalozzi. 1913.
Pons, J. Éducation en Angleterre entre 1750 et 1800. Paris, 1919. [With a bibliography. Influence of Rousseau.]
Porter, G. R. Statistical Enquiries into the Means of providing Education for Children [of the Working Classes]. [In Central Society of Education: Second Publication, 1838.]
Prideaux, E. B. R. A Survey of Elementary English Education. 1915.
Reyntiens, N. L'Enseignement primaire et professionnel en Angleterre et en Irlande. Paris, 1864.
Rich, R. W. The Training of Teachers during the Nineteenth Century. Cambridge, 1933. [Bibliographies.]
Roberts, R. D. Education in the Nineteenth Century. Cambridge, 1901.
Robson, A. H. The Education of Children engaged in Industry in England, 1833–76. 1931.
Roby, H. J. The Present State of the Schools: the Law of Charities as affecting Endowed Schools. [Chs. ii, iv of the Endowed Schools Report, 1867.] [See also Memoirs of Archbishop Temple, by Seven Friends, 1906.]
Rusk, R. R. History of Infant Education. 1933.
Sadler, Sir M. E. Continuation Schools in England and elsewhere. 1907. [With bibliography.]
—— Syllabus of a Course on the History of Education in England, 1800–1911. [In Outlines of an Education Course, Manchester, 1911.]
—— Progress in Education in England, 1823–1923. [In Birkbeck College Centenary Lectures, 1924.]
Salmon, D. and Hindshaw, W. Infant Schools: their History and Theory. 1904.
Selby-Bigge, Sir L. A. The Board of Education. [1927.]
Sexton, A. H. The First Technical College: a Sketch of the History of 'The Andersonian.' 1894.
Shuttleworth, U. J., Baron. Pioneering Work in Education. Postscript by D. H. S. Cranage. 1930. [The Gilchrist Trust.]
Smith, Frank. History of Elementary Education, 1760–1902. 1931. [Fully documented.]
[Stow, D.] Third Report of the Glasgow Educational Society's Normal Seminary, 1836. Glasgow, 1837.
Thompson, J. Forty four Years of the Education Question, 1870–1914. 1914.

Trimmer, S. The Oeconomy of Charity. 2 vols. 1801. [Greatly enlarged from the edn of 1786.]

Turner, D. M. History of Science Teaching in England. 1927.

University Extension.
 Mackinder, H. J. and Sadler, Sir M. E. University Extension, Past, Present and Future. 1891.
 Roberts, R. D. Eighteen Years of University Extension. Cambridge, 1891. [See Quart. Rev. CLXXII, 1891.]
 Draper, W. H. University Extension, a Survey of 50 years, 1873–1923. Cambridge, 1923.

Wellard, J. H. State of Reading among the Working Classes of England during the First Half of the Nineteenth Century. Library Quart. v, 1935.

Wood, Sir H. T. History of the Royal Society of Arts. 1913.

Wordsworth, E. Glimpses of the Past. Oxford, [1912].

The Working Men's College.
 Maurice, J. F. D. Learning and Working: Six Lectures. 1854.
 Litchfield, R. B. et al. The Working Men's College Magazine. Nos. 1–36, 1859–61; vols. I–III, 1859–62. [Short history of the College.]
 Furnivall, F. J. Early History of the Working Men's College. 1891.
 Davies, J. L. The Working Men's College, 1854–1904. 1904.
 Trevelyan, G. M. The Working Men's College, 1854–1904. 1904.

Wyse, Sir T. Education in the United Kingdom, its Progress and Prospects. [In Central Society of Education: First Publication, 1837.]

(2) ADULT EDUCATION

Duppa, B. F. A Manual for Mechanics' Institutes. 1839. [See also Mechanics' Institutes below, p. 134.]

Hodgen, M. Workers' Education in England and the United States. 1925.

Hole, J. History and Management of Literary, Scientific and Mechanics' Institutes. 1853.

Hudson, J. W. History of Adult Education. 1851.

Journal of Adult Education. Ed. J. D. Wilson and A. E. Heath, 1926–

Mansbridge, A. An Adventure in Working-Class Education. The W.E.A. 1903–1915. 1920.

Martin, G. C. The Adult School Movement. (National Adult School Movement.) 1924.

Parry, R. St J. et al. Cambridge Essays on Adult Education. Cambridge, 1920.

Peers, R. Adult Education in Practice. 1934.

Pole, T. History of the Origin and Progress of Adult Schools. 1816 (2nd edn).

Rowntree, J. W. and Binns, H. B. A History of the Adult School Movement. 1903.

Smith, G. C. M. The Story of the People's College, Sheffield. Sheffield, 1912.

Winks, J. F. History of Adult Schools. [Gainsborough?], 1821.

Yeaxlee, B. A. Lifelong Education. 1929. [See also Edinburgh Rev. XLII, 1825, XLVII, 1828, LXII, 1835; Quart. Rev. XXXIV, 1826, CXIII, 1863; and under University Extension and Working Men's College above.]

(3) PAMPHLETS

[Boade, W.] Observations on the Present System of Education: with some Hints for its Improvement. 1832; 1837 (4th edn); 1839 (6th edn).

Brief Hints in Aid of a Practical Solution of the Educational Problem. Glasgow, 1860.

Clements, J. The Farmer's Case with regard to Education, etc. 1851.

Collins, W. L. The Education Question. Revision a Necessity: a Voice from the Unassisted Schools. 1862.

Colquhoun, J. C. On the Measures to be now taken to secure a Good National Education. 1853.

—— Memorandum on a Bill to make further Provision for Education in Scotland. 1854.

—— Remarks on Pakington's Education Bill. 1855.

Davies, G. History and Mystery of the Scarborough Lancasterian Schools. Scarborough, 1840.

—— Sequel to the History [etc.]. 2 pts, 1842–3.

Denison, G. A. The Church of England and the Committee of Council on Education. 1849 (2nd edn).

Edwards, F. W. Technical Education, its Rise and Progress, including Recommendations to the Royal Commission. 1885. [See Quart. Rev. CLXV, 1887.]

—— Industrial Education. 1888.

—— Commercial Education, including a Review of Commercial Schools on the Continent. 1889.

The Education Controversy. 'Who should throw stones?' Dublin, 1860.

Educational Grants. 1849.

Fox, W. J. On the Educational Clauses in the Bill for the Education of Children in Factory Districts. 1843 (2nd edn). [Sir James Graham's bill.]

Fraser, J. The Revised Code of the Committee of Council on Education: its Principles, Tendencies and Details. 1861.

Fraser, J. National Education: a Sermon. 1868.

Fraser, W. National Education: Reasons for the Rejection in Britain of the Irish System: a Brief Exposition for Christian Educationists. 1861 (2nd edn). [See Quart. Rev. cxxxii, 1872.]

Garfit, A. Some Points of the Education Question, with Outline of the Progress of Popular Education. 1862.

—— The Conscience Clause and the Extension of Education in the Neglected Districts practically considered. 1868.

Grant, A. R. Remarks on the Revised Code. Cambridge, 1862.

Grote, J. A Few Words on the New Educational Code and the Report of the Education Commissioners. 1862.

Holland, H. W. Proposed National Arrangements for Primary Education. 1870 (3rd edn).

Inglis, Sir R. H. The Parochial Schools of Scotland: a Speech in the House of Commons, 4 June 1851.

L[ord?], E. Discursive Remarks on Modern Education. 1841.

Lowe, Robert. The Revised Code. Speech in the House of Commons, 13 February 1862. [See Quart. Rev. cxi, 1862.]

Manchester and Salford Education Bill, 1851–2.

Birley, W. A Letter to Archdeacon Denison in Reply to his Strictures. 1851.

Close, F. National Education. The Secular System, the Manchester Bill and the Government Scheme considered. 1852.

Denison, G. A. Supplement to Appendix B of a Reply to the Promoters of the Manchester and Salford Education Scheme. 1852.

Facts and Considerations on the Manchester and Salford Education Bill. 1853.

Hinton, J. H. A Review of the Evidence in relation to the State of Education in Manchester and Salford. 1852.

—— A Few Plain Words on the two Education Bills. 1852.

—— Case of the Manchester Educationists: State of Education in Manchester and Salford. 2 pts, 1852–4.

Newlands, H. Socinianism the Inevitable Result of the Manchester and Salford Scheme of National Education. 1851.

Richson, C. Sketch of some of the Causes which induced the Abandonment of the Voluntary System. 1851.

—— Educational Facts and Statistics, Evidence before the House of Commons. 1852.

[See also Parliamentary Papers, below, p. 120.]

Maynooth College.

The Crown and the Country: a Protest against Uncontrolled Endowment. 1845.

Brown, John. Some Considerations in favour of the Maynooth Grant. 1845.

Perceval, J. Letter on the Grant to Maynooth. 1845.

[Black, Adam.] Maynooth: in Three Letters. 1852.

[See also Quart. Rev. lxxvi, 1845, and Edinburgh Rev. cii, 1855.]

Melville, D. The Conscience Clause; Meaning, Authority, Use. 1865.

Menet, J. Letter on Mr. Walter's Motion. 1865. [See J. Walter below.]

Miller, J. C. Which? or Neither? An Examination of the Education Bills of Lord John Russell and Sir J. S. Pakington. 1855.

'One of Practical Experience.' Remarks on Popular Education in Reference to the New Code. Bradford, 1861.

Randolph, E. J. The Good Properties of the Revised Code. 1862.

Rigg, J. H. History and Present Position of Primary Education in England and in connexion with Wesleyan Methodism. [1870.]

—— Denominational and National Education. Reprinted from London Quarterly Rev. Jan. 1870. [1870].

Skeats, H. S. Results of Government Education. Reprinted from The Christian Spectator, April 1858. [1858].

Vaughan, C. J. The Revised Code dis-passionately considered. Cambridge, 1861.

Vaughan, H. Popular Education in England: the Conscience Clause, the Rating Clause and the Secular Current. 1868.

Walter, J. Correspondence relative to the Resolutions on the Educational Grant to be moved, May 5. 1863. [The unaided schools.]

Wyse, Sir T. Speech at the Opening of the New Mechanics' Institution, Liverpool. Liverpool, [1837].

(4) ILLUSTRATIVE MATTER

Baines, E. The Social, Educational and Religious State of the Manufacturing Districts. 1843.

Browning, E. B. The Cry of the Children. Blackwood's Mag. liv, 1843.

—— A Song for the Ragged Schools of London. 1854.

—— Aurora Leigh. 1857. [Feminine education.]

[Benson, A. C.] Memoirs of Arthur Hamilton. By Christopher Carr. 1886.

—— The Upton Letters. By T. B. 1905.

Besant, Sir W. All Sorts and Conditions of Men. 3 vols. 1882.

Brandl, A. Zwischen Inn und Themse. Berlin, 1936. [Teaching of German.]

[Brontë, C.] Jane Eyre. 1847.

Brown, John. A Memoir of Robert Blincoe, an Orphan Boy sent to endure the Horrors of a Cotton-mill. Manchester, 1832.

Central Society of Education: Publications. 3 vols. (all pbd), 1837–9.

Church, R. W. The Oxford Movement, 1833–1845. 1891.

Clarke, J. E. Plain Papers on the Social Economy of the People. 4 pts, 1858–60.

Cooper's Journal or Unfettered Thinker. Jan.–Oct. 1850. [Weekly.]

Couling, S. Our Labouring Classes, Intellectual, Social, Moral Condition. 1851.

Cruse, A. The Englishman and his Books. 1930.

Dickens, C. Nicholas Nickleby. 1838–9.

—— Dombey and Son. 1848.

—— David Copperfield. 1849–50.

—— Hard Times. 1854.

[See also the novels passim; education always interested Dickens.]

Dunlop, O. J. and Denman, R. D. English Apprenticeship and Child Labour. 1912.

'Eliot, George.' The Mill on the Floss. 3 vols. Edinburgh, 1860.

Farrar, F. W. Eric, or Little by Little. Edinburgh, 1858. [See Quart. Rev. CVIII, 1860.]

—— Julian Home, a Tale of College Life. Edinburgh, 1859.

Fearon, D. R. School Inspection. 1876.

Grant, P. The History of Factory Legislation, 1802–50, with a Warning. By the Earl of Shaftesbury. Manchester, 1866.

Hammond, J. L. and B. The Village Labourer, 1760–1832. 1911.

—— The Town Labourer. 1917.

—— The Skilled Labourer. 1919.

—— Lord Shaftesbury. 1923.

[Hughes, T.] Tom Brown's School Days. By an Old Boy. 1857. [See Quart. Rev. CII, 1857, and Edinburgh Rev. CVII, 1858.]

—— Tom Brown at Oxford. Cambridge, 1861.

Kay, J. The Condition of Poor Children. 1853.

Kendall, G. A Headmaster remembers. 1933. [Eton, Charterhouse, Oxford.]

Kingsley, C. Alton Locke. 1850.

Kipling, R. Stalky and Co. 1899.

Leavis, Q. D. Fiction and the Reading Public. 1932.

Marshall, A. Out and About: Random Reminiscences. 1933. [Trinity College, Cambridge, in the Nineties.]

Meredith, G. The Ordeal of Richard Feverel. 3 vols. 1859.

Meredith, G. The Adventures of Harry Richmond. 3 vols. 1871.

—— Lord Ormont and his Aminta. 3 vols. 1894. [Co-education.]

Mitford, M. R. Our Village: Sketches of Rural Character. 5 vols. 1824–32.

Nicholls, Sir G. History of the English Poor Law. 2 vols. 1854; 2 vols. 1898. [Vol. III, 'from 1834,' by T. Mackay, 1899.]

'Penny Fiction.' Quart. Rev. CLXXI, 1890. [See also Edinburgh Rev. CLXV, 1887.]

Polwhele, R. The Deserted Village-School. Edinburgh, 1812.

Rogers, F. Labour, Life and Literature. 1913.

'Rutherford, Mark.' The Autobiography of Mark Rutherford, Dissenting Minister. 1881.

—— The Early Life of Mark Rutherford. By Himself. 1913.

'An Old Schoolmaster.' A Letter respecting Pensions to Teachers addressed to a Member of Parliament. 1884. [Committee of Council Minutes, 1846.]

Cooper, A. A. (Earl of Shaftesbury). Speeches relating to the Labouring Classes. 1868.

Bready, J. W. Lord Shaftesbury and Social and Industrial Progress. [1926.] [See also P. Grant above.]

Sharpe, C. K. Letters to and from C. K. Sharpe. Ed. A. Allardyce, with Memoir by W. K. R. Bedford, 2 vols. 1888. [Christ Church, Oxford, 1798–1805.]

Simmons, G. The Working Classes: Moral, Social and Intellectual Condition. 1849.

Sneyd-Kynnersley, E. M. H.M.I.: Some Passages in the Life of One of H.M. Inspectors of Schools. 1908.

Society for the Diffusion of Useful Knowledge. The Penny Magazine. 1832.

—— The Penny Cyclopaedia. 27 vols. 3 supplementary vols. 1832–58.

—— The Quarterly Journal of Education. 10 vols. 1831–5.

—— Biographical Dictionary. 4 vols. 1842–4.

—— The Library of Entertaining Knowledge. 1829–40.

—— The Library of Useful Knowledge. [1827]–1854.

[See Edinburgh Rev. XLVI, 1827, XLIX, 1829, L, 1829, LI, 1830, LVII, 1833, LXXVI, 1842; and London Mag. VII, 1827.]

Southey, R. Essays, Moral and Political. 2 vols. 1832. [Essay IX, On the Means of Improving the People, 1818.]

Stephen, Sir L. The English Utilitarians. 3 vols. 1900.

Tollemache, L. A. Benjamin Jowett. [1895.]

Trail, H. D. et al. Social England. 6 vols. 1895–8; 6 vols. 1901–4. [Vol. I to accession of Edward I; vols. V, VI, George I to 1885.]

Ward, W. William George Ward and the Oxford Movement. 1889.

Williams, T. G. The Main Currents of Social and Industrial Change, 1870–1924. 1925.

Wood, Mrs Henry (née Ellen Price). Orville College. 1867.

Wordsworth, William. The Prelude [1805 and 1850]. Ed. E. de Selincourt, Oxford, 1926. [See also Legouis, p. 141 below.]

C. OFFICIAL DOCUMENTS

Adult Education Committee. (Ministry of Reconstruction. Cmd 321.) 1919.

Baines, E. Second Report, Congregational Board of Education. 1846.

Board of Education Reports.
Instruction and Training of Pupil Teachers. 1903–7.
Annual for 1910–11. [History of Elementary Curriculum.]
Annual for 1912–13. [Training College life in 1875.]
Modern Studies. 1918.
Teaching of English in England. 1921.
The Classics in Education. 1921.
Differentiation of Curricula between the Sexes in Secondary Schools. 1923.
Education of the Adolescent. 1926.
Training for Women Secondary School Teachers. Pamphlet No. 23.

Chance, Sir W. Children under the Poor Law. 1897.

Committee of Council on Education.
Minutes of the Committee. 1839–40, 1840–1, 1842, etc. [See Edinburgh Rev. LXXV, 1842, XCVII, 1853.]
Moseley, H. Report. 1845.
Report of Inquiry into the State of Education in Wales. 1847. [See Edinburgh Rev. XCVII, 1853.]
Arnold, M. Reports on Elementary Schools (1852–1882). Ed. Sir F. Sandford, 1889.
Revised Instructions to H.M. Inspectors. 1897, etc.

Elementary Education Act, 1870. Edinburgh Rev. CXXXIX, 1874.

Education Act, 1902. Edinburgh Rev. CXCVI, 1902.

The Educational Record of the British and Foreign School Society. 1848, etc.

International Conference on Education. 4 vols. 1884.

National Education League. First General Meeting. Birmingham, Oct. 1869.

National Education Union. Congress held in Manchester. 1869.

National Society. Church School Inquiry, 1856–7. 1858.

Parliamentary Papers.
Lower Orders: Reports, Select Committee, to inquire into the Education of the Lower Orders. (Brougham's Committee.) 12 pts, 1816–8. [See Quart. Rev. XIX, 1818, and Edinburgh Rev. XXX, XXXI, 1818–9.]
Education Inquiry (1833–5). [Lord Kerry's Return.] 3 vols. 1835.
Committee on providing Useful Education for the Poorer Classes. 1838.
Manchester and Salford. Educational Facts and Statistics. Evidence before the House of Commons. [See Edinburgh Rev. XCV, 1852.]
Report of Select Committee on Education in Manchester and Salford: with Evidence, Appendices and Index. 2 pts, 1852–3. [Voluntary System. Religious and secular instruction.]
Return relating to Endowed Grammar Schools in England and Wales. 1865.
Scientific Instruction, Report of Committee of British Association. 1867–8.
Technical Education. House of Commons Reports, LIV, 1867–8.
Technical Education in Various Countries: Letter of B. Samuelson to the Vice President. 1867.
Technical and Primary Education. Circular to H.M. Representatives abroad with Replies. 1868.
Chambers of Commerce on Technical Education: Letter from J. Behrens. 1868.
Select Committee on University Tests. 1870.
Special Reports on Educational Subjects. 1896, etc.

Poor Law Commission, Annual Reports. 1835, etc. [See also Chance, above.]

Society for Bettering the Conditions and increasing the Comforts of the Poor. Reports. 1797, etc.

Religious Teaching in Board Schools: Report. 1895. [See Edinburgh Rev. CLXXX, 1894.]

Archbishops' Commission on Religious Education. [1929.]

Royal Commissions' Reports.
Royal Commission to inquire concerning Charities for Education of the Poor. (Lord Brougham's Commission.) 44 vols. 818–42.
State of Universities and Colleges of Scotland. 4 vols. 1837. [See Edinburgh Rev. LIX, 1834.]
Analysis and Review. The Universities of King's College and Marischal College. Aberdeen, 1839.
State, Discipline, Studies and Revenues of the University and Colleges of Oxford. 2 pts, 1852. [See Edinburgh Rev. XCVI, 1852.]
State [etc.] of Cambridge. 2 pts, 1853.

D. UNIVERSITIES

(1) GENERAL WORKS

Royal Commissions' Reports.

Documents relating to the University and Colleges of Cambridge. 3 vols. 1852.

On Popular Education in England. (Newcastle Commission.) 6 vols. 1861. [Including reports by J. Fraser, Arnold and Pattison. See Edinburgh Rev. CXIV, 1861.]

Inquiry into the truth of the Report on the State of Popular Education in the County of Durham. Durham, 1862.

To inquire into Revenues and Management of Certain Colleges and Schools, and the Studies pursued. (Public Schools or Clarendon Commission.) 4 vols. 1864. [See Quart. Rev. CVIII, 1860, CXVI, 1864, and Edinburgh Rev. CXX, 1864.]

On the Schools in Scotland. (Argyll Commission.) 10 pts, 1865–7.

On Education given in Schools in England. .(Schools Inquiry or Taunton Commission.) 21 vols. 1868. [M. Arnold in vol. VI. See Quart. Rev. CXXVI, 1869.]

Schools Inquiry Commission on Technical Education. 1867.

On Scientific Instruction and the Advancement of Science. 10 pts, 1870–5. (Devonshire Commission.) [Full information respecting the whole range of instruction in science.]

Report of the Lords' Committee on Safeguards for the Maintenance of Religious Instruction and Worship in Oxford, Cambridge and Durham. 4 pts, 1870–1. [See Edinburgh Rev. CXXXV, 1872.]

On the Property and Income of Oxford and Cambridge. 3 vols. 1873.

On Technical Instruction. 5 vols. 1882–4.

On the Working of the Elementary Education Acts. (Cross Commission.) 10 vols. 1886–8. [See Quart. Rev. CLXV, 1887, and Edinburgh Rev. CLXXX, 1894.]

On Advancement of Higher Education in London. 1889.

Gresham University of London. 3 vols. 1894.

On Secondary Education. (Bryce Commission.) 9 vols. 1895. [See Quart. Rev. CLXXXV, 1897, and Edinburgh Rev. CLXXXV, 1897.]

On University Education in London. 1913.

Report of a Conference on Secondary Education held in Oxford. Oxford, 1893.

Shadwell, L. L. Enactments in Parliament specially concerning the Universities of Oxford and Cambridge, the Colleges and Halls and the Colleges of Winchester, Eton and Westminster. 4 vols. Oxford Hist. Soc. 1912. [Edward III–George V.]

Blakesley, J. W. The Studies of the University Essentially General. Cambridge, 1836.

—— Thoughts on the Recommendations of the Ecclesiastical Commission. 1837.

British Universities. Edinburgh Rev. CVII, 1858.

Caird, J. University Addresses on Academic Study. Glasgow, 1899.

Campbell, L. The Nationalisation of the Old English Universities. 1901.

Campion, W. M. Commissioners and Colleges. 1858.

Christie, W. D. Two Speeches in the House of Commons on the Universities. 1850. [25 May 1843 and 10 April 1845.]

Considerations on the Injuries arising from the Course of Education pursued in the Universities and Public Schools. 1832.

Emery, W. Past and Present Expenses and Social Conditions of University Education. [In British Association Report, 1862.]

English and Other Modern Literatures.
Quart. Rev. CLVI, 1883, CLXIV, 1887.
Nettleship, H. Study of Modern European Languages and Literatures in Oxford. 1887.
Collins, J. C. The Study of English Literature. 1891.
Firth, Sir C. H. The School of English Language and Literature. Oxford, 1909.

English Universities and their Reforms. Blackwood's Mag. LXV, 1849.

Fitch, J. G. The Universities and the Training of Teachers. Contemporary Rev. XXIX, 1876. [The 'Day Training College' anticipated.]

'A Graduate.' Enquiry into the Studies in the Universities preparatory to Holy Orders. 1824.

Griffiths, J. Enactments in Parliament concerning the Universities of Oxford and Cambridge. Oxford, 1869.

Haldane, R. B., Viscount. Universities and National Life. 1912.

Hamilton, Sir W. Discussions on Philosophy and Literature, Education and University Reform. Edinburgh, 1866 (3rd edn). [Education, III to VII and Appendix, Universities.]

Huber, V. A. The English Universities. Abridged trn, 2 vols. in 3, 1843. [See Quart. Rev. LXXII, 1843, and Edinburgh Rev. LXXXI, 1845.]

'A Layman'. The Independence of the Universities and Colleges. Oxford, 1838.

Lorimer, J. Universities of Scotland, Past, Present and Possible. Edinburgh, 1854.

[See also Scottish Universities, Edinburgh Rev. LXXXI, 1845, CXLIII, 1876, and J. Pillans below.]

Lyell, Sir C. Travels in North America. 2 vols. 1845. [Oxford and Cambridge: historical and critical, vol. I, pp. 271–316.]

Mansbridge, A. The Older Universities of England. 1923.

Morgan, A. Scottish University Studies. Oxford, 1933.

Mullinger, J. B. Universities. Ency. Brit. 11th edn, vol. XXVII, 1911.

Newman, J. H. Discourses on the Scope and Nature of University Education addressed to the Catholics of Dublin. Dublin, 1852; 1859.

—— Office and Work of the Universities. 1856.

—— Lectures and Essays on University Subjects. 1859. [The foregoing were incorporated in The Idea of a University Defined and Illustrated: I, in Nine Discourses addressed to the Catholics of Dublin; II, in Occasional Lectures and Essays addressed to Members of the Catholic University, 1873, etc.]

—— The Scope and Nature of University Education. Ed. A. R. Waller, Cambridge, 1901.

—— Select Discourses from The Idea of a University. Ed. M. Yardley, Cambridge, 1931.

Pillans, J. A Word for the Universities of Scotland. Edinburgh, 1848.

Quart. Rev. LXXIII, 1843, CXXIV, 1868, CXXXIV, 1873.

[Radnor.] An Historical Vindication of Earl Radnor's Bill to inquire respecting the Statutes and Administration of Oxford and Cambridge. 1837.

Raleigh, Sir W. A. Meaning of a University. 1911.

Roby, H. J. Remarks on College Reform. Cambridge, 1858.

Seeley, Sir J. Liberal Education in Universities. [In Essays on a Liberal Education, 1867.]

Sewell, W. Collegiate Reform. A Sermon. Oxford, 1838.

—— The Nation, the Church and the University of Oxford. Two Sermons. Oxford, 1849.

Smithells, A. From a Modern University. Oxford, 1921.

University Reform. Edinburgh Rev. LXXXIX, 1849.

Wilkins, A. Our National Universities. 1871.

(2) ADMISSION OF DISSENTERS

An Address to Dissenters. 1834.

Arnold, T. et al. Opinions on the Admission of Dissenters to the Universities and on University Reform. 1847.

Dalby, W. The Real Question at Issue. 1834.

Dicey, A. V. Lectures on the Relation between Law and Public Opinion. 1905; 1914. [University Tests, pp. 348 ff. and Appendix note III.]

Gray, J. H. The Admission of Dissenters into the Universities considered. Oxford, 1834.

Hamilton, Sir W. A Bill to remove certain Disabilities. Edinburgh Rev. LX, 1834.

Manning, W. O. Remarks upon Religious Tests at the English Universities. 1846.

Moberly, G. A Few Remarks on the proposed Admission of Dissenters. Oxford, 1834.

Opinions on the Admission of Dissenters and on University Reform. 1847. [Palmerston, Lord John Russell, Sir W. Hamilton, J. S. Mill and others.]

Pearson, G. Abrogating Religious Tests and Subscriptions. Cambridge, 1834.

Sedgwick, A. Admission of Dissenters to Academical Degrees. Cambridge Chronicle, 9 June 1834. [See also H. J. Rose's letter, Cambridge Chronicle, 10 June 1834.]

Select Committee on University Tests: Report to Parliament. 1870.

Selwyn, W. College Examinations in Divinity. Cambridge, 1834.

Sewell, W. Thoughts on the Admission of Dissenters to the University of Oxford. Oxford, 1834.

Smith, G. Plea for the Abolition of Tests in the University. Oxford, 1864.

Turton, T. Thoughts on the Admission of Persons, without Regard to their Religious Opinions, to certain Degrees in the Universities of England. Cambridge, 1834. [2nd edn, 1835, has 2 pp. of which the first is A Review of the Principal Dissenting Colleges. See also: Samuel Lee, Some Remarks on the Dean of Peterborough's Tract, 'Thoughts' [as above], Cambridge, 1834; C. Thirlwall, A Letter to the Revd Thos. Turton on the Admission of Dissenters to Academical Degrees, Cambridge, 1834; C. Thirlwall, A Second Letter to the Revd Thomas Turton, Cambridge, 1834; W. Whewell, Remarks on Some Parts of Mr Thirlwall's Letter, Cambridge, 1834; W. Whewell, Additional Remarks on Some Parts of Mr Thirlwall's Two Letters, Cambridge, 1834. See too Quart. Rev. LII, 1834, and Edinburgh Rev. LX, 1834–5.]

Wordsworth, C. On the Admission of Dissenters to reside and graduate. Cambridge, 1834.

(3) INDIVIDUAL UNIVERSITIES

Abrahams, H. M. and Bruce-Kerr, J. Oxford versus Cambridge. A Record of Inter-University Contests, 1827–1930. 1931.

Croome, A. C. M. *et al.* Fifty Years of Sport at Oxford, Cambridge and the Great Public Schools: arranged by Lord Desborough. 3 vols. 1913. [Vols. I, II, Oxford and Cambridge; vol. III, Eton, Harrow, Winchester.]

The Oxford and Cambridge Magazine. Conducted by Members of the two Universities. 1856.

Aberdeen

Aberdeen University Studies. Aberdeen, 1900.

Bulloch, J. M. History of the University of Aberdeen, 1495–1895. 1895.

Duff, Sir M. E. Grant. Inaugural Addresses delivered to the University of Aberdeen. Edinburgh, 1867.

Fasti Aberdonenses: Selections from the Records of the University and King's College of Aberdeen, 1494–1854. Spalding Club, 1854.

Maclean, N. N. Life at a Northern University. Ed. W. K. Leask, Aberdeen, 1906.

Rectorial Addresses delivered in the Universities of Aberdeen, 1835–1900. Aberdeen, 1902.

Birmingham

Lodge, Sir O. Address to Students by the Principal. 1900.

Smith, E. The Educational Work of the Birmingham and Midland Institute. 1870.

Cambridge

[See also the College histories, the more important of which are listed, vol. I, p. 370 above.]

Alma Mater, a Satire dedicated to the Collegiate Dignitaries. 1848. [Not to be confused with Alma Mater by J. M. F. Wright. See below, p. 124.]

Atkinson, T. D. Cambridge Described and Illustrated. Introduction by J. W. Clark. Cambridge, 1897.

Austen-Leigh, R. A. Bygone King's. Eton, 1907.

Benson, A. C. From a College Window. 1906.
—— The Upton Letters. 1907.

'A Brace of Cantabs.' Gradus ad Cantabrigiam, or New University Guide to the Academical Customs and Colloquial or Cant Terms. 1824.

Breul, K. Greek and its Humanistic Alternative. Cambridge, 1905. [See Quart. Rev. CLXXII, 1891.]

Bristed, C. A. Five Years in an English University. 1873 (3rd edn).

Browning, O. Memories of Sixty Years at Eton, Cambridge and Elsewhere. 1910.

Cambridge Essays contributed by Members of the University. 4 vols. 1855–8.

Cambridge University Reporter. On the Training of Teachers, 2 Nov. 1877, 20 Nov. 1878. Teachers' Training Syndicate, First Annual Report, 3 Dec. 1880.

Downs, B. W. Cambridge, Past and Present. 1926.

Dyer, G. The Privileges of the University of Cambridge. 1824.

'Eubulus' [Samuel Butler of Shrewsbury]. Thoughts on the Present System of Academic Education. 1822.
—— A Letter to Philograntus. 1822.

'Philograntus' [J. H. Monk]. A Letter on the Additional Examination of Students. 1822. [See 'Eubulus' above.]

Everett, W. On the Cam, Lectures on the University of Cambridge. 1866.

Gray, A. Cambridge and its Story. 1912.

Gunning, H. Ceremonies observed in the Senate House, Cambridge. 1828 (new edn).

Heitland, W. E. Cambridge in the Eighteen Seventies. [In The Eighteen Seventies, Royal Soc. of Literature, 1929.]

Historical Register of the University of Cambridge. 1917.

James, M. R. Eton and King's: Recollections, 1875–1925. 1926.

[Le Grice, C. V.] Conversations at Cambridge: Miscellaneous Pieces. Cambridge, 1836.

Leigh, A. A. A Record of College Reform. 1906.

Letters from Cambridge illustrative of the Studies, Habits and Peculiarities of the University. 1828.

Mann, E. An Englishman at Home and Abroad, 1792–1828. 1930. [John Scott, Fellow Commoner of Emmanuel College.]

Peacock, G. Observations on the Statutes of the University of Cambridge. 1841.

'Pembrochian.' Gradus ad Cantabrigiam, or a Dictionary of Terms used at the University of Cambridge. 1803.

Potts, R. Cantabrigiensis Liber: Aids afforded to Poor Students in the University: with Maxims designed for Learners. Cambridge, 1855.

Quart. Rev. XIX, 1818. [Botany professorship.]

'Resident Member of the University.' Hints for the Introduction of an Improved Course of Study in the University. Cambridge, 1835.

Roberts, S. C. Introduction to Cambridge. Cambridge, 1934.

Rolleston, Sir H. The Cambridge Medical School. Cambridge, 1932.

Sandys, Sir J. E. Orationes et Epistolae Cantabrigienses (1876–1909). 1910.

Sedgwick, A. A Discourse on the Studies of the University. Cambridge, 1833.
    Mill, J. S. Dissertations and Discussions. 4 vols. 1859–75. [On Professor Sedgwick's Discourse see vol. I, pp. 95–159.]

Selwyn, W. Extracts from College Examinations in Divinity with a Letter to the Lecturers and Examiners. Cambridge, 1834.

[Stephen, Sir L.] Sketches from Cambridge by a Don. 1865. Rptd 1932.

Stubbs, C. W. The Story of Cambridge. 1905.

Tillyard, A. I. A History of University Reform from 1800. Cambridge, 1913.

Trinity College. The King's Scholars and King's Hall: Six Hundredth Anniversary. 1917.

Venn, J. Biographical History of Gonville and Caius College 1349–1897. 3 vols. Cambridge, 1897–1901.

Venn, J. and J. A. Alumni Cantabrigienses. 1922–

Wainewright, L. The Literary and Scientific Studies pursued, encouraged and enforced in the University of Cambridge. 1815.

Walsh, B. D. A Historical Account of the University of Cambridge and its Colleges: in a Letter to the Earl of Radnor. 1837.

Whewell, W. On the Principles of University Education. 1837. [See Quart. Rev. LIX, 1837.]

—— Liberal Education, with particular reference to the University of Cambridge. 1845.

    Amos, A. Four Lectures on the Advantages of a Classical Education: with a Letter to Whewell. 1846.

    [Bain, A.] University Education. Westminster Rev. XLIX, 1848. [Reviewing Whewell's Liberal Education.]

Wilson, J. Memorabilia Cantabrigiae. 1803.

Wilson, J. M. Letter to St John's College on Sciences in relation to School and College. 1867.

Wright, H. et al. Cambridge University Studies, 1933.

[Wright, J. M. F.] Alma Mater, or Seven Years at the University of Cambridge by a Trinity-man. 1827. [See 'Alma Mater' above, p. 123, and London Mag. VII, 1827.]

Burnand, F. C. Personal Reminiscences of the A.D.C. 1880.

Byron, G. G., Baron. Thoughts suggested by a College Examination, 1806. Granta, a Medley, 1806. [In Hours of Idleness, 1807.]

Calverley, C. S. Complete Works. Biographical Notice by Sir W. J. Sendall. 1901.

Cambridge University Magazine. March 1839–Nov. 1840; Cambridge, 1840.

Ferguson, C. L. A History of the Magpie and Stump Debating Society. Cambridge, 1931. [Trinity College.]

[Gooch, R.] The Cambridge Tart. By Socius. 1823.

Hilton, A. C. et al. The Light Green: a Superior and High-class Periodical. Cambridge, 1872–3.

Lehmann, R. C. In Cambridge Courts. [1891.]

The Light Blue. 4 vols. 1866–70.

[Rice, J.] The Cambridge Freshman or Memoirs of Mr Golightly: By Martin Legrand. 1871.

Stephen, J. K. Lapsus Calami and other Verses. Ed. H. S., Cambridge, 1898.

Whibley, C. In Cap and Gown: Three Centuries of Cambridge Wit. 1889.

Dublin

Burtchaell, G. D. and Sadleir, T. U. Alumni Dublinenses, 1593–1860. Dublin, 1937.

Dixon, W. M. Trinity College, Dublin. Dublin, 1902.

Edinburgh Rev. LXXXVIII, 1848.

Hermathena: Papers by Members of T. C. D. Dublin, 1874–.

Hinkson, H. A. et al. Dublin Verses by Members of Trinity College. Dublin, 1925.

Stubbs, J. M. History of the University of Dublin. Dublin, 1889. [See Quart. Rev. CLXXV, 1892.]

Taylor, W. B. S. History of the University of Dublin. 1845.

Todd, J. H. University of Dublin: Remarks on Some Statements attributed to T. Wyse. 1844.

Tyrrell, R. Y. et al. Kottabos: a College Miscellany. Dublin, 1869, etc.

Vickers, R. Praelection on the University System of Education. Dublin, 1849.

Durham

Fowler, J. T. Durham University: Earlier Foundations and Present Colleges. 1904.

Whiting, C. E. The University of Durham, 1832–1932. 1933.

Edinburgh

Dalzel, A. History of the University of Edinburgh. 2 vols. Edinburgh, 1862.

Edinburgh Essays. 1858.

Geddes, P. et al. Viri Illustres Academiae Jacobi Sexti Scotiae Regis anno CCCmo. Edinburgh, 1884.

Grant, Sir A. The Story of the University of Edinburgh. 2 vols. 1884.

Rectorial Addresses delivered before the University, 1859–99. Ed. A. Stodart-Walker, 1900.

Turner, A. L. History of the University of Edinburgh, 1883–1933. Edinburgh, 1933.

Glasgow

Addison, W. I. *et al.* Roll of the Graduates of the University of Glasgow, 1727–1897: with Biographical Notes. Glasgow, 1898.

—— The Matriculation Albums of the University of Glasgow, 1728–1858. Glasgow, 1913.

Disraeli, B. (Earl of Beaconsfield). Inaugural Address delivered to the University of Glasgow. 1873. [See Edinburgh Rev. vol. cxxxix, 1874.]

Inaugural Addresses by Lords Rectors of the University. 1839. Ed. J. B. Hay, 1839.

Macaulay, T. B., Baron. Inaugural Address as Lord Rector. 1849.

Munimenta Alme Universitatis Glasguensis: Records of the University till 1727. 3 vols. in 4, Maitland Club, Glasgow, 1854.

Primrose, A. P. (Viscount Rosebery). Inaugural Address. 1900. [See Edinburgh Rev. cxcv, 1902.]

Remarks on a Pamphlet: 'A Memorial respecting the College of Glasgow.' Glasgow, 1835.

Ireland

Andrews, T. Address on Education to the Social Science Association. 1867.

—— Studium Generale, a Chapter of Contemporary History. 1867. [University of London, the new Irish universities, Maynooth.]

Corrigan, D. J. University Education in Ireland. Dublin, 1865.

Fathers of the Society of Jesus. A Page of Irish History: University College, Dublin, 1883–1909. Dublin, 1930.

'Nemo.' A Few Words on the New Irish Colleges. 1845.

Sullivan, W. K. University Education in Ireland. Dublin, 1866.

Walsh, W. J. The Irish University Question. Dublin, 1890.

[See also Quart. Rev. cxlviii, 1879, clxxxvii, 1898, cxcvii, 1903, and Edinburgh Rev. cxxxv, 1872, cxxxvii, 1873, clxxxvii, 1898, cxcv, 1902.]

London

Andrews, T. Studium Generale. 1867.

Bagehot, W. Matthew Arnold on the London University. Fortnightly Rev. ix, 1868. [See Arnold, above, p. 107.]

Beattie, W. Life and Letters of Thos. Campbell. 3 vols. 1849. [Vol. ii, ch. xiv.]

Campbell, T. Times, 9 Feb. 1824. [Letter.]

—— Suggestions respecting the Plan of an University in London. New Monthly Mag. xiii, 1825.

'Christianus.' Letter to Robert Peel on the London University. 1828. [See Quart. Rev. xxxix, 1829.]

Collins, Sir W. J. The University of London Fifty Years Ago. Contemporary Rev. Sept. 1935.

De Morgan, A. Thoughts suggested by the Establishment of the University of London. 1837.

Edinburgh Rev. xlii, 1825, xliii, 1826, xlviii, 1828, clxiv, 1886.

E., E. [Edwards, E.] The Metropolitan University: Remarks on a Central University Examining Board. 1836.

Gollancz, Sir H. A Contribution to the History of University College: to which is added Motives for the Present Founding an University in the Metropolis London, 1647. Oxford, 1930.

Grote, H. The Personal Life of George Grote. 1873.

Hoppus, John. Thoughts on Academical Education and Degrees in Arts. 1837.

Humberstone, T. L. University Reform in London. 1926.

Letter to a Member of the Senate relative to the B.A. Examination. 1838.

London University. Quart. Journ. of Education, vii, 1834.

The London University Press. Remarks upon a Popular System of Classical Instruction. Bath, 1828.

Prospectus of the Association for Promoting a Teaching University for London. 1886. [See Edinburgh Rev. clxiv, 1886.]

Quart. Rev. clxxiv, 1892. [London University Commission and Albert University Charter. By J. G. Fitch?]

Quart. Rev. clxiv, 1887, cxci, 1900.

The Proposed Teaching University for London. Times, 31 Jan. 1888.

Waller, A. D. Origins of the University of London. 1912.

Wetherell, Sir C. Substance of a Speech on Incorporating the University of London. 1834. [For Oxford; in opposition.]

Yates, J. Outlines of a Constitution for the University of London. 1832. [See also Yates, above p. 115.]

Beard, C. University College and Mr. Martineau. [1867.]

Bellot, H. H. University College, London, 1826–1926. 1929.

Centenary Addresses, University College, London. 1927.

['London University'] Prospectus. London Mag. v, 1826.

Morgan, J. M. Address to the Proprietors of the University of London. 1833. [Proposes a Chair of Education.]

Notes and Memorials for the History of University College, London. Ed. W. P. Ker, 1898.

'An Oxonian.' Proposals for Founding an University in London considered. 1825. Sewell, W. A Second Letter to a Dissenter on the Opposition of the University of Oxford to the Charter of the London College. Oxford, 1834. [See Edinburgh Rev. XLII, 1825.]

Quart. Rev. XXXIII, 1825.

Stähele, A. Letter to the Council of the University of London. 1828.

The Second Statement of the Council explanatory of the Plan of Instruction. 1828. [See Edinburgh Rev. XLVIII, 1828.]

Hearnshaw, F. J. C. et al. The Centenary History of King's College, London, 1828–1928. 1929.

Jelf, R. W. Grounds for laying before the Council of King's College, London, 'Theological Essays' by F. D. Maurice. 1853.

'A Subscriber.' Remarks to the Provisional Committee for the intended Establishment of King's College, London. 1828. [See also London Mag. I, 1828.]

Burns, C. D. A Short History of Birkbeck College. 1924.

Haldane, R. B., Viscount. Birkbeck College Centenary Lectures. 1924.

Becket, E. M. The History of University College, Nottingham. Nottingham, 1928.

Oxford

[See also the College histories, the more important of which are listed, vol. I, pp. 368–9 above.]

Academical Abuses disclosed by Initiated. 1832.

Acland, H. W. and Ruskin, J. The Oxford Museum. 1859.

Acland, Sir T. D. Some Account of the Origin and Objects of the new Oxford Examinations for the Title of Associate in Arts. 1858. [See also J. B. Atlay, Sir Henry Acland, A Memoir, 1903.]

Barrow, J. The Case of Queen's College. Oxford, 1854.

Barry, H. B. Remarks on the three Proposals for reforming the Constitution of the University. Oxford, 1854.

Bentham, J. Works. Ed. Sir J. Bowring, 11 vols. Edinburgh, 1843. [Vol. X, ch. ii, Westminster School and Oxford.]

'Beta' [T. E. Brown]. Christ Church Servitors in 1853 by One of Them. Macmillan's Mag. XIX, 1868.

[Boone, J. S.] The Oxford Spy, a Dialogue in Verse. Oxford, 1818. [With an appendix in prose on studies.]

Brasenose Quatercentenary Monographs. 2 vols. 1909.

Burgon, J. W. Historical Notices of Oxford Colleges. Oxford, 1888.

'A Cambridge Master of Arts.' Oxoniana, a Didactic Poem. 1812. [Study and examination for Oxford degrees.]

'Clericus' [A. Clissold]. A Letter to the Vice-Chancellor on Theology. 1856.

Coleridge, J. D., Baron. Memorials of Oxford. Oxford, 1844. [Verse.]

[Copleston, E.] A Reply to the Calumnies of the Edinburgh Review. Oxford, 1810. A Second Reply, Oxford, 1810. A Third Reply, Oxford, 1811. [See J. Davison below; Quart. Rev. IV, 1810; Edinburgh Rev. XIV, 1809, XVI. 1810; and D. K. Sandford to P. Elmslie in The Pamphleteer, vol. XXI, 1822.]

Courtney, J. E. An Oxford Portrait Gallery. 1931.

Cox, G. V. Recollections of Oxford. 1868.

Curzon of Kedleston, Marquis. Principles and Methods of University Reform. Oxford, 1909.

Davison, J. Remains and Occasional Publications. Oxford, 1840. [Includes Review of Replies to The Calumnies of the Edinburgh Rev. 1810. See J. H. Newman, Idea of a University, Discourse VI, 'Liberal Knowledge in relation to Professional.']

Edinburgh Rev. XIV, 1809, XVI, 1810, LIII, 1831, LIV, 1831, LXXVI, 1843, LXXXVIII, 1848, XCVI, 1852, CLXX, 1889, CXCVIII, 1903.

Edwards, C. E. H. An Oxford Tutor: Life of the Revd. Thomas Short. 1909.

English Literature at the Universities. Quart. Rev. CLXIII, 1886. [Discusses Petition for a School of Modern Literature, Oxford, 1886. See also Sir C. H. Firth, The School of English Language and Literature, 1909.]

Foster, J. Alumni Oxonienses, 1500–1886. Oxford, 1891.

Garbett, J. Dr Pusey and the University of Oxford. 1843.

Gordon, G. Three Oxford Ironies. 1927. [Copleston; Mansel.]

'A Graduate.' Thoughts on Reform at Oxford. Oxford, 1833.

Hamilton, Sir W. Discussions on Philosophy and Literature, Education and University Reform. Chiefly from the Edinburgh Review. 1866 (3rd edn).

Ingram, J. Apologia Academica. Oxford, 1831.

—— Memorials of Oxford. 3 vols. 1837.

[Jowett, B. and Stanley, A. P.] Suggestions for an Improvement of the Examination Statute. Oxford, 1848.

Lock, W. Oxford Memories. Oxford, 1932. [Keble College, 1870–1920.]

Macan, R. W. Oxford in the Eighteen Seventies. [In The Eighteen Seventies, Royal Soc. of Literature, 1929.]

Mackinder, H. J. and Sadler, Sir M. E. University Extension, Past, Present and Future. 1891 (3rd edn). [See Quart. Rev. CLXXII, 1891.]

Mackinnon, A. The Oxford Amateurs, a Short History. 1910.

Mansel, H. L. The Phrontisterion or Oxford in the Nineteenth Century. [A skit on the Royal Commission of 1850–2; in Letters, Lectures and Reviews, ed. H. W. Chandler, 1873.]

Maurice, J. F. D. The New Statute and Mr Ward. Oxford, 1845.

'A Member of Convocation' [V. Thomas]. The Legality of the Present Academical System asserted against the new Calumnies of the Edinburgh Review. Oxford, 1831. [See Edinburgh Rev. LIV, 1831, and under Thomas below.]

—— The Legality [etc.] reasserted. Oxford, 1832.

'A Member of the Oxford Convocation' [C. A. Row]. Letter to Lord John Russell on the Constitutional Defects of the University and Colleges of Oxford, with Suggestions for a Royal Commission. 1850.

'A Resident Member of Convocation' [A. C. Tait]. Hints on a Plan for the Revival of the Professorial System. Oxford, 1839.

'Members of the University.' Oxford Essays. 1855; 1856; 1857.

Our Memories: Shadows of Old Oxford. 2 sers. 1893–5.

Meyrick, F. Memoirs of Life at Oxford. 1905.

Moore, E. Frugal Education attainable under the existing Collegiate System. Oxford, 1867.

Moore, H. K. Reminiscences and Reflections. 1930. [Oxford in the 'Seventies.]

Morrah, H. A. The Oxford Union, 1823–1923. 1923.

Mozley, T. Reminiscences, chiefly of Oriel College and the Oxford Movement. 2 vols. 1882. [See Quart. Rev. CLIV, 1882.]

'A Nobleman.' Letters to his Son at Eton and Oxford. 2 vols. 1810.

Pattison, M. Suggestions on Academical Organization. Edinburgh, 1868.

—— Essays. Ed. H. Nettleship, 2 vols. Oxford, 1889. [See vol. I.]

Present State and Future Prospects of Mathematical and Physical Studies in the University. Oxford, 1832.

Price, B. Suggestions for the Extension of Professorial Teaching. 1850.

Prothero, R. E. (Baron Ernle). Balliol in the Seventies. Quart. Rev. April 1933.

Pusey, E. B. Collegiate and Professorial Teaching and Discipline. 1854. [See H. H. Vaughan below, p. 128.]

[Pycroft, J.] The Collegian's Guide or Recollections of College Days By the Revd. —, M.A.,— College. 1845 (anon.).

—— Oxford Memories. 2 vols. 1886.

Quart. Journ. of Education, I, II, IV, VII, 1831–4.

Quart. Rev. LII, 1834, LXI, 1838, CXXXVII, 1874.

Essays on the Endowment of Research. 1876. [By various writers.]

Rogers, J. E. T. Education in Oxford and its Methods. 1861.

Row, C. A. Letter to Sir Robert H. Inglis in reply to his Speech on University Reform. 1850.

'Country Schoolmaster.' A Letter to the Authors of 'Suggestions for an Improvement of the Examination Statute.' Oxford, 1848.

Selincourt, H. de. Oxford from Within. 1910.

Sewell, W. The Attack upon the University of Oxford in a Letter to Earl Grey. 1834 (2nd edn).

—— Suggestions for the Extension of the University. Oxford, 1850.

—— The University Commission, or Lord John Russell's Post-bag. Oxford, 1850 (anon.).

Sherwood, W. E. Oxford Yesterday. Memories of Seventy Years Ago. Oxford, 1927.

Skelton, J. Pietas Oxoniensis or Records of Oxford Founders. Oxford, 1828.

Skinner, J. The Journal of a Somerset Rector. 1772–1839. Ed. H. Coombs and A. N. Bax, 1930. [Winchester and Oxford.]

Smith, G. Oxford University Reform. 1858.

—— Re-organisation of the University. Oxford, 1868.

—— Oxford and her Colleges. 1894.

Stanley, E. L. [See above, p. 114.]

Stedman, A. M. M. Oxford, its Life and Schools. 1887.

[Tatham, E.] A New Address to Members of Convocation. Oxford, 1810.

—— An Address to the Chancellor upon Abuses. Oxford, 1811. [Both 'by the Rector of Lincoln College.']

Thomas, V. The Legality of the Academical System asserted. 2 pts, Oxford, 1853. [See also Edinburgh Rev. XCVI, 1852, and 'A Member of Convocation' above.]

Thompson, L. Christ Church. 1900.

Townsend, W. C. The Paean of Oxford: A Reply to the Charges against the University. 1826.

Tuckwell, W. Reminiscences of Oxford. 1900.

—— Pre-Tractarian Oxford: a Reminiscence of the Oriel 'Noetics.' 1909. [See also Quart. Rev. CLVI, 1883.]

Tutors' Association Reports, Oxford, 1853–4.
  1. Recommendations respecting Extension.
  2. Recommendations respecting the Constitution.
  3. Recommendations relating to the Professorial and Tutorial Systems.
  4. Recommendations respecting College Statutes.
[See also F. H. Dickinson and E. A. Freeman, Suggestions with regard to certain Proposed Alterations, Oxford, 1854, and J. W. Awdry and J. Patteson, Suggestions with regard to the Possibility of Legal Education, Oxford, 1854.]

Vaughan, H. H. Oxford Reform and Oxford Professors. 1854. [See E. B. Pusey above.]

Walker, J. Oxoniana. 4 vols. [1807].

Walker, R. A Letter on Improvements in the Present Examination Statute and the Studies of the University. Oxford, 1848.

Wells, J. et al. Oxford and Oxford Life. 1892.

Whittock, N. The Microcosm of Oxford. 1828.

Wilson, H. B. A Letter to the Chancellor of the University on University and College Reform. 1854.

'Bede, Cuthbert' [E. Bradley]. The Adventures of Mr Verdant Green, an Oxford Freshman. 1853.

[Caswell, E.] The Art of Pluck: By Scriblerus Redivivus. 1843.

'A Gentleman of the University.' A Poetical Essay on the Existing State of Things. [1811?]

Grand University Logic Stakes. 1849.

Maycock, A. L. An Oxford Note-Book. 1931.

'Nemo.' The Devil's Return from Oxford. Oxford, 1847.

The Newdigate [Prize Poem]. TLS. 14 June 1934.

Old Saints and New Demons. 1886.

The Oxford Sausage. 1814.

Reading

Childs, W. M. Making a University. 1933.

St Andrews

Anderson, J. M. Early Records of the University of St Andrews 1413–1579: and Matriculation Roll, 1473–1579. Edinburgh, 1926.

Donaldson, Sir J. Addresses delivered in the University of St Andrews from 1886 to 1910. Edinburgh, 1911.

Rectorial Addresses at St Andrews University, 1863–1893. Ed. W. Knight, 1894.

Votiva Tabella: Memorial Volume of St Andrews University, 1411–1911. 1911.

Sheffield

Floreamus! A Chronicle of University College, Sheffield, 1897. 1901.

Marshall, A. C. and Newbould, H. The History of Firth's, 1842–1918. 1924.

Papers to commemorate the Incorporation of University College. 1897. [Various authors.]

Victoria University, Manchester

Essays and Addresses by Professors of Owens College. 1874.

Hartog, P. J. Owens College, Manchester: a Brief History of the College. 1900.

Thompson, J. The Owens College, its Foundation and Growth and its Connection with the Victoria University, Manchester. Manchester, 1886.

Wales

Davies, W. C. and Jones, W. L. The University of Wales and its Colleges. 1905.

E. SCHOOLS, COLLEGES AND INSTITUTES

[The standard school histories, etc., which are listed, vol. i, pp. 372–4 and vol. ii, pp. 122–4 above, have not as a rule been repeated here.]

Johnston, M. Bibliography of the Registers (Printed) of the Universities, Inns of Court, Colleges and Schools of Great Britain and Ireland. Part ii. School Registers. Hist. Research Inst. Bulletin, ix, 1932.

Cotterill, C. C. Suggested Reforms in Public Schools. 1885.

Coulton, G. G. Public Schools and Public Needs. 1901.

Cowper, W. Tirocinium. [Pbd with The Task, 1785. See also Reply to Objections to Public Schools with particular reference to Tyrocinium, The Pamphleteer, vol. iv, 1814.]

David, A. A. Life and the Public Schools. 1932.

Farrar, F. W. On some Defects in Public School Education. 1857.

Gilbert, R. Parent's School and College Guide or Liber Scholasticus. 1843 (2nd edn). [Emoluments at Oxford, Cambridge, Durham, the Public and other endowed Schools and from City Companies.]

Grammar Schools and the Education of the Poor. Edinburgh Rev. xxxii, 1819.

Gray, H. B. The Public Schools and the Empire. 1913.

The Public Schools. Edinburgh Rev. xvi, 1810, li, 1830, liii, 1831, cxiii, 1861, cxx, 1864, cxlvi, 1877, clxxxv, 1897; Quart. Rev. xxv, 1821, xxxix, 1829, lii, 1834, cii, 1857, cviii, 1860, clxxvii, 1893, clxxxvii, 1898, clxxxix, 1899. [See also Sir J. T. Coleridge below, p. 131.]

The Public Schools from Within. 1906. [By various authors.]

[Smith, Sydney.] Edinburgh Rev. XVI, 1810. [Reviewing Remarks on the System of Education in Public Schools, 1809.]

Vincent, W. A Defence of Public Education. 1802. [See Remarks on Vincent's Defence. By A Layman, 1802; and An Attempted Reply to the Master of Westminster School. By D. Morrice, 1802.]

Buckler, J. C. Sixty Views of Endowed Grammar Schools. 1827.

Knox, V. Remarks on the Tendency in a Bill to degrade Grammar Schools. [The Pamphleteer, vol. XIX, 1822.]

Bousfield, W. et al. Elementary Schools: How to increase their Utility. Six Lectures. 1890.

Coombs, H. and Bax, A. N. The Journal of a Somerset Rector, John Skinner, 1772–1839. 1930. [Elementary and Sunday schools.]

Essay on the Institution and Management of Sunday Schools. 1805.

Moore, T. The Education Brief on behalf of Voluntary Schools. 1890.

Morley, C. R. Studies in London Board Schools. 1897.

Mozley, T. Reminiscences, chiefly of Towns, Villages, Schools. 2 vols. 1885 (2nd edn).

Newton, A. W. The English Elementary School. 1919.

Scots Parochial Schools. Edinburgh Rev. XLVI, 1827.

Philpott, H. B. London at School: the Story of the London School Board, 1874–1904. 1904.

Poole, J. The Village School Improved: the New System explained. 1813 (2nd edn); Oxford, 1815.

Sandford, J. Parochialia, or Church, School and Parish. 1845.

Schools for the Industrious Classes. [In Central Society of Education, Second Publication, 1838. Anon., B. F. Duppa taking responsibility for statement of facts.]

Sturge, J. The Story of Severn Street and Priory First Day Schools, Birmingham. 1895.

Wise, M. English Village Schools. 1931.

Airy, G. B. Statement on the History and Position of the Blue Coat Girls' School, Greenwich. 1867.

Cappe, C. An Account of two Charity Schools in York. York, 1800.

—— Observations on Charity Schools. York, 1805.

Cardwell, J. H. Story of a Charity School in Soho. 1899.

Charter, Act of Parliament, By-laws and Regulations of the Foundling Hospital. 1843.

Guthrie, T. Plea for Ragged Schools. Edinburgh, 1847.

—— Seed-Time and Harvest of Ragged Schools. Edinburgh, 1860. [See Edinburgh Rev. LXXXV, 1847.]

[Iffley.] Sarah Nowell's Endowed Charity School in Iffley. Oxford, 1854.

Ingram, R. A. A Sermon for the Charity School. Colchester, 1788.

—— Parochial Beneficence: the Baxted School of Industry. Colchester, [1800].

—— An Essay on Schools of Industry. [1808.]

A Short Account of the Marylebone Charity School. 1885.

Murray, A. M. Remarks on Education. 1847. [On Charity Schools. Miss Murray co-operated in founding Queen's College, London, 1848.]

Reformatory Schools. Edinburgh Rev. XCIV, 1851, CI, 1855.

Village Schools of Industry. 1831.

Rules for the Government of the Westminster New Charity School. 1818.

Westminster School of Industry. [An Ackermann colour print, c. 1840.]

History of Ackworth School during its first Hundred Years. By H. Thompson. 1879.

Aldenham School Register, 1836–1897. Ed. E. Beevor, [1897]; ed. E. Beevor and G. C. F. Mead, [1928] (6th edn).

St. Botolph Aldgate, he Story of a City Parish. Ed. A. G. B. Atkinson, 1898. [Sir John Cass School.]

Barrington School [Bishop Auckland]: Principles, Practices and Effects. By Sir T. Bernard. 1812.

Bath. The Grammar School of Edward VI. By K. E. Symons, Bath. 1934.

Bedales, a Pioneer School. By J. H. Badley, 1923.

History of Bedford School. By J. Sergeaunt and E. Hockliffe. 1925.

Bedford High School, History of. Ed. K. M. Westaway, Bedford, 1932.

Bingley Grammar School, History of. 1930.

Bishopsgate Schools, 1702–1889. By J. Avery. 1931 (priv. ptd).

Blackburn Grammar School, Records of. 3 vols. Chetham Soc. 1909.

Blackheath Proprietary School [1831–1907]. Blackheath. 1933.

Blundell's Worthies, 1604–1904. By M. L. Banks. 1904.

Visit to Borough Road Model School. By T. Coates. [In Central Soc. of Education, Second Publication, 1838.]

History of Bradfield College. By A. F. Leach. 1900.

Sampson, W. A. Bristol Grammar School, History of. Bristol, 1912.

—— History of the Red Maids' School. Bristol, 1908 (priv. ptd).

Bruce Castle, Tottenham, Junior School. By A. Fry. [In Central Society of Education, Second Publication, 1838.]

Bruce Castle Magazine. 1839.

The Brucian. 1851–2.

Bury St. Edmunds Grammar School: Biographical List, 1550–1900. 1908.

Memorials of King's School, Canterbury. By J. S. Sidebotham. 1865.

School for Clergymen's Daughters at Casterton. Tenth [etc.] Reports. Kirkby Lonsdale, 1838–53. [Associated with Charlotte Brontë and Dorothea Beale.]

Carthusian Memories and other Verses of Leisure. By W. Haig Brown. 1905.

Sertum Carthusianum Floribus Seculorum contextum 1620–1869. Ed. W. Haig Brown. 1870.

William Haig Brown of Charterhouse. Ed. by his Son. 1908.

Eardley Wilmot, E. P. and Streatfield, E. C. Charterhouse, Old and New. 1895.

Mozley, Thomas. Reminiscences. 2 vols. 1885 (2nd edn). [Charterhouse 1820–5.]

Chronicles of Charterhouse. By a Carthusian [W. J. D. Roper]. 1847.

'A Carthusian' [Robert Smythe]. Historical Account of the Charterhouse. 1808.

Charterhouse Register, 1872–1910. 2 vols. 1911.

'An Old Cheltonian.' Reminiscences of Cheltenham College. 1868.

Harper, A. History of the Cheltenham Grammar School from 1851. Cheltenham, 1856.

Christ's Hospital. By G. A. T. Allan. 1937.

Christ's Hospital: A Retrospect. By E. Blunden. [1923.]

Christ's Hospital from a Boy's Point of View. By W. M. D. La Touche. Cambridge, 1930.

Smith, Arthur Lionel, Master of Balliol, 1916–1924. By his Wife [M. F. Smith]. [1928.] [Christ's Hospital, 1856–69.]

Churcher's College, Petersfield and Life of Churcher. Petersfield, 1823.

Churcher's College, Petersfield. By J. H. Smith. Manchester, 1936.

Douglas-Smith, A. E. The City of London School. Oxford, 1937.

Clifton College Register, 1862–1887, compiled by E. M. Oakeley: Historical Preface by J. M. Wilson. 1887; 1890.

Clifton College Annals and Register, 1862–1912. Ed. F. Borwick. Introduction by J. E. King. Bristol, 1912.

[Newbolt, F. G.] Clifton College Forty Years ago: the Diary of a Praepostor. 1927.

Christie, O. F. Clifton School Days [1879–1885]. 1930.

—— A History of Clifton College. Bristol, 1935.

Mozley, J. R. Clifton Memories. Bristol, 1927.

Dulwich College Register, 1619–1926. By T. L. Ormiston. [1926.] [Re-organisations of 1858 and 1882.]

Young, W. The History of Dulwich College to 1857, with Life of Edward Alleyn. 2 vols. 1889.

Gilkes, A. H. A Day at Dulwich. 1905.

Downside Abbey and School, 1814–1914. By Dom L. Almond. Exeter, 1914.

—— Sketches of Old Downside. By Abbot T. B. Snow. 1903.

Durham School Register. C. S. Earle and L. A. Body. 1912.

History of the High School of Edinburgh. By W. Steven. 1849. [See Edinburgh Rev. xx, 1812.]

Edinburgh Academical Institution: Milton's Plan of Education with the Plan of the E.A.I. founded thereon. By William Scott. The Pamphleteer, vol. xvii, 1820.

Edinburgh Institution, 1832–1932. Ed. J. R. S. Young, Edinburgh, 1933.

Edinburgh Royal High School. Ed. W. C. A. Ross, Edinburgh, 1934.

Edinburgh Rev. li, 1830, cxiii, 1861, cxlvi, 1877, clxxxv, 1897.

Ely Cathedral Grammar School. Notes on the History of. By R. G. Ikin. Cambridge, 1931.

Emanuel School [Wandsworth], History of. By C. W. Scott-Giles. 1935.

Epsom College Register, 1855 to 1905. 1905.

History of the Foundling Hospital. By R. H. Nichols and F. A. Wray. Oxford, 1935.

Fasti Etonenses: Biographical History of Eton. Eton, 1899.

Eton of Old, or Eighty Years Since, 1811–1822. By An Old Colleger [W. H. Tucker]. 1892.

B., P. Eton Memories. By an Old Etonian. 1909. [Keate's time.]

Reminiscences of Eton [Keate's time]. By C. A. Wilkinson. 1888.

Reminiscences and Opinions, 1813–85. By Sir F. H. Doyle. 1886. [Eton and Christ Church, Oxford.]

Eton in 1829–30. By T. K. Selwyn. 1903. [Trn from the Greek and notes by E. Warre.]

Eton in the Forties. By A. D. Coleridge. 1898 (2nd edn).

Seven Years at Eton, 1857–64. Ed. J. B. Richards, 1883.

Eton in the Seventies. By G. Coleridge. 1912.

Eton in the Eighties. By E. Parker. 1914.

Eton under Hornby [1868–84]. By O. E. 1910.

Memories of By-gone Eton [1866–85]. By H. S. Salt. 1928.

The Nursery of Toryism: Reminiscences of Eton under Hornby. By H. S. Salt. 1911.

A Lawyer's Notebook. 1932. [Eton 1891–1906.]

Recollections of an Eton Colleger, 1898–1902. By C. H. M[alden]. Eton, 1905.

Shades of Eton. By P. Lubbock. 1929. [The Nineties and Warre.]

Etonensis.' Observations on an Article in the last Edinburgh Review [LI, 1830] entitled Public Schools of England. Eton, 1830.

Some Remarks upon the Present System of Eton School. By a Parent. [1834?] [See A Few Words in reply to 'Some Remarks' By Etonensis, 1834; The Eton System vindicated in Reply to some recent Publications, 1834. See also Quart. Rev. LII, 1834.]

Eton and King's: Recollections, 1875–1925. By M. R. James. 1926.

Eton and Elsewhere. By M. D. Hill. 1928.

Memories of Eton, Sixty Years Ago. By A. C. Ainger. 1917.

Eton in Prose and Verse. By A. C. Ainger. 1910. [Historical introduction.]

Recollections of Eton. By an Etonian. 1870.

Records of an Eton Schoolboy. By C. M. Gaskell. 1883.

'An Old Etonian.' Eton Memories. 1909.

Confessions of an Etonian. By J. E. M. 1846.

Memories of an Old Etonian, 1860–1912. By G. Greville. [1919.]

[Bankes, G. N.] A Day of my Life by an Eton boy. 1877.

—— An Eton Boy's Letters. 1901.

Browning, O. Memories of Sixty Years at Eton, Cambridge and Elsewhere. 1910.

Byrne, L. S. R. and Churchill, E. L. Changing Eton: since the Royal Commission of 1862. 1937.

Coleridge, Sir J. T. Public School Education: a Lecture at Tiverton. 1860. [See Edinburgh Rev. CXIII, 1861; Quart. Rev. CVIII, 1860; and see Paterfamilias below.]

Creasy, E. S. Some Account of Eton. 1848. [See Edinburgh Rev. CXIII, 1861.]

—— Memoirs of Eminent Etonians: with Notices on the Early History of Eton College. 1850.

Gambier-Parry, Ernest. Annals of an Eton House. 1907. [1839–1906.]

Johnson, W. (Cory). Eton Reform. 1861. [See Edinburgh Rev. CXIII, 1861.]

—— Hints for Eton Masters, 1862. 1898.

Johnson, W. (Cory). Extracts from the Letters and Journals of William Cory: selected by

F. W. Cornish. Oxford, 1897. [Eton, 1832–42, 1845–72; King's College, Cambridge, 1842–5.]

Leslie, S. The End of a Chapter. 1916. [Rev. and re-written, 1929. Eton and Cambridge.]

Lubbock, A. Memories of Eton and Etonians: with Boys' Chances at Eton by Robin Lubbock, 1854–63. 1899.

'Paterfamilias' [M. J. Higgins alias 'Jacob Omnium'?]. Letters. Cornhill Mag. May, Dec. 1860, March 1861.

Quart. Rev. XXV, 1821, LII, 1834, CLXXI, 1890, CLXXXVII, 1898. [On Eton.]

Edward Warre : a Biography. By C. R. L. Fletcher. 1922.

Lawrence, Sir J. The Etonian out of Bounds or Poetry and Prose. 2 vols. 1828.

Macnaghten, H. Fifty Years of Eton in Prose and Verse. 1924.

Stapylton, H. E. C. Eton School Lists 1791–1850. 1864. [Appendix 1853–6–9, Eton, 1868; Second Appendix 1862–5–8, 1871–4–7, 1884.]

Austen-Leigh, R. A. Eton Records. 1903.

—— Eton v. Winchester. 1903.

—— 'Upon St. Andrew's Day,' 1841–1901. Eton, 1902.

Stone, C. R. The Eton Glossary. Eton, 1903 (2nd edn).

The Etonian, a Magazine. I, II, Windsor, 1820–1, 1821–2; 1824 (4th edn). [See Quart. Rev. XXV, 1821.]

Some Unpublished Letters from A. H. Hallam. Ed. M. Zamick, John Rylands Lib. Bulletin, XVIII, 1934.

The Eton College Chronicle. No. 1, 14 May 1863; No. 1000, 5 March 1903.

Eton College Magazine. Eton, 1832.

Eton Addresses. Eton, 1840. [Verse.]

The Eton Observer, a Miscellany conducted by present Etonians. Eton, 1860.

The Kaleidoscope conducted by Eton Boys. Eton, 1833.

The Eton Book of the River. By L. S. R. Byrne and E. L. Churchill. 1935.

Alumni Felsted, Boys entering at Felsted School, 1852–1921. Felsted, 1921.

Fifty Years of Fettes: Memories of Old Fettesians, 1870–1920. Edinburgh, 1931.

The Godolphin School, 1726–1926. By M. A. Douglas and C. R. Ash. 1928.

Graham Street Memories. By B. Dunning. 1931. [Francis Holland School Jubilee.]

[Grey Coat Hospital.] An Old Westminster Endowment as recorded in the Minute Books. By E. S. Day. 1902.

Haileybury College, Past and Present. By L. S. Milford. 1909.

Memorials of Old Haileybury College. By F. C. Danvers and Others. Ed. Sir M.

Monier Williams, 1894. [See Edinburgh Rev. xxvii, 1816, and Quart. Rev. clxxix, 1894].

Haileybury Register, 1862–1922. Ed. L. A. Speakman, Haileybury, [1922].

Harrow School. By E. W. Howson and G. T. Warner. 1898. [See Quart. Rev. clxxxix, 1899.]

Harrow School Register, 1801–1900. Ed. R. C. Welch, rev. M. G. Dauglish, 1901.

Bowen, E. E. Harrow Songs and other Verses. 1886.

The Harrow Life of Henry Montagu Butler. By E. Graham. 1920.

Butler, J. E. Recollections of George Butler. Bristol, 1892. [Harrow and Cheltenham. See also under Winchester.]

Byron, G. G., Baron. On a Change of Masters at a Great Public School. [1805.] On a Distant View of Harrow. [1806.] [In Hours of Idleness, 1807.]

Concio apud Scholae Hergensis Gubernatores habita xj Kal. Jul. 1838.

Minchin, J. G. C. Old Harrow Days. 1898.

Moore, J. F. Fifty Years at Harrow. Cornhill Mag. Jan. 1932.

Recollections and Impressions of the Revd. John Smith of Harrow. By E. D. and G. H. Rendall. 1913.

Recollections of Schooldays at Harrow. Manchester, 1890.

Reminiscences of a Harrow Master. 1928. [1893 onwards.]

Robert Somervell, Chapters of Autobiography edited by his Sons. 1935. [Harrow, 1887–1911.]

Trollope, A. An Autobiography. [Ed. H. M. Trollope], 2 vols. Edinburgh 1883. [See also T. A. Trollope under Winchester below, p. 134, Harrow and Winchester.]

Vaughan, C. J. Letter to Viscount Palmerston on the Monitorial System. 1854 (2nd edn). [See Observations on the Abused Reform of the Monitorial System. By the Earl of Galloway, 1854; Remarks addressed to Dr. Vaughan. By Anti-Monitor, 1854; A Few Words on the Monitorial System. By One who was a Monitor, 1854.]

[Hill, M. D.] Plans for the Government and Liberal Instruction of Boys in Large Numbers as practized at Hazelwood School. 1822. [Title of 2nd edn, 1825, begins 'Public Education. Plans,' etc. (rptd 1894); ascribed to Arthur Hill and others. See Edinburgh Rev. xli, 1825 (by Jeffrey) and London Mag. ix, 1824 (by De Quincey).]

The Laws of Hazelwood School. By R. and F. Hill. 1827.

Sketch of the System of Education at Bruce Castle, Tottenham, and Hazelwood. 1833. [By Arthur Hill.]

The Pupils of Hill-Top School, Birmingham. By T. W. Hill. Birmingham, 1815. [Hill-Top, 1803–19, was the predecessor of the Hills' schools, Hazelwood, etc.]

Kelly College Register, 1877–1927. Tavistock, 1930. [Compiled by A. O. V. Penny.]

Why I helped to found King Alfred School [Hampstead]. By One who did. 1914.

Lyle, H. W. King's and some Kingsmen. 1935. [King's College, London Medical School.]

Kingswood School: History, Registers of Woodhouse Grove School. By Three Old Boys. 1898.

Lancing [College], 1848–1930. By B. W. T. Handford and Others. Oxford, 1933.

Register of the Leeds Grammar School, 1820–1896. 1897. [Compiled by J. H. D. Matthews and V. Thompson.]

Leeds Modern School, 1845–1931. By E. E. Bullus. Leeds, 1931.

Lichfield Grammar School: Short History. By P. Linthwaite. 1925.

Liverpool Collegiate Institution: Origin and Progress. Liverpool, 1843.

Short History of the Grammar School at Macclesfield, 1503 to 1910. By D. Wilmot. Macclesfield, 1910.

Manchester Free Grammar School: by an Old Scholar. 1849.

History of the Foundations in Manchester of Christ's College, Chetham's Hospital and the Free Grammar School. 3 vols. Manchester, 1828–33.

A History of Marlborough College. By A. G. Bradley, A. C. Champneys, J. W. Baines. 1893; rev. J. R. Taylor, H. Brentnall and G. C. Turner, 1923.

Other Days: Recollections of Rugby and Marlborough in the Sixties. By A. G. Bradley. 1913.

Lockwood, E. Early Days of Marlborough College. 1893. [See also Cotton, S. A. below.]

Marlborough College Register, 1843–1889. 1890.

Marlborough College Register, 1843–1904. 1905.

Marlborough in the Sixties. Quart. Rev. April 1933.

History of Mill Hill School, 1807–1907. [1909]; 1807–1923 (2nd edn). By N. G. B. James. Reigate, [1925].

Norwich Grammar School, History of. Norwich, 1932.

Statutes of Robert Johnson, Oakham and Uppingham. Uppingham, 1837.

Paston Grammar School. By C. R. Forder. N. Walsham, 1934.

The System pursued in the Pestalozzian Academy, South Lambeth: with some Remarks on Education. 1826. [The anon. author claims to have had daily intercourse with Pestalozzi at Yverdon.]

A History of Prior Park College and its Founder, Bishop Baines. By J. S. Roche. 1931.

A Year's Sermons preached in St. Peter's College, Radley. By W. Sewell. 2 vols. Oxford, 1854–69.

High Church Education, Delusive and Dangerous, being an Exposition of the System adopted by W. Sewell. By F. Close. 1855.

Memoir of George Wharton, Precentor of St. Peter's College, Radley. [1862–1914.] By R. Beddoes, Wallingford, 1932.

Latymer, H. B. M., Baron. Chances and Changes. Edinburgh, 1931. [Radley, 1889–95, Oxford, 1895–9.]

Foster, W. The Ratcliffe Charity, 1536–1936. 1936. [The Coopers Company's schools.]

Records and Reminiscences of Repton. By E. S. Messiter. Repton, 1907.

Repton and its Neighbourhood. By F. C. Hipkins. Repton, 1899 (2nd edn).

Repton Village, Church, Priory and School. By F. C. Hipkins. Derby, [1894].

Rivington and Blackwood Grammar School. By M. M. Kay. Manchester, 1931.

The Roffensian Register, 1835–1936. Rochester, 1937 (4th edn).

The Book of Rugby School, History and Daily Life. By E. M. Goulburn. 1856. [See Quart. Rev. CII, 1857.]

Cotton, S. A. Memoir of Geo. Edwd Lynch Cotton. 1871. [Rugby under Arnold; also Westminster 1825–32, and Marlborough.]

The School House, Rugby: Annals. By E. Davies. 1932.

Recollections of Rugby. By an Old Rugbeian [R. N. Hutton]. 1848.

Rugby Memoir of Archbishop Temple. By F. E. Kitchener. 1907.

Musings of an Old Schoolmaster. By T. Steele. Oxford, 1932. [Temple at Rugby.]

Rugby School Register, 1675–1904. 3 vols. 1881–1904.

Selfe, S. G. F. Notes on Tom Brown's Schooldays, with Information as to Rugby School, 1828–42. [Rugby?], 1909. [See also Hughes p. 119 above.]

The Leaflet. By Members of Rugby School. Rugby, 1883–1887.

Saint Martin's in the Fields High School. By D. H. Thomas. 1929.

St Leonard's School [St Andrews] 1877–1927. 1927.

The Admission Registers of St Paul's School. By R. B. Gardiner. Vol. II (1876–1905), 1906.

K., H. [Herbert Kynaston]. Lays of the Seven Half Centuries. 1859.

Reminiscences of a Public School Boy. By W. N. Marcy. 1932. [St Paul's under Walker.]

Saint Paul's School Fifty Years Ago. By L. Magnus. Cornhill Mag. May 1933.

Sams, Sir H. A. Pauline and Old Pauline, 1884–1931. Cambridge, 1933.

Sedbergh School and its Chapel. Leeds, 1897.

Sedgley Park School, History of. By F. C. Husenbeth. 1856.

Sevenoaks School and its Founder. By J. T. Lennox. Sevenoaks, 1932.

The Sherborne Register, 1550–1937. Sherborne, 1937.

Annals of Shrewsbury School. By G. W. Fisher and J. Spencer Hill. 1899.

Moss of Shrewsbury, a Memoir, 1841–1917. By his Wife. 1932.

Shrewsbury School: The Last Fifty Years. By W. J. Pendlebury and J. M. West. Shrewsbury, 1932.

Shrewsbury School: Recent Years. Shrewsbury, 1935 (rev. edn).

Shrewsbury. By J. M. West. 1937. [Foundation to 1936.]

Headmasters of Shrewsbury School. Shrewsbury, 1937.

Butler, S. A Letter to Henry Brougham, Esq. 1820.

A Sidcot Pageant. By E. Roberts. 1935. [Sidcot School, Somerset.]

Southwell Grammar and Song Schools. By W. A. James. Lincoln, 1927.

Stonyhurst College, 1592–1894. By J. Gerard. Belfast, 1894.

Memorials of Stonyhurst College. By J. G[erard]. 1881.

Stonyhurst, Past and Present. By J. Gruggen and J. Keating. 1901.

Stonyhurst Memories. By P. H. Fitzgerald. 1895.

The Old School Lists of Tonbridge School. Ed. W. G. Hart, 1933.

Tonbridge School, Register of, 1820–1893. Ed. W. O. Hughes-Hughes, 1893. [1826–1910, ed. H. E. Steed, 1911 (3rd edn).]

How not to do it as exemplified by the Skinners in their Government of Tonbridge School. By An Old Tonbridgean. [1873.]

The Endowed Schools Debate and the alleged neglect of the Skinners' Scheme. [1874.]

To the Governors of Tonbridge School. By J. C. Conybeare. [1877.] [See also Edinburgh Rev. XXXVI, 1822.]

Trent College, 1868–1927. By M. A. J. Tarver. 1930.

Toynbee Hall: Fifty Years of Social Progress. By T. A. R. Pimlott. 1935.

United Services College, 1874–1911. 1934 (priv. ptd).

University College School, London. Register 1831–1891: with Historical Introduction by T. Orme. [1892.]

From Gower Street to Frognal, University College School, 1830–1907. By F. W. Felkin. 1909.

Upper Sunbury School, Middlesex: for a limited Number of Persons of Distinction and Respectability. By W. H. Lauphier. 1816.

Uppingham School Roll, 1824 to 1894. 1894. [See also Statutes of Robert Johnson, above, p. 132.]

Forty Years of Uppingham: Memories and Sketches. By J. P. Graham. 1932.

Wellington College, The Making of. By J. L. Bevir. 1920.

The Trefoil. By A. C. Benson. 1923. [Wellington College, 1859–1873.]

A Short Account of the Discipline, Studies and Examinations, Prizes, etc. of Westminster School. [By Richard Williamson.] 1845 (anon.). [Rptd from Quart. Journ. of Education.]

Westminster School Register, 1764–1883. By G. F. R. Barker and A. H. Stenning. 1892.

The Record of Old Westminsters. 2 vols. 1928.

List of Queen's Scholars of St. Peter's College, Westminster since 1663. 1852.

The Works of Jeremy Bentham. Ed. J. Bowring, 11 vols. Edinburgh, 1843. [Vol. x, ch. ii, Westminster and Oxford. See The Education of Jeremy Bentham, below, p. 136.]

A Letter to the Edinburgh Review in answer to No. CV [LIII, 1831] respecting Westminster School. 1831.

A Very Short Letter from One Old Westminster to Another. 1829.

The Trifler, a Periodical Paper. March–Sept. 1817.

[See also W. Vincent above, p. 129.]

Whitgift Grammar School: History and Register. Croydon, 1892.

The Whitgift Foundation: a Sermon by E. H. Genge. Croydon, 1892.

History of Wigan Free Grammar School. By G. C. Chambers. Wigan, 1937 (2nd edn).

Winchester College and the Quarterly Review. Quart. Rev. CLXXVII, 1893.

Annals of my Early Life, 1806–46. By Charles Wordsworth. 1891. [Harrow, Oxford, Winchester.]

Vindiciae Wykehamicae: in a Letter to Henry Brougham. By W. L. Bowles.

1819 (2nd edn). [The Pamphleteer, vol. XIII; see Edinburgh Rev. XXXI, 1819.]

Winchester in 1867. By J. S. Furley. Winchester, 1936. [Ridding's headmastership.]

Some Account of Fagging at Winchester. By Sir A. Malet. 1828.

Letter to Sir Alexander Malet. By An Old Etonian. 1829. [See Quart. Rev. XXXIX, 1829.]

What I remember. By T. A. Trollope. 3 vols. 1877–9. [Harrow, 1818–20; Winchester, 1820–9; Oxford, 1829–32.]

The Barring Out. By M. Edgeworth. 1806. [Winchester 'rebellion,' of 1793.]

Letters (1807–1810) from Thomas Arnold when a School Boy at Winchester. Theology, June, July 1932.

Winchester Word Book. By R. G. Wrench. Winchester, 1891.

School-Life at Winchester College. [By R. B. Mansfield.] 1870.

Winchester in the Seventies. By J. E. Vincent, Cornhill Mag. Sept. 1909.

Winchester College Illustrated. By C. F. C. Hawkes. 1933.

The Woodard Schools. [See Nathaniel Woodard. By J. L. Otter, 1925.]

The Story of the Woodard Schools. By K. E. Kirk. 1937.

Wyggeston's Hospital, Hospital Schools and Grammar School, 1511–1893. By Geo. Cowie. Leicester, 1893.

Atkins, T. The History of St. John's College, Battersea. 1906.

City of London Literary and Philosophical Institution. [See Edinburgh Rev. XLVII, 1828.]

Davis, V. D. A History of Manchester College to its Establishment in Oxford. 1932.

Harrison, R. Sermons on Various Important Subjects: with Life of the Author by W. Harrison. Manchester, 1813.

Mansfield College, Oxford: Origin and Opening. By Various Authors. 1890.

Mechanics' Institutes and Libraries. [By Charles Baker in Central Society of Education, First Publication, 1837. See also Adult Education, above, p. 117 and Quart. Rev. XXXII, 1825.]

Naval Education. Quart. Rev. CXLV, 1878.

Queen's College, London. [See Quart. Rev. LXXXVI, 1850.]

Annals of Sandhurst: a Chronicle of the Royal Military College, with a Sketch of the History of the Staff College. By A. F. Mockler-Ferryman. 1900.

Royal Military College: H.M. Warrants and Statutes. 1802.

Social Science: Cassell's Prize Essays by Working Men and Women. 1861.

F. SCHOOL- AND TEXT-BOOKS: CHILDREN'S BOOKS

Bain, A. English Composition and Rhetoric. 1866.
—— On Teaching English. 1887.
Beattie, J. The Grammarian: or the English Writer and Speaker's Assistant. 1838.
Blair, Hugh. Lectures on Rhetoric and Belles Lettres. 3 vols. 1817.
Butterworth, J. Young Arithmetician's Instructor, Directions for Current Hand. Edinburgh, 1805.
Cassell's Popular Educator. 6 vols. 1852–5, 1862–4, 1867–70, 1872–5, 1876–9, 1880–4. [Various authors.]
The New Popular Educator. 8 vols. 1899, 1900–1, 1903, 1905, 1906, 1910; 6 vols. 1919.
Dalton, J. Elements of English Grammar. 1801.
Edgeworth, R. L. Poetry explained for Young People. 1802.
—— Early Lessons. 2 vols. 1815 (rev. edn).
—— Readings on Poetry. 1816.
Gaultier, A. E. C. Method of Making Abridgments or Rules for analysing Authors. 2 pts, 1800–1.
Greenwood, J. The London Vocabulary, English and Latin—Things as well as Words. 1802.
Hazlitt, W. A New and Improved Grammar of the English Language. 1810. [Rptd in Complete Works, ed. P. P. Howe, vol. II, 1931. See also G. Keynes, Hazlitt's Grammar Abridged, Library, XIII, 1932.]
Mavor, W. Universal Stenography. [1807.]
Newman, F.` W. Robilius Cruso: Robinson Crusoe in Latin: to lighten Tedium to a Learner. 1884. [An entirely different work is Robinson Crusoeus Latine scripsit F. J. Goffaux, Paris, 1807, which is a version of J. H. Campe's Robinson der Jüngere. There were London edns of 1820, 1823 and, by F. W. Grafton, in 1927. Also P. A. Barnett 'amended and re-arranged' Goffaux in 1907 (The Story of Robinson Crusoe in Latin).]
Penrose, Elizabeth (née Cartwright). Mrs Markham's History of England. 1823.
—— Mrs Markham's History of France. 1828.
—— Promiscuous Questions on Mrs Markham's History. By E. C. Hadwen. 1856.
Phonic Reading Books under the sanction of the Committee of Council on Education. [See Quart. Rev. LXXIV, 1844.]
Seeley, Sir J. English in Schools. [In Lectures and Essays, 1895.]
Thelwall, J. Selections for the Illustration of a Course of Instructions on the Rhythmus and Utterance of the English Language. 1812.

Thornton, R. J. Virgilius Maro, School Virgil whereby Boys will acquire Ideas as well as Words. 1812.
Whately, R. Rhetoric. 1828. [Rptd from the Encyclopaedia Metropolitana.]
Williams, A. M. The Scottish School of Rhetoric. 1897. [See Quart. Rev. XXXII, 1825.]

Children's Books

[See F. J. H. Darton, Children's Books in England, Cambridge, 1932, and the special section, pp. 564–79 below.]

Amey, Mlle. Atalinda ou l'Éducation mise en Practique pour la Jeunesse. 1812.
Argus, A. The Juvenile Spectator. Pt I (Tempers, Manners and Foibles of Young Persons), 1813.
Barry, F. V. A Century of Children's Books. [1922.]
The Child's Instructor, a First Book. 1828.
The Child's Magazine for 1826.
The Child's Own Book for 1839.
Cobbin, I. Elements of Arithmetic for Children. 1828.
Dutton, R. History of Ferocious and Foreign Quadrupeds 1806.
Edgeworth, M. The Parent's Assistant or Stories for Children. Pt I, 1796 (2nd edn); 6 vols. 1800 (3rd edn); ed. A. T. Ritchie, 1897 (selections). Tr. French, Geneva, [1826?].
Evans, J. The Juvenile Tourist through Great Britain. 1810.
Field, E. M. The Child and His Book. [1891.]
Hack, M. Harry Beaufoy: or the Pupil of Nature. 1821.
History of Young Edwin and Little Jessy: the Pleasant Walk which William and Winnifred took with Marjery who lives at the Foot of Parnassus. 1802.
Jones, M. A. The History of England from Julius Caesar to George IV. 1826.
Joyce, J. Scientific Dialogues for the Instruction and Amusement of Young People. 1840.
'A Lady.' A Peep at the Esquimaux to which is annexed a Polar Pastoral. 1825.
Matthews, Mrs C. The Lesson of Truth. York, 1806.
Matthews, E. Original Hymns and Poems for Children. 1835.
McDougall, Mrs. Letters from Sarawak addressed to a Child. 1854.
Olley, J. B. The Root of Grammar correctly taught in One Month, particularly recommended for the Nursery, Preparatory Schools and Parents. 1827.
[Peacock, T. L.] Sir Hornbook or Childe Lancelot's Expedition: a Grammatico-allegorical Ballad. 1814.

Phelps, Mrs. The Good Aunt, or a Summer in the Country. 1811.

The Pleasing Preceptor. Familiar Instructions in Natural History and Physics to inform and amuse. Chiefly from the German of G. A. Anthony Vieth. 1800–1. Quart. Rev. LXXIV, 1844, CLXXXIII, 1896.

Sandham, E. The History of William Selwyn. 1815.

Sherwood, M. M. History of the Fairchild Family: Stories to show the Importance of a Religious Education. 1818. [Many later edns to 1913.]

—— The History of Henry Milner, a Little Boy not brought up according to the Fashions of this World. 1822.

—— A Drive in the Coach through the Streets of London. 1830.

Taylor, I. Scenes in Africa for the Amusement and Instruction of Little Tarry-at-Home Travellers. 1821.

—— The Mine. 1832.

Taylor, J. and A. Original Poems for Infant Minds. 1807.

—— Essays in Rhyme and Manners. 1816.

Trimmer, S. The Ladder of Learning: edited and improved. 1849.

Tuer, A. W. Pages and Pictures from Forgotten Children's Books. 1898.

Turner, R. An Easy Introduction to the Arts and Sciences. 1807.

Ward, A. Some Aspects of Infant Education. [In Education in the Nineteenth Century, ed. R. D. Roberts, Cambridge, 1901.]

Welsh, C. On some Books for Children of the Last Century. Coloured Books for Children. Privately Printed Opuscula of the Sette of Odd Volumes. Nos. 11 (1886) and 13 (1887).

The Young Gentleman's Book: Choice Readings in Popular Science and Natural History. 1832 (2nd edn). [Dedication to Lord Brougham.]

G. MEMOIRS

Sir Henry Wentworth Acland, Regius Professor, Oxford. By J. B. Atlay. 1903.

Sir Thomas Dyke Acland, Memoir and Letters. Ed. A. H. D. Acland. 1902.

Almond of Loretto. Life and Selection from Letters. By R. J. Mackenzie. 1905.

Matthew Arnold. By G. W. E. Russell. 1904. [Ch. III.]

Matthew Arnold: a Critic of the Victorian Period. By C. H. Harvey. 1931. [Ch. III.]

Fitch, Sir J. G. Thomas and Matthew Arnold and their Influence on Education. 1897.

Thomas Arnold. Life and Correspondence. By A. P. Stanley. 1844. [See Edinburgh Rev. LXXXI, 1845.]

Findlay, J. J. Arnold of Rugby: his School Life and Contributions to Education. Cambridge, 1897.

Dr Arnold of Rugby. By S. G. F. Selfe. 1889.

Dr Arnold. [In Eminent Victorians. By G. L. Strachey. 1918.]

Arnold of Rugby. By A. Whitridge. Introduction by Sir M. E. Sadler. 1928.

William James Ashley. A Life. By Anne Ashley. 1932.

Austin, Alfred. Autobiography, 1835–1910. 1911. [St Edward's School, York, Stonyhurst and Oscott, 1843–53.]

Badley, J. H. A Schoolmaster's Testament. Oxford, 1937.

Alexander Bain. Autobiography. 1904.

Balfour, Arthur James, Earl of. Chapters of Autobiography. 1930. [Eton and Trinity College, Cambridge.]

Canon S. F. Barnett: Life, Work and Friends. By Henrietta Barnett. 1918. [Toynbee Hall.]

Andrew Bell. Life, comprising the History of the System of Mutual Tuition. By R. and C. C. Southey. 3 vols. 1844.

—— An Old Educational Reformer, Andrew Bell. By J. M. D. Meiklejohn. Edinburgh, 1881.

Edward White Benson, Archbishop of Canterbury. 2 vols. 1899. By A. C. Benson. [Wellington College.]

Benson, Frank. My Memoirs. 1930. [Brighton, Winchester, Oxford.]

Bentham, Jeremy. [In Sir L. Stephen, The English Utilitarians, 3 vols. 1900. Includes also James and John Stuart Mill.]

The Education of Jeremy Bentham. By C. W. Everett. New York, 1932.

Archbishop Bernard, Professor, Prelate and Provost. By R. H. Murray. 1931. [Trinity College, Dublin.]

Besant, Sir Walter. An Autobiography. 1902. [Cambridge and the People's Palace.]

George Birkbeck. Memoir and Review. By J. G. Godard. 1884.

W. J. Birkbeck: Life and Letters. By Rose K. Birkbeck. 1922. [Magdalen College, Oxford.]

Blair, Sir D. O. Hunter. A Medley of Memories. 1919. [May Place; Eton; Magdalen College, Oxford, 1864–75; Oxford, 1899–1903.]

Sir Nathan Bodington, first Vice-Chancellor of the University of Leeds. A Memoir. By W. H. Draper. 1912.

Edward Ernest Bowen. Memoir, with Essays, Songs and Verses. By W. E. Bowen. 1902. [King's College, London, 1852–4; Harrow, 1859–1901.]

Henry Bradshaw. Memoir. By G. W. Prothero. 1888. [Eton, 1843–50; King's College, Cambridge, 1850; University Librarian, 1875–86.]

W. C. Braithwaite [1862–1922]. By A. Ll. B. Thomas and E. B. Emmott. 1931. [Adult schools.]

Brodrick, G. C. Memories and Impressions, 1831–1900. 1900. [Balliol and Merton Colleges, Oxford.]

Brookfield, F. M. The Cambridge 'Apostles.' 1906.

Brougham, Henry, Baron. Life and Times written by Himself. 3 vols. Edinburgh, 1871.

Brougham and his Early Friends, 1798–1809. Ed. R. H. M. B. Atkinson and G. A. Jackson, 3 vols. 1908.

William Haig Brown. Short Biographical Memoir. Ed. H. E. Haig Brown, 1908.

Thomas Edward Brown: A Memorial Volume, 1830–1930. By various authors. Cambridge, 1930. [Oxford, 1849–53; Clifton.]

Oscar Browning. By H. E. Wortham. 1927. [Eton and King's College, Cambridge.]

Memorials of Edward Burne-Jones. By G. B.-J. [Lady Burne-Jones]. 2 vols. 1904. [King Edward's School, Birmingham, 1844–52; Exeter College, Oxford, 1853–5.]

Burrows, Montagu. Autobiography: with Notes by C. W. C. Oman. 1908.

Winfrid Burrows, 1858–1929. By Mary Moore. 1932. [Eton and Oxford.]

Arthur John Butler: Memoir. By Sir A. Quiller Couch. 1917. [Bradfield, 1852–7; Eton, 1857–63; Trinity College, Cambridge, 1863–70.]

Recollections of George Butler [1819–1890]. By Josephine E. Butler. Bristol, [1892]. [Harrow, Cambridge, Oxford, Durham, Liverpool.]

The Harrow Life of Henry Montagu Butler [1860–85]. By E. Graham. 1920.

Henry Montagu Butler, Master of Trinity College, Cambridge (1886–1918). By J. R. M. Butler. 1925.

Samuel Butler: Life and Letters. By Samuel Butler [his grandson]. 2 vols. 1896. [See Quart. Rev. CLXXXVII, 1898.]

Ingram Bywater: the Memoir of an Oxford Scholar, 1840–1914. By W. W. Jackson. 1917.

Sir Edwin Chadwick: 1800–1890. By Maurice Marston. 1925.

John Willis Clark. 'J.' A Memoir by A. E. Shipley. 1913. [Registrary, University of Cambridge, 1891–1910.]

Edward Daniel Clarke: Life and Remains. By W. Otter. 2 vols. 1825. ['Stone Clarke.']

Anne Jemima Clough. A Memoir. By B. A. Clough. 1897. [First Principal, Newnham College, Cambridge.]

Arthur Hugh Clough: Letters and Remains. 1865. [Rugby, 1829–36; Oxford, 1837–48; University Hall, London, 1849–52.]

Thomas Cooper. Cooper's Journal. 1850.
—— Life. By Himself. 1872.

Edward Copleston. Memoir with Selections from Diary and Correspondence. By W. J. Copleston. 1851.

Extracts from the Letters and Journals of William Cory [Johnson]. Ed. F. W. Cornish. Oxford, 1897. [Eton, 1832–42, 1845–72; King's College, Cambridge, 1842–5.]

Courtney, J. E. An Oxford Portrait Gallery. 1931. [Later 19th cent.]

Edward Byles Cowell. Life and Letters. By George Cowell. 1904. [Ipswich School, 1833–42; Oxford, 1850–6; Sanskrit Professor, Cambridge, 1867–1903.]

Mandell Creighton. Life and Letters. By Louise Creighton. 2 vols. 1904. [Carlisle and Durham Schools, 1852–62; Oxford, 1862–6; Dixie Professor, Cambridge, 1884–91.]

Richard Dawes. Biographical Notice. By W. C. Henry. 1867.

The Exemplary Mr Day, 1748–89. By Sir S. H. Scott. 1934.

Augustus De Morgan. Memoir by His Wife. 1882. [Private schools; Cambridge, 1823–7; Professor, University College, London, 1828–33 and 1836–66.]

Denison, G. A. Notes of My Life, 1805–78. Oxford, 1878 (2nd edn). [Eton and Christ Church.]

Catherine Isabella Dodd, 1860–1932. By E. C. Wilson. 1936.

Thomas William Dunn. By Various Writers. 1934. [Bath College.]

Maria Edgeworth. Life and Letters. Ed. Augustus J. C. Hare, 1894.

Richard Lovell Edgeworth. Memoirs. Begun by Himself and concluded by Maria Edgeworth. 1820.

Richard Lovell Edgeworth. By M. E. Sadler. 1911.

The Edgeworths and their Circle. By A. Watson. 1921.

The Edgeworths on Practical Education. By L. C. Miall. Journ. of Education, April 1894.

William Ellis. Life with Some Account of his Writings and Labours for the Improvement of Education. By E. K. Blyth. 1889.

Farnell, L. R. An Oxonian looks back. 1934. [City of London School, 1866–74; Oxford, 1874–1928.]

Henry Fawcett. Life. By Leslie Stephen. 1885. [King's College School, 1849–51; King's College, London, 1851–2; Cambridge, 1852, Professor of Political Economy, 1863–84.]

Sir Joshua Fitch. An Account of the Life and Work. By A. L. Lilley. 1906.

Lionel Ford. By C. Alington. 1934. [Eton, 1888–1901; Repton, 1901–10; Harrow, 1910–26.]

William Edward Forster. Life. By T. Wemyss Reid. 1889.

William Warde Fowler. By R. H. Coon. Oxford, 1934. [Marlborough and Oxford.]

H. W. Fowler. By G. G. Coulton. SPE. 1935.

W. Johnson Fox. Life. By R. and E. Garnett. 1909.

Francillon, R. E. Mid-Victorian Memories. [1913.] [Cheltenham College and Cambridge.]

James Fraser, second Bishop of Manchester, 1818–1885. By Thomas Hughes, Q.C. 1887.

Edward Augustus Freeman. Life and Letters. By W. R. W. Stephens. 2 vols. 1895. [Cheam, 1837–9; private tutor, 1839–41; Oxford, 1841, Regius Professor, 1884–92.]

Friedrich W. A. Froebel: Autobiography. Tr. and ed. E. Michaelis and H. K. Moore, 1886.

Furniss, Henry Sanderson (Baron Sanderson). Memories of Sixty Years. 1931. [Ruskin College.]

Frederick James Furnivall. A Volume of Personal Record. By Various Authors. Biography by John Munro. Oxford, 1911.

Gardner, P. Autobiographica. Oxford, 1933. [Cambridge, 1865–71, 1880–87; Oxford, 1887–1925.]

Herbert B. Garrod. A Memoir. By G. Garrod. 1913. [General Secretary, Teachers' Guild of Great Britain and Ireland.]

William Ewart Gladstone. Life. By John Morley. 3 vols. 1903. [Vol. I, Eton, 1821–7; Oxford, 1828–31.]

William Ewart Gladstone. Life. Ed. T. Wemyss Reid, 1899. [Eton and Christ Church, Oxford. By A. F. Robbins; Oxford Union Society. By F. W. Hirst; Gladstone as Scholar. By A. J. Butler.]

Graves, A. P. To return to All That: an Autobiography. 1930. [Inspector of Schools, 1875–1910.]

Gray of Bradfield: A Memoir. By Selina Gray. 1931. [Headmaster, 1880–1910.]

John Richard Green. Letters. Ed. Sir L. Stephen, 1901. [Magdalen College School, 1845–52; Jesus College, Oxford, 1855–9.]

Thomas Hill Green. Memoir. By R. L. Nettleship. 1906. [Rugby, 1850; Balliol College, 1855; Tutor, 1860; Assistant Commissioner, Schools Inquiry Commission, 1864–7; Professor, 1878–82.]

Robert Gregory. Autobiography. Ed. W. H. Hutton, 1912. [Corpus Christi College, Oxford, 1840–3; Elementary Education and Voluntary Schools.]

Gretton, F. E. Memory's Harkback through Half-a-Century, 1808 to 1858. 1889. [Shrewsbury, 1814; Cambridge, 1822.]

Hare, Augustus J. C. The Story of My Life. 6 vols. 1896, 1900. [Harrow, 1847–8; Oxford, 1853–7.]

Harrison, Frederic. Autobiographic Memoirs, 1831–1910. 2 vols. 1911. [King's College School, 1843–9; Oxford, 1849–55; 'Popular Lectures,' 1861.]

A Victorian Schoolmaster: Henry Hart of Sedbergh. By G. G. Coulton. 1923.

History of the Hawtrey Family. By Florence M. Hawtrey. 2 vols. 1903.

Edward Craven Hawtrey, Headmaster and afterwards Provost of Eton. By F. St J. Thackeray. 1896. [See Quart. Rev. CLXXXVII, 1898.]

Walter Headlam. Letters and Poems, with Memoir by Cecil Headlam. 1910. [Harrow; Cambridge, 1884–1908.]

Heitland, W. E. After Many Years: Experiences and Impressions. Cambridge, 1926. [Shrewsbury, 1862–7; Cambridge, 1867.]

Memorials of Lionel Helbert: Founder and Head of West Downs, Winchester [1897–1919]. 1926.

John Stevens Henslow: Memoir by L. Jenyns (afterwards Blomefield). 1862.

Frederic Hill. An Autobiography of Fifty Years in Times of Reform. Ed. C. Hill, 1894.

George Birkbeck Hill. Letters. Ed. L. Crump, 1906. [Bruce Castle, Tottenham; Oxford, 1855–8; Bruce Castle, 1858–78.]

Sir Rowland Hill. Life by G. Birkbeck Hill. 2 vols. 1880. [Hill-Top School and Hazelwood, vol. I, bk i.]

Thomas Wright Hill. Remains, with Notices of his Life [1763–1851]. By Himself and M. D. Hill. 1859. [Hill-Top School, Birmingham. See also The Pupils of Hill-Top School, above, p. 132.]

W. B. Hodgson. Life and Letters. By J. M. D. Meiklejohn. 1883.

Quintin Hogg. Biography. By E. M. Hogg. 1904.

How, F. D. Six Great Schoolmasters. 1905. [Hawtrey, Eton; Moberly, Winchester; Kennedy, Shrewsbury; Vaughan, Harrow; Temple, Rugby; Bradley, Marlborough.]

Howson of Holt, a Study in School-life. By James Herbert Simpson. 1925.

Thomas Henry Huxley. Life and Letters. By L. Huxley. 2 vols. 1900.

Henry Jackson, O.M., Vice Master of Trinity College, Cambridge, and Regius Professor of Greek. By R. St J. Parry. Cambridge, 1926.

Sir Richard Claverhouse Jebb. Life and Letters. By Caroline Jebb. 1907.

Francis Jenkinson. Memoir by H. F. Stewart, Cambridge, 1926. [Marlborough, 1865–72; Cambridge, 1872–1923.]

Margaret Dyne Jeune. Pages from the Diary of an Oxford Lady (1843–1862). Ed. M. J. Gifford, Oxford, 1932.

W. Stanley Jevons. Letters and Journals. Edited by his Wife. 1886. [University College School, 1850–1; University College, London, 1851–4 and 1859–80.]

Jones, E. E. Constance. As I remember, an Autobiographical Ramble. Preface by W. R. Inge. 1922. [Girton, 1875; Mistress of Girton College, 1903–16.]

Jones, Sir Henry. Old Memories: the Autobiography of Sir Henry Jones. 1922.

—— Life and Letters. By H. J. W. Hetherington. 1924.

John Viriamu Jones. Life. By K. V. Jones. 1915.

John Viriamu Jones and other Oxford Memories. By E. B. Poulton. 1911. [University College, London, 1872–5; Oxford, 1876–81; Firth College, Sheffield, 1881–3; Cardiff University College, 1883–1901.]

Benjamin Jowett. Life and Letters. By E. Abbott and L. Campbell. 2 vols. 1897.

Benjamin Jowett, a Personal Memoir. By Lionel A. Tollemache. [1895.]

Sir James Kay-Shuttleworth. Life and Work. By F. Smith. 1923.

Kilbracken, Viscount [Sir Arthur Godley]. Reminiscences. 1931. [Radley under Sewell, Rugby under Temple, Balliol and Jowett.]

Kitchin, D. B. Day of my Youth. 1936. [St Peter's School, York; Harrow; Cambridge.]

Knox, E. A., Bishop. Reminiscences of an Octogenarian. 1933. [St Paul's School, C.C.C. Oxon., Voluntary Schools Controversy.]

Lancaster, J. Epitome of Events and Transactions in his Life, and Rise and Progress of the Lancasterian System. By Himself. New Haven, Conn. 1833.

Joseph Lancaster. By D. Salmon. 1904.

Walter Leaf. Some Chapters of Autobiography: Memoir. By Charlotte M. Leaf. 1932. [Harrow and Cambridge.]

W. E. H. Lecky. Memoir. By his Wife. 1909. [Cheltenham, 1852–5; Trinity College, Dublin, 1856–9.]

Samuel Lee. A Scholar of a Past Generation, a Brief Memoir of Samuel Lee. By A. M. Lee. 1896.

Augustus Austen Leigh, Provost of King's College, Cambridge. By W. A. Leigh. 1906.

Lennox, Lord William Pitt. Drawn on my Memory. 2 vols. 1866. [Westminster School, 1808–14.]

Liddell, A. G. C. Notes from the Life of an Ordinary Mortal at School, College and the World. 1911. [Eton, 1859–64; Balliol College, 1865–9.]

Henry George Liddell. A Memoir. By H. L. Thompson. 1899. [Head Master, Westminster, 1846–55; Dean of Christ Church, Oxford, 1855–91.]

H. P. Liddon. Life and Letters. By John O. Johnston. 1904. [King's College School, 1844–6; Oxford, 1846–50 and 1859–82.]

Sir Norman Lockyer. Life and Work. By T. M. Lockyer and W. L. Lockyer. With Additions by Various Authors. 1928.

Lodge, Sir Oliver. Past Years, an Autobiography. 1931.

William Lovett. Life and Struggles [by Himself]. 1876; ed. R. H. Tawney, 2 vols. 1920.

Robert Lowe, Viscount Sherbrooke. Life and Letters. By A. P. Martin. 2 vols. 1893.

Lord Macaulay. Life and Letters. By G. O. Trevelyan. 2 vols. 1876. [Trinity College, Cambridge, 1818–24.]

Lord John Manners and his Friends. By C. Whibley. 2 vols. 1925. [Eton, 1831–5; Cambridge, 1835–8.]

Cardinal Manning. Life. By Edmund S. Purcell. 2 vols. 1895. [Harrow, 1822–6; Oxford, 1827–30. Vol. i, The Voluntary Schools in mid-century. Vol. ii, Education Act, 1870, University College, Kensington.]

Cardinal Manning. By A. W. Hutton. 1892. [Voluntary Schools, ch. vii.]

Charlotte M. Mason. In Memoriam. 1923. [By various authors.]

Frederick Denison Maurice. Life. By Sir F. Maurice. 2 vols. 1884 (3rd edn).

—— Founder of the Working Men's College. By B. H. Alford. 1909.

John McT. E. McTaggart. By G. Lowes Dickinson. Cambridge, 1931. [Clifton, 1882–6; Cambridge 1886–91 and 1899–1925.]

Meyrick, Frederick. Memories of Life at Oxford. 1905. [Oxford, 1842–59; Inspector of Schools, 1859–69.]

James Mill. Biography. By A. Bain. 1882.

John Stuart Mill. Autobiography. Ed. H. Helen Taylor, 1873. [See also Bentham above, p. 136, and Quart. Rev. cxxxvi, 1874.]

Richard Monckton Milnes, Lord Houghton. Life, Letters and Friendships. By T. W. Reid. 1890 (2nd edn). [Trinity College, Cambridge, 1827–30; London University, 1830; Cambridge 'Apostles.']

Sir Robert Morant. By B. M. Allen. 1934.

Morley, John, Viscount. Recollections. 2 vols. 1917. [University College School; Cheltenham College; Oxford, 1858–62.]

William Morris. Life. By J. W. Mackail. 2 vols. 1899. [Marlborough, 1848–51; Exeter College, Oxford, 1853–5.]

Murray, Lindley. Memoirs in Letters written by Himself. York, 1826.

Newbolt, Sir Henry. The World as in My Time 1862–1932. 1932. [Clifton and Oxford.]

Francis W. Newman. Memoir and Letters. Ed. J. G. Sieveking. 1909.

Okey, Thomas. A Basketful of Memories: an Autobiographical Sketch. 1930. [Toynbee Hall and Cambridge.]

Robert Owen. Life written by Himself, with Selections from his Writings and Correspondence. 1857.

Robert Owen. By F. Podmore. 2 vols. 1906.

Robert Owen. By G. D. H. Cole. 1925. [Ch. viii, Ideas on Education.]

Owen, R. D. Threading my Way. 1874.

Francis Paget, Bishop of Oxford. By S. Paget and J. M. C. Crum. 1912. [Shrewsbury, 1864–9; Christ Church, Oxford, 1869–83 and 1885–1901.]

Palmer, Roundell (Earl of Selborne). Memorials. 2 vols. in 4 pts, 1896–8. [Rugby, 1823–5; Winchester, 1825–30; Oxford, 1830–7. University Tests, Education Act, 1870 in vol. I, pt ii; Oxford Reform, 1854, in vol. II, pt ii.]

Parr, Samuel. Parriana. Ed. E. H. Barker, 1828–9.

—— Aphorisms, Opinions and Reflections of the late Dr. Parr. Ed. E. H. Barker. 1826.

Hubert Parry: Life and Work. By C. L. Graves. 2 vols. 1926. [Eton, 1861–6; Oxford, 1867–70.]

John Brown Paton. Biography. By J. L. Paton. 1914.

Pattison, Mark. Memoirs. 1885.

Charles Henry Pearson. Memorials by Himself, his Wife and his Friends. Ed. W. Stebbing, 1900.

Sir Robert Peel, from Private Papers and Correspondence. By C. S. Parker. 3 vols. 1891–9. [Harrow, 1801–4; Oxford, 1805–8.]

Life of Bishop [John] Percival. By W. Temple. 1921. [See also From Anne to Victoria. By H. M. Vaughan, 1931.] [Head Master, Clifton College, 1862–78.]

J. H. Pestalozzi. Memoir. By C. Mayo. 1828 (2nd edn). [Lecture delivered in 1826.]

Heinrich Pestalozzi and his Plan of Education. By E. Biber. 1831.

Life and Work of Pestalozzi. By J. A. Green. 1913.

Francis Place. Life. By G. Wallas. 1898; 1918.

Lyon Playfair. Memoirs and Correspondence. By T. W. Reid. 1899.

Thomas Poole and his Friends. By Mrs Henry Sandford. 2 vols. 1888.

George Pryme. Autobiographical Recollections. Ed. A. Bayne, Cambridge, 1870.

Robert Hebert Quick. Life and Remains. By F. Storr. 1899.

Reddie of Abbotsholme. By B. M. Ward. Introduction by J. J. Findlay. 1934.

Sir Harry Reichel, 1856–1931. By Sir J. E. Lloyd. 1934.

George Ridding. By Lady Laura Ridding. 1908. [Winchester, 1866–84.]

Roberts, Mrs E. S. Sherborne, Oxford and Cambridge: Recollections. 1934.

John Arthur Roebuck. Life and Letters. Ed. R. E. Leader, 1897.

Rogers, W. Reminiscences: compiled by R. H. Hadden. 1888.

Sir Samuel Romilly. Memoirs with Selection of his Correspondence. Edited by his Sons. 3 vols. 1840.

Thomas Godolphin Rooper. Selected Writings with Memoir. By R. G. Tatton. 1907.

Roscoe, Sir H. E. The Life and Experiences of, Written by himself. 1906.

The Rt. Hon. Sir H. E. Roscoe: a biographical Sketch. By Sir T. E. Thorpe. 1916.

Sanderson of Oundle. By various authors. 1923.

The Story of a Great Schoolmaster. By H. G. Wells. 1924. [F. W. Sanderson, Head Master, Oundle, 1892–1922.]

Sir John Edwin Sandys. By N. G. L. Hammond. Cambridge, 1933.

John Sargeaunt. [See Westminster Verse. By J. Gow, 1922.]

Adam Sedgwick. Life and Letters. By J. W. Clark and T. M. Hughes. Cambridge, 1890. [See Quart. Rev. CLXXII, 1891.]

Sewell, E. M. Autobiography. Ed. E. L. Sewell. 1907.

William Sewell in Ireland. Quart. Rev. CVIII, 1860.

Percy Bysshe Shelley. Life. By T. J. Hogg. 4 vols. 1858.

Life of Shelley. By E. Dowden. 1886. [Syon House Academy; Eton, 1804–10; Oxford, 1810–11.]

Henry Sidgwick. A Memoir. By A. and E. M. S[idgwick]. 1906.

Smith, Goldwin. Reminiscences. Ed. A. Haultain, New York, 1910. [Eton, 1831–40; Oxford, 1841–5, 1851–4; the University Commissions, 1854–8, Newcastle Commission, 1858–61; Regius Professor, 1858–68.]

Reginald Bosworth Smith. Memoir. By Lady Grogan. 1909. [Marlborough, 1855–8; Oxford, 1858–64; Harrow, 1864–1901.]

Spencer, Herbert. An Autobiography. 2 vols. 1904.

Arthur Penrhyn Stanley. By R. E. Prothero and G. G. Bradley. 1893. [Rugby, 1829–34; Oxford, 1834–63.]

Sir James Fitzjames Stephen. Life. By Sir L. Stephen. 1895. [Eton, 1842–5; King's College, London, 1845–7; Cambridge, 1847–51. 'The Apostles.']

Leslie Stephen. Life and Letters. By F. W. Maitland. 1906. [Eton, 1842–8; King's College, London, 1848–50; Cambridge, 1850–4 and 1854–64.]

David Stow. Memoir. By W. Fraser. 1868.

James L. Strachan-Davidson, Master of Balliol. By J. W. Mackail. Oxford, 1925. [Oxford, 1862–1916.]

Stuart, James. Reminiscences. 1911.

Sully, James. My Life and Friends. [1918.]

Archibald Campbell Tait, Archbishop of Canterbury. Life by R. T. Davidson and W. Benham. 2 vols. 1891 (3rd edn). [Edinburgh High School and Academy, 1821–7; Glasgow University, 1827–30; Oxford 1830–42; Rugby, 1842–50; Oxford University Commission, 1850, etc.]

Talbot, Edward Stuart. Memories of Early Life. 1924. [Charterhouse; Christ Church, Oxford, 1862–6; Keble College, 1870–88.]

Frederick Temple. Rugby Memoir, 1857–69. By Francis Elliot Kitchener. 1907.

—— Memoirs. By Seven Friends. 1906.

—— An Appreciation. By E. G. Sandford. 1907.

Thomson, J. J. Recollections and Reflections. 1936.

Edward Thring. Life, Diary and Letters. By Sir G. R. Parkin. 2 vols. 1898, [1900 (2nd edn, abridged). See Quart. Rev. CLXXXVII, 1898.]

—— A Memory of. By H. Skrine. 1889.

Edward Thring, Teacher and Poet By H. D. Rawnsley. 1889.

Edward Thring, Master of Uppingham School. By W. F. Rawnsley. 1926.

Arnold Toynbee. By F. C. Montague and P. L. Gell. [In Johns Hopkins University Studies, Baltimore, 1889. Toynbee Hall.]

Sarah Trimmer. Some Account of the Life and Writings, with Original Letters. 2 vols. 1814.

William Peveril Turnbull, H.M. Inspector of Schools. By H. W. Turnbull. 1919.

Edward Warre, D.D. By C. R. L. Fletcher. 1922.

Herbert Warren of Magdalen, 1853–1930. By Laurie Magnus. 1932.

William Whewell. Life and Correspondence. By Mrs Stair Douglas. 1881. [Cambridge, 1812–66; Master of Trinity College, 1841–66.]

William Henry Widgery, Schoolmaster. By W. K. Hill. 1894.

Sir George Williams. The Founder of the Red Triangle. By J. E. Hodder. 1918. [Founder of Y.M.C.A.]

Willoughby de Broke, Baron (Richard Greville Verney). The Passing Years. 1924. [Winton House, 1879–83; Eton, 1883–8; Oxford, 1888–91.]

James Maurice Wilson. An Autobiography, 1836–1931. Ed. A. T. K. and J. S. Wilson. 1932. [King William's College; Sedbergh; Cambridge, 1855–9; Rugby, 1859–79; Clifton, 1879–1890.]

Nathaniel Woodard. Memoir. By Sir J. L. Otter. [1925.]

Charles Wordsworth. Annals of my Early Life, 1806–46. 1891. [Harrow, Oxford, Winchester.]

—— Annals of my Life, 1847–56. Ed. W. E. Hodgson. 1893. [Trinity College, Glenalmond, 1846–54.]

La Jeunesse de William Wordsworth, 1770–1798. Étude sur le ' Prelude.' Par E. Legouis. Lyons, 1891; tr. Eng. 1897. [Hawkshead and Cambridge. See also Wordsworth above, p. 120.]

Joseph Wright. Life. By E. M. Wright. 2 vols. Oxford, 1932. [See also Joseph Wright, 1855–1930. By Sir C. H. Firth. Proc. British Academy, [1933].]

Young, R. The Life of an Educational Worker, Henrietta Busk. 1934.

H. EDUCATION OF WOMEN AND GIRLS

Beale, D. On the Education of Girls. Paper at the Social Science Congress. 1866.

—— Reports issued by the Schools Inquiry Commission on the Education of Girls. 1869.

—— On the Organisation of Girls' Day Schools. Paper at the Social Science Congress. 1873.

—— Work and Play in Girls' Schools. 1898. [With L. H. M. Soulsby and J. F. Dove.]

—— Addresses to Teachers. 1908.

[See also Cheltenham Ladies' College Magazine, 1890–1.]

Dorothea Beale of Cheltenham (1831–1905). By E. Raikes. 1908.

Dorothea Beale. By E. H. Shillito. 1020.

In the Days of Miss Beale: a Study of her Work and Influence. By F. C. Steadman. 1931.

Blease, W. L. The Emancipation of Englishwomen. 1910.

Booth, J. On the Female Education of the Industrious Classes. 1855.

Bremner, C. S. Education of Girls and Women in Great Britain. 1897.

Broadhurst, F. A Word in Favor of Female Schools. [The Pamphleteer, vol. XXVII, 1826.]

Broadhurst, T. Advice to Young Ladies on the Improvement of the Mind. 1808. [See Edinburgh Rev. xv, 1810.]

Browne, E. O. Fifty Years of the Alice Ottley School, Worcester. Worcester, 1933.

Bryant, S. An Account of the N. London Collegiate School. 1886. [See Edinburgh Rev. CLXVI, 1887.]

[Bülow, Baroness M. von.] Woman's Educational Mission: an Explanation of Froebel's Infant Gardens. 1855.

Burstall, S. A. and Douglas, M. A. Public Schools for Girls. 1911.

Burstall, S. A. Retrospect and Prospect: Sixty Years of Women's Education. 1933.

Frances Mary Buss and her Work for Education. By A. E. Ridley. 1895.

Frances Mary Buss Schools' Jubilee Record. By Eleanor M. Hill and Sophie Bryant. 1900. [See also under Gurney below.]

Frances Mary Buss: Leaves from her Note-Book. By S. G. Toplis. 1896.

Butler, J. et al. Women's Work and Women's Culture. 1869. [See Edinburgh Rev. cxxx, 1869.]

Butler, R. F. and Prichard, M. H. The Society of Oxford Home Students, Retrospects and Recollections, 1879–1921. Oxford, 1930 (priv. ptd).

Clough, A. J. Hints on the Organisation of Girls' Schools. Macmillan's Mag. Oct. 1866.

Cobbe, F. P. Female Education. Paper at Social Science Congress. 1862.

—— Life as told by Herself. 1904.

Courtney, J. E. The Ladies of Oxford. [In An Oxford Portrait Gallery, 1931.]

Cowdroy, C. J. H. Wasted Womanhood. Memoir by M. Bennell. 1933.

Davies, E. On secondary Instruction relating to Girls. 1864.

—— The Application of Funds to the Education of Girls. [1865.]

—— Higher Education of Women. 1866.

—— Women in the Universities of England and Scotland. 1896.

—— Thoughts on some Questions relating to Women, 1860–1908. 1910.

Emily Davies and Girton College. By B. Stephen. 1927.

'Domina' [Barbara Hofland?]. York House: Conversations in a Ladies' School, principally founded on Facts. 1813.

Dove, J. F. [See Beale above.]

[Duppa, B. F.] Scottish Institution for the Education of Young Ladies. [In Central Society of Education, First Publication, 1837.]

[Edgeworth, M.] Letters for Literary Ladies. 1795.

Female Education. Edinburgh Rev. xv, 1810.

Ellis, Lady M. The Education of Young Ladies for Other Occupations than Teaching. [In Central Society of Education, Second Publication, 1838.]

Faithful, L. M. In the House of My Pilgrimage. 1924.

Fawcett, M. G. Free Education in its Economic Aspect: Schools Inquiry Commission on the Education of Girls: Education of Women. [In Essays and Lectures on Social and Political Subjects. By Henry and M. G. Fawcett, Cambridge, 1872.]

Froebel. [See Bülow above.]

Gardner, A. A Short History of Newnham College. Cambridge, 1921.

Gray, F. R. 'And Gladly Wolde he Lerne and Gladly Teche': a Book about Learning and Teaching. [1931.]

Grey, Mrs W. [Maria Georgina Grey, born Shirreff]. The Education of Women. 1871.

Grey, Mrs W. and Shirreff, E. A. E. Thoughts on Self-culture addressed to Women. 2 vols. 1850.

Gurney, M. Are we to have Education for Middle-class Girls? The History of Camden Collegiate Schools. 1872.

Hamilton, E. Letters on the Elementary Principles of Education. 2 vols. Bath, 1801; 1818 (6th edn).

—— Hints addressed to Patrons and Directors of Schools. 1815. [Pestalozzi's principles.]

Hill, F. The Children of the State: the Training of Juvenile Paupers. 1868; 1889. [See Edinburgh Rev. CXLII, 1875.]

—— Education of Girls and Employment of Women of the Upper Classes. 1869 (2nd edn).

Hodgson, W. B. The Education of Girls considered in connexion with University Local Examinations. A Lecture. 1864.

Jones, E. E. C. Girton College. [1913.] [See also E. E. C. Jones above, p. 139.]

Lackington, J. Confessions. 1804.

Lumsden, Dame L. S. Yellow Leaves. 1933. [Hitchin, Girton, St Leonard's School.]

Maccarthy, M. A Nineteenth Century Childhood. 1924.

Maudsley, H. Sex and Mind in Education. 1874. [See Sex in Education (A Reply). By E. Garrett Anderson, 1874. See also Edinburgh Rev. CLXVI, 1887.]

Maurice, J. F. D. Queen's College, London, its Object and Method. 1848. [See Quart. Rev. LXXXIV, LXXXVI, 1848–50.]

—— A Letter to the Bishop of London in Reply to the Article in No. 172 [LXXXVI, 1850] of the Quarterly Review. 1850.

—— Plan of a Female College. Cambridge, 1855.

Maynard, C. L. From Early Victorian Schoolroom to University. Nineteenth Century, Nov. 1914.

Mill, J. S. The Subjection of Women. 1869. [See Edinburgh Rev. cxxx, 1869.]

More, Hannah.] Hints towards forming the Character of a Young Princess. 2 vols. 1805 (*bis*). [See Edinburgh Rev. vii, 1805.]

Neff, W. The Governess. [In Victorian Working Women, 1832–1850, 1929.]

Parkes, B. R. Remarks on the Education of Girls. 1854.

Pfeiffer, E. Women and Work; relation to Health and Physical Development of the Higher Education. 1888.

Pipe, H. E. Life and Letters (1831–96). By Anna M. Stoddart. 1908.

Quart. Rev. cxix, 1866, cxxvi, 1869, cxlvi, 1878, clxxxvi, 1897.

Remarks on Female Education adapted particularly to the Regulation of Schools. 1823.

Ruskin, J. Queens' Gardens. [In Sesame and Lilies, 1865.]

Sewell, E. M. Principles of Education applied to Female Education in the Upper Classes. 2 vols. 1865. [An abridgment in one vol. by Mrs G. J. Chitty and L. H. M. Soulsby, 1914.]

Mary Martha Sherwood. Life and Times. Ed. F. J. H. Darton, [1910]. [Reading Abbey School, 1791–3; private school for girls, Wick, Worcestershire, 1817–29.]

Shirreff, E. A. E. Intellectual Education and its Influence on Women. 1858.

—— The Kindergarten. Principles of Froebel's System and their Bearing on the Education of Women. 1876. [See also Mrs W. Grey above.]

Sinclair, C. Modern Accomplishments or the March of Intellect. 1836; 1837.

—— Modern Society: Conclusion of Modern Accomplishments. 1837.

Mary Somerville. Personal Recollections and Selections from Correspondence. By M. Somerville. 1873. [See Quart. Rev. cxxxvi, 1874.]

Stephens, B. Girton College, 1869–1932. Cambridge, 1933.

'An Experienced Teacher.' The Complete Governess; a Course of Mental Instruction for Ladies. 1826.

Tennyson, A. The Princess. 1847.

Frances, E. G., Countess of Warwick, *et al.* Progress in Women's Education in the British Empire. [In Report of the Education Section, Victorian Era Exhibition, 1897, 1898.]

West, J. Letters to a Young Lady. 3 vols. 1811.

Wolstenholme, E. C. The Education of Girls, its Present and Future. [In Women's Work and Women's Culture. By J. E. Butler, 1869.]

Wordsworth, E. Glimpses of the Past. [1912.]

—— Essays, Old and New. Oxford, 1919.

Women's Education. Edinburgh Rev. cix, 1859.

Zimmern, A. Renaissance of Girls' Education in England. 1898.

I. MANUSCRIPT MATERIAL.

[See note preceding the corresponding section, Education, 1660–1800, vol. ii, p. 132 above.]

Bentham MSS. [See Report on the Bentham MSS at University College, London, By B. T. Whitaker, [1892]. Case 18 has papers on Hazelwood School and drafts for Chrestomathia, 'London University,' etc.].

Place MSS (BM. Additional MSS, 27823, 27824). [Contain papers, ptd and MS, and letters relating to Joseph Lancaster, Lancasterian and 'Chrestomathic' schools, mechanics' institutes and the foundation of 'London University.']

J. W. A.

VI. THE POLITICAL AND SOCIAL BACKGROUND

Political History; Constitutional History; Social and Economic History; Political Speeches; Letters, Diaries and Autobiographies.

A. POLITICAL HISTORY

(1) GENERAL AND MISCELLANEOUS

(a) Sources

[Representative MS collections (all in BM.) are: Bentham MSS; F. Place, Additional MSS; Sir R. Wilson, Correspondence; Gladstone MSS. See also A. T. Milne, Catalogue of the Manuscripts of Jeremy Bentham in the Library of University College, London, 1937.]

The Annual Register. 1801–.

Cobbett, W. Parliamentary History of England. 1801–3. [Continued by Hansard; see below.]

Hansard's Parliamentary Debates. 1803–.

Journals of the House of Commons.

Journals of the House of Lords.

Parliamentary Papers and Reports.

Statutes of the United Kingdom. 1801–.

The Times. 1801–.

The Edinburgh Review. 1802–.

The Quarterly Review. 1809–.

Sheridan, R. B. Speeches. 5 vols. 1816.

D'Arblay, F. (Burney). Diary and Letters. Ed. A. Dobson, 6 vols. 1904–5.

State Trials. Ed. T. B. and T. J. Howell, 1817–.

Hazlitt, W. Spirit of the Age. 1825.

The Letters of King George IV, 1812–1830. Ed. A. Aspinall and C. K. Webster, 3 vols. Cambridge, 1938.

Brougham, H. P. (Baron Brougham and Vaux). Speeches. 4 vols. 1857.

Huskisson, W. Speeches. 1831.

Canning, G. Speeches. Ed. R. Therry, 6 vols. 1828.

O'Connell, D. Life and Speeches. Ed. J. O'Connell, 2 vols. Dublin, 1846.

O'Connell's Correspondence. Ed. W. J. Fitzpatrick, 1888.

Wellesley, A. (Duke of Wellington). Dispatches [1799–1818]. Ed. J. Gurwood, 12 vols. 1834–8. Supplementary Dispatches and Memoranda [1797–1818]. Ed. 2nd Duke of Wellington, 15 vols. 1858–72. Despatches, Correspondence and Memoranda [1818–32]. Ed. 2nd Duke of Wellington, 8 vols. 1867–80.

—— Parliamentary Speeches. Ed. J. Gurwood, 1854.

The Croker Papers. Ed. L. J. Jennings, 3 vols. 1884.

Grey, C., Earl. Correspondence [with] William IV. Ed. H., Earl Grey, 2 vols. 1867.

Lieven, Princess. Correspondence with Earl Grey. Ed. and tr. G. le Strange, 1890.

Report of the Poor Law Commissioners. 1834.

Report on Municipal Corporations. 1835.

Disraeli, B. (Earl of Beaconsfield). Runnymede Letters. 1836.

—— Lord George Bentinck. A Political Biography. 1852.

—— Selected Speeches. Ed. T. E. Kebbel, 2 vols. 1882.

—— Correspondence with his Sister. 1886.

Melbourne, W. Lamb, Viscount. Papers. Ed. L. C. Sanders, 1889.

Carlyle, T. Chartism. 1839.

The Peel Papers. Ed. C. S. Parker, 1891.

Macaulay, T. B., Baron. Speeches. 1854.

Bright, J. Speeches on Questions of Public Policy. Ed. J. E. T. Rogers, 2 vols. 1868.

—— Diaries. 1930.

Cobden, R. Speeches. Ed. J. E. T. Rogers, 1870.

Russell, J., Earl. Speeches and Despatches. 2 vols. 1870.

—— Early Correspondence. Ed. R. Russell, 1913.

—— Later Correspondence. Ed. G. P. Gooch, 1925.

Protests of the Lords. Ed. J. E. T. Rogers, 3 vols. Oxford, 1875.

Gladstone, W. E. Speeches and Public Addresses. Ed. A. W. Hutton and H. J. Cohen, 2 vols. 1892.

—— Gladstone's Speeches. Descriptive Index and Bibliography by A. T. Bassett. With a Preface by Viscount Bryce and Introductions to the Selected Speeches by Herbert Paul. 1916.

Victoria, H.M. Queen. Letters. Ed. A. C. Benson and R. Viscount Esher, 3 vols. 1907. Second Series. Ed. G. E. Buckle, 3 vols. 1926–8. Third Series. Ed. G. E. Buckle, 3 vols. 1930–2.

Blunt, W. S. My Diaries. 2 vols. 1919–20.

The Milner Papers. 1931.

Esher, R., Viscount. Journals and Letters. Ed. M. V. Brett and O. Brett (Viscount Esher), 4 vols. 1934–8.

[See also under Political Speeches, and Letters, Diaries and Autobiographies, pp. 149–55 below.]

(b) Later Works

Asquith, H. H. (Earl of Oxford and Asquith). Some Aspects of the Victorian Age. Oxford, 1918.

Bright, J. F. History of England. Vols. IV, V, 1875–1904.

Brinton, C. English Political Thought in the Nineteenth Century, 1933.

Brodrick, G. C. and Fotheringham, J. K. The Political History of England. Vol. XI (1801–1837), 1906.

Butler, J. R. M. History of England, 1815–1918. 1928.

—— The Passing of the Great Reform Bill. 1914.

Cambridge Modern History. Vols. IX–XII, Cambridge, 1906–10.

Cambridge History of the British Empire. Cambridge, 1929–.

Cambridge Shorter History of India. Ed. H. H. Dodwell, Cambridge, 1934.

Cornish, F. W. The English Church in the Nineteenth Century. 1899.

Davis, H. W. C. The Age of Grey and Peel. Oxford, 1929.

Dicey, A. V. Relations between Law and Opinion in England in the Nineteenth Century. 1905.

Egerton, H. E. A Short History of British Colonial Policy. 1897.

Ensor, R. C. K. England, 1870–1914. Oxford, 1935. (Oxford History of England, XIV.)

Firth, Sir C. H. English History in English Poetry, from the French Revolution to the Death of Queen Victoria. 1911.

Freemantle, G. F. England in the Nineteenth Century. 1929–.

Gretton, R. H. A Modern History of the English People, 1880–1910. 2 vols. 1912.

Halévy, E. A History of the English People. Tr. Eng. 3 vols. (1815–41), 1924. [Vol. I (Epilogue), 1895–1905, vol. II, 1905–14, 1934.]

—— The Growth of Philosophic Radicalism. Tr. Eng. 1928.

Hirst, F. W. Gladstone as Financier and Economist. 1931.

Hyde, L. Gladstone at the Board of Trade. 1934.

Knaplund, P. Gladstone's Colonial Policy. 1927.

Low, S. and Sanders, L. C. The Political History of England. Vol. XII (1837–1901), 1907.

Lucas, C. P. Introduction to a Historical Geography of the British Colonies. 1866.

—— Historical Geography of the British Colonies. 1888.

Mallet, B. British Budgets, 1887–1912. 1913.

Marriott, Sir J. A. R. England since Waterloo. 1913.

—— Queen Victoria and her Ministers. 1933.

—— Modern England: A History of My Own Times. 1934.

Martineau, H. History of the Thirty Years' Peace (1816–46). 4 vols. 1877 (rev.).

Overton, J. H. The English Church in the Nineteenth Century, 1800–33. 1894.

Paul, H. History of Modern England. 5 vols. 1904–6.

Robertson, Sir C. G. England under the Hanoverians. 1911.

Sharpe, R. London and the Kingdom. Vol. III, 1895.

Social and Political Ideas of the Victorian Age. Ed. F. J. C. Hearnshaw, 1933.

The History of The Times. Vol. I (1785–1841), 1935; vol. II (1841–84), 1939.

Trevelyan, G. M. British History in the Nineteenth Century. 1928.

Veitch, G. S. Genesis of Parliamentary Reform. 1913.

Walpole, Sir S. History of England from 1815. 6 vols. 1890.

—— The History of Twenty-five Years. 4 vols. 1904–8.

Williams, W. E. The Rise of Gladstone to the Leadership of the Liberal Party, 1859 to 1868. Cambridge, 1934.

Woodward, E. L. The Age of Reform, 1815–70. Oxford, 1938. (Oxford History of England, XIII.)

(c) Biographies, Memoirs and Family Correspondence

[Arranged chronologically according to the periods covered in each item.]

Dictionary of National Biography. Ed. Sir L. Stephen and Sir S. Lee, 63 vols. 1885–1900.

Rose, J. H. Life of William Pitt. 1923.

Hammond, J. L. Charles Fox, a Political Study. 1903.

Hyde, H. M. The Rise of Castlereagh. 1933.

Brougham, H. P., Baron. Life and Times, Written by himself. Edinburgh, 1871.

Aspinall, A. Lord Brougham, and the Whig Party. Manchester, 1928.

Garratt, G. T. Lord Brougham. 1935.

Campbell, J., Baron. Lives of the Lord Chancellors. 8 vols. 1845–69.

Cartwright, E. Life and Correspondence of Major Cartwright. 2 vols. 1926.

Coupland, R. Life of Wilberforce. Oxford, 1923.

Southey, R. Life of Nelson. 1813.

Mahan, A. Life of Nelson. 1897.

Guedalla, P. The Duke [of Wellington]. 1931.

Fortescue, Sir J. British Statesmen of the Great War, 1793–1814. Oxford, 1910.

The Marlay Letters, 1778–1820. Ed. R. W. Bond, 1937.

Carlyle, E. I. William Cobbett. 1904.

Cole, G. D. H. William Cobbett. 1924.

Brailsford, H. N. Shelley, Godwin and their Circle. 1913.

Wallas, G. Life of Francis Place. 1898.

Patterson, M. W. Sir Francis Burdett and his Times. 2 vols. 1931.

Temperley, H. W. V. Life of Canning. 1905.

Stockmar, C. F. von, Baron. Memoirs. 2 vols. 1872.

The Creevey Papers. Ed. Sir H. Maxwell, 2 vols. 1903.

Trevelyan, G. M. Lord Grey of the Reform Bill. 1920.

Melbourne, W. Lamb, Viscount. Memoirs. Ed. W. M. Torrens, 1890.

Newman, B. Life of Melbourne. 1930.

Bell, H. C. F. Lord Palmerston. 2 vols. 1936.

Thursfield, J. R. Peel. 1891.

Primrose, A. P. (Viscount Rosebery). Life of Peel. 1899.

Ramsay, A. A. W. Sir Robert Peel. 1928.

Clark, G. K. Peel and the Conservative Party. 1929.

Faber, G. C. Oxford Apostles. 1933.

Martin, Sir T. Life of His Royal Highness the Prince Consort. 5 vols. 1875–80.

Walpole, Sir S. Life of Russell. 1889.

Macaulay, T. B., Baron. Essays. [Collected Works, vols. VI, VII, 1866.]

Trevelyan, Sir G. O. Life and Letters of Lord Macaulay. 2 vols. 1876.

Lee, Sir S. Queen Victoria. 1904 (rev. edn).

Greville, C. C. F. Memoirs. Ed. H. Reeve, 8 vols. 1874–87; ed. L. Strachey and R. Fulford, 8 vols. 1938.

Bulwer, H. (Baron Dalling and Bulwer). Historical Characters. 2 vols. 1867.

Bagehot, W. Biographical Studies. 1889.

Villiers, G. A Vanished Victorian. George Villiers, Fourth Earl of Clarendon. 1938.

Harris, J. H. (Earl of Malmesbury). Memoirs of an Ex-Minister. 2 vols. 1884.

Trevelyan, G. M. Life of John Bright. 1913.

Morley, J., Viscount. Cobden. 1881.

Hobson, J. A. Richard Cobden. 1919.

Ward, W. Life of Cardinal Newman. 2 vols. 1912.

Hutton, A. W. Life of Cardinal Manning. 1892.

Purcell, E. S. Life of Cardinal Manning. 2 vols. 1895.

Froude, J. A. Lord Beaconsfield. 1890.

Monypenny, W. F. and Buckle, G. E. Life of Benjamin Disraeli, Earl of Beaconsfield. 2 vols. 1929 (rev. edn).

Morley, J., Viscount. The Life of W. E. Gladstone. 3 vols. 1903.

Eyck, E. Gladstone. Tr. Eng. 1938.

Holland, B. Life of Spencer Compton, eighth Duke of Devonshire. 2 vols. 1911.

Gwynn, S. and Tuckwell, G. M. Life of Sir Charles Dilke. 2 vols. 1917.

The Amberley Papers: the Letters and Diaries of Lord [1842–1876] and Lady Amberley. Ed. B. and P. Russell, 2 vols. 1937.

Cecil, G., Lady. Life of Lord Salisbury. 5 vols. 1921–31.

Garvin, J. L. Life of Joseph Chamberlain. 2 vols. 1932.

Acton, J. E. E., Baron. Letters to Mary Gladstone. Ed. H. Paul, 1904.

—— Selections from the Correspondence. Ed. J. N. Figgis and R. V. Lawrence, 1917.

Gasquet, F. A. Lord Acton and his Circle. 1906.

Morley, J., Viscount. Recollections. 2 vols. 1917.

Hirst, F. W. John Morley. Early Life and Letters. 1927.

Gooch, G. P. Life of Lord Courtney. 1920.

Dugdale, B. E. C. Arthur James Balfour. 2 vols. 1936.

Asquith, H. H. (Earl of Oxford and Asquith). Memories and Reflections, 1852–1927. 1928.

Spender, J. A. and Asquith, C. Life of Herbert Henry Asquith. 1932.

(2) FOREIGN RELATIONS

Cambridge Modern History. Vols. IX–XII, Cambridge, 1906–10.

Cambridge History of British Foreign Policy. 3 vols. Cambridge, 1923.

Fyffe, C. A. History of Modern Europe. 3 vols. 1895.

Lavisse, E. and Rambaud, A. Histoire Générale. Vols. XI, XII, Paris, 1901.

Stern, A. Geschichte Europas. 10 vols. Berlin, 1894–. Stuttgart, 1924.

Hertslet, Sir E. The Map of Europe by Treaty. 4 vols. 1875–91.

Marriott, Sir J. A. R. A History of Europe from 1815 to 1923. 1931.

Cecil, A. British Foreign Secretaries. 1926.

Fueter, E. World History 1815–1920. Tr. Eng. 1923.

Phillips, A. Modern Europe, 1815–99. 1901.

Mowat, R. B. History of European Diplomacy, 1815–1914. 1922.

Marvin, F. S. et al. England and the World. Oxford, 1925.

Fisher, H. A. L. A History of Europe. Vol. III, 1935.

Webster, C. K. The Congress of Vienna. 1918.

—— The Foreign Policy of Castlereagh, 1812–15. 1931.

Temperley, H. The Foreign Policy of Canning. 1925.

Phillips, A. The Confederation of Europe. 1914.

Mowat, R. B. The Concert of Europe. 1931.

Ashley, E. Life and Correspondence of Lord Palmerston. 2 vols. 1874.

Martin, B. K. The Triumph of Lord Palmerston. 1924.

Temperley, H. England and the Near East. The Crimea. 1936.

Dawson, W. H. Richard Cobden and Foreign Policy. 1926.

Fitzmaurice, Lord E. G. Life of Lord Granville. 1905.

Seton-Watson, R. W. Disraeli, Gladstone and the Eastern Question. 1935.

Gooch, G. P. A History of Modern Europe, 1878–1919. 1923.

Legh, T. W. (Baron Newton). Lord Lyons, a Record of British Diplomacy. 1913.

Mowat, R. B. Lord Pauncefote. 1928.

Baring, E. (Earl Cromer). Modern Egypt. 1908.

Zetland, Marquis of. Lord Cromer. 1932.

Pribram, A. F. Great Britain and the Policy of the European Powers, 1871–1914. 1931.

Gooch, G. P. and Temperley, H. British Documents on the Origins of the War, 1898–1914. Vol. I, 1928.

Documents diplomatiques français, 1871–1914. Paris, 1929.

Die grosse Politik der europäischen Kabinette, 1871–1914. 40 vols. in 54, Berlin, 1922–7.

Dugdale, E. T. S. German Diplomatic Documents, 1871–1914. 4 vols. 1928–31.

Fay, S. B. The Origins of the World War. Vol. I (1871–1914), New York, 1929.

Nicolson, H. Life of Lord Carnock. 1930.

Steed, H. W. Through Thirty Years. 1924.

Woodward, E. L. Great Britain and the German Navy. Oxford, 1935.

B. CONSTITUTIONAL HISTORY

Anson, Sir W. R. The Law and Custom of the Constitution. 2 vols. Oxford, 1907–8.

Bagehot, W. The English Constitution. 1872 (2nd edn).

Dicey, A. V. The Law of the Constitution. 1915 (8th edn).

Emden, C. S. The People and the Constitution. Oxford, 1933.

Eyre, E. European Civilization, Its Origin and Development. Vol. v (Economic History of Europe since the Reformation), Oxford, 1937.

Hardie, F. M. The Political Influence of Queen Victoria, 1861–1901. Oxford, 1935.

Jennings, W. I. Cabinet Government. Cambridge, 1936.

Keir, D. L. and Lawson, F. H. Cases in Constitutional Law. Oxford, 1928.

Keith, A. B. The Constitutional Law of the British Dominions. 1933.

Kennedy, W. P. M. Essays in Constitutional Law. 1934.

Lowell, A. L. The Government of England. 2 vols. New York, 1920.

Maitland, F. W. The Constitutional History of England. Cambridge, 1913.

May, Sir T. E. Constitutional History of England. 3 vols. 1889.

Pike, L. O. Constitutional History of the House of Lords. 1894.

Porritt, E. and A. The Unreformed House of Commons. 2 vols. Cambridge, 1909.

Port, F. J. Administrative Law. 1929.

Redlich, J. Procedure of the House of Commons. Tr. Eng. (introduction and supplementary chapter by Sir Courtney Ilbert), 3 vols. 1908.

Redlich, J. and Hirst, F. W. Local Government in England. 2 vols. 1903.

Robertson, Sir C. G. Select Statutes, Cases and Documents to illustrate English Constitutional History, 1660–1830. 1904.

Robson, W. A. Justice and Administrative Law. 1928.

Smellie, K. B. A Hundred Years of English Government. 1937.

Tilley, Sir J. A. C. and Gaselee, Sir S. The Foreign Office. 1933.

C. SOCIAL AND ECONOMIC HISTORY

Ashley, W. J. The Economic Organisation of England. 1914.

Bannington. English Public Health Administration. 1896.

Beer, M. History of British Socialism. 1920.

Booth, C. Life and Labour of the People in London. 17 vols. 1902–3 (3rd edn).

Clapham, J. H. An Economic History of Modern Britain. 3 vols. Cambridge, 1930–8.

Cobbett, W. Rural Rides. Ed. G. D. H. and M. Cole, 3 vols. 1930.

Cole, G. D. H. Robert Owen. 1925.

—— A Short History of the British Working Class Movement. 3 vols. 1925–7.

Coupland, R. The British Anti-Slavery Movement. 1933.

Cunningham, W. The Industrial Revolution. Cambridge, 1922.

Disraeli, B. (Earl of Beaconsfield). Sybil. 3 vols. 1845.

Dobbs, A. E. Education and Social Movements. 1919.

Early Victorian England. Ed. G. M. Young, 2 vols. Oxford, 1934.

Engels, F. Condition of the English Working Classes in 1844. Tr. Eng. 1892.

Fay, C. R. Life and Labour in the Nineteenth Century. 1920.

—— Great Britain from Adam Smith to the Present Day. 1927.

—— The Corn Laws and Social England. 1933.

Hammond, J. L. and B. The Village Labourer. 1911.

—— The Town Labourer. 1917.

—— The Skilled Labourer. 1919.

—— Life of Shaftesbury. 1923.

—— The Rise of Modern Industry. 1925.

—— The Age of the Chartists. 1929.

Hasbach, W. History of the English Agricultural Labourer. 1908.

Hobson, J. A. Evolution of Modern Capitalism. 1889.

Howell, M. The Chartist Movement. Manchester, 1918.

Hutchins, B. L. and Harrison, A. History of Factory Legislation. 1896.

Knowles, L. C. A. The Industrial and Commercial Revolutions in Great Britain during the Nineteenth Century. 1924 (3rd edn).

—— Economic Development of the British Overseas Empire. 2 vols. 1924–30.

Layton, T. An Introduction to the Study of Prices, with Special Reference to the History of the Nineteenth Century. 1912.

Lovett, W. Life and Struggles. 1876.

Mantoux, P. The Industrial Revolution. Tr. Eng. 1928.

Marx, K. Capital. Tr. Eng. 2 vols. 1889.

Owen, R. The Life. Written by Himself. 1857–8.

Podmore, F. Life of Robert Owen. 1923 (2nd edn).

Raven, C. E. Christian Socialism. 1920.

Redford, A. The Economic History of England, 1760–1860. 1931.

Redlich, J. and Hirst, F. W. Local Government in England. 2 vols. 1903.

Rees, J. F. A Short Fiscal and Financial History of England, 1815–1918. 1921.

Rees, J. F. Social and Industrial History of England, 1815–1918. 1923.

Russell, B., Earl. Freedom and Organization. 1934.

Shaw, G. B. The Commonsense of Municipal Trading. 1904.

Slater, G. The Making of Modern England. 1913.

Smart, William. Economic Annals of the Nineteenth Century. 2 vols. 1917.

Traill, H. D. et al. Social England. Vol. vi, 1897.

Wallas, G. Life of Francis Place. 1891.

Webb, B. The Co-operative Movement in Great Britain. 1891.

Webb, S. and B. English Local Government. 8 vols. 1904–29.

—— History of Trade Unionism. 1907.

—— Industrial Democracy. 1907.

West, J. The History of Chartism. 1920.

Williams, J. B. Guide to Printed Materials for English Economic History, 1750–1850. 2 vols. New York, 1926.

Wingfield-Stratford, E. C. The Victorian Tragedy. 1930.

—— The Victorian Sunset. 1932.

G. E. F.

D. POLITICAL SPEECHES

Grattan, Henry (1746–1820). Speeches in the Irish and in the Imperial Parliament. Ed. H. Grattan (jun.), 4 vols. 1822.

—— Speeches, to which is added his Letter on the Union. Ed. D. D. Madden, Dublin, 1845.

Erskine, Thomas, Baron (1750–1823). Speeches at the Bar on the Liberty of the Press and against Constructive Treason. 4 vols. 1810.

Windham, William (1750–1810). Speeches in Parliament. Ed. T. Amyot, 3 vols. 1812.

Sheridan, R. B. (1751–1816). Speeches. 5 vols. 1816.

Romilly, Sir Samuel (1757–1818). Speeches in the House of Commons. 2 vols. 1820.

Harrowby, Dudley Ryder, Earl (1762–1847). Speech on the Reform Bill, October 1831. 1831.

Plunket, William Conyngham, Baron (1764–1854). Speeches at the Bar and in the Senate. Ed. J. C. Hoey, 1865.

Wellesley, Arthur (Duke of Wellington) (1769–1852). Parliamentary Speeches. Ed. J. Gurwood, 1854.

Burdett, Sir Francis (1770–1844). [Speech prefixed to] Address to Prince Regent, House of Commons, 7 January 1812. 1812.

Canning, George (1770–1827). Speeches. Ed. R. Therry, 6 vols. 1828.

Huskisson, William (1770–1830). Speeches. 1831.

O'Connell, Daniel (1775–1847). Life and Speeches. Ed. J. O'Connell, 2 vols. 1846.

—— Speeches and Public Letters. Ed. M. F. Cusack, 2 vols. 1875.

Brougham and Vaux, Henry, Baron (1778–1868). Speech on Education of the Poor. 1820.

—— Speech on Present State of the Law of the Country. 1828.

—— Speech on Second Reading of Reform Bill. 1831.

—— Speeches upon Public Rights, Duties, etc. 4 vols. 1838.

Peel, Sir Robert (1788–1850). Speeches in the House of Commons. 4 vols. 1853.

Sheil, Richard Lalor (1791–1851). Speeches. Ed. T. MacNevin, 1845.

Russell, John, Earl (1792–1878). Selections from Speeches, 1817–1841 and from his Despatches, 1859–1865. 3 vols. 1870.

Macaulay, Thomas Babington, Baron (1800–1859). Speeches, Parliamentary and Miscellaneous. 2 vols. 1853.

—— Speeches on Reform, 1831–2. 1854.

—— Speeches, corrected by himself. 1854.

—— Works. Vol. viii (Speeches), 1866.

Bulwer-Lytton, E. L. (Baron Lytton) (1803–1873). Speeches, with some Political Writings. 2 vols. 1874.

Cobden, Richard (1804–1865). Speeches on Peace. 1849.

—— Speeches on Questions of Public Policy. Ed. J. Bright and J. E. T. Rogers, 2 vols. 1870.

Disraeli, Benjamin (Earl of Beaconsfield) (1804–1881). Selected Speeches. Ed. T. E. Kebbel, 2 vols. 1882.

Horsman, Edward (1807–1876). Five Speeches on Ecclesiastical Affairs delivered in the House of Commons, 1847–9. 1849.

—— Speech on the Present State of Parties. 1861.

Gladstone, W. E. (1809–1898). Speeches on Parliamentary Reform. 1866.

—— Speeches on Great Questions of the Day. 1870.

—— Political Speeches in Scotland, Nov.–Dec. 1879. March–April 1880. 2 vols. 1880.

—— Speeches delivered at Leeds, October 1881. 4 pts, 1881.

—— Fourth Midlothian Campaign: Political Speeches. 1885.

—— Speeches and Public Addresses. Ed. A. W. Hutton and H. T. Cohen. 2 vols. (1886–1891), 1892–4.

Herbert, Sidney (Baron Herbert of Lea) (1810–1861). Speech on the Conduct of the War, 12 December, 1854. 1854.

Bright, John (1811–1859). Speeches on Questions of Public Policy. Ed. J. E. T. Rogers, 2 vols. 1868.

—— Public Addresses. Ed. J. E. T. Rogers, 1879.

Lowe, Robert (Viscount Sherbrooke) (1811–1892). Speeches and Letters on Reform. 1867.

Palmer, Roundell (Earl of Selborne) (1812–1895). Speech on Our Judicial System, 22 February 1867. 1867.

Stanley, E. H. (Earl of Derby) (1826–1893). Speeches and Addresses on Political and Social Questions, 1870–91. 1893.

—— Speeches and Addresses. Selected by Sir T. H. Sanderson and E. S. Roscoe. 2 vols. 1894.

Cecil, R. A. T. G. (Marquis of Salisbury) (1830–1903). Life and Speeches. Ed. F. S. Pulling, 2 vols. 1885.

Fawcett, Henry (1833–1884). Speeches on some Current Political Questions. 1873.

Churchill, Lord Randolph (1849–1894). Speeches, 1880–8. Ed. L. W. Jennings, 2 vols. 1889.

E. LETTERS, DIARIES AND AUTOBIOGRAPHIES

[A brief representative selection. Other titles will be found under Literary Memoirs, Reminiscences and Letters (pp. 14–7 above), Education (pp. 136–41 above), Drama (pp. 580–5 below), The Literature of Sport (pp. 757–79 below), and elsewhere.]

Hutton, William (1723–1815). Life, written by Himself. Ed. C. Hutton, 1816; ed. L. Jewitt, 1872.

Cumberland, Richard (1732–1811). Memoirs, written by Himself. 2 vols. 1807.

Cartwright, John (1740–1824). Life and Correspondence. Ed. E. Cartwright, 2 vols. 1926.

Somerville, Thomas (1741–1830). My own Life and Times. Ed. W. Lee, Edinburgh, 1861.

Young, Arthur (1741–1820). Autobiography. Ed. M. Betham-Edwards, 1898.

Douglas, Sylvester (Baron Glenbervie) (1743–1823). Diaries. Ed. F. Bickley, 2 vols. 1928.

Rose, George (1744–1818). Diaries and Correspondence. Ed. L. V. Harcourt, 2 vols. 1860.

Hayley, William (1745–1820). Memoirs. Ed. J. Johnson, 1823.

Harris, James (Earl of Malmesbury) (1746–1820). Diaries and Correspondence. Ed. J. H. Harris (Earl of Malmesbury), 4 vols. 1844.

Northcote, James (1746–1831). Conversations. Ed. W. Hazlitt, 1830.

Fox, Charles James (1749–1806). Memorials and Correspondence. Ed. Lord John Russell, 4 vols. 1853–7. [The materials for

this had been collected by the third Lord Holland.]

Windham, William (1750–1810). Diary, 1784–1810. Ed. H. Baring, 1866.

—— The Windham Papers: The Life and Correspondence of William Windham, 1750–1810. With Introduction by the Earl of Rosebery. 2 vols. 1913.

Scott, John (Earl of Eldon) (1751–1838). Public and Private Life. With Selections from his Correspondence. Ed. H. Twiss, 1844.

Wraxall, Sir Nathaniel William (1751–1831). Historical and Posthumous Memoirs, 1772–1784. Ed. H. B. Wheatley, 5 vols. 1884.

D'Arblay, Frances (née Burney) (1752–1840). Diary and Letters. Ed. A. Dobson, 6 vols. 1904–5.

Rawdon-Hastings, Francis (Marquis of Hastings) (1754–1826). Private Journals. Ed. Marchioness of Bute, 2 vols. 1858.

Grant, Ann, of Lagan (1755–1838). Letters from the Mountains. 3 vols. 1806.

—— Memoirs and Correspondence. Ed. J. P. Grant, 3 vols. 1844.

Abbot, Charles (Baron Colchester) (1757–1829). Diary and Correspondence. 3 vols. 1861. [Speaker from 1802 to 1816.]

Addington, Henry (Viscount Sidmouth) (1757–1844). Life and Correspondence. Ed. G. Pellew, 3 vols. 1847.

Romilly, Sir Samuel (1757–1818). Memoirs. 1818.

—— Memoirs of the Life of, with Selections from his Correspondence. Edited by his Sons. 3 vols. 1840.

Angelo, Henry (1760–1839). Reminiscences. 2 vols. 1830; rptd 2 vols. 1904.

Dyott, William (1761–1847). Diary. Ed. R. W. Jefferey, 1907.

Cobbett, William (1762–1835). Rural Rides. 1830; ed. G. D. H. and Margaret Cole, 3 vols. 1930.

Berry, Mary (1763–1852). Journals and Correspondence. Ed. Lady T. Lewis, 3 vols. 1865.

Roberts, Samuel (1763–1848). Autobiography. 1849.

Rogers, Samuel (1763–1855). Reminiscences and Table-Talk. Ed. G. H. Powell, 1903.

Kelly, Michael (1764?–1826). Reminiscences. 2 vols. 1826. [Theatrical.]

Plunket, William Conyngham, Baron (1764–1854). Life, Letters and Speeches. Ed. Lord D. R. P. Rathmore. With a Preface by Lord Brougham. 1867.

Ward, Robert Plumer (1765–1846). Memoirs, with Selections from his Correspondence, Diaries and Remains. Ed. E. Phipps, 1850.

Pease, Edward (1767–1858). The Diaries of Edward Pease. Ed. A. Pease, 1907.

Creevey, Thomas (1768–1838). The Creevey Papers: a Selection from the Correspondence and Diaries of the late Thomas Creevey. Ed. Sir H. Maxwell, 2 vols. 1903–5.

Gunning, Henry (1768–1854). Reminiscences of the University, Town, and County of Cambridge. 2 vols. 1854, 1855.

Stewart, Robert (Viscount Castlereagh) (1769–1822). Memoirs and Correspondence. Ed. C. W. Stewart (Marquis of Londonderry), 12 vols. 1848–53.

Malcolm, Sir John (1769–1833). Life and Correspondence. Ed. Sir J. W. Kaye, 2 vols. 1856.

Fletcher, Eliza (1770–1858). Autobiography. 1875.

Wordsworth, William (1770–1850). Letters of the Wordsworth Family from 1787 to 1855. Ed. W. Knight, 1907.

Dibdin, Thomas John (1771–1841). Reminiscences. 2 vols. 1827. [Theatrical.]

Lingard, John (1771–1851). Life and Letters. Ed. M. Haile and E. Binney, 1911.

Owen, Robert (1771–1858). Life written by Himself, with Selections from his Writings and Correspondence. 1857.

Scott, Sir Walter (1771–1832). Journal. [Ed. D. Douglas], 2 vols. Edinburgh, 1890.

—— Letters. Ed. Sir H. J. C. Grierson, 10 vols. 1932–6.

Smith, Sydney (1771–1845). A Memoir by Lady Holland, with a Selection from his Letters. Ed. S. Austin, 2 vols. 1855.

Wordsworth, Dorothy (1771–1855). Journals. Ed. W. Knight, 2 vols. 1896.

Cockburn, Sir George (1772–1853). Diary. Boston, 1833. [Describing Napoleon's voyage to St Helena.]

Coleridge, Samuel Taylor (1772–1834). Letters, Conversations and Recollections. Ed. T. Allsop, 2 vols. 1836.

—— Letters. Ed. E. H. Coleridge, 2 vols. 1895.

—— Letters, hitherto Uncollected. Ed. W. F. Prideaux, 1913.

Skinner, John (1772–1839). The Journal of a Somerset Rector. Ed. H. Coombs and A. N. Bax, 1930.

Hunt, Henry (1773–1835). Memoirs. Written by Himself in H.M. Jail at Ilchester. 3 vols. 1820.

Southey, Robert (1774–1843). Life and Correspondence. Ed. C. C. Southey, 6 vols. 1849–50.

—— Correspondence with Caroline Bowles. Ed. E. Dowden, 1881.

Austen, Jane (1775–1817). Letters. Ed. R. W. Chapman, 2 vols. Oxford, 1932.

Bury, Lady Charlotte Susan Maria (née Campbell) (1775–1861). The Diary of a Lady in Waiting. Ed. A. F. Steuart, 2 vols. 1908.

Cochrane, Thomas (Earl of Dundonald) (1775–1860). Autobiography of a Seaman. 2 vols. 1860–1.

Lamb, Charles (1775–1834). Correspondence and Works. Ed. T. Purnell, 4 vols. 1870.

—— Works of Charles and Mary Lamb. Ed. E. V. Lucas, 7 vols. 1903–5.

Landor, Walter Savage (1775–1864). Letters. Ed. S. Wheeler, 1897.

O'Connell, Daniel (1775–1847). Speeches and Public Letters. Ed. M. F. Cusack, 2 vols. 1875.

—— O'Connell's Correspondence. Ed. W. J. Fitzpatrick, 1888.

Robinson, Henry Crabb (1775–1867). Diary, Reminiscences and Correspondence. Ed. T. Sadler, 3 vols. 1869.

—— Crabb Robinson in Germany, 1800–1805. Extracts from his Correspondence. Ed. E. J. Morley, 1929.

—— The Correspondence of Henry Crabb Robinson with the Wordsworth Circle, 1808–1866. Ed. E. J. Morley, 2 vols. Oxford, 1927.

White, Joseph Blanco (1775–1841). Life [autobiography]. Ed. J. H. Thom, 3 vols. 1845.

Knighton, Sir William (1776–1836). Memoirs of, including his Correspondence with Distinguished Personages. Ed. Dorothea Lady Knighton, 1838. [Knighton was keeper of the Privy Purse to George IV, and physician and private secretary to him as Regent and King.]

Stanhope, Lady Hester Lucy (1776–1839). Memoirs. Ed. C. L. Meryon, 1845.

Jones, William (1777–1821). Diary. Ed. O. F. Christie, 1929.

Raikes, Thomas (1777–1848). A Portion of the Journal kept by, 1831–47. 4 vols. 1856–7.

—— Private Correspondence of, with Duke of Wellington and Other Contemporaries. Ed. H. Raikes, 1861.

Brougham, Henry Peter (Baron Brougham and Vaux) (1778–1868). Life and Times, written by Himself. 3 vols. 1871.

Cockburn, Henry Thomas, Lord (1779–1854). Memorials of his Time. Edinburgh, 1856.

—— Journal and Letters. 2 vols. 1874.

—— Some Letters. Ed. H. A. Cockburn, Edinburgh, 1933.

Nugent, Lady Maria. Lady Nugent's Journal, Jamaica One Hundred Years Ago. Ed. F. Cundall, 1907.

Galt, John (1779–1839). Autobiography. 1833.

Lamb, William (Viscount Melbourne) (1779–1848). Lord Melbourne's Papers. Ed. L. C. Sanders, 1889.

Moore, Thomas (1779–1852). Memoirs, Journal and Correspondence. Ed. Lord John Russell, 8 vols. 1855.
—— Diary. Ed. J. B. Priestley, 1925. [Selections.]
Croker, John Wilson (1780–1857). The Croker Papers. Ed. L. J. Jennings, 3 vols. 1884. [Letters and diaries.]
Fry, Elizabeth (1780–1845). Memoir, with Extracts from her Journal and Letters. Edited by Two of her Daughters. 2 vols. 1847.
The Jerningham Letters (1780–1843). Excerpts from the Correspondence and Diaries of the Hon. Lady Jerningham and her Daughter Lady Bedingfield. Ed. E. Castle, 2 vols. 1896.
Clinton, Henry Fynes (1781–1852). Literary Remains. Ed. C. J. F. Clinton, 1854.
Martyn, Henry (1781–1812). Journals and Letters. Ed. S. Wilberforce, 2 vols. 1837.
Pryme, George (1781–1868). Autobiographical Recollections. Ed. A. Bayne, Cambridge, 1870. [Political economist.]
Sharpe, Charles Kirkpatrick (1781?–1851). Letters. Ed. A. Allardyce and W. K. R. Bedford, 2 vols. 1888.
Taylor, Ann (later Gilbert) (1782–1866). Autobiography. 1874.
Hunt, Leigh (1784–1859). Correspondence. Ed. T. Hunt, 2 vols. 1862.
—— Autobiography. 3 vols. 1850; ed. R. Ingpen, 2 vols. 1903; ed. E. Blunden, 1928 (World's Classics).
Temple, Henry John (Viscount Palmerston) (1784–1865). The Life of, with Selections from his Diary and Correspondence. Ed. Sir H. Lytton Bulwer (Baron Dalling and Bulwer) and A. E. M. Ashley, 5 vols. 1870–6. [Vol. I contains the short autobiography to 1830.]
De Quincey, Thomas (1785–1859). Collected Writings. Ed. D. Masson, 14 vols. Edinburgh, 1889–90.
—— Diary, 1803. Ed. H. A. Eaton, 1928.
Jackson, Sir George (1785–1861). Diaries and Letters. Ed. Lady Jackson, 4 vols. 1872–3.
Metcalfe, Charles Theophilus, Baron (1785–1846). Life and Correspondence. Ed. Sir J. W. Kaye, 2 vols. 1854.
Hawker, Peter (1786–1853). Diary, 1802–1853. Ed. Sir R. Payne-Gallwey, 2 vols. 1893.
Lucas, William. A Quaker Journal (1804–1861). Ed. G. E. Bryant and G. P. Baker, 2 vols. 1934.
Haydon, Benjamin Robert (1786–1846). Life. Ed. T. Taylor, 3 vols. 1853; ed. E. Blunden, 1927 (World's Classics).

Mitford, Mary Russell (1787–1855). The Life of [by W. Harness] related in a Selection from her Letters to her Friends. Ed. A. G. L'Estrange and H. Charters, 5 vols. 1870–2.
Procter, Bryan Waller (1787–1874) ('Barry Cornwall'). An Autobiographical Fragment and Biographical Notes, with Personal Sketches of Contemporaries. [Ed. C. Patmore], 1877.
Byron, George Gordon, Baron (1788–1824). Letters and Journals. Ed. R. E. Prothero, 6 vols. 1898–1904.
Gillies, Robert Pearce (1788–1858). Memoirs of a Literary Veteran. 3 vols. 1851.
Matthews, Henry (1789–1828). The Diary of an Invalid. 1819.
Stephen, Sir James (1789–1859). Letters, with Biographical Notes by his Daughter. 1906.
Wilson, Harriette (1789–1846). Memoirs. 1825; ed. J. Laver, 1929.
Senior, Nassau William (1790–1864). A Journal kept in Turkey and Greece (1857–8). 1859.
—— Journals, Conversations and Essays relating to Ireland. 2 vols. 1868.
—— Journals kept in France and Italy from 1848 to 1852. 2 vols. 1871.
—— Correspondence and Conversations with A. de Tocqueville. 2 vols. 1872.
—— Conversations with Thiers, Guizot, and other Distinguished Persons during the Second Empire. 2 vols. 1878.
—— Conversations with Distinguished Persons during the Second Empire, from 1860 to 1863. 2 vols. 1880.
—— Conversations and Journals in Egypt and Malta. 2 vols. 1882.
Vandenhoff, John (1790–1861). Dramatic Reminiscences. 1860. [Provincial actor.]
Knight, Charles (1791–1873). Passages of a Working Life, with Early Reminiscences. 3 vols. 1864–5.
Alison, Sir Archibald (1792–1867). Some Account of my Life and Writings. An Autobiography. Ed. Lady Alison, 2 vols. 1883.
[Carter, Thomas] (b. 1792). Memoirs of a Working Man. Ed. C. Knight, 1845.
—— Continuation of the Memoirs of a Working Man. 1850.
Franklin, Lady Jane (1792–1875). Life, Diaries, and Correspondence. Ed. W. F. Rawnsley, 1923.
Graham, Sir James Robert George (1792–1861). Life and Letters. Ed. C. S. Parker, 2 vols. 1907.
Lambton, John George (Earl of Durham) (1792–1840). Life and Letters. Ed. S. J. Reid, 2 vols. 1906.

Shelley, Percy Bysshe (1792–1822). Letters. Ed. R. Ingpen, 2 vols. 1912.
—— The Shelley Correspondence in the Bodleian Library. Ed. R. H. Hill, 1926.
—— Shelley's Lost Letters to Harriet. Ed. L. Hotson, 1930.
Trelawny, Edward John (1792–1881). Adventures of a Younger Son. 3 vols. 1831; ed. E. C. Mayne, 1925 (World's Classics).
—— Recollections of the Last Days of Shelley and Byron. 1858; ed. E. Dowden, 1906.
—— Letters. Ed. H. Buxton Forman, 1910.
Clare, John (1793–1864). Sketches in the Life of, Written by Himself. Ed. E. Blunden, 1931.
Fane, Priscilla Anne (Countess of Westmorland) (1793–1879). Correspondence. Ed. Lady R. Weigall, 1909.
Macready, William Charles (1793–1873). Diaries. Ed. W. Toynbee, 2 vols. 1912.
Ramsay, Edward Bannerman (1793–1872). Reminiscences of Scottish Life and Character. 1858.
Greville, Charles Cavendish Fulke (1794–1865). The Greville Memoirs. A Journal of the Reign of King George IV and King William IV. Ed. H. Reeve, 3 vols. 1874.
—— A Journal of the Reign of Queen Victoria from 1837 to 1852. 3 vols. 1885.
—— A Journal of the Reign of Queen Victoria from 1852 to 1860. 2 vols. 1887.
Lockhart, John Gibson (1794–1854). Life and Letters. Ed. A. Lang, 2 vols. 1897.
Carlyle, Thomas (1795–1881). Reminiscences. Ed. J. A. Froude, 2 vols. 1881.
—— Correspondence of Carlyle and R. W. Emerson. Ed. C. E. Norton, 1883.
—— Early Letters. Ed. C. E. Norton, 1887.
—— Letters, 1826–36. Ed. C. E. Norton, 1887.
—— New Letters. Ed. A. Carlyle, 2 vols. 1904–9.
—— Love Letters. Ed. A. Carlyle, 2 vols. 1909.
Keats, John (1795–1821). Letters. Ed. M. Buxton Forman, 2 vols. Oxford, 1931.
Shelley, Mary Wollstonecraft (1797–1851). Life and Letters. Ed. Mrs J. Marshall, 1889.
Keppel, George Thomas (Earl of Albemarle) (1799–1891). Fifty Years of my Life. 2 vols. 1876.
Lennox, Lord William Pitt (1799–1881). Drawn on my Memory. 2 vols. 1866. Memoirs of the Life of a Country Surgeon. 1845.
Bethell, Richard (Baron Westbury) (1800–1873). Life, with Selection from his Correspondence. Ed. T. A. Nash, 1881.
Denison, John Evelyn (Viscount Ossington) (1800–1873). Notes from Journal. Ed. L. E. Denison, 1899.

Lovett, William (1800–1877). Life and Struggles. 1876; ed. R. H. Tawney, 2 vols. 1920. [Chartist; autobiography.]
Macaulay, Thomas Babington, Baron (1800–1859). Life and Letters. Ed. Sir G. O. Trevelyan, 2 vols. 1876.
Mendelssohn and his Friends in Kensington. Letters from Fanny and Sophy Horsley, 1833–1836. Ed. R. B. Gotch, Oxford, 1934.
Taylor, Sir Henry (1800–1886). Autobiography. 2 vols. 1885.
—— Correspondence. Ed. E. Dowden, 1888.
Carlyle, Jane Welsh (1801–1866). Letters and Memorials. Ed. J. A. Froude, 3 vols. 1883.
—— New Letters and Memorials. Ed. A. Carlyle, 2 vols. 1903.
Greville, Henry William (1801–1872). Leaves from a Diary. Ed. Countess of Stratford, 6 vols. 1883–4.
Newman, John Henry (1801–1890). Apologia pro Vita sua. 1864; ed. W. Ward, 1913.
Owen, Robert Dale (1801–1877). Threading my Way. 1874.
Fox, Henry Edward (Baron Holland) (1802–1859). The Journal, 1818–30. Ed. G. S. H. Fox-Strangways (Earl of Ilchester), 1923.
Howard, George (Earl of Carlisle) (1802–1864). Extracts from Journals. [1869?] (priv. ptd).
Martineau, Harriet (1802–1876). Autobiography. Ed. M. W. Chapman, 3 vols. 1877.
Froude, Richard Hurrell (1803–1836). Remains. Ed. J. B. Mozley, 2 vols. 1837.
Hill, Frederic (1803–1896). An Autobiography of Fifty Years in Times of Reform. Ed. C. Hill, 1894.
Disraeli, Benjamin (Earl of Beaconsfield) (1804–1881). Letters, 1830–1852. Ed. [Ralph Disraeli], 1887.
—— Letters to Lady Bradford and Lady Chesterfield. Ed. Marquis of Zetland, 2 vols. 1929.
Cooper, Thomas (1805–1892). Life. By Himself. 1872. [Chartist.]
Newman, Francis William (1805–1897). Phases of Faith. 1850.
—— Memoir and Letters. Ed. I. G. Sieveking, 1909.
Wilberforce, Samuel (1805–1873). Life. 3 vols. 1879. [Vol. i by A. R. Ashwell, vols. ii, iii by R. G. Wilberforce. Includes letters.]
Browning, Elizabeth Barrett (1806–1861). Letters to R. H. Horne. Ed. S. R. T. Mayer, 2 vols. 1877.
—— Letters. Ed. F. G. Kenyon, 2 vols. 1897.
—— Letters to her sister. Ed. L. Huxley, 1929.
Mill, John Stuart (1806–1873). Autobiography. Ed. Helen Taylor, 1873; ed. J. J. Coss, New York, 1924 (from MS); ed. H. J. Laski, 1924 (World's Classics).

Mozley, Thomas (1806–1893). Reminiscences. 2 vols. 1882, 1885. [Anglo-Catholic journalist.]

Wordsworth, Charles (1806–1892). Annals of my Life. Ed. W. E. Hodgson, 1893.

Symonds, John Addington (1807–1871). John Addington Symonds. By Horatio Browne. 2 vols. 1895. [Includes letters.]

Manning, Henry Edward (1808–1892). Life. By E. S. Purcell. 2 vols. 1896. [Includes letters.]

Taylor, Philip Meadows (1808–1876). Story of My Life. 1877.

Darwin, Charles Robert (1809–1882). The Life and Letters, an Autobiographical Chapter. Ed. Sir F. Darwin, 3 vols. 1887.

FitzGerald, Edward (1809–1883). Letters and Literary Remains. Ed. W. A. Wright, 7 vols. 1902–3.

Gladstone, William Ewart (1809–1898). Life. By J. Morley. 3 vols. 1903. [Includes letters.]

Harris, George (1809–1890). Autobiography. 1888.

Kemble, Frances Anne (later Butler) (1809–1893). Records of a Girlhood. 3 vols. 1878.

—— Records of a Later Life. 3 vols. 1882.

Tennyson, Alfred, Baron (1809–1892). A Memoir. Ed. H., Baron Tennyson, 2 vols. 1897.

Tupper, Martin Farquhar (1810–1889). My Life as an Author. 1886.

Windham, Sir Charles (1810–1870). Crimean Diary and Letters. Ed. H. Pearse, 1897.

Bright, John (1811–1859). Public Letters. Ed. H. J. Leech, 1885.

—— Diaries. 1930.

Lowe, Robert (Viscount Sherbrooke) (1811–1892). Life and Letters. Ed. A. P. Martin, 2 vols. 1893.

Thackeray, William Makepeace (1811–1863). Letters, 1847–1855. Ed. J. O. Brookfield, 1887.

—— Letters to an American Family. Ed. L. W. Baxter, 1904.

—— Letters to Anne Thackeray Ritchie. Ed. H. Ritchie, 1924.

Browning, Robert (1812–1888). Letters to various Correspondents. Ed. T. J. Wise, 2 vols. 1895–6.

—— Letters of Robert Browning and Elizabeth Barrett Browning, 1845–1846. [Ed. R. B. Browning], 2 vols. 1899.

Burney, Fanny Anne (later Wood) (b. 1812). Extracts from the Journals, 1830–42. Ed. M. S. Rolt, 1926.

Dickens, Charles (1812–1870). Letters. Ed. G. Hogarth and M. Dickens, 3 vols. 1880–2.

Hope-Scott, James Robert (1812–1873). Memoirs, with Selections from his Correspondence. Ed. R. Ormsby, 2 vols. 1884.

Letters of Courtship between John Torr and Maria Jackson, 1838–43. Ed. E. F. Carritt, Oxford, 1933.

Smiles, Samuel (1812–1904). Autobiography. Ed. T. Mackay, 1905.

Pattison, Mark (1813–1884). Memoirs. 1883.

Sewell, Elizabeth Missing (1815–1906). Autobiography. Ed. E. L. Sewell, 1907. [Educational reformer.]

Trollope, Anthony (1815–1882). Autobiography. Ed. H. M. Trollope, 2 vols. 1883; ed. M. Sadleir, 1923 (World's Classics).

Brontë, Charlotte (1816–1855). Life and Letters. Ed. C. K. Shorter, 1908.

Hawkins, Sir Henry (Baron Brampton) (1817–1907). Reminiscences. 2 vols. 1904.

Jowett, Benjamin (1817–1893). The Life and Letters. Ed. E. Abbott and L. Campbell, 2 vols. 1897.

—— The Letters of Jowett. 1899.

Layard, Sir Austen Henry (1817–1894). Autobiography and Letters. 2 vols. 1903.

Bain, Alexander (1818–1903). Autobiography. 1904.

Jeune, Margaret Dyne (b. 1818). Pages from the Diary of an Oxford Lady (1843–62). Ed. M. J. Gifford, Oxford, 1932.

Northcote, Sir Stafford (Earl of Iddesleigh) (1818–1887). Life, Letters and Diaries. Ed. A. Lang, 2 vols. Edinburgh, 1890.

Burrows, Montagu (1819–1905). Autobiography. Ed. Sir C. W. C. Oman, 1908.

'Eliot, George' (1819–1880). George Eliot's Life as related in her Letters and Journals. Ed. G. W. Cross, 3 vols. 1885.

—— Letters to Elma Stuart, 1872–80. Ed. R. Stuart, 1909.

Fox, Caroline (1819–1871). Memories of Old Friends, being Extracts from the Journals and Letters. Ed. H. N. Pym, 1882.

Frith, William Powell (1819–1909). Reminiscences. 1887.

—— Further Reminiscences. 1888.

Gregory, Robert (1819–1911). Autobiography. Ed. W. H. Hutton, 1912.

Hole, Samuel Reynolds (1819–1904). A Little Tour in Ireland. 1859.

—— The Memories of Dean Hole. 1892.

—— More Memories: Thoughts about England spoken in America. 1894.

—— Letters. Ed. G. A. B. Dewar, 1907.

Kingsley, Charles (1819–1875). Letters and Memories. Edited by his Wife. 1877.

Lehmann, Rudolf (1819–1905). Reminiscences. 1894.

Ruskin, John (1819–1900). Praeterita: Outlines of my Past Life. 3 vols. Orpington, 1885–1900.

—— Letters to William Ward. Ed. T. J. Wise, 2 vols. 1893.

Ruskin, John (1819–1900). Letters to a College Friend, 1840–1845. 1894.

—— Letters to Ernest Clesneau. Ed. T. J. Wise, 1894.

—— Letters to Rev. J. P. Faunthorpe. Ed. T. J. Wise, 2 vols. 1895.

—— Letters to Rev. F. A. Malleson. Ed. T. J. Wise, 1896.

—— Letters to F. J. Furnivall. Ed. T. J. Wise, 1897.

—— Letters to M. G. and H. G. [Mary and Helen Gladstone]. 1903.

—— Letters to Charles Elict Norton. 2 vols. New York, 1905.

—— Letters to Dr John Brown of Edinburgh. 1907.

Shore, Margaret Emily (1819–1839). Journal. 1891.

Victoria, H.M. Queen (1819–1901). Leaves from a Journal of our Life in the Highlands. 1862.

—— More Leaves. 1883.

—— The Letters, 1837–1861. Ed. A. C. Benson and R. Viscount Esher, 3 vols. 1907.

—— The Letters, 1862–1901. Ed. G. E. Buckle, 2 sers. 6 vols. 1926–32.

Hollams, Sir John (1820–1910). Jottings of an old Solicitor. 1906.

Pell, Albert (1820–1907). Reminiscences of Albert Pell. Ed. T. Mackay, 1908.

Spencer, Herbert (1820–1903). Autobiography. 1904.

—— Life and Letters. Ed. D. Duncan, 1908.

Brookfield, Jane Octavia (née Elton) (1821–1894). Mrs. Brookfield and her Circle. By C. and F. Brookfield. 2 vols. 1905. [Mainly letters.]

Brown, Ford Madox (1821–1893). Praeraphaelite Diaries and Letters. Ed. W. M. Rosetti, 1900.

Locker-Lampson, Frederick (1821–1895). My Confidences, an Autobiographical Sketch. 1896.

Arnold, Matthew (1822–1888). Letters. Ed. G. W. E. Russell, 2 vols. 1898.

Cobbe, Frances Power (1822–1904). Autobiography. 2 vols. 1904.

Masson, David (1822–1907). Memories of London in the Forties. Ed. F. Masson, 1911.

Freeman, Edward Augustus (1823–1892). Life and Letters. Ed. W. R. W. Stephens, 2 vols. 1895.

Johnson (afterwards Cory), William (1823–1892). Extracts from the Letters and Journals. Ed. F. W. Cornish, Oxford, 1897.

Smith, Goldwin (1823–1910). Reminiscences. Ed. A. Haultain, New York, 1910.

—— A Selection from Goldwin Smith's Correspondence, comprising chiefly Letters to and from his English Friends between 1846 and 1910. Ed. A. Haultain, New York, 1913.

Wallace, Alfred Russel (1823–1913). My Life: a Record of Events and Opinions. 2 vols. 1905.

Stubbs, William (1825–1901). Letters. Ed. W. H. Hutton, 1904.

Beddoe, John (1826–1911). Memories of Eighty Years. Bristol, 1910.

Morier, Sir Robert Burnett David (1826–1893). Memoirs and Letters. 2 vols. 1912.

Hunt, William Holman (1827–1910). Pre-Raphaelitism and the Pre-Raphaelite Brotherhood. 2 vols. 1905.

Meyrick, Frederick (1827–1906). Memories of Life at Oxford. 1905.

Boyle, George David (1828–1901). Recollections. 1895.

Hardman, Sir William (1828–1890). A Mid-Victorian Pepys. The Letters and Memoirs. Ed. S. M. Ellis, 2 sers. 1923–5.

—— The Hardman Papers. A Further Selection (1865–8). Ed. S. M. Ellis, 1930.

Meredith, George (1828–1909). Letters. Ed. W. M. Meredith, 2 vols. 1912.

—— Letters to Edward Clodd and Clement Shorter. 1913.

—— Letters to R. H. Horne. Cape Town, 1919.

—— Letters to Alice Meynell, 1896–1907. 1923.

—— Letters to Various Correspondents. Pretoria, 1924.

Oliphant, Margaret Oliphant (née Wilson) (1828–1897). Memoir of Lawrence Oliphant and Alice Oliphant. 1892.

Rossetti, Dante Gabriel (1828–1882). Family Letters. Ed. W. M. Rossetti, 2 vols. 1895.

Grant Duff, Sir Mountstuart Elphinstone (1829–1906). Notes from a Diary (1851–1872). 2 vols. 1897. [Continued in successive sets of 2 vols. 1898, 1899, 1900, 1901, 1904 and 1905. The last vol. reaches the accession of King Edward VII, 23 Jan. 1901.]

G., H. S. (b. 1829). Autobiography of a Manchester Cotton Manufacturer. 1887.

Rumbold, Sir Horace (1829–1913). Recollections of a Diplomatist. 1902.

—— Further Recollections of a Diplomatist. 1903.

—— Final Recollections of a Diplomatist, 1885–1900. 1905.

Pearson, Charles Henry (1830–1894). Memorials by Himself, his Wife, and his Friends. Ed. W. Stebbing, 1900.

Stanley, Lady Augusta (née Bruce) (d. 1876). Letters of Lady Augusta Stanley, 1849–63. Ed. A. Baillie and H. Bolitho, 1927.

—— Later Letters, 1864–76. Ed. A. Baillie and H. Bolitho, 1929.

Wolff, Sir Henry Drummond Charles (1830–1908). Rambling Recollections. 2 vols. 1908.

Graham, Sir Gerald (1831–1899). Life, Letters and Diaries. Ed. R. H. Vetch, 1901.

Harrison, Frederic (1831–1923). Autobiographic Memoirs. 2 vols. 1911.

White, William Hale (1831–1913). The Autobiography of Mark Rutherford, Dissenting Minister. 1881.

—— Mark Rutherford's Deliverance. 1885.

—— Pages from a Journal. 1900. [More Pages, 1910; Last Pages, 1915.]

Stephen, Sir Leslie (1832–1904). Life and Letters. Ed. F. W. Maitland, 1906.

West, Sir Algernon (1832–1921). Recollections. 2 vols. 1899.

—— One City and Many Men. 1908.

—— Private Diaries. Ed. H. G. Hutchinson, 1922.

Gordon, Charles Gedge (1833–1885). Journals of General Gordon at Khartoum. Ed. A. E. Hake, 1885.

Wolseley, Garnet Joseph, Viscount (1833–1913). The Story of a Soldier's Life. 2 vols. 1903.

—— The Letters of Lord and Lady Wolseley, 1870–1911. Ed. Sir George Arthur, 1922.

Acton, John Emerich Edward Dalberg, Baron (1834–1902). Letters of Lord Acton to Mary, daughter of W. E. Gladstone. Ed. H. Paul, 1904.

—— Lord Acton and his Circle. Ed. F. A. Gasquet, 1906. [Letters.]

Baring-Gould, Sabine (1834–1924). Early Reminiscences, 1834–64. 1923.

Hamerton, Philip Gilbert (1834–1894). An Autobiography, 1834–58, and a Memoir by [E. Hamerton]. 1897.

Hare, Augustus John Cuthbert (1834–1903). Memorials of a Quiet Life. 3 vols. 1872–6.

—— The Story of my Life. 6 vols. 1896–1900.

Austin, Alfred (1835–1910). Autobiography. 2 vols. 1911.

Hill, George Birbeck (1835–1903). Letters. Ed. L. Crump, 1906.

Story, Robert Henry (1835–1907). Memoir. By his Daughter [and Lady F. Balfour]. Glasgow, 1909. [Includes letters.]

Besant, Sir Walter (1836–1901). An Autobiography. 1902.

Wilson, James Maurice (1836–1931). An Autobiography. Ed. [A. T. and J. S. Wilson], 1932.

Brackenbury, Sir Henry (1837–1914). Some Memories of my Spare Time. Edinburgh, 1909.

Browning, Oscar (1837–1923). Memories of Sixty Years at Eton, Cambridge and Elsewhere. 1910.

Burne, Sir Owen Tudor (1837–1909). Memories. 1907.

Green, John Richard (1837–1883). Letters. Ed. Sir L. Stephen, 1901.

Butler, Sir William Francis (1838–1910). Autobiography. 1911.

Morley, John, Viscount (1838–1923). Recollections. 2 vols. 1917.

Ball, Sir Robert Stawell (1840–1913). Reminiscences and Letters. Ed. V. Ball, 1915.

Blunt, Wilfred Seawen (1840–1922). My Diaries. 2 vols. 1912.

Creighton, Mandell (1843–1901). Life and Letters. By his Wife. 2 vols. 1904.

Campbell, John Douglas Sutherland (Duke of Argyll) (1845–1914). Passages from the Past. 2 vols. 1907.

Crane, Walter (1845–1915). An Artist's Reminiscences. 1907.

Besant, Annie (b. 1847). An Autobiography. 1893.

Gladstone, Mary (1847–1927). Diaries and Letters. Ed. L. Masterman, New York, 1930.

Hannington, James (1847–1885). Life. By C. E. Dawson. 1887. [Includes letters.]

Terry, Ellen (1847–1928). Memoirs. With Preface, Notes and Additional Biographical Chapters by Edith Craig and Christopher St John. 1933.

Jefferies, Richard (1848–1887). The Story of My Heart. 1883.

Gosse, Sir Edmund (1849–1928). Father and Son. 1907.

—— Life and Letters. Ed. E. Charteris, 1931.

Stevenson, Robert Louis (1850–1894). Letters. Ed. Sir S. Colvin, 4 vols. 1911.

Powell, Frederick York (1850–1904). A Life, with Selections from his Letters and Occasional Writings. Ed. O. Elton, 2 vols. Oxford, 1906.

Dolling, Robert William Radclyffe (1851–1902). Ten Years in a Portsmouth Slum. 1896.

Leaf, Walter (1852–1927). Some Chapters of Autobiography. Ed. C. M. Leaf, 1932.

2. THE POETRY

I. SURVEYS, CRITICAL STUDIES AND ANTHOLOGIES

[This section should be used in conjunction with the general lists of 19th cent. literary histories and critical studies on pp. 3–13 above. It will also be found partly to overlap the parallel section in vol. II (pp. 169–72). Some additional references are provided by: C. M. Gayley and F. N. Scott, An Introduction to the Methods and Materials of Literary Criticism, Boston, 1899 (chs. iv–vii); C. M. Gayley and B. P. Kurtz, Methods and Materials of Literary Criticism. Lyric, Epic, and Allied Forms of Poetry, Boston, 1920; E. Bernbaum, Guide through the Romantic Movement, New York, 1930.]

A. HISTORIES AND SURVEYS

(1) GENERAL

Griswold, R. W. The Poets and Poetry of England in the Nineteenth Century. Philadelphia, 1845 (2nd edn).

Moir, D. M. Sketches of the Poetical Literature of the Past Half-Century. Edinburgh, 1851.

Brandes, G. Hovedstrømninger i det 19de Aarhundredes Litteratur. 6 vols. Copenhagen, 1872–90; tr. Eng. 1901–5.

Sarrazin, G. Poètes modernes de l'Angleterre. Paris, 1885.

—— Renaissance de la Poésie anglaise, 1792–1889. Paris, 1889.

Saintsbury, G. A History of Nineteenth Century Literature (1780–1900). 1901.

Gosse, Sir E. A History of English Literature in the Nineteenth Century. 1906.

Payne, W. M. The Greater English Poets of the Nineteenth Century. New York, 1907.

Schelling, F. E. The English Lyric. Boston, 1907.

Walker, H. The Literature of the Victorian Era. Cambridge, 1910.

Dixon, W. M. English Epic and Heroic Poetry. 1912.

Rhys, E. Lyric Poetry. 1913.

Osmond, P. H. The Mystical Poets of the English Church. New York, 1919.

Cazamian, L. L'Évolution psychologique et la Littérature en Angleterre, 1660–1914. Paris, 1920. [How the romantic school arose out of the emotional reaction against intellect, but was influenced and antagonised by the positivist and utilitarian preoccupations of the age (Shelley the most striking example); how in its turn romanticism gave way before 'mid-victorian' neoclassicism, nationalism and realism.]

Darton, F. J. H. From Surtees to Sassoon. Some English Contrasts (1838–1928). 1931. [Hunting and war literature.]

Bateson, F. W. English Poetry and the English Language. Oxford, 1934. [Ch. iv.]

(2) THE ROMANTIC MOVEMENT

Talfourd, Sir T. N. An Attempt to Estimate the Poetical Talent of the Present Age, including a Sketch of the History of Poetry and the Characters of Southey, Crabbe. Scott, Moore, Lord Byron, Campbell, Lamb, Coleridge, and Wordsworth. 1815. [The Pamphleteer, vol. v.]

Oliphant, M. O. The Literary History of England in the End of the Eighteenth and the Beginning of the Nineteenth Century 3 vols. 1882.

Courthope, W. J. The Liberal Movement in English Literature. 1885.

—— History of English Poetry. Vol. VI, 1910.

Brandl, A. Samuel Taylor Coleridge and the English Romantic School. Tr. Eng. 1887.

Dixon, W. M. English Poetry from Blake to Browning. 1894.

Herford, C. H. The Age of Wordsworth. 1897.

Omond, T. S. The Romantic Triumph. Edinburgh, 1900.

Vaughan, C. E. The Romantic Revolt. Edinburgh, 1900.

Beers, H. A. A History of English Romanticism in the Nineteenth Century. New York, 1901.

Symons, A. The Romantic Movement in English Poetry. 1909.

Richter, H. Geschichte der englischen Romantik. 2 vols. Halle, 1911–6.

Elton, O. A Survey of English Literature, 1780–1830. 2 vols. 1912.

Sherwood, M. Undercurrents of Influence in English Romantic Poetry. Cambridge, U.S.A. 1934.

(3) VICTORIAN POETRY

Stedman, E. C. Victorian Poets. 1876; Boston, 1903 (rev. edn).

Oliphant, M. O. and F. R. The Victorian Age of English Literature. 2 vols. 1892.

Ritchie, A. I., Lady. Records of Tennyson, Ruskin and Robert and Elizabeth Browning. 1892.

Walker, H. The Greater Victorian Poets. 1893.
—— The Age of Tennyson. 1897.
—— The Literature of the Victorian Era. Cambridge, 1910.
Dixon, W. M. English Poetry from Blake to Browning. 1894.
Saintsbury, G. A History of Nineteenth Century Literature (1780–1900). 1901.
Smith, A. The Main Tendencies of Victorian Poetry. Birmingham, 1907.
Chesterton, G. K. The Victorian Age in Literature. 1913. (Home University Lib.)
Elton, O. A Survey of English Literature, 1830–1880. 2 vols. 1920.
Weatherhead, L. D. The After-World of the Poets. The Contribution of Victorian Poets to the Development of the Idea of Immortality. 1929.
Lucas, F. L. Eight Victorian Poets. Cambridge, 1930. [Tennyson, Browning, Arnold, Clough, Rossetti, Swinburne, Morris, Hardy.]

(4) LATE VICTORIAN POETRY

Austin, A. The Poetry of the Period. 1870. [Tennyson, Browning, Swinburne, Arnold, Morris.]
Forman, H. B. Our Living Poets. 1871.
Archer, W. Poets of the Younger Generation. 1902.
Brooke, S. A. A Study of Clough, Arnold, Rossetti, and Morris. With an Introduction on the Course of Poetry from 1822 to 1852. 1908.
Kennedy, J. M. English Literature, 1880–1905. 1912.
Jackson, H. The Eighteen-Nineties. 1913.
Burdett, O. The Beardsley Period. 1925.
Le Gallienne, R. The Romantic '90s. 1926.
Granville-Barker, H. et al. The Eighteen-Seventies. Cambridge, 1929.
de la Mare, W. et al. The Eighteen-Eighties. Cambridge, 1930.
Drinkwater, J. et al. The Eighteen-Sixties. Cambridge, 1932.
Wild, F. Die englische Literatur der Gegenwart seit 1870. Versdichtungen. Leipzig, 1931.
Walraf, E. Soziale Lyrik in England, 1880–1914. Leipzig, 1932.
Evans, B. I. English Poetry in the Later Nineteenth Century. 1933.
Mégroz, R. L. Modern English Poetry, 1882–1932. 1933.
Palmer, H. Post-Victorian Poetry. 1938.

B. CRITICAL STUDIES

(1) IDEALS AND POETIC THEORIES OF THE ROMANTIC SCHOOL

Wordsworth, W. Lyrical Ballads. 1800; 1815. [Preface. See A. J. George, Wordsworth's Prefaces and Essays on Poetry,

Boston, [1892], and H. Littledale, Lyrical Ballads. Ed. with Introduction and Appendix containing Wordsworth's Preface of 1800, 1911.]-
Bowles, W. L. Pope's Poetical Works. 10 vols. 1806. [Criticism of Pope's standards and methods prefixed. Discusses the relative value of subject and execution; believes that the nature of the theme is more important than the art with which it is presented.]
—— The Invariable Principles of Poetry. 1819.
—— Two Letters to Lord Byron. 1821.
Coleridge, S. T. Biographia Literaria. 2 vols. 1817. [See A. J. George, Coleridge's Principles of Criticism, Boston, n.d., an annotation of chs. of Biographia Literaria.]
—— Anima Poetae. From the Unpublished Notebooks of S. T. Coleridge. Ed. E. H. Coleridge, 1895.
Hazlitt, W. Lectures on the English Poets. 1818. [Especially on 'Poetry in general.' Though recognising the merits of the classical school, he defines poetry as 'the universal language which the heart holds with nature and itself.']
Campbell, T. An Essay on English Poetry. [Prefixed to Specimens of the British Poets, 7 vols. 1819. Upholds Pope's conceptions and method of 'first study nature.']
Byron, G., Baron. A Letter to [John Murray]. 1821.
—— Observations upon 'Observations.' 1821. [Maintains that the arts of presentation are more effective than the subject and nature of the theme.]
De Quincey, T. Letters to a Young Man whose Education has been neglected. III. London Mag. March 1823. [Literature of knowledge and of power.]
—— The Lake Poets: W. Wordsworth. Tait's Mag. Feb. 1839.
—— The Lake Poets: Southey, Wordsworth and Coleridge. Tait's Mag. Aug. 1839.
—— On Wordsworth's Poetry. Tait's Mag. Sept. 1845. [Rptd in De Quincey's Literary Criticism, ed. H. Darbishire, Oxford, 1909.]
—— Alexander Pope. North British Rev. Aug. 1848. [Review of edn by W. Roscoe, Literature of knowledge and of power.]
Heine, H. Zur Geschichte der neueren schönen Literatur in Deutschland. [In Europe littéraire, Paris, 1833. German version, Leipzig, 1833, 2nd German edn with addn of Bk III entitled Die romantische Schule, Leipzig, 1836; tr. Eng. 1883.]
Mill, J. S. Thoughts on Poetry and its Varieties. Monthly Repository, Jan., Oct. 1833. [Rptd in Dissertations and Discus

sions, vol. iv, 1875. Shelley and Wordsworth compared as exponents of the spontaneous and cultivated schools.]

Mill, J. S. Autobiography. 1873. [Ch. v.]

Wilson, J. M. The Enthusiast, with a Preliminary Chapter on Poetry. Edinburgh, 1834.

Hunt, J. H. L. Imagination and Fancy: or, Selections from the English Poets, Illustrative of those First Requisites of their Art. With an Essay in Answer to the Question 'What is Poetry?' 1844; ed. A. S. Cook, Boston, 1893.

Mackay, C. Egeria. 1850. [Includes essay on poetry.]

Lynch, T. T. On Poetry. [In Essays on some of the Forms of Literature, 1853.]

Lofft, C. Ernest. 1868. [Preface on nature of poetry.]

Shairp, J. Aspects of Poetry. Oxford, 1881. [Early nineteenth century.]

Watts-Dunton, T. Essay on Poetry. [In 9th edn of Encyclopaedia Britannica, 1884. Revised and re-edited by T. S. Baynes.]

—— The Sonnet. [In Chambers' Encyclopaedia, 1891.]

—— The Renascence of Wonder in English Poetry. [Introduction to vol. iii of Chambers' Cyclopaedia of English Literature, ed. D. Patrick, 1903. Germ of the idea in preface to Chatterton written for T. H. Ward's British Poets, 1880. Chatterton described as 'the renascence of wonder incarnate' because he 'refused to be imprisoned in the jar of eighteenth-century convention.']

—— Poetry and the Renascence of Wonder. With a Preface by T. Hake. 1916. [Based on the foregoing essays, which are rptd, and his contributions 1876–1902 to Athenaeum. Left unrevised at his death.]

Symonds, J. A. The Lyricism of the English Romantic Drama. [In the Key of Blue and Other Prose Essays, 1893.]

Herford, C. H. The Age of Wordsworth. 1897.

Texte, J. Keats et le Néo-Hellénisme dans la Poésie anglaise. [In Études de Littérature européenne, Paris, 1898.]

Campbell, O. W. Shelley and the Unromantics. 1923.

Gordon, G. Shelley and the Oppressors of Mankind. Oxford, 1923.

Gingerich, S. F. Essays in the Romantic Poets. New York, 1924. [Traces growth of their fundamental convictions.]

Murry, J. M. Romanticism and the Tradition. Criterion, April 1924.

Kauffmann, P. Defining Romanticism: a Survey and a Program. MLN. xl, 1925.

Powell, A. E. The Romantic Theory of Poetry. An Examination in the Light of Croce's Aesthetic. 1926.

Fairchild, H. N. The Noble Savage. A Study in Romantic Naturalism. New York. 1928.

—— The Romantic Quest. New York, 1931.

Chapman, J. A. Papers on Shelley, Wordsworth and Others. Oxford, 1929. [Directs attention to what is the supreme excellence of poetry.]

Elliott, G. R. The Cycle of Modern Poetry. Princeton, 1929.

Estève, E. Byron et le Romantisme français. Paris, 1929.

Praz, M. La Carne, la Morte e il Diavolo nella Letteratura Romantica. Florence, 1930; tr. Eng. 1933 (as The Romantic Agony).

Carr, P. Days with the French Romantics in the Paris of 1830. 1932. [Influence of Constable and Bonington in painting; Shakespeare and English actors in drama; Scott and Byron in Literature.]

Sickells, E. M. The Gloomy Egoist. Moods and Themes of Melancholy from Gray to Keats. New York, 1932.

Sherwood, M. Undercurrents of Influence in English Romantic Poetry. Cambridge, U.S.A. 1934.

Morley, E. J. The Life and Times of Henry Crabb Robinson. Oxford, 1935.

Bush, D. Mythology and the Romantic Tradition in English Poetry. Cambridge, U.S.A. 1937.

(2) French Revolution and Byronism

Goethe, J. W. von. Faust. Zweiter Theil. Stuttgart, 1833. [Especially Act iii, pbd separately, 1827, as Helena: Klassisch-romantische Phantasmagorie. Euphorion, son of Faust and Helen, symbolises Byron.]

Chasles, V. E. P. Vie et Influence de Byron sur son Époque. [In Études sur la Littérature et les Mœurs de l'Angleterre au XIXe Siècle, Paris, 1850.]

Courthope, W. J. The Liberal Movement in English Literature. 1885.

Dowden, E. The French Revolution and English Literature. 1897.

Hancock, A. E. The French Revolution and the English Poets. 1899.

Cestre, C. La Révolution française et les Poètes anglais. Dijon, 1906.

Graham, W. Politics of the Greater Romantic Poets. PLMA. xxxvi, 1921.

Chew, S. C. Byron in England. His Fame and Afterfame. 1924. [Decline of Byronism, revival, afterfame.]

Brinton, C. The Political Ideas of the English Romanticists. Oxford, 1926.

Estève, E. Byron et le Romantisme français. Paris, 1929.

Richter, H. Lord Byron. Persönlichkeit und Werk. Halle, 1929.

(3) POETIC FORMS

[See also Prosody and Prose Rhythm, vol. I, pp. 15–23, above.]

Gayley, C. M. and Scott, F. N. An Introduction to the Methods and Materials of Literary Criticism. Boston, 1899. [Ch. vii.]

Saintsbury, G. A History of English Prosody. Vol. III, 1910.

Reschke, H. Die Spenserstanze im neunzehnten Jahrhundert. Heidelberg, 1918. [Addns by R. A. Aubin, Imitations of Childe Harold, E. Studien, LXX, 1935.]

(a) The Sonnet

Hunt, J. H. L. The Book of the Sonnet. Edited [with an Essay on the Sonnet] by Leigh Hunt and [with an Essay on American Sonnets and Sonneteers by] S. A. Lee. 2 vols. Boston, 1867.

Tomlinson, C. The Sonnet. Its Origin, Structure and Place in Poetry. 1874.

Dennis, J. The English Sonnet. [In Studies in English Literature, 1876. The critic's office is to follow the poet, not to require the poet to follow him.]

Sharp, W. Sonnets of this Century. 1886.

Sanderlin, G. The Influence of Milton and Wordsworth on the Early Victorian Sonnet. ELH. v, 1938.

(b) The Lyric

Dennis, J. English Lyrical Poetry. [In Studies in English Literature, 1876.]

du Prell, C. Psychologie der Lyrik. Leipzig, 1880.

Sharp, W. Great Odes. English and American. Edited with Introduction. 1890.

Werner, R. M. Lyrik und Lyriker. Eine Untersuchung. Hamburg, 1890.

Peck, H. T. The Lyrics of Tennyson. [In Studies in Several Literatures, New York, 1909.]

Schelling, F. E. The English Lyric. Boston, 1910.

Hepple, N. Lyrical Forms in England. Cambridge, 1911.

Reed, E. B. English Lyrical Poetry. New Haven, 1912.

Rhys, E. Lyric Poetry. 1913.

Binyon, L. The English Ode. Trans. Royal Soc. Lit. II, 1922.

Grierson, Sir H. J. C. Lyrical Poetry from Blake to Hardy. 1928.

(c) Drawing-Room Verse

Locker-Lampson, F. Lyra Elegantiarum. 1867.

Hewlett, H. G. Poets of Society. Contemporary Rev. July 1872.

Smith, G. B. English Fugitive Poets. [In Poets and Novelists, 1875.]

Gosse, Sir E. A Plea for certain Exotic Forms of Verse. Cornhill Mag. July 1877.

Dobson, A. Notes on some Foreign Forms of Verse. [In Latter Day Lyrics, 1878.]

Lang, A. Letters on Literature. 1889. [2 letters on 'vers de société.']

Swinburne, A. C. Social Verse. [In Studies in Prose and Verse, New York, 1894.]

Walraf, E. Soziale Lyrik im England, 1880–1914. Leipzig, 1932.

(d) Ballads and Epics

Jordan, W. Epische Briefe. No. III. Frankfort, 1876. [Is the age of epic composition past?]

Beyer, V. Die Begründung der ernsten Ballade durch G. A. Bürger. QF. XCVII, 1905.

Bradley, C. B. On the Distinction between the Art-Epic and the Folk-Epic. University of California Chronicle, VIII, 1906, pp. 377–87.

Hamilton, C. Methods and Materials of Fiction. New York, 1908. [Novel v. poetry.]

Dixon, W. M. English Epic and Heroic Poetry. 1912.

Henderson, T. F. The Ballad in Literature. Cambridge, 1912.

Forsythe, R. S. Modern Imitations of the Popular Ballad. JEGP. XIII, 1914.

Elton, O. Poetic Romances after 1850. [In A Sheaf of Papers, 1922.]

Bond, W. The Art of Narrative Poetry. Trans. Royal Soc. Lit. IV, 1924.

(4) SCOPE AND RANGE OF NINETEENTH-CENTURY POETRY

[For discussion of later developments see pp. 161–2 below.]

(a) Philosophy and Religion

[See also under The Intellectual Background, pp. 46–70 above.]

Keble, J. Sacred Poetry. Quarterly Rev. XXXII, 1825. [Review of The Star in the East; with other Poems by J. Conder, 1824.]

Heine, H. Die romantische Schule. Leipzig, 1830. [See also p. 47 above.]

Shairp, J. C. Studies in Poetry and Philosophy. Edinburgh, 1868; 1887.

—— Aspects of Poetry. Oxford, 1881.

Brooke, S. A. Theology in the English Poets. 1874.

Courthope, W. J. The Liberal Movement in English Literature. 1885.

Dewey, J. Poetry and Philosophy. Andover Rev. XVI, 1891.

Dowden, E. Puritan and Anglican. 1900. [Ch. iv.]

Gingerich, S. F. Wordsworth, Tennyson and Browning: a Study in Human Freedom. Ann Arbor, 1911.

Vat, D. G. van der. The Fabulous Opera. Groningen, 1936. [Ideas in 19th cent. poets.]

(b) Nature and Landscape

Howitt, W. Homes and Haunts of the most eminent British Poets. 2 vols. 1847.

Dowden, E. Poetical Feeling for Nature. Contemporary Rev. ii, 1866.

Brandes, G. Hovedstrømninger i det 19de Aarhundredes Litteratur. 6 vols. Copenhagen, 1872–90; tr. Eng. 1901–5. [Vol. iv, Naturalism in England.]

Shairp, J. C. On the Poetic Interpretation of Nature. 1877.

Laprade, V. de. Histoire du Sentiment de la Nature. Paris, 1883.

Veitch, J. The Feeling for Nature in Scottish Poetry. 2 vols. Edinburgh, 1887.

Biese, A. Die Entwickelung des Naturgefühls im Mittelalter und in der Neuzeit. Leipzig, 1888.

Machie, A. Natural Knowledge in Modern Poetry. 1906.

Brooke, S. A. Naturalism in English Poetry. 1920.

Strong, A. T. An Essay on Nature in Wordsworth and Meredith. [Appended to Three Studies in Shelley, 1921.]

Foerster, N. Studies in the Modern View of Nature. New York, 1923.

Binyon, L. Landscape in English Art and Poetry. Tokyo, 1927.

Blunden, E. Nature in English Literature. 1929.

Huscher, H. Über Eigenart und Ursprung des englischen Naturgefühls. Leipzig, 1929.

Beach, J. W. The Concept of Nature in Nineteenth-Century English Poetry. New York, 1936.

(c) Science and Poetry

Peacock, T. L. The Four Ages of Poetry. 1820. [Rptd H. F. B. Brett-Smith, Oxford, 1921, with Shelley's Defense of Poetry (of which it was the provocation).]

Sonnenschein, E. A. Culture and Science. Macmillan's Mag. liii, 1885.

Scudder, V. D. Effect of the Scientific Temper in Modern Poetry. Andover Rev. viii, 1887.

Bourget, P. Science et Poésie. Fortnightly Rev. xlix, 1888.

Thomas, C. Poetry and Science. Open Court, iii, 1889.

—— Have we still Need of Poetry? Forum, xxv, 1900.

Watts-Dunton, T. Tennyson as a Nature Poet; Tennyson and the Scientific Movement. Nineteenth Century, May, Oct. 1893.

Brooke, S. A. Tennyson. His Art and Relation to Modern Life. 1894.

Elliott, G. R. The Arnoldian Lyric Melancholy. PMLA. xxxviii, 1923. ['In the chasm between the life of the centuries and the life in poetry lie the deepest waters of the Arnoldian melancholy.']

(5) Pre-Raphaelitism

Rossetti, W. M. et al. The Germ. 1850; ed. T. B. Mosher, 1898. [No. i, Thoughts towards Nature in Poetry, Literature and Art.]

Ruskin, J. Pre-Raphaelitism. 1851.

—— Ruskin as Literary Critic. Ed. A. H. R. Ball, Cambridge, 1928.

Buchanan, R. The Fleshly School of Poetry and other Phenomena of the Day; Mr D. G. Rossetti. Contemporary Rev. Oct. 1871; 1872.

Forman, H. B. Our Living Poets: An Essay in Criticism. 1871.

Rossetti, D. G. The Stealthy School of Criticism. Athenaeum, 16 Dec. 1871.

Hamilton, W. The Aesthetic Movement in England. 1882.

Myers, F. W. H. Rossetti and the Religion of Beauty. [In Essays: Modern, 1883.]

Wilde, O. Intentions. 1891.

Layard, G. S. Tennyson and his Pre-Raphaelite Illustrators. 1894.

Mosher, T. B. Ruskin, Rossetti and Preraphaelitism. 1899.

Hunt, W. H. Pre-Raphaelitism and the Preraphaelite Brotherhood. 2 vols. 1905.

Brooke, S. A. A Study of Clough, Arnold, Rossetti and Morris. With an Introduction on the Course of Poetry from 1822 to 1852. 1908.

Burdett, O. The Beardsley Period. An Essay in Perspective. 1925.

Vinciguerra, M. Romantici e Decadenti Inglesi. Foligno, 1926.

Reid, F. Illustrators of the Sixties. 1928.

Welby, T. E. The Victorian Romantics, 1850–1870. 1929.

Waller, R. D. The Rossetti Family, 1824–1854. Manchester, 1932.

(6) Post-Romantic Ideals and Theories of Poetry

Emerson, R. W. The Poet. [In Essays, ser. 2, Boston, 1844. Poetry is 'the expression of a sound mind speaking after the ideal and not the apparent.']

Poe, E. A. The Poetic Principle. Home Journ. (New York), 31 Aug. 1850. ['Inspired by an ecstatic prescience of the glories beyond the grave, we struggle by multiform combinations among the things and thoughts of Time, to attain a portion of that loveliness whose very elements perhaps appertain to eternity alone.' See also M. Alterton, Origin of Poe's Critical Theory, Iowa University Stud. II, 1925.

Brimley, G. Poetry and Criticism. [In Essays, 1858.]

Browning, R. [Introduction to forged Shelley letters, 1852. The poet 'is impelled to embody the thing he perceives, not so much with reference to the many below as to the One above him, the supreme Intelligence which apprehends all things in their absolute truth.']

Lewes, G. H. The Inner Life of Art. 1865.

Forman, H. B. Our Living Poets. 1871.

Dobell, S. T. The Nature of Poetry. [In Thoughts on Art, Philosophy and Religion, 1876.]

Selkirk, J. B. Ethics and Aesthetics of Modern Poetry. 1878.

Arnold, M. Wordsworth. Macmillan's Mag. May, July 1879. [Rptd in Essays in Criticism, ser. 2, 1888. 'His superiority arises from his powerful use in his best pieces, his powerful application to his subject of ideas "on man, on nature and on human life."']

—— The Study of Poetry. [In English Poets, ed. T. H. Ward, vol. IV, 1880. Rptd in Essays in Criticism, ser. 2, 1888. Poetry 'a criticism of life under the conditions fixed for such a criticism, by the laws of poetic truth and poetic beauty.']

—— Byron. Macmillan's Mag. March 1881. [Rptd in Essays in Criticism, ser. 2, 1888.]

—— Shelley. Nineteenth Century, Jan. 1888. [Rptd in Essays in Criticism, ser. 2 1888.]

Symonds, J. A. Matthew Arnold's Selections from Wordsworth. Fortnightly Rev. XXXII, 1879.

Austin, A. Old and New Canons of Criticism in Poetry. Contemporary Rev. XL, XLI, 1881–2. [Objects that there can be 'no consensus about the criticism of life.']

—— The Position and Prospects of Poetry. [Preface to 1889 edn of The Human Tragedy. Poetry is 'a transfiguration of life, in other words an imaginative representation of whatever men perceive, feel, think or do.']

Swinburne, A. C. Wordsworth and Byron. Nineteenth Century, April, May 1884. [Opposes Arnold, claims that poetry should combine imagination with humour and exhale a 'perceptible but indefinable charm.' See Sir H. J. C. Grierson, Lord Byron: Arnold and Swinburne, Warton Lecture, 1920.]

Courthope, W. J. The Liberal Movement in English Literature. 1885. [Criticises both Arnold and Swinburne and defines poetry as 'the art of producing pleasure by the just expression of imaginative thought and feeling in metrical language.']

Bain, A. On Teaching English, with an Inquiry into the Definition of Poetry. 1887. [Reviews definitions by Aristotle, Bacon, Wordsworth, Arnold, Austin. Discusses whether poetry is 'imitative' or 'effusive.' Defines poetry as 'a fine art, operating by means of thought conveyed in language.']

Cook, A. S. The Touchstones of Poetry. Selected from the Writings of Matthew Arnold and John Ruskin. With an Introduction. San Francisco, 1887.

Gurney, E. Tertium Quid. 2 vols. 1887. [Collection of essays. Deals with the Arnold, Austin, Swinburne controversy. As poetry possesses a 'non-reasonable' element, poets cannot be classed or analysed. He emphasises the 'magical element' and indefinable charm of 'quintessentially poetic passages,' which is partly a combination of 'mind-pleasure' and 'ear-pleasure.']

Everett, C. C. Poetry, Comedy and Duty. Boston, 1888. [Argues that the enjoyment of beauty, the independence of the spiritual life and obedience to the law of righteousness are interdependent and must be fused in art. Influenced by Schopenhauer and Hegel.]

Stedman, E. C. The Nature and Elements of Poetry. Boston, 1892. [Notices 'melancholia' of modern poetry and discriminates the 'self-consciousness' and the 'impersonality' of the poet.]

Dixon, W. M. English Poetry from Blake to Browning. 1894. [Poetry represents 'intenser spiritual life than the one in which we hourly move.']

Woodberry, G. E. The Appreciation of Literature. New York, 1907.

Herford, C. H. A Poetical View of the World. Warton Lecture, 1916.

Tucker, T. G. The Judgment and Appreciation of Literature. 1926. [Severe classicism; little toleration for modern experiments; prefers Browning to Tennyson.]

Brémond, H. La Poésie Pure: avec un Débat sur la Poésie, par R. de Souza. Paris, 1928. [Poetry is a mystic image, allied not to music but to prayer, speaking from the poet's 'underconsciousness to ours.']

(7) MODERNISM

Whitman, W. The Poetry of the Future. North American Rev. CXXXII, 1881.

Guyan, M.-J. L'Esthétique du Vers moderne. Revue Philosophique, xvii, 1884.

Davidson, J. W. The Poetry of the Future. New York, 1888. [Essential characteristic of English verse is rhythm.]

Henley, W. E. Views and Reviews. 2 vols. 1890–1902.

Symons, A. The Symbolist Movement in Literature. 1899.

van Bever, A. and Léautaud, P. Poètes d'Aujourd'hui, 1880–1900. Morceaux choisis, Accompagnés de Notices biographiques et d'un Essai de Bibliographie. Paris, 1901. [Contains examples of free verse and other experiments which influenced English poets.]

Archer, W. Poets of the Younger Generation. 1902.

Walker, H. The Literature of the Victorian Era. Cambridge, 1913.

Gosse, Sir E. The Future of English Poetry. [In Some Diversions of a Man of Letters, 1920.]

Olivero, F. Studies in Modern Poetry. 1921.

Clark, A. M. The Realist Revolt in Modern Poetry. Oxford, 1922.

Flecker, J. E. Critical Studies. [In Collected Prose, 1922.]

Lowes, J. L. Convention and Revolt in Poetry. Boston, 1922.

Buchan, J. The Old and New in Literature. Trans. Royal Soc. Lit. v, 1925.

Burdett, O. Critical Essays. 1925.

Williams, H. Modern English Writers: Being a Study of Imaginative Literature, 1890–1914. 1925.

Pelizzi, C. Romanticism and Regionalism. Oxford, 1929.

Decker, C. R. The Aesthetic Revolt against Naturalism in Victorian Criticism. PMLA. liii, 1938.

C. ANTHOLOGIES

(1) ANTHOLOGIES OF ENGLISH POETRY

Miles, A. H. et al. The Poets and the Poetry of the Century. 10 vols. [1891–7], 1898; 12 vols. 1905–7 (re-arranged, expanded and brought up to date as The Poets and the Poetry of the Nineteenth Century). [By far the fullest and most scholarly of the anthologies. Selections are included from some 300 writers, each being preceded by a biographical-bibliographical introduction either by Miles himself or some recognized authority. Referred to below as Miles.]

Dyce, A. Specimens of British Poetesses. 1825.

The Living Poets of England. [With] an Essay on English Poetry. 2 vols. Paris, 1827.

Hunt, J. H. L. Imagination and Fancy: or Selections from the English Poets, illustrative of these First Requisites of their Art. 1844.

Palgrave, F. T. The Golden Treasury of the Best Songs and Lyrical Poems in the English Language. 1861; 1891 (enlarged).

—— The Treasury of Sacred Song. Oxford, 1889.

—— The Golden Treasury. Second Series. 1897.

Savile, B. W. Lyra Sacra. Being a Collection of Hymns Ancient and Modern, Odes and Fragments of Sacred Poetry. 1861.

Hunt, J. H. L. and Lee, S. A. The Book of the Sonnet. 2 vols. Boston, 1867.

Blaikie, J. A. and Gosse, Sir E. Madrigals, Songs and Sonnets. 1870.

Ward, T. H. et al. The English Poets. 4 vols. 1880. [Vol. iv.]

Gosse, Sir E. English Odes. 1881. [Spenser–Swinburne.]

Waddington, S. English Sonnets by Poets of the Past and English Sonnets by Living Writers, selected and arranged, with a note on the History of the Sonnet. 1881.

Caine, Sir T. H. Sonnets of Three Centuries. 1882.

Sharp, W. Sonnets of this Century. 1886.

Henley, W. E. Lyra Heroica. A Book of Verse for Boys. 1892.

—— A London Garland. Selected from Five Centuries of English Verse. 1895.

—— English Lyrics. 1897.

Beeching, H. C. A Paradise of English Poetry. 2 vols. 1893.

—— Lyra Sacra. 1895.

—— A Book of Christmas Verse. 1895.

—— Lyra Apostolica. 1901.

Leonard, R. M. The Dog in British Poetry. 1893.

—— The Pageant of English Poetry. 1909.

—— A Book of Light Verse. Fourteenth to Nineteenth Century. 1910.

—— The Book-Lover's Anthology. 1911.

—— The Poetry of Peace. 1918.

Quiller-Couch, Sir A. T. The Oxford Book of English Verse, 1250–1900. Oxford, 1900.

—— The Oxford Book of Victorian Verse. Oxford, 1912.

Duff, Sir M. E. G. The Victorian Anthology. 1902.

Stone, C. Sea Songs and Ballads, 1400–1886. 1906.

Jerrold, W. The Book of Living Poets. 1907.

Jerrold, W. and Leonard, R. M. A Century of Parody and Imitation. 1913.

Knight, W. A Victorian Anthology. [1907.]

Dixon, W. M. and Grierson, Sir H. J. C. The English Parnassus. An Anthology of

Longer Poems (Chaucer to Omar Khayyam). Oxford, 1909.

Walker, Mrs H. A Book of Victorian Prose and Poetry. Cambridge, 1915.

Nicholson, D. H. S. and Lee, A. H. E. The Oxford Book of English Mystical Verse, Thirteenth to Twentieth Century. Oxford, 1916.

Methuen, Sir A. An Anthology of Modern Verse. 1921.

Newbolt, Sir H. An English Anthology of Prose and Poetry, showing the Main Stream of English Literature through Six Centuries. 1921.

Squire, Sir J. C. A Book of Women's Verse. Oxford, 1921.

Caldwell, T. The Golden Book of Modern English Poetry, 1870–1930. 1922.

Brie, F. Englisches Lesebuch: neunzehntes Jahrhundert. Heidelberg, 1923.

Binyon, L. The Golden Treasury of Modern Lyrics. 1924.

Smith, J. C. A Book of Modern Verse. Oxford, 1925.

Welby, T. E. The Silver Treasury of English Lyrics. 1925. [Supplements Palgrave.]

Crump, G. H. Poets of the Romantic Revival. 1927.

Lucas, E. V. The Joy of Life. 1927.

Williams, C. A Book of Victorian Narrative Verse. Oxford, 1927.

Wilson, J. D. The Poetry of the Age of Wordsworth. An Anthology of the Five Major Poets. Cambridge, 1927.

Milford, Sir H. S. The Oxford Book of Regency Verse, 1798–1837. Oxford, 1928.

Bernbaum, E. An Anthology of Romanticism. 5 vols. New York, 1929–30.

Woods, G. B. Poetry of the Victorian Period. Chicago, 1930.

Powley, E. B. A Hundred Years of English Poetry. Cambridge, 1931.

Sitwell, E. The Pleasures of Poetry: A Critical Anthology. Second Series. The Romantic Revival. 1931. [Third Series (the Victorian Age), 1932.]

Campbell, O. J., Pyre, J. F. A. and Weaver, B. Poetry and Criticism of the Romantic Movement. New York, 1932.

Hayward, J. Nineteenth-Century Poetry. An Anthology. 1932.

Stephens, J., Beck, E. L. and Snow, R. H. English Romantic Poets. New York, 1933.

Witts, W. An Anthology of Poetry from Spenser to Arnold. 1933. [8 of 12 poets represented belong to 19th century.]

Davidson, D. British Poetry of the Eighteen-Nineties. New York, 1937. [With bibliography.]

Henderson, W. Victorian Street Ballads. 1937.

(2) ANTHOLOGIES OF SCOTTISH POETRY

Johnson, J. The Scots Musical Museum. 5 vols. 1787–1803; rptd 6 vols. Edinburgh, 1833; ed. W. Stenhouse, D. Laing, and C. K. Sharpe, 4 vols. Edinburgh, 1853.

Thomson, G. Select Collection of Original Scottish Airs. With Select and Characteristic Verses by the most admired Scottish Poets. 5 vols. Edinburgh, 1799–1818.

The Caledonian Musical Museum. 1801.

The Nithsdale Minstrel. Dumfries, 1805.

The Caledonian Musical Repository. 1806; Edinburgh, 1809, 1811.

Cromek, R. H. Select Scottish Songs Ancient and Modern. 2 vols. 1810.

—— Remains of Nithsdale and Galloway Song. 1810; rptd Paisley, 1880.

Campbell, A. Albyn's Anthology. 2 vols. Edinburgh, 1816–8.

The Harp of Caledonia. 3 vols. Glasgow, 1819–81.

Motherwell, W. The Harp of Renfrewshire. Glasgow, 1820; rptd Paisley, 1872.

—— Minstrelsy Ancient and Modern. Glasgow, 1827; rptd Paisley, 1873.

Smith, R. A. The Scottish Minstrel. 6 vols. Edinburgh, 1821–4.

Cunningham, A. The Songs of Scotland, Ancient and Modern. 4 vols. 1825.

Songs of the Edinburgh Troop. Edinburgh, 1825.

Chambers, R. The Scottish Songs. 2 vols. 1829–32.

—— A Miscellany of Popular Scottish Songs. Edinburgh, 1841.

Whistle Binkie. Glasgow, 1832–47, etc.

A Miscellany of Popular Scottish Poems. Edinburgh, 1841.

Ayrshire Ballads and Songs. 2 sers. Ayr, 1846–, Edinburgh, 1847.

Rogers, C. The Modern Scottish Minstrel. 6 vols. Edinburgh, 1856–7.

Wilson, J. G. The Poets and Poetry of Scotland. 2 vols. 1876–7.

Edwards, D. H. Modern Scottish Poets. 16 vols. Brechin, 1880–97.

Douglas, Sir G. Poems of the Scottish Minor Poets. 1891.

—— The Book of Scottish Poetry. 1910.

Greig, J. Scots Minstrelsie. A National Monument of Scottish Song. 6 vols. Edinburgh, 1893.

Dixon, W. M. The Edinburgh Book of Scottish Verse. Edinburgh, 1910.

Buchan, J. The Northern Muse. 1924.

H. V. R.

II. THE EARLY NINETEENTH-CENTURY POETS

ROGERS, HOGG, WORDSWORTH, COLE-RIDGE, SOUTHEY, CAMPBELL, MOORE, BYRON, SHELLEY, CLARE, DARLEY, KEATS, HOOD

SAMUEL ROGERS (1763–1855)

(1) COLLECTED POEMS

The Poetical Works of Rogers, Campbell [and others]. Paris, 1829.
Italy: The Pleasures of Memory: Human Life, and Other Poems. [1845.]
The Poetical Works. Philadelphia, 1852.
The Poetical Works. 1856; ed. E. Bell, 1875 (Aldine edn).

(2) INDIVIDUAL PUBLICATIONS

An Ode to Superstition, with Some Other Poems. 1786 (anon.).
The Pleasures of Memory, a Poem in Two Parts. 1792 (4 edns); 1793; 1794 (illustrated by T. Stothard); 1806 (15th edn). Tr. French, Paris, 1825; German, Leipzig, 1836.
An Epistle to a Friend, with Other Poems. 1798 (bis).
Verses written in Westminster Abbey, after the Funeral of Charles James Fox. [1806.]
The Voyage of Columbus, a Poem. 1810; [1812].
Miscellaneous Poems [with E. C. Knight and others]. 1812.
Poems. 1812; 1814; 1816; 1820; 1822; 1834 (illustrated by J. M. W. Turner and T. Stothard); 2 vols. 1836; 1838; 1839; 1840; ed. S. Sharpe, 1860.
Jacqueline, a Poem. 1814 (bis, and with Byron's Lara).
Human Life, a Poem. 1819; Cambridge, U.S.A. 1820; tr. Italian, Turin, 1820.
Italy, a Poem. Part the First. 1822; 1823. Part the Second. 1828. [Both parts], 1830 (illustrated by J. M. W. Turner and T. Stothard); 1838.
Recollections of the Table-Talk of Samuel Rogers, with a Memoir [by A. Dyce]. 1856 (3 edns); 1887.
Recollections by Samuel Rogers. [Ed. W. Sharpe], 1859 (bis).
Reminiscences and Table-Talk of Samuel Rogers, collected [from the two preceding items] by G. H. Powell. 1903.

(3) BIOGRAPHY AND CRITICISM

Jeffrey, F., Lord. Edinburgh Rev. XXXI, 1819. [Human Life.]
Catalogue of the Celebrated Collection of Works of Art, the Property of Samuel Rogers; also the Extensive Library. [1856.]

Hayward, A. Biographical and Critical Essays. Vol. I, 1858.
Roscoe, W. C. Poems and Essays. Ed. R. H. Hutton, vol. II, 1860.
Martineau, H. Biographical Sketches. 1877.
Clayden, P. W. The Early Life of Samuel Rogers. 1887.
—— Rogers and his Contemporaries. 2 vols. 1889.
Eastlake, E., Lady. Quart. Rev. CLXVII, 1888. [Personal reminiscences.]
Schuyler, E. Italian Influences. 1901.
Roberts, R. Ellis. Samuel Rogers and his Circle. 1910.
Dobson, A. The Books of Samuel Rogers. [In De Libris, 1911 (2nd edn). Rogers as a book-collector.]
Adorno, C. 'Italy' di S. Rogers. Florence, 1925.
Boyle, E. Samuel Rogers, the Banker Poet. National Rev. LXXXV, 1925.
Harrold, C. F. Portrait of a Saurian: Samuel Rogers. Sewanee Rev. XXXVII, 1929.

R. W. K.

JAMES HOGG (1770–1835)

(1) BIBLIOGRAPHY

Batho, E. C. The Ettrick Shepherd. Cambridge, 1927. ['Bibliography' and 'List of Authorities,' pp. 183–224. Includes Hogg's contributions to periodicals, etc., many of which have not been rptd.]
—— Notes on the Bibliography of James Hogg. Library, XVI, 1935.

(2) COLLECTIONS AND SELECTIONS

The Poetical Works of James Hogg. 4 vols. Edinburgh, 1822.
Tales and Sketches. Including several pieces not before printed. 6 vols. 1837; 6 vols. 1852; 2 vols. 1880.
The Poetical Works. 5 vols. Glasgow, 1838–40.
The Works. Ed. T. Thomson, 2 vols. 1865; 2 vols. 1869. [A reprint of the two preceding items.]
The Poems. Selected by Mrs Garden. 1887.
The Poems. Selected by W. Wallace. 1903.

(3) SEPARATE POETICAL WORKS

Scottish Pastorals, Poems, Songs, etc. Mostly written in the Dialect of the South. Edinburgh, 1801.
The Mountain Bard; consisting of Ballads and Songs, founded on Facts and Legendary Tales. Edinburgh, 1807; Edinburgh, 1821 (3rd edn, 'greatly enlarged'); 1839, etc. (with The Forest Minstrel).

The Forest Minstrel: a Selection of Songs, few of them ever before published. Edinburgh, 1810.

The Queen's Wake: a Legendary Poem. Edinburgh, 1813 (re-issued as 2nd edn); Edinburgh, 1814 (re-issued 1815); Edinburgh, 1819 (*bis*); Edinburgh, 1842; [1867], etc.

The Hunting of Badlewe, a Dramatic Tale. By J. H. Edinburgh, 1814.

A Selection of German Hebrew Melodies: the poetry by James Hogg. [1815?]

The Pilgrims of the Sun; a Poem. Edinburgh, 1815.

The Ettricke Garland; being two Excellent New Songs on The Lifting of the Banner of the House of Buccleuch. Edinburgh, 1815. [One of the songs is by Hogg and the other by Sir W. Scott.]

The Poetic Mirror, or The Living Bards of Britain. 1816 (anon.); ed. T. E. Welby, 1929.

Mador of the Moor; a Poem. Edinburgh, 1816.

Dramatic Tales; by the author of 'The Poetic Mirror.' 2 vols. Edinburgh, 1817.

A Border Garland. [1819?]; n.d. (as The Border Garland).

The Royal Jubilee. A Scottish Mask. Edinburgh, 1822.

Queen Hynde. A Poem, in six books. 1825.

Select and Rare Scottish Melodies. [1829.]

Songs Now first collected. Edinburgh, 1831.

A Queer Book. Edinburgh, 1832.

(4) OTHER WRITINGS

The Shepherd's Guide: being a Practical Treatise on the Diseases of Sheep. Edinburgh, 1807.

The Spy. A Periodical Paper, of Literary Amusement and Instruction. 52 nos. Edinburgh, 1811. [Ed. and largely written by Hogg.]

The Long Pack. A Northumbrian Tale, An Hundred Years Old. Newcastle, 1817, 1818; Glasgow, n.d., etc.

The Brownie of Bodsbeck; and other Tales. 2 vols. Edinburgh, 1818.

The Jacobite Relics of Scotland. Collected and illustrated by James Hogg. 2 sers. Edinburgh, 1819–21; Paisley, 1874.

Winter Evening Tales, collected among the Cottagers in the South of Scotland. 2 vols. Edinburgh, 1820.

The Three Perils of Man; or, War, Women, and Witchcraft. A Border Romance. 3 vols. 1822.

The Three Perils of Women; or, Love, Leasing, and Jealousy. A Series of Domestic Scottish Tales. 3 vols. 1823; tr. French, Paris, 1825.

The Private Memoirs and Confessions of a Justified Sinner: written by himself: with a detail of curious traditionary facts, and other evidence, by the editor. 1824 (anon.); 1828 (as The Suicide's Grave); rptd 1895; ed. T. E. Welby, 1924.

The Shepherd's Calendar. 2 vols. Edinburgh, 1829.

Altrive Tales: collected among the peasantry of Scotland, and from foreign adventurers. Vol. I (all pbd), 1832.

A Series of Lay Sermons on Good Principles and Good Breeding. 1834.

The Domestic Manners and Private Life of Sir Walter Scott. With a memoir of the author, notes, etc. Glasgow, 1834; Edinburgh, 1882; ed. J. E. H. Thomson, Stirling, 1909.

The Works of Robert Burns. Edited by the Ettrick Shepherd, and William Motherwell. 5 vols. Glasgow, 1834–6, etc. [Vol. v is devoted to a 'Memoir of Burns' by Hogg.]

Tales of the Wars of Montrose. 3 vols. 1835.

A Tour in the Highlands in 1803: A Series of Letters by James Hogg to Sir Walter Scott. Paisley, 1888.

(5) BIOGRAPHY AND CRITICISM

Garden, Mrs. Memorials of James Hogg. Paisley, [1885]; 1887; Paisley, 1903.

Saintsbury, G. Essays in English Literature, 1780–1860. 1890.

Stephenson, H. T. The Ettrick Shepherd: a Biography. Bloomington, 1922.

Batho, E. C. The Ettrick Shepherd. Cambridge, 1927.

Strout, A. L. James Hogg's Familiar Anecdotes of Sir Walter Scott. Stud. Phil. XXXIII, 1936.

—— James Hogg's Forgotten Satire, John Paterson's Mare. PMLA. LII, 1937.

—— The Noctes Ambrosianae and James Hogg. RES. XIII, 1937.

—— Notes on James Hogg. N. & Q. 2 April 1938.

E. C. B.

WILLIAM WORDSWORTH (1770–1850)

(1) BIBLIOGRAPHIES

Wise, T. J. A Bibliography of the Writings in Prose and Verse of William Wordsworth. 1916 (priv. ptd).

—— Two Lake Poets. A Catalogue of Printed Books, Manuscripts, and Autograph Letters by Wordsworth and Coleridge, collected by Thomas James Wise. 1927 (priv. ptd).

Patton, C. H. The Amherst Wordsworth Collection; a Descriptive Bibliography. Amherst, 1936.

(2) Poetical Works

(a) Collected Poems

Poems. Including Lyrical Ballads, and the Miscellaneous Pieces of the Author. With Additional Poems, a New Preface, and a Supplementary Essay. 2 vols. 1815. [Does not include The Excursion. Adopts the arrangement of poems subsequently maintained by Wordsworth. In 1820 a third vol. was formed by binding together A Thanksgiving Ode, Peter Bell, The Waggoner and The River Duddon volumes.]

The Miscellaneous Poems. 4 vols. 1820; 4 vols. Boston, 1824. [Includes all pbd work except The Excursion, with the addn of some sonnets not previously pbd.]

The Poetical Works. Paris, 1826.

The Poetical Works. 5 vols. 1827. [Includes all 'published poems, for the first time collected in a uniform edition, with several new pieces interspersed.']

The Poetical Works. A new Edition. 4 vols. 1832. [Contains some poems previously unpbd.]

The Poetical Works. A New Edition. 6 vols. 1836–7, 1839, 1840 (with some variations), 1841; 7 vols. 1842 (vol. vii = Poems, Chiefly of Early and Late Years), 1843, 1845, 1846, 1849; 8 vols. 1851 (vol. viii = The Prelude).

Poems. Ed. H. Reed, Boston, 1837, 1851 (rev. and with the addn of all poems pbd to date).

The Poems. 1845. [Frequently rptd as the standard 1 vol. edn. The edns after 1850 include The Prelude, and the edn of 1869 includes 'nine additional poems,' dated 1846.]

The Poetical Works. 6 vols. 1849–50. [Vol. vi, The Excursion, was rptd separately, 1851, 1853, 1857. This edn was the last pbd in Wordsworth's lifetime and embodies his final revisions.]

Poetical Works. 7 vols. Boston, 1854, 1880. [With an unsigned memoir by James Russell Lowell.]

The Poetical Works. 6 vols. 1857, 1864, 1870, 1874, 1876, 1879, 1881, 1882. [Includes the Fenwick notes for the first time. The rpt of 1870 is the Centenary Edition.]

The Poetical Works. Ed. (with critical Memoir) W. M. Rosetti, [1870.] [The text is a re-issue of the edn of 1845, with the addn of The Prelude, but not of the poems of 1849–50. Rptd same year with slight differences.]

The Poetical Works. Ed. W. Knight, 8 vols. 1882–6, 1896. [The poems are arranged in chronological order. Some 'prose fragments' and a bibliography are in vol. viii. Knight's Life of Wordsworth was added in three supplementary vols. (ix–xi) in 1889.]

The Complete Poetical Works. With an Introduction by John Morley. 1888. [Notes and bibliography. Frequently rptd; Globe edn since 1924.]

Poetical Works. Ed. (with Memoir) E. Dowden, 7 vols. 1892–3. [Bibliography and chronological table of poems.] (Aldine edn.)

The Poetical Works. With Introductions and Notes. Ed. T. Hutchinson, 1895, 1904, 1910, 1917. Also 5 vols. 1895. [One of the introductions is a chronological table of Wordsworth's life.] (Oxford Poets.)

The Poems. Ed. (with Introduction and Notes) N. C. Smith, 3 vols. [1908].

(b) Selections

Selections from the Poems of William Wordsworth, Esq., chiefly for the use of schools and Young Persons. Ed. J. Hine, 1831; 1834 (in slightly different form).

Select Pieces from the Poems of William Wordsworth. 1843.

Selections. Ed. H. Reed, New York, 1843.

The Select Poetical Works of William Wordsworth. 2 vols. 1864. (Tauchnitz edn.)

A Selection from the Works of William Wordsworth. Ed. F. T. Palgrave, 1865, 1869, etc. (Moxon's Miniature Poets.)

Poems of Wordsworth. Ed. M. Arnold, 1879, etc. (Golden Treasury Ser.)

Selections from Wordsworth. Ed. J. S. Fletcher, 1883, 1885, etc.

Selections from Wordsworth. By William Knight and Other Members of the Wordsworth Society. With Preface and Notes. 1888.

Early Poems. 1889. [Selected by J. R. Tutin.]

Lyrics and Sonnets of Wordsworth. With Introduction by Clement Shorter. 1892.

Poems. A Selection. Ed. E. Dowden, Boston, 1897.

Poems dedicated to National Independence and Liberty. Reprinted on behalf of the Greek Struggle for the Independence of Crete. With an Introduction by Stopford A. Brooke. 1897.

Selections from Wordsworth. Ed. W. T. Webb, 1897.

Selections. With an Introduction by E. Caird. 1899.

Poems. With an Introduction by A. Meynell. 1903.

Poems. Ed. W. Knight, 1904.

Selections from Wordsworth, preceded by Lowell's Essay on Wordsworth and annotated by H. B. Cotterill. 1904.

Poems. Selected, with an Introduction, by Stopford A. Brooke. Illustrated by E. H. New. 1907.

Selections from Wordsworth. An Introduction to Romance in Literature. [With an introduction and notes] by Adam Fox. 1909.

A Decade of Years. Poems, 1797–1807. Selected by C. S. [i.e. T. J. Cobden-Sanderson]. Hammersmith, 1911.

The Patriotic Poetry of Wordsworth. Ed. A. H. D. Acland, Oxford, 1915.

Selections from the Poems. Ed. A. Hamilton Thompson, Cambridge, 1918.

Wordsworth. Select Poems. Ed. S. G. Dunn, Oxford, 1918.

Wordsworth. An Anthology. Ed. T. J. Cobden-Sanderson, 1920.

Wordsworth: Poetry and Prose. With Essays by Coleridge, Hazlitt, De Quincey. Ed. D. N. Smith, Oxford, 1921.

William Wordsworth. Poems. With Appendices containing A Letter to the Bishop of Llandaff and The Preface to the Lyrical Ballads, 1800. Ed. G. M. Harper, New York, 1923.

William Wordsworth. With an Introduction by Viscount Grey of Fallodon. [1924.]

Selections from Wordsworth. Poetry and Prose. Ed. B. I. Evans, 1935.

Wordsworth. A Selection. Ed. B. Groom, 1936.

Wordsworth: Representative Poems. Ed. A. Beatty, New York, 1937.

(c) Separate Poems or Collections of Poems

An Evening Walk. An Epistle; In Verse. Addressed to a Young Lady [Dorothy Wordsworth], from the Lakes of the North of England. 1793. [The 1793 version, never republished by Wordsworth in its original form, is rptd by Dowden, Hutchinson, and other editors.]

Descriptive Sketches. In Verse. Taken during a Pedestrian Tour in the Italian, Grison, Swiss, and Savoyard Alps. 1793. [Original version rptd as above.]

Lyrical Ballads, With A Few Other Poems. Bristol and London, 1798 (re-issued London, 1798); ed. facs. E. Dowden, 1890; ed. T. Hutchinson, 1898, 1920 (rev. edn); ed. H. Littledale, Oxford, 1911; rptd photo facs. 1927 and New York, 1934 (both from Bristol issue). [Both issues include Coleridge's The Rime of the Ancyent Marinere, The Foster Mother's Tale and The Dungeon. The London issue also includes Coleridge's The Nightingale. The Nightingale is found in some copies of the Bristol issue too, but in others its place is taken either by Lewti (by Coleridge) or Domiciliary Verses (by Dr Beddoes). See T. J. Wise's Bibliography,

pp. 14–34, and Hutchinson's edn, 1920, pp. ix–xvii, liii–lv. See also R. W. Daniel, The Publication of the Lyrical Ballads, MLR. xxxiii, 1938.]

Lyrical Ballads, with Other Poems. 2 vols. 1800 (actually pbd Jan. 1801) (2 issues of vol. ii; see T. J. Wise's Bibliography, pp. 47–50); 2 vols. 1802; 2 vols. Philadelphia, 1802; 2 vols. 1805; ed. G. Sampson, 1903. [Vol. i as in London issue of 1798, but Coleridge's Love substituted for The Convict, The Rime of the Ancyent Marinere revised and re-entitled 'The Ancient Mariner, A Poet's Reverie,' Preface added, and numerous changes of text and arrangement; vol. ii entirely new. On the cancel leaves see J. E. Wells, PMLA. liii, 1938. The 1802 edn introduces several changes. Vol. i, 1800 (but not vol. ii) is described as Second Edition, and vol. i, 1802 as Third Edition (vol. ii being Second Edition), but both vols., 1805, are Fourth Edition.]

Poems in Two Volumes. 1807; ed. T. Hutchinson, 2 vols. 1897; rptd 2 vols. Oxford, 1913; ed. H. Darbishire, Oxford, 1915. [For textual variants see B. I. Evans, TLS. 13 June 1936, p. 494.]

The Excursion, Being a Portion of The Recluse, A Poem. 1814; 1820; 1832. [Rptd in Poetical Works, vol. v, 1827, vol. iv, 1832, in Poetical Works, 1836–7, and subsequent edns. Frequently rptd separately; ed. E. E. Reynolds, 1935.]

The White Doe of Rylstone; or The Fate of the Nortons. A Poem. 1815; ed. M. T. Quinn, Madras, 1889; ed. W. Knight, Oxford, 1891. [The poem The Force of Prayer; or, The Founding of Bolton Priory. A Tradition, previously ptd, follows as an 'Appendage to the "White Doe."' Rptd separately 1859, 1867, 1889.]

Thanksgiving Ode, January 18, 1816. With Other Short Pieces, Chiefly referring to Recent Public Events. 1816. [Rebound to form part of vol. iii of Poems, Including Lyrical Ballads, 1815, in 1820.]

Peter Bell, A Tale in Verse. [With four sonnets.] 1819 (bis). [Rebound with A Thanksgiving Ode in 1820. The original version is rptd as an appendix to Hutchinson's edn of Lyrical Ballads.]

The Waggoner, A Poem. To which are added Sonnets. 1819. [Rebound with A Thanksgiving Ode in 1820.]

The Little Maid and the Gentleman: or, We are Seven. [1820?] [There are in existence at least three chapbook versions of We are Seven, one with the title as given above, pbd in York by J. Kendrew, n.d. The other two have the usual title: one was certainly, the other possibly, pbd by W. Davison,

Alnwick. All three seem to have been ptd from a text earlier than the revision of 1815. See H. S. Hughes, Two Wordsworthian Chapbooks, MP. xxv, 1927.]

The River Duddon, A Series of Sonnets: Vaudracour and Julia: and other Poems. To which is annexed, A Topographical Description of the Country of the Lakes, in the North of England. 1820. [Rebound with A Thanksgiving Ode in 1820. For A Topographical Description see under Separate Prose Works.]

Memorials of a Tour on the Continent, 1820. 1822.

Ecclesiastical Sketches. 1822; ed. A. F. Potts, New Haven, 1922. [Only 102 sonnets of a final total of 132 were here ptd. The title was changed in 1837 to Ecclesiastical Sonnets.]

Ode to the Memory of Charles Lamb. 1835 (priv. ptd).

Yarrow Revisited, And Other Poems. 1835; 1836; 1839. [Possibly intended as a supplementary fifth vol. to the collected edn of 1832.]

The Sonnets of William Wordsworth. Collected in One Volume, with A Few Additional Ones, now First Published. 1838; rptd 1884 (with an Essay on The History of the English Sonnet by R. C. Trench).

Poems, Chiefly of Early and Late Years; Including The Borderers, A Tragedy. 1842. [Rptd in 1843 as vol. vii of the collected edn of 1836–7.]

Poems on the Loss and Re-Building of St Mary's Church, Cardiff. Cardiff, 1842. [Includes one sonnet by Wordsworth and poems by James Montgomery, Thomas William Booker, and John Dix. There was possibly a separate issue of Wordsworth's poem. See T. J. Wise's Bibliography, p. 156.]

Grace Darling. [1843] (priv. ptd).

Verses Composed at the Request of Jane Wallis Penfold. [1844] (priv. ptd).

To the Queen. Kendal, 1846 (priv. ptd).

Ode, Performed in the Senate-House, Cambridge, On the Sixth of July, M.DCCC.XLVII. At the First Commencement after The Installation of His Royal Highness the Prince Albert, Chancellor of the University. Cambridge, 1847. [Also: Ode On the Installation of His Royal Highness Prince Albert as Chancellor of the University of Cambridge, [1847]. The first was the 'official' pbn; the second a public edn.]

The Prelude, Or Growth of a Poet's Mind; An Autobiographical Poem. 1850; 1851 (vol. viii of Poetical Works, 1849–50); rptd 1896, 1904, 1915, 1923; ed. E. de Selincourt, Oxford, 1926, 1934 (without *apparatus*

criticus); ed. E. E. Reynolds, 1932. [The de Selincourt edn prints on opposite pages the 1805–6 version—here pbd for the first time—and the version pbd in 1850, with notes showing all variations in the several MSS and fragments of MS recently discovered.]

The Recluse. 1888. [The law of copyright prevented the inclusion of this poem in many edns of Wordsworth's Collected Poems.]

(3) PROSE WORKS

(a) Collections

The Prose Works of William Wordsworth. For the first time collected, with Additions from Unpublished Manuscripts. Ed. A. B. Grosart, 3 vols. 1876.

Prose Works of William Wordsworth. Ed. W. Knight, 2 vols. 1896.

(b) Selections

Prose Writings of Wordsworth. Ed. W. Knight, [1893].

Wordsworth's Prefaces and Essays on Poetry, with Letter to Lady Beaumont, 1789–1845. Ed. A. J. George, Boston, [1892].

Wordsworth's Literary Criticism. Ed. Nowell C. Smith, 1905.

Coleridge's Biographia Literaria [chs. i–iv, xiv–xxii]: Wordsworth: Prefaces and Essays on Poetry, 1800–1815. Ed. G. Sampson (with Introductory Essay by Sir A. T. Quiller-Couch), Cambridge, 1920.

(c) Separate Prose Works

Concerning The Relations of Great Britain, Spain and Portugal, To each other, and to the Common Enemy, at this Crisis; and specifically as affected by the Convention of Cintra: etc. 1809 (originally ptd, but not pbd, with a different title-page); ed. A. V. Dicey, Oxford, 1915.

A Reply to 'Mathetes.' The Friend, nos. 17, 20, 14 Dec. 1809, 4 Jan. 1810.

Essay upon Epitaphs. The Friend, no. 25, 22 Feb. 1810. [Rptd by Wordsworth as a note to The Excursion, Bk v, l. 975 in 1814. Subsequently in all edns containing Wordsworth's notes.]

A Letter to A Friend of Robert Burns [James Gray]: occasioned by An intended Republication of The Account of the Life of Burns, by Dr Currie; and of the Selection made by him from his Letters. 1816.

Two Addresses to the Freeholders of Westmoreland. Kendal, 1818. [Portions had already appeared in the Kendal Chronicle and the Carlisle Patriot.]

A Description of the Scenery of the Lakes in the North of England. Third Edition (Now first published separately), With Additions, and Illustrative Remarks upon the Scenery of the Alps. 1822 (including the sonnet, 'A weight of awe not easy to be borne'); 1823 (adds an extract from The Recluse, 'Mark how the feathered tenant of the flood'); Kendal, 1835 ('with considerable additions,' as A Guide through the District of the Lakes in The North of England, with A Description of the Scenery. For the use of Tourists and Residents); 1842; 1843; 1846; 1853; 1859 (as part of A Complete Guide to the Lakes), etc.; ed. E. de Selincourt, 1906. [First ptd in part as Introduction to Joseph Wilkinson's Select Views in Cumberland, Westmoreland, and Lancashire, 1810. Rptd in rev. and enlarged form as appendix to The River Duddon, A Series of Sonnets, 1820, and in Poems, vol. III, 1820.]

Kendal and Windermere Railway. Two Letters, Re-printed from The Morning Post [11 and 20 Dec. 1844]. Revised, with Additions. Kendal, [1845]; [1845?]. [Includes the sonnet 'Is there no Nook of English Ground Secure?']

Memorials of Coleorton: being Letters from Coleridge, Wordsworth and his Sister, Southey, and Sir Walter Scott to Sir George and Lady Beaumont, 1803–1834. Ed. W. Knight, 2 vols. Edinburgh, 1887.

Letters from the Lake Poets to Daniel Stuart, Editor of The Morning Post and The Courier, 1800–1838. 1889 (priv. ptd). [Compiled by Mary Stuart; ed. E. H. Coleridge.]

Unpublished Letters of Wordsworth and Coleridge. Athenaeum, 8 Dec. 1894.

Letters of the Wordsworth Family, From 1787 to 1855. Ed. W. Knight, 3 vols. Boston, 1907.

The Law of Copyright. 1916 (priv. ptd). [Originally a letter to the Morning Post, 23 April 1838.]

The Hitherto Unpublished Preface to Wordsworth's Borderers. Ed. E. de Selincourt, Nineteenth Century, Nov. 1926. [Rptd in Oxford Lectures on Poetry, 1934.]

The Early Letters of William and Dorothy Wordsworth (1787–1805). Ed. E. de Selincourt, Oxford, 1935.

The Letters of William and Dorothy Wordsworth (1806–1820). Ed. E. de Selincourt, 2 vols. Oxford, 1937.

Later Letters of William and Dorothy Wordsworth (1821–1850). Ed. E. de Selincourt, 3 vols. Oxford, 1938.

(4) BIOGRAPHY AND CRITICISM

(a) Works of Reference, etc.

Catalogue of the Varied and Valuable, Historical, Poetical, Theological, and Miscellaneous Library of W. Wordsworth, which will be sold by auction at Rydal Mount, near Ambleside, July 1859, etc. [Preston], 1859.

Tutin, J. R. The Wordsworth Dictionary of Persons and Places. 1891.

—— An Index to the Animal and Vegetable Kingdoms of Wordsworth. 1892.

Cooper, L. A Concordance to the Poems of William Wordsworth. 1911.

(b) General Critical Works

Lamb, C. Works. Ed. E. V. Lucas, 7 vols. 1903–5. [For review of The Excursion, 1814, and letters.]

Coleridge, S. T. Biographia Literaria. 2 vols. 1817.

—— Table Talk. Ed. T. Ashe, 1884.

—— Letters. Ed. E. H. Coleridge, 2 vols. 1895.

Hazlitt, W. Lectures on the English Poets. 1818. [Rptd in Works, ed. A. R. Waller and A. Glover, vol. V, 1902.]

—— The Spirit of the Age: or Contemporary Portraits. 1825. [Rptd in Works, vol. IV, 1902.]

—— My First Acquaintance with Poets. [In The Plain Speaker, 1826. Rptd in Works, vol. XII, 1904.]

Landor, W. S. Southey and Porson. [In Imaginary Conversations, vol. I, 1824.]

Pichot, A. Voyage historique et littéraire en Angleterre et en Écosse. Vol. II, Paris, 1825, p. 363.

Cunningham, A. Biographical and Critical History of the British Literature of the Last Fifty Years. Paris, 1834.

Cottle, J. Early Recollections, chiefly relating to the late S. T. Coleridge in Bristol. 2 vols. 1837[–9]; 1847 (rev. and enlarged as Reminiscences of S. T. Coleridge and R. Southey).

Wilson, J. Recreations of Christopher North. 3 vols. 1842.

Horne, R. H. A New Spirit of the Age. Vol. I, 1844.

Taylor, Sir H. Wordsworth's Poetical Works; Wordsworth's Sonnets. [In Notes from Books, in Four Essays, 1849. Rptd in Works, 5 vols. 1877–8.]

Hunt, J. H. L. The Autobiography of Leigh Hunt. 3 vols. 1850; 1860 (rev. edn).

Wordsworth, Christopher. Memoirs of William Wordsworth. 2 vols. 1851. [Autobiographical memoranda dictated by Wordsworth, November 1847.]

13

Mitford, M. R. Recollections of a Literary Life. 1852.

Searle, J. Memoirs of William Wordsworth. 1852.

Emerson, R. W. English Traits. 1856.

Gilfillan, G. William Wordsworth. [In Galleries of Literary Portraits, vol. I, 1856.]

Hood, E. P. William Wordsworth: a Biography. 1856.

Lonsdale, H. W. Wordsworth. [In The Worthies of Cumberland, 1867, etc.]

Clough, A. H. Lecture on Poetry of Wordsworth. [In Poems and Prose Remains, vol. I, 1869, p. 307.]

Robinson, H. Crabb. Diary, Reminiscences, and Correspondence. 3 vols. 1869; 2 vols. 1872.

—— Blake, Coleridge, Wordsworth, Lamb, etc., being Selections from the Remains of Henry Crabb Robinson. Ed. E. J. Morley, Manchester, 1922.

—— The Correspondence of Henry Crabb Robinson with the Wordsworth Circle (1808–1866): the Greater Part now for the first time printed from the Originals. Ed. E. J. Morley, 2 vols. Oxford, 1927.

Lowell, J. R. Wordsworth. [In Among My Books, 1870.]

Brandes, G. Hovedstrømninger i det 19de Aarhundredes Litteratur. 6 vols. Copenhagen, 1872–90; tr. Eng. 1901–5. [Vol. IV.]

Shairp, J. C. Wordsworth, the Man and the Poet. [In Studies in Poetry and Philosophy, Edinburgh, 1872.]

—— Wordsworth as an Interpreter of Nature. [In The Poetic Interpretation of Nature, Edinburgh, 1877.]

—— The Three Yarrows; The White Doe of Rylstone. [In Aspects of Poetry, Oxford, 1881.]

Mill, J. S. Autobiography. Ed. H. Taylor, 1873.

Brooke, Stopford A. Wordsworth. [In Theology in the English Poets, 1874.]

—— Wordsworth, Shelley and Byron. [In Naturalism in English Poetry, 1920.]

Wordsworth, Dorothy. Recollections of a Tour made in Scotland, A.D. 1803. Ed. J. C. Shairp, Edinburgh, 1874.

—— Journals. Ed. W. Knight, 2 vols. 1897.

Masson, D. Wordsworth, Shelley, Keats, and other Essays. 1874.

Haydon, B. R. Correspondence and Table Talk. 2 vols. 1876.

—— Autobiography and Memoirs. Ed. A. D. Penrose, 1927.

Martineau, H. Autobiography. 3 vols. 1877.

Calvert, G. H. Wordsworth. A Biographic Aesthetic Study. Boston, 1878.

Dowden, E. The Prose Works of Wordsworth. [In Studies in Literature, 1789–1877, 1878.]

—— The Text of Wordsworth's Poems. Contemporary Rev. XXXIII, 1878.

—— The French Revolution and English Literature. 1897.

Knight, W. A. The English Lake District as Interpreted in the poems of Wordsworth. Edinburgh, 1878.

—— Wordsworthiana. 1889.

—— The Life of Wordsworth. 3 vols. (= IX–XI of Poetical Works, ed. Knight), 1889.

—— Coleridge and Wordsworth in the West Country; their Friendship, Work and Surroundings. 1913.

Bagehot, W. Wordsworth, Tennyson and Browning; or Pure, Ornate, and Grotesque Art in English Poetry. [In Literary Studies, vol. II, 1879.]

Myers, F. W. H. Wordsworth. 1881. (English Men of Letters ser.)

Shorthouse, J. H. On the Platonism of Wordsworth. Birmingham, [1881]. [Rptd in Trans. Wordsworth Soc. 1882–7.]

Graves, R. P. Life of Sir W. Rowan Hamilton. 3 vols. 1882–9.

Transactions of the Wordsworth Society. 1882–7.

Swinburne, A. C. Wordsworth and Byron. Nineteenth Century, April, May 1884. [Rptd in Miscellanies, 1886.]

de Vere, A. The Genius and Passion of Wordsworth; The Wisdom and Truth of Wordsworth's Poetry; Recollections of Wordsworth. [In Essays, chiefly on Poetry, vol. I, pp. 101, 174, vol. II, p. 275, 1887.]

Pater, W. H. Essay on Wordsworth. Fortnightly Rev. April 1887. [Rptd in Appreciations, 1889.]

Arnold, M. Wordsworth. [In Essays in Criticism, ser. 2, 1888. Rptd from Poems of Wordsworth, 1879.]

Sandford, M. Thomas Poole and His Friends. 2 vols. 1888.

De Quincey, T. William Wordsworth. [In Collected Writings, ed. D. Masson, vol. II, 1889. Literary Reminiscences, Boston, 1874, prints a different version of this essay.]

Stephen, Sir L. Wordsworth's Ethics. [In Hours in a Library, vol. II, 1892.]

—— Wordsworth's Youth. [In Studies of a Biographer, vol. I, 1898.]

Legouis, É. La Jeunesse de Wordsworth, 1770–1798. Paris, 1896; tr. Eng. (with a prefatory note by Sir L. Stephen), 1897, 1921 (with additional appendix).

—— Le Roman de William Wordsworth: sa Liaison avec Annette Vallon. Revue des Deux Mondes, April, May, 1922. [William Wordsworth and Annette Vallon, 1922, is rev. from the preceding articles.]

Herford, C. H. The Age of Wordsworth. 1897.
—— Goethe and Wordsworth. A Conversation. Contemporary Rev. CXXXVI, 1929.
—— Wordsworth. 1930.
Magnus, L. A Primer of Wordsworth. 1897.
White, W. H. A Description of the Wordsworth and Coleridge Manuscripts in the Possession of Mr T. N. Longman. 1897.
—— An Examination of the Charge of Apostasy against Wordsworth. 1898.
Raleigh, Sir W. A. Wordsworth. 1903.
Morley, J. Wordsworth. [In Literary Essays, 1906. Rptd from Preface to 1888 edn.]
Cooper, L. A Glance at Wordsworth's Reading. MLN. XXII, 1907. [Rptd with many alterations in Methods and Aims in the Study of Literature, 1915.]
Robertson, F. W. Wordsworth: a Criticism. [1907.]
Bradley, A. C. Wordsworth; the Long Poem in the Age of Wordsworth. [In Oxford Lectures on Poetry, 1909.]
—— English Poetry and German Philosophy in the Age of Wordsworth. Manchester, 1909. [Rptd in A Miscellany, 1929.]
Reynolds, M. The Treatment of Nature in English Poetry between Pope and Wordsworth. Chicago, 1909.
Strong, A. T. Nature—Meredith and Wordsworth. Being the Presidential Address to the Literature Society of Melbourne for 1910. Melbourne, 1910. [Rptd in Three Studies in Shelley, and an Essay on Nature in Wordsworth and Meredith, Oxford, 1921.]
Hepple, N. Lyrical Forms in English. Cambridge, 1011.
Suddard, S. J. M. L'Imagination de Wordsworth. [In Essais de Littérature anglaise, Cambridge, 1912. Also in English.]
Sneath, E. H. Wordsworth. Poet of Nature and Poet of Man. Boston, 1912.
Stewart, J. A. Platonism in English Poetry. [In English Literature and the Classics: Nine Lectures by G. Murray, J. A. Stewart, etc., Oxford, 1913.]
Hudson, W. H. Wordsworth and his Poetry. 1914.
Dicey, A. V. Wordsworth and the War. Nineteenth Century, May 1915.
—— Wordsworth on the Revolution. Nineteenth Century, Oct. 1915.
—— The Statesmanship of Wordsworth: an Essay. Oxford, 1917.
de Selincourt, E. English Poets and the National Ideal. Four Lectures on Shakespeare, Milton, Wordsworth, and English Poetry since 1815. Oxford, 1915.
—— Dorothy Wordsworth. Oxford, 1934.
—— The Early Wordsworth. English Ass. Lecture, 1936.

Harper, G. M. William Wordsworth, his Life, Works, and Influence. 2 vols. 1916, 1929 (rev. edn).
—— Wordsworth at Blois; Wordsworth's Love Poetry. [In John Morley and Other Essays, Princeton, 1920.]
—— Wordsworth's French Daughter. The Story of her Birth, with the Certificates of her Baptism and Marriage. Princeton, 1921.
—— Did Wordsworth Defy the Guillotine? Quart. Rev. CCXLVIII, 1927.
Wylie, L. J. The Social Philosophy of Wordsworth. [In Social Studies in English Literature, Boston, 1916.]
Barstow [afterwards Greenbie], M. L. Wordsworth's Theory of Poetic Diction: a Study of the Historical and Personal Backgrounds of the Lyrical Ballads. New Haven, 1917.
Beatty, A. Joseph Fawcett; 'the Art of War.' Madison, 1918.
—— William Wordsworth, his Doctrine and Art in their Historical Relations. Madison, 1922, 1927 (rev. edn).
Babbitt, I. Rousseau and Romanticism. Boston, 1919.
—— The Primitivism of Wordsworth. Bookman [U.S.A.], LXXIV, 1931.
Wordsworth, C. G. Boyhood of Wordsworth. Living Age, CCCV, 1920.
Campbell, O. J. Sentimental Morality in Wordsworth's Narrative Poetry. Madison, 1920.
Wells, J. E. The Story of Wordsworth's 'Cintra.' Stud. Phil. XVIII, 1921.
Bardi, P. La Poesia di Wordsworth, 1770–1808. Bari, 1922.
Williams, I. A. Wordsworth, Mrs Hemans, and Robert Perceval Graves. London Mercury, VI, 1922. [Letters.]
Fausset, H. I'A. Wordsworth. [In Studies in Idealism, 1923.]
—— Wordsworth. 1933.
Grey, E. (Viscount Grey of Fallodon). Wordsworth's Prelude. English Ass. Lecture, 1923.
Garrod, H. W. Wordsworth: Lectures and Essays. Oxford, 1923, 1927 (enlarged).
Swaen, A. E. H. Peter Bell. Ang. XLVII, 1923. [Appendix has Peter Bell the Second, The Two Asses, and The Examiner's review of the two Peter Bells.]
de Selincourt, B. Lord Grey and The Prelude. [In The English Secret, 1923.]
Woods, M. L. A Poet's Youth. 1923. [Early life of Wordsworth in novel form.]
Elton, O. Wordsworth. 1924. [Rev. ch. from A Survey of English Literature, 2 vols. 1912.]
Rice, R. A. Wordsworth since 1916. Northampton, 1924. [With a bibliography.]

Brinton, C. The Political Ideas of the English Romanticists. Oxford, 1926. [The discussion of Wordsworth includes précis of the Letter to the Bishop of Llandaff and the Tract on the Convention of Cintra.]

Campbell, O. J. and Mueschke, P. Guilt and Sorrow. A Study in the Genesis of Wordsworth's Aesthetic. MP. XXIII, 1926.

Clutton-Brock, A. The Problem of Wordsworth. [In Essays on Literature and Life, 1926.]

Darbishire, H. Wordsworth's Prelude. Nineteenth Century, May 1926.

Garstang, W. Wordsworth's Interpretation of Nature. Nature, Supplement, CXVII, Jan. 1926.

Powell, A. E. The Romantic Theory of Poetry: an Examination in the Light of Croce's Aesthetic. 1926.

Whiting, M. B. St Bega; a hitherto Unpublished Letter from Wordsworth. Bookman, LXXI, 1926.

Bickersteth, G. L. Leopardi and Wordsworth. Oxford, 1927.

Knaplung, P. Correspondence relating to the Grant of a Civil List Pension to William Wordsworth, 1842. MLN. XLII, 1927.

MacLean, C. M. Dorothy and William Wordsworth. Oxford, 1927.

—— Dorothy Wordsworth. The Early Years. 1932.

Whitehead, A. N. Science and the Modern World. Cambridge, 1927. [Ch. v.]

Graves, R. A Letter from William Wordsworth. Life and Letters, Aug. 1928.

Huxley, A. Wordsworth in the Tropics. Life and Letters, Oct. 1928.

Chapman, J. A. Papers on Shelley, Wordsworth and Others. Oxford, 1929.

Blunden, E. Nature in English Literature. 1929.

Read, H. Wordsworth. 1930.

Smith, E. An Estimate of William Wordsworth by his Contemporaries, 1793–1822. Oxford, 1932.

Batho, E. C. The Later Wordsworth. Cambridge, 1933.

Fairley, B. Wordsworth and Goethe. English Goethe Soc. Publications, X, 1934.

Gray, C. H. Wordsworth's First Visit to Tintern Abbey. PMLA. XLIX, 1934.

Hartman, H. Wordsworth's 'Lucy' Poems. PMLA. XLIX, 1934.

Leavis, F. R. Revaluations. VI. Wordsworth. Scrutiny, III, 1934. [Rptd in Revaluations, 1936.]

MacGillivray, J. R. The Date of Composition of The Borderers. MLN. XLIX, 1934. [See also J. H. Smith, PMLA. XLIX, 1934, pp. 922–30.]

Willey, B. Wordsworth's Beliefs. Criterion, XIII, 1934.

Bishop, D. H. Wordsworth's 'Hermitage': Racedown or Grasmere? Stud. Phil. XXXII, 1935. [See also R. D. Havens, Stud. Phil. XXXIII, 1936, pp. 55–6.]

Patton, C. H. The Rediscovery of Wordsworth. Boston, 1935.

Sperry, W. L. Wordsworth's Anti-Climax. Cambridge, U.S.A. 1935.

Burra, P. Wordsworth. 1936.

Grierson, Sir H. J. C. Milton and Wordsworth. Cambridge, 1937.

Stallknecht, N. P. Wordsworth's Ode to Duty. PMLA. LII, 1937.

—— Nature and Imagination in Wordsworth's Meditation upon Mt Snowdon. PMLA. LII, 1937.

Wright, H. G. Two Letters from Wordsworth to Robert Jones. RES. XIII, 1937.

Bradford, C. R. Wordsworth's White Doe of Rylstone and Related Poems. MP. XXXVI, 1938.

Willoughby, L. A. Wordsworth in Germany. [In German Studies presented to F. G. Fiedler, 1938.]

(c) Early Reviews

An Evening Walk. Monthly Rev. XI, p. 218; Critical Rev. VIII, p. 347; GM. LXIV, p. 252.

Descriptive Sketches. Monthly Rev. XII, p. 216; Critical Rev. VIII, p. 472.

Lyrical Ballads. Monthly Rev. XXIX, p. 202, XXXVIII, p. 209.

Poems in Two Volumes. Edinburgh Rev. XI, p. 214; Monthly Rev. LXXVIII, p. 225.

The White Doe of Rylstone. Edinburgh Rev. XXV, p. 355; Monthly Rev. LXXVIII, p. 235; GM. LXXXVII; Quarterly Rev. XIV, p. 201.

The Excursion. Quarterly Rev. XII, p. 100 (Lamb's review altered by Gifford. See Lamb's Works, ed. E. V. Lucas, vol. I, pp. 160, 446); Edinburgh Rev. XXIV, p. 1 (Jeffrey's 'This will never do'); Monthly Rev. LXXVI, p. 123.　　H. K. and E. de S.

SAMUEL TAYLOR COLERIDGE (1772–1834)

(1) BIBLIOGRAPHIES

Shepherd, R. H. The Bibliography of Coleridge. Rev. W. F. Prideaux, 1900.

Haney, J. L. A Bibliography of S. T. Coleridge. Philadelphia, 1903. [Still useful because of its list of books containing Coleridge marginalia and its list of critical references.]

Wise, T. J. A Bibliography of the Writings in Prose and Verse of S. T. Coleridge. Bibliog. Soc. 1913.

—— Coleridgiana. Being a Supplement to the Bibliography of Coleridge. Bibliog. Soc. 1919.

Wise, T. J. Two Lake Poets. A Catalogue of Printed Books, Manuscripts, and Autograph Letters by Wordsworth and Coleridge, collected by Thomas James Wise. 1927 (priv. ptd).

Kennedy, V. W. and Barton, M. N. Samuel Taylor Coleridge. A Selected Bibliography. Baltimore, 1935. [Very useful critical bibliography, supplementing Haney rather than Wise.]

(2) COLLECTED WORKS

¶See also the edns of separate works by Coleridge's children, Sara and Derwent, and the edns for Bohn's Standard Library by T. Ashe, listed below.]

Complete Works. Ed. W. G. T. Shedd, 7 vols. New York, 1853, 1884. [The claim to completeness in the title is not justified.]

(3) SELECTIONS

Coleridge: Poetry and Prose; with Essays by Hazlitt, Jeffrey, de Quincey, Carlyle, and Others. Ed. H. W. Garrod, 1925.

Coleridge: Select Poetry and Prose. Ed. S. Potter, 1933.

The Best of Coleridge. Ed. E. L. Griggs, New York, 1934.

The Political Thought of Samuel Taylor Coleridge. Ed. R. J. White, 1938.

(4) POETRY
(a) Collections

The Poetical Works. 3 vols. 1828.
The Poetical Works. 3 vols. 1829.
The Poetical Works of Coleridge, Shelley and Keats. Paris, 1829.
The Poetical Works. 3 vols. 1834.
Poems. 1844.
Poems. 1848.
Poems. Ed. D. and S. Coleridge, 1852, etc.
The Dramatic Works. Ed. D. Coleridge, 1852. [Frequently rptd.]
Poems. Ed. D. and S. Coleridge, 1863, etc. [The undated issue of 1870 added an introductory essay by Derwent Coleridge and restored the 1798 text of the Ancient Mariner.]
The Poetical Works. Ed. (with critical memoir) W. M. Rossetti, 1872.
The Poetical and Dramatic Works. [Ed. R. H. Shepherd], 4 vols. 1877 (re-issued with addns in 1880).
The Poetical Works. Ed. T. Ashe, 2 vols. 1885, etc. (Aldine edn).
The Poetical Works. Ed. J. D. Campbell, 1893. [Rptd 1899, etc. The excellent critical notes and the biographical introduction, which was the only reliable life of Coleridge, make this edn indispensable.]

Poems. With an Introduction by E. H. Coleridge. [1907.]

The Complete Poetical Works. Including Poems and Versions of Poems now published for the First Time. Ed. (with textual and bibliographical notes) E. H. Coleridge, 2 vols. Oxford, 1912. [The only complete text. Rptd in one vol. in the same year, by excluding certain materials of minor importance.]

(b) Selections

Christabel and the Lyrical and Imaginative Poems of S. T. Coleridge. Arranged and introduced by A. C. Swinburne. 1869. [Swinburne's introductory essay is rptd in his Essays and Studies, 1875.]

The Golden Book of Coleridge. Ed. S. A. Brooke, 1895, 1906 (Everyman's Lib.).

The Poetry of S. T. Coleridge. Ed. R. Garnett, 1898. (Muses' Lib.)

Coleridge's Poems. A Facsimile Reproduction of the Proofs and MSS. of some of the Poems. Ed. J. D. Campbell and W. H. White, 1899.

Poems. Ed. A. Symons, [1905.]

Poems. Ed. E. Dowden, Edinburgh, [1907].

'The Ancient Mariner' und 'Christabel,' mit literarhistorischer Einleitung und Kommentar. Ed. A. Eichler, Vienna, 1907.

(c) Individual Publications

[For the numerous poems first pbd in newspapers and periodicals, anthologies, or incidentally in other works, see E. H. Coleridge's Bibliographical Appendix, Coleridge's Complete Poetical Works, vol. II, Oxford, 1912.]

The Fall of Robespierre. An Historic Drama. Cambridge, 1794. [Act I by Coleridge, Acts II, III by Southey.]

Poems on Various Subjects. 1796; Bristol, 1797 ('To which are now added Poems by Charles Lamb and Charles Lloyd'); 1803 (omitting the contributions of Lamb and Lloyd).

Ode on the Departing Year. Bristol, 1796.

Sonnets from Various Authors. 1796 (priv. ptd). [4 sonnets by Coleridge, 24 by Bowles, Lamb, Lloyd, Southey, etc. The prefatory essay on the Sonnet was by Coleridge.]

Fears in Solitude. Written in 1798 during the alarm of an invasion. To which are added France, an Ode; and Frost at Midnight. 1798. [Rptd in The Poetical Register in 1812, and also privately in the same year.]

Lyrical Ballads, With A Few Other Poems [by Wordsworth and Coleridge]. Bristol and London, 1798. [See under Wordsworth, p. 167 above.]

Wallenstein. A Drama in Two Parts. 1800; rptd 1866, 1899 (Bohn's Standard Lib.). [*I.e.* The Piccolomini, 5 acts, and The Death of Wallenstein, 5 acts. The one-act prelude, Wallenstein's Lager, making up Schiller's original trilogy, was not translated.]

Remorse. A Tragedy in Five Acts. 1813 (3 edns). [This is the rev. version of Osorio, which Coleridge had sent to Sheridan as early as 1797. Osorio was ptd, ed. R. H. Shepherd, 1873.]

Christabel; Kubla Khan, a Vision; The Pains of Sleep. 1816 (3 edns).

Sibylline Leaves. A Collection of Poems. 1817. [The Rime of the Ancient Mariner was here acknowledged for the first time.]

Zapolya. A Christmas Tale in Two Parts. 1817.

A Hebrew Dirge, chaunted in the Great Synagogue, St James's Place, Aldgate, on the day of the funeral of her Royal Highness, the Princess Charlotte. By Hyman Hurwitz. With a translation in English verse by S. T. Coleridge. 1817.

The Tears of a Grateful People. A Hebrew Dirge and Hymn, chaunted in the Great Synagogue, St James's Place, Aldgate, on the day of the funeral of his late most Gracious Majesty King George III, of blessed memory. By Hyman Hurwitz. Translated into English verse by a friend [Coleridge]. [1820.]

The Devil's Walk, a Poem by Professor Porson. 1830. [Originally ptd anon. as The Devil's Thoughts, Morning Post, 6 Sept. 1799. The poem was by Coleridge and Southey, later (1827) amplified by Southey alone, with the new title, and rptd in 4 edns 1830, the first two as above, the third and fourth under the names of the true authors.]

Christabel. Illustrated by a Facsimile of the Manuscript and by Textual and Other Notes by E. H. Coleridge. 1907.

(5) PROSE

A Moral and Political Lecture delivered at Bristol. Bristol, [1795].

Conciones ad populum or Addresses to the People. [Bristol], 1795.

The Plot Discovered, or An Address to the People Against Ministerial Treason. Bristol, 1795.

An Answer to 'A Letter to Edward Long Fox, M.D.' Bristol, [1795].

The Watchman. 10 nos. Bristol, 1796.

The Friend. A literary, moral, and political weekly paper, excluding personal and party politics and the events of the day. 28 nos. Penrith, 1809–10 (re-issued with supplementary matter, 1812); 3 vols. 1818 (with alterations and a large amount of matter wholly new); ed. H. N. Coleridge, 3 vols. 1837, 1844, 1850; ed. H. N. Coleridge, 2 vols. 1863; rptd 1865, etc. (Bohn's Standard Lib.).

Omniana, or Horae Otiosiores. 2 vols. 1812. [Ed. by Southey with numerous articles by Coleridge. Rptd in Table-Talk and Omniana, ed. T. Ashe, 1884 (Bohn's Standard Lib.).]

The Statesman's Manual; or The Bible the Best Guide to Political Skill and Foresight. A Lay Sermon addressed to the Higher Classes of Society. 1816.

'Blessed are ye that sow beside all waters!' A Lay Sermon addressed to the Higher and Middle Classes on the Existing Distresses and Discontents. 1817. [This and the preceding Lay Sermon were rptd in 1839 with On the Constitution of the Church and State, and in 1865 with Biographia Literaria. The two Lay Sermons were rptd alone in 1852.]

Biographia Literaria, or Biographical Sketches of my Literary Life and Opinions. 2 vols. 1817; ed. (with long introduction and biographical supplement) H. N. and S. Coleridge, 2 vols. 1847; rptd 1865, etc. (with Two Lay Sermons in Bohn's Standard Lib.); ed. A. Symons [1906] (Everyman's Lib.); ed. (with the aesthetical essays) J. Shawcross, 2 vols. Oxford, 1907; ed. G. Sampson (with Wordsworth's prefaces and essays on poetry, 1800–15, and with an introductory essay by Sir A. T. Quiller-Couch), Cambridge, 1920 (chs. i–iv and xiv–xxii only).

On Method. [A preliminary treatise forming the General Introduction to the Encyclopaedia Metropolitana, 1818. A separate offprint, 1818. Rptd separately in 3 undated edns, 1849. 3 more edns, by 1854. Rptd with Whateley's Logic and Rhetoric under the title of Mental Science, 1855, 1873, 1875. Ed. (with MS fragments, detailed introduction and notes) A. D. Snyder, 1934.]

Remarks on the objections which have been urged against the principle of Sir Robert Peel's Bill. [1818.]

The Grounds of Sir Robert Peel's Bill vindicated. [1818.] [This and the preceding item were rptd privately in 1913.]

On the Prometheus of Aeschylus; an essay preparatory to a series of disquisitions respecting the Egyptian in connection with the sacerdotal theology, and in contrast with the mysteries of ancient Greece. 1825 (priv. ptd). [Rptd: Trans. Royal Soc. of Literature, II, 1834; Literary Remains, 1836; Notes and Lectures upon Shakespeare, 1849; Miscellanies, 1885.]

Aids to Reflection in the Formation of a Manly Character, on the Several Grounds of Prudence, Morality, and Religion; Illustrated by Select Passages from our Elder Divines, especially from Archbishop Leighton. 1825; 1831; 1836; ed. H. N. Coleridge, 1839; ed. H. N. Coleridge, 2 vols. 1843, 1848 (second vol. nearly all new material); ed. D. Coleridge, 1854, 1856; ed. T. Fenby, Liverpool, 1873; rptd (with Confessions of an Inquiring Spirit and Essays on Faith and the Book of Common Prayer, in Bohn's Standard Lib.) 1884, 1904, etc.

On the Constitution of the Church and State, according to the idea of each; with aids towards a right judgment on the late Catholic Bill. 1830 (bis); ed. H. N. Coleridge, 1839, 1852. [With the 3rd and 4th edns were rptd the two Lay Sermons.]

Specimens of the Table-Talk of the late Samuel Taylor Coleridge. [Ed. H. N. Coleridge], 2 vols. 1835, 1836 (with slight alterations); 1851; [1874], etc.; ed. H. Morley, 1884 (with Coleridge's three greatest poems); ed. (as Table-Talk and Omniana of S. T. Coleridge. With additional Table-Talk from Allsop's Recollections and manuscript matter not before printed) T. Ashe, 1884, etc. (Bohn's Standard Lib.).

The Literary Remains of Samuel Taylor Coleridge. Ed. H. N. Coleridge, 4 vols. 1836–9. [Vols. I–II are devoted to literature proper, and have been frequently rptd under different titles. Vols. III–IV deal chiefly with theological writers and have been rptd only in Notes on English Divines, and Notes Theological, Political, and Miscellaneous, 1853. All four vols. are based on MSS or marginal notes which were rev. and at times almost rewritten by the editor.]

Confessions of an Inquiring Spirit. Ed. ('from the Author's MS.') H. N. Coleridge, 1840; 1849; 1853; 1863; rptd (with Aids to Reflection in Bohn's Standard Lib.) 1884, etc.

Hints towards the Formation of a more comprehensive Theory of Life. Ed. S. B. Watson, 1848; ed. T. Ashe (in Miscellanies, Aesthetic and Literary, Bohn's Standard Lib. 1885).

Notes and Lectures upon Shakespeare and some of the old poets and dramatists, with other literary remains of S. T. Coleridge. Ed. Mrs H. N. Coleridge, 2 vols. 1849. [The text is rptd from Literary Remains, vols. I–II, with a few addns.]

Essays on His Own Times; Forming a Second Series of 'The Friend.' Ed. S. Coleridge, 3 vols. 1850.

Notes on English Divines. Ed. D. Coleridge, 2 vols. 1853. [A rpt of Literary Remains, vols. III–IV, with some addns.]

Notes Theological, Political, and Miscellaneous. Ed. D. Coleridge, 1853. [Nearly a third rptd from Literary Remains; the remainder new.]

Seven Lectures on Shakespeare and Milton, by the late S. T. Coleridge. Ed. J. P. Collier, 1856. [Collier's shorthand notes, at first unjustly suspected as a fabrication.]

Notes on Stillingfleet. 1875 (priv. ptd).

Lectures and Notes on Shakspere and other English Poets. Ed. T. Ashe, 1883, etc. (Bohn's Standard Lib.). [Text chiefly from Literary Remains, but with Collier's notes and reports of lectures from Bristol newspapers.]

Miscellanies, Aesthetic and Literary; to which is added 'The Theory of Life.' Collected and Arranged by T. Ashe. 1885, etc. (Bohn's Standard Lib.).

Critical Annotations. Being Marginal Notes inscribed in Volumes formerly in the Possession of Coleridge. Ed. W. F. Taylor, Harrow, 1889.

Anima Poetae. From the Unpublished Notebooks of Samuel Taylor Coleridge. Ed. E. H. Coleridge, 1895. [Like Literary Remains, rough notes largely rev. by the editor.]

Notizbuch aus den Jahren 1795–1798 (Gutch Memorandum Book). Archiv, xcvii, 1896.

Coleridge's Essays and Lectures on Shakspeare and some Other Old Poets and Dramatists. [1907.] (Everyman's Lib.)

Coleridge's Literary Criticism. Ed. J. W. Mackail, 1908.

Coleridge's Shakespearean Criticism. Ed. T. M. Raysor, 2 vols. Cambridge, U.S.A. 1930. [Vol. I, text directly from MSS; vol. II, reports of lectures. Some addns.]

Coleridge's Miscellaneous Criticism. Ed. T. M. Raysor, Cambridge, U.S.A. 1936. [Partly from MS.]

(6) CORRESPONDENCE

[For uncollected letters see T. J. Wise's Bibliography.]

Unpublished Letters from S. T. Coleridge to the Rev. John Prior Estlin. Communicated by H. A. Bright. Trans. Philobiblon Soc. xv, 1884; 1884 (priv. ptd).

Memorials of Coleorton: being Letters from Coleridge, Wordsworth and his Sister, Southey, and Sir Walter Scott to Sir George and Lady Beaumont of Coleorton, Leicestershire, 1803–1834. Ed. W. Knight, 2 vols. Edinburgh, 1887.

Letters from the Lake Poets to Daniel Stuart. 1889 (priv. ptd). [Compiled by Mary Stuart and ed. E. H. Coleridge.]

Letters. Ed. E. H. Coleridge, 2 vols. 1895.

Biographia Epistolaris: being the Biographical Supplement of Coleridge's Biographia Literaria, with Additional Letters, etc. Ed. A. Turnbull, 2 vols. 1911. [A collection second in usefulness only to the 1895 Letters.]

Letters hitherto Uncollected. Ed. W. F. Prideaux, 1913 (priv. ptd).

Unpublished Letters, including certain Letters republished from Original Sources. Ed. E. L. Griggs, 2 vols. 1932.

(7) BIOGRAPHY AND CRITICISM

[The following selected list may be amplified from V. W. Kennedy and M. N. Barton, Samuel Taylor Coleridge. A Selected Bibliography, Baltimore, 1935. See also the various introductions to Coleridge's works as before listed, and the bibliography of Wordsworth biography and criticism, pp. 169–72 above.]

Hazlitt, W. On the Living Poets. [In Lectures on the English Poets, 1818. Rptd in Works, ed. A. R. Waller and A. Glover, vol. v, 1902.]

—— My First Acquaintance with Poets. The Liberal, April 1823. [Rptd in Works, vol. xii, 1904.]

—— Mr Coleridge. [In The Spirit of the Age, 1825. Rptd in Works, vol. iv, 1902. See also index to Works for numerous other references.]

Lamb, C. Christ's Hospital Five and Thirty Years ago. The Two Races of Men. [In Elia, 1823, etc. Rptd in Works, ed. E. V. Lucas, vol. ii, 1903.]

—— Letters. Ed. E. V. Lucas, 2 vols. [1912].

Paris, J. A. The Life of Sir Humphry Davy. 2 vols. 1831.

Cergiel' [C. V. Le Grice?]. College Reminiscences of Mr Coleridge. GM. N.S. ii, 1834. [Rptd Penzance, 1842, and in J. Cottle, Reminiscences of Coleridge and Southey, 1847.]

Allsop, T. Letters, Conversations, and Recollections of S. T. Coleridge. 2 vols. 1836; 2 vols. 1858 (editor's name here first acknowledged); 2 vols. 1864.

Cottle, J. Early Recollections, chiefly relating to the Late S. T. Coleridge during his Long Residence in Bristol. 2 vols. 1837–9; 1847 (rev. and enlarged as Reminiscences of S. T. Coleridge and R. Southey).

Gillman, J. The Life of S. T. Coleridge. Vol. i (all pbd), 1838.

Stuart, D. Anecdotes of the Poet Coleridge.— The Late Mr Coleridge, the Poet. GM. N.S. ix, x, 1838.

[Ferrier, J. F.] The Plagiarisms of S. T. Coleridge. Blackwood's Mag. xlvii, 1840.

Southey, R. The Life and Correspondence of Robert Southey. Ed. C. C. Southey, 6 vols. 1849–50.

Southey, R. Selections from the Letters of Robert Southey. Ed. J. W. Warter, 4 vols. 1856.

Hunt, J. H. L. The Autobiography of Leigh Hunt. 3 vols. 1850; 1860 (rev. edn); ed. R. Ingpen, 1903.

Carlyle, T. Life of John Sterling. 1851. [Pt i, ch. viii, Coleridge.]

Coleridge, Hartley. Poems. Ed. (with memoir) D. Coleridge, 2 vols. 1851.

Carlyon, C. Early Years and Late Reflections. 4 vols. 1856–8.

Davy, Sir H. Fragmentary Remains. 1858.

Mill, J. S. Coleridge. [In Dissertations and Discussions, vol. i, 1859.]

Green, J. H. Spiritual Philosophy, founded on the Teaching of the late S. T. Coleridge. Ed. J. Simon, 2 vols. 1865.

Stirling, J. H. De Quincey and Coleridge upon Kant. Fortnightly Rev. viii, 1867.

Robinson, H. Crabb. Diary, Reminiscences, and Correspondence. Ed. T. Sadler, 3 vols. 1869; 2 vols. 1872.

—— Blake, Coleridge, Wordsworth, Lamb, etc., being Selections from the Remains of Henry Crabb Robinson. Ed. E. J. Morley, Manchester, 1922.

—— Correspondence with the Wordsworth Circle. Ed. E. J. Morley, 2 vols. Oxford, 1927.

Meteyard, E. A Group of Englishmen (1795 to 1815): being Records of the Younger Wedgwoods and their Friends. 1871.

Brandes, G. Hovedstrømninger i det 19de Aarhundredes Litteratur. 6 vols. Copenhagen, 1872–90; tr. Eng. 1901–5. [Vol. iv.]

Shairp, J. C. Coleridge. [In Studies in Poetry and Philosophy, Edinburgh, 1872.]

Coleridge, Sara. Memoir and Letters of Sara Coleridge. By her Daughter. 2 vols. 1873.

Brooke, S. A. Coleridge. [In Theology in the English Poets, 1874.]

Swinburne, A. C. Coleridge. [In Essays and Studies, 1875.]

[Zimmern, H.] Coleridge Marginalia. Blackwood's Mag. cxxxi, 1882.

Traill, H. D. Coleridge. 1884. (English Men of Letters ser.)

Brandl, A. Samuel Taylor Coleridge und die englische Romantik. Berlin, 1886; tr. Eng. 1887.

Caine, Sir T. H. H. Life of Samuel Taylor Coleridge. 1887. [With useful bibliography.]

Sandford, M. Thomas Poole and his Friends. 2 vols. 1888.

De Quincey, T. Coleridge. [In Collected Writings, ed. D. Masson, vol. ii, Edinburgh, 1889.]

—— Coleridge and Opium Eating. [In Collected Writings, vol. v, Edinburgh, 1890.]

—— Conversation and Coleridge. [In Posthumous Works, ed. A. H. Japp, vol. ii, 1893.]

Pater, W. H. Coleridge. [In Appreciations, 1889.]

Stephen, Sir L. Coleridge. [In Hours in a Library, vol. III, 1892.]

Campbell, J. D. Samuel Taylor Coleridge. A Narrative of the Events of his Life. 1894; 1896. [The standard life. Essentially a rpt of Campbell's biographical introduction to his edn of the poems. Campbell included in these books a good part, but by no means all, of the materials of his valuable articles in Athenaeum, 1884–5, 1887–93. These are over two score in number but may be listed here as a series, by reference to Haney's bibliography or index of Athenaeum for the years specified.]

Coleridge, E. H. Wordsworth on Wordsworth and Coleridge. Athenaeum, 24 Nov. 1894.

—— Coleridge. [In Chambers's Cyclopaedia of English Literature, vol. III, 1903.]

Wylie, L. J. Studies in the Evolution of English Criticism. Boston, 1894.

Dowden, E. Coleridge as a Poet. [In New Studies in Literature, 1895.]

—— The French Revolution and English Literature. 1897.

Gillman, A. W. The Gillmans of Highgate, with Letters from S. T. Coleridge, etc. [1895.]

Saintsbury, G. Coleridge and Southey. [In Essays in English Literature, ser. 2, 1895.]

Robertson, J. M. Coleridge. [In New Essays towards a Critical Method, 1897.]

White, W. H. A Description of the Wordsworth and Coleridge MSS. in the Possession of Mr T. Norton Longman. 1897.

Forman, H. B. Coleridge's Notes on Flögel. Cosmopolis, IX, X, 1898.

Lucas, E. V. Charles Lamb and the Lloyds. 1898.

Hancock, A. E. The French Revolution and the English Poets. New York, 1899.

Garnett, R. Essays of an Ex-Librarian. 1901.

Haney, J. L. The German Influence on S. T. Coleridge. Philadelphia, 1902.

—— The Marginalia of S. T. C. [In Schelling Anniversary Papers, New York, 1923.]

Machule, P Coleridge's Wallenstein-übersetzung. E. Studien, XXXI, 1902.

Litchfield, R. B. Tom Wedgwood, the First Photographer. An Account of his Life, his Discovery, and His Friendship with S. T. Coleridge, including the Letters of Coleridge to the Wedgwoods. 1903.

Cestre, C. La Révolution française et les Poètes anglais (1789–1809). Paris, 1906.

Aynard, J. La Vie d'un poète. Coleridge. Paris, 1907.

—— Notes inédites de S. T. Coleridge. Revue de Littérature comparée, II, 1922.

Helmholtz, A. A. The Indebtedness of S. T. Coleridge to A. W. von Schlegel. Madison, 1907.

Eagleston, A. J. Wordsworth, Coleridge, and the Spy. Nineteenth Century, LXIV, 1908.

Potts, R. A. A Forgotten Early Prose Work of Coleridge. Athenaeum, 2 May 1908. [Rpts Answer to a Letter to Fox.]

Ferrando, G. La Critica letteraria di S. T. Coleridge. Florence, 1909.

—— Coleridge: Studio critico. Florence, [1925].

Boas, F. S., Bradley, A. C., Jack, A. A., and de Selincourt, E. Short Bibliographies of Wordsworth, Coleridge, Byron, Shelley, Keats. English Ass. 1912. [Short critical bibliographies. Very useful.]

Towe, E. A. A Poet's Children, Hartley and Sara Coleridge. 1912.

Stork, C. W. The Influence of the Popular Ballad on Wordsworth and Coleridge. PMLA. XXIX, 1914.

Pizzo, E. S. T. Coleridge als Kritiker. Ang. XL, 1916.

Haller, W. The Early Life of Robert Southey, 1774–1803. New York, 1917.

Quiller-Couch, Sir A. T. Coleridge. [In Studies in Literature, Cambridge. 1918.]

Snyder, A. D. The Critical Principle of the Reconciliation of Opposites as Employed by Coleridge. Ann Arbor, 1918.

—— A Note on Coleridge's Shakespeare Criticism. MLN. XXXVIII, 1923.

—— Coleridge's Cosmogony: a Note on the Poetic 'World-View.' Stud. Phil. XXI, 1924.

—— Coleridge and Giordano Bruno. MLN. XLII, 1927.

—— Coleridge and the Watsons. TLS. 25 Aug. 1927.

—— Books Borrowed by Coleridge from the Library of the University of Göttingen, 1799. MP. XXV, 1928.

—— Coleridgeana. RES. IV, 1928.

—— Coleridge on Logic and Learning, with Selections from the Unpublished Manuscripts. New Haven, 1929.

—— Coleridge's Reading of Mendelssohn's 'Morgenstunden' and 'Jerusalem.' JEGP. XXVIII, 1929.

—— Coleridge on Böhme. PMLA. XLV, 1930.

Stewart, H. L. The Place of Coleridge in English Theology. Harvard Theological Rev. XI, 1918.

Hanford, J. H. Coleridge as a Philologian. MP. XVI, 1919.

Wilde, N. The Development of Coleridge's Thought. Philosophical Rev. XXVIII, 1919.

Gingerich, S. F. From Necessity to Transcendentalism in Coleridge. PMLA. XXXV, 1920.

Gingerich, S. F. Essays in the Romantic Poets. New York, 1924.

Murry, J. M. Coleridge's Criticism. [In Aspects of Criticism, 1920.]

—— The Metaphysic of Poetry. [In Countries of the Mind, ser. 2, 1931.]

Richter, H. Die philosophische Weltanschauung von S. T. Coleridge und ihr Verhältnis zur deutschen Philosophie. Ang. XLIV, 1920.

Graham, W. The Politics of the Greater Romantic Poets. PMLA. XXXVI, 1921.

—— Contemporary Critics of Coleridge the Poet. PMLA. XXXVIII, 1923.

Dunstan, A. C. The German Influence on Coleridge. MLR. XVII, XVIII, 1922–3.

Latymer, Lord. A Coleridge Note-Book. TLS. 11 Oct. 1923.

Howard, C. Coleridge's Idealism: a Study of its Relationship to Kant and to the Cambridge Platonists. Boston, 1924.

Kaufman, P. The Reading of Southey and Coleridge. The Record of their Borrowings from the Bristol Library, 1793–1798. MP. XXI, 1924.

Mackall, L. L. Coleridge Marginalia on Wieland and Schiller. MLR. XIX, 1924.

Ritter, O. Coleridgiana. E. Studien, LVIII, 1924.

Harper, G. M. Coleridge's Conversation Poems. Quarterly Rev. CCXLIV, 1925.

—— S. T. Coleridge. Quarterly Rev. CCLXIII, 1934.

Potter, G. R. Coleridge and the Idea of Evolution. PMLA. XL, 1925.

Watson, L. E. Coleridge at Highgate. 1925.

Raysor, T. M. Unpublished Fragments on Aesthetics by S. T. Coleridge. Stud. Phil. XXII, 1925.

—— Coleridge and 'Asra.' Stud. Phil. XXVI, 1929. [Coleridge's love for Sarah Hutchinson.]

Brinton, C. The Political Ideas of the English Romanticists. Oxford, 1926.

Drinkwater, J. The Notes of S. T. Coleridge in Milton's Poems [ed.] by Thomas Warton. London Mercury, XIV, 1926.

Fausset, H. I'A. Samuel Taylor Coleridge. 1926.

Greever, G. A Wiltshire Parson and His Friends. The Correspondence of William Lisle Bowles. Together with Four hitherto Unidentified Reviews by S. T. Coleridge. Boston, 1926.

Needham, J. S. T. Coleridge as a Philosophical Biologist. Science Progress, XX, 1926.

Powell, A. E. The Romantic Theory of Poetry. An Examination in the Light of Croce's Aesthetic. 1926.

Shafer, R. S. Coleridge. [In Christianity and Naturalism, New Haven, 1926.]

Stokoe, F. W. German Influence in the English Romantic Period, 1788–1818. Cambridge, 1926.

Thompson, F. T. Emerson's Indebtedness to Coleridge. Stud. Phil. XXIII, 1926.

White, H. O. The Ancient Mariner. TLS. 14 Jan. 1926.

Charpentier, J. Coleridge, le Somnambule sublime. Paris, 1927; tr. Eng. 1929.

Lowes, J. L. The Road to Xanadu. A Study in the Ways of the Imagination. Boston, 1927, 1930 (enlarged).

Morrill, D. I. Coleridge's Theory of Dramatic Illusion. MLN. XLII, 1927.

Nidecker, H. Notes marginales de S. T. Coleridge. Revue de Littérature comparée, VII, VIII, X, 1927–8, 1930.

Collins, H. P. The Criticism of Coleridge. New Criterion, V, 1927.

Rea, J. D. Coleridge's Intimations of Immortality from Proclus. MP. XXVI, 1928.

—— Coleridge's Health. MLN. XLV, 1930.

Babbitt, I. Coleridge and the Moderns. Bookman (U.S.A.), LXX, 1929.

—— Coleridge and Imagination. Nineteenth Century, CVI, 1929.

Bradley, A. C. A Miscellany. 1929. [Includes Coleridge-Echoes in Shelley's Poems; Coleridge's Use of Light and Colour.]

Carver, P. L. The Evolution of the Term 'Esemplastic.' MLR. XXIV, 1929.

Cobban, A. The Political Philosophy of Coleridge. [In Edmund Burke and the Revolt against the Eighteenth Century, 1929.]

Garrod, H. W. Coleridge. [In The Profession of Poetry and other Lectures, Oxford, 1929.]

Griggs, E. L. Hartley Coleridge, his Life and Work. 1929.

—— Coleridge and Byron. PMLA. XLV, 1930.

—— Coleridge and his Son. Stud. Phil. XXVII, 1930.

—— Coleridge and the Wedgwood Annuity. RES. VI, 1930.

—— Coleridge the Dragoon. MP. XXVIII, 1931.

—— Hartley Coleridge on His Father. PMLA. XLVI, 1931.

—— 'Diadestè,' a Fragment of an Unpublished Play by Samuel Taylor Coleridge. MP. XXXIV, 1937.

—— 'The Friend': 1809 and 1818 Editions. MP. XXXV, 1938.

Snell, A. L. F. The Meter of 'Christabel.' [In F. N. Scott Anniversary Papers, Chicago, 1929.]

Babcock, R. W. The Direct Influence of Late Eighteenth Century Shakespeare Criticism on Hazlitt and Coleridge. MLN. XLV, 1930.

—— The Genesis of Shakespeare Idolatry, 1766–1799. Chapel Hill, 1931.

Eugenia, Sister. Coleridge's Scheme of Pantisocracy and American Travel Accounts. PMLA. xLv, 1930.

Koszul, A. Coleridgiana. Revue anglo-américaine, vII, 1930.

Muirhead, J. H. Coleridge as Philosopher. 1930.

Stovall, F. Poe's Debt to Coleridge. Austin, Texas, 1930.

Dike, E. B. Coleridge Marginalia in Henry Brooke's The Fool of Quality. Huntington Lib. Bulletin, II, 1931.

Hartman, H. Hartley Coleridge, Poet's Son and Poet. 1931.

MacGillivray, J. R. The Pantisocracy Scheme and its Immediate Background. [In Studies in English by Members of University College, Toronto, 1931.]

Morley, E. J. Coleridge in Germany (1799). London Mercury, xxIII, 1931.

Wellek, R. Immanuel Kant in England, 1793–1838. Princeton, 1931.

McElderberry, B. R. Coleridge's Revision of The Ancient Mariner. Stud. Phil. xxIx, 1932.

Stallknecht, N. P. The Moral of the Ancient Mariner. PMLA. xLvII, 1932.

—— The Doctrine of Coleridge's 'Dejection' and its Relation to Wordsworth's Philosophy. PMLA. xLIx, 1934.

Gibbs, W. E. S. T. Coleridge's 'The Knight's Tomb' and 'Youth and Age.' MLR. xxvIII, 1933.

—— Unpublished Letters concerning Cottle's Coleridge. PMLA. xLIx, 1934.

Moore, J. R. Coleridge's Indebtedness to Paltock's Peter Wilkins. MP. xxxI, 1933.

Nitchie, E. The Moral of the Ancient Mariner Reconsidered. PMLA. xLvIII, 1933.

Strout, A. L. S. T. Coleridge and John Wilson of Blackwood's Magazine. PMLA. xLvIII, 1933.

Winkelmann, E. Coleridge und die Kantische Philosophie. Leipzig, 1933.

Abrams, M. H. The Milk of Paradise: The Effect of Opium Visions on the Works of De Quincey, Crabbe, Francis Thompson, and Coleridge. Cambridge, U.S.A. 1934. [Valuable pamphlet on 'The Ancient Mariner.']

Chambers, Sir E. K. Some Dates in Coleridge's 'Annus Mirabilis.' E. & S. xIx, 1934.

—— The Date of Coleridge's Kubla Khan. RES. xI, 1935.

—— Samuel Taylor Coleridge. Oxford, 1938.

Coburn, K. H. S. T. Coleridge's Philosophical Lectures of 1818–19. RES. x, 1934.

Coleridge: Studies by Several Hands on the Hundredth Anniversary of His Death. Ed. E. Blunden and E. L. Griggs, 1934.

Coleridge, Sara (Fricker). Minnow among Tritons, Mrs S. T. Coleridge's Letters to

Thomas Poole, 1799–1834. Ed. S. Potter, 1934.

Hearnshaw, F. J. C. Coleridge the Conservative. Nineteenth Century, cxvI, 1934.

Lindsay, J. Coleridge Marginalia in a Volume of Descartes. PMLA. xLIx, 1934.

—— Coleridge Marginalia in Jacobi's 'Werke.' MLN. L, 1935.

Richards, I. A. Coleridge on Imagination. 1934.

Stewart, J. I. M. Some Coleridge Letters. RES. x, 1934.

Willoughby, L. A. Coleridge and his German Contemporaries. English Goethe Soc. Publications, x, 1934.

—— Coleridge as a Philologist. MLR. xxxI, 1936.

Potter, S. Coleridge and S. T. C. 1935.

Sanders, C. R. Coleridge as a Champion of Liberty. Stud. Phil. xxxII, 1935.

—— Coleridge, F. D. Maurice and the Distinction between the Reason and the Understanding. PMLA. LI, 1936.

—— Maurice as a Commentator on Coleridge. PMLA. LIII, 1938.

Smith, F. M. The Relation of Coleridge's Ode on Dejection to Wordsworth's Ode on Intimations of Immortality. PMLA. L, 1935.

Weber, C. A. Bristols Bedeutung für die englische Romantik. Halle, 1935.

Isaacs, J. Coleridge's Critical Terminology. E. & S. xxI, 1936.

Klingender, F. D. Coleridge on Robinson Crusoe. TLS. 1 Feb. 1936. [Marginalia.]

McElderry, B. R. Coleridge's Plan for completing Christabel. Stud. Phil. xxxIII, 1936.

Potter, G. R. Unpublished Marginalia in Coleridge's Copy of Malthus's Essay on Population. PMLA. LI, 1936.

Waples, D. David Hartley in The Ancient Mariner. JEGP. xxxv, 1936.

de Selincourt, E. Coleridge's Dejection: an Ode. E. & S. xxII, 1937. [Prints earliest version.]

Evans, B. I. Coleridge on Slang. TLS. 29 May 1937. [Marginalia.]

Hamilton, M. P. Wordsworth's Relation to Coleridge's Osorio. Stud. Phil. xxxIV, 1937.

Shearer, E. A. Wordsworth and Coleridge Marginalia in a Copy of Richard Payne Knight's Analytical Inquiry into Taste. Huntington Lib. Quart. I, 1937.

Sherwood, M. Coleridge's Imaginative Conception of Imagination. Wellesley, 1937.

Hanson, L. The Life of S. T. Coleridge. 1938.

Tuttle, D. R. Christabel Sources in Percy's Reliques and the Gothic Romance. PMLA. LIII, 1938.

Coldicutt, D. Res. xv, 1939. [Attributions in Monthly Mag. 1796–9.]

T. M. R.

ROBERT SOUTHEY (1774–1843)

(1) BIBLIOGRAPHY

Haller, W. The Early Life of Robert Southey. New York, 1917. [Appendix A, 'Works of Robert Southey.']

(2) POETICAL WORKS

(a) Collected Editions

The Minor Poems. 3 vols. 1815, 1823. [A rpt of Poems, 1797–9, and Metrical Tales, 1805.]

The Poetical Works. Complete in One Volume. Paris, 1829; Paris, n.d.

The Poetical Works, collected by Himself. 10 vols. 1837–8; 10 vols. New York, 1839. [Each vol. has a separate preface by Southey. Frequently rptd, in whole or in part and dated and n.d., 1844–59; 1 vol. edns: Philadelphia, 1846; New York, 1848; 1850; New York, 1853, 1856; 1863; 1873.]

The Poetical Works, with a Memoir of the Author [by H. T. Tuckerman]. 10 vols. Boston, 1860.

Poems, chosen and arranged by E. Dowden. 1895.

Poems, containing Thalaba, the Curse of Kehama, Roderick, Madoc, A Tale of Paraguay, and Selected Minor Poems. Ed. M. H. Fitzgerald, 1909.

(b) Separate Poems

The Fall of Robespierre. An Historic Drama. Cambridge, 1794. [The first act by Coleridge, the second and third by Southey.]

Poems: containing The Retrospect, Odes, Elegies, Sonnets, &c. by Robert Lovell, and Robert Southey. Bath, 1795.

Joan of Arc, an Epic Poem. Bristol, 1796; 2 vols. Bristol, 1798; Boston, 1798; 1806; 1812; 2 vols. 1817; rptd 1853.

Poems. 2 vols. Bristol, 1797–9; Boston, 1799 (vol. I only); 2 vols. 1800; 2 vols. 1801; 2 vols. 1808–6. [Vol. I, 1797 is described as 'Second Edition,' being partly made up from Poems; 1795.]

Thalaba the Destroyer. 2 vols. 1801; 2 vols. 1809; Boston, 1812; 2 vols. 1814; 2 vols. 1821; 1846; 1853; 1860.

Madoc, a Poem, in two parts. 1805; 2 vols. Boston, 1806; 2 vols. 1807, 1812, 1815, 1825; 1853.

Metrical Tales, and Other Poems. 1805; Boston, 1811. [Poems rptd from The Annual Anthology, 1799–1800.]

The Curse of Kehama. 1810; New York, 1811; 2 vols. 1812; 2 vols. 1818; 1853; ed. H. Morley, 1886.

Roderick, The Last of the Goths. 1814; 2 vols. 1815 (bis); Philadelphia, 1815; 2 vols. 1816; 2 vols. 1818; 2 vols. 1826; rptd 1891. Tr. French, Paris, 1820; Dutch, Hague, 1823–4.

Odes to His Royal Highness The Prince Regent, His Imperial Majesty The Emperor of Russia, and His Majesty The King of Prussia. 1814; 1821 (as Carmen Triumphale, for the Commencement of the year, 1814).

The Poet's Pilgrimage to Waterloo. 1816 (12 large paper copies also issued) (bis); New York, 1816; Boston, 1816.

The Lay of the Laureate. Carmen Nuptiale. 1816. [On the marriage of the Princess Charlotte.]

Wat Tyler. A Dramatic Poem. 1817 (quotations from Southey on title-page; re-issued with quotations from Shakespeare substituted) (Sherwood, Neeley and Jones); 1817 (Fairburn); 1817 (Hone); 1817 (Sherwin); 1817 (Broom); Newcastle, [1820?], [1830?], [1835?].

A Vision of Judgement. 1821; 1822 (as The Two Visions; or Byron v. Southey. Containing the Vision of Judgement by Dr. Southey, LL.D.; also another Vision of Judgement, by Lord Byron); New York, 1823 (with Byron's travesty); 1824 (with Byron's).

A Tale of Paraguay. 1825; Boston, 1827; 1828.

All for Love; and The Pilgrim to Compostella. 1829.

The Devil's Walk, a poem by Professor Porson. 1830 (bis); 1830 (as by Coleridge and Southey) (bis). [By Coleridge and Southey. Originally ptd as The Devil's Thoughts, Morning Post, 6 Sept. 1799, and expanded (by Southey alone) in 1827.]

Oliver Newman: A New-England Tale (Unfinished): With Other Poetical Remains. [Ed. H. Hill], 1845.

Robin Hood: a Fragment. By the Late Robert Southey and Caroline Southey. With Other Fragments and Poems. Edinburgh, 1847.

(3) PROSE WORKS

The Flagellant. 9 nos. 1 March—26 April 1792. [Written by Southey and G. C. Bedford. The article on corporal punishment, for which Southey was dismissed the school, is in no. v.]

Letters written during a short residence in Spain and Portugal. With some Account of Spanish and Portuguese Poetry. Bristol, 1797; Bristol, 1799; 2 vols. 1808.

Letters from England: By Don Manuel Alvarez Espriella. Translated from the Spanish. 3 vols. 1807 (anon.); 2 vols. Boston, 1807; 3 vols. 1808; 2 vols. New York, 1808, 1836. Tr. French, Paris, 1817; German, Leipzig, 1818.

History of Brazil. 3 pts, 1810–29. [Pt I rptd 1822.]

Omniana, or Horae Otiosiores. 2 vols. 1812 (anon.). [Ed. by Southey with 45 articles by Coleridge.]

The Life of Nelson. 2 vols. 1813, etc. (at least 30 edns by 1900); ed. H. B. Butler, 1911; ed. G. A. R. Callender, New York, 1922; ed. A. D. Power, 1923; ed. Sir H. Newbolt, 1925.

A Letter to William Smith, Esq., M.P. 1817 (4 edns). [An occasion of certain strictures made by Smith in the House of Commons on the writings of Southey.]

The Life of Wesley; and the Rise and Progress of Methodism. 2 vols. 1820 (bis); New York, 1820; ed. C. C. Southey, 2 vols. 1846 (embodying notes by Coleridge and 'Remarks on Wesley' by A. Knox); 1858; 1864, etc.; ed. M. H. Fitzgerald, 2 vols. 1925; tr. German, 1828.

The Expedition of Orsua; and the Crimes of Aguirre. 1821. [Rptd from Edinburgh Annual Register, vol. III, pt 2.]

History of the Peninsular War. 3 vols. 1823–32; 6 vols. 1828–37.

The Book of the Church. 2 vols. 1824 (bis); 1825; Boston, 1825; 1837; 1841; 1848; 1859; 1869 (with notes from Vindiciae Ecclesiae Anglicanae); etc.

Vindiciae Ecclesiae Anglicanae. Letters to Charles Butler, Esq., Comprising Essays on the Romish Religion and vindicating the Book of the Church. 1826.

Sir Thomas More: or, Colloquies on the Progress and Prospects of Society. 2 vols. 1829; 2 vols. 1831; 1887.

Essays, Moral and Political. Now first collected. 2 vols. 1832.

Lives of the British Admirals, with an Introductory view of the Naval History of England. 5 vols. 1833–40 (vol. v continued by R. Bell); ed. D. Hannay, 1895 (as English Seamen).

Letter to John Murray, Esq., 'touching' Lord Nugent; in reply to a letter from his lordship, touching an article in the 'Quarterly Review.' By the Author of that Article. 1833 (anon.).

The Doctor. 7 vols. 1834–47 (anon.) (vols. I, II rptd 1835; vols. I–III rptd 1839; vols. VI, VII, ed. J. W. Warter); 2 vols. New York, 1836 (vols. I, II only); ed. J. W. Warter, 1848, 1849, 1853, 1862, 1864, 1865, etc.; ed. M. H. Fitzgerald, 1930 (abridged from 1848 edn).

The Life of the Rev. Andrew Bell. Comprising the History of the Rise and Progress of the System of Mutual Tuition. 3 vols. 1844. [Vol. I by Southey; vols. II, III by C. C. Southey.]

Select Biographies: Cromwell and Bunyan. 1844. [Cromwell rptd from Quart. Rev.; Bunyan from The Pilgrim's Progress, 1830.]

Southey's Common Place Book. Ed. J. W. Warter, 4 sers. 1849–51; 4 vols. 1876. [Ser. I, Choice Passages, 1849; ser. II, Special Collections, 1849; ser. III, Analytical Readings, 1850; ser. IV, Original Memoranda 1850.]

Review of Churchill's Poems. By the late Mr Southey. [1852] (priv. ptd). [Rptd from Annual Rev. 1804.]

Journal of a Tour in the Netherlands in the Autumn of 1815. Boston, 1902; ed. Sir W. R. Nicoll, 1903.

Journal of a Tour in Scotland in 1819. Ed. C. H. Herford, 1929.

(4) CORRESPONDENCE

The Life and Correspondence of the late Robert Southey. Ed. C. C. Southey, 6 vols. 1849–50.

Selections from the Letters of Robert Southey. Ed. J. W. Warter, 4 vols. 1856.

The Correspondence of Robert Southey with Caroline Bowles. To which are added: Correspondence with Shelley and Southey's Dreams. Ed. E. Dowden, Dublin, 1881.

Memorials of Coleorton: being Letters from Coleridge, Wordsworth and his Sister Southey, and Sir Walter Scott to Sir George and Lady Beaumont, 1803–1834. Ed. W Knight, 2 vols. Edinburgh, 1887.

Letters from the Lake Poets, to Daniel Stuart, Editor of the Morning Post and the Courier, 1800–1838. 1889 (priv. ptd). [Compiled by Mary Stuart and ed. by E. H. Coleridge. Southey's letters, pp. 387–434. Poems contributed to the Morning Post by Robert Southey, pp. 437–48.]

A House of Letters: being Excerpts from the Correspondence of Southey and Others with Matilda Betham. Ed. E. Betham, 1905.

Letters of Robert Southey. A Selection. Ed. M. H. Fitzgerald, 1912. (World's Classics.

(5) WORKS TRANSLATED AND EDITED BY SOUTHEY

On the French Revolution, by Mr Necker. Translated from the French. 2 vols. 1797. [Vol. II by Southey.]

The Annual Anthology. 2 vols. Bristol, 1799–1800. [Anon., but ed. and partly written by Southey.]

Amadis of Gaul, by Vasco Lobeira. 4 vols. 1803; rptd 1872 (3rd edn).

The Works of Thomas Chatterton. 3 vols. 1803. [Ed. by J. Cottle and Southey.]

Palmerin of England, by Francisco de Moraes. 4 vols. 1807. [Tr. by A. Munday, 1581, from the French version and extensively corrected by Southey from the original.]

Specimens of the Later English Poets, Preliminary Notices. 3 vols. 1807.

Chronicle of the Cid, from the Spanish. 1808;
1846; Lowell, Mass. 1846; 1868; 1883.
The Remains of Henry Kirke White. With
an Account of his Life. 3 vols. 1808–22;
3 vols. 1823 (10th edn), etc.
The Byrth, Lyf, and Actes of Kyng Arthur.
With an Introduction and Notes. 2 vols.
1817.
The Pilgrim's Progress. With a Life of John
Bunyan. 1830; Boston, 1832; New York,
1837; 1839; 1844; New York, 1846; 1847;
1881.
Attempts in Verse, by John Jones, an Old
Servant: with some Account of the Writer,
written by Himself: and an Introductory
Essay on the Lives and Works of our Uneducated Poets, by Robert Southey. 1831;
1836 (as Lives of Uneducated Poets, to
which are added Attempts in Verse).
[Southey's introductory essay has been
rptd as The Lives and Works of the Uneducated Poets, ed. J. S. Childers, 1925.]
Select Works of the British Poets, from Chaucer
to Jonson, with Biographical Sketches.
1831.
Horae Lyricae. By Isaac Watts. With a
Memoir of the Author. 1834; 1837; Boston,
1854.
The Works of William Cowper. With a Life
of the Author. 15 vols. 1835–7; 8 vols.
1853–5.

(6) BIOGRAPHY AND CRITICISM

Coleridge, S. T. Biographia Literaria. 2 vols.
1817; ed. J. Shawcross, 2 vols. Oxford,
1907.
The Changeling; a Poem in Two Cantos:
addressed to a Laureat. 1817. [Occasioned
by the pbn of Southey's Wat Tyler.]
Watson, R. Observations on Southey's Life
of Wesley. 1820.
Byron, G. G., Baron. The Vision of Judge-
ment. Liberal, i, 1822.
—— Letters and Journals. Ed. R. E.
Prothero, 6 vols. 1898–1901.
Tillbrook, S. Historical and Critical Remarks
upon the Modern Hexametrists, and upon
Mr Southey's Vision of Judgement. 1822.
Landor, W. S. Imaginary Conversations.
5 vols. 1824–9.
Benbow, W. A Scourge for the Laureate, in
Reply to his Letter Abusive of Lord Byron.
[1825?]
Hazlitt, W. The Spirit of the Age. 1825; ed.
A. Glover and A. R. Waller (Works,
vol. iv, 1902).
Macaulay, T. B. Southey's Colloquies. Edin-
burgh Rev. Jan. 1830. [Rptd in Critical
and Historical Essays, 3 vols. 1843, and
ed. F. C. Montague, 3 vols. 1903.]

Cottle, J. Early Recollections. 2 vols. 1837–9;
1847 (rev. and enlarged as Reminiscences
of S. T. Coleridge and R. Southey).
Lockhart, J. G. Life of Sir Walter Scott.
7 vols. Edinburgh, 1837–8.
Chorley, H. F. The Authors of England. 1838.
Robberds, J. W. A Memoir of the Life and
Writings of the late William Taylor, of
Norwich, Containing his Correspondence
with Robert Southey and Other Eminent
Literary Men. 2 vols. 1843.
Catalogue of the Valuable Library of the Late
Robert Southey, Esq. [1844.]
Browne, C. T. Life of Robert Southey. 1854.
Gilfillan, G. Robert Southey. [In Galleries of
Literary Portraits, vol. i, 1856.]
Thackeray, W. M. The Four Georges. 1861.
[See under George III.]
Jerdan, W. Men I have known. 1866.
Robinson, H. Crabb. Diary, Reminiscences,
and Correspondence. Ed. T. Sadler, 3 vols.
1869.
—— Correspondence with the Wordsworth
Circle. Ed. E. J. Morley, 2 vols. Oxford,
1927.
Dowden, E. Southey. 1874. (English Men of
Letters ser.)
—— The Early Revolutionary Group. [In The
French Revolution and English Literature,
1895.]
Dennis, J. Robert Southey. [In Studies in
English Literature, 1876.]
—— Robert Southey. The Story of his Life
written in his Letters. Boston, 1887.
Taylor, Sir H. Autobiography. 2 vols. 1885.
[Vol. i, ch. 17.]
De Quincey, T. Reminiscences of the Lake
Poets. [In Works, ed. D. Masson, Vol. ii,
Edinburgh, 1889.]
Smiles, S. A Publisher and his Friends.
Memoir of the late John Murray, with an
Account of the Origin and Progress of the
House, 1768–1843. 2 vols. 1891.
Scott, Sir W. Familiar Letters. Ed. D.
Douglas, 2 vols. Edinburgh, 1894.
Saintsbury, G. Coleridge and Southey. [In
Essays in English Literature, ser. 2, 1895.]
Stephen, Sir L. Southey's Letters. [In
Studies of a Biographer, vol. iv, 1902.]
Grannis, R. S. An American Friend of
Southey (Maria Gowen Brooks). 1913.
Haller, W. The Early Life of Robert Southey,
1774–1803. New York, 1917.
—— Southey's Later Radicalism. PMLA.
xxxvii, 1922.
Buceta, E. Una Traducción de Lope de Vega
hecha por Southey. Romanic Rev. xiii,
1922. [On The Madonna's Lullaby.]
Dolson, G. B. Southey and Landor and the
Consolations of Philosophy of Boethius.
AJ. Phil. xliii, 1922.

Graham, W. Robert Southey as Tory Reviewer. PQ. II, 1923.

Kaufman, P. The Reading of Southey and Coleridge. The Record of their Borrowings from the Bristol Library, 1793–1798. MP. XXI, 1924.

Knowlton, E. C. Southey's Eclogues. PQ. VII, 1928.

—— Southey's Monodramas. PQ. VIII, 1929.

Cobban, A. Edmund Burke and the Revolt against the Eighteenth Century. A Study of the Political and Social Thinking of Burke, Wordsworth, Coleridge and Southey. 1929.

Richter, H. Robert Southey. Ang. LIII, 1929.

Griggs, E. L. Robert Southey and the Edinburgh Review. MP. XXX, 1932.

Havens, R. D. Southey's Contributions to the Foreign Review. RES. VIII, 1932.

Marcus, H. Unterdrückte Revolutionsverse des jungen R. Southey. Archiv, CLXI, 1932.

Wright, H. G. Southey's Relations with Finland and Scandinavia. MLR. XXVII, 1932.

—— Three Aspects of Southey. RES. IX, 1933.

Ehrich, E. Southey und Landor. Göttingen, 1934.

Weber, C. A. Bristols Bedeutung für die englische Romantik. Halle, 1935.

Fletcher, I. K. Robert Southey and Miss Seton. TLS. 20 Nov., 4 Dec. 1937.

Curry, K. Uncollected Translations of Michaelangelo by Wordsworth and Southey. RES. XIV, 1938.

THOMAS CAMPBELL (1777–1844)

(1) COLLECTED POEMS

The Poetical Works of Thomas Campbell. Including a Biographical Sketch of the Author, by a Gentleman of New-York [Washington Irving]. 2 vols. Albany, 1810; Philadelphia, 1815.

The Poetical Works, now first collected. 2 vols. 1828, 1830, 1833, 1837 (illustrated by J. M. W. Turner); Edinburgh, 1837; 1838.

The Poetical Works of Rogers, Campbell [and others]. Paris, 1829.

The Poetical Works, with Notes and a Biographical Sketch by W. A. Hill, illustrated by J. M. W. Turner. 1851.

[Other edns: E. Sargent, Boston, 1854; C. Rogers, [1870]; W. M. Rossetti, [1871], 1880; W. A. Hill, with sketch of Campbell's life by W. Allingham, 1875, 1890; J. L. Robertson, Oxford, 1907.]

(2) SELECTIONS

Poems. Ed. J. Hogben, 1885.

Poems. Ed. L. Campbell, 1904.

(3) INDIVIDUAL PUBLICATIONS

The Pleasures of Hope, with other Poems. Edinburgh, 1799; Glasgow, 1800 (4th edn); Edinburgh, 1802 (6th edn); 1803 (7th edn; 'corrected and enlarged' by the inclusion of 'Hohenlinden,' 'The Soldier's Dream,' etc.); Edinburgh, 1807 (9th edn); Edinburgh, 1821 (illustrated by R. Westall); tr. German, Hamburg, 1838.

Poems. Edinburgh, 1803. ['Lochiel's Warning' and 'Hohenlinden' only.]

Poems. 1805. [Issued by subscription.]

Gertrude of Wyoming: a Pennsylvanian Tale, and Other Poems. 1809; 2 vols. 1810; 1814 (5th edn); 1825 (9th edn); ed. H. M. Fitzgibbon, Oxford, 1889; tr. German, Baden-Baden, 1882.

Specimens of the British Poets: with Biographical and Critical Notices, and An Essay on English Poetry. 7 vols. 1819; ed. P. Cunningham, 1841; ed. P. Cunningham, 1848 (essay and notices only).

Theodric: a Domestic Tale, and Other Poems. 1824 (bis).

Miscellaneous Poems. 1824.

Inaugural Discourse on being installed Lord Rector of the University of Glasgow. Glasgow, 1827. [Rptd in Inaugural Addresses by Lords Rectors of the University of Glasgow, ed. J. B. Hay, Glasgow, 1839, which contains also Campbell's address in 1828.]

Poland: a Poem, [and] Lines on the View from St Leonard's. 1831 (bis).

The Life of Mrs Siddons. 2 vols. 1834; 1839.

Letters from the South. 2 vols. 1837. [Prose.]

The Dramatic Works of Shakespeare, with remarks by T. Campbell. 1838, 1843, 1848.

The Life of Petrarch. 2 vols. 1841; 2 vols. 1843.

The Pilgrim of Glencoe, and Other Poems. 1842.

(4) PERIODICALS EDITED BY CAMPBELL

The New Monthly Magazine and Literary Journal. Ed. 1820–30.

The Metropolitan, a Monthly Journal. Ed. 1831–2.

The Scenic Annual for 1838.

(5) WORKS OF DOUBTFUL AUTHENTICITY

Annals of Great Britain from the Ascension of George III to the Peace of Amiens. 3 vols. Edinburgh, 1807.

Frederick the Great, his Court and Times. Edited with an introduction, by T. Campbell. 4 vols. 1842–3.

History of our own Times. By the author of The Court and Times of Frederick the Great. Vols. I, II, 1843–5.

(6) BIOGRAPHY AND CRITICISM

Jeffrey, F., Lord. Edinburgh Rev. XIV, 1809 (Gertrude of Wyoming), XXXI, 1819 (Specimens of the British Poets), XLI, 1825 (Theodric).

Hazlitt, W. The Spirit of the Age. 1825; ed. P. P. Howe (Complete Works, vol. XI, 1932).

Beattie, W. Life and Letters of Thomas Campbell. 3 vols. 1849, 1850.

Gilfillan, G. Galleries of Literary Portraits. Vol. I, 1856.

Redding, C. Literary Reminiscences and Memoirs of Thomas Campbell. 2 vols. 1860.

Taylor, Sir H. Thomas Campbell. [In The English Poets, ed. T. H. Ward, vol. IV, 1880.]

Hall, S. C. Retrospect of a Long Life. Vol. I, 1883.

Maginn, W. A Running Commentary on The Ritter Bann. [In Miscellanies, ed. R. W. Montagu, vol. II, 1885. A savage attack on Campbell.]

Saintsbury, G. Essays in English Literature, 1780–1860. Ser. 2, 1895.

Hadden, J. C. Thomas Campbell. Edinburgh, [1899].

Floryan, J. Polish Rev. I, 1917. [On Campbell's interest in Poland.]

Bierstadt, A. M. Gertrude of Wyoming. JEGP. XX, 1921.

—— Unacknowledged Poems by Thomas Campbell. MLN. XXXVII, 1922.

Turner, A. M. Wordsworth's Influence on Thomas Campbell. PMLA. XXXVIII, 1923.

Shumway, D. B. Thomas Campbell and Germany. [In Schelling Anniversary Papers, New York, 1923.]

Seton, W. Three Letters of Thomas Campbell. Nineteenth Century, XCVII, 1925.

Dixon, W. M. Thomas Campbell. An Oration. Glasgow, 1928.   R. W. K.

THOMAS MOORE (1779–1852)

(1) BIBLIOGRAPHIES

Power, J. A Catalogue of Vocal Music by Thomas Moore and Sir John Stevenson. 1814.

Gibson, A. Thomas Moore and his First Editions. A Lecture. Belfast, 1904.

Muir, P. H. Moore's Irish Melodies. Colophon, no. 15, 1933.

MacManus, M. J. A Bibliographical Hand-List of the First Editions of Thomas Moore. Dublin, 1934. [Rptd from Dublin Mag. VIII, 1933.]

(2) COLLECTED WORKS

The Works; with a Sketch of the Author's Life. 6 vols. Paris, 1819; 7 vols. Paris, 1820.

The Works. 6 vols. New York, 1825.

The Poetical Works. Complete in One Volume. Paris, 1827.

The Poetical Works. Ed. J. W. Lake, 6 vols. Paris, 1827.

The Poetical Works. Collected by Himself. 10 vols. 1840–1; ed. W. M. Rossetti, [1872]; ed. C. Kent, [1879]; rptd 1905; ed. A. D. Godley, 1910; rptd (from 1840–1 edn exactly, with introduction) Boston, 1930; tr. German, Leipzig, 1843 (2nd edn).

(3) SELECTIONS

The Poetical Works. Ed. J. Dorrian, 1888.

The Poetry. Ed. C. L. Falkiner, 1903.

Paradise and the Peri [part of Lalla Rookh]. Ed. K. Grosch, Karlsruhe, 1905.

Lyrics and Satires. Ed. S. O'Faoláin, Dublin, 1929.

(4) INDIVIDUAL PUBLICATIONS

Odes of Anacreon, translated into English Verse, with Notes. 1800; 1802; 1803; 1826 (8th edn); rptd [1869].

The Poetical Works of the Late Thomas Little, Esq. 1801; 1803 (3rd edn); Dublin, 1810; 1813 (11th edn); 1822 (15th edn).

Oh Lady Fair. A Ballad for three Voices. 1802.

A Candid Appeal to Public Confidence. 1803 (anon.).

Sequel to Oh Lady Fair! The Music and Words by Thomas Moore, Esqr. 1804.

Songs and Glees. The Music and Words by Thomas Moore, Esqr. 1804.

A Canadian Boat-Song, arranged for three Voices. 1805.

Epistles, Odes, and other Poems. 1806; 2 vols. 1807; 1814 (4th edn); 1822 (6th edn).

The Works of Sallust; translated into English by the late Arthur Murphy. 1807. [Life of Sallust by Moore.]

A Selection of Irish Melodies, With Symphonies and Accompaniments by Sir John Stevenson. 10 pts and supplement, [1808–34]. [For rpts, variant issues, etc. see P. H. Muir, Colophon, no. 15, 1933.]

Irish Melodies, and a Melologue upon National Music. Dublin, 1820, 1846. [Unauthorised edns of words only.]

Irish Melodies. With an Appendix, Containing the Original Advertisements, and the Prefatory Letter on Music. 1821 (first authorised edn of words only); Philadelphia, 1821; 1822; Brussels, 1822; Jersey, 1823; Paris, 1823; Pisa, [1823]; 1825 (6th edn); 1832 (10th edn); 1846 (illustrated by D. Maclise), 1866, 1873; ed. S. Gwynn, 1908 (Muses' Lib.). Tr. Swedish, Stockholm, 1825, Upsala, 1858; Latin, 1835;

Irish, Dublin, 1842; French, Paris, 1869; Spanish, New York, 1875; Italian, Pisa, 1880, Naples, 1893; German, Güstrow, 1884 (2nd edn).

Corruption and Intolerance. Two Poems, with Notes, addressed to an Englishman by an Irishman. 1808 (anon.); 1809.

The Sceptic: a Philosophical Satire. By the Author of 'Corruption and Intolerance.' 1809 (anon.).

A Letter to the Roman Catholics of Dublin. Dublin, 1810 (*bis*).

M.P.; or, The Blue Stocking: a Comic Opera in three Acts; composed and selected by Thomas Moore, Esqr. 1811. [Words and music.]

M.P.; or, The Blue-Stocking: a Comic Opera in three Acts. 1811. [Libretto only.]

Songs, Duets, Trios, Choruses, &c. in M.P.; or, The Blue-Stocking: a Comic Opera in three Acts. 1811.

A Melologue upon National Music. 1811. [Rptd with Irish Melodies.]

Parody of a Celebrated Letter [from the Prince Regent to the Duke of York]. 1812 (priv. ptd).

Intercepted Letters; or, The Twopenny Post-Bag. To which are added Trifles Reprinted. By Thomas Brown the Younger. 1813 (at least 11 edns); 1818 (16th edn).

Sacred Songs. 2 pts, 1816–24.

Lines on the Death of —— [*i.e.* R. B. Sheridan], from the Morning Chronicle of Monday, August 5, 1816. Ascribed to a Person of the Highest Poetical Talent. 1816 (anon.).

Lalla Rookh; an Oriental Romance. 1817; 1817 (6th edn); New York, 1817, 1818; 1829 (15th edn); 1844 (illustrated by R. Westall); 1861 (illustrated by Sir J. Tenniel). Tr. German, Vienna, 1825; Polish, Warsaw, 1826; Icelandic, Åbo, 1829–30; Dutch, Amsterdam, 1834; Italian, Milan, 1872, 1886; Danish, Copenhagen, 1878; French, Paris, [1888].

National Airs. 6 pts, 1818–27.

The Fudge Family in Paris, edited by Thomas Brown the Younger. 1818 (at least 8 edns). [Provoked several imitations, *e.g.* The Fudge Family in Edinburgh. By Nehemiah Nettlebottom, Edinburgh, 1820.]

Melodies, Songs, and Sacred Songs. 1818; 1849; 1856.

The World at Westminster. By Thomas Brown, the Younger. 2 vols. 1818.

Tom Crib's Memorial to Congress. With a Preface, Notes, and Appendix; by one of the Fancy. 1819 (at least 4 edns).

The Loves of the Angels. A Poem. 1823 (at least 5 edns); Philadelphia, 1823; Paris,

1823. Tr. French, Paris, 1837; Swedish, Upsala, 1864; Italian, Milan, 1886.

Fables for the Holy Alliance; Rhymes on the Road, &c. &c. By Thomas Brown, the Younger. 1823.

Irish Melodies. [No. 9.] 1824.

Memoirs of Captain Rock, the Celebrated Irish Chieftain, with some Account of his Ancestors. Written by himself. 1824 (at least 4 edns).

Memoirs of the Life of the Right Honourable Richard Brinsley Sheridan. 1825 (also issued in 2 vols.); 1827 (5th edn, with new preface).

Evenings in Greece. First [Second] Evening. 1826–32; tr. German, Darmstadt, 1846. [Words and music.]

The Epicurean. A Tale. 1827 (3 edns); Paris, 1828; 1839 (illustrated by J. M. W. Turner; with Alciphron); ed. J. Hannaford, 1900. Tr. French, Paris, 1827, 1865; German, Innsbruck, 1828; Dutch, Deventer, 1829; Spanish, Barcelona, 1832; Italian, Milan, 1836.

A Set of Glees. 1827.

Odes upon Cash, Corn, Catholics, and other Matters, selected from the Columns of The Times Journal. 1828; Philadelphia, 1828; Paris, 1829.

Legendary Ballads. 1828. [Words and music.]

Letters and Journals of Lord Byron; with Notices of his Life. 2 vols. 1830; 1831; 1833; tr. French, Paris, 1830.

The Life and Death of Lord Edward Fitzgerald. 2 vols. 1831; ed. M. MacDermott, 1897.

The Summer Fête. 1831; Paris, 1832. [A poem with songs and music.]

Travels of an Irish Gentleman in Search of a Religion; with Notes and Illustrations. By the Editor of 'Captain Rock's Memoirs.' 2 vols. 1833; ed. J. Burke, 1853.

Vocal Miscellany. 2 nos. 1834–5.

The Fudges in England: being a Sequel to the 'Fudge Family in Paris.' By Thomas Brown, the Younger. 1835 (*bis*); Philadelphia, 1835.

History. Ireland. [In D. Lardner's The Cabinet Cyclopedia, 4 vols. 1835–46; tr. German, Baden Baden, 1846.]

Alciphron: a Poem; with Vignette Illustrations by J. M. W. Turner. 1839.

Prose and Verse, Humorous, Satirical, and Sentimental; with Suppressed Passages from the Memoirs of Lord Byron; with Notes and Introduction by Richard Herne Shepherd. 1878.

[Moore was also a frequent contributor to periodicals, including The Times and Edinburgh Rev.]

(5) WORKS EDITED BY MOORE

The Works of the late Right Honourable Richard Brinsley Sheridan. 2 vols. 1821; Leipzig, 1833; ed. R. G. White, 3 vols. New York, 1883.
The Works of Lord Byron, with his Letters and Journals, and his Life by Thomas Moore. 17 vols. 1832–3. [See, however, under Byron, p. 187 below.]

(6) JOURNALS AND CORRESPONDENCE

Memoirs, Journals, and Correspondence. Ed. Lord J. Russell, 8 vols. 1853–6; abridged by Lord J. Russell, 1860. [See Correspondence between the Rt. Hon. J. W. Croker and the Rt. Hon. Lord John Russell on some Passages of Moore's Diary, 1854.]
The Letters of Thomas Moore. New York, 1854.
Notes from the Letters of Thomas Moore to his Music Publisher, James Power. Ed. T. C. Croker, New York, [1854].
'Thomas Moore' Anecdotes [from the Journals]. Ed. W. Harrison, 1899.
Summer in Bermuda, and Excerpts from Tom Moore's Bermudian Letters to his Mother. Ed. M. A. Bosworth, New York, [1912].
Tom Moore's Diary. A Selection. Ed. J. B. Priestley, Cambridge, 1925.

(7) BIOGRAPHY AND CRITICISM

(a) Books

Burke, J. The Life of Thomas Moore. 1852.
G., H. Notice of the Life of Thomas Moore [from Edinburgh Rev.]. 1854.
Montgomery, H. R. Thomas Moore, his Life, Writings, and Contemporaries. 1860.
Symington, A. J. Thomas Moore, his Life and Works. 1880.
Vallat, G. Étude sur la Vie et les Œuvres de Thomas Moore. Paris, 1886.
—— Thomas Moore et son Œuvre immortelle. Tours, 1895.
Gunning, J. P. Moore: Poet and Patriot. Dublin, 1900.
Gwynn, S. Thomas Moore. 1905; New York, 1924. (English Men of Letters ser.)
Clark, J. C. L. Tom Moore in Bermuda. Boston, 1909 (2nd edn).
Thomas, A. B. Moore en France [1819–30]. Paris, 1911.
Trench, W. F. Tom Moore. A Lecture. Dublin, 1934.
MacCall, S. Thomas Moore. Dublin, 1936.
Jones, H. M. The Harp that Once—a Chronicle of the Life of Thomas Moore. New York, 1937.
Strong, L. A. G. The Minstrel Boy. A Portrait of Tom Moore. 1937.

(b) Essays and Articles

Jeffrey, F., Lord. Edinburgh Rev. VIII, 1806 (Epistles, Odes, and Other Poems); XXIX, 1817 (Lalla Rookh); XLV, 1826 (Memoirs of Sheridan).
Darley, G. The Characteristic of the Present Age of Poetry. London Mag. IX, 1824. [Attacks the poetry of Moore and Byron.]
Hazlitt, W. The Spirit of the Age. 1825; ed. P. P. Howe (Complete Works, vol. XI, 1932).
—— On the Jealousy and the Spleen of Party. [In The Plain Speaker, vol. II, 1826, and ed. P. P. Howe (Complete Works, vol. XII, 1931). On Moore's view of Rousseau.]
Smith, Sydney. Memoirs of Captain Rock. Edinburgh Rev. XLI, 1825. [Rptd in Works, 3rd edn, vol. II, 1845.]
Macaulay, T. B., Baron. Edinburgh Rev. LIII, 1831. [On Moore's Byron. Rptd in Macaulay's Essays, vol. I, 1843.]
Southey, R. Quart. Rev. XLVI, 1832. [On Moore's Life of Fitzgerald.]
Gilfillan, G. Galleries of Literary Portraits. Vol. I, 1856.
Roscoe, W. C. Thomas Moore. [In Poems and Essays, ed. R. H. Hutton, vol. II, 1860.]
Gosse, Sir E. Thomas Moore. [In The English Poets, ed. T. H. Ward, vol. IV, 1880.]
—— Tom Moore in Wiltshire. [In Leaves and Fruit, 1927.]
Mahony, F. S. The Rogueries of Tom Moore. [In Works of Father Prout, ed. C. Kent, 1881; contains trns of 5 lyrics by Moore into Greek, Latin or French, jestingly presented as the 'originals.']
Saintsbury, G. Essays in English Literature, 1780–1860. 1890.
Baldensperger, F. Thomas Moore et Alfred de Vigny. MLR. I, 1906.
Previté-Orton, C. W. Political Satire in English Poetry. Cambridge, 1910. [Ch. vi.]
Hewlett, M. Bessy Moore [the poet's wife]. [In In a Green Shade, 1920.]
Mortimer, R. Thomas Moore. Dial, LXXI, 1921.
Monahan, M. Thomas Moore. Catholic World, vol. CXX, 1924.
Strahan, J. A. Byron's Biographer. Blackwood's Mag. CCXV, 1924.
Stockley, W. F. P. Essays in Irish Biography. Cork, 1933. [Includes 2 essays on Moore, both hostile in tone.]
Brown, W. C. Thomas Moore and English Interest in the East. Stud. Phil. XXXIV, 1937.
Parker, W. M. Moore in Wiltshire. TLS. 16 Oct. 1937.

R. W. K.

GEORGE GORDON BYRON, BARON
BYRON (1788–1824)

(1) BIBLIOGRAPHIES

Gerbel, N. V. O Russkikh Perevodakh iz
Byrona. 5 vols. Leningrad, 1864–7. [At
end of each vol.]
Anderson, J. P. Bibliography. [Appended to
R. Noel, Life of Lord Byron, 1890. Contains
the fullest lists of musical settings and of
magazine articles about Byron.]
Flaïschen, C. Lord Byron in Deutschland.
Centralblatt für Bibliothekswesen, VII,
1890, pp. 455–73.
Koelbing, E. Bibliographische Notizen. [The
Prisoner of Chillon and other Poems,
Weimar, 1898, pp. 55–96. Also contains a
list of volumes of illustrations of Byron's
Works.]
Lumbroso, A. Saggio di Bibliografia By-
roniana. [Il Generale Mengaldo, Lord
Byron, e l' 'Ode on the Star of the Legion
of Honour,' Rome, 1903; rptd in Pagine
Veneziane, Rome, 1905.]
Coleridge, E. H. A Bibliography of the Suc-
cessive Editions and Translations of Lord
Byron's Poetical Works. [The Works of Lord
Byron. Poetry, vol. VII, 1904, pp. 89–348. The
best general bibliography of the poems.]
Estève, E. Byron et le Romantisme français.
Paris, 1907, pp. 525–49.
Churchman, P. H. A Bibliography of Spanish
Translations of Byron. Revue Hispanique,
Dec. 1910.
Morvay, G. Byron Magyarországon. [In E.
Koeppel, Byron forditótta Esty Jánosné,
Budapest, 1913.]
Intze, O. Byroniana. [Birmingham, 1914.]
Griffith, R. H. and Jones, H. M. A Descriptive
Catalogue of an Exhibition of Manuscripts
and First Editions of Lord Byron. Austin
(Texas), 1924.
Chew, S. C. Byron in England. New York,
1924, pp. 353–407. [The fullest list of
Byroniana.]
Bibliographical Catalogue of First Editions,
Proof Copies, and Manuscripts of Books by
Lord Byron exhibited at the Fourth
Exhibition of the First Edition Club. 1925.
Wise, T. J. A Byron Library. 1928 (priv. ptd).
—— A Bibliography of the Writings in Verse
and Prose of Lord Byron. 2 vols. 1932–3
(priv. ptd). [The fullest discussion of the
issues of the first edns. See John Carter,
TLS. 27 April, 4 May 1933.]
Elkin Mathews Ltd. Byron and Byroniana.
A Catalogue of Books. 1930.
Nottingham Corporation. The Roe-Byron Col-
lection,Newstead Abbey. Nottingham,1937.
Pollard, G. Pirated Collections of Byron.
TLS. 16 Oct. 1937.

(2) COLLECTED EDITIONS

(a) Collected Works in English

The Poetical Works of Lord Byron. 2 vols.
Philadelphia, 1813; 2 vols. Boston, 1814;
3 vols. New York, 1815; 3 vols. Philadelphia,
1815; 2 vols. 1815; 4 vols. 1815 (bis); 3 vols.
Philadelphia, 1816; 5 vols. 1817; New York,
1817; Philadelphia, 1817; 6 vols. 1818;
vol. VII, 1819; vol. VIII, 1820; 6 vols. Paris,
1818; 6 vols. Zwickau, 1818–9; 13 vols.
Leipzig, 1818–22; 3 vols. 1819; 6 vols. Paris,
1819; 7 vols. Brussels, 1819; 4 vols. New
York, 1820; 5 vols. 1821; 5 vols. Paris,
1821; 16 vols. Paris, 1822–4 (with Life by
J. W. Lake); 4 vols. 1823; 12 vols. Paris,
1823; 12 vols. Paris, 1823–4 (with Life by
Sir Cosmo Gordon); 8 vols. Philadelphia,
1824; vols. V, VI, VII, 1824; 30 vols. Zwickau,
1824–5; 6 vols. 1825; 7 vols. Paris, 1825
(with Life by J. W. Lake); 8 vols. New York,
1825; 8 vols. Philadelphia, 1825; 33 vols.
Zwickau, 1825–38; 12 vols. Paris, 1826;
Paris, 1826 (with Life by J. W. Lake);
Frankfort, 1826; 6 vols. 1827; Paris, 1827
(with Life by J. W. Lake); 4 vols. 1828;
Paris, 1828 (with Life by J. W. Lake);
Frankfort, 1828; 6 vols. 1829; 4 vols.
1829; 2 vols. Philadelphia, 1829 (bis); Philadelphia, 1829; Frankfort, 1829; 4 vols.
1830; Paris, 1830; 6 vols. 1831 (bis);
Paris, 1831 (with abridged Life by J. W.
Lake); Philadelphia, 1831 (with Life by
J. W. Lake); 4 vols. Paris, 1832; The Works
of Lord Byron, with his Letters and
Journals, and his Life by Thomas Moore
[ed. John Wright], 17 vols. 1832–3 (the
earlier vols. several times rptd); New York,
1833 (with Life by FitzGreene Halleck);
Paris, 1835 (with Life by Henry Lytton
Bulwer); Paris, 1835 (with Life by John
Galt); 4 vols. Paris, 1835; 6 vols. New York,
1836–7 (with Life by T. Moore); 1837 (bis);
Frankfort, 1837; Paris, 1837 (with Life
by John Galt); Paris, 1837 (bis); 7 vols.
Mannheim, 1837; 1838; Paris, 1839;
Philadelphia, 1839; 8 vols. 1839; 4 vols.
Paris, 1840; Paris, 1841; 5 vols. Leipzig,
1842; 4 vols. Philadelphia, 1843 (with Life
by T. Moore); 1845; Frankfort, 1846; Paris,
1847; Hartford, 1847 (with Life by Fitz-
Greene Halleck); 1848; 2 vols. Edinburgh,
[1850] (with Life by William Anderson);
1850; Philadelphia, 1850; 1851 (with
Life by Henry Lytton Bulwer); Philadelphia, 1851; Frankfort, 1852 (with Life
by T. Moore); 2 vols. Philadelphia, 1853;
[1854] (with Life by Allan Cunningham);
Philadelphia, 1854; Boston, 1854; The
Illustrated Byron, [issued in parts 1854–5];
6 vols. 1855–6; Edinburgh, [1857] (with

'Objectionable Pieces' excluded); New York, 1857; 1857; 6 vols. 1857; 1859; Edinburgh, [1859]; Philadelphia, 1859; Leipzig, 1860; 3 vols. Leipzig, 1860; Edinburgh, 1861 (with Life by Alexander Leighton); 10 vols. Boston, 1861 (with Life by J. H. Lister); Halifax, 1863; Halifax, 1865 (*bis*); 1866; 1867; Edinburgh, [1868] (with Life by A. Leighton); 1868; 1869 (*bis*); Philadelphia, 1869; New York, 1869; 8 vols. 1870; [ed. W. M. Rossetti], 1870; Philadelphia, 1870; [ed. W. M. Rossetti], [1872]; 1873; [ed. W. B. Scott], [1874]; [1874]; Boston, 1874; 1876; [1878]; Boston, 1878; [ed. W. M. Rossetti], [1878]; [ed. W. M. Rossetti and T. Seccombe], [1880]; 3 vols. Leipzig, 1880; [1881]; Edinburgh, [1881] (with Life by A. Leighton); [ed. W. M. Rossetti and T. Seccombe], [1882]; [ed. W. B. Scott], 1883; 1883; 3 vols. 1883; 12 vols. 1885; New York [*c*. 1886]; [ed. Mathilde Blind], 1886 (*bis*); 1887; 2 vols. 1888; 1890; New York, [1890]; 12 vols. 1891–2; 3 vols. 1892; 12 vols. Philadelphia, 1892; Philadelphia, 1895; 4 vols. 1896; [1897] (*bis*); Edinburgh, 1897; 4 vols. Philadelphia, 1897; 13 vols. 1898–1904 (A New Revised and Enlarged Edition. Poetry, 7 vols. ed. Ernest Hartley Coleridge. Letters and Journals, 6 vols. ed. R. E. Prothero); 1904 (Poetical Works); [ed. E. H. Coleridge], 1905; [ed. P. E. More], New York, [1905]; 3 vols. 1906; [ed. W. P. Trent], [1910]; [ed. W. M. Rossetti and T. Seccombe], [1911]; [ed. N. H. Dole], New York, 1927.

(b) Translations of Collected Works

French. By 'A. E. de Chastopalli' (Amédée Pichot and Eusèbe de Salle), 10 vols. Paris, 1819–21; 5 vols. Paris, 1820–2; 15 vols. Paris, 1821–4; 8 vols. Paris, 1822–5; (Œuvres Nouvelles) 10 vols. Paris, 1824; 13 vols. Paris, 1823–4; 20 vols. Paris, 1827–31 (6th edn); 6 vols. Paris, 1830; 6 vols. Paris, 1830–5; 6 vols. Paris, 1836; Paris, 1837; Paris, 1842 (11th edn). By Paulin Paris, 3 vols. Paris, 1827; 13 vols. Paris, 1830–2; 13 vols. Paris, 1835. By Benjamin Laroche, 4 vols. Paris, 1836–7; Paris, 1837; Paris, 1838; 4 vols. Paris, 1840–1; Paris, 1842; 4 vols. Paris, 1847; 4 vols. Paris, 1850–1. By Orby Hunter and Pascal Ramé, 2 vols. Paris, 1841–2; 3 vols. Paris, 1845. By Louis Barré, Paris, 1856. By 'Daniel le Sueur' (Jeanne Loiseau), 2 vols. Paris, 1891–2.

German. By Julius Koerner, Wilhelm Reinhold, Heinrich Doering, August Schumann, Christian Karl Meissner, 31 vols. Zwickau, 1821–8. By G. N. Baermann, O. L. B. Wolff, K. L. Kannegiesser, A. Hungari, P. von Haugwitz, P. A. G. von Meyer, J. V. Adrian, 12 vols. Frankfort, 1830–1; 12 vols. Frankfort, 1837. By Gustav Pfizer, 4 vols. Stuttgart, 1836–9; Stuttgart, 1851. By E. Ortlepp, F. Kottenkamp, H. Kurtz, — Duttenhofer, — Bardili, Bernhard von Guseck, 10 vols. Stuttgart, 1839; 10 vols. Pforzheim, 1842; 10 vols. Stuttgart, 1845; 10 vols. Stuttgart, 1846; 12 vols. Stuttgart, 1856. By Adolf Boettger, Leipzig, 1840; 1841; 12 vols. 1842; 1844; 1845; 12 vols. 1847; 12 vols. 1850; 12 vols. 1852; 8 vols. 1854; 12 .vols. 1856; 12 vols. 1860; 12 vols. 1861; 8 vols. 1863; 8 vols. 1864; 8 vols. 1901. (All pbd Leipzig.) Ed. O. Gildemeister, 6 vols. Berlin, 1864; 6 vols. Berlin, 1866; 6 vols. Berlin, 1877; 6 vols. Berlin, 1888. By Alexander Neidhardt, 8 vols. Berlin, 1865. By Wilhelm Schaeffer, A. H. Janert, W. Gruezmacher, Heinrich Stadelmann, Adolf Strodtmann, 7 vols. Hildeburghausen, 1865–72. By Adolf Seubert, 3 vols. Leipzig, [1874]. By Adalbert Schroeter, 6 vols. Stuttgart, 1885–90. By Henry T. Tuckermann, 8 vols. Stuttgart, 1886.

Modern Greek. 3 vols. Athens, 1895 (anon.).

Italian. By Carlo Rusconi, 2 vols. Padua, 1842. By Giuseppe Gazzino, Giuseppe Nicolini, Pietro Isola, Pellegrino Rossi, Andrea Maffei, Marcello Mazzoni, P. G. B. Cereseto, Naples, 1853. By G. de Stefano, Naples, 1857. Naples, 1886 (anon.); rptd Naples, 1891.

Polish. By B. M. Wolff, Leningrad, 1857 (vol. I only, containing Childe Harold). By Piotr Chmielowski, Warsaw, 1895.

Russian. By N. V. Gerbel, M. Y. Lermontov, A. Pushkin, V. Jukovsky, K. Batinshkov, D. Minaev, I. Turgenev, L. Meya, P. Kozlov, I. Kozlov, N. Zorin and others, 5 vols. Leningrad, 1864–6; 4 vols. Leningrad, 1874–7; 3 vols. Leningrad, 1883–4. By P. I. Veinberg, Leningrad, 1876. By S. A. Vengerov (editor), V. Mazurkevitch, P. S. Kogan, S. A. Ilyin, A. M. Fedorov and others, 2 vols. Leningrad, 1904–5.

Spanish. Madrid, 1880 (anon.); rptd Madrid, 1898. By Francisco Gallach Palés, 5 vols. Madrid, 1930–1.

Swedish. By 'Talis Qualis' (C. W. A. Strandberg), 8 vols. Stockholm, 1854–6.

(3) PARTIAL COLLECTIONS
(a) Tales and Dramas

Tales. 2 vols. 1837; Halifax, 1845; 1853; Leipzig, 1857; [1859] (as Eastern Tales).

The Corsair, Lara. Paris, 1830; ed. M. F. Sweetzer, Boston, 1893. The Giaour, The Bride of Abydos. 1844; 1848. Beppo, Don Juan. 2 vols. 1853.

The Prisoner of Chillon, The Siege of Corinth. Ed. J. G. C. Schuler, Halle, 1886. The Prisoner of Chillon, Mazeppa, The Lament of Tasso. Oxford, [1929]. Dramas. Paris, 1832; 2 vols. 1837; 2 vols. 1853.

(b) Miscellaneous Collections

Three Poems not included in the Works of Lord Byron [Lines to Lady J[ersey], The Curse of Minerva, and The Enigma (by Catherine Maria Fanshawe)]. 1818. Suppressed Poems [English Bards, Ode to the Land of the Gaul, A Sketch, Windsor Poetics]. Paris, 1818 (2nd edn). The Works of Lord Byron [English Bards, The Curse of Minerva, Waltz, etc.]. 'Philadelphia,' 1820. The Miscellaneous Works [Werner, Heaven and Earth, Morgante Maggiore, The Age of Bronze, The Island, The Vision of Judgement, The Deformed Transformed]. 2 vols. 1824; 1830. Poems [Don Juan, Hours of Idleness, English Bards, Poems on his Domestic Circumstances]. 1825. Don Juan, complete, English Bards, Hours of Idleness, The Waltz, and all the other minor Poems. 1826; 1827; 2 vols. 1828; 2 vols. 1829. The Miscellaneous Poems [Hours of Idleness, English Bards, The Curse of Minerva, etc.]. 1829. Miscellanies. 3 vols. 1837; 2 vols. 1853.

(c) Translations of Partial Collections

Czech. (Corsair, Lara) by Čeněk Ibl, Prague, 1885.
Danish. (Dramas and Tales) by Edvard Lembcke, 2 vols. Copenhagen, 1873. (Manfred, The Prisoner of Chillon, Mazeppa) by Alfred Ipsen, Copenhagen, [1889?]. (Beppo, The Vision of Judgement) by Alfred Ipsen, Copenhagen, 1891.
Dutch. (Mazeppa, Parisina) by Nicholaas Beets (in his Gedichten), Haarlem, 1837; rptd Haarlem, 1848. (Poems) by J. J. L. Ten Kate, Leiden, [c. 1870].
French. (Childe Harold, Cantos III, IV, Prisoner of Chillon, The Corsair, Lara, The Giaour, The Lament of Tasso, The Siege of Corinth), Bibliothèque Universelle (Geneva), v–ix, May 1817–Dec.. 1818. (The Corsair, Mazeppa) by Lucien Méchin, Paris, 1848. (Manfred, Lara) by Hya du Pontavice de Henssey, Paris, 1856. (The Prisoner of Chillon, Lara, Parisina, Poems) by H. Gomont, Nancy, 1862. (The Corsair, Lara, The Siege of Corinth) by Paul Lorencin, Paris, 1868. (The Two Foscari, Beppo) by Achille Morisseau, Paris, 1881. (The Corsair, Lara), Paris, 1892.

German. (Tales) by J. V. Adrian, Frankfort, 1820. (The Prisoner of Chillon, Parisina) by Paul Graf von Haugwitz, Breslau, 1821. (Manfred, The Dream, etc.) by E. Koeppe, Berlin, 1835. (The Bride of Abydos, Mazeppa) by W. Gerhard, Leipzig, 1840. (The Giaour, Hebrew Melodies) by Friederike Friedmann, Leipzig, 1854. (Cain, Mazeppa) by Friederike Friedmann, Leipzig, 1855. (Manfred, The Prisoner of Chillon, Hebrew Melodies, etc.) by A. R. Nielo, Münster, 1857. (The Giaour, The Prisoner of Chillon), Dusseldorf, 1859 (anon.). (Mazeppa, The Corsair, Beppo) by Wilhelm Schaeffer, Leipzig, 1864. (Manfred, Cain, Heaven and Earth, Sardanapalus) by W. Gruezmacher, Hildburghausen, 1870. (The Bride of Abydos, The Dream) by Otto Riedel, Hamburg, 1872. (The Prisoner of Chillon, Mazeppa), Leipzig, [c. 1875]. (The Prisoner of Chillon, Parisina) by Otto Michaeli, Halle, 1890. (Tales) by A. Neidhardt, Halle, [1903].
Hungarian. (Mazeppa, The Dream, Poems) by Lázár Horváth, Budapest, 1842.
Icelandic. (The Prisoner of Chillon, etc.) by Steingrímur Thorsteinson. Copenhagen, 1866.
Italian. (The Prisoner of Chillon, Parisina, The Siege of Corinth, Lara) by Pietro Isola, Turin, 1827; (The Corsair, The Giaour) by Pietro Isola, Milan, 1830; (rptd together), 2 vols. Lugano, 1832. (The Bride of Abydos, Parisina, The Corsair, Lara) by Giuseppe Nicolini, Milan, 1834; rptd 2 vols. Milan, 1837; rptd, 2 vols. Milan, 1842. (Poems) by Giuseppe Zappala' Finocchiaro, Palermo, 1837. (Poems) by Marcello Mazzoni, Milan, 1838. (Dramas) by P. de Virgilii, Brussels, 1841. (Marino Faliero, The Two Foscari) by P. G. B. Cereseto, Savona, 1845. (Sardanapalus, Marino Faliero, The Two Foscari) by Andrea Maffei, Florence, 1862; (Cain, Parisina, etc.) by Andrea Maffei, Milan, 1886; (Mysteries, Tales, Poems) by Andrea Maffei, Florence, 1890. (Tales and Poems) Milan, 1882 (anon.). (Childe Harold, Parisina, Beppo, The Bride of Abydos) by Giacinto Casella (in his Opere Edite e Postume, vol. i), Florence, 1884. (Parisina, The Prisoner of Chillon) by Aldo Ricci, Florence, [1924].
Polish. (The Siege of Corinth, The Corsair) by B[runo hr] K[iciński] in Poemata i powieści, vol. i, Warsaw, 1820. (Mazeppa) by H. Dembiński (The Giaour, Parisina, etc.) by Wandy Maleckiéj, Warsaw, 1828; rptd, Warsaw, 1831. (Parisina, Calmar i Orla) by I. Szydlowski, Vilna, 1834. (The Giaour) by Adam Mickiewicz, (The Corsair) by A. E. Odyniec, Paris, 1835; rptd Wroclaw, 1839. (The Bride of Abydos) by A. E. Odyniec in Tlómaczenia, vol. ii, Leipzig, 1838; (The

Corsair, Heaven and Earth) by A. E. Odyniec
in Tlómaczenia, vol. III, Leipzig, 1841;
(Mazeppa) by A. E. Odyniec, in Tlómaczenia,
vol. v, Vilna, 1843. (The Lament of Tasso,
Werner, The Bride of Abydos, The Island)
by A. Zawadzki, Warsaw, 1846. (Manfred,
Mazeppa, The Siege of Corinth, Parisina, The
Prisoner of Chillon) by F. D. Morawski,
Leszno, 1853. (Parisina, Lara, Cain, Poems,
etc.) by Karol Kruzer (in his Przeklady i rymy
wlasne, vols. III and IV), Warsaw, 1876.

Portuguese. (Childe Harold, Sardanapalus)
by Francisco José Pinheiro Guimarães (in
Traduccões Poeticas), Rio de Janeiro, 1863.

Roumanian. (The Prisoner of Chillon,
Beppo, The Lament of Tasso) by T. Eliad,
Bucharest, 1834.

Russian. (Dramas) by I. A. Bunin and
N. A. Bryansky, Leningrad, 1922.

Spanish. (Ode to Napoleon, Napoleon's
Farewell, etc.) Paris, 1830 (anon.). (Lara,
The Siege of Corinth, Parisina, Childe Harold,
Mazeppa, The Lament of Tasso, Beppo) by
Ricardo Canales, Barcelona, [c. 1876]. (Parisina, The Prisoner of Chillon, The Lament of
Tasso, The Bride of Abydos) by Antonio
Sellen, New York, 1877. (Don Juan, The
Lament of Tasso) by J. A. R., Barcelona,
1883. (Dramas) by José Alcala Galiano,
Madrid, 1886.

(4) SELECTIONS

(a) *In English*

The Beauties of Byron. Ed. Thomas Parry,
1823; 1827.
Life and Select Poems. Ed. C. Hulbert,
Shrewsbury, [1828].
Beauties of Byron. Ed. B. F. French,
Philadelphia, 1828.
The Beauties of Byron. Ed. Alfred Howard,
[1829].
The Beauties of Byron. Ed. J. W. Lake,
Paris, 1829.
Select Works of Lord Byron. 6 vols. Frankfort, 1831–4.
Select Works. 1833.
Select Poetical Works, Paris, 1835; rptd Paris,
1836.
Lord Byron's Select Works. Berlin, 1837.
Select Works. 1837.
The Beauties of Byron. Ed. Alfred Howard,
1837.
The Beauties of Byron and Burns. Hull,
1837.
Byron's Select Works. Paris, 1843.
A Selection from Byron's Poetical Works.
Ed. Charles Graeser, Marienwerder, 1846.
Select Poetical Works. 1848.
Lord Byron's Select Works. Ed. F. Breier,
Oldenburg, 1848.

Selections from the Writings of Lord Byron
by a clergyman [Whitwell Elwin]. 1854.
Poems. 1855.
Poems. [1859.]
The Choice Works. Halifax, 1864.
A Selection from the Works of Lord Byron.
Ed. A. C. Swinburne, 1866.
Songs. 1872.
Selections. [Ed. W. Elwin], 1874.
Beautés de Byron. Ed. A. Biard, Paris,
1876.
Favourite Poems by Lord Byron. Boston,
1877.
The Byron Birthday Book. Ed. J. Burrows,
1879.
Poems. [1880.]
The Beauties of Byron. Stuttgart, [c. 1880].
The Poetry of Byron, chosen and arranged by
Matthew Arnold. 1881.
Selections. Ed. A. C. Swinburne, [1885].
Gems from Byron. Ed. H. R. Haweis, 1886.
Poems carefully selected. 2 vols. [1886].
Shorter Poems by Burns, Byron and Campbell. Ed. W. Murrison, 1893; rptd 1895.
Selections from Wordsworth, Byron, Shelley.
Ed. Adele Ellis, 1896.
Selections. Ed. F. I. Carpenter, New York,
1900; rptd 1908.
Poems selected by C. Linklater Thomson.
1901.
Poems. Ed. Arthur Symons, [1904].
Songs. 1904.
Selected Poetry. Ed. J. W. Duff, 1904.
Love Poems of Byron. 1905.
With Byron in Italy, a Selection of the Poems
and Letters. Ed. Anna B. McMahon,
Chicago, 1906.
Poems selected by Charles Whibley. [1907.]
Byron's Shorter Poems. Ed. Ralph Hartt
Bowles, 1907.
Selections from Byron. Ed. S. M. Tucker,
[1907].
Love Poems of Byron. 1911.
Selected Poems. 1913.
Selections. 1913.
Selected Poems. [Ed. William Robertson,
1913.]
Selections. Ed. A. Hamilton Thompson,
Cambridge, 1920.
Poems. Ed. Sir H. J. C. Grierson, 1923.
Selections. Ed. M. F. Dee, [1926].
With Byron in Love. Ed. Walter Littlefield,
New York, [1926].
An Introduction to Byron. Ed. Guy N.
Pocock, [1927].
Poems. Ed. Arthur Symons, [1927].
Selections. Ed. W. Roy Macklin, 1927.
Selections. [1927.]
The Shorter Poems. Ed. Ernest Rhys, 1927;
[1928].
Selections. Ed. Hamish Miles, 1930.

Selections. Ed. D. M. Walmsley, 1931.
Selections. Ed. John Bullocke, [1931].
Lyrical Poems. Ed. E. du Perron, Maastricht, 1933.
The Best of Byron. Ed. R. A. Rice, New York, 1933.
Byron, Satirical and Critical Poems. Ed. J. Bennett, Cambridge, 1937.

(b) Selections in Translation

Armenian.
Beauties of English Poets. Venice, 1852.
Lord Byron's Armenian Exercises and Poetry. Venice, 1870; Venice, 1886.

French.
Choix de Poésies de Byron, de W. Scott, et de Th. Moore. 2 vols. Geneva, 1820.
Beautés de Lord Byron. Tr. Charles Édouard de Léonville, Paris, 1825.
Les Beautés de Lord Byron. Tr. Amédée Pichot, Paris, 1838.
Écrin Poétique de Littérature Anglaise. Tr. D. Bonnefin, Paris, 1841.
Chefs d'Œuvre de lord Byron. Tr. Comte de Hautefeuille, Paris, 1847.
Rough Hewing of Lord Byron in French by Francis D'Autrey. 1869.
Chefs d'Œuvre de lord Byron. Tr. A. Regnault, 2 vols. Paris, 1874.

German.
Byrons Lieder. [Ed. A. Friederick], Carlsruhe, 1820.
Kleine Gedichte von Byron und Moore. [Ed. C. von K.], Berlin, 1829.
Lord Byrons Ausgewaehlte Dichtungen. Leipzig, 1838.
Dichtungen von Lord Byron. Ed. A. Rolein, Crefeld, 1841.
Schoenheiten aus Byrons Werken. Ed. Adolf Boettger, Leipzig, 1841.
Byron-Anthologie. Ed. Eduard Hobein, Schwerin, 1866.
Lord Byrons Lyrische Gedichte. Ed. H. Stadelmann, Hildburghausen, 1872.
Auswahl aus Byron. Ed. J. Hengesbach, [n.p.], 1892.

Italian.
A Miei Amici [by Pietro Isola]. [Novi, c. 1870.]

Russian.
Vuibor iz Sochineny. Ed. M. Kachenovsky, Moscow, 1821.

Spanish.
[Selections by various translators.] Barcelona, [1922].

(5) SEPARATE WORKS

[In this and the following section the word 'proof' is used to indicate that the work is known to have been put in type, whether a copy is now extant or not. The word 'counter-feit' is used to indicate editions indistinguish-able by normal methods of bibliographical description. Of Byron's earlier works many such were produced for commercial purposes before 1820.]

Fugitive Pieces. [Newark, 1806] (anon.; priv. ptd); ed. facs. H. Buxton Forman, 1886; ed. facs. M. Kessel, New York, 1933.
    Roe, Herbert C. The Rare Quarto Edition of Lord Byron's Fugitive Pieces de-scribed, with a Note on the Pigot Family. Nottingham, 1919 (priv. ptd).

Poems on Various Occasions. Newark, 1807 (anon.; priv. ptd). [Contains 50 pieces of which 12 are new.]

Hours of Idleness, A Series of Poems, Original and Translated. Newark, 1807 (1 counterfeit of larger size—see Athenaeum, 28 May 1898; T. M. B[lagg], Newark as a Publishing Town, Newark, 1898, pp. 20–35; T. J. Wise, Bibliography, I, pp. 9–10); 1822; Glasgow, 1825. [Contains 39 pieces of which 12 are new. Reviewed: Critical Rev. Sept. 1807 (by Henry Higgs Hunt); The Satirist, Oct. 1807; Edinburgh Rev. Jan. 1808 (by Henry Brougham; separately rptd 1820 (*bis*)); New Monthly Mag. Feb. 1819.]

Poems Original and Translated. Second Edition. Newark, 1808. [Contains 39 pieces of which 5 are new. 1 counterfeit (see Texas Exhibition, 1924, pp. 93–7). Rptd as Hours of Idleness, Paris, 1819; 1820 (4 edns); Paris, 1820; Paris, 1822.]

The British Bards. [Newark, 1808] (proof BM.). [Largely incorporated in the next entry.]

English Bards and Scotch Reviewers, A Satire. [1809] (2 variants; 3 counterfeits); 2nd edn ('with Considerable Additions and Alterations'), 1809; 3rd edn, 1810 (8 counter-feits); Philadelphia, 1811; 4th edn, 1810 (1 counterfeit); 4th edn, 1811 (6 counter-feits); Boston, 1814; ed. John Murray, Roxburghe Club, 1936 (facsimile of a copy with Byron's MS notes); 5th edn, ('with Additions'), 1816; New York, 1817; Paris, 1818; Paris, 1819; Brussels, 1819; Geneva, 1820; 1821; Paris, 1821; 1823 (*bis*); Glasgow, 1824; Glasgow, 1825; 1825; 1826; 1827 (*bis*); [c. 1830]; Halifax, 1834. Tr. French by — Raoul (as Les Poètes Anglais et les Auteurs de l'Edinburgh Review), Ghent, 1821.
    Koenig, Carl. Byrons 'English Bards and Scotch Reviewers' Entstehung und Be-ziehungen zur zeitgenoessischen Satire und Kritik. Berlin, [1914].

Hints from Horace. 1811 (proof BM.). [Extracts were pbd by R. C. Dallas in 1824 and by T. Moore in 1830; the full text was first pbd in the 6 vol. edn of Works, 1831, vol. v, pp. 273–327.]

Childe Harold's Pilgrimage, A Romaunt [Cantos I, II]. 1812 (5 edns); Philadelphia, 1812; 6th edn, 1813; 7th, 8th edns, 1814; 10th edn, 1815; 3rd American edn, Philadelphia, 1816; 11th edn, 1819.
Childe Harold's Pilgrimage, Canto the Third. 1816 (3 issues); Boston, 1817; Philadelphia, 1817.
Childe Harold's Pilgrimage, Canto the Fourth. 1818 (7 states. See W. H. McCarthy, The Printing of Canto IV of Childe Harold, Yale University Library Gazette, Jan. 1927); New York, 1818 (bis); Philadelphia, 1818 (with other poems).
Childe Harold's Pilgrimage. [Cantos I–IV.] 2 vols. 1819; 2 vols. Leipzig, 1820; 1825; 2 vols. Paris, 1825; 1826; 1827; Paris, 1827; 2 vols. Brussels, 1829; [c. 1831]; Nuremberg, [1831]; New York, 1836; 1837; Mannheim, 1837; 1839; 1841; 1842; ed. A. Mommsen, Hamburg, 1853, Berlin, 1885; 1853; ed. F. Brockerhoff, Berlin, 1854; 1859; 1860 (bis); Leipzig, 1862; ed. W. Spalding, [1866]; ed. P. Weeg, Münster, 1867; 1869; ed. W. Hiley, 1877; ed. J. Darmesteter, Paris, 1882; ed. A. Julien, Paris, 1883; ed. H. F. Tozer, Oxford, 1885, 1907; ed. W. J. Rolfe, Philadelphia, 1886; ed. M. Krummacher, Bielefeld, 1886, 1891, 1893; ed. H. G. Keene, 1893; ed. E. Chasles, Paris, 1893; ed. E. C. E. Owen, [1897]; ed. E. E. Morris, 2 vols. 1899; ed. A. J. George, New York, 1900; ed. H. Bennett, 1905; ed. A. Hamilton Thompson, Cambridge, 1913; ed. David Frew, 1918.

Selections: Glasgow, [1882]; ed. T. Morrison, [1882]; ed. E. D. A. Morshead, 1893, 1894, [1900]; ed. J. Downie, [1901]; ed. J. H. Fowler, 1906; ed. H. F. Tozer, Oxford, 1907; ed. J. C. Scrimgeour, Calcutta, 1914; ed. B. J. Hayes, [1932]; ed. G. A. Sheldon, 1933.

Tr. Armenian by Gheuond Alíshanian (Canto IV only), Venice, 1860, 1872. Czech by Eliška Krásnohorská [i.e. Jindřiška Pechová], Prague, 1890. Danish by Adolf Hansen, Copenhagen. 1880. French, [by Pauthier de Censay], Paris, 1828; by P. A. Deguer, Paris, 1828; by F. Ragon, Paris, 1833; by Eugène Quiertant (Canto I only), Paris, 1852; by Eugène Quiertant (Cantos I–IV), Paris, 1861; by Lucien Davésiès de Pontès, 2 vols. Paris, 1862; 1870; by V. R. Jones, St Quentin, 1862; by M. Ph. Alard, Dunkirk, 1869; by H. Bellet, Paris, 1881; by A. Julien, Paris, 1883; by M. A. Elwall, Paris, 1892; by D. Gibb, Paris, 1892. German by K. Baldamus, 3 vols. Leipzig, 1835; by J. C. von Zedlitz, Stuttgart, 1836; by Hermann von Pommer Esche, Stralsund, 1839; by C. D. (Canto I

only), Ansbach, 1845; by Adolf Boettger, Leipzig, 1846; by Alexander Buechner, Frankfort, 1853, 1855; by Erich von Monbart, Cologne, 1865; by A. H. Janert, Hildburghausen, 1868; by F. Schmidt, Berlin, 1869; by Adolf Seubert, 2 vols. Leipzig, 1871–6; by F. Dobbert, [Leipzig?], 1893. Hungarian by Johanna Bickersteth, Geneva, 1857. Italian by Michele Leoni (Canto IV only), [n.p.], 1819; by Giuseppe Gazzino, Genoa, 1836; by Melchior Missirini (Canto IV only), Milan, 1848; by F. Armenico, Naples, 1858; by Giovanni Giovio (Cantos I, II only), Milan, 1866; by Pietro Isola (Canto IV only), Novi, 1870; by Andrea Maffei (Canto IV only), Florence, 1872, 1874, 1897; by Carlo Faccioli, Florence, 1873; by Aldo Ricci, 3 vols. Florence, [1924–8]. Latin (part only, verse) by N. J. Brennan, Dublin, 1894. Polish by M. B. Wolff, Leningrad, 1857; by Wiktor z Baworow, Lwow, 1857; by Frederyk Krauze, [n.p.], 1865–71; by Jan Kasprowicz, Warsaw, 1895; by A. A. K[rajewski], Cracow, 1896. Russian by D. Minaev, Rosskoi Slovo, Leningrad, Jan., March, May, Oct. 1864; by A. Kozlov, Rosskaya Mysl, Moscow, Jan., Feb., Nov. 1890. Spanish, 4 vols. Paris, 1829 (anon.); (Canto I only) by Antonio Ledesma, Almeria, 1884. Swedish by A. F. Skjoldebrand, Stockholm, 1832.

[Reviewed: Edinburgh Rev. Feb. 1812 (by Francis Jeffrey); Quarterly Rev. March 1812 (by George Ellis); O Investigador Portuguez em Inglaterra, 6 April 1812; Quarterly Rev. Oct. 1816 (by Sir Walter Scott); Edinburgh Rev. Dec. 1816 (by Francis Jeffrey); Quarterly Rev. April 1818 (by Sir Walter Scott); Yellow Dwarf, 2 May 1818 (by William Hazlitt); Edinburgh Rev. June 1818 (by John Wilson).]
[Penn, Granville.] Lines to Harold. Stoke Park, Bucks. [1812] (priv. ptd); rptd Original Lines and Translations, 1815; rptd (as Address to Lord Byron on the Publication of Childe Harold) The Poetical Album, ser. 2, 1829.
Hobhouse, John Cam. Historical Illustrations of the Fourth Canto of Childe Harold. 1818 (bis); New York, 1818.
[Hodgson, Francis.] Childe Harold's Monitor; or, Lines occasioned by the last Canto of Childe Harold. 1818.
Koelbing, E. Zur Textueberlieferung von Byron's Childe Harold, Cantos I, II. Leipzig, 1896.
Moll, O. E. E. Der Stil von Byron's 'Childe Harold's Pilgrimage.' Berlin, 1911.

Maier, H. Entstehungsgeschichte von Byron's 'Childe Harold's Pilgrimage,' Cantos I, II. Berlin, 1911.

Dalgado, D. G. Childe Harold's Pilgrimage to Portugal critically examined. Lisbon, 1919.

Murray, John. Two Passages in Childe Harold, Canto IV. TLS. 25 Aug. 1921.

Lewis, Robert T. A Commentary and Questionnaire on Childe Harold, Cantos III, IV. 1927.

[Gillies, R. P.] Childe Alarique. A Poet's Reverie, and other Poems. 1813; Edinburgh, 1814.

The Baron of Falconberg; or, Childe Harold in prose by Mrs Bridget Bluemantle. 3 vols. 1815.

The Last Canto of Childe Harold's Pilgrimage, with Notes Not by Lord Byron. 1818.

The Soul's Pilgrimage: A Poem, written in reference to the sentiments of the Noble Author of Childe Harold's Pilgrimage. Cambridge, 1818.

Prodigious!!! or Childe Paddie in London. 3 vols. 1818.

Childe Albert, or the Misanthrope. Edinburgh, 1819.

Harold the Exile. [1819.]

Childe Harold in the Shades. An Infernal Romaunt. 1819.

[Deacon, W. F.] The Childe's Pilgrimage by Lord B. [In Warreniana, 1824.]

Bedford, J. H. Wanderings of Childe Harold. 3 vols. 1825.

Lamartine, Alphonse de. Le Dernier Chant du Pèlerinage d'Harold. Paris, 1825 (4 edns). Tr. Eng. by J. W. Lake, Paris, 1826. Another trn, 1827. Another, Dublin, 1848.

Verfèle, D. J. C. Les Pèlerinages d'un Childe Harold Parisien. Paris, 1825.

Carry, Aristide. Childe Harold aux Ruines de Rome. Paris, 1826.

The Pilgrimage of Ormonde; or, Childe Harold in the New World. Charleston, 1831.

Driver, H. A. Harold de Burun. 1835.

B., J. The Childe Harold and the Excursion. [1842.]

Euthanasia. [1812] (proof). [First pbd in the second (first 8vo) edn of Childe Harold (Cantos I, II), 1812; but a proof in 4to exists in the W. A. Clark Library at Pasadena: it was probably set up in this format for inclusion in the first (4to) edition of Childe Harold. See T. J. Wise, Bibliography, vol. I, pp. xx–xxii, vol. II, pp. xxx–xxxi).]

The Curse of Minerva. 1812 (anon.; priv. ptd); Philadelphia [= London?], 1815; Paris,

1818 (bis); Paris, 1820; Paris, 1821. [A slightly different text was first pbd in New Monthly Mag. April 1815, as The Malediction of Minerva, or the Athenian Marble Market and rptd under the original title by William Hone in the 8th edn of Poems on his Domestic Circumstances, 1816.]

Waltz: An Apostrophic Hymn. By Horace Hornem Esq. 1813; 1821 (bis); Paris, 1821; 1826.

The Giaour, A Fragment of a Turkish Tale. 1813; 1813 ('with some additions'); 3rd edn ('with considerable additions'), 1813; Boston, 1813; Philadelphia, 1813; 5th edn ('with considerable additions'), 1813; 6th edn, 1813; 7th edn ('with some additions'), 1813; 8th edn ('with some additions'), 1813; 9th–12th edns, 1814; 13th, 14th edns, 1815; 1825; 1842; [1844]. Tr. Dutch by J. J. Ten Kate, Haarlem, 1859. French by J. M. H. Bigeon, Paris, 1828; by Theodore Carlier (in Voyages Poétiques), Paris, 1830; by L. Joliet, Paris, 1833; by F. Le Bidau and A. Lejourdan, Marseilles, 1860. German, Berlin, 1819 (anon.); by 'A. von Nordstern' [i.e. G. A. E. von Nostiz-Jänkendorf], Leipzig, 1820; by Adolf Seubert, Leipzig, [1874]; by A. Strodtmann, Leipzig, 1887. Modern Greek by A. K. Dosios, Athens, 1873, [1898?]. Italian by Pellegrino Rossi, Genoa, 1817, Milan, 1818; by Andrea Maffei, Milan, 1884. Polish by Ladislaus hr Ostrowski, Pulawy, 1830; by Adam Mickiewicz, Paris, 1835, Wrocklaw, 1839, Zloczów, [1896]. Russian by M. Kachenovsky, Vyestnik Evropui (Moscow), nos. 15–17, 1821; by N. R., Moscow, 1822; by A. Voeikov, Novosti Literatur (Leningrad), Sept., Oct. 1826; by E. Mimel, Leningrad, 1862; by V. A. Petrov, Leningrad, 1873, 1874. Serbian by A. Popović, Novisad, 1860. Spanish, Paris, 1828. Swedish by 'Talis Qualis' [i.e. C. W. A. Strandberg], Stockholm, 1855. [Reviewed: Edinburgh Rev. July 1813 (by Francis Jeffrey); Quarterly Rev. Jan. 1814 (by George Ellis).]

Hoffmann, K. Ueber Lord Byrons 'The Giaour.' Halle, 1898.

The Bride of Abydos, A Turkish Tale. 1813 (2 issues); 2nd–5th edns, 1813; 6th–10th edns, 1814; Boston, 1814; Philadelphia, 1814; 11th edn, 1818; [1844]. Tr. Bulgarian by N. D. Katrapov, Moscow, 1850. Czech by Josef V. Frič, Prague, 1854. Dutch by J. van Lennep, Amsterdam, 1826. French by Léon Thiessé (as Zuleika et Selim), Paris, 1816; by August Clavereau, Ghent, 1823. German by J. V. Adrian, Frankfort, 1819; by Finck de Bailleul, Landau, 1843; by O. Riedel, Hamburg, 1872; by F. Kley, Halle, 1884. Hungarian by Tercsi, Budapest,

1884. Italian, Milan, 1828 (anon.); by Angelo Fava, Milan, 1832; by Giovanni Giovio, Milan, 1854. Polish by Ladislaus hr Ostrowski, Warsaw, 1828. Russian by M. Kachenovsky, Vyestnik Evropui (Moscow), nos. 18–20, 1821; by Ivan Kozlov, Leningrad, 1826, 1831; by M. Politkovsky, Moscow, 1859. Spanish, Paris, 1828 (anon.); by Joaquin Fiol, Palma de Mallorca, 1854. Swedish [by C. W. A. Strandberg], Stockholm, [1855].

[Reviewed: Edinburgh Rev. April 1814 (by Francis Jeffrey); Quarterly Rev. July 1814 (by George Ellis).

Dramatised: Dimond, William, The Bride of Abydos, A Tragick Play in Three Acts, 1818; New York, 1818; [1866]. O., W., The Bride of Abydos; a Tragedy in Five Acts, 1818. Parodied: The Outlaw. A Tale, by Erasmus, Edinburgh, 1818. Adapted: [Payne, J. W. H.] The Unfortunate Lovers; or, the affecting History of Selim and Almena; A Turkish Tale from the Bride of Abydos of Lord Byron, [c. 1821]; New York, 1822.]

The Corsair, A Tale. 1814 (3 issues); 2nd–7th edns, 1814; New York, 1814; Philadelphia, 1814; Boston, 1814; Baltimore, 1814; 8th, 9th edns, 1815; 10th edn, 1818; 1825; ed. J. W. Lake, Paris, 1830; Paris, 1835; [1844]; 1867. Tr. Czech by Čeněk Ibl, Prague, 1885. Danish by H. Schou, Copenhagen, 1855. French by Lucile Thomas, Paris, 1825. German by F. L. von Tschirsky, Berlin, 1816; by Elise von Hohenhausen, Altona, 1820; by Caroline Pichler, Vienna, 1820; by Friederike Friedmann, Leipzig, 1852; by Victor von Arentschild, Mainz, 1852; by Adolf Seubert, Leipzig, [1874]. Hungarian by Gésa Kacziány, Budapest, 1892. Italian by L. C. Turin, 1819, Milan, 1820, 1824 (anon.); by Giuseppe Nicolini, Milan, 1842; by Eritrio Migdonio, Florence, 1842; by Luigi Serenelli Honorati, Bologna, 1870; by Carlo Rosnati, Pavia, 1879. Polish by A. E. Odyniec, Paris, 1835; rptd Wroclaw, 1839. Russian by A. Boeikov, Novosti Literatur (Leningrad), Oct., Nov. 1825; by V. Olin, Leningrad, 1827. Spanish, Paris, 1827 (anon.); Valencia, 1832 (anon.); by Vicente W. Querol and T. Llorente, Valencia, 1863. Swedish by 'Talis Qualis' [i.e. C. W. A. Strandberg], Stockholm, 1868.

[Reviewed: Edinburgh Rev. April 1814 (by Francis Jeffrey); Quarterly Rev. July 1814 (by George Ellis).

Adapted or Dramatised: [Hone, William]. Conrad the Corsair; or, The Pirate's Isle. Adapted as a Romance. 1817; Boulay-Paty, E. F. C. and Lucas, H. J. J. Le Corsaire, Paris, 1830 (rptd Paris, 1901); Galzerani, G. Il Corsaro, Azione mimica, Milan, 1826;

Rossetti, G. (sen.). Il Corsaro, Scene melodrammatiche, [c. 1830]; Rossetti, G. (sen.). Medora e Corrado, Cantata Melodrammatica tratta dal Corsaro di Lord Byron, [c. 1832]; Ferretti, Giacopo. Il Corsaro, Melo-Dramma Romantico in Due Atti. Rome, [1831].]

Uhde, H. Zur Poetik von Byrons 'Corsair.' Leipzig, 1907.

Ode to Napoleon Buonaparte. 1814 (anon.); 2nd–9th edns, 1814 (anon.); Boston, 1814; New York, 1814; Philadelphia, 1814; 11th edn, 1815; 12th edn, 1816; 13th edn, 1818. Tr. Spanish, Paris, 1830 (anon.). [Reviewed: Morning Chronicle, 21 April 1814 (by James Perry); The Examiner, 24 April 1814 (by Leigh Hunt); Anti-Jacobin Rev. May 1814.]

Lara, A Tale. Jacqueline, A Tale. 1814 (anon. 2 issues; Jacqueline is by Samuel Rogers); 2nd, 3rd edns, 1814 (anon.); Boston, 1814 (anon.); 4th edn (1st separate and acknowledged edn), 1814; New York, 1814; 5th edn, 1817. Tr. Czech by Č. Ibl, Prague, 1885. French, Avallon, 1840 (anon.; priv. ptd). German by J. V. Adrian (in Versmaase des Originals), Frankfort, 1819; by W. Schaeffer and A. Strodtmann, Leipzig, 1886. Italian by Girolamo, Count Bazoldo, Paris, 1828; by Andrea Maffei, Milan, 1882. Polish by J. Korsak, Vilna, 1833. Serbian by Åtso Popović, Novisad, 1860. Spanish, Paris, 1828 (anon.). Swedish by 'Talis Qualis' [i.e. C. W. A. Strandberg], Stockholm, 1869. [Reviewed: Quarterly Rev. July 1814 (by George Ellis); The Plagiarisms of Lord Byron, by Alexander Dyce, GM. VI, 1818.]

Hebrew Melodies Ancient and Modern with Appropriate Symphonies and Accompaniments by I. Braham and I. Nathan, the Poetry written expressly for the work by Lord Byron. 2 pts, [1815]; 1815 (poetry without the music; 2 issues); Boston, 1815; New York, 1815; Philadelphia, 1815; 1823; 1825; 1829 (with addns in Fugitive Pieces and Reminiscences of Lord Byron by I. Nathan). Tr. Czech by Jaroslen Vrchlicky and J. V. Sládek, Prague, 1890. Danish by F. Andresen-Halmrast, Oslo, 1889. French by J. A. Delérue (in Méandres), Rouen, 1845. German by Franz Theremin, Berlin, 1820; by J. E. Hilscher, Laibach, 1833; by Eduard Nickles, Karlsruhe, 1863; by Heinrich Stadelmann, Memmingen, 1866. Hebrew by S. Mandelkern, Leipzig, 1890. Italian by P. P. Parzanese, Naples, 1837; Ivrea, 1855 (anon.). Russian by P. Kozlov, Leningrad, 1860. Spanish by Tomás Aguiló (in La Fe), Palma de Mallorca, 1844, rptd (in his Obras en Prosa y en Versa), Palma de Mallorca, 1883. Swedish by Theodor Lind, Helsingfors, [1862]. Yiddish by Nathan Horowitz, 1925;

[Reviewed: Christian Observer, Aug. 1815. Analectic Mag. (Philadelphia), Dec. 1815; Edinburgh Rev. Dec. 1816 (by Francis Jeffrey).]

Beutler, C. A. Ueber Lord Byrons 'Hebrew Melodies.' Leipzig, 1912.

There's not a Joy this World can give. A Ballad written by Lord Byron. Composed by Sir John Stevenson. [1815] (4 leaves with music). [Rptd in Poems, 1816.]

The Siege of Corinth, A Poem. Parisina, A Poem. 1816 (anon.); 2nd, 3rd edns, 1816 (anon.); New York, 1816; 4th edn, 1818; 1824; 1826. [Reviewed: Monthly Rev. Feb. 1816; Eclectic Rev. March 1816; European Mag. May 1816; Literary Panorama, June 1816.]

The Siege of Corinth [alone]. 1824; Paris, 1835; Luneburg, 1854; 1879; ed. J. G. C. Schuler, Halle, 1886; ed. K. Bandow, Bielefeld, [c. 1890]; ed. E. Koelbing, Berlin, 1893; ed. P. Hordern, 1914. Tr. Dutch by J. Van Lennep, Amsterdam, 1831. French by C. Mancel, Paris, 1820; (extracts only) by F. de Reiffenberg (in Poésies Diverses), Paris, 1825; by A. Giron, Brussels, 1827. German by A. Wollheim, Hamburg, [1817?]; [by F. L. Breuer], Leipzig, 1820; by G. E. Schumann, Hamburg, 1827. Italian by Vincenzo Padovan, Venice, 1838. Spanish, Madrid, 1818; Paris, 1826; Paris, 1828 (bis); Barcelona, 1838. Swedish [by C. W. A. Strandberg], Stockholm, [1854]. [Dramatised by — Soumet and — Balochi, Le Siège de Corinth, Tragédie Lyrique en Cinq Actes, Paris, 1826.]

Parisina [alone]. Tr. French by Adolphe Krafft, Paris, 1900. German by J. V. Cirkel (in Gedichte), Münster, 1826; by L. A. Frankel, Vienna, 1836. Italian, Milan, 1821 (anon.); by Andrea Maffei, Milan, 1853; by Carlo Dall' Oro, Mantua, 1854; by Paolo Pappalardo, Palermo, 1855; by A. Canepa, Genoa, 1864. Polish by I. Szydlowski, Vilna, 1834. Russian by V. Verderevsky, Leningrad, 1827. Spanish, Paris, 1830 (anon.); by H. de V[edia] (in El Seminario Pintoresco (pp. 339, 349)), Madrid, 1841. Swedish [by C. W. A. Strandberg], Stockholm, [1854]. [Adapted in Parisina, Poème imité de Lord Byron, Montpellier, 1829. Dramatised by F. Romani as Parisina, Dramma Serio, Bologna, 1836; as Parisina, Melodramma, Venice, 1838, Vercelli, [c. 1840], Turin, 1858; as Parisina, Tragedia Lirica, Milan, 1841.]

Wurzbach, W. von. Lord Byrons Parisina und ihre Vorgaengerinnen. E. Studien, xxv, 1898.

Fare Thee Well! 18 March 1816 (52 lines; proof, Murray); [4 April] (60 lines, priv. ptd); 7 April 1816 (60 lines, priv. ptd). [First pbd in The Champion, 14 April 1816. A list of later appearances in newspapers is given by E. H. Coleridge, Works, Poetry, vol. iii, pp. 532–5.]

A Reply to Fare Thee Well. Lines addressed to Lord Byron. 1816 (bis).

Lady Byron's Responsive Fare Thee Well. 1816 (3 edns); 1825.

Lines addressed to Lady Byron. 1817. [Attrib. to Mrs Cockle.]

Reply to Lord Byron's Fare Thee Well. 1817. [Also attrib. to Mrs Cockle.]

Reply to Fare Thee Well. Newcastle, 1817.

A Sketch from Private Life. 30 March 1816 (proof, Murray); [2 April] (priv. ptd). [First pbd in The Champion, 14 April 1816.]

A Sketch from Public Life, and A Farewell. By Tyro. 1816.

Lines on the Departure of a great Poet from his Country. 1816. [Attrib. to Charles Thomson.]

[Poems on his Domestic Circumstances.] Fare Thee Well. A Sketch from Private Life. Bristol, Barry and Son, 1816 (2 poems only); W. Espy, Dublin (2 poems); Fare Thee Well, A Sketch, etc. Napoleon's Farewell, On the Star of the Legion of Honour and Ode from the French. Sherwood, Neely and Jones, 1816 (5 poems); An Ode. On the Star of the Legion of Honour. New York, 1816 (the same 5 poems as the previous edn); Fare Thee Well, A Sketch from Private Life, with other Poems. Rodwell and Martin, 1816 (6 poems); Fare Thee Well and other Poems. Edinburgh, J. Robertson, 1816 (7 poems, 2 of which not by Byron); Poems on his Domestic Circumstances, William Hone, 1816 (20 edns, 7 poems, 2 of which not by Byron. 'Adieu to Malta' was added to the sixth Hone edn (its first appearance in print), and 'The Curse of Minerva' to the 8th edn; succeeding edns have the same title as Hone, except where noted); Richard Edwards, 1816 (10 edns); Effingham Wilson, 2nd edn, 1816; Bumpus, 1816 (2 edns, prefatory matter by J. Nightingale)· J. Fairburn; Boston, J. Eliot, 1816 (from Hone's 6th edn); Bristol, W. Sheppard, 2nd edn, 1816 (20 poems, of which 7 not by Byron); Lord Byron's Farewell to England and other Poems, Philadelphia, Moses Thomas, 1816; Hone, 23rd edn, 1817; Richard Edwards, 18th edn, 1818; J. Limbird, 1823 (24 poems of which 5 not by Byron); Miscellaneous Poems including Those on his Domestic Circumstances, S. Hodgson, 1823 (25 poems, of which 7 not by Byron); J. Bumpus, 1824 (same title as previous edn; 25 poems of which 7 not by Byron); Miscellaneous Poems on His Domestic and Other Circumstances, William Cole, 1825 (29 poems, as in the 1824 edn, with 4 genuine poems added). Tr. French by Aristide Guilbert, 1826 (Ode from the French only).

> Cook, Davidson. Byron's 'Fare Thee Well.' TLS. 18 Sept. 1937.
> Pollard, G. Pirated Collections of Byron. TLS. 16 Oct. 1937.

Poems. John Murray, 1816 (2 issues); 2nd edn, 1816.

The Prisoner of Chillon, and other Poems. 1816 (2 issues); Lausanne, 1818; Lausanne, 1822; 1824; [1825?]; Geneva, 1830; ed. Thomas Harvey, Paris, 1846; Lausanne, 1857; 1865; ed. R. S. Davies, [1877]; ed. F. Fischer, Berlin, 1884; ed. T. C. Cann, Florence, 1885; ed. Henry Evans, 1896; ed. E. Koelbing, Weimar, 1898; ed. J. W. Cousins, [1910]. Tr. Czech by Antonín Klásterský, Prague, 1895, 1922. Dutch by K. L. Ledeganck (in Gedichten), Ghent, 1856. French, Vevey, [c. 1870] (anon.); Geneva, 1892 (anon.). German by G. Kreyenberg, Lausanne, 1861; by M. von der Marwitz, Vevey, [1865]; by T. R., Berlin, 1886; by J. G. Hagmann, Leipzig, 1892. Icelandic by Steingrimur Thorsteinson, Copenhagen, 1866. Italian, [n.p.], 1830 (anon.); by Andrea Maffei, Milan, 1853. Russian by V. J[ukovsky], Leningrad, 1822; (Darkness only) by I. Turgenev, Peterburgskii Sbornik, 1846, p. 501. Polish by F. D. Morawski (in Poematów), Leszno, 1853, rptd separately Zloczów, 1893. Spanish, Paris, 1830 (anon.). Swedish [by C. W. A. Strandberg], Stockholm, [1854]. [Reviewed: Quarterly Rev. Oct. 1816 (by Sir Walter Scott); Edinburgh Rev. Dec. 1816 (by F. Jeffrey); Critical Rev. Dec. 1816; Eclectic Rev. March 1817. [The Dream, originally pbd in this collection, was pbd separately 1849.]

> Monti, G. Studi Critici. Florence, 1887.
> 'Amstel, A. van' (i.e. J. C. Neuman). The True Story of the Prisoner of Chillon. Nineteenth Cent. May 1900.

Monody on the Death of the Right Honourable R. B. Sheridan. 1816 (anon.; 2 issues); 1817; 1818.

The Lament of Tasso. 1817; 2nd–5th edns, 1817; New York, 1817; 6th edn, 1818. Tr. Dutch by J. van Lennep, Amsterdam, 1833. French by — Marvaud (in Huit Mésséniennes), Paris, 1824. Italian by Michele Leoni, Pisa, 1818; by P. M. (in Veglie di Torquato Tasso), Venice, 1826; by Gaetano Polidori (in La Magion del Terrore), 1843 (priv. ptd); by Guglielmo Godio, Turin, 1873. [Reviewed: GM. Aug. 1817; Scots Mag. Aug. 1817; Blackwood's Mag. Nov. 1817.]

Manfred. A Dramatic Poem. 1817 (3 issues); 2nd edn, 1817; Philadelphia, 1817; New York, 1817 (bis); 1824; 1825; Brussels, [c. 1830]; (as Manfred. A Choral Tragedy in 3 Acts), [1863]; ed. G. Ferrando, Florence, 1926. Tr. Croatian by Stjepan Mildtić, Zagreb, 1894. Czech by Josef V. Frič, Prague, 1882. Danish by P. F. Wulff, Copenhagen, 1820; by Edvard Lembcke, Copenhagen, 1843. Dutch by Johan Rudolph Steinmetz, Amsterdam, 1857; by W. Gosler, Heusden, 1882. French by the Comtesse de Lalaing, Brussels, 1833, 1852; by François Ponsard, Paris, 1837; by Émile Moreau, Paris, 1887; by C. Trébla, Toulouse, 1888. German by Adolf Wagner, Leipzig, 1819; by T. Armin, Gottingen, 1836; by 'Posgaru' (i.e. G. F. W. Suckow), Breslau, 1839; by O. S. Seeman, Berlin, 1843; Leipzig, 1853 (anon.); by Hermann von Koesen, Leipzig, 1858; by L. Freytag, Berlin, 1872; by Adolf Seubert, Leipzig, [1874]; (with music by Robert Schumann) Leipzig, [c. 1880]; by Thierry Preyer, Frankfort, 1883. Modern Greek by E. Green, Patras, 1864. Hungarian by Lázár Horváth, Budapest, 1842; by Imre Kludik, Szolnok, 1884; by Emil Abrányi, Budapest, 1891, 1897. Icelandic by Matthias Jochumsson, Copenhagen, 1875. Italian by Marcello Mazzoni, Milan, 1832; by Silvio Pellico, Florence, 1859; by Andrea Maffei, Florence, 1870. Polish by E. S. Bojanowski, Wroclaw, 1835; by F. D. Morawski in Poematów, Leszno, 1853, rptd separately Lwow, [1885]; by Michal Chodźkę, Paris, [1859]. Roumanian by T. M. Stoenescu, Bucharest, 1896. Russian by O., Moskovskii Vyestnik, Moscow, July 1825; by M. Bronchenko, Leningrad, 1828; by A. Borodin, Panteon, Leningrad, Feb.1841; by E. Zarin, Biblioteca dlya Chteniya, Leningrad, Aug. 1858; by D. Minaev, Russkoi Slovo, Leningrad, April 1863. Spanish, Paris, 1830 (anon.); by José Alcalá Galiano and Fernandez de las Peñas, Madrid, 1861; by Angel R. Chaves, Madrid, 1876. [Reviewed: Edinburgh Monthly Mag. June 1817 (by John Wilson); Critical Rev. June 1817; Day and New Times, 23 June 1817; Eclectic Rev. July 1817; Monthly Rev. July 1817; GM. July 1817; Edinburgh Rev. Aug. 1817 (by F. Jeffrey); Kunst und Alterthum (Weimar), June 1820 (by Goethe; rptd in Sämtliche Werke, vol. xxxvii, Stuttgart, 1907, pp. 184–7.)]

> B., F. H. Manfred. An Address to Lord Byron, with an Opinion on some of his Writings. 1817.

Duentzer, H. Goethes Faust in seiner Einheit und Ganzheit; ueber Byron's Manfred. Cologne, 1836.

Roetscher, H. Manfred in ihren inneren Zusammenhange entwickelt. Berlin, 1844; Bamberg, 1884.

Lord Byron's Manfred at Drury Lane Theatre. By a Dilettante behind the scenes. 1863.

Manfred: Poem and Drama. By the London Hermit. Dublin University Mag. April 1874.

Anton, H. S. Byrons Manfred. Erfurt, 1875.

Koelbing, E. Zu Byrons Manfred. E. Studien, XXII, 1898.

Manfred, dramatische Dichtung von Lord Byron von einem Theologen. Oldenburg, [1898].

Brandl, A. Goethes Verhaeltniss zur Byron. Goethe-Jahrbuch, XX, 1899.

Varnhagen, H. De Rebus quibusdam Compositionem Byronis Dramatis quod Manfred inscribitur praecedentibus. Erlangen, 1909.

Butterwick, J. C. A Note on the First Editions of Manfred. Book Collectors' Quart. June 1931.

Beppo. A Venetian Story. 1818 (anon.); 2nd–7th edns, 1818; Boston, 1818; New York, 1818; Paris, 1821; 1825.

Additional Stanzas to the First, Second, and Third Editions of Beppo. [1818] (single sheet). [These were first added to the 4th edn: the 5th edn was the first to bear Byron's name.] Tr. Danish by Alfred Ipsen, Copenhagen, 1891. Dutch by J. van Lennep, Amsterdam, 1894. French by S. Clogenson, Paris, 1865; by A. Morisseau, Paris, 1881. Russian by V. Lubich-Romanovich, Sine Otechestva (Leningrad), April 1842; D. Minaev, Sovremennik (Leningrad), Aug. 1863. Spanish, Paris, 1829 (anon.). Swedish by 'Talis Qualis' (i.e. C. W. A. Strandberg), Stockholm, [1854]. [Reviewed: Edinburgh Rev. Feb. 1818 (by F. Jeffrey); Monthly Rev. March 1818; Eclectic Rev. June 1818.]

A Poetical Epistle from Alma Mater to Lord Byron occasioned by lines in a tale called Beppo. Cambridge, 1819.

Beppo in London. A Metropolitan Story. 1819.

On John William Rizzo Hoppner born at Venice on 18 January 1818. [Padua, 1818.]

'My Boat is on the Shore.' 1818. [With music by H. R. Bishop. See TLS. 16 Oct. 1937.]

Mazeppa. A Poem. 1819 (2 issues); Paris, 1819; Boston, 1819; Paris, 1822; 1824; ed. H. M. Melford, Brunswick, 1834; [1854?]. Tr. Czech by Antonín Klásterský, Prague, [c. 1895], 1922. French by J. Adolphe (in

Manuel Anglais), Paris, 1830. German by T. Hell [i.e. Th. Winkler], Leipzig, 1820; by Everhard Brauns, Gottingen, 1836; by Otto Gildemeister, Bremen, 1858; by Ferdinand Freiligath, Stuttgart, 1883. Hungarian by Lázár Horváth, Budapest, 1842. Italian by Antonio Arioti, Palermo, 1847; by T. Virzi, Palermo, 1876; by Andrea Maffei, Milan, 1886. Polish by Michal Chodźke, Halle, 1860. Russian by M. Kachenovsky (in Vuibor iz Sochineny Lorda Byrona), Moscow, 1821; by A. Voeikov, Novosti Literatur (Leningrad), Nov. 1824; by Ya. Grot, Sovremennik (Leningrad), IX, 1838; by D. Michailovsky, Sovremennik (Leningrad), May 1858; by I. Gogniev, Repertyar i Panteon (Leningrad), Oct. 1844, rptd Dramatichesky Sbornik (Leningrad), April 1860. Spanish, Paris, 1828 (anon.), 1830; by J. M. R. Bárcena (in his Ultimas Poesías Líricas), Mexico, 1888. Swedish [by C. W. A. Strandberg], Stockholm, [1853].

Reviewed: Blackwood's Mag. July 1819; John Gilpin and Mazeppa [by W. Maginn], ibid.; Monthly Rev. July 1819; Eclectic Rev. Aug. 1819.

Adapted: Mazeppa Travestied, A Poem. 1820. Milner, H. M. Mazeppa, a romantic drama from Lord Byron's poem. [c. 1830]; 1874. Cortesi, A. Mazeppa, Ballo Storico. Milan, 1841. White, C. Mazeppa. An Equestrian Burlesque in two Acts. New York, [c. 1860].

Englaender, D. Lord Byrons Mazeppa. Berlin, 1897.

Don Juan. [Cantos I, II.] 1819 (anon.); 1819 (2 more edns); Paris, 1819; Philadelphia, 1819; 1820 (3 edns); Paris, 1821; 1822; 1823.

Don Juan. Cantos III, IV, and V. 1821 (anon.); 1821 (4 more edns); Paris, 1821; New York, 1821; 5th edn, 1822 (rev.).

Don Juan. Cantos VI, VII, and VIII. 1823 (anon.); 1823 (2 more edns); Paris, 1823; Philadelphia, 1823; 1825.

Don Juan. Cantos IX, X, and XI. 1823 (anon.); 1823; Paris, 1823; Philadelphia, 1823.

Don Juan. Cantos XII, XIII, and XIV. 1823 (anon.); 1823 (2 more edns); Paris, 1824; New York, 1824.

Don Juan. Cantos XV and XVI. 1824 (anon.); 1824 (2 more edns); Paris, 1824.

Dedication to Don Juan. 1833.

Don Juan. [Cantos I–V.] 1822 (4 edns); 1823 (bis); 1824; [1826?]. [Cantos V–XI.] 1823. [Cantos I–XVI.] 2 vols. 1826; 1826 (3 edns); 1827 (bis); 2 vols. 1828 (bis); 1828; 1832; Nuremberg, [1832]; 1833; 1834; 1835; 1836; 2 vols. 1837; Mannheim, 1838; 1845;

1849; [c. 1850]; Halifax, 1857; ed. E. H. Coleridge, 1906; ed. F. H. Ristine, New York, 1927; ed. L. I. Bredvold, New York, 1935.

The Beauties of Don Juan. 2 vols. 1828.

Tr. Danish by H. Schou (Canto I only), Fredericia, 1854; by Holger Drachmann, 2 vols. Copenhagen, 1880–1902. French by A[médée] P[ichot], 3 vols. Paris, 1827, 2 vols. Paris, 1866; by Paul Lehodey, Paris, [1869]; by Adolphe Fauvel, Paris, 1866, 1868, 1878. German (Cantos I–IV) by A. von Marées, Essen, 1839; by Otto Gildemeister, 2 vols. Bremen, 1845; by Adolf Boettger, Leipzig, 1849, 1858; by Wilhelm Schaeffer, 2 vols. Hildburghausen, 1867. Italian by A. Caccia, Turin, 1853; by Antonietta Sacchi, Milan, 1865; (part as Aidea, Episodio di Don Giovanni) by Vitorio Betteloni, Verona, 1875, Milan, 1880; by Enrico Casali, Milan, 1876. Polish by Wiktor z Baworow (Canto I only), Tarnopol, 1863; (part of Canto II) by the same, Cracow, 1877; (Canto III) by the same, Cracow, 1877; (Cantos II, III, IV) by the same, Tarnopol, 1879; by E. Porebowicz, Warsaw, 1885, 2 vols. 1922. Roumanian by I. Eliade (Cantos I, II) Bucharest, 1847. Russian by I. Jand, Leningrad, 1846; (Cantos I–X) by V. Lubich-Romanovich, 2 vols. Leningrad, [1847]; by N. A. Markevitch, Leipzig, 1862; (Cantos I–X) by D. Minaev, Sovremennik (Leningrad), Jan.–Oct. 1865; by P. Kozlov, 2nd edn, ed. P. Veinberg, 2 vols. Leningrad, 1889; by A. Kozlov, 2 vols. Leningrad, 1892. Serbian by O. Glumchevik, 2 vols. Belgrade, 1888. Spanish, 2 vols. Paris, 1829 (anon.); 3 vols. Madrid, 1843–4 (anon.); by F. Villalba, 2 vols. Madrid, 1876, 2 vols. [1916]; by J. A. R., Barcelona, 1883. Swedish (Canto I only), Stockholm, 1838 (anon.); by C. W. A. Strandberg, 2 vols. Stockholm, [1857–62].

Reviewed: Literary Gazette, 17, 24 July 1819; 11, 18 Aug. 1821; 19 July 1823; 6 Sept. 1823; 6 Dec. 1823; 3 April 1824; Monthly Rev. July 1819; Aug. 1821; July 1823; Oct. 1823; April 1824; New Monthly Mag. Aug. 1819; British Critic, Aug. 1819; Sept. 1821; British Rev. Aug. 1819; Dec. 1821; Blackwood's Mag. Aug. 1819; 'Don Juan Unread' [by William Maginn], Nov. 1819; Aug. 1821; July 1823; The Examiner, 31 Oct. 1819; 26 Aug. 1821; 14, 21 March 1824.

[Colton, Charles Caleb.] Remarks, Critical and Moral, on the talents of Lord Byron and the tendencies of Don Juan. 1819.

[Hone, William?] 'Don John' or Don Juan unmasked. 1819 (3 edns).

[Stacy, John?] A Critique on the Genius and Writings of Lord Byron, with remarks on Don Juan. Norwich, 1820.

Cottle, Joseph. An Expostulary Epistle to Lord Byron. 1820.

[Black, John?] A Letter to the Rt Hon. Lord Byron by John Bull. 1821. [See Athenaeum, 7 March 1903.]

Gordon. A Tale. A Poetical Review of Don Juan. 1821.

Goethe, J. W. von. Kunst und Alterthum, III, 1821. [Rptd Sämtliche Werke, vol. xxxvii, Stuttgart, 1907, pp. 188–91.]

Thomas, John W. An Apology for Don Juan. 1824; 1825; 1850 ('to which is added a Third Canto'); 1855 (as Byron and the Times; or an Apology for Don Juan).

[Burges, George.] Cato to Lord Byron on the Immorality of his Writings. 1824.

The Morality of Don Juan, by the London Hermit. Dublin University Mag. May 1875.

Bévotte, G. G. de. La Légende de Don Juan. Son Évolution dans la Litérature des Origines au Romantisme. Paris, 1906.

Pfeiffer, A. Thomas Hopes Anastasius und Byrons Don Juan. Munich, 1913.

Alonzo, S. Giorgio Byron. Attraverso 'Don Juan.' Acireale, 1931.

Continuations:

[Hone, William?] Don Juan. Canto the Third. 1819.

Don Juan: with a biographical account of Lord Byron. Canto III. 1819.

A New Canto. 1819.

Don Juan. Canto XI. 1820.

Don Juan. Canto III. 1821.

[Clason, Isaac Star?] Don Juan. Cantos IX, X, and XI. Albany, 1823.

Continuation of Don Juan. Cantos XVII and XVIII. Oxford, 1825; 1825.

Don Juan. Cantos XVII, XVIII. 1825.

[Clason, Isaac Star.] Don Juan. Cantos XVII–XVIII. New York, 1825.

Don Juan. Canto XVII. In The Rambler, July 1825.

Juan Secundus. Canto the First. 1825.

Don Giovanni. A Poem in Two Cantos. Edinburgh, 1825; 1825.

The Seventeenth Canto of Don Juan. 1829.

Don Juan. Canto XVII. Ravonspear. 1830.

[Clark, Charles?] Twenty Suppressed Stanzas of 'Don Juan' in reference to Ireland. [In Georgian Revel—ations! or 'The most Accomplished Gentleman's' Midnight Visit below Stairs, Great

Totham (Essex), 1838 (priv. ptd). Priv. rptd separately as Some Rejected Stanzas of Don Juan, Great Totham, 1845.]

Baxter, G. R. Wythen. Don Juan Junior: A Poem by Byron's Ghost. 1839.

C[owley], W[illiam]. Don Juan Reclaimed; or his peregrination continued from Lord Byron. 1840.

Morford, Henry. The Rest of Don Juan. New York, 1846.

[Daniel, H. J.?] Don Juan Continued. Canto XVII. 1849.

Wilberforce, Edward and Blanchard, Edmund Forster. Don Juan. Canto Seventeenth. [In Poems, 1857.]

Wetton, Harry W. The Termination of the Sixteenth Canto of Lord Byron's Don Juan. 1864.

The New Don Juan. The Introduction by Gerald Noel Byron. The last Canto of the Original Don Juan from the Papers of the Countess Guiccioli, by Lord Byron. Never before published. [1880.] [The whole book is by G. N. Byron.]

Imitations and Adaptations:

Milner, H. M. The Italian Don Juan; or, Memoirs of the Devil. 1820.

Thornton, Alfred. Don Juan. Volume the First. 1821.

—— Don Juan. Volume the Second, containing his Life in London. 1822.

The Sultana; or, A Trip to Turkey; a Melodrama in Three Acts, founded on Lord Byron's Don Juan. New York, 1822.

Coates, Henry. The British Don Juan. 1823.

Buckstone, J. B. Don Juan. A Romantic Drama in Three Acts. [1828]; rptd [1887].

—— A New Don Juan. 1828.

The Irish Avatar. [1821] (priv. ptd). [The only copy known is in the T. J. Wise Library. See Athenaeum, 26 June 1909. First pbd by Thomas Medwin in Conversations of Lord Byron, 1824.]

Marino Faliero, Doge of Venice. An Historical Tragedy in Five Acts, With Notes. The Prophecy of Dante. A Poem. 1821 (2 issues); 2nd edn, 1821; 3rd edn, 1823. [Reviewed: Blackwood's Mag. April 1821 (by John Wilson); Monthly Rev. May 1821; The Indicator, 2 May 1821 (by Leigh Hunt); Eclectic Rev. June 1821; Edinburgh Rev. July 1821 (by F. Jeffrey); Quarterly Rev. July 1821 (by Reginald Heber).]

Marino Faliero [alone]. Paris, 1821; Philadelphia, 1821 (bis); 1842; ed. F. Brockerhoff, Berlin, 1853. Tr. German by G. von Hardt, Paderborn, 1827; by Carl Deahna, Bayreuth, 1850; by Thierry Preyer, Frankfort, 1883; by A. Fitger, Oldenburg, [1886]. Italian by P. G. B. Cereseto, Savona, 1845. Spanish by Marcial Busquetz, Barcelona, 1868.

Letter to R. W. Elliston on the Injustice and Illegality of his Conduct in presenting Lord Byron's Tragedy Marino Faliero. [1821.]

Marino Faliero; or, The Doge of Venice. An Interesting Tale on which is founded the celebrated Tragedy of Lord Byron. [c. 1822] (3 edns).

Kaiser, —— Byrons und Delavignes Marino Faliero. Düsseldorf, 1870.

Schiff, Hermann. Ueber Lord Byrons Marino Faliero und seine anderen geschichtlichen Dramen. Marburg, 1910.

King, Lucile. The Influence of Shakespeare on Byron's Marino Faliero. Texas University Stud. no. 11, 1931.

The Prophecy of Dante [alone]. Paris, 1821; Philadelphia, 1821; 1825; ed. L. W. Potts, 1879 (Cantos I, II). Tr. French by Benjamin Laroche (in Œuvres de Dante), Paris, 1842. Italian by L. da Ponte, New York, 1821; by Giovanni Giovio, Milan, 1856; by Melchiore Missirini, Milan, 1858. Spanish by Antonio Maria Vizcayno, Mexico, 1850.

Sardanapalus, A Tragedy. The Two Foscari, A Tragedy. Cain, A Mystery. 1821; Boston, 1822. [Reviewed: Edinburgh Rev. Feb. 1822 (by Francis Jeffrey); Blackwood's Mag. Feb. 1822; British Rev. March 1822; Eclectic Rev. May 1822; The Examiner, 2 June 1822; Quarterly Rev. July 1822 (by Reginald Heber); The Portfolio, Philadelphia, Dec. 1822.]

Sardanapalus [alone]. Paris, 1822; New York, 1822; 1823; [c. 1825]; 1829; Arnsberg, 1849; [1853] (adapted for representation by Charles Kean); Manchester, [1875] (adapted by Charles Calvert). Tr. Czech by Frantisec Krsek, Prague, 1891. Danish by J. Ruesse, Copenhagen, 1827. French by L. Aloin, Brussels, 1834; by H. Becque, Paris, 1867; by M. P. Berton, Paris, 1882. German by Emma Herz, Posen, 1854; by C. J. Arnold, Bremen, 1854; by Adolf Boettger, Jena, 1888; by Josef Kainz, Berlin, 1897. Modern Greek by Christos A. Parmenidos, Athens, 1865. Italian, Milan, 1884 (anon.). Polish by Fryderyk Krauze, Warsaw, 1872. Russian by E. Zarin, Biblioteka dlya Chteniya (Leningrad), Dec. 1860; by O. N. Chiuminoi, Artist (Moscow), Sept., Oct. 1890. Spanish, Madrid, 1847 (anon.); (part only) by Andres Bello (in his Obras Completas, vol. III), Santiago de Chile, 1883. Swedish by Nils Arfvidsson, Stockholm, 1864.

Nieschlag, Hermann. Ueber Lord Byrons Sardanapalus. Halle, 1900.

The Two Foscari [alone]. Paris, 1822; New
York, 1822. Tr. French by Escudier Frères,
1849; by A. Morisseau, Paris, 1881. Italian
by P. G. B. Cereseti, Savona, 1845. Russian
by E. Zarin, Biblioteka dlya Chteniya
(Leningrad), Nov. 1861. Spanish by Manuel
Canete, Madrid, 1846; by Manuel Hiraldez
de Acosta, Barcelona, 1868.

Cain [alone]. 1822 (6 edns); Paris, 1822; New
York, 1822; 1824; ed. Harding Grant,
1830; 1832; Breslau, 1840; [1883]; ed.
B. Uhlemayr, Nuremberg, 1907. Tr. Czech
by Josef Durdík, Prague, 1871. Dutch by
S. A. Klok, Hague, 1906. Esperanto by
A. Kofman, Nuremberg, 1896. French by
Fabre D'Olivet, Paris, 1823 (D'Olivet's
version tr. Eng. by L. Redfield, New York,
1923). German by G. Parthey, Berlin,
1831; by Frederike Friedmann, Leipzig,
1855; by Adolf Seubert, Leipzig, [1874].
Hebrew by David Frishmann, Warsaw, 1900.
Hungarian by Ilona Gyory, [Budapest],
1895; by Lajos Mikes, Budapest, 1898.
Italian by Andrea Maffei, Milan, 1852.
Polish by Adam Pajgert, Lwow, 1868.
Russian by E. Baruishev, Leningrad, 1881;
by P. A. Kalenov, Moscow, 1883. Spanish
by J. G., Madrid, 1873.

[Todd, H. J.] A Remonstrance to Mr John
Murray respecting a recent publication.
By Oxoniensis. 1822.

A Letter to Sir Walter Scott in answer to
the remonstrance of Oxoniensis on the
publication of Cain. 1822.

A Vindication of the Paradise Lost from
the charge of exculpating 'Cain.' By
Philo-Milton. 1822.

Harness, William. The Wrath of Cain.
1822.

Revolutionary Causes; with a postscript
containing strictures on Cain. By
Britannicus. 1822.

A Letter of Expostulation to Lord Byron.
1822.

Uriel, A Poetical Address to Lord Byron.
1822; 1825.

Battine, William. Another Cain, A
Mystery. 1822.

Another Cain. A Poem. 1822 (anon.).

Adams, T. A Scourge for Lord Byron;
or 'Cain, A Mystery' unmasked. 1823.

Wilkinson, H. Cain, A Poem containing
an antidote to the impiety and blasphemy
of Lord Byron's 'Cain. 1824.

Goethe, J. W. von. Kunst und Alterthum,
v, 1824. (Rptd Sämtliche Werke, vol.
xxxvii, Stuttgart, 1907, pp. 263–7.]

A Layman's Epistle to a certain Nobleman. 1824.

Remarks on Cain. [c. 1825] (priv. ptd).

[Reade, John Edmund.] Cain the

Wanderer and other Poems. 1830.
Monthly Mag. May 1830; Fraser's Mag.
April 1831. [Reviews of Harding Grant's
edn.]

Schaffner, A. Lord Byrons Cain und
seine Quellen. Strasburg, 1880.

Blumenthal, F. Lord Byron's Mystery
Cain and its relation to Milton's Paradise
Lost and Gessner's Death of Abel.
Oldenburg, 1891.

Graf, A. La Poesia di Caino. Nuova
Antologia, 16 March, 1 April 1908.

Brooke, Stopford A. Byron's Cain.
Hibbert Journ. Oct. 1919.

Babcock, R. W. The Inception and
Reception of Byron's Cain. South
Atlantic Quart. April 1927.

Heaven and Earth. [1821] (proof; no copy
extant); Paris, 1823 (anon.); 1824 (anon.);
1825; [c. 1825]. [First pbd in The Liberal,
no. 2, 1823.] Tr. Danish by P. F. Wulff,
Copenhagen, 1827. French by A[médée]
P[ichot] (in Essai sur le Génie et le Caractère
de Lord Byron), Paris, 1824. Italian by
Andrea Maffei, Milan, 1853. [Reviewed:
Blackwood's Mag. Jan. 1823 (by J. Wilson);
Edinburgh Rev. Feb. 1823 (by F. Jeffrey).]

Mayn, Georg. Ueber Lord Byrons
'Heaven and Earth.' Breslau, 1887.

Zuch, Josef. Thomas Moores 'The Loves
of the Angels' und Lord Byrons 'Heaven
and Earth.' Eine Parallele. Vienna, 1905.

The Vision of Judgement. Paris, 1822; 1822
(with Southey's Vision of Judgement, as
The Two Visions); New York, 1823; 1824
(anon.); [c. 1830] (anon.); ed. E. M. Earl,
1929. [First pbd in The Liberal, no. 1, 1822.
Reviewed: The Courier, 16 Oct. 1822;
Literary Gazette, 19, 26 Oct., 2 Nov. 1822.]

The Age of Bronze; or, Carmen Seculare et
Annus haud Mirabilis. 1823 (anon.); 2nd,
3rd edns, 1823; Paris, 1823; New York,
1823; 1824; 1825. [Reviewed: The
Examiner, 30 March 1823; Scots Mag.
April 1823; Monthly Rev. April 1823;
Literary Chronicle, 5 April 1823; Literary
Gazette, 5 April 1823; Monthly Mag. May
1823.]

The Island, or, Christian and his Comrades.
1823; 2nd, 3rd edns, 1823; Paris, 1823;
New York, 1823; 1826 (bis). Tr. German
[by F. L. Breuer], Leipzig, 1827. Italian
by — Morrone, Naples, 1840. Polish by
Adam Pajgert, Cracow, 1859. Swedish [by
C. W. A. Strandberg], Stockholm, [1856].
[Reviewed: Literary Chronicle, 21 June
1823; Literary Gazette, 21 June 1823;
Monthly Rev. July 1823; Atlantic Mag.
(New York), April 1826.]

Lotze, Curt. Quellenstudien ueber Lord
Byrons 'The Island.' Leipzig, 1902.

Werner. A Tragedy. 1823 (2 issues); Paris, 1823; Philadelphia, 1823; ed. J. W. S. Howes, New York, 1848; 1865; 1866. Tr. French, Paris, 1844 (anon.). German by G. Lotz, Hamburg, 1823. Russian by Neizvustn, Leningrad, 1829. [Reviewed: Blackwood's Mag. Dec.1822 (by W. Maginn); Scots Mag. Dec. 1822; European Mag. Jan. 1823; Eclectic Rev. Feb. 1823.]

>Stoehsel, C. Lord Byrons Trauerspiel Werner und seine Quelle. Erlangen, 1891.
>Gower, F. Leveson. Did Byron write Werner? Nineteenth Cent. Aug. 1899.
>Kluge, W. Lord Byrons Werner. Eine dramentechnische Untersuchung mit Quellenstudien. Leipzig, 1913.
>Motter, T. H. Vail. Byron's Werner Re-estimated. [In The Parrott Presentation Volume by pupils of Prof. Thomas Marc Parrott, Princeton, 1935.]

The Deformed Transformed; A Drama. 1824 (2 variants); 2nd, 3rd edns, 1824; Paris, 1824; Philadelphia, 1824; [1883]. Tr. Hungarian by József Eotvos, Budapest, 1840. [Reviewed: London Mag. March 1824; Scots Mag. March 1824; Monthly Mag. March 1824; Westminster Rev. July 1824.]

>Varnhagen, H. Ueber Byrons drama-tisches Bruchstueck Der Umgestaltete Missgestaltete. Erlangen, 1905.

A Political Ode. 1880. [= An Ode to the Framers of the Frame Bill. First pbd in Morning Chronicle, 2 March 1812.]

A Version of Ossian's Address to the Sun. Cambridge, U.S.A. [1898] (priv. ptd). [Rptd Atlantic Monthly, Dec. 1898.]

(6) PROSE WRITINGS

Letter to my Grandmother's Review. 1819 (proof; Murray). [First pbd in The Liberal, no. 1, [15 Oct. 1822].]

Some Observations upon an Article in Black-wood's Magazine, no. xxiv, August, 1819. [1820] (proof; no copy extant). [First pbd in The Works of Lord Byron, ed. John Wright, vol. xv, 1833.]

A Letter to [John Murray] on the Rev. W. L. Bowles' Strictures on the Life and Writings of Pope. 1821 (2 issues); 2nd, 3rd edns, 1821; Paris, 1821. [Reviewed: Blackwood's Mag. May 1821; London Mag. June 1821 (by William Hazlitt).]

>Campbell, Thomas. Essay on English Poetry. [In Specimens of the British Poets, vol. I, 1819.]
>Bowles, W. L. Invariable Principles of Poetry in a Letter addressed to T. Campbell. 1819.

[D'Israeli, Isaac.] [Review of Spence's Anecdotes.] Quarterly Rev. July 1820.
Bowles, W. L. A Reply to the Charges brought by the Reviewer of Spence's Anecdotes. The Pamphleteer, xvii, Oct. 1820.
Gilchrist, O. G. Letter to the Rev. W. L. Bowles. Stamford, 1820.
Bowles, W. L. Observations on the Poetical Character of Pope. The Pamphleteer, xvii, 1820, xviii, 1821.
—— Two Letters to Lord Byron in answer to his lordship's Letter. 1821 (bis); 3rd edn (as Letters to Lord Byron on a Question of Poetical Criticism), 1822.
MacDermot, M. A Letter to the Rev. W. L. Bowles in reply to his Letter to T. Campbell, and to his two Letters to Lord Byron. 1822.
A Letter to Lord Byron protesting against the Immolation of Gray, Cowper, and Campbell at the shrine of Pope. By Fabius. 1823.
Bowles, W. L. A Final Appeal to the Literary Public relative to Pope. 1825.
Rennes, J. J. van. Bowles, Byron, and the Pope Controversy. Amsterdam, 1927.

Observations upon 'Observations.' A Second Letter to John Murray Esq. on the Rev. W. L. Bowles' Strictures on the Life and Writings of Pope. 1821 (proof; no copy extant). [First pbd in The Works of Lord Byron, ed. John Wright, vol. vi, 1832.]

The Parliamentary Speeches of Lord Byron. Printed from Copies prepared by his Lordship for Publication. 1824.

Correspondence of Lord Byron with a Friend, including Letters to his Mother written from Portugal, Spain, Greece, and the Shores of the Mediterranean in 1809, 1810, and 1811. Ed. A. R. C. Dallas, [1824] (suppressed before publication); 3 vols. Paris, 1825; 2 vols. Philadelphia, 1825. Tr. French, Paris, 1825 (bis).

Letters and Journals of Lord Byron, with Notices of his Life by Thomas Moore. 2 vols. 1830; 2 vols. New York, [1830]; Paris, 1831; 3 vols. 1832; 3 vols. 1833; 1837; 1847 (as The Life of Lord Byron with his Letters and Journals); 1850; 1860 (as The Life, Letters and Journals of Lord Byron); 1875. Tr. French by Louise Swanton Belloc, 5 vols. Paris, 1830. [Reviewed: Athenaeum, 25 Dec. 1830, 1, 8 Jan. 1831; Blackwood's Mag. Feb., March 1831; Quarterly Rev. Feb. 1831; Fraser's Mag. March 1831; Edinburgh Rev. June 1831.]

The Works of Lord Byron in Verse and Prose, including his Letters, Journals, etc. [Ed. FitzGreene Halleck], New York, 1833; Hartford, 1847.

15

A Facsimile of an Interesting Letter Written by Lord Byron 15 Jan. 1809. 1876.

Letters Written by Lord Byron during his Residence at Missolonghi, Jan.–April 1824, to Mr Samuel Barff at Zante. Naples, 1884 (priv. ptd).

The Works of Lord Byron. Vol. i: Letters, 1804–1813. Ed. W. E. Henley, 1897. [No more pbd.]

The Works of Lord Byron. Letters and Journals. Ed. R. E. Prothero [Baron Ernle], 6 vols. 1898–1904.

Poems and Letters of Lord Byron, edited, from the originals in the possession of W. K. Bixby, by W. N. C. Carlton. Chicago, Society of Dofobs, 1912 (priv. ptd).

Lord Byron's Correspondence, chiefly with Lady Melbourne, Mr Hobhouse, the Hon. Douglas Kinnaird, and P. B. Shelley. 2 vols. 1922.

The Ravenna Journal, mainly compiled at Ravenna in 1821. With an Introduction by Lord Ernle [R. E. Prothero]. The First Edition Club, 1928 (priv. ptd).

(7) SELECTIONS FROM LETTERS AND JOURNALS

Lord Byron. Discorso di Cesare Cantù. Aggiuntevi alcune traduzioni ed un serie di lettere dello stesso Lord Byron ove si narrano i suoi viaggi in Italia e nella Grecia. Milan, 1833. Tr. Eng. by A. Kinloch (as Lord Byron and his Works. A Biography and Essay), 1883.

Lord Byron. Eine Autobiographie nach Tagebuechern und Briefen, mit Einleitung und Erlaeuterungen von E. Engel. Berlin, 1876 (bis).

The Letters and Journals of Lord Byron selected by Mathilde Blind. 1886.

The Confessions of Lord Byron. A Collection of his private opinions of Men and Matters. Ed. W. A. L. Bettany, 1905.

Lord Byron in his Letters. Selections by V. H. Collins. 1927.

Selected Letters. Ed. V. H. Collins, Oxford, 1928.

The Letters of George Gordon, Lord Byron. Selected by R. G. Howarth. 1933; 1936. (Everyman's Lib.)

(8) POETICAL PIECES FIRST PUBLISHED IN PERIODICALS

Stanzas to Jessy. Monthly Literary Recreations, July 1807, p. 22. [Rptd in A Sketch from Private Life, and other Poems, (Rodwell & Martin), 1816.]

An Ode to the Framers of the Frame Bill. Morning Chronicle, 2 March 1812. [Rptd separately as A Political Ode, 1880.]

Stanzas on a Lady Weeping. Morning Chronicle, 7 March 1812. [Rptd in The Corsair, 2nd edn, 1814.]

Address spoken at the Opening of Drury Lane Theatre. Morning Chronicle, 12 Oct. 1812. [Rptd in The Genuine Rejected Addresses presented to Drury Lane Theatre, 1812.]

Parenthetical Address by Dr Plagiary. Morning Chronicle, 23 Oct. 1812. [Rptd in Works (Murray), vol. xvii, 1833.]

To Sarah, Countess of Jersey. The Champion, 31 July 1814. [Rptd in Three Poems not included in Byron's Works, 1818.]

Elegiac Stanzas on the Death of Sir Peter Parker. Morning Chronicle, 7 Oct. 1814. [Rptd in Hebrew Melodies, 1816.]

The Curse of Minerva [as The Malediction of Minerva, or the Athenian Marble Market]. New Monthly Mag. April 1815. [Priv. ptd in 1812.]

'Bright be the place of thy soul.' The Examiner, 4 June 1815. [Rptd with music by I. Nathan, [1815], and in Poems, 1816.]

Napoleon's Farewell. The Examiner, 30 July 1815. [Rptd in Poems, 1816.]

'We do not curse thee, Waterloo.' Morning Chronicle, 15 March 1816. [Rptd in Poems, 1816.]

On the Star of the Legion of Honour. The Examiner, 7 April 1816. [Rptd in Poems, 1816.]

Fare Thee Well. The Champion, 14 April 1816. [Rptd in Poems, 1816.]

A Sketch from Private Life. The Champion, 14 April 1816. [Rptd in Poems on his Domestic Circumstances, 1816.]

'My Boat is on the shore.' The Traveller, 8 Jan. 1821. [Rptd with music by H. R. Bishop, [1818], and in The Works of Byron, 'Philadelphia,' 1820.]

The Vision of Judgement. The Liberal, no. 1, [15 Oct. 1822.]

Epigrams on Lord Castlereagh. Ibid. [Rptd in Works (Murray), vol. xvii, 1833.]

Heaven and Earth, A Mystery. The Liberal, no. 2, [1 Jan. 1823.]

From the French ('Aegle, beauty and poet'). Ibid. [Rptd in Works (Murray), vol. xvii, 1833.]

Martial. Lib. i, Epig. i. Translation. Ibid. [Rptd in Works (Murray), vol. xvii, 1833.]

New Duet ('Why how now, Saucy Tom?'). Ibid.

'And dost thou ask the reason of my sadness?' The Nicnac, 25 March 1823. [Rptd in Works (Murray), vol. v, 1831.]

The Blues, A Literary Eclogue. The Liberal, no. 3, [26 April 1823]. [Rptd in Works (Murray), vol. v, 1831.]

Morgante Maggiore di Messer Luigi Pulci. The Liberal, no. 4, [30 July 1823]. [Rptd in Works (J. H. L. Hunt), vol. vi, 1824.] Lord Byron, Leigh Hunt, and The Liberal. Ed. L. P. Pickering, [1925]. [Selections from The Liberal.]

A Critique on The Liberal, 1822.

The Illiberal! Verse and Prose from the North. [1822.] [Improbably attrib. to William Gifford.]

On this day I complete my 36th year. Morning Chronicle, 29 Oct. 1824. [Rptd in Works (Murray), vol. vi, 1831.]

[Lines to Lady Blessington.] Annales Romantiques, Paris, 1827–8.

Lines on hearing that Lady Byron was ill. New Monthly Mag. Aug. 1832.

'Could Love for ever.' New Monthly Mag. Oct. 1832.

Question and Answer. Fraser's Mag. Jan. 1833.

'But once I dared to lift my eyes.' New Monthly Mag. March 1833.

Last Words on Greece. Murray's Mag. Feb. 1887.

'I watched thee when the foe was at our side.' Murray's Mag. Feb. 1887.

Farewell Petition to J. C. H[obhouse]. Murray's Mag. March 1887.

My Boy Hobbie O! Murray's Mag. March 1887.

[Epilogue on Wordsworth's Peter Bell.] Philadelphia Record, 28 Dec. 1891.

The King of the Humbugs. Good Words, xlv, Aug., Sept. 1904.

[Addition to English Bards and Scotch Reviewers.] TLS. 30 April 1931.

(9) POETICAL PIECES FIRST PUBLISHED IN BOOKS BY OTHER WRITERS

Hobhouse, J. C. Imitations and Translations from the Ancient and Modern Classics. 1809. [9 poems, pp. 185–230.]

The Genuine Rejected Addresses, presented to the Committee of Management for Drury Lane Theatre, preceded by that written by Lord Byron. 1812. [Reviewed in The Examiner, 18 Oct. 1812 (by Leigh Hunt).]

[Smith, James and Horace.] Rejected Addresses: or the New Theatrum Poetarum. 1812.

A Critique on the Address spoken at the Opening of the New Theatre Royal, Drury Lane. [1812.]

A Sequel to the 'Rejected Addresses' or the Theatrum Poetarum Minorum, by Another Author. 1813.

Williams, H. W. Travels in Italy, Greece, and the Ionian Isles. Edinburgh, 1820. [Vol. ii, p. 290. Lines written in the Travellers' Book at Orchomenus (or rather the Macri album at Athens. See TLS. 10 Dec. 1931).]

Foscolo, Ugo. Essays on Petrarch. 1823. [Pp. 215–217.]

Medwin, Thomas. Conversations of Lord Byron at Pisa, 1824. [Remember Thee (1st edn only); Stanzas to the Po; The Irish Avatar.]

Dallas, R. C. Recollections of the Life of Lord Byron. 1824. [Stanzas omitted from Childe Harold, Canto II.]

The Casket, A Miscellany consisting of Unpublished Poems. 1829. [Verses written in compliance with a Lady's request to contribute to her Album.]

Gardiner, Marguerite, Countess of Blessington. Conversations of Lord Byron. 1834. [See opposite, New Monthly Mag. 1832 and 1833.]

Hodgson, J. T. Memoir of the Rev. Francis Hodgson. 1878. [Newstead Abbey, vol. ii, p. 187.]

Noel, Roden. The Life of Lord Byron. 1890. [The Monk of Athos, pp. 206–7.]

Foster, Vere. The Two Duchesses. 1898. [To the Hon. Mrs George Lamb, p. 374.]

Milbanke, Ralph, Earl of Lovelace. Astarte, 1905 (priv. ptd). [Magdalén, Harmodia.]

(10) PROSE PIECES (INCLUDING LETTERS) FIRST PUBLISHED IN PERIODICALS AND IN BOOKS BY OTHER WRITERS

[Review of Wordsworth's Poems, 1807.] Monthly Literary Recreations, July 1807.

[Review of Gell's Geography of Ithaca.] Monthly Rev. Aug. 1811.

[Letter to the Editor.] Galignani's Messenger (Paris), May 1819. [Facs. rptd in Works (Galignani), Paris, 1826, 1 vol. edn.]

[Translations from the Armenian: The Epistle of the Corinthians to St Paul, etc.] A Grammar, Armenian and English, by Yarouthiun Augerean. Venice, 1819; Venice, 1832; Venice, 1873.

[Part of Journal for Sept. 1816.] London Mag. March 1820.

[Letter I.] Sir Charles Darell; or, The Vortex, by R. C. Dallas. 4 vols. 1820. |Vol. i, pp. 1–6. Rptd in Dallas, Recollections, 1824, pp. 259–63.]

[Letter on swimming the Hellespont.] Monthly Mag. April 1821. [Rptd The Traveller, 3 April 1821.]

Letter to My Grandmother's Review. The Liberal, no. 1, [15 Oct. 1822].

Notizie Estere. El Telegrafo Greco (Missolonghi), no. 5, 17 April 1824. [Rptd Nineteenth Cent. Sept. 1926.]

[Letter to E. D. Clarke.] The Life and Remains of E. D. Clarke. Ed. W. Otter, 1824. [P. 627.]

[Letter to M. H. Beyle, and others.] Conversations of Lord Byron at Pisa by Thomas Medwin. 1824.

[Letter to Andreas Londos, and others.] A Narrative of Lord Byron's Last Journey to Greece by Count Pietro Gamba. 1825.

[Letter to John Bowring.] Greece in 1823 and 1824 by L. F. C. Stanhope. 1825. [P. 550.]

[Letters to J. J. Coulmann.] Une Visite à Byron à Gênes, suivie d'une Lettre du Noble Lord sur l'Essai sur sa Vie et ses Ouvrages de M. A[médée] P[ichot]. Par J. J. Coulmann. Paris, 1826. Tr. Eng. Paul Pry, 1 April 1826.

[Letter to W. E. West.] The Literary Souvenir. 1827. [Preface p. x.]

[Letters to Thomas J. Dibdin.] Reminiscences of Thomas J. Dibdin. 1827. [Vol. II, pp. 65, 69–70.]

[Letters to Leigh Hunt.] Lord Byron and Some of his Contemporaries, by Leigh Hunt. 1828.

[Letter to Isaac D'Israeli.] The Literary Character by Isaac D'Israeli. 4th edn, 1828. [Preface.]

[Letters to Hon. Douglas Kinnaird.] The Keepsake, 1830. [Pp. 218–32.]

[Letter to Henry Angelo.] Reminiscences of Henry Angelo. Vol. II, 1830. [P. 132.]

[Letter to John Galt.] The Life of Lord Byron by John Galt. 1830. [Pp. 179–80.]

[Letters to Col. Duffie.] Conversations on Religion with Lord Byron by James Kennedy. 1830.

[Letters to Eugenius Roche.] London in a Thousand Years, with other Poems, by Eugenius Roche. 1830. [Pp. v–vi.]

[Letters to John Hunt.] Literary Guardian, 5 Dec. 1831–16 June 1832.

[Letters to the Earl of Blessington.] New Monthly Mag. July 1832.

[Letter to John Taylor.] Records of my Life by John Taylor. 1832. [Vol. II, p. 351.]

[Letter to Sir James Mackintosh.] Life of the Rt. Hon. Sir James Mackintosh, by R. J. Mackintosh. 1835. [Vol. II, p. 268 n.]

[Letter to Col. Wildman.] The Crayon Miscellany, no. II, Abbotsford and Newstead Abbey, by Washington Irving. Philadelphia, 1835; 1835.

[Letter to Lady Byron.] Memoirs, Journal, and Correspondence of Thomas Moore. Ed. Lord John Russell, vol. III, 1853. [Pp. 114, 115.]

[Letters to E. J. Trelawny.] Recollections of the Last Days of Shelley and Byron, by E. J. Trelawny. 1858.

[Letters to J. Ridge.] N. & Q. 10 Nov. 1860.

[Letters to Augusta Leigh.] Sharpe's London Mag. July, Aug. 1869.

[Letter on the Separation.] Academy, 9 Oct. 1869.

[Letters to William Harness.] The Literary Life of the Rev. William Harness by A. G. L'Estrange. 1871.

[Letter to Mrs Parker.] Lord Byron. A Biography, by Karl Elze. 1872. [Facs. p. 1.]

[Letter to Andrea Vacci.] Nuova Antologia (Florence), July 1874.

[Letters to Francis Hodgson.] Memoirs of the Rev. Francis Hodgson, by J. T. Hodgson. 2 vols. 1878.

[Letters.] Catalogue of the Collection of Autograph Letters formed by Alfred Morrison, [1st ser.]. Ed. A. W. Thibaudeau, vol. I, 1883 (priv. ptd). [Pp. 142–51.]

[Letters to Mary Shelley.] The Life and Letters of Mary Wollstonecraft Shelley, by Mrs Julian Marshall. 2 vols. 1889.

[Letters to Samuel Rogers.] Samuel Rogers and his Contemporaries, by P. W. Clayden. 2 vols. 1889.

[Letter to R. B. Hoppner.] The Archivist, April 1889.

[Letter to E. J. Dawkins.] Nineteenth Cent. Nov. 1891.

[Letter to C. J. Barry (28 : v : 1823).] E. Studien, XVII, 1892.

[Letter to Rev. R. Lowe.] Life and Letters of Robert Lowe, Viscount Sherbrooke, by A. P. Martin. 1893. [Vol. I, p. 46.]

[Letters.] The Collection of Letters formed by Alfred Morrison. [2nd ser.], vol. I, 1893. [Pp. 446–78.]

[Letter to Shelley (24 : iv : 1822).] E. Studien, XXII, 1895.

[Letters (Zehn Byroniana, ed. Eugen Koelbing).] E. Studien, XXV, 1898.

[Letter to C. Barry.] Ang. Bbl. April 1898.

[Letter to J. Ridge.] Newark Advertiser, 4 May 1898.

[Letters to Elizabeth, Duchess of Devonshire.] The Two Duchesses, by Vere Foster. 1898.

[Letters to John Murray.] Reference Catalogue of British and Foreign Autographs and MSS. Ed. T. J. Wise. Part VII. Byron. By John Murray. 1898. [Facs.]

[Dedication of Marino Faliero to Goethe.] Goethe-Jahrbuch, XX, 1899, pp. 33–6.

[Letter to the Earl of Clare.] Daily Chronicle, 19 April 1900.

[Letters to George Steevens, and others, ed. Clement K. Shorter.] The Sphere, 17 Sept. 1904.

[Letters to Lady Byron.] Astarte, by Ralph Milbanke, Earl of Lovelace. 1905 (priv. ptd).

[Letters.] Poems and Letters of Lord Byron. Ed. (from the original MSS in the possession of W. K. Bixby) W. N. C. Carlton, Chicago, Society of Dofobs, 1912 (priv. ptd).

[Letters.] Byroniana und anderes aus dem englischen Seminar in Erlangen. Erlangen, 1912.

[Letter to C. Barry.] Byroniana, by Ottokar Intze. [Birmingham, 1914.]

[Letter to W. Baldwin.] The Nation (New York), 18 April 1918.

[Letter to Hodgson (20 : i : 1811).] Annual Report of the British School at Athens, (1916–18), xxii, 1919, pp. 107–9. [Facs.]

[Letters to Augusta Leigh.] Astarte. 2nd edn with additional letters, ed. Mary Countess of Lovelace, 1921.

[Letters to Mrs Stith (Catherine Potter Stith and her meeting with Byron, by Adolph B. Benson).] South Atlantic Quart. Jan. 1923.

[Letters to Dallas, and to Hodgson.] A Descriptive Catalogue of an Exhibition of MSS and First Editions of Lord Byron, by R. H. Griffith and H. M. Jones. Austin (Texas), 1924.

[Letter to J. Webb (ed. A. Koszul).] Revue anglo-américaine, Aug. 1925.

[Letters to the Greek Committee.] Nineteenth Cent. Sept. 1926.

[Letters to Lady Byron.] The Life and Letters of Lady Byron, by E. C. Mayne. 1929.

[Letter to the Greek Committee (ed. W. H. McCarthy).] Yale University Lib. Gazette, Jan. 1934.

[Letters to Miss Mercer Elphinstone.] Cornhill Mag. April 1934.

Three Byron Letters. Ed. C. O. Parsons, N. & Q. 26 May 1934.

[Letters to Lord Holland.] The Home of the Hollands, by the Earl of Ilchester. [1937.]

(11) WORKS INCORRECTLY ASCRIBED
TO BYRON

[The spurious continuations of Don Juan have already been listed after the edns of that poem (see pp. 198–9) and are not here repeated.]

A Farrago Libelli. A Poem, chiefly Imitated from the First Satire of Juvenal. 1806. [See B. Dobell, English Rev. Aug. 1915; S. C. Chew, MLN. May 1916.]

Lord Byron's Farewell to England, with Three Other Poems. 1816. [Included in some later edns of Poems on his Domestic Circumstances. See Prothero, Prose Works, vol. iii, p. 337. Ascribed to John T. Agg. See H. M. Jones, The Author of Two Byron Apocrypha, MLN. Feb. 1926.]

Reflections on Shipboard by Lord Byron. 1816.

Lord Byron's Pilgrimage to the Holy Land. 1816; 2nd edn (without Byron's name), 1817. [See Prothero, vol. iv, p. 19. Ascribed to John T. Agg. See H. M. Jones, MLN. Feb. 1926.]

Clarke, Hewson. Lord Byron. The Legal Critics Refuted; or an Essay to prove from the arguments of Lord Byron's Counsel, that 'Childe Harold' and the 'Prisoner of Chillon' are Mercenary Forgeries, and that 'Pilgrimage to the Holy Land' is a genuine production. 1817.

Modern Greece. 1817. [By Felicia Hemans.]

Poems Written by Somebody. 1818.

Childe Harold's Pilgrimage to the Dead Sea; Death on the Pale Horse; and other Poems. 1818. [See Prothero, vol. iv, p. 474.]

The Vampyre. A Tale. 1819 (3 edns; first pbd in New Monthly Mag. April 1819). Tr. French by Amédée Pichot, Paris, 1830; dramatised in German by L. Ritter, Brunswick, 1822; tr. Spanish, Paris, 1829. [By J. W. Polidori. See Prothero, vol. iv, p. 286.]

Anastasius, or Memoirs of a Greek. 1819. [By Thomas Hope.]

Giuseppino, An Occidental Story. 1821 (bis); Philadelphia, 1822. [Rptd in Arnaldo, Gaddo, etc., 1836; by E. N. Shannon.]

La Mort de Napoléon. Dithyrambe traduit de l'anglais de Lord Byron. Paris, 1821 (7 edns).

Le Cri d'Angleterre au Tombeau de sa Reine, Dithyrambe de Lord Byron. Traduit de l'Anglais. Paris, 1821.

Irner par Lord Byron. 2 vols. Paris, 1821.

The Duke of Mantua. A Tragedy. 1823; 1833. [By John Roby; included in The Legendary and Poetical Remains of John Roby, 1854.]

My Wedding Night: The Obnoxious Chapter in Lord Byron's Memoirs. John Bull Mag. July 1824.

The Count Arezzi. 1824. [By Robert Eyres Landor.]

Lettre de Lord Byron au Grand Turc. Paris, 1824.

Arnaldo; Gaddo; and other unacknowledged poems by Lord Byron and some of his contemporaries. Ed. 'Odoardo Volpi,' Dublin, 1836.

The Incdited Works of Lord Byron, now first published from his Letters, Journals, and other MSS in the possession of his son Major Gordon Byron. 2 pts (all pbd), New York, 1849. [Some of this is a rpt of genuine originals already pbd.]

Don Leon. [Pbd abroad before 1853? See N. & Q. 15 Jan. 1853]; 1866 (bis); rptd 1934.

Leon to Annabella. An Epistle after the Manner of Ovid. [N.d.]; 1865; 1866 (as The Great Secret Revealed); Brussels, 1875; Paris, [c. 1900]; New York, 1922 (in Poetica Erotica, ed. T. R. Smith, vol. iii).

The Unpublished Letters of Lord Byron. Edited with a Critical Essay by H. S. Schultess-Young. 1872. [Suppressed before publication. The only letters in this book known to be authentic are those to Byron's mother; and these had been ptd previously.]

The Bride's Confession. Paris, 1916 (priv. ptd).

Seventeen Letters to an Unknown Lady, 1811–17. Ed. W. E. Peck, New York, 1930. [These letters derive from the Schultess-Young edn of 1872. Prothero, vol. vi, p. 460, did not accept them as authentic.]

(12) Biography and Criticism

(a) Biography

Hobhouse, J. C. (Baron Broughton). A Journey through Albania and Other Provinces of Turkey. 1813; 2 vols. 1813; 2 vols. 1855 (as Travels in Albania).

—— Lord Byron's Residence in Greece. Westminster Rev. July 1824.

—— [Review of] Dallas's Recollections and Medwin's Conversations. Westminster Rev. Jan. 1825.

—— Italy; Remarks made in Several Visits from 1816 to 1854. 2 vols. 1859.

—— Recollections of a Long Life. 5 vols. 1865 (priv. ptd); 6 vols, 1909–11.

—— Contemporary Account of the Separation of Lord and Lady Byron, also of the destruction of Lord Byron's Memoirs. 1870 (priv. ptd; reviewed in Edinburgh Rev. April 1871). [Rptd in Recollections of a Long Life, 2nd edn, vol. ii.]

A Narrative of the Circumstances which attended the separation of Lord and Lady Byron. 1816.

A Catalogue of Books the Property of a Nobleman [i.e. Byron] about to leave England, which will be sold by Auction by [Robert H.] Evans. 5 April [1816].

Shelley, P. B. History of a Six Weeks' Tour. 1817.

[Beyle, M. H.] Rome, Naples, et Florence en 1817 par M. de Stendhal. Paris, 1817; tr. Eng. 1818.

—— Lord Byron en Italie et en France. Revue de Paris, March 1830; tr. Eng. (as Reminiscences of Lord Byron in Italy), Mirror of Literature, 17, 24 April 1830. [Rptd in Racine et Shakespeare, Paris, 1854.]

[Watkins, John.] Memoirs of the Life and Writings of Lord Byron. 1822; tr. German, Leipzig, 1825.

El Telegrafo Greco (Missolonghi), 24 April 1824.

Full Particulars of the much Lamented Death of Lord Byron with a Sketch of his Life. 1824.

Gordon, Sir Cosmo. The Life and Genius of Lord Byron. 1824. [Rptd in The Pamphleteer, vol. xxiv, 1824.]

Medwin, Thomas. Journal of the Conversations of Lord Byron at Pisa. 1824 (3 edns). [Reviewed in Blackwood's Mag. Nov. 1824; GM. Nov. 1824.]

Murray, John. Notes on Capt. Medwin's Conversations of Lord Byron. 1824 (priv. ptd). [Rptd in The Works of Lord Byron (Murray), 1829.]

Capt. Medwin vindicated from the Calumnies of the Reviewers by Vindex. 1825.

—— The Angler in Wales. 2 vols. 1834.

Dallas, R. C. Recollections of the Life of Lord Byron, 1808–1814. 1824.

Belloc, Louise S. Lord Byron. Paris, 1824.

The Particulars of the Dispute between the late Lord Byron and Mr Southey. Edinburgh. 1824.

Tricoupi, Spiridion. Funeral Oration on Lord Byron, delivered at Missolonghi. 1825; 1836.

Gamba, Pietro. A Narrative of Lord Byron's Last Journey to Greece. 1825.

Parry, William. The Last Days of Lord Byron. 1825.

Blaquiere, Edward. Narrative of a Second Visit to Greece, including Facts connected with the Last Days of Lord Byron. 1825.

Stanhope, L. F. C. Greece in 1823 and 1824, to which is added Reminiscences of Lord Byron. 1825; Paris, 1825.

Clinton, George. Memoirs of the Life and Writings of Lord Byron. 1825.

Salvo, C. de. Lord Byron en Italie et en Grèce. Paris, 1825.

The Life, Writings, Opinions and Times of Lord Byron, including copious Recollections of the lately destroyed Memoirs by an English Gentleman in the Greek Military Service. 3 vols. 1825. [Ascribed to Matthew Iley.]

[Kilgour, Alexander.] Anecdotes of Lord Byron from Authentic Sources. 1825.

Albrizzi, Isabella Teotochi. Ritratti Scritti. Pisa, 1826.

Lake, J. W. The Life of Lord Byron. Paris, 1826; Frankfort, 1827. [First pbd in Galignani's edn of the Works of Lord Byron, Paris, 1822.]

Catalogue of the Library of the late Lord Byron which will be sold at Auction by R. H. Evans, 16 July 1827. Ed. G. H. Doane, [Nebraska] 1929 (priv. ptd).

Hunt, J. H. Leigh. Lord Byron and Some of his Contemporaries. 1828; 2 vols. 1828. [Reviewed: Athenaeum, 2, 23, 30 Jan. 1828; Quarterly Rev. March 1828.]
—— Autobiography. 3 vols. 1850; 1860 (rev.); ed. R. Ingpen, 1903.
Moore, Thomas. Letters and Journals of Lord Byron, with Notices of his Life. 2 vols. 1830; 2 vols. New York, [1830]; Paris, 1831; 3 vols. 1832; 3 vols. 1833; 1837; 1847; 1850; 6 vols. 1851; 1860; 1875; tr. French, Paris, 1830–1. [Reviewed: Blackwood's Mag. Feb., March 1830; Athenaeum, 25 Dec. 1830, 1, 8 Jan. 1831; Quarterly Rev. Jan. 1831 (by J. G. Lockhart); Fraser's Mag. March 1831; British Critic, April 1831 (by C. W. Le Bas); Edinburgh Rev. June 1831 (by T. B. Macaulay).]
[Byron, Isabella, Lady.] Remarks occasioned by Mr Moore's Notices of Lord Byron's Life. [1830] (priv. ptd; 3 edns).
Campbell, Thomas. [Lady Byron and Thomas Moore.] New Monthly Mag. April 1830.
Lord Byron Vindicated and Mr Campbell Answered. 1830.
Galt, John. The Life of Lord Byron. 1830; [1908]. [Reviewed: Athenaeum, 4 Sept. 1830; GM. Sept. 1830; Edinburgh Rev. Oct. 1830; Fraser's Mag. Oct. 1830.]
—— Pot versus Kettle. Fraser's Mag. Dec. 1830.
—— Prose and Verse, Humorous, Satirical, and Sentimental. Ed. R. H. Shepherd, 1878. [Contains rough notes for the Life.]
Kennedy, James. Conversations on Religion with Lord Byron and Others, held in Cephalonia, a Short Time previous to his lordship's Death. 1830.
Gordon, P. L. Personal Memoirs or Reminiscences. 1830.
Milligen, Julius. Memoirs of the Affairs of Greece with Various Anecdotes of Lord Byron, and an Account of his last Illness and Death. 1831.
Gardiner, Marguerite (Countess of Blessington). Conversations of Lord Byron. 1834; 1893 (rev.); tr. French, Paris, 1833. [First pbd in New Monthly Mag. July 1832–Dec. 1833.]
Bluemel, M. Die Unterhaltungen Lord Byrons mit der Gräfin Blessington als ein Beitrag zur Byronbiographie kritisch untersucht. Breslau, 1900.
—— The Idler in Italy. 3 vols. 1839–40.
Browne, J. Hamilton. Voyage from Leghorn to Cephalonia with Lord Byron in 1823. Blackwood's Mag. Jan. 1834.
—— Narrative of a Visit to Greece. Fraser's Mag. Sept. 1834.

Irving, Washington. The Crayon Miscellany. No. 2 (Abbotsford and Newstead Abbey). Philadelphia, 1835; 1835.
Niccolini, G. Vita di Giorgio, Lord Byron. Milan, 1835.
Conversations of an American with Lord Byron. New Monthly Mag. Oct., Nov. 1835.
Mordani, Filippo. La Vita di Giorgio Lord Byron. Bologna, 1839.
Dueringsfeld, Ida von. Byrons Frauen. Breslau, 1845.
Russell, Lord John. Memoirs, Journal, and Correspondence of Thomas Moore. 6 vols. 1853–6.
Rogers, Samuel. Recollections of the Table Talk of Samuel Rogers. 1856.
Trelawny, E. J. Recollections of the Last Days of Shelley and Byron. 1858; ed. E. Dowden, 1906.
—— Records of Shelley, Byron, and the Author. 2 vols. 1878; 1887; 1905.
—— The Relations of P. B. Shelley with his Two Wives and a Comment on the Character of Lord Byron. 1920 (priv. ptd).
—— The Relations of Lord Byron and Augusta Leigh. 1920 (priv. ptd).
Finlay, George. History of the Greek Revolution. 2 vols. 1861.
Gronow, R. H. Reminiscences: being Anecdotes of the Camp, the Court, and the Clubs. 1862.
—— Last Recollections, being the Fourth and Final Series. 1866.
Coulmann, J. J. Réminiscences. 3 vols. Strasburg, 1862–9.
Guiccioli, Teresa, Countess of (Mme de Boissy). Lord Byron jugé par les Témoins de sa Vie. Paris, 1868; tr. Eng. 1869, New York, 1869. [Reviewed in Belgravia, Feb. 1869, by W. Stigand.]
Martineau, Harriet. Biographical Sketches. 1869.
Stowe, Harriet Beecher. The True Story of Lady Byron's Married Life. Macmillan's Mag. Sept. 1869.
—— Lady Byron Vindicated: a History of the Byron Controversy. 1870.
Byron painted by his Compeers; or all about Lord Byron from his Marriage to his Death as given in the Various Newspapers of his day. 1869.
Austin, Alfred. A Vindication of Lord Byron. 1869.
Mackay, Charles. Medora Leigh. A History and an Autobiography. 1869.
[Fox, John.] Vindication of Lady Byron. Blackwood's Mag. Oct. 1869. [Separately rptd 1871.]
[Hayward, Abraham.] The Byron Mystery. Quarterly Rev. Oct. 1869, Jan. 1870. [Letters of Lady Byron.]

[Hayward, Abraham.] Sketches of Eminent Statesmen and Writers. 2 vols. 1880.

[Lucas, Samuel.] The Stowe-Byron Controversy. A Complete Résumé of all that has been written and said on the Subject. 1869.

Elze, Karl. Lord Byron. Berlin, 1870, 1881, 1886; tr. Eng. 1872 (with addns).

L'Estrange, A. G. The Literary Life of the Rev. William Harness. 1871.

[Haussonville, Comtesse de.] La Jeunesse de Lord Byron. Paris, 1872.

—— Les Dernières Années de Lord Byron. Paris, 1874.

Tribolati, Felice. Lord Byron a Pisa. Nuova Antologia, July 1874. [Rptd in Saggi Critici e Biografici, Pisa, 1891.]

Mackay, George E. Lord Byron at the Armenian Convent. Venice, 1876.

Torrens, W. M. Memoirs of William, 2nd Viscount Melbourne. 1878.

Hodgson, J. T. Memoirs of the Rev. Francis Hodgson. 2 vols. 1878.

Telles, Alberto. Lord Byron em Portugal. Lisbon, 1879.

Nichol, John. Byron. 1880. (English Men of Letters ser.)

Jeaffreson, J. C. The Real Lord Byron. 1883. [Reviewed: Fortnightly Rev. April 1883; Quarterly Rev. July 1883 (by Abraham Hayward); Nineteenth Cent. Aug. 1883 (by J. A. Froude).]

Dowden, Edward. Life of P. B. Shelley. 2 vols. 1886.

Jerningham, H. E. H. Reminiscences of an Attaché. 1886.

[Milbanke, Ralph (Viscount Wentworth, later Earl of Lovelace).] Lady Noel Byron and the Leighs: Some Authentic Records of Certain Circumstances in the Lives of Augusta Leigh and Others that concerned Anne Isabella Lady Byron. 1870 (priv. ptd).

—— Astarte. A Fragment of Truth concerning Lord Byron. 1905 (priv. ptd); ed. Mary, Countess of Lovelace, 1921 (with additional letters).

Megyery, A. Lord Byron. Budapest, 1889.

Noel, Roden. Life of Lord Byron. 1890.

Rabbe, Felix. Les Maîtresses authentiques de Lord Byron. Paris, 1890.

Bancroft, George. History of the Battle of Lake Erie and Miscellaneous Papers. New York, 1891.

Ross, Janet. Byron at Pisa. Nineteenth Cent. Nov. 1891.

Smiles, Samuel. A Publisher and his Friends. Memoir and Correspondence of the late John Murray. 2 vols. 1891.

Roe, John C. Some Obscure and Disputed Points in Byronic Biography. Leipzig, 1893.

Hayman, Henry. Lord Byron and the Greek Patriots. Harper's Mag. Feb. 1894.

Hamann, Albert. The Life and Works of Lord Byron. Berlin, 1895; Berlin, 1910.

Bleibtreu, Karl. Byron der Uebermensch, sein Leben und sein Dichten. Jena, [1896].

Graham, William. Last Links with Byron, Shelley, and Keats. 1898. [See N. & Q. 27 Oct. 1923.]

Foster, Vere. The Two Duchesses. 1898.

Biondi, Emilio. La Figlia di Lord Byron. Faenza, 1899.

Ackermann, Richard. Lord Byron. Sein Leben, seine Werke, sein Einfluss auf die deutsche Literatur. Heidelberg, 1901.

Williams, E. E. The Journal of Edward Ellerker Williams, companion of Shelley and Byron in 1821 and 1822. 1902.

Veselovsky, A. N. Byron. Moscow, 1902; Moscow, 1914.

Bulloch, J. M. House of Gordon. Gight. New Spalding Club, [1903] (priv. ptd).

Lumbroso, A. Il Generale Mengaldo, Lord Byron, e l' ' Ode on the Star of the Legion of Honour.' Rome, 1903. [Rptd in Pagine Veneziane, Rome, 1905.]

Koeppel, E. Lord Byron. Berlin, 1903; tr. Hungarian, Budapest, 1913.

Hoops, Johannes. Lord Byrons Leben und Dichten. Frankfort, 1903.

Wetz, W. Neuere Beiträge zur Byron-Biographie. Cologne, 1905.

Prothero, R. E. (Baron Ernle). The Goddess of Wisdom and Lady Caroline Lamb. Monthly Rev. June 1905.

—— The End of the Byron Mystery. Nineteenth Cent. Aug. 1921.

Murray, John [iv], Pember, E. H., and Prothero, R. E. Lord Byron and his Detractors. Roxburghe Club, 1906 (priv. ptd).

Edgecumbe, Richard. Byron. The Last Phase. 1909.

Churchman, P. H. Lord Byron's Experiences in the Spanish Peninsula in 1809. Bulletin Hispanique (Bordeaux), March, June 1909.

Lang, Andrew. Byron and Mary Chaworth. Fortnightly Rev. Aug. 1910.

Meneghetti, Nazzareno. Lord Byron a Venezia. Venice, [1910].

Miller, Barnette. Leigh Hunt's Relations with Byron, Shelley, and Keats. New York, 1910.

Polidori, J. W. The Diary. Ed. W. M. Rossetti, 1911.

Angeli, Helen Rossetti. Shelley and his Friends in Italy. 1911.

Shaw, W. A. The Authentic Portraits of Lord Byron. The Connoisseur, July, Aug. 1911.

Brecknock, Albert. The Pilgrim Poet. Lord Byron of Newstead. 1911.

—— Byron. A Study of the Poet in the Light of New Discoveries. [1926.]

Knott, John. The Last Illness of Lord Byron. St Paul (Minnesota), 1912.

Mayne, Ethel. Byron. 2 vols. 1912; [1924].

—— The Life and Letters of Anne Isabella, Lady Noel Byron. 1929.

Ward, James, and Napier, George G. Lord Byron's Lameness. Nottingham, 1915 (priv. ptd).

Fletcher, William. Lord Byron's Illness and Death as described in a Letter to Augusta Leigh. Nottingham, 1920 (priv. ptd).

Lord Teignmouth. Byron's Suliote Bodyguard. Nineteenth Cent. April 1924.

Berton, R. Une Confession de Byron en 1823. La Nouvelle Revue (Paris), 15 April 1924.

Cameron, H. C. The Mystery of Lord Byron's Club Foot. N. & Q. 19 April 1924.

Nicolson, Harold. Byron. The Last Journey. 1924.

Raymond, Dora N. The Political Career of Lord Byron. [1924.]

Bellamy, R. L. Byron the Man. 1924.

Symon, J. D. Byron in Perspective. [1924.]

Fox, Sir John C. The Byron Mystery. 1924.

Boutet de Monvel, Roger. La Vie de Lord Byron. Paris, 1924.

Rodocanachi, E. Byron, 1788–1824. Paris, [1924].

Blackett, John. Joseph Blackett and his Links with Byron. Quarterly Rev. Jan. 1925.

Drinkwater, John. The Pilgrim of Eternity. Byron—A Conflict. [1925.]

de Beer, E. S. and Seton, W. W. Byroniana. The Archives of the London Greek Committee. Nineteenth Cent. Sept. 1926.

Cantoni, F. La Prima Dimora di Lord Byron a Bologna. Il Comune di Bologna (Bologna), March, April 1926.

—— Byron e la Guiccioli a Bologna. Ibid. April, May 1927.

Gordon, Armistead G. Allegra. The Story of Byron and Miss Clairmont. New York, 1926.

Treimer, K. Byron und die Albanologie. Séminaire de Philologie albanoise (Belgrade), III, 1926.

Mayfield, J. S. Notes on Lord Byron's Infirmity. [Texas] 1927 (priv. ptd).

Rava, Luigi. Lord Byron e P. B. Shelley a Ravenna e Teresa Guiccioli Gamba. Rome, 1929.

Richter, Helene. Lord Byron. Persönlichkeit und Werk. Halle, 1929.

Engel, C. E. Byron et Shelley en Suisse et en Savoie, Mai–Oct. 1816. Chambéry, 1930.

'Maurois, André' (E. S. W. Herzog). Byron. Paris, 1930; tr. Eng. [1930].

—— Byron et les Femmes. Paris, 1934.

Kemble, James. Byron: his Lameness and Last Illness. Quarterly Rev. Oct. 1931.

Castelain, M. Byron. Paris, 1931.

Simmons, E. J. Byron and a Greek Maid. MLR. xxvii, 1932.

'Paston, G.' (Emily Morse Symonds). New Lights on Byron's Lovers. Cornhill Mag. April–Sept. 1934.

Clarke, Isabel C. Shelley and Byron. 1934.

Quennell, P. C. Byron. The Years of Fame. 1935.

—— Byron and Harriette Wilson. Cornhill Mag. April 1935.

Renzulli, M. Il Peccatore. Byron. Naples [1935].

Calvert, W. J. Byron. Romantic Paradox. Chapel Hill, 1935.

Foà, Giovanna. Lord Byron, Poeta e Carbonaro. Florence, 1935.

Origo, Iris. Allegra. 1935.

Caclamanos, D. Some Byron Relics. N. & Q. 11 June 1938.

Pope-Hennessy, U. Byron and an American. TLS. 23 April 1938.

(b) Byron in Poetry and Fiction (to 1837)

[Lamb, Lady Caroline.] Glenarvon. 3 vols. 1816 (3 edns); [1865] (as The Fatal Passion); tr. French, Paris, 1819.

[Barrett, Eaton Stannard.] Six Weeks at Long's, by a Late Resident. 3 vols. 1817.

Three Weeks at Fladong's, by a Late Visitant. 1817.

[Peacock, Thomas Love.] Nightmare Abbey. 1818.

An Account of Lord Byron's Residence in the Island of Mitylene. 1819. [See Prothero, vol. IV, p. 288; Byron and Col. Rooke [by F. W. Hasluck], Saturday Rev. 11 June 1921.]

Lamartine, Alphonse de. L'Homme: à Lord Byron. Méditations Poétiques. Paris, 1820; tr. Eng. by C. Hicks, Whitby, 1837. [Another English tr., 1843.]

Delavigne, Casimir. Messénienne sur Lord Byron. Paris, 1824 (bis). [Rptd in Nouvelles Messéniennes, Paris, 1824; tr. Eng. Marseilles, 1824.]

Vigny, Alfred de. Sur la Mort de Byron. La Muse Française (Paris), 15 June 1824.

Shelley, P. B. Julian and Maddalo. [In Posthumous Poems, 1824.]

Narrative of Lord Byron's Voyage to Corsica and Sardinia by Capt. Benson. 1824; Paris, 1825.

Bedford, J. H. Wanderings of Childe Harold. 3 vols. 1825.

[Shelley, Mary.] The Last Man. 3 vols. 1826.

—— Lodore. 3 vols. 1835.

Taylor, John. Byronna the Disappointed. [c. 1830.]

[Brydges, Sir S. E.] Modern Aristocracy, or the Bard's Reception. Geneva, 1831.

Driver, H. A. Harold de Burun. A Semi-Dramatic Poem. 1835.

Laube, H. Lord Byron, eine Reisenovelle. Mannheim, 1835.

Mitford, J. The Private Life of Lord Byron; comprising his Voluptuous Amours, Secret Intrigues, and Close Connection with Various Ladies of Rank. [1836]; tr. French, Paris, 1837.

Magnien, Édouard. Mortel, Ange, ou Démon. Paris, 1836.

[Disraeli, Benjamin.] Venetia, or the Poet's Daughter. 3 vols. 1837.

> Hamilton, Herbert Bruce. Inaugural Essay on the Portrayal of the Life and Character of Lord Byron in a Novel entitled Venetia. Leipzig, 1884.

Cipro, G. B. Lord Byron a Venezia. [Florence?] 1837. [Drama.]

(c) Criticism

[Reference should also be made to the numerous studies of Byron's influence on the Continent listed pp. 17–45 above.]

[Irving, Washington.] Lord Byron. Analectic Mag. (Philadelphia), July 1814. [Rptd in Poetical Works of Lord Byron, Boston, 1814.]

—— An Unwritten Drama of Lord Byron. The Gift for 1836 (New York), [1835]. [Separate rpt, ed. T. O. Mabbott, Metuchen (New Jersey), 1925.]

Hazlitt, William. Lectures on the English Poets. 1818.

—— The Spirit of the Age. 1825.

Wiffen, J. H. The Character and Poetry of Lord Byron. New Monthly Mag. May 1819.

The Radical Triumvirate; or Infidel Paine, Lord Byron, and Surgeon Lawrence colleaguing with the patriotic radicals to emancipate mankind from all laws, human and divine. By an Oxonian. 1820.

Vigny, Alfred de. Littérature Anglaise: Œuvres Complètes de Lord Byron. Le Conservateur Littéraire (Paris), Dec. 1820.

Watts, A. A. Lord Byron's Plagiarisms. Literary Gazette, 24 Feb.–31 March 1821.

Styles, John. Lord Byron's Works viewed in connection with Christianity and the Obligations of Social Life. 1824.

Brydges, Sir S. E. Letters on the Character and Poetical Genius of Lord Byron. 1824.

—— An Impartial Portrait of Lord Byron as a Poet and a Man. Paris, 1825.

Scott, Sir Walter. The Death of Lord Byron. Edinburgh Weekly Journ. 19 May 1824. [Rptd in Miscellaneous Prose Works, vol. I, Edinburgh, 1841.]

Hugo, Victor. Sur George Gordon, Lord Byron. La Muse Francaise, 15 June 1824.

Simmons, J. W. An Inquiry into the Moral Character of Lord Byron. New York, 1824; 1826.

[Phillips, W.] A Review of the Character and Writings of Lord Byron. Atlantic Monthly, Oct. 1825. [Separately rptd 1826; also attrib. to Andrews Norton.]

Byroniana: Bozzies and Piozzies. 1825.

Mérimée, Prosper. Mémoires de Lord Byron. Le National (Paris), 7 March 1830.

Macaulay, T. B. (Baron). Lord Byron. Edinburgh Rev. June 1831. [Rptd in Critical and Miscellaneous Works, vol. I, Philadelphia, 1841.]

'Sand, George' (A. A. L. Dudevant). Essai sur le Drame Fantastique: Goethe, Byron, Mickiewicz. Revue des Deux Mondes, 1 Dec. 1839. [Rptd in Autour de la Table, Paris, 1862.]

Villemain, A. F. Études de Littérature anciennes et étrangères. Paris, 1846.

Mazzini, Giuseppe. Byron e Goethe. Scritti Litterari d' un Italiano vivente. Lugano, 1847; tr. Eng. (Life and Writings of G. Mazzini, vol. VI, 1891).

Hohenhausen, Elise von. Rousseau, Goethe, Byron. Cassel, 1847.

Nisard, D. Lord Byron et la Société anglaise. Revue des Deux Mondes, 1 Nov. 1850.

Chasles, V. E. P. Vie et Influence de Byron sur son Époque. [In Études sur la Littérature et les Mœurs de l'Angleterre au XIXe Siècle, Paris, [1850].]

Kingsley, Charles. Thoughts on Shelley and Byron. Fraser's Mag. Nov. 1853. [Rptd in Miscellanies, vol. I, 1859.]

Hannay, J. Satire and Satirists. 1854.

Ferguson, J. C. Lecture on the Writings and Genius of Byron. Carlisle, 1856.

Mickiewicz, Adam. Goethe i Byron. Gazeta Codzienna (Warsaw), 29 April 1860; tr. French (Mélanges Posthumes, vol. I, Paris, 1872).

Mondot, Armand. Histoire de la Vie et des Écrits de Lord Byron. Paris, 1860.

Treitschke, Heinrich von. Lord Byron und der Radicalismus. Preussisches Jahrbuch, Berlin, 1863. [Rptd in Historische und politische Aufsaetze, Leipzig, 1865.]

Morley, John. Byron and the French Revolution. Fortnightly Rev. Dec. 1870. [Rptd in Miscellanies, vol. I, 1886.]

Blaze de Bury, H. Lord Byron et le Byronisme. Revue des Deux Mondes, 1 Oct. 1872.

Ruskin, John. Fiction, Fair and Foul. Nineteenth Cent. Sept. 1880. [Rptd in Works, ed. Sir E. T. Cook and A. D. O. Wedderburn, vol. XXXIV.]

'Rutherford, Mark' (William Hale White). Byron, Goethe, and Mr Matthew Arnold. Contemporary Rev. Aug. 1881. [Rptd in Pages from a Journal, 1901.]

Froude, J. A. A Leaf from the Real Life of Lord Byron. Nineteenth Cent. Aug. 1883.

Edgecumbe, Richard. History of the Byron Memorial. 1883.

Swinburne, A. C. Wordsworth and Byron. Nineteenth Cent. April, May 1884. [Rptd in Miscellanies, 1886.]

Jowett, B. Byron. [Oxford, 1884] (priv. ptd).

Weddigen, F. H. O. Lord Byrons Einfluss auf die europäische Literatur der Neuzeit. Hanover, 1884; Leipzig, 1901.

'Gerard, William' (William Gerard Smith). Byron re-studied in his Dramas. 1886.

Arnold, Matthew. Byron. [In Essays in Criticism, ser. 2, 1888. Rptd from The Poetry of Byron, 1881.]

Axon, W. E. A. Byron's Influence on European Literature. [In Stray Chapters on Literature, Folk-lore and Archaeology, 1888.]

Lombroso, Cesare. L' Uomo di Genio. Turin, 1888; tr. Eng. 1891.

Westenholz, F. Ueber Byrons historische Dramen. Stuttgart, 1890.

Dallois, Joseph. Études morales et littéraires à propos de Lord Byron. Paris, 1890.

Brandes, G. M. C. Shelley und Lord Byron. Zwei literarische Charakterbilder. Leipzig, 1894.

Maychrzak, F. Lord Byron als Uebersetzer. Altenburg, 1895.

Dowden, E. The French Revolution and English Literature. 1897.

Donner, J. O. E. Lord Byrons Weltanschauung. Helsingfors, 1897.

Holthausen, F. Skandinavische Byron-Übersetzungen. E. Studien, xxv, 1898.

Kraeger, H. Der Byronsche Heldentypus. Munich, 1898.

Phillips, Stephen. The Poetry of Byron. Cornhill Mag. Jan. 1898.

Woodberry, G. E. Makers of Literature. New York, 1900.

Clark, W. J. Byron und die romantische Poesie in Frankreich. Leipzig, 1901.

Ritter, O. Byron and Chateaubriand. Archiv, cix, 1902.

Muoni, G. La Fama del Byron e il Byronismo in Italia. Milan, 1903.

—— La Leggenda del Byron in Italia. Milan, 1907.

Pudbres, A. Lord Byron, the Admirer and Imitator of Alfieri. E. Studien, xxxiii, 1903.

Fuhrmann, L. Die Belesenheit des jungen Byron. Berlin, 1903.

Hoops, J. Lord Byrons Leben und Dichten. Frankfort, 1903.

Melchior, F. Heines Verhältnis zu Lord Byron. Berlin, 1903.

Coleridge, E. H. Lord Byron. Trans. Royal Soc. Lit. xxv, 1904.

Holzhausen, P. Bonaparte, Byron, und die Briten. Frankfort, 1904.

Zabel, E. Byrons Kenntnis von Shakespeare und sein Urteil über ihn. Halle, 1904.

Collins, J. C. The Works of Lord Byron. [In Studies in Poetry and Criticism, 1905.]

Leonard, W. E. Byron and Byronism in America. Boston, 1905.

Ochsenbein, W. Die Aufnahme Lord Byrons in Deutschland und sein Einfluss auf den jungen Heine. Berne, 1905.

Estève, Edmond. Byron et le Romantisme français. Paris, 1907; Paris, 1929.

Calcaño, J. Tres Poetas pessimistas del Siglo xix. Caracas, 1907.

Eimer, M. Lord Byron und die Kunst. Strasburg, 1907.

—— Die persönlichen Beziehungen zwischen Byron und den Shelleys. Heidelberg, 1910.

—— Byron und die Kosmos. Heidelberg, 1912.

Symons, Arthur. The Romantic Movement in English Poetry. 1909.

Churchman, P. H. Byron and Espronceda. Revue Hispanique (Paris), March 1909.

—— The Beginnings of Byronism in Spain. Revue Hispanique (Paris), Dec. 1910.

Simhart, Max. Lord Byrons Einfluss auf die italienische Litteratur. Munich, 1909.

Austin, A. Byron and Wordsworth. [In The Bridling of Pegasus, 1910.]

Chesterton, G. K. Twelve Types. 1910.

Dobosal, G. Lord Byron in Deutschland. Zwickau, 1911.

Spasowicz, W. Byronism u Pushkina i Lermontova. Vilna, 1911.

Fuess, C. M. Lord Byron as a Satirist in Verse. New York, 1912.

Byroniana und anderes aus dem englischen Seminar in Erlangen. Erlangen, 1912.

Windakiewicz, S. Walter Scott i Lord Byron w Odniesieniu do polskiej Poezyi romantycznij. Cracow, 1914.

Chew, Samuel C. The Dramas of Lord Byron. Göttingen, 1915.

—— Byron in England: his Fame and After-Fame. 1924.

Hearn, Lafcadio. Interpretations of Literature. New York, 1916.

Northup, C. S. Byron and Gray. MLN. May 1917.

Zacchetti, C. Lord Byron e l' Italia. Palermo, 1919.

Grierson, Sir H. J. C. Lord Byron: Arnold and Swinburne. Proc. British Academy, IX, 1921.

Reul, P. de. Byron. Revue de l'Université de Bruxelles, May, June 1921.

Goode, C. T. Byron as Critic. Weimar, 1923.

Porta, A. Byronismo italiano. Milan, 1923.

Ker, W. P. Byron: an Oxford Lecture. The Criterion, Oct. 1923. [Rptd in Collected Essays, ed. C. Whibley, vol. I, 1925.]

Byron the Poet. Essays by Viscount Haldane, Sir A. T. Quiller-Couch, H. J. C. Grierson, William Archer, Marie Corelli, [etc.]. Ed. W. A. Briscoe, 1924.

Sbornik Byron, 1824–1924. By P. S. Kogan, M. N. Pozanov, L. P. Grossman, E. D. Grimm. Moscow, 1924.

Garrod, H. W. Byron, 1824–1924. Oxford, 1924.

Henson, H. H. Byron. Cambridge, 1924.

Jirmunsky, V. M. Byron i Pushkin. Leningrad, 1924.

Castelain, M. Byron—en 1924. Revue anglo-américaine, Oct. 1924.

Elliott, G. R. Byron and the Comic Spirit. PMLA. XXXIX, 1924. [Rptd in The Cycle of Modern Poetry, Princeton, 1929.]

Prothero, R. E. (Baron Ernle). The Poetry of Byron. Quarterly Rev. April 1924.

Rice, R. A. Lord Byron's British Reputation. Northampton (Mass.), 1924.

Spender, H. Byron and Greece. 1924.

Farinelli, A. Byron e il Byronismo. Bologna, 1924.

—— Byron e il Byronismo nell' Argentina. Rome, 1928.

Elton, Oliver. The Present Value of Byron. RES. Jan. 1925.

Chambers, R. W. Ruskin (and Others) on Byron. English Ass. Lecture, 1925.

Robertson, J. G. Goethe and Byron. Publications of English Goethe Soc. II, 1925.

Praz, Mario. La Fortuna di Byron in Inghilterra. Florence, 1925.

Popma, T. Byron en het Byronisme in de nederlandsche Letterkunde. Amsterdam, 1928.

Flower, Robin E. W. Byron and Ossian. Nottingham, 1929.

Du Bos, Charles. Byron et le Besoin de la Fatalité. Paris, 1929; tr. Eng. [1932].

Doerken, Hildegard. Lord Byrons Subjectivismus in seinem Verhalten zur Geschichte. Leipzig, 1929.

Schults, U. Het Byronisme in Nederland. Utrecht, 1929.

Balslev, C. F. Lord Byron, Mennesket og Digteren. Copenhagen, 1930.

Griggs, E. L. Coleridge and Byron. PMLA. XLV, 1930.

Koch, J. Goethe und Byron. Archiv, CLXIII, 1933.

Eggert, G. Lord Byron und Napoleon. Leipzig, 1933.

Howarth, R. G. Allusions in Byron's Letters. N. & Q. 28 Nov. 1936–9 April 1938.

Brown, W. C. Byron and English Interest in the Near East. Stud. Phil. XXXIV, 1937.

Eliot, T. S. Byron. [In From Anne to Victoria, ed. B. Dobrée, 1937.]

Kaiser, R. René und Harold. Archiv, CLXX, 1937.

H. G. P.

PERCY BYSSHE SHELLEY (1792–1822)

(1) BIBLIOGRAPHIES

Forman, H. B. The Shelley Library. An Essay in Bibliography. I. Shelley's Own Books, Pamphlets, and Broadsides; Posthumous Separate Issues, and Posthumous Books wholly or mainly by him. Shelley Soc. 1886.

Granniss, R. S. A Descriptive Catalogue of the First Editions in Book Form of the Writings of Percy Bysshe Shelley. Grolier Club (New York), 1923.

Wise, T. J. A Shelley Library. 1924.

De Ricci, S. A Bibliography of Shelley's Letters, Published and Unpublished. Paris, 1927 (priv. ptd).

(2) COLLECTED WORKS

The Works. Ed. M. W. Shelley, 2 pts, 1847.

The Works. With a Memoir by Leigh Hunt. Ed. R. H. Shepherd, 4 sers. 1871–5.

The Works in Verse and Prose. Ed. H. B. Forman, 8 vols. 1880.

The Complete Works. Ed. R. Ingpen and W. E. Peck, 10 vols. 1926–30.

Relics of Shelley. Ed. R. Garnett, 1862.

Note Books of Percy Bysshe Shelley. From the Originals in the Library of W. K. Bixby. Ed. H. B. Forman, 3 vols. Bibliophile Soc. Boston, 1911.

The Shelley Notebook in the Harvard Library. Ed. G. E. Woodberry, Cambridge, U.S.A. 1930.

Verse and Prose from the Manuscripts of Percy Bysshe Shelley. Ed. Sir J. C. E. Shelley-Rolls and R. Ingpen, 1934 (priv. ptd).

(3) POETICAL WORKS

(a) Collected Editions

The Works of Percy Bysshe Shelley. Vol. I (5 pts, all pbd), 1826 (re-issued 1826 as Miscellaneous Poems).

The Poetical Works of Coleridge, Shelley and Keats. Paris, 1829. [With a memoir of Shelley by Cyrus Redding.]

The Works. 2 vols. 1834, 1836; 2 vols. 1839.
The Poetical Works. Ed. (with notes) M. W.
Shelley, 4 vols. 1839; 1840. [Rptd with
memoir by J. R. Lowell, 3 vols. Boston,
1855, 1889.]
The Poetical Works. Ed. (with memoir) W. M.
Rossetti, 2 vols. 1870; 3 vols. 1878.
The Poetical Works. Ed. W. B. Scott, [1874];
[1880].
The Poetical Works. Ed. H. B. Forman,
4 vols. 1876; 2 vols. 1882; 5 vols. 1892 (with
memoir; Aldine edn).
The Poetical Works. Ed. R. H. Shepherd,
3 vols. 1888; 2 vols. 1912.
The Poetical Works. Ed. E. Dowden, 1890;
1896; 1900.
The Complete Poetical Works. Ed. (with
memoir) G. E. Woodberry, 4 vols. 1892.
The Complete Poetical Works. Ed. T.
Hutchinson, Oxford, 1904; rev. B. P. Kurtz,
1934.
The Poems. Ed. C. D. Locock, 4 vols. 1906.
The Poems. With an Introduction by A.
Clutton-Brock. Ed. C. D. Locock, 2 vols.
1911.
The Lyrical [Dramatic, Narrative] Poems and
Translations, arranged in Chronological
Order. Ed. C. H. Herford, 4 vols. 1918–27.
[Shelley's poems were tr. into French by
F. Rabbe, 3 vols. Paris, 1885–7; into German
by J. Seybt, Leipzig, 1844, and A. Strodtmann,
Hildburghausen, 1866; into Italian, Milan,
1858, and Naples, 1878; into Russian, 1895,
etc.]

(b) Selections

Miscellaneous and Posthumous Poems. 1826.
The Beauties of Shelley. 1830; 1831; 1832;
1836. [Preface by C. Roscoe.]
A Selection from the Poems of P. B. Shelley.
Ed. M. Blind, 1872.
Poems from Shelley. Ed. Stopford A. Brooke,
1880, 1906. (Golden Treasury ser.)
Poems selected from Shelley. Ed. R. Garnett,
1880.
Lyric Poems. Ed. E. Rhys, 1895.
Poems. Ed. H. B. Forman, 1899. (Temple
Classics.)
Poems. Ed. Sir W. Raleigh, 1902.
Poems. Ed. A. Meynell, 1903.
Poems. Ed. J. C. Collins, 1907.
Select Poems. Ed. G. E. Woodberry, Boston,
1908.
Odes, Poèmes et Fragments lyriques choisis.
Ed. and tr. A. Fontaines, Paris, 1923.
Shelley. Ed. and tr. A. Koszul, Paris, 1930.
Poetry and Prose. With Essays by Browning,
Bagehot, Swinburne, and Reminiscences by
Others. Ed. A. M. D. Hughes, Oxford, 1931.
The Best of Shelley. Ed. N. I. White, New
York, 1932.

(c) Separate Poetical Works

Original Poetry. By Victor and Cazire [Percy
Bysshe Shelley and Elizabeth Shelley].
Worthing, 1810; ed. R. Garnett, 1898.
Posthumous Fragments of Margaret Nichol-
son: being poems found amongst the papers
of that noted female who attempted the
life of the king in 1786. Ed. 'John Fitz-
Victor,' Oxford, 1810; priv. rptd H. B.
Forman, 1877.
A Poetical Essay on the Existing State of
Things. By a Gentleman of the University
of Oxford. 1811.
The Devil's Walk; a Ballad. [1812.] [Broad-
side.]
Queen Mab; a Philosophical Poem. 1813.
Alastor; or The Spirit Of Solitude: and other
poems. 1816; ed. facs. B. Dobell, 1885; tr.
French, A. Beljame, Paris, 1895.
Laon and Cythna; or, The Revolution of The
Golden City: A Vision of the Nineteenth
Century. In The Stanza Of Spenser. 1818
(ptd 1817). [Suppressed and re-issued in a
rev. form as The Revolt of Islam; a Poem,
in twelve Cantos, 1818. The same sheets
issued again, with a new title-page, 1829.]
Rosalind and Helen, A Modern Eclogue; with
Other Poems. 1819; ed. type-facs. H. B.
Forman, Shelley Soc. 1888.
The Cenci. A Tragedy, in five acts. Italy,
1819; 1821; 1827; ed. A. and H. B. Forman
with prologue by J. Todhunter, Shelley Soc.
1886; ed. G. E. Woodberry, Boston, 1909.
Tr. French, 1883; German, 1837; Italian,
1892.
Prometheus Unbound A Lyrical Drama in
four acts With Other Poems. 1820; ed.
G. L. Dickinson, 1898 (Temple Dramatists);
ed. A. M. D. Hughes, Oxford, 1910. Tr.
German, 1876, 1887; Italian, 1892, 1894.
Oedipus Tyrannus; or, Swellfoot the Tyrant.
A Tragedy. In Two Acts. Translated From
The Original Doric. 1820 (anon.).
Epipsychidion: Verses Addressed To The
Noble And Unfortunate Lady, Emilia
V——, Now Imprisoned In The Convent
Of ——. 1821 (anon.); ed. facs. S. A.
Brooke, A. C. Swinburne and R. A. Potts,
Shelley Soc. 1887; rptd 1921. Tr. Italian,
1893; Polish, [1924].
Adonais An Elegy on the Death of John
Keats, Author Of Endymion, Hyperion,
Etc. Pisa, 1821; Cambridge, 1829; ed. type-
facs. T. J. Wise, Shelley Soc. 1886; ed. W. M.
Rossetti and A. O. Prickard, Oxford, 1903;
rptd photo-facs. 1927.
Hellas A Lyrical Drama. 1822; ed. T. J. Wise,
Shelley Soc. 1886.
Poetical Pieces. 1823.
Posthumous Poems. [Ed. M. W. Shelley,]
1824.

The Masque of Anarchy. A Poem. Now first published, with a Preface by Leigh Hunt. 1832. [Facs. of the holograph MS, ed. H. B. Forman, Shelley Soc. 1887.]

The Daemon of the World. The First Part as published in 1816 with Alastor. The Second Part deciphered and now first printed from his own Manuscript Revision and Interpolation in the newly discovered Copy of Queen Mab. Priv. ptd H. B. Forman, 1876.

The Wandering Jew. Ed. B. Dobell, Shelley Soc. 1887.

Shelley's Skylark. A Facsimile of the Original MS., with a Note on Other MSS. of Shelley in Harvard College Library. Cambridge, U.S.A. 1888.

The Celandine. Winchester, 1927.

(4) Prose Works
(a) Collected Editions and Selections

Essays, Letters from Abroad, Translations, and Fragments. Ed. M. W. Shelley, 2 vols. 1840; 2 vols. 1852.

The Prose Works. Ed. H. B. Forman, 4 vols. 1880.

Essays and Letters of Shelley. Ed. E. Rhys, 1886; 1905.

The Prose Works. Ed. R. H. Shepherd, 2 vols. 1888, 1912.

Shelley's Literary and Philosophical Criticism. Ed. J. Shawcross, 1909.

Shelley's Prose in the Bodleian MSS. Ed. A. H. Koszul, 1910.

(b) Separate Prose Works

Zastrozzi. A Romance. By P. B. S. 1810.

St Irvyne; or, The Rosicrucian. A Romance. By a Gentleman of the University of Oxford. 1811 (re-issued 1822).

The Necessity of Atheism. Worthing, [1811].

An Address to the Irish People. Dublin, 1812; ed. T. J. Wise (with introduction by T. W. Rolleston), Shelley Soc. 1890.

Proposals for an association of those philanthropists who, convinced of the inadequacy of the moral and political state of Ireland to produce benefits which are nevertheless attainable, are willing to unite to accomplish its regeneration. Dublin, [1812].

Declaration of Rights. [Dublin, 1812] (broadside); rptd Philobiblon Soc. Misc. vol. XII, 1868–9.

A Letter to Lord Ellenborough. [1812.]

A Vindication of Natural Diet. 1813; rptd Shelley Soc. 1884.

A Refutation of Deism, in a Dialogue. 1814.

A Proposal for putting Reform to the Vote throughout the Kingdom. By the Hermit of Marlow. 1817. [Facsimile of the holograph MS, ed. H. B. Forman, Shelley Soc. 1887.]

An Address to the People on the Death of the Princess Charlotte. [1817]; rptd [1843?].

History of a Six Weeks' Tour. 1817; ed. C. I. Elton, 1894. [Written in collaboration with Mrs Shelley.]

Notes on Sculptures in Rome and Florence: together with a Lucianic Fragment and a Criticism of Peacock's Poem Rhododaphne. Ed. H. B. Forman, 1879 (priv. ptd).

Review of Hogg's Memoirs of Prince Alexy Haimatoff. Together with an Extract from some Early Writings of Shelley. By E. Dowden. Ed. T. J. Wise, Shelley Soc. 1886.

A Philosophical View of Reform. Ed. T. W. Rolleston, 1920; ed. W. E. Peck, 1930 (priv. ptd).

On the Vegetarian System of Diet. Ed. R. Ingpen, 1929 (priv. ptd).

Plato's Banquet translated from the Greek, A Discourse on the Greeks, etc. Revised and enlarged from MSS. Ed. R. Ingpen, 1931 (priv. ptd).

(c) Letters

Southey, R. Correspondence with Caroline Bowles. Together with his Correspondence with Shelley, etc. Ed. E. Dowden, 1881.

Select Letters. With Introduction by R. Garnett. 1882.

Letters to Robert Southey and Other Correspondents. 1886 (priv. ptd).

Letters to Jane Clairmont. 1889 (priv. ptd).

Letters to Elizabeth Hitchener. 2 vols. 1890 (priv. ptd); ed. B. Dobell, 1909.

Letters to William Godwin. 2 vols. 1891 (priv. ptd).

Letters to Leigh Hunt. Ed. T. J. Wise, 2 vols. 1894 (priv. ptd).

Letters to T. J. Hogg. With notes by W. M. Rossetti and H. B. Forman. 1897 (priv. ptd).

The Letters of Shelley. Ed. R. Ingpen, 2 vols. 1909; 2 vols. 1912; 2 vols. 1914 (rev. edn).

The Shelley Correspondence in the Bodleian Library. Ed. R. H. Hill (with 'a list of other Shelley MSS and Relics in the Library'), Oxford, 1926.

Letters of Shelley Selected by R. B. Johnson. 1929.

Shelley's Lost Letters to Harriet. Ed. L. Hotson, 1930.

(5) Biography and Criticism
(a) General Works

[Further studies of Shelley's influence, etc. will be found in the section Literary Relations with the Continent, pp. 17–45 above.]

Reply to the Anti-Matrimonial Hypothesis and Supposed Atheism of Shelley, as Laid down in Queen Mab. 1821.

Barton, B. Verses on the Death of P. B. Shelley. 1822.

Brooke, A.' [*i.e.* J. C. Claris]. Elegy on the Death of P. B. Shelley. 1822.

Hunt, J. H. L. Lord Byron and Some of his Contemporaries. 1828.

—— The Autobiography of Leigh Hunt. 3 vols. 1850; 1860 (rev. edn).

Moore, T. Letters and Journals of Byron, with Notices of his Life. 2 vols. 1830.

Browning, R. Address to Shelley. [In Pauline, 1833.]

—— Essay on Shelley. [Prefixed to Letters of P. B. Shelley [for the most part spurious], 1852. Ed. W. T. Harden, Shelley Soc. 1888; ed. R. Garnett, 1903; ed. H. F. B. Brett-Smith, Oxford, 1921.]

Medwin, T. The Shelley Papers. Memoir of Percy Bysshe Shelley. By T. Medwin, Esq. And Original Poems and Papers by Percy Bysshe Shelley. Now first collected. 1833.

—— Life of Shelley. 2 vols. 1847; ed. H. B. Forman, Oxford, 1913.

White, W. The Calumnies of the 'Athenæum' exposed on the subject of the Byron, Shelley, and Keats MSS. 1852.

Gilfillan, G. P. B. Shelley. [In Galleries of Literary Portraits, vol. I, 1856.]

Hogg, T. J. Life of Shelley. 2 vols. 1858; ed. E. Dowden, 1906.

—— Shelley at Oxford. Ed. R. A. Streatfeild, 1904.

Middleton, C. S. Shelley and his Writings. 2 vols. 1858.

Trelawny, E. J. Recollections of the Last Days of Shelley and Byron. 1858; ed. E. Dowden, 1906.

—— Records of Shelley, Byron, and the Author. 1878; rptd 1005.

—— Letters. Ed. H. B. Forman, Oxford, 1910.

Shelley, J., Lady. Shelley Memorials. 1859; 1875 (3rd edn).

Hunt, Thornton. Shelley. Atlantic Monthly, XI, 1863.

Baynes, S. Edinburgh Rev. April 1871.

Brandes, G. Hovedströmninger i det 19de Aarhundredes Litteratur. 6 vols. Copenhagen, 1872–90; tr. Eng. 1901–5. [Vol. IV.]

MacCarthy, D. F. Shelley's Early Life from Original Sources. [1872.]

Masson, D. Wordsworth, Shelley, Keats, and other Essays. 1874.

Peacock, T. L. Memoirs of Shelley. [In Works, vol. III, 1875. Ed., with the letters to Peacock, H. F. B. Brett-Smith, Oxford, 1909.]

—— T. L. Peacock on the Portraits of Shelley. 1911.

Paul, C. K. William Godwin: his Friends and Contemporaries. 2 vols. 1876.

Sotheran, C. P. B. Shelley as a Philosopher and Reformer. 1876.

Smith, G. Barnett. Shelley: a Critical Biography. 1877.

Scott, R. P. The Place of Shelley among the English Poets of his Time. Cambridge, 1878.

Symonds, J. A. Shelley. 1878; 1887 (rev. edn). (English Men of Letters ser.)

Bagehot, W. Literary Studies. Vol. I, 1879.

Calvert, G. H. Coleridge, Shelley, Goethe. Boston, 1880.

Myers, F. W. H. Shelley. [In The English Poets, ed. T. H. Ward, vol. IV, 1880.]

Todhunter, J. A Study of Shelley. 1880.

Zanella, G. Shelley e G. Leopardi. Nuova Antologia, I, 1881. [Rptd in Paralleli letterari, Verona, 1885.]

Druskowitz, H. Percy Bysshe Shelley. Berlin, 1884.

Shelley Society Publications. 1884–8.

Jeaffreson, J. C. The Real Shelley. 2 vols. 1885.

Sarrazin, G. Poètes modernes de l'Angleterre. Paris, 1885.

Dowden, E. Life of Shelley. 2 vols. 1886; 1896 (rev. and condensed). [See Quart. Rev. April 1887; Athenaeum, 14 May 1887.]

—— Last Words on Shelley. [In Transcripts and Studies, 1888.]

Rossetti, W. M. Memoir of Shelley, with New Preface. 1886.

Salt, H. S. Shelley Primer. Shelley Soc. 1887.

—— Percy Bysshe Shelley: a Monograph. 1888.

—— Percy Bysshe Shelley: Poet and Pioneer. 1896.

Rabbe, F. Shelley: sa Vie, ses Œuvres. Paris, 1887; tr. Eng. 1888.

Sharp, W. Life of Shelley [with bibliography by J. P. Anderson]. 1887.

Arnold, M. Essays in Criticism. Second Series. 1888.

Ellis, F. S. An Alphabetical Table of Contents to Shelley's Poetical Works. Shelley Soc. 1888.

—— A Lexical Concordance to the Poetical Works of Shelley. 1892.

Hime, H. W. L. The Greek Materials of Shelley's Adonais. 1888.

Mayor, J. B. A Classification of Shelley's Metres. 1888.

Shelley, M. W. Life and Letters. By Mrs Julian Marshall. 2 vols. 1889.

Woodberry, G. E. Notes on the MS. Volume of Shelley's Poems in the Library of Harvard College. Cambridge, U.S.A. 1889.

Ackermann, R. Quellen zu Shelleys poetischen Werken. Erlangen, 1890.

—— Shelley in Frankreich und Italien. E. Studien, XVII, 1893.

—— Lucans Pharsalia in den Dichtungen Shelleys. Zweibrücken, 1896.

—— Percy Bysshe Shelley, der Mann, der Dichter, und seine Werke. Dortmund, 1906.

Biagi, G. Gli ultimi Giorni di P. B. Shelley. Florence, 1892; tr. Eng. 1898.

Stephen, Sir L. Godwin and Shelley. [In Hours in a Library, vol. III, 1892.]

Elton, C. I. An Account of Shelley's Visits to France, Switzerland and Savoy in the Years 1814 and 1816. 1894.

Platt, J. H. The Cosmic Sense as Manifested in Shelley and Whitman. The Conservator, v, 1894.

Swinburne, A. C. Les Cenci. [In Studies in Prose and Poetry, 1894.]

—— Shelley. [In Chambers's Cyclopaedia of English Literature, vol. III, 1903.]

Kellner, L. E. Studien, XXII 1895, pp. 295–8. [German trns of Prometheus Unbound.]

—— Shelley's 'Queen Mab' und Volney's 'Les Ruines.' E. Studien, XXII, 1895.

Graham, W. Last Links with Byron, Shelley, and Keats. 1898.

Kuhns, O. Dante's Influence on Shelley. MLN. XIII, 1898.

Richter, H. Percy Bysshe Shelley. 1898.

Edgar, P. A Study of Shelley. Toronto, 1899.

Chiarini, G. Studi e Ritratti letterari. Florence, 1900.

Cordier, H. P. B. Shelley. 1900.

Bernthsen, S. Der Spinozismus in Shelleys Weltanschauung. Ang. XXIV, 1901.

—— Über den Einfluss des Plinius in Shelleys Jugendwerken. E. Studien, XXX, 1902.

Chevrillon, A. La Nature dans la Poésie de Shelley. [In Études anglaises, Paris, 1901.]

Flügel, E. Shelley's Sophocles. Ang. XXIV, 1901.

Zettner, H. Shelleys Mythendichtung. Leipzig, [1902.]

Kroder, A. Shelleys Verskunst. Erlangen, 1903.

Locock, C. D. An Examination of the Shelley MSS. in the Bodleian Library. Oxford, 1903.

Slicer, J. R. P. B. Shelley. An Appreciation. 1903.

Yeats, W. B. The Philosophy of Shelley's Poetry. [In Ideas of Good and Evil, 1903.]

Jack, A. A. Shelley: an Essay. 1904.

Winstanley, L. Shelley as Nature Poet. E. Studien, XXXIV, 1904.

—— Platonism in Shelley. E. & S. IV, 1913.

Vaughan, P. Early Shelley Pamphlets. 1905.

Bradley, A. C. Notes on Passages in Shelley. MLR. I, 1906.

—— Shelley's View of Poetry. [In Oxford Lectures on Poetry, Oxford, 1909.]

—— On The Triumph of Life. MLR. IX, 1914.

—— A Miscellany. 1929. [Contains 3 essays on Shelley.]

Droop, A. Die Belesenheit P. B. Shelleys. Berlin, 1906.

Elsner, P. P. B. Shelleys Abhängigkeit von W. Godwins 'Political Justice.' Berlin, 1906.

Maurer, O. Shelley und die Frauen. Berlin, 1906.

Young, A. B. Shelley and M. G. Lewis. MLR. I, 1906.

—— Shelley and Peacock. MLR. II, 1907.

Brooke, S. A. The Lyrics of Shelley. [In Studies in Poetry, 1907, 1910.]

Calcaño, J. Tres Poetas pessimistas del Siglo XIX (Byron, Shelley, Leopardi). Caracas, 1907.

Yolland, A. B. Shelley's Poetry. Budapest, 1907.

Bates, E. S. A Study of Shelley's Drama The Cenci. New York, 1908.

Imelmann, R. Shelleys Alastor und Goethe. Zeitschrift für vergleichende Litteraturgeschichte, XVII, 1909.

Symons, A. The Romantic Movement in English Poetry. 1909.

Thompson, F. Shelley. 1909. [Written 1889.]

Clutton-Brock, A. Shelley, the Man and the Poet. 1910; 1923 (rev. edn).

Eimer, M. Die persönlichen Beziehungen zwischen Byron und den Shelleys. Heidelberg, 1910.

Koszul, A. H. La Jeunesse de Shelley. Paris, 1910.

—— Les Océanides et le Thème de l'Amour dans le Prométhée de Shelley. Revue anglo-américaine, June 1925.

Angeli, H. R. Shelley and his Friends in Italy. 1911.

Asanger, F. P. B. Shelleys Sprachstudien. Leipzig, 1911.

Godwin, W. The Elopement of Shelley and Mary Wollstonecraft Godwin, as narrated by W. Godwin. Ed. H. B. Forman, 1911 (priv. ptd).

Gribble, F. The Romantic life of Shelley, and the Sequel. 1911.

Polidori, J. The Diary of, 1816, relating to Byron, Shelley, etc. Ed. W. M. Rossetti, 1911.

Schmitt, H. Shelley als Romantiker. E. Studien, XLIV, 1911.

Elton, O. A Survey of English Literature (1780–1830). 2 vols. 1912.

Hughes, A. M. D. Shelley's Zastrozzi and St Irvyne. Shelley's Witch of Atlas. MLR. VII, 1912.

—— The Nascent Mind of Shelley. E. Studien, XLV, 1912.

Suddard, M. Keats, Shelley, and Shakespeare Studies. Cambridge, 1912.

Brailsford, H. N. Shelley, Godwin, and their Circle. [1913.]

Schelling, F. E. The English Lyric. Boston, 1913.

Vaughan, C. E. The Influence of English Poetry upon the Romantic Revival on the Continent. Proc. British Academy, VI, 1913–4.

Stawell, M. On Shelley's The Triumph of Life. E. & S. v, 1914.

Garnett, R. Letters about Shelley. 1917.

Ingpen, R. Shelley in England. New Facts and Letters. 1917.

Huscher, H. Studien zu Shelleys Lyrik. Leipzig, 1919.

Madariaga, S. de. Shelley and Calderón and other Essays. 1920; tr. Spanish, 1922.

Strong, A. T. Three Studies in Shelley. 1921.

White, N. I. Shelley's Swell-Foot the Tyrant in relation to Contemporary Political Satire. PMLA. xxxvi, 1921.

—— Shelley's Charles the First. JEGP. xxi, 1922.

—— Literature and the Law of Libel: Shelley and the Radicals of 1840–1842. Stud. Phil. xxii, 1925.

—— Shelley's Prometheus Unbound. PMLA. xl, 1925.

—— Shelley and the Active Radicals of the Early Nineteenth Century. South Atlantic Quart. xxix, 1930.

—— Shelley's Biography: the Primary Sources. Stud. Phil. xxxi, 1934.

—— The Unextinguished Hearth: Shelley and his Contemporary Critics. Durham (North Carolina), 1938.

Allen, L. H. Plagiarism, Sources and Influences in Shelley's Alastor. MLR. xviii, 1923.

Maurois, A. Ariel, ou la Vie de Shelley. 1923; tr. Eng. 1924.

Spira, T. Shelleys geistesgeschichtliche Bedeutung. Giessener Beiträge, i, 1923.

Campbell, O. W. Shelley and the Unromantics. 1924.

Liptzin, S. Shelley in Germany. New York, 1924.

Blunden, E. Shelley and Keats as they struck their Contemporaries. 1925.

Graham, W. Shelley's Debt to Leigh Hunt and the 'Examiner.' PMLA. xl, 1925.

—— Shelley and the 'Empire of the Nairs.' PMLA. xl, 1925.

Walker, A. S. Peterloo, Shelley and Reform. PMLA. xl, 1925.

Stokoe, F. W. German Influence in the English Romantic Period, 1788–1818, with special reference to Scott, Coleridge, Shelley and Byron. Cambridge, 1926.

Bald, M. A. Shelley's Mental Progress. E. & S. xiii, 1927.

Peck, W. E. Shelley his Life and Works. 2 vols. 1927.

King, R. W. Crabb Robinson's Opinion of Shelley. RES. iv, 1928.

O'Sullivan-Köhling, J. Shelley und die bildende Kunst. Halle, 1928.

Shelley–Leigh Hunt; Being Reviews and Leaders from the 'Examiner,' etc., with Letters between the Shelleys and Leigh Hunt. Ed. R. B. Johnson, 1928.

Solve, M. T. Shelley: His Theory of Poetry. Chicago, 1928.

Bates, E. S. Mad Shelley: a Study in the Origins of English Romanticism. [In Fred Newton Scott Anniversary Papers, Chicago, 1929.]

Carpenter, E. and Barnefield, G. The Psychology of the Poet Shelley. 1929.

Elliott, G. R. The Cycle of Modern Poetry. Princeton, 1929.

Marsh, G. L. The Early Reviews of Shelley. MP. xxvii, 1929.

Grabo, C. A Newton among Poets: Shelley's Use of Science in Prometheus Unbound. Chapel Hill, 1930.

—— The Meaning of The Witch of Atlas. Chapel Hill, 1935.

—— The Magic Plant: the Growth of Shelley's Thought. Chapel Hill, 1936.

Havens, R. D. Julian and Maddalo. Stud. Phil. xxvii, 1930.

—— Shelley's Alastor. PMLA. xlv, 1930.

—— Rosalind and Helen. JEGP. xxx, 1931.

Ullman, J. R. Mad Shelley. Princeton, 1930.

Stovall, F. Desire and Restraint in Shelley. Durham (North Carolina), 1931.

The Journal of Harriet Grove for 1809–1810. Ed. R. Ingpen, 1932 (priv. ptd).

Propst, L. An Analytical Study of Shelley's Versification. Iowa City, 1932.

Renzulli, M. La Poesia di Shelley. Rome, 1932.

Strout, A. L. 'Maga,' Champion of Shelley. Stud. Phil. xxix, 1932.

Weaver, B. Toward the Understanding of Shelley. Ann Arbor, 1932.

Clark, D. L. Shelley and Bacon. PMLA. xlviii, 1933.

Hofman, H. L. An Odyssey of the Soul: Shelley's Alastor. New York, 1933.

Jones, F. L. The Revision of Laon and Cythna. JEGP. xxxiii, 1933.

—— Hogg and The Necessity of Atheism. PMLA. lii, 1937.

Kurtz, B. P. The Pursuit of Death. A Study of Shelley's Poetry. New York, 1933.

Bailey, R. Shelley. 1934.

Clarke, I. C. Shelley and Byron. 1934.

Mueschke, P. and Griggs, E. L. Wordsworth as the Prototype of the Poet in Shelley's Alastor. PMLA. xlix, 1934. [See also PMLA. li, 1936, pp. 302–12.]

After Shelley. The Letters of T. J. Hogg to Jane Williams. Ed. S. Norman, Oxford, 1934.

Leavis, F. R. Revaluations. viii. Shelley. Scrutiny, iv, 1935. [Rptd in Revaluations, 1936.]

Peyre, H. Shelley et la France. Paris, 1935.

Du Bois, A. E. Alastor: The Spirit of Solitude. JEGP. xxxv, 1936.

Kapstein, I. J. The Symbolism in Shelley's Ode to the West Wind. PMLA. LI, 1936.

Mousel, M. E. Falsetto in Shelley. Stud. Phil. XXXIII, 1936.

Notopoulos, J. A. Shelley and Thomas Taylor. PMLA. LI, 1936.

Read, H. In Defence of Shelley and Other Essays. 1936.

Sen, A. Studies in Shelley. Calcutta, 1936.

Barnard, E. Shelley's Religion. Minneapolis, 1937.

Bush, D. Mythology and the Romantic Tradition in English Poetry. Cambridge, U.S.A. 1937.

Firkins, O. W. Power and Elusiveness in Shelley. Minneapolis, 1937.

Gates, E. J. Shelley and Calderón. PQ. XVI, 1937.

Blunden, E., de Beer, G. and Norman, S. On Shelley. Oxford, 1938.

(b) Early Reviews

[The following list is restricted to the more important notices. For a complete list, with summaries and quotations, see G. L. Marsh, The Early Reviews of Shelley, MP. XXVII, 1929. With some minor exceptions they are all rptd in N. I. White, The Unextinguished Hearth, Durham (North Carolina), 1938.]

Zastrozzi. GM. LXXX, Sept. 1810; Critical Rev. XXI, Nov. 1810.

Original Poetry. Literary Panorama and National Register, VIII, Oct. 1810; British Critic, XXXVII, April 1811; Poetical Register for 1810–11, 1814.

St Irvyne. British Critic, XXXVII, Jan. 1811.

Queen Mab. Literary Gazette, 19 May 1821; Monthly Mag. LI, June 1821; Literary Chronicle, 2 June 1821.

Alastor. Monthly Rev. LXXIX, April 1816; British Critic, N.S. V, May 1816; Eclectic Rev. N.S. VI, Oct. 1816; Blackwood's Mag. VI, Nov. 1819.

Revolt of Islam. Examiner, 1, 22 Feb., 1 March 1818 (by Hunt); Blackwood's Mag. IV, Jan. 1819; Quart. Rev. XXI, April 1819.

Rosalind and Helen. Examiner, 9 May 1819 (by Hunt); London Chronicle, CXXV, 1 June 1819; Blackwood's Mag. V, June 1819; Monthly Rev. XC, Oct. 1819.

The Cenci. Literary Gazette, 1 April 1820; [Gold's] London Mag. I, April 1820; Theatrical Inquisitor, XVI, April 1820; New Monthly Mag. XIII, 1 May 1820; London Mag. I, May 1820; Edinburgh Monthly Rev. III, May 1820; Indicator, 19, 26 July 1820; Independent, 17 Feb. 1821; British Rev. XVII, June 1821.

Prometheus Unbound. Blackwood's Mag. VII, Sept. 1820; Literary Gazette, 9 Sept.

1820; [Gold's] London Mag. II, Oct. 1820; Monthly Rev. XCIV, Feb. 1821; Quart. Rev. XXVI, Oct. 1821; Examiner, 20 Jan., 9, 16, 23 June 1822 (by Hunt).

Epipsychidion. Gossip, 23 June, 14 July 1821; Blackwood's Mag. XI, Feb. 1822.

Adonais. Literary Gazette, 8 Dec. 1821; Blackwood's Mag. X, Dec. 1821; Examiner, 7 July 1822 (by Hunt); European Mag. LXXXVII, April 1825.

Hellas. Paris Monthly Rev. II, Aug. 1822.

Posthumous Poems. Examiner, 13 June 1824; Edinburgh Mag. N.S. XV, July 1824; Edinburgh Rev. XL, July 1824 (by Hazlitt); Literary Gazette, 17 July 1824; Knight's Quart. Mag. III, Aug. 1824.

A. T. B., rev. R. I.

JOHN CLARE (1793–1864)

[MSS by or concerning Clare (some unpbd) are in: Peterborough Natural History Soc. Museum; Northampton Public Lib.; BM. (letters to Clare). These collections cover practically his whole literary life, except 1837–41. The poems of the Asylum period (1841–64) are available only in transcripts.]

(1) Selections

The Life and Remains of John Clare. Ed. J. L. Cherry, 1873.

Poems by John Clare. Ed. N. Gale, Rugby, 1901.

Poems by John Clare. Ed. A. Symons, 1908.

John Clare: Poems Chiefly from Manuscript. Ed. E. Blunden and A. Porter, 1920.

Madrigals and Chronicles: being newly found Poems written by John Clare. Ed. E. Blunden, 1924.

The Poems of John Clare. Ed. J. W. Tibble, 2 vols. 1935. [Fullest and best collection.]

(2) Separate Works

Proposals for Publishing a Collection of Trifles in Verse. Market Deeping, 1817.

Poems Descriptive of Rural Life and Scenery. By John Clare, a Northamptonshire Peasant. 1820 (3 edns); 1821.

The Village Minstrel and other Poems. 2 vols. 1821 (re-issued 1823).

The Shepherd's Calendar; with Village Stories, and other Poems. 1827.

The Rural Muse. 1835.

Sketches in the Life of John Clare, Written by Himself. 1930.

(3) Biography and Criticism

Gilchrist, O. Some Account of John Clare, an Agricultural Labourer and Poet. London Mag. Jan. 1820.

[Taylor, J.] A Visit to John Clare. London Mag. Nov. 1821.

Four Letters from the Rev. W. Allen, to the Right Honourable Lord Radstock, G.C.B., on the Poems of John Clare. 1824.

Prospectus of The Midsummer Cushion. Helpstone, 1832.

Elton, Sir C. A. Boyhood, with other Poems. 1835.

[Wilson, J.] The Rural Muse. Blackwood's Mag. Aug. 1835.

Hood, T. Literary Reminiscences. Hood's Own, May 1839.

De Quincey, T. Literary Reminiscences. Tait's Edinburgh Mag. Dec. 1840.

Allen, M. Appeal for Clare. Athenaeum, 8 May 1841.

Redding, C. Clare the Poet. English Journ. May 1841.

Hood, E. P. The Literature of Labour. 1851.

Baker, A. E. Northamptonshire Glossary. 2 vols. 1854.

Obituary. GM. July 1864.

James, T. The History and Antiquities of Northamptonshire. 1864.

Martin, F. The Life of John Clare. 1865.

Wainewright, T. G. Essays and Criticisms. Ed. W. C. Hazlitt, 1880.

Noel, R. John Clare. [In The Poets and Poetry of the Nineteenth Century, ed. A. H. Miles, vol. III, [1892], 1898, 1905.]

The John Clare Centenary Exhibition Catalogue. [Ed. C. Dack and J. W. Bodger], Peterborough, 1893.

Druce, G. C. Northamptonshire Botanologia: John Clare. Northampton. 1912. [Rptd in Flora of Northamptonshire, 1930.]

Thomas, Edward. A Literary Pilgrim in England. 1917.

Unpublished Writings of John Clare. Athenaeum, 9 April 1920.

[Murry, J. M.] The Poetry of John Clare. TLS. 13 Jan. 1921.

Gosse, Sir E. The Village Minstrel. Sunday Times, 23 Jan. 1921. [Rptd in Silhouettes, 1925.]

John Clare. Villager (New York), 20 Aug. 1921.

Porter, A. John Clare. Spectator, 23 Aug. 1924.

Notes for an Autobiography. By John Clare. Spectator, 19, 26 Sept., 3 Oct. 1925.

Blunden, E. More Footnotes to Literary History. Tokyo, 1926.

—— Nature in English Literature. 1929.

Abbott, C. C. Life of George Darley. 1928.

Brown, R. W. John Clare's Library. Northampton, 1929.

Kirby, H. T. The Clare Country. Saturday Rev. 14 March 1931.

—— Notes on John Clare. Bookmark, Spring 1935.

Tibble, J. W. and A. John Clare: A Life. 1932. [The full biography.]

Bell, A. The Village Minstrel. Spectator, 8 March 1935.

[Tomlinson, P.] Clare's Dream. TLS. 21 Feb. 1935.

E. BL.

GEORGE DARLEY (1795–1846)

(1) COLLECTED POEMS

The Complete Poetical Works. Ed. R. Colles, [1908]. (Muses' Lib.)

(2) SELECTION

Selections from the Poems of George Darley. Ed. R. A. Streatfeild, 1904.

(3) INDIVIDUAL PUBLICATIONS

The Errors of Ecstasie, a Dramatic Poem, with other pieces. 1822.

The Labours of Idleness: or Seven Nights Entertainments. By Guy Penseval. 1826. [Prose sketches, including 'Lilian of the Vale,' the basis of Sylvia.]

A System of Popular Geometry. 1826; 1844 (5th edn).

A System of Popular Algebra. 1827; 1836 (3rd edn).

A System of Popular Trigonometry. 1827.

Sylvia, or the May Queen. A Lyrical Drama. 1827; ed. J. H. Ingram, 1892.

The Geometrical Companion. 1828; 1848.

The New Sketch Book, by Geoffrey Crayon, Jun. 2 vols. 1829. [Prose sketches and essays; vol. II consists of the unused sheets of The Labours of Idleness.]

Familiar Astronomy. 1830.

Nepenthe. 1835 (priv. ptd); ed. R. A. Streatfeild, 1897.

Thomas à Becket, a Dramatic Chronicle. 1840.

The Works of Beaumont and Fletcher, with an Introduction by G. Darley. 2 vols. 1840.

Ethelstan; or the Battle of Brunanburh, a Dramatic Chronicle. 1841.

Poems of the late George Darley, a Memorial Volume printed for Private Circulation. Liverpool, [1890]. [Contains the first appearance of 'Lenimina Laborum.']

(4) CONTRIBUTIONS TO PERIODICALS AND ANNUALS

The London Magazine. [Ed. J. Taylor], Dec. 1822–March 1825. [Chief contributions: Letters to the Dramatists of the Day (6 articles, signed 'John Lacy'); The Characteristic of the Present Age of Poetry, April 1824; and some lyrics and 'dramaticles.']

The Anniversary. Ed. A. Cunningham, 1828. [A poem, The Sorrows of Hope.]

The Athenaeum. 1834–46. [Numerous reviews and articles on literature and fine art, and some lyrics.]

The Tribute. 1837. [6 Syren Songs.]
Bentley's Miscellany. 1844. [Short stories and poems.]
The Illuminated Magazine. [Ed. D. Jerrold and W. J. Linton], 1844. [Short stories and poems.]

(5) WORKS OF DOUBTFUL AUTHENTICITY

Essays and Sketches by the late R. Ayton, with a memoir [probably by Darley]. 1825.
The Works of Virgil, translated by Dryden. 2 vols. New York, 1825. [Contains a Life of Virgil signed G. D.]

(6) BIOGRAPHY AND CRITICISM

Streatfeild, R. A. A Forgotten Poet: George Darley. Quart. Rev. CXCVI, 1902.
Meynell, Alice. The Second Person Singular and Other Essays. 1921.
Looker, S. J. Cotton and Darley. TLS. 29 Jan. 1925.
Abbott, C. C. The Life and Letters of George Darley, Poet and Critic. Oxford, 1928. [Includes a bibliography.]
Blunden, E. George Darley and his Latest Biographer [C. C. Abbott]. TLS. 14 Feb. 1929. [Rptd in Votive Tablets, 1931.]
Greene, G. George Darley. London Mercury, XXIX, 1929.
Bridges, Robert. Collected Essays, Papers, etc. Vol. V, Oxford, 1931. [Written 1906.]
Wolff, L. George Darley, Poète et Critique d'Art. Revue anglo-américaine, Feb. 1931.

R. W. K.

JOHN KEATS (1795–1821)

(1) COLLECTED EDITIONS

The Poetical Works of Coleridge, Shelley, and Keats. Paris, 1829.
The Poetical Works. 1840; 1841; 1847; 1851.
The Poetical Works. With a Memoir by R. M. Milnes [Baron Houghton]. 1854; 1863; 1865 (rev. and enlarged); 1866; 1867.
The Poetical Works. Ed. W. M. Rossetti, [1872]; [1880].
The Poetical Works. Chronologically arranged, with a Memoir by Lord Houghton. 1876; 1879. (Aldine edn.)
The Poetical Works. Ed. W. B. Scott, [1880]; [1894].
The Poetical Works and Other Writings, now first brought together. Ed. H. B. Forman, 4 vols. 1883, 1889. [Supplement, 1890.]
The Poems, with the Annotations of Lord Houghton and a Memoir by J. G. Speed. 2 vols. New York, 1883.
The Poetical Works. Ed. H. B. Forman, 1884; 1898.
Poems. Ed. W. T. Arnold, 1884; 1907.

Poems. Ed. F. S. Ellis, 1894. (Kelmscott Press.)
Poems. Ed. G. Thorn-Drury, with Introduction by R. Bridges, 2 vols. 1896. (Muses' Lib.)
Poems. Ed. A. Bates, Boston, 1896.
Poems. Ed. Sir W. Raleigh, 1897.
Poems. Ed. C. J. Holmes. Decorations by C. Ricketts. 2 vols. 1898.
The Complete Works. Ed. H. B. Forman, 5 vols. Glasgow, 1900–1. [With textual and critical notes, and bibliography.]
The Poetical Works. Ed. W. S. Scott, 1902.
Poems. Ed. E. de Selincourt, 1905; 1926 (rev. edn). [With introduction, textual and critical notes, and an essay on the sources of Keats's vocabulary.]
The Poetical Works. Ed. (with introduction and textual notes) H. B. Forman, Oxford, 1906, 1907, 1908, 1914 (rev.), etc.
The Poetical Works. Ed. G. Sampson, 1906.
The Poems arranged in Chronological Order. Ed. Sir S. Colvin, 2 vols. 1915, 1920, 1924.
Complete Poetry. Ed. G. R. Elliott, New York, 1927.
Poems and Verses. Ed. J. M. Murry, 2 vols. 1930.
Complete Poetical Works. Ed. M. B. Forman and L. Bacon, New York, 1935.
The Poetical Works. Ed. H. W. Garrod, Oxford, 1939. [The definitive edn: new matter from MSS, full critical apparatus and introduction.]

(2) SELECTIONS

The Poetical Works. Ed. F. T. Palgrave, 1884.
Selected Poems. Ed. J. Hogben, 1885.
The Odes of Keats. Ed. A. C. Downer, Oxford, 1897.
Endymion and the Longer Poems. Ed. H. B. Forman, 1898. (Temple Classics.)
Poems. Ed. A. Meynell, 1903, 1923.
Poems. Ed. L. Binyon and J. Masefield, 1903.
Poems. Ed. A. Symons, 1907.
Poems of 1820. Ed. M. Robertson, 1909.
Odes, Lyrics, Sonnets. Ed. M. Hills (Robertson), 1916.
Endymion and Other Poems. Ed. W. T. Young, Cambridge, 1917.
Poetry and Prose with Essays by Lamb, Leigh Hunt, Bridges and Others. Ed. H. Ellershaw, Oxford, 1922.
Leben und Werke. Tr. M. Gothien, Halle, 1897.
Poèmes et Poésies. Traduction, précédée d'une Étude, par P. Gallimard. 1910.
Sonnets, Odes. Tr. M. Manent (preface by E. d'Ors), Barcelona, 1919.
John Keats. Traduction et Notes par L. Bocquet. Paris, 1923.

(3) SEPARATE WORKS

(a) Books

Poems. 1817; rptd photo-facs. 1927 and New York, 1934.

Endymion: A Poetic Romance. 1818; ed. type facs. C. E. Notcutt, Oxford, 1927.

Lamia, Isabella, The Eve of St. Agnes, and Other Poems. 1820; ed. type facs. M. Robertson, Oxford, 1909; rptd photo-facs. 1927 and New York, 1934.

Another Version of Keats's Hyperion. Ed. R. M. Milnes (Baron Houghton), Philobiblon Soc. Misc. vol. III, 1856–7.

Keatsii Hyperionis Libri tres. Latine reddidit C. Merivale. Cambridge, 1863.

Hyperion. Ed. J. Hoops, Berlin, 1899.

Hyperion. A Facsimile of Keats's Autograph Manuscript with a Transliteration of the Manuscript of The Fall of Hyperion a Dream. Ed. E. de Selincourt, Oxford, 1905.

Ode to a Nightingale. Ed. T. J. Wise, 1884 (priv. ptd).

Ode to a Nightingale. Facsimile of the Autograph Manuscript of the Original Version. [In Sir S. Colvin, A Morning's Work in a Hampstead Garden, Monthly Rev. March 1903. Rptd in The John Keats Memorial Volume, 1921.]

(b) Contributions to Periodicals

[The following list is restricted to Keats's life-time and poems not previously ptd elsewhere.]

Examiner, 5 May 1816. [Sonnet, signed J. K., beginning 'O Solitude! if I must with thee dwell.']

Examiner, 23 Feb. 1817. [Sonnet beginning 'After dark vapors have oppress'd our plains.']

Examiner, 9 March 1817. [2 sonnets to B. R. Haydon on the Elgin Marbles.]

Examiner, 16 March 1817. [Sonnet on The Floure and the Lefe.]

Champion, 7 Aug. 1817. [Sonnet 'On the Sea.']

Annals of the Fine Arts, IV, 1819. [Ode to a Nightingale and Ode on a Grecian Urn, both anon.]

Literary Pocket-Book. 1820. [2 sonnets: 'The Human Seasons'; 'To Ailsa Rock.']

Indicator, 10 May 1820. ['La Belle Dame sans Merci,' signed 'Caviare.']

Indicator, 28 June 1820. [Sonnet 'A Dream, after Reading Dante's Episode of Paulo and Francesca.']

(4) LETTERS, ETC.

Life, Letters, and Literary Remains. Ed. R. M. Milnes (Baron Houghton), 2 vols.

1848; 1852; 1867; 1906; rptd R. Lynd, 1928 (Everyman's Lib.); rptd 1931 (World's Classics).

Letters to Fanny Brawne written in 1819 and 1820. Ed. H. B. Forman, 1878; 1889 (rev. and enlarged).

The Letters. Ed. J. G. Speed, New York, 1883.

Letters. Ed. Sir S. Colvin, 1891.

The Letters. Ed. H. B. Forman, 1895.

The Keats Letters, Papers and Other Relics forming the Dilke Bequest in the Hampstead Public Library. Ed. facs. G. C. Williamson, T. Watts-Dunton and H. B. Forman, 1914.

The Letters. Ed. M. B. Forman, 2 vols. Oxford, 1931; Oxford, 1935 (rev., adds 10 further letters). [The definitive edn.]

Autobiography of John Keats: Compiled from his Letters and Essays. Ed. E. V. Weller, Palo Alto, 1933.

John Keats's Anatomical and Physiological Note Book. Ed. M. B. Forman, Oxford, 1934.

(5) BIOGRAPHY AND CRITICISM

(a) Concordance

Baldwin, D. L., Hebel, J. W., Broughton, L. N., Stelter, B. F., Evans, L. C., and Thayer, M. R. A Concordance to the Poems of John Keats. Washington, 1917.

(b) Books

Shelley, P. B. Adonais. An Elegy on the Death of John Keats. Pisa, 1821.

Medwin, T. Journal of the Conversations of Lord Byron. 1824.

—— The Life of Percy Bysshe Shelley. 2 vols. 1847.

Hunt, J. H. L. Lord Byron and Some of his Contemporaries. 1828; 2 vols. 1828; 3 vols. Paris, 1828.

—— Imagination and Fancy; or Selections from the English Poets. 1844; 1845; 1846; 1852; ed. Sir E. Gosse, 1907.

—— The Autobiography of Leigh Hunt; with Reminiscences of Friends and Contemporaries. 3 vols. 1850; 1860 (rev. edn); ed. R. Ingpen, 2 vols. 1903; ed. E. Blunden, 1928 (World's Classics).

Dendy, W. C. The Philosophy of Mystery. 1841.

Haydon, B. R. Life. Ed. T. Taylor, 3 vols. 1853; 3 vols. 1853 (enlarged); ed. E. Blunden, 1927 (World's Classics).

—— Correspondence and Table-Talk. With a Memoir by his Son. 2 vols. 1876.

Gilfillan, G. John Keats. [In Galleries of Literary Portraits, vol. I, 1856.]

Arnold, M. On the Study of Celtic Literature. 1867.

Arnold, M. John Keats. [In The English Poets, ed. T. H. Ward, vol. iv, 1880. Rptd in Essays in Criticism, Second Series, 1888.]

Masson, D. Wordsworth, Shelley, Keats, and Other Essays. 1874.

Dilke, C. W. The Papers of a Critic. 2 vols. 1875. [The Memoir by Sir C. W. Dilke contains letters from Keats, etc.]

Procter, B. W. ('Barry Cornwall'). An Autobiographical Fragment and Biographical Notes, with Personal Sketches of Contemporaries. [Ed. C. Patmore], 1877.

Owen, F. M. John Keats. A Study. 1880.

Richardson, B. W. The Asclepiad. A Book of Original Research and Observation. Vol. i, 1884. [Includes An Aesculapian Poet— John Keats.]

Sarrazin, G. Poètes modernes de l'Angleterre. Paris, 1885.

Dowden, E. The Life of Percy Bysshe Shelley. 2 vols. 1886.

Swinburne, A. C. Keats. [In Miscellanies, 1886.]

Colvin, Sir S. Keats. 1887. (English Men of Letters ser.)

—— John Keats: his Life and Poetry, his Friends, Critics and After-fame. 1917.

Rossetti, W. M. Life of John Keats. 1887. [Includes bibliography by J. P. Anderson.]

Angellier, A. De Joh. Keatsii Vita et Carminibus. Paris, 1892.

Sharp, W. The Life and Letters of Joseph Severn. 1892.

Watson, Sir W. Excursions in Criticism. 1893.

Bridges, R. John Keats. A Critical Essay. 1895 (priv. ptd). [Rptd as introduction to Poems of John Keats, ed. G. Thorn-Drury, vol. i, 1896 (Muses' Lib.), and in Collected Essays, Papers, etc., vol. iv, Oxford, 1929.]

Nicoll, Sir W. R. and Wise, T. J. Literary Anecdotes of the Nineteenth Century. Vol. ii, 1896.

Graham, W. Last Links with Byron, Shelley, and Keats. 1898.

Texte, J. Keats et le Néo-Hellénisme dans la Poésie anglaise. [In Études de Littérature européenne, Paris, 1898.]

Brooke, Stopford A. Studies in Poetry. 1907.

Geest, S. Der Sensualismus bei John Keats. Freiburg, 1908.

Hancock, A. E. John Keats. A Literary Biography. 1908.

Bradley, A. C. The Letters of Keats. [In Oxford Lectures on Poetry, 1909.]

Wolff, L. An Essay on Keats's Treatment of the Heroic Rhythm and Blank Verse. Paris, 1909.

—— John Keats, sa Vie et son Œuvre. Paris, 1910.

—— Keats. Paris, 1929.

Starick, O. P. Die Belesenheit von John Keats, und die Grundzüge seiner literarischen Kritik. Berlin, 1910.

Elton, O. A Survey of English Literature, 1780–1830. 2 vols. 1912.

Gay, H. N. John Keats e gli Inglesi a Roma. Rome, 1912.

Mackail, J. W. Lectures on Poetry. 1912.

Suddard, M. Keats, Shelley and Shakespeare. Cambridge, 1912.

Olivero, F. Saggi di Letteratura inglese. Bari, 1914.

Herford, C. H. Keats. CHEL. vol. xii, 1915.

Notcutt, H. C. An Interpretation of Keats's Endymion. Capetown, [1919].

—— The Story of Glaucus in Keats's Endymion. Capetown, 1921.

Rossetti, D. G. John Keats: Criticism and Comments. 1919. [5 letters to H. B. Forman.]

The John Keats Memorial Volume. Ed. G. C. Williamson, 1921. [Includes inter alia: L. Abercrombie, The Second Version of Hyperion; A. C. Bradley, Keats and 'Philosophy' (rptd in A Miscellany, 1929); C. H. Herford, Mountain Scenery in Keats; J. W. Mackail, The Composition of Keats's Endymion (rptd in Studies of English Poets, 1926).]

de Selincourt, E. Keats. British Academy Lecture, 1921. [Rptd in The John Keats Memorial Volume, 1921.]

Fausset, H. I'A. Keats, a Study in Development. 1922.

Cazamian, L. Histoire de la Littérature anglaise. Paris, 1924; tr. Eng. vol. ii, 1927

Blunden, E. Shelley and Keats as they struck their Contemporaries. 1925.

Ker, W. P. Keats. [In Collected Essays, vol. i, 1925.]

Lowell, A. John Keats. 2 vols. Boston, 1925.

Murry, J. M. Keats and Shakespeare. Oxford, 1925.

—— Studies in Keats. Oxford, 1930, 1938 (with 3 additional essays).

Garrod, H. W. Keats. Oxford, 1926.

The Keats House, Hampstead. Guide. [1926.]

Thorpe, C. de W. The Mind of John Keats. Oxford, 1926.

Lafourcade, G. Swinburne's Hyperion and Other Poems, with an Essay on Swinburne and Keats. 1928.

Spurgeon, C. F. E. Keats's Shakespeare. Oxford, 1928.

Weller, E. V. Poems of Mary Tighe with Parallel Passages from the Works of John Keats. New York, 1928.

Erlande, A. La Vie de John Keats. Paris, 1929; tr. Eng. 1929.

Orend-Schmidt, V. John Keats Schönheitsideal und Weltanschauung. Marburg, 1929.

Saito, T. Keats's View of Poetry. 1929.
Anders, H. Die Bedeutung Wordsworthscher Gedankengänge für das Denken und Dichten von John Keats. Breslau, 1932.
Forman, M. B. John Keats and his Family. A Series of Portraits. Edinburgh, 1933.
Evans, B. I. Keats. 1934.
Ridley, M. R. Keats's Craftsmanship: A Study in Poetic Development. Oxford, 1934.
Blunden, E. Keats's Publisher: a Memoir of John Taylor, 1781–1864. 1936.
Finney, C. L. The Evolution of Keats's Poetry. 2 vols. Cambridge, U.S.A. 1936.
Adami, M. Fanny Keats 1937.
Brown, Charles Armitage. The Life of John Keats. Ed. D. H. Bodurtha and W. B. Pope, Oxford, 1937.
Bush, D. Mythology and the Romantic Tradition in English Poetry. Cambridge, U.S.A. 1937.
Hewlett, D. Adonais: a Life of John Keats. 1937.
Letters of Fanny Brawne to Fanny Keats, 1820–1824. Ed. F. Edgcumbe, New York, 1937.
Some Letters and Miscellanea of Charles Brown. Ed. M. B. Forman, 1937.
Hale-White, Sir W. Keats, as Doctor and Patient. Oxford, 1938.

(c) Early Reviews

[For a more detailed list see G. L. Marsh and N. I. White, Keats and the Periodicals of his Time, MP. xxxii, 1934.]

Poems, 1817. Champion, 9 March 1817; Monthly Mag. xliii, April 1817; European Mag. lxxi, May 1817 (by G. F. Mathew?); Examiner, 1 June, 6, 13 July 1817 (by Leigh Hunt); Eclectic Rev. N.S. viii, Sept. 1817; Constable's Edinburgh Mag. i, Oct. 1817.
Endymion. Quart. Rev. xix, April 1818 (by J. W. Croker); Literary Journ. 17, 24 May 1818; British Critic, N.S. ix, June 1818; Oxford Herald, 6 June 1818 (by B. Bailey); Champion, 7 June 1818 (by John Scott?); Alfred, West of England Journ. 6 Oct. 1818 (by J. H. Reynolds); (Baldwin) London Mag. i, April 1820; Edinburgh Rev. xxxiv, Aug. 1820 (by F. Jeffrey).
Lamia, Isabella, the Eve of St. Agnes, and Other Poems. Monthly Rev. xcii, July 1820; New Times, 19 July 1820 (by C. Lamb); Literary Chronicle, 29 July 1820; (Gold's) London Mag. ii, Aug. 1820; Indicator, 2, 9 Aug. 1820 (by Leigh Hunt); Guardian, 6 Aug. 1820; Constable's Edinburgh Mag. vii, Aug., Oct. 1820; Eclectic Rev. N.S. xiv, Sept. 1820; British Critic,

N.S. xiv, Sept. 1820; New Monthly Mag. xiv, Sept. 1820; Monthly Mag. l, Sept. 1820; (Baldwin's) London Mag. ii, Sept. 1820.

(d) Articles in Periodicals

Hunt, J. H. L. Young Poets. Examiner, 1 Dec. 1816.
'Z.' (J. G. Lockhart?). On the Cockney School of Poetry. No. iv. Blackwood's Mag. iii, Aug. 1818.
Severn, J. The Vicissitudes of Keats's Fame. Atlantic Monthly, xi, 1863.
Clarke, C. Cowden. Recollections of John Keats. GM. N.S. xii, 1874. [Rptd with some changes in Recollections of Writers, by C. and M. Cowden Clarke, 1878.]
Hoops, J. Keats's Jugend und Jugendgedichte. E. Studien, xxi, 1895.
Keats Double Number. Bookman, Oct. 1906. [Facsimiles, photographs, critical studies, etc.]
MacCracken, H. The Source of Keats's Eve of St Agnes. MP. v, 1908.
Bulletin of the Keats-Shelley Memorial, Rome. Ed. R. Rodd (Baron Rennell) and H. N. Gay, 2 nos. 1910–3.
Rannie, D. W. Keats's Epithets. E. & S. iii, 1912.
Colvin, Sir S. New Notes on Keats. TLS. 18 Feb. 1915.
Elliott, G. R. The Real Tragedy of Keats. PMLA. xxxvi, 1921. [Rptd in The Cycle of Modern Poetry, Princeton, 1929.]
Shackford, M. H. The Eve of St Agnes and The Mysteries of Udolpho. PMLA. xxxvi, 1921.
—— Hyperion. Stud. Phil. xxii, 1925.
Toynbee, P. Keats and Cary's Dante. TLS. 16 June 1921.
Finney, C. L. Drayton's Endimion and Phoebe and Keats's Endymion. PMLA. xxxix, 1924.
—— Shakespeare and Keats's Hyperion. PQ. iii, 1924.
—— Keats's Philosophy of Beauty. PQ. v, 1926.
—— The Fall of Hyperion. JEGP. xxvi, 1927. [See however D. Bush, MLN. xlix, 1934, pp. 281–6.]
Cornelius, R. D. Two Early Reviews of Keats's First Volume. PMLA. xl, 1925.
Hale-White, Sir W. Keats as a Medical Student. 1925. [Rptd from Guy's Hospital Reports, vol. lxxv.]
Darbishire, H. Keats and Egypt. RES. iii, 1927.
Draper, W. A. A Literary Windfall. American Collector, v, 1927. [MS of La Belle Dame sans Merci.]

Milner, G. On some Marginalia made by Rossetti in a Copy of Keats's Poems. E. Studien, LXI, 1927.

Thorpe, C. de W. Wordsworth and Keats: a Study in Personal and Critical Impression. PMLA. XLII, 1927.

—— Keats's Interest in Politics and World Affairs. PMLA. XLVI, 1931.

Weller, E. V. Keats and Mary Tighe. PMLA. XLII, 1927.

Murry, J. M. The Birth of a Great Poem. Hibbert Journ. XXVII, 1928.

Evans, B. I. Keats's Approach to the Chapman Sonnet. E. & S. XVI, 1930.

—— Keats and Joseph Severn. London Mercury, XXX, 1934.

Brown, L. The Genesis, Growth, and Meaning of 'Endymion.' Stud. Phil. XXX, 1933.

Beach, J. W. Keats's Realms of Gold. PMLA. XLIX, 1934.

Forman, M. B. Keats and the Richards Family. TLS. 26 April 1934.

—— Keats's 'I stood tip-toe.' TLS. 27 Aug. 1938.

Marsh, G. L. and White, N. I. Keats and the Periodicals of his Time. MP. XXXII, 1934.

Olney, C. John Keats and Benjamin Haydon. PMLA. XLIX, 1934.

Havens, R. D. Unreconciled Opposites in Keats. PQ. XIV, 1935.

Roberts, J. H. The Significance of 'Lamia.' PMLA. L, 1935.

Caldwell, J. R. The Meaning of 'Hyperion.' PMLA. LI, 1936.

Leavis, F. R. Keats. Scrutiny, IV, 1936. [Rptd in Revaluations, 1936.]

Lowes, J. L. 'Hyperion' and the 'Purgatorio.' TLS. 11 Jan. 1936.

—— Moneta's Temple. PMLA. LI, 1936.

—— Keats, Diodorus Siculus and Rabelais. MP. XXXIV, 1937.

de Selincourt, E. Keats and Monkhouse. TLS. 23 Oct. 1937. [Unpbd letter.]

Garrod, H. W. An Unpublished Sonnet of Keats. TLS. 27 Nov. 1937.

Page, F. Keats and the Midnight Oil. Dublin Rev. CI, 1937.

Wagenblass, J. H. Keats and Lucretius. MLR. XXXII, 1937.

Birss, J. H. Fragment of a New Keats Letter. N. & Q. 26 Feb. 1938. E. de S.

THOMAS HOOD (1799–1845)

(1) COLLECTED WORKS

The Works of Thomas Hood: Comic and Serious, in Prose and Verse. Edited, with Notes, by his Son [T. Hood, jun.]. 7 vols. 1862.

The Works. Edited, with Notes, by his Son [T. Hood, jun.] and Daughter [F. F. Broderip]. 10 vols. 1869–73 (illustrated); 11 vols. 1882–4.

(2) COLLECTED POEMS

Poems [serious]. 2 vols. 1846 (*bis*); 1853 (6th edn); 1858 (10th edn). [This and the next item form the first collected edn of Hood's poems.]

Poems of Wit and Humour [excluding those in Hood's Own]. 1847; 1851 (3rd edn); 1856 (7th edn); [1872] (19th edn).

The Poetical Works, with some Account of the Author. Boston, 4 vols. 1856, 1857.

The Serious [Comic] Poems. Ed. S. Lucas, with Preface by T. Hood the Younger, 2 vols. [1867], 1876.

The Poetical Works. Ed. W. M. Rossetti, illustrated by G. Doré. 2 sers. [1871–5], [1880].

[Other edns: illustrated by Birket Foster, 1871; 1872; [1874]; [1875]; [1878]; [1880]; 2 vols. 1881; 2 vols. 1886; 2 vols. [1886]; [1887]; ed. J. Ashton, [1891]; ed. A. Ainger, 2 vols. 1897; ed. W. Jerrold, 1906, 1917 (World's Classics).]

(3) SELECTIONS

Humorous Poems. Ed. E. Sargent, Boston, 1856.

Selected Poems, translated into German by H. Harrys. Hanover, 1859.

Early Poems and Sketches. Edited by his Daughter. 1869.

The Poetical Works of Leigh Hunt and Thomas Hood. 1889.

Poems, chosen by Sir A. T. Quiller-Couch. [1912.]

(4) INDIVIDUAL PUBLICATIONS

Odes and Addresses to Great People. 1825 (anon.); 1826 (3rd edn). [In collaboration with J. H. Reynolds.]

Whims and Oddities: in Prose and Verse [illustrated]. 2 sers. 1826–7; 1829 (4th edn).

The Plea of the Midsummer Fairies, Hero and Leander, Lycus the Centaur, and Other Poems. 1827.

National Tales [in prose]. 2 vols. 1827.

The Epping Hunt. Illustrated by George Cruikshank. 1829; 1830.

The Dream of Eugene Aram. [First ptd in The Gem, 1829. First separate edn, with designs by W. Harvey, 1831. Tr. Welsh, Rhyl, 1853; German, Bromberg, 1861.]

Tylney Hall. A Novel. 3 vols. 1834, 1840, 1857, 1878.

Hood's Own, or Laughter from Year to Year [illustrated; contains the Literary Reminiscences]. 1839; 1846. Second Series, with Preface by his Son. 1861. [Both sers.] [1882].

Up the Rhine. 1840. Frankfort, 1840. [Prose; a few poems interspersed.]

The Loves of Sally Brown and Ben the Carpenter. [1840?] [A song; quarto, single sheet.]

The Song of the Shirt. Punch, Christmas No., 1843.

Whimsicalities: a Periodical Gathering. With Illustrations by Leech. 2 vols. 1844; 1870 (enlarged); [1878]. [Verse and prose.]

Lamia, a romance. [In verse; written about 1827. First ptd in W. Jerdan, Autobiography, vol. I, 1852.]

Fairy Land. By the late Thomas and Jane Hood, their Son and Daughter. 1861.

(5) Periodicals edited by Hood

The Gem, a Literary Annual. 1829. [Vol. I only.]

The Comic Annual. 11 vols. 1830–42. [Literary contributions mainly by Hood. No vols. issued for 1840–1.]

The New Monthly Magazine and Humorist. LXIII–LXVIII, 1841–3.

Hood's Magazine and Comic Miscellany. I–III, 1844–5. [Contains the first appearance of The Bridge of Sighs.]

(6) Other Works with contributions by Hood

The London Magazine. IV–VIII, July 1821–July 1823. [Ed. by John Taylor, with Hood as assistant and frequent contributor.]

Sporting, with literary contributions by T. Hood [and others]. Ed. 'Nimrod' (i.e. C. J. Apperley), 1838.

(7) Biography and Criticism

Horne, R. H. A New Spirit of the Age. Vol. II, 1844.

Gilfillan, G. Galleries of Literary Portraits. Vol. I, 1856.

[Broderip, F. F. and Hood, T., jun.] Memorials of Thomas Hood. Collected by his Daughter. With a Preface and Notes by his Son. 2 vols. 1860.

Masson, D. Thomas Hood. Macmillan's Mag. Aug. 1860.

Thackeray, W. M. On a Joke I once heard from the late T. Hood. [In Roundabout Papers, 1863.]

Elliot, A. Hood in Scotland. Dundee, 1885.

Ashton, J. The True Story of Eugene Aram. [In Eighteenth Century Waifs, 1887.]

Henley, W. E. Views and Reviews. 1890.

Saintsbury, G. Essays in English Literature, 1780–1860. Ser. 2, 1895.

Oswald, E. Thomas Hood und die soziale Tendenzdichtung seiner Zeit. Vienna, 1904.

Jerrold, W. Thomas Hood: His Life and Times. 1907.

—— Thomas Hood and Charles Lamb, the Story of a Friendship. 1930. [Includes rpt of the Literary Reminiscences.]

Shelley, H. C. Thomas Hood's Homes and Friends. [In Literary By-Paths in Old England, 1909.]

More, P. E. The Wit of Thomas Hood. [In Shelburne Essays, vol. VII, New York, 1910.]

Hudson, W. H. Thomas Hood: the Man, the Wit, and the Poet. [In A Quiet Corner in a Library, Chicago, 1915.]

The Exhibition of Hood MSS. at Bristol Reference Library. Bookman, LXIV, 1923.

Swann, J. H. The Serious Poems of Thomas Hood. Manchester Quart. LI, 1925.

Shaw, C. B. This Fellow of Infinite Jest. Poet-Lore, XL, 1929.

Blunden, E. Hood's Literary Reminiscences. [In Votive Tablets, 1931.]

Mabbott, T. O. Letters of Leigh Hunt, Thomas Hood, and Allan Cunningham. N. & Q. 23 May 1931.

Turnbull, J. M. Reynolds, the Hoods, and Mary Lamb. TLS. 5 Nov. 1931.

R. W. K.

III. MINOR VERSE, 1800–1835

[This section is restricted, with a few exceptions, to writers who were born between the years 1764 and 1800. The references to *Miles*, X (XI), etc., are to The Poets and Poetry of the Century, ed. A. H. Miles, the vol. nos. in brackets being those in the rev. edn of 1905–7.]

ROBERT ANDERSON (1770–1833)

Ballads in the Cumbrian Dialect. Carlisle, 1805; Wigton, 1808; Alnwick, [1840].

The Poetical Works [and autobiography]. 2 vols. Carlisle, 1820.

Anderson's Cumberland Ballads and Songs. Ed. T. Ellwood, Ulverston, 1904.

The Cumberland Dialect. Selections from the Cumberland Ballads of Robert Anderson. Ed. R. Crowther, Ulverston, 1907.

JOHN ANSTER (1793–1867)

Poems with some Translations from the German. Edinburgh, 1819.

Faustus, a Dramatic Mystery; the Bride of Corinth; the First Walpurgis Night. Translated from the German of Goethe. 1835. [Faustus (= Faust, pt I) has been frequently rptd, e.g. ed. H. Morley, 1883, and ed. Sir A. W. Ward, 1907 (World's Classics). Passages from it had appeared anon. in Blackwood's Mag. June 1820.]

Xeniola: Poems, including Translations from Schiller and De la Motte Fouqué. Dublin, 1837.

Faustus, the Second Part, from the German of Goethe. 1864; ed. H. Morley, 1886.

German Literature at the Close of the Last Century and the Commencement of the Present. [In Lectures on Literature and Art delivered in Dublin, ser. 2, 1864.]

[Anster was also a regular contributor, mainly on literary topics, to Dublin University Mag. 1837–56, and North British Rev. 1847–66.]

EDWIN ATHERSTONE (1788–1872)

The Last Days of Herculaneum. Poems. 1821.

A Midsummer Day's Dream, a Poem. 1824.

The Fall of Nineveh, a Poem. 2 vols, 1828–30; 1847 (enlarged); 1868 (further enlarged).

The Sea-Kings in England, an Historical Romance [in prose]. 3 vols. Edinburgh, 1830.

The Handwriting on the Wall. A Story [in prose]. 3 vols. 1858.

Israel in Egypt, a Poem. 1861.

The Poetical Works. Ed. M. E. Atherstone, 1888.

[See F., Lord Jeffrey, Edinburgh Rev. XLVIII, 1828, and J. Wilson, Blackwood's Mag. XXVII, 1830—favourable and unfavourable reviews respectively of The Fall of Nineveh; and A. H. Miles, *Miles*, II.]

JOANNA BAILLIE (1762–1851)

(a) Collected Works

The Complete Poetical Works. Philadelphia, 1832.

The Dramatic and Poetical Works, 1851; 1853 (includes memoir).

The Modern Scottish Minstrel. Ed. C. Rogers, 6 vols. Edinburgh, 1855. [Vol. I contains Joanna Baillie's songs and a memoir.]

(b) Individual Publications

Fugitive Verses. 1790; 1840 (enlarged); 1842.

A Series of Plays in which it is attempted to delineate the Stronger Passions. Vol. I: 1798 (anon.; includes De Montfort); 1799; 1800 (with author's name). Vol. II: 1802 (bis); 1806. Vol. III: 1812. Vols. I–III, 1821. Tr. German, Amsterdam, 1806 (vols. I, II). [Chiefly in verse.]

Miscellaneous Plays. 1804; 1805. [Chiefly in verse.]

The Family Legend, a Tragedy [in verse]. Edinburgh, 1810 (bis).

Metrical Legends of Exalted Characters. 1821 (bis).

Poetical Miscellanies. 1822. [Contains poems also by Sir W. Scott, Mrs Hemans, etc.]

A Collection of Poems from Living Authors. 1823. [Ed. by Joanna Baillie.]

The Martyr, a Drama [in verse]. 1826.

The Bride, a Drama [in verse]. 1828 (bis).

A View of the General Tenour of the New Testament regarding the Nature of Jesus Christ. 1831; 1838.

Dramas. 3 vols. 1836.

Ahalya Baee, a Poem. 1849 (priv. ptd).

(c) Biography and Criticism

Sadler, T. The Father seen in Christ. A Sermon on the Death of Mrs Joanna Baillie. 1851.

Gilfillan, G. Galleries of Literary Portraits. Vol. I, 1856.

Druskowitz. H. von. Drei englische Dichterinnen. Berlin, 1885. [Joanna Baillie, E. B. Browning and George Eliot.]

Whyte, W. *Miles*, VII (VIII).

Plarr, V. G. Sir Walter Scott and Joanna Baillie. Edinburgh Rev. CCXVI, CCXVII, 1912–3. [Previously unpbd correspondence.]

Meynell, A. The Second Person Singular and other Essays. 1921.

Carhart, M. S. The Life and Work of Joanna Baillie. New Haven, 1923. [Includes a bibliography.]

Carswell, D. Sir Walter, a Four-Part Study in Biography. 1930. [Scott's relations with Hogg, Lockhart and Joanna Baillie.]

Sutton, D. Joanna Baillie and Sir George Beaumont. N. & Q. 26 Feb. 1938.

JOHN BANIM (1798–1842)

[See p. 387 below.]

RICHARD HARRIS BARHAM (1788–1845)

(a) Works

Baldwin, or a Miser's Heir, a Serio-Comic Tale. By an Old Bachelor. 1820. [In prose.]

The Ingoldsby Legends, or Mirth and Marvels, by Thomas Ingoldsby, Esquire. 3 sers. 1840 –7, etc.; ed. (with memoir) R. H. D. Barham, [1860]; illustrated by G. Cruikshank, J. Leech and J. Tenniel, 1864; ed. E. A. Bond, 3 vols. 1894; ed. J. B. Atlay, 2 vols. 1903. Selections, ed. Sir H. Newbolt, [1910]. [First ptd in Bentley's Monthly Misc. and New Monthly Mag. from 1837 on.]

Some Account of My Cousin Nicholas. 3 vols. 1841; 1846. [A novel, rptd from Blackwood's Mag. 1834.]

Ingoldsby Lyrics, by Thomas Ingoldsby, edited by his Son. 1881. [Partly from The Ingoldsby Legends, partly from other sources.]

(b) Biography and Criticism

Horne, R. H. A New Spirit of the Age. Vol. I, 1844.

Barham, R. H. D. The Life and Letters of Richard Harris Barham. 2 vols. 1870; 1899.

Saintsbury, G. Three Humourists—Hook, Barham, Maginn. [In Essays in English Literature, 1780–1860, ser. 2, 1895.]

Harper, C. G. The Ingoldsby Country: Literary Landmarks. 1904.

Ellis, S. M. Bookman, LI, 1917. [Illustrated.]

Elwin, M. Victorian Wallflowers. 1934.

The Ingoldsby Legends. TLS. 26 Dec. 1936.

EATON STANNARD BARRETT (1786–1820)

[See p. 388 below.]

BERNARD BARTON (1784–1849)

(a) Selection

Selections from the Poems and Letters of Bernard Barton. Ed. L. Barton, 1849, 1853. [With memoir by E. FitzGerald.]

(b) Individual Publications

Metrical Effusions. 1812.

The Triumph of the Orwell. Woodbridge (Suffolk), [1817].

The Convict's Appeal. 1818.

Poems by an Amateur. 1818.

A Day in Autumn, a Poem. 1820.

Poems. 1820; 1821; 1822; 1825.

Napoleon, and Other Poems. 1822.

Verses on the Death of P. B. Shelley. 1822.

Minor Poems. 1824.

Poetic Vigils. 1824.

Devotional Verses: Founded on, and Illustrative of, Select Texts of Scripture. 1826.

A Missionary's Memorial, or Verses on the Death of J. Lawson. 1826.

A Widow's Tale and Other Poems. 1827.

A New Year's Eve, and Other Poems. 1828.

Bible Letters for Children [by Lucy Barton], with Introductory Verses by B. Barton. 1831; [1857?] (6th edn).

Fisher's Juvenile Scrap-Book. 1836. [Ed. by Barton; the 1837 and 1839 nos. were ed. by Barton and Agnes Strickland.]

The Reliquary. With a Prefatory Appeal for Poetry and Poets. 1836. [With Lucy Barton.]

Household Verses. 1845.

Sea-Weeds, gathered at Aldborough. Woodbridge, [1846] (priv. ptd).

A Memorial of J. J. Gurney [in verse]. 1847.

Birthday Verses at Sixty-Four. Woodbridge, 1848.

Ichabod! Woodbridge, 1848. [Poems.]

On the Signs of the Times. Woodbridge, 1848. [Poems.]

The Natural History of the Holy Land [by Lucy Barton], with Poetical Illustrations by B. Barton. [1856.]

(c) Biography and Criticism

[Lamb, C.?] London Mag. II, 1820. [A review of Poems, 1820.]

Lucas, E. V. Bernard Barton and his Friends. 1893.

Miles, A. H. Miles, x (XI).

Ritchie, J. E. Christopher Crayon's Recollections. 1898.

Unpublished Letters from Edward FitzGerald to Bernard Barton. Scribner's Mag. LXXII, 1922.

THOMAS HAYNES BAYLY (1797–1839)

(a) Collected Poems

Songs, Ballads, and Other Poems. Ed. (with memoir) Mrs T. H. Bayly, 2 vols. 1844.

Songs of the Affections. Selected by W. L. Hanchant. 1932.

(b) Individual Publications

Rough Sketches of Bath [in verse]. 1819 (4th edn).

Parliamentary Letters, and Other Poems, by Q in the Corner. 1819; 1820.

Erin, and Other Poems. Dublin, 1822.

Fifty Lyrical Ballads. Bath, 1829 (priv. ptd).

Musings and Prosings. Boulogne, 1833.

Flowers of Loveliness, by Various Artists, with Poetical Illustrations by T. H. Bayly. 1837.

Kindness in Women. Tales [prose]. 3 vols. 1837; 1862.

Weeds of Witchery. 1837. [Songs.]

Songs and Ballads. [1837?]

[Bayley also pbd: (a) numerous dramatic pieces, including the farce Perfection (1836); (b) several novels, including The Aylmers (3 vols. 1827); (c) single-sheet quarto issues of popular songs, e.g. 'I'd be a butterfly.']

(c) Criticism

Lang, A. Essays in Little. 1891 (rev. edn).

Miles, A. H. Miles, IX (X).

ROBERT BLOOMFIELD (1766–1823)

The Farmer's Boy. A Rural Poem. 1800 (3 edns); 1801 (5th edn); ed. C. Lofft, 1810; 1827 (15th edn); rptd Darlington, 1898; tr. (in part) Latin, Ipswich, 1804.

Rural Tales, Ballads, and Songs. 1802; 1803 (3rd edn); 1806; 1826 (10th edn).

Good Tidings, or News from the Farm. A Poem. 1804.

Wild Flowers; or Pastoral and Local Poetry. 1806; 1809; 1816; 1819.

The Banks of Wye. A Poem. 1811; 1823 (3rd edn).

May Day with the Muses. 1822.

Hazelwood-Hall: a Village Drama [in prose]. 1823.

The Remains of Robert Bloomfield. [Ed. J. Weston], 2 vols. 1824.

The Poems. 3 vols. 1827; 1831.

The Poetical Works. 1835; ed. W. B. Rands, [1855]; illustrated by Birket Foster, 1857, 1864.

Selections from the Correspondence of Robert Bloomfield. Ed. W. H. Hart, 1870.

Miles, A. H. *Miles*, I. [Selection and criticism.]

SIR ALEXANDER BOSWELL (1775–1822)

Songs Chiefly in the Scottish Dialect. Edinburgh, 1803.

The Spirit of Tintoc or Johnny Bell and the Kelpie. Edinburgh, 1803.

Epistle to the Edinburgh Reviewers, by A. B. Edinburgh, 1803.

Clan Alpin's Vow. A Fragment. Edinburgh, 1811; 1813; 1817.

The Tyrant's Fall. A Poem on Waterloo. Auchinleck, 1815.

Sheldon Haugh's or the Sow Flitted. Auchinleck, 1816.

The Woo' Creel or the Bill o' Bashan. Auchinleck, 1816.

Song for the Harveian Anniversary. Edinburgh, 1816.

Elegiac Ode to the Memory of Dr Harvey. [In Andrew Duncan's Tribute to Raeburn, Edinburgh, 1824.]

The Poetical Works. Ed. S. H. Smith, Glasgow, 1871.

[Boswell also ed. or rptd several 16th century rarities, mainly at the Auchinleck press under the title Frondes Caducae, 1816–8.]

CAROLINE ANNE BOWLES later SOUTHEY (1786–1854)

[See also under Robert Southey, pp. 180–3 above.]

(a) *Works*

Ellen Fitzarthur, a Metrical Tale. 1820; 1822.

The Widow's Tale. 1822. [Poems.]

Solitary Hours. Edinburgh, 1826; 1839. [Prose and verse.]

Chapters on Churchyards. 2 vols. Edinburgh, 1829. [Prose tales, originally pbd in Blackwood's Mag.]

Tales of the Factories [in verse]. 1833.

The Birthday, a Poem in Three Parts. To which are added, Occasional Verses. Edinburgh, 1836.

Robin Hood: a Fragment. By the late Robert Southey and Caroline Southey. With Other Fragments and Poems by R. S. and C. S. Edinburgh, 1847.

The Poetical Works. 1867.

[The following attributions in the BM. Catalogue are probably erroneous: Tales of the Moors [in prose], 1828; Olympia Morata, her Times, Life and Writings, 1834; Selwyn in Search of a Daughter, and Other Tales, 3 vols. 1835.]

(b) *Biography and Criticism*

Coleridge, H. N. Modern English Poetesses. Quart. Rev. LXVI, 1840. [Caroline Bowles, Sara Coleridge and others.]

The Correspondence of Robert Southey with Caroline Bowles. Ed. E. Dowden, Dublin, 1881.

Miles, A. H. *Miles*, VII (VIII).

SIR JOHN BOWRING (1792–1872)

(a) *Poems*

Specimens of the Russian Poets. With Preliminary Remarks and Biographical Notices. 1820; 2 pts, 1821–3 (enlarged).

Matins and Vespers: with Hymns and Occasional Devotional Pieces. 1823; 1824 (enlarged); 1841 ('altered and enlarged'); 1851; Boston, 1853.

Batavian Anthology; or, Specimens of the Dutch Poets; with Remarks on the Poetical Literature and Language of the Netherlands, to the End of the Seventeenth Century. 1824. [With H. S. Van Dyk.]

Ancient Poetry and Romances of Spain: selected and translated. 1824.

Hymns. 1825.

Servian Popular Poetry. Translated, 1827.

Specimens of the Polish Poets, with Notes and Observations on the Literature of Poland. 1827.

Poetry of the Magyars, preceded by a Sketch of the Language and Literature of Hungary and Transylvania. 1830.

Cheskian [*i.e.* Czech] Anthology; being a History of the Poetical Literature of Bohemia; with Translated Specimens. 1832.

Manuscript of the Queen's Court. A Collection of Old Bohemian Lyrico-Epic Songs, with other Ancient Bohemian Poems. Prague, 1843.

Ode to the Deity. Translated from the Russian of [G. R.] Derzhavin. [Brighton? 1861.]

Translations from A. [or rather, S.] Petöfi, the Magyar Poet. 1866.

A Memorial Volume of Sacred Poetry; to which is prefixed a Memoir of the Author, by Lady Bowring. 1873.

(b) *Prose Writings*

Observations on the State of Religion and Literature in Spain. 1820.

Peter Schlemihl: from the German of La Motte Fouqué [or rather, of Chamisso]. 1824.

Sketch of the Language and Literature of Holland: being a Sequel to his Batavian Anthology. Amsterdam, 1829.

Minor Morals for Young People, illustrated in Tales and Travels. With Engravings by G. Cruikshank and W. Heath. 3 pts, 1834–9.

Autobiographical Recollections; with a Brief Memoir by L. B. Bowring. 1877.

[Bowring pbd a number of other prose works, on politics, literature, etc. as well as editing The Westminster Review, 1824, and Bentham's collected Works, 1838–43.]

(c) Biography and Criticism

The Oratory of Sir John Bowring. Fraser's Mag. XXXIV, 1846.

Moor, L. Bowring, Cobden and China: a Memoir. 1857.

Miles, A. H. Miles, x (xi).

Nesbitt, G. L. Benthamite Reviewing. New York, 1934.

HENRY BOYD (d. 1832)

(a) Writings

A Translation of the Inferno of Dante in English Verse. To which is added, a Specimen of a New Translation of the Orlando Furioso of Ariosto. 1785.

Poems chiefly Dramatic and Lyric. Dublin, 1793.

The Divina Commedia. Translated into English Verse. 3 vols. 1802.

The Penance of Hugo. A Vision on the French Revolution. In the Manner of Dante. Translated from Vincenzo Monti. 1805.

The Woodman's Tale, after the Manner of Spenser. To which are added Other Poems, chiefly Narrative and Lyrical; and The Royal Message: a Drama. 1805.

The Triumphs of Petrarch. 1807.

Remarks on the Fallen Angels of Milton. [In The Poetical Works of Milton, ed. H. Todd, 1809.]

(b) Criticism

Toynbee, P. Dante in English Literature. 2 vols. 1909. [Vol. i, pp. 410–9.]

BARBARINA BRAND, Lady DACRE (1768–1854)

(a) Poems and Plays

Ina. A Tragedy [in verse]. 1815 (3 edns).

Le Canzoni di Petrarca. [1815?] (priv. ptd). [With trns.]

Due Canzoni del Petrarca. Rome, 1818 (priv. ptd). [With trns.]

[Due Canzoni del Petrarca.] Naples, 1819 (priv. ptd). [With trns.]

Dramas, Translations, and Occasional Poems. 2 vols. 1821 (priv. ptd). [Includes Ina and the trns from Petrarch. The latter were rptd in Ugo Foscolo's Essays on Petrarch, 1823.]

Translations from the Italian. 1836 (priv ptd).

Frogs and Bulls: a Lilliputian Piece in Three Acts. 1838.

[Lady Dacre also ed. and rev. the writings of her daughter, Arabella Sullivan.]

(b) Biography

A Family Chronicle. Ed. Mrs J. Lyster, 1908.

SIR SAMUEL EGERTON BRYDGES (1762–1837)

[See pp. 662–3 below.]

CHARLES BUCKE (1781–1846)

[See pp. 663–4 below.]

ALFRED BUNN (1796–1860)

[See pp. 587–8 below.]

JEREMIAH JOHN CALLANAN (1795–1829)

[See p. 1051 below.]

GEORGE CANNING (1770–1827)

[See vol. II, p. 356 above.]

HENRY FRANCIS CARY (1772–1844)

(a) Works

An Irregular Ode to General Elliott. Birmingham, [1788].

Sonnets and Odes. 1788.

Ode to General Kosciusko. 1797.

The Inferno of Dante. With a Translation in Blank Verse, Notes, and a Life of the Author. 2 vols. 1805–6.

The Vision, or Hell, Purgatory, and Paradise, of Dante. Translated, 3 vols. 1814; 3 vols. 1819; Philadelphia, 2 vols. 1822; 1831; 1844, etc.; illustrated by G. Doré, 1866; ed. P. Toynbee, 1900–3; ed. E. Gardner, 1908 (Everyman's Lib.); illustrated by J. Flaxman, 1910; with drawings by Botticelli, and the Italian text, 1928.

The Birds of Aristophanes. Translated. 1824.

Pindar in English Verse. 1833.

Lives of English Poets, from Johnson to Kirke White. 1846. [Rptd from London Mag. Aug. 1821–Dec. 1824.]

The Early French Poets. Notices and Translations. 1846; ed. T. E. Welby (without the French texts), 1923. [Rptd from London Mag. Nov. 1821–April 1824.]

(b) Biography and Criticism

Foscolo, Ugo. Edinburgh Rev. XXIX, 1818. [On the Dante; Sir J. Mackintosh and Samuel Rogers assisted Foscolo.]

Coleridge, H. N. Cary's Pindar. Quart. Rev. LI, 1834.

Cary, H. Memoir of the Rev. H. F. Cary. 2 vols. 1847.

Toynbee, P. Dante in English Literature from Chaucer to Cary. 2 vols. 1909.

—— The Centenary of Cary's Dante. MLR. VII, 1912.

Farinelli, A. Dante in Inghilterra. [In Dante in Spagna, Francia, etc., Turin, 1922.]

King, R. W. The Translator of Dante. The Life, Work, and Friendships of H. F. Cary. 1925.

Gosse, Sir E. Cary's Early French Poets. [In Silhouettes, 1925.]

JOHN CASTILLO (1792–1845)

Awd Isaac, The Steeple Chase, and Other Poems. Whitby, 1843.

The Bard of the Dales, or Poems partly in the Yorkshire Dialect. Kirby Moorside, 1850; Stokesley, 1858.

Jacob's Ladder. Filey, 1858. [A sermon.]

Poems in the North Yorkshire Dialect. Ed. G. M. Tweddell, Stokesley, 1878.

RICHARD COBBOLD (1797–1877)

[See p. 491 below.]

HARTLEY COLERIDGE (1796–1849)

[See also under Samuel Taylor Coleridge, pp. 176–9 above.]

(a) Collected Works

Poems, with a Memoir by his Brother [Derwent Coleridge]. 2 vols. 1851; 1851.

The Complete Poetical Works. Ed. R. Colles, [1908]. (Muses' Lib.)

Letters of Hartley Coleridge. Ed. G. E. and E. L. Griggs, 1937.

(b) Selections

The Poetical Works of Bowles, Lamb, and Hartley Coleridge. Ed. W. Tirebuck, 1887.

Poems. Ed. W. Bailey-Kempling, Ulverston, 1903.

Poems. 1907.

Essays on Parties in Poetry and on the Character of Hamlet. Ed. J. Drinkwater, Oxford, 1925.

(c) Individual Publications

Poems. Vol. I (all pbd), Leeds, 1833 (re-issued as Poems, Songs and Sonnets).

Biographia Borealis, or Lives of Distinguished Northerns. Leeds, 1833; [ed. D. Coleridge], 3 vols. 1852 (as Lives of Northern Worthies).

Lives of Illustrious Worthies of Yorkshire. Hull, 1835. [Part of the Biographia Borealis re-issued with new title page.]

The Dramatic Works of Massinger and Ford, with an Introduction by H. Coleridge. 1840 (re-issued 1848, 1851).

Essays and Marginalia. Ed. [D. Coleridge], 2 vols. 1851.

Life of Andrew Marvell. Hull, 1853.

Ascham, R. The Scholemaster. With Memoir by H. Coleridge. 1884.

(d) Biography and Criticism

Horne, R. H. A New Spirit of the Age. Vol. I, 1844.

Bagehot, W. Literary Studies. Vol. I, 1879.

Waddington, S. Miles, III.

Bradshaw, J. Material for a Memoir of Hartley Coleridge. [In Primitiae: Essays by Students of the University of Liverpool, Liverpool, 1912.]

Towle, E. A. A Poet's Children: Hartley and Sara Coleridge. 1912.

Turner, A. M. Wordsworth and Hartley Coleridge. JEGP. XXII, 1923.

Williams, S. T. Hartley Coleridge as a Critic of Literature. In Southern Atlantic Quart. XXIII, 1924.

Hall, W. C. Manchester Quart. LI, 1925.

Pomeroy, M. J. The Poetry of Hartley Coleridge. Washington, 1927.

Griggs, E. L. Hartley Coleridge, his Life and Work. 1929. [Includes bibliography.]

—— Coleridge and his Son. Stud. Phil. XXVII, 1930.

—— Hartley Coleridge on his Father. PMLA. XLVI, 1931.

—— Hartley Coleridge's Unpublished Correspondence. London Mercury, XXIV, 1931.

Blunden, E. Coleridge the Less. [In Votive Tablets, 1931.]

Hartman, H. Hartley Coleridge, Poet's Son and Poet. 1931. [Includes bibliography.]

Rea, J. D. Hartley Coleridge and Wordsworth's Lucy. Stud. Phil. XXVIII, 1931.

GEORGE COLMAN the younger (1762–1836)

[See vol. II, p. 463 above.]

JOSIAH CONDER (1789–1855)

(a) Poems

The Associate Minstrels. 1810 (anon.); 1813. [Poems by Conder and others; ed. by Conder.]

Gloria in Excelsis Deo. 1812.

The Star in the East; with Other Poems. 1824.

The Congregational Hymn-Book. 1834; 1836.

The Choir and the Oratory; or, Praise and Prayer. 1837. [A collection of poems.]

The Psalms of David imitated, by Isaac Watts; the Whole carefully revised by Josiah Conder. 1851.

Hymns of Prayer, Praise, and Devout Meditation. Prepared for Publication by the Author. Ed. E. R. Conder, 1856.

(b) Prose

The Law of the Sabbath, Religious and Political. 1830; 1852.

The Modern Traveller. 30 vols. 1830.

Italy. 3 vols. 1831.

Illustrations of the Pilgrim's Progress; with a Sketch of the Life and Writings of Bunyan. [1836.]

The Literary History of the New Testament. 1845 (anon.).

[Conder wrote a number of other works on religious, political, geographical and literary subjects.]

(c) Biography and Criticism

Keble, J. Sacred Poetry. Quart. Rev. XXXII, 1825. [Rptd in Occasional Papers and Reviews, ed. E. B. Pusey, 1877, and in English Critical Essays (Nineteenth Century), ed. E. D. Jones, 1916 (World's Classics). A review of The Star in the East.]

Conder, E. R. Josiah Conder: a Memoir. 1857.

Horder, W. G. Miles, x (xi).

LOUISA STUART COSTELLO (1799–1870)

The Maid of the Cyprus Isle and other Poems. 1815 (bis).

Redwald, a Tale of Mona, and other Poems. Brentford, 1819.

Songs of a Stranger. 1825.

Specimens of the Early Poetry of France, from the Time of the Troubadours and Trouvères to the Reign of Henri Quatre. 1835.

The Lay of the Stork, a Poem. 1856.

[Louisa Costello also pbd books of travel and historical memoirs, mainly concerned with France.]

JOSEPH COTTLE (1770–1853)

Poems: containing John the Baptist; Sir Malcolm and Alla, a Tale; War, a Fragment. With a Monody to John Henderson; and a Sketch of his Character. Bristol, 1795.

Malvern Hills: a Poem. 1798; 1802 (3rd edn); 2 vols. 1829 (adds an appendix of essays in prose).

John the Baptist, a Poem. 1801.

Alfred, an Epic Poem. 1801; 2 vols. 1802; 2 vols. Newburyfort, 1814; 2 vols. 1816; 1850.

The Fall of Cambria: a Poem. 1809; 2 vols. 1811.

Messiah: a Poem. 1815.

Dartmoor, and Other Poems. 1823.

Hymns and Sacred Lyrics. 1828.

Early Recollections, chiefly relating to the late Samuel Taylor Coleridge. 2 vols. 1837; 1847 (as Reminiscences of Coleridge and Southey).

[Cottle also pbd some miscellaneous prose.]

JOHN WILSON CROKER (1780–1857)

[See p. 665 below.]

GEORGE CROLY (1780–1860)

(a) Works

Paris in 1815. A Poem. 1817; 1818. Second Part, with Other Poems. 1821.

Lines on the Death of Princess Charlotte. 1818.

The Angel of the World, an Arabian Tale, Sebastian, a Spanish Tale, with Other Poems. 1820.

Gems, principally from the Antique. Drawn by Richard Dagley, with Illustrations in Verse by George Croly. 1822.

Catiline, a Tragedy. With Other Poems. 1822.

May Fair. In Four Cantos. 1827. [A satire in verse.]

Salathiel: A Story [in prose], of the Past, the Present, and the Future. 3 vols. 1828; 1829; 1855 (rev. edn); ed. L. Wallace, Toronto, 1901; ed. I. K. F., New York, 1901.

Tales [in prose] of the Great St Bernard. 3 vols. 1828; 1858 (rev. edn).

The Poetical Works of the Rev. George Croly. 2 vols. 1830.

The Modern Orlando. Cantos i to vii [all pbd]. 1846; 1855. [A poem.]

Marston, or the Soldier and Statesman [a novel]. 3 vols. 1846; 1860.

Scenes from Scripture, with Other Poems. 1851.

Psalms and Hymns for Public Worship. 1854. [Partly original, partly compiled.]

The Book of Job. With a Memoir by F. W. Croly. 1863.

[Croly also pbd: (a) numerous sermons and other theological works, e.g. The Apocalypse of St John, a New Interpretation, 1827; (b) historical and biographical works, e.g. on George IV, 1830, and Burke, 1840, and edns of Jeremy Taylor and of Pope's poems; (c) voluminous contributions to periodicals, including Blackwood's Mag., Literary Gazette, etc.]

(b) Biography and Criticism

Herring, R. A Few Personal Recollections of George Croly, with Extracts from his Speeches and Writings. 1861.

A Dictionary of Hymnology. Ed. J. Julian, 1892.

ALLAN CUNNINGHAM (1784–1842)
[See p. 391 below.]

THOMAS MOUNSEY CUNNINGHAM (1776–1834)

The Modern Scottish Minstrel: or, the Songs of Scotland of the Past Half Century. Ed. C. Rogers, 6 vols. Edinburgh, 1855. [Cunningham's works and life in vol. II.]

ROBERT CHARLES DALLAS (1754–1824)
[See p. 392 below.]

GEORGE DANIEL (1789–1864)
[See p. 666 below.]

THOMAS DERMODY (1775–1803)

(a) Works

Poems. Dublin, 1789; 1800 (as Poems, Moral and Descriptive).
Poems, consisting of Essays, Lyric, Elegiac, etc. Dublin, 1792.
The Rights of Justice. [Dublin?], 1793. [Prose.]
Poems on Various Subjects. 1802.
The Harp of Erin, containing the Poetical Works of the late Thomas Dermody. [Ed. J. G. Raymond], 2 vols. 1807.

(b) Biography and Criticism

Raymond, J. G. The Life of Thomas Dermody. 2 vols. 1806.
Jeffrey, F., Lord. Edinburgh Rev. VIII, 1806.
Morgan, S., Lady. Memoirs. Ed. W. H. Dixon and G. E. Jewsbury, 2 vols. 1862. [Many references to Dermody.]
Mabbott, T. O. Thomas Dermody: Three Letters. N. & Q. 26 May 1934.

SIR AUBREY DE VERE (originally HUNT) (1788–1846)

Julian the Apostate, a Dramatic Poem. 1822; 1858 (with The Duke of Mercia).
The Duke of Mercia, a Drama; and Other Poems. 1823.
A Song of Faith, Devout Exercises, and Sonnets. 1842.
Mary Tudor, a Drama. 1847; with Memoir by A. T. De Vere, 1884.
Sonnets. A New Edition [with memoir by A. T. De Vere]. 1875.
Bell, M. Miles, II. [Selection and criticism.]
[For further criticism see under A. T. De Vere, p. 1052 below.]

CHARLES DIBDIN the Younger (1768–1833)
[See p. 588 below.]

THOMAS JOHN DIBDIN (1771–1841)
[See p. 589 below.]

ISAAC D'ISRAELI (1766–1848)
[See pp. 667 below.]

THOMAS DOUBLEDAY (1790–1870)

(a) Poems

Sixty-five Sonnets; with Prefatory Remarks on the Accordance of the Sonnet with the Powers of the English Language. 1818 (anon.).
The Italian Wife. A Tragedy. 1823 (anon.).
Babington. A Tragedy. 1825.
Dioclesian. A Dramatic Poem. 1829.
Caius Marius, the Plebeian Consul: a Historical Tragedy. 1836.
The Coquet-Dale Fishing Songs, now first collected and edited by a North Country Angler [i.e. Doubleday]. 1852.

(b) Miscellaneous Prose

The Political Life of Sir Robert Peel. 2 vols. 1856.
The Eve of St Mark: a Romance of Venice. 2 vols. 1857; 1864.
The Touchstone: a Series of Letters on Social, Literary and Political Subjects, originally published in the 'Newcastle Daily Chronicle' under the Signature of Britannicus. 1863.
Matter for Materialists: a Series of Letters in Vindication and Extension of the Principles regarding the Nature and Existence of Dr [George] Berkeley. 1870.
[Doubleday also pbd several works on population, and on other political and social subjects.]

GEORGE DYER (1755–1841).

(a) Works

Inquiry into the Nature of Subscription to the 39 Articles. [1789]; 1792 (enlarged).
Poems, consisting of Odes and Elegies. 1792.
The Complaints of the Poor People of England. 1793 (bis).
Account of New South Wales and State of the Convicts. 1794.
A Dissertation on the Theory and Practice of Benevolence. 1795. [Rptd in The Pamphleteer, vols. XIII, XIV, 1813.]
Memoirs of the Life and Writings of Robert Robinson. 1796.
The Poet's Fate, a Poetical Dialogue. 1797 (bis).
An Address to the People of Great Britain on the Doctrines of Libel. 1799.
Poems. 2 vols. 1802.
Poems and Critical Essays. 1802.
Poetics, or a Series of Poems and Disquisitions on Poetry. 2 vols. 1812.

Four Letters on the English Constitution. 1812; 1817 (3rd edn, enlarged). [Rptd in The Pamphleteer, vol. XII, 1813.]
History of the University and Colleges of Cambridge. 2 vols. 1814.
The Privileges of the University and Colleges of Cambridge. 2 vols. 1824.
Academic Unity. 1827.

[Dyer also contributed to Analytical Rev., Critical Rev., Reflector, and Monthly Mag.]

(b) Biography

Lucas, E. V. The Life of Charles Lamb. 2 vols. 1905.

CHARLOTTE ELLIOTT (1789–1871)

(a) Selections

Selections from the Poems of Charlotte Elliott, with a Memoir by E. B[abington]. [1873.]
[The memoir was re-issued [1875].]
Words of Hope and Grace. With Biographical Sketch. [1914.]

(b) Individual Publications

The Invalid's Hymn Book. 1834; 1841; 1854 (6th edn). [Includes 'Just as I am.']
Hours of Sorrow. 1836; 1856 (5th edn); 1869 (7th edn).
Morning and Evening Hymns for a Week. 1839 (priv. ptd); 1842.
Thoughts in Verse on Sacred Subjects. 1869; 1871.
Leaves from the Unpublished Journals, Letters and Poems of Charlotte Elliott. [1874.]

[Charlotte Elliot also contributed hymns to Psalms and Hymns, ed. H. V. Elliott, Brighton, 1835, and to The Christian Remembrancer Pocket Book, 1834, which she edited herself.]

(c) Biography and Criticism

Winslow, O. The King in his Beauty: a Tribute to the Memory of Miss Charlotte Elliott. [1872.]
A Dictionary of Hymnology. Ed. J. Julian, 1892. [Information on the hymns.]
Miles, A. II. Miles, x (xi).

EBENEZER ELLIOTT (1781–1849)

(a) Works

The Vernal Walk. 1801.
Night, a Descriptive Poem. 1818.
Love, a Poem. 1823; 1831.
The Village Patriarch. 1829; 1831.
Corn-Law Rhymes. 1831 (3 edns).
The Splendid Village; Corn-Law Rhymes; and Other Poems. 3 vols. 1833–5.
Poetical Works. Edinburgh, 1840; 3 vols. 1844; ed. E. Elliott, 2 vols. 1876.

More Verse and Prose by the Corn-Law Rhymer. 2 vols. 1850.

(b) Biography and Criticism

Carlyle, T. Corn Law Rhymes. Edinburgh Rev. LV, 1832. [Rptd in Critical and Miscellaneous Essays, 1839.]
Wilson, J. Blackwood's Mag. XXXV, 1834. [Chiefly on The Village Patriarch. Rptd in Works, vol. VI, Edinburgh, 1856.]
Watkins, J. The Life, Poetry, and Letters of Ebenezer Elliott. 1850. [Includes an autobiographical fragment.]
'Searle, J.' [i.e. G. S. Phillips]. The Life of Ebenezer Elliott. 1850; 1852.
King, J. W. Ebenezer Elliott, a Sketch. Sheffield, 1854.
Miles, A. H. Miles, II.
Odom, W. Two Sheffield Poets: James Montgomery and Ebenezer Elliott. [1929.]

THOMAS ERSKINE, Baron ERSKINE (1750–1823)

[See p. 668 below.]

CATHERINE MARIA FANSHAWE (1765–1834)

A Collection of Poems from living authors. Ed. J. Baillie, 1823. [Includes a few poems by Catherine Fanshawe ptd for the first time.]
Memorials of Miss C. M. Fanshawe. [Ed. W. Harness], Westminster [1865] (priv. ptd). [Includes most of her poems.]
Literary Remains [Poems]. With Notes by W. Harness. 1876.

JOHN HOOKHAM FRERE (1769–1846)

[See vol. II, p. 362 above.]

JOHN GALT (1779–1839)

[See p. 394 below.]

WILLIAM GILBERT (1760?–1825?)

(a) Poems

The Hurricane. A Theosophical and Western Eclogue. To which is subjoined, a Solitary Effusion in a Summer's Evening. Bristol, 1796.

(b) Biography and Criticism

Retrospective Rev. x, 1824. [Gives extracts from Gilbert's poems.]
Cottle, J. Reminiscences of Coleridge and Southey. 1847. [Pp. 42–7, brief biographical notice.]

ROBERT GILFILLAN (1798–1850)

Original Songs. Edinburgh, 1831; Edinburgh, 1835 (enlarged, as Songs); Edinburgh, 1839 (as Poems and Songs); Edinburgh, 1851 (with Memoir [by W. Anderson]).

17

WILLIAM GLEN (1787–1826)

Poems chiefly Lyrical. Glasgow, 1815.
The Star of Brunswick. Lanark, 1818.
Poetical Remains. Ed. C. Rogers, Edinburgh, 1874.

JAMES GRAHAME (1765–1811)

[See vol. II, p. 991 above.]

SIR ROBERT GRANT (1779–1838)

Sacred Poems. [Ed. Charles, Lord Glenelg], 1839; 1844; 1868.
Dictionary of Hymnology. Ed. J. Julian, 1892. [Information on Grant's hymns.]
Miles, A. H. *Miles*, x (XI). [Selection and criticism.]

[Grant contributed hymns to The Christian Observer, 1806–15, and to Psalms and Hymns, ed. H. V. Elliott, Brighton, 1835. His only separate pbns during his life were a few prose writings on the East India Company, *e.g.* a sketch of its history (1813).]

HENRY MONTAGUE GROVER (1791–1866)

(a) Poems

Anne Boleyn, a Tragedy [in five acts and in verse]. 1826.
Socrates, a Dramatic Poem [in five acts, with notes]. 1828.

(b) Prose

The History of the Resurrection authenticated. A Review of the Four Gospels on the Resurrection. 1841.
Analogy and Prophecy, Keys of the Church; Showing the Progress of the Dispensation and the Interpretation of the Prophecies by Analogies derived from the Mosaic Creation. 1846.
A Voice from Stonehenge. Pt 1, 1847.
Changes of the Poles and the Equator, Considered as a Source of Error in the Present Construction of the Maps and Charts of the Globe. 1848.
A Catechism for Sophs. 1848. [A 'summary of scriptural doctrine.']
Soundings of Antiquity: a New Method of applying the Astronomical Evidences to the Events of History; and an Assignment of True Dates to the Epochs of the Church. 1862.

JANET HAMILTON (1795–1873)

Poems and Essays. Glasgow, 1863.
Poems of purpose and sketches in prose. Glasgow, 1865.
Poems and Ballads. Glasgow, 1868.
Poems, Essays, and Sketches. [Ed. J. Hamilton], Glasgow, 1880, 1885.

[See J. Veitch, Janet Hamilton, the Poetess of Langloan, Good Words, xxv, 1884.]

REGINALD HEBER (1783–1826)

(a) Works

A Sense of Honour, a Prize Essay. Oxford, 1805.
Palestine, a Prize Poem. Oxford, 1807; 1809; 1810; tr. Welsh, 1822; Latin, Leamington, 1844.
Europe; Lines on the Present War. 1809 (*bis*).
Poems and Translations. 1812; 1829.
Hymns, written and adapted to the Weekly Church Service of the Year. [Ed. A. Heber], 1827; 1828 (4th edn); 1834 (10th edn).
Select Portions of Psalms and Hymns. With some Compositions of a late Distinguished Prelate [*i.e.* Heber]. 1827.
Narrative of a Journey through India, 1824–5. [Ed. A. Heber], 2 vols. 1828; 3 vols. 1828 (3rd edn); 2 vols. 1844. [Selection, ed. P. R. Krishnaswami, 1923.]
Sermons preached in England. [Ed. A. Heber], 1829 (*bis*).
Sermons preached in India. [Ed. A. Heber], 1829.
The Poetical Works of Reginald Heber. 1841; 1842; 1852; [1861]; [1881].
Blue-Beard. A Serio-Comic Oriental Romance in One Act [in verse]. 1868; [1874].

[A number of sermons and charges were also pbd separately. Some hymns were first ptd in The Christian Observer, 1811–6.]

(b) Biography and Criticism

Kaye, J. A Valedictory Address to the Bishop of Calcutta, with his Lordship's Reply. 1823.
Blunt, J. J. The Church in India—Bishop Heber. Quart. Rev. xxxv, 1827. [Biographical and critical.]
Milman, H. H. Heber's Hymns. Quart. Rev. xxxviii, 1828.
Jeffrey, F., Lord. Edinburgh Rev. xlviii, 1828. [On the Narrative of a Journey.]
Robinson, T. The Last Days of Bishop Heber. Madras, 1829; 1830.
Some Account of the Life of Reginald Heber. 1829.
Heber, A. Life of Reginald Heber, by his Widow. 2 vols. 1830.
Smyth, T. S. The Character and Religious Doctrines of Bishop Heber. 1831.
Bonner, G. Memoir of Heber. Cheltenham, 1833.
Taylor, T. Memoirs of Heber. 1836 (3rd edn).
Chambers, J. Bishop Heber and Indian Missions. 1846.
A Dictionary of Hymnology. Ed. J. Julian, 1892. [Information on the hymns.]
Miles, A. H. *Miles*, x (XI).
Smith, G. Bishop Heber: Poet and Missionary. 1895.

FELICIA DOROTHEA HEMANS (born
　BROWNE) (1793–1835)

(a) Collections and Selections

The Poetical Works. Ed. — Norton, Phila-
delphia, 1825; 1832; 1837; 1842.
The Works. Ed. (with memoir) by her Sister
[Mrs Hughes]. 7 vols. Edinburgh, 1839;
chronologically arranged, Edinburgh, 1849
(many re-issues); ed. R. W. Griswold,
Philadelphia, 1850 ('with an essay on her
genius' by H. T. Tuckerman); ed. W. M.
Rossetti, [1873]; rptd Oxford, 1914.
Select Poetical Works. 1865.
Favorite Poems. Boston, 1877.
The Hemans Birthday Book. Ed. R. G. B.,
Edinburgh, [1884].
Selections. [1911.]

(b) Individual Publications

Poems. Liverpool, 1808.
England and Spain. 1808. [Poem.]
The Domestic Affections, and Other Poems.
1812; 1843; 1844.
The Restoration of the Works of Art to Italy.
Oxford, 1816 (*bis*). [Poem.]
Modern Greece, a Poem. 1817; 1821.
Translations from Camoens and Other Poets.
Oxford, 1818.
Tales and Historic Scenes, in Verse. 1819; 1824.
Wallace's Invocation to Bruce: a Poem.
Edinburgh, 1819.
The Sceptic. 1820; 1821 (with the following).
[Poem.]
Stanzas to the Memory of the late King.
1820; 1821 (with The Sceptic).
Dartmoor, a Poem. 1821.
Welsh Melodies. 1822.
Vespers of Palermo. 1823; [1883]. [Tragedy
in verse.]
The Siege of Valencia, a Dramatick Poem. The
Last Constantine, With Other Poems. 1823.
The Forest Sanctuary, and Other Poems.
1825; Edinburgh, 1829; tr. German, Stutt-
gart, 1871.
Lays of Many Lands. 1825.
Records of Woman, with Other Poems.
1828 (*bis*); 1837 (5th edn).
Songs of the Affections, with Other Poems.
Edinburgh, 1830.
Hymns on the Works of Nature for the Use
of Children. 1833.
Hymns for Childhood. Dublin, 1834; Dublin,
1839.
National Lyrics and Songs for Music. Dublin,
1834; Dublin, 1836.
Scenes and Hymns of Life, with Other Re-
ligious Poems. Edinburgh, 1834.
Poetical Remains [with memoir by Δ, *i.e.*
D. M. Moir]. Edinburgh, 1836.

Early Blossoms. With a Life of the Authoress.
1840. [Juvenile poems.]
[Mrs Hemans also contributed to numerous
periodicals, including Blackwood's, Colburn's,
and the Edinburgh Monthly Mag.]

(c) Biography and Criticism

(i) Books

A Short Sketch of the life of Mrs Hemans.
1835.
Chorley, H. F. Memorials of Mrs Hemans.
2 vols. 1836; Philadelphia, 1836.
Ritchie, A. T., Lady. Felicia Felix. [In
Blackstick Papers, 1908.]
Ledderbogen, W. Felicia Hemans Lyrik.
Heidelberg, 1913.
Duméril, E. Une Femme Poète au Déclin du
Romantisme anglais: Felicia Hemans.
Toulouse, 1929.

(ii) Essays and Articles

Jeffrey, F., Lord. Edinburgh Rev. L, 1829.
Robinson, E. S. English Poetesses. 1883.
[Ch. vi, a short account, with specimens of
the lyrics.]
Bell, M. *Miles*, VII (VIII).
Walford, L. B. Twelve English Authoresses.
1893.
Williams, I. A. Wordsworth, Mrs Hemans,
and R. P. Graves. London Mercury, VI,
1922.
Rupprecht, W. K. Felicia Hemans und die
englischen Beziehungen zur deutschen
Literatur. Ang. XLVIII, 1924.

JOHN ABRAHAM HERAUD (1799–1887)

(a) Works

The Legend of St Loy, with Other Poems.
1820.
Tottenham, a Poem. 1820.
The Descent into Hell. 1830; 1835 (rev. and
other poems added).
An Oration on the Death of Coleridge. 1834.
The Judgment of the Flood. 1834; 1854 (rev.).
[Poem.]
The Substance of a Lecture on Poetic Genius.
1837.
Salvator, the Poor Man of Naples. 1845 (priv.
ptd). [A dramatic poem.]
Videna, or the Mother's Tragedy [in verse].
1854.
Shakespeare; his Inner Life. 1865.
The Wreck of the London, a Lyrical Ballad.
1866.
The In-Gathering. 1870. [Poems.]
The War of Ideas, a Poem. 1871.
Uxmal; Macée de Léodepart. 1877. [Tales in
prose and verse.]

[Only the more important of Heraud's
writings in prose are listed here. He ed. The

Sunbeam, 1838–9; and The Monthly Magazine, 1839–42. He also contributed to Quart. Rev., Athenaeum, Fraser's Mag. and others.]

(b) Biography

Heraud, E. Memoirs of John Abraham Heraud. 1898.

WILLIAM HERBERT (1778–1847)

Ossiani Darthula Graece reddita. 1801.
Select Icelandic Poetry, translated from the Originals with Notes. 2 pts, 1804–6.
Translations from the German, Danish, etc. To which is added Miscellaneous Poetry. 1804.
Translations from the Italian, Spanish, Portuguese, German, etc. To which is added Miscellaneous Poetry. Part Second. 1806.
Helga: a Poem in Seven Cantos. 1815; 1816.
Hedin: or the Spectre of the Tomb. A Tale [in verse]. From the Danish History. 1820.
Pia della Pietra. 1820.
Iris. York, 1820. [A Latin ode.]
The Guahiba: a Tale [in verse]. 1822.
The Winged Wanderer of Jutland. A Tragedy. 1822. [Includes also: Julia Montalban, a Tale. Both in verse.]
Attila, or the Triumph of Christianity. 1838. [An epic.]
Works. 3 vols. 1842.
The Christian. 1846. [A poem.]

[Herbert also pbd sermons, and books and articles on botanical subjects, *inter alia* contributing notes to edns of Gilbert White's Selborne.]

THEODORE EDWARD HOOK (1788–1841)

[See p. 399 below.]

MARY HOWITT (1799–1888)

[See p. 672 below.]

JAMES HENRY LEIGH HUNT (1784–1859)

[See p. 643 below.]

JAMES HYSLOP (1798–1827)

Poems. With a Sketch of his Life, and Notes on his Poems, by P. Mearns. Glasgow, 1887.

WILLIAM HENRY IRELAND (1777–1835)

(a) Poems

Ballads, in Imitation of the Ancient. 1801.
Mutius Scaevola; or the Roman Patriot: an Historical Drama. 1801.
A Ballade, wrotten on the Feastynge and Merrimentes of Easter Maunday, laste paste. By Paul Persius, a Learnedd Clerke. 1802.
Rhapsodies. 1803.
The Angler: a Didactic Poem. 1804.

All the Blocks! or, an Antidote to 'All the Talents.' A Satirical Poem. 1807.
Stultifera Navis. The Modern Ship of Fools. 1807.
The Fisher Boy: a Poem. 1808.
Effusions of Love from Chatelar to Mary, Queen of Scotland. Interspersed with Songs, Sonnets, and Notes, by the Translator. 1808.
The Sailor Boy: a Poem. 1809; 1822.
Neglected Genius: a Poem; illustrating the Untimely and Unfortunate Fate of Many British Poets, containing Imitations of their Different Styles. 1812.
Chalcographimania; or, the Portrait-Collector and Printseller's Chronicle. A Humorous Poem. 1814.
Jack Junk; or, the Sailor's Cruise on Shore. 1814.
Scribbleomania; or, the Printer's Devil's Polichronicon. 1815.
The Maid of Orleans. 1822. [From Voltaire.]

(b) Shakespeare Forgeries

Miscellaneous Papers and Legal Instruments under the Hand and Seal of William Shakespeare. 1796.
An Authentic Account of the Shakesperian Manuscripts. 1796.
Vortigern, an Historical Tragedy; and Henry the Second, an Historical Drama, supposed to be written by the Author of Vortigern. 2 pts, 1799. [Vortigern was rptd 1832 with facs. of portions of the forged MS.]
The Confessions of William Henry Ireland, containing the Particulars of his Fabrication of the Shakespeare Manuscripts; together with Anecdotes and Opinions of Many Distinguished Persons. 1805; ed. R. G. White, New York, 1874. [An expansion of the Authentic Account.]

[Ireland also pbd several novels and romances and much miscellaneous hackwork. His writings, including the above, were almost all anon. or pseudonymous.]

(c) Criticism

Ingleby, C. M. The Shakespeare Fabrications [of J. P. Collier]. With an Appendix on the Authorship of the Ireland Forgeries. 1859.
The Shakespeare Forgeries of W. H. Ireland. Fraser's Mag. LXII, 1860.
Libbis, G. H. Notes on Samuel and William Henry Ireland and the Shakespeare Fabrications. N. & Q. 21, 28 March 1931, 2, 16 April 1932.
Mair, J. The Fourth Forger. 1938.

[For contemporary pamphlets on Ireland's forgeries see R. W. Lowe, A Bibliographical Account of English Theatrical Literature, 1888.]

JOHN KEBLE (1792–1866)

[See p. 857 below.]

JOHN KENYON (1784–1856)

(a) Poems

A Rhymed Plea for Tolerance. 1833.
Poems, for the Most Part Occasional. 1838
A Day at Tivoli, with Other Verses. 1849.

(b) Biography and Criticism

Poems by John Kenyon. Blackwood's Mag.
Dec. 1838. [Long and complimentary review.]
Crosse, Mrs A. Temple Bar, April 1890, Jan. 1892.

HERBERT KNOWLES (1798–1817)

Lines written in the Churchyard of Richmond,
Yorkshire. [Composed Oct. 1816; ptd in
N. Carlisle, The Endowed Grammar Schools
in England and Wales, vol. II, 1818,
pp. 880–2. Rptd in Chambers's Cyclopaedia of English Literature, ed. D. Patrick,
vol. II, 1903, p. 788. The original title was
The Three Tabernacles.]

JAMES SHERIDAN KNOWLES (1784–1862)

[See p. 590 below.]

WILLIAM LAIDLAW (1780–1845)

Poems, chiefly on Jedburgh and Vicinity.
With a Selection from his Prose Writings
and a Biographical Sketch by Sir G. B.
Douglas. [1901.]

LADY CAROLINE LAMB (1785–1828)

[See p. 404 below.]

CHARLES LAMB (1775–1834)

[See p. 631 below.]

ROBERT EYRES LANDOR (1781–1869)

(a) Selection

Selections from Robert Eyres Landor. Ed.
E. Partridge, 1927.

(b) Separate Works

The Count Arezzi, a Tragedy [in verse]. 1824
(anon.).
The Impious Feast: a Poem in Ten Books.
1828.
The Earl of Brecon: a Tragedy. 1841. [Con-
taining also Faith's Fraud: a Tragedy, and
The Ferryman: a Tragedy.]
The Farm of Sertorius. 1846. [A novel.]
The Fountain of Arethusa. 2 vols. 1848.

(c) Biography and Criticism

Partridge, E. Robert Eyres Landor. A
Biographical and Critical Sketch. 1927.

WALTER SAVAGE LANDOR (1775–1864)

[See p. 637 below.]

CHARLES VALENTINE LE GRICE (1773–1858)

(a) Bibliography

Boase, G. C. and Courtney, W. P. Bibliotheca
Cornubiensis. Vol. I, 1874.

(b) Works

An Imitation of Horace's First Epistle.
Cambridge, 1793; Penzance, 1824; Truro,
1850.
The Tineum. Cambridge, 1794. [Mock-heroic
pieces in prose and verse.]
Analysis of Paley's Principles of Philosophy.
Cambridge, 1795; Cambridge, 1796; 1822
(8th edn).
Daphnis and Chloe. Now first selectly trans-
lated. Penzance, 1803.
Petition of an Old Uninhabited House in
Penzance to its Master in Town. Penzance,
[1811]; 1823; 1858. [Poem.]
College Reminiscences of Mr Coleridge.
Reprinted from the Gentleman's Magazine,
Dec. 1834, by desire. Penzance, [1842].
[Also rptd in J. Cottle, Reminiscences of
Coleridge and Southey, 1847.]
[Not here listed: a number of poems ptd
separately as single sheets, and a few of the
slighter prose pbns.]

MATTHEW GREGORY LEWIS (1775–1818)

[See p. 406 below.]

JOHN LEYDEN (1775–1811)

(a) Works

Scenes of Infancy. Edinburgh, 1803; Jed-
burgh, 1844; rptd Edinburgh, 1875 (with
memoir by W. W. Tulloch).
Scottish Descriptive Poems. Edinburgh,
1803. [An anthology; ed. by Leyden.]
Poetical Remains. Ed. (with memoir) J.
Morton, 1819.
Poems and Ballads. Ed. R. White, Kelso,
1858, 1875.
The Poetical Works. 1875.

[Leyden also contributed to M. G. Lewis's
Tales of Wonder, 1801, and assisted Sir W.
Scott with the earlier vols. of Minstrelsy of the
Scottish Border, 1802. He was an authority
on several oriental languages, publishing trea-
tises and trns.]

(b) Biography and Criticism

Aiyangar, S. An Anglo-Indian Poet, John
Leyden. Madras, 1912.
Reith, J. Life of Dr John Leyden. 1923.

CHARLES LLOYD (1775–1839)

(a) Works

Poems on Various Subjects. Carlisle, 1795.
Poems on the Death of Priscilla Farmer, by
her Grandson. 1796.

Poems, by S. T. Coleridge. Second Edition. To which are now added Poems by Charles Lamb, and Charles Lloyd. Bristol, 1797. [28 poems by Lloyd.]

Blank Verse. By Charles Lloyd and Charles Lamb. 1798.

Edmund Oliver. Bristol, 1798. [Novel.]

Lines suggested by the Fast appointed on Wednesday, February 27, 1799. Birmingham, 1799.

The Tragedies of Vittorio Alfieri. Translated. 3 vols. 1815.

Nugae Canorae. Poems. Third Edition, with Additions. 1819. [More than half the book was new.]

Isabel, a Tale [in prose]. 2 vols. 1820.

Desultory Thoughts in London; Titus and Gisippus, with Other Poems. 1821.

Poetical Essays on the Character of Pope as a Poet and Moralist; and on the Language and Objects most fit for Poetry. 1821.

The Duke D'Ormond, a Tragedy; and Beritola, a Tale [in verse]. 1822.

Poems. 1823.

(b) Biography and Criticism

Southey, R. Alfieri's Life and Writings. Quart. Rev. xiv, 1816. [Includes remarks on and specimens of Lloyd's trn.]

Lamb, C. Examiner, 24–25 Oct. 1819. [Rptd in Works, ed. T. Hutchinson, vol. i, 1908. A review of Nugae Canorae.]

De Quincey, T. Society of the Lakes, i: C. Lloyd. Tait's Mag. March 1840. [Rptd in Reminiscences of the Lake Poets, 1907 (Everyman's Lib.).]

Lucas, E. V. Charles Lamb and the Lloyds. 1898.

SAMUEL LOVER (1797–1868)

[See p. 407 below.]

HENRY LUTTRELL (1765?–1851)

(a) Poems

Lines written at Ampthill Park in the Autumn of 1818. 1819; 1822 (with Letters to Julia).

Advice to Julia. A Letter in Rhyme. 1820 (bis).

Letters to Julia, in Rhyme. Third Edition. To which are added Lines written at Ampthill-Park. 1822. [The Advice to Julia is rehandled and considerably enlarged.]

Crockford-House, a Rhapsody. In Two Cantos. A Rhymer in Rome. 1827.

(b) Biography and Criticism

Dobson, A. A Forgotten Poet of Society. St James's Mag. xxxiii, 1878. [Rptd as Luttrell's Letters to Julia in A Paladin of Philanthropy, 1899.]

Crosse, A. An Old Society Wit. Temple Bar, civ, 1895.

HENRY FRANCIS LYTE (1793–1847)

(a) Works

Tales in Verse Illustrative of the Lord's Prayer. 1826; 1829.

Poems, chiefly Religious. 1833; 1845 (enlarged).

The Spirit of the Psalms. 1834; 1836 (enlarged); [1864].

The Poems of Henry Vaughan, with a Memoir [by Lyte]. 1846.

Remains, with Memoir [by his daughter, Mrs Hogg]. 1850.

Miscellaneous Poems. 1868. [A rpt of Poems, chiefly Religious, 1845, with 'Abide with me' added.]

The Poetical Works. Ed. J. Appleyard, 1907.

(b) Biography and Criticism

Julian, J. A Dictionary of Hymnology. 1892. [Detailed information on the hymns.]

Miles, A. H. Miles, x (xi).

WILLIAM MAGINN (1793–1842)

[See p. 677 below.]

RICHARD MANT (1776–1848)

(a) Works

Verses to the Memory of Joseph Warton. Oxford, 1800.

The Poetical Works of Thomas Warton, with a Memoir by R. Mant. 2 vols. Oxford, 1802.

The Country Curate. Oxford. 1804. [Poems.]

Poems. Oxford, 1806.

The Slave. Oxford, 1806. [Poems.]

The Book of Psalms, in an English Metrical Version. 1824.

The Holydays of the Church; with Metrical Sketches. 2 vols. 1828–31.

The Gospel Miracles: Poetical Sketches. 1832.

The Happiness of the Blessed [in prose]; Musings on the Church [in verse]. 1833; 1837 (4th edn); 1870.

Christmas Carols. 1833.

The British Months, a Poem. 2 vols. 1835.

Ancient Hymns from the Roman Breviary. 1837; 1871. [Also original hymns by Mant.]

The Sundial of Armoy, a Poem. Dublin, 1847.

The Matin Bell. Oxford, 1848. [Poem.]

The Youthful Christian Soldier [in prose]. With Spiritual Songs and Hymns. Dublin, 1848.

[Mant also pbd numerous sermons and other prose works, including a History of the Church of Ireland (2 vols. 1840) still held in some repute.]

(b) Biography and Criticism

Berens, E. Memoir of Bishop Mant. 1849.

Mant, W. B. Memoirs of Richard Mant. Dublin, 1857.

A Dictionary of Hymnology. Ed. J. Julian, 1892. [Information on the hymns.]

Miles, A. H. *Miles*, x (xi).

JOHN HERMAN MERIVALE (1779–1844)

(a) Collected Poems

Poems Original and Translated, now first Collected. 2 vols. 1828–38; 1844 ('corrected').

(b) Individual Publications

Translations chiefly from the Greek Anthology, with Tales and Miscellaneous Poems. 1806. [With R. Bland.]

Collections from the Greek Anthology. By R. Bland and Others [including Merivale]. 1813; 1833 (3rd edn).

Orlando in Roncesvalles, a Poem. 1814.

The Two First Cantos of Richardetto, from the original of N. Fortiguerra. 1820.

The Minor Poems of Schiller, translated. 1844.

Leaves from the Diary of a Literary Amateur. Ed. E. H. A. Koch, Hampstead, 1911.

[Not here listed: (a) a few pbns on legal subjects; (b) contributions to periodicals, including Quart. Rev., New Monthly Mag. and GM.]

(c) Biography and Criticism

Coleridge, H. N. Quart. Rev. XLIX, 1833. [A notice of the 3rd edn of Collections from the Greek Anthology.]

RICHARD ALFRED MILLIKEN (1767–1815)
[See p. 1051 below.]

HENRY HART MILMAN (1791–1868)
[See p. 887 below.]

THOMAS MITCHELL (1783–1845)
[See p. 995 below.]

JOHN MITFORD (1781–1859)

(a) Works

Agnes, with Other Poems. 1811.

A Letter to R. Heber, Esq., on Mr Weber's Edition of Ford. 1812.

Sacred Specimens from the Early English Poets. With Prefatory Verses. 1827.

Lines suggested by a Fatal Shipwreck. 1855; Woodbridge [Suffolk], 1856.

Cursory Notes on Beaumont and Fletcher, as edited by A. Dyce. 1856.

Miscellaneous Poems. 1858.

The Rev. John Mitford on Cricket. Ed. F. S. Ashley-Cooper, Nottingham, 1921. [Writings rptd from GM.]

[Mitford ed. The Gentleman's Magazine, 1834–50, contributing frequently to it; he also ed. numerous rpts of the English poets, chiefly in the Aldine ser. 1830–9.]

(b) Biography

Houstoun, M. C. Sylvanus Redivivus, the Rev. John Mitford. 1889 (re-issued 1891 as Letters and Reminiscences of John Mitford).

MARY RUSSELL MITFORD (1787–1855)
[See p. 409 below.]

DAVID MACBETH MOIR (1798–1851)
[See p. 410 below.]

WILLIAM THOMAS MONCRIEFF (1794–1857)
[See p. 992 below.]

JAMES MONTGOMERY (1771–1854)

(a) Collected Poems

The Poetical Works. 3 vols. 1819; 3 vols. 1825, 1828, 1836.

The Poetical Works of Rogers, James Montgomery [and others]. Paris, 1829.

The Poetical Works. Collected by Himself, with Notes. 4 vols. 1841; 1850; 1855; 1858; 1863; [1874]; [1878]; [1879]; Edinburgh, [1881].

The Poetical Works. Ed. (with memoir) R. Carruthers, Boston, 5 vols. 1860.

Poems, selected by R. A. Willmot. Illustrated by Birket Foster. 1860; 1861.

(b) Individual Publications

Prison Amusements. By Paul Positive. 1797. [Poems.]

The Ocean. 1805. [Poem.]

The Wanderer of Switzerland, and Other Poems. 1806; Edinburgh, 1815 (7th edn).

Poems on the Abolition of the Slave Trade. 1809. [With J. Grahame and E. Benger.]

The West Indies and Other Poems. 1810; 1828 (7th edn). [Includes his contributions to the preceding.]

The World before the Flood, a Poem, with Other Occasional Pieces. 1813; 1823 (6th edn); 1826 (7th edn).

The State Lottery. 1817. [By various writers; includes Thoughts on Wheels, a poem by Montgomery.]

Verses to the Memory of Richard Reynolds. 1817.

Greenland, and Other Poems. 1819.

Abdallah and Labat. 1821. [Poem.]

Songs of Zion. 1822; 1828 (3rd edn). [Hymns.]

The Chimney-sweeper's Friend. 1824. [Ed. by Montgomery and with poems by him.]

Prose. By a Poet. 2 vols. 1824.

The Christian Psalmist, or Hymns Selected and Original. Glasgow, 1825; Glasgow, 1826 (4th edn); 1857 (10th edn).

The Christian Poet. Glasgow, 1825; Glasgow, 1828 (3rd edn).

The Pelican Island, and Other Poems. 1826; 1828.
Lectures on Poetry. 1833; New York, 1846.
A Poet's Portfolio, or Minor Poems. 1835.
Lives of Literary and Scientific Men of Italy, Spain, etc. 3 vols. 1835–7. [Part of D. Lardner, The Cabinet Cyclopedia. Ariosto, Dante, and Tasso by Montgomery.]
Poems on the Loss of St Mary's Church, Cardiff. 1842. [By various writers; includes a poem by Montgomery.]
Original Hymns. 1853; ed. J. Holland, New York, 1854.

[Not here listed: (a) minor prose works; (b) a few poems issued in single-sheet or pamphlet form; (c) many hymns contributed to collections ed. by W. B. Collyer (1812), T. Cotterill (8th edn, 1819), and others. Montgomery was editor and proprietor of The Sheffield Iris, 1795–1825.]

(c) Biography and Criticism

(i) Independent Works

The Trial of J. Montgomery for a Libel on the War. Sheffield. 1795.
Holland, J. and Everett, J. Memoirs of James Montgomery. 7 vols. 1854–6.
King, J. W. James Montgomery, a Memoir. 1858.
Ellis, S. The Life, Times, and Character of James Montgomery. 1864.
Wissmann, P. Die grösseren Dichtungen von James Montgomery. Königsberg, 1914.
Odom, W. Two Sheffield Poets: James Montgomery and Ebenezer Elliott. [1929.]

(ii) Essays and Articles

Jeffrey, F., Lord. Edinburgh Rev. ix, 1807. [Severe critique of The Wanderer of Switzerland.]
Southey, R. Quart. Rev. vi, 1811, xi, 1814. [Favourable notices of poems.]
Wilson, J. Sacred Poetry. [In Recreations of Christopher North. 1842. Chs. i and ii chiefly on Wordsworth and Montgomery.]
A Dictionary of Hymnology. Ed. J. Julian, 1892. [Full information on the hymns.]
Miles, A. H. Miles, x (xi).

SYDNEY OWENSON, Lady MORGAN (1783?–1859)
[See p. 412 below.]

WILLIAM MOTHERWELL (1797–1835)
Poems, Narrative and Lyrical. Glasgow, 1832.
The Works of Robert Burns. Edited by the Ettrick Shepherd, and William Motherwell. 5 vols. Glasgow, 1834–6, etc.
The Poetical Works. Ed. J. M'Conechy, Glasgow, 1847 (2nd and enlarged edn); Paisley, 1881.

Ingram, J. H. Miles, iii. [Selection and criticism.]

JOHN MOULTRIE (1799–1874)
(a) Collected Poems
Poems, with Memoir by Prebendary [Derwent] Coleridge. 2 vols. 1876.

(b) Individual Publications
Poems. 1837; 1852 (3rd edn). [Includes My Brother's Grave and Godiva, both written in 1820.]
The Dream of Life, and Other Poems. 1843.
Saint Mary, the Virgin and the Wife. 1850 (bis); 1856. [Poem.]
The Black Fence, a Lay of Modern Rome. 1850; 1851 (4th edn).
Psalms and Hymns. 1851; 1860. [Compiled by Moultrie and including about 20 of his hymns.]
The Song of the Rugby Church-Builders. [1851.]
A Pentecostal Ode. 1852.
The Poetical Remains of William Sidney Walker, with a Memoir [by Moultrie]. 1852.
Sermons. 1852.
Altars, Hearths, and Graves. 1854. [Poems.]
[Moultrie also contributed poems to The Etonian, 1820–1, and to Knight's Quart. Mag. 1823–4.]

(c) Criticism
A Dictionary of Hymnology. Ed. J. Julian, 1892. [Information on the hymns.]

CAROLINA, Baroness NAIRNE (1766–1845)
[See vol. ii, p. 991 above.]

JOHN NICHOLSON (1790–1843)
(a) Collected Works
Poems, Collected and Edited with Memoir by J. James. 1844; ed. W. Dearden, Bingley, 1859; ed. A. Holroyd, Bingley, 1876; ed. W. G. Hird, 1876.

(b) Individual Publications
The Siege of Bradford. Bradford, 1821; 1831. [A play in verse.]
Airedale in Ancient Times, and Other Poems. 1825 (bis).
Lines on the Grand Musical Festival. Bradford, 1825.
The Airedale Poet's Walk. Knaresborough, 1826. [Poem.]
The Lyre of Ebor, and Other Poems. 1827.

WILLIAM NICHOLSON (1782?–1849)
Tales in Verse and Miscellaneous Poems. Edinburgh, 1814; Edinburgh, 1828.
The Poetical Works with a Memoir by M. M'L. Harper. Dalbeattie, 1895.

AMELIA OPIE (1769–1853)
[See p. 411 below.]

HENRY JOHN TEMPLE, Viscount PALMERSTON
(1784–1865)
[See p. 677 below.]

THOMAS PARK (1759–1834)
[See p. 1027 below.]

THOMAS LOVE PEACOCK (1785–1866)
[See p. 384 below.]

JAMES ROBINSON PLANCHÉ (1796–1880)
[See p. 592 below.]

ROBERT POLLOK (1798–1827)

(a) Works

Ralph Gemmel, a Tale [in prose]. [1825?]; Edinburgh, 1829 (3rd edn).

Helen of the Glen, a Tale for Youth [in prose]. [1825?]; Glasgow, 1830 (4th edn); 1870.

The Course of Time: a Poem in Ten Books. 2 vols. Edinburgh, 1827; Edinburgh, 1829 (9th edn); 1867 (25th edn); 1868; tr. German, Hamburg, 1830.

Tales of the Covenanters [in prose]. Edinburgh, 1833; Edinburgh, 1836; ed. A. Thomson, Edinburgh, 1895; rptd Kilmarnock, [1928].

(b) Biography and Criticism

Pollok, D. Life of Robert Pollok. 1843.
Miles, A. H. Miles, x (xi).
Masson, R. O. Pollok and Aytoun. [1898.]

THOMAS PRINGLE (1789–1834)

The Autumnal Excursion, or Sketches in Teviotdale; with Other Poems. Edinburgh, 1810.

Ephemerides; or Occasional Poems. Written in Scotland and South Africa. 1828.

African Sketches. 1834. [Poems, with a prose Narrative of his Residence in South Africa. The latter was rptd in 1835 with a biographical sketch by J. Conder.]

The Poetical Works of Thomas Pringle. With a Sketch of his Life by L. Ritchie. 1838.

Afar in the Desert: and Other South African Poems. Ed. J. Noble, 1881.

Poems. Ed. W. Hay, Capetown, 1912.

[Pringle also pbd some miscellaneous prose and edited various newspapers, Scottish and African.]

BRYAN WALLER PROCTER ('BARRY CORNWALL') (1787–1874)

(a) Collected Poems

The Poetical Works of Barry Cornwall. 3 vols. 1822.

The Poetical Works of Milman, Barry Cornwall [and others]. Paris, 1829.

(b) Individual Publications

Dramatic Scenes, and Other Poems. 1819; 1820; enlarged, and illustrated by Birket Foster, Tenniel, and others, 1857.

A Sicilian Story, and Other Poems. 1820 (bis); 1821.

Marcian Colonna, An Italian Tale with Three Dramatic Scenes and Other Poems. 1820.

Mirandola, a Tragedy [in verse]. 1821 (bis).

The Flood of Thessaly, the Girl of Provence, and Other Poems. 1823.

Effigies Poeticae, or the Portraits of the British Poets. 1824.

English Songs. 1832. New ed. 1844, 1851.

The Life of Edmund Kean. 2 vols. 1835; tr. German, Hamburg, 1836.

The Works of Ben Jonson, with a Memoir [by Procter]. 1838.

The Works of Shakespeare, with a Memoir and Essay on his Genius [by Procter]. 1843; 1853; 1857; 1875.

Essays and Tales in Prose. 2 vols. Boston, 1853.

Selections from Robert Browning. [Ed. B. W. Procter and J. Forster], 1863.

Charles Lamb: a Memoir. 1866. [Rptd in Essays of Elia, with a Memoir of Lamb, 1879.]

Bryan Waller Procter. An Autobiographical Fragment. Ed. C. Patmore, 1877; ed. R. W. Armour, Boston, 1936.

[Procter also made numerous contributions to periodicals, including Literary Gazette, London Mag. and Edinburgh Rev.]

(c) Biography and Criticism

Jeffrey, F., Lord. Edinburgh Rev. XXXII, 1820. [Favourable notice of A Sicilian Story.]

[Lamb, C.?] New Times, 22 July 1820. [Rptd in Works of Lamb, ed. W. Macdonald, vol. III, 1903. A review of Marcian Colonna.]

Darley, G. The Characteristic of the Present Age of Poetry. London Mag. IX, 1824. [An attack on Procter, Moore, and Byron.]

Fields, J. T. Old Acquaintance. Barry Cornwall and Some of his Friends. Boston, 1876.

Martineau, H. Biographical Sketches, 1852–1875. 1877.

Stedman, E. C. Victorian Poets. 1887 (rev. edn).

Miles, A. H. Miles, II.

Becker, F. Bryan Waller Procter. Vienna, 1912.

Armour, R. W. Barry Cornwall: a Biography of Bryan Waller Procter; with a Selection of hitherto Unpublished Letters. Boston, 1935.

EDWARD QUILLINAN (1791–1851)

(a) Collected Poems

Poems, with a Memoir by W. Johnston. 1853.

(b) Works privately printed at the Lee Priory Press, Kent

Dunluce Castle, a Poem. 1814.
Stanzas, 1814.
Consolation, a Poem. 1815.
The Sacrifice of Isabel, a Poem. 1816.
Elegiac Verses, Addressed to a Lady. 1817.
Wood Cuts and Verses, edited with a Preface by E. Quillinan. 1820.

(c) Other Publications

Ball-Room Votaries. 1810 (bis). [Satirical verses.]
Monthermer, a Poem. 1815.
The Sacrifice of Isabel, a Poem. 1816.
The Retort Courteous. 1821. [A pamphlet replying to T. Hamilton's attack in Blackwood's Mag. on Dunluce Castle.]
Carmina Brugesiana: Domestic Poems. Geneva, 1822 (priv. ptd).
The Conspirators. 3 vols. 1841. [A novel.]
The Lusiad [of Camoens], Books i–v. Translated. Ed. J. Adamson, 1853.

(d) Biography

Quillinan, Dorothy. Journal of a Few Months' Residence in Portugal. 2 vols. 1847.
The Correspondence of Henry Crabb Robinson with the Wordsworth Circle. Ed. E. J. Morley, 2 vols. Oxford. 1927. [Contains about 70 letters from Quillinan, and a rpt (from Blackwood's Mag. April 1843) of an article by Quillinan defending Wordsworth against Landor.]

ANN RADCLIFFE (1764–1823)

[See p. 414 below.]

JOHN HAMILTON REYNOLDS (1796–1852)

(a) Bibliography

Marsh, G. L. The Writings of Keats's Friend Reynolds. Stud. Phil. xxv, 1928. [Lists Reynolds's contributions to periodicals, including Champion, London Mag. (1815–25), Athenaeum, and New Monthly Mag. (1830–48).]

(b) Selection

John Hamilton Reynolds: Poetry and Prose. Ed. G. L. Marsh, 1928. [Includes a detailed biographical introduction.]

(c) Poems and Plays

Safie. An Eastern Tale. 1814.
The Eden of Imagination. A Poem. 1814.
An Ode. 1815 (anon.).

The Naiad: a Tale. With Other Poems. 1816 (anon.).
Peter Bell: a Lyrical Ballad. 1819 (3 edns). [Signed W. W. An anticipatory parody of Wordsworth's poem.]
Benjamin, the Waggoner, a Ryghte Merrie and Conceitede Tale in Verse. A Fragment. 1819 (anon.). [A further burlesque of Wordsworth's Peter Bell.]
The Fancy: a Selection from the Poetical Remains of the late Peter Corcoran, of Gray's Inn, Student-at-law. With a Brief Memoir of his Life. 1820; ed. J. Masefield, 1905.
The Garden of Florence and Other Poems. 1821.
Odes and Addresses to Great People. 1825 (anon.); 1826 (3rd edn). [In collaboration with Thomas Hood.]
One, Two, Three, Four, Five: by Advertisement, a Musical Entertainment in one Act. [Acted 1815. Ptd as anon. in J. Cumberland's British Theatre, vol. xxxi, 1829.]
Confounded Foreigners. A Farce in One Act. [1838.]

(d) Biography and Criticism

Dilke, C. W. Papers of a Critic. 1875.
Gosse, Sir E. Gossip in a Library. 1891. [Articles on Peter Bell and The Fancy.]
Shelley, H. C. Literary By-Paths in Old England. 1909. [Chs. viii and x deal with Reynolds's relations with Keats and with Hood.]
Swaen, A. E. H. Peter Bell. Ang. xlvii, 1923. [Reprints Reynolds's burlesque and gives a full account of its relation to Wordsworth's poem.]
Gates, W. B. A Sporting Poet of the Regency. Sewanee Rev. xxxv, 1927.
Marsh, G. L. New Data on Reynolds. MP. xxv, 1928. [Biographical.]
Turnbull, J. M. Keats, Reynolds, and The Champion. London Mercury, xix, 1929.
Blunden, E. Friends of Keats. [In Votive Tablets, 1931. On Reynolds and G. F. Mathew.]
Pope, W. B. John Hamilton Reynolds. Wessex, iii, 1935.

ALEXANDER RODGER (1784–1846)

Scotch Poetry; consisting of Songs, Odes, Anthems, and Epigrams. 1821.
Peter Cornclips, a Tale of Real Life; with other Poems. 1827.
Poems and Songs, Humorous and Satirical. 1838; ed. R. Ford, 1897; 1901.
Stray Leaves from the Portfolios of Alisander the Seer, Andrew Whamp, and Humphrey Henkeckle. 1842 (2nd edn). [Verse and prose.]

Songs. [In C. Rogers, The Modern Scottish Minstrel, vol. III, 1855.]

WILLIAM STANLEY ROSCOE (1782–1843)

Poems. 1834.

[See The Poems of W. S. Roscoe, Blackwood's Mag. XXXVII, 1835. For biographical material see under William Roscoe, p. 887 below.]

WILLIAM STEWART ROSE (1775–1843)

A Naval History of the Late War. Vol. I (all pbd), 1802.

Amadis de Gaul. Freely translated from the First Part of the French version. 1803.

Partenopex de Blois. Freely translated from the French. 1807.

The Crusade of St Lewis, and King Edward the Martyr. 1810. [Ballads.]

The Court of Beasts. Translated [or rather freely adapted] from the Animali Parlanti of Giambattista Casti. A Poem. 1816 (anon.); 1819 (with name).

Letters from the North of Italy. Addressed to Henry Hallam, Esq. 2 vols. 1819.

The Orlando Innamorato. Translated into Prose. Edinburgh, 1823. [Abridged and with passages in verse.]

Orlando Furioso, translated, with Notes. 8 vols. 1823–31; 2 vols. 1858 (with brief memoir by C. Townsend); 2 vols. 1864.

Thoughts and Recollections [in prose]. 1825.

Apology addressed to the Travellers' Club, or Anecdotes of Monkeys. 1825 (anon.). [Authenticity doubtful.]

To the Right Honorable J. H. Frere. Brighton, [1834]. [No title page; a rhymed epistle.]

Rhymes. Brighton, 1837 (priv. ptd). [Includes the preceding.]

[Some verses to Byron (1818) were first ptd in Works of Byron, Letters, ed. R. E. Prothero, vol. IV, 1900, pp. 212–4.]

FRANCIS BARRY BOYLE ST LEGER (1799–1829)

[See p. 415 below.]

HORATIO (HORACE) SMITH (1779–1849) and JAMES SMITH (1775–1839)

(a) Collaborations

Rejected Addresses, or, the New Theatrum Poetarum. 1812 (anon.); 1813 (9th edn); 1813 (13th edn); 1833 (18th edn, 'carefully revised'); ed. P. Cunningham, 1851; ed. E. Sargent, New York, 1871 (with memoirs); ed. P. Fitzgerald, 1890; ed. A. D. Godley, 1904; ed. A. Boyle, 1929 (with bibliography).

Horace in London: consisting of Imitations of the First Two Books of the Odes of Horace. 1813 (bis); 1815 (4th edn). [Rptd from Monthly Mirror.]

[For the poems, novels; etc. of Horace Smith alone, together with his edn of James Smith's Comic Miscellanies in Prose and Verse, see p. 417 below.]

(b) Criticism

Jeffrey, F., Lord. Edinburgh Rev. XX, 1812. [Rejected Addresses.]

Hayward, A. Biographical and Critical Essays. Vol. I, 1858.

Whyte, W. Miles, IX (X).

Lowe, R. W. The Real Rejected Addresses. Blackwood's Mag. CLIII, 1893. [The actual competition which provided the occasion for the Smiths' burlesque.]

Beavan, A. H. James and Horace Smith. 1899.

Jerrold, W. C. The Centenary of the Rejected Addresses. Fortnightly Rev. XCIV, 1912.

Blunden, E. The Rejected Addresses. [In Votive Tablets, 1931.]

WILLIAM SOTHEBY (1757–1833)

(a) Works

Poems, consisting of Sonnets, Odes, etc. Bath, 1790; 1794 (as A Tour through Parts of Wales, Sonnets, and other Poems).

Oberon, a Poem, from the German of Wieland. 1798; 1805 (illustrated by H. Fuseli).

The Battle of the Nile, a Poem. 1799.

The Georgics of Virgil, translated. 1800; 1815; 1827; 1830.

The Siege of Cuzco, a Tragedy [in verse]. 1800.

The Cambrian Hero. [1800?] [A tragedy in verse; authenticity doubtful.]

A Poetical Epistle to Sir George Beaumont. 1801.

Julian and Agnes, a Tragedy [in verse]. 1801; 1814 (as The Confession); 1816 (as Ellen, or the Confession).

Orestes, a Tragedy [in verse]. 1802.

Oberon, a Mask [in verse] and Orestes. 1802.

Saul, a Poem. 1807.

Constance de Castile, a Poem. 1810.

A Song of Triumph. 1814.

Tragedies. 1814. [The Confession, Orestes, and three others—all in verse.]

Ivan, a Tragedy [in verse]. 1816.

Farewell to Italy, and Occasional Poems. 1818; 1825 (rev. and enlarged as Poems); 1828 (as Italy and Other Poems).

The First Book of the Iliad [and two other] Specimens of a New Version of Homer. 1830.

The Iliad of Homer, translated. 1831.

The Odyssey of Homer, translated. 1834.

Lines suggested by the Third Meeting of the British Association. With a Short Memoir of his Life. 1834.

(b) Criticism

Wilson, J. Homer and his Translators. Blackwood's Mag. XXIX–XXXI, 1831–2, XXXV, 1834. [Rptd in Works, vol. VIII, Edinburgh, 1859.]

WILLIAM ROBERT SPENCER (1769–1834)

Leonora, translated from the German of G. A. Bürgher. Illustrated. 1796; Dublin, 1799; 1809.
Urania, a Comedy [in prose]. 1802.
The Year of Sorrow. 1804. [A poem.]
Poems. 1811; 1835 (enlarged and with memoir).
Miscellaneous Poems. 1812.
Miles, A. H. *Miles*, IX (X). [Selection and criticism.]

ROBERT STORY (1795–1860)

The Harvest, a Poem. 1816.
Craven Blossoms. 1826. [Poems.]
The Magic Fountain, with Other Poems. 1829.
The Isles are Awake. 1834. [Poems.]
The Outlaw, a Drama [in verse]. 1839.
Love and Literature: Reminiscences of a Poet in Humble Life. 1842.
Songs and Lyrical Poems. Liverpool, [1845?]; 1849 (3rd edn, as Songs and Poems).
Guthrum the Dane, a Tale [in verse]. 1852; 1853.
The Third Napoleon, an Ode. 1854; 1855 (enlarged).
The Poetical Works. Newcastle, 1857.
The Alloway [Burns] Centenary Festival, an Ode. 1859.
The Lyrical and Other Minor Poems of Robert Story, with a Sketch of his Life and Writings by J. James. 1861.

CHARLES STRONG (1785–1864)

(a) Poems

Specimens of Sonnets from the most Celebrated Italian Poets. With Translations. 1827 (anon.).
Sonnets, by the Author of Specimens of Sonnets from the most Celebrated Italian Poets, with Translations. 1829.
Sonnets. 1835; 1862 (with fifteen additional Sonnets by a friend, C. L.).

(b) Criticism

The Sonnets of Charles Strong. Blackwood's Mag. XLIX, 1841.

SIR THOMAS NOON TALFOURD (1795–1854)

[See p. 596 below.]

ROBERT TANNAHILL (1774–1810)

The Soldier's Return, with other Poems. Paisley, 1807.
Poems and Songs. Glasgow, 1807.

Poems, with Life. Glasgow, 1815 (*bis*); 1817 (4th edn, enlarged).
The Poetical Works. Glasgow, 1825.
The Works. Edinburgh, 1835; 1857 (with Life).
Poems and Songs, with Life of Tannahill and of Robert A. Smith [responsible for musical settings]. Glasgow, 1838; ed. D. Semple, Paisley, 1874 (best edn).
Political Songs, Ballads and Fragments. Ed. A. Laing, Brechin, n.d.
Whyte, W. *Miles*, II. [Selection and criticism.]

ANN TAYLOR, later GILBERT (1782–1866) and JANE TAYLOR (1783–1824)

[See p. 565 below.]

WILLIAM TAYLOR (1765–1836)

[See p. 680 below.]

WILLIAM TENNANT (1784–1848)

Anster Fair. Edinburgh, 1812 (anon.); Edinburgh, 1814 (other poems added); Edinburgh, 1815; 1821; 1838 (with memoir).
Elegy on Trottin' Nanny. Edinburgh, 1814.
The Thane of Fife. Edinburgh, 1822.
Cardinal Beaton: a Drama in Five Acts. Edinburgh, 1823.
Papistry Stormed or the Dingin' doun o' the Cathedral. Edinburgh, 1827.
John Baliol: a Historical Drama. Edinburgh, 1828.
The Life and Writings. Ed. M. F. Conolly, 1861.
Miles, A. H. *Miles*, II. [Selection and criticism.]

[Tennant also pbd edns of Allan Ramsay and works on some of the oriental languages.]

JOHN THELWALL (1764–1834)

Poems on Various Subjects. Vol. I consisting of Tales. [Vol. II, consisting of a Dramatic Poem, Miscellanies, etc.] 2 vols. 1787.
Poems written in Close Confinement in the Tower and Newgate upon a Charge of Treason. 1795.
Poems chiefly written in Retirement: The Fairy of the Lake, a Dramatic Romance; Effusions of Relative and Social Feelings; and Specimens of The Hope of Albion, an Epic Poem. With Notes and Memoirs of the Life of the Author. Hereford, 1801; Hereford, [1805?].
Monody on the Right Hon. Charles James Fox. 1806 (*bis*).
The Poetical Recreations of the Champion, and his Literary Correspondents: with a Selection of Essays, Literary and Critical, which have appeared in the 'Champion' Newspaper. 1822. [Ed. by Thelwall; includes 12 poems by C. Lamb.]

[Thelwall also pbd many miscellaneous lectures and tracts, mainly on elocution and political subjects. He was proprietor and editor of The Champion, 1818.]

WILLIAM THOM (1798?–1848)

Rhymes and Recollections of a Hand Loom Weaver. 1844; 1845 (enlarged); ed. W. Skinner, Paisley, 1880.
Miles, A. H. *Miles*, III. [Selection and criticism.]

EDWARD THURLOW, afterwards HOVELL-THURLOW, Baron Thurlow (1781–1829)

(a) Poems

The Defence of Poesy. By Sir Philip Sidney. 1810. [Ed., with five original sonnets, by Thurlow.]
Verses prefixed to the Defence of Poesy; the Induction to an Heroic Poem; also Verses dedicated to the Prince Regent. 1812 (anon.).
Hermilda in Palestine; with Other Poems. 1812 (anon.).
Poems on Several Occasions. 1813; 1813 (enlarged). An Appendix to Poems on Several Occasions; being a Continuation of the Sylva. 1813.
Ariadne: a Poem. 1814; 1822.
Carmen Britannicum; or, The Song of Britain: written in Honour of his Royal Highness, George Augustus Frederick, Prince Regent. 1814.
Moonlight; The Doge's Daughter; Ariadne; Carmen Britannicum, or the Song of Britain; Angelica, or the Rape of Proteus. 1814.
Moonlight, a Poem; with Several Copies of Verses. 1814. [A different collection from the preceding.]
The Sonnets of Edward, Lord Thurlow. Brussels, 1819 (priv. ptd).
Select Poems. Chiswick, 1821 (priv. ptd).
Angelica; or, The Rape of Proteus: a Poem. 1822.
Arcita and Palamon; after Geoffrey Chaucer. 1822.

(b) Biography and Criticism

[Moore, T.] The Poems of Lord Thurlow. Edinburgh Rev. XXIII, 1813.
Obituary. GM. XCIX, ii, 1829.

MARY TIGHE, née BLACHFORD (1772–1810)

Psyche, or the Legend of Love. 1805 (priv. ptd). [Written c. 1795. There is said to be an edn of Psyche ptd in that year.]
Psyche, with Other Poems. 1811; 1812 (4th edn); Philadelphia, 1812; 1816; 1843. [Also rptd in trn of Apuleius' Works, 1853.]

Keats and Mary Tighe. The Poems of Mary Tighe, with Parallel Passages from the Works of John Keats. Ed. E. V. Weller, New York, 1928.

WILLIAM SIDNEY WALKER (1795–1846)

[See p. 1028 below.]

WILLIAM WATT (1793–1859)

Comus and Cupid. Glasgow, 1835; Glasgow, 1844; Glasgow, 1860 (as Poems and Songs).

ALARIC ALEXANDER WATTS (1797–1864)

(a) Works

Poetical Sketches. 1822 (priv. ptd).
Poetical Sketches: The Profession; The Broken Heart, etc. With Stanzas for Music, and Other Poems. 1823; 1824; 1828.
Scenes of Life and Shades of Character. 2 vols. 1831. [Prose.]
Lyrics of the Heart. 1851.

[A few minor prose writings and numerous contributions to periodicals are not listed.]

(b) Periodicals and Annuals edited by Watts

The Leeds Intelligencer. 1822–5.
The Manchester Courier. 1825–6.
The Literary Souvenir. 1825–35.
The Cabinet of British Art. 1835–8. [A continuation of The Literary Souvenir.]
The Poetical Album. 1828–9.
The United Services Gazette. 1833–47.
Men of the Time. 1856.

(c) Biography

Watts, A. Alfred. Alaric Watts: a Narrative of his Life. 2 vols. 1884.

CHARLES JEREMIAH WELLS (1800–1879)

(a) Works

Stories after Nature [in prose]. 1822; ed. W. J. Linton, 1891.
Joseph and his Brethren, a Scriptural Drama [in verse]. 1824; ed. A. C. Swinburne, 1876, 1908 (World's Classics). [Pbd under the pseudonym 'H. L. Howard.' Swinburne's introduction is virtually rptd from his article An Unknown Poet, Fortnightly Rev. XXIV, 1875.]
A Dramatic Scene. Ed. H. B. Forman (in Literary Anecdotes of the Nineteenth Century, ed. Sir W. R. Nicoll and T. J. Wise, vol. I, 1895). [Written c. 1876; intended for insertion in Joseph and his Brethren.]
Forman, H. B. *Miles*, III. [Selection and criticism.]

(b) Biography and Criticism

Gosse, Sir E. Academy, 1 March 1879. [Obituary.]

HENRY KIRKE WHITE (1785–1806)

(a) Bibliography

Catalogue of Portraits, Books, MSS., etc., relating to Henry Kirke White [exhibited in Nottingham, Nov. 1906]. Ed. J. T. Godfrey, Nottingham, 1906.

(b) Works

Clifton Grove: a Sketch in Verse, with Other Poems. 1803.

The Remains of Henry Kirke White; with an Account of his Life by Robert Southey. Vols. I, II: 1807; 1811 (5th edn, 'corrected'); 1813; 1816; 1823 (10th edn). Vol. III: 1822. Vols. I–III: 1853, etc. [Other edns: with a Biographical Preface by R. A., 4 vols. 1825; with a Life, 1828; Boston, 1829; with a Memoir, Glasgow, 1844.]

The Poetical Works of Rogers, Kirke White [and others]. Paris, 1829.

The Poetical Works, with a Memoir by Sir H. Nicolas. 1830; 1837; Boston, 1854. (Aldine edn.)

The Poetical Works of Henry Kirke White and James Grahame. Ed. G. Gilfillan, Edinburgh, 1856.

Poems, Letters, and Prose Fragments. Ed. J. Drinkwater, [1907]. (Muses' Lib.)

[The above are only the more important collections. There were many others.]

(c) Biography and Criticism

Piggott, S. Guide for Families. 1818 (2nd edn). [Includes an account of White.]

Cary, H. F. Lives of the English Poets from Johnson to Kirke White. 1846.

A Dictionary of Hymnology. Ed. J. Julian, 1892. [Information on the hymns.]

Miles, A. H. *Miles*, x (XI).

Godfrey, J. T. and Ward, J. Homes and Haunts of Henry Kirke White. 1908. [Illustrated; incorporates Southey's memoir.]

JOSEPH BLANCO WHITE (1775–1841)

[See p. 847 below.]

JEREMIAH HOLMES WIFFEN (1792–1836)

(a) Works

Poems by Three Friends. 1813; 1815. [With T. Raffles and J. B. Brown.]

Elegiac Lines. 1818. [With B. B. Wiffen.]

Aonian Hours and Other Poems. 1819; 1820.

Julia Alpinula, with Other Poems. 1820 (*bis*).

Jerusalem Delivered. Book the Fourth. 1821. [Specimen of projected verse translation of Tasso, with dissertation on existing ones.]

The Works of Garcilasso de la Vega, translated [in verse]. 1823.

Jerusalem Delivered. Translated. 2 vols. 1824–5; 1826; 1830; 1846; 1854.

Verses on the Alameda at Ampthill Park. 1827 (priv. ptd).

Historical Memoirs of the House of Russell. 2 vols. 1833.

Appeal for the Injured African [in verse]. Newcastle-on-Tyne, 1833.

Verses written at Woburn Abbey. 1836 (priv. ptd).

[A few minor prose writings have not been listed.]

(b) Biography and Criticism

Quart. Rev. XXXIV, 1826. [Contains an able comparison between Wiffen's Tasso and earlier versions.]

The Brothers Wiffen [J. H. and B. B. Wiffen]. Memoirs. Ed. S. R. Pattison, 1880. [With selections from their poems.]

ALEXANDER WILSON (1766–1813)

[See vol. II, p. 991 above.]

JOHN WILSON (1774–1855)

[See p. 682 below.]

CHARLES WOLFE (1791–1823)

(a) Works

The Burial of Sir John Moore. [Written 1816, first ptd in The Newry Telegraph (Co. Armagh, Ireland), 19 April 1817. A skilful French version, jestingly presented as the 'original,' is in Works of Father Prout (*i.e.* F. S. Mahony), ed. C. Kent, 1881.]

Remains of the late Rev. Charles Wolfe. Ed. J. A. Russell, 2 vols. Dublin, 1825; 1826; 1829 (4th edn); 1838 (7th edn); 1846. [Contains about 15 short poems, a number of sermons, and a memoir by Russell.]

The Burial of Sir John Moore, with Other Poems [and a memoir]. 1825.

Poems. 1903; 1909. [With memoir by C. L. Falkiner and facsimile of the MS of The Burial.]

(b) Biography and Criticism

[O'Sullivan, S.] College Recollections. 1825. [Contains a personal sketch of Wolfe as 'Waller.']

Newick, R. C. The Writer of 'The Burial of Sir John Moore' discovered. 1908. [Attributes the poem (erroneously) to Joseph Wolfe.]

FRANCIS WRANGHAM (1769–1842)

(a) Poems

The Restoration of the Jews: a Poem. Cambridge, 1795.

The Destruction of Babylon. 1795.

Poems. 1795 (priv. ptd, only pbd c. 1802).
The Holy Land. Cambridge, 1800.
The Raising of Jaïrus' Daughter. A Poem; to which is annexed a Short Memoir, interspersed with a Few Poetical Productions, of the late Caroline Symmons. 1804.
A Poem on the Restoration of Learning in the East. Cambridge, 1805.
A Volunteer Song. York, [1805] (anon.). [A collection of 11 pieces in verse.]
Trafalgar: a Song. [1805?] (priv. ptd). [Rptd from previous item.]
The Sufferings of the Primitive Martyrs. A [Seatonian] Prize Poem. Cambridge, 1812.
Joseph made known to his Brethren. A [Seatonian] Prize Poem. Cambridge, 1812.
On the Death of Saul and Jonathan. 1813 (no copy extant?).
Poetical Sketches of Scarborough. 1813 (bis, anon.). [By Wrangham and others.]
Poems. [1814?] (priv. ptd).
Virgil's Bucolics translated. Scarborough, 1815.
A few [40] Sonnets attempted from Petrarch in Early Life. Lee Priory, 1817.
Quintus Horatius Flaccus: Carmina. Selections. Specimens of a Version of Book III of Horace's Odes attempted in Octosyllabic Verse. 1820.
The Lyrics of Horace, being the First Four Books of his Odes. York, 1821; Chester, [1832?].
Scarborough Castle: a Poem. Scarborough, 1823.
Psychae; or, Songs on Butterflies, by T. H. Bayly, attempted in Latin Rhyme. 1828.
Homerics. 1834. [Trns of Odyssey v and Iliad III.]
Epithalamia tria Mariana &c. Chester, 1837. [Trns from George Buchanan and others.]
A Few Epigrams attempted in Latin Translations by an Old Pen nearly worn to its Stump. [Chester, 1842.]

(b) Theological Writings

Thirteen Practical Sermons; founded upon Doddridge's Rise and Progress of Religion in the Soul [with two more sermons]. 1800; 1802 (2nd edn).
Sermons Practical and Occasional; Dissertations, Translations, including new versions of Virgil's Bucolica, and of Milton's Defensio Secunda; Seaton Poems &c. 3 vols. 1816.
The Pleiad; or, A Series of Abridgements of Seven Distinguished Writers, in Opposition to the Pernicious Doctrines of Deism. 7 pts, 1820; Edinburgh, 1828.

[Also sundry sermons, charges, etc.]

(c) Miscellaneous Writings

Reform. A Farce modernised from Aristophanes by Samuel Foote, Jun. 1792.
A Dissertation on the Best Means of civilizing the Subjects of the British Empire in India, and of diffusing the Light of the Christian Religion throughout the Eastern World. 1805.

[Also several other pieces and much edited matter. For a fuller list see M. Sadleir, Archdeacon Francis Wrangham, Bibliog. Soc. 1937 (supplement, Library, XIX, 1939, pp. 422–61).]

R. W. K.

IV. THE MID-NINETEENTH CENTURY POETS

PRAED, BEDDOES, THE BROWNINGS, FITZGERALD, TENNYSON, CLOUGH, ARNOLD, PATMORE, AND THE ROSSETTIS.

WINTHROP MACKWORTH PRAED (1802–1839)

(1) COLLECTED POEMS

The Poetical Works, now first collected by R. W. Griswold. New York, 1844, 1853.
Lillian and Other Poems, now first collected [by R. W. Griswold]. New York, 1852.
The Poetical Works. Ed. W. A. Whitmore, New York [?], 1859.
Poems, with a Memoir by Derwent Coleridge. 2 vols. 1864. [The authorised and standard edn.]
Poems. Revised and Complete Edition. 2 vols. New York, 1885.

(2) SELECTIONS

Charades. New York, 1752 (for 1852).
A Selection from the Works. Ed. Sir G. Young, 1866.
Poems. Ed. F. Cooper, 1866.
Political and Occasional Poems. Ed. Sir G. Young, 1888.
Select Poems. Ed. A. D. Godley, 1909.
Poems. Ed. F. Greenslet, Boston, 1909.

(3) INDIVIDUAL PUBLICATIONS

Carmen Graecum numismate annuo dignatum, 1822. (Pyramides Aegyptiacae.) [Cambridge, 1822.]
Epigrammata numismate annuo dignata, 1822. (Nugae seria ducunt in mala.) [Cambridge, 1822.]
Carmen Graecum numismate annuo dignatum, 1823. (In Obitum T. F. Middleton, Episcopi Calcuttensis.) [Cambridge, 1823.]
Lillian, a Fairy Tale [in verse]. 1823.
Australasia. A Poem which Obtained the Chancellor's Medal. Cambridge, 1823.

Athens. A Poem which Obtained the Chancellor's Medal. Cambridge, 1824. [Rptd, with the preceding, in Cambridge Prize Poems, 1828 (4th edn).]

Epigrammata numismate annuo dignata, 1824. (Scribimus indocti doctique.) [Cambridge, 1824.]

The Ascent of Elijah, a Poem. Cambridge, 1831.

Intercepted Letters about the Infirmary Bazaar. N.d. [4 leaflets of 4 pp. each, in verse and ptd on light green paper.]

Speech in Committee on the Reform Bill, on moving an amendment. 1832.

Trash dedicated without respect to J. Halse, Esq. M.P. Penzance, 1833.

Essays, Collected and Arranged by Sir G. Young. 1887. (Morley's Universal Lib.)

(4) PERIODICALS WITH CONTRIBUTIONS BY PRAED

The Etonian. 2 vols. 1821. [Ed. and largely written by Praed and W. Blunt, Oct. 1820–Aug. 1821.]

Knight's Quarterly Magazine. 1823–4.

The Brazen Head. 1826. [4 nos. only; written and ed. by Praed, C. Knight and J. B. B. St Leger.]

[Praed also contributed to The Albion (1830–2), The Morning Post (1832–4), The Times and other papers, The Literary Souvenir, ed. A. A. Watts, 1825 ff., and other poetical annuals.]

(5) BIOGRAPHY AND CRITICISM

Saintsbury, G. Essays in English Literature, 1780–1860. 1890.

Kraupa, M. Winthrop Mackworth Præd, sein Leben und seine Werke. Vienna, 1910.

Previté-Orton, C. W. Political Satire in English Poetry. Cambridge, 1910. [Ch. vi.]

Hudson, D. A Poet in Parliament. 1939.

R. W. K.

THOMAS LOVELL BEDDOES (1803–1849)

(1) COLLECTED WORKS

The Poems posthumous and collected of Thomas Lovell Beddoes. 2 vols. 1851. [Vol. II includes Death's Jest-Book, 1850. Also issued in one vol. without Death's Jest-Book, as Poems by the late Thomas Lovell Beddoes, author of Death's Jest-Book or The Fool's Tragedy. With a Memoir [by T. F. Kelsall], 1851.]

The Poetical Works. Ed. (with memoir) Sir E. Gosse, 2 vols. 1890. [Memoir rptd in Critical Kit-Kats, 1896.]

The Poems. Ed. R. Colles, 1907. (Muses' Lib.)

The Complete Works. Ed. (with memoir) Sir E. Gosse, 2 vols. 1928.

The Works. Ed. H. W. Donner, Oxford, 1935. [Includes complete and variorum Death's Jest-Book, new poetry and prose in English and German, *apparatus criticus*, commentary, and bibliography.]

(2) SELECTION

Thomas Lovell Beddoes. An Anthology. Ed. F. L. Lucas, Cambridge, 1932. [Introduction rptd in Studies French and English, 1934.]

(3) INDIVIDUAL PUBLICATIONS

The Comet. Morning Post, 6 July 1819. [Signed E. D. Bodes.]

The Improvisatore, in three fyttes, with Other Poems. Oxford, 1821.

The Brides' Tragedy. 1822.

The Romance of the Lily. Album, Aug. 1823 (anon.).

Philosophic Letters by F. Schiller. Oxford Quarterly Mag. I, 1825 (anon.).

Letter from Cassel. Leigh Hunt's Companion, 2 April 1828 (anon.).

Love's Last Messages and Fragment of An Apotheosis. Athenaeum, 7 July 1832.

Lines written in the 'Prometheus Unbound.' Athenaeum, 18 May 1833.

Antistraussianischer Gruss an einen Herrn Antistes von Struthio Camelus. [Zurich, 1839.]

Death's Jest-Book or The Fool's Tragedy. 1850 (anon.).

Cupid, Death, and Psyche. Examiner, 8 Oct. 1864.

The Letters of Thomas Lovell Beddoes. Ed. Sir E. Gosse, 1894.

Two Unpublished Fragments. Spectator, 27 Feb. 1932.

(4) BIOGRAPHY AND CRITICISM

Monthly Rev. June 1821. [Review of Improvisatore.]

Monthly Rev. Jan. 1823. [Review of Brides' Tragedy.]

Procter, B. W. London Mag. Feb. 1823, March 1824.

—— Edinburgh Rev. Feb. 1823.

—— An Autobiographical Fragment. 1877.

Darley, G. London Mag. Dec. 1823, May 1824.

Wilson, John. Blackwood's Mag. Dec. 1823.

Bayerisches Volksblatt (Würzburg), 29 March (speech for Poland), 16 June (speech for political freedom), 24 July, 30 Aug. 1832 (deportation from Bavaria).

Der Freisinnige, 9 July 1832. [Speech for political freedom.]

Nürnberger Correspondent, 25, 30 July 1832. [Deportation from Bavaria.]

Der Volksbote (Zurich), 23 Jan. (report of performance of Henry IV), 7 Dec. 1838 (formation of Booing Society), 3 May 1839 (Strauss feud).

Scherr, I. T. Beobachtungen, Bestrebungen und Schicksale. Vols. III, IV, St Gall, 1840.

Spectator, 6 July 1850. [Review of Death's Jest-Book.]

Forster, J. Examiner, 20 July 1850.

—— Examiner, 27 Sept. 1851.

Spectator, 13 Sept. 1851. [Review of Poems posthumous and collected.]

Blackwood's Mag. Oct. 1856.

Kelsall, T. F. Fortnightly Rev. July 1872.

Collins, Mabel. A Poet not Laureate. Dublin University Mag. Nov. 1879.

Gosse, Sir E. Athenaeum, 20 Oct. 1883.

—— TLS. 11 March 1909.

Symons, A. Academy, 15 Aug. 1891. [Rptd in Figures of Several Centuries, 1916.]

Crosse, Mrs A. Temple Bar, March 1894.

Elton, O. A Survey of English Literature, 1780–1830. Vol. II, 1912, pp. 299–304.

Feller, A. Thomas Lovell Beddoes. Marburg, 1914.

Strachey, L. The Last of the Elizabethans. [In Books and Characters, 1922.]

Potter, G. R. Did T. L. Beddoes believe in the Evolution of the Species? MP. XXI, 1923.

Rickword, E. London Mercury, IX, 1923.

Moldauer, Grete. Thomas Lovell Beddoes. Vienna, 1924.

Snow, R. H. Thomas Lovell Beddoes. Eccentric and Poet. New York, 1928.

Fugô, S. Beddoes Ron-kô (Studies on Beddoes). Tokyo, 1930.

Blunden, E. Votive Tablets. 1931.

Günther, Leo. Würzburger Chronik, III, 1932, pp. 620–2, 638, 648.

Weber, C. A. Literarisches Bristol. Seine Bedeutung für den provinziellen Ursprung der englischen Romantik und für die deutsch-englischen Beziehungen. Halle, 1935.

Donner, H. W. The Browning Box or The Life and Works of Thomas Lovell Beddoes as reflected in Letters by his Friends and Admirers. Oxford, 1935.

—— Thomas Lovell Beddoes: the Making of a Poet. Oxford, 1935.   H. W. D.

ELIZABETH BARRETT BROWNING
(1806–1861)

(1) BIBLIOGRAPHY

Forman, H. B. Elizabeth Barrett Browning and her Scarcer Books. 1896 (priv. ptd). [Also included in Literary Anecdotes of the Nineteenth Century, ed. Sir W. R. Nicoll and T. J. Wise, vol. II, 1896.]

Wise, T. J. A Bibliography of the Writings in Prose and Verse of Elizabeth Barrett Browning. 1918 (priv. ptd).

Ehrsam, T. G. and Deily, R. H. Bibliographies of Twelve Victorian Authors. New York, 1936.

(2) COLLECTED POEMS

Poems. 2 vols. 1844; rptd 1 vol. [with a prefatory note by R. B., i.e. Robert Browning], 1887, etc.

Poems. New Edition [greatly enlarged]. 1850; 2 vols. 1853; 3 vols. 1856; 3 vols. 1862; 4 vols. 1864.

The Poetical Works of Elizabeth Barrett Browning [= 7th edn of Poems]. 5 vols. 1866; 6 vols. 1889; rptd 1890, etc.

The Poetical Works. With a Memoir. 2 vols. New York, 1871.

The Poetical Works. Corrected by the Last London Edition. New York, 1877.

The Poetical Works, from 1826 to 1844. Ed. (with memoir) J. H. Ingram, [1887].

The Poetical Works. [Ed. Sir F. G. Kenyon,] 1897.

The Poetical Works. 1904. (Oxford Complete edn.)

The Complete Poems. 2 vols. [1904].

(3) SELECTED POEMS

A Selection from the Poetry of Elizabeth Barrett Browning [made with the assistance of Robert Browning]. Ser. 1 (with a foreword by Robert Browning), 1866; ser. 2, 1880.

The Earlier Poems of Elizabeth Barrett Browning, 1826–1833. Ed. R. H. Shepherd, 1878.

(4) SEPARATE PUBLICATIONS
(a) Poetry

The Battle of Marathon. A Poem. 1820; ed. facs. H. B. Forman, 1891 (priv. ptd).

An Essay on Mind; with other Poems. 1826.

Prometheus Bound, translated from the Greek of Aeschylus: and Miscellaneous Poems. By the Translator, Author of an Essay on Mind; with Other Poems. 1833; ed. A. Meynell, 1896.

The Seraphim and Other Poems. 1838.

A Drama of Exile: and Other Poems. 2 vols. New York, 1845.

Sonnets. By E. B. B. Reading, 1847 (priv. ptd). [For an attack on the authenticity of this edn see J. Carter and G. Pollard, Nineteenth Century Pamphlets, 1934. The sonnets were included in the 1850 edn of Poems, under the title Sonnets from the Portuguese, and afterwards issued separately in numerous edns under this title. For the bibliographical history of the Sonnets, see Literary Anecdotes of the Nineteenth Century, ed. Sir W. R. Nicoll and T. J. Wise, vol. II, 1895, pp. 90 ff.]

The Runaway Slave at Pilgrim's Point. 1849. [Also a forgery? See J. Carter and G. Pollard, Nineteenth Century Pamphlets, 1934.]

Casa Guidi Windows. A Poem. 1851.

Two Poems. (A Plea for the Ragged Schools of London. The Twins: Give and It-shall-be-given-unto-you [the latter by Robert Browning].) 1854.

Aurora Leigh. 1857 (3 edns); 1859; 1860 (with several corrections); ed. A. C. Swinburne, 1898; ed. H. B. Forman, 1899 (Temple Classics).

Poems before Congress. 1860. [Rptd under title of Napoleon III in Italy, and Other Poems, New York, 1860.]

Last Poems. 1862 (bis).

Psyche Apocalypté: A Lyrical Drama. Projected by E. B. Browning and R. H. Horne. 1876 (priv. ptd). [Rptd from St James's Mag. and United Empire Rev. Feb. 1876.]

New Poems by Robert Browning and Elizabeth Barrett Browning. Ed. Sir F. G. Kenyon, 1914.

The Poets' Enchiridion. A hitherto Unpublished Poem with an Inedited Address to Uvedale Price, an Early Invocation to Sleep and a Preliminary Draft of the Renowned Poem Catarina to Camoens. Bibliophile Soc. Boston, 1914.

Hitherto Unpublished Poems and Stories. With an Inedited Autobiography. Bibliophile Soc. Boston, 1914.

(b) Prose (other than Letters)

The Greek Christian Poets and the English Poets. 1863. [Consisting of a series of articles ptd in Athenaeum, 1842.]

Charles Dickens and other 'Spirits of the Age.' 1919 (priv. ptd).

Edgar Allan Poe. A Criticism. With Remarks on the Morals and Religion of Shelley and Leigh Hunt. 1919 (priv. ptd).

Alfred Tennyson. Notes and Comments. With a defence of the Rhyme System of 'The Dead Pan.' 1919 (priv. ptd).

A Note on William Wordsworth, with a Statement on Spiritualism. 1919 (priv. ptd).

[Mrs Browning also contributed Queen Annelida and False Arcite to The Poems of Geoffrey Chaucer, Modernised, 1841. Much material was supplied by her for R. H. Horne's A New Spirit of the Age (2 vols. 1844; ed. W. Jerrold, 1907) of which the essay on Carlyle, freed from Horne's emendations and interpolations, is ptd in Literary Anecdotes of

the Nineteenth Century, ed. Sir W. R. Nicoll and T. J. Wise, vol. II, 1896, pp. 105 ff., under the title Carlyle: A Disentangled Essay. For her contributions to American periodicals, see MLN. xxxv, 1920.]

(5) LETTERS

Letters of Elizabeth Barrett Browning addressed to Richard Hengist Horne. Ed. S. R. T. Mayer, 2 vols. 1877.

Kind Words from a Sick-Room. Greenock, 1891 (priv. ptd). [4 letters from Mrs Browning, 1845–6, and 1 from Browning, 1883.]

The Religious Opinions of Elizabeth Barrett Browning. Ed. Sir W. R. Nicoll, 1896 (priv. ptd); 1906 (pbd). [3 letters to W. Merry. Also included in Literary Anecdotes of the Nineteenth Century, ed. Sir W. R. Nicoll and T. J. Wise, vol. II, 1896.]

The Letters of Elizabeth Barrett Browning. Ed. Sir F. G. Kenyon, 2 vols. 1897.

The Letters of Robert Browning and Elizabeth Barrett Browning, 1845–6. 2 vols. 1899; 1923; 2 vols. New York, 1930.

Letters to Robert Browning and Other Correspondents. Ed. T. J. Wise, 1916 (priv. ptd).

Elizabeth Barrett Browning. Letters to her Sister, 1846–1859. Ed. L. Huxley, 1929.

Twenty-two Unpublished Letters of Elizabeth Barrett Browning and Robert Browning addressed to Henrietta and Arabella Moulton-Barrett. New York, 1935.

From Robert and Elizabeth Browning: a further Selection of the Barrett-Browning Family Correspondence. Ed. W. R. Benét, 1936.

(6) BIOGRAPHY AND CRITICISM

[For literature relating to both the Brownings jointly, see the separate list of Browningiana below, p. 251.]

(a) Biographical Studies

Selden, C. Elizabeth Browning. [In Portraits des Femmes, Paris, 1877.]

Stedman, E. C. Elizabeth Barrett Browning. 1877.

Ingram, J. H. Elizabeth Barrett Browning. 1888.

Merlette, G. M. La Vie et l'Œuvre d'Elizabeth Barrett Browning. Paris, 1905.

Viterbi, B. B. Elisabetta Barrett-Browning. Bergamo, 1913.

Willis, I. C. Elizabeth Barrett Browning. 1928.

Clarke, I. C. Elizabeth Barrett Browning: a Portrait. 1929.

Boas, L. S. Elizabeth Barrett Browning. New York, 1930.

Huxley, L. Mrs Browning and her Father's Forgiveness. Cornhill Mag. LXXIV, 1933.
Woolf, V. Flush: a Biography. 1933.

(b) Critical Studies

Gilfillan, G. Galleries of Literary Portraits. Vol. I, 1856.
Smith, G. B. Poets and Novelists. 1875.
Bayne, P. Two Great Englishwomen: Mrs Browning and Charlotte Brontë. 1881.
Des Guerrois, C. Étude sur E. Browning. Paris, 1885.
Druskowitz, H. Drei englische Dichterinnen. Berlin, 1885. [Essays on Joanna Baillie, Mrs Browning and George Eliot.]
Montégut, E. Écrivains modernes de l'Angleterre. Ser. 2, Paris, 1885.
Pluviannes, H. et al. Hommage français à Elizabeth Barrett Browning à l'Occasion de son Centenaire. Vals-les-Bains, 1906.
Nicati, W. Femme et Poète. Elizabeth Browning. Paris, 1912.
Royds, K. E. Elizabeth Barrett Browning and her Poetry. 1912.
Bald, M. A. Women-Writers of the Nineteenth Century. Cambridge, 1923.
Shackford, M. H. E. B. Browning; R. H. Horne. Two Studies. Wellesley, 1935.

(c) Special Studies

Gosse, Sir E. The Sonnets from the Portuguese. [In Critical Kit-Kats, vol. III, 1896.]
Lubbock, P. Elizabeth Barrett Browning in her Letters. 1906.
Jacobi, B. Elizabeth Barrett Browning als Übersetzerin antiker Dichtungen. Münster, 1908.
Minckwitz, M. J. Zu den 'Casa Guidi Windows.' Ang. N.S. XXXVIII, 1926.
[Woolf, V.] Aurora Leigh. TLS. 2 July 1931.
Drachmann, A. G. E. B. Browning and Hans Andersen. Edda, XXXIII, 1933.

(7) BROWNINGIANA

Sarrazin, G. Poètes modernes de l'Angleterre. Paris, 1885.
Ritchie, A., Lady. Records of Tennyson, Ruskin and the Brownings. 1892.
Nicoll, Sir W. R. and Wise, T. J. Literary Anecdotes of the Nineteenth Century. 2 vols. 1895–6.
Zampini-Salazar, F. Roberto ed Elisabetta Browning. Naples, 1896.
—— La Vita e le Opere di Roberto Browning ed Elisabetta Browning. Turin, 1907.
Darmesteter (afterwards Duclaux), A. M. F. Grands Écrivains d'Outre-Manche. Paris, [1901].
Stephen, Sir L. The Browning Letters. [In Studies of a Biographer, ser. 2, vol. III, 1902.]

Cunliffe, J. W. Elizabeth Barrett's Influence on Browning's Poetry. PMLA. XXIII, 1908.
de Fonblanque, E. Influence of Italy on the Poetry of the Brownings. Fortnightly Rev. XCII, 1909.
Whiting, L. The Brownings: their Life and Art. Boston. 1911.
The Browning Collections. 1913. [Sale catalogue of the Brownings' libraries.]
Symons, A. Some Browning Reminiscences. North American Rev. CCIV, 1916.
Elton, O. A Survey of English Literature, 1830–1880. Vol. I, 1920.
Jones, Sir H. Robert Browning and Elizabeth Barrett Browning. [In Essays on Literature and Education, 1924.]
Burdett, O. The Brownings. 1928.
Wise, T. J. A Browning Library. 1929 (priv. ptd).
Sim, F. M. Robert Browning and Elizabeth Barrett. 1930.
Letters from Owen Meredith to Robert and Elizabeth Barrett Browning. Ed. A. B. and J. L. Harlan, Waco (Texas), 1937.

G. A. P. B., rev. J. P. C.

EDWARD FITZGERALD (1809–1883)

(1) BIBLIOGRAPHIES

A Chronological List of the More Important Issues of Edward FitzGerald's Version of the Rubáiyát of Omar Khayyám, and of Other Books, written, translated, edited or owned by him; with Autograph Letters, etc.; and with Ana, other Versions of the Rubáiyát [etc.]. 1899.
Prideaux, W. F. Notes for a Bibliography of Edward FitzGerald. 1901. [List of separate publications to 1900 and of contributions by FitzGerald to books and periodicals. Notes, critical and bibliographical, to each item listed.]
Potter, A. G. A Bibliography of the Rubáiyát of Omar Khayyám together with Kindred Matter in Prose and Verse pertaining thereto. 1929.
Ehrsam, T. G. and Deily, R. H. Bibliographies of Twelve Victorian Authors. New York, 1936.

(2) COLLECTED WORKS AND LETTERS

Works. Reprinted from the Original Impressions, with some Corrections derived from his own Annotated Copies. 2 vols. New York, 1887.
Letters and Literary Remains. Ed. W. A. Wright, 3 vols. 1889.
Letters. Ed. W. A. Wright, 2 vols. 1894.
Letters to Fanny Kemble, 1871–1883. Ed. W. A. Wright, 1895.

Miscellanies. Ed. W. A. Wright, 1900.

More Letters. Ed. W. A. Wright, 1901.

The Variorum and Definitive Edition of the Poetical and Prose Writings of Edward FitzGerald, including a Complete Bibliography and Interesting Personal and Literary Notes. Ed. (with preface by Sir E. Gosse) G. Bentham, 7 vols. New York, 1902.

Letters and Literary Remains. Ed. W. A. Wright, 7 vols. 1902–3. [Absorbs the previous collections of letters made by Wright.]

Edward FitzGerald and 'Posh' 'Herring Merchants,' including a Number of Letters from Edward FitzGerald to Joseph Fletcher or 'Posh' not hitherto published. Ed. J. Blyth, 1908.

Some New Letters. With a Foreword by Viscount Grey. Ed. F. R. Barton, 1923.

Letters to Bernard Quaritch, 1853–1883. Ed. C. Q. Wrentmore, 1926.

A FitzGerald Friendship. Letters from Edward FitzGerald to William Bodham Donne. Ed. N. C. Hannay, 1932.

(3) SEPARATE WORKS

Euphranor: a Dialogue on Youth. 1851; 1855; ed. F. Chapman, 1906.

Polonius: a Collection of Wise Saws and Modern Instances. 1852; 1854.

Six Dramas of Calderón freely translated. 1853; 1854; ed. H. Oelsner, 1903; rptd [1928] (Everyman's Lib.).

Salámán and Absál: an Allegory freely translated from the Persian of Jámí. 1856; 1871; 1879 (together with 4th edn of the Rubáiyát).

Rubáiyát of Omar Khayyám, the Astronomer-Poet of Persia, rendered into English Verse. 1859 (anon.); 1868 (rev.); 1872 (rev.); 1879 (rev., with the Salámán and Absál of Jámí), etc.; ed. N. H. Dole, 2 vols. 1898 (includes French, German, Italian and Danish versions, with voluminous critical material); ed. T. Williams, Philadelphia, 1898 (text of 4th and 1st edns); ed. H. M. Batson and Sir E. D. Ross, 1900; ed. R. A. Nicholson, 1900 (text of 1st edn); ed. E. Heron-Allen, 1908 (text of 2nd edn); ed. F. H. Evans, 1914 (variorum text); rptd photofacs. (from 1st edn) New York, 1934; ed. C. Ganz and Sir E. D. Ross, 1938 (with unpbd fragmentary trn into 'Monkish Latin' by FitzGerald).

Tutin, J. R. A Concordance to FitzGerald's Translation of the Rubáiyát. 1900.

The Mighty Magician and Such Stuff as Dreams are made of. Two Plays translated from Calderón. 1865.

Agamemnon, a Tragedy taken from Aeschylus. [1876] (priv. ptd).

Readings in Crabbe's 'Tales of the Hall.' [1879] (priv. ptd); 1882; 1883 (with enlarged introduction).

The Downfall and Death of King Oedipus, a Drama in Two Parts, chiefly taken from the Oedipus Tyrannus and Coloneus of Sophocles. 1880–1 (priv. ptd).

Euphranor, A May-Day Conversation at Cambridge, "Tis Forty Years Since.' [1882] (priv. ptd).

The Two Generals. I. Lucius Aemilius Paullus. II. Sir Charles Napier. [Two poems. Priv. ptd. Date uncertain.]

Occasional Verses. 1891 (priv. ptd).

Eight Dramas of Calderón, freely translated. 1906. [Consists of Six Dramas, 1853, and The Mighty Magician and Such Stuff as Dreams, 1865.]

Dictionary of Madame de Sevigny. Ed. M. E. FitzGerald, 2 vols. 1914.

A FitzGerald Medley. Ed. C. Ganz, 1933.

[For contributions by FitzGerald to books and periodicals, see W. F. Prideaux, Notes for a Bibliography of Edward FitzGerald, pp. 57–72.]

(4) BIOGRAPHY AND CRITICISM

[For personal memoirs of FitzGerald, see W. F. Prideaux, Notes for a Bibliography of Edward FitzGerald, pp. 72–4.]

Groome, F. H. Two Suffolk Friends. 1895. [FitzGerald and Archdeacon Groome.]

Nicoll, Sir W. R. and Wise, T. J. Literary Anecdotes of the Nineteenth Century. 2 vols. 1895–6. [Vol. II includes 'An Old Commonplace Book of Edward FitzGerald's.']

Heron-Allen, E. Some Sidelights upon Edward FitzGerald's Poem The Rubáiyát of Omar Khayyám. 1898.

—— Edward FitzGerald's Rubáiyát of Omar Khayyám with their Original Persian Sources. 1899.

Jackson, H. Edward FitzGerald and Omar Khayyám. An Essay and a Bibliography. 1899.

More, P. E. Shelburne Essays. Ser. 2, New York, 1899.

Glyde, J. The Life of Edward FitzGerald, with an Introduction by E. Clodd. 1900.

Campbell, G. Edward and Pamela FitzGerald, being Some Account of their Lives compiled from the Letters of those who knew them. 1904.

Wright, T. The Life of Edward FitzGerald. 2 vols. 1904.

Benson, A. C. Edward FitzGerald. 1905. (English Men of Letters ser.)

Dutt, W. H. Some Literary Associations of East Anglia. [1907.] [Ch. 1, The Homes and Haunts of Edward FitzGerald.]

Edward FitzGerald, 1809–1909. Centenary Celebrations Souvenir. Ipswich, 1909.

The Book of the Omar Khayyám Club, 1892–1910. 1910 (priv. ptd).

Adams, M. Omar's Interpreter. A New Life of Edward FitzGerald. 1911 (rev. edn).

—— In the Footsteps of Borrow and Fitz-Gerald. 1913.

Bailey, J. FitzGerald. [In Poets and Poetry, Oxford, 1911.]

Nicholson, R. A. Omar Khayyám, Some Facts and Fallacies. Aberdeen University Rev. Feb. 1914.

Browning, R. Edward FitzGerald and Elizabeth Barrett Browning. 1919 (priv. ptd). [3 letters from Browning to his son.]

Elton, O. A Survey of English Literature, 1830–1880. Vol. II, 1920.

Birrell, A. FitzGerald's Letters. Empire Rev. May 1924.

Thonet, J. M. H. Étude sur E. FitzGerald et la Littérature persane. Liége, 1929.

Campbell, A. Y. Edward FitzGerald. [In Great Victorians, ed. H. J. and H. Massingham, 1932.]

G. A. P. B., *rev.* J. P. C.

ALFRED, BARON TENNYSON (1809–1892)

(1) BIBLIOGRAPHIES

[Shepherd, R. H.] The Bibliography of Tennyson. A Bibliographical List of the Published and Privately Printed Writings of Alfred Lord Tennyson, with his Contributions to Annuals, Magazines, Newspapers and Other Periodical Publications, and a Scheme for a Final and Definitive Edition of the Poet's Works. 1896.

Chronological List of the Works of Tennyson. Grolier Club, 1897.

L[ivingston], L. S. A Bibliography of the First Editions of Tennyson in Book Form. New York, 1901.

W[ise], T. J. A Bibliography of the Writings of Alfred, Lord Tennyson. 2 vols. 1908 (priv. ptd).

Ehrsam, T. G. and Deily, R. H. Bibliographies of Twelve Victorian Authors. New York, 1936.

(2) COLLECTED POEMS

(a) Early Collections, 1827–65

Poems by Two Brothers [Alfred and Charles Tennyson; Frederick Tennyson also contributed 4 poems]. 1827; rptd 1893 (with preface by Hallam Tennyson, and facs. of five leaves of the original MS; also four additional poems and rpt of Timbuctoo).

Poems, chiefly Lyrical. 1830.

Poems. 1833 [1832].

Poems. 2 vols. 1842; 2 vols. 1843; 2 vols. 1845; 2 vols. 1846; 1848; 1850; 1851; 1853, etc. (16 more edns up to 1872, after which date no further numbered edns, but poems incorporated in the various Collected Works); 1857 (illustrated); ed. J. C. Collins, 1900 (with critical introduction, commentaries and notes, various readings, transcript of poems temporarily and finally suppressed and a bibliography); ed. A. M. D. Hughes, Oxford, 1914 (with introduction and notes).

A Selection from the Works. 1865. [Contains 5 new poems.]

(b) Tennyson's Works, 1870–1907

Miniature Edition. 13 vols. 1870–7. [Between 1870 and 1883 the several vols. of this edn were frequently rptd under various dates; 1870–4 they bore imprint of Strahan & Co., 1874–8 that of Henry S. King & Co., 1878–83 that of C. Kegan Paul & Co. Vols. I–XII were rptd in shilling edn (12 vols.) 1878, to which vol. XIII was added in 1882.]

Imperial Library Edition. 6 vols. 1872–3 (Strahan); re-issued 7 vols. 1877 (King).

Cabinet Edition. 13 vols. 1874–81. [1874–83 the several vols. of this edn were frequently rptd under various dates; 1874–8 imprint of King, 1878–83 imprint of Kegan Paul.]

Author's Edition. 7 vols. 1874–81. [1874–83 the several vols. of this edn were frequently rptd under various dates; 1874–8 imprint of King, 1878–83 imprint of Kegan Paul.]

Crown Edition. 1878. [Rptd frequently up to Jan. 1884, when replaced by Macmillan's 1 vol. edn.]

[Macmillan's 1 vol. edn.] 1884. [Rev. by Tennyson. Rptd, with slight corrections, 1884 ff. In Sept. 1894 this edn became the complete 1 vol. edn. Rptd 1895 ff.]

[Edition-de-luxe.] 12 vols. 1898–9. [Vols. I–IV, Memoir by Hallam Tennyson; vols. V–XII, Poems.]

Eversley Edition. Ed. Hallam Tennyson, 9 vols. 1907–8; 1 vol. 1913. [Annotated by Tennyson.]

[For Macmillan's various collected edns, 1884–1907, see T. J. Wise's Bibliography, vol. II, pp. 41–52.]

(3) SELECTED POEMS

Lyrical Poems, selected and annotated by F. T. Palgrave. 1885.

Lyrics and Poems. Ed. E. A. Sharp, 2 vols. 1899. [With biographical introduction and appendix of comparative readings.]

Selections from Tennyson. Ed. R. S. Sheppard, Madras, 1899. [Introduction, full notes, appendices and index.]
In Memoriam, The Princess and Maud. Ed. J. C. Collins, 1902. [Critical introductions, commentaries and notes, various readings.]
Poems. Chosen by H. Van Dyke. 1903; 1920.
Suppressed Poems, 1830–62. Ed. J. C. Thomson, 1904.
Tennyson's Shorter Poems and Lyrics, 1833–42. [English Idyls and Other Poems, 1842–55.] Ed. B. C. Mulliner, Oxford, 1909.
Tennyson, Fifty Poems, 1830–64. Ed. J. H. Lobban, Cambridge, 1910.
Poems, 1830–70. With an Introduction by T. H. Warren. Illustrated with Two Pictures in Colour after G. F. Watts, and Ninety-one Illustrations by Millais, Rossetti, Maclise and Others. 1912. [Also, unillustrated, in World's Classics, 1910.]
Selected Poems. The Lotus-Eaters, Ulysses, Death of the Duke of Wellington, The Coming of Arthur, The Passing of Arthur. Ed. C. B. Wheeler and F. A. Cavenagh, Oxford, 1916.
Unpublished Early Poems. Ed. C. B. L. Tennyson, 1931.

(4) POEMS SEPARATELY PUBLISHED

[Comprising poems separately pbd as first edns and those that originally appeared in collected edns and were afterwards ptd singly. Titles in alphabetical order.]

The Antechamber. 1906 (priv. ptd). [An earlier version of The Gardener's Daughter. Ptd from a MS of 1834.]
Aylmer's Field. With Introduction (by F. J. Rowe and W. T. Webb) and Notes by W. T. Webb. 1891.
Ballads and Other Poems. 1880.
Becket. A Tragedy. [Trial edn, 1879.] 1884 (probably a forgery); arranged for the stage by Henry Irving [revised by Tennyson], 1893.
[The Birth of Arthur, etc. 1868.] [See T. J. Wise's Bibliography. vol. I, p. 197.]
The Brook. 1887.
Carmen Seculare, an Ode [on Queen Victoria's Jubilee, 1887]. [1887] (priv. ptd). [A forgery? See J. Carter and G. Pollard, An Enquiry into the Nature of Certain Nineteenth-Century Pamphlets, 1934.]
The Charge of the Light Brigade. [1855.]
Child-Songs. 1880.
The Cup. 1881 (priv. ptd). [A forgery? See J. Carter and G. Pollard, as above. The Cup was acted at the Lyceum Theatre, 1881.]
The Cup and the Falcon. [Trial edn, 1882.] 1884; ed. H. B. Cotterill, 1903.

The Day-Dream, and Other Poems. Ed. A. Wilson, 1899.
The Death of the Duke of Clarence and Avondale. [1892.]
The Death of Oenone, Akbar's Dream, and Other Poems. 1892 (bis).
Demeter, and Other Poems. 1889. [20,000 copies sold in first week.]
The Devil and the Lady. Ed. C. B. L. Tennyson, 1930.
Dora, and Other Poems. Ed. A. Wilson, 1899.
A Dream of Fair Women. 1892.
Early Spring. 1883.
England and America in 1782. 1872.
Enid and Nimuë: The True and the False. 1857; rptd Guildford, 1902.
Enoch Arden. Idylls of the Hearth. 1864; 1866 (illustrated); ed. W. T. Webb, 1891; ed. H. Marwick, Oxford, 1914.
Epilogue to the Queen. 1873 (priv. ptd). [Probably a forgery.]
The Falcon. 1879 (priv. ptd). [A forgery? See J. Carter and G. Pollard, as above. Produced at St James's Theatre 1879.]
The Foresters. Robin Hood and Maid Marion. 1892. [Trial edn, 1881. Produced at Daly's Theatre, New York, same year.]
The Gardener's Daughter, and Other Poems. Edinburgh, [1910].
Gareth and Linette. 1872 (trial edn). Gareth and Lynette [i.e. The Last Tournament]. 1872; ed. G. C. Macaulay, 1892. [See also under Idylls of the King.]
Gordon Boys' Morning and Evening Hymns. The Words edited by Alfred, Lord Tennyson. [1885.]
Hands All Round, A National Song. The Music by C. Villiers Stanford. [1882.]
Harold. A Drama. 1877 [1876].
Helen's Tower, Clandeboye. [1861] (priv. ptd).
The Holy Grail, and Other Poems. 1870 [1869]; ed. G. C. Macaulay, 1893. [See also under Idylls of the King.]
Idylls of the Hearth. 1864. [See also under Enoch Arden.]
Idylls of the King. (Enid, Vivien, Elaine, Guinevere.) 1859 (bis); 1861; 1862; 1863; 1865; 1868; 1869.
Idylls of the King. (The Coming of Arthur [ed. C. B. Wheeler, Oxford, 1909], Geraint and Enid, Merlin and Vivien, Lancelot and Elaine, The Holy Grail, Pelleas and Ettarre, Guinevere, The Passing of Arthur.) 1869 (9th edn); 1870.
Idylls of the King. (The Coming of Arthur, The Round Table: Gareth and Lynette, The Marriage of Geraint [ed. G. C. Macaulay, 1892], Balin and Balan, Merlin and Vivien, Lancelot and Elaine, The Holy Grail, Pelleas and Ettarre, The Last Tournament, Guinevere [ed. G. C. Macaulay, 1895], The

Passing of Arthur.) 1889, etc.; ed. W. Broughton, Boston, [1913]; ed. B. Wheeler, 1913.

In Memoriam. 1850 (3 edns); 1851 (bis); 1855; 1856; 1880; 1885; ed. H. C. Beeching, 1900, 1923; ed. A. W. Robinson, Cambridge, 1901; 1905 ('annotated by the author'); ed. H. M. Percival, 1907. [See The Love Story of In Memoriam: Letters from A. H. Hallam to Emily Tennyson, 1916.]

The Lady of Shalott. Illustrated by a Lady. Nottingham, 1852.

The Last Tournament. 1868 (trial edn); 1871 (priv. ptd). [The 1871 edn is probably a forgery. See J. Carter and G. Pollard, as above. See also under Idylls of the King.]

Locksley Hall, and the Talking Oak. Boston, 1877.

Locksley Hall Sixty Years after. 1886.

The Lotos Eaters. 1901.

The Lover's Tale. 1833 (trial edn); 1870 (a forgery? See J. Carter and G. Pollard, as above); 1875 (pirated by R. H. Shepherd); 1879.

Lucretius. Cambridge, U.S.A. 1868 (priv. ptd). [A forgery? See J. Carter and G. Pollard, as above.]

Mariana. With Etchings. Worthing, [1863].

Maud, and Other Poems. 1855 (bis); 1856; 1857; 1858; 1859, etc. (17 further edns up to 1893); ed. Elizabeth Wordsworth, 1899.

The May Queen. Illustrated. 1861 [1860].

The Miller's Daughter. Illustrated. [1858.]

Morte d'Arthur; Dora; and other Idyls. 1842. [A forgery? See J. Carter and G. Pollard, as above.] Morte d'Arthur, The Lady of Shalott. Ed. A. Wilson, 1899.

Ode: May the First, 1862, for the Opening of the International Exhibition. 1862. [A forgery? See J. Carter and G. Pollard, as above.]

Ode on the Death of the Duke of Wellington. 1852; 1853; ed. W. K. Leask, 1905.

Ode on the Opening of the Colonial and Indian Exhibition, Tuesday, 4 May 1886. [1886.]

The Princess; a Medley. 1847; 1848; 1850; 1851; 1853; 1854; 1856; 1860 (1st illustrated edn); 1882; 1884 (2nd illustrated edn); ed. P. M. Wallace, 1892; ed. H. Allsopp, Oxford, 1910.

The Promise of May. A Rustic Drama. In Three Acts. 1882 (a forgery? See J. Carter and G. Pollard, as above); 1883.

Property. [1864]. [Afterwards pbd in The Holy Grail and Other Poems, 1870, under amended title of 'Northern Farmer. New Style.']

Queen Mary. A Drama. 1875 (bis). [Produced at Lyceum Theatre, 1876.]

Rifle-Clubs. New York, 1899.

Ring out, wild Bells. [1911.]

The Sailor Boy. 1861. [A forgery? See J. Carter and G. Pollard, as above.]

St Agnes' Eve. [1911.]

The Silent Voices. 1892 (bis; 1 edn with music by Lady Tennyson).

The Throstle. 1889.

Timbuctoo. A Poem which obtained the Lord Chancellor's Medal at Cambridge Commencement, 1829. [Also included in Prolusiones, Cambridge, 1829.]

Tiresias and Other Poems. 1885.

To H.R.H. Princess Beatrice. 1885 (bis) (priv. ptd).

The True and the False. Four Idylls of the King. 1859.

The Victim. Canford Manor (Dorset), 1867 (priv. ptd).

A Welcome to Alexandra. 1863 (bis); 1863 (illustrated).

A Welcome to Her Royal Highness Marie Alexandrovna, Duchess of Edinburgh. 1874 (priv. ptd). [A forgery? See J. Carter and G. Pollard, as above.]

The Window, Or the Loves of the Wrens. Canford Manor (Dorset), 1867 (priv. ptd). First published edn [with music by Sir Arthur Sullivan], 1871 [1870].

[For poems contributed to miscellanies, etc., see T. J. Wise's Bibliography, vol. i, pp. 303 ff.]

(5) CORRESPONDENCE

Alfred Lord Tennyson and Lord Kirby: Unpublished Correspondence. Ed. L. A. Pierce, Toronto, 1929.

[See also the various biographical material, especially that collected by Hallam Tennyson.]

(6) BIOGRAPHY AND CRITICISM

(a) Biographical Studies

Jennings, H. J. Tennyson, a Biographical Sketch. 1884; 1892.

Napier, G. G. Homes and Haunts of Tennyson. 1892.

Ritchie, A. I., Lady. Records of Tennyson, Ruskin and the Brownings. 1892.

Brookfield, Mrs W. H. Early Recollections of Tennyson. Temple Bar, CI, 1894.

Tennyson, H., Baron. Alfred, Lord Tennyson: a Memoir. 2 vols. 1897; 4 vols. 1898–9; 1899.

Cary, E. L. Tennyson. His Homes, his Friends, and his Work. Illustrated. 1898.

Cuthbertson, E. J. Tennyson: the Story of his Life. 1898.

Stephen, Sir L. The Life of Tennyson. [In Studies of a Biographer, vol. ii, 1898.]

Fischer, T. A. Leben und Werke Tennysons. Gotha, 1899.

Rawnsley, H. D. Memories of the Tennysons. Glasgow, 1900; 1912.

Lang, A. Alfred Tennyson. 1901.

Lyall, Sir A. Tennyson. 1902. (English Men of Letters ser.)

MacCabe, W. G. Personal Recollections of Tennyson. 1902.

Chesterton, G. K. and Garnett, R. Tennyson. 1903; 1906.

Weld, A. G. Glimpses of Tennyson and of Some of his Relations and Friends. 1903.

Benson, A. C. Alfred Tennyson. 1904.

di Silvestris Falconieri, F. Lord Tennyson. Rome, 1911.

Turnbull, A. Life and Writings of Alfred Lord Tennyson. 1914.

Lounsbury, T. R. The Life and Times of Tennyson from 1809 to 1850. Ed. W. L. Cross, New Haven, 1915.

Nicolson, H. Tennyson: Aspects of his Life, Character and Poetry. 1923; 1925.

Rawnsley, W. F. Personal Recollections of Tennyson. Nineteenth Century, Jan., Feb. 1925.

Howe, M. A. de W. The Tennysons at Farringford: A Victorian Vista. Drawn from the Unpublished Papers of Mrs James T. Fields. Cornhill Mag. Oct. 1927.

Gosse, Sir E. A First Sight of Tennyson. [In Selected Essays, vol. I, 1928.]

Abercrombie, L. Tennyson. [In Revaluations. Studies in Biography, 1931.]

Tennyson, C. Tennyson Papers. Cornhill Mag. CLIII, 1936.

(b) Critical Studies

Horne, R. H. A New Spirit of the Age. Vol. II, 1844.

Brimley, G. Alfred Tennyson's Poems. [In Cambridge Essays for 1855. Rptd in Essays, ed. W. G. Clark, Cambridge, 1858.]

Gilfillan, G. Galleries of Literary Portraits. Vol. I, 1856.

Dowden, E. Mr Tennyson and Mr Browning. [In Studies in Literature 1789–1877, 1878.]

Bagehot, W. Wordsworth, Tennyson and Browning; or, Pure, Ornate and Grotesque Art in English Poetry. [In Literary Studies, vol. II, 1879. Written 1864.]

Bayne, P. Lessons from my Masters, Carlyle, Tennyson, and Ruskin. 1879.

Swinburne, A. C. Tennyson and Musset. [In Miscellanies, 1886.]

Hutton, R. H. Tennyson. [In Literary Essays, 1888.]

Robertson, J. M. The Art of Tennyson. [In Essays towards a Critical Method, 1889.]

Henley, W. E. Tennyson. [In Views and Reviews, 1890.]

Collins, J. C. Illustrations of Tennyson. 1891.

Waugh, A. Alfred, Lord Tennyson. A Study of his Life and Work. 1892; 1893.

Innes, A. D. Seers and Singers. A Study of Five English Poets. 1893.

Ince, M. New Studies in Tennyson, including a Commentary on Maud. Clifton [1893] (2nd edn).

—— A Handbook to the Works of Alfred Lord Tennyson. 1896; 1902.

Parsons, E. Tennyson's Life and Poetry. Chicago, 1893.

Walters, J. C. Tennyson: Studies. 1893.

Brooke, Stopford A. Tennyson. His Art and Relation to Modern Life. 1894; 2 vols. 1900.

Saintsbury, G. Tennyson. [In Corrected Impressions, 1895.]

—— Tennyson. [In The Later Nineteenth Century, Edinburgh, 1907.]

Barera, E. A Critical Essay on the Works of Alfred, Lord Tennyson. 1896.

Dixon, W. M. A Primer of Tennyson. 1896; 1902.

Jacobs, J. Literary Studies: George Eliot, Tennyson, Browning. 1896.

Van Dyke, H. G. The Poetry of Tennyson. 1898. [With a bibliography.]

Gwynn, S. L. Tennyson: a Critical Study. 1899.

Harrison, F. Tennyson, Ruskin, Mill, and Other Literary Estimates. 1899.

Koeppel, E. Tennyson. Berlin, 1899.

Elton, O. Tennyson. An Inaugural Lecture. Liverpool, 1901. [Rptd in Modern Studies, 1907.]

—— A Survey of English Literature, 1830–1880. Vol. I, 1920.

Blöndal, S. Alfred Tennyson. Reykjavik, 1903.

Jones, Sir H. Tennyson. Proc. British Academy, IV, 1909. [Rptd in Essays on Literature and Education, 1924.]

Ker, W. P. Tennyson: the Leslie Stephen Lecture. 1909. [Rptd in Collected Essays, vol. I, 1925.]

Rawnsley, W. F. Tennyson 1809–1909. A Lecture. 1909.

Sidgwick, A. Tennyson. (A Paper read in Trinity College Chapel, Cambridge, 19 Oct. 1909.) [1909.]

Warren, Sir T. H. The Centenary of Tennyson, 1809–1909. A Lecture. Oxford, 1909. [Rptd in Oxford Lectures on Literature, 1907–1920, 1921.]

Roz, F. Tennyson. Paris, 1911.

Johnson, R. B. Tennyson and his Poetry. 1913.

Browning, E. B. Alfred Tennyson: Notes and Comments. 1919 (priv. ptd).

Browning, R. An Opinion of the Writings of Alfred Lord Tennyson. 1920 (priv. ptd).

Fausset, H. I'A. Tennyson: a Modern Portrait. 1923.

Boas, G. Tennyson and Browning contrasted. 1925.

Mackail, J. W. Tennyson. [In Studies of English Poets, 1926.]

Macnaughton, G. F. A. Tennyson: an Interview. Glasgow, [1928].

Orsini, G. N. G. La Poesia di Alfred Tennyson. 1928.

Lucas, F. L. Tennyson. [In Eight Victorian Poets, Cambridge, 1930.]

Scaife, C. H. O. The Poetry of Alfred Tennyson. 1930.

Wolfe, H. Tennyson. 1930.

Noyes, A. Tennyson. Edinburgh, 1932.

Eliot, T. S. In Memoriam. [In Essays Ancient and Modern, 1936.]

(c) Special Studies

(i) Studies and Reviews of Particular Poems

Poems, chiefly Lyrical

[Bowring, Sir J.] Westminster Rev. Jan. 1831.

[Hallam, A. H.] Englishman's Mag. Aug. 1831. [Rptd in part in Remains in Verse and Prose, 1863.]

[Hunt, Leigh.] Tatler, 24, 26 Feb. 1831.

[Wilson, J.] ('Christopher North'). Blackwood's Mag. XXXI, 1832. [Rptd in Essays Critical and Imaginative, vol. II, 1866. See A. L. Strout, 'Christopher North' on Tennyson, RES. XIV, 1938.]

Poems (1833)

[Croker, J. W.] Quart. Rev. XLIX, 1833. [Often ascribed to J. G. Lockhart; but see Sir H. J. C. Grierson, TLS. 24 April 1937.]

[Mill, J. S.] Tennyson's Poems. London and Westminster Rev. XXX, 1835.

Carlson, C. L. A French Review of Tennyson's 1830 and 1832 Volumes. ELH. III, 1936.

Howell, A. C. Tennyson's 'Palace of Art'—an Interpretation. Stud. Phil. XXXIII, 1936.

Poems (1842)

M[ilnes], R. M. (Baron Houghton). Westminster Rev. Oct. 1842.

[Sterling, J.] Quart. Rev. LXX, 1842. [Rptd in Essays and Tales, ed. J. C. Hare, vol. I, 1848.]

[Mill, J. S.] Westminster Rev. Feb. 1843. [Rptd in Famous Reviews, ed. R. B. Johnson, 1914.]

[Spedding, J.] Edinburgh Rev. April 1843. [Rptd in Reviews and Discussions, 1879.]

Guiliano, A. Essai sur 'Locksley Hall' et 'Locksley Hall Sixty Years After' d'Alfred Tennyson. [In Commentaires et Comparaisons, Turin, 1907.]

Richardson, R. K. The Idea of Progress in 'Locksley Hall.' Trans. Wisconsin Academy, XXVIII, 1933.

Brie, F. Tennysons Ulysses. Ang. LIX, 1935. [See also H. Jensen in Deutschbein Festschrift, Leipzig, 1936.]

In Memoriam

[Kingsley, C.] Fraser's Mag. Sept. 1850. [Rptd in Miscellanies, vol. I, 1859.]

Gatty, A. A Key to Tennyson's In Memoriam. 1881; 1885 (3rd edn).

Chapman, E. R. A Companion to In Memoriam. 1888.

Bradley, A. C. A Commentary on Tennyson's In Memoriam. 1901; 1902 (rev. edn).

Jennings, J. G. An Essay on Metaphor in Poetry, with an Appendix on the Use of Metaphor in Tennyson's In Memoriam. 1915.

Dixon, J. M. The Spiritual Meaning of In Memoriam. New York, 1920.

Maud

Mann, R. J. Maud Vindicated. 1856.

Idylls of the King

[Gladstone, W. E.] Quart. Rev. CVI, 1859. [Rptd in Gleanings of Past Years, vol. II, 1879, and in Famous Reviews, ed. R. B. Johnson, 1914.]

Alford, H. The Idylls of the King. Contemporary Rev. XIII, 1870.

Elsdale, H. Studies in the Idylls. 1878.

Littledale, H. Essays on Lord Tennyson's Idylls of the King. 1893.

Maccallum, M. W. Tennyson's Idylls and Arthurian Story from the Sixteenth Century. 1894.

Jones, R. The Growth of the Idylls of the King. Philadelphia, 1895.

Pallen, C. B. The Meaning of the Idylls of the King. 1904.

Dhaleine, L. A Study on Tennyson's Idylls of the King. 1905.

MacEwen, V. Knights of the Holy Eucharist. [1912.]

Boas, F. S. The Idylls of the King in 1921. Trans. Royal Soc. Literature, 1922.

Lucretius

Jebb, Sir R. C. On Mr Tennyson's Lucretius. Macmillan's Mag. XVIII, 1868.

(ii) Concordances and Reference Books

Langley, S. Concordance to the Works of Alfred Tennyson. 1870.

Baker, A. E. A Concordance to the Poetical and Dramatic Works of Alfred Lord Tennyson. 1914. [Supplement, 1931.]

Baker, A. E. A Tennyson Dictionary; the Characters and Place-Names contained in the Poetical and Dramatic Works of the Poet, alphabetically arranged and described. [1916.]

Catalogue of Autograph MSS. by Lord Tennyson sold by Auction. 1930. [Property of C. B. L. Tennyson.]

(iii) Miscellaneous Studies

S[hepherd], R. H. Tennysoniana. Notes Bibliographical and Critical on Early Poems of Alfred and Charles Tennyson. Opinions of Contemporary Writers. In Memoriam: Various Readings. Various Readings in Later Poems. The Tennyson Portraits. Bibliographical List of Tennyson's Volumes and his Contributions to Periodical Publications. 1866[-75]; 1879 (rev. and enlarged).

Myers, F. W. H. Tennyson as Prophet. Nineteenth Century, xxv, 1889.

Walters, J. C. In Tennyson Land, being a Brief Account of the Home and Early Surroundings of the Poet and an Attempt to identify the Scenes and trace the Influences of Lincolnshire in his Works. 1890.

Salt, H. S. Tennyson as a Thinker. [1893.]

Layard, G. S. Tennyson and his pre-Raphaelite Illustrators. 1894.

The Trees and Flowers of Tennyson. Temple Bar, ciii, 1894.

Nicoll, Sir W. R. and Wise, T. J. Literary Anecdotes of the Nineteenth Century. 2 vols. 1895-6. [Vol. i includes letters about Tennyson from A. H. Hallam to Leigh Hunt, and 'An Opinion on Tennyson' by E. B. Browning. Vol. ii includes 'The Building of the Idylls' and various 'Tennysoniana.']

Masterman, C. F. G. Tennyson as a Religious Teacher. 1900.

Sneath, E. H. The Mind of Tennyson. 1900.

Paul, H. W. The Classical Poems of Tennyson. [In Men of Letters, 1901.]

Ainger, A. The Death of Tennyson. [In Lectures and Essays, 1905.]

Dyboski, R. Über Wortbildung und Wortgebrauch bei Tennyson. Berlin, 1905.

—— Tennysons Sprach und Stil. Vienna, 1907.

Gordon, W. C. The Social Ideals of Alfred Tennyson as related to his Time. 1906.

Leveloh, P. Tennyson und Spenser. Spenser's Einfluss auf Tennyson mit Berücksichtigung von Keats. Marburg, 1909.

Stork, C. W. Heine and Tennyson: an Essay in Comparative Criticism. [In Haverford Essays prepared in Honour of F. B. Gummere, 1909.]

Jurczyk, O. Tennyson. Eine kritische Würdigung zur 100. Wiederkehr seines Geburtstages. E. Studien, xli, 1910.

Lauvrière, E. Repetition and Parallelism in Tennyson. 1910.

Lockyer, Sir N. and W. L. Tennyson as a Student and Poet of Nature. 1910.

Way, A. S. Tennyson and Quintus Calaber. Journ. English Stud. i, 1912-3.

Olivero, F. Sulla Lirica di Alfred Tennyson. Bari, 1915.

Anandasan, K. Kant and Tennyson and Kant and Browning. 1917.

Cross, T. P. Alfred Tennyson as a Celticist. MP. xviii, 1921.

Pyre, J. F. A. The Formation of Tennyson's Style. Madison, 1921.

Staines, de W. T. The Influence of Carlyle upon Tennyson. Texas Rev. vi, 1921.

Japikse, C. G. H. The Dramas of Alfred, Lord Tennyson. Amsterdam, 1926.

Postma, J. Tennyson as seen by his Parodists. Amsterdam, 1926.

Wright, H. G. Tennyson and Wales. E. & S. xiv, 1928.

Bradley, A. C. The Reaction against Tennyson. [In A Miscellany, 1929.]

Bowden, M. M. Tennyson in France. Manchester, 1930.

Tennyson, C. B. L. Tennyson's Unpublished Poems. Nineteenth Century, March–June 1931.

Evans, B. I. Tennyson and the Origins of the Golden Treasury. TLS. 8 Dec. 1932.

[Quiller-Couch, Sir A. T.] Tennyson in 1833. TLS. 14 Sept. 1933. [Rptd in The Poet as Citizen, and Other Papers, Cambridge, 1934.]

Bush, D. The Personal Note in Tennyson's Classical Poems. Toronto University Quart. iv, 1935.

—— Mythology and the Romantic Tradition in English Poetry. Cambridge, U.S.A. 1937.

Roy, P. N. Italian Influence on the Poetry of Tennyson. Benares, 1936.

Weygandt, C. The Time of Tennyson. New York, 1936. [Influence in U.S.]

Potter, G. R. Tennyson and the Biological Theory of Mutability in Species. PQ. xvi, 1937.   G. A. P. B., rev. J. P. C.

ROBERT BROWNING (1812–1889)

(1) Bibliographies

Furnivall, F. J. Bibliography of Robert Browning from 1833 to 1881. Browning Soc. Papers, i, 1881-4.

Anderson, J. P. Bibliography. [In W. Sharp's Life of Robert Browning, 1890.]

Cooke, G. W. A Guide Book to the Poetic and Dramatic Works of Robert Browning. Boston, 1891.

Wise, T. J. A Complete Bibliography of the Writings in Prose and Verse of Robert Browning. 1897 (priv. ptd). [Also included in Literary Anecdotes of the Nineteenth Century, vol. I, 1895, as Materials for a Bibliography of Robert Browning.]

Brooks, A. E. Browningiana in Baylor University. Baylor Bulletin, XXIV, [1921]. [Contains a comprehensive bibliography of criticism, periodical and otherwise.]

(2) COLLECTED WORKS

Poems. A New Edition. 2 vols. 1849. [The first collected edn, comprising Paracelsus and Bells and Pomegranates.]

The Poetical Works. Third Edition. 3 vols. 1863; 6 vols. 1868; 17 vols. 1888–94; [ed. A. Birrell and Sir F. G. Kenyon], 2 vols. 1896; 2 vols. 1898.

The Complete Poetic and Dramatic Works. Boston, 1895. (Cambridge edn.)

The Complete Works. Ed. (with introductions and notes) C. Porter and H. A. Clarke, 12 vols. New York, [1898]. (Florentine edn.)

Poems, containing Dramatic Lyrics, Dramatic Romances, Men and Women, Dramas, Pauline, Paracelsus, Christmas Eve and Easter-Day and Sordello. 1905. (Oxford edn.)

The Works. Ed. (with detailed introduction) Sir F. G. Kenyon, 10 vols. 1912. (Centenary edn.)

The Complete Poetical Works. Ed. A. Birrell, New York, 1915; 2 vols. 1919. [The most nearly complete edn.]

(3) SELECTIONS

Selections from the Poetical Works of Robert Browning. 1863. [Selected by John Forster; authorized by Browning.]

A Selection from the Works of Robert Browning. 1865. [Browning's selection; omits pieces ptd by Forster.]

Selections from the Poetical Works of Robert Browning. 2 sers. 1872–80; 1884. [Browning's selection.]

Pomegranates from an English Garden. Ed. J. M. Gibson, New York, 1885.

Pocket Volume of Selections from the Poetical Works of Robert Browning. 1890. [Arranged chronologically.]

Selections from the Early Poems. Ed. W. H. Griffin, 1902.

A Selection of Poems (1835–1864). Ed. W. T. Young, Cambridge, 1911.

Poems and Plays. Ed. H. E. Joyce, New York, 1922.

Robert Browning: Humanist. A Selection from Browning's Poetry. Ed. A. Compton-Rickett, 1924.

Poems. Ed. F. W. Robinson, 1926.

Selections from the Poems. Ed. H. A. Needham, [1931].

The Shorter Poems of Robert Browning. Ed. W. C. De Vane, New York, 1934.

The Reader's Browning: Selected Poems. Ed. W. Graham, New York, 1934.

(4) SEPARATE PUBLICATIONS

(a) Poetry and Drama

Pauline: A Fragment of a Confession. 1833; ed. T. J. Wise, 1886; ed. N. H. Wallis, 1931.

Paracelsus. 1835; ed. M. L. Lee and K. B. Locock, 1909.

Strafford: an Historical Tragedy. 1837; ed. E. H. Hickey and S. R. Gardiner, 1884.

Sordello. 1840; 1863; ed. H. B. Forman, 1902 (Temple Classics); ed. A. J. Whyte, 1913; tr. French and ed. P. de Reul, Brussels, 1936.

Bells and Pomegranates. 8 nos. 1841–6. [Pippa Passes, 1841; King Victor and King Charles, 1842; Dramatic Lyrics, 1842; The Return of the Druses, 1843; A Blot in the 'Scutcheon, 1843; Colombe's Birthday, 1844; Dramatic Romances and Lyrics, 1845; Luria; and a Soul's Tragedy, 1846. Each no. was pbd separately; when completed the entire series was issued in 1 vol. entitled Bells and Pomegranates, 1846; rptd 2 sers. 1896–7 (ser. 1 with Preface and notes by T. J. Wise).]

Christmas Eve and Easter-Day. A Poem. 1850.

Two Poems. By Elizabeth Barrett Browning and Robert Browning. 1854. [A Plea for the Ragged Schools of London (by Elizabeth Barrett Browning). The Twins. Give and It-shall-be-given-unto-you (by Robert Browning).]

Cleon. 1855. [A forgery? See J. Carter and G. Pollard, An Enquiry into the Nature of Certain Nineteenth Century Pamphlets, 1934. The poem is ptd in Men and Women, 1855.]

The Statue and the Bust. 1855. [Another forgery? See J. Carter and G. Pollard, as above. The poem is also ptd in Men and Women, 1855.]

Men and Women. 2 vols. 1855; ed. H. B. Forman, 1899 (Temple Classics); ed. G. E. Hadow, Oxford, 1911.

Gold Hair: A Legend of Pornic. 1864. [Another forgery? See J. Carter and G. Pollard, as above. The poem is ptd in Dramatis Personae, where it attains its final form in the 2nd edn.]

Dramatis Personae. 1864 (bis).

The Ring and the Book. 4 vols. 1868–9; ed. E. Dowden, 1912 (Oxford edn).

The Old Yellow Book, Source of The Ring and the Book. Ed. facs. and tr. C. W. Hodell, Carnegie Inst. Washington, 1908; [1911] (Everyman's Lib.). [See also E. Koeppel, Ang. xliv, 1912. The original is in the library of Balliol College.]

Balaustion's Adventure; including a Transcript from Euripides [i.e. a trn of the Alcestis]. 1871; ed. E. A. Parker, 1929.

Prince Hohenstiel-Schwangau, Saviour of Society. 1871.

Fifine at the Fair. 1872.

Red Cotton Nightcap Country, or Turf and Towers. 1873.

Aristophanes' Apology; including a Transcript from Euripides: Being the Last Adventure of Balaustion. 1875.

The Inn Album. 1875.

Pacchiarotto, and How He Worked in Distemper; with other Poems. 1876.

The Agamemnon of Aeschylus. Transcribed. 1877.

La Saisiaz: The Two Poets of Croisic. 1878.

Dramatic Idyls. First Series. 1879. Second Series. 1880.

Jocoseria. 1883.

Ferishtah's Fancies. 1884.

Parleyings with Certain People of Importance in their Day. Introduced by a Dialogue between Apollo and the Fates: concluded by another between John Fust and his Friends. 1887.

Asolando: Fancies and Facts. 1890 [1889].

New Poems by Robert Browning and Elizabeth Barrett Browning. Ed. Sir F. G. Kenyon, 1914.

[For full list of poems which first appeared in periodicals, see bibliography by J. P. Anderson attached to William Sharp's Life of Browning, 1890. For early trns of Browning into German and French respectively, see W. L. Phelps, Browning in Germany, MLN. xxviii, 1913, and Browning in France, MLN. xxxi, 1916. See also A. J. Armstrong, Browning the World Over (1. Browning's International Influence; 2. A Bibliography of Foreign Browningiana), Waco (Texas), 1933.]

(b) Prose (other than Letters)

Introductory Essay. [Prefixed to the forged Letters of Percy Bysshe Shelley, 1852.] Ed. F. J. Furnivall, Browning Soc. 1881 (as On the Poet, Objective and Subjective); ed. W. T. Harden, Shelley Soc. 1888; ed. R. Garnett, 1914; ed. H. F. B. Brett-Smith, Oxford, 1921.

The Divine Order, and Other Sermons and Addresses, by Thomas Jones. Ed. B. Jones, 1884. [Short introduction by Browning.]

Robert Browning's Prose Life of Strafford. 1892; ed. Sir C. H. Firth and F. J. Furnivall, Browning Soc. 1892.

(5) Letters

[For letters to or from Elizabeth Barrett Browning, see p. 250 above.]

Letters from Robert Browning to Various Correspondents. Ed. T. J. Wise. Ser. 1. 2 vols. 1895 (priv. ptd). Ser. 2, 2 vols. 1907–8 (priv. ptd).

Letters to T. J. Wise and Other Correspondents. 1912 (priv. ptd).

Letter to Sarianne Browning on the Death of Elizabeth Barrett Browning. 1916 (priv. ptd).

The Browning Society. Being Letters from Robert Browning to James Dykes Campbell. [With an introduction by C. K. Shorter.] 1917.

Letters to my Son. [With an introduction by C. K. Shorter.] 1917.

The Last Hours of Elizabeth Barrett Browning [a letter] by Robert Browning. 1919 (priv. ptd).

Edward FitzGerald and Elizabeth Barrett Browning. 1919 (priv. ptd). [3 letters from Browning to his son on FitzGerald's criticism of Mrs Browning.]

Critical Comments on A. C. Swinburne and D. G. Rossetti. With an Anecdote relating to W. M. Thackeray. 1919 (priv. ptd).

Letters from Le Croisic. [With an introduction by Sir E. Gosse.] 1919 (priv. ptd).

Some Records of Walter Savage Landor [in 3 letters from Browning to Isa Blagden]. 1919 (priv. ptd).

Reflections on the Franco-Prussian War. 1919 (priv. ptd).

An Opinion on the Writings of Alfred Lord Tennyson, with a Statement of his Changed Views regarding Percy Bysshe Shelley. 1920 (priv. ptd).

Letters to his Son R. W. B. Browning and his Daughter-in-Law Fanny Browning. 1920 (priv. ptd).

Deux Lettres inédites à Joseph Milsand. Ed. W. Thomas, Revue Germanique, xii, 1921, xiv, 1923.

An Account of the Illness and Death of his Father, Robert Browning the second. With Further Records of Walter Savage Landor. 1921 (priv. ptd).

Letters to Miss Isa Blagden. Ed. A. J. Armstrong, Waco (Texas), 1923.

Letters of Robert Browning. Collected by Thomas J. Wise. Ed. T. L. Hood, New Haven, 1933. [Includes all the items previously priv. ptd by Wise.]

Intimate Glimpses from Browning's Letter File; selected from Letters in the Baylor University Browning Collection. Ed. R. A. Young, Waco (Texas), 1934.

Twenty-two Unpublished Letters of Elizabeth Barrett Browning and Robert Browning addressed to Henrietta and Anabella Moulton-Barrett. New York, 1935.

From Robert and Elizabeth Browning: a further Selection of the Barrett-Browning Family Correspondence. Ed. W. R. Benét, 1936.

Robert Browning and Julia Wedgwood: a Broken Friendship as revealed in their Letters. Ed. R. Curle, 1937.

(6) BIOGRAPHY AND CRITICISM

[For literature relating to the Brownings jointly, see Browningiana, p. 251 above.]

(a) Biographical Studies

Gosse, Sir E. Robert Browning: Personalia. 1890.

Sharp, W. Life of Robert Browning. 1890.

Orr, A. (Mrs Sutherland). Life and Letters of Robert Browning. 1891; rev. Sir F. G. Kenyon, 1908.

Waugh, A. Robert Browning. 1900.

Chesterton, G. K. Browning. 1903. (English Men of Letters ser.)

Dowden, E. The Life of Robert Browning. 1904; [1915] (Everyman's Lib.).

Kenyon, Sir F. G. Robert Browning and Alfred Domett. 1906.

Griffin, W. H. and Minchin, H. C. The Life of Robert Browning. With Notices of his Writings, his Family, and his Friends. [1910]; 1938 (rev.).

Sim, F. M. Robert Browning, the Poet and the Man, 1833–1846. 1912; 1923.

—— Robert Browning, Poet and Philosopher, 1850–1889. 1923; 1925.

—— Robert Browning. [1931.]

Drinkwater, J. Some Letters from Matthew Arnold to Robert Browning. Cornhill Mag. Dec. 1923.

Holt, O. S. A Visitor to the Brownings at Casa Guidi. Cornhill Mag. Jan. 1924.

Browning, Fanny (Mrs R. W. B. Browning). Some Memories of Robert Browning. New York, 1928.

Hood, T. L. Browning and Lady Ashburton. Yale Rev. xxi, 1932.

Moore, T. Sturge. Michael Field and Robert Browning. Cornhill Mag. Jan., Feb. 1932.

Hovelaque, H.-L. La Jeunesse de Browning. Paris, 1932.

Howe, M. L. Robert Browning and William Allingham. Stud. Phil. xxxi, 1934.

(b) Critical Studies

[Early reviews, etc. are listed and quoted in F. J. Furnivall's bibliography, Browning Soc. Papers, i, 1881–4, pp. 89–108, 125–50.]

Horne, R. H. A New Spirit of the Age. Vol. ii, 1844.

Nettleship, J. T. Essays on Robert Browning's Poetry. 1868; 1890 (expanded as Robert Browning. Essays and Thoughts); 1895.

Dowden, E. Mr Tennyson and Mr Browning. [In Studies in Literature 1789–1877, 1878.]

Bagehot, W. Wordsworth, Tennyson and Browning; Or, Pure, Ornate, and Grotesque Art in English Poetry. [In Literary Studies, vol. ii, 1879. Written 1864.]

Browning Society's Papers. 1881–95.

Birrell, A. The Alleged Obscurity of Mr Browning's Poetry. [In Obiter Dicta, 1885.]

Orr, A. (Mrs Sutherland). A Handbook to the Works of Browning. 1885; 1887 (rev. edn).

Chicago Browning Society. Robert Browning's Poetry. Outline Studies. Chicago, 1886.

Symons, A. An Introduction to the Study of Browning. 1886; 1906.

Fotheringham, J. Studies in the Poetry of Robert Browning. 1887; 1888.

—— Studies of the Mind and Art of Robert Browning. 1898; 1900 (4th cdn).

Corson, H. An Introduction to the Study of Robert Browning's Poetry. Boston, 1888, 1903 (rev.).

Hutton, R. H. Mr Browning. [In Literary Essays, 1888 (rev. edn).]

—— Robert Browning. [In the Footsteps of the Poets, by D. Masson and others, [1893].]

MacCormick, W. S. The Poetry of Robert Browning. [In Three Lectures on English Literature, 1889.]

Jacobs, J. George Eliot, Matthew Arnold, Browning, Newman. Essays and Reviews from the 'Athenaeum.' 1891.

Innes, A. D. Seers and Singers: a Study of Five English Poets. 1893.

Saintsbury, G. Browning. [In Corrected Impressions, 1895.]

Berdoe, E. et al. Browning Studies. Being Select Papers by Members of the Browning Society. 1895.

Jusserand, J.-J. Histoire abregée de la Littérature anglaise. Paris, 1896.

Thomson, James. Notes on the Genius of Robert Browning. [In Biographical and Critical Studies, 1896.]

Quayle, W. A. The Poet's Poet, Robert Browning. Cincinnati, 1897.

Boston Browning Society Papers, selected to represent the Work of the Society from 1886 to 1897. 1897.

Cary, E. L. Browning, Poet and Man. A Survey. 1899.

Little, M. Essays on Robert Browning. 1899.

Santayana, G. The Poetry of Barbarism. [In Interpretations of Poetry and Religion, 1900.]

Pater, W. Robert Browning. [In Essays from The Guardian, 1901.]

Pigou, A. C. Robert Browning as a Religious Teacher. 1901.

Brooke, S. A. The Poetry of Robert Browning. 1902; 2 vols. 1905.

Flew, J. Studies in Browning. 1904; 1915.

Parrott, T. M. The Vitality of Browning. [In Studies of a Book Lover, 1904.]

Herford, C. H. Robert Browning. 1905.

More, P. E. Why is Browning Popular? [In Shelburne Essays, ser. 3, New York, 1905.]

Inge, W. R. The Mysticism of Robert Browning. [In Studies of English Mystics, 1906.]

Ker, W. P. Browning. E. & S. i, 1910. [Rptd in Collected Essays, vol. i, 1925.]

Schmidt, K. Robert Browning als Dichter und Mensch. Tauberbischofsheim, 1910.

Gingerich, S. F. Wordsworth, Tennyson and Browning. Ann Arbor, 1911.

Berger, P. Robert Browning. Paris, 1912.

Koeppel, E. Robert Browning. Berlin, 1912.

Pellegrini, L. Studi sulla Poesia di Roberto Browning. Naples, 1912.

Rhys, E. Browning and his Poetry. 1914.

Phelps, W. L. Browning: How to know him. Indianapolis, 1915, 1932 (rev. edn).

Scott, Dixon. The Homeliness of Browning. [In Men of Letters, 1916.]

Skemp, A. Robert Browning. 1916.

Powell, J. W. The Confessions of a Browning-Lover. [1918.]

Woodberry, G. E. Late Victorian Verse: Browning, Swinburne, Tennyson. [In Studies of a Litterateur, 1921.]

Winchester, C. Browning. [In An Old Castle and Other Essays, New York, 1922.]

Hearn, L. Studies in Browning. [In Pre-Raphaelite and Other Poets, ed. J. Erskine, New York, 1923.]

Grierson, Sir H. J. C. Tennyson, Browning and some Others. [In Lyrical Poetry from Blake to Hardy, 1928.]

Reul, P. de. L'Art et la Pensée de Robert Browning. Brussels, 1929.

Russell, F. T. One More Word on Browning. Palo Alto, 1929.

Lucas, F. L. Eight Victorian Poets. Cambridge, 1930.

Duckworth, F. R. G. Browning: Background and Conflict. New York, 1931.

Brockington, A. A. Browning and the Twentieth Century. Oxford, 1932.

De Vane, W. C. A Browning Handbook. New York, 1935. [With selective bibliography, list of uncollected poems, etc.]

Charlton, H. B. Browning: the Poet's Aim. John Rylands Lib. Bulletin, xxii, 1938.

—— Browning as Dramatist. John Rylands Lib. Bulletin, xxiii, 1939.

(c) Special Studies
(i) Studies of Particular Works

Pauline.

Wallis, N. H. A Study of Pauline. [In The Ethics of Criticism, 1924.]

Phelps, W. L. Notes. MLN. xlvii, 1932.

Paracelsus.

Raymond, W. O. Browning's Conception of Love as represented in Paracelsus. Papers of Michigan Academy of Sciences, iv, 1924.

Goldschmidt, E. Der Gedankengehalt von Robert Browning's Paracelsus. E. Studien, lxviii, 1933.

Boas, F. S. Quart. Rev. cclxv, 1935.

Strafford.

Somervell, D. C. London Mercury, xlii, 1927.

Sordello.

Dowden, E. Mr Browning's Sordello. [In Transcripts and Studies, 1896 (2nd edn).]

Omond, T. S. Browning's Sordello: a Commentary. 1906.

Thomson, E. H. The Tragedy of a Troubadour. An Appreciation and Interpretation of Browning's Sordello. 1914.

Brocher, H. La Jeunesse de Browning et le Poème de Sordello. Geneva, 1930.

De Vane, W. C. Stud. Phil. xxvii, 1930.

Heuer, H. Zum Formproblem in Browning's Sordello. E. Studien, lxvii, 1933.

Hovelaque, H.-L. Browning's English in Sordello. Paris, 1933.

Holmes, S. W. The Sources of Browning's Sordello. Stud. Phil. xxxiv, 1937.

Pippa Passes.

Gabriel, M. The Jules-Phene Episode. Papers of Michigan Academy of Sciences, xii, 1930.

A Toccata of Galuppi's.

Bitzkat, F. Robert Browning's A Toccata of Galuppi's. E. Studien, lvii, 1923, lix, 1925.

Childe Roland.

Gloder, H. Childe Roland. PMLA. xxxix, 1924.

De Vane, W. C. The Landscape of Childe Roland. PMLA. xl, 1925.

The Pied Piper of Hamelin.

Thompson, S. P. The Pied Piper of Hamelin. Sette of Odd Volumes, No. 53, 1905. [An enquiry into the sources.]

Dickson, A. Browning's Source for The Pied Piper of Hamelin. Stud. Phil. xxiii, 1926.

A Grammarian's Funeral.

Heuer, H. [In Deutschbein Festschrift, Leipzig, 1936.]

Porphyria's Lover.

Tracy, C. R. MLN. lii, 1937.

My Last Duchess.

Bitzkat, F. Zeitschrift für französische und englische Unterricht, xxiv, 1925.

Rea, J. D. Stud. Phil. xxix, 1932.

Friedland, L. S. Ferrara and My Last Duchess. Stud. Phil. xxxiii, 1936.

Luria—A Tragedy.

Ruete, E. Browning's Luria. Bremen, 1910.

A Soul's Tragedy.

Tupper, J. W. A Soul's Tragedy. A Defence of Chiappino. E. Studien, xliv, 1912.

Christmas-Eve and Easter-Day.

Göritz, K. 'Christmas-Eve and Easter-Day' und Das Leben Jesu von D. F. Strauss. Archiv, cxlvii, 1924.

Crawford, A. W. Methodist Rev. cx, 1927.

Cleon.

Crawford, A. W. JEGP. xxvi, 1927.

Saul.

Crawford, A. W. Queen's Quart xxxiv, 1927.

Nykoff, G. S. A Possible Source. PQ. vii, 1928.

Epilogue to Dramatis Personae.

Kirkconnell, W. MLN. xli, 1926.

Gold Hair.

Dominique, J. Le Poète Browning à Sainte-Marie-de-Pornic. La Légende de la Chevelure d'Or. Vannes, 1900. [An historical account of the facts about the poem 'Gold Hair' and Browning's visit to Sainte-Marie-de-Pornic.]

Caliban upon Setebos.

Tracy, C. R. Stud. Phil. xxxv, 1938.

The Ring and the Book.

Meyer-Franck, H. Robert Browning, 'The Ring and the Book.' Eine Interpretation. Göttingen, 1912.

Treves, Sir F. The Country of the Ring and the Book. 1913.

Cook, A. K. A Commentary upon Browning's The Ring and the Book. 1920.

Shaw, J. E. The 'Donna Angelicata' in the Ring and the Book. PMLA. xli, 1926.

Phelps, W. L. Yale Rev. xviii, 1928.

Raymond, W. O. MLN. xliii, 1928.

Snitslaar, L. Sidelights on The Ring and the Book. Amsterdam, 1934.

Pettigrew, H. P. The Early Vogue of The Ring and the Book. Archiv, clxix, 1936.

McElderry, B. R. TLS. 22 May 1937. [Contemporary reviews.]

Fifine at the Fair.

De Vane, W. C. The Relation between Rossetti's Jenny and Browning's Fifine. Stud. Phil. xxix, 1932.

Raymond, W. O. Browning's Dark Mood: a Study of Fifine. Stud. Phil. xxxi, 1934.

Aristophanes' Apology.

Jackson, C. N. Classical Elements in Browning's Aristophanes' Apology. Harvard Stud. in Classical Philology, xx, 1909.

Tisdel, F. M. Missouri University Stud. ii, 1927.

Cenciaja.

Knickerbocker, K. C. PQ. xiii, 1934.

Ferishtah's Fancies.

Bevan, T. W. Holborn Rev. July 1928.

Parleyings with Certain People.

De Vane, W. C. Browning's Parleyings. The Autobiography of a Mind. New Haven, 1927.

(ii) Concordances and Books of Reference

Berdoe, E. The Browning Cyclopaedia, a Guide to the Study of the Works of Robert Browning: with Copious Explanatory Notes and References on All Difficult Passages. 1892; 1905 (3rd edn).

Molineux, M. A. A Phrase-Book from the Poetic and Dramatic Works of Robert Browning. To which is added an Index containing the Significant Words not elsewhere noted. Cambridge, U.S.A. 1900.

Broughton, L. N. and Stelter, B. F. A Concordance to the Poems of Robert Browning. 2 vols. New York, 1924–5.

(iii) Miscellaneous Studies

Westcott, B. F. On some Points in Browning's View of Life. A Paper read at Cambridge. 1883.

Furnivall, F. J. How the Browning Society came into being. With some Words on Browning's Early and Late Work. 1884.

—— Robert Browning's Ancestors. [1890.] [See also Furnivall's various contributions to the Browning Soc. papers, bibliographical and miscellaneous.]

Berdoe, E. Browning's Message to his Time. His Religion, Philosophy and Science. 1890; 1897 (4th edn).
—— Browning and the Christian Faith. 1896.
Forster, J. Four Great Teachers: John Ruskin, Thomas Carlyle, R. W. Emerson and Robert Browning. 1890.
Jones, Sir H. Browning as a Philosophical and Religious Teacher. 1891; 1912.
Stefánnson, J. Robert Browning: et Literaturbillede fra det moderne England. Copenhagen, 1891. [See O. Jespersen, Dr J. Stefánnson's Bog om Robert Browning, Copenhagen, 1893.]
Parrott, T. M. An Examination of the Non-Dramatic Poems of Robert Browning's First and Second Periods. Leipzig, 1893.
Lawton, W. C. The Classical Element in Browning's Poetry. AJ. Phil. xvii, 1896.
Machen, M. G. The Bible in Browning. New York, 1903.
Stephen, Sir L. Browning's Casuistry. Living Age, 31 Jan. 1903.
Naish, E. M. Browning and Dogma. Seven Lectures on Browning's Attitude towards Dogmatic Religion. 1906.
Stubbs, C. W. The Christ of English Poetry. (Cynewulf, Langland, Shakespeare and Browning.) 1906.
Berger, P. Quelques Aspects de la Foi moderne dans les Poèmes de Robert Browning. Paris, 1907.
Campbell, L. B. The Grotesque in the Poetry of Robert Browning. Austin, [1907].
Clarke, Helen A. Browning's Italy. New York, 1907.
Curry, S. S. Browning and the Dramatic Monologue. Boston, 1908.
Ell'ott, G. R. Shakespeare's Significance for Browning. Ang. xxxii, 1909.
—— The Whitmanism of Browning. [In The Cycle of Modern Poetry, Princeton, 1929.]
Schmidt, Karl. Robert Brownings Verhältnis zu Frankreich. Berlin, 1909.
Albrecht, R. Robert Brownings Verhältnis zu Deutschland. Munich, 1912.
Lounsbury, T. R. The Early Literary Career of Robert Browning. Four Letters. 1912.
Mayne, E. C. Browning's Heroines. 1913.
Phelps, W. L. Browning in Germany. MLN. xxviii, 1913.
—— Browning in France. MLN. xxxi, 1916.
—— Robert Browning on Spiritualism. Yale Rev. xxiii, 1933.
Hogrefe, P. Browning and Italian Art and Artists. Kansas University Bulletin, 1914.
Anandasan, K. B. D. Kant and Tennyson and Kant and Browning. 1917.
Palmer, G. H. The Monologue of Browning. Harvard Theological Rev. April 1918.

Bonnell, J. K. Touch Images in the Poetry of Robert Browning. PMLA. xxxvii, 1922.
Hood, T. H. Browning's Ancient Classical Sources. Harvard Stud. in Classical Philology, xxxiii, 1922.
Burt, E. J. The Seen and Unseen in Browning. Oxford, 1923.
Pottle, F. A. Shelley and Browning. A Myth and some Facts. Chicago, 1923.
Drinkwater, J. Browning's Diction. [In Victorian Poetry, 1924.]
Jones, R. M. Mysticism in Browning. New York, 1924.
Wenger, C. N. The Aesthetics of Robert Browning. Ann Arbor, 1924.
Babington, P. L. Browning and Calverley: or Poem and Parody. 1925.
Boas, G. Tennyson and Browning contrasted. 1925.
Du Bos, C. Notes sur Browning en France. [In Approximations, ser. 2, Paris, 1925.]
Massey, B. W. A. Browning's Vocabulary. N. & Q. 8, 15 Aug., 12 Sept., 10 Oct. 1925.
Lengefield, H. von. Die Lyrik Robert Brownings vor 1868. Marburg, 1925.
Cressman, E. D. Classical Poems of Robert Browning. Classical Journ. xxiii, 1927.
Hatcher, H. H. The Versification of Robert Browning. Columbus, 1928.
Raymond, W. O. Browning and Higher Criticism. PMLA. xliv, 1929.
Somervell, D. C. The Reputation of Robert Browning. E. & S. xv, 1929.
Spindler; R. Robert Browning und die Antike. Leipzig, 1930.
Alekseev, M. Zur Entstehungsgeschichte der 'Dramatic Idylls.' E. Studien, lxvi, 1931.
Lieberman, J. B. Robert Browning and Hebraism. Jerusalem, 1934.
Heuer, H. Browning und die englische Romantik. Zeitschrift für neusprachlichen Unterricht, xxxiv, 1935.
—— Browning und Donne. E. Studien, lxxii, 1938.
Knickerbocker, K. L. Browning and his Critics. Sewanee Rev. xliii, 1935.
Du Bois, A. E. Robert Browning, Dramatist. Stud. Phil. xxxiii, 1936.
Roberts, W. W. Music in Browning. Music and Letters, xvii, 1936.
Tracy, C. R. Browning's Heresies. Stud. Phil. xxxiii, 1936.

ARTHUR HUGH CLOUGH (1819–1861)

(1) COLLECTED WORKS

Poems. With a Memoir [by F. T. Palgrave]. 1862; 1863; 1871; 1883; 1888 (rev. edn); ed. C. Whibley, 1913.
Poems. With an Introduction by C. E. Norton. Boston, 1862.

Letters and Remains of A. H. Clough. 1865.
The Poems and Prose Remains of A. H.
Clough. With a Selection from his Letters
and a Memoir. Edited by his Wife. 2 vols.
1869; 1870. [Prose Remains rptd separately
1888.]
The Poetical Works of A. H. Clough. With a
Memoir by F. T. Palgrave. [1906.] (Muses'
Lib.)

(2) SELECTED POEMS

Selections from the Poems of A. H. Clough.
1894. (Golden Treasury Ser.)
The Bothie and Other Poems. Ed. E. Rhys,
1896.
Poems of Clough, including Ambarvalia, Both
Versions of the Bothie, Amours de Voyage,
etc. Ed. H. S. Milford, 1910.

(3) SEPARATE PUBLICATIONS

The Longest Day. A Poem written at Rugby
School. [1836.]
A Consideration of Objections against the
Retrenchment Association. Oxford, 1847.
The Bothie of Toper-na-Fuosich. A Long-
Vacation Pastoral. Oxford, 1848; Cam-
bridge, U.S.A. 1849.
Ambarvalia. Poems. By T. Burbidge and
Arthur H. Clough. 1849. [Separate issue
of Clough's contributions, [1850].]
Greek History from Themistocles to Alex-
ander in a series of Lives from Plutarch.
Revised and arranged [with a preface] by
A. H. Clough. 1860.
Plutarch's Lives. The Translation called
Dryden's, corrected from the Greek and
revised [with an introduction] by A. H.
Clough. 5 vols. Boston, 1864; 1874; 1876;
1902; ed. E. Rhys, 3 vols. 1910 (Everyman's
Lib.).

(4) BIOGRAPHY AND CRITICISM

Sidgwick, H. The Poems and Prose Remains
of Arthur Hugh Clough. Westminster Rev.
Oct. 1869. [Rptd in Miscellaneous Essays
and Addresses, 1904.]
Hutton, R. H. Essays, Theological and
Literary. Vol. II, 1877.
—— Literary Essays. 1888 (3rd edn).
—— Brief Literary Criticisms. 1906.
Bagehot, W. The Poems of Clough. [In
Literary Studies, vol. II, 1879.]
Waddington, S. Arthur Hugh Clough; a
Monograph. 1883.
Hudson, W. H. Studies in Interpretation. 1896.
Robertson, J. M. New Essays towards a
Critical Method. 1897.
Huth, A. Über A. H. Clough's 'The Bothie of
Toper-na-Fuosich.' Ein Beitrag zur engli-
schen Literaturgeschichte des 19. Jahr-
hunderts. Leipzig, 1911.

Lutonsky, Paula. Arthur Hugh Clough.
Vienna, 1912.
Brooke, S. A. Four Poets: Clough, Arnold,
Rossetti, Morris. 1913.
Guyot, E. Essai sur la Formation philoso-
phique du Poète Clough: Pragmatisme et
Intellectualisme. Paris, 1913.
Osborne, J. I. Arthur Hugh Clough. 1920.
Williams, S. T. Studies in Victorian Litera-
ture. New York, [1923].
Turner, A. M. A Study of Clough's Mari
Magno. PMLA. XLIV, 1929.
Lucas, F. L. Clough. [In Eight Victorian
Poets, Cambridge, 1930.]
Garrod, H. W. Clough. [In Poetry and the
Criticism of Life, Oxford, 1931.]
The Letters of Matthew Arnold to A. H.
Clough. Ed. H. F. Lowry, 1932.
Ehrsam, T. G. and Deily, R. H. Bibliographies
of Twelve Victorian Authors. New York,
1936. [Books and articles about Clough.]
Levy, G. Arthur Hugh Clough. 1938.

G. A. P. B., rev. J. P. C.

MATTHEW ARNOLD (1822–1888)*

(1) BIBLIOGRAPHY

Smart, T. B. The Bibliography of Matthew
Arnold. 1892. [Rev. and expanded in The
Works, vol. XV, 1904, but omitting the list of
criticisms and reviews of Arnold's writings.]
Wise, T. J. Catalogue of the Ashley Library.
Vol. I, 1922.

(2) COLLECTED WORKS

The Works of Matthew Arnold. (Edition de
Luxe.) 15 vols. 1903–4.

(3) POETICAL WORKS

(a) Collected Poems

Poems. A New and Complete Edition.
Boston, 1856.
Poems. 2 vols. 1869. [Vol. I, Narrative and
Elegiac Poems; vol. II, Dramatic and Lyric
Poems.]
Poems. New and Complete Edition. 2 vols.
1877; New York, [1880?]; 2 vols. 1881;
2 vols. New York, 1883.
Poems. (Library Edition.) 3 vols. 1885;
3 vols. 1888; 3 vols. 1895. [Vol. I, Early
Poems, Narrative Poems, and Sonnets;
vol. II, Lyric and Elegiac Poems; vol. III,
Dramatic and Later Poems. The first com-
plete collection and the last supervised by
Arnold himself.]
The Poetical Works. 1890. (Globe edn.)
Alaric at Rome and Other Poems [1840–69].
Ed. R. Garnett, 1896; 1913.

* Revised by Professor T. H. V. Motter.

19

The Strayed Reveller, Empedocles on Etna and Other Poems. Ed. W. Sharpe, 1896. [Includes contents of 1852 and 1853 collections.]

Poems. Ed. A. C. Benson, 1900.

Poems, Narrative, Elegiac and Lyric. Ed. H. B. Forman, 1900. (Temple Classics.)

Dramatic and Early Poems. Ed. H. B. Forman, 1902. (Temple Classics.)

Poems (prior to 1864). Ed. L. Magnus, [1906]. (Muses' Lib.)

Dramas and Prize Poems. Ed. L. Magnus, [1906]. (Muses' Lib.)

The Poems, 1849–1864. Ed. Sir A. T. Quiller-Couch, 1906; rev. G. St Quintin, 1926. (World's Classics.)

The Poems, 1840–1866. Ed. R. A. Scott-James, 1908. (Everyman's Lib.)

The Poems, 1840–1867. With an Introduction by Sir A. T. Quiller-Couch. Ed. H. S. M[ilford], 1909, etc. (Oxford edn.)

(b) Selected Poems

Selected Poems. 1878, etc. [Selected by Arnold himself.]

Poems. Ed. G. C. Macaulay, 1896; 1928 (enlarged edn).

Selected Poems. Ed. A. Waugh, 2 vols. 1905.

Sohrab and Rustum, and Other Poems. Ed. W. P. Trent and W. T. Brewster, Boston, 1906.

Selected Poems. Ed. H. B. George and A. M. Leigh, Oxford, 1909.

(c) Separate Publications

Alaric at Rome. A Prize Poem, recited in Rugby School, June xii, MDCCCXL. Rugby, 1840; ed. type-facs. T. J. Wise, 1893 (priv. ptd).

Cromwell: a prize poem. Recited in the Theatre, Oxford, 28 June 1843. Oxford, 1843; 1863; 1891. [Also rptd in Oxford Prize Poems, 1846.]

The Strayed Reveller, and Other Poems. By A. 1849.

Empedocles on Etna, and Other Poems. By A. 1852.

Poems. A New Edition. 1853. [Of the 23 poems, or groups of poems, included 15 were rptd, often in rev. form, from the two preceding collections. 'Sohrab and Rustum' and 'The Scholar Gipsy' were among the new poems. There was also a long critical 'Preface.']

Poems. Second Edition. 1854. [Drops 5 of the poems in the 1853 collection and re-arranges some of the others, adding 'A Farewell' (already ptd in the 1852 collection) to the 'Switzerland' group and an additional 'Preface.']

Poems. Second Series. 1855. [Largely made up out of poems in the earlier collections rejected in Poems, 1854; but includes 'Balder Dead' and 1 other new poem.]

Poems. Third Edition. 1857. [A rpt of 1854, adding only a new piece to the 'Switzerland' group.]

Merope. A Tragedy. 1858; ed. J. C. Collins, Oxford, 1906 (with a trn of Sophocles' Electra by R. Whitelaw), 1917 (rev. edn).

Saint Brandan. 1867. [A forgery? See J. Carter and G. Pollard, An Enquiry into the Nature of Certain Nineteenth Century Pamphlets, 1934. 'Saint Brandan' had been ptd in Fraser's Mag. July 1860, and was rptd in New Poems, 1867.]

New Poems. 1867; Boston, 1867; 1868; Boston, 1868. [Includes 26 poems, or groups of poems, not previously collected, together with 6 poems rptd, or re-cast, from the 1852 collection.]

Geist's Grave. 1881 (priv. ptd). [A forgery? See J. Carter and G. Pollard, as above. The poem appeared in Fortnightly Rev. Jan. 1881.]

Kaiser Dead: a Poem. [Philadelphia, 1887.] [Rptd from Fortnightly Rev. July 1887.]

Sohrab and Rustum. Ed. H. W. B. Moreno, 1909.

[For poems first ptd in periodicals and miscellanies, see The Works, vol. xv, 1904, pp. 354–5.]

(4) Prose Works

(a) Selected Prose

Passages from the Prose Writings of Matthew Arnold. 1880. [Selected by Arnold himself.]

Essays Literary and Critical. Ed. G. K. Chesterton, [1906]. (Everyman's Lib.)

Essays, including Essays in Criticism 1865, On Translating Homer (with F. W. Newman's Reply), and Five Other Essays now for the First Time Collected. 1914. (Oxford edn).

Selected Essays. Ed. H. G. Rawlinson, 1924.

Selections from Matthew Arnold's Prose. Ed. D. C. Somervell, 1924.

Representative Essays. Ed. E. K. Brown, Toronto, 1936.

(b) Separate Publications

England and the Italian Question. 1859.

The Popular Education of France, with notices of that of Holland and Switzerland. 1861.

On Translating Homer. Three Lectures given at Oxford. 1861; ed. W. H. D. Rouse, 1905.

On Translating Homer: Last Words. A Lecture given at Oxford. 1862. [Popular edn, 1896, comprises the two works issued in 1861 and 1862 respectively.]

Heinrich Heine. Philadelphia, 1863. [Rptd from Cornhill Mag. Aug. 1863.]

A French Eton; or, Middle Class Education and the State. 1864. [Rptd 1892 in vol. containing also Schools and Universities in France, being part of a volume on 'Schools and Universities on the Continent' pbd in 1868.]

Essays in Criticism. [Ser. 1], 1865; 1869 (condenses 'Preface' and enlarges 'Spinoza' as 'Spinoza and the Bible'); 1875 (adds A Persian Passion Play); 1884, etc.; rptd 1907 ('with the addition of two essays [viz. Dante and Beatrice, The Jewish Church] not hitherto reprinted'); ed. C. A. Miles and L. Smith, Oxford, 1918.

On the Study of Celtic Literature. 1867; New York, 1883; ed. A. Nutt, 1910; ed. E. Rhys, 1910 (with other critical essays and a supplement by Lord Strangford and D. W. Nash) (Everyman's Lib.)

Schools and Universities on the Continent. 1868. [Part relating to Germany rptd separately as Higher Schools and Universities in Germany, 1874, 1882.]

Culture and Anarchy: an Essay in Political and Social Criticism. 1869; 1875; 1882; New York, 1883; 1889; ed. J. D. Wilson, Cambridge, 1931.

St Paul and Protestantism; with an introduction on Puritanism and the Church of England. 1870 (bis); 1875; New York, 1883; 1887.

Friendship's Garland: being the Conversations, Letters and Opinions of the late Arminius, Baron Von Thunder-Ten-Tronckh. Collected and Edited with a Dedicatory Letter to Adolescens Leo, Esq. of the Daily Telegraph. 1871; 1897; 1903.

Literature and Dogma. An Essay towards a better apprehension of the Bible. 1873 (3 edns); New York, 1873; 1874; 1876 (references to all Bible quotations supplied for the first time); New York, 1877; 1883; New York, 1883; tr. French, Paris, 1876.

God and the Bible: a review of objections to Literature and Dogma. 1875; New York, 1883; 1884.

Last Essays on Church and Religion. 1877; 1903.

Mixed Essays. 1879; 1880; New York, 1880; 1903.

Irish Essays and Others. 1882; 1891.

Emerson. New York, 1884; [Cambridge, U.S.A. 1884] ('from the author's MS for his use in the lecture room').

Discourses in America. 1885; 1889; 1896; New York, 1902.

Education Department. Special Report on Certain Points connected with Elementary Education in Germany, Switzerland and France. 1886; 1888 (issued by Education Reform League).

General Grant; an Estimate. Boston, 1887.

Essays in Criticism. Second Series. 1888; 1889; 1891; 1895, etc. (Eversley Ser.)

Civilization in the United States. First and Last Impressions of America. Boston, 1888 (4 edns).

Reports on Elementary Schools, 1852–1882. Ed. Sir F. Sandford, 1889; ed. F. S. Marvin, 1908. [This work is not rptd in any collected edn.]

On Home Rule for Ireland. Two Letters to the Times. 1891 (priv. ptd).

Matthew Arnold's Note Books, with a Preface by Mrs Wodehouse. 1902.

Essays in Criticism: third series. Boston, 1910.

Letters of an Old Playgoer. Ed. B. Matthews, New York, 1919. [Rptd from Pall Mall Gazette. Previously priv. ptd by C. K. Shorter, 1903.]

[For contributions to periodicals and letters to the press, see The Works, vol. xv, 1904, pp. 378–87, and for Arnold's 13 Reports on Training Colleges, ibid, p. 372 (footnote).]

(c) Letters

Letters, 1848–1888. Ed. G. W. E. Russell, 2 vols. 1895; 2 vols. 1901 (Eversley Ser.)

Letters to John Churton Collins. 1910 (priv. ptd). [On the subject of education at the Universities.]

Unpublished Letters. Ed. A. Whitridge, New Haven, 1923.

Letters to Arthur Hugh Clough. Ed. H. F. Lowry, Oxford, 1932.

[See also under Biography and Criticism below for stray letters, and T. H. V. Motter, A Check List of Matthew Arnold's Letters, Stud. Phil. xxxi, 1934.]

(d) Works Arranged and Edited by Arnold, or Containing Contributions by him

A Bible-Reading for Schools. The Great Prophecy of Israel's Restoration (Isaiah, chapters xl–lxvi). 1872 (bis); 1875; 1889.

Isaiah xl–lxvi. With the Shorter Prophecies allied to it. 1875. [A Bible-Reading for Schools rptd with appendix and rev. introduction.]

The Six Chief Lives [Milton, Dryden, Swift, Addison, Pope, Gray] from Johnson's Lives of the Poets, with Macaulay's Life of Johnson. 1878; 1879; 1881; 1886 (with new preface and notes); 1889.

Poems of Wordsworth. 1879; 1879 (with additional poems); 1880, etc. (Golden Treasury Ser.).

The Hundred Greatest Men. Vol. i, 1879. [Introduction (on poetry).]

The English Poets. Ed. T. H. Ward, 4 vols. 1880.

Poetry of Byron. 1881; 1890; 1892. (Golden Treasury Ser.)

Letters, Speeches and Tracts on Irish Affairs by Edmund Burke. 1881.

The Natural Truth of Christianity. Selections from the Select Discourses of John Smith, M.D. 1882.

Isaiah of Jerusalem in the Authorised Version with an Introduction, Corrections and Notes. 1883.

The Encyclopaedia Britannica. 1886 (9th edn).

The Reign of Queen Victoria. Ed. T. H. Ward, 1887.

Wordsworthiana. A Selection from Papers read to the Wordsworth Society. Ed. W. Knight, 1889.

(5) Biography and Criticism

(a) Books

Newman, F. W. Homeric Translation in Theory and Practice. A Reply to Matthew Arnold. 1861.

Wright, I. C. A Letter to the Dean of Canterbury on the Homeric Lectures of Matthew Arnold. 1864.

Austin, A. The Poetry of the Period. 1870.

Forman, H. B. Our Living Poets. 1871.

Stedman, E. C. Matthew Arnold. [In Victorian Poets, 1876.]

Hutton, R. H. The Poetry of Matthew Arnold. [In Literary Essays, 1877 (2nd edn).]

—— Essays on some of the Modern Guides in Matters of Faith. 1887.

—— Mr Arnold's Sublimated Bible. Matthew Arnold as Critic. [In Criticisms on Contemporary Thought and Thinkers, vol. i, 1894.]

Mallock, W. H. The New Republic. 1877.

Galton, A. Urbana Scripta: Studies of Five Living Poets. 1885.

—— Two Essays upon Matthew Arnold (with some of his Letters to the Author). 1897.

Lund, T. W. M. Matthew Arnold. The Message and Meaning of his Life. 1888.

Watson, R. A. Gospels of Yesterday. Drummond, Spenser, Arnold. 1888.

Henley, W. E. Arnold. [In Views and Reviews, 1890.]

Robertson, J. M. Modern Humanists: Sociological Studies of Carlyle, Mill, Emerson, Arnold, Ruskin and Spencer. 1891.

—— Modern Humanists Reconsidered. 1927.

Birrell, A. Matthew Arnold. [In Res Judicatae, 1892.]

Burroughs, J. Indoor Studies. 1895.

Saintsbury, G. Matthew Arnold. [In Corrected Impressions, 1895.]

—— Matthew Arnold. 1899.

—— A History of Criticism. Vol. iii, Edinburgh, 1904.

Walker, H. The Greater Victorian Poets. 1895.

Hudson, W. H. Studies in Interpretation. 1896.

Fitch, Sir J. G. Thomas and Matthew Arnold. 1897.

Tovey, D. C. Reviews and Essays on English Literature. 1897.

Traill, H. D. The New Fiction and Other Essays on Literary Subjects. 1897.

Worsfold, W. B. The Principles of Criticism. 1897.

Dixon, W. M. The Poetry of Mathew Arnold. [In In the Republic of Letters, 1898.]

Stephen, Sir Leslie. Studies of a Biographer. Vol. ii, 1898.

White, G. Matthew Arnold and the Spirit of the Age. New York, 1898.

Gates, L. E. Matthew Arnold. [In Three Studies in Literature, New York, 1899.]

Harrison, F. Matthew Arnold. [In Tennyson, Ruskin, Mill and Other Literary Estimates, 1899.]

Woodberry, G. E. Makers of Literature. New York, 1900.

Brownell, W. C. Victorian Prose Masters. New York, 1901.

Mustard, W. P. Homeric Echoes in 'Balder Dead.' [In B. L. Gildersleeve Studies, Baltimore, 1902.]

Paul, H. W. Matthew Arnold. 1902. (English Men of Letters ser.)

Dawson, W. H. Matthew Arnold and his Relation to the Thought of Our Time. 1904.

Russell, G. W. E. Matthew Arnold. 1904.

Brooke, S. A. Clough, Arnold, Rossetti, and Morris. 1908.

Benson, A. C. The Leaves of the Tree. 1911.

Bickley, F. L. Matthew Arnold and his Poetry. 1911.

Hobohm, J. Matthew Arnold als Naturschilderer. Halle, 1913.

Kelso, A. P. Matthew Arnold on Continental Life and Literature. Oxford, 1914.

Sherman, S. P. Matthew Arnold. New York, 1917.

Goldmark, R. The Hellenism of Matthew Arnold. [In Studies in the Influence of the Classics on English Literature, New York, 1918.]

Quiller-Couch, Sir A. T. Matthew Arnold. [In Studies in Literature, Cambridge, 1918.]

Grierson, Sir H. J. C. Lord Byron: Arnold and Swinburne. British Academy, 1921.

Houghton, R. E. C. The Influence of the Classics on the Poetry of Matthew Arnold. Oxford, 1923.

Ker, W. P. Matthew Arnold. [In The Art of Poetry, Oxford, 1923.]

Raleigh, Sir W. Matthew Arnold. [In Some Authors, Oxford, 1923.]

Williams, S. T. Studies in Victorian Literature. New York, [1923].

Elton, O. Tennyson and Matthew Arnold. 1924. [Rev. from his Survey of English Literature, 1830–1880.]

Murry, J. M. Matthew Arnold the Poet. [In Discoveries, 1924.]

Leach, H. G. The Forsaken Merman. [In Essays in Memory of Barrett Wendell, Cambridge, U.S.A. 1926.]

Hille, H. Die Kulturgedanken M. Arnold's und ihre Verwirklichung in die Pädagogik. Halle, 1928.

Kingsmill, H. Matthew Arnold. 1928.

Orrick, J. B. Matthew Arnold and Goethe. English Goethe Soc. 1928.

Lucas, F. L. Arnold. [In Eight Victorian Poets, Cambridge, 1930.]

Elias, O. Matthew Arnolds politische Grundanschauungen. Leipzig, 1931.

Garrod, H. W. Poetry and the Criticism of Life. Oxford, 1931. [3 lectures on Arnold.]

Blunden, E. Matthew Arnold. [In Great Victorians, ed. H. J. and H. Massingham, 1932.]

Chambers, Sir E. K. Matthew Arnold. British Academy Lecture, 1932. [Rptd in English Critical Essays (Twentieth Century), ed. P. M. Jones, 1933 (World's Classics).]

Steinmetz, M. S. Die ideengeschichtliche Bedeutung Matthew Arnolds. Schramberg, 1932.

Brown, E. K. Studies in the Text of Matthew Arnold's Prose Works. Paris, 1935.

Sells, I. E. Matthew Arnold and France. Cambridge, 1935.

Trilling, L. Matthew Arnold. 1939.

(b) Articles in Periodicals

[Other early reviews and articles are listed in T. B. Smart's Bibliography, 1892, and in T. G. Ehrsam and R. H. Deily, Bibliographies of Twelve Victorian Authors, New York, 1936.]

Rossetti, W. M. The Strayed Reveller and Other Poems. Germ, Feb. 1850.

[Clough, A. H.] Recent English Poetry. North American Rev. LXXVII, 1853. [Rptd in The Poems and Prose Remains, 1869.]

Arnold's Poems. Westminster Rev. LXI, 1854.

S[pedding], J. Arnold on Translating Homer. Fraser's Mag. LXIII, 1861. [Rptd in Reviews and Discussions, 1879.]

Sidgwick, H. The Prophet of Culture. Macmillan's Mag. Aug. 1867. [Rptd in Miscellaneous Essays and Addresses, 1904.]

Swinburne, A. C. Mr Arnold's New Poems. Fortnightly Rev. Oct. 1867. [Rptd in Essays and Studies, 1875.]

Gosse, Sir E. Matthew Arnold's Earliest Publication. Athenaeum, 28 April 1888.

—— Matthew Arnold and Swinburne. TLS. 12 Aug. 1920. [6 letters from Arnold.]

Whitman, W. New York Herald, 16 April 1888. [On Arnold's death. See MLN. XLVII, 1932, pp. 316–7.]

Smart, T. B. Sainte-Beuve and Matthew Arnold. Athenaeum, 3 Sept. 1898.

Omond, T. S. Matthew Arnold and Homer. E. & S. III, 1912.

Mott, L. F. Renan and Matthew Arnold. MLN. XXXIII, 1918.

Powell, A. F. Sainte-Beuve and Matthew Arnold: an Unpublished Letter. French Quart. Sept. 1921.

White, H. C. Matthew Arnold and Goethe. PMLA. XXXVI, 1921.

Drinkwater, J. Some Letters from Matthew Arnold to Robert Browning. Cornhill Mag. Dec. 1923. [Rptd in A Book for Bookmen, 1926.]

Elliott, G. R. The Arnoldian Lyric Melancholy. PMLA. XXXVIII, 1923. [Rptd in The Cycle of Modern Poetry, Princeton, 1929.]

Ingram, F. L. Matthew Arnold, the Educator. Education, XLIV, 1923.

Koszul, A. Une Lettre inédite de M. Arnold à Ed. Reuss. Revue de Littérature comparée, Oct. 1923.

Sadler, Sir M. Matthew Arnold. Nineteenth Century, Feb., March 1923.

Gummere, R. M. Matthew Arnold. Quart. Rev. Jan. 1924.

Reuschel, K. Matthew Arnolds 'The Forsaken Merman' und sein deutsches Vorbild. Germanisch-romanische Monatsschrift, XII, 1924.

Harper, G. M. Matthew Arnold and the Zeit-Geist. Virginia Quart. II, 1926. [Rptd in Spirit of Delight, New York, 1928.]

Romer, Mrs C. Matthew Arnold and some French Poets. Nineteenth Century, June 1926.

Tristram, H. Newman and Matthew Arnold. Cornhill Mag. March 1926.

Phillips, E. M. English Friendships of Sainte-Beuve. Mod. Humanities Research Ass. Bulletin, I, 1927.

Orrick, J. B. Hebraism and Hellenism. New Adelphi, II, 1928.

—— Matthew Arnold and America. London Mercury, XX, 1929.

Rivvallan, A. Matthew Arnold en Bretagne. Bulletin de l'Association France-Grande-Bretagne, Nov. 1928.

McCallum J. D. The Apostle of Culture meets America. New England Quart. II, 1929.

Discipline and Standards. TLS. 28 March 1929. [Arnold's notebooks.]

Woods, M. L. Matthew Arnold. E. & S. xv 1929. [Personal reminiscences.]

Yvon, P. L'Inspiration poétique chez Matthew Arnold à propos du 'Scholar Gipsy.' Revue anglo-américaine, April 1929.

Bonnerot, L. La Jeunesse de Matthew Arnold. Revue anglo-américaine, Aug. 1930.

Eliot, T. S. Arnold and Pater. Bookman (U.S.A.), LXXII, 1930. [Rptd in Selected Essays, 1932.]

Brown, E. K. The French Reputation of Matthew Arnold. [In Studies in English by Members of University College, Toronto, 1931.]

—— Matthew Arnold and the Elizabethans. Toronto University Quart. I, 1932.

—— The Scholar Gipsy, an Interpretation. Revue anglo-américaine, Feb. 1935.

Laurence, E. P. An Apostle's Progress: Matthew Arnold in America. PQ. x, 1931.

Harris, A. Matthew Arnold. The 'Unknown Years.' Nineteenth Century, April 1933.

Motter, T. H. V. A New Arnold Letter and an Old Swinburne Quarrel. TLS. 31 Aug. 1933.

Tinker, C. B. Arnold's Poetic Plans. Yale Rev. xxii, 1933.

Angell, J. W. Matthew Arnold's Indebtedness to Renau's 'Essais de Morale et de Critique.' Revue de Littérature comparée, Oct. 1934.

Whitridge, A. Matthew Arnold and Sainte-Beuve. PMLA. LIII, 1938.

Wickelgren, F. L. Matthew Arnold's Literary Relations with France. MLR. XXXIII, 1938.

COVENTRY KERSEY DIGHTON PATMORE
(1823–1896)
(1) BIBLIOGRAPHIES

Page, F. Courage in Politics and Other Essays, 1885–1896. 1921. [Includes a list of Patmore's prose contributions to periodicals.]

Patmore, D. Selected Poems of Coventry Patmore. 1931. [Bibliography, pp. 157–60.]

(2) COLLECTED WORKS

Poems. 4 vols. 1879. [Vol. I, Amelia, Tamerton Church-Tower, etc.; vol. II, The Angel in the House; vol. III, The Victories of Love; vol. IV, The Unknown Eros.]

Poems. 2 vols. 1886; 2 vols. 1887.

Poems. 1887. [Includes poems by Henry Patmore.]

A New Uniform Edition. 5 vols. 1897.

Poems. Ed. B. Champneys, 1906, 1909, 1915, 1921, 1928.

(3) SELECTED POEMS

Florilegium Amantis. Ed. R. Garnett, 1879.

The Poetry of Pathos and Delight. Ed. A. Meynell, 1895.

The Angel in the House [and other poems]. Ed. A. Meynell, 1905.

Selected Poems. Ed. D. Patmore, 1931. [Detailed introduction.]

(4) SEPARATE PUBLICATIONS
(a) Poems

Poems. 1844.

Tamerton Church Tower and Other Poems. 1853; 1854.

The Angel in the House. The Betrothal. 1854; Boston, 1856.

The Angel in the House. The Espousals. 1856.

The Angel in the House. 2 vols. 1858; 1860; 1863; 1878; 1885; 1887; 1888 (with other poems); 1896; 1905, etc. [A rpt of the 2 preceding items with revisions.]

Faithful for Ever. 1860; 1866.

The Victories of Love. 1863; 1878; 1888 (rev. with Faithful for Ever).

The Angel in the House. 2 vols. 1863; 1866 (rev. text), etc. [A rpt of the 3 preceding items, with a selection of earlier poems.]

Odes. 1868 (priv. ptd).

The Unknown Eros and Other Odes. 1877 (Odes I–XXXI); 1878 (Odes I–XLVI); 1890 (rev. text).

Amelia. 1878 (priv. ptd in black letter).

Amelia, Tamerton Church-Tower, etc. with Prefatory Study on English Metrical Law. 1878.

Seven Unpublished Poems to Alice Meynell. 1922.

(b) Prose and Editions

The Children's Garland from the Best Poets. 1862; 1873. (Golden Treasury Ser.) [Ed. by Patmore.]

Bryan Waller Procter (Barry Cornwall). An Autobiographical Fragment. 1877. [Ed. by C. P(atmore).]

Saint Bernard on the Love of God. Translated by M. C. and Coventry Patmore. 1881; 1884 (with Three Rosaries of Our Lady, and Marianna Caroline Patmore).

How I Managed and Improved My Estate. 1886.

Hastings, Lewes, Rye, and the Sussex Marshes. 1887.

Principle in Art. 1889. [Essays rptd from St James's Gazette.]

Religio Poetæ. 1893.

The Rod, the Root, and the Flower. 1895.

Courage in Politics, and Other Essays, 1885–1896. Ed. F. Page, 1921.
Further Letters of Gerard Manley Hopkins. Ed. C. C. Abbott, Oxford, 1937. [Includes Patmore's letters to Hopkins.]

(5) BIOGRAPHY AND CRITICISM

Brimley, G. Essays. Cambridge, 1858.
Garnett, R. Coventry Patmore. *Miles*, v.
Meynell, A. The Poetry of Coventry Patmore. Athenaeum, 12 Dec. 1896.
Nicoll, Sir W. R. and Wise, T. J. Literary Anecdotes of the Nineteenth Century. Vol. II, 1896. [For Emily Patmore.]
Symons, A. Studies in Two Literatures. 1897.
—— Figures of Several Centuries. 1916.
Champneys, B. Memoirs and Correspondence of Coventry Patmore. 1900; 1901.
Gosse, Sir E. Coventry Patmore. 1905.
Poèmes de Coventry Patmore. Paris, 1912. [Translated by .Paul Claudel; introduction by Valéry Larbaud.]
Harris, Frank. Contemporary Portraits. Ser. 3, 1920.
Burdett, O. The Idea of Coventry Patmore. Oxford, 1921.
Baum, P. F. Coventry Patmore's Literary Criticism. University of California Chronicle, xxv, 1923.
Page, F. Coventry Patmore. Dublin Rev. CLXXIII, 1923.
—— Patmore. A Study in Poetry. Oxford, 1933.
Leslie, S. Studies in Sublime Failure. 1932.
McCarthy, D. Criticism. 1932.
Read, H. Coventry Patmore. [In The Great Victorians, ed. II. J. and II. Massingham, 1932.]
Evans, B. I. English Poetry in the Later Nineteenth Century. 1933.
Patmore, D. Portrait of my Family, 1783–1896. 1935.   B. I. E.

DANTE GABRIEL ROSSETTI (1828–1882)

(1) BIBLIOGRAPHIES

Anderson, J. P. Bibliography. [Appended to J. Knight's Life of Dante Gabriel Rossetti, 1887; includes a list of articles on Rossetti.]
Rossetti, W. M. Bibliographer (New York), I, II, 1902–3. [Addns by W. F. Prideaux, Bibliographer (New York), II, 1903.]
—— A Bibliography of the Works of Dante Gabriel Rossetti. 1905.
Vaughan, C. E. Bibliographies of Swinburne, Morris, Rossetti. English Ass. 1914.
Ehrsam, T. G. and Deily, R. H. Bibliographies of Twelve Victorian Authors. New York, 1936.

(2) COLLECTED WORKS

The Collected Works of Dante Gabriel Rossetti. Ed. W. M. Rossetti, 2 vols. 1886, 1890, 1897, 1901. [Includes contents of Poems (1881) and Dante and his Circle (1874), and prose-tales, schemes for poems, critical essays and notes.]
The Poetical Works. Ed. W. M. Rossetti, 1891, 1898.
Ballads and Narrative Poems. 1893 (Kelmscott Press).
Sonnets and Lyrical Poems. 1894 (Kelmscott Press).
The Siddal Edition. Ed. W. M. Rossetti, 7 vols. 1898–1901.
The Poems. With Illustrations from his own Pictures and Designs. Ed. W. M. Rossetti, 2 vols. 1904. [Contains 4 pieces not included in The Collected Works, 1886.]
The Works. Ed. W. M. Rossetti, 1911. [Authoritative text, with dates of composition and first publication of each item.]
Poems and Translations, 1850–1870. 1913. (Oxford edn.)
Dante Gabriel Rossetti. An Anthology. Chosen by F. L. Lucas. Cambridge, 1933.

(3) SEPARATE PUBLICATIONS

Sir Hugh the Heron: a legendary tale in four parts. By Gabriel Rossetti, Junior. 1843 (priv. ptd by G. Polidori).
The Germ: Thoughts towards Nature in Poetry, Literature and Art. Nos. 1, 2, Jan., Feb. 1850. [Continued as] Art and Poetry: being Thoughts towards Nature. Conducted principally by artists. Nos. 3, 4, March, April 1850. Nos. 1–4, ed. facs. W. M. Rossetti, 1901. [Ed. by W. M. Rossetti. No. 1 contains 1 poem and 1 prose-tale by D. G. Rossetti, no. 2 1 poem, no. 3 2 poems, no. 4 8 pieces.]
The Düsseldorf Artists' Album. Ed. M. Howitt, 1854; ed. facs. M. Foerster, Leipzig, 1929. [Contains Rossetti's 'Sister Helen,' signed H. H. H.]
The Oxford and Cambridge Magazine, conducted by members of the two universities. 1856. [Ed. W. Fulford and W. Morris. No. 8 contains 'The Burden of Nineveh,' no. 11 the second version of 'The Blessed Damozel,' no. 12 'The Staff and Scrip.']
Sister Helen; a ballad. Oxford, 1857. [A forgery? See J. Carter and G. Pollard, An Enquiry into the Nature of Certain Nineteenth Century Pamphlets, 1934.]
The Early Italian Poets from Ciullo d' Alcamo to Dante Alighieri 1100–1200–1300 in the original metres together with Dante's Vita Nuova. 1861; 1874 (rev. and rearranged,

with 1 new trn, as Dante and his Circle); ed. E. G. Gardner, 1904; rptd Stratford-on-Avon, 1921.

Poems. 1870 (3 edns); 1872 (6th edn). [Contains 50 sonnets and 11 songs towards 'The House of Life,' and 51 other pieces of which 36 appeared for the first time.]

Verses. 1881 (priv. ptd). [A forgery? See J. Carter and G. Pollard, as above.]

Ballads and Sonnets. 1881 (*bis*). [The ballads were 'Rose Mary,' 'The White Ship' and 'The King's Tragedy.' 'The House of Life' sonnets, transferred from Poems, were now increased to 101 and there were 39 other pieces.]

Poems. New edition. 1881. [A rpt of the 1870 edn, but excluding 'The House of Life' sonnets and adding 7 new pieces.]

Bürger's Lenore. Ed. W. M. Rossetti, 1900.

The Ballad of Jan van Hunks. Ed. T. J. Wise, 1912; ed. M. Bell, 1929.

The House of Life, a Sonnet-Sequence. Ed. P. F. Baum, Cambridge, U.S.A. 1928.

Dante Gabriel Rossetti. An Analytical List of Manuscripts in the Duke University Library with hitherto Unpublished Verse and Prose. Ed. P. F. Baum, Durham, North Carolina, 1931.

Some Unpublished Stanzas by Rossetti. Ed. M. L. Howe, MLN. XLVIII, 1933.

The Blessed Damozel. The Unpublished Manuscript, Texts and Collation. Ed. P. F. Baum, Chapel Hill, 1938.

Rossetti's Sister Helen. Ed. J. C. Troxell, New Haven, 1939.

(4) LETTERS

Letters of Dante Gabriel Rossetti to William Allingham. Ed. G. B. Hill, 1897. [Contains 65 letters.]

Ruskin: Rossetti: Preraphaelitism. Papers, 1854–62. Ed. W. M. Rossetti, 1899. [Contains 40 letters by Rossetti.]

Praeraphaelite Diaries and Letters. Ed. W. M. Rossetti, 1900. [Contains 24 letters by Rossetti.]

Rossetti Papers, 1862–70. Ed. W. M. Rossetti, 1903. [Contains 60 letters by Rossetti.]

The Letters of Dante Gabriel Rossetti to his Publisher, F. S. Ellis. Ed. O. Doughty, 1928. [Contains 92 letters by Rossetti.]

Letters of Dante Gabriel Rossetti to Miss Alice Boyd. Ed. J. Purves, Fortnightly Rev. 1 May 1928. [Contains 16 letters by Rossetti.]

Three Rossettis: Unpublished Letters to and from Dante Gabriel, Christina, William. Ed. J. C. Troxell, Cambridge, U.S.A. 1937.

[9 letters from Rossetti to Swinburne are ptd in A. Compton-Rickett's Portraits and Personalities, 1937.]

(5) BIOGRAPHY AND CRITICISM

(*a*) Books

Caine, Sir T. H. Hall. Recollections of Dante Gabriel Rossetti. 1882; 1928 (rev. edn).

Sharp, W. Dante Gabriel Rossetti. A Record and a Study. 1882.

Knight, J. Life of Dante Gabriel Rossetti. 1887. [With bibliography by J. P. Anderson.]

Stephens, F. G. Dante Gabriel Rossetti. 1894.

Rossetti, W. M. Dante Gabriel Rossetti: His Family Letters, with a Memoir. 2 vols. 1895.

Cary, E. L. The Rossettis. New York, 1900.

Benson, A. C. Rossetti. 1904. (English Men of Letters ser.)

Hunt, W. Holman. Preraphaelitism and the Preraphaelite Brotherhood. 2 vols. 1905.

Singer, H. W. Rossetti. Berlin, 1905.

Horn, K. H. Studien zum dichterischen Entwicklungsgange Dante Gabriel Rossettis. Berlin, 1909.

Boas, H. O'B. Rossetti and his Poetry. 1914.

Watts-Dunton, T. Old Familiar Faces. 1916.

Dupré, H. Un Italien d'Angleterre. Paris, 1921.

Hearn, L. Pre-Raphaelite and Other Poets. New York, 1922.

Davies, C. Dante Gabriel Rossetti. 1925. [With bibliography.]

Mégroz, R. L. Dante Gabriel Rossetti. 1928.

Waugh, E. Rossetti: His Life and Works. 1928.

Ghose, S. Dante-Gabriel Rossetti and Contemporary Criticism, 1849–1882. Dijon, 1929.

Hunt, V. The Wife of Rossetti. 1932.

Waller, R. D. The Rossetti Family, 1824–1854. Manchester, 1932.

Larg, D. Trial by Virgins. Fragment of a Biography. 1933.

Winwar, F. Poor Splendid Wings. The Rossettis and their Circle. Boston, 1933.

Wolff, L. Dante Gabriel Rossetti. Paris, 1934.

Vincent, E. R. Gabriele Rossetti in England. Oxford, 1936.

(*b*) Articles and Essays

Swinburne, A. C. The Poems of Dante Gabriel Rossetti. Fortnightly Rev. XIII, 1870. [Rptd in Essays and Studies, 1875.]

Forman, H. B. Our Living Poets: an Essay in Criticism. 1871.

'Maitland, Thomas' (*i.e.* R. Buchanan). The Fleshly School of Poetry. Contemporary Rev. XVIII, 1871. [Rptd in The Fleshly School of Poetry and Other Phenomena of the Day, 1872.]

Stedman, E. C. Victorian Poets. Boston, 1876.

Pater, W. Dante Gabriel Rossetti. [In The English Poets, ed. T. H. Ward, vol. IV, 1880. Rptd in Appreciations, 1889.]

Hamilton, W. The Aesthetic Movement in England. 1882.

Myers, F. W. H. Rossetti and the Religion of Beauty. Cornhill Mag. XLVII, 1883. [In Essays: Modern, 1883.]

Sarrazin, G. Poètes modernes de l'Angleterre. Paris, 1885.

Caine, L. H. A Child's Recollections of Rossetti. New Rev. XI, 1894.

Raleigh, Sir W. Rossetti. [In Chambers's Cyclopedia of English Literature, vol. III, 1903.]

Brooke, Stopford A. A Study of Clough, Arnold, Rossetti and Morris. 1908.

Routh, J. Parallels in Coleridge, Keats and Rossetti. MLN. xxv, 1910.

Suddard, M. Studies and Essays. Cambridge, 1912. [The House of Life.]

Tisdel, F. M. Rossetti's House of Life. MP. xv, 1917.

Schücking, L. L. Rossettis Persönlichkeit. E. Studien, LI, 1917.

Trombly, A. E. Rossetti Studies. South Atlantic Quart. XVIII–xx, 1919–21.

Holthausen, F. Dante Gabriel Rossetti und die Bibel. Germanisch-romanische Monatschrift, XIII, XIV, 1925.

Block, L. Dante Gabriel Rossetti der Malerdichter. Giessener Beiträge, II, 1925.

Horn, K. 'The Staff and Scrip' von D. G. Rossetti. Zeitschrift für französische und englische Unterricht, XXVI, 1927.

Shine, W. H. The Influence of Keats upon Rossetti. E. Studien, LXI, 1927. [Includes rpt of marginalia in copy of Keats, ed. G. Milner, Manchester Quart. II, 1883, and combats J. Routh.]

Tietz, E. Das Malerische in Rossettis Dichtung. Ang. Bbl. xxxIx, 1927.

Turner, A. M. Rossetti's Reading and his Critical Opinions. PMLA. XLII, 1927.

Wallerstein, R. C. Personal Experience in Rossetti's House of Life. PMLA. XLII, 1927.

—— The Bancroft Manuscript of Rossetti's Sonnets. MLN. XLIV, 1929.

Hamilton, G. R. Dante Gabriel Rossetti: a Review of his Poetry. Criterion, VII, 1928.

Wolff, L. Rossetti et le Moyen-Âge. Revue anglo-américaine, June 1928.

Foerster, M. Die älteste Fassung von D. G. Rossetti's Ballade 'Sister Helen.' Die Leipziger Neunundneunzig, xxv, 1929.

Symons, A. Studies in Strange Souls. 1929. [Rossetti and Swinburne.]

—— Notes on Two Manuscripts. English Rev. LIV, 1932.

Lucas, F. L. Eight Victorian Poets. Cambridge, 1930.

Morse, B. J. A Note on the Autobiographical Elements in Rossetti's 'Hand and Soul.' Ang. LIV, 1930.

—— Dante Gabriel Rossetti and William Blake. E. Studien, LXVI, 1932.

—— Dante Gabriel Rossetti and Dante Alighieri. E. Studien, LXVIII, 1933.

Waller, R. D. 'The Blessed Damozel.' MLR. XXVI, 1931.

Cecil, Lord D. Gabriel Charles Dante Rossetti. [In Great Victorians, ed. H. J. and H. Massingham, 1932.]

De Vane, W. C. The Harlot and the Thoughtful Young Man. A Study of the Relation between Rossetti's 'Jenny' and Browning's 'Fifine at the Fair.' Stud. Phil. xxIx, 1932.

Knickerbocker, K. L. Rossetti's 'The Blessed Damozel.' Stud. Phil. xxIx, 1932.

Buck, J. C. Charles Augustus Howell and the Exhumation of Rossetti's Poems. Colophon, pt xv, 1933.

Evans, B. I. English Poetry in the Later Nineteenth Century. 1933.

Las Vergnas, R. Le Britannisme de Rossetti. Revue anglo-américaine, XI, 1933.

Howe, M. L. MLN. XLIX, 1934. [Rossetti on 'Maud'; a skit by Rossetti.]

Angeli, H. R. Correspondence of D. G. Rossetti. Dublin Rev. Oct. 1937.

Howarth, R. G. On Rossetti's 'Jenny.' N. & Q. 10 July 1937.

Sanford, J. A. The Morgan Library Manuscript of Rossetti's The Blessed Damozel. Stud. Phil. xxxv, 1938.

Troxell, J. C. The 'Trial Books' of D. G. Rossetti. Colophon, Spring 1938.

J. B. G.

CHRISTINA GEORGINA ROSSETTI
(1830–1894)

(1) BIBLIOGRAPHIES

Anderson, J. P. [Pp. 377–90 of H. T. M. Bell's Christina Rossetti, 1898.]

Ehrsam, T. G. and Deily, R. H. Bibliographies of Twelve Victorian Authors. New York, 1936.

(2) COLLECTED AND SELECTED POEMS

The Poetical Works of Christina Georgina Rossetti. With Memoirs and Notes by W. M. Rossetti. 1904, etc.

Selections. Ed. W. M. Rossetti, 1904, etc. (Golden Treasury Ser.)

Selected Poems. With an Introduction by Alice Meynell. 1910.

Selected Poems. Ed. C. B. Burke, New York, n.d.

Selected Poems. Ed. W. de la Mare, Newtown, 1930.

(3) SEPARATE PUBLICATIONS

(a) Poems, and Books containing Poems

To my Mother on the Anniversary of her Birth, April 27, 1842. [1842.] [A single sheet priv. ptd by G. Polidori.]

Verses by Christina G. Rossetti dedicated to her mother. 1847 (priv. ptd by G. Polidori); rptd J. D. Symon, 1906.

Goblin Market and other poems. 1864; 1865.

The Prince's Progress and other poems. 1866. [Rptd with Goblin Market as Poems, Boston, 1866.]

'Consider.' New York, 1866. [Single sheet ptd as a 'text' for illuminating.]

Commonplace and other short stories. 1870. [Prose, but 'Hero' contains the poem rptd in The Poetical Works as 'Father and Lover.']

Sing-Song. A Nursery Rhyme Book. 1872; 1893 (adds 5 poems).

Annus Domini: a prayer for each day of the year. 1874. [Includes the poem later rptd (with an extra stanza) as 'Wrestling.']

Goblin Market, The Prince's Progress and other poems. 1875, etc. [2 poems omitted and 2 titles changed from Goblin Market, 1864; 2 poems also omitted and 2 titles changed from The Prince's Progress, 1866. 37 new pieces added.]

A Pageant and Other Poems. 1881.

Called to be Saints: the Minor Festivals devotionally studied. 1881. [Prose, but includes 13 poems.]

Time Flies: a reading diary. 1885. [Verse and prose; 130 poems.]

Poems. 1890. [A rpt of Goblin Market, 1875, adding A Pageant, 1881, and 13 new poems.]

The Face of the Deep: a devotional commentary on the Apocalypse. 1892. [Prose, but contains over 200 poems and verse-fragments.]

Verses reprinted from 'Called to be Saints,' 'Time Flies,' 'The Face of the Deep.' 1893. [Some of the poems are modified or given new titles; a few pieces were added.]

New Poems Hitherto unpublished or uncollected. Ed. W. M. Rossetti, 1896.

Maude, a story for girls. With an introduction by W. M. Rossetti. 1897. [Prose, but includes 6 poems, 2 ptd for the first time.]

(b) Prose Works (other than those included above)

Speaking Likenesses. 1874.

Seek and Find, a double series of short studies of the Benedicite. 1879.

Letter and Spirit. Notes on the Commandments. 1883.

(c) Books and Periodicals containing Poems and Articles by Christina Rossetti. [A select list.]

The Germ. Pts I–III, Jan.–March 1850. [7 poems signed 'Ellen Alleyn.']

The Imperial Dictionary of Universal Biography. Ed. J. F. Waller, 1857–60. [Contains unreprinted articles by Christina Rossetti on: Giovanni, Count Giraud; Goldoni; Rosa Govona; Domenico da Gravina; Galeazzo Priorato-Gualdo; Giovanni Battista Guarini (1425–1513); Francesco Inghirami; Jacopone da Todi; Leopardi; Liutprando; Vincenzo Monti; Francesco Morosini; Ludovico Antonio Muratori; Giovanni Battista Niccolini; Giulio Pacio; Sforza Pallavicino; Onofrio Panvino; Giuseppe Parini; Domenico Passionei; Silvio Pellico; Petrarca (her longest and most important contribution); Ottavio Piccolomini; Modesta Pozzo; Angelo Maria Quirini; Ottavio Rinuccini; Roger I of Sicily; Jacopo Sadoleto; Jacopo Sannazaro; the house of Sforza; Bernardo Tasso; Girolamo Tiraboschi; Giovanni Pierio Valeriano; and Lorenzo Valla. W. M. Rossetti also contributed to this book.]

Macmillan's Mag. III, IV, VII, VIII, IX, XI, XII, XIII, XIV, XV, XVII, XVIII, XIX, XLVII, 1861–83. [Poems by Christina Rossetti were pbd in all these vols.; some she revised on publishing them in book form.]

Poems: an offering to Lancashire. 1863. [This contains A Royal Princess with some stanzas which were later omitted, and others which were revised.]

Lyra Eucharistica. 1863; 1864. Lyra Messianica. 1864; 1865. Lyra Mystica. 1865. [In these collections, all ed. by O. Shipley, 13 of Christina Rossetti's poems were pbd.]

Churchman's Shilling Mag. II, 1867. [Includes an unreprinted article 'Dante an English Classic.']

New and Old, VII, 1879. [Unreprinted article 'A Harmony on First Corinthians.']

Dawn of Day. May, June 1882. [2 unreprinted articles 'True in the Gain.']

The Century, Feb. 1884. [Unreprinted article 'Dante. The Poet illustrated out of the Poem.']

(d) Books containing Letters by Christina Rossetti

Christina Rossetti by Mackenzie Bell. 1898.

Ruskin, Rossetti and Preraphaelitism. Ed. W. M. Rossetti, 1899.

Rossetti Papers. Ed. W. M. Rossetti, 1903.

The Family Letters of Christina Georgina Rossetti. Ed. W. M. Rossetti, 1908.

Three Rossettis: Unpublished Letters to and from Dante Gabriel, Christina, William. Ed. J. C. Troxell, Cambridge, U.S.A. 1937.

(4) BIOGRAPHY AND CRITICISM

[See also under D. G. Rossetti, p. 272 above.]

Forman, H. B. Our Living Poets. 1871.
Nash, J. J. G. A Memorial Sermon. 1895.
Noble, J. A. Impressions and Memories. 1895.
Proctor, E. A. A Brief Memoir of Christina G. Rossetti. 1895.
'Thirlmere, Rowland' [John Walker]. Vita Aeterna. In Memoriam Christinae G. Rossetti. [c. 1895.]
Benson, A. C. Essays. 1896.
Gosse, Sir E. Critical Kit-Kats. 1896.
Symons, A. Studies in Two Literatures. 1897.
Bell, H. T. M. Christina Rossetti, a Biographical and Critical Study. 1898.
Westcott, B. F. An Appreciation of the late Christina G. Rossetti. 1899.
Breme, I. Christina Rossetti und der Einfluss der Bibel auf ihre Dichtung. Münster, 1907.
More, P. E. Shelburne Essays. Ser. 3, New York, 1907.
Ford, F. M. Memories and Impressions. 1911.
Venkatesan, N. K. Christina Georgina Rossetti. An Essay. 1914.
Watts-Dunton, T. Old Familiar Faces. 1916.
Bald, M. A. Woman-Writers of the Nineteenth Century. Cambridge, 1923.
De la Mare, W. Christina Rossetti. Trans. Royal Soc. Literature, VI, 1926.
Clutton-Brock, A. More Essays on Religion. 1928.
Birkhead, E. Christina Rossetti and her Poetry. 1930.
Rossetti, G. W. Christina Rossetti. Criterion, x, 1930.
Sandars, M. F. The Life of Christina Rossetti. 1930.
Shove, F. Christina Rossetti. Cambridge, 1930.
Stuart, D. M. Christina Rossetti. 1930. (English Men of Letters ser.)
—— Christina Rossetti. English Ass. 1931.
Morse, B. J. Some Notes on Christina Rossetti and Italy. Ang. LV, 1931.
Thomas, E. W. Christina Georgina Rossetti. New York, 1931.
Waller, R. D. The Rossetti Family, 1824–1854. Manchester, 1932.
Woolf, V. 'I am Christina Rossetti.' [In The Common Reader, ser. 2, 1932.]
Dubslaff, F. Die Sprachform der Lyrik Christina Rossettis. Halle, 1933.
Evans, B. I. The Sources of Christina Rossetti's Goblin Market. MLR. XXVIII, 1933.

Evans, B. I. English Poetry in the Later Nineteenth Century. 1933.
Curti, M. E. A Letter of Christina Rossetti. MLN. LI, 1936.

R. G.-H.

V. MINOR VERSE, 1835–1870

[This section has been restricted, with one or two exceptions, to writers born after 1799 and before 1831. The abbreviation *Miles* has been used to refer to The Poets and Poetry of the Century, ed. A. H. Miles, 10 vols. [1891–7] and 1898, 12 vols. 1905–7 (rev. and enlarged) —an elaborate anthology, in which most of these poets are included, and generally also providing detailed biographical and bibliographical information.]

SARAH FULLER ADAMS, née FLOWER
(1805–1848)

(a) Bibliography

Stephenson, H. W. The Author of Nearer, My God, to Thee. 1922. [Includes a dated list of Mrs Adams's contributions to periodicals and a full list of references to her.]

(b) Poems

Hymns and Anthems. Ed. W. J. Fox, 1841. [Contains 13 pieces by Mrs Adams, including 'Nearer, my God, to Thee.' This hymn was rptd separately 1884 with a brief memoir signed H. L. F. (*i.e.* Jane Borthwick), and ed. facs. J. Julian, 1911.]
Vivia Perpetua: a Dramatic Poem. In Five Acts. 1841; 1893 (priv. ptd, with the hymns and a memoir by E. F. Bridell-Fox).
The Flock at the Fountain. 1845. [A religious catechism interspersed with poems both in prose and in verse.]
A Summer Recollection. A Poem. [In Appendix II of The Centenary History of the South Place Society by M. D. Conway, 1894. The poem, a long one, is prefaced by a letter from E. F. Bridell-Fox, describing the Craven Hill circle.]

(c) Biography and Criticism

Fox, W. J. Lectures Addressed chiefly to the Working Classes. 4 vols. 1845–9. [Lecture IX, vol. IV, is on Miss Barrett and Mrs Adams.]
Taylor, Emily. Memories of Some Contemporary Poets. 1868. [Includes selected poems by Mrs Adams.]
Garnett, R. Sarah Flower Adams. *Miles*, VII (VIII).
Stephenson, H. W. The Author of Nearer, my God, to Thee. 1922.

THOMAS AIRD (1802–1876)

(a) Collected Poems

The Poetical Works of Thomas Aird. 1848;
1878 (5th edn, with Memoir by J. Wallace).

(b) Separate Poems

Murtzoufle; a Tragedy in Three Acts: with
Other Poems. 1826.
The Captive of Fez: a Poem, in Five Cantos.
Edinburgh, 1830.
Othuriel and Other Poems. 1839.

(c) Other Writings

Religious Characteristics. Edinburgh, 1827.
[Didactic essays.]
The Old Bachelor in the Old Scottish Village.
Edinburgh, 1845; 1857 (rev. and enlarged).
[A description of life in Scotland.]
Memoir of D. M. Moir. 1852. [Prefixed to the
Poetical Works of D. M. Moir, ed. T. Aird,
2 vols. 1852.]

(d) Criticism

Gilfillan, G. Galleries of Literary Portraits.
Vol. I, Edinburgh, 1856.

WILLIAM ALEXANDER (1824–1911)

(a) Selection

Selected Poems of William Alexander and
Cecil Frances Alexander. Ed. A. P. Graves,
1930.

(b) Poems

Specimens, Poetical and Critical. 1867 (priv.
ptd).
St Augustine's Holiday, and Other Poems. 1886.
Tenebrae. [1896.]
The Finding of the Book, and Other Poems.
1900.

(c) Other Works

Popular Lectures and General Reading. A
Lecture. 1862.
Victor Hugo as a Poet. [In The Afternoon
Lectures on English Literature, 1864.]
Matthew Arnold's Poetry. [In The Afternoon
Lectures on English Literature, 1867.]

[Alexander also wrote and edited a number
of theological works.]

(d) Biography and Criticism

Garrod, H. B. The Poems of William
Alexander. Academy, 15 Jan. 1887.
Julian, J. A Dictionary of Hymnology. 1907.
Primate Alexander, Archbishop of Armagh. A
Memoir. Ed. E. Alexander, 1913.

HENRY ALFORD (1810–1871)

(a) Collected Poems

The School of the Heart, and Other Poems.
2 vols. Cambridge, 1835; 2 vols. 1845 (as
The Poetical Works of Henry Alford); 1851

(as Select Poetical Works, with Several
Pieces not before published); 1865 ('containing many pieces now first collected');
1868.

(b) Poems

Poems and Poetical Fragments. Cambridge,
1833 (anon.).
The Abbot of Muchelnaye, Sonnets. 1841.
Psalms and Hymns adapted to the Sundays
and Holydays throughout the Year; to
which are added some Occasional Hymns.
1844.
The Odyssey of Homer in Hendecasyllabic
Verse. Books I–XII. 1861.
The Year of Praise: being Hymns, with Tunes,
for the Sundays and Holidays of the Year.
Edited by Henry Alford; assisted in the
Musical Part by R. Hake and T. E. Jones.
1867.

(c) Miscellaneous Prose

Chapters on the Poets of Ancient Greece.
1841.
The Greek Testament. For the Use of Theological Students and Ministers. 4 vols.
1849–61.
The Queen's English: Stray Notes on Speaking
and Spelling. 1864; Cambridge, 1864; 1870
(rev. and enlarged).
Letters from Abroad. 1865.
Life, Journals and Letters of Henry Alford.
Ed. F. Alford, 1873; 1874 (3rd edn).

[Alford was a very prolific writer, and his
numerous sermons, etc. are here omitted.]

(d) Biography and Criticism

Moon, G. W. A Defence of the Queen's
English. In Reply to A Plea for the Queen's
English, by the Dean of Canterbury. 2 pts,
1863.
The Poems of Henry Alford. Eclectic Rev.
CXXIII, 1866.
Miles, A. H. Miles, x (XI).
Hare, A. J. C. Biographical Sketches. 1895.
D[avidson], J. A Dictionary of Hymnology.
Ed. J. Julian, 1907.

WILLIAM ALLINGHAM (1824–1889)

(a) Bibliography

Kropf, H. William Allingham und seine
Dichtung. Biel, 1928. [Includes a list of
articles on, and references to, Allingham.]

(b) Collected and Selected Works

Works. 6 vols. 1890.
Sixteen Poems. Selected by W. B. Yeats.
Dundrum, 1905.
Poems. Selected and Arranged by Helen
Allingham. 1912. (Golden Treasury Ser.)

(c) Poems

Poems. 1850.

Day and Night Songs. 1854; 1855 (rev. and enlarged as The Music Master, a Love Story; and Two Series of Day and Night Songs. With Woodcuts by Arthur Hughes, D. G. Rossetti, and J. E. Millais); 1884 (re-arranged and some addns). [Some of the poems were first ptd in Household Words and other periodicals.]

Peace and War. 1854. [An ode rptd from Daily News.]

Laurence Bloomfield in Ireland. A Modern Poem. 1864; 1869 (adds a preface, and subtitle: 'or, the New Landlord').

Fifty Modern Poems. 1865.

Songs, Ballads and Stories. [Including many now first collected. The rest revised and re-arranged.] 1877.

Ashby Manor. A Play in Two Acts. 1883. [Rptd in Thought and Word, a Book of Poems, 1890.]

The Fairies. A Child's Song. 1883; 1912 (entitled in this edn and all later ones 'Up the Airy Mountain'). [Rptd from Day and Night Songs.]

Evil May-Day. 1883. [A poem on the relation of religion to dogma and science.]

Blackberries picked off many Bushes by D. Pollex and Others. Put in a Basket by William Allingham. 1884.

Irish Songs and Poems. 1887.

Rhymes for the Young Folk. 1887.

Flower Pieces and Other Poems. 1888. [With 2 designs by D. G. Rossetti.]

Life and Phantasy. Poems. 1889.

Thought and Word. 1890. [Poems; includes Ashby Manor.]

By the Way. Verses, Fragments and Notes arranged by Helen Allingham. 1912.

(d) Other Writings

Rambles in England and Ireland. 1873. [Essays under the pseudonym 'Patricius Walker.']

Varieties in Prose. 3 vols. 1893. [Vols. I and II contain Rambles by Patricius Walker. Vol. III contains Irish Sketches, Hopgood and Co. (a play), and Essays on Modern Prophets, Painter and Critic, Poetry, Disraeli's Monument to Byron, Some Curiosities of Criticism and Baudelaire.]

William Allingham. A Diary. Ed. H. Allingham and D. Radford, 1907.

Letters from William Allingham to Robert and Elizabeth Barrett Browning. 1914.

[Allingham also edited Thomas Campbell's poems and ballad and lyric anthologies.]

(e) Biography and Criticism

Critic, 15 Oct. 1850. [A long review of Allingham's poems, ascribed by Kropf to Rossetti.]

Yeats, W. B. William Allingham. Miles, v.

Letters of D. G. Rossetti to William Allingham, 1854–1870. Ed. G. Birbeck Hill, 1897. [A large selection from these letters originally appeared in Atlantic Monthly, July, Aug. 1896.]

Johnson, Lionel. [In A Treasury of Irish Poetry, ed. S. A. Brooke and T. W. Rolleston, bk v, 1900.]

Letters to William Allingham. Ed. H. Allingham and E. B. Williams, 1911. [Only one letter from Rossetti is given as Birbeck Hill had already published the others.]

Graves, A. P. William Allingham. Trans. Royal Soc. Lit. xxxII, 1914.

Kropf, H. William Allingham und seine Dichtung. Biel, 1928.

Howe, M. L. Notes on the Allingham Canon. PQ. xII, 1933.

WILLIAM EDMONDSTOUNE AYTOUN
(1813–1865)

(a) Poems

Poland, Homer, and Other Poems. 1832 (anon.).

The Book of Ballads. Edited by Bon Gaultier. 1845; 1849 (enlarged and with illustrations by A. H. Forrester, R. Doyle and J. Leech); 1903 (16th edn). [By Aytoun and Sir Theodore Martin.]

Lays of the Scottish Cavaliers and Other Poems. 1849; 1849 (adds Appendix on Macaulay, also issued separately); ed. H. Morley, 1891. [There have been numerous selections from the Lays for school use.]

Firmilian: or, the Student of Badajoz: a Spasmodic Tragedy. Edinburgh, 1854. [Pbd under the pseudonym 'T. Percy Jones.' Ridicules the Spasmodic School of poets, including A. Smith, P. J. Bailey and S. Dobell.]

Bothwell. A Poem in Six Parts. 1856; Edinburgh, 1858 (3rd edn, rev.).

Poems and Ballads of Goethe. 1859; 1860 (rev. and enlarged); 1877. [Translated by Aytoun and Sir Theodore Martin. Many of the poems were first ptd in Blackwood's Mag.]

Nuptial Ode on the Marriage of the Prince of Wales. 1863.

Poems of William Edmonstoune Aytoun. 1921. (Oxford Poets.)

(b) Other Writings

Our Zion; or, Presbyterian Popery. By Ane of that Ilk. Edinburgh, 1840 (anon.). [Written against the Veto Act. Attrib. to Aytoun in BM. Catalogue.]

The Life and Times of Richard the First, King of England. 1840.

The Glenmutchkin Railway. [A short story rptd from Blackwood's Mag. in Tales from Blackwood, vol. i, 1858.]

Inaugural Address. Edinburgh, 1861. [On rhetoric and the art of public speaking.]

Norman Sinclair. A Novel. 3 vols. 1861.

Endymion or A Family Party of Olympus. [In Ixion in Heaven and Endymion. Disraeli's skit and Aytoun's burlesque, ed. with foreword by E. Partridge, 1927. Rptd from Blackwood's Mag.]

(c) Biography and Criticism

Martin, Sir T. Memoir of W. E. Aytoun. 1867. [The appendix contains several sketches and essays of Aytoun's which are inaccessible elsewhere.]

Bell, H. William Edmondstoune Aytoun. Miles, iv.

Whyte, W. Aytoun—Martin. 'Bon Gaultier.' Miles, ix (x).

Masson, R. Pollok and Aytoun. Edinburgh, 1898.

TLS. 25 Aug. 1921. [A long review of the Oxford edn of Aytoun's poems.]

PHILIP JAMES BAILEY (1816–1902)

(a) Poems

Festus. A Poem. 1839; 1845 (with additions and a selection of press notices); 1864 (7th edn, enlarged); 1889 (adds long preface). [By 1889 the bulk of The Angel World (1850), The Mystic (1855) and Universal Hymn (1867) had been included in Festus. In 1884 'A Student' issued The Beauties of Festus, with a Descriptive Index.]

The Angel World, and Other Poems. 1850.

The Mystic, and Other Poems. 1855.

The Age; a Colloquial Satire. 1858. [A verse trialogue between author, critic and friend.]

Universal Hymn. 1867.

Nottingham Castle, an Ode. 1878.

Causa Britannica, a Poem in Latin Hexameters with English Paraphrase. Ilfracombe, 1883.

(b) Other Writings

The International Policy of the Great Powers. 1861.

(c) Biography and Criticism

Powell, T. Pictures of the Living Authors of Britain. 1851.

Gilfillan, G. Galleries of Literary Portraits. Vol. i, Edinburgh, 1856.

Brown, J. H. Philip James Bailey. Miles, iv.

Nicoll, Sir W. R. and Wise, T. J. Literary Anecdotes of the Nineteenth Century. 2 vols. 1895–6. [Vol. ii, The Author of Festus.]

Obituary. Athenaeum, 13 Sept. 1902.

Gosse, Sir E. Philip James Bailey. Fortnightly Rev. Nov. 1902.

Ward, James. Philip James Bailey, Personal Recollections. Nottingham, 1905 (priv. ptd).

McKillop, A. D. A Victorian Faust. PMLA. XL, 1925. [On Festus.]

Goldschmidt, E. Der Gedankengehalt von Bailey's 'Festus.' E. Studien, LXVII, 1932.

Black, G. A. P. J. Bailey's Debt to Goethe's Faust in his Festus. MLR. XXVIII, 1933.

WILLIAM BARNES (1801–1886)

(a) Collected and Selected Poems

Poems of Rural Life in the Dorset Dialect. 1879; 1883.

Select Poems. Chosen and Edited with a Preface and Glossarial Notes by T. Hardy. 1908.

A Selection of Poems of Rural Life in the Dorset Dialect. Ed. W. M. Barnes, 1909.

Twenty Poems in Common English. Ed. J. Drinkwater, Oxford, 1925.

(b) Poems

Orra, a Lapland Tale. Dorchester, 1822. [No copy extant?]

'Sabbath Days': Six Sacred Songs. 1844.

Poems of Rural Life, in the Dorset Dialect: with a Dissertation and Glossary. 1844; 1847; 1848 ('The Dissertation and Glossary enlarged'); 1862; 1866.

Poems, partly of Rural Life, (In National English.) 1846.

Hwomely Rhymes; a Second Collection of Poems in the Dorset Dialect. 1859; 1863 (as Poems of Rural Life in the Dorset Dialect. Second Collection).

Poems of Rural Life in the Dorset Dialect. Third Collection. 1862; 1869.

Poems of Rural Life in Common English. 1868; Boston, 1868.

(c) Other Works

An Etymological Glossary. Shaftesbury, 1829.

A Catechism of Government in General, and of England in Particular. Shaftesbury, 1833.

The Mnemonic Manual. 1833.

A few Words on the Advantages of a more Common Adoption of the Mathematics as a Branch of Education. 1834.

A Mathematical Investigation of the Principle of Hanging Doors, Gates, Swing Bridges, and other Heavy Bodies. Dorchester, 1835.

An Arithmetical and Commercial Dictionary, containing a Simple Explanation of Commercial and Mathematical Terms and Arithmetical Operations. To which are added 100 Practical Questions. 1840.

An Investigation of the Laws of Case in Language, exhibited in a System of Natural Cases; with some Observations on Prepositions, Tense and Voice, etc. 1840.

A Pronouncing Dictionary of Geographical Names. 1841.

The Elements of English Grammar, with a Set of Questions and Exercises. 1842.

The Elements of Linear Perspective and the Projection of Shadows. 1842.

Exercises in Practical Science. Dorchester, 1844.

Outlines of Geography and Ethnography for Youth. Dorchester, 1847.

Se Gefylsta (the Helper): an Anglo-Saxon Delectus, serving as a First Class-book of the Language. 1849; 1866.

A Philological Grammar, grounded upon English, and formed from a Comparison of more than Sixty Languages. 1854.

Notes on Ancient Britain and the Britons. 1858.

Views of Labour and Gold. 1859.

The Song of Solomon in the Dorset Dialect. 1859 (priv. ptd).

Tiw; or, a View of the Roots and Stems of the English as a Teutonic Tongue. [1861.]

A Grammar and Glossary of the Dorset Dialect, with the History, Outspreadings and Bearings of South-Western English. 1864.

A Guide to Dorchester. Dorchester, 1864.

Poole, J. A Glossary of the Old Dialect of the English Colony in the Baronies of Forth and Bargy. Ed. W. Barnes, 1867.

Early England and the Saxon English; with some notes on the Father-Stock of the Saxon English, the Frisians. 1869.

An Outline of English Speech-Craft. 1878.

An Outline of Rede-Craft (Logic), with English Wording. 1880.

A Glossary of the Dorset Dialect, with a Grammar of its Word Shapening and Wording. 1886.

[Barnes was also a voluminous contributor to GM., Hone's Year Book, Retrospective Rev., Macmillan's Mag., Fraser's Mag., etc. See L. Baxter, The Life of William Barnes, 1887, pp. 350–6.]

(d) Biography and Criticism

William Barnes, Dorsetshire Poet. Chambers's Journ. xxxix, 1862, xlv, 1868.

Doyle, Sir F. H. C. Provincial Poetry. [In Lectures, 1869.]

Hardy, T. Obituary. Athenaeum, 16 Oct. 1886. [Rptd in Lionel Johnson's The Art of Thomas Hardy, 1894.]

Palgrave, F. T. William Barnes. National Rev. viii, 1886.

Patmore, C. William Barnes, Dorset Poet. Fortnightly Rev. xlvi, 1886.

Baxter, L. The Life of William Barnes. By his Daughter. 1887. [With appended lists of pbd and unpbd writings.]

Sayle, C. William Barnes. Miles, iii.

Powys, L. William Barnes, the Dorset Poet. Freeman, 12 July 1922.

Grey, P. William Barnes. London Mercury, vii, 1923.

Pinto, V. de S. William Barnes. An Appreciation. Wessex, June 1930.

CHARLES DENT BELL (1818–1898)

(a) Poems

The Four Seasons at the Lakes. 1878.

Songs in the Twilight. 1881.

Hymns for the Church and the Chamber. 1882.

Songs in Many Keys. 1884.

Verses for Christmas and the New Year. 1885. [6 poems on Christmas and 6 on the New Year. The title-page has the words 'No. iv.' It has not been possible to discover whether this refers to a series or to works of this nature by Bell.]

Poems Old and New. 1893. [A selection from earlier volumes, with new poems added.]

Diana's Looking-Glass and Other Poems. 1894.

(b) Other Writings

Blanche Nevill; a Record of Married Life. 1853 (anon). [A novel.]

Henry Martyn. 1880. [A biography.]

Reminiscences of a Boyhood in the Early Part of the Century. 1889 (anon.).

Some of Our English Poets. 1895. [Gray, Goldsmith, Cowper, Scott, Coleridge, Wordsworth.]

Tales told by the Fireside. 1896. [7 short stories.]

[Bell also pbd books of travel, sermons and devotional works.]

WILLIAM COX BENNETT (1820–1895)

[Poems.] [1849] (priv. ptd; no title-page).

Poems. 1850.

The Triumph for Salamis, a Lyrical Ballad. Greenwich, [1850?] (priv. ptd).

War Songs. 1855.

Queen Eleanor's Vengeance and Other Poems. 1857.

Baby May, and other Poems on Infants. 1859; 2 pts, 1875 (also includes The Worn Wedding-Ring and other Home Poems and Narrative Poems and Ballads).

Songs by a Song-Writer. First Hundred. 1859; 1876 (adds nearly 50 lyrics).

The Worn Wedding-Ring, and Other Poems. 1861.

Eight Poems. 1865.

Our Glory-Roll and other Poems. 1867.

Proposals for and Contributions to a Ballad History of England and the States sprung from her. 1868. [Includes several ballads by Bennett himself. The preface had originally appeared in 1866 as Shall we have a National History for the English People?]

Songs for Sailors. 1872.

Prometheus the Fire-Giver. An Attempted Restoration of the Lost First Part of the Prometheian Trilogy of Aeschylus. 1877.

Sea Songs. 1878.

[For Bennett and his writings, and a selection from his poems, see A. H. Miles, *Miles*, v.]

ALEXANDER BETHUNE (1804–1843)

Tales and Sketches of the Scottish Peasantry. Edinburgh, 1838.

Lectures on Practical Economy. 1839. [With J. Bethune.]

Poems by the late J. Bethune, with a Sketch of the Author's Life, by his Brother. 1841.

The Scottish Peasant's Fireside: a Series of Tales and Sketches. Edinburgh, 1843.

Tales of the Scottish Peasantry, by A. and J. Bethune. With Biography of the Authors by J. Ingram. 1884. [Reprints both the Tales and Sketches and the Scottish Peasant's Fireside.]

[See W. MacCombie, Memoirs of Alexander Bethune, Aberdeen, 1845.]

EDWARD HENRY BICKERSTETH (1825–1906)

(a) Poems

The Two Brothers. 1845 (anon.).

Poems. Cambridge, 1849.

Nineveh: a Poem. 1851.

Ezekiel: a Seatonian Prize Poem. 1854.

Psalms and Hymns, based on the Christian Psalmody of Edward Bickersteth. Compiled anew by E. H. Bickersteth. [1858]; [1860].

The Tower of London; Caubul; Caesar's Invasion of Britain. [In A Complete Collection of the English Poems which have obtained the Chancellor's Gold Medal, Cambridge, 1859.]

Winged Words. 20 pts, [1861].

Yesterday, To-Day and For Ever: a Poem in Twelve Books. 1866; 1867; 1869; 1870; 1871 (*bis*); 1885 (17th edn); tr. German, Gotha, 1887.

The Hymnal Companion to the Book of Common Prayer. 1870; 1880 (rev. and enlarged); 1906.

Ode on the National Thanksgiving for the Recovery of the Prince of Wales. 1872.

The Shadow of the Rock, and other Poems [selected from various authors]. Ed. E. H. Bickersteth, 1873.

Songs in the House of Pilgrimage. Hampstead, [1880?].

From Year to Year. Poems and Hymns for all the Sundays and Holy Days of the Church. 1884; 1896 (3rd edn, rev. and enlarged). [Contains 'Peace, Perfect Peace.']

[Bickersteth also pbd many sermons and tracts.]

(b) Biography and Criticism

Miles, A. H. Edward Henry Bickersteth. *Miles*, x (xii).

Obituary. Times, 17 May 1906.

Aglionby, F. K. The Life of Edward Henry Bickersteth. 1907.

Julian, J. A Dictionary of Hymnology. 1907.

JOHN STANYAN BIGG (1828–1865)

(a) Writings

The Sea King; a Metrical Romance. 1848.

Night and the Soul: a Dramatic Poem. 1854.

Alfred Staunton. A Novel. 1860.

Shifting Scenes, and Other Poems. 1862.

(b) Criticism

Athenaeum, 28 Oct. 1854. [A long, unfavourable review of Night and the Soul.]

Gilfillan, G. Galleries of Literary Portraits. Vol. i, Edinburgh, 1856.

JOHN STUART BLACKIE (1809–1895)

(a) Selected Works

Rogers, C. The Modern Scottish Minstrel. Vol. vi, Edinburgh, 1855. [Gives a selection of Blackie's poems, with a memoir.]

The Selected Poems of John Stuart Blackie. Ed. A. S. Walker, 1896.

The Day-Book of John Stuart Blackie. Selected and Transcribed from the MSS. by A. S. Walker. 1901.

(b) Poems and Translations

[Goethe's] Faust [pt I], translated into English Verse, with Notes and Preliminary Remarks. 1834.

The Lyrical Dramas of Aeschylus translated into English Verse. 2 vols. 1850; rptd 1906 and 1911 (Everyman's Lib.).

Lays and Legends of Ancient Greece, with Other Poems. Edinburgh, 1857.

Lyrical Poems. Edinburgh, 1860.

Homer and the Iliad. 4 vols. Edinburgh, 1866. [Vols. I, IV, Dissertations and Notes; vols. II, III, Translation in Ballad Metre.].

Musa Burschicosa: a Book of Songs for Students. Edinburgh, 1869.

War Songs of the Germans; with Historical Illustrations of the Liberation War and the Rhine Boundary Question. Edinburgh, 1870.

Lays of the Highlands and Islands. 1871.

Songs of Religion and Life. 1876.

Messis Vitae. Gleanings of Song from a Happy Life. 1886.

A Song of Heroes. 1890.

(c) Other Writings

On Beauty: Three Discourses. Edinburgh, 1858.

The Gaelic Language. Edinburgh, 1864.

Four Phases of Morals: Socrates, Aristotle, Christianity, Utilitarianism. Edinburgh, 1871.

On Self Culture. Edinburgh, 1874.

The Language and Literature of the Highlands. Edinburgh, 1876.

The Wise Men of Greece. Dramatic Dialogues. 1877.

The Wisdom of Goethe. Edinburgh, 1883. [A critical estimate, with selections, translated by Blackie, from Goethe's prose and verse.]

Life of Robert Burns. 1887.

Scottish Song. Edinburgh, 1889. [Short essays with illustrations.]

The Letters of John Stuart Blackie to his Wife. With a Few Earlier Ones to his Parents. Ed. A. S. Walker, 1909.

Notes of a Life. Ed. A. S. Walker, 1910. [Letters and part of an unfinished autobiography.]

[Blackie also pbd much miscellaneous prose, mainly lectures, on educational, philological, political and religious questions as well as some school books.]

(d) Biography and Criticism

Whyte, W. John Stuart Blackie. *Miles*, IV.

Kennedy, H. A. Professor Blackie, His Sayings and Doings. 1895.

Stoddart, A. M. John Stuart Blackie. A Biography. 2 vols. 1895.

RICHARD DODDRIDGE BLACKMORE (1825–1900)

[See p. 474 below.]

HELEN SELINA BLACKWOOD, LADY DUFFERIN (1807–1867)

[See p. 1052 below.]

SAMUEL LAMAN BLANCHARD (1804–1845)

(a) Collected Works

Sketches from Life. Ed. (with memoir) Sir E. Bulwer Lytton, 3 vols. 1846. [Collected essays.]

The Poetical Works. Ed. (with memoir) B. Jerrold, 1876.

(b) Individual Publications

Lyric Offerings. 1828.

Life and Literary Remains of L. E. Landon. 2 vols. 1841.

Corporation Characters. 1855. [Prose sketches, illustrated by J. Kenny Meadows.]

[Blanchard also contributed to Monthly Mag., Examiner, and other periodicals.]

(c) Biography and Criticism

Thackeray, W. M. A Brother of the Press on the History of a Literary Man, Laman Blanchard, and the Chances of the Literary Profession. Fraser's Mag. XXXIII, 1846. [Rptd in Works, ed. A. T. Ritchie, vol. XIII, 1899.]

Japp, A. H. Laman Blanchard. *Miles*, III.

HORATIUS BONAR (1808–1889)

(a) Selection

Hymns; selected and arranged by H. N. Bonar. With a Brief History of some of the Hymns. 1904; 1908.

(b) Poems

Songs for the Wilderness. 1843–4.

The Bible Hymn-Book. 1845.

Hymns Original and Selected. 1846.

Hymns of Faith and Hope. 3 sers. 1857–66; 1867.

The Nun; or, Convent Life. [1869.]

The Song of the New Creation, and Other Pieces. 1872.

My Old Letters. 1877.

Hymns of the Nativity, and Other Pieces. 1879.

Communion Hymns. 1881.

Songs of Love and Joy. Poems. 1888.

Crowned with Light. A Poem. 1889.

Until the Day Break, and Other Hymns and Poems left behind. [Ed. H. N. Bonar], 1890.

[Bonar also pbd many sermons, books of travel, religious tracts, translations, etc.]

(c) Biography and Criticism

Horatius Bonar, D.D. A Memorial. 1889. [Includes an autobiographical fragment.]

Andrew A. Bonar, D.D. Diary and Letters. Ed. M. Bonar, 1894.

Bell, M. Horatius Bonar. *Miles*, X (XI).

Bonar, J. A Dictionary of Hymnology. Ed. J. Julian, 1907.
Memories of Dr Horatius Bonar by Relatives and Public Men: Addresses delivered at the Centenary Celebrations. 1909.

EMILY BRONTË (1819–1848)
[See p. 461 below.]

CHARLES SHIRLEY BROOKS (1816–1874)
[See p. 600 below.]

ROBERT BARNABAS BROUGH (1828–1860)
[See p. 601 below.]

THOMAS EDWARD BROWN (1830–1897)

(a) Bibliography

Radcliffe, W. [In Thomas Edward Brown, A Memorial Volume, Cambridge, 1930. Includes an annotated list of Brown's contributions to periodicals and of articles about him.]
Cubbon, W. Thomas Edward Brown: a Bibliography. Douglas, 1935.

(b) Collected and Selected Poems

Collected Poems. Ed. H. F. Brown, H. G. Dakyns and W. E. Henley, 1900; 1901 (adds Introduction by W. E. Henley).
Poems. Selected and Arranged, with Introduction and Notes by H. F. B[rown] and H. G. D[akyns]. 1908. (Golden Treasury Ser.)
Twenty-three Poems. 1931. (Augustan Books of Poetry.)

(c) Separate Publications

Betsy Lee, a Fo'c'sle Yarn. 1873 (anon.); 1881 (enlarged as Fo'c'sle Yarns, including Betsy Lee and Other Poems).
The Doctor and Other Poems. 1887.
The Manx Witch and Other Poems. 1889.
Kitty of the Shenagh Vane and The Schoolmaster. 1891. [Rptd from The Doctor and Other Poems.]
Old John and Other Poems. 1893.
Letters. Ed. (with Memoir) S. T. Irwin, 2 vols. 1900.

(d) Biography and Criticism

Storr, W. T. E. Brown. New Rev. Dec. 1897. [Also includes a poem, In Memoriam, by W. E. Henley.]
T. E. Brown. Macmillan's Mag. April, Oct. 1900, Jan. 1901.
Whibley, C. T. E. Brown, Poet and Letter Writer. [In Musings without Method, 1902.]
Strachan, L. R. M. The Poet of Manxland. E. Studien, xxxiv, 1904.
Simpson, S. G. Thomas Edward Brown, the Manx Poet: an Appreciation. 1906.

Tarver, J. C. T. E. B. Manxman, Scholar, Poet. Nineteenth Century, Dec. 1920.
Caine, W. R. H. T. E. Brown. The Last Phase. Douglas, 1924 (priv. ptd).
Spender, C. The Poetry of T. E. Brown. Contemporary Rev. March 1925.
Boas, F. S. T. E. Brown. 1930. [In The Eighteen-Eighties, Royal Soc. Lit. 1930; differs from the essay in Thomas Edward Brown, A Memorial Volume, 1930.]
Thomas Edward Brown, A Memorial Volume, 1830–1930. Cambridge, 1930. [Includes Memoir by Sir A. T. Quiller-Couch, personal recollections and impressions by various friends, some unpublished letters, bibliography, etc.]

JOHN WILLIAM BURGON (1813–1888)
[See p. 856 below.]

JAMES DRUMMOND BURNS (1823–1864)

(a) Poems

The Vision of Prophecy, and other Poems. Edinburgh, 1854; Edinburgh, 1858.
The Heavenly Jerusalem; or, Glimpses within the Gates. 1856.
The Evening Hymn. 1857. [A collection of hymns and prayers.]
[See also under J. Hamilton, below.]

(b) Biography and Criticism

Reminiscences of the Late J. D. Burns; from the Weekly Review of Dec. 17, 1864. [1864.]
Hamilton, James. Memoir and Remains of J. D. Burns. 1869. [The Remains include hymns and other verse.]
Grosart, A. B. James Drummond Burns. Miles, x (xii).
Mearns, J. A Dictionary of Hymnology. Ed. J. Julian, 1907.

WATHEN MARK WILKS CALL
(1817–1890)

(a) Writings

Lyra Hellenica. 1842. [Metrical trns of the Prometheus of Æschylus and some of the Homeric Hymns.]
Reverberations. 1849; 1876 (rev. edn). [Poems.]
Golden Histories. 1871. [Poems.]
Final Causes: a Refutation. [1891.]

(b) Biography and Criticism

The Poems of W. M. W. Call. Westminster Rev. xcvii, 1871.
Wathen Mark Wilks Call. Athenaeum, 30 Aug. 1890.

Conway, M. D. Religion and Progress. Interpreted by the Life and Last Work of Wathen M. W. Call. Monist, II, 1891–2. [A full-length study of Call.]

Japp, A. H. Wathen Mark Wilks Call. *Miles*, IV.

Griffiths, P. Wathen Mark Wilks Call. N. & Q. 18 Jan. 1936.

GEORGE DOUGLAS CAMPBELL, DUKE OF ARGYLL (1823–1900)

The Burdens of Belief, and Other Poems. 1894.

George Douglas, Eighth Duke of Argyll. Autobiography and Memoirs. Ed. the Dowager Duchess of Argyll, 2 vols. 1906.

[The Duke of Argyll was a prolific writer on politics, economics, theology and popular science. See also p. 862 below.]

EDWARD CASWALL (1814–1878)

(a) Poems and Hymns

Lyra Catholica, containing all the Breviary and Missal Hymns; with Others from Various Sources. Translated by E. Caswall. 1849; New York, 1851; 1884.

The Masque of Mary, and Other Poems. 1858; [1887].

L'Incoronata: a Tale of May. Birmingham, 1860.

A May Pageant, and Other Poems. 1865.

Hymns and Poems, Original and Translated. 1872; ed. (with biographical preface) E. Bellasis, 1908.

A Tale of Tintern. 1873. [This is A May Pageant with every line reduced by two syllables.]

(b) Humorous Writings

A New Art, teaching how to be plucked, being a Treatise after the Fashion of Aristotle writ for the Use of Students in the University. By Scriblerus Redivivus. Oxford, 1835; Oxford, 1874 (12th edn).

Pluck Examination Papers for Candidates at Oxford and Cambridge in 1836. By Scriblerus Redivivus. Oxford, 1836 (*bis*).

Sketches of Young Ladies: in which these Interesting Members of the Animal Kingdom are classified according to their Several Instincts, Habits and General Characteristics. By Quiz. Illustrated by Phiz [H. K. Browne]. 1837; 1838 (6th edn); [1869] (with Sketches of Young Couples, and Young Gentlemen by Dickens); tr. Spanish, Cadiz, 1842.

Morals from the Churchyard, in a Series of Cheerful Fables. 1838. [Signed E. C.]

(c) Devotional Works

The Child's Manual: Forty Days' Meditations on the Chief Truths of Religion as contained in the Church Catechism. 1846.

Sermons on the Seen and the Unseen. 1846.

[Caswall became a Roman Catholic in 1847, and wrote and translated various other devotional works.]

ELIZABETH CHARLES, née RUNDLE (1828–1896)

(a) Selections

Selections from the Writings of the Author of The Schönberg-Cotta Family. 1877.

Thoughts and Characters. Selections from the Writings of the Author of The Schönberg-Cotta Family. 1878.

Comfort and Counsel for Every Day from the Writings of E. R. Charles, by two of her Friends. With a Preface by B. Champneys. 1898.

(b) Poems

The Voice of Christian Life in Song. 1858.

The Three Wakings. 1859.

The Women of the Gospels, the Three Wakings and Other Verses. 1868.

Songs Old and New. 1894.

(c) Religious and Miscellaneous Works

Rest in Christ; or, the Crucifix and the Cross. 1848.

Tales and Sketches of Christian Life in Different Lands and Ages. 1850.

The Two Vocations; or, The Sisters of Mercy at Home. 1853.

The Cripple of Antioch, and Other Scenes from Christian Life in Early Times. 1856.

The Martyrs of Spain. 1862.

Chronicles of the Schönberg-Cotta Family. 1864.

Sketches of Christian Life in England in the Olden Time. 1864.

On both Sides of the Sea: a Story of the Commonwealth and the Restoration. 1868.

The Victory of the Vanquished. 1871.

Lapsed, but not Lost. 1877.

Joan the Maid. 1879.

Three Martyrs of the Nineteenth Century: Livingstone, Gordon and Patteson. 1885.

The True Vine. 1885.

Martyrs and Saints of the First Twelve Centuries. 1887.

Early Christian Missions of Ireland, Scotland, and England. 1893.

Ecce Ancilla Domini. Mary the Mother of Our Lord. Studies in the Christian Ideal of Womanhood. 1894.

Ecce Homo, Ecce Rex. Pages from the Story of the Moral Conquests of Christianity. [1895.]

Our Seven Homes: Autobiographical Reminiscences. [Ed. M. Davidson], 1896.

[Mrs Charles also translated and arranged some selections from Luther, and, besides the above-listed, wrote a number of other devotional books.]

(d) Criticism

Miller, J. Singers and Songs of the Church. 1869 (2nd edn).

Julian, J. A Dictionary of Hymnology. 1907.

MARY COWDEN CLARKE (1809–1898)

[See p. 711 below.]

CAROLINE CLIVE (1801–1873)

[See p. 479 below.]

SARA COLERIDGE (1802–1852)

[See also under S. T. Coleridge, pp. 176–9 above.]

(a) Individual Publications

Account of the Abipones, translated from the Latin of M. Dobrizhöffer. 3 vols. 1821.

Memoirs of the Chevalier Bayard, by the Loyal Servant, translated from the French. 1825.

Pretty Lessons in Verse for Good Children. 1834; 1845 (4th edn); 1853; 1875; rptd 1927.

Phantasmion. 1837; ed. Lord Coleridge, 1874. [A fairy tale with lyrics.]

(b) Biography and Criticism

[Coleridge, H. N.] Quart. Rev. LXVI, 1840. [Long review of Sara Coleridge, Caroline Bowles, Elizabeth Barrett, and others.]

Memoir and Letters of Sara Coleridge. Ed. E. Coleridge, 2 vols. 1873; 1874 (abridged edn).

Garnett, R. Sarah Coleridge. Miles, VII (VIII).

Towle, E. A. A Poet's Children: Hartley and Sara Coleridge. 1912.

Wilson, M. These Were Muses. 1924.

Broughton, L. N. Sara Coleridge and Henry Read. Ithaca, 1937.

MORTIMER COLLINS (1827–1876)

[See p. 479 below.]

JOHN CONINGTON (1825–1869)

(a) Poems and Verse Translations

The Victory of Suffering. A Prize Poem. 1842.

The Agamemnon [of Aeschylus], with a Translation into English Verse and Notes by J. C. 1848.

The Odes and Carmen Saeculare of Horace. 1863.

The Aeneid of Virgil, translated. 1866.

The Satires, Epistles and Art of Poetry of Horace, translated into English Verse. 1870.

(b) Prose Translations and Editions

The Works of Virgil, with a Commentary. 3 vols. 1858.

The Satires of A. Persius Flaccus, with a Translation and Commentary. Ed. H. Nettleship, Oxford, 1872. [With a lecture on the life and writings of Persius.]

The Poems of Virgil. Translated. 1882. [Rptd from the Miscellaneous Writings.]

(c) Other Writings

The University of Oxford and the Greek Chair. Oxford, 1863.

The Style of Lucretius and Catullus as compared with that of the Augustan Poets. A Lecture. 1867.

The Poetry of Pope. [Essay I in Oxford Essays, 1858.]

Miscellaneous Writings. Ed. J. A. Symonds, with a Memoir by H. J. S. Smith, 2 vols. 1872. [King Lear, Hamlet, The English Translators of Virgil, Six Lectures on Latin Literature, The Poems of Virgil translated into English Prose, Fables of Babrius, etc.]

ELIZA COOK (1812–1889)

(a) Collected and Selected Works

Poems. 4 vols. 1846–53.

Poems. 3 vols. [1858?]

Poems. 1859.

Poems. Selected and Edited by the Author. 1861.

Auswahl englischer Gedichte der Eliza Cook. Leipzig, 1865.

Poems. 1870. (Chandos Classics.)

(b) Poems

Lays of a Wild Harp: a Collection of Metrical Pieces. 1835.

Melaia, and Other Poems. 1838.

Poems. Second Series. 1845.

New Echoes, and Other Poems. 1864.

(c) Other Writings

Eliza Cook's Journal. 1849–54. [A periodical edited and partly written by Eliza Cook.]

Jottings from my Journal. 1860. [Short essays on topics of general interest, many of them rptd from Eliza Cook's Journal.]

Diamond Dust. 1865. [A collection of aphorisms.]

(d) Biography and Criticism

Notable Women of Our Own Times. [1883?] [Has a ch. on Eliza Cook.]

Ingram, J. H. Eliza Cook. Miles, VII (VIII).

THOMAS COOPER (1805–1892)

(a) Poems

The Purgatory of Suicides. A Prison-Rhyme. 1845; 1847; 1851; 1853. [A poem in ten books, written in Stafford Gaol and addressed to the working class.]

The Baron's Yule Feast; a Christmas Rhyme.
1846.
The Paradise of Martyrs: a Faith Rhyme.
1873. [The poem is in five books.]
Poetical Works. 1877. [The Purgatory of
Suicides; Smaller Prison Rhymes; The
Paradise of Martyrs; Early Pieces.]

(b) Other Writings

Wise Saws and Modern Instances. 2 vols.
1845; 1874 (enlarged as Old-Fashioned
Stories). [A collection of short stories and
sketches.]
The Land for the Labourers. [1848.]
The Life and Character of Henry Hethering-
ton. 1849. [Abridged from Cooper's éloge
(delivered 20 Aug. 1849) by G. J. Holyoake.]
Captain Cobler; or, the Lincolnshire Rebellion:
an Historical Romance of the Reign of
Henry VIII. 1850.
Eight Letters to the Young Men of the
Working Classes. 1851. [Rptd from The
Plain Speaker. Advice on the art of living.]
Alderman Ralph; or, the History of the
Borough of Willowacre. By Adam Horn-
book. 2 vols. 1853. ['Hornbook' is a
pseudonym for Cooper.]
The Family Feud. A Tale. 1855. [Under the
pseudonym of 'Adam Hornbook.']
The Bridge of History over the Gulf of Time.
1871.
The Life of Thomas Cooper: written by
Himself. 1872.
God, the Soul, and a Future State. 1873.
Evolution, the Stone Book, and the Mosaic
Record of Creation. 1878.
Thoughts at Fourscore, and Earlier. A
Medley. 1885. [Includes the Letters to the
Young Working Men.]

[Cooper also pbd sermons and theological
works.]

(c) Biography and Criticism

Holyoake, G. J. Thomas Cooper Delineated
as Convert and Controversialist. [1861?]
Cazamian, L. Kingsley et Thomas Cooper,
Étude sur une Source d'Alton Locke. Paris,
1903.
Conklin, R. J. Thomas Cooper, the Chartist.
1936.

DINAH MARIA MULOCK, later CRAIK
(1826–1887)
[See p. 498 below.]

WILLIAM DAVIES (1830–1896)
(a) Poems
Songs of a Wayfarer. 1869.
The Shepherd's Garden. 1873.

(b) Other Works

The Pilgrimage of the Tiber, from its Mouth
to its Source: with some Account of its
Tributaries. 1873.
A Fine Old English Gentleman, exemplified in
the Life and Character of Lord Collingwood.
1875.

[Davies also edited the works and letters of
James Smetham.]

THOMAS OSBORNE DAVIS (1814–1845)
[See p. 1052 below.]

AUBREY THOMAS DE VERE (1814–1902)
[See p. 1052 below.]

SYDNEY THOMPSON DOBELL (1824–1874)
(a) Collected and Selected Works
Poetical Works. With Introductory Notice and
Memoir by J. Nichol. 2 vols. 1875.
The Poems of Sydney Dobell, With an
Introductory Memoir. 1887.
Home in War Time. Poems selected by
W. G. Hutchison. 1900.

(b) Poems
The Roman. A Dramatic Poem. 1850. [Ptd
under the pseudonym 'Sydney Yendys.']
Balder. Part the First. 1853; 1854 (adds
preface). [Pt II was never completed.
Fragments of it are ptd at the end of
Thoughts on Art, Philosophy and Religion,
1876.]
Sonnets on the War. 1855. [In collaboration
with Alexander Smith.]
England in Time of War. 1856.
Love. To a Little Girl. 1863.

(c) Other Writings
Of Parliamentary Reform: a Letter to a
Politician. 1865.
Thoughts on Art, Philosophy and Religion;
selected from the Unpublished Papers of
Sydney Dobell. With Introductory Note
by J. Nichol. 1876. [Includes the lecture
on the Nature of Poetry, the Pamphlet on
Reform, and the Fragments of the Pro-
jected Continuation of Balder.]

(d) Biography and Criticism
Balder. Fraser's Mag. L, 1854.
'Jones, T. Percy' (i.e. W. E. Aytoun).
Firmilian: or the Student of Badajoz: a
Spasmodic Tragedy. Edinburgh, 1854.
[Ridicules Dobell and the Spasmodic School
of poetry.]
Gilfillan, G. Sydney Yendys. [In A Third
Gallery of Literary Portraits, Edinburgh,
1854.]
J[olly], E. The Life and Letters of Sydney
Dobell. 2 vols. 1878.

Buchanan, R. W. A Look round Literature. 1887. [Has a chapter on Sydney Dobell and the Spasmodic School.]

Garnett, R. Sydney Dobell. *Miles*, v.

ALFRED DOMETT (1811–1887)

(a) Poems

Venice. 1839.

Ranolf and Amohia: a South-Sea Day Dream. 1872; 2 vols. 1883 (rev. text).

Flotsam and Jetsam: Rhymes Old and New. 1877.

(b) Other Writings

Narrative of the Wairoan Massacre. 1843.

Petition to the House of Commons for the Recall of Governor Fitzroy. 1845.

(c) Biography and Criticism

Gisborne, W. New Zealand Rulers and Statesmen, 1840–1885. 1886. [Has an account of Domett.]

—— Alfred Domett. *Miles*, iv.

Robert Browning and Alfred Domett. Ed. Sir F. Kenyon, 1906. [Letters from Browning to Domett.]

SIR FRANCIS HASTINGS CHARLES DOYLE (1810–1888)

(a) Poems

Miscellaneous Verses. 1834.

The Two Destinies. A Poem. 1844.

Oedipus, King of Thebes. 1849. [Translated from the Oedipus Tyrannus of Sophocles into English verse.]

The Vision of Er, the Pamphylian. A Poem. [1850?]

The Duke's Funeral: a Poem. 1852.

The Return of the Guards, and Other Poems. 1866.

Robin Hood's Bay, an Ode. 1878.

(b) Other Writings

Lectures delivered before the University of Oxford, 1868. 1869. [Inaugural Lecture; Provincial Poetry; Dr Newman's Dream of Gerontius.]

Lectures on Poetry, delivered at Oxford. Second Series. 1877. [Lectures on Wordsworth, Scott and Shakespeare. 14 original poems at end.]

Reminiscences and Opinions, 1813–1885. 1886. [An autobiography.]

(c) Biography and Criticism

Japp, A. H. Sir Francis Hastings Doyle. *Miles*, iv.

ROWLAND EYLES EGERTON-WARBURTON (1804–1891)

Poems. Chester, 1833.

Hunting Songs, Ballads, etc. By R. E. E. W. 1834; 1846 (enlarged); 1859 (rev. and enlarged); 1860; 1873 (enlarged again); ed. Sir H. E. Maxwell, Liverpool, 1912; rptd 1925.

The Hawkstone Bow-Meeting. 1835.

Cheshire Chivalry. 1838. [Verses describing a hunt by the Cheshire Hounds.]

Rhymes on the Rules of the Cheshire Bowmen. Northwich [1840?].

Three Hunting Songs. Illustrated by H. K. Browne. Chester, 1855.

Four New Songs. 1859.

Epigrams and Humorous Verses. By Rambling Richard. 1867.

A Looking-Glass for Landlords. 1875.

Poems, Epigrams and Sonnets. 1877.

Songs and Verses on Sporting Subjects. 1879.

Twenty-two Sonnets; with Illustrations. 1883.

JANE FRANCESCA ELGEE, later LADY WILDE (1826–1896)

[See p. 1054 below.]

'GEORGE ELIOT' (1819–1880)

[See p. 465 below.]

JOHN ELLERTON (1826–1893)

(a) Hymns

Hymns for Schools and Bible Classes. Brighton, 1859.

Hymns, Original and Translated. 1888.

[Ellerton also pbd sermons and devotional works.]

(b) Biography and Criticism

John Ellerton. Being a Collection of his Writings on Hymnology, together with a Sketch of his Life and Works by H Housman. 1896.

Julian, J. A Dictionary of Hymnology. 1907.

SARAH ELLIS (1810?–1872)

[See p. 483 below.]

HENRY ELLISON (1811–1880)

Madmoments, or First Verseattempts by a Bornnatural. Malta, 1833; 2 vols. 1839.

Touches on the Harp of Nature. 1839.

The Poetry of Real Life. A New Edition, much Enlarged and Improved. (First Series.) 1844; 1851.

Stones from the Old Quarry; or, Moods of Mind. By Henry Browne. 1875. [Mainly sonnets. 'Henry Browne' is a pseudonym.]

[For Ellison's life and writings, with a selection from his poems, see John Brown's Henry Vaughan (in Horae Subsecivae, ser. 1, Edinburgh, 1882) and A. B. Grosart, *Miles*, x (xi).]

ANNE EVANS (1820–1870)

Poems and Music. With a Memorial Preface by Anne Thackeray Ritchie. 1880.

SEBASTIAN EVANS (1830–1909)

Sonnets on the Death of the Duke of Wellington. Cambridge, 1852.
Brother Fabian's Manuscripts; and Other Poems. 1865.
In the Studio. A Decade of Poems. 1875.
To the Memory of W. M. Thackeray. A Poem. [Appended to Mr Thackeray's Writings in 'The National Standard' and 'Constitutional,' 1899.]
In Quest of the Holy Graal: an Introduction to the Study of the Legend. 1898.

[Evans also pbd translations and political tracts. For his life and writings, and selected poems, see J. Knight, *Miles*, v.]

FREDERICK WILLIAM FABER (1814–1863)

(a) Collected Works

Works, Prose and Verse. 11 vols. 1914.

(b) Poems

The Knights of St John. 1836. [Newdigate Prize Poem.]
The Cherwell Water-Lily, and Other Poems. 1840.
The Styrian Lake and Other Poems. 1842.
Sir Lancelot. A Poem. 1844.
The Rosary and Other Poems. 1845.
Hymns. Derby, 1848; 1849 (much enlarged, as Jesus and Mary: or, Catholic Hymns); 1852 (enlarged); 1854 (enlarged, as The Oratory Hymn Book); 1861 (complete edn; contains 150 hymns).
Poems. 1856. [A large selection from Faber's earlier poems.]
Ausgewählte englische Gedichte von Dr Friedrich Wilhelm Faber. Ed. W. Bottmann, Regensburg, 1859. [The poems are in English, with notes in German.]
Gedichte von F. W. Faber aus dem englischen von C. Schüter und A. Jüngst. Münster, 1870. [With a lengthy biographical and critical introduction.]
Heavenly Promises. A Selection of Devotional Poetry from the Writings of F. W. Faber. 1898.
Selected Poetry of Father Faber. With Introduction by John Fitzpatrick. 1907.

(c) Other Writings

Sights and Thoughts in Foreign Churches and among Foreign Peoples. 1842.
All for Jesus: or, The Easy Ways of Divine Love. 1853; 1854 (4th edn, rev. and rearranged).
Growth in Holiness: or, the Progress of the Spiritual Life. 1854.

The Blessed Sacrament: or, the Works and Ways of God. 1855.
The Creator and the Creature, or, The Wonders of Divine Love. 1856.
Ethel's Book; or, Tales of the Angels. 1858. [Stories for children.]
The Foot of the Cross: or, The Sorrows of Mary. 1858.
Spiritual Conferences. 1859.
The Precious Blood; or, The Price of Our Salvation. 1860.
Bethlehem. 1860.
Notes on Doctrinal and Spiritual Subjects. Ed. J. E. Bowden, 2 vols. 1866. [Selected from Faber's papers after his death.]
Thoughts on Great Mysteries. 1884.
Characteristics from the Writings of Father Faber. Arranged by John Fitzpatrick. 1903. [A comprehensive selection.]
The Life Beautiful: a Selection of Passages from Faber. 1907.
The Spirit of Father Faber. With a Preface by Wilfrid Meynell. 1914.

[Faber also pbd numerous sermons and religious tracts, as well as contributing 9 lives to the Lives of the English Saints, 1844–5.]

(d) Biography and Criticism

Bowden, J. E. The Life and Letters of Frederick William Faber. 1869.
Faber, F. A. A Brief Sketch of the Early Life of the late F. W. Faber. 1869; 1901 (rev. edn).
Hall-Patch, W. Father Faber. 1914.
Plus, R. Frédéric William Faber. Études, CVII, 1931.
Faber, G. C. Oxford Apostles. 1933.

JULIAN HENRY CHARLES FANE (1827–1870)

(a) Poems

Monody on the Death of Adelaide the Queen Dowager. A Poem which obtained the Chancellor's Medal, 1850. [Cambridge, 1850.]
Poems. 1852; 1852 ('with additional poems').
Poems by Heinrich Heine; translated. 1854.
Julian Fane, ad Matrem. 1849–1857. [1857] (priv. ptd).
Tannhäuser; or, The Battle of the Bards. By Neville Temple [J. Fane] and Edward Trevor [E. R. B. Lytton]. 1861.

(b) Biography and Criticism

Obituary. Times, 21 April 1870.
Lytton, E. R. B. (Earl of Lytton). Julian Fane: a Memoir. 1871.

SIR SAMUEL FERGUSON (1810–1886)

[See p. 1052 below.]

CHARLES ROBERT FORRESTER (1803–1850)

(a) Poems

Absurdities in Prose and Verse. Written and illustrated by Alfred Crowquill. 1827. [Illustrations by A. H. Forrester.]

The Battle of the Annuals. A Fragment. 1835 (anon.).

(b) Other Writings

Castle Baynard; or, The Days of John. By Hal Willis. 1824.

Eccentric Tales from the German of W. F. von Kosewitz [C. R. Forrester] with Illustrations by G. Cruikshank, from Sketches by A. Crowquill. 1827.

Sir Roland: a Romance of the Twelfth Century. By Hal Willis. 4 vols. 1827.

The Lord Mayor's Fool. 1840.

Phantasmagoria of Fun. Edited and illustrated by Alfred Crowquill. 2 vols. 1843. [Illustrations by A. H. Forrester.]

(c) Biography and Criticism

Obituary. GM. May 1850.

Miles, A. H. Charles R. Forrester. Miles, IX (X).

LADY GEORGIANA FULLERTON (1812–1885)

[See p. 483 below.]

THOMAS HORNBLOWER GILL (b. 1819)

(a) Poems

The Fortunes of Faith; or, Church and State. A Poem. 1841.

The Anniversaries. Poems in Commemoration of Great Men and Great Events. Cambridge, 1858.

The Golden Chain of Praise. Hymns. [1868]; 1894 (greatly enlarged).

(b) Other Writings

The Papal Drama. A Historical Essay. 1866.

The Triumph of Christ. Memorials of Franklin Howorth. 1883.

Richard Serjeant: a Biographical Sketch. 1885.

(c) Biography and Criticism

Horder, W. G. Thomas Hornblower Gill. Miles, x (xi).

Julian, J. and Horder, W. G. A Dictionary of Hymnology. Ed. J. Julian, 1907.

DORA GREENWELL (1821–1882)

(a) Poems

Poems. 1848.

Stories that might be True, with Other Poems. 1850.

Poems. Edinburgh, 1861; 1867 (omits some earlier poems and adds a few later ones).

Carmina Crucis. 1869; ed. C. L. Maynard, 1906.

Songs of Salvation. 1873.

The Soul's Legend. 1873.

Camera Obscura. 1876.

Poems. Selected and with Biographical Introduction by W. Dorling. 1889.

Selected Poems, with Introduction by C. L. Maynard. 1906.

(b) Other Writings

A Present Heaven. 1855; 1867 (as The Covenant of Life and Peace). [Letters on the Gospel.]

The Patience of Hope. 1860; 1862 (with Preface by J. G. Whittier). [A treatise on the spiritual life.]

Two Friends. 1862; ed. C. L. Maynard, 1926. [Essays on the spiritual life.]

Essays. 1866. [Our Single Women; Hardened in Good; Prayer; Popular Religious Literature; Christianos ad Leones.]

Lacordaire. Edinburgh, 1867.

On the Education of the Imbecile. 1869. [Rptd from North British Rev. and ed. for Royal Albert Idiot Asylum, Lancaster.]

Colloquia Crucis. A Sequel to Two Friends. 1871.

John Woolman. 1871.

Liber Humanitatis. 1875. [8 essays.]

A Basket of Summer Fruit. 1877. [8 essays.]

(c) Biography and Criticism

Dorling, W. Memoirs of Dora Greenwell. 1885.

Japp, A. H. Dora Greenwell. Miles, VII (VIII).

McC., L. S. Dora Greenwell. Academy, 12 Aug. 1905.

Maynard, C. L. The Life of Dora Greenwell. 1926.

Bett, H. Studies in Literature. 1929. [Has a chapter on Dora Greenwell.]

GERALD GRIFFIN (1803–1840)

[See p. 485 below.]

THOMAS GORDON HAKE (1809–1895)

(a) Poems

Poetic Lucubrations; containing the Misanthrope and Other Effusions. 1828.

The Piromides: a Tragedy. 1839.

The World's Epitaph. 1866 (priv. ptd).

Madeline; with Other Poems and Parables. 1871. [Partly rptd from The World's Epitaph.]

Parables and Tales. 1872; ed. T. Hake, 1917.

New Symbols. 1876.

Legends of the Morrow. 1879.

Maiden Ecstasy. 1880.

The Serpent Play; a Divine Pastoral. 1883.

The New Day. Sonnets. Ed. (with long critical preface) W. G. Hodgson, 1890.

The Poems of Thomas Gordon Hake. Selected and with Prefatory Note by Alice Meynell. 1894.

(b) Other Writings

Vates: or the Philosophy of Madness: being an Account of the Life, Actions, Passions and Principles of a Tragic Writer. 4 pts, 1840.
On the Powers of the Alphabet. 1. A Tonic Scale of Alphabetic Sounds. 1883. [A short treatise on phonetics. Only pt 1 appears to have been pbd.]
Memoirs of Eighty Years. 1892.

[Hake also pbd two medical works.]

(c) Biography and Criticism

Rossetti, D. G. Dr. Hake's Poems. Fortnightly Rev. xix, 1873. [Rptd in Rossetti's Collected Works, vol. ii, 1886, etc.]
Bayne, T. Thomas Gordon Hake. Miles, iv.
Rossetti, W. M. Memoir of D. G. Rossetti. [Prefixed to D. G. Rossetti's Family Letters, 2 vols. 1895.]
Symons, A. Thomas Gordon Hake. [In Studies in Two Literatures, 1897.]
Watts-Dunton, T. Old Familiar Faces. 1916.

ARTHUR HENRY HALLAM (1811–1833)
[See p. 716 below.]

SIR WILLIAM ROWAN HAMILTON
(1805–1865)
[See p. 941 below.]

SIR JOHN HANMER, afterwards BARON
HANMER (1809–1881)

(a) Poems

Proteus, and Other Poems. 1833 (2nd edn).
Poems on Various Subjects. 1836 (priv. ptd).
Era Cipolla, and Other Poems. 1839.
Sonnets. 1840.
A Memorial of the Parish and Family of Hanmer in Flintshire. 1877 (priv. ptd). [With an Appendix of Sonnets and Epigrams.]

(b) Biography and Criticism

Obituary. Times, 11, 15 March 1881.

ROBERT STEPHEN HAWKER (1803–1875)

(a) Collected Poems

Poetical Works. Ed. J. G. Godwin, 1879.
The Poetical Works. Ed. A. Wallis, 1899. [Includes full bibliography.]

(b) Selections

Twenty Poems. Ed. J. Drinkwater, Oxford, 1925.

A Selection of Robert Stephen Hawker's Cornish Ballads. Ed. F. C. Hamlyn, Truro, [1928].
Hawker of Morwenstow. 1931. (Augustan Books of Poetry.)

(c) Individual Publications

Tendrils. By Reuben. Cheltenham, 1821. [Poems.]
Pompeii, a Prize Poem. Oxford, [1827]. [Rptd in Oxford English Prize Poems, 1828.]
Records of the Western Shore. First Series. Oxford, 1822; Camelford [Cornwall], 1868. [Poems.]
Poems. Stratton [Cornwall], 1836. [Contains 3rd edn of Pompeii, 2nd edn of Records, ser. 1, and 1st edn of Records, ser. 2.]
Minster Church. 1836 (priv. ptd). [Poems.]
A Welcome to the Prince Albert [in verse]. Oxford, 1840.
Ecclesia: a Volume of Poems. Oxford, 1840.
The Poor Man and his Parish Church. Plymouth, 1843 (2nd edn). [Poems.]
Reeds Shaken with the Wind. 1843. [Poems.]
Reeds Shaken with the Wind. Second Cluster. Derby, 1844.
Echoes from Old Cornwall. 1846. [Poems.]
A Voice from the Place of S. Morwenna. 1849.
The Quest of the Sangraal. Chant the First. Exeter, 1864 (priv. ptd).
Cornish Ballads and Other Poems. Oxford, 1869 (including 2nd edn of The Quest); 1884; ed. C. E. Byles, 1904.
Footprints of Former Men in Far Cornwall. 1870; ed. C. E. Byles, [1903]. [Prose sketches, with some verses.]
Prose Works. [Ed. J. G. Godwin], 1893. [A new edn of Footprints, with addns.]
Stones Broken from the Rocks. Extracts from Note-Books. [Ed. E. R. Appleton and C. E. Byles,] Oxford, 1922.

[Hawker also issued a number of single poems as leaflets.]

(d) Biography and Criticism

Gould, S. Baring. The Vicar of Morwenstow. 1875; 1876 (rev. edn), etc.
Lee, F. G. Memorials of Robert Stephen Hawker. 1876.
Noble, J. A. Robert Stephen Hawker. Miles, iii.
—— Hawker of Morwenstow. [In The Sonnet in England and Other Essays, 1893.]
Byles, C. E. Life and Letters of Robert Stephen Hawker. 1905.
Burrows, M. F. Robert Stephen Hawker. A Study of his Thought and Poetry. Oxford, 1926.
Hawker of Morwenstow. TLS. 20 Dec 1934.

RICHARD HENRY (or HENGIST) HORNE
(1803–1884)

(a) Individual Publications

Exposition of the False Medium and Barriers excluding Men of Genius from the Public. 1833 (anon.).

The Spirit of Peers and People: a National Tragi-Comedy. 1834.

Cosmo de' Medici, an Historical Tragedy [in verse]. 1837; 1875 (adds some other poems).

The Death of Marlowe, a Tragedy [in prose and verse]. 1837; 1870 (5th edn). [Rptd in Works of Marlowe, ed. A. H. Bullen, vol. III, 1885.]

Gregory VII, a Tragedy in One Act [in verse]. 1840; 1849 (3rd edn). [Includes an Essay on Tragic Influence.]

Poems of Chaucer Modernized. 1841. [By various writers. Horne contributed the introduction and three tales.]

The History of Napoleon. 2 vols. 1841; rev. S. R. T. Mayer, 1879.

Orion. An Epic Poem in Three Books. 1843 (3 edns, each sold at a farthing); Melbourne, 1854 (adds preface); 1872 (9th and definitive edn); ed. E. Partridge, 1928.

A New Spirit of the Age. Edited [and largely written] by R. H. Horne. 2 vols. 1844 (bis); ed. W. Jerrold, 1907 (World's Classics).

Ballad Romances. 1846.

Judas Iscariot, a Miracle Play. With Other Poems. 1848. [Rptd in Bible Tragedies, [1881].]

The Dreamer and the Worker, a Story of the Present Time. 2 vols. 1851.

Australian Facts and Prospects. 1859. [Includes 'the Author's Australian Autobiography.']

Prometheus, the Fire Bringer. A Drama in Verse. Edinburgh, 1864; Melbourne, 1864.

The South-Sea Sisters; a Lyric Masque, written for the Opening of the Inter-Colonial Exhibition of Australasia. Melbourne, 1866.

The Great Peace-Maker, a Sub-Marine Dialogue With a Preface by H. B. Forman. 1872. [Poem; rptd from Household Words.]

Ode to the Mikado of Japan. 1873.

Letters of Elizabeth Barrett Browning, addressed to R. H. Horne. Ed. S. R. T. Mayer, 2 vols. 1877. [With a connecting narrative by Horne.]

Laura Dibalzo; or, the Patriot Martyrs. A Tragedy. 1880.

King Nihil's Round Table, or, the Regicide's Symposium. A Dramatic Scene. 1881.

Bible Tragedies. 1881. [3 pieces in prose and verse.]

Soliloquium Fratris Rogeri Baconis [in verse]. 1882 (priv. ptd). [Rptd from Fraser's Mag.]

The Last Words of Cleanthes, a Poem. [1883.] [Rptd from Longman's Mag.]

[Horne also pbd much miscellaneous prose.]

(b) Biography and Criticism

Poe, E. A. R. H. Horne. Graham's Mag. (Philadelphia), March 1844. [Rptd in Works, ed. C. F. Richardson, New York, vol. VI, 1902. A full and favourable notice of Orion.]

Powell, T. Pictures of the Living Authors of Britain. 1851. [Chiefly on Gregory VII and Orion. Some personal details.]

Forman, H. B. Our Living Poets. 1871, pp. 427–46.

—— Literary Anecdotes of the Nineteenth Century. Ed. Sir W. R. Nicoll and T. J. Wise, vol. I, 1895.

Richard Henry Horne. Miles, III.

Gosse, Sir E. 'Orion' Horne. [In Portraits and Sketches, 1912.]

Letters from A. C. Swinburne to R. H. Horne. 1920 (priv. ptd). [18 pp. only.]

Dickens, C. Notes and Comments on Certain Writings by R. H. Horne. 1920 (priv. ptd). [6 letters from Dickens to Horne.]

Partridge, E. Literary Sessions. 1932.

WILLIAM WALSHAM HOW (1823–1897)

(a) Writings

Psalms and Hymns. Compiled by T. B. Morrell and W. Walsham How. 1854; 1860; 1872.

Poems. Enlarged Edition. [1886.]

Public Worship. [1894.]

A Sermon in a Children's Ward in a Hospital. 1896.

A Souvenir of the Late Bishop Walsham How. [1898.] [A poem To a Mother on the Death of her Boy.]

[How was one of the compilers of Church Hymns, 1871, and pbd many sermons and tracts.]

(b) Biography and Criticism

Miles, A. H. William Walsham How. Miles X, (XII).

How, F. D. Bishop Walsham How: a Memoir. 1898.

—— William Walsham How, first Bishop of Wakefield. 1909.

Julian, J. A Dictionary of Hymnology. 1907.

CECIL FRANCES HUMPHREYS, afterwards
ALEXANDER (1818–1895)

(a) Collected and Selected Works

Poems. Ed. W. Alexander, 1896.
Selected Poems of William Alexander and
Cecil Frances Alexander. Ed. A. P. Graves,
1930.

(b) Poems and Hymns

[Nearly all the following works were issued
under the initials C. F. H. or (after 1850)
C. F. A.]
Verses for Holy Seasons. 1846. [With a
preface by W. F. Hook.]
Hymns for Little Children. 1848. [With a
brief preface by John Keble.]
Moral Songs. 1849.
Narrative Hymns for Village Schools. 1853.
Poems on Subjects in the Old Testament. 1854.
Hymns Descriptive and Devotional. 1858.
The Legend of the Golden Prayers and Other
Poems. 1859.
Hymns for Children. 1894.
Quireach Phádruig, or St Patrick's Breast-
plate. 1902. [Rptd from The Irish Church
Hymnal. Mrs Alexander's trn is ptd along-
side the Irish text.]

(c) Fiction

The Lord of the Forest and his Vassals. An
Allegory. 1848.
The Baron's Little Daughter and Other
Tales. 1875 (4th edn).

[Mrs Alexander also pbd religious works.]

(d) Criticism

Dublin University Mag. Oct. 1858, Sept.
1850.
Obituary. Times, 14, 19 Oct. 1893.
Gwynn, S. Sunday Mag. Jan. 1896.
Davidson, J. A Dictionary of Hymnology.
Ed. J. Julian, 1907.

JOHN WILLIAM INCHBOLD (1830–1888)

Annus Amoris. 1876. [Sonnets.]

[For obituary see Athenaeum, 4 Feb. 1888.]

JEAN INGELOW (1820–1897)

(a) Poems

A Rhyming Chronicle of Incidents and
Feelings. Edited by Edward Harston.
1850 (anon.).
Poems. 1863 (23 edns by 1880).
Home Thoughts and Home Scenes. In
Original Poems by J. I. 1865.
A Story of Doom and Other Poems. 1867
(6 edns by 1880).
Poems. 2 vols. 1880; 2 vols. 1893. [Vol. I rptd
from 23rd edn of Poems (1863) with
additional matter; vol. II rptd with many

addns from 6th edn of A Story of Doom and
Other Poems.]
Poems. Third Series. 1885; 1888.
Poems of the Old Days and the New. Boston,
1885.
Lyrical and Other Poems. Selected from the
Writings of Jean Ingelow. 1886.
Poetical Works. 1898. [Rptd from Poems,
2 vols. 1893, and Poems: Third Series,
1888.]
Poems. 1906. (Muses' Lib.)
Poems. With an Introduction by Alice
Meynell. 1908.
Poems. Selected and Arranged by Andrew
Lang. 1908.
Poems, 1850–1869. 1913. (Oxford edn.)

(b) Fiction

Allerton and Dreux; or, the War of Opinion.
2 vols. 1851 (anon.).
Tales of Orris. Bath, 1860; 1865 (as Stories
told to a Child; omits one story). [The
Grandmother's Shoe; The Golden Oppor-
tunity; Little Rie and the Rosebuds; Two
Ways of telling a Story; The Moorish Gold;
Life of Mr John Smith; Can and Could;
Deborah's Book, etc. Many of these stories
were subsequently rptd separately.]
Studies for Stories. 2 vols. 1864 (anon.).
[Short stories. The Cumberers; My Great-
Aunt's Picture; Mr Deane's Governess;
The Stolen Treasure; Emily's Ambition.]
A Sister's Bye-Hours. 1868 (anon.). [Short
stories. Laura Richmond; Marked; Up and
Down; The Black Polyanthus; Widow
Maclean; The Clouded Intellect; Muscha-
chito Mio.]
Mopsa the Fairy. 1869. [A long fairy story.]
The Little Wonder-Horn. 1872. [Forms the
second series of Stories told to a Child.
The Ouphe of the Wood; The Fairy who
judged her Neighbours; The Snowflake;
The Water Lily; A Lost Wand; Muscha-
chito Mio, etc. Many of these stories were
subsequently rptd separately.]
Fated to be Free. 3 vols. 1875. [Rptd from
Good Words, where it appeared in serial
form in 1875.]
Off the Skelligs. 4 vols. 1877.
Sarah de Berenger. A Novel. 1879; 3 vols.
1880.
Don John: a Story. 3 vols. 1881.
John Jerome: his Thoughts and Ways. A
Book without Beginning. 1886.
Very Young and Quite Another Story. 1890.
[One story in two parts.]

(c) Biography and Criticism

Forman, H. B. Our Living Poets. 1871,
pp. 87–102.

Robertson, E. S. English Poetesses. 1883, pp. 359–67.

Bell, M. Jean Ingelow. *Miles*, VII (VIII).

Obituary. Times, 21 July 1897; Athenaeum, 24 July 1897.

Some Recollections of Jean Ingelow. 1901.

Hearn, L. Appreciations of Poetry. Ed. J. Erskine, New York, 1916.

JOHN KELLS INGRAM (1823–1907)

[See p. 1053 below.]

WILLIAM JOSIAH IRONS (1812–1883)

(a) *Poems*

Hymn for Advent. Dies Irae [of Thomas de Celano]. Translated [as Day of Wrath! O Day of Mourning!]. The Music by H. E. Havergal. [1854.]

Psalms and Hymns for the Church. [1875.]

(b) *Theological and Philosophical Works*

The Idea of a National Church. [In Replies to 'Essays and Reviews,' 1862.]

Analysis of Human Responsibility. Being Three Papers read before the Victoria Institute. [1869.]

Christianity as taught by S. Paul, considered in eight Lectures preached on the Foundation of the Rev. J. Bampton. To which is added an Appendix of the Continuous Sense of S. Paul's Epistles. Oxford, 1870.

[Irons was a prolific writer, mainly of theological tracts and sermons.]

(c) *Biography and Criticism*

Obituary. Times, 20 June 1883.

Miles, A. H. William Josiah Irons. *Miles*, x, (xII).

Julian, J. A Dictionary of Hymnology. 1907.

GEORGE PAYNE RAINSFORD JAMES (1799–1860)

[See p. 402 below.]

JOHN HENEAGE JESSE (1815–1874)

[See p. 899 below.]

WILLIAM JOHNSON, later CORY (1823–1892)

(a) *Poems*

Ionica. 1858 (anon.).

Plato. [Written 1843. In A Complete Collection of the English Poems which have obtained the Chancellor's Gold Medal in the University of Cambridge, vol. I, Cambridge, 1859.]

Ionica II. 1877 (anon. and priv. ptd).

Ionica. 1891. [A rpt of Ionica (1858) and Ionica II, with 85 additional poems, and a biographical introduction and notes by A. C. Benson.]

(b) *Other Writings*

Eton Reform. 2 vols. 1861. [Two short essays on the principles of education.]

On the Education of the Reasoning Faculties. [Essay VIII in Essays on a Liberal Education, ed. F. W. Farrar, 1867.]

Nuces: Exercises in the Syntax of the Public School Latin Primer. 3 vols. 1867–70.

Lucretilis. An Introduction to the Art of Writing Latin Lyric Verses. 2 vols. 1871.

Iophon: an Introduction to the Art of Writing Greek Iambic Verses. 1873.

A Guide to Modern English History [1815–35]. 2 vols. 1880–2.

Extracts from the Letters and Journals of William Cory. Selected and Arranged by F. W. Cornish. Oxford, 1897 (priv. ptd).

Hints for Eton Masters. 1898. [A short practical essay on the art of teaching and managing boys. Pbd under the initials W. J.]

(c) *Biography and Criticism*

Nicoll, Sir W. R. and Wise, T. J. Literary Anecdotes of the Nineteenth Century. Vol. II, 1896.

Paul, H. Stray Leaves. 1906. [Has an essay on The Author of Ionica, which consists mainly of personal reminiscences of Johnson at Eton and afterwards.]

Notes of the Table Talk of William Cory. [In Gathered Leaves from the Prose of Mary E. Coleridge, ed. E. Sichel, 1910.]

Esher, R., Viscount. Ionicus. 1923. [A biography and appreciation of Johnson. Contains many letters by Johnson, and in appendices, extracts from and notes on Ionica and Lucretilis.]

Madan, G. William Cory. Cornhill Mag. Aug. 1928.

EBENEZER JONES (1820–1860)

(a) *Writings*

Studies of Sensation and Event, Poems. 1843; ed. R. H. Shepherd, 1879 (with memorial notices by S. Jones and W. J. Linton).

The Land Monopoly, the Suffering and Demoralization caused by it, and the Justice and Expediency of its Abolition. 1849.

(b) *Biography and Criticism*

Shepherd, R. H. Forgotten Books Worth Remembering. 1878. [A series of monographs. No. 1 is on Ebenezer Jones.]

Athenaeum, 14 Sept. 1878. [A lengthy review of R. H. Shepherd's brochure.]

Watts, T. Athenaeum, 21, 28 Sept., 12 Oct. 1878. [Jones's life and work.]

Linton, W. J. Ebenezer Jones. *Miles*, v.

ERNEST CHARLES JONES (1819–1868)

(a) Poems

The Battle-Day: and Other Poems. 1855.
The Song of the Lower Classes. A Song of
Cromwell's Time. 1856.
Songs of Democracy. 1856. [Song of the Day
Labourers; A Song of Resurrection; The
Marriage Feast; Song of the Factory Slave.
Pbd separately as flysheets.]
The Emperor's Vigil, and the Waves and the
War. 1856.
The Revolt of Hindustan; or, the New World:
a Poem. 1857.
Corayda; a Tale of Faith and Chivalry, and
Other Poems. 1860.

(b) Fiction

The Wood-Spirit: a Novel. 2 vols. 1841.
The Maid of Warsaw, or the Tyrant Czar: a
Tale of the Last Polish Revolution. 1854.
The Lass and the Lady: a Tale. 1855.
Woman's Wrongs: a Series of Tales. 1855.
[The Working Man's Wife; The Young
Milliner; The Tradesman's Daughter; The
Girl with Red Hands; The Lady of Title.]

[Jones also pbd lectures on social and
political subjects.]

(c) Biography and Criticism

Obituary. Times, 27, 29 Jan., 31 March 1868.
Miles, A. H. Ernest Charles Jones. *Miles*, IV.

ROBERT DWYER JOYCE (1830–1883)
[See p. 1054 below.]

FRANCES ANNE KEMBLE, afterwards
BUTLER (1809–1893)

(a) Poems and Plays

Francis the First, an Historical Drama. 1832.
The Star of Seville. 1837. [A play.]
Poems. Philadelphia, 1844.
Poems. 1844. [The contents are in the main
identical with those in the American edn,
but the arrangement is different. Subse-
quent edns follow the American edn.]
Plays. 1863. [An English Tragedy; Mary
Stuart (tr. from the German of Schiller);
Mademoiselle de Belle Isle (tr. from the
French of Alexandre Dumas).]
Poems. 1866. [One or two poems rptd from
the earlier collection, but the bulk of the
work is new.]
The Poetical Works. 1883.
Adventures of John Timothy Homespun in
Switzerland. 1889. [A play 'stolen from
the French of Tartarin de Tarascon.']

(b) Other Writings

Journal. 2 vols. 1835. [An edn in 1 vol. with
the title Journal of a Residence in America
was pbd in the same year in Brussels.]

A Year of Consolation. 2 vols. 1847. [An
autobiographical account of a year spent
travelling in Italy.]
Journal of a Residence on a Georgian Planta-
tion in 1838–1839. 1863.
Record of a Girlhood. An Autobiography.
3 vols. 1878. [Rptd in part from Atlantic
Monthly.]
Records of Later Life. 3 vols. 1882.
Notes upon Some of Shakespeare's Plays.
1882. [On the Stage; Notes on Macbeth,
Henry VIII, the Tempest and Romeo and
Juliet.]
Far Away and Long Ago. 1889. [A novel.]
Further Records. 1848–1883. 2 vols. 1890.
[A series of letters forming a sequel to
Record of a Girlhood and Records of Later
Life.]
On the Stage. With Introduction by George
Arliss and Notes by B. M. New York, 1926.
[Rptd from Notes upon Some of Shake-
speare's Plays.]

(c) Biography and Criticism

Craven, P. M. A. A. La Jeunesse de F.
Kemble. Paris, 1880.
James, Henry. Essays in London and Else-
where. New York, 1893. [Has an essay on
Fanny Kemble.]
Japp, A. H. Frances Anne Kemble. *Miles*,
VII (VIII).
Letters of Edward FitzGerald to Fanny
Kemble, 1871–1883. Ed. W. A. Wright, 1895.
Pope-Hennessy, U. Three English Women in
America. 1929. [Fanny Trollope, Fanny
Kemble, and Harriet Martineau.]
Bobbé, D. Fanny Kemble. New York, 1931.
[Includes a full list of books and articles on
Fanny Kemble and her period.]
Armstrong, M. Fanny Kemble. 1938.

CHARLES RANN KENNEDY (1808–1867)

Ode on the Birth of the Prince. 1842.
Poems, Original and Translated. 1843; 1857
(re-arranged and enlarged).
Specimens of Greek and Latin Verse, chiefly
Translations. 1853. [English verse trans-
lated into Greek and Latin.]
Francis Beaumont: a Tragedy. Birmingham,
[1860?].
The Works of Virgil. 1861.
Hannibal: a Poem. [1866.]

[Kennedy also wrote on classical and legal
subjects and translated Demosthenes (see
p. 999 below).]

CHARLES KINGSLEY (1819–1875)

[See p. 487 below.]

LETITIA ELIZABETH LANDON, afterwards
MACLEAN (1802–1838)

(a) Collected Works

The Miscellaneous Poetical Works of L. E. L.
1835.
The Works. 2 vols. Philadelphia, 1838.
The Poetical Works. 4 vols. 1839.
The Poetical Works. 2 vols. Philadelphia, 1845.
Poetical Works: with a Memoir of the Author.
2 vols. 1850; 2 vols. 1855; 2 vols. 1867.
The Poetical Works. Ed. W. B. Scott, [1873].

(b) Poems

The Fate of Adelaide: a Swiss Romantic
Tale; and Other Poems. 1821.
The Improvisatrice; and Other Poems. By
L. E. L. 1824; 1825 (6th edn).
The Troubadour; Catalogue of Pictures; and
Historical Sketches. By L. E. L. 1825 (3
edns).
The Golden Violet, with its Tales of Romance
and Chivalry: and Other Poems. By
L. E. L. 1827.
The Venetian Bracelet, The Lost Pleiad, a
History of the Lyre, and Other Poems.
By L. E. L. 1828.
The Vow of the Peacock, and Other Poems.
1835.
A Birthday Tribute [in verse], addressed to
the Princess Alexandrina Victoria, on
attaining her Eighteenth Year. By L. E. L.
[1837].
Flowers of Loveliness. Twelve Groups of
Female Figures emblematic of Flowers; with
Poetical Illustrations by L. E. L. 1838;
[1854] (with similar collections by Lady
Blessington and T. H. Bayly).
The Easter Gift: a Religious Offering. By
L. E. L. [1838].
The Zenana, and Minor Poems of L. E. L.
With a Memoir by Emma Roberts. 1839.

(c) Other Works

Romance and Reality. By L. E. L. 3 vols.
1831. [A novel.]
Francesco Carrara. By L. E. L. 3 vols. 1834.
[A novel.]
Traits and Trials of Early Life. By L. E. L.
1836; 1844. [Tales, with poems interspersed.]
Ethel Churchill; or, The Two Brides. By the
Author of The Improvisatrice. 3 vols.
1837. [A novel.]
Lady Anne Granard; or, Keeping up Appear-
ances. 3 vols. 1842. [A novel.]

[L. E. L. also edited, or contributed to,
various annuals, scrapbooks, etc., as well as
writing numerous articles and reviews for
W. Jerdan's Literary Gazette from c. 1820.]

(d) Biography and Criticism

Blanchard, S. L. Life and Literary Remains
of L. E. L. 2 vols. 1841. [Vol. II consists of
unpbd works by L. E. L.]
S[heppard], S. Characteristics of the Genius
and Writings of L. E. L. With Illustrations
from her Works and from Personal Recol-
lection. 1841.
Elwood, A. K. Memoirs of the Literary Ladies
of England. Vol. II, 1843, pp. 304–32.
Hall, S. C. and A. M. Memories of Authors.
Miss Landon. Atlantic Monthly, xv, 1865.
Robertson, E. S. English Poetesses. 1883,
pp. 212–26.
Bates, W. The Maclise Portrait-Gallery of
'Illustrious Literary Characters.' 1883.
Bell, M. Laetitia Elizabeth Maclean. Miles,
VII (VIII).
Le Fèvre-Deumier, J. Célébrités anglaises.
Essais et Études biographiques et littéraires.
Paris, 1895. [Includes essay on L. E. L.]
Enfield, D. E. L. E. L.: a Mystery of the
Thirties. 1928.

EDWARD LEAR (1812–1888)
[See p. 567 below.]

PERCIVAL LEIGH (1813–1889)
[See p. 719 below.]

ROBERT LEIGHTON (1822–1869)
Poems by Robin. 1855.
Rhymes and Poems. 1861 (bis).
Poems. Liverpool, 1866; Liverpool, 1869.
Scotch Words, and The Bapteesement o' the
Bairn. 1869 (3 edns). [Biography prefixed.]
Reuben, and Other Poems. 1875.
Records, and Other Poems. 1880.

[The two last-named together constitute
the collected works.]

WILLIAM JAMES LINTON (1812–1898)

(a) Collected and Selected Works

Prose and Verse. Written and Published in the
Course of Fifty Years. 1836–1886. 20 vols.
[Cuttings from newspapers, periodicals,
pamphlets, etc., arranged and bound by
Linton and presented to the British
Museum.]
Poems and Translations. 1889. [Includes
Love Lore, with selections from Claribel and
other pieces from Linton's translations.]

(b) Poems

Bob Thin or the Poor-House Fugitive. 1845
(priv. ptd). [A satire.]
The Plaint of Freedom. Newcastle-on-Tyne,
1852.
Claribel and Other Poems. 1865. [Claribel is
a dramatic poem in two acts.]

Ireland for the Irish. Rhymes and Reasons against Landlordism. New York, 1867. [With a lengthy preface on Fenianism and Republicanism.]

The House that Tweed built. Boston, [1874?] (anon.). [A political lampoon.]

Famine, a Masque. Hamden, Connecticut, 1875.

Pot-Pourri. 1875. [Parodies on the poems of E. A. Poe.]

Adventures of Ulysses. Exposed in Modest Hudibrastic Measure by Abel Reid and A. N. Broome. Washington, 1876. [Reid and Broome are pseudonyms for Linton.]

Voices of the Dead. [1879?] [Verse dialogues between Charlotte Corday and Marat, and between Mazzini and the Countess Ossoli, and a short monologue by Delescluze on the Barricade.]

Love-Lore. Hamden, Connecticut, 1887; 1895 (adds other poems, early and late).

Catoninetales. A Domestic Epic by Hattie Brown. 1891. [Parodies.]

Heliconundrums. Hamden, Connecticut, 1892 (priv. ptd).

A Christmas Carol. 1893.

Ultima Verba. 1895 (priv. ptd).

(c) Other Writings

The Life of Thomas Paine. 1840.

The People's Land, and an Easy Way to recover it. 1850. [Letters to the editor of The Nation showing how famine may be prevented in Ireland.]

The Ferns of the English Lake Country. 1865.

The Flower and the Star and Other Stories. Boston, 1868; 1891. [6 stories for children.]

The Religion of Organization. An Essay. Boston, 1869. [Rptd from The Radical.]

The Paris Commune. Boston, 1871. [Rptd from The Radical. A reply to the calumnies of New York Tribune.]

James Watson. A Memoir. Hamden, Connecticut, 1879 (priv. ptd); Manchester, 1880 (for general circulation).

Reminiscences of Eben Jones. [Prefixed to Jones's Studies of Sensation and Event, 1879.]

Some Practical Hints on Wood-engraving, for the Instruction of Reviewers and the Public. Boston, 1879.

The History of Wood-Engraving in America. Boston, 1882.

Wood-Engraving: a Manual of Instruction. Boston, 1884.

The Masters of Wood-Engraving. 1889.

European Republicans. Recollections of Mazzini and Friends. 1893.

Life of J. G. Whittier. 1893.

Memories. 1895.

Darwin's Probabilities. Hamden, Connecticut, 1896. [A review of The Descent of Man.]

(d) Biography and Criticism

Kitton, F. G. W. J. Linton. Engraver, Poet, and Political Writer. English Illustrated Mag. April 1891.

Bullen, A. H. William James Linton. Miles, IV.

Obituary. Times, 3 Jan. 1898; Athenaeum, 8, 15 Jan. 1898.

Layard, G. S. Life of Mrs Lynn Linton. 1901. [Chs. viii and ix are on Linton.]

Hopson, W. F. Side Lights on William James Linton, 1812–97. Bibliog. Soc. of America Papers, XXVII, 1933.

FREDERICK LOCKER-LAMPSON (1821–1895)

(a) Bibliography

Livingston, F. V. Bookman's Journ. May, July, Aug., Sept. 1924. [A detailed account of all the edns of Locker-Lampson's works.]

(b) Writings

London Lyrics. 1857; 1862 (with alterations and omissions; adds 20 new poems); 1868 (adds 6 new poems but omits others); 1870 (adds 6 new poems); 1872 (adds 10 new poems); 1874 (adds 8 new poems); 1876 (final revision; 6 poems added); 1882 (as London Rhymes, omitting much but with 9 new poems); New York, 1883 (pirated as Poems); New York, 1884 (authorized edn, as Poems and differing slightly from 1876 edn); ed. A. D. Godley, 1903 (from 1857 edn); ed. A. Dobson, 1904 (definitive edn).

A Selection from the Works of Frederick Locker. 1865. [Includes 20 unpbd pieces and the remainder in rev. form.]

My Confidences. An Autobiographical Sketch addressed to my Descendants. Ed. A. Birrell, 1896.

(c) Compilations and Anthologies

Lyra Elegantiarum. 1867 (suppressed); 1867 (new and rev. edn); 1891 (rev. and enlarged with the assistance of Coulson Kernahan). [A collection of some of the best specimens of vers de société and vers d'occasion in the English language, with a prefatory essay.]

Patchwork. 1879 (priv. ptd for Philobiblon Soc.); 1879 (for general circulation). [A commonplace book. The volume contains 5 poems by Locker-Lampson, of which 3 are new.]

The Rowfant Library. A Catalogue of the Printed Books, Manuscripts, Autograph Letters, Drawings and Pictures collected by F. Locker-Lampson. 1886. [An appendix to the catalogue, with preface by A. Birrell and memorial verses by A. Dobson, A. Lang, Lord Crewe and Wilfred Scawen Blunt was pbd separately in 1900.]

(d) Biography and Criticism

Dobson, A. Frederick Locker-Lampson. *Miles*, v.

Swinburne, A. C. Studies in Prose and Poetry. 1894. [The essay on social verse is a review of Lyra Elegantiarum.]

Birrell, A. Frederick Locker-Lampson. A Character Sketch. 1920.

Locker-Lampson, O. Frederick Locker-Lampson, with some unpublished Sketches and Poems. Scribner's Mag. April 1921.

—— Recollections of Frederick Locker-Lampson. Cornhill Mag. Jan., Feb. 1921.

Kernahan, C. Austin Dobson and Lyra Elegantiarum. Quart. Rev. Jan. 1922.

CAPEL LOFFT (1806–1873)

(a) Writings

The Whigs, their Prospects and Policy. 1835.

Self-Formation; or, the History of an Individual Mind. 2 vols. 1837 (anon.). [A mental autobiography.]

Ernest or Political Regeneration. A Poem. 1839 (anon.); 1868 (as Ernest: the Rule of Right. Adds a long preface on the nature of poetry, and many alterations and additions). [The poem, a long one, represents the growth, struggles and triumph of Chartism.]

New Testament: Suggestions for Reformation of Greek Text on Principles of Logical Criticism. 1868. [Under the pseudonym 'R. E. Storer.']

(b) Criticism

Quart. Rev. LXV, 1840. [Long review of 'Ernest.']

THOMAS TOKE LYNCH (1818–1871)

(a) Poems

Memorials of Theophilus Trivial, Student. 1850; 1869 (3rd edn, enlarged). [The Thoughts, Poems, Meditations and Observations of Theophilus Trivial. There are 54 poems in the 1st edn and 81 poems in the 1869 edn.]

The Rivulet: a Contribution to Sacred Song. 1855; 1868 (3rd edn, enlarged). [For an account of the controversy over this work see W. White's memoir of T. T. Lynch, 1874.]

Songs Controversial. By Silent Long. 1856. [15 songs protesting against the review of The Rivulet which appeared in British Banner.]

(b) Other Writings

Thoughts on a Day. 1844 (anon.); 1856 (adds a morning and an evening hymn).

Essays on Some of the Forms of Literature. 1853. [On Poetry, its Sources and Influence; On Biography, Autobiography and History; On Fictions and Imaginative Prose; On Criticism and Writings of the Day.]

Lectures in Aid of Self Improvement, addressed to Young Men and Others. 1853. [On Self-Improvement, and the Motives to it; Religion as a Study; On Books, and on Reading Them; On Conversation and Discussion; On Manners and Social Respectability; On Circumstance and Character.]

The Ethics of Quotation, with a Preliminary Letter to the Secretaries of the Congregational Union. By Silent Long. 1856. [This pamphlet together with Songs Controversial constitutes Lynch's reply to the attack made on The Rivulet in British Banner.]

The Mornington Lecture: Thursday Evening Addresses. 1870. [George Fox; Bunyan; John Foster; Edward Irving; The Browns of Haddington; Almsgiving; Our Lord's Last Labours; Temper and Temperament; Jerusalem the Old and New, etc.]

[Lynch also pbd sermons and religious works.]

(c) Biography

White, William. Memoir of T. T. Lynch. 1874. [White describes himself as the editor of this work, but appears to be its author. Includes a list of Lynch's writings.]

Horder, W. G. Thomas Toke Lynch. *Miles*, x (xi).

EDWARD GEORGE EARLE LYTTON BULWER-LYTTON, BARON LYTTON (1803–1873)

[See p. 475 below.]

DENIS FLORENCE MACARTHY (1817–1882)

[See p. 1053 below.]

THOMAS BABINGTON, BARON MACAULAY (1800–1859)

[See p. 683 below.]

GEORGE MACDONALD (1824–1905)

[See p. 494 below.]

CHARLES MACKAY (1814–1889)

(a) Collected and Selected Poems

Selected Poems. With Memoir by Francis Bennoch. [In the Modern Scottish Minstrel, ed. C. Rogers, vol. VI, 1857.]

Collected Songs. 1859. [Includes One Hundred Songs here pbd for the first time.]

Poetical Works. 1876. [With an introductory essay on poetry rptd from Egeria and Other Poems, 1850.]

Selected Poems and Songs. 1888. [The introduction consists of short criticisms by Douglas Jerrold, George Combe and A. B. Reach, with a long anonymous review rptd from St James's Mag.]

(b) Separate Poems

Songs and Poems. 1834.

The Hope of the World, and Other Poems. 1840.

The Salamandrine; or, Love and Immortality. 1842.

Legends of the Isles and Other Poems. Edinburgh, 1845; 1857 (as Legends of the Isles and Highland Gatherings). [Some of the poems were rptd 1856 as Ballads and Lyrical Poems.]

Voices from the Crowd; and Other Poems. 1846; 1857 (5th edn, rev.). [Rptd from Daily News.]

Voices from the Mountains. 1847.

Town Lyrics and Other Poems. 1848.

Egeria, or the Spirit of Nature; and Other Poems. 1850. [With an introductory essay on poetry.]

Songs for Music. 1856.

The Lump of Gold: and Other Poems. 1856.

Under Green Leaves. 1857.

A Man's Heart: a Poem. 1860.

Studies from the Antique and Sketches from Nature. 1864.

Interludes and Undertones; or, Music at Twilight. 1884.

Gossamer and Snowdrift. Posthumous Poems. Ed. E. Mackay, 1890.

[Some of Mackay's poems were also rptd singly.]

(c) Other Writings

A History of London from its Foundation by the Romans to the Accession of Queen Victoria, with Sketches of the Manners and Customs of the People. 1838.

The Thames and its Tributaries; or, Rambles among the Rivers. 2 vols. 1840.

Longbeard, Lord of London: a Romance. 3 vols. 1841; 1850 (entitled Longbeard: or, the Revolt of the Saxons).

Memoirs of Extraordinary Popular Delusions. 3 vols. 1841. [The Mississippi Scheme, the South Sea Bubble, the O.P. Mania, the Witch Mania, the Slow Poisoners, Haunted Houses, the Crusades, the Alchymists, Fortune Telling, the Magnetisers, etc.]

Education of the People, and the Necessity for the Establishment of a National System: in a Series of Letters to Viscount Morpeth. Glasgow, 1846.

The Scenery and Poetry of the English Lakes. A Summer Ramble. 1846.

The World as It is. 3 vols. 1850–4. [In collaboration with W. C. Taylor. A comprehensive system of modern geography, physical, political and commercial.]

Life and Times of Sir Robert Peel from the Date of his Final Retirement to his Premature Death. 1851. [Forms vol. IV of the Life and Times of Sir Robert Peel carried to the end of vol. III by Cooke Taylor.]

The Mormons: or, Latter-Day Saints. With Memories of the Life and Death of Joseph Smith, the 'American Mahomet.' 1851.

Life and Liberty in America: or, Sketches of a Tour in the United States and Canada, in 1857–8. 2 vols. 1859.

The History of the United States of America, continued to the Southern Secession. 2 vols. 1861. [Issued in shilling parts.]

The Gouty Philosopher; or the Opinions, Whims and Eccentricities of John Wagstaffe, Esq. 1862. [On Tobacco, Paying the Piper, Stupidity, Critics and Criticism, Ugly People, Tradesmen, Manhood Suffrage, etc.]

Street Tramways for London. 1868.

Under the Blue Sky. 1871. [Papers rptd from All the Year Round, Robin Goodfellow and other periodicals.]

Lost Beauties of the English Language: an Appeal to Authors. 1874.

Forty Years' Recollections of Life, Literature, and Public Affairs. From 1830 to 1870. 2 vols. 1877.

The Gaelic Etymology of the Languages of Western Europe and more especially of the English and Lowland Scotch. 1877.

The Liberal Party, its Present Position and Future Work. 1880.

Luck; and what came of It. A Tale of Our Times. 3 vols. 1881.

The Poetry and Humour of the Scottish Language. Paisley, 1882. [Rptd in part from Blackwood's Mag.]

New Light on Some Obscure Words and Phrases in the Works of Shakespeare and his Contemporaries. 1884.

The Founders of the American Republic. A History and Biography, with a Supplementary Chapter on Ultra-Democracy. Edinburgh, 1885.

A Glossary of Obscure Words and Phrases in the Writings of Shakespeare and his Contemporaries, traced Etymologically to the Ancient Language of the British People. 1887.

Through the Long Day, or, Memorials of a Literary Life during Half a Century. 2 vols. 1887.

A Dictionary of Lowland Scotch with an introductory chapter on the Poetry, Humour and Literary History of the Scottish Language. 1888. [With an appendix of Scottish proverbs.]

(d) Biography and Criticism

Powell, T. Pictures of the Living Authors of Britain. 1851.

Miles, A. H. Charles Mackay. *Miles*, IV.

Wykoff, G. S. England's Forgotten Civil War Correspondent. South Atlantic Quart. Jan. 1927.

FRANCIS SYLVESTER MAHONY (1804–1866)
[See p. 719 below.]

JAMES CLARENCE MANGAN (1803–1849)
[See p. 1051 below.]

JOHN WESTLAND MARSTON (1819–1890)
[See p. 604 below.]

SIR THEODORE MARTIN (1816–1909)

(a) Poems

Disputation between the Body and the Soul. 1838. [Signed T. M. With other poems by Martin signed E. N., Martinus Scriblerus and I. G.]

The Book of Ballads. Edited by Bon Gaultier. 1845; [1849] (with several new ballads, illustrated by A. Crowquill [*i.e.* A. H. Forrester], R. Doyle and J. Leech); 1857 (5th edn); 1903 (16th edn). [By Martin and W. E. Aytoun.]

Madonna Pia: a Tragedy in Verse. 1855 (priv. ptd).

Poems; Original and Translated. 1863 (priv. ptd).

(b) Biographies and Other Prose

Memoir of W. E. Aytoun; with an Appendix. 1867.

Horace. 1870.

The Life of His Royal Highness the Prince Consort. 5 vols. 1875–80.

A Life of Lord Lyndhurst, from Letters and Papers in Possession of his Family. 1883.

Sketch of the Life of Princess Alice. 1885.

Shakespeare or Bacon? Reprinted from Blackwood's Magazine, with Additions. Edinburgh, 1888.

Helena Faucit (Lady Martin). Edinburgh, 1900.

Monographs: Garrick, Macready, Rachel and Baron Stockmar. 1906.

Queen Victoria as I knew her. 1908.

(c) Translations

Hertz. King René's Daughter. 1850.

Öhlenschläger. Correggio; a Tragedy; with Notes. 1854.

Öhlenschläger. Aladdin; or, The Wonderful Lamp. A Dramatic Poem. 1857.

Goethe. Poems and Ballads. 1859; 1860 (rev. and enlarged); 1877. [By Martin and W. E. Aytoun.]

The Odes of Horace translated into English Verse. 1860; 1861.

The Poems of Catullus translated into English Verse, with an Introduction and Notes. 1861.

Dante. The Vita Nuova, with an Introduction and Notes. 1862; 1871.

Goethe. Faust. Part I. 1865; 1866; 1877. Parts I and II, 1870.

Schiller. Complete Works. Ed. C. J. Hempel. [Vol. I, William Tell, 1870, by Martin.]

Heine. Poems and Ballads. 1878; 1894; 1907.

Schiller. The Song of the Bell, and Other Translations. 1889.

Virgil. The Æneid, Books I–VI [in English verse]. 1896.

Leopardi. Poems. 1904.

[Martin produced several other trns, addresses, etc.]

(d) Biography and Criticism

Theodore Martin, with Portrait. Dublin University Mag. XC, 1877.

Whyte, W. Aytoun-Martin. 'Bon Gaultier.' *Miles*, IX (x).

Obituary. Blackwood's Mag. CLXXXVI, 1909.

Parsons, C. O. The Friendship of Theodore Martin and William Harrison Ainsworth. N. & Q. 23 June 1934.

GERALD MASSEY (1828–1907)

(a) Poems

Poems and Chansons. Tring, 1848.

Voices of Freedom and Lyrics of Love. 1850.

The Ballad of Babe Christabel: with Other Lyrical Poems. 1854; 1854 (4th edn, enlarged); 1855.

War Waits. 1855. [Poems on the Crimean war.]

Craigcrook Castle. 1856. [7 poems forming one long narrative poem.]

The Complete Poetical Works. Boston, 1857; 1861 (with Biographical Sketch by Samuel Smiles, rptd from Eliza Cook's Journal, 1851).

Robert Burns: a Centenary Song and Other Lyrics. 1859.

Havelock's March and Other Poems. 1861. [Poems on the Indian Mutiny.]

In Memory of John William Spencer, Earl Brownlow. 1869 (priv. ptd).

A Tale of Eternity, and Other Poems. 1870.

Carmen Nuptiale. [1880?] (priv. ptd).

My Lyrical Life: Poems Old and New. 2 vols. 1889.

(b) Other Writings

Shakespeare's Sonnets never before Interpreted. 1866; 1888 (re-written and entitled The Secret Drama of Shakespeare's Sonnets). [Re-written and greatly enlarged from an article contributed to Quart. Rev.]

Concerning Spiritualism. 1871. [Subsequently withdrawn by Massey.]
A Book of the Beginnings. 2 vols. 1881. [An attempt to recover the lost origins of myths and mysteries, types and symbols, religion and language, with Egypt for the mouthpiece and Africa as the birthplace. The preface was rptd separately with extracts, 1881.]
The Natural Genesis. 2 vols. 1883. [Pt II of A Book of the Beginnings.]
Ancient Egypt the Light of the World: a Work of Reclamation and Restitution in Twelve Books. 2 vols. 1907.

[Massey also expounded his theories in a number of priv. ptd lectures.]

(c) Biography and Criticism

Dixon, H. Athenaeum, 4 Feb. 1854. [A long review of Babe Christabel.]
Miles, A. H. Gerald Massey. Miles, v.
Collins, J. C. Studies in Poetry and Criticism. 1905. [Includes an essay on Massey.]
Milne, J. A Silent Singer. Book Monthly, July 1905.
—— Poet and Thinker. Book Monthly, Sept. 1907.
Wright, D. Gerald Massey. Open Court, Aug. 1924.
Evans, B. I. English Poetry in the Later Nineteenth Century. 1933. [Ch. xvi.]

GEORGE MEREDITH (1828–1909)
[See p. 467 below.]

HUGH MILLER (1802–1856)
[See p. 721 below.]

THOMAS MILLER (1807–1874)
Songs of the Sea Nymphs. 1832.
A Day in the Woods: Tales and Poems. 1836.
Poems. 1841.
The Poetical Language of Flowers; or, the Pilgrimage of Love. 1847.
Original Poems for My Children. 2 sers. 1852.
Birds, Bees and Blossoms: Poems for Children. [1858.]
Songs of the Seasons for My Children. 1865.

[Miller also pbd novels and children's books.]

WILLIAM MILLER (1810–1872)
Willie Winkie, and Other Songs and Poems. 1902.

RICHARD MONCKTON MILNES, BARON HOUGHTON (1809–1885)
(a) Collected and Selected Works
Memorials of Many Scenes. (Poems, legendary and historical.) 2 vols. 1844. [Selected from Memorials of a Tour in Greece,

Memorials of a Residence on the Continent and Poetry for the People, with some new poems.]
Selections from the Poetical Works of R. M. Milnes. 1863.
A Selection from the [poetical] Works of Lord Houghton. 1867.
The Poetical Works. 2 vols. 1876. [Includes songs pbd as flysheets and not here mentioned separately.]

(b) Poems
Memorials of a Tour in Some Parts of Greece: chiefly Poetical. 1834.
Memorials of a Residence on the Continent, and Historical Poems. 1838.
Poems of Many Years. 1838 (priv. ptd); 1840 (for general circulation).
Poetry for the People, and Other Poems. 1840.
Palm Leaves. 1844. [Poems written during and about a tour in the East.]
Good Night and Good Morning. A Ballad. 1859.

(c) Other Writings
The Influence of Homer. A Prize Essay. 1829.
One Tract More. By a Layman. 1841. [In support of the Anglo-Catholic movement.]
The Life, Letters, and Literary Remains of John Keats. 2 vols. 1848; ed. R. Lynd, 1927 (Everyman's Lib.); rptd 1931 (World's Classics). [Also prefixed, in an abridged form, to Keats's Poetical Works, 1854, etc.]
Miscellanies of the Philobiblon Society. 15 vols. 1853–1884. [Ed. by Milnes and including numerous contributions by him.]
On the Present Social Results of Classical Education. [In Essays on a Liberal Education, ed. F. W. Farrar, 1867.]
Monographs. Personal and Social. 1873. [Suleiman Pasha; Alexander von Humboldt at the Court of Berlin; Cardinal Wiseman; W. S. Landor; The Berrys; Lady Ashburton; Sydney Smith; The Last Days of Heinrich Heine.]

[Milnes also wrote on political and social questions of the day.]

(d) Biography
Reid, T. W. The Life, Letters and Friendships of Richard Monckton Milnes, First Lord Houghton. 2 vols. 1890.
Gibbs, H. J. Lord Houghton. Miles, iv.
Fischer, W. Die Briefe Richard Monckton Milnes, ersten Barons Houghton an Varnhagen von Ense. Heidelberg, 1922.

ROBERT MONTGOMERY (1807–1855)
[For a fuller bibliography of Montgomery's writings see GM. 1856, i, p. 312.]

(a) Collected Poems

The Poetical Works of Robert Montgomery. 6 vols. 1839–40; 6 vols. 1841–3; ed. J. Twycross, 1853.

(b) Selected Poems

Selections from the Poetical Works of Robert Montgomery. With Introductory Remarks, and an Appendix. 1836; 1837.
The Poetical Works. 3 vols. Glasgow, 1839.
Religion and Poetry. Ed. S. J. H., 1847.
Lyra Christiana. 1851. [Selected by Montgomery himself.]
Christian Poetry. Ed. E. Farr, [1856].

(c) Individual Publications

The Stage-Coach. A Poem. 1827.
The Age Reviewed. A Satire in Two Parts. 1827; 1828 (rev. edn).
The Omnipresence of the Deity. A Poem. 1828. [28 edns by 1855.]
The Puffiad. A Satire. 1828 (anon.).
A Universal Prayer; Death; A Vision of Heaven; and A Vision of Hell. 1828; 1829 (4th edn); 1846.
Satan. A Poem. 1830 (bis); Glasgow 1841, (8th edn); 1842 (10th edn).
Oxford. A Poem. Oxford, 1831; Oxford, 1835 (4th edn, adding recollections of Shelley); 1843 (6th edn).
The Messiah. A Poem in Six Books. 1832; 1836 (5th edn); 1842 (8th edn).
Woman, the Angel of Life. A Poem. 1833; 1841 (5th edn).
Ellesmere Lake. Poems. 1836.
Sacred Meditations in Verse. 1842; [1847] (3rd edn).
Luther. A Poem. 1842 (bis); 1852 (6th and rev. edn).
Scarborough. A Poetic Glance. 1846.
The Christian Life. A Manual of Sacred Verse. 1849; [1855] (7th edn).
The Hero's Funeral. A Poem. 1852 (3 edns). [On the Duke of Wellington.]
The Sanctuary. A Companion in Verse for the Prayer Book. 1855.

[Montgomery also pbd numerous sermons and theological works.]

(d) Criticism

[Macaulay, T. B.] Edinburgh Rev. LI, 1830. [The famous attack on The Omnipresence and Satan.]
Clarkson, E. Robert Montgomery and his Reviewers. With some Remarks on the Present State of English Poetry and on the Laws of Criticism. 1830 (bis). [Defends Montgomery against Macaulay.]
—— The Reviewers Reviewed. [1830?]

Horne, R. H. A New Spirit of the Age. Vol. II, 1844. [Severe criticism of Satan and Woman.]
Maginn, W. A Gallery of Illustrious Literary Characters. Ed. W. Bates, [1873].

EDWARD MOXON (1801–1858)
(a) Poems

The Prospect, and Other Poems. 1826.
Christmas, a Poem. 1829.
Sonnets. 2 pts, 1830–5 (priv. ptd); 1837 (priv. ptd); 1843; 1871.

[Moxon edited The Englishman's Mag. Aug.–Oct. 1831.]

(b) Biography and Criticism

Lamb, C. Athenaeum, 13 April 1833. [Rptd in Works, ed. E. V. Lucas, vol. I, 1903. On the Sonnets.]
[Croker, J. W.] Quart. Rev. LIX, 1837. [A contemptuous review of the Sonnets.]
White, N. I. Literature and the Law of Libel. Stud. Phil. XXII, 1925. [Deals with Moxon's trial for blasphemous libel in 1841.]

ARTHUR JOSEPH MUNBY (1828–1910)
(a) Poems

Benoni: Poems. 1852.
Elegiacs. [In The Burns Centenary Poems, 1859.]
Verses New and Old. 1865.
Dorothy, a Country Story in Elegiac Verse. 1880.
Vestigia Retrorsum: Poems. 1890.
Vulgar Verses, by Jones Brown [i.e. A. J. Munby]. [1890.]
Susan: a Poem. 1893.
Ann Morgan's Love. A Pedestrian Poem. 1896.
Poems, chiefly Lyric and Elegiac. 1901.
Relicta: Verses. 1909.

(b) Other Works

A Memorial of Joseph Munby, of Clifton Holme. [1875.]
Faithful Servants: Epitaphs and Obituaries. Ed. A. J. Munby, 1891.

(c) Biography and Criticism

Bayne, T. The Poetry of Arthur Munby. GM. LXXIII, 1870, p. 503.
Marston, P. B. A. J. Munby, a Realistic Poet. Atlantic Monthly, XLIX, 1881.

JOSEPH JOHN MURPHY (1827–1894)
(a) Poems

Sonnets and Other Poems, chiefly Religious. 1890.

[Murphy also wrote several prose works on religious matters.]

(b) *Biography and Criticism*

Grosart, A. B. Joseph John Murphy. *Miles*, x (xii).

JOHN MASON NEALE (1818–1866)

(a) *Selections*

Selections from the Writings of John Mason Neale. 1884.

Collected Hymns, Sequences and Carols. [Ed. M. S. Lawson], 1914.

(b) *Poems (including collections and translations of Latin hymns)*

The Fisherman's Song. Speed the Plough! Work over. [1840?]

Hymns for Children, in Accordance with the Catechism. 1843; 2 pts, 1844–5 (rev. edn); 3 sers. 1848 (rev. and corrected).

Hymns for the Sick. 1843.

Songs and Ballads for the People. 1843.

A Mirror of Faith. Lays and Legends of the Church in England. 1845.

Songs and Ballads for Manufacturers. 1850.

The Hymnal Noted. 2 pts, 1851–4. [Mainly translated by Neale.]

Hymni Ecclesiae, a Breviariis quibusdam et Missalibus Gallicanis, Germanis, Hispanis, Lusitanis desumpti. Collegit et recensuit Joannes M. Neale. 1851.

Mediaeval Hymns and Sequences. 1851; 1863 ('with very numerous additions and corrections').

Sequentiæ ex Missalibus Germanicis, Anglicis, Gallicis, aliisque medii ævi collectæ. 1852.

Carols for Christmas Tide. 1853.

Carols for Easter Tide. 1854.

Judith. A Seatonian Poem. 1856.

Egypt. A Seatonian Prize Poem. 1858.

The Disciples at Emmaus. A Seatonian Prize Poem. 1859.

The Rhythm of Bernard de Morlaix on the Celestial Country. 1859.

Ruth. A Seatonian Poem. 1860.

Hymns of the Eastern Church. 1862; 1882 (4th edn, with Music from Greek and other Sources, Verifications, Various Readings and prose trns by S. G. Hatherly).

King Josiah. A Seatonian Poem. 1862.

Christ was born on Christmas Day. A Carol. 1864.

Seatonian Poems. 1864.

The Celestial Country. 1865. Trn of a portion of Bernard de Morlaix's De Contemptu Mundi; a metrical trn of the Vexilla Regis of Fortunatus, and of the Cantemus Cuncti of Gotteschalcus.]

Hymns, chiefly Mediaeval, on the Joys and Glories of Paradise. 1865.

Hymn for Use during the Cattle Plague. 1866.

Sequences, Hymns, and Other Ecclesiastical Verses. [1866.]

Hymns suitable for Invalids. Selected by R. F. Littledale. 1867.

The Dissolution of the Religious Houses, A.D. 1536. The Curse of the Abbeys. [1886.] [Two historical poems.]

Good King Wenceslas. A Carol. Pictured by A. J. Gaskin. With Introduction by W. Morris. 1895.

(c) *Other Works*

A History of the Jews. 1841. [Supplement, 1842.]

Agnes de Tracy: a Tale of the Times of S. Thomas of Canterbury. 1843.

The Triumphs of the Cross. Tales and Sketches of Christian Heroism. 1845.

Annals of Virgin Saints. 1846.

Duchenier; or the Revolt of La Vendée. 1848.

The Egyptian Wanderers: a Story for Children of the Great Persecution. 1854.

Theodora Phranza; or the Fall of Constantinople. 1857; ed. E. Rhys, [1913].

A Commentary on the Psalms; from Primitive and Mediaeval Writers. By John Mason Neale and R. F. Littledale. 1860.

The Daughters of Pola. [1861.]

A History of the Holy Eastern Church. 5 vols. 1847–1873.

Letters of John Mason Neale. Ed. M. S. Lawson, 1910.

[Neale was a most prolific writer. Besides the above works in prose he pbd many sermons, commentaries, historical novels for children, etc.]

(d) *Biography and Criticism*

St Margaret's Mag. I–IV, 1887–95. [Issued in half-yearly parts. A memoir begins in pt I and is continued in each pt to end of vol. IV. A complete account of Neale's life and writings.]

Towle, E. A. John Mason Neale, D.D.: a Memoir. 1906. [Appendix II is a complete list of Neale's writings.]

Julian, J. A Dictionary of Hymnology. 1907.

CHARLES NEAVES, LORD NEAVES (1800–1876)

(a) *Poems*

Songs and Verses, Social and Scientific. Edinburgh, 1868.

(b) *Other Writings*

A Glance at Some of the Principles of Comparative Philology as illustrated in the Latin and Anglican Forms of Speech. 1870.

The Greek Anthology. 1870. [An account, with specimens in English.]

Some Helps to the Study of Scoto-Celtic Philology. 1872.

[Neaves also pbd two or three didactic works.]

FRANCIS WILLIAM NEWMAN (1805–1897)

(a) Poems

The Odes of Horace translated. 1853.
The Iliad of Homer translated. 1856.
Hiawatha: rendered into Latin. 1862.
Translations of English Poetry into Latin Verse. 1868.

(b) Other Writings (select list)

Lectures on Logic. 1838.
History of the Hebrew Monarchy. 1847.
The Soul; her Sorrows and her Aspirations. 1849.
Phases of Faith. 1850.
Theism, Doctrinal and Practical. 1858.
Homeric Translation in Theory and Practice. A Reply to Matthew Arnold, Esq. 1861. [Rptd in Essays by Matthew Arnold, 1914 (Oxford edn).]
A Handbook of Modern Arabic. 1866.
Miscellanies: chiefly Addresses, Academical and Historical. 3 vols. 1869–89.
A Dictionary of Modern Arabic. 1871.
Hebrew Theism: the Common Basis of Judaism, Christianity, and Mohammedism. 1874.
Comments on the Text of Æschylus. 1884.
Robilius Crusoe. 1884. [Robinson Crusoe in Latin.]
Contributions chiefly to the Early History of the late Cardinal Newman. 1891.

(c) Biography and Criticism

Arnold, M. On Translating Homer. 1861.
—— On Translating Homer. Last Words. 1862.
Gribble, F. Francis W. Newman. Fortnightly Rev. LXXXIV, 1905.
Harrison, F. Collected Essays. Vol. IV, 1908. [Includes an essay on Newman.]
Sieveking, I. G. Memoir and Letters of Francis W. Newman. 1909.

JOHN HENRY NEWMAN (1801–1890)

[See p. 686 below.]

ROBERT NICOLL (1814–1837)

(a) Writings

Poems and Lyrics. Edinburgh, 1835; Edinburgh, 1842 (enlarged and with memoir by C. I. Johnstone); Glasgow, 1852; Paisley, 1877; rptd Paisley, 1914.
Marion Wilson: a Tale of the Persecuting Times. [In C. I. Johnstone's The Edinburgh Tales, vol. II, Edinburgh, 1846.]

(b) Biography and Criticism

Kingsley, C. Robert Nicoll. North British Rev. XVI, 1851.
Smiles, S. The Life and Work of Robert Nicoll. Good Words, XVI, 1875.

Drummond, P. R. The Life of Robert Nicoll, with some hitherto Uncollected Pieces. 1884.

CAROLINE ELIZABETH SARAH NORTON, née SHERIDAN and afterwards LADY STIRLING-MAXWELL (1808–1877)

(a) Poems

The Sorrows of Rosalie; a Tale. With Other Poems. 1829 (anon.).
The Undying One, and Other Poems. 1830.
Poems. Boston, 1833.
A Voice from the Factories. 1836.
The Dream, and Other Poems. 1840.
Lines [on Queen Victoria]. [1840.]
The Child of the Islands. A Poem. 1845.
Aunt Carry's Ballads for Children. Adventures of a Wood Sprite. The Story of Blanche and Brutikin. 1847.
Love Not. [1850?] [A song.]
The Centenary Festival. [In G. Anderson and J. Finlay, The Burns Centenary Poems, 1859.]
The Lady of La Garaye. Cambridge, [1861].
Bingen on the Rhine. [1888.]

(b) Novels

Stuart of Dunleath, a Story of Modern Times. 3 vols. 1851.
Lost and Saved. 3 vols. 1863.
Old Sir Douglas. 3 vols. [1867].

[Mrs Norton also wrote several short works on sociological subjects and edited various annuals, etc.]

(c) Biography and Criticism

The Writings of the Hon. Mrs Norton. Littell's Museum of Foreign Literature, XLI, 1840.
[Coleridge, H. N.] Quart. Rev. LXVI, 1845. [Long review.]
[Lockhart, J. G.] Mrs Norton's Child of the Islands. Quart. Rev. LXXVI, 1845.
Mrs Norton's The Lady of La Garaye. Edinburgh Rev. CXV, 1861.
Maginn, W. A Gallery of Illustrious Literary Characters. Ed. W. Bates, [1873].
Mrs Norton and her Writings. Temple Bar, LII, 1877.
Roberison, E. S. English Poetesses. 1883, pp. 240–6.
Miles, A. H. Hon. Mrs Norton. Miles, VII (VIII).
Alexander, A. H. Mrs Norton. [In Women Novelists of Queen Victoria's Reign, 1897.]
Hector, A. F. Mrs Norton. 1897.
Perkins, J. G. The Life of Mrs Norton. 1909.

JOHN WALKER ORD (1811–1853)

(a) Poems

England: a Historical Poem. 2 vols. 1834–5.
The Bard, and Minor Poems. 1841.

Rural Sketches, and Poems, chiefly relating to Cleveland. 1845.

(b) Other Works

Remarks on the Sympathetic Connection existing between the Body and the Mind especially during Disease. 1836.
The History and Antiquities of Cleveland. 1846.

(c) Biography and Criticism

Whellan, T. York and the North Riding. Vol. II, 1859, p. 206.

GEORGE OUTRAM (1805–1856)

(a) Poems

Legal Lyrics; or, Metrical Illustrations of the Law of Scotland. By Quizdom Rumfunidos. 1871 (priv. ptd); ed. H. G. Bell, Edinburgh, 1874; ed. J. H. Stoddard, Edinburgh, 1887; rptd 1916 ('containing a number of new pieces').

(b) Biography and Criticism

White, W. George Outram. Miles, IX (x).

JOHN OXENFORD (1812–1877)

[See p. 605 below.]

HENRY NUTCOMBE OXENHAM (1829–1883)

(a) Poems

The Sentence of Kaïres, and Other Poems. 1854; 1871 (3rd edn, as Poems).

[Oxenham pbd or translated a number of controversial and devotional works from the Roman Catholic standpoint.]

(b) Biography and Criticism

The Rev. Henry N. Oxenham. Saturday Rev. LXV, 1887.

FRANCIS TURNER PALGRAVE (1824–1897)

(a) Poems

Idyls and Songs. 1854.
The Passionate Pilgrims, or Eros and Anteros. 1858.
Hymns. 1867.
Lyrical Poems. 1871.
A Lyme Garland. Lyme, [1874].
The Visions of England. 1881.
Amenophis and Other Poems. 1892. [Includes all the earlier poems Palgrave wished to preserve, as well as some new poems.]

(b) Anthologies

The Golden Treasury. 1861; 1896 (rev. and enlarged), etc.
The Golden Treasury. Second Series. 1897.
The Children's Treasury of English Song. 1875.
The Treasury of Sacred Song. 1889.

(c) Other Works

Preciosa: a Tale. 1852.
Essay on the First Century of Italian Engraving. [In F. T. Kugler's Handbook of Painting, 1855.]
Handbook to the Fine Art Collection in the International Exhibition of 1862. 1862.
Essays on Art. 1866.
The Five Days' Entertainments at Wentworth Grange. 1868.
Gems of English Art of this Century; with Illustrative Texts. 1869.
The Life of Jesus Christ illustrated from the Italian Painters of the 14th, 15th and 16th Centuries. 1885.
Landscape in Poetry, from Homer to Tennyson. 1897.

[Palgrave was also responsible for numerous edns and selections of the poets.]

(d) Biography and Criticism

Wedmore, Sir T. F. F. T. Palgrave as an Art Critic. Colburn's New Monthly Mag. CXXXVII, 1865.
Chambers, Sir E. K. Academy, 14 Jan. 1893. [Review of Amenophis.]
Palgrave, G. F. Francis Turner Palgrave: his Journals and Memories of his Life. 1899.
Horder, W. G. A Dictionary of Hymnology. Ed. J. Julian, 1907.
Evans, B. I. Tennyson and the Origins of the Golden Treasury. TLS. 8 Dec. 1932.

SIR JOSEPH NOEL PATON (1821–1901)

Poems. By a Painter. 1861.
Spendrift. 1867. [Poems.]
[See Miles, v.]

EMILY PFEIFFER, née DAVIS (1827–1890)

(a) Poems

Margaret; or, the Motherless. 1861.
Gerard's Monument; and Other Poems. 1873; 1878 (enlarged).
Poems. 1876.
Glân-Alarch, his Silence and Song. 1877.
Quarterman's Grace and Other Poems. 1879.
Sonnets and Songs. 1880; 1886 (rev. and enlarged).
Under the Aspens: Lyrical and Dramatic. [1881.]
The Rhyme of the Lady of the Rock, and how it grew. 1884. [Prose and verse.]
Flowers of the Night. 1889.

(b) Other Works

Valisneria; or, a Midsummer Night's Dream. A Tale. 1857.
Flying Leaves from East and West. 1885.
Women and Work. An Essay. [1887.]

(c) Biography and Criticism

Robertson, E. S. English Poetesses. 1883, pp. 348–53.

Obituary. Academy, 1 Feb. 1890; Athenaeum, 1 Feb. 1890.

Emily Pfeiffer. Western Mail, 8 Oct. 1895.

EDWARD HAYES PLUMPTRE (1821–1891)

(a) Poems

Lazarus, and Other Poems. 1864; 1884 (4th edn).

The Tragedies of Sophocles: a New Translation, with a Biographical Essay. 2 vols. 1865; 1867 (rev. edn).

Master and Scholar. 1866.

The Tragedies of Æschylos. A New Translation, with a Biographical Essay, and an Appendix of Rhymed Choral Odes. 2 vols. 1868.

Samples of a New Translation of the Divina Commedia. 1883.

Things New and Old. [1884.]

The Commedia and Canzoniere of Dante: a New Translation. 2 vols. 1886–7.

(b) Other Writings

The Life of Thomas Ken, Bishop of Bath and Wells. With Illustrations by E. Whymper. 2 vols. 1888.

[Plumptre also pbd many sermons and other theological works, and contributed a few articles on Dante to Quart. Rev. and Contemporary Rev.]

(c) Biography and Criticism

C[otton], J. S. Dean Plumptre. Academy, 7 Feb. 1891.

Obituary. Times, 12 Feb. 1891.

Horder, W. G. Edward Hayes Plumptre. Miles, x (xii).

Julian, J. A Dictionary of Hymnology. 1907.

JOHN CRITCHLEY PRINCE (1808–1866)

(a) Collected Poems

The Poetical Works of J. C. Prince. Ed. R. A. D. Lithgow, 2 vols. 1880.

(b) Separate Poems

Hours with the Muses. [1841]; 1842 (3rd edn, enlarged); 1847 (enlarged).

Dreams and Realities, in Verse and Prose. 1847.

The Poetic Rosary. 1851.

Autumn Leaves: Original Poems. Hyde, 1856; [1865] (with additional poems).

Miscellaneous Poems. Manchester, [1861].

(c) Biography and Criticism

Ossoli, M. F. Art, Literature and the Drama. 1874.

Lithgow, R. A. D. The Life of J. C. Prince. 1880.

ADELAIDE ANNE PROCTER (1825–1864)

(a) Collected and Selected Works

Ausgewählte Gedichte. Nach dem Englischen herausgegeben von C. Schlüter und H. Brinckmann. Cologne, 1867.

Poems. 1905. (Muses' Lib.)

The Complete Poetical Works. With Introduction by Charles Dickens. 1905. [Including one poem hitherto unpbd.]

Selected Poems. 1911.

Legends and Lyrics together with A Chaplet of Verses. With Introduction by Charles Dickens. 1914. (Oxford Standard Authors.)

(b) Poems

Legends and Lyrics. 2 vols. 1858–61; 2 vols. 1866 (with addns and introduction by Charles Dickens); 1895 (with additional poems); rptd 1906 (Everyman's Lib.; omits the introduction by Dickens). [Most of the poems had appeared first in Household Words.]

A Chaplet of Verses. 1862.

(c) Biography and Criticism

Robertson, E. S. English Poetesses. 1883, pp. 226–39.

Gibbs, H. J. Adelaide Anne Procter. Miles, VII (VIII).

Julian, J. A Dictionary of Hymnology. 1907.

Janku, F. A. A. Procter: Ihr Leben und ihre Werke. Vienna, 1912.

Duméril, E. Un Poète catholique anglais au XIXe Siècle: A. A. Procter. Nouvelle Revue des Jeunes, 25 May 1930.

WILLIAM BRIGHTY RANDS (1823–1882)

(a) Poems

Chain of Lilies and Other Poems. 1857.

Lilliput Levee. 1864.

Lilliput Lectures. 1871.

Lilliput Revels. 1871.

Lilliput Legends. 1872.

(b) Other Works

Robert Bloomfield: a Sketch of his Life and Writings. [1855.]

Tangled Talk. An Essayist's Holiday. By Thomas Talker [i.e. W. B. Rands]. 1864.

Views and Opinions. By Matthew Browne [i.e. W. B. Rands]. 1866.

Chaucer's England. By Matthew Browne [i.e. W. B. Rands]. 2 vols. 1869.

[Rands also pbd fairy-tales, essays, etc. under his own name and under several pseudonyms. For his life and writings, and a selection from his poems, see A. H. Japp, Miles, v.]

BENJAMIN BICKLEY ROGERS (1828–1919)
[See p. 1009 below.]

WILLIAM CALDWELL ROSCOE (1823–1859)

(a) Collected Works

Poems and Essays. Ed. (with memoir) R. H. Hutton, 2 vols. 1860.
Poems. Ed. E. M. Roscoe, 1891.

(b) Dramatic Works

Eliduc, Count of Yoeloc. 1846.
Violenzia: a Tragedy. 1851.

(c) Biography and Criticism

The Poems of William Caldwell Roscoe. National Rev. XI, 1860.
The Writings of William Caldwell Roscoe. Dublin University Mag. LVIII, 1860.
Le Gallienne, R. William Caldwell Roscoe. Miles, V.

JOHN RUSKIN (1819–1900)
[See p. 691 below.]

WILLIAM BELL SCOTT (1811–1890)

(a) Poems

Hades; or, The Transit: and The Progress of Mind. Two Poems. 1838.
The Year of the World; a Philosophical Poem on Redemption from the Fall. Edinburgh, 1846.
Poems. 1854.
Poems. Ballads, Studies from Nature, Sonnets, etc. 1875.
A Poet's Harvest Home: being One Hundred Short Poems. 1882; 1893 ('with an Aftermath of Twenty Short Poems').

(b) Other Works

Memoir of David Scott, containing his Journal in Italy, Notes on Art and Other Papers. 1850.
Albert Dürer: his Life and Works. 1869.
The Little Masters. (Altdorfer, Beham, [etc.].) 1879.
Autobiographical Notes of the Life of William Bell Scott, 1830–1882. Ed. W. Minto, 2 vols. 1892.

[Scott also produced a number of collections of works of art, and edited Byron, Coleridge, Mrs Inchbald, Keats, 'L. E. L.,' Scott, Shakespeare and Shelley.]

(c) Biography and Criticism

Forman, H. B. Our Living Poets. 1871, pp. 287–308.

Rossetti, W. M. William Bell Scott and Modern English Poetry. Macmillan's Mag. XXXIII, 1875.
Obituary. Athenaeum, 29 Nov. 1890.
Knight, J. William Bell Scott. Miles, IV.
Evans, B. I. English Poetry in the Later Nineteenth Century. 1933. [Ch. V.]

JOHN CAMPBELL SHAIRP (1815–1885)
[See p. 725 below.]

LOUISA CATHERINE SHORE (1824–1895)

War Lyrics. 1855; 1855 (enlarged). [With Arabella Shore.]
Gemma of the Isles. 1859. [With Arabella Shore.]
Hannibal: a Drama. 2 pts, 1861; ed. A. Shore, 1898.
Fra Dolcino. 1870. [With Arabella Shore.]
Elegies and Memorials. 1890. [With Arabella Shore.]
Poems by A[rabella] and L[ouisa Shore]. 1897.
Poems; with a Memoir by Arabella Shore and an Appreciation by Frederic Harrison. 1897.

MENELLA BUTE SMEDLEY (1820–1877)

(a) Poems

Lays and Ballads from English History. [1856.]
The Story of Queen Isabel, and Other Verses. 1863.
Poems. 1868.
Poems written for a Child. By Two Friends [M. B. Smedley and Mrs E. A. Hart]. 1868.
Child-World. By [M. B. Smedley and Mrs E. A. Hart]. 1869.
Two Dramatic Poems [Blind Love; Cyril]. 1874.

(b) Other Works

The Maiden Aunt. [1849.]
A Very Woman. [In Seven Tales by Seven Authors, 1849.]
The Use of Sunshine: a Christmas Narrative. 1852.
Nina: a Tale for the Twilight. 1853.
Twice Lost. 1863.
A Mere Story. 1865.
Other Folks' Lives. 1869.
Linnet's Trial. 1871.
Boarding-out and Pauper Schools especially for Girls. [From] the Blue-Book for 1873–74. Ed. M. B. Smedley, 1875.

(c) Biography and Criticism

Forman, H. B. Our Living Poets. 1871, pp. 71–86.

Robertson, E. S. English Poetesses. 1883, p. 335.

Japp, A. H. Menella Bute Smedley. *Miles*, VII (VIII).

JAMES SMETHAM (1821–1889)

(a) Writings

Essay on Blake, from the London Quarterly Review. [In A. Gilchrist's Life of William Blake, vol. II, 1880.]

Letters, with an Introductory Memoir. Ed. S. Smetham and W. Davies, 1891.

The Literary Works of James Smetham. Ed. W. Davies, 1893.

(b) Biography and Criticism

Beardmore, W. G. James Smetham, Painter, Poet, Essayist. [1906.]

ALEXANDER SMITH (1829–1867)

(a) Collected Poems

A Life Drama, City Poems, etc. Ed. R. E. D. Sketchley, [1901].

The Poetical Works. Ed. W. Sinclair, Edinburgh, 1909.

(b) Separate Poems

Poems. 1853 (*bis*); 1854; 1856.

Sonnets on the War. 1855. [With Sydney Dobell.]

City Poems. Cambridge, 1857.

Edwin of Deira. Cambridge, 1861.

(c) Other Writings

Dreamthorp: a Book of Essays written in the Country. 1863; 1881; ed. J. Hogben, 1906; ed. H. Walker and F. A. Cavenagh, 1914; ed. H. Walker, 1914 (with selection from Last Leaves).

A Summer in Skye. 2 vols. 1865; 1885; ed. L. M. Watt, [1907] (with unpublished letter); ed. W. F. Gray, Edinburgh, 1912.

Alfred Hagart's Household. 2 vols. 1866.

Miss Oona McQuarrie. [1866.]

Last Leaves. Sketches and Criticisms. Ed. (with memoir) P. P. Alexander, Edinburgh, 1868.

[Smith also supervised an edn of Burns's poems and wrote introductions for a rpt of Bunyan's Divine Emblems and J. W. S. Howe's Golden Leaves from the American Poets.]

(d) Biography and Criticism

Kingsley, C. Alexander Smith and Alexander Pope. Fraser's Mag. XLVIII, 1853.

Aytoun, W. E. Firmilian, or the Student of Badajoz. [1854.] [Parodies Smith's poems.]

Gilfillan, G. Galleries of Literary Portraits. Vol. I, Edinburgh, 1856.

Brisbane, T. The Early Years of Alexander Smith. 1869.

Japp, A. H. Alexander Smith. *Miles*, v.

Looker, S. J. Alexander Smith. Poetry Rev. May, June 1921.

Grimsditch, H. B. Alexander Smith, Poet and Essayist. London Mercury, XII, 1925.

Alexander Smith. TLS. 25 Dec. 1930.

WALTER CHALMERS SMITH (1824–1908)

(a) Poems

The Bishop's Walk. 1860.

Hymns of Christ and the Christian Life. 1867.

Olrig Grange. 1872.

Borland Hall. 1874.

Hilda among the Broken Gods. 1878.

Raban; or, Life Splinters. Glasgow, 1880.

North Country Folk. Glasgow, 1883.

Kildrostan: a Dramatic Poem. Glasgow, 1884.

Thoughts and Fancies for Sunday Evenings. Glasgow, 1887.

A Heretic, and Other Poems. [1890.]

Selections from the Poems of Walter Chalmers Smith. Glasgow, 1893.

The Poetical Works. 1902.

[Smith also pbd a Life of Thomas Chalmers, and lectures and sermons.]

(b) Biography and Criticism

Saintsbury, G. W. C. Smith's North-Country Folk. Academy, XXIII, 1882, p. 206.

The Poems of Walter Chalmers Smith. Scottish Rev. I, 1883.

Horder, W. G. Walter Chalmers Smith. *Miles*, x (XII).

ARTHUR PENRHYN STANLEY (1815–1881)

[See p. 901 below.]

EDWARD GEORGE GEOFFREY SMITH STANLEY, EARL OF DERBY (1799–1869)

(a) Poems

Translations of Poems, Ancient and Modern. 1862 (priv. ptd). [Trns from poems in Greek, Latin, French, Italian and German.]

The Iliad of Homer rendered into English Blank Verse. 2 vols. 1864; ed. F. M. Stawell, [1910] (Everyman's Lib.).

(b) Other Writings

Journal of a Tour in America 1824–1825. 1930 (priv. ptd).

[Many of Lord Derby's speeches were also ptd.]

(c) Biography and Criticism

Henkel, W. Ilias und Odyssee, und ihre Übersetzer in England von Chapman bis auf Lord Derby. Hersfeld, 1867.

Kebbel, T. E. Life of the Earl of Derby, K.G. 1890. [This life has a chapter on Lord Derby as a man of letters.]

Saintsbury, G. The Earl of Derby. 1892. [Has a chapter on Lord Derby's literary work.]

JAMES BRUNTON STEPHENS (1835–1902)
[See p. 1094 below.]

JOHN STERLING (1806–1843)
[See p. 680 below.]

THOMAS TOD STODDART (1810–1880)

(a) Poems

The Death-Wake, or Lunacy. A Necromaunt in Three Chimeras. Edinburgh, 1831; ed. A. Lang, 1895.

Angling Songs. 1839; 1889.

Songs and Poems. In Three Parts. Edinburgh, 1839.

An Angler's Rambles and Angling Songs. Edinburgh, 1866, 1889 (with memoir by A. M. Stoddart).

Songs of the Seasons; and Other Poems. Edinburgh, 1873; Kelso, 1881 (with autobiographical sketch).

(b) Other Works

The Art of Angling as practised in Scotland. Edinburgh, 1835.

Angling Reminiscences. Edinburgh, 1837; 1887.

Abel Massinger: or the Aëronaut: a Romance. 1846.

The Angler's Companion to the Rivers and Lochs of Scotland. Edinburgh, 1847; 1853; ed. Sir H. Maxwell, 1923.

Rambles by Tweed. [In H. C. Pennell, Fishing Gossip, 1866.]

(c) Biography and Criticism

Wilson, J. G. The Poets and Poetry of Scotland. Vol. II, 1876, p. 326.

Thomas Tod Stoddart. Scottish Angler. Chambers's Journ. LVIII, 1881.

Lang, A. Thomas Tod Stoddart: a Scottish Romanticist of 1830. [In Adventures among Books, 1905.]

LADY EMMELINE CHARLOTTE ELIZABETH STUART-WORTLEY (1806–1855)

(a) Poems

Poems. 1833.

London at Night; and Other Poems. 1834.

Unloved of Earth; and Other Poems. 1834.

The Knight and the Enchantress; with Other Poems. 1835.

Travelling Sketches in Rhyme. 1835.

The Village Churchyard; and Other Poems. 1835.

The Visionary; a Fragment, with Other Poems. 2 pts, 1836–9.

Fragments and Fancies. 1837.

Hours at Naples; and Other Poems. 1837.

Impressions of Italy; and Other Poems. 1837.

Lays of Leisure Hours. 2 vols. 1838.

Queen Berengaria's Courtesy, and Other Poems. 3 vols. 1838.

Sonnets, written chiefly during a Tour through Holland, Germany, Italy, Turkey and Hungary. 1839.

Eva; or The Error. A Play in Five Acts. 1840.

Jairah, a Dramatic Mystery; and Other Poems. 1840.

Alphonzo Algarves. A Play in Five Acts. 1841.

Angiolina del' Albano; or, Truth and Treachery: a Play in Five Acts. 1841.

Lillia-Bianca. A Tale of Italy. 1841.

The Maiden of Moscow: a Poem in Twenty-One Cantos. 1842.

Adelaida; or Letters, etc. of Madame von Regenburg. To which are added Poems. 1843.

The Great Exhibition. Honour to Labour; a Lay of 1851. [1851.]

On the Approaching Close of the Great Exhibition, and Other Poems. 1851.

(b) Other Works

Moonshine: a Comedy, in Five Acts. 1843.

Ernest Mountjoy; a Comedietta. 1844.

Travels in the United States, etc. during 1849 and 1850. 3 vols. 1851.

Sketches of Travel in America. 1853.

A Visit to Portugal and Madeira. 1854.

[Lady Emmeline Stuart-Wortley edited The Keepsake in 1837 and 1840.]

(c) Biography and Criticism

[Coleridge, H. N.] Quart. Rev. LXVI, 1840. [Long review.]

Bethune, G. W. The British Female Poets. 1848, p. 376.

Lady E. Stuart-Wortley's Travels in America. Littell's Living Age, XXIX, 1851.

Lady Emmeline Stuart-Wortley. Chambers's Journ. XIX, 1852.

Obituary. GM. Feb. 1856.

HENRY SEPTIMUS SUTTON (1825–1901)

(a) Poems

Clifton Grove Garland. Nottingham, 1848.

Quinquenergia; or, Proposals for a New Practical Theology. 1854. [Contains 'Rose's Diary,' poems.]

Poems. Glasgow, 1886.

A Sutton Treasury. Manchester, 1899; 1909.

Fragments of Verse. [1916.]

[Sutton also pbd several works on the Swedenborgian theology.]

(b) Biography and Criticism

Obituary. Manchester Guardian, 3 May 1901;
Times, 6 May 1901.
Horder, W. G. Henry Septimus Sutton.
Miles, x (xii).
Davis, V. D. A Dictionary of Hymnology.
Ed. J. Julian, 1907.

CHARLES SWAIN (1801–1874)

(a) Collected and Selected Poems

The Poems of Charles Swain. Ed. (with a
short life) C. C. Smith, Boston, 1857.
Selections from Charles Swain, compiled by
his Third Daughter (C. S. D.). 1906.

(b) Individual Publications

Metrical Essays. 1827; 1828.
Beauties of the Mind, a Poetical Sketch. With
Lays. 1831. [Title poem recast and much
enlarged in the following.]
The Mind and Other Poems. 1832 (bis);
1841; 1870 (5th edn); 1873.
Dryburgh Abbey, a Poem on the Death of
Sir Walter Scott. 1832; 1868 (with other
poems).
Memoir of Henry Liverseege. 1835; 1864.
Cabinet of Poetry and Romance. 1844.
Rhymes for Childhood. 1846.
Dramatic Chapters, Poems, and Songs. 1847;
1850.
English Melodies. 1849.
Letters of Laura d'Auverne. 1853. [Poems.]
Art and Fashion, with Other Poems. 1863.
Songs and Ballads. 1867; 1877 (5th edn).

SIR HENRY TAYLOR (1800–1886)

(a) Collected Works

The Poetical Works of Sir Henry Taylor.
3 vols. 1864. [Plays and poems.]
The Works. 5 vols. 1877–8.

(b) Individual Publications

Isaac Comnenus. 1827; 1845 (adds Edwin the
Fair); 1852; 1875. [Verse tragedy.]
Philip van Artevelde, a Dramatic Romance
[in verse]. 2 vols. 1834; 1844 (3rd edn);
1852 (6th edn); 1872; tr. German, Leipzig,
1852.
The Statesman. 1836; ed. H. J. Laski, Cam-
bridge, 1927. [Prose.]
Edwin the Fair, an Historical Drama [in
verse]. 1842. [For later edns see Isaac
Comnenus.]
The Eve of the Conquest, and Other Poems.
1847. [Rptd in A Sicilian Summer, 1875.]
Notes from Life, in Six [prose] Essays. 1847;
1848; 1854 (4th edn).
Notes from Books, in Four Essays. 1849.
[Chiefly from Quart. Rev.; two papers are
on Wordsworth.]

The Virgin Widow, a Play [chiefly in verse].
1850; 1875 (as A Sicilian Summer).
St Clement's Eve, a Play [in verse]. 1862.
Crime Considered. 1869. [A letter to Glad-
stone, on the criminal code.]
A Sicilian Summer [i.e. The Virgin Widow].
With the Eve of the Conquest and Minor
Poems. 1875.
Autobiography, 1800–1875. 1877 (priv. ptd);
2 vols. 1885.
[Taylor also wrote a little for London Mag.
c. 1823 and for Quart. Rev., his contributions
to the latter being mostly rptd in Notes from
Books, 1849.]

(c) Biography and Criticism

[Lockhart, J. G.] Quart. Rev. LI, 1834. [A
favourable notice of Philip van Artevelde.]
Horne, R. H. A New Spirit of the Age.
Vol. II, 1844.
Powell, T. Pictures of the Living Authors of
Britain. 1851.
Forman, H. B. Our Living Poets. 1871,
pp. 447–66.
De Vere, A. Essays, chiefly on Poetry.
Vols. I, II, 1887. [Five papers on Taylor's
plays and minor poems.]
Correspondence. Ed. E. Dowden, 1888.
Japp, A. H. Sir Henry Taylor. Miles, III.
Knanth, R. Henry Taylors Leben und Werke.
Strasburg, 1913.
Taylor, U. Guests and Memories. 1924. [Deals
chiefly with Taylor's later life and friend-
ships.]
Abercrombie, L. Sir Henry Taylor. [In The
Eighteen-Sixties, ed. J. Drinkwater, Royal
Soc. of Literature, 1932.]

CHARLES TENNYSON, afterwards TURNER (1808–1879)

(a) Poems

Poems by Two Brothers. 1827. [See p. 253
above, under Alfred Tennyson.]
Sonnets and Fugitive Pieces. Cambridge, 1830.
Sonnets. 1864.
Small Tableaux. 1868.
Sonnets, Lyrics, and Translations. 1873.
Collected Sonnets, Old and New. 1880; 1898.
[With a preface by Hallam Tennyson, and
an introductory essay by J. Spedding, rptd
from Nineteenth Cent.]

(b) Biography and Criticism

S[hepherd], R. H. Tennysoniana. Notes
Bibliographical and Critical on Early Poems
of Alfred and Charles Tennyson. 1866[–75].
Japp, A. H. Charles Tennyson Turner.
Miles, IV.
Jelinek, K. A. A. Charles Tennyson-Turners
Leben und Werke. Leipzig, 1909.

FREDERICK TENNYSON (1807–1898)

(a) Poems

Poems by Two Brothers. 1827. [See p. 253 above under Alfred Tennyson.]

ΑΙΓΥΠΤΟΣ. Carmen Graecum Numismate Annuo dignatum et in Curia Cantabrigiensi recitatum Comitiis maximis A.D. MDCCCXXVIII. [In Prolusiones Academicae, Cambridge, 1828.]

Days and Hours. 1854.

The Isles of Greece. Sappho and Alcaeus. 1890.

Daphne and Other Poems. 1891.

Poems of the Day and Year. 1895.

The Shorter Poems of Frederick Tennyson. Ed. C. B. L. Tennyson, 1913.

(b) Biography and Criticism

Mr Frederick Tennyson's Poems. Fraser's Mag. XLIX, 1854.

Japp, A. H. Frederick Tennyson. Miles, IV.

Rawnsley, H. D. Memories of the Tennysons. Glasgow, 1912.

Letters to Frederick Tennyson. Ed. H. J. Schonfield, 1930.

WILLIAM MAKEPEACE THACKERAY (1811–1863)

[See p. 429 below.]

GEORGE WALTER THORNBURY (1828–1876)

(a) Poems

Lays and Legends, or Ballads of the New World. 1851.

Songs of the Cavaliers and Roundheads, Jacobite Ballads, etc. With Illustrations by H. S. Marks. 1857.

The Fables of La Fontaine. Translated into English Verse. [1867.]

Historical and Legendary Ballads and Songs. Illustrated by J. Whistler, F. Walker, John Tenniel and Many Others. [1875.]

(b) Other Works

The Monarchs of the Main; or, Adventures of the Buccaneers. 3 vols. 1855; 1858.

Art and Nature at Home and Abroad. 2 vols. 1856.

Shakspere's England; or Sketches of our Social History in the Reign of Elizabeth. 2 vols. 1856.

Every Man his own Trumpeter. 3 vols. 1858.

Life in Spain, Past and Present. 2 vols. 1859.

British Artists from Hogarth to Turner; being a Series of Biographical Sketches. 2 vols. [1860].

The Life of J. M. W. Turner, R.A. Founded on Letters and Papers furnished by his Friends and Fellow Academicians. 2 vols. [1861]; 1877 (rev. and mostly rewritten).

Haunted London. Illustrated by F. W. Fairholt. 1865.

Two Centuries of Song; or Lyrics, Madrigals, Sonnets and Other Occasional Verses of the English Poets of the Last Two Hundred Years. With Critical and Biographical Notes. 1867.

A Tour round England. 2 vols. 1870.

Criss-Cross Journeys. 2 vols. 1873.

Old and New London. 6 vols. 1873–8, etc. [Vols. I, II by Thornbury.]

[Thornbury also produced several novels, collections of tales, topographical works and trns, etc. He was associated with Dickens on Household Words and All the Year Round.]

(c) Biography and Criticism

The Writings of G. W. Thornbury. Dublin University Mag. L, 1859.

Kent, C. George Walter Thornbury. Athenaeum, 17 June 1876.

Ingram, J. H. Walter Thornbury. Miles, V.

RICHARD CHENEVIX TRENCH (1807–1886)

(a) Poems

The Story of Justin Martyr, and Other Poems. 1835.

Sabbation; Honor Neale, and Other Poems. 1838.

Poems. 1841.

Genoveva: a Poem. 1842.

Poems from Eastern Sources: The Steadfast Prince, and Other Poems. 1842.

Poems from Eastern Sources: Genoveva, and Other Poems. 1851.

Alma: and Other Poems. 1855.

Poems, Collected and Arranged anew. Cambridge, 1865.

In Time of War: Poems. With Preface by F. W. H. Myers. 1900.

(b) Anthologies

Sacred Latin Poetry, chiefly Lyrical. 1849–64.

A Household Book of English Poetry. 1868.

(c) Philological Writings

On the Study of Words: Five Lectures. 1851; ed. A. S. Palmer, 1904.

English, Past and Present: Five Lectures. 1855; rev. A. L. Mayhew, 1889; ed. A. S. Palmer, 1905.

On Teaching by Words. 1855.

On Some Deficiencies in our English Dictionaries. 1857.

A Select Glossary of English Words, used formerly in Senses Different from their Present. 1859.

(d) Theological and Other Writings

Notes on the Parables of Our Lord. 1841.

The fitness of Holy Scripture for unfolding the Spiritual Life of Men. (Hulsean Lectures, 1845.) 1845.

Notes on the Miracles of Our Lord. 1846.
On the Lessons in Proverbs: Five Lectures.
1853; ed. (with bibliography of proverbs)
A. S. Palmer, 1905.
Synonyms of the New Testament. 1854.
The History of the English Sonnet. 1863.
Gustavus Adolphus. Social Aspects of the
Thirty Years' War. 1865.
Studies in the Gospels. 1867.
Plutarch: his Life, his Lives and his Morals.
1873.
Lectures on Medieval Church History, etc.
1877.
Brief Thoughts and Meditations on some
Passages in Holy Scripture. 1884.

(e) Biography and Criticism

Myers, F. W. H. The Poems of R. C. Trench.
Nineteenth Century, II, 1877.
De Vere, A. The Poems of R. C. Trench.
Nineteenth Century, XXIII, 1887.
Silvester, J. Archbishop Trench: a Sketch of
his Life and Character. [1891.]
Gibbs, H. J. Richard Chenevix Trench.
Miles, IV.
Julian, J. A Dictionary of Hymnology. 1907.

MARTIN FARQUHAR TUPPER (1810–1889)

(a) Selections

Cithara: a Selection from the Lyrics of Martin
F. Tupper. 1863.
A Selection from the Works of Martin
Farquhar Tupper. 1866.
Select Miscellaneous Poems of Martin Farquhar
Tupper. [1874.]

(b) Poems

Sacra Poesis. 1832. [No copy traceable.]
Geraldine: a Sequel to Coleridge's Christabel,
with Other Poems. 1838.
Proverbial Philosophy. A Book of Thoughts
and Arguments, originally treated. 1838.
[Complete edn, 4 sers. [1876?].]
A Modern Pyramid, to commemorate a
Septuagint of Worthies. 1839. [A sonnet
and an essay on each of seventy famous
men.]
St Martha's: near Guildford, Surrey. 1841.
A Thousand Lines: now first offered to the
World we live in. 1845.
Hactenus. 1848.
The Loving Ballad to Brother Jonathan.
[1848.]
King Alfred's Poems, turned into English
Metres. 1850.
Half a Dozen No-Popery Ballads. [1851.]
A Hymn for All Nations. 1851.
A Dirge for Wellington. 1852.
Half a Dozen Ballads for Australian Emi-
grants. 1853.
A Batch of War Ballads. 1854.

A Dozen Ballads for the Times about Church
Abuses. 1854.
A Dozen Ballads for the Times about White
Slavery. 1854.
Lyrics of the Heart and Mind. 1855.
A Missionary Ballad. [1855?]
Some Verse and Prose about National Rifle-
Clubs. 1859.
Three Hundred Sonnets. 1860.
Translation of T. Sullivan's 'La Bannière sur
le Char de la Victoire.' [1866.]
Translation of J. Sullivan's 'Élégie sur la
Mort de Lord Palmerston.' 1866.
Our Canadian Dominion: Half a Dozen Ballads
about a King for Canada. 1868.
Twenty-one Protestant Ballads published in
'The Rock.' 1868.
Plan of the Ritualistic Campaign. [1869.]
A Creed, etcetera. 1870.
Washington: a Drama in Five Acts. 1876.
Jubilate! An Offering for [Queen Victoria in]
1887. [1887.]
[Tupper was also a prolific prose writer, but
nothing of interest survives except his Auto-
biography, 1886.]

(c) Biography and Criticism

Tupper's Geraldine. Blackwood's Mag. Dec.
1838. [Long unfavourable review.]
Drinkwater, J. Martin Tupper. [In The
Eighteen-Eighties, ed. W. de la Mare,
Royal Soc. of Literature, 1930.]

THOMAS WADE (1805–1875)

(a) Individual Publications

Tasso, and the Sisters. Poems. 1825.
Woman's Love, or the Triumph of Patience, a
Drama [in prose and verse]. 1829.
The Phrenologists, a Farce [in prose]. 1830.
The Jew of Arragon, a Tragedy [in verse]. 1830.
Mundi et Cordis, de Rebus sempiternis et
temporariis, Carmina. 1835. [Lyrics and
sonnets, in English.]
The Contention of Love and Death. 1837. [A
poem; rptd in H. B. Forman's second
article mentioned below.]
Helena, a Poem. 1837.
The Shadow-Seeker, a Poem. 1837.
Prothanasia, and Other Poems. 1839.
What does 'Hamlet' mean? A Lecture.
Jersey, [1855?].
[Wade edited Bell's Weekly Messenger for
some time, c. 1838, and later The British Press,
Jersey, for many years. The MS of his unpublished trn of Dante's Inferno (executed
1845–6) is in the Macauley Collection, University of Pennsylvania; specimens are given
in Forman's second article mentioned below.]

(b) Biography and Criticism

Forman, H. B. Thomas Wade. *Miles*, III.
—— Thomas Wade, the Poet and his Surroundings. [In Literary Anecdotes of the Nineteenth Century, ed. W. R. Nicoll and T. J. Wise, vol. I, 1895. Includes sonnets and other poems, many previously unpublished.]

EDWARD WALSH (1805–1850)

[See p. 1051 below.]

ANNA LAETITIA WARING (1823–1910)

(a) Poems

Hymns and Meditations. By A. L. W. 1850 (*bis*); 1852; 1854; 1855; 1856; 1858; 1860; 1863 (*bis*); 1870. [Most of the edns contain a certain amount of new matter.]
Additional Hymns. 1858.

[Miss Waring also wrote a few tracts.]

(b) Biography and Criticism

Horder, W. G. *Miles*, x (XI).
Crawford, G. A. A Dictionary of Hymnology. Ed. J. Julian, 1907.
Talbot, M. S. In Remembrance of Anna Letitia Waring. With Portrait. 1911. [Contains additional hymns and other verses.]

EDWIN WAUGH (1817–1890)

(a) Collected Works

Waugh's Complete Works. 10 vols. 1881–3.

(b) Selections

Poesies from a Country Garden. Selections from the Works of Edwin Waugh. 2 pts, 1866.
Samples of Lancashire Wares, being Selections from the Works of Edwin Waugh, Ben Brierley, etc. [1879.]

(c) Poems

Come whoam to thy Childer an' me. [Manchester?], 1856.
What ails thee, my son Robin? [1856.]
Chirrup. 1858.
Poems, and Lancashire Songs. 1859; 1870 (3rd edn, with addns); 1876 (4th edn, with addns).
Lancashire Songs. 1863; [1892] (6th edn).
Prince's Theatre, Manchester. The Grand Comic Christmas Pantomime, for 1866 and 1867, of Robin Hood and ye Merrie Men of Sherwood. [1866.]
Rambles and Reveries. 1872.
Poems and Songs. (Second Series.) Liverpool, 1889; ed. G. Milner, [1893] (with an introductory essay on the dialect of Lancashire considered as a vehicle for poetry).

(d) Other Works

Sketches of Lancashire Life and Localities. 1855.
Irish Sketches. 1869.
Around the Yule-Log. [1879.]
The Chimney Corner. 1879; ed. G. Milner, [1892]. [Sketches, mostly in the Lancashire dialect.]
Fireside Tales. 1885.
Besom Ben Stories. Ed. G. Milner, [1892].
Lancashire Sketches. Ed. G. Milner, 2 pts, [1892].
Tufts of Heather from the Lancashire Moors. Ed. G. Milner, 2 sers. [1892].
Rambles in the Lake Country and other Travel Sketches. Ed. G. Milner, 2 sers. [1893].

[Waugh pbd other Lancashire tales, sketches, etc. The above edns, ed. G. Milner, 1892–3, constitute a liberal selection, and are given as the most accessible forms of various works which were pbd separately at various dates.]

(e) Biography and Criticism

Edwin Waugh's Besom Ben Stories. Saturday Rev. LIII, 1882, p. 576.
Lamb, R. Obituary. Leisure Hour, XXXIX, 1890.
Obituary. Athenaeum, 10 May 1890; Temple Bar, XC, 1890.
Watson, Sir W. Edwin Waugh, Lancashire Laureate. National Rev. XV, 1890.
Espinasse, F. Manchester Memories: Edwin Waugh. [In Literary Recollections and Sketches, 1893.]

THOMAS WESTWOOD (1814–1888)

(a) Poems

Poems. 1840.
Beads from a Rosary. 1843.
The Burden of the Bell, and Other Lyrics. 1850.
Berries and Blossoms: a Verse-Book for Young People. 1855.
A Stream in Arden—Hey for Coquet! A Lay of the Sea. [In H. C. Pennell, Fishing Gossip, 1866.]
The Sword of Kingship, a legend of the 'Mort d'Arthure.' 1866 (priv. ptd).
The Quest of the Sancgreall, the Sword of Kingship, and Other Poems. 1868.
Gathered in the Gloaming. 1881 (priv. ptd).
In Memoriam Izaak Walton, obiit 15th December 1683. Twelve Sonnets and an Epilogue. 1884.

(b) Other Works

A New Bibliotheca Piscatoria; or, General Catalogue of Angling and Fishing Literature. With Biographical Notes and Data. 1861; rev. T. Westwood and T. Satchell, 1883.

The Chronicle of the Compleat Angler of Izaak Walton and Charles Cotton. Being a Bibliographical Record of all its Various Phases and Mutations. 1864. [The reminiscences of Lamb, together with the further articles by Westwood in N. & Q., are rptd in E. V. Lucas, Life of Charles Lamb, vol. II, 1905, chs. xlv, l.]

The Secrets of Angling. By J. D. A Reprint, with Introduction, by Thomas Westwood. 1883.

A Literary Friendship. Letters to Lady Alwyne Compton, 1869–1881. 1914. [With a preface by Lady Alwyne Compton and a memoir of Westwood by Rosa Westwood.]

(c) Biography and Criticism

Obituary. Athenaeum, 24 March 1888.
Watkins, M. G. Obituary. Academy, 31 March 1888.
Miles, A. H. Thomas Westwood. Miles, IV.

CHARLES WHITEHEAD (1804–1862)

(a) Collected Poems

The Solitary and Other Poems. 1849. [Includes The Cavalier.]

(b) Individual Publications

The Solitary, a Poem. 1831.
The Autobiography of Jack Ketch. 1834. [Prose burlesque.]
The Lives and Exploits of English Highwaymen. 2 vols. 1834.
The Cavalier, a Drama [in verse]. 1836.
Victoria Victrix. 1838. [A poem.]
Richard Savage. 3 vols. 1842; ed. H. Orrinsmith, 1896; rptd 1903. [Prose romance partly based on Dr Johnson's Life of Savage.]

[Whitehead also made numerous contributions to periodicals, particularly Bentley's Miscellany; and pbd a few minor prose works, including a revision (1846) of Grimaldi's Memoirs as originally edited by Dickens (1838).]

(c) Biography and Criticism

Bell, H. T. M. A Forgotten Genius: Charles Whitehead. 1884.
—— Charles Whitehead. Miles, III.

GEORGE JOHN WHYTE-MELVILLE (1821–1878)

[See p. 511 below.]

ISAAC WILLIAMS (1802–1865)

(a) Poems

Lyra Apostolica. 1836; ed. H. S. Holland and H. C. Beeching, 1899. [Williams contributed 9 poems.]

The Cathedral, or the Catholic and Apostolic Church of England. 1838; 1859 (8th edn); ed. W. Benham, 1889.
Thoughts in Past Years. 1838; 1852 (6th edn, enlarged).
Hymns translated from the Parisian Breviary. 1839.
Ancient Hymns for Children. 1842.
The Baptistery, or the Way of Eternal Life. 2 vols. Oxford, 1842–4.
Hymns on the Catechism. 1843.
Sacred Verses, with Pictures. 2 pts, 1845.
The Altar: or Meditations in Verse on the Great Christian Sacrifice. 1847 (anon.); 1849.
The Christian Scholar. 1849.
The Seven Days, or the Old and New Creation. 1850.
The Christian Seasons. 1854.

(b) Other Works

Some Meditations and Prayers selected from The Way of Eternal Life, in order to illustrate and explain the Pictures by Boetius a Bolswert, for the Same Work. Translated from the Latin [of A. Sucquet]. 1845.
A Series of Sermons on the Epistle and Gospel for each Sunday in the Year, and on some of the Chief Festivals. 1853–5.
Female Characters of Holy Scripture; in a Series of Sermons. 1859.
Devotional Commentary on the Gospel Narrative. 8 vols. 1869–70.
The Autobiography of Isaac Williams. Ed. Sir G. Prevost, 1892; 1893 (3rd edn).

[Williams pbd a number of other sermons, religious tracts, and 'harmonies' of the Gospels. He wrote nos. 80, 86 and 87 of Tracts for the Times.]

(c) Biography and Criticism

Griswold, R. W. Sacred Poets of England and America. 1859.
Miller, Josiah. Singers and Songs of the Church. 1869 (2nd edn).
Isaac Williams and the Oxford Movement. Church Quart. Rev. XXXIV, 1892.
Overton, J. H. A Dictionary of Hymnology. Ed. J. Julian, 1907.

ALEXANDER WILSON (d. 1852)

The Songs of the Wilsons. 1865; 1866; [1873]. [Poems by M. T. and Alexander Wilson.]

RICHARD WILTON (1827–1903)

Wood-Nuts and Church-Bells. 1873.
Lyrics, Sylvan and Sacred. 1878.
Sungleams: Rondeaux and Sonnets. [1882.]
Benedicite and Other Poems. [1889.]

Lyra Pastoralis: Songs of Nature, Church and Home. 1902.

[Wilton also assisted A. B. Grosart in translating into English verse the sacred Latin poems of George Herbert and Richard Crashaw. For Wilton's life and writings, with a selection from his poems, see A. H. Miles, *Miles*, x (xii).]

DAVID WINGATE (1828–1892)

(a) Poems

Poems and Songs. 1862.
Annie Weir, and Other Poems. 1866.
Lily Neil. A Poem. 1879.

(b) Criticism

David Wingate's Poems and Songs. Blackwood's Mag. xci, xcii, 1862.
Wilson, J. G. The Poets and Poetry of Scotland. Vol. ii, 1877, pp. 459–65.

CATHERINE WINKWORTH (1827–1878)

(a) Hymns

Lyra Germanica. Hymns for the Sundays and Chief Festivals of the Christian Year. Translated from the German. 1855.
Lyra Germanica. Second Series. The Christian Life. 1858.
A Selection of Hymns from the Lyra Germanica. 1859.
The Chorale Book for England. 1863. [Trns of German hymns with the original music.]
Lyra Germanica. [1906.] [A collected edn.] (Muses' Lib.)

[Catherine Winkworth also pbd trns of German prose, and an account of The Christian Singers of Germany, 1866.]

(b) Biography and Criticism

Julian, J. A Dictionary of Hymnology. 1907.
Shaen, M. J. Memorials of Two Sisters, Susanna and Catherine Winkworth. 1908.

THOMAS WOOLNER (1825–1892)

(a) Poems

My Beautiful Lady. [Ptd in The Germ, Jan. 1850, and, separately, in expanded form, in 1863.]
Pygmalion. 1881.
Silenus. 1884.
Tiresias. 1886.
My Beautiful Lady; [and] Nelly Dale. 1887.
Poems. Nelly Dale. Children. 1887.

(b) Biography and Criticism

Forman, H. B. Our Living Poets. 1871, pp. 273–86.

Tupper, J. L. Thomas Woolner. Portfolio, ii, 1871.
Meynell, A. Thomas Woolner's Pygmalion. Art Journ. xxxiv, 1882.
Garrod, H. B. Academy, 29 May 1886. [Review of Tiresias.]
Stephens, F. G. Thomas Woolner. Art Journ. xlvi, 1894.
Le Gallienne, R. Thomas Woolner. *Miles*, v.
Woolner, A. Thomas Woolner, his Life and Letters. 1917.
Evans, B. I. English Poetry in the Later Nineteenth Century. 1933. [Ch. v.]

CHRISTOPHER WORDSWORTH (1807–1885)

(a) Poems

The Druids. Chancellor's Medal Poem. Cambridge, 1827.
The Invasion of Russia by Napoleon Buonaparte. A Poem which obtained the Chancellor's Medal. Cambridge, 1828.
Ode at Cambridge on 7 July 1835 after the Installation of the Chancellor of the University. 1835.
The Druids; Invasion of Russia by Napoleon Buonaparte. [In Cambridge Prize Poems, 1859.]
The Holy Year; or, Hymns for Sundays, Holydays, and other Occasions; with Tunes. Ed. W. H. Monk, 1862.
Additional Hymns for the Holy Year. 1864.

(b) Other Works

Athens and Attica. 1836.
Greece, Pictorial, Descriptive and Historical. Illustrated by Copley Fielding. 1839.
Memoirs of William Wordsworth. 2 vols. 1851.
The Inspiration of the Bible. Five Lectures. 1861.
The Interpretation of the Bible. Five Lectures. 1861.
Church History up to A.D. 451. 4 vols. 1881–3.

[Wordsworth also pbd a Commentary on the whole Bible, numerous sermons, religious tracts, etc.]

(c) Biography and Criticism

Overton, J. H. and Wordsworth, E. Christopher Wordsworth, Bishop of Lincoln. 1888.
Overton, J. H. A Dictionary of Hymnology. Ed. J. Julian, 1907.

R. D. C. and H. B. C.

VI. THE LATER NINETEENTH CENTURY POETS

MORRIS, JAMES THOMSON, SWINBURNE, BRIDGES, HOPKINS, HOUSMAN AND FRANCIS THOMPSON

WILLIAM MORRIS (1834–1896)

(1) BIBLIOGRAPHIES

Forman, H. B. The Books of William Morris described, with Some Account of his Doings in Literature and in the Allied Crafts. 1897.

Scott, T. A Bibliography of the Works of William Morris. 1897.

Vallance, A. William Morris, his Art, his Writings and his Public Life. 1897. [Includes a classified bibliography.]

Cockerell, S. C. A Note by William Morris on his Aims in Founding the Kelmscott Press. [Kelmscott Press], 1898. [Includes a description of the Press and its pbns.]

Vaughan, C. E. Bibliographies of Swinburne, Morris, Rossetti. English Ass. 1914.

Tomkinson, G. S. A Select Bibliography of Modern Presses. 1928, pp. 104–31.

Ehrsam, T. G. and Deily, R. H. Bibliographies of Twelve Victorian Authors. New York, 1936.

(2) COLLECTED AND SELECTED WORKS

The Collected Works of William Morris, with Introductions by May Morris. 24 vols. 1910–5.

The Defence of Guenevere, the Life and Death of Jason, and Other Poems. 1914. (World's Classics.)

William Morris. Selected by Henry Newbolt. 1923.

Selections from the Prose Works. Ed. A. H. R. Ball, Cambridge, 1931.

Stories in Prose and Verse, Shorter Poems, Lectures and Essays. Ed. G. D. H. Cole, 1934.

(3) SEPARATE PUBLICATIONS
(a) Poems

The Oxford and Cambridge Magazine. 1856. [Morris's contributions are: No. 1, Winter Weather; No. 5, Riding Together; No. 6, Hands; No. 9, The Chapel in Lyoness; No. 10, Pray but one prayer for me.]

The Defence of Guenevere and Other Poems. 1858. [Kelmscott Press edn, 1892.]

The Life and Death of Jason. 1867. [Kelmscott Press edn, 1895.]

The Earthly Paradise: a Poem. 3 vols. 1868–70. [Kelmscott Press edn, 8 vols. 1896–7.]

Love is Enough, or the Freeing of Pharamond. A Morality. 1873. [Kelmscott Press edn, 1898.]

The Aeneids of Virgil, done into English verse. 1876 [end of 1875].

The Two Sides of the River, Hapless Love, and The First Foray of Aristomenes. 1876. [Unauthorised publication of doubtful date.]

The Story of Sigurd the Volsung and the Fall of the Niblungs. 1877 [Nov. 1876]. [Kelmscott Press edn, 1898.]

The Pilgrims of Hope. 1886. [Rptd from The Commonweal, 1885.]

The Odyssey of Homer, done into English verse. 1887.

Poems by the Way. 1891. [First ptd at the Kelmscott Press, 1891.]

The Order of Chivalry. [Kelmscott Press], 1893. [L'Ordene de Chevalerie, with trn into English verse.]

The Tale of Beowulf, done out of the Old English Tongue by William Morris and A. J. Wyatt. Kelmscott Press, 1895.

(b) Prose

The Oxford and Cambridge Magazine. 1856. [Morris's contributions are: No. 1, The Story of the Unknown Church; No. 2, The Churches of North France. (No. 1.) Shadows of Amiens; No. 3, A Dream. Men and Women, by Robert Browning [review]; No. 4, Frank's Sealed Letter; Nos. 7, 8, Gertha's Lovers; No. 8, Death the Avenger and Death the Friend. Svend and his Brethren; No. 9, Lindenborg Pool; Nos. 9, 10, The Hollow Land, a tale; No. 12, Golden Wings. The greater number of these tales and articles were rptd in The Hollow Land and Other Contributions to The Oxford and Cambridge Magazine, 1903.]

Grettis Saga, translated by E. Magnússon and W. Morris. 1869.

Volsunga Saga, translated by E. Magnússon and W. Morris. 1870.

Three Northern Love Stories, translated from the Icelandic by Eiríker Magnússon and William Morris. 1875.

The Decorative Arts, their relation to Modern Life and Progress, an address delivered before the Trades' Guild of Learning. 1878. [Rptd in Hopes and Fears for Art, 1882.]

Hopes and Fears for Art: five Lectures. 1882.

The Tables Turned, or Nupkins Awakened. A Socialist Interlude. 1887.

Signs of Change: seven Lectures. 1888.

A Dream of John Ball and A King's Lesson. 1888. [Rptd from The Commonweal. Kelmscott Press edn, 1892.]

A Tale of the House of the Wolfings and all the Kindreds of the Mark, written in prose and in verse. 1889.

The Roots of the Mountains, wherein is told somewhat of the lives of the men of Burgdale, their friends, their neighbours, their foemen and their fellows in arms. 1890.

News from Nowhere, or an Epoch of Rest, being some chapters from a Utopian romance. 1891. [Kelmscott Press edn, 1892.]

The Story of the Glittering Plain, which has also been called the Land of Living Men or the Acre of the Undying. 1891. [First book ptd at the Kelmscott Press after serial pbn in English Illustrated Mag.]

Under an Elm-tree, or Thoughts in the Country-side. Aberdeen, 1891.

An Address on the collection of paintings of the English pre-Raphaelite school delivered in the [Birmingham] museum and art gallery. Birmingham, 1891.

The Saga Library. Ed. William Morris and E. Magnússon, 5 vols. 1891–5.

Gothic Architecture, a lecture for the Arts and Crafts Exhibition Society. [Kelmscott Press], 1893.

The Tale of King Florus and the Fair Jehane. Kelmscott Press, 1893.

Of the Friendship of Amis and Amile, done into English by W. M. [Kelmscott Press, 1894.]

The Tale of the Emperor Coustans, and of Over Sea, done out of ancient French into English by William Morris. Kelmscott Press, 1894.

The Wood beyond the World. Kelmscott Press, 1894.

Child Christopher and Goldilind the Fair. 2 vols. [Kelmscott Press], 1805.

The Well at the World's End. [Kelmscott Press], 1896. [Ordinary edn ptd at the Chiswick Press, 2 vols. 1894, but not issued until 1896, with a new title-page.]

Old French Romances, done into English by William Morris. 1896. [The 3 trns mentioned above as ptd separately at the Kelmscott Press.]

The Water of the Wondrous Isles. [Kelmscott Press], 1897.

The Sundering Flood. [Kelmscott Press], 1898.

A Note by William Morris on his aims in founding the Kelmscott Press. [Kelmscott Press], 1898. [With description of the press and list of books by S. C. Cockerell.]

Lectures printed at the Chiswick Press in the Golden type of the Kelmscott Press. (1) Address delivered at the distribution of prizes to students of the Birmingham municipal school of art on 21 Feb. 1894. 1898. (2) Art and the Beauty of the Earth. 1898. (3) Some hints on pattern-designing. 1899. (4) Architecture and History; and

Westminster Abbey. 1900. (5) Art and its producers, and the arts and crafts of to-day. 1901.

Architecture, Industry and Wealth: collected papers. 1902.

(4) Biography and Criticism

[See also under Bibliographies, p. 314 above.]

Forman, H. B. Our Living Poets. 1871, pp. 375–426.

Stedman, E. C. Latter-Day British Poets. Scribner's Mag. Feb. 1875.

Swinburne, A. C. Morris's Life and Death of Jason. [In Essays and Studies, 1875.]

Saintsbury, G. Corrected Impressions. 1895.

Symons, A. Studies in Two Literatures. 1897.

Mackail, J. W. The Life of William Morris. 2 vols. 1899. [Also various addresses, each pbd separately, on Morris and his circle, 1901–14.]

Lethaby, W. R. Morris at Work. A Lecture. 1901.

Cary, E. L. William Morris, Poet, Craftsman, Socialist. 1902.

B[urne]-J[ones], G. Memorials of Sir Edward Burne-Jones. 2 vols. 1904.

Brooke, Stopford A. A Study of Clough, Arnold, Rossetti and Morris. 1908.

Jackson, Holbrook. William Morris, Craftsman-Socialist. 1908.

Noyes, A. William Morris. 1908. (English Men of Letters ser.)

Brief Sketch of the Morris Movement. Written to commemorate the Firm's 50th Anniversary. 1911.

Drinkwater, J. William Morris, a Critical Study. 1912.

Compton-Rickett, A. William Morris. A Study in Personality. With an Introduction by R. B. Cunninghame Graham. 1913.

Clutton-Brock, A. William Morris, his Work and Influence. 1914. (Home University Lib.)

Watts-Dunton, T. Old Familiar Faces. 1916.

Pennell, E. R. Some Memories of William Morris. American Mag. of Art, xi, 1920.

Glasier, J. B. William Morris and the Early Days of the Socialist Movement. With a Preface by May Morris. 1921.

Sparling, H. H. The Kelmscott Press and William Morris. 1924.

Wilson, S. P. William Morris and France. South Atlantic Quart. xxiii, 1924.

Wolff, L. Le Sentiment médiéval en Angleterre au XIXe Siècle et la première Poésie de William Morris. Revue anglo-américaine, Aug., Oct. 1924.

Evans, B. I. William Morris and his Poetry. 1925.

—— English Poetry in the Later Nineteenth Century. 1933. [Ch. iv.]

Tea, E. William Morris e Giacomo Boni. I Libri del Giorno, Oct. 1926. [Quotes unpbd letters.]

Fritzsche, G. William Morris: Socialismus und anarchistischer Kommunismus. Leipzig, 1927.

Helmholtz-Phelan, A. von. The Social Philosophy of William Morris. Durham, North Carolina, 1927.

A Chronological List of the Books printed at the Kelmscott Press with Illustrated Material from a Collection made by William Morris and Henry C. Marillier, now in the Library of Marsden J. Perry. Boston, 1928.

Kuester, E. C. Mittelalterliche und Antike bei William Morris. Berlin, 1928.

Parry, J. J. A Note on the Prosody of William Morris. MLN. XLIV, 1929.

Lucas, F. L. Eight Victorian Poets. Cambridge, 1930.

Cole, G. D. H. William Morris. [In Revaluations, ed. A. C. Ward, 1931.]

Davies, F. J. J. William Morris's Sir Peter Harpdon's End. PQ. XI, 1932.

Murry, J. M. The Greatness of William Morris. Adelphi, IV, 1932.

—— The Return to Fundamentals: Marx and Morris. Adelphi, V, 1932.

Bloomfield, P. William Morris. 1934.

Some Appreciations of William Morris. Ed. G. E. Roebuck, 1934.

Tillotson, G. Morris and Machines. Fortnightly Rev. CXLI, 1934.

Weekley, M. William Morris. 1934.

Litzenberg, K. William Morris and Scandinavian Literature: Bibliographical Essay. Scandinavian Stud. XIII, 1935.

—— Scandinavian Stud. XIV, 1936, pp. 17–24, 33–9, 40–1. [Notes on Morris and various sagas.]

—— William Morris and the Reviews. RES. XII, 1936.

Walton, T. A French Disciple of W. Morris (Jean Lahor). Revue de Littérature comparée, Sept. 1935.

Morris, May. William Morris, Artist, Writer, Socialist. With an Account of William Morris as I knew him, by Bernard Shaw. 2 vols. Oxford, 1936.

Bush, D. Mythology and the Romantic Tradition in English Poetry. Cambridge, U.S.A. 1937.

Hoare, A. D. M. The Works of Morris and Yeats in relation to Early Saga Literature. Cambridge, 1937.

Löhmann, O. Die Rahmenerzählung von Morris 'Earthly Paradise.' Archiv, CLXXII, 1937.

Riddehough, G. B. William Morris's Translation of the Aeneid. JEGP. XXXVI, 1937.

S. C. C.

JAMES THOMSON (1834–1882)

[Wrote under the pseudonym 'B. V.']

(1) COLLECTED AND SELECTED WORKS

Selections from the Original Contributions of James Thomson to Cope's Tobacco Plant. Ed. W. Lewin, 1889.

The Poetical Works of James Thomson. Ed. (with memoir) B. Dobell, 2 vols. 1895.

The City of Dreadful Night [and a selection of other poems]. Ed. B. Dobell, 1910.

Poems. Selected. Ed. G. H. Gerould, New York, 1927.

The City of Dreadful Night and Other Poems. Ed. E. Blunden, 1932.

(2) SEPARATE PUBLICATIONS
(a) Poems

The City of Dreadful Night and Other Poems. 1880. [The City of Dreadful Night first appeared in The National Reformer, 22 March to 17 May 1874.]

Vane's Story, Weddah and Om-el-Bonain, and Other Poems. 1881 [1880].

A Voice from the Nile and Other Poems. With a Memoir by B. Dobell. 1884 [1883].

[For Shelley, a Poem, see below under Prose.]

(b) Prose

Essays and Phantasies. 1881.

The Story of a famous Old Jewish Firm, etc. Leek Bijou Freethought Reprints, No. 6. 1881.

Satires and Profanities: with a Preface by G. W. Foote. 1884.

Shelley, a Poem: with Other Writings relating to Shelley by the late James Thomson ('B. V.') to which is added an Essay on the Poems of William Blake by the Same Author. 1884 (priv. ptd with a prefatory note by B. Dobell).

Biographical and Critical Studies. Ed. B. Dobell, 1896.

Essays, Dialogues and Thoughts of Giacomo Leopardi. [1905.] [Translated, with a memoir of Leopardi, by Thomson.]

James Thomson on George Meredith. 1910 (priv. ptd).

Walt Whitman, the Man and the Poet. Ed. B. Dobell, 1910.

(3) BIOGRAPHY AND CRITICISM

Marston, P. B. James Thomson. [In The English Poets, ed. T. H. Ward, vol. IV, 1883.]

Noel, R. James Thomson. [In The Poets and Poetry of the Century, ed. A. H. Miles, vol. V, [1893], etc.]

Symons, A. Studies in Two Literatures. 1897.

Salt, H. S. The Life of James Thomson. 1898; 1914 (rev. and enlarged).

Weissel, J. James Thomson der jüngere. Vienna, 1906.
Dobell, B. The Laureate of Pessimism. 1910.
Meeker, J. E. The Life and Poetry of James Thomson. 1917.
Hoffman, H. An Angel in The City of Dreadful Night. Sewance Rev. xxxii, 1924.
Peyre, R. Les Sources du Pessimisme de Thomson. Revue anglo-américaine, Dec. 1924, Feb. 1925.
Hirsch, A. James Thomson: ses Traducteurs et ses Critiques en France. Revue de l'Enseignement des Langues Vivantes, Feb. –April 1925.
Evans, B. I. English Poetry in the Later Nineteenth Century. 1933. [Ch. ix.]
Black, G. A. James Thomson: his Translations of Heine. MLR. xxxi, 1936.
Rebora, P. James Thomson e la Poesia di Leopardi in Inghilterra. Bolletino degli Studi inglesi in Italia, July 1937.
B. I. E.

ALGERNON CHARLES SWINBURNE
(1837–1909)
(1) BIBLIOGRAPHIES

Wise, T. J. A Bibliography of the Writings of A. C. Swinburne. 2 vols. 1919–20.
—— Catalogue of the Ashley Library. Vols. vi and (Supplements) vii, viii, ix, x, 1925–30. [Vol. vi rptd separately as A Swinburne Library, 1925.]
—— The Complete Works of A. C. Swinburne. Vol. xx, 1927. (Bonchurch edn.)

(2) POETICAL AND DRAMATIC WORKS
(a) Collected Editions

Poetical Works including Most of the Dramas. New York, 1884.
Poems. 6 vols. 1904 (with Atalanta and Erechtheus); 1904; 1909; 1910; 1912, etc.
Tragedies. 5 vols. 1905.
Chastelard and Mary Stuart, with a Preface by Watts Dunton. Leipzig, 1908. (Tauchnitz edn.)
The Golden Pine Edition. 7 vols. 1917, etc. [Includes Poems and Ballads, i, ii, iii, Atalanta and Erechtheus, Songs before Sunrise, Tristram, A Study of Shakespeare, William Blake.]
Collected Poetical Works. 2 vols. 1924; 1927.
Complete Works. 20 vols. 1925–7. (Bonchurch edn.) [Vols. i–x, Poetry and Dramas.]

(b) Selections

Selections from the Poetical Works. Ed. R. H. Stoddard, New York, 1884.
Selections. 1887.
[Selected] Lyrical Poems [including Atalanta]. Ed. W. Sharp Leipzig, 1901. (Tauchnitz edn.)
The Springtide of Life, Poems on Childhood. Ed. Sir E. Gosse, 1918.
Selections. Ed. Sir E. Gosse and T. J. Wise, 1919.
Golden Book of Swinburne's Lyrics. Ed. E. H. Blakeney, 1922.
Selections. Ed. H. M. Burton, 1927.
Selections. Ed. H. Wolfe, 1928.

(c) Poems

[The pbn of a poem in a paper, review, etc. is only recorded when the said poem was not included by Swinburne in any of his later collections. All poems pbd separately as a book or pamphlet are included.]
The Sundew. Spectator, 26 July 1862. [Rptd in Poems and Ballads, i, but with important modifications.]
Laus Veneris. 1866. [A forgery? See J. Carter and G. Pollard, An Enquiry into the Nature of Certain Nineteenth Century Pamphlets, 1934.]
Poems and Ballads. 1866 (re-issued 1866); 1866; 1867; 1868; 1871; 1873, etc.
Cleopatra. 1866. [A forgery? See J. Carter and G. Pollard, as above.]
Regret. Fortnightly Rev. Sept. 1867. [Rptd as Pastiche with considerable alterations in Poems and Ballads, ii.]
Dolores. 1867. [A forgery? See J. Carter and G. Pollard, as above.]
A Song of Italy. 1867 (re-issued 1868).
An Appeal to England. 1867. [Probably a forgery? See J. Carter and G. Pollard, as above.]
Siena. 1868 (a forgery? See J. Carter and G. Pollard, as above); Philadelphia, 1868.
Ode on the French Republic. 1870.
Tristram and Iseult: Prelude of an Unfinished Poem. [In Pleasure: a Holiday Book of Prose and Verse, 1871; rptd with alterations in Tristram.]
Songs before Sunrise. 1871; 1874; 1877, etc.; 1909 (Florence Press edn).
Le Tombeau de Théophile Gautier. 1873. [The Greek epigrams have never been rptd.]
Songs of Two Nations. 1875; 1893.
Poems and Ballads, Second Series. 1878 (bis); 1880; 1882, etc.
An Election. 1879. [A lithographed leaflet.]
Songs of the Springtides. 1880 (bis); 1891; 1902.
Studies in Song. 1880; 1896; 1907.
Euthanatos. 1881.
Tristram and other Poems. 1882 (bis); 1884, etc.

A Century of Roundels. 1883 (bis); 1892; 1909.

Dolorida, In the Album of Adah Menken. 1883. [A leaflet, ptd also in Walnuts on Wine, a Christmas annual, 1883.]

A Midsummer Holiday and Other Poems. 1884 (bis); 1889.

The Commonweal, A Song for Unionists. 1886.

A Word for the Navy. 1887 (bis); 1896.

The Question. 1887.

The Jubilee. 1887. [Rptd as The Commonweal: 1887, in Poems and Ballads, III.]

Gathered Songs. 1887.

The Whippingham Papers. 1888.

The Bride's Tragedy. 1889.

A Logical Ballad of Home Rule. St James's Gazette, 2 March 1889.

Ballad of Dead Men's Bay. 1889.

Poems and Ballads, III. 1889 (bis); 1892, etc.

The Brothers. 1889.

Sonnets on the Death of Browning. 1890.

Russia: an Ode. 1890.

Eton: an Ode. [In Catalogue of Objects of Interest connected with the History of Eton, 1891, ptd by R. I. Drake.]

Music: an Ode. 1892; 1893.

Grace Darling. 1893.

The Ballad of Bulgarie. 1893.

Astrophel and Other Poems. 1894 (bis).

A February Roundel. Saturday Rev. 22 Feb. 1896.

Robert Burns. 1896.

A Roundel of Rabelais. [In The Pageant, ed. C. H. Shannon and J. W. G. White, 1896. Rptd in A Channel Passage and Other Poems.]

A Tale of Balen. 1896.

A Channel Passage. 1899.

A Channel Passage and Other Poems. 1904 (3 edns).

Lord Soulis. 1909 (priv. ptd). [Rptd with six other ballads, Boston, 1912.]

In the Twilight. 1909 (priv. ptd).

To W. T. W. D. 1909 (priv. ptd).

Lord Scales. 1909 (priv. ptd).

Burd Margaret. 1909 (priv. ptd).

The Worm of Spindlestonheugh. 1909 (priv. ptd).

Border Ballads. 1909 (priv. ptd).

Saviour of Society. 1909 (priv. ptd). [Rptd from Examiner and Spectator.]

Ode to Mazzini. 1909 (priv. ptd).

The Ballade of Truthful Charles, etc. 1910 (priv. ptd).

Blest and the Centenary of Shelley. 1912 (priv. ptd). [Rptd from Athenaeum, etc.]

Lady Maisie's Bairn and Other Poems. 1915 (priv. ptd).

The Death of Sir John Franklin. 1916 (priv. ptd).

The Triumph of Gloriana. 1916 (priv. ptd).

Poetical Fragments. 1916 (priv. ptd).

Wearieswa'. 1917 (priv. ptd).

Posthumous Poems. 1917.

Rondeaux Parisiens. 1917 (priv. ptd).

The Italian Mother and Other Poems. 1918 (priv. ptd).

The Ride from Milan. 1918 (priv. ptd).

The Two Knights and Other Poems. 1918 (priv. ptd).

A Lay of Lilies and Other Poems. 1918 (priv. ptd).

Queen Yseult. Poem in 6 Cantos. 1918 (priv. ptd). [Rptd in part from Undergraduate Papers, Dec. 1857.]

Undergraduate Sonnets. 1918 (priv. ptd).

Lancelot, The Death of Rudel and Other Poems. 1918 (priv. ptd).

The Queen's Tragedy. 1919 (priv. ptd).

French Lyrics. 1919 (priv. ptd).

William the Ranter on William the Canter. New York Times, 9 Feb. 1919.

Ballads of the English Border. Ed. W. A. MacInnes, 1925.

Swinburne's Hyperion and Other Poems. Ed. (with Essay on Swinburne and Keats) G. Lafourcade, 1928.

The Temple of Janus. [Ptd in vol. II of Lafourcade's Jeunesse de Swinburne, 1928.]

(d) Parodies

The Monomaniac's Tragedy. Undergraduate Papers, no. 2, Part III, Feb., March 1858. [Unsigned.]

The Heptalogia. 1880; Portland, Maine, 1898.

The Cannibal Catechism. 1913 (priv. ptd).

Félicien Cossu. 1915 (priv. ptd).

Burlesque Lines on Robert Buchanan. Star, 19 March 1917.

(e) Tragedies

The Queen Mother and Rosamond. 1860 (re-issued 1866); 1868; 1896; 1907; 1908.

A Pilgrimage of Pleasure. [In Mary Gordon's Children of the Chapel, 1864. Rptd 1875, 1910 and (separately) 1913 (Boston).]

Atalanta in Calydon. 1865; 1865 (re-issued 1866); 1866; 1868; 1875, etc.; Kelmscott Press edn, 1894; Riccardi Press edn, 1923. [Facs. of first edn with preface by G. Lafourcade, 1930.]

Chastelard. 1865 (re-issued 1866, 1868); 1868; 1878, etc.

The First Act of Bothwell. 1871 (priv. ptd). [An early version.]

Bothwell. 1874 (bis); 1882; 1900.

Erechtheus. 1876 (bis); 1887, etc.

Mary Stuart. 1881; 1898; 1909.

Marino Faliero. 1885; 1907.

Locrine. 1887; 1896.

The Sisters. 1892.
Rosamund, Queen of the Lombards. 1899; 1900.
The Duke of Gandia. 1908.

(f) Translations

The Ballad of Villon and Fat Madge. 1910 (priv. ptd).
Poems from Villon. 1916 (priv. ptd).

(3) PROSE WORKS

[The pbn of prose works in periodicals, etc., is only recorded when such works were not included in any of the collections pbd in Swinburne's life-time. Most of these, but not all, were included in vols. XI–XVIII of the Bonchurch edn. All prose works which were pbd separately are included.]

(a) Collected Edition

[See, under Poetical Works, Bonchurch edn, vols. XI–XVIII.]

(b) Prefaces, Controversial Pamphlets, etc.

Notes on Poems and Reviews. 1866 (bis); Portland, Maine, 1899.
Under the Microscope. 1872; Portland, Maine, 1899.
The Devil's Due by Thomas Maitland [i.e. Swinburne]. 1875.
Testimonial in favour of John Nichol. 1885.
A Record of Friendship. 1910.

(c) Literary Criticism

William Congreve. [In The Imperial Dictionary, ed. J. F. Waller, 1857, p. 1107; rptd in Pericles and other Studies, 1914.]
Marlowe and Webster. Undergraduate Papers, Oxford, no. 1, Dec. 1857. [Unsigned.]
Modern Hellenism. Undergraduate Papers, Oxford, no. 1, Dec. 1857. [Unsigned.]
Byron. 1866. [A preface to a vol. of selections.]
The Imaginative Literature of England. 1866. [Report on the Anniversary of the Royal Literary Fund.]
William Blake. 1868 (re-issued 1868); 1896; 1906.
Christabel and the poems of S. T. Coleridge [with an introduction]. 1869.
George Chapman. 1875. [Introduction to the Works of Chapman.]
Essays and Studies. 1875; 1876; 1887, etc.
Joseph and his Brethren. 1876. [An introduction to the rpt of C. Wells's play.]
A Note on Charlotte Brontë. 1877 (bis); 1894.
William Congreve. Ency. Brit. 1877. [No connection with previous article in Imperial Dictionary.]
A Study of Shakespeare. 1880 (bis); 1895; 1902, etc.
Les Cenci. Paris, 1883. [An introduction, in French, to a trn of the play.]

Christopher Marlowe. Ency. Brit. 1883.
Mary Queen of Scots. Ency. Brit. 1883.
Wordsworth and Byron. Nineteenth Century, April–May 1884. [Rptd with an important omission in Miscellanies.]
Miscellanies. 1886; 1895; 1911.
A Study of Victor Hugo. 1886; 1909.
Thomas Middleton. 1887. [An introduction to a vol. of the Mermaid Ser.]
Cyril Tourneur. Ency Brit. 1888.
A Study of Ben Jonson. 1889.
Robert Herrick. 1891. [Preface to a vol. of the Muses' Lib.]
Studies in Prose and Poetry. 1894; 1897; 1906; 1915.
Aurora Leigh. 1898. [Prefatory Note to a New Edition of the Poem. Rptd in Pericles, etc.]
Victor Hugo. Ency. Brit. 1902.
Percy Bysshe Shelley. Philadelphia, 1903. [Also ptd in Chambers's Cyclopedia of Literature, vol. III, 1903.]
Pericles. 1907. [In vol. XIII of the Complete Works of Shakespeare (Harrap).]
The Age of Shakespeare. 1908.
Shakespeare. 1909.
Three Plays of Shakespeare. 1909.
Les Fleurs du Mal and Other Studies. 1913 (priv. ptd). [Rptd from The Spectator, 1862, etc.]
Charles Dickens. 1913. [First part ptd in Quart. Rev. July 1902.]
A Study of Les Misérables. 1914 (priv. ptd). [Rptd from The Spectator, 1862.]
Pericles and Other Studies. 1914 (priv. ptd).
Thomas Nabbes. 1914 (priv. ptd).
Sappho [a fragment]. Saturday Rev. 21 Feb. 1914.
Christopher Marlowe in relation to Greene, Peele and Lodge. 1914 (priv. ptd).
Theophile. 1915 (priv. ptd).
The Character and Opinions of Dr Johnson. 1918 (priv. ptd). [A student's essay.]
The Contemporaries of Shakespeare. 1919.

(d) Parodies and Burlesques

Critical Condition of Lord Sherbrooke. St James's Gazette, 5 May 1885.
Ernest Clouet. 1916 (priv. ptd).
A Vision of Bags. 1916 (priv. ptd).

(e) Art Criticism

Notes on the Royal Academy Exhibition. 1868. [Rptd with omissions in Essays and Studies.]
Mr Prudhomme at the International Exhibition. 1909.
Mr Whistler's Lecture on Art. Boston, 1913. [Also in Pericles and Other Studies, 1914; rptd from Fortnightly Rev. June 1888.]

(f) Political Pamphlets, etc.

Church Imperialism. Undergraduate Papers, March, April 1858. [Unsigned. Only rptd in Lafourcade's Jeunesse de Swinburne, vol. II.]

Note on the Muscovite Crusade. 1876.

On Liberty and Loyalty. 1909 (priv. ptd).

The Saviour of Society. 1909. [Contains a letter on Christianity and Imperialism rptd from Examiner, 7 July 1873.]

(g) Tales and Novels

Dead Love. Once a Week, Oct. 1862. [Rptd as a pamphlet 1864 and 1904. On the authenticity of the 1864 edn see J. Carter and G. Pollard, An Enquiry into the Nature of Certain Nineteenth Century Pamphlets, 1934.]

Lesbia Brandon. [Ptd 1877. Unpbd.]

A Year's Letters. 1877. [First pbd by instalments in Tatler, 25 Aug.–29 Dec. 1877. Rptd Portland, Maine, 1901, and 1905 as Love's Cross Currents (3 edns including Tauchnitz edn).]

The Marriage of Monna Lisa. 1909 (priv. ptd).

The Portrait. 1909 (priv. ptd).

The Chronicle of Queen Fredegond. 1909 (priv. ptd).

A Criminal Case. 1910 (priv. ptd).

(h) Letters

[Most, but by no means the whole, of the contents of the priv. ptd collections of letters mentioned below were included in The Letters of A. C. Swinburne, 1918, and in vol. XVIII of the Bonchurch edn. Many unpbd letters are preserved in the library of Mr T. J. Wise.]

A Word of Protest. Spectator, 10 July 1880. [On a review of Swinburne's Study of Shakespeare.]

Cats of History. Spectator, 17 Aug. 1881.

A Letter from Swinburne. World, 6 Dec. 1882. [On Swinburne's residence at Etretat.]

Ercole Strozzi or Aldo Romano? Spectator, 3 May 1884.

A Letter on Marino Faliero. Pall Mall Gazette, 11 April 1885.

Monna Vanna and S. Maria Aegyptiaca. Times, 25 June 1902.

Letters to T. J. Wise. 1909 (priv. ptd).

Letters on the Works of George Chapman. 1909 (priv. ptd).

Letters to John Churton Collins. 1910 (priv. ptd).

Letters on William Morris, etc. 1910 (priv. ptd).

Letters on the Elizabethan Dramatists. 1910 (priv. ptd).

Letters to A. H. Bullen. 1910 (priv. ptd).

Letters to Thomas Purnell. 1910 (priv. ptd).

Letters concerning Edgar Allan Poe. 1910 (priv. ptd).

Letters to Edmund Gosse. 5 sers. 1910–1 (priv. ptd).

Letters to Edmund Clarence Stedman. 1912 (priv. ptd).

Letters to Sir Richard Burton. 1912 (priv. ptd).

Letters to Sir Henry Taylor. 1912 (priv. ptd).

Letters to F. Locker-Lampson, etc. 1912 (priv. ptd).

Letters to the Press. 1912 (priv. ptd).

Letters to Sir Edward Lytton Bulwer. 1913 (priv. ptd).

Letters to Frederick Locker. 1913 (priv. ptd).

Letters to Stéphane Mallarmé. 1913 (priv. ptd).

Letters to John Morley. 1914 (priv. ptd).

Letters to Edward Dowden. 1914 (priv. ptd).

Letters to Lord Houghton. 1915 (priv. ptd).

Letters to Lady Trevelyan. 1916 (priv. ptd).

Early Letters to John Nichol. 1917.

Letters to Victor Hugo. 1917 (priv. ptd).

The Boyhood of A. C. Swinburne. Ed. Mrs D. Leith, 1917.

A Letter to Ralph Waldo Emerson. 1918 (priv. ptd).

Letter to P. Hamilton Hayne. Boston Evening Transcript, 16 Oct. 1918.

The Letters of A. C. Swinburne. Ed. A. C. Ricket and T. Hake-Murray, 1918.

The Letters of A. C. Swinburne. Ed. Sir E. Gosse and T. J. Wise, 2 vols. 1918.

A Romance of Literature. 1919 (priv. ptd).

Letters to Richard Hengist Horne. 1920 (priv. ptd).

Autobiographical Notes. 1920 (priv. ptd).

Swinburne's Mystifications [letter to H. G. Fielder]. TLS. 14 Aug. 1920.

The Complete Works of A. C. Swinburne. Vol. XVIII, 1927. Bonchurch edn.)

[See also under T. J. Wise's Bibliographies listed above.]

(4) MANUSCRIPTS

[Among unpbd MSS of Swinburne mention should be made of 4 unfinished pastiches of the Elizabethan drama (all in BM.): The Unhappy Revenge (1849); The Laws of Corinth (1858); Laugh and Lie Down; The Loyal Servant (1860). La Fille du Policeman (1861; a burlesque novel in French) and The Flogging Block (1862–5) are also in BM. Many letters, fragments, school or college essays, etc. are preserved in BM., Brotherton Lib., Nat. Lib. Wales, etc.]

(5) BIOGRAPHY AND CRITICISM

(a) General Works

Mr Swinburne's Poetry. Westminster Rev. April 1867.

Austin, A. The Poetry of the Period. 1870.

Friswell, J. H. Modern Men of Letters honestly criticised. 1870.

Forman, H. B. Our Living Poets. 1871, pp. 333–73.

Buchanan, R. W. The Fleshly School of Poetry. 1872.

Blémont, E. Swinburne. La Renaissance (Paris), I, 1872.

Stedman, E. C. Latter-Day British Poets. Scribner's Mag. Feb. 1875.

—— Victorian Poets. Boston, 1876.

Harvey, H. (probably Swinburne himself). Swinburne. République des Lettres (Paris), 18 Feb. 1877.

Clifford, W. K. Cosmic Emotion. [In Lectures and Essays, 1879.]

Courtney, W. L. Mr Swinburne's Poetry. Fortnightly Rev. XXXVII, 1885.

Sarrazin, G. Poètes modernes de l'Angleterre. Paris, 1885.

Graham, P. A. Mr Swinburne's Poetry. Contemporary Rev. II, 1886.

Villiers de l'Isle Adam, A. Le Sadisme anglais. [In Histoires insolites, Paris, 1888.]

Patmore, C. Principle in Art. 1889.

Lang, A. Letters on Literature. 1889.

Maupassant, Guy de. Notes sur A. C. Swinburne. [A preface to Mourey's trn of Poems and Ballads, I, 1891.]

Shindler, R. The Theology of Swinburne's Poems. GM. CCLXXI, 1891.

Waugh, A. Reticence in Literature. Yellow Book, I, 1894.

Saintsbury, G. Corrected Impressions. 1895.

—— History of English Prosody. 1910.

Who should be Laureate? Idler, VII, 1895.

Douglas, J. Swinburne. [In Chambers' Cyclopaedia of English Literature, vol. III, 1903.]

Barlow, G. On the Spiritual Side of Swinburne's Genius. Contemporary Rev. LXXXVIII, 1905.

Woodberry, G. E. Swinburne. New York, 1905.

Elton, O. Modern Studies. 1907.

—— A Survey of English Literature, 1830–1880. Vol. II, 1920.

Mackail, J. W. Swinburne, a Lecture. 1909.

Nicoll, Sir W. R. A. C. Swinburne. Contemporary Rev. I, 1909.

Genius and Influence of Swinburne. Bookman, June 1909.

Meynell, A. Swinburne's Lyrical Poetry. Dublin Rev. CXLV, 1909.

Hardy, T. A Singer Asleep. English Rev. V, 1910.

Thomas, E. Swinburne. 1912.

Drinkwater, J. Swinburne. 1913.

Welby, T. E. Swinburne. 1914.

—— A Study of Swinburne. 1926.

Harris, F. Swinburne: the Poet of Youth and Revolt. [In Contemporary Portraits, 1915.]

Lyall, Sir A. C. Characteristics of Swinburne's Poetry. [In Studies in Literature and History, 1915.]

Bennett, A. Books and Persons. 1917.

Gosse, Sir E. The Life of A. C. Swinburne. 1917. [Rptd with modifications as vol. XIX of the Bonchurch edn.]

—— An Essay on Swinburne. 1925. [Rptd from Det Nittende Aarhundrede, 1875.]

Symons, A. A. C. Swinburne. Fortnightly Rev. CLXI, 1917.

—— Studies in Strange Souls. 1929.

Bailey, J. Swinburne. Quart. Rev. CCXXI, 1917.

Hearn, L. History of English Literature. Vol. II, Tokyo, 1917.

Fehr, B. Studien zu Oscar Wildes Gedichten. Berlin, 1918. [Ch. III.]

—— Englische Literatur des 19. und 20. Jahrhunderts. Potsdam, 1923. [Ch. XXIV.]

—— Ang. Bbl. XI, 1929.

Pound, E. Swinburne. Poetry, XI, 1918.

Quiller-Couch, Sir A. T. Studies in Literature. Cambridge, 1919.

Kernahan, C. Swinburne as I knew him. 1919.

Eliot, T. S. Swinburne as Poet. [In The Sacred Wood, 1920.]

Squire, Sir J. C. Books in General. Ser. 2, 1920.

Grierson, Sir H. J. C. Lord Byron, Arnold and Swinburne, a Lecture. British Academy, 1921.

—— RES. VI, 1930, pp. 77–87.

Watts-Dunton, C. The Home Life of Swinburne. 1922.

Reul, P. de. L'Œuvre de Swinburne. 1922.

—— Revue Belge de Philosophie et d'Histoire, VIII, 1929.

Praz, M. Swinburne. La Cultura (Bologna), I, 1922.

—— La Carne, la Morte e il Diavolo nella Litteratura Romantica. Florence, 1930; tr. Eng. 1933.

Galimberti, A. L' Aedo d' Italia. Rome, 1925.

Nicolson, H. Swinburne. 1926. (English Men of Letters ser.)

Lafourcade, G. Revue anglo-américaine, IV, 1926.

—— La Jeunesse de Swinburne. 2 vols. Paris, 1928.

—— Swinburne. A Literary Biography. 1932.

—— Le Triomphe du Temps, où la Réputation de Swinburne. Études anglaises, I, 1937.

—— Le Centenaire de Swinburne. Études anglaises, II, 1938.

Chew, S. C. Swinburne. Boston, 1929.

Saurat, D. Litteris, VI, 1929.

Galland, R. L'Inspiration de Swinburne. Revue anglo-américaine, VI, 1929.

Lucas, F. L. Eight Victorian Poets. Cambridge, 1930.

Rutland, W. R. Swinburne. A Nineteenth Century Hellene. Oxford, 1931.

Hyder, C. K. Swinburne's Literary Career and Fame. Durham, North Carolina, 1933.

Winwar, F. The Rossettis and their Circle. Boston, 1934.

Bush, D. Mythology and the Romantic Tradition in English Poetry. Cambridge, U.S.A. 1937.

(b) Special Studies

[Milnes, R. M. (Baron Houghton).] Swinburne's Atalanta. Edinburgh Rev. CXXII. 1865.

—— Swinburne's Chastelard. Fortnightly Rev. IV, 1866.

Buchanan, R. W. Athenaeum, 4 Aug. 1866. [Review of Poems and Ballads I.]

[Morley, J.] Mr Swinburne's New Poems. Saturday Rev. 4 Aug. 1866.

Rossetti, W. M. Swinburne's Poems and Ballads, a Criticism. 1866.

Étienne, L. Swinburne et Keats. Revue des Deux-Mondes, 15 May 1867.

Bayne, P. Mr Arnold and Mr Swinburne. Contemporary Rev. IV, 1867.

Conway, M. D. Fortnightly Rev. III, 1868. [Review of William Blake.]

Lowell, J. R. My Study Window. Boston, 1871. [Reviews of Chastelard and Atalanta.]

Watts[-Dunton], T. Athenaeum, 6 July 1878. [Review of Poems and Ballads II.]

—— Athenaeum, 22 July 1882. [Review of Tristram.]

Thomson, J. The Swinburne Controversy. [In Satires and Profanities, 1884.]

Ethics of Swinburne's Poetry. Saturday Rev. LXXXI, 1896.

Reul, P. de. Swinburne et la France. Revue de l'Université de Bruxelles, Jan. 1904.

Russell, C. E. Swinburne and Music. North American Rev. CLXXXVI, 1907.

Keys, F. V. The Elizabethans and Mr Swinburne. North American Rev. CLXXXIX, 1909.

Serner, G. The Language of Swinburne's Lyrics and Epics. Lund, 1910.

Wilde, O. Reviews. Vol. II, 1910. [Poems and Ballads III.]

Kado, M. Swinburne's Verskunst. Berlin, 1911.

Richter, L. Swinburnes Verhältnis zur Frankreich und Italien. Leipzig, 1911.

Aubry, J. Baudelaire et Swinburne. Mercure de France, CXXV, 1917.

Henderson, W. B. D. Swinburne and Landor. 1918.

Gosse, Sir E. The First Draft of Anactoria. MLR. July 1919.

Waugh, A. The Swinburne Letters. [In Tradition and Change, 1919.]

Wier, M. C. The Influence of Aeschylus and Euripides on Atalanta in Calydon and Erechtheus. Ann Arbor, 1920.

Olivero, F On Swinburne's Atalanta in Calydon. [In Studies in Modern Poetry, 1921.]

Praz, M. La Trilogia di Maria Stuarda. La Cultura (Bologna), 15 Feb. 1921.

—— Le Fonti dell' Atalanta, Atene e Roma. Roma, July–Sept. 1922.

—— Il Manoscritto dell' Atalanta. La Cultura (Bologna), July 1929.

Lafourcade, G. Swinburne et Baudelaire. Revue anglo-américaine, I, 1924.

—— Atalanta: Le Manuscrit, les Sources. Revue anglo-américaine, I, 1925.

—— Swinburne and Lord Morley. TLS. 1 July 1926.

—— Swinburne and Walt Whitman. MLR. Jan. 1927.

—— Swinburne's Death of Sir John Franklin. TLS. 9 Feb. 1928.

—— L'Algolagnie de Swinburne. Hippocrate (Paris), March, April 1935.

—— Swinburne Romancier. Minotaure (Paris), VII, 1935. [La Fille du Policeman.]

Nicolson, H. Swinburne and Baudelaire, a Lecture. Trans. Royal Soc. of Literature, VI, 1925. [Rptd with modifications, 1930.]

Dottin, P. La Littérature, les Legendes et l'Histoire anciennes dans la Poésie de Swinburne. Revue de l'Enseignement des Langues Vivantes, XLII, 1925.

Löhrer, A. Swinburne als Kritiker der Literatur. Zurich, 1925.

Viereck, G. S. Freudian Glimpses of Swinburne. Stratford Monthly, Jan. 1925.

Delattre, F. A. C. Swinburne et la France. Revue des Cours et Conférences, 28 Feb. 1926.

—— Baudelaire et le jeune A. C. Swinburne. [In Mélanges Baldensperger, Paris, 1930.]

Galland, R. Emerson, Swinburne et Meredith. Revue anglo-américaine, Oct. 1928.

Hyder, C. K. Swinburne's Laus Veneris and the Tannhäuser Legend. PMLA. XLV, 1930.

—— The Medieval Background in Swinburne's The Leper. PMLA. XLVI, 1931.

—— Swinburne and the Popular Ballad. PMLA. XLIX, 1934.

Falk, B. The Naked Lady. 1934. [Adah Menken.]

Wright, H. G. Unpublished Letters from Theodore Watts-Dunton to Swinburne. RES. X, 1934.

Child, R. C. Swinburne's Mature Standards of Criticism. PMLA. LII, 1937.

Knaplund, P. Swinburne and the Poet-Laureateship, 1892. Toronto University Quart. VI, 1937.

G. L.

ROBERT SEYMOUR BRIDGES (1844–1930)

(1) BIBLIOGRAPHIES

[Useful bibliographical notes by Bridges will be found in each vol. of Poetical Works, 1898–1905, and in many of the separate vols. of prose and verse. The Oxford Mag. (1895) and Modern Authors (1921) bibliographies were supervised by Bridges.]

[Daniel, C. H. O.] Notes on a Bibliography of Bridges to 1895. Oxford Mag. 19 June 1895, p. 445.

The Daniel Press, 1845–1919. Oxford, 1921. [Bibliography by F. Madan, pp. 37 ff.]

Bibliographies of Modern Authors. No. 1, Robert Bridges. 1921.

McKay, G. L. Bibliography of Robert Bridges. New York, 1933.

(2) COLLECTED WORKS

Poetical Works. 6 vols. 1898–1905. [Vol. I, 1898: Prometheus; Eros and Psyche; Growth of Love. Vol. II, 1899: Shorter Poems (Bks i–v); New Poems. Vol. III, 1901, vols. IV, V, 1902, vol. VI, 1905: Dramas.]

Poetical Works excluding the eight Dramas. 1912; 1936 (enlarged). [1st edn contains vols. I and II of previous entry, Demeter, Later Poems and Poems in Classical Prosody. 2nd edn adds contents of October and Other Poems (omitting some war poems) and New Verse, and 3 unpbd pieces.]

Collected Essays, Papers, etc. [I, 1927: Influence of Audience on Shakespeare's Drama. II, III, 1928: Humdrum and Harum-Scarum; Poetic Diction. IV, 1929: Critical Introduction to Keats. V, 1930: George Darley. VI, VII, 1931: Poems of Mary Coleridge; Lord de Tabley's Poems. VIII–X, 1932: Dante in English Literature; Poems of Emily Brontë; Dryden on Milton. XI–XV, 1933: Studies in Poetry; Springs of Helicon; Wordsworth and Kipling; Word-Books; Letter on English Prosody. XVI–XX, 1934: The Bible; Bunyan's Pilgrim's Progress; Sir Thomas Browne; George Santayana; The Glamour of Grammar. XXI–XXVI, 1935: The Musical Setting of Poetry; Some Principles of Hymn-Singing; About Hymns; English Chanting; Chanting; Psalms Noted in Speech Rhythm. XXVII–XXX, 1936: An Address to the Swindon W.E.A.; The Necessity of Poetry; Poetry; An Account of the Casualty Department. Nos. v and following ed. by M. M. Bridges.]

(3) SEPARATE PUBLICATIONS

(a) Poems and Plays

Poems. 1873 (suppressed by author). [Partly rptd as Poems by the Author of The Growth of Love, First Series, Second Edition, 1880 (anon.); partly rptd in Poems, 1884; author's 'final selection' forms bk I of Shorter Poems, 1890.]

The Growth of Love, in twenty-four Sonnets. 1876 (anon.); Daniel Press (Oxford), 1889 (79 sonnets, rev.; anon.); 1890 (black letter); Portland, Maine, 1894 (pirated). [69 sonnets included, in rev. form, in Poetical Works, vol. I, 1898.]

Carmen Elegiacum de Nosocomio Sti. Bartolomaei Londiniensi. 1876; 1877 (rev. text).

Poems by the Author of The Growth of Love (Second Series). 1879 (anon.). [Partly rptd in Poems, 1884.]

Poems by the Author of The Growth of Love, Third Series. 1880 (anon.). [Partly rptd in Poems, 1884.]

The Garland of Rachel by [Bridges and] Divers Kindly Hands. Daniel Press, 1881; Portland, Maine, 1902 (pirated).

Prometheus the Firegiver, a Mask. Daniel Press, 1883 (4to); 1884 (8vo, rev. text).

Poems. Daniel Press, 1884. [Mostly included in Shorter Poems, 1890.]

Nero, an Historical Tragedy. Part I. 1885. Part II. [1894.]

Eros and Psyche, a Narrative Poem. 1885; 1894 (rev. and partly re-written).

The Feast of Bacchus, a Comedy. Daniel Press, 1889; [1894] (rev. text).

Shorter Poems. 1890 (4 bks); Daniel Press, [1893]–1894 (rev. and 5th bk added); 1894; 1896 (rev.); ed. M. M. Bridges, Oxford, 1931 (enlarged edn).

Palicio, a Romantic Drama. 1890.

The Return of Ulysses, a Drama. 1890.

The Christian Captives, a Tragedy. 1890.

Achilles in Scyros, a Drama. 1890 (4to); 1892 (8vo, rev.).

Eden, an Oratorio. 1891 (with and without music by Sir C. V. Stanford).

November Drear. 1892. [Off-print from Songs of Sundry Natures, by W. Byrd, Oxford, 1892.]

Founder's Day, a Secular Ode on the Ninth Jubilee of Eton College. [Daniel Press, 1893] (anon.). [Included in Shorter Poems, bk v, 1893.]

Shorter Poems, Book v. [Daniel Press, 1893]; 1894. [See also Shorter Poems, 1890, above.]

The Humours of the Court, a Comedy. [1893] (4to); 1893 (8vo, as The Humours of the Court and Other Poems, i.e. bk v of Shorter Poems).

Invocation to Music, an Ode in Honour of Purcell. 1895 (with music by Sir C. H. H. Parry); 1896 ('largely re-written' as Purcell Commemoration Ode with Other Poems and Preface, Mathews' Shilling Garland, no. II). [The Ode is rptd in Later Poems, 1912; the other poems are rptd in New Poems, 1899.]

A Song of Darkness and Light. 1898 (with music by Sir C. H. H. Parry). [Rptd as A Hymn of Nature in Later Poems, 1912.]

New Poems. [First collected in Poetical Works, vol. II, 1899.]

Now in Wintry Delights. Daniel Press, 1903. [Rptd in Poems in Classical Prosody, 1912.]

Peace, an Ode by R. B. Daniel Press, 1903. [Rptd in Poems in Classical Prosody, 1912.]

Demeter, a Mask. Oxford, 1905. [Rptd in Poetical Works, 1912.]

Eton Memorial Ode. 1908 (with music by Sir C. H. H. Parry). [Included in Later Poems, 1912.]

Sonnet XLIV of Michelangelo Buonarroti, translated. 1912 (priv. ptd).

Later Poems and Poems in Classical Prosody. [First collected in Poetical Works, 1912.]

Poems written in 1913. Ashendene Press, 1914. [Included in October and Other Poems, 1920.]

Shakespeare Tercentenary Ode. 1916 (priv. ptd). [Rptd in Shakespeare's England, 2 vols. Oxford, 1916.]

Lord Kitchener. 1916 (priv. ptd).

The Chivalry of the Sea, a Naval Ode. 1916 (with music by Sir C. H. H. Parry). [Included in October and Other Poems, 1920.]

Ibant Obscuri, an Experiment in the Classical Hexameter. Oxford, 1916. [Enlarged from article in New Quart. Jan. 1909; trns from Virgil rptd from Poems in Classical Prosody, 1912, and trns from Homer and notes added.]

Britannia Victrix. Oxford, 1918. [Included in New Verse, 1925.]

October and Other Poems. 1920 (re-issued Oxford, [1929]).

Poor Poll. 1923 (priv. ptd). [Included in New Verse, 1925.]

The Tapestry. 1925 (priv. ptd). [Partly rptd from October, 1920; partly rptd in New Verse, 1925.]

New Verse written in 1921 and Earlier Pieces. Oxford, 1925; 1926 (rev. text).

The Testament of Beauty. 5 pts, [1927–9] (large 4to, priv. ptd); Oxford, 1929 (rev. and pbd, 4to and 8vo); 1930 ('with final corrections,' small 4to).

On receiving Trivia from the Author. Mill House Press (Stanford Dingley, Berks.), 1930.

Verses written for Mrs Daniel. With an Introduction by George Gordon. Oxford, 1932.

[For Bridges's contributions to The Yattendon Hymnal see under 'Edited Matter' below.]

(b) Prose Works

An Account of the Casualty Ward. [1878.] [Rptd from St Bartholomew's Hospital Reports, vol. XIV.]

On the Elements of Milton's Blank Verse. [1887] (anon.). [Off-print from Paradise Lost, bk I, ed. H. C. Beeching, Oxford, 1887.]

On the Prosody of Paradise Regained and Samson Agonistes. Oxford, 1889 (anon.).

Milton's Prosody. Oxford, 1893; 1894; Oxford, 1901 (enlarged and adds Classical Metres in English Verse, by W. J. Stone); Oxford, 1921 (with further addns).

John Keats, a Critical Essay. 1895 (priv. ptd; re-issued in Poems of Keats, ed. G. Thorn Drury, vol. I, 1896). [Rev. and rptd in Poetical Works of Keats, ed. L. Binyon, [1916].]

A Practical Discourse on Hymn-Singing. Oxford, 1901.

About Hymns. 1911. (Church Music Society papers, no. II.)

On the Present State of English Pronunciation. Oxford, 1913. [Rptd from E. & S. I, 1910.]

An Address to the Swindon Branch of the W.E.A. Oxford, 1916.

The Necessity of Poetry. Oxford, 1918.

Dedication at Unveiling of Memorial, St Bartholomew's School, Newbury, 1921 (priv. ptd).

The Influence of the Audience. New York, 1926 (priv. ptd). [Rptd from Works of Shakespeare, ed. A. H. Bullen, vol. X, Stratford-on-Avon, 1907.]

Henry Bradley, a Memoir. Oxford, 1926. [Rptd in Collected Papers of H. Bradley, Oxford, 1928, and in Three Friends, 1932.]

Poetry. 1929. [Broadcast lecture.]

Three Friends. 1932. [Memoirs of D. M. Dolben (rptd from Poems of Dolben; see below), R. W. Dixon (rptd from Poems by R. W. Dixon; see below) and H. Bradley (rptd from Collected Papers).]

[For Bridges's SPE. tracts see under 'Edited Matter' below.]

(c) Edited Matter

The Yattendon Hymnal. Ed. R. Bridges and H. E. Wooldridge, 4 pts, Oxford, 1895–9; 1899 (complete); Oxford, 1920. Yattendon Hymns [Bridges's words only]. Oxford, 1897 [1898]. Hymns from the Yattendon Hymnal. Daniel Press, 1899. The Small Hymn Book [words only]. Oxford, 1899; 1914; 1920.

Yattendon Four-part Chants. [1897] (4to and folio, priv. ptd).

Last Poems of R. W. Dixon. 1905.

Poems by R. W. Dixon, with a Memoir. 1909.

The Poems of Digby Mackworth Dolben, with memoir. 1911; 1915 (rev.).

Society for Pure English. [The following tracts are wholly or principally by Bridges: Prospectus, 1913; I, Preliminary Announcement, 1919; II, English Homophones, 1919; v, Dialectal Words in Blunden's Poems, 1921; VIII, What is Pure French? By M. Barnes (pseud.), 1922; XIV, Briton, British, Britisher (by H. Bradley and Bridges), 1923; xv, Pictorial, Picturesque, etc., 1923; XVIII, Poetry in Schools, etc., 1924; XXI, The Society's Work, 1925. Contributions by Bridges appear also in tracts III, IV, VI, VII, IX, X, XI, XIII, XVI, XVII, XIX, XXII, XXIII, XXIV, XXVI, XXVIII, XXX and XXXII.]

The Spirit of Man, an Anthology in English and French. 1916.

Poems of Gerard Manley Hopkins. 1918.

The Chilswell Book of English Poetry for Schools. 1924.

Selection from the Letters of Sir Walter Raleigh. Ed. Lady Raleigh, [1928]. [Introduction by Bridges.]

Collected Papers of Henry Bradley, with Memoir. Oxford, 1928.

(d) *Unreprinted Pieces*

[A full list of Bridges's articles and letters in Musical Antiquary, Speaker and Times (with supplements) is given in G. L. McKay's Bibliography.]

Severe Case of Rheumatic Fever. [St Bartholomew's Hospital Reports, vol. XII, 1876, pp. 175–81.]

Gerard Hopkins. [The Poets and Poetry of the Century, ed. A. H. Miles, vol. VIII, 1893, pp. 161–4; rptd 1898, 1906.]

English Music. Monthly Rev. XVI, 1904, pp. 105–10.

To —— [alcaics in Stone's phonetic prosody]. Academy, 6 May 1905, p. 492.

Henry John Newbolt. [The Poets and Poetry of the Nineteenth Century, ed. A. H. Miles, vol. VII, 1906.]

Theobaldus Stampensis. [Oxford Pageant Book, 1907, pp. 29–34.]

[Address.] [Verhaeren Commemoration Addresses, Royal Soc. of Literature, 1917, pp. 23–7.]

Two Essays [Affection; Deliberation]. Forum, LXIX, 1923, pp. 1649–51.

(4) BIOGRAPHY AND CRITICISM

Warren, Sir T. H. Robert Bridges. [In The Poets and Poetry of the Century, ed. A. H. Miles, vol. VIII, 1893, etc.]

Warren, Sir T. H. Robert Bridges, Poet Laureate. A Lecture. Oxford, 1913.

Dowden, E. New Studies in Literature. 1895.

Young, F. E. B. Robert Bridges, A Critical Study. 1914.

Hearn, L. Appreciations of Poetry. Ed. J. Erskine, New York, 1916.

Fox, A. W. Robert Bridges: Poet Laureate. Manchester Quart. CLXVII, 1923.

Davison, E. Robert Bridges, Poet Laureate of England. English Journ. XIV, 1925.

—— In Praise of the Poet Laureate. Fortnightly Rev. CXXX, 1928.

Dackweiler, C. Robert Bridges, Poète-lauréat. Humanitas, II, 1927.

The Testament of Beauty. TLS. 24 Oct. 1929.

de Selincourt, E. The Testament of Beauty. Hibbert Journ. XXVIII, 1930.

MacCarthy, D. Notes on the Poetry of Robert Bridges. Life and Letters, IV, 1930.

Magnus, L. The Testament of Beauty. Cornhill Mag. LXIX, 1930; Trans. Royal Soc. of Literature, X, 1931.

Sasaki, T. On the Language of Robert Bridges in Poetry. Tokio, 1930.

Waugh, A. Robert Bridges. Fortnightly Rev. June 1930.

Garrod, H. W. Poetry and the Criticism of Life. Oxford, 1931.

Smith, L. P. Robert Bridges. SPE. XXXV, 1931. [Includes a section by E. Daryush on Bridges' work on the English language.]

Smith, N. C. Notes on the Testament of Beauty. Oxford, 1931, 1932 (rev.).

Elton, O. Robert Bridges and The Testament of Beauty. English Ass. 1932.

Gordon, G. S. Robert Bridges. (Rede Lecture.) Cambridge, 1932.

Evans, B. I. English Poetry in the Later Nineteenth Century. 1933. [Ch. x.]

The Letters of Gerard Manley Hopkins to Robert Bridges. Ed. C. C. Abbott, Oxford, 1935.

Lipscomb, H. C. Lucretius and The Testament of Beauty. Classical Journ. XXXI. 1935.   S. N. S.

GERARD MANLEY HOPKINS (1844–1889)

(1) WRITINGS

Gerard Hopkins. [Selected poems, with a critical-biographical introduction by R. Bridges. In The Poets and Poetry of the Century, ed. A. H. Miles, vol. VIII, [1893], etc.]

The Spirit of Man. An Anthology. Ed. R. Bridges, 1916. [Includes 6 poems by Hopkins.]

Poems of Gerard Manley Hopkins. Ed. R. Bridges, 1918; rev. C. Williams, 1930 (with additional poems).

A Vision of the Mermaids. A Prize Poem dated Christmas, 1862, and now for the First Time printed in full. 1929.

The Letters of Gerard Manley Hopkins to Robert Bridges. (The Correspondence of Gerard Manley Hopkins and Richard Watson Dixon.) Ed. C. C. Abbott, 2 vols. Oxford, 1935.

Further Letters of Gerard Manley Hopkins. Ed. C. C. Abbott, Oxford, 1937. [To and from Coventry Patmore and others.]

The Note-Books and Papers of Gerard Manley Hopkins. Ed. H. House, Oxford, 1937.

(2) BIOGRAPHY AND CRITICISM

Porter, A. Difficult Beauty. Spectator, 13 Jan. 1923.

Lahey, G. F. Gerard Manley Hopkins. 1930. [A biography.]

Grisewood, H. Gerard Manley Hopkins, S.J. Dublin Rev. CLXXXIX, 1931.

Leavis, F. R. Gerard Manley Hopkins. [In New Bearings in English Poetry, 1932.]

Phare, E. E. The Poetry of Gerard Manley Hopkins; a Survey and Commentary. Cambridge, 1933.

Read, H. The Poetry of Gerard Manley Hopkins. [In English Critical Essays (Twentieth Century), ed. P. M. Jones, 1933 (World's Classics).]

Stonier. G. W. Gerard Manley Hopkins. [In Gog Magog and Other Critical Essays, 1933.]

Brémond, A. La Poésie naïve et savante de Gerard Hopkins. Études, 5 Oct. 1934.

Fletcher, J. G. Gerard Manley Hopkins. American Rev. VI, 1936.

Gardner, W. H. A Note on Hopkins and Duns Scotus. Scrutiny, V, 1936.

—— The Wreck of the Deutschland. E. & S. XXI, 1936.

—— The Religious Problem in Gerard Manley Hopkins. Scrutiny, VI, 1937.

ALFRED EDWARD HOUSMAN (1859–1936)
(1) POEMS

A Shropshire Lad. 1896.

Last Poems. 1922.

Three Poems: The Parallelogram, The Amphisbaena, The Crocodile. 1935. [Rptd from Union Mag., University College, London.]

More Poems. [Ed. L. Housman], 1936.

[Some 30 more poems, parodies, etc. are included in L. Housman's biography, 1937.]

(2) OTHER WRITINGS

Introductory Lecture delivered [at] University College, London. Cambridge, 1892, 1933 (priv. ptd); Cambridge, 1937 (pbd). [On the study of the classics.]

Nine Essays by Arthur Platt. With a Preface by A. E. Housman. Cambridge, 1927.

The Name and Nature of Poetry. The Leslie Stephen Lecture delivered at Cambridge, May 9, 1933. Cambridge, 1933.

[Housman also pbd critical edns of Manilius, Juvenal and Lucan. See Gow below.]

(3) BIOGRAPHY AND CRITICISM

Gale, N. Some Volumes of Verse. Academy, 11 July 1896.

Archer, W. Poets of the Younger Generation. 1901.

TLS. 19 Oct. 1922. [A long review of Last Poems.]

Ellis, S. M. Fortnightly Rev. Jan. 1923. [A long review of Last Poems.]

Macdonald, J. F. The Poetry of A. E. Housman. Queen's Quart. Oct.–Dec. 1923.

Priestley, J. B. Figures in Modern Literature. 1924. [Contains an essay on Housman.]

Collins, H. P. A. E. Housman: a Retrospective Note. Adelphi, III, 1925.

Sparrow, J. Echoes in the Poetry of A. E. Housman. Nineteenth Century, CXV, 1934. [Supplemented by L. R. Lind, Classical Weekly, 9 Dec. 1935.]

Tinker, C. B. Housman's Poetry. Yale Rev. XXV, 1935.

Gow, A. S. F. A. E. Housman. A Sketch, together with a List of his Writings and Indexes to his Classical Papers. Cambridge, 1936.

Symons, K. E. Memories of A. E. Housman. Bath, 1936.

Housman, L. A. E. H., some Poems, some Letters and a Personal Memoir. 1937. [Includes pp. 273–5 complete list of dated poems.]

Pollet, M. A. E. Housman. Études anglaises, I, 1937.

Tillotson, G. The Publication of A. E. Housman's Comic Poems. English, I, 1937.

Wilson, Edmund. The Triple Thinker. 1938.

FRANCIS THOMPSON (1859–1907)
(1) BIBLIOGRAPHY

Stonehill, C. A. and H. W. Bibliographies of Modern Authors. (Second Series.) 1925.

(2) COLLECTED AND SELECTED WORKS

Selected Poems. 1908. [With A Biographical Note by W. Meynell.]

The Works of Francis Thompson. [Ed. W. Meynell], 3 vols. [1913]. [Vols. I, II, poems; vol. III, prose essays. Poems rptd in 1 vol. 1938.]

The Collected Poetry of Francis Thompson. 1913.

(3) SEPARATE PUBLICATIONS

(a) Poems

The Child Set in the Midst. By Modern Poets. Ed. W. Meynell, [1892]. [Contains 4 poems by Thompson.]

Poems. 1893.

Sister-Songs. An Offering to Two Sisters. 1895. [Also priv. ptd 1895 as Songs Wing to Wing: An Offering to Two Sisters.]

St Anthony of Padua. By Father Leopold de Chérance. Rendered into English by Father Marianus. [1895.] [Contains Thompson's poem, To St Anthony of Padua.]

New Poems. 1897.

Victorian Ode for Jubilee Day, 1897. 1897 (priv. ptd.)

Eyes of Youth. A Book of Verse. With Four Early Poems by Francis Thompson. [1909.]

Uncollected Verse. By Francis Thompson. 1917 (priv. ptd).

(b) Prose

The Life and Labours of Blessed John Baptist de la Salle, Founder of the Brothers of the Christian Schools, and Father of Modern Popular Education. [1891]; 1911 (with preface by W. Meynell).

Health & Holiness. A Study of the Relations between Brother Ass, the Body, and his Rider, the Soul. With a Preface by George Tyrrell. 1905.

Shelley. With an Introduction by George Wyndham. 1909. [Written 1889.]

Saint Ignatius Loyola. Ed. J. H. Pollen, 1909. [With preface by W. Meynell.]

A Renegade Poet and Other Essays. With an Introduction by Edward J. O'Brien. Boston, 1910.

Sir Leslie Stephen as a Biographer. [1915] (priv. ptd).

(4) BIOGRAPHY AND CRITICISM

Archer, W. Poets of the Younger Generation. 1902.

Delattre, F. Le Poète Francis Thompson. Paris, 1909. [Rptd from Revue Germanique, v, 1000.]

Beacock, G. A. Francis Thompson. Marburg, 1912.

Thomson, John. Francis Thompson, the Preston Poet. Preston, 1912; 1922 (rev. edn).

Jackson, Holbrook. The Eighteen Nineties. 1913. [Ch. xii.]

Meynell, E. The Life of Francis Thompson. 1913; 1926. [The standard biography.]

Rooker, K. Francis Thompson. 1913. [A French dissertation.]

Hodgson, G. E. A Study of Illumination. 1914.

Haecker, T. Über Francis Thompson und Sprachkunst. Hochland, XXII, 1924.

Finberg, H. P. R. Francis Thompson. English Rev. XLI, 1925.

Symons, A. Dramatis Personae. 1925.

Hutton, J. A. Guidance from Francis Thompson in Matters of Faith. 1926.

Shuster, G. N. Notes for a Literary Study of The Hound of Heaven. Catholic Educational Rev. XXIV, 1926.

Mégroz, R. L. Francis Thompson, the Poet of Earth in Heaven. 1927.

Wright, T. H. Francis Thompson and his Poetry. 1927.

Peterson, E. L. Francis Thompson: a Picture Biography. Virginia Quart. IV, 1928.

Chapman, J. A. Shelley and Francis Thompson. [In Papers on Shelley, Wordsworth, and Others, 1929.]

Tardivel, F. L'Expérience poétique et l'Expérience religieuse de Francis Thompson. Revue Anglo-Américaine, Dec. 1930.

De la Gorce, A. Francis Thompson et les Poètes Catholiques d'Angleterre. Paris, 1932; tr. Eng. 1933.

Gautrey, R. M. 'This Tremendous Lover.' An Exposition of Francis Thompson's Hound of Heaven. 1932.

Evans, B. I. English Poetry in the Later Nineteenth Century. 1933. [Ch. vi.]

McNabb, V. Francis Thompson and Other Essays. 1935.

Olivero, F. Francis Thompson. Brescia, 1935; tr. Eng. Turin, 1938.

D'Alessio, E. Francis Thompson. Milan, 1937.

B. I. E.

VII. MINOR VERSE, 1870–1900

[This section has been restricted, with one or two exceptions, to writers born after 1830 and before 1865. The abbreviation *Miles* has been used to refer to The Poets and Poetry of the Century, ed. A. H. Miles, 10 vols. [1891–7], 1898, 12 vols. 1905–7 (rev. and enlarged).]

ALEXANDER ANDERSON (1845–1909)

(a) Poems

A Song of Labour and Other Poems. Dundee, 1873.

The Two Angels, and Other Poems. With an Introductory Sketch by G. Gilfillan. 1875.

Songs of the Rail. 1878.

Ballads and Sonnets. 1879. [Partly rptd from A Song of Labour and The Two Angels, but with many new poems.]

Later Poems of Alexander Anderson, 'Surface man.' Ed. (with biographical sketch) A. Brown, Glasgow, 1912.

(b) Biography and Criticism

Cuthbertson, D. The Life-History of Alexander Anderson. Inveresk, 1929 (priv. ptd).

Evans, B. I. English Poetry in the Later Nineteenth Century. 1933. [Ch. xvi.]

SIR EDWIN ARNOLD (1832–1904)

(a) Collected and Selected Poems

Edwin Arnold Birthday Book. Ed. K. L. and C. Arnold, 1885. [Compiled from The Works of Edwin Arnold, with new and additional poems written expressly therefor.]

Poems, National and Non-Oriental, with Some New Pieces, selected from the Works of Sir E. Arnold. 1888.

Poetical Works. 8 vols. 1888.

Oriental Poems. Selected by J. M. Watkins. 1904.

Indian Poetry and Indian Idylls. 1915.

The Arnold Poetry Reader. Selections. With Memoir and Notes by E. L. Arnold. 1920.

(b) Separate Poems and Plays

The Feast of Belshazzar. A Prize Poem. Oxford, 1852.

Poems, Narrative and Lyrical. Oxford, 1853. [Includes The Feast of Belshazzar.]

Griselda, a Tragedy, and Other Poems. 1856.

The Wreck of the Northern Belle. A Poem. Hastings, 1857.

The Light of Asia, or, the Great Renunciation. 1879, etc.; ed. Sir E. D. Ross, 1926.

Indian Poetry. 1881.

Pearls of the Faith, or Islam's Rosary. 1883.

The Secret of Death, with Some Collected Poems. 1885. [The Secret of Death is from the Sanskrit.]

Lotus and Jewel. 1887.

With Sa'di in the Garden, or, The Book of Love. 1888. [A long poem based on Ishk, or the third chapter of the Bôstân of the Persian poet Sa'di.]

In my Lady's Praise. Being Poems, Old and New, written in the Honour of Fanny, Lady Arnold, and now collected for her Memory. 1889.

The Light of the World, or the Great Consummation. A Poem. 1891; tr. Dutch, 1892.

Potiphar's Wife and Other Poems. 1892.

Adzuma; or, the Japanese Wife. A Play in Four Acts. 1893.

The Tenth Muse, and Other Poems. 1895. [Many of these poems are 'from the Sanskrit.']

The Voyage of Ithobal. A Poem. 1901.

(c) Other Writings

Education in India. A Letter from the Ex-Principal of an Indian Government College to his Appointed Successor. 1860.

The Marquis of Dalhousie's Administration of British India. 2 vols. 1862–5.

The Poets of Greece. 1869.

A Simple Transliteral Grammar of the Turkish Language with Dialogues and Vocabulary. 1877.

India Revisited. 1886. [Rptd with 'Additions Descriptive and Poetical,' from Daily Telegraph. Essays on India, mostly of a descriptive kind.]

Death—and afterwards. 1887. [An essay rptd from Fortnightly Rev. A supplement is added.]

Seas and Lands. 1891. [Rptd from Daily Telegraph, where these essays appeared as letters entitled By Sea and Land. Descriptive essays on America, Africa, but mainly on Japan.]

Japonica. 1892. [Essays rptd from Scribner's Mag.]

Wandering Words. 1894. [Essays on Egypt, India, Japan, etc.; rptd from Daily Telegraph and other periodicals.]

East and West. 1896. [Papers rptd from Daily Telegraph and other sources.]

Victoria, Queen and Empress. The Sixty Years. 1896. [Rptd from Daily Telegraph.]

The Queen's Justice: a true Story of Indian Village Life. 1899. [A novel founded on official facts.]

(d) Biography and Criticism

The Two Arnolds. Blackwood's Mag. March 1854. [A long review comparing Matthew Arnold and Sir Edwin Arnold.]

Bell, M. Sir Edwin Arnold. *Miles*, v.

Obituary. Times, 26 March 1904.

THOMAS ASHE (1836–1889)

(a) Poems

Poems. 1859.

Dryope, and Other Poems. 1861.

Pictures, and Other Poems. 1865.

The Sorrows of Hypsipyle. A Poem. 1867.

Edith, or Love and Life in Cheshire. A Poem. 1873.

Songs Now and Then. 1876.

Poems. Complete Edition. 1886.

Songs of a Year. 1888 (priv. ptd).

[Ashe also edited several of Coleridge's works.]

(b) Biography and Criticism

Ellis, H. Thomas Ashe's Poems. Westminster Rev. April 1886.

—— Thomas Ashe. *Miles*, vi.

ALFRED AUSTIN (1835–1913)

(a) Selected Works

Days of the Year. A Poetic Calendar from the Works of Alfred Austin. With an Introduction by William Sharp. 1886.

English Lyrics. Ed. Sir W. Watson, 1890.
Love Poems. 1912.

(b) Poems

Randolph. A Poem in Two Cantos. 1854;
1877 (re-cast as Leszko the Bastard: a Tale
of Polish Grief).
The Season: a Satire 1861; 1861 (rev., adds
Preface); 1869 (rev.). [A satire on the
follies of the London season.]
The Human Tragedy. A Poem. 1862 (with-
drawn from circulation); 1876 (rev. and
expanded); 1889 (rev. edn; adds preface On
the Position and Prospects of Poetry);
1891 (omits preface).
The Golden Age. A Satire in Verse. 1871.
Interludes. 1872.
Madonna's Child. 1873. [Incorporated in
The Human Tragedy, 1876, as Act II.]
Rome or Death! A Poem. 1873. [Forms
Act III of The Human Tragedy, 1876.]
The Tower of Babel. A Poetical Drama. 1874.
Savonarola; a Tragedy. 1881.
Soliloquies in Song. 1882.
At the Gate of the Convent, and Other Poems.
1885.
Prince Lucifer. 1887; 1887 (adds essay on
The End and Limits of Objective Poetry);
1891 (omits essay).
Love's Widowhood, and Other Poems. 1889.
Lyrical Poems. 1891.
Narrative Poems. 1891. [In the Heart of the
Forest, At the Gate of the Convent, Love's
Widowhood, etc., but also many new poems.]
Fortunatus the Pessimist. A Dramatic
Poem. 1892.
England's Darling. 1896. [In subsequent.
edns the poem was entitled Alfred the
Great, England's Darling.]
The Conversion of Winckelmann, and Other
Poems. 1897.
Victoria. June 20, 1837, June 20, 1897. 1897.
Songs of England. 1898; 1900 (enlarged);
1900 (enlarged); 1900 (enlarged).
Polyphemus. 1901.
A Tale of True Love, and Other Poems. 1902.
Flodden Field. A Tragedy. 1903.
The Door of Humility. A Poem. 1906.
Sacred and Profane Love, and Other Poems.
1908.

(c) Other Writings

Five Years of it. A Novel. 2 vols. 1858.
An Artist's Proof. A Novel. 3 vols. 1864.
Won by a Head. A Novel. 3 vols. 1866.
A Vindication of Lord Byron. 1869. [In
reply to Mrs Stowe's article in Macmillan's
Mag.]
The Poetry of the Period. 1870. [Papers rptd
from Temple Bar Mag.: Tennyson, Brown-
ing, Swinburne, Arnold, Morris, Roman
Catholic Poets, etc.]

The Garden that I Love. 2 sers. 1894–1907.
[Written in the form of a diary.]
In Veronica's Garden. 1895. [In the form of a
diary.]
Lamia's Winter Quarters. 1898. [An account
of a holiday in Italy, told in the form of a
story.]
Spring and Autumn in Ireland. 1900. [Rptd
with alterations from two papers in Black-
wood's Mag. A long descriptive essay on
Ireland.]
Haunts of Ancient Peace. 1902. [An account
of a ramble through England, written in the
form of a story.]
The Poet's Diary. Edited by Lamia. 1904.
The Bridling of Pegasus. 1910. [The Es-
sentials of Great Poetry, The Feminine Note
in English Poetry, Milton and Dante,
Byron and Wordsworth, Poetry and
Pessimism, Tennyson, Literature and
Politics, A Conversation with Shakespeare
in the Elysian Fields, Dante.]
Autobiography. 2 vols. 1911.

[Austin also pbd several political and
controversial pamphlets.]

(d) Biography and Criticism

Whyte, W. Alfred Austin. *Miles*, VI.
O., J. Alfred Austin. Athenaeum, 7 June
1913.
Sherman, S. P. The Complacent Toryism of
Alfred Austin. [In On Contemporary
Literature, New York, 1917.]
Welby, T. E. Alfred Austin. Bookman, Dec.
1930.
May, J. L. A Neglected Poet. Dublin Rev.
no. 402, 1937.

ADA BARTRICK BAKER (b. 1854)

A Palace of Dreams, and Other Verse. Edinburgh, 1901.

[For biography and criticism, and a selection from the poems, see A. H. Miles, *Miles*,
(IX).]

JOHN EVELYN BARLAS (1860–1914)

[Several volumes were pbd under the pseudonym 'Evelyn Douglas.']

(a) Poems

Poems Lyrical and Dramatic. 1884.
Queen of the Hid Isle. 1885.
Punchinello and his Wife Judith: a Tragedy.
Chelmsford, 1886.
Phantasmagoria: Dream Fugues. Chelmsford,
1887.
Bird-Notes. Chelmsford, 1887.
Holy of Holies: Confessions of an Anarchist.
Chelmsford, 1887.
Love Sonnets. Chelmsford, 1889.

Songs of a Bayadere and Songs of a Trouba-
dour. Dundee, 1893 (priv. ptd).
Selections. Ed. (with introduction) H. S.
Salt, 1925. [With a bibliography.]

(b) Biography and Criticism

Lowe, D. John Barlas: Sweet Singer and
Socialist. Cupar, 1915. [With a bibliography.]

GEORGE BARLOW (1847–1913)

(a) Collected and Selected Works

The Poetical Works of George Barlow. 11
vols. 1902–14.
Selected Poems. 1921. [With introductory
note, signed C. W., a bibliography and a
short life.]

(b) Poems

A Life's Love. 1873. [Sonnets.]
An English Madonna. By James Hinton.
1874.
Under the Dawn. 1875.
The Gospel of Humanity; or, the Connection
between Spiritualism and Modern Thought.
1876.
The Marriage before Death, and Other Poems.
1878.
Through Death to Life. 1878.
Love-Songs. 1880.
Time's Whisperings. Sonnets and Songs.
1880.
Song-Bloom. 1881. [At the end are ptd
extracts from contemporary reviews.]
Song-Spray. 1882.
An Actor's Reminiscences, and Other Poems.
1883.
Love's Offering. By James Hinton. 1883.
Poems Real and Ideal. 1884.
Loved beyond Words. 1885.
The Pageant of Life. An Epic Poem in Five
Books. 1888.
From Dawn to Sunset. 1890.
A Lost Mother. 1892.
The Crucifixion of Man. A Narrative Poem.
1893.
To the Women of England and Other Poems.
1901.
A Coronation Poem. 1902.
Vox Clamantis. Sonnets and Poems. 1904.
A Man's Vengeance and Other Poems. 1908.
Songs of England Awaking. 1909.

(c) Plays

The Two Marriages: a Drama in Three Acts.
1878.
Jesus of Nazareth. 1896. [A tragedy in prose
and verse.]

[Barlow also pbd a novel and various
miscellaneous essays.]

(d) Biography and Criticism

Miles, A. H. George Barlow. *Miles*, VIII (VII).
Bennett, E. T. The Poetical Work of George
Barlow: a Study. 1903.

JANE BARLOW (1857–1917)

[See p. 1056 below.]

AUBREY VINCENT BEARDSLEY (1872–1898)

(a) Bibliography

Gallatin, A. E. Aubrey Beardsley's Drawings.
1903. [Gives list of books and articles on,
and references to, Beardsley, both as artist
and writer.]

(b) Miscellaneous Writings

Under the Hill and Other Essays in Prose and
Verse. 1904. [Rptd from The Yellow Book
and The Savoy. Under the Hill, The Three
Musicians (a poem), The Ballad of a
Barber (a poem), Carmen CI (a poem),
Table Talk of Beardsley, 2 letters.]
Last Letters. With an Introductory Note by
John Gray. 1904.
The Story of Venus and Tannhäuser. A
Romantic Novel. 1907 (priv. ptd). [The
original, unexpurgated version of Under
the Hill.]

(c) Biography and Criticism

Symons, A. Aubrey Beardsley. 1897; 1905
(rev. and enlarged).
Gallatin, A. E. Whistler's Art Dicta and
Other Essays. 1904. [2 essays on Beards-
ley.]
Ross, R. Aubrey Beardsley. 1909. [A life.]
King, A. W. An Aubrey Beardsley Lecture.
With Introduction by R. A. Walker. 1924.
[Includes 10 letters.]
Macfall, H. Aubrey Beardsley. The Man and
his Work. 1928.

HENRY CHARLES BEECHING (1859–1919)

(a) Bibliography

Stephen, G. A. Bibliography of H. C.
Beeching. Norwich Public Library Readers'
Guide, VII, 1919.

(b) Poems

Mensae Secundae. Oxford, 1879. [By
Beeching, J. W. Mackail and J. B. B.
Nichols.]
Love in Idleness. 1883; 1891 (with addns and
omissions, as Love's Looking Glass. Anon.)
[By Beeching, J. W. Mackail and J. B. B.
Nichols.]
In a Garden, and Other Poems. 1895.
St Augustine at Ostia: Oxford Sacred Poem
1896.

(c) Biographical, Critical and Miscellaneous Writings

Pages from a Private Diary. 1898 (anon.); 1903 (by Urbanus Sylvan).
Conferences on Books and Men. 1900 (anon.). [Cowley, Sir John Davies, H. D. Traill, Cowper, Chaucer, etc.]
Two Lectures Introductory to the Study of Poetry. Cambridge, 1901.
Religio Laici: a Series of Studies addressed to Laymen. 1902.
Provincial Letters and Other Papers. 1906 (anon.). [7 provincial letters; essays on Atterbury, Alaric Watts, Shakespeare, etc.]
William Shakespeare, Player, Playmaker and Poet. 1908. [Anti-Baconian theory.]
Francis Atterbury. 1909.

[Beeching also pbd numerous sermons, lectures and addresses, and edited Milton's poems and several devotional series.]

(d) Biography and Criticism

Archer, W. Poets of the Younger Generation. 1902.
Greenwood, Sir G. G. In Re Shakespeare. Beeching versus Greenwood. Rejoinder on Behalf of the Defendant. 1909.
Lee, Sir S. Norwich Public Library Readers' Guide, vii, 1919.
Huxley, L. Obituary. Cornhill Mag. April 1919.

HENRY THOMAS MACKENZIE BELL

(a) Collected and Selected Poems

Collected Poems. 1901.
The Poems of Mackenz; Bell. 1909.
Selected Poems. 1921.

(b) Separate Poems

The Keeping of the Vow, and Other Verses. 1879.
Verses of Varied Life. 1882.
Old Year Leaves: being Old Verses revived. 1883; 1886.
Spring's Immortality, and Other Poems. 1893; 1895; 1896.
Pictures of Travel, and Other Poems. 1898.
The Taking of the Flag, and Other Recitations. With an Introduction by the Rev. J. J. Nesbitt. 1900.
'John Clifford.' A Poem. [1908.]
The Heart's Summer, and Other Poems. [1913.]
Holy Quietude, and Other Poems. [1913.]
Lyrics of Consolation. [1913.]
Poetical Pictures of the Great War. 4 sers. 1917.

(c) Critical Writings

A Forgotten Genius: Charles Whitehead. A Critical Monograph. 1884; 1899.
Christina Rossetti: a Biographical and Critical Study. 1898.
Half Hours with Representative Novelists of the Nineteenth Century. 3 vols. 1927.

[Bell also edited some of the Pre-Raphaelites, as well as contributing several notices to Miles.]

ARTHUR CHRISTOPHER BENSON (1862–1925)

[See p. 734 below.]

LOUISA SARAH BEVINGTON afterwards GUGGENBERGER (b. 1845)

Key Notes. By Arbor Leigh. 1876; 1879 (under own name).
Poems, Lyrics and Sonnets. 1882.

[For biography and criticism, and a selection from the poems, see A. H. Miles, Miles (ix).]

ROBERT LAURENCE BINYON (b. 1869)

(a) Collected and Selected Works

Selected Poems. 1926. (Augustan Books of Modern Poetry.)
A Lawrence Binyon Anthology. 1927.
Collected Poems. 2 vols. 1931.

(b) Poems

Four Poems. 1890. [In Primavera. Poems by L. Binyon, Stephen Phillips, Manmohan Ghose, and A. S. Cripps.]
Lyric Poems. 1894.
Poems. Oxford, 1895.
London Visions. 1896 (bk i); 1896 (12 poems, of which 5 are rptd from Pall Mall Gazette and Poems, Oxford, 1895); 1899 (bk ii); 1908 (collected edn; rptd from Poems, Oxford, 1895, and from Porphyrion and Other Poems; adds some new poems).
The Praise of Life. Poems. 1896.
Porphyrion, and Other Poems. 1898.
Odes. 1901; 1913 (re-arranged and rev.).
The Death of Adam, and Other Poems. 1903.
Dream come True. 1905.
Penthesilea: a Poem. 1905.
England, and Other Poems. 1909.
Auguries. 1913.
The Winnowing-Fan: Poems on the Great War. 1914.
The Anvil and Other Poems. 1916.
The Cause: Poems of War. [1917?]
The New World: Poems. 1918.
The Four Years. War Poems collected and newly augmented. 1919.
Six Poems on Bruges. 1919. [Specially written for 6 colour prints of Bruges by Frank Brangwyn.]

The Secret: Sixty Poems. 1920.
The Sirens. An Ode. Chelsfield, 1924; 1925.
The Wonder Night. 1927. [4 pp. leaflet.]
The Idols. An Ode. 1928.
The Inferno of Dante. Translated into English Verse. 1933.

(c) Dramatic Works

The Supper. A Lyrical Scene. 1897 (priv. ptd).
Paris and Œnone. 1906.
Attila: a Tragedy. 1907.
Bombastes in the Shades: a Play in One Act: [In Oxford Pamphlets, 1914–1915, 1915.]
Arthur. A Tragedy. 1923.
Ayuli. A Play in Three Acts and an Epilogue. Oxford, 1923.
Boadicea. A Play in Eight Scenes. 1927.
Sophro the Wise. A Play for Children. 1927.
Three Short Plays: Godstow Nunnery, Love in the Desert, Memnon. 1930. [In verse.]
The Young King. 1935.
Brief Candles. 1938.

(d) Other Writings

Dutch Etchers of the Seventeenth Century. 1895.
John Crome and John Sell Cotman. 1897.
Western Flanders: a Medley of Things Seen, Considered and Imagined. 1899. [Anecdotes and descriptions drawn from a holiday in Flanders. With 10 etchings by William Strang.]
Thomas Girtin. His Life and Works. An Essay. 1900.
English Poetry in its Relation to Painting and the Other Arts. British Academy, 1918.
Poetry and Modern Life. 1918. [A paper read before the Royal Institution of Great Britain.]
The English Ode. Trans. Royal Soc. of Literature, II, 1922.
Tradition and Re-Action in Modern Poetry. English Ass. 1926.
Landscape in English Art and Poetry. Tokyo, 1930; 1931.
[Since 1900 Mr Binyon has also pbd several important works on oriental art.]

(e) Criticism

Streatfeild, R. A. Two Poets of the New Century, Stephen Phillips and Laurence Binyon. A Critical Appreciation. 1901.
Archer, W. Poets of the Younger Generation. 1902.
Williams, H. H. Modern English Writers. 1918. [Ch. iii, Binyon and his Contemporaries.]
Maynard, T. Our Best Poets: English and American. 1924.

Twitchett, E. G. The Poetry of Lawrence Binyon. London Mercury, Sept. 1930.
Southworth, J. G. Laurence Binyon. Sewanee Rev. XLIII, 1935.

MATHILDE BLIND (1841–1896)

(a) Collected and Selected Works

A Selection from the Poems of Mathilde Blind. Ed. A. Symons, 1897.
The Poetical Works. Edited by Arthur Symons, with a Memoir by Richard Garnett. 1900.

(b) Poems

Poems by Claude Lake. 1867.
The Prophecy of St Oran and Other Poems. 1881.
The Heather on Fire: a Tale of the Highland Clearances. 1886.
The Ascent of Man. 1889; 1899 (with introduction by A. R. Wallace).
Dramas in Miniature. 1891.
Songs and Sonnets. 1893.
Birds of Passage. Songs of the Orient and Occident. 1895.
Shakespeare Sonnets. 1902.

(c) Other Writings

Shelley. A Lecture. 1870.
George Eliot. 1883.
Tarantella. A Prose Romance. 2 vols. 1885.
Madame Roland. 1886.
Shelley's View of Nature contrasted with Darwin's. 1886 (priv. ptd).
A Study of Marie Bashkirtseff. [An essay in A. Theuriet, Jules Bastien-Lepage, 1892, one of four essays by different writers.]
[Miss Blind also translated D. F. Strauss's The Old Faith and the New, 1873, and the Journal of Marie Bashkirtseff, 1890.]

(d) Biography and Criticism

Garnett, R. Mathilde Blind. Miles, VII (XI).

WILFRID SCAWEN BLUNT (1840–1922)

(a) Collected and Selected Works

The Poetry of Wilfrid Blunt. Selected and arranged by W. E. Henley and G. Wyndham. 1898.
Love Poems. 1902.
Poetical Works. 2 vols. 1914.
Poems. 1923. [Selected by Floyd Dell.]

(b) Poems

Sonnets and Songs by Proteus. 1875.
The Love Sonnets of Proteus. 1880.
The Wind and the Whirlwind. 1883. [A poem on the British intervention in Egypt.]
In Vinculis. 1889.

A New Pilgrimage and Other Poems. 1889.
The Celebrated Romance of the Stealing of
the Mare. 1892; 1930. [Tr. from Arabic by
Lady Anne Blunt; done into verse by W. S.
Blunt.]
Esther, Love Lyrics and Natalia's Resurrec-
tion. 1892; Boston, 1895 (as Esther and
The Love Sonnets of Proteus).
The Love Lyrics and Songs of Proteus.
[Kelmscott Press], 1892. [Most of the
poems in the 1875 and 1880 vols. are here
rptd, but in their full text. Many sonnets
omitted from the earlier vols. are included
in this one.]
Griselda. 1893.
Satan Absolved. A Victorian Mystery. A
Poem. 1899.
Mu'allakāt. The Seven Golden Odes. 1903.
[Done into English verse.]

(c) Other Writings

Proteus and Amadeus: A Correspondence.
Ed. A. de Vere, 1878. [A correspondence
between Blunt and Wilfrid Meynell on
questions of religion and philosophy.]
The Future of Islam. 1882. [Essays rptd
from Fortnightly Rev.]
Ideas about India. 1885.
Atrocities of Justice under British Rule in
Egypt. 1906; 1907 (with a new preface).
The Secret History of the English Occupation
of Egypt. Being a Personal Narrative of
Events. 1907; 1907 (with special appen-
dices).
India under Ripon: a Private Diary. 1909.
Gordon at Khartoum: being a Personal
Narrative of Events. 1911.
The Land War in Ireland. 1912.
My Diaries. 2 vols. 1919–20; 1922 (with
preface by Lady Gregory).

(d) Biography and Criticism

Le Gallienne, R. Wilfred Scawen Blunt.
Miles, VI.
'Ouida' (M. L. de la Ramée). Critical Studies.
1900.
Cunninghame Graham, R. B. W. S. Blunt.
English Rev. Dec. 1922.
Symons, A. Wilfred Scawen Blunt. [In The
Café Royal, 1923.]
Lytton, N. S. The English Country Gentle-
man. 1925. [Has a ch. on Blunt containing
many anecdotes and reminiscences.]
MacCarthy, D. Portraits. 1931. [Has a
character sketch of Blunt.]
Leslie, S. Men were Different. 1937. [In-
cludes an essay on Blunt.]
Finch, E. Wilfrid Scawen Blunt. 1938.

FRANCIS WILLIAM BOURDILLON (1852–1921)

(a) Poems

Among the Flowers, and Other Poems. 1878.
Young Maids and Old China. 1889.
Where Lilies live and Waters wind away.
1889.
Ailes d'Alouette. 2 sers. Oxford, 1890–1902
(priv. ptd).
A Lost God. 1891.
Sursum Corda. Poems. 1893.
Minuscula: Lyrics of Nature, Art and Love.
1897.
Through the Gateway. 1902.
Preludes and Romances. 1908.
Ode in Defence of the Matterhorn against the
Proposed Railway to its Summit. 1910.
Moth-Wings. 1913. [Selected poems rptd
from Ailes d'Alouette, sers. 1 and 2. Later
verses added.]
Christmas Roses for Nineteen Hundred and
Fourteen. 1914.
Easter Lilies for Nineteen Hundred and
Fifteen. 1915.
Russia Re-born. Poems. 1917.

(b) Other Writings

Aucassin and Nicolette. A Love Story. 1887
(trn accompanied by the Old French text,
introduction, notes and bibliography);
1897 (rev.); 1913 (trn only. A rev. and freer
rendering).
Nephelé. 1896. [A tale.]
The Early Editions of the Roman de la Rose.
Bibliog. Soc. 1906.
Gerard and Isabel. 1921. [A romance.]

(c) Biography and Criticism

Obituary. Times, 14 Jan. 1921.

ERASMUS H. BRODIE

Euthanasia: a Poem in Four Cantos of
Spenserian Metre on the Discovery of the
North-West Passage by Sir John Franklin.
1866.
Translations from the Lyrics of Horace, in
English Verse. 1868.
Sonnets. 1885.
Lyrics of the Sea; Varieties in Verse Transla-
tions; Sonnets. 1887.

OLIVER MADOX BROWN (1855–1874)
[See p. 539 below.]

ROBERT WILLIAMS BUCHANAN (1841–1901)

(a) Bibliography

Jay, H. Robert Buchanan. 1903. [Biblio-
graphy appended.]

(b) Poems and Plays

Undertones. 1863.
Idylls and Legends of Inverburn. 1865.
London Poems. 1866.
Ballad Stories of the Affections. 1867.
[Adapted into English verse from the Scandinavian.]
North Coast and Other Poems. 1868.
The Book of Orm. A Prelude to the Epic. 1870.
Napoleon Fallen: a Lyrical Drama. 1871.
The Drama of Kings. 1871.
Saint Abe and his Seven Lovers. 1872; 1896 (adds a bibliographical note on the poem).
White Rose and Red. A Love Story. 1873.
The Poetical Works. 3 vols. 1874.
Balder the Beautiful: a Song of Divine Death. 1877.
Ballads of Life, Love and Humour. 1882.
Selected Poems. 1882.
The Poetical Works. 1884; 2 vols. 1901 (enlarged as The Complete Poetical Works of Robert Buchanan).
The Earthquake, or Six Days and a Sabbath. 1885.
The City of Dream. An Epic Poem. 1888.
The Outcast. A Rhyme for the Time. 1891.
The Buchanan Ballads, Old and New. 1892. [Vol. i in Buchanan's Poems for the People. A selection from Buchanan's ballad books with a few new ballads added.]
The Piper of Hamelin. A Fantastic Opera in Two Acts. 1893.
The Wandering Jew. A Christmas Carol. 1893.
The Devil's Case. A Bank Holiday Interlude. 1896. [A long narrative poem.]
The Ballad of Mary the Mother: a Christmas Carol. 1897. [Includes other poems.]
The New Rome: Poems and Ballads of Our Empire. 1899.
Sweet Nancy: a Comedy in Three Acts. 1914.

(c) Novels

The Shadow of the Sword. 3 vols. 1876; 3 vols. 1883 (adds Preface); Liverpool, 1919.
A Child of Nature. A Romance. 3 vols. 1881.
God and the Man. 1881. [Dedicated to D. G. Rossetti.]
Foxglove Manor: a Novel. 3 vols. 1881.
The Martyrdom of Madeleine. A Novel. 3 vols. 1882.
Love me for ever: a Romance. 1883.
Annan Water. A Romance. 3 vols. 1883.
The New Abelard: a Romance. 3 vols. 1884.
The Master of the Mine. A Novel. 2 vols. 1885.
Malt. A Story of a Caravan. 1885.
Stormy Waters. A Story of To-day. 3 vols. 1885.

That Winter Night, or Love's Victory. 1886; 1887 (rev. and enlarged).
The Heir of Linne. A Novel. 2 vols. 1888.
The Moment After; a Tale of the Unseen. 1890.
Come, Live with Me and Be my Love. A Novel. 2 vols. 1891.
Woman and the Man. A Story. 2 vols. 1893.
Red and White Heather. 1894. [North country tales and ballads in prose.]
Rachel Dene: a Tale of the Deepdale Mills. 2 vols. 1894.
Lady Kilpatrick. A Novel. 1895.
Diana's Hunting. A Novel. 1895.
A Marriage by Capture: a Romance of To-day. 1896.
Effie Hetherington. A Novel. 1896.
The Rev. Annabel Lee: a Tale of To-morrow. 1898.
Father Anthony: a Romance of To-day. 1898.
Andromeda: An Idyll of the Great River. 1900.

(d) Other Writings

David Gray, and Other Essays, chiefly on Poetry. 1868. [The Poet or Seer; David Gray; The Student, and his Vocation; Walt Whitman; Herrick's Hesperides; Literary Morality; On a Passage in Heine; My own Tentatives.]
The Land of Lorne, including The Cruise of the 'Tern' to the Outer Hebrides. 2 vols. 1871; 1883 (as The Hebrid Isles).
The Fleshly School of Poetry, and Other Phenomena of the Day. 1872. [An attack on the Pre-Raphaelites rptd from Contemporary Rev.]
Master-Spirits. 1873. [Criticism as One of the Fine Arts; Dickens; Tennyson, Heine, De Musset; Browning; Hugo; George Heath; William Miller; Scandinavian Studies, etc.]
A Poet's Sketch-Book. Selections from the Prose Writings of Robert Buchanan. 1883.
A Look round Literature. 1887. [From Aeschylus to Victor Hugo; The Character of Goethe; Free Thought in America; Dante Rossetti; Sidney Dobell and the Spasmodic School of Poetry; George Eliot; Flotsam and Jetsam; From Pope to Tennyson; A Last Look Round.]
On Descending into Hell: a Letter to the Home Secretary concerning the proposed Suppression of Literature. 1889.
The Coming Terror and Other Essays and Letters. 1891. [Includes On Descending into Hell.]

(e) Biography and Criticism

Rossetti, D. G. The Stealthy School of Criticism. Athenaeum, 16 Dec. 1871. [A reply to Buchanan's attack on Rossetti in The Fleshly School of Poetry.]

Smith, G. Barnett. Poets and Novelists. 1875.

Stedman, E. C. Latter-Day British Poets. Scribner's Mag. Feb. 1875.

Walkley, A. B. Playhouse Impressions. 1892.

Noble, J. A. Robert Buchanan. *Miles*, VI.

Obituary. Athenaeum, 15 June 1901.

Murray, Henry. Robert Buchanan: a Critical Appreciation. 1901.

Walker, A. S. Robert Buchanan: the Poet of Modern Revolt. An Introduction to his Poetry. 1901.

Jay, H. Robert Buchanan. 1903. [A memoir.]

Symons, A. Studies in Verse and Prose. 1904.

Hearn, L. Appreciations of Poetry. Ed. J. Erskine, New York, 1916.

Letters from D. G. Rossetti to A. C. Swinburne regarding the Attacks made upon Both by Robert Buchanan. 1921 (priv. ptd).

Blodgett, H. Whitman and Buchanan. American Literature, May 1930.

ARTHUR HENRY BULLEN (1857–1920)

[See p. 1037 below.]

CHARLES STUART CALVERLEY, earlier BLAYDS (1831–1884)

(a) Collected Works

Complete Works. With a Biographical Notice by Sir W. J. Sendall. 1901. [A bibliography is prefixed.]

Verses, Translations and Fly Leaves. 1904.

Verses and Translations. Ed. Sir O. Seaman, 1905.

(b) Poems and Translations

Verses and Translations. 1862; 1865 (3rd edn, rev.); 1871 (4th edn, rev.).

Translations into English and Latin. Cambridge, 1866; 1885 (rev. edn). [Trns from Homer, Virgil, Horace into English verse and from Milton, Herbert, Tennyson, Trench, Landor, Cowley, Pope and others into Latin verse.]

Theocritus translated into English Verse. Cambridge, 1869; 1883 (rev. edn).

Fly Leaves. Cambridge, 1872; 1885 (as Verses and Fly Leaves). [Humorous poems, parodies, etc.]

The Literary Remains of C. S. Calverley. With a Memoir by W. J. Sendall. 1885.

(c) Criticism

Whyte, W. C. S. Calverley. *Miles*, IX (X).

Babington, P. L. Browning and Calverley, or Poem and Parody. An Elucidation. 1925. [The Cock and the Bull on one side of each page and extracts from The Ring and the Book on the other.]

Ince, R. B. Calverley and Some Cambridge Wits of the Nineteenth Century. 1929.

WILLIAM CANTON (1845–1926)

(a) Collected and Selected Poems

Nineteen Poems. 1925.

Poems. Ed. (with biographical sketch) G. D. Canton, 1927.

(b) Poems

A Lost Epic, and Other Poems. 1887.

The Comrades: Poems, Old and New. 1902.

(c) Children's Books

The Invisible Playmate: a Story of the Unseen. 1894; 1912 (Everyman's Lib.).

W. V. Her Book, and Various Verses. 1896. [W. V. is his daughter, Winifred Veda.]

A Child's Book of Saints. 1898; 1906 (Everyman's Lib.).

In Memory of W. V. 1901.

[Canton also pbd A History of the British and Foreign Bible Society, 5 vols. 1904–10, as well as several other children's books.]

(d) Biography and Criticism

Noble, J. A. William Canton. *Miles*, VIII (VII).

de M., S. The Poetry of William Canton. Contemporary Rev. May 1927.

EDWARD CARPENTER (1844–1929)

[See p. 736 below.]

'LEWIS CARROLL' (1832–1898)

[See p. 513 below.]

HARRY CHOLMONDELEY-PENNELL (1836–1915)

Puck on Pegasus. Illustrated by Leech, Portch, [etc.]. 1861; 1862 (4th edn, 'completely revised and enlarged'); 1869 (6th edn).

Crescent? and Other Lyrics. 1864.

The Oxford and Cambridge Boat Race. [1871.]

Modern Babylon, and Other Poems. [1872.]

The Muses of Mayfair. Selections from Vers de Société of the Nineteenth Century. 2 pts, 1874.

Pegasus Re-saddled. With Illustrations by Du Maurier. 1877; 1884 (rev. edn).

From Grave to Gay. A Volume of Selections from the Complete Poems of H. C. Pennell. 1884.

[Pennell also pbd fairy tales and several books on fishing. For his writings, and a selection from the poems, see A. H. Miles, *Miles*, IX (X).]

EDMUND BROWN VINEY CHRISTIAN
(b. 1864)

The Lays of a Limb of the Law, by John
Popplestone. Edited with a Memoir and
Postscript, by E. B. V. Christian. 1889.

[Mr Christian has also written several books
on lawyers and on cricket.]

HERBERT EDWIN CLARKE (b. 1852)

Songs in Exile and Other Poems. Belfast, 1879.
Storm-Drift. 1882.
Poems and Sonnets. 1895.
Tannhäuser and Other Poems. 1896.

[For criticism and selected poems see A. H.
Miles, *Miles*, VIII (VII).]

MARY ELIZABETH COLERIDGE (1861–1907)

(a) *Poems*

Fancy's Following. 1896. [Pbd under the
pseudonym 'Aνόδos.]
Fancy's Guerdon. 1897. [Partly rptd from
Fancy's Following, but with many addns.]
Poems. Ed. Sir H. Newbolt. 1908. [With a
preface containing an exact account of how
the poems originally appeared.]

(b) *Other Writings*

The Seven Sleepers of Ephesus. 1893. [A
novel.]
The King with Two Faces. 1897. [A historical
romance.]
Non Sequitur. 1900. [Essays.]
The Fiery Dawn. 1901. [A novel.]
The Shadow on the Wall. 1904. [A romance.]
The Lady on the Drawingroom Floor. 1906.
[A novel.]
Holman Hunt. 1908.
Gathered Leaves from the Prose of Mary E.
Coleridge. With a Memoir by Edith Sichel.
1910. [Also includes 6 unpublished poems.
Appendix A consists of Notes of the Table
Talk of William Cory.]

(c) *Biography and Criticism*

Binyon, L. Mary Coleridge. [In The English
Poets, ed. T. H. Ward, vol. v, 1918.]
Bridges, R. Collected Essays, VI. 1931. [An
essay rptd from Cornhill Mag.]
Evans, B. I. English Poetry in the Later
Nineteenth Century. 1933. [Ch. x.]

WILLIAM JOHN COURTHOPE (1842–1917)

[See p. 738 below.]

ISA CRAIG, later KNOX (1831–1903)

(a) *Poems*

Poems by Isa. Edinburgh, 1856.
Duchess Agnes, etc. 1864. [A short verse
drama and a collection of lyrics.]
Songs of Consolation. 1874.

(b) *Other Writings*

Esther West. A Story. 1870.
The Little Folks' History of England. 1872.
Tales on the Parables. 2 sers. 10 vols. 1872–3.

(c) *Biography and Criticism*

Japp, A. H. Isa Craig (Knox). *Miles*, VII (IX).
Anderson, G. and Finlay, J. The Burns
Centenary Poems. 1859. [See preface for
Isa Craig's prize poem.]

THOMAS WILLIAM HODGSON CROSLAND
(1865–1924)

(a) *Poems*

The Pink Book. Being Verses Good, Bad and
Indifferent. Brighton, 1894.
Other People's Wings. 1899. [Parodies and
other verses.]
The Absent-minded Male and Other Oc-
casional Verses. 1899.
The Finer Spirit and Other Poems. 1900.
Pleasant Odes. 1900.
Outlook Odes. 1902.
The Five Notions. 1903. [A parody of The
Five Nations by Rudyard Kipling.]
Red Rose. A Poem. 1905.
The First Stone. 1912. [A satire on Oscar
Wilde, written 'on Reading the Unpublished
Parts of De Profundis.']
Sonnets. 1912.
A Chant of Affection and Other War Verses.
1915.
War Poems by X. 1916.
Collected Poems. 1917.
Last Poems. 1928.

(b) *Satires*

The Unspeakable Scot. 1902.
The Egregious English. 1903; 1925. [Originally
pbd under the pseudonym 'Angus McNeill.']
A Looking-Glass for Mr Chamberlain. 1904.
The Lord of Creation. 1904; 1925 (with an
appreciation by Henry Savage).
Lovely Woman. 1904.
Wisdom for the Holidays. 1905.
The Suburbans. 1905.
The Wild Irishman. 1905.
The Wicked Life. 1905.
The Country Life. 1906.
The Beautiful Teetotaller. 1907.
Who goes Racing? 1907.
Taffy was a Welshman. 1912.
Find the Angels. The Showman. A Legend of
the War. 1915. [A short parody of The
Angels of Mons by Arthur Machen.]
The Fine Old Hebrew Gentleman. 1922.
Pop goes the Weasel. 1924. [A sequel to The
Unspeakable Scot.]
The Rogue. 1926. [A satirical novel.]

(c) Other Writings

Literary Parables. 1898.
Fifty Fables. 1899.
The Truth about Japan. 1904.
Little Stories. 1907.
The English Sonnet. 1917.

(d) Biography and Criticism

Brown, W. S. The Life and Genius of T. W. H. Crosland. 1928.

OLIVE CUSTANCE, afterwards LADY DOUGLAS

Opals. 1897. [Poems.]
Rainbows. 1902. [Poems.]
The Blue Bird, and Other Poems. 1905.
The Inn of Dreams and Other Poems. 1911.

[For Lady Douglas see Lord A. Douglas's Autobiography, 1929.]

JOHN DAVIDSON (1857–1909)

(a) Bibliography

Stonehill, C. A. and H. W. Bibliographies of Modern Authors. Second Series. 1925.

(b) Poems

Diabolus Amans. A Dramatic Poem. Glasgow, 1885.
In a Music-Hall, and Other Poems. 1891.
Fleet Street Eclogues. 2 sers. 1893–6.
Ballads and Songs. 1894.
St George's Day: A Fleet Street Eclogue. New York, 1895. [Afterwards included in Fleet Street Eclogues, ser. 2.]
New Ballads. 1897.
The Last Ballad, and Other Poems. 1899.
The Testament of a Vivisector. 1901.
The Testament of a Man Forbid. 1901.
The Testament of an Empire-Builder. 1902.
The Testament of a Prime Minister. 1904.
Selected Poems. 1905.
Holiday and Other Poems, with a Note on Poetry. 1906.
The Testament of John Davidson. 1908.
Fleet Street and Other Poems. 1909.
Seventeen Poems. 1925. (Augustan Books of Modern Poetry).

(c) Dramatic Works

Bruce. Glasgow, 1886. [In verse.]
Smith. A Tragedy. Glasgow, 1888.
Plays. Greenock, 1889 (An Unhistorical Pastoral; A Romantic Farce; Scaramouch in Naxos); 1894 (adds Bruce and Smith; frontispiece by Aubrey Beardsley).
Godfrida. 1898.
Self's the Man. A Tragi-Comedy. 1901.
The Knight of the Maypole. 1903. [A comedy in four acts, in prose and in verse.]
A Rosary. 1903.
The Theatrocrat. A Tragic Play of Church and State. 1905.

God and Mammon. 1907. [Davidson intended this work to be a trilogy, but in fact only completed pt 1, The Triumph of Mammon, and pt 2, Mammon and his Message.]

(d) Fiction

The North Wall. Glasgow, 1885. [A novel.]
Perpervid: the Career of Ninian Jamieson, 1890.
The Great Men and a Practical Novelist. 1891. [A collection of tales.]
Laura Ruthven's Widowhood. A Novel. 1892. [In collaboration with C. J. Wills.]
Baptist Lake. A Novel. 1894.
A Full and True Account of the Wonderful Mission of Earl Lavender. 1895. [A satirical novel.]
Miss Armstrong's and Other Circumstances. 1896. [A collection of tales.]

(e) Other Writings

Persian Letters. 1892. [A trn of Montesquieu.]
Sentences and Paragraphs. 1893. [Essays and epigrams.]
A Random Itinerary. 1894. [In Expectation of Rain, Parks and Squares, etc.]
For the Crown. 1896. [A trn of Coppée.]
A Rosary. 1903. [Essays on Shakespeare, Literature and Philosophy, Critic and Author, Ibsen, Sappho, Chaucer, Blake, Contemporary Poetry, Meredith and Nature, The Poet, etc.]
A Queen's Romance. 1904. [A trn of Hugo's Ruy Blas.]

(f) Biography and Criticism

Archer, W. Poets of the Younger Generation. 1902.
Jackson, Holbrook. The Eighteen Nineties. 1913.
Fineman, H. John Davidson; a Study of the Relation of his Ideas to his Poetry. Philadelphia, 1916.
Johnson, Lionel. Reviews and Critical Papers. Ed. R. Shafer, 1921.
Petzold, G. von. John Davidson und sein geistiges Werden unter dem Einfluss Nietzsches. Leipzig, 1928.
Bett, H. Studies in Literature. 1929.
Evans, B. I. English Poetry in the Later Nineteenth Century. 1933.
Thouless, P. Modern Poetic Drama. Oxford, 1934.

THOMAS DAVIDSON (1838–1870)

The Life of a Scottish Probationer; being a Memoir of Thomas Davidson, with his Poems and Extracts from 'his Works. Glasgow, 1877; Glasgow, 1908 (4th edn). [The life is by J. Brown.]

WILLIAM JAMES DAWSON (1854–1928)

(a) Poems

Arvelon: a First Poem. 1878.
A Vision of Souls, with Other Ballads and Poems. 1884.
Poems and Lyrics. 1893.

(b) Other Writings

Quest and Vision: Essays on Life and Literature. 1886.
The Makers of Modern English. A Popular Handbook to the Greater Poets of the Century. 1890.
The Makers of English Fiction. 1905.
The Autobiography of a Mind. [1925.]

[Dawson also pbd many sermons, tales, etc. (mainly works of edification). With C. W. Dawson he edited The Great English Essayists, 1909.]

(c) Biography and Criticism

Miles, A. H. William James Dawson. Miles, VIII (VII).
Middleton, C. The Rev. W. J. Dawson at Home. Sunday Mag. xxv, 1896.

RICHARD WATSON DIXON (1833–1900)

(a) Poems

Christ's Company and Other Poems. 1861.
Historical Odes and Other Poems. 1864.
Mano: a Poetical History in Four Books. 1883. [A long narrative poem.]
Odes and Eclogues. Oxford, 1884 (priv. ptd).
Lyrical Poems. Oxford, 1887 (priv. ptd).
The Story of Eudocia and her Brothers. Oxford, 1888 (priv. ptd). [With a preface on the use of the five-beat couplet verse in serious narrative poems.]
Songs and Odes. Ed. R. Bridges, 1896.
The Last Poems of R. W. Dixon. Ed. Robert Bridges (with preface by Mary Coleridge), 1905.
Poems. A Selection, with a Memoir by Robert Bridges. 1909.

(b) Other Writings

The Close of the Tenth Century of the Christian Era. Oxford, 1858. [Prize essay.]
Essay on the Maintenance of the Church of England as an Established Church. 1874. [Essay II of the Three Peek Prize Essays, 1874.]
The Life of James Dixon, D.D. 1874.
The History of the Church of England from the Abolition of the Roman Jurisdiction. 6 vols. 1878–1902. [Memoir of Dixon by H. Gee prefixed to vol. v, 1900.]
The Monastic Comperta, so far as they regard the Religious Houses of Cumberland and Westmorland. Kendal, 1879.

Mackail, J. W. The Life of William Morris. Vol. I, 1899. [Dixon contributed reminiscences.]
The Correspondence of Gerard Manley Hopkins and Richard Watson Dixon. Ed. C. C. Abbott, Oxford, 1935.

(c) Biography and Criticism

Miles, A. H. Richard Watson Dixon. Miles, v.
Coleridge, Mary. Non Sequitur. 1900. [The essay entitled The Last Hermit of Warkworth is on Dixon.]
Lahey, G. F. Gerard Manley Hopkins. 1930.
Evans, B. I. English Poetry in the Later Nineteenth Century. 1933. [Ch. x.]

AUSTIN DOBSON (1840–1921)

[See p. 739 below.]

DIGBY MACKWORTH DOLBEN (1848–1867)

The Poems. Ed. (with memoir and letters) R. Bridges, 1911, 1915 (rev. and enlarged edn). [The memoir is rptd in Three Friends, 1932.]

CHARLES MONTAGU DOUGHTY (1843–1926)

(a) Poems and Plays

Under Arms. 1900.
The Dawn in Britain. 6 vols. 1906. [Selected Passages, ed. B. Fairley, 1935.]
Adam Cast Forth. 1908. [A sacred drama in five songs.]
The Cliffs. 1909. [A play in verse.]
The Clouds. 1912. [A poetic drama.]
The Titans. 1916.
Mansoul, or The Riddle of the World. 1920; 1922 (rev.).

(b) Other Writings

On the Jöstedal-Brae Glaciers in Norway. 1866. [A geological paper.]
Documents épigraphiques recueillis dans le Nord de l'Arabie. Paris, 1884. [Introduction by Ernest Renan, a long note on his journey by Doughty, the inscriptions, copies, translations and notes.]
Travels in Arabia Deserta. 2 vols. Cambridge, 1888; 2 vols. 1921 (new preface and introduction by T. E. Lawrence).
Wanderings in Arabia with an Introduction by Edward Garnett. 2 vols. 1908. [An abridgement of Travels in Arabia Deserta.]
Hogarth's 'Arabia.' 1922 (priv. ptd). [A review rptd from The Observer.]
Passages from Arabia Deserta. Selected by Edward Garnett. 1931.

(c) Biography and Criticism

Burton, Sir R. Academy, 28 July 1888. [An adverse review of Arabia Deserta.]

Edinburgh Rev. April 1908. [A review of Wanderings in Arabia and The Dawn in Britain.]

Chew, S. C. The Poetry of C. M. Doughty. North American Rev. Dec. 1925.

Charles Montague Doughty. TLS. 11 Feb. 1926.

Armstrong, M. The Works of Charles Doughty. Fortnightly Rev. Jan. 1926.

Freeman, J. Charles Montague Doughty. Bookman, March 1926; London Mercury, Aug. 1926.

Fairley, B. Charles M. Doughty. A Critical Study. 1927.

Hogarth, D. G. The Life of Charles M. Doughty. 1928.

Treneer, A. Charles M. Doughty: a Study of his Prose and Verse. 1935.

Taylor, Walt. Doughty's English. SPE. 1939.

LORD ALFRED DOUGLAS (b. 1870)

(a) Bibliography

Braybrooke, P. Lord Alfred Douglas, his Life and Work. 1931. [Appendix B, Bibliography.]

(b) Poems and Satires

Poems. (Poèmes.) Paris, 1896. [Poems in English and French.]

Tails with a Twist. 1898.

The City of the Soul. 1899.

The Duke of Berwick. 1899; 1925.

The Placid Pug, and Other Rhymes. 1906.

The Pongo Papers and the Duke of Berwick. 1907. [The rhymes in Pongo Papers are rptd from Vanity Fair.]

Sonnets. 1909.

The Rossiad. Galashiels, [1916?]. [A lampoon.]

Eve and the Serpent. Galashiels, 1917. [A lampoon.]

Collected Poems. 1919.

In Excelsis. 1924. [A sonnet sequence.]

Nine Poems. 1926 (priv. ptd).

Select Poems. 1926. (Augustan Books of Modern Poetry.)

Collected Satires. 1926.

Complete Poems, including the Light Verse. 1928.

(c) Other Writings

Salome. 1894. [A trn of Wilde's French.]

Oscar Wilde and Myself. 1914.

The Autobiography of Lord Alfred Douglas. 1929.

The True History of Shakespeare's Sonnets. 1933.

Without Apology. 1938.

(d) Biography and Criticism

Brown, W. Sorley. Lord Alfred Douglas: the Man and the Poet. 1918.

Ellis, S. M. An Authentic Poet: Lord Alfred Douglas. [In Mainly Victorian, 1925.]

Braybrooke, P. Lord Alfred Douglas. His Life and Work. 1931.

EDWARD DOWDEN (1843–1913)

[See p. 740 below.]

ERNEST CHRISTOPHER DOWSON (1867–1900)

(a) Bibliography

Stonehill, C. A. and H. W. Bibliographies of Modern Authors. Ser. 2, 1925.

(b) Collected Works

Poems. With a Memoir by Arthur Symons. 1905.

Complete Poems. New York, 1929.

The Poetical Works. Ed. D. Flower, 1934. [Includes 40 unpbd poems.]

(c) Poems

The Book of the Rhymers' Club. 1892. [Contains 6 poems by Dowson; The Second Book, 1894, contains 6 more poems.]

Verses. 1896.

The Pierrot of the Minute. A Dramatic Phantasy in One Act. 1897; Grolier Club, 1923.

Decorations in Verse and Prose. 1899.

(d) Fiction

A Comedy of Masks. A Novel. 3 vols. 1893; 1896. [With Arthur Moore.]

Dilemmas. Stories and Studies in Sentiment. 1895.

Adrian Rome. 1899. [With Arthur Moore.]

(e) Translations

Couperus. Majesty. 1894. [With A. Texeira de Mattos.]

Zola. La Terre. 2 vols. 1895 (priv. ptd).

Balzac. La Fille aux Yeux d'Or. 1896.

Laclos. Les Liaisons Dangereuses. 2 vols. 1898 (priv. ptd).

Memoirs of Cardinal Dubois. 2 vols. 1899.

Voltaire. La Pucelle. 2 vols. 1899.

Goncourt, E. de. The Confidantes of a King: the Mistresses of Louis XV. 2 vols. 1907.

The Story of Beauty and the Beast. 1908.

(f) Biography and Criticism

Sherard, R. H. Obituary. Author, May 1900.

Jepson, E. The Real Ernest Dowson. Academy, Nov. 1907.

Plarr, V. Ernest Dowson, 1888–1897. Reminiscences, Unpublished Letters and Marginalia. 1914. [With bibliography by H. G. Harrison.]

Huxley, A. Ernest Dowson. [In The English Poets, ed. T. H. Ward, vol. v, 1918.]

Wheatley, K. Ernest Dowson's 'Extreme Unction.' MLN. xxxviii, 1923.

Thomas, W. R. Ernest Dowson at Oxford. Nineteenth Century, ciii, 1928.

Evans, B. I. English Poetry in the Later Nineteenth Century. 1933. [Ch. xv.]

GEORGE DU MAURIER (1834–1896)

[See p. 543 below.]

LADY CHARLOTTE ELLIOT (1839–1880)

Medusa and Other Poems. 1878.

JOSEPH ELLIS

(a) Poems

Meletae. Poems. 1869.

Caesar in Egypt; Costanza; and Other Poems. 1876; 1885 (3rd edn).

(b) Biography and Criticism

Mackay, [G.] E. Vox Clamantis. A Comparison, Analytical and Critical, between the 'Columbus at Seville' of Joseph Ellis and the 'Columbus' of [Tennyson]. [1887.]

ROBINSON ELLIS (1834–1913)

The Poems and Fragments of Catullus. Translated in the Metres of the Original. 1871.

[Ellis also pbd Latin verses, but his life work lay in the editing and commentary of Catullus, Ovid and the lesser Latin poets.]

FRANCIS ROBERT ST CLAIR ERSKINE, EARL OF ROSSLYN (1833–1890)

Sundry Sonnets, Various Verses and Trifling Translations. [1871] (priv. ptd).

Sonnets. Edinburgh, 1883.

Sonnets and Poems. [Ed. W. E. Hodgson], 1889.

'MICHAEL FIELD' [i.e. KATHERINE HARRIS BRADLEY (1846–1913) and EDITH EMMA COOPER (1862–1914)]

(a) Selected Works

Selections. Compiled by T. Sturge Moore. 1923.

(b) Poems

The New Minnesinger, and Other Poems. By Arran Leigh. 1875.

Bellerophôn and Other Poems. By Arran and Ilsa Leigh. 1881.

Long Ago. 1889. [Founded on the fragments of Sappho.]

Sight and Song. 1892.

Underneath the Bough. A Book of Verses. 1893; 1893 (rev. and reduced edn); Portland, Maine, 1898 (adds some new poems and restores some poems deleted from the 2nd edn).

Wild Honey from Various Thyme. Poems. 1908.

Poems of Adoration. 1912.

Mystic Trees. 1913.

Dedicated: an Early Work of Michael Field. 1914.

Whym Chow, Flame of Love. 1914 (priv. ptd).

The Wattlefold. Unpublished Poems. Collected by E. C. Fortey. Oxford, 1930.

(c) Plays, etc.

Callirrhoë. Fair Rosamund. 1884; 1897 (Fair Rosamund ptd separately).

The Father's Tragedy. William Rufus. Loyalty or Love. 1885.

Brutus Ultor. A Play in Verse. 1886.

Canute the Great. The Cup of Water. 1887.

The Tragic Mary. 1890.

Stephania. A Trialogue. 1892.

A Question of Memory. A Play in Four Acts. 1893.

Attila, my Attila! A Play in Verse. 1896.

The World at Auction. A Drama in Verse. 1898.

Noontide Branches. Oxford, 1899 (priv. ptd).

Anna Ruina. A Drama in Verse. 1899.

The Race of Leaves. 1901.

Julia Domna. A Drama in Verse. 1903.

Borgia: a Period Play. 1905.

Queen Mariamne. A Play. 1908.

The Tragedy of Pardon. Diane. 1911.

The Accuser. Tristran de Léonois. A Messiah. 1911.

Deidre, A Question of Memory, and Ras Byance. 1918.

In the Name of Time: a Tragedy. 1919.

Works and Days. Extracts from the Journals of Michael Field. Ed. T. and D. C. Sturge Moore, 1934.

(d) Biography and Criticism

Johnson, L. Michael Field. Miles, viii (ix).

Sturgeon, M. Studies of Contemporary Poets. 1920 (rev. edn). [Has an essay on Michael Field which supplements her memoir, 1922.]

—— Michael Field. 1922. [With bibliography.]

Symons, A. Michal Field. Forum, lxix, 1923.

Smith, L. P. Michael Field. Dial, lxxviii, 1925. [Rptd in Reperusals and Recollections, 1936.]

Boas, F. S. Two Unpublished Poems by Michael Field. London Mercury, xii, 1925.

WILLIAM FREELAND

Love and Treason. A Novel. 3 vols. 1872.

A Birth Song, and Other Poems. Glasgow, 1882.

Ballads and Other Poems. With Memoir by Henry Johnston. Glasgow, 1904.

NORMAN ROWLAND GALE (b. 1862)

(a) Poems

Cricket Songs and Other Trifling Verses.
Rugby, 1890 (anon.).
Here be Blue and White Violets. Rugby, n.d.
A Country Muse. 2 sers. 1892–3; 1894; 1895.
Orchard Songs. 1893.
A Verdant County. [In A. Hayes, A Fellow-
ship in Song, 1893.]
Cricket Songs. 1894.
On Two Strings. Rugby, 1894 (priv. ptd).
[With R. K. Leather.]
Songs for Little People. 1896.
More Cricket Songs. 1905.
A Book of Quatrains. Rugby, [1909].
Song in September. 1912.
Country Lyrics, selected from 'A Country
Muse' and 'Orchard Songs.' [1913.]
Collected Poems. 1914.
A Merry-go-round of Song. 1919.
Verse in Bloom. [1924.]
A Flight of Fancies. [1926.]
Messrs Bat and Ball. 1930.

(b) Other Writings

A June Romance. Rugby, 1892 (priv. ptd);
Rugby, 1894.
Barty's Star. [1903.]
Solitude. 1913.

(c) Biography and Criticism

Tomson, G. R. A Country Muse. Academy,
XLII, 1892.
Noble, J. A. Norman Gale. Miles, VIII (VII).

RICHARD GARNETT (1835–1906)

[See p. 742 below.]

SIR WILLIAM SCHWENCK GILBERT
(1836–1911)

[See p. 610 below.]

SIR EDMUND GOSSE (1849–1928)

[See p. 742 below.]

DAVID GRAY (1838–1861)

(a) Poems

The Luggie and Other Poems. With a Memoir
by James Hedderwick and a Prefatory
Notice by R. M. Milnes. Cambridge, 1862;
1874 (enlarged).

(b) Biography and Criticism

David Gray. Cornhill, IX, 1863.
Buchanan, R. W. David Gray and Other
Essays. 1868.
Noble, J. A. David Gray. Miles, VI.
Russell, G. W. E. Selected Essays. 1914.
Evans, B. I. English Poetry in the Later
Nineteenth Century. 1933. [Ch. xvi.]

JOHN GRAY

Silverpoints. 1893.
The Blue Calendar. 3 pts, 1895–7 (priv. ptd).
[Carols.]
Spiritual Poems, chiefly done out of Several
Languages. 1896.
Ad Matrem. Poems. 1904.
The Long Road. Oxford, 1926.
Sound: a Poem. 1926 (priv. ptd).
Poems. 1931.
Park. 1932.

[Gray also pbd trns from Bourget, Couperus,
Goethe and Nietzsche and edns of the poems
of Campion, Constable, Drayton and Sidney,
as well as devotional works and anthologies.]

ALEXANDER BALLOCH GROSART (1835–1899)

[See p. 1038 below.]

WILLIAM HALL (b. 1838)

The Victory of Defeat, and Other Poems,
chiefly on Hebrew Themes. 1896.
The Way of the Kingdom, and Other Poems.
1899.
Renunciation, and Other Poems. 1902.
Via Crucis. 1906.
Poems of a Riper Experience, Devotional and
Reflective. [1922.]
Nunc Dimittis. Poems. 1926.

[For Hall's life and writings, and a selection
from the poems, see A. H. Miles, Miles, X
(XII).]

PHILIP GILBERT HAMERTON (1834–1894)

[See p. 744 below.]

THOMAS HARDY (1840–1928)

[See p. 516 below.]

ISABELLA HARWOOD (1840–1888)

(a) Poems and Plays

[All written under pseudonym 'Ross Neil.']
Lady Jane Grey. Inez; or, The Bride of
Portugal. 1871.
The Cid. The King and the Angel. Duke for a
Day; or, The Tailor of Brussels. 1874.
Elfinella; or, Home from Fairyland. Lord and
Lady Russell. 1876.
Arabella Stuart. The Heir of Lynne. Tasso.
1879.
Andrea the Painter. Claudia's Choice.
Orestes. Pandora. 1883.

(b) Novels

[Pbd under her own name.]
Abbot's Cleve. 1864.
Carleton Grange. [1866.]
Raymond's Heroine. 1867.
Kathleen. 1869.
The Heir Expectant. 1870.

(c) Biography and Criticism

Garnett, R. Isabella Harwood. *Miles*, VII (IX).

WILLIAM HASTIE (1842–1893)

The Glory of Nature in the Land of Lorn, a Sonnet Sequence. Edinburgh, 1903.

[Some theological writings by Hastie were pbd after his death; he was an industrious translator of German philosophy and theology.]

FRANCES RIDLEY HAVERGAL (1836–1879)
(a) Selections

Ivy Leaves; selections from the Poems of F. R. Havergal [by Frances A. Shaw]. 1884.
Gems from Havergal. Poetry. Selected by Frances A. Shaw. [1912.]
Gems from Havergal. Prose. Selected by Beatrice Havergal Shaw. [1912.]

(b) Poems

The Ministry of Song. 1869.
Under the Surface. 1874.
Loyal Responses; or, Daily Melodies for the King's Minstrels. 1878. [Hymns.]
Life Echoes. 1883.

[Miss Havergal also wrote a great deal of religious verse and some prose.]

(c) Biography and Criticism

List of Works by F. R. Havergal. [1873?]
F. R. Havergal. A Biographical Sketch. [1881.]
Miles, A. H. Frances Ridley Havergal. *Miles*, X (XII).
Bullock, C. 'Near the Throne.' Frances Ridley Havergal, the Sweet Singer and Royal Writer. [1902.]
Chappell, J. Women who have worked and won. The Life Story of F. R. Havergal, etc. [1904.]
Enock, E. E. Frances Ridley Havergal. [1929.]

ALFRED HAYES (b. 1857)

The Last Crusade, and Other Poems. Birmingham, 1887.
Welcome to the Queen. Birmingham, 1887.
David Westren. Birmingham, 1888.
The March of Man, and Other Poems. 1891.
A Fellowship in Song. Alfred Hayes, Richard Le Gallienne, Norman Gale. 3 pts, Rugby, 1893.
The Vale of Arden, and Other Poems. 1895; Birmingham, 1897.
The Cup of Quietness. 1911.
Simon de Montfort: an Historical Drama in Five Acts. 1918.
Borís Godunór, by Pushkin, rendered into English Verse. [1918.]

The Mayflower. 1920. [With W. E. Stirling.]
Czar Feodor Ioannovich, by Tolstoi, rendered into English Verse. 1924.
The Death of Ivan the Terrible, by Tolstoi, rendered into English Verse. 1926.
[See J. A. Noble, *Miles*, VIII (VII).]

WILLIAM ERNEST HENLEY (1849–1903)
(a) Bibliography

Chesterton, G. K. English Illustrated Mag. XXIX, 1903.

(b) Collected Works

The Works of W. E. Henley. 7 vols. 1908.
The Works of W. E. Henley. 5 vols. 1921.

(c) Poems

A Book of Verses. 1888.
The Song of the Sword and Other Verses. 1892.
London Voluntaries and Other Verses. 1893.
London Types. 1898. [Quatorzains by W. E. Henley; illustrations by Sir W. Nicholson.]
Poems. 1898.
Hawthorn and Lavender: Songs and Madrigals. 1899; 1901 (with other verses).
For England's Sake: Verses and Songs in Time of War. 1900.
A Song of Speed. 1903. [Rptd from The World's Work.]
Selected Poems. 1931. (Augustan Books of Poetry.)

(d) Plays

Deacon Brodie. 1880 (priv. ptd); 1888 (finished version). [In collaboration with R. L. Stevenson.]
Admiral Guinea. 1884. [In collaboration with R. L. Stevenson.]
Beau Austin. 1884. [In collaboration with R. L. Stevenson.]
Macaire. 1885. [In collaboration with R. L. Stevenson.]
Mephisto. A New and Original Travestie by Byron M'Guiness. 1887.
Collected Plays. 1892 (3 plays); 1896 (complete edn).

(e) Other Writings

Pictures at Play by Two Art-Critics. 1888. [Andrew Lang and W. E. Henley.]
Catalogue of Pictures by the French and Dutch Romanticists of this Century. With an Introduction and Biographical Notes of Artists. 1889.
Views and Reviews: Essays in Appreciation. Literature. 1890. [Dickens, Thackeray, Disraeli, Dumas, Meredith, Byron, Hugo, Heine, Arnold, Homer and Theocritus, Rabelais, Shakespeare, Sidney, Tourneur, Walton, Herrick, Berlioz, George Eliot,

Borrow, Balzac, Longfellow, Tennyson, Landor, Hood, Gay, Boswell, Congreve, Tolstoi, etc.]

Dictionary of Slang and its Analogues. 1894–1904. [In collaboration with J. S. Farmer.]

Burns. Life, Genius, Achievement. An Essay. Edinburgh, 1898. [Originally prefixed to The Poetry of Robert Burns, ed. W. E. Henley and T. F. Henderson, vol. i, Edinburgh, 1896.]

Views and Reviews: Essays in Appreciation. Art. 1902.

[Henley also produced several anthologies of English verse and prose, as well as editing some or all of the works of Blunt, Burns, Byron, Fielding, Shakespeare and Smollett.]

(f) Biography and Criticism

Meynell, A. Mr W. E. Henley's Poems. Merry England, xi, 1888.

Noble, J. A. William Ernest Henley. *Miles*, viii (vii).

Archer, W. Study and Stage. 1899.

—— W. E. Henley. Pall Mall Gazette, xxxi, 1903.

Thompson, Francis. W. E. Henley. Academy, 18 July 1903.

Cornford, L. C. William Ernest Henley. 1913.

Lucas, E. V. The Colvins and their Friends. 1928.

Williamson, Kennedy. W. E. Henley. A Memoir. 1930.

Schappes, M. U. William Ernest Henley's Principles of Criticism. PMLA. xlvi, 1931.

Evans, B. I. English Poetry in the Later Nineteenth Century. 1933. [Ch. xii.]

Niven, F. Henley. Library Rev. no. 27, 1934.

McCarthy, M. Handicaps. 1936. [Includes essay on Henley.]

EMILY HENRIETTA HICKEY (1845–1924)

(a) Poems

A Sculptor, and Other Poems. 1881.

Verse-Tales, Lyrics and Translations. 1889.

Michael Villiers, Idealist: and Other Poems. 1891.

Poems. 1896.

Ancilla Domini: Thoughts in Verse on the Life of the Blessed Virgin Mary. [1898] (priv. ptd).

Our Lady of May, and Other Poems. 1902.

Havelok the Dane. An Old English Romance rendered into Later English. 1902.

Later Poems. 1913.

Devotional Poems. 1922.

Jesukin, and Other Christmastide Poems. 1924.

(b) Other Works

Browning, R. Strafford. With Notes by E. H. Hickey. 1884.

Noel, R. B. W. Livingstone in Africa. With Preface by E. H. Hickey. 1895.

Our Catholic Heritage in English Literature. 1910.

(c) Biography and Criticism

Miles, A. H. Emily H. Hickey. *Miles*, viii (ix).

Dinnis, E. M. Emily Hickey: Poet, Essayist, Pilgrim. A Memoir. [1927.] [With a selection of poems and a portrait.]

ARTHUR CLEMENT HILTON (1851–1877)

The Light Green. 1872. [Parodies, mainly by Hilton.]

The Works. Together with his Life and Letters. [Ed. Sir R. Pearce-Edgcumbe], 1904.

EDMOND GORE ALEXANDER HOLMES (b. 1850)

(a) Poems

Poems. 1876.

Poems. Second Series. 1879.

The Silence of Love. 1899; 1901.

The Triumph of Love. 1903. [Sonnets.]

The Creed of my Heart, and Other Poems. 1912.

Sonnets to the Universe. 1918.

Sonnets and Poems, selected and arranged by T. J. Cobden-Sanderson. 1920.

(b) Other Writings

What is Poetry? 1900.

Walt Whitman's Poetry. A Study and a Selection. 1902.

In Quest of an Ideal: an Autobiography. 1920.

[Mr Holmes has also written on educational and philosophical topics.]

LAURENCE HOUSMAN (b. 1865)

(a) Poems

Green Arras. 1896.

Spikenard: a Book of Devotional Love-Poems. 1898.

The Little Land, with Songs from its Four Rivers. 1899.

Rue. 1899.

Selected Poems. 1908.

(b) Other Writings (to 1900)

A Farm in Fairyland. 1894.

The House of Joy. [1895.] [Fairy tales.]

All-Fellows. Seven Legends of Lower Redemption. With Insets in Verse. 1896.

Gods and their Makers. 1897.

The Field of Clover. 1898. [Tales.]

The Story of the Seven Young Goslings. [1899.]

An Englishwoman's Love-Letters. 1900.
The Unexpected Years. 1937. [Autobiography.]

[Since 1900 Mr Housman has pbd some fifty works, including many plays and dramatic dialogues, and poems, novels, fairy-tales, etc.]

(c) Biography and Criticism

Archer, W. Poets of the Younger Generation. 1902.
Pennell, E. R. Laurence Housman. Nation (New York), LXXVI, 1902.
Rudolf, A. Die Dichtung von Laurence Housman. Breslau, 1930.

HENRY NEWMAN HOWARD (b. 1861)

Footsteps of Proserpine, and Other Verses and Interludes. 1897.
Kiartan the Icelander. A Tragedy. 1902 [1901].
Savonarola. A City's Tragedy. 1904.
Constantine the Great: a Tragedy. 1906.
Collected Poems. 1913.

[For biography and criticism, and a selection from the poems, see A. H. Miles, *Miles*, (VII).]

DOUGLAS HYDE (b. 1860)

[See p. 1056 below.]

SELWYN IMAGE (1849–1930)
(a) Writings

Poems and Carols. 1894.
[Collected] Poems. Ed. A. H. Mackmurdo, 1932.

[Image's letters were pbd 1932. He had also pbd several lectures and introductions to books.]

(b) Biography and Criticism

Miles, A. H. Selwyn Image. *Miles*, x (XII).
Obituary. Times, 22 Aug. 1930.

LIONEL PIGOT JOHNSON (1867–1902)
(a) Collected and Selected Works

Twenty-one Poems. Selected by William Butler Yeats. Dundrum, 1904.
Selections from the Poems, including some now collected for the First Time. With a Prefatory Memoir [by C. K. Shorter]. 1908.
Some Poems. Selected, with an Introduction by L. I. Guiney. 1912.
Poetical Works. With an Introduction by Ezra Pound. 1915.
The Religious Poems. Selected by G. F. Engelbach. With a Preface by Wilfrid Meynell. 1916.
A New Selection from the Poems. Compiled by H. V. Marrot. 1927.

(b) Poems

Sir Walter Raleigh in the Tower. A Prize Poem. Chester, 1885.
The Book of the Rhymers' Club. 1892. [Contains 6 poems by Johnson; The Second Book, 1894, contains 6 more poems.]
Poems. 1895.
Ireland, with Other Poems. 1897.

(c) Critical Writings

The Fools of Shakespeare. An Essay. [In Noctes Shakesperianae, Winchester College Shakspere Soc. 1887.]
The Art of Thomas Hardy. 1894 (with a bibliography by J. Lane); 1923 (adds a chapter on Hardy's poetry by J. E. Barton).
James Clarence Mangan. [In A Treasury of Irish Poetry, ed. S. A. Brooke and T. W. Rolleston, 1900. This is not the same as the review in Post Liminium, prefixed to the prose writings of J. C. Mangan.]
Poetry and Ireland: [Two] Essays by W. B. Yeats and Lionel Johnson. Dundrum, 1908. [A preliminary note, presumably by Elizabeth C. Yeats, the publisher, gives a character-sketch of Johnson and describes his manner of reading poetry.]
Post Liminium. Essays and Critical Papers. Ed. T. Whittemore, 1911. [Papers on Pater, Charlotte Brontë, Savonarola, Blake, Bacon, Boswell, Pascal, Newman, etc.]
Reviews and Critical Papers. Ed. R. Shafer, 1921. [Reviews of books by Kipling, Stevenson, J. Davidson, Morris, Mrs H. Ward, Meredith, A. Dobson, Richard Le Gallienne, etc.]

(d) Other Writings

The Gordon Riots. Catholic Truth Soc. 1893.
Bits of Old Chelsea. 1894. [Etchings by W. W. Burgess, with descriptions by Johnson and R. Le Gallienne.]
Some Winchester Letters. 1919.

(e) Biography and Criticism

Obituary. Athenaeum, 18 Oct. 1902.
Guiney, L. I. Obituary. Atlantic Monthly, Dec. 1902.
Waugh, A. Tradition and Change. 1919. [Has a ch. on Johnson.]
TLS. 7 July, 1921.
Tynan, K. Memories. 1924. [A ch. on Johnson as mediaevalist.]
Weygandt, C. Tuesdays at Ten. Philadelphia, 1928. [Contains a ch. on Johnson.]
Evans, B. I. English Poetry in the Later Nineteenth Century. 1933. [Ch. xv.]

MAY KENDALL (b. 1861)
(a) Poems

Dreams to Sell. 1887.
Songs from Dreamland. 1894.

(b) Fiction

That Very Mab. 1885. [Anon. In collaboration with Andrew Lang.]
From a Garret. 1887.
Such is Life. 1889.
White Poppies. A Novel. 1893.
Turkish Bonds. [1898.] [Short stories.]

(c) Biography and Criticism

Miles, A. H. Mary Kendall. *Miles*, IX (x).

HARRIET ELEANOR HAMILTON KING (1840–1920)

(a) Poems

Aspromonte and Other Poems. 1869.
The Disciples. 1873.
A Book of Dreams. 1888.
Ballads of the North and Other Poems. 1889.
The Prophecy of Westminster. 1895.
The Hours of Passion. 1902.

[Harriet King's Letters and Recollections of Mazzini were ed. by G. M. Trevelyan, 1912.]

(b) Biography and Criticism

Robertson, E. S. English Poetesses. 1883, pp. 367–74.
Hickey, E. H. Harriet Eleanor Hamilton-King. *Miles*, VII (IX).
—— Two Catholic Poetesses. Dublin Rev. Jan. 1921.

RUDYARD KIPLING (1865–1936)

[See p. 527 below.]

MARY MONTGOMERIE LAMB, later SINGLETON, later LADY CURRIE (1843–1905)
[Pseudonym 'Violet Fane']

(a) Collected Works

Collected Verses. 1880.
Poems. 2 vols 1892. [With critical introduction.]
Collected Essays. 1902.

(b) Poems

From Dawn to Noon. Poems. 1872.
Denzil Place, a Story in Verse. 1875.
The Queen of the Fairies, and Other Poems. 1876.
Anthony Babington. 1877. [A play, in prose and verse.]
Autumn Songs. 1889.
Under Cross and Crescent. Poems. 1896.
Betwixt Two Seas. Poems and Ballads written at Constantinople and Therapia. 1900.

(c) Novels and Essays

Edwin and Angelina Papers. 1878. [Essays rptd from The World; pbd under the initial 'V.']

Sophy; or, the Adventures of a Savage. 3 vols. 1881.
Thro' Love and War. 3 vols. 1886.
The Story of Helen Davenant. 3 vols. 1889.
Two Moods of a Man. With Other Papers and Short Stories. 1901.

(d) Biography and Criticism

Japp, A. H. Mary M. Singleton. *Miles*, VII (IX).
Obituary. Times, 16 Oct. 1905.

ANDREW LANG (1844–1912)

[See p. 747 below.]

FRANCIS BURDETT THOMAS COUTTS-NEVILL, BARON LATYMER (1852–1923)

(a) Poems

The Girls of England. A Battle Call. 1882.
Poems. 1896. [Includes An Essay in a Brief Model.]
The Alhambra and Other Poems. 1898.
The Revelation of St Love the Divine. A Poem. 1898.
The Mystery of Godliness. 1900.
The Nut Brown Maid. 1901. [A new version of the old ballad.]
Musa Verticordia. 1905.
The Song of Songs. 1906. [The Song of Solomon re-arranged in dramatic form.]
The Heresy of Job. 1907. [With Blake's engravings.]
The Romance of King Arthur. 1907. [Uther Pendragon, A Poem; Merlin, A Play; Launcelot du Lake, A Drama; The Death of Launcelot, A Poem.]
Egypt, and Other Poems. 1912.
Psyche. A Poem. 1912.
A Ballad of the War. 1915.
The Spacious Times, and Others. 1920.
Selected Poems. 1923.

[Latymer also edited Flowers of Parnassus, 27 vols. 1900–6.]

(b) Other Writings

The Training of the Instinct of Love. With a Preface by E. Thring. 1885.
Two Heirs Presumptive. A Tale. 1894.
The Poet's Charter, or the Book of Job. 1903.
The Royal Marines. 1915.
Ventures in Thought. 1915. [Essays.]
Well. 1922. [A Yorkshire village. With F. Redmayne.]

(c) Biography and Criticism

Archer, W. Poets of the Younger Generation. 1902.
Obituary. Times, 9 June 1923.

EMILY LAWLESS (1845–1913)

[See p. 1055 below.]

EUGENE JACOB LEE-HAMILTON (1845–1907)

(a) Poems

Poems and Transcripts. 1878.
Gods, Saints and Men. 1880.
The New Medusa and Other Poems. 1882.
Apollo and Marsyas, and Other Poems. 1884.
Imaginary Sonnets. 1888.
The Fountain of Youth. A Fantastic Tragedy. 1891.
Sonnets of the Wingless Hours. 1894.
Forest Notes. 1899. [In collaboration with Mrs Lee-Hamilton.]
Dramatic Sonnets, Poems and Ballads: Selections from the Poems of E. Lee-Hamilton. With an Introduction by William Sharp. 1903.
Minima Bella. With Preface by Annie E. Lee-Hamilton. 1909.

(b) Fiction

The Lord of the Dark Red Star. 1903.
The Romance of the Fountain. 1905.

(c) Biography and Criticism

Symonds, J. A. Eugenè Lee-Hamilton. *Miles*, VIII (VII).
Obituary. Times, 11 Sept. 1907.

EDWARD CRACROFT LEFROY (1855–1891)

(a) Poems

Echoes from Theocritus. Blackheath, 1883; 1885 (adds Sonnets); 1922 (adds a selection from Lefroy's other poems and a short introduction by J. A. Symonds).
Cytisus and Galingale. A Series of Sonnets. Blackheath, 1883.
Windows of the Church, and Other Sonnets. Blackheath, 1883.
Sketches and Studies, and Other Sonnets. Blackheath, 1884. [32 sonnets.]

[Lefroy also pbd sermons and addresses. His articles in Oxford and Cambridge Undergraduates' Journ. 1876–7 were rptd Oxford, 1878, as Undergraduate Oxford.]

(b) Biography and Criticism

Miles, A. H. Edward Cracroft Lefroy. *Miles*, VIII (VII).
Gill, W. A. E. C. Lefroy: his Life and Poems. With a Critical Estimate of the Sonnets by J. A. Symonds. 1897. [Includes selected poems and 30 sonnets pbd for the first time.]

RICHARD LE GALLIENNE (b. 1866)

[See p. 551 below.]

HENRY SAMBROOKE LEIGH (1837–1883)

Carols of Cockayne. 1869. [Light verse illustrated by Alfred Concanen and John Leech.]

Gillott and Goosequill. 1871. [Light verse.]
A Town Garland. A Collection of lyrics. 1878.
Fatinitza. 1878. [A comic opera adapted from the German.]
Strains from the Strand. Trifles in Verse. 1882.
The Brigands. 1884. [A play adapted from the French.]
Lurette. A Comic Opera. [The lyrics are by Leigh and the music by Offenbach. Not ptd?]

AMY LEVY (1861–1889)

(a) Poems

Xantippe and Other Verse. Cambridge, 1881.
A Minor Poet and Other Verses. 1884. [Partly rptd from Xantippe and Other Verse.]
A London Plane-Tree and Other Verse. 1889.

(b) Fiction

Reuben Sachs. A Sketch. 1888.
The Romance of a Shop. 1888.
Miss Meredith: a Tale. 1889.

SIR ALFRED COMYN LYALL (1835–1911)

(a) Poems

Verses written in India. 1889; 1907 (rev. and enlarged as Poems).

(b) Other Writings

Asiatic Studies, Religious and Social. 1882; 2 vols. 1899 (one essay omitted, but adds a long essay on history and fable).
Warren Hastings. A Biography. 1889.
The Rise of the British Dominion in India. 1893; 1910 (5th edn, corrected and enlarged).
Tennyson. 1902. (English Men of Letters ser.)
The Life of the Marquis of Dufferin and Ava. 2 vols. 1905.
Some Aspects of Asiatic History. 1910.
Studies in Literature and History. Ed. J. O. Miller, 1915. [English Letter-Writing, Thackeray, The Anglo-Indian Novelist, Heroic Poetry, Byron, The English Utilitarians, Swinburne's Poetry, etc.]
[See also p. 932 below.]

(c) Biography and Criticism

Miles, A. H. Sir Alfred Lyall. *Miles*, v.
Prothero, G. W. Commemorative Address. 1912. [In Commemorative Addresses of the Academic Committee, Royal Soc. Lit. 1912.]
Ubert, Sir C. P. Sir Alfred Lyall. Proc. British Academy, v, 1911–2.
Durand, Sir H. M. The Life of Sir Alfred Comyn Lyall. Edinburgh, 1913.

EDWARD ROBERT BULWER LYTTON,
EARL OF LYTTON (1831–1891)

[Lytton generally wrote under the pseudonym 'Owen Meredith.']

(a) Collected and Selected Works

Poetical Works of Owen Meredith. 2 vols. 1867.
Owen Meredith's Poems. 2 vols. Boston, 1869.
The Imperial Bouquet of Pretty Flowers. Ed. N. A. Chick, Calcutta, 1877. [A selection from Lytton's poems and public speeches in India, with a critique on his poetry rptd from The Pioneer.]
Poems of Owen Meredith. Selected by M. Betham-Edwards. 1890.
Selected Poems. With an Introduction by Lady [B.] Balfour. 1894.

(b) Poems

Clytemnestra, the Earl's Return, the Artist, and Other Poems. 1855.
The Wanderer. 1857; 1893 (rev. text; adds an unsigned preface, and discards pseudonym).
Lucile. 1860; 1893 (3rd edn, adds preface). [A novel in verse.]
Tannhäuser; or, The Battle of the Bards. By Neville Temple and Edward Trevor. 1861. [Really by Julian Fane and Lytton.]
Serbski Pesme or National Songs of Servia. 1861; ed. G. H. Powell, 1917. [Free versions of Serbian songs and ballads.]
Chronicles and Characters. 2 vols. 1868. ['An attempt at a poetic history of the education of man.']
Orval or The Fool of Time; and Other Imitations and Paraphrases. 1869. [Founded on the Infernal Comedy by Krazinski. Many of the Serbski Pesme are rptd in an appendix.]
Fables in Song. 2 vols. Edinburgh, 1874; tr. French, 1891.
King Poppy: a Story without End. 1875 (priv. ptd); 1892 (greatly rev.). [A long narrative poem.]
Glenaveril; or, the Metamorphoses. A Poem in Six Books. 2 vols. 1885; tr. French, 1888.
After Paradise; or, Legends of Exile, with Other Poems. 1887.
Marah. 1892. [Preface signed E. L. *i.e.* Edith, Lady Lytton.]

(c) Other Writings

The Ring of Amasis. From the Papers of a German Physician (Dr N——). 2 vols. 1863; 1890 (shortened and re-cast in the form of a novel).
Julian Fane. A Memoir. 1871.
Memoir of Edward, Lord Lytton. 1874. [Prefixed to Speeches of Edward, Lord Lytton, vol. I, 1874. Distinct from the longer biography of 1883.]

The Life, Letters and Literary Remains of Edward Bulwer, Lord Lytton. 2 vols. 1883.
Baldine and Other Tales. 2 vols. 1886. [Translated by Lytton from the German of K. E. Edler.]
Personal and Literary Letters. Ed. Lady B. Balfour, 2 vols. 1906.
Letters from Owen Meredith to Robert and Elizabeth Barrett Browning. Ed. A. B. and J. L. Harlan, Waco (Texas), 1937.

(d) Biography and Criticism

Obituary. Times, 25, 26 Nov. 1891.
'Owen Meredith.' Athenaeum, 28 Jan. 1893.
Whyte, W. Robert Earl of Lytton. *Miles*, v.
Balfour, Lady B. The History of Lord Lytton's Indian Administration, 1876 to 1880. 1899.
Sadleir, M. Bulwer: a Panorama. 1931.

JAMES MACFARLAN (1832–1862)

Poems. 1854.
City Songs and Other Poetical Pieces. Glasgow, 1855.
Lyrics of Life. 1856. [With a sketch of the author's life signed A. A.]
Poem on the Centenary of Robert Burns. [In The Burns Centenary Poems, ed. G. Anderson and J. Finlay, Glasgow, 1859.]
The Wanderer of the West. A Poem. [Glasgow, 1860?]
Poems contributed to All the Year Round. Glasgow, [1870?].
The Poetical Works, with a Memoir by C. Rae-Brown. Glasgow, 1882.

[Macfarlan also pbd in prose The Attic Study. Brief Notes on Nature, Men and Books, 1862.]

DOLLIE MAITLAND, afterwards RADFORD (b. 1858)

A Light Load. 1891.
Songs for Somebody. 1893.
Good Night. 1895.
Songs and other Verses. 1895.
One Way of Love: an Idyll. 1898.
Sea-Thrift: a Fairy Tale. 1904.
The Young Gardener's Kalendar. 1904.
A Ballad of Victory, and Other Poems. 1907.
The Young Gardener's Year. 1908.
Poems. 1910.

[For criticism, and a selection from the poems, see A. Symons, *Miles*, VIII (IX).]

WILLIAM HURRELL MALLOCK (1849–1923)

[See p. 554 below.]

PHILIP BOURKE MARSTON (1850–1887)

(a) Poems

Song-Tide and Other Poems. 1871; ed. (with memoir) W. Sharp, 1888. [The 2nd edn was enlarged into a representative selection.]

All in All: Poems and Sonnets. 1875.
Wind-Voices. 1883.
Garden Secrets. Ed. L. C. Moulton, Boston, 1887.
A Last Harvest: Lyrics and Sonnets from the Book of Love. 1891. [With a biographical sketch by L. C. Moulton.]
Collected Poems. With a Biographical Sketch by Louise Chandler Moulton. 1892.

[Marston's For a Song's Sake and Other Stories was edited by William Sharp, with a memoir, 1887. The 2nd edn of Song-Tide also included this memoir and a critical estimate.]

(b) Biography and Criticism

Swinburne, A. C. Fortnightly Rev. Jan. 1891.
Kernahan, C. Philip Bourke Marston. *Miles*, VIII (VII).
—— Celebrities. 1923.
Drinkwater, J. Philip Bourke Marston. [In The English Poets, ed. T. H. Ward, vol. v, 1918.]
Osborne, C. C. Philip Bourke Marston. 1926 (priv. ptd).
Evans, B. I. English Poetry in the Later Nineteenth Century. 1933. [Ch. v.]

THEOPHILUS JULIUS HENRY MARZIALS (b. 1850)

Passionate Dowsabella. A Pastoral. 1872.
The Gallery of Pigeons, and Other Poems. 1873.
Esmeralda: an Opera. [1890.]

ANNIE MATHESON (1853–1924)

The Religion of Humanity and Other Poems. 1890.
Love's Music and Other Poems. 1894.
Love Triumphant, and Other New Poems. 1898.
Selected Poems: Old and New. 1899; 1900 (with addns); 1918 (rev. and enlarged as Roses, Loaves and Old Rhymes).

[Miss Matheson also pbd a number of children's books, etc. For her poems see A. H. Miles, *Miles*, (IX).]

HERMAN CHARLES MERIVALE (1839–1906)
[See p. 626 below.]

ALICE MEYNELL, née THOMPSON (1850–1922)

(a) Bibliographies

Tuell, A. K. Mrs Meynell and her Literary Generation. New York, 1925. [Bibliography appended.]
Stonehill, C. A. and H. W. Bibliographies of Modern Authors. Ser. 2, 1925.

(b) Collected and Selected Works

Poems. Collected Edition. 1913.
Essays. 1914.
The Poems. Complete Edition. 1923.

Selected Essays. 1926.
Selected Poems and Prose. Ed. A. A. Cock, 1928.
Selected Poems. Ed. W. M[eynell], 1930.

(c) Poems

Preludes. By A. C. Thompson. 1875. [Pbd before marriage.]
Poems. 1893.
Other Poems. 1896 (priv. ptd).
Later Poems. 1902; 1914 (as The Shepherdess and Other Poems; 2 poems omitted).
Ten Poems, 1913–1915. 1915.
Poems on the War. 1916.
A Father of Women, and Other Poems. 1917.
Aenigma Christi. [In O. R. Vassall-Phillips, The Mother of Christ, 1920. Never rptd.]
Last Poems. 1923.

(d) Other Writings

G. H. Boughton, A.R.A. 1883. J. L. E. Meissonier. 1883. [In Some Modern Artists and Their Work, ed. W. Meynell, 1883.]
The Poor Sisters of Nazareth. An Illustrated Record of Life at Nazareth House, Hammersmith. 1889.
The Life and Work of Holman Hunt. 1893. [With W. Farrar.]
Rhythm of Life, and Other Essays. 1893. [O. W. Holmes, J. R. Lowell, Coventry Patmore's Odes, etc.]
The Colour of Life, and Other Essays. 1896.
The Children. 1897. [Essays.]
London Impressions. 1898.
The Spirit of Place, and Other Essays. 1899.
John Ruskin. A Biography. 1900.
Children of Old Masters. 1903.
The Red Letter Poets. 12 vols. 1903. [Introductions to 10 of the 12 vols., on Arnold, Browning, E. B. Browning, Keats, Christina Rossetti, Shelley, Tennyson, and Wordsworth.]
Ceres' Runaway, and Other Essays. 1909.
Mary, the Mother of Jesus. An Essay. 1912.
Childhood. 1913.
Francis Thompson. By Everard Meynell. 1913. [Contains letters and articles by Mrs Meynell.]
Hearts of Controversy. [1917.] [Tennyson, Dickens, Swinburne, Charlotte and Emily Brontë, Charmian, etc.]
Second Person Singular, and Other Essays. 1921. [Robert Green, Arabella Stuart, To Italy with Evelyn, Sterne, Gibbon's Style, Anna Seward, Joanna Baillie, Classic Novelists, T. L. Beddoes, G. Darley, Dobell, Patmore, Meredith, G. Gallina, etc.]

[Mrs Meynell also translated Daniel Barbé's Lourdes, Yesterday, To-day and To-morrow, 1894; Adolfo Venturi's The Madonna, 1901; and René Bazin's The Nun, 1908.]

(e) Biography and Criticism

Noble, J. A. Alice Meynell. *Miles*, (IX).
Archer, W. Poets of the Younger Generation. 1902.
The Letters of George Meredith to Alice Meynell, 1896–1907. 1923. [Annotated; rpts Meredith's article on Alice Meynell's prose, etc.]
Chesterton, G. K. Alice Meynell. Dublin Rev. CLXXII, 1923.
Noyes, A. Some Aspects of Modern Poetry. 1924. [Contains an essay on Alice Meynell.]
Tuell, A. K. Mrs Meynell and her Literary Generation. New York, 1925.
Newbolt, Sir H. Studies Green and Gray. 1926. [Contains a paper on Mrs Meynell.]
Meynell, V. Alice Meynell. A Memoir. 1929.
Galland, R. Alice Meynell. Revue anglo-américaine, June 1930.
Hall, W. C. Alice Meynell. Papers of Manchester Literary Club, LVI, 1930.
Tynan, K. A Shrine to Alice Meynell. Commonweal, 21, 28 Jan. 1931.
Evans, B. I. English Poetry of the Later Nineteenth Century. 1933. [Ch. v.]

WILLIAM COSMO MONKHOUSE (1840–1901)

(a) Poems

A Dream of Idleness and Other Poems. 1865.
Corn and Poppies. 1890. [Partly rptd from Mag. of Art.]
The Christ upon the Hill. A Ballad. 1895.
To Our Sovereign Lady, Queen Victoria. June 22, 1897. 1897.
Pasiteles the Elder, and Other Poems. With Preface by Austin Dobson. 1901. [Includes The Christ upon the Hill.]
Nonsense Rhymes. 1902. [Illustrated by G. K. Chesterton.]

(b) Other Writings

A Question of Honour. A Novel. 3 vols. 1868.
Masterpieces of English Art, with Sketches of Some of the Most Celebrated of the Deceased Painters of the English School. 1869.
Sir Charles Eastlake. [A long biographical and critical sketch prefixed to Pictures by Sir Charles Eastlake, 1875.]
Joseph Mallord William Turner. 1879; rev. H. Shipp and F. Kendrick, 1929.
The Italian Pre-Raphaelites. 1887.
The Earlier English Water-Colour Painters. 1890; 1897 (adds preface).
Life of Leigh Hunt. 1893.
In the National Gallery. 1895. [Papers rptd from The Monthly Packet.]
British Contemporary Artists. 1899. [Rptd from Scribner's Mag. Watts, Millais,

Leighton, Burne-Jones, Orchardson, Alma-Tadema, Poynter.]
A History and Description of Chinese Porcelain. With Preface and Notes by S. W. Bushell. 1901.
Sir John Tenniel. 1901. [Forms a complete no. of The Art Annual, the Easter no. of Art Journ.]

(c) Biography and Criticism

Le Gallienne, R. Cosmo Monkhouse. *Miles*, VI.
Lee, Sir S. Athenaeum, 27 July 1901. [Gives an account of Monkhouse's contributions to the DNB.]
Gosse, Sir E. Cosmo Monkhouse as an Art Critic. Art Journ. 1902.

SIR LEWIS MORRIS (1833–1907)

(a) Collected and Selected Poems

The Poetical Works. 3 vols. 1882; 1907 (rev. and enlarged. [Songs Unsung, 1883, and Songs of Britain (4th edn) are sometimes counted as vols. IV and V of the 1st edn of the collected works.]
Selections. 1897.
Poems. 1904. [Authorised selection.]

(b) Separate Poems

Songs of Two Worlds. 3 sers. 1871–5; 1878.
The Epic of Hades. 1876 (bk II only); 1877 (bks I and III); 1877 (complete edn).
Gwen. A Drama in Monologue. 1879.
The Ode of Life. 1880.
Songs Unsung. 1883.
Gycia. A Tragedy. 1886. [Mostly in verse.]
Songs of Britain. 1887.
A Vision of Saints. 1890.
Odatis: an Old Love-Tale. A Poem. 1892.
Love and Sleep and Other Poems. 1893.
Ode on the Marriage of H.R.H. the Duke of York and H.S.H. Princess Victoria Mary of Teck. 1893.
Meliora. A Poem. 1894.
Songs without Notes. 1894.
Idylls and Lyrics. 1896.
The Diamond Jubilee. An Ode. 1897. [Rptd from Times.]
Harvest-Tide. 1901.
The Life and Death of Leo the Armenian (Emperor of Rome): a Tragedy. 1904.

(c) Other Writings

The New Rambler: from Desk to Platform. 1905. [Essays including A New Criticism of Poetry and Some Thoughts on Modern Poetry.]

(d) Biography and Criticism

Rees, J. R. Lewis Morris. *Miles*, V.
Obituary. Times, 13 Nov., 24 Dec. 1907; Athenaeum, 16 Nov. 1907.

ROBERT FULLER MURRAY (1863–1894)

The Scarlet Gown: being Verses by a St Andrew's Man. 1891; 1909 (with additional poems and an introduction by A. Lang); ed. J. H. Baxter, 1932.
Robert F. Murray, his Poems, with a memoir by Andrew Lang. 1894.

ERNEST JAMES MYERS (1844–1921)

(a) Poems

The Puritans. 1869. [A one-act play.]
Poems. 1877.
The Defence of Rome and Other Poems. 1880.
The Judgment of Prometheus and Other Poems. 1886.
Gathered Poems of Ernest Myers. 1904.
Selected Poems. 1931. (Augustan Books of Poetry.)

(b) Other Works

Aeschylus. An Essay. 1880. [In Hellenica, ed. E. Abbott, 1880.]
The Iliad of Homer done into English Prose. 1883. [With A. Lang and W. Leaf.]
Lord Althorp. A Biography. 1890.

(c) Biography and Criticism

Miles, A. H. Ernest Myers. Miles, VIII (VII).
Obituary. Times, 28 Nov. 1921.

FREDERIC WILLIAM HENRY MYERS
(1843–1901)

(a) Poems

[Burns Centenary Poem.] [In The Burns Centenary Poems, ed. G. Anderson and J. Finlay, 1859.]
The Distress in Lancashire. Chancellor's Medal Poem. Cambridge, 1863.
Saint Paul. 1867.
Poems. 1870.
The Renewal of Youth, and Other Poems. 1882.
Fragments of Prose and Poetry. Ed. E. Myers, 1904.
Collected Poems, with Autobiographical and Critical Fragments. Ed. E. Myers, 1921.
Saint John the Baptist. [1927.]

(b) Other Writings

Greek Oracles. [In E. Abbott's Hellenica, 1880.]
Wordsworth. 1881. (English Men of Letters ser.)
Essays Classical and Modern. 2 vols. 1883.
Phantasms of the Living. 1886. [With E. Gurney and F. Podmore.]
Science and a Future Life: with Other Essays. 1893.
Human Personality and its Survival of Bodily Death. 2 vols. 1903.

(c) Biography and Criticism

Morshead, E. D. A. The Poems of F. W. H. Myers. Academy, XXII, 1882.
Anderson, M. B. F. W. H. Myers. Dial, IV, 1884.
Symonds, J. A. Frederic W. H. Myers. Miles, VIII (VII).
Mallock, W. H. The Gospel of F. W. H. Myers. Nineteenth Century, LIII, 1902.
Muirhead, J. H. Myers on Personality and its Survival. Contemporary Rev. LXXXIV, 1903.
Sidgwick, A. The Posthumous Works of F. W. H. Myers. Independent Rev. v, 1904.
Benson, A. C. The Leaves of the Tree: Studies in Biography. 1911.

CONSTANCE CAROLINE WOODHILL NADEN
(1858–1889)

(a) Writings

Songs and Sonnets of Springtime. 1881.
What is Religion? A Vindication of Free Thought. Annotated by Robert Lewins. 1883 (anon.).
A Modern Apostle, the Elixir of Life, and Other Poems. 1887.
Induction and Deduction [and other essays]. Ed. R. Lewins (with Memoir by M. M. Daniell), 1890.
Further Reliques. Ed. G. M. McCrie, 1891.
Selections from the Philosophical and Poetical Works of C. C. W. Naden. Compiled by Emily and Edith Hughes. With Introduction by G. M. McCrie. 1893.
Complete Poetical Works. With Fore-word by Robert Lewins. 1894.

(b) Biography and Criticism

Hughes, W. R. Constance Naden: A Memoir. With Introduction by Professor Lapworth and Additions by Professor Tilden and Robert Lewins. 1890.
Dale, R. W. Constance Naden. Contemporary Rev. April 1891. [This article is rptd as Appendix I in Further Reliques, 1891.]
Brewer, E. C. Constance Naden and Hylo-Idealism. 1891.
Garnett, R. Constance Naden. Miles, (IX).
A Modern Interpreter. Temple Bar, CIII, 1894.

EDITH NESBIT, afterwards BLAND
(1858–1924)

(a) Poems

Lays and Legends. 2 sers. 1886–92.
The Lily and the Cross. [1887.]
Leaves of Life. 1888.
Corals, Sea Songs, etc. [1889.]
Life's Sunny Side. 1890. [By E. Nesbit and others.]
Songs of Two Seasons. [1890.]

Sweet Lavender. [1892.]
Our Friends and all about them. [1893.]
The Star of Bethlehem. [1894.]
A Pomander of Verse. 1895.
Rose Leaves. [1895.]
Songs of Love and Empire. 1898.
The Rainbow and the Rose. 1905.
Ballads and Lyrics of Socialism, 1883–1908.
1908.
Jesus in London. With Seven Pictures by
Spencer Pryse. [1908.]
Ballads and Verses of the Spiritual Life. 1911.
Many Voices. Poems. [1922.]

(b) Fiction

Doggy Tales. [1895.]
The Red House: a Novel. 1902.
The Phoenix and the Carpet. [1904.]
The Incomplete Amorist: a Novel. 1906.
Harding's Luck. 1909.
The Magic World. 1912. [Tales.]
To the Adventurous. [1923.]
The Complete History of the Bastable Family.
1928. [The Story of the Treasure Seekers;
The Wouldbegoods; New Treasure Seekers.]

[And many other novels and tales—
mainly for children.]

(c) Biography and Criticism

Japp, A. H. Miles, (ix), 1907.
Moore, D. L. E. Nesbit. A Biography. 1933.

SIR HENRY JOHN NEWBOLT (1862–1937)

(a) Collected and Selected Works

Collected Poems. 1897–1907. 1910.
Prose and Poetry. Selected by the Author.
1920.

(b) Poems

Mordred. A Tragedy. 1895.
Admirals All and Other Verses. 1897.
The Island Race. 1898.
The Sailing of the Long Ships and Other
Poems. 1902.
Clifton Chapel and Other School Poems.
1908.
Songs of Memory and Hope. 1909.
Poems, New and Old. 1912.
Drake's Drum and Other Songs of the Sea.
1914.
St George's Day and Other Poems. 1918.
The Linnet's Nest. 1927.
A Child is Born. 1931.

(c) Fiction

Taken from the Enemy. A Novel. 1892.
The Old Country. A Romance. 1906.
The New June. 1909.
The Twymans. A Tale of Youth. Edinburgh,
1911.
Aladore. Edinburgh, 1914.
Tales of the Great War. 1916.

(d) Critical Writings

A New Study of English Poetry. 1917.
[Poetry, Chaucer, The Approach to Shake-
speare, Milton, British Ballads, Poets and
their Friends.]
Poetry and Time. 1919. (Warton Lecture on
English Poetry.)
Studies Green and Gray. 1926. [Camden's
Elizabeth, Shakespeare, John Inglesant, A
New Departure in English Poetry, Poetry
and Time, Peacock, Scott and Robin Hood,
A. Meynell, Some Devotional Poets, etc.]
The Idea of an English Association. English
Ass. 1928.

(e) Historical Writings, etc.

The Year of Trafalgar. 1905.
The Book of the Blue Sea. 1914.
The Story of the Oxfordshire and Bucking-
hamshire Light Infantry, the Old 43rd and
52nd Regiments. 1915.
The War and the Nations. 1915. [Rptd from
Fortnightly Rev.]
The Book of the Thin Red Line. 1915.
The Book of the Happy Warrior. 1917.
Submarine and Anti-Submarine. 1918.
The Book of the Long Trail. 1919.
The Book of Good Hunting. 1920.
A Naval History of the War, 1914–1918.
5 vols. 1920–31.
The Book of the Grenvilles. 1921.
Days to Remember. 1923. [Stories of the
European War in collaboration with John
Buchan.]
The Building of Britain. 1927. [A description
of a series of historical paintings in St
Stephen's Hall, Westminster.]
My World as in My Time. 1932.

[Newbolt also edited and contributed to
The Teaching of English Series, 1925–32.]

(f) Biography and Criticism

Archer, W. Poets of the Younger Generation.
1902.
Bridges, R. Henry John Newbolt. Miles,
(vii).
Kernahan, C. Six Famous Living Poets. 1922.

ROSA NEWMARCH (b. 1857)

Horae Amoris. Songs and Sonnets. 1903.
Songs to a Singer, and Other Verses. 1906.

[Miss Newmarch has also written on Russia
and on music. For her poems see A. H. Miles,
Miles, (ix).]

JOHN NICHOL (1833–1894)

The Death of Themistocles, and Other Poems.
Glasgow, 1881.

JAMES ASHCROFT NOBLE (1844–1896)

(a) Poems

Verses of a Prose-Writer. Edinburgh, 1887.

(b) Other Writings

The Pelican Papers: Reminiscences and Remains of a Dweller in the Wilderness. 1873.
Morality in English Fiction. Liverpool, [1887].
The Sonnet in England, and other Essays. 1893. [Only 50 copies printed.]
From Coal Pit to Pulpit. Anecdotes and Incidents from the Life of the Rev. Peter Mackenzie. 1895.
Impressions and Memories. 1895.

[Noble contributed regularly to Spectator, New Age and Academy, and wrote many of the notices in *Miles*.]

(c) Biography and Criticism

C[otton], J. S. James Ashcroft Noble. Academy, 11 April 1896.

EDWARD HENRY NOEL (d. 1884)

Poems. 1884.

[Noel also pbd a trn from J. P. Richter. A brief appreciation will be found in W. Sharp's Sonnets of this Century, 1886.]

RODEN BERKELEY WRIOTHESLEY NOEL
(1834–1894)

(a) Selected and Collected Works

Selections; with Prefatory Notice by R. Buchanan. 1892.
Selected Poems. With a Biographical and Critical Essay by P. Addleshaw. 1897.
The Collected Poems. Ed. J. A. Symonds, 1902.

(b) Poems

Behind the Veil; and Other Poems. 1863.
Beatrice and Other Poems. 1868.
The Red Flag, and Other Poems. 1872.
Livingstone in Africa. 1874.
The House of Ravensburg. 1877. [A drama in verse.]
A Little Child's Monument. 1881.
Songs of the Heights and Deeps. 1885.
A Modern Faust, and Other Poems. 1888.
Poor People's Christmas: a Poem. 1890.
My Sea, and Other Poems. With an Introduction by Stanley Addleshaw. 1896.

(c) Other Writings

Syrian Travel and Syrian Tribes. 1861.
A Philosophy of Immortality. 1882.
Essays on Poetry and Poets. 1886.
Life of Lord Byron. 1887.

[Noel also edited selections from Spenser and Otway.]

(d) Biography and Criticism

The Poems of Roden Noel. British Quart. Rev. LXXVIII, 1883.
Monkhouse, W. C. Roden Noel's 'Songs of the Heights and Deeps.' Academy, XXVII, 1884, p. 179.
Symonds, J. A. A Modern Faust. Academy, XXXV, 1888, p. 33.
—— Hon. Roden Noel. *Miles*, VI.
Gale, N. The Poetry of Roden Noel. Academy, XLIII, 1892, pp. 306, 328.
Roden Noel. Saturday Rev. 2 June 1894.
Ellis, S. M. Mainly Victorian. [1925.]

ELLEN O'LEARY (1831–1889)

Lays of Country, Home and Friends. Dublin, 1891. [With a Biographical Sketch by T. W. Rolleston and criticism by Sir C. Gavan Duffy.]

[See also W. B. Yeats, *Miles*, VII (IX).]

JOHN BOYLE O'REILLY (1844–1890)

[See p. 1055 below.]

ARTHUR O'SHAUGHNESSY (1844–1881)

[See p. 1055 below.]

JOHN PAYNE (1842–1916)

(a) Bibliography

Wright, T. The Life of John Payne. 1919. [Bibliography appended.]

(b) Poems

The Masque of Shadows and Other Poems. 1870.
Intaglios. 1871.
Songs of Life and Death. 1872.
Lautrec. 1878.
New Poems. 1880.
The Descent of the Dove. 1902. [Subsequently included in Songs of Consolation, 1904.]
The Poetical Works. 2 vols. 1902.
Vigil and Vision. 1903. [A supplement containing 12 Sonnets de Combat was priv. ptd in the same year.]
Songs of Consolation. 1904.
Hamid the Luckless and Other Tales in Verse. 1904. [Rptd from Flowers from Syrian Gardens (Collected Poems, vol. I, pp. 322–59) with the difference that no. 2, The Scavanger of Baghdad, is omitted, Hamid the Luckless taking its place.]
Sir Winfrith, and Other Poems. Olney, 1905.
Selections from the Poetry of John Payne. Made by Tracy and Lucy Robinson. New York, 1906.
Verses for the Newton-Cowper Centenary. 1907.

The Quatrains of Ibn El-Tefrid. 1908 (priv.
ptd); 1909 (with omissions); 1921 (with
introduction by T. Wright). [An original
poem in the Persian manner.]
Carol and Cadence. 1908.
Flower o' the Thorn. 1909.
The Way of the Winepress. Olney, 1920.
Nature and her Lover, and Other Poems.
With an Introduction by T. Wright. Olney,
1922. [Largely rptd from Carol and
Cadence.]

(c) Translations

The Poems of Master François Villon. 1878.
The Book of the Thousand Nights and One
Night. 9 vols. 1882–4.
The Book of the Thousand Nights and One
Night: its History and Character. 1884
(priv. ptd). [Rptd from vol. IX of Payne's
trn of the complete work.]
Tales from the Arabic. 4 vols. 1884–5. [Vol.
IV is formed by Alaeddin and Zein ul
Asuam, 1885, which is sometimes referred
to as a separate work.]
The Decameron of Boccaccio. 3 vols. 1886.
The Novels of Matteo Bandello. 6 vols.
1890.
The Quatrains of Omar Kheyyam of Nisha
Pour. 1898. [With a critical introduction.]
The Poems of Shemseddin Mohammed Hafiz.
3 vols. 1901. [With a biographical and
critical introduction.]
Abou Mohammed the Lazy and Other Tales
from the Arabian Nights. 1906.
Flowers of France. The Romantic Period.
2 vols. 1906. The Renaissance Period. 1907.
The Latter Days. Nineteenth and Twentieth
Centuries. 2 vols. 1913. The Classic Period.
1914.
The Poetical Works of Heinrich Heine. 3 vols.
1911.

(d) Other Writings

Humoristica. 3 sers. 1909–[1910?] (priv. ptd).
The Autobiography of John Payne. With
Preface and Annotations by T. Wright.
1926.

(e) Biography and Criticism

Forman, H. B. Our Living Poets. 1871.
[Pp. 503–7.]
Garnett, R. John Payne. Miles, VIII (VII).
Wright, T. The Life of John Payne. 1919.
[Appendix III gives names and dates of
articles by Wright on Payne in various
periodicals, from 1906 onwards.]
Evans, B. I. English Poetry in the Later
Nineteenth Century. 1933. [Ch. v.]

STEPHEN PHILLIPS (1864–1915)

[See p. 627 below.]

VICTOR GUSTAVE PLARR (1863–1929)

(a) Poems

Scenes from the Alcestis of Euripides. 1886
(priv. ptd).
The Book of the Rhymers' Club. 1892.
[Contains 6 pieces by Plarr; The Second
Book, 1894, contains 6 more poems by him.]
In the Dorian Mood. Verses, 1896.
Nine Poems. [In The Garland of New Poetry
by Various Writers, 1899.]
The Tragedy of Asgard. 1905.

(b) Other Writings (select list)

Literary Etiquette. 1903. [Advice to authors
and to publishers.]
Ernest Dowson, 1888–1897: Reminiscences,
Unpublished Letters and Marginalia. 1914.
Plarr's Lives of the Fellows of the Royal
College of Surgeons of England. Rev. Sir
D'A. Power, W. G. Spencer and G. E. Gask,
2 vols. 1930. [Includes a memoir of Plarr.
Plarr's version was not pbd, being too
diffuse, but the work is substantially his.]

SIR FREDERICK POLLOCK (1845–1937)

(a) Poems

Leading Cases done into English. By an
Apprentice of Lincoln's Inn. 1876 (2nd
edn).
Leading Cases done into English, and Other
Diversions. 1892.
Outside the Law. Diversions partly Serious.
1927. [Prose and verse.]

(b) Other Writings

Spinoza, his Life and Philosophy. 1880.
Essays in Jurisprudence and Ethics. 1882.
An Introduction to the History of the Science
of Politics. 1890.
Oxford Lectures, and Other Discourses. 1890.
For my Grandson: Remembrances of an
Ancient Victorian. 1933.

[Pollock also wrote a number of important
works on legal subjects.]

WALTER HERRIES POLLOCK (1850–1926)

(a) Poems

The Poet and the Muse. 1880. [A version (not
a trn), in verse, of de Musset's La Nuit de
Mai, La Nuit d'Août, and La Nuit d'Octobre.]
Songs and Rhymes: English and French.
1882.
Verses of Two Tongues. 1884.
Old and New. 1890.
Sealed Orders and Other Poems. 1907.
Icarian Flights. 1920. [Trns into English
verse of some of the Odes of Horace. In
collaboration with Francis Coutts.]

(b) Other Writings

Lectures on French Poets. 1879. [Pierre Jean de Béranger, A. de Musset, Victor Hugo, and a lecture on romanticism.]

He. By the Authors of It, King Solomon's Wives, Bess, etc. 1887. [A parody of Sir H. Rider Haggard's novel 'She,' written in collaboration with Andrew Lang.]

Jane Austen, her Contemporaries and Herself. An Essay in Criticism. 1899.

Impressions of Henry Irving. With an Introduction by H. B. Irving. 1908.

[Pollock also pbd novels, short stories, plays, and miscellaneous writings.]

MAY PROBYN

(a) Poems

Poems. 1881.

A Ballad of the Road, and Other Poems. 1883.

Pansies. A Book of Poems. [1895.]

(b) Fiction

Once! Twice! Thrice! and Away! A Novel. 1878.

Robert Tresilian. 1880.

Who Killed Cock Robin? [1880.]

WILLIAM JEFFERY NICHOLAS PROWSE (1836–1870)

(a) Poems

Nicholas's Notes, and Sporting Prophecies, with some Miscellaneous Poems, Serious and Humorous. Ed. (with brief biographical notice) T. Hood, [1870].

(b) Other Works

England's Workshops. By G. L. M. Strauss and W. J. Prowse. 1864.

The Key of the Study. [In T. Hood, A Bunch of Keys, 1865.]

Like to Like. The Water-rate's Story. [In T. Hood, Rates and Taxes, 1866.]

[For Prowse's life and writings, and a selection from his poems, see A. H. Miles, *Miles*, ix (x).]

SIR ARTHUR QUILLER-COUCH (b. 1863)

[See p. 556 below.]

ERNEST RADFORD

(a) Poems

Translations from Heine and Other Verses. 1882.

Measured Steps. 1884.

Chambers Twain. 1890.

The Book of the Rhymers' Club. 1892. [Contains 5 pieces by Radford; The Second Book, 1894, contains 9 pieces.]

Old and New: a Collection of Poems. 1895.

A Collection of Poems. 1906.

Johnson and the Literary Club. [1907.]

Songs in the Whirlwind. 1918. [With A. Radford.]

(b) Other Writings

Syllabus of a Course of Twelve Lectures upon the Method of Art Study. 1885–86. [1885.]

Dante Gabriel Rossetti. [1905.]

SIR WALTER RALEIGH (1861–1922)

[See p. 752 below.]

HARDWICKE DRUMMOND RAWNSLEY (1850–1920)

(a) Poems

A Book of Bristol Sonnets. 1877.

'The Miners' Rescue.' Troedyrhin Colliery, Rhondda Vale, Glamorganshire, April 20, 1877. A Poem. 1877.

Sonnets at the English Lakes. 1881.

Sonnets round the Coast. 1887.

Poems, Ballads and Bucolics. 1890.

Notes for the Nile; together with a Metrical Rendering of the Hymns of Ancient Egypt and of the Precepts of Ptah-Hotep,—the Oldest Book in the World. 1892.

The Undoing of De Harcla. A Ballad of Cumberland. 1892.

Tennyson, and Other Memorial Poems. Glasgow, 1893.

Idylls and Lyrics of the Nile. 1894.

Ballads of Brave Deeds. With a Frontispiece and Preface by G. F. Watts. 1896.

Sonnets in Switzerland and Italy. 1899.

Ballads of the War. 1900.

A Sonnet Chronicle, 1900–1906. Glasgow, 1906.

Poems at Home and Abroad. Glasgow, 1909.

The European War, 1914–1915. Poems. [1915.]

(b) Writings on the English Lake Country

A Coach Drive at the Lakes. Windermere to Keswick. Keswick, 1890.

Literary Associations of the English Lakes. 2 vols. Glasgow, 1894.

Life and Nature at the English Lakes. Glasgow, 1899.

Ruskin and the English Lakes. Glasgow, 1901.

A Rambler's Note-Book at the English Lakes. Glasgow, 1902.

Lake Country Sketches. Glasgow, 1903.

Months at the Lakes. Glasgow, 1906.

Wordsworth. Tennyson. 1906. (Homes and Haunts of Famous Authors.)

Round the Lake Country. Glasgow, 1909.

By Fell and Dale at the English Lakes. Glasgow, 1911.

Chapters at the English Lakes. Glasgow, 1913.

Past and Present at the English Lakes. Glasgow, 1916.

[Rawnsley also pbd a number of sermons, biographies, and miscellaneous works.]

(c) Biography and Criticism

Noble, J. A. Hardwick Drummond Rawnsley. *Miles*, VIII (VII).

Rawnsley, E. F. Canon Rawnsley. An Account of his Life. Glasgow, 1923.

JAMES RHOADES (1841–1923)

(a) Collected Poems

Collected Poems. Ed. L. N. P[arker], 1925.

(b) Poems

Poems. 1870.

Timoleon: a Dramatic Poem. 1875.

The Georgics of Virgil, translated into English Verse. 1881.

Dux Redux; or, a Forest Tangle. A Comedy. 1887.

The Æneid of Virgil, Books I–VI. Translated into English Verse. 1893.

Teresa (a Tragedy in One Act) and Other Poems. 1893.

The Little Flowers of St Francis of Assisi. Rendered into English Verse. 1904; rptd 1925 (World's Classics).

Out of the Silence. 1907.

The Æneid of Vergil; translated into English Verse. 1907.

O Soul of Mine! 1912.

The City of the Fire Gates. 1913.

Words by the Wayside. 1915.

The Poems of Virgil, translated into English Verse. 1921. (World's Classics.)

(c) Other Work

The Training of the Imagination. 1908.

(d) Biography and Criticism

Layard, G. S. James Rhoades (1841–1923). Bookman, LXIV, 1923.

ERIC SUTHERLAND ROBERTSON

(a) Poems

The Dreams of Christ, and Other Verses. Lahore, 1891 (priv. ptd).

From Alleys and Valleys: Verses. 1918.

(b) Other Writings

English Poetesses. A Series of Critical Biographies, with Illustrative Extracts. 1883.

Life of H. W. Longfellow. 1887.

[Robertson also pbd theological and topographical works.]

JAMES LOGIE ROBERTSON (1846–1922)

(a) Poems

Poems. Dundee, 1878.

Orellana and Other Poems. Edinburgh, 1881.

Our Holiday among the Hills. Edinburgh, 1882. [With Janet Logie Robertson.]

Horace in Homespun. By Hugh Haliburton. Edinburgh, 1886; 1925 (adds other Scots poems, with memoir by Janet L. Robertson.) [The last edn was pbd under the author's own name.]

New Songs of Innocence. Edinburgh, 1889.

Ochil Idylls and Other Poems. By Hugh Haliburton. 1891.

Petition to the Deil, and Other War Verses. Paisley, 1917.

(b) Fiction, Essays and Sketches

The White Angel of the Polly Ann and Other Stories. Edinburgh, 1886.

'For Puir Auld Scotland's Sake.' By Hugh Haliburton. Edinburgh, 1887. [Essays on Fergusson, Allan Ramsay, Burns, Authorship of Christ's Kirk on the Green, A Plea for Scottish Literature at the Universities, etc.]

In Scottish Fields. By Hugh Haliburton. 1890. [William Dunbar, 5 Essays on Burns, etc.]

Furth in Field. By Hugh Haliburton. 1895. [Essays on the Life, Language and Literature of Old Scotland, including Thomson and Burns.]

(c) Educational Writings

A History of English Literature for Secondary Schools. Edinburgh, 1894.

Outlines of English Literature for Young Scholars. Edinburgh, 1897.

Nature in Books. A Literary Introduction to Natural Science. 1914.

[Robertson also edited Burns's letters and poems.]

AGNES MARY FRANCES ROBINSON, afterwards DARMESTETER, afterwards DUCLAUX (b. 1857)

(a) Poems

A Handful of Honeysuckle. 1878.

The Crowned Hippolytus of Euripides; with New Poems. 1881.

The New Arcadia, and Other Poems. 1884.

An Italian Garden. A Book of Songs. 1886.

Songs, Ballads, and a Garden Play. 1888.

Poésies, traduites de l'anglais par James Darmesteter. 1888.

Lyrics, selected from the Works of A. M. F. Robinson. 1891.

Retrospect, and Other Poems. 1893.

Collected Poems, Lyrical and Narrative. With a Preface. 1902.
The Return to Nature. Songs and Symbols. 1904.
Images and Meditations. Poems. 1923.

(b) Other Writings

Margaret of Angoulême, Queen of Navarre. 1886.
The End of the Middle Ages. Essays and Questions in History. [1888.]
Marguerites du Temps passé. 1892. [Tales; tr. Eng. May Tomlinson, as A Mediaeval Garland, 1898.]
Froissart. 1894. [In French; tr. Eng. by E. F. Poynter, 1895.]
The Life of Ernest Renan. 1897; tr. French, 1898.
Grands Écrivains d'Outre-Manche. Les Brontë—Thackeray—Les Browning—Rossetti. [1901.]
The Fields of France. Little Essays in Descriptive Sociology. 1903; 1905 (enlarged).
The French Procession: a Pageant of Great Writers. 1909.
The French Ideal. Pascal, Fénelon, and Other Essays. 1911.
A Short History of France, from Caesar's Invasion to the Battle of Waterloo. 1918.
Twentieth Century French Writers. Reviews and Reminiscences. [1920.]
Victor Hugo. [1921.]
The Life of Racine. 1925.
Victor Hugo. Paris, 1925.
Portrait of Pascal. 1927.

[Madame Duclaux has also written introductions to edns of Browning (in French), Mrs Browning, Madame de Sévigné (in both French and English), to Renan's Souvenirs et Impressions, to the Journal of Marie Lenéru and to two books by her first husband, James Darmesteter, whose Nouvelles Études anglaises she translated in 1896.]

(c) Biography and Criticism

Robertson, E. S. English Poetesses. 1883, pp. 376–81.
Watson, Sir W. The Poetry of Agnes Mary Frances Robinson. Academy, XXXIX, 1890, p. 179.
Symons, A. A. Mary F. Darmesteter. Miles, VIII (VII).
Lynch, H. The Writings of A. Mary F. Robinson. Fortnightly Rev. LXXVII, 1902.

JAMES RENNELL RODD, BARON RENNELL (b. 1858)

(a) Poems

Newdigate Prize Poem. Raleigh. [1880.]
Songs in the South. 1881.

Poems in Many Lands. 1883; 1886.
Feda, with Other Poems, chiefly Lyrical. 1886.
The Unknown Madonna and Other Poems. 1888.
The Violet Crown, and Songs of England. 1891; 1913 ('with several new poems').
Ballads of the Fleet, and Other Poems. 1897; 1901 ('with several additional pieces').
Myrtle and Oak. 1902.
Love, Worship and Death: some Renderings from the Greek Anthology. 1916.
Trentaremi, and Other Moods. 1923.

(b) Other Works

Frederick, Crown Prince and Emperor. A Biographical Sketch. With an Introduction by H.M. the Empress Frederick. 1888.
Sir Walter Raleigh. 1889.
The Customs and Lore of Modern Greece. 1892.
The Princes of Achaia and the Chronicles of Morea: a study of Greece in the Middle Ages. 2 vols. 1907.
Social and Diplomatic Memories. 3 sers. 1922–5.
Homer's Ithaca. A Vindication of Tradition. 1927.
Diplomacy. 1929.
Rome of the Renaissance and of To-Day. 1932.

[Lord Rennell has also written several pamphlets and introductions.]

(c) Biography and Criticism

Williams, F. H. The Poems of Rennell Rodd. American, V, 1882.
Miles, A. H. Rennell Rodd. Miles, VIII (VII).

GEORGE JOHN ROMANES (1848–1894)

Poems. 1889 (priv. ptd).
A Selection from the Poems of G. J. Romanes; with an Introduction by T. H. Warren. 1896.

[Romanes wrote chiefly on physiology and biology, and produced several works on his theological standpoint; see p. 872 below.]

GEORGE RUSSELL (1867–1935)

[See p. 1058 below.]

WILLIAM SHARP (1855–1905)

[See p. 552 below.]

DORA SIGERSON SHORTER (1866–1918)

[See p. 1057 below.]

GEORGE AUGUSTUS SIMCOX (b. 1841)

(a) Poems

Prometheus Unbound. A Tragedy. 1867.
Poems and Romances. 1869.

(b) Other Works

Recollections of a Rambler. 1874.
A History of Latin Literature from Ennius to Boethius. 2 vols. 1883.

[Simcox also edited the Greek Testament, Demosthenes, Juvenal and Thucydides. For his life and writings and a selection from his poems, see A. H. Miles, *Miles*, VIII (VII).]

JOSEPH SKIPSEY (1832–1903)
(a) Poems

Poems, Songs and Ballads. 1862.
The Collier Lad, and Other Lyrics. 1864 (priv. ptd).
Poems. 1871.
A Book of Miscellaneous Lyrics. Bedlington, 1878; 1881 (rev. as A Book of Lyrics, including Songs, Ballads and Chants).
Carols from the Coal-fields: and Other Songs and Ballads. 1886. [With a biographical note on Skipsey by R. S. Watson.]
Songs and Lyrics, Collected and Revised. 1892.
[Skipsey also edited the first 6 vols. of the 'Canterbury Poets.']

(b) Biography and Criticism

Watts[-Dunton], T. Joseph Skipsey's Miscellaneous Lyrics. Athenaeum, 16 Nov. 1878.
Lewin, W. Joseph Skipsey's Songs and Lyrics. Academy, XLII, 1892, p. 147.
Watson, R. S. Joseph Skipsey: his Life and Work. [1908.]
Runciman, J. F. Joseph Skipsey, Poet of the Northumbrian Pits. Living Age, CCLXII, 1909.
Miles, A. H. Joseph Skipsey. *Miles*, v.
Evans, B. I. English Poetry of the Later Nineteenth Century. 1933. [Ch. xvi.]

DOUGLAS BROOKE WHEELTON SLADEN (b. 1856)

Frithjof and Ingebjorg, and Other Poems. 1882.
Australian Lyrics. Melbourne, 1883.
A Poetry of Exiles, and Other Poems. 1884 (2 vols. announced, but only 1 appeared); 1885 (2nd edn rev. Vol. I only).
A Summer Christmas, and a Sonnet upon the S.S. Ballaarat. 1884.
In Cornwall and Across the Sea; with Poems written in Devonshire. 1885.
Edward the Black Prince. An Epic Drama. 1887.
A Ballad for the Tercentenary of the Spanish Armada. Penzance, 1888.
Lestee the Loyalist. A Romance of the Founding of Canada. Tokio, 1890.

[Sladen has also pbd novels, biographies and books of travel, and Twenty Years of my Life, 1915, and My Long Life, 1939.]

JAMES KENNETH STEPHEN (1859–1892)
(a) Poems

Lapsus Calami. Cambridge, 1891; 1891 (3rd edn, with considerable omissions and addns).
Quo Musa Tendis? Cambridge, 1891.
Lapsus Calami and Other Verses. With Introduction by Sir Herbert Stephen. 1896.
Select Poems. 1926. (Augustan Books of Modern Poetry.)

(b) Critical and Legal Writings

International Law and International Relations. 1884.
The Living Languages. A Defence of the Compulsory Study of Greek at Cambridge. Cambridge, 1891.

(c) Biography and Criticism

Miles, A. H. J. K. Stephen. *Miles*, IX (X).
J. K. S. Academy, 19 Aug. 1905.
Benson, A. C. The Leaves of the Tree: Studies in Biography. 1911.
Evans, B. I. English Poetry in the Later Nineteenth Century. 1933. [Ch. xi.]

JOSEPH ASHBY STERRY (b. 1838)
(a) Poems

Boudoir Ballads. 1876.
The Lazy Minstrel. 1886; 1888 (4th edn).
A Tale of the Thames. With Illustrations in Verse by the Author. 1896.
The River Rhymer. 1913.

(b) Other Writings

Katharine and Petruchio; or, The Shaming of the True. 1870.
The Shuttlecock Papers. A Book for an Idle Hour. 1873.
Tiny Travels, 1874.
[Sterry also pbd other novels and humorous works.]

(c) Biography and Criticism

Miles, A. H. Ashby Sterry. *Miles*, IX (X).

ROBERT LOUIS STEVENSON (1850–1894)
[See p. 520 below.]

SAMUEL JOHN STONE (1839–1900)
(a) Poems

Lyra Fidelium. Twelve Hymns on the Twelve Articles of the Apostles' Creed. 1866.
The Knight of Intercession and Other Poems. 1872; [1881] (5th edn, enlarged).

Sonnets of the Sacred Year. [1875.]
Order of the Consecutive Church Service for Children, with Original Hymns by S. J. Stone. [1884.]
Hymns. [1886.]
The Rationalistic Chicken. [1890.]
Lays of Iona, and Other Poems. 1897.
Poems and Hymns. With Memoir by F. G. Ellerton. 1903.

[Stone also pbd a few sermons, tracts, etc.]

(b) Biography and Criticism

Miles, A. H. Samuel John Stone. *Miles*, x (XII).
Kernahan, C. The Noblest Man I have known: S. J. Stone, the Hymn-Writer. London Quart. Rev. CXXIV, 1915.

JOHN ADDINGTON SYMONDS (1840–1893)

(a) Bibliography

Babington, P. L. A Bibliography of the Writings of J. A. Symonds. 1925.

(b) Poems

The Escorial. Oxford, 1860. [Newdigate Prize Poem.]
Seven Pamphlets. N.d. [A collection of poems, anon. and priv. ptd over several years, bound together by Symonds in 1880. Largely rptd in Many Moods.]
Many Moods. 1878.
New and Old. 1880.
Animi Figura. 1882. [Sonnets.]
Fragilia Labilia. 1884 (priv. ptd); Portland, Maine, 1902.
Vagabunduli Libellus. 1884. [Sonnets.]
Miscellanies: Parts 1 and 2. 1885 (priv. ptd). [Poems and translations afterwards largely rptd in accessible works.]
Midnight at Baïae. 1893. [Originally ptd in Seven Pamphlets.]

(c) Translations

The Sonnets of M. A. Buonarrotti and T. Campanella. 1878.
Wine, Women and Song. 1884. [Verse trns of Latin songs of mediaeval students with long preface on Goliardic literature.]
Autobiography of Benvenuto Cellini. 2 vols. 1888.
The Autobiography of Count Carlo Gozzi. 2 vols. 1890. [Translation accompanied by long essay on Italian impromptu comedy.]

(d) Other Writings

The Renaissance. Oxford, 1863. [A prize essay.]
Memoir of J. A. Symonds, M.D., F.R.S. 1871. [Prefixed to Miscellanies by the elder Symonds.]

Introduction to the Study of Dante. 1872. [Lectures given at Clifton.]
The Renaissance of Modern Europe. A Review of the Scientific, Artistic, Rationalistic, Revolutionary Revival, dating from the 15th Century. A Lecture. 1872.
Studies of the Greek Poets. 2 sers. 1873–6. [Lectures delivered at Clifton.]
Sketches in Italy and Greece. 1874. [Largely rptd from Cornhill Mag. and Fortnightly Rev.]
Renaissance in Italy. 7 vols. 1875–86; 1893 (abridged edn).
Shelley. 1878. (English Men of Letters ser.)
Sketches and Studies in Italy. 1879. [Largely rptd from Cornhill Mag. and Fortnightly Rev.]
Italian By-ways. 1883. [Largely rptd from Cornhill Mag., Fortnightly Rev. and Fraser's Mag.]
A Problem in Greek Ethics: being an Inquiry into the Problem of Sexual Inversion. 1883 (priv. ptd).
Shakspere's Predecessors. 1884.
Life of Ben Jonson. 1886.
Sir Philip Sidney. 1886. (English Men of Letters ser.)
Essays, Speculative and Suggestive. 2 vols. 1890. [Four essays on style, The Philosophy of Evolution, Elizabethan and Victorian Poetry, and Discussions on Literary Aesthetics.]
A Problem in Modern Ethics. [1891] (anon. and priv. ptd). [Partly rptd in Sexual Inversion, by Havelock Ellis and J. A. Symonds, 1897.]
Our Life in the Swiss Highlands. 1892. [Partly rptd from Fortnightly Rev. and with 5 papers by Margaret Symonds.]
In the Key of Blue. 1893. [E. Cracroft Lefroy, Fletcher's Valentinian, La Bête Humaine, Culture, The Lyrism of the Romantic Drama, etc.]
The Life of Michelangelo Buonarroti. 2 vols. 1893.
Walt Whitman: a Study. 1893.
Blank Verse. 1894. [Originally pbd in small type as appendix to Sketches and Studies in Italy.]
On the English Family of Symonds. Oxford, 1894 (priv. ptd). [Later included in the Life of Symonds, vol. II, by H. F. Brown.]
Giovanni Boccaccio, Man and Author. 1895.
Sexual Inversion. 1897. [In Collaboration with Havelock Ellis. Includes A Problem in Greek Ethics, some portions of A Problem in Modern Ethics, and much new matter.]
Sketches and Studies in Italy and Greece. Ed. H. F. Brown, 3 sers. 1898. [Rpt of Sketches in Italy and Greece, Sketches and Studies in Italy and Italian Byways.]

Last and First. Being two Essays: The New Spirit and Arthur Hugh Clough. New York, 1919. [Rptd from Fortnightly Rev. 1893 and 1868.]

Letters and Papers. Ed. H. F. Brown, 1923.

(e) Biography and Criticism

Men and Women Who Write. No. 1. Mr John Addington Symonds. Pall Mall Gazette, 17 May 1890.

Warren, Sir T. H. John Addington Symonds. Miles, VI.

Brown, H. F. J. A. Symonds. A Biography Compiled from his Papers and Correspondence. 2 vols. 1895.

Symons, A. Studies in Two Literatures. 1897.

—— A Study of John Addington Symonds. Fortnightly Rev. Feb. 1924.

Harrison, Tennyson, Ruskin, Mill and Other Literary Estimates. 1899.

Symonds, M. Last Days of J. A. Symonds. 1906.

—— Out of the Past. 1925.

Brooks, Van W. John Addington Symonds: a Biographical Study. 1914.

ARTHUR SYMONS (b. 1865)

(a) Bibliographies

Danielson, H. Bibliographies of Modern Authors. 1921.

Welby, T. E. Arthur Symons. 1925. [Bibliography appended.]

(b) Collected Works

Poems. 2 vols. 1902.

Poésies. Bruges, 1907. [Collected, and for the most part translated, with an essay on Symons, by Louis Thomas.]

The Works. 9 vols. 1924. [Incomplete.]

(c) Poems

Days and Nights. 1889; 1924 (with original notice by Walter Pater).

Silhouettes. 1892; 1896 (rev.).

London Nights. 1895; 1897 (rev.).

Amoris Victima. 1897.

Images of Good and Evil. 1899.

The Loom of Dreams. 1901 (priv. ptd).

A Book of Twenty Songs. 1905.

The Fool of the World, and Other Poems. 1906.

Knave of Hearts, 1894–1908. 1913.

Lesbia and Other Poems. New York, 1920.

Love's Cruelty. 1923.

From Catullus. Chiefly Concerning Lesbia. 1924. [Latin and English.]

Jezebel Mort, and Other Poems. 1931.

(d) Plays

Tragedies. 1916. [The Death of Agrippina; Cleopatra in Judaea; The Harvesters.]

Tristran and Iseult. 1917.

The Toy Cart. 1919.

Cesare Borgia, Iseult of Brittany, The Toy Cart. New York, 1920.

(e) Translations

Zola. L'Assommoir. 1894 (included in the works of Zola); 1928 (separately, with an Introduction by Symons).

Verhaeren. The Dawn. 1898; 1916 (in the Plays of Émile Verhaeren).

d'Annunzio. The Child of Pleasure. 1898. [Only the verses translated by Symons.]

—— The Dead City. 1900.

—— Giocunda. 1901.

—— Francesca da Rimini. 1902.

Baudelaire. Poems in Prose. 1905. [Subsequently included in Les Fleurs du Mal, 1925.]

—— Les Fleurs du Mal, Petits Poèmes en Prose, Les Paradis artificiels. 1925.

—— The Letters of Charles Baudelaire to his Mother. 1928.

Pignata. The Adventures of Giuseppe Pignata. 1930.

(f) Critical and Other Writings

An Introduction to the Study of Browning. 1886; 1906 (rev. and enlarged).

Studies in Two Literatures. 1897. [Studies in the Elizabethan Drama, Studies in Contemporary Literature, Notes and Impressions; English Writers, French Writers, R. Jefferies, J. Thomson, T. G. Hake, J. A. Symonds, etc.]

Aubrey Beardsley. 1898; 1905 (rev.).

The Symbolist Movement in Literature. 1899.

Cities. 1903. [Rome, Venice, Naples, Seville, Prague, Moscow, Budapest, Belgrade, Sofia, Constantinople.]

Plays, Acting and Music. 1903; 1909 (rev.). [Technique and the Artist, Nietzsche on Tragedy, Dolmetsch, Bernhardt, Coquelin and Molière, Stephen Phillips, Pachmann, Duse, etc.]

Studies in Prose and Verse. 1904. [Partly rptd from Studies in Two Literatures, Balzac, Mérimée, Gautier, De Quincey, Hawthorne, Pater, W. Morris, Maupassant, Daudet, Crackanthorpe, R. Buchanan, Yeats, A. Dobson, Dowson, Gorki, etc.]

Spiritual Adventures. 1905. [A Prelude to Life, Esther Kahn, Christian Trevalga, An Autumn City, Seaward Lackland, and other Sketches.]

Studies in Seven Arts. 1906. [Rodin, Painting of the Nineteenth Century, Moreau, Watts, Whistler, Beethoven, Wagner, R. Strauss, A Symbolist Farce, The World as Ballet, etc.]

Cities of Italy. 1907.

Great Acting in English. 1907 (priv. ptd).

William Blake. 1907.

London. A Book of Aspects. 1909 (priv. ptd).

The Romantic Movement in English Poetry. 1909.

Dante Gabriel Rossetti. 1910.

Figures of Several Centuries. 1916. [Augustine, Lamb, Villon, Casanova, Donne, Poe, Beddoes, Flaubert, Léon Cladel, Hardy, Huysmans, Patmore, etc.]

Cities and Sea-Coasts and Islands. 1917. [Includes London: a Book of Aspects, Seville, Painters of Seville, Toledo, Núñez de Arce, Dieppe, Cornwall, Cornish Sketches, Winchelsea, Aran, etc.]

Colour Studies in Paris. 1918. [Montmartre and the Latin Quarter, Yvette Guilbert, La Mélinite, Leon Bloy, Victor Hugo and Words, Pétrus Borel, Notes on Paris and Paul Verlaine, Odilon Redon, etc.]

Charles Baudelaire. 1920.

Studies in the Elizabethan Drama. 1920. [Rptd, with addns, from Studies in Two Literatures, Middleton and Rowley, Shakespeare, Massinger, John Day, etc.]

Carlo Goldoni. An Essay. [Prefixed to The Good-Humoured Ladies, translated by Richard Aldington, 1923.]

Dramatis Personae. Indianopolis, 1923; 1925 (corrected). [Conrad, Emily Brontë, Maeterlinck, Francis Thompson, Decadent Movement in Literature, English and French Fiction, Russian Ballets, Réjane, Da Vinci, etc.]

The Café Royal, and Other Essays. 1923. [Proust, Some American Poets, Marlowe, Rimbaud and his Biographer, W. S. Blunt, Duse.]

Notes on Joseph Conrad. With Some Unpublished Letters. 1925.

Studies on Modern Painters. New York, 1925. [Painting of the Nineteenth Century, Genius of Augustus John, Whistler, Gordon Craig, Watts, French Pictures at the International Exhibition.]

Eleonora Duse. 1926. [Distinct from the essay in The Café Royal.]

Parisian Nights. 1926. [Lautrec and the Moulin-Rouge, Aristide Bruant, Guys, Forain, Daumier, On Cats and Clowns, etc.]

A Study of Thomas Hardy. 1927.

Studies in Strange Souls. 1929. [Rossetti and Swinburne.]

From Toulouse-Lautrec to Rodin, with some Personal Impressions. 1929. [Dégas, Guys, Daumier, Forain, de Groux, Monticelli, Beardsley, Whistler and Manet, etc.]

Confessions. A Study in Pathology. New York, 1930.

A Study of Oscar Wilde. 1930.

Mes Souvenirs. Chapelle-Réanville, 1931. [Written in English. Verlaine, Bohemian Chelsea, The Magic of the East.]

Wanderings. 1931. [In France, Italy, Switzerland, Germany, Constantinople and Sofia and at Home.]

[Mr Symons has also pbd edns and anthologies of the English poets.]

(g) Biography and Criticism

Waugh, A. Tradition and Change. 1919. [Has chs. on Symons's tragedies and criticism.]

Welby, T. E. Arthur Symons. 1925.

Yeats, W. B. Autobiographies. 1926. [Particularly the ch. 'The Tragic Generation.']

Wildi, M. Arthur Symons als Kritiker der Literatur. Heidelberg, 1929.

JOHN TODHUNTER (1839–1916)

[See p. 1054 below.]

GRAHAM ROSAMUND TOMSON, later MARRIOTT WATSON (1860–1911)

(a) Poems

The Bird-Bride; a Volume of Ballads and Sonnets. 1889.

A Summer Night. 1891.

The Patchwork Quilt: A Poem. 1891.

Vespertilia and Other Verses. 1895.

After Sunset. 1904.

The Poems. 1912. [Contains many poems pbd for the first time.]

(b) Essays and Fiction

The Art of the House. 1897. [Essays on furnishing and decoration.]

An Island Rose. 1900. [A novel.]

The Heart of a Garden. 1905. [Essays and poems.]

HENRY DUFF TRAILL (1842–1912)

[See p. 755 below.]

HERBERT TRENCH (1865–1923)

[See p. 1057 below.]

KATHARINE TYNAN (1861–1931)

[See p. 1057 below.]

CHRISTINA CATHERINE FRASER TYTLER, afterwards LIDDELL (b. 1848)

(a) Poems

Songs in Minor Keys. 1881.

Songs of the Twilight Hours. [1909.]

(b) Novels

Jasmine Leigh. 1871.
Jonathan. A Novel. 2 vols. 1876.
The Other Half of the World. [1881.]

[Mrs Liddell wrote some 8 novels or collections of short stories altogether, and a few other works.]

(c) Biography and Criticism

Miles, A. H. C. C. Fraser Tytler-Liddell. *Miles*, (IX), 1907.

MARGARET VELEY (1843–1887)

For Percival. A Novel. 3 vols. 1878.
Damocles. A Novel. 3 vols. 1882.
Mitchelhurst Place: a Novel. 2 vols. 1884.
A Garden of Memories. Mrs Austin. Lizzie's Bargain. 2 vols. 1887.
A Marriage of Shadows, and Other Poems. With a Biographical Preface by Leslie Stephen. 1888.

SAMUEL WADDINGTON (1844–1923)

(a) Poems

Sonnets and Other Verse. 1884.
A Century of Sonnets. 1889.
Poems. 1896.
Collected Poems. 1902.
[Collected] Sonnets. 1906.

(b) Anthologies

English Sonnets by Living Writers. 1881; 1884 (enlarged). [With a long note on the history of the sonnet.]
English Sonnets by Poets of the Past. 1882.
The Sonnets of Europe: a Volume of Translations. Selected and Arranged, with Notes. 1886.

(c) Other Writings

Arthur Hugh Clough; a Monograph. 1883.
Chapters of my Life: an Autobiography. 1909.
Some Views respecting a Future Life. 1917.

(d) Biography and Criticism

Le Gallienne, R. Samuel Waddington. *Miles*, VIII (VII).

ARTHUR EDWARD WAITE (b. 1860)

Israfel. Letters, Visions and Poems. 1886.
A Soul's Comedy. 1887.
Lucasta: Parables and Poems. 1889.
A Book of Mystery and Vision. 1902.
Strange Houses of Sleep. 1906.
Collected Poems. 2 vols. 1914.
The Book of the Holy Grail. 1921. [Poems.]

[Mr Waite has also written on alchemy, freemasonry, the Rosicrucians and cognate subjects.]

FREDERICK WILLIAM ORDE WARD (1843–1922)

(a) Poems

The Cry of the Woman-Child. 1886. [This and the following, up to and including English Roses, were pbd under the pseudonym 'Harald Williams.']
Women must Weep. 1888.
'Twixt Kiss and Lip, or, Under the Sword. 1890.
Confessions of a Poet. 1894.
Matin Bells and Scarlet and Gold. 1897.
English Roses. 1899.
New Century Hymns for the Christian Year. [1901.]
The Prisoner of Love. 1904.
The Last Crusade: Patriotic Poems. [1917.]
Songs for Sufferers, from a Sick-Room. [1917.]
Selected Poems by F. W. Orde Ward. Ed. C. O. O. Ward and R. Markland, 1924.

[Ward also pbd theological works and a short paper on Shelley.]

(b) Biography and Criticism

Miles, A. H. Frederick William Orde Ward. *Miles*, (XII).
TLS. 18 Dec. 1924. [Review of Selected Poems.]

JOHN BYRNE LEICESTER WARREN, BARON DE TABLEY (1835–1895)

(a) Selected Poems

Poems, Dramatic and Lyrical. 2 sers. 1893–5.
Collected Poems. 1903.
Select Poems. Ed. J. Drinkwater, 1924.

(b) Separate Poems

Poems. 1859. [With G. Fortescue.]
Ballads and Metrical Sketches. 1860.
The Threshold of Atrides. 1861.
Glimpses of Antiquity. 1862.
Praeterita. 1863.
Eclogues and Monodramas. 1864.
Studies in Verse. 1865.
Philoctetes: a Metrical Drama. 1866.
Orestes: a Metrical Drama. 1867.
Rehearsals: a Book of Verses. 1870.
Searching the Net: a Book of Verses. 1873.
The Soldier of Fortune: a Tragedy. 1876.
Orpheus in Thrace, and Other Poems. Ed. E., Lady Leighton-Warren, 1901.

(c) Other Works

An Essay on Greek Federal Coinage. 1863.
On Some Coins of Lycia under the Rhodian Domination, and of the Lycian League. 1863.
A Screw Loose: a Novel. 1868.
Ropes of Sand: a Novel. 1869.
A Guide to the Study of Book Plates. 1880.

The Flora of Cheshire. Ed. S. Moore, 1899. [Includes letters and memoir by Sir M. G. Duff.]

(d) Biography and Criticism

Le Gallienne, R. The Poetry of Lord de Tabley. Nineteenth Century, XXXIII, 1892.

Miles, A. H. Lord de Tabley. *Miles*, VI.

Monkhouse, C. The Poetry of Lord de Tabley. Academy, XLVII, 1894.

Gosse, Sir E. Lord de Tabley. Contemporary Rev. LXIX, 1895. [Rptd in Critical Kit-Kats, 1896.]

Watts[-Dunton], T. Lord de Tabley. Athenaeum, 30 Nov. 1895. [Rptd in Old Familiar Faces, 1916.]

Hearn, L. Life and Literature. New York, 1917.

Bridges, R. Collected Essays, VII. Lord de Tabley's Poems. Oxford, 1931.

Lord de Tabley. TLS. 25 April 1935.

SIR THOMAS HERBERT WARREN (1853–1930)

By Severn Sea, and Other Poems. Oxford, 1897; 1898.

SIR WILLIAM WATSON (1858–1935)
(a) Poems

The Prince's Quest and Other Poems. 1880 (re-issued 1892).

Epigrams of Art, Life and Nature. Liverpool, 1884. [With a note on the epigram.]

Wordsworth's Grave, and Other Poems. 1890; 1892 (as Poems; adds 26 short poems).

Lachrymae Musarum. 1892 (priv. ptd); 1892 (adds other poems). [Lachrymae Musarum is a collection of verses on the death of Tennyson.]

Shelley's Centenary. 1892 (priv. ptd).

The Eloping Angels. A Caprice. 1893.

Odes and Other Poems. 1894.

The Father of the Forest, and Other Poems. 1895.

Ode for the Centenary of the Death of Burns. 1895.

The Purple East. A Series of Sonnets on England's Desertion of Armenia. 1896.

The Lost Eden. New York, 1897.

The Year of Shame. With an Introduction by the Bishop of Hereford. 1897.

The Hope of the World, and Other Poems. 1898.

Collected Poems. 1898.

New Poems. Greenfield, Massachusetts, 1902; 1909.

Ode on the Day of the Coronation of King Edward VII. 1902.

Selected Poems. 1903.

For England. Poems written during Estrangement. 1904.

[Collected] Poems. With Introduction by J. A. Spender. 2 vols. 1905.

Sable and Purple, with Other Poems. 1910.

The Heralds of the Dawn. 1912. [A play. Includes a bibliography of Watson's writings.]

The Muse in Exile. 1913. [With an address on the poet's place in the scheme of life.]

The Man Who Saw, and Other Poems arising out of the War. 1917.

Retrogression and Other Poems. 1917.

The Superhuman Antagonists, and Other Poems. 1919.

Ireland Arisen. 1921.

Ireland Unfreed. 1921.

A Hundred Poems by Sir W. Watson, selected from his Various Volumes. 1922.

Poems Brief and New. 1925.

Poems, selected, with Notes, by the Author. 1928.

The Poems of Sir William Watson, 1878–1935. 1936.

(b) Other Writings

Excursions in Criticism. Being some Prose Recreations of a Rhymer. 1893. [Keats and Mr Colvin, R. H. Hutton, Saintsbury, Edwin Waugh, A. Dobson, Meredith, Lowell, Coleridge, etc.]

Pencraft: a Plea for the Older Ways. 1917.

(c) Criticism

Noble, J. A. William Watson. *Miles*, VIII (VII).

Archer, W. Poets of the Younger Generation. 1902.

Macfie, R. C. Sir William Watson's Poems. Bookman, March 1923.

Kernahan, C. Five More Famous Living Poets. 1928. [Has a ch. on Watson.]

Harper, G. M. Literary Appreciations. Indianapolis, 1937.

THEODORE WATTS-DUNTON (1836–1914)

[See p. 756 below.]

AUGUSTA WEBSTER, née DAVIES (1837–1894)
(a) Selection

Selections from the Verse of Augusta Webster. 1893.

(b) Poems

Blanche Lisle, and Other Poems. By Cecil Home [*i.e.* Augusta Webster]. 1860.

Lilian Gray. 1864.

Dramatic Studies. 1866.

The Prometheus Bound of Æschylus, literally translated. 1866.

The Medea of Euripides, literally translated into English Verse. 1867.

A Woman Sold, and Other Poems. 1867.

Portraits. 1870; 1893 (enlarged).

The Auspicious Day. 1872. [A play.]

Yu-Pe-Ya's Lute. A Chinese Tale in English Verse. 1874.

Disguises. A Drama. 1879.
A Book of Rhyme. 1881.
In a Day. A Drama. 1882.
The Sentence. A Drama. 1887.
Mother and Daughter. An Uncompleted
Sonnet-Sequence. With an Introductory
Note by W. M. Rossetti. To which are added
Seven, her Only Other, Sonnets. 1895.

(c) Other Works

A Housewife's Opinions. [1878.]
Parliamentary Franchise for Women Rate-
payers. Reprinted from the Examiner. 1878.
Daffodil and the Croäxaxicans: a Romance of
History. 1884. [A story for children.]

(d) Biography and Criticism

Forman, H. B. Our Living Poets. 1871,
pp. 169–84.
Robertson, E. S. English Poetesses. 1883,
pp. 354–8.
Obituary. Athenaeum, 15 Sept. 1894.

OSCAR WILDE (1856–1900)

[See p. 620 below.]

SARAH WILLIAMS (1841–1868)
[Pseudonym 'Sadie']

Twilight Hours: a Legacy of Verse. With a
Memoir by E. H. Plumptre. 1868; ed. H. A.
Page, 1872 (enlarged).

[For biography and criticism, and a selection from the poems, see A. H. Japp, *Miles*,
VII (IV).]

JAMES CHAPMAN WOODS

A Child of the People, and Other Poems.
1879. [Woods also pbd guide-books, travel
books, etc.]

MARGARET LOUISA WOODS (b. 1856)

[See p. 563 below.]

PHILIP STANHOPE WORSLEY (1835–1866)
(a) Poems and Translations

The Temple of Janus. A [Newdigate] Prize
Poem. 1857.
The Odyssey of Homer translated into English
Verse. 1861.
Poems and Translations. 1863; ed. E. Worsley,
1875 (enlarged).
The Iliad of Homer [the first 12 bks] trans-
lated into English Verse. 1865.

(b) Biography and Criticism

S[pedding], J. Homeric Translations. Fraser's
Mag. LXV, 1862.
Austin, S. Obituary. Athenaeum, 19 May
1866.
Obituary. GM. June 1866.

THEODORE WRATISLAW (1871–1933)
(a) Writings

Love's Memorial. Rugby, 1892 (anon.).
Some Verses. Rugby, 1892 (anon.).
Caprices. Poems. 1893.
The Pity of Love. A Tragedy. 1895.
Orchids. Poems. 1896.
Love in a Mist. Adapted as a Comedietta by
Mrs Francis Ward. Worcester, 1903.
Two Ballads transcribed from the French of
Master François Villon. Rugby, 1933.
Selected Poems of Theodore Wratislaw. Ed.
(with brief biographical note) J. Gaws-
worth, 1935.

[Wratislaw also pbd a study of Swinburne,
1900.]

(b) Biography and Criticism

Ellis, S. M. A Poet of the Nineties: Theodore
Wratislaw. [In Mainly Victorian, 1925.]

WILLIAM BUTLER YEATS (1865–1939)

[See p. 1059 below.]

R. D. C. and H. B. G.

3. PROSE FICTION

I. BIBLIOGRAPHIES, HISTORIES AND CRITICAL STUDIES

(1) BIBLIOGRAPHIES

Baker, E. A. and Packman, J. A Guide to the Best Fiction in English. 1913; 1932 (rev. and enlarged edn).

Nield, J. Guide to Historical Novels. 1913.

Parrish, M. L. Victorian Lady Novelists. 1933. [George Eliot, Mrs Gaskell, the Brontës.]

Block, A. The English Novel, 1740–1850. A Catalogue including Prose Romances, Short Stories and Translations of Foreign Fiction. 1939.

(2) HISTORIES AND SURVEYS

Brandes, G. Hovedströmninger i det 19. Aarhundredes Literatur. Copenhagen, 1875; tr. Eng. 6 vols. 1901–5.

Tuckerman, B. A History of English Prose Fiction. 1882.

Lanier, S. The English Novel. New York, 1883.

Minto, W. The Literature of the Georgian Era. 1894. [Contains chs. on the novelists from Mrs Radcliffe to Bulwer-Lytton.]

Saintsbury, G. A History of Nineteenth Century Literature. 1896.

—— The English Novel. 1913.

Women Novelists of Queen Victoria's Reign. A Book of Appreciations, 1897. [By A. Sergeant, C. M. Yonge and others.]

Beers, H. A. A History of English Romanticism in the Eighteenth Century. New York, 1898, 1910 (rev.).

—— A History of English Romanticism in the Nineteenth Century. New York, 1901.

Cross, W. L. The Development of the English Novel. New York, 1899.

Chambers' Cyclopaedia of English Literature. Ed. D. Patrick, 3 vols. 1901–3.

Cazamian, L. Le Roman social en Angleterre (1830–1850). Paris, 1904.

Walker, H. The Literature of the Victorian Era. Cambridge, 1910.

Elton, O. A Survey of English Literature, 1780–1830. 2 vols. 1912.

—— A Survey of English Literature, 1830–1880. 2 vols. 1920.

Chesterton, G. K. The Victorian Age in Literature. [1913.] (Home University Lib.)

The Cambridge History of English Literature. Vols. XI–XIV, 1914–6.

Phelps, W. L. The Advance of the English Novel. New York, 1916. [Chs. iv–vii.]

Baker, E. A. The History of the English Novel. 9 vols. 1924–38. [Vols. v–ix.]

Legouis, E. and Cazamian, L. Histoire de la Littérature anglaise. Paris, 1924; tr. Eng. 2 vols. 1926–7.

Weygandt, C. A Century of the English Novel. New York, 1925.

Prothero, R. E. (Baron Ernle). The Light Reading of Our Ancestors. Chapters on the Growth of the English Novel. 1927. [To Scott.]

Wild, F. Die englische Literatur der Gegenwart seit 1870. Drama und Roman. Wiesbaden, 1928.

Tompkins, J. M. S. The Popular Novel in England, 1770–1800. 1932.

Edgar, P. The Art of the Novel. New York, 1933. [Chs. vii–xvi.]

(3) CRITICAL ESSAYS AND SPECIAL STUDIES

[The collections of critical essays listed pp. 7–12 above will also be found to include many occasional studies of 19th cent. novelists.]

Famous Reviews. Ed. R. B. Johnson, 1914.

Novelists on Novels. Ed. R. B. Johnson, 1928.

Stephen, Sir J. F. The Relation of Novels to Life. [In Cambridge Essays, 1855.]

Jeaffreson, J. C. Novels and Novelists. 2 vols. 1858.

Masson, D. British Novelists and their Styles. Cambridge, 1859.

Sensation Novels. Quarterly Rev. CXIII, 1863.

Senior, N. W. Essays on Fiction. 1864. [Scott, Lytton, Thackeray.]

Watt, J. C. Great Novelists. Scott, Thackeray, Dickens, Lytton. Edinburgh, 1880.

Besant, Sir W. The Art of Fiction. 1884.

James, Henry. The Art of Fiction. [In Partial Portraits, 1888.]

Howells, W. D. Criticism and Fiction. Boston, 1891.

Saintsbury, G. The Present State of the English Novel. [In Miscellaneous Essays, 1892.]

—— Corrected Impressions. Studies in Victorian Writers. 1895.

Crawford, F. M. The Novel. 1893.

Gosse, Sir E. Questions at Issue. 1893. [The Tyranny of the Novel; The Limits of Realism in Fiction.]

On the Art of Writing Fiction. [1894.] [Essays by Baring-Gould, 'Lanoe Falconer,' L. T. Meade, and others.]

My First Book. Ed. J. K. Jerome, 1894. [Essays by Besant, Payn, Russell, Allen, Hall Caine, Ballantyne, Kipling, Stevenson, Marie Corelli and other novelists.]

Bridges, R. Novels that Every-body read. [In Suppressed Chapters and Other Bookishness, New York, 1895.]

Harrison, F. Studies in Early Victorian Literature. 1895. [Disraeli, Thackeray, Dickens, C. Brontë, C. Kingsley, Trollope, George Eliot.]

Lilly, W. S. Four English Humourists of the Nineteenth Century. 1895. [Dickens, Thackeray, George Eliot, Carlyle.]

Douglas, Sir G. The Blackwood Group. 1897.

Murray, D. C. My Contemporaries in Fiction. 1897. [Dickens—George Moore.]

Traill, H. D. The New Fiction. 1897. [Reprinted essays, mainly on 19th cent. fiction.]

Scudder, V. D. Social Ideals in English Letters. 1898.

Oliphant, J. Victorian Novelists. 1899.

Brownell, W. C. Victorian Prose Masters. New York, 1901.

Machen, A. Hieroglyphics. 1902.

Möbius, H. The Gothic Romance. Leipzig, 1902.

—— Die englischen Rosenkreuzerromane und ihre Vorläufer, während des 18. und 19. Jahrhunderts. Hamburg, 1911.

Courtney, W. L. The Feminine Note in Fiction. 1904.

Williams, A. M. Early Female Novelists. 1904.

Dawson, W. J. Makers of English Fiction. 1905.

Stevenson, R. L. Essays in the Art of Writing. 1905.

'Melville, Lewis.' Victorian Novelists. 1906.

Baker, E. A. History in Fiction. 2 vols. 1907.

Chandler, F. W. The Literature of Roguery. 2 vols. Boston, 1907. [Contains invaluable bibliographies.]

Courtney, W. P. The Secrets of Our National Literature. 1908. [Anon. and pseudonymous fiction.]

Jackson, Holbrook. Great English Novelists. [1908.]

—— The Eighteen-Nineties. A Review of Art and Ideas at the Close of the Nineteenth Century. 1913.

Canby, H. S. The Short Story in English. New York, 1909.

Zeidler, K. J. Beckford, Hope und Morier als Vertreter des orientalischen Romans. Leipzig, 1909.

Dibelius, W. Englische Romankunst. Die Technik des englischen Romans in achtzehnten und zu Anfang des neunzehnten Jahrhunderts. 2 vols. Berlin, 1910.

Phelps, W. L. Essays on Modern Novelists. New York, 1910.

Williams, Harold. Two Centuries of the English Novel. 1911.

—— Modern English Writers. 1918; 1925 (rev. edn).

James, H. The New Novel. [In Notes on Novelists, 1914.]

Binbert, D. Historische Romane vor Walter Scott. Berlin, 1915.

Gregory, A. The French Revolution and the English Novel. 1915.

Waugh, A. Reticence in Literature and Other Papers. 1915. [Contains Fiction in the Nineteenth Century.]

—— Tradition and Change. 1919.

Hearn, L. Interpretations of Literature. 2 vols. 1916. [Vol. i contains 2 chs. on English Fiction in the Nineteenth Century.]

Scarborough, D. The Supernatural in Modern English Fiction. New York, 1917.

Johnson, R. B. Women Novelists. 1918.

Whiteford, R. N. Motives in English Fiction. 1918.

Phillips, W. C. Dickens, Reade and Collins—Sensation Novelists. A Study in the Conditions and Theories of Novel Writing in Victorian England. New York, 1919.

Birkhead, E. The Tale of Terror. 1921.

Ditchfield, P. H. The Parson in Literature. Trans. Royal Soc. Lit. i, 1921.

Lubbock, P. The Craft of Fiction. 1921.

Villard, L. La Femme anglaise au dix-neuvième Siècle et son Évolution d'après le Roman anglais contemporain. Paris, 1921.

Cazamian, M. L. Le Roman et les Idées en Angleterre. [i]: L'Influence de la Science (1860–90). ii: L'Anti-Intellectualisme et l'Esthétisme (1880–1900). Strasburg, 1923–Paris, 1935.

Oster, E. Das Verhältnis von Mutter und Kind im englischen Roman von 1700–1860. Bonn, 1923.

Gutermuth, E. Das Kind im englischen Roman von Richardson bis Dickens. Giessener Beiträge, ii, 1924.

Killen, A. M. Le Roman Terrifiant ou Roman Noir. Paris, 1924.

Speare, M. E. The Political Novel. New York, 1924.

Burdett, O. The Beardsley Period. An Essay in Perspective. 1925.

Ellis, S. M. Mainly Victorian. [1925.] [Short essays—mainly on minor Victorian novelists.]

—— Wilkie Collins, Le Fanu and Others. 1931.

Frierson, W. C. L'Influence du Naturalisme français sur les Romanciers anglais de 1885 à 1900. Paris, [1925].

—— The English Controversy over Realism in Fiction, 1885–95. PMLA. xliii, 1928.

Priestley, J. B. The English Comic Characters. 1925.
—— The English Novel. 1927.
Quiller-Couch, Sir A. T. Charles Dickens and Other Victorians. Cambridge, 1925. [Dickens, Thackeray, Disraeli, Mrs Gaskell, Trollope.]
Walpole, H. The English Novel. 1925.
Wharton, E. The Writing of Fiction. 1925.
Drew, E. The Modern Novel. 1926.
Jansonius, H. Some Aspects of Business Life in Early Victorian Fiction. Amsterdam, 1926.
Williams, O. Some Great English Novels. 1926.
de Vooys, S. The Psychological Element in the English Sociological Novel of the Nineteenth Century. Amsterdam, 1927.
Forster, E. M. Aspects of the Novel. 1927.
Myers, W. L. The Later Realism. A Study of Characterization in the British Novel. Chicago, 1927.
Railo, E. The Haunted Castle. A Study of the Elements of English Romanticism. 1927.
Wortham, H. E. 'The Constant Nymph' and the Musical Novel. Nineteenth Century, Feb. 1927.
Brauchli, J. Der englische Schauerroman um 1800. Weida, 1928.
Collins, A. S. The Profession of Letters, 1780–1832. 1928.
Muir, E. The Structure of the Novel. 1928.
Taylor, H. W. Some Nineteenth Century Critics of Realism. Texas University Bulletin, 8 July 1928.
de la Mare, W. Some Women Novelists of the 'Seventies. [In The Eighteen-Seventies, ed. H. G. Barker, Royal Soc. Lit. 1929.]
Devonshire, M. G. The English Novel in France, 1830–70. 1929.
Proper, C. B. A. Social Elements in English Prose Fiction between 1700 and 1832. Amsterdam, 1929.
Rotter, A. Der Arbeiterroman in England seit 1880. Reichenburg, 1929.
Somervell, D. C. English Thought in the Nineteenth Century. 1929. [The Novelists.]
Cruse, A. The Englishman and his Books in the Early Nineteenth Century. 1930.
—— The Victorians and their Books. 1935.
—— After the Victorians. 1938.
Dane, C. The Writer's Partner. Trans. Royal Soc. Lit. IX, 1930.
Ford, F. M. The English Novel. 1930.
Reid, F. Minor Fiction in the 'Eighties. [In The Eighteen-Eighties, ed. W. de la Mare, Royal Soc. Lit. 1930.]
Gibson, B. H. History from 1800–1832 of English Criticism of Prose Fiction. Urbana, 1931.

Rogers, W. H. Portraits of Romantic Poets in Contemporary Minor Fiction. Western Reserve University Bulletin, XXXIV, 1931.
—— The Reaction against Melodramatic Sentimentality in the English Novel, 1796–1830. PMLA. XLIX, 1934.
Sadleir, M. Bulwer. A Panorama. 1931. [Contains a ch. on The Novel of the Period.]
Baker, J. E. The Novel and the Oxford Movement. Princeton, 1932.
Collins, N. Facts of Fiction. 1932.
Darton, F. J. H. Children's Books in England. Cambridge, 1932.
Leavis, Q. D. Fiction and the Reading Public. 1932.
The Great Victorians. Ed. H. J. and H. Massingham, 1932.
Watt, W. W. Shilling Shockers of the Gothic School. A Study of Chapbook Gothic Romances. Cambridge, U.S.A. 1932.
Singer, G. F. The Epistolary Novel. Philadelphia, 1933.
Cecil, Lord D. Early Victorian Novelists. 1934.
Elwin, M. Victorian Wallflowers. 1934. ['Christopher North'—'Ouida.']
—— Old Gods Falling. 1939. [Moore, Stevenson, Lang, Haggard, etc.]
New Paths in Book Collecting. Ed. J. Carter, 1934. [Yellow books, detective stories, etc.]
Smith, Warren H. Architecture in English Fiction. New Haven, 1934.
Ernst, G. Die Rolle des Geldes im englischen Roman des neunzehnten Jahrhunderts. Villingen, 1936.
Rosa, M. W. The Silver-Fork School: Novels of Fashion preceding 'Vanity Fair.' New York, 1936.
Shepperson, A. B. The Novel in Motley. A History of the Burlesque Novel in English. Cambridge, U.S.A. 1936.
König, G. Die viktorianische Schulroman. Berlin, 1937.
Utter, R. P. and Needham, G. B. Pamela's Daughters. New York, 1937.
Wright, W. F. Sensibility in English Prose Fiction, 1760–1814. Urbana, 1937.

S. J. L.

II. THE EARLY NINETEENTH-CENTURY NOVELISTS

MARIA EDGEWORTH, SCOTT, JANE AUSTEN, PEACOCK, MARRYAT

MARIA EDGEWORTH (1767–1849)

(1) BIBLIOGRAPHY

Slade, B. C. Maria Edgeworth: a Bibliographical Tribute. 1937.

(2) COLLECTED WORKS

[Works.] 12(?) vols. Boston, 1822–5; 20 vols. in 10, New York, 1835–6.

Tales and Miscellaneous Pieces. 14 vols. 1825.
Tales and Novels. 18 vols. 1832–3, 1848, 1856.
Tales and Novels. 10 vols. 1893; 12 vols. 1893.

(3) SELECTED WORKS

Tales from Maria Edgeworth. 1903. [Introduction by A. Dobson, illustrated by H. Thomson.]
Selection from the Works of Maria Edgeworth. By Gerald Griffin. [1918.]
Selections from the Works of Maria Edgeworth. Ed. M. C. Seton, [1919].

(4) FICTION

The Parent's Assistant; or, Stories for Children. 3 vols. 1795 (anon.; no copies extant?); 3 vols. 1796 (adds The Barring-Out; no complete sets located); 6 vols. 1800 (signed; adds Simple Susan and omits 8 stories transferred to Early Lessons); 6 vols. 1800 (illustrated); Cork, 1800 (3 stories only); Drogheda, 1802 (selection); 8 vols. Georgetown, 1809; 7 vols. 1815–27 (adds Little Plays); 2 vols. 1853, etc.; 1897 (introduction by A. T. Ritchie); tr. French, Paris, 1820, Geneva, [1826?], etc. [One or more stories often rptd separately.]
Castle Rackrent, An Hibernian Tale. Taken from Facts, and from the Manners of the Irish Squires, before the Year 1782. 1800 (anon.; *bis*); Dublin, 1800; 1801; Dublin, 1802; Newbern (North Carolina), [*c.* 1802] (no copy traced); 1804; 1810, etc.; 1895 (introduction by A. T. Ritchie).
Belinda. 3 vols. 1801; 2 vols. Dublin, 1801; 4 vols. Paris, 1802 ('corrected'); 2 vols. Dublin, 1802; 2 vols. 1810 (rev.); 3 vols. 1811; 1896 (introduction by A. T. Ritchie); tr. French, Paris, 1802.
Harry and Lucy. Part I. Being the First Part of Early Lessons. By the Author of The Parent's Assistant. 1801; pt II, 1801. Rosamond, Part I; containing [3 stories, including The Purple Jar from The Parent's Assistant]. 1801; pt II (3 stories), 1801; pt III (The Rabbit), 1801. Frank. Part I. 1801; pt II, 1801; pt III, 1801; pt IV, 1801. The Little Dog Trusty; The Orange Man [both from The Parent's Assistant]; and the Cherry Orchard: being the tenth part of Early Lessons. 1801 (re-issued 1802). [Complete work.] 10 vols. 1803 (copies of pts 1, 2, 4, 5, 6 not traced); 10 (?) vols. Philadelphia, 1805–8 (pt 10 not traced); 10 vols. 1809 (signed; only 4 pts located); 2 vols. 1813; 4 vols. 1835; 4 vols. 1855; 1856 (illustrated by Birket Foster), etc.; tr. French, 1803.
Moral Tales for Young People. 5 vols. 1801; 3 vols. 1802; 3 vols. 1806; 1809; 3 vols.

Philadelphia, 1810; 3 vols. New York, 1819; Philadelphia, 1846; 1856, etc. [With a preface by R. L. Edgeworth. Separate tales often tr. and rptd.]
Popular Tales. 3 vols. 1804; 3(?) vols. Philadelphia, 1804; 3 vols. 1805; 3 vols. 1811; 2 vols. Poughkeepsie, 1813; 1856, etc.; 1895 (introduction by A. T. Ritchie). [Separate tales often tr. and rptd.]
The Modern Griselda. A Tale. 1805 (*bis*, 2nd edn 'corrected'); 1810; Georgetown, 1810; 1813; tr. French, Paris, 1813.
Leonora. 2 vols. 1806; 2 vols. New York, 1806; 2 vols. 1815; tr. French, 1807.
Tales of Fashionable Life. Ser. 1, 3 vols. 1809; 2 vols. Georgetown, 1809. [Containing Ennui, Madame de Fleury, The Dun, Manœuvring, and Almeria.] Ser. 2, 3 vols. 1812; 3 vols. Boston, 1812. [Containing The Absentee, Vivian, and Emilie de Coulanges.] Both sers. 6 vols. 1809–12 (*bis*); 6 vols. 1815; tr. French (in part), Paris, 1813.
Patronage. 4 vols. 1814 (*bis*); 4 vols. 1815; 3 vols. Philadelphia, 1815; tr. French, Paris, 1816.
Continuation of Early Lessons. 2 vols. 1814; 2 vols. 1815; 2 vols. Boston, 1815. [Contains Frank, Rosamond, Harry and Lucy.]
Harrington, a Tale; and Ormond, a Tale. 3 vols. 1817 (*bis*, 2nd edn 'corrected'); New York, 1817; tr. French, Paris, 1817. [Preface by R. L. Edgeworth. Ormond was rptd 1895 with introduction by A. T. Ritchie.]
Rosamond A Sequel to Early Lessons. 2 vols. 1821; 2 vols. Philadelphia, 1821; 2 vols. 1822; 2 vols. 1830.
Frank A Sequel to Frank in Early Lessons. 3 vols. 1822; 2 vols. New York, 1822; 2 vols. Cambridge, U.S.A. 1822; tr. Italian, Milan, 1839.
Harry and Lucy Concluded; being the Last Part of Early Lessons. 4 vols. 1825; 4 vols. 1827 ('corrected'); 3 vols. 1840 (rev.).
Garry Owen; or, the Snow-Woman; and Poor Bob, the Chimney-Sweeper. 1832; tr. French, Paris, 1835.
Helen, A Tale. 3 vols. 1834 (*bis*); Paris, 1834; 2 vols. Philadelphia, 1834; [1838]; [1877]; [1879]; [1880]; [1883]; [1884]; 1896 (introduction by A. T. Ritchie). Tr. French, Paris, 1834; Swedish, Stockholm, 1836–7.
Orlandino. Edinburgh, 1848; Boston, 1848; Paris, 1849; Edinburgh, 1853; 1865.
The most Unfortunate Day of my Life. Being a hitherto Unpublished Story by Maria Edgeworth, together with The Purple Jar and Other Stories by the Same Author. 1931.

(5) EDUCATIONAL AND MISCELLANEOUS
WRITINGS

Letters for Literary Ladies, To Which is added
an Essay on the Noble Science of Self-
Justification. 1795; 1799 ('corrected and
much enlarged'); 1805; Georgetown, 1810;
1814.
Practical Education. 2 vols. 1798; 3 vols.
1801 (rev.); 2 vols. New York, 1801; 2 vols.
1811 (as Essays on Practical Education);
2 vols. Providence, 1815; 2 vols. 1815;
3 vols. 1822; tr. French, Geneva, 1801.
[With R. L. Edgeworth.]
A Rational Primer. 1799. [With R. L. Edge-
worth.]
Essay on Irish Bulls. 1802; 1803 ('corrected');
Philadelphia, 1803; New York, 1803; 1808;
1823. [With R. L. Edgeworth.]
Essays on Professional Education, by R. L.
Edgeworth, Esq. [and Maria Edgeworth].
1809; 1812 (rev.).
Cottage Dialogues among the Irish Peasantry.
By Mary Leadbeater. With Notes and a
Preface by Maria Edgeworth. 1811; Phila-
delphia, 1811.
Readings on Poetry. 1816; 1816 ('cor-
rected'); New York, 1816. [With R. L.
Edgeworth.]
Comic Dramas in Three Acts. 1817; 1817
('corrected'); Philadelphia, 1817; Boston,
1817.
Memoirs of Richard Lovell Edgeworth, con-
cluded by Maria Edgeworth. 2 vols. 1820;
2 vols. 1821 ('corrected'); 1844 (rev.).
Little Plays for Children. 1827; Philadelphia,
1827; New York, 1827. [Vol. VII of The
Parent's Assistant.]
Maria Edgeworth. Chosen Letters. Ed.
F. V. Barry, 1931.

(6) BIOGRAPHY AND CRITICISM

(a) Books

Edgeworth, [F. A.]. A Memoir of Maria
Edgeworth, with a Selection from her
Letters. By Mrs Edgeworth, edited by her
Children. 3 vols. 1867 (priv. ptd).
Oliver, G. A. A Study of Maria Edgeworth.
With Notices of her Father and Friends.
Boston, 1882.
Zimmern, H. Maria Edgeworth. 1883.
Hare, A. J. C. The Life and Letters of Maria
Edgeworth. 2 vols. 1894.
Lawless, E. Maria Edgeworth. 1904. (Eng-
lish Men of Letters ser.)
Hill, C. Maria Edgeworth: her Circle in the
Days of Buonaparte and Bourbon. 1910.
Paterson, A. The Edgeworths. 1914.
Michael, E. F. Die irischen Romane von
Maria Edgeworth. Dresden, 1918.

The Black Book of Edgeworthstown and
Other Edgeworth Memories, 1585–1817.
Ed. H. J. and H. E. Butler, 1927.
Romilly-Edgeworth Letters: 1813–1818. Ed.
S. H. Romilly, 1936.

(b) Chapters in Books and Articles
in Periodicals

Tales of Fashionable Life. Quarterly Rev. II,
1809. [On this and several later reviews of
Edgeworth works, see K. G. Pfeiffer, PQ.
XI, 1932, pp. 97–108.]
[Croker, J. W.] Miss Edgeworth's Tales of
Fashionable Life. Quarterly Rev. VII,
1812.
[Foster, J.] Eclectic Rev. VIII, 1812. [A
denunciation of Tales of Fashionable Life;
rptd in Critical Essays, 1856.]
Miss Edgeworth's Patronage. Edinburgh Rev.
XXII, 1814. [Has been attrib. both to
Jeffrey and Scott.]
Lockhart, J. G. Memoirs of the Life of Sir
Walter Scott. 2 vols. Edinburgh, 1837–
8.
Hall, A. M. Edgeworthstown: Memories of
Maria Edgeworth. Art Journ. I, 1849.
Hall, A. M. and S. C. Memories of the
Authors of the Age. Art Journ. XVIII, 1866,
pp. 345–9.
Hayward, A. Miss Edgeworth. Edinburgh
Rev. CXXVI, 1867. [Rptd in Biographical
and Critical Essays, 5 vols. 1858–74.]
Ritchie, A. T. A Book of Sybils. 1883.
Repplier, A. Essays in Miniature. New York,
1892.
Francis, S. M. Maria Edgeworth. Atlantic
Monthly, XCVI, 1905.
Grey, R. Society According to Maria Edge-
worth. Fortnightly Rev. Aug. 1907.
—— Heavy Fathers. Fortnightly Rev. July
1909.
—— Maria Edgeworth and Étienne Dumont.
Dublin Rev. Oct. 1909.
The Correspondence of Ricardo with Maria
Edgeworth. Economic Journ. Sept. 1907.
Ward, W. Moral Fiction a Hundred Years
Ago. Dublin Rev. April 1909.
Colum, P. Maria Edgeworth and Ivan
Turgenev. British Rev. XI, 1915.
Dobson, A. De Libris. 1923.
Woolf, V. The Common Reader. 1925.
Maria Edgeworth. English Rev. Jan.
1927.
Butler, H. J. and H. E. Some Unpublished
Letters. Sir Walter Scott and Maria
Edgeworth. MLR. XXIII, 1928.
Baker, E. A. The History of the English
Novel. Vol. VI, 1935. [Chs. i, ii.]

S. J. L.

SIR WALTER SCOTT (1771–1832)

(1) MANUSCRIPTS

[Scott's Journal, much of his correspondence, the collections of ballad versions utilised for the Minstrelsy of the Scottish Border, miscellaneous MSS including unpbd trns of German dramas, and his notes as a law student, are preserved at Abbotsford. The MSS of most of Scott's poems and novels are in existence, the majority in private hands. The MS of The Fortunes of Nigel is at Brantwood; the BM. possesses most of the MS of Kenilworth, various letters to George Thomson, with verses for his Scottish airs, the proofsheets of Woodstock, with Scott's corrections and addns, 18 letters of James Ballantyne, a copy of the Life of Napoleon with MS corrections and notes by Scott, and a portion of an edn of Swift's works used by Scott, with his MS notes. The National Lib. of Scotland possesses the MSS of Marmion, Waverley, and the Minstrelsy of the Scottish Border. The University of Edinburgh possesses portions of Kenilworth and The Legend of Montrose, letters and verses belonging to Scott, and letters from Scott. Messrs A. and C. Black, London, possess Scott's annotated edn of the Waverley Novels with textual corrections by him.]

(2) BIBLIOGRAPHIES

Anderson, J. P. Bibliography. [In C. D. Yonge, Life of Sir Walter Scott, 1888.]

Ball, M. Bibliography. [In Sir Walter Scott as a Critic of Literature, New York, 1907.]

Caplan, A. The Bibliography of Sir Walter Scott, Bart. Philadelphia, 1928. [Inaccurate.]

Worthington, G. Bibliography of the Waverley Novels. 1930.

van Antwerp, W. C. A Collector's Comment on his First Editions of the Works of Sir Walter Scott. San Francisco, 1932.

Ruff, W. A Bibliography of the Poetical Works of Sir Walter Scott, 1796–1832. Trans. Edinburgh Bibliog. Soc. I, 1937–8. [Includes the miscellanies, annuals, etc. with verse by Scott.]

(3) POETRY

(a) Collected Editions

The Poetical Works. 6 vols. Edinburgh, 1806–8. [The Minstrelsy, Sir Tristrem, Lay of the Last Minstrel, Marmion.]

The Poetical Works. 12 vols. Edinburgh, 1820; 10 vols. Edinburgh, 1821; 8 vols. Edinburgh, 1822; 10 vols. Edinburgh, 1823; 10 vols. Edinburgh, 1825. [The 1821, 1823 and 1825 edns were all re-issued 1830 with new introductory matter to each vol. and a new vol. XI including the plays. Another

vol. XI also appeared in 1830 including both the plays and all the new introductions.]

The Poetical Works. 7 vols. Paris, 1821, 1827.

The Poetical Works. Ed. J. G. Lockhart (with illustrations on steel from drawings by Turner), 12 vols. Edinburgh, 1833–4, 1848.

The Poetical Works. 9 vols. Boston, 1857.

The Poetical Works. Ed. G. Gilfillan, 3 vols. Edinburgh, 1857.

The Poetical Works. Ed. F. T. Palgrave, London, 1866, etc. (Globe edn). [Omits a few short poems, and some notes and introductions (the copyright of A. and C. Black, Ltd).]

The Poetical Works. Ed. W. M. Rossetti (illustrated by T. Seccombe), 1870; 1882 (without illustrations).

The Poetical Works. Ed. W. Sharp, 2 vols. 1885–6.

The Poetical Works. Ed. W. Minto, 2 vols. 1887.

The Poetical Works. Ed. J. Dennis, 5 vols. 1892.

The Poetical Works. Ed. A. Lang, 1895.

The Poetical Works. Ed. H. E. Scudder, Boston, 1900.

The Poetical Works. Ed. J. L. Robertson, 1904, etc. (Oxford edn.)

(b) Separate Poems, Dramatic Sketches, and Early Translations from the German

[For single priv. ptd short poems, contributions to miscellanies and books of songs, etc., see W. Ruff's Bibliography (listed above).]

The Chase, and William and Helen: two ballads from the German of Gottfried Augustus Bürger. Edinburgh, 1796 (anon.; re-issued 1807).

Goetz of Berlichingen, With The Iron Hand: A Tragedy. Translated from the German of Goethé. 1799.

Tales of Terror. Kelso, 1799 (re-issued as An Apology for Tales of Terror). [Includes Scott's trns from Bürger, and some ballads, with 4 ballads by M. G. Lewis, later ptd in Tales of Wonder (see below), 2 ballads by R. Southey, and 1 anon. ballad.]

The Eve of St John. A Border Ballad. Kelso, 1800. Tr. German, 1816 (with the Bridal of Triermain); Dutch, 1834; Polish, 1835.

Tales of Wonder; Written and Collected by M. G. Lewis. 2 vols. 1801 (bis); 1817. [William and Helen, The Wild Huntsman, The Fire King, Frederick and Alice, Glenfinlas, The Eve of St John.]

The Lay of the Last Minstrel. 1805 (bis, 2nd edn rev.); 1806 (3 edns); 1807; 1808 (8th edn, with Ballads and Lyrical Pieces; a few copies have an appendix of poetical pieces by Scott not ptd elsewhere); 1808; 1809; 1810; 1811; 1812; 1814; 1816 (15th edn); 1821; 1823. Tr. German, 1820; Dutch, 1840; Spanish, 1843.

Ballads and Lyrical Pieces. Edinburgh, 1806 (*bis*); Boston, 1807; Edinburgh, 1810; Baltimore, 1811; Edinburgh, 1812; Edinburgh, 1819; Zwickau, 1825.

Marmion; A Tale of Flodden Field. Edinburgh, 1808 (4 edns); Philadelphia, 1808; 1810; 2 vols. Edinburgh, 1810, 1811 (*bis*), 1815, 1821, 1825 (*bis*, 12th edn re-issued 1830); Paris, 1827; tr. French, 1820.

The Lady of the Lake; A Poem. Edinburgh, 1810 (6 edns, 2nd rev., 5th re-issued as 'Sixth Edition' and 6th as 'Eighth'); Edinburgh, 1811; Baltimore, 1812; Edinburgh, 1814; Edinburgh, 1816; Edinburgh, 1819; Paris, 1822; Edinburgh, 1825 (*bis*); 1830; Edinburgh, 1832. Tr. German, 1819; Polish, 1828; Swedish, 1828; Portuguese, 1842; Danish, 1871.

The Vision of Don Roderick. Edinburgh, 1811 (priv. ptd and *bis*); Philadelphia, 1811; Edinburgh, 1821 (with The Field of Waterloo); tr. German, 1816.

Rokeby; A Poem. Edinburgh, 1813 (5 edns, 2nd rev.); Edinburgh, 1815; Edinburgh, 1821; Paris, 1827; tr. German, 1822.

The Bridal of Triermain, or The Vale of St John. Edinburgh, 1813 (3 edns); 1814; 1815; Edinburgh, 1817; Edinburgh, 1819 (with Harold the Dauntless); tr. German, 1816.

The Lord of the Isles, A Poem. 1815 (5 edns, 2nd rev.); Paris, 1827. Tr. German, 1822; Spanish, 1830; Portuguese, 1839; Italian, 1884.

The Field of Waterloo; A Poem. Edinburgh, 1815 (3 edns); Boston, 1815; Paris, 1815; tr. German, 1825.

Harold the Dauntless; A Poem, In Six Cantos. Edinburgh, 1817; tr. German, 1817.

The Bridal of Triermain and Harold the Dauntless. Edinburgh, 1819.

Miscellaneous Poems. Edinburgh, 1820. [Contains smaller pieces pbd previously as well as the first issue of the preceding item. For the bibliographical niceties, re-issues, etc. consult Ruff's Bibliography (listed above).]

The Poetry, Contained in the Novels, Tales and Romances, of the Author of 'Waverley.' Edinburgh, 1822 (re-issued *c.* 1827 in Scott's name).

Halidon Hill; A Dramatic Sketch from Scottish History. Edinburgh, 1822 (re-issued same year as 2nd edn).

The Doom of Devorgoil, A Melo-drama. Auchindrane; or, the Ayrshire Tragedy. Edinburgh, 1830; Paris, 1830.

New Love Poems by Sir Walter Scott. Ed. D. Cook, Oxford, 1932.

(4) Novels and Tales

(a) Collected Editions

Novels and Tales of the Author of Waverley. 12 vols. Edinburgh, 1820. Historical Romances, etc. 6 vols. Edinburgh, 1823. Novels and Romances. 7 vols. Edinburgh, 1824. Tales and Romances. 14 vols. Edinburgh, 1827. Introductions, Notes, and Illustrations. 2 vols. Edinburgh, 1833. [In all 41 vols. Edinburgh, 1819–33. Also 53 vols. Edinburgh, 1821–33; and 41 vols. Edinburgh, 1823–33.]

Waverley Novels. 43 vols. Boston, 1829.

Waverley Novels. Author's Favourite Edition. Illustrated. 48 vols. Edinburgh, 1830–4.

Waverley Novels. Cabinet Edition. 25 vols. Edinburgh, 1841–3.

Waverley Novels. Abbotsford Edition. 12 vols. Edinburgh, 1842–7.

Waverley Novels. 5 vols. 1846–9, 1850–1.

Waverley Novels. Library Edition. 25 vols. Edinburgh, 1852–3.

Waverley Novels. Roxburghe Edition. 48 vols. Edinburgh, 1859–61.

Waverley Novels. Centenary Edition. 25 vols. Edinburgh, 1870–1.

Waverley Novels. Illustrated by G. Cruikshank, [etc.]. 23 vols. 1875–6.

Waverley Novels. Edition de Luxe. Illustrated by French Artists. 25 vols. 1882–98.

Waverley Novels. Edinburgh Edition. 25 vols. Edinburgh, 1887.

Waverley Novels. Dryburgh Edition. 25 vols. 1890–1900.

Waverley Novels. Border Edition. 48 vols. 1892–4, etc.

Waverley Novels. 48 vols. 1895–6.

Waverley Novels. Temple Edition. 48 vols. 1897–9.

Waverley Novels. Melrose Edition. 25 vols. 1897.

Waverley Novels. Scott Centenary Edition. 48 vols. 1898.

Waverley Novels. Edinburgh Edition. 48 vols. 1901–3.

Waverley Novels. Soho Edition. 25 vols. 1903–5.

Waverley Novels. Everyman's Edition. 25 vols. 1906, etc.

Waverley Novels. Oxford Edition. 24 vols. Oxford, 1914, etc.

(b) Separate Novels and Tales

Waverley, or 'Tis Sixty Years Since. 3 vols. Edinburgh, 1814 (4 edns), 1815, 1816, 1817. Tr. French, 1818; Italian, 1823; Spanish, 1836; Dutch, 1872; Polish, 1875.

Guy Mannering, or The Astrologer. By the Author of Waverley. 3 vols. Edinburgh, 1815 (3 edns), 1817. Tr. French, 1816; Spanish, 1835; Portuguese, 1842.

The Antiquary. By the Author of Waverley and Guy Mannering. 3 vols. Edinburgh, 1816, 1818 (5th edn). Tr. Dutch, 1825; Swedish, 1827; Polish, 1828; Spanish, 1831 (Castilian, 1834); Russian, 1845; French, 1854; Danish, 1856–8.

Tales of my Landlord. Collected and arranged by Jedidiah Cleisbotham. 4 vols. Edinburgh, 1816, 1817 (bis), 1818, 1819; Paris, 1821. The Black Dwarf: tr. Portuguese, 1838; Spanish, 1844. Old Mortality: tr. French, 1817; Portuguese, 1837. [The Black Dwarf and Old Mortality.]

The Search after Happiness, or The Quest of The Sultan of Serendib. The Sale-Room, Nos. 1–28. Edinburgh, 4 Jan.–12 July 1817.

Tales of my Landlord. Second Series. 4 vols. Edinburgh, 1818 (bis); Paris, 1828. Tr. French, 1818; Swedish, 1824; Italian, 1824; Spanish, 1831; Portuguese, 1844. [The Heart of Midlothian.]

Rob Roy. By the Author of Waverley. 3 vols. Edinburgh, 1818 (3 edns); Paris, 1822. Tr. French, 1818; Spanish, 1828.

Tales of my Landlord. Third Series. 4 vols. Edinburgh, 1819 (3 edns); Paris, 1823. Tr. French, 1819; Spanish, 1831. [The Bride of Lammermoor and The Legend of Montrose.]

Ivanhoe. A Romance. By the Author of Waverley. 3 vols. Edinburgh, 1820 (bis), 1821; Paris, 1821; Boston, 1827. Tr. French, 1820; Spanish, 1826 (Castilian, 1825); German, 1826; Portuguese, 1808; Italian, 1840; Greek, 1847; Polish, 1865.

The Monastery. A Romance. By the Author of Waverley. 3 vols. Edinburgh, 1820; New York, 1820; Paris, 1821. Tr. French, 1820; Portuguese, 1842; Spanish, 1845.

The Abbot. By the Author of Waverley. 3 vols. Edinburgh, 1820; Philadelphia, 1820; Paris, 1820, 1832. Tr. French, 1822, 1829; Portuguese, 1844; Spanish, 1845.

Kenilworth. A Romance. By the Author of Waverley. 4 vols. Edinburgh, 1821; Paris, 1821, 1823, 1832. Tr. French, 1821, 1822, 1828; Spanish, 1832; Polish, 1870.

The Pirate. By the Author of Waverley. 3 vols. Edinburgh, 1822 (bis); Paris, 1822. Tr. French, 1822; Russian, 1865.

The Fortunes of Nigel. By the Author of Waverley. 4 vols. Edinburgh, 1822. Tr. French, 1836; Spanish, 1845.

Peveril of the Peak. By the Author of Waverley. 4 vols. Edinburgh, 1822; Paris, 1823, 1832. Tr. French, 1823; Spanish, 1836.

Quentin Durward. By the Author of Waverley. 3 vols. Edinburgh, 1823; Paris, 1823, 1827, 1832. Tr. French, 1823; Spanish, 1827.

St Ronan's Well. By the Author of Waverley. 3 vols. Edinburgh, 1824 (bis); Paris, 1824; tr. French, 1824.

Redgauntlet: a tale of the eighteenth century. By the Author of Waverley. 3 vols. Edinburgh, 1824 (bis); Paris, 1824; tr. French, Paris, 1824, Brussels, 1827.

Tales of the Crusaders. 4 vols. Edinburgh, 1825; Paris, 1825; tr. French, 1825. The Talisman: tr. German, 1825; Spanish, 1826. [Vols. I–II, The Betrothed; vols. III–IV, The Talisman.]

Woodstock: or, The Cavalier. A tale of the year Sixteen Hundred and Fifty-One. By the Author of Waverley. 3 vols. Edinburgh, 1826. Tr. French, Brussels, 1827; Portuguese, 1843.

Chronicles of the Canongate. 2 vols. Edinburgh, 1827. [The Highland Widow, The Two Drovers, and The Surgeon's Daughter. With an introduction by Scott acknowledging the authorship of the Waverley Novels. The Morning Chronicle, 22 Oct. 1827, contains an abridgment of The Two Drovers.]

My Aunt Margaret's Mirror. The Tapestried Chamber. The Laird's Jock. [In The Keepsake, 1828. My Aunt Margaret's Mirror: tr. Spanish, 1830 (Castilian, 1838); French, 1897.]

Chronicles of the Canongate. Second Series. 3 vols. Edinburgh, 1828. [St Valentine's Day: or The Fair Maid of Perth.]

Anne of Geierstein: or The Maiden of the Mist. By the Author of Waverley. 3 vols. Edinburgh, 1829. Tr. Portuguese, 1843; Italian, 1882.

Tales of my Landlord. Fourth and Last Series. 4 vols. Edinburgh, 1832. Castle Dangerous: tr. Portuguese, 1842. [Count Robert of Paris and Castle Dangerous.]

(5) MISCELLANEOUS PROSE WORKS

(a) Collected Editions

Miscellaneous Prose Works of Sir Walter Scott. 6 vols. Edinburgh, 1827. [Life of Swift; Life of Dryden; Lives of the Novelists; other biographies; Chivalry; Romance and the Drama; Paul's Letter to his Kinsfolk, etc.]

The Prose Works of Sir Walter Scott. 9 vols. 1827–34; 8 vols. Paris, [1840?].

The Introductions, Notes, and Illustrations to the Novels, Tales, and Romances of the Author of Waverley. 8 vols. Edinburgh, 1833.

The Miscellaneous Prose Works of Sir Walter Scott. 30 vols. 1834–71; 3 vols. 1847.

The Miscellaneous Works of Sir Walter Scott, Bart. Edinburgh, 1836. [Introductory Remarks on Popular Poetry, prefixed to an edn of the Minstrelsy of the Scottish Border; new introductions to the Lay of the Last Minstrel, Marmion, The Lady of the Lake, Rokeby, and The Lord of the Isles; Macduff's Cross; The Doom of Devorgoil; The Ayrshire Tragedy.]

(b) Separate Works

Edinburgh Rev. III–VII, IX, XXX. London Quart. Rev. I–III, V, XIV, XVI, XVIII, XIX, XXX, XXXIII, XXXIV, XXXVI–XXXIX, XLI, XLIII, XLIV. Foreign Quart. Rev. I, II. [Details are given in Lockhart's Life of Scott and in Alibone's Dictionary.]

Biographical Memoir of John Leyden, M.D. Edinburgh Annual Register, IV. 1811. [Rptd in Poems and Ballads by John Leyden, M.D. Kelso, 1858.]

The Eyrbiggia Saga. [In H. Weber's Illustrations of Northern Antiquities, 1814.]

Chivalry. The Drama. [In Encyclopaedia Britannica, 1814.]

The Border Antiquities of England and Scotland. 2 vols. 1814–7.

Quart. Rev. Oct. 1815. [Review of Jane Austen's Emma; rptd in Famous Reviews, ed. R. B. Johnson, 1914.]

Edinburgh Annual Register, 1814–5. [Historical Sketches for 1814, 1815.]

Paul's Letters to his Kinsfolk. Edinburgh, 1816 (3 edns). Tr. French, 1822; German, 1822.

Provincial Antiquities of Scotland. 10 pts, 1819–26; 2 vols. Edinburgh, 1826.

Description of the Regalia of Scotland. 1819; 1824, etc. [Rptd from Provincial Antiquities.]

Account of the Coronation of George III. 1821.

Lives of the Novelists, prefixed to Ballantyne's Novelists' Library. 4 vols. 1821–4; 2 vols. Paris, 1825; ed. G. Saintsbury, 1910 (Everyman's Lib.). Tr. French, 1825; German, 1826.

Hints addressed to the Inhabitants of Edinburgh, and others, in prospect of His Majesty's Visit. By an old Citizen. Edinburgh, 1822.

Sketch of the Life and Character of the late Lord Kinneder. Edinburgh, 1822 (priv. ptd).

Romance. [In Encyclopaedia Britannica, 1822.]

Character of the late Lord Byron. [In The Pamphleteer, vol. XXIV, 1824.]

Thoughts on the proposed change of currency. Three letters to the editor of the Edinburgh Weekly Journal from Malachi Malagrowther, Esqr. Edinburgh, 1826. [The letters were ptd separately, Edinburgh, 1826 (bis).]

Sykes, J. An Account of the Death of Frederick, Duke of York. To which is subjoined Sir Walter Scott's Character of His Royal Highness. Newcastle, 1827.

The Life of Napoleon Buonaparte, Emperor of the French. With a Preliminary View of the French Revolution. By the Author of Waverley. 9 vols. Edinburgh, 1827. Tr. French, 1827; Italian, 1827; Spanish, 1827; German, 1827; Dutch, 1865.

Religious Discourses. By a Layman. 1828.

Tales of a Grandfather. Being Stories taken from Scottish History. Humbly inscribed to Hugh Littlejohn, Esqr. 3 vols. Edinburgh, 1828 (5 edns); Paris, 1828; tr. French, 1828. Second Series, 3 vols. Edinburgh, 1829; Paris, 1829; tr. French, 1829. Third Series. Edinburgh, 1830; Paris, 1830; tr. French, 1830.

History of Scotland. 2 vols. [Lardner's Cabinet Cyclopaedia, 1829–30; tr. German, 1830.]

Essays on Ballad Poetry. Edinburgh, 1830.

Letters on Demonology and Witchcraft, addressed to J. G. Lockhart, Esqr. Edinburgh, 1830; Paris, 1830. Tr. French, 1832; Spanish, 1876.

Tales of a Grandfather. Being Stories taken from the History of France. Inscribed to Master John Hugh Lockhart. 3 vols. Edinburgh, 1831; Paris, 1831; tr. French, 1831.

Essays on Chivalry, Romance, and the Drama. 1868.

Memoirs of Samuel Pepys. Pepys Club Occasional Papers, vol. II, 1925.

(6) Correspondence

Letters of Sir Walter Scott addressed to the Rev. R. Polwhele, D. Gilbert, Esq., Francis Douce, Esq., etc. 1832.

Letters between James Ellis, Esq., and Walter Scott, Esq. Newcastle, 1850.

Memorials of Coleorton, being Letters from Sir Walter Scott [and others] to Sir George and Lady Beaumont of Coleorton. Ed. W. Knight, 2 vols. Edinburgh, 1887.

Journal (1825–32). From the Original MS. at Abbotsford. Ed. D. Douglas, 2 vols. Edinburgh, 1890; 1891; 1927.

Tales of Adventure and Stories of Travel 50 Years Ago. 1893. [P. 76, Letter from Sir Walter Scott to Sir Adam Ferguson.]

Familiar Letters. Ed. D. Douglas, 2 vols. Edinburgh, 1894.

The Letters of Sir Walter Scott and Charles Kirkpatrick Sharpe to Robert Chambers, 1821–45. 1904.

Letters of Sir Walter Scott's Family to their Governess. Ed. F. A. W. Henderson, 1905.

Cook, D. Murray's Mysterious Contributor. Nineteenth Century, April 1927. [Includes unpbd letters.]

—— Lockhart's Treatment of Scott's Letters. Nineteenth Century, Sept. 1927.

Butler, H. J. and H. E. Sir Walter Scott and Maria Edgeworth: some Unpublished Letters. MLR. July 1928.

Stirton, J. Leaves from my MS. Portfolio. 1929. [P. 269, Letter from Scott dated 9 Nov. 1811.]

Partington, W. The Private Letter-Books of Sir Walter Scott. 1930. [Selections from the Abbotsford MSS.]

Some Unpublished Letters of Sir Walter Scott. From the Collection in the Brotherton Library. Ed. J. A. Symington, Oxford, 1932.

Sir Walter's Postbag: More Stories and Side-lights from his Unpublished Letter-Books. Ed. W. Partington, 1932.

The Letters of Sir Walter Scott. Ed. Sir H. J. C. Grierson, D. Cook, and others, 12 vols. 1932–7. [Complete and standard edn.]

The Correspondence of Sir Walter Scott and Charles Robert Maturin. Ed. F. E. Ratchford and W. M. McCarthy, Austin, 1937.

(7) WORKS EDITED BY SCOTT

Minstrelsy of the Scottish Border: Consisting of Historical and Romantic Ballads. 2 vols. Kelso, 1802; 3 vols. Edinburgh, 1803 (enlarged); 3 vols. Edinburgh, 1806, 1810 (with alterations), 1812, 1821 (re-issued 1830 with 2 introductory essays added); ed. J. G. Lockhart, 1833 (from Scott's interleaved copy of the Minstrelsy with MS annotations and additions); ed. T. F. Henderson, 4 vols. Edinburgh, 1902, 1932; ed. A. Noyes, Edinburgh, 1908; ed. T. Henderson, 1931.

Sir Tristrem; a Metrical Romance of the Thirteenth Century; by Thomas of Ercildoune. Edited from the Auchinleck MS. Edinburgh, 1804, 1806, 1811, 1819.

Original Memoirs written during the Great Civil War: being the Life of Sir H. Slingsby and Memoirs of Captain Hodgson. Edinburgh, 1806.

The Works of John Dryden, now first collected. Illustrated with notes, historical, critical and explanatory, and a life of the author. 18 vols. London, 1808, 1821; rev. G. Saintsbury, 18 vols. Edinburgh, 1882–93.

Life of John Dryden. Edinburgh, 1808 (50 copies only, for presentation).

Queenhoo Hall, a Romance; and Ancient Time, a Drama, by the late Joseph Strutt. 4 vols. Edinburgh, 1808.

Memoirs of Capt. George Carleton, written by himself. Edinburgh, 1808.

Memoirs of Robert Carey, and Fragmenta Regalia: being a History of Queen Elizabeth's Favourites, by Sir R. Naunton. Edinburgh, 1808.

A Collection of Scarce and Valuable Tracts. Vols. I–III, 1809; vols. IV–X, 1812. [Known as the Somers Tracts.]

The Life of Edward, Lord Herbert of Cherbury, written by himself. With a Prefatory Memoir [by Scott]. Edinburgh, 1809.

The State Papers and Letters of Sir Ralph Sadler. Edited by A. Clifford. To which is added, a memoir of the Life of Sir Ralph Sadler, with Historical Notes, by Walter Scott, Esqr. 3 vols. Edinburgh, 1809.

Memoirs of the Duke of Sully. With a brief Historical Introduction [attrib. to Scott]. 1810; 1812.

English Minstrelsy. Being A Selection of Fugitive Poetry From the Best English Authors; with some Original Pieces Hitherto Unpublished. 2 vols. Edinburgh, 1810.

The Ancient British Drama. 3 vols. 1810. [Anon., but notes, etc. generally attrib. to Scott.]

The Poetical Works of Anna Seward. With extracts from her literary correspondence. 3 vols. Edinburgh, 1810.

Memoirs of Count Grammont. 1811; 2 vols. 1818 (rev.). [A revision, with notes, of A. Boyer's trn of 1714.]

The Castle of Otranto. With a Critical Introduction. 1811.

Secret History of the Court of James the First. 2 vols. Edinburgh, 1811.

Memoirs of the Reign of King Charles I. By Sir Philip Warwick. Edinburgh, 1813.

The Works of Jonathan Swift, containing additional letters, tracts and poems not hitherto published. With notes and a life of the author. 19 vols. Edinburgh, 1814, 1824. [Memoirs of Swift pbd separately, Paris, 1826.]

Illustrations of Northern Antiquities. With Translations of Metrical Tales, notes and illustrations, by H. Weber, J. Jamieson, and Walter Scott. Edinburgh, 1814.

The Letting of Humours Blood in the Head Vaine. By S. Rowlands. Edinburgh, 1814, 1815. [With an advertisement by Scott.]

Memoirs of the Somervilles. 2 vols. Edinburgh, 1815.

Criminal Trials. Illustrative of the Tale entitled The Heart of Midlothian. Edinburgh, 1818. [Preface by Scott, who perhaps edited the work.]

Burt's Letters from Scotland. Edinburgh, 1818. [With R. Jamieson.]

Letter from a Gentleman in the North of Scotland. With the History of Donald the Hammerer. Edinburgh, 1818.

Memorials of the Haliburtons. Edinburgh, 1820 (priv. ptd).

Trivial Poems and Triolets. Written in Obedience to Mrs Tomkin's Commands. By Patrick Carey. 29th Aug. 1651. Edinburgh, 1820.

Northern Memoirs, calculated for the Meridian of Scotland. Writ in the year 1655, by Richard Franck. Edinburgh, 1821.

Chronological Notes of Scottish Affairs from 1688 till 1701; being chiefly taken from the diary of Lord Fountainhall. Edinburgh, 1822.

Military Memoirs of the Great Civil War, being the Military Memoirs of J. Gwynne; and an account of the Earl of Glencairn's Expedition. Edinburgh, 1822.

Lays of the Lindsays, being Poems by the Ladies of the House of Balcarres. Edinburgh, 1824. [Suppressed.]

Auld Robin Gray, A Ballad. By the Rt. Honourable Lady Anne Barnard, born Lady Anne Lindsay of Balcarres. Bannatyne Club, Edinburgh, 1825.

Memoirs of the Marchioness de la Rochejaquelin. Translated from the French. [In Constable's Miscellany, vol. v, Edinburgh, 1827.]

The Bannatyne Miscellany. Vol. I, Bannatyne Club, Edinburgh, 1827. [Edited by Scott and D. Laing.]

Proceedings in the Court Martial held upon John, Master of Sinclair. Roxburghe Club, Edinburgh, 1828.

Memorials of George Bannatyne, 1545–1608. With a Memoir. Bannatyne Club, Edinburgh, 1829.

Papers relative to the Regalia of Scotland. Bannatyne Club, Edinburgh, 1829.

The Trial of Duncan Terig alias Clerk, and Alexander Bane Macdonald for the murder of Arthur Davis, serjeant in General Guise's Regiment of Foot. June, A.D. 1754. Edinburgh, 1831.

Kinmont Willie: A Border Ballad. With an historical introduction by Sir Walter Scott. Edinburgh, 1841.

The Novels and Miscellaneous Works of Daniel Defoe. With Prefaces and Notes including those attributed to Sir Walter Scott. 1854.

Memoirs of the Insurrection in 1715, by John Master of Sinclair. Abbotsford Club, Edinburgh, 1858.

The Image of Ireland. By John Dericke, 1581. Edited with the notes of Sir Walter Scott, by J. Small. 1883.

(8) BIOGRAPHY AND CRITICISM

(a) Biographies

Taylor, J. The Caledonian Comet. A Satirical Poem. 1810.

Sellon, Mary A. The Caledonian Comet Elucidated. 1810. [Reply to above.]

Letter to Sir W. S. Bart., on the Moral and Other Characteristics of the Ebony and Shandryan Schools. Edinburgh, 1820.

Jacob, C. G. Walter Scott. Ein biographisch-literarischer Versuch. Cologne, 1827.

Impromptu adressé à M. Alexandre, par Sir Walter Scott, pendant une Visite qu'il lui fit à son Château d'Abbotsford. Paris, 1827. [With trn.]

Lacroix, P. Soirées de Walter Scott à Paris. Paris, 1829.

Biographical Memoirs. Paris, 1830.

Autobiography of Sir Walter Scott. Philadelphia, 1831.

Vedder, D. Memoir of Sir Walter Scott. 1832.

Knowles, J. S. A Masque (on the death of Sir Walter Scott). 1832.

Naylor, B. S. Memoir of the Life and Writings of Walter Scott. 1833.

Allan, G. Life of Sir Walter Scott, Baronet; with Critical Notices of his Writings. Edinburgh, 1834.

Chambers, R. Life of Sir Walter Scott. Edinburgh, 1834; 1871 (3rd edn, with notanda on Scott and his factor by R. Carruthers).

Cunningham, A. Biographical and Critical History of British Literature of the Last Fifty Years. Paris, 1834.

Hogg, J. Domestic Manners and Private Life of Sir Walter Scott. Glasgow, 1834; Edinburgh, 1882, 1909.

Soirées d'Abbotsford. Chroniques et Nouvelles recueillies dans les Salons de Walter Scott. Paris, 1834.

Weir, A. and Albany, G. Life of Sir Walter Scott. 1834.

Irving, W. Abbotsford and Newstead Abbey. 1835.

Martineau, H. Miscellanies. 2 vols. Boston, 1836.

Periodical Criticisms of Sir Walter Scott. Edinburgh, 1836.

Gillies, R. P. Recollections of Sir Walter Scott, Bart. 1837.

Lockhart, J. G. Memoirs of the Life of Sir Walter Scott, Bart. 2 vols. Edinburgh, 1837–8; 7 vols. Edinburgh, 1837; 10 vols. Edinburgh, 1839. Abridged, 1871; tr. German, 1839–41.

—— The Ballantyne-Humbug Handled. Edinburgh, [1838].

Bucke, C. A. A Letter intended (one day) as a Supplement to Lockhart's Life of Scott. 1838.

Cochrane, J. G. Catalogue of the Library at Abbotsford. Bannatyne Club, 1838.

[Ballantyne, A.] Refutation of the Mistatements and Calumnies contained in Mr Lockhart's Life of Sir Walter Scott, respecting Messrs Ballantyne. By the Trustees and Son of the late Mr James Ballantyne. Edinburgh, 1838.

—— Reply to Mr Lockhart's Pamphlet entitled The Ballantyne-Humbug Handled. Edinburgh, 1839.

Chorley, H. F. The Authors of England. A Series of Medallion Portraits. 1838; 1861 (rev. edn).

Blanchard, L. Life and Literary Remains of L. E. L[andon]. 2 vols. 1841.

Scott, J. (of Gala). Journal of a Tour to Waterloo and Paris with Sir Walter Scott. 1842.

Robberds, J. W. Memoir of the Life of W. Taylor of Norwich. 2 vols. 1843.

Howitt, W. Homes and Haunts of the Most Eminent British Poets. 2 vols. 1847; 1857 (3rd edn).

Grant, G. Life of Sir Walter Scott. 1849.

Particulars and Conditions of Sale of Copyrights, etc., of the Works of Sir Walter Scott. 1851.

Cockburn, H. T., Lord. Life of Lord Jeffrey. 2 vols. Edinburgh, 1852.

—— Memorials of his Time. Edinburgh, 1856.

—— Journal (1831–1854). Edinburgh, 1874.

Macleod, D. Life of Sir Walter Scott. 1852.

[Matthews, G. K.] Abbotsford and Sir Walter Scott. 1853.

Willis, N. P. Famous Persons and Famous Places. 1854.

Mason, E. T. Personal Traits of British Authors. 2 vols. New York, 1855.

Rogers, S. Recollections of the Table-Talk of Samuel Rogers. 1856.

White, J. Robert Burns and Sir Walter Scott: Two Lives. 1858.

Eberty, F. Walter Scott: Ein Lebensbild. 2 vols. Breslau, 1860, 1871.

Leslie, C. R. Autobiographical Recollections. 2 vols. 1860.

Elze, K. Sir Walter Scott. Dresden, 1864.

Gilfillan, G. Life of Sir Walter Scott. Edinburgh, 1870, 1871.

History of the Ballantyne Press and its Connection with Sir Walter Scott. Edinburgh, 1871.

Catalogue of the Scott Exhibition. Edinburgh, 1871.

Gibson, J. Reminiscences of Sir Walter Scott. Edinburgh, 1871.

Gleig, G. R. The Life of Sir Walter Scott. Edinburgh, 1871.

Lockhart, C. S. M. Centenary Memorials of Sir Walter Scott. 1871.

Mackay, C. Forty Years' Recollections. 2 vols. 1871.

Mackenzie, R. S. Sir Walter Scott: The Story of his Life. 1871.

Constable, T. Archibald Constable, and his Literary Correspondents. 3 vols. 1873.

Ticknor, G. Life, Letters and Journals. 2 vols. 1876.

Lennox, Lord W. P. Celebrities I have known. Second Series, 2 vols. 1877.

Rogers, G. Genealogical Memoirs of the Family of Scott. Grampian Club, Royal Hist. Soc. 1877.

Hutton, R. H. Sir Walter Scott. 1878. (English Men of Letters ser.)

Rossetti, W. M. Lives of Famous Poets. 1878.

Colston, T. History of the Scott Monument. Edinburgh, 1881.

Jennings, J. L. Correspondence and Diaries of J. W. Croker. 3 vols. 1885 (2nd edn).

Wood, J. The Life of Sir Walter Scott. 1886.

Yonge, C. D. Life of Sir Walter Scott. 1888.

Smiles, S. A Publisher [John Murray] and his Friends. 2 vols. 1891.

Masson, D. In the Footsteps of the Poets. 1893.

Maxwell-Scott, M. M. Abbotsford: The Personal Relics and Antiquarian Treasures of Sir Walter Scott. 1893.

—— The Making of Abbotsford. 1897.

Swinburne, A. C. Journal of Sir Walter Scott (1825–32). [In Studies in Prose and Poetry, 1894.]

Lang, A. Sir Walter Scott. 1896.

—— Life and Letters of J. G. Lockhart. 2 vols. 1896.

Scott, A. The Story of Sir Walter Scott's First Love. 1896.

Napier, G. C. Homes and Haunts of Scott. 1897.

Hay, J. Speech at the Unveiling of the Bust of Scott in Westminster Abbey, May 21, 1897. 1897.

—— Sir Walter Scott. 1899.

Saintsbury, G. Sir Walter Scott. [1897.]

Dickens, C. Sir Walter Scott and his Publishers. [In To Be Read at Dusk, 1898.]

Memoirs of a Highland Lady. (1797–1833.) 1898.

Stephen, Sir L. The Story of Scott's Ruin. [In Studies of a Biographer, vol. II, 1898.]

Neuburger, E. Goethe und Walter Scott. Frankfurt, 1900.

Hudson, W. H. Sir Walter Scott. 1901.

Rosel, L. K. Die litterarischen und persönlichen Beziehungen Sir Walter Scotts zu Goethe. Leipzig, 1902.

Crockett, W. S. and Caw, T. L. Sir Walter Scott. 1903.

Memorials of James Hogg. Ed. Mrs M. G. Gardner, Paisley, 1903.

Hughes, M. A. Letters and Recollections of Sir Walter Scott. 1904; 1909.

O'Donoghue, D. J. Sir Walter Scott's Tour in Ireland in 1825. Glasgow, 1905.

Laidlaw, W. Recollections of Sir Walter Scott (1802–1804). Ed. J. Sinton, Trans. Hawick Archaeological Soc. 1905.

Fyfe, W. T. Edinburgh under Sir Walter Scott. 1906.

Gondielock, H. J. The Lodge of Sir Walter Scott. A Historical Sketch of Lodge St David. No. 36. Edinburgh, 1906.

Wyndham, G. Sir Walter Scott. 1908.

The Ballantyne Press and its Founders. 1909.

Skene, J. Memories of Sir Walter Scott. Ed. B. Thomson, 1909.

MacGunn, F. Sir Walter Scott's Friends. Edinburgh, 1909.

MacGregor, M. Scott. 1910.

Norgate, G. Le G. Life of Sir Walter Scott. 1913.

Cruse, A. Sir Walter Scott. 1915.

Chisholm, J. Sir Walter Scott as a Judge. 1918.

Withington, R. Scott's Contributions to Pageantic Developement. A Note on the Visit of George IV to Edinburgh in 1822. Stud. Phil. April 1920.

The Scotts in France. Texas Rev. July 1920.

Stalker, A. The Intimate Life of Sir Walter Scott. 1921.

Emerson, O. F. The Early Literary Life of Sir Walter Scott. JEGP. Jan., April, July 1924.

Harris, D. F. Sir Walter Scott and the West Port Atrocities. Cornhill Mag. Jan. 1927.

Cook, D. Murray's Mysterious Contributor. Nineteenth Century, April 1927. [Includes unpbd letters.]

—— Lockhart's Treatment of Scott's Letters. Nineteenth Century, Sept. 1927.

Butler, H. J. and H. E. Sir Walter Scott and Maria Edgeworth: Some Unpublished Letters. MLR. xxiii, 1928.

Grierson, H. J. C. Scott and Carlyle. E. & S. xiii, 1928.

Boas, L. C. A Great Rich Man: The Romance of Sir Walter Scott. 1929.

Johnston, Sir C. N. (Lord Sands). Sir Walter Scott's Congé. 1929; 1930 (with supplementary chapter).

Dickson, W. K. Sir Walter Scott and the Parliament House. 1930.

Gwynn, S. The Life of Sir Walter Scott. 1930; 1932.

Carswell, D. Sir Walter: a Four-Part Study in Biography. 1930; 1932.

Bayne, M. Sir Walter Scott: the Wizard of the North. 1931.

Cook, E. J. Sir Walter Scott's Dogs. 1931.

Gray, W. F. Scott in Sunshine and Shadow. The Tribute of his Friends. 1931.

Buchan, J. Sir Walter Scott. 1932.

Patten, J. A. Sir Walter Scott: A Character Study. 1932.

Pope-Hennessy, U. The Laird of Abbotsford. 1932.

Pagan, E. T. Scott and his Times. 1935.

Strout, A. L. James Hogg's Familiar Anecdotes of Sir Walter Scott. Stud. Phil. xxxiii, 1936.

Tait, J. G. The Missing Tenth of Sir Walter Scott's Journal. Edinburgh, 1936.

—— Sir Walter Scott's Journal and its Editors. Edinburgh, 1938.

Grierson, Sir H. J. C. The Story of Scott's Early Love. Blackwood's Mag. cxli, 1937.

—— Sir Walter Scott, Bart. A New Life. 1938.

(b) General Critical and Topographical Works

[For topography of the Waverley Novels see under (d) below, p. 378.]

'Stendhal' (i.e. H. Beyle). Walter Scott et la Princesse de Clèves. [In Racine et Shakespeare, Paris, 1823.]

Weston, S. The Praise of W[alter] S[cott]. 1823.

Hazlitt, W. The Spirit of the Age. 1825.

Ritchie, L. Scott and Scotland. 1835.

A Parallel between Shakespeare and Scott. 1835.

Carlyle, T. Sir Walter Scott. Westminster Rev. xxviii, 1838. [Rptd in Critical and Miscellaneous Essays, 4 vols. 1839.]

Hagberg, C. A. Cervantes et Walter Scott. 1838.

The Genius and Wisdom of Sir Walter Scott. 1839.

Jeffrey, F., Lord. Contributions to the Edinburgh Review. 4 vols. 1844.

Prescott, W. H. Critical and Historical Essays. 1850.

Miller, H. Essays. Edinburgh, 1862.

—— Leading Articles. Edinburgh, 1870.

Rushton, W. The Classical and Romantic School of English Literature. 1863.

Senior, N. W. Essays on Fiction. 1864. [Scott, pp. 1–188.]

Harkon, J. M. Sir Walter Scott, the Character of his Genius, and the Moral Influence his Works are fitted to exercise. 1867.

Schmidt, J. Walter Scott und seine Bedeutung für unsere Zeit. Westmans Monatshefte, xxvi, 1869.

The Centenary Garland. Pictorial Illustrations by G. Cruikshank, etc. Ed. C. Rogers, Edinburgh, 1871.

Hunnewell, J. F. The Lands of Scott. Edinburgh, 1871.

Gottshall, R. von. Die deutsche National-litteratur des 19. Jahrhunderts. Vol. IV, Leipzig, 1872.

Yonge, C. D. Three Centuries of English Literature. 1872.

Stephen, Sir L. Hours in a Library. Ser. 1, 1874, 1877 (enlarged).

Keble, J. Occasional Papers and Reviews. Oxford, 1877.

Stevenson, R. L. A Gossip on Romance. Longman's Mag. Feb. 1882. [Rptd in Memories and Portraits, 1887.]

Oliphant, M. O. The Literary History of England in the End of the Eighteenth and the Beginning of the Nineteenth Century. Vol. II, 1882.

Courthope, W. J. The Liberal Movement in English Literature. 1885.

Lang, A. Letters to Dead Authors. 1886.

—— Scott and the Border Minstrelsy. 1910.

Hannay, D. Glimpses of the Land of Scott. 1887.

Waille, V. Le Romantisme de Manzoni. Algiers, 1890.

Howells, W. D. Criticism and Fiction. 1891.

Masson, D. Edinburgh Sketches. 1892.

Walker, H. Three Centuries of Scottish Literature. Vol. II, Glasgow, 1893.

Minto, W. The Literature of the Georgian Era. Edinburgh, 1894.

Saintsbury, G. A History of Nineteenth Century Literature (1780–1895). 1896.

Herford, C. H. The Age of Wordsworth. 1897.

Hallays, A. Walter Scott et le Romantisme français. Journal des Débats, 26 July 1898.

Maigron, L. Le Roman historique à l'Époque romantique. Essai sur l'influence de Walter Scott. Paris, 1898. [See Quart. Rev. cxc, 1899.]

—— Walter Scott. Paris, 1920.

Omond, T. S. The Romantic Triumph. Edinburgh, 1900.

Hudson, W. H. Sir Walter Scott. 1901.

Crockett, W. S. The Scott Country. Edinburgh, 1902, 1921, 1930.

—— The Footsteps of Scott. Edinburgh, 1907.

—— The Scott Originals. Edinburgh, 1912.

Freye, W. The Influence of Gothic Literature on Sir Walter Scott. Rostock, 1902.

Armour, A. Sir Walter Scott. 1904.

Ainger, A. Some Leaders in the Poetic Revival of 1760–1820. [In Lectures and Essays, vol. I, 1905.]

Wenger, K. Historische Romaner deutscher Romantiker. (Untersuchungen über den Einfluss Walter Scotts.) Berne, 1905.

Fyfe, W. G. Edinburgh under Sir Walter Scott. Edinburgh, 1906.

Vaughan, C. E. The Romantic Revolt. Edinburgh, 1907.

Des Granges, C. M. Le Romantisme et la Critique. Le Presse littéraire sous la Restauration, 1815–30. Paris, 1907.

Ball, M. Sir Walter Scott as a Critic of Literature. New York, 1907.

Williams, A. M. Scott as a Man of Letters. E. Studien, XXXVII, 1907.

Wyndham, G. Sir Walter Scott. 1908.

Elton, O. A Survey of English Literature, 1780–1830. 2 vols. 1912. [Ch. on Scott pbd separately, 1924.]

Findlay, J. P. Sir Walter Scott, the Great Unknown. [1912.]

Olcott, C. S. Country of Sir Walter Scott. 1913.

Grierson, E. Sir Walter Scott. 1913.

Thomas, E. A Literary Pilgrim in England. 1917.

Mukhopadhyaya, H. The Supernatural in Scott. 1917.

Shears, L. A. The Influence of Walter Scott on the Novels of Theodor Fontane. 1922.

Ker, W. P. Sir Walter Scott's Scotland. 1922.

Churchman, P. H. and Peers, E. A. A Survey of the Influence of Sir Walter Scott in Spain. Revue Hispanique, LV, 1922.

Vissink, H. Scott and his Influence on Dutch Literature. 1922.

C., A. J. Notes on the Influence of Sir W. Scott on G. Eliot. 1923.

Croce, B. Sir Walter Scott. Critica, Jan. 1923. [Rptd in European Literature in the Nineteenth Century, 1924.]

Draper, F. W. M. The Rise and Fall of French Romantic Drama, with Special Reference to the Influence of Sir Walter Scott. 1923.

Buchan, J. Some Notes on Sir Walter Scott. English Ass. 1924.

—— Homilies and Recreations. 1926.

Jones, Sir H. Essays on Literature and Education. 1924.

Newbolt, Sir H. Peacock, Scott, and Robin Hood. Trans. Royal Soc. Lit. IV, 1924.

Fletcher, C. R. L. Sir Walter Scott. Quart. Rev. Jan. 1925.

Ker, W. P. Collected Essays. Vol. I, 1925.

Macintosh, W. Scott and Goethe: German Influence on the Writings of Sir Walter Scott. Galashiels, 1925.

Tearle, C. In Edinburgh and the Scott Country with Mr Fairfield. 1925.

Garnand, H. J. The Influence of Sir Walter Scott on the Works of Balzac. 1926.

Stokoe, F. W. German Influence in the English Romantic Period, with Special Reference to Scott, Coleridge, Shelley, and Byron. 1926.

Brinton, C. Political Ideas of the English Romanticists. 1926.

Baldensperger, F. La grande Communion romantique de 1827: Sous le Signe de Walter Scott. Revue de Littérature comparée, Jan. 1927.

Barkie, J. The Charm of the Scott Country. 1927.

Smith, F. E. (Earl of Birkenhead). Law, Life and Letters. Vol. i, 1927.

The Sir Walter Scott Quarterly. Ed. W. F. Gray, April 1927–Jan. 1928.

Hartland, R. W. Walter Scott et le Roman frénétique. Paris, 1928.

Batho, E. C. Sir Walter Scott and the Sagas. MLR. xxiv, 1929.

Fraser, J. A. L. Scott and Stevenson. 1929.

Ker, J. I. The Land of Scott. 1931.

Sir Walter Scott Today. Some Retrospective Essays and Studies. Ed. Sir H. J. C. Grierson, 1932.

Scott Centenary Articles. Essays from the Times Literary Supplement. Oxford, 1932.

Gray, W. F. The Scott Centenary Handbook. Edinburgh, 1932.

Cecil, Lord D. Sir Walter Scott. 1933.

Marshall, D. Sir Walter Scott and Scots Law. Edinburgh, 1933.

Dargan, E. P. Scott and the French Romantics. PMLA. xlix, 1934.

Stuart, D. M. Sir Walter Scott: some Centenary Reflections. English Ass. lecture, 1934.

Muir, E. Scott and Scotland. The Predicament of the Scottish Writer. 1936.

Korn, M. Sir Walter Scott und die Geschichte. Ang. lxi, 1937.

(c) Criticism of Scott's Poetry

Illustrations of the Lay of the Last Minstrel: with Anecdotes and Descriptions. 1808.

'Pry, Peter.' Marmion travestied. A Tale of Modern Times. 1809.

[Roby, J.] Jokeby: a Burlesque on Rokeby. 1813; 1820 (10th edn).

The Lay of the Poor Fiddler. A Parody on the Lay of the Last Minstrel. By an Admirer of Walter Scott. 1814.

The Lay of the Scottish Fiddle. A Poem, in Five Cantos. Supposed to be written by W— S—, Esq. First American, from the Fourth Edinburgh Edition [actually first English edn]. 1814.

Turner, J. M. W. Descriptive Catalogue of Drawings especially made for Sir Walter Scott's Poetical Works. 1833.

Moir, D. M. Sketches of the Poetical Literature of the Last Half Century. Cambridge, 1851.

Jellett, J. H. The Poetry of Sir Walter Scott. Dublin, 1869.

Sproat, G. M. Sir Walter Scott as a Poet. 1871.

Airy, G. B. On the Topography of The Lady of the Lake. [1875?]

Doyle, Sir F. H. Lectures on Poetry. Second Series. 1877.

Rehdans, W. J. An Exact Account and Critical Examination of The Lady of the Lake. Culm, 1878. [Continuation, Strasburg, 1880.]

Shairp, J. C. The Homeric Spirit in Sir Walter Scott. [In Aspects of Poetry, being Lectures delivered at Oxford. Oxford, 1881.]

Sarrazin, G. Les Poètes modernes d'Angleterre. Paris, 1885.

Veitch, J. The Feeling for Nature in Scottish Poetry. Vol. ii, Edinburgh, 1887.

Staake, P. Critical Introduction to Sir Walter Scott's Lay of the Last Minstrel. Meerane, 1888.

Winch, R. F. Glossary and Notes on Old Mortality. 1894.

Palgrave, F. T. Landscape in Poetry. 1896.

Benner, F. Poetik W. Scotts in seiner 'Lady of the Lake' mit Hinweisen auf Byrons 'Siege of Corinth' und Burns 'Poems.' Ludwigslust, 1899.

Williams, A. M. Some Characteristics of Scott's Poetry. [In Our Early Female Novelists, Glasgow, 1904.]

Brooke, S. A. Studies in Poetry. 1907.

Franke, P. W. Der Stil in den epischen Dichtungen Walter Scotts. Berlin, 1909.

Courthope, W. J. History of English Poetry. Vol. vi, 1910.

Streizle, A. Personifikation und poetische Beseelung bei Scott und Burns. Heidelberg, 1911.

Watt, L. M. Scottish Life and Poetry. 1912.

Morgan, A. E. Scott and his Poetry. 1913.

Hoffmann, —. Entstehungsgeschichte von Sir Walter Scotts Marmion. Königsberg, 1913.

Draat, P. F. van. The Poetry of Sir Walter Scott. Inaugural Lecture. Utrecht, 1924.

Grady, R. M. Sources of Scott's Eight Long Poems. Urbana, 1934.

Parsons, C. O. Scott's Translation of Bürger's 'Das Lied von Treue.' JEGP. xxxiii, 1934.

Burr, A. Sir Walter Scott: an Index. Placing the Short Poems in his Novels and in his Long Poems and Dramas. Cambridge, U.S.A. 1936.

Mennie, D. M. Sir Walter Scott's Unpublished Translations of German Plays. MLR. xxxiii, 1938.

(d) Criticism of Scott's Novels

Quart. Rev. July 1814. [Review of Waverley; rptd in Famous Reviews, ed. R. B. Johnson, 1914.]

Quart. Rev. Jan. 1817. [Review of Tales of my Landlord; rptd in Famous Reviews, ed. R. B. Johnson, 1914.]

Grahame, J. Vindication of the Scottish Presbyterians and Covenanters against the Aspersions of the Author of The Tales of my Landlord. Glasgow, 1817.

Criminal Trials, Illustrative of the Tale entitled The Heart of Midlothian. Edinburgh, 1818. [Preface by Scott, who perhaps edited the work.]

'Touchstone, Timothy.' A Letter to the Author of Waverley, on the Moral Tendency of those Popular Works. 1820.

Allan, W. Illustrations of the Novels and Tales [to 1819]. Edinburgh, 1820. A New Series, [1820–1]. Edinburgh, 1823. Illustrations, [1822–3]. Edinburgh, 1825.

[Adolphus, J. L.] Letters to Richard Heber, Esq. containing Critical Remarks on the Series of Novels beginning with Waverley, and an Attempt to ascertain their Author. 1821; 1822.

Aiton, W. History of the Rencounter at Drumclog, and Battle at Bothwell Bridge, with an Account of what is Correct, and what is Fictitious in The Tales of My Landlord. Hamilton, 1821.

Warner, R. Illustrations, Critical, Historical, Biographical, and Miscellaneous, of Novels by the Author of Waverley. 3 vols. 1821, 1823–4.

Wilks, M. Historical Notices of E. and W. Christian, Two Characters in Peveril of the Peak. 1822.

Illustrations of the Novels and Tales of the Author of Waverley, with Biographical Notes. 1823.

Historical Illustrations of Quentin Durward, selected from the Memoirs of Phillip de Commines and Other Authors. 1823.

Chambers, R. Illustrations of the Author of Waverley: being Notices and Anecdotes of Real Characters and Incidents supposed to be described in his Works. Edinburgh, 1825.

'Dreadnought, D.' Familiar Epistles, addressed to Malachi Malagrowther. 1826.

Skene, J. Sketches of the Existing Localities alluded to in the Waverley Novels. Edinburgh, 1829.

Auction Catalogues of the Original MSS. of the Waverley Novels. 1831.

F. The Waverley Anecdotes. 2 vols. 1833; 1884.

Du Roman historique en France et en Angleterre. Revue Britannique, Nov. 1834.

Wright, C. N. Landscape-Historical Illustrations of Scotland and the Waverley Novels, from Drawings by J. M. W. Turner. 1836–8.

A Letter containing some Remarks on the Tendency and Influence of the Waverley Novels on Society. From a Clergyman of the Church of England. 1838.

Scott, A. Ivanhoe! or The Jew of York. [1840.]

The Waverley Gallery of the Principal Female Characters in Sir Walter Scott's Romances. 1841.

MacCrie, T. Vindication of the Covenanters in a Review of The Tales of My Landlord. Edinburgh, 1845. [Rptd in M'Crie's Works, vol. VII, 1856.]

Terry, D. The Waverley Dramas, from the Novels of Sir Walter Scott. 1845.

The Female Characters of Scott. 1848.

Bartlett, A. D. Historical Account of Cumnor Place, Berks. followed by some Remarks on the Statements in Kenilworth. 1850.

A Series of One Hundred and Twenty Engravings illustrating the Abbotsford Edition of the Novels of Sir Walter Scott. Edinburgh, 1851.

Beautés de Walter Scott. Magnifiques Portraits des Héroïnes de Walter Scott, Accompagnés chacun d'un Portrait littéraire par MM. A. Dumas, Carmouche, etc. Paris, 1852.

French, G. J. Parallel Passages from Two Tales elucidating the Origin of the Plot of Guy Mannering. Manchester, 1855.

—— An Inquiry into the Origin of the Authorship of some of the Earlier Waverley Novels. Boston, 1856.

F[itzpatrick], W. J. Who wrote the Earlier Waverley Novels? 1856.

Jeafferson, J. C. Novels and Novelists from Elizabeth to Victoria. Vol. II, 1858.

Bagehot, W. The Waverley Novels. National Rev. VI, 1858. [Rptd in Literary Studies, vol. II, 1879.]

Masson, D. British Novelists and their Styles. Cambridge, 1859.

Senior, N. W. Essays on Fiction. 1864.

Freeman, E. The Norman Conquest. 1867–79. [Note 2 (on Ivanhoe) in Appendix.]

Cornish, S. W. The Waverley Manual. A Handbook of the Chief Characters in the Waverley Novels. Edinburgh, 1871.

Rogers, M. The Waverley Dictionary. Chicago, 1879.

Canning, A. S. G. The Philosophy of the Waverley Novels. 1879.

—— History in Fact and Fiction. 1897.

—— History in Scott's Novels. 1905.

—— Sir Walter Scott studied in Eight Novels. 1910.

Watt, J. C. Great Novelists. 1880.

Grey, H. Key to the Waverley Novels. 1881; 1884 (rev. edn).

Tuckerman, R. A History of English Prose Fiction. New York, 1882.

Dickson, N. The Bible in Waverley, or Sir Walter Scott's Use of the Sacred Scriptures. 1884.

Eastman, C. W. Wilhelm Hauff's Lichtenstein [compared with Ivanhoe]. America Germanica, III–IV, 1890–1900.

Saintsbury, G. The Historical Novel. [In Essays in English Literature (1780–1860), ser. 2, 1895.]

Burgess, S. The Law in Scott. 1896.

Jack, A. A. Essays on the Novel as illustrated by Scott and Miss Austen. 1897.

Novels and Novelists. Chapters on the Waverley Novels. 1898.

Bouchier, J. A Waverley Mosaic. (An Imaginary Letter from the Laird of Dumbiedikes to Dandie Dinmont.) 1898 (priv. ptd).

Sidney, P. Who killed Amy Robsart? Being some Account of her Life and Death: with Remarks on Sir Walter Scott's Kenilworth. 1901.

Schüler, F. M. Quellenforschung zu Scotts Roman Rob Roy. Leipzig, 1901.

Gaebel, K. Beiträge zur Technik der Erzählung in den Romanen Walter Scotts. Marburger Studien zur Englischen Philologie, II, 1901.

Abramczyk, R. L. A. Über die Quellen zu Walter Scotts Roman Ivanhoe. Halle, 1903.

Wolf, M. Walter Scott's Kenilworth. Eine Untersuchung über sein Verhältnis zur Geschichte und zu seinen Quellen. Leipzig, 1903.

Siebert, A. Untersuchungen zu Walter Scotts Waverley. 1903.

Carruth, W. H. The Relation of Hauff's Lichtenstein to Scott's Waverley. PMLA. XVIII, 1903.

Gärdes, J. Walter Scott als Characterzeichner in 'The Heart of Midlothian.' Vegesack, 1904.

Agnoli, G. Gli Albori del Romanzo storico in Italia e i primi Imitatori di Walter Scott. Piacenza, 1906.

Gest, J. M. Law and Lawyers of Sir Walter Scott. 1906.

Young, C. A. The Waverley Novels: An Appreciation. Glasgow, 1907.

Korff, H. A. Scott und Alexis (G. W. H. Haering). Eine Studie zur Technik des historischen Romans. Heidelberg, 1907.

Jackson, H. Great English Novelists. [1908.]

Ruskin, J. Fiction, Foul and Fair. [In Works, ed. Sir E. T. Cook, vol. XXXIV, 1908.]

Hofer, E. Sir Walter Scotts Einfluss auf Ph. J. von Rehfues. Mähr-Weisskirchen, 1909.

Husband, M. F. A. Dictionary of Characters in the Waverley Novels. 1910.

Thompson, G. W. Wilhelm Hauff's Specific Relation to Walter Scott. PMLA. XXVI, 1911.

Watson, J. ('Ian Maclaren'). The Waverley Novels. 1911.

Crockett, W. S. The Scott Originals. 1912.

Lorenzon, H. L. Peveril of the Peak. Ein Beitrag zur literarischen Würdigung Sir Walter Scotts. Berlin, 1912.

Müller, K. A. P. Die Quellen zu Walter Scotts Roman 'The Fortunes of Nigel.' Leipzig, 1913.

Knothe, K. Untersuchungen zu Redgauntlet. Görlitz, 1913.

Steiger, O. Die Verwendung des schottischen Dialekts in Sir Walter Scotts Romanen. Darmstadt, 1913

Verrall, A. W. The Prose of Sir Walter Scott. [In Collected Literary Essays, Cambridge, 1913.]

Watson, G. Literary Blunders of the Author of Waverley. Trans. Hawick Archaeological Soc. 1914.

Miller, F. Andrew Crosbie, Advocate, a Reputed Original of Paulus Playdell in Guy Mannering. 1919.

Saintsbury, G. Scott and Dumas. [In Modern English Essays, 1922.]

Lindström, E. Walter Scott och den historiska romanen och novellen i Sverige intill 1850. Göteborgs Högskolas Årsskrift, XXXI, 1925.

Brewer, W. Shakespeare's Influence on Sir Walter Scott. Boston, 1925.

Weygandt, C. A Century of the English Novel. New York, 1925.

Scott's Diary and Woodstock. TLS. 27 May 1926.

White, H. A. Sir Walter Scott's Novels on the Stage. New Haven, 1927.

Haber, T. B. The Chapter-Tags in the Waverley Novels. PMLA. XLV, 1930.

Boatright, M. C. Witchcraft in the Novels of Sir Walter Scott. Texas University Stud. XIII, XIV, 1933–4.

—— Scott's Theory and Practice concerning the Use of the Supernatural in Prose Fiction in Relation to the Chronology of the Waverley Novels. PMLA. L, 1935.

Parsons, C. O. Demonological Background of 'Donnerhugel's Narrative' and 'Wandering Willie's Tale.' Stud. Phil. XXX, 1933.

—— Character Names in the Waverley Novels. PMLA. XLIX, 1934.

Baker, E. A. The History of the English Novel. Vol. VI, 1935. [Chs. vi–ix.]

Millett, F. B. The Date and Literary Relations of Woodstock. Chicago, 1935.

Randall, D. A. Waverley in America. Colophon, summer 1935.

Hillhouse, J. T. The Waverley Novels and their Critics. Minneapolis, 1936.

Muir, E. Sir Walter Scott. [In The English Novelists, ed. D. Verschoyle, 1936.]

D. H.

JANE AUSTEN (1775–1817)*

(1) BIBLIOGRAPHY

Keynes, G. L. Jane Austen. A Bibliography. 1929.

(2) COLLECTED EDITIONS

Novels by Miss Jane Austen. 5 vols. 1833 (also issued separately), 1866, 1869; 6 vols. 1878–9 (vol. VI is J. E. Austen-Leigh's Memoir, originally pbd 1870). [Prefixed to vol. I is a memoir by 'the author's brother,' *i.e.* Henry Austen, dated 5 Oct. 1832.]

Jane Austen's Works. Steventon Edition. 6 vols. 1882, 1886. [Vol. VI is J. E. Austen-Leigh's Memoir.]

Jane Austen's Novels. Ed. R. B. Johnson, 10 vols. 1892.

Jane Austen's Novels. 12 vols. Boston, 1892.

The Novels of Jane Austen. Ed. R. B. Johnson, 10 vols. 1898.

The Novels of Jane Austen. Winchester Edition. 10 vols. 1898.

The Novels of Jane Austen. Hampshire Edition. 6 vols. 1902.

The Novels of Jane Austen. 6 vols. 1922. [Introductory notes by R. B. Johnson.]

The Adelphi Edition of The Works of Jane Austen. 7 vols. [1923]. [Vol. VII, Lady Susan and The Watsons.]

The Novels of Jane Austen. The Text based on Collation of the Early Editions by R. W. Chapman. With Notes, Indexes and Illustrations from Contemporary Sources. 5 vols. Oxford, 1923, 1926, 1933 (with some addns); 2 vols. Oxford, 1934. [The standard edn.]

The Works of Jane Austen. Georgian Edition. 5 vols. 1927. [Introductions by J. Bailey.]

The Complete Novels of Jane Austen. With an Introduction by J. C. Squire. [1928.]

[For what are virtually collected edns of the novels in the Everyman's Lib. and World's Classics sers., and ed. A. Dobson, 1895–7, see below under the separate novels.]

(3) THE NOVELS

Sense and Sensibility: A Novel. By A Lady. 3 vols. 1811; 3 vols. 1813 (embodies minor corrections by Jane Austen); 1833; 2 vols. Philadelphia, 1833; 1847; 1852; 1856; New York, 1857 (also includes Persuasion), etc.; ed. A. Dobson, 1896; ed. R. B. Johnson, 1906 (Everyman's Lib.); ed. Lord D. Cecil, 1931 (World's Classics); ed. P. Quennell, 1933; tr. French, 1815 (as Raison et Sensibilité, ou les deux manières d'aimer). [Originally written in letters *c.* 1795 as

Elinor and Marianne; re-written 1797–8 as Sense and Sensibility; revised 1809–10.]

Pride and Prejudice: A Novel. By The Author Of 'Sense And Sensibility.' 3 vols. 1813 (*bis*); 2 vols. 1817; 2 vols. Philadelphia, 1832 (as Elizabeth Bennet; or, Pride and Prejudice); 1833; 1839; 1844; Boston, 1848; 1852; 1856; New York, 1857 (also includes Northanger Abbey), etc.; ed. G. Saintsbury, 1894; ed. A. Dobson, 1895; ed. E. V. Lucas, 1900; ed. R. B. Johnson, 1906 (Everyman's Lib); ed. K. M. Metcalfe, Oxford, 1912; ed. R. W. Chapman, 1929 (World's Classics); tr. French, 1822 (as Orgueil et Prévention and as Orgueil et Préjugé). [Originally written 1796–7 as First Impressions, revised 1812.]

Mansfield Park: A Novel. By The Author Of 'Sense And Sensibility,' and 'Pride And Prejudice.' 3 vols. 1814; 3 vols. 1816 (embodies minor corrections by Jane Austen); 2 vols. Philadelphia, 1832; 1833; Belfast, 1846; 1851; 1857; New York, 1857, etc.; ed. A. Dobson, 1897; ed. R. B. Johnson, 1906 (Everyman's Lib.); ed. M. Lascelles, 1929 (World's Classics); tr. French, 1816 (as Le Parc de Mansfield, ou Les Trois Cousines).

Emma: A Novel. By The Author Of 'Pride And Prejudice,' &c. &c. 3 vols. 1816; 1833; 2 vols. Philadelphia, 1833; 1849; 1856; 1857; New York, 1857, etc.; ed. A. Dobson. 1896; ed. R. B. Johnson, 1906 (Everyman's Lib.); ed. E. V. Lucas, 1907 (World's Classics); tr. French, 1816 (as La Nouvelle Emma, ou les Caractères Anglais du Siècle).

Northanger Abbey: and Persuasion. By The Author Of 'Pride And Prejudice,' 'Mansfield Park,' etc. With A Biographical Notice Of The Author [by Henry Austen]. 4 vols. 1818; 4 vols. Philadelphia, 1833–2; 1833; 1850; 1856; 1857, etc.; ed. A. Dobson, 1897; ed. E. V. Lucas, 1901; ed. R. B. Johnson, 1906 (Everyman's Lib.); ed. K. M. Metcalfe, Oxford, 1923 (Northanger Abbey only); ed. M. Sadleir, 1930 (World's Classics; Northanger Abbey only); ed. F. Reid, 1930 (World's Classics; Persuasion only); tr. French, 1824 (L'Abbaye de Northanger) and 1821 (La Famille Elliot, ou L'Ancienne Inclination). [Northanger Abbey was written 1797–8 as Susan, revised *c.* 1803 and prepared for publication, 1816, as Catherine, but laid aside. A chapter of Persuasion, cancelled 1816, is in J. E. Austen-Leigh's Memoir, 1871 (2nd edn), and in R. W. Chapman's edn of The Novels, vol. V.]

* Revised by Dr R. W. Chapman.

(4) JUVENILIA AND FRAGMENTS

[Arranged in order of composition.]

Volume the First. Now First Printed from the Manuscript in the Bodleian Library. [Ed. R. W. Chapman], Oxford, 1933. [Jane Austen collected her juvenilia in 3 MS vols. *c*. 1793. Vol. II is Love and Freindship; vol. III is extant, but has not been pbd except for the specimens given in W. and R. A. Austen-Leigh, Jane Austen, her Life and Letters, 1913, p. 55.]

Love and Freindship and Other Early Works now first printed from the Original MS. with a Preface by G. K. Chesterton. 1922. [Love and Freindship (1790); Lesley Castle; The History of England (1791); A Collection of Letters; scraps.]

Lady Susan. Ed. R. W. Chapman, Oxford, 1925. [Written *c*. 1805; first ptd in J. E. Austen-Leigh, A Memoir of Jane Austen, 1871 (2nd edn).]

The Watsons. A Fragment. Now reprinted from the MS. Ed. R. W. Chapman, Oxford, 1927; ed. E. and F. Brown, 1928. [Written 1805 or later; first ptd in Memoir, 1871. The 1928 edn includes a completion of the story based on a family tradition that The Younger Sister, 1850, by Catherine Hubback (Jane Austen's niece) embodies the projected plot of The Watsons. See however TLS. 17 May 1928, p. 375.]

Plan of a Novel. According to Hints from Various Quarters; with Opinions on Mansfield Park and Emma, and Other Documents. [Ed. R. W. Chapman], Oxford, 1926. [Written *c*. 1816?]

Sanditon, Fragment of a Novel written January–March, 1817. Ed. R. W. Chapman, Oxford, 1925. [Extracts only in Memoir, 1871.]

Sanditon; The Watsons; Lady Susan, and Other Miscellanea. Ed. R. B. Johnson, 1934.

(5) LETTERS

Austen-Leigh, J. E. A Memoir of Jane Austen. By her Nephew. 1870; 1871 (enlarged); ed. R. W. Chapman, Oxford, 1926 (with brief notes, index and account of extant MSS).

Letters of Jane Austen. Edited with an Introduction and Critical Remarks by Edward, Lord Brabourne. 2 vols. 1884. [Not used in the Memoir.]

Hubback, J. H. and E. C. Jane Austen's Sailor Brothers. 1906. [Includes unpbd letters to Francis Austen.]

Austen-Leigh, W. and R. A. Jane Austen, her Life and Letters. A Family Record. 1913. [Quotes largely from the letters.]

Five Letters from Jane Austen to her Niece Fanny Knight. Ed. facs. R. W. Chapman, Oxford, 1924.

The Letters of Jane Austen. Selected by Brimley Johnson. [1925.]

Jane Austen's Letters. Ed. R. W. Chapman, 2 vols. Oxford, 1932. [The only complete edn, containing a few unpbd letters and correcting the text of most from the originals, together with a brief commentary, full indexes and a chronology of Jane Austen's life. A further letter to Martha Lloyd is added in a few copies.]

(6) BIOGRAPHY AND CRITICISM

[For further titles see J. P. Anderson's Bibliography appended to Goldwin Smith's Life of Jane Austen, 1891, and G. L. Keynes's Bibliography, 1929.]

(a) Books

Austen-Leigh, J. E. A Memoir of Jane Austen. By her Nephew. 1870; 1871 (enlarged; see under Juvenilia and Fragments above); ed. R. W. Chapman, Oxford, 1926.

Ritchie, A. T., Lady. Jane Austen. [In Toilers and Spinsters, 1874; rptd with alterations in A Book of Sibyls, 1883.]

'Tytler, Sarah' (*i.e.* H. Keddie). Jane Austen and her Works. [1880.]

Oliphant, M. O. The Literary History of England. Vol. III, 1882. [Ch. VI, Maria Edgeworth, Jane Austen, Susan Ferrier.]

Malden, S. F. Jane Austen. 1889.

Smith, Goldwin. Life of Jane Austen. 1890.

Adams, O. F. The Story of Jane Austen's Life. Chicago, 1891; Boston, 1897 (rev.).

Charades, etc. written a Hundred Years ago by Jane Austen and her Family. [1895.]

Jack, A. A. Essays on the Novel as Illustrated by Scott and Miss Austen. 1897.

Pollock, W. H. Jane Austen, her Contemporaries and Herself. 1899.

Bonnell, H. H. Charlotte Brontë, George Eliot, Jane Austen. New York, 1902.

Hill, C. Jane Austen, her Homes and her Friends. 1902.

Mitton, G. E. Jane Austen and her Times. [1905.]

Hubback, J. H. and E. C. Jane Austen's Sailor Brothers, Francis Austen and Charles Austen. 1906.

Helm, W. H. Jane Austen and her Country-House Comedy. 1909.

Austen-Leigh, W. and Knight, M. G. Chawton Manor and its Owners. A Family History. 1911.

Fitzgerald, P. Jane Austen, a Criticism and Appreciation. 1912.

Sackville, Lady M. Jane Austen. 1912.

Austen-Leigh, W. and R. A. Jane Austen, her Life and Letters. A Family Record. 1913. [The authoritative life, based on a full knowledge of almost all the extant letters (given only in extract) and other family MSS and traditions; a book of exceptional accuracy.]

Cornish, F. W. Jane Austen. 1913. (English Men of Letters ser.)

Villard, L. Jane Austen, sa Vie et son Œuvre. Paris, 1915; tr. Eng. (in part) 1924.

Austen-Leigh, M. A. Personal Aspects of Jane Austen. 1920.

Meynell, A. The Classic Novelist. [In The Second Person Singular, 1921.]

Walkley, A. B. Pastiche and Prejudice. 1921. [This collection of essays rptd from Times, with its sequels (More Prejudice, 1923; Still More Prejudice, 1925), contains several on Jane Austen.]

Birrell, A. 'Elementary Jane.' [In More Obiter Dicta, 1924.]

Thomson, C. L. Jane Austen. A Survey. 1929.

Johnson, R. B. Jane Austen, her Life, her Work, her Family and her Critics. [1930.]

Canby, H. S. Emma and Mr Knightley. A Critical Essay. New York, 1931.

Rawlence, G. Jane Austen. 1934.

Baker, E. A. The History of the English Novel. Vol. VI, 1935. [Chs. iii–v.]

Cecil, Lord D. Jane Austen. Cambridge, 1935. (Leslie Stephen Lecture.)

Bowen, E. Jane Austen. [In The English Novelists, ed. D. Verschoyle, 1936.]

Haferkorn, R. Zum Begriff des Sentimentalen. [In M. Deutschbein Festschrift, Leipzig, 1936.]

Austen-Leigh, E. Jane Austen and Steventon. 1937.

Bühler, W. Die 'Erlebte Rede' in englischen Roman. Zurich, 1937.

Seymour, B. K. Jane Austen: Study for a Portrait. 1937.

Jenkins, E. Jane Austen. 1938.

Wilson, M. Jane Austen and some Contemporaries. 1938.

(b) Early Reviews*

Sense and Sensibility. Critical Rev. Feb. 1812; British Critic, May 1812.

Pride and Prejudice. British Critic, Feb. 1813; Critical Rev. March 1813.

Emma. Quart. Rev. Oct. 1815 (by Sir W. Scott; rptd in Famous Reviews, ed. R. B. Johnson, 1914); British Critic, July 1816; Monthly Rev. July 1816.

Northanger Abbey and Persuasion. British Critic, March 1818; Edinburgh Mag. and Literary Misc. May 1818; Quart. Rev. Jan.

1821 (by R. Whately; rptd in Famous Reviews, ed. R. B. Johnson, 1914).

(c) Articles in Periodicals

[Lewes, G. H.] The Lady Novelists. Westminster Rev. July 1852.

—— The Novels of Jane Austen. Blackwood's Mag. LXXXVI, 1859.

[Kirk, J. F.] Jane Austen. North American Rev. LXXVII, 1853.

[Pollock, Sir W. F.] British Novelists. Richardson, Miss Austen, Scott. Fraser's Mag. LXI, 1860.

Boucher, L. Le Roman classique en Angleterre. Jane Austen. Revue des deux Mondes, XXIX, 1878.

Dodge, R. E. N. The Note of Provinciality in Jane Austen. Harvard Monthly, VIII, 1889.

Verrall, A. W. On some Passages in Jane Austen's Mansfield Park. Cambridge Rev. XV, 1893. [See also N. & Q. 11 July 1936, pp. 20–2.]

Bradley, A. C. Jane Austen. E. & S. II, 1911. [Rptd in A Miscellany, 1929.]

McKillop, A. D. Jane Austen's Gothic Novels, N. & Q. 5 Nov. 1921.

[Chapman, R. W.] Jane Austen's Methods. TLS. 9 Feb. 1922.

—— Jane Austen and her Publishers. London Mercury, XXII, 1930.

—— Jane Austen. A Reply to Mr Garrod. Trans. Royal Soc. Lit. X, 1931.

—— Jane Austen's Library. Book Collectors' Quart. XI, 1933.

—— Jane Austen's Text. TLS. 13 Feb. 1937.

Woolf, V. Jane Austen at Sixty. Nation, 15 Dec. 1923. [Rptd in The Common Reader, 1925.]

Forster, E. M. 'Jane, how shall we ever recollect?' Nation, 5 Jan. 1924.

—— Sanditon. Nation, 21 March 1925.

—— Miss Austen and Jane Austen. TLS. 10 Nov. 1932. [A depreciation. Forster's articles are all rptd in Abinger Harvest, 1936.]

Walkley, A. B. The Novels of Jane Austen. Edinburgh Rev. CCXXXIX, 1924.

Edmonds, J. L. Jane Austen: a Bibliography. Bulletin of Bibliography, XII, 1925.

Hopkins, A. B. Jane Austen's Love and Freindship: a Study in Literary Relations. South Atlantic Quart. XXIV, 1925.

—— Jane Austen the Critic. PMLA. XL, 1925.

MacKinnon, Sir F. D. Topography and Travel in Jane Austen's Novels. Cornhill Mag. LIX, 1925.

Rowland-Brown, L. Jane Austen Abroad. Nineteenth Century, XCVIII, 1925.

* This section has been contributed by Mr C. B. Hogan.

Howe, M. A. de W. A Jane Austen Letter with Other 'Janeana' from an Old Book of Autographs. Yale Rev. xv, 1926.

Brown, E. C. The Date of The Watsons. Spectator, 11 June 1927.

Pink, M. A. Jane Austen and a Forgotten Dramatist. Nineteenth Century, cii, 1927.

Sadleir, M. The Northanger Novels: a Footnote to Jane Austen. Edinburgh Rev. ccxlvi, 1927; English Ass. 1927.

Alexander, S. The Art of Jane Austen. John Rylands Lib. Bulletin, xii, 1928. [Also issued separately.]

Garrod, H. W. Jane Austen: a Depreciation. Trans. Royal Soc. Lit. viii, 1928.

Hubback, J. H. Pen-Portraits in Jane Austen's Novels. Cornhill Mag. lxv, 1928.

Balfour, Lady. The Servants in Jane Austen. Cornhill Mag. lxvii, 1929.

Wanklyn, C. Jane Austen and Lyme Regis. Dorset Chronicle, 29 Dec. 1932.

Butler, E. M. Mansfield Park and Kotzebue's Lovers' Vows. MLR. xxviii, 1933. [See however H. W. Husbands, MLR. xxix, 1934, pp. 176–9.]

Garnett, D. 'Dear Jane.' Saturday Rev. of Lit. 14 Jan. 1933.

Reitzel, W. Mansfield Park and Lovers' Vows. RES. ix, 1933.

Lascelles, M. Miss Austen and some Books. London Mercury, xxix, 1934.

—— Some Characteristics of Jane Austen's Style. E. & S. xxii, 1937.

Lockwood, E. M. Jane Austen and some Drawing-Room Music of her Time. Music and Letters, xv, 1934.

THOMAS LOVE PEACOCK (1785–1866)

(1) Collected Editions

The Works of Thomas Love Peacock, with a Preface by Lord Houghton, [and] a Biographical Notice by his Granddaughter Edith Nicolls. Ed. H. Cole, 3 vols. 1875

Novels, Calidore and Miscellanea. Ed. R. Garnett, 10 vols. 1891.

Novels and Rhododaphne. Ed. G. Saintsbury, 5 vols. 1895–7.

Poems. Ed. R. B. Johnson, [1906]. (New Universal Lib. and Muses' Lib.)

Plays published for the First Time. Ed. A. B. Young, 1910. [BM. Add. MS 36816.]

Letters to Edward Hookham and Percy B. Shelley with Fragments of Unpublished MS. Ed. R. Garnett, Boston, 1910.

Works. Halliford Edition. Ed. H. F. B. Brett-Smith and C. E. Jones, 10 vols. 1924–34. [The standard edn, with a biographical introduction that supersedes the earlier lives and full bibliographical and textual notes.]

(2) Selections

Thomas Love Peacock. Ed. W. H. Helm, [1911].

Selections from Thomas Love Peacock. Ed. H. F. B. Brett-Smith, 1928.

(3) Separate Works
(a) Verse

The Monks of St Mark. 1804.

Palmyra, and Other Poems. 1806.

The Genius of the Thames. A Lyrical Poem in Two Parts. 1810.

The Genius of the Thames, Palmyra and Other Poems. 1812. [Adds 2 poems.]

The Philosophy of Melancholy, a Poem in Four Parts, with a Mythological Ode. 1812.

Sir Hornbook; or, Childe Launcelot's Expedition. A Grammatico-allegorical Ballad. 1814; 1815 (bis), etc.

Sir Proteus. A Satirical Ballad. By P. M. Donovan, Esq. 1814.

The Round Table; or, King Arthur's Feast. [1817.]

Rhododaphne: or the Thessalian Spell. A Poem. 1818.

Paper Money Lyrics, and Other Poems. 1837 (priv. ptd).

A Bill for the Better Promotion of Oppression on the Sabbath Day. 1926 (priv. ptd).

(b). Novels

Headlong Hall. 1816 (bis); 1822; 1837 (with new Preface, Nightmare Abbey, Maid Marian and Crotchet Castle, as vol. 57 of Bentley's Standard Novel ser.).

Melincourt. By the Author of Headlong Hall. 3 vols. 1817; 1856 (with new Preface).

Nightmare Abbey. By the Author of Headlong Hall. 1818; 1837 (see above under Headlong Hall); ed. C. E. Jones, 1923.

Maid Marian. By the Author of Headlong Hall. 1822; 1837 (see above under Headlong Hall). Tr. German, Jena, 1823; French, Paris, 1826, Brussels, 1855.

The Misfortunes of Elphin. By the Author of Headlong Hall. 1829.

Crotchet Castle. By the Author of Headlong Hall. 1831; 1837 (see above under Headlong Hall).

Gryll Grange. By the Author of Headlong Hall. 1861. [First ptd serially in Fraser's Mag. lxi, lxii, 1860.]

(c) Other Writings

The Four Ages of Poetry. Ollier's Literary Miscellany, No. 1 (only issue), 1820; ed. H. F. B. Brett-Smith, Oxford, 1921 (with Shelley's Defence of Poetry and Browning's Essay on Shelley, as No. 3 of the Percy Reprints).

Memoirs of Percy Bysshe Shelley. Fraser's Mag. LVII, LXI, 1858, 1860 (supplementary notice, *ibid.* LXV, 1862); ed. H. F. B. Brett-Smith, 1909 (with Shelley's letters to Peacock).

Gl' Ingannati: the Deceived. A Comedy performed at Siena in 1531; and Aelia Laelia Crispis. 1862.

(4) BIOGRAPHY AND CRITICISM

[Spedding, J.] Headlong Hall, [etc.]. Edinburgh Rev. LXVIII, 1839.

[Hannay, J.] Recent Humorists: Aytoun, Peacock, Prout. North British Rev. XLV, 1866.

Smith, G. B. Thomas Love Peacock. Fortnightly Rev. XIV, 1873. [Rptd in Poets and Novelists, 1875.]

[Cole, H.] Thomas Love Peacock. Biographical Notes. [1874?] (priv. ptd).

Davies, J. Thomas Love Peacock. Contemporary Rev. XXV, 1875.

Buchanan, R. Thomas Love Peacock: a Personal Reminiscence. New Quart. Mag. IV, 1875.

G[osse], [Sir] E. Thomas Love Peacock. London Society, XXVII, 1875.

The Works of Thomas Love Peacock. Edinburgh Rev. CXLII, 1875.

Saintsbury, G. Thomas Love Peacock. Macmillan's Mag. LIII, 1886. [Rptd in Essays in English Literature 1780–1860, 1890, and Collected Essays and Papers, Vol. II, 1923.]

Paul, H. The Novels of Peacock. Nineteenth Century, LIII, 1903. [Rptd in Stray Leaves, 1906.]

Young, A. B. The Life and Novels of Thomas Love Peacock. Norwich, 1904 (priv. ptd).

van Doren, C. The Life of Thomas Love Peacock. 1911.

Freeman, A. M. Thomas Love Peacock. A Critical Study. 1911.

Burdett, O. Thomas Love Peacock. London Mercury, VIII, 1923.

Newbolt, Sir H. Peacock, Scott and Robin Hood. Trans. Royal Soc. Lit. IV, 1924.

Wright, H. The Associations of Thomas Love Peacock with Wales. E. & S. XII, 1926.

Priestley, J. B. Thomas Love Peacock. 1927. (English Men of Letters ser.)

Digeon, A. T. L. Peacock, Ami de Shelley. Revue anglo-américaine, Feb. 1928.

Dannenberg, F. Peacock in seinem Verhältnis zu Shelley. Germanisch-romanische Monatsschrift, XX, 1932.

Able, A. H. Meredith and Peacock. A Study in Literary Influence. Philadelphia, 1933.

Brett-Smith, H. F. B. The L'Estrange-Peacock Correspondence. E. & S. XVIII, 1933.

Mayoux, J. J. Un Épicurien anglais: Thomas Love Peacock. Paris, 1933.

Fedden, H. R. Peacock. [In The English Novelists, ed. D. Verschoyle, 1936.]

Cellini, B. T. L. Peacock. Rome, 1937.

C. E. J.

FREDERICK MARRYAT (1792–1848)

(1) BIBLIOGRAPHY

Sadleir, M. Excursions in Victorian Bibliography. 1922. [Contains a bibliography of Marryat; a rev. edn. is in preparation.]

(2) COLLECTED WORKS

The Novels of Marryat. Author's Copyright Edition. 8 pts, [1875].

Captain Marryat's Novels. The King's Own Edition. 10 vols. 1896–8. [Introduction to each vol. by W. L. Courtney.]

The Novels of Captain Marryat. Ed. R. Brimley Johnson, 24 vols. 1896–8; 26 vols. 1929–30.

(3) FICTION

The Naval Officer; or, Scenes and Adventures in the Life of Frank Mildmay. 3 vols. 1829; 1836; 1839; Paris, 1840; [1873] (memoir by Florence Marryat), etc.

The King's Own. 3 vols. 1830; 3 vols. 1836; 1838; Paris, 1840; 1856; 1873; [1874]; 1874 (memoir by Florence Marryat); [1880], etc.; tr. French, 1837.

Newton Forster; or, the Merchant Service. 3 vols. 1832; 1838; Paris, 1840; 1855; 1873; [1874]; [1880]; 1897 (illustrations by E. J. Sullivan), etc.

Peter Simple. 3 vols. 1834; 3 vols. 1837; 1838; 1856; 1870; 1873; [1874]; [1876]; [1878]; [1880]; [1881]; [1888], etc.; 2 vols. 1929 (with biographical essay by M. Sadleir); tr. French, Paris, 1834. [First appeared in Metropolitan Mag. June 1832–Dec. 1833.]

Jacob Faithful. 3 vols. 1834 (*bis*); 3 vols. 1835; 3 vols. 1837; 1838; 1856; 1873; [1874]; [1877]; [1878]; [1881]; [1883], etc.; 2 vols. 1928 (introduction by G. Saintsbury). [First appeared in Metropolitan Mag., Sept. 1833–Dec. 1834.]

The Pacha of Mary Tales. 3 vols. 1835 (*bis*); 1838; 1856; 1873; 1874; [1880], etc.; tr. French, Paris, 1837. [The stories appeared intermittently in Metropolitan Mag. between June 1831 and May 1835.]

The Diary of a Blasé. Philadelphia, 1836. [Previously but incompletely pbd in Metropolitan Mag. to July 1836.]

The Pirate and the Three Cutters. With Illustrations by Clarkson Stanfield. 1836; 15 pts, 1845; 1877 (with memoir); [1880]; [1886], etc; 1924 (illustrated by E. J. Sullivan); tr. French, Paris, 1837 (as Caïn le Pirate).

Japhet in Search of a Father. 3 vols. 1836 (*bis*); 1838; 1857; 1873; [1881]; [1883]; 1895, etc. [First appeared in Metropolitan Mag., Oct. 1834–Jan. 1836.]

Stories of the Sea. New York, 1836. [Contains Moonshine, which originally appeared in The Keepsake and was not pbd separately.]

Mr Midshipman Easy. 3 vols. 1836; 1838; 1856; 1873; [1879]; [1880]; [1881]; [1883]; 1888; etc. [One instalment appeared in Metropolitan Mag. in July 1836, but serialization was never completed.]

Snarleyow or, the Dog Fiend. 3 vols. 1837; Paris, 1837; 1847 (as The Dog Fiend); 1856; 1873; [1880]; 1897, etc. [First appeared in Metropolitan Mag. Feb. 1836– July 1837.]

The Phantom Ship. 3 vols. 1839; Paris, 1839; 1847; 1856; 1874; 1880; 1896; etc. [First appeared in New Monthly Mag. during 1837.]

Poor Jack. 12 monthly pts, Jan.–Dec. 1840 (with illustrations by Clarkson Stanfield); 1840; Paris, 1841; 1880; [1883]; 1895, etc.; tr. French, Paris, 1841.

Olla Podrida. 1840; 1842; 1849; 1874; [1875]; [1880], etc. [Diary on the Continent first appeared in Metropolitan Mag. 1836 as Diary of a Blasé and the shorter pieces partly in the same journal, partly in New Monthly Mag., and Moonshine in The Keepsake.]

Masterman Ready; or, the Wreck of the Pacific. Written for Young People. 3 vols. 1841–2; 1845; 1850; 2 vols. 1851; 1875; 1878; 1885; [1886]; 1887; [1893], etc.

Joseph Rushbrook or the Poacher. 3 vols. 1841; Paris, 1841; 1846 (as The Poacher); 1856; [1873]; [1880]; [1883], etc. [First appeared in The Era.]

Percival Keene. 3 vols. 1842; Paris, 1842; 1848; 1857 (with a memoir); [1873]; [1875]; [1880] (with a memoir), etc.; tr. French, Paris, 1843.

Narrative of the Travels and Adventures of Monsieur Violet in California, Sonora and Western Texas. 3 vols. 1843; 1849; 1874; [1875]; [1880], etc.

The Settlers in Canada. Written for Young People. 2 vols. 1844; 1886; 1887; 1895, etc.

The Mission; or, Scenes in Africa. 2 vols. 1845; 1884; 1887, etc.

The Privateer's-man, One Hundred Years Ago. 2 vols. 1846; [1888], etc. [First appeared in New Monthly Mag.]

The Children of the New Forest. 2 vols. [1847] (with illustrations by Frank Marryat); [1848?]; 1849; 1850; 1853; 1888; 1889; 1894, etc. [Planned for part-issue; pt 1 (all issued?) [1847].]

The Little Savage. 2 pts, 1848–9; 1853; 1889; 1893 (illustrated by A. W. Cooper and Sir J. Gilbert), etc. [Ed. by Frank S. Marryat. Of pt 2 Frederick Marryat only wrote 2 chs.]

Valerie: an Autobiography. 2 vols. 1849; 1852; [1875]; [1880], etc. [First appeared (to the end of vol. ii, ch. iii) in New Monthly Mag. during 1846 and 1847. Finished by another hand, owing to Marryat's illness.]

[Marryat owned and edited Metropolitan Mag. from 1832 to 1835. In 1836 he rev. and transformed a work by his sub-editor, E. G. G. Howard—Rattlin the Reefer. The following by Howard, were until recently attrib. to Marryat: The Old Commodore; Outward bound; Memoirs of Admiral Sir Sydney Smith; Jack Ashore; Sir Henry Morgan, the Buccaneer; The Marine Coast (in Tales from Bentley, vol. i).]

(4) OTHER WRITINGS

A Code of Signals for the Use of Vessels Employed in the Merchant Service. 1817; 1837 (rev.); 1841 (last edn rev. by Marryat).

A Suggestion for the Abolition of the Present System of Impressment in the Naval Service. 1822.

The Floral Telegraph. A New Mode of Communication by Floral Signals. With Plates. 1836 (anon.; re-issued, with Marryat's name on the title-page, 1850). [Attrib. to Marryat.]

A Diary in America, with Remarks on its Institutions. 2 pts, 6 vols. 1839.

(5) BIOGRAPHY AND CRITICISM

Marryat's Novels. Fraser's Mag. xvii, 1837.

Horne, R. H. The New Spirit of the Age. 2 vols. 1844.

Whitehead, C. Marryat. Bentley's Misc. xxiv, 1848.

Marryat, Florence. Life and Letters of Captain Marryat. 2 vols. 1872.

The Sea Novels of Captain Marryat. Cornhill Mag. xxvii, 1873.

Poe, E. A. The Works. Ed. J. H. Ingram, 4 vols. 1874–5.

Hutton, L. Literary Landmarks in London. 1885.

Wotton, M. E. Word Portraits. 1887.

Hannay, D. Life of Frederick Marryat. 1889. [Contains a bibliography by J. P. Anderson.]

Wilson, R. R. Foreign Authors in America. Bookman (New York), xiii, 1901.

Conrad, J. Tales of the Sea. 1919. [A criticism of Marryat and Cooper.]

Dorling, H. T. Men O'War. St Vincent, Marryat, [etc.]. 1929.

McGrath, M. A Century of Marryat. Nineteenth Century, cvi, 1929.

Meyerstein, E. H. W. Captain Marryat and the Ariadne. Mariners' Mirror, XXI, 1935.

Bader, A. L. Captain Marryat and the American Pirates. Library, XVI, 1935.

—— Marryat's The Ocean Wolf. PQ. XV, 1936.

Lloyd, C. Captain Marryat and the Old Navy. 1939. S. J. L.

III. MINOR FICTION, 1800–1835*

[This section has been restricted, with one or two exceptions, to writers who were born between the years 1760 and 1800.]

JOHN BANIM (1798–1842)

[The pseudonym 'The O'Hara Family' was used sometimes by John and Michael Banim collaborating and sometimes by either separately.]

(a) Fiction

Tales by the O'Hara Family. Ser. 1, 3 vols. 1825. [Crohoore of the Bill-Hook by M. Banim; The Fetches by J. Banim; John Doe in collaboration.] Ser. 2, 3 vols. 1826. [The Nowlans by J. Banim; Peter of the Castle in collaboration.] Both sers. 3 pts, 1846; Crohoore of the Bill-Hook and The Fetches, 1848; John Doe, 1853; The Nowlans, 1853; The Peep O'Day, or John Doe. And Crohoore of the Billhook, Dublin, 1865 (ed. M. Banim); Peter of the Castle and The Fetches, Dublin, 1866 (ed. M. Banim); Crohoore of the Bill-Hook, tr. French, Paris, 1829; tr. German, Hamburg, 1828.

The Boyne Water. By the O'Hara Family [John Banim alone]. 3 vols. 1826; ed. M. Banim, Dublin, 1865; tr. French, Paris, 1829.

The Anglo-Irish of the Nineteenth Century. A Novel. 3 vols. 1828 (anon.).

The Denounced. By the Authors of Tales of the O'Hara Family [really John Banim]. 3 vols. 1830; ed. M. Banim, Dublin, 1866.

The Smuggler. A Tale. By the Author of Tales by the O'Hara Family, The Denounced, etc. [i.e. John Banim]. 3 vols. 1831; 1833; 1850.

The Bit o' Writin', and Other Tales. By the O'Hara Family [i.e. John and Michael Banim]. 3 vols. 1838; ed. M. Banim, Dublin, 1865.

Father Connell. By the O'Hara Family, [i.e. John and Michael Banim]. 3 vols. 1842; 1849; Dublin, 1858 (with introduction and notes).

(b) Other Writings

The Celt's Paradise, in Four Duans. 1821. [A poem.]

Damon and Pythias. A Tragedy in Five Acts. 1821; [1825?] (in J. Duncombe's British Theatre, vol. LXI); 1865 (in British Theatre, vol. III); [1883] (in J. Dicks, Standard Plays). [R. L. Sheil had a small share in this play.]

A Letter to the Committee appointed to appropriate a Fund for a National Testimonial Commemorative of His Majesty's First Visit to Ireland. Dublin, 1822.

Revelations of the Dead Alive. 1824 (anon.); 1845 (as London and its Eccentricities in the Year 2023, or Revelations of the Dead Alive, by the author of Boyne Water). [Essays.]

Chaunt of the Cholera. Songs for Ireland. By the Authors of the O'Hara Tales [i.e. John and Michael Banim]. 1831.

[John Banim also wrote the following plays: The Prodigal, a Tragedy (all trace lost); Turgesius; The Moorish Wife; Sylla (adapted from M. Jouy); and the novel The Dwarf Bride, 1829–31 (MS lost).]

(c) Biography and Criticism

Griffin, D. The Life of Gerald Griffin. 1843.

Horne, R. H. A New Spirit of the Age. Vol. II, 1844.

John Banim. Irish Quart. Rev. IV, V, VI, 1854–6.

Murray, P. J. The Life of John Banim. 1857.

Steger, A. John Banim, ein Nachahmer Walter Scotts. Erlangen, 1935.

MICHAEL BANIM (1796–1874)

[This bibliography comprises only works by Michael Banim alone. For books written in collaboration with John Banim, or in which the brothers severally wrote different tales, see under John Banim above.]

The Croppy. A Tale of 1798. By the Authors of O'Hara Tales [really Michael Banim]. 1828; tr. French, 4 vols. Paris, 1833.

The Ghost-Hunter and his Family. By John [really Michael] Banim. 1833; 1851; 1863; [1870] (as Joe Wilson's Ghost); rptd [1913]; tr. French, 2 vols. Paris, 1833.

The Mayor of Wind-Gap, and Canvassing. By the O'Hara Family. 3 vols. 1835; ed. M. Banim, Dublin, 1865. [Canvassing is by Miss Martin.]

Clough Fion. 1852. [Pbd in Dublin University Mag.]

The Town of the Cascades. 2 vols. 1864.

[For biography and criticism see under John Banim.]

* This section has been revised by Mr Michael Sadleir.

RICHARD HARRIS BARHAM (1788–1845)
[See p. 226 above.]

EATON STANNARD BARRETT (1786–1820)

The Rising Sun. A Serio-Comic Satiric Romance. By Cervantes Hogg, F.S.M. 2 vols. 1807.
The Second Titan War against Heaven. A Satirical Poem. By the Author of The Rising Sun. 1807.
All the Talents. A Satirical Poem in Three Dialogues. By Polypus. 1807 (at least 19 edns).
The Mis-led General. A Serio-Comic, Satiric, Mock-Heroic Romance. By the Author of the Rising Sun. 1808 (*bis*).
Woman. A Poem. 1810; 1819 (3rd edn).
The Heroine, or Adventures of a Fair Romance Reader. 3 vols. 1813; 3 vols. 1815 (3rd edn); 3 vols. 1816; rptd 1909 (introduction by Sir W. Raleigh); rptd 1927 (introduction by M. Sadleir).
Six Weeks at Long's. By a Late Resident. 3 vols. 1817 (*bis*). [Satirical novel.]
Henry Schultze. A Tale. The Savoyard, a French Republican's Story, with Other Poems. 1821 (anon.). [Sometimes attrib. to Barrett.]

[For The Hero; or, the Adventures of a Night (incorrectly attrib. to Barrett) see A. D. McKillop, MLN. LIII, 1938. For letters of Barrett to his bookseller see J. C. Mendenhall, University of Pennsylvania General Mag. xxx, 1927, pp. 10–14.]

THOMAS HAYNES BAYLY (1797–1839)
[See p. 227 above.]

AGNES MARIA BENNETT (c. 1750–1808)

Anna, or Memoirs of a Welch Heiress, interspersed with Anecdotes of a Nabob. 4 vols. 1785 (anon.); 4 vols. 1786; rptd 1854; tr. French, Paris, 1788.
Juvenile Indiscretions. A Novel. 5 vols. 1786 (anon.); tr. French, Paris, 1788.
Agnes de Courcy. A Domestic Tale. 4 vols. 1789; tr. French, Paris, 1789.
Ellen, Countess of Castle Howell. A Novel. 4 vols. 1794; 2 vols. Dublin, 1794; 4 vols. 1805; tr. French, Paris, 1822.
Henry Bennett and Julia Johnson. [1794?]; tr. French, Paris, 1794.
The Beggar Girl and her Benefactors. A Novel. 7 vols. 1797; 3 vols. Dublin, 1798; 5 vols. 1799; Philadelphia, 1801; 5 vols. 1813 (3rd edn).
Vicissitudes Abroad, or the Ghost of my Father. 6 vols. 1806; tr. French, Paris, 1809.

ELIZABETH BENNETT

Faith and Fiction, or Shining Lights in a Dark Generation. A Novel. 5 vols. 1816; tr. French, Paris, 1816.
Emily, or the Wife's First Error; and Beauty and Ugliness, or the Father's Prayer and the Mother's Prophecy. Two Tales. 4 vols. 1819.

MARGUERITE, COUNTESS OF BLESSINGTON, née POWER (1789–1849)

(a) Fiction

The Repealers. 3 vols. 1833; 3 vols. 1834 (as Grace Cassidy, or the Repealers).
The Two Friends. 3 vols. 1835.
The Confessions of an Elderly Gentleman. 1836.
The Victims of Society. 3 vols. 1837.
The Confessions of an Elderly Lady. 1838.
The Governess. 2 vols. 1839; Paris, 1840.
The Lottery of Life. 3 vols. 1842.
Meredith. 3 vols. 1843.
Strathern or Life at Home and Abroad. 4 vols. 1845.
The Memoirs of a Femme de Chambre. 3 vols. 1846.
Lionel Deerhurst, or Fashionable Life under the Regency. 1846.
Country Quarters. 3 vols. 1850. [With a Memoir by Miss Power.]

(b) Other Writings

The Magic Lantern, or Sketches of Scenes in the Metropolis. 1822 (anon.).
Sketches and Fragments. 1822.
Conversations of Lord Byron with the Countess of Blessington. 1834; rptd 1893.
The Works of Lady Blessington. 2 vols. Philadelphia, 1838. [Contains items not collected elsewhere in book form.]
The Idler in Italy. 3 vols. 1839–40.
Desultory Thoughts and Reflections. 1839.
The Belle of a Season. 1840. [In verse.]
The Idler in France. 2 vols. 1841.

[Lady Blessington edited various gift-books. She was also for many years both editor and principal contributor to The Book of Beauty and The Keepsake.]

(c) Biography and Criticism

Madden, R. R. The Literary Life and Correspondence of the Countess of Blessington. 3 vols. 1855.
Maginn, W. A Gallery of Illustrious Literary Characters. Ed. W. Bates, [1873].
Sadleir, M. Blessington–D'Orsay. 1933.
Rosa, M. W. The Silver Fork School: Novels of Fashion preceding Vanity Fair. New York, 1936.

CAROLINE ANNE BOWLES, later SOUTHEY
(1786–1854)
[See p. 228 above.]

ANNA ELIZA BRAY, née KEMPE,
first married name STOTHARD (1790–1883)

(a) Collected Novels

The Novels and Romances of Anna Eliza
Bray. 10 vols. 1845–6; 12 vols. 1884 (rev.
edn).

(b) Separate Novels

De Foix, or Sketches of the Manners and
Customs of the Fourteenth Century. An
Historical Romance. 3 vols. 1826.
The White Hoods. An Historical Romance.
3 vols. 1828; tr. French, Paris, 1828.
The Protestant. A Tale of the Reign of
Queen Mary. By the Author of De Foix,
The White Hoods, etc. 1828.
Fitz of Fitz-ford. A Legend of Devon. 3 vols.
1830.
The Talba, or Moor of Portugal. A Romance.
3 vols. 1830.
Warleigh or the Fatal Oak. A Legend of
Devon. 3 vols. 1834.
Trelawney of Trelawne, or the Prophecy. A
Legend of Cornwall. 3 vols. 1837.
Trials of the Heart. 3 vols. 1839.
Henry de Pomeroy, or the Eve of St John.
A Legend of Cornwall and Devon. 3 vols.
1842.
Courtenay of Wabreddon. A Romance of the
West. 3 vols. 1844.
Trials of Domestic Life. 3 vols. 1848.
Hartland Forest. A Legend of North Devon.
1871.
Roseteague or the Heir of Treville Crewse.
2 vols. 1874.
Silver Linings, or Light and Shade. 1880.

(c) Other Writings

Letters written during a Tour through
Normandy, Britanny, and Other Parts of
France in 1818; with Engravings after
Drawings by C. Stothard. 1820.
Memoirs, including Original Journals, Letters,
Papers, and Antiquarian Tracts, of the late
C. A. Stothard; and some Account of a
Journey in the Netherlands. 1823.
A Description of the Part of Devonshire
bordering on the Tamar and the Tavy in a
Series of Letters to Robert Southey, Esq.
3 vols. 1836; 3 vols. 1838 (as Traditions,
Legends, Superstitions and Sketches of
Devonshire); 2 vols. 1879 (as The Borders
of the Tamar and the Tavy).
The Mountains and Lakes of Switzerland;
with Descriptive Sketches of Other Parts of
the Continent. 3 vols. 1841.

The Life of Thomas Stothard; with Personal
Reminiscences. 1851.
A Peep at the Pixies; or, Legends of the West.
With Illustrations by H. K. Browne. 1854.
Handel: his Life, Personal and Professional.
With Thoughts on Sacred Music. 1857.
The Good St Louis and his Times. 1870.
The Revolt of the Protestants of the Cevennes;
with some Account of the Huguenots in the
Seventeenth Century. 1870.
Joan of Arc, and the Times of Charles VII,
King of France. 1874.
Autobiography of Anna Eliza Bray [to 1843].
Ed. J. A. Kempe, 1884.

(d) Biography and Criticism

Anna Eliza Bray. Spectator, LVII, 1884, p. 519.
Boase, G. C. Anna Eliza Bray and her
Writings. Library Chronicle, I, 1884.

MARY BRUNTON née BALFOUR (1778–1818)

Self Control. A Novel. 3 vols. Edinburgh,
1811 (3 edns).
Discipline. A Novel. By the Author of Self
Control. 3 vols. Edinburgh, 1814.
Emmeline, with some Other Pieces. To which
is prefixed a Memoir of her Life, including
some Extracts from her Correspondence.
Edinburgh, 1819. [The memoir is by her
husband, Alexander Brunton.]

SIR SAMUEL EGERTON BRYDGES
(1762–1837)

[See p. 662 below.]

LADY CHARLOTTE SUSAN MARIA BURY,
née CAMPBELL (1775–1861)

(a) Fiction

Self Indulgence. A Tale of the Nineteenth
Century. 2 vols. Edinburgh, 1812 (anon.).
Conduct is Fate. 3 vols. Edinburgh, 1822
(anon.).
Alla Giornata, or To the Day. 3 vols. 1826
(anon.).
Flirtation. A Novel. 3 vols. 1827 (anon.);
1828 (bis).
A Marriage in High Life [by Caroline Lucy,
Lady Scott]. Edited by the Authoress of
Flirtation. 1828 (anon.); 1857. Tr. French,
Paris, 1832; German, Vienna, 1837.
Journal of the Heart. Edited by the Authoress
of Flirtation. 2 sers. 1830–5.
The Separation. A Novel. By the Authoress
of Flirtation. 3 vols. 1830.
The Disinherited and the Ensnared. By the
Authoress of Flirtation. 3 vols. 1834.
The Devoted. By the Authoress of The Disin-
herited, Flirtation, etc. 3 vols. 1836.
The Divorced. A Tale. 2 vols. 1837 (anon.);
1858.
Love. 3 vols. 1837 (anon.); 1860.

The History of a Flirt, related by herself. 3 vols. 1840 (anon.); [1857?].

Family Records, or the Two Sisters. 3 vols. 1841.

The Manœuvring Mother. By the Author of the History of a Flirt. 3 vols. 1842; 1858.

The Lady of Fashion. By the Author of the History of a Flirt. 3 vols. 1856.

The Two Baronets. A Novel of Fashionable Life. 1864.

[Lady Charlotte also edited Memoirs of a Peeress, or the Days of Fox, by Mrs C. F. Gore, 1837. The Exclusives, 3 vols. 1830 (anon.), though often attrib. to Lady Charlotte, is probably not by her.]

(b) Other Writings

Poems on Several Occasions, by a Lady. Edinburgh, 1797 (anon.).

Suspirium Sanctorum, or Holy Breathings. A Series of Prayers for Every Day of the Month. By a Lady. 1826 (anon.).

The Three Great Sanctuaries of Tuscany: Valombrosa, Camaldoli, Laverna. A Poem, with Historical and Legendary Notices. Illustrated by E. Bury. 1833.

Diary illustrative of the Times of George the Fourth, interspersed with Original Letters from the Late Queen Caroline and Other Distinguished Persons. 2 vols. 1838 (anon.); 4 vols. 1838 (expanded, vols. III–IV ed. John Galt; copy in BM. contains pages that were suppressed); ed. A. F. Steuart, 2 vols. 1908.

(c) Biography and Criticism

Lady Charlotte Bury. New Monthly Mag. XLIX, 1837.

Rosa, M. W. The Silver Fork School: Novels of Fashion preceding Vanity Fair. New York, 1936.

WILLIAM CARLETON (1794–1869)
(a) Selected Works

Stories from Carleton. With an Introduction by W. B. Yeats. [1889.]

Stories from Carleton. With an Introduction by Tighe Hopkins. [1905.]

Carleton's Stories of Irish Life. With an Introduction by Darrell Figgis. [1918.]

(b) Fiction

Traits and Stories of the Irish Peasantry. 2 sers. 5 vols. Dublin, 1830–3; 2 vols. Dublin, 1843 (illustrated by 'Phiz,' Harvey, Gilbert, etc.); 1853; 1864; [1872]; 1875; [1876]; 1877; [1880]; [1881].

Tales of Ireland. 1834; 1848.

Fardorougha the Miser; or, the Convicts of Lisnamona. Dublin, 1839; 1846; 1848. [Rptd from Dublin University Mag.]

The Fawn of Spring-Vale; The Clarionet, and Other Tales. 3 vols. Dublin, 1841. [Several tales rptd under various titles 1843, 1850 and later.]

Parra Sastha; or, the History of Paddy Go-Easy and his Wife Nancy. Dublin, 1845.

Roddy the Rover; or, the Ribbon Man. 1845.

Valentine McClutchy, the Irish Agent; or, Chronicles of the Castle Cumber Property. 3 vols. Dublin, 1845; Dublin, 1846 (with The Pious Aspirations of Solomon M'Slime).

Denis O'Shaughnessy going to Maynooth. 1845.

The Black Prophet. A Tale of Irish Famine. 1847; 1847 (illustrated); 1899 (introduction by D. J. O'Donoghue).

Art Maguire, or the Broken Pledge. Dublin, 1847.

The Emigrants of Ahadarra, A Tale of Irish Life. 1848.

The Tithe-Proctor. 1849.

The Clarionet; the Dead Boxer; and Barry Branagan. 1850.

Red Hall; or, the Baronet's Daughter. 3 vols. 1852; 1858 (as The Black Baronet).

The Squanders of Castle Squander. 2 vols. 1852.

Willy Reilly and his Dear Cooleen Bawn. A Tale founded upon Fact. 3 vols. 1855.

The Evil Eye; or, the Black Spectre. A Romance. Dublin, 1860.

Redmond, Count O'Hanlon; the Irish Rapparee. An Historical Tale. Dublin, 1862.

The Double Prophecy; or, Trials of the Heart. 2 vols. 1862. [Rptd from Duffy's Hibernian Mag.]

The Silver Acre and Other Tales. 1862.

The Fair of Emyvale and the Master and Scholar. 1870.

The Poor Scholar; Frank Martin and the Fairies; The Country Dancing Master; and Other Tales. [1870?]

The Red Haired Man's Wife. Dublin, 1889.

Tubber Derg; or, the Red Well-party Fight and Funeral-Dandy Kehoe's Christening and Other Irish Tales. N.d.

(c) Other Writings

Father Butler, the Lough Dearg Pilgrim, Being Sketches of Irish Manners. Dublin, 1829; Dublin, 1839.

Characters and Sketches of Ireland and the Irish by Carleton, Lover, and Mrs Hall. Dublin, 1845.

(d) Biography and Criticism

O'Donoghue, D. J. The Life of William Carleton. 2 vols. 1896.

Shaw, Rose. Carleton's Country. 1930.

FREDERICK CHAMIER (1796–1870)

(a) Fiction

The Life of a Sailor. 3 vols. 1832; 1850.
The Unfortunate Man. 3 vols. 1835.
Ben Brace: the Last of Nelson's Agamemnons. 3 vols. 1836; 1839 (3rd edn, rev. and corrected).
The Saucy Arethusa. 1836.
Walsingham, the Gamester. 3 vols. 1837.
Jack Adams. 1838.
The Spitfire. A Tale of the Sea. 3 vols. 1840.
Tom Bowling. A Tale of the Sea. 3 vols. 1841.
Count Königsmark. 1845.
Jack Malcolm's Log. 1846.

[Chamier also 'edited' Passion and Principle, 3 vols. 1842.]

(b) Other Writings

Review of the French Revolution of 1848. 2 vols. 1849.
My Travels. An Unsentimental Journey Through France, Switzerland and Italy. 3 vols. 1855.

MARY CHARLTON

The Parisian or Genuine Anecdotes of Distinguished and Noble Personages. 2 vols. 1794 (anon.).
Phedora, or the Forest of Minski. 4 vols. 1798.
Rosella, or Modern Occurrences. A Novel. 4 vols. 1799; 2 vols. Dublin, 1800.
The Wife and the Mistress. A Novel. 4 vols. 1802.
Pathetic Poetry for Youth. 1815.
Grandeur and Meanness, or Domestic Persecution. A Novel. 3 vols. 1824.
Past Events, or the Treacherous Guide. A Romance. 3 vols. 1830.

[Mary Charlton also wrote: The Pirate of Naples, 3 vols., Andronica; Ammorin and Zallida, 2 vols.—but copies have not been located. She translated: The Reprobate, 2 vols. 1802 (from La Fontaine's German); The Philosophic Kidnapper, 3 vols. 1803 (from French).]

RICHARD COBBOLD (1797–1877)

(a) Narrations

The History of Margaret Catchpole, a Suffolk Girl. With Illustrations [by Cobbold himself]. 3 vols. 1845; 2 vols. 1845; 1847; 1852; [1856]; [1858] (enlarged); [1878]; rptd 1907 (World's Classics).
Mary Ann Wellington, the Soldier's Daughter, Wife, and Widow. With Illustrations [by Cobbold]. 3 vols. 1846; 3 vols. 1853 ('improved'); [1875].

Zenon the Martyr, a Record of the Piety, Patience and Persecution of the Early Christian Nobles. 3 vols. 1847; 1855; [1874].
Freston Tower, or the Early Days of Cardinal Wolsey. With Illustrations [by Cobbold]. 3 vols. 1850; [1880]; rptd 1913.
Courtland. A Novel. By the Daughter of Mary Ann Wellington. 3 vols. 1852. [Edited, and largely written, by Cobbold.]
John H. Steggall: a Real History of a Suffolk Man. Narrated by Himself. Edited by the Author of 'Margaret Catchpole.' 1857; 1859; n.d. (in picture boards as The Suffolk Gipsy).

(b) Other Writings

Original, Serious and Religious Poetry. Ipswich, 1827.
Valentine Verses, or Lines of Truth, Love, and Virtue. With Illustrations [by Cobbold]. Ipswich, 1827.
The Spirit of the Litany of the Church of England. Eye, 1833. [Poem.]
Men and Women. 1843 (anon.).
The Bottle, or Cruikshank Illustrated. A Poem. 1848.
The Character of Woman: a Lecture delivered April 1848. Diss, n.d.
Geoffrey Gambado. By a Humourist Physician. With Illustrations after Bunbury. N.d.

[Cobbold also pbd sermons and devotional works.]

GEORGE CROLY (1780–1860)

[See p. 281 above.]

ALLAN CUNNINGHAM (1784–1842)

(a) Fiction

Traditional Tales of the English and Scotch Peasantry. 2 vols. 1822; ed. H. Morley, 1887.
Paul Jones. A Romance. 3 vols. Edinburgh, 1826.
Sir Michael Scott. A Romance. 3 vols. 1828.
Lord Roldan. A Romance. 3 vols. 1836.

[Cunningham also contributed to Andrew Picken's The Club Book, 3 vols. 1831 and wrote a memoir of Burns, prefixed to his edn of that poet, 1834, etc.]

(b) Other Writings

The Magic Bridle. N.d.
Songs, chiefly in the Rural Language of Scotland. 1813.
Sir Marmaduke Maxwell. A Dramatic Poem. 1822.
The Songs of Scotland, Ancient and Modern. With Introduction and Notes, Historical and Critical, and Characters of the Lyric Poets. 4 vols. 1825.

Lives of the most Eminent British Painters, Sculptors and Architects. 6 vols. 1829–33; 6 vols. 1830–7; 5 vols. New York, 1844; ed. W. Sharp, 1886 (selections), [1893].

The Maid of Elvar, a Poem in Twelve Parts. 1833.

The Cabinet Gallery of Pictures, selected from the Collections of Art, Public and Private, which adorn Great Britain. With Biographical and Critical Descriptions. 2 vols. 1833–4.

Biographical and Critical History of the British Literature of the Last Fifty Years. Paris, 1834.

The Life and Correspondence of Robert Burns. 1836.

The Life of Sir David Wilkie. With his Journals, Tours and Critical Remarks on Works of Art, and a Selection from his Correspondence. [Ed. P. Cunningham], 3 vols. 1843.

Poems and Songs. Ed. P. Cunningham, 1847; 1875.

(c) Biography and Criticism

Gilfillan, G. Galleries of Literary Portraits. Vol. I, Edinburgh, 1856.

Hall, S. C. Allan Cunningham. Art Journ. XVIII, 1866.

Hogg, D. The Life of Allan Cunningham, With Selections from his Works and Correspondence. Dumfries, 1875.

Elton, O. A Survey of English Literature, 1780–1830. Vol. I, 1912, pp. 132–3.

T. J. HORSLEY CURTIES

Ancient Records, or the Abbey of Saint Oswythe. A Romance. 4 vols. 1801; tr. French, Paris, 1813.

The Scottish Legend; or, The Isle of St Clothair. 4 vols. 1801.

Ethelwina or the House of Fitz-Auburne. 3 vols. [?]; tr. French, Paris, 1802.

The Watch Tower, or the Sons of Ulthona. An Historical Romance. 5 vols. 1804.

St Botolph's Priory, or the Sable Mask. An Historic Romance. 5 vols. 1806.

The Monk of Udolpho. 4 vols. 1807.

THE MISSES CUTHBERTSON

Romance of the Pyrenees. 4 vols. 1803; 4 vols. 1807 (3rd edn); 4 vols. 1822 (5th edn); 1844.

Santo Sebastiano; or, the Young Protector. By the Author of The Romance of the Pyrenees. 5 vols. 1806; 5 vols. 1809.

Forest of Montalbano. A Novel. By the author of Santo Sebastiano, etc. 4 vols. 1810.

Adelaide or the Countercharm. By the Author of Santo Sebastiano, etc. 5 vols. 1813.

Rosabella; or, A Mother's Marriage. By the Author of The Romance of the Pyrenees. 5 vols. 1817.

The Hut and the Castle: a Romance. By the Author of The Romance of the Pyrenees. 4 vols. 1823.

Sir Ethelbert or the Dissolution of the Monasteries. By the Author of Santo Sebastiano, etc. 3 vols. 1830.

CHARLOTTE DACRE, afterwards BYRNE

The Confessions of the Nun of St Omer. A Tale. By Rosa Matilda. 3 vols. 1805.

Hours of Solitude. A Collection of Original Poems. By Charlotte Dacre, better known by the Name of Rosa Matilda. 2 vols. 1805.

Zofloya, or the Moor. By Charlotte Dacre, better known as Rosa Matilda. 1806; ed. M. Summers, 1928; tr. French, 1812.

The Libertine. By Charlotte Dacre, better known as Rosa Matilda. 4 vols. 1807 (bis); tr. French, Paris, 1816.

The Passions. By Rosa Matilda. 4 vols. 1811.

ROBERT CHARLES DALLAS (1754–1824)
(a) Collected Works

The Miscellaneous Works and Novels of R. C. Dallas, Esq. 7 vols. 1813.

(b) Novels

Percival; or, Nature Vindicated. A Novel. 4 vols. 1801.

Aubrey. A Novel. 4 vols. 1804.

The Morlands. Tales Illustrative of the Simple and Surprising. 4 vols. 1805.

The Knights. Tales Illustrative of the Marvellous. 3 vols. 1808.

Sir Francis Darrell; or, The Vortex. A Novel. 4 vols. 1820.

(c) Poems and Miscellaneous Writings

Miscellaneous Writings, consisting of Poems; Lucretia, a Tragedy; and Moral Essays; with a Vocabulary of the Passions. 1797.

Elements of Self-knowledge. An Anatomical Display of the Human Frame and an Enquiry into the Genuine Nature of the Passions. 1802; 1805 (rev.).

The History of the Maroons, from their Origin to the Establishment of their Chief Tribe at Sierra Leone; 2 vols. 1803.

Not at Home: a Dramatic Entertainment. 1809.

The New Conspiracy against the Jesuits detected and exposed. 1815; tr. French, Brussels, 1816.

A Letter to C. Butler, Esq. relative to the New Conspiracy against the Jesuits. 1817.

Ode to the Duke of Wellington, and Other Poems. 1819.

Adrastus, a Tragedy; Amabel or the Cornish Lovers; and Other Poems. 1823.

Recollections of the Life of Lord Byron from the Year 1808 to the end of 1814. [Ed. A. R. C. Dallas], 1824.

[Dallas also edited some of Byron's letters (1824 and 1825) and made a number of trns from the French, including The Siege of Rochelle or the Christian Heroine. By Mad. de Genlis, 3 vols. 1808.]

SELINA DAVENPORT

The Hypocrite, or the Modern Janus. A Novel. 5 vols. 1814.

Donald Monteith, the Handsomest Man of the Age. A Novel. 5 vols. 1815; 1832.

The Original of the Miniature. A Novel. 4 vols. 1816.

Leap Year; or, Woman's Privilege. A Novel. 5 vols. 1817.

An Angel's Form and a Devil's Heart. A Novel. 4 vols. 1818.

Preference. A Novel. 2 vols. 1824.

Italian Vengeance and English Forbearance. A Romance. 3 vols. 1828.

The Queen's Page. A Romance. 3 vols. 1831.

The Unchanged. A Novel. 3 vols. 1832.

Personation. A Novel. 3 vols. 1834.

ISAAC D'ISRAELI (1766–1848)

[See p. 667 below.]

EMILY EDEN (1797–1869)

Portraits of the Princes and Peoples of India. 1844.

The Semi-Detached House. Ed. Lady T. Lewis, 1859 (anon.); 1860; 1872; ed. A. Eden, 1928.

The Semi-Attached Couple. By E. E., the Author of The Semi-Detached House. 2 vols. 1860; 1865; ed. J. Gore, 1927; rptd 1934.

'Up the Country.' Letters written to her Sister from the Upper Provinces of India. 2 vols. 1866; 1867; ed. E. Thompson, 1930.

Letters from India. Ed. Eleanor Eden, 2 vols. 1872.

Miss Eden's Letters. Ed. V. Dickinson, 1919.

PIERCE EGAN (1772–1849)

[See p. 668 below.]

SUSAN EDMONDSTONE FERRIER (1782–1854)

(a) Collected Works

Miss Ferrier's Novels. 6 vols. 1882. [Marriage, Destiny, The Inheritance.]

Miss Ferrier's Novels. Ed. R. B. Johnson, 6 vols. 1894.

The Works of Susan Ferrier. With an Introduction by Lady Margaret Sackville. 4 vols. 1928. [Vols. I–III, the novels; vol. IV, Doyle's Memoir.]

(b) Fiction

Marriage, a Novel. 3 vols. Edinburgh, 1818 (anon.); 2 vols. Edinburgh, 1826 (3rd edn); 1841; [1856]; [1873]; [1878]; 2 vols. 1902 (with biographical preface by A. Goodrich-Freer and critical notices by Walter, Earl of Iddesleigh), etc.; tr. French, 4 vols. Paris, 1825.

The Inheritance. By the Author of Marriage. 3 vols. Edinburgh, 1824; 3 vols. 1825; 1841; [1856]; [1873]; [1878] (as The Inheritance, or True Love wins); 2 vols. 1903 (with biographical preface by A. Goodrich-Freer and critical notices by Walter, Earl of Iddlesleigh).

Destiny, or the Chief's Daughter. By the Author of Marriage and Inheritance. 3 vols. Edinburgh, 1831; 1841; [1873]; [1878], etc.

(c) Biography and Criticism

[Lockhart, J. G.] Noctes Ambrosianae. LVIII. Blackwood's Mag. XXX, 1831.

Edinburgh Rev. LXXIV, 1842. [Essay on Susan Ferrier's novels.]

Miss Ferrier's Novels. Temple Bar, LIV, 1878.

Hamilton, C. J. Women Writers, their Works and Ways. Ser. 1, 1892. [Ch. xiv.]

Douglas, Sir G. The Blackwood Group. [1897.]

Memoir and Correspondence of Susan Ferrier, 1782–1854. Based on her Private Correspondence, collected by her Grand-nephew John Ferrier. Ed. J. A. Doyle, 1898.

Elton, O. A Survey of English Literature, 1780–1830. Vol. I, 1912, pp. 366–9.

Johnson, R. B. The Women Novelists. [1918], pp. 131–40.

Birrell, A. More Obiter Dicta. 1924.

JAMES BAILLIE FRASER (1783–1856)

(a) Fiction

The Kuzzilbash. A Tale of Khorasan. 3 vols. 1828 (anon.).

The Persian Adventurer. Being the Sequel to the Kuzzilbash. 3 vols. 1830.

The Highland Smugglers. By the Author of Adventures of a Kuzzilbash. 3 vols. 1832.

Tales of the Caravanserai: The Khan's Tale. 1833; 1850.

Allee Neemroo, the Buchtiaree Adventurer. A Tale of Louristan. 3 vols. 1842.

The Dark Falcon. A Tale of the Attruck. 4 vols. 1844.

27

(b) Other Writings

Journal of a Tour through Part of the Himālā Mountains and to the Sources of Jumna and Ganges. 1820.

Narrative of a Journey into Khorasan, 1821–22. Including Accounts of Countries N.E. of Persia. 1825.

Travels and Adventures in the Persian Provinces on the South Banks of the Caspian Sea. With Notices on the Geology and Commerce of Persia. 1826.

History and Descriptive Account of Persia, including Descriptions of Afghanistan and Beloochistan. 1834.

Narrative of the Residence of the Persian Princes in London, 1835–36. With an Account of their Journey from Persia and Subsequent Adventures. 2 vols. 1838.

A Winter's Journey (Tārtar), from Constantinople to Jeheran, with Travels through Various Parts of Persia. 2 vols. 1838.

Travels in Koordistan, Mesopotamia, etc. 2 vols. 1840.

Mesopotamia and Assyria. 1842.

Military Memoirs of Colonel James Skinner. 2 vols. 1851.

JOHN GALT (1779–1839)

(a) Bibliography

Lumsden, H. The Bibliography of John Galt. Records of Glasgow Bibliog. Soc. IX, 1931. [Admittedly incomplete, several of Galt's earlier works being only traceable in advertisements. Includes contributions to periodicals, miscellanies, etc.]

(b) Collected Works

The Works of John Galt. Ed. D. S. Meldrum and W. Roughead, 10 vols. Edinburgh, 1936.

(c) Fiction

The Majolo. A Tale. 2 vols. 1816 (anon.).

The Earthquake. A Tale. 3 vols. Edinburgh, 1820 (anon.).

The Wandering Jew, or the Travels and Observations of Hareach the Prolonged. By the Rev. T. Clark. 1820. [The 'Rev. T. Clark' was Galt's pseudonym.]

The Ayrshire Legatees; or, the Pringle Family. Edinburgh, 1821 (anon.); 1823 (adds The Gathering of the West); ed. D. S. Meldrum and S. R. Crocket, Edinburgh, 1895. [Frequently rptd with Annals of the Parish. First pbd in Blackwood's Mag. 1820–1.]

Annals of the Parish, or the Chronicle of Dalmailing, during the Ministry of the Rev. Micah Balwhidder. Edinburgh, 1821 (anon.); 1822, etc.; ed. D. S. Meldrum and S. R. Crockett, Edinburgh, 1895; ed. G. S. Gordon, 1908.

Sir Andrew Wylie, of That Ilk. By the Author of Annals of the Parish, etc. 3 vols. Edinburgh, 1822 (bis); 1841; 1850; 1854; 1868, etc.; ed. D. S. Meldrum and S. R. Crockett, 2 vols. Edinburgh, 1895.

The Provost. Edinburgh, 1822 (anon.) (bis); New York, 1822; ed. D. S. Meldrum and S. R. Crockett, 2 vols. Edinburgh, 1896. [Rptd with The Steamboat and The Omen, Edinburgh, 1842, 1850, 1869.]

The Steamboat. By the Author of Annals of the Parish [etc.]. Edinburgh, 1822; New York, 1823. [Rptd with the Provost and The Omen, Edinburgh, 1842, 1850, 1869.]

The Gathering of the West. 1823 (anon.).

The Entail; or, the Lairds of Grippy. By the Author of Annals of the Parish [etc.]. 3 vols. Edinburgh, 1823; 1842; ed. D. S. Meldrum and S. R. Crockett, 2 vols. Edinburgh, 1895; ed. J. Ayscough, 1913 (World's Classics).

Ringan Gilhaize; or, the Covenanters. 3 vols. Edinburgh, 1823 (anon.); Glasgow, [1870?]; ed. Sir G. Douglas, 1899.

The Spaewife. A Tale of the Scottish Chronicles. 3 vols. Edinburgh, 1823 (anon.); [1880?].

Rothelan, A Romance of the English Histories. By the Author of Annals of the Parish, etc. 3 vols. Edinburgh, 1824; 2 vols. New York, 1825.

The Last of the Lairds; or, the Life and Opinions of Malachi Mailings, Esq. of Auldbiggings. By the Author of Annals of the Parish, etc. Edinburgh, 1826; New York, 1827; rptd 1926.

The Omen. Edinburgh, 1826 (anon.). [Rptd with The Provost and The Steamboat, 1842, 1850, 1869.]

Lawrie Todd; or, the Settlers in the Woods. 3 vols. 1830 (bis); New York, 1830; 1832; 1849 (rev.); [1880?].

Southennan. 3 vols. 1830; New York, 1830.

Bogle Corbet; or, the Emigrants. 3 vols. [1831].

The Club-Book. Ed. A. Picken, 3 vols. 1831. [Includes 5 tales by Galt, all rptd separately 1841.]

The Member. An Autobiography. 1832 (reissued 1833 with The Radical as The Reform).

The Radical. An Autobiography. 1832 (reissued 1833 with The Member as The Reform).

Stanley Buxton, or the Schoolfellows. 3 vols. 1832; 2 vols. Philadelphia, 1833.

Eben Erskine, Or the Traveller. 3 vols. 1833.

The Stolen Child. A Tale of the Town. 1833. [Preface signed J. G.]

Stories of the Study. 3 vols. 1833.

Efforts. By an Invalid. Greenock, 1835; 1835.

The Howdie and Other Tales. Ed. W. Roughead, Edinburgh, 1923.

A Rich Man and Other Stories. Ed. W. Roughead, 1925.

(d) Other Writings

The Battle of Largs. A Gothic Poem With Several Miscellaneous Pieces. 1804 (anon.).

Cursory Reflections on Political and Commercial Topics as connected with the Regent's Accession to Royal Authority. 1812.

Voyages and Travels in the years 1809, 1810 and 1811. Containing Statistical, Commercial and Miscellaneous Observations On Gibraltar, Sardinia, Sicily, Malta, Serigo and Turkey. 1812.

The Life and Administration of Cardinal Wolsey. 1812; 1817; 1846.

The Tragedies of Maddelen, Agamemnon, Lady Macbeth, Antonia and Clytemnestra. 1812.

Letters from the Levant: containing Views of the State of Society, Manners, Opinions and Commerce; in Greece and the Archipelago. 1813.

Naval History of Great Britain. By Dr John Campbell. 8 vols. 1813. [Galt contributed the anon. lives of Hawke, Byron and Rodney, vols. v, vi.]

The New British Theatre. Edited by John Galt. 4 vols. 1814–5. [Contains several of Galt's own dramas, including The Witness, afterwards performed and ptd at Edinburgh as The Appeal.]

The Life and Studies of Benjamin West. 2 pts, 1816–20.

The Crusade. 1816. [A poem.]

All the Voyages Round the World. By Samuel Prior. 1820. ['Samuel Prior' was another of Galt's pseudonyms.]

A Tour of Europe and Asia. By Rev. T. Clark [i.e. Galt]. 2 vols. 1820.

George the Third, his Court and Family. 2 vols. 1820.

Pictures, Historical and Biographical, drawn from English, Scottish and Irish History. 2 vols. 1821 (re-issued 1824).

Modern Geography and History. By the Rev. T. Clark [i.e. Galt]. 1823.

The Bachelor's Wife. A Selection of Curious and Interesting Extracts, with Cursory Observations. Edinburgh, 1824. [Essays.]

The Life of Lord Byron. 1830 (3 edns); 1831 (5th edn); 1832; New York, 1835.

The Lives of the Players. 2 vols. 1831; 1886.

The Canadas as they at Present commend themselves to the Enterprise of Emigrants, Colonists and Capitalists. Compiled and condensed from Original Documents furnished by John Galt. By Andrew Picken. 1832.

The Autobiography of John Galt. 2 vols. 1833. [Galt's works listed, vol. ii, pp. 410–2.]

Poems. 1833.

The Literary Life, and Miscellanies. 3 vols. Edinburgh, 1834. [Essays, poems, tales, etc.]

A Contribution to the Greenock Calamity Fund. Greenock, 1835. [Poems.]

Diary [by Lady C. Bury] Illustrative of the Times of George IV. 4 vols. 1838–9. [Vols. iii–iv ed. by Galt.]

The Demon of Destiny and Other Poems. Greenock, 1839.

[The Canadian Boat Song first appeared in Noctes Ambrosianae in Blackwood's Mag. Sept. 1829, without the author's name and was included in The Republic of Letters, vii, 1831, a compilation edited by A. Whitelaw. Galt's authorship, although generally accepted, is open to some doubt. See E. Mac-Curdy, A Literary Enigma, Stirling, 1936, who attributes to Moir and Lockhart, Galt only providing the initial hint. Galt contributed a Life of John Wilson to Scottish Descriptive Poems, 1803, and a preface to A. Graydon's Memoirs, 1822. He was a frequent contributor to Fraser's and Blackwood's Mags. 1829–36.]

(e) Biography and Criticism

[Jeffrey, F.] Secondary Scottish Novels. Edinburgh Rev. Oct. 1823.

[Maginn, W.] John Galt. Fraser's Mag. Dec. 1830. [Rptd in A Gallery of Illustrious Literary Characters, ed. W. Bates, [1873].]

Cunningham, A. Biographical and Critical History of the Literature of the Last Fifty Years. Paris, 1834.

[Moir, D. M.] Biographical Memoir of [John Galt]. Edinburgh, 1841. [Prefixed to The Annals of the Parish and The Ayrshire Legatees, Blackwood's Standard Novels, vol. i.]

Douglas, Sir G. The Blackwood Group. [1897.]

Gordon, R. K. John Galt. Toronto, 1920. [With bibliography.]

Aberdein, J. W. John Galt. Oxford, 1936.

THOMAS GASPEY (1788–1871)

The Mystery, or Forty Years ago. A Novel. 3 vols. 1820.

Calthorpe, or Fallen Fortunes. A Novel. By the Author of The Mystery. 3 vols. 1821.

The Lollards. A Tale. By the Author of The Mystery. 3 vols. 1822.

Other Times, or The Monks of Leadenhall. By the Author of The Lollards. 3 vols. 1823.

The Witch Finder, or the Wisdom of our Ancestors. A Romance. By the Author of The Lollards. 3 vols. 1824.

Richmond, or Scenes in the Life of a Bow Street Officer, drawn up from his Private Memoranda. 3 vols. 1827 (anon.). [Also attrib. to T. S. Surr.]

The History of George Godfrey, written by himself. 3 vols. 1828 (anon.).

The Self Condemned. A Romance. By the Author of The Lollards. 3 vols. 1836.

'Many Coloured Life,' or Tales of Woe and Touches of Mirth. By the Author of The Lollards, etc. 1842.

Laurence Stark: a Family Picture. Translated [from J. J. Engel] by Thomas Gaspey. Heidelberg, 1843.

The Life and Times of the Good Lord Cobham. 2 vols. 1843.

The Pictorial History of France. 1843.

Glory. A Tale of Morals drawn from History. 1844.

The Dream of Human Life. By the Author of The Lollards. 2 vols. 1849.

The History of Smithfield. 1852.

WILLIAM NUGENT GLASCOCK (1787?–1847)

The Naval Sketch Book, or the Service afloat and ashore. With Characteristic Reminiscences, Fragments, and Opinions on Professional, Colonial and Political Subjects, interspersed with Copious Notes by an Officer of Rank. 2 vols. 1826.

Sailors and Saints, or Matrimonial Manœuvres. 3 vols. 1829.

Tales of a Tar. 1830.

The Naval Sketch Book. Second Series. By the Author of Tales of a Tar. 2 vols. 1834.

The Naval Service, or Officer's Manual for Every Grade in His Majesty's Ships. 2 vols. 1836; 1848.

Land Sharks and Sea Gulls. 3 vols. 1838.

GEORGE ROBERT GLEIG (1796–1888)

(a) Fiction

The Subaltern. Edinburgh, 1825; Edinburgh, 1826 (bis); Edinburgh, 1872 (rev. and corrected).

Tales of a Voyage to the Arctic Ocean. 3 vols. 1826.

The Chelsea Pensioners. 3 vols. 1829; 3 vols. 1833; 1841.

The Country Curate. 2 vols. 1830; 1834; 1856.

Allan Breck. A Novel. By the Author of The Subaltern. 3 vols. 1834.

The Chronicles of Waltham. By the Author of The Subaltern. 3 vols. 1835.

The Hussar. By the Author of The Subaltern. 2 vols. 1837.

The Light Dragoon. 2 vols. 1844.

With the Harrises Seventy Years Ago. By the Author of The Subaltern, The Chronicles of Waltham. 1889.

[Gleig also edited Katherine Randolph, or Self-Devotion, 1847.]

(b) Other Writings

Narrative of the Campaigns at Washington and New Orleans, 1814–15. 1821.

Sermons, Doctrinal and Practical. 1829.

The Life of Sir Thomas Munro. 3 vols. 1830.

The History of the Bible. 2 vols. 1830–1.

Lives of British Military Commanders. 3 vols. [In D. Lardner's The Cabinet Cyclopaedia, 1831–2.]

History of the British Empire in India. 4 vols. 1830–5.

Chelsea Hospital and its Traditions. 3 vols. 1838.

Germany, Bohemia, Hungary. 3 vols. 1839.

Memoirs of the Life of Warren Hastings. 3 vols. 1841.

The Veterans of Chelsea Hospital. 3 vols. 1844.

A Sketch of the Military History of Great Britain. 1845.

Sale's Brigade in Afghanistan. 1846.

Story of the Battle of Waterloo. 1847.

The Life of Robert, First Lord Clive. 1848.

The Leipsic Campaign. 1852.

India and its Army. 1857.

Essays, Biographical, Historical and Miscellaneous. Contributed chiefly to the Edinburgh and Quarterly Reviews. 2 vols. 1858.

The Life of The Duke of Wellington. 1862.

The Life of Sir Walter Scott. 1871.

The History of the Reign of George III to the Battle of Waterloo. 1873.

The Great Problem. Can It Be Solved? 1876.

Personal Reminiscences of the 1st Duke of Wellington. Ed. M. E. Greig, 1904.

(c) Biography and Criticism

Maginn, W. A Gallery of Illustrious Literary Characters. Ed. W. Bates, [1873].

CATHERINE GRACE FRANCES GORE, née MOODY (1799–1861)

(a) Original Fiction

Theresa Marchmont, or the Maid of Honour. A Tale. 1824. [Rptd in vol. I of The Edinburgh Tales, 1845.]

Richelieu, or the Broken Heart. 1826. [Attrib. to Mrs Gore.]

The Lettre de Cachet. A Tale; The Reign of Terror. A Tale. 1827. [The Reign of Terror alone, 1827.]

Hungarian Tales. By the Author of The Lettre de Cachet. 1829. [Selection rptd in The Edinburgh Tales, vol. II, 1845.]

Romances of Real Life. By the Author of Hungarian Tales. 3 vols. 1829; 1859.

Women as They are, or the Manners of the Day. 3 vols. 1830 (bis).

Pin-Money. A Novel. By the Authoress of The Manners of the Day. 3 vols. 1831; 1854.

The Tuileries. A Tale. By the Authoress of Hungarian Tales. 3 vols. 1831; 1841 (as The Soldier of Lyons).

Mothers and Daughters. A Tale of the Year 1830. 3 vols. 1831; 1834 (anon.).

The Opera. A Novel. By the Authoress of Mothers and Daughters. 3 vols. 1832.

The Fair of Mayfair. 3 vols. 1832 (anon.).

The Sketch Book of Fashion. By the Authoress of Mothers and Daughters. 3 vols. 1833.

Polish Tales. By the Authoress of Hungarian Tales. 3 vols. 1833.

The Hamiltons, or the New Era. 3 vols. 1834; 1850 (sub-title: Official Life in 1830).

The Diary of a Désennuyée. 2 vols. 1836 (anon.).

Mrs Armytage, or Female Domination. By the Authoress of Mothers and Daughters. 3 vols. 1836.

Memoirs of a Peeress, or the Days of Fox. Ed. Lady C. Bury, 3 vols. 1837; 1859.

Stokeshill Place, or the Man of Business. By the Authoress of Mrs Armytage. 3 vols. 1837.

The Heir of Selwood, or three Epochs of a Life. 3 vols. 1838; 1855.

Mary Raymond and Other Tales. 3 vols. 1838.

The Woman of the World. By the Authoress of the Diary of a Désennuyée. 3 vols. 1838.

The Cabinet Minister. By the Authoress of Mothers and Daughters. 3 vols. 1839.

The Courtier of the Days of Charles II. With Other Tales. Paris, 1839; 1847.

The Dowager, or the New School for Scandal. 3 vols. 1840.

Preferment, or My Uncle the Earl. 3 vols. 1840.

Greville, or a Season in Paris. 3 vols. 1841; Paris, 1841; 3 vols. 1844.

Cecil. Adventures of a Coxcomb. 3 vols. 1841; 1845.

Cecil a Peer. A Sequel to Cecil or the Adventures of a Coxcomb by the same Author. 3 vols. 1841; 1842 (as Ormington: or Cecil, a Peer, with a Word from the Author).

Fascination, and Other Tales. Edited by Mrs Gore. 3 vols. 1842.

The Man of Fortune and Other Tales. 3 vols. [1842].

The Ambassador's Wife. 3 vols. 1842; 1863.

The Money-Lender. 3 vols. 1843; 1854.

Modern Chivalry, or a New Orlando Furioso. 2 vols. 1843 (anon., with illustrations by George Cruikshank). ['Edited' by W. H. Ainsworth.]

The Banker's Wife, or Court and City. A Novel. 3 vols. 1843; 1859.

Agathonia. A Romance. 1844 (anon.).

The Birthright, and Other Tales. 3 vols. 1844.

The Popular Member, The Wheel of Fortune [etc.]. 3 vols. 1844.

Self. By the Author of Cecil. 3 vols. 1845; 1856.

The Story of a Royal Favourite. 3 vols. 1845.

The Snow Storm, A Christmas Story. With Illustrations by George Cruikshank. [1845.]

Peers and Parvenus. A Novel. 3 vols. 1846; 1859.

New Year's Day. A Winter's Tale. With Illustrations by George Cruikshank. [1846.]

Men of Capital. 3 vols. 1846.

The Débutante, or the London Season. 3 vols. 1846.

Castles in the Air. A Novel. 3 vols. 1847.

Temptation and Atonement, and Other Tales. 3 vols. 1847; [1860?].

The Inundation, or Pardon and Peace. A Christmas Story. With Illustrations by George Cruikshank. [1848.]

The Diamond and the Pearl. A Novel. 3 vols. 1849; [1859] (rev.).

The Dean's Daughter, or the Days we live in. 3 vols. 1853.

The Lost Son. A Winter's Tale. [1854.]

Progress and Prejudice. 3 vols. 1854.

Mammon, or the Hardships of an Heiress. 3 vols. 1855.

A Life's Lessons. A Novel. 3 vols. 1856.

The Two Aristocracies. A Novel. 3 vols. 1857.

Heckington. A Novel. 3 vols. 1858.

[Mrs Gore also contributed The Abbey of Laach to Tales of All Nations, 1827, and to The Tale Book, Königsberg, 1859.

(b) Translated Fiction

Picciola; or, Captivity Captive. Translated from the French. 1837.

The Lover and the Husband. From the French of Gerfaut, by Charles de Bernard. Edited by Mrs Gore. 3 vols. 1841.

Modern French Life. Edited by Mrs Gore. 3 vols. 1842. [A collection of tales tr. from the French.]

The Queen of Denmark. An Historical Novel. Translated from the Danish of T. C. Heiberg; edited by Mrs Gore. 1846.

(c) Other Writings

The Bond. A Dramatic Poem. 1824.

The Historical Traveller. Comprising Narratives connected with European History. 2 vols. 1831.

The Rose Fancier's Manual. 1838.

Dacre of the South, or the Olden Time. A Drama. 1840.

The Maid of Croissey; or Theresa's Vow. A Drama, in Two Acts. [In B.N.Webster, The Acting National Drama, vol. vi, [1840].]

A Good Night's Rest, or Two in the Morning. A Farce, in One Act. [In J. Duncombre, British Theatre, vol. xxxix, [1840?].]

King O'Neil, or the Irish Brigade. A Comedy in Two Acts. [In B. N. Webster, The Acting National Drama, vol. vii, [1840].]

Paris in 1841. With Engravings after T. Allom. 1842. [Heath's Picturesque Annual for 1842.)

Quid Pro Quo, or the Day of Dupes. [1844.] [A comedy.]

Sketches of English Character. 2 vols. 1846.

Adventures in Borneo. 1849.

(d) Biography and Criticism

Catherine Frances Gore. Colburn's New Monthly Mag. xlix, 1837.

Horne, R. H. A New Spirit of the Age. Vol. i, 1844.

The Works of Mrs Gore. Colburn's New Monthly Mag. xcv, 1852.

Obituary. Athenaeum, 9 Feb. 1861. [Addns 16, 23 Feb.]

Rosa, M. W. The Silver Fork School: Novels of Fashion Preceding Vanity Fair. New York, 1936.

THOMAS COLLEY GRATTAN (1792–1864)
(a) Fiction

Highways and Byways, or Tales of the Roadside, picked up in the French Provinces by a Walking Gentleman. Ser. 1, 1823. Ser. 2, 3 vols. 1825. Ser. 3, 3 vols. 1827. [Sers. 1, 2 rptd 1847, 1848.]

Traits of Travel, or Tales of Men and Cities. 3 vols. 1829.

The Heiress of Bruges. A Tale of the Year Sixteen Hundred. 4 vols. 1830; 1834.

Jacqueline of Holland; A Historical Tale. 3 vols. 1831, 1843 (rev. edn).

Agnes de Mansfeldt. A Historical Tale. 3 vols. 1835; 1847.

The Forfeit and Other Tales. [1847?]

The Curse of the Black Lady and Other Tales. [1847?]

The Cagot's Hut and the Conscript's Bride. 1852.

(b) Other Writings

Philibert, a Poetical Romance [in 6 cantos with notes]. 1819.

Ben Nazir the Saracen. A Tragedy. 1827.

History of the Netherlands. 1830.

Legends of the Rhine and of the Low Countries. 1832; 1849.

Civilized America. 2 vols. 1859.

England and the Disrupted States of America. 1861.

Beaten Paths and those who trod them. 2 vols. 1862.

SARAH GREEN

The History of the Tankerville Family. 3 vols. 1806.

The Private History of the Court of England. 2 vols. 1808.

Tales of the Manor. 2 vols. 1809.

The Festival of St Jago. 2 vols. 1810.

The Reformist. 2 vols. 1810.

Romance Readers and Romance Writers. 3 vols. 1810. [Preceded by a critical 'Literary Retrospection' partly rptd in Novelists on Novels, ed. R. B. Johnson, 1928.]

The Royal Exile, or Victims of Human Passions. 4 vols. 1811 (bis).

Good Men of Modern Date. A Satirical Tale. 3 vols. 1812.

Raphael; or, A Peaceful Life. From the German. 2 vols. 1812.

Deception, a Fashionable Novel. 3 vols. 1813.

BASIL HALL (1788–1844)
[See p. 670 below.]

ELIZABETH HAMILTON (1758–1816)
(a) Fiction

Translation of the Letters of a Hindoo Rajah, to which is prefixed a Preliminary Dissertation on the Hindoos. 2 vols. 1796. [Essays in fictional form.]

Memoirs of Modern Philosophers. 3 vols. 1800 (bis); 3 vols. 1801; 2 vols. Dublin, 1801. [A novel.]

Memoirs of the Life of Agrippina, Wife of Germanicus. 3 vols. [Bath], 1804; 2 vols. 1811.

The Cottagers of Glenburnie. [Edinburgh], 1808.

(b) Other Writings

Letters on Education. [Bath], 1801; 1824 (7th edn).

Letters on the Elementary Principles of Education. 2 vols. [Bath], 1802.

Letters Addressed to the Daughter of a Nobleman on the Formation of the Religious and the Moral Principle. 2 vols. 1806.

Exercises in Religious Knowledge. [Edinburgh], 1809.

Popular Essays on the Elementary Principles of the Human Mind. 1812.

Hints addressed to the Patrons and Directors of Public Schools. 1815.

(c) Biography

Benger, E. O. Memoirs of Mrs Elizabeth Hamilton, with Selections from her Correspondence and Unpublished Writings. 1818

THOMAS HAMILTON (1789–1842)

The Youth and Manhood of Cyril Thornton. 3 vols. 1827.

Annals of the Peninsular Campaigns, 1808–14. 3 vols. 1829; rev. F. Hardman, 1849.

Men and Manners in America. 2 vols. 1833.

[For Hamilton see Sir G. Douglas, The Blackwood Group, 1897.]

ELIZABETH HELME (d. 1816)

(a) Novels

St Margaret's Cave, or the Nun's Story. An Ancient Legend. 4 vols. 1801.

St Clair of the Isles, or, the Outlaws of Barra. A Scottish Tradition. 4 vols. 1803; 1825; 1867; [1889].

The Pilgrim of the Cross, or the Chronicles of Christabelle de Mowbray. An Ancient Legend. 4 vols. Brentford, 1805.

Modern Times or the Age we Live in. A Posthumous Novel. 3 vols. Brentford, 1814; 1817.

[L. G. Michaud, Biographie universelle, mentions another posthumous novel, Madeleine or the Penitent of Godstow, 3 vols. n.d. For novels and trns pbd before 1801 see vol. II, pp. 549, 550, 560, 566 above.]

(b) Works of Instruction

Plutarch's Lives abridged. 1795.

Instructive Rambles in London and the Adjacent Villages. 2 vols. 1798, 1800; 1806 (4th edn); 1808; 1812. [Instructive Rambles extended, 2 vols. 1800.]

Maternal Instruction; or, Family Conversations on Moral and Entertaining Subjects. 2 vols. 1802; 1810 (3rd edn); 1815.

The History of England, related in Familiar Conversations, by a Father to his Children. 2 vols. 1805.

The History of Scotland, related in Familiar Conversations, by a Father to his Children. 2 vols. Brentford, 1806.

The Fruits of Reflection, or Moral Remembrances on Various Subjects. 2 vols. Brentford, 1809.

A Preparatory Exercise on the Road leading to the Land of Learning. Brentford, 1816.

[Also several trns.]

WILLIAM BROWNE HOCKLEY (1792–1860)

Pandurang Hari, or Memoirs of a Hindoo. 3 vols. 1826; 2 vols. 1873 (with introduction by Sir H. B. E. Frere).

The Zenana: or a Nawab's Leisure Hours. By the Author of Pandurang Hari. 3 vols. 1827; rptd Lord Stanley of Alderley, 2 vols. 1874.

The English in India. 3 vols. 1828.

The Vizier's Son. 3 vols. 1831.

The Memoirs of a Brahmin, or the Fatal Jewels. 3 vols. 1843.

BARBARA HOFLAND (1770–1844)

[See Barbara Hoole below.]

JAMES HOGG (1770–1835)

[See p. 164 above.]

JAMES HOOK (1771–1828)

Pen Owen. A Novel. 3 vols. Edinburgh, 1822 (anon.); 1842; 1849.

Percy Mallory. By the Author of Pen Owen. 3 vols. Edinburgh, 1824.

[Hook also pbd various pamphlets, sermons, etc.]

THEODORE EDWARD HOOK (1788–1841)

(a) Selected Works

Theodore Hooks ausgewählte Romane. Aus dem Englischen von E. A. Moriarty und J. Seybt. 16 pts, Leipzig, 1842–3.

The Choice Humorous Works, Ludicrous Adventures, Bon Mots, Puns and Hoaxes of Theodore Hook. With a New Life of the Author, Portraits by Maclise and D'Orsay, Caricatures and Facsimiles. [1873.]

Bon-Mots of Samuel Foote and Theodore Hook. Ed. W. Jerrold, 1894.

(b) Fiction

The Man of Sorrow, by Alfred Allendale. 3 vols. 1808.

Sayings and Doings. A Series of Sketches from Life. 3 sers. 9 vols. 1824–8 (ser. 1 rptd 1824) (anon.); 3 vols. 1836, 1838; tr. French, Paris, 1828.

Maxwell. By the Author of Sayings and Doings. 3 vols. 1830; 1834; 1854 (rev.); [1878].

Love and Pride. By the Author of Sayings and Doings. 3 vols. 1833; 1842 (as The Widow and the Marquess, or Love and Pride).

The Parson's Daughter. By the Author of Sayings and Doings. 3 vols. 1833; 1835 (rev. and corrected); 1867.

Gilbert Gurney. By the Author of Sayings and Doings. 3 vols. 1836; Paris, 1836; 1841; tr. French, Paris, 1861.

Jack Brag. By the Author of Sayings and Doings. 3 vols. 1837; Paris, 1837; 1839; 1847.

Gurney Married: a Sequel to Gilbert Gurney. By the Author of Sayings and Doings. 3 vols. 1838; 3 vols. 1839; 1842; [1863].

Births, Deaths, and Marriages. By the Author of Sayings and Doings. 3 vols. 1839; 1842 (as All in the Wrong; or, Births, Deaths, and Marriages); [1863] (as All in the Wrong).

Precepts and Practice. 3 vols. 1840; [1863].

Fathers and Sons. A Novel. 3 vols. 1842; [1860].

Peregrine Bunce, or Settled at Last. A Novel. 3 vols. 1842; 1857.

Ned Musgrave, or the most Unfortunate Man in the World. A Comic Novel. N.d.; 1854.

(c) Plays

The Soldier's Return, or What can Beauty do? A Comic Opera. 1805 (anon.).

Catch him who can. A Musical Farce. 1806.

The Invisible Girl. A Piece in One Act. 1806.

Tekeli, or the Siege of Montgatz. A Melodrama in Three Acts. 1806.

The Fortress. A Melo-drama, from the French. 1807.

Music-Mad. A Dramatic Sketch. 1808.

Killing No Murder. A Farce in two acts. 1809 (2nd edn, together with a Preface, and the Scene suppressed by the Lord Chamberlain); 1811 (5th edn).

Safe and Sound. An Opera in Three Acts. 1809.

Darkness Visible. A Farce. 1811 (bis).

The Trial by Jury. A Comic Piece in Two Acts. 1811.

Exchange no Robbery, or the Diamond King. A Comedy. 1820.

(d) Other Writings

Facts illustrative of the Treatment of Napoleon Buonaparte in Saint Helena. 1819 (anon.); 1910.

Tentamen, or an Essay towards the History of Whittington. By Vicesimus Blinkinsop. 1820. [A satire on Sir Matthew Wood, the partisan of Queen Caroline.]

Life of General Sir David Baird. 2 vols. 1832.

The Ramsbottom Letters. 1872; [1874] (as The Ramsbottom Papers; complete and unabridged).

[Hook also edited Reminiscences of Michael Kelly, 1826, and J. A. Bernard's The French Stage and the French People, 1841, as well as the following novels: A. Dumas' Pascal Bruno, 1837; J. T. J. Hewlett's Peter Priggins, 3 vols. 1841, and The Parish Clerk, 3 vols. 1841; and H. M. G. Smythies's Cousin Geoffrey, the Old Bachelor, 3 vols. 1840. He was editor of John Bull from 1820 to about 1825, and of The New Monthly Magazine and Humourist from vol. XLIX to LXII.]

(e) Biography and Criticism

Memoir. New Monthly Mag. LXIII, 1841. [With portrait.]

[Lockhart, J. G.] Peregrine Bunce. Quarterly Rev. May 1843.

—— Theodore Hook. A Sketch. 1852 (3 edns); 1853.

Horne, R. H. A New Spirit of the Age. Vol. II, 1844.

Theodore Edward Hook. Chambers's Journ. V, 1846.

A Graybeard's Gossip about his Literary Acquaintance. No. VI. New Monthly Mag. LXXX, 1847.

Barham, R. H. D. The Life and Remains of Theodore Edward Hook. 2 vols. 1849; 1853 (rev. and corrected); 1877 (rev.).

Hall, A. M. and S. C. Memories of Authors, Theodore Hook and his Friends. Atlantic Monthly, XV, 1865.

Maginn, W. A Gallery of Illustrious Literary Characters. Ed. W. Bates, [1873].

Saintsbury, G. Theodore Hook. Macmillan's Mag. LXIX, 1894.

Theodore Hook, Satirist and Novelist. Temple Bar, CIII, 1894.

Waugh, F. G. Unpublished Letters of Theodore Hook. GM. LVI, 1896.

St Cyres, S. H. N. Theodore Hook. Cornhill Mag. LXXXIX, 1904.

Brightfield, M. F. Theodore Hook and his Novels. Cambridge, U.S.A. 1928.

Repplier, A. The Laugh that failed. Atlantic Monthly, CLVIII, 1936.

BARBARA HOOLE, afterwards HOFLAND, née WREAKS (1770–1844)

(a) Novels

The History of an Officer's Widow and her Young Family. 1809 (anon.); 1814; 1834.

The History of a Clergyman's Widow and her Young Family. 1812 (anon.).

The Son of a Genius: a Tale, for the Use of Youth. 1812; 1816; 1819; 1821; 1822; 1841 (14th edn); tr. French, Paris, 1817.

Says she to her Neighbour, What? By an Old-Fashioned Englishman. 4 vols. 1812.

Patience and Perseverance, or the Modern Griselda. By the Author of Says she to her Neighbour, What? 4 vols. 1813.

Iwanonna, or, the Maid of Moscow. 1813 (anon.).

A Father as he should be. A Novel. 4 vols. 1815.

The Affectionate Brothers. A Tale. 2 vols. 1816; 1829; [1835?]; 1863.

Matilda; or, The Barbadoes Girl. A Tale. 1816 (anon.); [1825?] (5th edn); 1866.

The Good Grandmother and her Offspring. A Tale. 1817.

The Blind Farmer and his Children. 1819 (2nd edn); [1830?] (6th edn).

Ellen the Teacher. 1819 (2nd edn); 1822; 1833; [1879].

Tales of the Priory. 4 vols. 1820.

Tales of the Manor. 4 vols. 1822.

Adelaide, or the Intrepid Daughter. A Tale. 1823 (anon.); [1825?] (3rd edn).

The Daughter of a Genius. A Tale for Youth. 1823 (bis); 1848; [1879].

Integrity. A Tale. 1823; 1840; 1868.

The History of a Merchant's Widow and her Young Family. 1823 (anon.); 1867; tr. French, Paris, 1831.

Decision. A Tale. 1824.

Patience. A Tale. 1824.

Alfred Campbell, the Young Pilgrim, containing Travels in Egypt and the Holy Land. 1825.

A Reflection. A Tale. 1826.

The Young Pilgrim, or, Alfred Campbell's Return to the East. 1826.

William and his Uncle Ben. A Tale. 1826; [1865].

Self-Denial. A Tale. 1827.

Katharine. A Tale. 1828.

Beatrice. A Tale founded on Facts. 3 vols. 1829.

The Daughter-in-law, her Father and Family. 1829.

Elizabeth and her Three Beggar Boys. [1830?]

The Sisters. A Domestic Tale. [1830?]; 1866; tr. French, Paris, 1832.

The Stolen Boy. An Indian Tale. [1830?]

Theodore; or, The Crusaders. 1833 (6th edn); [1879].

The Captives in India: a Tale; and A Widow and a Will. 3 vols. 1834.

Fortitude: a Tale. 1835.

Rich Boys and Poor Boys, and Other Tales. [1836?]; [1840?].

The Young Cadet; or, Henry Delamere's Voyage to India. 1836 (new edn, 'revised and altered by the author').

Humility: a Tale. 1837.

Energy: a Tale. 1838.

Farewell Tales. 1840.

The Young Crusoe. A Tale. [1840?] (new edn); 1876; ed. A. Gardiner, Manchester, [1894].

Alicia and Her Aunt; or, Think before you speak. [1841] (new edn).

The Czarina: an Historical Romance of the Court of Russia. 3 vols. 1842.

The Godmother's Tales. 1842.

The King's Son. A Romance of English History. 3 vols. 1843.

Emily's Reward, or the Holiday Trip to Paris. 1844.

(b) Other Writings

Poems. Sheffield, [1805].

Little Dramas for Young People, on Subjects taken from English History. 1810.

A Season at Harrogate; in a series of poetical epistles from Benjamin Blunderhead, Esquire, to his mother. Knaresborough, 1812; Harrogate, 1838 (rev. edn).

A Descriptive Account of the Mansions and Gardens of White Knights; with Twenty-Three Engravings from Pictures by T. J. Hofland. [1819] (priv. ptd).

The Panorama of Europe, or a New Game of Geography. 1824 (4th edn).

Africa Described, in its Ancient and Present State. 1828; 1834.

The Young Northern Traveller, or the Invalid restored; containing a Tour through Northern Europe, with Anecdotes. [1830?] (new edn with addns); tr. French, Paris, 1834.

Richmond and the Surrounding Scenery; with Letterpress by Mrs Hofland. 1832.

The Illustrated Alphabet; with Poetry by Mrs Hofland. 1839.

(c) Biography and Criticism

Ramsay, Thomas. The Life and Literary Remains of Barbara Hofland. 1849.

L'Estrange, A. G. K. The Friendships of Mary Russell Mitford, as recorded in Letters from her Literary Correspondents. 1882.

THOMAS HOPE (1770–1831)

Observations on the Plans by James Wyatt for Downing College. 1804.

Household Furniture and Interior Decorating. 1807.

The Costume of the Ancients. 2 vols. 1809; 2 vols. 1812 (enlarged).

Designs of Modern Costumes. 1812.

Anastasius, or Memoirs of a Modern Greek, written at the Close of the Eighteenth Century. 3 vols. 1819 (anon.); 3 vols. 1820 (bis); 1836.

An Essay on the Origins and Prospects of Man. 3 vols. 1831.

An Historical Essay on Architecture. 2 vols. 1835.

[For Hope's Anastasius see K. J. Zeidler, Beckford, Hope und Morier als Vertreter des orientalischen Romans, Leipzig, 1909.]

EDWARD GEORGE GRANVILLE HOWARD (d. 1841)

Rattlin the Reefer. 3 vols. 1836. [Edited by Marryat and illustrated by Hervieu.]

The Old Commodore. 3 vols. 1837.

Outward Bound, or a Merchant's Adventures. 3 vols. 1838; tr. French, Paris, 1838.

Jack Ashore. 3 vols. 1840; tr. French, Paris, 1841.

Sir Henry Morgan the Buccaneer. 3 vols. 1842.

[For Howard see T. Hood, New Monthly Mag. LXIV, 1842, pp. 438–41.]

MARY HOWITT, née BOTHAM (1799–1888)

[See p. 672 below.]

WILLIAM HOWITT (1792–1879)

[See p. 673 below.]

CATHERINE HUTTON (1756–1846)

[See p. 674 below.]

MRS ISAACS

Ariel, or the Invisible Monitor. 4 vols. 1801 (anon.).

Glenmore Abbey, or the Lady of the Rock. By the Author of Ariel. 3 vols. 1805.

The Wood Nymph. 3 vols. [1807?]

Ella St Laurence or the Village of Selwood and its Inhabitants. A Novel. 4 vols. 1809.

The Wanderings of Fancy: consisting of Miscellaneous Pieces in Prose and Verse. 1812.

Tales of To-day. 3 vols. 1816; tr. French, Paris, 1817.

Earl Osric or the Legend of Rosamond. 4 vols. 1820.

GEORGE PAYNE RAINSFORD JAMES (1799–1860)

(a) Collected Works

The Works, revised and corrected by the Author. With an Introductory Preface. 21 vols. 1844–9. [Not complete.]

(b) Fiction

Adra, or the Peruvians. 1829.

Richelieu. A Tale of France. 3 vols. 1829.

Darnley, or the Field of the Cloth of Gold. 3 vols. 1830; 1836; 1850.

De L'Orme. By the Author of Richelieu and Darnley. 3 vols. 1830; 1837; 1856.

Philip Augustus, or the Brothers in Arms. By the Author of Darnley, De L'Orme, etc. 3 vols. 1831; 1837; 1851.

Bertrand de la Croix, or the Siege of Rhodes. 1841. [First ptd in The Club Book, 1831.]

Henry Masterton, or the Adventures of a Young Cavalier. By the Author of Richelieu, Darnley, 3 vols. 1832; 1837; 1851.

The String of Pearls. By the Author of Darnley, etc. 2 vols. 1832.

Delaware, or the Ruined Family. A Tale. 3 vols. Edinburgh, 1833; 1855.

Mary of Burgundy, or the Revolt of Ghent. By the Author of Darnley. 3 vols. 1833; 1850.

The Life and Adventures of John Marston Hall. By the Author of Darnley. 3 vols. 1834; 1851.

The Gipsey. A Tale. By the Author of Richelieu. 3 vols. 1835; 1850.

My Aunt Pontypool. 3 vols. 1835.

One in a Thousand, or the Days of Henry Quatre. By the Author of The Gipsey. 3 vols. 1835; 1850.

The Desultory Man. By the Author of Richelieu. 3 vols. 1836.

Attila. A Romance. By the Author of The Gipsey. 3 vols. 1837.

The Robber. A Tale. By the Author of Richelieu. 3 vols. 1838; 1850.

Henry of Guise, or the States of Blois. 3 vols. 1839.

The Huguenot. A Tale of the French Protestants. By the Author of The Gipsey. 3 vols. 1839; 1853.

Charles Tyrrell, or the Bitter Blood. 1839; 1851.

The Gentleman of the Old School. A Tale. 3 vols. 1839; 1852.

The King's Highway. A Novel. 3 vols. 1840; 1851.

The Man at Arms, or Henri de Cerons. A Romance. 1840; 1844.

Corse de Leon, or the Brigand. A Romance. 3 vols. 1841; 1851.

The Ancient Regime. A Tale. 3 vols. 1841; 1850 (as Castlenau).

The Jacquerie, or the Lady and the Page. An Historical Romance. 3 vols. 1841; 1852.

Morley Ernstein, or the Tenants of the Heart. 3 vols. 1842; 1850.

The Commissioner, or De Lunatico Inquirendo. With Twenty-Eight Illustrations by Phiz. 1843 (anon.).

Forest Days. A Romance of Old Times. 3 vols. 1843; 1852.

The False Heir. 3 vols. 1843.

Eva St Clair and Other Collected Tales. 2 vols. 1843.

Agincourt. A Romance. 3 vols. 1844; 1852.

Arabella Stuart. A Romance from English History. 3 vols. 1844.

Rose D'Albret, or Troublous Times. 3 vols. 1844; 1856.

Arrah Neil, or Times of Old. 3 vols. 1845; 1853.

The Smuggler. A Tale. 3 vols. 1845.

Beauchamp, or the Error. 3 vols. 1848. [First appeared serially in New Monthly Mag. 1845–6.]

The Stepmother, or Evil Doings. 1845 (priv. ptd); 3 vols. 1846 (as The Stepmother); 1855.

Heidelberg. A Romance. 3 vols. 1846; 1852.

The Castle of Ehrenstein, its Lords, Spiritual and Temporal, its Inhabitants, Early and Unearthly. 3 vols. 1847; 1855.

A Whim and its Consequences. 3 vols. 1847 (anon.); 1853.

The Convict. A Tale. 3 vols. 1847; 1851.

Russell. A Tale of the Reign of Charles II. 3 vols. 1847.

Margaret Graham. A Tale Founded on Facts. 2 vols. 1848. [Pbd serially in New Monthly Mag. during 1847.]

The Last of the Fairies. With Eleven Illustrations by John Gilbert. 1848.

Sir Theodore Broughton, or Laurel Water. 3 vols. 1848; 1853.

Gowrie, or the King's Plot. 1848 (as vol. XVII of Collected Works); 1851.

The Forgery, or Best Intentions. 3 vols. 1849; 1853.

John Jones's Tales for Little John Joneses. 2 vols. 1849.

The Woodman. A Romance of the Times of Richard III. 3 vols. 1849; 1857.

The Old Oak Chest. A Tale of Domestic Life. 3 vols. 1850.

Henry Smeaton. A Jacobite Story of the Reign of George the First. 3 vols. 1851.

The Fate. A Tale of Stirring Times. 3 vols. 1851.

Revenge. A Novel. 3 vols. 1852.

Adrian, or the Clouds of the Mind. A Romance. 2 vols. 1852. [With M. B. Field.]

Pequinillo. A Tale. 3 vols. 1852.

The Bride of Landeck. New York, 1878. [First pbd in Harper's New Monthly Mag. June–Nov. 1852.]

Agnes Sorrel. An Historical Romance. 3 vols. 1853.

The Vicissitudes of a Life. A Novel. 3 vols. 1853.

Ticonderoga, or the Black Eagle. A Tale of Times not long Past. 3 vols. 1854.

Prince Life. A Story for my Boy. 1856.

The Old Dominion, or the Southampton Massacre. A Novel. 3 vols. 1856.

Leonora D'Orco. A Historical Romance. 3 vols. 1857.

Lord Montagu's Page. A Historical Romance. 3 vols. 1858.

The Cavalier. An Historical Novel. Philadelphia, 1859; 2 vols. 1864 (as Bernard Marsh, a Novel).

[James also contributed to Seven Tales by Seven Authors, ed. F. E. Smedley, 1849, 1860.]

(c) Historical Writings

The History of Chivalry. 1830.

Memoirs of Great Commanders. 3 vols. 1832.

France, in the Lives of her Great Men. The History of Charlemagne. 1832.

A History of the Life of Edward the Black Prince and of Various Events connected therewith which occurred during the Reign of Edward III, King of England. 2 vols. 1836.

The Cabinet Cyclopædia. Ed. D. Lardner. Biography: Eminent Foreign Statesmen. By G. P. R. James. 1836. [Vols. II, III, IV, V.]

Memoirs of Celebrated Women. Ed. G. P. R. James, 2 vols. 1837.

The Life and Times of Louis the Fourteenth. 4 vols. 1838.

A Brief History of the United States Boundary Question, drawn up from Official Papers. 1839.

Letters illustrative of the Reign of William III from 1696 to 1708, addressed to the Duke of Shrewsbury by James Vernon, Secretary of State. Now First Published. 3 vols. 1841.

A History of the Life of Richard Cœur-de-Lion, King of England. 4 vols. 1842–9.

The Life of Henry the Fourth, King of France and Navarre. 3 vols. 1847.

An Investigation of the Circumstances Attending the Murder of John, Earl of Gowrie and Alexander Ruthven. 1849.

Rizzio, or Scenes in Europe during the Sixteenth Century. By the Late Mr [W. H.] Ireland. Ed. G. P. R. James, 3 vols. 1849. [James's memoir is of interest.]

Dark Scenes of History. 3 vols. 1849.

An Oration on the Character and Services of the Late Duke of Wellington. Boston, 1853.

(d) Other Writings

The Ruined City. A Poem. 1828 (priv. ptd).

On the Educational Institutions of Germany. 1835.

Blanche of Navarre. A Play. 1839.

A Book of the Passions. With Sixteen Engravings. 1839.

Some Remarks on the Corn Laws, with Suggestions for an Alteration in the Sliding Scale. In a Letter to Colonel Charles Wyndham, M.P. 1841.

Camaralzaman. A Fairy Drama. 1848.

(e) Biography and Criticism

The Novels of G. P. R. James. Dublin University Mag. XIX, 1842.

Horne, R. H. A New Spirit of the Age. Vol. I, 1844.

Recollections of G. P. R. James. Bentley's Misc. XLIX, 1861.

Frost, W. A. The Novels and Short Stories of G. P. R. James. N. & Q. 26 Aug. 1916. [Annotated list.]

Ellis, S. M. The Solitary Horseman, or the Life and Adventures of G. P. R. James. 1927. [With bibliography.]

CHRISTIAN ISOBEL JOHNSTONE (1781–1857)

(a) Fiction

Clan-Albin. A National Tale. 4 vols. Edinburgh, 1815.

Elizabeth de Bruce. A Novel. 3 vols. 1827.

Nights of the Round Table; or, Stories of Aunt Jane and her Friends. 2 pts, Edinburgh, 1832.

The Edinburgh Tales, conducted by Mrs Johnstone. 3 vols. Edinburgh, 1845–6.

(b) Other Writings

The Cook and Housewife's Manual. Containing the most Approved Modern Receipts for making Soups, Gravies, Sauces. By Margaret Dods. Edinburgh, 1826 (10 edns by 1854).
The Students; or, Biography of Grecian Philosophers. 1827.
The Diversions of Hollycot; or, the Mother's Art of Thinking. 1828.
Scenes of Industry displayed in the Beehive and the Ant-hill. [1829?]; 1830.
The Wars of the Jews, adapted to Young Persons. 1832.
True Tales of the Irish Peasantry, as related by themselves, selected from the Report of the Poor-Law Commissioners. 1836.
Rational Reading Lessons. 1842.
Poems by Robert Nicoll. With a Memoir of the Author by C. I. Johnstone. 1842.

ISABELLA KELLY, later HEDGELAND

(a) Novels

Madeline, or the Castle of Montgomery. A Novel. 4 vols. 1794 (anon.); 4 vols. 1799.
The Abbey of St Asaph. A Novel. By the Author of Madeline, or the Castle of Montgomery. 3 vols. 1795.
The Ruins of Avondale Priory. A Novel. 3 vols. 1796.
Joscelina, or the Rewards of Benevolence. A Novel. 2 vols. 1797.
Eva. A Novel. 3 vols. 1799; tr. French, Paris, 1803.
Ruthinglenne or the Critical Moment. A Novel. 3 vols. 1801.
The Baron's Daughter: a Gothic Romance. 4 vols. 1802.
A Modern Incident in Domestic Life. 2 vols. Brentford, 1803.
The Secret. A Novel. 4 vols. Brentford, 1805.
Jane de Dunstanville or Characters as they are. A Novel. 4 vols. 1813.

(b) Other Writings

A Collection of Poems and Fables. 1794.
Poems. 1802.
[Isabella Kelly also pbd some educational works.]

JAMES SHERIDAN KNOWLES (1784–1862)
[See p. 590 below.]

LADY CAROLINE LAMB, née PONSONBY (1785–1828)

(a) Fiction

Glenarvon. 3 vols. 1816 (anon.); 3 vols. 1816 (contains an important new preface); 3 vols. 1816; 1865 (as The Fatal Passion).

Verses from Glenarvon: to which is prefixed the Original Introduction not published with the Early Editions of that Work. 1816.
Graham Hamilton. 2 vols. 1822 (anon.).
Ada Reis. A Tale. 3 vols. 1823 (anon.).

(b) Other Writings

A New Canto. 1819 (anon.).
Fugitive Pieces and Reminiscences of Lord Byron with some Original Poetry, Letters and Recollections of Lady Caroline Lamb. Ed. I. Nathan, 1829.

FRANCIS LATHOM (1777–1832)

(a) Novels

The Castle of Ollada. 2 vols. [1794?].
The Midnight Bell. A German Story founded on Incidents in Real Life. 3 vols. 1798 (anon.); 3 vols. 1825; tr. French, Paris, [1799?].
Men and Manners. A Novel. 4 vols. 1799; 1800.
Mystery. A Novel. 2 vols. 1800; tr. French, German, n.d.
Astonishment!!! A Romance of a Century Ago. 2 vols. 1802.
Very Strange but Very True, or the History of an Old Man's Young Wife. A Novel. 4 vols. 1803.
Ernestina: a Tale from the French. 2 vols. 1803.
The Impenetrable Secret: find it out! 2 vols. 1805.
The Mysterious Freebooter; or, The Days of Queen Bess. A Romance. 4 vols. 1806.
Human Beings. A Novel. 3 vols. 1807.
The Fatal Vow; or, St Michael's Monastery. A Romance. 2 vols. 1807.
The Unknown; or, The Northern Gallery. 3 vols. 1808.
London; or, Truth without Treason. 4 vols. 1809.
The Romance of the Hebrides; or, Wonders Never Cease! 3 vols. 1809.
Italian Mysteries; or, More Secrets than One. A Romance. 3 vols. 1820; tr. French, Paris, 1823.
The One Pound Note, and Other Tales. 2 vols. 1820.
Puzzled and Pleased; or, The Two Old Soldiers: and Other Tales. 3 vols. 1822.
Live and Learn; or, The First John Brown, his Friends, Enemies and Acquaintances, in Town and Country. A Novel. 4 vols. 1823.
The Polish Bandit; or, Who is my Bride? and Other Tales. 3 vols. 1824.
Young John Bull; or, Born Abroad and Bred At Home. 3 vols. 1828.
Fashionable Mysteries; or, The Rival Duchesses and Other Tales. 3 vols. 1829.

Mystic Events; or, The Vision of the Tapestry. A Romantic Legend of the Days of Anne Boleyn. 4 vols. 1830.

(b) Plays

All in a Bustle. A Comedy. By the Author of The Castle of Ollada. Norwich, 1795; Norwich, 1800.

The Dash of the Day. A Comedy. Norwich, 1800 (2nd edn).

Holiday Time; or, The School Boy's Frolic. A Farce. Norwich, 1800.

Curiosity. A Comedy. 1801. [Adapted from the French of Madame de Genlis.]

The Wife of a Million. A Comedy. Norwich, [1802?].

Orlando and Seraphina; or, The Funeral Pile. A Drama. [1804?]. [Founded on Tasso's Gerusalemme Liberata.]

THOMAS PIKE LATHY

(a) Novels

Usurpation, or the Inflexible Uncle. A Novel. 3 vols. 1805.

The Paraclete. A Novel. 5 vols. 1805.

The Invisible Enemy, or the Mines of Wielitska. A Polish Legendary Romance. 4 vols. 1806.

Gabriel Forrester, or the Deserted Son. 4 vols. 1807.

The Misled General. 1807 (anon.).

Love, Hatred and Revenge: a Swiss Romance. 3 vols. 1809.

[The Biographical Dictionary of Living Authors, 1816, also lists The Rising Sun, 3 vols. 1807, and The Setting Sun, 3 vols. 1809 (anon.).]

(b) Miscellaneous Writings

Reparation, or the School for Libertines. A Dramatic Piece in Three Acts. Boston, 1800.

The Angler: a Poem in Ten Cantos. With Proper Instructions in the Art, Rules to choose Fishing Rods, Lines, Hooks, etc. 1819; 1820. [Almost entirely plagiarised from The Anglers, by Thomas Scott of Ipswich, 1758.]

Memoirs of the Court of Louis XIV, comprising Biography and Anecdotes of the Most Celebrated Characters of that Period. 3 vols. 1819.

SIR THOMAS DICK LAUDER (1784–1848)

Lochandu. A Tale of the Eighteenth Century. 3 vols. Edinburgh, 1825.

The Wolfe of Badenoch. An Historical Romance. 1827.

Highland Rambles and Legends to shorten the Way. 2 vols. 1837.

Legendary Tales of the Highlands. 3 vols. 1841.

The Edinburgh Tales. Ed. C. I. Johnstone, 3 vols. 1845–6. [Lauder contributed The Story of Farquharson of Inverarey to vol. I and Donald Lamont, the Braemar Drover, to vol. III.]

[Lauder edited Sir U. Price's Essays on the Picturesque, to which he contributed an essay On the Origin of Taste, and Gilpin's Forest Scenery. With Thomas Brown and William Rhind he issued The Miscellany of Natural History, 2 vols. 1833–4. He also pbd some topographical works.]

HARRIET LEE (1757–1851)

(a) Novels

The Canterbury Tales. 5 vols. 1797–1805 (vols. I, II rptd 1799); 2 vols. 1826; 2 vols. 1832 (rev. and with new Preface). [In 1st edn Harriet Lee's name appears alone on title-page of vols. I, IV, V; not at all on vol. II; jointly with Sophia Lee's on vol. III. Vol. III was rptd separately Dublin, 1799, as The Officer's Tale and Clergyman's Tale; vol. IV was also often rptd separately (5th edn, 1823) as Kruitzner or the German's Tale. The latter was dramatised by Byron in 1822 as Werner.]

[For novels pbd before 1801 see vol. II, pp. 549, 551 above.]

(b) Plays

The New Peerage, or Our Eyes may deceive us. A Comedy. 1787; Dublin, 1788.

The Mysterious Marriage; or, The Heirship of Roselva. A Drama. 1798.

The Three Strangers. 1826. [A dramatisation of Kruitzner.]

(c) Biography and Criticism

Obituary. Bristol Journ. 9 Aug. 1851.

Mrs Harriet Lee. Littell's Living Age, XXXI, 1851.

SOPHIA LEE (1750–1824)

(a) Novels

The Canterbury Tales. 5 vols. 1797–1805; 2 vols. 1826, 1831. [Mainly by Harriet Lee. Sophia contributed 2 tales to vols. II and III, and the introduction to vol. I.]

The Life of a Lover; in a Series of Letters. 6 vols. 1804.

Ormond, or the Debauchee. 3 vols. 1810.

[For Sophia Lee's novels pbd before 1801 see vol. II, pp. 548, 551 above.]

(b) Other Writings

The Chapter of Accidents. A Comedy. 1780 (bis); Dublin, 1781; 1781, etc.; tr. German, Augsburg, [1788?]. [Based on Diderot's Père de Famille.]

A Hermit's Tale, recorded by his own Hand and found in his Cell. By the Author of The Recess. 1787 (anon.); Dublin, 1787.

Almeyda, Queen of Granada. A Tragedy. 1796; Dublin, 1796. [Partly from Shirley's The Cardinal.]

[Sophia Lee's comedy The Assignation, acted Drury Lane, 1807, was apparently not ptd. For Sophia Lee's novels see J. M. S. Tompkins, The Popular Novel, 1932.]

MATTHEW GREGORY LEWIS (1775–1818)
(a) Fiction

The Monk. A Romance. 3 vols. 1796 (bis); 2 vols. Dublin, 1796; Waterford, '1796' (watermarked 1818); 3 vols. 1797; 2 vols. Dublin, 1797; 3 vols. 1798 (expurgated, as Ambrosio or the Monk), etc.; ed. E. A. Baker, 1907. Tr. French, 1803; Spanish, 1822.

The Bravo of Venice. A Romance, translated from the German [of J. H. D. Zschokke]. 1805; 1807; 1809; 1830; 1834; [1844]; 1856; 1857, etc.

Feudal Tyrants, or the Counts of Carlsheim and Sargans. A Romance. Taken from the German. 4 vols. 1806.

Romantic Tales. 4 vols. 1808; 1838. [Also many rpts of separate tales.]

Tales of Mystery. Ed. G. Saintsbury, 1891. [Selections from Mrs Radcliffe, Lewis and Maturin.]

[Lewis also translated, with others, Anthony Hamilton's Fairy Tales and Romances, 1849. In 1899 appeared an edn of his trn of Hamilton's Les Quatre Facardins, with continuations by Lewis and the Duc de Lévis. Les Mystères de la Tour Saint-Jean, 4 vols. Paris, 1819, is described on title-page as 'par Lewis, auteur du Moine,' but cannot be identified as a trn of any known work of his.]

(b) Plays

The Minister. A Tragedy. Translated from the German of Schiller. 1797.

The Castle Spectre. A Drama. 1798 (7 edns); Dublin, 1798; 1799.

Rolla, or the Peruvian Hero. A Tragedy. Translated from the German of Kotzebue. 1799 (4 edns).

The East Indian. A Comedy. 1800 (bis); Dublin, 1800 (as Rivers, or the East Indian).

Adelmorn the Outlaw. A Romantic Drama. 1801; Dublin, 1801; tr. German, Prague, 1829. [Songs in Adelmorn the Outlaw, 1801.]

Alfonso, King of Castile. A Tragedy. 1801; 1802.

Rugantino, or the Bravo of Venice. A Grand Romantic Melodrama. 1805.

Adelgitha, or the Fruits of a Single Error. A Tragedy. 1806 (4 edns); 1817, etc.

Venoni, or the Novice of St Mark's. A Drama. 1809; 1829 (in J. Cumberland's British Theatre, vol. XXXVIII).

Timour the Tartar. A Grand Romantic Melodrama. [1811]; 1829 (in J. Cumberland's British Theatre, vol. XXIX); 1868.

One O'Clock! or, the Knight and the Wood Daemon. A Grand Musical Romance. [1811], etc.

(c) Other Writings

Tales of Terror. Kelso, 1799 (also issued as An Apology for Tales of Terror). [For Lewis's share see under Scott, p. 369 above.]

The Love of Gain. A Poem imitated from the Thirteenth Satire of Juvenal. 1799.

Alonzo the Brave, and Fair Imogene. A Ballad. To which is added a Description of a Beauty at —— Races. A Ballad. Glasgow, [1800?] (anon.); [1810?]; [1820?]; [1830?].

Tales of Wonder [in verse]. Written and Collected by M. G. Lewis, Esq., M.P. 2 vols. 1801 (bis); 2 vols. Dublin, 1801; 3 vols. Vienna, 1805; 1836; [1869]. [Includes contributions by Southey and Scott.]

Tales of Terror [in verse], with an Introductory Dialogue. 1801 (anon.); 1808 (with additional ballad); Dublin, 1808. [Generally attrib. to Lewis; see however E. Church, A Bibliographical Myth, MP. XIX, 1922, who shows that these ballads are actually an anon. parody of Lewis.]

The Wild Wreath. Ed. Mary Elizabeth Robinson, 1804. [Contains 4 poems by Lewis.]

Poems. 1812.

The Isle of Devils. A Historical Tale [in verse] founded on an Anecdote in the Annals of Portugal. Kingston, Jamaica, 1827; rptd 1912.

Crazy Jane [by M. G. Lewis, with other songs]. Waterford, [1830?] (anon.); Manchester, [1835?].

Journal of a West India Proprietor, kept during a Residence in the Island of Jamaica. 1834; 1845 (as Journal of a Residence among the Negroes in the West Indies); ed. M. Wilson, 1929.

(d) Biography and Criticism

Gossip about 'Monk' Lewis. Colburn's New Monthly Mag. LXXXII, 1829.

[Baron-Wilson, M.] The Life and Correspondence of Matthew Gregory Lewis. With Many Pieces never before published. 2 vols. 1839.

Bortone, G. Fra il Voto e l'Amore. Note critiche sul Monaco del Lewis, [etc.]. Naples, 1908.

Birkhead, E. The Tale of Terror. 1921, pp. 63–72.

Killen, A. M. Le Roman terrifiant de Walpole à Anne Radcliffe, et son Influence sur la Littérature française jusqu'en 1840. Paris, 1923.

Taylor, A. The Three Sins of the Hermit. MP. xx, 1923. [On the ultimate sources of The Monk.]

Emerson, O. F. Monk Lewis and the Tales of Terror. MLN. xxxviii, 1923.

Schneider, Rudolf. Der Mönch in der englischen Literatur bis auf Lewis's 'Monk,' 1795. Berlin, 1927.

Cook, D. Robert Burns did not write The Hermit. Bookman, lxxxv, 1934.

Coykendall, F. A Note on the Monk. Colophon, N.S. no. 1, 1935. [Detailed bibliographical analysis.]

JOHN GIBSON LOCKHART (1794–1854)
[See p. 676 below.]

SAMUEL LOVER (1797–1868)
(a) Fiction

Legends and Stories of Ireland. 2 sers. 1831–4 (ser. 1 rptd Dublin, 1832); 1844; [1861]; [1893]; ed. D. J. O'Donoghue, 1899.

Rory O'More. A National Romance. Fifteen Illustrations by the Author. 3 vols. 1837; 1839 (rev.); [1879] (bis); [1891]; [1893]; ed. D. J. O'Donoghue, 1898. [A dramatisation, produced at the Adelphi, is in B. N. Webster's Acting National Drama, vol. iii, 1837, and J. Dicks's Standard Plays, 1883.]

Handy Andy. A Tale of Irish Life. 1842; 1884 (bis); [1886]; [1890]; ed. C. Whibley, 1896; ed. D. J. O'Donoghue, 1898. [A stage adaptation by H. W. Montgomery was produced at Wallack's, New York, in 1862.]

Treasure Trove. The First of a Series of Accounts of Irish Heirs. A Romantic Tale of the Last Century. 1844; [1856] (as He would be a Gentleman, or Treasure Trove); [1862]; [1887]; 1890.

Further Stories of Ireland. Ed. D. J. O'Donoghue, 1899.

(b) Plays

The White Horse of the Peppers. A Comic Drama in two Acts. [1838] (in B. Webster's Acting National Drama, vol. v).

The Hall Porter; a Comic Drama in two Acts. [1839] (in B. N. Webster's Acting National Drama, vol. vii).

The Happy Man. An Extravaganza in one Act. [1839] (in B. N. Webster's Acting National Drama, vol. vii).

The Greek Boy. A Musical Drama in two Acts. [1840] (in B. N. Webster's Acting National Drama, vol. ix).

Il Paddy Whack in Italia. An Operetta in one Act. [1842?] (in J. Duncombe's British Theatre, vol. xliv).

MacCarthy More, or Possession Nine Points of the Law. A Comic Drama in Two Acts. [1861] (in T. H. Lacy's Acting Edition of Plays, vol. li).

Barney the Baron, a Farce in one Act; [and] The Happy Man, an Extravaganza in one Act. [1883] (J. Dicks's Standard Plays).

(c) Other Writings, and Works edited

The Parson's Horn-book. 2 pts, Dublin, 1831 (anon.; bis). [Satires in prose and verse on the Established Church in Ireland, by Lover and others.]

Popular Tales and Legends of the Irish Peasantry. With Illustrations by Samuel Lover. Dublin, 1834; Dublin, 1837. [Ed. by Lover.]

Songs and Ballads. 1839.

Characteristic Sketches of Ireland and the Irish. By Carleton, Lover, and Mrs Hall. Dublin, 1845. [Lover's contributions are Paddy Mullonney's Travels in France; A Legend of Clanmacnoise; Ballads and Ballad Singers.]

The Lyrics of Ireland. Edited and annotated by Samuel Lover. 1858; 1884 (as Poems of Ireland, to which is added Lover's Metrical Tales).

Rival Rhymes in Honour of Burns; with Curious Illustrative Matter. Collected and edited by Ben Trovato [Samuel Lover]. 1859.

Metrical Tales and Other Poems. 1860; 1884 (with Poems of Ireland).

Original Songs for the Rifle Volunteers. 1861. [With C. Mackay and T. Miller.]

The Poetical Works. [1880.]

(d) Biography and Criticism

Samuel Lover. Dublin University Mag. xxxvii, 1851.

The Life and Writings of Samuel Lover. Temple Bar, xxiv, 1868.

Bernard, W. B. The Life of Samuel Lover, Artistic, Literary, and Musical, with Selections from his Unpublished Papers and Correspondence. 2 vols. 1874.

Symington, A. J. Samuel Lover. A Biographical Sketch, with Selections from his Writings and Correspondence. 1880.

—— Samuel Lover. [In The Poets and the Poetry of the Century, ed. A. H. Miles, vol. ix, 1894. Precedes a selection from Lover's poems.]

Layard, G. S. Samuel Lover as a Graphic Humourist. Mag. of Art, XIX, 1896.
Schmid, F. Samuel Lover. Century Mag. XXXI, 1897.
'Melville, Lewis.' Victorian Novelists. 1906.

WILLIAM MAGINN (1793–1842)
[See p. 677 below.]

CHARLES ROBERT MATURIN (1782–1824)

(a) Fiction

Fatal Revenge, or the Family of Montorio. By Dennis Jasper Murphy. 3 vols. 1807; 4 vols. 1824; 1841.
The Wild Irish Boy. By the Author of Montorio. 3 vols. 1808; 1814; 1839.
The Milesian Chief. A Romance. By the Author of Montorio and The Wild Irish Boy. 4 vols. 1812.
Women, or Pour et Contre. A Tale by the Author of Bertram, etc. 3 vols. Edinburgh, 1818.
Melmoth the Wanderer. A Tale by the Author of Bertram. 4 vols. Edinburgh, 1820; 4 vols. Edinburgh, 1821; 3 vols. 1892 (with memoir and bibliography); tr. French, Paris, 1821.
The Albigenses. A Romance. By the Author of Bertram, etc. 4 vols. 1824.
Tales of Mystery. Ed. G. Saintsbury, 1891. [Selections from Mrs Radcliffe, Lewis and Maturin.]

(b) Other Writings

Bertram, or The Castle of St Aldobrand. A Tragedy. 1816 (7 edns); 1817 (8th edn); 1829; 1865; 1884.
Manuel. A Tragedy in Five Acts, as performed at the Theatre Royal, Drury Lane. By the Author of Bertram. 1817.
Fredolfo. A Tragedy in Five Acts. 1819.
Sermons. 1819; 1821.
Extracts from some Unpublished Scenes of Manuel. New Monthly Mag. XI, 1819.
Six Sermons of the Errors of the Roman Catholic Church. Dublin, 1824; 1826.

[The Universe, a Poem, 1821, bears Maturin's name, but was really by James Wills.]

(c) Biography and Criticism

[Review of Melmoth.] Edinburgh Rev. July 1821. [Rptd in part in Famous Reviews, ed. R. B. Johnson, 1914.]
The Writings of Maturin. London Mag. III, 1821.
The Conversations of Maturin. Colburn's New Monthly Mag. XIX, 1827.
Elton, O. A Survey of English Literature, 1780–1830. Vol. I, 1912, pp. 217–22.

Maturin and the Novel of Terror. TLS. 26 Aug. 1920.
Birkhead, E. The Tale of Terror. 1921, pp. 80–93.
Idman, N. Charles Robert Maturin, his Life and Works. Helsingfors, 1923.
Scholten, W. Charles Robert Maturin, the Terror-Novelist. Amsterdam, 1933.
Baker, E. A. The History of the English Novel. Vol. v, 1934, pp. 219–25.

WILLIAM HAMILTON MAXWELL (1792–1850)

(a) Fiction

O'Hara, or 1798. 2 vols. 1825 (anon.).
Stories of Waterloo and Other Tales. 3 vols. 1829; 1834.
Wild Sports of the West, with Legendary Tales and Local Sketches. 1832.
The Dark Lady of Doona. 1834.
My Life. By the Author of Stories of Waterloo, etc. 3 vols. 1835; 1838 (as The Adventures of Captain Blake).
The Bivouac; or, Stories of the Peninsular War. 3 vols. 1837; 1839.
Rambling Recollections of a Soldier of Fortune. Dublin, 1842.
The Fortunes of Hector O'Halloran and his Man Mark Anthony O'Toole. Illustrated by John Leech. [1842]; 1851.
Wanderings in the Highlands and Islands, with Sketches taken on the Scottish Border. Being a Sequel to Wild Sports in the West. 2 vols. 1844.
Captain O'Sullivan; or, Adventures, Civil, Military and Matrimonial of a Gentleman on Half-pay. 3 vols. 1846.
Hillside and Border Sketches. 2 vols. 1847.
Brian O'Linn; or, Luck in Everything. 3 vols. 1848; 1856 (as Luck in Everything; or, the Adventures of Brian O'Linn).
Erin-go-Bragh; or, Irish Life Pictures. With a Life of the Author by William Maginn. 2 vols. 1859.
Terence O'Shaughnessy's First Attempt to get Married. [In Tales from Bentley, vol. I, 1859.]

(b) Other Works

The Hamilton Wedding. A Humorous Poem. 1833.
The Field-Book; or, Sports and Pastimes of the United Kingdom. 1833.
The Victories of the British Armies. 1839.
Life of Field-Marshal the Duke of Wellington. 3 vols. 1839–41, etc.
The Naval and Military Almanack. 1840. [Ed. by Maxwell.]
Sporting. By Nimrod. 1840. [Contains contributions by Maxwell.]
Hints to a Soldier on Service. 2 vols. 1845.

History of the Irish Rebellion in 1798. With Memoirs of the Union and Emmett's Insurrection in 1803. 1845.

Peninsular Sketches. By Actors on the Scene. 2 vols. 1845. [Ed. by Maxwell.]

The Irish Movements, their Rise, Progress and Certain Termination. With a Few Broad Hints to Patriots and Pikemen. 1848.

[For appreciations of Maxwell see Bentley's Misc. VII, 1840, and Dublin University Mag. XVIII, 1841; there are obituaries in Times, 16 Jan. 1851 and GM. XXXV, 1851.]

MARY MEEKE (d. 1816?)

Count St Blancard, or the Prejudiced Judge. A Novel. 3 vols. 1795.

The Abbey of Clugny. 3 vols. 1795.

The Mysterious Wife. By Gabrielli. 4 vols. 1797.

Palmira and Ermance. 3 vols. 1797.

Ellesmere. A Novel. 4 vols. 1799.

Harcourt. By Gabrielli. 4 vols. 1799.

Anecdotes of the Altamont Family. By the Author of The Sicilian, etc. 4 vols. 1800.

Which is the Man? A Novel. 4 vols. 1801.

What shall be, shall be. A Novel. 4 vols. 1801.

The Mysterious Husband. By Gabrielli. 4 vols. 1801.

Independence. By Gabrielli. 4 vols. 1802.

Midnight Weddings. A Novel. 3 vols. 1802; tr. French, Paris, 1820.

Amazement! 3 vols. 1804.

The Old Wife and the Young Husband. 3 vols. 1804.

Murray House. 3 vols. 1804.

The Nine Days' Wonder. 3 vols. 1804.

Something Odd. By Gabrielli. 3 vols. 1804.

Something Strange. By Gabrielli. 4 vols. 1806.

Ellen, Heiress of the Castle. 3 vols. 1807.

Julian, or My Father's House. 4 vols. 1807. [Listed in Biographical Dictionary of Living Authors, 1816, but no copy located.]

'There's a Secret; find it out.' A Novel. 4 vols. 1808.

Laughton Priory. By Gabrielli. 4 vols. 1809.

Matrimony the Height of Bliss or Extreme of Misery. 4 vols. 1811.

Stratagems Defeated. A Novel. By Gabrielli. 4 vols. 1811.

Conscience. A Novel. 4 vols. 1814.

The Spanish Campaign, or the Jew. A Novel. 3 vols. 1815.

The Veiled Protectress, or the Mysterious Mother. 5 vols. 1819.

[Mrs Meeke also translated a number of works from French and German, including several novels, Mme Du Deffand's Unpublished Correspondence (1810) and the completion of Mrs Collyer's trn of Klopstock's Messiah (1811).]

MARY RUSSELL MITFORD (1787–1855)

(a) Fiction

Our Village. Sketches of Rural Character and Scenery. 5 vols. 1824–32; 2 vols. Paris, 1839; 2 vols. 1852; 1879; 1893 (introduction by Lady Ritchie), etc.

Stories of American Life by American Writers. 3 vols. 1830.

Lights and Shadows of American Life. 3 vols. 1832.

Belford Regis, or Sketches of a Country Town. 3 vols. 1835; 1846; 1849.

Country Stories. 1837.

The Edinburgh Tales. Ed. C. I. Johnstone, 3 vols. 1845–6. [Miss Mitford contributed The Freshwater Fisherman to vol. I, Country Town Life, Christmas Amusements, Stories and Charades—Old Master Green, to vols. II and III.]

Atherton and Other Tales. 3 vols. 1854.

(b) Other Writings

Poems. 1810; 1811 (with addns).

Christina, the Maid of the South Seas. A Poem. 1811.

Blanche of Castile. 1812.

Watlington Hill, A Poem. 1812.

Narrative Poems on the Female Character. Vol. I, 1813. [No more pbd.]

Julian. A Tragedy in Five Acts. 1823.

Foscari. A Tragedy. 1826.

Foscari and Julian. Tragedies. 1827.

Dramatic Scenes, Sonnets and Other Poems. 1827.

Rienzi. A Tragedy. 1828.

Mary, Queen of Scots. A Scene in English Verse. 1831.

Charles the First. An Historical Tragedy in Five Acts. 1834.

Sadak and Kalasrade, or the Waters of Oblivion. A Romantic Opera. [1835.]

Recollections of a Literary Life; or Books, Places, and People. 3 vols. 1852; 1883 (as Recollections of a Literary Life and Selections from my Favourite Poets and Prose Writers).

Dramatic Works. 2 vols. 1854.

The Life of Mary Russell Mitford in a Selection from her Letters. Ed. A. G. L'Estrange, 3 vols. 1870.

The Letters of Mary Russell Mitford. Second Series. Ed. H. F. Chorley, 2 vols. 1872.

The Friendships of Mary Russell Mitford in Letters from her Literary Correspondents. Ed. A. G. L'Estrange, 2 vols. 1882.

Correspondence with C. Boner and J. Ruskin. Ed. E. Lee, [1914].

(c) Biography and Criticism

Oliphant, M. O. Mary Russell Mitford. Blackwood's Mag. June 1854.
—— Miss Austen and Miss Mitford. Blackwood's Mag. March 1870.
Kettle, R. M. Memoirs and Letters With Letters of Mary Russell Mitford to him during Ten Years. 2 vols. 1871.
Maginn, W. A Gallery of Illustrious Literary Characters. Ed. W. Bates, [1873].
Martineau, H. Biographical Sketches, 1852–1875. 1877.
Roberts, W. J. Mary Russell Mitford. The Tragedy of a Blue-Stocking. 1913.
Hill, C. Mary Russell Mitford and her Surroundings. 1920.
Woolf, V. The Common Reader. 1925.
Astin, M. Mary Russell Mitford; her Circle and her Books. 1930.
Carter, J. and Pollard, G. An Enquiry into the Nature of certain XIX Century Pamphlets. 1934.

DAVID MACBETH MOIR (1798–1851)
(a) Fiction

The Legend of Geneviève. With Other Tales and Poems. By Delta. Edinburgh, 1824.
The Life of Mansie Waugh, Taylor in Dalkeith, written by himself. Edinburgh, 1828 (anon.); 1839 (rev., illustrated by G. Cruikshank); 1853, etc. [First pbd in Blackwood's Mag.]
The Bridal of Borthwick. [In The Club Book, ed. A. Picken, 3 vols. 1831; rptd in The Romancist and Novelists' Library, ed. W. Hazlitt, vol. IV, 1841.]

(b) Other Writings

The Bombardment of Algiers, and Other Poems. Edinburgh, 1816 (anon.).
Biographical Memoir of the Author [John Galt]. Edinburgh, 1841. [113 pp. signed Δ, prefixed to The Annals of the Parish and The Ayrshire Legatees, Blackwood's Standard Novels, vol. I.]
Domestic Verses. By Δ. Edinburgh, 1843 (priv. ptd); Edinburgh, 1843; Edinburgh, 1871.
Sketches of the Poetical Literature of the Past Half-Century, in Six Lectures. Edinburgh, 1851.
The Poetical Works. Ed. (with memoir) T. Aird, 2 vols. 1852.
The Roman Antiquities of Inveresk. Edinburgh, 1860. [First pbd in the Statistical Account of Scotland, 1845.]

[Moir also wrote several medical works, the final chs. of John Galt's The Last of the Lairds, nearly 400 contributions to Blackwood's Mag. and various memoirs and periodical articles. For his claim to The Canadian Boat Song see under Galt, p. 395 above.]

(c) Biography and Criticism

[Maginn, W.] Gallery of Literary Characters, No. XI, Dr Moir. Fraser's Mag. VIII, 1833. [Rptd in A Gallery of Illustrious Literary Characters, ed. W. Bates, [1873].]
Obituary. Blackwood's Mag. LXX, 1851.
[Review of The Poetical Works.] Eclectic Rev. XCVI, 1852.
Gilfillan, G. Galleries of Literary Portraits. Vol. II, Edinburgh, 1856.
Douglas, Sir G. The Blackwood Group. [1897.]
MacCurdy, E. A Literary Enigma. The Canadian Boat Song. Stirling, 1936. [Attributes to Moir and Lockhart.]

SYDNEY, LADY MORGAN (1776–1859)
[See under Owenson below.]

JAMES JUSTINIAN MORIER (1780–1849)
(a) Fiction

The Adventures of Hajji Baba of Ispahan. 3 vols. 1824 (bis, 2nd edn with long Preface); 1835 (rev.); 1856; 1863 (rev. and illustrated with notes), etc.; 1895 (introduction by G. Curzon); ed. C. J. Wills, 1897; rptd 1914 (Everyman's Lib.); ed. C. W. Stewart, 1923 (World's Classics).
The Adventures of Hajji Baba of Ispahan in England. 2 vols. 1828; 1835 (rev.); rptd 1925 (World's Classics).
Zohrab the Hostage. By the Author of Hajji Baba. 3 vols. 1832 (bis); 3 vols. 1833 (rev. with notes); 1836; 1864.
Ayesha, the Maid of Kars. By the Author of Zohrab. 3 vols. 1834; 1846.
Abel Allnutt. A Novel. By the Author of Hajji Baba. 3 vols. 1837.
An Oriental Tale. By the Author of Hajji Baba. Brighton, [1839]. [Ptd (not pbd) for sale in aid of the funds of the Sussex County Hospital.]
The Mirza. 3 vols. 1841.
Misselmah. A Persian Tale. Brighton, 1847 (anon.).
Martin Toutrond. A Frenchman in London in 1831. 1849 (anon.); 1849 (signed); 1852. [Written in French by Morier and translated by himself.]

[Morier also 'edited' with a preface W. Hauff's The Banished, 3 vols. 1839, and St Roche, a Romance from the German, 3 vols. 1847.]

(b) Other Writings

Journey through Persia, Armenia and Asia Minor to Constantinople, 1808–9. Including an Account of the Mission under Sir Harford Jones to the Shah of Persia. 1812.

Second Journey Through Persia, Armenia and Asia Minor to Constantinople, 1810–16. With a Voyage by the Brazils and Bombay to the Persian Gulf and an Account of the Embassy under Sir G. Ouseley. 1818.

The Adventures of Tom Spicer, who advertised for a Wife. A Poem. 1840 (priv. ptd).

Literary Contributions by Various Authors in aid of the Funds of the Hospital for Consumption and Diseases of the Chest. Edited by Mrs Leicester Stanhope. 1846. [Contains contributions by Morier.]

(c) Biography and Criticism

[Scott, Sir W.] Quarterly Rev. xxxix, 1829, pp. 73–96. [Review of Hajji Baba.]

James Morier. Fraser's Mag. vii, 1852.

Maginn, W. A Gallery of Illustrious Literary Characters. Ed. W. Bates, [1873].

Zeidler, K. J. Beckford, Hope und Morier als Vertreter des orientalischen Romans. Leipzig, 1909.

WILLIAM MUDFORD (1782–1848)

(a) Fiction

Augustus and Mary, or the Maid of Buttermere. A Domestic Tale. 1803.

The Five Nights of St Albans. Edinburgh, 3 vols. 1829 (anon.); [1878].

The Premier. 3 vols. 1831 (anon.).

Stephen Dugard. A Novel. By the Author of Five Knights [sic] of St Albans. 3 vols. 1840 (anon.); [1860].

The Iron Shroud, or Italian Revenge. [1840?] (anon.).

Arthur Wilson: a Study. 3 vols. 1872 (anon.).

(b) Other Writings

A Critical Enquiry into the Moral Writings of Dr Samuel Johnson. 1802 (anon.); 1803.

Nubilia in Search of a Husband; including Sketches of Modern Society, and interspersed with Moral and Literary Disquisitions. 1809 (anon.); 1809 (4th edn, containing 2 additional chs.).

The Contemplatist, or a Series of Essays upon Morals and Literature. 1811.

The Life and Adventures of Paul Plaintive, Esq., an Author. Compiled from Original Documents, and interspersed with specimens of his Genius, in Prose and Poetry, by Martin Gribaldus Swammerdam (his Nephew and Executor). 2 vols. 1811.

A Critical Examination of the Writings of Richard Cumberland, Esq. 2 vols. 1812.

An Historical Account of the Campaign in the Netherlands, in 1815. 1817.

Tales and Trifles, from Blackwood's and Other Popular Magazines. 2 vols. 1849.

[Mudford also wrote a life of James Beattie (1809), and a critique of Goldsmith (1804). He translated several works from the French, including Helvétius's De l'Esprit. He edited several papers at different times, and was a frequent contributor to Blackwood's Mag.]

AGNES MUSGRAVE

Cicely; or, The Rose of Raby. A Novel. 4 vols. [1796?] (anon.); 4 vols. 1796; 4 vols. 1797; 1831.

Edmund of the Forest, an Historical Novel. By the Author of Cicely, or the Rose of Raby. 4 vols. 1797.

The Solemn Injunction. A Novel. 4 vols. 1798.

The Confession. A Novel. 5 vols. 1801.

William de Montfort; or, The Sicilian Heiress. A Novel. 3 vols. 1808.

AMELIA OPIE, née ALDERSON (1769–1853)

(a) Collected Works

Miscellaneous Tales. 12 vols. 1845–7.

Works. 3 vols. Philadelphia, 1848.

(b) Fiction

The Dangers of Coquetry. A Novel. 2 vols. [1790] (anon.). [Only known copy is in Harvard College Lib.]

The Father and Daughter. A Tale in Prose, with an Epistle from the Maid of Corinth to her Lover, and Other Poetical Pieces. 1801 (2nd edn); 1804 (4th edn); 1819 (8th edn); 1844 (10th edn).

Adeline Mowbray, or the Mother and Daughter. A Tale. 3 vols. 1804; 1805; 1810; 1844 (with The Welcome Home and The Quaker and the Young Man of the World).

Simple Tales. 4 vols. 1806 (bis); 4 vols. 1815 (4th edn).

Temper, or Domestic Scenes. A Tale. 3 vols. 1812; 4 vols. 1813 (3rd edn); tr. French, Paris, 1813.

Tales of Real Life. 3 vols. 1813; 1816 (3rd edn); tr. French, Paris, 1814.

Valentine's Eve. 3 vols. 1816 (bis); tr. French, Paris, 1816.

New Tales. 4 vols. 1818; 4 vols. 1819 (3rd edn); tr. French, Paris, 1818.

Tales of the Heart. 4 vols. 1820.

Madeline. A Tale. 2 vols. 1822.

Illustrations of Lying, in all its Branches. 2 vols. 1825; New York, 1827; Exeter, New Hampshire, 1832.

Tales of the Pemberton Family, for the Use of Children. 1825; 1826.

(c) Other Writings

Poems. 1802; 1803; 1804; 1806; 1808; 1811.

An Elegy to the Memory of the Late Duke of Bedford, written on the Evening of his Interment. 1802.

The Warrior's Return and Other Poems. 1808.

The Black Man's Lament, or how to make Sugar. 1826. [Verse.]

Detraction Displayed. 1828. [A manual showing how to defeat calumny.]

Lays for the Dead. 1834; 1840.

[Mrs Opie also contributed a Memoir to Lectures on Painting by her husband, John Opie, 1809. She pbd a number of tales, poems, etc. in Friendship's Offering, European Mag. and other periodicals between 1795 and 1841. To Mrs Margaret Roberts's Duty, a Novel, 1814, she contributed a character of the author.]

(d) Biography and Criticism

Brightwell, C. L. Memorials of the Life of Amelia Opie, from her Letters, Diaries and Other Manuscripts. Norwich, 1854.

—— Memoir of Amelia Opie. 1855.

Hall, S. C. Memories of Mrs Opie. Art Journ. vi, 1854.

—— Retrospect of a Long Life. 2 vols. 1883.

Kavanagh, J. English Women of Letters. Vol. ii, 1863.

Martineau, H. Biographical Sketches, 1852–1875. 1877.

Mrs Opie. Cornhill Mag. xlviii, 1883.

Robertson, E. S. English Poetesses. 1883, pp. 104–19.

Thackeray, A. I. (later Lady Ritchie). A Book of Sibyls: Mrs Barbauld, Miss Edgeworth, Mrs Opie, Miss Austen. 1883.

Ross, Janet A. Three Generations of Englishwomen. Memoirs and Correspondence of Mrs John Taylor, Mrs Sarah Austin and Lady Duff Gordon. 2 vols. 1888.

Amelia Opie. Temple Bar, xcviii, 1893.

Earland, A. John Opie and his Circle. 1911.

Macgregor, Margaret E. Amelia Alderson Opie, Worldling and Friend. Northampton, Massachusetts, 1933. [With a bibliography.]

Menzies-Wilson, J. and Lloyd, H. Amelia. The Tale of a Plain Friend. Oxford, 1937.

SYDNEY OWENSON, afterwards LADY MORGAN (1776–1859)

(a) Novels

St Clair, or the Heiress of Desmond. By S. O. 1803; Philadelphia, 1807; 1812 (3rd edn); tr. Dutch, Amsterdam, 1816.

The Novice of St Dominick. 4 vols. 1805; 4 vols. 1806; 4 vols. 1808; 4 vols. 1823.

The Wild Irish Girl. 3 vols. 1806; 3 vols. 1813 (5th edn); 1846.

Woman; or, Ida of Athens. 4 vols. 1809.

The Missionary: an Indian Tale. 3 vols. 1811 (4 edns); 1859 (altered and remodelled by the author, as Luxima, the Prophetess. A Tale of India).

O'Donnel. A National Tale. 3 vols. 1814; 3 vols. 1815; 1836.

Florence Macarthy. An Irish Tale. 4 vols. 1818; 4 vols. 1819 (5th edn); 1839.

The O'Briens and the O'Flahertys: a National Tale. 4 vols. 1827; 4 vols. 1828; tr. French, 6 vols. Paris, 1828.

The Princess; or, The Beguine. 3 vols. 1835.

Woman and her Master. 2 vols. 1840.

(b) Other Writings

Poems. Dublin, 1801.

The Lay of an Irish Harp; or, Metrical Fragments. 1807; 1808.

Patriotic Sketches of Ireland, written in Connaught. 2 vols. 1807.

France. 1817; 2 vols. 1818 (3rd edn with additional notes); 2 vols. 1818; tr. French, 2 vols. Paris, 1817.

Italy. 2 vols. 1821; 3 vols. 1821 (text differs in part from that of the 2 vols. edn); New York, 2 vols. 1821. Tr. French, Brussels, 1821; Weimar, 1821. [Notes on law, statistics, and on literary disputes, with appendix on the state of medicine by Sir Thomas Charles Morgan.]

The Life and Times of Salvator Rosa. 2 vols. 1824; 1855.

Absenteeism. 1825.

The Book of the Boudoir. 2 vols. 1829 (bis). [Autobiographical sketches.]

France in 1829–30. 2 vols. 1830.

Dramatic Scenes from Real Life. 2 vols. 1833.

The Book without a Name. 2 vols. 1841. [With Sir T. C. Morgan.]

Passages in my Autobiography. 1859.

Lady Morgan's Memoirs: Autobiography, Diaries and Correspondence. [Ed. W. H. Dixon], 2 vols. 1862; 1863; 2 vols. 1863.

[Both France and Italy aroused considerable controversy, to which Lady Morgan replied.]

(c) Biography and Criticism

Fitzpatrick, W. J. The Friends, Foes, and Adventures of Lady Morgan. Dublin, 1859.

Jewsbury, G. E. Lady Morgan. Cornhill Mag. vii, 1863.

Kavanagh, J. English Women of Letters. Vol. ii, 1863.

Maginn, W. A Gallery of Illustrious Literary Characters. Ed. W. Bates, [1873].

'Paston, George.' Little Memoirs of the Nineteenth Century. 1902.

Wilson, Mona. These were Muses. 1924.

Stevenson, L. The Wild Irish Girl. The Life of Sydney Owenson, Lady Morgan. 1936.

ELIZA PARSONS (d. 1811)

Murray House. 'A plain unvarnished tale.' 3 vols. Brentford, 1804.

The Convict, or Navy Lieutenant. A Novel. Brentford, 1807.

[For Mrs Parsons's novels pbd before 1801 see vol. II, p. 550 above. She also adapted one of Molière's farces and in 1804 pbd six tales from La Fontaine as Love and Gratitude.]

CONSTANTINE HENRY PHIPPS, MARQUIS OF NORMANBY (1797–1863)

(a) Fiction

The English in Italy. A Novel. 3 vols. 1825 (anon.). [A collection of romances.]

Matilda. A Tale of the Day. 2 vols. 1825 (3 edns); 4 vols. Paris, 1826.

Historiettes, or Tales of Continental Life. 3 vols. 1827.

The English in France. 3 vols. 1828.

Yes and No. A Tale of the Day. By the Author of Matilda. 2 vols. 1828.

Clarinda, or the Necklace of Pearls. The Tale of a Bystander. [In The Keepsake, 1829.]

The Contrast. By the Author of Matilda, Yes and No, etc. 3 vols. 1832.

(b) Other Writings

A Year of Revolution, From a Journal kept in Paris, 1848. 2 vols. 1857; 2 vols. Paris, 1858.

The Congress and the Cabinet. 1859; Paris, 1860.

An Historical Sketch of Louise de Bourbon, Duchess Regent of Parma. 1861.

A Vindication of the Duke of Modena from the Charges of Mr Gladstone. From Official Documents. 1861.

[Several of the Marquis of Normanby's speeches were also pbd.]

(c) Biography and Criticism

The Marquis of Normanby. Fraser's Mag. XVIII, 1838.

Greville, C. C. F. The Greville Memoirs. 8 vols. 1888. [Allusions in vols. IV, VI, VIII.]

ANDREW PICKEN (1788–1833)

Tales and Sketches of the West of Scotland. By Christopher Keelivine. 1824. [Mary Ogilvie rptd from above, 1840 (6th edn), illustrated by R. Cruikshank.]

The Sectarian, or the Church and the Meeting-House. 3 vols. 1829.

The Dominie's Legacy. 3 vols. 1830.

Travels and Researches of Eminent English Missionaries, including an Historical Sketch of the Progress of Protestant Missions of Late Years. 1831.

The Club Book. Edited by the Author of The Dominie's Legacy. 3 vols. 1831. [Picken contributed The Deer-stalker, and The Three Kearneys. The other contributors included Galt, Hogg, Cunningham, James, Jerdan and Moir.]

Waltham. A Novel. 1832.

The Canadas as they at present commend themselves to the Enterprise of Emigrants, Colonists, and Capitalists. Compiled and condensed from Original Documents furnished by John Galt. 1832.

Traditionary Stories of Old Families and Legendary Illustrations of Family History. With Historical and Biographical Notes. 2 vols. 1833.

The Black Watch. 3 vols. 1834.

[Picken also wrote A Life of John Wesley and a narrative entitled Experience of Life, which remain unpbd. See Robert Brown, Memoirs of Ebenezer Picken, Poet, and of Andrew Picken, Novelist, Paisley, 1879.]

JOHN WILLIAM POLIDORI (1795–1821)

(a) Fiction

The Vampyre. A Tale. 1819 (anon.); tr. Italian, 1829.

Ernestus Berchtold, or the Modern Œdipus. A Tale. 1819 (anon.).

(b) Other Writings

On the Punishment of Death. [In The Pamphleteer, vol. VIII, 1816.]

An Essay upon the Source of Positive Pleasure. 1818.

Ximenes, the Wreath, and Other Poems. 1819.

ROBERT POLLOK (1798–1838)

[See p. 241 above.]

JOHN POOLE (1786?–1872)

[See p. 594 below.]

ANNA MARIA PORTER (1780–1832)

(a) Fiction

Artless Tales. 2 vols. 1795 (anon.).

The Lake of Killarney. A Novel. 3 vols. 1804; 1856 (as Rose de Blaquière).

A Sailor's Friendship and a Soldier's Love. 2 vols. 1805.

The Hungarian Brothers. 3 vols. 1807; 3 vols. 1819 (4th edn); 3 vols. 1832 (rev.).

Don Sebastian, or the House of Braganza. An Historical Romance. 4 vols. 1809; 1838.

The Recluse of Norway. 4 vols. 1814.

Tales of Pity on Fishing, Shooting and Hunting, intended to inculcate in the Mind of Youth Sentiments of Humanity toward the Brute Creation. 1814.

The Knight of St John. A Romance. 3 vols. 1817 (bis).

The Fast of St Magdalen. A Romance. 3 vols. 1818.

The Village of Mariendorpt. A Tale. 4 vols. 1821.

Roche-Blanche, or the Hunters of the Pyrenees. A Romance. 3 vols. 1822.

O'Hara, or 1798. 2 vols. 1825.

Honor O'Hara. A Novel. 3 vols. 1826.

Tales round a Winter Hearth. By Jane and Anna Maria Porter. 2 vols. 1826. [Anna Maria contributed Glenawan, Lord Howth, Jeanie Halliday.]

Coming Out. By Jane and Anna Maria Porter. 3 vols. 1828.

The Barony. 3 vols. 1830.

Walsh Colville, or a Young Man's First Entrance into Life. 1833; 1840.

Octavia. 3 vols. 1833.

[Miss Porter also pbd Ballad Romances and Other Poems, 1811.]

(b) Biography and Criticism

Elwood, A. K. Memoirs of the Literary Ladies of England. Vol. II, 1843.

De La Mare, W. The Material of Fiction. 1933.

JANE PORTER (1776–1850)
(a) Writings

Thaddeus of Warsaw. 4 vols. 1803; 4 vols. 1809 (5th edn); 4 vols. 1812; 4 vols. 1816; 1831 (rev. with preface).

Sketch of the Campaign of Count A. Suwarrow Ryminski. 1804.

Aphorisms of Sir Philip Sidney with Remarks. 2 vols. 1807.

The Scottish Chiefs. A Romance. 5 vols. 1810; 5 vols. 1811; 5 vols. 1820 (4th edn); 2 vols. 1831 (rev.).

The Pastor's Fire-Side. A Novel. 3 vols. 1815; 4 vols. 1817; 2 vols. 1832 (with new introduction); [1846] (rev., with note by ·a friend of the author's' and appendix).

Duke Christian of Luneburg, or Traditions from the Hartz. 3 vols. 1824 (bis); tr. French, 1824.

Tales round a Winter Hearth. By Jane and Anna Maria Porter. 2 vols. 1826.

Coming Out. By Jane and Anna Maria Porter. 3 vols. 1828.

The Field of the Forty Footsteps. 3 vols. 1828.

Sir Edward Seaward's Narrative of his Shipwreck and Consequent Discovery of Certain Islands in the Caribbean Sea; with a Detail of Many Extraordinary and highly Interesting Events of his Life from 1733 to 1749 as written in his Own Diary. Edited by Jane Porter. 3 vols. 1831; 1852 (abridged). [In reality written by Jane Porter.]

Young Hearts. By a Recluse. Preface by Jane Porter. 1834.

(b) Biography and Criticism

Miss Jane Porter. Fraser's Mag. XI, 1835.

Hall, A. M. Memoirs of Jane Porter. Art Journ. II, 1850.

Maginn, W. A Gallery of Illustrious Literary Characters. Ed. W. Bates, [1873].

Wilson, Mona. A Romantic Novelist. [In These were Muses, 1924.]

ANN RADCLIFFE, née WARD (1764–1823)
(a) Writings

The Castles of Athlin and Dunbayne. A Highland Story. 1789; 1793 (bis); Philadelphia, 1796; Boston, 1797; 1811; 1824; 1827, etc.

A Sicilian Romance. 1790; 2 vols. 1792; 1809 (4th edn); 1818; 1821; 1826.

The Romance of the Forest, interspersed with some Pieces of Poetry. 3 vols. 1791 (anon.); 3 vols. 1792 (bis); 2 vols. Dublin, 1792; 3 vols. 1794, 1796, 1816 (8th edn), etc.

The Mysteries of Udolpho. A Romance, interspersed with some Pieces of Poetry. 4 vols. 1794 (bis); 4 vols. 1795; Boston, 1795; Worcester (Massachusetts), 1795; Dublin, 1800; 4 vols. 1803, 1806, etc. (11 more edns by 1832); tr. French, 1808.

A Journey made in the Summer of 1794 through Holland and the Western Frontier of Germany. 1795.

The Italian, or the Confessional of the Black Penitents. A Romance. 3 vols. 1797 (bis); 2 vols. Dublin, 1797; 3 vols. 1811, etc.

The Female Advocate, or an Attempt to recover the Rights of Women from Male Usurpation. 1799.

The Poems of Ann Radcliffe. 1816; 1834; 1845. [An unauthorized rpt of the poetical pieces in the novels.]

Novels by Ann Radcliffe, to which is prefixed a Memoir of the Life of the Author by Sir Walter Scott. 1821.

Gaston de Blondeville, or the Court of Henry III keeping Festival in Ardenne. A Romance. St Alban's Abbey. A Metrical Tale. With some Poetical Pieces. To which is prefixed a Memoir of the Author [by W. Radcliffe?] with Extracts from her Journals. 4 vols. 1826.

Tales of Mystery. Ed. G. Saintsbury, 1891. [Selections from Mrs Radcliffe, Lewis and Maturin.]

(b) Biography and Criticism

Summers, M. A Great Mistress of Romance: Ann Radcliffe. Trans. Royal Soc. Lit. [1917].

MacIntyre, C. F. Ann Radcliffe in Relation to her Time. New Haven, 1920.

Birkhead, E. The Tale of Terror. 1921. [Ch. iii.]

Killen, A. M. Le Roman terrifiant ou Roman noir, de Walpole à Anne Radcliffe, et son Influence sur la Littérature française jusqu'en 1840. Paris, 1923.

Wieten, A. S. S. Mrs Radcliffe—her Relation towards Romanticism. Amsterdam, 1926. [Contains an appendix on the novels falsely ascribed to her.]

Tompkins, J. M. S. The Popular Novel in England, 1770–1800. 1932. [Ch. viii and Appendix III (Mrs Radcliffe's Sources).]

Baker, E. A. The History of the English Novel. Vol. v, 1934, pp. 192–204.

REGINA MARIA ROCHE, née DALTON (1764?–1845)

The Vicar of Lansdowne, or Country Quarters. 1789.

The Maid of the Hamlet. 2 vols. 1793; Dublin, 1802.

The Children of the Abbey. A Tale. 4 vols. 1796; 4 vols. 1800 (4th edn); 4 vols. 1810 (6th edn); 2 vols. Hartford, 1822; 4 vols. 1825 (10th edn).

Clermont. A Tale. 4 vols. 1798; Philadelphia, 1802.

The Nocturnal Visit. 4 vols. 1800.

Alvondown Vicarage. A Novel. 2 vols. 1807 (anon.).

The Discarded Son, or the Haunt of the Banditti. 5 vols. 1807.

The Houses of Osma and Almeria, or the Convent of St Ildefonso. 3 vols. 1810.

The Monastery of St Colomba. 5 vols. 1812.

Trecothiek Bower, or the Lady of the West Country. 3 vols. 1813.

London Tales. 2 vols. 1814 (anon.).

The Munster Cottage Boy. 4 vols. 1819.

The Bridal of Dunamore and Lost and Won. Two Tales. 3 vols. 1823.

The Tradition of the Castle, or Scenes in the Emerald Isle. 4 vols. 1824.

The Castle Chapel. 3 vols. 1825.

Contrast. 3 vols. 1828.

The Nun's Picture. 3 vols. 1834.

'ROSALIA ST CLAIR'

The Son of O'Donnel. A Novel. 3 vols. 1819.

The Highland Castle and the Lowland Cottage. A Novel. 4 vols. 1820.

Clavering Tower. A Novel. 4 vols. 1822.

The Banker's Daughter of Bristol; or, Compliance and Decision. A Novel. 3 vols. 1824.

Fashionables and Unfashionables. A Novel. 3 vols. 1827.

The First and Last Years of Wedded Life. A Novel. 4 vols. 1827.

Ulrica of Saxony. A Romantic Tale of the Fifteenth Century. 3 vols. 1828.

Eleanor Ogilvie, the Maid of the Tweed. A Romantic Legend. 3 vols. 1829.

The Sailor Boy; or, The Admiral and his Protégée. A Novel. 4 vols. 1830.

The Pauper Boy. A Novel. 3 vols. 1834.

Marston. A Novel, by a Lady. 3 vols. 1835.

FRANCIS BARRY BOYLE ST LEGER (1799–1829)

Remorse and Other Poems. 1821 (priv. ptd).

Some Account of the Life of the Late Gilbert Earle, Esq., written by himself. 1824 (anon.).

Mr Blount's Manuscripts, being Selections from the Papers of a Man of the World. 2 vols. 1826 (anon.).

Tales of Passion; Lord Lovel's Daughter; The Bohemian; Second Love. 3 vols. 1829.

Froissart and his Times. Stories From Froissart. 3 vols. 1832.

[St Leger also edited The Album from 1822 and The Brazen Head, 1826.]

WILLIAM PITT SCARGILL (1787–1836)

(a) Fiction

Elizabeth Evanshaw, the Sequel of Truth, a Novel. 3 vols. 1827. [Truth was not by Scargill.]

Blue-Stocking Hall. 3 vols. 1827.

Truckleborough Hall. A Novel. 3 vols. 1827.

Penelope, or Love's Labour Lost. A Novel. 3 vols. 1828.

Rank and Talent. A Novel. By the Author of Truckleborough Hall. 3 vols. 1829.

Tales of my Time. By the Author of Blue-Stocking Hall. 3 vols. 1829.

Atherton. A Tale of the Last Century. By the Author of Rank and Talent. 3 vols. 1831.

The Usurer's Daughter. By a Contributor to Blackwood's Magazine. 3 vols. 1832.

The Autobiography of a Dissenting Minister. 1832; 1835.

The Puritan's Grave. By the Author of The Usurer's Daughter. 3 vols. 1833.

Provincial Sketches. By the Author of The Usurer's Daughter. 1835.

(b) Other Writings

Essays on Various Subjects. 1815.

Moral Discourses principally intended for Young People. 1816.

The Peace of the County. A Letter to the Freeholders of Suffolk. 1830.

A Reformer's Reasons for voting for Earl Jermyn. [1832.]

The Widow's Offering. A Selection of Tales and Essays. Ed. M. A. Scargill, 2 vols. 1837; 1856 (unauthorised, as The English Sketch Book); 1857 (authorised 2nd edn, as Essays and Sketches).

MICHAEL SCOTT (1789–1835)

Tom Cringle's Log. Paris, 1836 (anon.); Edinburgh, 1842; [1875]; [1876]; 1895; ed. M. Morris, 1895, etc. [First pbd anon. in Blackwood's Mag. 1829–33.]

The Cruise of the Midge. By the Author of 'Tom Cringle's Log.' Paris, 1836 (anon.); 2 vols. Edinburgh, 1836; Edinburgh, 1842; 1878; 1895, etc. [First pbd anon. in Blackwood's Mag. 1834–5.]

[For Scott see Sir G. Douglas, The Blackwood Group, 1897.]

SIR MARTIN ARCHER SHEE (1769–1850)

[See p. 595 below.]

MARY WOLLSTONECRAFT SHELLEY, née GODWIN (1797–1851)

(a) Fiction

Frankenstein or the Modern Prometheus. 1818 (anon.); 2 vols. 1823; [1831]; [1856]; 1882; ed. H. R. Haweis, 1886; 1888.

Valperga or the Life and Adventures of Castruccio Prince of Lucca. By the Author of Frankenstein. 3 vols. 1823.

The Last Man. By the Author of Frankenstein. 3 vols. 1826 (bis).

The Fortunes of Perkin Warbeck. A Romance. By the Author of Frankenstein. 3 vols. 1830; 1830 ('revised, corrected, and illustrated with a new introduction by the author'); 1857.

Lodore. By the Author of Frankenstein. 3 vols. 1835.

Falkner: a Novel. By the Author of Frankenstein. 3 vols. 1837.

The Swiss Peasant. [In The Tale Book, by C. A. Bowles, J. S. Knowles, M. W. Shelley, etc., Königsberg, 1859.]

Tales and Stories by Mary Wollstonecraft Shelley, now first collected with an Essay by R. Garnett. 1891.

(b) Other Writings

History of a Six Weeks' Tour through a Part of France, Switzerland, Germany, and Holland. 1817 (anon.). [By P. B. and M. W. Shelley.]

Lives of the Most Eminent Literary and Scientific Men of France. [By Mary Shelley and others. In D. Lardner's Cabinet Cyclopaedia, 1838.]

Lives of the Most Eminent Literary and Scientific Men of Italy, Spain and Portugal. [By J. Montgomery, Mary Shelley and others. In D. Lardner's Cabinet Cyclopaedia, 3 vols. 1835–7.]

Rambles in Germany and Italy in 1840, 1842 and 1843. 2 vols. 1844.

The Choice. A Poem on Shelley's Death. Ed. H. B. Forman, 1876 (priv. ptd).

The Romance of Mary W. Shelley, John Howard Payne and Washington Irving. Boston, 1907. [The Payne-Shelley letters, with remarks by F. B. Sanborn.]

Letters, mostly Unpublished. Ed. H. H. Harper, Boston, 1918.

Proserpine and Midas. Mythological Dramas. Ed. A. Koszul, 1922.

[Mary Shelley also edited Shelley's Poems, in 1830. In 1824 she brought out his Posthumous Poems and in 1840 his Essays, Letters from Abroad, Translations and Fragments. In 1886 the Shelley Soc. pbd an edn of Hellas with notes by Mary Shelley and others.]

(c) Biography and Criticism

Gilfillan, G. Galleries of Literary Portraits. Vol. I, Edinburgh, 1856.

Moore, Helen. Mary Wollstonecraft Shelley. Philadelphia, 1886.

Marshall, F. A. The Life and Letters of Mary Wollstonecraft Shelley. 2 vols. 1889.

Rossetti, L. M. Mrs Shelley. 1890.

Eimer, M. Die persönlichen Beziehungen zwischen Byron und den Shelleys. Eine kritische Studie. Heidelberg, 1901.

Vohl, M. Die Erzählungen der Mary Shelley und ihre Urbilder. Heidelberg, 1912.

Wise, T. J. A Shelley Library. A Catalogue of Printed Books, Manuscripts, and Autograph Letters by Percy Bysshe Shelley and Mary Wollstonecraft Shelley. 1924.

Church, R. Mary Shelley. 1928.

Dodd, C. I. Eagle-Feather. 1933. [A biography of Mary Shelley.]

Jones, F. L. Letters of Mary W. Shelley in the Bodleian Library. Bodleian Quart. Record, VIII, 1937.

Booth, B. A. 'The Pole': a Story by Clare Claremont? ELH. V, 1938.

Grylls, R. G. Mary Shelley. 1938.

Norman, S. On Shelley. 1938.

MARY MARTHA SHERWOOD, née BUTT (1775–1851)

(a) Fiction

The Tradition. 1794.

Margarita. 1802.

Susan Gray. 1802.

The Infant's Progress. [1814?]

The History of Lucy Clare. 1815.

The Indian Pilgrim. An Allegory adapted to Native Experience. 1815.

The Lady and her Ayah. 1816.

Memoirs of Sergeant Dale. 1816.

The History of the Fairchild Family, or the Child's Manual, being a Collection of Stories calculated to show the Importance and Effects of a Religious Education. 3 pts, 1818–47 (frequently rptd). [Pt 3 was partly written by Streeten Butt.]

The History of Theophilus and Sophia. 1818.

The Hedge of Thorns, etc. 1819.

The Governess, or the Little Female Academy. Wellington, 1820.

Dudley Castle. A Tale. [1820?]

The Welsh Cottage. 1820.

The Infant's Progress from the Valley of Destruction to Everlasting Glory. 1821.

The Potter's Common. 4 pts, 1822.

The History of Henry Milner. 4 pts, 1822–37.

Mary Anne. [1823?]

The History of Mrs Catherine Crawley. Wellington, 1824.

Waste Not, Want Not. 4 pts, 1824.

Juliana Oakley. 1825.

The Lady of the Manor. 4 vols. 1825–9; 7 vols. 1842; 5 vols. 1860.

My Uncle Timothy. 1825.

My Three Uncles and the Swiss Cottage. [1825?]

Two Dolls. 1826.

The Two Sisters. 1827.

The Lady in the Arbour. [1827?]

The Idiot Boy. A Tale. 1828.

The Rainbow. A Tale. Wellington, 1828.

Home. A Tale. 1828.

My Aunt Kate. Wellington, 1828.

Arzoomund. Wellington, 1829 (2nd edn).

The Orange Grove. Wellington, 1829.

Roxobel. 3 vols. 1830.

The Oddingley Murders. 1830.

Sequel to the Oddingley Murders. 1830.

Obedience. Berwick, 1830.

Maria and the Ladies and Other Tales. 6 pts, [1830?].

Ermina. 1831.

Little Henry and his Bearer. 1832.

The Little Morière. 1833.

Victoria. 1833.

The Nun. 1833.

The Monk of Cimiés. [1837?]

Sea-Side Stories. [1838?]

The Flowers of the Forest. 1839 (5 edns).

The Druids of Britain. [1840?]

The Christmas Carol. [1840?]

The History of John Milner. A Sequel to Henry Milner. 1844.

Caroline Mordaunt, or the Governess. [1845?]

The De Cliffords. An Historical Tale. 1847. [By Mrs Sherwood and Streeten Butt.]

The Golden Garland of Inestimable Delights. By Mrs Sherwood and her Daughter. 1849.

The Two Knights, or Delancey Castle. A Tale of the Civil Wars. 1851.

The Mirror of Maidens in the Days of Queen Bess. By Mrs Sherwood and her Daughter. 1851.

Boys Will Be Boys. By Mrs Sherwood and Her Daughter. 1854.

(b) Other Writings

An Introduction to Astronomy for Children. 1817.

An Introduction to Geography. Wellington, 1818.

Biography Illustrated. [1836.]

The Life and Times of Mrs Sherwood (1775–1851). From the Diaries of Captain [Henry] and Mrs Sherwood. Ed. F. J. H. Darton, 1910.

[Mrs Sherwood also wrote The Little Woodman and his Dog Caesar (very popular and frequently rptd); The Young Forester; The Bitter Sweet; The Hop Picking; The History of Mary Saunders; Henry Marten; Little Arthur; The Busy Bee; Charles Lorraine; The Blind Man and Little George; The Gipsy Babes; The Red Book; The Rose. A Fairy Tale; Social Tales for the Young; Stories Explanatory of the Church Catechism; The Wishing Cap; The Thunderstorm; The Poor Man of Colour; The Parson's Case of Jewels; The Rosebuds; The Story Book of Wonders; The Orphans of Normandy.]

(c) Biography

Kelly, S. Life of Mrs Sherwood. 1854.

HORATIO SMITH (1779–1849)

(a) Novels and Short Stories

The Runaway, or the Seat of Benevolence. 4 vols. 1800.

Trevanion, or Matrimonial Ventures. 4 vols. 1801.

Horatio, or Memoirs of the Davenport Family. 1807.

Gaieties and Gravities [in prose and verse]. 3 vols. 1825. [Mainly rptd from London Mag. and New Monthly Mag.]

The Tor Hill. 3 vols. 1826.

Brambletye House, or Cavaliers and Roundheads. 3 vols. 1826 (3 edns).

Reuben Apsley. 3 vols. 1827.

Zillah. A Tale of the Holy City. 4 vols. 1828; 3 vols. 1828.

The New Forest. A Novel. 3 vols. 1829.

Walter Colyton. A Tale of 1688. 3 vols. 1830.

The Midsummer Medley for 1830. A Series of Comic Tales. 1830.

Tales of the Early Ages. 3 vols. 1832.

Gale Middleton. A Story of the Present Day. 3 vols. 1833.

The Involuntary Prophet. A Tale of the Early Ages. 1835.

Jane Lomax, or a Mother's Crime. 3 vols. 1838.

Oliver Cromwell. An Historical Romance. 3 vols. 1840.

The Moneyed Man, or the Lesson of a Life. 3 vols. 1841.

Massaniello. A Historical Romance. 3 vols. 1842.

Adam Brown, the Merchant. 3 vols. 1843.

Arthur Arundel. A Tale of the English Revolution. 3 vols. 1844.

Love and Mesmerism. 3 vols. 1845.

(b) Other Works

[For Smith's parodies, in collaboration with his brother James, see p. 243 above.]

First Impressions, or Trade in the West. A Comedy. 1813; 1816.

Amarynthus, the Nympholept. A Pastoral Drama. With Other Poems. 1821.

Festivals, Games, and Amusements, Ancient and Modern. 1831.

The Tin Trumpet; or Heads and Tales, for the Wise and Waggish, to which are added, Poetical Selections by the late Paul Chatfield M.D. Edited by Jefferson Saunders Esq. 2 vols. 1836 (anon.); rptd 1890.

Memoirs, Letters, and Comic Miscellanies in Prose and Verse of the Late James Smith. Edited by his brother Horace Smith. 2 vols. 1840; 2 vols. 1841.

The Poetical Works of Horace Smith. 2 vols. 1846 (re-issued 1 vol. 1851).

(c) Biography

Sargent, E. Rejected Addresses. New York, 1871. [A memoir of Smith is prefixed.]

Beavan, A. H. James and Horace Smith. 1899.

GEORGE SOANE (1790–1860)

[See p. 595 below.]

LOUISA SIDNEY STANHOPE

Striking Likenesses; or, The Votaries of Fashion. A Novel. 4 vols. 1808.

The Age we live in. A Novel. 3 vols. 1809.

Di Montranzo; or, The Novice of Corpus Domini. A Romance. 4 vols. 1810.

The Confessional of Valombre. A Romance. 4 vols. 1812.

Madelina. A Novel. 4 vols. 1813.

Treachery; or, The Grave of Antoinette. A Romance. 4 vols. 1815.

The Nun of Santa Maria di Tindaro. A Tale. 3 vols. 1818.

The Crusaders. An Historical Romance of the Twelfth Century. 5 vols. 1820.

The Festival of Mora. An Historical Romance. 4 vols. 1821.

The Siege of Kenilworth. An Historical Romance. 4 vols. 1824.

Runnemede. An Ancient Legend. 3 vols. 1825.

The Bandit's Bride, or the Maid of Saxony. 4 vols. 1827 (3rd edn).

The Seer of Teviotdale. A Romance. 4 vols. 1827.

The Corsair's Bride. A Legend of the Sixteenth Century. 3 vols. 1830.

Sydney Beresford. A Tale. By the Author of The Bandit's Bride. 3 vols. 1835.

[R. Watt, Bibliotheca Britannica, vol. II, 1824, also gives Montbrasil Abbey, 2 vols. n.d.]

CATHERINE, LADY STEPNEY, née POLLOK, first married name MANNERS (d. 1845)

Castle Nuovier, or Henry and Adelina. 2 vols. 1806.

The Lords of Erith. A Romance. 3 vols. 1809.

The New Road to Ruin. A Novel. 3 vols. 1833.

The Heir Presumptive. 3 vols. 1835.

The Courtier's Daughter. A Novel. 3 vols. 1838; 3 vols. 1841.

The Three Peers. 3 vols. 1841.

[For Lady Stepney's life and writings see Colburn's New Monthly Mag. LI, 1837, and GM. XXIV, 1845.]

AGNES STRICKLAND (1796–1874)

[See p. 897 below.]

THOMAS SKINNER SURR (1770–1847)

(a) Novels

George Barnwell. A Novel. 3 vols. 1798; 3 vols. Dublin, 1798; 1834 (6th edn); 1834 (6th edn); tr. French, [1799].

Splendid Misery. 3 vols. 1801; 3 vols. 1807 (4th edn).

A Winter in London, or Sketches of Fashion. A Novel. 3 vols. 1806 (5 edns); 1824 (14th edn); tr. French, Paris, 1810.

The Magic of Wealth. A Novel. 3 vols. 1815.

Richmond or Scenes in the Life of a Bow Street Officer. 3 vols. 1827 (anon.). [Also attrib. to T. Gaspey.]

(b) Other Writings

Christ's Hospital: a Poem. 1797.

Refutation of Certain Misrepresentations relative to the Nature and Influence of Bank Notes and of the Stoppage of Specie at the Bank of England on the Price of Provisions. 1801.

EDWARD JOHN TRELAWNY (1792–1881)

[See p. 681 below.]

FRANCES TROLLOPE, née MILTON
(1780–1863)

(a) Fiction

The Refugee in America. A Novel. 3 vols. 1832.
The Abbess. A Romance. 3 vols. 1833.
Tremordyn Cliff. 3 vols. 1835.
The Life and Adventures of Jonathan Jefferson Whitlaw, or Scenes on the Mississippi. 3 vols. 1836; [1857] (as Lynch Law).
The Vicar of Wrexhill. 3 vols. 1837; 1840; [1860].
A Romance of Vienna. 3 vols. 1838.
The Widow Barnaby. 3 vols. 1839; 1840; 1856; [1860]; [1881]; tr. French, Paris, 1877.
The Life and Adventures of Michael Armstrong, the Factory Boy. 3 vols. 1840.
One Fault. A Novel. 3 vols. 1840; 1858.
The Widow Married. A Sequel to The Widow Barnaby. 3 vols. 1840.
Charles Chesterfield, or the Adventures of a Youth of Genius. 3 vols. 1841. [With illustrations by 'Phiz.']
The Ward of Thorpe Combe. 3 vols. 1841; 1857; tr. French, Paris, 1858.
The Blue Belles of England. 3 vols. 1842.
The Barnabys in America, or Adventures of the Widow Wedded. With Illustrations by John Leech. 3 vols. 1843; [1859] (as Adventures of the Barnabys in America).
Hargrave, or the Adventures of a Man of Fashion. 3 vols. 1843.
Jessie Phillips. A Tale of the Present Day. With Illustrations by John Leech. 3 vols. 1843; 1844.
The Laurringtons, or Superior People. 3 vols. 1844.
Young Love. A Novel. 3 vols. 1844.
The Attractive Man. A Novel. 3 vols. 1846.
The Robertses on their Travels. 3 vols. 1846.
Father Eustace. A Tale of the Jesuits. 3 vols. 1847.
The Three Cousins. A Novel. 3 vols. 1847; [1858].
Town and Country. A Novel. 3 vols. 1848; [1857] (as The Days of the Regency).
The Young Countess, or Love and Jealousy. 3 vols. 1848.
The Lottery of Marriage. A Novel. 3 vols. 1849.
The Old World and the New. A Novel. 3 vols. 1849.
Petticoat Government. A Novel. 3 vols. 1850; 1857.
Mrs Mathews, or Family Mysteries. A Novel. 3 vols. 1851; 1864.
Second Love, or Beauty and Intellect. A Novel. 3 vols. 1851.
Uncle Walter. A Novel. 3 vols. 1852.
The Young Heiress. A Novel. 3 vols. 1853; 1864.

The Life and Adventures of a Clever Woman, illustrated with Occasional Extracts from her Diary. 3 vols. 1854.
Gertrude, or Family Pride. 3 vols. 1855; 1864.
Fashionable Life, or Paris and London. 3 vols. 1856.

(b) Other Writings

Domestic Manners of the Americans. 2 vols. 1832 (4 edns); New York, 1832; 1839; ed. M. Sadleir, 1927; tr. French, Paris, 1841 (3rd edn).
The Mother's Manual, or Illustrations of Matrimonial Economy. An Essay in Verse. 1833 (anon.).
Belgium and Western Germany in 1833. 2 vols. 1834; 2 vols. Paris, 1834.
Paris and the Parisians in 1835. 2 vols. 1836; tr. French, Paris, [1911].
Vienna and the Austrians, with Some Account of a Journey through Swabia, Bavaria, the Tyrol, and the Salzbourg. 2 vols. 1838.
A Visit to Italy. 2 vols. 1842.
Travels and Travellers. A Series of Sketches. 2 vols. 1846.

[Mrs Trollope also ed. T. A. Trollope's A Summer in Brittany, 2 vols. 1840 and his A Summer in Western France, 2 vols. 1841.]

(c) Biography and Criticism

[Lockhart, J. G.] Domestic Manners of the Americans. By Mrs Trollope. Quarterly Rev. XLVII, 1832.
Frances Trollope. New Monthly Mag. LV, 1839.
Horne, R. H. A New Spirit of the Age. Vol. I, 1844.
Trollope, A. An Autobiography. 2 vols. Edinburgh, 1883.
Trollope, T. A. What I remember. 3 vols. 1887–9.
Trollope, F. E. Frances Trollope, her Life and Literary Works from George III to Victoria. 2 vols. 1895.
Wilson, Mona. These were Muses. 1924.
Sadleir, M. Trollope, a Commentary. 1927. [Appendix contains a calendar of events in the life of Frances Trollope and a bibliography.]
Pope-Hennessy, U. Three English Women in America. 1929. [F. Trollope, F. Kemble, H. Martineau.]

GEORGE WALKER (1772–1847)

(a) Novels

Don Raphael. 3 vols. 1803.
Two Girls of Eighteen. 2 vols. 1806.
The Adventures of Timothy Thoughtless, or the Misfortunes of a Little Boy who ran away from Boarding-School. 1813.
The Travels of Sylvester Tramper. 1813 (anon.).

The Midnight Bell. 3 vols. 1824. [For Walker's novels pbd before 1801 see vol. II, p. 551 above.]

(b) Poems

Poems. 1801.

The Battle of Waterloo. A Poem. 1815.

ROBERT WARD, afterwards PLUMER WARD (1765–1846)

(a) Fiction

Tremaine, or the Man of Refinement. 3 vols. 1825 (anon.); 3 vols. 1827 (4th edn); 2 vols. 1835.

De Vere, or the Man of Independence. 4 vols. 1827; 3 vols. 1833.

Illustrations of Human Life. By the Author of Tremaine. 3 vols. 1837; 1843. [Includes three novels: Atticus; St Laurence; Fielding, or Society.]

De Clifford, or the Constant Man. 4 vols. 1841.

(b) Other Writings

An Inquiry into the Foundation and History of the Law of Nations in Europe from the Time of the Greeks and Romans to the Age of Grotius. 1795.

A Treatise of the Relative Rights and Duties of Belligerents and Neutral Powers in Maritime Affairs, in which the Principles of the Armed Neutralities and the Opinions of Hübner and Schlegel are fully discussed. 1801; 1875.

An Essay on Contraband. Being a Continuation of the Treatise of the Relative Rights and Duties. 1801.

A View of the Relative Situations of Mr Pitt and Mr Addington previous to and on the Night of Mr Patten's Motion. 1803.

An Enquiry into the Manner in which the Different Wars of Europe have commenced during the last two Centuries. 1804.

An Historical Essay on the Real Character and Amount of the Precedent of the Revolution of 1688. In which the Opinions of Mackintosh, Price, Hallam and Locke are initially considered. 2 vols. 1838.

The Reviewer Reviewed. 1838 (anon.). [An answer to a review of An Historical Essay in Edinburgh Rev.]

Pictures of the World at Home and Abroad. 3 vols. 1839.

[Ward also edited P. G. Patmore's Chatsworth, or the Romance of a Week, 1844.]

(c) Biography and Criticism

Phipps, E. Memoirs of the Political and Literary Life of Robert Plumer Ward. With Selections from his Correspondence, Diaries, and Unpublished Literary Remains. 2 vols. 1850.

Robert Plumer Ward. Bentley's Misc. XXVIII, 1850.

Patmore, P. G. My Friends and Acquaintances. 3 vols. 1855. [Contains a number of letters by Ward.]

JANE WEST (1758–1852)

(a) Novels

The Advantages of Education; or, The History of Maria Williams. A Tale for very Young Ladies (by Mrs Prudentia Homespun). 2 vols. 1793; 2 vols. 1803.

A Gossip's Story, and a Legendary Tale. By the Author of the Advantages of Education. 2 vols. 1796; 2 vols. 1797 (bis); 1804 (5th edn); Cork, 1799.

A Tale of the Times. By the Author of A Gossip's Story. 3 vols. 1799.

The Infidel Father. By the Author of A Tale of the Times. 3 vols. 1802.

The Refusal. By the Author of A Tale of the Times. 3 vols. 1810.

The Loyalists: an Historical Novel. By the Author of Letters to a Young Man. 3 vols. 1812.

Alicia de Lacy: an Historical Romance. 4 vols. 1814.

Ringrove; or, Old Fashioned Notions. By the Author of Letters to a Young Man. 2 vols. 1827.

(b) Other Writings

Miscellaneous Poems, Translations and Imitations. 1780.

Miscellaneous Poetry, written at an Early Period of Life. 1786.

The Humours of Brighthelmstone. 1788. [A poem.]

Miscellaneous Poems, and a Tragedy [Edmund surnamed Ironside]. York, 1791; 1797; 1804.

Elegy on the Death of the Right Honourable Edmund Burke. 1797.

Poems and Plays. 4 vols. 1799–1805. [Includes the tragedies Adela and The Minstrel, and the comely How will it end?].

Letters addressed to a Young Man on his First Entrance into Life. 3 vols. 1801; 1802; 1806 (4th edn); 1818 (6th edn).

Letters to a Young Lady, in which the Duties and Character of Women are considered. 3 vols. 1806 (bis); 1811 (4th edn).

The Mother: a Poem in Five Books. 1809; 1810.

Select Translation of the Beauties of Massillon. 1812.

Scriptural Essays adapted to the Holydays of the Church of England; with Meditations on the Prescribed Services. 2 vols. 1816; 1817.

JOHN WILSON (1785–1854)

[See p. 682 below.]

S. J. L. and H. B. G.

IV. THE MID-NINETEENTH CENTURY NOVELISTS

BORROW, DISRAELI, MRS GASKELL, THACKERAY, DICKENS, READE, TROLLOPE, THE BRONTËS, GEORGE ELIOT, MEREDITH

GEORGE HENRY BORROW (1803–1881)

(1) BIBLIOGRAPHY

Wise, T. J. A Bibliography of the Writings in Prose and Verse of George Henry Borrow. 1914.

Stephen, G. A. Borrow House Museum. A Brief Account of the Life of George Borrow and his Norwich Home. With a Bibliography. Norwich, 1927.

[There are also bibliographies in W. I. Knapp's Life, Writings and Correspondence of George Borrow, 1899, in Edward Thomas's George Borrow, the Man and his Books, 1912, by G. A. Stephen in Norwich Public Library Readers' Guide, 1913, and by G. F. Black in Gypsy Lore Soc. Monographs, I, 1914.]

(2) COLLECTED WORKS

The Works of George Borrow. 4 vols. 1900–2. [Contains only Lavengro, The Bible in Spain, The Romany Rye, and The Zincali.]

The Works of George Borrow. 5 vols. [1906]. (New Universal Lib.)

The Works of George Borrow. Edited, with much hitherto Unpublished Manuscript, by Clement Shorter. 16 vols. 1923–4. (Norwich edn.)

(3) SELECTED WORKS

The Pocket George Borrow. Passages chosen from the Works of Borrow by Edward Thomas. 1912.

Readings from George Borrow. Selected by S. A. Richards. 1921. (King's Treasuries of Literature.)

Borrow: Selections. With Essays by Richard Ford, Leslie Stephen, and George Saintsbury; with an Introduction and Notes by H. S. Milford. Oxford, 1924.

Selections from George Borrow. Chosen by W. E. Williams. 1927.

(4) ORIGINAL PROSE

The Zincali; or, An Account of the Gypsies of Spain. With an Original Collection of their Songs and Poetry, and a Copious Dictionary of their Language. 2 vols. 1841; 1843 (*bis*); 1846; 1870; 1882; 1888, etc.; 1901 (definitive edn); Italian epitome, Milan, 1878.

The Bible in Spain; or, The Journeys, Adventures, and Imprisonments of an English-

man, in an Attempt to circulate the Scriptures in the Peninsula. 3 vols. 1843 (6 edns); 1896 (18th edn), etc.; ed. E. Thomas, 1906 (Everyman's Lib.); rptd 1906 (World's Classics). Tr. German, Breslau, 1844; Spanish, Madrid, [1921].

Lavengro; The Scholar—the Gypsy—the Priest. 3 vols. 1851; 1872; 1888; 1896, etc.; ed. T. Watts[-Dunton], 1893; ed. [W. I. Knapp], 1900; ed. F. H. Groome, 2 vols. 1901; rptd 1904 (World's Classics); ed. T. Seccombe, 1906 (Everyman's Lib.); tr. French, Paris, 1892.

The Romany Rye; a Sequel to Lavengro. 2 vols. 1857; 1858; 1872; 1888; 1896; ed. T. Watts[-Dunton],[1900];ed. [W.I.Knapp], 1900; ed. J. Sampson, 1903; rptd 1906 (Everyman's Lib.); rptd 1906 (World's Classics).

Wild Wales: its People, Language and Scenery. 3 vols. 1862; 1865; 1888; 1901 (authoritative edn), etc.; rptd 1906 (Everyman's Lib.); rptd 1920 (World's Classics).

Romano Lavo-Lil: Word-Book of the Romany; or, English Gypsy Language. With Many Pieces in Gypsy, illustrative of the Way of Speaking and Thinking of the English Gypsies; with Specimens of their Poetry, and an Account of Certain Gypsyries or Places inhabited by them, and of Various Things relating to Gypsy Life in England. 1874; 1888; 1905; 1907; 1908.

Letters to the British and Foreign Bible Society. Ed. T. H. Darlow, 1911.

Letters to his Wife, Mary Borrow. 1913 (priv. ptd).

Letters to his Mother, Ann Borrow, and Other Correspondents. 1913 (priv. ptd).

A Supplementary Chapter to The Bible in Spain, inspired by Ford's Hand-book for Travellers in Spain. 1913 (priv. ptd).

Wild Wales: Suppressed Chapters. Ed. H. Wright, Welsh Outlook, IX, X, 1922–3.

Celtic Bards, Chiefs and Kings. Ed. H. G. Wright, 1928. [Probably written between 1857 and 1860.]

(5) WORKS EDITED BY BORROW

Celebrated Trials, and Remarkable Cases of Criminal Jurisprudence, from the Earliest Records to the Year 1825. 6 vols. 1825; ed. and rev. E. H. Bierstadt, 1928.

Mousei echen Isus Gheristos i tuta puha itche ghese. St Petersburg, 1835.

El Nuevo Testamento, traducido al Español. Madrid, 1837.

Evangelioa San Lucasen Guissan. El Evangelio segun S. Lucas, traducido al Vascuence. Madrid, 1838.

(6) Translations in Verse and Prose

Faustus: his Life, Death, and Descent into Hell; translated from the German [of F. M. von Klinger]. 1825 (anon.).

Romantic Ballads, translated from the Danish; and Miscellaneous Pieces. Norwich, 1826; 1826; rptd Norwich, 1913; rptd 1926.

Targum; or, Metrical Translations from Thirty Languages and Dialects. St Petersburg, 1835. [Rptd facs. in Targum, and The Talisman; with Other Pieces, [1892].]

The Talisman; from the Russian of Alexander Pushkin; with Other Pieces. St Petersburg, 1835. [Rptd facs. in Targum, and The Talisman, [1892].]

Embéo e Majaró Lucas. Brotoboro randado andré la chipe griega, acana chibado andré o Romano, ó chipe es Zincales de Sesé. El Evangelio segun S. Lucas, traducido al Romaní, ó Dialecto de los Gitanos de España. [Madrid], 1837; 1871; 1872.

The Sleeping Bard; or, Visions of the World, Death and Hell, by Elis Wyn; translated from the Cambrian British. 1860.

The Turkish Jester; or, The Pleasantries of Cogia Nasr Eddin Effendi; translated from the Turkish. Ipswich, 1884.

The Death of Balder; from the Danish of Johannes Ewald (1773). 1889.

Welsh Poems and Ballads; with an Introduction by Ernest Rhys. 1915.

Ballads of All Nations. Translated by George Borrow. A Selection by R. Brimley Johnson. 1927.

(7) Privately Printed Ballads, Poems and Tales

Marsk Stig: a Ballad. 1913.
The Serpent Knight, and Other Ballads. 1913.
The King's Wake, and Other Ballads. 1913.
The Dalby Bear, and Other Ballads. 1913.
The Mermaid's Prophecy, and Other Songs relating to Queen Dagmar. 1913.
Hafbur and Signe: a Ballad. 1913.
The Story of Yvashka with the Bear's Ear; translated from the Russian. 1913.
The Verner Raven; The Count of Vendel's Daughter, and Other Ballads. 1913.
The Return of the Dead, and Other Ballads. 1913.
Axel Thordson and Fair Valborg: a Ballad. 1913.
King Hacon's Death; and Bran and the Black Dog: two Ballads. 1913.
Marsk Stig's Daughters, and other Songs and Ballads. 1913.
The Tale of Brynild, and King Valdemar and his Sister: two Ballads. 1913.
Proud Signild, and Other Ballads. 1913.
Ulf Van Yern and Other Ballads. 1913.

Ellen of Villenskov, and Other Ballads. 1913.
The Songs of Ranild. 1913.
Niels Ebbesen, and Germand Gladenswayne: two Ballads. 1913.
Child Maidelvold, and Other Ballads. 1913.
Ermeline: a Ballad. 1913.
The Giant of Bern, and Orm Ungerswayne: a Ballad. 1913.
Little Engel: a Ballad; with a Series of Epigrams from the Persian. 1913.
Alf the Freebooter, Little Danneved and Swayne Trost, and Other Ballads. 1913.
King Diderik and the Fight between the Lion and Dragon; and Other Ballads. 1913.
The Nightingale, The Valkyrie and Raven, and Other Ballads. 1913.
Grimmer and Kamper; The End of Sivard Snaren-Swayne, and Other Ballads. 1913.
The Fountain of Maribo, and Other Ballads. 1913.
Queen Berngerd, The Bard and the Dreams, and Other Ballads. 1913.
Finnish Arts; or, Sir Thor and Damsel Thure: a Ballad. 1913.
Brown William, The Power of the Harp, and Other Ballads. 1913.
The Song of Deirdra, King Byrge and his Brothers, and Other Ballads. 1913.
Signelil: a Tale from the Cornish, and Other Ballads. 1913.
Young Swaigder; or, The Force of Runes, and Other Ballads. 1913.
Emelian the Fool: a Tale; translated from the Russian. 1913.
The Story of Tim; translated from the Russian. 1913.
Mollie Charane, and Other Ballads. 1913.
Grimhild's Vengeance: Three Ballads; edited, with an Introduction, by Edmund Gosse. 1913.
The Brother Avenged, and Other Ballads. 1913.
The Gold Horns; translated from the Danish of Adam Gottlob Oehlenschläger; edited, with an Introduction, by Edmund Gosse. 1913.
Tord of Hafsborough, and Other Ballads. 1914.
The Expedition to Birting's Land, and Other Ballads. 1914.

(8) Biography and Criticism

(a) Books

Dutt, W. A. George Borrow in East Anglia. 1896.

Knapp, W. I. Life, Writings, and Correspondence of George Borrow; derived from Official and Other Authentic Sources. 2 vols. 1899.

Walling, R. A. J. George Borrow: the Man and his Work. 1908.

Blaesing, B. George Borrow. Berlin, 1910.

Thomas, Edward. George Borrow: the Man and his Books. 1912.

Jenkins, Herbert. The Life of George Borrow, compiled from Unpublished Official Documents, his Works, Correspondence, etc. 1912.

Shorter, C. K. George Borrow and his Circle; wherein may be found many hitherto Unpublished Letters of Borrow and his Friends. 1913.

—— The Life of George Borrow. [1920.]

Adams, M. In the Footsteps of Borrow and FitzGerald. [1914.]

Hopkins, R. T. George Borrow, Lord of the Open Road. [1922.]

Elam, S. M. George Borrow. New York, 1929.

Dearden, S. The Gypsy Gentleman. 1939.

(b) Articles in Periodicals, Pamphlets and Chapters of Books

[For further titles, to 1927, see G. A. Stephen's bibliography.]

[Lockhart, J. G.] The Bible in Spain. Quart. Rev. Dec. 1842.

[Ford, R.] The Bible in Spain. Edinburgh Rev. Feb. 1843.

Elwin, W. Mr Borrow. Athenaeum, 6 Aug. 1881. [Obituary.]

Hake, A. E. Recollections of George Borrow. Athenaeum, 13 Aug. 1881.

—— George Borrow. Macmillan's Mag. xlv, 1882.

Stephen, Sir L. Hours in a Library. Vol. iii, 1881.

Watts[-Dunton], T. Reminiscences of George Borrow. Athenaeum, 3, 10 Sept. 1881. [Rptd in Old Familiar Faces, 1916.]

Saintsbury, G. George Borrow. Macmillan's Mag. liii, 1886. [Rptd in Essays in English Literature, 1780–1860, 1890.]

Montégut, E. Écrivains modernes de l'Angleterre: deuxième Série: Mrs Gaskell; Mrs Browning; George Borrow; Alfred Tennyson. Paris, 1889.

Birrell, A. The Office of Literature. [In Obiter Dicta, ser. 2, 1890.]

—— Res Judicatæ. 1892.

Henley, W. E. Borrow. [In Views and Reviews, Literature, 1890.]

Harvey, E. George Borrow: Personal Recollections. Eastern Daily Press, 1 Oct. 1892.

Groome, F. H. George Borrow. Bookman, iii, 1893.

Findlater, J. H. George Borrow. Cornhill Mag. lxxx, 1899.

Herzfeld, G. George Borrow. Archiv, cvii, 1901.

Seccombe, T. George Borrow: his Homes and Haunts. Bookman, xxi, 1902.

Euren, H. F. Norwich Notables, viii: George Borrow. Norwich Mercury, 4, 18 July, 1903.

Doyle, Sir A. C. Through the Magic Door. 1907.

Jenkins, H. George Borrow in Russia. National Rev. liv, 1910.

Cantrill, T. C. and Pringle, J. George Borrow's Second Tour in Wales. Y Cymmrodor, xxii, 1910. [Also separately, 1911.]

Baldrey, S. H. George Borrow Reminiscences: New Biographical Material. Eastern Daily Press, 31 July 1913.

Shorter, C. K. George Borrow in Scotland. Fortnightly Rev. xcix, 1913.

Ralli, A. The Works of George Borrow. Fortnightly Rev. civ, 1915.

Rhys, E. Unpublished Prose Miscellanies of George Borrow. Y Cymmrodor, xxv, 1915.

Thomas, Edward. George Borrow. [In Literary Pilgrims in England, 1917.]

Elton, O. Borrow. [In A Survey of English Literature, 1830–80, vol. i, 1920.].

Jerrold, W. George Borrow's Joseph Sell. Cornhill Mag. l, 1921.

Hustvedt, S. B. George Borrow and his Danish Ballads. JEGP. xxii, 1923.

Rye, W. The Inaccuracies of George Borrow. History Teachers' Misc. ii, 1923–4.

Speck, W. A. George Borrow and Goethe's Faust. PMLA. xli, 1926.

Boyle, A. Portraiture in Lavengro. Cornhill Mag. lxv, 1928.

More, P. E. The Demon of the Absolute. Princeton, 1928. [Pp. 127–42 are on Borrow.]

Wright, H. G. Was George Borrow ever in Denmark? MLR. xxiii, 1928.

—— Borrow and Grundtvig. TLS. 12 June 1930.

—— Influence of George Borrow in Norway and Sweden. MLR. xxix, 1934.

H. B. G.

BENJAMIN DISRAELI, EARL OF BEACONSFIELD (1804–1881)

(1) BIBLIOGRAPHIES

Contributions to a Bibliography of Benjamin Disraeli, Earl of Beaconsfield. N. & Q. 29 April–8 July 1893.

Sadleir, M. Excursions in Victorian Bibliography. 1922. [Contains a bibliography of Disraeli.]

(2) COLLECTED WORKS

Collected Edition of the Novels of Benjamin Disraeli. 10 vols. 1870–1. [Preface by Disraeli.]

Novels and Tales. Collected Edition. 10 vols. 1871–81.

Novels and Tales. With a Portrait and Sketch of his Life. 11 vols. 1881. (Hughenden edn.)

The Bradenham Edition of the Novels and Tales of Benjamin Disraeli. With Introductions by Philip Guedalla. 12 vols. 1926–7.

The Novels of Benjamin Disraeli. 11 vols. 1927–8.

(3) FICTION

Vivian Grey. Vols. I, II, 1826; vols. III–v, 1827; 1853 (with preface); [1888] (introduction by Earl of Iddesleigh); ed. L. Wolf, 2 vols. 1904. [Key to Vivian Grey, 1827 (10th edn).]

The Voyage of Captain Popanilla. By the Author of Vivian Grey. 1828; ed. W. S. Northcote (Earl of Iddesleigh), 1906 (with Alroy, etc.).

The Young Duke. 3 vols. 1831; [1888]; [1894]; ed. W. S. Northcote (Earl of Iddesleigh), 1906.

Contarini Fleming: A Psychological Autobiography. 4 vols. 1832; 4 vols. 1834 (2nd edn); 3 vols. 1846; 1853; [1888]; ed. W. S. Northcote (Earl of Iddesleigh), 1905.

The Wondrous Tale of Alroy and The Rise of Iskander. 3 vols. 1833; 1846; [1888]; ed. W. S. Northcote (Earl of Iddesleigh), 1906.

Henrietta Temple: A Love Story. 3 vols. 1837; 1853; [1888]; ed. W. S. Northcote (Earl of Iddesleigh), 1906.

Venetia. 3 vols. 1837; 1853; 2 vols. 1858; [1888]; ed. W. S. Northcote (Earl of Iddesleigh), 1905.

Coningsby: Or the New Generation. 3 vols. 1844 (bis); 2 vols. Paris, 1846; [1888]; ed. F. Hitchman, 1888–9; 1891, etc.; ed. B. N. Langdon-Davies, [1911]; ed. A. Maurois, 1931 (World's Classics).

> Anti-Coningsby: Or, the New Generation Grown Old. By An Embryo M.P. 1844.
> Strictures on Coningsby, With Remarks On the Present State of Parties and the Character of the Age. 1844.
> A Key To The Characters In Coningsby. 1844.
> A New Key to the Characters in Coningsby. [1845.]

Sybil: Or, The Two Nations. 3 vols. 1845; 1853; Paris, 1859; [1888]; ed. H. D. Traill, 1895; ed. W. S. Northcote (Earl of Iddesleigh), 1905; [1913]; ed. W. Sichel, 1925; 1925 (World's Classics); ed. V. Cohen, 1934.

Tancred: Or The New Crusade. 3 vols. 1847; ed. W. S. Northcote (Earl of Iddesleigh), 1905; Berlin, 1914 (with a postscript by Oscar Levy).

Ixion In Heaven, The Infernal Marriage, Popanilla, Count Alarcos. 1853; ed. W. S.

Northcote (Earl of Iddesleigh), 1906. [Ixion in Heaven and The Infernal Marriage had both been ptd in Colburn's New Monthly Mag. 1832–4. Ixion was rptd separately 1925 and, with W. E. Aytoun's Endymion, 1927; The Infernal Marriage was rptd separately 1929.]

Lothair. 3 vols. 1870 (7 edns); 2 vols. Leipzig, 1870; 2 vols. Paris, 1872; 4 vols. Leipzig, 1874; [1877]; 2 vols. Budapest, 1878; [1915].

> Lothaw, Or The Adventures of A Young Gentleman In Search Of A Religion. By Mr Benjamins [F. Bret Harte]. [1871.]
> Lothair, the Critics and the Rt Hon. Benjamin Disraeli's General Preface to all His Works. By E. W. [1872.]
> Lothair Its Beauties and Blemishes. By G. E. [1873.]
> Lothair's Children. By H. R. H. [Campbell MacKellar]. 1890.

Endymion. By the Author of Lothair. 3 vols. 1880; 1880; 1881; 3 vols. Leipzig, 1881.

> A Key To The Characters Of Endymion. New York, [1881].
> Ben D'Ymion and Other Parodies, by H. F. Lester. 1887.

Tales And Sketches By The Right Hon. Benjamin Disraeli, Earl of Beaconsfield With A Prefatory Memoir by J. Logie Robertson. 1891. [Contains for the first time in book form: A True Story, The Carrier Pigeon, The Consul's Daughter, Walstein, The Speaking Harlequin, The Midland Ocean, Ibrahim Pacha, The Court of Egypt, The Valley of Thebes, Egyptian Thebes, Shoubra, The Bosphorus, An Interview With A Great Turk, Munich.]

(4) POEMS

The Revolutionary Epick: The Work Of Disraeli The Younger. 2 vols. 1834; 1864 (rev.).

The Tragedy Of Count Alarcos. 1839. [Rptd with Ixion, 1853, and ed. W. S. Northcote (Earl of Iddesleigh), with Alroy, 1906.]

The Revolutionary Epick and Other Poems. Ed. W. D. Adams, 1904.

The Dunciad Of To-Day; A Satire (Here Attributed to Disraeli) and, The Modern Aesop, first published in the Star Chamber, With an Introduction by Michael Sadleir. 1928.

(5) POLITICAL WRITINGS

An Enquiry Into the Plans, Progress and Policy of American Mining Companies. 1825.

Lawyers And Legislators: Or Notes On The American Mining Companies. 1825.

The Present State of Mexico: As Detailed in a Report presented to the General Congress by the Secretary of State for the Home Department and Foreign Affairs at the Opening of the Session in 1825. 1825.

England and France: Or A Cure For The Ministerial Gallomania. 1832.

What Is He? 1833; 1833 (rev.); ed. F. Hitchman, [1884].

The Crisis Examined. 1834.

Vindication Of The English Constitution In A Letter To A Noble And Learned Lord. By Disraeli the Younger. 1835; ed. F. A. Hyndman, [1895].

The Letters Of Runnymede. 1836; ed. F. Hitchman, 1885; ed. F. Bickley, [1923]. [Rptd from The Times, Jan.–May 1836.]

The Spirit of Whiggism. 1836; ed. F. Bickley, 1923 (with The Letters of Runnymede).

Lord George Bentinck: A Political Biography. 1852 (4 edns); 1858; 1872 (8th edn, rev.); ed. C. Whibley, 1905.

Mr Disraeli to Colonel Rathbone. [1858.] [Letters on the annexation of Oude.]

Whigs and Whiggism: Political Writings. Ed. W. Hutcheon, 1913. [Includes What is He?, The Crisis Examined, Vindication of the English Constitution, Letters of Runnymede, The Spirit of Whiggism, together with various unreprinted articles from The Times (1837–41), Morning Post (1835), The Press (1853), and Fraser's Mag. (1835–6).]

(6) SPEECHES

Speech in the House Of Commons Friday, 15th May 1846. 1846.

England and Denmark, Speech in the House of Commons 19th April 1848. 1848.

The Parliament and the Government. Speech on the Labours of the Session, August 30th, 1848. [1848.]

The New Parliamentary Reform. Speech in the House of Commons. Tuesday, June 20th, 1848. 1848.

Financial Policy. Speech in the House of Commons. June 30th, 1851. 1851.

Address Delivered to the Members of the Manchester Athenaeum on the 23rd October 1844 on the Importance of Literature to Men of Business. 1852.

Parliamentary Reform. House of Commons, 25th March 1852. 1852.

Parliamentary Reform. House of Commons, February 28th 1859. 1859.

Public Expenditure. Speech in the House of Commons. June 3rd, 1862. 1862.

Mr Gladstone's Finance, 1853–1862. 1862. [Speeches in the House of Commons, 24 Feb. 1860, 8 April 1862.]

Church Policy, Speech to the Oxford Diocesan Society. October 30th, 1862. 1862.

Speech at Public Meeting of the Oxford Diocesan Society for the Augmentation of Small Livings in the Sheldonian Theatre, November 25, 1864. 1864.

'Church and Queen.' Five Speeches 1860–64. Edited with a Preface by A Member of the University of Oxford. 1865.

Two Speeches in the City of Edinburgh on 29th and 30th October 1867. 1867.

Speeches on Parliamentary Reform (1848–1866). Ed. M. Corry, 1867.

The Prime Minister On Church and State. Speech at the Hall of the Merchant Taylors Company, June 17th, 1868. [1868.]

Speeches on the Conservative Policy of the Last Thirty Years. Ed. J. F. Bulley, [1870].

Speech at the Banquet of the National Union of Conservative and Constitutional Associations at the Crystal Palace, Monday, June 24th, 1872. 1872.

Speech at Free Trade Hall, Manchester, April 3rd 1872. [1872.] [Rptd in Representative British Orations, ed. C. Adams, vol. III, 1884.]

Mr Osborne Morgan's Burials Bill Speech by Disraeli moving the Rejection, House of Commons, March 26th, 1873. 1873.

Inaugural Address Delivered to the University of Glasgow, November 19th, 1873. 1873.

Speech At Aylesbury, 20th September 1876. 1876. [On the Eastern question.]

Selected Speeches. With Notes By T. E. Kebbel. 2 vols. 1882.

(7) BOOKS EDITED BY DISRAELI

The Life of Paul Jones. From Original Documents in the possession of John Henry Sherburne, Register of the Navy of the United States. 1825. [Disraeli contributed an anon. preface.]

The Works of Isaac Disraeli. Edited With Introductions by Benjamin Disraeli. 9 vols. 1849–59.

(8) LETTERS

Home Letters, 1830–31. [Ed. R. Disraeli], 1885 (bis).

Correspondence with his Sister. [Ed. R. Disraeli], 1886; Paris, 1889. [Rptd with the earlier collection as Lord Beaconsfield's Letters, 1830–1852, in 1887, and ed. A. Birrell, 1928.]

A New Sheaf of Disraeli Letters. Hitherto Unpublished Correspondence with his Sister Sarah. Ed. C. I. Freed, American Hebrew, 15 April 1927.

Letters of Disraeli to Lady Bradford and Lady Chesterfield. Ed. Marquis of Zetland, 2 vols. 1929.

Some Early Letters of Lord Beaconsfield. Ed. E. T. Cook, Saturday Rev. 21, 28 May 1932.

Letters to Frances Anne, Marchioness of Londonderry, 1837–1861. 1938.

(9) BIOGRAPHY AND CRITICISM

(a) Books

Francis, G. H. The Rt Hon. Benjamin Disraeli. A Critical Biography. 1852.

MacKnight, T. Disraeli. A Literary and Political Biography. 1854.

MacGilchrist, J. Life of Benjamin Disraeli. [1868.]

O'Connor, T. P. and Foggo, A. Benjamin Disraeli, Earl of Beaconsfield. A Biography. 2 vols. 1878–81.

Hitchman, F. The Public Life of Beaconsfield. 1879.

Brandes, G. Beaconsfield. Tr. Eng. 1880.

Manners, J. (Duchess of Rutland). Some Personal Recollections of the Later Years of the Earl of Beaconsfield. 1881.

Ewald, [A. C.] Disraeli and his Times. 1883.

O'Connor, T. P. Lord Beaconsfield. 1884.

Kebbel, T. E. The Life of Lord Beaconsfield. 1888.

—— Lord Beaconsfield and Other Tory Memories. 1907.

Froude, J. A. Lord Beaconsfield. 1890.

Fraser, Sir W. A. Disraeli and his Day. 1891.

Lake, H. Personal Reminiscences of Beaconsfield. [1891.]

Meynell, W. Benjamin Disraeli. An Unconventional Biography. 1903; 1927 (rev. edn).

Sichel, W. Disraeli. 1904.

Monypenny, W. F. and Buckle, G. E. The Life of Benjamin Disraeli, Earl of Beaconsfield. 6 vols. 1910–20; 2 vols. 1929 (rev.). [The standard life.]

Baring, E. (Earl of Cromer). Disraeli. 1912.

'Raymond, E. T.' Disraeli, the Alien Patriot. 1925.

Somervell, D. C. Disraeli and Gladstone. 1925.

Clarke, Sir E. G. Benjamin Disraeli, 1804–1881. 1926.

Maurois, A. La Vie de Disraeli. Paris, 1927; tr. Eng. 1928.

Murray, D. L. Disraeli. 1927.

Rühl, H. Disraelis Imperialismus und die Kolonialpolitik seiner Zeit. Leipzig, 1935.

Beeley, H. Disraeli. 1936.

Thane, E. Young Mr Disraeli. New York, 1936.

(b) Articles in Periodicals, Essays and Chapters of Books

Gilfillan, G. Galleries of Literary Portraits. Vol. II, Edinburgh, 1856.

Stephen, Sir L. Mr Disraeli's Novels. [In Hours in a Library, ser. 2, 1876.]

Collins, Mortimer. Pen Sketches. Vol. I, 1879.

Greg, W. R. Miscellaneous Essays. Vol. I, 1882.

Sichel, W. Disraeli as a Landscape Painter. Time, XVIII, 1885.

Harrison, F. The Choice of Books. 1886.

—— Studies in Early Victorian Literature. 1895.

Saintsbury, G. Disraeli. Mag. of Art, IX, 1886.

Shelton, Sir J. The Table Talk of Shirley. 1895. [Includes reminiscences of Disraeli.]

Traill, H. D. The Political Novel. [In The New Fiction, 1897.]

Whibley, C. Disraeli the Younger. [In The Pageantry of Life, 1900.]

Bryce, J., Viscount. Studies in Contemporary Biography. 1903.

Cazamian, L. Le Roman social en Angleterre (1830–1850). Paris, 1904. [Ch. vi.]

'Melville, Lewis.' The Novels of Disraeli. Fortnightly Rev. LXXXII, 1904. [Rptd in Victorian Novelists, 1906.]

Cecil, A. Disraeli. The First Two Phases. Quarterly Rev. CCXVIII, 1913.

More, P. E. Disraeli and Conservatism. Atlantic Monthly, LXXXV, 1915.

Sherman, S. P. Points of View. New York, 1921.

George, R. E. G. The Novels of Disraeli. Nineteenth Century, XCVI, 1924.

Speare, M. E. The Political Novel. New York, 1924.

Brandl, A. Zur Quelle von Disraelis Alroy. Archiv, CXLVIII, 1925.

Hever, E. Entstehungsgeschichte von Disraelis Vivian Grey. Berlin, 1925.

Quiller-Couch, Sir A. T. Charles Dickens and Other Victorians. Cambridge, 1925.

Bjerre, B. Den tredje Markisen av Hertford i Coningsby. Edda, XXV, 1927.

Swinnerton, F. Disraeli as a Novelist. Bookman, April 1927; London Mercury, XVII, 1928; Yale Rev. XVII, 1928.

Caspar, M. Disraelis Vivian Grey II als politischer Schlüsselroman. Archiv, CLIII, 1928.

Segalowitsch, B. Benjamin Disraelis Orientalismus. Berlin, 1930.

Jean-Aubry, G. Disraeli et le Solitaire de Bath. Figaro, 5 Dec. 1931. [Beckford's marginal notes on Alroy.]

Baumann, A. A. Benjamin Disraeli. [In Great Victorians, ed. H. J. and H. Massingham, 1932.]

'Paston, George.' The Young Disraeli and his Adventures in Journalism. Cornhill Mag. LXXIII, 1932.

Seibat, H. Die Romankunst Disraelis. Jena, 1933.

Modder, F. M. The Alien Patriot in Disraeli's Novels. London Quart. Rev. CLIX, 1934.

Clive, C. L. Disraeli's Only Venture in Dramatic Composition. Texas University Stud. XVI, 1936.

Rosa, M. W. The Silver Fork School: Novels of Fashion preceding Vanity Fair. New York, 1936.

Thomas, W. Deux Chefs-d'Œuvre de Raillerie sociale et politique. Revue de l'Enseignement des Langues vivantes, Aug., Nov. 1936.

Hudson, R. L. Poe and Disraeli. American Lit. VIII, 1937.
S. J. L.

ELIZABETH CLEGHORN GASKELL, NÉE STEVENSON (1810–1865)

(1) BIBLIOGRAPHIES

Green, J. A. A Bibliographical Guide to the Gaskell Collection in the Moss Side Library. Manchester, 1911.

Sadleir, M. Excursions in Victorian Bibliography. 1922.

Northup, C. S. [Bibliography appended to G. De W. Sanders, Elizabeth Gaskell, New Haven, 1929. Very full; includes contributions to periodicals as well as reviews, books and articles on Mrs Gaskell.]

Whitfield, A. S. Mrs Gaskell: her Life and Work. 1929. [Bibliography appended.]

Parrish, M. L. Victorian Lady Novelists. First Editions in the Library at Dormy House, New Jersey. 1933.

(2) COLLECTED WORKS

The Novels and Tales of Mrs Gaskell. 7 vols. [1872–3], [1887–92], [1889–93], [1894]. [Illustrated (except frontispiece to vol. V) by G. du Maurier. The shorter stories were re-arranged for this edn, several being omitted.]

Pocket Edition of Mrs Gaskell's Works. 8 vols. [1897]. [Contents identical with the earlier collections.]

The Works of Mrs Gaskell. Ed. Sir A. W. Ward, 8 vols. 1906 (Knutsford edn). [Vol. I contains an elaborate Biographical Introduction.]

The Novels and Tales of Mrs Gaskell. Ed. C. K. Shorter, 11 vols. 1906–19. (World's Classics.) [The fullest edn.]

(3) NOVELS AND TALES

Life in Manchester. By Cotton Mather Mills, Esq. Manchester, 1848. [Includes: Libbie Marsh's Three Eras (rptd separately [1850] and tr. French, 1854); The Sexton's Hero; Christmas Storms and Sunshine (rptd 1850, 1855, with The Sexton's Hero). The stories were all originally pbd in

William Howitt's Journal of Literature and Popular Progress, I–III, 1847–8, and were rptd in Lizzie Leigh and Other Stories, 1855, and later collections.]

Mary Barton, a Tale of Manchester Life. 2 vols. 1848 (anon.); 2 vols. 1849 (bis); Leipzig, 1849; 1854 (5th edn; includes 2 lectures by W. Gaskell on the Lancashire dialect); 1861; New York, 1864; 1865; 1866; 1867; 1869, etc.; ed. T. Seccombe, 1912 (Everyman's Lib.). Tr. French, 1856; Hungarian, 1875; Spanish, 1879. [Dramatised by D. Boucicault as The Long Strike, 1867.]

The Moorland Cottage. By the Author of 'Mary Barton.' With Illustrations by Birket Foster. 1850; New York, 1868.

Ruth, A Novel. By the Author of 'Mary Barton.' 3 vols. 1853; 2 vols. Leipzig, 1853; 1855; Boston, [1855]; 2 vols. [1857]; 1861; 1867 (8th edn), etc.; tr. French, 1856.

Cranford. By the Author of 'Mary Barton,' 'Ruth,' &c. 1853 (bis); New York, 1853; 1855; 1858 (bis); 1864; 1867; 1870, etc.; ed. A. T., Lady Ritchie, 1891 (illustrated by Hugh Thomson); ed. E. V. Lucas, 1899. Tr. French, 1856; German, [1857?]; Hungarian, 1884. [First pbd in Household Words, 13 Dec. 1851–21 May 1853.]

Lizzie Leigh and Other Tales. 1854; 1855; Leipzig, 1855; 1865; 1871 (bis), etc.; tr. French, 1882. [Lizzie Leigh was first pbd in Household Words from 30 March 1850. Most of the other stories included had also appeared in Household Words, 1850–4. Lizzie Leigh was dramatised by W. R. Waldron in 1872.]

Hand and Heart and Bessy's Troubles at Home. By the Author of 'Mary Barton.' 1855. [Rptd from Lizzie Leigh.]

North and South. By the Author of 'Mary Barton,' 'Ruth,' 'Cranford,' &c. 2 vols. 1855 (bis); Leipzig, 1855; New York, 1855; 1859 (4th edn); New York, 1864; 1865; 1867; 1869; 1870, etc.; ed. E. A. Chadwick, 1914 (Everyman's Lib.); tr. French, 1859. [First pbd in Household Words, 2 Sept. 1854–27 Jan. 1855.]

My Lady Ludlow. A Novel. New York, 1858.

Round the Sofa. By the Author of 'Mary Barton,' 'Life of Charlotte Brontë,' &c. &c. 2 vols. 1859 (bis); 1861 (as My Lady Ludlow, and other tales included in 'Round the Sofa'); 1866, etc.; tr. French, 1860. [Introduction, links, and 6 stories, including My Lady Ludlow, all first pbd in Household Words or Harper's Mag. 1855–8.]

Right at Last, and Other Tales. By the Author of 'Mary Barton,' 'Life of Charlotte Brontë,' 'Round the Sofa,' &c. &c. 1860; New York, 1860; 1867. [Right at Last was first pbd in Household Words, 27 Nov. 1858, as The Sin of a Father. The other stories included were rptd from Household Words, All the Year Round, and Littell's Living Age.]

Lois the Witch and Other Tales. Leipzig, 1861. [Lois the Witch was rptd from Right at Last; some of the other stories included only appeared in the later English collections.]

A Dark Night's Work. 1863 (illustrated by G. du Maurier); Leipzig, 1863; New York, 1863; 1871, etc. Tr. German, 1865; French, 1879. [First pbd in All the Year Round, 24 Jan.–21 Feb. 1863.]

Sylvia's Lovers. 3 vols. 1863 (illustrated by G. du Maurier) (bis); 2 vols. Leipzig, 1863; New York, 1863; 1870, etc.; ed. T. Seccombe, 1910. Tr. German, 1863–4; French, 1865.

The Cage at Cranford. [First pbd in All the Year Round, Nov. 1863; only rptd in World's Classics edn, 1907.]

Cousin Phillis. A Tale. New York, 1864. [First pbd in Cornhill Mag. Nov. 1863–Feb. 1864.]

Cousin Phillis and Other Tales. 1865 (illustrated by G. du Maurier); Leipzig, 1867; 1870; ed. T. Seccombe, 1908, 1912 (Everyman's Lib.); tr. French, 1867.

The Grey Woman and Other Tales. 1865 (illustrated by G. du Maurier); 1871 (bis), etc. [The Grey Woman was first pbd in All the Year Round, 5, 12, 19 Jan. 1861; it had already been rptd in Lois the Witch and Other Tales, Leipzig, 1861.]

Wives and Daughters. An Every-Day Story. 2 vols. 1866 (illustrated by G. du Maurier); 2 vols. Leipzig, 1866; New York, 1866; 1869; 1870, etc.; ed. T. Seccombe, 1912. Tr. German, 1867; French, 1868. [First pbd in Cornhill Mag. Aug. 1864–Jan. 1866, the last number being completed by F. Greenwood.]

Two Fragments of Ghost Stories. [First pbd in Knutsford edn, vol. VII, 1906.]

(4) OTHER WRITINGS

Sketches among the Poor. No. 1. Blackwood's Mag. XLI, 1837. [A poem, by Mrs Gaskell and her husband; rptd Biographical Introduction to vol. I, Knutsford edn, and World's Classics edn, vol. X.]

Account of Clopton Hall, Warwickshire. [In William Howitt's Visits to Remarkable Places, 1840, pp. 130–46. Originally a letter to Howitt; rptd Knutsford edn, vol. I.]

Bran. Household Words, 22 Oct. 1853. [A poem; rptd World's Classics edn, vol. X.]

The Scholar's Story. Household Words, 25 Dec. 1853. [William Gaskell's trn of the Breton ballad of the Vicomte de la Ville-

marqué with an introduction by Mrs Gaskell (rptd World's Classics edn, vol. X).]

A Christmas Carol. Household Words, 27 Dec. 1856. [Rptd World's Classics edn, vol. X.]

The Life of Charlotte Brontë, Author of 'Jane Eyre,' 'Shirley,' 'Villette' &c. 2 vols. 1857 (3 edns, 3rd 'revised and corrected'); 2 vols. New York, 1857; 1858; 2 vols. New York, 1858; 2 vols. Leipzig, 1859; 1859; 1860; 1862; 1871, etc.; ed. C. K. Shorter, 1900; ed. T. Scott and B. W. Willett, 1901; ed. M. Sinclair, 1908 (Everyman's Lib.); tr. French, 1877.

Mabel Vaughan. By the Author of The Lamplighter [Maria S. Cummins]. 1857; Leipzig, 1857. [Edited with a preface by Mrs Gaskell.]

Garibaldi at Caprera. By Colonel [C. A.] Vecchj. Translated from the Italian [by L. and M. Ellis]. With Preface by Mrs Gaskell. Cambridge, 1862.

Letters on Charlotte Brontë. [1916] (priv. ptd).

'My Diary.' The Early Years of My Daughter Marianne. 1923 (priv. ptd). [Written 10 March 1835–28 Oct. 1838.]

Letters of Mrs Gaskell and Charles Eliot Norton (1855–1865). Ed. J. Whitehill, Oxford, 1932.

Letters. Ed. R. D. Waller, John Rylands Lib. Bulletin, Jan. 1935.

(5) BIOGRAPHY AND CRITICISM
(a) Books

Chadwick, E. A. Mrs Gaskell: Haunts, Homes and Stories. 1910.

Dullemen, J. J. van. Mrs Gaskell. Novelist and Biographer. Amsterdam, 1924.

Payne, G. A. Mrs Gaskell. A Brief Biography. Manchester, 1929.

Whitfield, A. S. Mrs Gaskell: her Life and Work. 1929.

Sanders, G. De W. Elizabeth Gaskell. New Haven, 1930.

Haldane, E. Mrs Gaskell and her Friends. 1930.

(b) Biographical Sources

Green, Henry. Knutsford: its Traditions and History. 1859.

Forster, J. The Life of Charles Dickens. 3 vols. 1872–4.

Dickens, C. Letters. Ed. G. Hogarth and M. E. Dickens, 3 vols. 1880–2.

—— Letters to Wilkie Collins. Ed. L. Hutton, 1892.

Howitt, Margaret. Mary Howitt. An Autobiography. 2 vols. 1889.

—— Stray Notes about Mrs Gaskell. Good Words, Sept. 1895.

Browning, E. B. Letters. Ed. Sir F. G. Kenyon, 2 vols. 1898.

Holland, M. S. Letters. Ed. B. Holland, 1898.

Shaen, M. J. Memorials of Two Sisters: Susanna and Catherine Winkworth. 1908.

Norton, C. E. Letters. Ed. S. Norton and M. A. de W. Howe, 1913.

Shorter, C. K. Charlotte Brontë and her Circle. 1914 (rev. edn).

(c) Critical Essays and Articles

Greg, W. R. Mary Barton. Edinburgh Rev. April 1849. [Another review of Mary Barton (from Edinburgh Rev. July 1857) is rptd in Mistaken Aims, 1876.]

Landor, W. S. Last Fruit off an Old Tree. 1853. [Epistle CCLXVIII, To the Author of Mary Barton.]

Montégut, E. Revue des Deux Mondes, 1853–5. [Various reviews of Mrs Gaskell; rptd in Écrivains modernes de l'Angleterre, ser. 2, Paris, 1889.]

Dicey, E. Mrs Gaskell. Nation (New York), 7 Dec. 1865.

Milnes, R. M. (Baron Houghton). Mrs Gaskell. Pall Mall Gazette, 14 Nov. 1865.

S[mith], G. B. Mrs Gaskell and her Novels. Cornhill Mag. XXIX, 1874.

Minto, W. Mrs Gaskell's Novels. Fortnightly Rev. XXX, 1878.

'Lyall, Edna' (A. E. Bayly). Mrs Gaskell. [In Women Novelists of Queen Victoria's Reign, 1897.]

Cazamian, L. Le Roman social en Angleterre (1830–50). Paris, 1904, pp. 380 435.

Ritchie, A. T., Lady. The Author of Cranford. Cornhill Mag. XCIV, 1906. [Rptd in Blackstick Papers, 1908.]

More, P. E. Shelburne Essays. Ser. 5, New York, 1908.

Coleridge, M. E. Gathered Leaves. 1910.

Herford, C. H. Mrs Gaskell. Manchester Guardian, 29 Sept. 1910.

'Melville, Lewis.' The Centenary of Mrs Gaskell. Nineteenth Century, LXVIII, 1910.

Seccombe, T. Elizabeth Cleghorn Gaskell. Bookman, XXXVIII, 1910.

Ward, Sir A. W. Disraeli, Charles Kingsley, Mrs Gaskell, 'George Eliot.' CHEL. XIII, 1916.

Bald, M. A. Women-Writers of the Nineteenth Century. 1923.

Quiller-Couch, Sir A. T. Charles Dickens and Other Victorians. Cambridge, 1925.

Cecil, Lord D. Early Victorian Novelists. 1934.

Hopkins, A. B. Mrs Gaskell in France, 1849–1890. PMLA. LIII, 1938.

A. S. W.

WILLIAM MAKEPEACE THACKERAY
(1811–1863)

(1) BIBLIOGRAPHIES

Shepherd, R. H. The Bibliography of Thackeray: the Published Writings in Prose and Verse and the Sketches and Drawings from 1829–1880. 1881. [Also appended, in a rev. and enlarged form, to Sultan Stork and Other Stories, 1887.]

Johnson, C. P. Hints to Collectors of Original Editions of the Works of William Makepeace Thackeray. 1885.

—— The Earlier Writings of William Makepeace Thackeray. 1888.

Anderson, J. P. [Bibliography appended to H. C. Merivale and Sir F. T. Marzials, Life of William Makepeace Thackeray, 1891.]

Spielmann, M. H. Thackeray's hitherto Unidentified Contributions to Punch. With a Complete Bibliography from 1845 to 1848. 1899.

Dickson, F. S. Bibliography of Thackeray in the United States. [In J. G. Wilson's Thackeray in the United States, vol. II, 1904.]

'Melville, Lewis.' William Makepeace Thackeray. 2 vols. 1910. [Bibliography, vol. II, pp. 143–376. Very thorough; supersedes and incorporates the bibliography in The Life of William Makepeace Thackeray, 2 vols. 1899.]

Catalogue of an Exhibition commemorating the Hundredth Anniversary of the Birth of William Makepeace Thackeray. Grolier Club, 1912.

Van Duzer, H. S. A Thackeray Library. A Complete Thackeray Bibliography. New York, 1919.

(2) COLLECTED WORKS

Thackeray's Works. 22 vols. 1867–9 (Library edn). [2 supplementary vols. added 1885–6, consisting mainly of miscellaneous articles rptd from Fraser's Mag. and Punch.]

Thackeray's Works. 24 vols. 1877–9 (cheaper illustrated edn).

Thackeray's Works. 26 vols. 1878–86 (De Luxe edn). | With memoir by Sir L. Stephen.]

Thackeray's Works. 27 vols. 1887–93 (Pocket edn).

Thackeray's Works. Ed. H. E. Scudder, 22 vols. Boston, 1889. [Considerably fuller than the English edns.]

Thackeray's Works. With Biographical Introductions by Anne Thackeray Ritchie. 13 vols. 1898–9 (Biographical edn); 26 vols. 1910–1 (enlarged as Centenary Biographical edn). [Includes Sir L. Stephen's memoir.]

Thackeray's Works. 14 vols. 1899–1900 (New Century Lib.).

Thackeray's Prose Works. Ed. W. Jerrold, 30 vols. 1901–3.
Thackeray's Works. Ed. (from vol. VIII) 'Lewis Melville,' 20 vols. 1901–7, 1911. [Rptd from first edns and including much new matter.]
Thackeray's Works. 13 vols. 1903 (London edn). [Vol. XIII is 'Lewis Melville's' Life of Thackeray (first pbd 2 vols. 1899). Vols. I–XII have topographical introductions by J. McVicar.]
Thackeray's Works. 17 vols. 1908 (Oxford edn). [Critical introductions to each vol. by G. Saintsbury; includes much matter not to be found in earlier collected edns.]

(3) Novels

The Luck of Barry Lyndon. A Romance of the Last Century, by Fitz-Boodle. Fraser's Mag. Jan.–Dec. 1844 (12 nos.); 2 vols. New York, 1852; 1856 (rev. as The Memoirs of Barry Lyndon, Esq.). [Also rptd as Memoirs of Barry Lyndon in Miscellanies, vol. III, 1856.]
Vanity Fair: Pen and Pencil Sketches of English Society. 20 monthly nos. Jan. 1847–July 1848; 1848 (bis) (as Vanity Fair, A Novel without a Hero); 2 pts, New York, 1848; 3 vols. Leipzig, 1849; 1853 (rev. edn); 1863 (2nd rev. edn); ed. J. E. Wells, 2 vols. New York, 1928; ed. P. E. More, 2 vols. Garden City, 1935.
The History of Pendennis. His Fortunes and Misfortunes, His Friends and His Greatest Enemy. 24 monthly nos. Nov. 1848–Dec. 1850; 2 vols. 1849–50; 3 vols. Leipzig, 1849–50; 2 vols. 1850; 2 vols. New York, 1850; 1856; 1863 (rev. edn).
The History of Henry Esmond, Esq. A Colonel in the Service of her Majesty Q. Anne. Written by Himself. 3 vols. 1852; 2 vols. Leipzig, 1852; New York, 1852; 1858 (rev. edn); ed. G. Saintsbury, 1909.
The Newcomes. Memoirs of a Most Respectable Family. Edited by Arthur Pendennis, Esqre. 24 monthly nos. Oct. 1853–Aug. 1855; Harper's Mag. Nov. 1853–Oct. 1855; 2 vols. 1854–5; 4 vols. Leipzig, 1854–5; 2 vols. New York, 1855; 1860; 1863 (final rev. edn).
The Virginians. A Tale of the Last Century. 24 monthly nos. Nov. 1857–Sept. 1859; Harper's Monthly Mag. Dec. 1857–Nov. 1859; 2 vols. 1858–9; 12 vols. Leipzig, 1858–9; New York, 1859; 1863 (rev.); ed. G. Saintsbury and J. L. Robertson, 1911.
Lovel the Widower. Cornhill Mag. Jan.–June 1860; Harper's Mag. Feb.–July 1860; 1861 (rev.).
The Adventures of Philip on his Way Through the World, Shewing who Robbed Him, who Helped Him, and who Passed Him By.

Cornhill Mag. Jan. 1861–Aug. 1862 (20 nos.); Harper's Mag. Feb. 1861–Sept. 1862; 3 vols. 1862; New York, 1862; 2 vols. Leipzig, 1862; Columbia, 1864.
Denis Duval. Cornhill Mag. March–June 1864 (4 nos.); Harper's Monthly Mag. April, May, July, Aug. 1864; New York, 1864; 1867; Leipzig, 1867.

(4) Miscellanies

Comic Tales and Sketches. Edited and Illustrated by Mr Michael Angelo Titmarsh, Author of the 'Paris Sketch Book,' etc. 2 vols. 1841 (re-issued 1848). [Vol. I, The Yellowplush Correspondence; vol. II, Some Passages in the Life of Major Gahagan, The Professor, The Bedford Row Conspiracy, Stubbs's Calendar.]
Miscellanies: Prose and Verse. Vol. I, Leipzig, 1849. [The Great Hoggarty Diamond; The Book of Snobs.]
Miscellanies: Prose and Verse. Vol. II, Leipzig, 1851. [The Kickleburys Abroad; A Legend of the Rhine; Rebecca and Rowena; The Second Funeral of Napoleon; The Chronicle of the Drum.]
The Confessions of Fitz-Boodle; and Some Passages in the Life of Major Gahagan. New York, 1852.
A Shabby Genteel Story, and Other Tales. New York, 1852, 1853 (enlarged). [Includes also: The Professor, The Bedford Row Conspiracy, A Little Dinner at Timmins's (incomplete in 1852 edn).]
Jeames's Diary, A Legend of the Rhine, and Rowena and Rebecca. New York, 1853.
Mr Brown's Letters to a Young Man about Town; with the Proser, and other Papers. New York, 1853. [Rptd from Punch, 1845–50.]
Punch's Prize Novelists, The Fat Contributor, and Travels in London. New York, 1853. [Rptd from Punch, 1844–50, except for Going to See a Man Hanged (in Travels in London) which is from Fraser's Mag. XXII, 1840.]
Miscellanies: Prose and Verse. Vol. I, 1855; 1861 (re-issued 1865). [The Book of Snobs, The Fatal Boots (i.e. Stubbs's Calendar), Cox's Diary (i.e. Barber Cox), The Tremendous Adventures of Major Gahagan (i.e. Some Passages in the Life of Major Gahagan), Ballads.]
The Fatal Boots, and Cox's Diary. 1855.
Miscellanies: Prose and Verse. Vol. II, 1856; 1861 (re-issued 1865). [The Memoirs of Mr Yellowplush, Diary of C. Jeames de la Pluche, Esq., Novels by Eminent Hands, Sketches and Travels in London (combining Mr Brown's Letters to a Young Man with Travels in London), Character Sketches.]

Memoirs of Mr C. J. Yellowplush and The Diary of C. Jeames de la Pluche, Esq. 1856.

Novels by Eminent Hands, and Character Sketches. 1856. [Character Sketches included Captain Rook and Mr Pigeon (rptd from Corsair, 28 Sept. 1839), The Fashionable Authoress (rptd from Heads of the People, 1841), The Artist (*ibid.*).]

Miscellanies, Prose and Verse. Vol. III, 1856; 1861 (re-issued 1865). [Memoirs of Barry Lyndon, A Legend of the Rhine, Rebecca and Rowena, A Little Dinner at Timmins's, The Bedford Row conspiracy.]

Burlesques. A Legend of the Rhine; Rebecca and Rowena. 1856.

A Little Dinner at Timmins's and The Bedford-Row Conspiracy. 1856.

Miscellanies: Prose and Verse. Vols. III–VIII, Leipzig, 1856–7. [Contents of London Miscellanies but excluding works already rptd in Leipzig Miscellanies.]

Miscellanies: Prose and Verse. Vol. IV, 1857; 1861 (re-issued 1865). [The Fitz-Boodle Papers, Men's Wives, A Shabby Genteel Story, The History of Samuel Titmarsh and the Great Hoggarty Diamond.]

The Fitz-Boodle Papers: and Men's Wives. 1857.

Christmas Books. 1857. [Mrs Perkins's Ball, Our Street, and Dr Birch.]

Miscellanies. 6 vols. New York, 1864. [Paris Sketch Book, Yellowplush Papers, Book of Snobs, Men's Wives, Barry Lyndon, A Shabby Genteel Story and Other Tales, Confessions of Fitz-Boodle, Major Gahagan, Jeames's Diary, Legend of the Rhine, Rowena and Rebecca, Mr Brown's Letters and Other Papers, Punch's Prize Novelists, etc. All rptd from the New York edns of 1852–3.]

Early and Late Papers, hitherto Uncollected. Ed. J. T. Fields, Boston, 1867. [Rptd from Fraser's Mag., Quarterly Rev., Cornhill Mag., etc. 1841–63.]

Miscellanies. v. Catherine, Titmarsh among Pictures and Books, Fraser Miscellanies, Christmas Books, Ballads, etc. Boston, 1870.

The Student's Quarter, or, Paris Five and Thirty Years Since. 1870. [Articles originally contributed to Corsair (New York) in 1839 and rptd, except 'More Aspects of Paris Life,' in rev. form in The Paris Sketch Book, 1840.]

The Orphan of Pimlico, and Other Sketches, Fragments, and Drawings. 1876. [Notes by I. A. Thackeray.]

Sultan Stork, and other Stories and Sketches (1829–44), now first collected [by R. H. Shepherd]. 1887. [Contributions to The Snob, 1829; Elizabeth Brownrigge, Fraser's Mag. Aug., Sept. 1829 (not by Thackeray?);

contributions to The National Standard, 1833–4; review of Carlyle's French Revolution, Times, 3 Aug. 1837; Dickens in France, Fraser's Mag. March 1842, etc.]

Loose Sketches, An Eastern Adventure, etc. 1894. [Loose Sketches by M. A. Titmarsh, rptd from Britannia, 1 May–5 July 1841; An Eastern Adventure of the Fat Contributor, from Punch's Pocket-Book, 1847; preface to Sketches after English Landscape Painters by L. Marvy, 1850.]

The Hitherto Unidentified Contributions of W. M. Thackeray to Punch, with a Complete Authoritative Bibliography from 1845 to 1848, by M. H. Spielmann. 1899.

Mr Thackeray's Writings in The National Standard and The Constitutional. 1899.

Stray Papers, being Stories, Reviews, Verses, and Sketches (1829–1851). Ed. 'Lewis Melville,' 1901.

W. M. Thackeray, The New Sketch Book, being Essays now first collected from The Foreign Quarterly Review. Ed. R. S. Garnett, 1906.

(5) MINOR FICTION AND OTHER WRITINGS

The Professor. A Tale. Bentley's Misc. Sept. 1837. [Rptd in Comic Tales and Sketches, vol. II, 1841, as by Goliah Gahagan, and with A Shabby Genteel Story, etc., New York, 1852, 1853.]

The Yellowplush Correspondence. Fraser's Mag. Nov. 1837–Aug. 1838; Philadelphia, 1838 (incomplete); New York, 1852 (as The Yellowplush Papers). [Rptd with omissions and addns in Comic Tales and Sketches, vol. I, 1841, and as Memoirs of Mr C. J. Yellowplush both in Miscellanies, vol. II, 1856, and separately with The Diary of C. Jeames de la Pluche, Esqr. 1856.]

Some Passages in the Life of Major Gahagan. New Monthly Mag. Feb. 1838–Feb. 1839 (title changed first to Historical Recollections. By Major Gahagan, and then to Major Gahagan's Historical Reminiscences); [Philadelphia, 1839?] (as Reminiscences of Major Gahagan). [Rptd as Some Passages in the Life of Major Gahagan both in Comic Tales and Sketches, vol. II, 1841, and with The Confessions of Fitz-Boodle, New York, 1852, and as The Tremendous Adventures of Major Gahagan in Miscellanies, vol. I, 1855.]

Catherine, a Story, by Ikey Solomons, Esq., junior. Fraser's Mag. May 1839–Feb. 1840. [Rptd in Thackeray's Works, vol. XXII, 1869 (Library edn), and later collections.]

The Loving Ballad of Lord Bateman. With eleven Plates by George Cruikshank. 1839. [See also Harper's Mag. Dec. 1892, pp. 124–9, for additional illustrations by Thackeray and comment by A. T., Lady Ritchie.]

Stubbs's Calendar; or, the Fatal Boots. Cruikshank's Comic Annual, 1839. [Rptd in Comic Tales and Sketches, vol. II, 1841, and separately New York, 1850, and as The Fatal Boots both in Miscellanies, vol. I, 1854, and with Cox's Diary, 1855.]

The Bedford Row Conspiracy. New Monthly Mag. Jan.–April 1840. [Rptd with A Shabby Genteel Story, etc. New York, 1852, 1853, in Comic Tales and Sketches, vol. II, 1841, in Miscellanies, vol. III, 1856, and with A Little Dinner at Timmins's, 1856.]

The Paris Sketch Book: by Mr Titmarsh. With numerous Designs by the Author on copper and wood. 2 vols. 1840; 2 vols. New York, 1852. [Various sketches already ptd in Corsair (New York) and elsewhere and much new matter.]

A Shabby Genteel Story. Fraser's Mag. June–Oct. 1840. [Rptd with The Professor, etc. New York, 1852, 1853, separately 1857, and in Miscellanies, vol. IV, 1857.]

An Essay on the Genius of George Cruikshank. 1840; éd. W. E. Church, 1884. [Rptd from Westminster Rev. June 1840.]

Barber Cox and the Cutting of His Comb. With twelve Illustrations by George Cruikshank. Cruikshank's Comic Annual, 1840. [Rptd as Cox's Diary both in Miscellanies, vol. I, 1855, and with The Fatal Boots, 1855.]

The History of Samuel Titmarsh and the Great Hoggarty Diamond. Fraser's Mag. Sept.–Dec. 1841; New York, 1848 (as The Great Hoggarty Diamond); 1849 (under original title). [Rptd in Miscellanies, vol. IV, 1857.]

The Second Funeral of Napoleon: in Three Letters to Miss Smith, of London. And the Chronicle of the Drum. By Mr M. A. Titmarsh. 1841. [The Chronicle of the Drum is rptd with the Ballads in Miscellanies, vol. I, 1855, and from the original MS in Cornhill Mag. XIII, 1866.]

Sultan Stork; Being the One Thousand and Second Night. By Major G. O'Gahagan, H.E.I.C.S. Ainsworth's Mag. Feb., May 1842. [Rptd by R. H. Shepherd with other stories and sketches, 1887, and in Thackeray's Works, ed. H. E. Scudder, vol. XX, Boston, 1889.]

[The Fitz-Boodle Papers.] Fraser's Mag. June 1842–Feb. 1843. [Rptd as The Confessions of Fitz-Boodle, New York, 1852 (with Some Passages in the Life of Major Gahagan). First 2 instalments rptd as The Fitz-Boodle Papers both in Miscellanies, vol. IV, 1857, and with Men's Wives, 1857. Remainder rptd in Thackeray's Works, vols. XXII, XXIII, 1869–85 (Library edn).]

Miss Tickletoby's Lectures on English History. Punch, 2 July–1 Oct. 1842. [Rptd for the first time in Thackeray's Works, vol. XXIV, 1885 (Library edn).]

[Men's Wives.] Confessions of George Fitz-Boodle; Men's Wives. Fraser's Mag. March–Nov. 1843; New York, 1852. [Rptd, without The —'s Wife, both in Miscellanies, vol. IV, 1857, and with The Fitz-Boodle Papers, 1857.]

The Irish Sketch-Book. By Mr M. A. Titmarsh. With numerous Engravings on wood, drawn by the Author. 2 vols. 1843 (dedication signed W. M. Thackeray); New York, [1844]; 2 vols. 1845; 1857.

Bluebeard's Ghost. By M. A. Titmarsh. Fraser's Mag. Oct. 1843. [Rptd in Early and Late Papers, Boston, 1867 and in Thackeray's Works, vol. XXIII, 1885 (Library edn).]

The History of the Next French Revolution. From a Forthcoming History of Europe. Punch, 24 Feb.–20 April 1844.

Wanderings of our Fat Contributor. Punch, 3 Aug. 1844. Travelling Notes. By our Fat Contributor. Punch, 10 Aug.–14 Dec. 1844. [Rptd with other pieces from Punch, in Punch's Prize Novelists, etc. New York, 1853.]

A Legend of the Rhine. By Michael Angelo Titmarsh. George Cruikshank's Table-Book, June–Dec. 1845. [Rptd with Jeames's Diary and Rebecca and Rowena, New York, 1853, in Miscellanies, vol. III, 1856, and with Rebecca and Rowena, 1856.]

Jeames's Diary. Punch, 8 Nov. 1845–7 Feb. 1846; New York, 1846 (as Jeames's Diary; or, Sudden Wealth. By Michael Angelo Titmarsh, Esq.). [Rptd, with A Legend of the Rhine and Rebecca and Rowena, New York, 1853, and as The Diary of C. Jeames de la Pluche, Esq. both in Miscellanies, vol. II, 1856, and with The Memoirs of Mr C. J. Yellowplush, 1856. 3 additional papers from Punch, 1845–6, first rptd in Thackeray's Works (Library edn).]

Notes of a Journey from Cornhill to Grand Cairo. By Way of Lisbon, Athens, Constantinople, and Jerusalem: Performed in the Steamers of the Peninsula and Oriental Company. By Mr M. A. Titmarsh. 1846 (bis, 2nd edn adds Postscript signed W. M. T.); New York, 1846, 1852.

The Snobs of England, by one of themselves. Punch, 28 Feb. 1846–27 Feb. 1847; 1848 (as The Book of Snobs, omitting chs. xvii–xxiii); New York, 1852 (complete); 1855 (incomplete); ed. G. K. Chesterton, 1911. [Also rptd in Miscellanies, vol. I, 1855. The omitted chs. were restored in Thackeray's Works, vol. XXIII, 1885 (Library edn).]

Punch's Prize Novelists. Punch, 3 April–9 Oct. 1847. [Rptd with The Fat Contributor and Travels in London, New York, 1853, in Miscellanies, vol. ii, 1856, and with Character Sketches, 1856, under the title Novels by Eminent Hands.]

Travels in London. Punch, 20 Nov. 1847–25 March 1848 (signed 'Spec.'). [Rptd, with other pieces from Punch, New York, 1853, and as Sketches and Travels in London both in Miscellanies, vol. ii, 1856 and separately 1856.]

Mrs Perkins's Ball. By M. A. Titmarsh. 1847 (3 edns); rptd facs. 1898. [Rptd in Christmas Books, 1857.]

A Little Dinner at Timmins's. Punch, 27 May–29 July 1848. [Rptd with A Shabby Genteel Story, etc. New York, 1852 (incomplete) and 1853 (complete); also rptd in Miscellanies, vol. iii, 1856, and with The Bedford Row Conspiracy, 1856.]

'Our Street,' By Mr M. A. Titmarsh. 1848 (bis). [Rptd in Christmas Books, 1857.]

Mr Brown's Letters to a Young Man About Town. Punch, 31 March–18 Aug. 1849. [Rptd with other pieces from Punch, New York, 1853.]

Doctor Birch and his Young Friends. By Mr M. A. Titmarsh. 1849; New York, 1853. [Rptd in Christmas Books, 1857.]

An Interesting Event. By M. A. Titmarsh. 1849. [A forgery? See J. Carter and G. Pollard, An Enquiry into the Nature of Certain Nineteenth Century Pamphlets, 1934. First ptd in The Keepsake, 1849.]

The Proser. Essays and Discourses by Dr Solomon Pacifico. Punch, 20 April–3 Aug. 1850. [3 papers rptd with Mr Brown's Letters, etc. New York, 1853.]

Rebecca and Rowena. A Romance upon Romance. By Mr M. A. Titmarsh. 1850; Paris, 1850. [A revision of Proposals for a Continuation of 'Ivanhoe,' Fraser's Mag. Aug., Sept. 1846. Rptd with Jeames's Diary and A Legend of the Rhine, New York, 1853, in Miscellanies, vol. iii, 1856, and in Burlesques, 1856.]

Sketches after English Landscape Painters. By L. Marvy. With Short Notices by W. M. Thackeray. 1850.

The Kickleburys on the Rhine. By Mr M. A. Titmarsh. 1850; 1851 (preface added, 'being an Essay on Thunder and Small Beer'); Frankfort, 1851; New York, 1851; 1866.

The English Humourists of the Eighteenth Century. A Series of Lectures Delivered in England, Scotland, and the United States of America. 1853; Leipzig, 1853; New York, 1853; 1858; ed. W. L. Phelps, 1913. [Notes by George Hodder.]

Ballads. 1855; Boston, 1856; 1866.

The Rose and the Ring: or, the History of Prince Giglio and Prince Bulbo. A fire-side Pantomime for Great and Small Children. By Mr M. A. Titmarsh. 1855; New York, 1855.

The Four Georges: Sketches of Manners, Morals, Court and Town Life. New York, 1860 (bis); 1861; Leipzig, 1861; ed. G. Meredith and T. Bayne, 1903. [First pbd in Cornhill Mag. July–Oct. 1860, Harper's Mag. Aug.–Nov. 1860, and Littell's Living Age, 11 Aug.–10 Nov. 1860.]

A Leaf out of a Sketch-Book. 1861 (priv. ptd). [A forgery? See J. Carter and G. Pollard, An Enquiry into the Nature of Certain Nineteenth Century Pamphlets, 1934. First pbd in The Victoria Regia, ed. A. A. Procter, 1861.]

Roundabout Papers. 1863; New York, 1863; ed. (from MSS) J. E. Wells, New York, 1925. [First pbd in Cornhill Mag. Jan. 1860–Feb. 1863 (28 nos.). The early edns are incomplete.]

(6) LETTERS

A Collection of Letters of William Makepeace Thackeray, 1847–55. Ed. J. O. Brookfield, 1887.

Thackeray's Letters to an American Family. With an Introduction by Lucy W. Baxter. 1904.

Letters of Dr John Brown, M.D. of Edinburgh. With Letters from Ruskin, Thackeray and Others. 1907.

Some Family Letters of W. M. Thackeray, together with Recollections by his Kinswoman B. W. Cornish. 1911.

Unpublished Letters. Ed. C. K. Shorter, 1916 (priv. ptd).

W. M. Thackeray and Edward FitzGerald, a Literary Friendship. Unpublished Letters and Verses by W. M. Thackeray. With an Introduction by Lady Ritchie. Ed. C. K. Shorter, 1916 (priv. ptd).

Letters of Anne Thackeray Ritchie. With Forty-two Additional Letters from her Father, William Makepeace Thackeray. Ed. H. T. Ritchie, 1924.

(7) BIOGRAPHY AND CRITICISM
(a) Books

Yates, E. Mr Thackeray, Mr Yates, and the Garrick Club. The Correspondence and Facts. 1859 (priv. ptd); 1895.

Hannay, J. A Brief Memoir of the Late Mr Thackeray. 1864.
—— Studies on Thackeray. 1869.

Reed, W. B. Haud Immemor. A Few Personal Recollections of Mr Thackeray in Philadelphia. 1864. [With extracts from correspondence.]

'Taylor, Theodore' (J. C. Hotten or J. Grego). Thackeray: the Humourist and the Man of Letters. 1864; New York, 1864 (enlarged).

Grego, J. Thackerayana, Notes and Anecdotes illustrated by nearly Six Hundred Sketches by William Makepeace Thackeray. 1875; 1901.

Stoddard, R. H. Anecdote Biographies of Thackeray and Dickens. New York, 1875.

Etchings by the late William Makepeace Thackeray, while at Cambridge, illustrative of University Life. 1878.

Trollope, A. Thackeray. 1879. (English Men of Letters ser.)

Johnson, C. P. The Early Writings of William Makepeace Thackeray. 1888.

Merivale, H. C. and Marzials, Sir F. T. Life of W. M. Thackeray. 1891.

Crowe, Sir E. With Thackeray in America. 1893.

—— Thackeray's Haunts and Homes. 1897.

Jack, A. A. Thackeray: a Study. 1895.

Hunter, Sir W. W. The Thackerays in India. 1897.

'Melville, Lewis.' The Life of William Makepeace Thackeray. 2 vols. 1899; 1927.

—— The Thackeray Country. 1905.

—— William Makepeace Thackeray. A Biography, including hitherto Uncollected Letters and Speeches and a Bibliography of 1300 Items. 2 vols. 1910. [A list of Thackeray speeches, portraits, MSS, authorities, etc. in vol. II, pp. 63–142, and a full bibliography, pp. 143–376.]

—— Some Aspects of Thackeray. 1911.

Whibley, C. William Makepeace Thackeray. 1903.

Wilson, J. G. Thackeray in the United States, 1852–3, 1855–6. 2 vols. 1904.

Werner, R. M. Der Einfluss der deutschen Literatur auf W. M. Thackeray. Teplitz-Schönau, 1907.

Jïva-Ratnam, M. Thackeray's Henry Esmond. A Criticism. 1910.

Romilly, A. J. Thackeray Studies. 1912.

Vogel, G. Thackeray als historischer Romanschriftsteller. Leipzig, 1920.

Chancellor, E. B. The London of Thackeray. 1923.

Steuerwald, C. Die Londoner Vulgärsprache in Thackeray's 'Yellowplush Papers.' Leipzig, 1930.

Saintsbury, G. A Consideration of Thackeray. Oxford, 1931. [Introductions rptd from Oxford edn of Thackeray's Works.]

Bancke, L. Die Erzählkunst in Thackerays 'Vanity Fair.' Hamburg, 1932.

Elwin, M. Thackeray: a Personality. 1932.

Las Vergnas, R. W. M. Thackeray: l'Homme, le Penseur, le Romancier. Paris, 1932.

Gulliver, H. S. Thackeray's Literary Apprenticeship; a Study of the Early Newspaper and Magazine Work. Valdosta, 1934 (priv. ptd).

Wethered, H. N. The Art of Thackeray. 1938.

(b) Essays, Pamphlets and Chapters of Books

[For biographies and autobiographies with passing references to Thackeray see 'Lewis Melville,' William Makepeace Thackeray, vol. II, 1910, pp. 133–42, and DNB.]

Gilfillan, G. Galleries of Literary Portraits. Vol. II, Edinburgh, 1856.

Senior, N. W. Essays on Fiction. 1864.

Taine, H. A. Notes on England. Tr. Eng. 1872.

Smith, G. B. Poets and Novelists. 1875.

Pryme, J. T. and Bayne, A. Memorials of the Thackeray Family. 1879.

Watt, J. C. Great Novelists: Scott, Thackeray, Dickens, Lytton. [1885.]

FitzGerald, Edward. Letters. Ed. W. A. Wright, vol. I, 1889.

Lang, A. Lost Leaders. 1889.

Ritchie, A. T., Lady. Chapters from Some Memoirs. 1894.

—— Blackstick Papers. 1908.

Harrison, Frederic. Studies in Early Victorian Literature. 1895.

Spielmann, M. H. The History of Punch. 1895.

Saintsbury, G. Corrected Impressions. 1895; 1898 (rev. edn).

Brownell, W. C. Victorian Prose Masters. New York, 1901.

Brookfield, C. and F. Mrs Brookfield and her Circle. 2 vols. 1905.

Carr, J. C. Some Eminent Victorians. 1908.

Thompson, A. H. Thackeray. CHEL. vol. XIII, 1916.

Bailey, J. Thackeray and the English Novel. [In The Continuity of Letters, Oxford, 1923.]

Elton, O. Dickens and Thackeray. 1924. [Rptd, with addns, from A Survey of English Literature, 1830–1880, 2 vols. 1920.]

Quiller-Couch, Sir A. T. Charles Dickens and Other Victorians. Cambridge, 1925.

Forsythe, R. S. A Noble Rake. The Life of Charles, Lord Mohun. Cambridge, U.S.A. 1928. [For Esmond.]

Swinnerton, F. William Makepeace Thackeray. [In Great Victorians, ed. H. J. and H. Massingham, 1932.]

Ellis, G. U. Thackeray. 1933.

Cecil, Lord D. Early Victorian Novelists. 1934.

Baker, E. A. The History of the English Novel. Vol. VII, 1936.

(c) Articles in Periodicals

[Rigby, E. (later Lady Eastlake).] Quarterly Rev. Dec. 1848. [Review of Vanity Fair and Jane Eyre. Rptd in Famous Reviews, ed. R. B. Johnson, 1914.]

Oxford and Cambridge Mag. I, 1856, pp. 323–35. [Charlotte Brontë and Thackeray.]

Brown, John. Thackeray. North British Rev. XL, 1864. [Rptd as Thackeray's Death in Horae Subsecivae, vol. III, 1882.]

Dickens, C. In Memoriam W. M. T. Cornhill Mag. Feb. 1864.

Taylor, Bayard. William Makepeace Thackeray. Atlantic Monthly, XIII, 1864.

Boyes, J. F. A Memorial of Thackeray's Schooldays. Cornhill Mag. XI, 1865.

Bedingford, R. Recollections of Thackeray. Cassell's Mag. II, 1870.

Lunt, G. Recollections of Thackeray. Harper's Mag. LIV, 1877.

D., D. Some Few Thackerayana. National Rev. XIII, 1889.

Ritchie, A. T., Lady. The Boyhood of Thackeray. St Nicholas Mag. XVII, 1889.

—— The First Number of the Cornhill. Cornhill Mag. July 1896.

Kitton, F. G. The Portraits of Thackeray. Mag. of Art, XIV, 1891.

Davies, G. S. Thackeray as Carthusian. Grey Friar, II, 1892.

Irvine, J. W. A Study for Colonel Newcome. Nineteenth Century, XXXIV, 1893.

Thackeray, F. St J. Reminiscences of William Makepeace Thackeray. Temple Bar, July 1893.

Vulpius, W. Thackeray in Weimar. Century Mag. LIII, 1897.

Smith, G. M. Our Birth and Parentage. Cornhill Mag. Jan. 1901. [Thackeray and Cornhill Mag.]

Elwin, W. Thackeray's Boyhood. Thackeray at Cambridge. Thackeray in Search of a Profession. Monthly Rev. June, Sept., Oct. 1904.

Thackeray as a Sub-Editor. GM. CCCI, 1906.

Ely, C. B. The Psychology of Becky Sharp. MLN. XXXV, 1920.

Jerrold, W. Cynic or Sentimentalist? New World, May 1921.

Matthews, B. Thackeray and the Theatre. Scribner's Mag. LXIX, 1921.

Gibson, E. C. S. Thackeray and Charterhouse. Cornhill Mag. June 1922.

Sandwith, H. Becky Sharp and Emma Bovary. Nineteenth Century, Jan. 1922.

Sutcliffe, E. G. Thackeray's Romanticism. South Atlantic Quart. XXI, 1922.

Knaphe, W. Die Geschichte der Ermordung der Karoline von Braunschweig-Wolfenbüttel. Ang. Bbl. XXXIV, 1923. [On Barry Lyndon.]

Buttler, P. Die Ausländer in den Romanen Thackerays. Giessener Beiträge, II, 1924.

Patterson, J. M. Thackeray's Diary. Bookman (New York), Dec. 1924.

Schild, B. Die Personencharakterisierung bei Thackeray. Giessener Beiträge, II, 1924.

Weill, M. Thackeray et la Société anglaise du XVIIIe Siècle. Revue anglo-américaine, Oct. 1924.

'Melville, Lewis.' On an Unreprinted Article by Thackeray. New Criterion, Oct. 1926.

Hubbell, J. B. Thackeray and Virginia. Virginia Quart. III, 1927.

Knislinaswami, P. R. Some Thackeray Originals. I. Who was Colonel Newcome? II. James Binnie. III. Rummun Loll. IV. The Rev. Charles Honeyman. Cornhill Mag. Dec. 1927–March 1928.

Minchin, H. C. Thackeray in the Temple. Cornhill Mag. Sept. 1928.

Hirst, W. A. The Chronology in Thackeray's Novels. Cornhill Mag. Nov. 1929.

Wells, C. W. Thackeray and the Victorian Compromise. [In Essays in Criticism by Members of the Department of English (University of California), Berkeley, 1929.]

Enzinger, P. Thackeray, Critic of Literature. North Dakota University Quart. Journ. XX, XXI, 1930–1.

Simpson, V. A. Thackeray's Last Heroine. Cornhill Mag. May 1930.

Whitton, F. E. Thackeray and the Army. Nineteenth Century, Nov. 1931.

Digeon, A. Sur un Chapitre des Newcomes. Revue anglo-américaine, June 1932.

Forsythe, R. S. Thackeray, Critic of Literature. North Dakota University Quart. Journ. XXII, 1932.

Smith, S. N. In Defence of Thackeray. Nineteenth Century, July 1933.

Stevenson, A. L. Vanity Fair and Lady Morgan. PMLA. XLVIII, 1933.

Wells, J. E. On a Sheet of Thackeray Manuscript. Cornhill Mag. LXXIV, 1933.

Thackeray, C. B. Thackeray and the Melancholy Humorist: the Gentle Art of 'Debunking.' Cornhill Mag. CLII, 1935.

A. H. T., rev. A. K. H. J.

CHARLES DICKENS (1812–1870)

(1) BIBLIOGRAPHIES AND CATALOGUES

(a) Manuscripts and Relics

[Most of the MSS of Dickens's works are in the Forster Collection, at the Victoria and Albert Museum, London; a small quantity, including a few leaves of Pickwick, in the BM.; the MS of Great Expectations in the Wisbech Museum; and a few in private hands.

The Forster Collection includes corrected proof-sheets and similar matter. A considerable number of letters, many still unprinted, are in private collections. For a convenient summary of a few of the chief miscellaneous documents in private hands see B. Currie, Fishers of Books, Boston, .1931. Dickens's private life, which entered largely into his work, is illustrated in various museums connected with his name, and in exhibitions of books, relics, documents, etc., held from time to time. The sale catalogues of his effects have also been ptd and annotated.]

Dickens Memento. Catalogue with Purchasers' Names and Prices Realised of the Pictures, Drawings, and Objects of Art of the Late Charles Dickens, sold by Auction on July 9th, 1870. Introduction by Francis Phillimore, and Hints to Collectors, by John F. Dexter. [1884.] [The Hints are bibliographical details of great value. The catalogue has been rptd 1935 with the sale-catalogue of Dickens's library.]

An Interesting Dickens Collection. [W. R. Hughes of Birmingham.] Reprinted from The Birmingham Daily Mail. 1887.

Victoria and Albert Museum, South Kensington. Catalogue of the Printed Books bequeathed by John Forster. 1888. Catalogue of the Paintings, Manuscripts, etc. bequeathed by John Forster. 1893. Catalogue of Dickens Exhibition, March to Oct. 1912. [1912.]

Portsmouth. Dickens Birthplace Museum. Catalogue. 1904.

New Dudley Gallery, London. Dickens Exhibition, September 1908. Catalogue. [1908.] [Illustrated, with introductions by Percy Fitzgerald and J. W. T. Ley.]

St Louis. Franklin Club. Catalogue of an Exhibition of Books, Prints, Drawings, Manuscripts and Letters Commemorative of the Centenary of Charles Dickens. 1912.

New York. Grolier Club. Catalogue of an Exhibition of the Works of Charles Dickens. With an Introduction by Royal Cortissoz. 1913.

The Dickensian, July, Aug. 1917. [Contains a list of extant MSS and their whereabouts, as known at that time.]

Harvard University. Catalogue of the Writings of Charles Dickens in the Harry Elkins Widener Memorial Library. 1918.

Suzannet, A. de. Catalogue d'un Choix de Livres Imprimés et Manuscrits, Lettres, Autographes, Dessins Originaux et Gravures. 4 vols. Biarritz, 1925 (priv. ptd). [Vol. I, Œuvres de Charles Dickens. A Catalogue raisonné of the Comte de Suzannet's private collection, containing scarce edns and unpbd letters.]

[The Dickens House, 48 Doughty Street, London, W.C. 1, vested in trustees and administered through the Dickens Fellowship, has a copious National Dickens Library and contains a number of personal relics. It issues two guides: a short history of the house and a souvenir guide to the Collection.]

(b) Printed Writings

[Bibliographies and kindred compilations dealing with single works only, or special subjects, are included in the appropriate sections below. Many biographies (see below) also contain partial bibliographies.]

Cook, James. Bibliography of the Writings of Charles Dickens, with many Particulars relating to his Works. 1879.

Shepherd, R. H. The Bibliography of Dickens. Manchester, [1880]; 1884.

Johnson, C. P. Hints to Collectors of Original Editions of the Works of Charles Dickens. 1885. [Certain details given are now incorrect, but some works are recorded and collated which do not appear in other bibliographies and are in few libraries.]

Kitton, F. G. Dickensiana. A Bibliography of the Literature relating to Charles Dickens and his Writings. 1886.

—— The Novels of Charles Dickens. A Bibliography and Sketch. 1897. [Narrative and tabular form combined.]

—— The Minor Writings of Charles Dickens. A Bibliography and Sketch. 1900. [Narrative and tabular form combined. Includes Sketches by Boz, and Hard Times; plagiarisms; and a note on the Edwin Drood 'problem.']

Anderson, J. P. Bibliography. [Attached to Sir F. T. Marzials' Life of Charles Dickens, 1887.]

Slater, J. H. Early Editions of some Popular Modern Authors. 1894.

Chapman and Hall, Ltd. The Works of Charles Dickens and of Thomas Carlyle. With Full Particulars of Each Edition and Biographical Introductions. [1900.]

Thomson, Joseph C. Bibliography of the Writings of Charles Dickens. Warwick, 1904.

The Dickensian. 1905–. [In progress; pbd monthly to 1914, subsequently at more infrequent intervals, now quarterly. Includes in each issue a list of edns of Dickens's works and books and magazine articles dealing with him, which have appeared since the previous issue. The more important works are criticised, and independent biographical and bibliographical notes appear in the pages of the magazine, which is illustrated.]

Layard, G. S. Suppressed Plates. 1907. [Includes 2 chs. with illustrations, on Dickens's works.]

Hammerton, Sir J. A. The Dickens Companion, 1910. [Vol. xviii of The Charles Dickens Library. Contains short-title list of pbd books and contributions to periodicals, and a list of biographies, reminiscences, etc., which mention Dickens, with short extracts.]

Wilkins, W. G. First and Early American Editions of the Works of Charles Dickens. Iowa, 1910 (priv. ptd). [Some portions first pbd in The Dickensian.]

Eckel, J. C. The First Editions of Charles Dickens. 1913; 1932 (greatly rev. and enlarged). [Gives full collations and many facsimiles, and details of variants in early issues. Includes also magazine contributions and chief auction prices of rare copies. For criticism of some defects, see TLS. 26 Jan. 1933, and The Dickensian, Spring No., 1933.]

Stonehouse, J. H. Sikes and Nancy [from Oliver Twist]. A Reading by Charles Dickens. Reprinted from the privately printed Edition, with an Introduction and a General Bibliography of the Reading Editions [as arranged and written by Dickens himself]. 1921. [For the separately pbd edns, see below under each work.]

Spencer, W. Forty Years in my Bookshop. 1923. [Includes 4 chs. on Dickens bibliography.]

British Museum, Department of Printed Books. Charles Dickens: an Excerpt from the General Catalogue. 1926. [Contains the General Catalogue entries of all works by Dickens, biographies, and Dickensiana in the Library in 1926.]

Sawyer, C. J. and Darton, F. J. H. English Books (1475–1900). 2 vols. 1927. [Vol. ii, ch. 7, Charles Dickens. Mainly from a collector's standpoint, but includes collation of certain works.]

Anderson Galleries, New York. Catalogue of the Library of Jerome Kern, New York City. 1929. [Sale catalogue. Lots 360 to 472, fully described, are a Dickens collection, including first edns and some MSS.]

Waugh, Arthur. A Hundred Years of Publishing; being the Story of Chapman and Hall Ltd. 1930.

Hatton, T. and Cleaver, A. H. A Bibliography of the Periodical Works of Charles Dickens. 1934.

(2) COLLECTED WORKS

[During Dickens's lifetime and the duration of the chief copyrights, the only authorised collected edns issued in England were pbd by Chapman and Hall. These edns were expanded from time to time, and in due course furnished with introductory or critical matter. After Dickens's death similarly annotated edns were issued by other firms, and new artists were procured for the illustrations; only the more important of these edns are given here. The authorised edns themselves are not all included, because some varied merely in title, price, and other technical details. Rpts of any kind not containing new material are not included. For texts now available, see Reference Catalogue of Current Literature.]

(a) Editions published by Chapman and Hall

The Works of Charles Dickens. 17 vols. 1847–68. [The first systematic re-issue, known as the 'first cheap edition.' Frontispiece illustrations only. Contains some specially written prefaces and similar addresses to the reader (see, e.g., Pickwick Papers, below).]

Library Edition. 22 vols. 1858–9. [Frontispiece illustrations only. Re-issued in 30 vols. (including later works), 1861–74, with new title-pages, and illustrations, including the original ones and addns by Marcus Stone, John Leech, Clarkson Stanfield, and others. Issued in the first instance jointly by Chapman and Hall and Bradbury and Evans.]

Charles Dickens Edition. 21 vols. 1867–[74]. [Mainly rpt of foregoing, with slight addns and revisions by Dickens.]

Household Edition. 21 vols. [1873–9]. [With new illustrations by F. Barnard, J. Mahoney and others.]

Gadshill Edition. Ed. A. Lang, 36 vols. 1897–[1908]. [Contains all the original illustrations, with many additional ones by Charles Green, Harry Furniss, Maurice Greiffenhagen, and others. Vols. xxxv, xxxvi, Miscellaneous Papers (not previously collected), ed. B. W. Matz. Rptd in edn de luxe, 1903, with Forster's Life of Dickens added. The fullest 'standard' and 'authorised' edn.]

The Authentic Edition. 21 vols. 1901–[6]. [With the original illustrations.]

Oxford India Paper Dickens. 17 vols. 1901–2. [In conjunction with Henry Frowde (afterwards Humphrey Milford). Copyright text, on thin paper, with the original illustrations.]

Biographical Edition. Ed. A. Waugh, 20 vols. 1902–3. [With the original illustrations.]

Fireside Edition. 23 vols. 1903–7. [Includes Forster's Life.]

The National Edition. 40 vols. 1906–8. [Includes newly collected articles, letters,

speeches, plays and poems, and Forster's Life, together with the original illustrations, and portraits, facsimiles and drawings.]
Centenary Edition. 36 vols. 1910–11. [With original illustrations.]
Universal Edition. 22 vols. n.d. [740 illustrations from the originals, and 2 portraits. Each work complete in one vol.]

(b) Other Editions

The Works of Charles Dickens. 20 vols. 1892–5. [Rpts of 1st edns, with biographical and bibliographical introductions by C. Dickens, jun.]
Temple Edition. Ed. W. Jerrold, 35 vols. 1899–1903. [Incomplete.]
Rochester Edition. 9 vols. (all pbd), 1900–1. [Introductions by George Gissing and notes by F. G. Kitton.]
Imperial Edition. 16 vols. 1901–2. [Incomplete; includes a critical study by George Gissing and topographical illustrations by F. G. Kitton.]
Complete Works. Ed. F. G. Kitton, 1903–8. [Only 6 works pbd. Original and later illustrations, introductions by various writers, bibliographical and topographical notes.]
Everyman's Library. 22 vols. [1906–21]. [Introductions to Barnaby Rudge and A Tale of Two Cities by Walter Jerrold, to remainder by G. K. Chesterton.]
The Charles Dickens Library. Ed. Sir J. A. Hammerton, 18 vols. [1910]. [1200 illustrations in all, including the original ones and 500 specially drawn by Harry Furniss. Vol. XVII, The Dickens Picture Book (a compendium of information about illustrators of Dickens); vol. XVIII, The Dickens Companion (a biographical narrative with extracts, list of authorities, and short-title bibliography).]
Waverley Edition. 30 vols. 1913–8. [With character-study illustrations by Charles Pears and coloured versions of F. Barnard's illustrations.]
The Nonesuch Dickens. Ed. A. Waugh, W. Dexter, T. Hatton and H. Walpole, 23 vols. 1938. [Illustrations from original plates and blocks (over 800) bought from Chapman and Hall. Each work complete in 1 vol. Fullest collection of letters.]

(3) THE NOVELS

[Almost all the first edns of Dickens's works, major and minor, contain small textual discrepancies or technical variations in production which determine, whenever they can be established with final certainty, priority of publication as between one copy or set of copies and another. (For some causes, see under Pickwick Papers below.) These minutiae are of importance to book-collectors, but affect the material state of the various works rather than the contents, and there is still considerable disagreement between experts about points of detail. Such points cannot be enumerated here in full. They have been dealt with exhaustively in J. C. Eckel's The First Editions of Dickens, 1932, The Dickensian, etc. The following entries do not include either rpts of separate works pbd after Dickens's death (unless they contain critical or introductory matter, or illustrations, of recognised value), or selections, abridgments, and school edns. Sequels, imitations and dramatisations are included (up to 1900) only if they utilised Dickens's own scenes and characters or very close imitations of them, and were clearly meant to share the popularity of the original work, or to adapt it legitimately. Dickens's own 'reading versions' are given.]

Sketches by Boz

Sketches by 'Boz.' Illustrative of Every-Day Life, and Every-Day People. Illustrated by George Cruikshank. 2 vols. 1836. The Second Series. 1836. [The ptd title-page of ser. 2 is dated 1837, the engraved, 1836. It was actually pbd on 17 Dec. 1836. There are variants in both sers. The Sketches appeared originally at intervals in Monthly Mag., Evening Chronicle, Bell's Life in London, Morning Chronicle, Library of Fiction, Carlton Chronicle, and London Weekly Mag. (late The Thief). The earliest —Dickens's first appearance in print as an author—was A Dinner at Poplar Walk (called Mr Minns and his Cousin in ser. 2) in Monthly Mag. Dec. 1833. After the first edn Dickens transferred the work from John Macrone to Chapman and Hall.]
Sketches by 'Boz.' [Both sers.] 20 monthly pts, 1 Nov. 1837–1 June 1839 (variants); 1839 (the monthly pts in 1 vol.; known as the first 8vo edn; variants); 2 vols. Philadelphia, 1836 (ser. 1 only, as Watkins Tottle, and other Sketches, illustrative of Every-Day Life and Every-Day People; variants); Calcutta, 1837 (20 sketches from ser. 2, as The New Series of Sketches by Boz).
'Bos' [Thomas Peckett Prest or Edward Lloyd?]. The Sketch Book. Embellished with seventeen elegant engravings. [1837?] [Ostensibly, and partly in fact, a close imitation of Sketches by Boz, but from internal evidence written when Pickwick was advanced in monthly publication and Oliver Twist begun.]
A Dinner at Poplar Walk. Being [Dickens's] First Effusion 'in all the glory of print.' Reproduced in Facsimile

from the Monthly Magazine, December, 1833. 1933 (priv. ptd). [With facs. of page of 1847 Pickwick preface corrected by Dickens.]

Darton, F. J. H. Dickens; Positively the First Appearance. A Centenary Review. With a Bibliography of Sketches by 'Boz' [by J. E. S. Sawyer and F. J. H. Darton]. 1933. [Includes original text of A Dinner at Poplar Walk.]

Pickwick Papers

(i) Bibliographies

Fitzgerald, P. H. The History of Pickwick. With a Bibliography. 1891.

Davis, G. W. The Posthumous Papers of the Pickwick Club. Some New Bibliographical Discoveries. 1928.

Eckel, J. C. Prime Pickwicks in Parts. A Census with Complete Collation. With a Foreword by A. Edward Newton, and 11 plates. New York, 1928. [See note on the same author's First Editions of Dickens, above, under Bibliography.]

The Lombard Street Edition of Dickens: The Pickwick Papers. With [biographical and bibliographical] Introduction by John Harrison Stonehouse. [In monthly pts] 1932–3. [A rpt of the original text, with plates and wrappers (except date and imprint) in facsimile, including the suppressed plates; •modern advertisements inserted in the same style as in the original pts.]

The Dickensian. Autumn No. 1933. [See also subsequent nos.]

Miller, W. and Strange, E. H. A Centenary Bibliography of the Pickwick Papers. 1936.

(ii) Principal Separate Editions

The Posthumous Papers of the Pickwick Club Containing a faithful Record of the Perambulations, Perils, Travels, Adventures and Sporting Transactions of the corresponding Members. Edited by 'Boz.' [20 (as 19) monthly pts from 31 March 1836 (illustrated successively by Robert Seymour, d. April 1836, Robert W. Buss, superseded after one no. and Hablot Knight Browne, 'Phiz'); 1 vol. 1837 (Buss's illustrations omitted).]

[These are the bare facts of first issue. There are innumerable variants in the earliest copies, and the exact bibliographical details are still undecided, owing to (i) inequality of demand for each part in the early stages, and consequent use of material in various states of production, (ii) textual and pictorial changes made in the course of serial issue, though the main body was unaltered, (iii) insertion in bound-up copies of discarded or extra plates (see below), (iv) the binding-up or improvisa-

tion of 'perfect' copies out of different-state but genuine monthly parts. The whole question is discussed elaborately in the bibliographies, etc.]

The Posthumous Papers of the Pickwick Club. With Illustrations, after Phiz. Launceston (Tasmania), 1838; Philadelphia, 1838 ('With illustrations by Sam Weller, Jr. [T. H. Onwhyn] and Alfred Crowquill' [Alfred Henry Forrester]); 1847 (frontispiece by C. R. Leslie and preface describing origin of the Pickwick Papers and Dickens's relations with Robert Seymour; first 'cheap' edn).

The Posthumous Papers of the Pickwick Club. Ed. C. Dickens, jun., 2 vols. 1886 (with valuable notes); 2 vols. 1887 (with facsimiles of original illustrations, including Buss's, and additional drawings by John Leech); ed. C. Van Noorden, B. W. Matz, and C. P. Johnson, 2 vols. 1909 (original illustrations and prefaces, 223 additional pictures, introduction, notes, etc.).

(iii) Extra Illustrations

[Onwhyn, T., possibly aided by others.] Thirty-two Illustrations by Mr Samuel Weller. 1837. [Issued in 8 pts.]

Heath, W. Pickwickian Illustrations [20]. 1837.

'Crowquill, Alfred' (A. H. Forrester). Pictures Picked from the Pickwick Papers. 1837. [Issued in pts.]

Sibson, T. Racy Sketches of Expeditions from The Pickwick Club. 1838.

Plates to illustrate the Cheap Edition. From original Designs by John Gilbert. [1847.] [32 plates.]

Six Original Illustrations. Engraved on wood. By Phiz [H. K. Browne]. [1847] (re-issued, 1847). [The above two pbns were apparently recognised by Dickens and his publishers.]

Pickwick Pictures. [1847.] [Pbd by W. Strange; issued in 4 pts.]

Onwhyn, T. Twenty-Four Illustrations to the Pickwick Club. [Executed in 1847, but not pbd till 1894.]

Dulcken, A. Scenes from the Pickwick Papers, designed and drawn on stone. [1861.] [4 large oblong folio plates and a decorated title-page, produced as a book.]

Pailthorpe, F. W. Illustrations to the Pickwick Club. 1882. [24, including engraved title-page.]

Grego, J. Pictorial Pickwickiana. Charles Dickens and his Illustrators. 2 vols. 1899. [350 reproductions, with notes and commentary. Includes supposititious productions.]

New Dudley Gallery, London. The Pickwick Exhibition, July, 1907. Catalogue. [1907.] [Illustrated.]

(iv) Reading Versions (by Dickens himself)

Bardell and Pickwick; Mr Chops, the Dwarf [from A Christmas Carol]; Mr Bob Sawyer's Party: Three Readings, each in One Chapter. [1866] (priv. ptd).

Bardell and Pickwick. As condensed by [Dickens] himself, for his Readings. Boston, 1868.

Mr Bob Sawyer's Party. Boston, 1868.

(v) Imitations and Sequels

The Pickwick Gazette. Illustrated by Robert Cruikshank. 1837. [2 issues only, June and July.]

The Beauties of Pickwick. By Sam Weller. 1838; rptd facs. 1883 (with introduction on original of Sam Weller, note on piracies, and other comments, 'by a lover of Charles Dickens's works'). [Partly quotation, partly invention.]

Reynolds, G. W. M. Pickwick Abroad; or, The Tour in France. Illustrated. 1839; 1864. [Appeared serially, 1837-8, in Monthly Mag., of which Reynolds was then editor. Also issued in monthly pts from Jan. 1839. The vol. issue contains a long preface defending the imitation. 41 steel engravings by 'Alfred Crowquill' (A. H. Forrester) and John Phillips, and 33 woodcuts by G. W. Bonner (views of Paris).]

—— The Marriage of Mr Pickwick. [In Master Timothy's Book Case, 1842. A tale occupying over one-fifth of a long work.]

'Bos.' The Post-humourous Notes of the Pickwickian Club. 2 vols. [1839?]. [Issued weekly at 1d. as The Penny Pickwick, and 4d. monthly; illustrated.]

—— Pickwick in America! [1840.]

[Besant, Sir W. and Rice, J.] The Death of Samuel Pickwick. [In The Case of Mr Lucraft; and Other Tales, 2 vols. 1876.]

(vi) Dramatisations, etc.

Rede, W. L. The Peregrinations of Pickwick. [In Duncombe's British Theatre, n.d.; acted 1836.]

Stirling, E. The Pickwick Club. A Burletta in Three Acts. [In Duncombe's British Theatre, n.d.; produced 1837.]

'Moncrieff, William Thomas' (W. T. Thomas). Sam Weller; or, the Pickwickians. A Drama. 1837. [Adapted for Lacy's Acting Edition of Plays as The Pickwickians; or, the Peregrinations of Sam Weller, [1872].]

Russell, H. The Ivy Green. [1844]; 1846, etc. [Song from ch. vi, arranged for the piano.

Also arranged for other instruments and for use as an air for quadrilles.]

Emson, F. E. The Weller Family. A Comedy. 1878.

Gem, T. H. Bardell versus Pickwick; versified. Leamington, [1881]. [With music by F. Spinney.]

The Great Pickwick Case, arranged as a Comic Opera. Songs by Robert Pollitt. Manchester. [1884.]

Burnand, Sir F. C. A Dramatic Cantata. [1889.]

Parker, J. M. An Evening with Pickwick. A Literary and Musical Dickens Entertainment. New York, 1889.

(vii) Studies and Commentaries

Calverley, C. S. An Examination Paper [on The Pickwick Papers]. [1857.] [Rptd in Fly-Leaves, 1866.]

Seymour, Mrs [Robert]. An Account of the Origin of the 'Pickwick Papers.' N.d. (priv. ptd and apparently not circulated); ed. F. G. Kitton, 1901 (priv. ptd).

Hassard, J. R. G. A Pickwickian Pilgrimage. Boston, 1881. [Chiefly on London scenes.]

Lockwood, Sir F. The Law and Lawyers of Pickwick. [1894]; [1896].

Fitzgerald, P. H. Pickwickian Manners and Customs. [1897.]

—— Bardell v. Pickwick. With Notes and Commentaries. 1902.

—— The Pickwickian Dictionary and Cyclopaedia. [1903.]

—— Pickwick Riddles and Perplexities. 1912.

Neale, C. M. An Index to Pickwick. 1897.

Hall, Hammond. Mr Pickwick's Kent. 1899.

The Eatanswill Gazette. Official Organ of the Eatanswill Club, Sudbury, Suffolk. A Journal devoted to Eatanswillian, Pickwickian, and Dickensian Humour and Research. 4 nos. Sudbury, 1907-8. [Founded chiefly to defend the theory that Eatanswill in the Pickwick Papers represents Sudbury, but contains other minutiae.]

Matz, B. W. The Inns and Taverns of Pickwick. [1921.]

Lambert, S. W. When Mr Pickwick went Fishing. 1925. [Deals with Seymour's claim to origin of Pickwick. See The Dickensian, July 1925.]

Dexter, W. Mr Pickwick's Pilgrimages. 1926.

Clendening, L. A Handbook to Pickwick Papers. New York, 1936.

Dexter, W. and Ley, J. W. T. The Origin of Pickwick. New Facts. 1936.

A Pickwick Portrait Gallery: From the Pens of Divers Admirers, Friends and Enemies. 1936.

Oliver Twist

Oliver Twist; or, the Parish Boy's Progress. By 'Boz.' 3 vols. 1838, 1839, 1840, 1841 (with new preface). [All illustrated by G. Cruikshank. Variants in first issue. First appeared serially in Bentley's Misc. Feb. 1837–March 1839. Re-issue in 10 monthly pts (as The Adventures of Oliver Twist) from Jan. 1846; parts as 1 vol. 1846. First 'cheap' edn, 1846.]

The Adventures of Oliver Twist. With 26 water-colour Drawings by George Cruikshank. 1895; [ed. J. Grego], [1903] (selections). [Coloured drawings done specially by Cruikshank for a friend, F. W. Cosens, in 1866, though similar in design to the earlier line engravings. The 1903 edn contains in full Cruikshank's claim to have invented the substance of the novel. The 2 edns differ widely in colour reproduction.]

Sikes and Nancy. A Reading. [1866] (priv. ptd; only known copy has MS addns by Dickens); ed. J. H. Shorthouse, 1921. [See E. Yates, Mr Charles Dickens's New Reading, Tinsley's Mag. Feb. 1869.]

Almar, G. Oliver Twist. A Serio-Comic Burletta. [1839] (in B. N. Webster's Acting National Drama, with engravings by Pierce Egan, Jun.); Leipzig, 1842 (in L. Hilsenberg's Modern English Comic Theatre); 1884 (in Dicks's Standard Plays). [Produced 1838.]

'Bos' [T. P. Prest or E. Lloyd?]. The Life and Adventures of Oliver Twiss, the Workhouse Boy. [1839.]

Barnett, C. Z. Oliver Twist, or the Parish Boy's Progress. A Domestic Drama. N.d. [Produced 1838.]

Oliver Twist; or, the Parish Boy's Progress. A Drama. [1858]; n.d. (in T. H. Lacy's Acting Edition of Plays).

Emson, F. R. Bumble's Courtship. A Comic Interlude. [1874] (in T. H. Lacy's Acting Edition of Plays).

Nicholas Nickleby

(i) Principal Editions

The Life and Adventures of Nicholas Nickleby Containing a Faithful Account of the Fortunes, Misfortunes, Uprisings, Downfallings, and Complete Career of the Nickleby Family. Edited by 'Boz.' With Illustrations by 'Phiz.' [Title on wrapper. On title-page, The Life and Adventures of Nicholas Nickleby. By Charles Dickens.] 20 (as 19) monthly pts (with variants), from April 1838; 1 vol. Oct. 1839 (with portrait of Dickens by Daniel Maclise, as The Life and Adventures of Nicholas Nickleby); 1848 (first 'cheap' edn).

Nicholas Nickleby at the Yorkshire School: a Reading in Four Chapters. [1866] (priv. ptd); Boston, 1868 (rev. and 'In Three Chapters'); Boston, 1868 ('In four Chapters').

(ii) Imitations, Dramatisations and Sequels

'Bos' [T. P. Prest or E. Lloyd?]. Nickelas Nickelbery. Containing the Adventures of the Family of Nickelbery. Embellished with forty-two Engravings. [1838?] [In 8-page nos.]

Nickleby Married. With 22 plates by Quiz. John Williams. 1840.

Stirling, E. Nicholas Nickleby. A Farce. [1838] (in B. N. Webster's Acting Drama); Leipzig, 1841 (in L. Hilsenberg's Modern English Comic Theatre). [Produced 1838. The ptd text contains a preface and dedication to Dickens.]

—— The Fortunes of Smike; or, a sequel to Nicholas Nickleby. N.d. (in B. N. Webster's Acting Drama); Leipzig, 1841 (in L. Hilsenberg's Modern English Comic Theatre). [Produced 1840.]

Simms, H. Nicholas Nickleby. A Drama in four Acts. [1883] (in Dicks's Standard Plays).

(iii) Studies and Commentaries

Thackeray, W. M. Dickens in France. Fraser's Mag. March 1842. [On a Parisian stage version of Nicholas Nickleby. Illustrated by Thackeray himself.]

Elliot, W. H. The Country and Church of the Cheeryble Brothers. Selkirk, 1893.

—— The Story of the 'Cheeryble' Grants. Manchester, 1906.

Pascoe, C. E. Dickens in Yorkshire. Being Notes of a Journey to the Delightful Village of Dotheboys, near Greta Bridge. [1912.]

Wackford Squeers and Pecksniff: an Unpublished Letter. [1915] (priv. ptd). [Foreword by C. K. Shorter.]

Clark, Cumberland. Charles Dickens and the Yorkshire Schools. 1918 (priv. ptd). [With facsimile of an unpbd letter.]

Darton, F. J. H. Vincent Crummles. His Theatre and his Times. 1926. [Illustrated.]

Master Humphrey's Clock, Old Curiosity Shop, Barnaby Rudge

Master Humphrey's Clock. By 'Boz.' With Illustrations by G. Cattermole and H. K. Browne. 88 weekly pts and 20 monthly nos. from April 1840; 3 vols. 1841 ('by Charles Dickens'); ed. Sir F. T. Marzials, [1891] (with other early pieces). [The Old Curiosity Shop began in the course of

monthly pt I, and ended in Feb. 1841, when
Barnaby Rudge began. Some variants in
the periodical issues. The 'Clock' setting
was not retained when the two long stories
were pbd as separate works, and in the
more modern collected edns is usually included in a 'miscellany' vol.]
> 'Bos' [T. P. Prest or E. Lloyd?]. Mister
> Humfries' Clock. 'Bos,' maker. A mis-
> cellany of striking matter. 1840.
> Cooper, F. F. Master Humphrey's Clock.
> A Domestic Drama. N.d. (in Duncombe's
> British Theatre). [Produced 1840.]

The Old Curiosity Shop. 1841 (with the
original illustrations; first separate edn);
1848 (cheap edn; 4 extra illustrations by
H. K. Browne issued separately).
> Stirling, E. The Old Curiosity Shop. A
> Drama. N.d. (in T. H. Lacy's Acting
> Edition of Plays). [Produced 1840.]
> Lander, G. The Old Curiosity Shop. A
> Drama. [1885] (in Dicks's Standard
> Plays).
> FitzGerald, E. Little Nell's Wanderings.
> ['A short abstract, leaving out the
> travelling, etc.' In A Fitzgerald Medley,
> ed. C. Ganz, 1933.]

Barnaby Rudge; a Tale of the Riots of
'Eighty. 1841 (with the original illustrations; first separate edn); 1849 (cheap edn;
4 extra illustrations by H. K. Browne
issued separately).
> Selby, C. and Melville, C. Barnaby Rudge.
> A Domestic Drama. Leipzig, 1841 (in L.
> Hilsenberg's Modern English Comic
> Theatre); [1875]. [Produced 1841.]
> Higgie, T. H. Barnaby Rudge, or, the
> Murder at the Warren. A Drama. [1854.]
> The King's Head, Chigwell. A Short
> Account of the Historic 'Maypole' of
> Charles Dickens in 'Barnaby Rudge.'
> With Illustrations. [1912.]

Martin Chuzzlewit

The Life and Adventures of Martin Chuzzle-
wit, His Relatives, Friends, and Enemies.
Comprising All His Wiles and His Ways,
With an Historical Record of What He
Did, and What He Didn't; Showing, more-
over, Who Inherited the Family Plate,
Who came in For the Silver Spoons, and
Who for the Wooden Ladles. The Whole
Forming a Complete Key to the House of
Chuzzlewit. Edited by 'Boz.' With Illus-
trations by 'Phiz.' [Title on wrapper. On
title-page and for vol. issue, The Life and
Adventures of Martin Chuzzlewit, by
Charles Dickens]. 20 (as 19) monthly pts
from Jan. 1843 (with variants); 1 vol.
1844; 1850 (first cheap' edn).

Mrs Gamp. A Reading. 1858 (priv. ptd, with
Boots at the Holly-Tree Inn and The Poor
Traveller); Boston, 1868 (Mrs Gamp only).
An Account of a late Expedition into the
North, for an Amateur Theatrical Benefit,
written by Mrs Gamp. [Fragment com-
posed for use on theatrical tour on behalf of
Leigh Hunt, 1847. Not pbd in Dickens's
lifetime, but included in Forster's Life,
Book VI, and priv. ptd from MS as Mrs
Gamp With the Strolling Players An Un-
finished Sketch By Charles Dickens, New
York, 1899.]
> Stirling, E. Martin Chuzzlewit. A
> Drama. N.d. (in Duncombe's British
> Theatre); n.d. (in T. H. Lacy's Acting
> Edition of Plays). [Produced 1844.]
> —— Mrs Harris. A Farce. N.d.
> Webster, B. Mrs Sarah Gamp's Tea and
> Turn Out; a Bozzian Sketch. N.d.
> [Produced 1846.]
> Higgie, T. and Lacy, T. H. Martin
> Chuzzlewit; or, his Wills and his Ways.
> A Drama. [1872] (pbd in T. H. Lacy's
> Acting Edition of Plays). [Produced
> 1844.]
> Dilley, J. J. and Clifton, L. Tom Pinch.
> A Domestic Comedy. [1884.] [Produced
> 1881.]
> Butler, Samuel. A Translation, attempted
> in consequence of a Challenge. Cambridge,
> [1894]. [Rptd from The Eagle. A trn of
> an utterance of Mrs Gamp's (Ch. xix of
> Martin Chuzzlewit) into Greek Homeric
> hexameters.]

Dombey and Son

Dealings with the Firm of Dombey and Son
Wholesale, Retail, and for Exportation.
With Illustrations by H. K. Browne. [Title
on wrapper. On title-page and for vol.
issue, Dombey and Son.] 20 (as 19)
monthly pts from Oct. 1846 (with variants);
1 vol. 1848; 1858 (first 'cheap' edn). [After
Martin Chuzzlewit, Dickens for a time
transferred his new works from Chapman
and Hall to Bradbury and Evans. But
Chapman and Hall pbd 12 separate extra
illustrations to Dombey and Son, by 'Phiz,'
2 pts, 1848.]
The Story of Little Dombey, as condensed by
[Dickens] Himself, for his Readings. 1858,
1862 (priv. ptd); Boston, 1868.
> 'Buz.' Dolby and Father. New York,
> 1868. [Parody, in part, of Dombey and
> Son, with introduction of characters from
> other works by Dickens and some serious
> attacks upon him.]
> Brougham, J. Dombey and Son. [1885]
> (in Dicks's Standard Plays). [Dramati-
> sation produced, New York, 1848.]

David Copperfield

The Personal History, Adventures, Experiences, and Observation of David Copperfield the Younger. Of Blunderstone Rookery. (Which He never meant to be Published on any Account.) With Illustrations by H. K. Browne. [Title on wrapper. On title-page and for vol. issue, The Personal History of David Copperfield.] 20 (as 19) monthly pts, from May 1849 (variants); 1 vol. 1850; 1858 (first 'cheap' edn).

David Copperfield. A Reading, in Five Chapters. [1866] (priv. ptd); Boston, 1868; 1921 (with a note by J. H. Stonehouse summarising the Maria Beadnell correspondence and the relation between David Copperfield and Dickens's own life).

Halliday, A. Little Emily ('David Copperfield'). A Drama. New York, n.d.

Brougham, J. David Copperfield. A Drama. [1885] (in Dicks's Standard Plays).

Cooper, T. P. The Real Micawber, with a Batch of his Remarkable Letters. [1922.] [Suggests a Yorkshire original.]

Graves, R. The Real David Copperfield. 1933. [Dickens's text revised at full length to 'sort what is true from what is false,' with critical introduction by way of justification.]

The Personal History of David Copperfield. Ed. H. S. Hughes, 2 vols. Garden City, 1936.

Bleak House

Bleak House. With Illustrations by H. K. Browne. 20 (as 19) monthly pts from March 1852 (slight variants); 1 vol. 1853.

Simpson, J. P. Lady Dedlock's Secret. [1885] (in French's Acting Edition of Plays). [Produced 1874.]

Lander, G. Bleak House; or, Poor Jo. A Drama. [1885] (in Dicks's Standard Plays). [Produced 1876.]

Denman, T., Baron. Uncle Tom's Cabin, Bleak House, Slavery and Slave Trade. Six articles reprinted from The Standard. 1853.

Brimley, G. Dickens's Bleak House. [In Essays by the Late George Brimley, 1858. Rptd from Spectator, 24 Sept. 1853.]

Leigh Hunt and Harold Skimpole: an Unpublished Letter by Charles Dickens. [1915] (priv. ptd). [With foreword by C. K. Shorter.]

Brewer, L. A. Leigh Hunt and Charles Dickens. The Skimpole Caricature. [Cedar Rapids], 1930 (priv. ptd).

Hard Times

Hard Times. For These Times. 1854. [No illustrations. Not issued in pts, but pbd serially in Household Words, 1 April—12 Aug. 1854.]

Yates, E. H. and Brough, R. B. Hard Times. (Refinished.) By Charles Diggins. [One of a collection of parodies in Our Miscellany, 1857.]

Ruskin, J. ' Unto This Last: ' Four Essays on the First Principles of Political Economy. 1862. [Long note on Hard Times in Essay I, The Roots of Honour.]

Little Dorrit

Little Dorrit. With Illustrations by H. K. Browne. 20 (as 19) monthly pts from Dec. 1855 (variants); 1 vol. 1857.

Tale of Two Cities

A Tale of Two Cities. With Illustrations by H. K. Browne. [Appeared simultaneously in All the Year Round (from April) and in 8 (as 7) monthly pts from June 1859. 1 vol. 1859. Variants. For full collation of pts, see C. J. Sawyer and F. J. H. Darton, English Books, vol. II, 1927.]

The Bastille Prisoner: a Reading. [1866] (priv. ptd). [Arranged by Dickens, but never used.]

Rivers, H. J. The Tale of Two Cities; a Drama. [1862.]

Taylor, T. A Tale of Two Cities. A Drama. N.d. (in Lacy's Acting Edition of Plays).

Wills, F. The Only Way: a Tale of Two Cities. [A play produced in London and New York; text not ptd.]

Great Expectations

Great Expectations. 3 vols. 1861. [Pbd serially in All the Year Round, Dec. 1860–July 1861. No issue in pts, no illustrations. Variants in vol. issue.]

Great Expectations. By Charles Dickens. ('Boz.') With thirty-four Illustrations by John McLenan. Printed from the Manuscript and Early Proof-sheets purchased from the Author, for which Charles Dickens has been paid in Cash, the Sum of One Thousand Pounds Sterling. T. B. Peterson and Brothers, Philadelphia. [New York, 1860]; [Philadelphia, 1861].

Great Expectations: a Reading. In Three Stages. [1886] (priv. ptd). [Never used.]

Pailthorpe, F. W. Great Expectations. 1885. [21 plates including title-page.]

Scott, Shafto. My Unknown Friend. (Being a dramatised version of Great

Expectations). [1886] (in Dicks's Standard Plays).

Gadd, W. L. The Great Expectations Country. [1929.]

Our Mutual Friend

Our Mutual Friend. With Illustrations By Marcus Stone. 20 (as 19) monthly pts from May 1864; 2 vols. 1865.

Edwin Drood

The Mystery of Edwin Drood. With twelve Illustrations by S. L. Fildes, and a Portrait. Monthly pts from April 1870 (ended at 6th pt by Dickens's death); 1 vol. 1870.

The Complete Edwin Drood. [Full text with] The History, Continuations, and Solutions (1870–1912). By J. Cuming Walters. With a Portrait, Illustrations by Sir Luke Fildes, R.A., F. G. Kitton, Facsimiles, and a Bibliography. 1912.

> Kerr, O. C. The Cloven Foot: being an adaptation [of Edwin Drood] to American Scenes, Characters, Customs, and Nomenclature. New York, 1870. [Complete adaptation with a conclusion, and a critical introduction.]

> [Morford, H. and others.] John Jasper's Secret. A Sequel to Charles Dickens' unfinished Novel. 1871.

> 'Vase, Gillan' (Mrs Richard Newton). A Great Mystery solved: being a Sequel to The Mystery of Edwin Drood. 1878; [1914].

> Proctor, R. A. Watched by the Dead: a loving Study of Dickens' half-told Tale. 1887.

> Lang, A. The Puzzle of Dickens's Last Plot. 1905.

> Walters, J. C. Clues to Dickens's Mystery of Edward Drood. 1905.

> Charles, E. Keys to the Drood Mystery. 1908; 1915.

> J[ackson], H[enry]. About Edwin Drood. Cambridge, 1911.

> Nicoll, Sir W. R. The Problem of Edwin Drood. [1912.] [With a bibliography by B. W. Matz, rev. from The Dickensian, 1911.]

> Fennell, C. A. M. 'The Opium-Woman' and 'Datchery' in The Mystery of Edwin Drood. Cambridge, 1913.

> Trial of John Jasper for the Murder of Edwin Drood. Verbatim Report of the Proceedings by J. W. T. Ley. 1914. [Report of a mock trial, G. K. Chesterton as judge.]

> C., W. E. The Mystery of Edwin Drood completed. Ed. M. L. C. Grant, [1914]. [21 additional chs.]

> Saunders, M. The Mystery in the Drood Family. Cambridge, 1914.

> Kavanagh, M. A New Solution of the Mystery of Edwin Drood. 1919.

> Carden, P. T. The Murder of Edwin Drood. An Attempted Solution. 1920.

> Squire, Sir J. C. The Great Unfinished. [In Life and Letters, [1920].]

> Dickens' Mystery of Edwin Drood, completed by a Loyal Dickensian. 1927.

> Harris, E. John Jasper's Gatehouse. A Sequel. Rochester, 1931.

> Graeme, B. Epilogue. 1933. [A novel treating the Drood mystery as the basis of a detective story.]

(4) Christmas Books and Christmas Numbers

(a) Christmas Books

A Christmas Carol. In prose. Being A Ghost Story of Christmas. With illustrations by John Leech. 1843. [The variants of the title-page and end-papers of the 'first issue' are a matter of controversy. See J. C. Eckel, The First Editions of Charles Dickens, 1932; C. J. Sawyer and F. J. H. Darton, English Books, vol. II, 1927, ch. 7; The Bookman, Christmas No., 1931; TLS. 14, 28 Jan. 1932.]

A Christmas Carol. Ed. facs. (from original MS) F. G. Kitton, 1890, 1897 (without introduction); ed. facs. (from original edn) G. K. Chesterton and B. W. Matz, 1922. [Principal later illustrated edns: S. Eytinge, Boston, 1869; Charles Pears, [1905]; John Leech and F. Barnard (from Household edn of Works), with introduction by Sir W. P. Treloar, 1907.]

A Christmas Carol. Reading Edition. 1858; Boston, 1868; [1886] (priv. ptd in part, with 2 Pickwick readings, as Mr Chops, the Dwarf)

> Barnett, C. Z. A Christmas Carol; or, the Miser's Warning. [1872] (in T. H. Lacy's Acting Edition of Plays). [Dramatisation.]

> Wallace, J. A Christmas Carol. Adapted for Platform Performance. Manchester, [1898.]

> Jaques, E. T. Charles Dickens in Chancery, being an Account of his Proceedings in respect of the Christmas Carol. 1914.

> Newton, A. E. The Greatest Book in the World and Other Papers. Boston, [1925]. [Facsimile and criticism.]

> Osborne, E. A. The Facts about A Christmas Carol. 1937 (priv. ptd).

The Chimes: A Goblin Story of Some Bells that Rang An Old Year Out And A New

Year In. 1845 (for 1844). [Illustrated by Daniel Maclise, John Leech, Richard Doyle and Clarkson Stanfield. Slight variants.]

The Chimes. Reading Edition. 1858; [1866] (priv. ptd with Sikes and Nancy, from Oliver Twist).

Lemon, M. and à Beckett, G. A. The Chimes; a Drama in Four Quarters. [1844] (in B. N. Webster's Acting National Drama). [Produced 19 Dec. 1844.]

The Cricket on the Hearth. A Fairy Tale Of Home. 1846 (for 1845). [Illustrated by Daniel Maclise, John Leech, Richard Doyle, Clarkson Stanfield, and Edwin Landseer.]

The Cricket on the Hearth. Reading Edition. 1858.

Smith, Albert R. The Cricket on the Hearth. A Drama, in Three Acts. By the Express Permission of the Author. [1885] (in Dicks's Standard Plays); n.d. (in S. French's American edn). [Produced Dec. 1845.]

Stirling, E. The Cricket on the Hearth, a Fairy Tale of Home. [1847] (in B. N. Webster's Acting National Drama). [Produced Jan. 1846.]

The Cricket on the Hearth. A Fairy Tale of Home in Three Chirps. N.d. (in T. H. Lacy's Acting Edition of Plays).

The Battle of Life. A Love Story. 1846. [Dickens's name on ptd title-page, not on engraved. Illustrated by Daniel Maclise, John Leech, Richard Doyle, and Clarkson Stanfield. Variants.]

Smith, Albert [R.] The Drama founded on the new Christmas Annual of Charles Dickens, Esq., called The Battle of Life. From early Proofs of the Work, by the Express Permission of the Author. As performed at the Theatre Royal, Lyceum, Monday, December 21, 1846. [1846]; [1888]; [1890].

The Haunted Man And The Ghost's Bargain. A Fancy for Christmas Time. 1848. [Illustrated by John Leech, Clarkson Stanfield, John Tenniel and F. Stone. Variant.]

The Haunted Man, and the Ghost's Bargain. 1848. [A reading prepared but not used by Dickens himself: cited by J. H. Stonehouse from a sale catalogue of 1879.]

(b) Christmas Numbers

[Issued as special nos. of Household Words and All the Year Round and not entirely by Dickens. Usually included in Collected Works under the title Christmas Stories. Frequently rptd singly or in groups of two or three.]

Christmas Stories from the Household Words. 9 pts, 1860. From All the Year Round.

9 pts, n.d. Both sers. 5 pts, 1898. [The authorised collections.]

Household Words:

1850. A Christmas Tree. [The whole issue is called simply Christmas Number.]

1851. What Christmas is as we Grow Older. [Whole issue called Extra Number for Christmas.]

1852. The Poor Relation's Story; The Child's Story. [In A Round of Stories By the Christmas Fire.]

1853. The Schoolboy's Story; Nobody's Story. [In Another Round of Stories.]

1854. Introductory matter; The First Poor Traveller; The Road. [In The Seven Poor Travellers.]

The Poor Traveller. 1858 (with Boots at the Holly Tree Inn, and Mrs Gamp); 1858 (another version, with MS alterations by Dickens). [Reading edns.]

1855. Introductory matter [The Guest, also called later Myself]; The Boots; The Bill. [In The Holly-Tree Inn. Remainder by Wilkie Collins.]

Boots at the Holly-Tree Inn. 1858 (with The Poor Traveller, and Mrs Gamp); Boston, 1868. [Reading edn.]

1856. The Wreck of The Golden Mary. [The Wreck mainly by Dickens, Wilkie Collins collaborating and writing most of remainder.]

1857. The Perils of Certain English Prisoners, and Their Treasure in Women, Children, Silver and Jewels. [Chs. i, iii by Dickens, ch. ii by Wilkie Collins.]

1858. Going Into Society. [In A House To Let.]

[Household Words ceased to appear after 1858.]

All The Year Round:

1859. The Mortals in the House; The Guest in Master B.'s Room; The Ghost in The Corner Room; connecting links. [In The Haunted House.]

1860. A Message From The Sea. [Chs. i, ii, v by Dickens, remainder by Wilkie Collins considerably edited by Dickens.]

A Message from the Sea. A Drama In Three Acts. By Charles Dickens and Wilkie Collins. 1861 [1860]. [Persons of the Drama and Outline of the Plot only. Pbd for copyright purposes.]

Brougham, J. A Message from the Sea. (A Drama founded on Charles Dickens's Tale.) [1883] (in Dicks's Standard Plays).

1861. Tom Tiddler's Ground. [Chs. i, vi, vii.]

1862. Somebody's Luggage. [i, His Leaving It Till Called For; ii, His Boots; part of iii; vii, His Brown-Paper Parcel; x, His Wonderful End.]

1863. Mrs Lirriper's Lodgings. [i, viii.]
Mrs Lirriper's Lodgings, a Reading.
[1866] (priv. ptd). [Never used.]
1864. Mrs Lirriper's Legacy. [i, vii.]
1865. Dr Marigold's Prescriptions. [i, vi and viii.]
Doctor Marigold: a Reading. In Two Parts. [1866] (priv. ptd); Boston, 1868.
1866. Mugby Junction. [Barbox Brothers; Barbox Brothers & Co.; Main Line, The Boy at Mugby; No. 1 Branch Line, The Signal Man.]
The Barbox Brothers; The Boy at Mugby, and The Signalman: Three Readings, each in one Chapter. [1866] (priv. ptd).
1867. No Thoroughfare. [In close collaboration with Wilkie Collins; Overture and Act III entirely by Dickens, Act II entirely by Collins. See also Plays, below.]
No Thoroughfare by C—S D—S, Bellamy Brownjohn, and Domby. Boston, 1868. [A parody with reference also to Dickens's readings and American Notes.]

(5) MINOR WORKS AND REPRINTED PAPERS

[Lists of Dickens's contributions to periodicals are given in J. C. Eckel's The First Editions of Dickens, 1932, F. G. Kitton's The Minor Writings of Dickens, 1900, J. A. Hammerton's Dickens Companion, 1910, and R. H. Shepherd's The Speeches of Dickens, 1884. The majority are included in various edns of the complete Works in one vol. or more, as Reprinted Pieces. Only separate rpts issued in Dickens's own lifetime, or subsequently pbd with comment or other supplementary matter, are included here.]

Sunday Under Three Heads. As it is; As the Sabbath Bills Would Make it; As it Might Be Made. By Timothy Sparks. 1836 (illustrated by H. K. Browne); rptd facs. 1884 (with introduction); rptd facs. Manchester, [1884].

The Mudfog Papers. [Serially in Bentley's Misc. 1837–8. Now usually included in Works in vol. containing Sketches by Boz. Rptd with preface by G. Bentley, 1880 (bis), and, in part, as The Public Life of Mr Tubrumble, once Mayor of Mudfog. By Boz. With other tales and sketches, from Bentley's Miscellany, and The Library of Fiction, Philadelphia, 1837. Only one contribution by Dickens; remainder by Lover, Peacock, Douglas Jerrold, and other writers.]

Memoirs of Joseph Grimaldi. Edited by 'Boz.' With Illustrations by George Cruikshank. 2 vols. 1838 (variants); rev. C. Whitehead, 1846, 1853, 1866, 1884; ed. P.

Fitzgerald, 1903. [Dickens rewrote Grimaldi's MS; 'he has not swelled the quantity of matter, but materially abridged it' (Preface).]

Sketches of Young Gentlemen. Dedicated to the Young Ladies: With Six Illustrations. By 'Phiz.' 1838 (anon.).

Sketches of Young Couples; With an Urgent Remonstrance to the Gentlemen of England (Being Bachelors or Widowers), On the Present Alarming Crisis. By The Author of 'Sketches of Young Gentlemen.' With Six Illustrations by 'Phiz.' 1840. [Sketches of Young Couples and Young Gentlemen were issued in one vol. with Sketches of Young Ladies as the work of 'Quiz' (Edward Caswall?) and illustrations by 'Phiz' to all three works, in 1869. 'Quiz's' Sketches of Young Ladies was first pbd in 1837.]

American Notes For General Circulation. 2 vols. 1842. [Variants. A suppressed ch. is given in Forster's Life of Dickens.]
'Quickens, Quarles' (Poe, E. A.?). English Notes, intended for very extensive circulation! Boston, 1842; ed. J. Jackson and G. H. Sargent, New York, 1920. [A parody and retort to American Notes.]
'Buz.' Current American Notes. [London] n.d. [A close parody of Dickens; evidently almost contemporary with American Notes.]
[Cary, T. G.] Letter to a Lady in France with Answers to Enquiries concerning the Books of Capt. Marryat and Mr Dickens. Boston, 1843, 1844.
[Wood, Henry.] Change for the American Notes: in Letters from London to New York. By an American Lady. 1843.
Spedding, J. Dickens's American Notes. [In Reviews and Discussions, Literary, Political, and Historical, 1879. Rptd with addns from Edinburgh Rev. Jan. 1843.]
Some Notes on America to be rewritten: suggested, with respect, to Charles Dickens, Esq. Philadelphia, 1868.

Pictures from Italy. The vignette Illustrations on Wood by Samuel Palmer. 1846. [Appeared in part as letters in Daily News, 1846, as Travelling Sketches—Written on the Road.]

A Child's Dream of A Star. With Illustrations By Hammatt Billings. Boston, 1871. [From Household Words, 6 April 1850.]

A Child's History of England. With a Frontispiece by F. W. Topham [in each vol.]. Vol. I, 1852; Vol. II, 1853; Vol. III, 1854. [Slight variants. Originally appeared intermittently in Household Words, 25 Jan. 1851–10 Dec. 1853. Illustrated by Marcus Stone, 1873.]

To Be Read at Dusk. 1852 (priv. rptd from The Keepsake, 1852); [ed. F. G. Kitton],

1898 (with 'other stories, sketches, and essays. Now first collected'). [The 1852 edn is probably a forgery; see J. Carter and G. Pollard, An Enquiry into the Nature of certain Nineteenth-Century Pamphlets, 1934.]

A Curious Dance Round a Curious Tree. [1860?] [Variants. Main text has title preceded by 1852; the article itself is followed by an extract from The Times headed 1860 and an appeal for St Luke's Hospital headed Contrast between 1852 and 1860. Dickens's paper originally appeared in Household Words, Feb. 1852.]

Post Office Money Orders. [By W. H. Wills, or by Wills and Dickens conjointly? Rptd from Household Words, 20 March 1852 in W. H. Wills's Old Leaves, 1860, and (in part) in Methods of Employment (anon.), 1852, as Remarks by Charles Dickens, Esq.]

Gone Astray. With Illustrations by Ruth Cobb, from Old Prints, and from Photographs, and Introduction by B. W. Matz. 1912. [Originally in Household Words, 13 Aug. 1853.]

The Late Mr Justice Talfourd. [?] [Recorded by J. C. Eckel, The First Editions of Charles Dickens (1932), as a rare rpt of an article in Household Words, 25 March, 1854.]

The Lazy Tour of Two Idle Apprentices. [In collaboration with Wilkie Collins. Originally appeared in Household Words, 3–31 Oct. 1857. Rptd in part in Joseph Sly's King's Arms and Royal Hotel, Lancaster, [1875]. With No Thoroughfare and The Perils of Certain English Prisoners (see Christmas Numbers, above). Illustrated, 1890.]

Pavilionstone. With an Introduction by Percy Fitzgerald. [1902.] [Dickens's Out of Town (Household Words, Sept. 1859) with a biographical preface describing Folkestone and the writing of Little Dorrit.]

Hunted Down: A Story. With Some Account of Thomas Griffiths Wainewright, The Poisoner. [1870.] [Originally in The New York Ledger, 20, 27 Aug., 3 Sept. 1859; also in All The Year Round, 4, 11 April 1860. With The Uncommercial Traveller, in Tauchnitz Collection of British Authors, Leipzig, 1860; and with The Lamplighter, and Other Nouvellettes, Philadelphia [1861]. The Account of Wainewright is by John Camden Hotten.]

The Uncommercial Traveller. 1861. [17 articles contributed to All The Year Round during 1860; rptd 1865 (dated 1866) with frontispiece by G. J. Pinwell, and 11 additional articles; and 1875 in the Illustrated Library edn of Works, with 8 further additional articles.]

The Gad's Hill Gazette. [1862–6.] [A family magazine to which Dickens contributed. Produced partly in MS and partly on a small private press, for domestic use only. See The Dickensian, July 1910 (facsimile of page) and Recreations of a Literary Man, by Percy Fitzgerald, vol. i, facsimile.]

East London Hospital for Children. Reprinted By Permission Of Charles Dickens, Esq., From All The Year Round, Dec. 19th, 1868. N.d. [Original magazine title, New Uncommercial Samples: A Small Star in the East.]

On Mr Fechter's Acting. Leeds, [1872]. [Rptd from Atlantic Monthly, Aug. 1869.]

Payne, E. F. and Harper, H. H. The Charity of Charles Dickens. Boston Bibliophile Soc. 1929. [Narrative embodying some correspondence and a short pamphlet by Dickens about the foundation, with the aid of Miss Burdett-Coutts, of a Home for Fallen Women.]

The Readings of Charles Dickens as arranged and read by himself. With illustrations. 1883; ed. J. Hollingshead, 1907. [The complete 'authorized' edn; 10 readings. For separate issues, see Novels and Christmas Books, above, under the works themselves, and J. H. Stonehouse's edn of Sikes and Nancy, 1921.]

Field, Kate. Pen Photographs of Charles Dickens's Readings, taken from Life. (Illustrated.) [1868]; 1871 (enlarged). [Deals with American reading tours.]

Kent, W. C. M. Charles Dickens as a Reader. 1872.

Dolby, G. Charles Dickens as I knew Him: The Story of the Reading Tours in Great Britain and America (1866–1870). 1885; 1912.

The Life of our Lord. Written for his own Children, 1849. 1934.

A Review and Other Writings. Ed. (from MSS) M. Tyson, John Rylands Lib. Bulletin, xviii, 1934.

(6) PLAYS AND POEMS

(a) Plays

The Strange Gentleman; A Comic Burletta, In Two Acts. By 'Boz.' First performed at The St James's Theatre, on Thursday, September 29, 1836. 1837 (with frontispiece by 'Phiz'); 1871 (without frontispiece). [Variants; in some copies extra frontispiece by F. W. Pailthorpe. J. C. Eckel, The First Editions of Charles Dickens (1932), mentions another rpt, but gives no data.]

The Strange Gentleman. [1883] (in Dicks's Standard Plays); 2 pts, 1904; 1928 (priv.

ptd, 'illustrated with reproductions from original drawings by John Leech, John Orlando Parry, etc.').

[This is Dickens's first publicly produced play, written before Pickwick began to appear. A version of it as a short story, The Great Winglebury Duel, appeared in Sketches by 'Boz,' First Series, 1836.]

The Village Coquettes: A Comic Opera. In Two Acts. The Music by John Hullah. 1836; 1837 (theatre edn); Leipzig, 1845 (in L. Hilsenberg's Modern English Comic Theatre); Amsterdam, [1868?] (in Modern English Comedies and Farces, No. 1); rptd facs.[1878]; 1883 (in Dicks's Standard Plays). [Written 1835. The following songs were pbd separately (Hullah's music, Dickens's words): 'The Child and the Old Man,' 1836; 'Some folks who have grown old,' 1836; 'How beautiful at eventide,' 1836; 'No light bound of stag,' 1836; 'My fair home,' 1851; 'In rich and lofty station shine,' 1858; 'The cares of the day,' 1858; 'Autumn Leaves,' 1871.]

Is She His Wife? Or Something Singular. A Comic Burletta In One Act. [1872?] [The only known 1st edn. A unique copy of the real 1st edn—date unknown; presumably about 1837—was destroyed by fire in 1879. A rpt of the text had been made from it and was issued at Boston, in 1877. Play produced at St James's Theatre, London, 6 March 1877. See R. H. Shepherd, A Lost Work of Charles Dickens, The Pen, Oct. 1880, and J. C. Eckel, The First Editions of Charles Dickens (1932).]

The Lamplighter A Farce by Charles Dickens (1838) now first printed from a Manuscript in the Forster Collection at the South Kensington Museum. 1879; ed. W. L. Phelps, New York, 1926 (with The Lamplighter's Story). [Discovered and ptd by R. H. Shepherd. Never produced or ptd in Dickens's lifetime. Written as a farce for Macready, but withdrawn. The substance was turned into a tale and included in The Pic Nic Papers (see below) as The Lamplighter's Story.]

The Patrician's Daughter, a tragedy in five Acts by J. Westland Marston. 1841. [Play produced Dec. 10, 1842. Prologue in rhymed couplets by Dickens.]

Mr Nightingale's Diary: A Farce. In One Act. By — [Dickens and Wilkie Collins]. 1851 (priv. ptd); Boston, 1877 (some copies with frontispiece by F. W. Pailthorpe). [Produced at Devonshire House, 16 May 1851, both authors in the cast.]

Collins, W. Wilkie. The Lighthouse. [Not pbd? Acted at Dickens's Tavistock House

Theatre in 1856. Prologue and The Song of the Wreck by Dickens; text of play revised by him during rehearsal.]

The Frozen Deep. A Drama. In Three Acts. By Wilkie Collins. [Not published.] 1866. ['Not published' is part of the title-page. The play was produced at Dickens's house in 1857. His MS copy proves that in supervising rehearsals he rewrote much of the play himself. See Introduction to Collins's version of it as a story-reading, Readings and Writings in America, 2 vols. 1874.]

No Thoroughfare. A Drama. In Five Acts. (Altered from the Christmas Story, for Performance on the Stage.) By Charles Dickens and Wilkie Collins. 1867. [Produced Dec. 26, 1867. Possibly variants. See above, Christmas Numbers, 1867.]

(b) Poems

[Dickens's poems are collected from his works and from periodicals in the vol. edited by R. H. Shepherd and F. G. Kitton mentioned below. The following appeared independently in periodicals.]

The Examiner, 1841. [The Fine Old English Gentleman (7 Aug.). The Quack Doctor's Proclamation (14 Aug.). Subjects for Painters (21 Aug.).]

The Keepsake, 1844. [A Word in Season (rptd in Forster's Life).]

The Daily News, 1846. [The British Lion. A New Song, but an Old Story (24 Jan.; signed 'Catnach'), The Hymn of the Wiltshire Labourers (14 Feb.; signed Charles Dickens).]

All The Year Round, 20 April 1859. [The Blacksmith.]

(c) Collections and Commentaries

The Plays and Poems of Charles Dickens with a Few Miscellanies in Prose now first collected. Ed. R. H. Shepherd, 2 vols. 1885. [An earlier edn, 1882, was withdrawn through copyright difficulties.]

The Poems and Verses of Charles Dickens Collected and Edited, with Bibliographical Notes, by F. G. Kitton. 1903.

Pemberton, T. E. Charles Dickens and the Stage. 1888.

Fitzgerald, S. J. A. Dickens and the Drama. 1910.

Woollcott, A. Mr Dickens goes to the Play. New York, 1922. [On Dickens's various stage connections.]

van Amerongen, J. B. The Actor in Charles Dickens. 1926. [Illustrated. List of authorities at end.]

(7) Works Associated with or in Part by Dickens

(a) Periodicals edited by Dickens

Bentley's Miscellany. 1837–9. [Monthly.]

Household Words. 1850–1859. [Weekly. Charles Dickens, jun., revived the magazine and title in 1881.]

All the Year Round. 1859. [Weekly. Household Words was incorporated in this by Dickens, who edited it until his death in 1870. It continued in existence until it was incorporated in 1895 in the revived Household Words.]

The Daily News. [Dickens was the first editor. It appeared on 21 Jan. 1846. He resigned on 9 Feb. of that year.]

(b) Prefaces, Edited Matter, etc.

The Loving Ballad Of Lord Bateman. Illustrated by George Cruikshank. 1839. [Authorship uncertain; ballad possibly by W. M. Thackeray. According to Cruikshank, Dickens wrote the Preface.]

The Pic Nic Papers. By Various Hands. Edited by Charles Dickens. With Illustrations by George Cruikshank, Phiz, etc. 3 vols. 1841. [Variants. Preface and The Lamplighter's Story by Dickens.]

Overs, John. Evenings of a Working Man. With a Preface Relative to the Author. By Charles Dickens. 1844.

Royal Literary Fund. The Case of The Reformers In The Literary Fund; Stated By Charles W. Dilke, Charles Dickens and John Forster. [1858.] [Followed by a Summary of Facts, by the R.L.F. Committee, and an Answer to the Committee by the same three members.]

Old Leaves: Gathered From Household Words. By W. Henry Wills. 1860. [Contributions edited, revised, and in part written by Dickens.]

Procter, A. A. Legends and Lyrics. With an Introduction by Charles Dickens. New edition, with additions. Illustrated. 1866. [The Introduction was included in later edns and also in The Complete Works, 1905.]

Religious Opinions Of The Late Reverend Chauncey Hare Townshend. Published As Directed In His Will, By His Literary Executor [Charles Dickens]. 1869.

(8) Letters and Speeches

[Letters dealing with particular works or themes, pbd separately or in small special collections, are entered under the appropriate works above.]

Speeches, Letters, and Sayings of Charles Dickens. To which is added a Sketch of the Author by George Augustus Sala, and Dean Stanley's Sermon. New York, 1870. [Contains also some of the poems, a note on the readings, and a biographical introduction.]

Speeches Literary and Social By Charles Dickens. Now First Collected. With Chapters on Charles Dickens As a Letter Writer, Poet and Public Reader. [Ed. R. H. Shepherd], 1870.

The Newsvendors' Benevolent and Provident Institution. Speeches In Behalf of The Institution. By the Late Charles Dickens, President. [1871.] [5 speeches 1849–1870.]

Fields, J. T. Yesterdays with Authors. 1872. [Contains 24 letters from Dickens not in the authorised collected edn.]

Clarke, Charles and Mary Cowden. Recollections of Writers. 1878. [Contains 16 letters from Dickens not in the authorised collected edn.]

The Letters of Charles Dickens. Edited by his sister-in-law [Georgina Hogarth] and his eldest daughter [Mamie Dickens]. 3 vols. 1880–2; 2 vols. 1882; 1893.

Heaphy, T. A Wonderful Ghost Story, being Mr H.'s own Narrative, reprinted from All The Year Round; with [3] Letters hitherto Unpublished of Charles Dickens respecting it. 1882.

The Speeches of Charles Dickens [1841–1870]. Ed. R. H. Shepherd, 1884. [With bibliography including sections dealing with letters and with biographies, criticisms, references in current volumes of reminiscence, and magazine articles.]

Hans Christian Andersen's Correspondence. Ed. F. Crawford, [1891]. [Letters to and from Dickens.]

Letters of Charles Dickens to Wilkie Collins, 1851–1870. Selected by Miss G. Hogarth. Ed. L. Hutton, 1892.

Lewes, G. Dr Southwood Smith. A Retrospect. 1898. [Ch. vi deals with Dickens's support in philanthropic work and amateur theatrical performances in aid. Letters, one in facsimile.]

Charles Dickens and Maria Beadnell. Ed. (with notes by J. H. Stonehouse) G. P. Baker, Boston Bibliophile Soc. 1908; St Louis, 1908 (priv. ptd for W. K. Bixby, owner of the MS letters). [See Piccadilly Notes (Henry Sotheran), No. iv, 1933, for history of the letters and their discovery by J. H. Stonehouse. See also The Dickensian, Spring No., 1933.]

The Dickens-Kolle Letters. Supplemental to the letters from Charles Dickens to Maria Beadnell. Ed. H. B. Smith and H. H. Harper, Boston Bibliophile Soc. 1910.

Payne, E. F. and Harper, H. H. The Romance of Charles Dickens and Maria Beadnell

Winter. Boston Bibliophile Soc. 1929. [A commentary on the foregoing and other newly discovered material.]

Charles Dickens as Editor: being Letters written by him to William Henry Wills, his Sub-editor. Ed. R. C. Lehmann, 1912.

Letters to Mark Lemon. Ed. T. J. Wise, 1917.

The Unpublished Letters of Charles Dickens to Mark Lemon. Ed. W. Dexter, 1927.

Clark, Cumberland. Charles Dickens and his Jewish Characters. 1918. [Unpublished letters, with commentary.]

—— The Story of a Great Friendship. Charles Dickens and Clarkson Stanfield. With Seven Unpublished Letters. 1918.

—— Charles Dickens' Letter to Henry Colburn [about W. S. Landor and The Pic Nic Papers]. A Note. 1918.

—— Dickens and Talfourd, with Three Unpublished Letters [on copyright]. 1919.

—— Dickens and the Begging-Letter Writer: with a Letter. 1923.

An Account of the First Performance of Lytton's Comedy 'No So Bad as We Seem,' with Other Matters of Interest. 1919 (priv. ptd). [A letter from Dickens to R. H. Horne, dated 1853, with postscript by W. H. Wills.]

Notes and Comments on certain Writings in Prose and Verse by Richard Henry Horne. [Six letters.] 1920 (priv. ptd). [6 letters.]

An American Note Never Intended For General Circulation. [Cambridge, U.S.A.], 1924 (priv. ptd). [A letter, dated 13 March 1842, from Dickens to Charles Sumner.]

S[awyer], C[harles] J. and D[arton], F. J. H[arvey]. Dickens v. Barabbas, Forster Intervening. A Study based upon some hitherto Unpublished Letters. With Facsimiles. 1930.

The Letters of Charles Dickens to the Baroness Burdett-Coutts. Ed. C. C. Osborne, 1931. [Partial text of a large collection now in U.S.A., with running commentary. A portion appeared in Cornhill Mag. LXX, LXXI, 1931.]

Dickens to His Oldest Friend. Some Unpublished Letters to Thomas Beard. With a Foreword by Sir Henry Fielding Dickens. 1931 (priv. ptd). [5 ptd letters, one unprinted facsimile, and A Fable in facsimile, with brief comment.]

Dickens to his Oldest Friend. The Letters of a Lifetime. Ed. W. Dexter, 1932. [The whole available correspondence with notes, introduction and facsimiles.]

Dexter, W. Dickens to his First Publisher, John Macrone. Some hitherto Unpublished Letters. 1931 (priv. ptd). [Also in The Dickensian, Dec. 1931. With facsimiles.]

Dickens's Letters to Charles Lever. Ed. F. V. Livingston and H. E. Rollins, New York, 1933.

Mr. and Mrs. Charles Dickens. His Letters to Her. Ed. W. Dexter, 1935.

The Love Romance of Charles Dickens, told in his Letters to Maria Beadnell (Mrs. Winter). Ed. W. Dexter, 1936.

The Speeches of Charles Dickens. Ed. B. Darwin, 1937.

The Letters of Charles Dickens. Ed. W. Dexter, 3 vols. 1938. [Fullest collection. Part of Nonesuch Dickens (see p. 438 above).]

Rolfe, F. P. The Dickens Letters in the Huntington Library. Huntington Lib. Quart. I, 1938.

[Many of Dickens's speeches were pbd separately, the majority in America; and some appeared with other matter relevant to their occasion. The following, recorded by J. C. Eckel, The First Editions of Charles Dickens (1932), as ptd, are not included in the collections mentioned above:]

At the [Annual] Festivals—2nd, 4th, 5th, 7th, 8th, 10th, 11th, 12th, 13th, 18th, 21st, 25th—of the General Theatrical Fund. [All pbd in U.S.A.]

The Public Health a Public Question. First Report of The Metropolitan Sanitary Association. 1850.

At the Opening of the Manchester Free Library. Manchester, [1852].

At the Royal Hospital Dinner, [London], May 26, 1857.

At the First Festival Dinner of the Playground and General Recreation Society, June 1st, 1858.

At the Anniversary Festival Dinner of the Royal Free Hospital. N.d. [Delivered 1863; pbd 1870.]

At the Anniversary Dinner of the London or University Hospital, April 12th, 1864.

The Charles Dickens Dinner. An Authentic Record Of The Public Banquet on Nov. 2nd, 1867, Prior To His Departure For The United States. With A Report Of The Speeches. With A Preface By [William] C[harles] [Mark] K[ent]. 1867. [Speeches by Dickens, Lytton, Trollope and others.]

At the Birmingham and Midland Institute, Sept. 27th, 1869. Birmingham, 1869.

(9) BIOGRAPHY AND CRITICISM
(i) Biographies
1. General Works

Forster, John. The Life of Charles Dickens. 3 vols. 1872–4 (13th edn of vol. I, 1873); 2 vols. 1876 (Library edn); 1879 (illustrated); rev. G. Gissing, 1903 (abridged) ed. B. W. Matz, 2 vols. 1911 (500 portraits, facsimiles, etc.); ed. G. K. Chesterton, 2 vols. 1927 (Everyman's Lib.); ed. J. W. T. Ley, [1928] (notes embody much new matter).

[Hotten, J. C., or Grego, J.?] Charles Dickens. The Story of his Life, by the Author of the 'Life of Thackeray.' [1870]; [1873].

Sala, G. A. Charles Dickens. [1870.]

Mackenzie, R. S. Life of Charles Dickens. Philadelphia, [1870].

Jerrold, W. B. The Best of All Good Company: a [monthly] Series. 1871–2. [Pt ɪ, A Day with Charles Dickens, June, 1871. Includes short life, personal appreciation, account of friendships, and facs. of handwriting.]

Stoddard, R. H. Anecdote Biographies of Thackeray and Dickens. New York, 1874.

Langton, R. Charles Dickens and Rochester. 1880. [Rptd with addns from Papers of Manchester Literary Club. Partly incorporated in following work.]

—— The Childhood and Youth of Charles Dickens. With Retrospective Notes and Elucidations, from his Books and Letters. Manchester, 1883; 1891 (enlarged and rev.); 1912 (with memoir of author. [Supplements and controverts Forster.]

Jones, C. H. A Short Life of Charles Dickens. With Selections from his Letters. New York, 1880.

Ward, Sir A. W. Charles Dickens. 1882. (English Men of Letters ser.)

Dickens, Mary. Charles Dickens. By his Eldest Daughter. 1885; 1911.

—— My Father as I recall him. [1897.]

Marzials, Sir F. T. Life of Charles Dickens. 1887.

Kitton, F. G. Charles Dickens by Pen and Pencil. Including Anecdotes and Reminiscences collected by his Friends and Companions. 1890; 1891.

Matz, B. W. Charles Dickens. The Story of his Life and Writings. [1902.] [Rptd from Household Words, 14 June 1902.]

Shore, W. T. Dickens. 1904; 1910.

—— Charles Dickens and his Friends. 1909.

Fitzgerald, P. H. The Life of Charles Dickens as revealed in his Writings. 2 vols. 1905.

—— Memoirs of Charles Dickens. 1913.

Chesterton, G. K. Charles Dickens. 1906.

Ellison, O. Charles Dickens, Novelist. [1908.]

Dark, S. Charles Dickens. 1919.

Dexter, W. Dickens: the Story of the Life of the World's Favourite Author. 1927.

Dickens, Sir H. F. Memories of my Father. 1928.

Straus, R. Dickens: a Portrait in Pencil. 1928. [Based partly on unpbd material.]

Stonehouse, J. H. Green Leaves: New Chapters in the Life of Charles Dickens. 1930–1 (priv. ptd); 1931 (rev.).

Darwin, B. Charles Dickens. 1933.

Leacock, S. Dickens. 1933.

'Kingsmill, Hugh.' The Sentimental Journey. A Life of Charles Dickens. 1934.

Wright, T. The Life of Charles Dickens. 1935.

2. *Special Periods and Aspects*

'Morna' (T. M. O'Keefe). The Battle of London Life; or, Boz and his Secretary. With six [five] Designs on Stone by George Sala. 1849.

Yates, E. Mr Thackeray, Mr Yates and The Garrick Club. The Correspondence and Facts. 1859 (priv. ptd). [See also In Memoriam, W. M. T., by Charles Dickens, Cornhill Mag. Feb. 1864, rptd in American (not English) edn of Thackeray the Humorist and the Man of Letters. By Theodore Taylor (*i.e.* J. C. Hotten or J. Grego), New York, 1864.]

Stanley, A. P. A Sermon preached in Westminster Abbey the Sunday following the Funeral of Charles Dickens. 1870.

Fields, J. T. In and Out of Doors with Charles Dickens. Boston, 1876. [In part rptd from Yesterdays with Authors, 1872.]

Fitzgerald, P. H. Recreations of a Literary Man. 2 vols. 1882. [Vol. ɪ, ch. 4, Charles Dickens as an Editor; ch. 5, Charles Dickens at Home.]

—— John Forster, by One of his Friends. 1903.

Payn, James. The Youth and Middle Age of Charles Dickens. 1883. [Rptd from Chambers's Journ.]

—— Some Literary Recollections. 1884.

Hone, P. The Diary of Philip Hone. Ed. B. Tuckerman, 2 vols. New York, 1889. [Vol. ɪɪ, intimate account of Dickens's reception in U.S.A. in 1842.]

Axon, W. E. A. Charles Dickens and Shorthand. [1892.] [Dickens as a reporter.]

Wilkins, W. G. Charles Dickens in America. 1911.

Renton, R. John Forster and his Friendships. 1912.

Ley, J. W. T. The Dickens Circle. A Narrative of the Novelist's Friendships. 1918.

Langstaff, J. B. David Copperfield's Library. 1924. [An account of Dickens's residence in boyhood at 13 Johnson Street, Camden Town, London, now held as a national trust and used as a children's library.]

Humphreys, Arthur. Charles Dickens and his First Schoolmaster [*i.e.* William Giles, of Chatham]. 1926.

Carlton, W. J. Charles Dickens, Shorthand Writer. 1926.

Payne, E. F. Dickens Days in Boston. A Record of Daily Events. Boston, 1927.

Gray, W. F. The Edinburgh Relatives and Friends of Dickens. [1927.] [Rptd from The Dickensian.]

3. *Personal Recollections and Memoirs*

[References to Dickens occur in numerous contemporary biographies and vols. of reminiscence. They can be traced through his more intimate friendships, for which see J. W. T. Ley, The Dickens Circle, 1918, and W. T. Shore, Charles Dickens and his Friends, 1909. A number of extracts are given in J. A. Hammerton, The Dickens Companion, 1910. The following select list includes only writers not specially mentioned already whose personal contacts with Dickens have more than casual interest.]

Ainger, A. Mr Dickens's Amateur Theatricals. [1870.] [In Lectures and Essays, vol. II, 1905.]

Ainsworth, W. H. William Harrison Ainsworth and his Friends. By S. M. Ellis. 2 vols. 1911.

Andersen, H. C. Pictures of Travel. New York, 1871. [Pp. 267–93, A Visit at Charles Dickens's House. See also R. N. Bain's Life of Andersen, 1895.]

Berger, F. Reminiscences, Impressions, and Anecdotes. [1913.] [Ch. 3.]

Browning, R. Life and Letters. Ed. Mrs S. Orr, 1908 (rev. edn).

Carlyle, T. Thomas Carlyle, a History of His Life in London, 1834–1881. By J. A. Froude. 2 vols. 1884.

Clarke, C. and M. C. Recollections of Writers. 1878. [See also Mary Cowden Clarke's My Long Life, 1896.]

Collier, J. P. An Old Man's Diary, Forty Years ago. 4 pts, 1871–2 (priv. ptd).

Frith, W. P. My Autobiography and Reminiscences. 3 vols. 1887–8.

Grant, James. The Newspaper Press. 3 vols. 1871[–2].

Hall, S. C. A Book of Memories of Great Men and Women of the Age, from Personal Acquaintance. 1870.

—— Retrospect of a Long Life: from 1815 to 1883. 2 vols. 1883.

Hodder, G. Memories of My Time including Personal Reminiscences of Eminent Men. 1870.

Hood, T. Thomas Hood: His Life and Times. By Walter Jerrold. 1907.

Jeaffreson, J. C. A Book of Recollections. 2 vols. 1894.

Jeffrey, F. (Lord Jeffrey). Life of, with a Selection from his Correspondence. By Lord Cockburn. 2 vols. 1852. [Vol. II, 10 letters to Dickens.]

Jerdan, W. Autobiography. 4 vols. 1852–3.

Jerdan, W. Personal Reminiscences. [Ed. R. H. Stoddard], 1874.

Lever, C. J. Life of, by W. J. Fitzpatrick. 2 vols. 1879.

Linton, E. (Mrs Lynn Linton). My Literary Life. 1899.

Mackay, Charles. Forty Years' Recollections of Life, Literature, and Public Affairs. From 1830 to 1870. 2 vols. 1877.

Macready, W. C. Reminiscences, and Selections from his Diaries and Letters. Ed. Sir F. Pollock, 2 vols. 1875.

—— The Diaries. Ed. W. Toynbee, 2 vols. 1912.

Marryat, Frederick. Life and Letters, by Florence Marryat. 2 vols. 1872.

Mason, E. T. Personal Traits of British Authors. 3 vols. New York, 1885. [Extracts from contemporary personal impressions, with brief comment. Dickens in vol. III.]

Ritchie, A. T., Lady. Charles Dickens as I remember him. [In From the Porch, 1913.]

Storey, G. Dickens and Daughter. 1939.

Thackeray, W. M. [Many allusions and criticisms in essays and letters. See especially Dickens in France (1842), Jerome Paturot (1843), in various edns of Collected Works; A Collection of Letters, 1847–1855, 1887; Letters of Anne Thackeray Ritchie. With 42 Additional Letters from her Father, 1924.]

Willis, N. P. Ephemera. New York, 1854.

Yates, E. Recollections and Experiences. 2 vols. 1884.

(ii) Critical Studies
1. *Books*

Fitzgerald, P. H. Two English Essayists: Charles Lamb and Charles Dickens. 1863.

Canning, A. S. G. Philosophy of Charles Dickens. 1880.

—— Dickens and Thackeray studied in Three Novels [Pickwick, Nicholas Nickleby, Vanity Fair]. 1911.

—— Dickens studied in Six Novels. 1912.

Gissing, G. Charles Dickens: a Critical Study. 1898; 1926.

—— Dickens. 1906.

—— Critical Studies of the Works of Charles Dickens. Ed. T. Scott, 1924.

—— The Immortal Dickens. 1925. [9 introductions, from Works ed. by Gissing.]

Hughes, James L. Dickens as an Educator. New York, 1900.

Chesterton, G. K. and Kitton, F. G. Charles Dickens. 1903.

Saunders, Margaret B. The Philosophy of Dickens: a Study of his Life and Teaching as a Social Reformer. 1905.

Leffmann, H. About Dickens: being a Few Essays on Themes suggested by the Novels. Philadelphia, 1908 (priv. ptd).

Pugh, E. W. Charles Dickens. The Apostle of the People. 1908; 1910.
—— The Charles Dickens Originals. 1912.
Chesterton, G. K. Appreciations and Criticisms of the Works of Charles Dickens. 1911; 1933.
—— The Victorian Age in Literature. [1913]; 1925.
Moses, B. Charles Dickens and his Girl Heroines. 1911.
Walters, J. C. Phases of Dickens. The Man, his Message, and his Mission. 1911.
Thomson, W. R. In Dickens Street. 1912. [Studies in Dickens characters.]
Whipple, E. P. Charles Dickens: the Man and his Work. 2 vols. Boston, 1912.
Swinburne, A. C. Charles Dickens. With Preface and Illustrative Notes by the Editor [T. Watts-Dunton]. 1913. [Rptd with addns from Quarterly Rev. July 1902, with an unpbd section on Oliver Twist.]
Crotch, W. W. Charles Dickens, Social Reformer. 1913.
—— The Pageant of Dickens. 1915; 1916.
—— The Soul of Dickens. 1916.
—— The Secret of Dickens. 1919.
—— The Touchstone of Dickens. 1920.
Charles Dickens. A Bookman Extra Number. 1914. [By various writers: chiefly reprints of prefaces, essays, etc., and numerous illustrations, previously pbd in other forms.]
Burton, R. E. Dickens: how to know him. Indianapolis, 1919.
Phillips, W. C. Dickens, Reade, and Collins, Sensation Novelists. A Study in the Conditions and Theories of Novel Writing in Victorian England. New York, 1919.
Nicoll, Sir W. R. Dickens's Own Story. Sidelights on his Life and Personality. 1923. [Rptd criticisms.]
Clark, Cumberland. The Dogs in Dickens. 1926.
—— Dickens and Democracy, and Other Studies. 1930.
Roberts, C. E. B. ('Ephesian'). This Side Idolatry. 1928. [Biography in the form of a novel.]
Wagenknecht, E. The Man Charles Dickens. 1929.
Kent, W. Dickens and Religion. 1930.
Procter, W. C. Christian Teaching in the Novels of Charles Dickens. [1930.]
Chancellor, E. B. Dickens and his Times. [1932.]
Sitwell, O. Dickens. 1932.
Jackson, T. A. Charles Dickens: the Progress of a Radical. 1937.

2. Shorter Appreciations

[Unreprinted articles are not included, nor are special chs. in general histories of English literature. The Dickensian has recorded these as they have appeared from 1905 onwards, and has also rptd earlier pieces from time to time.]

Horne, R. H. A New Spirit of the Age. Vol. I, 1844. [See also E. B. Browning's 2 letters to Horne, 1844, priv. ptd 1919 as Charles Dickens and Other 'Spirits of the Age.']
[Cruikshank, George.] A Letter from Hop-o'-my-Thumb to Charles Dickens, Esq. [1854.] [Rptd from George Cruikshank's Magazine, Feb. 1854.]
Ham, J. P. Parables of Fiction: A Memorial Discourse on Charles Dickens. 1870.
Trollope, A. Charles Dickens. The Dickensian, June 1910. [Rptd from The St Paul's Mag. July 1870.]
Harte, F. B. Dickens in Camp. [In Poetical Works, Boston, 1871, etc.]
—— The Haunted Man. A Christmas Story. By Ch–r–s D–c–k–n–s. [In Sensation Novels Condensed, [1871], etc.]
Bagehot, W. Charles Dickens. [In Literary Studies, vol. II, 1879. Written 1858.]
Watt, J. C. Great Novelists. Scott, Thackeray, Dickens, Lytton. Edinburgh, 1880.
Lang, A. Dickens. [In Essays in Little, 1891.]
Harrison, Frederic. Studies in Early Victorian Literature. 1895.
Lilly, W. S. Four English Humourists of the Nineteenth Century. 1895. [Dickens, Thackeray, George Eliot and Carlyle.]
Saintsbury, G. Corrected Impressions. Studies in Victorian Writers. 1895. [2 papers on Dickens.]
Rideal, C. F. Charles Dickens' Heroines and Women-Folk. [1896] (rev. edn).
Murray, David C. First, the Critics, and then a Word on Dickens. [In My Contemporaries in Fiction, 1897.]
Machen, A. Hieroglyphics. 1902. [On Pickwick and Vanity Fair.]
Hutton, R. H. The Genius of Dickens. [In Brief Literary Criticisms selected from The Spectator, 1906.]
Barlow, G. The Genius of Dickens. [1909.] [Rptd from Contemporary Rev.]
Beerbohm, M. Dickens. By G**rge M**re. [In A Christmas Garland, 1912. A parody of George Moore which is also an oblique criticism of Dickens.]
Leacock, S. Fiction and Reality: A Study of the Art of Charles Dickens. [In Essays and Literary Studies, 1916.]
Meynell, A. Dickens as a Man of Letters. [In Hearts of Controversy, [1917].]
Darwin, Sir F. Charles Dickens. [In Springtime and Other Essays, 1920.]
Zweig, S. Drei Meister. Balzac, Dickens, Dostoievsky. Leipzig, 1920; tr. Eng. 1930.
Santayana, G. Dickens. [In Soliloquies in England, and Later Soliloquies, 1922.]

Elton, O. Dickens and Thackeray. 1924. [Separate issue of chs. from A Survey of English Literature, 1830–1880, 2 vols. 1920, with some addns.]

Furniss, H. Charles Dickens. [In Some Victorian Men, 1924. Mainly Dickens as an actor.]

Priestley, J. B. The English Comic Characters. 1925. [The Two Wellers, Dick Swiveller, Mr Micawber.]

Quiller-Couch, Sir A. T. Charles Dickens and Other Victorians. Cambridge, 1925.

Williams, Orlo. Martin Chuzzlewit. [In Some Great English Novels. Studies in the Art of Fiction, 1926.]

Maurois, A. Études anglaises. Paris, 1927.
—— Dickens. Tr. Eng. 1934.

Baker, E. A. The History of the English Novel. Vol. vii, 1936. [Chs. v, vi.]

(iii) Special Studies

1. *Works of Reference*

Pierce, G. A. The Dickens Dictionary. A Key to the Characters and Scenes of the Novels and Miscellaneous Works alphabetically arranged. With Additions by W. A. Wheeler. Boston, 1872; 1878.

McSpadden, J. W. Synopses of Dickens's Novels. [1905]; [1909].

Williams, Mary. The Dickens Concordance: being a Compendium of Names and Characters and Principal Places mentioned in all the Works of Charles Dickens. 1907.

Philip, Alexander J. A Dickens Dictionary: the Characters and Scenes of the Novels and Miscellaneous Works alphabetically arranged. 1909; 1928 (rev. and enlarged in collaboration with W. L. Gadd).

Fyfe, T. A. Who's Who in Dickens. A Complete Dickens Repertory in Dickens' Own Words. 1912.

Stevens, J. S. Quotations and References in Charles Dickens. Boston, 1929.

2. *Topographical Studies*

Pemberton, T. E. Dickens's London. Guildford, 1876.

Frost, T. In Kent with Charles Dickens. 1880.

Rimmer, A. About England with Dickens. 1883.

Allbut, R. London Rambles 'en zigzag' with Charles Dickens. [1886.]
—— Rambles in Dickens Land. 1899; 1903 (rev.).

Hughes, William R. A Week's Tramp in Dickens-Land, together with Personal Reminiscences. 1891.

Fitzgerald, P. H. Bozland. Dickens' Places and People. 1895.
—— Boz and Bath. Bath, 1905.

[See also Minor Works, Pavilionstone.]

Trumble, A. In Jail with Charles Dickens. 1896. [A study of the prisons described by Dickens.]

'Miltoun, Francis' (F. M. Milburg). Dickens' London. With Many Illustrations and Plans. 1904.

Ward, H. S. and C. W. B. The Real Dickens Land. With an Outline of Dickens's Life. 1904.

Bowes, C. C. The Associations of Charles Dickens with Liverpool. With an Introduction by Edgar A. Browne. Liverpool, 1905.

Kitton, F. G. The Dickens Country. 1905; 1911; 1925.

Harris, Edwin. Gad's Hill Place and Charles Dickens. Rochester, 1910.

Nicklin, J. A. Dickens-Land. Pictured by E. W. Haslehurst. 1911.

Smith, Francis H. In Dickens' London. 1914. A Dickens Pilgrimage. 1914. [Rptd from The Times.]

Matz, B. W. Dickensian Inns and Taverns. 1922.

Hopkins, A. A. and Read, N. F. A Dickens Atlas. New York, 1923.

Miller, Leonard. References in the Works of Charles Dickens to Rochester, Chatham and Neighbourhood and to Persons resident therein. A Paper read at the Grand Pump Room, Bath, Oct. 2nd, 1923. Bath, [1923].

Clark, Cumberland. Dickens' London: a Lecture. 1923.

Dexter, W. The London of Dickens. 1923; 1930 (3rd edn).
—— The Kent of Dickens. 1924.
—— The England of Dickens. 1925.
—— Days in Dickensland. 1933. [Chiefly London and Kent.]

Cooper, T. P. With Dickens in Yorkshire. With an Introduction by B. W. Matz. York, [1923], 1924 (rev.).

Hayward, A. L. The Dickens Encyclopaedia. 1924.
—— The Days of Dickens. [1926.]

Kent, W. With Charles Dickens in the Borough. [1926.]
—— The George Inn, Southwark. [1932.]

Moreland, A. Dickens in London. 47 Drawings with Descriptive Notes. 1928.
—— Dickens Landmarks in London. 1931.

Wilson, S. G. F. Canterbury and Charles Dickens. Canterbury, [1928].

Barnes, A. W. A Dickens Guide. 1929.

3. *Dickens's Illustrators and Illustrations*

[For extra illustrations to particular works, see under Novels and Minor Works, above. The following entries include only (1) general collections of illustrations or commentaries on them; (2) works dealing with an illustrator's relations with Dickens; not general biographies of the artists.]

Archer, T. Charles Dickens: A Gossip about his Life, Works, and Characters. With Eighteen Full-page Character Sketches (reproduced in photogravure) by Frederick Barnard, and Other Illustrations by Well-known Artists. In Six Sections for Subscribers only. [1894?]; [1902].

Scenes and Characters from the Works of Charles Dickens. Being 866 drawings [by various artists] printed from the Original Woodblocks engraved for 'The Household Edition.' 1898. [With an introductory note.]

Grego, J. Pictorial Pickwickiana. Charles Dickens and his Illustrators. With 350 Drawings and Engravings [by various artists who illustrated original or early edns of Dickens]. 2 vols. 1899. [Commentary and bibliographical notes are not confined to The Pickwick Papers.]

Kitton, F. G. Dickens and his Illustrators. 1899. [All the recognised illustrators, with 22 portraits and 70 unpbd illustrations, and bibliography.]

Hammerton, Sir J. A. The Dickens Picture-Book, A Record of the Dickens Illustrations. [1910]. [Vol. XVII of The Charles Dickens Library. See above, Collected Works.]

Nonesuch Dickensiana. 1937. [I. A. Waugh, Charles Dickens and his Illustrators; II. T. Hatton, A Bibliographical List of the Original Illustrations to the Works of Charles Dickens.]

Kitton, F. G. 'Phiz' (Hablot Knight Browne). A Memoir. 1882. [Quotes unpbd letters from Dickens.]

Browne, Edgar A. Phiz and Dickens. 1913. [By the artist's son.]

Cohn, A. M. George Cruikshank: a Catalogue Raisonné. 1924.

Barnard, Frederick. A Series of Character Sketches from Dickens. [Lithographed. 6 plates. Re-issued in photogravure in 1887 uniformly with 2 further sers. (6 plates each) pbd in 1884 and 1885 respectively. All the 18 plates, in photogravure, were re-issued later in six sections for subscribers, with letterpress by T. Archer (see above).]

Gibson, C. D. People of Dickens. New York, 1897. [6 plates.]

Crowdy, W. L. Famous Dickens Pictures. [1912.] [Reproduction of 12 illustrations by Charles Green, with brief introduction.]

Lewin, F. G. Characters from Dickens. A Portfolio of 20 Vandyck Gravures from the Drawings of F. G. L., with an Introduction by B. W. Matz. 1912.

Fraser, C. L. Characters from Dickens. [1924.] [18 coloured plates, and decorations. Foreword by H. Macfall.]

Reynolds, Frank. The Buchanan Portfolio of Characters from Dickens. Glasgow, [1925]. [14 coloured plates.]

4. Miscellaneous Works

Christian, E. B. V. Leaves of the Lower Branch. The Attorney in Life and Letters. 1909.

Fyfe, T. A. Charles Dickens and the Law. 1910.

Lightwood, J. T. Charles Dickens and Music. 1912; 1916.

Gordon, E. H. The Naming of Characters in the Works of Charles Dickens. Lincoln, Nebraska, 1917.

Wilkins, W. G. Dickens in Cartoon and Caricature. With an Introduction by B. W. Matz. Boston Bibliophile Soc. 1924. [Facsimiles with notes and comment.]

Delattre, F. Dickens et la France. Paris, 1927. [Includes unpbd letters.]

Holdsworth, Sir W. S. Charles Dickens as a Legal Historian. New Haven, 1928.

Newton, A. E. This Book-Collecting Game. Boston, 1928.

Darwin, B. The Dickens Advertiser. A Collection of the Advertisements in the Original Parts of Novels by Charles Dickens. 1930. [A narrative and criticism with facsimiles.]

Sennewald, C. Die Namengebung bei Dickens; eine Studie über Lautsymbolik. Leipzig, 1936.   F. J. H. D.

CHARLES READE (1814–1884)

(1) Bibliographies

Sadleir, M. Excursions in Victorian Bibliography. 1922. [Contains a bibliography of Reade.]

Elwin, M. Charles Reade. A Biography. 1930. [Contains a bibliographical list.]

(2) Collected Works

The Uniform Library Edition. 17 vols. 1895.
The Popular Edition in Uniform Binding. 21 vols. [Various dates.]

(3) Novels and Tales

Peg Woffington: A Novel. 1853; 1857; 1868; [1872]; 1899; [1901], etc.

Christi Johnstone: a Novel. 1853; 1854 (3rd edn); 1857; 1868; 1872, etc.

Clouds and Sunshine and Art: a Dramatic Tale. Boston, 1855.

It Is Never Too Late To Mend: a Matter of Fact Romance. 3 vols. 1856 (bis); 2 vols. Leipzig, 1856; 1857; 1868; [1872]; 1893; 1900, etc. [Reade wrote a pamphlet defending his novel under the title: It Is Never Too Late To Mend. Proofs of Its Prison Revelations, 1859.]

The Course Of True Love Never Did Run Smooth. 1857; 1868; [1873]. [First pbd in Bentley's Misc.]

White Lies. A Story. 3 vols. 1857; 1868 (as The Double Marriage, Or White Lies); [1872]. [First pbd in London Journ.]

The Box Tunnel. Boston, 1857. [This short story was pbd in Bentley's Misc. Nov. 1853, and only issued in book form in America.]

Cream. 1858; [1873]. [Contains: Jack of All Trades, a Matter of Fact Romance (first pbd in Illustrated London News, 1856); The Autobiography of a Thief.]

'Love Me Little Love Me Long.' 2 vols. 1859; Leipzig, 1859; 1868; [1873].

A Good Fight and Other Tales. With Illustrations by Charles Keene. New York, 1859; ed. A. Lang, 1910. [A Good Fight, first pbd in Once a Week, 1859, is the earliest version of The Cloister and the' Hearth.]

The Eighth Commandment. 1860.

The Cloister and the Hearth: A Tale of the Middle Ages. 4 vols. 1861; 1862; 2 vols. Leipzig, 1864; 1868; 1873; ed. Sir W. Besant, 4 vols. 1894; 1900; 1901; 1902; 1903; ed. A. C. Swinburne, 1905, 1906, 1907; 1909, etc.; ed. C. B. Wheeler, 1915 (Oxford edn).

Hard Cash: A Matter of Fact Romance. 3 vols. 1863; 3 vols. 1864; 3 vols. Leipzig, 1864; 1868; [1872]; 1898; [1906]; 1909. [First pbd in All The Year Round as Very Hard Cash.]

Griffith Gaunt: Or Jealousy. 3 vols. 1866 (*bis*); 3 vols. 1867; 1868 (5th edn); 1869; [1872]. [First pbd in The Argosy.]

Foul Play. 3 vols. 1868; rptd 1927. [First pbd in Once a Week, 1868.]

Put Yourself in His Place. 3 vols. 1870; 1871; 1876. [First pbd in Cornhill Mag.]

A Terrible Temptation. 3 vols. 1871. [First pbd in Cassell's Mag. Reade's pamphlet To the Editor of The Daily Globe, Toronto. A Reply to Criticism, 1871, deals with this book.]

A Simpleton: a Story of the Day. 3 vols. 1873. [First pbd in London Society.]

Trade Malice: a Personal Narrative, and The Wandering Heir: a Matter of Fact Romance. 1875. [The Wandering Heir was first pbd in The Graphic, 1872; it has been rptd 1905 and [1924].]

A Woman Hater. 3 vols. 1877.

Golden Crowns: Sunday Stories. Manchester, 1877.

Single Heart and Double Face: a Matter of Fact Romance. 1884. [First pbd in Harper's Mag.]

Good Stories of Man and Other Animals. 1884.

The Jilt: and Other Stories. With Four Illustrations by Joseph Nash. 1884.

A Perilous Secret. 2 vols. 1884; 1885; 1891. [First pbd in Temple Bar Mag.]

(4) PLAYS

Peregrine Pickle. [1834–5?] (priv. ptd).

The Ladies' Battle: or Un Duel en Amour. A Comedy. [1851]; 1877 (rev.).

Angelo: a Tragedy in Four Acts. 1851.

The Lost Husband: a Drama in Four Acts Written and Adapted from the French. 1852. [Based on Les Dames de la Halle.]

Gold: a Drama. [1853]; 1899 (Dicks's Standard Plays).

The Courier of Lyons: or The Attack Upon The Mail: a Drama in Four Acts. Translated from the French of MM. Moreau, Siraudin and Delacourt. 1854.

Masks and Faces: or Before and Behind the Curtain: a Comedy in Two Acts by Tom Taylor and Charles Reade. 1854.

Two Loves and A Life: a Drama in Four Acts. By Tom Taylor and Charles Reade. 1854.

The King's Rival: a Drama in Five Acts. By Tom Taylor and Charles Reade. 1854.

Poverty and Pride: a Drama in Five Acts. Being the Authorised English Version of Les Pauvres de Paris, a Drama by Edward Brisebarre and Eugene Nus. 1857.

The Hypochondriac. Adapted to the English Stage from the Malade Imaginaire of Molière. 1857.

Le Faubourg Saint-Germain. Paris, 1859.

Dora: a Pastoral Poem in Three Acts. Founded on Mr Tennyson's Poem. 1867. [For this see Reade's pamphlet Dora: or the History of a Play, 1877.]

The Double Marriage. A Drama. In Five Acts. By Auguste Maquet and Charles Reade. [1867.] [Based on Maquet's Le Château Grantier.]

Kate Peyton: or Jealousy. [1869?]; 1883 (slightly different text).

It's Never Too Late To Mend. A Drama in Five Acts. 1872. [Also an unauthorised edn of Reade's dramatisation of his novel. N.d.]

The Well-Born Workman: or A Man of the Day. 1878.

Foul Play. A Drama. 1883. [With D. Boucicault. Produced 1868.]

Love and Money; an Original Drama in a Prologue and Four Acts. By Charles Reade and Henry Pettitt. 1883.

The Countess and the Dancer: or High Life in Vienna; a Comedy Drama in Four Acts. Altered from a Comedy Masterpiece of Victorien Sardou. 1883.

(5) PAMPHLETS AND OTHER WRITINGS

It is Never Too Late to Mend. Proofs of its Prison Revelations. 1859.

Monopoly Versus Property. 1860.

The Prurient Prude. 1866.

To the Editor of The Daily Globe, Toronto. A Reply to Criticism. 1871.

The Legal Vocabulary. 1872.

A Hero and A Martyr: a True and Accurate Account of the Heroic Feats and Sad Calamity of James Lambert. 1874.

Dora; Or the History of a Play. 1877.

Readiana: Comments on Current Events. 1883.

Bible Characters. 1888.

[The London Lib. possesses 32 vols. folio commonplace books, containing cuttings, suggestions for plots, reviews and opinions by Reade.]

(6) Principal Contributions to Periodicals

[For the novels and stories later pbd separately see above.]

Bentley's Miscellany. [Clouds and Sunshine, June–Sept. 1854.]

The Times. [Facts Must Be Faced, Aug. 1871.]

The Pall Mall Gazette. [Ancient Musical Instruments, 5 June 1872; The Rights and Wrongs of Authors, 13 letters Sept.–Oct. 1875.]

Belgravia. [A Special Constable, July 1876; Suspended Animation, Aug. 1876; Lambert's Leap, Sept. 1876; The Two Lears, Sept. 1876; Doubles, 1877.]

The Daily Telegraph. [Hang In Haste, Repent At Leisure, 6 letters 29 Sept.–13 Oct. 1877; The Coming Man, March 1878.]

Life. [The Knightsbridge Mystery, May–June 1882.]

Harper's New Monthly Magazine. [Tit For Tat, Jan. 1883; Rus, June 1883; Born To Good Luck, July 1883; There's Many a Slip 'Twixt the Cup and the Lip, Dec. 1883; The Picture, April 1884.]

(7) Biography and Criticism

(a) Books

Reade, C. L. and C. Charles Reade: Dramatist, Novelist, Journalist. A Memoir compiled chiefly from his Literary Remains. 2 vols. 1887.

Coleman, J. Charles Reade as I knew him. 1903.

Phillips, W. C. Dickens, Reade and Collins: Sensation Novelists. New York, 1919.

Elwin, M. Charles Reade. A Biography. 1931.

(b) Essays, Articles and Chapters of Books

Charles Reade. Blackwood's Mag. cvi, 1869.

Archer, W. English Dramatists. 1882.

Besant, Sir W. The Novels of Reade. GM. xxix, 1882.

'Ouida' (M. L. de la Ramée). Charles Reade. GM. xxix, 1882.

Littledale, R. F. Charles Reade. Academy, 19 April 1884.

Swinburne, A. C. Miscellanies. [1886], pp. 271–302.

Buchanan, R. A Look Round Literature. 1887.

Courtney, W. L. Charles Reade's Novels. [In Studies New and Old, 1889.]

Howells, W. D. My Literary Passions. New York, 1895.

Moulton, R. G. Four Years Novel Reading. Boston, 1895.

Quiller-Couch, Sir A. T. Adventures in Criticism. 1896.

Lord, W. F. The Mirror of the Century. 1906.

Hornung, E. W. Charles Reade. London Mercury, iv, 1921.

Turner, A. M. Another Source for the Cloister and the Hearth. PMLA. xl, 1925. [See also O. R. Kuehne, Classical Weekly, 25 April 1932, pp. 177–81.]

—— Charles Reade and Montaigne. MP. xxx, 1933.

—— The Making of The Cloister and the Hearth. Chicago, 1938.

Hruby, A. Zur Darstellungstechnik des englischen Romans. Die Personen in Charles Reades 'Matter of Fact' Romanen. Vienna, 1928.

Sutcliffe, E. G. Charles Reade's Notebooks. Stud. Phil. xxvii, 1930.

—— The Stage in Reade's Novels. Stud. Phil. xxvii, 1930.

—— Femina Vera in Charles Reade's Novels. PMLA. xlvi, 1931.

—— Plotting in Reade's Novels. PMLA. xlvii, 1932.   S. J. L.

ANTHONY TROLLOPE (1815–1882)

(1) Bibliographies

Lavington, M. [Bibliography appended to T. H. S. Escott's Anthony Trollope, 1913.]

Sadleir, M. Excursions in Victorian Bibliography. 1922.

—— Trollope. A Bibliography. 1928.

Irwin, M. L. Anthony Trollope. A Bibliography. New York, 1926.

(2) Collected Works

The Barsetshire Novels. Ed. F. Harrison, 8 vols. 1906, 1923, 1928.

The Shakespeare Head Edition of Anthony Trollope. Group i, The Barchester Novels. Ed. M. Sadleir, 14 vols. Oxford, 1929.

31

(3) NOVELS AND TALES

The Macdermots of Ballycloran. 3 vols. 1847 (re-issued 1848 as The Macdermots of Ballycloran. A Historical Romance); 1859; 1865; 1866; rptd [1905].

The Kellys and the O'Kellys: A Tale of Irish Life. 3 vols. 1848; 1859; 1865 (5th edn); 1866; rptd 1929 (World's Classics).

La Vendée: An Historical Romance. 3 vols. 1850; 1875.

The Warden. 1855; 1858; 1859; Leipzig, 1859; 1866; 1870; 1886; 1902, etc.; rptd 1918 (World's Classics).

Barchester Towers. 3 vols. 1857; 1858; 2 vols. Leipzig, 1859; 1866; 1870; 1886; 1902; 1903; [1906], etc.; rptd 1925 (World's Classics).

The Three Clerks. 3 vols. 1858; 1859; 1860; 1865; 1878; 1884; 1891; 1900; 1903; 1904; ed. W. T. Shore, 1907 (World's Classics).

Doctor Thorne. 3 vols. 1858 (bis); 2 vols. Leipzig, 1858; 1859; 1865; [1901]; 1906, etc.; rptd 1926 (World's Classics).

The Bertrams. 3 vols. 1859; 2 vols. Leipzig, 1859; 3 vols. 1859; 1860; 1861; 1866; [1904].

Castle Richmond. 3 vols. 1860; 1860; 2 vols. Leipzig, 1860; 1866; [1905].

Tales of All Countries. 1861. Second Series 1863. Both sers. 1864; 1866; rptd 1931 (World's Classics).

Framley Parsonage. With Six Illustrations by J. E. Millais. 3 vols. 1861; 1861; 2 vols. Leipzig, 1861; 1869; 1872; 1879; 1886; 1890; 1903; [1904]; 1906; [1907], etc.; rptd 1926 (World's Classics). [First pbd in Cornhill Mag. Jan. 1860–April 1861.]

Orley Farm. 20 monthly pts, March 1861–Oct. 1862; 2 vols. 1862; 3 vols. Leipzig, 1862; 1868; 1871; 2 vols. 1906; rptd 2 vols. 1935 (World's Classics).

The Struggles of Brown, Jones and Robinson By one of the Firm. New York, 1862 (pirated); 1870 (authorized). [First pbd in Cornhill Mag. Aug. 1861–March 1862.]

Rachel Ray. 2 vols. 1863; 2 vols. Leipzig, 1863; 1864 (7th edn); 1866; rptd 1924 (World's Classics).

The Small House at Allington With Eighteen Illustrations by J. E. Millais. 2 vols. 1864; 1864; 3 vols. Leipzig, 1864; 1869; 1872; 1877; 2 vols. 1879; 1903; 2 vols. 1906; [1909]; 1914; rptd 2 vols. 1938 (World's Classics). [First pbd in Cornhill Mag. Sept. 1862–April 1864.]

Can You Forgive Her? 20 monthly pts, Jan. 1864–Aug. 1865; 2 vols. 1864; 3 vols. Leipzig, 1865; 1866; 1868; 1869; 1871; 1873; 1889; 2 vols. [1907]; rptd 2 vols. 1938 (World's Classics).

Miss MacKenzie. 2 vols. 1865; 1866 (illustrated); 1868; [1876]; rptd 1924 (World's Classics).

The Belton Estate. 3 vols. 1866 (3 edns); 2 vols. Leipzig, 1866; 1866 (illustrated); 1868; rptd 1923 (World's Classics). [First pbd in Fortnightly Rev. 15 May 1865–1 Jan. 1866.]

Nina Balatka: The Story of a Maiden of Prague. 2 vols. 1867 (remainder 2 vols. in 1 1879); Leipzig, 1867. [First pbd Blackwood's Mag. July 1866–Jan. 1867.]

The Last Chronicle of Barset. With Thirty-Two Illustrations by George H. Thomas. 32 weekly pts, 1 Dec. 1866–6 July 1867; 2 vols. 1867; 3 vols. Leipzig, 1867; 2 vols. 1869; 1872; 2 vols. 1879; 2 vols. 1906; 2 vols. [1909]; 2 vols. 1910; 1914, etc.; rptd 2 vols. 1932 (World's Classics).

The Claverings. With Sixteen Illustrations by M. Ellen Edwards. 2 vols. 1867; 2 vols. Leipzig, 1867; 1871; 1872; rptd 1924 (World's Classics). [First pbd in Cornhill Mag. Feb. 1866–May 1867.]

Lotta Schmidt and Other Stories. 1867; 1870; 1882.

Linda Tressel. 2 vols. 1868; 1879. [First pbd in Blackwood's Mag. 1867–May 1868.]

Phineas Finn, The Irish Member. With Twenty Illustrations by J. E. Millais. 2 vols. 1869; 3 vols. Leipzig, 1869; 1870; 1871; 2 vols. 1911, etc. [First pbd in St Paul's Mag. Oct. 1867–May 1869.]

He Knew He was Right. With Sixty-four Illustrations by Marcus Stone. 32 weekly pts, 17 Oct. 1868–22 May 1869; 2 vols. 1869; 3 vols. Leipzig, 1869; 1870; 1871.

The Vicar Of Bullhampton. With Thirty Illustrations by H. Woods. 11 monthly pts, July 1869–May 1870; 1870; 2 vols. Leipzig, 1870; 1871; 1875; rptd 1924 (World's Classics).

An Editor's Tales. 1870; 1871; 1873; 1876. [First pbd in St Paul's Mag. Oct. 1869–May 1870.]

Sir Harry Hotspur Of Humblethwaite. 1871; Leipzig, 1871; rptd 1928 (World's Classics). [First pbd in Macmillan's Mag. May 1870–Dec. 1870.]

Ralph the Heir. 19 monthly pts, Jan. 1870–July 1871; 3 vols. 1871; 2 vols. Leipzig, 1871; 1871 (illustrated by F. A. Fraser); 1872; 1878.

The Golden Lion of Granpere. 1872 (illustrated by F. A. Fraser); Leipzig, 1872; 1873; 1873 (with illustrations); 1885, etc. [First pbd in Good Words, Jan. 1872–Aug. 1872.]

The Eustace Diamonds. 3 vols. 1873; 1875; 2 vols. [1873]; rptd 1930 (World's Classics). [First pbd in Fortnightly Rev. July 1871–Feb. 1873.]

Lady Anna. 2 vols. Leipzig, 1873; 2 vols. 1874; 1875. [First pbd in Fortnightly Rev. April 1873–April 1874.]

Phineas Redux. With Illustrations Engraved on Wood. 2 vols. 1874; 3 vols. [1874]; 1874; 1875; 2 vols. 1913. [First pbd in Graphic, 19 July 1873–10 Jan. 1874.]

Harry Heathcote of Gangoil. A Tale Of Australian Bush Life. 1874; Leipzig, 1874; 1874 (illustrated); 1883. [Pbd as Christmas no. of Graphic on 25 Dec. 1873, with six illustrations.]

The Way We Live Now. With Forty Illustrations. 20 monthly pts, Feb. 1874–Sept. 1875; 2 vols. 1875; 4 vols. Leipzig, 1875; 2 vols. 1876; 1879.

The Prime Minister. 8 monthly pts, Nov. 1875–June 1876; 4 vols. 1876; 4 vols. Leipzig, 1876; Toronto, 1876; 1877 (with frontispiece); 1878; rptd 2 vols. 1938 (World's Classics).

The American Senator. 3 vols. 1877; 3 vols. Leipzig, 1877; 1877; 1878; 1886; rptd 1931 (World's Classics). [First pbd in Temple Bar, May 1876–July 1877.]

Christmas at Thompson Hall. (With Eight Illustrations.) New York, 1877; 1885. [First pbd in Graphic Christmas no. 1876.]

Is He Popenjoy? 3 vols. 1878; 3 vols. Leipzig, 1878; 1 vol. 1879. [First pbd in All The Year Round, 13 Oct. 1877–13 July 1878.]

How The 'Mastiffs' Went To Iceland. With Illustrations by Mrs Hugh Blackburn. 1878 (priv. ptd).

The Lady of Launay. New York, 1878.

An Eye For An Eye. 2 vols. 1879; Leipzig, 1879; 1879 (rev.). [First pbd in Whitehall Rev. 24 Aug. 1878–1 Feb. 1879.]

John Caldigate. 3 vols. 1879; 3 vols, Leipzig, 1879; 1880; 1885. [First pbd in Blackwood's Mag. April 1878–June 1879.]

Cousin Henry. 2 vols. 1879; Leipzig, 1879; 1880; rptd 1929 (World's Classics). [First pbd in Manchester Weekly Times Supplement, 8 March 1879–24 May 1879.]

The Duke's Children. 3 vols. 1880; 1880; 3 vols. Leipzig, 1880. [First pbd in All the Year Round, 4 Oct. 1879–24 July 1880.]

Dr Wortle's School. 2 vols. 1881; Leipzig, 1881; 1881; rptd 1928 (World's Classics). [First pbd in Blackwood's Mag. May 1880–Dec. 1880.]

Ayala's Angel. 3 vols. 1881; 3 vols. Leipzig, 1881; 1881; 1882; 1884; rptd 1929 (World's Classics).

Why Frau Frohmann Raised Her Prices and Other Stories. 1882; Leipzig, 1883.

The Fixed Period. 2 vols. 1882; Leipzig, 1882. [First pbd in Blackwood's Mag. Oct. 1881–March 1882.]

Marian Fay. 3 vols. 1882; 2 vols. Leipzig, 1882; 1884. [First pbd in Graphic 3 Dec. 1881–3 June 1882.]

Kept In The Dark. 2 vols. 1882; Leipzig, 1882; 1883. [First pbd in Good Words, May 1882–Dec. 1882.]

Mr Scarborough's Family. 3 vols. 1883; 1883. [First pbd in All the Year Round, 27 May–16 June 1883.]

The Landleaguers. 3 vols. 1883; 1884. [First pbd in Life, 16 Nov. 1882–4 Oct. 1883.]

An Old Man's Love. 2 vols. 1883; Leipzig, 1884.

(4) OTHER WRITINGS

The West Indies and the Spanish Main. 1859; Leipzig, 1860; 1860 (3rd edn); 1862; 1869.

The Civil Service As A Profession. [1861] (priv. ptd). [Lecture.]

North America. 2 vols. 1862; 3 vols. Leipzig, 1862; 1864; 1866.

The Present Condition of the Northern States of the American Union. [1862?] (priv. ptd). [Lecture.]

Hunting Sketches. 1865; 1866; ed. J. Boyd, 1934. [First pbd in Pall Mall Gazette, 9 Feb.–20 March 1865.]

Travelling Sketches. 1866. [First pbd in Pall Mall Gazette, 3 Aug.–6 Sept. 1865.]

Clergymen of the Church of England. 1866. [First pbd in Pall Mall Gazette, 20 Nov. 1865–25 Jan. 1866.]

British Sports and Pastimes, 1868. Edited by Anthony Trollope. 1868.

Higher Education of Women. [1868] (priv. ptd). [Lecture.]

Did He Steal It? A Comedy In Three Acts. 1869 (priv. ptd).

On English Prose Fiction As A Rational Amusement. [1870] (priv. ptd). [Lecture.]

The Commentaries of Caesar. 1870.

Australia and New Zealand. 2 vols. 1873; 4 pts, 1874; 2 vols. 1876; 6 pts, Melbourne, 1873; 3 vols. Leipzig, 1873.

Iceland. 1878 (priv. rptd from Fortnightly Rev. Aug. 1878).

South Africa. 2 vols. 1878; 2 vols. Leipzig, 1878; 1879 (abridged and in part rewritten).

Thackeray. 1879; 1892. (English Men of Letters ser.)

The Life of Cicero. 2 vols. 1880.

English Political Leaders. Lord Palmerston. 1882; 1883.

An Autobiography. 2 vols. 1883; Leipzig, 1883; ed. M. Sadleir, 1923 (World's Classics).

The Noble Jilt. A Comedy. Ed. M. Sadleir, 1923.

London Tradesmen. Ed. M. Sadleir, 1927. [First pbd in Pall Mall Gazette, July–Sept. 1880.]

Four Lectures. Ed. M. L. Parrish, 1938.

(5) Contributions to Periodicals

[A select list of unreprinted articles.]

W. M. Thackeray. Cornhill Mag. Feb. 1864.

On Anonymous Literature. Fortnightly Rev. 1 July 1865.

The Irish Church. Fortnightly Rev. 15 Aug. 1865.

Public Schools. Fortnightly Rev. 1 Oct. 1865.

An Essay on Carlylism. St Paul's Mag. Dec. 1867.

Mr Freeman on the Morality of Hunting. Fortnightly Rev. 1 Dec. 1869.

Charles Dickens. St Paul's Mag. July 1870.

Cicero As A Politician. Fortnightly Rev. 1 April 1877.

Cicero As A Man Of Letters. Fortnightly Rev. 1 Sept. 1877.

George Henry Lewes. Fortnightly Rev. 1 Jan. 1879.

Novel Reading. Nineteenth Century, Jan. 1879.

The Genius Of Hawthorne. North American Rev. Sept. 1879.

Longfellow. North American Rev. April 1881.

[Trollope edited from Oct. 1867 to July 1869 Saint Paul's Magazine, which contains serials and signed and unsigned articles by him, the last instalment of the last serial appearing in April 1871.]

(6) Biography and Criticism

(a) Books

Escott, T. H. S. Anthony Trollope: his Work, Associates and Literary Originals. 1913.

Sadleir, M. Trollope. A Commentary. 1927.

Walpole, H. Anthony Trollope. 1928. (English Men of Letters ser.)

Koets, C. C. Female Characters in the Works of Anthony Trollope. Amsterdam, 1933.

(b) Essays, Pamphlets and Chapters of Books

Friswell, J. H. Modern Men of Letters. 1870.

Cooper, T. Men of Mark. 6 vols. 1876–82. [Vol. III.]

Heywood, J. C. How They Strike Me. Philadelphia, 1877.

Wilman, G. Living Celebrities. 1882.

Hawthorne, J. Confessions. Boston, 1887.

Wotton, M. E. Word Portraits. 1887.

James, H. Partial Portraits. 1888.

Harrison, F. Studies in Early Victorian Literature. 1895.

Saintsbury, G. Corrected Impressions. 1895.

—— Trollope Revisited. E. & S. VI, 1920.

Stephen, Sir L. Studies of A Biographer. Vol. IV, 1902.

Street, G. S. A Book of Essays. 1902.

Bryce, J., Viscount. Studies in Contemporary Biography. 1903.

Nichols, S. van B. The Significance of Anthony Trollope. New York, 1925.

Quiller-Couch, Sir A. T. Charles Dickens and Other Victorians. Cambridge, 1925.

More, P. E. My Debt to Trollope. [In The Demon of the Absolute, Princeton, 1929.]

MacCarthy, D. Portraits. 1931.

Cecil, Lord D. Early Victorian Novelists. 1934.

(c) Articles in Periodicals

Freeman, E. A. Anthony Trollope. Macmillan's Mag. XLVII, 1882.

Anthony Trollope. Blackwood's Mag. CXXXIII, 1882.

The Novels of Anthony Trollope. Dublin Rev. XCII, 1882.

Pollock, W. H. Trollope. Harper's Mag. LXVI, 1882.

Trollope's Mode of Work. London Society, XLIV, 1883.

Trollope. Good Words, XXIV, 1883.

Anthony Trollope. Westminster Rev. CXXI, 1883.

Last Reminiscences of Trollope. Temple Bar, LXX, 1883.

MacLeod, N. Trollope. Good Words, XXV, 1884.

English Character and Manners as Portrayed by Trollope. Westminster Rev. CXXIII, 1884.

Trollope Compared with Daudet. Atlantic Monthly, LIV, 1884.

Lord, W. F. The Novels of Trollope. Nineteenth Century, XLIX, 1900.

Bettany, F. G. In Praise of the Novels of Trollope. Fortnightly Rev. LXXXIII, 1904.

Escott, T. H. S. An Appreciation and Reminiscence of Trollope. Fortnightly Rev. LXXXVI, 1906.

Trollope's Political Novel. Spectator, 3 May 1913.

Randell, W. L. Anthony Trollope and his Work. Fortnightly Rev. Sept. 1920.

Sadleir, M. A Guide to Anthony Trollope. Nineteenth Century, April 1922.

—— A Trollope Love-Story, Mary Thorne. Nineteenth Century, Sept. 1924.

—— Anthony Trollope and his Publishers. Library. V, 1924.

—— The Victorian Woman as Trollope knew her. Bermondsey Book, March 1925.

Whibley, C. Trollope's Autobiography. English Rev. XXXVII, 1923.

Newbolt, Sir F. Reg. versus Mason. Nineteenth Century, XCV, 1924. [Orley Farm.]

Payne, G. H. Belles Lettres in Ballot Boxes, a Forgotten Statesman [Plantagenet Palliser]. Forum, Feb. 1925.

Grey, R. Anthony Trollope and his Mother. Cornhill Mag. Nov. 1926.

Gwynn, S. Trollope and Ireland. Contemporary Rev. cxxix, 1926.

Ellis, S. M. Trollope and Mid-Victorianism. Fortnightly Rev. cxxviii, 1927.

Priestley, J. B. In Barsetshire. Saturday Rev. 12 Nov. 1927.

Belloc, H. Anthony Trollope. London Mercury, xxvii, 1932.

Huxley, L. Anthony Trollope on 'The Cornhill.' Cornhill Mag. lxxii, 1932.

Waugh, A. Trollope after Fifty Years. Fortnightly Rev. cxxxvii, 1932.

Pavey, L. A. Anthony Trollope. [In The English Novelists, ed. D. Verschoyle, 1936.]

Baker, E. A. The History of the English Novel. Vol. viii, 1937.

Trollope's House of Commons. TLS. 20 March 1937.

Sampson, A. Trollope in the Twentieth Century. London Mercury, xxxv, 1937.

S. J. L.

THE BRONTËS

(1) BIBLIOGRAPHIES AND CATALOGUES

Anderson, J. P. [Bibliography appended to A. Birrell's Charlotte Brontë, 1887.]

Museum of Brontë Relics. A Descriptive Catalogue of Brontë Relics now in the Possession of R. and F. Brown. [1890?]

Wood, B. A Bibliography of the Works of the Brontë Family. Brontë Soc. 1895.

Catalogue of the Gleave Brontë Collection at the Moss Side Free Library. Manchester, 1905.

Catalogue of Autograph Letters, Manuscripts and Relics of Charlotte Brontë, sold at Sotheby's 19 June 1914. [1914.]

Wise, T. J. A Bibliography of the Writings in Prose and Verse of the Brontë Family. 1917 (priv. ptd).

—— A Brontë Library. A Catalogue of Printed Books, Manuscripts and Autograph Letters by the Members of the Brontë Family. 1929 (priv. ptd).

(2) COLLECTED AND COMPOSITE WORKS

Poems By Currer, Ellis, and Acton Bell. 1846 (re-issued 1848 but still dated 1846); Philadelphia, 1848.

The Life [by Mrs Gaskell] and Works of Charlotte Brontë and her Sisters. 7 vols. 1872–3.

The Works of Charlotte, Emily and Anne Brontë. 12 vols. 1893, 1901.

The Life [by Mrs Gaskell] and Works of Charlotte Brontë and her Sisters. Ed. Mrs H. Ward and C. K. Shorter, 7 vols. 1899–1900 (Haworth edn).

The Works of the Brontës. 12 vols. 1901. (Temple edn).

The Novels of the Sisters Brontë. Ed. T. Scott, 12 vols. 1901. (Thornton edn.) [Includes Mrs Gaskell's Life of Charlotte Brontë, ed. T. Scott and B. W. Willet.]

The Novels and Poems of Charlotte, Emily and Ann Brontë. 7 vols. 1901–7. (World's Classics.) [General introduction by T. Watts-Dunton prefixed to The Professor.]

Poems By Charlotte, Emily, and Anne Brontë now for the First Time printed. New York, 1902.

The Complete Works of Charlotte Brontë and her Sister. 7 vols. [1905]. (Book Lovers' edn.)

Brontë Poems: Selections from the Poetry of Charlotte, Emily, Anne and Branwell Brontë. Ed. A. C. Benson, 1915.

The Orphans and Other Poems by Charlotte, Emily, and Branwell Brontë. 1917 (priv. ptd).

The Shakespeare Head Brontë. Ed. T. J. Wise and J. A. Symington, 20 vols. Oxford, 1932– . [Novels, 11 vols.; Life and Letters, 4 vols.; Miscellaneous and Unpublished Writings, 2 vols.; Poems, 2 vols.; Bibliography, 1 vol.]

(3) CHARLOTTE BRONTË, later NICHOLLS (1816–1855). [Pseudonym 'Currer Bell']

Jane Eyre. An Autobiography. Edited by Currer Bell. 3 vols. 1847; 3 vols. 1848 (as 'By Currer Bell'; adds dedication to Thackeray and preface); 3 vols. 1848; 1850; 2 vols. Leipzig, 1850; 1857; 1858, etc.; ed. C. K. Shorter, [1889]; ed. Sir W. R. Nicoll, 1902 (also includes The Moores); ed. M. Sinclair, 1908 (Everyman's Lib.).

Shirley, A Tale. By Currer Bell. 3 vols. 1849; 2 vols. Leipzig, 1849; 1852; 1857; 1860; 1862, etc.; ed. M. Sinclair, 1908 (Everyman's Lib.).

Villette. By Currer Bell. 3 vols. 1853; Leipzig, 1853; 1855; 1857; 1858; 1860; 1861; 1866; 1867, etc.; ed. M. Sinclair, 1909 (Everyman's Lib.).

The Professor, A Tale. By Currer Bell. 2 vols. 1857 (preface by A. B. Nicholls); 1860 (also includes Emma and Poems by Currer, Ellis and Acton Bell); 1860; 1862, etc.; ed. M. Sinclair, 1910 (Everyman's Lib.).

Emma. Cornhill Mag. April 1860. [Fragment, preceded by a brief notice by Thackeray. Rptd with The Professor, 1860.]

Unpublished Letters of Charlotte Brontë. Hours at Home, ii, 1870. [Letters to Ellen Nussey.]

The Story of the Brontës: Their Home, Haunts, Friends, and Works. Part Second —Charlotte's Letters. Bradford, 1889. [Ptd but not pbd owing to copyright difficulties. Consists of Charlotte's Letters to Ellen Nussey.]

The Adventures of Ernest Alembert. A Fairy Tale. Ed. T. J. Wise, 1896 (priv. ptd). [Rptd in Literary Anecdotes of the Nineteenth Century, ed. Sir W. R. Nicoll and T. J. Wise, vol. II, 1896.]

The Moores. [Fragment ptd with Jane Eyre, ed. Sir W. R. Nicoll, 1902.]

Richard Cœur de Lion and Blondell. A Poem. Ed. C. K. Shorter, 1912 (priv. ptd).

The Love Letters of Charlotte Brontë to Constantin Heger. Ed. M. H. Spielmann, Times, 29 July 1913; Trans. Brontë Soc. XXIV, 1914; 1914 (priv. ptd).

Letters Recounting the Deaths of Emily, Anne and Branwell Brontë By Charlotte Brontë. To which are added Letters signed 'Currer Bell' and 'C. B. Nicholls.' 1913 (priv. ptd).

Saul and Other Poems. 1913 (priv. ptd).

Lament befitting these 'Times of Night.' Ed. G. E. MacLean, Cornhill Mag. Aug. 1916; 1916.

Unpublished Essays in Novel Writing by Charlotte Brontë. Ed. G. E. MacLean, 1916.

The Violet. A Poem written at the Age of Fourteen. Ed. C. K. Shorter, [1916] (priv. ptd).

The Red Cross Knight and Other Poems. 1917 (priv. ptd).

The Swiss Emigrant's Return and Other Poems. 1917 (priv. ptd).

The Four Wishes. A Fairy Tale. Ed. C. K. Shorter, 1918 (priv. ptd).

Latest Gleanings: being a Series of Unpublished Poems from Early Manuscripts. Ed. C. K. Shorter, 1918 (priv. ptd).

Napoleon and the Spectre. A Ghost Story. 1919 (priv. ptd).

Thackeray and Charlotte Brontë: being some hitherto Unpublished Letters by Charlotte Brontë. 1919 (priv. ptd).

Darius Codomannus. A Poem. Written at the Age of Eighteen Years. 1920 (priv. ptd).

The Complete Poems of Charlotte Brontë. Ed. C. K. Shorter and C. W. Hatfield, 1923.

An Early Essay by Charlotte Brontë. Ed. M. H. Spielmann, Brontë Soc. 1924.

Conversations. (A Dialogue Playlet in Prose and Verse.) Ed. D. Cook, Bookman, Dec. 1925.

The Twelve Adventurers and Other Stories. Ed. C. K. Shorter, 1925.

Miniature Magazines of Charlotte Brontë. With Unpublished Poems. Ed. D. Cook, Bookman, Dec. 1926.

The Spell, an Extravaganza. Ed. G. E. MacLean, Oxford, 1931.

Legends of Angria. Compiled from the Early Writings of Charlotte Brontë. Ed. F. E. Ratchford and W. C. De Vane, New Haven, 1933.

(4) EMILY JANE BRONTË (1818–1848).
[*Pseudonym 'Ellis Bell'*]

Wuthering Heights a novel, by Ellis Bell. 3 vols. 1847. [Vols. I, II, Wuthering Heights; vol. III, Agnes Grey. A Novel, by Acton Bell, *i.e.* Anne Brontë.]

Wuthering Heights and Agnes Grey. By Ellis and Acton Bell. A New Edition revised, with A Biographical Notice of the Authors, A Selection from their Literary Remains, and a Preface by Currer Bell. 1850 (also issued 1851); Leipzig, 1851; 1858, etc.

Poems of Emily Brontë. Ed. A. Symons, 1906.

The Complete Works of Emily Brontë. Ed. C. K. Shorter and Sir W. R. Nicoll, 2 vols. 1910–1.

The Complete Poems of Emily Jane Brontë. Ed. C. K. Shorter and C. W. Hatfield, 1924.

Wuthering Heights. Ed. R. Macaulay, New York, 1926; ed. H. W. Garrod, 1930.

Gondal Poems, now first published from the Manuscript in the British Museum. Ed. H. Brown and J. Mott, Oxford, 1938.

(5) ANNE BRONTË (1820–1849).
[*Pseudonym 'Acton Bell'*]

Agnes Grey. [See under Emily Brontë above.]

The Tenant of Wildfell Hall. By Acton Bell. 3 vols. 1848 (also re-issued as 2nd edn with new Preface); 1854; 1859; 1867, etc.; ed. M. Sinclair, 1914 (Everyman's Lib.).

Self-Communion. A Poem By Anne Brontë. Ed. T. J. Wise, 1900 (priv. ptd).

Dreams and Other Poems. 1917 (priv. ptd).

The Complete Poems of Anne Brontë. Ed. C. K. Shorter and C. W. Hatfield, 1923.

(6) BIOGRAPHY AND CRITICISM
(a) Books

Gaskell, E. C. The Life of Charlotte Brontë. 2 vols. 1857 (3 edns, 3rd 'revised and corrected'); ed. C. K. Shorter, 1900; ed. T. Scott and B. W. Willett, 1901 (Thornton edn of novels); ed. M. Sinclair, 1908 (Everyman's Lib.).

Reid, Sir T. W. Charlotte Brontë. A Monograph. 1877.

Turner, J. H. Haworth Past and Present. Brighouse, 1879.

—— Brontëana. The Rev. Patrick Brontë, his Collected Works and Life. 1898.

Robinson, A. M. F. Emily Brontë. 1883.

Scruton, W. The Birthplace of Charlotte Brontë. 1884.

—— Thornton and the Brontës. 1898.

Leyland, F. A. The Brontë Family with Special Reference to Patrick Branwell Brontë. 2 vols. 1886.

Birrell, A. Life of Charlotte Brontë. 1887.

Holroyd, A. Currer Bell. [1887.]

Wright, W. The Brontës in Ireland. 1893.

Transactions and Publications of the Brontë Society. Bradford [later Haworth], 1895–.

Shorter, C. K. The Brontës and their Circle. 1896.

—— The Brontës. Life and Letters. 2 vols. 1908.

Mackay, A. M. The Brontës. Fact and Fiction. 1897.

Yates, W. W. The Father of the Brontës. With a Chapter on Currer Bell. 1897.

Dimnet, E. Les Sœurs Brontë. Paris, 1910; tr. Eng. 1927.

Masson, F. The Brontës. 1912.

Sinclair, M. The Three Brontës. 1912; 1914 (rev. edn).

Chadwick, E. A. In the Footsteps of the Brontës. 1914.

Richardson, F. (later Macdonald). The Secret of Charlotte Brontë. Followed by some Reminiscences of the Real Monsieur and Madame Heger. 1914.

Charlotte Brontë, 1816–1916. A Centenary Memorial prepared by the Brontë Society, Foreword by Mrs Humphry Ward. 1917.

Law, A. Patrick Branwell Brontë. [1924.]

Kuhlman, R. Natur-Paganismus in der Weltanschauung von Emily Brontë. Schloppe, 1926.

Wilson, Romer. All Alone. The Life and Private History of Emily Jane Brontë. 1928.

Hale, W. T. Anne Brontë: her Life and Writings. Bloomington, 1929.

Simpson, Charles. Emily Brontë. 1929.

Sugden, K. A. R. A Short History of the Brontës. Oxford, 1929.

Romieu, E. and G. La Vie des Sœurs Brontë. Paris, 1930; tr. Eng. 1931.

Benson, E. F. Charlotte Brontë. 1932.

Wise, T. J. and Symington, J. A. The Brontës: their Lives, Friendships and Correspondence. 4 vols. Oxford, 1932. [The fullest and most authoritative account. Part of the Shakespeare Head Brontë.]

Ratchford, F. E. Emily Brontë. Two Poems: Leve's Rebuke and Remembrance; with the Gondal Background of her Poems and Novel. Austin, 1934.

The Brontës: their Lives recorded by their Contemporaries. Ed. E. M. Delafield, 1935.

Wroot, H. E. Persons and Places: Sources of Charlotte Brontë's Novels. Brontë Soc. 1935.

Cooper-Willis, I. The Authorship of Wuthering Heights. 1936.

Moore, V. The Life and Eager Death of Emily Brontë. 1936.

Schulte, C. Genie im Schatten. Das Leben der Charlotte Brontë. Dresden, 1936.

Dry, F. S. The Sources of Wuthering Heights. Cambridge, 1937.

Harrison, G. E. Haworth Parsonage: a Study of Wesley and the Brontës. 1937.

Wells, A. L. Les Sœurs Brontë et l'Étranger. Paris, 1937.

White, W. B. The Miracle of Haworth. 1937.

(b) Essays, Pamphlets and Chapters of Books

P., W. P. Jottings on Currer, Ellis, and Acton Bell. 1856.

Shepheard, H. A Vindication of the Clergy Daughters' School from the Remarks in the Life of Charlotte Brontë. Kirkby Lonsdale, 1857.

Bayne, P. Ellis, Acton, and Currer Bell. [In Essays, Biographical, Critical, and Miscellaneous, 1859.]

—— Two Great Englishwomen : Mrs Browning and Charlotte Brontë. With an Essay on Poetry. 1881.

Roscoe, W. C. Poems and Essays. Vol. II, 1860.

'Selden, Camille.' Charlotte Brontë et la Vie morale en Angleterre. [In L'Esprit des Femmes de notre Temps, Paris, 1865.]

Smith, G. B. The Brontës. [In Poets and Novelists, 1875.]

Martineau, H. Biographical Sketches, 1852–75. 1877.

Swinburne, A. C. A Note on Charlotte Brontë. 1877.

—— Emily Brontë. [In Miscellanies, 1886.]

Grundy, F. H. Pictures of the Past. 1879.

Stephen, Sir L. Charlotte Brontë. [In Hours in a Library, ser. III, 1879.]

Skelton, Sir J. Essays in History and Biography. Edinburgh, 1883.

Montégut, E. Écrivains modernes de l'Angleterre. Ser. 1, Paris, 1885. [Pp. 183–354, Charlotte Brontë.]

Ritchie, A. T., Lady. Chapters from Some Memories. 1894.

Harrison, F. Studies in Early Victorian Literature. 1895.

Saintsbury, G. Three Mid-Century Novelists. [In Corrected Impressions, 1895.]

Oliphant, M. O. The Sisters Brontë. [In Women Novelists of Queen Victoria's Reign, 1897.]

Stead, J. J. A Chronology of the Principal Events in the Lives of the Brontës. Brontë Soc. 1897.

Fotheringham, J. The Works of Emily Brontë and the Brontë Problem. Brontë Soc. 1900.

Bonnell, H. H. Charlotte Brontë, George Eliot, Jane Austen: Studies in their Works. New York, 1902.

Gosse, Sir E. The Challenge of the Brontës. 1903 (priv. ptd). [Rptd in Selected Essays, ser. 2, 1928.]

Spielmann, M. H. The Inner History of the Brontë-Heger Letters. 1919.

Kavanagh, C. The Symbolism of Wuthering Heights. [1920.]

Bald, M. A. Women-Writers of the Nineteenth Century. Cambridge, 1923.

Symons, A. Emily Brontë. [In Dramatis Personae, 1923.]

Law, A. Emily Brontë and the Authorship of Wuthering Heights. Altham, 1925.

Woolf, V. Jane Eyre and Wuthering Heights. [In The Common Reader, 1925.]

S., C. P. The Structure of Wuthering Heights. 1926.

Bradby, G. F. The Brontës and Other Essays. Oxford, 1932.

Morgan, C. Emily Brontë. [In Great Victorians, ed. H. J. and H. Massingham, 1932.]

West, R. Charlotte Brontë. [In Great Victorians, ed. H. J. and H. Massingham, 1932.]

Cecil, Lord D. Early Victorian Novelists. 1934.

Baker, E. A. The History of the English Novel. Vol. VIII, 1937. [Chs. i, ii.]

(c) Articles in Periodicals

Dobell, S. Athenaeum, 4 July 1846. [Review of Poems by Currer, Ellis and Acton Bell.]

—— Currer Bell. Palladium, Sept. 1850. [Wuthering Heights. Rptd in The Life and Letters of Sydney Dobell, vol. I, 1878.]

[Lewes, G. H.] Fraser's Mag. XXXVI, 1847. [Jane Eyre.]

—— Edinburgh Rev. XCI, 1850. [Shirley.]

Christian Remembrancer, XV, 1848. [Jane Eyre.]

Dublin University Mag. XXXI, 1848. [Jane Eyre.]

[Rigby, E. (Lady Eastlake).] Quarterly Rev. Dec. 1848. [Jane Eyre and Vanity Fair. Rptd in Famous Reviews, ed. R. B. Johnson, 1914.]

Forçade, E. Revue des Deux Mondes, XXIV, 1849. [Jane Eyre.]

—— Revue des Deux Mondes. XL, 1849. [Shirley.]

Christian Remembrancer, XXV, 1853. [Villette.]

Oxford and Cambridge Mag. I, 1856, pp. 323–35. [Charlotte Brontë and Thackeray.]

Christian Remembrancer, XXXIV, 1857. [Mrs Gaskell's Life.]

Waring, S. M. Charlotte Brontë and Lucy Snowe. Harper's Mag. XXXII, 1865.

'E.' [Ellen Nussey]. Reminiscences of Charlotte Brontë. Scribner's Mag. II, 1871.

Trafton, A. Charlotte Brontë. A Visit to her School at Brussels. Scribner's Mag. III, 1871.

Lang, A. Charlotte Brontë. Good Words, 1889.

Candy, F. H. Some Reminiscences of the Author of Jane Eyre. GM. CCLXVII, 1889.

Howells, W. D. Jane Eyre. Harper's Bazaar, Dec. 1900.

Lord, W. F. The Brontë Novels. Nineteenth Century, March 1903.

Mackay, A. M. The Brontës at Cowan Bridge. Bookman, Oct. 1904.

Smith, G. C. Moore. The Brontës at Thornton. Bookman, Oct. 1904.

Hobson, E. Shirley Land. Westminster Rev. July 1906.

Meynell, A. Charlotte and Emily Brontë. Dublin Rev. April 1911.

Harper, J. Charlotte Brontë and the Heger Family. Blackwood's Mag. April 1912.

Ralli, A. Self-Expression in Charlotte Brontë's Books. Fortnightly Rev. Sept. 1913.

—— Emily Brontë. The Problem of Personality. North American Rev. March 1925.

Smith, J. C. Emily Brontë. A Reconsideration. E. & S. V, 1914.

Brown, L. R. Charlotte Brontë and Belgium. Nineteenth Century, April 1916.

Spielmann, M. H. Charlotte Brontë in Brussels. TLS. 13 April 1916.

Chadwick, E. A. Patrick Branwell Brontë, a Vindication. Nineteenth Century, Aug. 1918.

Crichton-Browne, Sir J. Patrick Branwell Brontë. An Extenuation. Fortnightly Rev. July 1918.

Masson, J. The Brontës as seen Through French Eyes. London Quarterly Rev. Jan. 1919.

Sandwith, M. T. E. Jane Eyre and Eugénie Grandet. Nineteenth Century, Aug. 1922.

Dodds, M. H. Gondaliand. MLR. XVIII, 1923. [Emily Brontë's poems.]

—— A Second Visit to Gondaliand. MLR. XXI, XXII, 1926–7.

Mirsky, D. S. Emily Brontë. London Mercury, Jan. 1923.

Read, H. Charlotte and Emily Brontë. Yale Rev. July 1925.

Cook, D. Emily Brontë's Poems: Textual Corrections and Unpublished Verses. Nineteenth Century, Aug. 1926.

Green, J. Charlotte Brontë et. ses Sœurs. Revue hebdomadaire, July 1926; tr. Eng. Virginia Quart. V, 1929.

Bell, H. K. Charlotte Brontë's Husband. Cornhill Mag. Jan. 1927.

Tompkins, J. M. S. Jane Eyre's 'Iron Shroud.' MLR. XXII, 1927.

Ratchford, F. E. Charlotte Brontë's Angrian Cycle of Stories. PMLA. XLIII, 1928.

Ratchford, F. E. The Brontës' Web of Dreams. Yale Rev. xxi, 1931.

Spens, J. Charlotte Brontë. E. & S. xiv, 1928.

Haldane, E. S. The Brontës and their Biographers. Nineteenth Century, Dec. 1932.

Charlier, G. The Brussels Life in Villette. Contemporary Rev. Nov. 1933.

Gary, F. Charlotte Brontë and George Henry Lewes. PMLA. li, 1936.

GEORGE ELIOT,' *i.c.* MARY ANN EVANS, LATER CROSS (1819–1880)

(1) BIBLIOGRAPHIES

Sutton, C. W. George Eliot. A Bibliography. Papers of Manchester Literary Club, 1881, pp. 97–107.

Anderson, J. P. [Bibliography appended to O, Browning's Life of George Eliot, 1890.]

Muir, P. H. A Bibliography of the First Editions of Books by George Eliot. Bookman's Journ. Supplement, 1927–8.

Parrish, M. L. Victorian Lady Novelists. First Editions in the Library at Dormy House, New Jersey. 1933.

(2) COLLECTED WORKS

George Eliot's Novels. 6 vols. 1867–[78]. (Illustrated edn.)

George Eliot's Works. 20 vols. 1878–80. (Cabinet edn.)

George Eliot's Works. 12 vols. Edinburgh, 1901–3. (Warwick edn.)

George Eliot's Works. 12 vols. Toronto, 1902. (Foleshill edn.)

George Eliot's Works. 21 vols. [1908–11]. (Illustrated copyright edn.)

(3) NOVELS AND TALES

Scenes of Clerical Life. 2 vols. Edinburgh, 1858; 2 vols. Edinburgh, 1859, 1860; 1863 (with Silas Marner); 1868, etc.; ed. W. W. Fowler and E. Limouzin, 1916. Tr. German, 1885; French, 1886 (in part). [First pbd in Blackwood's Mag.: The Sad Fortunes of the Rev. Amos Barton, Jan., Feb. 1857; Mr Gilfil's Love Story, March–June 1857; Janet's Repentance, July–Nov. 1857.]

Adam Bede. 3 vols. Edinburgh, 1859 (7 edns); 1862 (10th edn); [1873], etc. Tr. German, 1860; French, 1861; Dutch, 1870; Hungarian, 1888.

The Lifted Veil. Blackwood's Mag. July 1859. [Rptd with Silas Marner in Works, 1878, and separately [1924]; tr. French, 1880.]

The Mill on the Floss. 3 vols. Edinburgh, 1860 (*bis*); Edinburgh, 1862 (5th edn); Edinburgh, 1867; 2 vols. Edinburgh, 1878, etc.; ed. R. O. Morris, 1913. Tr. German, 1861; French, 1863; Dutch, 1870.

Silas Marner: the Weaver of Raveloe. Edinburgh, 1861 (7 edns); 1863 (with Scenes of Clerical Life); 1868, etc. Tr. German, 1861; French, 1862; Hungarian, 1885.

Romola. 3 vols. 1863 (*bis*); 2 vols. Leipzig, 1863; 1865 (illustrated); 2 vols. 1880, etc.; ed. G. Biagi, 2 vols. 1907; ed. C. B. Wheeler, 1916. Tr. German, 1864; Dutch, 1864; French, 1887. [First pbd, illustrated by Leighton, Cornhill Mag. July 1862–Aug. 1863.]

Brother Jacob. Cornhill Mag. July 1864. [Rptd with Silas Marner in Works, 1878; tr. Italian, 1880.]

Felix Holt the Radical. 3 vols. Edinburgh, 1866; 2 vols. Edinburgh, 1866; 2 vols. Leipzig, 1867; Edinburgh, 1868; Edinburgh, 1878, etc. Tr. German, 1867; Dutch, 1867; Hungarian, 1874.

Middlemarch, a Study of Provincial Life. 4 vols. Edinburgh, 1871–2; 4 vols. 1873; 1874, etc. Tr. German, 1872–3; Dutch, 1873; Hungarian, 1874–5.

Daniel Deronda. 4 vols. Edinburgh, 1876 (*bis*), etc. Tr. German, 1876; Swedish, 1878; Italian, 1882–3; Hebrew, 1892.

(4) POEMS

The Spanish Gypsy, a Poem. Edinburgh, 1868 (3 edns); 1875 (5th edn).

Agatha. 1869 (priv. ptd) (*bis*). [2nd edn a forgery? For this and the next item see J. Carter and G. Pollard, An Enquiry into the Nature of Certain Nineteenth Century Pamphlets, 1934.]

Brother and Sister. Sonnets by Marian Lewes. 1869 (priv. ptd). [A forgery?]

How Lisa loved the King. Boston, 1869; 1883.

The Legend of Jubal and other Poems. Edinburgh, 1874; tr. Dutch, 1888.

The Complete Poetical Works of George Eliot. New York, 1888.

George Eliot's Complete Poems. Ed. M. Browne, Boston, [1889].

(5) OTHER WRITINGS

The Life of Jesus critically examined. By Dr David Friedrich Strauss. Translated from the fourth German edition. 3 vols. 1846. [Begun by Mrs Charles Hennell and completed by George Eliot.]

The Essence of Christianity. By Ludwig Feuerbach. Translated from the second German edition by Marian Evans. 1854.

Impressions of Theophrastus Such. Edinburgh, 1879; tr. German, 1880 (in part).

Essays and Leaves from a Note-Book. [Ed. C. L. Lewes], Edinburgh, 1884. [Includes 6 articles rptd from Westminster Rev. and elsewhere, 1855–66.]

Early Essays. 1919 (priv. ptd).

(6) Letters

George Eliot's Life as related in her Letters and Journals. Arranged and edited by her Husband, J. W. Cross. 3 vols. Edinburgh, 1885.
Letters from George Eliot to Elma Stuart, 1872–80. Ed. R. Stuart, 1909.
The Letters of George Eliot. Selected by R. Brimley Johnson. 1926.

(7) Biography and Criticism

(a) Books

[Briddon, J.?] Seth Bede, 'The Methody': his Life and Labours, chiefly written by himself. Ryde, 1859.
Roslyn, G. George Eliot in Derbyshire. 1876.
Blind, M. George Eliot. 1883.
Cooke, G. W. George Eliot. A Critical Study. 1883.
Cross, J. W. George Eliot's Life as related in her Letters and Journals. Arranged and edited by her Husband. 3 vols. 1885; 3 vols. 1886.
Wolzogen, E. von. George Eliot: eine biographisch-kritische Studie. Leipzig, 1885.
Lonsdale, M. George Eliot: Thoughts upon her Life, her Books, and herself. 1886.
Conrad, H. George Eliot: ihr Leben und Schaffen dargestellt nach ihren Briefen und Tagebüchern. Berlin, 1887.
Parkinson, S. Scenes from the George Eliot Country. Leeds, 1888.
Browning, O. Life of George Eliot. 1890.
Negri, G. George Eliot: la sua Vita e i suoi Romanzi. 2 vols. Milan, 1891.
Bender, H. George Eliot: ein Lebensbild. Hamburg, 1893.
Westermarck, H. George Eliot och den engelska naturalistiska Romanen. Helsingfors, 1894.
Thomson, C. L. George Eliot. [1901.]
Stephen, Sir L. George Eliot. 1902. (English Men of Letters ser.)
Mottram, W. The Story of George Eliot in Relation to Adam Bede. 1905.
Richter, H. George Eliot: fünf Aufsätze. Berlin, 1907.
Olcott, C. S. George Eliot: Scenes and People in her Novels. New York, 1910.
Rhotert, C. Die Frau bei George Eliot. Berlin, 1915.
Berle, L. W. George Eliot and Thomas Hardy: a Contrast. New York, 1917.
Zuber, E. Kind und Kindheit bei George Eliot. Frauenfeld, 1919.
Mudge, I. G. and Sears, M. E. A George Eliot Dictionary. New York, 1924.
Pfeiffer, S. George Eliots Beziehungen zu Deutschland. Heidelberg, 1925.

Summers, A. L. The Homes of George Eliot; with an Appreciative Commentary on her Characteristics and Philosophy. 1926.
Haldane, E. S. George Eliot and her Times: a Victorian Study. 1927.
Pond, E. J. Les Idées morales et religieuses de George Eliot. Paris, 1927.
Paterson, A. George Eliot's Family Life and Letters. 1928.
Simon-Baumann, L. Die Darstellung der Charaktere in George Eliots Romanen: eine literarästhetische Wertkritik. Leipzig, 1929.
May, J. L. George Eliot. A Study. 1930.
Romieu, E. and G. La Vie de George Eliot. Paris, 1930; tr. Eng. 1932.
Buckrose, J. E. Silhouette of Mary Ann. A Novel about George Eliot. 1931.
Toyoda, M. Studies in the Mental Development of George Eliot in Relation to the Science, Philosophy and Theology of her Day. Tokyo, 1932.
Bourl'honne, P. George Eliot: Essai de Biographie intellectuelle et morale, 1819–1854. Paris, 1933.
Kitchel, A. T. George Lewes and George Eliot. New York, 1933.
Williams, Blanche C. George Eliot. A Biography. 1936.

(b) Essays, Pamphlets and Chapters in Books

Scheerer, E. H. A. Études critiques sur la Littérature contemporaine. 10 vols. Paris, 1863–95. [Vols. I, V and VIII contain essays on George Eliot.]
Hutton, R. H. Essays, Theological and Literary. Vol. II, 1871.
—— Essays on some of the Modern Guides of English Thought. 1887.
McCarthy, Justin. Modern Leaders: being a Series of Biographical Sketches. New York, 1872.
Axon, W. E. A. George Eliot's Use of Dialect. English Dialect Soc. Misc. 1876–87.
Dowden, E. Studies in Literature, 1789–1877. 1878.
Taylor, Bayard. Critical Essays and Literary Notes. New York, 1880.
Myers, F. W. H. Essays Classical; Essays Modern. 2 vols. 1883. [George Eliot in vol. II.]
Druskowitz, H. Drei englische Dichterinnen. Berlin, 1885. [Joanna Baillie, Elizabeth Barrett Browning, and George Eliot.]
Montégut, E. Écrivains modernes de l'Angleterre. Ser. 1, Paris, 1885.
Harrison, Frederic. The Choice of Books, and Other Literary Pieces. 1886. [Contains The Life of George Eliot, rptd from Fortnightly Rev.]

Harrison, Frederic. Studies in Early Victorian Literature. 1895.

Dawson, William J. Quest and Vision: Chapters in Life and Literature. 1886.

Barine, A. Portraits de Femmes: Madame Carlyle: George Eliot; Une Détraquée [Mary Wollstonecraft]. Paris, 1887.

James, Henry. Partial Portraits. 1888.

—— The Poetry of George Eliot. [In Views and Reviews, 1908.]

Jacobs, Joseph. George Eliot, Matthew Arnold, Browning, Newman. Essays and Reviews from the Athenaeum. 1891.

Scherer, W. George Eliot und das Judentum. [In Kleine Schriften, vol. II, Berlin, 1893.]

Lilly, W. S. Four English Humourists of the Nineteenth Century. 1895. [Dickens, Thackeray, George Eliot and Carlyle.]

Saintsbury, G. Corrected Impressions. 1895.

Newdigate-Newdegate, A. E., Lady. The Cheverels of Cheverel Manor. 1899.

Brownell, W. C. Victorian Prose Masters. New York, 1901.

Bonnell, H. H. Charlotte Brontë, George Eliot, Jane Austen: Studies in their Works. New York, 1902.

Gould, G. M. Biographic Clinics: the Origin of the Ill-Health of De Quincey, Carlyle [and others]. 6 vols. Philadelphia, 1903–9. [Vol. II, 1904, on George Eliot.]

Paul, H. Stray Leaves. 1906.

Ward, Sir A. W. The Political and Social Novel. CHEL. vol. XIII, 1916.

Gosse, Sir E. Aspects and Impressions. 1922.

Bald, M. A. Women-Writers of the Nineteenth Century. Cambridge, 1923.

C., A. J. Notes on the Influence of Sir Walter Scott on George Eliot. Edinburgh, 1923.

Cazamian, M. L. Le Roman et les Idées. L'Influence de la Science. Strasburg, 1923.

Imelmann, R. Briefe Lord Actons über George Eliot. [In Festschrift für Johannes Hoops, Heidelberg, 1925.]

Woolf, V. The Common Reader. 1925.

Sackville-West, V. George Eliot. [In Great Victorians, ed. H. J. and H. Massingham, 1932.]

Cecil, Lord D. Early Victorian Novelists. 1934.

Baker, E. A. The History of the English Novel. Vol. VIII, 1937.

(c) Articles in Periodicals

Quarterly Rev. Oct. 1860. [Review of Scenes of Clerical Life, Adam Bede, Mill on the Floss. Rptd in Famous Reviews, ed. R. B. Johnson, 1914.]

Browne, M. George Eliot as a Poet. Contemporary Rev. VIII, 1868.

George Eliot and Comtism. London Quarterly Rev. XLVII, 1877.

Bryce, J., Viscount. George Eliot and Carlyle. Nation (New York), XXXII, 1881.

Kebbel, T. Village Life according to George Eliot. Fraser's Mag. CIII, 1881.

Simcox, E. George Eliot. Nineteenth Century, IX, 1881.

Ward, R. Scepticism in George Eliot. Journ. of Science, XVIII, 1881.

Whipple, E. P. The Private Life of George Eliot. North American Rev. CXLI, 1885.

Ireland, A. I. George Eliot and Jane Welsh Carlyle. GM. XL, 1887.

Whiting, M. B. George Eliot as a Character Artist. Westminster Rev. July, Dec. 1892.

Damon, L. T. George Eliot's Theory of Realism. Harvard Monthly, XV, 1893.

Ponsonby, M. E. George Eliot and George Sand. Nineteenth Century, L, 1901.

Clifford, L. Remembrance of George Eliot. Nineteenth Century, LXXIV, 1913.

—— George Eliot. Some Personal Recollections. Bookman, LXXIII, 1927.

Isenbarth, M. Die Psychologie der Charaktere in George Eliots 'The Mill on the Floss.' Die neueren Sprachen, XXI, 1913.

Parry, E. A. The Humour of George Eliot. Fortnightly Rev. CXII, 1919.

Rowland-Brown, L. The Boys of George Eliot. Nineteenth Century, LXXXVI, 1919.

Cross, W. L. George Eliot in Retrospect. Yale Rev. IX, 1920.

Gardner, C. George Eliot's Quarries. Atlantic Monthly, CXXXVI, 1925.

Lusky, A. E. George Eliot's The Mill on the Floss and Storm's Immensee. Modern Language Journ. X, 1926.

Lösch, O. Das Naturgefühl bei George Eliot und Thomas Hardy. Beiträge zur Erforschung der Sprache und Kultur Englands und Nordamerikas, V, 1928.

Parlett, M. George Eliot and Humanism. Stud. Phil. XXVII, 1930.

—— The Influence of Contemporary Criticism on George Eliot. Stud. Phil. XXX, 1933.

Simon-Baumann, L. George Eliot über Heinrich Heine. Ang. LV, 1931.

Sparrow-Simpson, W. J. The Religion of George Eliot. Church Quarterly Rev. CXII, 1931.

Williams, B. C. George Eliot and John Chapman: a Fragment. Colophon, I, 1935.

Diekhoff, J. S. The Happy Ending of Adam Bede. ELH. III, 1936. H. B. G.

GEORGE MEREDITH (1828–1909)

(1) BIBLIOGRAPHIES

Esdaile, A. J. K. Bibliography of the Writings in Prose and Verse of George Meredith. 1907.

—— A Chronological List of George Meredith's Publications, 1849–1911. 1914.

Forman, M. B. A Bibliography of the Writings in Prose and Verse of George Meredith. 1922.
—— Meredithiana, being a Supplement to the Bibliography of Meredith. 1924.

(2) COLLECTED WORKS

The Works of George Meredith. 34 vols. 1896–8, 1910–1.
New Popular Edition. 18 vols. 1897–8, 1902–5.
Memorial Edition. 27 vols. 1909–11. [Vol. xxvii Bibliography by A. J. K. Esdaile.]
Standard Edition. 15 vols. 1914–20.
Mickleham Edition. 18 vols. 1922–4.

(3) POEMS

Poems. 1851.
Modern Love, and Poems of the English Roadside, with Poems and Ballads. 1862; ed. E. Cavazza, Portland, Maine, 1891; 1892 (adds The Sage Enamoured and The Honest Lady); Portland, Maine, 1898.
Poems and Lyrics of the Joy of Earth. 1883.
Ballads and Poems of Tragic Life. 1887.
A Reading of Earth. 1888.
Jump-to-Glory Jane. A Poem. 1889 (priv. ptd); ed. H. Quilter, 1892 (illustrated by L. Housman).
Poems. The Empty Purse. With Odes to the Comic Spirit, to Youth in Memory, and Verses. 1892.
Odes in Contribution to the Song of French History. 1898.
A Reading of Life, with Other Poems. 1901.
Last Poems. 1909.
Milton. 1909. [A poem on the tercentenary of Milton's birth.]
The Poetical Works of George Meredith. With some Notes by G. M. Trevelyan. 1912.

(4) PROSE WORKS

The Shaving of Shagpat. An Arabian Entertainment. 1856 [1855].
Farina: a Legend of Cologne. 1857.
The Ordeal of Richard Feverel. A History of Father and Son. 3 vols. 1859; 1899 (rev. edn); tr. Italian, Milan, 1873.
Evan Harrington. 3 vols. 1861.
Emilia in England. 3 vols. 1864; 1889 (as Sandra Belloni); tr. French, Paris, 1866.
Rhoda Fleming. A Story. 3 vols. 1865.
Vittoria. 3 vols. 1867.
The Adventures of Harry Richmond. 3 vols. 1871 (bis).
Beauchamp's Career. 3 vols. 1876.
The House on the Beach. A Realistic Tale. New York, 1877.
On the Idea of Comedy and the Uses of the Comic Spirit. (A Lecture delivered at the London Institution, February 1st, 1877.) [1877.]

The Egoist. A Comedy in Narrative. 3 vols. 1879; tr. French, Paris, 1904.
The Tragic Comedians. A Study in a Well-known Story. Enlarged from the Fortnightly Review. 2 vols. 1880; 2 vols. 1881; 1892 (rev. and corrected, with Introductory Note on Ferdinand Lassalle by C. K. Shorter); tr. German, 1909.
Diana of the Crossways. A Novel. Considerably enlarged from The Fortnightly Review. 3 vols. 1885; New York, [1885]. [26 chs. were originally pbd in Fortnightly Rev. xxxv, xxxvi, 1881.]
The Case of General Ople and Lady Camper. New York, [1890].
The Tale of Chloe: an Episode in the History of Beau Beamish. New York, [1890]. [Rptd in London with The House on the Beach and The Case of General Ople and Lady Camper, 1894, and by itself, 1900.]
One of our Conquerors. 3 vols. 1891.
Lord Ormont and his Aminta. A Novel. 3 vols. 1894.
The Amazing Marriage. 2 vols. 1895.
Celt and Saxon. 1910.
Up to Midnight. A Series of Dialogues contributed to The Graphic, now reprinted for the first time. Boston, 1913.
The Contributions of George Meredith to the Monthly Observer, January–July 1849. Ed. M. B. Forman, 1928 (priv. ptd).

(5) PREFACES

Gordon, L. D., Lady. Letters from Egypt. New Introduction by George Meredith. 1902.
Thackeray, W. M. The Four Georges. With an Introduction by George Meredith. [1903.]
Okakura, Y. The Japanese Spirit. With an Introduction by George Meredith. 1905.
Sigerson, afterwards Shorter, D. M. Collected Poems. With an Introduction by George Meredith. 1907.

(6) LETTERS

Letters of George Meredith, collected and edited by his son [W. M. Meredith]. 2 vols. 1912.
Letters to E. Clodd and C. K. Shorter. 1913 (priv. ptd).
Letters to R. H. Horne. Cape Town, 1919 (priv. ptd).
Letters to A. C. Swinburne and T. Watts-Dunton. Cape Town, 1922 (priv. ptd).
Letters to Alice Meynell, with Annotations thereto. 1923.
Letters to Various Correspondents. Pretoria, 1924 (priv. ptd).

(7) BIOGRAPHY AND CRITICISM

(a) Books

Le Gallienne, R. George Meredith: some Characteristics; with a Bibliography by J. Lane [and some Notes on Meredith in America by W. M. Fullerton]. 1890.

Lynch, H. George Meredith: a Study. 1891.

Jerrold, W. George Meredith: an Essay towards Appreciation. 1902.

Trevelyan, G. M. The Poetry and Philosophy of George Meredith. 1906.

Henderson (afterwards Gretton), M. S. George Meredith, Novelist, Poet, Reformer. 1907.

—— The Writings and Life of George Meredith. 1926.

Short, T. S. On Some of the Characteristics of George Meredith's Prose-Writing. 1907.

Curle, R. H. P. Aspects of George Meredith. 1908.

Barrie, Sir J. M. George Meredith. 1909.

Forman, M. B. George Meredith: some Early Appreciations. 1909.

Hammerton, Sir J. A. George Meredith in Anecdote and Criticism. 1909.

Moffatt, J. George Meredith: a Primer to the Novels. 1909.

Sclater, J. R. P. The Sons of Strength. 1909. [On some religious ideas in Meredith's poems.]

Thomson, James. James Thomson ('B. V.') on George Meredith. 1909.

Bailey, E. J. The Novels of George Meredith. New York, 1910.

Dick, E. George Meredith: drei Versuche. Berlin, 1910.

Frey, E. Die Dichtung George Merediths. Zurich, 1910.

—— Die Romane George Merediths. Ein Versuch. Winterthur, 1913.

MacKechnie, J. Meredith's Allegory, The Shaving of Shagpat, interpreted. 1910.

Photiadès, C. George Meredith: sa Vie—son Imagination—son Art—sa Doctrine. Paris, 1910; tr. Eng. 1913.

Beach, J. W. The Comic Spirit of George Meredith. New York, 1911.

Benedetti, A. George Meredith, Poeta: Fiona Macleod. Studi letterari. Palermo, 1913.

Bedford, H. The Heroines of George Meredith. 1914.

Crees, J. H. E. George Meredith: a Study of his Works and Personality. Oxford, 1918.

—— Meredith Revisited. [1921.]

Torretta, L. George Meredith, Romanziere, Poeta, Pensatore. Naples, 1918.

Butcher, A. M., Lady. Memories of George Meredith. 1919.

Ellis, S. M. George Meredith: his Life and Friends. 1919.

Watson, A. F. Meredith and Italy. 1919.

Galland, R. George Meredith and British Criticism. 1923.

—— George Meredith: les Cinquante Premières Années. Paris, 1923.

Wolff, Lucien. George Meredith, Poète et Romancier. Paris, 1924.

Chislett, W. George Meredith: a Study and an Appraisal. [1925.]

Milnes, G. T. Meredith and the Cosmic Spirit. 1925.

Priestley, J. B. George Meredith. 1926. (English Men of Letters ser.)

Gamper, F. Die Sprache George Merediths. Mulhouse, 1927.

Senft, O. George Meredith als Pädagog. Langensalza, 1928.

Sencourt, R. E. The Life of George Meredith. 1929.

Alberts-Arndt, B. Die englische Gesellschaft im Spiegel der Romane von George Meredith. Karlsruhe, 1931.

Coolidge, B. A Catalogue of the Altschul Collection of George Meredith in the Yale University Library. New Haven, 1931.

Peel, Robert. The Creed of a Victorian Pagan. Cambridge, U.S.A. 1931.

Able, A. H. George Meredith and Thomas Love Peacock. Philadelphia, 1933.

Mackay, M. E. Meredith et la France. Paris, 1937.

Woods, A. George Meredith as Champion of Women and Progressive Education. Oxford, 1937.

(b) Essays and Chapters in Books

McCarthy, J. 'Con Amore, or Critical Studies. 1868. [Novels with a Purpose.]

—— Reminiscences. 2 vols. 1899.

Henley, W. E. Views and Reviews. 1890.

Stewart, J. A. Letters to Living Authors. 1890.

Gosse, Sir E. Gossip in a Library. 1891. [The Shaving of Shagpat, pp. 319–29.]

Watson, Sir W. Excursions in Criticism. 1893. [Mr Meredith's Poetry.]

Bridges, R. Overheard in Arcady. 1894. [Meredith, pp. 81–93.]

Monkhouse, A. Books and Plays. 1894. [Mr Meredith's Novels, pp. 1–46; Mr Meredith's Poems, pp. 47–79.]

Dowden, E. New Studies in Literature. 1895. [Mr Meredith in his Poems, pp. 33–60.]

Schwob, M. Spicilège. Paris, 1896.

Street, G. S. Quales Ego. 1896.

Dixon, W. M. In the Republic of Letters. 1898. [The Poetry of George Meredith, pp. 32–63; The Novels of George Meredith, pp. 159–82.]

Escott, T. H. S. Personal Forces of the Period. 1898.

Oliphant, J. Victorian Novelists. 1899. [Ch. vii: George Meredith, pp. 143–208.]

Wilson, S. L. The Theology of Modern Literature. 1899.

Brownell, W. C. Victorian Prose Masters. New York, 1901.

Legras, C. Chez nos Contemporains d'Angleterre. Paris, 1901.

Sharp, W. Literary Geography. 1904.

More, P. E. Shelburne Essays. Second Series. New York, 1905. [The Novels of George Meredith.]

Quiller-Couch, Sir A. T. From a Cornish Window. 1906. [Meredith's Poetry, pp. 261–290.]

Elton, O. Modern Studies. 1907.

Bailey, John. Poets and Poetry: being Articles reprinted from the Literary Supplement of The Times. 1911. [Meredith's Poetry, pp. 206–17.]

Jack, A. A. Poetry and Prose: being Essays on Modern English Poetry. 1911. [Meredith—Intellectual Poetry, pp. 201–43.]

Figgis, D. Studies and Appreciations. 1912. [George Meredith: the Philosopher in the Artist, pp. 169–98.]

Trevelyan, G. M. Clio: a Muse, and Other Essays. 1913.

Verrall, A. W. Collected Literary Essays, Classical and Modern. 1913. [Diana of the Crossways, pp. 276–88.]

Symons, A. Figures of Several Centuries. 1916. [George Meredith as a Poet, pp. 141–52.]

Morley, J., Viscount. Recollections. 2 vols. 1917. [Vol. I, ch. iv: Two Early Friends and Teachers, I: Meredith.]

Sherman, S. P. On Contemporary Literature. New York, 1917.

Thomas, Edward. A Literary Pilgrim in England. 1917.

Quiller-Couch, Sir A. T. Studies in Literature. Cambridge, 1918. [The Poetry of George Meredith, pp. 168–88.]

Sully, J. My Life and Friends. 1918.

'Raymond, Ernest.' Portraits of the Nineties. 1921.

Strong, Sir A. T. Three Studies in Shelley, and an Essay on Nature in Wordsworth and Meredith. 1921.

'Lee, Vernon.' The Handling of Words. 1923.

Fernandez, R. Messages. Paris, 1926; tr. Eng. 1927.

Lowes, J. L. Of Reading Books. 1930.

MacCarthy, D. Portraits. 1931.

Thomas, Sir W. B. George Meredith. [In Great Victorians, ed. H. J. and H. Massingham, 1932.]

Evans, B. I. English Poetry in the Later Nineteenth Century. 1933.

Dobrée, B. George Meredith. [In The English Novelists, ed. D. Verschoyle, 1936.]

Baker, E. A. The History of the English Novel. Vol. VIII, 1937. [Chs. vii–ix.]

Bush, D. Mythology and the Romantic Tradition in English Poetry. Cambridge, U.S.A. 1937.

(c) Articles in Periodicals

Shore, A. The Novels of George Meredith. British Quarterly Rev. LXX, 1879.

Courtney, W. L. George Meredith's Novels. Fortnightly Rev. XLV, 1886.

Lathrop, G. P. George Meredith. Atlantic Monthly, LXI, 1888.

[Sergeant, A.] George Meredith's Views of Women. Temple Bar, LXXXVI, 1889.

Dolman, F. George Meredith as a Journalist. New Rev. VIII, 1893.

George Meredith. Temple Bar, XCVII, 1893.

Mr Meredith's Novels. Edinburgh Rev. CLXXXI, 1895.

Smith, G. The Women of George Meredith. Fortnightly Rev. LXV, 1896.

Mr Meredith's Early Poetry. An Appreciation. Academy, 22 Oct. 1898.

Freiligrath-Kroeker, K. George Meredith. Litterarisches Echo (Berlin), 15 Sept. 1899.

Olivier, S. George Meredith's Writings: a Side-View on Democratic Tendency. Humane Rev. I, 1900.

Leonard, R. M. Politics in George Meredith's Novels. New Liberal Rev. II, 1901.

Samuel Richardson and George Meredith. Macmillan's Mag. LXXXV, 1902.

O., H. Mr George Meredith on the Future of Liberalism, Home Rule and Imperialism, Education and the Use of Votes. Manchester Guardian, 2 Feb. 1903.

Stead, W. T. Character Sketch: George Meredith. Review of Reviews, XXIX, 1904.

Moffatt, J. Mr Meredith on Religion. Hibbert Journ. III, 1905.

Pigou, A. C. The Optimism of Browning and Meredith. Independent Rev. VI, 1905.

Trevelyan, G. M. Optimism and Mr Meredith: a Reply. Independent Rev. VI, 1905.

Legouis, E. 'L'Égoïste' de George Meredith. Revue germanique, I, 1905.

Cordelet, H. La Femme dans l'Œuvre de Meredith. Revue germanique, II, 1906.

Henderson, M. S. Some Thoughts underlying George Meredith's Poems. International Journ. of Ethics, XVI, 1906.

Cecchi, E. Giorgio Meredith. Nuova Antologia, CXXV, 1906.

de Selincourt, B. George Meredith's 'Hymn to Colour.' Independent Rev. XI, 1906.

Greene, H. C. George Meredith. Atlantic Monthly, XCIX, 1907.

Edgar, P. George Meredith. National Rev. L, 1907.

—— The Poetry of George Meredith. National Rev. L, 1907.

Magnus, L. The Succession of Mr Meredith. Fortnightly Rev. LXXXVIII, 1907.

Roz, F. Romanciers anglais contemporains: George Meredith. Revue des Deux Mondes, XLIII, 1908.

George Meredith and the Jews. Jewish Chronicle, 14 Feb. 1908.

The Novels of George Meredith. TLS. 20 May 1909.

The Metres of George Meredith. TLS. 27 May 1909.

Henriot, P. Un Romancier anglais: George Meredith. Revue hebdomadaire, 5 June 1909.

Davray, H. D. George Meredith: Souvenirs et Réflexions. Mercure de France, LXXIX, 1909.

Chesterton, G. K. The Moral Philosophy of Meredith. Contemporary Rev. XCVI, 1909.

Clodd, E. George Meredith: some Recollections. Fortnightly Rev. XCII, 1909.

Tuell, A. K. George Meredith. Atlantic Monthly, CIV, 1909.

Matz, B. W. George Meredith as Publisher's Reader. Fortnightly Rev. XCII, 1909.

Lubbock, P. The Collected Works of George Meredith. Quart. Rev. CCXII, 1910.

Watson, F. George Meredith and Education. Nineteenth Century, LXVII, 1910.

Cunliffe, J. W. Modern Thoughts in Meredith's Poems. PMLA. XXVII, 1912.

Jones, D. M. English Writers and the Making of Italy. London Quarterly Rev. CXVIII, 1912.

Collins, J. P. Conversations with George Meredith. Pall Mall Mag., L, 1912.

Foote, G. W. George Meredith: Freethinker. English Rev. XIII, 1913.

Hartog, W. G. George Meredith, France and the French. Fortnightly Rev. CII, 1914.

Grey, R. Certain Boys of Meredith. Fortnightly Rev. CX, 1918.

Watson, A. F. Meredith and Italy. Fortnightly Rev. CXI, 1919.

Dimond, C. Music in the Novels of George Meredith. Nineteenth Century, LXXXVII, 1920.

Galland, R. Meredith et l'Allemagne; quelques Traductions inconnues. Revue de Littérature comparée, July 1923.

Symons, A. George Meredith: with some Unpublished Letters. Fortnightly Rev. CXIII, 1923.

Brewer, E. V. Unpublished Aphorisms by George Meredith. Yale Rev. XIV, 1925.

—— The Influence of Jean Paul Richter on George Meredith's Conception of the Comic. JEGP. XXIX, 1930.

Krusemeyer, M. Der Einfluss Goethes auf George Meredith. E. Studien, LIX, 1925.

George, R. E. G. Unpublished Letters of George Meredith. Nineteenth Century, CIII, 1928.

Hardy, T. G. M.: a Reminiscence. Nineteenth Century, CIII, 1928.

Fiedler, H. G. Notes by George Meredith on Grillparzer's 'Ahnfrau.' MLR. XXVI, 1931.

Dobrée, B. Some Novels of Meredith. National Rev. XCVIII, 1932.

Roberts, W. W. Music in Meredith. Music and Letters, XIII, 1932.

Simpson, H. George Meredith translates. Spectator, 9 Nov. 1934.

Mainland, W. F. A German Source for The Shaving of Shagpat. MLR. XXXI, 1936.

Zipf, G. K. New Facts in the Early Life of George Meredith. Harvard Stud. XX, 1938.

Robinson, E. A. Meredith's Literary Theory and Science. PMLA. LIII, 1938.

H. B. G.

V. MINOR FICTION, 1835–1870

[This section has been restricted, with one or two exceptions, to novelists born after 1799 and before 1831.]

WILLIAM HARRISON AINSWORTH
(1805–1882)

(a) Bibliography

Locke, Harold. A Bibliographical Catalogue of the Published Novels and Ballads of William Harrison Ainsworth. 1925.

(b) Collected Works

The Works of William Harrison Ainsworth. 14 vols. 1850–1. [With a memoir by S. L. Blanchard.]

The Collected Works. 16 vols. 1875; 31 vols. 1878–80; 12 vols. 1923.

[There is no complete edn of Ainsworth's writings.]

(c) Novels

Sir John Chiverton. A Romance. 1826 (anon.). [In collaboration with J. P. Aston.]

Rookwood. A Romance. 3 vols. 1834 (bis, 1st edn anon.); 1835; 1836; Paris, 1836; 1837; Leipzig, 1837; 1851; 1857; 1875, etc.

Crichton. 3 vols. 1837; Paris, 1837; 3 vols. 1849 (rev. edn); 1853; 1854, etc.

Jack Sheppard. A Romance. 1839; 15 weekly pts, 1840; 1840; 1854; 1856; 1862; 1865; 1884, etc. [First pbd in Bentley's Misc. 1839–40.]

The Tower of London. 13 monthly pts, 1840; 1840; 1842 (bis); 1843; 1844; 1845; 1853; 1854; 1878; 1882, etc.

Guy Fawkes, or the Gunpowder Treason. An Historical Romance. 3 vols. 1841; 1857; 1878; 1884; 1891. [First pbd in Bentley's Misc. Jan. 1840–Nov. 1841.]

Old Saint Paul's. A Tale of the Plague and the Fire. 12 monthly pts, 1841; 3 vols. 1841; 1847; 1855; 1857; 1884; 1891, etc. [First pbd in Sunday Times, Jan.–Dec. 1841.]

The Miser's Daughter. A Tale. 3 vols. 1842; 3 vols. 1843; 1848; 1855; 1879; 1886; 1892. [First pbd in Ainsworth's Mag. 1842.]

Modern Chivalry, or a New Orlando Furioso. 2 vols. 1843. [In collaboration with Catherine Gore.]

Windsor Castle. An Historical Romance. 3 vols. 1843; 1843; 11 pts, 1843–4; 1844; 1847; 1853; 1878; 1884, 1891, etc. [First pbd in Ainsworth's Mag. 1842–3.]

Saint James's, or the Court of Queen Anne. An Historical Romance. 3 vols. 1844; 3 vols. 1846; 1853; 1879; 1889. [First pbd in Ainsworth's Mag. 1844.]

James the Second, or the Revolution of 1688. An Historical Romance. 3 vols. 1848; 1854; 1890.

The Lancashire Witches. A Novel. 1849 (priv. ptd); 3 vols. 1849 (as The Lancashire Witches. A Romance of Pendle Forest); 1854; 1878; 1884. [First pbd in Sunday Times, 1848.]

Life and Adventures of Mervyn Clitheroe. 16 monthly pts, Dec. 1851–March 1852, Dec.–June 1858; 1858 (as Mervyn Clitheroe).

The Star Chamber. An Historical Romance. 2 vols. 1854; 1857; 1861; 1879; 1889; 1892. [First pbd in Home Companion, 1853.]

The Flitch of Bacon, or the Custom of Dunmow. 1854; 1855; 1874; 1879; 1889; 1892. [First pbd in New Monthly Mag. 1853–4.]

The Spendthrift. A Tale. 1857; 1879; 1889; 1892. [First pbd in Bentley's Misc. 1855–7.]

Ovingdean Grange. A Tale of the South Downs. 1860; 1879; 1891. [First pbd in Bentley's Misc. 1859–60.]

The Constable of the Tower. An Historical Romance. 3 vols. 1861; 1880; 1906. [First pbd in Bentley's Misc. 1861.]

The Lord Mayor of London, or City Life in the Last Century. 3 vols. 1862; 1880; 1906. [First pbd in Bentley's Misc. 1862.]

Cardinal Pole, or the Days of Philip and Mary. An Historical Romance. 3 vols. 1863; 1864; 1881, etc. [First pbd in Bentley's Misc. 1862–3.]

John Law, the Projector. 3 vols. 1864; 1866; 1881. [First pbd in Bentley's Misc. 1863–4.]

The Spanish Match, or Charles Stuart at Madrid. 3 vols. 1865 (bis); 1880; 1894. [First pbd in Bentley's Mag. 1864–5, as The House of Seven Chimneys.]

Auriol, or the Elixir of Life. 1865 (with The Old London Merchant, and A Night's Adventure in Rome—2 short stories): [1875]; 1875; 1881; 1890; 1892. [First pbd in Ainsworth's Mag. and New Monthly Mag. 1844–6.]

The Constable de Bourbon. 3 vols. 1866; 1880. [First pbd in Bentley's Misc. 1865–6.]

Old Court. A Novel. 3 vols. 1867; 1880. [First pbd in Bentley's Misc. 1866–7.]

Myddleton Pomfret. A Novel. 3 vols. 1868; 1881. [First pbd in Bentley's Misc. 1867–8.]

Hilary St Ives. A Novel. 3 vols. 1870; 1881. [First pbd in New Monthly Mag. 1869.]

The South Sea Bubble. A Tale of the Year 1720. [1871]; 1902. [First pbd in Bow Bells, 1868.]

Talbot Harland. 1871. [First pbd in Bow Bells, 1870.]

Tower Hill. [1871.] [First pbd in Bow Bells, 1871.]

Boscobel, or the Royal Oak. A Tale of the Year 1651. 3 vols. 1872, 1874; 1875; 1879; 1889. [First pbd in New Monthly Mag. 1872.]

The Good Old Times. The Story of the Manchester Rebels of '45. 3 vols. 1873; 1874 (as The Manchester Rebels of the Fatal '45); 1880; 1884; 1890; 1892; 1893.

Merry England, or Nobles and Serfs. 3 vols. 1874; [1875]. [First pbd in Bow Bells, 1874.]

The Goldsmith's Wife. A Tale. 3 vols. 1875; [1875]. [First pbd in Bow Bells, 1874.]

Preston Fight, or the Insurrection of 1715. A Tale. 3 vols. 1875; 1879.

Chetwynd Calverley. A Tale. 3 vols. 1876; [1877]. [First pbd in Bow Bells, 1876.]

The Leaguer of Lathom. A Tale of the Civil War in Lancashire. 3 vols. 1876; 1880.

The Fall of Somerset. 3 vols. 1877; [1878]. [First pbd in Bow Bells, 1877–8.]

Beatrice Tyldesley. 3 vols. 1878; [1879]. [First pbd in Bow Bells, 1878.]

Beau Nash, or Bath in the Eighteenth Century. 3 vols. [1879]; 1880; 1881; 1889.

Stanley Brereton. 3 vols. [1881]; 1882; 1884. [First pbd in Bolton Weekly Journ. 1881.]

(d) Other Writings

Poems. By Cheviot Tichburn. 1822.

Monody on the Death of John Philip Kemble. Manchester, 1823.

December Tales. 1823.

The Boeotian. Manchester, 1824.

The Works of Cheviot Tichburn. Manchester, 1825.

A Summer Evening Tale. 1825.

Consideration on the Best Means of affording Immediate Relief to the Operative Classes in the Manufacturing Districts. 1826.

Letters from Cockney Lands. 1826; 1827.

May Fair. In Four Cantos. 1827.

Ballads: Romantic, Fantastical, and Humorous. 1855; [1872] (with memoir of Ainsworth by J. Crossley, and adding The Combat of the Thirty). [Rptd from the novels.]

The Combat of the Thirty from a Breton Lay of the Fourteenth Century. 1859.

[Ainsworth edited Bentley's Miscellany from March 1840, and from 1842 began the publication of Ainsworth's Magazine which lasted until 1853, when he bought The New Monthly Magazine. From 1821 to 1881 Ainsworth contributed many stories and serials, with a few poems, to Arliss's Pocket Mag., Edinburgh Mag., European Mag., London Mag., Keepsake and other annuals, Fraser's Mag., Bentley's Misc., Sunday Times, Ainsworth's Mag., New Monthly Mag., Home Companion, and Bow Bells.]

(e) Biography and Criticism

Horne, R. H. A New Spirit of the Age. Vol. II, 1844.

Friswell, J. H. Modern Men of Letters. 1870.

Maginn, W. A Gallery of Illustrious Characters, 1830–1838. Ed. W. Bates, [1873].

Evans, John. The Early Life of William Harrison Ainsworth. 1882.

Axon, W. E. A. William Harrison Ainsworth. A Memoir. 1902.

Gribble, F. Estimate of William Harrison Ainsworth. Fortnightly Rev. March 1905.

Shelley, H. C. Untrodden English Ways. 1910.

Ellis, S. M. William Harrison Ainsworth and his Friends. 2 vols. 1911. [Includes bibliography.]

Elwin, M. Victorian Wallflowers. 1934.

Parsons, C. O. The Friendship of Theodore Martin and William Harrison Ainsworth. N. & Q. 23 June 1934.

WILLIAM EDMONDSTOUNE AYTOUN (1813–1865)

[See p. 277 above.]

'A. J. BARROWCLIFFE' i.c. ALBERT JULIUS MOTT

Amberhill, or Guilty Peace. 2 vols. 1856; 1862.

Trust for Trust. 3 vols. 1859.

Normanton. 1862; 1865.

'CUTHBERT BEDE,' i.e. EDWARD BRADLEY (1827–1889)

The Adventures of Mr Verdant Green, an Oxford Freshman; with Numerous Illustrations designed and drawn on the Wood by the Author. 'A College Joke to cure the Dumps.' 1853.

The Further Adventures of Mr Verdant Green, an Oxford Undergraduate: being a Continuation of the Adventures of Mr Verdant Green, an Oxford Freshman. With Illustrations by the Author. 1854.

Mr Verdant Green married and done for; being the Third and Concluding Part of the Adventures of Mr Verdant Green, an Oxford Freshman. 1857. [The 3 pts have been frequently rptd together as Mr Verdant Green, with Illustrations by the Author.]

Motley: Prose and Verse, Grave and Gay; with Illustrations by the Author. 1855.

Love's Provocations; being Extracts taken in the most Unmanly and Unmannerly Manner from the Diary of Miss Polly C — . Illustrations by the Author. 1855.

Photographic Pleasures popularly portrayed with Pen and Pencil. 1855.

Medley. [1856.]

The Shilling Book of Beauty. Edited and Illustrated by Cuthbert Bede. 1856.

Tales of College Life. 1856; 1862 (as College Life).

Nearer and Dearer: a Tale out of School. A Novelette. Illustrated by the Author. 1857.

Fairy Fables; with Illustrations by Alfred Crowquill. 1858.

Funny Figures. By A. Funnyman. 1858. ['One Shilling Plain: Two Shillings Coloured,' the latter with 24 coloured pictures.]

Happy Hours at Wynford Grange. A Story for Children. With Coloured Illustrations. 1859.

Glencreggan, or a Highland Home in Cantire. Illustrated from the Author's Drawings. 2 vols. 1861.

Our New Rector, or the Village of Norton. Edited by Cuthbert Bede. 1861.

The Curate of Cranston; with Other Prose and Verse. 1862.

A Tour in Tartan-Land. 1863.

The Visitor's Handbook to Rosslyn and Hawthornden. 1864.

The White Wife; with Other Stories, Supernatural, Romantic, Legendary. Collected and Illustrated by Cuthbert Bede. 1865.

The Rook's Garden: Essays and Sketches. 1865.

Mattins and Muttons, or the Beauty of Brighton. A Love Story. 2 vols. 1866.

Round the Peat Fire at Glenbrechy. With Illustrations by the Author. [Christmas no. of Once a Week, 1869.]

Little Mr Bouncer and his Friend, Verdant Green. With Illustrations by the Author. 1873.

Figaro at Hastings, St Leonards. With Illustrations by the Author. 1877.

Humour, Wit, and Satire; containing I. Book of Beauty, II. Motley, III. Medley. With Numerous Illustrations by the Author. 1885.

Fotheringay and Mary Queen of Scots; being an Account, Historical and Descriptive, of Fotheringay Castle, the Last Prison of Mary

Queen of Scots and the scene of her Trial and Execution. With Illustrations by the Author. 1886. [First pbd in The Leisure Hour, 1865.]

Betrothal Ring of Mary Queen of Scots, 1565. A Description of the Darnley Ring discovered in 1820 by a Labourer, Robert Wyatt, when digging in the Eastern Mound on which stood the Eastern Keep of Fotheringay Castle. Printed for the Ter-Centenary of Mary Queen of Scots Exhibition held at Peterborough. 1887.

Argyll's Highlands, or MacCailein Mor and the Lords of Lorne; with Traditional Tales. Ed. J. Mackay, Glasgow, 1902.

['Cuthbert Bede' was a frequent contributor to Punch, All the Year Round, The Field, GM., Once a Week, St James's Mag., London Rev., The Quiver, Boy's Own Paper, Illustrated London News, and N. & Q.]

RICHARD DODDRIDGE BLACKMORE
(1825–1900)
(a) Bibliography

Keogh, A. [In Essays on Modern Novelists by W. L. Phelps, New York, 1910, pp. 265–7.]

(b) Fiction

Clara Vaughan. A Novel. 3 vols. 1864; 1872 (rev.).

Cradock Nowell. A Tale of the New Forest. 3 vols. 1866; 1873 (rev.). [First pbd in Macmillan's Mag. May 1865–Aug. 1866.]

Lorna Doone. A Romance of Exmoor. 3 vols. 1869; 1873 (6th edn); ed. H. S. Ward, New York, 1908; ed. Sir H. Warren, 1914 (World's Classics); ed. R. O. Morris, 1920.

The Maid of Sker. 3 vols. Edinburgh, 1872; Edinburgh, 1873. [First pbd in Blackwood's Mag. Aug. 1871–July 1872.]

Alice Lorraine. A Tale of the South Downs. 3 vols. 1875; 1876 (6th edn, rev.). [First pbd in Blackwood's Mag. March 1874–April 1875.]

Cripps the Carrier. A Woodland Tale. 3 vols. 1876; 1877.

Erema, or my Father's Sin. 3 vols. 1877; 1878. [First pbd in Cornhill Mag. Nov. 1876–Nov. 1877.]

Mary Anerley. A Yorkshire Tale. 3 vols. 1880; 1881. [First pbd in Fraser's Mag. July 1879–Sept. 1880.]

Christowell. A Dartmoor Tale. 3 vols. 1882; 1882. [First pbd in Good Words, Jan.–Dec. 1881.]

The Remarkable History of Sir Thomas Upmore, Bart., M.P. formerly known as 'Tommy Upmore'. 2 vols. 1884 (bis); 1885.

Springhaven. A Tale of the Great War. 3 vols. 1887. [First pbd in Harper's Mag. April 1886–April 1887.]

Kit and Kitty. A Story of West Middlesex. 3 vols. 1890; New York, n.d.; 1890.

Perlycross. A Tale of the Western Hills. 3 vols. 1894; New York, 1894; 1894.

Tales from the Telling House. 1896.

Dariel. A Romance of Surrey. 1897; New York, 1897.

(c) Poems

Poems by Melanter. 1854.

Epullia [and other poems]. By the Author of Poems by Melanter. 1854.

The Bugle of the Black Sea, or the British in the East. By Melanter. 1855.

The Fate of Franklin. 1860.

The Farm and Fruit of Old. A Translation in Verse of the First and Second Georgics of Virgil. By a Market-Gardener. 1862.

The Georgics of Virgil, translated. 1871; ed. R. S. Conway, 1932.

Fringilla. Some Tales in Verse. 1895.

(d) Biography and Criticism

[For a much fuller list see Q. G. Burris, Richard Doddridge Blackmore, Urbana, 1930, pp. 212–6.]

Smith, G. B. Mr Blackmore's Novels. International Rev. VII, 1879.

The Novels of Mr Blackmore. Blackwood's Mag. CLX, 1896.

Snell, F. J. The Blackmore Country. 1906.

Phelps, W. L. Lorna Doone. [In Essays on Modern Novelists, New York, 1910.]

Bernbaum, E. Richard Doddridge Blackmore and American Cordiality. Southwest Rev. XI, 1925.

—— On Blackmore and Lorna Doone. A Selected Bibliography, with Brief Comments. Library Journ. 15 June 1925.

Burris, Q. G. Richard Doddridge Blackmore: his Life and Novels. Urbana, 1930.

Elwin, M. Victorian Wallflowers. 1934.

'ROLF BOLDREWOOD,' i.e. THOMAS ALEXANDER BROWNE (1826–1915)

[See p. 1096 below.]

ARCHIBALD BOYD

The Duchess, or Woman's Love and Woman's Hate. A Romance. 3 vols. 1850 (anon.).

The Crown Ward. A Novel. 3 vols. 1856.

The Cardinal. A Romance. 3 vols. 1858.

CHARLES WILLIAM SHIRLEY BROOKS
(1816–1874)

[See p. 600 below.]

ROBERT BARNABAS BROUGH (1828–1860)

[See p. 601 below.]

FRANCES BROWNE

(a) Fiction

The Ericksons; the Clever Boy, or Consider one another. Edinburgh, 1852.
Granny's Wonderful Chair and its Tales of Fairy Times. 1857.
Our Uncle the Traveller. Stories. 1859.
The Young Foresters. [1860.]
The Orphans of Elfholm. [1860.]
My Share of the World: an Autobiography. A Novel. 3 vols. 1861.
The Castleford Case. 3 vols. 1862.
The Hidden Sin. A Novel. 3 vols. 1866 (anon).
The Exile's Trust, A Tale of the French Revolution, and Other Stories. [1869.]
The Nearest Neighbour and Other Stories. [1875.]
The Dangerous Guest. A Story of 1745. [1886.]
The Foundling of the Fens. A Story of a Flood. [1886.]
The First of the African Diamonds. [1887.]

(b) Poems

The Star of Attéghéi; the Vision of Schwartz; and Other Poems. 1844.
Lyrics and Miscellaneous Poems. Edinburgh, 1848.
Pictures and Songs of Home. [1856.]

EDWARD GEORGE EARLE LYTTON
BULWER-LYTTON, BARON LYTTON
(1802–1873)

(a) Collected Works

The Novels. 10 vols. 1840.
The Dramatic Works. 1841; 1859; 1863; 1873; [1887]; [1890]. [Includes (in addn to The Duchess de la Vallière, The Lady of Lyons, Richelieu, and Money) Odes on Elizabeth, Cromwell and Nelson.]
The Critical and Miscellaneous Works. 2 vols. Philadelphia, 1841.
The Poems. Collected and arranged by C. Donald Macleod. New York, 1845.
The Poetical and Dramatic Works. 5 vols. 1848; 5 vols. 1852–4.
The Novels. 41 vols. 1859–62; 22 vols. 1877–8. (Library edn.)
The Poetical Works. 1859; 1865; 1873.
Novels and Romances. 43 vols. 1864; 23 vols. 1867; 11 vols. 1868.
Miscellaneous Prose Works. 3 vols. 1868.
The Speeches of Edward, Lord Lytton. With Memoir by his Son. 2 vols. 1874.
The Works. 38 vols. 1874; 26 vols. 1877–8. (Knebworth edn.)
The Novels. 29 vols. 1895–8. (New Knebworth edn.)

(b) Fiction

Falkland. 1827; 2 vols. Paris, 1833; [1876], etc.
Pelham, or the Adventures of a Gentleman. 3 vols. 1828; 1839; 1854; 1860; 1873; 2 vols. Paris, 1874; 1877, etc.
The Disowned. 4 vols. 1828; 3 vols. 1829; 1831; 2 vols. 1835; 1852; 1855; 2 vols. Paris, 1858; 1874, etc.
Devereux. A Tale. 3 vols. 1829; 1831; 1836; 1839; 1841; 1852; 1855; Paris, 1859; 1861; 1874; 1879, etc.
Paul Clifford. 3 vols. 1830; 1835; Stockholm, 1835; 1854; 2 vols. Paris, 1858; 1860; 1861; 1874; 1878; [1879]; 1880, etc.
Eugene Aram. 3 vols. 1832; 2 vols. Paris, 1832; 1849; 1854; 1861; [1873]; 2 vols. Paris, 1873; 1877; 1878; 1879; [1881], etc.
Godolphin. 3 vols. 1833 (anon.); 1850; 1854; 1860; 1862; 1874; 1879, etc.
The Pilgrims of the Rhine. 1834; Frankfort, 1838; 1840; 1850; 1854; 1860; 1861; 1865, etc.
The Last Days of Pompeii. 3 vols. 1834; 1835 ('revised and corrected'); 2 vols. Brussels, 1837; 1839; 1850; 1854; 1856; 1861; 1872; 1873; [1879]; 1880; [1881]; [1883]; [1884], etc.
Rienzi, the Last of the Roman Tribunes. 3 vols. 1835; 2 vols. Milan, 1836; 1837; 1854; 2 vols. Paris, 1859; 1861; 1874; 1878; [1879]; [1883]; [1885], etc.
Ernest Maltravers. 3 vols. 1837; 1851; 1854; Paris, 1859; 1861; 1873; 1876; 1877; 1879; 1880, etc.
Leila, or the Siege of Granada. Berlin, 1837; 1838; 1847; 0 pts, 1850 (as Leila and Calderon the Courtier); 1855; 1862; 1878 (original title); 1879.
Alice, or the Mysteries. 3 vols. 1838; 1852; 1854; 1860; 1873; 1875; [1879]; 1880, etc.
Night and Morning. 3 vols. 1841; 1851; 1854; 2 vols. 1876; 1878; Paris, 1879; [1880]; [1889], etc.
Zanoni. 3 vols. 1842; 1853; 1856; Paris, 1858; 1860; 1862; [1880]; [1892], etc.
The Last of the Barons. 3 vols. 1843; 1850; 1854; 1860; 1874; 1878; 1884; [1888], etc.; ed. F. C. Romilly, 1913.
Lucretia, or the Children of Night. 3 vols. 1846; 2 vols. Leipzig, 1846; 1847; 1853; 1855; 1860; 2 vols. 1863; 1874; 1877; 1889.
Harold, the Last of the Saxons. 3 vols. 1848 (bis); 1853; 1855; 1866; 1874; 1892, etc.; ed. G. L. Gomme, [1906].
The Caxtons. A Family Picture. 3 vols. 1849; 2 vols. 1849; 1853; 1854; 1855; 1874; 1890; 1892; 1896; [1898]; [1899], etc. [First pbd anon. in Blackwood's Mag.]

'My Novel,' by Pisistratus Caxton, or Varieties
in English Life. 4 vols. 1853; 1854; 1856;
1861; 2 vols. Paris, [1861]; 2 vols. 1892, etc.
[First pbd in Blackwood's Mag.]
The Haunted and the Haunters. 1857; 1905,
etc.
What Will He Do With It? By Pisistratus
Caxton. 4 vols. 1859; 1860; 2 vols. Paris,
1860; 1864; 2 vols. 1875; 2 vols. 1892; 2 vols.
1902. [First pbd in Blackwood's Mag.]
A Strange Story. 2 vols. 1862 (3 edns); 1863
(rev.); 1864; 1865; 1875; 1892. [First pbd
in All the Year Round.]
The Coming Race. 1871 (anon.); 1872; 1873;
1874; 1875; 1886; Madrid, 1893; 1928.
[First pbd in Blackwood's Mag.]
The Parisians. 4 vols. 1873; 4 vols. Edinburgh,
[1873]; 2 vols. 1876; 2 vols. 1878; 2 vols.
[1890]; 2 vols. 1892. [First pbd in Blackwood's Mag.]
Kenelm Chillingly, his Adventures and
Opinions. 3 vols. 1873; 1874; 1875; [1876];
1878; 1892; 1904, etc.
Pausanias the Spartan. 1876. [An unfinished
historical romance ed. by Lytton's son.]

(c) Plays

The Duchess de la Vallière. 1836.
The Lady of Lyons. 1838; 1839 (8th edn);
1851; 1860; 1879; [1880]; [1883]; [1885],
etc.
The Sea Captain, or the Birthright. A Drama.
1839; Paris, 1840; [1885].
Richelieu, or the Conspiracy. 1839; 1850;
1873; [1881]; [1885]; Paris, 1897.
Money. A Comedy. 1840; 1848; 1851; 1873;
1874; [1883]; [1885], etc.
Not So Bad As We Seem, or Many Sides to a
Character. A Comedy. 1851; 1853.
The Rightful Heir. 1868; Leipzig, 1869.
Walpole, or Every Man has his Price. 1869.

(d) Poems

Ismael, an Oriental Tale, with Other Poems.
1820.
Delmour, or the Tale of a Sylphid and Other
Poems. 1823 (anon.).
Sculpture. A Poem which obtained the
Chancellor's Medal, July 1825. Cambridge,
1825; [Cambridge, 1825].
Weeds and Wildflowers. By E. G. L. B.
Paris, 1826 (priv. ptd).
O'Neill, or the Rebel. 1827; Paris, 1829.
The Siamese Twins, A Satirical Tale of the
Times. 1831.
Eva, The Ill-omened Marriage and Other
Poems. 1842.
Poems of Schiller. 2 vols. 1844; 1852; 1859;
1870; 1877; [1887]; [1889].
The New Timon. 1846.

King Arthur, an Epic Poem, 3 pts, 1848–9;
2 vols. 1849; 1870 (rev.); [1888].
St Stephen's. A Poem. 1860. [First pbd in
Blackwood's Mag.]
The Boatman. By Pisistratus Caxton. 1864.
[First pbd in Blackwood's Mag.]
The Odes and Epodes of Horace. A Metrical
Translation into English. 1869; 1872;
[1887]; 1894.

[Lytton also pbd the following poems in
Knight's Quarterly Mag. under the pseudonym
'Edmund Bruce': Poems to Zoe (June 1823);
The First Songstresses in Town (Oct. 1823);
Narenor; A Tale, I, Sonnet to A. T. on her
Birthday (April 1824); Madame Catalani,
Sonnet written on the First Leaf of Keats'
Poems, Despair, Song, To M---- (Jan. 1824);
Narenor II (Aug. 1824).]

(e) Other Writings

England and the English. 2 vols. 1833; Paris,
1833; 1834 (3rd edn, with new preface);
1840; 1874; [1887].
Asmodeus at Large. 1833; Philadelphia,
1833.
A Letter to a Late Cabinet Minister on the
Crisis. [1834] (20 edns).
The Student. A Series of Papers. 2 vols.
1835; 1840.
Literary Remains of William Hazlitt, with
Thoughts on his Genius and Writings.
2 vols. 1836.
Athens: its Rise and Fall. 2 vols. 1837; 1874;
2 vols. n.d.
Confessions of a Water Patient. In a Letter to
W. Harrison Ainsworth. 1846.
The Works of Laman Blanchard. Sketches
from Life. 3 vols. 1846. [Contains a long
introduction by Lytton.]
A Word to the Public. 1847.
Letters to John Bull Esquire. 1851.
Outlines of the Early History of the East. A
Lecture, delivered at the Royston Me-
chanics' Institute. Royston, 1852.
Caxtoniana. 2 vols. 1863; 1875.
Lost Tales of Miletus. 1866; 1870.
The Princess Alexandra Gift Book. Ed. J.
Sherer, 1868. [Contains contributions by
Lytton.]
Pamphlets and Sketches. 1875.
Quarterly Essays. 1875.
A Letter of Bulwer Lytton to Macready.
Carteret Book Club, New Jersey, 1911.

The New Monthly Magazine. [Vols. xxxi–
xlviii, were ed. by Lytton and contain
many articles, poems and sketches from his
pen. For a list see appendix to M. Sadleir,
Bulwer, A Panorama, 1931.]

(f) Speeches

To the Independent Freemen and Electors of the City of Lincoln. Lincoln, [1848]. [2 addresses.]

Address to the Associated Societies of the University of Edinburgh, On his Installation as their Honorary President and his Speech at the Public Dinner, January 20th, 1854. Edinburgh, 1854.

Speech delivered at the Leeds Mechanics' Institution. 1854.

Speech On the Representation of the People Bill, delivered in the House of Commons, March 22nd, 1859. 1859.

The New Reform Bill, Speech delivered in the House of Commons, Revised and Corrected by the Author. 1860.

The Inaugural Address of Lord Lytton, delivered at the Congress of the British Archaeological Association at The Town Hall, St Albans, 1869. Ed. T. Wright, Hertford, [1880].

(g) Biography and Criticism

(i) Books

Cooper, Thomson. Lord Lytton. A Biography. 1873.

Frost, W. A. Lord Lytton: the Man and the Author. 1873.

—— Bulwer Lytton: Errors of his Biographers. 1913.

Jowett, B. Lord Lytton, the Man and the Author; to which is attached a Biography by M. Marsden. 1873.

Ten Brink, J. E. G. Bulwer-Lytton, Biografie en Kritick. Haarlem, 1873.

The Life, Letters and Literary Remains. Edited by his Son. 2 vols. 1883.

Letters of the Late Edward Bulwer, Lord Lytton, to his Wife, published in Vindication of her Memory. Ed. L. Devey, 1884.

Escott, T. H. S. Edward Bulwer, First Baron Lytton of Knebworth. 1910.

The Life of Edward Bulwer, First Lord Lytton, By his Grandson. 2 vols. 1913.

Sadleir, M. Bulwer, A Panorama. i, Edward and Rosina, 1803–1835. 1931.

(ii) Essays, Pamphlets and Chapters of Books

Laube, H. Bulwer und das Saint-Simonismus. [In Moderne Charakteristiken, 2 vols. Mannheim, 1835.]

Carlyle, T. The Dandiacal Body. [In Sartor Resartus, Boston, 1836. First pbd in Fraser's Mag. Aug. 1834.]

Planché, Gustave. Portraits littéraires. Vol. i, Paris, 1836.

Chorley, H. F. The Authors of England. 1838.

Horne, R. H. A New Spirit of the Age. Vol. ii, 1844.

Powell, T. Pictures of the Living Authors of England. 1851.

Gilfillan, G. Galleries of Literary Portraits. Vol. ii, Edinburgh, 1856.

'Rochester, Mark' (i.e. C. Kent). The Derby Ministry, A Series of Cabinet Pictures. 1858.

Senior, N. W. Essays on Fiction. 1864.

Friswell, J. H. Modern Men of Letters. 1870.

Reid, T. W. Cabinet Portraits. 1872.

Maginn, W. A Gallery of Illustrious Characters, 1830–1838. Drawn by Daniel Maclise, and accompanied by Notices chiefly by the late William Maginn. Ed. W. Bates, [1873].

Heywood, J. C. How they strike me. Philadelphia, 1877.

'Lytton, Lady.' A Blighted Life. 1880. [Authorship denied by R sina Bulwer-Lytton.]

Lennox, W. P. Plays and Players. 2 vols. 1881.

Walsh, W. S. Pen Pictures of Victorian Authors. New York, 1884.

Watt, J. C. Great Novelists. [1885.]

Devey, L. The Life of Rosina Lady Lytton. 1887.

Griswold, H. T. The Home Life of Great Authors. Chicago, 1887.

Matthews, W. Men, Places and Things. Chicago, 1887.

Jeaffreson, J. C. Novels and Novelists. 2 vols. 1888.

Cooke, P. J. Bulwer-Lytton's Plays. [1894.]

McCarthy, J. Portraits of the Sixties. 1903.

'Melville, Lewis.' Victorian Novelists. 1906.

Bell, E. G. An Introduction to the Prose Romances, Plays and Comedies of E. Bulwer. Chicago, 1914.

The Unpublished Letters of Lady Bulwer Lytton to A. E. Chalon. Ed. S. M. Ellis, 1914.

Stewart, C. N. Bulwer-Lytton as an Occultist. 1927.

Maurois, A. Les Derniers Jours de Pompéi. Paris, 1928; tr. Eng. Southwest Rev. xvi, 1930. [A study of Lytton and his wife.]

Liljegren, S. B. Quelques Romans anglais, Source partielle d'une Religion nouvelle. [Lytton and theosophy. In Mélanges Baldensperger, vol. ii, Paris, 1930.]

Sheppard, A. T. The Art and Practice of Historical Fiction. 1930.

Seifert, H. Bulwers Verhältnis zur Geschichte. Leipzig, 1935 (priv. ptd).

Rosa, M. W. The Silver Fork School: Novels of Fashion preceding Vanity Fair. New York, 1936.

(iii) Reviews of the Novels

Pelham. North American Rev. xxix, 1829. [By W. Phillips.]

Devereux. Colburn's New Monthly Mag. xxvi, 1829.

Paul Clifford. Christian Examiner (Boston), ix, 1830. [By J. T. Austin.]

Eugene Aram. Fraser's Mag. Feb. 1832. ['A Good Tale badly told'.]

The Disowned. Colburn's New Monthly Mag. xlv, 1835.

The Last Days of Pompeii. Dublin University Mag. v, 1835; North American Rev. xl, 1835 (by G. H. Devereux).

Rienzi. Dublin Rev. i, 1836.

Ernest Maltravers. Eclectic Rev. lxviii, 1838; Tait's Edinburgh Mag. v, 1838.

Alice, Or the Mysteries. Tait's Edinburgh Mag. v, 1838.

Night and Morning. Tait's Edinburgh Mag. viii, 1841.

Zanoni. Tait's Edinburgh Mag. x, 1842.

The Last of the Barons. Monthly Rev. clx, 1843; Tait's Edinburgh Mag. x, 1843.

Lucretia. Bentley's Misc. xxi, 1847; Colburn's New Monthly Mag. lxxix, 1847; Dublin University Mag. xxix, 1847.

Harold. Fraser's Mag. xxxviii, 1848.

The Caxtons. Westminster Rev. lii, 1849; Fraser's Mag. liii, 1856.

My Novel. New Quarterly Rev. ii, 1853.

What will he do with it? North American Rev. lxxxviii, 1859. [By M. J. M. Sweat.]

A Strange Story. Christian Remembrancer, xliii, 1862.

The Coming Race. Blackwood's Mag. cx, 1871.

Kenelm Chillingly. Blackwood's Mag. cxiii, 1873. [By Mrs Oliphant.]

(iv) Articles in Periodicals

'North, Christopher.' Noctes Ambrosianae. Blackwood's Mag. March 1829.

[Landon, L. E.] Bulwer as a Man and a Novelist. New Monthly Mag. May 1831.

Bulwer. Quarterly Rev. Dec. 1832. [An attack and violent criticism.]

'Yellowplush, C. J.' (i.e. W. M. Thackeray). Epistle to Sir Edward Lytton Bulwer, Bart. Fraser's Mag. Jan. 1840. [Rptd in Thackeray's Works in The Yellowplush Correspondence.]

Lowell, J. R. The New Timon. North American Rev. lxiv, 1847.

Oliphant, M. O. Bulwer. Blackwood's Mag. Feb. 1855.

Böddeker, K. Über Bulwers Übersetzungen Schillerischer Gedichte. Archiv, xlix, 1872.

Tawle, G. M. Reminiscences of Lytton. Appleton's Journ. ix, 1873.

Saintsbury, G. The Poetry of Lytton. Forum, xxii, 1896.

Howells, W. D. Nydia. Harper's Bazaar, 25 Aug. 1900.

Lord, W. F. The Novels of Lytton. Nineteenth Century, Sept. 1901.

—— The Wand of Prospero. Nineteenth Century, Jan. 1924.

Lytton. A Sketch from Memory. MacMillan's Mag. lxxxiii, 1901.

The Last Days of Pompeii: Contemporary Criticism. Bookman (New York), July 1903.

Wilstack, P. Dramatisations of Lytton. Bookman (New York), July 1903.

A Visit to Bulwer-Lytton at Knebworth in 1857. Blackwood's Mag. Jan. 1905.

Gosse, Sir E. The Life of Edward Bulwer. Fortnightly Rev. Dec. 1913.

Messac, R. Bulwer-Lytton et Dostoievski: de Paul Clifford à Raskolnikof. Revue de Littérature comparée, Oct. 1926.

Qualia, C. B. French Dramatic Sources of Bulwer-Lytton's Richelieu. PMLA. xlii. 1927.

Stevenson, L. Stepfathers of Victorianism. Virginia Quart. April 1930.

Bangs, A. R. Mephistophiles in England, or the Confessions of a Prime Minister. PMLA. xlvii, 1932. [Here attrib. to Lytton.]

Watts, H. H. Lytton's Theories of Prose Fiction. PMLA. l, 1935.

ROSINA, LADY BULWER-LYTTON, née WHEELER (1804–1882)

(a) Fiction

Cheveley, or the Man of Honour. 3 vols. 1839 (3 edns).

The Budget of the Bubble Family. 3 vols. 1840.

The Prince-Duke and the Page. An Historical Novel. 3 vols. 1841.

Bianca Cappello. An Historical Romance. 3 vols. 1843.

Memoirs of a Muscovite. 3 vols. 1844.

The Peer's Daughters. A Novel. 3 vols. 1849.

Miriam Sedley, or the Tares and the Wheat. A Tale of Real Life. 3 vols. 1851.

The School for Husbands, or Molière's Life and Times. 3 vols. 1852.

Behind the Scenes. A Novel. 3 vols. 1854.

Very Successful! 3 vols. 1856; [1859].

The World and his Wife, or a Person of Consequence. A Photographic Novel. 3 vols. 1858.

The Household Fairy, [etc.]. 1870.

(b) Other Writings

Lady Bulwer Lytton's Appeal to the Justice and Charity of the English Public. [1857.]

Shells from the Sands of Time. 1876. [Essays.]

[Rosina Bulwer-Lytton did *not* write A Blighted Life, which was pbd in her name in 1880.]

(c) Biography

Sadleir, M. Bulwer, A Panorama. i. Edward and Rosina, 1803–1836. 1931.

HENRY FOTHERGILL CHORLEY (1808–1872)

[See p. 710 below.]

CHARLES CLARKE

Charlie Thornhill, or the Dunce of the Family. A Novel. 3 vols. 1863.
A Box for the Season. A Sporting Sketch. 2 vols. 1864.
Which is the Winner? Or the First Gentleman of his Family. 3 vols. 1864.
Crumbs from a Sportsman's Table. 2 vols. 1865; [1869].
The Flying Scud: a Sporting Novel. 2 vols. 1867 (anon.); 1868 (3rd edn).
Tom Crackenthorpe: Hunting and Steeple-Chasing. 1867.
The Beauclercs, Father and Son. A Novel. 3 vols. 1867.
Lord Falconberg's Heir. A Novel. 2 vols. 1868.
A Forecastle Frolic. Being a Round of Stories for Christmas. Conducted by Charles Clarke. [1868.]
Myra Gray, or sown in Tears, reaped in Joy. A Novel. 3 vols. 1870.
Calcraft's Confessions; or, Coward-Conscience. 1870.
Chips from an Old Block. [1871.]

MARY COWDEN CLARKE (1809–1897)

[See p. 711 below.]

CAROLINE CLIVE, née MEYSEY-WIGLEY (1801–1873)

(a) Novels

Paul Ferroll. A Tale. By the Author of IX Poems by V. 1855; rptd 1929.
Year after Year. A Tale. 1858.
Why Paul Ferroll killed his Wife. 1860.
John Greswold. 2 vols. 1864.

(b) Poems

IX Poems by V. 1840; 1841 (enlarged); ed. (with biographical introduction) E. Partridge, 1928.
I Watched the Heavens. A Poem by V. 1842.
Saint Oldooman. A Myth of the Nineteenth Century. 1845 (anon.). [A satire on Newman's Lives of the English Saints.]
The Queen's Ball. A Poem by V. 1847.
The Valley of the Rea. A Poem. 1851.

The Morlas. A Poem by V. 1853.
Poems by the Author of Paul Ferroll. 1856; 1872; ed. A. Greathed, 1890.

(c) Criticism

[Coleridge, H. N.] Quarterly Rev. LXVI, 1840. [Review of IX Poems by V.]
Brown, John. Henry Vaughan. [In Horae Subsecivae, ser. i, Edinburgh, 1882. The essay includes an appreciation of IX Poems by V.]
Sergeant, A. Mrs Archer Clive. [In Women Novelists of Queen Victoria's Reign, 1897.]

HENRY COCKTON (1807–1853)

The Life and Adventures of Valentine Vox, the Ventriloquist. 1840; 1853 (rev.).
Stanley Thorn. 3 vols. 1841.
George St George Julian, the Prince of Swindlers. 1841; 1844.
Sylvester Sound the Somnambulist. 1844.
The Love Match. 1845.
The Steward. A Romance of Real Life. 1850.
The Sisters, or the Fatal Marriage. 1851.
Lady Felicia. A Novel. 1852.
Percy Effingham, or the Germ of the World's Esteem. 3 vols. 1853.

CHARLES ALSTON COLLINS (1828–1873)

A New Sentimental Journey. 1859. [First pbd in All the Year Round, June, July 1859.]
The Eyewitness, his Evidence about Many Wonderful Things. 1860. [First pbd in All the Year Round, 1859–60.]
A Cruise upon Wheels. The Chronicles of some Autumn Wanderings among the Deserted Post Roads of France. 2 vols. 1862; 1863; rptd 1926.
The Bar Sinister. A Tale. 2 vols. 1864.
Strathcairn, A Novel. 2 vols. 1864.
At the Bar. A Tale. 2 vols. 1866.

[For Collins, see S. M. Ellis, Wilkie Collins and Others, 1931.]

MORTIMER COLLINS (1827–1876)

(a) Fiction

Who is the Heir? A Novel. 3 vols. 1865.
Sweet Anne Page. 3 vols. 1868.
The Ivory Gate. 2 vols. 1869.
The Vivian Romance. 3 vols. 1870.
Marquis and Merchant. 3 vols. 1871.
The Princess Clarice. A Story of 1871. 2 vols. 1872.
Two Plunges for a Pearl. 3 vols. 1872. [First pbd in London Society, Jan.–Nov. 1871.]
Squire Silchester's Whim. 3 vols. 1873.
Miranda. A Midsummer Madness. 3 vols. 1873.
Mr Carington. A Tale of Love and Constancy. 3 vols. 1873. [Pbd as 'By Robert Turner Cotton.']

Transmigration. 3 vols. 1874.

Frances. 3 vols. 1874.

Sweet and Twenty. 3 vols. 1875.

Blacksmith and Scholar and From Midnight to Midnight. 3 vols. 1876. [From Midnight to Midnight rptd separately, 1883.]

A Fight with Fortune. 3 vols. 1876.

You play me False. A Novel. By Mortimer and Frances Collins. 3 vols. 1878.

The Village Comedy. By Mortimer and Frances Collins. 3 vols. 1878.

(b) Poems

Idyls and Rhymes. Dublin, 1855.

Summer Songs. 1860.

A Letter to the Right Honourable Benjamin Disraeli, M.P. 1869.

The Inn of Strange Meetings and Other Poems. 1871.

The British Birds. A Communication from the Ghost of Aristophanes. 1872.

Selections from the Poetical Works of Mortimer Collins. Ed. F. P. Cotton, 1886.

(c) Other Writings

The Secret of Long Life. 1871. [Essays.]

Pen Sketches from a Vanished Hand, from the Papers of the Late Mortimer Collins. Edited by Tom Taylor, with Notes by the Editor and Mrs Mortimer Collins. 2 vols. 1879.

Thoughts in My Garden. Edited by Edmund Yates, with Notes by the Editor and Mrs Mortimer Collins. 2 vols. 1880.

(d) Biography and Criticism

Collins, Frances. Mortimer Collins: his Letters and Friendships, with Some Account of his Life. 2 vols. 1877.

Ellis, S. M. Wilkie Collins, Le Fanu and Others. 1931

WILLIAM WILKIE COLLINS (1824–1889)*

(a) Fiction

Antonina: Or the Fall of Rome. A Romance of the Fifth Century. 3 vols. 1850.

Mr Wray's Cash Box: Or the Mask and the Mystery: A Christmas Sketch. 1852.

Basil: A Story of Modern Life. 3 vols. 1852; 1862 (presents important modifications both in preface and the text).

Hide and Seek. 3 vols. 1854.

After Dark. 2 vols. 1856. [6 stories with connecting narrative: A Terribly Strange Bed; A Stolen Letter; Sister Rose; The Lady of Glenwith Grange; Gabriel's Marriage; The Yellow Mask. All originally pbd in Household Words, 1853–5.]

The Dead Secret. 2 vols. 1857. [First pbd in Household Words from 3 Jan. 1857.]

The Queen of Hearts. 3 vols. 1859. [11 stories with connecting narrative: The Black Cottage; The Family Secret (first pbd in National Mag. 1857, as Uncle George or the Family Mystery); The Dream-Woman (first pbd in Household Words, Christmas No. 1855); The Holly-Tree Inn (first pbd ibid. as The Ostler; see also The Frozen Deep below); Mad Monkton; The Dead Hand (first pbd in Household Words, 1857, in The Lazy Tour; see below); The Biter Bit; The Parson's Scruple; A Plot in Private Life; Fauntleroy (first pbd in Household Words, 1858); Anne Rodway (first pbd in Household Words, 1856). 5 stories from The Queen of Hearts were rptd as A Plot in Private Life and Other Tales, Leipzig, 1859.]

The Woman in White. 3 vols. 1860; 1861 (contains correction of all dates in latter part of Marion Halcombe's Diary in consequence of criticism in Times). [First pbd in All the Year Round from 26 Nov. 1859.]

No Name. 3 vols. 1862. [First pbd in All the Year Round from 15 March 1862.]

Armadale. 2 vols. 1866. [First pbd in Cornhill Mag. and Harper's Mag. 1864–5.]

The Moonstone: A Romance. 3 vols. 1868. [First pbd in All the Year Round from 4 Jan. 1868.]

Man and Wife: A Novel. 3 vols. 1870.

Poor Miss Finch: A Novel. 3 vols. 1872. [First pbd in Cassell's Mag. 1871.]

The New Magdalen: A Novel. 2 vols. 1873. [First pbd in Temple Bar, 1872.]

Miss or Mrs? And Other Stories in Outline. 1873. [Miss or Mrs? (first pbd in Graphic); Blow up with the Brig! (first pbd in All the Year Round, Christmas No. 1859); The Haunted House (as The Ghost in the Cupboard Room); The Fatal Cradle (first pbd in All the Year Round, Christmas No. 1861); Tom Tiddler's Ground (as Picking up Waifs at Sea).]

The Frozen Deep: And Other Stories. (Readings and Writings in America.) 2 vols. 1874. [The Frozen Deep (story version of play, first pbd in Temple Bar); The Dream Woman (story from The Queen of Hearts, transferred from the first person into the third and with a conclusion added to render it suitable for public reading); John Jago's Ghost (first pbd in Home Journ.).]

The Law and the Lady: A Novel. 3 vols. 1875.

The Two Destinies: A Romance. 2 vols. 1876.

The Haunted Hotel: A Mystery of Modern Venice, to which is added My Lady's Money. 2 vols. 1879. [First pbd in Belgravia, 1875.]

* The bibliography of Wilkie Collins has been contributed by Miss Dorothy L. Sayers.

A Rogue's Life: From his Birth to his Marriage. 1879. [First pbd in Household Words, from 1 March 1856. Text slightly revised.]

The Fallen Leaves. First Series. 3 vols. 1879. [Not successful, and contemplated sequel never written. First pbd in Canadian Monthly, 1878.]

Jezebel's Daughter. 3 vols. 1880. [Book version of play, The Red Vial.]

The Black Robe. 3 vols. 1881. [First pbd in Canadian Monthly, 1880.]

Heart and Science: A Story of the Present Time. 3 vols. 1883. [First pbd in Belgravia, 1882.]

I Say No. 3 vols. 1884.

The Evil Genius: A Domestic Story. 3 vols. 1886. [Ch. I also pbd separately under same title, Bolton, 1885.]

The Guilty River. 1886 (Arrowsmith's Christmas Annual).

Little Novels. 3 vols. 1887. [Mrs Zant and the Ghost; Miss Morris and the Stranger; Mr Cosway and the Landlady; Mr Medhurst and the Princess; Mr Lismore and the Widow; Miss Jeromette and the Clergyman; Miss Minor and the Groom; Mr Lepel and the Housekeeper; Mr Captain and the Nymph; Mr Marmaduke and the Minister; Mr Percy and the Prophet; Miss Bertha and the Yankee; Miss Dulane and My Lord; Mr Policeman and the Cook. Most or all were originally pbd in various periodicals under quite different titles. Mrs Zant and the Ghost was pbd with My Lady's Money as The Ghost's Touch, Leipzig, 1879; Miss Minor and the Groom as A Shocking Story, New York, 1878; Miss Morris and the Stranger originally appeared as Why I Married Him.]

The Legacy of Cain. 3 vols. 1889.

Blind Love. 3 vols. 1890. [Preface by Sir Walter Besant. First pbd in Illustrated London Mag. 1889. By Collins up to the end of the 18th weekly part, when the onset of his last illness obliged him to hand it over to Besant for completion. Besant's work begins at ch. xlix, and is based throughout on a very complete synopsis drawn up by Collins.]

The Lazy Tour of Two Idle Apprentices. No Thoroughfare. The Perils of Certain English Prisoners. 1890. [In collaboration with Dickens, The Lazy Tour was first pbd in Household Words, 1857, in 5 pts, of which Collins wrote pt 1 (top of p. 316, column 2 to end), pt 2 (beginning to break in p. 340, column 2), pt 3 (reflections of Mr Idle, pp. 363–5), whole of pt 5. No Thoroughfare was first pbd in All the Year Round, Christmas No. 1867, Collins writing whole of Act 2 and contributing to Acts 1 and 4.

Perils was first pbd in Household Words, Christmas No. 1857, Collins writing all except pts 1 and 2.]

[The following magazine stories by Collins have not been rptd in book form: The Chief Mate's Story, The Deliverance (Household Words, Christmas No. 1856, The Wreck of the Golden Mary); Over the Way, Trottles' Report, Let at Last (with Dickens) (Household Words, Christmas No. 1858, A House To Let); A New Mind (Household Words, New Year Extra No. 1859); ch. 4 and portions of chs. 2, 5 of A Message from the Sea (All the Year Round, Christmas No. 1860); The Devil's Spectacles (unidentified, 1879); Fie ! Fie! or The Fair Physician (Pictorial World, Christmas Supplement, 23 Dec. 1882).]

(b) Plays

A Message from the Sea: A Drama in Three Acts. 1861. [In collaboration with Dickens.]

No Name: A Drama in Five Acts. 1863.

Armadale: A Drama in Three Acts. 1866.

The Frozen Deep: A Drama in Three Acts. [Not pbd; ptd 1866.]

No Thoroughfare: A Drama in Five Acts. 1867. [In collaboration with Dickens. Also issued 1867 with a different text from Act IV, scene 3 to end.]

Black and White: A Love Story in Three Acts. 1869. [In collaboration with Charles Fechter.]

No Name: A Drama in Four Acts. 1870. [A different text from that pbd in 1863.]

The Woman in White: A Drama in Prologue and Four Acts. 1871.

The New Magdalen: A Dramatic Story in a Prologue and Three Acts. 1873.

Miss Gwilt: A Drama in Five Acts. [Not pbd; ptd 1875.]

The Moonstone: A Dramatic Story in Three Acts. 1877 (priv. ptd).

(c) Other Writings

Memoirs of the Life of William Collins, R.A.: With Selections from his Journals and Correspondence. 2 vols. 1848.

Rambles beyond Railways: Or, Notes in Cornwall Taken A-Foot. 1851; 1861 (adds The Cruise of the Tomtit, first pbd in Household Words, 1855).

My Miscellanies. 2 vols. 1863. [Various articles and sketches, all first pbd in Household Words.]

Considerations on the Copyright Question Addressed to an American Friend. 1880.

(d) Articles not Reprinted in Book Form

Illuminated Magazine. The Last Stage-Coachman (Aug. 1843).

Household Words. The National Gallery and the Old Masters (25 Dec. 1856); A Fair Penitent (18 July 1857); The Debtor's Best Friend (19 Sept. 1857); A Deep Design on Society (2 Jan. 1858); The Little Huguenot (9 Jan. 1858); Thanks to Doctor Livingstone (23 Jan. 1858); Strike! (6 Feb. 1858); A Sermon for Sepoys (27 Feb. 1858); Dramatic Grub Street (6 March 1858); A Shy Scheme (20 March 1858); Awful Warning to Bachelors (27 March 1858); Sea-Breezes with a London Smack (4 Sept. 1858); Highly Proper! (2 Oct. 1858); A Clause for the New Reform Bill (with Charles Dickens) (9 Oct. 1858); Dr Dulcamara, M.P. (with Charles Dickens) (18 Dec. 1858); Pity a Poor Prince (15 Jan. 1859); Burns Viewed as a Hat-Peg (12 Feb. 1859); A Column to Burns (26 Feb. 1859); A Breach of British Privilege (19 March 1859); A Dramatic Author (28 May 1859).

All the Year Round. Sure to be Healthy, Wealthy and Wise (30 April 1859); The Royal Academy in Bed (28 May 1859); My Advisers (?) (18 June 1859); A New View of Society (20 Aug. 1859); Cooks at College (?) (29 Oct. 1859); The Tattlesnivel Bleater (??) (21 Dec. 1859); My Boys (?) (28 Jan. 1860); My Girls (?) (17 Feb. 1860); Boxing-Day (22 Dec. 1860); A Night in the Jungle (certainly by Collins) (3 Aug. 1861); An Unreported Speech (16 Nov. 1861); A Trial at Toulouse (?) (15 Feb. 1862); Notes of Interrogation (?) (10 May 1862); Suggestions from a Maniac (13 Feb. 1864); To Let (18 June 1864); Going into Housekeeping (8 July 1865). [The office-book of All the Year Round appears to be no longer in existence. Although it is certain that Collins contributed largely to the earlier numbers, his work can only be identified by internal evidence, and the above attributions are advanced with the utmost caution. My Advisers, My Boys, and My Girls are attrib. to Collins by analogy with My Spinsters, which he contributed to Household Words and rptd in My Miscellanies.]

Pall Mall Gazette. Books Necessary for a Liberal Education (11 Feb. 1886).

Universal Review. Reminiscences of a Story-Teller (I, 1888, p. 182).

(e) Biography and Criticism

Forster, J. Life of Charles Dickens. 3 vols. 1872–4; ed. J. W. T. Ley, 1928.

Letters of Charles Dickens. Ed. G. Hogarth, 2 vols. London, 1880.

Wolzogen, E. von. Wilkie Collins. Ein biographisch-kritischer Versuch. Leipzig, 1885.

Lang, A. Contemporary Rev. Jan. 1890. [Obituary.]

Swinburne, A. C. Fortnightly Rev. Nov. 1890. [Obituary.]

Y[ates], E. Temple Bar, Aug. 1890. [Obituary.]

Letters of Charles Dickens to Wilkie Collins, 1851–1870. Ed. G. Hogarth, 1892.

Quilter, H. Preferences in Art, Life and Literature. 1892.

Beard, N. Some Recollections of Yesterday. Temple Bar, July 1894.

Reeve, W. Recollections of Wilkie Collins. Chambers' Journ. IX, 1905–6.

Winter, W. Old Friends. New York, 1907.

Caine, Sir T. H. My Story. 1908.

Lehmann, R. C. Memories of Half a Century. 1908.

—— Charles Dickens as Editor. 1912.

Shore, W. T. Charles Dickens and his Friends. 1909.

Phillips, Walter C. Dickens, Reade and Collins: Sensation Novelists. New York, 1919.

Ellis, S. M. Wilkie Collins, Le Fanu and Others. 1931.

Sehlbach, H. Untersuchungen über die Romankunst von Wilkie Collins. Jena, 1931.

de la Mare, W., The Early Novels of Wilkie Collins. [In The Eighteen-Sixties, Royal Soc. Lit. 1932.]

Flower, D. Authors and Copyright in the Nineteenth Century, with Unpublished Letters from Wilkie Collins. Book-Collector's Quart. July–Sept. 1932.

Elwin, M. Victorian Wallflowers. 1934.

Sayers, D. L. Wilkie Collins. [In preparation.]

THOMAS COOPER (1805–1892)

[See p. 284 above.]

CATHERINE CROWE, née STEVENS
(1800?–1876)

(a) Fiction

Adventures of Susan Hopley, or the Adventures of a Maid Servant. 3 vols. 1841.

Men and Women, or Manorial Rights. 3 vols. 1844.

The Seeress of Prevorst. 1845. [From the German of A. J. C. Kerner.]

The Story of Martha Guinnis and her Son. [In The Edinburgh Tales, ed. C. I. Johnstone, vol. I, 1845.]

The Story of Lilly Dawson. 3 vols. 1847.

Pippie's Warning, or Mind your Temper. 1848.

Light and Darkness, or Mysteries of Life. 3 vols. 1850.

Adventures of a Beauty. 3 vols. 1852.
Uncle Tom's Cabin adapted for Young Persons. 1853. [From the novel by Harriet Beecher Stowe.]
Linny Lockwood. A Novel. 2 vols. 1854.
Ghosts and Family Legends. A Volume for Christmas. 1859.
The Story of Arthur Hunter and his First Shilling; with Other Tales. [1861.]
The Adventures of a Monkey. 1862.

(b) Other Writings

Aristodemus. A Tragedy. 1838.
The Night Side of Nature, or Ghosts and Ghost Seers. 2 vols. 1848.
The Cruel Kindness. A Romantic Play. 1853.
Spiritualism and the Age we live in. 1859.

(c) Criticism

Sergeant, A. Mrs Crowe. [In Women Novelists of Queen Victoria's Reign, 1897.]
Clapton, G. T. Baudelaire and Catherine Crowe. MLR. xxv, 1930.
Hughes, R. Une Étape de l'Ésthétique de Baudelaire: Catherine Crowe. Revue de Littérature comparée, xvii, 1937.

SARAH ELLIS, née STICKNEY (1810?–1872)

(a) Fiction

Pictures of Private Life. 3 sers. 1833–7.
Home, or the Iron Rule. A Domestic Story. 3 vols. 1836.
Look to the End, or the Bennets abroad. 2 vols. [1845].
Temper and Temperament, or Varieties of Character. 2 vols. [1846].
Prevention Better than Cure, or the Moral Wants of the World we live in. [1847.]
Social Distinction, or Hearts and Homes. 3 vols. [1848–9].
Fireside Tales for the Young. 4 vols. [1849?].
Pique. A Novel. 3 vols. 1850; [1869].
The Mother's Mistake. A Tale. [1856.]
The Widow Green and the Three Nieces. 1859.
The Brewer's Family. [1863.]
William and Mary, or the Fatal Blow. [1865.]
Share and Share alike, or the Grand Principle. 1865.
Northern Roses. A Yorkshire Story. 3 vols. 1868.
The Brewer's Son. A Story. [1881.]

(b) Other Writings (Selected)

The Poetry of Life. 2 vols. 1835.
The Women of England, their Social Duties and Domestic Habits. [1839.]
The Sons of the Soil. A Poem. [1840.]
The Island Queen. A Poem. 1846.

Friends at their own Firesides, or Pictures of the Private Life of the People called Quakers. 2 vols. 1858.
Janet: one of Many. A Story in Verse. 1862.

[For biography see The Home Life and Letters of Mrs Ellis, compiled by her Nieces, [1893].]

LADY GEORGIANA CHARLOTTE FULLERTON (1812–1885)

(a) Fiction

Ellen Middleton. A Tale. 3 vols. 1844.
Grantley Manor. A Tale. 3 vols. 1847.
Lady-Bird. A Tale. 3 vols. 1852.
Laurentia. A Tale of Japan. 1861.
Rose Leblanc. 1862.
Too Strange not to be True. 3 vols. 1864.
Constance Sherwood. An Autobiography of the Sixteenth Century. 3 vols. 1865.
A Stormy Life. 3 vols. 1867.
Mrs Gerald's Niece. A Novel. 3 vols. 1869.
Seven Stories. 1873.
A Will and a Way. 3 vols. 1881.

[Lady Georgiana Fullerton also translated 7 novels from the French.]

(b) Other Writings

The Old Highlander and Other Verses. 1849 (priv. ptd).
The Life of St Frances of Rome. 1855.
La Comtesse de Bonneval: her Life and Letters. 2 vols. 1857.
Our Lady's Little Books. 4 nos. 1860–1. [Edited by Lady Georgiana Fullerton.]
The Helpers of the Holy Souls. 1868.
The Gold-Digger and Other Verses. Edinburgh, 1872.
Dramas from the Lives of the Saints: Germaine Cousin, the Shepherdess of Pibrac. [1872.]
Life of Luisa de Carvajal. 1873.
A Sketch of the Life of the Late Father H. Young. 1874.
The Life of Mère Marie de la Providence. 1875.
The Miraculous Medal. Life and Visions of Catherine Labouré. 1880.
The Fire of London. A Play. [1882.]
The Life of Elisabeth Lady Falkland, 1585–1639. 1883.

[Lady Georgiana Fullerton also translated several biographies from the French and Italian.]

(c) Biography and Criticism

Craven, A. The Life of Lady Georgiana Fullerton. Translated from the French by H. J. Coleridge. 1888.
Yonge, C. M. Lady Georgiana Fullerton. [In Women Novelists of Queen Victoria's Reign, 1897.]

Taylor, F. M. The Inner Life of Lady Georgiana Fullerton, with Notes of Retreat and Diary. [1899.]

MARGARET GATTY (1807–1873)

The Fairy Godmother and Other Tales. 1851.

Parables from Nature. 5 sers. 1855–71. [Frequently rptd, especially the earlier sers., and tr. into German, Swedish, French, Danish, Russian and Italian, 1856–80. Sers. 1. 2 rptd 1885 with memoir by J. H. Ewing.]

'Worlds not Realized.' 1856; 1869 (with next item).

Proverbs Illustrated. 1857; 1869 (with preceding item).

The Poor Incumbent. A Tale. 1858.

Legendary Tales. 1858.

Aunt Judy's Tales. 1859.

The Human Face Divine and Other Tales. 1860.

Aunt Judy's Letters. 1862.

British Seaweeds. Drawn from Professor Harvey's Phycologia Britannica. 1863; 2 vols. 1872.

Domestic Pictures and Tales. 1866.

Waifs and Strays of Natural History. 1871.

A Book of Emblems. With Interpretations thereof. 1872.

The Book of Sundials. 1872.

[Mrs Gatty also founded, and contributed constantly to, Aunt Judy's Magazine for Children, from May 1866.]

JAMES GRANT (1822–1887)

(a) Fiction

The Romance of War, or the Highlanders in Spain [France and Belgium]. 4 vols. 1846–7.

Adventures of an Aide-de-Camp, or A Campaign in Calabria. 3 vols. 1848.

Memoirs and Adventures of Sir William Kirkaldy of Grange. Edinburgh, 1849.

The Scottish Cavalier. An Historical Romance. 3 vols. 1850.

Memoirs and Adventures of Sir John Hepburn. 1851.

Jane Seton, or the King's Advocate. A Scottish Historical Romance. 3 vols. 1853.

Bothwell, or the Days of Mary Queen of Scots. [1854.]

Philip Rollo, or the Scottish Musketeers. 2 vols. 1854.

Frank Hilton, or the Queen's Own. 1855.

The Yellow Frigate, or the Three Sisters. [1855.]

Harry Ogilvie, or the Black Dragoons. New Edition. 1856.

The Phantom Regiment, or Stories of 'Ours.' [1856]; [1864].

The Highlanders of Glen Ora. 1857; 1862 (as Laura Everingham, or the Highlanders of Glen Ora).

Memoirs of James, Marquis of Montrose. 1858.

Arthur Blane, or the Hundred Cuirassiers. [1858.]

Hollywood Hall. A Tale of 1715. 1859; 1861 (as Lucy Arden, or Hollywood Hall).

Legends of the Black Watch, or Forty-Second Highlanders. 1859.

Mary of Lorraine. An Historical Romance. 1860.

Oliver Ellis, or the Fusiliers. 1861.

Jack Manly: his Adventures by Sea and Land. 1861.

Dick Rodney, or the Adventures of an Eton Boy. [1862.]

The Captain of the Guard. 1862.

Letty Hyde's Lovers, or The Household Brigade. 1863.

Second to None. A Military Romance. 3 vols. 1864.

Adventures of Rob Roy. 1864.

The King's Own Borderers. A Military Romance. 3 vols. 1865.

The White Cockade, or Faith and Fortitude. 3 vols. 1867.

First Love and Last Love. A Tale of the Indian Mutiny. 3 vols. 1868.

The Girl he Married. A Novel. 3 vols. 1869.

The Secret Dispatch, or the Adventures of Captain Balgonie. 1869.

Lady Wedderburn's Wish. A Tale of the Crimean War. 3 vols. 1870.

Only an Ensign: the Retreat from Cabul. 3 vols. 1871.

Under the Red Dragon. 3 vols. 1872.

Fairer than a Fairy. A Novel. 3 vols. 1874.

Shall I win her? The Story of a Wanderer. 3 vols. 1874.

The Queen's Cadet and Other Tales. 1874.

One of the Six Hundred. A Novel. 3 vols. 1875.

Did she love him? A Novel. 3 vols. 1876.

Morley Ashton. A Story of the Sea. 3 vols. 1876.

Six Years ago. A Novel. 2 vols. 1877.

Vere of Ours, the Eighth or King's. A Novel. 3 vols. 1878.

The Ross-shire Buffs. A Novel. [1878.]

The Lord Hermitage. A Novel. 3 vols. 1878.

The Royal Regiment and Other Novelettes. 1879.

The Duke of Albany's Own Highlanders. A Novel. 3 vols. 1880.

Lady Glendonwyn. A Novel. 3 vols. 1881.

Derval Hampton. A Story of the Sea. 2 vols. 1881.

The Cameronians. A Novel. 3 vols. 1881.

Violet Jermyn, or Tender and True. 1882.

The Scot's Brigade and Other Tales. 1882.

Jack Chaloner, or the Fighting Forty-Third. [1883.]
The Dead Tryst, and a Haunted Life. [1883.]
Miss Cheyne of Essilmont. A Novel. 3 vols. 1883.
The Master of Aberfeldie. A Novel. 3 vols. 1884.
Colville of the Guards. 3 vols. 1885.
The Royal Highlanders, or The Black Watch in Egypt. A Novel. [1885.]
Dulcie Carlyon. A Novel. 3 vols. 1886.
Playing with Fire. A Story of the Soudan War. 3 vols. 1887.
Love's Labour Lost. A Novel. 3 vols. 1888; 1889.

(b) Other Writings

Sketches in London. 1838. [Illustrated by Phiz and others.]
Memorials of the Castle of Edinburgh. 1850; Edinburgh, 1862.
The Cavaliers of Fortune, or British Heroes in Foreign Lands. 1859.
The Constable of France and Other Military Historiettes. 1866.
British Battles on Land and Sea. 3 vols. [1873–5]; 4 vols. [1884–8]; 4 vols. [1896–7].
Cassell's Illustrated History of India. 2 vols. [1876–7].
Cassell's Old and New Edinburgh. 3 vols. [1880–3].
Cassell's History of the War in the Soudan. 6 vols. [1885–6].
The Tartans of the Clans of Scotland. 1886.

(c) Criticism

Ellis, S. M. Mainly Victorian. [1925.]

GERALD GRIFFIN (1803–1840)
(a) Collected Works

The Works. 8 vols. 1842–3. [Vol. i, Life, vol. ii, The Collegians; vol. iii, Card Drawing; vol. iv, Holland-Tide; vol. v, Tales of the Munster Festivals; vol. vi, The Duke of Monmouth; vol. vii, Talis Qualis, or Tales of the Jury Room; vol. viii, Poetical Works.]

(b) Fiction

Holland-Tide, or Munster Popular Tales. 1827; 1857.
Tales of the Munster Festivals. 3 vols. 1827.
The Collegians, or the Colleen Bawn. A Tale of Garryowen. 3 vols. 1829; 1861; 1887; ed. P. Colum, 1918. [For the dramatisation by Dion Boucicault, see p. 600 below.]
The Rivals. Tracy's Ambition. 3 vols. 1830.
The Christian Physiologist. Tales Illustrative of the Five Senses. 1830; Dublin, 1854 (as The Offering of Friendship, or Tales of the Five Senses).

The Invasion. 4 vols. 1832.
Tales of my Neighbourhood. 3 vols. 1835.
The Duke of Monmouth. 1836.
The Kelp-Gatherer. An Irish Tale. Dublin, 1854.
The Beautiful Queen of Leix, or the Self-Consumed. An Irish Tale. Dublin, 1854.
A Story of Psyche. Dublin, 1854.
The Day of Trial. An Irish Tale. Dublin, 1854.
Card-Drawing, the Half Sir, and Suil Dhur the Coiner. Dublin, 1857.

(c) Other Writings

Gisippus. A Play. 1842.
The Poetical Works of Gerald Griffin. 1851.
The Poetical Works of Gerald Griffin. Dublin, 1926. [Includes Gisippus.]

(d) Biography

Griffin, Daniel. The Life of Gerald Griffin. 1843.

ANNA MARIA HALL, née FIELDING (1800–1881)
(a) Writings

Sketches of Irish Character. 3 vols. 1829. Ser. 2, 1831.
Chronicles of a Schoolroom. 1830.
The Buccaneer. 3 vols. 1832 (anon.).
The Outlaw. An Historical Romance. 1835.
Tales of a Woman's Trials. 1835.
Uncle Horace. 1837 (anon.).
Lights and Shadows of Irish Life. 3 vols. 1838. [First pbd in New Monthly Mag.]
The Hartopp Jubilee, or Profit from Play. 1840.
Marian, or a Young Maid's Fortunes. 3 vols. 1840.
Number One. A Tale. 1844.
Little Chatterbox. A Tale. 1844.
Characteristic Sketches of Ireland and the Irish. By Carleton, Lover, and Mrs S. C. Hall. 1845.
The Whiteboy: Ireland in 1822. 2 vols. 1845.
The Forlorn Hope. A Story of Old Chelsea. [1846.]
Uncle Sam's Money Box. 1848, etc.
Grandmamma's Pockets. 1848.
Midsummer Eve. A Fairy Tale of Love. 1848; 1870. [First pbd in Art Journ.]
The Whisperer. 1848, etc.
Seven Tales. By Seven Authors. Ed. F. E. Smedley, 1849; 1860. [Contains The Last in the Lease by Mrs S. C. Hall.]
The Swan's Egg. A Tale. 1850.
Stories of the Irish Peasantry. 1851. [First pbd in Chambers' Journ.]
Stories of the Governess. 1852.
The Worn Thimble. A story of Woman's Duty and Woman's Influence. 1853.

The Drunkard's Bible. 1854.
Popular Tales and Sketches. 1856.
The Two Friends. A Temperance Sketch.
[1856.]
A Woman's Story. 3 vols. 1857.
The Lucky Penny and Other Tales. 1857.
Turns of Fortune. A Tale. 1858.
There is no Hurry and Deeds not Words.
Tales. 1858.
The Unjust Judge. 1858.
All is not Gold that Glitters. A Tale. 1858.
Cleverness. A Tale. 1858.
The Governess. A Tale. 1858.
Wives and Husbands. A Tale. 1858.
The Tale Book. Königsberg, 1859. [Contains
The Dispensation by Mrs S. C. Hall.]
Daddy Dacre's School. A Story for the
Young. 1859.
Mamma Milly. A Story. [1860.]
Fanny's Fancies. [1860.]
The Golden Casket. By M. Howitt. [1861.]
[Contains William and his Teacher by
Mrs S. C. Hall.]
Can Wrong be Right? A Tale. 2 vols. 1862.
Building a House with a Teacup. [1863.]
The Village Garland. Tales and Sketches.
1863.
Nelly Nawlan and Other Stories. 1865.
Ronald's Reason, or the Little Cripple.
[1865.]
The Cabman's Cat. [1865.]
The Playfellow and Other Illustrated Stories.
1866.
The Way of the World and Other Stories.
1866.
The Prince of the Fairy Family. A Fairy Tale.
[1867.]
Alice Stanley and Other Stories. 1868.
The Fight of Faith. A Story. 2 vols. 1869.
The Rift in the Rock. A Tale. [1871.]
Digging a Grave with a Wine Glass. 1871.
Chronicles of a Cosy Nook. 1875.
Boons and Blessings. Stories and Sketches to
Illustrate the Advantages of Temperance.
1875.
Ann Leslie and Other Stories. 1877.

[Mrs Hall also conducted The St James's
Mag. 1861, and Sharpe's London Mag. from
1845. In addn to her novels and tales she pbd
plays and miscellaneous hack-work as well as
several books of travel in collaboration with
her husband S. C. Hall.]

(b) *Biography and Criticism*

Maginn, W. A Gallery of Illustrious Literary
Characters. Ed. W. Bates, [1873].
Hall, S. C. Retrospect of a Long Life. 1883.

JAMES HANNAY (1827–1873)
[See p. 717 below.]

SIR ARTHUR HELPS (1813–1875)
[See p. 718 below.]

THOMAS HUGHES (1822–1896)

(a) *Fiction*

Tom Brown's School Days. By an Old Boy.
Cambridge, 1857 (3 edns); 1861; 1868; 1869;
1871; 1882; 1896; 1897; 1903 (*bis*); [1904];
ed. V. Rendall, 1904; 1905 (*bis*); 1906;
1907, etc.; ed. F. Sidgwick, 1913.
The Scouring of the White Horse, or the Long
Vacation Ramble of a London Clerk.
Illustrated by Richard Doyle. 1859 (*bis*);
1889 (with The Ashen Faggot, a Tale for
Christmas), etc.
Tom Brown at Oxford. By the Author of
Tom Brown's Schooldays. 3 vols. Cambridge, 1861; 1864; 1865; 1869; 1871; 1872;
1874; 1875; 1877 (*bis*); 1879; 1880; 1883;
1886; 1889; 1905, etc.

(b) *Other Writings*

History of the Working Tailor's Association.
[1850.] [Tracts on Christian Socialism, XI.]
A Lecture on the Shop System, especially as
it bears upon the Females engaged in it.
Delivered at Reading. 1852.
Account of the Lock-out of Engineers, 1851–
52, prepared for the National Association
for the Promotion of Social Science.
Cambridge, 1860.
Tracts for Priests and People. No. 1: Religio
Laici. Cambridge, 1861 (4 edns). [After-
wards included in Tracts for Priests and
People, ser. 1.]
The Struggle for Kansas. [Appended to J. M.
Ludlow, A Sketch of the History of the
United States, Cambridge, 1862.]
The Cause of Freedom. Which is its Champion
in America, the North or the South?
[1863.]
A Layman's Faith. 1868.
Alfred The Great. 3 pts, 1869; [1871]; 1873;
1874; 1877; 1881; 1887; 1898, etc.
Memoir of a Brother. 1873 (*bis*).
Lecture on the History and Objects of Co-
operation. Delivered at Manchester. Man-
chester, 1878.
The Old Church: what shall we do with it?
1878.
The Manliness of Christ. 1879; 1880; 1907.
Rugby, Tennessee; being some Account of the
Settlement founded on the Cumberland
Plateau by the Board of Aid to Land Owner-
ship. 1881.
Memoir of Daniel MacMillan. 1882; 1882
(corrected); 1883.
Address by Thos. Hughes on the Occasion of
the Presentation of a Testimonial of his
Services to the Cause of Co-operation, 6th
December 1884. Manchester, 1885.

Life and Times of Peter Cooper. 1886 (priv. ptd).

James Fraser, Second Bishop of Manchester. A Memoir, 1818–1885. 1887; 1888; 1889.

Co-operative Production. An Address delivered at the Annual Co-operative Congress, Carlisle. Manchester, [1887].

Church Reform and Defence. An Address delivered in Wadham College Hall, Oxford. 1887.

David Livingstone. 1889 (bis).

Co-operative Faith and Practice. An Address. [1890.]

Vacation Rambles. 1895.

Early Memories for the Children. 1899 (priv. ptd).

Fragments of Autobiography. Ed. H. C. Shelley, Cornhill Mag. March–May 1925.

[Hughes also wrote introductions to James Lowell's Biglow Papers, 1859, J. F. D. Maurice's Christian Socialism, 1898, and other works.]

(c) Biography and Criticism

Ritchie, J. E. British Senators. 1869.

Cooper, T. Men of Mark. 6 vols. 1876–82. [Ch. on Hughes in vol. IV.]

Hinton, R. J. English Radical Leaders. New York, 1887.

Ludlaw, J. M. Thomas Hughes and Septimus Hansard. Economic Rev. July 1896.

Thomas Hughes. Macmillan's Mag. LXXIV, 1896.

Tollemache, L. A. Essays and Mock Essays and Character Sketches. 1898.

Selfe, S. Chapters from the History of Rugby School. Together with Notes on the Characters and Incidents depicted in Tom Brown's Schooldays. 1910.

Some Letters of Thomas Hughes. Economic Rev. Oct. 1914.

Hamer, M. B. Thomas Hughes and his American Rugby. [1928.]

Parrish, M. L. and Mann, B. K. Charles Kingsley and Thomas Hughes. First Editions in the Library at Dormy House. 1936.

JEAN INGELOW (1820–1897)

[See p. 291 above.]

DOUGLAS JERROLD (1803–1857)

[See p. 602 below.]

GERALDINE ENDSOR JEWSBURY (1812–1880)

(a) Writings

Zoe: the History of Two Lives. 3 vols. 1845.
The Half-Sisters. A Tale. 2 vols. 1848.
Marian Withers. 3 vols. 1851.
The History of an Adopted Child. 1853.

Constance Herbert. 3 vols. 1855.
The Sorrows of Gentility. 2 vols. 1856.
Angelo, or the Pine Forest in the Alps. 1856.
A Selection from the Letters of Geraldine Jewsbury to Jane Welsh Carlyle. Ed. Mrs A. Ireland, 1892.

(b) Criticism

[Woolf, V.] Geraldine and Jane. TLS. 28 Feb. 1929. [See also subsequent correspondence.]

JULIA KAVANAGH (1824–1877)

(a) Fiction

The Montyon Prizes. [1846.]
The Three Paths. A Story for Young People. 1848.
Madeleine. A Tale of Auvergne. 1848.
Nathalie. A Tale. 3 vols. 1850.
Daisy Burns. A Tale. 3 vols. 1853.
Grace Lee. A Tale. 3 vols. 1855.
Rachel Gray. A Tale founded on Fact. 1856.
Adèle. A Tale. 3 vols. 1858.
Seven Years and Other Tales. 3 vols. 1860.
Queen Mab. A Novel. 3 vols. 1863.
Beatrice. A Novel. 3 vols. 1865.
Sybil's Second Love. A Novel. 3 vols. 1867.
Dora. A Novel. 3 vols. 1868.
Silvia. 1870.
Bessie. A Novel. 3 vols. 1872.
John Dorrien. A Novel. 3 vols. 1875.
The Pearl Fountain and Other Fairy Tales. 1876.
Two Lilies. A Novel. 3 vols. 1877.
Forget-me-nots. 3 vols. 1878. [Short stories.]

(b) Other Writings

Woman in France during the Eighteenth Century. 2 vols. 1850.
Women of Christianity Exemplary for Acts of Piety and Charity. 1852.
A Summer and Winter in the Two Sicilies. 2 vols. 1858.
French Women of Letters: Biographical Sketches. 2 vols. 1862.
English Women of Letters: Biographical Sketches. 2 vols. 1863.

(c) Criticism

Macquoid, K. S. Julia Kavanagh. [In Women Novelists of Queen Victoria's Reign, 1897.]

CHARLES KINGSLEY (1819–1875)

(a) Collected Works

The Works of Charles Kingsley. 28 vols. 1880–5, 1888–9.
The Life and Works of Charles Kingsley. 19 vols. 1901–3.

(b) Novels and Tales

Alton Locke, Tailor and Poet. An Autobiography. 2 vols. 1850 (anon.); 1852; 1856 (with 'Preface Addressed to the Working Men of Great Britain'); 1862 (with a new preface 'To the Undergraduates of Cambridge'); 1875; 1876 (with a prefatory memoir by Thomas Hughes); 1877; 1879; 2 vols. 1881 (with Hughes's memoir); 1889; 1892; [1893], etc.

Yeast, a Problem. 1851(anon.); 1859 (4th edn, with a new preface); 1867; 1875; 1877; 1879; 1881; 1888; 1893; 1895, etc. [First pbd Fraser's Mag. July–Dec. 1848.]

Hypatia, or New Foes with an Old Face. 2 vols. 1853; 1856; 1863; 1874; 1876; 1879; 2 vols. 1881; 1889; 1895; 1897; 1899; 1903, etc. [First pbd Fraser's Mag. Jan. 1852–April 1853.]

Westward Ho! or the Voyages and Adventures of Sir Amyas Leigh, Knight, of Burrough, in the County of Devon, in the Reign of her most Glorious Majesty Queen Elizabeth. Rendered into Modern English by Charles Kingsley. 3 vols. Cambridge, 1855 (bis); 1861; 1865; 1869; 1873; 1876; 1879; 2 vols. 1881; 1894; 2 vols. 1896; 1898; ed. W. K. Leask, 1899; [1900]; [1901]; 2 vols. 1901; 2 vols. 1902; [1903]; 1904; 1905, etc.

The Heroes, or Greek Fairy Tales for my Children. With 8 Illustrations by the Author. Cambridge, 1856; 1862; 1864; 1868; 1873; 1875; 1879; 1885; 1887; 1889; 1899; 1900; 1902; 1903; 1904; 1905; 1906, etc.

Two Years Ago. A Novel. 3 vols. Cambridge, 1857; 1859; 1877; 1879; 2 vols. 1881; 1889; 1902; 1903; [1904], etc.

The Water-Babies. A Fairy Tale for a Land-Baby with Two Illustrations by J. Noel Paton. 1863; 1869; 1871; 1872; 1878; 1879; 1885 (with 100 llustrations by Linley Sambourne); 1889; 1903; 1904; 1905; [1905]; 1906; [1907]; [1908]; 1908; 1909 (3 edns); 1912; 1913, etc.

Hereward the Wake, 'Last of the English.' 2 vols. 1866; 1867; 1877; 1879; 2 vols. 1881; 1908; [1909]; 1911 (introduction and notes); 1912; 1914, etc. [First pbd in Good Words, Jan.–Dec. 1865.]

The Hermits. 3 pts, [1868]; 1878; 1880.

Prose Idylls, New and Old. 1873; 1880; 1889.

The Tutor's Story. By the late Charles Kingsley, revised and completed by his Daughter, Lucas Malet. 1916; 1920. [This story of which c. 150 foolscap pages were left in MS by Kingsley seems to have been written about 1863.]

(c) Poems

The Saint's Tragedy. With a Preface by Professor Maurice. 1848; 1859; 1861.

Andromeda and Other Poems. 1858; 1862.

Ode performed in the Senate-House, Cambridge, composed for the Installation of his Grace the Duke of Devonshire, Chancellor of the University. Cambridge, 1862.

Poems. Collected Edition. 1872; 1878 (enlarged); 1879; 1880 (enlarged as vol. 1 of The Works); 2 vols. 1884 (enlarged); 1889; 1913; 1927.

(d) Sermons, Lectures, Essays and Pamphlets

On English Composition. On English Literature. [In Introductory Lectures delivered at Queen's College, London, 1849.]

Twenty-Five Village sermons. 1849; 1857; 1861 (with other sermons, under the title Town and Country Sermons); 1867; 1868; 1872; 1877; 1880, etc.

Cheap Clothes and Nasty. By Parson Lot. 1850; 1851.

The Application of Associative Principles and Methods to Agriculture. A Lecture. 1851.

Who are the Friends of Order? 1852.

Phaethon: or, Loose Thoughts for Loose Thinkers. Cambridge, 1852; 1854; 1859.

Sermons on National Subjects. 1852; 1872 (as The King of the Earth, and Other Sermons preached in a Village Church); 1873.

Alexandria and her Schools. Cambridge, 1854.

Sermons on National Subjects. Second Series. 1854; 2 vols. 1872; 1880.

Who causes Pestilence? 1854.

Glaucus, or the Wonders of the Shore. Cambridge, 1855; Cambridge, 1856 (3rd edn, corrected and enlarged); 1859 (enlarged); 1862; 1873; 1879; 1886; 1904. [First pbd in North British Rev. Nov. 1854.]

Sermons for the Times. 1855; 1858; 1872; 1878.

Sermons for Sailors. [1855]; 1885 (as Sea Sermons).

The Country Parish. A Lecture. [In Lectures to Ladies on Practical Subjects, Cambridge, 1855, 1857.]

The Massacre of the Innocents. An Address. [1859.]

The Good News of God: Sermons. 1859; 1866; 1872; 1878; 1881, etc.

Miscellanies. Reprinted chiefly from Fraser's Magazine and the North British Review. 2 vols. 1859.

The Limits of Exact Science as applied to History. Inaugural Lecture. Cambridge, 1860.

Speech of Lord Dundreary on the Great Hippocampus Question. Cambridge, 1862.

The Gospel of the Pentateuch. A Set of Parish Sermons. 1863; 1864; 1872; 1878; 1881.

Hints to Stammerers. By a Minute Philosopher. 1864 (also issued as The Irrationale of Speech).

The Roman and the Teuton. A Series of Lectures delivered before the University of Cambridge. Cambridge, 1864; ed. F. M. Müller, 1875, 1879.

Mr Kingsley and Dr Newman. A Correspondence on the Question whether Dr Newman teaches that Truth is no Virtue. 1864.

'What, then, does Dr Newman mean?' A Reply to a Pamphlet lately published by Dr Newman. 1864; ed. W. Ward, Oxford, 1913 (with Newman's Apologia).

David: Four Sermons delivered before the University of Cambridge. 1865; 1874 (5 Sermons).

Three Lectures delivered at the Royal Institution, on the Ancien Régime before the French Revolution. 1867.

The Water of Life and Other Sermons. 1867; 1872; 1879.

Discipline and Other Sermons. 1868; 1872; 1881.

Madam How and Lady Why, or First Lessons in Earth-Lore for Children. 1870; 1872; 1880; 1889; 1897, etc. [First pbd in Good Words for the Young, Nov. 1868–Oct. 1869.]

At Last: A Christmas in the West Indies. With Illustrations. 2 vols. 1871; 1872; 1880; 1889; 1910.

Town Geology. 1872; 1879.

Plays and Puritans, and Other Historical Essays. 1873; 1880.

Westminster Sermons. 1874; 1877.

Health and Education. 1874.

Lectures delivered in America in 1874. 1875.

Letters to Young Men on Betting and Gambling. 1877.

True Words for Brave Men. 1878; 1879; 1914.

All Saints Day and Other Sermons. Ed. W. Harrison, 1878.

Historical Lectures and Essays. 1880 (The Works, vol. XVII); 1889.

Sanitary and Social Lectures and Essays. 1880 (The Works, vol. XVII); 1899.

Literary and General Lectures and Essays. 1880 (The Works, vol. XX).

Scientific Lectures and Essays. 1885 (The Works, vol. XIX).

From Death to Life. Fragments of Teaching to a Village Congregation, with Letters on the Life after Death, edited by his Wife. 1887.

Words of Advice to Schoolboys, collected from hitherto Unpublished Notes and Letters. Ed. E. F. Johns, 1912.

[Kingsley also contributed prefaces, etc. to the following: C. B. Mansfield, Paraguay, Brazil and the Plate, edited with a Sketch of the Author's Life, 1856; The History and Life of J. Tauler with 25 of his Sermons, 1857; H. Brooke, The Fool of Quality, 1859; The Pilgrim's Progress, 1860. Separately ptd sermons and short tracts have been omitted here. These and Kingsley's articles in periodicals are listed in full in M. F. Thorp's biography (1937).]

(e) Biography and Criticism

(i) Books

Charles Kingsley. His Letters and Memories of his Life. Edited by his Wife. 2 vols. 1877; 1878; 1883. [Rptd as vols. I–IV of Life and Works, 1901–2. Abridged 2 vols. 1879.]

Nielsen, F. Charles Kingsley og den 'Kristelige Socialisme' i England. Copenhagen, 1888.

Kaufmann, M. Charles Kingsley, Christian Socialist and Social Reformer. 1892.

Groth, E. Charles Kingsley als Dichter und Sozial-reformer. Leipzig, 1893.

Stubbs, C. W. Charles Kingsley and the Christian Social Movement. 1899.

Keller, Ludwig. Charles Kingsley und die religiös-sozialen Kämpfe in England im 19. Jahrhundert. Berlin, [1911].

Brown, W. H. Charles Kingsley: the Work and Influence of 'Parson Lot.' Manchester, 1924.

(ii) Articles in Periodicals, Essays and Chapters of Books

Kingsley as a Lyric Poet. Chambers' Journ. XXIII, 1854.

Brimley, G. Essays. 1858.

Masson, D. British Novelists and their Styles. Cambridge, 1859.

Greg, W. R. Literary and Social Judgments. 1868.

Friswell, J. H. Modern Men of Letters. 1870.

Phillips, Samuel. Essays from the Times. 2 vols. 1871.

Helps, A. Charles Kingsley. Macmillan's Mag. XXXI, 1874.

Senior, W. Charles Kingsley in the Saddle. GM. XIV, 1874.

Recollections of Kingsley. Good Words, XVI, 1875.

Boyd, A. K. H. Charles Kingsley. Fraser's Mag. 1876.

James, Henry. Life and Letters of Charles Kingsley. Nation (New York), XXIV, 1876.

Page, H. A. The Chartism of Kingsley. Good Words, XVII, 1876.

Stephen, Sir L. Hours in a Library. Ser. III, 1879.

Henley, W. E. Charles Kingsley. [In The English Poets, ed. T. H. Ward, vol. IV, 1880.]

Rigg, J. H. Modern Anglican Theology. 1880 (3rd edn). [Includes Memoir of Kingsley.]

Watkins, M. G. Kingsley as a Fisherman. GM. xxv, 1880.

Stanley, A. P. Sermons at Westminster. 1882.

Müller, Max. Biographical Essays. 1884.

Davies, G. J. Successful Preachers. 1884.

Tulloch, J. Movements of Religious Thought in the Nineteenth Century. 1885.

Mallock, M. M. Charles Kingsley. Dublin Rev. xxiv, 1890.

Martineau, J. Essays. 4 vols. 1890–1.

Lang, A. Essays in Little. 1891.

Marriott, Sir J. A. R. Charles Kingsley, Novelist. 1892.

Groser, H. G. Charles Kingsley. [Prefixed to a selection from the poems in The Poets and the Poetry of the Century, ed. A. H. Miles, vol. v, 1893, etc.]

Harrison, Frederic. Studies in Early Victorian Literature. 1895.

Cazamian, L. Le Roman Social en Angleterre (1830–1850). Paris, 1904, pp. 436–531.

Lord, W. F. Kingsley's Novels. Nineteenth Century, June 1904.

Benson, A. C. The Leaves of the Tree. Studies in Biography. 1911.

Chape, R. P. The Historical Basis of Kingsley's Westward Ho. [1912.]

Jacobson, Anna. Charles Kingsleys Beziehungen zu Deutschland. Heidelberg, 1917.

Courtney, J. E. Charles Kingsley. Fortnightly Rev. June 1919.

'Melville, Lewis.' The Centenary of Charles Kingsley. Contemporary Rev. June 1919.

Williams, S. T. Yeast. A Victorian Heresy. North American Rev. ccxii, 1920.

Brunner, K. Charles Kingsley als christlichsozialer Dichter. Ang. xlvi, xlvii, 1922–3.

Brown, W. H. Maurice, Kingsley and Hughes. Manchester Quart. li, 1925.

Juhnke, E. Charles Kingsley als sozialreformatorischer Schriftsteller. Ang. xlix, 1925.

Geffcken, J. Kingsleys Hypatia und ihr geschichtlicher Hintergrund. Neue Jahrbücher für Wissenschaft- und Jugendbildung, ii, 1926.

Sedgwick, J. H. A Mid-Victorian Nordic. North American Rev. ccxxv, 1928.

Partington, W. Westward Ho! with Charles Kingsley. Colophon, iii, 1933.

Baldwin, S. E. Charles Kingsley. Ithaca, 1934.

Parrish, M. L. and Mann, B. K. Charles Kingsley and Thomas Hughes. First Editions in the Library at Dormy House. 1936.

Hanawalt, M. Charles Kingsley and Science. Stud. Phil. xxxiv, 1937.

Thorp, M. F. Charles Kingsley. Princeton, 1937. [With bibliography.]

HENRY KINGSLEY (1830–1876)

(a) Bibliography

Ellis, S M. Henry Kingsley. 1931. [Bibliography appended, including Kingsley's contributions to magazines.]

(b) Collected Works

The Novels of Henry Kingsley. 7 vols. 1872, 1885.

The Novels of Henry Kingsley. Ed. C. K. Shorter, 8 vols. 1894–5.

(c) Novels and Short Stories

The Recollections of Geoffrey Hamlyn. 3 vols. 1859; 1860; 1872; 1885; [1891] (with memoir by C. K. Shorter); 1909, etc.; rptd 1924 (World's Classics).

Ravenshoe. 3 vols. 1861; 1862; 1864; 1872; 1875; 1885; 1903; 1906; 1909; 1910, etc.; rptd 1925 (World's Classics).

Austin Elliott. 2 vols. 1863 (3 edns); 1866; 1872; 1885; rptd 1932 (World's Classics).

The Hillyars and the Burtons. A Story of Two Families. 3 vols. 1865; 1866; 1870; 1895 (with a note on Old Chelsea Church by C. K. Shorter).

Leighton Court. A Country House Story. 2 vols. 1866; 1867.

Silcote of Silcotes. 3 vols. 1867; 1869.

Mademoiselle Mathilde. 3 vols. 1868; 1870; 1885. [First pbd in GM.]

Stretton. 3 vols. 1869; 1870; 1879; 1885.

The Boy in Grey and Other Stories and Sketches. 1871.

Hetty and Other Stories. 1871; 1885.

The Lost Child. 1871.

Old Margaret and Other Stories. 2 vols. 1871; 1872; 1885; 1895.

Valentin. A French Boy's Story of Sedan. 2 vols. 1872; [1874] (rev.); 1885.

The Harveys. 2 vols. 1872; 1873; 1885.

Hornby Mills and Other Stories. 2 vols. 1872; 1873; 1885.

Oakshott Castle. By Mr Granby Dixon. Edited by Henry Kingsley. 3 vols. 1873; 1878. ['Granby Dixon' was Kingsley's pseudonym.]

Reginald Hetherege. 3 vols. 1874; 1875.

Number Seventeen. 2 vols. 1875; 1876; 1879.

The Grange Garden. A Romance. 3 vols. 1876.

The Mystery of the Island. 1877.

(d) Other Writings

Tales of Old Travel re-narrated. 1869; 1871.

Fireside Studies. 2 vols. 1876.

[Kingsley also edited Robinson Crusoe, 1868, 'with a Biographical Introduction.']

(e) Biography and Criticism

Geoffrey Hamlyn. North British Rev. xxxi, 1859.

The Hillyars and the Burtons. North American Rev. ci, 1865.

Quiller-Couch, Sir A. T. Adventures in Criticism. 1896.

'Melville, Lewis.' Victorian Novelists. 1906.

Russell, G. W. E. Selected Essays. 1914.

Sadleir, M. Henry Kingsley. A Portrait. Edinburgh Rev. Oct. 1924.

Henry Kingsley. TLS. 2 Jan. 1930.

Ellis, S. M. Henry Kingsley, 1830–1876. Towards a Vindication. 1931.

WILLIAM HENRY GILES KINGSTON (1814–1880)

The Circassian Chief. A Romance of Russia. 3 vols. 1843.

The Prime Minister. An Historical Romance. 3 vols. 1845.

The Albatross, or Voices from the Ocean. A Tale of the Sea. 3 vols. 1849; 1853; 1877.

The Pirate of the Mediterranean. A Tale of the Sea. 3 vols. 1851.

Peter the Whaler; his Early Life and Adventures in the Arctic Regions. 1851, etc.

Manco, the Peruvian Chief; or an Englishman's Adventures in the Country of the Incas. 1853.

The Emigrant's Home, or how to settle. A Story of Australian Life. 1856.

Digby Heathcote, or the Early Days of a Country Gentleman's Son and Heir. 1860.

Ernest Bracebridge, or Schooldays. 1860; [1871].

Will Weatherhelm, or the Yarn of an Old Sailor about his Early Life and Adventures. 1860; 1879 (enlarged).

The Fire-ships. A Tale of the Last Naval War. 3 vols. 1862; 1867; [1871].

Count Ulrich von Lindburg. A Tale of the Reformation in Germany. [1868.]

The Royal Merchant, or Events in the Days of Sir Thomas Gresham, as Narrated in the Diary of E. Verner, whilom his Page and Secretary during the Reigns of Queens Mary and Elizabeth. 1870; [1880] (as The Golden Grasshopper).

Millicent Courtenay's Diary, or the Experiences of a Young Lady at Home and Abroad. [1873.]

Eldol the Druid, or the Dawn of Christianity in Britain. [1874.]

Jovinian, or the Early Days of Papal Rome. A Tale. 1877.

The Rival Crusoes. 1879.

The Ferryman of Brill, and Other Stories. [1880.]

[The above is only a brief, though representative, selection from Kingston's 100 or more stories, mainly for boys and of the sea. He also translated Jules Verne and edited the following periodicals: The Colonist; The Colonial Magazine and East India Review; Kingston's Annual for Boys; Kingston's Magazine for Boys; The Union Jack.]

LETITIA ELIZABETH LANDON (1802–1838)

[See p. 294 above.]

GEORGE ALFRED LAWRENCE (1827–1876)

(a) Writings

The Marriage of Marie Antoinette with the Dauphin. A Prize Poem recited in Rugby School, June 20. MDCCCXLV. Rugby, 1845.

Songs of Feast, Field and Fray. By Λ. 1853.

Guy Livingstone, or 'Thorough.' 1857 (anon.); 1863 (6th edn); ed. S. Kaye-Smith, 1928.

Sword and Gown. 1859. [First pbd in Fraser's Mag.]

Barren Honour. A Tale. 2 vols. 1862. [First pbd in Fraser's Mag.]

Border and Bastille. 1863; New York, 1866. [Includes Songs of Feast, Field and Fray.]

A Bundle of Ballads. 1864.

Maurice Dering, or the Quadrilateral. A Novel. 2 vols. 1864; Leipzig, 1864.

Sans Merci, or Kestrels and Falcons. 3 vols. 1866; 1866.

Brakespeare, or the Fortunes of a Free Lance. 3 vols. 1868.

Breaking a Butterfly, or Blanche Ellerslie's Ending. 3 vols. 1869.

Anteros. A Novel. 3 vols. 1873.

Silverland. 1873.

Hagarene. 3 vols. 1874.

(b) Criticism

Edinburgh Rev. Oct. 1858. [Review of Guy Livingstone.]

Montégut, E. Guy Livingstone. [In Écrivains modernes de l'Angleterre, ser. 1, Paris, 1885.]

Roberts, W. G. A. Lawrence's Songs of Feast, Field and Fray. TLS. 4, 18 July 1935.

'HOLME LEE,' i.e. HARRIET PARR (1828–1900)

(a) Fiction

Maude Talbot. 3 vols. 1854.

Thorney Hall. A Story of an Old Family. 1855.

Gilbert Massenger. 1855.

Kathie Brande. A Fireside History of a Quiet Life. 2 vols. 1856.

Sylvan Holt's Daughter. 3 vols. 1858.

Against Wind and Tide. 3 vols. 1859.

Hawksview. A Family History. 1859.

Legends from Fairyland, narrating the History of Prince Glee and Princess Trill, [and] the Cruel Persecutions of Aunt Spite. 1860.

The Wortlebank Diary and some Old Stories from Kathie Brande's Portfolio. 3 vols. 1860.

The Wonderful Adventures of Tuflongbo and his Elfin Company, in their Journey of Little Content through the Enchanted Forest. 1861.

Warp and Woof, or the Reminiscences of Doris Fletcher. 3 vols. 1861.

Tuflongbo's Journey in Search of Ogres, with some Account of his Early Life. 1862.

Annie Warleigh's Fortunes. 3 vols. 1863.

The True Pathetic History of Poor Match. 1863; [1863] (as Poor Match, his Life, Adventures and Death).

Mrs Wynward's Ward. 2 vols. 1867.

Basil Godfrey's Caprice. 3 vols. 1868.

Contrast, or the Schoolfellows. 1868.

For Richer, for Poorer. 3 vols. 1870.

Her Title of Honour. 1871.

The Beautiful Miss Barrington. 3 vols. 1871.

Echoes of a Famous Year. 1872.

Country Stories, Old and New, in Prose and Verse. 2 vols. 1872.

Katherine's Trial. 1873.

The Vicissitudes of Bessie Fairfax. 3 vols. 1874.

This Work-a-day World. 3 vols. 1875.

Ben Milner's Wooing. 1876.

Straightforward. 3 vols. 1878.

Mrs Denys of Cote. 3 vols. 1880.

A Poor Squire. 2 vols. 1882.

Loving and Serving. 3 vols. 1883.

(b) Other Writings

In the Silver Age. Essays—that is, Dispersed Meditations. 2 vols. 1864.

Life and Death of Jeanne d'Arc. 2 vols. 1866.

Maurice and Eugénie Guérin. A Monograph. 1870.

JOSEPH SHERIDAN LE FANU (1814–1873)

(a) Fiction

The Cook and Anchor; being a Chronicle of Old Dublin City. 3 vols. Dublin, 1845 (anon.); 1873 (as Morley Court); ed. B. S. Le Fanu, [1895].

The Fortunes of Colonel Torlogh O'Brien. Dublin, 1847 (anon.); 1855; n.d.; 1896.

Ghost Stories and Tales of Mystery. Dublin, 1851.

The House by the Church-Yard. 3 vols. 1863; 1866; [1870]; Dublin, 1904.

Wylder's Hand. A Novel. 3 vols. 1864; [1870]; [1903].

Uncle Silas. A Tale of Bartram-Haugh.

3 vols. 1864; 3 vols. 1865; 1865; 2 vols. Leipzig, 1865; [1871]; Dublin, 1904; [1913].

Guy Deverell. 3 vols. 1865; 2 vols. Leipzig, 1865; 1866; [1869].

All in the Dark. 2 vols. 1866; [1869].

The Tenants of Malory. A Novel. 3 vols. 1867; [1872].

A Lost Name. 3 vols. 1868.

Haunted Lives. A Novel. 3 vols. 1868.

The Wyvern Mystery. A Novel. 3 vols. 1869; 1889; [1904].

Checkmate. 3 vols. 1871.

The Rose and the Key. 3 vols. 1871.

Chronicles of Golden Friars. 3 vols. 1871.

In a Glass darkly. 3 vols. 1872; 1884; rptd 1923, 1929.

Willing to die. 3 vols. 1873; [1895?].

The Purcell Papers. With a Memoir by Alfred Perceval Graves. 3 vols. 1880.

The Watcher and Other Weird Stories. [1894.]

The Evil Guest. [1895.]

Madam Crowl's Ghost and Other Tales of Mystery. Ed. M. R. James, 1923.

(b) Other Writings

The Poems of J. S. Le Fanu. Ed. A. P. Graves, 1896.

[Le Fanu joined the staff of the Dublin University Mag. in 1837 and many of his tales and novels were originally pbd there. He was editor and proprietor, 1869–72.]

(c) Biography and Criticism

Kenton, E. A Forgotten Creator of Ghosts. Bookman (New York), July 1929.

Benson, E. F. Sheridan Le Fanu. Spectator, 21 Feb. 1931.

Ellis, S. M. Wilkie Collins, Le Fanu and Others. 1931. [With bibliography, including partial list of Le Fanu's contributions to periodicals.]

CHARLES JAMES LEVER (1806–1872)*

(a) Collected Works

The Military Novels of Charles Lever. Illustrated by George Cruickshank and 'Phiz.' 9 vols. n.d.

The Works. 34 vols. 1876–8. (Harry Lorrequer edn.)

The Novels. Edited by his Daughter [Julia Kate Neville]. 37 vols. 1897–9.

(b) Fiction

The Confessions of Harry Lorrequer. Dublin, 1839; 1845; 1882; 1884; ed. 'Lewis Melville,' [1907] (Everyman's Lib.).

Diary and Notes of Horace Templeton, Late Secretary of Legation. Philadelphia, [1840?]; 2 vols. 1848; [1878].

* The bibliography of Lever has been contributed by Mr A. M. Cohn.

Charles O'Malley, the Irish Dragoon. Edited by Harry Lorrequer. 2 vols. Dublin, 1841; 2 vols. 1842; 2 vols. 1845; 3 vols. Leipzig, 1848; 2 vols. 1857; 1876.

Our Mess. 3 vols. Dublin, 1843–4; 1857; 1876; 1885. [Vol. I, Jack Hinton; vols. II, III, Tom Burke of 'Ours.']

Arthur O'Leary: his Wanderings and Ponderings in Many Lands. 3 vols. 1844; 1845; 1856 (as Adventures of Arthur O'Leary); 1877; 1886.

St Patrick's Eve. 1845; 1871 (with A Rent in the Cloud, etc.).

Nuts and Nutcrackers. 1845.

Tales of the Trains. 1845.

The O'Donoghue. A Tale of Ireland Fifty Years Ago. Dublin, 1845; 1858; 1868; 1876.

The Knight of Gwynne. A Tale of the Time of the Union. 1847; 1858; 1867; 1877; 1889.

The Martins of Cro' Martin. 1847; 1856; 1856; 1878.

Confessions of Con Cregan, the Irish Gil Blas. 2 vols. [1849]; 1854; 1876; 1891.

Roland Cashel. 1850; 1858; 1864.

The Daltons, or Three Roads in Life. 2 vols. 1850–2; 1859; 1876.

Maurice Tiernay, the Soldier of Fortune. 1852; [1855]; 2 vols. 1861; 1878.

The Dodd Family Abroad. 2 vols. 1852–4; 1859; 1877.

Sir Jasper Carew, his Life and Experiences. [1855]; 1878.

The Fortunes of Glencore. 3 vols. 1857; 1878.

Davenport Dunn, or the Man of the Day. 1859.

One of Them. 1861; 1877.

A Day's Ride. 2 vols. 1863; 1878.

Barrington. 1863; 2 vols. Leipzig, 1863; 1878.

Cornelius O'Dowd upon Men, Women and Other Things in General. 3 sers. 1864–5; 1874. [First pbd in Blackwood's Mag.]

Luttrell of Arran. 1865; 1877.

A Rent in a Cloud. [1865]; 1878 (with St Patrick's Eve, etc.).

Tony Butler. 3 vols. Edinburgh, 1865; 1878.

Sir Brook Fossbrooke. 3 vols. 1866; 1867; 1878.

The Bramleighs of Bishop's Folly. 3 vols. 1868; 1877.

Paul Gosslett's Confessions in Law and the Civil Service. 1868; rptd 1924. [First pbd in Saint Paul's Mag.]

That Boy of Norcott's. 1869; 1878 (with A Rent in a Cloud, etc.).

Lord Kilgobbin. A Tale of Ireland in Our Own Time. 3 vols. 1872; 1877; 1906.

Gerald Fitzgerald the Chevalier. 1899. [First pbd in Dublin University Mag.; rptd 27 years after Lever's death.]

[Lever edited The Dublin University Mag. 1835–72, and from 1835 was also a regular contributor to Blackwood's Mag.]

(c) Biography and Criticism

The Works of Charles Lever. Blackwood's Mag. April 1862; 1866.

Friswell, J. H. Modern Men of Letters. 1870.

Fitzpatrick, W. J. Life of Charles Lever. 2 vols. 1879.

Downey, E. Charles Lever: Life in his Letters. 2 vols. 1906.

Rolfe, F. P. Letters of Charles Lever to his Wife and Daughter. Huntington Lib. Bulletin, Oct. 1936.

Stevenson, L. Dr Quicksilver. 1939.

GEORGE HENRY LEWES (1817–1878)

[See p. 869 below.]

ELIZA LYNN LINTON, née LYNN (1822–1898)

(a) Fiction

Azeth the Egyptian. 3 vols. [1846].

Amymone. A Romance of the Days of Pericles. 3 vols. 1848.

Realities. A Tale. 3 vols. 1851.

Witch Stories. 1861. [First pbd in All the Year Round.]

Grasp your Nettle. A Novel. 3 vols. 1865.

Lizzie Norton of Greygrigg. A Novel. 3 vols. 1866.

Sowing the Wind. 3 vols. 1867.

The True History of Joshua Davidson. 1872; 1873.

Patricia Kemball. A Novel. 3 vols. 1874.

The Mad Willoughby's and Other Tales. 1875.

The Atonement of Leam Dundas. A Novel. 3 vols. 1877.

The World well Lost. 2 vols. 1877.

Under which Lord? A Novel. 1879.

The Rebel of the Family. 3 vols. 1880.

With a Silken Thread and Other Stories. 3 vols. 1880.

My Love. A Novel. 3 vols. 1881.

Jane. A Novel. 1883.

The Autobiography of Christopher Kirkland. 3 vols. 1885.

Stabbed in the Dark. A Tale. [1885.]

The Rift in the Lute. A Tale. Glasgow, [1885.]

Paston Carew, Millionaire and Miser. A Novel. 3 vols. 1886.

Through the Long Night. 3 vols. 1888.

An Octave of Friends; with Other Silhouettes and Stories. 1891.

The One Too Many. 3 vols. 1894.

In Haste and at Leisure. 3 vols. 1895.

Dulcie Everton. 2 vols. 1896.

Twixt Cup and Lip, [etc.]. 1896. [Short stories.]

The Second Youth of Theodora Desanges. With an Introduction by G. S. Layard. 1900.

(b) Other Writings

The Lake Country. Illustrated by W. J. Linton. 1864.
Ourselves: Essays on Women. 1869; 1870; 1884.
At Night in a Hospital. 1879. [Rptd from Belgravia.]
The Girl of the Period and Other Essays from the Saturday Review. 2 vols. 1883.
About Ireland. 1890.
About Ulster. 1892.
My Literary Life; with a Prefatory Note by Beatrice Harraden. 1899.

(c) Biography

Tweedie, Mrs A. A Chat with Mrs Lynn Linton. Temple Bar, CIII, 1894.
Linton, W. J. Autobiographical Memories. 1895. [By the husband of Mrs Lynn Linton.]
Layard, G. S. Eliza Lynn Linton: her Life, Letters and Opinions. 1901.

THOMAS HENRY LISTER (1800–1842)

(a) Fiction

Granby. A Novel. 3 vols. 1826 (3 edns); 1838.
Herbert Lacy. 3 vols. 1828.
Arlington. A Novel. 3 vols. [1832].
Flirtation. 3 vols. [1833?]
Romance of Real Life. 3 vols. [1833?].
Yes and No. 2 vols. 1834.
Anne Grey. A Novel. By Harriet Lister. Edited by the Author of 'Granby.' 3 vols. 1834.
Hulse House. 1860.

(b) Other Writings

Epicharis. An Historical Tragedy. 1829.
The Life and Administration of Edward, First Earl of Clarendon; with Original Correspondence and Authentic Papers never before published. 3 vols. 1837–8.
An Answer to the Misrepresentations contained in an Article [by J. W. Croker] on the Life of Clarendon in No. CXXIV of the Quarterly Review. 1839.

GEORGE MACDONALD (1824–1905)

(a) Collected Works

Works of Fancy and Imagination. 10 vols. 1871.

(b) Fiction

Phantastes: A Faerie Romance for Men and Women. 1858.
David Elginbrod. 3 vols. 1863.
Adela Cathcart. 3 vols. 1864.

The Portent. A Story of the Inner Vision of the Highlanders commonly called the Second Sight. 1864. [First pbd in Cornhill Mag. 1860.]
Alec Forbes of Howglen. 3 vols. 1865.
Annals of a Quiet Neighbourhood. 3 vols. 1867. [First pbd anonymously in Sunday Mag. 1866.]
Dealings with the Fairies. 1867.
Guild Court. 3 vols. 1868. [First pbd in Good Words, 1867.]
Robert Falconer. 3 vols. 1868. [First pbd in The Argosy, 1867.]
The Seaboard Parish. 3 vols. 1868.
At the Back of the North Wind. 1871. [First pbd in Good Words for the Young.]
Ranald Bannerman's Boyhood. 1871. [First pbd in Good Words for the Young.]
The Princess and the Goblin. 1872.
The Vicar's Daughter. 3 vols. 1872.
Wilfrid Cumbermede. 3 vols. 1872.
Gutta Percha Willie: the Working Genius. 1873.
Malcolm. 3 vols. 1875.
The Wise Woman, A Parable. 1875; 1895 (as The Lost Princess or the Wise Woman).
Thomas Wingfold, Curate. 3 vols. 1876.
St George and St Michael. 3 vols. 1876.
The Marquis of Lossie. 3 vols. 1877.
Sir Gibbie. 3 vols. 1879.
Paul Faber, Surgeon. 3 vols. 1879.
Mary Marston. 3 vols. 1881.
Castle Warlock. A Homely Romance. 3 vols. 1882.
Weighed and Wanting. 3 vols. 1882.
The Gifts of the Christ Child and Other Tales. 2 vols. 1882. [Later pbd as Stephen Archer and Other Tales, n.d.]
Donal Grant. 3 vols. 1883.
The Princess and Curdie. 1883.
What's Mine's Mine. 3 vols. 1886.
Cross Purposes, and the Shadows. Two Fairy Stories. 1886. [Rptd from Dealings with the Fairies.]
Home Again. A Tale. 1887.
The Elect Lady. 1888.
A Rough Shaking. A Tale. 1890.
The Light Princess and Other Fairy Stories. 1890. [Rptd from Dealings with the Fairies.]
There and back. 3 vols. 1891.
The Flight of the Shadow. 1891.
Heather and Snow. 2 vols. 1893.
Lilith. A Romance. 1895.
Salted with Fire. A Tale. 1897.

(c) Other Writings

Within and Without. A Poem. 1855.
Poems. 1857.
The Disciple and Other Poems. 1867.
Unspoken Sermons. 3 sers. 1867–89.
The Miracles of Our Lord. 1870.

England's Antiphon. 1874.

Exotics. A Translation of the Spiritual Songs of Novalis, the Hymn Book of Luther and Other Poems from the German and Italian. 1876. [Verse.]

A Book of Strife, in the Form of the Diary of an Old Soul. 1880; 1909; 1913.

Orts. 1882; 1893 (enlarged, as A Dish of Orts).

A Threefold Cord. Poems by Three Friends. 1883 (priv. ptd). [Edited by MacDonald.]

The Tragedie of Hamlet. With a Study of the Text of the Folio of 1623. 1885.

A Cabinet of Gems, cut and polished by Sir Philip Sidney, now for their More Radiance presented without their Setting by George MacDonald. 1891.

The Hope of the Gospel. 1892.

The Poetical Works of George MacDonald. 2 vols. 1893.

Rampolli: Growths from a Long-planted Root, being Translations chiefly from the German, along with a Year's Diary of an Old Soul. 1897. [Poems.]

(d) Biography and Criticism

Geddes, Sir W. D. George MacDonald as a Poet. Blackwood's Mag. March 1891.

Johnson, J. George MacDonald. A Biography and Critical Appreciation. 1906.

MacDonald, Ronald. Essays from a Northern Window. [1911.] [Contains an essay on George MacDonald by his son.]

MacDonald, Greville. George MacDonald and his Wife. With An Introduction by G. K. Chesterton. 1924.

Evans, B. I. English Poetry in the Later Nineteenth Century. 1933. [Ch. xvi.]

ANNE MANNING (1807–1879)

(a) Fiction

Stories from the History of Italy, from the Invasion of Alaric to the Present Time. 1831.

Village Bells. 3 vols. 1838; 1859.

The Maiden and Married Life of Mary Powell, afterwards Mistress Milton. 1849; 1855; 1859 (with Deborah's Diary); 1860; 1866; 1874. [First pbd in Sharpe's Mag. 1849.]

The Household of Sir Thomas More. 1851; 1860; 1870; 1887; 1896, etc. [First pbd in Sharpe's Mag.]

Queen Philippa's Golden Rule. 1851.

The Colloquies of Edward Osborne, Citizen and Cloth Worker of London. 1852.

Cherry and Violet. A Tale of the Plague. 1853.

The Provocations of Madame Palissy. 1853.

Jack and the Tanner of Wymondham. 1854.

Claude the Colpasteur. 1854.

Some Account of Mrs Clarida Singlehart. 1855.

Stories from the History of the Caliph Haroun al Raschid. 1855.

A Sabbath at Home. 1855.

The Old Chelsea Bun House. A Tale. 1855.

Tasso and Leonora. The Commentaries of Ser Pantaleone degli Gambacorti. 1856.

The Good Old Times. A Tale of Auvergne. 1857.

Helen and Olga. A Russian Story. 1857.

Deborah's Diary. 1858. [Sequel to Mary Powell.]

The Year Nine. A Tale of the Tyrol. 1858.

The Ladies of Bever Hollow. 2 vols. 1858.

Poplar House Academy. 2 vols. 1859.

Autobiography of Valentine Duval. 1860.

Town and Forest. 1860.

Family Pictures. 1861.

Chronicle of Ethelfled. 1861.

Bessy's Money. A Tale. 1863.

Meadowleigh. 1863.

The Duchess of Trajetto. 1863.

An Interrupted Wedding. 1864.

Belfast. A Tale. 1865.

Selvaggio. A Tale of Italian Country Life. Edinburgh, 1865.

Miss Biddy Frobisher. A Saltwater Story. 1866.

The Lincolnshire Tragedy. Passages in the Life of the Faire Gospeller, Mistress Anne Askewe, recounted by Nicholas Moldwarp. 1866.

The Masque at Ludlow and Other Romanesques. 1866.

Diana's Crescent. 2 vols. 1868.

Jacques Bonneval. 1868.

The Spanish Barber. A Tale. 1869.

Margaret More's Tagebuch. 1870.

One Trip more. 1870.

Compton Friars. 1872.

The Lady of Limited Income. 2 vols. 1872.

Lord Harry Bellair. 2 vols. 1874.

Monk's Norton. 2 vols. 1874.

An Idyll of the Alps. 1876.

(b) Other Writings

A Sister's Gift. Conversations on Sacred Subjects. 1826.

The Drawing Room Table Book. 1852.

Chronicles of Merry England. 1854.

The Hill Side. Illustrations of some of the Simplest Terms used in Logic. 1854.

The Week of Darkness. A Short Manual for the Use and Comfort of Mourners. 1856.

Lives of Good Servants. 1857.

An English Girl's Account of a Moravian Settlement. 1858. [Edited by Anne Manning.]

The Day of Small Things. 1860.

The Cottage History of England. 1861.

A Noble Purpose nobly won. 2 vols. 1862. [On Joan of Arc.]

Heroes of the Desert. The Story of the Lives of Moffat and Livingstone. 1875.

[From 1868 to 1876 Anne Manning contributed articles and stories to Golden Hours, a magazine ed. by Dr Whittemore. The following serials, not rptd, were pbd there: Madame Prosni and Madame Bleay, 1868; Rosita, 1869; On the Grand Tour, 1870; Octavia Solaro, 1871; Illusions Dispelled, 1871; the only book pbd under her own name was Stories from the History of Italy, 1831.]

(c) Criticism

Yonge, C. M. Anne Manning. [In Women Novelists of Queen Victoria's Reign, 1897.]

ANNE MARSH, later MARSH-CALDWELL, née CALDWELL (1791–1874)

Two Old Men's Tales: The Deformed, and The Admiral's Daughter. 2 vols. 1834 (bis).
Tales of the Woods and Fields. A Second Series of Two Old Men's Tales. 3 vols. 1836; 1846; 1850.
The Triumphs of Time. 1844; 1849.
Mount Sorel, or the Heiress of the de Veres. 2 vols. 1845; [1856].
Emilia Wyndham. 3 vols. 1846; 1848; 2 vols. Leipzig, 1852.
Father Darcy. 2 vols. 1846; [1857].
Norman's Bridge, or the Modern Midas. 1847; 1850; [1855].
The Protestant Reformation in France, or the History of the Hugonots. 1847.
Angela. A Novel. 3 vols. 1848; [1855]; [1875].
Mordaunt Hall, or a September Night. 3 vols. 1849; 1853.
Tales of the First French Revolution. 1849.
Lettice Arnold. A Tale. 1850; [1856]; [1876].
The Wilmingtons. 3 vols. 1850; 1852.
Ravenscliffe. 3 vols. 1851; 2 vols. Leipzig, 1851.
Time the Avenger. 3 vols. 1851; 1853.
Castle Avon. 3 vols. 1852; 2 vols. Leipzig, 1852; [1855].
The Longwoods of the Grange. 1853; 1862.
Aubrey. 3 vols. 1854; 2 vols. Leipzig, 1854; [1857]; [1875].
The Heiress of Houghton, or the Mother's Secret. 3 vols. 1855; 2 vols. Leipzig, 1855; [1858].
Woman's Devotion. A Novel. 3 vols. 1855.
Evelyn Marston. 3 vols. 1856; 2 vols. Leipzig, 1856; [1860].
Margaret and her Bridesmaids. 1856; [1860].
The Rose of Ashurst. 3 vols. 1857; 2 vols. Leipzig, 1857; 1859.
Mr and Mrs Asheton. 3 vols. 1860; 1864.
The Ladies of Lovel-Leigh. 3 vols. 1862.
Chronicles of Dartmoor. 3 vols. 1866.

Lords and Ladies. 1866.

[Anne Marsh also pbd 2 trns from the French.]

JOHN WESTLAND MARSTON (1819–1890)

[See p. 604 below.]

HARRIET MARTINEAU (1802–1876)

(a) Fiction

Five Years of Youth, or Sense and Sentiment. 1831.
Illustrations of Political Economy. 9 vols. 1832–4. [Contains inter alia: Life in the Wilds; Ellin of Gavreloch; A Manchester Strike; Cousin Marshall; The Loom and the Lugger; Sowers not Reapers, etc.]
Poor Laws and Paupers Illustrated. 1. The Parish, a Tale. 2. The Hamlets, a Tale. 3. The Town, Tale. 4. The Land's End, a Tale. 4 pts, 1833–4.
Illustrations of Taxation. 1834. [Contains inter alia: The Park and the Paddock; The Scholars of Arneside.]
Deerbrook. A Novel. 3 vols. 1839.
The Rioters. N.d.; 1842 (unauthorized). [Short story.]
The Hour and the Man. An Historical Romance. 3 vols. 1841.
The Playfellow. A Series of Tales. 4 vols. 1841. [The Settlers at Home (rptd separately 1856); The Peasant and the Prince (rptd separately 1856); Feats on the Fiord (rptd separately 1844, 1856, 1883, etc.); The Crofton Boys (rptd separately 1856).]
Forest and Game-Law Tales. 3 vols. 1845–6.
Dawn Island. A Tale. Manchester, 1845. [Pbd on behalf of the Anti-Corn Law League.]
The Billow and the Rock. 1846.
Merdhen, the Manor and the Eyrie, and Old Landmarks and Old Laws. 1852.
The Hampdens. An Historiette. 1880 (illustrations by Sir J. E. Millais).

(b) Other Writings

Devotional Exercises for the Use of Young Persons. 1823; 1832 (enlarged as Devotional Exercises, to which is added a Guide to the Study of the Scriptures).
Addresses with Prayers and Original Hymns for the Use of Families. By a Lady. 1826.
Traditions of Palestine. 1830. [Edited by Harriet Martineau.]
Essential Faith of the Universal Church deduced from the Sacred Records. 1831.
The Faith as unfolded by Many Prophets. An Essay Addressed to the Disciples of Mohammed. 1832.
Providence as manifested through Israel. 1832.
Miscellanies. 2 vols. [Boston], 1836.

Society in America. 3 vols. 1837.
A Retrospect of Western Travel. 3 vols. 1838.
How to observe. Morals and Manners. 1838.
Guides to Service. [1839?]
The Martyr Age of the United States of America. 1840.
Life in the Sick-Room, or Essays by an Invalid. 1844.
Letters on Mesmerism. 1845.
The Land we live in. 1847. [With Charles Knight.]
Eastern Life, Past and Present. 3 vols. 1848.
Household Education. 1849.
History of England During the Thirty Years' Peace, 1816-46. 2 vols. 1849-50; 1855 (rev. as History of the Peace, 1816-1846); 4 vols. [1877-8].
Two Letters on Cow-Keeping. [1850?]
Letters on the Laws of Man's Nature and Development. 1851. [With H. G. Atkinson.]
Introduction to the History of the Peace from 1800 to 1815. 1851; 1878.
Half a Century of the British Empire: a History of the Kingdom and the People, from 1800 to 1850. Pt I (all pbd), [1851].
Letters from Ireland. 1853. [Rptd from Daily News.]
The Positive Philosophy of August Comte freely translated and condensed. 2 vols. 1853.
Complete Guide to the Lakes. 1854.
Guide to Windermere, with Tours to the Neighbouring Lakes and Other Interesting Places. Windermere, [1854] (bis); [1856].
The Factory Controversy. A Warning against Meddling Legislation. Manchester, 1855.
A History of the American Compromises. 1856. [Rptd in part from Daily News.]
Corporate Traditions and National Rights. Local Dues on Shipping. [1857.]
Guide to Keswick and its Environs. Windermere, [1857].
Suggestions towards the Future Government of India. 1858.
Endowed Schools of Ireland. 1859. [Rptd from Daily News.]
England and her Soldiers. 1859.
Survey of the Lake District. 1860.
Health, Husbandry and Handicraft. 1861.
Biographical Sketches. 1869; 1877 (enlarged and with autobiographical sketch). [Rptd from Daily News.]
Harriet Martineau's Autobiography. With Memorials by Maria Weston Chapman. 3 vols. 1877.

[Harriet Martineau also wrote over 1600 articles for Daily News, 1851-66, as well as contributing to Edinburgh Rev. from 1859.]

(c) Biography and Criticism

[Lockhart, J. G.] Quarterly Rev. April 1833. [An attack on Harriet Martineau.]

Horne, R. H. A New Spirit of the Age. Vol. II, 1844.
Maginn, W. A Gallery of Illustrious Literary Characters. Ed. W. Bates, [1873].
Oliphant, M. O. Harriet Martineau. Blackwood's Mag. April 1877.
Miller, Mrs Fenwick. Harriet Martineau. 1884.
Payn, James. Literary Recollections. 1884.
Hamilton, Catherine J. Harriet Martineau. 1894.
Escher, E. Harriet Martineaus sozialpolitische Novellen. Zurich, 1925.
Bosanquet, T. Harriet Martineau. 1927.
Marvin, F. S. Harriet Martineau: Triumph and Tragedy. Hibbert Journ. July 1927.
Pope-Henessy, U. Three English Women in America [Fanny Trollope, Fanny Kemble, Harriet Martineau]. 1929.
Calkins, E. E. Harriet Martineau: Deaf Blue Stocking. Colophon, pt 14, 1933.
Ruenberg, N. E. Harriet Martineau: an Example of Victorian Conflict. Philadelphia, 1933.
Stearns, B.-M. Miss Sedgwick observes Harriet Martineau. New England Quart. VII, 1934.
Bloore, S. Miss Martineau speaks out. New England Quart. IX, 1936.
Ratcliffe, S. K. Eccentric Englishwomen. VI. Harriet Martineau. Spectator, 21 May 1937.

AUGUSTUS SEPTIMUS MAYHEW (1826-1875)

(a) Fiction by A. S. Mayhew

Kitty Lamere, or a Dark Page in London Life. A Tale. 1855.
Paved with Gold, or the Romance and Reality of London Streets. An Unfashionable Novel. Illustrated by H. K. Browne. 1858.
The Finest Girl in Bloomsbury. A Serio-comic Tale of Ambitious Love. 1861.
Blow Hot—Blow Cold. A Love Story. 1862.
Faces for Fortunes. 3 vols. 1865.

(b) Fiction in Collaboration with Henry Mayhew

The Greatest Plague of Life. Adventures of a Lady in Search of a Good Servant. Illustrated by George Cruikshank. [1847.]
The Good Genius that turned Everything into Gold, or the Queen Bee and the Magic Dress. A Christmas Fairytale. 1847.
Whom to marry and how to get married. Illustrated by George Cruikshank. [1848.]
The Image of his Father, or One Boy is more Trouble than a Dozen Girls. Illustrated by 'Phiz.' 1848.

The Magic of Kindness, or the Wondrous Story of the Good Huan. Illustrated by George Cruikshank and Kenny Meadows. [1849]; [1869] (illustrated by Walter Crane).
Living for Appearances. A Tale. 1855.
The Comic Almanack. 1870, etc.

JOHN MILLS

(a) Novels

The Old English Gentleman, or the Fields and the Woods. 3 vols. 1841 (bis); 1854.
The Stage Coach, or the Road of Life. 3 vols. 1843.
D'Horsay; or, The Follies of the Day. By a Man of Fashion. 1844; ed. J. Grego, 1902 (with introduction, sketch of D'Orsay's career, key to the characters mentioned in the satire and bibliography of works written by Mills).
The English Fireside: a Tale of the Past. 3 vols. 1844.
The Days of Old. [In The Edinburgh Tales, vol. II, 1845.]
The Old Hall, or Our Hearth and Homestead. 3 vols. 1845.
Christmas in the Olden Time, or the Wassail Bowl. [1846.]
A Capful of Moonshine, or 'tis not all Gold that Glitters. 1849.
Our County. 3 vols. 1850.
The Belle of the Village. 3 vols. 1852.
The Wheel of Life. 1855.
Too Fast to last. 3 vols. 1881; [1882].
On the Spur of the Moment. 3 vols. 1884.
Jack Cherton of Sydney. [1906.]

(b) Sporting Books

The Sportsman's Library. Edinburgh, 1845.
The Life of a Foxhound. 1848; 1849; 1861; 1892; [1910]; 1921.
The Life of a Race-Horse. 1854; 1861.
The Flyers of the Hunt. Illustrated by J. Leech. 1859; 1865.
Stable Secrets, or Puffy Doddles, his Sayings and Sympathies. 1863.

DINAH MARIA MULOCK, later CRAIK (1826–1887)

(a) Fiction

The Ogilvies. A Novel. 3 vols. 1849; 1875.
Cola Monti, or the Story of a Genius. [1849]; [1866] (rev.); [1883].
Olive. 3 vols. 1850.
The Head of the Family. 3 vols. 1851.
Alice Learmont. A Fairy Tale. 1852; 1884 (rev.).
Bread upon the Waters: a Governess's Life. 1852.
Avillion and Other Tales. 3 vols. 1853.
Agatha's Husband. A Novel. 3 vols. 1853.
A Hero. Philip's Book. 1853.

John Halifax, Gentleman. 3 vols. 1856; 2 vols. Leipzig, 1857; 1859; [1898]; [1900]; 1903; [1906], etc.
Nothing New. Tales. 1857.
A Life for a Life. 3 vols. 1859.
Romantic Tales. 1859.
Domestic Stories. [1859?]
Our Year. A Child's Book. 1860.
Studies from Life. 1861.
Mistress and Maid. 2 vols. 1863.
The Fairy Book: the Best Popular Fairy Stories selected and rendered anew. 1863.
Christian's Mistake. 1865.
A New Year's Gift for Sick Children. 1865.
A Noble Life. 2 vols. 1866.
How to win Love, or Rhoda's Lesson. A Story for the Young. 1866[?]
Two Marriages. 2 vols. 1867.
The Woman's Kingdom. 3 vols. 1869.
A Brave Lady. 3 vols. 1870.
The Unkind Word and Other Stories. 2 vols. 1870.
Little Sunshine's Holiday. 1871.
Hannah. 2 vols. 1872.
Is it True? Tales Curious and Wonderful. 1872.
The Adventures of a Brownie. 1872.
My Mother and I. 1874.
The Little Lame Prince. 1875.
Will Denbigh, Nobleman. 1877.
The Laurel Bush. 1877.
Young Mrs Jardine. 3 vols. 1879.
His Little Mother and Other Tales. 1881.
Miss Tommy. 1884.
King Arthur—not a Love Story. 1886.
An Unknown Country. 1887.

(b) Other Writings

A Woman's Thoughts about Women. 1858.
Poems. [1859.]
Home Thoughts and Home Scenes. 1865.
Fair France. Impressions of a Traveller. 1871.
Sermons out of Church. 1875.
Thirty Years. Poems New and Old. 1881; 1888 (as Poems by the Author of John Halifax, Gentleman).
Children's Poetry. 1881.
Plain Speaking. 1882.
An Unsentimental Journey through Cornwall. 1884.
About Money and Other Things. 1886.
Work for the Idle Hands [in Ireland]. 1886.
Fifty Golden Years: Incidents in the Queen's Reign. [1887.]
Concerning Men and Other Papers. 1888.

[Mrs Craik also edited various works as well as publishing trns from the French.]

(c) Biography and Criticism

Miles, A. H. Dinah Maria Craik. [In The Poets and the Poetry of the Century, vol. VII, 1893, vol. VIII, 1906.]

Parr, [Louisa]. Dinah Mulock. [In Women Novelists of Queen Victoria's Reign, 1897.]
—— The Author of John Halifax, Gentleman. A Memoir. 1898.
Reade, A. L. The Mellards and their Descendants; with Memoirs of Dinah Maria Mulock. 1915.
Johnson, R. B. The Women Novelists. [1918], pp. 186–8.

SIR CHARLES AUGUSTUS MURRAY (1806–1895)

(a) Novels

The Prairie-Bird. 3 vols. 1844; 1845; 1857; [1874].
Hassan, or the Child of the Pyramid. An Egyptian Tale. 2 vols. 1857; 1901.
Nom-ed-dyn, or the Light of the Faith. An Eastern Fairy Tale. [1883.]

(b) Other Writings

Travels in North America during the Years 1834, 1835, and 1836, including a Summer Residence with the Pannee Tribe of Indians and a Visit to Cuba and the Azore Islands. 2 vols. 1839; 2 vols. 1854 (rev.).
A Short Memoir of Mohammed Ali, Founder of the Vice-Royalty of Egypt. Ed. Sir H. Maxwell, 1898.

(c) Biography

Maxwell, Sir H. The Hon. Sir Charles Murray, K.C.B. A Memoir. 1898.

JOHN MASON NEALE (1818–1866)
[See p. 301 above.]

WILLIAM JOHNSON NEALE (1812–1893)

(a) Fiction

Cavendish, or the Patrician at Sea. 1831.
The Port Admiral. A Tale of the War. 3 vols. 1833.
Will-Watch, from the Auto-biography of a British Officer. 3 vols. 1834.
The Priors of Prague. 3 vols. 1836.
Gentleman Jack. A Naval Story. 1837.
The Flying Dutchman. A Legend of the High Seas. 3 vols. 1839.
Paul Periwinkle, or the Pressgang. 1841 (illustrated by 'Phiz').
The Naval Surgeon. 3 vols. 1841.
The Captain's Wife. 3 vols. 1842.
The Lost Ship, or the Atlantic Steamer. 3 vols. 1843.
Scapegrace at Sea. 3 vols. 1863 (2nd edn).

(b) Other Writings

The Lauread. A Satire. 1833.
The Law of Parliamentary Elections. 1839.
History of the Mutiny at Spithead and the Nore. 1842.

A Letter to the Attorney General, Sir W. W. Follett, suggesting some Amendments in the Proposed New County Courts Bill. 1844.

JOHN HENRY NEWMAN (1801–1890)
[See p. 686 below.]

CAROLINE NORTON (1808–1877)
[See p. 302 above.]

LAURENCE OLIPHANT (1829–1888)

(a) Novels

Piccadilly. A Fragment of Contemporary Biography. 1866; Edinburgh, 1870; 1874; ed. M. Sadleir, 1928. [First pbd in Blackwood's Mag. 1865.]
Altiora Peto. 2 vols. Edinburgh, 1883.
Masollam. A Problem of the Period. 3 vols. Edinburgh, 1886.

(b) Other Writings

A Journey to Katmandu [capital of Nepaul] with the Camp of Jung Bahadoor, including a Sketch of the Nepaulese Ambassador at Home. 1852.
The Russian Shores of the Black Sea in the Autumn of 1852, with a Voyage down the Volga, and a Tour through the Country of the Don Cossacks. Edinburgh, 1853; 1853 (enlarged); 1854.
The Coming Campaign. Edinburgh, 1855.
Minnesota and the Far West. Edinburgh, 1855.
The Trans-Caucasian Provinces the Proper Field of Operation for a Christian Army. Edinburgh, 1855.
The Trans-Caucasian Campaign of the Turkish Army under Omar Pasha. A Personal Narrative. Edinburgh, 1856.
Narrative of the Earl of Elgin's Mission to China and Japan in the Years 1857, 58, 59. 2 vols. Edinburgh, 1859.
Patriots and Filibusters. Incidents of Political and Exploratory Travel. Reprinted from Blackwood's Magazine with Corrections and Additions. Edinburgh, 1860.
Universal Suffrage and Napoleon the Third. 1860.
On the Present State of Political Parties in America. Edinburgh, 1866.
The Land of Gilead, with Excursions in the Lebanon. Edinburgh, 1880.
The Land of Khemi. Up and down the Middle Nile. Edinburgh, 1882.
Traits and Travesties, Social and Political. Edinburgh, 1882. [Largely rptd from Blackwood's Mag. Includes The Autobiography of a Joint-Stock Company, The Adventures of a War Correspondent, and other sketches and essays.]

A Trip to the North-East of Lake Tiberias in Jaulan. 1885.

Haifa, or Life in Modern Palestine. 1885; Edinburgh, 1887.

Sympneumata, or Evolutionary Forces now Active in Man. Edinburgh, 1885.

Episodes in a Life of Adventure, or Moss from a Rolling Stone. Edinburgh, 1887. [Rptd from Blackwood's Mag.]

Fashionable Philosophy and Other Sketches. Edinburgh, 1887. [Rptd from Nineteenth Century and Blackwood's Mag. Dramatic sketches and stories, mainly satirical.]

The Star in the East. 1887. [A pamphlet written for Mohammedans.]

Scientific Religion, or Higher Possibilities of Life and Practice through the Operation of Natural Forces. With an Appendix by a Clergyman of the Church of England [Haskett Smith]. 1888.

(c) Biography

Liesching, L. F. Personal Reminiscences of Laurence Oliphant. [1891.]

Oliphant, M. O. Memoir of Laurence Oliphant and of Alice Oliphant, his Wife. Edinburgh, 2 vols. 1891.

Scott, C. N. Laurence Oliphant. Supplementary Contributions to his Biography. 1895.

Owen, R. D. My Perilous Life in Palestine. 1928. [By Oliphant's second wife.]

MARGARET OLIPHANT OLIPHANT, née WILSON (1828–1897)

(a) Fiction

Passages in the Life of Mrs Margaret Maitland. 3 vols. 1849.

Caleb Field. 1851.

Merkland. A Story of Scottish Life. 3 vols. 1851.

Memoirs and Resolutions of Adam Graeme of Mossgray. 3 vols. 1852.

Katie Stewart. 1853.

Harry Muir. A Story of Scottish Life. 3 vols. 1853.

Quiet Heart. A Story. 1854.

Magdalen Hepburn. A Story of the Scottish Reformation. 1854.

Lilliesleaf. Conclusion of 'Margaret Maitland.' 3 vols. 1855.

Zaidee. A Romance. 3 vols. 1856.

The Athelings, or the Three Gifts. 3 vols. 1857.

The Days of my Life. 1857.

Sundays. 1858.

The Laird of Nordlaw. 3 vols. 1858.

Orphans. A Chapter in Life. 1858.

Agnes Hopetoun's Schools and Holidays. 1859.

Lucy Crofton. 1860.

The House on the Moor. 1861.

The Last of the Mortimers. 1862.

The Rector and the Doctor's Family. 3 vols. 1863 (anon.). (Chronicles of Carlingford.)

Salem Chapel. 2 vols. 1863 (anon.). (Chronicles of Carlingford.)

Heart and Cross. 1863.

The Perpetual Curate. 3 vols. 1864 (anon.). (Chronicles of Carlingford.)

Agnes. 3 vols. 1866.

Miss Marjoribanks. 3 vols. 1866 (anon.). (Chronicles of Carlingford.)

A Son of the Soil. 1866.

Madonna Mary. 3 vols. 1867.

The Brownlows. 3 vols. 1868.

The Minister's Wife. 1869.

John. A Love Story. 2 vols. 1870.

The Three Brothers. 3 vols. 1870.

Squire Arden. 3 vols. 1871.

At his Gates. 3 vols. 1872.

Ombra, [etc.]. 3 vols. 1872.

May. 3 vols. 1873.

Innocent. A Tale of Modern Life. 1873.

A Rose in June. 2 vols. 1874.

For Love and Life. 3 vols. 1874.

The Story of Valentine and his Brother. 3 vols. 1875.

Whiteladies. 3 vols. 1875.

The Curate in Charge. 2 vols. 1876.

Phoebe, Junior. A Last Chronicle of Carlingford. 3 vols. 1876 (anon.).

Young Musgrave. 3 vols. 1877.

Mrs Arthur. 3 vols. 1877.

Carita. 3 vols. 1877.

The Primrose Path. A Chapter in the Annals of the Kingdom of Fife. 3 vols. 1878.

Within the Precincts. 3 vols. 1879.

The Two Mrs Scudamores. 1879. [Tales from Blackwood's Mag.]

The Greatest Heiress in England. 3 vols. 1879.

A Beleaguered City. 1880.

He that will not when he may. 3 vols. 1880.

Harry Joscelyn. 3 vols. 1881.

In Trust. A Story of a Lady and her Lover. 3 vols. 1882.

A Little Pilgrim in the Unseen. 1882.

Hester. A Story of a Contemporary Life. 3 vols. 1883.

It was a Lover and his Lass. 3 vols. 1883.

The Ladies Lindores. 3 vols. 1883.

Sir Tom. 3 vols. 1884.

The Wizard's Son. 3 vols. 1884.

Two Stories of the Seen and Unseen. 1885.

Madam. 3 vols. 1885.

Oliver's Bride. A True Story. 1886.

A Country Gentleman and his Family. 3 vols. 1886.

Effie Ogilvie. 2 vols. 1886.

A House divided against itself. 3 vols. 1886.

The Son of his Father. 3 vols. 1887.

The Land of Darkness, along with some Fur-
ther Chapters in the Experience of the Little
Pilgrims. 1888.
Joyce. 3 vols. 1888.
The Second Son. 3 vols. 1888.
Cousin Mary. 1888.
Neighbours on the Green. A Collection of
Stories. 1889.
A Poor Gentleman. 3 vols. 1889.
Lady Car. The Sequel of a Life. 1889.
Kirsteen. A Story of a Scottish Family
Seventy Years ago. 1890.
The Duke's Daughter and the Fugitives.
3 vols. 1890.
Sons and Daughters. 1890.
The Mystery of Mrs Blencarrow. 1890.
The Railway Man and his Children. 3 vols.
1891.
Janet. 3 vols. 1891.
The Cuckoo in the Nest. 3 vols. 1892.
Diana Trelawny. The Story of a Great Mis-
take. 2 vols. 1892.
The Marriage of Elinor. 3 vols. 1892.
The Heir Presumptive and the Heir Apparent.
3 vols. 1892.
Lady William. 3 vols. 1893.
The Sorceress. 3 vols. 1893.
A House in Bloomsbury. 2 vols. 1894.
Who was lost and is found. 1894.
The Prodigals and their Inheritance. 2 vols.
1894.
Two Strangers. 1895.
Sir Robert's Fortune. A Story of a Scotch
Moor. 1895.
The Unjust Steward, or the Minister's Debt.
1896.
The Two Marys. 1896.
Old Mr Tredgold. 1896.
The Lady's Walk. 1897.
The Ways of Life. Two Stories. 1897.
A Widow's Tale and Other Stories. 1898.
That Little Cutty; and Two Other Stories.
1898.

(b) Other Writings

The Life of Edward Irving. 2 vols. 1862.
Francis of Assisi. 1868.
Historical Sketches of the Reign of George II.
2 vols. 1869.
Memoirs of the Count de Montalembert. A
Chapter of Recent French History. 1872.
Dress. 1876.
The Makers of Florence: Dante, Giotto,
Savonarola, and their City. 1876.
Dante. 1877. (Foreign Classics for English
Readers.)
Molière. 1879. (Foreign Classics for English
Readers.) [With F. Tarver.]
Cervantes. 1880. (Foreign Classics for English
Readers.)

Literary History of England in the End of
the Eighteenth and Beginning of the Nine-
teenth Century. 3 vols. 1882.
Sheridan. 1883. (English Men of Letters ser.)
The Makers of Venice: Doges, Conquerors,
Painters, and Men of Letters. 1887.
Memoir of the Life of John Tulloch. 1888.
Royal Edinburgh: her Saints, Kings, Prophets
and Poets. 1890.
Jerusalem: its History and Hope. 1891.
Memoirs of the Life of Laurence Oliphant, and
Alice Oliphant, his Wife. 1891.
The Victorian Age of English Literature.
2 vols. 1892. [With F. R. Oliphant.]
Thomas Chalmers, Preacher, Philosopher, and
Statesman. 1893.
Historical Sketches of the Reign of Queen
Anne. 1894.
A Child's History of Scotland. 1895.
The Makers of Modern Rome. 1895.
Jeanne d'Arc: her Life and Death. 1896.
The Sisters Brontë. 1897.
Annals of a Publishing House. William Black-
wood and his Sons: their Magazine and
Friends. 2 vols. 1897.

[Mrs Oliphant also wrote considerably over
200 articles and stories for Blackwood's Mag.
between July 1852 and June 1897, as well as
introductions to several books.]

(c) Biography and Criticism

Coghill, A. L. The Autobiography and Letters
of Mrs Oliphant. 1899 (3 edns). [Includes
(except in 3rd edn) a complete list of Mrs
Oliphant's contributions to Blackwood's
Mag.]
'Melville, Lewis.' Victorian Novelists. 1906.
Ritchie, A. T., Lady. From the Porch. 1913.
Johnson, R. B. The Women Novelists.
[1918], pp. 188–99.

FRANCIS EDWARD PAGET (1806–1882)
[See p. 859 below.]

JAMES PAYN (1830–1898)
(a) Fiction
Stories from Boccaccio. 1852.
Stories and Sketches. 1857.
The Foster Brothers. 1859.
The Bateman Household. 1860. [Rptd from
Chambers's Journ.]
Richard Arbour, or the Family Scapegrace.
Edinburgh, 1861; [1869] (as The Family
Scapegrace, or Richard Arbour).
Meliboeus in London. Cambridge, 1862.
Lost Sir Massingbird. A Romance of Real
Life. 2 vols. 1864. [First pbd in Chambers's
Journ.]
Married beneath him. 3 vols. 1865.
Mirk Abbey. 1866.

The Clyffards of Clyffe. 3 vols. 1866.
Carlyon's Year. 2 vols. 1868.
Blondel Parva. 2 vols. 1868.
Bentinck's Tutor: One of the Family. A Novel. 1868.
A Perfect Treasure, An Incident in the Early Life of Marmaduke Drake Esq. 1869.
A County Family. A Novel. 3 vols. 1869.
Not wooed but won. A Novel. 1871.
Like Father, like Son. A Novel. 1871.
A Woman's Vengeance. 1872.
Gwendoline's Harvest. A Novel. 3 vols. 1872.
Cecil's Trust. A Novel. 3 vols. 1872.
Murphy's Master and Other Stories. 2 vols. 1873.
The Best of Husbands. 3 vols. 1874.
At her Mercy. 3 vols. 1874.
Walter's Word. A Novel. 3 vols. 1875.
Halves, a Novel; and Other Tales. 3 vols. 1876.
Fallen Fortunes. 3 vols. 1876.
What he cost her. 3 vols. 1877.
By Proxy. A Novel. 2 vols. 1878.
Less Black than we're painted. A Novel. 3 vols. 1878.
Under One Roof, an Episode in a Family History. 3 vols. 1879.
High Spirits, being Certain Stories written in them. 3 vols. 1879.
A Confidential Agent. 3 vols. 1880.
From Exile. A Novel. 3 vols. 1881.
A Grape from a Thorn. A Novel. 3 vols. 1881.
For Cash only. A Novel. 3 vols. [1882].
Thicker than Water. A Novel. 3 vols. 1883.
Kit. A Memory. 3 vols. 1883.
The Canon's Ward. A Novel. 3 vols. 1884.
The Talk of the Town. A Novel. 2 vols. 1885.
The Luck of the Darrells. A Novel. 3 vols. 1885.
In Peril and Privation, Stories of Marine Disaster retold. 1885.
The Heir of the Ages. A Novel. 3 vols. 1886.
Glow-Worm Tales. 3 vols. 1887.
The Eavesdropper. An Unparalleled Experience. 1888.
A Prince of the Blood. A Novel. 3 vols. 1888.
The Mystery of Mirbridge. 3 vols. 1888.
The Word and the Will. A Novel. 3 vols. 1890.
The Burnt Million. A Novel. 3 vols. 1890.
Sunny Stories and some Shady Ones. 1891.
A Stumble on the Threshold. A Novel. 2 vols. 1892.
A Modern Dick Whittington, or a Patron of Letters. 2 vols. 1892.
A Trying Patient. 1893. [Short stories.]
In Market Overt. A Novel. 1895.
The Disappearance of George Driffell. 1896.
Another's Burden. 1897.

(b) Other Writings

Poems. Cambridge, 1853.
Leaves from Lakeland. [1858.]
Furness Abbey and its Neighbourhood. Windermere, [1858].
A Handbook to the English Lakes. [1859.]
People, Places and Things. 1865.
The Lakes in Sunshine, being Photographic and Other Pictures of the Lake District of Westmoreland and North Lancashire with Descriptive Letterpress by James Payn. 2 vols. Windermere, 1867–70.
Lights and Shadows of London Life. 1867.
Maxims by a Man of the World. 1869.
Some Private Views, being Essays from the Nineteenth Century Review with some Occasional Articles from the Times. 1881.
Some Literary Recollections. 1884; 1885.
Holiday Tasks, being Essays written in Vacation Time. 1887.
Notes from the News [Illustrated London News]. 1890.
Gleams of Memory with some Reflections. 1894.
The Backwater of Life or Essays of a Literary Veteran. With a Biographical Introduction by Sir Leslie Stephen. 1899.

[From 1859 to 1874 Payn was editor of Chambers's Journ. and from 1882 to 1896 of Cornhill Mag.]

(c) Criticism

'Melville, Lewis.' Victorian Novelists. 1906.
Russell, G. W. E. Selected Essays. 1914.

SAMUEL PHILLIPS (1814–1854)

Caleb Stukely. A Novel. 3 vols. Edinburgh, 1844; 1854; 1862.
Letters from the Orient. By Countess Hahn-Hahn. Translated by the Author of Caleb Stukely. 1845 (The Novel Times, vol. i).
The Literature of the Rail. 1851.
Essays from the Times, being a Selection from the Literary Papers, which have appeared in that Journal. 1851. Ser. 2, 1854. Both sers. 2 vols. 1871.
Memoirs of the Duke of Wellington. 1852 (anon.); 1856. [Usually attrib. to Phillips.]
Guide to the Crystal Palace and Park. 1854.
The Portrait Gallery of the Crystal Palace. 1854.
We're All Low People there. 1854.

[Phillips was also editor of The Literary Gazette; for his career see the Times obituary, 17 Oct. 1854.]

WATTS PHILLIPS (1825–1874)

[See p. 606 below.]

THOMAS MAYNE REID (1818–1883)

(a) *Fiction*

The Rifle Rangers, or Adventures of an Officer in Southern Mexico. 2 vols. 1850; 1853; [1857]; [1871]; 1891, etc.

The Scalp Hunters, or Romantic Adventures in Northern Mexico. 3 vols. 1851; 1852; [1886]; 1892, etc.

English Family Robinson. 1851.

The Desert Home, or the Adventures of a Lost Family in the Wilderness. 1852; [1884].

The Boy Hunters, or Adventures in Search of a White Buffalo. 1852; [1884]; [1892].

The Young Voyageurs, or the Boy Hunters in the North. [1853]; [1884]; Paris, [1877].

The Forest Exiles, or the Perils of a Peruvian Family amid the Wilds of the Amazon. [1854.]

The White Chief. A Legend of Northern Mexico. 3 vols. 1855; [1871].

The Hunter's Feast, or Conversations around the Camp Fire. [1855]; [1860]; [1871].

The Quadroon, or a Lover's Adventures in Louisiana. 3 vols. 1856; Paris, 1858.

The Bush Boys, or the Adventures of a Cape Farmer and his Family in the Wild Karoos of Southern Africa. 1856; [1884].

The Young Jägers, or a Narrative of Hunting Adventures in Southern Africa. 1857; 1884; Paris, 1859.

The Plant Hunters, or Adventures among the Himalaya Mountains. 1857; Paris, 1859; [1884]; [1892].

The War Trail, or, the Hunt of the Wild Horse. 1857; Paris, 1861.

Ran away to Sea. 1858; 1884.

Oceola the Seminole. New York, 1858; 3 vols. 1859; [1861]; Paris, 1873; [1890].

The Boy Tar, or a Voyage in the Dark. 1859; Paris, 1861; [1884].

Bruin, or the Great Bear Hunt. 1860; Paris, 1863; [1884].

The Wild Huntress. 3 vols. 1861; 1865; 1871; Paris, [1875]; [1890].

The Maroon. A Novel. 3 vols. 1862; [1864]; Paris, [1874]; [1891].

The Tiger Hunter. 1863.

The Cliff Climbers, or the Lone Home in the Himalayas. [1864]; Paris, 1865; [1872]; [1888].

Ocean Waifs. 1864; [1871]; tr. French, Paris, [1869?].

The White Gauntlet. A Romance. 3 vols. [1864]; [1865]; Paris, 1865; [1872].

Lost Lenore. 3 vols. 1864; 1865; [1872]; [1888]; [1908]. [Pbd under the pseudonym 'Charles Beach.']

The Boy Slaves. [1865]; Paris, [1869]; [1872].

The Headless Horseman. A Strange Tale of Texas. 2 vols. 1866; [1868]; [1874]; [1888].

Afloat in the Forest. 1866; [1868].

The Bandolero, or a Marriage among the Mountains. 1866; [1867] (as The Mountain Marriage, or the Bandolero); [1873].

The Guerilla Chief and Other Tales. 1867; [1871]; [1891].

The Giraffe Hunters. 3 vols. 1867; [1868]; Paris, [1869].

The Child Wife. A Tale of the Two Worlds. 3 vols. 1868; 1888.

The Fatal Cord. A Tale of Backwood Retribution. [1869]; [1872] (with The Falcon Rover).

The Yellow Chief. A Romance of the Rocky Mountains. [1870.]

The Castaways. A Story of Adventure in the Wilds of Borneo. 1870; Paris, [1872].

The White Squaw and the Yellow Chief. 2 pts, [1871].

The Lone Ranche. A Tale of the 'Staked Plain.' 2 vols. 1871.

The Finger of Fate. A Romance. 2 vols. 1872; Paris, 1873.

The Death Shot. A Romance of Forest and Prairie. 3 vols. 1873; 1884.

Gaspar the Gaucho, A Tale of the Gran Chaco. Paris, [1874]; [1879]; [1884].

The Half Blood. 1875.

The Flag of Distress. A Story of the South Sea. 3 vols. 1876; 1879.

Gwen Wynn. A Romance of the Wye. 3 vols. 1877; 1889.

The Queen of the Lakes. A Romance of the Mexican Valley. 1879.

The Free Lances. A Romance of the Mexican Valley. 3 vols. 1881; [1888].

The Chase of Leviathan, or Adventures in the Ocean. Paris, 1882; 1885.

The Lost Mountain. A Tale of Sonora. Paris, [1883]; 1884.

The Land of Fire. A Tale of Adventure. [1884]; Paris, 1885.

The Vee Boers. A Tale of Adventure in Southern Africa. Paris, [1884]; [1885]; [1907].

The Pierced Heart and Other Stories. [1885.]

The Star of Empire. A Romance. 1886; [1888].

No Quarter. 3 vols. 1888.

The Naturalist in Siluria. 1889.

[Mayne Reid also translated 2 novels from the French of L. de Bellemare and edited The Cadet Button, by Frederick Whittaker.]

(b) *Other Writings*

Quadrupeds: what they are, and where found. A Book of Zoology for Boys. [1860]; 1867.

Odd People. Being a Popular Description of Singular Races of Men. 1860; Paris, 1862; [1884].

Croquet. 1863; 1865; 1866; New York, 1869.

Garibaldi Rebuked by one of his Best Friends. Being a Letter addressed to him by Captain Mayne Reid. 1864.

A Zigzag Journey through Mexico. [1872.]

Love's Martyr. A Tragedy. Perth, [1884].

Stories of Bold Deeds and Brave Men. By Mayne Reid and Others. Beeton's Annual, [1893].

A Dashing Dragoon, The Murat of the American Army (Philip Kearny). New York, 1913. [Mag. of History, extra no. 22.]

(c) Biography

Reid, Elizabeth. Mayne Reid. A Memoir of his Life. 1890.

—— Captain Mayne Reid: his Life and Adventures. 1900.

GEORGE WILLIAM McARTHUR REYNOLDS
(1814–1879)

(a) Fiction (dated)

The Youthful Impostor. 3 vols. Paris, 1835.

Grace Darling, or the Heroine of the Fern Islands. A Tale founded on Recent Facts. 1839.

The Appointment. A Tale. [In The Isis, I, 1839.]

The Last Day of a Condemned. By Victor Hugo. 1840. [From the French.]

Alfred, or the Adventures of a French Gentleman. [1840]; 1846.

Sister Anne, A Novel. By Paul de Kock. 1840. [From the French.]

The Drunkard's Progress. A Tale. 1841.

Master Timothy's Bookcase. 1842.

The Steam-Packet. A Tale of the River and the Ocean. 1844.

Alfred de Rosanne. 1846.

Faust. A Romance of the Second Empire. [1847.]

The Parricide, or the Youth's Career of Crime. 1847.

Mary Price. 2 vols. 1852.

Soldier's Wife. 1853.

Joseph Wilmot, or the Memoirs of a Man Servant. 2 vols. 1854.

Rosa Lambert. 1854.

Ciprina, or the Secrets of the Picture Gallery. Philadelphia, [1855].

Loves of the Harem. 1855; 1871.

Agnes, or Beauty and Pleasure. 2 vols. 1857; 1858.

Ellen Percy, or the Memoirs of an Actress. 2 vols. 1857.

Wagner the Werewolf. 1857; 1872.

The Empress Eugenie's Boudoir. 1857.

Canonbury House, or the Queen's Prophecy. 1870.

Bronze Statue, or the Virgin's Kiss. 1872.

(b) Fiction (undated)

[The bibliography of Reynolds is extremely obscure. It is impossible to trace the dates of pbn in many cases. His books were often issued in cheap edns of which no records are available.]

Agnes Evelyn

The Banker's Daughter.

Caroline of Brunswick.

Catherine Volman, or a Father's Revenge.

Coral Island or the Hereditary Curse.

Count Chrisoval.

The Countess of Lascelles.

The Days of Hogarth, or the Mysteries of Old London.

The Duke of Marchmont.

Edgar Montrose.

Eustace Quentin.

Gipsy Chief.

Isabella Vincent.

Karaman, or the Bandit Chief.

Kenneth, A Romance of the Highlands.

Leila.

Life in Paris.

Lord Saxondale.

Margaret, or the Discarded Queen.

Mary Middleton.

Massacre of Glencoe.

The Necromancer.

Omar Pasha or the Vizier's Daughter.

Pope Joan, or the Female Pontiff.

Robert Bruce.

Rose Foster.

The Rye House Plot.

The Seamstress.

The Soldier's Wife.

Venetian Trelawny.

Vivian Bertram.

Wallace; the Hero of Scotland.

The White Lady. A Romance of Love and War.

The Young Duchess.

(c) Other Writings

Songs of Twilight. By Victor Hugo. 1836. [From the French.]

Pickwick Abroad, or the Tour in France. 1839.

Modern Literature of France. 2 vols. 1839; 1841.

Robert Macaire in England. Illustrated by 'Phiz.' 3 vols. 1840.

Sequel to Don Juan. [1843]; 1845.

The French Self Instructor. 1846.

Mysteries of London. 2 vols. 1847. Ser. 2, 2 vols. n.d.

The Mysteries of the Court of London. 8 vols. 1849–56.

Mysteries of the Court of Naples. N.d.
Mary Stuart, Queen of Scots. N.d.

[Reynolds edited Reynolds's Miscellany, 1847 and Reynolds's Political Instructor, 1849–50.]

(d) Criticism

Mischievous Literature. Bookseller, July 1868. [A long article dealing with Reynolds and including an incomplete list of his works, without dates.]
G. W. M. Reynolds and Penny Fiction. TLS. 24 Jan. 1924.

LEITCH RITCHIE (1800?–1865)

(a) Fiction

Head-Pieces and Tale-Pieces by a Travelling Artist. 1826. [Short stories.]
Tales and Confessions. 1829.
The Game of Life. 2 vols. 1830.
Schinderhannes, the Robber of the Rhine. 1833; 1878 (as The Robber of the Rhine).
The Magician. 3 vols. 1836.
Wearyfoot Common. A Tale. 1855.
The New Shilling. 1857.
The Midnight Journey [by Ritchie] and Other Tales [by Mrs Crowe and others] reprinted from Chambers's Journal. 1871.

[Ritchie also contributed The Cheatrice Packman to The Club-Book, ed. A. Picken, 3 vols. 1831, and The Storm Lights of Anzasia to The Tale Book, Königsberg, 1859.]

(b) Other Writings

Friendship's Offering. 1824–44. [Ed. by Ritchie, 1842–4.]
The Romance of History: France. 3 vols. 1831; [1872] (with illustrations by T. Landseer).
The Library of Romance. 15 vols. 1833–5. [Ed. by Ritchie.]
Wanderings by the Seine. [1835?] (illustrated by J. M. W. Turner).
Beauty's Costume. A Series of Female Figures in the Dresses of All Times and Nations with Descriptions by Leitch Ritchie. 1838.
The Poetical Works of Thomas Pringle with a Sketch of his Life by Leitch Ritchie. 1838.
The Wye and its Associations. A Picturesque Ramble. 1839.
A View of the Opium Trade, Historical, Moral, and Commercial. 1843.
The British World in the East. 2 vols. 1846.
Winter Evenings. 2 vols. 1859.

[Ritchie also contributed the letterpress to 9 of Heath's Picturesque Annuals, 1832–40.]

EMMA ROBINSON

Richelieu in Love. 1844.
Whitefriars, or the Days of Charles II. 3 vols. [1844].

Whitehall, or the Days of Charles I. 3 vols. 1845.
Caesar Borgia. An Historical Romance. 3 vols. 1846.
Owen Tudor. An Historical Romance. 3 vols. 1849.
The Maid of Orleans. 1849.
The Gold Worshipper, or the Days we live in. A Future Historical Novel. 3 vols. 1851.
Westminster Abbey, or the Days of the Reformation. 3 vols. 1854.
The City Banker, or Love and Money. 3 vols. 1856.
Mauleverer's Divorce. 1858.
Which wins, Love or Money? 1862.
Cynthia Thorold. 3 vols. 1862.
Epithalamium in Honour of the Marriage of their Royal Highnesses the Prince and Princess of Wales. 1863.
Madeleine Graham. 3 vols. 1864.
Christmas at Old Court. 3 vols. 1864.
Dorothy Firebrace, or the Armourer's Daughter of Birmingham. 3 vols. 1865.
The Matrimonial Vanity Fair. 1868.

GEORGE HERBERT BUONAPARTE RODWELL (1800–1852)

[See p. 607 below.]

'JOHN RUFFINI' [GIOVANNI DOMENICO RUFFINI] (1807–1881)

(a) Fiction

Lorenzo Benoni, or Passages from the Life of an Italian, edited by a Friend. 1853.
Doctor Antonio. A Tale. 1855.
The Paragreens on a Visit to the Paris Universal Exhibition. 1856. [Illustrated by John Leech.]
Lavinia. 3 vols. 1860.
Vincenzo, or Sunken Rocks. 3 vols. 1863.
A Quiet Nook in the Jura. 1867.
Carlino. 1870.

(b) Biography and Criticism

Linaker, A. Ruffini. 1882.
Nota, A. Ruffini. 1899.

GEORGE AUGUSTUS HENRY SALA (1828–1896)

(a) Fiction

How I tamed Mrs Cruiser. By Benedict Cruiser. Illustrated by 'Phiz.' 1858.
The Baddington Peerage; who won and who wore it. A Story of the Best and Worst Society. Illustrated by 'Phiz.' 3 vols. 1860. [First pbd in H. Vizetelly's Illustrated Times.]
Make your Game, or the Adventures of the Stout Gentleman, the Slim Gentleman, and the Man with the Iron Chest. A Narrative of the Rhine and thereabouts. 1860.

The Seven Sons of Mammon. 3 vols. 1862. [First pbd in Temple Bar.]

The Two Prima Donnas. The Dumb Door Porter. 1862.

The Ship Chandler and Other Tales. 1862.

The Strange Adventures of Captain Dangerous. 3 vols. 1863.

The Perfidy of Captain Slyboots and Other Tales. 1863.

Quite Alone. 3 vols. 1864. [Finished by another hand; first ptd in All the Year Round.]

The Late M. D. — and Other Tales. [1870.]

The Story of the Count de Chambord. A Trilogy. 1873.

Stories with a Vengeance. [1883.] [By Sala and others.]

Dead Men tell no Tales, but Live Men do. Nine Stories. [1884.]

Mrs General Mucklestrap's Four Tall Daughters. [1887.]

Not a Friend in the World and Other Stories. [1890.]

Margaret Foster. A Dream within a Dream. 1897.

(b) Other Writings

The Great Exhibition. 1850.

Grand National, Historical and Chivalric Pantomime, ye Belle Alliance, or Harlequin Good Humour and ye Field of ye Clothe of Golde. [1856.] [Verse.]

A Journey due North; being Notes of a Residence in Russia in the Summer of 1856. 1858. [First pbd in Household Words.]

Gaslight and Daylight; with some London Scenes they shine upon. 1859.

Twice round the Clock, or the Hours of the Day and Night in London. [1859.] [First pbd in H. Vizetelly's The Welcome Guest.]

Looking At Life, or, Thoughts and Things. 1860.

Lady Chesterfield's Letters to her Daughter. 1860.

Dutch Pictures. With some Sketches in the Flemish Manner. 1861; 1883 (with Pictures done with a Quill).

Accepted Addresses. 1862.

Breakfast in Bed, or Philosophy between the Sheets, A Series of Indigestible Discourses. 1863.

After Breakfast, or Pictures done with a Quill. 2 vols. 1864. [First pbd in All the Year Round and Household Words.]

Robson [the actor]. A Sketch. 1864.

My Diary in America in the Midst of War. 2 vols. 1865. [First pbd in Daily Telegraph.]

William Hogarth: Essays on the Man, the Work, and the Time. 1866. [First pbd in Cornhill Mag.]

A Trip to Barbary by a Roundabout Route. 1866.

From Waterloo to the Peninsula. Four Months' Hard Labour in Belgium, Holland, Germany, Spain. 2 vols. 1867.

Banter. 1868.

The Complete Correspondence and Works of Charles Lamb. With an Essay on his Life and Genius by George Augustus Sala. Vol. I (all pbd), 1868.

The Battle of the Safes, or British Invincibles versus Yankee Ironclads. 1868.

Notes and Sketches of the Paris Exhibition. 1868.

Rome and Venice; with Other Wanderings in Italy, 1866–7. 1869.

Wat Tyler M.P. 1869. [An 'Operatic Extravaganza.']

Charles Dickens. An Essay. [1870.]

Under the Sun. Essays, mainly written in Hot Countries. 1872.

Papers Humorous and Pathetic, being Selections from the Works of George Augustus Sala, revised and abridged by the Author for Public Reading. 1872.

India and the Prince of Wales. [1875.]

Paris herself again, in 1878–9. 2 vols. 1879.

The Hats of Humanity historically, humorously, and aesthetically considered. [1880.]

America Revisited. 2 vols. 1882.

Living London. Echoes re-echoed. 1883.

Echoes of the Year 1883. [1884.]

A Journey due south. 1885. [First pbd in Daily Telegraph.]

Right round the World. [1887.] [First pbd in Daily Telegraph.]

Dublin Whiskey. An Essay. [1888.]

Things I have seen and People I have known. 2 vols. 1894.

London up to Date. 1894.

Brighton as I have known it. 1895.

The Life and Adventures of George Augustus Sala. 2 vols. 1895.

The Thorough Good Cook. A Series of Chats on the Culinary Art and Nine Hundred Recipes. [1895.]

[Sala also edited Temple Bar from 1860 to 1866.]

(c) Criticism

Friswell, J. H. Modern Men of Letters. 1870.

MARMION W. SAVAGE (1803–1872)

The Falcon Family, or Young Ireland. 1845; 1854.

The Bachelor of the Albany. 1848; ed. B. Dobrée, 1927.

My Uncle the Curate. A Novel. 3 vols. 1849.

Rueben Medlicott, or the Coming Man. 3 vols. 1852.

Sketches, Legal and Political. By the Rt. Hon. R. L. Sheil. 1855. [Ed. by Savage.]

Clover Cottage. 1856. [Tom Taylor's Comedietta, Nine Points of the Law, was founded on this.]

The Woman of Business, or the Lady and the Lawyer. A Novel. 3 vols. 1870.

ELIZABETH MISSING SEWELL (1815–1906)

(a) Fiction

Amy Herbert. By a Lady. 1844. [Ed. by W. Sewell.]

Gertrude. 1846.

Laneton Parsonage. A Tale for Children on the Practical Use of a Portion of the Church Catechism. 3 pts, 1846–8.

Margaret Percival. 1847.

The Sketches. Three Tales. 1848.

Was It A Dream? 1849.

Margaret Percival in America. A Tale. 1850.

The Earl's Daughter. 1850. [Ed. by W. Sewell.]

Stories Illustrative of the Lord's Prayer. 1851.

The Experience of Life. 1853.

Katharine Ashton. 1854.

Cleve Hall. 1855.

Ivors. 1856.

Ursula. A Tale. 1858.

Tales by the Author of Amy Herbert. 1858.

A Glimpse of the World. 1863.

Uncle Peter's Fairy Tale for the Nineteenth Century. 1869. [Ed. by E. M. Sewell.]

The Giant. Edited by the Author of 'Amy Herbert.' 1871.

(b) Other Writings

The Child's First History of Rome. 1849.

A Journal kept during a Summer Tour. 1852.

A First History of Greece. 1852.

History of the Early Church from the First Preaching of the Gospel to the Council of Nicea. 1859.

Impressions of Rome, Florence and Turin. 1862.

Ancient History of Egypt, Assyria and Babylonia. 1862.

The Principles of Education Drawn From Nature and Revelation and Applied to Female Education in the Upper Classes. 2 vols. 1865; rev. Mrs G. J. Chitty and L. H. M. Soulsby, 1914.

The Journal of a Home Life. 1867.

After Life. 1868. [A sequel to the preceding. The two vols. were pbd together in 1891 under title Home and After Life.]

Thoughts for the Age. 1870.

What can be done for our Young Servants? [1873.]

Some Questions of the Day. 1875.

Popular History of France to the Death of Louis XIV. 1876.

Notebooks of an Elderly Lady. 1881. [Rptd from Monthly Packet.]

Letters on Daily Life. 1885. [Rptd from Monthly Packet.]

Outline History of Italy From the Fall of the Western Empire. 1895 (preface by L. H. M. Soulsby).

Conversations between Youth and Age. 1896.

The Autobiography of Elizabeth M. Sewell. Edited by her Niece, Eleanor L. Sewell. 1907.

[Elizabeth Sewell also pbd devotional works and text-books.]

ELIZABETH SARA SHEPPARD (1830–1862)

Charles Auchester. A Memorial. 3 vols. 1853.

Counterparts, or the Cross of Love. 3 vols. 1854.

The Double Coronet. 2 vols. 1856.

Rumour. 3 vols. 1858.

Almost a Heroine. 3 vols. 1859.

[Elizabeth Sheppard also edited My First Season, by Beatrice Reynolds, 1855.]

JOHN PALGRAVE SIMPSON (1807–1887)

[See p. 608 below.]

CATHERINE SINCLAIR (1800–1864)

(a) Fiction

Modern Accomplishments, or the March of Intellect. 1836.

Modern Society, or the March of Intellect. Conclusion of 'Modern Accomplishments.' 1837.

Holiday House. A Series of Tales. Edinburgh, 1839; [1856] (as Holiday House, a Book for the Young), etc.

Shetland and the Shetlanders, or the Northern Circuit. 1840.

Scotland and the Scotch, or the Western Circuit. 2 pts, 1840; 1859 (rev.).

Modern Flirtations, or a Month at Harrowgate. 3 vols. Edinburgh, 1841.

Jane Bouverie, or Prosperity and Adversity. Edinburgh, 1840; 1855 (as Jane Bouverie and how she became an Old Maid).

The Journey of Life. 1847.

The Business of Life. 2 vols. 1848.

Sir Edward Graham, or Railway Speculators. 3 vols. 1849; 1854 (as The Mysterious Marriage, or Sir Edward Graham).

Lord and Lady Harcourt, or Country Hospitalities. 1850; [1856] (as Country Hospitalities, or Lord and Lady Harcourt).

Beatrice, or the Unknown Relatives. 3 vols. 1852. [Preface also rptd separately as a tract (Modern Superstition, 1857).]

Frank Vansittart, or the Model Schoolboys. 1853.

Lady Mary Pierrepoint. 1853.

London Homes; including the Murder Hole, the Drowning Dragon, the Priest and the Curate, Lady Mary Pierrepoint and Frank Vansittart. 6 pts, 1853.

The Priest and the Curate, or the Two Diaries. 1853.

Cross Purposes. A Novel. 3 vols. 1855; [1857] (as Porchester Abbey, or Cross Purposes, a Tale).

The Cabman's Holiday. A Tale. 1855.

Charlie Seymour, or the Good and Bad Choice. 1856 (4th edn).

The First of April Picture Letter. Edinburgh, 1864.

(b) Other Writings

Hill and Valley, or Hours in England and Wales. Edinburgh, 1838.

Scotch Courtiers and the Court. Edinburgh, 1842. [A poem on the Queen's visit to Scotland.]

The Lives of the Caesars, or the Juvenile Plutarch. [1847]; [1862] (abbreviated as Anecdotes of the Caesars).

The Kaleidoscope of Anecdotes and Aphorisms. 1851.

Popish Legends, or Bible Truths. 1852.

A Letter on the Principles of the Christian Faith. By Hannah Sinclair. 1852. [Ed. by Catherine Sinclair.]

Memoirs of the English Bible. [1858.]

Sketches and Stories of Wales and the Welsh. [1860] (3 edns).

Letters for Children with Pictures. 6 nos. Edinburgh, 1863–4. ['Hieroglyphic' stories in letter-form.]

FRANCIS EDWARD SMEDLEY (1818–1864)

Seven Tales by Seven Authors. 1849; 1850. [Ed. by Smedley, and includes his Mysteries of Redgrave Court.]

Frank Fairleigh, or Scenes from the Life of a Private Pupil. 1850 (illustrated by G. Cruikshank); 1854; 1866; 1878; 1892; 1904.

Lewis Arundel, or the Railroad of Life. Illustrated by 'Phiz.' 1852; [1855]; 2 vols. 1892; 1898.

The Fortunes of the Colville Family. A Christmas Story. 1853.

Harry Coverdale's Courtship and all that came of it. Illustrated by 'Phiz.' 1855.

Mirth and Metre. 1855. [With E. H. Yates.]

Gathered Leaves; being a Collection of the Poetical Writings of the Late F. E. Smedley. With a Memorial Preface by Edmund Yates. 1865.

Last Leaves from Beechwood. Ed. W. Brailsford, Enfield, 1867. [Poems.]

The 'Wicked Lady Ferrers.' A Legend of Markyate Cell in Flamstead; (being the Poem of F. E. Smedley entitled 'Maude Allinghame,' extracted from 'Mirth and Metre'). With an Introductory Note, forming an Attempt to solve the Mystery of 'The Lady Highwayman' by W. B. Gerish. Bishop's Stortford, 1911.

[Smedley also edited George Cruikshank's Mag. 1854. For criticism see S. M. Ellis, Mainly Victorian, [1925].]

MENELLA BUTE SMEDLEY (1820–1877)

[See p. 305 above.]

ALBERT RICHARD SMITH (1816–1860)

Beauty and the Beast. Illustrated by Alfred Crowquill. [1843?]

The Wassail Bowl. 2 vols. 1843. [Comic Sketches from the Wassail Bowl, 1848.]

The Adventures of Mr Ledbury and His Friend Jack Johnson. 3 vols. 1844; 1847.

The Adventures of Jack Holyday; with Something about his Sister. 1844.

The Fortunes of the Scattergood Family. 3 vols. 1845; 1853.

The Marchioness of Brinvilliers, the Poisoner of the Seventeenth Century. A Romance of Old Paris. Etchings by John Leech. 1846; 1856; 1860; 1886.

The Physiology of Evening Parties. [1846?]; 1849 (as The Natural History of Evening Parties); 1872.

The Man in the Moon. 5 vols. 1847–9.

The Natural History of Stuck-up People. 1847; 1872.

The Natural History of the Ballet Girl. 1847; 1872.

The Natural History of the Gent. 1847; 1872.

The Natural History of the Flirt. 1848; 1872.

The Natural History of the Idler upon Town. 1848; 1872.

The Struggles and Adventures of Christopher Tadpole at Home and Abroad. Illustrated by John Leech. 1848; 1853; 1864; 1897.

A Bowl of Punch. 1848.

A Pottle of Strawberries to Beguile a Short Journey or a Long Half-Hour. 1848.

The Pottleton Legacy. A Story of Town and Country Life. 1849 (illustrated by H. K. Browne).

Gavarni in London. Sketches of Life and Character; with Illustrative Essays by Popular Writers. Edited by Albert Smith. 1849; 1859 (as Sketches of London Life and Character).

A Month at Constantinople. 1850.

Comic Tales and Sketches. 1852.

Pictures of Life at Home and Abroad. 1852.

The Momentous Question. A Lay in Three Fyttes. 1852 (priv. ptd).
The Story of Mont Blanc. 1853; 1854 (enlarged); 1860 (with a life by E. H. Yates).
The English Hotel Nuisance. 1855.
To China and Back; being a Diary kept out and home. [1859.]
Wild Oats and Dead Leaves. 1860.
The London Medical Student. Edited by Albert Smith. 1861.

ALEXANDER SMITH (1829-1867)
[See p. 306 above.]

JOHN STERLING (1806-1844)
[See p. 680 below.]

ROBERT SMITH SURTEES (1803-1864)

(a) Collected Works

Sporting Novels; with All the Coloured Plates from the Original Editions. 6 vols. n.d. (priv. ptd); 6 vols. [1926].
The Novels of Surtees. 10 vols. 1930.

(b) Novels

[Surtees's novels were all anon.]

Jorrocks' Jaunts and Jollities, or the Hunting, Racing, Driving, Sailing, Eating, Eccentric and Extravagant Exploits of that Renowned Sporting Citizen, Mr John Jorrocks of St Boltoph Lane and Great Coram Street; with Illustrations by Phiz. 1838; 1839; 1843; 1869 (rev. and enlarged; illustrated by Henry Alken); 1874, etc. [First pbd in New Sporting Mag. July 1831-Sept. 1834.]
Handley Cross, or the Spa Hunt. A Sporting Tale. 3 vols. 1843 (no illustrations); 17 monthly pts, March 1853-Oct. 1854 (expanded as Handley Cross, or Mr Jorrocks's Hunt; illustrated by John Leech); 1854; 1888 (new illustrations); 1891; 1892, etc.
Hillingdon Hall, or the Cockney Squire. A Tale of Country Life. 3 vols. 1845; 1888 (with coloured illustrations), etc. [Portions first pbd in New Sporting Mag.]
Hawbuck Grange, or the Sporting Adventures of Thomas Scott Esq. 1847 (illustrated by 'Phiz'); [1888]; 1891; 1892, etc. [First pbd in Bell's Life, 1846-7.]
Mr Sponge's Sporting Tour. 13 monthly pts, 1853 (illustrated by John Leech); 1853; [1888]; 1892; 1893 (as Soapey Sponge's Sporting Tour), etc.
Ask Mamma, or the Richest Commoner in England. 13 monthly pts, 1858 (illustrated by John Leech); 1858; [1888]; 1892; 1903; 1904, etc.
Plain or Ringlets? 13 monthly pts, 1860 (illustrated by John Leech); 1860; [1888]; 1892; 1900, etc.

Mr Romford's Hounds. 12 monthly pts, 1865 (illustrated by John Leech and 'Phiz'); 1865 (as Mr Facey Romford's Hounds); 1892; 1911.

(c) Other Writings

The Horseman's Manual; being a Treatise on Soundness, the Law of Warranty and Generally on the Laws relating to Horses. 1831.
The Analysis of the Hunting Field; being a Series of Sketches of the Principal Characters that compose one; the Whole forming a Slight Souvenir of the Season 1845-6. 1846 (anon.; illustrated by Henry Alken); 1869, etc.

[Surtees also helped to found The New Sporting Magazine, which he edited 1831-6.]

(d) Biography and Criticism

Frith, W. P. John Leech. 1891. [Chs. xv, xvii.]
Neill, M. O. Novels by Surtees. Blackwood's Mag. April 1913.
—— The Author of Jorrocks. Blackwood's Mag. June 1924.
Cuming, E. D. Handley Cross behind the Scenes. Blackwood's Mag. Oct. 1924.
—— Robert Smith Surtees, Creator of Jorrocks. 1924.
Surtees, H. C. and Leighton, H. R. The Family of Surtees. Newcastle, 1926.
Robert Smith Surtees. TLS. 27 March 1930.
Steel, Anthony. Jorrocks's England. 1932.
Watson, Frederick. Robert Smith Surtees. A Critical Study. 1933.

JEMIMA, BARONESS TAUTPHOEUS, née MONTGOMERY (1807-1893)

The Initials. A Novel. 3 vols. 1850; 1853; 2 vols. Leipzig, 1854; 1858 (6th edn).
Cyrilla. A Tale. 3 vols. 1853; 2 vols. Leipzig, 1853; 1872; tr. German, Leipzig, 1854.
Quits. A Novel. 3 vols. 1857; 2 vols. Leipzig, 1858; 1860; 1864; tr. German, Leipzig, [1863].
At Odds. A Novel. 2 vols. 1863; 2 vols. Leipzig, 1863; 1873.

PHILIP MEADOWS TAYLOR (1808-1876)

(a) Novels

Confessions of a Thug. 3 vols. 1839; 1858; 1873, etc.; rptd 1917 (World's Classics).
Tippoo Sultaun. A Tale of the Mysore War. 3 vols. 1840; 1880.
Tara. A Mahratta Tale. 3 vols. 1863; 1874; 1881.
Ralph Darnell. 3 vols. 1865; 1879.
Seeta. 3 vols. 1872; 1880; 1890.
A Noble Queen. A Romance of Indian History. 3 vols. 1878; 1880; 1890.

(b) Other Writings

Sketches in the Deccan. 1837.
Letters from Meadows Taylor Esq. during the Indian Rebellion, 1857. 1857 (priv. ptd).
The People of India. 6 vols. 1868–72.
A Student's Manual of the History of India from the Earliest Period to the Present. 1870; 1871; 1896.
The Story of my Life. Edited by His Daughter. Edinburgh, 1877; 1878; 1920 (with introduction and notes).

THOMAS ADOLPHUS TROLLOPE (1810–1892)

(a) Fiction

La Beata. A Tuscan Romeo and Juliet. 2 vols. 1861.
Marietta. A Novel. 2 vols. 1862.
Giulio Malatesta. A Novel. 3 vols. 1863.
Beppo the Conscript. A Novel. 2 vols. 1864.
Lindisfarne Chase. A Novel. 3 vols. 1864.
Gemma. A Novel. 3 vols. 1866.
Artingale Castle. 3 vols. 1867.
Leonora Casaloni. A Novel. 2 vols. 1868.
The Dream Numbers. A Novel. 3 vols. 1868.
The Garstangs of Garstang Grange. 3 vols. 1869.
A Siren. 3 vols. 1870.
Durnton Abbey. A Novel. 3 vols. 1871.
The Stilwinches of Combe Mavis. A Novel. 3 vols. 1872.
Diamond cut Diamond, a Story of Tuscan Life and Other Stories. 2 vols. 1875.
A Family Party in the Piazza of St Peter and Other Stories. 3 vols. 1877.

(b) Other Writings

A Summer in Brittany. Ed. F. Trollope, 2 vols. 1840.
A Summer in Western France. Ed. F. Trollope, 2 vols. 1841.
Impressions of a Wanderer in Italy, Switzerland, France, Spain. 1850.
The Girlhood of Catherine de Medici. 1856.
A Decade of Italian Women. 2 vols. 1859.
Tuscany in 1849 and in 1859. 1859.
Filippo Strozzi: a History of the Last Days of the Old Italian Liberty. 1860.
Paul the Pope [Paul V] and Paul the Friar [Paolo Sarpi]. A Story of an Interdict. 1861.
A Lenten Journey in Umbria and the Marches. 1862.
History of the Commonwealth of Florence to 1531. 4 vols. 1865.
The Papal Conclaves as they were and as they are. 1876.
A Peep Behind the Scenes at Rome. 1877. [First pbd in part in The Standard.]
Story of the Life of Pius IX. 2 vols. 1877.
Sketches from French History. 1878. [First pbd in St Paul's Mag.]

Homes and Haunts of Italian Poets. By F. E. Trollope and T. A. Trollope. 1881.
What I Remember. 3 vols. 1887–9.
The General Election. A Working Man's Advice. 1892.

ELIOT WARBURTON (1810–1852)

[See p. 727 below.]

SAMUEL WARREN (1807–1877)

(a) Collected Works

The Works of Samuel Warren. 5 vols. 1854–5.

(b) Fiction

Passages from the Diary of a Late Physician. With Notes and Illustrations by the Editor. 2 vols. New York, 1831 (pirated); 2 vols. 1832 (anon.; vol. III, signed, 1838); 1841; 1842; 1848; 1853; 1864; [1884]. [First pbd in Blackwood's Mag. 1830–7.]
Adventures of an Attorney in Search of Practice. 1839.
Ten Thousand a Year. 3 vols. 1841; 1845; 1849; 1854; 1855; [1884]; [1887]; 1899. [First pbd in Blackwood's Mag.; dramatized by R. B. Peake, [1886].]
Now and then. 1847.

(c) Other Writings

A Popular and Practical Introduction to Law Studies. 1835; 1845 (rewritten and enlarged); 2 vols. 1863 (rewritten and enlarged).
Select Extracts from Blackstone's Commentaries. 1837.
The Opium Question. 1840.
The Moral, Social and Professional Duties of Attorneys and Solicitors. 1848.
Letter to the Queen on a Late Court Martial (Captain G. Douglas). 1850.
The Lily and the Bee. An Apologue of the Crystal Palace. 1851; 1854 (rev.).
The Queen or the Pope? Edinburgh, 1851 (6 edns).
A Manual of the Parliamentary Election Law. 1852.
The Intellectual and Moral Development of the Present Age. Edinburgh, 1853 (2nd edn).
The Law and Practice of Election Committees. 1853.
Miscellanies, Critical, Imaginative and Juridical, contributed to Blackwood's Magazine. 2 vols. 1855.
An Abridgement of Blackstone's Commentaries. 1855; 1856.
Labour: its Rights, Difficulties, Dignity and Consolations. 1856.

EDWIN WAUGH (1817–1890)

[See p. 311 above.]

CHARLES WHITEHEAD (1804–1862)
[See p. 312 above.]

GEORGE JOHN WHYTE-MELVILLE
(1821–1878)

(a) Collected Works

The Works of G. J. Whyte-Melville. Ed. Sir H. Maxwell, 24 vols. 1898–1902.
The Works of G. J. Whyte-Melville. 25 vols. n.d. (Library edn).

(b) Fiction

Captain Digby Grand. An Autobiography. 2 vols. 1853.
Tilbury Nego, or Passages in the Life of an Unsuccessful Man. 1854.
General Bounce, or the Lady and the Locusts. 2 vols. 1855.
Kate Coventry. An Autobiography. 1856.
The Interpreter. A Tale of the War. 1858.
Holmby House. 2 vols. 1860.
Market Harborough, or how Mr Sawyer went to the Shires. 1861.
Good for Nothing, or all Down Hill. 2 vols. 1861.
The Queen's Maries. 2 vols. 1862.
The Gladiators. A Tale of Rome and Judaea. 3 vols. 1863.
The Brookes of Bridlemere. 3 vols. 1864.
Cerise, a Tale of the Last Century. 3 vols. 1866.
'Bones and I,' or the Skeleton at Home. 1868.
The White Rose. 3 vols. 1868.
M. or N. 2 vols. 1869.
Sarchedon. A Tale of the Great Queen. 3 vols. 1871.
Contraband, or a Losing Hazard. 2 vols. 1871.
Satanella. A Story of Punchestown. 2 vols. 1872.
Uncle John. 3 vols 1874.
Katerfelto. A Story of Exmoor. 1875.
Sister Louise, or the Story of a Woman's Repentance. 1876.
Rosine. 1877.
Roy's Wife. A Novel. 2 vols. 1878.
Black but Comely, or the Adventures of Jane Lee. 3 vols. 1879.

(c) Other Writings

Horace translated into English Verse. 1850.
The Arab's Ride to Cairo. A Legend of the Desert. Edinburgh, [1857?]. [Verse.]
Songs and Verses. 1869; rptd 1924.
The True Cross. A Legend of the Church. 1873. [Verse.]
Riding Recollections. 1878.
The Bones at Rothwell. A Lecture. [Rothwell, 1903.]
Hunting Poems. 1911

(d) Biography and Criticism

'Melville, Lewis.' Victorian Novelists. 1906.
Ellis, S. M. Mainly Victorian. [1925.]
Fortescue, Sir J. George Whyte-Melville. [In The Eighteen-Sixties, Royal Soc. Lit. 1932.]

WILLIAM GORMAN WILLS (1828–1891)
[See p. 609 below.]

MRS HENRY WOOD, née ELLEN PRICE
(1814–1887)

(a) Fiction

Danesbury House. Glasgow, 1860.
East Lynne. 3 vols. 1861; 1862; 1888; 1895; 1903; [1906]; 1907, etc.
The Golden Casket. Ed. M. Howitt, [1861]. [Contains The Elchester College Boys by Mrs Henry Wood.]
Mrs Halliburton's Troubles. 3 vols. 1862.
The Channings. 3 vols. 1862.
The Shadow of Ashlydyat. 3 vols. 1863.
The Foggy Night at Offord. A Christmas Gift for the Lancashire Fund. 1863.
Verner's Pride. 3 vols. 1863.
William Allair, or Running away to Sea. 1864.
Lord Oakburn's Daughters. 3 vols. 1864.
Oswald Cray. 3 vols. Edinburgh, 1864.
Trevlyn Hold, or Squire Trevlyn's Heir. 3 vols. 1864.
Mildred Arkell. A Novel. 3 vols. 1865.
St Martin's Eve. A Novel. 3 vols. 1866.
Elster's Folly. A Novel. 3 vols. 1866.
Lady Adelaide's Oath. 3 vols. 1867; 1889 (as Lady Adelaide).
A Life's Secret. 2 vols. 1867.
Orville College. A Story. 2 vols. 1867.
Mixed Sweets from Routledge's Annual. By Mrs Henry Wood and Others. [1867.] [Prose and verse.]
Castle Wafer, or the Plain Gold Ring. New York, [1868?].
The Red Court Farm. A Novel. 3 vols. 1868.
Anne Hereford. A Novel. 3 vols. 1868.
Roland Yorke. A Novel. 3 vols. 1869. [A sequel to The Channings.]
Bessy Rane. A Novel. 3 vols. 1870.
George Canterbury's Will. A Novel. 3 vols. 1870.
Dene Hollow. A Novel. 3 vols. 1871.
Within the Maze. A Novel. 3 vols. 1872.
The Master of Greylands. 3 vols. 1873.
Johnny Ludlow. 6 sers. (12 vols.) 1874–89.
Told in the Twilight. 3 vols. 1875. [Contains Parkwater and 9 shorter stories.]
Bessy Wells. 1875.
Adam Grainger. A Tale. 1876.
Edina. A Novel. 3 vols. 1876.
Parkwater, with Four Other Tales. 1876. [First pbd in Told in the Twilight, 1875.]

Our Children. 1876.

Pomeroy Abbey. A Romance. 3 vols. 1878.

Court Netherleigh. A Novel. 3 vols. 1881.

About Ourselves. 1883.

Lady Grace and Other Stories. 3 vols. 1887.

The Story of Charles Strange. A Novel. 3 vols. 1888.

Featherston's Story. 1889.

The Unholy Wish and Other Stories. 1890.

Edward Burton. Boston, 1890.

Summer Stories from the Argosy. By Mrs Henry Wood and Other Authors. 2 pts. 1890.

The House of Halliwell. A Novel. 3 vols. 1890.

Ashley and Other Stories. 1897.

(b) Biography and Criticism

Wood, C. W. Memorials of Mrs Henry Wood. 1894.

Sergeant, A. Mrs Henry Wood. [In Women Novelists of Queen Victoria's Reign, 1897.]

Elwin, M. Victorian Wallflowers. 1934.

CHARLOTTE MARY YONGE (1823–1901)

(a) Collected Works

Novels and Tales. New Editions. 15 vols. 1879–80.

(b) Selected Fiction

Abbeychurch, or Self-Control and Self-Conceit. 1844; 1872.

Scenes and Characters, or Eighteen Months at Beechcroft. 1847.

Kenneth, or the Rearguard of the Grand Army. 1850.

The Two Guardians, or Home in this World. 1852; 1861 (4th edn).

The Heir of Redclyffe. 2 vols. 1853; 1854 (5th edn); 1868 (17th edn), etc.

The Herb of the Field. 1853; 1887. [First pbd in Mag. for the Young.]

The Little Duke, or Richard the Fearless. 1854; 1857; 1891, etc.

The Castle Builders, or the Deferred Confirmation. 1854; 1859.

Heartsease, or the Brother's Wife. 1854; 1862.

The Lances of Lynwood. 1855; 1857; 1894 (abridged).

The History of Sir Thomas Thumb. 1855; 1859.

The Daisy Chain, or Aspirations. A Family Chronicle. 2 vols. 1856; 1868 (9th edn), etc.

Dynevor Terrace. 2 vols. 1857; 1858; 1860.

Hopes and Fears, or Scenes from the Life of a Spinster. 2 vols. 1860; 1861.

The Pigeon Pie. 1860; 1861.

The Stokesley Secret. 1861; 1862; rptd 1892 (with Countess Kate).

Countess Kate. 1862.

The Trial: More Links of the Daisy Chain. 1864; 1868 (4th edn); 2 vols. 1870.

The Clever Woman of the Family. 2 vols. 1865; 1867.

The Dove in the Eagle's Nest. 2 vols. 1866; 1870.

The Six Cushions. 1867; 1869.

The Pillars of the House, or under Wode under Rode. 4 vols. 1873; 2 vols. 1875.

Burnt Out. A Story for Mothers' Meetings. 1879; 1880.

Bye-words. A Collection of Tales Old and New. 1880.

Frank's Debt. 1881; 1882.

Unknown to History. A Story of the Captivity of Mary of Scotland. 2 vols. 1882; 1884.

Chantry House. 2 vols. 1886; 1887.

More Bye-words. 1890. [Tales and poems.]

The Patriots of Palestine. A Story of the Maccabees. 1898.

[The above represents less than a quarter of Charlotte M. Yonge's pbd fiction.]

(c) Other Writings

History of Christian Names. 2 vols. 1863; 1884.

A Book of Golden Deeds of all Times and all Lands. 1864; 1871, etc.

Historical Dramas. 1864.

Cameos from English History. 1868; 2 vols. 1871.

Musings over the Christian Year and Lyra Innocentium, together with a Few Gleanings of Recollections of the Rev. J. Keble, gathered by Several Friends. 1871.

Life of J. C. Patteson, Missionary Bishop of the Melanesian Islands. 2 vols. 1873; 2 vols. 1878 (6th edn).

Eighteen Centuries of Beginnings of Church History. 2 vols. 1876; 1876.

Life of H.R.H. the Prince Consort. 1890.

John Keble's Parishes: a History of Hursley and Otterbourne. 1898.

[Charlotte M. Yonge also pbd many historical and religious schoolbooks, sometimes as 'Aunt Charlotte,' as well as miscellaneous leaflets, etc. She edited the following periodicals: The Monthly Packet, 1851–99; Monthly Papers of Sunday Teaching, 1860–75; Mothers in Council, 1890.]

(d) Biography and Criticism

Coleridge, C. R. Charlotte Mary Yonge: her Life and Letters. 1903. [Includes bibliography.]

Bailey, S. Charlotte Mary Yonge. Cornhill Mag. Aug. 1934.

Cruse, A. The World of Charlotte Yonge. [In The Victorians and their Books, 1935.]

S. J. L.

VI. THE LATER NINETEENTH CENTURY NOVELISTS

LEWIS CARROLL, HARDY, STEVENSON, GISSING, MOORE, KIPLING

'LEWIS CARROLL,' i.e. CHARLES LUTWIDGE DODGSON (1832–1898)

(1) BIBLIOGRAPHIES

Collingwood, S. D. The Life and Letters of Lewis Carroll. 1898.
Williams, S. H. A Bibliography of the Writings of Lewis Carroll. 1924; Oxford, 1931 (rev. in collaboration with F. Madan). [Addenda, by F. Madan, 1935.]
Parrish, M. L. List of the Writings of Lewis Carroll collected by Morris L. Parrish. 1928. [Supplementary List, 1933.]
Catalogue of an Exhibition at Columbia University to commemorate the One Hundredth Anniversary of the Birth of Lewis Carroll. New York, 1932.
Livingston, F. V. The Harcourt Armory Collection of Lewis Carroll in the Harvard College Library. Cambridge, U.S.A. 1932 (priv. ptd).
Madan, F. and Hartley, H. Lewis Carroll Centenary Exhibition Catalogue. 1932.

(2) BOOKS PUBLISHED UNDER THE NAME 'LEWIS CARROLL'

Alice's Adventures in Wonderland. 1865 (reissued New York, 1866); 1866; 1867; 1869 (bis), etc.
Through the Looking-Glass. 1872. [Frequently rptd both separately and with Alice's Adventures in Wonderland.]
[Plays and charades were made from both books, and verses set to music, 1870, 1880, 1890.]
To all Child Readers of 'Alice in Wonderland.' Christmas Greeting. 1871.
Easter Greeting to Every Child who Loves 'Alice.' 1876; 1880. [5 or more edns; rptd in later edns of Through the Looking-Glass.]
Jabberwocky. Cambridge, 1881. [From Through the Looking-Glass; in English and Latin. Latin version by A. A. Vansittart.]
[Circular sent to hospitals and other institutions offering the 'Alice' books, 1890.]
[List of Institutions to which the 'Alice' books were to be offered, 1890.]
[Advertisement asking that Through the Looking-Glass be returned to be sent to Hospitals, Mechanics' Institutes, etc. 1893.]

[Circular requesting the return of the 60,000th issue of Through the Looking-Glass to be exchanged for the next issue, 1894.]
Alice's Adventures Under Ground. 1886; New York, 1932. [Facs. of original MS from which Alice in Wonderland was rewritten and enlarged.]
The Nursery Alice with text adapted to Nursery Readers. 1889; 1890, etc.
Alice in Wonderland adapted for very little children. 1903.
Phantasmagoria and Other Poems. 1869, etc. [Rptd in Rhyme? and Reason? 1883.]
Some Popular Fallacies about Vivisection. 1875. [Rptd from Fortnightly Rev.]
The Hunting of the Snark. 1876, etc. [Rptd in Rhyme? and Reason? 1883, and in The Hunting of the Snark and Other Poems, 1903.]
Love Among the Roses. [Broadside poem, dated 3 Jan. 1878.]
A Charade. [Written with a cyclostyle, dated 8 April 1878.]
Word-Links, A Game for two players. [Leaflet written with a cyclostyle, dated 11 April 1878. This developed into the Doublets, ptd in Vanity Fair, 1879–80.]
Doublets, A Word Puzzle. 1879. [A New Puzzle (29 March); Doublets (19 April); Doublets already Set (3 May) issued separately from the types of Vanity Fair.]
Doublets. 1879 (first complete edn); 1880 (bis).
New Method of Scoring for Doublets. 1880.
[Two circulars, asking for a list of Shakespeare's Plays suitable for girls, and suggesting an expurgated edn of Shakespeare for girls, 1882.]
Dreamland. [1882.] [Song with words composed especially for it by 'Lewis Carroll.']
Rhyme? and Reason? 1883. [Phantasmagoria, Hunting of the Snark, Other Poems.]
Christmas Greeting from a Fairy to a Child. 1884. [Rptd in Phantasmagoria, 1889, and other collections of poems.]
Profits of Authorship. 1884.
A Tangled Tale. 1885. [10 knots rptd from Monthly Packet, April 1880–Nov. 1884. These and the answers were also issued separately.]
The Game of Logic. 1886; 1887 (with variations). [The dedication 'To my Child Friend' was issued separately in 1875.]
Children in Theatres. [1887.] [Rptd from St James's Budget, 23 July 1887.]
Circular Billiards, For Two Players. 1889, etc.
Sylvie and Bruno. 1889. Sylvie and Bruno Concluded. 1893. The Story of Sylvie and Bruno. 1904; 1914. [Portions referring to Sylvie and Bruno, ed. E. H. Hodgson.]

The Stranger Circular. [1890.] [Protesting against letters being addressed to him in the name of 'Lewis Carroll.']

Eight or Nine Wise Words about Letter-Writing. 1890; 1897, etc.

The Wonderful Postage-Stamp Case. [To accompany Eight or Nine Wise Words.] [1890], etc. [Issued in a pink envelope, at least in 3 forms.]

[Circular asking for addresses of stationers likely to sell the Wonderful Postage-Stamp Case, 1890.]

Syzygies. A Word Puzzle. 1891. [Rptd from The Lady, 23, 30 July.]

Syzygies. 1893 (priv. ptd).

Syzygies and Lanrick. A Word Puzzle and a Game for Two Players. 1893.

A Logical Paradox. [Off-print from Mind, July 1894.]

Fascinating Mental Recreation for the Young. Symbolic Logic. November, 1895. Part I. [The advance notice of Symbolic Logic. The 2nd issue, May 1896, contains additional paragraphs and lacks the Postscript.]

Symbolic Logic. 1896 (3 edns); 1897. [Accompanied by an envelope containing 9 counters, 4 red, 5 grey.]

Three Sunsets and Other Poems. 1898.

Lewis Carroll Picture Book. Ed. S. D. Collingwood, 1899.

Feeding the Mind. 1907. [Rptd from Harper's Mag. May 1906.]

Six Letters by Lewis Carroll. 1924.

Some Rare Carrolliana. Ed. S. H. Williams, 1924 (priv. ptd).

Novelty and Romancement. Boston, 1925. [Rptd from The Train, 1856.]

Collected Verses of Lewis Carroll. Ed. J. F. McDermott, 1929.

[Inscribed in Hunting of the Snark given to Marion Terry.] Edinburgh, 1930.

New Lewis Carroll Letters written to Harry Furniss. Ed. D. Furniss, Pearson's Mag., Christmas no., 1930.

To Mab. [Inscribed in Alice, 1866, given to Marion Terry.] Birmingham, 1931.

The Lewis Carroll Book. Ed. Richard Herrick, 1931.

La Guida di Bragia. The Queen, 18 Nov. 1931.

A Charade. [Dedicated to Marion Terry.] Birmingham, 1932.

Two Letters to Marion. Bristol, 1932.

The Rectory Umbrella and Mischmasch. Ed. F. Milner, 1932.

Further Nonsense in Verse and Prose. Ed. Langford Reed, 1932.

The Collected Verse of Lewis Carroll. 1932.

For the Train. Five Poems and a Tale. Being Contributions to the 'Train,' 1856–1857. Ed. H. J. Schonfield, 1932.

A Selection from the Letters of Lewis Carroll to his Child-Friends. Ed. E. M. Hatch, 1933.

Logical Nonsense: the Works of Lewis Carroll. Ed. P. C. Blackburn and L. White, 1935.

(3) BOOKS PUBLISHED UNDER THE NAME C. L. DODGSON OR UNSIGNED

(a) Mathematical Works

A Syllabus of Plane Algebraical Geometry. Part I. 1860.

Notes on the first two books of Euclid. 1860.

Notes on the first part of Algebra. 1861.

The Formulae of Plane Trigonometry. 1861.

[Letter to Mathematical Friends.] 1862.

Enunciations of the Propositions and Corollaries [of] Euclid, with questions. Books I and II. 1863.

General List of Mathematical Subjects and Cycle for working Examples. 1863.

Guide to the Mathematical Student in Reading, Reviewing and Working Examples. Part I. Pure Mathematics. 1864.

Condensation of Determinants. 1866.

Elementary Treatise on Determinants. 1867.

Fifth Book of Euclid treated Algebraically. 1868; 1874.

Algebraical Formulae for Responsions. 1868.

Algebraical Formulae and Rules. 1870.

Symbols, etc. to be used in Euclid Books I and II. 1872.

Number of Propositions in Euclid. 1872.

Enunciations. Euclid Books I to IV. 1873.

Preliminary Algebra, and Euclid Book V. 1874.

Euclid. Book V. Proved Algebraically. 1874.

Examples in Arithmetic. 1874.

Euclid. Books I and II. 1875 (not pbd); 1882.

Syllabus of Plane Geometry. Euclid books I to IV. 1875.

Responsions of Hilary Term. 18 April 1877.

Euclid and his Modern Rivals. 1879–85. [Appendix IV, (1879), ptd separately, 1881. Supplement to Euclid and his Modern Rivals, 1885.]

Analysis of Responsions Lists, 1873–1881. 1882.

Notes on Questions. 1885.

Divisibility by Seven. 1885.

Curiosa Mathematica. Part I. New Theory of Parallels. 1888; 1890 (3rd edn).

Curiosa Mathematica. Part II. Pillow Problems. 1894.

Logical Nomenclature. Desiderata. June, 1895.

(b) Other Writings

[Examination Questions of the Pickwick Club.] 1857.

List of Photographs. 1860.

Rules for Court Circulars. 1860; 1862.

Endowment of the Greek Professorship. 1861.

Index to In Memoriam. 1862; 1878. [Notice on Concordance to In Memoriam, 1881.]

Croquet Castles for Five Players. 1863.

Examination Statute. 1864.

New Examination Statute. 1864.

American Telegrams. Summary. 1865.

New Method of Evaluation as applied to π. 1865.

Dynamics of a Particle with an excursus on the new method of Evaluation as applied to π. 1865.

Castle-Croquet for Four Players. 1866.

Elections to the Hebdomadal Council. 1866.

Deserted Parks. 1867.

Offer of the Clarendon Trustees. 1868.

The New Belfry. 1872.

Vision of the Three T's. 1873.

Blank Check. 1874.

Facts, Figures and Fancies. 1874. [Elections to the Hebdomadal Council, Deserted Parks, Offer of the Clarendon Trustees.]

Notes by an Oxford Chiel. 1874 (bis). [New Method of Evaluation, Dynamics of a Particle, Elections to the Hebdomadal Council, Deserted Parks, Offer of the Clarendon Trustees, The New Belfry, and Vision of the Three T's. 2nd edn adds The Blank Check.]

Enigma. 1866.

Explanation of the Enigma. 1866.

Telegraph Cypher. 1868.

Alphabet Cypher. 1868.

Objections Submitted to the Governing Body of Christ Church, Oxford, against alterations in the Quadrangle. 1873.

Discussion of the Various Methods of Procedure in Conducting Elections. 1873.

Suggestions as to the Best Method of taking Votes. 1874.

Method of taking Votes on more than Two Issues. 1876.

Professorship of Comparative Philology. 4 February, 1876. [Supplementary Letter, 12 Feb.; Supplementary Letter, 14 Feb. 1876.]

Fame's Penny Tribute. 1876.

Letter and Questions to Hospitals. 1876.

[Poem to Rachel Daniel, in Garland of Rachel, 1881.]

On Catching Colds. 1881.

[Two circulars, Purifying the Stage, and The School of Dramatic Art, 1881.]

Mischmasch. 1882.

Rules for Reckoning Postage. 1883.

Lawn Tennis Tournament. 1883.

Parliamentary Elections. 1884.

Principles of Parliamentary Representation. 1884; 1885. [Supplement, and Postscript, 1885.]

Twelve Months in a Curatorship. 1884. [Supplement, and Postscript, 1884.]

Proposed Procuratorial Cycle. 24 October. 1885.

Procuratorial Cycle to be voted. 10 November. 1885.

Suggestions as to the Elections of Proctors. 1885; 1886.

Three Years in a Curatorship. 1886.

First Paper on Logic. 1886.

Observations on Mr Sampson's New Proposal. 1886.

Remarks on Mr Sampson's Proposal. 1886.

Questions in Logic. 1887.

Second, Third, Fourth, Fifth, Sixth Papers on Logic. 1887.

Special Meeting of the Common Room. 1889.

[Registration of parcels.] 1890.

Postal Problem. 1891. [Supplement, 1891; Supplement with blanks, 1891.]

Curiossima Curatoria. 1892.

Seventh, Eighth, Ninth Papers on Logic. 1892.

Notes on Eighth and Ninth Papers on Logic. 1892.

[Circular on resignation of Curatorship.] 1892.

Unparliamentary Words. 1892.

Second Hand Books. 1893.

Disputed Points in Logic. April, May. 1894.

Logical Puzzle. Sept. 1894.

[Circular for Mechanics' Institute.] 1894.

Theorem in Logic. 1894.

Symbolic Logic. 1894. [Conclusions, 1894. Questions, i and ii, 1894.]

[Seven printed Diagrams. Quadriliteral, Quinqueliteral Diagrams.] 1894.

What the Tortoise said to Achilles. Mind, Dec. 1894.

Resident Women-Students. 1896.

Tour in 1867. Ed. M. L. Parrish, 1929.

(4) BIOGRAPHY AND CRITICISM

Collingwood, S. D. The Life and Letters of Lewis Carroll. 1898.

Bowman, I. The Story of Lewis Carroll told for Young People by the Real Alice. 1899.

Furniss, H. Recollections of Lewis Carroll. Strand Mag. Jan. 1908.

Moses, B. Lewis Carroll in Wonderland and at Home: the Story of his Life. New York, 1910.

Parry, E. A. The Early Writings of Lewis Carroll. Cornhill Mag. April 1924.

Milner, F. Mathematics and Fun. St Nicholas, Nov. 1927.

Arnold, E. M. Reminiscences of Lewis Carroll. Atlantic Monthly, June 1929.

De la Mare, W. Lewis Carroll. [In The Eighteen-Eighties, Royal Soc. Lit. 1930.]

—— Lewis Carroll. 1932.

Reed, Langford. The Life of Lewis Carroll. 1932.

De Sousmarez, F. B. Early Theatricals at Oxford; with Prologues by Lewis Carroll. Nineteenth Century, cxi, 1932.

Leslie, S. Lewis Carroll and the Oxford Movement. London Mercury, xxviii, 1933.

Empson, W. Some Versions of Pastoral. 1935.

Fontenoy, H. Présentation de Lewis Carroll. Nouvelle Revue Française, Aug. 1935.

Ayres, H. M. Carroll's Alice. New York, 1936.   F. V. L.

THOMAS HARDY (1840–1928)

(1) Bibliographies

Danielson, H. The First Editions of the Writings of Thomas Hardy and their Values. A Bibliographical Handbook. 1916.

Webb, A. P. A Bibliography of the Works of Thomas Hardy, 1865–1915. 1916.

Lane, J. Thomas Hardy. A Bibliography of First Editions, 1865–1922. [Appended to L. Johnson, The Art of Thomas Hardy, 1923.]

(2) Collected Works

Thomas Hardy's Works. 18 vols. 1895–1913.

The Works of Thomas Hardy in Prose and Verse. With Prefaces and Notes. 23 vols. 1912–3. (Wessex edn.)

The Works of Thomas Hardy. 37 vols. 1919–20. (Mellstock edn.)

(3) Fiction

Desperate Remedies. A Novel. 3 vols. 1871 (anon.); 1889; 1892, etc.

Under the Greenwood Tree. A Rural Painting of the Dutch School. 2 vols. 1872 (anon.); 1876; 1878; 1891; 1892; 1893; 1902, etc.; tr. French, Paris, 1923.

A Pair of Blue Eyes. A Novel. 3 vols. 1873; 1877; 1884; 1888; 1890; 1892; 1893, etc. [First pbd in Tinsley's Mag. xi, xii, 1872–3.]

Far from the Madding Crowd. 2 vols. 1874 (bis); 1877; 1878; 1882; 1884; 1889; 1892; 1893; 1899, etc.; ed. C. J. Weber, New York, 1937; tr. French, Paris, 1901. [First pbd, anon., in Cornhill Mag. xxix, xxx, 1874, dramatic version (with Comyns Carr), Prince of Wales' Theatre, Liverpool, 27 Feb. 1882.]

The Hand of Ethelberta. 2 vols. 1876; 1877; 1878; 1882; 1888; 1890; 1892; 1893, etc. [First pbd in Cornhill Mag. xxxii, xxxiii, 1875–6.]

The Return of the Native. 3 vols. 1878; 1879; 1880; 1884; 1890; 1893, etc.; tr. French, Paris, [1923]. [First pbd in Belgravia, xxxiv–xxxvii, 1878.]

The Trumpet-Major. A Tale. 3 vols. 1880; 1881; 1887; 1890; 1892; 1893, etc.; ed. J. H. Fowler, 1929 (abridged by C. F.

Knox). [First pbd in Good Words, Jan.–Dec. 1880.]

A Laodicean, or the Castle of the De Stancys. A Story of To-Day. 3 vols. 1881; 1882; 1890 (bis); 1893, etc. [First pbd in Harper's Mag., European edn, i–iii, 1880–1.]

Two on a Tower. A Romance. 3 vols. 1882; 1883 (bis); 1888; 1890; 1891; 1893. [First pbd in Atlantic Monthly, xlix, l, 1882.]

The Romantic Adventures of a Milkmaid. New York, 1884. [First pbd in The Graphic, summer no. 1883.]

The Mayor of Casterbridge: the Life and Death of a Man of Character. 2 vols. 1886; 1887; 1888; 1889; 1892; 1893, etc.; tr. French, Paris, 1922. [First pbd in The Graphic, 2 Jan.–15 May 1886.]

The Woodlanders. 3 vols. 1887 (bis); 1889, etc. [First pbd in Macmillan's Mag. liv, lv, 1886–7.]

Wessex Tales; Strange, Lively and Commonplace. 2 vols. 1888; 1889; 1893, etc. [The Distracted Young Preacher (first pbd in New Quarterly Mag. i, 1879); Fellow-Townsmen (ibid. iii, 1880); The Three Strangers (Longman's Mag. March 1883); Interlopers at the Knap (English Illustrated Mag. ii, 1884–5); The Withered Arm (Blackwood's Mag. Jan. 1888).]

Three Notable Stories. 1890. [Includes The Melancholy Hussar, by Hardy.]

Tess of the D'Urbervilles: a Pure Woman faithfully presented. 3 vols. 1891 (4 edns); 1892 (5th edn; adds preface); 1900, etc.; ed. C. J. Weber, New York, 1935. Tr. Danish, Copenhagen, [1924]; French, Paris, 1924; Spanish, Madrid, 1924. [Main portion, modified, first pbd in The Graphic, 4 July–26 Dec. 1891; other chapters 'more especially addressed to adult readers' in Fortnightly Rev. and National Observer, as episodic sketches. Dramatic version by H. A. Kennedy, St James's Theatre, 2 March 1897; by L. Illica, 1909; dramatic version by Hardy produced at Dorchester Corn Exchange, 26 Nov. 1924.]

A Group of Noble Dames. 1891; tr. Finnish, Helsingfors, 1906. [First pbd, in different form, in The Graphic, Christmas no. 1890; The First Countess of Wessex had been pbd in Harper's Mag. Dec. 1889 and The Lady Penelope in Longman's Mag. xv, 1890.]

Life's Little Ironies. A Set of Tales. With some Colloquial Sketches entitled A Few Crusted Characters. 1894; tr. French, Paris, 1921. [First pbd separately at various dates.]

Jude the Obscure. 1896; Tr. French, Paris, [1913]; Danish, Copenhagen, 1926. [First pbd in abridged and modified form in

Harper's Mag. XXIX, XXX, 1894–5. See Hardy's Defence of Jude the Obscure, priv. ptd, Edinburgh, 1928 and H. H. Ellis, Concerning Jude the Obscure, 1931.]

In Scarlet and Grey. Stories of Soldiers and Others by Florence Henniker, and The Spectre of the Real by Thomas Hardy and Florence Henniker. 1896.

The Well-Beloved. A Sketch of a Temperament. 1897; tr. Spanish, Madrid, [1921]. [First pbd in Illustrated London News, 1 Oct.–17 Dec. 1892, as The Pursuit of the Well-Beloved.]

A Changed Man, The Waiting Supper, and Other Tales; concluding with The Romantic Adventures of a Milkmaid. 1913. [First pbd separately at various dates.]

The Short Stories of Thomas Hardy. 1928.

An Indiscretion in the Life of an Heiress. 1934 (priv. ptd); ed. C. J. Weber, Baltimore, 1935. [First pbd in New Quarterly Mag. April–Oct. 1878; see Sir S. Cockerell, TLS. 14 March 1935, p. 160.]

(4) POEMS

(a) Collected and Selected Poems

Wessex Poems and Other Verses. With Thirty Illustrations by the Author. 1898.

Poems of the Past and the Present. 1901; 1902.

Time's Laughingstocks, and Other Verses. 1909; 1915.

Satires of Circumstance: Lyrics and Reveries. With Miscellaneous Pieces. 1914.

Selected Poems. 1916.

Moments of Vision, and Miscellaneous Verses. 1917.

The Poetical Works. 2 vols. 1919–21; 1923 (vol. I only); tr. French, Paris, 1925. [Vol. I, Collected Poems; vol. II, The Dynasts.]

Selected Poems. With Portrait by William Nicholson. 1921.

Late Lyrics and Earlier. With Many Other Verses. 1922.

Human Shows, Far Phantasies. Songs and Trifles. 1925.

Winter Words, in Various Moods and Metres. 1928.

Collected Poems. 1932.

(b) Separate Poems

The Convergence of the Twain. 1912. [For the 'Titanic' Disaster Fund Matinée.]

Song of the Soldiers. [1914] (priv. ptd). [First pbd in The Times, 9 Sept. 1914.]

Before Marching and After. [1915] (priv. ptd).

The Oxen. Hove, 1915 (priv. ptd). [First pbd in The Times, 24 Dec. 1915.]

In Time of 'the Breaking of Nations.' 1916 (priv. ptd).

To Shakespeare after Three Hundred Years. 1916 (priv. ptd).

'When I weekly knew.' 1916 (priv. ptd).

A Call to National Service; An Appeal to America; Cry of the Homeless. 1917 (priv. ptd).

The Fiddler's Story; A Jingle on the Times. 1917 (priv. ptd).

Domicilium. 1918 (priv. ptd). [Hardy's earliest known poem; written between 1857 and 1860; not previously ptd.]

Compassion. An Ode in Celebration of the Centenary of the Royal Society for the Prevention of Cruelty to Animals. [In E. G. Fairholme and W. Pain, A Century of Work for Animals, 1924.]

Yuletide in a Younger World. [1927.]

[Most of the above poems were ptd in very small private edns.]

(5) PLAYS

The Three Wayfarers. A Pastoral Play in One Act. (Terry's, 3 June 1893.) New York, 1893; New York, 1930. [Dramatized from The Three Strangers.]

The Dynasts. A Drama of the Napoleonic Wars. 3 pts, 1903–8; 1910; [1914] (the Prologue and Epilogue); 2 vols. 1924 (with The Famous Tragedy of the Queen of Cornwall); 3 vols. 1927; ed. J. H. Fowler, 1928 (selections). [Pt I was originally pbd at end of 1903, but only a few copies bear that date, the vol. being re-issued Jan. 1904 bearing that date; abridged version produced by H. Granville Barker, 25 Nov. 1914.]

The Play of 'Saint George,' as aforetime acted by the Dorsetshire Christmas Mummers. Based on the Version in 'The Return of the Native' and completed from Other Versions and from Local Tradition. Cambridge, 1921 (priv. ptd); New York, [1928] (with modernized version by R. S. Loomis).

The Famous Tragedy of the Queen of Cornwall at Tintagel in Lyonness. 1923; 1924 (rev.). [With facs. of MS title-page and 2 plates by Hardy.]

(6) PAMPHLETS AND CONTRIBUTIONS TO PERIODICALS

[Excluding letters, reviews, and work later rptd.]

How I built myself a House. Chambers's Journ. March 1865 (anon.).

The Dorsetshire Labourer. Longman's Mag. II, 1883.

The Dorset Farm Labourer, Past and Present. Dorchester, 1884.

Candour in English Fiction. New Rev. II, 1890.

The Science of Fiction. New Rev. III, 1891.

Why I don't write Plays. Pall Mall Gazette, 31 Aug. 1892.
Ancient Earthworks at Casterbridge. English Illustrated Mag. Christmas 1893.
Memories of Church Restoration. Cornhill Mag. July 1906.
Letters on the War. 1914 (priv. ptd).
The War and Literature. Book Monthly, April 1915.

[Hardy also edited selections from William Barnes's Poems, 1908, and wrote several prefaces, etc.]

(7) BIOGRAPHY AND CRITICISM

[See also T. G. Ehrsam and R. H. Deily, Bibliographies of Twelve Victorian Authors, New York, 1936.]

(a) Books

Johnson, Lionel. The Art of Thomas Hardy; with Bibliography. 1894; 1923 (with ch. on the poetry by J. E. Barton and bibliography by J. Lane).
Macdonell, A. Thomas Hardy. 1894.
Sherren, W. The Wessex of Romance. 1902; 1908 (rev.). [With bibliography.]
Windle, B. C. A. The Wessex of Thomas Hardy. 1902.
Harper, C. G. The Hardy Country. Literary Landmarks of the Wessex Novels. 1904; 1911; 1925.
Lea, H. A Handbook to the Wessex Country of Thomas Hardy's Novels and Poems. [1906.]
—— Thomas Hardy's Wessex. 1913; 1925.
Hedgcock, F. A. Essai de Critique: Thomas Hardy, Penseur et Artiste. 1911.
Saxelby, F. O. A Thomas Hardy Dictionary. 1911.
Abercrombie, L. Thomas Hardy. A Critical Study. 1912.
Child, H. Thomas Hardy. 1916.
Duffin, H. C. Thomas Hardy. A Study of the Wessex Novels. 1916; 1921 (with appendix on the poems and The Dynasts).
Berle, L. W. George Eliot and Thomas Hardy. A Contrast. 1917.
Chew, S. C. Thomas Hardy, Poet and Novelist. Bryn Mawr, 1921; 1928.
Whitfield, A. S. Thomas Hardy: the Artist, the Man, and the Disciple of Destiny. 1921.
Beach, J. W. The Technique of Thomas Hardy. 1922.
Hopkins, R. T. Thomas Hardy's Dorset. 1922.
Döll, M. Die Verwendung der Mundart bei Thomas Hardy. Giessen, 1923.
Brennecke, E. Thomas Hardy's Universe. A Study of a Poet's Mind. 1924.
—— The Life of Thomas Hardy. 1925.

Parker, W. M. On the Track of the Wessex Novels. 1924.
Williams, R. The Wessex Novels of Thomas Hardy. 1924.
Grimsditch, H. B. Character and Environment in the Novels of Thomas Hardy. 1925.
Chase, M. E. Thomas Hardy from Serial to Novel. Minneapolis, 1927.
Symons, A. A Study of Thomas Hardy. 1927.
Weltzien, E. Die Gebärden der Furcht in Thomas Hardys Wessexromanen. Berlin, 1927.
Braybrooke, P. Thomas Hardy and his Philosophy. 1928.
Catalogne, G. de. Le Message de Thomas Hardy. Paris, 1928.
Collins, V. H. G. Talks with Thomas Hardy. 1928.
Exideuil, P. d'. Le Couple humain dans l'Œuvre de Thomas Hardy. Paris, 1928; tr. Eng. 1930.
Fowler, J. H. The Novels of Thomas Hardy. English Ass. Lecture, 1928.
Hardy, F. E. The Early Life of Thomas Hardy, 1840–1891. 1928.
—— The Later Years of Thomas Hardy, 1892–1928. 1930.
Hommage à Thomas Hardy. Paris, 1928. [Special no. of La Revue nouvelle, containing trns of various passages, a short bibliography, and short articles by M. Proust, R. Boylesve, E. Phillpotts, J. Joyce, J. M. Murry, E. Jaloux, J. Schlumberger, J. L. Vaudoyer, R. Fernandez, G. D'Hangest, P. d'Exideuil, F. Hellens, C. Du Bos.]
Maxwell, D. The Landscape of Thomas Hardy. 1928.
Sime, J. G. Thomas Hardy of the Wessex Novels. An Essay and Biographical Note. Montreal, 1928.
Zachrisson, R. E. Thomas Hardy as Man, Writer and Philosopher. An Appreciation, with a Swedish Hardy Bibliography. Stockholm, 1928.
Olivero, F. An Introduction to Hardy. Turin, 1930.
Firor, R. A. Folk-ways in Thomas Hardy. Philadelphia, 1931.
Hickson, E. C. The Versification of Thomas Hardy. Philadelphia, 1931.
MacDowall, A. S. Thomas Hardy. A Critical Study. 1931.
Rutland, W. R. Thomas Hardy. Conférence inaugurale. Montreux, [1932]. [English.]
Hiller, H. Thomas Hardy: seine Entwicklung als Romancier. Tübingen, 1933.
Holland, C. Thomas Hardy, O.M.: the Man, his Works, and the Land of Wessex. 1933.
Ridder-Barzin, L. de. Le Pessimisme de Thomas Hardy. Brussels, 1933.

Weber, C. J. In Thomas Hardy's Workshop. Waterville (Maine), 1934.
—— Colby Notes on Far from the Madding Crowd. Waterville (Maine), 1935.
—— Hardy at Colby; a Check-List of the Writings by and about Thomas Hardy now in the Library of Colby College. Waterville (Maine), 1936.
Elliott, A. P. Fatalism in the Works of Thomas Hardy. Philadelphia, 1935.
Hänsch, M.-L. Die sprach-künstlerische Gestaltung bei Thomas Hardy: Stilstudien zu 'Tess of the d'Urbervilles.' Marburg, 1936.
Castelli, A. Thomas Hardy Poeta. Milan, 1937.
Chakravarty, A. C. The Dynasts and the Post-War Age in Poetry. 1938.
Rutland, W. R. Thomas Hardy. Oxford, 1938.

(b) Books containing Chapters on Hardy

Watson, Sir W. Excursions in Criticism. 1893.
Murray, D. C. My Contemporaries in Fiction. 1897.
Cross, W. L. The Development of the English Novel. New York, 1899.
Howells, W. D. Heroines of Fiction. 1901.
Cunliffe, J. W. English Literature during the Last Half-Century. New York, 1908; New York, 1923 (rev.).
Frye, P. H. Literary Reviews and Criticisms. Boston, 1908.
Scott-James, R. A. Modernism and Romance. 1908.
Phelps, W. L. Essays on Modern Novelists. New York, 1910. [With bibliographies.]
Beerbohm, M. A Christmas Garland. 1912.
Sharp, W. Papers Critical and Reminiscent. [1913.]
Powys, J. C. Visions and Revisions. 1915.
Freeman, John. The Moderns. 1916.
Canby, H. S. Definitions. Essays in Contemporary Criticism. 1922.
Cazamian, M. L. Le Roman et les Idées. L'Influence de la Science. Strasburg, 1923.
'Lee, Vernon.' The Handling of Words, and Other Studies in Literary Psychology. 1923.
Anglica. Unterschrift zur englischen Philologie, Alois Brandl zum 70. Geburtstage überreicht. Leipzig, 1925. [A. Steinbach, Thomas Hardy und Schopenhauer.]
Gosse, Sir E. Selected Essays. Ser. 1, 1928.
Dobrée, B. The Lamp and the Lute. Studies in Six Modern Authors. Oxford, 1929.
Elliott, G. R. The Cycle of Modern Poetry. Princeton, 1929.
Lowes, J. L. Of Reading Books. Four Essays. 1930.

Lucas, F. L. Eight Victorian Poets. Cambridge, 1930.
Du Bos, C. Approximations. Ser. 4, Paris, 1930.
Norman, S. Thomas Hardy. [In Great Victorians, ed. H. J. and H. Massingham, 1932. Appended are notes of conversations with Hardy by E. Blunden.]
Evans, B. I. English Poetry in the Later Nineteenth Century. 1933. [Ch. viii.]
Strong, Sir A. Four Studies. 1933. [The Poetry of Thomas Hardy.]
Baker, E. A. The History of the English Novel, Vol. ix, 1938. [Chs. i, ii.]

(c) Articles in Periodicals

Mr Hardy's Novels. New Quarterly Mag. ii, 1879.
Mr Hardy's Novels. British Quarterly Rev. lxxiii, 1881.
Barrie, Sir J. M. Thomas Hardy: the Historian of Wessex. Contemporary Rev. lvi, 1889.
Trent, W. P. The Novels of Thomas Hardy. Sewanee Rev. i, 1893.
—— Thomas Hardy as a Novelist. Citizen, i, 1896.
Butler, A. J. Mr Hardy as a Decadent. National Mag. xxvii, 1896.
Tyrrell, R. Y. Jude the Obscure. Fortnightly Rev. lxv, 1896.
Ellis, Havelock. Concerning 'Jude the Obscure.' Savoy, October 1896.
Le Gallienne, R. Jude the Obscure. Idler, ix, 1896.
Kendall, M. Pessimism in the Poems of Thomas Hardy. London Quarterly Rev. xci, 1899.
Archer, W. Thomas Hardy. Pall Mall Mag. xxiii, 1901.
Turnbull, M. M. Thomas Hardy and William Barnes. GM. n.s. lxxi, 1903.
Beerbohm, M. The Dynasts. Saturday Rev. xcvii, 1904.
—— Thomas Hardy as a Panoramatist. Littell's Living Age, ccxl, 1904.
MacFall, H. Thomas Hardy. A Portrait. Canadian Mag. xxiii, 1904.
Noyes, A. The Poetry of Hardy. North American Rev. cxciv, 1911.
Beach, J. W. Hardy's 'Romantic Adventures of a Milkmaid' and its History. Nation (New York), xciv, 1912.
—— Bowdlerized Versions of Hardy. PMLA. xxxvi, 1921.
Whibley, C. The Work of Hardy. Blackwood's Mag. cxciii, 1913.
Williams, H. The Wessex Novels of Thomas Hardy. North American Rev. cxcix, 1914.
Binyon, L. The Art of Thomas Hardy. Bookman, Feb. 1915.

Courtney, W. L. Mr Thomas Hardy and Æschylus. Fortnightly Rev. cvii, 1917.

Meibergen, C. R. The Woodlanders. E. Studien, li, 1917.

Fairley, B. Notes on the Form of The Dynasts. PMLA. xxxiv, 1919.

—— Thomas Hardy's Lyrical Poems. Canadian Bookman, ii, 1920.

Symons, A. Thomas Hardy. Dial, lxviii, 1920.

Baum, P. F. As to Sources. Literary Rev. 9 Sept. 1922.

Grey, R. Certain Women of Thomas Hardy. Fortnightly Rev. cxviii, 1922.

—— Woman in the Poetry of Thomas Hardy. Fortnightly Rev. cxxv, 1926.

Hone, J. M. The Poetry of Mr Hardy. London Mercury, v, 1922.

Powys, L. Glimpses of Thomas Hardy. Dial, lxxii, 1922.

Arns, K. Bemerkungen zu Hardys Lyrik. Zeitschrift für französischen und englischen Unterricht, xxii, 1923.

Hutchins, M. Selected List of References on Thomas Hardy's Works. Bulletin of Bibliography (Boston), xii, 1923-4.

Zachrisson, R. E. Stil och Personlighet i Thomas Hardy's Diktning. Edda, i, 1923.

Aldington, R. Conrad and Hardy. Literary Rev. v, 1924.

Fletcher, J. G. The Spirit of Thomas Hardy. Yale Rev. xiii, 1924.

Fournier-Pargoire, J. La Poésie de Thomas Hardy. Revue de l'Enseignement des Langues Vivantes, 1924, pp. 297–300.

Muir, E. The Novels of Mr Hardy. Literary Rev. iv, 1924.

Parker, W. M. Christmas with Thomas Hardy: Christmas Readings. Fortnightly Rev. cxxii, 1924.

—— The Jubilee of 'Far from the Madding Crowd.' Cornhill Mag. lvi, 1924.

Stewart, A. The Dynasts: a Psychological Interpretation. English Rev. xxxviii, 1924.

Tomlinson, M. Jude the Obscure. South Atlantic Quarterly, xxiii, 1924.

Veldkamp, J. The Tristram-Legend and Thomas Hardy. Neophilologus, ix, 1924.

West, R. Interpreters of their Age. Saturday Rev. of Lit. i, 1924.

Whitmore, C. E. Mr Hardy's Dynasts as Tragic Drama. MLN. xxxix, 1924.

Darton, F. J. H. Thomas Hardy's Birthplace. Living Age, cccxxiv, 1925.

Hall, J. A. The 'Thing' of Mr Hardy's Poetry. Adelphi, iii, 1925.

Van Doren, C. Anatole France and Thomas Hardy. Century, cix, 1925.

Valakis, A. P. D. Moira of Æschylus and the Immanent Will of Thomas Hardy. Classical Journ. xxi, 1926.

Mayeux, J. J. La Fatalité intérieure dans les Romans de Thomas Hardy. Revue anglo-américaine, Feb. 1927.

Davray, H. D. Thomas Hardy et son Temps. Mercure de France, ccii, 1928.

Ellis, S. M. Thomas Hardy: some Personal Recollections. Fortnightly Rev. cxxix, 1928.

Freeman, J. Thomas Hardy. London Mercury, xvii, 1928.

Murry, J. M. The Supremacy of Thomas Hardy. New Adelphi, i, 1928.

Sime, A. H. M. Thomas Hardy and Music. Musical Opinion, Sept. 1928.

Bensusan, S. L. Thomas Hardy. Quarterly Rev. ccliii, 1929.

Weltzien, E. Thomas Hardys Anschauung vom immanenten Willen. Neue Jahrbücher für Wissenschaft und Jugendbildung, v, 1929.

Scripture, E. W. Versformeln und Betonungsprinzipien bei Hardy und Kipling. Die Neueren Sprachen, xxxviii, 1930.

Grove, F. P. Thomas Hardy. A Critical Examination of a Typical Novel and his Shorter Poems. University of Toronto Quart. i, 1932.

Lawrence, D. H. Six Novels of Thomas Hardy and the Real Tragedy. Book-Collector's Quart. pt 5, 1932.

Webster, H. C. Borrowings in 'Tess of the D'Urbervilles.' MLN. xlviii, 1933.

Weber, C. J. RES. x, 1934, pp. 456–9; Classical Journ. xxix, 1934, pp. 533–5; Revue anglo-américaine, xii, 1935, pp. 520–3; MLN. l, 1935, pp. 41–3; ELH. ii, 1935, pp. 242–5; Colby Mercury, vi, 1936, pp. 64–7, 89–93; Colophon, i, ii, 1936–7. [Miscellaneous brief notes.]

—— Chronology in Hardy's Novels. PMLA. liii, 1938.

Chapman, F. Revaluations. iv. Hardy the Novelist. Scrutiny, iii, 1934.

Ford, F. M. Thomas Hardy. American Mercury, xxxviii, 1936.

Wright, W. An Index to Hardy's Poems. Colby Mercury, vi, 1936.　　　　H. B. G.

ROBERT LOUIS STEVENSON (1850–1894)

[No attempt has been made here to record either Stevenson's juvenilia, toy-books and trifles, or his contributions to periodicals and other books.]

(1) Bibliographies

Prideaux, W. F. A Bibliography of the Works of Robert Louis Stevenson. New York, 1903; rev. F. V. Livingston, 1917.

Slater, J. H. A Bibliography of R. L. S. 1914.

First Editions of the Works of Robert Louis Stevenson, 1850–1894. With Other Stevensoniana exhibited Nov. 5–28, 1914. Grolier Club, 1914.

(2) Collected Works

Edinburgh Edition. Ed. Sir S. Colvin, 28 vols. 1894–8.
Thistle Edition. 26 vols. New York, 1902.
Pentland Edition. Ed. Sir E. Gosse, 20 vols. 1906–7.
Swanston Edition. 25 vols. 1911–2. [Introduction by A. Lang.]
Vailima Edition. Ed. L. Osbourne and F. Van de G. Stevenson, 26 vols. 1922–3.
Tusitala Edition. 35 vols. 1923–4.

(3) Novels and Short Stories

The Story of a Lie. 1882. [A forgery? See J. Carter and G. Pollard, An Enquiry into the Nature of Certain Nineteenth Century Pamphlets, 1934. First pbd in New Quarterly Mag. Oct. 1879.]
New Arabian Nights. 2 vols. 1882. [Vol. i: The Suicide Club; The Rajah's Diamond. Vol. ii: The Pavilion on the Links; A Lodging for the Night; The Sire de Malétroit's Door; Providence and the Guitar. The contents of vol. i had already appeared in London, 8 June–26 Oct. 1878, as Latter-Day Arabian Nights. The stories in vol. ii were rptd from Cornhill Mag., Temple Bar and London.]
Treasure Island. 1883. [First pbd in slightly different form in Young Folks, 1 Oct. 1881–28 Jan. 1882, as by 'Captain George North.' For Stevenson's own account of the writing of this book see Essays in the Art of Writing, 1905.]
Prince Otto. A Romance. 1885. [First pbd in Longman's Mag. April–Oct. 1885.]
More New Arabian Nights. The Dynamiter. 1885. [With Fanny Van de Grift Stevenson, who was entirely responsible for The Destroying Angel and The Fair Cuban.]
Strange Case of Dr Jekyll and Mr Hyde. 1886.
Kidnapped. Being Memoirs of the Adventures of David Balfour In the Year 1751: How he was Kidnapped and Castaway; his Sufferings in a Desert Isle; his Journey in the Wild Highlands; his Acquaintance with Alan Breck Stewart and other notorious Highland Jacobites; with all that he Suffered at the Hands of his Uncle, Ebenezer Balfour of Shaws, falsely so-called: Written by Himself and now set forth By Robert Louis Stevenson. 1886. [This edn was preceded by a small priv. ptd edn to secure copyright. Kidnapped was first pbd in Young Folks, 1 May–13 July 1886.]

The Merry Men and Other Tales and Fables. 1887. [The Merry Men; Will o' the Mill; Markheim; Thrawn Janet; Olalla; The Treasure of Franchard—all first pbd in Cornhill Mag. and other periodicals.]
The Black Arrow: A Tale of the Two Roses. New York, 1888; 1888. [First pbd in Young Folks, 30 June–20 Oct. 1883, as The Black Arrow: a Tale of Tunstall Forest, by Captain George North.]
The Misadventures of John Nicholson. A Christmas Story. New York, 1889. [Piratically rptd from Yule-Tide, Cassell's Christmas Annual for 1887.]
The Master of Ballantrae. A Winter's Tale. 1889. [This·edn was preceded by a small priv. ptd edn in 1888 to secure copyright. The story was first pbd in Scribner's Mag. Nov. 1888–Oct. 1889.]
The Wrong Box. 1889. [With Lloyd Osbourne.]
The Wrecker. 1892. [With Lloyd Osbourne. First pbd in Scribner's Mag. Aug. 1891–July 1892.]
Island Night's Entertainments, consisting of The Beach of Falesá, The Bottle Imp, The Isle of Voices. 1893. [The stories were first pbd in: Illustrated London News, 2 July–6 Aug. 1892; Black and White, 28 March, 4 April 1891; National Observer, 4–25 Feb. 1893. They had been priv. ptd in 1892.]
Catriona. A Sequel to Kidnapped. Being Memoirs of the Further Adventures of David Balfour at Home and Abroad In which are set forth his Misfortunes anent the Appin Murder; his Troubles with Lord Advocate Grant; Captivity on the Bass Rock; Journey into Holland and France; and singular Relations with James More Drummond or MacGregor, a son of the notorious Rob Roy, and his Daughter Catriona. Written by Himself, and now set forth by Robert Louis Stevenson. 1893. [First pbd in Atalanta, Dec. 1892–Sept. 1893, as David Balfour. Memoirs of his Adventures at Home and Abroad.]
The Ebb-Tide. A Trio and Quartette. Chicago, 1894; 1894. [With Lloyd Osbourne. First pbd in To-Day, 11 Nov. 1893–3 Feb. 1894.]
The Body-Snatcher. New York, 1895. [First pbd in Pall Mall Christmas no. 1884.]
The Strange Case of Dr Jekyll and Mr Hyde with other Fables. 1896. [The fables were first pbd in Longman's Mag. Aug., Sept. 1895.]
Weir of Hermiston. An Unfinished Romance. 1896. [This edn was preceded by a copyright edn, Chicago, 1896. The story was first pbd in Cosmopolis, Jan.–April 1896.]
St Ives. Being the Adventures of a French Prisoner in England. New York, 1897;

1898. [Completed by Sir A. T. Quiller-Couch, the first 30 chs. only being by Stevenson. First pbd in Pall Mall Mag. Nov. 1896–Nov. 1897.]

Tales and Fantasies. 1905. [The Misadventures of John Nicholson; The Body-Snatcher; The Story of a Lie.]

The Waif Woman. 1916. [First pbd in Scribner's Mag. Dec. 1914.]

When the Devil was Well. Hitherto Unpublished Story. Ed. W. P. Trent, Bibliophile Soc. (Boston), 1921.

Ticonderoga. A Legend of the West Highlands. New York, 1923.

(4) Poems and Plays

Deacon Brodie, or, The Double Life: A Melodrama, founded on Facts In Four Acts and Ten Tableaux. Edinburgh, 1880 (priv. ptd); Edinburgh, 1888 (rev.; priv. ptd). [With W. E. Henley.]

Beau Austin: A Play in Four Acts. Edinburgh, 1884 (priv. ptd). [With W. E. Henley.]

Admiral Guinea. A Melodrama in Four Acts. Edinburgh, 1884 (priv. ptd). [With W. E. Henley.]

Macaire. A Melodramatic Farce in Three Acts. Edinburgh, 1885 (priv. ptd). [With W. E. Henley.]

A Child's Garden of Verses. 1885. [39 of the 64 poems were priv. ptd in 1883 as Penny Whistles, which also included 9 poems omitted from A Child's Garden of Verses. These 9 poems were priv. rptd by L. S. Livingston in 1912 as Verses by R. L. S.]

Underwoods. 1887. [38 poems in English and 16 in Scots.]

Ticonderoga. Edinburgh, 1887 (priv. ptd). [First pbd in Scribner's Mag. Dec. 1887; rptd in Ballads, 1890.]

Ballads. 1890. [The Song of Rabéro; The Feast of Famine; Ticonderoga; Heather Ale; Christmas at Sea—each (except Christmas at Sea) with notes.]

Three Plays. Deacon Brodie, Beau Austin, Admiral Guinea. 1892.

The Plays of W. E. Henley and R. L. Stevenson. Deacon Brodie, Beau Austin, Admiral Guinea, Robert Macaire. 1896.

Songs of Travel and other Verses. 1896. [44 poems first pbd in Edinburgh edn, vol. XIV, 1895.]

Three Short Poems. 1898 (priv. ptd); Chicago, 1902.

R. L. S. Teuila. 1899 (priv. ptd). [20 poems.]

The Poems and Ballads of Robert Louis Stevenson. Complete Edition. New York, 1913.

The Hanging Judge. A Drama in Three Acts and Six Tableaux. Ed. Sir E. Gosse, 1914 (priv. ptd). [With Fanny Van de Grift Stevenson.]

Poetical Fragments. [1915] (priv. ptd).

An Ode of Horace. Book II. Ode III. Experiments in Three Metres. [1916] (priv. ptd).

Poems. Hitherto Unpublished. Ed. G. S. Hellmann, Bibliophile Soc. (Boston), 1916.

New Poems and Variant Readings. 1918.

Stevenson's Workshop. Ed. W. P. Trent, Bibliophile Soc. (Boston), 1921. [MSS and variant readings of the poems.]

(5) Essays and Miscellaneous Writings

An Inland Voyage. 1878; 1881.

Edinburgh. Picturesque Notes. With Etchings. 1879; 1888. [First pbd in The Portfolio, June–Dec. 1878.]

Travels with a Donkey in the Cévennes. 1879 (bis).

Virginibus Puerisque And Other Papers. 1881; 1887. [12 essays, all (except 'Some Portraits by Raeburn') rptd from Cornhill Mag., MacMillan's Mag. and London.]

Familiar Studies of Men and Books. 1882. [9 essays rptd from Cornhill Mag. and other periodicals.]

The Silverado Squatters. Sketches from a Californian Mountain. 1883. [First pbd in Century Mag. Nov., Dec. 1883. An edn of 10 copies of the first instalment was produced in 1883 for copyright reasons.]

Some College Memories. Edinburgh, 1886. [A forgery? See J. Carter and G. Pollard, as above. First pbd in The New Amphion, being the Book of the Edinburgh University Union Fancy Fair, Edinburgh, 1886.]

Thomas Stevenson Civil Engineer. 1887 (priv. ptd). [Also pbd in Contemporary Rev. June 1887.]

Memories & Portraits. 1887. [16 essays, including Some College Memories and Thomas Stevenson, mainly rptd from Cornhill Mag. and Longman's Mag.]

The Papers of H. Fleeming Jenkin; with a Memoir by R. L. Stevenson. 2 vols. 1887. [Memoir rptd alone New York, 1887.]

Father Damien. An Open Letter to the Reverend Dr Hyde of Honolulu. 1890. [This edn was preceded by a priv. ptd edn at Sidney and a second at Edinburgh. The letter was first pbd in Scots Observer, 3, 10 May 1890.]

Across the Plains with other Memories and Essays. 1892. [12 essays mainly rptd from Scribner's Mag.]

A Footnote to History. Eight Years of Trouble in Samoa. 1892.

War in Samoa. 1893 (priv. ptd). [First pbd in Pall Mall Gazette, 4 Sept. 1893.]

The Amateur Emigrant from the Clyde to Sandy Hook. Chicago, 1895. [First ptd in Edinburgh edn of Works, vol. III, 1895.]

In the South Seas. New York, 1896; 1900. [15 of the 35 letters were priv. ptd in 1890 as The South Seas: A Record of Three Cruises. The letters were first pbd in the Sun (New York), 1891.]

Familiar Epistle in Verse and Prose [to Charles Baxter]. 1896 (priv. ptd). [Written 1872.]

A Mountain Town in France. A Fragment. New York, 1896.

The Morality of The Profession of Letters. New York, 1899. [First pbd in Fortnightly Rev. April 1881.]

A Stevenson Medley. Ed. Sir S. Colvin, 1899. [Includes the Davos-Platz booklets, mainly ptd from the original blocks.]

Essays and Criticisms. Boston, 1903.

Prayers Written at Vailima. With An Introduction By Mrs Stevenson. 1905. [First pbd in Edinburgh edn of Works, vol. XXI.]

Essays of Travel. 1905.

Essays in the Art of Writing. 1905.

Essays. Selected by W. L. Phelps. New York 1906.

Lay Morals And Other Papers. 1911. [10 essays.]

Records of a Family of Engineers. 1912.

Memoirs of Himself. Philadelphia, 1912 (priv. ptd).

On the Choice of a Profession. 1916. [First pbd in Scribner's Mag. Jan. 1915.]

Confessions of a Unionist. An Unpublished Talk on Things Current. Written in 1888. Ed. F. V. L[ivingston], Cambridge, U.S.A. 1921.

Selected Essays. Ed. H. G. Rawlinson, 1923.

The Manuscripts of Robert Louis Stevenson's Records of a Family of Engineers: the Unfinished Chapters. Chicago, 1930.

(6) LETTERS

Vailima Letters. Being Correspondence addressed by Robert Louis Stevenson to Sidney Colvin November 1890–October 1894. 1895.

The Letters of Robert Louis Stevenson to his Family and Friends selected and edited with Notes and Introductions by Sidney Colvin. 2 vols. 1899; 4 vols. 1911 (enlarged).

Some Letters By Robert Louis Stevenson. Ed. H. Townsend, New York, 1902. [5 letters to A. T. Haddon, 1879–84.]

Three Letters. 1902.

Letters to an Editor [C. K. Shorter]. [1914] (priv. ptd).

Letters To Charles Baxter. [1914] (priv. ptd).

Some Letters of Robert Louis Stevenson. Ed. L. Osbourne, 1914.

New Letters. Ed. Sir S. Colvin, Scribner's Mag. LXXIII, LXXIV, 1923.

(7) BIOGRAPHY AND CRITICISM

[See also T. G. Ehrsam and R. H. Deily, Bibliographies of Twelve Victorian Authors, New York, 1936.]

(a) Books

Armour, M. The Home and Early Haunts of Robert Louis Stevenson. 1895.

Fraser, Marie. In Stevenson's Samoa. 1895.

Raleigh, Sir W. Robert Louis Stevenson. 1895.

Black, M. M. Robert Louis Stevenson. [1898.]

Geddie, J. The Home Life of Robert Louis Stevenson. 1898.

Simpson, E. B. R. L. S.'s Edinburgh Days. 1898.

—— Robert Louis Stevenson. 1906.

—— The R. L. S. Originals. 1912.

Cornford, L. C. Robert Louis Stevenson. 1899.

Baildon, H. B. Stevenson. 1901.

Balfour, Graham. The Life of Robert Louis Stevenson. 2 vols. 1901.

Hammerton, Sir J. A. Stevensoniana. 1903.

Strong, I. and Osbourne, Lloyd. Memories of Vailima. 1903.

Japp, A. H. Robert Louis Stevenson. An Estimate. 1905.

Johnstone, A. Recollections of Stevenson in the Pacific. 1905.

Stevenson, M. I. Letters from Samoa. 1906.

Moors, H. J. With Stevenson in Samoa. 1910.

Strong, I. Robert Louis Stevenson. 1911.

Webster, Alexander. R. L. S. and Henry Drummond. 1912.

Masson, R. O. Robert Louis Stevenson. 1914.

—— The Life of Robert Louis Stevenson. 1923.

Swinnerton, F. Robert Louis Stevenson. A Critical Study. 1914.

Cruse, A. Robert Louis Stevenson. 1915.

Eaton, C. A Last Memory of Robert Louis Stevenson. [1916.]

Chalmers, Stephen. The Penny Piper of Saranac. An Episode in Stevenson's Life. 1916.

Clayton, H. In the Trail of Stevenson. [1916.]

Fletcher, C. B. Stevenson's Germany. 1920.

Guthrie, C. J. (Lord Guthrie). Robert Louis Stevenson: some Personal Recollections. Edinburgh, 1920.

Harper, H. H. Robert Louis Stevenson. An Appreciation. Boston, [1920].

Balfour, M. I. Stevenson's Baby Book; being a Record of the Sayings and Doings of R. L. S. 1922.

Adcock, A. St J. et al. Robert Louis Stevenson; his Work and his Personality. 1924.

Osborne, Lloyd. An Intimate Portrait of R. L. S. New York, 1924.

Sarolea, C. Robert Louis Stevenson and France. 1924.

Steuart, J. A. Robert Louis Stevenson: Man and Writer. A Critical Biography. 2 vols. [1924].

Hellman, G. S. The True Stevenson. A Study in Clarification. Boston, 1925.

Cunningham, A. Cummy's Diary. A Diary kept by Robert Louis Stevenson's Nurse on the Continent during 1863. Ed. R. T. Skinner, 1926.

Boodle, A. A. R. L. S. and his Sine Qua Non. Flashlights from Skerrynore. 1926.

Chesterton, G. K. Robert Louis Stevenson. 1927.

MacCulloch, J. A. Robert Louis Stevenson and the Bridge of Allan. With Other Stevenson Essays. 1927.

Morris, D. B. Robert Louis Stevenson and the Scottish Highlanders. Stirling, 1929.

MacPherson, H. D. R. L. Stevenson. A Study in French Influence. New York, 1930.

Carré, J.-M. Robert Louis Stevenson: the Frail Warrior. Tr. Eng. 1931.

Dark, S. Robert Louis Stevenson. 1931.

Lockett, W. G. Robert Louis Stevenson at Davos. 1934.

Dalglish, D. N. Presbyterian Pirate: a Portrait of Stevenson. Oxford, 1937.

Field, I. This Life I've loved. 1937.

Smith, Janet A. R. L. Stevenson. 1937.

(b) Essays, Articles and Chapters of Books

Archer, W. R. L. S.: his Style and Thought. Time, Nov. 1885.

—— R. L. S. at Skerryvore. Critic, Nov. 1887.

—— In Memoriam R. L. S. New Rev. Jan. 1895.

James, Henry. Partial Portraits. 1888.

—— Notes on Novelists. 1914.

Lang, A. Essays in Little. 1891.

—— Adventures among Books. 1905.

Lowe, C. Robert Louis Stevenson. A Reminiscence. Bookman, Nov. 1891.

Walkley, A. B. Playhouse Impressions. 1892. [On the Stevenson-Henley plays.]

Crockett, S. R. The Apprenticeship of Robert Louis Stevenson. Bookman, March 1893.

Gosse, Sir E. Questions at Issue. 1893.

—— Critical Kit-Kats. 1896.

—— Stevenson's Relations with Children. Chamber's Journ. July 1899.

Gwynn, S. Robert Louis Stevenson. A Critical Study. Fortnightly Rev. Dec. 1894.

—— The Posthumous Works of Robert Louis Stevenson. Fortnightly Rev. April 1898.

With Stevenson in Samoa. Cornhill Mag. July 1894.

Quiller-Couch, Sir A. T. Adventures in Criticism. 1896.

Symons A. Studies in Two Literatures. 1897.

—— Studies in Prose and Verse. [1904.]

Primrose, A. P. (Earl of Rosebery). Appreciations and Addresses. 1899.

Robert Louis Stevenson. By Two of his Cousins. English Illustrated Mag. May 1899.

Henley, W. E. 'R. L. S.' Pall Mall Mag. Dec. 1901.

Colvin, Sir S. Robert Louis Stevenson at Hampstead. Hampstead Annual, Dec. 1902.

Lennox, C. James Chalmers of New Guinea. 1902. [Ch. xxi, With Robert Louis Stevenson.]

Muirhead, J. H. Robert Louis Stevenson's Philosophy of Life. [In Philosophy and Life, 1902.]

Stephen, Sir L. Studies of a Biographer. Vol. iv, 1902.

Pinero, Sir A. W. Robert Louis Stevenson: the Dramatist. A Lecture. 1903; ed. C. Hamilton, New York, 1914.

Nevinson, H. W. From Leith to Samoa. 1905.

Phelps, W. L. Essays on Modern Novelists. New York, 1910. [With bibliographies by A. Keogh.]

Lansing, R. R. Robert Louis Stevenson's French reading as shown in his Correspondence. Poet Lore, March 1918.

Robertson, S. Sir Thomas Browne and R. L. Stevenson. JEGP. xx, 1921.

Freeman, J. Robert Louis Stevenson. London Mercury, April 1922.

'Lee, Vernon.' The Handling of Words. 1923.

Pears, Sir E. R. Some Recollections of Robert Louis Stevenson. Scribner's Mag. Jan. 1923.

Noyes, A. Some Aspects of Modern Poetry. 1924.

Benson, E. F. The Myth of Robert Louis Stevenson. London Mercury, July, Aug. 1925.

Torossian, A. Stevenson as a Literary Critic. California University Chronicle, Jan. 1925.

Fraser, James A. L. Stevenson and the Jacobite Tradition. [1927.]

—— Scott and Stevenson. A Lecture. [1929.]

Masson, R. O. R. L. S. at Pitlochry. Cornhill Mag. March 1927.

Bonnerot, L. Quelques Notes sur l'Exotisme de Stevenson. Revue anglo-américaine, June 1928.

Garrod, H. W. The Poetry of R. L. Stevenson. [In The Profession of Poetry, Oxford, 1929.]

Carré, J.-M. R. L. Stevenson et la France. [In Mélanges Baldensperger, vol. i, Paris, 1930.]

Muir, E. Robert Louis Stevenson. Bookman (New York), Sept. 1931.

Tomlinson, H. M. Robert Louis Stevenson. [In Great Victorians, ed. H. J. and H. Massingham, 1932.]

Evans, B. I. English Poetry in the Later Nineteenth Century. 1933. [Ch. xii.]

Heanley, K. The Mystery of Lettermore. Cornhill Mag. LXXIV, 1933.

S. J. L.

GEORGE ROBERT GISSING (1857–1903)

(1) BIBLIOGRAPHY

Scott, Temple. [Bibliography prefixed to Critical Studies of the Works of Charles Dickens, New York, 1924.]

(2) NOVELS AND SHORT STORIES

Workers in the Dawn. A Novel. 3 vols. 1880.
The Unclassed. A Novel. 3 vols. 1884.
Demos. A Story. 1886.
Isabel Clarendon. 2 vols. 1886.
Thyrza. A Tale. 3 vols. 1887.
A Life's Morning. 3 vols. 1888.
The Nether World. A Novel. 3 vols. 1889.
The Emancipated. A Novel. 3 vols. 1890.
New Grub Street. A Novel. 3 vols. 1891.
Born in Exile. A Novel. 3 vols. 1892.
Denzil Quarrier. A Novel. 3 vols. 1892.
The Odd Women. 3 vols. 1893.
In the Year of Jubilee. 3 vols. 1894.
Eve's Ransom. 1895.
The Paying Guest. 1895.
Sleeping Fires. 1895.
The Whirlpool. 1897.
Human Odds and Ends: Stories and Sketches. 1898.
The Town Traveller. 1898.
The Crown of Life. 1899.
Our Friend the Charlatan. 1901.
Veranilda: a Romance. 1904. [Preface by Frederic Harrison.]
Will Warburton: a Romance of Real Life. 1905.
The House of Cobwebs and Other Stories, 1906.
A Victim of Circumstance and Other Stories. 1927.
Brownie, now first Reprinted from the Chicago Tribune, together with Six Other Stories attributed to [Gissing]. Ed. G. E. Hastings, V. Starrett and T. O. Mabbott, New York, 1931.

(3) CRITICAL AND MISCELLANEOUS WRITINGS

Charles Dickens. A Critical Study. 1898; 1902 (with topographical notes by F. G. Kitton).

The Rochester Edition of the Works of Charles Dickens. 9 vols. (all pbd), 1900–1. [Introductions by Gissing, notes by F. G. Kitton.]

By the Ionian Sea. Notes of a Ramble in Southern Italy. 1901; ed. V. Woolf, 1933.

Forster's Life of Dickens. Abridged and Revised. 1903.

The Private Papers of Henry Ryecroft. 1903.

Dickens. [In Homes and Haunts of Famous Authors, 1906.]

Critical Studies of the Works of Charles Dickens. Ed. T. Scott, New York, 1924. [Consists of the introductions to the Rochester edn, including 3 not previously pbd.]

Selections, Autobiographical and Imaginative, from the Works of George Gissing. With Biographical and Critical Notes by his Son [A. C. Gissing]. With an Introduction by Virginia Woolf. 1929.

Hope in Vain. [Winchester], 1930 (priv. ptd). [A poem.]

(4) LETTERS

Letters to Edward Clodd. 1914 (priv. ptd).

Letters to an Editor [C. K. Shorter]. 1915 (priv. ptd).

Letters to Members of his Family. Collected and arranged by Algernon and Ellen Gissing. 1927.

Autobiographical Notes, with Comments on Tennyson and Huxley. In Three Letters to Edward Clodd. Edinburgh, 1930 (priv. ptd).

(5) BIOGRAPHY AND CRITICISM

Sichel, E. George Gissing, Philanthropic Novelist. Murray's Mag. III, 1888.

Wells, H. G. George Gissing. Contemporary Rev. LXXII, 1897.

—— George Gissing: an Impression. Monthly Rev. XVI, 1904.

Dolman, F. The Novels of George Gissing. National Rev. XXX, 1897.

White, G. George Gissing. Sewanee Rev. VI, 1898.

Findlater, J. H. The Spokesman of Despair. National Rev. XLIV, 1904–5.

Waugh, A. George Gissing. Fortnightly Rev. LXXXI, 1904.

Wedd, N. George Gissing. Independent Rev. II, 1904.

Harrison, A. George Gissing. Nineteenth Century, LX, 1906.

Seccombe, T. The Work of George Gissing: an Introductory Survey. [Prefixed to Gissing's House of Cobwebs, 1906.]

More, P. E. George Gissing. [In Shelburne Essays, ser. 5, New York, 1908.]

Roberts, Morley. The Private Life of Henry Maitland. 1912. [Novel based on Gissing's life.]
—— The Letters of George Gissing. Virginia Quart. VII, 1931.
Swinnerton, F. George Gissing: a Critical Study. 1912.
Björkman, E. Voices of To-Morrow. New York, 1914.
Alden, S. George Gissing: Humanist. North American Rev. CCXVI, 1922.
Yates, M. George Gissing: an Appreciation. Manchester, 1922.
Cazamian, M. L. Le Roman et les Idées. L'Influence de la Science. Strasburg, 1923.
Gissing, E. George Gissing: a Character Sketch. Nineteenth Century, CII, 1927.
—— Some Personal Recollections of George Gissing. Blackwood's Mag. CCXXV, 1929.
Gissing, A. C. George Gissing: some Aspects of his Life and Work. National Rev. XCIII, 1929.
Roberts, G. George Gissing. Queen's Quart. XXXVII, 1930.
Rotter, A. Frank Swinnerton und George Gissing: eine kritische Studie. Brünn, 1930.
Weber, Anton. George Gissing und die soziale Frage. Leipzig, 1932.
McKay, R. C. George Gissing and his Critic Frank Swinnerton. Philadelphia, 1933.
Gapp, S. V. George Gissing: Classicist. Philadelphia, 1936.
Baker, E. A. The History of the English Novel. Vol. IX, 1938.   H. B. G.

GEORGE MOORE (1857–1933)

(1) BIBLIOGRAPHIES

Williams, I. A. Bibliographies of Modern Authors. No. 3. George Moore. 1921.
Danielson, H. George Moore. A Bibliography, 1878–1921. [In J. Freeman, A Portrait of George Moore, 1922.]

(2) COLLECTED WORKS

The Works of George Moore. Uniform Edition. 1932– .
The Works of George Moore. Ebury Edition. 20 vols. 1937.

(3) FICTION

A Modern Lover. 3 vols. 1883. [Re-written as Lewis Seymour and some Women, 1917.]
A Mummer's Wife. 1885; tr. French, Paris, 1888.
A Drama in Muslin. A Realistic Novel. 1886; 1915 (largely rewritten, as Muslin).
A Mere Accident. 1887. [John Norton, in Celibates, 1895, is a re-writing of this.]
Spring Days. A Realistic Novel. A Prelude to 'Don Juan.' 1888; [1912] (with preface).

Mike Fletcher. A Novel. 1889.
Vain Fortune. [1890]; 1895 (rev.).
Esther Waters. A Novel. 1894; 1920 (rev. and priv. ptd). [Dramatic version, 1913.]
Celibates. 1895. [3 tales: Mildred Lawson; John Norton; Agnes Lahens.]
Evelyn Innes. 1898.
Sister Teresa. 1901; [1928] (entirely rewritten).
The Untilled Field. 1903. [Short stories; part of the book first pbd in Irish, Dublin, 1902.]
Memoirs of my Dead Life. 1905; 1921 (rev. and enlarged).
The Lake. 1905.
The Brook Kerith. A Syrian Story. 1916; 1921 (5th edn, rev.); 1927 (7th edn, rev.).
Lewis Seymour and some Women. 1917. [A re-writing of A Modern Love.]
A Story-Teller's Holiday. 1918 (priv. ptd); 2 vols. 1928 (rev., with additional tales).
Héloïse and Abélard. 2 vols. 1921 (priv. ptd); 1925. [Some 'Fragments,' i.e. addns and corrections, were priv. ptd 1921.]
In Single Strictness. 1922; 1927 (as Celibate Lives). [Stories.]
Ulick and Soracha. 1926.
A Flood. New York, 1930.
Aphrodite in Aulis. 1930; 1931 (rev.).
Peronnik the Fool. With Engravings by Stephen Gooden. 1933.

(4) OTHER WRITINGS

Worldliness. A Comedy in Three Acts. [c. 1874.] ['The author believes, and hopes, that, no copy of this, his first published work, now exists.'—I. A. Williams.]
Flowers of Passion. 1878. [Poems.]
Martin Luther. A Tragedy in Five Acts. 1879. [Verse; with Bernard Lopez.]
Pagan Poems. 1881.
Literature at Nurse, or Circulating Morals. [1885.] [Pamphlet on the selection of books at Mudie's Library.]
Parnell and his Island. 1887. [Sketches.]
Confessions of a Young Man. 1888; 1904 (ed. and annotated by Moore); 1917 (ed. and annotated by Moore); 1926 (rev.).
Impressions and Opinions. 1891.
Modern Painting. 1893; 1898 (enlarged).
The Strike at Arlingford. A Play in Three Acts. 1893.
The Royal Academy, 1895. 1895. [New Budget Extra, No. 1.]
The Bending of the Bough. A Comedy in Five Acts. 1900.
Literature and the Irish Language. [In Ideals in Ireland, ed. Lady Gregory, 1901.]
Reminiscences of the Impressionist Painters. Dublin, 1906.
'Hail and Farewell!' A Trilogy. 3 vols. 1911-4. [Pt I, Ave; Pt 2, Salve; pt 3, Vale.]

The Apostle. A Drama in Three Acts. Dublin, 1911.

Elizabeth Cooper. A Comedy in Three Acts. Dublin, 1913.

Avowals. 1919.

The Coming of Gabrielle. A Comedy. 1920 (priv. ptd).

Conversations in Ebury Street. 1924; 1930 (rev.).

The Pastoral Loves of Daphnis and Chloe. Done into English. 1924. [From Longus.]

Pure Poetry. An Anthology. 1924.

The Making of an Immortal. A Play in One Act. New York, 1927.

Letters from George Moore to Ed. Dujardin, 1866–1922. New York, 1929. [From the French, tr. J. Eglinton.]

The Passing of the Essenes. A Drama in Three Acts. 1930; 1931 (rev.).

A Communication to my Friends. 1933.

[Moore also wrote introductions to Zola's Piping Hot! 1885, Dostoevsky's Poor Folk, 1894, and several other books.]

(5) BIOGRAPHY AND CRITICISM

Murray, D. C. My Contemporaries in Fiction. 1897.

Mitchell, S. L. George Moore. 1916.

Lucas, E. V. His Fatal Beauty, or the Moore of Chelsea. 1917 (priv. ptd). [Dramatic satire, played at Chelsea Palace, 20 March 1917.]

Sherman, S. P. On Contemporary Literature. New York, 1917.

—— The Main Stream. New York, 1927.

Freeman, J. A Portrait of George Moore in a Study of his Work. 1922.

Jean-Aubry, G. George Moore and Émile Zola. Bookman's Journ. XI, 1924.

Hergesheimer, J. Lyrical Mr George Moore. Saturday Rev. of Literature, 3 Jan. 1925.

Blanche, J. E. George Moore. Nouvelles Littéraires, 16, 23 June 1928. [Recollections.]

Gosse, Sir E. Selected Essays. 2 sers. 1928. [Ser. 2, pp. 7–16: The Carpet and the Clock.]

Goodwin, G. Conversations with George Moore. 1929.

—— Call Back Yesterday. 1933.

Bock, H. George Moore, The Brook Kerith. Eine kritische Studie. Die neueren Sprachen, XXXIX, 1931.

MacCarthy, D. Portraits. 1931. [Pp. 192–203.]

Wolfe, H. George Moore. 1931.

Sechler, R. P. George Moore: 'A Disciple of Walter Pater.' Philadelphia, 1932.

Weferling, H. Das religiöse Gefühl bei George Moore. Bottrop, 1932.

Burdett, O. George Moore. London Mercury, XXVII, 1933.

Davray, H. S. George Moore. Mercure de France, 15 March 1933.

Ford, F. M. Contrasts. Memories of John Galsworthy and George Moore. Atlantic Monthly, CLI, 1933.

Gilomen, W. George Moore. Jugendwerk, Naturalismus und Abkehr. Zurich, 1933.

—— George Moore and his Friendship with W. B. Yeats. E. Studien, XIX, 1937.

Whitall, G. George Moore. Bookman (New York), LXXVI, 1933.

—— English Years. New York, 1935.

Dixon, P. J. Letters from George Moore: the Greek Background of Aphrodite in Aulis. London Mercury, XXI, 1934.

Ferguson, W. D. The Influence of Flaubert on George Moore. Philadelphia, 1934.

Steward, S. M. J.-K. Huysmans and George Moore. Romanic Rev. XXV, 1934.

Morgan, C. Epitaph on George Moore. 1935.

Hone, J. M. The Life of George Moore. 1936.

Yeats, W. B. Dramatis Personae, 1896–1902, and Other Papers. 1936.

Baker, E. A. The History of the English Novel. Vol. IX, 1938.   S. J. L.

RUDYARD KIPLING (1865–1936)

(1) BIBLIOGRAPHIES

Martindell, E. W. A Bibliography of the Works of Rudyard Kipling. 1923 (rev. edn).

Livingston, F. V. Bibliography of the Works of Rudyard Kipling. New York, 1927. [Supplement, 1938.]

Chandler, L. H. A Summary of the Works of Rudyard Kipling, including Items ascribed to him. Grolier Club, New York, 1930.

Catalogue of the Works of Rudyard Kipling exhibited at the Grolier Club, 1929. Grolier Club, New York, 1930.

Catalogue of the Ellis Ames Ballard Kipling Collection. Philadelphia, 1935.

(2) COLLECTED WORKS

The Outward Bound Edition. New York, 1897–.

The Edition de Luxe. 1897–1920.

The Trade Edition. New York, 1898–.

The Uniform Edition. 1899–.

The Bombay Edition. 1913–29.

The Seven Seas Edition. Garden City, 1913–26.

The Sussex Edition. 1937–8.

(3) PRINCIPAL WORKS

Schoolboy Lyrics. Lahore, 1881.

Echoes. By Two Writers. Lahore, 1884. [32 poems by Rudyard Kipling, 7 poems by Alice [Trix] Kipling.]

Quartette. By Four Anglo-Indian Writers. Lahore, 1885. [Prose and verse by J. Lockwood Kipling, Mrs Kipling, Rudyard and Alice Kipling.]

Departmental Ditties and Other Verses. [Lahore], 1886; Calcutta, 1886 (5 new poems); Calcutta, 1888 (10 new poems); 1890 (10 new poems); 1891 (with glossary); 1897 (illustrated).

Plain Tales from the Hills. Calcutta, 1888. [40 stories, 32 rptd from The Civil and Military Gazette.]

Plain Tales from the Hills. New York, 1899 (pirated edn). [The Last Relief is not rptd elsewhere.]

Soldiers Three. Allahabad, 1888; 1890 (rev.). [7 stories, 6 rptd from The Week's News.]

The Story of the Gadsbys. Allahabad, 1888; 1890 (rev.). [8 stories, 6 rptd from The Week's News.]

In Black and White. Allahabad, 1888; 1890 (rev.). [8 stories, 7 rptd from The Week's News.]

Under the Deodars. Allahabad, 1888; 1890 (rev.). [6 stories, 5 rptd from The Week's News.]

The Phantom 'Rickshaw and Other Tales. Allahabad, 1888; 1890 (rev.). [4 stories rptd from Quartette and The Week's News.]

Wee Willie Winkie and Other Child Stories. Allahabad. 1888; 1890 (rev.). [4 stories, 3 rptd from The Week's News.]

Departmental Ditties, Barrack-Room Ballads, and Other Verses. New York, 1890. [The Ballads and Other Verses were rptd from the Scots Observer and English Illustrated Mag.]

The Courting of Dinah Shadd. New York, 1890 (bis). [6 stories rptd from magazines. 2nd edn substitutes The Record of Badalia Herodsfoot for Krishna Mulvaney.]

The Light That Failed. New York, 1890 (unhappy ending; 12 chs.); New York, 1890 (happy ending as ptd in Lippincott's Mag.; 14 chs.); 1891 (15 chs.; dedicatory poem and preface); 1898 (rev., Outward Bound edn).

City of Dreadful Night and Other Sketches. Allahabad, 1890 (suppressed). [18 stories rptd from The Civil and Military Gazette, and The Pioneer.]

City of Dreadful Night and Other Places. Allahabad, 1891 (suppressed); 1891. [11 stories rptd from The Pioneer.]

Smith Administration. Allahabad, 1891 (suppressed). [20 articles rptd from The Civil and Military Gazette, and The Pioneer.]

Letters of Marque. Allahabad, 1891 (suppressed); 1891 (Part i; suppressed). [Rptd from The Pioneer.]

American Notes. New York, 1891. [Rptd from The Pioneer.]

Mine Own People. New York, 1891. [12 stories, 6 rptd from The Courting of Dinah Shadd.]

Life's Handicap. 1891. [10 stories from Mine Own People, 14 new ones rptd from Indian and English newspapers and magazines, 1 poem.]

Naulahka. By Rudyard Kipling and Wolcott Balestier. 1892; New York, 1892. [Chapter headings were ptd separately for copyright.]

Barrack-Room Ballads and Other Verses. London, 1892. [Poems from Departmental Ditties, etc., 1890, 15 rptd from newspapers and magazines, 3 rptd from Lyra Heroica, and Beast and Man in India, 1891.]

Ballads and Barrack-Room Ballads. New York, 1893. [4 new poems.]

Many Inventions. 1893. [14 stories, 2 poems; 10 stories were rptd from magazines, 2 were issued separately for copyright.]

The Jungle Book. 1894. [7 stories rptd from magazines, 7 poems.]

Second Jungle Book. 1895. [8 stories rptd from magazines, 8 poems.]

Out of India. New York, 1895. [City of Dreadful Night, and Letters of Marque, 1891.]

Soldiers Three, The Story of the Gadsbys, In Black and White. New York, 1895. [Rev., 2 new stories from The Civil and Military Gazette not in English edn, 1895.]

Wee Willie Winkie, Under the Deodars, The Phantom 'Rickshaw. New York, 1895. [Rev., 2 new stories from The Civil and Military Gazette not in English edn, 1895.]

Seven Seas. 1896. [3 poems from Ballads, New York, 1893; many poems rptd from newspapers and magazines; 3 poems ptd separately for copyright.]

Soldiers Tales. 1896. [7 stories rptd from other books.]

The Kipling Birthday Book. 1896. [Many quotations from The Civil and Military Gazette; plates by J. L. Kipling.]

Captains Courageous. 1897.

Almanac of Sports. 1897.

Day's Work. 1898. [12 stories rptd from magazines.]

A Fleet in Being. 1898. [Rptd from The Morning Post.]

Recessional and Other Poems. 1899. [4 poems rptd from newspapers.]

Departmental Ditties and Ballads and Barrack-Room Ballads. New York, 1899. [Departmental Ditties with rev. text.]

Stalky and Co. 1899. [9 stories rptd from magazines. The Complete Stalky, 1929, includes 4 additional stories and 3 poems rptd from other books and magazines.]

From Sea to Sea. New York, 1899; 1900. [Letters of Marque, City of Dreadful Night, Smith Administration.]

Occasional Poems. Boston, 1900. [16 poems rptd from newspapers and magazines.]

With Number Three, Surgical and Medical, and New Poems. Santiago de Chile, 1900. [Rptd from newspapers and magazines.]

Kim. 1901.

Railway Reform in Great Britain. New York, 1901.

Sin of Witchcraft. 1901. [Rptd from The Times.]

Science of Rebellion. 1901. [Written for Imperial South African Ass.]

Just So Stories. 1902. [12 stories, 11 rptd from magazines, and 9 poems.]

Five Nations. 1903. [Many poems rptd from newspapers and magazines; 14 poems were ptd separately.]

Traffics and Discoveries. 1904. [11 stories rptd from newspapers and magazines, 11 poems.]

Puck of Pook's Hill. 1906. [10 stories rptd from magazines, 16 poems.]

Letter on a Possible Source of The Tempest. Providence, 1906.

South Africa ['A shame of a Majuba Hill']. New York, 1906. [Copyright edn; not rptd.]

Collected Verse. New York, 1907; 1912. [Adds 1 new poem.]

Speech [at the] Artists' Benevolent Institution. 1907.

Doctors. 1908.

Letters to the Family. Toronto, 1908, 1910. [Rptd from newspapers.]

Actions and Reactions. 1909. [8 stories rptd from magazines, 8 poems.]

Abaft the Funnel. New York, 1909 (pirated); New York, 1909 (authorized). [Rptd from Indian newspapers.]

Rewards and Fairies. 1910. [11 stories, 10 rptd from magazines; 23 poems, 3 rptd from magazines; 10 stories were ptd separately for copyright.]

The History of England. 1911; 1912 (rev.). [With C. R. L. Fletcher; 23 poems.]

Songs from Books. New York, 1912. [Many new poems.]

Songs from Books. 1913. [Additional poems from The Jungle Book, Just So Stories, History of England.]

Kipling Reader for Elementary Grades. New York, 1912. [How to bring up a Lion, not rptd elsewhere.]

The New Army in Training. 1915. [6 pts rptd from the Daily Mail.]

France at War. 1915. [6 pts rptd from the Daily Mail.]

Fringes of the Fleet. 1915. [6 pts rptd from the Daily Telegraph.]

Tales of the Trade. 1916. [3 pts rptd from the Times.]

Sea Warfare. 1916. [Fringes of the Fleet, Tales of the Trade, Destroyers at Jutland, all rptd from newspapers; The Neutral ptd separately.]

Diversity of Creatures. 1917. [12 stories rptd from magazines, 1 ptd separately, 13 poems.]

The Eyes of Asia. New York, 1918. [4 pts rptd from Saturday Evening Post.]

War in the Mountains. Milan, 1918 (in Italian). [5 pts ptd in London, New York, Paris, and Milan newspapers.]

Twenty Poems. 1918. ['Sons of Martha,' and 'Holy War' with other rptd poems.]

Graves of the Fallen. Imperial War Graves Commission. 1919.

The Years Between. 1919. [46 poems, 11 new and 31 rptd from magazines and newspapers; 21 were ptd separately.]

Verse Inclusive Edition. 3 vols. 1919.

Verse Inclusive Edition. New York, 1919. [Does not include 'Mowgli's Song at the Council Rock.']

Verse Inclusive Edition. New York, 1921. ['Philadelphia,' 'When 'Omer Smote 'is Bloomin' Lyre' not in previous edns.]

Verse Inclusive Edition. 1921. ['Great Heart' omitted; 'Philadelphia,' 'When 'Omer Smote 'is Bloomin' Lyre' and 12 poems rptd from magazines and newspapers added.]

Verse Inclusive Edition. 1927. [Verses from Debits and Credits, 7 rptd from newspapers and magazines, and 'A Song in the Desert' added.]

Verse Inclusive Edition. 1933. [Brazilian Verses, and 8 other new poems added.]

Letters of Travel. 1920. [From Tideway to Tideway, Letters to the Family, Egypt of the Magicians rptd from newspapers and magazines.]

Select Stories. New York, 1921. [13 stories rptd from books.]

The First Assault on the Sorbonne. New York, 1922.

The King's Pilgrimage. 1922. [Rptd from The Times.]

Kipling Anthology. Verse. 1922.

Kipling Anthology. Prose. 1922.

Land and Sea Tales. 1923. [11 stories rptd from newspapers and magazines, 1 new story, 7 new poems.]

The Irish Guards. 2 vols. 1923.

Kipling Calendar. 1923.

The Two Jungle Books. 1924.

Songs of Youth. 1924. [55 poems rptd from other collections.]

Choice of Songs. 1925. [30 poems rptd from other collections, 1 new poem.]

'They' and Brushwood Boy. 1925.

Sea and Sussex. 1926. [1 new poem.]

Letter to Conrad. 1926.

Debits and Credits. 1926. [14 stories rptd from magazines, 20 new poems.]

On Dry-Cow Fishing. Cleveland, 1926. [Rptd from The Fishing Gazette, Dec. 1890.]

Songs of the Sea. 1927. [11 poems rptd from books, 1 new poem.]

One Volume Kipling. New York, 1928. [Ballads and Barrack-Room Ballads, The Light That Failed, City of Dreadful Night, Plain Tales From the Hills, Soldiers Three, Mine Own People, In Black and White, Phantom 'Rickshaw, Under the Deodars, Wee Willie Winkie, Story of the Gadsbys, Departmental Ditties, and 3 uncollected stories rptd from magazines.]

A Book of Words. 1928. [31 speeches, 13 ptd separately, others rptd from newspapers.]

Kipling Stories for Children. New York, 1928. [12 rptd stories.]

Supplication of the Black Aberdeen. 1929. [Rptd from Strand Mag.]

Poems, 1886–1929. 3 vols. 1929. [Rev. text, 4 new poems.]

Thy Servant a Dog. 1930. [3 stories, 2 rptd from magazines.]

Selected Poems. 1931. [30 poems rptd.]

Humorous Tales. 1931. [16 tales, 7 poems rptd.]

The Jungle Book. New York, 1932. ['How to say the names' added.]

Animal Stories. 1932. [12 stories, 7 poems rptd.]

Limits and Renewals. 1932. [14 stories (3 new ones), 19 poems (12 new ones).]

Souvenirs of France. 1933.

All the Mowgli Stories. 1933. [10 stories, 3 poems rptd.]

Collected Dog Stories. 1934. [7 stories, 5 poems rptd, 1 new story.]

A Kipling Pageant. New York, 1935.

All the Puck Stories. 1935.

Two Forewords. New York, 1935.

The King and the Sea. 1935.

Something of Myself, for My Friends known and unknown. 1936.

(4) Separate Stories, Poems and Speeches

[This list does not include the 120 or more items ptd separately for copyright purposes or the hundreds of pirated rpts.]

Song of the Women. 1890.

'Cleared.' 1890.

Kipling's Regrets. 1896.

The Vampire. 1897, etc.

Recessional. 1897, etc.

The Brushwood Boy. 1899; 1907.

The Absent-minded Beggar. 1899, etc.

[Auld Lang Syne.] 1900.

The Settler. 1903.

The Gipsy Trail. 1904; 1909.

'They.' 1904; 1906.

The Army of a Dream. 1905.

With the Night Mail. 1909.

The Song of the English. 1909; 1915.

If. 1910, etc.

The Dead King. 1910.

The Female of the Species. 1910.

France. 1914.

Ulster. 1914.

Some Aspects of Travel. Paris, 1914. [In French.]

Hymn before Action. 1914, etc.

Secret Bargain and the Ulster Plot. 1914.

Indictment of the Government. 1914.

The Children's Song. 1914, etc.

Call to the Nation. 1914.

National Bands. 1915.

Fringes of the Fleet. Boston, 1915.

The Holy War. 1917.

Kipling's Message. 1918.

Justice. 1918.

'Mother o' Mine.' 1918.

The Irish Guards. 1918.

The Feet of the Young Men. 1920.

England and the English. 1921.

Independence. 1924.

The Janeites. 1924.

Shipping Industry. 1925.

The Art of Fiction. 1926.

Supplication of the Black Aberdeen. 1927.

His Apologies. 1932.

The Fox Meditates. 1933.

Hymn of the Breaking Strain. 1934.

The Religion of War. 1935.

(5) Contributions to Books not reprinted elsewhere

Fame's Tribute to Children. Chicago, 1892. [Poem: 'Old Johnny Grundy.']

Library of Edmund Gosse. 1893; 1924. [Poem.]

My First Book. 1894. [Prose: 'Departmental Ditties.']

Book of Beauty. 1897. [Poem: 'The Quest.']

War's Brighter Side. By Julian Ralph. 1901. [Prose and poems.]

Helio-Trope. 1904. [Poem.]

From Pillar to Post. By Col. H. C. Lowther. 1911. [Poem.]

King's Book of Quebec. Ottawa, 1911. [Prose.]

The Merry Thought. 1911. [Story ('Why Snow falls at Vernet') and letter.]

Collected Poems of James Whitcomb Riley. 1913. [Poem.]

War. By W. Douglas Newton. 1914. [Preface.]

Britain and the War. By André Chévrillon. 1917. [Preface.]

Q. Horati Flacci Carminum Librum Quintum a Rudyardo Kipling et Carolo Graves Anglice redditum edidit Aluredus D. Godley. Oxford, 1920, 1922.

An Historical Event at Stationer's Hall. 1926. [Speech.]

St Andrews. By Rudyard Kipling and Walter de la Mare. 1926. [Poem.]

The Legion Book. 1929. [Poem.]

Story of a Surgeon. By Sir John Bland-Sutton. 1930. [Introduction.]

Five Hundred Points of Good Husbandry by Thomas Tusser. 1931. [Benediction by Kipling.]

The Authors' Bulletin. Montreal, 1933. [Toast of the Canadian Authors' Association.]

Ant Antics. 1933. ['Mr Wu of Peking.']

India and the Report of the Joint Committee. [1933.] [Message from Mr Kipling.]

Cecil Rhodes by Herbert Baker. 1934. [Poem.]

Princess Elizabeth's Gift Book. 1934. [Ham and the Porcupine.]

(6) PERIODICALS CONTAINING UN-REPRINTED MATTER

The United Services College Chronicle. Bideford, 1881–98.

The Civil and Military Gazette.

The Pioneer Mail.

The Pioneer.

The Week's News.

The Calcutta Review. 1885–6.

'Turnovers.' Lahore, 1888–90.

St James's Gazette. 1889–92.

The Spectator. [Various dates.]

The Friend. Bloemfontein, 1900.

The Daily Mail. 1900.

The Near East. May 1912.

(7) LETTERS

Year Boke of the Sette of Odd Volumes. 1892.

Letters to A. P. Watt. 1893; 1897; 1902.

The Tenth Island. By Beckles Wilson. Newfoundland, 1897.

The School Budget. No. 13. Horsmonden School. 1898.

The Cruise of the 'Cachalot.' By Frank T. Bullen. 1898.

Ken of Kipling. By Will M. Clemens. 1899.

Kipling Primer. By F. W. Knowles. 1899.

An Attempt at Appreciation by G. F. Monkshood [W. J. Clarke]. 1899.

Eccentricities of Genius. By Major J. H. Pond. 1900.

Life and Letters of Sir Arthur Sullivan. By Arthur Lawrence. 1900.

The Complete Motorist. By A. Filson Young. 1904.

Through Isle and Empire. By the Vicomte Robert D'Humières. 1905. [Letter, Daily Mail, 10 Sept. 1904.]

'The Times' and the Publisher. 1906.

The Surplus. Salvation Army. 1909; 1924.

Life and Letters of Edmund Clarence Stedman. 1910.

Letters. La Revue de Paris, 1 Nov. 1915, 1 Jan. 1916. [Concerning 'Britain and the War.']

Life and Letters of Joel Chandler Harris. 1918.

Guynemer. By Henry Bordeau. 1918. [Not in American edn.]

Americanization of Edward Bok. 1920.

Proceedings of the American Academy of Arts and Letters. W. D. Howells Memorial Meeting. New York, 1921.

The Log of the H.M.A. R. 34, Journey to America and back by Commodore Maitland. 1921.

Remembered Yesterdays. By Robert Underwood Johnson. 1923.

Life of Mrs Humphry Ward. 1923.

Life and Letters of Sir Mark Sykes. By Shane Leslie. 1923.

Life of Sir William Osler. By Harvey Cushing. 1925.

The Sunlight Hours. By Theodore A. Cook. 1926.

The India We Served. By Sir Walter R. Lawrence. 1928.

The Days of My Life. By Rider Haggard. 1928.

Life in Letters to W. D. Howells. 1928.

South Africa and Other Poems. By A. Vine Hall. N.d. [Not in 2nd edn, 1926.]

Among my Books. Paul Lemperly. Cleveland, 1929.

The Ashley Library. Collected by T. J. Wise. Vol. x, 1930. [Letters to Sir Edmund Gosse.]

Life and Letters of Henry Arthur Jones. 1930.

A Few Significant and Important Kipling Items. W. M. Carpenter. Chicago, 1930. [Letters to Julian Ralph.]

Letters of James Whitcomb Riley. 1931.

Books of Association Interest, Manuscripts, Letters, etc. Alwin J. Scheuer. 1931. [Letters to W. H. Phillips ('Sitting Fox').]

(8) BIOGRAPHY AND CRITICISM

(a) Books

Forster's Note Book of Kipling. Birmingham, 1898.

Graz, F. Beiträge zu eine Kritick Rudyard Kipling. Leipzig, 1898.

Clemens, W. M. Ken of Kipling. 1899.

Lawton, W. C. Rudyard Kipling, the Artist. 1899.

Livingston, L. S. Rudyard Kipling's First Book. New York, 1899.

—— The Works of Rudyard Kipling. 1901.

Mansfield, M. F. Kipling Note Book. Kiplingiana. 1899; 1900.

'Monkshood, G. F.' [W. J. Clarke] and Gamble, G. Rudyard Kipling. The Man and his Work. 1899; 1902.

Norton, C. E. A Biographical Sketch. 1899.

Parker, W. P. The Religion of Mr Kipling. 1899.

Robertson, W. Kipling Guide Book. Birmingham, 1899.

Buchanan, Robert and Besant, Sir W. The Voice of the Hooligan. 1900.

Knowles, F. L. Kipling Primer. 1900.

Le Gallienne, R. Criticism; Bibliography by John Lane. 1900.

Wyzewa, T. de. Stalky and Co. Paris, 1900.

Dalrymple, C. M. Kipling's Prosa. Marburg, 1905.

Löwe, Ernst. Beiträge zur Metrik Rudyard Kipling. Marburg, 1906.

Loeb-Lundberg, C. Word-Formation in Kipling. Lund, 1909.

Charles, Cecil. Rudyard Kipling. 1911.

Young, W. A. Kipling Dictionary. 1911.

Becher, J. A. Untersuchungen über Kipling's Erzählungskunst. Marburg, 1913.

Durant, R. Handbook of Poetry. 1914.

Falls, C. Rudyard Kipling. A Critical Study. 1915.

Munson, A. I. Kipling's India. 1915.

Palmer, J. W. Rudyard Kipling. 1915.

Hopkins, R. T. A Literary Appreciation. 1916.

—— Rudyard Kipling. 1930.

'Monkshood, G. F.' Less Familiar Kipling and Kiplingiana. 1917.

Hart, W. M. Kipling the Story Teller. Berkeley, 1918.

Worster, W. Merlin's Isle. 1921.

Ferguson, J. De L. Rudyard Kipling's Revisions of his Published Works. Urbana, 1923.

Braybrook, P. Kipling and his Soldiers. 1925.

Around the World with Kipling. Garden City, 1926. [Contributions by W. L. Phelps, R. Le Gallienne, A. Chévrillon, etc.]

The Kipling Society Journal. 1927–

Dunsterville, L. C. Stalky's Reminiscences. 1928.

Brion, M. Rudyard Kipling. Paris, 1929.

Marquardt, H. Kipling und Indien. Breslau, 1931.

MacMunn, Sir G. Kipling's Women. 1933.

—— Rudyard Kipling, Craftsman. 1937.

Nazari, E. Rudyard Kipling. Saggio critico. Palermo, 1933.

Tapp, H. A. United Services College. 1933.

Beresford, G. C. Schooldays with Kipling. 1936.

Rice, H. C. Rudyard Kipling in New England. Brattleboro, 1936.

Seillière, E. Notice sur la Vie et les Travaux de M. Rudyard Kipling. Paris, 1936.

Mason, J. S. A Yale Footnote to Kipling. New Haven, 1937.

(b) Essays and Chapters of Books

Lang, A. Essays in Little. 1891.

Dawson, W. J. Quest and Vision. 1892.

Oliphant, M. O. and F. R. English Literature. 1892.

Gosse, Sir E. Questions at Issue. 1893.

—— Short History of Modern Literature. 1893.

Bridges, R. Overheard in Arcady. 1894.

Nicoll, Sir W. R. and Wise, T. J. Literary Anecdotes of the Nineteenth Century. Vol. I, 1895.

Rideing, W. H. Boyhood of Famous Authors. 1897.

Shorter, C. K. Victorian Literature. 1897.

Burton, Sir R. Literary Likings. 1898.

Griswold, H. T. Personal Sketches of Recent Authors. Chicago, 1898.

Adams, Francis. Essays in Modernity. 1899.

Bangs, J. K. Peeps at People. 1899.

McCarthy, J. Reminiscences. 1899.

Oliphant, J. Victorian Novelists. 1899.

Bell, F. W. The South African Conspiracy. 1900.

Castelnuovo, E. Un Apostolo della Forza. Venice, 1900.

Jeanroy, F. V. Études de Littérature étrangère. Paris, 1900.

Chévrillon, A. Études Anglaises. 1901.

—— Nouvelles Études Anglaises. 1910.

—— Three Studies in English Literature. Tr. Eng. 1923.

Murray, Henry. Robert Buchanan and Other Essays. 1901.

'Stephen, Sidney' and 'Lee, Leslie.' Lives of the 'Lustrious. A Dictionary of Irrational Biography. 1901.

Archer, W. Poets of the Younger Generation. 1902.

Muirhead, J. H. Philosophy and Life. 1902.

Vogué, E. M., Vicomte de. Pages d'histoire. Paris, 1902.

Disraeli; les Romans de Rudyard Kipling. Paris, 1902.

Little, J. S. Progress of the British Empire in the Century. 1903.

McNeill, A. Egregious English. 1903.

Findlater, J. H. Stones from a Glass House. The Art of Narration. 1904.

Chesterton, G. K. Heretics. 1905.

—— What's Wrong with the World. 1910.

—— The Victorian Age in Literature. 1913.

More, P. E. Shelburne Essays. Ser. 2, New York, 1905.

Beeching, H. C. Provincial Letters and Other People. 1906.

Worsfold, W. B. Lord Milner's Work in South Africa. 1906.

James, Henry. Views and Reviews. 1908.

Murray, D. C. Recollections. 1908.

Oaten, E. F. Sketches of Anglo-Indian Literature. 1908.

Magnus, L. English Literature of the Nineteenth Century. 1909.

Roz, F. Romanciers anglais contemporains. Paris, 1909.

—— Le Roman anglais. Paris, 1909.

Chapman, E. M. English Literature in Account with Religion. 1910.

Fuller, T. E. The Right Honourable Cecil Rhodes. 1910.

Phelps, W. L. Essays on Modern Novelists. New York, 1910.

—— Advance of the Novel. 1916.

—— Advance of English Poetry in the Twentieth Century. 1918.

Previté-Orton, C. W. Political Satire in English Poetry. Cambridge, 1910.

Rivett-Carnac, J. H. Many Memories in India, at Home and Abroad. 1910.

Cooper, F. T. Some English Story Tellers. 1912.

Fitch, G. H. Modern English Books of Power. San Francisco, 1912.

Holliday, C. English Fiction. 1912.

Kennedy, J. M. English Literature, 1880–1905. 1912.

Scott-James, R. A. Personality in Literature. 1913.

Gardiner, A. G. Proofsheets, Priests, and Kings. 1914.

McClure, S. S. My Autobiography. 1914.

Simon, J. D. The Press and its Story. 1914.

Harris, Frank. Contemporary Portraits. 1915.

Mason, E. Book of Preferences in Literature. 1915.

Russell, George ('A. E.') Imaginations and Reveries. 1915.

Leslie, S. The End of the Chapter. 1916.

Scott, Dixon. Men of Letters. 1916.

Bennett, Arnold. Books and Persons. 1917.

Cestre, C. France, England and European Democracy, 1215–1915. 1918.

Jessup, A. and Canby, H. S. The Book of Short Stories. 1918.

Legouis, E. and Chislett, W. Classical Influence. 1918.

McSpadden, J. W. Famous Ghost Stories. 1918.

Murphy, W. S. The Genesis of War Poetry. 1918.

Ward, A. C. Aspects of the Short Story. 1918.

Williams, Harold. Modern English Writers. 1918.

Cross, W. L. The Development of the English Novel. New York, 1919.

Cunliffe, J. W. English Literature during the Last Half Century. New York, 1919.

Ellsworth, W. W. The Golden Age of Authors. 1919.

Hudson, W. H. English History of the Nineteenth Century. 1919.

Lynd, R. Old and New Masters. 1919.

Thompson, E. R. All and Sundry. 1919.

Waugh, A. Tradition and Change. 1919.

The Country Life Press. Garden City, 1919.

Gerould, K. F. Modes and Morals. 1920.

Hutchinson, H. G. Portraits of the Eighties. 1920.

Jones, Kennedy. Fleet Street and Downing Street. 1920.

Muddiman, B. Men of the Nineties. 1920.

Brown, R. W. The Writer's Art. 1921.

Chevalley, A. Le Roman anglais de notre Temps. Paris, 1921.

Hind, C. L. Authors and I. 1921.

Hueffer, F. M. Thus to Revisit. Some Remembrances. 1921.

Johnson, Lionel. Reviews and Critical Papers. Ed. R. Shafer, 1921.

Jackson, H. The Eighteen Nineties. 1922.

Kernahan, C. Six Famous Living Poets. 1922.

Adcock, A. St J. Gods of Modern Grub Street. 1923.

Hubbell, J. B. and Beatty, J. O. An Introduction to Poetry. 1923.

'Lee, Vernon.' The Handling of Words. 1923.

Nevins, A. American Social History as recorded by English Travellers. 1923.

Serra, R. Scritti Inediti. Florence, 1923.

Squire, Sir J. C. Essays on Poetry. 1923.

Doyle, Sir A. C. Memories and Adventures. 1924.

Springfield, L. Some Piquant People. 1924.

'Lacon.' Lectures to Living Authors. 1925.

[Pearson, H.] The Whispering Gallery. 1926.

Cazamian, J. History of English Literature. Tr. Eng. 1927.

Cummings, Sir J. G. Historical Biography relating to India. 1927.

Guedalla, P. Men of Letters. 1927.

Hutton, M. Many Minds. 1927.

McKnight, G. H. Modern English in the Making. 1928.

Rickword, E. et al. Scrutinies by Various Writers. 1928.

Dobrée, B. The Lamp and the Lute. Oxford, 1929.

Mitchell, S. W. Life and Letters by Anna Robeson Burr. 1929.

Roberts, R. E. Reading for Pleasure and Other Essays. 1929.

Williams, Charles. Poetry at Present. Oxford, 1930.

Thirkell, A. Three Houses. 1931.

Maurois, A. Magicians and Logicians. 1936.

Gerould, K. F. Side Lines. 1937.

F. V. L.

VII. MINOR FICTION, 1870–1900

[This section has been restricted to writers born between 1830 and 1865 whose more important works were written before 1900. Novelists whose reputation depends mainly or wholly on their 20th-century productions have been deliberately excluded.]

GRANT ALLEN, *i.e.* CHARLES GRANT BLAIRFINDIE ALLEN (1848–1899)

(a) *Fiction*

Philistia. 3 vols. 1884. [Pbd under the pseudonym 'Cecil Power.']

Strange Stories. 1884.

Babylon. 3 vols. 1885. [Pbd under the pseudonym 'Cecil Power.']

Kalee's Shrine. Bristol, 1886. [With May Cotes.]

In all Shades. 3 vols. 1886.

The Sole Trustee. [1886.]

For Maimie's Sake. A Tale of Love and Dynamite. 1886.

The Beckoning Hand, and Other Stories. 1887.

A Terrible Inheritance. [1887.]

This Mortal Coil. A Novel. 3 vols. 1888.

The White Man's Foot. 1888.

The Devil's Die. A Novel. 3 vols. 1888.

The Tents of Shem. A Novel. 3 vols. 1889. [Contains 16 stories first pbd in Cornhill Mag., Longman's Mag. and Belgravia, under the pseudonym 'J. Arbuthnot Wilson.']

Dr Palliser's Patient. 1889.

The Jaws of Death. [1889.]

A Living Apparition. [1889.]

The Great Taboo. 1890.

Recalled to Life. Bristol, [1891].

What's Bred in the Bone. 1891.

Dumaresq's Daughter. A Novel. 3 vols. 1891.

The Duchess of Powysland. A Novel. 3 vols. 1892.

The Scallywag. 3 vols. 1893.

Michael's Cray. 1893.

Ivan Greet's Masterpiece and Other Stories. 1893.

Blood Royal. A Novel. 1893.

An Army Doctor's Romance. [1893.]

At Market Value. 2 vols. 1894.

The British Barbarians. A Hill-Top Novel. 1895.

The Woman who did. 1895.

Under Sealed Orders. A Novel. 3 vols. 1895.

Moorland Idylls. 1896.

A Splendid Sin. 1896.

An African Millionaire. 1897.

Tom Unlimited. A Story for Children. 1897. [Pbd under the pseudonym 'Martin Leach Warborough.']

The Type-Writer Girl. 1897. [Pbd under the pseudonym 'Olive Pratt Rayner.']

Linnet. A Romance. 1898.

The Incidental Bishop. [1898.]

Rosalba: the Story of her Development. 1899. [Pbd under the pseudonym 'Olive Pratt Rayner.']

Miss Cayley's Adventures. 1899.

Twelve Tales. Selected Stories. 1899.

Hilda Wade. 1900. [First pbd in Strand Mag.]

Sir Theodore's Guest and Other Stories. Bristol, 1902.

The Desire of the Eyes and Other Stories. N.d.

(b) *Other Writings*

Physiological Aesthetics. 1877.

The Colour-Sense: its Origin and Development. 1879.

Early Britain: Anglo-Saxon Britain. [1881.]

The Evolutionist at large. 1881.

Vignettes from Nature. 1881.

The Colours of Flowers, as illustrated in the British Flora. 1882.

Colin Clout's Calendar, April–October. 1883.

Flowers and their Pedigrees. 1883.

Nature Studies. [1883.] [With Andrew Wilson, Thomas Foster, Edward Clodd and R. A. Proctor.]

Biographies of Working Men. 1884.

Darwin. 1885.

The Miscellaneous and Posthumous Works of H. T. Buckle. [1885.] [Ed. by Allen.]

Commonsense Science. Boston, 1887.

Force and Energy. A Theory of Dynamics. 1888.

Falling in Love. With Other Essays. 1889.

Science in Arcady. 1892.

The Tidal Thames. 1892.

The Attis of Caius Valerius Catullus, translated into English Verse. 1892.

The Lower Slopes. 1894. [Poems.]

Post-Prandial Philosophy. 1894. [First pbd in Westminster Gazette.]

In Memoriam G. P. Macdonell. 1895.

The Story of the Plants. 1895.

The Evolution of the Idea of God. 1897.

Cities of Belgium. 1897.

Florence. 1897.

Paris. 1897.

Venice. 1898.

The European Tour. A Handbook for Americans and Colonists. 1899.

Flashlights on Nature. 1899.

The Natural History of Selborne. By Gilbert White. 1900. [Ed. by Allen.]
In Nature's Workshop. 1901.
Evolution in Italian Art. Rev. J. W. Cruikshank, 1908.

(c) Biography

Harrison, Frederic. Grant Allen. 1899.
Clodd, Edward. Grant Allen; A Memoir, with a List of Writings. 1900.
Le Gallienne, R. Attitudes and Avowals. 1910.

'F. ANSTEY,' i.e. THOMAS ANSTEY GUTHRIE (1856–1934)

(a) Bibliography

Turner, M. J. A Bibliography of the Works of F. Anstey (Thomas Anstey Guthrie). 1931 (priv. ptd).

(b) Selected Works

Humour and Fantasy. 1931. [Contents: Vice Versa, The Tinted Venus, A Fallen Idol, The Brass Bottle, The Talking Horse, and Salted Almonds.]

(c) Novels, Sketches and Miscellaneous Writings

Vice Versa, or a Lesson to Fathers. 1882; 1883 (rev.).
The Giants' Robe. 1884.
The Black Poodle and Other Tales. 1884.
The Tinted Venus. 1885.
A Fallen Idol. 1886.
Mr Punch's Young Reciter. 1888; 1889 (enlarged as Burglar Bill and Other Pieces); 1931 (rev. as The Young Reciter and Model Music-Hall).
The Parish. 3 vols. 1889.
Voces Populi. 2 sers. 1890–2. [From Punch.]
Tourmalin's Time Cheques. 1891; 1905 (as The Time Bargain, or Tourmalin's Time Cheques).
The Travelling Companions. 1892.
Mr Punch's Model Music Hall Songs and Dramas. 1892.
The Talking Horse and Other Tales. 1892.
Mr Punch's Pocket Ibsen. 1893.
The Man from Blankley's and Other Sketches. 1893. [From Punch.]
Under the Rose. A Story in Scenes, from Punch. [1894.]
Lyre and Lancet. A Story in Scenes. 1895.
Puppets at Large. Scenes and Subjects from Mr Punch's Show. 1897.
Baboo Jabberjee, B.A. 1897.
Love among the Lions. 1898.
Paleface and Redskin and Other Stories for Boys and Girls. 1898.
The Brass Bottle. 1900.

A Bayard from Bengal. 1902.
Only Toys. 1903.
Salted Almonds and Other Tales. 1906.
In Brief Authority. 1915.
Percy and Others. Sketches, mainly reproduced from Punch. 1915.
The Last Load. Stories and Essays. 1925.
Four Molière Comedies, freely adapted. 1931.
Three Molière Plays, freely adapted. 1933.
A Long Retrospect. Oxford, 1936.

SABINE BARING-GOULD (1834–1924)

(a) Fiction

The Path of the Just. Tales of Holy Men and Children. 1857.
Through Flood and Flame. A Novel. 3 vols. 1868.
In Exitu Israel. An Historical Novel. 2 vols. 1870.
Ernestine. A Novel. By Wilhelmine von Hillern. 1879. [From the German by Baring-Gould.]
Mehalah. A Story of the Salt Marshes. 2 vols. 1880.
John Herring. A West of England Romance. 3 vols. 1883; 1884.
Please tell me a Tale. A Collection of Short Original Stories for Children. 1885. [Baring-Gould contributed 'Gottlob's Picture.']
Just One More Tale. A Second Collection of Stories for Children, being a Companion Volume to 'Please tell me a Tale.' 1886. [Baring-Gould contributed 'Wow Wow.']
Court Royal. 3 vols. 1886.
Little Tu'penny. 1887.
Jack Frost's Little Prisoners. 1887. [With other stories.]
Red Spider. 2 vols. 1887.
The Gaverocks. A Tale of the Cornish Coast. 3 vols. 1887.
Richard Cable, the Lightshipman. 3 vols. 1888.
Eve. A Novel. 2 vols. 1888.
The Pennycomequicks. A Novel. 3 vols. 1889.
Grettir the Outlaw. A Story of Iceland. 1889.
Arminell. A Social Romance. 3 vols. 1890.
Jacquetta and Other Stories. 1890.
My Prague Pig and Other Stories for Children. 1890.
Urith. A Tale of Dartmoor. 3 vols. 1891.
Margery of Quether and Other Stories. 1891.
In the Roar of the Sea. A Tale of the Cornish Coast. 3 vols. 1892.
Through all the Changing Scenes of Life. A Tale. [1892.]
Mrs Curgenven of Curgenven. A Novel. 3 vols. 1893.
Cheap Jack Zita. 3 vols. 1893.
The Queen of Love. A Novel. 3 vols. 1894.

Kitty Alone. A Story of Three Fires. 3 vols. 1894.

The Icelander's Sword, or the Story of Oraefadal. 1894.

A Book of Fairy Tales, retold. 1894.

Noemi. 1895.

Dartmoor Idylls. 1896.

The Broom Squire. 1896.

Perpetua. A Story of Nimes in A.D. 213. 1897.

Guasvas the Tinner. 1897.

Bladys of the Stewponey. 1897.

Domitia. A Tale. 1898.

Pabo the Priest. 1899.

The Crock of Gold. [1899.] [Fairy tales.]

Furze Bloom. Tales of the Western Moors. 1899.

Winefred. A Story of the Chalk Cliffs. 1900.

In a Quiet Village. Tales. 1900.

The Frobishers. A Story of the Staffordshire Potteries. 1901.

Royal Georgie. 1901.

Nebo the Nailer. 1902.

Miss Quillet. A Novel. 1902.

Chris of all Sorts. 1903.

Amazing Adventures. Drawn by H. B. Neilson and written by S. Baring-Gould. [1903.]

Siegfried. A Romance. 1904. [Founded on Wagner's operas.]

In Dewisland. A Novel. 1904.

Monsieur Pichelmère and Other Stories. 1905.

(b) Other Writings

Iceland: its Scenes and Sagas. 1863.

The Book of Were Wolves; being an Account of a Terrible Superstition. 1865.

Post-Mediaeval Preachers. 1865.

Curious Myths of the Middle Ages. 2 sers. 1866-8.

The Silver Store, collected from Mediaeval, Christian and Jewish Mines. 1868; 1887 (with addns); 1898 (with addns). [Poems.]

Curiosities of the Olden Times. [1869.]

Origin and Development of Religious Belief. 2 pts, 1869-70.

The Lives of the Saints. 17 vols. 1872-89; 16 vols. 1897-8 (rev.).

Yorkshire Oddities, Incidents and Strange Events. 2 vols. 1874.

Some Modern Difficulties. 1875.

The Vicar of Morwenstow. Life of R. S. Hawker. 1876; 1876 (rev.); 1899 (rev.).

Germany Past and Present. 2 vols. 1879.

Germany. 1886; [1905] (rev.); 1921 (rev. and enlarged by J. MacCabe).

Historic Oddities and Strange Events. [Freaks of Fanaticism and Other Strange Events.] 2 vols. 1889-91.

Old Country Life. 1890.

In Troubadour Land. Provence and Languedoc. 1891.

Strange Survivals. 1892.

The Tragedy of the Caesars. 2 vols. 1892.

The Deserts of Southern France. 2 vols. 1894.

Colour in Composition. [In On the Art of writing Fiction, [1894].]

English Minstrelsie. 1895-9.

A Book of Nursery Songs and Rhymes. [1895.] [Ed. by Baring-Gould.]

A Garland of Country Song: English Folk Song. 1895.

Fairy Tales from Grimm. 1895. [Introduction by Baring-Gould.]

Life of Napoleon. 1897.

A Study of St Paul. 1897.

An Old English Home and its Dependencies. 1898.

A Book of the West. Introduction to Devon and Cornwall. 2 vols. 1899.

A Book of Dartmoor. 1900.

A Book of Brittany. 1901.

Bath Waters. By Preston King. With an Historical Sketch by S. Baring-Gould. [1901.]

Brittany. 1902.

A Book of North Wales. 1903.

A Book of Ghosts. 1904.

A Book of South Wales. 1905.

A Book of the Riviera. 1905.

A Book of the Rhine. 1906.

Lives of the British Saints. 1907. [With J. Fisher.]

A Book of the Cevennes. 1907.

A Book of the Pyrenees. 1907.

Devonshire Characters and Strange Events. 1908.

Cornish Characters and Strange Events. 1909.

A History of Sarawak under its Two White Rajahs, 1839-1908. 1909.

Family Names and their Story. 1910.

The Land of Teck and its Neighbourhood. 1911.

Cliff Castles and Cave Dwellings of Europe. 1911.

Sheepstor. [Plymouth], 1912.

A Book of Folk Lore. [1913.]

Early Reminiscences, 1834-64. 1923.

Further Reminiscences, 1864-94. 1925.

[Baring-Gould also wrote a number of devotional and theological works, and contributed introductions to several books on folk-lore and theology. A few ephemeral works are unrecorded here.]

(c) Criticism

Ellis, S. M. Mainly Victorian. [1925.]

Powys, L. A Devonshire Gentleman. North American Rev. ccxxi, 1925.

SIR JAMES MATTHEW BARRIE (1860-1937)

[See p. 623 below.]

ARTHUR CHRISTOPHER BENSON (1862–1925)
[See p. 734 below.]

SIR WALTER BESANT (1836–1901)

(a) Fiction (by Besant alone)

The Revolt of Man. 1882.
All Sorts and Conditions of Men. 3 vols. 1882.
All in a Garden Fair. 3 vols. 1883.
The Captain's Room. 3 vols. 1883.
Dorothy Forster. 3 vols. 1884.
Uncle Jack [etc.]: 1885. [5 tales.]
Children of Gibeon. 3 vols. 1886.
Katherine Regina. Bristol, [1887].
The World went very well then. 3 vols. 1887.
Herr Paulus. 3 vols. 1888.
The Inner House. Bristol, 1888.
The Doubts of Dives. Bristol, [1889]. [Rptd in Verbena Camellia Stephanotis, etc., 1892.]
The Bell of St Paul's. 3 vols. 1889.
For Faith and Freedom. 3 vols. 1889.
To call her mine, etc. 1889.
Armorel of Lyonesse. 3 vols. 1890.
The Demoniac. Bristol, [1890].
The Holy Rose, etc. 1890.
St Katherine's by the Tower. 3 vols. 1891.
Verbena Camellia Stephanotis, etc. 1892. [The Doubts of Dives and 2 short stories.]
The Ivory Gate. 3 vols. 1892.
The Rebel Queen. 3 vols. 1893.
Beyond the Dreams of Avarice. 1895.
In Deacon's Orders, etc. 1895.
The City of Refuge. 3 vols. 1896.
The Master Craftsman. 2 vols. 1896.
A Fountain sealed. 1897.
The Changeling. 1898.
The Orange Girl. 1899.
The Fourth Generation. 1900.
The Lady of Lynn. 1901.
A Five Year's Tryst and Other Stories. 1902.

(b) Fiction (in collaboration with James Rice)

Ready-Money Mortiboy. 3 vols. 1872. [Dramatic version, as Ready Money, by Rice and W. Maurice, was produced at the Court Theatre, 12 March 1874.]
My Little Girl. 3 vols. 1873.
The Golden Butterfly. 3 vols. 1876.
The Case of Mr Lucraft and Other Tales. 2 vols. 1876.
This Son of Vulcan. 3 vols. 1876.
With Harp and Crown. 1877.
Such a Good Man. 1877.
The Monks of Thelema. 3 vols. 1878. [First pbd in The World.]
By Celia's Arbour. 3 vols. 1878. [First pbd in The Graphic.]
'Twas in Trafalgar Bay, and Other Stories. 1879.

The Seamy Side. 3 vols. 1880. [First pbd in Time.]
The Chaplain of the Fleet. 3 vols. 1881.
Sir Richard Whittington. 1881.
The Ten Years' Tenant and Other Stories. 3 vols. 1881.

(c) Other Writings (by Besant alone, except where noted)

Studies in Early French Poetry. 1868.
Jerusalem: the City of Herod and Saladin. 1871. [With E. H. Palmer.]
The French Humourists. 1873.
The Literary Remains of C. F. T. Drake. 1877. [Ed., with a memoir, by Besant.]
Constantinople. 1879. [With W. J. Brodribb.]
Gaspard de Coligny. 1879.
Rabelais. 1879.
The Survey of Western Palestine. By C. R. Condor. 1881. [Ed. by E. H. Palmer and Besant.]
The Life and Achievements of E. H. Palmer. 1883.
Life in an Hospital. An East End Chapter. [1883.]
Readings in Rabelais. 1883.
The Art of Fiction. A Lecture. 1884.
Twenty-One Years' Work, 1865–1886. Palestine Exploration Fund, 1886; 1895 (with addns).
The Eulogy of Richard Jefferies. 1888.
Fifty Years Ago. 1888.
Captain Cook. 1890.
London. 1892.
The History of London. 1893.
The Society of Authors. 1893.
Westminster. 1895.
The Charm, and Other Drawing Room Plays. 1896. [With W. Pollock.]
The Rise of the Empire. [1897.]
Alfred. A Lecture. 1898.
The Pen and the Book. 1899.
South London. 1899.
East London. 1901.
The Story of King Alfred. 1901.
Autobiography. 1902.
London in the Eighteenth Century. 1902.
The Fascination of London Series. 11 vols. 1902–6. [Ed. by Besant, who collaborated with G. E. Mitton for the Strand, Westminster and Holborn–Bloomsbury vols.]
No Other Way. 1902.
The Survey of London. 10 vols. 1902–12. [Ed. by Besant.]
London in the Time of the Stuarts. 1903.
As we are and as we may be. 1903. [Essays.]
Essays and Historiettes. 1903.
The Thames. 1903.
London in the Time of the Tudors. 1904.
Mediaeval London. 2 vols. 1906.

Early London: Prehistoric, Roman, Saxon and Norman. 1908.

London in the Nineteenth Century. 1909.

London South of the Thames. 1912.

[Besant also contributed introductions to works by Charles Reade, Defoe, J. H. Round and others. For criticism of his novels see 'Lewis Melville,' Victorian Novelists, 1906.]

WILLIAM BLACK (1841–1898)

(a) Collected Works

New and Revised Edition of the Novels of William Black. 28 vols. 1892–8.

(b) Fiction

Love or Marriage. 3 vols. 1868.

In Silk Attire. 3 vols. 1869.

Kilmeny. 3 vols. 1870.

The Monarch of Mincing Lane. 3 vols. 1871.

A Daughter of Heth. 3 vols. 1871.

The Strange Adventures of a Phaeton. 2 vols. 1872.

A Princess of Thule. 3 vols. 1874.

The Maid of Killeena and Other Stories. 1874; 1892 (as The Maid of Killeena and the Marriage of Moira Fergus).

Three Feathers. 3 vols. 1875.

Madcap Violet. 3 vols. 1876.

Lady Silverdale's Sweetheart and Other Stories. 1876.

Green Pastures and Piccadilly. 3 vols. 1877.

Macleod of Dare. 3 vols. 1878.

White Wings. 3 vols. 1880.

Sunrise. 3 vols. 1881.

The Beautiful Wretch; The Four Macnicols; The Pupil of Aurelius. 3 vols. 1881.

Yolande. 3 vols. 1883.

Adventures in Thule. Three Stories for Boys. 1883.

Shandon Bells. 3 vols. 1883.

Judith Shakespere. 3 vols. 1884.

White Heather. 3 vols. 1885.

Sabina Zembra. 3 vols. 1887.

In Far Lochaber. 3 vols. 1888.

Strange Adventures of a House-Boat. 3 vols. 1888.

The Penance of John Logan and Two Other Stories. 1889.

Nanciebel. A Tale of Stratford-on-Avon. New York, 1889.

The New Prince Fortunatus. 3 vols. 1890.

Stand fast, Craig Royston! 3 vols. 1890.

Donald Ross of Heimra. 3 vols. 1891.

Wolfenburg. 3 vols. 1892.

The Magic Inkstand and Other Tales. 1892.

The Handsome Humes. 3 vols. 1893.

Highland Cousins. 3 vols. 1894.

Briseis. 1896.

Wild Eelin. 1898.

(c) Other Writings

Mr Pisistratus Brown, M.P. in the Highlands. 1871. [Rptd from Daily News with addns.]

Oliver Goldsmith. 1878. (English Men of Letters ser.)

The Wise Women of Inverness and Other Miscellanies. 1885.

With the Eyes of Youth, and Other Sketches. 1903.

(d) Biography and Criticism

Reid, Sir T. W. William Black, Novelist. A Biography. 1902.

'Melville, Lewis.' Victorian Novelists. 1906.

MARY ELIZABETH BRADDON, later MAXWELL (1837–1915)

(a) Fiction

Three Times Dead, or the Secret of the Heath. [1854]; 1861 (as The Trail of the Serpent, or the Secret of the Heath). [First ptd in penny pts, undated.]

Lady Lisle. 1861.

Captain of the Vulture. 1862.

Lady Audley's Secret. 3 vols. 1862. [First ptd in Robin Goodfellow and Sixpenny Mag.]

Ralph the Bailiff and Other Tales. [1862.]

Eleanor's Victory. 3 vols. 1863.

Aurora Floyd. 3 vols. 1863.

John Marchmont's Legacy. 3 vols. 1863.

The Doctor's Wife. 3 vols. 1864.

Henry Dunbar. The Story of an Outcast. 2 vols. 1864.

Only a Clod. 3 vols. 1865.

Sir Jasper's Tenant. 3 vols. 1865.

The Lady's Mile. 3 vols. 1866.

Birds of Prey. 3 vols. 1867.

Rupert Godwin. 3 vols. 1867.

Dead Sea Fruit. 3 vols. 1868.

Charlotte's Inheritance. 3 vols. 1868.

Run to Earth. 3 vols. 1868.

Fenton's Quest. A Novel. 3 vols. 1871.

The Lovels of Arden. 3 vols. 1871.

Robert Ainsleigh. 3 vols. 1872.

To the Bitter End. 3 vols. 1872.

Lucius Davoren, or Publicans and Sinners. A Novel. 3 vols. 1873.

Milly Darrell and Other Tales. 3 vols. 1873.

Strangers and Pilgrims. 3 vols. 1873.

Taken at the Flood. A Novel. 3 vols. 1874.

Lost for Love. A Novel. 3 vols. 1874.

Hostages to Fortune. 3 vols. 1875.

A Strange World. 3 vols. 1875.

Dead Men's Shoes. 3 vols. 1876.

Put to the Test. 1876. [Ed. by Miss Braddon.]

Joshua Haggard's Daughter. 3 vols. 1876.

Weavers and Weft, and Other Tales. 3 vols. 1877.

Only a Woman. 1878. [Ed. by Miss Braddon.]

An Open Verdict. 3 vols. 1878.

The Cloven Foot. A Novel. 3 vols. [1879.]
Vixen. A Novel. 3 vols. 1879.
Aladdin, or the Wonderful Lamp. [1880.] [Rev. by Miss Braddon.]
Just as I am. A Novel. 3 vols. [1880].
The Story of Barbara. A Novel. 3 vols. [1880].
Asphodel. 3 vols. 1881.
Mount Royal. A Novel. 3 vols. 1882.
Phantom Fortune. 3 vols. 1883.
Married in Haste. [1883.]
The Golden Calf. A Novel. 3 vols. 1883.
Under the Red Flag. 1884.
Ishmael. 3 vols. [1884].
Wyllard's Weird. 3 vols. [1885].
One Thing Needful. A Novel. 3 vols. 1886.
Cut by the County. 1886.
Mohawks. 3 vols. [1886].
Like and Unlike. 3 vols. 1887.
The Fatal Three. 3 vols. [1888].
The Day will come. 3 vols. [1889].
One Life, One Love. 3 vols. 1890.
Gerard, or the World, the Flesh and the Devil. A Novel. 3 vols. 1891.
The Venetians. 3 vols. 1892.
All along the River. A Novel. 3 vols. 1893.
Thou art the Man. 3 vols. [1894].
Sons of Fire. 3 vols. [1896].
London Pride, or When the World was Younger. [1896.]
Under Love's Rule. 1897.
Rough Justice. [1898.]
In High Places. 1898.
His Darling Sin. [1899.]
The Infidel. A Story of the Great Revival. [1900.]
The Conflict. 1903.
A Lost Eden. 1904.
The Rose of Life. 1905.
The White House. 1906.
Her Convict. 1907.
Dead Love has Chains. 1907.
During her Majesty's Pleasure. 1908.
Our Adversary. 1909.
Beyond these Voices. 1910.
The Green Curtain. 1911.
Miranda. 1913.
Mary. 1916.
Flower and Weed, and Other Tales. N.d.

(b) Other Writings

Garibaldi and Other Poems. 1861.
The Summer Tourist. A Book for Long and Short Journeys. 1871. [Ed. by Miss Braddon.]
The Missing Witness. An Original Drama in Four Acts. [1880.]
Dross, or the Root of Evil. A Comedy in Four Acts. [1882.]
Married Beneath him. A Comedy in Four Acts. [1882.]

Marjorie Daw. A Household Idyl in Two Acts. [1882.]

[Miss Braddon also edited Belgravia from 1866, the Belgravia Annual from 1867, and The Mistletoe Bough from 1878. For an appreciation, see M. Sadleir, Mary Elizabeth Braddon, TLS. 2 Oct. 1937.]

RHODA BROUGHTON (1840–1920)

Not wisely, but too well. 3 vols. 1867.
Cometh up as a Flower. 2 vols. 1867.
Red as a Rose is she. 3 vols. 1870.
'Goodbye, Sweetheart.' A Tale. 3 vols. 1872.
Nancy. A Novel. 3 vols. 1873.
Tales for Christmas Eve. 1873; 1879 (as Twilight Stories).
Joan. A Tale. 3 vols. 1876.
Second Thoughts. 2 vols. 1880.
Belinda. 3 vols. 1883.
Doctor Cupid. A Novel. 3 vols. 1886.
Alas! A Novel. 3 vols. 1890.
A Widower indeed. 1891. [With E. Bisland.]
Mrs Bligh. A Novel. 1892.
A Beginner. 1894.
Scylla or Charybdis? A Novel. 1895.
Dear Faustina. 1897.
The Game and the Candle. 1899.
Foes in Law. 1900.
Lavinia. 1902.
A Waif's Progress. 1905.
Mamma. 1908.
The Devil and the Deep Sea. 1910.
Between two Stools. [1912.]
Concerning a Vow. [1914.]
A Thorn in the Flesh. 1917 (3rd edn).
A Fool in her Folly. [1920.] [With an appreciation by Mrs Belloc Lowndes.]

OLIVER MADOX BROWN (1855–1874)
(a) Writings

Gabriel Denver. A Novel. 1873.
The Dwale Bluth, Hebditch's Legacy and Other Literary Remains. With a Memoir of the Author. Ed. W. M. Rossetti and F. Hueffer, 2 vols. 1876. [Prefixed is a Lament by P. B. Marston. Contains the original version of Gabriel Denver, under the title of The Black Swan. Vol. II contains 13 lyrics.]

(b) Biography and Criticism

Marston, P. B. Oliver Madox Brown, Scribner's Mag. July 1876.
Ingram, J. H. Oliver Madox Brown. A Biographical Sketch. 1883.
—— Oliver Madox Brown. [In The Poets and Poetry of the Century, ed. A. H. Miles, vol. VIII, 1893, etc.]

ROBERT BUCHANAN (1841–1901)

[See p. 333 above.]

SAMUEL BUTLER (1835–1902)
[See p. 728 below.]

SIR THOMAS HENRY HALL CAINE
(1853–1931)

(a) Fiction

The Shadow of a Crime. 3 vols. 1885.
The Deemster. 3 vols. 1887.
A Son of Hagar. 3 vols. 1887.
The Bondman. A New Saga. 3 vols. 1890.
The Scapegoat. 2 vols. 1891.
Capt'n Davy's Honeymoon and Other Stories. 1893.
The Manxman. 1894.
The Christian. 1897.
The Eternal City. 1901.
The Prodigal Son. 1904.
The White Prophet. 2 vols. 1909.
The Woman Thou Gavest me. 1913.
The Master of Man. 1921.
The Woman of Knockaloe. 1923.

(b) Other Writings

Richard III and Macbeth. A Dramatic Study. 1877.
Recollections of D. G. Rossetti. 1882; 1929 (rev.).
Sonnets of Three Centuries. 1882. [Ed. by Hall Caine.]
Cobwebs of Criticism. 1883.
Life of Coleridge. 1887.
The Little Manx Nation. 1891.
My Story. 1908.
King Edward. A Prince and a Great Man. [Rptd from Daily Telegraph, 1910.]
King Albert's Book. 1914. [Ed. by Hall Caine.]
The Drama of 365 Days. Scenes in the Great War. 1915. [Rptd from Daily Telegraph.]
Our Girls: their Work for the War. 1916.
Life of Christ. 1938.

[2 sonnets by Hall Caine are included in W. Sharp, Sonnets of the Century, 1886.]

(c) Biography and Criticism

Kenyon, C. F. Hall Caine: the Man and the Novelist. 1901.
MacCarthy, D. Portraits. 1931. [Pp. 226–33.]

MARY CHOLMONDELEY (d. 1925)

The Danvers Jewels. [1887.]
Sir Charles Danvers. A Novel. 2 vols. 1889.
Diana Tempest. 3 vols. 1893.
The Devotee. An Episode in the Life of a Butterfly. 1897.
Red Pottage. 1899.
Moth and Rust; together with Geoffrey's Wife and The Pitfall. 1902.
Prisoners (Fast Bound in Misery and Iron). 1906.

The Lowest Rung. With The Hand on the Latch, St Luke's Summer and The Understudy. 1908.
Notwithstanding. 1913.
Under One Roof. A Family Record. [1918.]
The Romance of his Life, and Other Romances. 1921.

[For biography see P. Lubbock, Mary Cholmondeley, a Sketch, 1928. See also M. Kent, A Novelist of Yesterday, Cornhill Mag. CLI, 1936.]

MARY COLERIDGE (1861–1907)
[See p. 336 above.]

'HUGH CONWAY' i.e. FREDERICK JOHN FARGUS (1847–1885)

Called Back. Bristol, [1883]; Bristol, 1885 (with life of the author).
Bound Together. Tales. 2 vols. 1884.
Chewton Abbot and Other Tales. [1884.]
Dark Days. Bristol, 1884.
Slings and Arrows. Bristol, 1885.
At what Cost and Other Stories. [1885.]
A Family Affair. 3 vols. 1885.
A Cardinal Sin. 3 vols. 1886.
Carriston's Gift; A Fresh Start; Julian Vanneck, and A Dead Man's Face. Bristol, 1886.
'Somebody's Story.' [1886.] [An exact reproduction of Conway's original MS.]
Living or Dead. [1886.]
A Life's Idylls and Other Poems. Bristol, 1887.

MARIE CORELLI (1864–1924)

(a) Fiction

A Romance of Two Worlds. 2 vols. 1886.
Vendetta, or the Story of One Forgotten. A Novel. 3 vols. 1886.
Thelma. A Society Novel. 3 vols. 1887.
Ardath. The Story of a Dead Self. 3 vols. 1889.
My Wonderful Wife. A Study in Smoke. 1889.
Wormwood. A Drama of Paris. 3 vols. 1890.
The Silver Domino. 1892 (anon.).
The Soul of Lilith. 3 vols. 1892.
Barabbas. A Dream of the World's Tragedy. 3 vols. [1893].
The Sorrows of Satan, or the Strange Experience of one Geoffrey Tempest, Millionaire. A Romance. 1895.
The Murder of Delicia. 1896.
The Mighty Atom. 1896.
Cameos. Short Stories. 1896.
Zisha. The Problem of a Wicked Soul. 1897.
Jane. A Social Incident. 1897.
Boy. A Sketch. 1900.
The Master Christian. 1900.

'Temporal Power.' A Study in Supremacy.
1902.
God's Good Man. A Simple Love Story. 1904.
The Strange Visitation of Josiah McNason.
A Christmas Ghost Story. 1904.
The Treasure of Heaven. A Romance of
Riches. 1906.
Holy Orders. 1908.
The Devil's Motor. 1910.
The Life Everlasting. A Reality of Romance.
1911.
Innocent: her Fancy and his Fact. A Novel.
1914.
Eyes of the Sea. 1917.
The Young Diana. An Experience of the
Future. 1918.
My Little Bit. 1919.
The Love of long ago, and Other Stories. 1920.
The Secret Power. 1921.
Love and the Philosopher. 1923.
Open Confession to a Man from a Woman.
1925.

(b) Other Writings

A Christmas Greeting of Various Thoughts,
Verses and Fancies. 1901.
The Vanishing Gift. An Address on the Decay
of the Imagination, delivered before the
Philosophical Institution, Edinburgh.
[1902.]
The Plain Truth of the Stratford-on-Avon
Controversy, concerning the fully-intended
Demolition of Old Houses in Henley Street
and the Changes proposed to be effected on
the National Ground of Shakespeare's
Birthplace. 1903.
Free Opinions freely expressed on Certain
Phases of Modern Social Life and Conduct.
1905.
Woman or Suffragette? A Question of
National Choice. 1907.
Poems. Ed. B. Vyver, 1925.

(c) Biography and Criticism

Carr, K. Miss Marie Corelli. 1901.
Murray, H. Robert Buchanan and Other
Essays. 1901.
Coates, T. F. G. and Bell, R. S. W. Marie
Corelli; the Writer and the Woman. 1903.
Vyver, B. Memoirs of Marie Corelli. With an
Epilogue by J. Cuming Walters. [1930.]

HUBERT CRACKANTHORPE (d. 1897)

Wreckage. Seven Studies. 1893.
Sentimental Studies and a Set of Village Tales.
1895.
Vignettes. A Miniature Journal of Whim and
Sentiment. 1896.
Last Studies. 1897.

[For criticism see W. C. Frierson, Hubert
Crackanthorpe, Analyst of the Affections,
Sewanee Rev. XXXVI, 1928.]

SAMUEL RUTHERFORD CROCKETT
(1860–1914)

(a) Fiction

The Stickit Minister and some Common Men.
1893. [Stories.]
The Play-Actress. 1894.
The Lilac Sunbonnet. 1894.
Mad Sir Uchtred of the Hills. 1894.
The Raiders. 1894.
Bog-Myrtle and Peat. Tales, chiefly of
Galloway. 1895.
The Men of the Moss Hags. 1895.
Sweetheart Travellers. 1895.
The Grey Man. 1896.
The Smugglers of the Clone. 1896.
Cleg Kelly, Arab of the City. 1896.
The Surprising Adventures of Sir Toady Lion
with those of General Napoleon Smith.
1897.
Lad's Love. Tales. 1897.
Lochinvar. 1897.
The Standard Bearer. 1898.
The Red Axe. 1898.
The Black Douglas. 1899.
Kit Kennedy. 1899.
Ione March. 1899.
Joan of the Sword Hand. 1900.
The Stickit Minister's Wooing. 1900.
Little Anna Mark. 1900.
Love Idylls. 1901.
The Silver Skull. 1901.
Cinderella. 1901.
The Firebrand. 1901.
The Dark o' the Moon; being Certain Further
Histories of Folk called 'Raiders.' 1902.
Flower o'-the-Corn. 1902.
The Banner of Blue. 1903.
The Loves of Miss Anne. 1904.
Strong Mac. 1904.
The Cherry Riband. 1905.
Sir Toady Crusoe. 1905.
Maid Margaret of Galloway. 1905.
Kid McGhie. 1906.
Fishers of Men. 1906.
The White Plumes of Navarre. 1906.
Me and Myn. 1907.
Little Esson. 1907.
Vida, or the Iron Lord of Kirktown. 1907.
Deep Moat Grange. 1908.
Princess Penniless. 1908.
The Bloom o' the Heather. 1908.
The Men of the Mountain. 1909; 1910.
Rose of the Wilderness. 1909.
The Seven Wise Men. 1909.
Dew of their Youth. 1910.
Young Nick and Old Nick. [1910.]
The Lady of the Hundred Dresses. 1911.
Love in Pernicketty Town. [1911.]
Anne of the Barricades. [1912.]
The Moss Troopers. 1912.

Sweethearts at Home. [1912.]
Sandy's Love Affair. 1913.
A Tatter of Scarlet. 1913.
Silver Sand. 1914.
Hal o' the Ironsides. 1915.
The Azure Hand. [1917.]
The White Pope. 1920.
Rogue's Island. 1926.

(b) Other Writings

Dulce Cor; being the Poems of Ford Berêton. 1886. ['Ford Berêton' was Crockett's pseudonym.]
The Adventurer in Spain. 1903.
Raiderland. All about Grey Galloway. 1904.
Red Cap Tales. 2 vols. 1904–8. [Abbreviated versions of some of Scott's novels.]
The Smugglers, Chronicles of the Last Raiders of Solway. [1911.]

[Crockett also wrote forewords to Carlyle's Montaigne and Other Essays, 1897, and several other works.]

(c) Biography and Criticism

Dudgeon, F. Glossaries to S. R. Crockett's The Stickit Minister, The Raiders, The Lilac Sunbonnet. 1895.
Harper, M. M. Crockett and Grey Galloway. The Novelist and his Works. [1907.]

JOHN DAVIDSON (1857–1909)

[See p. 337 below.]

'GEORGE DOUGLAS,' i.e. GEORGE DOUGLAS BROWN (1869–1902)

(a) Fiction

Love and a Sword. 1899. [Pbd under the pseudonym 'Kennedy King.']
The House with the Green Shutters. 1901.

(b) Biography and Criticism

Lennox, C. George Douglas Brown. A Memoir. And Reminiscences of Brown by Andrew Melrose. 1903.
Muir, E. Latitudes. 1924.

ERNEST DOWSON (1867–1900)

[See p. 339 above.]

SIR ARTHUR CONAN DOYLE (1859–1930)

(a) Bibliography

Locke, H. A Bibliographical Catalogue of the Writings of Sir Arthur Conan Doyle, 1879–1928. 1928. [Incomplete.]

(b) Collected and Selected Works

Works. The Author's Edition. 12 vols. 1903. [Incomplete.]

The Principal Works of Fiction of Conan Doyle. 20 vols. 1913.
Tales of Adventure and Medical Life. A Selection. 1922.
Tales of Terror and Mystery. A Selection. 1922.
Tales of Twilight and the Unseen. A Selection. 1922.
Tales of Long Ago. A Selection. 1922.
Tales of Pirates and Blue Water. A Selection. 1922.
Tales of the Ring and the Camp. A Selection. 1922.
Collected Poems. 1922.
The Conan Doyle Historical Romances. 2 vols. 1931–2.

(c) Fiction

A Study in Scarlet. [In Beeton's Christmas Annual. Twenty-Eighth Season, [1887].]
The Mystery of Cloomber. 1889.
Micah Clarke. 1889.
Mysteries and Adventures. 1889; 1893 (as The Gully of Bluemansdyke and Other Stories).
The Sign of Four. 1890. [First pbd in Lippincott's Mag. Feb. 1890.]
The Captain of the Polestar and Other Tales. 1890.
The Firm of Girdlestone. 1890.
The White Company. 3 vols. 1891. [First pbd in Cornhill Mag. Jan.–Dec. 1891.]
The Doings of Raffles Haw. 1892.
The Great Shadow. 1892.
Beyond the City. 1892.
The Adventures of Sherlock Holmes. 1892. [First pbd in Strand Mag. July 1891–June 1892.]
The Refugees. 3 vols. 1893. [First pbd in Harper's Mag. 1893.]
The Memoirs of Sherlock Holmes. 1894. [First pbd in Strand Mag. Dec. 1892–Dec. 1893.]
Round the Red Lamp. Being Facts and Fancies of Medical Life. 1894.
The Parasite. 1894.
The Stark Munro Letters. 1895. [First pbd in Idler Mag. 1894–5.]
The Exploits of Brigadier Gerard. 1896. [First pbd in Strand Mag. 1894–5.]
Rodney Stone. 1896. [First pbd in Strand Mag. 1896.]
Uncle Bernac. A Memory of the Empire. 1897.
The Tragedy of the Korosko. 1898. [First pbd in Strand Mag. May–Dec. 1897.]
A Duet with an Occasional Chorus. 1899.
The Green Flag and Other Stories of War and Sport. 1900. [The Croxley Master was first pbd in Strand Mag. 1900, and was later rptd separately, New York, 1907.]

The Hound of the Baskervilles. 1902. [First pbd in Strand Mag. 1901–2.]

Adventures of Gerard. 1903. [The separate stories were all first pbd in Strand Mag. 1900–3, but some under different titles from those in 1st edn.]

The Return of Sherlock Holmes. 1905. [First pbd in Strand Mag. Oct. 1903–Dec. 1904.]

Sir Nigel. 1906. [First pbd in Strand Mag. July 1905–Dec. 1906.]

Through the Magic Door. 1907. [First pbd in Cassell's Mag. Nov. 1906–Oct. 1907.]

Round the Fire Stories. 1908.

The Last Galley. 1911.

The Lost World. 1912. [First pbd in Strand Mag. 1912.]

The Poison Belt. 1913. [First pbd in Strand Mag. 1913.]

The Valley of Fear. 1915. [First pbd in Strand Mag. 1914–5.]

His Last Bow. 1917. [The separate stories were all first pbd in Strand Mag. at various dates 1893–1917.]

Danger! and Other Stories. 1918.

Three of them. 1923.

The Land of Mist. 1926.

The Case-Book of Sherlock Holmes. 1927. [The separate stories were all first pbd in Strand Mag.]

Pheneas Speaks. 1927.

The Maracot Deep and Other Stories. 1929.

(d) Poems

Songs of Action. 1898.

Songs of the Road. 1911.

The Guards came through, and Other Poems. 1919.

(e) Writings on Spiritualism

The New Revelation, or What is Spiritualism? 1918.

The Vital Message. 1919.

The Wanderings of a Spiritualist. 1921.

The Case for Spirit Photography. 1922.

The Coming of the Fairies. 1922.

The Spiritualist's Reader. 1924.

The History of Spiritualism. 2 vols. 1926.

(f) Miscellaneous Writings

The Great Boer War. 1900.

The War in South Africa: its Cause and Conduct. 1902.

The Crime of the Congo. 1909.

The German War: Sidelights and Reflections. 1914.

The British Campaign in France and Flanders. 6 vols. 1916–9.

A Visit to Three Fronts. 1916.

Our American Adventure. 1923.

Our Second American Adventure. 1924.

Memories and Adventures. 1924.

The Mystery of Joan of Arc. 1924. [From the French of Léon Denis.]

Our African Winter. 1929.

(g) Biography and Criticism

Knox, R. Essays in Satire. 1928.

Lamond, J. Arthur Conan Doyle. A Memoir. 1931.

Roberts, S. C. Doctor Watson. 1931.

Bell, H. W. Sherlock Holmes and Dr Watson. 1932.

Blakeney, T. S. Sherlock Holmes. Fact or Fiction? 1932.

Baker Street Studies. Ed. H. W. Bell, 1934.

Starrett, V. The Private Life of Sherlock Holmes. 1934.

GEORGE LOUIS PALMELLA BUSSON DU MAURIER (1834–1896)

(a) Writings

English Society at Home. 1880.

Peter Ibbetson. 2 vols. 1892. [First pbd in Harper's Mag.]

Trilby. 3 vols. 1894. [First pbd in Harper's Mag.]

The Martian. A Novel. 1897.

Social Pictorial Satire. 1898.

A Legend of Camelot. 1898.

(b) Biography and Criticism

Gilder, J. L. and J. B. Trilbyana. The Rise and Progress of a Popular Novel. 1895.

Armstrong, T. Reminiscences of Du Maurier. 1912.

Wood, T. M. Du Maurier, the Satirist of the Victorians. A Review of his Art and Personality. 1913.

Lucas, E. V. George du Maurier at Thirty-Three. Cornhill Mag. CL, 1935. [Rptd in All of a Piece, 1937.]

Du Maurier, D. The Du Mauriers. 1937.

Feipel, L. N. The American Issues of Trilby. Colophon, II, 1937.

JULIANA HORATIA EWING (1841–1885)

(a) Collected Works

Uniform Edition. 18 vols. 1894–6. [Complete, vol. XVII, Miscellanea (later called Tales of the Khoja), consisting of uncollected articles, tales and trns from Aunt Judy's Mag., London Society, etc. Vol. XVIII is H. K. F. Eden's life.]

Jackanapes, Daddy Darwin's Dovecot, and The Story of a Short Life. 1916. (Everyman's Lib.)

Mrs Overtheway's Remembrances and Other Stories by Mrs Ewing. 1916. (Everyman's Lib.)

(b) Separate Writings

Melchior's Dream and Other Tales. 1862. [Edited by Mrs Gatty. First pbd in Monthly Packet, 1861.]

Mrs Overtheway. 1869. [First pbd in Aunt Judy's Mag. 1866–8.]

The Brownies and Other Tales. 1870. [First pbd in Aunt Judy's Mag. 1865–70, and Little Folks.]

A Flat Iron for a Farthing. 1872. [First pbd in Aunt Judy's Mag. 1870–1.]

Lob-lie-by-the-Fire, or the Luck of Lingborough, and Other Tales. 1874. [4 of the 5 stories were first pbd in Aunt Judy's Mag.; 'Lob' had not appeared before.]

Six to Sixteen. 1875. [First pbd in Aunt Judy's Mag. 1872.]

Jan of the Windmill. 1876. [First pbd in Aunt Judy's Mag. 1872–3, as 'The Miller's Thumb.']

A Great Emergency and Other Tales. 1877. [First pbd in Aunt Judy's Mag. 1873–5.]

We and the World. 1880. [First pbd in Aunt Judy's Mag. 1877–9.]

Old Fashioned Fairy Tales. 1882. [First pbd in Aunt Judy's Mag. 1870–6.]

Brothers of Pity and Other Tales. 1882. [First pbd in Aunt Judy's Mag. 1876–9.]

Blue and Red. 1883. [First pbd in Aunt Judy's Mag. 1881.]

Jackanapes. 1883. [First pbd in Aunt Judy's Mag. Oct. 1879.]

Daddy Darwin's Dovecot. 1884. [First pbd in Aunt Judy's Mag. 1881.]

The Story of a Short Life. 1885. [First pbd in Aunt Judy's Mag. as 'Laetus Sorte Mea.']

Mary's Meadow. 1886. [First pbd in Aunt Judy's Mag. 1883–4.]

Dandelion Clocks and Other Tales. 1887. [First pbd in Monthly Packet, 1871, and Aunt Judy's Mag. 1875–7.]

The Peace Egg. A Christmas Mumming Play. 1887. [First pbd in Aunt Judy's Mag. 1884.]

Snapdragon and Old Father Christmas. 1888. ['Snapdragon' was first pbd in Monthly Packet, 1870; 'Old Father Christmas,' first pbd in Little Folks, had already been collected in The Brownies and Other Tales.]

Verses for Children. 3 vols. 1888. ['The Blue Bells on the Lea,' 'Mother's Birthday Review,' and 'A Soldier's Children' was first pbd in Aunt Judy's Mag. 1880–3. The verses were originally issued, 1883–5, in 24 quarto vols. with coloured illustrations.]

[Mrs Ewing also assisted in editing Aunt Judy's Magazine, 1874–6, and contributed a memoir of Mrs Gatty to the latter's Parables from Nature, sers. 1, 2, 1885.]

(c) Biography and Criticism

Eden, H. K. F. Juliana Horatia Ewing and her Books. 1885.

Marshall, E. Mrs Ewing. [In Women Novelists of Queen Victoria's Reign, 1897.]

'MICHAEL FAIRLESS,' i.e. MARGARET FAIRLESS BARBER (1869–1901)

(a) Writings

The Gathering of Brother Hilarius. 1901.

The Roadmender and Other Papers. 1902; ed. (with additional matter) N. E. Dowson, 1926. [First pbd in The Pilot.]

The Child King: Four Christmas Writings. 1902.

The Grey Brethren and Other Fragments in Prose and Verse. 1905.

Stories told to Children. Ed. 'M. E. D[owson],' 1914.

(b) Biography and Criticism

'Dowson, M. E.' (William Scott Palmer) and Haggard, A. M. Michael Fairless: her Life and Writings. 1913.

'LANOE FALCONER,' i.e. MARY ELIZABETH HAWKER (1848–1908)

(a) Fiction

Mademoiselle Ixe. 1891 (for 1890).

Cecilia de Noël. 1891.

The Hôtel d'Angleterre and Other Stories. 1891.

Shoulder to Shoulder. A Tale of Love and Friendship. [1891.]

The Wrong Prescription. [In Tavistock Tales by Gilbert Parker, etc. 1893.]

Old Hampshire Vignettes. 1907.

['Lanoe Falconer' also contributed 'The Short Story' to On the Art of writing Fiction, 1894.]

(b) Biography and Criticism

Phillipps, E. M. Lanoe Falconer. Cornhill Mag. Feb. 1912.

—— Lanoe Falconer (Author of 'Mademoiselle Ixe'). 1915.

'VIOLET FANE' (1843–1905)

[See p. 345 above.]

BENJAMIN LEOPOLD FARJEON (1838–1903)

(a) Fiction

Grif: a Story of Australian Life. Dunedin (New Zealand), 1866; 2 vols. 1870.

Shadows on the Snow: a Christmas Story. [Dunedin (New Zealand), 1866]; [1904].

Joshua Marvel. 3 vols. 1871.

London's Heart. 3 vols. 1873.

Christmas Stories: Blade o' Grass; Golden Grain; and Bread and Cheese and Kisses. 3 pts, 1874.

Jessie Trim. A Novel. 3 vols. 1874.
Love's Victory. A Novel. 2 vols. 1875.
At the Sign of the Silver Flagon. 3 vols. 1876.
The Duchess of Rosemary Lane. A Novel. 3 vols. 1876.
The House of White Shadows. A Novel. 3 vols. 1884.
The Shield of Love. 1884. (Arrowsmith's Christmas Annual.)
Christmas Angel. [1885.]
Great Porter Square: a Mystery. 3 vols. 1885.
The Sacred Nugget. A Novel. 3 vols. 1885.
Self-Doomed. [1885.]
The Golden Land, or Links from Shore to Shore. 1886.
In a Silver Sea. 1886.
The Nine of Hearts. [1886.]
A Secret Inheritance. 3 vols. 1887.
The Tragedy of Featherstone. A Novel. 3 vols. 1887.
Devlin the Barber. 1888.
Miser Farebrother. A Novel. 3 vols. 1888.
Toilers of Babylon. 3 vols. 1888.
The Blood White Rose. [1889.]
Doctor Glennie's Daughter. A Story of Real Life. 1889.
A Strange Enchantment. 1889.
A Young Girl's Life. A Novel. 3 vols. 1889.
Basil and Annette. A Novel. 3 vols. 1890.
The Mystery of M. Felix. A Novel. 3 vols. 1890.
The Peril of Richard Pardon. A Novel. 1890.
A Very Young Couple. A Novel. 1890.
For the Defence. A Realistic Story. 1891.
The March of Fate. A Novel. 3 vols. 1893.
The Last Tenant. [1893.]
Something Occurred. 1893.
Aaron the Jew. A Novel. 3 vols. 1894.
The Betrayal of John Fordham. 1896.
Miriam Rozella. 1898.
Samuel Boyd of Catchpole Square: a Mystery. 1899.
The Mesmerists. 1900.
The Pride of Race. In Five Panels. 1901.
The Mystery of the Royal Mail. 1902.
The Amblers. 1904.
The Clairvoyante. 1905.
Mrs Dimmock's Worries. 1906.

[Stories by Farjeon also appeared in the following collections: In Australian Wilds, ed. P. Mennell, 1889; Seven Xmas Eves, 1894, and Fifty-Two Stories of the British Empire, ed. A. H. Miles, 1900.]

(b) Biography and Criticism

B. L. Farjeon. Victoria Mag. xxxii, 1879.
Bok, E. W. B. L. Farjeon. Author (Boston), iii, 1891.
Obituary. Times, 24 July 1903.

FREDERIC WILLIAM FARRAR (1831–1903)

(a) Fiction

Eric, or Little by Little. A Tale of Roslyn School. Edinburgh, 1858.
Julian Home. A Tale of College Life. Edinburgh, 1859.
St Winifred's, or The World of School. 1862.
The Three Homes. A Tale for Fathers and Sons. 1873 (under the pseudonym 'F.T.L.'); 1896 (under own name).
Darkness and Dawn, or Scenes in the Days of Nero. An Historic Tale. 2 vols. 1891.
Gathering Clouds. A Tale of the Days of St Chrysostom. 2 vols. 1895.
Allegories. 1898.

[Farrar also pbd many sermons and theological works, the more important of which are listed p. 848 below.]

(b) Biography and Criticism

Farrar, R. The Life of Frederick William Farrar. 1904.
Russell, G. W. E. Sketches and Snapshots. 1910.
'Kingsmill, Hugh.' After Puritanism, 1850–1900. 1929.

PERCY HETHERINGTON FITZGERALD (1834–1925)

(a) Fiction

The Night Mail: its Passengers, and how they fared at Christmas. 1862.
Bella Donna, or the Cross before the Name. A Romance. 2 vols. 1864. [Pbd under the pseudonym 'Gilbert Dyce.']
Fairy Alice. 2 vols. 1865.
Never Forgotten. A Novel. 3 vols. 1865.
The Second Mrs Tillotson. A Story. Reprinted from All the Year Round. 3 vols. 1866.
Jenny Bell. A Story. 3 vols. 1866.
School Days at Saxonhurst. Illustrated by 'Phiz.' 1867.
Seventy-Five Brooke Street. A Story. 3 vols. 1867.
The Dear Girl. 3 vols. 1868.
Diana Gay, or the History of a Young Lady. 3 vols. 1868. [First pbd in Belgravia.]
Beauty Talbot. 3 vols. 1870.
The Rev. Alfred Hoblush and his Curacies. [1870.]
Two Fair Daughters. 3 vols. 1871.
The Middle-Aged Lover. A Story. 2 vols. 1873.
The Parvenu Family, or Phoebe, Girl and Wife. 3 vols. 1876.
Little Dorinda: who won and who lost her! [1878.]
A Little Life. 1880.

Young Coelebs. A Novel. 3 vols. 1881.
Puppets. A Romance. 3 vols. 1884.
Fatal Zero. 1886.
Three Weeks at Mopetown. 1891.
The Bachelor's Dilemma. 1892.
Lady Jean. 1904.
Josephine's Troubles. A Story. [1907.]
Worldlyman. A Modern Morality of our Day. [1913.]

(b) Other Writings

Roman Candles. 1861.
Words for the Worldly. [1861.]
Two English Essayists: Charles Lamb and Charles Dickens. 1863.
The Life of Laurence Sterne. 2 vols. 1864.
A Famous Forgery. The Story of Dr Dodd. 1865.
Charles Townshend, Wit and Statesman. 1866.
Charles Lamb: his Friends, his Haunts and his Books. 1866.
The Life of David Garrick from Original Family Papers. 2 vols. 1868; 1899 (rev.).
Proverbs or Comediettas written for Private Representation. 1869.
Principles of Comedy and Dramatic Effect. 1870.
The Kembles: an Account of the Kemble Family. 2 vols. [1871].
Life and Adventures of Alexander Dumas. 2 vols. 1873.
Kings and Queens of an Hour. Records of Love, Romance, Oddity and Adventure. 2 vols. 1873.
The Romance of the English Stage. 2 vols. 1874.
The Life of Samuel Johnson [by Boswell], edited with New Notes. 3 vols. 1874 (reissued 1888).
The Life, Letters and Writings of Charles Lamb, edited with Notes. 1876.
Croker's Boswell and Boswell: Studies in the Life of Johnson. 1880.
The Life of George IV. 2 vols. 1881.
The World behind the Scenes. 1881.
The Life and Writings of Charles Lamb. 4 vols. 1882.
A New History of the English Stage. 2 vols. 1882.
The Royal Dukes and Duchesses of the Family of George III. A View of their Life and Manners for Seventy Years, 1760–1830. 2 vols. 1882.
Recreations of a Literary Man, or does Writing pay? 2 vols. 1882.
The Life and Times of William IV. 2 vols. 1884.
The Art of the Stage as set out in Lamb's Dramatic Essays. With a Commentary. 1885.

Lives of the Sheridans. 2 vols. 1886.
The Book Fancier. 1886.
A Day's Tour. 1887.
Chronicles of Bow Street. 2 vols. 1888.
The Life of John Wilkes. 2 vols. 1888.
Life of Mrs Catherine Clive. 1888.
Music Hall Land. [1890.]
King Theodore of Corsica. 1890.
The Story of 'Bradshaw's' Guide. [1890.]
Life of James Boswell. 2 vols. 1891.
Editing à la Mode. An Examination [of G. Birkbeck Hill's Boswell]. [1891.]
History of Pickwick. 1891.
The Art of Acting. 1892.
Henry Irving. 1893; 1895 (rev.).
Memoirs of an Author. 2 vols. 1894.
The Savoy Opera. 1894.
Bozland. 1895.
Pickwickian Manners and Customs. [1897.]
A Critical Examination of Dr G. Birkbeck Hill's 'Johnsonian' Edition. 1898.
The Good Queen Charlotte. 1899.
John Forster. 1903.
The Pickwickian Dictionary. [1903.]
Lightning Tours. 1903.
Pickwickian Wit and Humour. 1903.
The Garrick Club. 1904.
Robert Adam. 1904.
The Life of Charles Dickens, traced in his Works. 2 vols. 1905.
Sir Henry Irving. A Biography. 1906.
Shakespearian Representation. 1908.
Samuel Foote. 1910.
Jane Austen. 1912.
Pickwick Riddles and Perplexities. 1912.
Memories of Charles Dickens. 1913.

[Fitzgerald also wrote a number of books on Roman Catholicism, London, and other miscellaneous subjects.]

RICHARD GARNETT (1835–1906)
[See p. 742 below.]

SIR EDMUND GOSSE (1845–1928)
[See p. 742 below.]

NAT GOULD (1857–1919)
[See p. 764 below.]

'SARAH GRAND,' i.e. FRANCES ELIZABETH MACFALL, née CLARKE (b. 1862).

(a) Fiction

Ideala. A Study from Life. 1888 (anon.).
A Domestic Experiment. By the Author of Ideala. 1891.
The Heavenly Twins. 3 vols. 1893.
Singularly Deluded. By the Author of Ideala. 1893.
Our Manifold Nature. 1894. [Stories.]

The Beth Book. 1898.
Babs the Impossible. 1901.
Emotional Moments. 1908. [Stories.]
Adnam's Orchard. A Prologue. 1912.
The Winged Victory. 1916.
Variety. 1922. [Stories.]

(b) Other Writings

The Modern Man and Maid. 1898.
The Human Quest. Being some Thoughts in Contribution to the Subject of the Art of Happiness. 1900.

[Mrs MacFall also wrote a preface to 'Bartholomew's' As they are, 1908, and a personal sketch of Matilda B. B. Edwards, prefixed to that writer's Mid-Victorian Memories, 1919.]

(c) Biography and Criticism

Sarah Grand. Critic (New York), XXIII, 1893.
Cotton, J. J. Sarah Grand. Macmillan's Mag. LXXXII, 1900.
Foerster, E. Die Frauenfragen in den Romanen englischer Schriftstellerinnen der Gegenwart. (George Egerton, Mona Caird, Sarah Grand.) Marburg, 1907.

SIR HENRY RIDER HAGGARD (1856–1925)

(a) Bibliography

McKay, G. L. A Bibliography of the Writings of Rider Haggard. 1930.

(b) Fiction

Dawn. 3 vols. 1884.
The Witch's Head. 3 vols. 1884.
King Solomon's Mines. 1885.
She. 1887. [First pbd in The Graphic, 1886–7.]
Jess. 1887. [First pbd in Cornhill Mag. 1886–7.]
Allan Quatermain. 1887. [First pbd in Longman's Mag. 1887.]
A Tale of Three Lions. New York, 1887. [First pbd in Atalanta, 1887.]
Mr Meeson's Will. 1888. [First pbd in Illustrated London News, Summer no. 1888.]
Maiwa's Revenge, or the War of the Little Hand. 1888.
My Fellow Laborer and The Wreck of the 'Copeland.' New York, 1888. [First pbd in Collier's Once a Week, 1888.]
Colonel Quaritch, V.C. 3 vols. 1888.
Cleopatra. 1889. [First pbd in Illustrated London News, 1889.]
Allan's Wife and Other Tales. 1889.
Beatrice. 1890.
The World's Desire. 1890. [With Andrew Lang; first pbd in New Rev. 1890.]
Eric Brighteyes. 1891.

Nada the Lily. 1892.
Montezuma's Daughter. 1893.
The People of the Mist. 1894.
Joan Haste. 1895.
Heart of the World. 1896.
The Wizard. Bristol, 1896.
Dr Therne. 1898.
Swallow. 1899.
Black Heart and White Heart, and Other Stories. 1900.
Lysbeth. 1901.
Pearl-Maiden. 1903.
Stella Fregelius. 1904.
The Brethren. 1904.
Ayesha. The Return of She. 1905.
The Way of the Spirit. 1906.
Benita. 1906.
Fair Margaret. 1907.
The Ghost Kings. 1908.
The Yellow God. 1908.
The Lady of Blossholme. 1909.
Morning Star. 1910.
Queen Sheba's Ring. 1910.
Red Eve. 1911.
The Mahatma and the Hare. 1911.
Marie. 1912.
Child of Storm. 1913.
The Wanderer's Necklace. 1914.
The Holy Flower. 1915.
The Ivory Child. 1916.
Finished. 1917.
Love Eternal. 1918.
Moon of Israel. 1918.
When the World Shook. 1919.
The Ancient Allan. 1920.
Smith and the Pharaohs, and Other Tales. Bristol, 1920.
She and Allan. 1921.
The Virgin of the Sun. 1922.
Wisdom's Daughter. 1923.
Heu-Heu. 1924.
Queen of the Dawn. 1925.
Treasure of the Lake. 1926.
Allan and the Ice Gods. 1927.
Mary of Marion Isle. 1929.
Belshazzar. 1930.

(c) Other Writings

Cetywayo and his White Neighbours. 1882; 1888 (with new material).
Church and State. 1895.
A Farmer's Year. 1899. [First pbd in Longman's Mag. 1898–9.]
The Last Boer War. 1899.
The Spring of a Lion. New York, 1899.
The New South Africa. 1900.
A Winter Pilgrimage. 1901. [First pbd in The Queen, 1901.]
Rural England. 2 vols. 1902.
A Gardener's Year. 1905. [First pbd in The Queen, 1904.]

Report on Salvation Army Colonies. 1905.
Regeneration: an Account of the Social Work of the Salvation Army. 1910.
Rural Denmark. 1911.
A Call to Arms. 1914 (priv. ptd).
The After-War Settlement and Employment of Ex-Service Men. 1916.
The Days of my Life. 2 vols. 1926. [First pbd in Strand Mag. 1926, but expanded in book form.]

PHILIP GILBERT HAMERTON (1834–1894)
[See p. 744 below.]

BEATRICE HARRADEN (b. 1864)
Things will take a Turn. 1889; 1915 (rev.).
Master Roley. 1889.
Ships that pass in the Night. 1893.
In Varying Moods. Short Stories. 1894.
Untold Tales of the Past. 1897.
A New Book of the Fairies. 1897.
The Fowler. 1899.
The Scholar's Daughter. 1906.
Hilda Strafford and the Remittance Man. 1906.
Interplay. 1908.
Out of the Wreck I rise. 1912.
The Guiding Thread. 1916.
Where your Treasure is. 1918.
Spring shall plant. 1920.
Thirteen all told. Tales. 1921.
Patuppa. 1923.
Youth Calling. 1924.
Rachel. 1926.
Katherine Frensham. 1927.
Search will find it out. 1928.

JOSEPH HATTON (1841–1907)
(a) Fiction
Provincial Papers; being a Collection of Tales and Sketches. 1861.
Bitter Sweets. A Love Story. 3 vols. 1865. [Dramatic version as Two May Days, 1871.]
Against the Stream. 3 vols. 1866.
The Tallants of Barton. A Tale of Fortune and Finance. 3 vols. 1867.
Not in Society: a Posthumous Story by Vaughan Morgan edited by Joseph Hatton. 1868. [Rptd [1877] with other tales by Hatton.]
Christopher Kenrick. 2 vols. 1869.
Behind a Mask. A Romance of Real Life. 1870.
Kites and Pigeons. A Novelette. [1872.] [Dramatic version as Birds of a Feather; a Serio-Comic Play, [1872].]
The Valley of Poppies. 2 vols. 1872.
In the Lap of Fortune. A Story 'Stranger than Fiction.' 3 vols. 1873.
Clytie. A Novel of Modern Life. 3 vols. 1874. [Dramatic version, [1874].]

The Queen of Bohemia. A Novel. 2 vols. 1877.
Cruel London. A Novel. 3 vols. 1878.
Liz. A Drama. [1879.]
Three Recruits and the Girls they left behind them. 3 vols. 1880.
The Dove's Nest. 1883.
A Modern Ulysses. A Novel. 3 vols. 1883.
John Needham's Double. A Story founded upon Fact. [1885.]
The Old House at Sandwich. 2 vols. 1887.
The Park Lane Mystery. Bristol, [1887].
The Gay World. 3 vols. 1887.
Captured by Cannibals. 1888.
By Order of the Czar. 3 vols. 1890 (2nd edn).
The Princess Mazaroff. A Romance. 2 vols. 1891.
The Fate of Fenella. By Twenty-four Authors. 1892.
Under the Great Seal. 3 vols. 1893.
Tom Chester's Sweetheart. A Tale of the Press. [1895.]
When Greek meets Greek. 1895.
The Banishment of Jessop Blythe. 1895.
A World afloat. [1897.]
The Dagger and the Cross. A Novel. 1897.
The Vicar. A Novel. 1898.
The White King of Manoa. An Anglo-Spanish Romance. 1899.
When Rogues fall out. 1899.
In Male Attire. 1900.
A Vision of Beauty. 1902.

(b) Other Writings
Pippins and Cheese. 1868.
With a Show in the North. Reminiscences of Mark Lemon. With Lemon's Revised Text of Falstaff. 1871.
Romantic Caroline. A Comedy founded upon the Comedy of Barrière and Thiboust. [1874.]
Much Too Clever. A Comedy. [1879.] [With J. Oxenford.]
To-day in America. 2 vols. 1881.
'The New Ceylon.' British North Borneo. 1881.
Journalistic London. 1882.
Henry Irving's Impressions of America. 2 vols. 1884.
Old Lamps and New. [1890.]
Club-Land, London and Provincial. 1890.
Cigarette Papers for After-Dinner Smoking. 1892. [Essays and sketches.]
In Jest and Earnest. A Book of Gossip. 1893.
The Life and Work of Alfred Gilbert. 1903.

[Hatton also wrote works on cocoa, tobacco, etc., and edited E. W. Streeter's Great Diamonds, 1882, and J. L. Toole's Reminiscences, 1889.]

'JOHN OLIVER HOBBES' *i.e.* PEARL MARY
TERESA CRAIGIE (1867–1906)

(a) Fiction

Some Emotions and a Moral. 1891.
The Sinner's Comedy. 1892.
A Bundle of Life. 1893.
A Study in Temptations. 1893.
The Gods, some Mortals and Lord Wicken-
ham. 1895.
The Tales of John Oliver Hobbes. [1895.]
The Herb Moon. 1896.
The School for Saints. 1897.
Robert Orange. 1900. [Sequel to The School
for Saints.]
The Serious Wooing. 1901.
Tales about Temperaments. 1902.
Love and the Soul Hunters. 1902.
The Vineyard. 1904.
The Flute of Pan. [1905.] [Originally written
as a play and on its failure in that form
converted into a novel.]
The Dream and the Business. 1906.

(b) Other Writings

The Ambassador. A Comedy in Three Acts.
1898.
Osbern and Ursyne. A Drama in Three Acts.
1900.
The Wisdom of the Wise. 1901. [A comedy.]
Imperial India. Letters from the East. 1903.
The Artist's Life. 1904. [Critical essays.]
Letters from a Silent Study. 1904.

(c) Biography

The Life of John Oliver Hobbes, told in her
Correspondence with her Friends. With
Biographical Sketch by J. M. Richards and
Introduction by Bishop [J. C.] Welldon.
1911.

'ANTHONY HOPE,' *i.e.* SIR ANTHONY HOPE
HAWKINS (1863–1933)

(a) Fiction

A Man of Mark. 1890.
Father Stafford. 1891.
Mr Witt's Widow. 1892.
A Change of Air. 1893.
Half a Hero. 2 vols. 1893.
Sport Royal and Other Stories. 1893.
The Dolly Dialogues. 1894.
The God in the Car. 2 vols. 1894.
The Indiscretion of the Duchess. 1894.
The Prisoner of Zenda. 1894.
The Chronicle of Count Antonio. 1895.
Comedies of Courtship. 1896.
The Heart of Princess Osra and Other Stories.
1896.
Phroso. 1897.

Rupert of Hentzau. Being a Sequel to a
Story by the Same Writer entitled The
Prisoner of Zenda. Bristol, [1898].
Simon Dale. 1898.
The King's Mirror. 1899.
Quisanté. 1900.
Tristram of Blent. 1901.
The Intrusions of Peggy. 1902.
Double Harness. 1904.
A Servant of the Public. 1905.
Sophy of Kravonia. 1906.
Tales of Two People. 1907.
The Great Miss Driver. 1908.
Second String. 1910.
Mrs Maxon protests. 1911.
A Young Man's Year. 1915.
Captain Dieppe. 1918.
Beaumaroy home from the Wars. 1919.
Lucinda. 1920.
Little Tiger. 1925.

(b) Other Writings

Dialogue. English Ass. lecture, 1909.
The New (German) Testament. Some Texts
and a Commentary. [1914.]
Militarism, German and British. 1915.
Why Italy is with the Allies. 1917.
Memories and Notes. [1927.]

(c) Biography

Mallet, Sir C. Anthony Hope and his Books.
Being the Authorized Life of Sir Anthony
Hope Hawkins. 1935.

WILLIAM HENRY HUDSON (1841–1922)

(a) Bibliography

Wilson, G. F. A Bibliography of the Writings
of W. H. Hudson. 1922.

(b) Collected and Selected Works

The Collected Works. 24 vols. 1922–3.
A Hudson Anthology. Arranged by Edward
Garnett. 1924.
W. H. Hudson's South American Romances:
The Purple Land; Green Mansions; El
Ombú, [etc.]. 1930.
Birds of Wing and Other Wild Things. Selec-
tions from the Works of W. H. Hudson by
H. F. B. Fox. 1930.

(c) Fiction

The Purple Land that England lost. Travels
and Adventures in the Banda Oriental,
South America. 2 vols. 1885.
A Crystal Age. 1887 (anon.); 1906 (with
signed preface).
Ralph Herne. Youth, XII, 1888. [Hudson's
first story; not separately rptd, but included in Collected Works, 1922–3.]
Fan. The Story of a Young Girl's Life. 3 vols.

1892. [Pbd under the pseudonym 'Henry Harford.']

El Ombú [and other tales]. 1902; 1909 (as South American Sketches).

Green Mansions. A Romance of the Tropical Forest. 1904.

A Little Boy lost. 1905.

Dead Man's Plack, and An Old Thorn. 1920.

(d) Writings on Ornithology, Nature Study, etc.

The Naturalist in La Plata. 1892.

Birds in a Village. 1893; [1920] (with Poems of Birds by various writers).

Idle Days in Patagonia. 1893.

British Birds. With a Chapter on Structure and Classification by Frank E. Beddard. 1895.

Birds in London. 1898.

Nature in Downland. 1900.

Birds and Man. 1901.

Hampshire Days. 1903.

The Land's End. A Naturalist's Impressions in West Cornwall. 1908.

Afoot in England. 1909.

A Shepherd's Life. Impressions of the South Wiltshire Downs. 1910.

Adventures among Birds. 1913.

Far away and long ago. A History of my Early Life. 1918; 1931 (rev.).

Birds in Town & Village. 1919.

The Book of a Naturalist. [1919.]

Birds of La Plata. 2 vols. 1920.

A Traveller in Little Things. 1921.

A Hind in Richmond Park. Ed. M. Roberts, 1922.

Rare, Vanishing & Lost British Birds. 1923. [Compiled from Hudson's notes by L. Gardiner.]

153 Letters. Ed. (with introduction and explanatory notes) E. Garnett, 1923; 1925 (as Letters from W. H. Hudson to Edward Garnett).

Men, Books and Birds. With Notes, some Letters, and an Introduction by Morley Roberts. 1925.

[Hudson also contributed notes to P. L. Sclater's Argentine Ornithology, 2 vols. 1888–9, and a preface to P. Fountain's The Great Deserts and Forests of North America, 1901; he pbd a few periodical articles, and a number of pamphlets, the latter mostly for the Society for the Protection of Birds.]

(e) Biography and Criticism

The Work of W. H. Hudson. English Rev. II, 1909.

Rhys, E. W. H. Hudson, Rare Traveller. Nineteenth Century, LXXXVIII, 1920.

Curle, R. W. H. Hudson. Fortnightly Rev. CXVIII, 1922.

Massingham, H. J. Untrodden Ways. Adventures on English Coasts, Heaths and Marshes and also among the Works of Hudson, Crabbe, and Other Country Writers. 1923.

Hughes, M. Y. A Great Skeptic: W. H. Hudson. University of California Chronicle, XXVI, 1924.

Roberts, Morley. W. H. Hudson. A Portrait. 1924.

Nicholson, E. M. W. H. Hudson's 'Birds in a Village.' Cornhill Mag. LIX, 1925.

Salt, H. S. W. H. Hudson, as I saw him. Fortnightly Rev. CXIX, 1926.

Harper, G. M. Spirit of Delight. 1928. [P. 70, Hardy, Hudson, Housman.]

Fletcher, J. V. The Creator of Rima, W. H. Hudson: a Belated Romantic. Sewanee Rev. XLI, 1933.

Charles, R. H. The Writings of W. H. Hudson. E. & S. XX, 1935.

Ford, F. M. W. H. Hudson. American Mercury, XXXVII, 1936.

RICHARD JEFFERIES (1848–1887)

(a) Selected Writings

Out-of-Doors with Richard Jefferies. An Anthology. Ed. E. F. D[aglish], 1935.

Richard Jefferies: Selections of his Work. Ed. H. Williamson, 1937.

Jefferies' England. Nature Essays by Richard Jefferies. Ed. S. J. Looker, 1937.

(b) Fiction

Jack Bass, Emperor of England. Swindon, 1873.

The Scarlet Shawl. A Novel. 1874.

Restless Human Hearts. 3 vols. 1875.

The World's End. 3 vols. 1877.

Green Ferne Farm. 1880.

Wood Magic. A Fable. 2 vols. 1881.

Bevis. The Story of a Boy. 3 vols. 1882; ed. E. V. Lucas, 1904.

The Dewy Morn. A Novel. 2 vols. 1884.

After London, or Wild England. I. The Relapse into Barbarism. II. Wild England. 2 pts, 1885.

Amaryllis at the Fair. A Novel. 1887.

The Early Fiction of Richard Jefferies. Ed. G. Toplis, 1896.

T. T. T. Wells, 1896. [An early romance rptd from North Wilts Herald.]

(c) Other Writings

Reporting, Editing and Authorship. Swindon, [1873].

A Memoir of the Goddards of North Wilts. Swindon, [1873].

Suez-cide!! Or how Miss Britannia bought a Dirty Puddle and lost her Sugarplums. 1876.

The Gamekeeper at Home. Sketches of Natural History and Rural Life. 1878.
Wild Life in a Southern County. 1879.
The Amateur Poacher. 1879.
Hodge and his Masters. 2 vols. 1880.
Round about a Great Estate. 1880.
Nature near London. 1883.
The Story of my Heart: my Autobiography. 1883.
Red Deer. 1884.
The Life of the Fields. 1884.
The Open Air. 1885.
Field and Hedgerow; being the Last Essays of Richard Jefferies. Collected by his Widow. 1889.
The Toilers of the Field. 1892.
The Hills and the Vale. Ed. E. Thomas, 1909.
[Jefferies also edited Gilbert White's Natural History of Selborne, 1887.]

(d) Biography and Criticism

Besant, Sir W. The Eulogy of Richard Jefferies. 1888.
Salt, H. S. Richard Jefferies. A Study. 1894.
—— The Faith of Richard Jefferies. 1906. [Pamphlet.]
Symons, A. Studies in Two Literatures. 1897.
Thomas, Edward. Richard Jefferies: his Life and Work. 1909.
Masseck, C. J. Richard Jefferies. Étude d'une Personalité. Paris, 1913; tr. Eng. St Louis, 1914. |With bibliography.]
Thom, A. F. The Life Worship of Richard Jefferies. [1920.]
Arkell, R. Richard Jefferies. 1933.

JEROME KLAPKA JEROME (1859–1927)

(a) Fiction

Three Men in a Boat (to say Nothing of the Dog). Bristol, 1889.
Told after Supper. 1891. [Ghost stories.]
John Ingerfield and Other Stories. 1894.
Sketches in Lavender, Blue and Green. 1897.
Three Men on the Bummel. 1900.
The Observations of Henry. 1901.
Paul Kelver. 1902.
Tommy and Co. 1904.
The Passing of the Third Floor Back, and Other Stories. 1907. [Dramatized version of The Passing of the Third Floor Back, 1910.]
The Angel and the Author and Others. 1908.
Malvina of Brittany. 1916.
Anthony John. 1923.

(b) Other Writings

Idle Thoughts of an Idle Fellow. 1886.
On the Stage and Off. 1888.
Stageland. 1889.

Diary of a Pilgrimage (and Six Essays). Bristol, 1891.
Novel Notes. 1893. [Rptd from The Idler.]
The Second Thoughts of an Idle Fellow. 1898.
Tea-Table Talk. 1903.
Idle Ideas in 1905. 1905.
They and I. 1909.
All Roads lead to Calvary. 1919.
A Miscellany of Sense and Nonsense from the Writings of Jerome K. Jerome; selected by the Author. 1923.
My Life and Times. 1926.
[Jerome also produced some 19 plays, of which only 4 or 5 however seem to have been ptd.]

(c) Biography and Criticism

Walkley, A. B. Playhouse Impressions. 1892.
Moss, A. Jerome K. Jerome: his Life and Works. 1929.

MAY KENDAL (b. 1861)

[See p. 344 above.]

ANDREW LANG (1844–1912)

[See p. 747 below.]

EMILY LAWLESS (1845–1913)

[See p. 1055 below.]

'VERNON LEE' (1856–1935)

[See p. 749 below.]

RICHARD LE GALLIENNE (b. 1866)

(a) Fiction

The Student and the Body-Snatcher. [1890.] [With R. K. Leather.]
The Book-Bills of Narcissus. An Account Rendered. [Derby], 1891; 1895 (3rd edn, rev.).
Young Lives. 1893.
Limited Editions, a Prose Fancy; together with Confessio Amantis, a Sonnet. 1893 (priv. ptd).
Prose Fancies. 2 sers. 1894–6.
The Quest of the Golden Girl. 1896.
If I were God. 1897.
The Romance of Zion Chapel. 1898.
The Worshipper of the Image. 1899.
Sleeping Beauty and Other Prose Fancies. 1900.
The Life Romantic. 1901.
Perseus and Andromeda. The Story retold. New York, 1903.
Little Dinners with the Sphinx and Other Prose Fancies. 1909.
The Maker of Rainbows, and Other Fairy-Tales and Fables. 1912.
Pieces of Eight. 1918.
Old Love Stories retold. 1924.

(b) Other Writings

My Lady's Sonnets. [Liverpool], 1887 (priv. ptd).
Volumes in Folio. 1889. [Poems.]
George Meredith: some Characteristics. 1890.
English Poems. 1892.
A Fellowship in Song. [Rugby, 1893.] [With Alfred Hayes and Norman Gale.]
The Religion of a Literary Man. 1893.
Bits of Old Chelsea. 1894. [With Lionel Johnson.]
Robert Louis Stevenson and Other Poems. 1895.
Retrospective Reviews. 2 vols. 1896.
Rubáiyát of Omar Khayyám. A Paraphrase. 1897.
The Beautiful Lie of Rome. 1900.
Rudyard Kipling. A Criticism. 1900.
Travels in England. 1900.
Odes from the Divan of Hafiz freely rendered. 1903.
An Old Country House. 1903.
The Burial of Romeo and Juliet. 1904.
How to get the Best out of Books. 1904.
Romances of Old France. New York, 1905.
Omar Repentant. 1908. [Poems.]
Painted Shadows. 1908.
Attitudes and Avowals. With some Retrospective Reviews. 1910.
New Poems. 1910.
Orestes. A Tragedy. New York, 1910.
The Loves of the Poets. New York, 1911.
October Vagabonds. 1911.
The Lonely Dancer and Other Poems. 1914.
The Highway to Happiness. 1914.
Vanishing Roads and Other Essays. 1915.
The Silk-Hat Soldier and Other Poems. 1915.
The Junk Man and Other Poems. New York, 1920.
A Jongleur strayed. New York, 1922.
The Romantic Nineties. 1926.
There was a Ship. [New York], 1930.

[Le Gallienne also edited Hazlitt's Liber Amoris, 1893, A. H. Hallam's Poems, 1893, and Walton's Compleat Angler, 1896, and tr. Wagner's Tristan into verse, 1909.]

(c) Criticism

Archer, W. Poets of the Younger Generation. 1902.
Johnson, Lionel. Reviews and Critical Papers. Ed. R. Shafer, 1921.

AMY LEVY (1861–1889)

[See p. 346 above.]

'EDNA LYALL,' i.e. ADA ELLEN BAYLY (1857–1903)

(a) Fiction

Won by Waiting. A Story of Home Life in France and England. 1879; 1886 (rev.).

Donovan. A Novel. 3 vols. 1882.
We Two. A Novel. 3 vols. 1884.
In the Golden Days. A Novel. 3 vols. 1885.
Autobiography of a Slander. 1887.
Knight-Errant. A Novel. 3 vols. 1887.
Their Happiest Christmas. 1889.
Derrick Vaughan, Novelist. 1889.
A Hardy Norseman. A Novel. 3 vols. 1890.
Max Hereford's Dream. A Tale. 1891.
To right the Wrong. 3 vols. 1894.
Doreen. The Story of a Singer. 1894.
How the Children Raised the Wind. A Tale. 1896.
The Autobiography of a Truth. 1896.
Wayfaring Men. A Novel. 1897.
Hope the Hermit. A Novel. 1898.
In Spite of all. A Novel. 1901.
The Hinderers. A Story of the Present Time. 1902.

(b) Other Writings

Mrs Gaskell. [In Women Novelists of Queen Victoria's Reign, 1897.]
The Burges Letters. A Record of Child Life in the Sixties. 1902. [Autobiography.]

(c) Biography and Criticism

Payne, G. A. Edna Lyall. An Appreciation. With Biographical and Critical Notes. [1903.]
Escreet, J. M. The Life of Edna Lyall (Ada Ellen Bayly). 1904.

'FIONA MACLEOD,' i.e. WILLIAM SHARP (1855–1905)

(a) Collected Works

The Writings of Fiona Macleod. Uniform Edition. Arranged by Mrs William Sharp. 7 vols. 1909–10.
Selected Writings of William Sharp. Arranged by Mrs William Sharp. 5 vols. 1912.
The Writings of Fiona Macleod. Pocket Edition. 8 vols. 1927.

(b) Writings published under the Pseudonym 'Fiona Macleod'

Pharais. A Romance of the Isles. Derby, 1894.
The Mountain Lovers. 1895.
The Sin Eater and Other Tales. Edinburgh, 1895.
The Washer of the Ford and Other Legendary Moralities. Edinburgh, 1896.
Green Fire. A Romance. 1896.
From the Hills of Dream. Mountain Songs and Island Runes. 1896; Edinburgh, [1897]. [Poems.]
The Laughter of Peterkin. A Retelling of Old Tales of the Celtic Wonderland. 1897.

The Shorter Stories of Fiona MacLeod, Re-arranged, with Additional Tales. 3 vols. Edinburgh, [1897].

The Dominion of Dreams. 1899.

The Divine Adventure; Iona; By Sundown Shores. Studies In Spiritual History. 1900.

The House of Usna. A Drama. 1903.

The Winged Destiny. Studies in the Spiritual History of the Gael. 1904.

Where the Forest Murmurs. Nature Essays. 1906.

From the Hills of Dream. Threnodies and Songs, and Later Poems. 1907.

The Immortal Hour. A Drama. 1908.

A Little Book of Nature. Selected from the Writings of Fiona MacLeod by Mrs William Sharp. 1909.

(c) Other Writings

(i) Fiction

Jack Noel's Legacy. A Story for Boys. [A serial in Young Folks, 1886.]

Under the Banner of St James. A Romance of the Discovery of the Pacific. [A serial in Young Folks, 1887.]

The Secret of the Seven Fountains. A Story for Boys. [A serial in Young Folks, 1888.]

The Sport of Chance. A Novel. 3 vols. 1888. [First pbd in The People's Friend (Dundee), 1887, as A Deathless Hate.]

Children of To-morrow. A Romance. 1889.

A Fellowe and his Wife. 1892. [With B. W. Howard.]

The Red Rider. A Romance of the Garibaldian Campaign in the Two Sicilies. [A serial in Weekly Budget, 1892.]

The Last of the Vikings, Being the Adventures in the East and West of Sigurd, the Boy King of Norway. [A serial in Old and Young, 1893.]

Ecce Puella and Other Prose Imaginings. 1896.

Madge o' the Pool, the Gypsy Christ and Other Tales. 1897.

Wives in Exile. A Comedy in Romance. 1898.

Silence Farm. A Novel. 1899.

(ii) Poems

The Human Inheritance, the New Hope, Motherhood. 1882.

Earth's Voices, Transcripts from Nature, Sospitra, and Other Poems. 1884.

Euphrenia, or the Test of Love. A Poem. 1884.

Romantic Ballads and Poems of Phantasy. 1888; 1889 (with 2 additional poems).

Sospiri di Roma. 1891.

Songs and Poems, Old and New. 1909.

(iii) Biographical and Miscellaneous Works

D. G. Rossetti. A Record and a Study. 1882.

Life of P. B. Shelley. 1887.

Life of Heinrich Heine. 1888.

Life of Robert Browning. 1890.

The Life and Letters of Joseph Severn. 1892.

The Pagan Review. Edited by W. H. Brooks. No. 1 (all pbd), Aug. 1892. [Written entirely by Sharp under various pseudonyms.]

Fair Women in Painting and Poetry. 1894.

Vistas. Derby, 1894.

Literary Geography. 1904.

[From May 1879 to Dec. 1905 Sharp contributed articles, sketches and poems to Fortnightly Rev., Nineteenth Century, Examiner, Chambers's Journ., Good Words, Athenaeum, Academy, Portfolio, Art Journ., National Rev., Atlantic Monthly, Literature, Harper's Mag., Century Mag., Quarterly Rev., Pall Mall Mag., Evergreen, Savoy, Dome, English Illustrated Mag., Literature, Contemporary Rev., Country Life, and North American Rev., both under his own name and (1895–1905) as 'Fiona Macleod.' He also edited several vols. in the Canterbury Poets Ser. as well as 3 anthologies.]

(d) Biography and Criticism

Rhys, [Ernest]. The New Mysticism. Fortnightly Rev. LXXIII, 1900.

Yeats, W. B. The Later Work of Fiona Macleod. North American Rev. CLXXV, 1902.

Noyes, A. Fiona MacLeod. Bookman, Jan. 1906.

Tynan, K. Fiona Macleod. Fortnightly Rev. LXXXV, 1906.

Sharp, E. A. William Sharp (Fiona MacLeod). A Memoir. Compiled by his Wife. 1910; 2 vols. 1912. [Contains a list of Sharp's writings.]

More, P. E. Shelburne Essays. Ser. 8, New York, 1913.

Evans, B. I. English Poetry in the Later Nineteenth Century. 1933. [Ch. v.]

Fiechter, S. Von William Sharp zu Fiona Macleod. Tübingen, 1936.

Waugh, A. Fiona Macleod: a Forgotten Mystery. Spectator, 14 Aug. 1936.

'LUCAS MALET' i.e. MARY ST LEGER KINGSLEY, later HARRISON (d. 1931)

Mrs Lorimer. 2 vols. 1882.

Colonel Enderby's Wife. 3 vols. 1885.

A Counsel of Perfection. 1888.

Little Peter. 1888.

The Wages of Sin. A Novel. 3 vols. 1891.

The Carissima. 1896.

The Gateless Barrier. 1900.

The History of Sir Richard Calmady. A Romance. 2 vols. 1901.

The Far Horizon. 1906.
The Score. 1909.
Adrian Savage. 1911.
The Tutor's Story. An Unpublished Novel by
Charles Kingsley, revised and completed by
Lucas Malet. 1916.
Damaris. 1916.
Deadham Hard. 1919.
The Tall Villa. 1920.
Da Silva's Widow and Other Stories. 1922.
The Survivors. 1923.
The Dogs of Want. 1924.
The Private Life of Mr Justice Syme. 1932.
[Left unfinished at her death and completed
by Gabrielle Vallings.]

WILLIAM HURRELL MALLOCK (1849–1923)

(a) Fiction

The New Republic, or Culture, Faith and
Philosophy in an English Country House.
2 vols. 1877.
The New Paul and Virginia, or Positivism
on an Island. 1878.
A Romance of the Nineteenth Century. 2 vols.
1881.
The Old Order Changes. A Novel. 3 vols.
1886.
A Human Document. A Novel. 3 vols. 1892.
The Heart of Life. A Novel. 3 vols. 1895.
The Individualist. A Novel. 1899.
The Veil of the Temple, or from Night to
Twilight. 1904.
An Immortal Soul. 1908.

(b) Other Writings

Poems. 1867 (priv. ptd).
The Parting of the Ways. A Poetic Epistle.
1867.
Newdigate Prize Poem. The Isthmus of Suez.
Oxford, 1871.
Everyman His Own Poet, or the Inspired
Singer's Recipe Book. Oxford, 1872 (anon.).
Lucretius. 1878.
Is Life worth living? 1879.
Poems. 1880.
Social Equality. A Short Study in a Missing
Science. 1882.
Atheism and the Value of Life. Five Studies
in Contemporary Literature. 1884.
Property and Progress, or a Brief Enquiry
into Contemporary Social Agitation in
England. 1884. [A reply to H. George's
Progress and Poverty.]
The Landlords and the National Income. A
Chart showing the Proportion borne by the
Rental of the Landlords to the Gross In-
come of the People. 1884.
In an Enchanted Island, or a Winter Retreat
in Cyprus. 1889.
Verses. 1893. [Partly rptd from the 1880
collection.]

Labour and the Popular Welfare. 1893;
1894 (with Appendix).
Studies of Contemporary Superstition. 1895.
Classes and Masses, or Wealth, Wages and
Welfare in the United Kingdom. A Hand-
book of Social Facts for Political Thinkers
and Speakers. 1896.
Aristocracy and Evolution: a Study of the
Rights, the Origin and the Social Functions
of the Wealthier Classes. 1898.
Doctrine and Doctrinal Disruption: being an
Examination of the Intellectual Position of
the Church of England. 1900.
Lucretius on Life and Death. 1900. [A very
free adaptation of Lucretius in the metre
of Omar Khayyám.]
The Fiscal Dispute Made Easy, or a Key to
the Principles involved in the Opposite
Policies. 1903.
Religion as a Credible Doctrine. 1903.
The Reconstruction of Belief. 1905.
A Critical Examination of Socialism. New
York, 1907.
The Nation as a Business Firm. An Attempt
to cut a Path through Jungle. 1910.
Social Reform as related to Realities and
Delusions. An Examination of the Increase
and Distribution of Wealth from 1801 to
1910. 1914
The Limits of Pure Democracy. 1918; 1924
(abridged as Democracy, with an Intro-
duction by the Duke of Northumberland).
Capital, War and Wages: Three Questions in
Outline. 1918.
Memoirs of Life and Literature. 1920.

(c) Biography and Criticism

Shaw, G. B. Socialism and Superior Brains.
A Reply to Mr Mallock. 1909.
Obituary. The Times, 5 April 1923.
Adams, A. B. The Novels of William Hurrell
Mallock. Orono, 1934.

HELEN BUCKINGHAM MATHERS, later
REEVES (1853–1920)

(a) Fiction

Comin' thro' the Rye. A Novel. 1875 (anon.)
As he comes up the Stair. By the Author of
Comin' thro' the Rye. 1878.
Cherry Ripe! A Romance. By the Author of
Comin' thro' the Rye. 3 vols. 1878.
Land o' the Leal. 1878 (anon.).
My Lady Green Sleeves. By the Author of
Comin' thro' the Rye. 3 vols. 1879.
Story of a Sin. By the Author of Comin' thro'
the Rye. 1882.
Sam's Sweetheart. 3 vols. 1883.
Eyre's Acquittal: a Sequel to Story of a Sin.
3 vols. 1884.
Jock o' Hazelgreen. 1884.

Found Out. By the Author of Comin' thro' the Rye. [1885.]

Murder or Manslaughter? A Novel. [1885.]

The Fashion of this World. [1886.]

Blind Justice. A Story. 1890.

The Mystery of No. 13. A Novel. 1891.

My Jo, John. A Novel. 1891.

The Fate of Fenella. 1892.

T'other Dear Charmer. A Novel. [1892.]

A Study of a Woman, or Venus Victrix. A Novel. 1893.

What the Glass told. A Novel. 1893.

A Man of To-day. A Novel. 3 vols. 1894.

The Lovely Malincourt. A Novel. 1895.

The Juggler and the Soul. 1896.

The Sin of Hagar. 1896.

David Lyall's Love Story. By the Author of The Land o' the Leal. 1897.

Bam Wildfire: a Character Sketch. 1898.

Becky. 1900.

Cinders. A Novel. 1901.

'Honey.' 1902.

Venus Victrix, and Other Stories. 1902.

Dahlia, and Other Stories. 1903.

Dimples. 1903.

The Face in the Mirror, and Other Stories. 1903.

Griff of Griffithscourt. 1903.

The New Lady Teazle, and Other Stories. 1903.

'Side-Shows.' 1904.

The Ferryman. 1905.

Tally Ho! 1906.

Pigskin and Petticoat. 1907.

The Pirouette, and Other Stories. 1907 (2nd edn).

Gay Lawless. 1908.

Love, the Thief. 1909.

Man is Fire: Woman is Tow, and Other Stories. [1912.]

(b) Other Writings

The Token of the Silver Lily. 1877. [A poem.]

[Mrs Reeves also contributed a preface to Miss H. Killick's Life's Orchestra, 1904.]

LEONARD MERRICK, originally MILLER (1864–1938)

(a) Collected Works

The Works of Leonard Merrick. 12 vols. 1918–9. [Introductions to each vol. by M. Hewlett, W. D. Howells, N. Munro, H. G. Wells, etc.]

(b) Fiction

Mr Bazalgette's Legacy. 1888.

Violet Moses. 3 vols. 1891.

The Man who was Good. 2 vols. 1892.

This Stage of Fools. 1896.

Cynthia; a Daughter of the Philistines. 2 vols. 1896; 1897.

One Man's View. 1897.

The Actor Manager. 1898.

The Worldlings. 1900.

When Love flies out of the Window. 1902.

Conrad in Quest of his Youth. 1903.

Quaint Companions. 1903.

Whispers about Women. 1906.

The House of Lynch. 1907.

The Man who understood Women, and Other Stories. [1908.]

All the World wondered, and Other Stories. 1911.

The Position of Peggy Harper. 1911.

While Paris laughed. 1914.

The Chair on the Boulevard. Short Stories. 1919.

To tell you the Truth. [1922.]

The Call from the Past, and Other Stories. 1924.

Four Stories. 1925.

'HENRY SETON MERRIMAN,' i.e. HUGH STOWELL SCOTT (1862–1903)

(a) Collected Works

The Works of Henry Seton Merriman. 14 vols. 1909–10.

(b) Fiction

Young Mistley. 2 vols. 1888 (anon.).

The Phantom Future. 2 vols. 1888.

Suspense. 3 vols. 1890.

Prisoners and Captives. 3 vols. 1891.

The Slave of the Lamp. 2 vols. 1892.

From One Generation to another. 2 vols. 1892.

With Edged Tools. 3 vols. 1894.

The Grey Lady. 1895.

Flotsam. The Study of a Life. 1896.

The Money-Spinner and Other Character Notes. 1896. [With S. G. Tallentyre.]

The Sowers. 1896.

In Kedar's Tents. 1897.

Roden's Corner. 1898.

Dross. 1899.

The Isle of Unrest. 1900.

The Velvet Glove. 1901.

The Vultures. 1902.

Barlasch of the Guard. 1903.

The Last Hope. 1904.

Tomaso's Fortune and Other Stories. 1904.

WILLIAM MINTO (1845–1893)

[See p. 750 below.]

EDITH NESBIT (1858–1924)

[See p. 350 above.]

LADY AUGUSTA NOEL (1838–1902)

Effie's Friends, or Chronicles of the Woods and Shore. 1865 (anon.).
The Story of Wandering Willie. 1870.
The Life and Times of Conrad the Squirrel. A Story for Children. 1872.
Owen Gwynne's Great Work. 2 vols. 1875.
From Generation to Generation. A Novel. 2 vols. 1879; ed. (with biographical and critical introduction) J. Gore, 1929.
Faith and Unfaith. [In In a Good Cause. A Collection of Stories, 1885.]
Hithersea Mere. 3 vols. 1887.
The Wise Man of Sterncross. 1901.

'OUIDA,' *i.e.* MARIE LOUISE DE LA RAMÉE (1839–1908)

(a) Fiction

Held in Bondage. 3 vols. 1863. [First pbd in New Monthly Mag. as Granville de Vigne: a Tale of the Day, Jan. 1861–June 1863.]
Strathmore. 3 vols. 1865. [First pbd in New Monthly Mag.]
Chandos. 1866.
Under Two Flags. 3 vols. 1867.
Cecil Castlemaine's Gage and Other Novelettes. 1867. [First ptd in Bentley's Misc.]
Idalia. 3 vols. 1867. [First pbd in New Monthly Mag. March 1865–Feb. 1867.]
Tricotrin. 2 vols. 1869.
Puck. 3 vols. 1870.
Folle Farine. 3 vols. 1871.
A Dog of Flanders and Other Stories. 1872. [First pbd in Lippincott's Mag.]
Pascarel. 3 vols. 1873.
Two Little Wooden Shoes. 1874.
Signa. 3 vols. 1875.
In a Winter City. 1876.
Ariadne. The Story of a Dream. 3 vols. 1877.
Friendship. 3 vols. 1878.
Moths. 3 vols. 1880.
Pipistrello, and Other Stories. 1880
A Village Commune. 2 vols. 1881.
In Maremma. 3 vols. 1882.
Bimbi. Stories for Children. 1882.
Frescoes: Dramatic Sketches. 1883.
Wanda. 3 vols. 1883.
Princess Napraxine. 3 vols. 1884.
A Rainy June. [1885.]
Othmar. 3 vols. 1885.
Don Gesualdo. 1886.
A House Party. 1887.
Guilderoy. 3 vols. 1889.
Ruffino, etc. 1890. [Contents: Ruffino; An Orchard; Trottolino; The Bullfinch.]
Syrlin. 3 vols. 1890.
Santa Barbara. 1891. [Tales.]
The Tower of Taddeo. 3 vols. 1892.
Two Offenders and Other Tales. 1894.

The Silver Christ, and A Lemon Tree. 1894.
Toxin. 1895.
Le Selve and Other Tales. 1896.
An Altruist. 1897.
The Massarenes. 1897.
La Strega and Other Stories. 1899.
The Waters of Edera. 1900.
Street Dust and Other Stories. 1901.
Helianthus. 1908. [Unfinished.]

(b) Other Writings

The New Priesthood. A Protest against Vivisection. 1893.
Views and Opinions. 1895. [Essays.]
Critical Studies. 1900.

[Ouida contributed various articles from 1897 onwards to Fortnightly Rev., Nineteenth Century, North American Rev. and other journals. She also wrote several articles in Italian for Nuova Antologia.]

(c) Biography and Criticism

Burnand, Sir F. C. Strapmore! A Romance by Weeder. 1878. [First pbd in Punch, 1878.]
Street, G. S. An Appreciation of Ouida. [In Quales Ego, 1896.]
Beerbohm, M. More. 1899.
Lee, Elizabeth. Ouida: a Memoir. 1914.
Elwin, M. Victorian Wallflowers. 1934.
Macaulay, R. Eccentric Englishwomen. IV. Ouida. Spectator, 7 May 1937.
ffrench, Y. Ouida. 1938.

WALTER PATER (1839–1894)

[See p. 731 below.]

'Q,' *i.e.* SIR ARTHUR THOMAS QUILLER-COUCH (b. 1863)

(a) Collected and Selected Works

Selected Stories by Q. Chosen by the Author [1921.]
The Duchy Edition of Tales and Romances by Q. 30 vols. 1928.
Collected Poems. 1929.

(b) Fiction

Dead Man's Rock. 1887.
The Astonishing History of Troy Town. 1888.
The Splendid Spur. 1889.
Noughts and Crosses. Stories. 1891.
A Blot of Ink. By René Bazin. 1892. [Tr. from the French by Quiller-Couch and P. M. Francke.]
I saw Three Ships, and Other Winter's Tales. 1892.
The Blue Pavilions. 1892.
The Delectable Duchy. Stories. 1893.
Wandering Heath. Stories. 1895.

Fairy Tales, Far and Near. 1895.

Ia. 1896.

St Ives. By Robert Louis Stevenson. 1898. [Completed from ch. xxxi by Quiller-Couch.]

The Ship of Stars. 1899.

Old Fires and Profitable Ghosts. Stories. 1900.

The Laird's Luck and Other Fireside Tales. 1901.

The Westcotes. 1902.

The White Wolf and Other Fireside Tales. 1902.

The Adventures of Harry Revel. 1903.

Two Sides of the Face. Tales. 1903.

The Collaborators, or the Comedy that wrote itself. 1903.

Hetty Wesley. 1903.

Fort Amity. 1904.

Shakespeare's Christmas and Other Stories. 1905.

Shining Ferry. 1905.

Sir John Constantine. 1906.

The Mayor of Troy. 1906.

Major Vigoureux. 1907.

Poison Island. 1907.

Merry-Garden and Other Stories. 1907.

True Tilda. 1909.

Corporal Sam and Other Stories. 1910.

Lady Good for Nothing. 1910.

The Sleeping Beauty and Other Tales from the Old French. Illustrated by Edmund Dulac. [1911.]

Brother Copas. 1911.

Hocken and Hunken. 1912.

In Powder and Crinoline. Old Fairy Tales retold. [1913.]

News from the Duchy. 1913.

Nicky-Nan, Reservist. 1915.

Mortallone and Aunt Trinidad. Tales of the Spanish Main. 1917.

Foe-Farrell. 1918.

(c) Poems

Athens. A Poem. [Bodmin], 1881.

Green Bays. Verses and Parodies. 1893.

Poems and Ballads. 1896.

The Vigil of Venus and Other Poems. 1912.

(d) Critical and Miscellaneous Prose

The Warwickshire Avon. 1892.

Adventures in Criticism. 1896.

From a Cornish Window. 1906.

Poetry. 1914.

On the Art of Writing. Cambridge, 1916.

Memoir of A. J. Butler. 1917.

Shakespeare's Workmanship. 1918.

Studies in Literature. 3 sers. Cambridge, 1918–29.

On the Art of Reading. Cambridge, 1920.

Charles Dickens and Other Victorians. Cambridge, 1925.

Honourable Men—Livingstone; Lincoln; Gordon. 1925. [Rptd from The Roll Call of Honour.]

Victors of Peace—Florence Nightingale; Pasteur; Father Damien. [1926.] [Rptd from The Roll Call of Honour.]

The Age of Chaucer. 1926.

A Lecture on Lectures. 1927.

The Poet as Citizen and Other Papers. Cambridge, 1934.

(e) Works Edited

The Golden Pomp. Lyrics from Surrey to Shirley. 1895.

The Story of the Sea. 2 vols. 1895–6.

Historical Tales from Shakespeare. 1899; 1905.

The Oxford Book of English Verse, 1250–1900. 1900.

The World of Adventure. A Collection of Stirring Scenes. 6 vols. 1904.

The Pilgrim's Way. A Little Book of Good Counsel for Travellers. 1906.

Select English Classics. 1908– .

The Oxford Book of Ballads. 1910.

The Roll Call of Honour. 1912.

The Oxford Book of Victorian Verse. 1912.

The King's Treasuries of Literature. 1920– .

The Works of Shakespeare. Cambridge, 1921– . (New Cambridge edn.) [The comedies edited by Quiller-Couch and J. D. Wilson, the tragedies and histories by Wilson alone.]

The Oxford Book of English Prose. 1925.

(f) Criticism

Archer, W. Poets of the Younger Generation. 1902.

JAMES RICE (1843–1882)

[See under Sir Walter Besant, p. 537 above.]

MRS J. H. RIDDELL, i.e. CHARLOTTE ELIZABETH LAWSON COWAN (1832–1906)

Zuriel's Grandchild. [1855?]; 1873 (as Joy after Sorrow).

The Ruling Passion. 3 vols. 1857; 1896. [Pbd under the pseudonym 'Rainey Hawthorne.']

The Moors and the Fens. 3 vols. 1858. [Pbd under the pseudonym 'F. G. Trafford.']

The Rich Husband. 3 vols. [1858?] (anon.).

Too much alone. By F. G. Trafford. 3 vols. 1860.

City and Suburb. By F. G. Trafford. 3 vols. 1861.

The World in the Church. By F. G. Trafford. 3 vols. 1863 (2nd edn).

George Geith of Fen Court. A Novel. By F. G. Trafford. 3 vols. 1864.

Maxwell Drewitt. A Novel. By F. G. Trafford. 3 vols. 1865.

Phemie Keller. A Novel. By F. G. Trafford. 3 vols. 1866.

The Race for Wealth. A Novel. 3 vols. 1866. [First pbd in Once A Week.]

Far above Rubies. A Novel. 3 vols. 1867 (2nd edn),

The Miseries of Christmas. [In Routledge's Christmas Annual, 1867.]

Austin Friars. A Novel. 3 vols. 1870.

A Life's Assize. A Novel. 3 vols. 1871. [First pbd in St James's Mag. April 1868–Feb. 1870.]

The Earl's Promise. A Novel. 3 vols. 1873.

Home, Sweet Home. A Novel. 3 vols. 1873.

Mortomley's Estate. A Novel. 3 vols. 1874.

Frank Sinclair's Wife and Other Stories. 3 vols. 1874.

The Uninhabited House. [Routledge's Christmas Annual, 1875.]

Above Suspicion. A Novel. 3 vols. 1876.

Her Mother's Darling. A Novel. 3 vols. 1877.

The Haunted River. A Christmas Story. [Routledge's Christmas Annual, 1877.]

Fairy Water. A Christmas Story. 1878. [First pbd as Routledge's Christmas Annual, 1873.]

The Disappearance of Mr Jeremiah Redworth. [Routledge's Christmas Annual, 1878.]

The Mystery in Palace Gardens. A Novel. 3 vols. 1880. [First pbd in London Society.]

Alaric Spenceley, or a High Ideal. 3 vols. 1881.

The Senior Partner. A Novel. 3 vols. 1881. [First pbd in London Society.]

The Curate of Lawood, or Every Man has his Golden Chance. [1882.]

Daisies and Buttercups. A Novel. 3 vols. 1882.

The Prince of Wales's Garden Party and Other Stories. 1882.

Idle Tales. 1882.

A Struggle for Fame. 3 vols. 1883.

Susan Drummond. A Novel. 3 vols. 1884. [First pbd in London Society, 1883, as Three Wizards and a Witch.]

Weird Stories. 1884.

Berna Boyle. A Love Story of the County Down. 3 vols. 1884.

Mitre Court. A Tale of the Great City. 3 vols. 1885. [First pbd in Temple Bar.]

For Dick's Sake. 1886.

Miss Gascoigne. A Novel. 1887.

The Nun's Curse. 3 vols. 1888.

Princess Sunshine and Other Stories. 2 vols. 1889.

The Head of the Firm. A Novel. 3 vols. 1892.

The Rusty Sword, Or Thereby hangs a Tale. 1894. [First pbd in Dawn of Day, 1893.]

A Silent Tragedy. A Novel. 1893.

The Banshee's Warning and Other Tales. 1894.

Did he deserve it? 1897.

A Rich Man's Daughter. 1897.

Handsome Phil and Other Stories. 1899.

The Footfall of Fate. 1900.

Poor Fellow. 1902.

[Mrs Riddell also collaborated with A. H. Norway in The Government Official, 3 vols. 1887. She revised Sir C. P. Roney's How to spend a Month in Ireland, 1874, and wrote A Mad Tour, or a Journey undertaken in an Insane Moment through Central Europe on Foot, 1891. For criticism see Helen C. Black, Notable Women Authors of the Day, 1893, and S. M. Ellis, Wilkie Collins and Others, 1931.]

WILLIAM CLARK RUSSELL (1844–1911)

(a) Fiction

The Hunchback's Charge. A Romance. 3 vols. 1867.

Is she a Wife? 3 vols. 1871. [Pbd under the pseudonym 'Sydney Mostyn.']

Memoirs of Mrs Laetitia Boothby. 1872.

Perplexity. 3 vols. 1872. [Pbd under the pseudonym 'Sydney Mostyn.']

The Surgeon's Secret. By Sydney Mostyn. 1872.

Which Sister? By Sydney Mostyn. 2 vols. 1873.

Kitty's Rival. By Sydney Mostyn. 3 vols. 1873.

John Holdsworth, Chief Mate. 3 vols. 1875.

Is he the Man? 3 vols. 1876.

Captain Fanny. 3 vols. 1876.

The Lady Maud. 3 vols. 1876.

The Wreck of the 'Grosvenor.' 3 vols. 1877.

The Frozen Pirate. 2 vols. 1877.

Auld Lang Syne. 2 vols. 1878.

The Little Loo. By Sydney Mostyn. 3 vols. 1878; 1883 (as Little Loo). ['Little Loo' is the name both of a ship and a personage; hence the slight change of title in 2nd edn.]

A Sailor's Sweetheart. The Wreck of the Waldershare. 3 vols. 1880.

An Ocean Tragedy. 3 vols. 1881.

An Ocean Free-lance. 3 vols. 1881.

My Watch below. Yarns. 1882. [First pbd in Daily Telegraph.]

A Sea Queen. 3 vols. 1883.

Round the Galley Fire. Stories. 1883. [First pbd in Daily Telegraph.]

On the Fo'c'sle Head. 1884.

Jack's Courtship. A Sailor's Yarn of Love and Shipwreck. 3 vols. 1884.

A Strange Voyage. 3 vols. 1885.

In the Middle Watch. 1885.

A Voyage to the Cape. 1886.

A Book for the Hammock. 1887. [Tales.]

The Golden Hope. 3 vols. 1887.

The Death Ship. 3 vols. 1888.

The Mystery of the Ocean Star. A Collection of Maritime Sketches. 1888.

Marooned. 3 vols. 1889.

My Shipmate Louise. 3 vols. 1890.

The Romance of Jenny Harlowe; and Sketches of Maritime Life. 1890.

Master Rockafellar's Voyage. 1891.

My Danish Sweetheart. A Novel. 3 vols. 1891.

A Marriage at Sea. 2 vols. 1891.

A Strange Elopement. 1892.

Alone on a Wide Wide Sea. 3 vols. 1892.

The Emigrant Ship. 3 vols. 1893.

List, ye Landsmen! 3 vols. 1893.

The Tragedy of Ida Noble. 1893.

The Good Ship Mohock. 2 vols. 1894.

Miss Parson's Adventure. 1894. [Stories by Russell and others.]

The Convict Ship. 3 vols. 1895.

Heart of Oak. 3 vols. 1895.

The Phantom Death and Other Stories. 1895.

The Honour of the Flag and Other Stories. 1896.

The Tale of the Ten. 3 vols. 1896.

What Cheer! 1896.

A Noble Haul. 1897.

The Two Captains. 1897.

The Last Entry. 1897.

A Tale of Two Tunnels. 1897.

Romance of a Midshipman. 1898.

The Pretty Polly. 1900.

Rose Island. 1900.

A Voyage at Anchor. 1900.

The Sequel. 1901.

The Ship's Adventure. 1901.

Overdue. 1903.

Abandoned. 1904.

Wrong Side out. 1904.

An Atlantic Tragedy and Other Stories. 1905.

His Island Princess. 1905.

The Yarn of Old Harbour Town. 1905.

(b) Other Writings

The Book of Authors. [1871.]

Representative Actors. [1872.]

The Book of Table Talk. Selections from the Conversations of Poets, Philosophers, Statesmen and Divines. Notes and Memoirs by Clark Russell. 1874.

Sailor's Language. A Collection of Sea-terms and their Definitions. 1883.

Betwixt the Forelands. Historical Essays. [1889.]

William Dampier. 1889.

Nelson and the Naval Supremacy of England. 1890. [With W. H. Jaques.]

Nelson's Words and Deeds. 1890. [Edited by Russell.]

Collingwood. 1891.

The British Seas. Picturesque Notes. 1892. [By Russell and others.]

Pictures from the Life of Nelson. 1897.

The Ship: her Story. 1899.

The Life of Nelson in a Series of Episodes. 1905.

The Turnpike Sailor, or Rhymes on the Road. 1907.

The Father of the Sea and Other Verses. 1911.

'MARK RUTHERFORD,' i.e. WILLIAM HALE WHITE (1831–1913)*

(a) Bibliography

Nowell Smith, S. Mark Rutherford: a Bibliography of the First Editions. 1930.

(b) Works published pseudonymously

[The following appeared as 'by Mark Rutherford,' the first 6 being 'edited by his friend Reuben Shapcott.']

The Autobiography of Mark Rutherford, Dissenting Minister. 1881.

Mark Rutherford's Deliverance, being the Second Part of his Autobiography. 1885. [Rptd 1888 in rev. and expanded form, with The Autobiography.]

The Revolution in Tanner's Lane. 1887.

Miriam's Schooling and Other Papers. 1890.

Catharine Furze. 2 vols. 1893.

Clara Hopgood. 1896.

Pages from a Journal, with Other Papers. 1900; 1910 (expanded); 1930 (World's Classics).

More Pages from a Journal. 1910.

Last Pages from a Journal. Ed. D. V. White, 1915.

(c) Other Writings

An Argument for an Extension of the Franchise. Letter to G. J. Holyoake. 1866.

Benedict de Spinoza. Ethic. 1883. [Tr. by White.]

A Dream of Two Dimensions. 1884 (anon. and priv. ptd). [Later included in Last Pages from a Journal.]

Benedict de Spinoza. Tractatus de Intellectus Emendatione. Translation [by White] revised by Amelia H. Stirling. 1895.

The Inner Life of the House of Commons, by William White. Preface by Justin McCarthy. Introduction by the Author's Son [i.e. White]. 2 vols. 1897.

A Description of the Wordsworth and Coleridge MSS. in the Possession of Mr T. Norton Longman. 1897.

An Examination of the Charge of Apostasy against Wordsworth. 1898.

Coleridge's Poems. A Facsimile Reproduction of the Proofs and MSS. of some of the Poems. Edited by the late James Dykes Campbell. With Preface and Notes by W. Hale White. 1899.

* The bibliography of 'Mark Rutherford' has been contributed by Mr S. Nowell Smith.

John Bunyan. By the Author of 'Mark Rutherford.' 1905.

Selections from Dr Johnson's 'Rambler.' 1907. [Ed. by White.]

The Life of John Sterling. By Thomas Carlyle. 1907. (World's Classics.) [Ed. by White.]

The Early Life of Mark Rutherford (W. Hale White). By Himself. 1913. [Preface by White's son.]

Letters to Three Friends. [Ed. D. V. White], 1924.

(d) Biography and Criticism

Taylor, A. E. The Novels of Mark Rutherford. E. & S. v, 1914.

Massingham, H. W. Memorial Introduction. [Prefixed to The Autobiography of Mark Rutherford, 1923.]

Nicoll, Sir W. R. Introduction to the Novels of Mark Rutherford. [1924.] [Pamphlet.]
—— Memories of Mark Rutherford. 1924.

White, Dorothy V. The Groombridge Diary. 1924.

Klinke, H. William Hale White. Frankfort, 1931. [A dissertation in German.]

OLIVE SCHREINER (1865–1920)

(a) Fiction

The Story of an African Farm. A Novel. 2 vols. 1883. [First pbd under the pseudonym 'Ralph Iron.']

Dreams. 1891.

Dream Life and Real Life. Tales by Ralph Iron. 1893.

Trooper Peter Halket of Mashonaland. 1897.

From Man to Man, or perhaps only. 1926. [With introduction by S. C. Schreiner.]

Undine. 1928. [With introduction by S. C. Schreiner.]

(b) Other Writings

The Political Situation in Cape Colony. 1896. [With S. C. Schreiner.]

An English-South African's View of the Situation. Words in Season. 1899.

Closer Union. A Letter on the South African Union and the Principles of Government. 1909.

Woman and Labour. 1911.

Thoughts on South Africa. 1923.

The Letters of Olive Schreiner. Ed. S. C. Schreiner, 1924.

(c) Biography

Schreiner, S. C. The Life of Olive Schreiner. 1924.

Chapin, A. le B. Their Trackless Way. 1931. [Contains some memories of Olive Schreiner.]

GEORGE BERNARD SHAW (b. 1856)

[See p. 617 below.]

JOSEPH HENRY SHORTHOUSE (1834–1903)

(a) Collected Works

Collected Edition of the Novels. 6 vols. 1891–4.

(b) Fiction

John Inglesant. A Romance. Birmingham, 1880 (priv. ptd); 2 vols. 1881.

The Little Schoolmaster Mark. A Spiritual Romance. 2 pts, 1883–4.

Sir Percival. A Story of the Past and Present. 1886.

A Teacher of the Violin, and Other Tales. 1888.

The Countess Eve. 1888.

Blanche, Lady Falaise. A Tale. 1891.

[Shorthouse also pbd a paper On the Platonism of Wordsworth, 1882, and wrote introductions for George Herbert's The Temple and for several devotional works.]

(c) Biography and Criticism

Gardiner, S. R. John Inglesant. Fraser's Mag. cv, 1882.

John Inglesant. Dublin Rev. xc, 1882.

'Lee, Vernon.' The Little Schoolmaster Mark. Academy, 29 Dec. 1883.

West, H. E. 'John Inglesant' and 'Sartor Resartus.' Two Phases of Religion. [1884.]

Wilson, H. S. The Philosophy of Shorthouse. Modern Rev. v, 1884.

Sir Percival. Blackwood's Mag. cxl, 1886.

Linnell, C. The True Story of John Inglesant. Athenaeum, 27 July, 17 Aug. 1901.

Hutton, E. The Work of Shorthouse. Blackwood's Mag. clxxiii, 1903.

Montgomery, J. D. Personal Recollections of Shorthouse. Temple Bar, cxxvii, 1903.

Acton, C. E. D. (Baron). Letters to Mary Gladstone. With Introduction by Herbert Paul. 1904. [Contains a discussion of Shorthouse's historical point of view.]

The Life and Letters of J. H. Shorthouse. Edited by his Wife [Sarah]. With an Introduction by John Hunter Smith. 2 vols. 1905. [Also contains Literary Remains.]

Durham, J. Marius the Epicurean and John Inglesant. [1905.]

More, P. E. Shelburne Essays. Ser. 3, New York, 1906.

Gosse, Sir E. Portraits and Sketches. 1912.

Coats, R. H. Birmingham Mystics of the Mid-Victorian Era. Hibbert Journ. xvi, 1918.

Fleming, W. K. Some Truths about John Inglesant. Quarterly Rev. ccxlv, 1925.

Polak, M. The Historical, Philosophical and Religious Aspects of John Inglesant. Oxford, 1934.

HENRY HAWLEY SMART (1833–1893)

Breezie Langton: a Story of Fifty-Two to Fifty-Five. 3 vols. 1869.

Bitter is the Rind. 3 vols. 1870; [1909] (as Bit and Bridal).

A Race for a Wife. A Novel. 1870.

Cecile; or, Modern Idolaters. 3 vols. 1871.

False Cards. 3 vols. 1873.

Broken Bonds. 3 vols. 1874.

Two Kisses. 3 vols. 1875.

Courtship in Seventeen Hundred and Twenty, in Eighteen Hundred and Sixty. 2 vols. 1876.

Bound to Win: a Tale of the Turf. 3 vols. 1877.

Play or Pay. A Novelette. 1878.

Sunshine and Snow. A Novel. 3 vols. 1878.

Social Sinners. A Novel. 3 vols. 1880.

Belles and Ringers. A Novelette. 1880.

The Great Tontine. A Novel. 3 vols. 1881.

At Fault. 3 vols. 1883.

Hard Lines. A Novel. 3 vols. 1883.

From Post to Finish. A Novel. 3 vols. 1884.

Salvage. A Collection of Stories. [1884.]

Tie and Trick: a Melodramatic Story. 3 vols. 1885.

Lightly Lost. 1885.

Struck Down: 'a Tale of Devon.' 1886.

Plucked: a Tale of a Trap; [with] Other Contributions by Annie Thomas. [1886.]

Bad to Beat. A Novel. [1886.]

The Outsider. A Novel. 2 vols. 1886.

A False Start. A Novel. 3 vols. 1887.

Cleverly Won. A Romance of the Grand National. A Novelette. 1887.

The Pride of the Paddock. 1888.

The Master of Rathkelly. A Novel. 2 vols. 1888.

Saddle and Sabre. A Novel. 3 vols. 1888.

The Last Coup. A Novelette. 1889.

Long Odds. A Novel. 3 vols. 1889.

A Black Business. A Novelette. [1890.]

Without Love or Licence. A Tale of South Devon. 3 vols. 1890.

Thrice Past the Post. A Novel. 1891.

Beatrice and Benedick: a Romance of the Crimea. 2 vols. 1891.

'The Plunger.' A Turf Tragedy of Five-and-Twenty Years ago. 2 vols. 1891.

A Member of Tattersall's: a Novel. 1892.

Vanity's Daughter. A Novel. 1893.

A Racing Rubber. A Novel. 1895.

ANNE ISABELLA THACKERAY, later LADY RITCHIE (1837–1923)

(a) Fiction

The Story of Elizabeth. 1863; 1895 (with Two Hours and From an Island).

The Village on the Cliff. 1867.

Five Old Friends; and a Young Prince. 1868.

To Esther, and Other Sketches. 1869.

Old Kensington. 1873.

Bluebeard's Keys and Other Stories. 1874.

Miss Angel. 1875.

Miss Williamson's Divagations. 1881.

Mrs Dymond. 1885.

Jack Frost's Little Prisoners. 1887.

(b) Other Writings

Toilers and Spinsters and Other Essays. 1874.

Madame de Sévigné. 1881.

A Book of Sibyls. Mrs Barbauld, Mrs Opie, Miss Edgeworth, Miss Austen. 1883.

Records of Tennyson, Ruskin and Robert and Elizabeth Browning. 1892.

Lord Tennyson and his Friends. 1893.

Lord Amherst and the Advance to Burma. 1894. [With R. Evans.]

Chapters from some Memoirs. 1894.

Blackstick Papers. 1908.

A Discourse on Modern Sibyls. English Ass. Lecture, 1913.

From the Porch. 1913. [Essays.]

W. M. Thackeray and Edward FitzGerald: a Literary Friendship. Unpublished Letters and Verses by W. M. Thackeray; with an Introduction by Lady Ritchie. 1916.

From Friend to Friend. Edited by Emily Ritchie. 1919. [Reminiscences and a short story, 'Binnie.']

Letters of Anne Thackeray Ritchie. Ed. H. Ritchie, 1924.

[Lady Ritchie also edited or contributed introductions to works by Thackeray, Mary Russell Mitford, Mrs Gaskell, Miss Edgeworth, etc.]

(c) Biography and Criticism

Earl, E. The Author of The Story of Elizabeth: Anne Thackeray Ritchie. Cornhill Mag. March 1927.

Kent, M. Anne Thackeray Ritchie. Cornhill Mag. CLV, 1937

HENRY DUFF TRAILL (1842–1900)

[See p. 755 below.]

KATHARINE TYNAN (1861–1931)

[See p. 1057 below.]

C. C. FRASER TYTLER (b. 1848)

[See p. 360 above.]

MARGARET VELEY (1843–1887)

[See p. 361 above.]

MRS HUMPHRY WARD, i.e. MARY AUGUSTA WARD, née ARNOLD (1851–1920)

(a) Collected Works

The Writings of Mrs Humphry Ward. With Introductions by the Author. 16 vols. 1911–2 (Westmorland Edn).

(b) Fiction

Milly and Olly, or a Holiday among the Mountains. 1881.

Miss Bretherton. 1884.

Robert Elsmere. 3 vols. 1888.

The History of David Grieve. 3 vols. 1892 (6 edns, the 6th with a prefatory letter answering certain criticisms).

Marcella. 3 vols. 1894.

The Story of Bessie Costrell. 1895. [First pbd in Cornhill Mag. May–July 1895.]

Sir George Tressady. 1896. [First pbd in Century Mag. Nov. 1895–Oct. 1896.]

Helbeck of Bannisdale. 1898.

Eleanor. 1900. [First pbd in Harper's Mag. Jan.–Dec. 1900.]

Lady Rose's Daughter. 1903. [First pbd in Harper's Mag. May 1902–April 1903.]

The Marriage of William Ashe. 1905. [First pbd in Harper's Mag. June 1904–May 1905.]

Fenwick's Career. 1906.

Diana Mallory. 1908. [First pbd in Harper's Mag. Nov. 1907–Oct. 1908, as The Testing of Diana Mallory.]

Daphne, or Marriage à la Mode. 1909. [First pbd in McClure's Mag. Jan.–June 1909.]

Canadian Born. 1910.

The Case of Richard Meynell. 1911.

The Mating of Lydia. 1913.

The Coryston Family. 1913.

Delia Blanchflower. 1915.

Eltham House. 1915.

A Great Success. 1916.

Lady Connie. 1916.

'Missing.' 1917.

Cousin Philip. 1919.

Harvest. 1920; 1929 (as Love's Harvest).

(c) Other Writings

Amiel's Journal Intime. Translated with Introduction and Notes. 2 vols. 1885.

University Hall; Opening Address. 1891.

Unitarians and the Future. The Essex Hall Lecture, 1894. 1894.

Play-Time of the Poor. 1906. [Rptd from The Times.]

William Thomas Arnold, Journalist and Historian. Manchester, 1907. [With C. E. Montague. Originally pbd as preface to W. T. Arnold's Fragmentary Studies on Roman Imperialism, 1907.]

Letters to my Neighbours on the Present Election. 1910.

England's Effort. With a Preface by the Earl of Rosebery. 1916.

Towards the Goal. With an Introduction by Theodore Roosevelt. 1917.

The War and Elizabeth. 1918.

A Writer's Recollections. 1918.

Fields of Victory. The Journey through the Battlefields of France. 1919.

(d) Biography and Criticism

Phelps, W. L. Essays on Modern Novelists. New York, 1910. [Includes a bibliography of Mrs H. Ward's writings by A. Keogh.]

Walters, J. S. Mrs Humphry Ward: her Work and Influence. 1912.

Gwynn, S. Mrs Humphry Ward. 1917.

Johnson, Lionel. Reviews and Critical Papers. Ed. R. Shafer, 1921.

Trevelyan, J. P. Life of Mrs Humphry Ward. 1923.

THEODORE WATTS-DUNTON (1832–1914)

[See p. 756 below.]

SIR FREDERICK WEDMORE (1844–1921)

[See p. 756 below.]

STANLEY JOHN WEYMAN (1855–1928)

(a) Collected Works

The Novels of Stanley Weyman in Thin Paper and arranged Chronologically. With an Introduction in the First Volume by the Author. 21 vols. 1911; 21 vols. 1922.

(b) Fiction

The House of the Wolf. 1890.

The New Rector. 2 vols. 1891.

The Story of Francis Cludde. 1891.

A Gentleman of France. Being the Memoirs of Gaston de Bonne, Sieur de Marsac. 3 vols. 1893.

The Man in Black. 1894.

My Lady Rotha. 1894.

Under the Red Robe. 2 vols. 1894.

From the Memoirs of a Minister of France. 1895.

The Red Cockade. 1895.

The Castle Inn. 1898.

Shrewsbury. A Romance. 1898.

Sophia. 1900.

Count Hannibal. 1901.

In Kings' Byways. 1902. [Short stories.]

The Long Night. 1903.

The Abbess of Vlaye. 1904.

Starvecrow Farm. 1905.

Chippinge. 1906.

Laid up in Lavender. 1907. [Stories.]

The Wild Geese. [1908.]

The Great House. 1919.

Ovington's Bank. 1922.

The Traveller in the Fur Cloak. 1924.

Queen's Folly. 1925.

The Lively Peggy. 1928.

OSCAR WILDE (1856–1900)

[See p. 620 below.]

EMMA CAROLINE WOOD (LADY WOOD)

Rosewarn. A Novel. 3 vols. 1866. [Pbd under the pseudonym 'C. Sylvester.']
Sorrow on the Sea. A Novel. 3 vols. 1868.
Sabina. A Novel. 3 vols. 1868.
On Credit. 2 vols. 1870.
Seadrift. A Novel. 3 vols. 1871.
Cloth of Frieze. A Novel. 3 vols. 1872.
Wild Weather. A Novel. 2 vols. 1873.
Up Hill. A Novel. 3 vols. 1873.
Ruling the Roast. A Novel. 3 vols. 1874.
Below the Salt. A Novel. 3 vols. 1876.
Through Fire and Water. A Novel. 2 vols. 1876.
Sheen's Foreman. A Novel. 3 vols. 1877.
Youth on the Prow. A Novel. 3 vols. 1879.

[Lady Wood also pbd an anthology, Leaves from the Poet's Laurels, 1869.]

MARGARET LOUISA WOODS, née BRADLEY (b. 1856)

(a) Fiction

A Village Tragedy. 1887.
Esther Vanhomrigh. 3 vols. 1891.
The Vagabonds. 1894.
Weeping Ferry and Other Stories. 1898.
Sons of the Sword. A Romance of the Peninsular War. 1901.
The Princess of Hanover. 1902.
The King's Revoke. 1905.
The Invader. 1907.
Come unto these Yellow Sands. [1915.]
A Poet's Youth. 1923.
The Spanish Lady. 1927.

(b) Other Writings

Lyrics and Ballads. 1889.
Songs. Oxford, 1896 (priv. ptd).
Aëromancy and Other Poems. 1896.
Wild Justice. 1896.
Poems Old and New. 1907.
Pastels under the Southern Cross. 1911. [Essays of travel.]
Collected Poems. 1914.

EDMUND HODGSON YATES (1831–1894)

(a) Fiction

Broken to Harness. A Story of English Domestic Life. 3 vols. 1864.
For better, for worse. A Romance of the Affections. 2 vols. 1864.
Running the Gauntlet. A Novel. 3 vols. 1865.
Kissing the Rod. A Novel. 3 vols. 1866.
Land at Last. A Novel in Three Books. 3 vols. 1866.
Black Sheep. A Novel. 3 vols. 1867.
The Rock ahead. A Novel. 3 vols. 1868.
Wrecked in Port. A Novel. 3 vols. 1869.

A Righted Wrong. A Novel. 3 vols. 1870.
Dr Wainwright's Patient. 3 vols. 1871.
Castaway. A Novel. 3 vols. 1872.
The Yellow Flag. A Novel. 3 vols. Dublin, 1872.
A Waiting Race. A Novel. 3 vols. 1872.
Nobody's Fortune. A Novel. 3 vols. 1872.
The Impending Sword. 3 vols. 1874.
Two by Tricks. A Novel. 2 vols. 1874.
A Silent Witness. A Novel. 3 vols. 1875.

(b) Other Writings

My Haunts and their Frequenters. 1854.
Mirth and Metre. 1855. [With F. E. Smedley.]
Our Miscellany. Containing Contributions by W. H. Painsworth, G. P. R. Jacobus, T. B. Macawley and Other Eminent Authors. 1857. [Ed. by Yates and R. B. Brough.]
Mr Thackeray, Mr Yates and the Garrick Club. The Correspondence and Facts, stated by Edmund Yates. 1859 (priv. ptd).
The Life and Correspondence of Charles Matthews the Elder, Comedian, by Mrs Matthews, abridged and condensed by Edmund H. Yates. 1860.
After Office Hours. [1861.]
The Business of Pleasure. 2 vols. 1865. [Essays.]
Pages in Waiting. 1865. [Rptd from Temple Bar.]
Celebrities at Home. Sers. 1–3 (all pbd), 1877–9. [Rptd from The World.]
Edmund Yates: his Recollections and Experiences. 2 vols. 1884.

[Yates also contributed a memoir of Albert Smith to that writer's Mont Blanc, 1860, and of F. E. Smedley to Gathered Leaves, 1865; he edited M. Collins's Thoughts in my Garden, 1880, and was successively editor of Temple Bar from 1860, Tinsley's Mag. from 1867, Time from 1879, and The World.]

(c) Biography

The Last Days of Edmund Yates. Temple Bar, CII, 1894.

ISRAEL ZANGWILL (1864–1926)

(a) Collected Works

The Works of Israel Zangwill. 14 vols. 1925.

(b) Fiction

The Premier and the Painter. 1888. [With Louis Cowen.]
The Bachelor's Club. 1891.
The Big Bow Mystery. 1892.
Children of the Ghetto. 3 vols. 1892.
The Old Maid's Club. 1892.
Ghetto Tragedies. 1893.
Merely Mary Ann. 1893.

The King of Schnorrers. Grotesques and Fantasies. 1894.
Joseph the Dreamer. 1895.
The Master. 1895.
The Celibates' Club. 1898.
Dreamers of the Ghetto. 1898.
'They that walk in Darkness.' 1899.
The Mantle of Elijah. 1900.
The Grey Wig. Stories and Novelettes. 1903.
Ghetto Comedies. 1907.
Italian Fantasies. 1910.
Jinny the Carrier. 1919.

(c) Other Writings

Without Prejudice. Reprinted Articles. 1896.
Blind Children. 1903. [Poems.]
The War God. A Tragedy. 1911.
The Next Religion. 1912. [A play.]
The Melting Pot. A Drama. 1914.
The War for the World. 1916.
The Principles of Nationalities. 1917. (Conway Memorial Lecture.)
Chosen Peoples: Hebraic Ideal versus the Teutonic. With a Foreword by H. Samuel. 1918. (Davis Memorial Lecture.)
Hands off Russia. A Speech delivered at the Royal Albert Hall, February 8th, 1919. 1919.
The Voice of Jerusalem. 1920.   S. J. L.

VIII. CHILDREN'S BOOKS

[The following types of book are not included: (i) Alphabets, as such; (ii) Didactic works of all kinds, including such as were merely meant to convey knowledge in a domestic or familiar manner; (iii) Works in which pictures purposely predominate over text (but see note on Illustrators, p. 577 below); (iv) Anthologies, with a few special exceptions, particularly in respect of Fairy Tales. The more voluminous writers are represented only by a typical selection.]

(1) HISTORY, BIBLIOGRAPHY AND CRITICISM

Trimmer, Sarah. The Guardian of Education. 1802–4. [Criticism of current works for children, with account of and comment on many earlier works. The greater part written by Mrs Trimmer, though in magazine form.]
[Kendrew, J. (publisher, of York).] A Collection of the Publications of J. Kendrew [with notes by his family]. [In BM.]
Children's Books. Quarterly Rev. LXXIV, June 1844.
'Titmarsh, Michael Angelo' (W. M. Thackeray). On Some Illustrated Children's Books. Fraser's Mag. April 1846.

Yonge, C. M. Children's Literature of the Last Century [1769 to 1869]. Macmillan's Mag. xx, 1869.
—— A Storehouse of Stories. 2 vols. 1870. [Selections, 18th and 19th centuries, with historical introduction.]
Mackarness, Mrs H. Children of the Olden Time. 1874.
'Tytler, Sarah' (H. Keddie). Childhood a Hundred Years Ago. 1877.
Tuer, A. W. 1000 Quaint Cuts from Books of Other Days. [1886.]
—— The History of the Horn-Book. 2 vols. 1896.
—— Pages and Pictures from Forgotten Children's Books. 1898–9.
—— Stories from Old-Fashioned Children's Books. 1899–1900.
Welsh, C. On Coloured Books for Children. 1887. [No. XII of priv. ptd Opuscula of the Sette of Odd Volumes.]
Hewins, C. The History of Children's Books [early English and American works]. Atlantic Monthly, LXI, 1888.
Salmon, E. Juvenile Literature as it is. 1888.
Pearson, E. Banbury Chapbooks and Nursery Toy Book Literature of the Eighteenth and early Nineteenth Centuries. 1890 (priv. ptd).
Field, L. F. The Child and his Book. [1891.]
Children Yesterday and To-day. Quarterly Rev. CLXXXIII, 1896.
White, Gleeson. Children's Books and their Illustrators. Studio Special Number, 1897–8.
'Tallentyre, S. G.' (E. B. Hall). The Road to Knowledge a Hundred Years Ago. Cornhill Mag. IX, 1900.
The Imprint. 1901. [Short contributions by Walter Crane, Alice and Everard Meynell and others, with some facsimiles, chiefly to show typographical requirements and methods of reproduction.]
Lucas, E. V. Old Fashioned Tales. 1905. [Selections, with introduction.]
—— Forgotten Tales of Long Ago. 1906. [Selections, with introduction.]
Dodd, C. I. Some Aspects of Children's Books. National Rev. Jan. 1905.
Moses, M. J. Children's Books and Reading. New York, 1907. [English books as well as American.]
H.M. Stationery Office. Catalogue of the British Section of the International Exhibition of the Book Industry and Graphic Arts, Leipzig, 1914. [Special section devoted to Children's Books. With introductions by Arthur Rackham and F. J. H. Darton.]
Barry, F. V. A Century of Children's Books. 1922.

Babenroth, A. C. English Childhood. New York, 1922. [Chs. iii, iv, v.]

Andreae, G. The Dawn of Juvenile Literature in England. Amsterdam, 1925.

Sawyer, C. J. and Darton, F. J. H. English Books, 1475–1900. 2 vols. 1927. [Vol. i, ch. 7 and Vol. ii, ch. 4.]

Newton, A. E. This Book-Collecting Game. Boston, 1928. [Chs. iii, iv.]

[Gumuchian et Cie.] Les Livres de l'Enfance du XVe au XIXe Siècle. Préface de Paul Gavault. Paris, [1930]. [Many facsimiles. A bookseller's catalogue which is virtually a bibliography. English collations, etc. in English.]

Fulham Public Libraries. Catalogue of an Exhibition of Children's Books of Long Ago. With Foreword by F. E. Hansford. [1931.]

Sayers, W. C. B. A Manual of Children's Libraries. 1932. [Chs. i, ii.]

Darton, F. J. H. Children's Books in England. Five Centuries of Social Life. Cambridge, 1932.

Rosenbach, A. S. W. Early American Children's Books. With a Bibliographical Description of the Books in his Private Collection. Foreword by A. Edward Newton. Portland, Maine, 1933 (priv. ptd). [Contains bibliography of earlier English edns.]

James, Philip. Children's Books of Yesterday. Ed. C. G. Holme, 1933. [Studio Special Number.]

König, G. Der viktorianische Schulroman. Berlin, 1937.

(2) Principal Writers

Taylor, Isaac ('of Ongar'; 1759–1829). Scenes in Europe; for the Amusement and Instruction of little Tarry-at-home Travellers. 1819 (bis); 1823 (6th edn).

—— Scenes of British Wealth. 1823.

—— Bunyan Explained to a Child. 2 pts, 1824; 1825.

—— The Biography of a Brown Loaf. 1829.

—— The Ship. 1830.

Taylor, Ann (née Martin; 1757–1830: 'of Ongar'). The Family Mansion. A Tale. 1819; 1820.

Taylor, Ann (née Martin) and Jane. Correspondence between a Mother and her Daughter at School. 1817; 1818 (4th edn); 1821 (6th edn). [Narrative of school life in letter-form.]

Taylor, Ann (afterwards Gilbert; 1782–1866). The Wedding among the Flowers. 1808. [See below, under William Roscoe. For Ann Taylor see Autobiography and Other Memorials of Mrs Gilbert, ed. Josiah Gilbert, 2 vols. 1874, 1878.]

Taylor, Jane (1783–1824). Display. A Tale for Young People. 1815; 1818.

—— Contributions of Q. Q. 2 vols. 1824.

[For Jane Taylor see Memoirs and Poetical Remains, with Extracts from Correspondence, ed. Isaac Taylor, 2 vols. 1825; Mrs H. C. Knight, Jane Taylor; her Life and Letters, 1880; and L. B. Walford, Four Biographies from 'Blackwood,' 1888.]

Taylor, Ann (afterwards Gilbert) and Jane. Original Poems for Infant Minds, by Several Young Persons [i.e. Ann and Jane Taylor, Isaac Taylor (their father), Isaac Taylor (their brother), Bernard Barton (see p. 227 above), and Adelaide O'Keeffe (see below)]. 2 vols. 1804–5; 1808 (7th edn); 1818 (18th edn); 1834 (30th edn); 1875 (complete edn, containing Mrs Gilbert's final revision); ed. E. V. Lucas, [1903] (contains also Rhymes for the Nursery and other matter). [Selections and single poems —especially 'My Mother'—were issued in many forms with and without authority. See especially Little Ann and other poems, illustrated by Kate Greenaway, [1883], and Meddlesome Mattie, and Other Poems for Infant Minds, ed. E. Sitwell, 1925.]

Taylor, Ann (afterwards Gilbert) and Jane. Rhymes for the Nursery. 1806; 1818 (11th edn); 1835 (27th edn); 1857; 1878 (illustrated by Sir John Gilbert).

—— City Scenes. 1806. Country Scenes. 1806. [Rev. versions of older works composed by the publisher, William Darton. Illustrations drawn and engraved by Jane Taylor.]

—— Hymns for Infant Minds. 1808; 1810; 1823 (10th edn); 1844 (35th edn, 'containing many hymns never before published'); 1868 (47th edn).

—— Signor Topsy-Turvy's Wonderful Magic Lantern; or, the World turned upside down. 1810. [By Ann, Jane, and possibly Jefferys Taylor.]

Taylor, Jefferys (1792–1853). Harry's Holiday. 1818 (with preface by Jane Taylor); 1822 (3rd edn).

—— Ralph Richards, the Miser. 1821.

—— Aesop in Rhyme. 1822.

The Family Pen. Memorials, Biographical and Literary, of the Taylor Family of Ongar. By [Canon] Isaac Taylor. 2 vols. 1867. [Contains recollections by editor's father, memoir of Jane Taylor, short pieces by various members of the family not all pbd elsewhere, and List of Works by them all. See also Hereditary Genius, by Sir Francis Galton, 1869, D. M. Armitage, The Taylors of Ongar, Cambridge, 1938, and lists of works in DNB. under each author.]

[Roscoe, William (1753–1831).] The Butter-fly's Ball and the Grasshopper's Feast. 1807, etc. [See also p. 887 below.]

[Dorset, Catherine Ann (née Turner; 1750?–1817?).] The Peacock 'At Home': a Sequel to the Butterfly's Ball. 1807, etc.

[The above two works produced many imitations. The chief are mentioned in C. Welsh's facs. rpts (1883) of them and of The Lion's Masquerade (by Mrs Dorset?), 1807, and The Elephant's Ball (by W. B.), 1807. Addenda: The Lion's Parliament, [1808?] (illustrated by W. Mulready?); The Rose's Breakfast, 1808; The Tyger's Theatre (by Samuel James Arnold, 1774–1852), 1808; The Butterfly's Funeral (by J. L. B.), 1808; Flora's Gala, 1808; The Feast of the Fishes (by 'Theresa Tyro'), 1808; The Ape's Concert (by 'A. Tabby'), 1808; The Council of Dogs, 1808; The Horse's Levee, 1808; The Wedding among the Flowers (by Ann Taylor), 1808; The Butterfly's Birthday (by W. Roscoe), 1809; La Fête de la Rose (by B. Hoole, Mrs Hofland), [1809?].]

Turner, Elizabeth (d. 1846). The Daisy, or Cautionary Stories in Verse, adapted to the Ideas of Children, from four to eight years old. 1806; 1816 (6th edn); 1840 (25th edn); ed. C. Welsh, 1883; rptd 1900.

—— The Cowslip. 1811; 1817 (5th edn); 1842 (22nd edn); ed. C. Welsh, 1883.

—— The Pink. 1811; 1842 (22nd edn); ed. (with addns), Mary Howitt, 1835.

[Also The Crocus, 1844 (not 1st edn?), The Rose (——?), The Blue-Bell; or, Tales and Fables, 1838, and Short Poems for Young Children, 1859 (not 1st edn?). Selections are Mrs Turner's Cautionary Stories, ed. E. V. Lucas, 1897 (The Dumpy Books), and Grand-mamma's Book of Rhymes, ed. G. K. Chesterton, 1927. See also 'F. Anstey' (F. Anstey Guthrie), Mr Punch's Model Music Hall Songs and Dramas, 1892.]

Barbara Hoole (afterwards Hofland, née Wreaks; 1770–1844). [See p. 400 above.]

Lamb, Charles (1775–1834). The King and Queen of Hearts. 1805.

Lamb, Charles and Mary Ann (1764–1847). Tales from Shakespeare. 2 vols. 1807 [1806].

[See also pp. 631, 675 below. The children's books by Charles and Mary Lamb are all contained, with bibliographical notes, in vol. III of Collected Works, ed. E. V. Lucas, 1903–5.]

Sherwood, Mary Martha (née Butt; 1775–1851). [See p. 416 above.]

Hack, Maria (née Barton; 1777–1844). Winter Evenings, or Tales of Travellers. 4 vols. 1818–9; 1853 (rev.).

—— English Stories. 3 sers. 1820–5; rev. D. M. Smith, 1872 (sers. 1, 2 only).

Hack, Maria (née Barton; 1777–1844). Harry Beaufoy, or the Pupil of Nature. 1821; 1830 (3rd edn).

Elliott, Mary (née Belson). Precept and Example, or Midsummer Holidays. 1812 (2nd edn).

—— The Orphan Boy, or a Journey to Bath. [1814.]

—— Simple Truths, in Verse. 1816; [1850?] (7th edn).

—— The Modern Goody Two-Shoes; exemplifying the Good Consequences of Early Attention to Learning and Virtue. 1819.

—— Rural Employment, or a Peep into Village Concerns. 1820.

Robson, Mary (afterwards Hughs). Aunt Mary's Tales for the Entertainment and Improvement of Little Girls. 1813 (bis); 1822 (6th edn).

—— The Alchemist. 1818.

—— The Ornaments Discovered. 1819.

—— The Orphan Girl. A Moral Tale. 1819.

—— The Metamorphoses. 1822.

Cameron, Lucy Lyttelton (née Butt; 1781–1858). The History of Margaret Whyte. N.d. [Written in 1798 but not pbd till later.]

—— The Polite Little Children. 1822 (6th edn); 1836 (12th edn).

—— The Two Lambs. 1821.

[See Life, ed. C. Cameron, 1862, and rev. G. T. Cameron, [1873]. Mrs Cameron was the sister of Mrs Sherwood (see p. 416 above).]

Howitt, William (1792–1879). [See p. 673 below.]

Marryat, Frederick (1792–1848). Masterman Ready, or the Wreck of the Pacific. 3 vols. 1841–2. [See also p. 385 above.]

'Parley, Peter.' [The inventor of this pseudonym was an American, Samuel Griswold Goodrich (1793–1860), but the name was at once adopted by English writers and publishers. Goodrich claimed, in Recollections of a Lifetime, 1857, to have compiled 116 'Parley' books (see his List), but their titles also were used, and their text often adapted freely, in English edns by rivals. It is impossible in many instances to say whether such works were English or American or hybrid. For summary of the books and authors, see F. J. H. Darton, Children's Books in England, Cambridge, 1932, ch. xiii, and Peter Parley and the Battle of the Children's Books, Cornhill Mag. Nov. 1932. Goodrich's first 'Parley' book was Tales of Peter Parley about America, Boston, 1827. Peter Parley's Magazines and Peter Parley's Annuals, containing little genuine work by the originator, appeared in various forms simultaneously from c. 1835 to c. 1865. The writers who can be certainly identified as having produced original work under this pseudonym, or as 'edited by Peter Parley' (*i.e.* really written by them), are:]

Mogridge, George (1787–1854; also wrote as 'Alan Gray,' 'Aunt Mary,' 'Aunt Newbury,' 'Aunt Upton,' 'Grandfather Gregory,' 'Grandmamma Gilbert,' 'Ephraim Holding,' 'Old Humphrey,' 'The Traveller,' 'Uncle Adam,' 'Uncle Newbury'). The Juvenile Moralists. 1829. The Juvenile Culprits. 1829.
[See Life, Character, and Writings, by C. Williams, 1856; and John Strong the Boaster and other Pithy Papers [by Mogridge], with a Short Biography by A. R. Buckland, 1904.]

Martin, William (1801–1867). The Parlour Book. [1835?]
—— The Book of Sports. [1837?]
—— The Hatchups of Me and My Schoolfellows. 1858.
—— Holiday Tales. 1860.

Clark, Samuel (1810–1875). Peter Parley's Wonders of the Earth, Sea and Sky. [1837.]
[See Memorials, from Journals and Letters, edited by his Wife, 1878.]

Strickland, Agnes (1796–1874). The Moss-House. 1822 (anon.).
—— The Rival Crusoes. 1826.
[See also p. 897 below.]

Corner, Julia (1798–1875). The Village School; with the History, and what became of some of the Scholars. [1848.]
—— The Child's Own Sunday Book. 1850.
—— The Cow Boy, or the Reward of Honesty. [1854.]
—— Little Plays for Little Actors. [1854.]

[Jerram, Jane Elizabeth.] The Child's Own Story Book. 1837; [1843] (3rd edn).

Howitt, Mary (née Botham; 1799–1888). [See p. 672 below.]

Hall, Anna Maria (née Fielding; 1800–1881). The Hartopp Jubilee. [1840?] [See also p. 485 above.]

Sinclair, Catherine (1800–1864). Holiday House. A Book for the Young. 1839.
—— Charlie Seymour. 1856 (4th edn).
—— Letters. 6 nos. 1861–4. ['Hieroglyphic' stories in letter-form.]
[See also p. 507 above.]

[Bevan, Favell Lee (afterwards Mortimer; 1802–1878).] The Peep of Day. 1833. [Later issues with text mitigated. For her more scholastic and historical works for children, see The Times, 27 June 1933 (A Law-giver in the Nursery, by Edwyn Bevan).]

Martineau, Harriet (1802–1876). The Playfellow. 1841. [4 pts: The Settlers at Home, The Peasant and the Prince, Feats on the

Fiord, The Crofton Boys. See also p. 496 above.]

Howard, Edward Granville George (d. 1841). Rattlin the Reefer. 1836. [Ed. by F. Marryat. See also p. 401 above.]

Gatty, Margaret (née Scott; 1807–1873). [See p. 484 above.]

Lemon, Mark (1809–1870). The Enchanted Doll. 1849. [Illustrated by Richard Doyle. See also p. 603 below.]

Thackeray, William Makepeace (1811–1863). The Rose and the Ring. 1855. [See also p. 429 above.]

Dickens, Charles (1812–1870). Holiday Romance. 1868. [See also p. 435 above.]

Lear, Edward (1812–1888). A Book of Nonsense. 1846; 1861 (enlarged); 1863 (enlarged).
—— Nonsense Songs, Stories, Botany and Alphabets. 1871.
—— More Nonsense Pictures, Rhymes, Botany, etc. 1872.
—— Laughable Lyrics. A Fresh Book of Nonsense Poems, Songs, Botany, Music, etc. 1877.
—— Queery Leary Nonsense. Compiled by Lady Strachey and with an Introduction by the Earl of Cromer. 1911. [Selection from earlier books with some new matter.]
[Lear also pbd books of travel. See his Letters, ed. Lady C. Strachey, 1907–11, and Sir E. Strachey, Nonsense as a Fine Art, Quarterly Rev. Oct. 1888, and Talk at a Country House, 1895. Also: W. B. O. Field, Edward Lear on My Shelves, New York, 1933 (detailed bibliography); A. Davidson, Edward Lear, 1938.]

Macleod, Norman (1812–1872). The Gold Thread. 1861; 1904; ed. D. Macleod, 1907. [Macleod also edited Good Words for the Young (see under Periodicals, p. 578 below).]

Smiles, Samuel (1812–1904). Self-Help; with Illustrations of Character and Conduct. 1859. [See also p. 925 below.]

Kingston, William Henry Giles (1814–1880). [See p. 491 above.]

Browne, Frances (b. 1816). Granny's Wonderful Chair and its Tales of Fairy Times. 1857. [See short biography and List of Works in Everyman's Lib. edn, 1906.]

[Hawkshaw, Mrs.] Aunt Effie's Rhymes for Little Children. Illustrated by H. K. Browne. [1852]; 1878.
—— Aunt Effie's Gift to the Nursery. 1854; 1876.

[Charlesworth, Maria Louisa (1819–1880).] Ministering Children. 1854; 1857. [Sequel, 1862.]

Kingsley, Charles (1819–1875). The Water Babies. 1863. [See also p. 487 above.]

Ruskin, John (1819–1900). The King of the Golden River. 1851. [Written 1841 for private use. See also p. 691 below.]

Ingelow, Jean (1820–1897). Stories Told to a Child. 1865. [See also p. 291 above.]

Rossetti, Christina (1820–1894). Sing-Song. 1872. [See also p. 273 above.]

Sewell, Anna (1820–1878). Black Beauty: the Autobiography of a Horse. 1877; [1878] (5th edn). [No other works. See edn in Everyman's Lib. 1921.]

St John, Percy Bolingbroke (1821–1889). The Arctic Crusoe. [1854.]

—— The Coral Reef. [1868.]

—— The Sailor Crusoe. [1876.]

Hughes, Thomas (1822–1896). Tom Brown's School Days. 1857. [See also p. 486 above.]

Patmore, Coventry Kersey Dighton (1823–1806). The Children's Garland from the best Poets. 1862. [Ed. by Patmore. See also p. 270 above.]

Rands, William Brighty (1823–1882). Lilliput Levee. 1864. [Illustrated by J. E. Millais and G. J. Pinwell. See also p. 304 above.]

Macdonald, George (1824–1905). At the Back of the North Wind. 1871. [Macdonald also edited Good Words for the Young (see under Periodicals, p. 578 below). See also p. 494 above.]

Palgrave, Francis Turner (1824–1897). The Children's Treasury of English Song. 2 pts, 1875. [Ed. by Palgrave. See also p. 303 above.]

Ballantyne, Robert Michael (1825–1894). Snowflakes and Sunbeams, or the Young Fur Traders. 1855.

—— Three Little Kittens. [1856.] [With music.]

—— Ungava. A Tale of Esquimaux-Land. 1857.

—— Martin Rattler, or a Boy's Adventures in the Forests of Brazil. 1858.

—— The Coral Island. 1858; ed. E. Rhys, 1907 (Everyman's Lib.); ed. Sir J. M. Barrie, 1913.

—— The Robber Kitten. 1860.

—— The Dog Crusoe. A Tale of the Western Prairies. 1860.

—— The Gorilla Hunters. 1861.

—— Fighting the Flames. A Tale of the London Fire Brigade. 1867.

—— Deep Down. A Tale of the Cornish Mines. 1868.

—— Erling the Bold. A Tale of the Norse Sea-Kings. 1869.

—— The Iron Horse, or Life on the Line. 1871.

—— The Pirate City. An Algerian Tale. 1875.

—— The Middy and the Moors. 1888.

[See Personal Reminiscences in Book-Making, n.d. For Ballantyne's early life see Hudson's Bay; or, Every-Day Life in the Wilds of North America, during Six Years' residence in the territory of the Hudson's Bay Company, 1845 (2nd edn), rptd 1902.]

Keary, Annie (1825–1879). Little Wanderlin and Other Fairy Tales. 1865.

—— Sidney Grey, or a Year from Home. 1876.

Keary, Annie and Eliza. The Heroes of Asgard. 1857. [See Memoir of Annie Keary, by her sister, 1882, and Letters (selected), 1883.]

'A. L. O. E.' ('A Lady of England,' i.e. Charlotte Maria Tucker, 1825–1893). The Claremont Tales; or, Illustrations of the Beatitudes. [1854.]

—— Wings and Stings. A Tale for the Young. 1855.

—— Upwards and Downwards, or the Sluggard and the Diligent. A Story for Boys. 1856.

—— The Rambles of a Rat. 1857.

—— The Story of a Needle. 1858.

—— Fairy Know-a-Bit. 1866.

—— The Little Maid. [1874.]

—— Life in the Eagle's Nest. A Tale of Afghanistan. [1883.]

[For over 140 other works, see A Lady of England: the Life and Letters of Charlotte Maria Tucker. By Agnes Giberne, 1895.]

Mackarness, Matilda Anne (née Planché; 1826–1881). Old Joliffe. 1845.

—— A Trap to Catch a Sunbeam. 1849; 1850 (10th edn).

—— The Golden Rule. 1859.

Church, Alfred John (1829–1912). Stories from Homer. 1878.

—— The Chantry Priest of Barnet. A Tale of the Two Roses. 1885.

—— The Count of the Saxon Shore. A Tale of the Departure of the Romans from Britain. 1887.

—— The Crusaders. 1905.

[Church also pbd other works, especially edns and adaptations of classics. See his Memories of Men and Books, 1908.]

Marshall, Emma (née Martin; 1830–1899). Happy Days at Fernbank. 1861.

—— Life's Aftermath. 1876.

—— Bristol Diamonds. 1888.

—— Under Salisbury Spire. 1890.

[See Beatrice Marshall's Emma Marshall, a Biographical Sketch, 1900.]

Farrar, Frederic William (1831–1903). Eric, or Little by Little. 1858. [See also p. 545 above.]

Fenn, George Manville (1831–1909). Hollow-dell Grange, or Holiday Hours in a Country House. 1866.
—— Nat the Naturalist. 1882.
—— Bunyip Land. 1884.
—— The Silver Cañon. 1884.
—— Brownsmith's Boy. 1886.
—— Mother Carey's Chicken. 1888.
—— The Queen's Scarlet. 1895.
—— Marcus: the Young Centurion. [1904.]
'Carroll, Lewis' (Charles Lutwidge Dodgson, 1832–1898). [See p. 513 above.]
Henty, George Alfred (1832–1902). Out on the Pampas, or the Young Settlers. 1868.
—— The Young Franc-Tireurs. 1872.
—— Winning his Spurs. A Tale of the Crusades. 1882.
—— Facing Death. 1883.
—— Under Drake's Flag. 1883.
—— With Clive in India. 1884.
—— The Lion of the North. A Tale of the Times of Gustavus Adolphus. 1886.
—— The Young Carthaginian. 1887.
—— The Cat of Bubastes. 1889.
—— One of the 28th. A Tale of Waterloo. 1889.
—— The Lion of St Mark. A Tale of Venice. 1889.
—— By Right of Conquest, or with Cortez in Mexico. 1891.
—— Beric the Briton. 1893.
—— With Roberts to Pretoria. 1902.
—— With Kitchener in the Sudan. 1903.
—— With the Allies to Pekin. 1904.
[Henty also edited The Union Jack, 1880 to 1883, and contributed to other magazines. See G. M. Fenn, George Alfred Henty: the Story of an Active Life, 1907. DNB. enumerates over 30 (out of nearly 90) titles of works, and a letter in Fenn's Life gives 45.]
'Stretton, Hesba' (Sarah Smith; 1832–1911). Jessica's First Prayer. 1867.
—— Alone in London. 1869.
—— The King's Servants. 1873.
—— Lost Gip. 1873.
—— The Wonderful Life [of Christ]. 1875.
—— The Sweet Story of Old. [1884.]
Ker, David. On the Road to Khiva. 1874.
—— The Boy Slave in Bokhara. 1875.
—— The Wild Horseman of the Pampas. 1876.
—— Lost among White Africans. 1886.
—— Vanished! Or the Strange Adventures of Arthur Hawksleigh. 1895.
—— O'er Tartar Deserts. 1898.
Molesworth, Mary Louisa (née Stewart; d. 1921). Carrots. 1876.
—— The Tapestry Room. 1879.
—— Two Little Waifs. 1883.
—— Little Miss Peggy. 1887.
'Thorn, Ismay' (Edith Caroline Pollock). Pinafore Days. [1878.]

'Thorn, Ismay' (Edith Caroline Pollock). A Six-years' Darling, or Trix in Town. [1880.]
—— Over the Wall. [1881.]
—— Sister Sue. 1884.
—— Quite Unexpected. [1889.]
—— Max or Baby. The Story of a Very Little Boy. [1889.]
—— Courage. 1899.
Stables, William Gordon (1840–1910). Aileen Aroon. A Memoir [of a Dog]. [1884.]
—— 'Twixt School and College. 1891.
—— Facing Fearful Odds. [1893.]
—— A Fight for Freedom. 1897.
—— In Quest of the Giant Sloth. 1902.
—— Leaves from the Log of a Sailor. 1906.
Ewing, Juliana Horatia (née Gatty; 1841–1885). [See p. 543 above.]
Montgomery, Florence (1843–1923). A Very Simple Story. 1867.
—— Misunderstood. 1869.
—— Moral Tales for Children. 1886 (new edn).
Lang, Andrew (1844–1912). The True Story Book. 1893. [Ed. by Lang. See also p. 747 below and below under Fairy Tales.]
Greenaway, Catherine (Kate) (1846–1901). Under the Window. [1879.] [Kate Greenaway also illustrated many works by other writers. See Kate Greenaway, by M. H. Spielmann and G. S. Layard, 1905.]
'Hope, Ascott' (A. R. Hope-Moncrieff, 1846–1927). A Book about Boys. 1868.
—— A Peck of Troubles. [1874.]
—— The Pampas. A Story of Adventure. 1876.
—— The Wigwam and the Warpath. 1884.
—— A String of Stories. [1891.]
—— Ups and Downs. 1895.
[And nearly 200 other works.]
Jefferies, Richard (1848–1887). Bevis. 1882. [See also p. 550 above.]
Burnett, Frances Hodgson (1849–1924). Little Lord Fauntleroy. 1886.
Stevenson, Robert Louis (1850–1894). Treasure Island. 1882. [First pbd in Young Folks (see under Periodicals, p. 578, below), Oct. 1881–Jan. 1882. See also p. 520 above.]
Reed, Talbot Baines (1852–1893). The Adventures of a Three-Guinea Watch. 1880.
—— The Cock-house of Fellsgarth. 1891.
—— Kilgorman. 1894. [With memoir of author, by John Sime.]
Clifford, Lucy. Anyhow Stories, Moral and Otherwise. 1882; 1899 (enlarged).
'Meade, L. T.' (Elizabeth Thomasina Meade, afterwards Toulmin Smith; d. 1914). The Children's Pilgrimage, 1883.
—— A World of Girls. The Story of a School. 1886.
—— Daddy's Boy. 1888.
—— A Young Mutineer. 1893.

'Meade, L. T.' (Elizabeth Thomasina Meade, afterwards Toulmin Smith; d. 1914). Betty, a School Girl. 1895.
['L. T. Meade' also edited Atalanta (see p. 578 below under Periodicals).]
'Anstey, F.' (Thomas Anstey Guthrie; 1856–1934). Vice Versa. A Lesson for Fathers. 1882. [See also p. 535 above.]
Haggard, Sir Henry Rider (1856–1925). King Solomon's Mines. 1885. [See also p. 547 above.]
Wilde, Oscar Fingall O'Flahertie Wills (1856–1900). The Happy Prince, and Other Tales. 1888. [See also p. 620 below.]
'Lyall, Edna' (Ada Ellen Bayly; 1857–1903). How the Children raised the Wind. 1896. [See also p. 552 above.]
Nesbit, E[dith] (afterwards Bland and Bland-Tucker; 1858–1924). The Story of the Treasure Seekers. 1899.
—— The Book of Dragons. 1900.
[For other works see bibliography in E. Nesbit, a Biography, by Doris Langley Moore, 1933, and p. 350 above.]
Phillpotts, Eden (b. 1862). The Human Boy. 1899.
Quiller-Couch, Sir Arthur Thomas (b. 1863). Dead Man's Rock. 1887. [See also, under Anonymous Works, This World of Adventure; and p. 556 above.]
Housman, Laurence (b. 1865). A Farm in Fairyland. 1894.
—— The House of Joy. [1895.]
—— The Story of the Seven Young Goslings. [1899.]
[See also p. 343 above.]
Kipling, Rudyard (1865–1936). The Jungle Book. 1894. The Second Jungle Book. 1895.
—— Stalky and Co. 1899.
[See also p. 527 above.]
Lucas, Edward Verrall (1868–1938). The Flamp, The Ameliorator, and The School boys' Apprentice. 1897.
[Lucas also edited The Dumpy Books, 6 vols. 1897–1900 (re-issued with addns, 1932). Original series contained: The Flamp (by E. V. Lucas); Mrs Turner's Cautionary Stories; The Bad Family and other Stories (by Eliza Fenwick); The Story of Little Black Sambo (by Helen Bannerman); A Cat Book (by E. V. Lucas and H. Officer Smith); and The Bountiful Lady (by Thomas Cobb). For Lucas's other writings see A. Lucas, A Memoir of E. V. Lucas, 1938.]
Cresswell, Beatrix F. The Royal Progress of King Pepito. Illustrated by Kate Greenaway. [1889.]
Sharp, Evelyn (afterwards Nevinson). The Making of a School Girl. 1897.
—— Wymps, and Other Fairy Tales. 1897.

Sharp, Evelyn (afterwards Nevinson). All the Way to Fairyland. 1898.
—— The Youngest Girl in the School. 1901.
[See also Fairy Tales, as they are, as they were, and as they should be, Brighton, [1889]; and Unfinished Adventure. Selected Reminiscences, 1933.]
Upton, Bertha. The Adventures of Two Dutch Dolls and a Golliwogg. [1895.] [Many sequels.]
B[elloc], H[ilaire] (b. 1870). The Bad Child's Book of Beasts. 1896.
—— More Beasts for Worse Children. 1897.
—— Cautionary Tales for Children. [1908.]
Turner, Ethel (later Curlewis; b. 1872). Seven Little Australians. 1894.
—— The Family at Misrule. 1895.

(3) MINOR WRITERS

Porter, Jane (1776–1850). The Two Princes of Persia. Addressed to Youth. 1801. [See also p. 414 above.]
Somerville, Elizabeth. The Village Maid, or Dame Burton's Moral Stories. 1801.
—— My Birthday, or Moral Dialogues and Stories. 1802.
—— Aurora and Maria, or the Advantages of Adversity. 1809.
Aikin, Lucy (1781–1864). Poetry for Children. 1803. [An anthology, with valuable preface.]
—— An English Lesson Book. 1828. [Short Stories, or 'Christmas Tales,' rptd as Holiday Stories for Young Readers, 1858.]
Barton, Bernard (1784–1849). [See p. 227 above, and under Ann and Jane Taylor, Original Poems, immediately above, and p. 577 below, under Periodicals, The Juvenile Scrap Book.]
Hurry, Mrs Ives (née Mitchell). Tales of Instruction and Amusement. [c. 1803.]
—— The Faithful Contrast, or Virtue and Vice accurately delineated, in a Series of Moral and Instructive Tales. 1804.
—— National Amusement for Leisure Hours. 1804.
—— Moral Tales. 1807.
Bingley, William (1774–1823). Animal Biography. 3 vols. 1804, 1805 (3rd edn, enlarged); 4 vols. 1820 (5th edn).
—— Useful Knowledge. 3 vols. 1816; 1852 (7th edn).
—— Travels in Africa. 1819.
Taylor, Joseph. The General Character of the Dog; illustrated by a Variety of Anecdotes. 1804.
—— The Wonders of the Horse, recorded in Anecdotes. 1813; New York, 1836.
—— Tales of the Robin and Other Small Birds. 1815. [An anthology.]

'Baldwin, Edward' (William Godwin; 1756–1836). Fables Ancient and Modern. Adapted for the Use of Children. 1805; 1821 (9th edn). [See also vol. II, p. 654 above.]

Fenwick, Eliza. A Visit to the Juvenile Library [i.e. B. Tabart's bookshop]. 1805.
—— Infantine Stories. 1810.
—— Lessons for Children, or Rudiments of Good Manners, Morals, and Humanity. N.d. [Selection, ed. E. V. Lucas, 1898 (The Dumpy Books).]

Monget, M. Moral Playthings, or Tales for Children. 1806.

Ventum, Harriet. Tales for Domestic Instruction. 1806.
—— Charles Leeson, or the Soldier. 1810.

Cockle, Mary. The Juvenile Journal, or Tales of Truth. 1807.

Day, Isaac. Scenes for the Young. 1807.

Carey, John (1756–1826). Learning Better than House or Land, as exemplified in the History of Harry Johnson and Dick Hobson. 1808; 1813 (3rd edn, improved); 1864 (omits some characteristic passages).

O'Keeffe, Adelaide (1776–1855). Original Poems calculated to Improve the Mind of Youth and Allure it to Virtue. 1808.
—— Zenobia, Queen of Palmyra. 1814.
—— National Characters exhibited in 40 Geographical Poems. 1818.
—— Poems for Young Children. [1849?] [See also under Ann and Jane Taylor, p. 565 above.]

Parkinson, James. Dangerous Sports. A Tale addressed to Children. 1808 (2nd edn).

Richardson, Mrs. Original Poems intended for the Use of Young Persons. On a Plan recommended by the Rev. Dr Isaac Watts. 1808.

Argas, Arabella (pseudonym?). The Juvenile Spectator. 1810; 1813.
—— The Adventures of a Donkey. 1813. [Many edns to 1872, and a sequel.]
—— Ostentation and Liberality. A Tale. 1821. [Possibly earlier.]

Mant, Alicia Catherine. Ellen, or the Young Godmother. 1812; 1815 (3rd edn).
—— The Canary Bird. 1817.
—— The Cottage in the Chalk-Pit. 1822; 1825; 1857 (6th edn).
—— Tales for Ellen. 1825.

Barnard, Caroline. The Parent's Offering, or Tales for Children. 2 vols. 1813.
—— The Prize, or the Lace Makers of Missenden. 1817.

[Peacock, Thomas Love (1785–1866).] Sir Hornbook, or Childe Launcelot's Expedition. A Grammatico-Allegorical Ballad.

1814. [Rptd in 'Felix Summerly's' Home Treasury, 1841, 1843, 1855. See also p. 384 above.]

Cecil, Sabina (pseudonym?). Little John, or the Picture Book. 1815. [Also, uniform, but n.d. or various dates up to 1822, Little Ann, Charles, Charlotte, Edward, Eliza, George, Henry, James, Jane, Mary, Sally, Thomas, and William. Prose and verse mixed, evidently to fit older illustrations (woodcuts, hand-coloured, by Piggott) which bear various dates from 1799 onwards.]

Leonard, Eliza Lucy. The Ruby Ring, or the Transformations. 1815.
—— The Miller and his Golden Dream. Wellington, 1822.

Vaux, Frances Bowyer. Henry. A Story for Little Boys and Girls. 2 pts, 1815–6.
—— Domestic Pleasures, or the Happy Fireside. 1816.
—— The Dew-drop, or the Summer Morning's Walk. 1818.

Mister, Mary. The Adventures of a Doll. 1816.
—— Mungo, or the Little Traveller. Dublin, 1817.
—— Little Anecdotes for Little People. 1817; [1830].

Sullivan, William Francis. The History of Mr Rightway and his Pupils. 1816.
—— Pleasant Stories, or the Histories of Ben the Sailor and Ned the Soldier. [1818.]
—— Young Wilfred, or the Punishment of Falsehood. 1821.

Bloomfield, Robert (1766–1823). The History of Little Davy's New Hat. 1817 (bis); 1824; 1878. [See also p. 227 above.]

Clark, Emily. Tales at the Fireside, or a Father and Mother's Stories. 3 vols. Brentford, 1817.

Crichton, A. The Festival of Flora. A Poem, with Botanical Notes. 1818 (2nd edn).

Marshall, Mrs. Henwick Tales: designed to amuse the Mind of Youth. 1818 (3rd edn).
—— Ida, or Living for Others. A Story for the Young. [1865.]
—— Grannie's Wardrobe, or the Lost Key. [1867.]

'Blackford, Martha' (Isabella Stoddart). The Eskdale Herdboy. A Scottish Tale. 1819.
—— The Scottish Orphans. A Moral Tale. 1822.
—— Arthur Monteith. A Moral Tale, being a Continuation of The Scottish Orphans. 1823.

Hedge, Mary Ann. Affection's Gift to a Beloved God-child. 1819.
—— Samboe, or the African Boy. 1823.
—— Radama, or the Enlightened African [King Radama of Madagascar]. 1824; 1826.

Barton, R. C. Chrysallina, or the Butterfly's Gala. An Entertaining Poem, addressed to Children. 1820.

Upton, W. The School Girl. The School Boy. 1820.

White, E. Gertrude, or Thoughtlessness and Inattention Corrected. 1823.

[Benson, Edward White.] Education at Home, or a Father's Instruction. Miscellaneous Pieces for the Young. 1824.

Copley, Esther (née Hewlett; living in 1859). The Old Man's Head, or Youthful Recollections. [1824.] [Not biography.]

—— The Young Reviewers, or the Poems Dissected. [c. 1830.]

[For other works, especially on domestic economy, see incomplete list at end of My Mother's Stories, 1838.]

Baker, M. Emily and her Cousins. A Tale of Real Life for Little Girls. 1828.

Taylor, Emily (1795–1872). Tales of the Saxons. 1832.

—— The Boy and the Birds. 1835.

[For other works, see Sir Francis Galton's Hereditary Genius, 1869, and DNB. (s.v. Edgar Taylor).]

Barwell, Louisa Mary (1800–1885). The Value of Time. A Tale for Children. 1834.

—— Good in every Thing, or the Early History of Gilbert Harland. 1852.

Coleridge, Sara (1802–1852). Pretty Lessons in Verse, for Good Children. 1834. [See also p. 284 above.]

Bruce, Carlton. The Boy's Friend, or the Maxims of a Cheerful Old Man. 1835; 1837.

Tytler, Margaret Fraser. Tales of the Great and Brave. 1838.

—— Tales of Many Lands. 1839.

—— The Wonder-Seeker. 1846.

—— Little Fanny's Journal. 1855.

Webb, Mrs J. B. The Travels and Adventures of Charles Durand. 1839.

—— A Tale of the Vaudois. 1841.

—— Naomi, or the Siege of Jerusalem. 1841; 1853 (11th edn).

Tytler, Ann Fraser. Mary and Florence, or Grave and Gay. N.d.

—— Leila, or the Island. 1839.

Barth, C. G. Winter Evening Stories. [c. 1840.]

Bingley, Thomas. Tales about Travellers. 1840.

—— Tales about Birds. 1840 (2nd edn); 1864.

Kelty, Mary Ann (1789–1873). Mamma and Mary, discoursing upon Good and Evil. 1840.

—— Gentle Gertrude. A Tale for Youth. [1843?]

Richmond, Legh (1772–1827). The Young Cottager, and Other Tales. [c. 1840.]

Smythe, Elizabeth Ann. The History of Mary the Beggar Girl. [c. 1840.]

Wilberforce, Samuel (1805–1873). Agathos, and Other Sunday Stories. 1840 (2nd edn); 1865; 1901; ed. A. J. Mason, Cambridge, 1908; 1918.

Gresley, William (1801–1876). Holyday Tales. 1842.

Neale, John Mason (1818–1866). Hymns for the Young. 2 pts, 1843. [See also p. 301 above.]

Paget, Francis Edward (1806–1882). The Juvenile Englishman's Library. 21 vols. 1845–9. [Included J. M. Neale's Triumphs of the Cross; A Selection of Popular Tales from the German; Tales of the Village Children, chiefly by the editor; and The Hope of the Katzekopfs, by 'William Churne' (F. E. Paget).] [See also p. 859 below.]

'Myrtle, Harriet' (Lydia Falconer Miller, née Fraser; 1811?–1876). Little Amy's Birthday, and Other Tales. A Story-Book for Autumn. 1846.

—— Home and its Pleasures: Simple Stories for Young People. 1852. [Illustrated by H. K. Browne.]

—— The Ocean Child, or Showers and Sunshine. A Tale of Girlhood. 1857.

Bunbury, Selina. The Triumph of Truth, or Henry and his Sister. [1847?]

—— The Blind Clergyman and his Little Guide. 1850.

de Chatelain, Catherine. The Silver Swan. A Fairy Tale. 1847. [Illustrated by John Leech, but his name is only in advertisements, not in the book.]

—— Merry Tales for Little Folk. 1851.

—— The Lilliputian Library. New Series. Guben, [1861?]. [No complete set found. Apparently a miscellany in several vols., containing translations and original work.]

Burden, Mrs. The Three Baskets, or how Henry, Richard and Charles were occupied, while Papa was away. [c. 1850.]

—— The Favourite Dog and the Idle Cat. [1854.]

—— Little Miss Fanny and her Visit to the Sea Shore. [1854.]

—— The Stray Child. [1854.]

—— The Faithful Dog. [1857.]

Clarke, Mary Victoria Cowden (1809–1898). The Girlhood of Shakespeare's Heroines. 3 vols. 1851–2. [See also p. 711 below.]

Crewdson, Jane. Aunt Jane's Verses for Children. 1851; 1871 (3rd edn, with addns).

B[oyle], Eleanor Vere. Child's Play. [1852]; 1853; 1859; 1865.

Crompton, Sarah. Tales that are True. 1853.

—— Fairy Tales and Fables in Short Words. [1872.]

Maitland, Julia Charlotte. The Doll and Her Friends. 1854. [Illustrated by H. K. Browne.]
—— Cat and Dog, or Memoirs of Puss and the Captain. 1854.
Bishop, James. The Painted Picture Play-Book. [1855.] Ser. 2, 1856.
—— Pictures and Knowledge. Pretty Pages, to make all Good Little Folks as Wise as Sages. By Uncle Know-all. [1862.]
Bowman, Anne. Charade Dramas for the Drawing Room. 1855.
—— The Castaways. 1857.
—— The Boy Voyagers, or the Pirates of the East. 1859; 1876.
—— Among the Tartar Tents. 1861; 1875.
—— The Boy Foresters. [1868]; [1905].
Landells, E. Home Pastime, or the Child's Own Toy-Maker. 2 pts, [1858].
Betham-Edwards, Matilda Barbara (d. 1919). Charles and Ernest, or Play and Work. A Story of Hazlehurst School. Edinburgh, 1859.
[Leathley, Mrs.] Chick-Seed without Chick-Weed. N.d.; 1860.
Walks Abroad and Evenings at Home. 1861. [Natural History disguised as fiction.]
Balfour, Clara Lucas. Passages in the History of a Shilling. [1862.]
—— Lame Dick's Lantern. A Story for Children. 1874.
Bethell, Augusta. Maud Latimer. A Tale for Young People. 1863.
—— Among the Fairies. [1883.]
Lushington, Henrietta, Lady (née Prescott; d. 1875). The Happy Home, or the Children at the Red House. 1864.
—— Hacco the Dwarf, and Other Tales. 1865.
[Noel, Lady Augusta (1838–1902).] Effie's Friends, or Chronicles of the Woods and Shore. 1865. [See also p. 556 above.]
'Quiz, Roland' (Richard M. H. Quittenton). Juvenile Rhymes and Little Stories. [1865.] [See also below (under Periodicals) The People's Pocket Story Books.]
Gilbert, William (1804–1890). The Magic Mirror. A Round of Tales for Young and Old. With Illustrations by W[illiam] S[chwenk] Gilbert. 1866.
—— King George's Middy. Illustrated by W. S. Gilbert. 1869.
'Tytler, Sarah' (Henrietta Keddie). Girlhood and Womanhood. The Story of some Fortunes and Misfortunes. 1868.
—— A Houseful of Girls. 1889.
[Tuckett, Elizabeth.] Our Children's Story. By One of their Gossips. 1870.
—— The Children's Journey, and Other Stories. 1872.
Cobb, James Francis. Silent Jim. A Cornish Story. [1871]; 1892.

Cobb, James Francis. The Watchers on the Longships. 1878; [1883] (11th edn).
—— Off to California. [1885.] [A free adaptation of Hendrik Conscience's Het Goudland, 1862.]
Knatchbull-Hugessen, Edward Hugessen, Baron Brabourne (1829–1893). Tales at Tea-Time. 1872.
—— Higgledy-Piggledy. 1875.
Havergal, Francis Ridley (1836–1879). Brucy: a Little Worker for Christ. 1873 (2nd edn). [See also p. 342 above.]
Stebbing, Beatrice (afterwards Batty). Effie and her Ayah, or the Faithful Monkey and his Little White Mistress. [1873.]
—— Stories of my Pets. 1886.
—— The Life and Adventures of a Very Little Monkey. 1888.
Giberne, Agnes. Drusie's Own Story. 1874.
—— The Hillside Children. 1878.
—— A Modern Puck. A Fairy Story for Children. 1898.
Pollock, Juliet, Lady, Clifford, William Kingdon (1848–1879; see p. 942 below), and Pollock, Walter Herries (1850–1926; see p. 353 above). The Little People, and Other Tales. 1874.
Austin, Stella. Stumps. A Story For Children. 1875; 1900 (10th edn).
—— Somebody. 1875; 1900 (7th edn).
—— For Old Sake's Sake. 1877; 1898 (4th edn).
—— Great-Grandmother's Shoes. 1882 (2nd edn).
—— Tom the Hero. 1887.
Mulock, Dinah Maria (afterwards Craik; 1826–1887). The Little Lame Prince. 1875. [See also p. 498 above.]
Potter, Frederick Scarlett. Erling, or the Days of St Olaf. [1876.]
—— Cousin Flo. [1877.]
—— Princess Myra, and her Adventures among the Fairy-Folk. [1880.]
—— Talby's Travels told by Herself. [1880.]
—— A Venturesome Voyage. [1898.]
'Garrett, Edward' (Isabella Fyvie, afterwards Mayo). Doing and Dreaming. A Tale for the Young. 1877.
—— The Magic Flower-Pot, and Other Stories. [1878.]
'Stuart, Esmé' (Miss Leroy). The Little Brown Girl. 1877.
—— The Unwelcome Guest. A Story for Girls. 1886.
—— Harum Scarum. A Poor Relation. 1896. [Sequel, 1909 and 1912.]
'Author of Honour Bright' (Evelyn Whitaker). Two Blackbirds. N.d.
—— Honour Bright, or the Four-leaved Shamrock. [1879]; 1893 (6th edn).
—— Peasblossom. 1883.
—— N. or M. 1885.

Coleridge, Christabel. The Girls of Flaxby. 1882.

Allingham, William (1824–89). The Fairies. [1883.] [See also p. 276 above.]

Corkran, Alice (d. 1916). The Adventures of Mrs Wishing-to-be. 1883.

—— Down the Snow Stairs. 1887.

—— Margery Merton's Girlhood. 1888.

—— Mischievous Jack, and Other Stories. [1888.]

—— Joan's Adventures at the North Pole. 1889.

Overton, Robert (1859–1924). Me and Bill. 1883.

—— The King's Pardon! 1895.

—— Far From Home. 1896.

Green, Evelyn Everett. Uncle Roger, or a Summer of Surprises. [1885.]

—— A Difficult Daughter. [1885.]

—— The Head of the House. [1886.]

—— Dulcie's Little Brother. 1887.

—— Molly Melville. A Tale for Girls. 1897.

Adams, William Henry Davenport (1828–1891). Master Minds in Art, Science, and Letters. A Book for Boys. [1886.]

—— Sunshine and Shadow, or Stories from Cragford. For the Young Folk. 1888. [See also p. 1077 below.]

Miles, Alfred Henry. Fifty-two Stories for Boys [by various writers]. [1889.]

Field, Louise Frances. Bryda. [1890.]

—— Master Magnus, or the Prince, the Princess, and the Dragon. [1895.]

Baring-Gould, Sabine (1834–1924). Grettir the Outlaw. 1890. [See also p. 535 above.]

Hueffer, Ford H. Madox (afterwards Ford, b. 1873). The Feather. 1892.

—— The Queen who flew. 1894.

Hyne, Charles John Cutcliffe Wright (b. 1866). The Captured Cruiser. 1893.

Landor, Owen. Whither Bound? A Story of Two Lost Boys. [1894]; [1902].

Marchant, Bessie (afterwards Comfort; b. 1862). The Old House by the Water. [1894.]

—— Weasel Tim. [1896.]

—— The Rajah's Daughter, or the Half-Moon Girl. 1899.

—— Winning his Way. A Story for Boys. [1899.]

Meredith, Hal. [Author of the Sexton Blake series of 'penny dreadfuls' (1894 and later). See below, Periodicals, The Union Jack Library of High-Class Fiction. Contributed also to the 'Halfpenny Marvel' Library.]

Crockett, Samuel Rutherford (1840–1914). Sweetheart Travellers. 1895 (3 edns). [See also p. 541 above.]

Edwardes, Charles. The New House-Master. A School Story. [1895.]

—— Dr Burleigh's Boys. A Tale of Misrule. [1897.]

Farrow, George Edward. The Wallypug of Why. 1895. [Several sequels.]

—— The Missing Prince. 1896.

—— The Little Panjandrum's Dodo. 1899.

'A. Nobody' (Frederick Gordon Browne; d. 1932). Nonsense for Somebody, Anybody or Everybody. Written and Illustrated by A. Nobody. [1895.]

—— Some More Nonsense. 1896.

—— A. Nobody's Scrap Book. 1900.

O'Grady, Standish (1846–1928). The Chain of Gold, or, In Crannied Rocks. A Boys' Tale of Adventure. 1895. [See also p. 1050 below.]

Parry, Sir Edward Abbott (b. 1863). Katawampus. 1895.

—— Butterscotia, or a Cheap Trip to Fairy Land. 1896.

—— The First Book of Krab. 1897.

Whishaw, Frederick J. Boris the Bear-Hunter. 1895; 1903.

—— Gubbins Minor and some Other Fellows; a Story of School Life. [1897]; 1913.

—— The Adventures of a Stowaway. [1897]; 1916.

Haverfield, Eleanor Louisa (b. 1870). The Doctor's Little Dot. 1898.

—— Our Vow. A Story for Children. 1899. [Sequel: Blind Loyalty, 1900.]

Le Feavre, Amy. Bulbs and Blossoms. [1898.]

—— His Big Opportunity. 1898.

—— Bunny's Friends. [1899.]

Kearton, Richard. Our Bird Friends. A Book for All Boys and Girls. 1900.

(4) ANONYMOUS WORKS

[Including those under unidentified pseudonyms.]

Summer Rambles, or Conversations Instructive and Amusing, for the use of Children. By a Lady. 1801.

A Cup of Sweets that can never Cloy; or, Delightful Tales for Good Children. By a London Lady. 1804.

A True History of a Little Old Woman who found a Silver Penny. 1805.

W., S. A Visit to a Farm-house. 1805 (2nd edn); 1815 (6th edn).

—— A Visit to London. 1808; 1820 ('with Additions and Improvements,' by T. H.).

—— The Warren Family, or Scenes at Home. 1813.

Rhyme and Picture Books, 1806–1808. [A large number of ephemeral works much alike in scope and design appeared during these years: only a few have had a long life. The chief are:]

Cobler, Stick to your Last, or the Adventures of Joe Dobson. N.d.

The Talking Bird, or Dame Trudge and her Parrot. N.d.

Whimsical Incidents, or the Power of Music. N.d.

The Comic Adventures of Old Mother Hubbard and her Dog. N.d.

Dame Trot and her Comical Cat. N.d.

Dame Partlet's Farm; containing an Account of the Great Riches she obtained by Industry, the Good Life she led, and alas, Good Reader! Her Sudden Death. 1806.

T., B. A. The History of Mother Twaddle, and the Marvellous Atchievements of her Son Jack. By B. A. T. 1807. [A rhymed version of Jack and the Beanstalk.]

The Book of Trades, or the Library of the Useful Arts. 1807. [Many edns in various forms, with valuable illustrations.]

The Adventures of the Little Girl in the Wood. 1808. [Coloured plates.]

The History of Little Henry, exemplified in a Series of Figures. 1810. [Verses; coloured illustrations with movable heads. Similar works issued at the same time: The Young Roscius; Frank Feignwell; Little Fanny; Lauretta the Little Savoyard. See Paper Dolls and Other Cut-out Toys (Description of collection of W. M. Stone), Newark, Pennsylvania, 1931 (priv. ptd).]

Felissa, or, The Life and Opinions of a Kitten of Sentiment. 1811; rptd 1903.

My Real Friend; or, Incidents in Life, founded on Truth. 1812.

Verses for Little Children: Written by a Young Lady for the Amusement of her Junior Brothers and Sisters. 1813.

Buds of Genius, or some Account of the Lives of Celebrated Characters. 1816; 1818.

The Little Warbler of the Cottage, and her Dog Constant. By a Lover of Children. 1816.

H., M. The Winter Scene; to amuse and instruct the Rising Generation. 1818.

Motherless Mary. A Tale. Shewing that Goodness even in Poverty is sure of meeting its Proper Reward. 1818. [The same author also wrote: Arthur and Alice, or the Little Wanderers; Whim and Contradiction, or the Party of Pleasure; Walter and Hubert, n.d. (all 1816 or earlier).]

Nursery Morals; chiefly in Monosyllables. 1818.

Rhyme and Picture Books, 1821-3. [A large number appeared at this time, following a fashion. Few had long life. The chief are:] The History of Sixteen Wonderful Old Women. 1821. [Supposed first use of 'limerick' metre. Also, uniform, but n.d., Anecdotes and Adventures of Fifteen Young Ladies, and Anecdotes and Adventures of Fifteen Gentlemen.]

Aldiboronti phoskyphorniostikos: a Round Game for Merry Parties. [c. 1822.] [Illustrated by R. Stennet. A nonsense story for reading aloud.]

Deborah Dent and her Donkey. 1823; ed. A. W. Tuer, 1887.

The Dame and her Donkeys Five. 1823; ed. A. W. Tuer, 1888.

[Sharpe, R. S. and Pearson, Mrs ?] Dame Wiggins of Lee and her Seven Wonderful Cats. A Humorous Tale. Written principally by a Lady of Ninety. 1823 (illustrated by R. Stennet?); ed. (with addns) J. Ruskin, 1885 (extra-illustrated by Kate Greenaway); ed. facs. A. W. Tuer, 1887.

Always Happy! Or, Anecdotes of Felix and his sister Serena. 1823 (5th edn).

The Tell-Tale: an Original Collection of Moral and Amusing Stories. 1823.

Town and Country Tales. Intended for the Amusement and Moral Instruction of Youth. 1824.

The Milkmaid, a Fable. By a Lady. [1825?] [Illustrated by D. Dighton; lithographs.]

Interesting Walks of Henry and his Tutor. 1827.

Edith Vernon's Life Work. [1864]; [1872] (3rd edn).

Little Songs for me to Sing. 1865. Songs for Little Folks. 1865. [By various writers. Illustrated by Sir J. E. Millais, with music by Henry Leslie. Editor unidentified.]

'Quiz, Ronald.' The Fatal Phantom. 1868. [Also Felix the Hunchback, 1868; The Divorced Queen, 1868; and other 'penny dreadfuls.']

The World of Adventure. 3 vols. 1888-91, 1896, 1899. [Chiefly edited by Sir A. T. Quiller-Couch (see above, p. 556).]

(5) FAIRY TALES

[The stories already accumulated—traditional, and the translated tales by Perrault, D'Aulnoy and others (see vol. II, pp. 565-6 above)—became a common repertory which editors and publishers varied and used at will. The chief collection made before fresh matter appeared was: Popular Stories for the Nursery. By Benjamin Tabart, [4 vols.?], 1809; re-issued [1818] as Popular Fairy Tales; or, a Liliputian [sic] Library. (One or more tales were issued separately at various dates.) A great increase in the common stock was made by trns of Grimm, Andersen, and others (see under Translations, below), by wider investigation of folk-lore, by the use of Edwin Lane's version of the Arabian Nights (3 vols. 1839-41, rev. H. W. Dulcken, 1863-5), and by the invention of new tales. The principal general collections only are included here.]

The Court of Oberon, or Temple of the Fairies.
1823.
Croker, Thomas Crofton. Fairy Legends and
Traditions of the South of Ireland. 3 pts,
1825–8; ed. T. Wright, 1882.
Keightley, Thomas. Fairy Mythology. 1828;
1847 (enlarged).
'Summerly, Felix' (Sir Henry Cole). The
Home Treasury. 1841–9. [Original edn
12 vols. afterwards regrouped into 5. In-
cluded ballads and other matter. For con-
tents see F. J. H. Darton, Children's Books
in England, Cambridge, 1932, ch. xiii.]
'Merton, Ambrose' (William John Thoms).
Gammer Gurton's Famous Histories. Newly
Revised and Amended. [1846.] [Guy of
Warwick and other romances.]
—— Gammer Gurton's Famous Stories.
Newly Revised and Amended. [1846.] [A
miscellany of fairy tales and ballads.]
Montalba, Anthony. Fairy Tales of All Na-
tions. 1849. [Illustrated by Richard
Doyle.]
[Cundall, Joseph.] A Treasury of Pleasure
Books for Young and Old. 1849.
Burkhardt, C. B. Fairy Tales and Legends of
Many Nations. Dublin, 1849.
George Cruikshank's Fairy Library. 4 vols.
1853–64. [Old fairy tales altered in the
interests of total abstinence.]
Bechstein, Ludwig. The Old Story-Teller.
1854. [German tales.]
Planché, James Robinson. Four and Twenty
[French] Fairy Tales. 1858.
Mulock, Dinah Maria (later Craik). The Fairy
Book. 1863.
Lang, Andrew. The Blue Fairy Book. 1889.
[Also annual volumes under the title of the
cover colour.]
Jacobs, Joseph. English Fairy Tales. 1890.
[Also Celtic Fairy Tales, 1891; Indian Fairy
Tales, 1892; The Book of Wonder Voyages,
1896.]

(6) Translations

Andersen, Hans Christian. Eventyr og
Historier. 5 sers. 1835–72. [Select tales:
Charles Boner 1846 (Cundall edn) Mary
Howitt, 1846; Caroline Peachey, 1846 (Pick-
ering edn); Catherine de Chatelain, 1852;
H. W. Dulcken, 1866 (Dalziel edn); Augusta
Plesner and S. Rugeley-Powers, 1867;
Mrs H. B. Paull, 1867; A. Wehnert, 1869;
H. L. D. Ward and Augusta Plesner, 1872;
Mrs Edgar Lucas, 1899; H. L. Braekstad,
1900 (introduction by Sir E. Gosse); M. R.
James, 1930.]
Asbjörnsen, Peter Christian and Moe, Joergen.
Norske Folkeeventyr. 2 sers. 1842–71.
[Translated by Sir George Webbe Dasent as

Popular Tales from the Norse, 1859, and
Tales from the Fjeld, 1874; also by H. L.
Braekstad in Round the Yule Log, 1881.]
Carové, Friedrich Wilhelm. [The Story with-
out an End. Translated by Sarah Austin,
1834.]
Chamisso, Adelbert von. Peter Schlemihl.
1813. [Various trns, usually as The Shadow-
less Man; by William Howitt (c. 1850), and
others anon. and n.d.]
Cottin, Sophie. Élisabeth, ou Les Exilés de
Sibérie. 1806. [Translated (anon.: attrib.
to Fanny Burney), as Elizabeth; or, the
Exiles of Siberia, 1807; 1809 (3rd edn).
Translated by Mary Meeke, as Elizabeth; or,
the Exiles of Siberia, 1817, 1822, 1825,
1831, 1864, 1868.]
Fouqué, Friedrich Heinrich Carl de La Motte,
Baron. [Aslauga's Knight. Translated by
Thomas Carlyle, 1827. Sintram and his
Companions. Translated by Julius Charles
Hare, 1820. Undine. Translated by G.
Soane, 1818; by T. Tracy, 1841; by Sir
Edmund Gosse, 1896.]
Grimm, Jacob Ludwig Carl and Wilhelm Carl.
Kinder-und Haus-Märchen. 3 vols. 1819–22.
[Anon. trn by Edgar Taylor, 2 vols. 1823–6;
2nd edn, as Gammer Grethel, 1839; rptd
with introduction by John Ruskin, [1869],
and as Grimm's Goblins, 1876. All illus-
trated by George Cruikshank. Principal
other trns: by Mrs H. B. Paull, [1872]; by
L. Crane (illustrated by Walter Crane), 1882;
by M. Hunt (introduction by Andrew Lang),
1884; by Mrs Edgar Lucas (illustrated by
Arthur Rackham), 1884; by Beatrice
Marshall, 1900.]
[Hoffman, Heinrich.] Lustige Geschichten
und drollige Bilder. [Translated [1848?] as
Shock-headed Peter. Also n.d. as The
English Struwelpeter; or, Pretty Stories and
Funny Pictures. Many edns and many
parodies and adaptations.]
Lossius, Caspar Friedrich. Gumal und Lina.
[Gumal and Lina, or the African Children.
Translated (from a French version) by
Simon Bernelot Moens,1817,1839(4th edn).]
Verne, Jules. Cinq Semaines en Ballon. 1862.
—— Voyage au Centre de la Terre. 1864.
—— De la Terre à la Lune. 1865.
—— Vingt mille Lieues sous les Mers. 1869.
—— Les Anglais au Pole nord. 1870.
—— Voyage autour du Monde en quatre-
vingt Jours. 1872.
[English trns, most of them anon. (a few by
W. H. G. Kingston, see p. 491 above), ap-
parently began with Five Weeks in a Balloon,
serially in The Youth's Play-Hour, 1871 (see
Periodicals, p. 578 below). Many stories
appeared in English boys' magazines (in-
cluding The Boy's Own Paper) between 1872

and 1900. The majority of the trns were un-
dated in book-form, and went into many edns.
See Introduction to Everyman's Lib. edn of
Five Weeks in a Balloon.]

Wyss, Johann David Rudolf. Der Schweizerische Robinson. 2 pts, 1812–3. [English
versions chiefly from the French trns by
Mme de Montholieu (1814), who expanded
the original. Anon. 1814 (apparently two
issues, 1 vol. and 2 vols., containing Wyss's
1st pt only). Complete version (anon.),
1816. Translated or revised by W. H. G.
Kingston, 1849; translated by W. H.
Davenport Adams, 1869–70.]

Keene, Henry George. Persian Fables, for
Young and Old. 1833. [From various
sources.]
—— Persian Stories. 1835; 1844 (7th edn).
The Saga of Burnt Njal [Icelandic]. Trans-
lated by Sir George Webb Dasent. 1861.
Frere, Mary. Old Deccan Days; or, Hindoo
Fairy Legends, Current in Southern India.
Collected from Oral Tradition. Introduction
by Sir Bartle Frere. 1868; 1870; 1881;
1889 (rev.).

(7) ILLUSTRATORS

[The majority of 19th cent. children's books
were illustrated, and there also appeared
early in the period books whose chief attraction was pictures. These however are not
literature, strictly speaking. A few are
inserted in the section Anonymous Works
above, as being typical. Some of the principal
illustrators of original books are also mentioned in the appropriate entries. Many older
books, stories, or poems were rptd with fresh
illustrations, and these have some historical
and aesthetic importance, but do not come
fully within the scope of this Bibliography.
They were particularly developed during the
period known for convenience as 'the 'Sixties.'
Three artists devoted themselves specially to
children's books—Kate Greenaway (see above,
Principal Writers), Randolph Caldecott, and
Walter Crane. Their work in colour had a
valuable influence in improving the general
standard. The wood-engravers, and artists
whose work was reproduced on wood—
Millais, Boyd Houghton, Pinwell, the Brothers
Dalziel, C. H. Bennett, Ernest Griset, and
others of the same period—did a like service in
black-and-white. They should however be
studied in the literature of art. For general
purposes reference should be made to F. Reid,
Illustrators of the 'Sixties, 1928, and F. J. H.
Darton, Children's Books in England, Cambridge, 1932, ch. xiv.]

(8) PERIODICALS

The Youth's Monthly Visitor. 1822–3.
[Monthly; rptd as The Youth's Miscellany
of Knowledge and Entertainment, 3 vols.
1823. See also Juvenile Essays which
obtained Prizes offered by The Youth's
Monthly Visitor, ed. H. F. Burder, 1825.]
The Child's Companion; or Sunday Scholars
Reward. 1824–. [In progress; from 1846
as The Child's Companion and Juvenile
Instructor.]
The Children's Friend. Kirkby Lonsdale,
1826–60. [Edited by W. Carus Wilson.]
The Christmas Box. Ed. T. C. Croker, 1828–9.
[Annual vol.]
The Juvenile Forget Me Not. A Christmas and
New Year's Gift, or Birthday Present. Ed.
A. M. Hall, 1829–37. [Annual. Prose and
verse by many writers, with steel engrav-
ings.]
Fisher's Juvenile Scrap-Book. 1836–50.
[Editors: 1836, Bernard Barton; 1837, 1839,
Agnes Strickland and Bernard Barton;
1843–48, Mrs Ellis; 1849, Jane Strickland;
1850, Mrs Milner. Other years anon.
Annual: prose and verse, with steel en-
gravings. Also, on change of publisher, as
The Juvenile Scrap Book. A Gage d'Amour
for the Young.]
Peter Parley's Annual. c. 1840–70. [See
above, Principal Writers, 'Peter Parley.']
The Teacher's Offering: or, Sunday-School
Monthly Visitor. 1840 (Jan.)–64.
The Sunday School Magazine. 1842–50. [In-
corporated in The Sunday School Teachers'
Magazine, 1850–7.]
The Child's Own Annual. 1843–4.
The Juvenile Miscellany of Facts and Fiction,
with Stray Leaves from Fairy Land. 1844
(Jan.)–5 (June). [Monthly. Ed. by M. A. B.]
Green's Nursery Annual. 1847–8.
The Charm. Ed. J[oseph] C[undall?], 1852–4.
The Juvenile. A Penny Magazine for Children.
1852 (Jan.)–4 (Dec.). [From Feb. 1853 as
The Pictorial Juvenile.]
The Halfpenny Picture Magazine for Little
Children. Ed. J. F. Winks, 1854–65. [1855–8
as The Pictorial Magazine for Little Children;
1859–62 as The Little Child's Picture Maga-
zine; 1863–5 as The Picture Magazine.]
The Boy's Own Magazine. Ed. S. O. Beeton,
1855–74. [Incorporating, 1857, The Boy's
Own Journal, and 1858, The Youth's In-
structor.]
The Boy's Own Journal. 1856–7. [Incor-
porated in The Boy's Own Magazine.]
The Boys' and Girls' Companion for Leisure
Hours. Ed. John and Mary Bennett, 1857–
61. [From 1858 as The Companion for
Youth.]

The Youth's Instructor. 1858. [9 months only; then incorporated in The Boy's Own Magazine.]

The Boy's Journal: a Magazine of Literature, Science, and Amusement. 1863–71. [Incorporated 1871 in The Youth's Play Hour, 1870–2.]

The Boy's Penny Magazine. 1863–7. [Monthly: from Jan. 1864 as The Boy's Monthly Magazine. Ed. by S. O. Beeton.]

The Boy's Yearly Book. 1863. [One year only; ed. by S. O. Beeton.]

The Children's Prize. Founded by J. Erskine Clarke. 1864–. [In progress; from 1876 as The Prize for Girls and Boys.]

Golden Hours. A Magazine for Sunday Reading. 1864–84.

Aunt Judy's Magazine. 1866–85. [Founded by Margaret Gatty and edited by her till 1873. 1874–6, ed. by H. K. F. Gatty and J. H. Ewing; 1877–85, ed. by H. K. F. Gatty.]

Beeton's Annual; a Book for the Young. 1866. [One year only; ed. by S. O. Beeton.]

Boys of England. A Magazine of Sport, Sensation, Fun and Instruction. 1866–1906 (?). [First editor C. Stevens; from vol. II, E. J. Brett. Incorporated in or restarted with The Surprise, 1906. Incorporated Jack Harkaway's Journal for Boys, 1894. See also Boys of England Pocket Novelettes, 1880–3. Weekly; also collected into vols. of 10 stories each. Colloquially known as 'penny dreadfuls.' Chief contributor Bracebridge Heming (pseudonym?), author of the Jack Harkaway series.]

Chatterbox. Founded by J. Erskine Clarke. 1866–. [In progress. See F. J. H. Darton, The Birth of a Children's Magazine, Cornhill Mag. May 1932.]

Father William's Stories. 1866–7. [Continued as The Children's Treasury, 1868–81. Continued as Our Darlings; in progress.]

The Infant's Magazine. Ed. W. Carus Wilson, 1866–. [In progress.]

Kind Words for Boys and Girls. 1866–. [In progress; from 1880 as Young England.]

The People's Pocket Story Books. 1867–8. [Monthly complete stories, colloquially known as 'penny dreadfuls.' Chief writer 'Roland Quiz' (Richard M. H. Quittenton), see under Minor Writers, p. 573 above.]

Good Words for the Young. 1869–77. [Ed. by Norman Macleod and afterwards by George Macdonald. From 1873 as Good Things Annual.]

The Youth's Play-hour. 1870–2. [Incorporated The Boy's Journal in 1871. Jules Verne's first translated story, Five Weeks in a Balloon, appeared in it in 1871.]

Little Folks. 1871–1933.

Young Folks. Ed. James Henderson, 1871–97. [Titles successively: 1871, Our Young Folks' Weekly Budget; 1876, Young Folks' Weekly Budget; 1879, Young Folks (Treasure Island, by R. L. Stevenson, appeared in it in this period); 1884, Young Folks' Paper; 1891, Old and Young; 1896, Folks at Home.]

Sunday. Reading for the Young. 1872–1926. [In 1914 as Sunday and Everyday. From 1915 as Everyday.]

The Boy's Own Paper. 1879 (Jan.)–. [Monthly. In progress. Annually as The Boy's Own Annual. Founded by J. M. Macaulay, but first and chief editor, 1879–1912, George Andrew Hutchinson. The Jubilee Volume (1930) of The Boy's Own Paper contains an historical and literary retrospect of the magazine's past.]

The Girl's Own Paper. 1880–1908. [In 1908 became The Girl's Own Paper and Woman's Magazine, and in 1928 The Woman's Magazine; in progress.]

The Union Jack. A Magazine of Healthy Stirring Tales for Boys. 1880–3. [Edited by W. H. G. Kingston, 1880, and afterwards by G. A. Henty.]

Our Little Ones: Illustrated Stories and Poems for Little People. William T. Adams (Oliver Optie), Editor. 1881–3.

Bo-peep. A Magazine for the Nursery. 1882–. [In progress.]

The Boy's Comic Journal. Stories, Fun, and Adventure. Ed. Edwin J. Brett, 1883–98. [Weekly, and as annual vol.]

Atalanta. Ed. 'L. T. Meade' (E. T. Meade, later Toulmin Smith) and A. A. Leith, 1887–98. [For girls.]

Boys and Girls. Conducted by G. Rayner. 1887–8. [Also as Boys of the United Kingdom.]

Our Boys' Magazine. Edited by University Men. 1887–. [Monthly. In progress, as The Boys' Magazine.]

Our Little Dots. Pretty Pictures and Stories for Little Girls and Boys. 1887–1922. [In progress as Little Dots.]

Boys. 1892 (July 16)–1894 (Sept.). [Then incorporated in The Boy's Own Paper. Weekly and monthly.]

Chums. 1892–. [In progress.]

Jack Harkaway's Journal for Boys. Ed. E. J. Brett, 1893. [Weekly. Chief contributor Bracebridge Heming (pseudonym?). Incorporated in Boys of England.]

The 'Halfpenny Marvel' Library. 1893–1922. [Weekly; after No. 3 as the 'Halfpenny Marvel'; after 1898 as The Marvel. Allied to The Union Jack Library of High-Class Fiction.]

The Halfpenny Surprise. Ed. E. J. Brett, 1894–1906. [Weekly, later as The Surprise; later sub-title A Journal for Youths. Main contents one complete story, with short editorial matter and picture pages. Incorporated in 'new' Boys of England, 1906.]

The Union Jack Library of High-Class Fiction. 1894–1933. [Weekly. Includes the Sexton Blake series of tales. A 'long complete novel' in each number with a few brief editorial notes.]

The Girl's Realm. 1898–1915. [Then incorporated in The Woman at Home.]

Tiny Tots. A Magazine for very Little Folks. 1899–. [In progress.]

F. J. H. D.

4. THE DRAMA

I. GENERAL INTRODUCTION

Bibliographies and Reference-Books; Dramatic and Theatrical Histories and Biographies; Theatrical Periodicals; Collections of Plays.

(1) BIBLIOGRAPHIES AND REFERENCE-BOOKS

Jones, Stephen. Biographia Dramatica. 3 vols. in 4, 1812.

[Genest, J.] Some Account of the English Stage, from 1660 to 1830. 10 vols. Bath, 1832.

Lowe, R. W. A Bibliographical Account of English Theatrical Literature. 1888.

Cameron, J. A Bibliography of Scottish Theatrical Literature. Trans. Edinburgh Bibliog. Soc. I, 1896. [Supplement *ibid.*]

Adams, W. D. A Dictionary of the Drama. Vol. I (A–G), 1904.

'Clarence, R.' (H. J. Eldridge). 'The Stage' Cyclopaedia. A Bibliography of Plays. 1909. [An alphabetical list of plays, giving theatres and dates of first London productions.]

O'Neill, J. J. A Bibliographical Account of Irish Theatrical Literature. Dublin, 1920.

Firkins, I. T. E. Index to Plays, 1800–1926. New York, 1927.

Nicoll, A. A History of Early Nineteenth Century Drama, 1800–1850. 2 vols. Cambridge, 1930. [Vol. II contains a play-list covering the whole dramatic output of the years 1800–50, and giving theatres and dates of first provincial and/or London productions. For some addenda see R. C. Rhodes, Library, XVI, 1935, pp. 91–112, 210–31.]

Parker, John. Who's Who in the Theatre. 1930 (rev. edn). [Contains list of long 'runs' and much other valuable information.]

Gilder, R. and Freedley, G. Theatre Collections in Libraries and Museums. An International Handbook. New York, 1936.

(2) HISTORIES AND BIOGRAPHIES (DRAMATIC AND THEATRICAL)

[For further titles, particularly for accounts of provincial theatres, etc., the parallel sections 1660–1800, vol. II, pp. 392–410 above, should be referred to.]

Angus, J. K. A Scotch Playhouse; being the Historical Records of the Old Theatre Royal, Marischal Street, Aberdeen. Aberdeen, 1878.

Archer, Frank. An Actor's Note-Books. [1912.]

Archer, W. English Dramatists of To-Day. 1882.

—— Henry Irving, Actor and Manager. A Critical Study. 1883.

—— About the Theatre. 1886.

—— William Charles Macready. 1890.

—— The Theatrical 'World.' 5 vols. 1893–7.

—— Study and Stage, a Yearbook of Criticism. 1899.

—— The Old Drama and the New. 1923.

Archer, W. and Lowe, R. W. The Fashionable Tragedian. Edinburgh, 1877.

—— Dramatic Essays. Leigh Hunt, William Hazlitt, John Forster and George Henry Lewes. 3 vols. 1894–6.

Armstrong, C. F. A Century of Great Actors: 1750–1850. 1912.

Arnold, Matthew. Letters of an Old Playgoer. Ed. B. Matthews, New York, 1919.

Baker, H. B. Our Old Actors. 1881.

—— History of the London Stage: 1576–1903. 1904 (rev. edn).

Baker, W. T. The Manchester Stage: 1800–1900. 1903.

Bancroft, Lady (M. E.) and Sir S. Mr and Mrs Bancroft on and off the Stage. Written by Themselves. 2 vols. 1888.

—— The Bancrofts: Recollections of Sixty Years. 1909.

Bancroft, Sir S. and Archer, W. Byron on the Stage. [In Byron, the Poet, ed. W. A. Briscoe, 1924.]

Barnes, J. H. Forty Years on the Stage. 1914.

Barrington, R. Rutland Barrington. By Himself. With a Preface by W. S. Gilbert. 1908.

Baynham, W. The Glasgow Stage. [1892.]

Bedford, P. J. Recollections and Wanderings. 1864.

Beerbohm, M. Herbert Beerbohm Tree. 1921.

Bergholz, H. Die Neugestaltung des modernen englischen Theaters, 1870–1930. Berlin, 1933.

Boaden, J. Memoirs of the Life of John Philip Kemble. 2 vols. 1825.

—— Memoirs of Mrs Siddons. 2 vols. 1827.

Board, M. E. The Story of the Bristol Stage, 1490–1925. Bristol, 1925.

Borsa, M. Il Teatro inglese contemporaneo. Milan, 1906; tr. Eng. 1908.

Bowley, V. E. A. English Versions of Victor Hugo's Plays. French Quart. June 1928.

Brereton, A. Dramatic Notes. 1881–2.
—— Some Famous Hamlets. 1884.
—— The Lyceum and Henry Irving. 1903.
—— The Life of Henry Irving. 1908.
Broadbent, R. J. A History of Pantomime. [1901.]
—— Stage Whispers. [1901.]
—— Annals of the Liverpool Stage. Liverpool, 1908.
Bunn, A. The Stage. 3 vols. 1840.
Burley, T. L. G. Playhouses and Players of East Anglia. Norwich, 1928.
Byrne, M. St C. 'Stalls and Places in the Orchestra.' TLS. 24 Nov. 1932.
—— Supplement to the Playbill. TLS. 29 June 1933.
Calvert, A. H. Sixty-eight Years on the Stage. 1911.
Calvert, W. Sir Henry Irving and Miss Ellen Terry. 1897.
Campbell, L. B. A History of Costuming on the English Stage between 1660 and 1823. Wisconsin University Stud. II, 1918.
Campbell, Mrs P. My Life and Some Letters. 1922.
Carré, J. M. Goethe en Angleterre. Paris, 1920.
Carter, Huntley. The New Spirit in Drama and Art. 1912.
Chandler, F. W. Aspects of Modern Drama. New York, 1914.
Chapman, J. K. A Complete History of Theatrical Entertainments, Dramas, Masques, and Triumphs, at the English Court. [1849.]
Chew, S. C. The Relation of Lord Byron to the Drama of the Romantic Period. Baltimore, 1914.
Child, H. Nineteenth-Century Drama. CHEL. vol. XIII, 1916. [Ch. viii.]
Clapp, H. A. Reminiscences of a Dramatic Critic. With an Essay on the Art of Henry Irving. 1902.
Cole, J. W. The Life and Theatrical Times of Charles Kean. 2 vols. 1859.
Coleman, J. Players and Playwrights I have known. 2 vols. 1888.
Compton, C. and E. Memoir of Henry Compton. 1879.
Cook, Dutton. A Book of the Play. 2 vols. 1876.
—— Hours with the Players. 2 vols. 1881.
—— Nights at the Play. 2 vols. 1883.
—— On the Stage. 2 vols. 1883.
—— Memoirs of Samuel Phelps. 1886.
Cooke, J. The Stage. [1840.]
Cooke, W. M. Schiller's Robbers in England. MLR. April 1916.
'Cornwall, Barry' (B. W. Procter). The Life of Edmund Kean. 2 vols. 1835.

Cotton, W. The Story of the Drama in Exeter. Exeter, 1887.
Courtney, W. L. The Idea of Tragedy in Ancient and Modern Drama. With a Prefatory Note by Sir A. W. Pinero. 1900.
Craig, E. G. The Art of the Theatre. Edinburgh, 1905.
—— Henry Irving. 1930.
Cunliffe, J. W. Modern English Playwrights: a Short History of the English Drama from 1825. New York, 1927.
Dawson, J. The Autobiography of James Dawson. Truro, 1865.
Day, W. C. Behind the Footlights. 1885.
Desultory Thoughts on the National Drama, Past and Present. By an Old Playgoer. 1850.
Dibdin, C. History and Illustrations of the London Theatres. 1826.
Dibdin, J. C. The Annals of the Edinburgh Stage. 1888.
Dibdin, T. J. Reminiscences of Thomas Dibdin, of the Theatres Royal, Covent Garden, Drury Lane, etc. 2 vols. 1827.
Dickens, C. Memoirs of Joseph Grimaldi. With Illustrations by G. Cruickshank. 2 vols. 1838; ed. C. Whitehead and P. Fitzgerald, 1903.
—— Macready as Benedict. Examiner, 4 March 1843.
—— The Amusements of the People. Household Words, 30 March, 30 April 1850. [A vivid picture of the early Victorian London cheap theatres; see also Great Expectations, chs. xxxi, xlvii, and for its provincial parallel, Nicholas Nickleby, chs. xx–xxv, xxix, xlviii.]
—— The Guild of Literature and Art. Household Words, 10 May 1851.
—— Gaslight Fairies. Household Words, 10 Feb. 1855.
—— On Mr Fechter's Acting. Atlantic Monthly, Aug. 1869.
—— Miscellaneous Papers. Ed. B. W. Matz (vols. xxxv, xxxvi of Gadshill edn of Dickens's Works, 1897–1908). [Includes the articles listed above. See also J. Forster's Life of Dickens, 2 vols. 1911 (Memorial edn).]
Dickinson, T. H. The Contemporary Drama of England. 1920.
Dimmick, R. C. Our Theatres Today and Yesterday. 1913.
Disher, M. W. Clowns and Pantomimes. 1925.
—— Greatest Show on Earth: Astley's. 1937.
—— Winkles and Champagne. 1938. [A history of the 19th-century music halls.]
Donaldson, W. A. Recollections of an Actor. 1865.

Doran, J. 'Their Majesties' Servants.' Annals of the English Stage, from Betterton to Kean. 2 vols. 1864; rev. R. W. Lowe, 3 vols. 1888.

A New Drama; or, We faint!!! Decline of the Drama!!! Review of the Actors!!! Reprinted from Bentley's Monthly Review. 1853.

'Dramaticus.' An Impartial View of the Stage. 1816.

—— The Stage as it is. 1847.

Dubois, A. E. Shakespeare and 19th-Century Drama. ELH. i, 1934.

—— Beginnings of Tragic Comedy in the Drama of the Nineteenth Century. Baltimore, 1934.

Dukes, A. Modern Dramatists. [1911.]

Dyer, R. Nine Years of an Actor's Life. 1833.

The Eighteen-Seventies. Royal Soc. Lit. 1929. [Includes Sir A. Pinero, The Theatre in the 'Seventies, and H. Granville-Barker, Tennyson, Swinburne, Meredith and the Theatre.]

Ellehauge, M. The Initial Stages in the Development of the English Problem Play. E. Studien, LXVI, 1932.

—— Striking Figures amongst Modern English Dramatists. Copenhagen, 1931.

Ellerslie, A. The Diary of an Actress. 1885.

Elton, O. A Survey of English Literature, 1780–1830. Vol. II, 1912. [Ch. xxi.]

Fairfax, W. Robert Browning and the Drama. 1891.

Field, Kate. Adelaide Ristori, a Biography. 1867.

Filon, A. The English Stage: an Account of the Victorian Drama. 1897.

Fitzball, Edward. Thirty Five Years of a Dramatic Author's Life. 2 vols. 1859.

Fitzgerald, P. H. Principles of Comedy and Dramatic Effect. Bungay, 1870.

—— The Book of Theatrical Anecdotes. 2 vols. 1874.

—— The Romance of the English Stage. 2 vols. 1874.

—— The World behind the Scenes. 1881.

—— A New History of the English Stage. [1660–1842]. 2 vols. 1882.

—— Henry Irving. A Record of Twenty Years at the Lyceum. 1893.

—— The Garrick Club. 1904.

—— Sir Henry Irving. 1906.

Fornelli, G. Tendenze e Motivi nel Dramma inglese moderno e contemporaneo. Florence, [1930].

Frank, M. A. Ibsen in England. 1919.

Frohman, D. Memories of a Manager. Reminiscences of the Old Lyceum and of some Players of the Last Quarter Century. 1911.

Fyvie, J. Tragedy Queens of the Georgian Era. 1903.

—— Comedy Queens of the Georgian Era. 1906.

G., G. M. The Stage Censor. An Historical Sketch: 1544–1907. 1908.

Gillet, J. E. A Forgotten German Creditor of the English Stage. Nineteenth Century, April 1912.

Glover, J. M. Jimmy Glover his Book. 1911.

—— Jimmy Glover and his Friends. 1913.

Goddard, A. Players of the Period. A Series of Anecdotal, Biographical and Critical Monographs of the Leading English Actors of the Day. 2 vols. 1891.

Goldman, E. The Social Significance of Modern Drama. 1914.

Goodman, W. The Keelys. On Stage and at Home. 1895.

Gosse, Sir E. The Revival of Poetic Drama. Atlantic Monthly, xc, 1902.

Grau, R. Forty Years' Observation of Music and Drama. 1909.

Gregory, Lady (I. A.). Our Irish Theatre. 1914.

Grein, J. T. Dramatic Criticism. 3 vols. 1899–1903.

Grundy, S. The Play of the Future. 1914.

Hadow, W. H. The Use of Comic Episodes in Tragedy. 1915.

Hale, E. E. Dramatists of To-Day. 1906.

Hamilton, C. The Theory of the Theatre. 1910.

Hamilton, C. and Baylis, L. The Old Vic. 1926.

Hannam-Clark, T. Drama in Gloucestershire. 1928.

Harcourt, B. The Theatre Royal, Norwich. 1903.

Hastings, C. Le Théâtre français et anglais. Paris, 1900; tr. Eng. 1901.

Hatton, J. Reminiscences of Mark Lemon. 1872.

Hawkins, F. W. The Life of Edmund Kean. 1869.

Hazlitt, W. A View of the English Stage. 1818; ed. W. Archer and R. W. Lowe, 1895.

Henderson, Archibald. The Changing Drama. 1914.

Heraud, J. A. The Present Position of the Dramatic Poet. 1841.

Hiatt, C. Ellen Terry and her Impersonations. 1898.

Hillebrand, H. N. Edmund Kean. New York, 1933.

Hingston, E. P. The Siddons of Modern Italy: Adelaide Ristori. 1856.

Hogarth, G. Memoirs of the Musical Drama. 1838.

Holbrook, A. C. The Dramatist: or, Memoirs of the Stage. Birmingham, 1809.

Hollingshead, J. Gaiety Chronicles. 1890.

Holman, L. E. Lamb's 'Barbara S—.' The Life of Frances Maria Kelly, Actress. 1935.

Hook, T. Reminiscences of Michael Kelly. 2 vols. 1826.

Horne, R. H. A New Spirit of the Age. 2 vols. 1844.

Howe, P. P. Dramatic Portraits. 1913.

Huber, R. Ibsens Bedeutung für das englische Drama. Marburg, 1914.

Huneker, J. G. Iconoclasts: a Book of Dramatists. 1905.

Hunt, Leigh. Critical Essays on the Performers of the London Theatres. 1807.

Idman, N. Charles Robert Maturin. Helsingfors, 1923.

'Irving, Sir H. The Stage. 1878.

Jackson, Holbrook. The Eighteen-Nineties. 1923.

Jerome, J. K. On the Stage—and off. 1885.

Joannides, A. La Comédie Française de 1860 à 1900. Paris, 1901.

Jones, F. M. On the Causes of the Decline of the Drama. Edinburgh, 1834.

Jones, H. A. The Renascence of the English Drama. 1895.

Kemble, F. A. Record of a Girlhood. 3 vols. 1878.

Kendal, Madge. The Drama. [1884.]

—— Dramatic Opinions. 1890.

Knight, J. Theatrical Notes. 1893.

—— The History of the English Stage during the Reign of Victoria. 1901.

Lawrence, J. Dramatic Emancipation. 1813.

Lawrence, W. J. The Elizabethan Playhouse and Other Studies. 2 sers. Stratford-on-Avon, 1912–3.

—— Old Theatre Days and Ways. 1935.

Lawson, R. The Story of the Scottish Stage. Glasgow, 1917.

Lee, Henry. Memoirs of a Manager. 2 vols. Taunton, 1830.

Lennox, Lord W. P. Plays, Players and Playhouses. 2 vols. 1881.

Levey, R. M. and O'Rorke, J. Annals of the Theatre Royal, Dublin. Dublin, 1880.

Lewes, G. H. On Actors and Acting. 1875.

Lingwood, H. R. Ipswich Playhouses. Chapters of Local Theatrical History. [Ipswich, 1936.]

Macready, W. C. Reminiscences. Ed. Sir F. Pollock, 1875.

Mantzius, K. Skuespilkunstens Historie. 5 vols. Copenhagen, 1897–1907; tr. Eng. 6 vols. 1903–21. [Vol. vi.]

Marston, J. W. Our Recent Actors. 2 vols. 1888.

Martin, Sir T. Essays on the Drama. 1874.

—— Helen Faucit—Lady Martin. 1900.

Mathews, Mrs. Memoirs of Charles Mathews. 4 vols. 1838–9.

Matthews, J. B. French Dramatists of the Nineteenth Century. 1882.

Maude, C. The Haymarket Theatre. 1903.

Meeks, L. H. Sheridan Knowles and the Theatre of his Time. Bloomington, 1933.

Meredith, G. An Essay on Comedy and the Use of the Comic Spirit. 1897.

Miller, Anna I. The Independent Theatre in Europe. 1931.

Molloy, J. F. The Romance of the Irish Stage. 2 vols. 1897.

Morgan, A. E. Tendencies of Modern English Drama. 1923.

Morgan, B. Q. A Bibliography of German Literature in English Translation. Madison, 1922.

Morley, H. The Journal of a London Playgoer, 1851–1866. 1866.

Morris, M. Essays in Theatrical Criticism. 1882.

Munden, T. S. Memoirs of Joseph Shepherd Munden. By his Son. 1844.

Nag, U. C. The English Theatre of the Romantic Revival. Nineteenth Century, Sept. 1928.

Neville, H. The Stage: its Past and Present in Relation to Fine Art. 1875.

Nicholson, W. The Struggle for a Free Stage. 1906.

Nicoll, A. British Drama. 1925.

—— The Development of the Theatre. 1927; 1937 (rev.).

—— A History of Early Nineteenth Century Drama: 1800–1850. 2 vols. Cambridge, 1930.

—— The English Theatre. A Short History. 1936.

Odell, G. C. D. Shakespeare from Betterton to Irving. 2 vols. New York, 1920.

Oliver, D. E. The English Stage: its Origins and Modern Developments. [1912.]

Oxberry, W. Oxberry's Dramatic Biography. 1825–7.

Palmer, J. The Censor and the Theatres. 1913.

Pascoe, C. E. Dramatic Notes. 1870.

—— Our Actors and Actresses. The Dramatic List. 1880.

'Paterson, P.' (J. G. Bertram). Behind the Scenes: being the Confessions of a Strolling Player. 1858.

Peake, R. B. Memoirs of the Colman Family. 2 vols. 1841.

Pearce, C. E. Madame Vestris and her Times. 1923.

Pellizzi, C. Il Teatro inglese. Milan, 1934; tr. Eng. 1935 (as English Drama, the Last Great Phase). [Vol. iii of Il Teatro del Novecento.]

Pemberton, T. E. Charles Dickens and the Stage. 1888.

—— The Birmingham Theatres [1862–79]. Birmingham, [1890].

—— The Kendals. 1900.

—— The Theatre Royal, Birmingham, 1774–1901. Birmingham, 1901.

—— Ellen Terry, and her Sisters. 1902.

Penley, B. S. The Bath Stage. 1892.

Perugini, M. E. The Omnibus Book, being Digressions on Social and Theatrical Life, 1830–1850. 1933.

Phelps, W. M. and Forbes-Robertson, J. The Life and Life-work of Samuel Phelps. 1886.

Poel, W. William Poel and his Stage Productions. 1933 (priv. ptd).

Porter, H. C. A History of the Theatres of Brighton from 1774 to 1885. Brighton, 1886.

Powell, G. R. The Bristol Stage. 1919.

[Purnell, T.] Dramatists of the Present Day. By 'Q.' 1871.

Quinlan, M. A. Poetic Justice in the Drama. The History of an Ethical Principle in Literary Criticism. Notre Dame (Indiana), 1912.

Raymond, G. Memoirs of R. W. Elliston. 1845.

Rea, T. Schiller's Poems and Dramas in England. 1906.

Reade, C. The Eighth Commandment. 1860.

Reynolds, E. Early Victorian Drama, 1830–1870. Cambridge, 1936.

Rhodes, R. C. The Theatre Royal, Birmingham, 1774–1924. 1924.

Rubinstein, H. F. The English Drama. 1928.

Russell, Sir Edward R. The Theatre and Things Said about it. Liverpool, 1911.

Russell, W. Clark. Representative Actors. [1872.]

Ryan, R. Dramatic Table Talk. 3 vols. 1825–30.

Ryley, S. W. The Itinerant. 3 vols. 1808.

Salvini, T. Leaves from the Autobiography of Tommaso Salvini. 1893.

Schelling, F. E. English Drama. 1914. [Ch. xii.]

Scott, Clement W. From The Bells to King Arthur. A Critical Record of First-Night Productions at the Lyceum Theatre from 1871 to 1895. 1896.

—— The Drama of Yesterday and To-day. 2 vols. 1899.

—— Ellen Terry. New York, 1900 (rev. edn).

—— Some Notable Hamlets of the Present Time. 1905.

Sellier, W. Kotzebue in England. Leipzig, 1901.

Senior, W. The Old Wakefield Theatre. Wakefield, 1894.

Sharp, R. F. A Short History of the English Stage to 1908. 1909.

Sharp, R. F. Travesties of Shakespeare's Plays. Library, June 1920.

Shaw, G. B. The Quintessence of Ibsenism. 1891; 1913 (rev.).

—— Dramatic Opinions and Essays. 2 vols. 1907.

Sheppard, T. Evolution of the Drama in Hull and District. Hull, 1917.

Sherson, E. London's Lost Theatres of the Nineteenth Century. 1925.

Sillard, R. S. Barry Sullivan and his Contemporaries. 1901.

Simpson, H. and Brown, Mrs C. A Century of Famous Actresses, 1750–1850. [1913.]

Smythe, A. J. The Life of William Terriss. 1898.

Spence, E. F. Our Stage and its Critics. 1910.

Sper, F. The Periodical Press of London: Theatrical and Literary, excluding the Daily Newspaper, 1800–1830. Boston, 1938.

Stahl, E. Das englische Theater im 19. Jahrhundert. Munich, 1914.

Stirling, E. Old Drury Lane; Fifty Years' Recollections. 2 vols. 1881.

Stokoe, F. W. German Influence in the English Romantic Period, 1788–1818. Cambridge, 1926.

Syles, L. D. Essays in Dramatic Criticism. 1898.

Taylor, T. The Theatre in England. 1871.

Terry, Ellen. The Story of My Life. 1908.

—— Memoirs, with Additional Chapters by E. Craig and C. St John. 1933.

Thackeray, T. J. On Theatrical Emancipation and the Rights of Dramatic Authors. 1832.

Thompson, L. F. Kotzebue: a Survey of his Progress in England and France. Paris, 1928.

Thorndike, A. H. English Comedy. New York, 1929.

Thorp, W. The Stage Adventures of some Gothic Novels. PMLA. XLIII, 1928.

Thouless, P. Modern Poetic Drama. Oxford, 1934.

Tomkins, F. G. A Brief View of the English Drama. 1840.

Toole, J. L. Reminiscences of J. L. Toole, related by himself and chronicled by J. Hatton. 2 vols. 1889.

Vandenhoff, J. M. Dramatic Reminiscences. 1860.

Waitzkin, L. The Witch of Wych Street. A Study of the Theatrical Reforms of Madame Vestris. Cambridge, U.S.A. 1933.

Walbrook, H. M. Nights at the Play. 1911.

Walkley, A. B. Playhouse Impressions. 1892.

—— Frames of Mind. 1899.

—— Drama and Life. 1907.

Ward, G. Genevieve Ward. A Biographical Sketch. [1881.]

Watson, E. B. Sheridan to Robertson. Cambridge, U.S.A. 1926.

Watts, G. T. Theatrical Bristol. Bristol, 1915.

Webster, B. The Series of Dramatic Entertainments performed by Royal Command at Windsor Castle, 1848–9. [1849.]

White, H. A. Sir Walter Scott's Novels on the Stage. New Haven, 1927.

Williams, M. Some London Theatres Past and Present. 1883.

Wray, E. English Adaptations of French Drama between 1780 and 1815. MLN. XLIII, 1928.

Wyndham, H. S. The Annals of Covent Garden Theatre, 1732–1897. 2 vols. 1906.

Wynne, A. The Growth of English Drama. Oxford, 1914.

Young, C. M. A Memoir of Charles Mayne Young. 2 vols. 1891.

(3) THEATRICAL PERIODICALS

[See also F. Sper, The Periodical Press of London: Theatrical and Literary, 1800–1830, Boston, 1938.]

The Covent Garden Theatrical Gazette. 140 nos. 1816–7. [Weekly.]

The Drama; or Theatrical Pocket Magazine. 7 vols. 1821–5. New ser. vol. I, 1825. [Monthly.]

The Era. 30 Sept. 1839 onwards. [Weekly.]

The London Entr'acte. [10 July 1869?]– 17 Feb. 1872. [Weekly. Continued as Entr'acte, 24 Feb. 1872–26 April 1907.]

The Theatre. 1877–97. [Monthly. Ed. by Clement Scott (1878–90), B. E. J. Capes, Charles Rolleston (1890–7).]

The Stage Directory. 1 Feb. 1880–1 March 1881. [Monthly. Continued weekly as The Stage, 25 March 1881 onwards.]

(4) COLLECTIONS OF PLAYS

[The following list is largely based on 2 articles by R. C. Rhodes, Library, XVI, 1935.]

The London Theatre. A Collection of the most Celebrated Dramatic Pieces. Ed. T. J. Dibdin, 26 vols. 1815–8.

The New English Drama. Ed. W. Oxberry, 20 vols. (100 plays, each with separate title-page), 1818–25. (Oxberry.)

[John] Duncombe's New Acting Drama. 12 nos. (1 play each), 1821–5.

[Thomas] Dolby's British Theatre. 12 vols. (84 plays, each with separate title-page), 1823–5. [Continued as Cumberland (see below).]

The British Drama. A Collection of the most Esteemed Tragedies, Comedies, Operas, and Farces in the English Language. 2 vols. 1824–6; 2 vols. Philadelphia, 1837–8.

The London Stage. A Collection of the most Reputed Tragedies, Comedies, Operas, Melodramas, Farces and Interludes. 4 vols. [1824–7].

[John] Duncombe's British Theatre. 67 vols. (also issued in 540 separate nos.), [1825–52]. (Duncombe.)

[John] Cumberland's British Theatre; with Remarks Biographical and Critical [by D. G., i.e. George Daniel]. 48 vols. (398 plays, each with separate title-page, but including several originally issued in Cumberland Minor), 1826–[1861]. (Cumberland.)

[Thomas] Richardson's New Minor Drama; with Remarks Biographical and Critical by W. T. Moncrieff. 4 vols. 1828–31. (Richardson.)

[John] Cumberland's Minor Theatre; with Remarks Biographical and Critical [by D. G., i.e. George Daniel]. 17 vols. 1828–43. (Cumberland Minor.)

The Acting Drama. 1834.

[John Duncombe's] Minor British Drama. 24 nos. (1 play each), [1834]. (Duncombe Minor.)

The Acting National Drama. Ed. B. N. Webster, 18 vols. 1837–[1859]. [Sponsored by the Dramatic Authors' Soc.] (Webster.)

The London Acting Drama. 31 (at least) nos. (1 play each), 1837–8.

Pattie's Play or Weekly Acting Drama. 45 nos. (often several to each play), [1838–9].

[James] Pattie's Universal Stage or Theatrical Prompt-Book. 100 nos. (1 play each), [1839–45]. [No. 32 onwards pbd by William Barth.]

The Modern English Comic Theatre. Ed. L. Hilsenberg, J. A. Diezemann and C. Albrecht, 6 sers. Leipzig, 1843–[1890?]. [Notes in German.]

[T. H.] Lacy's Acting Edition of Plays, Dramas, Extravaganzas, Farces, etc. 165 vols. [1849–1917]. [From vol. CI the collection becomes French's Acting Edition. For contents see Lacy's List of Plays wholly or partially the Property of T. H. Lacy, 1864, and Samuel French's Descriptive Catalogue of Plays and Dramatic Works, from c. 1891.] (Lacy.) (French.)

The British Drama. Illustrated. 12 vols. 1864–72.

[John Dicks'] The British Drama. 12 vols. (each 14–20 plays), [1866–?].

[John] Dicks' Standard Plays. [1875–1908.] (Dicks.)

Representative British Dramas, Victorian and Modern. Ed. M. J. Moses, Boston, 1918.

A. N.

II. THE EARLY NINETEENTH-CENTURY DRAMA, 1800–1835

[This section has been restricted, with a few exceptions, to writers born between 1760 and 1800. Moreover here, and in the following sections, cross-references have not usually been included to the unacted poetic dramas of the period, which will be found under Poetry, pp. 156–363 above. The following abbreviations have been adopted: B. (=burlesque), C. (= comedy), D. (=drama or melodrama), Ext. (= extravaganza), F. (= farce), O. (= opera), P. (= pantomime), Spec. (= spectacle), T. (= tragedy), CG. (= Covent Garden Theatre), DL. (= Drury Lane Theatre), Hay. (= Haymarket Theatre). Italicized forms like *Cumberland*, *Dicks*, etc. refer to their collections of plays (listed in full p. 585 above), and references to vol. II of A. Nicoll's Early Nineteenth Century Drama, Cambridge, 1930, have been abbreviated as 'Nicoll.' It should be added that the plays are listed in the order of their production, not of their publication.]

SAMUEL JAMES ARNOLD (1774–1852)

(a) Plays

Auld Robin Gray. A Pastoral Entertainment. O. (Hay. 29 July 1794.) 1794.

The Shipwreck. A Comic Opera in Two Acts. (DL. 19 Dec. 1796.) 1797; New York, 1805; *Oxberry*, IX, 1820.

The Veteran Tar, or A Chip of the Old Block. A Comic Opera in Two Acts. (DL. 29 Jan. 1801.) 1801.

'Foul Deeds will rise.' A Musical Drama. (Hay. 18 July 1804.) 1804.

Man and Wife, or More Secrets than One. C. (DL. 5 Jan. 1809.) 1809 (8 edns); New York, 1809; Boston, 1855.

The Woodman's Hut. A Melo-dramatic Romance, in Three Acts. (DL. 12 April 1814.) 1814; *Oxberry*, IV, 1814; [1822]; [1859].

The Devil's Bridge. An Opera in Three Acts. (Lyceum, 6 May 1812.) Dublin, 1820; [1825?]; *Cumberland*, XLII, [1842?]. Songs, Duets, Chorusses. 1815; 1818.

Free and Easy. A Musical Farce in Two Acts. (Opera House, 16 Sept. 1816.) *Cumberland*, XLII, [1842?].

[Nicoll also lists 2 other musical pieces in his Late Eighteenth Century Drama and 17 (also mainly musical) in his Early Nineteenth Century Drama.]

(b) Other Writings

The Creole, or the Haunted Island. 3 vols. 1796. [A novel.]

A Letter to all the Proprietors of Drury-Lane Theatre, excepting Peter Moore, Esq. 1818.

Forgotten Facts in the Memoirs of Charles Mathews, Comedian, recalled in a Letter to Mrs Mathews, his Biographer. [1839.]

JOANNA BAILLIE (1762–1851).

[See p. 226 above.]

EDWARD BALL, afterwards FITZBALL (1792–1873)

(a) Plays

The Innkeeper of Abbeville, or the Ostler and the Robber. D. (Norwich Theatre, 1821; Surrey, 1822.) 1822.

Peveril of the Peak. D. (Surrey, 6 Feb. 1823.) [1823.] [From Scott's novel.]

The Floating Beacon; or, The Norwegian Wreckers. (Surrey, 19 April 1824.) *Cumberland Minor*, II, [1828?]; *Lacy*, LXXV, [1867].

The Pilot, or a Tale of the Sea. C. (Adelphi, 31 Oct. 1825.) 1825. [From Fenimore Cooper's novel.]

The Flying Dutchman, or the Phantom Ship. O. (Adelphi, 1 Jan. 1827.) *Cumberland Minor*, II, [1828?]; *Lacy*, LXXI, [1867].

Jonathan Bradford, or the Murder at the Roadside Inn. D. (Surrey, 12 June 1833.) *Lacy*, LV, [1862]; *Dicks*, 370, [1883].

Zazezizozu. B. (CG. 4 April 1836.) *Duncombe*, XXI, [1836?]. [From the French.]

The Miller of Derwent Water. D. (Olympic, 2 May 1853.) *Lacy*, XII, [1854].

[Fitzball was one of the most prolific writers the English stage has seen. Nicoll, pp. 302–7, lists 118 pieces, and these are not all. He adapted many novels (especially by Sir W. Scott) to the stage and wrote a large number of songs, of which the most famous is 'The Bloom is on the Rye' ('My Pretty Jane'). Further, he wrote the libretti for such well-known operas as The Daughter of the Regiment and Maritana.]

(b) Other Writings

Thirty-five Years of a Dramatic Author's Life. 2 vols. 1859.

JOHN BANIM (1798–1842)

[See p. 387 above.]

WILLIAM BARRYMORE (d. 1845)

The Dog of Montargis, or the Forest of Bondy. D. (CG. 30 Sept. 1814.) *Dicks*, 163, [1883]. [From Guilbert de Pixérécourt's Le Chien de Montargis.]

Trial by Battle, or Heaven defend the Right. Spec. (Royal Coburg, 11 May 1818.) *Duncombe*, VIII, [1830?]; [1854].

Wallace, the Hero of Scotland. D. (Royal Amphitheatre, 6 Oct. 1817.) *Duncombe Minor*, I, [1834]; Boston, [1856?]; *Lacy*, LXXIII, [1867?]; *Dicks*, 953, [1888].

El Hyder, the Chief of the Ghaut Mountains. Spec. (Royal Coburg, 7 Dec. 1818.) *Lacy*, VI, [1852]; *Dicks*, 140, [1883].

Gilderoy, or the Bonnie Boy. D. (Royal Coburg, 25 June 1822.) *Richardson*, II, [1829]; *Cumberland Minor*, VIII, [1835?].

The Secret. B. (Royal Amphitheatre, 11 May 1824.) [1854]; *Lacy*, XLVIII, [1861?].

The Two Sisters. D. *Duncombe*, LXVI, [1852?].

The Fatal Snowstorm. D. (Astley's.) *Cumberland Minor*, XIII, [1838?].

[Nicoll also lists 7 other pieces.]

THOMAS HAYNES BAYLY (1797–1839)
[See p. 227 above.]

SAMUEL BEAZLEY (1786–1851)
(a) Plays

The Boarding-House, or Five Hours at Brighton. A Musical Farce. (Lyceum, 26 Aug. 1811.) 1811; 1816.

Is he Jealous? O. (English Opera House, 2 July 1816.) 1816; *Oxberry*, III, [1818]; *Dicks*, 774, [1886].

My Uncle. O. (English Opera House, 23 June 1817.) 1817.

Jealous on all Sides, or the Landlord in Jeopardy. O. (English Opera House, 19 Aug. 1818.) 1818.

The Steward, or Fashion and Feeling. C. (CG. 15 Sept. 1819.) *Dicks*, 539, [1884].

Love's Dream. O. (English Opera House, 5 July 1821.) *Duncombe*, VIII, [1830?].

The Lottery Ticket, or, the Lawyer's Clerk. F. (DL. 13 Dec. 1826.) *Lacy*, LXVIII, [1866]; *Dicks*, 226, [1883].

You know what. F. (Sadler's Wells, 28 Nov. 1842.) *Dicks*, 653, [1885].

[Nicoll, p. 253–4, lists 19 further pieces (mainly musical), only 3 of which were pbd.]

(b) Novels

The Roué. 3 vols. 1828.

The Oxonians. A Glance at Society. 3 vols. 1830.

JAMES BOADEN (1762–1839)
(a) Plays

Osmyn and Daraxa. A Musical Romance. (DL. Company at Opera House, 1793.) Songs and Chorusses. [1793.]

Fontainville Forest. A Play in Five Acts. (CG. 25 March 1794.) 1794 (*bis*). [A dramatic version of Ann Radcliffe's novel, The Romance of the Forest.]

The Secret Tribunal. A Play in Five Acts. (CG. 3 June 1795.) 1795. [In verse.]

The Italian Monk. A Play in Three Acts. (Hay. 15 Aug. 1797.) 1797 (*bis*). [A dramatic version of Ann Radcliffe's novel, The Italian, in prose and verse.]

Cambro-Britons. An Historical Play in Three Acts. (Hay. 21 July 1798.) 1798. [Verse and prose.]

Aurelio and Miranda. D. (DL. 29 Dec. 1798.) 1798; 1799 (3rd edn). [Founded on Matthew Gregory Lewis's novel, The Monk. In verse.]

The Voice of Nature. A Play in Three Acts. (Hay. 31 July 1802.) 1803. [Founded on Le Jugement de Salomon of L. C. Caigniez.]

The Maid of Bristol. A Play [in three acts]. (Hay. 24 Aug. 1803.) 1803.

(b) Other Writings

A Letter to George Steevens; containing a critical examination of the papers of Shakspeare [forged by W. H. Ireland and] published by Samuel Ireland: to which are added Extracts from 'Vortigern.' 1796.

An Inquiry into the Authenticity of Various Pictures and Prints which have been offered to the Publick as Portraits of Shakspeare. 1824.

Memoirs of the Life of John Philip Kemble, including a History of the Stage from the Time of Garrick to the Present Period. 2 vols. 1825.

Memoirs of Mrs Siddons; interspersed with Anecdotes of Authors and Actors. 2 vols. 1827.

The Life of Mrs Jordan, including Original, Private Correspondence, and Numerous Anecdotes of her Contemporaries. 2 vols. 1831.

Memoirs of Mrs Inchbald; including her Familiar Correspondence with the most Distinguished Persons of her time. To which are added The Massacre and A Case of Conscience; now first published from her Autograph Copies. 2 vols. 1833.

On the Sonnets of Shakespeare: identifying the Persons to whom they are addressed, and elucidating Several Points in the Poet's History. 1837.

[Boaden also wrote 2 novels.]

ALFRED BUNN (1796–1860)
(a) Plays

Kenilworth. An Historical Drama in Two Acts. (CG. 8 March 1821.) [1821]; *Duncombe*, X, [1831?]; *Lacy*, XCVIII, [1874]. [In collaboration with T. Dibdin, and after Sir W. Scott.]

My Neighbour's Wife. F. (CG. 7 Oct. 1833.) *Lacy*, XVIII, [1855]; *Dicks*, 316, [1883].

The Minister and the Mercer. C. (DL. 8 Feb. 1834.) 1834. [An adaptation of Scribe's Bertrand et Raton.]

The Bohemian Girl. O. (DL. 27 Nov. 1843.) [1872.] [Tr. by Bunn; music by M. W. Balfe.]

The Daughter of St Mark. O. (DL. 27 Nov. 1844.) [1845.] [Tr. by Bunn; music by M.W. Balfe.]

The Enchantress. (DL. 14 May 1845.) [1845.] [Tr. by Bunn; music by M. W. Balfe.]

The Bondman. (DL. 11 Dec. 1846.) [1847.] [Tr. by Bunn; music by M. W. Balfe.]

[9 more pieces (mostly operas played at Drury Lane) are noted by Nicoll, p. 266.]

(b) Other Writings

Poems. 1816.

Tancred, a Tale, and Other Poems. 1819 (anon.).

A Letter to the Rev. J. A. James. With Notes, Critical, Religious, and Moral. Birmingham, 1824.

Songs, Duets, etc. in the Opera of the Bronze Horse, adapted from Scribe's Drama of 'le Cheval de Bronze.' [1836.]

The Stage; both before and behind the Curtain. 3 vols. 1840.

A Word with Punch. No. 1 (all pbd), [1847]. [A satire upon G. A. A'Beckett, D. W. Jerrold and M. Lemon, with extracts from their writings.]

Old England and New England, in a Series of Views taken on the Spot. 2 vols. 1853.

JOHN C. CROSS
(a) Collected Plays

Circusiana, or a Collection of the Most Favourite Ballets, Spectacles, Melodrames, etc. performed at the Royal Circus, St George's Fields. 2 vols. 1809 (re-issued 1812, as The Dramatic Works of J. C. Cross).

(b) Separate Plays

The Purse, or Benevolent Tar. A Musical Drama. (Hay. 8 Feb. 1794.) 1794 (bis); Dublin, 1794; 1797.

The Apparition! A Musical Dramatic Romance. (CG. 29 April 1794.) 1794.

The Raft, or Both Sides of the Water. A Musical Drama. (CG. 31 March 1798.) 1798.

The Enchanted Harp, or Harlequin for Ireland. P. (Royal Circus, 22 April 1802.) 1802.

The Rival Statues, or Harlequin Humourist. P. (Royal Circus, 11 April 1803.) 1803.

John Bull and Buonaparte, or a Meeting at Dover. Spec. (Royal Circus, 8 Aug. 1803.)

Pedler's Acre, or Harlequin Mendicant. (Royal Circus, 2 July 1804.) 1804.

The False Friend, or Assassin of the Rocks. (Royal Circus, 25 Aug. 1806.) [In Circusiana, 1809.]

[For other pieces by Cross, pbd and unpbd, see Nicoll (pp. 276–7, and Late Eighteenth Century Drama, pp. 249–50).]

(c) Other Writings

The Insolvent Debtor. A Simple Pathetic Tale [in verse], founded on Facts. To which is added a Small Collection of Miscellaneous Poetry. Salisbury, 1793.

Parnassian Bagatelles; being a Miscellaneous Collection of Poetical Attempts. 1796. [Contains 2 plays, both acted 1796.]

CHARLES DANCE (1794–1863)

A Match in the Dark. F. (Olympic, 21 Feb. 1833.) 1836.

The Beulah Spa. C. (Olympic, 18 Nov. 1833.) 1833.

Pleasant Dreams. F. (CG. 24 May 1834.) Lacy, LXXX, [1868]; Dicks, 590, [1884].

The Bengal Tiger. B. (Olympic, 18 Dec. 1837.) Leipzig, 1843 (in The Modern English Comic Theatre, ed. L. Hilsenberg, vol. I); Dicks, 366, [1883].

Naval Engagements. B. (Olympic, 3 May 1838.) Webster, IV, 1838; Dicks, 351, [1883].

Delicate Ground, or Paris in 1793. C. (Lyceum, 27 Nov. 1849.) Dicks, 1008, [1896].

A Morning Call. C. (DL. 17 March 1851.) Lacy, XXII, [1855].

Marriage a Lottery. C. (Strand, 20 May 1858.) Lacy, XXXVI, [1858].

[Nicoll lists 42 pieces by Dance (up to 1850 only) and particulars of some others are in DNB.]

CHARLES ISAAC MUNGO DIBDIN (1768–1833). [Known as CHARLES DIBDIN, Jr.]
(a) Plays

Wizard's Wake, or Harlequin's Regeneration. P. (Sadler's Wells, 23 Aug. 1802.) [1803.]

The Little Gipsies. O. (Sadler's Wells, 2 April 1804.) [1804.]

Harlequin and the Water Kelpe. P. (Sadler's Wells, 14 April 1806.) 1806.

The Wild Man, or the Water Pageant. O. (Sadler's Wells, 22 May 1809.) 1809.

The Council of Ten, or the Lake of the Grotto. O. (Sadler's Wells, 3 June 1811.) 1811.

The Farmer's Wife. O. (CG. 1 Feb. 1814.) 1814. Dicks, 110, [1883].

My Spouse and I. O. (DL. 7 Dec. 1815.) 1815; 1816; Dicks, 180, [1883].

Life in London, or the Day and Night Adventures of Logic, Tom and Jerry. Ext. (Olympic, 12 Nov. 1821.) 1821.

[Dibdin was enormously productive. Nicoll (pp. 280–6) lists 205 pieces by him. Most were pantomimes, operatic farces and melodramas, and only a few were ever ptd.]

(b) Other Writings

Mirth and Metre: consisting of Poems, Serious, Humorous, and Satirical. 1807.

Young Arthur, or the Child of Mystery. A Metrical Romance. 1819.

Comic Tales and Lyrical Fancies; including the Chessiad, a Mock Heroic, in Five Cantos; and the Wreath of Love, in Four Cantos. 1825.

History and Illustrations of the London Theatres. Comprising an Account of the Origin and Progress of the Drama in England. 1826.

THOMAS JOHN DIBDIN (1771–1841)

(a) Plays

The Mouth of the Nile, or the Glorious First of August. A Musical Entertainment. (CG. 6 April 1798.) 1798.

The Jew and the Doctor. F. (CG. 1800.) 1800; 1809 (in Mrs Inchbald's Collection of Farces, vol. ii); Cumberland, xxxiv, [1834?].

Il Bondocani, or the Caliph Robber. (CG. 15 Nov. 1800.) 1801.

The Cabinet. O. (CG. 9 Feb. 1802.) Dublin, 1802 (pirated); 1805; New York, 1809.

Two Faces under a Hood. O. (CG. 17 Nov. 1807.) [1807.]

Harlequin Harper, or a Jump from Japan. P. (DL. 27 Dec. 1813.) 1813.

Ivanhoe, or the Jew's Daughter. D. (Surrey, 20 Jan. 1820.) 1820; Cumberland Minor, ii, [1828?]; Lacy, xcii, [1872]. [From Sir W. Scott's novel.]

The Fate of Calas. D. (Surrey, 3 April 1820.) 1820; n.d.

[According to DNB. Dibdin wrote nearly 200 plays. Nicoll (pp. 286–95) notes 227. They include dramatic versions of several of Scott's novels.]

(b) Other Works

A Metrical History of England, or Recollections in Rhyme of some of the most Prominent Features in our National Chronology. 2 vols. 1813.

The Reminiscences of Thomas Dibdin. 2 vols. 1827.

Thomas Dibdin's Penny Trumpet. 1832. [A periodical, of which only 4 nos. appeared.]

Bunyan's Pilgrim's Progress metrically condensed. 1834.

[Dibdin also wrote many songs, and several collections were pbd.]

WILLIAM DIMOND (1780?–1836?)

The Sea-Side Story. O. (CG. 12 May 1801.) 1801.

The Hunter of the Alps. D. (Hay. 3 July 1804.) 1804; Cumberland, xxxix, [1839?]; Lacy, xci, [1872]; Dicks, 961, [1888].

The Foundling of the Forest. (Hay. 10 July 1809.) 1809; Philadelphia, 1810; Cumberland, xl, [1840?]; Lacy, xcix, [1874]; Dicks, 74, [1883].

Gustavus Vasa. O. (CG. 29 Nov. 1810.) 1811. [From his own melodrama, The Hero of the North, produced DL. 19 Feb. 1803.]

Brother and Sister. O. (CG. 1 Feb. 1815.) 1829; Lacy, xlvi, [1860].

The Lady and the Devil. O. (DL. 3 May 1820.) 1820; Cumberland, xlvi, [1846?]; Lacy, xc, [1871]; Dicks, 435, [1883]. [From La Dama Duende of Calderon.]

The Nymph of the Grotto, or a Daughter's Vow. O. (CG. 15 Jan. 1829.) 1829.

Stage Struck. F. (English Opera House, 12 Nov. 1835.) Lacy, x, [1853]; Dicks, 324, [1883].

[Nicoll, pp. 296–7, notes 23 further pieces by Dimond, mainly comic operas produced at Drury Lane and Covent Garden.]

JOHN THOMAS HAINES (1799?–1843)

The Idiot Witness, or a Tale of Blood. D. (Coburg, 6 Oct. 1823.) Duncombe, v, [1829?]; Lacy, xlvi, [1860].

Jacob Faithful, the Lighter Boy. A Tale of the Thames. D. (Surrey, 14 Dec. 1834.) Duncombe, xvi [1835?]; Dicks, 507, [1884].

My Poll and my Partner Joe. D. (Surrey, 31 Aug. 1835.) Lacy, lxxi, [1866]; Dicks, 500, [1884].

The Ocean of Life, or Every Inch a Sailor. D. (Surrey, 4 April 1836.) Lacy, lxix, [1866]; Dicks, 634, [1885].

Richard Plantagenet, or a Legend of Walworth. D. (Victoria, 1 Dec. 1836.) Dicks, 449, [1883].

Angeline de Lis. D. (St James's, 29 Sept. 1837.) Webster, iii, [1838]; Dicks, 669, [1885].

The Rye House Plot, or the Maltster's Daughter. D. (Sadler's Wells, 4 June 1838.) Dicks, 426, [1883].

Ruth, or the Lass that loves a Sailor. D. (Victoria, 23 Jan. 1843.) Lacy, xliv, [1860]; Dicks, 625, [1888].

[Nicoll, pp. 312–3, lists 33 further plays by Haines. Most were dramas and melodramas, nautical or of the 'blood-and-thunder' type, and the majority were produced either at the Surrey or the Victoria Theatre.]

JAMES HAYNES

(a) Plays

Conscience, or the Bridal Night. T. (DL. 2 Feb. 1821.) 1821.

Durazzo. T. (CG. Nov. 1838.) 1823.

Mary Stuart. T. (DL. 22 Jan. 1840.) 1840; Dicks, 749, [1886].

(b) Criticism

James Haynes's Conscience, or the Bridal Night. London Mag. III, 1821.

CHARLES KEMBLE (1775–1854)

(a) Plays

The Point of Honour. D. (Hay. 15 July 1800.) 1800; 1801; 1805; *Cumberland*, XXVIII, [1831?]; *Dicks*, 791, [1886]. [From L. S. Mercier's Le Deserteur.]
The Wanderer, or the Rights of Hospitality. D. (CG. 12 Jan. 1808.) 1808; [1809]. [Adapted from A. F. F. von Kotzebue's Eduard in Schottland. A rev. version was produced at CG. on 26 Nov. 1829 as The Royal Fugitive, with music by J. Stansbury.]
Plot and Counterplot, or the Portrait of Michael Cervantes. F. (Hay. 30 June 1808.) 1808; 1812; *Cumberland*, XLI, [1841?]; *Lacy*, XC, [1871]. [From Dieulafoi's Le Portrait de Michel Cervantes.]

[Nicoll, p. 324, gives 3 more plays, produced but not pbd.]

(b) Biography

Kemble (afterwards Butler), F. A. Record of a Girlhood. An Autobiography. 3 vols. 1878.
—— Records of Later Life. 3 vols. 1882.

JAMES KENNEY (1780–1849)

(a) Plays

Raising the Wind. F. (CG. 5 Nov. 1803.) 1803; 1804; *Dicks*, 208, [1883]; *Lacy*, Supplement, vol. II, [1857].
False Alarms, or my Cousin. O. (DL. 12 Jan. 1807.) 1807.
The World. C. (DL. 31 March 1808.) 1808.
Turn Him Out! O. (Lyceum, 7 March 1812.) 1812.
The Portfolio, or the Family of Anglade. D. (CG. 1 Feb. 1816.) 1816.
Sweethearts and Wives. D. (Hay. 7 July 1823.) 1823; *Webster*, XV, [1849]; *Dicks*, 228, [1883].
Spring and Autumn, or the Bride at Fifty. F. (Hay. 6 Sept. 1827.) *Lacy*, XXIV, [1856]; *Dicks*, 708, [1886].
The Sicilian Vespers. T. (Surrey, 21 Sept. 1840.) 1840. [From C. Delavigne's Les Vêpres siciliennes.]

[Nicoll lists a further 39 plays by Kenney (pp. 326–8).]

(b) Other Writings

Society, a Poem in Two Parts, with Other Poems. 1803.
Valdi, or the Libertine's Son. A Poem. 1820.

(c) Biography

Clayden, P. W. Rogers and his Contemporaries. 2 vols. 1889.

JAMES SHERIDAN KNOWLES (1784–1862)

(a) Collected Works

The Dramatic Works of James Sheridan Knowles. With a Memoir by R. Shelton Mackenzie. Baltimore, 1835; Calcutta, 1838.
Plays. The Hunchback, The Wife, The Beggar of Bethnal-Green, The Daughter. 1838. [Separate plays bound together, with a general title.]
The Dramatic Works. 3 vols. 1841; 2 vols. 1856; [1883].
Various Dramatic Works of James Sheridan Knowles. 2 vols. 1874 (priv. ptd).

(b) Separate Plays

Brian Boroihme, or the Maid of Erin. D. (Belfast, 1811; CG. 20 April 1837.) *Webster*, VIII, [1840]; *French*, CIX, [1878]; *Dicks*, 670, [1885]. [Adapted from D. O'Meara.]
Caius Gracchus. T. (Belfast, 13 Feb. 1815; DL. 18 Nov. 1823.) Glasgow, 1823; *Cumberland*, VI, [1827?]; *Dicks*, 298, [1883].
Virginius, or the Liberation of Rome. T. (Glasgow, 1820; CG. 17 May 1820.) 1820 (bis); 1824 (in Dolby's British Theatre, vol. XII); *Cumberland*, VI, [1827?]; *Dicks*, 246, [1883]; ed. M. J. Moses (in Representative British Dramas, Boston, 1918).
William Tell. D. (DL. 11 May 1825.) 1825; *Cumberland*, XXII, [1830?]; *Lacy*, LXXXIII, [1869]; *Dicks*, 238, [1883].
The Beggar's Daughter of Bethnal Green. C. (DL. 22 Nov. 1828.) 1828; *Dicks*, 695, [1885]. [Rev. and played at the Victoria in 1834 as The Beggar of Bethnal Green. Pbd 1834.]
The Hunchback. C. (CG. 5 April 1832.) 1832 (bis); 1836 (9th edn); *Lacy*, LXVII, [1866]; New York, [1876?]; tr. German, Vienna, 1838.
The Wife. A Tale of Mantua. (CG. 24 April 1833.) 1833 (6 edns); *French*, CIX, [1878]. [Charles Lamb wrote a prologue and an epilogue for this play.]
The Love-Chase. C. (Hay. 9 Oct. 1837.) 1837; *Cumberland*, XLI, [1840?]; *Lacy*, LXVIII, [1866]; *Dicks*, 322, [1883].

(c) Miscellaneous Works

The Welch Harper. A Ballad. 1796.
Fugitive Pieces. 1810.
The Elocutionist: a Collection of Pieces in Prose and Verse, peculiarly adapted to display the Art of Reading. Belfast, [1823?]; Belfast, 1831 (7th edn); New York, 1844; [1883] (28th edn).

Fortescue. A Novel. 1846 (priv. ptd); 3 vols. 1847.

George Lovell. A Novel. 3 vols. 1847.

The Rock of Rome, or the Arch Heresy. 1849.

The Idol demolished by its own Priest. An Answer to Cardinal Wiseman's Lectures on Transubstantiation. Edinburgh, 1851.

The Gospel attributed to Matthew is the Record of the whole original Apostlehood. 1855.

Old Adventures. [In The Tale Book, by Knowles and others, Königsberg, 1859.]

Lectures on Dramatic Literature. (Lectures on Oratory, Gesture and Poetry. To which is added a Correspondence with Four Clergymen in Defence of the Stage.) Ed. S. W. Abbott, and F. Harvey, 2 vols. 1873 (priv. ptd).

Tales and Novelettes. Rev. and ed. F. Harvey, 1874 (priv. ptd).

(d) Biography and Criticism

Hazlitt, W. The Spirit of the Age. 1825.

Horne, R. H. A New Spirit of the Age. Vol. II, 1844.

James Sheridan Knowles. Blackwood's Mag. XCIV, 1863.

Knowles, R. B. The Life of James Sheridan Knowles. Rev. and ed. F. Harvey, 1872 (priv. ptd).

Maginn, W. A Gallery of Illustrious Characters. Ed. W. Bates, [1873]; 1883. [Essay on Knowles first pbd, with drawing by Maclise, in Fraser's Mag. XIV, 1836.]

Hasberg, L. James Sheridan Knowles' Leben und dramatische Werke. Lingen, 1883.

Klapp, W. Sheridan Knowles' Virginius und sein angebliches französisches Gegenstück. Rostock, 1904.

Meeks, L. H. Sheridan Knowles and the Theatre of his Time. Bloomington, 1933. [With bibliography.]

MICHAEL ROPHINO LACY (1795–1867)

Love and Reason. C. (CG. 22 May 1827.) 1827. [Adapted from Scribe's Bertrand et Suzette.]

The Two Friends. C. (Hay. 11 July 1828.) Cumberland, XXXVII, [1835?]; Dicks, 679, [1885].

The Maid of Judah, or the Knights Templars. O. (CG. 7 March 1829.) Cumberland, XXV, [1829?]. [An adaptation of Scott's Ivanhoe.]

Robert the Devil, or the Fiend Father. O. (CG. 2 Feb. 1830.) Lacy, XXXI, [1857]. [According to Nicoll this appeared as Robert the Devil, Duke of Normandy, and was from L'Anneau de la Fiancée, attributed

by Genest to Raymond. The title given is from BM. catalogue which attributes the original to A. E. Scribe and G. Delavigne.]

Cinderella, or the Fairy-Queen and the Glass Slipper. O. (CG. 13 April 1830.) Lacy, XVIII, [1855].

Fra Diavolo, or the Inn of Terracina. (CG. 3 Nov. 1831.) 1831. [An adaptation of A. E. Scribe's Fra Diavolo, with music by Auber.]

Doing for the Best. D. (Sadler's Wells, 13 Nov. 1861.) Lacy, LV, [1862].

Doing my Uncle. F. (Surrey, 8 Sept. 1866.) Lacy, LXXII, [1867].

[Nicoll, p. 330, lists 7 other pieces by Lacy. According to DNB. he provided the first English adaptations of Semiramide, Cinderella, William Tell, Fra Diavolo, and others less famous. He wrote an oratorio called The Israelites in Egypt, for music by Handel and Rossini and collaborated in Schälcher's Life of Handel.]

MATTHEW GREGORY LEWIS (1775–1818)

[See p. 406 above.]

SAMUEL LOVER (1797–1868)

[See p. 407 above.]

CHARLES ROBERT MATURIN (1782–1824)

[See p. 408 above.]

HENRY M. MILNER

Barmecide, or the Fatal Offspring. D. (DL. 3 Nov. 1818.) 1818.

The Bandit of the Blind Mine. D. (Coburg, 15 Oct. 1821.) [1821.]

Frankenstein, or the Demon of Switzerland. D. (Coburg, 18 Aug. 1823.) Duncombe, II [1827?]; Lacy, LXXV, [1867]. [Based on Mrs Shelley's book of the same name.]

Alonzo the Brave and the Fair Imogene, or the Spectre Bride. D. (Coburg, 19 June 1826.) Duncombe, II, [1827?].

The Gambler's Fate, or a Laps of Twenty Years. D. (DL. 15 Oct. 1827.) 1827; Dicks, 308, [1883]. [Based on V. Ducange, Trente Ans, ou la Vie d'un Joueur.]

Mazeppa, or the Wild Horse of Tartary. D. (Royal Amphitheatre, 4 April 1831.) Cumberland Minor, V, [1831?]; New York, n.d.; Dicks, 620, [1885]. [Based on Byron's poem.]

Gustavus of Sweden, or the Masked Ball. D. (Victoria, 8 Nov. 1833.) Duncombe, XIII, [1834?]; Dicks, 630, [1885].

Dick Turpin's Ride to York. 'D. (Surrey, 30 Aug. 1841.) Dicks, 632, [1885].

[Nicoll, pp. 346–7, lists 22 further works by Milner. They were mostly melodramas, and were produced at various theatres.]

MARY RUSSELL MITFORD (1787–1855)
[See p. 409 above.]

WILLIAM THOMAS MONCRIEFF (1794–1857)

(a) Selected Works

Selections from the Dramatic Works of William Thomas Moncrieff. 3 vols. 1851.

(b) Plays

All at Coventry, or Love and Laugh. B. (Olympic, 8 Jan. 1816.) [1816]; *Richardson*, II, [1829]; *Lacy*, LIX, [1864].

Wanted a Wife, or a Cheque on my Banker's. C. (DL. 3 May 1819.) 1819.

The Spectre Bridegroom, or a Ghost in Spite of Himself. F. (DL. 2 July 1821.) 1821; New York, 1821; *Cumberland*, XVI, [1828?]; *Lacy*, XXXV, [1858]; *Dicks*, 353, [1883].

Tom and Jerry, or Life in London. CO. (Adelphi, 26 Nov. 1821.) 1826; *Cumberland*, XXXIII, [1834?]; *Lacy*, LXXXVIII, [1871]; *Dicks*, 82, [1883]. [Based on Pierce Egan's Life in London.]

The Cataract of the Ganges! or, The Rajah's Daughter. D. (DL. 27 Oct. 1823.) 1823; *Richardson*, III, [1830]; *Cumberland*, XXXIII, [1834?].

The Somnambulist, or the Phantom of the Village. D. (CG. 19 Feb. 1828.) 1828; *Cumberland*, V, [1827?]; *Lacy*, LXXXVI, [1870]; *Dicks*, 224, [1883]. [Founded on the ballet by A. E. Scribe and Aumer, called La Somnambule.]

Eugene Aram, or St Robert's Cave. D. (Surrey, 8 Feb. 1832.) *Cumberland Minor*, X; *French*, CIII, [1875]; *Dicks*, 312, [1883].

The Scamps of London, or the Cross Roads of Life. D. (Sadler's Wells, 13 Nov. 1843.) 1851; *Lacy*, LXXXI, [1869]; *Dicks*, 472, [1883].

[DNB. credits Moncrieff with upwards of 170 dramatic pieces. Nicoll (p. 348–51) lists 69, of very varied types.]

(c) Other Writings

Prison-Thoughts. Elegy written in the King's Bench, in imitation of Gray. 1821.

The New Guide to the Spa of Leamington Priors. To which is added Historical Notices of Warwick and its Castle. 1822; 1824.

Excursion to Stratford upon Avon; with a Compendious Life of Shakespeare, Account of the Jubilee, Catalogue of the Shakespeare Relics. Leamington, 1824.

Songs, Duets and Glees sung at the Royal Gardens, Vauxhall, [1827].

Poems. 1829. [Priv. ptd at the author's own press.]

The March of Intellect. A Comic Poem. 1830.

Old Booty! A Serio-Comic Sailor's Tale [in verse]. 1830.

The Triumph of Reform. A Comic Poem. With Six Plates by R. Seymour. [1832.]

An Original Collection of Songs, sung at the Theatres Royal, etc. [1850.]

[Moncrieff also edited Richardson's New Minor Drama, 4 vols. 1828–31.]

RICHARD BRINSLEY PEAKE (1792–1847)

(a) Plays

Amateurs and Actors. F. (English Opera House, 29 Aug. 1818.) 1818. *Cumberland*, XVI, [1828?]; *Dicks*, 962, [1888].

The Duel, or my Two Nephews. F. (CG. 18 Feb. 1823.) 1823; *Cumberland*, XXII, [1830?].

Jonathan in England. F. (English Opera House, 3 Sept. 1824.) *Dicks*, 589, [1884] (as Americans Abroad).

The Middle Temple, or 'Which is my Son?' (English Opera House, 27 June 1829.) *Webster*, I, 1837; *Dicks*, 692, [1885].

In the Wrong Box. F. (Olympic, 3 Feb. 1834.) 1834; *Dicks*, 737, [1886].

The Chain of Gold, or a Daughter's Devotion. B. (Adelphi, 29 Sept. 1834.) *Dicks*, 694, [1885].

Ten Thousand a Year. D. (Adelphi, 29 March 1844.) *Cumberland Minor*, XVI, [1840]; *Dicks*, 445, [1883].

The Title Deeds. C. (Adelphi, 21 June 1847.) [1847]; *Webster*, XIV, [1849]; *Dicks*, 1013, [1896].

[Nicoll, pp. 359–61, lists a further 40 pieces by Peake.]

(b) Other Writings

French Characteristic Costumes. 1816.

Snobson's Seasons, being Annals of Cockney Sports. [1838?]

Memoirs of the Colman Family, including their Correspondence with the most Distinguished Personages of their Time. 2 vols. 1841.

Cartouche, the Celebrated French Robber. 3 vols. 1844.

JAMES ROBINSON PLANCHÉ (1796–1880)

(a) Collected Plays

The Extravaganzas of J. R. Planché, 1825–1871. Ed. T. F. D. Croker and S. Tucker, 5 vols. 1879.

(b) Separate Plays

The Vampyre, or the Bride of the Isles. D. (English Opera House, 9 Aug. 1820.) 1820; *Cumberland*, XXVII, [1831?]; *French*, CVII, [1877]; *Dicks*, 875, [1887]. [Adapted from the French.]

Maid Marian, or the Huntress of Arlingford. O. (CG. 3 Dec. 1822.) [1822.] [Based on T. L. Peacock's novel.]

A Woman never Vext, or the Widow of Cornhill. C. (CG. 9 Nov. 1824.) [1824]; *Dicks*, 880, [1887]. [Based on Rowley's play.]

The Jenkinses, or Boarded and Done For. F. (DL. 9 Dec. 1830.) *Lacy*, VIII, [1853]; *Dicks*, 899, [1887].

Olympic Devils, or Orpheus and Eurydice. B. (Olympic, 26 Dec. 1831.) 1836; *Lacy*, XLI, [1859]. [Written with Charles Dance.]

Court Favour, or Private and Confidential. (Olympic, 29 Sept. 1836.) *Webster*, II, 1838; *Dicks*, 883, [1887].

Riquet with the Tuft. B. (Olympia, 26 Dec. 1836.) *Webster*, I, 1837 (with biographical sketch by B. Webster).

The Captain of the Watch. D. (CG. 25 Feb. 1841.) [1841]; *Lacy*, XVIII, [1855]. [Based on M. Lockroy's Le Chevalier du Guet.]

The King of the Peacocks. E. (Lyceum, 26 Dec. 1848.) [1849]; *Lacy*, XIX, [1856].

[Planché wrote 72 original pieces and adapted some 96 from the French, Spanish, Italian and German and from old English authors. A list to 1850 (154 items) will be found in Nicoll, pp. 366–73.]

(c) Other Writings

Costumes of Shakespeare's King John, [etc.] selected from the Best Authorities with Biographical, Critical and Explanatory Notices by J. R. Planché. 5 pts, 1823–5.

Shere Afkun, the First Husband of Nourmahal. A Legend of Hindoostan. 2 pts, 1823. [Poem.]

Descent of the Danube from Ratisbon to Vienna, during the Autumn of 1827. With Anecdotes and Recollections, Historical and Legendary. 1828.

History of British Costume. 1834; 1847; 1874.

Regal Records, or a Chronicle of the Coronation of the Queens Regnant of England. 1838.

The Pursuivant of Arms, or Heraldry founded upon Facts. 1852; [1859] (rev. edn); [1874].

The Recollections and Reflections of J. R. Planché: A Professional Autobiography. 2 vols. 1872.

William with the Ring. A Romance in Rhyme. 1873.

The Conqueror and his Companions. 2 vols. 1874.

A Cyclopaedia of Costume, or Dictionary of Dress: including Notices of Contempor-aneous Fashions on the Continent, and a General Chronological History of the Costumes of the Principal Countries of Europe. 2 vols. 1876–9.

Suggestions for establishing an English Art Theatre. 1879.

[Planché also wrote several other works on armoury, archaeology and cognate subjects, and tr. or ed. French and German fairy-tales, books on heraldry, etc.]

(d) Biography and Criticism

Obituary. Athenaeum, 5 June 1880.

Obituary. Journ. British Archaeological Ass. XXXVI, 1880.

Simpson, J. P. J. R. Planché. Theatre, Aug. 1880.

MacMillan, D. Planché's Early Classical Burlesques. Stud. Phil. XXV, 1928.

—— Burlesques with a Purpose, 1830–70. PQ VIII, 1929.

Rhodes, R. C. Library, XVI, 1935, pp. 96–103.

ISAAC POCOCK (1782–1835)

Hit or Miss! O. (Lyceum, 26 Feb. 1810.) 1810 (3 edns); 1811; 1816 (Dibdin's London Theatre, vol. VI); 1818; *Cumberland*, XXXIV [1834?].

The Miller and his Men. D. (CG. 21 Oct. 1813.) 1813; 1816; 1820; *Cumberland*, XXVI, [1831?]; Boston, 1856.

The Magpie or the Maid? D. (CG. 15 Sept. 1815.) [1815]; [1816]; Baltimore, 1831; *Cumberland*, XXVIII, [1831?]; *Lacy*, LXXXVII, [1870]. [Based on L. C. Caigniez, La Pie Voleuse.]

Robinson Crusoe, or the Bold Buccaneers. D. (CG. 7 April 1817.) 1817; *Cumberland*, XXVIII, [1831?]; *Lacy*, LXXXIX, [1871]. [Based on R. C. Guilbert de Pixérécourt, Robinson Crusoe.]

Rob Roy Macgregor, or Auld Lang Syne! O. (CG. 12 March 1818.) 1818 (*bis*); *Oxberry*, X, [1821]; *Lacy*, III, [1851]. [Based on Sir W. Scott's novel.]

Montrose, or the Children of the Mist. O. (CG. 14 Feb. 1822.) 1822; Baltimore, 1822. [Based on Sir W. Scott's Legend of Montrose.]

Nigel, or the Crown Jewels. D. (CG. 28 Jan. 1823.) 1823. [Based on Sir W. Scott's novel.]

The Robber's Bride. D. (CG. 22 Oct. 1829.) *Cumberland Minor*, XI, [1836?]; Boston, 1856; *Dicks*, 362, [1883].

[43 pieces in all are listed by Nicoll (pp. 373–5). They include a number of adaptations of Scott's novels in addition to those given above. Pocock was also a painter of note.]

JOHN POOLE (1786–1872)

(a) Plays

Hamlet Travestie. B. (New, 24 Jan. 1811.)
1810; 1811; 1817 (6th edn); Lacy, x, [1853];
New York, 1866.
The Hole in the Wall. F. (DL. 23 June 1813.)
1813; New York, 1813.
A Short Reign and a Merry One. F. (CG.
19 Nov. 1819.) 1819.
Simpson and Co. C. (DL. 5 Dec. 1822.) New
York, 1823; 1827; Cumberland, XLIII,
[1845?]; Lacy, LXXIV, [1867].
'Twould Puzzle a Conjuror. F. (Hay. 11
Sept. 1824.) Lacy, XIV, [1854]; Dicks,
648, [1885].
Paul Pry. C. (Hay. 13 Sept. 1825.) Dun-
combe, I, [1825]; New York, 1826; Lacy,
xv, [1854]; Dicks, 321, [1883]. Tr. German,
Stuttgart, 1854; Hungarian, Budapest, 1882.
Lodgings for Single Gentlemen. F. (Hay.
15 June 1829.) French, cxv, [1879]; Dicks,
403, [1883].
Patrician and Parvenu, or Confusion Worse
Confounded. C. (DL. 21 March 1835.)
1835.

[Nicoll, pp. 376–7, lists 23 further pieces,
mainly farces and comedies, and for the most
part produced at the Haymarket, Covent
Garden and Drury Lane.]

(b) Other Writings

Byzantium. A Dramatic Poem. N.d.
Crotchets in the Air; or, an [Un]scientific
Account of a Balloon-Trip, in a Familiar
Letter to a Friend. 1838 (bis).
Little Pedlington and the Pedlingtonians.
2 vols. 1839; 1860.
Phineas Quiddy, or Sheer Industry. 3 vols.
1843.
Christmas Festivities. Tales, Sketches, and
Characters, with Beauties of the Modern
Drama in Four Specimens. 1845–8.
The Comic Miscellany for 1845. 1845. [Ed. by
Poole.]
The Comic Sketch-Book or Sketches and
Recollections. 1859 ('new edn').

(c) Biography and Criticism

Fitzgerald, P. John Poole, Author of Paul
Pry. GM. XIII, 1874.

RICHARD JOHN RAYMOND

The Castle of Paluzzi, or the Extorted Oath.
D. (CG. 27 May 1818.) 1818.
Cherry Bounce. F. (Sadler's Wells, 27 Aug.
1821.) Lacy, LXIX, [1866]; Dicks, 360,
[1883].
Robert the Devil, or the Wizard's Ring.
(Coburg, 21 June 1830.) 1830; Cumberland,
XXXIII, [1834?].

The Deuce is in her. F. (Adelphi, 28 Aug.
1830.) Duncombe, VII [1830?]; Dicks, 993,
[1888].
The Farmer's Daughter of the Severnside, or
the Broken Heart. (Coburg, 11 April 1831.)
Lacy, XXVI, [1856].
The Old Oak Tree. D. (English Opera
House, 24 Aug. 1835.) Duncombe, XVIII,
[1835?].
Mrs White. O. (English Opera House, 23
June 1836.) Duncombe, XXII, [1836?];
Lacy, LV, [1862]; Dicks, 360, [1883].
The Discarded Daughter. (Surrey, 5 April
1847.) Duncombe, LIX, [1847?].

[Nicoll, pp. 378–9, lists 12 further pieces,
farces and dramas, played at various theatres.]

WILLIAM BARNES RHODES (1772–1826)

(a) Play

Bombastes Furioso. A Burlesque Tragic
Opera, in One Act. (Hay. 7 Aug. 1810.)
[Dublin], 1813; 1822 (bis, a pirated and the
first authorised edn); 1830; Duncombe,
XLVIII, [1845?]; Cumberland, XLIII, [1845?];
Lacy, III, [1851]; Dicks, 222, [1883].

(b) Other Writings

The Satires of Juvenal translated into English
Verse. 1801.
Epigrams, in Two Books. 1803.
Eccentric Tales in Verse. By Cornelius
Crambo. 1808.

(c) Biography

Bibliotheca Dramatica. A Catalogue of the
Dramatic Library of W. B. Rhodes, Esq.,
which will be sold by Auction by Mr
Sotheby. [1825.]
Obituary. GM. 1826, II, p. 471.

LORD JOHN RUSSELL, EARL RUSSELL
(1792–1878)

Don Carlos, or Persecution. A Tragedy, in
Five Acts. (Surrey, 8 June 1848.) 1822
(6 edns). [Trn of Schiller's drama.]
Caius Gracchus. Translated from T. Monti.
[1830.]

[For Russell's other writings, biographical,
political, historical and miscellaneous (including the suppressed story The Nun of
Arouca, 1822), see S. Walpole, The Life of
Lord John Russell, 2 vols. 1889, and p. 897
below.]

THOMAS JAMES SERLE

(a) Plays

Raffaelle Cimaro. T. (Unacted.) 1819.
The Man in the Iron Mask, or the Secrets of
the Bastille. D. (Coburg, 16 Jan. 1832.)
Duncombe Minor, 22, [1834]; Dicks, 428,
[1883].

The Merchant of London. D. (DL. 26 April 1832.) 1832; *Dicks*, 1033, [1897].
The Gamester of Milan. D. (Victoria, 21 April 1834.) *Duncombe*, xiv, [1834?].
The Ghost Story. D. (Adelphi, 4 Jan. 1836.) 1836.
The Parole of Honour. D. (CG. 4 Nov. 1837.)
Joan of Arc, the Maid of Orleans. D. (CG. 28 Nov. 1837.) 1837; *Duncombe*, xxxiv, [1838?]; *Dicks*, 1029, [1897].
Master Clarke. D. (Hay. 26 Sept. 1840.) *Dicks*, 1031, [1897].
[Nicoll, pp. 389–90, lists 15 further plays by Serle, mainly dramas and melodramas, played at Covent Garden and elsewhere.]

(b) Other Writings

Joan of Arc, the Maid of Orleans. 3 vols. 1841.
The Players, or the Stage of Life. 3 vols. 1847.

SIR MARTIN ARCHER SHEE (1769–1850)

(a) Play

Alasco. T. (Surrey, 5 April 1824.) 1824.

(b) Other Writings

Rhymes on Art, or the Remonstrance of a Painter; with Notes and a Preface, including Strictures on the State of the Arts, Criticism, Patronage, and Public Taste. 1805; 1805 (with additional preface, and notes).
Elements of Art. A Poem in Six Cantos; with Notes and a Preface; including Strictures on the State of the Arts, Criticism, Patronage and Public Taste. 1809.
The Commemoration of Reynolds, in Two Parts, with Notes and Other Poems. 1814.
Oldcourt. A Novel. 1829.
Cecil Hyde. A novel. 1834.

(c) Biography and Criticism

Shee, M. A. The Life of Sir Martin Archer Shee, President of the Royal Academy. 2 vols. 1860.

RICHARD LALOR SHEIL (1791–1851)

(a) Plays

Adelaide, or the Emigrants. T. (Dublin, Crow Street, 19 Feb. 1814.) Dublin, 1814; 1816.
The Apostate. T. (CG. 3 May 1817.) 1817 (4 edns); 1818.
Bellamira, or the Fall of Tunis. T. (CG. 22 April 1818.) 1818 (3 edns).
Evadne, or the Statue. T. (CG. 10 Feb. 1819.) 1819 (5 edns); *Dicks*, 25, [1883]. [An adaptation of Shirley's The Traitor.]
Damon and Pythias. T. (CG. 28 May 1821.) 1821; *Dicks*, 19, [1883]. [This play was by John Banim, but was altered and revised for the stage by Sheil.]

[Sheil also wrote 2 plays called Montoni, or the Phantom and The Huguenot, produced at Covent Garden in May 1820 and Dec. 1822 respectively. Neither was pbd. In 1824 he adapted Massinger's Fatal Dowry for Drury Lane.]

(b) Other Writings

The Speeches of the Right Honourable Richard Lalor Sheil, M.P., with a Memoir. Ed. T. MacNevin, Dublin, 1845.
Sketches of the Irish Bar. With Memoir and Notes by R. S. Mackenzie. 2 vols. New York, 1854–6. [W. H. Curran was joint-author of these. Sheil's own contributions, with other papers, were later rptd as Sketches, Legal and Political, ed. M. W. Savage, 2 vols. 1855.]

(c) Biography and Criticism

The Writings of Richard Lalor Sheil. Quart. Rev. xvii, 1817.
Richard Lalor Sheil. Fraser's Mag. xxxiii, 1846.
MacCullagh, afterwards MacCullagh Torrens, W. T. Memoirs of the Rt. Hon. Richard Lalor Sheil. 1855.

GEORGE SOANE (1790–1860)

(a) Plays

The Innkeeper's Daughter. D. (DL. 7 April 1817.) 1817; *Duncombe*, xliii, [1842?]; *French*, cxiv, [1879].
Self-Sacrifice; or The Maid of the Cottage. D. (English Opera House, 19 July 1819.) 1819.
The Hebrew. D. (DL. 2 March 1820.) 1820. [In verse. Based on Sir Walter Scott's Ivanhoe.]
Faustus. D. (DL. 16 May 1825.) 1825; *Cumberland*, xxxiii, [1834?]. [In verse.]
Pride shall have a Fall, or the Ladder of Life. C. (Coburg, 30 July 1832.) 1824.
Zarah, D. (Queen's, 7 Sept. 1835.) *Cumberland*, xxxv, [1835?]; *Lacy*, xcii, [1872]; *Dicks*, 357, [1883].
The Syren. O. (Princess's, 14 Oct. 1844.) [1844.] [Based on A. E. Scribe's La Sirène; music by Auber.]
Haydee, or the Secret. O. (Strand, 3 April 1848.) 1848. [Based on A. E. Scribe's Haydée; music by Auber.]
[Nicoll, pp. 393–4, lists 14 further dramatic works.]

(b) Other Writings

Knight Damon and a Robber Chief. 1812.
The Eve of St Marco. A Novel. 1813.
Specimens of German Romance. Selected and translated from Various Authors. 1826.

The Frolics of Puck. 1834.
Life of the Duke of Wellington, compiled from his Grace's Despatches, and Other Authentic Records and Original Documents. 2 vols. 1839–40.
The Last Ball, and Other Tales. 3 vols. 1843.
January Eve. A Tale of the Times. 1847.
New Curiosities of Literature, and Book of the Months. 2 vols. 1847.

CHARLES A. SOMERSET

Crazy Jane. D. (Surrey, 19 June 1827.) *Cumberland Minor*, II, [1828?].
The Roebuck, or Guilty and not Guilty. C. (Surrey, 1 Oct. 1827.) *Duncombe*, II, [1827?]; *Dicks*, 544, [1885]. [Adapted from Kotzebue.]
A Day after the Fair, or the Roadside Cottage. F. (Olympic, 5 Jan. 1829.) *Cumberland Minor*, III, [1829?]; New York, 1828 (for 1829?); *Lacy*, LXXVI, [1867]; *Dicks*, 415, [1883].
Home Sweet Home! or the Ranz des Vaches. D. (CG. 19 March 1829.) 1829; *Duncombe*, III, [1829?]; *Dicks*, 296, [1883]. [Adapted from the German.]
Shakespeare's Early Days. D. (CG. 29 Oct. 1829.) *Cumberland*, XXVIII, [1831?]; *Lacy*, XCIII, [1872]; *Dicks*, 792, [1886]. [First called The Life of William Shakespeare.]
The Female Mascaroni, or the Fair Brigands. O. (Surrey, 12 Feb. 1831.) *Cumberland Minor*, XIII, [1838?].
The Mistletoe Bough, or the Fatal Chest. (Garrick, 1834.) *Cumberland Minor*, XII, [1837?] (as The Mistletoe Bough, or Young Lovel's Bride); *Lacy*, C, [1874].
The Sea. D. (Queen's, 1834). *Cumberland Minor*, VII, [1834?]; *French*, CV, [1875].

[Nicoll, pp. 394–5, notes 17 further pieces, mainly burlettas and melodramas, and indicates that there were other plays after 1850.]

SIR THOMAS NOON TALFOURD (1795–1854)

(a) Collected Plays

Tragedies; to which are added a few Sonnets and Verses. 1844; 1852 (11th edn).

(b) Separate Plays

Ion. T. (CG. 26 May 1836.) [1835] (priv. ptd); [1835] (priv. ptd, with a few sonnets); 1836 (3 edns); 1837 (4 edns); New York, 1837; *Dicks*, 319, [1883].
The Athenian Captive. T. (Hay. 4 Aug. 1838.) 1838; New York, 1838; *Dicks*, 327, [1883].
Glencoe, or the Fate of the Macdonalds. T. (Hay. 23 May 1840.) 1839 (priv. ptd); 1840; *Dicks*, 323, [1883].
The Castilian. T. (Unacted?) 1853.

(c) Other Writings

Poems on Various Subjects. Including a Poem on the Education of the Poor; an Indian Tale; and the Offering of Isaac, a Sacred Drama. 1811.
The Letters of Charles Lamb, with a Sketch of his Life by T. N. Talfourd. 1837.
Speech delivered in the House of Commons on moving for Leave to bring in a Bill to consolidate the Law relating to Copyright and to extend the Term of its Duration. 1837.
Three Speeches in Favour of a Measure for an Extension of Copyright. 1840.
Speech for the Defendant in the Prosecution of the Queen v. Moxon for the Publication of Shelley's Works. 1841.
Recollections of a first Visit to the Alps, in August and September, 1841. [1842?] (priv. ptd).
Vacation Rambles and Thoughts. 2 vols. 1845; 1851 (3rd edn). [Supplement to Vacation Rambles, consisting of Recollections of a Tour through France to Italy, and homewards by Switzerland, in the Vacation of 1846, 1854.]
Final Memorials of Charles Lamb, consisting chiefly of his Letters not before published. By T. N. Talfourd. 1848; 1850.
Encyclopaedia Metropolitana. Ed. E. Smedley. [Contributions to The History of Greece, and of Rome, and on Early Greek Poetry, by Talfourd, c. 1848–50.]
The Importance of Literature to Men of Business: an Address delivered to Members of the Manchester Athenaeum. 1852.

[Talfourd also contributed important reviews and critical essays to The Pamphleteer, New Monthly Mag., and Retrospective Rev., 1816–25, and later to other periodicals.]

(d) Biography and Criticism

Horne, R. H. A New Spirit of the Age. Vol. I, 1844.
Dickens, C. The late Mr Justice Talfourd. Household Words, 25 March 1854.
A Memoir of Mr Justice Talfourd. By a Member of the Oxford Circuit. 1854.
Brain, J. A. An Evening with T. N. Talfourd. Reading, [1889]. [Lecture.]

BENJAMIN THOMPSON (1776?–1816)

(a) Plays

The Stranger. D. (DL. 24 March 1798). 1801, etc.; *Lacy*, XXII, [1855]; *Dicks*, 12, [1883]. [From the German of Kotzebue's Menschenhass und Reue.]

The German Theatre. 6 vols. 1800; 1801; 1811 (4th edn). [Contains trns of 19 plays, by Kotzebue, Goethe, Schiller and others.]

Ignes de Castro. T. (Unacted.) 1800. [From the Portuguese of Domingo Quita.]

Rokeby, or the Buccaneer's Revenge. D. (Unacted.) [Dublin], 1814.

Oberon's Oath, or the Paladin and the Princess. O. (DL. 21 May 1816.) 1816 (includes a memoir of Thompson).

[Thompson translated several other dramas of Kotzebue besides those included in The German Theatre. His own opera, Godolphin, was put on at Drury Lane on 12 Oct. 1813.]

(b) Other Writings

The Florentines, or Secret Memoirs of the Noble Family D. C.**. 1808.

An Account of the Introduction of Merino Sheep into the Different States of Europe and at the Cape of Good Hope. 1810.

JOHN TOBIN (1770–1804)

(a) Plays

The Honey Moon. C. (DL. 31 Jan. 1805.) 1805; 1807; Lacy, xvi, [1854], [etc.].

The Curfew. D. (DL. 19 Feb. 1807.) 1807 (7 edns), [etc.].

The School for Authors. C. (CG. 5 Dec. 1808.) 1808.

The Faro Table, or the Guardians. C. (DL. 5 Nov. 1816.) 1816.

[The farce All's Fair in Love (CG. 29 April 1803) is not in BM. The operatic farce Yours or Mine? (CG. 23 Sept. 1816) was pbd in 1820 with several other pieces, by E. O. Benger.]

(b) Biography and Criticism

Benger, E. O. Memoirs of John Tobin, with a Selection from his Unpublished Writings. 1820.

BENJAMIN NOTTINGHAM WEBSTER (1797–1882)

High Ways and By Ways. F. (DL. 15 March 1831.) Cumberland, xxviii, [1831?]. [From the French.]

Paul Clifford, the Highwayman of 1770, or Crime and Ambition. D. (Coburg, 12 March 1832.) Cumberland Minor, vi, [1832?]. [From Lytton's novel.]

The Modern Orpheus or Music the Food of Love. F. (CG. 15 April 1837.) Webster, i, 1837.

The Village Doctor, or the Hind's Disease. C. (Hay. 24 July 1839.) Webster, vii, [1840].

Caught in a Trap. F. (Hay. 25 Nov. 1843.) Webster, x, [1844].

Pierrot (the Married Man) and Polichinello (the Gay Single Fellow). B. (Adelphi, 27 Dec. 1847.) Webster, xiv, [1849].

Belphegor, the Mountebank, or Pride of Bath. D. (Adelphi, Jan. 1851.) Webster, xvii, [1853].

The Man of Law. D. (Hay. 9 Dec. 1851.) Webster, xvii, [1853].

[Webster wrote, adapted or translated about a hundred plays in all. A memoir of him will be found in his Acting National Drama, vol. iv, 1838.] H. B. G.

III. THE MID-NINETEENTH CENTURY DRAMA

ROBERTSON AND OTHER DRAMATISTS, 1835–1870

THOMAS WILLIAM ROBERTSON (1829–1871)

(1) COLLECTED PLAYS

The Principal Dramatic Works of T. W. Robertson. With a Memoir by his Son [T. W. S. Robertson]. 2 vols. 1889.

(2) ORIGINAL PLAYS

The Half Caste, or the Poisoned Pearl. D. (Surrey, 8 Sept. 1856.) Lacy, xcvii [1872].

The Cantab. F. (Strand, 14 Feb. 1861.) Lacy, L, [1861].

Society. C. (Liverpool, 1865; Prince of Wales's, 11 Nov. 1865.) Lacy, lxxi, [1866].

Ours. C. (Prince of Wales's, Liverpool, 23 Aug. 1866; Prince of Wales's, 16 Sept. 1866.) New York, [1879]; French, cxxxii, [1890].

Caste. C. (Prince of Wales's, 6 April 1867.) New York, [1878]; French, cxxxi, [1897?]; ed. M. J. Moses (in Representative British Dramas, Boston, 1918).

Play. C. (Prince of Wales's, 15 Feb. 1868.) French, cxxxii, [1890].

School. C. (Prince of Wales's, 16 Jan. 1869.) New York, [1879]; French, cxxxiii, [1891]; Philadelphia, 1903.

A Breach of Promise. F. (Globe, 10 April 1869.) French, cxxviii, [1888].

My Lady Clara. D. (Alexandra, Liverpool, 22 Feb. 1869; Gaiety, 27 March 1869, as Dreams.) New York, [1875?]; French, cxxxi, [1890] (as Dreams).

The Nightingale. D. (Adelphi, 15 Jan. 1870.) French, cxxxii, [1890].

M.P. C. (Prince of Wales's, 23 April 1870.) French, cxxxii, [1890].

Birth. C. (Bristol, New Theatre Royal, 5 Oct 1870.) French, cxxxi, [1890].

War. D. (St James's, 16 Jan. 1871.) French, cxxxiii, [1891].

Birds of Prey, or a Duel in the Dark. D. (Unacted?) *Lacy*, xciii, [1872].

Not at all Jealous. F. (Court, 29 May 1871.) *Lacy*, xci, [1872].

A Row in the House. F. (Toole's, 30 Aug. 1883.) *French*, cxxviii, [1888]. [Written about 1854.]

Peace at any Price. F. (Unacted?) *Lacy*, xcv, [1872].

(3) TRANSLATIONS OR ADAPTATIONS

The Chevalier de St George. From the French of M. Mélesville and R. de Beauvoir. D. (Princess's, 20 May 1845.) [1870?]

Noémie. From the French of A. D'Ennery and Clément. D. (Princess's, 14 April 1846.) *Lacy*, xxiii, [1856]; New York, n.d. [Played as Ernestine.]

Faust and Marguerite. From the French of M. Carré. D. (Princess's, April 1854.) *Lacy*, xv, [1854].

The Ladies' Battle. From the French of A. E. Scribe and Legouvé. C. (Unacted?) Boston, [1856?]; *Lacy*, Supplement, i, [1867].

My Wife's Diary. Adapted from 'Les Mémoires de Deux Jeunes Mariées' of A. D'Ennery and Clairville. F. (Olympic, 1854.) *Lacy*, xviii, [1855]. [Played as A Wife's Journal.]

Two Gay Deceivers, or Black, White and Grey. From E. M. Labiche's 'Deux profonds Scélérats.' F. (Strand, 1858?) *Lacy*, xxiii, [1856]. [In collaboration with T. H. Lacy.]

David Garrick. From the French of M. Mélesville's 'Sullivan.' C. (Prince of Wales's, Birmingham, April 1864; Hay. 30 April 1864.) New York, [1870?]; *French*, cxvii, [1881]; Philadelphia, 1903.

Robinson Crusoe. After A. E. Scribe's 'Un Verre d'Eau.' B. (Unacted?) [1865?]

Home. Founded on G. V. E. Augier's 'L'Aventurière.' C. (Hay. 14 Jan. 1869.) New York, [1879]; *French*, cxxxi, [1890]; New York, [1890?].

Progress. Founded on V. Sardou's 'Les Ganaches.' C. (Globe, 18 Sept. 1869.) *French*, cxxxiii, [1891].

The Star of the North. From the French. D. (Unacted?) *Lacy*, xciii, [1872].

[DNB. notes a number of other plays, which have remained unprinted.]

(4) OTHER WRITINGS

David Garrick. A Love Story. 1865. [A novel.]

Dazzled not Blinded. [?] [A novel.]

Stephen Caldrick. [?] [A novel.]

The Ring. [In A Bunch of Keys, ed. T. Hood, 1865.]

The Poor-Rate. [In Rates and Taxes, ed. T. Hood, 1866.]

Exceptional Experiences. [In A. Halliday, The Savage Club Papers for 1868.]

(5) BIOGRAPHY AND CRITICISM

The Comedies of T. W. Robertson. Broadway, vi, 1870.

Friswell, J. H. Modern Men of Letters. 1870.

Thomas William Robertson and the Modern Theatre. Temple Bar, xliv, 1875.

Jones, W. W. Thomas W. Robertson as a Dramatist. Theatre, 1879, i.

Pemberton, T. E. The Life and Writings of T. W. Robertson. 1893.

Hawkins, F. Academy, 3 June 1893. [Review of preceding item.]

Shaw, G. B. T. W. Robertson's 'Caste.' Saturday Rev. lxxxiii, 1897, p. 685.

Grein, K. Thomas William Robertson (1829–1871). Ein Beitrag zur Geschichte des neueren englischen Dramas. Marburg, 1911.

Armstrong, C. F. Shakespeare to Shaw. Studies in the Life's Work of Six Dramatists of the English Stage. 1913.

Harrison, D. Tom Robertson. A Century of Criticism. Contemporary Rev. April 1929.

Rahill, F. A Mid-Victorian Regisseur. Theatre Arts Monthly, Nov. 1929.

Bulloch, J. M. Dame Madge Kendal's Robertson Ancestors. N. & Q. 3, 10, 17 Dec. 1932.   H. B. G.

OTHER DRAMATISTS (1835–1870)

GILBERT ABBOTT À BECKETT (1811–1856)

(a) Plays

The Man with the Carpet Bag. F. (Strand, 1835.) *Cumberland Minor*, xiii, [1838?]; *Lacy*, lxviii, [1866].

The Postillion. B. (St James's, 13 March 1837.) *Cumberland*, xliii, [1845?].

Don Caesar de Bazan. D. (Princess's, 8 Oct. 1844.) *Lacy*, xii, [1853]; *Dicks*, 800, [1884]. [With M. Lemon; based on the play by Dumanois and Dennery.]

The School for Sentiment, or the Tar! the Tear!! and the Tilbury!!! (In Scenes from the Rejected Comedies for B. Webster's £500 Prize.) 1844.

The Chimes, or a Goblin Tale. D. (Adelphi, 19 Feb. 1844.) *Webster*, xi, [1845]. [From Dickens's novel; in collaboration with M. Lemon.]

St George and the Dragon. B. (Adelphi, 24 March 1845.) *Webster*, xi, [1845]. [With M. Lemon.]

Peter Wilkins, or the Loadstone Rock and the Flying Indians. D. (Adelphi, 9 April 1846.) *Webster*, xii, [1846]. [With M. Lemon.]

The Castle of Otranto. B. (Hay. 24 April 1848.) *Webster*, xiv, [1848]. [In verse.]

[à Beckett is supposed to have written '50 or 60' pieces. Nicoll lists 42 (pp. 239–41), mainly burlesques and farces.]

(b) Comic Histories, etc.

The Comic Blackstone. 1844; 1846 (with illustrations by G. Cruikshank).

The Quizziology of the British Drama. 1846.

The Comic History of England, with Coloured Etchings and Woodcuts by John Leech. 2 vols. 1847–8; 1894; [1897?].

The Comic History of Rome. Illustrated by John Leech. 1852; [1897].

(c) Biography and Criticism

A'Beckett, A. W. The à Becketts of 'Punch': Memories of Father and Sons. 1903.

GEORGE ALMAR

The Rover's Bride, or the Bittern's Swamp. D. (Surrey, 30 Oct. 1830.) *Cumberland Minor*, xi, [1836?].

Pedlar's Acre, or the Wife of Seven Husbands. D. (Surrey, 22 Aug. 1831.) *Cumberland Minor*, ix [1835?]; *Lacy*, lxxxiv, [1867]; *Dicks*, 280, [1884].

The Tower of Nesle. D. (Surrey, 17 Sept. 1832.) *Cumberland Minor*, vi [1832?]; *Lacy*, xci, [1872]; *Dicks*, 234, [1883].

The Knights of St John, or the Fire Banner. D. (Sadler's Wells, 26 Aug. 1833.) *Duncombe*, xii, [1833]; *Lacy*, lvi, [1863].

The Clerk of Clerkenwell, or, the Three Black Bottles. D. (Sadler's Wells, 27 Jan. 1834.) *Cumberland Minor*, vii, [1834?].

The Bull-Fighter, or the Bridal Ring. D. (Surrey, 8 Oct. 1838.) *Cumberland Minor*, xiv, [1838?].

Oliver Twist, or the Parish Boy's Progress. D. (Surrey, 19 Nov. 1838.) *Webster*, vi, [1840]; *Dicks*, 293, [1884]. [After Dickens.]

Jane of the Hatchet, or the Siege of Beauvais. Spec. (Surrey, 20 July 1840.) *Duncombe*, xli, [1840?].

[Almar's 17 pbd and 34 unpbd plays, chiefly melodramas, are listed in Nicoll, pp. 242–3.]

MORRIS BARNETT (1800–1856)

The Bold Dragoons. B. (Adelphi, 9 Feb. 1830.) *Lacy*, ix, [1853]; *Dicks*, 509, [1884?].

Tact, or the Wrong Box. F. (Queen's, 21 Feb. 1831.) *Duncombe*, xiii, [1833?].

Mrs G. of the Golden Pippin. A Musical Entertainment. (Queen's, 14 March 1831.) *Duncombe*, viii, [1831?].

The Spirit of the Rhine. D. (Queen's, 22 Sept. 1835.) *Duncombe*, xix, [1836?].

The Yellow Kids. B. (Adelphi, 19 Oct. 1835.) *Duncombe*, xviii, [1835?]; *Dick*, 967, [1888].

Monsieur Jacques. B. (St James's, 13 Jan. 1836.) *Dicks*, 503, [1884?]; *Lacy*, xxviii, [1857]. [From Cogniard's Le Pauvre Jacques.]

The Serious Family. F. (Hay. 30 Oct. 1849.) *Dicks*, 1007, [1896?]. [From Le Mari à la Campagne.]

Sarah the Creole, or a Snake in the Grass. D. (Olympic.) *Lacy*, xxxi, [1858].

[BM. Catalogue gives 6 other plays, and Nicoll (p. 251) notes an early unpbd burletta.]

THOMAS LOVELL BEDDOES (1803–1849)

[See p 248 above.]

WILLIAM BAYLE BERNARD (1807–1875)

(a) Plays

The Four Sisters. F. (Strand, 3 May 1832.) *Lacy*, xxiii, [1855].

Lucille, or the Story of a Heart. D. (Lyceum, 4 April 1836.) 1836. [Founded on Lytton's Pilgrims of the Rhine.]

Marie Ducange. An Original Domestic Drama. (Hay. 29 May 1841.) *Lacy*, xxxii, [1857].

The Round of Wrong, or a Fireside Story. D. (Hay. 19 Dec. 1846.) *Dicks*, 1000, [1888].

The Passing Cloud. A Romantic Drama. (DL. 8 April 1850.) *Lacy*, i, [1852].

The Evil Genius. C. (Hay. 8 March 1856.) *Lacy*, xxvi, [1856].

A Life's Trial. D. (Hay. March 1857.) *Lacy*, xxx, [1857].

The Tide of Time. C. (Hay. 13 Dec. 1858.) *Lacy*, xxxviii, [1859].

[Bernard wrote some 40 plays, most of which are listed in Nicoll, pp. 255–6.]

(b) Other Work

The Life of Samuel Lover, Artistic, Literary and Musical, with Selections from his Unpublished Papers and Correspondence. 2 vols. 1874.

EDWARD LITT LEMAN (LAMAN) BLANCHARD (1820–1889)

(a) Plays

The Artful Dodge. F. (Olympic, 21 Feb. 1842.) *Lacy*, xlii, [1859].

Pork Chops. Ext. (Olympic, 13 Feb. 1843.) *Lacy*, xlv, [1860] (as Pork Chops, or a Dream at Home).

Faith, Hope and Charity, or Chance and Change. D. (Surrey, 7 July 1845.) *Duncombe*, liv, [1845?].

Adam Buff, or the Man without a ——! F. (Surrey, 4 March 1850.) *Duncombe*, lxv, [1850?].

Cherry and Fair Star, or the Singing Apple, the Talking Bird, and the Dancing Waters. P. (Sadler's Wells, Dec. 1861.) [1862.]

Harlequin and the House that Jack built. P. (DL.) [1862.]

Riquet with the Tuft, or Harlequin and Old Mother Shipton. P. (Princess's.) [1863.]

An Induction. The Three Temptations. [In Drawing-Room Plays, ed. C. Scott, 1870.]

[Blanchard also wrote many other pieces, mainly DL. pantomimes, some of which are recorded in Nicoll (pp. 258–9) and W. D. Adams, A Dictionary of the Drama, vol. i, 1904.]

(b) Other Writings

Adams's Illustrated Descriptive Guide to the Watering-Places of England, and Companion to the Coast. 2 vols. 1848.

The Stranger's and Visitor's Conductor through London. 1851; 1857 (as Bradshaw's Guide through London and its Environs).

A Handy Book on Dinners. Dinners and Diners at Home and Abroad. With Piquant Plates and Choice Cuts. 1860.

(c) Biography and Criticism

Scott, C. and Howard, C. The Life and Reminiscences of E. L. Blanchard. 2 vols. 1891.

DIONYSIUS LARDNER BOUCICAULT
(1822–1890)

(a) Plays

London Assurance. C. (CG. 4 March 1841.) 1841 (bis); Lacy, XXXIV, [1858]; Dicks, 1044, [1898]; ed. M. J. Moses (in Representative British Dramas, Boston, 1918).

The Old Guard. D. (Princess's, 9 Oct. 1843.) Dicks, 1056, [1900].

Old Heads and Young Hearts. C. (Hay. 18 Nov. 1844.) [1845.]

The Knight of Arva. C. (Hay. 22 Nov. 1848.) New York, [1868?].

The Queen of Spades. D. Adapted from La Dame de Pique [of A. E. Scribe]. (DL. 29 March 1851.) Lacy, XXIV, [1856].

The Colleen Bawn, or the Brides of Garryowen. D. (New York, Dec. 1859; Adelphi, 10 Sept. 1860.) Lacy, LXIII, [1865]; Dicks, 389, [1884]. [Founded on G. Griffin's novel, The Collegians. In 1862 made into the opera (The Lily of Killarney) by O. Benedict.]

Arragh-na-Pogue, or the Wicklow Wedding. (Theatre Royal, Dublin, 5 Nov. 1864; Princess's, 22 March 1865.) [1865]; Chicago, n.d.

The Shaughraun. D. (DL. 4 Sept. 1875.) Lacy, CXXIII, [1885]; New York, [1885?].

[Boucicault wrote, in all, over 50 pieces, either alone or in collaboration.]

(b) Biography and Criticism

Dion Boucicault on Himself. Theatre, Nov. 1879.

Dion Boucicault as a Dramatist. Saturday Rev. LXI, 1886.

Dion Boucicault. Critic (New York), IX, 1886.

Leaves from the Diary of Dion Boucicault. North American Rev. CXLIX, 1889.

Obituary. Athenaeum, 27 Sept. 1890.

Walsh, T. The Career of Dion Boucicault. [1915.]

CHARLES WILLIAM SHIRLEY BROOKS
(1816–1874)

(a) Plays

The Wigwam. B. (Lyceum, 25 Jan. 1847.) Dicks, 1004, [1890].

The Creole, or Love's Fetters. D. (Lyceum, 8 April 1847.) Lacy, I, [1852]; Dicks, 1009, [1896].

Anything for a Change. F. (Lyceum, 7 June 1848.) Lacy, IV, [1852]; [1872?].

The Daughter of the Stars. D. (Strand, 5 Aug. 1850.) Lacy, II, [1851].

The Exposition. A Scandinavian Sketch [in verse]. (Strand, 28 April 1851.) Lacy, III, [1851].

The Guardian Angel. F. (Hay. 1852?) Lacy, V, [1852?].

Timour the Tartar! or the Iron Master of Samarkand-by-Oxus. (Olympic, 26 Dec. 1860.) Lacy, XLIX, [1861]. [With J. Oxenford.]

[Brooks produced 3 other plays (Nicoll, p. 261) which have apparently not been pbd.]

(b) Other Writings

The Opera. The Coulisses. Foreign Gentlemen in London. [In A. R. Smith's Gavarni in London, 1849.]

The Russians of the South. 1854.

Aspen Court. A Story of Our Own Time. 3 vols. 1855; 1857 (rev.).

The Gordian Knot. A Story of Good and Evil. With Illustrations by J. Tenniel. [1858]–1860.

The Silver Cord. A Story. 3 vols. 1861.

Sooner or Later. With Illustrations by G. du Maurier. 2 vols. 1868.

The Naggletons, and Miss Violet and her 'Offers.' 1875.

Wit and Humour. Poems from 'Punch.' 1875. [Ed. by Brooks.]

[Brooks also contributed regularly to Punch from 1851, becoming editor in 1870.]

(c) Biography and Criticism

Jerrold, B. Shirley Brooks. GM. XII, 1874.
Layard, G. S. A Great 'Punch' Editor: being the Life, Letters and Diaries of Shirley Brooks. 1907.

ROBERT BARNABAS BROUGH (1828–1860)

(a) Plays

The Enchanted Isle, or 'Raising the Wind' on the most Approved Principles. A Drama without the Smallest Claim to Legitimacy, Consistency, Probability, or Anything else but Absurdity, in which will be found much that is unaccountably Coincident with Shakspere's 'Tempest.' Ext. (Amphitheatre, Liverpool, 1848; Adelphi, 20 Nov. 1848.) [1848]; Webster, XIV, [1849]. [With W. Brough.]
Camaralzaman and Badoura, or the Peri who loved the Prince. Ext. (Hay. 26 Dec. 1848.) Webster, XV, [1849]. [With W. Brough.]
The Sphinx. Ext. (Hay. 9 April 1849.) Webster, XV, [1849]. [With W. Brough.]
The Second Calendar. An Extravaganza in Two Acts. (Hay.?) Webster, XVI, [1851]. [With W. Brough.]
A Cracker Bon-Bon for Christmas Parties. 1852. [Includes 3 short plays (unacted) and Christmas miscellanies in prose and verse.]
The Siege of Troy. A Burlesque in One Act. (Unacted?) 1858.
Alfred the Great, or the Minstrel King. Ext. (Olympic, 26 Dec. 1859.) Lacy, XLIII, [1860]. [With W. Brough.]

[Other extravaganzas by the brothers Brough will be found in Lacy, VI, XIV, XV, XXVII, XXIX, XXXII, LIII, LXXXVIII and Supplement, II.]

(b) Fiction

The Alain Family. A Tale. 1853. [Tr. by Brough from the French of J. B. A. Karr.]
The Life of Sir John Falstaff. With a Biography of the Knight, from Authentic Sources. 1857–8. [Illustrated by George Cruikshank. Issued in 10 pts at one shilling each and subsequently bound up to form one vol.]
Alf the Minstrel or The Princess Diamonducky and the Hazel Fairy. A Dragon Story for Christmas. 1859.
Miss Brown. A Romance; and Other Tales in Prose and Verse. 1860. [Rptd from The Welcome Guest, a periodical ed. by Brough for a short time.]
Which is Which? or, Miles Cassidy's Contract. 2 vols. 1860.
Marston Lynch. A Personal Biography. With a Memoir of the Author by G. A. Sala. 1860. [First pbd in The Train, 1856–7.]

Shadow and Substance. By C. H. Bennett and R. B. Brough. 1860.
Character Sketches. By C. H. Bennett and R. B. Brough. [1872.]

(c) Poems

Songs of the Governing Classes and Other Lyrics. 1855; 1890.
Béranger's Songs. Translated into English Verse. 1856.

(d) Criticism

Archer, W. Robert Brough. [In The Poets and the Poetry of the Century, ed. A. H. Miles, vol. V, 1893.]

JOHN BALDWIN BUCKSTONE (1802–1879)

(a) Plays

Luke the Labourer, or the Lost Son. D. (Adelphi, 17 Oct. 1826.) Cumberland Minor, II, [1828]; Lacy, LXIX, [1866]; Dicks, 830, [1887]; ed. A. E. Morgan (in English Plays, 1660–1820, 1935).
The May Queen, or Sampson the Serjeant. B. (Adelphi, 9 Oct. 1828.) 1834; Dicks, 818, [1886].
Ellen Wareham. D. (Hay. 24 April 1833.) Dicks, 837, [1887].
Agnes de Vere, or the Wife's Revenge. D. (Adelphi, 10 Nov. 1834.) 1836; Lacy, CVI, [1876]; Boston, 1885.
The Green Bushes, or a Hundred Years Ago. (Adelphi, 27 Jan. 1845.) Webster, XI, [1846]; Boston, [1857?]; Dicks, 827, [1887].
The Flowers of the Forest. A Gipsy Story. D. (Adelphi, 11 March 1847.) Webster, XIII, [1847]; Boston, [1857?]; Dicks, 1002, [1896].
Nine too Many. B. (Adelphi, 11 March 1847.) Dicks, 1004, [1890].
An Alarming Sacrifice. F. (Hay. 12 July 1849.) Boston, [1885?]; Dicks, 1012, [1892].

[Nicoll (pp. 262–5) lists 80 works by Buckstone (comedies, dramas, farces, etc.), mostly produced at the Adelphi and the Haymarket, to 1850 only.]

(b) Biography and Criticism

John Baldwin Buckstone. Once a Week, XXVII, 1872.
Maginn, W. A Gallery of Illustrious Characters. Ed. W. Bates, [1873]; 1883. [The essay on Buckstone was first pbd, with a drawing by Maclise, in Fraser's Mag. XIV, 1836.]
Taylor, T. Impressions of John Baldwin Buckstone. Theatre, Dec. 1879.

JOSEPH STIRLING COYNE (1803–1868)

(a) Plays

The Queer Subject. F. (Adelphi, 28 Nov. 1836.) Webster, I, [1837]; Dicks, 782, [1886].

Valsha, or the Slave Queen. B. (Adelphi, 30 Oct. 1837.) *Webster*, II, [1838]; *Dicks*, 702, [1886]. [Adapted from La Guerre des Servantes.]

How to settle Accounts with your Laundress. F. (Adelphi, 26 July 1847.) *Webster*, XIV, [1849]; *Dicks*, 1006, [1896].

The Hope of the Family. C. (Hay. 3 Dec. 1853.) *Lacy*, XIII, [1854].

The Secret Agent. C. (Hay. 10 March 1855.) *Lacy*, XVIII, [1855]. [Partly from the German.]

The Man of Many Friends. C. (Hay. 1 Sept. 1855.) *Lacy*, XXIII, [1855]; New York, 1855.

The Love-Knot. C. (DL. 8 March 1858.) *Lacy*, XXXV, [1858]; Boston, [1858?].

The Woman in Red. A Drama, in a Prologue and Three Acts. Adapted and altered from La Tireuse des Cartes. (St James's, 13 April 1868.) *Lacy*, XCII, [1872].

[According to DNB. Coyne wrote 'upwards of fifty-five' pieces. 26 are noted by Nicoll (to 1850 only, pp. 274–5). He also wrote plays in collaboration with H. C. Coape, H. Hamilton and F. Talfourd.]

(b) Other Writings

The Barmaid. The Potato Can. [In Albert R. Smith's Gavarni in London, 1849.]

Pippins and Pies, or Sketches out of School. 1855.

Sam Spangles, or the History of a Harlequin. 1866.

'Oil is better for a Wig than Vinegar.' A Dramatic Proverb. [In Mixed Sweets from Routledge's Annual, [1867].]

'HENRY THORNTON CRAVEN,' *i.e.* HENRY THORNTON (1818–1905)

Done Brown. F. (Adelphi, Edinburgh, 1845.) *Duncombe*, LVI, [1846?]; *Lacy*, LXXXI, [1869].

Bletchington House, or the Surrender. D. (City of London, 20 April 1846.) *Duncombe*, LVI, [1846?].

The Village Nightingale. O. (Strand, 12 June 1851.) *French*, CVIII, [1877].

Bowl'd out, or a Bit of Brummagem. F. (Princess's, 9 July 1860.) *Lacy*, XLVII, [1860].

The Chimney Corner. D. (Olympic, 21 Feb. 1861.) *Lacy*, L, [1861].

Miriam's Crime. D. (Strand, 9 Oct. 1863.) *Lacy*, LX, [1864].

Milky White. A Serio-Comic Drama. (Prince of Wales's, Liverpool, 20 June 1864; Strand, 28 Sept. 1864.) *Lacy*, LXXXV, [1870].

Meg's Diversion. D. (Royalty, 17 Oct. 1866.) *Lacy*, LXXIII, [1867].

[BM. catalogue notes 10 other plays and one novel.]

CHARLES DICKENS (1812–1870)
[See p. 447 above.]

RICHARD HENGIST HORNE (1803–1884)
[See p. 290 above.]

DOUGLAS WILLIAM JERROLD (1803–1857)

(a) Collected Works

The Writings of Douglas Jerrold. 8 vols. 1851–4.

The Works of Douglas Jerrold. With an Introductory Memoir by his Son, W. B. Jerrold. 4 vols. 1863–4.

(b) Plays

Paul Pry. F. (Coburg, 27 Nov. 1827.) *Lacy*, XLVII, [1860]; *Dicks*, 982, [1888].

Fifteen Years of a Drunkard's Life. D. (Coburg, 24 Nov. 1828). *Duncombe*, III, [1829?]; *Dicks*, 220, [1883].

Black-Eyed Susan, or All in the Downs. D. (Surrey, 8 June 1829.) *Duncombe*, IV [1829?]; *Lacy*, XXIII, [1855]; Boston, [1857?]; *Dicks*, 230, [1883]; ed. M. J. Moses (in Representative British Dramas, Boston, 1918).

The Mutiny at the Nore, or British Sailors in 1797. D. (Royal Pavilion, 7 June 1830.) *Lacy*, LXXVIII, [1868]; *Dicks*, 795, [1886].

The Bride of Ludgate. C. (DL. 8 Dec. 1831.) *Cumberland*, XXX, [1832?]; *Lacy*, XCIII, [1872]; *Dicks*, 530, [1884].

The Rent Day. D. (DL. 25 Jan. 1832.) 1832. *Lacy*, XV, [1854]; *Dicks*, 210, [1883].

Beau Nash, the King of Bath. C. (Hay. 16 July 1834.) 1834; *Dicks*, 554, [1884].

Time works Wonders. C. (Hay. 26 April 1845.) 1845; *Lacy*, XCII, [1872]; *Dicks*, 851, [1887].

[Nicoll (to 1850 only, pp. 321–3) notes 53 further plays by Jerrold, and DNB. 4 more. Most were comedies or melodramas.]

(c) Other Writings

Men of Character. 3 vols. 1838.

Heads of the People. Drawn by Kenny Meadows, described by Douglas Jerrold [and others]. 2 vols. 1840–1.

Punch's Letters to his Son. 1843.

The Story of a Feather. 1844.

Punch's Complete Letter Writer. 1845.

The Chronicles of Clovernook; with Some Account of the Hermit of Bellyfulle. 1846.

Mrs Caudle's Curtain Lectures. 1846, etc.; ed. W. Jerrold, 1907 (World's Classics). Tr. Hungarian, Kolozsvarth, 1860; French, Paris, 1865; German, Leipzig, 1869; Swedish, Stockholm, 1872; Italian, Bologna, 1885.

A Man made of Money. 1849.

Cakes and Ale. 1852. [Tales and essays.]

The Brownrigg Papers. Ed. B. Jerrold, 1860.
Other Times: being Liberal Leaders contributed to Lloyd's Weekly Newspaper by Douglas and Blanchard Jerrold. 1868.
The Barber's Chair; and the Hedgehog Letters. Ed. B. Jerrold, 1874. [Rptd from Douglas Jerrold's Weekly Newspaper.]
Tales, now first collected, with a Biographical Notice by J. L. Robertson. 1891.

(d) Biography and Criticism

Horne, R. H. A New Spirit of the Age. Vol. I, 1844.
Powell, T. Pictures of the Living Authors of Britain. 1851.
Hannay, J. Douglas Jerrold. Atlantic Monthly, I, 1858.
Jerrold, W. B. The Life and Remains of Douglas Jerrold. 1859.
Phillips, G. S. Douglas Jerrold. North American Rev. LXXXIX, 1859.
Stirling, J. H. Jerrold, Tennyson and Macaulay. Edinburgh, 1868.
Bedford, H. Douglas Jerrold. Month, XII, 1870.
Copping, E. Douglas Jerrold. New Rev. VII, 1892.
Fyvie, J. Douglas Jerrold. Macmillan's Mag. LXXXVII, 1903.
Jerrold, W. Douglas Jerrold and 'Punch.' 1910.
—— Douglas Jerrold, Dramatist and Wit. 2 vols. [1914].

MARK LEMON (1809–1870)
(a) Plays

P.L.; or 30 Strand. F. (Strand, 25 April 1836.) Duncombe, XXII, [1836?]; Dicks, 977, [1888].
The M.P. for the Rotten Borough. F. (English Opera House, 27 July 1838.) Dicks, 719, [1886].
A Familiar Friend. B. (Olympic, 8 Feb. 1840.) [1840]; Dicks, 981, [1888].
The Gentleman in Black, or the Loves of the Devils. (Olympic, 9 Dec. 1840.) [1840?]; Dicks, 776, [1886].
What will the World say? (CG. 25 Sept. 1841.) 1841.
Grandfather Whitehead. C. (Hay. 31 Sept. 1842.) Webster, x, [1844]; Dicks, 505, [1885].
Hearts are Trumps. F. (Strand, 30 July 1849.) [1863]; Dicks, 1058, [1900].
The Railway Belle. F. (Adelphi, 20 Nov. 1854.) Lacy, XVII, [1855].

[Nicoll lists 45 further pieces up to 1850. DNB. gives Lemon's total output as some 60 plays. Most were of a farcical nature and were produced at various theatres (chiefly the English Opera House, Adelphi, Strand and Olympic).]

(b) Other Writings

The Enchanted Doll. A Fairy Tale for Little People. The Illustrations by R. Doyle. 1849.
Prose and Verse. 1852.
A Christmas Hamper. 1860. [Tales.]
Wait for the End. A Story. 3 vols. 1863.
Legends of Number Nip. 1864. [From the German of J. C. A. Musaeus.]
The Jest Book. The Choicest Anecdotes and Sayings, selected and arranged by Mark Lemon. Cambridge, 1864.
Loved at Last. A Story. 3 vols. 1864.
Tom Moody's Tales. Edited [or rather written] by Mark Lemon. Illustrated by H. K. Browne. 1864.
Falkner Lyle, or the Story of Two Wives. 3 vols. 1866.
Leyton Hall and Other Tales. 3 vols. 1867.
Golden Fetters. 3 vols. 1867. [A novel.]
Up and down the London Streets. 1867. [Historical and descriptive lectures.]
Fairy Tales. With Illustrations by R. Doyle and C. H. Bennett. 1868.
Tinykin's Transformations. A Child's Story. 1869.
The Small House over the Water, and Other Stories. With Portrait and Illustrations by G. Cruikshank. 1888.

[Lemon, with Henry Mayhew, founded Punch, the first number of which appeared on 17 July 1841. He remained editor until his death in 1870.]

(c) Biography and Criticism

Friswell, J. H. Modern Men of Letters. 1870.
Hatton, J. Reminiscences of Mark Lemon. GM. V, VI, 1870–1.
—— The True Story of 'Punch.' London Society, XXVIII, XXX, 1875–6.
Spielmann, M. H. The History of 'Punch.' 1895.

LEOPOLD DAVID LEWIS (1828–1890)

The Mask. A Humorous and Fantastic Review. Edited by Leopold Lewis and Alfred Thompson [and entirely written by them]. Feb.–Dec. 1868.
The Bells. A Drama in Three Acts. (Lyceum, 25 Nov. 1871.) Lacy, XCVII, [1872]; New York, 1872. [Adapted from Le Juif polonais of Erckmann-Chatrian.]
A Peal of Merry Bells. 3 vols. [1880]. [A novel.]

[Lewis wrote 3 other plays, two of which were produced at the Adelphi and one at Sadler's Wells, but these have apparently not been pbd.]

GEORGE WILLIAM LOVELL (1804–1878)

The Provost of Bruges. T. (DL. 10 Feb. 1836.) 1836; *Dicks*, 681, [1885]. [Founded on The Serf, a story in Leitch Ritchie's Romance of History.]

Love's Sacrifice, or the Rival Merchants. D. (CG. 12 Sept. 1842.) *Lacy*, LXVII, [1866]; *Dicks*, 650, [1885].

Look before you Leap, or Wooings and Weddings. C. (Hay. 29 Oct. 1846.) *Webster*, XIII, [1847]; *Dicks*, 998, [1888].

The Wife's Secret. D. (Park Theatre, New York, 12 Oct. 1846; Hay. 17 Jan. 1848.) *Lacy*, LXXXII, [1869]; *Dicks*, 1005, [1896].

[Lovell also wrote two dramas which have not been pbd, produced respectively at the Surrey in 1835 and the Princess's in 1852. He pbd a novel, The Trustee, in 1841.]

E. G. E. L. BULWER-LYTTON, BARON LYTTON (1803–1873)

[See p. 475 above.]

W. R. S. MARKWELL

Louis XI. An Historical Drama in Three Acts, adapted from C. Delavigne. (Unacted?) *Lacy*, IX, [1853].

The Prophet's Curse. A Play in Three Acts. (Unacted?) 1862. [In verse.]

JOHN WESTLAND MARSTON (1819–1890)

(a) Collected Works

The Dramatic and Poetical Works of Westland Marston. 2 vols. 1876. [Includes all the following plays (some, *e.g.* Strathmore, very much rev.) except The Heart and the World (fragments only) and Trevanion.]

(b) Plays

The Patrician's Daughter. T. (DL. 10 Dec. 1842.) 1841; 1842 (3 edns); Boston, 1856; *Lacy*, XLIII, [1859].

Borough Politics. F. (Hay. 27 June 1846.) *Webster*, XII, [1847].

The Heart and the World. D. (Hay. 4 Oct. 1847.) 1847.

Strathmore. T. (Hay. 20 June 1849.) 1849; *Lacy*, LVI, [1863]. [Based on Scott's Old Mortality.]

Trevanion, or the False Position. D. (Surrey, 22 Oct. 1849.) [1849.] [With W. Bayle Bernard.]

Philip of France and Marie de Méranie. T. (Olympic, 5 Nov. 1850.) 1850.

Anne Blake. D. (Princess's, 28 Oct. 1852.) 1852; Boston, [1856?]; *Lacy*, XLIX, [1861].

A Life's Ransom. D. (Lyceum, 16 Feb. 1857.) *Lacy*, LIV, [1861]; Boston, [1861?].

A Hard Struggle. A Domestic Drama. (Lyceum, 1 Feb. 1858.) *Lacy*, XLVIII, [1860]; Boston, [1860?].

The Wife's Portrait. A Household Picture, under Two Lights. D. (Hay. 10 March 1862.) *Lacy*, LIV, [1862].

Pure Gold. D. (Sadler's Wells, 9 Nov. 1863.) *Lacy*, LXI, [1864].

Donna Diana. C. (Princess's, 2 Jan. 1864.)

The Favourite of Fortune. C. (Hay. 2 April 1866.)

Life for Life. D. (Lyceum, 6 March 1869.)

(c) Poetical and Critical Works

Poetry as an Universal Nature: a Lecture, to which is added The Poet, an Ode. 1838.

Poetic Culture: an Appeal to those interested in Human Destiny. 1839.

Gerald, a Dramatic Poem, and Other Poems. 1842.

The Death-Ride. A Tale of the Light Brigade. 1855.

A Lady in her own Right. A Novel. 1860.

The Family Credit, and Other Tales. 1862.

The Wife's Portrait, and Other Tales. [1870.]

Our Recent Actors: being Recollections of Late Distinguished Performers. With some Incidental Notices of Living Actors. 2 vols. 1888.

[Marston also edited (with J. Saunders) The National Magazine, 1857–64.]

(d) Biography and Criticism

Horne, R. H. A New Spirit of the Age. Vol. II, 1844.

Powell, Thomas. Pictures of the Living Authors of Britain. 1851.

Obituary. Athenaeum, 11 Jan. 1890.

Clarke, H. E. John Westland Marston. [In The Poets and the Poetry of the Century, ed. A. H. Miles, vol. IV, [1891].]

CHARLES JAMES MATHEWS (1803–1878)

(a) Plays

My Wife's Mother. C. (Hay. 3 July 1833.) *Lacy*, XXIII, [1855]; *Dicks*, 659, [1885].

Truth, or a Glass Too Much. B. (Adelphi, 10 March 1834.) *Webster*, III, [1838].

The Hump-backed Lover. F. (Olympic, 7 Dec. 1835.) *Cumberland Minor*, XII, [1837?]; *Dicks*, 660, [1885].

Why did you Die? B. (Olympic, 20 Nov. 1837.) *Webster*, II, [1838]; *Dicks*, 662, [1885].

The Black Domino. B. (Olympic, 18 Jan. 1838.) *Webster*, III, [1838]. [Adapted from A. E. Scribe's Le Domino noir, with music by Auber.]

Patter versus Clatter. F. (Olympic, 21 May 1838.) *French*, 1755, [1883]; *Dicks*, 660, [1885].

Married for Money. C. (DL. 10 Oct. 1855.)
French, 117, [1881].
My Awful Dad. C. (Gaiety, 13 Sept. 1875.)
French, 117, [1881].
[The Life, ed. C. Dickens, contains a list of
Mathews's pieces and those in which he ap-
peared as an actor. Nicoll (pp. 343–4) lists 21,
mainly farces and comedies, but only covers
the period to 1850.]

(b) Other Writings

Lettre aux Auteurs dramatiques de la France.
1852; tr. Eng. (by Mathews himself), 1852.
The Life of Charles James Mathews [chiefly
autobiographical]. Ed. C. Dickens, 2 vols.
1879.

(c) Biography and Criticism

Mathews, A. Memoirs of Charles Mathews,
Comedian. 4 vols. 1838–9; abridged by E.
Yates, 1860. [Covers early years of Charles
James Mathews.]
Biographical Sketch. Webster, III, [1838].

JOHN MADDISON MORTON (1811–1891)

(a) Plays

My Husband's Ghost. F. (Hay. 26 April
1836.) Boston, [1857?]; Lacy, XCIII, [1872].
Chaos is Come Again, or the Race-Ball. F.
(CG. 19 Nov. 1838.) Webster, VI, [1839].
The Thumping Legacy. F. (DL. 11 Feb.
1843.) [1843]; Lacy, V, [1852].
The Mother and Child are doing well. F.
(Adelphi, 24 Feb. 1845.) Webster, XI, [1846].
Done on Both Sides. F. (Lyceum, 24 Feb.
1847.) Duncombe, LXI, [1848?]; Lacy,
XXVI, [1856].
Box and Cox. F. (Lyceum, 1 Nov. 1847.)
Lacy, V, [1852]; Dicks, 1059, [1900].
John Dobbs, or a Dab at Anything. F.
(Strand, 23 April 1849.) Duncombe, LXIV,
[1849?]; Lacy, VII, [1853].
Where there's a Will there's a Way. F.
(Strand, 6 Sept. 1849.) Duncombe, LXIV,
[1849?]; Lacy, IX, [1853].
Comediettas and Farces. New York, 1886.
[7 pieces.]
[Morton wrote a great number of plays,
mostly farces, and nearly all (according to
DNB.) adapted from the French. DNB. lists
89, without pretending to completeness, and
Nicoll (pp. 351–3) gives 46 to 1850. I. T. E.
Firkins, Index to Plays, 1927, lists 110 pieces
(including collaborations).]

(b) Biography and Criticism

Scott, C. John Maddison Morton. London
Society, XLIX, [1886].

JOHN OXENFORD (1812–1877)

(a) Plays

My Fellow Clerk. F. (English Opera House,
20 April 1835.) 1835; Dicks, 558, [1884].
The Dice of Death. D. (English Opera House,
14 Sept. 1835.) Duncombe, XXVIII, [1839?];
French, CX, [1878]; Dicks, 592, [1884].
Twice Killed. B. (Olympic, 26 Nov. 1835.)
Duncombe, XXI, [1836?]; Lacy, XXIV, [1855];
Dicks, 531, [1884].
A Day Well Spent, or Three Adventures. O.
(English Opera House, 4 April 1836.)
Duncombe, XXXI, [1836?]; Lacy, XXXIV,
[1858]; Dicks, 531, [1884].
A Quiet Day. F. (Unacted.) Duncombe,
XXXIV, [1837?]; Dicks, 987, [1888].
No Followers. F. (Strand, 4 Sept. 1837.)
Duncombe, XXXIV, [1837?]; Dicks, 987,
[1888].
Doctor Dilworth. F. (Olympic, 15 April
1839.) Webster, VII, [1840]; Boston, [1857?];
Dicks, 558, [1884].
The Reigning Favourite. D. (Strand, 9 Oct.
1849.) Lacy, I, [1851].
[Oxenford wrote some 60 more pieces at
least, chiefly farces and libretti of operas. The
text of Der Freischutz, of which the trn is
attrib. to him by Nicoll and BM. Catalogue,
cannot be his since it was played in 1824,
when he was only 12 years old. He collaborated
in one play each with D. Boucicault, S. Brooks,
J. Hatton and H. Wigan.]

(b) Translations

The Autobiography of Goethe. 1848; 1888.
Eckermann, J. P. Conversations of Goethe
with Eckermann and Soret. 1850; 1874.
Callery, J. M. and Yvan, M. History of the
Insurrection in China. With a Supple-
mentary Chapter. 1853.
Molière. Tartuffe. Webster, XVII, [1853].
Bürger, G. A. Lenora. 1855.
The Illustrated Book of French Songs from
the Sixteenth to the Nineteenth Century.
Translated by John Oxenford. 1855.
Jacobs, F. C. W. Hellas, or the Home, History,
Literature, and Art of the Greeks. 1855.
Fischer, Kuno. Francis Bacon of Verulam.
1857.
Cormon, E. and Carré, M. Lara, an Opera.
[1865.]
Wagner Festival, Royal Albert Hall, May
1877. Selections from the German Texts of
Der Ring des Nibelungen, Rienzi, etc. With
English Versions by Dr Hueffer and J.
Oxenford.
[According to DNB. Oxenford also translated
Calderón's Vida es Sueño and a large portion
of Boiardo's Orlando Innamorato. He was a
translator of outstanding merit.]

(c) Other Writings

Music in the Drawing Room. [In A. R. Smith's Gavarni in London, 1849.]

Flügel's Complete Dictionary of the German and English Languages. With Additions and Improvements by John Oxenford. 1857; [1880].

[From 1850 Oxenford was dramatic critic to The Times for more than 25 years. An essay by him on Schopenhauer (Iconoclasm in German Philosophy, Westminster Rev. III, 1853) was the foundation of Schopenhauer's fame.]

WATTS PHILLIPS (1825–1874)

(a) Plays

The Dead Heart. D. (Adelphi, 10 Nov. 1859.) Lacy, LXXXII, [1869]. [This play had considerable renown, and was revived by Irving at the Lyceum in 1889. On it were founded two novels: The Dead Heart, a Tale of the Bastille, by C. Gibbon, 1865, and Love in Death, by A. R. Phillips, 1889.]

His Last Victory. C. (St James's, 21 June 1862.) Lacy, LIX, [1864].

Camilla's Husband. D. (Olympic, 10 Nov. 1862.) Lacy, LIX, [1864].

Paul's Return. C. (Princess's, 15 Feb. 1864.) Lacy, LXII, [1865].

Theodora, Actress and Empress. D. (New Surrey, 9 April 1866.) Lacy, LXXIV, [1867].

Lost in London. D. (Adelphi, 16 March 1867.) Lacy, LXXX, [1868].

Maud's Peril. D. (Adelphi, 23 Oct. 1867.) Lacy, LXXX, [1868].

Not Guilty. D. (Queen's, 13 Feb. 1869.) Lacy, LXXXIV, [1869].

[Joseph Knight in DNB. credits Phillips with more than 26 plays, some of which remained unacted, and with 'innumerable' novels in Family Herald, etc. He was also a popular illustrator.]

(b) Other Writings

The Model Republic, or Cato Potts in Paris. [1848?] [Etchings.]

Showing how the Honourable Mr Teddington Locke, M.P., was not returned for the Incorruptible Borough of Bubengrub. Drawn and etched by Watts Phillips, from Notions by Edward Grant. [1850?]

The Wild Tribes of London. 1855. [An account of the slums.]

The Hooded Snake. A Story of the Secret Police. [1860.]

Amos Clark, or the Poor Dependent. A Story of Country Life in the Seventeenth Century. 1862.

Canary Bird. A Story of Town Life in the Seventeenth Century. A Sequel to Amos Clark. 1862.

Who will Save Her? A Novel. 3 vols. 1874.

(c) Biography and Criticism

Phillips, E. W. Watts Phillips: Artist and Playwright. 1891.

GEORGE DIBDIN PITT

The Monster of the Eddystone, or the Lighthouse Keepers. D. (Sadler's Wells, 7 April 1834.) Cumberland Minor, X, [1836?]; Lacy, LXIX, [1866].

The Jersey Girl, or the Red Robbers. D. (Surrey, 9 Feb. 1835.) Lacy, XXVI, [1856]; Dicks, 512, [1884].

The Twins, Paul and Philip. B. (Queen's, 21 Jan. 1836.) Dicks, 419, [1884].

The Last Man, or the Miser of Eltham Green. D. (Unacted?) Duncombe, XXIV, [1837?].

Simon Lee, or the Murder of the Five Fields Copse. D. (Royal City of London, 1 April 1839.) Lacy, LXXVIII, [1868].

Susan Hopley, or the Vicissitudes of a Servant Girl. (Victoria, 31 May 1841.) Lacy, LXIX, [1866].

The Beggar's Petition, or a Father's Love and a Mother's Care. D. (City; 18 Oct. 1841.) Lacy, LXXXVII, [1870]; Dicks, 514, [1884].

Marianne, the Child of Charity, or the Head of a Lawyer. (Victoria, 30 Dec. 1844.) French, CXIX, [1883]; Dicks, 825, [1887].

[Nicoll (pp. 362–6) notes 95 further pieces by Pitt (all save 3 unpbd) and says he had many other plays produced after 1850. Most were of a melodramatic nature and appeared at various theatres, but more at the Britannia than elsewhere.]

CHARLES READE (1814–1884)

[See p. 455 above.]

WILLIAM LEMAN REDE (1802–1847)

(a) Plays

The Rake's Progress. D. (City, 28 Jan. 1833). Duncombe, XII, [1833?]; New York, [1856?]; Lacy, XXXII, [1857]; Dicks, 240, [1883].

An Affair of Honour. F. (Olympic, 12 March 1835.) 1835; Cumberland, XLIV, [1845?]; Lacy, LXXVIII, [1868]; Dicks, 517, [1884].

Come to Town, or Next Door Neighbours. F. (Strand, 25 April 1836.) Duncombe, XXI, [1836?].

The Flight to America; or, Ten Hours in New York. D. (Adelphi, 7 Nov. 1836.) Duncombe, XXIV, [1837?]; New York, [1840?].

The Peregrinations of Pickwick, or, Boz-i-a-na. F. (Adelphi, 3 April 1837.) Duncombe, XXXIII, [1837?].

Jack in the Water, or the Ladder of Life. D. (Olympic, 25 April 1842.) *Cumberland Minor*, XVI, [1840]; *Dicks*, 574, [1884].

Our Village, or Lost and Found. D. (Olympic, 17 April 1843.) *Lacy*, LXXXVIII, [1871]; *Dicks*, 711, [1886].

La Somnambula, or the Somnambulist. O. (CG. 1848.) [1848.]

[Nicoll, pp. 379–81, gives 28 further pieces, chiefly farces and burlesques.]

(b) Other Writings

The Royal Rake [George IV], and the Adventures of Alfred Chesterton. 1842 (priv. ptd). [A satirical romance.]

[Rede started Judy in 1842 as a rival to Punch, but only 2 issues appeared.]

(c) Biography and Criticism

Obituary. Era, 11 April 1847.

Recollections of W. L. Rede. New Monthly Mag. LXXX, 1847.

GEORGE HERBERT BUONAPARTE RODWELL (1800–1852)

(a) Plays

Where shall I dine? F. (Olympic, 17 Feb. 1819.) [1819]; Dicks, 973, [1888].

Freaks and Follies, or a Match for the Old One. F. (Adelphi, 5 Nov. 1827.) *Dicks*, 988, [1888].

Teddy the Tiler. F. (CG. 8 Feb. 1830.) *Cumberland*, XXV, [1830?]; *Dicks*, 784, [1886]. [Based on Pierre le Couvreur.]

Was I to Blame? B. (Adelphi, 18 Dec. 1830.) *Lacy*, XXXII, [1857].

I'll be your Second. F. (Olympic, 10 Oct. 1831.) *Lacy*, III, [1851].

My Wife's Out. F. (CG. 2 Oct. 1843.) *Lacy*, XLV, [1860]; *Dicks*, 699, [1885].

The Pic Nic, or Husbands, Wives and Lovers. (Adelphi, 4 Dec. 1843.) *Dicks*, 561, [1884].

The Seven Maids of Munich, or the Ghost's Tower. (Princess's, 19 Dec. 1846.) 1846 (Songs, Duets, Choruses only.)

[Rodwell, besides writing many other stage pieces, was a musical composer of note, his most famous work in this kind being The Flying Dutchman. His principal librettist was Edward Fitzball, but in some cases he wrote both scores and libretti.]

(b) Other Writings

The First Rudiments of Harmony. 1831.

A Letter to the Musicians of Great Britain, containing a Prospectus of Proposed Plans for the Better Encouragement of Native Musical Talent, and for the Erection and Management of a Grand National Opera in London. 1833.

A Catechism of Music. [1840?] (21st edn).

A Catechism on Harmony. [1841?]

Memoirs of an Umbrella. [1845.] [A novel.]

Woman's Love. A Romance of Smiles and Tears. [1846.]

Old London Bridge. A Romance of the Sixteenth Century. [1848–9.]

The Devil's Ring, or Fire, Water, Earth and Air. A Grand Musical Fairy Romance in Three Acts and Four Elements. [1850.] [In verse.]

CHARLES SELBY (1802?–1863)

(a) Plays

A Day in Paris. O. (Strand, 18 July 1832.) *Duncombe*, XVI, [1838?]; *Dicks*, 425, [1883].

The Married Rake. C. (Queen's, 9 Feb. 1835.) *Duncombe*, XVI, [1835?]; *Lacy*, LXXI, [1866]; *Dicks*, 676, [1885].

Robert Macaire, or the Exploits of a Gentleman at Large. B. (Adelphi, 2 March 1835.) *Dicks*, 325, [1883].

Little Sins and Pretty Sinners. B. (Queen's, 12 Jan. 1836.) *Duncombe*, XXX, [1836?]; *Dicks*, 957, [1888].

The Loves of Lord Bateman and the Fair Sophia. (Strand, 3 July 1839.) *Duncombe*, XXXVII, [1839?].

The Boots at the Swan. F. (Strand, 8 June 1842.) *Duncombe*, XLV, [1842?]; *Dicks*, 564, [1884].

The Mysterious Stranger. D. (Adelphi, 30 Oct. 1844.) *Webster*, X, [1844]; Boston, 1855 (as Satan in Paris, or the Mysterious Stranger); *Dicks*, 798, [1886].

Taken in and done for. F. (Strand, 10 May 1849.) *Lacy*, III, [1851].

[Selby is credited by DNB. with over 70 plays. 54, chiefly farces and burlettas, are listed by Nicoll, pp. 387–9.]

(b) Other Writings

Maximums and Specimens of William Muggins, Natural Philosopher and Citizen of the World. 1841; 1859.

Events to be remembered in the History of England; forming a Series of Interesting Narratives of the most Remarkable Occurrences in Each Reign. 1851; 1891 (28th edn).

The Dinner Question. By Tabitha Tickletooth. 1860.

JOHN PALGRAVE SIMPSON (1807–1887)

(a) Plays

Second Love. C. (Hay. 23 July 1856.) Lacy, XXVIII, [1856]; Boston, [1856].

Daddy Hardacre. D. (Olympic, 26 March 1857.) Lacy, C, [1874].

World and Stage. C. (Hay. 12 March 1859.) Lacy, XCVII, [1872].

A School for Coquettes. C. (Strand, 4 July 1859.) Lacy, XLI, [1859].

A Scrap of Paper. C. (St James's, 22 April 1861.) Lacy, LI, [1861]. [Adapted from V. Sardou's Pattes de Mouche.]

Court Cards. C. (Olympic, 25 Nov. 1861.) Lacy, LIII, [1862]. [Adapted from J. Barbier and M. Carré, La Fileuse.]

Sybilla, or Step by Step. C. (Olympic, 29 Oct. 1864.) Lacy, LXIV, [1865].

Alone. C. (Court, 25 Oct. 1873.) French, CIII, [1875]. [In collaboration with H. C. Merivale.]

[According to DNB. Simpson produced upwards of 60 dramatic pieces, including comedies, melodramas, farces, operas and extravaganzas.]

(b) Fiction and Miscellaneous Works

Second Love, and Other Tales from the Notebook of a Traveller. 3 vols. 1846.

Gisella. 1847.

Letters from the Danube. 1847.

Pictures from Revolutionary Paris, sketched during the First Phases of the Revolution of 1848. Edinburgh, 1848.

The Lily of Paris, or the King's Nurse. 3 vols. 1849.

Carl Maria von Weber. The Life of an Artist. From the German by J. P. Simpson. 2 vols. 1865.

For Ever and Never. A Novel. 2 vols. 1884.

EDWARD STIRLING

The Pickwick Club, or the Age we live in. B. (City of London, 27 March 1837.) Duncombe, XXVI, [1837?]. [Based on Dickens.]

The Wreck at Sea, or the Fern Light. D. (Adelphi, 3 Dec. 1838.) Webster, VI, [1839] (as Grace Darling); French, CVI, [1877].

The Little Back Parlour. F. (English Opera House, 17 Aug. 1839.) Duncombe, XXXVIII, [1839?]; French, CXI, [1878].

The Serpent of the Nile. B. (Adelphi, 20 April 1840.) Duncombe, XLI, [1840?].

The Bohemians, or the Rogues of Paris. (Adelphi, 6 Nov. 1843.) [1870?] (in The British Drama. Illustrated, vol. x); Dicks, 98, [1883]. [Based on E. Sue, Les Mystères de Paris.]

Lestelle, or the Wrecker's Bride. D. (Surrey, 21 Aug. 1845.) Duncombe, LIV, [1845?].

The Jockey Club. E. (Adelphi, 19 Oct. 1846.) Webster, XIII, [1847].

The Bould Soger Boy. F. (Olympic, 6 Nov. 1848.) French, CXI, [1878].

[Stirling's 77 further pieces are listed by Nicoll, pp. 396–9.]

SIR HENRY TAYLOR (1800–1886)

[See p. 308 above.]

TOM TAYLOR (1817–1880)

(a) Plays

A Trip to Kissingen. B. (Lyceum, 14 Nov. 1844.) Dicks, 881, [1887].

Plot and Passion. D. (Olympic, 17 Oct. 1853.) Lacy, XIII, [1854]; New York, [1870?].

Still Waters Run Deep. C. (Olympic, 14 May 1855.) Lacy, XXII, [1855]; Boston, [1856?].

Going to the Bad. C. (Olympic, 5 June 1858.) Lacy, XXXVII, [1859].

The Fool's Revenge. D. (Sadler's Wells, 18 Oct. 1859.) Lacy, XLIII, [1859]; New York, [1863?]. [Adapted from Victor Hugo's Le Roi s'amuse. A version in novel form, by H. L. Williams, was pbd in 1883.]

Up at the Hills. C. (St James's, 29 Oct. 1860.) Lacy, L, [1861].

The Ticket-of-Leave Man. D. (Olympic, 27 May 1863.) Lacy, LIX, [1864]. [Founded on Le Retour du Melun, by É. Brisebarre and E. Nus. A version in novel form, by H. L. Williams, was pbd in 1870.]

Sense and Sensation, or the Seven Sisters of Thule. A Morality [in verse]. (Olympic, 16 May 1864.) Lacy, LXIII, [1865].

Historical Dramas. 1877. [7 plays.]

[DNB. notes 32 further stage pieces, some of them adapted from the French or the German and several written in collaboration with other authors.]

(b) Other Writings

Birket Foster's Pictures of English Landscape. With Pictures in Words by Tom Taylor. 1863 [1862].

Handbook of the Pictures in the International Exhibition of 1862. 1862.

The Railway Station, painted by W. P. Frith, described by Tom Taylor. 1862.

A Marriage Memorial. Verse and Prose. Commemorative of the Wedding of the Prince and Princess of Wales, March 10, 1863. [1863].

Life and Times of Sir Joshua Reynolds. Commenced by C. R. Leslie, continued by Tom Taylor. 2 vols. 1865.

English Painters of the Present Day. Essays by J. B. Atkinson, [etc.] and Tom Taylor. 1871.

The Theatre in England: some of its Shortcomings and Possibilities. 1871.

English Artists of the Present Day. Essays by J. B. Atkinson, [etc.] and Tom Taylor. 1872.

Leicester Square: its Associations and its Worthies. With a Sketch of Hunter's Scientific Character and Works by Richard Owen. 1874.

Storm at Midnight, and other Poems. Ed. J. H. Burn, Mintlaw, 1893.

[Taylor edited Punch from 1874 until his death in 1880. Besides the above works, he edited C. R. Leslie's Autobiographical Recollections, 1860, B. R. Haydon's Life, 1853, and Mortimer Collins's Pen Sketches by a Vanished Hand, 2 vols. 1879.]

(c) Biography and Criticism

Sheehan, J. Tom Taylor. Dublin University Mag. xc, 1877.

Hughes, T. In Memoriam Tom Taylor. Macmillan's Mag. XLII, 1880.

ALFRED, BARON TENNYSON (1809–1892)

[See p. 253 above.]

CHARLES WHITEHEAD (1804–1862)

[See p. 312 above.]

ALFRED SYDNEY WIGAN (1814–1878)

A Model of a Wife. F. (Lyceum, 27 Jan. 1845.) Lacy, LXI, [1864].

The Loan of a Wife. F. (Lyceum, 7 July 1846.) Duncombe, LVI, [1846?]. [From the French.]

Five Hundred Pounds Reward. C. (Lyceum, 28 Jan. 1847.) Duncombe, LVIII, [1847?]. [Adapted from Le Capitaine de Voleurs.]

Tit for Tat. C. By Francis Talfourd and Alfred Wigan. (Olympic, 22 Jan. 1855.) Lacy, XVII, [1855].

[Wigan wrote or adapted many other plays; DNB. states that no list is obtainable.]

THOMAS EGERTON WILKS

The Wolf and the Lamb. C. (Hay. 23 June 1832.) Duncombe, XXXII, [1837?]; Dicks, 968, [1888].

The Seven Clerks, or The Three Thieves and the Dreamer. D. (Surrey, 3 Nov. 1834.) Duncombe, XV, [1835?]; Lacy, XL, [1859]; Dicks, 923, [1888].

The King's Wager, or the Camp, the Cottage and the Court. B. (Victoria, 5 Dec. 1837.) [1837]; Duncombe, XXXIV, [1838?]; Lacy, LXII, [1865]; Dicks, 501, [1884].

The Wren Boys. F. (City of London, 8 Oct. 1838.) Duncombe, XXXII, [1838?]; Lacy, LII, [1861]; Dicks, 404, [1883].

Ben the Boatswain, or Sailors' Sweethearts! D. (Surrey, 19 Aug. 1839.) Duncombe, XXXVIII, [1839?]; Lacy, XXVIII, [1856].

Bamboozling. F. (Olympic, 16 May 1842.) Duncombe, XLI, [1842?]; Lacy, XXVIII, [1856]; Dicks, 627, [1885].

Sixteen String Jack, or the Knave of Knaves' Acre. D. (Sadler's Wells, 28 Nov. 1842.) Duncombe, LXIII, [1849?]; French, CV, [1875].

Kennyngton Crosse, or the Old Farm House on the Common. D. (Surrey, 12 June 1848.) Lacy, LXXV, [1867].

[Nicoll, pp. 410–1, lists 43 further plays, and mentions that several were produced after 1850.]

WILLIAM GORMAN WILLS (1828–1891)

(a) Plays

The Man o' Airlie. D. (Princess's, 20 July 1867.) [Not ptd.]

Medea in Corinth. T. (Lyceum, June 1872.) [Not ptd.]

Charles the First. T. (Lyceum, 28 Sept. 1872.) Edinburgh, 1873. [In verse.]

Olivia. D. (Court, 28 March 1873.) [Based on The Vicar of Wakefield. Not ptd.]

Drawing Room Dramas. By W. G. Wills and the Hon. Mrs Greene. Edinburgh, 1873. [In verse.]

[DNB. notes some 23 further dramatic pieces, all unptd and nearly all of an historical nature.]

(b) Other Writings

Old Times. A Novel. With Illustrations by the Author. [1856–]1857.

Life's Foreshadowings. A Novel. 3 vols. 1859.

Notice to Quit. 3 vols. 1861.

The Wife's Evidence. 3 vols. 1864.

David Chantry. 3 vols. 1865.

The Three Watches. 3 vols. 1865.

The Love that Kills. A Novel. 3 vols. 1867.

Melchior. 1885. [A poem in blank verse.]

(c) Biography and Criticism

Archer, W. English Dramatists of To-Day. 1882.

Wills, F. W. G. Wills, Dramatist and Painter. 1898.

H. B. G.

IV. THE LATE NINETEENTH-CENTURY DRAMA

GILBERT, JONES, PINERO, SHAW, WILDE, BARRIE, AND OTHER DRAMATISTS, 1870–1900.

[This section has been restricted to writers born after 1830 whose reputations as dramatists had been thoroughly established by 1900. The abbreviations employed (C., DL., *French*, etc.) are explained on p. 586 above.]

SIR WILLIAM SCHWENCK GILBERT
(1836–1911)

(1) BIBLIOGRAPHY

Searle, T. A Bibliography of Sir William Schwenck Gilbert; with Bibliographical Adventures in the Gilbert and Sullivan Operas. Introduction by R. E. Swartwout. 1931 (priv. ptd; re-issued 1931, by publisher, under title: Sir William Schwenck Gilbert a Topsy-Turvy Adventure).

(2) COLLECTED PLAYS

Original Plays. Ser. 1, 1876; ser. 2, 1881; ser. 3, 1895; ser. 4, 1911, 1920 (enlarged).

(3) SEPARATE PLAYS

Ruy Blas: a Burlesque. (Unacted?) [In Warne's Christmas Annual, 1866, illustrated by Gilbert.]

A New and Original Extravaganza entitled Dulcamara, or the Little Duck and the Great Quack. (St James's, 29 Dec. 1866.) 1866.

The Pretty Druidess, or the Mother, the Maid, and the Mistletoe Bough. An Extravaganza. (Charing Cross [later Toole's], 19 June 1869.) 1869.

An Old Score. An Original Comedy-Drama, in Three Acts. (Gaiety, 19 July 1869.) *Lacy*, LXXXV, 1869.

The Princess. A Whimsical Allegory. (Being a Respectful Perversion of Mr Tennyson's Poem.) (Olympic, 8 Jan. 1870.) *Lacy*, LXXXVII, 1870.

The Palace of Truth. A Fairy Comedy. In Three Acts. (Hay. 19 Nov. 1870.) *Lacy*, LXXXVIII, 1870.

A Medical Man. A Comedietta. (Unacted?) [In C. W. Scott's Drawing-Room Plays and Parlour Pantomimes, 1870.]

Randall's Thumb. An Original Comedy. In Three Acts. (Court, 25 Jan. 1871.) *Lacy*, XCI, 1871.

Pygmalion and Galatea. An entirely Original Mythological Comedy in Three Acts. (Hay. 9 Dec. 1871.) *French*, CIII, 1871.

On Guard. An entirely Original Comedy in Three Acts. (Court, 28 Oct. 1872.) *Lacy*, XCVIII, 1872.

The Wicked World. An entirely Original Fairy Comedy, in Three Acts and One Scene. (Hay. 4 Jan. 1873.) [1873] (priv. ptd); *French*, CXXVI, [1887].

The Happy Land. A Burlesque Version of The Wicked World. By F. Tomline [*i.e.* W. S. Gilbert] and G. A'Beckett. (Royal Court, 3 March 1873. Prohibited by the Lord Chamberlain 7 March 1873.) 1873.

The Wedding March. ('Le Chapeau de Paille d'Italie.') An Eccentricity, in Three Acts. (Court, 15 Nov. 1873.) *French*, CXIV, 1873.

Charity. An entirely Original Play, in four Acts. D. (Hay. 3 Jan. 1874. Denounced as immoral and withdrawn.) *French*, CXXIII, 1874.

Topsyturvydom. Original Extravaganza. (Criterion, 1874.) Oxford, 1931.

Sweethearts. An Original Dramatic Contrast, in Two Acts. (Prince of Wales', 7 Nov. 1874.) *French*, CXI; [1878].

Tom Cobb, or Fortune's Toy. An entirely Original Comedy in Three Acts. (St James's 24 April 1875.) *French*, CXVII, [1880].

Broken Hearts. An entirely Original Fairy Play. In Three Acts. (Court, 9 Dec. 1875.) *French*, CXVIII, [1881].

Dan'l Druce, Blacksmith. A New and Original Drama, in Three Acts. (Hay. 11 Sept. 1876.) *French*, CXVIII, [1881].

On Bail. A Farcical Comedy, in Three Acts. Adapted from 'Le Reveillon' [of H. Meilhac and L. Halévy]. (Criterion, 2 Feb. 1877.) *French*, CXVII, [1881]. [A re-written version of Committed for Trial, played Globe 24 Jan. 1874 as by 'F. L. Tomline,' condemned as 'unfit for public presentation,' and never pbd.]

Engaged. An entirely Original Farcical Comedy, in Three Acts. (Hay. 3 Oct. 1877.) *French*, CXVII, [1881].

The Ne'er-do-Weel. An entirely Original Play in Three Acts. (Olympic, 25 Feb. 1878.) [1878] (priv. ptd).

Gretchen. A Play, in Four Acts. C. (Olympic, 24 March 1879.) 1879.

Foggerty's Fairy. A Comedy. (Criterion, 23 April 1881.) 1881 (priv. ptd).

Comedy and Tragedy. An Original Drama in One Act. (Lyceum, 26 Jan. 1884.) *French*, CXXXIX, [1895].

An entirely New and Original Drama, in Four Acts, entitled Brantinghame Hall. (St James's, 1888.) 1888 (priv. ptd).

Rosencrantz and Guildenstern. A Tragic Episode, in Three Tableaux, founded on an Old Danish Legend. (Vaudeville, 3 June 1891.) *French*, CXXXIII, [1893]. [A travesty of Shakespeare's Hamlet.]

The Fortune Hunter. An Original Play in Three Acts. C. (Birmingham, 27 Sept. 1897.) [1897?] (priv. ptd).

The Fairy's Dilemma. A Domestic Pantomime. (Garrick, 3 May 1904.) [1904?] (priv. ptd).

A Stage Play. With Introduction by W. Archer. (Unacted?) 1916.

A Colossal Idea. An Original Farce. With Introduction and Decorations by T. Searle. 1932. [Written 1873; unacted.]

[Searle's Bibliography also lists the following plays and pantomimes, which have not been printed: Robinson Crusoe (with H. J. Byron, T. Hood, H. S. Leigh and A. Sketchley), 1867; Allow Me to explain, 1867; Highly Improbable, 1867; Great Expectations, 1871; Topsy-Turvydom, 1873; The Realm of Joy, 1873; Ought We to Visit Her? (with Mrs A. Edwards); Committed for Trial, 1874; Ali Baba and the Forty Thieves (with H. J. Byron, F. C. Burnand and R. Reece), 1878.]

(4) COLLECTED OPERAS

Original Comic Operas. Containing The Sorcerer; Patience; H.M.S. Pinafore; Princess Ida; The Pirates of Penzance; The Mikado; Iolanthe; Trial by Jury. [1890.]

Original Comic Operas. Second Series. Containing The Gondoliers; The Grand Duke; The Yeomen of the Guard; His Excellency; Utopia, Limited; Ruddigore; The Mountebanks; Haste to the Wedding. [1896?]

The Savoy Operas; being the Complete Text of the Gilbert and Sullivan Operas. 1926.

(5) SELECTED OPERAS, ETC.

The Gilbert and Sullivan Birthday Book. Compiled by A. Watson. 1888 [1887].

Selected Operas. 2 sers. 1928.

Scenes and Songs from the Savoy Operas, and some Bab Ballads. Selected by J. Compton. 1930.

(6) SEPARATE OPERAS, WITH MUSIC BY SIR A. SULLIVAN

Thespis: or, The Gods grown Old. Grotesque Opera in two Acts. (Gaiety, 23 Dec. 1871.) 1871. [Full musical score never pbd.]

Trial by Jury. A Novel and Original Dramatic Cantata. (Royal, 23 March 1875.) 1875; 1888 (full score).

The Sorcerer. An entirely Original Modern Comic Opera in Two Acts. (Opéra Comique, 17 Nov. 1877.) [1877]; [1884?] (with addns and alterations; Savoy, 11 Oct. 1884).

H.M.S. Pinafore: or, The Lass that loved a Sailor. An entirely Original Nautical Comic Opera, in Two Acts. (Opéra Comique, 25 May 1878.) [1878.]

The Pirates of Penzance: or, The Slave of Duty. An entirely Original Comic Opera in Two Acts. (Fifth Avenue Theater, New York, 31 Dec. 1879; Opéra Comique, 3 April 1880.) [1887?]

An entirely New and Original Æsthetic Opéra, in Two Acts, entitled Patience; or, Bunthorne's Bride! (Opéra Comique, 23 April 1881.) [1881.]

An entirely Original Fairy Opera, in Two Acts, entitled Iolanthe; or, The Peer and the Peri. (Savoy, 25 Nov. 1882.) [1885?]

A Respectful Operatic Per-Version of Tennyson's 'Princess,' in Two Acts, entitled Princess Ida; or, Castle Adamant. (Savoy, 5 Jan. 1884.) [1884.]

An entirely New and Original Japanese Opera, in two Acts, entitled The Mikado; or, The Town of Titipu. (Savoy, 14 March 1885.) [1885]. Tr. Danish, 1887; German, Chicago, [1887].

An entirely Original Supernatural Opera, in Two Acts, entitled Ruddygore; or, The Witch's Curse! (St James's, 22 Jan. 1887.) [1887] [Spelling of title altered to Ruddigore four days after production, because of objections.]

A New and Original Opera, in Two Acts, entitled The Yeomen of the Guard; or, The Merryman and his Maid. (Savoy, 31 Oct. 1888.) [1888.]

An entirely Original Comic Opera, in Two Acts, entitled The Gondoliers; or, The King of Barataria. (Savoy, 7 Dec. 1889.) [1889.]

An Original Comic Opera, in Two Acts, entitled Utopia (Limited); or, The Flowers of Progress. (Savoy, 7 Oct. 1893.) 1893.

The Grand Duke; or, The Statutory Duel. A Comic Opera in Two Acts. (Savoy, 7 March 1896.) 1896.

(7) SEPARATE OPERAS AND MUSICAL PLAYS, WITH COMPOSERS OTHER THAN SULLIVAN

La Vivandière; or, True to the Corps! An Operatic Extravaganza founded on Donizetti's Opera 'La Figlia del Regimento.' (St James's Hall, Liverpool, 15 June 1867; Queen's, 22 Jan. 1868.) Liverpool, 1867; 1868.

Harlequin, Cock-Robin and Jenny Wren: or, Fortunatus and the Water of Life, the Three Bears, the Three Gifts, the Three Wishes, and the Little Man who woo'd the Little Maid. Grand Comic Christmas Pantomime. (Lyceum, 26 Dec. 1867.) 1867.

The Merry Zingara; or, The Tipsy Gipsy and the Pipsy Wipsy. A Whimsical Parody on the 'Bohemian Girl.' (Royalty, 21 March 1868.) 1868.

Robert the Devil; or, The Nun, the Dun and the Son of a Gun. An Operatic Extravaganza. (Gaiety, 21 Dec. 1868.) 1868.

No Cards: a Musical Piece in one Act for four Characters; with Music by L. Elliott. (Gallery of Illustration, 29 March 1869.) [1901.]

Ages Ago. Opera in One Act. The Music by F. Clay. (Gallery of Illustration, 22 Nov. 1869.) 1869 (vocal score); 1895 (libretto). [Afterwards expanded into Ruddigore.]

The Gentleman in Black, an Original Musical Legend. In two Acts. Music by F. Clay. (Charing Cross, 26 May 1870.) *Lacy*, LXXXVIII, 1870.

A Sensation Novel. In three Volumes. [Operetta with music by] F. Pascal. (Gallery of Illustration, 30 Jan. 1871.) 1912.

Creatures of Impulse. A Musical Fairy Tale in One Act. Music by A. Randegger. (Royal Court, 15 April 1871.) *Lacy*, XCI, 1871.

Les Brigands: Opéra Bouffe en trois Actes, par H. Meilhac et L. Halévy. Musique de J. Offenbach. L'Adaptation anglaise par W. S. Gilbert. (Played 1896.) 1871; 1884. [Text in French and English.]

Happy Arcadia. Music by F. Clay. (Gallery of Illustration, 28 Oct. 1872.) 1872.

Eyes and No Eyes; or, The Art of Seeing. [Music] by F. Pascal. (St George's Hall, 5 July 1875.) 1896. [Adapted from Hans Andersen's The Emperor's New Clothes.]

Princess Toto. Comic Opera in three Acts. Music by F. Clay. (Strand, 2 Oct. 1876.) [1876?]

An entirely Original Comic Opera, in Two Acts, entitled The Mountebanks. [Music] by A. Callier. (Lyric, 4 Jan. 1892.) 1892.

A Musical Version of 'Le Chapeau de Paille d'Italie,' in Three Acts. Entitled Haste to the Wedding. Music by G. Grossmith. (Criterion, 27 July 1892.) 1892.

His Excellency. An entirely Original Comic Opera in Two Acts. Music by O. Carr. (Savoy, 7 Oct. 1894.) 1894.

An Original Opera in two Acts, entitled Fallen Fairies; or, The Wicked World. [Music] by [Sir] E. German. (Garrick 11 Dec. 1909.) 1909.

[Searle's Bibliography also lists the following operetta, which has not been pbd: Our Island Home, 1870.]

(8) Prose Fiction

The Key of the Strong Room. [In T. Hood's A Bunch of Keys, 1865.]

The Income-Tax. [In T. Hood's Rates and Taxes, 1866.]

Foggerty's Fairy and Other Tales. 1890.

(9) Verse

The 'Bab' Ballads. Much Sound and Little Sense. With Illustrations by the Author. 1869; 1870.

More 'Bab' Ballads. With Illustrations by the Author. [1873.]

The 'Bab' Ballads and More 'Bab' Ballads. Much Sound and Little Sense. With Illustrations by the Author. Complete. 1874.

Songs of a Savoyard. Illustrated by the Author. 1890. [Lyrics from the Operas performed at the Savoy Theatre.]

The Bab Ballads, with which are included Songs of a Savoyard. With 350 Illustrations by the Author. 1898.

Lost Bab Ballads. Collected and illustrated by T. Searle. 1932.

[Gilbert also illustrated several books by other authors. Various songs and other *ephemera* were also pbd separately.]

(10) Biography and Criticism

Adams, W. D. Mr Gilbert as a Dramatist. Belgravia, XLV, 1881.

Archer, W. English Dramatists of To-day. 1882.

—— Real Conversations. 1904.

William Schwenck Gilbert. An Autobiography. Theatre, April 1883.

Marshall, A. F. The Spirit of Gilbert's Comedies. Month, LV, 1885.

Grossmith, G. A Society Clown. 1888.

W. S. Gilbert at Home. Critic (New York), XIX, 1891.

Fitzgerald, P. H. The Savoy Opera and the Savoyards. 1894.

Bulloch, J. M. The Work of W. S. Gilbert. Book Buyer, XVII, 1898.

—— The Anatomy of the 'Bab' Ballads. N. & Q. 14, 28 Nov. 1936, 22 May 1937.

—— W. S. Gilbert's Father. N. & Q. 19 Dec. 1936.

Beerbohm, M. W. S. Gilbert as Humorist. Saturday Rev. XCVII, 1904.

Browne, Edith A. W. S. Gilbert. [In J. T. Grein, Stars of the Stage, 1907.]

Sichel, W. The English Aristophanes. Fortnightly Rev., XCVI, 1911.

Goldberg, I. Sir William S. Gilbert. A Study in Modern Satire. A Handbook on Gilbert and the Gilbert and Sullivan Operas. Boston, [1913].

—— The Story of Gilbert and Sullivan. 1929.

Cellier, F. A. and Bridgeman, C. Gilbert, Sullivan, and D'Oyly Carte. Reminiscences of the Savoy and the Savoyards. 1914.

Newman, E. The Gilbert and Sullivan Operas. Littell's Living Age, CCCIII, 1919.

Baring, M. Gilbert and Sullivan. Fortnightly Rev. cxviii, 1922.

Rowland-Brown, H. The Gilbertian Idea. Cornhill Mag. lii, 1922.

Wilkinson, C. Gilbert and Sullivan. London Mercury, v, 1922.

Dark, S. and Grey, R. W. S. Gilbert: his Life and Letters. 1923.

Wilson, A. C. W. S. Gilbert. Manchester Quart. li, 1925.

Godwin, A. H. Gilbert and Sullivan. A Critical Appreciation of the Savoy Operas; with an Introduction by G. K. Chesterton. 1926.

Hamilton, Edith. W. S. Gilbert: a mid-Victorian Aristophanes. Theatre Arts Monthly, xi, 1927.

Lytton, Sir H. A. Secrets of a Savoyard. [1927.]

Perry, H. T. E. The Victorianism of W. S. Gilbert. Sewanee Rev., xxxvi, 1928.

Du Bois, A. E. W. S. Gilbert, Practical Classicist. Sewanee Rev. xxxvii, 1929.

—— Additions to the Bibliography of W. S. Gilbert's Contributions to Magazines. MLN. xlvii, 1932.

Quiller-Couch, Sir A. T. Studies in Literature, Ser. 3, Cambridge, 1929.

Lambton, G. Gilbertian Characters, and a Discourse on W. S. Gilbert's Philosophy in the Savoy Operas. 1931.

Barker, H. Granville. Exit Planché, enter Gilbert. London Mercury, xxv, 1932.

Ellehauge, M. Initial Stages in the Development of the English Problem-Play: the Savoy Opera. E. Studien, lxvi, 1932.

Kendal, Madge. W. S. Gilbert. Cornhill Mag. cxlviii, 1933.

Halton, F. J. Gilbert and Sullivan Operas: a Concordance. New York, 1935.

Pearson, H. Gilbert and Sullivan: a Biography. 1935.

Dunn, G. E. A Gilbert and Sullivan Dictionary. 1936. H. B. G.

HENRY ARTHUR JONES (1851–1929)

(1) Bibliography

Jones, J. D. The Life and Letters of Henry Arthur Jones. 1930. [Appendices A and B.]

(2) Collected Plays

Representative Plays. Ed. (with historical, biographical, and critical introductions) C. Hamilton, 4 vols. 1926. [Vol. i: The Silver King; The Middleman; Judah; The Dancing Girl. Vol. ii: The Crusaders; The Tempter; The Masqueraders; The Case of Rebellious Susan. Vol. iii: Michael and his Lost Angel; The Liars; Mrs Dane's Defence; The Hypocrites. Vol. iv: Dolly reforming herself; The Divine Gift; Mary goes First; The Goal; Grace Mary.]

[There is a uniform (but not complete) demy 8vo edn of 24 of Jones's plays pbd by Samuel French. The vols. are undated and Messrs French are unable to supply dates.]

(3) Separate Plays

Hearts of Oak: a Domestic Drama in Two Acts. (Theatre Royal, Exeter, 29 May 1879.) Lacy, cxxii, [1885]. [Re-written with fuller dialogue as Honour Bright, 1879, but unacted in this form. Priv. ptd by J. Tait, Ilfracombe.]

Harmony: a Domestic Drama in One Act. (Grand, Leeds, 13 Aug. 1879, as Harmony Restored; Strand, 14 June 1884.) Lacy, cxix, [1883]. [Played as It's only Round the Corner, Theatre Royal, Exeter, 11 Dec. 1879; and as The Organist, Lyceum, New York, May 1892.]

Elopement: a Comedy in Two Acts. (Theatre Royal, Oxford, 19 Aug. 1879.) Lacy, cxxii, [1885].

A Drive in June. (Unacted.) [Ilfracombe], 1879 (priv. ptd).

A Clerical Error: a Comedy in One Act. (Court, 16 Oct. 1879.) Lacy, clii, [1904].

A Garden Party. A Play in Three Acts. (Unacted.) [Ilfracombe], 1880 (priv. ptd).

Humbug. A Play in Three Acts. (Unacted.) Ilfracombe, 1881 (priv. ptd).

An Old Master. A Comedy in One Act. (Princess's, 6 Nov. 1880.) Lacy, cxix, [1883].

Lady Caprice. A Comedy in Three Acts. (Unacted.) [Ilfracombe], 1880 (priv. ptd).

A Bed of Roses. A Comedy in One Act. (Globe, 26 Jan. 1882.) Lacy, cxix, [1883].

The Silver King. A Drama in Four Acts. (Princess's, 16 Nov. 1882.) [1907]; French, 1675, [1921]. [With H. A. Herman.]

The Wedding Guest. A Play in One Act. (Unacted.) [Ilfracombe], 1882 (priv. ptd).

Breaking a Butterfly. A Play in Three Acts. (Prince's, 3 March 1884.) [1884] (priv. ptd). [With Henry A. Herman; founded on Ibsen's Doll's House.]

Saints and Sinners: a New and Original Drama of Modern English Middle-Class Life. In Five Acts. (Prince of Wales's, Greenwich, 17 Sept. 1884; Vaudeville, 25 Sept. 1884.) 1891.

The Middleman. A Play in Four Acts. (Shaftesbury, 27 Aug. 1889.) [1907.]

Judah: an Original Play in Three Acts. (Shaftesbury, 21 May 1890.) New York, 1894. [With a preface by Joseph Knight.]

Sweet Will. A Comedy in One Act. (Shaftesbury, 25 July 1890.) *Lacy*, cxxxi, [1893]. [According to 'The Stage' Cyclopædia this play was first performed at the New Club, Covent Garden, on 5 March 1887.]

The Deacon: a Comedy-Sketch in Two Acts. (Shaftesbury, 27 Aug. 1890.) *Lacy*, cxxxiii, [1891].

The Dancing Girl: a Drama in Four Acts. (Hay. 15 Jan. 1891.) [1907.]

The Crusaders: an Original Comedy of Modern London Life. (Avenue, 2 Nov. 1891.) 1893.

The Bauble Shop: a Play in Four Acts. (Criterion, 26 Jan. 1893.) [1893?]

The Tempter: a Tragedy in Verse. (Hay. 30 Sept. 1893.) 1898.

The Masqueraders: a Play in Four Acts. (St James's, 28 April 1894.) [1894] (priv. ptd); 1899.

The Case of Rebellious Susan: a Comedy in Three Acts. (Criterion, 3 Oct. 1894.) 1897.

Grace Mary. (Unacted.) [1895] (priv. ptd). [Rptd in The Theatre of Ideas, 1915.]

The Triumph of the Philistines. A Comedy in Three Acts. (St James's, 11 May 1895.) 1899.

Michael and his Lost Angel. A Play in Five Acts. (Lyceum, 15 Jan. 1896.) 1896. [With a preface by Joseph Knight.]

The Rogue's Comedy. A Play in Three Acts. (Garrick, 21 April 1896.) 1898.

The Physician. An Original Play in Four Acts. (Criterion, 26 March 1897.) 1899.

The Liars. An Original Comedy in Four Acts. (Criterion, 6 Oct. 1897.) New York, 1901.

The Manœuvres of Jane. An Original Comedy in Four Acts. (Hay. 29 Oct. 1898.) 1904.

Carnac Sahib. An Original Play in Four Acts. (Her Majesty's, 12 April 1899.) 1899.

The Lackey's Carnival. Play in Four Acts. (Duke of York's, 26 Sept. 1900.) 1900 (priv. ptd).

Mrs Dane's Defence. A Play in Four Acts. (Wyndham's, 9 Oct. 1900). 1905.

James the Fogey. A Play in Four Acts. (Unacted.) [1902] (priv. ptd).

The Princess's Nose. A Comedy in Four Acts. (Duke of York's, 11 March 1902.) [1902] (priv. ptd).

Chance the Idol. A Play in Four Acts. (Wyndham's, 9 Sept. 1902.) [1902] (priv. ptd).

Whitewashing Julia. A Comedy in Three Acts, and an Epilogue. (Garrick, 2 March 1903.) 1905.

Chrysold. A Play in Five Acts. (Unacted.) [1904] (priv. ptd).

Joseph Entangled. A Comedy in Three Acts. (Hay. 19 Jan. 1904.) [1906.]

The Chevaleer. A Comedy in Three Acts. (Garrick, 27 Aug. 1904.) [1905?]

The Sword of Gideon. A Play in Four Acts. (Unacted.) [1905?] (priv. ptd).

The Heroic Stubbs. Comedy in Four Acts. (Terry's, 24 Jan. 1906.) [1906?] (priv. ptd).

The Hypocrites. A Play in Four Acts. (Hudson, New York, 30 Aug. 1906; Hicks's, London, 27 Aug. 1907.) [1908.]

The Evangelist. A Tragi-Comedy in Two Acts. (Knickerbocker, New York, 30 Sept. 1907.) [1908?] (as The Galilean's Victory).

Dolly Reforming Herself. A Comedy in Four Acts. (Hay. 3 Nov. 1908.) [1913.] [Samuel French and Co. also pbd in New York a one-act version called Dolly's Little Bills.]

The Knife. A Play in One Act. (Palace, 20 Dec. 1909.) [New York, 1909?]

Fall in, Rookies. A Play in Two Scenes. (Alhambra, 24 Oct. 1910.) [1910?] (priv. ptd).

We can't be as Bad as All That. A Play in Three Acts. (Nazimova's, 39th Street, New York, 30 Dec. 1910; Croydon Hippodrome, 4 Sept. 1916.) New York, 1910 (priv. ptd).

The Ogre. A Play in Three Acts. (St James's, 11 Sept. 1911.) [1911?]

Lydia Gilmore. A Play in Four Acts. (Lyceum, New York, 1 Feb. 1912.) [1912?]

The Divine Gift. A Play in Three Acts. (Unacted.) 1913.

Her Tongue. A Play in One Act. (Unacted.) [In The Theatre of Ideas, 1915.]

Mary goes First. A Comedy in Three Acts and an Epilogue. (Playhouse, 18 Sept. 1913.) 1913.

The Goal. A Play in One Act. (Princess's, New York, 26 Oct. 1914; Palace, London, 20 May 1919.) [In The Theatre of Ideas, 1915.]

The Lie. A Play of English Life in Four Acts. (Harris, New York, 24 Dec. 1914; New, London, 13 Oct. 1923.) New York, 1915.

The Pacifists. A Parable in Farce in Three Acts. (St James's, 4 Sept. 1917.) [1917?] (priv. ptd).

[Doris Jones's Bibliography also records 26 plays which have not been pbd and 4 film scenarios, written in 1920, which were neither used nor ptd.]

(4) MISCELLANEOUS WORKS

The Renascence of the English Drama. Essays, Lectures and Fragments relating to the Modern English Stage, 1883–94. 1895.

The Foundations of a National Drama. A Collection of Lectures, Essays and Speeches, delivered and written in the Years 1896–1912, revised and corrected, with Additions. 1913.

The Theatre of Ideas, a Burlesque Allegory; and Three One-Act plays: The Goal; Her Tongue; Grace Mary. 1915.

Patriotism and Popular Education. 1919.

My Dear Wells. A Manual for the Haters of England. Being a Series of Letters upon Bolshevism, Collectivism, Internationalism, and the Distribution of Wealth, addressed to Mr H. G. Wells. [1921.]

What is Capital? An Inquiry into the meaning of the Words 'Capital' and 'Labour.' 1925.

[Jones also produced some pamphlets—*e.g.* one of some length on the question of dramatic censorship, and was a frequent contributor to the periodical press (usually on some aspect of the drama).]

(5) BIOGRAPHY AND CRITICISM

Walkley, A. B. Playhouse Impressions. 1892.
—— Drama and Life. 1907.

Bettany, W. A. L. Henry Arthur Jones and Modern English Drama. Theatre, xxxi, 1893.

Blathwayt, R. Henry Arthur Jones. Idler, iv, 1893.

Hamilton, J. A. Henry Arthur Jones. Munsey's Mag. xi, 1894.

Newton, H. C. Henry Arthur Jones. Theatre, xxxvi, 1896.

Bulloch, J. M. Henry Arthur Jones; with Bibliography of his Plays. Book Buyer, xvi, 1898.

Beerbohm, M. The Popular Success of Henry Arthur Jones. Saturday Rev. xc, 1900.

Tarpey, W. K. Henry Arthur Jones's Work as a Dramatist. Critic, xxxvii, 1900.

Grein, J. T. Dramatic Criticism. Vol. iii, 1902.

Matthews, J. B. A Study of the Drama. Boston, 1910.

Arthur Jones's Confusion. Blackwood's Mag. cxciv, 1913.

Grossmith, W. From Studio to Stage. 1913.

Howe, P. P. Dramatic Portraits. 1913.

Winter, W. The Wallet of Time. Vol. ii, 1913.

Chandler, F. W. Aspects of Modern Drama. New York, 1914.

Dickinson, T. H. Henry Arthur Jones and the Dramatic Renascence. North American Rev. ccii, 1915.

Wauchope, G. A. Henry Arthur Jones and the New Social Drama. Sewanee Rev. xxix, 1921.

Archer, W. The Old Drama and the New. 1923.

Henry Arthur Jones, Dramatist, self-revealed; a Conversation on the Art of writing Plays with Archibald Henderson. Nation, 5, 12 Dec. 1925.

Shorey, P. Henry Arthur Jones. New York, 1925.

Allen, P. Henry Arthur Jones. Fortnightly Rev. cxxxi, 1929.

Obituary. London Mercury, xix, 1929.

Shelley, H. C. Henry Arthur Jones. Bookman, lxxv, 1929.

Jones, Doris Arthur. The Life and Letters of Henry Arthur Jones. 1930.

Cordell, R. A. Henry Arthur Jones and the Modern Drama. 1932.

Ellehauge, M. Intitial Stages in the Development of the English Problem-Play. E. Studien, lxvi, 1932.   H. B. G.

SIR ARTHUR WING PINERO (1855–1934)

(1) SELECTED PLAYS

The Social Plays of Arthur Wing Pinero. Ed. (with General Introduction and Critical Preface to each play) C. Hamilton, 4 vols. New York, 1917–1922. [Vol. i: The Second Mrs Tanqueray; The Notorious Mrs Ebbsmith. Vol. ii: The Gay Lord Quex; Iris. Vol. iii: Letty; His House in Order. Vol. iv: The Thunderbolt; Mid-Channel.]

(2) SEPARATE PLAYS

[The subjoined plays marked * constitute a uniform (but not complete) edn in 15 vols., with introductory notes by M. C. Salaman.]

Hester's Mystery. A Comedy in One Act. (Folly, 5 June 1880.) *Lacy*, cxxxvi, 1893.

The Money Spinner. An Original Comedy in Two Acts. (Prince's, Manchester, 5 Nov. 1880; St James's, 8 Jan. 1881.) *Lacy*, cxlvi, [1900].

The Squire. An Original Comedy in Three Acts. (St James's, 29 Dec. 1881.) [1905.]

The Rocket. An Original Comedy in Three Acts. (Prince of Wales's, Liverpool, 30 July 1883; Gaiety, 10 Dec. 1883.) [1905.]

In Chancery. An Original Fantastic Comedy in Three Acts. (Lyceum, Edinburgh, 19 Sept. 1884; Gaiety, 24 Dec. 1884.) [1905.]

*The Magistrate. A Farce in Three Acts. (Royal Court, 21 March 1885.) 1892.

*The Schoolmistress. A Farce in Three Acts. (Royal Court, 27 March 1886.) 1894.

*The Hobby-Horse. A Comedy in Three Acts. (St James's, 23 Oct. 1886.) 1892.

*Dandy Dick. A Farce in Three Acts. (Royal Court, 27 Jan. 1887.) 1893.

*Sweet Lavender. A Domestic Drama in Three Acts. (Terry's, 21 March 1888.) 1893.

*The Weaker Sex. A Comedy in Three Acts. (Royal Court, 16 March 1889.) 1894.

*The Profligate. A Play in Four Acts. (Garrick, 24 April 1889.) 1892.

*The Cabinet Minister. A Farce in Four Acts. (Royal Court, 23 April 1890.) 1892.

*Lady Bountiful. A Story of Years. A Play in Four Acts. (Garrick, 7 March 1891.) 1892.

*The Times. A Comedy in Four Acts. (Terry's, 24 Oct. 1891.) 1891.
*The Amazons. A Farcical Romance in Three Acts. (Royal Court, 7 March 1893.) 1895.
*The Second Mrs Tanqueray. A Play in Four Acts. (St James's, 27 May 1893.) 1895.
*The Notorious Mrs Ebbsmith. A Drama in Four Acts. (Garrick, 13 March 1895.) 1895.
*The Benefit of the Doubt. A Comedy in Three Acts. (Comedy, 16 Oct. 1895.) 1896.
*The Princess and the Butterfly, or the Fantastics. A Comedy in Five Acts. (St James's 29 March 1897.) 1898.
Trelawny of the 'Wells.' A Comedietta. (Court, 20 Jan. 1898.) New York, 1898; 1899.
The Beauty Stone. An Original Romantic Musical Drama. By A. W. Pinero, J. C. Carr and A. Sullivan. (Savoy, 28 May 1898.) 1898.
The Gay Lord Quex. C. (Globe, 8 April 1899.) 1900.
Iris. D. (Garrick, 21 Sept. 1901.) 1902.
Letty. D. (Duke of York's, 8 Oct. 1903.) 1904.
A Wife without a Smile. A Comedy in Disguise. (Wyndham's, 12 Oct. 1904.) 1905.
His House in Order. C. (St James's, 1 Feb. 1906.) 1906.
The Thunderbolt. C. (St James's, 9 May 1908.) 1909.
Mid-Channel. (St James's, 2 Sept. 1909.) 1910.
Preserving Mr Panmure. A Comic Play in Four Acts. (Comedy, 19 Jan. 1911.) 1912.
The 'Mind the Paint' Girl. A Comedy in Four Acts. (Duke of York's, 17 Feb. 1912.) 1913.
Playgoers. A Domestic Episode. (St James's, 31 March 1913.) French, 2507, 1913.
The Big Drum. A Comedy in Four Acts. (St James's, 1 Sept. 1915.) 1915.
The Freaks. An Idyll of Suburbia. A Comedy in Three Acts. (New, 14 Feb. 1918.) 1922.
A Seat in the Park. C. (Winter Garden, 21 Feb. 1922.) French, 2618, [1922].
The Enchanted Cottage. A Fable in Three Acts. (Duke of York's, 1 March 1922.) 1922.
A Private Room. A Play in Two Parts. (Little, 14 May 1928.) French, 852, [1928].
Two Plays. 1930. [Dr Harmer's Holidays. A Contrast in Nine Scenes. (Shubert-Belasco, Washington, 16 March 1931); Child Man. A Sedate Farce in Three Acts. (Unacted).]

[The following were also produced but remain unpbd: Lords and Commons, C. (Hay. 24 Nov. 1883); Low Water, C. (Globe, 12 Jan. 1884); A Cold June, C. (Duchess, 20 May 1932).]

(3) CRITICAL WORKS

Robert Louis Stevenson: the Dramatist. A Lecture. 1903.
Robert Louis Stevenson as a Dramatist. With an Introduction (and Bibliographical Appendix) by Clayton Hamilton. New York, 1914.

(4) BIOGRAPHY AND CRITICISM

Archer, W. English Dramatists of To-Day. 1882.
—— The Theatrical 'World.' 5 vols. 1893–7.
—— Real Conversations. 1904.
—— The Old Drama and the New. 1923.
Cook, D. Plays, Plagiarisms and Mr Pinero. Theatre, v, 1882.
—— The Case of Mr Pinero. Theatre, v, 1882.
Sharp, R. F. A. W. Pinero and Farce. Theatre, xx, 1892.
Walkley, A. B. Playhouse Impressions. 1892.
—— Frames of Mind. 1899.
Mr Pinero and the Literary Drama. Theatre, xxii, 1893.
Hamilton, J. A. A. W. Pinero. Munsey's Mag. x, 1894.
Fyfe, H. H. Mr Pinero's Plays as Literature. Theatre, xxvi, 1895.
—— Arthur Wing Pinero, Playwright. A Study. 1902. [With casts.]
—— Sir Arthur Pinero's Plays and Players. 1930.
Wilson, H. S. The Notorious Mrs Ebbsmith. 1895.
Courtney, W. L. The Idea of Comedy and Mr Pinero's New Play [The Princess and the Butterfly]. Fortnightly Rev. LXVII, 1897.
—— Realistic Drama. Fortnightly Rev. xcix, 1913.
Kobbé, G. The Plays of Arthur Wing Pinero. Forum, xxvi, 1898–9.
Frohman, D. Memories of a Manager. 1899.
Hamelius, J. P. Arthur W. Pinero und das englische Drama der Jetztzeit. Brussels, 1900.
Tarpey, W. K. English Dramatists of To-day. (A. W. Pinero.) Critic, xxxvii, 1900.
Beers, H. A. The English Drama of To-day. North American Rev. CLXXX, 1905.
Hale, E. E. Dramatists of To-day. New York, 1905.
A. W. Pinero's Skill as a Dramatist. Nation (New York), 6 Sept. 1906.
Rideing, W. H. Some Women of Pinero's. North American Rev. CLXXXVIII, 1908.
Stöcker, W. Pineros Dramen. Marburg, 1911.
Walbrook, H. H. Nights at the Play. 1911.
Armstrong, C. F. Shakespeare to Shaw. Studies in the Life's Work of Six Dramatists of the English Stage. 1913.

Howe, P. P. Dramatic Portraits. 1913.

Moore, G. Impressions and Opinions. 1913.

Chandler, F. W. Aspects of Modern Drama. New York, 1914.

Pinero as a Playwright. New Republic, XIII, 1917.

Phelps, W. L. Sir Arthur Pinero. Bookman (New York), XLVII, 1918.

Krutch, J. W. Pinero the Timid. Nation (New York), 19 Nov. 1924.

Wilson, E. Sixty-five years of Realism. New Republic, XLIII, 1925.

Cunliffe, J. W. Modern English Playwrights. New York, 1927.

Holt, E. A Dramatist's Jubilee. Fortnightly Rev. CXXIX, 1928.

Ellehauge, M. Initial Stages in the Development of the English Problem-Play. E. Studien, LXVI, 1932. H.B.G.

GEORGE BERNARD SHAW (b. 1856)

(1) BIBLIOGRAPHIES

Wells, G. H. A Bibliography of the Books and Pamphlets of George Bernard Shaw. With Occasional Notes by G. B. Shaw. 1925–9. [Supplement to Bookman's Journ.]

Broad, C. L. and V. M. Dictionary to the Plays and Novels of Bernard Shaw; with Bibliography of his Works and of the Literature concerning him. With a Record of the Principal Shavian Play Productions. 1929.

Holmes, M. Some Bibliographical Notes on the Novels of George Bernard Shaw. With some Comments by Bernard Shaw. [1929.]

(2) COLLECTED AND SELECTED WORKS

Selected Passages from the Works of Bernard Shaw. Chosen by Charlotte F. Shaw. 1912.

Cabinet Collection of the Plays. 1926.

The Works of Bernard Shaw. 1930– .

Collected Works. 21 vols. New York, 1930–1.

The Complete Plays. 1931.

Prefaces. 1934. [Includes all the prefaces, with any added notes made by the author up to 1934. Among the more important prefaces are: Getting Married (Getting Married); Parents and Children (Misalliance); Epistle Dedicatory, The Revolutionist's Handbook, Maxims for Revolutionists (Man and Superman); [On prostitution and censorship of plays] (Mrs Warren's Profession); On Doctors (The Doctor's Dilemma); Imprisonment (S. and B. Webb, English Local Government); The Infidel Half Century (Back to Methuselah); On the Prospects of Christianity (Androcles and the Lion); Saint Joan (Saint Joan); Mainly about Myself (Plays Unpleasant).]

Short Stories, Scraps and Shavings. 1934. [Includes The Adventures of the Black Girl, various short stories rptd from periodicals 1885–1916, and some unpbd dramatic fragments, etc.]

(3) PLAYS

Widowers' Houses. A Comedy. (Royalty, 9 Dec. 1892.) 1893.

Plays, Pleasant and Unpleasant. 2 vols. 1898. [Vol. I: Plays Unpleasant: Widowers' Houses (Royalty, 9 Dec. 1892); Mrs Warren's Profession (Stage Soc. at New Lyric, 5 Jan. 1902); The Philanderer. (Cripplegate Institute, 20 Feb. 1905; Court, 5 Feb. 1907.) Vol. II: Plays Pleasant: Arms and the Man (Avenue, 21 April 1894); Candida (Theatre Royal, South Shields, 30 March 1895); The Man of Destiny (Grand Theatre, Croydon, 1 July 1897); You never can tell (Stage Soc. at Royalty, 26 Nov. 1899).]

Three Plays for Puritans: The Devil's Disciple (Bayswater Bijou, 17 April 1897), Caesar and Cleopatra (Theatre Royal, Newcastle-on-Tyne, 15 March 1899), and Captain Brassbound's Conversion (Stage Soc. at Strand, 16 Dec. 1900). 1901.

Man and Superman. A Comedy and a Philosophy. (Court, 23 May 1905.) 1903. [Includes Epistle Dedicatory, The Revolutionist's Handbook, and Maxims for Revolutionists.]

Mrs Warren's Profession. A Play in Four Acts. 1903. [Stage Soc. edn, with author's apology; first pbd in Plays, Pleasant and Unpleasant, 1898; the Apology alone, with introduction by J. Corbin, The Tyranny of Police and Press, New York, 1905.]

Passion, Poison, and Petrifaction, or the Fatal Gazogene. A Tragedy. (Booth in Regent's Park, 14 July 1905.) [1905.] [Burlesque melodrama, first pbd in Harry Furniss's Christmas Annual, 1905.]

John Bull's Other Island (Court, 1 Nov. 1904) and Major Barbara (Court, 28 Nov. 1905); also How he lied to her Husband (Berkeley Lyceum, New York, 26 Sept. 1904). 1907.

Interlude at the Playhouse. (Playhouse, 28 Jan. 1907.) [In Daily Mail, 29 Jan. 1907; not rptd.]

Press Cuttings. A Topical Sketch compiled from the Editorial and Correspondence Columns of the Daily Papers. (Court, 9 July 1909.) 1909.

The Doctor's Dilemma (Court, 20 Nov. 1906), Getting Married (Haymarket, 12 May 1908) and The Shewing-up of Blanco Posnet (Abbey Theatre, Dublin, 25 Aug. 1909). 1911.

41

Misalliance (Duke of York's, 23 Feb. 1910), the Dark Lady of the Sonnets (Haymarket, 24 Nov. 1910), and Fanny's First Play (Little, 19 April 1911). With a Treatise on Parents and Children. 1914.

Androcles and the Lion (St James's, 1 Sept. 1913), Overruled (Duke of York's, 14 Oct. 1912), Pygmalion (Lessing Theatre, Berlin, 1 Nov. 1913; His Majesty's, 11 April 1914). 1916.

Heartbreak House (Court, 18 Oct. 1921), Great Catherine (Vaudeville, 18 Nov. 1913), and Playlets of the War. 1919. [The Playlets are: O'Flaherty, V.C. (Lyric, Hammersmith, 20 Dec. 1920); The Inca of Perusalem (Birmingham Repertory, 9 Oct. 1916); Augustus does his Bit (Stage Soc. at Court, 21 Jan. 1917); Annajanska, the Bolshevik Empress (Coliseum, 21 Jan. 1918).]

Back to Methuselah. A Metabiological Pentateuch. (Birmingham Repertory, 9 Oct. 1923.) 1921. [Includes preface on 'Creative Evolution as the Creed of the Twentieth Century.']

Saint Joan. A Chronicle Play in Six Scenes and an Epilogue. (Theatre Guild, New York, 28 Dec. 1923; New, 26 March 1924.) 1924.

Translations and Tomfooleries. 1926. [Contents: Jitta's Atonement; adapted from the German of S. Trebitsch (Shubert Theatre, New York, 6 Jan. 1923); The Admirable Bashville, or Constancy Unrewarded; Press Cuttings; The Glimpse of Reality (Arts, 20 Nov. 1927); Passion, Poison and Petrifaction, or the Fatal Gazogene; The Fascinating Foundling; The Music Cure (Little, 28 Jan. 1914).]

The Apple Cart. A Political Extravaganza. (Polish Theatre, Warsaw, 29 June 1929; Malvern Festival, Aug. 1929.) 1930.

Too True to be Good (Colonial Theatre, Boston, 29 Feb. 1932; Malvern Festival, Aug. 1932), Village Wooing (Tunbridge Wells Repertory, 30 April 1934) and On the Rocks (Winter Garden, 25 Nov. 1933). 1934.

The Simpleton of the Unexpected Isles. (Malvern Festival, 29 July 1935.) 1935.

Three New Plays: The Simpleton of the Unexpected Isles, The Six of Calais (Regent's Park, 17 July 1934), The Millionairess. 1936.

(4) NOVELS

Cashel Byron's Profession. A Novel. 1886; [1889] (rev.); 1901 (newly rev. as Novels of his Nonage, no. 4). [First pbd in To-day, 1885–6; for dramatic version see under Plays, The Admirable Bashville.]

An Unsocial Socialist. 1887. [First pbd in To-day, 1884.]

Love among the Artists. Chicago, 1900; 1914. [First pbd in Our Corner, 1887–8.]

The Irrational Knot. Being the Second Novel of his Nonage. 1905. [First pbd in Our Corner, 1885–7.]

(5) LITERARY, DRAMATIC AND MUSICAL CRITICISM

The Quintessence of Ibsenism. 1891; 1913 (completed to the death of Ibsen).

The Perfect Wagnerite. A Commentary on the Ring of the Niblungs. 1898.

Dramatic Opinions and Essays; with an Apology. Containing as well a Word on the Dramatic Opinions and Essays of Bernard Shaw by James Huneker. 2 vols. 1907. [Selected from Saturday Rev. 5 Jan. 1895–21 May 1898.]

The Sanity of Art. An Exposure of the Current Nonsense about Artists being Degenerate. 1908. [A criticism of Max Nordau's Entartung; rptd from Liberty, New York, 1895.]

London Music in 1888–89 as heard by Corno di Bassetto (later known as Bernard Shaw). With some Further Autobiographical Particulars. 1937.

(6) SOCIOLOGICAL AND MISCELLANEOUS WRITINGS

The Common Sense of Municipal Trading. 1904; 1908 (with new preface).

Socialism and Superior Brains. A Reply to Mr [W. H.] Mallock. 1909. [From Fortnightly Rev. 1894.]

Common Sense about the War. [Supplement to New Statesman, 14 Nov. 1914.]

How to settle the Irish Question. Dublin, 1917.

Peace Conference Hints. 1919.

Ruskin's Politics. 1921.

Table-Talk of G. B. S. Conversations on Things in General between Bernard Shaw and his Biographer. By Archibald Henderson. 1925.

Letters from George Bernard Shaw to Miss Alma Murray. Edinburgh, 1927 (priv. ptd).

The Intelligent Woman's Guide to Socialism and Capitalism. 1928.

Bernard Shaw and Karl Marx. A Symposium, 1884–1889. New York, 1930. [Articles on Marx by Shaw, and controversy between Shaw and P. H. Wicksteed; ed. by R. W. Ellis.]

Ellen Terry and Bernard Shaw. A Correspondence. 1931. [With preface by Shaw; see also E. Gordon Craig, Ellen Terry and her Secret Self, 1931.]

What I really wrote about the War. 1931.

The Adventures of the Black Girl in her Search for God. 1932.

The Political Madhouse in America and Nearer Home. A Lecture. 1933.

[Mr Shaw has also pbd many pamphlets (especially for the Fabian Society), lectures, reports of debates, and periodical articles, and has edited or contributed introductions to numerous works by other authors; his works have been translated into French, German, Spanish, Swedish, Danish, Hungarian and Polish.]

(7) BIOGRAPHY AND CRITICISM
(a) Books

Mencken, H. L. George Bernard Shaw: his Plays. 1905.

Castren, G. G. Bernard Shaw. Helsingfors, 1906.

Jackson, Holbrook. Bernard Shaw. 1907.

Chesterton, G. K. George Bernard Shaw. 1909.

Deacon, R. M. Bernard Shaw as Artist-Philosopher. 1910.

Caro, J. George Bernard Shaw und Shakespeare. Frankfort, 1912.

Cestre, C. Bernard Shaw et son Œuvre. Paris, 1912.

Hamon, A. F. A. Le Molière du XXe Siècle: Bernard Shaw. Paris, 1913; tr. Eng. 1916.

Norwood, G. Euripides and Mr Shaw. An Address to the Newport (Mon.) Literary Society, December 1912. 1913.

Richter, Helene. Die Quintessenz des Shawismus. Leipzig, 1913.

MacCabe, J. George Bernard Shaw. A Critical Study. 1914.

Howe, P. P. Bernard Shaw. A Critical Study. 1915.

Palmer, J. Bernard Shaw, Harlequin or Patriot? 1915.

Burton, R. Bernard Shaw, the Man and the Mask. 1916.

Lord, D. A. George Bernard Shaw. 1916.

Skimpole, H. Bernard Shaw. 1918.

Duffin, H. C. The Quintessence of Bernard Shaw. 1920; 1939 (expanded).

Engel, F. Bernard Shaw und seine besten Bühnenwerke. Berlin, 1921.

Shanks, E. Bernard Shaw. 1924.

Collis, J. S. Shaw. 1925. [With annotations by Shaw.]

Eulenberg, H. Gegen Shaw. Eine Streitschrift, mit einer Shaw-Parodie des Verfassers. Dresden, 1925.

Robertson, J. M. Mr Shaw and the Maid. 1925.

Rider, D. Adventures with Bernard Shaw. [1929.]

Wagenknecht, E. A Guide to Bernard Shaw. New York, 1929.

De Casserers, B. Mencken and Shaw. New York, [1930].

Brinser, A. The Respectability of Mr Bernard Shaw. Cambridge, U.S.A., 1931.

Harris, Frank. Frank Harris on Bernard Shaw. An Unauthorised Biography based on Firsthand Information. With a Postscript by Mr Shaw. 1931.

Henderson, Archibald. Bernard Shaw, Playboy and Prophet. Authorized. 1932. [The official biography. 1st edn 1911.]

Lengnick, P. Ehe und Familie bei Bernard Shaw. Königsberg, 1933.

Moore, Mina. Bernard Shaw et la France. Paris, 1933.

Rattray, R. F. Bernard Shaw. A Chronicle and an Introduction. 1934.

Gupta, S. C. S. The Art of Bernard Shaw. 1936.

Heydet, X. Shaw-Kompendium: Verzeichnis und Analyse seiner Werke. Paris, 1936.

Knowlton, T. A. Economic Theory of George Bernard Shaw. Orono, 1936.

Saxe, J. Bernard Shaw's Phonetics. Copenhagen, 1936.

Hackett, J. P. Shaw, George versus Bernard. 1937.

(b) Chapters in Books and Periodical Articles

Mallock, W. H. A Socialist in a Corner. Fortnightly Rev. LXI, 1894.

Walkley, A. B. Frames of Mind. 1899.

Street, G. S. Shaw and Sheridan. Blackwood's Mag. CLXVII, 1900.

Hale, E. E. Dramatists of To-day. New York, 1905.

Huneker, J. G. Iconoclasts. A Book of Dramatists. [1906.]

Boynton, H. W. Shaw as a Critic. Atlantic Monthly, XCIX, 1907.

Hankin, St J. Bernard Shaw as a Critic. Fortnightly Rev. 1907.

Dukes, A. Modern Dramatists. 1911.

—— The Youngest Drama. 1924.

—— A Doll's House and the Open Door; with Two Letters from George Bernard Shaw. Theatre Arts Monthly, XII, 1928.

Montague, C. E. Dramatic Values. 1911; 1925 (rev.).

Armstrong, C. F. Shakespeare to Shaw. Studies in the Life's Work of Six Dramatists of the English Stage. 1913.

Henderson, Archibald. European Dramatists. 1914.

Palmer, J. Bernard Shaw: an Epitaph. Fortnightly Rev. CIII, 1915. [Also separately.]

Parker, D. C. Bernard Shaw as a Musical Critic. Opera Mag. (New York), June 1915.

Scott, Dixon. Men of Letters. 1916.

Slosson, E. E. Six Major Prophets. 1917.

Phelps, W. L. Essays on Modern Dramatists. 1921.

Jones, H. A. Bernard Shaw as a Thinker. English Rev. xxxvi, xxxvii, 1923.

Guedalla, P. A Gallery. 1924.

Cammaerts, E. Molière and Bernard Shaw. Nineteenth Century, Sept. 1926.

Gardiner, A. G. Certain People of Importance. 1926.

Grein, J. T. Notes about Bernard Shaw. Illustrated London News, Aug. 1926.

Shaws Selbstbildnis, oder wie Frank [Harris] es hätte schreiben sollen. Deutsche Neue Rundschau, xxxvii, 1926.

D'Angelo, E. Bernard Shaw's Theory of Stage Representation. Quarterly Journ. of Speech, xv, 1929.

Wainger, B. M. Henry Sweet—Shaw's Pygmalion. Stud. Phil. xxvii, 1930.

Welby, T. E. Frank Harris: Bernard Shaw. An Antithesis. Fortnightly Rev. cxxxvii, 1932.

Burdett, O. A Critical Stroll through Bernard Shaw. London Mercury, xxviii, 1933.

Maurois, A. Bernard Shaw. Revue Hebdomadaire, 16, 23 March 1935.

Sobra, A. Les Femmes dans le Théâtre de G. Bernard Shaw. Revue de l'Enseignement des Langues vivantes, 1936.

H. B. G.

OSCAR FINGALL O'FLAHERTIE WILLS WILDE (1856–1900)

(1) BIBLIOGRAPHY

'Mason, Stuart' (C. S. Millard). A Bibliography of the Poems of Oscar Wilde. 1907.
—— Bibliography of Oscar Wilde. 1908 (priv. ptd); [1914].

(2) COLLECTED WORKS

The Poems of Oscar Wilde. 2 vols. New York, 1906.

[Works.] 14 vols. 1908. [13 vols. pbd by Methuen, London: the remaining vol., The Picture of Dorian Gray, pbd by Charles Carrington, Paris.]

[Works. Ed. R. B. Ross,] 12 vols. 1909; 14 vols. Boston, 1910; 14 vols. 1911.

Werke. Herausgegeben und eingeleitet von Arnold Zweig. 2 vols. Berlin, [1930].

The Works of Oscar Wilde. With drawings by Donia Nachshen. [1931.]

Complete Works of Oscar Wilde. 4 vols. Paris, 1936.

(3) SELECTED WORKS

Oscariana: Epigrams. 1895 (priv. ptd). [Rptd 1895, 1910, 1912, all priv. ptd.]

The Best of Oscar Wilde: being a Collection of the Best Poems and Prose Extracts of the

Writer. Collected by Oscar Hermann. Ed. W. W. Massee, New York, [1905].

Epigrams and Aphorisms by Oscar Wilde. Boston, 1905.

The Wisdom of Oscar Wilde; selected with Introduction and Index by Temple Scott. New York, 1906.

The Oscar Wilde Calendar. With some Unrecorded Sayings selected by Stuart Mason. 1910; 1911 (rev.); 1914 (rev.).

Selected Poems, including the Ballad of Reading Gaol. 1911; 1925 (13th edn). [Selected by R. B. Ross.]

Charmides, and Other Poems. 1913.

Aphorisms of Oscar Wilde. Selected and arranged by G. N. Sutton. 1914.

(4) PLAYS

Vera; or, The Nihilists. A Drama, in a Prologue and Four Acts. (New York, Union Square, 20 Aug. 1883.) 1880 (priv. ptd); 1882 (priv. ptd); 1902 (priv. ptd).

The Duchess of Padua: a Tragedy of the XVI Century. Written in Paris in the XIX Century. (New York, Broadway, 26 Jan. 1891—played under title of Guido Ferranti.) [New York, 1883] (priv. ptd); 1907 (prefatory letter by R. B. Ross).

Lady Windermere's Fan: a Play about a Good Woman. C. (St James's, 20 Feb. 1892.) 1893. Tr. Italian, Naples, 1912; Spanish, Madrid, 1920.

A Woman of no Importance. C. (Hay. 19 April 1893.) 1894.

An Ideal Husband. D. (Hay. 3 Jan. 1895.) 1899; [ed. R. B. Ross, 1914].

The Importance of being Earnest: a Trivial Comedy for Serious People. (St James's, 14 Feb. 1895.) 1899; tr. Spanish, Madrid, 1920.

Salomé: drame en un Acte. (Paris, Théâtre de l'Œuvre, 11 Feb. 1896; London, Bijou Theatre—New Stage Club, 10 May 1905.) Paris, 1893. Tr. Eng. [by Lord Alfred B. Douglas], 1894 (pictured by Aubrey Beardsley); Dutch, Amsterdam, 1918; Spanish, Madrid, 1919.

A Florentine Tragedy. (Literary Theatre Society, 10 June 1906.) [Written 1893–4; MS lost or stolen; first pbd in the first collected edn of the Works, 1908, with an opening scene by T. Sturge Moore, replacing one lost. Rptd in subsequent collected edns.]

For Love of the King. A Burmese Masque. [1922.]

(5) POEMS

Newdigate Prize Poem. Ravenna. Recited in the Theatre, Oxford, June 26, 1878. Oxford, 1878.

Poems. 1881.

The Sphinx. With Decorations by Charles Ricketts. 1894; 1910 (with notes by R. B. Ross).

The Ballad of Reading Gaol. By C.3.3. 1898. Tr. French, Paris, 1898; German, Leipzig, [1907]; Hungarian, 1912; Norwegian, Christiania, [1915]; Russian, Moscow, 1919; Swedish, Åbo, 1907.

To M[argaret] B[urne] J[ones]. [1920] (priv. ptd). [With note by 'Stuart Mason.']

(6) FICTION

The Happy Prince, and Other Tales. Illustrated by Walter Crane and Jacomb Hood. 1888; tr. Spanish, Madrid, 1922.

The Picture of Dorian Gray. 1891; 1891 (with 6 new chs.). Tr. Czech, Prague, [1905]; Danish, Copenhagen, 1905; Dutch, Amsterdam, [1893]; Finnish, Porvoosa, 1906; French, Paris, 1895; German, Leipzig, [1901]; Modern Greek, Athens, [1912]; Hungarian, Budapest, 1907; Italian, Palermo, [1906]; Polish, Warsaw, 1906; Russian [Moscow, 1905]; Swedish, Stockholm, [1905]; Yiddish, [1912]. [First pbd in Lippincott's Mag. July 1890.]

Lord Arthur Savile's Crime, and Other Stories. 1891. Tr. Spanish, Madrid, [1922].

A House of Pomegranates. The Design and Decoration by C. Ricketts and C. H. Shannon. 1891. Tr. Spanish, Madrid, [1922]; German, Leipzig, 1914.

(7) MISCELLANEOUS PROSE

Intentions. 1891. Tr. French, Paris, 1905; Spanish, Madrid, [1926].

The Soul of Man. 1895 (priv. ptd); 1912 (as The Soul of Man under Socialism; with preface by R. B. Ross). [Originally pbd under the longer title in Fortnightly Rev. Feb. 1891.]

The Portrait of Mr W. H. Portland, Maine, 1901. [Originally pbd in Blackwood's Mag. July 1889. Later rptd with Lord Arthur Savile's Crime.]

De Profundis. 1905 (preface by R. B. Ross); New York, 1909 (80 pp. of new matter). Tr. German, Berlin, 1905; French, Paris, 1905; Spanish, Madrid, [1925].

The Suppressed Portion of 'De Profundis' now for the First Time published by his Literary Executor, Robert [B.] Ross. New York, 1913 (priv. ptd).

Wilde v. Whistler. Being an Acrimonious Correspondence on Art between Oscar Wilde and J. A. MacN. Whistler. 1906 (priv. ptd).

Resurgam: Unpublished Letters. [Ed. C. K. Shorter], 1917 (priv. ptd).

After Reading. Letters to Robert Ross. 1921.

After Berneval. Letters to Robert Ross. 1922.

Letters to the Sphinx [Ada Leverson]; with Reminiscences of the Author by Ada Leverson. 1930.

Sixteen Letters. Ed. J. Rothenstein, 1930.

[There have been various other collections and recombinations of essays by Wilde, pbd England, America, and elsewhere. Also very large numbers of trns of his different works into many foreign languages.]

(8) BIOGRAPHY AND CRITICISM

(a) Books and Pamphlets

Gómez Carillo, E. Esquisses. Siluetas de Escritores y Artistas. Madrid, 1892.

Archer, W. The Theatrical 'World.' 5 vols. 1893–7.

'Y.T.O.' (L. C. M. S. Amery, F. W. Hirst and H. A. A. Cruso). Aristophanes at Oxford. Oxford, 1894. [A satire, in verse.]

Young, Dal. Apologia pro Oscar Wilde. [1895.]

Grein, J. T. Dramatic Criticism. Vol. III, 1902.

Sherard, R. H. Oscar Wilde: the Story of an Unhappy Friendship. 1902 (priv. ptd); 1905.

—— The Life of Oscar Wilde. With a Full Reprint of the Famous Revolutionary Article, 'Jacta Alea est,' by Jane Francesca Elgee, Mother of Oscar Wilde. 1906. [Supplemented by The Real Oscar Wilde, 1917.]

—— Oscar Wilde Twice Defended. Chicago, 1934.

—— Bernard Shaw, Frank Harris and Oscar Wilde. New York, 1936.

Gide, A. Oscar Wilde. [In Prétextes, Reflexions critiques sur quelques Points de Littérature et de Morale, Paris, 1903; tr. Eng. 'Stuart Mason,' 1905 (with introduction, notes and bibliography).

—— Oscar Wilde: In Memoriam. (Souvenirs): le 'De Profundis,' 1910.

Hagemann, Carl. Oscar Wilde. Studien zur modernen Weltliteratur. Minden, 1904.

Blei, F. In Memoriam Oscar Wilde. Leipzig, 1905.

La Jeunesse, E. Recollections of Oscar Wilde, by E. La Jeunesse, A. Gide and F. Blei. Translated by P. Pollard. Greenwich, Connecticut, 1905.

Young, John M. S. Osrac; the Self-Sufficient, and Other Poems, with a Memoir of the late Oscar Wilde. 1905.

Glaenzer, R. B. Decorative Art in America: a Lecture by Oscar Wilde; together with Letters, Reviews and Interviews. New York, 1906.

The Trial of Oscar Wilde, from the Shorthand Reports. 1906.

Ingleby, L. C. Oscar Wilde. 1907.

—— Oscar Wilde. Some Reminiscences. 1912.

Weisz, E. Psychologische Streifzüge über Oscar Wilde. Leipzig, 1908. [With introduction by R. Foerster.]

Balen, C. L. van. Manner en Vrouwen van Beteekenis in onze Dagen. Haarlem, 1910.

Brémont, A. Oscar Wilde and his Mother. A Memoir. 1911.

Henderson, A. Interpreters of Life and the Modern Spirit. 1911.

Crosland, T. W. H. The First Stone. On reading the Unpublished Parts of 'De profundis.' [Priv. ptd.]

Kenilworth, W. W. A Study of Oscar Wilde. New York, 1912.

Ransome, A. Oscar Wilde. A Critical Study. 1912.

Oscar Wilde, Three Times Tried. 1912.

Bock, E. J. Walter Pater's Einfluss auf Oscar Wilde. Bonn, 1913.

Hopkins, R. T. Oscar Wilde. A Study of the Man and his Work. With Introduction by Sir T. M. Williams. 1913.

Howe, P. P. Dramatic Portraits. 1913.

Bendz, E. The Influence of Pater and Matthew Arnold in the Prose Writings of Oscar Wilde. Gothenburg, 1914.

—— Oscar Wilde: a Retrospect. Vienna, 1921.

Birnbaum, M. Oscar Wilde: Fragments and Memories. 1914.

Douglas, Lord Alfred. Oscar Wilde and Myself. 1914.

'Mason, Stuart' (C. S. Millard). Oscar Wilde: Art and Morality. A Defence of The Picture of Dorian Gray. 1915. [With the correspondence called forth by the book, and bibliography.]

—— Oscar Wilde and the Æsthetic Movement. Dublin, 1920.

—— Who wrote 'For Love of the King'? Birmingham, 1926.

Fehr, B. Studien zu Oscar Wilde's Gedichten. Berlin, 1918.

Harris, Frank. Oscar Wilde: his Life and Confessions. Together with Memories of Oscar Wilde, by Bernard Shaw. 2 vols. New York 1918. [See also Harris's Contemporary Portraits, vol. I, 1915.]

Engel, Fritz. Oscar Wilde und seine besten Bühnenwerke. Eine Einführung. Berlin, 1922.

Duthuit, G. Le Rose et le Noir. De Walter Pater à Oscar Wilde. Paris, 1923.

Housman, L. Écho de Paris. A Study from Life. 1923. [Recollections of a conversation between the author, Oscar Wilde, and others.]

Powys, J. C. Suspended Judgments. New York, 1923.

Jackson, Holbrook. The Eighteen Nineties. 1923.

González-Ruano, C. Notas sobre Oscar Wilde. Madrid, 1925.

Choisy, L. F. Oscar Wilde. Paris, 1927.

Maurois, A. Études anglaises—Dickens, Walpole, Ruskin et Wilde. Paris, 1927.

Davray, H. D. Oscar Wilde: la Tragédie finale. Suivi d'Épisodes et Souvenirs et des Apocryphes. Paris, 1928.

Braybrooke, P. Oscar Wilde: a Study. 1930.

Herzog, Alice. Die Märchen Oscar Wildes. Mulhouse, 1930.

Symons, A. A Study of Oscar Wilde. 1930.

Thompson, Vance. The Two Deaths of Oscar Wilde. San Francisco, 1930.

Lemonnier, L. La Vie d'Oscar Wilde. Paris, 1931.

Cooper-Prichard, A. H. Conversations with Oscar Wilde. 1931.

Ricketts, C. S. Oscar Wilde. Recollections by Jean Paul Raymond and Charles Ricketts. 1932.

Evans, B. I. English Poetry in the Later Nineteenth Century. 1933. [Ch. xiv.]

Renier, G. J. Oscar Wilde. 1933.

Zanco, A. Oscar Wilde. Genoa, 1934.

Lewis, L. and Smith, J. Oscar Wilde discovers America. New York, 1936.

O'Sullivan, V. Aspects of Wilde. 1936.

Brasol, B. Oscar Wilde. 1938.

(b) Articles in periodicals

Leadman, W. M. The Literary Position of Oscar Wilde. Westminster Rev. CLXVI, 1906.

Hankin, St J. The Collected Plays of Oscar Wilde. Fortnightly Rev. LXXXIX, 1908.

Woodbridge, H. E. Oscar Wilde as a Poet. Poet Lore (Boston), XIX, 1908.

Esdaile, A. J. K. The New Hellenism. Fortnightly Rev. LXXXVIII, 1910.

Wood, A. I. P. Oscar Wilde as a Critic. North American Rev. CCII, 1915.

Richter, H. Oscar Wilde's Persönlichkeit in seinen Gedichten. E. Studien, LIV, 1920.

Fehr, B. Das gelbe Buch in Oscar Wildes Dorian Gray. E. Studien, LV, 1921.

Le Gallienne, R. Oscar Wilde and Willie Hughes. Bookman (New York), LIV, 1921.

Lintot, B. Oscar Wilde as a Letter-writer. Littell's Living Age, CCCXX, 1924.

Shanks, E. Oscar Wilde. London Mercury, X, 1924.

Rudwin, M. Oscar Wilde et Barbey d'Aurévilly. Révue anglo-américaine, April 1927.

Cook, H. Lucius. French Sources of Wilde's Picture of Dorian Gray. Romanic Rev. XIX, 1928.

Temborius, H. Neuromantische Wesenzüge bei Oscar Wilde. Zeitschrift für französichen und englischen Unterricht, XXVII, 1928.

Atkinson, G. T. Oscar Wilde at Oxford. Cornhill Mag. LXVI, 1929.

Eichbaum, G. Die persönlichen und literarischen Beziehungen zwischen Oscar Wilde und James MacNeill Whistler. Bibliographie für englischen Studien, LXV, 1931.

Ellehauge, M. Initial Stages in the Development of the English Problem-Play. E. Studien, LXVI, 1932.

Herbert Spencer and Oscar Wilde; from Works and Days, the Diary of Michael Field. Ed. T. S. Moore, Cornhill Mag. LXXII, 1932.

Silver, R. G. Oscar makes a Call [on Whitman]. Colophon, pt 20, 1935.

Flanagan, J. T. Oscar Wilde's Twin City Appearances. Minnesota History, XVII, 1936.

Saix, G. de. Oscar Wilde et le Théâtre. Mercure de France, 1937, pp. 513–49.

Ullmann, S. Von. Synästhesien in den dichterischen Werken von Oscar Wilde. E. Studien, LXXII, 1938.

H. B. G.

SIR JAMES MATTHEW BARRIE (1860–1937)

(1) BIBLIOGRAPHIES

Garland, H. A Bibliography of the Writings of Sir James Matthew Barrie. 1928.

Cutler, B. D. Sir James M. Barrie. A Bibliography, with Full Collations of the American Unauthorized Editions. [1931.]

Block, A. Sir J. M. Barrie: his First Editions; Points and Values. 1933.

(2) COLLECTED AND SELECTED WORKS

The Novels, Tales and Sketches. 12 vols. New York, 1896–1902. (Thistle edn.)

The Kirriemuir Edition of the Works. 10 vols. 1913; 1922.

The Uniform Edition of the Plays. 10 vols. 1918–38. [The following are 1st edns of plays not so far (1938) separately pbd: What Every Woman knows (Duke of York's, 3 Sept. 1908), 1918; Alice Sit-by-the-Fire (Duke of York's, 5 April 1905), 1919; A Kiss for Cinderella (Wyndham's, 3 March 1916), 1920; Dear Brutus (Wyndham's, 17 Oct. 1917), 1922; Mary Rose (Haymarket, 22 April 1920), 1924; Peter Pan, or the Boy who would not grow up (Duke of York's, 27 Dec. 1904), 1928; The Boy David (His Majesty's, Dec. 1936), 1938 (preface by H. G[ranville]-B[arker]).]

The Works of J. M. Barrie. 10 vols. New York, 1918.

The Works of J. M. Barrie. [1925– .]

Representative Plays. With an Introduction by William Lyon Phelps. New York, 1926. [Contents: Quality Street; The Admirable Crichton; What Every Woman Knows; Dear Brutus; The Twelve-Pound Look; The Old Lady shows her Medals.]

The Plays of J. M. Barrie. 1928.

Selections from the Plays. 1929.

Selections from the Prose Works. 1929.

The Works of J. M. Barrie, Peter Pan Edition. 14 vols. New York, 1929.

(3) PLAYS

Richard Savage. A Play in Four Acts. (Criterion, 16 April 1891.) 1891 (priv. ptd). [With H. B. Marriott Watson.]

Walker, London. A Farcical Comedy in Three Acts. (Toole's, 25 Feb. 1892.) 1907.

Jane Annie, or the Good Conduct Prize. A New and Original English Comic Opera. (Savoy, 13 May 1893.) 1893. [With Sir A. Conan Doyle; music by E. Ford.]

The Wedding Guest. A Play in Four Acts. (Garrick, 27 Sept. 1900.) 1900 (pbd as a supplement to Fortnightly Rev.); New York, 1900.

Quality Street. A Comedy in Four Acts. (Vaudeville, 17 Sept. 1902.) 1913; New York, 1918.

The Admirable Crichton. (Duke of York's, 4 Nov. 1902.) 1914; New York, 1918; tr. French, Paris, 1920.

Der Tag. A Play. (Coliseum, 21 Dec. 1914.) 1914; New York, 1914; New York, 1919 (with Half Hours).

Half Hours. 1914; New York, 1914; New York, 1919 (with Der Tag). [Contents (all produced at Duke of York's Theatre): Pantaloon (5 April 1905); The Twelve-Pound Look (1 March 1910); Rosalind (14 Oct. 1912); The Will (4 Sept. 1913).]

Shakespeare's Legacy. F. (Drury Lane, 14 April 1916.) 1916 (priv. ptd).

Echoes of the War. 1918. [Contents: The Old Lady shows her Medals (7 April 1917); The New Word (22 March 1915); Barbara's Wedding (Apollo, 23 Aug. 1927); A Well-Remembered Voice (28 June 1918).]

Shall we join the Ladies? (Royal Dramatic Academy's Theatre, 27 March 1921). [First act of an unfinished play; first pbd in C. Asquith, The Black Cap: New Stories of Murder and Mystery, 1927.]

[For Dear Brutus, Mary Rose, Peter Pan, and other plays first pbd in the uniform edn, see under Collected and Selected Works, above. The following have not been pbd: The Professor's Love-Story (Comedy, 25 June 1894); Little Mary (Wyndham's, 24 Sept. 1903); The Adored One (Duke of York's, 4 Sept. 1913); Rosy Rapture, or the Pride of the Beauty Chorus (Duke of York's, 22 March 1915); Old Friends (Duke of York's, 1 March 1910).]

(4) FICTION

[In many cases there were numerous pirated American edns, which as a rule are not noted.]

Better Dead. 1888 (*bis*); New York, 1896 (1st authorised American edn).

Auld Licht Idylls. 1888; New York, 1891; 1895; 1898 (11th edn). [Based on articles first pbd in St James's Gazette, 1884–5.]

When a Man's Single. A Tale of Literary Life. 1888; New York, 1889 (etc., pirated); New York, 1896 (1st authorised American edn).

A Window in Thrums. 1889; New York, 1892; 1898 (16th edn). [Ch. i separately rptd, 1895, as The Sabbath Day.]

The Little Minister. 3 vols. 1891 (*bis*); New York, 1891 (*bis*); 2 vols. Leipzig, 1891; 1892; New York, 1892; New York, 1897; 1898; 1903; 1905; 1907. [First pbd in Good Words, Jan.–Dec. 1891; dramatic version, Haymarket Theatre, 6 Nov. 1897.]

A Lady's Shoe. New York, 1893 (unauthorised 1st edn, with The Inconsiderate Waiter); 1894 (in Miss Parson's Adventure, by W. C. Russell, and Other Stories by Other Writers); New York, 1898.

A Powerful Drug; and Other Stories. New York, 1893.

Sentimental Tommy: the Story of his Boyhood. 1896; New York, 1896; 1897; tr. Czech, Prague, 1902.

Jess. Boston, [1898]. [Unauthorised collection of the first 16 stories in A Window in Thrums.]

Tommy and Grizel. 1900; New York, [1900]; Toronto, 1900.

The Little White Bird. 1902; New York, 1902; Toronto, 1902. [First pbd in Scribner's Mag. Aug.–Nov. 1902.]

Peter Pan in Kensington Gardens. (From 'The Little White Bird'). With Drawings by Arthur Rackham. 1906; New York, 1906; 1912; tr. French, Paris, 1917.

Peter and Wendy. 1911; New York, 1911; 1915, 1921 (as Peter Pan and Wendy); New York, 1921; tr. Spanish, Barcelona, 1925. [Many adaptations of Peter Pan pbd, chiefly for young children; one of these, The Peter Pan Picture Book, tr. French, London, 1916.]

Farewell, Miss Julie Logan. 1932. [First pbd as Christmas supplement to The Times, 24 Dec. 1931.]

(5) MISCELLANEOUS WRITINGS

An Edinburgh Eleven. Pencil Portraits from College Life. 1889; New York, 1892. [First pbd in British Weekly, 1888.]

My Lady Nicotine. 1890; New York, 1896 (1st authorised American edn).

A Holiday in Bed, and Other Sketches. With a Short Biographical Sketch of the Author. New York, 1892. [Unauthorised collection of periodical articles.]

A Tillyloss Scandal. New York, [1893] (*bis*), 1894, 1915? [Unauthorised collection of periodical articles.]

Two of them. New York, 1893. [Unauthorised collection of periodical articles.]

An Auld Licht Manse and Other Sketches. New York, 1893. [Unauthorised collection of periodical articles.]

Allahakbarries C[ricket] C[lub]. 1893 (priv. ptd).

Scotland's Lament. A Poem on the Death of Robert Louis Stevenson, December 3rd, 1894. 1895 (priv. ptd); 1918 (priv. ptd).

Margaret Ogilvy. By her Son, J. M. Barrie. 1896; New York, 1896.

The Allahakbarrie Book of Broadway Cricket for 1899. 1899 (priv. ptd).

Life in a Country Manse. 1899. [Unauthorised. First pbd in British Weekly, July–Aug. 1891; rptd in A Holiday in Bed and Other Sketches, 1892, and in A Tillyloss Scandal, [1893].]

George Meredith. 1909; Chicago, 1910 (as Neither Dorking nor the Abbey); Portland, Maine, 1911, 1912, 1914 (all 3 pirated). [First pbd in Westminster Gazette, 26 May 1909, as Neither Dorking nor the Abbey.]

Charles Frohman. A Tribute. 1915 (priv. ptd). [First pbd in Daily Mail, 10 May 1915.]

Who was Sarah Findlay? By Mark Twain. With a Suggested Solution of the Mystery by J. M. Barrie. 1917 (priv. ptd).

The Rectorial Address delivered at St Andrews University, May 3rd 1922. Courage. 1922 (*bis*); New York, 1922. [First pbd in St Andrews University Mag. XVII, 1922.]

Neil and Tintinnabulum. 1925 (priv. ptd).

The Greenwood Hat. 1930 (priv. ptd); 1937.

[Several speeches by Sir James Barrie have also been pbd (now collected in M'Connachie and J.M.B., 1938); he wrote numerous articles in periodicals (listed in H. Garland's Bibliography) and contributed prefaces to various books, including Daisy Ashford's The Young Visiters, 1919.]

(6) BIOGRAPHY AND CRITICISM

(a) Books

Hammerton, Sir J. A. J. M. Barrie and his Books. Biographical and Critical Studies. 1900.

—— Barrie. The Story of a Genius. 1929.

The Bookman Autumn Double Number, 1910.

—— Special Christmas Number, 1920.

Walbrook, H. M. J. M. Barrie and the Theatre. 1922.

Braybrooke, P. J. M. Barrie. A Study in Fairies and Mortals. [1924.]

Goitein, P. L. A New Approach to an Analysis of 'Mary Rose.' [1926.]

Moult, T. Barrie. 1928.

Darton, F. J. H. Barrie. 1929.

Eschenauer, W. Sir James Barrie als Dramatiker. Würzburg, 1930.

Kennedy, John. Thrums and the Barrie Country. 1930.

Roy, J. A. James Matthew Barrie. 1937.

Chalmers, P. R. The Barrie Inspiration. 1938.

Darlington, W. A. J. M. Barrie. 1938.

(b) Periodical Articles and Chapters in Books

Beerbohm, M. Barrie as a Child. Saturday Rev. xcix, 1905, p. 13.

Browne, E. A. Barrie's Dramatic and Social Outlook. Fortnightly Rev. lxxxv, 1906.

Howe, P. P. Dramatic Portraits. 1913.

Scott, Dixon. Men of Letters. 1916. [Pp. 63–77, The Ambition of Sir James M. Barrie, Bart.]

Parker, W. M. Modern Scottish Writers. Edinburgh, 1917.

Herford, O. The Question of the Moment: Did Barrie write The Young Visiters? Bookman (U.S.A.), l, 1919.

Hind, C. L. Authors and I. 1921.

Phelps, W. L. Essays on Modern Dramatists. New York, 1921. [Pp. 1–66.]

Vernon, F. The Twentieth Century Theatre. 1924.

Frith, J. C. How James Matthew Barrie 'commenced author.' Bookman's Journ. xi, 1925.

A Barrie Bibliography. TLS. 15 Nov. 1928.

Delavenay, E. 'Mary Rose' et le Problème de la Personnalité chez Barrie. Revue anglo-américaine, vi, 1929.

Kaplan, I. B. A Scot in America. Colophon, i, 1936.

S. J. L. and H. B. G.

OTHER DRAMATISTS (1870–1900)

[For Synge, Yeats and the other Anglo-Irish dramatists of the 'nineties and after see p. 1059 below.]

JAMES ALBERY (1838–1889)

Two Roses. An Original Comedy. (Vaudeville, 4 June 1870.) French, cxviii, [1881].

The Pink Dominos. Founded on the Comedy of [A.] Hennequin and [A.] Delacour. (Criterion, 31 March 1877.) [1878.]

The Dramatic Works of James Albery. Ed. W. Albery, 2 vols. 1939. [Includes memoir, chronological table, correspondence and newspaper reports in full; many plays here first pbd.]

HENRY JAMES BYRON (1834–1884)
(a) Plays

George de Barnwell. A Burlesque Pantomime Opening [in verse]. (Adelphi, 26 Dec. 1862.) Lacy, lvii, [1863].

War to the Knife. C. (Prince of Wales, 10 June 1865.) Lacy, lxvii, [1866].

Cyril's Success. C. (Globe, 28 Nov. 1868.) Lacy, lxxxix, [1871].

Partners for Life. C. (Globe, 7 Oct. 1871.) Lacy, cviii, [1876].

Old Soldiers. C. (Strand, 25 Jan. 1873.) Lacy, cxiii, [1879].

Weak Woman. C. (Strand, 6 May 1875.) Lacy, cxii, [1878].

Our Boys. C. (Vaudeville, 16 Jan. 1875.) Lacy, cxvi, [1880].

£20 a Year—all found. F. (Folly, 17 April 1876.) Lacy, cxvi, [1880].

[Byron was an enormously prolific writer. DNB. gives a chronological list, which 'omits little of importance,' of 136 pieces, chiefly farces, burlesques and comedies.]

(b) Novel

Paid in Full. 3 vols. 1865. [First pbd in Temple Bar.]

(c) Biography and Criticism

Wrey, P. H. J. Byron. London Society, xxvi, 1874.

Archer, W. Dramatists of To-Day. 1882.

Obituary. Era, 19 April 1884.

ROBERT BUCHANAN (1841–1901)
[See p. 333 above.]

'HENRY VERNON ESMOND,' i.e. HENRY VERNON JACK (1869–1922)

In and out of a Punt. Duologue. (St James's, 9 March 1896.) French, cxlviii, [1902].

One Summer's Day. C. (Comedy, 16 Sept. 1897.) New York, [1901].

The Wilderness. C. (St James's, 11 April 1901.) New York, 1901.

When We were Twenty-one. C. (Comedy, 2 Sept. 1901.) New York, 1903.

Billy's Little Love Affair. C. (Criterion, 2 Sept. 1903.) [1904?]

Her Vote. C. (Playhouse, 18 May 1909.) French, clviii, [1910].

Eliza Comes to Stay. F. (Criterion, 12 Feb. 1913.) French, 2510, [1913].

The Law Divine. C. (Wyndham's, 29 Aug. 1918.) *French*, 1035, [1922].

[About a dozen more plays by Esmond were produced, but only one of them, A Woman in Chains, seems to have been ptd.]

'MICHAEL FIELD'

[See p. 340 above.]

SYDNEY GRUNDY (1848–1914)

(a) *Plays*

The Snowball. F. (Strand, 2 Feb. 1879.) *French*, CXXXI, [1890].

In Honour Bound. C. (Prince of Wales's, 25 Sept. 1880.) *French*, CXXIII, [1885]. [From Scribe's Une Chaîne.]

The Silver Shield. C. (Strand, 19 May 1885.) *French*, CXLII, [1899].

A Fool's Paradise. C. (Prince of Wales's, Greenwich, 7 Oct. 1887.) *French*, CXLII, [1899].

A Pair of Spectacles. C. (Garrick, 22 Feb. 1890.) *French*, CXLII, [1899]. [Adapted from Les Petits Oiseaux of Labiche and Delacour.]

Haddon Hall. O. (Savoy, 24 Sept. 1892.) 1892. [Music by Sir A. Sullivan.]

Sowing the Wind. C. (Comedy, 30 Sept. 1893.) *French*, CXLVIII, [1902].

A Bunch of Violets. C. (Hay. 25 April 1894.) *French*, CXLVIII, [1902]. [Founded on Octave Feuillet's Montjoye.]

[Grundy wrote 10 other pieces, several of them adaptations from the French.]

(b) *Other Works*

The Days of his Vanity: a Passage in the Life of a Young Man. 1894.

The Play of the Future. By a Playwright of the Past. A Glance at 'The Future of the Theatre' by John Palmer. 1914.

(c) *Biography and Criticism*

Watson, Sir W. Sydney Grundy and the Critics. Theatre, XXXIII, 1894.

Beerbohm, M. Degenerates. Saturday Rev. LXXXVIII, 1899.

ISABELLA HARWOOD (1840?–1888)

[See p. 341 above.]

'JOHN OLIVER HOBBES' (1867–1906)

[See p. 549 above.]

HENRY SAMBROOKE LEIGH (1837–1883)

[See p. 346 above.]

PAUL MERITT (d. 1895)

(a) *Plays*

Glin Gath, or the Man in the Cleft. D. (Grecian, 1 April 1872.) *French*, XCIX, [1874].

Linked by Love. C. (Grecian, 29 July 1872.) *French*, CXXVIII, [1888].

'British Born.' D. (Grecian, 17 Oct. 1872.) *French*, CIX, [1878]. [With H. Pettitt.]

Velvet and Rags. A Spanish Romance of the Present Day. (Grecian, 6 April 1873.) *French*, CXII, [1878]. [With G. Conquest.]

Chopsticks and Spikins. F. (Grecian, 25 Sept. 1873.) *French*, CIX, [1878] (with his drama, Seven Sins, written with G. Conquest, acted Grecian, 27 Aug. 1874.)

Hand and Glove. D. (Grecian, 25 May, 1874.) *French*, CIX, [1878]. [With G. Conquest.]

The Word of Honour. A Jersey Love Story. D. (Grecian, 22 Oct. 1874.) *French*, CXIII, [1878].

The Golden Plough. A Melo-Dramatic Romance. (Adelphi, 11 Aug. 1877.) *French*, CXI, [1878].

(b) *Other Writings*

New Babylon, or Daughters of Eve. By Paul Merritt and W. H. Poole. 3 vols. 1882.

Loaded Dice. A Story of Modern Life. [In The Round Table Annual, [1891].]

[The above comprises the whole of Meritt's work in BM. He wrote a number of other plays which do not seem to have been pbd.]

(c) *Biography and Criticism*

Archer, W. English Dramatists of To-Day. 1882.

Pleasure. By Paul Meritt and A. Harris. Theatre, XIX, 1887.

HERMAN CHARLES MERIVALE (1839–1906)

(a) *Plays*

A Son of the Soil. Founded on the 'Lion Amoureux' of Ponsard. D. (Court, 4 Sept. 1872.) *Lacy*, XCVII, [1873].

A Husband in Clover. F. (Lyceum 26 Dec. 1873.) *French*, C, [1875].

The White Pilgrim. The Legend by G. A'-Beckett. T. (Court, 14 Feb. 1874.) 1874 (priv. ptd); *French*, CXIII, [1879]; 1883 (with other poems). [In verse.]

Peacock's Holiday. F. (Court, 16 April 1874.) *French*, CXV, [1879].

The Lady of Lyons Married and Settled. F. (Gaiety, 5 Oct. 1878.) *French*, CXV, [1879].

Florien. A Tragedy in Five Acts, and Other Poems. (Unacted?) 1884.

[Merivale wrote a number of other plays, mostly farces, some of which are listed in DNB.]

(b) *Other Works*

Faucit of Balliol. A Story in Two Parts. 3 vols. 1882.

Binko's Blues. A Tale for Children of All
Growths. 1884.
Life of W. M. Thackeray. 1891. [Completed
by Sir F. T. Marzials.]
Bar, Stage and Platform. Autobiographic
Memories. 1902.

(c) Biography and Criticism

Adams, W. D. Herman Merivale. Theatre,
XXIV, 1890.
Bancroft, Sir S. B. and E. The Bancrofts:
Recollections of Sixty Years. 1909.

T. A. PALMER

Too Late to save, or Doomed to die. D.
(Theatre Royal, Exeter, 1861.) 1878.
Among the Relics. C. (Theatre Royal, Ply-
mouth, 22 Nov. 1869.) *French*, CVIII,
[1877].
Rely on my Discretion. F. (Royalty, 17 Jan.
1870.) *French*, CVI, [1877].
Insured at Lloyd's. D. (New Queen's, Man-
chester, 5 Nov. 1870.) *French*, CX, [1878].
A Dodge for a Dinner. F. (Strand, 28 Dec.
1872.) *French*, C, [1874].
The Last Life. D. (Greenwich, 9 Feb. 1874.)
French, CIII, [1875]. [Adapted from one of
Mrs S. C. Hall's Stories of Irish Life.]
East Lynne. A Domestic Drama in a Pro-
logue and Four Acts. (Nottingham, 19 Nov.
1874.) *French*, CIII, [1875]. [Adapted from
Mrs Henry Wood's novel of the same name.]
Woman's Rights. C. (Grand, Douglas, Aug.
1882.) *French*, CXXI, [1885].

STEPHEN PHILLIPS (1864–1915)
(a) Plays (in verse)

Herod. T. (Her Majesty's, 31 Oct. 1900.)
1901.
Ulysses. D. (His Majesty's, 1 Feb. 1902.)
1902.
Paolo and Francesca. T. (St James's, 6
March 1902.) 1900.
The Sin of David. D. (Stadttheater, Düssel-
dorff, 30 Sept. 1905; Savoy, July 1914.)
1904; 1912 (rev.).
Nero. T. (His Majesty's, 25 Jan. 1906.) 1906.
[Part omitted appears as 1-act play (Nero's
Mother) in Lyrics and Dramas, 1913.]
Faust. T. (His Majesty's, 5 Sept. 1908.) 1908.
[With J. Comyns Carr.]
Pietro of Siena. D. (Studio, 10 Oct. 1911.)
1910.
Iole. D. (Cosmopolis, June 1913.) [Pbd in
New Poems, 1908.]
The King. D. (Unacted.) 1912. [Subsequently
included in Lyrics and Dramas, 1913.]
Armageddon: a Modern Epic Drama. (New
Theatre, 1 June 1915.) 1915. [Partly in

verse and partly in prose. Rptd from
Lyrics and Dramas, 1913.]
Harold. A Chronicle Play. (Unacted.)
Poetry Rev. Jan., March 1916; ed. A.
Symons, 1927.

[The Last Heir, also called The Bride of
Lammermoor, though acted, was never pbd.
The Adversary, included in Lyrics and Dramas,
1913, was never acted.]

(b) Poems

Orestes and Other Poems. 1884 (priv. ptd).
Primavera. Poems by Four Authors. Oxford,
1890. [16 Poems, of which 4 are by
Phillips.]
Eremus: a Poem. 1894.
Christ in Hades. 1896; ed. C. L. Hind,
1917.
Poems. 1897; 1898 (enlarged and rev.).
Marpessa: a Poem. 1900; 1928.
New Poems. 1908.
The New Inferno. 1911.
Lyrics and Dramas. 1913.
Panama and Other Poems, Narrative and
Occasional. 1915.

(c) Biography and Criticism

Academy, 1 Jan. 1898. [Long review of
Poems, 1897.]
Farrer, R. J. Herod through the Opera Glass.
1901. [A parody of Phillips's Herod.]
Streatfield, R. A. Two Poets of the New
Century: Stephen Phillips and Laurence
Binyon. 1901. [Rptd from Monthly Rev.]
Archer, W. Poets of the Younger Generation.
1902.
—— Real Conversations. 1904.
Hale, E. E. Dramatists of To-Day. 1906.
Kyle, Galloway. 'Edited by Stephen Phillips.'
Poetry Rev. Jan.–Feb. 1916.
Meynell, A. Stephen Phillips. Poetry Rev.,
Jan.–Feb. 1916.
Waugh, A. Stephen Phillips. Fortnightly
Rev. Jan. 1916. [Afterwards included in
Tradition and Change, 1919.]
Kernahan, C. In Good Company. 1917.
—— Celebrities. 1923.
Colvin, Sir S. Stephen Phillips. [In The Eng-
lish Poets, ed. T. H. Ward, vol. v, 1918.]
Liljegren, S. B. Die Dichtung Stephen Phil-
lipps. E. Studien, LVII, 1923.
Weygandt, C. Tuesdays at Ten. Philadelphia,
1928.

ROBERT REECE (1838–1891)
(a) Plays

Prometheus, or the Man on the Rock! B.
(Royalty, 23 Dec. 1865.) *Lacy*, LXVIII,
[1866].

Whittington, Junior, and his Sensation Cat. B. (Royalty, 23 Nov. 1870.) *Lacy*, LXXXIX, [1871].

Dora's Device. C. (Royalty, 11 Jan. 1871). *Lacy*, XC, [1871].

Paquita, or Love in a Frame. O. (Royalty, 21 Oct. 1871.) *Lacy*, XCIV, [1872].

The Very Last Days of Pompeii. B. (Vaudeville, 13 Feb. 1872.) *Lacy*, XCV, [1872].

May, or Dolly's Delusion. D. (Strand, 4 April 1874.) *French*, CXXVI, [1887].

Green Old Age. O. (Vaudeville, 31 Oct. 1874.) *French*, CIII, [1875].

Valentine and Orson. B. (Gaiety, 23 Dec. 1882.) 1882.

[DNB credits Reece with at least 22 pieces of his own and 15 in collaboration with Henry Brougham Farnie. Most were of a burlesque or farcical nature.]

(b) Biography and Criticism

Archer, W. English Dramatists of To-Day. 1882.

Obituary. Era, 11 July 1891.

ROBERT LOUIS STEVENSON (1850–1894)

[See p. 520 above.]

H. B. G.

5. CRITICAL AND MISCELLANEOUS PROSE

[For anthologies and surveys of 19th century critics, essayists and miscellaneous prosewriters see p. 13 above. As this section has been used as a rag-bag of the less easily classifiable writers and subjects, cross-references have been introduced more sparingly than elsewhere, except in the one case of literary critics.]

I. THE EARLY NINETEENTH-CENTURY ESSAYISTS

COBBETT, LAMB, LANDOR, HAZLITT, HUNT, DE QUINCEY, CARLYLE

WILLIAM COBBETT (1762–1835)

(1) COLLECTED WORKS AND SELECTIONS

Porcupine's Works; containing various Writings and Selections exhibiting a Faithful Picture of the United States of America. 12 vols. 1801.

Selections from Cobbett's Political Works: with Notes, Historical and Explanatory. By John M. Cobbett and James P. Cobbett. 4 vols. 1835.

The Last of the Saxons: Light and Fire from the Writings of William Cobbett. Ed. E. P. Hood, 1854.

William Cobbett. Selections, with Hazlitt's Essay, and Other Critical Estimates, with an Introduction and Notes, by A. M. D. Hughes. Oxford, 1923.

(2) SEPARATE WORKS

Observations on Priestley's Emigration, to which is added, A Story of a Farmer's Bull. Philadelphia, 1794 (anon.); Birmingham, 1794; Philadelphia, 1796; 1798.

A Bone to gnaw for the Democrats, or Observations on a Pamphlet entitled, 'The Political Progress of Great Britain.' Philadelphia, 1795 (Jan.) (anon.); Philadelphia, 1796; 1797.

Part II. A Bone to Gnaw for the Democrats, containing 1st, Observations on a patriotic pamphlet entitled 'Proceedings of the United Irishmen'; 2ndly, Democratic Principles exemplified by Example. 3rdly, Democratic Memoires. Philadelphia, 1795 (March).

A Little Plain English, addressed to the People of the United States, on the Treaty negociated with his Brittanic Majesty. Philadelphia, 1795 (Aug.); 1795.

A New Year's Gift to the Democrats, or Observations on a Pamphlet entitled 'A Vindication of Mr. Randolph's Resignation.' Philadelphia, 1796 (Jan.).

The Life and Adventures of Peter Porcupine, with a full and fair account of all his Authoring Transactions. Philadelphia, 1796 (Aug.); 1797; ed. G. D. H. Cole, 1927.

The Scarecrow; being an Infamous Letter sent to Mr. John Oldden, threatening destruction to his house and Violence to the Person of his Tenant, William Cobbett; with remarks. Philadelphia, 1796.

The Bloody Buoy, thrown out as a Warning to the Political Pilots of America, or a Faithful Relation of a Multitude of Horrid Barbarities, such as the Eye never witnessed until the Commencement of the French Revolution. Philadelphia, 1796; 1797 (as The Bloody Buoy, thrown out as a Warning to the Political Pilots of All Nations); Cambridge, 1797 (as The Annals of Blood, By an American).

Porcupine's Gazette. Philadelphia, 1797–1800. [Issued daily from 5 March 1797 to Oct. 1799. A 'Farewell Number' issued from New York, Jan. 1800.]

The Democratic Judge; or, the Equal Liberty of the Press, as Exhibited, Explained, and Exposed, in the Prosecution of William Cobbett. Philadelphia, 1798 (March); 1798 (as The Republican Judge, With an Address to the People of England).

The American Rush-Light, by which Britons may see a complete specimen of the baseness of Republicans. 1800. [First issued in fortnightly pamphlets in New York, 15 Feb. to 31 March 1800.]

The Porcupine. Nos. 1–333. 30 Oct. 1800–24 Nov. 1801. [From No. 299 called The Porcupine and Anti-Gallican Monitor.]

The Trial of Republicanism proving the injurious and debasing consequences of republican government and written constitutions. 1801.

A Collection of Facts and Observations, relative to the Peace with Bonaparte including Mr. Cobbett's Letters to Lord Hawkesbury. 1801 (2 Nov.); Philadelphia, 1802.

Letters to the Right Honourable Henry Addington, Chancellor of His Majesty's Exchequer, on the fatal effects of the peace with Buonaparte. 1802 (Jan.).

Cobbett's Weekly Political Register. Vols. I–LXXXVIII, 1802–1835. [There is a short break in the series from 5 April to 12 July 1817.]

Paper Against Gold: being an Examination of the Report of the Bullion Committee: in a Series of Letters to the Tradesmen and Farmers in and near Salisbury. Political Register, 1 Sept. 1810–3 Aug. 1811 (29 letters); 2 vols. 1815 (as Paper Against Gold and Glory against Prosperity, or An Account of the Rise and Present State of the Funds and of the Paper Money of Great Britain, brought down to the end of the year 1814); 15 nos. 1817; 1821; 1828 (with dedication to the Duke of Wellington, First Lord of the Treasury).

Letters on the Late War between the United States and Great Britain. New York, 1815.

A Year's Residence in the United States of America. 3 pts, New York, 1818–9; 1819; 1821; 1822; 1828; ed. J. Freeman, 1923.

A Grammar of the English Language, in a Series of Letters. Intended for the use of schools and young persons in general; but, more especially for the use of soldiers, sailors, apprentices, and ploughboys. New York, 1818; 1818; 1819; 1820; 1823 (To which are added, Six Lessons, intended to prevent Statesmen from using false grammar); 1824; 1826; 1829; 1831; ed. J. P. Cobbett, 1866; ed. A. Ayres, New York, 1888; ed. H. L. Stephen, 1906.

The American Gardener; or, a treatise on the situation, soil, fencing, and laying-out of gardens. Claremont, New Hampshire, 1819; 1821.

Cobbett's Cottage Economy. 1822; 1823; 1824; 1831; rptd 1916; ed. G. K. Chesterton, 1926. [Originally issued in 7 monthly pts, 1 Aug. 1821–1 March 1822.]

Cobbett's Sermons, on 1. Hypocrisy and Cruelty. 2. Drunkenness. 3. Bribery. 4. Oppression. 5. Unjust Judges. 6. The Sluggard. 7. Murder. 8. Gaming. 9. Public Robbery. 10. The Unnatural Mother. 11. Forbidding Marriage. 12. Parsons and Tithes. 1822. [Issued in monthly pts from March to May 1821 as Cobbett's Monthly Religious Tracts, and from June 1821 to March 1822, Feb. excepted, as Cobbett's Monthly Sermons. Rptd 1828 and New York, 1834 (as Thirteen Sermons).]

A History of the Protestant 'Reformation' in England and Ireland. In a Series of Letters Addressed to all sensible and just Englishmen. 2 pts, 1824 (actually 1826)–7; 1829; 1846; ed. F. A. Gasquet, 1896. [Pt I was issued in 16 monthly pts from 29 March 1824 to 31 March 1826.]

The Woodlands; or, a Treatise on Forest Trees and Underwoods. 1825 (actually 1828).

[Issued irregularly in pts, Dec. 1825–March 1828.]

Big O and Sir Glory, or 'Leisure to Laugh.' A Comedy in Three Acts. 1825. [Rptd from Political Register, XXIV, Sept. 1825.]

Cobbett's Poor Man's Friend; or, Useful Information for the Working Classes. In a series of Letters addressed to the Working Classes of Preston. 1827. [Issued in 5 pts, 1826–Oct. 1827.]

A Treatise on Cobbett's Corn. 1828.

The English Gardener, with a Kalendar. Andover, 1829.

The Emigrant's Guide. 1829.

Advice to Young Men, and (incidentally) to Young Women, in the Middle and Higher Ranks of Life. In a Series of Letters addressed to a Youth, a Bachelor, a Lover, a Husband, a Father, a Citizen or a Subject. Andover, 1829 (actually 1830); New York, 1831; 1842; ed. H. Morley, 1887; ed. P. Snowden, 1926; ed. E. E. Fisk, 1930. [Issued in 14 pts, 1 June 1829–1 Sept. 1830.]

History of the Regency and Reign of King George the Fourth. 2 vols. 1830 (actually 1834)–4. [Issued in pts at irregular intervals, 1830–4.]

Rural Rides in the Counties of Surrey, Kent, Sussex, Hampshire, Wiltshire, Gloucestershire, Herefordshire, Worcestershire, Somersetshire, Oxfordshire, Berkshire, Essex, Suffolk, Norfolk, and Hertfordshire: with Economical and Political Observations. 1830; ed. J. P. Cobbett, 1853; ed. P. Cobbett, 2 vols. 1885; ed. J. H. Lobban, Cambridge, 1908; rptd 1914 (Everyman's Lib.); ed. G. D. H. and M. Cole, 3 vols. 1930 (with Tour in Scotland, and Letters from Ireland).

Eleven Lectures on the French and Belgian Revolutions and English Boroughmongering. Delivered in the Theatre of the Rotunda, Blackfriars Bridge. 1830. [Delivered between 30 Aug.–7 Oct. 1830. First issued in single pamphlets, separately paged.]

Good Friday, or the Murder of Jesus Christ by the Jews. 1830. [Usually occurs as No. 13 of Cobbett's Sermons.]

A Spelling Book, with appropriate Lessons in Reading, and with a Stepping Stone to English Grammar. 1831.

Cobbett's Two-penny Trash. 2 vols. 1831–2. [Issued monthly from July 1830–July 1832, excepting March 1832.]

Cobbett's Manchester Lectures, in Support of his Fourteen Reform Propositions: delivered in the Minor Theatre, in that town, on the six last days of the year 1831. 1832.

Cobbett's Tour in Scotland, and in the four northern counties of England; in the autumn of the year 1832. 1832 (actually Jan. 1833).

Life of Andrew Jackson, President of the United States of America. 1834.

Cobbett's Legacy to Labourers, or What is the Right which the Lords, Baronets, and 'Squires have to the Lands of England? In Six Letters, addressed to the Working People of England. 1834; ed. J. M. Cobbett, 1872.

Three Lectures on the Political State of Ireland, delivered in the Fishamble Street Theatre, Dublin. Dublin, 1834.

Surplus Population: and Poor Law Bill. A Comedy in Three Acts. 1835. [First pbd in Political Register, LXXII, 28 May 1831.]

Cobbett's Legacy to Parsons; or, Have the Clergy of the Established Church an equitable right to the Tithes? In Six Letters. 1835; ed. W. Cobbett, jun. 1869.

Cobbett's Legacy to Peel. In Six Letters. 1836. [Rptd from Political Register, 24 Jan.–28 Feb. 1835.]

A History of the Last Hundred Days of English Freedom. Ed. J. L. Hammond, 1921. [Extracted from the Political Register, 1817.]

Letters from William Cobbett to Edward Thornton, written in the Years 1797 to 1800. Ed. G. D. H. Cole, Oxford, 1937.

(3) BIOGRAPHY AND CRITICISM

(a) Biographies

[Hone, William?] The Life of William Cobbett, author of The Political Register. Written by Himself. 1816. [A rpt with slight alterations of the English edn of 1797 of Life and Adventures of Peter Porcupine.]

The Life of William Cobbett, Esq., M.P. for Oldham. Written by Himself. [1835.] [Prints death notices from various newspapers, rpts part of The Life of 1816, extracts material from the Advice to Young Men.]

The Life of William Cobbett. 1835.

Huish, R. Memoirs of the Late William Cobbett, Esq. 2 vols. 1836.

Smith, Edward. William Cobbett: a Biography. 2 vols. 1879.

Carlyle, E. I. William Cobbett. A Study of his Life as shown in his Writings. 1904.

'Melville, Lewis' (L. S. Benjamin). The Life and Letters of William Cobbett in England and America. 2 vols. 1913.

Cole, G. D. H. The Life of William Cobbett. 1924.

Chesterton, G. K. William Cobbett. 1925.

The Progress of a Ploughboy to a Seat in Parliament, as exemplified in the History of the Life of William Cobbett, M.P. for Oldham. Ed. W. Reitzel, 1933. [The auto-

biographical passages arranged as a connected narrative.]

Bowen, M. Peter Porcupine. 1935.

(b) Essays, Pamphlets and Chapters in Books

Hazlitt, W. The Spirit of the Age. 1825.

Gilfillan, G. Galleries of Literary Portraits. Vol. II, Edinburgh, 1857.

Bulwer, Sir H. L. Political Characters. Vol. II, 1868.

Rogers, J. E. T. Historical Gleanings. 1869.

Stephen, Sir J. F. Cobbett's Political Works. [In Horae Sabbaticae, vol. III, 1892.]

Smith, Thomas. William Cobbett, a Literary and Political Study. 1906.

Freeman, J. William Cobbett. [In English Portraits and Essays, 1924.]

Cole, G. D. H. William Cobbett. Westminster, 1925.

Johnson, D. C. Pioneers of Reform. Cobbett, Owen, Place, 1925.

Saintsbury, G. Collected Essays. Vol. I, 1925.

Blunden, E. Rural Rides. [In Votive Tablets, 1931.]

(c) Articles in Periodicals

Cobbett's Political Register. Edinburgh Rev. July 1807.

William Cobbett, Esq., M.P. GM. Aug. 1835.

Cobbett, J. M. Obituary. Political Register, LXXXVIII, 1835.

Grant, J. Editors and Newspaper Writers of the Last Generation. Fraser's Mag. Feb. 1862.

Chesterton, G. K. William Cobbett. Trans Royal Soc. Lit. III, 1923.

Woolf, L. 'An Englishman.' Nation, 25 Aug. 1923.

Sellers, E. Cobbett on Choosing a Wife. Contemporary Rev. CXXXIII, 1928.

Beresford, J. Cobbett and the Reverend Beresford. TLS. 29 Jan. 1931.

Reitzel, W. Cobbett and Philadelphia Journalism, 1794–1800. Pennsylvania Mag. LIX, 1935. W. R.

CHARLES LAMB (1775–1834)

(1) BIBLIOGRAPHIES

Ireland, A. List of the Writings of William Hazlitt and Leigh Hunt. Preceded by a Chronological List of the Works of Charles Lamb. 1868.

North, E. D. Bibliography. [In B. E. Martin, In the Footprints of Charles Lamb, 1891, pp. 147–93.]

Dodd, Mead and Co. Descriptions of a Few Books from Charles Lamb's Library, and of some Presentation Copies and First Editions of his Rarer Books. New York, 1899. [A sale catalogue.]

Livingston, L. S. A Bibliography of the First Editions in Book Form of the Writings of Charles and Mary Lamb, published prior to Charles Lamb's Death in 1834. New York, 1903.

Thomson, J. C. Bibliography of the Writings of Charles and Mary Lamb. Hull, 1908.

Hutchinson, T. Bibliographical List (1794–1834). [In The Works, ed. T. Hutchinson, vol. I, 1908, pp. xvii–xlvii.]

American Art Association. The Literary Treasures of Walter Thomas Wallace. New York, 1920. [A sale catalogue; Lamb, nos. 755–804.]

Wise, T. J. The Ashley Library Catalogue. Vol. III, 1923. [Describes more than 40 Lamb items.]

Tregaskis, J. An Important Collection of some of the Rarer Works of Charles Lamb, together with some Lambiana. 1927. [A bookseller's catalogue.]

Griffith, R. H. Charles Lamb. An Exhibition of Books and Manuscripts in the Library of the University of Texas. Austin, 1935.

(2) Collected Works

The Works of Charles Lamb. 2 vols. 1818.

The Poetical Works of Rogers, Lamb, [etc.]. Paris, 1829. [Unauthorized.]

The Prose Works. 3 vols. 1835.

The Poetical Works. 1836; 1848.

The Works. [Ed. Sir T. N. Talfourd], 5 pts, 1840.

The Works. 4 vols. 1850 (vols. I and II new edns of Letters and Final Memorials); 1852; 2 vols. New York, 1852; 4 vols. 1855.

Complete Correspondence and Works. Ed. T. Purnell, 4 vols. 1870.

Complete Works. Ed. R. H. Shepherd, 1874.

Life, Letters and Writings. Ed. P. Fitzgerald, 6 vols. 1875; 1895; 1924.

The Works. Ed. C. Kent, 1876.

The Works. Ed. A. Ainger, 7 vols. 1878–88.

Life and Works. Ed. A. Ainger, 12 vols. 1899–1900.

The Works. Ed. E. V. Lucas, 7 vols. 1903–5; 6 vols. 1912 (including rev. edn of Letters, 2 vols., but omitting Dramatic Specimens).

The Works. Ed. T. Hutchinson, 2 vols. 1908.

(3) Selections

The Best of Lamb. Ed. E. V. Lucas, 1914.

Lamb: Prose and Poetry. Ed. G. S. Gordon, Oxford, 1921.

Lamb's Criticism. A Selection. Ed. E. M. W. Tillyard, Cambridge, 1923.

Everybody's Lamb. Ed. A. C. Ward, 1933.

Essays and Letters. Ed. J. M. French, New York, 1937.

(4) Separate Works
(a) Poems and Plays

Poems on Various Subjects, by S. T. Coleridge, Late of Jesus College, Cambridge. 1796. ['The Effusions [4 sonnets] signed C. L. were written by Mr. Charles Lamb, of the India House.']

[Sonnets. 1796. An anthology without title, priv. ptd for the editor, S. T. Coleridge. Includes 4 sonnets by Lamb.]

Poems on the Death of Priscilla Farmer, by her grandson, Charles Lloyd. 1796. [With Lamb's 'The Grandam.']

Poems, by S. T. Coleridge. Second edition. To which are now added Poems by Charles Lamb, and Charles Lloyd. Bristol, 1797. [Poems by Charles Lamb of the India House, pp. 215–240.]

Blank Verse, by Charles Lloyd and Charles Lamb. 1798.

John Woodvil, a Tragedy. To which are added, Fragments of Burton, the Author of 'The Anatomy of Melancholy.' 1802.

Mr H., or Beware a Bad Name. Philadelphia, 1813; Philadelphia, 1825.

The Poetical Recreations of 'The Champion.' 1822. [Ed. and pbd by J. Thelwall. Many contributions by Lamb.]

Album Verses, with a Few Others. 1830.

Satan in Search of a Wife, and Who Danced at the Wedding. By an Eye-Witness. 1831.

(b) Elia and Eliana

Elia. Essays which have appeared under that Signature in the London Magazine. 1823 (anon.). [First copies issued before the end of 1822.]

Elia. 2 sers. Philadelphia, 1828. [Unauthorized; see Hutchinson's bibliography.]

The Last Essays of Elia. Being a Sequel to Essays published under that Name. 1833 (anon.).

Elia. Both sers. 2 vols. 1835. [Moxon's first collected edn.]

Essays of Elia, [and miscellaneous prose writings]. Paris, 1835. [Unauthorized.]

Eliana: being the Hitherto Uncollected Writings. [Ed. J. E. Babson,] Boston, 1866–7.

[The following later edns may be noted among the innumerable rpts: Essays of Elia, 2 sers. ed. A. Ainger, 1883; ed. N. L. Hallward and S. C. Hill, 2 vols. 1895–1900; ed. W. J. Craig, 1897; Essays of Elia, ed. O. C. Williams, Oxford, 1911; ed. A. H. Thompson, 2 vols. Cambridge, 1913; Last Essays, ed. F. Page, Oxford, 1929; 2 sers. (with engravings adapted from contemporary prints) 2 vols. Newtown, 1929–30. Saggi di Elia. Traduzione, introduzione e note di Mario Praz,

Lanciano, [1924]. The Old Benchers of the Inner Temple. Ed. Sir F. D. Mackinnon, Oxford, 1927.]

(c) Miscellaneous Prose

Original Letters, &c. of Sir John Falstaff and his Friends; now first made public by a Gentleman, a Descendant of Dame Quickly, from Genuine Manuscripts. 1796; ed. R. H. Shepherd, 1877; ed. Sir I. Gollancz, 1907. [By James White assisted by Lamb.]

A Tale of Rosamund Gray and Old Blind Margaret. Birmingham, 1798.

Recollections of Christ's Hospital. 1835. [First ptd GM. 1813.]

[Lamb also revised for press P. S. Dupuy, Sentimental Tablets of the Good Pamphile, 1795. See his letter to Coleridge, 14 June 1796.]

(d) Books for Children

The King and Queen of Hearts. 1805 (anon.); 1806 (re-issued 1808); ed. facs. E. V. Lucas, 1902.

Tales from Shakespear, designed for the Use of Young Persons. 2 vols. 1807, 1809, 1816, 1822, 1831, 1837, 1838, 1844; 1856 (11th edn); ed. F. J. Furnivall, 2 vols. 1901. Tr. German, 1842, 1843; French, 1847; Swedish, 1851; Spanish, 1893; Polish, 1893. [With Mary Lamb, whose name did not appear on the title-pages of the first 6 edns. Some of the Tales were issued separately; see Hutchinson's Bibliography.]

Mrs. Leicester's School, or the History of Several Young Ladies, related by Themselves. 1809 (anon.); 1809; 1825 (9th edn); ed. A. Ainger, 1885 (with other writings).

The Adventures of Ulysses. 1808; 1819; 1839; 1848; ed. A. Lang, 1890; ed. E. A. Gardner, Cambridge, 1921.

Poetry for Children, entirely original. By the Author of Mrs. Leicester's School. 1809 (anon., 84 poems); Boston, 1812 (81 poems); ed. R. H. Shepherd, 1872.

Prince Dorus, or Flattery put out of Countenance. A Poetical Version of an Ancient Tale. 1811 (anon.); ed. facs. A. W. Tuer, 1889; ed. J. P. Briscoe, Nottingham, 1896.

Beauty and the Beast, or a Rough Outside with a Gentle Heart. 1811 (anon.); 1825.

(e) Specimens

Specimens of English Dramatic Poets who Lived about the Time of Shakespear; with Notes. 1808 (re-issued 1813); 2 vols. 1835, 1844, 1854 (with added Extracts from the Garrick Plays); ed. Sir I. Gollancz, 2 vols. 1893; ed. J. D. Campbell, 1907.

[Lamb also had a hand in G. Burnett's Specimens of English Prose-Writers to the Close of the Seventeenth Century, 3 vols. 1807. 'Your friend George Burnett calls as usual for Charles to *point out* something for him,' M. Lamb to S. Stoddart, April 1806.]

(f) Periodicals

[Lamb's early journalism (c. 1800) for Morning Chronicle, Morning Post, Albion and perhaps other newspapers awaits final investigation. Subsequently he contributed chiefly to Hunt's Reflector (1810–2), Examiner (1812–21) and Indicator (1819–21); London Magazine (1820–5); New Monthly Magazine (1825–7); Hone's Every-Day Book (1825–6), Table Book (1827), Year Book (1831); Blackwood's Mag. (1828–30); Moxon's Englishman's Mag. 1831; Athenaeum (1832–4).]

(g) Letters

Letters, with a sketch of his Life. Ed. Sir T. N. Talfourd, 2 vols. 1837.

Final Memorials; consisting chiefly of his Letters not before published. Ed. Sir T. N. Talfourd, 2 vols. 1848.

Letters. Ed. W. C. Hazlitt, 2 vols. 1886.

Letters. Ed. A. Ainger, 2 vols. 1888.

Letters. Ed. W. Macdonald, 2 vols. 1903; 2 vols. 1906 (Everyman's Lib.).

Letters. Ed. E. V. Lucas. 2 vols. 1905; 2 vols. 1912.

Letters. Ed. H. H. Harper, 5 vols. Boston, 1905 (priv. ptd). [Vol. I contains facsimiles.]

Some Lamb and Browning Letters to Leigh Hunt. Ed. L. A. Brewer, Cedar Rapids, Iowa, 1924. [With facsimiles.]

Seven Letters to Charles Ryle of the East India House, 1828–1832. Oxford, 1931.

The Letters of Charles Lamb, to which are added those of his Sister, Mary Lamb. The First Complete Edition. Ed. E. V. Lucas, 3 vols. 1935. [Incorporating the projected edn by the late Mrs G. A. Anderson, and unrestricted by former difficulties of copyright. For some further letters see TLS. 13 Feb., 8 May 1937.]

(h) Works attributed to Lamb

[Mainly books for children: King and Queen of Clubs; of Spades; of Diamonds. 3 pts, n.d. The Book of the Ranks and Dignities of Society, chiefly intended for the Instruction of Young Persons. [1806?]; rptd 1924. Felissa, or the Life and Opinions of a Kitten of Sentiment. 1811. The New Year's Feast on his Coming of Age. 1824. (A rhyming version of an Essay of Elia.) And some others; none of them appears to deserve the attribution, on internal or external evidence, or the money that has been paid for them. The late W. Jerrold (Cornhill Mag. Nov. 1924) attempted to claim for Lamb an anthology of wit entitled The Laughing Philosopher, 1825, 1835.]

(5) BIOGRAPHY AND CRITICISM

(a) *Books and Chapters in Books*

Dyer, G. The Poet's Fate. 1797.

[Canning, G.] The Beauties of the Anti-Jacobin. 1799.

Coleridge, S. T. Sibylline Leaves. 1817.

Wilson, J. I. The History of Christ's Hospital. 1821.

Lloyd, C. Desultory Thoughts in London. 1821.

Hazlitt, W. Table Talk. 2 vols. 1821–2.

—— The Spirit of the Age. 1825.

—— The Plain Speaker. 2 vols. 1826.

—— Literary Remains. 2 vols. 1836.

Hunt, Leigh. Lord Byron and Some of his Contemporaries. 1828.

—— Autobiography. 3 vols. 1850; 1860 (rev.).

—— Correspondence. 2 vols. 1862.

Barton, B. A New Year's Eve. 1828.

—— Selections from Poems and Letters. 1849.

[Scargill, W. P.] Recollections of a Blue-Coat Boy. Swaffham, 1829.

Trollope, W. History of Christ's Hospital. 1834.

Cunningham, A. Biographical and Critical History of the Last Fifty Years. Paris, 1834.

Moxon, E. Charles Lamb. 1835 (priv. ptd).

—— Sonnets. 2 pts, 1835.

Wordsworth, W. [To the Memory of Charles Lamb. Poem without title, priv. ptd 1835.]

Willis, N. P. Pencillings by the Way. 3 vols. 1835.

Cottle, J. Early Recollections. 2 vols. 1837.

Chorley, H. F. The Authors of England. 1837–8.

Talfourd, Sir T. N. [Sketch of Lamb's Life in] Letters. 2 vols. 1837. [See for this R. S. Newdick, Ohio State University Contributions in English, no. 3, 1935.]

—— Critical and Miscellaneous Writings. Philadelphia, 1842.

—— Tragedies. To which are added a Few Sonnets and Verses. 1846.

—— Final Memorials. 2 vols. 1848.

Hall, S. C. The Book of Gems. Modern Poets. 1838.

—— A Book of Memories. 1871.

Hood, T. Hood's Own. 1839.

Mathews, C. Memoirs. 4 vols. 1839.

Macaulay, T. B. Critical and Miscellaneous Essays. 5 vols. Philadelphia, 1841–4.

Munden, T. S. Memoirs of J. S. Munden, Comedian. 1846.

Blanchard, S. L. Sketches from Life. 3 vols. 1846.

—— Poetical Works. 1876.

Gutch, J. M. A Lytell Geste of Robyn Hode. 1847.

Richardson, D. L. Literary Chit-Chat. 1848.

Le Grice, C. V. Sonnet on C. Lamb leading his Sister to the Asylum. 1849. [Broadside.]

Powell, T. Living Authors of England. New York, 1849.

Tuckerman, H. T. Characteristics of Literature. New York, 1849.

Southey, R. Life and Correspondence. 6 vols. 1849.

—— Selections from Letters. 4 vols. 1856.

Haydon, B. R. Life, from his Autobiography and Journals. 3 vols. 1853–4.

—— Correspondence and Table-Talk. 2 vols. 1876.

Patmore, P. G. My Friends and Acquaintance. 3 vols. 1854.

Balmanno, M. Pen and Pencil. 1858.

Leslie, C. R. Autobiographical Recollections. 2 vols. 1860.

Irving, P. M. Life of Washington Irving. 4 vols. 1862.

De Quincey, T. Leaders in Literature. 1862.

Daniel, G. Love's Last Labour Not Lost. 1863. [Recollections of Lamb rptd separately, 1927.]

Robinson, H. C. Diary. Ed. T. Sadler, 3 vols. 1866.

—— Blake, Coleridge, Wordsworth, Lamb. Ed. E. J. Morley, 1922.

—— Henry Crabb Robinson on Books and their Writers. Ed. E. J. Morley, 3 vols. 1938.

Procter, B. W. ('Barry Cornwall'). Charles Lamb. A Memoir. 1866; 1869.

—— An Autobiographical Fragment. 1877.

Fitzgerald, P. Charles Lamb: his Friends, his Haunts, and his Books. 1866.

—— Memoirs of an Author. 2 vols. 1895.

Ollier, E. A Few Reminiscences. [Prefixed to Elia, ser. 1, [1867].]

Craddock, T. Charles Lamb. 1867.

Mitford, M. R. The Life of in a Selection from her Letters. Ed. A. G. L'Estrange, 3 vols. 1870.

—— The Friendships of as recorded in Letters from her Literary Correspondents. Ed. A. G. L'Estrange, 2 vols. 1882.

Hazlitt, W. C. Mary and Charles Lamb. 1874.

—— Offspring of Thought in Solitude. 1884.

—— The Lambs. 1897.

—— Lamb and Hazlitt. 1900.

Bates, W. [and Maginn, W.]. The Maclise Portrait Gallery. 1874.

Fields, J. T. Underbrush. Boston, 1877.

Clarke, C. C. and M. C. Recollections of Writers. 1878.

Wainewright, T. G. Essays and Criticisms. Ed. W. C. Hazlitt, 1880.

Main, D. M. A Treasury of English Sonnets. 1880.

Beatty, P. Three Women of the People; and other Poems. 1881.

Carlyle, T. Reminiscences. 2 vols. 1881.

Ainger, A. Charles Lamb. 1882.

—— Lectures and Essays. 2 vols. 1905.

Gilchrist, A. Mary Lamb. 1883.

Robertson, E. S. English Poetesses. 1883.

Swinburne, A. C. Miscellanies. 1886.

Birrell, A. Obiter Dicta. Ser. 2, 1887.

Pater, W. Appreciations. 1889.

Harrison, W. Memorable London Houses. 1890 (3rd edn).

Martin, B. E. In the Footprints of Charles Lamb. 1891.

Watson, Sir W. Lacrimae Musarum. 1892.

Lucas, E. V. Bernard Barton and his Friends. 1893.

—— Charles Lamb and the Lloyds. 1898.

—— Life of Charles Lamb. 1905; 1910 (5th edn); 1921 (rev.). [The standard Life.]

—— At the Shrine of St Charles. 1934.

— — Coleridge, Lamb and the Year 1834. 1934. [Pamphlet issued in connection with N.P.G. Centenary Exhibition.]

Clarke, M. C. My Long Life. 1896.

—— Letters to an Enthusiast. N.d.

Johnson, R. B. Christ's Hospital: Recollections of Lamb, Coleridge and Leigh Hunt. 1896.

[British Museum.] Facsimiles of Autographs. 2 sers. 1896.

[Welford, C.] A Descriptive Catalogue of the Library of Charles Lamb. New York, 1897.

Pearce, E. H. Annals of Christ's Hospital. 1901.

Dobell, B. Sidelights on Charles Lamb. 1903.

Lake, B. A General Introduction to Charles Lamb. Leipzig, 1903.

Rees, J. R. With Elia and his Friends. 1903.

Wilson, J. G. Thackeray in America. 2 vols. New York, 1904.

Derocquigny, A. Charles Lamb; sa Vie et ses Œuvres. Lille, 1904.

Betham, E. A House of Letters. 1905.

Jerrold, W. Charles Lamb. 1905.

—— Thomas Hood and Charles Lamb. 1930.

Symons, A. The Romantic Movement in English Poetry. 1909.

—— Figures of Several Centuries. 1916.

Bensusan, S. L. Charles Lamb. 1910.

Ellis, S. M. William Harrison Ainsworth and his Friends. 2 vols. 1911.

Elton, O. A Survey of English Literature, 1780–1830. 2 vols. 1912.

Williams, O. The Life of John Rickman. 1912.

—— Charles Lamb. 1934.

Strong, A. T. Peradventure. 1912.

Masson, F. Charles Lamb. 1913.

London County Council. Indication of Houses of Historical Interest in London. Part xv. 64 Duncan Terrace. (C. Lamb.) [1914.]

[Westwood, T.] A Literary Friendship. 1914.

Howe, P. P. The Life of William Hazlitt. 1922; 1928 (rev.).

Blunden, E. Christ's Hospital: a Retrospect. 1923.

—— Leigh Hunt's 'Examiner examined. 1929.

—— Charles Lamb and his Contemporaries. Cambridge, 1933.

—— Charles Lamb, Recorded by his Contemporaries. 1934.

Roberts, H. A. Records of the Amicable Society of Blues. 1924 (priv. ptd).

Foster, Sir William. The East India House. 1924.

Wilson, D. A. Carlyle to The French Revolution. 1924.

Wherry, G. E. Cambridge and Charles Lamb. Cambridge, 1925.

Graveson, W. Charles and Mary Lamb 'in Hearty, Homely, Loving Hertfordshire.' Hertford, 1925.

Anderson, G. A. The Letters of Thomas Manning to Charles Lamb. 1925.

Birkhoff, B. As Between Friends. Criticism of Themselves and One Another in the Letters of Coleridge, Wordsworth and Lamb. Cambridge, U.S.A. 1930.

Fulton, M. G. Charles Lamb in Essays and Letters. New York, 1930.

Rich, S. M. The Elian Miscellany. 1931.

Morley, F. V. Lamb before Elia. 1932.

May, J. L. Charles Lamb; a Study. 1934.

Ward, A. C. The Frolic and the Gentle. 1934.

Roberts, R. E. Lamb. Trans. Royal Soc. Lit. xiii, 1934.

Henry Sotheran Ltd. Piccadilly Notes: The Charles Lamb Centenary Number. 1934. [A bookseller's catalogue.]

Johnson, E. C. Lamb Always Elia. 1935.

Holman, L. E. Lamb's 'Barbara S——'; the Life of Frances Maria Kelly, Actress. 1935.

The Thunderer in the Making, 1785–1841. 1935.

Morley, E. J. The Life and Times of Henry Crabb Robinson. 1935.

Christ Church, Greyfriars. Charles Lamb. Dedication of the Centenary Memorial. 5 Nov. 1935.

Iseman, J. S. A Perfect Sympathy: Charles Lamb and Sir Thomas Browne. Cambridge, U.S.A. 1937.

(b) Articles in Periodicals

[Jeffrey, F.] John Woodvil. Edinburgh Rev. April 1803.

Lamb's Specimens. Annual Rev. 1808.

Hunt, L. Harry Brown's Letter to C. L. Examiner, 25 Aug. 1816. [Verse.]
—— The Works of Charles Lamb. Examiner, March 1819; Indicator, 31 Jan., 7 Feb. 1821.
—— Charles Lamb. Leigh Hunt's London Journ. 7 Jan. 1835.
—— Sayings of Charles Lamb. Leigh Hunt's London Journ. 17 Oct. 1835.
Works of Charles Lamb. Blackwood's Mag. Aug. 1818.
Works of Charles Lamb. Monthly Rev. Nov. 1819.
Letter of Timothy Tickler to Christopher North. Blackwood's Mag. Sept. 1823.
Manifesto. Blackwood's Mag. Oct. 1823.
[Talfourd, Sir T. N.] Remarks on the Writings of Charles Lamb. New Monthly Mag. Aug. 1820.
Coleridge, H. N. On Charles Lamb's Poetry. Etonian, March 1821.
[Elton, C. A.] Epistle to Elia. London Mag. Aug. 1821.
[Clare, J.] To Elia. London Mag. Aug. 1822. [Sonnet.]
On Meyer's Portrait of Lamb. New Monthly Mag. May 1827.
[Jerdan, W.] Album Verses. Literary Gazette, 10 July 1830.
—— The Baa-Lamb School. Literary Gazette, 8 Dec. 1832. [Review of Tennyson's poems.]
—— Last Essays of Elia. Literary Gazette, 2 March 1833.
Southey, R. To Charles Lamb, on the Review of his 'Album Verses' in the Literary Gazette. Times, 6 Aug. 1830.
[Hunter, J.] To Elia. Friendship's Offering, 1832. [Sonnet.]
Mitford, J. Sonnet to Mr Charles Lamb on his Poem called 'Leisure.' Raw's Ladies' Fashionable Repository, 1832.
[Maginn, W.] Charles Lamb, Esq. Fraser's Mag. Jan. 1835.
[Procter, B. W.] Charles Lamb; Recollections of Charles Lamb. Athenaeum, 3, 24 Jan., 7 Feb. 1835.
[Forster, J.] Lamb on Coleridge, an Autobiographic Sketch. New Monthly Mag. Feb.–April 1835.
[Dyer, G.] Memoir of Lamb. GM. March 1835.
[Flower, S.] An Evening with Charles Lamb and Coleridge. Monthly Repository, March 1835.
Landor, W. S. To the Sister of Charles Lamb. Leigh Hunt's London Journ. 13 June 1835. [Verse.]
Last Essays. Quarterly Rev. July 1835.
[Patmore, P. G.] Reminiscences, with Original Letters. Court Mag. March, Dec. 1835.
[Field, B.] Ch. Lamb Esq. Annual Biography, 1836.

[De Quincey, T.] Recollections of Charles Lamb. Tait's Mag. April, June 1838.
—— Charles Lamb and his Friends. North British Rev. Nov. 1848.
[Lewes, G. H.] Charles Lamb and his Friends. British Quarterly Rev. Nov. 1848.
Final Memorials. Westminster Rev. Jan. 1849.
Dramatic Treasure-Trove. Fraser's Mag. Jan. 1859.
[Symonds, W. L.] Charles Lamb and Sydney Smith. Atlantic Monthly, March 1859.
Charles Lamb. Edinburgh Rev. July 1866.
Westwood, T. Recollections of Charles Lamb. N. & Q. 22 Sept. 1866.
—— Two Unpublished Poems. N. & Q. 4 June 1870.
—— 'Witches and other Night-Fears.' N. & Q. 23 Nov. 1872.
[Lytton, Sir E. B.] Lamb and Some of his Companions. Quarterly Rev. Jan. 1867.
[Hazlitt, W. C.] Charles Lamb: Gleanings After His Biographers. Macmillan's Mag. April 1867.
Massey, G. Charles Lamb. Fraser's Mag. May 1867.
Palgrave, F. T. Lamb as a Letter-Writer. Macmillan's Mag. March 1868.
Latin and English lines on Haydon's Picture 'Christ's Entry into Jerusalem.' N. & Q. 5 April 1873.
Cox, H. F. Charles Lamb at Edmonton. Dublin University Mag. Oct. 1878.
Hendriks, F. Bernard Barton's Inmost Opinion of Charles Lamb. N. & Q. 18 Oct. 1879.
Black, Algernon. Charles Lamb. Macmillan's Mag. March 1879. [Anecdotes of Lamb at the India House.]
Russell, J. F. Lamb's Notes on a Metrical Novel. N. & Q. 17 Sept., 5 Nov. 1881.
—— Charles Lamb at Home. N. & Q. 1 April 1882.
[Payne, J. H.] Lamb's Correspondence with him. Century Mag. Oct. 1882.
'A.' 'Mr H——' and the Dramatic Students. N. & Q. 28 Nov. 1885.
W., M. E. Charles Lamb. Temple Bar, July 1886. [A poem.]
Stephen, J. Letters of Charles Lamb and Henry Taylor. Reflector, 7 April 1888.
An Unpublished Letter [to C. Chambers]. Strand Mag. ii, 1891.
Unpublished Letters of Charles and Mary Lamb. Cornhill Mag. Dec. 1892.
Campbell, J. D. Lamb's Specimens. Athenaeum, 25 Aug. 1894.
Mr Charles Lamb of the India House. Macmillan's Mag. Nov. 1896.
Lucas, E. V. Two Notes on Charles Lamb. Fortnightly Rev. April 1901.

Lucas, E. V. A New Book by Charles Lamb. Athenaeum, 2 Nov. 1901.
—— Charles Lamb: 1775–1834. Times, 7 Nov. 1934.
—— Recollections of Charles Lamb [by Walter Wilson]. London Mercury, Dec. 1934.
Lamb's Letters. Athenaeum, 3 June 1905.
Paul, H. Charles Lamb. Independent Rev. Nov. 1905.
Symons, A. Charles Lamb. Monthly Rev. Nov. 1905.
Rees, J. R. Lamb, Dyer and Primrose Hill. N. & Q. 19 Oct. 1907.
—— Charles Lamb's Captain Starkey. N. & Q. 27 March 1909.
—— Charles Lamb's Cancellarius Magnus. N. & Q. 8 Nov. 1913.
Ellis, S. M. Some New Charles Lamb Letters. Saturday Rev. 12, 19 June 1915.
Butterworth, S. Coleridge's 'Marine Sonnet.' Bookman, Nov. 1920.
Blunden, E. New Sidelights on Keats, Lamb and Others. From Letters to J. Clare. London Mercury, IV, 1921.
—— Clare on the Londoners. London Mercury, Feb. 1923.
—— Elia's G. D. Nation, 5 May 1928.
—— Charles Lamb, an Appreciation. Argosy, Jan. 1935.
—— Elia and Christ's Hospital. E. & S. XXII, 1937.
Anderson, G. A. Some Unpublished Letters of Lamb. London Mercury, Nov. 1922.
—— Edward White of the India House. Bookman, April 1924.
—— Lamb and the Two G. D.'s. London Mercury, XI, 1925.
—— On the Dating of Lamb's Letters. London Mercury, XVIII, 1928.
Smith, H. B. Charles Lamb's Album. Scribner's Mag. LXXIV, 1923.
King, R. W. Charles Lamb, Cary and the London Magazine. Nineteenth Century, XCIV, 1923.
Turnbull, J. M. Lamb's 'Poor Relations.' Bookman, Feb. 1924.
—— Charles Lamb and Griffiths Wainewright. Bookman, May 1925.
—— Wordsworth's Part in the Production of Lamb's 'Specimens.' N. & Q. 18 Feb. 1928.
—— Charles Lamb. Some Sidelights from Barry Cornwall. Bookman, LXXVIII, 1930.
Burriss, E. E. The Classical Culture of Charles Lamb. Classical Weekly, 6 Oct. 1924.
Wright, D. Charles Lamb and George Dyer. English Rev. XXXIX, 1924.
Green, Julien. La Vie mélancolique de Charles Lamb. Revue Universelle, 15 Oct. 1926.
Frend, G. G. The Lambs, Fanny Kelly and Some Others. Bookman, Nov. 1926.

Griswold, L. The Diction of Charles Lamb. Quarterly Journ. of University of N. Dakota, XVII, 1927.
Riddell, W. R. Letters from Charles and Mary Lamb to Fanny Kelly. Trans. Royal Soc. of Canada, XXIII, 1929.
Hard, F. Lamb on Spenser. Stud. Phil. XXVIII, 1931.
—— Lamb and Spenser again. Stud. Phil. XXX, 1933.
Waters, A. W. Lamb and the Directors of the East India Company. N. & Q. 29 Aug. 1931.
Wells, J. E. 'John Gilpin' and Charles Lamb. E. Studien, LXVII, 1932.
Draper, M. C. Charles Lamb and Thomas Stackhouse. Bookman, LXXXV, 1933.
French, J. M. Lamb and Spenser. Stud. Phil. XXX, 1933.
—— Lamb and Milton. Stud. Phil. Jan. 1934.
Mabbott, T. O. and Birss, J. H. Some Uncollected Letters of Charles Lamb. N. & Q. 28 Oct. 1933.
Tillett, N. S. Elia and 'The Indicator.' South Atlantic Quart. July 1934.
Temple, J. Charles Lamb Centenary. Sphere, 28 July 1934.
French, J. M. Lamb and Milton. Stud. Phil. XXXI, 1934.
Knox, R. S. Charles Lamb, 1834–1934. University of Toronto Quart. Oct. 1934.
Lawrence, C. E. Elia. Quarterly Rev. Oct. 1934.
—— Charles Lamb. Cornhill Mag. Dec. 1934.
Coleridge-Lamb Centenary. The Blue, Christ's Hospital, Dec. 1934.
Law, A. Charles Lamb. Contemporary Rev. Dec. 1934.
Praz, M. Charles Lamb. Pan (Milan), Dec. 1934.
Evans, B. I. Charles Lamb. Nineteenth Century, Dec. 1934.
Kempling, W. B. Centenary of Lamb. St Martin's Rev. Dec. 1934.
'Elian.' A Defence of Elia. Life and Letters, Jan. 1935.
The Charles Lamb Society. Monthly Bulletin. Ed. S. M. Rich, May 1935– . [In progress.]
[Rendall, V.] Wordsworth and Lamb. N. & Q. 1 June 1935.
Johnson, E. C. Lamb and Coleridge. American Scholar, VI, 1937. E. BL.

WALTER SAVAGE LANDOR (1775–1864)

(1) BIBLIOGRAPHIES

Wise, T. J. and Wheeler, S. A Bibliography of the Writings in Prose and Verse of Walter Savage Landor. Bibliog. Soc. 1919.
Wise, T. J. A Landor Library. A Catalogue of Printed Books, MSS. and Autograph Letters. 1928 (priv. ptd).

(2) Collected and Selected Works

The Works of Walter Savage Landor. 2 vols. 1846. [Vol. i, Imaginary Conversations, adding to those included in vol. i, 1826, a 2nd Conversation of Southey and Porson, and to those of vol. ii, 1826, a 2nd Conversation of Johnson and Tooke. Peleus and Thetis is incorporated in Epicurus, Leontion and Ternissa, and 19 poems are added to Pericles and Aspasia. Vol. ii includes all except 13 of the shorter poems in Gebir, Count Julian, and Other Poems, 1831, the rest of the 'Miscellaneous' poems being new.]

The Works of Walter Savage Landor and Life by John Forster. 8 vols. 1876. [Vol. i, The Life, is a condensation of Forster's Walter Savage Landor, 1869. Adds *inter alia*: (ĩ) to Roman Conversations, Virgil and Horatius, Asinius Pollio and Licinius Calvus (2 Conversations); (2) to Dialogues of Literary Men, Hare and Landor, Milton and Marvel (2 Conversations); (3) to Miscellaneous Dialogues, Louis Philippe and Guizot, Thiers and Lamartine, Nicholas and Nesselrode. Overlooks 10 Imaginary Conversations in Fraser's Mag., Examiner, etc. and omits many poems in The Last Fruit, 1853, Dry Sticks, 1858, and Heroic Idylls, 1863. Forster's text is uncritical.]

Selections from the Writings of Landor. Ed. Sir S. Colvin, 1882. (Golden Treasury ser.)

Imaginary Conversations. 6 vols. Poems, Dialogues in Verse, and Epigrams. 2 vols. The Longer Prose Works. 2 vols. Ed. G. C. Crump, 1891–3. [Supplies 5 of the 10 Conversations overlooked by Forster. Some variant readings are recorded, but includes only a selection from the poems.]

Imaginary Conversations. A Selection. Ed. E. de Selincourt, 1915. (World's Classics.)

The Complete Works of Walter Savage Landor. Ed. T. E. Welby and S. Wheeler. 16 vols. 1927–36. [Adds further Conversations, as well as High and Low Life in Italy (from Monthly Repository, Aug. 1837–April 1838). Includes elaborate bibliographical and textual apparatus. Prose works (vols. i–xii), ed. T. E. Welby; poems (vols. xiii–xvi and separately 3 vols. Oxford, 1937), ed. S. Wheeler.]

Imaginary Conversations and Poems. A Selection. Ed. H. Ellis, 1933. (Everyman's Lib.)

Imaginary Conversations. Selected by T. E. Welby. Ed. F. A. Cavenagh and A. C. Ward, Oxford, 1934.

(3) Principal Publications

The Poems of Walter Savage Landor. 1795. [Suppressed by Landor.]

Moral Epistle, Respectfully Dedicated to Earl Stanhope. 1795.

Gebir; A Poem, in Seven Books. 1798; Oxford, 1803 (rev. text); 1831 (with omissions and further rev. in Gebir, Count Julian, and Other Poems); ed. (from 1798 text) A. Symons, 1907 (with Hellenics).

Poems from the Arabic and Persian; with Notes By the Author of Gebir. Warwick, 1800; rptd facs. 1927. [Rptd in Dry Sticks, Fagoted, 1858.]

Poetry By The Author of Gebir. 1802. [Ptd in 1800, but only pbd (with the last 47 pp. deleted) 1802. Includes 'From the Phoceans' (omitted in Works, 1846 and 1876).]

Gebirus, Poema. Oxford, 1803. [Landor's own Latin version of Gebir. Text altered in Poemata et Inscriptiones, 1847.]

Simonidea. Bath, 1806.

The Dun Cow; An Hyper-Satirical Dialogue, in Verse. With Explanatory Notes. 1808 (anon.). [Landor's reply to an attack on Dr Parr in Guy's Porridge Pot; the entry in the catalogue of Parr's library is the only external evidence for Landor's authorship.]

Three Letters, Written in Spain, to D. Francisco Riguelme. 1809.

Ode ad Gustavum Regem. Ode ad Gustavum Exulem. 1810.

Count Julian: A Tragedy. 1812. [Rptd in Gebir, Count Julian, and Other Poems, 1831.]

Commentary on Memoirs of Mr. Fox [by J. B. Trotter]. 1812 (anon.); ed. S. Wheeler. 1907. [Suppressed by Landor.]

Letters Addressed to Lord Liverpool, and The Parliament, on the Preliminaries of Peace. By Calvus. 1814. [Suppressed by Landor, who marked a copy (now in BM.) for a new edn, but never issued it.]

Idyllia Nova Quinque Heroum atque Heroidum, &c. Oxford, 1815. [Idylls rptd, with changes, in Idyllia Heroica, 1820; all the contents, except 3 pieces, in Poemata et Inscriptiones, 1847.]

Idyllia Heroica Decem [etc.]. Pisa, 1820. [Adds 4 further Idylls and 52 Hendecasyllabi.]

Imaginary Conversations of Literary Men and Statesmen. 3 vols. 1824–8 (vols. i, ii 'corrected and enlarged' 1826). Second Series. 2 vols. 1829.

Gebir, Count Julian, and Other Poems. 1831. [The 'Other Poems' include dialogues, 'Poems Addressed to Ianthe,' 'Miscellaneous Poems' and 'On the Dead.' A certain number were rptd from Simonidea, 1806.]

Citation and Examination of William Shakespeare touching deer-stealing to which is added a Conference of Edmund Spenser with the Earl of Essex. 1834.

Terry Hogan, An Eclogue. Edited by Phelim Octavius Quarle. 1836 (anon.). [Only external evidence of Landor's authorship. Augustus De Morgan's inscription in BM. copy.]

A Satire on Satirists, and Admonition to Detractors. 1836. [Not rptd by Landor, Forster or Crump.]

The Letters of a Conservative: In which are shown the only means of saving what is left of the English Church. 1836.

Pericles and Aspasia. 2 vols. 1836; 2 vols. Philadelphia, 1839. [Rptd with 24 new letters and some changes in The Works, 1846.]

The Pentameron and Pentalogia. 1837. [3 of the Pentalogia pieces (The Parents of Luther, The Death of Clytemnestra, The Madness of Orestes) had appeared in miscellanies, 1836–7.]

Andrea of Hungary, and Giovanna of Naples. 1839.

Fra Rupert: The Last Part of a Trilogy. The first being Andrea of Hungary, the second being Giovanna of Naples. 1840.

The Hellenics of Walter Savage Landor. Enlarged and Completed. 1847; Edinburgh, 1859 (rev. and adds Acon and Rhodope, Sophocles to Poseidon, The Last of Ulysses, Silenus, and Regeneration); ed. A. Symons, 1907 (with Gebir).

Poemata et Inscriptiones. 1847. [Includes, with much new matter: 12 poems from The Philological Museum, Cambridge, 1832–3; all but 1 of the Hendecasyllabi in Idyllia, 1820; the odes Ad Gustavum, 1810; and, with some changes, pieces from Simonidea, 1806. Of the 28 Inscriptiones, 6 are from Imaginary Conversations, vol. II, 1824.]

Imaginary Conversation of King Carlo Alberto and The Duchess Belgioioso. 1848. [Rptd in The Last Fruit off an Old Tree, 1853.]

The Italics of Walter Savage Landor. 1848.

Popery: British and Foreign. 1851. [Rptd in The Last Fruit off an Old Tree, 1853.]

Imaginary Conversations of Greeks and Romans. 1853. [Adds 3 Greek Conversations (Achilles and Helena, Xerxes and Artabanus, Alcibiades and Xenophon) and 1 Roman (Tibullus and Messala).]

The Last Fruit off an Old Tree. 1853. [Includes 18 further Conversations, essays on Theocritus, Catullus and Petrarca rptd from Foreign Quarterly Rev. 1842–3, and Five Scenes rptd from Fraser's Mag. 1851.]

Letters of an American, mainly on Russia and Revolution. Edited by Walter Savage Landor. 1854. [By Landor.]

Antony and Octavius. Scenes for the Study. 1856.

Letter from W. S. Landor to R. W. Emerson. Bath, 1856. [Rptd in Literary Anecdotes of the Nineteenth Century, ed. Sir W. R. Nicoll and T. J. Wise, vol. II, 1896; not rptd by Forster or Crump.]

Dry Sticks, Fagoted. 1858.

Savonarola E Il Priore di San Marco. Florence, 1860. [English versions, by Landor himself, in London Rev. 22 Sept. 1860, and in Letters and Other Unpublished Writings, ed. S. Wheeler, 1897.]

Heroic Idylls, with additional poems. 1863. [First appearance of most of the Latin poems.]

Letters and Other Unpublished Writings of Walter Savage Landor. Ed. S. Wheeler, 1897. [Contains many minor pieces not previously ptd.]

Letters of Walter Savage Landor Private and Public. Ed. S. Wheeler, 1899.

Walter Savage Landor. Last Days, Letters and Conversations. Ed. H. C. Minchin, 1934.

(4) MINOR AND PRIVATELY PRINTED WORKS

Iambi (Incerto Auctore). Oxford, 1800 (priv. ptd). [Only extant copy in BM.]

Letter from Mr. Landor to Mr. Jervis. [1814.] [Only extant copy in Forster Lib., South Kensington.]

Sponsalia Polyxenae. Pistoia, 1819. [Rptd in Idyllia Heroica Decem, 1820.]

Poche Osservazioni sullo stato attuale di que' popoli che vogliono governarsi per mezzo delle rappresentanze. [Naples,] 1821.

Imaginary Conversation. Solon and Pisistratus. [1832] (priv. ptd).

To Robert Browning. 1845 (priv. ptd by Browning's father).

Epistola ad Romanos. Bath, [1849?] (priv. ptd).

Statement of Occurrences at Llanbedr. Bath, [1849].

On Kossuth's Voyage to America. [1851.] [Broadside.]

Tyrannicide. Published for the benefit of the Hungarians. [1851.] [Broadside.]

Walter Savage Landor and the Honourable Mrs Yescombe. [Bath, 1857.]

Mr. Landor Threatened. Bath, [1857] (bis).

Mr. Landor's Remarks On a Suit preferred against him. 1859.

An Address to the Fellows of Trinity College, Oxford, on the Alarm of Invasion. 1917 (priv. ptd).

To Elizabeth Barrett Browning and Other Verses. 1917 (priv. ptd).

A Modern Greek Idyl. 1917 (priv. ptd).

Garibaldi and the President of the Sicilian Senate. (An Imaginary Conversation.) 1917 (priv. ptd).

[For Landor's lost works see Wise and Wheeler's Bibliography, pp. 232–4; for his numerous contributions to periodicals and miscellanies, and his many letters to newspapers, see the complete list in Wise and Wheeler, pp. 239–365.]

(5) BIOGRAPHY AND CRITICISM

Horne, R. H. A New Spirit of the Age. Vol. I, 1844.

Madden, R. R. The Literary Life and Correspondence of the Countess of Blessington. 3 vols. 1855.

Emerson, R. W. English Traits. 1856.

Field, Kate. Landor's Last Years in Italy. Atlantic Monthly, April–June 1856.

Gilfillan, G. Galleries of Literary Portraits. Vol. II, Edinburgh, 1857.

De Quincey, T. Works. Vols. VIII, IX, XI, Edinburgh, 1862–3.

Forster, J. Walter Savage Landor. A Biography. 2 vols. 1869. [Reviewed by Dickens, All the Year Round, 24 July 1869.]

Colvile, F. L. Worthies of Warwickshire. 1869.

Robinson, H. C. Diary, Reminiscences, and Correspondence. Ed. T. Sadler, 3 vols. 1869.
—— Henry Crabb Robinson on Books and their Writers. Ed. E. J. Morley, 3 vols. 1938.

Linton, E. Lynn. Reminiscences of Walter Savage Landor. Fraser's Mag. July 1870.

Milnes, R. M. (Baron Houghton). Monographs, Personal and Social. 1873.

Stephen, Sir L. Landor's Imaginary Conversations. [In Hours in a Library, ser. 3, 1879.]

Colvin, Sir S. Landor. 1881. (English Men of Letters ser.)

Bulwer-Lytton, R. (Lady Lytton). Reminiscences of Walter Savage Landor. Tinsley's Mag. June 1883.

Swinburne, A. C. Miscellanies. 1886. [The essay on Landor rptd from Ency. Brit. 9th edn, 1882.]

De Vere, A. Landor's Poetry. [In Essays chiefly on Poetry, vol. II, 1887.]

Crosse, Mrs A. Red Letter Days of my Life. 1892.

Evans, E. W. Walter Savage Landor. A Critical Study. New York, 1892.

Saintsbury, G. Essays in English Literature, 1780–1860. Ser. 2, 1895.

Thompson, Francis. Landor. Academy, 27 Feb. 1897.

Woodberry, G. E. Makers of Literature. New York, 1900.

Betham, E. The Llanthony Maze. [In A House of Letters, 1905.]

Whiting, L. The Florence of Landor. 1905.

Schlaak, R. Entstehungs- und Textgeschichte von Landor's Gebir. Halle, 1909.

Symons, A. The Romantic Movement in English Poetry. 1909.

Duke, R. E. H. Pedigree of the Paternal Ancestry of W. S. Landor. 1912.

Bradley, W. The Early Poems of Walter Savage Landor. 1914.

Henderson, W. B. D. Swinburne and Landor. 1918.

Elton, O. A Survey of English Literature, 1830–1880. Vol. I, 1920.

Williams, S. T. The Story of Gebir. PMLA. XXXVI, 1921. [On the sources and variants of the theme.]
—— The Sources of Landor's Gebir. MLN. XXXVI, 1921.
—— Walter Savage Landor as a Critic of Literature. PMLA. XXXVIII, 1923.

'Lee, Vernon.' The Rhetoric of Landor. [In The Handling of Words, 1923.]

Aldington, R. Landor's 'Hellenics.' [In Literary Studies and Reviews, 1924.]

Mason, A. H. Walter Savage Landor, Poète lyrique. Paris, 1924.

Fornelli, G. W. S. Landor e l' Italia. Forlì, 1930.

de Selincourt, E. Classicism and Romanticism in the Poetry of Walter Savage Landor. [In England und die Antike: Vorträge der Bibliothek Warburg, 1930–1, Berlin, 1932.]

Hawkes, C. P. The Spanish Adventure of Walter Savage Landor. Cornhill Mag. LXXIV, 1933.

Elkin, F. Walter Savage Landor's Studies of Italian Life and Literature. Philadelphia, 1934.

Minchin, H. C. Walter Savage Landor. Last Days, Letters and Conversations. 1934.

Ashley-Montagu, M. F. Three Unknown Portraits of Landor. Colophon, II, 1937.

Super, R. H. Forster as Landor's Literary Executor. MLN. LII, 1937.
—— An Unknown Child of Landor's. MLN. LIII, 1938.

Becker, G. J. Landor's Political Purpose. Stud. Phil. xxxv, 1938.

T. E. W.

WILLIAM HAZLITT (1778–1830)

(1) BIBLIOGRAPHIES

Ireland, A. List of the Writings of William Hazlitt and Leigh Hunt. 1868.

Douady, J. Liste Chronologique des Œuvres de William Hazlitt. Paris, 1907.

Keynes, G. Bibliography of William Hazlitt. 1931.

(2) COLLECTED WORKS

The Collected Works. Ed. A. R. Waller and A. Glover, 12 vols. and Index, 1902–6. [Introduction by W. E. Henley.]

The Complete Works. Ed. P. P. Howe, 20 vols. and Index, 1930–4. [A re-issue of the Waller-Glover edn with additional notes, The Life of Napoleon, and other uncollected matter.]

[The 12 vols. edited by Hazlitt's son, 1838–51, were part of a projected collected edn that was to include all the ptd works with addns from MS and other sources. The 7 vols. edited by W. C. Hazlitt, 1869–86, represent part of a similar project.]

(3) SELECTIONS

Essays of William Hazlitt. Ed. F. Carr, 1889.

William Hazlitt, Essayist and Critic. Ed. A. Ireland, 1889.

Hazlitt. Essays on Poetry. Ed. D. N. Smith, 1901.

Essays. Ed. C. Whibley, [1906].

Hazlitt on English Literature. Ed. J. Zeitlin, New York, 1913. [Important biographical-critical introduction.]

Selections. Ed. W. D. Howe, Boston, 1913.

Hazlitt. Selected Essays. Ed. G. Sampson, Cambridge, 1917.

Twenty-Two Essays. Ed. A. Beatty, Boston, 1920.

The Best of Hazlitt. Ed. P. P. Howe, 1923.

Essays. Ed. P. van D. Shelly, New York, 1924.

William Hazlitt. Twenty Selected Essays. Ed. A. J. Wyatt, 1925.

Essays. Ed. C. H. Gray, New York, 1926.

Selected Essays. Ed. G. Keynes, 1930. [The most comprehensive selection.]

(4) SEPARATE WORKS

An Essay on the Principles of Human Action: being an Argument in favour of the Natural Disinterestedness of the Human Mind. To which are added, some Remarks on the Systems of Hartley and Helvetius. 1805 (anon.); ed. (with additional essay on Abstract Ideas) W. Hazlitt, jun. [1836].

Free Thoughts on Public Affairs: or Advice to a Patriot; in a Letter addressed to A Member of the Old Opposition. 1806 (anon.); ed. W. C. Hazlitt (with The Spirit of the Age, 1885).

An Abridgment of The Light of Nature Pursued, by Abraham Tucker. 1807 (anon.).

The Eloquence of the British Senate; or, Select Specimens from the Speeches of the most distinguished Parliamentary Speakers, from the beginning of the Reign of Charles I. With Notes. 2 vols. 1807 (re-issued 1808 and 1812); 2 vols. Brooklyn, 1809–10.

A Reply to the Essay on Population, by the Rev. T. R. Malthus. In a Series of Letters. 1807 (anon.). [Letters 1–3 first pbd in Cobbett's Political Register, 14 March, 16, 23 May 1807.]

A New and Improved Grammar of the English Tongue: for the use of schools. To which is added, A New Guide to the English Tongue [by Godwin]. 1810. [Rptd only in The Complete Works, ed. P. P. Howe. Outlines of English Grammar, 1810, is an abridgment by Godwin.]

Memoirs of the late Thomas Holcroft, Written by himself and continued to the time of his death [by Hazlitt]. 3 vols. 1816; 1852 (abridged); ed. E. Colby, 2 vols. 1925; rptd 1926 (World's Classics).

The Round Table: A Collection of Essays on Literature, Men and Manners. 2 vols. Edinburgh, 1817 (includes 12 essays by Leigh Hunt); ed. W. Hazlitt, jun. 1841 (adds 3 uncollected essays from The Liberal 1822–3); 1869; ed. W. C. Hazlitt, 1871 (with Northcote's Conversations and Characteristics). [Hazlitt's essays mainly first pbd in Examiner, May 1814–Jan. 1817; some portions had appeared in Morning Chronicle, 1813–4.]

Characters of Shakespear's Plays. 1817; 1818; Boston, 1818; ed. W. Hazlitt, jun., 1838, 1848, 1854; ed. W. C. Hazlitt, 1869 (with Lectures on the Dramatic Literature of the Age of Elizabeth); rptd 1906 (Everyman's Lib.); ed. J. H. Lobban, 1908; ed. Sir A. T. Quiller-Couch, 1917 (World's Classics); tr. German, Leipzig, [1838].

A View of the English Stage; or, a Series of Dramatic Criticisms. 1818 (re-issued 1821); ed. W. Hazlitt, jun., 1851 (selection); ed. W. Archer and R. W. Lowe, 1895 (as Dramatic Essays); ed. W. S. Jackson, 1906 (text from original articles; adds 3 uncollected critiques from Examiner). [Originally contributed to Morning Chronicle, Champion, Examiner, and Times, 1814–8.]

Lectures on the English Poets. Delivered at the Surrey Institution. 1818; Philadelphia, 1818; 1819; ed. W. Hazlitt, jun., 1841 (adds further matter in 4 appendixes); ed. W. C. Hazlitt, 1869 (with Lectures on the English Comic Writers); ed. A. R. Waller, 1910 (Everyman's Lib.); rptd 1924 (World's Classics); ed. F. W. Baxter, 1929.

A Letter to William Gifford, Esq. from William Hazlitt, Esq. 1819 (re-issued 1820); ed. W. C. Hazlitt, 1886 (with The Spirit of the Age). [First draft in Examiner, 15 June 1818.]

Lectures on the English Comic Writers. Delivered at the Surry Institution. 1819; Philadelphia, 1819; ed. W. Hazlitt, jun., 1841 (expands, mainly from prefaces originally contributed by Hazlitt to Oxberry's New English Drama, 1818–9); ed. W. C. Hazlitt, 1869 (with Lectures on the English Poets); ed. A. Dobson, 1900 (Temple Classics); ed. R. B. Johnson, 1907 (World's Classics); rptd 1910 (Everyman's Lib., introduction by W. E. Henley from Waller-Glover Collected Works, with miscellaneous essays from New Monthly Mag. and Monthly Mag.).

Political Essays, with Sketches of Public Characters. 1819 (re-issued 1822). [Mainly rptd from articles in various periodicals, 1813–8, but including extracts from The Eloquence of the British Senate, 1807, and A Reply to Malthus, 1807.]

Lectures chiefly on the Dramatic Literature of the Age of Elizabeth. Delivered at the Surry Institution. 1820 (re-issued 1821); ed. W. Hazlitt, jun., 1840; ed. W. C. Hazlitt, 1869 (with Characters of Shakespear's Plays).

Table Talk; or, Original Essays. 2 vols. 1821–2; 2 vols. 1824; ed. W. Hazlitt, jun., 2 vols. 1845–6, 1857–61; ed. W. C. Hazlitt, 1869, 1878; rptd 1901 (World's Classics); rptd 1908 (Everyman's Lib.). [Some of the essays rptd from London Mag. and New Monthly Mag.; 1845–6 edn adds On Travelling Abroad (from MS) and On the Spirit of Controversy (from London Weekly Rev.).]

Liber Amoris; or, the New Pygmalion. 1823 (anon.); rptd 1884; ed. R. Le Gallienne, 1893; ed. (with much additional matter) R. Le Gallienne [and W. C. Hazlitt], 1894 (priv. ptd).

Characteristics: in the Manner of Rochefoucault's Maxims. 1823 (re-issued 1837, with introduction by R. H. Horne); rptd 1927.

Sketches of the Principal Picture-Galleries in England. With a Criticism on 'Marriage a-la-Mode.' 1824. [Originally contributed to London Mag. 1822–3, except the Hogarth essay which is rptd from The Round Table, 1817.]

Select British Poets, or New Elegant Extracts from Chaucer to the Present Time, with critical remarks. 1824 (withdrawn owing to infringements of copyright in the contemporary section); 1825 (omitting copyright matter, as Select Poets of Great Britain).

The Spirit of the Age: or Contemporary Portraits. 1825 (bis, 2nd edn enlarging Coleridge and adding Cobbett from Table Talk); 2 vols. Paris, 1825 (re-arranged, omitting Moore and Irving and adding Canning and Knowles); ed. W. Hazlitt, jun., 1858; ed. W. C. Hazlitt, 1886 (with Letter to Gifford and Free Thoughts). [Partly rptd from London Mag. and New Monthly Mag.]

Table-Talk: or, Original Essays. 2 vols. Paris, 1825; 2 vols. New York, 1845–6. [A selection, made by Hazlitt himself, from Table Talk, 1821–2, and essays later collected in The Plain Speaker, 1826.]

The Plain Speaker: Opinions on Books, Men, and Things. 2 vols. 1826; ed. W. Hazlitt, jun., 1851; ed. W. C. Hazlitt, 1870; ed. P. P. Howe, 1928 (Everyman's Lib.). [Essays mainly rptd from London Mag. and New Monthly Mag. 1820–5.]

Notes of a Journey through France and Italy. 1826; Philadelphia, 1833.

The Life of Napoleon Buonaparte. 4 vols. 1828–30 (vols. I, II re-issued 1830); 3 vols. New York, 1847–8; rev. W. Hazlitt, jun., 4 vols. 1852; rptd 6 vols. Grolier Soc. [1910]; tr. German, Leipzig, 1835.

Conversations of James Northcote, Esq., R.A. 1830; ed. W. C. Hazlitt, 1871 (with Round Table); ed. Sir E. Gosse, 1894. [Rptd from New Monthly Mag. Aug. 1826–March 1827, London Weekly Rev., 1829, Atlas, March–Nov. 1829, and Court Journ. 1830.]

Literary Remains of the late William Hazlitt. With a notice of his life, by his son, and thoughts on his genius and writings, by E. L. Bulwer, Esq., M.P. and Mr Sergeant Talfourd, M.P. 2 vols. 1836; New York, 1836. [22 essays mainly rptd from various periodicals.]

Painting [by B. R. Haydon], and the Fine Arts [by Hazlitt]. Edinburgh, 1838. [Rptd from Ency. Brit. 7th edn, Supplement, vol. I, 1816.]

Sketches and Essays. Now first collected by his son. 1839; 1852 (as Men and Manners); ed. W. C. Hazlitt, 1872 (with Winterslow); rptd 1902 (World's Classics). [18 essays rptd from various periodicals.]

Criticisms on Art: and Sketches of the Picture Galleries of England. Edited by his Son. 2 sers. 1843–4; ed. W. C. Hazlitt, 1873 (expanded as Essays on the Fine Arts).

Winterslow: Essays and Characters written there. Collected by his son. 1850; ed. W. C. Hazlitt, 1872 (with Sketches and Essays); rptd 1902 (World's Classics). [Partly rptd from Literary Remains, but mainly from various periodicals.]

Memoirs of William Hazlitt, with Portions of his Correspondence. Ed. W. C. Hazlitt, 2 vols. 1867.

Lamb and Hazlitt. Further Letters. Ed. W. C. Hazlitt, 1900.

Unpublished Letters. Ed. P. P. Howe, Athenaeum, 8, 15 Aug. 1919.

A Reply to Z. Ed. C. Whibley, 1923. [Unpbd retort to article signed 'Z.' in Blackwood's Mag. Aug. 1818.]

New Hazlitt Letters. Ed. P. P. Howe, London Mercury, March 1923, May 1924, Aug. 1925.

New Writings of William Hazlitt. Ed. P. P. Howe, 2 sers. 1925–7. [Articles rptd from various periodicals and Oxberry's New English Drama.]

(5) BIOGRAPHY AND CRITICISM

[For some further titles see under Lamb, pp. 634–7 above.]

(a) Books

Hazlitt, W. C. Memoirs of William Hazlitt, with Portions of his Correspondence. 2 vols. 1867.

—— Four Generations of a Literary Family. 2 vols. 1897.

—— The Hazlitts: an Account of their Origin and Descent. With Autobiographical Particulars of William Hazlitt. 2 vols. Edinburgh, 1911–2 (priv. ptd).

Birrell, A. William Hazlitt. 1902. (English Men of Letters ser.)

Douady, J. Vie de William Hazlitt, l'Essayiste. Paris, 1907.

Howe, P. P. The Life of William Hazlitt. 1922; 1928 (rev.). [The standard biography.]

Stephenson, H. W. William Hazlitt and Hackney College. 1930.

Schneider, E. The Aesthetics of William Hazlitt. Philadelphia, 1933.

Pearson, H. The Fool of Love. 1934.

(b) Chapters in Books and Articles in Periodicals

[Early criticisms will be found in the following: Blackwood's Mag. Feb., March, April, June, Aug. 1818; July, Aug. 1822; July 1824; March 1825. Edinburgh Rev. Aug. 1817; Nov. 1820. London Mag. Feb. 1820; April, May 1821; June 1823; June 1825. Quarterly Rev. April 1817; Jan., Dec. 1818; July 1819; Oct. 1821.]

Procter, B. W. ('Barry Cornwall'). My Recollections of the Late William Hazlitt. New Monthly Mag. Nov. 1830.

Patmore, P. G. My Friends and Acquaintances. 3 vols. 1854.

Gilfillan, G. William Hazlitt; Hazlitt and Hallam. [Both in Galleries of Literary Portraits, vol. II, Edinburgh, 1856.]

Stephen, Sir L. Hours in a Library. Ser. 2, 1876.

De Quincey, T. Works. Ed. D. Masson, vols. IX, XI, Edinburgh, 1889–90.

Saintsbury, G. Essays in English Literature (1780–1860). 1890.

Smiles, S. A Publisher [John Murray] and his Friends. 2 vols. 1891.

Stoddard, R. H. Personal Recollections of Lamb, Hazlitt and Others. 1903.

More, P. E. Shelburne Essays. Ser. 2, New York, 1905.

Irwin, S. T. Hazlitt and Lamb. Quarterly Rev. CCIV, 1906.

Elton, O. A Survey of English Literature, 1780–1830. Vol. II, 1912.

Howe, P. P. Hazlitt and Liber Amoris. Fortnightly Rev. CV, 1916.

—— Hazlitt's Second Marriage. Fortnightly Rev. CVI, 1916.

—— Hazlitt and Blackwood's Magazine. Fortnightly Rev. CXII, 1919.

Ker, W. P. Hazlitt. E. & S. VIII, 1922. [Rptd in Collected Essays, vol. I, 1925.]

Chase, S. P. Hazlitt as a Critic of Art. PMLA. XXXIX, 1924.

Clark, E. M. The Kinship of Hazlitt and Stevenson. Texas University Stud. IV, 1924.

Newdick, R. S. Coleridge on Hazlitt. Texas Rev. IX, 1924.

Carver, P. L. Hazlitt's Contributions to The Edinburgh Review. RES. IV, 1928.

Garrod, H. W. The Place of Hazlitt in English Criticism. [In the Profession of Poetry, and Other Lectures, Oxford, 1929.]

Babcock, R. W. The Direct Influence of Late Eighteenth Century Criticism on Hazlitt and Coleridge. MLN. XLV, 1930.

Olney, C. William Hazlitt and Benjamin Robert Haydon. N. & Q. 5, 12 Oct. 1935.

Strout, A. L. Hunt, Hazlitt and 'Maga.' ELH. IV, 1937.

Vigneron, R. Stendhal et Hazlitt. MP. XXXV, 1938.

P. P. H.

LEIGH HUNT (1784–1859)

(1) BIBLIOGRAPHIES

[Alexander Ireland's List of the Writings of William Hazlitt and Leigh Hunt, 1868, is still consulted. In Bookman's Journ. XV, no. 1, 1927, Alexander Mitchell has published a specimen of his more precise A Bibliography of the Writings of Leigh Hunt. With Critical Notes. L. A. Brewer, of Cedar Rapids, Iowa, has described very fully his great collection of Huntiana in My Leigh Hunt Library: First Editions, 1932. But the most useful bibliography of Hunt is that by L. Landré, appended to his Leigh Hunt, vol. II, Paris, 1936, pp. 483–595.]

(2) COLLECTED EDITIONS

(a) Poems

Poetical Works. 3 vols. 1819. [5 separate publications bound together with collective title-pages.]

Poetical Works of Leigh Hunt. 1832. [In spite of the title, it is in fact a cautious selection.

Poetical Works of Leigh Hunt; containing many pieces now first collected. 1844. [Another selective edn.]

Poetical Works of Leigh Hunt; now first entirely collected. Ed. S. Adams Lee, 2 vols. Boston, 1857.

The Poetical Works of Leigh Hunt. Now Finally Collected, Revised by Himself, and Edited by his Son, Thornton Hunt. 1860. ['The reader holds in his hand the Poetical Works of Leigh Hunt, collected and arranged with his own final judgment.']

The Poetical Works of Leigh Hunt. Ed. H. S. Milford, 1923. [The definitive edn, containing far more of Hunt's verse than any other, with variants from MS and ptd sources. A few pieces remain uncollected in periodicals, to some of which Milford provides references; he omits Juvenilia as of no value, and the trn Amyntas from considerations of space.]

(b) Prose

[Nothing approaching a collected edn exists. In 1857 an attempt was made in America in 4 vols. The full collection would perhaps require 40. In 1870 Smith, Elder published a uniform reprint, in 7 vols., of some of Hunt's later prose works.]

(3) SELECTIONS

A Tale for a Chimney Corner, and other Essays. Ed. E. Ollier, [1869].

Essays. Ed. A. Symons, 1887.

Leigh Hunt as Poet and Essayist. Ed. C. Kent, 1889.

The Poetical Works of Leigh Hunt and Thomas Hood (Selected). Ed. J. H. Panting, [1889].

Essays, and Poems. Ed. R. B. Johnson, 2 vols. 1891.

Dramatic Essays. Ed. W. Archer and R. W. Lowe, 1894.

Essays and Sketches. Ed. R. B. Johnson, [1907].

Selections in Prose and Verse. Ed. J. H. Lobban, 1909.

Leigh Hunt. Ed. E. Storer, [1911]. [Prose and verse.]

Prefaces, mainly to his Periodicals. Ed. R. B. Johnson, 1927.

Essays (Selected). Ed. J. B. Priestley, 1929. (Everyman's Lib.)

(4) SEPARATE WORKS

(a) Poems

Juvenilia; or, a Collection of Poems. Written between the ages of twelve and sixteen. By J. H. L. Hunt. 1801 (bis); 1802; 1803.

The Feast of the Poets, with Notes; and other pieces in verse. By the editor of the Examiner. 1814 (2 issues, with different imprints); 1815 ('amended and enlarged').

The Descent of Liberty, a Mask. 1815; 1816.

The Story of Rimini. 1816; 1817; 1819.

Foliage; or Poems Original and Translated. 1818.

Hero and Leander, and, Bacchus and Ariadne. 1819.

Amyntas, a Tale of the Woods; from the Italian of Torquato Tasso. 1820. [Apparently issued in two forms, with and without illustrations.]

Ultra-Crepidarius; a Satire on William Gifford. 1823.

Bacchus in Tuscany, a Dithyrambic Poem, from the Italian of Francesco Redi. 1825.

Captain Sword and Captain Pen, a Poem. 1835; 1839; 1849 (with a new Preface).

A Legend of Florence. A Play. In Five Acts. 1840; 1840 (with an added preface). [Rptd in G. H. Lewes's Modern British Dramatists, 1867.]

The Poems of Geoffrey Chaucer Modernized. 1840. [Edited by R. H. Horne, although Thomas Powell, the Z.A.Z. of the book, also claims the editorship. The contributors included Wordsworth, Miss Barrett and Hunt, who modernized the Tales of the Squire and the Friar.]

The Palfrey; a Love-Story of Old Times. 1842.

Stories in Verse. Now first collected. 1855.

Ballads of Robin Hood; with some manuscript reproductions. Ed. L. A. Brewer, Cedar Rapids, Iowa, 1922.

[Bodleian MS Eng. Poet. e. 38 is a notebook containing unptd draft poems by Hunt.]

(b) Prose

Critical Essays on the Performers of the London Theatres, including general observations on the practice and genius of the stage. By the author of the theatrical criticisms in the weekly paper called the News. 1807.

An Attempt to Shew the Folly and Danger of Methodism; in a series of essays first published in the weekly paper called the Examiner, and now enlarged with a preface and additional notes. By the editor of the Examiner. 1809.

The Reformist's Answer to the Article entitled 'State of Parties' in the last Edinburgh Review (No. 30). By the editor of the Examiner, in which paper it first appeared. 1810.

The Prince of Wales v. the Examiner. A full report of the trial of John and Leigh Hunt. To which are added, Observations on the trial, by the editor of the Examiner. 1813.

Musical Copyright. Whitaker versus Hume. To which are subjoined observations on the defence made by Sergeant Joy, by Leigh Hunt. 1816.

The Round Table: a Collection of Essays. 2 vols. 1817. ['The Round Table,' in the Examiner, was intended to be written by Hazlitt, T. Barnes, and Hunt in turn. In the end, Hazlitt monopolized it; but of the 52 papers collected in vol. form, 10 were by Leigh Hunt.]

The Months descriptive of the Successive Beauties of the Year. 1821; ed. W. Andrews, 1897; ed. R. H. Bath, 1929. [Founded on articles in the Literary Pocket-Book.]

The Keepsake for 1828. 1827. [Hunt contributed anon. 'Dreams on the Borders of the Land of Poetry' and 'Pocket Books and Keepsakes.']

Lord Byron and Some of his Contemporaries; with Recollections of the Author's Life, and of his Visit to Italy. 1828; 2 vols. 1828; 3 vols. Paris, 1828 (with additional matter). [Hunt's Autobiography, 1850, was partly a reconstruction of this work.]

Sir Ralph Esher; or, Adventures of a Gentleman of the Court of Charles II. 3 vols. 1832 (anon.); 1850 (4th edn, with preface). [A novel. Some copies are dated 1830, but reviews show that the date of publication was 1832.]

Christianism; or Belief and Unbelief Reconciled: being exercises and meditations. 1832 (anon.). [Expanded, for general circulation, into The Religion of the Heart; see below.]

The Indicator, and the Companion; a Miscellany for the Fields and the Fireside. 2 vols. 1834; 1840; 1845. [Hunt's selection from the two periodicals named.]

The Seer; or, Common-Places Refreshed. 1840-1; 1850. [A similar selection.]

Heads of the People: or, Portraits of the English. Drawn by Kenny Meadows. With original essays by distinguished writers. 1840. [Hunt's contributions are 'The Monthly Nurse' and 'The Omnibus Conductor.']

Notice of the late Mr. Egerton Webbe. 1840. [Rptd from Morning Chronicle.]

Imagination and Fancy; with an essay in answer to the question 'What is Poetry?' 1844; 1845; 1846; 1852; ed. Sir E. Gosse, 1907.

Wit and Humour, with an Illustrative Essay. 1846 (bis).

Stories from the Italian Poets; with Lives of the Writers. 2 vols. 1846; 2 vols. 1854. [An excerpt entitled 'Dante's Divine Comedy. The Book and its Story. By Leigh Hunt' was pbd by Newnes c. 1903.]

Men, Women and Books; a selection of Sketches, Essays and Critical Memoirs, from his uncollected Prose Writings. 2 vols. 1847; 2 vols. 1852.

A Jar of Honey from Mount Hybla. 1848; 1852.

The Town; its Memorable Characters and Events. 2 vols. 1848; 1859; ed. A. Dobson, 1907 (World's Classics).

The Autobiography of Leigh Hunt; with Reminiscences of Friends and Contemporaries. 3 vols. 1850; 1860 ('revised by the Author; with further revision, and an introduction by his Eldest Son'); ed. R. Ingpen, 2 vols. 1903; ed. E. Blunden, 1928 (World's Classics).

Table Talk. To which are added Imaginary Conversations of Pope and Swift. 1851.

The Religion of the Heart. A Manual of Faith and Duty. 1853.

The Old Court Suburb; or, Memorials of Kensington. 2 vols. 1855; 1855 (enlarged); 1860; ed. A. Dobson, 2 vols. 1902.

A Saunter through the West End. 1861.

A Day by the Fire; and other papers, hitherto uncollected. Ed. J. E. Babson, 1870.

The Wishing-Cap Papers. Now first collected [by J. E. Babson]. Boston, 1873.

Tales. Now first collected, with a prefatory memoir by William Knight. 1891. [Many of Hunt's 'Tales' had been rptd in 'The Romanticist and Novelist's Library,' 1839-40.]

The Love of Books. Ed. L. A. and E. T. Brewer, Cedar Rapids, Iowa, 1923.

(c) Correspondence

The Correspondence of Leigh Hunt. Edited by his Eldest Son. 2 vols. 1862.

Six Letters addressed to W. W. Story, 1850-1856. 1913.

Letter on Hogg's Life of Shelley. With Other Papers. [Ed. L. A. Brewer,] Cedar Rapids, Iowa, 1927.

My Leigh Hunt Library: The Holograph Letters. Ed. L. A. Brewer, Iowa City, 1938. [900 letters and MS scraps, most not previously ptd.]

(d) Anthologies and Edited Matter

Classic Tales, Serious and Lively: with Critical Essays on the Merits and Reputations of the Authors. 5 vols. 1806–7; 5 vols. 1895. [The critical papers were chiefly by Hunt, who wrote on Henry Mackenzie, Goldsmith, Henry Brooke, Voltaire, and Dr Johnson.]

The Masque of Anarchy, a Poem by Percy Bysshe Shelley. Now first published, with a preface by Leigh Hunt. 1832.

The Dramatic Works of R. B. Sheridan. With a Biographical and Critical Sketch. 1840; 1846; 1851.

The Dramatic Works of Wycherley, Congreve, Vanbrugh and Farquhar. With Biographical and Critical Notices. 1840; 1851.

One Hundred Romances of Real Life. 1843; 1888.

The Foster Brother: a Tale of the Wars of Chiozza. 3 vols. 1845. [A romance by Thornton Hunt. Edited with an introduction by Leigh Hunt.]

Readings for Railways. 1849; ser. 2, 1853 (with J. B. Syme).

A Book for a Corner; or selections in prose and verse, from authors the best suited to that mode of enjoyment, with comments on each, and a general introduction. 2 vols. 1849; 1858.

Beaumont and Fletcher; or the finest scenes, lyrics and other beauties of those two poets, now first selected. 1855.

The Book of the Sonnet. Edited by Leigh Hunt and S. Adams Lee. 2 vols. Boston, 1867. [Includes an essay on the Sonnet by Hunt.]

(e) Periodicals

The Examiner, a Sunday Paper. 1808–21. [Hunt's editorial work actually ended in 1821, but he considered himself on the editorial staff some time after that; he contributed until 1825, when the dispute over proprietorship between him and his brother excluded him. He appeared among the correspondents of The Examiner at the time of the controversy caused by his book on Byron; his final reappearance in the journal he helped to make famous was in 1836, on the performance of Talfourd's tragedy Ion.]

The Reflector, a Quarterly Magazine. 1810–1. [Re-issued, on its termination, as The Reflector, a Collection of Essays on Miscellaneous Subjects, 2 vols.]

The Literary Pocket-Book; or, Companion for the Lover of Nature and Art. 1818–22 (for 1819–23). [Resuscitated for 1827; but without reference to Hunt. An annual.]

The Indicator. 76 nos. Every Wednesday 13 Oct. 1819–21 March 1821; 2 vols. in one,

1822. [Some further Indicators appeared in The Literary Examiner 1823, and no. 89 and last (apparently) in New Monthly Mag. May 1832.]

The Liberal. Verse and Prose from the South. 1822–3. [4 nos., collected as 2 vols.]

The Literary Examiner. 1823. [Mentioned here because commonly included among Leigh Hunt's editorial works; probably edited by John Hunt.]

The Companion. Every Wednesday, 9 Jan. 1828–23 July 1828.

The Chat of the Week. Every Saturday, 28 June 1830–28 Aug. 1830.

The Tatler. A Daily Journal of Literature and the Stage. 4 Sept. 1830–13 Feb. 1832.

Leigh Hunt's London Journal. Every Wednesday, 2 April 1834–26 Dec. 1835.

The Monthly Repository. July 1837–April 1838.

Leigh Hunt's Journal; a miscellany for the cultivation of the memorable, the progressive and the beautiful. Weekly. 7 Dec. 1850–29 March 1851.

[No register has yet been made of Hunt's very numerous and often anon. contributions to periodicals other than those which he edited. The following references may be found useful (so far as uncollected writings are concerned): papers signed 'Mr Town, Junior' in Traveller (before 1805); theatre articles in News (1805–7); papers in Statesman (1806); notices of plays in Times (Aug. 1807); essays and verses in New Monthly Mag. (particularly 1825–6, and occasionally until 1850); Atlas, (c. 1828–30); True Sun, and Weekly True Sun (c. 1833–4); Spectator (1858–9); Morning Chronicle at intervals throughout his life. See also the article in DNB. which points out some of Hunt's contributions to musical criticism. In short, one can hardly be surprised when Browning mentions, to Elizabeth Barrett, that Hunt is writing for Church of England Quart.]

(5) DUBIOUS ASCRIPTIONS

[Among the publications sometimes attrib. to Hunt, there is no doubt that the Reminiscences of Michael Kelly the singer (2 vols. 1826) should not stand. This work was prepared by Theodore Hook. The Rebellion of the Beasts; or 'The Ass is Dead! Long live the Ass!' (1825), by 'a late Fellow of St John's College, Cambridge,' may or may not be Hunt's. It is nowhere mentioned in his available Letters. Dictionary of Anonymous and Pseudonymous English Literature, ed. J. Kennedy, W. A. Smith and A. F. Johnson, describes Florentine Tales, 1847, as 'largely by Thomas Powell, but after his death by J. H. Leigh Hunt.' Powell, however, was sufficiently alive in 1849 to emigrate to New York (pursued by the execrations of Browning). A poem in Ollier's Literary Miscellany, 1820,—'The Universal Pan'—signed L., is more the fault of 'Barry Cornwall' than Leigh Hunt. As a rule, everything in the autograph of any of Hunt's family is entered in booksellers' lists as Leigh Hunt's.]

(6) Biography and Criticism

(a) Books

Keats, J. Poems. 1817.

Shelley, P. B. The Cenci. 1821. [Dedication.]

—— Letters to Leigh Hunt. Ed. T. J. Wise, 2 vols. 1894.

[Kent, E.] Flora Domestica. 1823.

—— Sylvan Sketches. 1825.

Hazlitt, W. The Spirit of the Age. 1825.

Brougham, H. P. (Baron Brougham and Vaux). Speeches. 4 vols. 1837.

Hall, S. C. The Book of Gems. The Modern Poets and Artists of Great Britain. 1838. [Here, besides a notice of Hunt, occur memoranda by Hunt on Shelley, Keats, and Tennyson.]

—— A Book of Memoirs. [1876.]

Horne, R. H. A New Spirit of the Age. Vol. i, 1844.

—— Letters of E. B. Browning. 2 vols. 1877.

Howitt, W. Homes and Haunts of the British Poets. 2 vols. 1847.

Haydon, B. R. Autobiography and Journals. 3 vols. 1853.

Moore, Thomas. Memoirs, Journals and Correspondence. 8 vols. 1853–6. [See especially vol. viii.]

Dickens, C. Bleak House. 1853.

—— Letters. 3 vols. 1880–2.

Hawthorne, N. Our Old Home. 1863.

Kent, C. Footprints on the Road. 1864.

Bates, William. A Gallery of Illustrious Literary Characters (1830–1838) drawn by the late Daniel Maclise R.A., and accompanied by notices chiefly by the late William Maginn, LL.D. [1876.]

Procter, B. W. An Autobiographical Fragment. 1877.

Clarke, Charles and Mary Cowden. Recollections of Writers. 1878.

Dowden, E. The Life of Percy Bysshe Shelley. 2 vols. 1886.

Saintsbury, G. Essays in English Literature, 1780–1860. 1890.

—— A History of Criticism. Vol. iii, 1904.

Monkhouse, W. C. Life of Leigh Hunt. 1893.

Johnson, R. B. Leigh Hunt. 1896.

—— Shelley–Leigh Hunt. 1928.

Punchard, C. D. Helps to the Study of Leigh Hunt's Essays. 1899.

Allingham, W. Diary. 1907.

Miller, Barnette. Leigh Hunt's Relations with Byron, Shelley and Keats. 1910.

Moebus, Otto. Leigh Hunts Kritik der Entwicklung der englischen Literatur bis zum Ende des 18. Jahrhundert. Strasburg, 1916.

Howe, P. P. Life of William Hazlitt. 1922; 1928 (rev. edn).

Brewer, L. A. Some Lamb and Browning Letters to Leigh Hunt. Cedar Rapids, 1924.

—— The Joys and Sorrows of a Book Collector. Cedar Rapids, 1928.

—— Some Letters from my Leigh Hunt Portfolios. Cedar Rapids, 1929.

Blunden, E. Leigh Hunt's 'Examiner' Examined. 1928.

—— Leigh Hunt: a Biography. 1930.

Munby, A. N. L. Letters to Leigh Hunt from his Son Vincent. 1934.

Landré, L. Leigh Hunt (1784–1859). Contribution à l'Histoire du Romantisme anglais. 2 vols. Paris, 1936.

[Numerous references to Hunt will also be found in the standard edns of the Works, or Letters, of Byron, Hazlitt, Keats and Shelley.]

(b) Articles

Hunt, Leigh. [Autobiographical paper.] Monthly Mirror, April 1810.

'Z.' The Cockney School of Poetry. Blackwood's Mag. Oct. 1817–Jan. 1818.

'A.' Mr Hunt's Hero and Leander. London Mag. July 1820.

[Lamb, C.] Letter of Elia to Robert Southey, Esq. London Mag. Oct. 1823.

[Lytton, E. B.] Sir Ralph Esher. New Monthly Mag. March 1832.

[Macaulay, T. B.] Comic Dramatists of the Restoration. Edinburgh Rev. Jan. 1841.

[Ireland, A.] The Genius and Writings of Leigh Hunt. Manchester Examiner, July 1847.

[Ollier, E.] The Occasional. Spectator, 3 Sept. 1859.

—— Correspondence of Leigh Hunt. Spectator, 22 March 1862.

—— A Literary Life. All the Year Round, 12 April 1862.

[Dickens, C.] Leigh Hunt. A Remonstrance. All the Year Round, 24 Dec. 1859.

[Hunt, Thornton L.] A Man of Letters of the Last Generation. Cornhill Mag. Jan. 1860.

[Carlyle, T.] Memoranda concerning Mr Leigh Hunt. Macmillan's Mag. July 1862.

Collier, J. P. The Late Duke of Devonshire and Leigh Hunt. Athenaeum, 8 March 1862.

[Mayer, S. R. T.] Selections from Leigh Hunt's Correspondence with B. R. Haydon, Charles Ollier, and Southwood Smith. St James's Mag. 1874–5.

—— Leigh Hunt and Lord Brougham. With Original Letters. Temple Bar, XLVII, 1876.

Forman, M. B. Leigh Hunt: some Unfamiliar Apologists. London Mercury, June 1926.

Roberts, M. Leigh Hunt's Place in the Reform Movement, 1808–10. RES. Jan. 1935.

Kishimoto, J. Leigh Hunt's Marginalia on Shakespeare. Stud. Eng. Lit. (Tokio), Jan. 1936.

Brawner, J. P. Leigh Hunt and his Wife Marianne. West Virginia University Stud. III, 1937.

Strout, A. L. Hunt, Hazlitt, and 'Maga.' ELH. IV, 1937.

E. BL.

THOMAS DE QUINCEY (1785–1859)

(1) BIBLIOGRAPHIES

Masson, D. The Collected Writings of Thomas De Quincey. Vol. XIV. Appendix, Chronological and Bibliographical. 1890.

Green, J. A. Thomas De Quincey. A Bibliography based upon the De Quincey Collection in the Moss Side Library (Manchester). 1908.

Axon, W. E. A. The Canon of De Quincey's Writings, with some References to his Unidentified Articles. Trans. Royal Soc. Lit. XXXII, 1912.

(2) COLLECTED WORKS

De Quincey's Writings. 24 vols. Boston, 1851–9; 22 vols. in 11, Boston, 1873 (as Author's Library Edn). [Ed. by J. T. Fields, with the consent of De Quincey; contents rptd directly from magazines without revision by the author.]

Selections Grave and Gay, from Writings, Published and Unpublished, of Thomas De Quincey. Revised and arranged by himself. (Author's Collected Edition.) 14 vols. Edinburgh, 1853–60. [From 1853 until his death in 1859, De Quincey was chiefly occupied in recasting and revising for this edn the works already pbd. The following is a list of the vols. with their separate titles, with notes of the new material: I. Autobiographic Sketches. 1853. (Revision, recast, and enlargement of articles in Tait's Mag., Blackwood's Mag. and Hogg's Instructor.) II. Autobiographic Sketches. 1854. (New: Laxton, Northamptonshire, and The Priory, Chester.) III. Miscellanies. 1854. (New: Postscript [to the System of the Heavens] On the True Relations of the Bible to Merely Human Science.) IV. Miscellanies. 1854. (New: Postscript [to On Murder Considered as One of the Fine Arts].) V. Confessions of an English Opium Eater. 1856. (Much enlarged, and including The Daughter of Lebanon.) VI. Sketches, Critical and Biographic. 1857. (New: Notes to Whiggism in its Relations to Literature.) VII. Studies on Secret Records, Personal and Historic. With other Papers. 1858. (New: Supplementary note on The Essenes appended to the article on Secret Societies.) VIII. Essays Sceptical and Antisceptical, on Problems Neglected or Misconceived. 1858. (With addns to some of the articles.) IX. Leaders in Literature, with a Notice of Traditional Errors affecting them. 1858. (With postscripts to some of the articles.) X. Classic Records Reviewed or Deciphered. 1859. (With addn to article on Milton, viz. Postscript on Dr. Johnson's Life of Milton.) XI. Critical Suggestions on Style and Rhetoric, with German Tales, and other Narrative Papers. 1859. XII–XIII. Speculations, Literary and Philosophic, with German Tales and other Narrative Papers. 1859. XIV. Letters to a Young Man whose Education has been neglected, and Other Papers. 1860. (Partly prepared before De Quincey's death, Dec. 8, 1859, and pbd posthumously. In vol. XIV was included Traditions of the Rabbins by George Croly which through De Quincey's forgetfulness had been ptd by J. T. Fields in the Boston edn. It continued to be rptd as De Quincey's up to 1873 (the 2nd American edn) and 1878 (the 4th Edinburgh edn).)]

Works. 17 vols. Edinburgh, 1862–3 (to have been completed in 15 vols.; 2 vols. added in course of pbn); 16 vols. Edinburgh, 1871 (vols. retain earlier dates, 1862–3; there are addns to last 4); 16 vols. Edinburgh, 1878 (all vols. save 1st are dated 1862 or 1863; 3 essays added).

Writings. Riverside Edition. 11 vols. Boston, 1877 (3rd edn). [With notes and general index; has been several times rptd.]

The Collected Writings. New and Enlarged Edition by David Masson. 14 vols. Edinburgh, 1889–90. [With introductions and notes; considerable new material now first collected. This has remained the standard edn and has been several times rptd.]

The Uncollected Writings. With Preface and Annotations by James Hogg. 2 vols. 1890.

(3) SELECTIONS

Selected Essays. Ed. D. Masson, 2 vols. 1888.

Essays. Ed. C. Whibley, 1903.

Joan of Arc, the English Mail-Coach, and the Spanish Military Nun. Ed. C. M. Newman, 1906.

The English Mail-Coach and Other Essays. 1914. (Everyman's Lib.)
The Ecstasies of Thomas De Quincey. Ed. T. Burke, 1928.
Selected Writings of Thomas De Quincey. Ed. P. Van D. Stern, New York, 1937.

(4) Books and Contributions to Books

Translation from Horace, Ode 22, Lib. 1. (Third Prize Translation.) Juvenile Lib. i, 1800.
Concerning the Relations of Great Britain, Spain and Portugal, as affected by the Convention of Cintra. 1809. [By Wordsworth. Appendix on the Letters of Sir J. Moore by De Quincey.]
Close Comments upon a Straggling Speech. 1818. [Unique copy at Tullie House, Carlisle; never rptd.]
Confessions of an English Opium Eater. 1822 (rpt of the 2 pts from London Mag. Sept.–Oct. 1821, with appendix 30 Sept. 1822); 1823; Edinburgh, 1856 (greatly enlarged); ed. R. Garnett, 1885 (rpt of 1st edn, with De Quincey's Conversations with Richard Woodhouse, a note on De Quincey and Musset, etc.); ed. A. W. Pollard, 1901; ed. D. Masson, 1904; ed. Sir G. Douglas, 1907 (Everyman's Lib.); ed. G. Saintsbury, 1927. Tr. French, C. Baudelaire, Paris, 1860, A. de M[usset], Paris, 1878 (with addns by de Musset) and V. Descreux, Paris, 1903 (première Traduction intégrale); German, Stuttgart, 1886; Italian, Milan, 1889.
Popular Tales and Romances of the Northern Nations. 3 vols. 1823. [De Quincey contributed a trn from the German of J. A. Apel, The Fatal Marksman.]
Walladmor. A Novel. Freely translated from the English of Sir Walter Scott, and now freely translated from the German into English. 2 vols. 1825. [A German forgery, very freely done into English; see De Quincey's paper on Walladmor, 1838.]
Klosterheim,* or the Masque. Edinburgh, 1832.
The Gallery of Portraits. Ed. A. T. Malkin, 7 vols. 1832–7. [De Quincey contributed a Life of Milton to vol. i.]
Encyclopaedia Britannica. 7th edn, 1827–42. [Articles on Goethe, 1835; Pope, 1837–8; Schiller, 1838; Shakespeare, 1838.]
The Logic of Political Economy. Edinburgh, 1844.
China. 1857. [Rev. rpt from articles in Titan, with preface and addns.]
The Wider Hope. Essays on Future Punishment, with a Paper on the Supposed Scriptural Expression for Eternity. 1890.

De Quincey Memorials. Being Letters and Other Records here first published. With Communications from Coleridge, the Wordsworths, Hannah More, Professor Wilson, and Others. Ed. A. H. Japp, 2 vols. 1891.
The Posthumous Works, edited from the Original MSS. with Introductions and Notes, by A. H. Japp. 2 vols. 1891. [Vol. i: Suspiria de Profundis, with Other Essays, Critical, Biographical, Philosophical, Imaginative and Humorous. Vol. ii: Conversation and Coleridge, with Other Essays, etc.]
A Diary of Thomas De Quincey, 1803. Here reproduced in Replica, as well as in Print, from the Original Manuscript in the possession of the Rev. C. H. Steel. Ed. H. A. Eaton, 1927.
De Quincey at Work: as seen in One Hundred and Thirty New and newly edited Letters. Ed. W. H. Bonner, Buffalo, 1936.

(5) Contributions to Periodicals

Westmorland Gazette. [De Quincey was editor 11 July, 1818–5 Nov. 1819.]
London Magazine. [De Quincey contributed irregularly 1821–5 some 45 articles: Confessions of an English Opium Eater, Sept.–Oct. 1821; On the Knocking at the Gate in Macbeth, Oct. 1823.]
Knight's Quarterly Magazine, 1824–5. [2 stories from the German: The Incognito, or Count Fitz-Hum, and The Love Charm of Tieck.]
Blackwood's Magazine, 1826–8. [6 articles: On Murder considered as One of the Fine Arts, Feb. 1827.]
Edinburgh Literary Gazette, 1829. [Sketch of Prof. Wilson, 3 articles, 6, 20 June, 11 July.]
Blackwood's Magazine, 1830–4. [14 articles: Richard Bentley, 1830; Dr. Parr and his Contemporaries, 1831; The Caesars 1832–4, Also several political articles (not rptd and only partly identifiable).]
Tait's Magazine, 1833–41. [Some 40 articles: Sketches of Life and Manners: from the Autobiography of an English Opium Eater (27 articles); Samuel Taylor Coleridge, 1834–5 (4 articles); Lake Reminiscences, 1839 (5 articles).]
Blackwood's Magazine, 1837–45. [28 articles: Revolt of the Tartars, 1837; Casuistry, 1839–40; On Murder Considered as One of the Fine Arts, second part, 1839; On the Essenes, 1840; Style, 1840–1; Homer and the Homeridae, 1841; The Pagan Oracles, 1842; Coleridge and Opium Eating, 1845; Suspiria de Profundis, 1845.]
Tait's Magazine, 1845–8. [Some 30 articles: On Christianity as an Organ of Political Movement, 1846; System of the Heavens

as Revealed by Lord Rosse's Telescopes, 1846; Joan of Arc, 1847; Secret Societies, 1847; Conversation, 1847.]

The Glasgow Athenaeum Album, 1848. [2 articles.]

North British Review, 1848. [3 articles: Reviews of Forster's Goldsmith; Roscoe's Pope; Talfourd's Final Memorials of Charles Lamb.]

Blackwood's Magazine, 1849. [2 articles: The English Mail-coach; The Vision of Sudden Death.]

Hogg's Instructor, 1850–3. [24 articles: Conversation (final part), 1850; The Sphinx's Riddle, 1850; A Sketch from Childhood, 1851–2; Judas Iscariot, 1853.]

Tait's Magazine, 1851. [Lord Carlisle on Pope (3 articles).]

Titan, 1856–7. [6 articles.]

The Archivist and Autograph Review, June 1888. [An Essay on Novels.]

The New Review, Dec. 1890. Two Newly-discovered Papers. [The Dark Interpreter, and The Loveliest Sight for Woman's Eyes.]

The New Review, Jan. 1891. Further Newly-discovered Papers. [On Miracles; Why the Pagans could not Invest their Gods with any Iota of Grandeur; Great Forgers: Chatterton, Walpole, and 'Junius.']

The Independent, 15 Jan. 1914. Lessons of the French Revolution: an Unpublished Paper by Thomas De Quincey.

(6) Biography and Criticism

(a) Books and Chapters in Books

Gillies, R. P. Memoirs of a Literary Veteran. 3 vols. 1851.

Masson, D. Essays, Biographical and Critical. 1855.

—— Wordsworth, Shelley, Keats and Other Essays. 1874.

—— De Quincey. 1881. (English Men of Letters ser.)

Gilfillan, G. Galleries of Literary Portraits. 2 vols. Edinburgh, 1856–7.

Bayne, P. Essays in Biography and Criticism. 2 vols. 1857–8.

Baudelaire, C. Les Paradis artificiels, Opium et Hachisch. Paris, 1860.

Gordon, Mary. Christopher North: a Memoir of John Wilson, by his Daughter. 2 vols. Edinburgh, 1862.

Burton, J. H. The Book-hunter. 1862.

'Christopher North' (J. Wilson), et al. Noctes Ambrosianae. 4 vols. 1864.

Knight, C. Passages of a Working Life during Half-a-century. 3 vols. 1864–5.

Stirling, J. H. Jerrold, Tennyson, and Macaulay. 1868.

Martineau, H. Biographical Sketches. 1869.

Fields, J. T. Yesterdays with Authors. 1872.

Robinson, H. C. Diary, Reminiscences and Correspondence. Ed. T. Sadler, 2 vols. 1872.

—— Henry Crabb Robinson on Books and their Writers. Ed. E. J. Morley, 3 vols. 1938.

Espinasse, F. Lancashire Worthies. 2 vols. 1874–7.

Stephen, Sir L. Hours in a Library. 3 sers. 1874–9.

Proctor, B. W. Autobiographical Fragment and Biographical Notes. 1877.

Mackay, C. Forty Years' Recollections of Life, Literature and Public Affairs. 2 vols. 1877.

'Page, H. A.' (H. A. Japp). Thomas De Quincey: his Life and Writings; with Unpublished Correspondence. 2 vols. 1877; 1890 (rev., re-arranged, and with addns). [Appendix by W. C. B. Eatwell, A Medical View of Mr De Quincey's Case.]

Hill, R. and F. Memoir of Matthew Davenport Hill. 1878 (priv. ptd).

Carlyle, T. Reminiscences. Ed. J. A. Froude, 2 vols. 1881.

—— Letters, 1826–36. Ed. C. E. Norton, 1889.

Hodgson, S. H. Outcast Essays, and Verse Translations. 1881.

Froude, J. A. Life of Thomas Carlyle. 2 vols. 1884.

Woodhouse, R. Notes of Conversations with Thomas De Quincey. [In R. Garnett's rpt of Confessions of an English Opium Eater, 1885.]

Mason, E. T. Personal Traits of British Authors. 4 vols. 1885.

Payn, J. Some Literary Recollections. 1885.

Brandl, A. Samuel Taylor Coleridge und die englische Romantik. Berlin, 1886; tr. Eng. 1887.

Findlay, J. R. Personal Recollections of Thomas De Quincey. 1886.

Ingleby, C. M. Essays: Edited by his Son. 1888.

Salt, H. S. Literary Sketches. 1888.

—— De Quincey. 1904.

Sandford, Mrs H. Thomas Poole and his Friends. 2 vols. 1888.

Stuart, D. Letters from the Lake Poets, S. T. Coleridge, Wordsworth, Southey to Daniel Stuart. Ed. E. H. Coleridge, 1889 (priv. ptd).

Pollitt, C. De Quincey's Editorship of the Westmorland Gazette, with Selections from his Work on that Journal from July, 1818 to November, 1819. 1890.

Saintsbury, G. Essays in English Literature (1780–1860). 1890.

—— The Landors, Leigh Hunt, De Quincey. CHEL. vol. xii, 1915.

Bertram, J. Some Memories of Books, Authors and Events. 1893.

Fields, Mrs J. T. A Shelf of Old Books. 1894.

Hogg, J. De Quincey and his Friends. Personal Recollections, Souvenirs and Anecdotes. 1895.

Hill, G. B. Talks about Autographs. 1896.

Lang, A. The Life and Letters of John Gibson Lockhart. 2 vols. 1897.

Oliphant, M. O. W. Annals of a Publishing House: William Blackwood and Sons. 3 vols. 1897–8.

Hitchcock, R. Thomas De Quincey. A Study. 1899.

Dunn, W. A. Thomas De Quincey's Relation to German Literature and Philosophy. Strasburg, 1900.

Birrell, A. Essays about Men, Women and Books. 1901.

Cooper, L. Prose-Poetry of Thomas De Quincey. Leipzig, 1902.

Gould, G. M. Biographic Clinics: the Origin of the Ill-Health of De Quincey, Carlyle, Darwin, Huxley and Browning. Vol. I, Philadelphia, 1903.

Symons, A. Studies in Prose and Verse. 1904.

Dawson, W. J. Makers of Modern Prose. 1905.

Guerrier, P. Étude médico-psychologique sur Thomas De Quincey. Lyons, 1907.

Sellar, Mrs E. M. Recollections and Impressions. 1907.

Priestley, E., Lady. The Story of a Lifetime. 1908.

Armitt, M. L. Rydal. 1916.

MacFarlane, C. Reminiscences of a Literary Life. 1917.

'Lee, Vernon.' The Syntax of De Quincey. [In The Handling of Words, 1923.]

Marks, J. Genius and Disaster: Studies in Drugs and Genius. New York, 1925.

Powell, A. E. The Romantic Theory of Poetry. 1926.

Clapton, G. T. Baudelaire et De Quincey. Paris, 1931.

Abrams, M. H. The Milk of Paradise. The Effect of Opium Visions on the Works of De Quincey, Crabbe, Francis Thompson, and Coleridge. Cambridge, U.S.A. 1934.

Elwin, M. De Quincey. 1935.

Eaton, H. A. Thomas De Quincey. A Biography. Oxford, 1936.

Sackville-West, E. A Flame in Sunlight. The Life and Work of Thomas De Quincey. 1936.

(b) Articles in Periodicals

'Monkshood' (Francis Jacox?). Thomas De Quincey. Bentley's Misc. xxxvii, 1855.

S., H. W. Life and Writings of Thomas De Quincey. Fraser's Mag. lxi, 1860.

Kebbel, T. E. Quarterly Rev. cx, 1861. [Review of Selections Grave and Gay.]

Alden, H. M. Thomas De Quincey. Atlantic Monthly, xii, 1863.

Masson, D. Dead Men I have Known: Dr Samuel Brown, Hugh Miller, De Quincey. Macmillan's Mag. xii, 1865.

Lathrop, G. P. Some Aspects of De Quincey. Atlantic Monthly, xl, 1877.

Conway, M. D. The English Lakes and their Genii. Harper's Mag. lxii, 1880.

Japp, A. H. Early Intercourse of the Wordsworths and De Quincey. Century Mag. xli, 1891.

Contades, G. de. Le Jeanne d'Arc de Thomas De Quincey. Revue des Deux Mondes, cxv, 1893.

L., P. Emerson's Meeting with De Quincey. Blackwood's Mag. clv, 1894.

Dowden, E. How De Quincey worked. Saturday Rev. lxxix, 1895.

Jarvis, J. B. Neglect shown to De Quincey. Monthly Mag. cviii, 1906.

Robinson, H. P. De Quincey and the 'Grand Style.' Academy, lxx, 1906.

Durand, W. Y. De Quincey and Carlyle in their Relation to the Germans. PMLA. xxii, 1907.

Green, J. A. Notes on the Portraits of De Quincey. Manchester Quart. July 1913.

Eaton, H. A. De Quincey's Love of Music. JEGP. xiii, 1914.

—— The Letters of De Quincey to Wordsworth, 1803–1807. ELH. iii, 1936.

Fairbrother, E. H. De Quincey and the War Office. N. & Q. 9 Oct. 1915.

Duckers, J. S. The De Quincey Family. TLS. 21 Oct. 1920.

Paull, H. M. De Quincey's Style. Fortnightly Rev. cxviii, 1922.

Fowler, J. H. De Quincey as Literary Critic. English Ass. 1922.

Richter, H. Thomas De Quincey. E. Studien, lviii, 1924.

Gray, W. F. De Quincey as Lady Nairne's Tenant. Chambers Journ. xvi, 1926.

Impassioned Prose. TLS. 16 Sept. 1926.

Bostock, J. R. Johanna d'Arc als Nationalistin und Protestantin. E. Studien, lxii, 1928.

Burke, T. De Quincey the Goblin. Nineteenth Century, ciii, 1928.

—— The Obsequies of Mr. Williams: New Light on De Quincey's Famous Tale of Murder. Bookman (U.S.A.), lxviii, 1928.

Salt, H. S. The Depreciation of De Quincey. National Rev. cxliii, 1928.

Griggs, E. L. Coleridge, De Quincey, and Nineteenth Century Editing. MLN. xlvii, 1932.

Moore, E. H. Some Unpublished Letters of Thomas De Quincey. RES. ix, 1933.

Parsons, C. O. The Woes of Thomas De Quincey. RES. x, 1934.

Scott, C. A. De Quincey and Lamb. TLS. 24 Jan. 1935.

Astre, G. A. Balzac et De Quincey. Revue de Littérature comparée, Dec. 1935.

Forward, K. 'Libellous Attack' on De Quincey. PMLA. LII, 1937.

Galinsky, H. K. Is Thomas De Quincey Author of The Love-Charm? MLN. LII, 1937.

H. A. E.

THOMAS CARLYLE (1795–1881)

(1) Bibliographies

Lane, W. C. The Carlyle Collection. A Catalogue of Books on Oliver Cromwell and Frederick the Great bequeathed by Thomas Carlyle to Harvard College Library. Cambridge, U.S.A. 1888.

Wead, M. E. A Catalogue of the Dr Samuel A. Jones Carlyle Collection. University of Michigan. Ann Arbor, 1919.

Dyer, I. W. A Bibliography of Thomas Carlyle's Writings and Ana. Portland, Maine, 1928.

(2) Collected Works

Collected Works. 16 vols. 1857–8.

Library Edition. 34 vols. 1869–71.

People's Edition. 37 vols. 1871–4.

Edition de Luxe. 20 vols. Boston, 1884.

Sterling Edition. 20 vols. Boston, 1885.

People's Edition. 20 vols. in 10, Boston, 1885.

Ashburton Edition. 17 vols. (with 3 supplementary vols.), 1885–8.

Collected Works. 12 vols. New York, 1885. [Pbd by J. B. Alden.]

Collected Works. 20 vols. in 10, New York, [1887]. [Pbd by National Book Co.]

Copyright Edition. 37 vols. 1888; 20 vols. 1894.

Centenary Edition. Ed. (with Introductions) H. D. Traill, 30 vols. 1896–9, New York, 1896–1901. [Most complete edn.]

Chelsea Edition. 11 vols. [1900]; 11 vols. [1900?] ('cheap issue').

Edinburgh Edition. 30 vols. New York, 1903; 15 vols. 1903.

Centennial Edition. Ed. W. J. Rolfe, 26 vols. Boston, n.d.

Standard Edition. 18 vols. New York, 1905.

(3) Selections

Passages Selected from the Writings of Thomas Carlyle. With a Biographical Memoir by T. Ballantyne. 1855.

Ausgewählte Schriften. Ed. A. Kretschmar, 6 vols. Leipzig, 1855–6.

The Carlyle Anthology. Selected and Arranged by E. Barrett. New York, 1876.

Thomas Carlyle. Ein Lebensbild; und Goldkörner aus seinen Werken. Leipzig, 1882.

The Socialism and Unsocialism of Thomas Carlyle. 2 vols. New York, [1891].

Rescued Essays. Ed. P. Newberry, [1892].

Readings from Carlyle. Ed. W. K. Leask, 1894.

Sozialpolitische Schriften. Ed. P. Hensel and tr. German E. von Pfannkuche, 3 vols. Göttingen, 1894–8.

Thoughts on Life, by Thomas Carlyle. Ed. R. Duncan, 1895.

Outline of the Doctrines of Thomas Carlyle. 1896.

Arbeiten und nicht Verzweifeln. Auszüge aus Carlyles Werken. Tr. German and ed. A. Kretschmar and M. Kühn, Düsseldorf, 1902.

Zerstreute historische Aufsätze. Tr. German and ed. T. A. Fischer, Leipzig, 1905.

Pages Choisies des Grands Écrivains. Carlyle. Tr. French and ed. É. Masson, Paris, 1905.

Arbeta och Förtvifla icke. Lefvande Ord ur Thomas Carlyle. Tr. Swedish and ed. E. Ryding, Stockholm, 1906.

Essais Choisis de Critique et de Morale. Tr. French and ed. E. Barthélemy, Paris, 1907.

Short Passages from the Works of Thomas Carlyle. Selections by Lady Sarah Spencer. 1908.

Pocket Carlyle. Ed. R. Gardner, 1908.

Pen Portraits from Thomas Carlyle. [1908]

Masters of Literature. Carlyle. Ed. A. W. Evans, 1909.

Selected Essays of Thomas Carlyle. Ed. A. S. Pringle-Pattison, 1909.

Nouveaux Essais Choisis de Critique et de Morale. Du Genre Biographique. Tr. French and ed. E. Barthélemy, Paris, 1909.

Lavora, non Disperarti. Brani scelti delle sue Opere. Tr. Italian and ed. V. Morali, Turin, 1910.

Carlyles Skrifter. Tr. Danish U. Birkedal, Copenhagen, 1916.

Thomas Carlyle a Faithful Friend of Germany: Eine Auswahl. Ed. J. Bube, Leipzig, 1919.

Pagine Scelte. Tr. Italian and ed. G. Valori, Milan, 1920.

The Best of Carlyle. Ed. T. O. Glencross, 1923.

(4) Separate Works
(a) Books

Elements of Geometry and Trigonometry; with notes. Translated from the French of A. M. Legendre. Edinburgh, 1824. [The trn and the introductory ch. on Proportion are by Carlyle.]

Wilhelm Meister's Apprenticeship. A Novel from the German of Goethe. 3 vols. Edinburgh, 1824 (anon.); 1839; Philadelphia, 1840; 1842; Boston, 1851; 1858; Boston, 1865, etc.; ed. E. Dowden, 1890; ed. N. H. Dole, Boston, 1901.

The Life of Schiller, comprehending an examination of his Works. 1825; Boston, 1833; 1845. [First pbd as Schiller's Life and Writings, London Mag. 1823-4 (see below). Tr. German, with an introduction by Goethe, as Leben Schillers, aus dem Englischen, Frankfort, 1830.]

German Romance. Specimens of its Chief Authors; with biographical and critical notices. By the Translator of Wilhelm Meister, and the Author of the Life of Schiller. 4 vols. Edinburgh, 1827. [Vol. I, Musaeus and Fouqué; vol. II, Tieck and Hoffman; vol. III, Richter; vol. IV, Goethe. Rptd 2 vols. 1874, as Tales by Musaeus, Tieck, Richter.]

Sartor Resartus; the Life and Opinions of Herr Teufelsdröckh. In Three Books. With Preface by R. W. Emerson. Boston, 1836; 1838; 1841; 1849; ed. E. Dowden, 1896; ed. A. MacMechan, Boston, 1896 (most thoroughly edited); ed. J. A. S. Barrett, 1897, 1905 (rev. edn); ed. J. Wood, 1902; ed. P. C. Parr, 1913; ed. C. S. Northup, New York, 1921; ed. A. H. Thorndike, New York, [1921] (Modern Student's Lib.); ed. W. S. Johnson, Boston, 1924; ed. F. W. Roe, New York, 1927. Tr. Dutch, Amsterdam, 1880; German, Leipzig, 1882; French, Paris, 1899. [First pbd in Fraser's Mag. 1833–4.]

The French Revolution. A History. 3 vols. 1837; 3 vols. 1839; 3 vols. 1848; ed. C. R. L. Fletcher, 3 vols. 1902; ed. J. H. Rose, 3 vols. 1902; ed. C. F. Harrold, New York, 1937. Tr. German, Leipzig, 1844; French, Paris, 1865, 1888. [Reviews: J. S. Mill, London and Westminster Rev. XXVII, 1837, p. 179; W. M. Thackeray, Times, 3 Aug. 1837; P. Chasles, Revue des Deux Mondes, XXIV, 1840, pp. 109–26. See also R. T. Kerlen, Contemporary Criticism of Carlyle's French Revolution, Sewanee Rev. XX, 1912.]

Lectures on German Literature. [Delivered 1837, not pbd; see Spectator, 6 May 1837, for condensed report.]

Lectures on the History of Literature. 1838; ed. J. R. Greene, 1892; ed. R. P. Karkaria, Bombay, 1892. [See E. Dowden, Transcripts and Studies, 1887; Spectator, LXVIII, 1892, pp. 494–531, LXIX, p. 621.]

Six Lectures on Revolutions in Modern Europe. [Delivered 1839, not pbd. See R. H. Shepherd, Memoirs of the Life and Writings of Thomas Carlyle, vol. I, 1881, pp. 197–214, for a report of the lectures.]

Critical and Miscellaneous Essays. 4 vols. Boston, 1838; 4 vols. New York, 1839; 4 vols. 1839; 5 vols. 1840; 4 vols. 1847; 4 vols. 1857. [The individual essays of the collection will be found enumerated, p. 654 below.]

Chartism. 1840; Boston, 1840; 1842.

On Heroes, Hero-Worship, and the Heroic in History. Six Lectures. Reported with Emendations and Additions. 1841; 1842; 1846; ed. A. MacMechan, Boston, 1901 (best edn); ed. J. C. Adams, Boston, 1907; ed. P. C. Parr, 1910; ed. H. M. Buller, 2 vols. 1926. Tr. French, Paris, 1888; Spanish, Madrid, 1893; German, Leipzig, 1895; Italian, Florence, 1897.

Preface to R. W. Emerson's Essays. 1841; 1844; 1853.

Past and Present. 1843; Boston, 1843; 1845; ed. O. Smeaton, 1902 (Temple Classics); ed. F. Harrison, [1903]; ed. E. Mims, New York, 1918 (Modern Student's Lib.); ed. A. M. D. Hughes, Oxford, 1921; ed. J. Paton, New York, 1927; ed. E. Rhys, n.d. (Everyman's Lib., with Emerson's review). [See R. B. E., Thoughts on Thomas Carlyle; or a Commentary on the 'Past and Present,' 1843; F. Schneider, Carlyles 'Past and Present' und der 'Chronica Jocelini de Brakelonda,' Halle, 1911; Dial, July 1843 (Emerson's review).]

Oliver Cromwell's Letters and Speeches: With Elucidations. 2 vols. 1845; 2 vols. New York, 1845; 3 vols. 1846 (enlarged); 4 vols. 1850; ed. S. C. Lomas, 1904; ed. W. A. Shaw, [1907] (Everyman's Lib.); ed. E. Sanderson, New York [1924] (abridged). [See C. Remusat, De Cromwell selon M. Carlyle et M. de Lamartine, Revue des Deux Mondes, V, 1854, pp. 1073–1112; J. B. Mozley, Essays Historical and Theological, vol. I, Oxford, 1878; H. Mazel, Le Cromwell de Carlyle, Mercure de France, XCIV, Nov. 1911.]

Latter-Day Pamphlets. 1850; New York, 1850; 1855; 1858. [Eight pamphlets, as follows: I (Feb.), The Present Time; II (March), Model Prisons; III (April), Downing Street; IV (April), The New Downing Street; V (May), Stump-Orator; VI (June), Parliaments; VII (July), Hudson's Statue; VIII (Aug.), Jesuitism. For reviews, etc., see Athenaeum, 1850, pp. 126–7, 227–8, 704–5, 894–5; Blackwood's Mag. LXVII, 1850, pp. 641–58; J. Hanay, Blackwood v. Carlyle. A Vindication by a Carlylian, 1850; Revue des Deux Mondes, VI, 1850, pp. 1083–1111; Eclectic Rev. XXVIII, 1850, pp. 385–409.]

Life of John Sterling. 1851; 1852; ed. W. H. White, 1907 (World's Classics). [For reviews, etc., see Athenaeum, 1851, pp. 1088–90; British Quarterly Rev. XV, 1852, pp. 240–53; Eclectic Rev. II, 1851, pp. 717–29; North British Rev. XVI, 1852, pp. 359–89; Revue des Deux Mondes, XV, 1852, pp. 133–

64; Tait's Edinburgh Mag. xviii, 1851, pp. 699–707; Westminster Rev. lvii, 1852, pp. 247–51 (George Eliot's review).]

The History of Friedrich II of Prussia, called Frederick the Great. 6 vols. 1858–65; 13 vols. Leipzig, 1858–65; 6 vols. New York, 1858–66; 6 vols. New York, 1863–71; 7 vols. 1869; 10 vols. 1872–3; ed. C. Ransome, New York, 1892 (abridged); ed. E. Sanderson, 1909 (abridged); ed. A. M. D. Hughes, Oxford, 1916 (abridged); tr. German, Berlin, 1858–69. [For reviews, etc., see Athenaeum, 1862, pp. 585–8, 1864, pp. 369–71, 1865, pp. 413–4; Atlantic Monthly, x, 1862, p. 643; Blackwood's Mag. lxxxv, 1859, pp. 127–54, xcviii, 1865, pp. 38–56; Dublin Rev. xlvii, 1859, pp. 132–68, li, 1862, pp. 408–28; Eclectic Mag. (New York), lxii, 1864, pp. 321–31; Eclectic Rev. ii, 1862, pp. 499–523, vi, 1864, pp. 703–14, ix, 1865, pp. 299–324; Edinburgh Rev. cx, 1859, pp. 376–410; Fraser's Mag. lviii, 1858, pp. 631–49, lxix, 1864, pp. 539–50, lxxii, 1865, pp. 778–810; Harper's New Monthly Mag. xviii, 1858, pp. 86–95, xxv, 1862, pp. 523–82; National Rev. vii, 1858, pp. 247–9; North American Rev. lxxxviii, 1859, pp. 503–47, cii, 1866, pp. 419–45; North British Rev. xxx, 1859, pp. 22–43, xliii, 1865, pp. 79–126; Preussischer Jahrbücher, ii, 1858, pp. 542–55. Quarterly Rev. cv, 1859, pp. 275–304, cxviii, 1865, pp. 225–54; Revue des Deux Mondes, ciii, 1873, pp. 269–303; Westminster Rev. xv, 1859, pp. 174–208. See also H. H. Lancaster, Carlyle's Frederick the Great, in Essays and Reviews, Edinburgh, 1876.]

Inaugural Address at Edinburgh, April 2nd, 1866. On the Choice of Books. With a Memoir of Thomas Carlyle by J. C. Hotten. 1866; 1869 ('with a new Life of the Author').

The Early Kings of Norway: Also an Essay on the Portraits of John Knox. 1875. [Rptd from Fraser's Mag. 1875. See J. Drummond, The Portraits of John Knox and George Buchanan, Trans. Antiquarian Soc. Edinburgh, 1875.]

Reminiscences. Ed. J. A. Froude, 2 vols. 1881; ed. C. E. Norton, 2 vols. 1887, 1932 (Everyman's Lib.); tr. German, Göttingen, 1897. [For reviews, see Edinburgh Rev. cliii, 1881, pp. 469–97; A. Hayward, Quarterly Rev. cli, 1881, pp. 385 ff.; H. Larkin, British Quarterly Rev. lxxiv, 1881, pp. 28–84; Sir Henry Taylor, Nineteenth Century, ix, 1881, pp. 1009–25; A. Lang, Fraser's Mag. ciii, 1881, pp. 515–28; Blackwood's Mag. cxxxii, 1882, pp. 18–35; Cornhill Mag. lxvi, 1881, pp. 349–58; Fortnightly Rev. xxxv, 1881, pp. 456–66; In-

quirer, March, April 1881. See also I. W. Dyer, Carlyle Bibliography, pp. 209–18.]

Reminiscences of my Irish Journey in 1849. 1882.

Last Words of Thomas Carlyle on Trades-Unions, Promoterism, and The Signs of the Times. Ed. J. C. Aitken, Edinburgh, 1882.

Letters and Memorials of Jane Welsh Carlyle, Prepared for Publication by Thomas Carlyle. Ed. J. A. Froude, 3 vols. 1883. [For Mrs Carlyle, see Reminiscences; Mrs A. E. Ireland, Life of Jane Welsh Carlyle, 1891; Elizabeth Drew, Jane Welsh and Jane Carlyle, 1928. See also p. 656 below.]

Last Words of Thomas Carlyle. Wotton Reinfred: A Romance. Excursion (Futile Enough) to Paris. Letters. 1892; New York, 1892 (with introduction on Wotton Reinfred).

New Letters and Memorials of Jane Welsh Carlyle. Annotated by Thomas Carlyle. Ed. A. Carlyle and Sir J. Crichton-Browne, 2 vols. 1903. [For reviews see Academy, lxvi, 1903, p. 448; Athenaeum, l, 1903, pp. 585–6; Fortnightly Rev. lxxix, 1903, pp. 1000–9, lxxx, 1903, pp. 180–92; Nineteenth Century, liii, 1903, pp. 813–20.]

Historical Sketches of Notable Persons and Events in the Reigns of James I and Charles I. Ed. A. Carlyle, 1898. [Written 1842–3.]

Two Notebooks of Thomas Carlyle from 23rd March 1822 to 16th May 1832. Ed. C. E. Norton, Grolier Club, New York, 1898.

(b) Contributions to Magazines and Miscellanies

Articles in the Edinburgh Encyclopaedia. Vol. xiv (1820): Montaigne; Lady Montagu; Montesquieu; Montfaucon; Dr John Moore; Sir John Moore. Vol. xv (1822): Necker; Nelson; Netherlands; Newfoundland; Norfolk; Northamptonshire; Northumberland. Vol. xvi (1823): Mungo Park; Pascal (see I. W. Dyer, Carlyle Bibliography, p. 201); William Pitt, Earl of Chatham; William Pitt the Younger. [Rptd in Montaigne, and Other Essays, Chiefly Biographical, By Thomas Carlyle, ed. S. R. Crockett, 1897.]

Joanna Baillie's Metrical Legends. New Edinburgh Rev. i, Oct. 1821.

Goethe's Faust. New Edinburgh Rev. ii, April 1822. [Ed. R. Garnett, Publications of English Goethe Soc. iv, 1888, pp. 85 ff.]

Schiller's Life and Writings. London Mag. viii–x, 1823–4. [Rptd in book-form, 1825; see p. 653 above.]

Jean Paul Friedrich Richter. Edinburgh Rev. xlvi, June 1827.

State of German Literature. Edinburgh Rev. XLVI, Oct. 1827.

Life and Writings of Werner. Foreign Rev. I, Jan. 1828.

Goethe's Helena. Foreign Rev. I, April 1828.

Goethe. Foreign Rev. II, July 1828.

Life of Heyne. Foreign Rev. II, Oct. 1828.

Burns. Edinburgh Rev. XLVIII, Dec. 1828.

German Playwrights. Foreign Rev. III, Jan. 1829.

Voltaire. Foreign Rev. III, April 1829.

Signs of the Times. Edinburgh Rev. XLIX, June 1829.

Novalis. Foreign Rev. IV, July 1829.

Jean Paul Friedrich Richter Again. Foreign Rev. V, Jan. 1830.

Jean Paul Friedrich Richter's Review of Madame de Staël's De l'Allemagne. Fraser's Mag. I, Feb., May 1830.

Cui Bono? And Four Fables by Pilpay Junior. Fraser's Mag. II, Sept. 1830.

Thoughts on History. Fraser's Mag. II, Nov. 1830.

Luther's Psalm. Fraser's Mag. II, Jan. 1831.

Cruthers and Jonson. Fraser's Mag. II, Jan. 1831.

Peter Nimmo: a Rhapsody. Fraser's Mag. III, Feb. 1831.

The Beetle. Fraser's Mag. III, Feb. 1831.

Taylor's Historic Survey of German Poetry. Edinburgh Rev. LIII, March 1831.

Schiller. Fraser's Mag. III, March 1831.

The Sower's Song. Fraser's Mag. III, April 1831.

The Niebelungen Lied. Westminster Rev. XV, July 1831.

Tragedy of the Night-Moth. Fraser's Mag. IV, Aug. 1831.

German Literature of the Fourteenth and Fifteenth Centuries. Foreign Quarterly Rev. VIII, Oct. 1831.

Characteristics. Edinburgh Rev. LIV, Dec. 1831.

Schiller, Goethe, and Madame de Staël, and Goethe's Portrait. Fraser's Mag. V, March 1832.

Goethe's Portrait. Fraser's Mag. V, March 1832.

Biography. Fraser's Mag. V, April 1832.

Boswell's Life of Johnson. Fraser's Mag. V, May 1832.

Death of Goethe. New Monthly Mag. XXXIV, June 1832.

Corn Law Rhymes. Edinburgh Rev. LV, July 1832.

Goethe's Works. Foreign Quarterly Rev. X, Aug. 1832.

The Tale, by Goethe. Fraser's Mag. VI, Oct. 1832.

Novelle, by Goethe. Fraser's Mag. VI, Nov. 1832.

Diderot. Foreign Quarterly Rev. XI, April 1833.

Quae Cogitavit on History Again. Fraser's Mag. VII, May 1833.

Count Cagliostro. Fraser's Mag. VIII, July, Aug. 1833.

Sartor Resartus. Fraser's Mag. VIII–X, Nov. 1833–Aug. 1834. [See p. 653 above.]

Death of Edward Irving. Fraser's Mag. XI, Jan. 1835.

Mirabeau. Westminster Rev. XXVI, Jan. 1837.

The Diamond Necklace. Fraser's Mag. XV, Jan., Feb. 1837.

Parliamentary History of the French Revolution. Westminster Rev. XXVII, April 1837.

Sir Walter Scott. Westminster Rev. XXVIII, Jan. 1838.

Varnhagen von Ense's Memoirs. Westminster Rev. XXXII, Dec. 1838.

Petition on the Copyright Bill. Examiner, 7 April 1839.

On the Sinking of the Vengeur. Fraser's Mag. XX, July 1839.

Baillie the Covenanter. Westminster Rev. XXXVII, Jan. 1842.

Dr Francia. Foreign Quarterly Rev. XXXI, July 1843.

An Election to the Long Parliament. Fraser's Mag. XXX, Oct. 1844.

Thirty-five Unpublished Letters of Oliver Cromwell. Fraser's Mag. XXXVI, Dec. 1847. [See p. 653 above.]

Louis Philippe. Examiner, 4 March 1848.

Repeal of the Union. Examiner, 29 April 1848.

Legislation for Ireland. Examiner, 13 May 1848.

Ireland and the British Chief Governor. Irish Regiments (of the new era). Spectator, 13 May 1848.

Death of Charles Buller. Examiner, 2 Dec. 1848.

Occasional Discourse on the Nigger Question. Fraser's Mag. XL, Dec. 1849. [Rptd separately, 1853.]

From Mr. Bramble's Unpublished Arboretum Hibernicum. Nation (Dublin), 1 Dec. 1849.

Two Hundred and Fifty Years Ago; A Fragment about Duels. Leigh Hunt's Journ. 7, 21 Dec. 1850, 11 Jan. 1851.

The Opera. Keepsake, 1852.

The Prinzenraub. Westminster Rev. VII, Jan. 1855.

Suggestions for a National Exhibition of Scottish Portraits. Proc. Soc. of Antiquaries of Scotland, I, Edinburgh, 1855.

Memoranda Concerning Mr. Leigh Hunt. Macmillan's Mag. VI, July 1862.

Ilias (Americana) in Nuce. The American Iliad in a Nutshell. Macmillan's Mag. VIII, Aug. 1863.

Shooting Niagara: and After? Macmillan's Mag. xvi, Aug. 1867.

Letters on the War between Germany and France. By T. Mommsen, D. F. Strauss, F. Max Müller and T. Carlyle. 1871.

Early Kings of Norway. Fraser's Mag. xi, Jan. Feb., March 1875. [See p. 654 above.]

Portraits of John Knox. Fraser's Mag. xi, April 1875. [See p. 654 above.]

(c) Collected Correspondence

Letters to Mrs. B. Montagu and B. W. Procter. 1881; Lakeland, Michigan, 1907.

Conway, M. D. Thomas Carlyle. 1881. [Contains 24 letters, 1824–8; 6 letters to Leigh Hunt, etc.]

Correspondence of Carlyle and Emerson. Ed. C. E. Norton, 2 vols. 1883.

Early Letters of Carlyle (1814–1821). Ed. C. E. Norton, 2 vols. 1886.

Correspondence between Goethe and Carlyle. Ed. C. E. Norton, 1887; ed. H. Oldenberg, Berlin, 1887; ed. G. Hecht, Dachau, [1913]. [See F. Max Müller, Goethe and Carlyle, Contemporary Rev. June 1886, English Goethe Soc. 1886; E. Flügel, Der Briefwechsel zwischen Goethe und Carlyle, Grenzboten, xlvi, 1887; H. Grimm, Goethes und Carlyles Briefwechsel, Deutsche Rundschau, Oct. 1887; H. H. Boyesen, Goethe and Carlyle, in Essays on German Literature, 1892; O. Baumgarten, Carlyle und Goethe, Tübingen, 1906.]

Letters of Thomas Carlyle (1826–1836). Ed. C. E. Norton, 2 vols. 1888.

Briefe T. Carlyles an Varnhagen von Ense. Ed. R. Preuss, Berlin, 1892. [Letters from Carlyle to Varnhagen von Ense are included in Last Words of Thomas Carlyle, 1892.]

Early Letters of Jane Welsh Carlyle, together with a Few of Later Years and some of Thomas Carlyle. Ed. D. G. Ritchie, 1899.

Letters of Carlyle to his Youngest Sister. With an Introductory Essay by C. T. Copeland. Boston, 1899.

New Letters of Thomas Carlyle. Ed. A. Carlyle, 2 vols. 1904.

Quelques Lettres inédites de Thomas Carlyle. Ed. C. Pitollet, Revue Germanique, iv, 1905.

Carlyle Intime. Lettres de Thomas Carlyle à sa Mère, dont plusieurs inédites, revues sur les Originaux par A. Carlyle. Tr. French E. Masson, Paris, 1907.

Love Letters of Carlyle and Jane Welsh. Ed. A. Carlyle, 2 vols. 1909. [For reviews see I. W. Dyer, Carlyle Bibliography, pp. 141–2.]

Quelques Lettres inédites de William Taylor, Coleridge, Carlyle à H. C. Robinson sur la Littérature allemande. Ed. J. M. Carré, Revue Germanique, viii, 1912.

Letters of Thomas Carlyle to John Stuart Mill, John Sterling, and Robert Browning. Ed. A. Carlyle, 1923.

Jane Welsh Carlyle: Letters to her Family (1839–1863). Ed. L. Huxley, 1924.

New Letters of Carlyle to Eckermann. Ed. W. A. Speck, Yale Rev. xv, 1926.

(5) Biography and Criticism

(a) Biographical Works

Conway, M. D. Thomas Carlyle. 1881.

Nicoll, H. J. Thomas Carlyle. Edinburgh, 1881.

Shepherd, R. H. and Williamson, C. N. Memoirs of Carlyle with Personal Reminiscences and Selections from his Private Letters. 2 vols. 1881.

Fischer, T. A. Thomas Carlyle. Leipzig, 1882.

Froude, J. A. Thomas Carlyle. A History of the First Forty Years of his Life, 1795–1835. 2 vols. 1882. [See also Froude's The Early Life of Thomas Carlyle, Nineteenth Century, x, 1881, pp. 1–42.]

—— Thomas Carlyle. A History of his Life in London, 1834–1881. 2 vols. 1884; tr. German (with preceding item), Gotha, 1887. [For reviews see British Quarterly Rev. lxxxi, 1885, pp. 143–59; Dublin Rev. xiii, 1885, pp. 63–90; Blackwood's Mag. cxxxii, 1882, pp. 18–35; Fortnightly Rev. xxxix, 1883, pp. 622–42, xlii, 1884, pp. 594–604; Macmillan's Mag. li, 1884, pp. 62–70; North American Rev. cxl, 1885, pp. 9–21; Quarterly Rev. clix, 1885, pp. 76–112; Westminster Rev. cxxviii, 1887, pp. 211–24. See also J. Wedgewood, Mr Froude as a Biographer, Contemporary Rev. xxxix, 1881, pp. 821–42. On the 'Froude-Carlyle controversy,' see further: J. A. Froude, My Relations with Carlyle; with a Letter from Sir James Stephen, 1903; Sir James Crichton-Browne, Froude and Carlyle: The Imputation Considered Medically, British Medical Journ. 27 June 1903 (rptd as pamphlet same year); Sir J. Crichton-Browne and A. Carlyle, The Nemesis of Froude: a Rejoinder to J. A. Froude's My Relations with Carlyle, 1903; D. A. Wilson, Mr. Froude and Carlyle, 1898; D. A. Wilson, The Truth about Carlyle, 1913; W. H. Dunn, Froude and Carlyle, 1930.]

Masson, D. Carlyle Personally and in his Writings. Two Lectures. 1885.

—— Edinburgh Sketches and Memories. 1892.

—— Memories of London in the 'Forties. 1908.

Garnett, R. Life of Thomas Carlyle. 1887.

Arnold, A. S. The Story of Thomas Carlyle. 1888.

Duffy, C. G. Conversations with Carlyle. 1892.

Nichol, J. Thomas Carlyle. 1892. (English Men of Letters ser.)
Blunt, R. The Carlyles' Chelsea Home. 1895.
MacPherson, H. C. Thomas Carlyle. Edinburgh, [1896].
Matz, B. W. Thomas Carlyle, a Brief Account of his Life and Writings. 1902.
Sloan, J. M. The Carlyle Country, with a Study of his Life. 1904.
Craig, R. S. The Making of Carlyle. An Experiment in Biographical Explication. 1908.
Archibald, R. C. Carlyle's First Love: Margaret Gordon, Lady Bannerman. 1910.
Wilson, D. A. Life of Thomas Carlyle. Vol. I, Carlyle till Marriage, 1795–1826. 1923. Vol. II, Carlyle till the French Revolution, 1826–1837. 1924. Vol. III, Carlyle on Cromwell and Others, 1837–1847. 1925. Vol. IV, Carlyle at his Zenith, 1848–1853. 1927. Vol. V, Carlyle to Threescore-and-Ten, 1853–1865. 1929. Vol. VI, Carlyle in Old Age. 1934 (completed by D. W. MacArthur).
Burdett, O. The Two Carlyles. 1930.

(b) Critical Works

Alexander, P. P. Mill and Carlyle. An Examination of Mr. John Stuart Mill's Doctrine of Causation in Relation to Moral Freedom. With an Occasional Discourse on Sauerteig, by Smelfungus. Edinburgh, 1866.
—— Carlyle Redivivus, Being an Occasional Discourse on Sauerteig, by Smelfungus. Glasgow, 1881.
Hodge, D. Thomas Carlyle: the Man and the Teacher. Edinburgh, [1870].
Hood, E. P. Thomas Carlyle, Philosophic Thinker, Theologian, Historian, and Poet. 1875.
Mead, E. D. The Philosophy of Carlyle. Boston, 1881.
Wylie, W. H. Thomas Carlyle, the Man and his Books. 1881.
Francison, A. National Lessons from the Life and Works of Carlyle. [1881.]
Oswald, E. Thomas Carlyle. Ein Lebensbild; und Goldkörner aus seinen Werken. Leipzig, 1882.
Larkin, H. Carlyle and the Open Secret of his Life. 1886.
Flügel, E. Thomas Carlyles religiöse und sittliche Entwicklung und Weltanschauung. Leipzig, 1887; tr. Eng. New York, 1891.
Schulze-Gaevernitz, G. von. Thomas Carlyles Welt und Gesellschaftsanschauung. Dresden, 1893.
Streuli, W. Thomas Carlyle als Vermittler deutscher Litteratur und deutsches Geistes. Zürich, 1895.

Barthélemy, E. Thomas Carlyle: Essai biographique et critique. Paris, 1900 (2nd edn).
Gildemeester, F. von. Thomas Carlyle. Nijkerk, [1900].
Hensel, P. Thomas Carlyle. Stuttgart, 1901.
Baumgarten, O. Carlyle und Goethe. Tübingen, 1906.
Shelley, H. C. In Carlyle's Country. [In Literary By-Paths in Old England, Boston, 1906.]
Johnson, W. S. Thomas Carlyle: a Study of his Literary Apprenticeship, 1814–1831. New Haven, 1911.
Cazamian, L. Carlyle. Paris, 1913; tr. Eng. 1932.
Perry, B. Thomas Carlyle: How to Know Him. Indianapolis, [1915].
Ralli, A. Guide to Carlyle. 2 vols. [1920].
Neff, E. Carlyle and Mill: Mystic and Utilitarian. New York, 1924.
—— Carlyle. 1932.
Hagberg, K. Thomas Carlyle: Romantik och Puritanism i Sartor Resartus. Stockholm, 1925.
Hamilton, M. A. Thomas Carlyle. [1926.]
Young, N. Carlyle: his Rise and Fall. [1927.]
Lehman, B. H. Carlyle's Theory of the Hero: Its Sources, Development, History, and Influence on Carlyle's Work. Durham, North Carolina, 1928.
Taylor, A. C. Carlyle: sa première Fortune littéraire en France (1825–65). Paris, 1929.
—— Carlyle et la Pensée latine. Paris, 1937.
Sagar, S. Round by Repentance Tower. A Study of Carlyle. 1930. [From Roman Catholic standpoint.]
Harrold, C. F. Carlyle and German Thought, 1819–1834. New Haven, 1934.
Basch, V. Carlyle. Paris, 1938.

(c) Articles, Essays, Chapters of Books, Pamphlets, and Monographs

Sterling, J. On the Writings of Thomas Carlyle. London and Westminster Rev. XXXIII, 1839, pp. 1–68. [Rptd in Essays and Tales, 1848.]
Mazzini, J. On the History of the French Revolution by Thomas Carlyle. Monthly Chronicle, V, 1840, pp. 71–84. On the Genius and Tendency of the Writings of Thomas Carlyle. British and Foreign Rev. XVI, 1844, pp. 262–93. [Both essays rptd in Life and Writings of Joseph Mazzini, vol. IV, 1867.]
Grant, J. Carlyle. [In Portraits of Public Characters, vol. II, 1841.]
Horne, R. H. Thomas Carlyle. [In A New Spirit of the Age, vol. II, 1844.]

Gilfillan, G. Carlyle and Sterling. [In A Gallery of Literary Portraits, Edinburgh, 1845.]

Lester, J. W. Carlyle. [In Criticisms, 1847.]

Montégut, E. Thomas Carlyle: Sa Vie et Ses Écrits. Revue des Deux Mondes, vi, 1849, pp. 278–314.

—— Littérature Américaine: Du Culte des Héros, Carlyle et Emerson. Revue des Deux Mondes, vii, 1850, pp. 722–37.

—— Thomas Carlyle et John Sterling. Revue des Deux Mondes, xv, 1852, pp. 133–64.

Emerson, R. W. English Traits. 1856. [See also Emerson's Impressions of Thomas Carlyle, Scribner's Mag. May 1881. Rptd in Lectures and Biographical Sketches, 1884.]

Schmidt, J. Übersicht der englischen Literatur des 19. Jahrhunderts. Leipzig, 1856.

—— Porträts aus dem neunzehnten Jahrhundert. Berlin, 1878.

Brimley, G. Essays by the Late George Brimley. Ed. W. G. Clark, Cambridge, 1858. [Carlyle's Life of Sterling.]

Häusser, L. Macaulay's Friedrich der Grosse mit einem Nachtrag über Carlyle. Historische Zeitschrift, i, 1859, pp. 43–107.

McNicoll, T. Carlyle. [In Essays on English Literature, 1861.]

Stephen, Sir J. F. Carlyle. [In Essays from the Saturday Review, 1862.]

Kebbel, T. E. Essays upon History and Politics. 1864.

Taine, H. A. L'Idéalisme anglais: Étude sur Carlyle. Paris, 1864.

—— Histoire de la Littérature anglaise. Vol. iv, Paris, 1864; tr. Eng. Edinburgh, 1871.

Japp, A. H. Three Great Teachers of our Own Times: Carlyle, Tennyson, and Ruskin. 1865.

Althaus, F. Thomas Carlyle: Eine biographisch-literarische Characteristik. [In Unsere Zeit, vol. ii, Leipzig, 1866.]

—— Englische Characterbilder. Vol. i, Berlin, 1869.

Thoreau, H. D. Carlyle and his Works. [In A Yankee in Canada, Boston, 1866.]

Smith, Alexander. Last Leaves. Sketches and Criticisms. Edinburgh, 1868.

Greg, W. R. Kingsley and Carlyle. [In Literary and Social Judgments, 1869 (2nd edn).]

Morley, J. Carlyle. [In Critical Miscellanies (First Series), 1871.]

Sillem, J. A. De Klaagliedern van Thomas Carlyle. De Gids (Amsterdam), Aug. 1871.

—— Thomas Carlyle's Leerjaren. De Gids, Sept. 1881.

Lowell, J. R. My Study Windows. Boston, 1871.

Mr Carlyle and Père Bouhours. Catholic World, xiii, 1871, pp. 820–5.

Stephen, Sir L. Some Words about Sir Walter Scott. [Review of Carlyle's essay on Scott. In Hours in a Library, ser. 1, 1874.]

—— Historians and Essayists. New York, 1899.

—— Studies of a Biographer. Vol. iii, 1902. [On Froude.]

—— Some Early Impressions. 1924.

McCrie, G. The Religion of Our Literature: Essays upon Carlyle, Browning, Tennyson. 1875.

Davey, S. Darwin, Carlyle, and Dickens; with Other Essays. [1876.]

Dowden, E. The Transcendental Movement and Literature. [In Studies in Literature, 1789–1877, 1878.]

—— Carlyle's Lectures on Periods of European Culture. Nineteenth Century, ix, 1881, pp. 856–79. [Rptd in Transcripts and Studies, 1888.]

Bayne, P. Lessons from My Masters: Carlyle, Tennyson, and Ruskin. 1879.

Courtney, W. L. Carlyle's Political Doctrines. Fortnightly Rev. xxxii, 1879, pp. 817–28.

Crozier, J. B. Carlyle. [In The Religion of the Future, 1880.]

—— Civilization and Progress. 1885.

—— My Inner Life. 1898.

—— The Wheel of Wealth. 1906.

Grant, C. Thomas Carlyle als Moralist. Deutsche Rundschau, xxiv, 1880, pp. 417–31.

Boglietti, G. Tommaso Carlyle. Nuova Antologia, lvi, 1881, pp. 541–74.

'Valbert, G.' (C. V. Cherbuliez). Carlyle. Revue des Deux Mondes, xliv, 1881, pp. 209–20.

Hamley, Sir E. B. Thomas Carlyle: an Essay from Blackwood's Magazine. Edinburgh, 1881.

James, H. (the elder). Some Personal Recollections of Carlyle. Atlantic Monthly, May 1881. [Rptd in Literary Remains, Boston, 1885.]

Knighton, W. Conversations with Carlyle. Contemporary Rev. June 1881.

Larkin, H. Carlyle and Mrs. Carlyle. A Ten Years' Reminiscence. British Quarterly Rev. July 1881.

Oliphant, M. O. Thomas Carlyle. Macmillan's Mag. April 1881.

Reid, S. J. Thomas Carlyle: His Work and Worth, with some Personal Reminiscences. An Address. Manchester, [1881].

Shairp, J. C. Carlyle. [In Aspects of Poetry, being Lectures delivered at Oxford, Oxford, 1881.]

Shepherd, R. H. Thomas Carlyle. GM. March 1881.

Stanley, A. P. Sermon on Thomas Carlyle, preached at Westminster Abbey, February 6, 1881. 1881.

Symington, A. J. Some Personal Reminiscences of Thomas Carlyle. New York Independent, May, June 1881; Paisley, 1886.

Saintsbury, G. Thomas Carlyle: his Life and Writings. Westminster Rev. April 1881.

—— Specimens of English Prose Style from Malory to Macaulay. 1885.

—— Corrected Impressions. 1895.

—— History of Nineteenth Century Literature. 1896.

—— Essays in English Literature (1780–1860). 1896.

—— History of Criticism. 3 vols. 1904.

—— History of English Prose Rhythm. 1912.

Scherer, E. Études Critiques de Littérature. Paris, 1882.

—— Essays on English Literature. Tr. G. Saintsbury, 1891.

Harrison, F. Histories of the French Revolution. North American Rev. cxxxvii, 1883, pp. 388–402. [Rptd in The Choice of Books, 1886.]

—— Studies in Early Victorian Literature. 1895.

—— Carlyle and the London Library. 1906. [Ed. by Harrison.]

Krummacher, M. Notizen über den Sprachgebrauch Carlyles. E. Studien, vi, 1883, pp. 352–98.

—— Sprache und Stil in Carlyle's 'Friedrich II.' E. Studien, xi, 1888, pp. 67–91, 433–57.

Birrell, A. Obiter Dicta. 1884.

Breitinger, H. Thomas Carlyle: ein Nachahmer Jean Pauls? Die Gegenwart, xxviii, 1885, pp. 21–4.

Burroughs, J. Mr. Carlyle's Country. [In Fresh Fields, Boston, 1885.]

—— Indoor Studies. Boston, 1889.

Smith, J. C. Thomas Carlyle. [In Writings by the Way, Edinburgh, 1885.]

Tulloch, J. Carlyle as a Religious Teacher. [In Movements of Religious Thought in Britain during the Nineteenth Century, 1885.]

Nencioni, E. Le Letture su gli Eroi. Nuova Antologia, xc, 1886, pp. 615–32.

Müller, F. M. Goethe and Carlyle. An Inaugural Address. English Goethe Soc. 1886.

Dawson, G. Carlyle. [In Biographical Lectures, 1886.]

Hutton, R. H. Carlyle. [In Essays on Some of the Modern Guides to English Thought in Matters of Faith, 1887.]

—— Criticisms on Contemporary Thought and Thinkers. 1894.

Browning, O. Carlyle as an Historian. Athenaeum 10 Nov. 1888, p. 625.

Conrad, H. Carlyle und Schiller. Vierteljahrschrift für Litteraturgeschichte, ii, 1889, pp. 195–228.

—— Carlyle und Jean Paul. Die Gegenwart, xxxix, 1891, pp. 309–11.

James, L. G. Carlyle's Philosophy of History. Westminster Rev. cxxxii, 1889, p. 414.

Robertson, J. M. Essays Towards a Critical Method. 1889.

—— Modern Humanists: Sociological Studies of Carlyle, [etc.]. 1891.

—— Modern Humanists Reconsidered. 1927.

Troye, V. Thomas Carlyle hans Liv og hans Vaerk. Bergen, 1889.

Forster, J. Four Great Teachers: Ruskin, Carlyle, [etc.]. 1890.

—— Great Teachers: Burns, Carlyle, etc. 1898.

Smalley, G. W. London Letters and Some Others. 1890.

—— Mr. Froude. [In Studies of Men, New York, 1895.]

Dilthey, W. Thomas Carlyle. Archiv für Geschichte der Philosophie, iv, 1891, pp. 260–85.

Rose, H. The New Political Economy: the Social Teaching of Carlyle, [etc.]. 1891.

Boyeson, H. H. Carlyle and Goethe. [In Essays on German Literature, New York, 1892.]

Caird, E. The Genius of Thomas Carlyle. [In Essays on Literature, Glasgow, 1892.]

Gibbins, H. de B. English Social Reformers. 1892.

Espinasse, F. The Carlyles and a Segment of their Circle. [In Literary Recollections and Sketches, 1893.]

Lilly, W. S. Four English Humorists of the Nineteenth Century. 1895.

Aronstein, P. Dickens und Carlyle. Ang. xviii, 1896, pp. 360–70.

Schröder, R. Carlyles Abhandlung über den Goetheschen Faust. Archiv, xcvi, 1896, pp. 241–68.

Kellner, L. Goethe und Carlyle. Die Nation (Berlin), 21, 28 March 1896, pp. 380–3, 400–3.

—— Macht ist Recht. Die Nation, 21 July 1906, pp. 666–9.

—— Die englische Literatur im Zeitalter der Königin Viktoria. Leipzig, 1909.

—— Die englische Literatur der Neuesten Zeit. Leipzig, 1921.

Wilson, H. S. Carlyle and Taine on the French Revolution. Goethe and Carlyle. [In History and Criticism, 1896.]

Mackinnon, J. Carlyle and Goethe. [In Leisure Hours in the Study, 1897.]

Walker, H. The Age of Tennyson. 1897.

—— The Literature of the Victorian Era. Cambridge, 1910.

—— The English Essay and Essayists. [1915.]

Wilhelmi, J. H. Thomas Carlyle und Friedrich Nietzsche: Wie sie Gott suchten und was für einen Gott sie fanden. Göttingen, 1897.

Schmidt, F. J. Thomas Carlyle. Preussische Jahrbücher, LXXXIX, 1897, pp. 413–30.

Scudder, V. D. Social Ideals in English Letters. Boston, 1898.

Gosse, Sir E. Carlyle and Macaulay. Littell's Living Age, CCXVII, 1898, p. 491.

Kraeger, H. Carlyles deutsche Studien und der Wotton Reinfred. Ang. Bbl. 1898, pp. 193–219.

—— Byron und Carlyle. [In Der Byronische Heldentypus, Munich, 1898.]

—— Carlyles Stellung zur deutschen Sprache und Literatur. Ang. XXII, 1899, pp. 145–343.

—— Zu Carlyles Sartor Resartus. Ang. Bbl. x, 1899, pp. 12–3.

Wilson, P. Carlyle and Emerson. [In Leaders in Literature, Edinburgh, 1898.]

Traill, H. D. Social England. Vol. VI, 1898.

Maulsby, D. L. The Growth of Sartor Resartus. Malden, Massachusetts, 1899.

Trevelyan, G. M. Carlyle as an Historian. Nineteenth Century, XLVI, 1899, p. 493; Life and Letters, v, 1930.

Thayer, W. R. Throne Makers. New York, 1899.

Wells, J. T. Thomas Carlyle: His Religious Experiences as Reflected in Sartor Resartus. Edinburgh, 1899.

Wilson, S. L. The Theology of Thomas Carlyle. [In The Theology of Modern Literature, Edinburgh, 1899.]

Schmeding, O. Über Wortbildung bei Carlyle. Halle, 1900.

Brownell, W. C. Victorian Prose Masters. New York, 1901.

Ward, M. A. Prophets of the Nineteenth Century. Boston, 1901.

'Bos, Camille' (H. Bœuf). Le Kantisme de Carlyle. Archiv für Geschichte der Philosophie, xv, 1902, pp. 32–41.

Chesterton, G. K. Carlyle. [In Twelve Types, 1902.]

—— Varied Types. 1903.

—— The Victorian Age in Literature. [1913.]

Gazeau, J. L'Impérialisme anglais: Son Évolution. Carlyle-Seely-Chamberlain. Paris, 1903.

Gould, G. M. Biographic Clinics: The Origin of the Ill Health of De Quincey, Carlyle, [etc.]. Vol. I, Philadelphia, 1903, pp. 222 ff.

Küchler, F. Carlyle und Schiller. Ang. XXVI, 1903, pp. 1–93, 393–446.

Ravenna, G. La Teoria dell' Eroe in T. Carlyle e F. Nietzsche. Nuova Antologia, cxc, 1903, pp. 249–60.

Wiecki, E. von. Carlyle's 'Helden' und Emerson's 'Repräsentanten.' Königsberg, 1903.

Batt, M. Carlyle's Life of Schiller. MP. I, 1904.

Cazamian, L. Le Roman Social en Angleterre (1830–1850). Paris, 1904.

—— L'Angleterre moderne: Son Évolution. Paris, 1911; tr. Eng. 1912.

—— L'Évolution psychologique et la Littérature en Angleterre (1860–1914). Paris, [1920].

Lincke, O. Über die Wortzusammensetzung in Sartor Resartus. Berlin, 1904.

Lyttleton, A. T. Carlyle's Life and Works. [In Modern Poets of Faith, Doubt, and Paganism, and Other Essays, 1904.]

Oswald, E. Thomas Carlyle noch einmal. Archiv, CXII, 1904, pp. 317–27.

Pape, H. Jean Paul als Quelle von Thomas Carlyles Anschauung und Stil. Rostock, 1904.

Sharp, W. The Country of Carlyle. [In Literary Geography, 1904.]

Warner, P. Thomas Carlyle: the Man and his Influence. 1904.

Fletcher, J. B. Newman and Carlyle. Atlantic Monthly, xcv, 1905.

Nevinson, H. W. Wedded Genius. Carlyle's Letters. [In Books and Personalities, 1905.]

More, P. E. The Spirit of Carlyle. [In Shelburne Essays, ser. 1, New York, 1905.]

Durand, W. Y. De Quincey and Carlyle in their Relation to the Germans. PMLA. XXII, 1907.

MacCunn, J. Six Radical Thinkers: Bentham, Mill, Cobden, Carlyle, Mazzini, T. H. Green. 1907.

Schmidt, W. Der Kampf um den Sinn des Lebens von Dante bis Ibsen. Vol. II, Berlin, 1907.

Goodwin, E. J. Ethics of Carlyle. International Journ. of Ethics, xv, 1908.

Krauske, O. Macaulay und Carlyle. Historische Zeitschrift (Munich), III, 1908; Berlin, 1909.

Ströle, A. Thomas Carlyle's Anschauung vom Fortschritt in der Geschichte. Gütersloh, 1909.

Wedgewood, J. A Study of Carlyle. [In Nineteenth Century Teachers and Other Essays, 1909.]

Lehmann, E. Die Religion Thomas Carlyles. Deutsche Rundschau, CXLIII, April, June 1910.

Luntowski, A. Menschen: Carlyle, Whitman, [etc.]. Leipzig, 1910.

Roe, F. W. Thomas Carlyle as a Critic of Literature. New York, 1910.

—— Social Philosophy of Carlyle and Ruskin. New York, 1921.

Vaughan, C. E. Carlyle and his German Masters. E. & S. I, 1910.

Stawell, F. M. Goethe's Influence on Carlyle. International Journ. of Ethics, XXI, 1911.

Moisant, X. L'Individualisme de Carlyle. Revue de Philosophie, xix, 1911.
—— L'Optimisme au XIXe Siècle. Beauchesne, 1911.
Brandl, A. Chartisten, Sozialisten, und Carlyle. Deutsche Rundschau, cli, April, June 1912.
Kure, J. Thomas Carlyle og hans Hustru med en Sammentraengt Gennemgang af hans Udvikling og Livsanskuelse. Copenhagen, 1912.
Cestre, C. La Doctrine sociale de Carlyle. Revue du Mois, xvi, Nov. 1913.
Hildebrand, A. Carlyle und Schiller. Berlin, 1913.
Fehr, B. Der deutsche Idealismus in Carlyles Sartor Resartus. Germanisch-Romanische Monatsschrift, v, 1913.
Gooch, G. P. Carlyle and Froude. [In History and Historians in the Nineteenth Century, 1913.]
Norton, C. E. Letters, with Biographical Comment by his Daughter. Ed. S. Norton and M. A. de Wolfe Howe, Boston, 1913.
Lorenz, A. C. Diogenes Teufelsdröckh und Thomas Carlyle. Leipzig, 1913.
Meyer, M. Carlyles Einfluss auf Kingsley in sozialpolitischer und religiös-ethischer Hinsicht. Weimar, 1914.
Hearn, L. On the Philosophy of Sartor Resartus. [In Interpretations of Literature, ed. J. Erskine, New York, i, 1916.]
Klein, A. Die Weltanschauung Carlyles. Neue Jahrbücher für das klassische Altertum, xxxviii, 1916.
Morgan, W. Carlyle and German Thought. Queen's Quart. xxiii, 1916.
Robertson, J. G. Carlyle. CHEL. vol. xiii, 1916.
Stewart, H. L. Carlyle's Conception of History. Political Science Quart. xxxii, 1917.
—— Carlyle's Conception of Religion. American Journ. of Theology, xxi, 1917.
—— Alleged Prussianism of Carlyle, International Journ. of Ethics, xxviii, 1918.
—— Carlyle and his Critics. Nineteenth Century, lxxxvi, 1919.
—— Carlyle's Place in Philosophy. Monist, xxix, 1919.
—— Declining Fame of Thomas Carlyle. Royal Soc. of Canada Proc. iii, 1920.
Kemper, E. Carlyle als Imperialist. Zeitschrift für Politik, xi, 1918.
Upham, A. H. Rabelaisianism in Carlyle. MLN. xxxiii, 1918.
Besch, J. Sprecher Gottes in unserer Zeit: Schleiermacher, Carlyle, Tolstoi. Stuttgart, 1919.
Carré, J. M. Goethe en Angleterre. Paris, 1920.

Elton, O. A Survey of English Literature (1830–1880). Vol. ii, 1920.
Hohlfeld, A. R. Poems in Carlyle's Translation of Wilhelm Meister. MLN. xxxvi, 1921.
Bruce, H. L. Blake, Carlyle and the French Revolution. [In Gayley Anniversary Papers, Berkeley, 1922.]
Leopold, W. Die religiöse Wurzel von Carlyles literarischer Wirksamkeit: Dargestellt an seinem Aufsatz 'State of German Literature' (1827). Halle, 1922.
—— Thomas Carlyle and Franz Horn. JEGP. xxviii, 1929.
Morley, E. J. Carlyle in the Diary, Reminiscences and Correspondence of H. C. Robinson. London Mercury, vi, 1922.
Williams, S. T. Carlyle's Life of John Sterling. Carlyle's Past and Present: A Prophecy. [In Studies in Victorian Literature, New York, [1923].]
Schanck, N. Die sozial-politischen Anschauungen Coleridges und sein Einfluss auf Carlyle. Bonn, 1924.
Thrall, M. M. A Phase of Carlyle's Relation to Fraser's Magazine. PMLA. xxxix, 1924.
—— Two Articles attributed to Carlyle. MLN. xlvi, 1931.
Liljegren, S. B. The Origin of Sartor Resartus. [In Anglica, Leipzig, 1925.]
Marx, O. Carlyle's Translation of Wilhelm Meister. Baltimore, 1925.
Mott, F. L. Carlyle's American Public. PQ. iv, 1925.
Geissendoerfer, T. Carlyle and Jean Paul Friedrich Richter. JEGP. xxv, 1926.
Hess, O. Carlyles Stellung zum Germantum. Freiburg, 1926.
Willcocks, M. P. Between the Old World and the New. New York, 1926.
Blankenagel, J. C. Carlyle as a Critic of Grillparzer. PMLA. xlii, 1927.
Brie, F. Imperialistische Strömungen in der englischen Literatur. Halle, 1928, pp. 101–13.
Harrold, C. F. Carlyle's Interpretation of Kant. PQ. vii, 1928.
—— Two Critics of Democracy: Carlyle and H. L. Mencken. South Atlantic Quart. xxvii, 1928.
—— Carlyle's General Method in the French Revolution. PMLA. xliii, 1928.
—— The Translated Passages in Carlyle's French Revolution. JEGP. xxvii, 1928.
—— Carlyle and Novalis. Stud. Phil. xxvii, 1930.
—— The Mystical Element in Carlyle (1827–34). MP. xxix, 1932.
—— The Nature of Carlyle's Calvinism. Stud. Phil. xxxiii, 1936.
—— Remembering Carlyle. A Visit with his Nephew. South Atlantic Quart. xxxvi, 1937.

Tristram, H. Two Leaders: Newman and Carlyle. Cornhill Mag. LXV, 1928.

Fischer, W. Thomas und Jane Carlyle im Spiegel der Briefe Amely Böltes an Varnhagen von Ense (1844–1853). E. Studien, LXIV, 1929.

Murray, R. H. Carlyle the Romantic Radical. [In Studies in the English Social and Political Thinkers of the Nineteenth Century, vol. I, Cambridge, 1929.]

Stockley, V. German Literature as known in England (1750–1830). 1929.

Wellek, R. Carlyle and German Romanticism. [In Zvláštní otisk z Xenia Pragensia, 1929.]
—— Kant in England. Princeton, 1931.

Storrs, M. The Relation of Carlyle to Kant and Fichte. Bryn Mawr, Pennsylvania, 1929.

Howe, S. Carlyle and Wilhelm Meister. [In Wilhelm Meister and his English Kinsmen, New York, 1930.]

Barrett, J. A. S. Carlyle's Debt to Goethe. Hibbert Journ. xxx, 1931.

Lotter, K. Carlyle und die deutsche Romantik. Nuremberg, 1931.

Muirhead, J. H. Carlyle's Transcendental Symbolism. [In The Platonic Tradition in Anglo-Saxon Philosophy, 1931.]

Sarolea, C. The Tragedy of Thomas Carlyle. English Rev. LII, 1931.

Strachey, L. Portraits in Miniature. 1931.

Dunn, W. H. Wilson's Carlyle. Sewanee Rev. XL, 1932.
—— Lectures on Three Eminent Victorians. Claremont, California, 1933.

Huxley, L. Carlyle and Huxley: Early Influences. Cornhill Mag. LXXII, 1932.

Tilby, W. Carlyle. [In The Great Victorians, ed. H. and H. J. Massingham, 1932.]

Suzannet, A. de. Mérimée et Carlyle. Bulletin du Bibliophile, Aug. 1932.

Dyer, I. W. Carlyle Reconsidered. Sewanee Rev. XLI, 1933.

Ralli, A. Carlyle and Shakespeare. [In Later Critiques, 1933.]

Lammond, D. Carlyle. 1934.

Shine, H. Carlyle and the German Philosophy Problem during the Year 1826–1827. PMLA. L, 1935.
—— Articles in Fraser's Magazine attributed to Carlyle. MLN. LI, 1936.
—— Carlyle and 'Fraser's' Letter on the Doctrine of St Simon. N. & Q. 24 Oct. 1936.
—— Carlyle's Views on the Relation between Religion and Poetry up to 1832. Stud. Phil. XXXIII, 1936.
—— Carlyle's Fusion of Poetry, History and Religion by 1834. Stud. Phil. XXXIV, 1937. [Rptd separately with previous item, Chapel Hill, 1937.]

Murphy, E. M. Carlyle and the Saint-Simonians. Stud. Phil. XXXIII, 1936.

Smith, Logan P. Reperusals and Recollections. 1936.

Vance, W. S. Carlyle in America before Sartor Resartus. American Lit. VII, 1936.

Flower, R. Letters of William Somerville and Thomas Carlyle. British Museum Quart. XI, 1937.

Gray, W. F. Carlyle and John Forster: an Unpublished Correspondence. Quarterly Rev. CCLXVIII, 1937.

C. F. H.

II. MINOR CRITICS AND ESSAYISTS, 1800–1835

[This section has been restricted, with one or two exceptions, to critics, essayists and miscellaneous writers born between 1765 and 1800. Cross-references, however, have only been included to *critical* writings appearing elsewhere; the inclusion of essays and miscellaneous writings would have multiplied them disproportionately. And no cross-references have been given to the section on English Scholarship (pp. 1021–44 below). Studies and anthologies of 19th century essays and criticism are listed, pp. 18–4 above.]

JOHN ANSTER (1793–1867)
[See p. 225 above.]

JAMES BOADEN (1762–1839)
[See p. 587 above.]

SIR JOHN BOWRING (1792–1872)
[See p. 228 above.]

SIR SAMUEL EGERTON BRYDGES (1762–1837)

(a) Bibliography

Woodworth, M. K. The Literary Career of Sir Samuel Egerton Brydges. Oxford, 1935. [Bibliography, pp. 167–88, which includes MSS, books written or edited by Brydges, some of his contributions to periodicals, and books about Brydges. Some minor addenda will be found in TLS. 16 Nov. 1935, p. 744.]

(b) Bibliographical and Antiquarian Writings

The Topographer, containing a variety of original articles, illustrative of the Local History and Antiquities of England. 4 vols. 1789–91. [With Lawrence Stebbing Shaw.]

Topographical Miscellanies. 1792.

Censura Literaria. Containing Titles, Abstracts, and Opinions of Old English Books, with Original Disquisitions, Articles of Biography, and Other Literary Antiquities. 10 vols. 1805–9; 10 vols. 1815 (articles rearranged chronologically).

The British Bibliographer. 4 vols. 1810–4.

Restituta; or Titles, Extracts, and Characters of Old Books in English Literature, Revived. 4 vols. 1814–16.

Excerpta Tudoriana; or Extracts from Elizabethan Literature, with a Critical Preface. 2 vols. Lee Priory, 1814–8 (priv. ptd).

Archaica. Containing a Reprint of Scarce Old English Tracts. With Prefaces, Critical and Biographical. 2 vols. 1815 (priv. ptd).

Res Literariae: Bibliographical and Critical. 3 nos. Naples, Rome, Geneva, 1820–2.

[Also a large number of genealogical works. Brydges edited (in addn to matter included in the above) one or more works by the following: Edward Phillips (Theatrum Poetarum Anglicanorum), Duchess of Newcastle, Greene, Raleigh, Thomas Stanley, Breton, Drayton, Henry Wotton, William Browne, Wither, Brathwait, William Hammond, John Hall (of Durham), Chapman, William Collins, Milton, several minor 17th-century poets, and some Latin and Italian writers.]

(c) Poems, Novels and Miscellaneous Writings

Sonnets and Other Poems, with a Versification of the Six Bards of Ossian. 1785 (anon.); 1785 (signed and expanded); 1795; 1807 (further expanded, as Poems).

Mary de Clifford: a Story. Interspersed with many poems. 1792 (anon.); 1800.

Verses on the Late Unanimous Resolutions to Support the Constitution [with] some other poems. Canterbury, 1794.

Arthur Fitz Albini: A novel. 2 vols. 1798; 2 vols. 1799; 2 vols. 1810.

Le Forester, A Novel. 3 vols. 1802.

The Sylvan Wanderer; consisting of A Series of Moral, Sentimental, and Critical Essays. 4 pts, Lee Priory, 1813–21 (priv. ptd).

The Ruminator: containing A Series of Moral, Critical, and Sentimental Essays. 2 vols. 1813.

Occasional Poems, written in the year MDCCCXI. Lee Priory, 1814 (priv. ptd).

Select Poems. Lee Priory, 1814 (priv. ptd).

Bertram, a Poetical Tale. Lee Priory, 1814 (priv. ptd); 1816.

Desultoria: or Comments of a South-Briton on Books and Men. Lee Priory, 1815 (priv. ptd).

Lord Brokenhurst, or A Fragment of Winter Leaves. Geneva, 1819. [Rptd in Tragic Tales, 1820.]

Coningsby. Paris, 1819. [Rptd in Tragic Tales, 1820.]

Sir Ralph Willoughby: an historical tale of the sixteenth century. Florence, 1820.

The Hall of Hellingsley; A Tale. 3 vols. 1821.

Odo, Count of Lingen; a poetical tale in six cantos. Geneva, 1824; Paris, 1826.

Gnomica: Detached Thoughts, Sententious, Axiomatic, Moral and Critical. Geneva, 1824.

Letters on the Character and Poetical Genius of Lord Byron. 1824.

An Impartial Portrait of Lord Byron, as a Poet and a Man. Paris, 1825.

Recollections of Foreign Travel on Life, Literature and Self-knowledge. 2 vols. 1825.

Modern Aristocracy or the Bard's Reception. Geneva, 1831. [Poem on Byron.]

The Lake of Geneva, a poem moral and descriptive. 2 vols. Geneva, 1832.

Imaginative Biography. 2 vols. 1834.

The Autobiography, Times, Opinions, and Contemporaries of Sir Egerton Brydges. 2 vols. 1834.

Moral Axioms in Single Couplets: for the use of the young. 1837.

Human Fate, and An Address to the Poets Wordsworth & Southey: Poems. Great Totham, 1846 (priv. ptd).

[Also a number of books on economic and social questions (summarised by M. K. Woodworth, Appendix) and numerous pamphlets.]

(d) Biography and Criticism

Woodworth, M. K. The Literary Career of Sir Samuel Egerton Brydges. Oxford, 1935.

CHARLES BUCKE (1781–1846)

(a) Miscellaneous Writings

The Philosophy of Nature or the Influence of Scenery on the Mind and Heart. 2 vols. 1813; 4 vols. 1821 (as On the Beauties, Harmonies and Sublimities of Nature; with Occasional Remarks on the Laws, Customs, Manners, and Opinions of Various Nations); 3 vols. 1837 (enlarged); New York, 1843 (with notes, commentaries, and illustrations; selected and rev. by W. P. Page).

Amusements in Retirement. 1816.

The Fall of the Leaf, and Other Poems. 1819.

A Classical Grammar of the English Language; with a Short History of its Origin and Formation. 1829.

On the Life, Writings and Genius of Akenside: with some Account of his Friends. 1832.

A Book of Human Character. 2 vols. 1837.

A Letter intended (one day) as a Supplement to Lockhart's Life of Sir Walter Scott. 1838 (priv. ptd). [On Scott's mention of Bucke's dispute with Kean.]

The Life of John, Duke of Marlborough. 1839.
Ruins of Ancient Cities; with General and Particular Accounts of their Rise, Fall, and Present Condition. 2 vols. 1840; New York, 1875.

(b) Plays

The Italians, or The Fatal Accusation. A Tragedy. 1819 (7 edns); 1820 (with the prefaces to the 1st, 3rd, 6th, 7th and 8th edns). [Produced Drury Lane, 3 April 1819.]
Julio Romano, or the Force of the Passions. An Epic Drama in Six Books. 1830.

(c) Biography and Criticism

The Assailant Assailed. Being a Vindication of Mr. Kean [with regard to his conduct in connection with 'The Italians']. 1819.
A Defence of Edmund Kean, Esq. Being a Reply to Mr. Buck's Preface, and Remarks on his Tragedy of 'The Italians.' [1819.]
Charles Bucke's 'Julio Romano.' Monthly Rev. cxxii, 1830.

THOMAS CAMPBELL (1777–1844)

[See p. 183 above.]

ROBERT CARRUTHERS (1799–1878)

(a) Critical Writings

The Poetry of Milton's Prose. Selected from his Various Writings, with Notes and an Introductory Essay. 1827.
Chambers's Cyclopaedia of English Literature. [1857.] [New edn by Carruthers.]
The Life of Alexander Pope, including Extracts from his Correspondence. 1857.

[Carruthers edited the following: Pope's Poetical Works, 4 vols. 1853, 1853–4; 1858 (rev.); Boswell's Tour to the Hebrides, 1852; Falconer's Shipwreck, 1858; James Montgomery's Poetical Works, 1860; Chambers's Household Edition of Shakespeare, 1861–3 (with W. Chambers); R. Chambers's Life of Sir W. Scott, 1871; and Gray's Select Poems, 1876.]

(b) Writings on Local History

The History of Huntingdon. 1824.
The Highland Note-Book, or Sketches and Anecdotes. Edinburgh, 1843.

(c) Biography and Criticism

Obituary. Scotsman, 28 May 1878.
Mackay, C. Robert Carruthers. Eclectic Mag. civ, 1884.

HENRY FRANCIS CARY (1772–1844)

[See p. 229 above.]

CHARLES COWDEN CLARKE (1787–1877)

Readings in Natural Philosophy. 1828.
Tales from Chaucer in Prose, designed chiefly for the Use of Young Persons. 1833; 1870.
Adam the Gardener. 1834. [A boys' book.]
The Riches of Chaucer. 1835; 1870.
Carmina Minima. 1859.
Shakespeare Characters, chiefly those Subordinate. 1863.
Molière-Characters. Edinburgh, 1865.
On the Comic Writers of England. GM. April–Dec. 1871. [Chaucer; Jonson; Beaumont and Fletcher; Butler; Addison and Steele; Swift; Burlesque Writers; English Satirists; Wycherley and Congreve.]

[Cowden Clarke also edited Nyren's Young Cricketers' Tutor, and the poems of Herbert, Burns, Cowper, Pope, etc., etc. For his collaborations with his wife Mary Cowden Clarke, and for her Biographic Sketch of him, see p. 711 below.]

HARTLEY COLERIDGE (1796–1849)

[See p. 230 above.]

HENRY NELSON COLERIDGE (1798–1843)

Six Months in the West Indies in 1825. 1826 (anon.); 1832; 1841; tr. Dutch, 1826.
Introductions to the Study of the Greek Classic Poets. Pt 1 (all pbd), 1830; 1834. [On Homer.]
Specimens of the Table-Talk of the late Samuel Taylor Coleridge. 2 vols. 1835; 2 vols. 1836 (with slight alterations); 1851, etc.

[For H. N. Coleridge's edns of his uncle's Literary Remains, Aids to Reflection, Confessions of an Inquiring Spirit, Biographia Literaria, etc. see under S. T. Coleridge, p. 175 above. His pseudonymous and anon. critical essays and reviews in The Etonian, British Critic and Quarterly Rev. are summarised in W. Graham's Henry Nelson Coleridge, Expositor of Romantic Criticism, PQ. iv, 1925.]

EDWARD COPLESTON (1776–1849)

(a) Writings

Advice to a Young Reviewer. With a Specimen of the Art. 1807; ed. J. C. Collins, 1903 (in Critical Essays and Literary Fragments); ed. G. S. Gordon, 1927 (in Three Oxford Ironies; with bibliographical notes); Oxford, 1927 (with note on the author by V. M. D.).
The Examiner examined. 1809.
A Reply to the Calumnies of the Edinburgh Review against Oxford. Containing an Account of the Studies pursued in that University. Oxford, 1810. [A Second

Reply, Oxford, 1810; A Third Reply, Oxford, 1811.]
Praelectiones Academicae Oxonii Habitae. Oxford, 1833. [35 Latin lectures on poetry.]
Remains of the late Edward Copleston. With an Introduction Containing Some Reminiscences of his Life. Ed. R. Whately, 1854.

[Copleston also pbd An Inquiry into the Doctrines of Necessity and Pre-destination, in Four Discourses, 1821, and a number of sermons, charges and pamphlets.]

(b) Biography and Criticism

Copleston, W. J. Memoir of Edward Copleston with Selections from his Diary and Correspondence. 1851. [Includes bibliography.]
Tuckwell, W. Pre-Tractarian Oxford. A Reminiscence of the Oriel 'Noetics.' 1909. [Has a ch. on Copleston.]

GEORGE LILLIE CRAIK (1798–1866)

(a) Critical and Philological Writings

Sketches of the History of Literature and Learning in England from the Norman Conquest. 6 vols. 1844–5; 2 vols. 1861 (much enlarged, as A Compendious History of English Literature and Language from the Conquest); 1862 (abridged); ed. Sir H. Craik, 1883 (abridged edn, with ch. on recent literature by Sir H. Craik, as A Manual of English Literature and of the History of the English Language).
Spenser and his Poetry. 3 vols. 1845.
Bacon: his Writings and his Philosophy. 3 vols. 1846–7.
Outlines of the History of the English Language for the Use of Junior Classes. 1851; 1864 (5th edn, rev. and improved).
The English of Shakespeare illustrated by a Philological Commentary on Julius Caesar. 1856.

(b) Historical Writings

The New Zealanders. 1830 (anon.).
The Pursuit of Knowledge under Difficulties, illustrated by Anecdotes. 2 vols. 1830–1 (anon.); 2 vols. 1844; 3 vols. 1845; 2 vols. 1858 (rev. and enlarged); 1865 (rev. and enlarged); Edinburgh, 1881; rptd 1906 (rev. and enlarged).
Paris and its Historical Scenes. 2 vols. 1831–2 (anon.).
The Pictorial History of England. Being a History of the People as well as a History of the Kingdom. 4 vols. 1837–41 (to the Accession of George III); 4 vols. 1841–4 (during the Reign of George III); 9 vols. 1850 (vol. IX contains Index by H. C. Hamilton). [With C. MacFarlane.]

The History of British Commerce from the Earliest Times. 3 vols. 1844. [Rptd from The Pictorial History of England by Craik and MacFarlane.]
The Pursuit of Knowledge under Difficulties, illustrated by Female Examples. 1847. [A Supplement to the first work of the same title.]
The Romance of the Peerage, or Curiosities of Family History. 4 vols. 1848–50.
Paris and its Historical Buildings. 1849.

JOHN WILSON CROKER (1780–1857)

(a) Historical and Miscellaneous Writings

A Sketch of the State of Ireland. 1808 (anon.).
A Key to the Orders in Council. 1812.
A Letter on the Fittest Style and Situation for the Wellington Testimonial about to be erected in Dublin. 1815.
Stories for Children from the History of England. 1817.
Substance of the Speech in the House of Commons on the Roman Catholic Question. 1819.
An Answer to O'Meara's Napoleon in Exile. New York, 1823. [Rptd from Quarterly Rev.]
Royal Memoirs, or the French Revolution. With Historical and Biographical Illustrations. 1823. [Trns of two memoirs by Madame Royale, Duchess of Angoulême, and the Narrative of Journey to Brussels and Coblenz by Louis XVIII.]
Progressive Geography for Children. 1828.
The Life of Samuel Johnson, LL.D. by James Boswell. 5 vols. 1831; 5 vols. 1835; 1848 ('thoroughly revised, with much additional matter').
Speech on the Reform Question. 1831.
Speech on the Question that 'The Reform Bill do pass.' 1831.
Resolutions moved by Mr. Croker on the Report of the Reform Bill. 1832.
Robespierre. 1835. [Rptd from Quarterly Rev.]
History of the Guillotine. 1853. [Revised from Quarterly Rev.]
Correspondence with the Right Honourable Lord John Russell on Some Passages of Moore's Diary. With a Postscript by Mr. Croker explanatory of Mr. Moore's Acquaintance and Correspondence with him. 1854.
Essays on the Early Period of the French Revolution. 1857. [Rptd, with addns and corrections, from Quarterly Rev.]
The Croker Papers. The Correspondence and Diaries of John Wilson Croker. Ed. (with memoir) L. J. Jennings, 3 vols. 1884, 1885 (rev.).

(b) Poems

Familiar Epistles on the State of the Irish Stage. 1804; ed. W. Donaldson, 1875. [Letters in verse addressed to F. Jones.]

An Intercepted Letter from Canton. Dublin, 1804. [A satire on the state of society in Dublin.]

Songs of Trafalgar. Dublin, 1804.

The Amazoniad, or Figure and Fashion. A Scuffle in High Life. 2 pts, Dublin, 1806 (anon.). [A satirical poem.]

The Battles of Talavera. 1809; 1812 (9th edn, as Talavera. To which are Added, Other Poems).

(c) Biography and Criticism

Macaulay, T. B. (Baron). Critical and Historical Essays Contributed to the Edinburgh Review. 3 vols. 1843.

Answers to Mr. Macaulay's Criticism on Mr. Croker's Edition of Boswell's Life of Johnson. 1856. [Selected from Blackwood's Mag.]

Maginn, W. A Gallery of Illustrious Characters. Ed. W. Bates, [1873].

Quarterly Rev. Oct. 1884.

ALLAN CUNNINGHAM (1785–1842)

[See p. 391 above.]

GEORGE DANIEL (1789–1864)

(a) Criticism, Essays and Sketches

Cumberland's British Theatre, with Remarks, Biographical and Critical, by D. G. 48 vols. 1826–[1861]. [Daniel contributed a critical preface to each play.]

Cumberland's Minor Theatre, with Remarks Biographical and Critical, by D. G. 17 vols. 1828–43. [Daniel contributed a critical preface to each farce, etc.]

Garrick in the Green Room. 1829. [A biographical and critical analysis of a picture, painted by Hogarth and engraved by W. Ward.]

Merrie England in the Olden Time. 2 vols. 1842; 1874. [Illustrated by Leech and Cruikshank; rptd from Bentley's Misc.]

An Elizabethan Garland. A Descriptive Catalogue of Seventy Black-Letter Ballads printed between 1559 and 1597. 1856 (priv. ptd).

Love's Last Labour not Lost. 1863. [Includes Recollections of Charles Lamb, Robert Cruikshank, a Reply to Macaulay's Essay on Dr Johnson, and other essays in prose and verse.]

Recollections of Charles Lamb. 1927. [Rptd from Love's Last Labour not Lost.]

[Daniel also pbd a novel, The Adventures of Dick Distich, 3 vols. 1812 (anon.).]

(b) Poems and Plays

Stanzas on Lord Nelson's Death and Victory. By G. D. and E[dwin] B[entley]. 1806.

The Times, or the Prophecy. 1811 (anon.); 1813 (enlarged).

Miscellaneous Poems. 1812. [Includes Woman, and other poems rptd from Ackermann's Mag., mostly satirical.]

R–y–l Stripes, or a Kick from Yar–th to Wa–s. A Poem by P— P—, Poet Laureate. 1812. [Suppressed, and bought up by order of the Prince Regent. Only 6 copies known to be in existence.]

The Ghost of R–L Stripes. A Poem by P— P—, Poet Laureate. 1812.

Sophia's Letters to the B–r–n Ger–b, or Whiskers in the Dumps. By P— P—, Poet Laureate. 1812.

Suppressed Evidence on R–l Intriguing. 1813. By P— P—, Poet Laureate.

The R–l First Born. By P— P—, Poet Laureate. 1814.

Virgil in London. 1814.

The Modern Dunciad. A Satire. With Notes, Biographical and Critical. 1814; 1835 (with Virgil in London, and other poems).

London and Dublin. An Heroic Epistle to Counsellor Phillips, the Celebrated Irish Orator. 1817. [Probably by Daniel.]

Doctor Bolus. A Serio-Comick-Bombastick-Operatick Interlude. 1818.

Sworn at Highgate. A Farce. [In Cumberland's Minor Theatre, vol. VI, 1828.]

The Disagreeable Surprise. A Farce. [In Cumberland's British Theatre, vol. XIV, 1829.]

Ophelia Kean. A Dramatic Legendary Tale. 1829. [An attack on Charles Kean's private life; suppressed.]

The Missionary. A Religious Poem. 1847.

Democritus in London. With the Mad Pranks and Comical Conceits of Motley and Robin Good-Fellow. To which are added Notes Festivous, [etc.]. 1852. [A verse continuation of Merrie England. Contains also The Stranger Guest, a religious poem.]

(c) Biography and Criticism

Obituary. Athenaeum, 9 April 1864.

Catalogue of the most Valuable, Interesting, and Highly Important Library of the Late George Daniel, Esq. 1864.

GEORGE DARLEY (1795–1846)

[See p. 219 above.]

CHARLES WENTWORTH DILKE (1789–1864)

Old English Plays, being a Selection from the Early Dramatic Writers. 6 vols. 1814–5. [Ed. by Dilke; supplements Dodsley's collection.]

The Papers of a Critic, selected from the Writings of the late Charles Wentworth Dilke, with a Biographical Sketch by his Grandson, Sir Charles Wentworth Dilke. 2 vols. 1875. [Essays on Pope, Lady M. W. Montagu, 'Junius,' Wilkes, 'Peter Pindar,' etc. rptd from Athenaeum.]

[Dilke was for many years editor of Athenaeum and contributed regularly 1848–64; his best earlier writing was for Retrospective Rev. 1820–5.]

ISAAC D'ISRAELI (1766–1848)

(a) Collected Works

Miscellanies of Literature. 1841. [The words 'A New Edition, Revised and Corrected' seem to apply to the separate works here collected. Miscellanies of Literature; Quarrels of Authors; Calamities of Authors; The Literary Character; Character of James I; Literary Miscellanies (not the same as earlier work of this title); Goldsmith and Johnson; Molière; Racine; Sterne; Hume, etc.]

Works. Edited with Memoir and Notes, by the Right Honourable Benjamin Disraeli. 7 vols. 1858–9.

(b) Essays and Chapters of Literary History

Curiosities of Literature. Consisting of Anecdotes, Characters, Sketches and Dissertations, Literary, Critical and Historical. [Ser. 1]: 1791; 3 vols. 1793–1817; 5 vols. 1823. Ser. 2: 3 vols. 1823 (containing the Secret Histories). Both sers.: 6 vols. 1834; 3 vols. 1849 (with memoir by B. Disraeli); 3 vols. 1858; 1866; 3 vols. 1881; 3 vols. 1927.

A Dissertation on Anecdotes. 1793.

An Essay on the Manners and Genius of the Literary Character. 1795; 1818 (rev. and enlarged as The Literary Character); 1822 (rev. and enlarged); 1859, 1881 (with Literary Miscellanies and The Character of James the First; with new Preface by the Author and ed. B. Disraeli); ed. B. Disraeli, 1927.

Miscellanies, or Literary Recreations. 1796; 1801 (as Literary Miscellanies; adds The Dissertation on Anecdotes).

Calamities of Authors. Including some Inquiries Respecting their Moral and Literary Characters. 2 vols. 1812; ed. B. Disraeli, 1859, 1881.

Quarrels of Authors, or Some Memoirs for our Literary History. 3 vols. 1814; 1881 (with Calamities of Authors; ed. B. Disraeli). [Warburton; Pope and Curll; Pope and Cibber; Addison; Lintot's Account Book; Boyle; Bentley; Jonson; Dekker, etc.]

Amenities of Literature. Consisting of Sketches and Characters of English Literature. 3 vols. 1841; ed. B. Disraeli, 1859, 1881. [A history of English literature from the beginnings to Bacon, with some chapters on contemporary literary affairs.]

(c) Historical Writings

Inquiry into the Literary and Political Character of James I. 1816.

Commentaries on the Life and Reign of Charles the First, King of England. 5 vols. 1828–31; 2 vols. 1851 (rev. by the author and ed. by B. Disraeli).

Eliot, Hampden, and Pym. 1832.

Genius of Judaism. 1833.

(d) Poems

A Defence of Poetry. 1790.

Narrative Poems. 1803.

(e) Fiction

Vaurien. A Sketch of the Times. 2 vols. 1797.

Mejnoun and Leila, the Arabian Petrarch and Laura. 1797; 1799 (adds Love and Humility, The Lovers, and a Poetical Essay on Romance); 1801 (adds The Daughter).

Romances. 1799.

Flim-Flams! or the Life and Errors of my Uncle, and the Amours of my Aunt! With an Illuminating Index! 3 vols. 1805; 1806 (rev. and enlarged).

Despotism, or the Fall of the Jesuits. 1811.

(f) Biography and Criticism

Corney, B. Curiosities of Literature. With Ideas on Controversy: deduced from the Practice of a Veteran. 1838. [An attack on D'Israeli.]

Disraeli, B. (Earl of Beaconsfield). The Life and Writings of Mr. Disraeli By his Son. [Prefixed to The Works of Isaac D'Israeli, vol. I, 1858.]

Maginn, W. A Gallery of Illustrious Characters. Ed. W. Bates, [1873].

Axon, W. E. A. D'Israeli the Novelist. GM. CCLXVII, 1889.

Monypenny, W. F. and Buckle, G. E. The Life of Benjamin Disraeli. 2 vols. 1929 (rev. edn). [Vol. I has a ch. on Isaac D'Israeli.]

NATHAN DRAKE (1766–1836)

The Speculator. 26 nos. 27 March–22 June 1790; 1791; Dublin, 1791. [By Drake and another (unidentified).]

Literary Hours, or Sketches Critical and Narrative. Sudbury, 1798: 2 vols. Sudbury, 1800 (enlarged); 3 vols. 1804; 3 vols. 1820.

The Old Abbey Tale. [In Canterbury Tales, by C. F. Barrett, Drake and others, 1802.]

Essays Biographical, Critical, and Historical, Illustrative of the 'Tatler,' 'Spectator,' and 'Guardian.' 3 vols. 1805; 3 vols. 1814.

Essays Biographical, Critical, and Historical, Illustrative of the 'Rambler,' 'Adventurer,' 'Idler,' [etc., 1715–1800]. 2 vols. 1809–10.

The Gleaner: a Series of Periodical Essays, Selected and Arranged from Scarce and Neglected Volumes. 4 vols. 1811.

Shakespeare and his Times. 2 vols. 1817; Paris, 1843.

Winter Nights, or Fire-Side Lucubrations. 2 vols. 1820.

Evenings in Autumn: a Series of Essays. 2 vols. 1822.

Noontide Leisure, or Sketches in Summer, including a Tale of the Days of Shakespeare. 2 vols. 1824.

Mornings in Spring, or Retrospections, Biographical, Critical, and Historical. 2 vols. 1828.

Memorials of Shakespeare, or Sketches of his Character and Genius by Various Writers. 1828.

The Harp of Judah, or Songs of Sion, being a Metrical Translation of the Psalms. 1837.

JOHN COLIN DUNLOP (d. 1842)

The History of Fiction. Being a Critical Account of the most Celebrated Prose Works of Fiction from the Earliest Greek Romances to the Novels of the Present Age. 3 vols. Edinburgh, 1814, 1816; 1845; rev. and ed. H. Wilson, 2 vols. 1888; tr. German, Berlin, 1851. [Reviewed by Hazlitt, Edinburgh Rev. Nov. 1814.]

History of Roman Literature from its Earliest Period to the Augustan Age. 3 vols. 1823–8.

Memoirs of Spain during the Reigns of Philip IV and Charles II, from 1621 to 1700. 2 vols. Edinburgh, 1834.

Selections from the Latin Anthology, translated into English Verse. Edinburgh, 1838. [Reviewed by 'Christopher North' (John Wilson), Edinburgh Rev. April 1838.]

GEORGE DYER (1755–1841)

[See p. 232 above.]

PIERCE EGAN (1772–1849)

(a) Writings on Sport

Boxiana, or Sketches of Antient and Modern Pugilism. 4 vols. 1818–24.

Sporting Anecdotes, Original and Selected. 1820. [See G. L. Marsh, Stud. Phil. xxviii, 1931, pp. 784–9.]

Life in London, or the Day and Night Scenes of Jerry Hawthorn, Esq. and Corinthian Tom. With thirty-six Scenes from Real Life, designed and etched by I. R. and G.

Cruikshank. 1821; 1823. [There were many imitations and parodies and several dramatic versions; Egan's own stage adaptation was produced at Sadler's Wells in 1822.]

Finish to the Adventures of Tom, Jerry and Logic in their Pursuits through Life in and out of London. With Coloured Illustrations by R. Cruikshank. [1828]; ed. J. C. Hotten, [1871].

Anecdotes of the Turf, the Chase, the Ring, and the Stage, embellished with Thirteen Coloured Plates by T. Lane. 1827.

The Show Folks. With Nine Designs on Wood by Mr Theodore Lane. To which is added a Sketch of the Life of Mr Theodore Lane. 1831. [A poem.]

Pierce Egan's Book of Sports and Mirror of Life. 1832.

(b) Miscellaneous Writings

The Mistress of Royalty, or the Loves of Florizel and Perdita. 1814 (anon.). [Attack on the Prince Regent and Mrs Robinson.]

Account of the Trial of J. Thurtell and J. Hunt. With an Appendix. With Portraits and Many Other Illustrative Engravings. 1824.

The Life of an Actor. 1825.

The Pilgrims of the Thames in Search of the National. Illustrations on Wood by Pierce Egan the Younger. 1838.

[Egan also wrote several other accounts of trials, a few guide-books, some slang terms for F. Grose's Classical Dictionary of the Vulgar Tongue, etc.]

THOMAS ERSKINE, BARON ERSKINE (1750–1823)

(a) Selections

The Beauties of Erskine; consisting of selections from his prose and poetry, by A. Howard. [1834?]

(b) Collected Speeches

The Speeches (at length) of the Rt. Hon. C. J. Fox, T. Erskine, [etc.]. 1797.

Speeches of J. P. Curran. With the Speeches of Grattan, Erskine and Burke. 2 vols. New York, 1809.

The Speeches of the Hon. Thomas Erskine, when at the Bar, on Subjects connected with the Liberty of the Press, and against Constructive Treasons. Collected by J. Ridgway. 4 vols. 1810; 1812; Georgetown, 1813; 4 vols. 1813–6; 4 vols. 1847 (with prefatory memoir by Lord Brougham); 2 vols. 1870 (with memoir by E. Walford).

The Modern Orator. The most Celebrated Speeches of the Earl of Chatham, R. B. Sheridan, Lord Erskine and Edmund Burke. 1847.

(c) Miscellaneous Prose

Plain Thoughts of a Plain Man, addressed to the Common Sense of the People of Great Britain. 1797.

A View of the Causes and Consequences of the Present War with France. 1797 (35 edns); tr. French, London, [1797] (23 edns at least).

Cruelty to Animals. The Speech of Lord Erskine, in the House of Peers, on the Second Reading of the Bill for preventing Malicious and Wanton Cruelty to Animals. 1809; 1824.

Armata. A Fragment. 1817 (anon., 4 edns). The Second Part of Armata. 1817 (3 edns). [A political romance.]

A Short Defence of the Whigs against the Imputations attempted to be cast upon them during the Late Election for Westminster. 1819 (bis).

A Letter to 'An Elector of Westminster,' Author of 'A Reply to the Short Defence of the Whigs.' 1819.

The Defences of the Whigs. 1819. [Rpts of the two preceding.]

A Letter to the Earl of Liverpool on the Subject of the Greeks. 1822 (2nd edn).

Age of Reason. Erskine's Defence of the Cause of Newton, Boyle, Locke, Hale, and Milton, versus T. Paine. [1831.]

Erskine's Opinion of Paine's 'Age of Reason.' [1831.]

[The above constitute only a representative selection from a considerable body of pbd speeches and pamphlets.]

(d) Poems

The Farmer's Vision. By E. 1819 (priv. ptd).

The Poetical Works. With a Biographical Memoir. 1823.

(e) Biography and Criticism

A Sketch of the Character of the Late Lord Erskine. The Pamphleteer, vol. XXIII, 1823.

Campbell, John, Baron. The Lives of the Lord Chancellors. Ser. 3, vol. VI, 1847.

Duméril, H. Lord Erskine: Étude sur le Barreau anglais à la Fin du XVIIIe Siècle. Paris, 1883.

Fraser, J. A. L. Erskine. Cambridge, 1932.

JOHN FOSTER (1770–1843)

(a) Essays

Essays in a Series of Letters to a Friend. 2 vols. 1805; 2 vols. 1806 (rev.) (bis); 1830 (9th edn, embodying final revisions); ed. J. M., 1876 (as Decision of Character and Other Essays). [On a Man's writing Memoirs of Himself; On Decision of

Character; On the Application of the Epithet Romantic; On some of the Causes by which Evangelical Religion has been rendered less Acceptable to Persons of Cultivated Taste.]

An Essay on the Evils of Popular Ignorance. 1820; 1821 (with a Discourse on the Communication of Christianity to the People of Hindoostan); 1846 (rev. and enlarged).

Contributions, Biographical, Literary and Philosophical, to the Eclectic Review. 2 vols. 1844; ed. J. E. Ryland, 1856.

Fosteriana: consisting of Thoughts, Reflections and Criticisms, of John Foster. Selected from Periodical Papers not hitherto Published in a Collected Form. Ed. H. G. Bohn, 1858.

An Essay on the Improvement of Time: and Other Literary Remains. With a Preface by John Sheppard. Ed. J. E. Ryland, 1863; 1886 (with Notes of Sermons and Other Pieces).

[An important introductory essay by Foster is prefixed to the 1825 and later rpts of Doddridge's The Rise and Progress of Religion.]

(b) Other Writings

Discourse on Missions. 1818.

Lectures delivered at Broadmead Chapel, Bristol. Ed. J. E. Ryland, 2 sers, 1844–7; 2 vols. 1853 (with addns).

The Life and Correspondence of John Foster. Edited by J. E. Ryland. With Notices of Mr. Foster as a Preacher and a Companion by John Sheppard. 2 vols. 1846.

A Brief Memoir of Miss Sarah Saunders, with Nine Letters addressed to her during her Last Illness. 1847.

Letters from John Foster to Thomas Coles, M.A. Now First Published with an Appendix by Henry Coles. 1864.

[Foster also pbd various sermons, religious discourses and controversial works. He was a regular contributor to Eclectic Rev. 1806–39.]

(c) Biography and Criticism

Hall, Robert. Reviews. 1825. [Includes a review of Foster's Essays.]

Gilfillan, G. Galleries of Literary Portraits. Vol. II, Edinburgh, 1856.

Whately, E. Life and Writings of the Late John Foster, the Essayist. [In The Afternoon Lectures on English Literature, Dublin, 1863.]

Everts, W. W. Life and Thoughts of John Foster. 1868.

Bayne, P. Six Christian Biographies. 1887.

Kaufman, P. John Foster's Pioneer Interpretation of the Romantic. MLN. XXXVIII, 1923.

BASIL HALL (1788–1844)

(a) Writings on Travel

Account of a Voyage of Discovery to the West Coast of Corea, and the Great Loo-Choo Island. With an Appendix and a Vocabulary of the Loo-Choo Language, by H. I. Clifford. 1818; 1820 (with plates); 1826; 1840 (with an Interview with Napoleon Bonaparte at St Helena).

Extracts from a Journal written on the Coasts of Chili, Peru, and Mexico, in the Years 1820, 1821, 1822. 2 vols. 1823; 2 vols. Edinburgh, 1824; 2 vols. Edinburgh, 1825 (4th edn). Tr. Portuguese, Santiago, 1906; Spanish, Buenos Aires, 1920.

Hall's Voyages. 3 vols. Edinburgh, 1826–7.

Travels in North America in the Years 1827 and 1828. 3 vols. Edinburgh, 1829; 2 vols. Philadelphia, 1829; tr. French, Paris, [1841?].

Fragments of Voyages and Travels. Ser. 1, 3 vols. 1832 (2nd edn). Ser. 2, 3 vols. Edinburgh, 1832 (2nd edn). Ser. 3, 3 vols. Edinburgh, 1833, 1834. Tr. French, Paris, 1858. [Autobiographical sketches from this work were separately pbd as The Midshipman, and The Lieutenant and Commander, 1862.]

Voyages and Travels. 1895. [With biographical preface.]

Travels in India, Ceylon and Borneo. Selected and edited, with Biographical Introduction, by H. G. Rawlinson. 1931. (Broadway Travellers ser.)

(b) Fiction

Schloss Hainfeld, or A Winter in Lower Styria. Edinburgh, 1836 (bis).

Patchwork. 3 vols. 1841.

[Hall also produced several ephemeral pieces.]

HENRY HALLAM (1777–1859)

[See p. 880 below.]

JULIUS CHARLES HARE (1795–1855)

(a) Bibliography

GM. April 1855. [Incomplete but very accurate bibliography, giving much information unobtainable elsewhere.]

(b) Miscellaneous Writings

Guesses at Truth. By Two Brothers. Ser. 1: 1827; 1838 (with addns); 1840 (rev.). Ser. 2: 1848 (title-page states: '2nd edition with large additions,' but preface explains that '2nd edition' means that part of ser. 1 is included). Both sers: 1866; 1871 (with memoir of J. C. Hare by E. H. Plumptre);

rptd 1905. [With A. W. Hare, until his death; essays, epigrams, etc.]

A Vindication of Niebuhr's History of Rome. Cambridge, 1829.

Memoir of John Sterling. [Prefixed to Essays and Tales of John Sterling, collected and edited by Hare, 2 vols. 1848.]

Thou shalt not bear false witness against thy Neighbour. A Letter to the Editor of the English Review. With a Letter from Professor Maurice to the Author. 1849.

The Life of Luther in Forty-Eight Historical Engravings by G. Koenig. 1855. [Text by Hare: continued by S. Winkworth.]

Fragments of Two Essays in English Philology. Ed. J. E. B. Mayor, 1873.

(c) Translations

La Motte Fouqué. Sintram and his Companions. 1820.

Niebuhr. The History of Rome. 3 vols. 1828–42. [Vols. I, II by Hare and Connop Thirlwall. Vol. III by W. Smith and L. Schmitz; a 2nd edn of vols. I and II, rev. and rearranged by Hare appeared 1829–32.]

The Old Man of the Mountain; The Love-charm; and Pietro of Abano. Tales from the German of Tieck. 1831.

Schiller. Poems. 1847. [Translated, with some poems by Goethe, into English hexameters.]

(d) Theological Writings

The Victory of Faith, and other Sermons. Cambridge, 1840; ed. E. H. Plumptre, 1874 (introductory notices by J. F. D. Maurice and A. P. Stanley, the latter rptd from Quarterly Rev. July 1855).

The Mission of the Comforter, and Other Sermons. With Notes. 2 vols. 1846; Cambridge, 1850 (rev.); ed. E. H. Plumptre, 1876. [Vindication of Luther ptd separately, 1855.]

Charges to the Clergy of the Archdeaconry of Lewes, 1840–1854, with Notes on Events affecting the Church during that Period. With a Memoir of the Author by F. D. Maurice. 3 vols. 1856.

[Hare also pbd a number of sermons, charges, and tracts on ecclesiastical subjects.]

(e) Biography and Criticism

Rigg, J. H. Modern Anglican Theology. 1857.

Hare, A. J. C. Memorials of a Quiet Life. 1872.

Galinsky, H. K. Is Thomas De Quincey the Author of The Love-Charm? MLN. LII, 1937. [Really by Hare?]

BENJAMIN ROBERT HAYDON (1786-1846)

(a) *Critical Writings*

The Judgment of Connoisseurs upon Works of Art compared with that of Professional Men; in Reference more particularly to the Elgin Marbles. 1816.

New Churches considered with Respect to the Opportunities they afford for the Encouragement of Painting. 1818.

Some Enquiry into the Causes which have obstructed the Advance of Historical Painting for the Last Seventy Years in England. 1829.

On Academies of Art (more particularly the Royal Academy); and their Pernicious Effect on the Genius of Europe. Lecture XIII. 1839.

Thoughts on the Relative Value of Fresco and Oil Painting, as applied to the Architectural Decorations of the Houses of Parliament. 1842.

Lectures on Painting and Design. 2 vols. 1844-6.

(b) *Autobiography and Letters*

The Life of Benjamin Robert Haydon, from his Autobiography and Journals. Edited and compiled by Tom Taylor. 3 vols. 1853; 3 vols. 1853 (with additional appendix and index by W. R. S. Ralston); ed. A. Huxley, 2 vols. 1926; ed. A. P. D. Penrose, 1927; ed. E. Blunden, 1927 (World's Classics).

Benjamin Robert Haydon: Correspondence and Table-Talk. With a Memoir by his Son, F. W. Haydon. With Facsimile Illustrations from his Journals. 1876.

(c) *Biography and Criticism*

Benjamin Robert Haydon and Wilkie. Fraser's Mag. xxxvi, 1847.

The Autobiography of Benjamin Robert Haydon. Fraser's Mag. xLVIII, 1853.

The Life of Benjamin Robert Haydon. Edinburgh Rev. xcviii, 1853.

Taylor's Life of Benjamin Robert Haydon. Quarterly Rev. xciii, 1853.

Benjamin Robert Haydon. Temple Bar, xciv, 1891.

'Paston, G.' Little Memoirs of the Nineteenth Century. 1902.

—— B. R. Haydon and his Friends. 1905.

Forman, H. B. Keats and Haydon. Athenaeum, 21 May 1904.

Sargant, F. W. Benjamin Haydon, Forerunner. Nineteenth Century, xciii, 1923.

Woolf, V. The Genius of Benjamin Robert Haydon. New Republic, xlix, 1926.

Walker, F. R. The Diary of a Defeated Painter. Independent, cxviii, 1927.

Blunden, E. Haydon outside his Autobiography. Nation, 7 April 1928.

JOHN ABRAHAM HERAUD (1799-1887)

[See p. 235 above.]

WILLIAM HONE (1780-1842)

(a) *Bibliographies*

Stephens, F. G. Memoir of G. Cruikshank. 1891. [Includes list of Hone's works illustrated by Cruikshank.]

Jerrold, B. Life of G. Cruikshank. 1891. [Includes Supplementary List of Hone's Works Illustrated by Cruikshank.]

(b) *Collected Squibs*

Facetiae and Miscellanies with One Hundred and Twenty Engravings drawn by George Cruikshank. 1827 (2nd edn). [12 of Hone's most successful political pamphlets; includes The Political House that Jack Built, The Queen's Matrimonial Ladder and The Political Showman.]

(c) *Separate Works*

The Rules and Regulations of an Institution called Tranquillity commenced as an Economical Bank. 1807.

The King's Statue at Guildhall. 1815. [Broadside.]

Report of the Coroner's Inquest on Jane Watson. 1815.

The Case of Elizabeth Fenning. 1815.

Appearance of an Apparition to James Sympson Commanding him to do Strange Things in Pall Mall, and what he did. With Coloured Illustrations by G. Cruikshank. 1816.

View of the Regent's Bomb, now Uncovered in St. James's Park. 1816. [Broadside.]

An Authentic Account of the Royal Marriage, Containing Memoirs of Prince Leopold and Princess Charlotte. 1816.

Four Trials at Kingston, with 10 Questions to Mr. Espinasse respecting Elizabeth Fenning. 1816.

An Account of Christian Slavery in Algiers. 1816.

An Account of the Riots in London, Dec. 2, 1816. 3 pts, 1816.

The Reformists' Register and Weekly Commentary. [Issued from 1 Feb. 1816 to 25 Oct. 1817. Edited and owned by Hone, who was the largest contributor.]

The Life of William Cobbett, written by Himself. 1816. [Cobbett indignantly denied authorship. Little doubt that Hone was responsible.]

Another Ministerial Defeat. The Trial of the Dog for Biting the Noble Lord [Castlereagh]. 1817. [With woodcut by G. Cruikshank.]

Official Account of the Noble Lord's Bite and his Dangerous Condition. 1817. [With woodcut by G. Cruikshank.]

Bag Nodle's Feast, or the Partition and Re-Union of Turkey. 1817. [A ballad on the alleged meanness of Lord and Lady Eldon.]

The Late John Wilkes's Catechism. 1817.

The Political Litany. 1817. [For this and the 2 following parodies Hone was prosecuted, but defended himself successfully and was acquitted; see The Trials of William Hone.]

The Sinecurist's Creed. 1817.

A Political Catechism, dedicated without Permission to His Most Serene Highness Omar, Bashan Dey, etc., etc., of Algiers. By an Englishman. 1817.

The Political House that Jack built. 1819. [With 13 cuts by George Cruikshank.]

The Radical House that Jack Built. 1819.

The Queen's Matrimonial Ladder, a National Toy. 1819. [With 14 'stepscenes' and illustrations in verse, with 18 other cuts by G. Cruikshank.]

Hone's Political Showman—at Home! [1819?]

The Queen's Budget Opened. 1820.

The Man in the Moon. 1820. [With 15 illustrations by Cruikshank.]

The Midnight Intruder, or Old Nick at Carlton House. 3 pts, 1820. [A poem.]

The Englishman's Mentor, the Picture of the Palais Royal. [1820?]

The Form of Prayer, with Thanksgiving to Almighty God, to be used Daily for the Happy Deliverance of Queen Caroline from the Late most Traitorous Conspiracy. 1820.

The Bank-Restriction Barometer. 1820. [Originally ptd as a large open half-sheet, as an envelope for Cruikshank's 'Banknote not to be Imitated.']

The Apocryphal New Testament. Being All the Gospels, Epistles and other Pieces now Extant, attributed in the first four Centuries to Jesus Christ, His Apostles and Companions, and not included in the New Testament. 1820. [Fiercely attacked in Quarterly Rev. and as furiously defended by Hone.]

The Right Divine of Kings to Govern Wrong. 1821. [An adaptation, with addns and alterations, of Defoe's Jure Divino, 1706. With a preface by Hone and 2 woodcuts by G. Cruikshank.]

An Imaginary Interview between W. Hone and a Lady. 1822.

A Slap at Slop and the Bridge St. Gang. 1822; [A burlesque on Stoddart's The New Times; inspired and illustrated by Cruikshank.]

The Ancient Mysteries Described. 1823. [Old English miracle plays and other early dramas found by Hone in MS in the BM. and pbd with notes and illustrations, the latter by G. Cruikshank.]

The Every-Day Book: or Everlasting Calendar of Popular Amusements. With Four Hundred and Ninety Engravings [by G. Cruikshank and others]. 2 vols. 1826–7.

The Table Book. 2 vols. 1827–8. [With 116 engravings by Cruikshank and others.]

Full Annals of the Revolution in France. 1830.

The Year-Book of Daily Recreation and Information concerning Remarkable Men and Manners, Times and Seasons. 1832. [Illustrations by George Cruikshank, and others.]

The Early Life and Conversion of William Hone by Himself. Edited by his Son. 1841.

Some Account of the Conversion of the Late W. Hone, with further Particulars of his Life and Extracts from his Correspondence. 1853.

(d) Biography and Criticism

The Three Trials of William Hone, for publishing Three Parodies. 1818; ed. W. Tegg, 1876. [The Trials were pbd separately in 1817.]

Hackwood, F. W. William Hone: his Life and Times. 1912.

MARY HOWITT, née BOTHAM
(1799–1888)

[For works written in collaboration with her husband see William Howitt, below.]

(a) Popular Natural History

Sketches of Natural History. 1834; [1851] (7th edn, enlarged); [1864]; [1872].

Wood Leighton, or a Year in the Country. 3 vols. 1836.

Birds and Flowers and Other Country Things. [1855.]

Our Four-Footed Friends. [1867.]

Birds and their Nests. [1872.]

(b) Children's Books

Sowing and Reaping, or What will come of it? 1841 (bis).

No Sense like Common Sense, or Some Passages in the Life of Charles Middleton. 1843.

The Children's Year. 1847.

Our Cousins in Ohio. 1849.

The Picture Book for the Young. 1855.

Tales in Prose for Young People. [1864.]

Tales for all Seasons. [1881.]

(c) Poems

Hymns and Fireside Verses. 1839.

Fireside Verses. [1845.]

Ballads and other Poems. [1847.]

Marion's Pilgrimage, a Fire-side Story, and Other Poems. [1859.]

Tales in Verse for Young People. [1865.]

(d) Fiction and History

Strive and thrive. A Tale. 1840.
Work and Wages, or Life in Service. [1842.]
Love and Money. An Every Day Tale. [1843.]
The Heir of Wast-Waylan. 1847.
A Popular History of the United States of America, from the Discovery of the American Continent to the present time. 2 vols. 1859.
The Cost of Caergwyn. 3 vols. 1864.
Stories of Stapleford. 2 pts, 1864.
Vignettes of American History. [1869]; [1876].

[Mrs Howitt wrote, edited, or translated some 110 works. Among her more notable trns are various tales from the Danish of Hans Andersen and the novels of Fredrika Bremer, from the Swedish, in 18 vols.]

(e) Biography and Criticism

[Wilson, J.] Noctes Ambrosianae, xxxix, lvi. Blackwood's Mag. Nov. 1828, April 1831.
Mary Howitt. An Autobiography. Ed. Margaret Howitt, 1889; [1891].
Britten, J. Mary Howitt. [1890.] [A biography.]

WILLIAM HOWITT (1792–1879)

(a) Writings on Country Life and Travel

The Book of the Seasons, or the Calendar of Nature. 1831.
The Rural Life of England. 2 vols. 1838.
The Boy's Country-Book. Being the Real Life of a Country Boy. 1839.
Visits to Remarkable Places, Old Halls, Battlefields, and Scenes Illustrative of Striking Passages in English History and Poetry. 1840. [Ser. 2, 'chiefly in the Counties of Durham and Northumberland,' 1842.]
The Student Life of Germany. By Dr. Cornelius. 1841. [Really by Howitt.]
The Rural and Domestic Life of Germany, with Characteristic Sketches of its Cities and Scenery, collected in a General Tour, and during a Residence in the Country in 1840, 41 and 42. 1842.
German Experiences: addressed to the English, both Stayers at Home and Goers abroad. 1844.
Homes and Haunts of the most Eminent British Poets. 2 vols. 1847; 1857 (3rd edn).
The Hall and the Hamlet, or Scenes and Characters of Country Life. 2 vols. 1848.
The Year-Book of the Country, or the Field, the Forest, and the Fireside. 1850.
A Boy's Adventures in the Wilds of Australia, or Herbert's Note-Book. 1854.

Land, Labour, and Gold, or Two Years in Victoria: with Visits to Sydney and Van Diemen's Land. 2 vols. 1855.
Tallangetta, the Squatter's Home. A Story of Australian Life. 2 vols. 1857.
The History of Discovery in Australia, Tasmania, and New Zealand, from the Earliest Date to the Present Day. 1865.

(b) Writings on Religion and History

A Popular History of Priestcraft in all Ages and Nations. 1833; 1834 (4th edn, enlarged); [1834] (abridgement).
Pantika, or Traditions of the Most Ancient Times. 2 vols. 1835.
Colonization and Christianity. A Popular History of the Treatment of the Natives by the Europeans in all their Colonies. 1838.
Cassell's Illustrated History of England. The Text to Edward I by J. F. Smith and [thence] by W. Howitt. 8 vols. [1856]–64.
The History of the Supernatural in All Ages and Nations, and in All Churches, Christian and Pagan, demonstrating a Universal Faith. 2 vols. 1863.
The Northern Heights of London, or Historical Associations of Hampstead, Highgate, Muswell Hill, Hornsey, and Islington. 1869.

(c) Fiction

The Life and Adventures of Jack of the Mill, commonly called Lord Othmill. A Fire-side Story. 2 vols. 1844.
Madam Dorrington of the Dene. The Story of a Life. 3 vols. 1851.
The Man of the People. 3 vols. 1860.
Woodburn Grange. A Story of English Country Life. 3 vols. 1867.

[Howitt also pbd some shorter tales.]

(d) Poems

A Poet's Thoughts at the Interment of Lord Byron. 1824.
The Mad War-Planet and Other Poems. 1871.

(e) Works written with Mary Howitt

(i) Poems

The Forest Minstrel, and Other Poems. 1823. [With notes.]
The Desolation of Eyam: the Emigrant, a Tale of the American Woods, and Other Poems. 1827.

(ii) Prose

Howitt's Journal of Literature and Popular Progress. 1847–9.
The Literature and Romance of Northern Europe: constituting a Complete History of the Literature of Sweden, Denmark, Norway and Iceland. 2 vols. 1852.

Stories of English and Foreign Life. 1853.
Ruined Abbeys and Castles of Great Britain. 2 sers. 1862–4. [Separate extracts from the above were brought out—Yorkshire, 1863; the Wye, 1863; the Border, 1865.]

[Howitt also produced a number of trns, including von Chamisso de Boncourt's History of Peter Schlemihl, 1843, and J. Ennemoser's History of Magic, 1854; he wrote a number of minor works and many contributions to periodicals, including about 100 articles on spiritualism in Spiritual Mag.]

(f) Biography and Criticism

Horne, R. H. William and Mary Howitt. [In A New Spirit of the Age, vol. I, 1844.]
Brown, Cornelius. The Worthies of Nottinghamshire. 1883.
Hall, S. C. Retrospect of a Long Life. 2 vols. 1883.
Howitt, later Watts, A. M. The Pioneers of the Spiritual Reformation. Life and Works of D. J. Kerner: William Howitt, and his Work for Spiritualism. Biographical Sketches. 1883.
Mary Howitt: an Autobiography. Ed. Margaret Howitt, 1889. [With a ch., describing his youth, by W. Howitt.]

CATHERINE HUTTON (1756–1846)
(a) Writings

The Miser Married. A Novel. 1813.
The Life of William Hutton, by Himself; Conclusion by Catherine Hutton. 1816; 1817; 1841.
The Welsh Mountaineer. A Novel. 3 vols. 1817.
The History of Birmingham. By William Hutton. Continued to the Present Time by Catherine Hutton. 1819.
Oakwood Hall. A Novel. 3 vols. 1819.
The Tour of Africa: containing a Concise Account of all the Countries in that Quarter of the Globe hitherto visited by Europeans. Selected from the Best Authors and arranged by Catherine Hutton. 3 vols. 1819–21.
Reminiscences of a Gentlewoman of the Last Century: Letters of Catherine Hutton. Ed. C. H. Beale, Birmingham, 1891.
Catherine Hutton and her Friends. Ed. C. H. Beale, Birmingham, 1895. [Letters.]

(b) Biography and Criticism

Miss Catherine Hutton. GM. April, May 1846.
Colvile, F. L. The Worthies of Warwickshire who lived between 1500 and 1800. Warwick, [1870].
Jewitt, Ll. The Life of William Hutton. [1872.]

ANNA BROWNELL JAMESON, née MURPHY (1794–1860)
(a) Miscellaneous Writings

Cadijah, or the Black Palace. A Tragedy in Five Acts. 1825.
A First or Mother's Dictionary for Children; containing upwards of 3,800 Words. [1825?]
A Lady's Diary. 1826; 1826 (as Diary of an Ennuyée); Paris, 1836 (with Diary of a Désennuyée).
The Loves of the Poets. 1829.
Memoirs of Celebrated Female Sovereigns. 2 vols. 1831.
Characteristics of Women, Moral, Poetical and Historical; with Etchings. 2 vols. 1832; 2 vols. 1833 (corrected and enlarged). [This work comprises Shakespeare's Heroines, frequently rptd under that title.]
Beauties of the Court of King Charles the Second. A Series of Portraits, illustrating the Diaries of Pepys, Evelyn, Clarendon and other Contemporary Writers, with Memoirs Biographical and Critical. The Portraits from Copies made by Mr. Murphy. 1833.
Visits and Sketches at home and abroad. With Tales and Miscellanies now first collected, and a New Edition of the Diary of an Ennuyée. 4 vols. 1834.
The Romance of Biography, or Memoirs of Women loved and celebrated by the Poets; from the Days of the Troubadours to the Present Age. 2 vols. 1837 (3rd edn).
Sketches of Germany. Art—Literature—Character. Frankfort, 1837.
Winter Studies and Summer Rambles in Canada. 3 vols. 1838.
A Handbook to the Public Galleries of Art in and near London. 2 pts, 1842.
Companion to the most Celebrated Private Galleries of Art in London. With a Prefatory Essay on Art, Artists, Collectors and Connoisseurs. 1844.
Memoirs of the Early Italian Painters, and of the Progress of Painting in Italy. From Cimabue to Bassano. 2 vols. 1845; 1859 (much enlarged).
Memoirs and Essays, Illustrative of Art, Literature and Social Morals. 1846.
Sacred and Legendary Art. 2 vols. 1848; ed. E. M. Hurll, 2 vols. Boston, 1896.
Legends of the Monastic Orders, as represented in the Fine Arts: forming the Second Series of Sacred and Legendary Art. 1850; 1852 (enlarged).
Legends of the Madonna, as represented in the Fine Arts: forming the Third Series of Sacred and Legendary Art. Illustrated. 1852.

A Commonplace Book of Thoughts, Memories, and Fancies, Original and Selected. 1854.
Sisters of Charity, Catholic and Protestant, abroad and at home. 1855.
The Communion of Labour, A Second Lecture on the Social Employments of Women. 1856.
The History of Our Lord as exemplified in Works of Art. Commenced by Mrs. Jameson; completed by Lady Eastlake. 2 vols. 1864.
Letters of Anna Jameson to Ottilie von Goethe. Ed. G. H. Needler, 1939.

[Several ephemeral handbooks, etc. are omitted.]

(b) Biography and Criticism

Horne, R. H. The New Spirit of the Age. Vol. II, 1844.
Kingsley, C. The Poetry of Sacred and Legendary Art. Fraser's Mag. XXXIX, 1848.
Powell, T. Pictures of the Living Authors of Britain. 1851.
The Writings of Mrs. Anna Jameson. New Monthly Mag. XCIX, 1853.
Macpherson, Gerardine. Memoirs of the Life of Anna Jameson; with Postscript by Mrs. M. O. Oliphant. 1878.
Mrs. Anna Jameson. Blackwood's Mag. CXXV, 1878.
Hamilton, C. J. Women Writers. Vol. II, 1893, p. 24.
Erskine, Mrs S. Anna Jameson: Letters and Friendships, 1812–1860. 1915.

FRANCIS, LORD JEFFREY (1773–1850)

(a) Critical Writings

Essay on Beauty. [Rptd from Edinburgh Rev. with addns in Ency. Brit. Supplement, 1824, 1841; rptd 1844 in Contributions to the Edinburgh Rev. vol. I.]
Eulogium of James Watt. 1839. [Rptd from Ency. Brit. and included in the Life of Watt by D. F. J. Arago, 1839.]
Two Inaugural Addresses and a Parting Address delivered at Glasgow University. [First 3 Addresses in Inaugural Addresses by Lords Rectors of the University of Glasgow, ed. J. B. Hay, Glasgow, 1839.]
Contributions to the Edinburgh Review. 4 vols. 1844; 3 vols. 1846; Philadelphia, 1848; 1853.
Samuel Richardson. 1853. [Pamphlet.]
Jonathan Swift. 1853. [Pamphlet.]
Jeffrey's Literary Criticism. Ed. (with introduction) D. Nichol Smith, 1910. [Gives list of Jeffrey's articles in Edinburgh Rev.]

(b) Political and Miscellaneous Writings

Observations on Mr. Thelwall's Letter to the Editor of the Edinburgh Review. 1804.

A Summary View of the Rights and Claims of the Roman Catholics of Ireland. Edinburgh, 1808. [Rptd from Edinburgh Rev.]
Combinations of Workmen. A Speech. Edinburgh, 1825.
Corrected Report of the Speech of the Lord Advocate of Scotland upon the Motion of Lord John Russell, in the House of Commons, for Reform of Parliament. 1831.
Peter and His Enemies. Edinburgh, 1859 (2nd edn). [A story exposing abuses in the law.]
The Letters of Francis Jeffrey to Ugo Foscolo. Ed. J. Purves, Edinburgh, 1934.

(c) Biography and Criticism

Cockburn, Lord H. T. Life of Lord Jeffrey· With a Selection from his Correspondence. 2 vols. Edinburgh, 1852 (bis); 1872 (Works of Lord Cockburn, vol. I). [Includes list of Jeffrey's articles in Edinburgh Rev.]
Gilfillan, G. Galleries of Literary Portraits. Vol. II, Edinburgh, 1856.
Carlyle, T. Lord Jeffrey. [In Reminiscences, ed. J. A. Froude, 2 vols. 1881.]
Taylor, James. Lord Jeffrey and Craigcrook. Edinburgh, 1892. [With a sketch of Jeffrey's character and Craigcrook life by Lord Moncreif.]
Gates, L. E. Three Studies in Literature. New York, 1899. [Jeffrey, Newman and Arnold.]
Elsner, R. Francis Jeffrey und seine kritischen Prinzipien. Berlin, 1908.
Hughes, M. Y. The Humanism of Francis Jeffrey. MLR. XVI, 1921.
Beatty, J. M. Lord Jeffrey and Wordsworth. PMLA. XXXVIII, 1923.
Bald, R. C. Francis Jeffrey as a Literary Critic. Nineteenth Century, XCVII, 1925.

MARY ANN LAMB (1764–1847)

(a) Bibliographies

[See L. S. Livingston, 1903, and J. C. Thomson, 1908, under Charles Lamb, p. 632 above.]

(b) Writings

Helen. [Poem, pbd with Charles Lamb's John Woodvil, 1802.]
Mrs. Leicester's School, or the History of Several Young Ladies, related by Themselves. 1807 (anon.); 1809; 1825 (9th edn); 1827; ed. A. Ainger, 1885 (with other writings). [With Charles Lamb.]
Tales from Shakespear, designed for the Use of Young Persons. 2 vols. 1807; 1809; ed. F. J. Furnivall, 2 vols. 1901. [With Charles Lamb; Mary's name did not appear on title-page of 1st edn.]

(c) Biography and Criticism

Hazlitt, W. C. Mary and Charles Lamb. 1874.

Gilchrist, A. Mary Lamb. 1883.

Anderson, G. A. 'Poems,' by a Sister (1812), wrongly attributed to Mary Lamb. TLS. 21 Aug. 1924.

Frend, G. G. The Lambs, Fanny Kelly and some Others. Bookman, LXXI, 1926.

Riddell, W. R. The Tragedy of Mary Lamb. Trans. Royal Soc. of Canada, XXII, 1928.

[See also under Charles Lamb, p. 634 above, *passim*.]

CHARLES LLOYD (1775–1839)

[See p. 237 above.]

JOHN GIBSON LOCKHART (1794–1854)

(a) Biographical, Critical and Miscellaneous Writings

Ancient Spanish Ballads, Historical and Romantic, translated, with Notes. Edinburgh, 1823; 1841 (rev.); New York, 1856 (rev., with memoir); 1870.

Janus; or, The Edinburgh Literary Almanack. Edinburgh, 1826. [With John Wilson.]

Life of Robert Burns. Edinburgh, 1828 (*bis*); Edinburgh, 1830; New York, 1831; 1838; 1847; 1871; 1872, etc.; ed. W. S. Douglas, 1882, 1890 (rev. J. H. Ingram); ed. E. Rhys, 1907 (Everyman's Lib.).

The History of Napoleon Buonaparte. 1829 (anon.); 2 vols. New York, 1843; 1867; 1878 (abridged by W. Tegg); Edinburgh, 1885 (abridged); 1889; rptd 1906 (Everyman's Lib.); ed. J. H. Rose, 1916 (Oxford edn).

The History of the Late War; including Sketches of Buonaparte, Nelson and Wellington. For Children. 1832. [Preface signed 'J. G. L.']

Memoirs of the Life of Sir Walter Scott, Bart. 7 vols. Edinburgh, 1837–8; 10 vols. Edinburgh, 1839; 2 vols. Edinburgh, 1848, 1853 (abridged as Narrative of the Life of Sir Walter Scott); Edinburgh, 1871 (abridged, with letter by J. R. H. Scott); rptd 5 vols. 1900; ed. J. M. Sloan, 1904 (abridged); ed. O. L. Reid, 1914 (abridged); tr. German, 1839–41.

The Ballantyne-Humbug handled. Edinburgh, 1839. [Reply to criticisms of the life of Scott by James Ballantyne's trustees and son.]

The Noctes Ambrosianae of 'Blackwood.' 4 vols. Philadelphia, 1843; ed. R. S. Mackenzie, 5 vols. New York, 1866. [First pbd in Blackwood's Mag. 1822–35. Mainly by John Wilson, but Lockhart wrote several of the earlier papers.]

Theodore Hook. A Sketch. 1852. [First pbd in Quarterly Rev. May 1843.]

Lockhart's Literary Criticism. With Introduction and Bibliography by M. Clive Hildyard. Oxford, 1931.

[Lockhart also supplied copious notes and an essay on the Life and Writings of Cervantes to the rpt of Motteux's Don Quixote, 5 vols. 1822. For a list of his contributions to Blackwood's Mag. April 1817–May 1846, and Quarterly Rev. (which he edited), March 1826–June 1852, see M. C. Hildyard's selection.]

(b) Novels

Peter's Letters to His Kinsfolk. By Peter Morris the Odontist. 3 vols. Edinburgh, 1819.

Valerius. A Roman Story. 3 vols. Edinburgh, 1821; 1842 (rev.).

Some Passages in the Life of Mr. Adam Blair, Minister of the Gospel at Cross Meikle. A Novel. Edinburgh, 1822; 1843 (with Matthew Wald).

Reginald Dalton. A Story of English University Life. 3 vols. Edinburgh, 1823; 1842; [1880].

The History of Matthew Wald. A Novel. Edinburgh, 1824; 1843 (with Adam Blair).

(c) Biography and Criticism

Gleig, G. R. Quarterly Rev. Oct. 1864.

Maginn, W. A Gallery of Illustrious Characters. Ed. W. Bates, [1873].

Croker, J. W. The Croker Papers. Ed. L. J. Jennings, 3 vols. 1884.

Smiles, S. A Publisher and his Friends. 2 vols. 1891.

Lang, A. The Life and Letters of John Gibson Lockhart. 2 vols. [1897].

Birrell, A. The Biographer of Sir Walter Scott. [In Et Cetera, a Collection, 1930.]

Hildyard, M. C. John Gibson Lockhart. Cornhill Mag. LXXII, 1932.

Ewen, F. John Gibson Lockhart, Propagandist of German Literature. MLN. XLIX, 1934.

Swann, E. Christopher North (John Wilson). Edinburgh, 1934.

Macbeth, G. John Gibson Lockhart. A Critical Study. Urbana, 1935. [With bibliography.]

MacCurdy, E. A Literary Enigma. The Canadian Boatsong. Stirling, 1936.

Strout, A. L. John Gibson Lockhart. N. & Q. 15, 22, 29 Oct., 3 Dec. 1938. [New letters, etc.]

[See also under Sir Walter Scott, pp. 374–80 above.]

WILLIAM MAGINN (1793–1842)

(a) Collected and Selected Works

Miscellaneous Writings. Ed. R. S. Mackenzie, 5 vols. New York, 1855–7. [Vols. I, II, The O'Doherty Papers; vol. III, Shakespeare Papers; vol. IV, Homeric Ballads and Comedies of Lucian; vol. V, The Fraserian Papers, with a Life of the Author.]

Miscellanies, Prose and Verse. Ed. R. W. Montague [Johnson], 2 vols. 1885. [With memoir.]

Ten Tales. 1933. [Preface signed W. B.]

(b) Essays and Miscellaneous Writings

Magazine Miscellanies. [1841.] [Tales, verses, maxims, etc.]

The Noctes Ambrosianae of 'Blackwood.' 4 vols. Philadelphia, 1843; ed. R. S. Mackenzie, 5 vols. Philadelphia, 1854. [First pbd in Blackwood's Mag. 1822–35. Mainly by John Wilson, but some papers by Maginn, J. G. Lockhart, James Hogg, and others.]

Maxims of Sir Morgan O'Doherty. Edinburgh, 1849. [A parody of La Rochefoucauld.]

Shakespeare Papers. Pictures Grave and Gay. 1859; 1860 (adds paper on Hamlet and a sketch of Maginn signed B.).

A Gallery of Illustrious Literary Characters (1830–1838) drawn by Daniel Maclise and accompanied by Notices, chiefly by William Maginn. Republished from Fraser's Magazine. Ed. W. Bates, [1873].

(c) Fiction

Whitehall, or the Days of George IV. [1827] (anon.).

The City of Demons. [In A. A. Watts, The Literary Souvenir, 1828.]

John Manesty, the Liverpool Merchant. With Illustrations by George Cruikshank. 2 vols. 1844.

Jochonan in the City of Demons. [In Light from the East, ed. G. Measom, 1856.]

A Story without a Tail. 1858 (in Tales from Blackwood, vol. II); ed. G. Saintsbury, 1928. [First pbd in Blackwood's Mag. 1834.]

[The anon. The Military Sketch Book, 2 vols. 1827, and Tales of Military Life. By the Author of 'The Military Sketch Book,' 3 vols. 1829, have also occasionally been attrib. to Maginn. It is, however, most improbable that they are by him.]

(d) Translations and Adaptations

Memoirs of Vidocq, translated from the French [of E. Morice and L. F. L'Héritier]. 4 vols. 1828–9. Memoirs of Madame Du Barri. Translated from the French [of E. L. de La Mothe Langon], by the Translator of 'Vidocq.' 4 vols. 1830–1. [Respectively vols. XXV–XXVIII and XXIX–XXXII of Autobiography. A Collection of the most Instructive and Amusing Lives ever published. Vol. IV of Memoirs of Vidocq has a 'Sequel' appended (apparently by the translator) signed H. T. R. Both trns are conjecturally attrib. to Maginn by Halkett and Laing. They have also been assigned to George Borrow.]

Homeric Ballads, with Translations and Notes. 1850.

[Maginn also wrote a great deal in Blackwood's Mag., Fraser's Mag. and other journals.]

(e) Biography and Criticism

[Lockhart, J. G.] The Doctor. Fraser's Mag. Jan. 1831. [Rptd in A Gallery of Illustrious Characters, ed. W. Bates, [1873].]

Kenealy, E. V. and Moir, D. M. William Maginn, LL.D. Dublin University Mag. XXIII, 1844.

Hall, S. C. A Book of Memories of Great Men and Women of the Age, from Personal Acquaintance. 1871.

Sadleir, M. Bulwer. A Panorama, 1803–1836. 1931. [Appendix IV consists of a bibliography of Maginn's writings.]

Elwin, M. Victorian Wallflowers. 1934.

Thrall, M. Rebellious Fraser's. New York, 1934.

JOHN MITFORD (1781–1859)

[See p. 239 above.]

JAMES MONTGOMERY (1771–1854)

[See p. 239 above.]

WILLIAM MUDFORD (1782–1848)

[See p. 411 above.]

HENRY JOHN TEMPLE, VISCOUNT PALMERSTON (1784–1865)

(a) Speeches and Writings

The New Whig Guide. 1819; 1824. [By Palmerston and others; edited by 'E.']

Speech in the House of Commons on 1 June 1829, upon the Motion of Sir J. Macintosh respecting the Relations of England with Portugal. [1829.]

Speech in the House of Commons on 16 February 1842, on Lord John Russell's Motion against a Sliding Scale of Duties on the Importation of Foreign Corn. 1842.

Speech in the House of Commons on 25 June 1850, on Mr. Roebuck's Motion on the Foreign Policy of the Government. 1850; tr. French, Paris, 1850.

Opinions and Policy of Viscount Palmerston. With a Memoir by G. H. Francis. 1852. [Selections from speeches.]

Selections from [Palmerston's] Diaries and Correspondence. [In H. L. E. Bulwer's Life, 5 vols. 1871–6; tr. French, Paris, 1878–9.]

Selection from Private Journals of Tours in France in 1815 and 1818. 1871.

The Palmerston Papers: Gladstone and Palmerston. Being the Correspondence of Lord Palmerston with Mr. Gladstone, 1851–1865. Ed. P. Guedalla, 1928.

[The speeches given above are selected from a considerable number ptd.]

(b) Biography and Criticism

The Oratory of Lord Palmerston. Fraser's Mag. xxxiii, 1846.

Bulwer, H. L. E. (Baron Dalling and Bulwer). The Life of Henry John Temple, Viscount Palmerston, with Selections from his Diaries and Correspondence. 5 vols. 1871–6. [With A. E. M. Ashley, who wrote part of vol. iii and the whole of vols. iv, v; the whole rev. and abridged by A. E. M. Ashley, 2 vols. 1879, as The Life and Correspondence of Henry John Temple, Viscount Palmerston.]

Bell, H. C. F. Lord Palmerston. 2 vols. 1936.

PETER GEORGE PATMORE (1786–1855)

Letters on England. By Victoire, Count de Soligny. 1823. [By Patmore.]

British Galleries of Art. 1824.

Mirror of the Months. 1826. [A novel.]

Rejected Articles. 1826 (bis); 1844 (4th edn, as Imitations of Celebrated Authors, or Imaginary Rejected Articles). [Parodies.]

Sir Thomas Lawrence's Cabinet of Gems, with Biographical and Descriptive Memorials by Peter George Patmore. 1837.

Finden's Gallery of Beauty, or Court of Queen Victoria. Ed. P. G. Patmore, [1841].

Chatsworth, or the Romance of a Week. 1844 (anon.). [Ed. by R. Plumer Ward.]

Marriage in May Fair. A Comedy in Five Acts. 1854 (2nd edn).

My Friends and Acquaintances. Being Memorials, Mind-Portraits, and Personal Recollections of Deceased Celebrities of the Nineteenth Century. 3 vols. 1855. [Reviewed in New Quarterly Rev. iii, 1854.]

[Patmore edited The New Monthly Magazine, 1841–53.]

BRYAN WALLER PROCTER (1787–1874)

[See p. 241 above.]

HENRY CRABB ROBINSON (1775–1867)

(a) Writings

Strictures [by T. Clarkson] on a Life of W. Wilberforce, by the Rev. W. Wilberforce and the Rev. S. Wilberforce; with a Correspondence between Lord Brougham and Mr Clarkson; also a Supplement. 1838. [Ed. by Robinson.]

Exposure of Misrepresentations contained in the Preface to the Correspondence of William Wilberforce. 1840.

The Diary, Reminiscences and Correspondence of Henry Crabb Robinson. Ed. T. Sadler, 3 vols. 1869; 2 vols. 1872 (adds Augustus De Morgan's 'Recollections' of Robinson).

Blake, Coleridge, Wordsworth, etc., being Selections from the Remains of Henry Crabb Robinson. Ed. E. J. Morley, Manchester, 1922.

The Correspondence of Henry Crabb Robinson with the Wordsworth Circle (1808–66). Ed. E. J. Morley, 2 vols. Oxford, 1927.

Crabb Robinson in Germany, 1800–5. Extracts from his Correspondence. Ed. E. J. Morley, Oxford, 1929.

Henry Crabb Robinson on Books and their Writers. Ed. E. J. Morley, 3 vols. 1938.

(b) Biography and Criticism

Bagehot, W. Literary Studies. Vol. ii, 1879.

Wright, H. G. Henry Crabb Robinson's 'Essay on Blake.' MLR. xxii, 1927.

King, R. W. Crabb Robinson's Opinion of Shelley. RES. iv, 1928.

Larg, D. G. Mme de Staël et Henry Crabb Robinson. Revue de Littérature comparée, viii, 1928.

—— Henry Crabb Robinson and Madame de Staël. RES. v, 1929.

Norman, P. Henry Crabb Robinson and Goethe. 2 pts, English Goethe Soc. 1930–1.

Morse, B. J. Crabb Robinson and Goethe in England. E. Studien, lxvii, 1932.

Morley, E. J. The Life and Times of Henry Crabb Robinson. 1935.

Baker, J. M. Henry Crabb Robinson of Bury, Jena, the 'Times' and Russell Square. 1937.

Gilbert, M. E. Two Little-known References to Henry Crabb Robinson. MLR. xxxiii, 1938.

THOMAS ROSCOE (1791–1871)

(a) Topographical Writings

The Tourist in Switzerland and Italy. 1830. [The 1st pt of his Landscape Annual, in which the following subsequently appeared: Italy, 1832–3; France, 1834; Spain, 3 vols. 1835–7; Spain and Morocco, 1838.]

Wanderings and Excursions in North Wales. 1836; 1853. [Illustrations after Cox and others.]

Wanderings and Excursions in South Wales; including the Scenery of the River Wye. [1837.] [With L. A. Twamley, later Meredith; illustrations after Cox and others.]

Windsor Castle and its Environs, illustrated with Historical Sketches by Thomas Roscoe and Engravings by J. Carter. Pt 1 (all pbd), 1838.

The London and Birmingham Railway, with the Home and Country Scenes on each Side of the Line. Historical Details by P. Lecount. [1839.]

The Book of the Grand Junction Railway. Being a History and Description of the Line from Birmingham to Liverpool and Manchester. 1839.

Belgium in a Picturesque Tour. 1841.

Summer Tour to the Isle of Wight, including Portsmouth, Southampton, Winchester, etc. 1843.

(b) Fiction and Miscellaneous Writings

Gonzalo, the Traitor. A Tragedy in Five Acts. 1820. [Verse.]

The King of the Peak. 3 vols. 1823 (anon.).

Owain Goch. A Tale of the Revolution. 3 vols. 1827 (anon.).

Life of Michael Angelo Buonaroti. [In Lives of Eminent Persons, 1833.]

Legends of Venice. 1841.

Lives of the Kings of England, from the Norman Conquest. Vol. i (all pbd), 1846. [On William I.]

The Last of the Abencerages, and Other Poems. 1850.

[Roscoe also revised his father William's Leo X and Lorenzo de' Medici, and contributed memoirs of the following authors to edns of their works: Fielding, Hurtado de Mendoza, Cervantes, Swift. He edited The Juvenile Keepsake, 1828–30 and The Novelists' Library, 12 vols. 1831–2.]

(c) Translations

Cellini, Benvenuto. Memoirs; with the Notes and Observations of G. P. Carpani. 1822; 1847; rptd L. Ricci, 1904 (rev.).

Simonde de Sismondi, J. C. L. Historical View of the Literature of the South of Europe; with Notes. 4 vols. 1823; 1846.

The German Novelists. Tales selected from Ancient and Modern Authors in that Language. Translated with Critical and Biographical Notices. 4 vols. 1826; [1880].

Lanzi, L. A. The History of Painting in Italy. 6 vols. 1828.

Potter, L. J. A. de. Memoirs of S. de Ricci. 2 vols. 1829.

The Spanish Novelists. A Series of Tales, from the Earliest Period to the Close of the Seventeenth Century. Translated with Critical and Biographical Notices. 3 vols. 1832.

Pellico, Silvio. My Imprisonments. 1833.

—— The Duties of Men. 1834.

Fernandez de Navarette, M. The Life and Writings of Miguel de Cervantes Saavedra 1839.

Kohl, J. G. Travels in England and Wales. [1845.]

WILLIAM ROSCOE (1753–1831)

[See p. 887 below.]

NASSAU WILLIAM SENIOR (1790–1864)

[See p. 872 below.]

SYDNEY SMITH (1771–1845)

(a) Collected and Selected Works

Works. 4 vols. 1839–40 (bis); 3 vols. 1845; 3 vols. 1854; 2 vols. 1859; 1869.

Selections from the Writings of Sydney Smith. 2 vols. 1855.

Wit and Wisdom of the Rev. Sydney Smith. With a Biographical Memoir and Notes by E. A. Duyckuick. New York, 1858. [Long extracts almost forming an abridgement of the works.]

The Wit and Wisdom of the Rev. Sydney Smith. 1860. [A different selection from the American one; short complete extracts.]

Selections. Ed. E. Rhys, 1892.

Bon-Mots of Sydney Smith and R. Brinsley Sheridan. Ed. W. Jerrold, 1893.

The Letters of Peter Plymley, with Other Selected Writings, Sermons and Speeches. Ed. G. C. Heseltine, 1929.

(b) Separate Writings

Six Sermons. Edinburgh, 1800; 2 vols. 1801 (enlarged).

Elementary Sketches of Moral Philosophy. 1804, 1805, 1806 (priv. ptd); 1850 (public issue). [Lectures at the Royal Institution, 1804–6.]

The Letters of Peter Plymley to my Brother Abraham who lives in the Country. 1807–8; 1808 (the 9 letters collected); ed. H. Morley, 1886 (with Selected Essays); ed. G. C. Heseltine, 1929 (with other selected writings).

A Sermon upon the Conduct to be observed by the Established Church towards Catholics and other Dissenters. 1807.

Extracts from the Edinburgh Review. [1810?] [On Methodism; Indian Missions; Proceedings of the Society for the Suppression of Vice.]

The Lawyer that tempted Christ. A Sermon. York, 1824 (priv. ptd).
Catholic Claims. A Speech. 1825.
A Sermon on Religious Charity. York, 1825.
A Letter to the Electors, upon the Catholic Question. York, 1826.
Mr. Dyson's Speech to the Freeholders on Reform. 1831. ['Dyson' was Sydney Smith.]
Speech at the Taunton Reform Meeting. 1831.
The New Reign. The Duties of Queen Victoria. A Sermon. 1837.
A Letter to Archdeacon Singleton, on the Ecclesiastical Commission. 1837.
A Letter to Lord John Russell on the Church Bills. 1838.
Second Letter to Archdeacon Singleton, being the Third of the Cathedral Letters. 1838.
Third Letter to Archdeacon Singleton. 1839.
Ballot. 1839. [Against the secret ballot.]
Letters on American Debts. 1844 (2nd edn). [Rptd from Morning Chronicle.]
A Fragment on the Irish Roman Catholic Church. 1845.
Essays, 1802–[1827]. 2 vols. 1874–80. [Rptd from Edinburgh Rev.]
Essays, Social and Political, 1802–1825. 1874; 1877 (adds Essays from Edinburgh Rev. and Letters of Peter Plymley; with a brief memoir by S. O. Beeton). [Necker; Suppression of Vice; Bentham; Education; English Public Schools; C. J. Fox; Poor-Laws; Prisons; Reviews, etc.]
Nine Letters. Ed. E. Cheney, Philobiblon Soc. Misc. vol. xv, 1877–84.

(c) Biography and Criticism

Horne, R. H. A New Spirit of the Age. Vol. i, 1844.
Holland, S., Lady. A Memoir of Sydney Smith by his Daughter. With a Selection from his Letters. Ed. Mrs Austin, 1855. [Contains list of his articles in Edinburgh Rev.]
Gilfillan, G. Galleries of Literary Portraits. Vol. ii, Edinburgh, 1856.
Vaughan, R. A. Essays and Remains. 2 vols. 1858.
Maginn, W. A Gallery of Illustrious Characters. Ed. W. Bates, [1873].
Milnes, R. M. (Baron Houghton). Monographs. 1873.
Hayward, Abraham. Selected Essays. Vol. i, 1878.
Reid, S. J. A Sketch of the Life and Times of Sydney Smith. 1884.
Chevrillon, A. Sydney Smith et la Renaissance des Idées libérales en Angleterre au XIXe Siècle. Paris, 1894.
Russell, G. W. E. Sydney Smith. 1905. (English Men of Letters ser.)

Saint Clair, O. Sydney Smith: a Biographical Sketch. 1913.
Biron, Sir H. C. A Victorian Prophet. Fortnightly Rev. Jan. 1921.
Williams, S. T. The Literary Criticism of Sydney Smith. MLN. xxxviii, 1923.
Burdett, O. The Rev. Smith, Sydney. 1934.
Pearson, H. The Smith of Smiths. 1934.
Murphy, J. Some Plagiarisms of Sydney Smith. RES. xiv, 1938.

JOHN STERLING (1806–1844)
(a) Miscellaneous Writings

FitzGeorge. A Novel. 3 vols. 1832 (anon.).
Arthur Coningsby. A Novel. 3 vols. 1833 (anon.).
Poems. 1839.
The Election. A Poem in Seven Books. 1841 (anon.).
Strafford. A Tragedy. 1843.
Essays and Tales. Collected and Edited with a Memoir of his Life by Julius Charles Hare. 2 vols. 1848. [Vol. i, historical and critical essays ('Christabel,' Napier's 'War in the Peninsula,' Montaigne, Carlyle, Tennyson, etc.); vol. ii, aphorisms, apologues, etc.]
Letters to a Friend [William Coningham]. Brighton, [1848]; 1851 (as Twelve Letters); Bath, [1872].

(b) Biography and Criticism

Gilfillan, G. Galleries of Literary Portraits. Vol. ii, Edinburgh, 1856.
Carlyle, T. The Life of John Sterling. 1857; ed. W. H. White, 1907 (World's Classics).
Ince, R. B. Calverley and some Cambridge Wits of the Nineteenth Century. 1929. [Includes a study of Sterling's career.]

WILLIAM TAYLOR (1765–1836)
(a) Critical and Miscellaneous Writings

A Letter concerning the Two First Chapters of Luke. 1810 (anon.).
English Synonyms Discriminated. 1813; 1850; tr. German, 1851.
Some Biographic Particulars of the late Dr Sayers. [Prefixed to Frank Sayers's Collective Works, Norwich, 1823.]
Historic Survey of German Poetry. Interspersed with Various Translations. 3 vols. 1828–30.
A Memoir of the late Philip Meadows Martineau, Surgeon. 1831. [With F. Elwes.]
[Taylor's 1754 articles and reviews were largely in Monthly Rev. 1793–1824.]

(b) Translations

Lessing. Nathan the Wise. Written originally in German. Norwich, 1791 (priv. ptd); 1805; ed. H. Morley, 1886.

Goethe. Iphigenia in Tauris. A Tragedy. 1793 (priv. ptd); 1794.

Wieland. Dialogues of the Gods. 1795.

Bürger. Ellenore. 1796. [Rptd with some alterations from Monthly Mag. March 1796.]

Select Fairy Tales from the German of Wieland. 1796.

Tales of Yore. 3 vols. 1810. [From French and German.]

(c) Biography and Criticism

Carlyle, T. Taylor's Historic Survey of German Poetry. Edinburgh Rev. March 1831.

Robberds, J. W. A Memoir of the Life and Writings of the Late William Taylor of Norwich, containing his Correspondence. 2 vols. 1843.

Herzfeld, G. William Taylor von Norwich. Eine Studie über den Einfluss der neueren deutschen Literatur in England. Halle, 1897.

EDWARD JOHN TRELAWNY (1792–1881)

(a) Writings

The Adventures of a Younger Son. 3 vols. 1831; 1835; 1848; ed. E. Garnett, 1890; ed. H. N. Brailsford, 1914; ed. E. C. Mayne, 1925 (World's Classics).

Recollections of the Last Days of Shelley and Byron. 1858; 1878 (with addns, as Records of Shelley, Byron and the Author); ed. E. Dowden, 1906.

Letters of Edward John Trelawny. Ed. H. Buxton Forman, 1910.

The Relations of Percy Bysshe Shelley with his Two Wives, Harriet and Mary, and a Comment on the Character of Lady Byron. 1920 (priv. ptd).

The Relations of Lord Byron and Augusta Leigh. With a Comparison of the Characters of Byron and Shelley, and a Rebuke to Jane Clairmont on her Hatred of the Former. 1920 (priv. ptd). [4 letters.]

(b) Biography and Criticism

Garnett, R. Shelley's Last Days. Fortnightly Rev. XXIX, 1878.

Mathilde Blind. Whitehall Rev. 10 Jan. 1880. [Record of conversation.]

Rossetti, W. M. Talks with Trelawny, 1879–1880. Athenaeum, 15, 29 July, 5 Aug. 1882.

Edgcumbe, R. Edward Trelawny. A Biographical Sketch. Plymouth, 1882.

Sharp, William. The Life and Letters of Joseph Severn. 1892.

Miller, Joaquin. Trelawny with Shelley and Byron. 1922.

Massingham, H. J. The Friend of Shelley. A Memoir of Edward John Trelawny. 1930.

RICHARD WHATELY (1787–1863)

(a) Selections

Detached Thoughts and Apophthegms, extracted from some of the Writings of Archbishop Whately. Ser. 1, 1854.

Selections from the Writings of Dr. Whately. 1856 [1855].

Miscellaneous Remains from the Commonplace Book of Richard Whately. Being a Collection of Notes and Essays made during the Preparation of his Various Works. Ed. E. J. Whately, 1864; 1865 (with addns).

(b) Theological Writings

Historic Doubts relative to Napoleon Bonaparte. 1819 (anon.); 1863 (13th edn). [A travesty of the higher criticism.]

Essays on some of the Peculiarities of the Christian Religion. Oxford, 1825; 1846 (5th edn, rev.).

Sermons on Various Subjects. 1835; 1849 (adds 4 sermons); 1854–62 (enlarged, as Sermons on the Principal Christian Festivals and on Other Occasions).

Historic Certainties respecting the Early History of America. By Rev. Aristarchus Newlight [i.e. Whately]. 1851.

(c) Philosophical and Miscellaneous Writings

Elements of Logic, comprising the Substance of the Article in the Encyclopaedia Metropolitana, with Additions. 1826; 1832 (4th edn, rev.); 1836 (6th edn, rev.); 1840 (rev.); 1844 (rev.).

Elements of Rhetoric. 1828; 1836 (5th edn, rev.); 1846 (7th edn, rev.). [Rptd from Encyclopaedia Metropolitana.]

Introductory Lectures on Political Economy. 2 pts, 1831–2; 1847 (3rd edn, rev.); 1855 (rev. and enlarged).

Miscellaneous Lectures and Reviews. 1861.

[Whately also edited: Thomas Whately's Remarks on some of the Characters of Shakespeare, 1839; E. Copleston's Remains, 1854; Bacon's Essays, 1856; W. Paley's Moral Philosophy, and Evidences, 1859. The foregoing entries constitute only a brief selection from a voluminous output which fills more than 10 columns of BM. Catalogue.]

(d) Biography and Criticism

Blanco, afterwards White, J. M. The Life of the Rev. Blanco White, written by Himself; with Portions of his Correspondence. Ed. J. H. Thom, 3 vols. 1845.

'An Old Oxonian.' Recollections of Archbishop Whately. Christian Observer, LXIII, 1863.

Fitzpatrick, W. J. Memoirs of Archbishop Richard Whately of Dublin; with a Glance at his Contemporaries and Times. 2 vols. 1864.

Archbishop Whately. Eclectic Rev. VII, 1864.

Memoirs of Richard Whately. Blackwood's Mag. XCVI, 1864.

Whately, E. J. Life and Correspondence of Richard Whately. 2 vols. 1866; 1875 (with additional correspondence).

Parrish, W. M. Whately and his Rhetoric. Quart. Journ. of Speech, XV, 1929.

JOHN WILSON ('CHRISTOPHER NORTH') (1785–1854)

(a) Collected Works

The Works of Professor Wilson of the University of Edinburgh. Edited by his Son-in-Law Professor Ferrier. 12 vols. Edinburgh, 1855–8.

(b) Critical and Miscellaneous Writings

Janus; or, The Edinburgh Literary Almanack. Edinburgh, 1826. [With Lockhart.]

Some Illustrations of Mr McCullogh's Principles of Political Economy. By Mordecai Mullion, Private Secretary to Christopher North. Edinburgh, 1826.

The Land of Burns. A Series of Landscapes and Portraits Illustrative of the Life and Writings of the Scottish Poet. 2 vols. Glasgow, 1840. [Illustrated by D. O. Hill with letterpress by Robert Chambers and Wilson.]

The Recreations of Christopher North. 3 vols. Edinburgh, 1842; Philadelphia, 1850; 2 vols. 1864.

The Noctes Ambrosianae of 'Blackwood.' 4 vols. Philadelphia, 1843; 4 vols. Edinburgh, 1864; ed. R. S. Mackenzie, 5 vols. New York, 1866 (best edn); 4 vols. 1868. [Mainly by Wilson, but some papers by J. Hogg, J. G. Lockhart, W. Maginn and others; first pbd in Blackwood's Mag. 1822–35. Selections: ed. J. Skelton, Edinburgh, 1876; ed. J. S. Moncrieff and J. H. Millar, 1904.]

The Works of Robert Burns; with Dr Currie's Memoir of the Poet, and an Essay on his Genius and Character by Professor Wilson. Vol. I, Glasgow, 1843. [Wilson's essay was rptd separately New York, 1845, Philadelphia, 1854, and New York, 1861.]

Scotland Illustrated by John C. Brown, and Other Scottish Artists; with Letter-Press Descriptions and an Essay on the Scenery of the Highlands by Professor Wilson. 1845. [Wilson's essay is rptd in A History of the Scottish Highlands, ed. J. S. Keltie, vol. I, Edinburgh, 1875.]

Specimens of the British Critics by Christopher North. Philadelphia, 1846.

Essays Critical and Imaginative. 4 vols. Edinburgh, 1866.

(c) Poems

A Recommendation of the Study of the Remains of Ancient Grecian and Roman Architecture, Sculpture and Painting. A Prize Poem. Oxford, 1807.

Lines Sacred to the Memory of the Rev. James Grahame. Glasgow, 1811.

The Isle of Palms, and Other Poems. Edinburgh, 1812.

The Magic Mirror. Addressed to Walter Scott, Esq. Edinburgh, 1812.

The City of the Plague, and Other Poems. Edinburgh, 1816.

Poems. A New Edition. 2 vols. 1825.

The Poetical Works of Milman, Bowles, Wilson, and Barry Cornwall. Paris, 1829.

The Poetical Works of Professor Wilson. Edinburgh, 1865, 1874.

(d) Fiction

Translation from an Ancient Chaldee Manuscript. From No. VII of Blackwood's Magazine. [Edinburgh, 1817.]

Lights and Shadows of Scottish Life. A Selection from the Papers of the Late Arthur Austin. Edinburgh, 1822; Edinburgh, 1853; tr. French, Geneva, 1826.

Little Hannah Lee. A Winter Story. 1823. [From Lights and Shadows of Scottish Life.]

The Trials of Margaret Lyndsay. By the Author of Lights and Shadows of Scottish Life. Edinburgh, 1823; Edinburgh, 1854; Glasgow, [1879]; [1886].

The Foresters. By the Author of Lights and Shadows of Scottish Life and The Trials of Margaret Lyndsay. Edinburgh, 1825; Edinburgh, 1852.

Blind Allan. A Tale. 1840; [Falkirk? 1850?]. [From Lights and Shadows of Scottish Life.]

Tales by Professor Wilson. Lights and Shadows. Margaret Lyndsay. The Foresters. Edinburgh, 1865.

(e) Biography and Criticism

Lockhart, J. G. Peter's Letters to his Kinsfolk. 3 vols. Edinburgh, 1819.

Professor Wilson. A Memorial and Estimate by One of his Students. Edinburgh, 1854.

Gilfillan, G. Galleries of Literary Portraits. Vol. II, Edinburgh, 1856.

Heart-break. The Trials of Literary Life, or Recollections of Christopher North. 1859. [A story introducing recollections of Wilson.]

Gordon, Mary. Christopher North. A Memoir of John Wilson, compiled from Family Papers and Other Sources. 2 vols. Edinburgh, 1862.

Hannay, J. Professor Wilson. [In Characters and Criticisms, Edinburgh, 1865.]

Maginn, W. A Gallery of Illustrious Characters. Ed. W. Bates, [1873].

Saintsbury, G. Essays in English Literature, 1780–1860. Ser. 1, 1890.

Oliphant, M. O. W. Annals of a Publishing House. William Blackwood and his Sons. 3 vols. 1897.

Douglas, Sir G. The Blackwood Group. 1897.

Masson, D. Christopher North. [In Memories of Two Cities, Edinburgh, 1911.]

Struve, H. von. John Wilson (Christopher North) als Kritiker. Leipzig, 1922.

Elwin, M. Christopher North. [In Victorian Wallflowers, 1934.]

Strout, A. L. John Wilson, 'Champion' of Wordsworth. MP. xxxi, 1934.

—— Purple Patches in the 'Noctes Ambrosianae.' ELH. ii, 1935.

—— Concerning the 'Noctes Ambrosianae.' MLN. li, 1935. [See also RES. xiii, 1937, pp. 46–63, 177–89.]

Swann, E. Christopher North (John Wilson). Edinburgh, 1934. [Includes, pp. 239–52, lists of Wilson's works and of books and articles about him.]

DOROTHY WORDSWORTH (1771–1855)

(a) Miscellaneous Writings

Recollections of a Tour made in Scotland, A.D. 1803. Ed. J. C. Shairp, Edinburgh, 1874 (bis); Edinburgh, 1894.

Letters to Sir George and Lady Beaumont. [In W. Knight, Memorials of Coleorton, 2 vols. 1887.]

Journals of Dorothy Wordsworth. Ed. W. Knight, 2 vols. 1897; 1924.

Letters of the Wordsworth Family from 1787 to 1855. Collected by W. Knight. 3 vols. 1907.

The Letters of William and Dorothy Wordsworth. Ed. E. de Selincourt, 6 vols. Oxford, 1935–8.

(b) Biography and Criticism

[The section on Wordsworth, pp. 169–72 above, should also be consulted.]

Chambers, W. William and Dorothy Wordsworth. Chambers's Journ. lxi, 1874.

Lee, E. Dorothy Wordsworth. 1886.

Maclean, C. M. Dorothy and William Wordsworth. 1927.

—— Dorothy Wordsworth: the Early Years. 1932. [With a bibliography.]

de Selincourt, E. Dorothy Wordsworth. A Biography. 1933.

R. D. C. and H. B. G.

III. THE MID-NINETEENTH CENTURY ESSAYISTS

MACAULAY, NEWMAN AND RUSKIN

THOMAS BABINGTON MACAULAY, BARON MACAULAY (1800–1859)

(1) COLLECTED WORKS

Œuvres, traduites par M. G. Guizot. 6 vols. Paris, 1862–85.

The Works of Lord Macaulay. Complete. Edited by his Sister Lady Trevelyan. 8 vols. 1866.

The Works of Lord Macaulay. 12 vols. 1898. (Albany edn.)

The Works of Lord Macaulay. 9 vols. 1905–7. [Vols. iv–viii, The History of England, ed. T. F. Henderson.]

(2) SELECTED WORKS

Scenes and Characters from the Writings of Thomas Babington Macaulay. New York, 1846.

Selections from Macaulay's Essays and Speeches. 2 vols. 1856.

Selections from the Writings of Lord Macaulay. Ed. Sir G. O. Trevelyan, 1876.

Morceaux choisis de l'Histoire d'Angleterre et des Chants de l'ancienne Rome. Accompagnés d'une Notice, d'Arguments analytiques et de Notes par W. Battier. Paris, 1892.

Selections from the Prose of Macaulay. Ed. L. H. Holt, Boston, [1916].

Readings from Macaulay. Ed. H. Hayens, [1925].

Selections from Macaulay's Prose. Ed. E. Jackson, 1925.

Selections from Macaulay. Ed. E. V. Downs and G. L. Davies, 1930.

The Reader's Macaulay. A Selection from his Essays, Letters and History of England. Ed. W. H. French and G. D. Sanders, New York, 1936.

(3) CRITICAL AND HISTORICAL WRITINGS

Critical and Miscellaneous Essays. 5 vols. Philadelphia, 1841–4. [Unauthorised.]

Critical and Historical Essays, contributed to The Edinburgh Review. 3 vols. 1843; 1848; 1850; 3 vols. 1853; 2 vols. 1854; 5 vols. New York, 1857; 1861; 1872, etc.; ed. G. T. Bettany, 1892; rptd 5 vols. 1900 (Temple Classics); ed. F. C. Montague, 3 vols. 1903 (best edn); rptd 2 vols. 1907 (Everyman's Lib.); rptd 2 vols. 1913 (Oxford edn). Tr. Italian, 5 vols. Turin, 1859–66; French, Paris, 1860; Dutch, 2 vols. Haarlem, 1865; Spanish, Madrid, 1880. [Authorised selection; Macaulay's other contributions to

Edinburgh Rev. were collected in The Miscellaneous Writings. The numerous rpts of one or more of the Essays, chiefly for school use, have not been listed. Vol. I: Preface; Milton (Aug. 1825); Machiavelli (March 1827); Hallam (Sept. 1828); Southey's Colloquies (Jan. 1830); Mr Robert Montgomery (April 1830); Civil Disabilities of the Jews (Jan. 1831); Moore's Life of Lord Byron (June 1831); Samuel Johnson (Sept. 1831); John Bunyan (Dec. 1830); John Hampden (Dec. 1831). Vol. II: Burleigh and his Times (April 1832); War of the Succession in Spain (Jan. 1833); Horace Walpole (Oct. 1833); William Pitt, Earl of Chatham (Jan. 1834); Sir James Mackintosh (July 1835); Lord Bacon (July 1837); Gladstone on Church and State (April 1839). Vol. III: Sir William Temple (Oct. 1838); Lord Clive (Jan. 1840); Von Ranke (Oct. 1840); Leigh Hunt (Jan. 1841); Lord Holland (July 1841); Warren Hastings (Oct. 1841). In later edns the Essays were rearranged in more strictly chronological order and the following addns made: Frederic the Great (April 1842); Madame D'Arblay (Jan. 1843); The Life and Writings of Addison (July 1843); The Earl of Chatham (Oct. 1844).]
The History of England from the Accession of James II. Vols. I, II, 1849; vols. III, IV, 1855; vol. V, ed. H., Lady Trevelyan, 1861; 8 vols. 1858–62 (with memoir by H. H. Milman), etc.; rptd 3 vols. 1906 (Everyman's Lib.); ed. T. F. Henderson, 5 vols. 1931 (World's Classics). Tr. Danish, Copenhagen, 1852–8; Hungarian, Pest, 1853; Polish, Posen, 1854–61; French, Paris, 1861; Czech, Prague, 1862–5; German, Brunswick, 1863 (5th edn); Finnish, Helsingissä, 1866; Dutch, Amsterdam, 1868; Greek, Athens, 1897–1902; Spanish, Madrid, 1905–6.
The Miscellaneous Writings of Lord Macaulay. Ed. T. F. E[llis], 2 vols. 1860; 1865; 1871 (Speeches added); [1874]; 4 vols. 1880 (Speeches and Poems added), etc.; rptd 1910 (Everyman's Lib., with Lays). [Vol. I: Contributions to Knight's Quarterly Mag. (June 1823–Nov. 1824); Contributions to Edinburgh Rev. (Jan. 1828–Oct. 1829). Vol. II: Contributions to Edinburgh Rev. (July 1830–April 1844); Contributions to Ency. Brit. (8th edn) (Francis Atterbury, John Bunyan, Oliver Goldsmith, Samuel Johnson, William Pitt); Miscellaneous Poems, Inscriptions, etc. (1812–47).]
Biographies by Lord Macaulay contributed to the Encyclopaedia Britannica. With Extracts from his Letters and Speeches. Edinburgh, 1860.

Were Human Sacrifices in Use among the Romans? Correspondence between Mr. Macaulay, Sir Robert Peel and Lord Mahon. 1860.
Marginal Notes by Lord Macaulay. Selected and arranged by Sir George Otto Trevelyan. 1907.
What did Macaulay say about America? Text of Four Letters to Henry S. Randall. Ed. H. M. Lydenberg, New York, 1925.

(4) SPEECHES

[Several of Macaulay's speeches were originally ptd separately when delivered.]

Speeches, Parliamentary and Miscellaneous. 2 vols. 1853; 2 vols. New York, 1853. [Unauthorised; inaccurate text.]
Speeches of the Right Honourable Thomas Babington Macaulay, corrected by himself. 1854; 1866; tr. Spanish, Madrid, 1885.
Speeches. Ed. G. M. Young, 1935. (World's Classics.)

(5) MINUTES ON INDIAN AFFAIRS

The Indian Civil Service. Report to the Rt. Hon. Sir C. Wood, Bart., by T. B. Macaulay, Lord Ashburton, the Rev. H. McCrill, B. Jowett and the Speaker of the House of Commons. 1855.
The Indian Education Minutes of Lord Macaulay now first collected from Records in the Department of Public Instruction. Ed. H. Woodrow, Calcutta, 1862.

(6) POEMS

Pompeii. A Poem which obtained the Chancellor's Medal, 1819. [Cambridge, 1819.]
Evening. A Poem which obtained the Chancellor's Medal, 1821. Cambridge, 1821.
Lays of Ancient Rome. 1842; 1847; 1848 (with Ivry and The Armada); 1881; 1882; 1884 (3 edns, one with Selections from the Essays); 1886 (bis); 1887; 1888; Glasgow, 1889; 1892, etc.; rptd 1902 (Temple Classics); 1903 (World's Classics); ed. G. M. Trevelyan, 1928. Tr. German, Leipzig, 1853; Italian, Florence, 1869.
The Miscellaneous Writings of Lord Macaulay. Ed. T. F. E[llis], 2 vols. 1860, etc. [Vol. II includes various uncollected Miscellaneous Poems.]
Hymn by Lord Macaulay. An Effort of his Early Childhood, hitherto Unpublished. Ed. L. Horton-Smith, Cambridge, 1902. [Facs. of original MS.]

(7) BIOGRAPHY AND CRITICISM

[The following list may be supplemented by the useful Bibliographical Note appended to Arthur Bryant's Macaulay, 1932, pp. 172–84.]

(a) Books

Spedding, J. Evenings with a Reviewer, or a Free and Particular Examination of Mr. Macaulay's Article on Lord Bacon. 2 vols. 1848 (priv. ptd); ed. G. S. Venables, 2 vols. 1881.

Paget, John. An Inquiry into the Evidence relating to the Charges brought by Lord Macaulay against William Penn. 1858.

—— The New 'Examen,' or An Inquiry into the Evidence relating to Certain Passages in Lord Macaulay's History. Edinburgh, 1861; rptd 1934.

—— Paradoxes and Puzzles, Historical, Judicial and Literary. Edinburgh, 1874.

Macaulay: the Historian, Statesman and Essayist. Anecdotes of his Life and Literary Labours. 1860.

Lançon, X. Études d'Histoire et d'Éloquence au XIXᵉ Siècle. Lord Macaulay: ses Essais, ses Discours et son Histoire d'Angleterre. Lyon, 1861.

Arnold, F. The Public Life of Lord Macaulay. 1862.

Milman, H. H. A Memoir of Lord Macaulay. Reprinted from the Papers of the Royal Society. 1862.

Trevelyan, Sir G. O. The Life and Letters of Lord Macaulay. By his Nephew. 2 vols. 1876; 1877; 1878; 1881; 1908; [1913]; rptd 2 vols. 1932 (World's Classics).

Canning, A. S. G. Lord Macaulay, Essayist and Historian. 1882; [1913] (rev. and enlarged).

Morison, J. C. Macaulay. 1882 (English Men of Letters ser.).

Buelow, G. Thomas Babington Macaulay: sein Leben und seine Werke. Schweidnitz, [1901].

Walcha, G. Macaulay als Geschichtschreiber. Leipzig, 1931.

Bryant, A. Macaulay. 1932.

Firth, Sir C. A Commentary on Macaulay's History of England. 1938.

(b) Pamphlets and Chapters in Books

Horne, R. H. A New Spirit of the Age. Vol. II, 1844.

Impey, E. B. A Life of Sir Elijah Impey. 1846.

Powell, T. The Living Authors of England. New York, 1849.

Dixon, W. H. Life of Penn. 1851.

Clements, H. G. J. Lord Macaulay: his Life and Writings. Two Lectures delivered at Sidmouth. 1860.

Dareste de la Charanne, A. E. C. Macaulay et l'Histoire contemporaine. Discours. Lyon, [1860].

Letters of Hannah More to Zachary Macaulay, Esq., containing Notices of Lord Macaulay's Youth. Ed. A. Roberts, 1860.

Mignet, F. A. M. Éloges historiques: T. Jouffroy, Baron De Gerando, Laromiguière, Lakanal, Schelling, Comte Portalis, Hallam, Lord Macaulay. Paris, 1864.

Taine, H. A. Histoire de la Littérature anglaise. Vol. IV, Paris, 1864; tr. Eng. Edinburgh, 1871.

Stirling, J. H. Jerrold, Tennyson and Macaulay, with other Critical Essays. Edinburgh, 1868.

Morley, J., Viscount. Critical Miscellanies. Vol. II, 1877. [Rptd from Fortnightly Rev. xxv, 1876.]

Bagehot, W. Literary Studies. Ed. R. H. Hutton, vol. II, 1879.

Gladstone, W. E. Gleanings of Past Years. Vol. II, 1879. [Essay on Macaulay rptd from Quarterly Rev. CXLII, 1876.]

Kinkel, J. G. Macaulay: sein Leben und sein Geschichtswerk. Basle, 1879.

Napier, Macvey. Selections from the Correspondence of. 1879.

Stephen, Sir L. Hours in a Library. Ser. 3, 1879.

Skelton, Sir J. Essays in History and Biography. Edinburgh, 1883.

Stephen, Sir J. F. The Story of Nuncomar. 2 vols. 1885.

Laurie, W. F. B. Sketches of some Distinguished Anglo-Indians. 1888. [Includes Macaulay's minute on Education.]

Harrison, Frederic. Macaulay's Place in Literature. 1894. [Rptd in Studies in Early Victorian Literature, 1895.]

Jebb, Sir R. C. Macaulay. A Lecture. Cambridge, 1900.

Macgregor, D. H. Lord Macaulay. 1901.

Paul, H. Men and Letters. 1901.

Trevelyan, G. M. Clio: A Muse. 1913.

Hassard, A. R. A New Light on Lord Macaulay. Toronto, 1918.

Kellett, E. E. Macaulay's Lay Figures. [In Suggestions, Cambridge, 1923.]

—— Macaulay and the Authorised Version. [In Reconsiderations, Cambridge, 1928.]

Roberts, S. C. Lord Macaulay, the Pre-eminent Victorian. English Ass. 1927. [Rptd in An Eighteenth Century Gentleman and Other Essays, Cambridge, 1930.]

Willoughby, D. Lord Macaulay. [In The Great Victorians, ed. H. J. and H. Massingham, 1932.]

(c) Articles in Periodicals

Mill, J. S. Macaulay's Lays of Ancient Rome. Westminster Rev. XXXIX, 1843. [Rptd in R. B. Johnson, Famous Reviews, 1914.]

Croker, J. W. Quarterly Rev. March 1849. [Review of Macaulay's History, vols. I, II; rptd in R. B. Johnson, Famous Reviews, 1914.]

Macaulay as a Translator. Colburn's New Monthly Mag. CXIX, 1860.

[Thackeray, W. M.] A Few Words on Junius and Macaulay. Cornhill Mag. March 1860.

Froude, J. A. Macaulay. Fraser's Mag. XCIII, 1876.

Macaulay and Sir Elijah Impey. Macmillan's Mag. LII, 1885.

Dicey, A. V. Macaulay and his Critics. Nation (New York), LXXIV, 1902.

Blakely, T. E. Macaulay's English. Harper's Mag. CV, 1902.

Chislett, W. Macaulay's Classical Reading. Classical Journ. XI, 1915.

Hopman, F. J. Notes on Macaulay. E. Studies, V, 1923.

Williams, S. T. Macaulay's Reading and Literary Criticism. PQ. III, 1924.

Sampson, G. Macaulay and Milton. Edinburgh Rev. CCXLII, 1925.

Alston, Dorothy. Some Personal Recollections of Lord Macaulay. London Mercury, XVIII, 1928.

Wells, J. Macaulay as a Man of Letters. Fortnightly Rev. Oct. 1928.

Abbot, W. C. Macaulay and the New History. Yale Rev. XVIII, 1929.

Carver, P. L. The Sources of Macaulay's Essay on Milton. RES. VI, 1930.

Strachey, Lytton. Portraits in Miniature. 1931.

Ottley, R. R. Macaulay Reconsidered. National Rev. Oct. 1932.

Dobrée, B. Macaulay. Criterion, XII, 1933.

Rolfe, J. C. Macaulay's Lays of Ancient Rome. Classical Journ. XXIX, 1934.

JOHN HENRY NEWMAN (1801–1890)

(1) BIBLIOGRAPHIES

Guibert, J. Le Réveil du Catholicisme en Angleterre au XIXᵉ Siècle. Paris, 1907. [Bibliographies, pp. 311–335 of Newman and pp. 336–350 of the Oxford Movement.]

Delattre, F. La Pensée de J. H. Newman. Paris, [1914]. [Pp. 297–302 selective bibliography.]

Guitton, J. La Philosophie de Newman. Paris, 1933. [Pp. 195–230 good classified bibliography.]

(2) COLLECTED WORKS

Works. 36 vols. 1868–81. [Incomplete.]

Cardinal Newman's Works. 40 vols. 1874–1921. [Index by J. Rickaby.]

(3) SELECTIONS

Miscellanies from the Oxford Sermons and other Writings of J. H. Newman. 1870.

Six Selections from the Writings of J. H. Newman, by a Late Member of Oriel College, Oxford [W. S. Lilly]. 1874.

Characteristics from the Writings of J. H. Newman: being Selections, Personal, Historical, Philosophical and Religious, from his Various Works. Arranged by W. S. Lilly. 1875.

Echoes from the Oratory. Selections from the Poems of John Henry Newman. New York, 1884.

Sayings of Cardinal Newman. [1890.]

Select Essays of John Henry, Cardinal Newman. Ed. G. Sampson, [1903].

University Sketches. Ed. G. Sampson, [1903].

Sermons for the Festivals. [1904.]

Le Chrétien: Choix de Discours extraits des Sermons de Newman. Traduction et Préface par R. Saleilles. Paris, 1906.

Cardinal Newman. Ed. W. Meynell, [1907].

Literary Selections from Newman. With Introduction and Notes by a Sister of Notre Dame. 1913.

The Spirit of Cardinal Newman. With a Preface by C. C. Martindale. 1914.

La Pensée de J. H. Newman. Extraits choisis et traduits par Floris Delattre, avec une Introduction, une Bibliographie et le Texte anglais correspondant. Paris, [1920].

Readings from Newman. Ed. G. O'Neill, 1923.

A Newman Synthesis. Arranged by Erich Przywara. 1930. [An abridgement, in the original English, of Christentum: ein Aufbau, vol. IV.]

(4) THEOLOGICAL AND DEVOTIONAL WRITINGS (PROSE)

Suggestions on Behalf of the Church Missionary Society. 1830.

The Arians of the Fourth Century; their Doctrine, Temper and Conduct, chiefly as exhibited in the Councils of the Church, between A.D. 325 & A.D. 381. 1833; ed. G. H. Forbes, 1854; 1871; 1876.

Tracts for the Times; by Members of the University of Oxford. 6 vols. 1834–41. [The following are by Newman: vol. I, nos. 1, 2, 6, 7, 8, 10, 11, 19, 20, 21, 34, 38, 41, 45; vol. II, no. 47; vol. III, nos. 71, 73, 75; vol. IV, nos. 79, 82; vol. V, nos. 83, 85, 88; vol. VI, no. 90 (Remarks on Certain Passages in the Thirty-Nine Articles). No. 90 has been frequently rptd separately: ed. J. J. Frew, 1855; ed. E. B. Pusey, 1865 (with appendix by J. Keble); ed. A. W. Evans, 1933; tr. German, Göttingen, 1844.]

Parochial Sermons. 6 vols. 1834–42; ed. W. J. Copeland, 8 vols. 1868 (as Parochial and Plain Sermons); 8 vols. 1872–9; 8 vols. 1881–4. [Selection adapted to the Seasons of the Ecclesiastical Year, ed. W. J. Copeland, 1878; Twelve Sermons, selected from the Parochial and Plain Sermons, [1908].]

The Restoration of Suffragan Bishops recommended as a Means of effecting a more Equal Distribution of Episcopal Duties as contemplated by His Majesty's Recent Ecclesiastical Commission. 1835.

Letter to Parishioners on Laying the First Stone of the Church at Littlemore. 1835.

Elucidations of Dr. Hampden's Theological Statements. 1836 (anon.).

Letter to the Margaret Professor of Divinity on Mr. R. H. Froude's Statements on the Holy Eucharist. Oxford, 1836.

Make Ventures for Christ's Sake. A Sermon. 1836 (anon.).

Lectures on the Prophetical Office of the Church, viewed relatively to Romanism and Popular Protestantism. 1837.

A Letter to the Rev. Godfrey Faussett, on certain Points of Faith and Practice. Oxford, 1838.

Lectures on Justification. 1838; 1874 (3rd edn); 1885.

The Church of the Fathers. 1840 (anon.); 1868 (4th edn).

The Tamworth Reading Room. Letters on an Address delivered by Sir Robert Peel, Bart., on the Establishment of a Reading Room at Tamworth. By Catholicus. 1841. [Rptd in Discussions and Arguments, 1872.]

A Letter addressed to the Rev. R. W. Jelf in Explanation of No. 90 in the Series called The Tracts for the Times. Oxford, 1841 (bis). [Signed J. H. N.]

A Letter to Richard [Bagot], Bishop of Oxford, on Occasion of No. 90 in the Series called The Tracts for the Times. Oxford, 1841.

Plain Sermons by Contributors to the 'Tracts for the Times.' [Vol. v (anon.) by Newman, 1843.]

Sermons bearing on Subjects of the Day. 1843; 1844; ed. W. J. Copeland, 1869; 1879; 1885.

Sermons, chiefly on the Theory of Religious Belief, preached before the University of Oxford. 1843; 1872 (3rd edn); tr. French, Paris, 1850.

The Cistercian Saints of England. [Continued as Lives of the English Saints. Pts I, II, 1844–5, ed. by Newman, who wrote the prose portion of St Bettelin; St Edilwald, and St Gundleas. The whole series appeared in 4 vols.; ed. A. W. Hutton, 6 vols. 1900–1.]

An Essay on the Development of Christian Doctrine. 1845; 1846; 1878; tr. French (in part), Paris, 1847.

Dissertatiunculae quaedam critico-theologicae (ex nupera Oxoniensi Bibliotheca Patrum maxima ex parte desumpta; Latine autem liberius reddita). Rome, 1847.

Discourses addressed to Mixed Congregations. 1849.

Christ upon the Waters. A Sermon preached on Occasion of the Establishment of the Catholic Hierarchy in this Country. Birmingham, 1850 (3 edns); Birmingham, [1852]; [1898].

Lectures on Certain Difficulties felt by Anglicans in submitting to the Catholic Church. 1850; 1872 (with rpt of Letter to Pusey); tr. French, Paris, 1851.

Lectures on the Present Position of Catholics in England: addressed to the Brothers of the Oratory. 1851; [1880] (5th edn); 9 pts, 1890–1905 (with Life by W. Barry); tr. German, Regensburg, 1853.

Remarks on the Oratorian Vocation. 1856 (priv. ptd).

Sermons preached on Various Occasions. 1857; 1870 (3rd edn); 1881 (5th edn).

Mr. Kingsley and Dr. Newman: a Correspondence on the Question whether Dr. Newman teaches that Truth is no Virtue. 1864.

Apologia pro Vita Sua: being a Reply to a Pamphlet [by Charles Kingsley] entitled 'What, then, does Dr. Newman mean?' 1864; 1865 (as History of my Religious Opinions); 1873 (as Apologia pro Vita Sua: being a History of his Religious Opinions), etc.; ed. C. Sarolea, 1912 (Everyman's Lib.); ed. W. Ward, 1913 (2 versions of 1864 and 1865, preceded by Newman's and Kingsley's pamphlets); ed. J. Gamble, 2 vols. [1913]; tr. French, Paris, 1865.

A Letter to the Rev. E. B. Pusey, D.D., on his Recent Eirenicon. 1866 (bis); 1872; 1876. Tr. French, Paris, 1866; German, Cologne, 1866.

The Pope and the Revolution: a Sermon preached in the Oratory Church, Birmingham. 1866.

An Essay in Aid of a Grammar of Assent. 1870; 1881 (5th edn). Tr. French, Paris, 1907; German, Munich, 1921.

Two Essays on Scripture Miracles and on Ecclesiastical. 1870. [Rptd respectively from Encyclopaedia Metropolitana and from Fleury's Ecclesiastical History.]

Causes of the Rise and Success of Arianism. 1872.

Discussions and Arguments on Various Subjects. 1872. [Rpts of short papers and periodical articles.]

The Heresy of Apollinaris. 1874.

Tracts, Theological and Ecclesiastical. 1874.

A Letter addressed to his Grace the Duke of Norfolk on Occasion of Mr. Gladstone's Recent Expostulation [on the Vatican Decrees]. 1875; 1875 (with Postscript on Mr. Gladstone's 'Vaticanism'); 1876.

The Via-Media of the Anglican Church. Illustrated in Lectures, Letters and Tracts, written between 1830 and 1841. With a Preface and Notes. 2 vols. 1877.

Two Sermons preached in the Church of S. Aloysius, Oxford, on Trinity Sunday, 1880. Oxford, [1880] (priv. ptd).

What is of Obligation for a Catholic to believe concerning the Inspiration of the Canonical Scriptures; being a Postscript to an Article in the 'Nineteenth Century Review,' in Answer to Professor Healey. [1884.]

Meditations and Devotions. 1893; 3 pts, 1908. Tr. French, Paris, 1905; German, Mainz, 1919. [Preface by W. P. Neville.]

The Mission of St. Philip Neri. An Instruction. Rome, 1901.

The Fitness of the Glories of Mary. [1904.]

The Glories of Mary for the Sake of her Son. [1904.]

Addresses to Cardinal Newman, with his Replies, 1879–81. Ed. W. P. Neville, 1905.

The Mission of the Benedictine Order. 1908.

Sermon Notes of John Henry, Cardinal Newman, 1849–78. Edited by the Fathers of the Birmingham Oratory. 1913; tr. French, Paris, 1914.

Cardinal Newman on the Benedictine Order. With Introduction by Dom Henry Norbert Birt. 1914. [2 essays rptd from Atlantis.]

(5) EDUCATIONAL AND MISCELLANEOUS WRITINGS

Loss and Gain. 1848 (anon.); rptd 1904. Tr. Italian, Milan, 1857; Paris, 1857.

Discourses on the Scope and Nature of University Education, addressed to the Catholics of Dublin. Dublin, 1852; 1859 (rev. and altered, and with new titles to several of the discourses, as The Scope and Nature of University Education); 1873 (with some titles of discourses again altered, and with addn of 10 further essays, as The Idea of a University defined and illustrated. I. In Nine Discourses addressed to the Catholics of Dublin. II. In Occasional Lectures and Essays addressed to the Members of the Catholic University); ed. A. R. Waller, 1903; ed. W. Ward, 1915 (Everyman's Lib.). [Select Discourses, ed. M. Yardley, Cambridge, 1931.]

Lectures on the History of the Turks in its Relation to Christianity. By the Author of 'Loss and Gain.' 1854 (anon.).

Callista: a Sketch of the Third Century. [1856] (anon.); 1881; rptd [1901], 1904, [1906]. Tr. Czech, Prague, 1887; French, Limoges, [1890].

The Office and Work of the Universities. 1856.

Lectures and Essays on University Subjects. 1859.

Essays, Critical and Historical. 2 vols. 1872.

Historical Sketches. 3 vols. 1872–3.

[Newman also wrote accounts of Cicero, Apollonius Tyanaeus, the Miracles of Scripture for the Encyclopaedia Metropolitana, etc. and contributed much to periodicals. Among his numerous prefaces to works by other writers may be mentioned that to Hurrell Froude's Remains, 1838, and that on miracles prefixed to a trn of C. Fleury's Ecclesiastical History, 1843. Certain funeral sermons and other ephemerae have been omitted.]

(6) POEMS AND HYMNS

St. Bartholomew's Eve; a Tale of the Sixteenth Century. 1821. [With J. W. Bowden.]

Memorials of the Past. 1832. [Dedication signed J. H. N.]

Lyra Apostolica. Derby, 1836; Derby, 1838 (3rd edn); Derby, 1843 (6th edn); 1879. [Poems by J. W. Bowden, R. H. Froude, J. Keble, J. H. Newman, R. Wilberforce and I. Williams; signed respectively $\alpha, \beta, \gamma, \delta, \epsilon,$ and ζ.]

Verses on Religious Subjects. Dublin, 1853 (anon.).

Hymns for the Use of the Birmingham Oratory. Dublin, 1854.

Hymn Tunes of the Oratory, Birmingham. 1860 (anon., priv. ptd).

Verses for Penitents. 1860 (anon., priv. ptd).

The Dream of Gerontius. 1866 (Dedication signed J. H. N.); 1866; 1888 (23rd edn), etc.; ed. E. Caswall, 1909 (with facs. of MS.); 1914 (with other poems; Oxford edn); ed. W. F. P. Stockley, [1923]. Tr. French, Caen, 1869; German, Mainz, 1885.

Verses on Various Occasions. 1868; 1874; 1880.

(7) LETTERS

Letters and Correspondence of J. H. Newman during his Life in the English Church. With a Brief Autobiography. Ed. Anne Mozley, 2 vols. 1891.

Correspondence of John Henry Newman with John Keble and Others, 1839–1845. Edited at the Birmingham Oratory. 1917.

A Set of Unpublished Letters. [In F. L. Cross, John Henry Newman, 1933.]

Cardinal Newman and William Froude, F.R.S.: a Correspondence. Ed. G. H. Harper, Baltimore, 1933.

(8) Translations

The Devotions of Bishop [Lancelot] Andrewes. 2 pts, Oxford, 1842–4; rptd 1920. [Pt 1 tr. from the Greek and arranged by Newman; pt 2 tr. from the Latin by J. M. Neale. Newman's pt had previously appeared, in 1840, as no. 88 of Tracts for the Times.]

Select Treatises of S. Athanasius in Controversy with the Arians, translated, with Notes and Indices. 2 vols. Oxford, 1842–4; 1881 (as Select Treatises of St. Athanasius in Controversy with the Arians. Freely translated by John Henry Cardinal Newman).

The Ecclesiastical History of M. L'Abbé [Claude] Fleury, from the Second Ecumenical Council to the End of the Fourth Century; translated, with Notes, and an Essay on the Miracles of the Period. Oxford, 1842. The Ecclesiastical History, from A.D. 400 to A.D. 429. Oxford, 1843. The Ecclesiastical History, from A.D. 429 to A.D. 456. Oxford, 1844.

(9) Biography and Criticism

(a) Books

Gondon, J. Notice biographique sur le R. P. Newman. Paris, 1853.

Jennings, H. J. Cardinal Newman. 1882.

Fletcher, J. S. A Short Life of Cardinal Newman. 1890.

Meynell, W. John Henry Newman, the Founder of Modern Anglicanism and a Cardinal of the Roman Church. 1890; 1907 (rev.).

Hutton, R. H. Cardinal Newman. 1891.

Lockhart, W. Cardinal Newman. 1891.

Newman, F. W. Contributions chiefly to the Early History of Cardinal Newman. 1891.

Abbott, E. A. The Anglican Career of Cardinal Newman. 2 vols. 1892.

Joye, D. Théorie du Cardinal Newman sur le Développement du Dogme chrétien. Paris, 1896.

Thureau-Dangin, P. La Renaissance catholique en Angleterre au XIXe Siècle. 3 vols. Paris, 1899–1906; tr. Eng. 2 vols. 1914.

—— Newman Catholique, d'après des Documents nouveaux. Paris, 1912.

Carry, E. Les Années anglicanes du Cardinal Newman. Trois Conférences. Geneva, 1901.

Faure, afterwards Goyau, L. F. Newman: sa Vie et ses Œuvres. Paris, 1901.

Waller, A. R. and Burrow, G. H. S. John Henry Cardinal Newman. [1901.]

Grappe, G. J. H. Newman. Essai de Psychologie religieuse. Préface de P. Bourget. Paris, 1902.

Barry, W. Newman. 1904; [1927] (rev.).

Blennerhassett, C. J., Lady. John Henry Kardinal Newman. Ein Beitrag zur religiösen Entwicklungsgeschichte der Gegenwart. Berlin, 1904.

Gout, R. Du Protestantisme au Catholicisme: John-Henry Newman. Anduze, 1904.

Brémond, H. Newman: Essai de Biographie psychologique. Paris, [1906]; tr. Eng. 1907.

Williams, W. J. Newman, Pascal, Loisy and the Catholic Church. 1906.

Saroléa, C. Cardinal Newman and his Influence on Religious Life and Thought. 1908.

Ward, W. P. The Life of John Henry Cardinal Newman, based on his Private Journals and Correspondence. 2 vols. 1912; 2 vols. 1913; 2 vols. 1927.

Stoel, H. Kardinal Newman. Groningen, 1915.

Bellasis, E. Coram Cardinali. 1916.

Bloss, W. E. Twixt the Old and the New: a Study in the Life and Times of John Henry Cardinal Newman. 1916.

Przywara, E. and Karrer, O. Christentum: ein Aufbau. 8 vols. Freiburg, 1922. [Selections. Vol. IV by E. Przywara, Einführung in Newmans Wesen und Wert.]

Battistini, P. J.-H. Newman dans le Mouvement d'Oxford, 1833–1839. Paris, 1924.

Newman, Bertram. Cardinal Newman: a Biographical and Literary Study. 1925.

Reilly, J. J. Newman as a Man of Letters. New York, 1925.

Folghera, J. D. Newman Apologiste. Paris, 1927; tr. Eng. [1929].

Juergens, S. P. Newman on the Psychology of Faith in the Individual. 1928.

May, J. L. Cardinal Newman. 1929.

Atkins, Gaius G. Life of Cardinal Newman. New York, 1931.

Cross, F. L. John Henry Newman; with a Set of Unpublished Letters. 1933.

Faber, G. C. Oxford Apostles. A Character Study of the Oxford Movement. 1933.

Flood, J. M. Cardinal Newman and Oxford. 1933.

Guitton, J. La Philosophie de Newman. Essai sur l'Idée de Développement. Paris, 1933.

Ross, John Elliot. John Henry Newman. [1933.]

Stockley, W. F. P. Newman, Education, and Ireland. [1933.]

Tristram, H. Newman and his Friends. 1933.

Dark, S. Newman. 1934.

Cronin, J. F. Cardinal Newman: his Theory of Knowledge. Washington, 1935.

Tardivel, F. La Personnalité littéraire de Newman. Paris, 1937.

—— John Henry Newman, Éducateur. Paris, 1937.

(b) Pamphlets, Chapters in Books, and Periodical Articles

[See also 'The Oxford Movement,' pp. 854–60 below.]

Achilli v. Newman. A Full and Authentic Report of the Above Prosecution for Libel tried before Lord Campbell and a Special Jury, June 1852. With Introductory Remarks by the Editor of 'The Confessional Unmasked.' [1852.]

Martineau, J. Dr. Newman and Present Theology. National Rev. III, 1856.

Dr. Newman and Charles Kingsley. London Quarterly Rev. XXIII, 1865.

Vaughan, E. T. Dr. Newman as a Preacher. Contemporary Rev. X, 1869.

The Poems of John Henry Newman. Blackwood's Mag. CVIII, 1870.

Stephen, Sir L. The Theory of Belief of Dr. Newman. Fortnightly Rev. XXVIII, 1877.

Dr. Newman and Mr. Froude. Month, XLI, 1881.

Earle, J. C. Dr. Newman as a Man of Letters. American Catholic Quart. VII, 1882.

Froude, J. A. Short Studies on Great Subjects. Vol. IV, 1883.

Capecelatro, A. Commemorazione del Cardinale G. E. Newman nei solenni Funerali fattigli dai Confratelli dell' Oratorio di Napoli il 6 Novembre, 1890. Rome, 1891.

Jacobs, Joseph. George Eliot, Matthew Arnold, Browning, Newman. Essays and Reviews from the 'Athenaeum.' 1891.

Bellasis, E. Cardinal Newman as a Musician. 1892.

Birrell, A. Res Judicatae. 1892. [Newman's English style.]

Barry, W. Cardinal Newman and Renan. National Rev. XXIX, 1897.

—— John Henry Newman. [In Catholic Encyclopaedia, vol. X, New York, 1911.]

Gates, L. E. Three Studies in Literature. New York, 1899. [Newman as a prose-writer.]

Donaldson, A. B. Five Great Oxford Leaders: Keble, Newman, Pusey, Liddon, and Church. 1900.

Ridder, A. de. La Renaissance catholique en Angleterre. Louvain, [1900?].

Fletcher, J. B. Newman and Carlyle: an Unrecognized Affinity. Atlantic Monthly, XCV, 1905.

Dawson, W. J. Makers of English Prose. New York, 1906.

Hutton, J. A. Pilgrims in the Region of Faith: Amiel, Tolstoy, Pater, Newman. 1906.

Guibert, J. Le Réveil du Catholicisme en Angleterre au XIXe Siècle: Conférences Prêchées dans l'Église Saint-Sulpice, 1901–1906. Paris, 1907.

Morley, J., Viscount. Miscellanies. Ser. 4, 1908.

Castle, W. R. Newman and Coleridge. Sewanee Rev. XVII, 1909.

Cecil, A. Six Oxford Thinkers: Edward Gibbon; John Henry Newman; R. W. Church; James Anthony Froude; Walter Pater; Lord Morley of Blackburn. 1909.

Groot, J. V. de. Denkers van onzen Tijd. Herbert Spencer, Edm. du Bois-Reymond, Louis Pasteur, Ferdinand Brunetière, John Henry Newman. Amsterdam, 1910.

More, P. E. Cardinal Newman. [In Shelburne Essays, ser. 8, The Drift of Romanticism, New York, 1913.]

Cadman, S. P. The Three Religious Leaders of Oxford and their Movements: John Wycliffe; John Wesley; John Henry Newman. New York, 1916.

Chesterton, C. The Art of Controversy: Macaulay, Huxley and Newman. Catholic World (New York), CV, 1917.

Coleman, A. I. du P. John Henry Newman. [In J. Hastings, Encyclopaedia of Religion and Ethics, vol. IX, 1917.]

Strachey, Lytton. Eminent Victorians: Cardinal Manning; Florence Nightingale; Dr. Arnold; General Gordon. 1918.

Williams, S. T. Newman's Literary Preferences. Sewanee Rev. XXVIII, 1920.

Brickel, A. G. The Newman Revival in Germany. Catholic World (New York), CXVII, 1923.

Janssens, A. Anglicaansche Bekeerlingen. Antwerp, 1928.

Burgum, E. B. Cardinal Newman and the Complexity of Truth. Sewanee Rev. XXXVIII, 1930.

Olivero, F. La Teoria poetica di Newman. Milan, 1930.

Tristram, H. and Bacchus, F. John Henry Newman. [In J. Vacant, E. Mangenot, and É. Amann, Dictionnaire de Théologie catholique, vol. XI, Paris, 1931.]

Leslie, Shane. Studies in Sublime Failure: Cardinal Newman; Charles Stewart Parnell; Coventry Patmore; Lord Curzon; Moreton Frewen. 1932.

Thirlwall, J. C. Cardinal Newman's Literary Preferences. MLN. XLVIII, 1933.

Young, G. M. Daylight and Champagne. 1937.

(c) *Books, Pamphlets, etc., relating to Separate Works by Newman*

Pusey, E. B. The Articles treated on in Tract 90 reconsidered. 1841.

Ward, W. G. A Few More Words in Support of No. 90 of the Tracts for the Times. 1841.

Harper, F. W. A Few Observations on the Teaching of Mr. Newman concerning Justification. 1842.

Bricknell, W. S. Oxford: Tract No. 90; and Ward's Ideal of a Christian Church. A Practical Suggestion respectfully submitted to Members of Convocation. With an Appendix containing the Testimonies of Twenty-Four Prelates against Tract No. 90, and a Series of Extracts from Ward's Ideal. Oxford, 1844.

Barter, W. B. A Postscript to The English Church not in Schism: containing a Few Words on Mr. Newman's Essay on Development. 1846.

Crosthwaite, J. C. Modern Hagiology: an Examination of the Nature of Some Works published under the Sanction of John Henry Newman. 1846. [On The Lives of the English Saints.]

Irons, W. J. The Theory of Development examined with Reference specially to Mr. Newman's Essay. 1846.

Maurice, J. F. D. The Epistle to the Hebrews; with a Preface containing a Review of Mr. Newman's Theory of Development. 1846.

Mithridates; or, Mr. Newman's Essay on Development its own Confutation. By a Quondam Disciple. 1846.

Minton, S. An Exposure of the Inconsistencies, Fictions and Fallacies of Dr. Newman's Lectures [on the Position of Catholics in England]. 1851.

Hare, J. C. Vindication of Luther against his Recent English Assailants. 1855. [Newman's Lectures on Justification.]

Kingsley, C. 'What, then, does Dr. Newman mean?' A Reply to a Pamphlet lately published by Dr. Newman. 1864.

—— Mr. Kingsley and Dr. Newman: a Correspondence on the Question whether Dr. Newman teaches that Truth is no Virtue? 1864.

Meyrick, F. But isn't Kingsley Right after all? A Letter to Dr. Newman. 1864.

—— On Dr. Newman's Rejection of Liguori's Doctrine of Equivocation. 1864.

D[arby], J. N. Analysis of Dr. Newman's Apologia pro Vita Sua. 1866.

Goode, W. Tract XC. historically refuted. 1866.

Harper, T. N. Difficulties touching Certain Philosophical Theories propounded in Dr. Newman's 'Grammar of Assent.' [1871?]

Pearson, S. Conscience and the Church in their Relations to Christ and Caesar. Thoughts suggested by Dr. J. H. Newman's Pamphlet on the Vatican Decrees. 1875.

A Study on Cardinal Newman's Grammar of Assent. 1889.

Abbott, E. A. Philomythus: an Antidote against Credulity. A Discussion of Cardinal Newman's Essay on Ecclesiastical Miracles. 1891.

Toohey, J. J. An Indexed Synopsis of An Essay in Aid of a Grammar of Assent. 1906.

Tristram, H. Lead, Kindly Light—June 16, 1833. Dublin Rev. cxciii, 1933.

—— Two Suppressed Passages from Newman's Autobiographical Memoirs, now first published. Revue anglo-américaine, xi, 1934.

Sabry, P. Newman en zijn 'Idea of a University.' Brussels, 1934.   H. B. G.

JOHN RUSKIN (1819–1900)

[The works of Ruskin, as pbd before 1868, went out of copyright in 1907, and all edns pbd since then, with the exception of those issued by Ruskin's publisher, George Allen (or by arrangement with him, as World's Classics and Tauchnitz edns) are based on the early and in many cases unrevised text. There were no copyright edns of Ruskin pbd in America before the Brantwood edn of the Collected Works (1891), with the exception of the New York edn of the Lectures on Art (1870). An attempt has been made to list here all the non-copyright edns to 1900; it is, however, certain that many have been overlooked.]

(1) BIBLIOGRAPHIES

Allibone, S. A. A Critical Dictionary of English Literature, and British and American Authors. Vol. ii, Philadelphia, 1870, pp. 1894–6. [Useful for contemporary reviews and American edns.]

[Shepherd, R. H.] The Bibliography of Ruskin from 1834 to the Present Time. [1878]; 1881 (5th edn).

Axon, W. E. A. John Ruskin: A Bibliographical Biography. Manchester, 1879, 1881 (enlarged). [Rptd from Papers of Manchester Literary Club, vol. v.]

Kennedy, W. S. A Bibliography of Ruskin. Literary World (Boston), 13 June 1885.

Wise, T. J. and Smart, J. P. A Bibliography of the Writings in Prose and Verse of John Ruskin. 19 pts, 1889–93 (priv. ptd). [This is the most minute account of the various early edns of Ruskin, and lists some of the more important early reviews.]

Jameson, M. E. A Bibliographical Contribution to the Study of John Ruskin. Cambridge, U.S.A. 1901. [The fullest list of American edns, but at second hand and careless.]

Copyright and Copy-wrong. The Authentic and the Unauthentic Ruskin. 1907. [Not a bibliography, but a summary of the controversy that arose when those of Ruskin's Works that were ptd before 1865 went out of copyright in 1907, and were rptd in large numbers in their unrevised form.]

Cook, E. T. and Wedderburn, A. D. O. The Works of John Ruskin. Library Edition. Vol. xxxviii. Bibliography. 1912. [This is much the most comprehensive and reliable bibliography, although much of it is references to the detailed bibliographies prefixed to each work separately in the earlier vols. of the set.]

Carter, J. and Pollard, G. An Enquiry into the Nature of Certain Nineteenth Century Pamphlets. 1934. [8 of the pamphlets discussed are by Ruskin.]

(2) COLLECTED WORKS

Collected Works. 15 vols. New York, 1861–3; 13 vols. New York, 1861–3.

Collected Works. 11 vols. 1871–80. [Vol. i, Sesame and Lilies, 1871; vol. ii, Munera Pulveris, Keston, 1872; vol. iii, Aratra Pentelici, Keston, 1872; vol. iv, The Eagle's Nest, Keston, 1872; vol. v, Time and Tide, Keston, 1872; vol. vi, The Crown of Wild Olive, Orpington, 1873; vol. vii, Ariadne Florentina, Orpington, 1876; vol. viii, Val d'Arno, Orpington, 1874; vol. ix, The Queen of the Air, Orpington, 1874; vol. x, The Two Paths, Orpington, 1878; vol. xi, A Joy for Ever, Orpington, 1880.]

Collected Works. 30 vols. New York, 1876; 20 vols. New York, 1876; 25 vols. New York, 1884 (Library edn); 12 vols. New York, 1885 (New edn); 19 vols. New York, 1886 (Popular edn); 18 vols. New York, 1886; 26 vols. New York, 1897 (New Popular edn); 13 vols. (including life by J. A. Hobson); New York, 1899 (St Mark's edn); Albany [c. 1900]; 26 vols. Boston, 1900 (bis; illustrated); 13 vols. Boston, 1900 (bis; illustrated).

Selected Works. 8 vols. New York, 1885; 4 vols. Chicago, 1900.

Collected Works. Brantwood Edition. With Introductions by Prof. C. E. Norton. 22 vols. New York, 1891–2. [First authorised American edn.]

Ausgewählte Werke von John Ruskin. Ed. C. Broicher and W. Scholermann, 15 vols. Leipzig, 1900–4.

The Works of John Ruskin. Library Edition. Ed. Sir E. T. Cook and A. D. O. Wedderburn, 39 vols. 1902–12. [The only complete edn, reprinting almost every word Ruskin is known to have written and edited with meticulous care. The following works were first ptd here: Reply to Blackwood's Criticism of Turner (1836)—the first draft of Modern Painters; Letters on Painted Glass (1844); Notes on the Louvre (1844, 1849, 1854); An Essay on Baptism (1850–1); Letters on Politics (1852); Notes on German Galleries (1859); The Rede Lecture at Cambridge (1867); The Aesthetic and Mathematical Schools of Art in Florence (1874); Studies in the Discourses of Sir Joshua Reynolds (1875); Final Lectures at Oxford (1884); The Grammar of Silica (undated); Letters to his Father (various dates). Important additional passages or projected continuations to the following works were also included: Modern Painters; The Seven Lamps of Architecture; The Stones of Venice; The Queen of the Air; Fors Clavigera; Aratra Pentelici; Love's Meinie; Mornings in Florence; Proserpina; Deucalion; Bibliotheca Pastorum; Fiction, Fair and Foul; 'Our Fathers have told us' (pt iii, Ara Coeli); The Pleasures of England; Praeterita; Dilecta.]

Collected Works. Routledge's New Universal Edition. 15 vols. 1907. [Non-copyright; works as pbd before 1865.]

The Ruskin House Edition. 4 vols. 1907. (World's Classics.)

(3) SELECTIONS AND EXTRACTS

The True and the Beautiful in Nature, Art, Morals and Religion, selected from the Writings of John Ruskin with a Notice of the Author. Ed. L. C. Tuthill, New York, 1858 (2nd edn), etc.

Selections from the Writings of John Ruskin. [Ed. W. S. Williams], 1861, etc.

Selections from the Writings of John Ruskin. Ed. W. G. Collingwood, 2 vols. Orpington, 1893, etc. [Vol. i is practically identical with the preceding item.]

Ruskin on Music. Ed. A. M. Wakefield, Orpington, 1894.

Ruskin on Education. Ed. W. Jolly, Orpington, 1894, etc.

The Ruskin Reader. [Ed. W. G. Collingwood], Orpington, 1895, etc.

Studies in Both Arts: being ten subjects Drawn and Described by John Ruskin. [Ed. W. G. Collingwood], Orpington, 1895.

Was wir lieben und pflegen müssen. Eine Sammlung Natur-Ansichten und Schilderungen aus den Werken des John Ruskin. Ed. J. Feis, Strasburg, 1895.

Turner and Ruskin. An Exposition of Turner from the Writings of Ruskin. Ed. Sir F. Wedmore, 2 vols. 1900.

Ruskin on Pictures. A Collection of Criticisms by John Ruskin not heretofore reprinted. Ed. Sir E. T. Cook, 1902.

Obras Escogidas. Ed. E. Gonzalez-Blanco, 2 vols. Madrid, [1906].

Ruskin. Pages Choisies. Avec une Introduction de Robert de la Sizeranne. Paris, 1909, etc.

Selections from Ruskin. Ed. A. C. Benson, Cambridge, 1923.

Ruskin as Literary Critic. Ed. A. H. R. Ball, Cambridge, 1928.

(4) POEMS

Salsette and Elephanta: A Prize Poem. Oxford, 1839; Orpington, 1879. [Rptd in Oxford Prize Poems, Oxford, 1839, 1846.]

The Scythian Guest: A Poem. 1849. [A forgery executed between 1880 and 1890. See Collected Works, ed. Sir E. T. Cook and A. D. O. Wedderburn, vol. II, pp. 101–2; and J. Carter and G. Pollard, An Enquiry into the Nature of Certain Nineteenth Century Pamphlets, 1934, pp. 225–6. The poem was first ptd in Friendship's Offering, 1840, pp. 52–60.]

Poems. J. R. Collected. 1850 (priv. ptd for J. J. Ruskin, senior). [An unauthorised selection from this vol. ed. by J. O. Wright was pbd at New York in 1882.]

The Poems of John Ruskin: now first collected from original manuscript and printed sources; and Edited in chronological order, with Notes, Biographical and Critical, by W. G. Collingwood. 2 vols. Orpington, 1891.

Poems, Collected and Edited by James Osborne Wright. New York, [1894?].

Poems, with an Essay on the Author by G. K. Chesterton. 1906. (Muses' Lib.)

A Walk in Chamouni and Other Poems. [Ed. J. R. Tutin], Hull, 1908.

(5) WRITINGS IN PROSE

[Ruskin's various catalogues of drawings, minerals, etc. 1857–89, and his St George's Guild pbns, 1878–85, have not been included in the following list. For them and for such Ruskiniana as catalogues of St George's Museum and pbns and magazines of Ruskin Societies the bibliographies of T. J. Wise and J. P. Smart and of Sir E. T. Cook and A. D. O. Wedderburn should be consulted. Some offprints from periodical articles by Ruskin have been included in the next section (p. 700 below).]

Modern Painters: their Superiority in the Art of Landscape Painting to all the Ancient Masters proved by Examples of the True, the Beautiful, and the Intellectual, from the works of Modern Artists, especially those of J. M. W. Turner. By a Graduate of Oxford. 1843; 1844 (with new preface); 1846 (with new preface); New York, 1847; 1848; 1851 (with Ruskin's name for the first time); 1857; 1867. Vol. II, 1846 (anon.); 1848; 1851 (with Ruskin's name for the first time); 1856; 1869; 2 vols. Orpington, 1883 (rev. and rearranged); New York, 1883; Orpington, 1885, 1888, 1891. Vol. III, 1856; 1867. Vol. IV, 1856; 1868. Vol. V, 1860. 5 vols. New York, 1865; 5 vols. 1873 (Autograph edn); 5 vols. New York, 1876, 1882; 2 vols. New York, 1884; 5 vols. New York, 1885; 5 vols. Orpington, 1888; 5 vols. New York, 1889; 5 vols. Orpington, 1892; 2 vols. Boston, 1894; 5 vols. New York, 1894; 5 vols. Orpington, 1897, 1898, etc.; ed. L. Cust, 5 vols. 1907 (Everyman's Lib.; text from 1st edns); 5 vols. 1907 (text from 1st edns); tr. German, Leipzig, 1902–4.

Frondes Agrestes. Readings in 'Modern Painters.' Orpington, 1875; New York, 1876 (bis); Orpington, 1876, 1878, 1879, 1880; New York, 1880; Orpington, 1883, 1884, 1886, 1889, 1890, 1891, 1893, 1895 (bis), 1896, 1898, 1899; New York, 1899, 1900; 1900; 1902.

Ruskin on Painting, with a biographical Sketch. New York, 1879.

In Montibus Sanctis. Studies of Mountain Form and of its visible causes. Collected and Completed out of 'Modern Painters.' 2 pts, Orpington, 1884–5. [Rptd with Hortus Inclusus, New York, 1894.]

Coeli Enarrant. Studies of Cloud Form and of its visible causes. Collected and Completed out of 'Modern Painters'. Pt 1 (all pbd), Orpington, 1885. [Rptd with Hortus Inclusus, New York, 1894.]

Modern Painters. A Volume of Selections. 1909.

Modern Painters. Abridged and Edited by A. J. Finberg. 1927.

Wedderburn, A. D. O. Modern Painters. General Index, Bibliography and Notes. Orpington, 1888.

The Seven Lamps of Architecture. With Illustrations drawn and etched by the Author. 1849; New York, 1849; 1855; New York, 1876; Orpington, 1880; New York, 1880; Orpington, 1883; New York, 1884, 1885 (bis); Orpington, 1886; New York, 1889; Orpington, 1890, 1891, 1894, 1895, 1897, 1898, 1899; ed. R. Sturgie, New York, 1899; New York, 1900 (9 edns), etc.; ed. S. Image, 1907 (Everyman's Lib.; text from 1st edn); ed. A. Meynell, 1910 (text from 1st edn). Tr. French, Paris, 1900; German, Leipzig, 1900. [Index by A. D. O. Wedderburn, 1890 (priv. ptd).]

The King of the Golden River; or the Black Brothers: A Legend of Styria. Illustrated by Richard Doyle. 1851 (3 edns); 1856; Boston, 1856 (in Curious Stories); 1859; New York, 1860; 1863; 1867; Boston, 1875 (in Little Classics, ed. R. Johnson, vol. x); Boston, 1876; New York, 1876; Orpington, 1882; New York, 1882; 1885 (bis); Boston, 1885; Orpington, 1886, 1888; New York, 1888 (bis); Boston, 1888 (bis); New York, 1890 (bis); Orpington, 1892; New York, 1895; Boston, 1895; 1899; New York, 1899; 1900, etc.; rptd 1907 (Everyman's Lib.). Tr. German, Dresden, 1861, Stuttgart, 1861; Italian, 1891; Welsh, Denbigh, 1909.

The Stones of Venice. Vol. i. The Foundations. With Illustrations drawn by the Author. 1851; 1858. Vol. ii. The Sea Stories. With Illustrations drawn by the Author. 1853; 1867. Vol. iii. The Fall. With Illustrations drawn by the Author. 1853; 1867. 3 vols. New York, 1865; 3 vols. 1874; 3 vols. Orpington, 1886, 1898, 1900; etc.; ed. L. M. Phillipps, 3 vols. 1907 (Everyman's Lib.). Tr. German, Leipzig, 1903; Hungarian, Budapest, 1907.

Examples of the Architecture of Venice. Selected and drawn to measurement from the edifices. By John Ruskin. 1851; 1887.

On the Nature of Gothic: and herein the True Functions of the Workman in Art. Being the greater part of the Sixth Chapter of the Second Volume of Mr Ruskin's Stones of Venice. 1854 (bis); 1892 (Kelmscott Press); Orpington, 1899, 1900. Tr. French, Paris, 1907, 1908 (2 versions); Swedish, [c. 1908]; Danish, Copenhagen, 1917.

Notice of the Paintings by Tintoretto, in the Scuola di San Rocco, at Venice. Extracted from Mr Ruskin's 'Stones of Venice,' Vol. iii. Arundel Soc. [1857].

The Stones of Venice: Introductory Chapters and Local Indices for the Use of Travellers, while staying in Venice and Verona. 2 vols. Orpington, 1879–81, 1881–5, 1884–8, 1888–90, 1890, 1894, 1896, 1897, 1900, 1902, 1904, 1905; Leipzig, 1906; 1907. Tr. French, Paris, 1905 (with preface, also ptd separately, by R. de la Sizeranne).

Selections from the Stones of Venice. Ed. E. A. Parker, 1925.

[Wedderburn, A. D. O.] The Stones of Venice. Index. 1886 (priv. ptd).

Something on Ruskinism; with a 'Vestibule' in Rhyme. By an Architect. 1851. [Parody.]

Notes on the Construction of Sheepfolds. 1851 (bis); Orpington, 1875; New York, 1876; Orpington, 1879. [Rptd in On the Old Road, vol. ii, 1885.]

Two Letters concerning 'Notes on the Construction of Sheepfolds' Addressed to the Rev. F. D. Maurice by John Ruskin in 1851. Ed. F. J. Furnivall, 1890 (priv. ptd).

Dyce, W. Notes on Shepherds and Sheep. 1851.

A Reply to 'Notes on the Construction of Sheepfolds' by A Graduate of the University of Cambridge. 1851.

Maurice, F. D. Three Letters concerning Ruskin's 'Notes on the Construction of Sheepfolds.' [In Literary Anecdotes of the Nineteenth Century, ed. Sir W. R. Nicoll and T. J. Wise, vol. ii, 1896; also ptd separately.]

Pre-Raphaelitism. By the Author of Modern Painters. 1851; 1862 (with Ruskin's name); New York, 1876 (with other essays by Ruskin); New York, 1891; ed. W. M. Rossetti, Boston, 1899; ed. L. Binyon, 1907 (Everyman's Lib.; with other essays by Ruskin). [Also rptd in On the Old Road, vol. i, 1885.]

Rippingille, E. V. A Reply to the Author of Modern Painters in his defence of 'Pre-Raphaelitism.' 1852.

Young, Edward. Art, its constitution and capacities. Bristol, 1854.

—— Pre-Raffaelitism; or, a Popular Enquiry into some newly-asserted Principles of Art. 1857.

Ballantyne, John. What is Pre-Raphaelitism? Edinburgh, 1856.

Thomas, W. C. Pre-Raphaelitism tested by the Principles of Christianity. 1861.

The National Gallery. Two Letters to the Editor of 'The Times' By the Author of 'Modern Painters.' 1852. [A forgery executed 1880–90; see Collected Works, ed. Sir E. T. Cook and A. D. O. Wedderburn, vol. xii, p. 396, and J. Carter and G. Pollard, An Enquiry into the Nature of Certain Nineteenth Century Pamphlets, 1934, pp. 227–9. The letters appeared in The Times, 4 Jan. 1847, 29 Dec. 1852, and were rptd in The Arrows of the Chace, vol. i, 1880.]

'Verax.' The Abuses of the National Gallery. 1847. [Includes Ruskin's first letter.]

Moore, Morris. Revival of Vandalism at the National Gallery; a Reply to Messrs Ruskin, Heaphy and Wornum's Letters in 'The Times.' 1853.

Giotto and his Works in Padua: being an explanatory Notice of the series of woodcuts executed for the Arundel Society after the Frescoes in the Arena Chapel. 1854. [Really 3 pts, 1853, 1854, 1860, which were bound up as 1 vol. 1877 (rptd New York, 1890, Orpington, 1900, 1905).]

Lectures on Architecture and Painting Delivered at Edinburgh in November, 1853. With Illustrations drawn by the Author. 1854; New York, 1854; 1855; New York, 1885; Orpington, 1891; ed. C. E. Norton, New York, 1892; Orpington, 1899; 1902, etc.; rptd 1907 (Everyman's Lib.; with other essays by Ruskin).

The Opening of the Crystal Palace Considered in some of its Relations to the Prospects of Art. 1854. [Rptd in On the Old Road, vol. I, 1885.]

Notes on some of the Principal Pictures exhibited in the Rooms of the Royal Academy: 1855. 1855 (5th edn); 1855 (with supplement); rptd 1907 (Everyman's Lib.; with other essays by Ruskin). [Modern Painters, vol. II (2nd edn) had included as 'Addenda': Notes on Pictures exhibited in the Royal Academy. 1848. The later Notes (listed immediately below) are all included in the Everyman's Lib. vol. (1907) as above.]

    Notes on some of the Principal Pictures exhibited in the Rooms of the Royal Academy, and the Society of Painters in Water Colours. No. II.—1856. 1856 (bis); 1856 (adds Postscript; 4 edns).

    Notes on some of the Principal Pictures exhibited in the Rooms of the Royal Academy, and the Society of Painters in Water Colours No. III.—1857. 1857 (bis).

    Notes on some of the Principal Pictures exhibited in the Rooms of the Royal Academy, the Old and New Societies of Painters in Water Colours, and the French Exhibition. No. IV.—1858. 1858.

    Notes on some of the Principal Pictures exhibited in the Rooms of the Royal Academy, the Old and New Societies of Painters in Water Colours, the Society of British Artists, and the French Exhibition. No. v.—1859. 1859.

    Notes on some of the Principal Pictures exhibited in the Rooms of the Royal Academy: 1875. Orpington, 1875 (4 edns).

    Notes on so much of the Catalogue of the present Exhibition of the Royal Academy as relates to the Works of the Members. 1855 (priv. ptd). [A reply to Ruskin.]

Hamley, Sir Edward. Mr Dusky's Opinions on Art. Blackwood's Mag. LXXXIV, July 1858. [Rptd in Shakespeare's Funeral, 1889. A parody.]

[Morgan, John.] [Index to Notes on the Royal Academy.] Aberdeen, 1888 (priv. ptd), 1890.

The Harbours of England. Engraved by Thomas Lupton, from original drawings made expressly for the work by J. M. W. Turner. With Illustrative Text by J. Ruskin. 1856; [1857?]; [1859?]; 1872; 1877; [ed. T. J. Wise], Orpington, 1895; 1900, etc.

Notes on the Turner Gallery at Marlborough House. 1856. 1857 (5 edns, 4th adds Preface, 5th rev.); rptd [1907] (Everyman's Lib., with other essays).

The Elements of Drawing; in Three Letters to Beginners. Illustrated by the Author. 1857; New York, 1857; 1857 (adds Appendix); 1859; 1860; 1861; New York, 1876; 1887; 1892; Orpington, 1892, 1895, 1898, 1900, etc.; rptd 1907 (Everyman's Lib., with The Elements of Perspective). Tr. Italian, Turin, 1898; German, Strasburg, [1901] (abridged). [Partly rptd in R. St J. Tyrwhitt, Our Sketching Club. Letters and Studies in Landscape Art with an authorised reproduction of the Lessons and Woodcuts in Professor Ruskin's 'Elements of Drawing,' 1874, 1875, 1882, 1886, Boston, 1874.]

The Political Economy of Art being the substance (with Additions) of Two Lectures delivered at Manchester, July 10th and 13th, 1857. 1857; 1867; 1868; New York, 1876; ed. Sir O. Lodge, 1907 (Everyman's Lib., with Unto this Last); ed. C. F. G. Masterman, 1907. [Rptd with 3 supplementary papers, (1) 'Education in Art' (first pbd in Trans. National Assoc. for Promotion of Social Science, 1858, pp. 811 6), (2) 'Remarks addressed to the Mansfield Art Night Class. Oct. 14th [1873],' (3) 'Social Policy must be based on the Scientific Principle of Natural Selection' (read before Metaphysical Soc. 11 May 1875; priv. ptd 1875), in Collected Works, vol. XI, Orpington, 1880, as 'A Joy for Ever'; (and its price in the market). Later rptd in this form: New York, 1885; Orpington, 1887, 1889; New York, 1890; Orpington, 1893, 1895, 1897, 1899; New York, 1899; Orpington, 1900, etc.]

Cambridge School of Art. Mr Ruskin's Inaugural Address. Delivered at Cambridge, Oct. 29, 1858. Cambridge, 1858; Orpington, 1879. [Also ptd in Cambridge School of Art. Inaugural Soirée, Cambridge, 1858.]

The Oxford Museum. By Henry W. Acland and John Ruskin. 1859; 1860; 1866, 1867 (omitting Ruskin's contributions); 1893 (adds new Preface by Ruskin). [Ruskin's original contributions are rptd in Arrows of the Chace, vol. I, 1880.]

The Unity of Art. Delivered at the Annual Meeting of the Manchester School of Art, Feb. 22nd, 1859. Manchester, 1859. [Largely rptd in The Two Paths, 1859.]

The Two Paths: Being Lectures on Art, and its application to Decoration and Manufacture, delivered in 1858–9. 1859; Orpington, 1884, 1887; New York, 1889; 1891; 1896; 1898; 1900, etc.; ed. G. Wallas, 1907; ed. Sir O. Lodge, 1907 (Everyman's Lib., with other Ruskin essays).

The Elements of Perspective arranged for the use of schools, and intended to be read in connexion with the first three books of Euclid. 1859; 1876; 1907 (Everyman's Lib., with The Elements of Drawing); 1910 (rev.).

'Unto this Last.' Four Essays on the First Principles of Political Economy. 1862; New York, 1866; 1876; Orpington, 1877, 1882, 1884; New York, 1885; Orpington, 1887, 1888, 1890, 1892, 1893, 1895, 1896, 1898, 1899, 1900, etc.; ed. J. A. Hobson, 1907; ed. Sir O. Lodge, 1907 (Everyman's Lib., with The Political Economy of Art and Munera Pulveris). Tr. French, Paris, 1902; German, Leipzig, 1902; Italian, Bari, 1902; Danish, Copenhagen, 1917. [First pbd in Cornhill Mag. Aug.–Nov. 1860 and Harper's Mag. Sept.–Dec. 1860.]

   The Rights of Labour according to John Ruskin, arranged by Thomas Barclay. Leicester, [1887], [1888?]; 1889.

   Papajewski, H. Zur Erkenntniss des Gehalts von Ruskin's 'Unto this Last.' Breslau, 1930.

Sesame and Lilies. Two Lectures delivered at Manchester in 1864. 1. Of Kings' Treasuries. 2. Of Queens' Gardens. 1865; New York, 1865; 1865 (adds Preface); 1866; 1867; Orpington, 1882 (with new Preface), 1884; New York, 1884, 1885; Orpington, 1886, 1887, 1888; New York, 1888; Chicago, 1889; Orpington, 1889, 1890, 1891; New York, 1891, 1892; Philadelphia, 1892; Orpington, 1892; 1894; 1896; 1897; 1898 (bis); New York, 1898; 1900 (bis); New York, 1900 (10 edns); Cambridge, U.S.A. 1900, etc.; ed. Sir O. Lodge, 1907 (Everyman's Lib., with The Two Paths, etc.) ed. T. Cartwright, 1908; ed. A. E. Roberts, 1910. Tr. Swedish, Stockholm, 1900; German, Leipzig, 1900; French, Paris, 1906 (by Marcel Proust); Spanish, Madrid, 1907; Italian, Milan, 1907; Hungarian, Budapest, 1911. [Also rev. and enlarged with new Preface and a third lecture 'The Mystery of Life and its Arts' as Collected Works, vol. I, Keston, 1871. Rptd in this form: New York, 1876; Orpington, 1876, 1880; New York, 1880; Orpington, 1883, 1887; New York,

1889, 1890; Orpington, 1893, 1894, 1895; New York, 1895; 1896; 1897; Toronto, 1897, 1898; New York, 1898; 1898 (bis); 1899; 1900; New York, 1900 (4 edns); Portland, Maine, 1900, etc.; ed. A. H. Bates, New York, 1909.]

   Warren, P. W. T. Notes on Ruskin's 'Sesame and Lilies.' Cape Town, 1898.
   —— Reader's Companion to 'Sesame and Lilies.' 1899.
   Booth, J. B. Notes on 'Sesame and Lilies.' St George, IV, v, 1901–2.

Of Kings' Treasuries. New York, 1899; 1902; ed. E. D. Jones, 1907.

The Queen's Gardens. A Lecture delivered at the Town Hall, Manchester. On Wednesday, Dec. 14, 1864. Manchester, 1864. [A forgery executed between 1880 and 1890; see Collected Works ed. Sir E. T. Cook and A. D. O. Wedderburn, vol. XVIII, pp. 13–5, and J. Carter and G. Pollard, An Enquiry into the Nature of Certain Nineteenth Century Pamphlets, 1934, pp. 232–5.]

Of Queens' Gardens. New York, 1899; 1902.

The Mystery of Life and its Arts. New York, 1869. [First pbd in The Afternoon Lectures on Literature and Art, ser. 5, Dublin, 1869.]

An Inquiry into some of the Conditions at present affecting the Study of Architecture in our Schools. New York, 1865; New York, 1866, 1876. [First pbd in The Sessional Papers of the Royal Institute of British Architects, pt 3, 1864–5; rptd in On the Old Road, vol. I, 1885.]

The Ethics of the Dust. Ten Lectures to Little Housewives on the Elements of Crystallisation. 1866; New York, 1866, 1876; Orpington, 1877 (with new Preface), 1883; New York, 1885; Orpington, 1886, 1888; New York, 1889, 1890; Orpington, 1890; New York, 1891; Orpington, 1892; Philadelphia, 1893; Orpington, 1894 (adds Index), 1896, 1898, 1900, etc.; ed. G. Rhys, 1908 (Everyman's Lib.); ed. R. O. Morris, 1914.

The Crown of Wild Olive. Three Lectures on Work, Traffic and War. 1866 (3 edns); New York, 1866, 1876; Orpington, 1882 (vol. VI of Collected Works; rev. and adding both a 4th lecture 'The Future of England' and 'Notes on the Political Economy of Russia'); New York, 1885; Orpington, 1886, 1889; New York, 1889, 1890 (bis); Orpington, 1890; New York, 1891; Orpington, 1892, 1894 (adds Index), 1895, 1897; ed. J. C. Saul and D. M. Duncan, Toronto, 1897; 1898; 1899; 1900; New York, 1900 (14 edns); Boston, 1900; Philadelphia, 1900; Chicago, 1900, etc.; ed. C. Bax, 1907 (Everyman's

Lib.); ed. W. F. Melton, New York, 1919 (with The Queen of the Air). Tr. French, Paris, 1900; German, Leipzig, 1901.
War. A Lecture delivered at the Royal Military Academy, Woolwich. 1866 (priv. ptd).
[The Future of England.] A Paper read at the Royal Artillery Institution, Woolwich, Dec. 14, 1869. Woolwich, 1869. [This title appears on the wrapper. An unauthorised type facs. without wrappers is discussed by J. Carter and G. Pollard, An Enquiry into the Nature of Certain Nineteenth Century Pamphlets, 1934, pp. 238–9.]
Time and Tide By Weare and Tyne. Twenty-Five Letters to a Working Man of Sunderland on the Laws of Work. 1867 (bis); New York, 1868; New York, 1876, 1884, 1885 (bis); Orpington, 1886, 1891; New York, 1891; 1894 (with Index); 1897; 1899; 1900, etc.; rptd 1910 (Everyman's Lib., with other Ruskin essays; ed. P. Kaufman, New York, 1928; tr. Swedish, Stockholm, 1903. [First pbd in Leeds Mercury, 1 March–4 May 1867, Manchester Daily Examiner and Times, 1 March–7 May 1867; Letters i, ii, Scotsman, 27 Feb., 4 March 1867; Letter v, Pall Mall Gazette, 1 March 1867.]
Leoni: A Legend of Italy. By J. R. 1868. [A forgery executed between 1880 and 1890; see Collected Works, ed. Sir E. T. Cook and A. D. O. Wedderburn, vol. i, p. 288, and J. Carter and G. Pollard, An Enquiry into the Nature of Certain Nineteenth Century Pamphlets, 1934, pp. 236–7. Originally pbd in Friendship's Offering, 1837.]
First Notes on the General Principles of Employment for the Destitute and Criminal Classes. 1868 (priv. ptd); 1868 (enlarged and with 'First' omitted from title). [Rptd with further addns in The Queen of the Air, 1869. Portions of the 2nd version were ptd in Daily Telegraph, 26 Dec. 1868, together with a letter from Ruskin. These are rptd together with the complete text of the pamphlet in Arrows of the Chace, vol. ii, 1880.]
The Queen of the Air; being a Study of the Greek Myths of Cloud and Storm. 1869 (bis); New York, 1869; New York, 1876, 1885 (bis); Orpington, 1887; New York, 1889; 1890; New York, 1891; 1892; 1895 (adds Index); 1898; 1900; Chicago, 1900, etc.; tr. German, Strasburg, 1905. [Rptd in part from the preceding item and from passages in The Cestus of Aglaia (see below). For a critical study see R. W. Bond, St George, vi, Jan. 1903, pp. 46–74.]
Samuel Prout. Oxford, 1870 (priv. ptd). [A forgery? See J. Carter and G. Pollard, An

Enquiry into the Nature of Certain Nineteenth Century Pamphlets, 1934, pp. 240–1. First pbd in Art Journ. March 1849, rptd in On the Old Road, vol. i, 1885, and in Ruskin on Painting, 1902.]
Lectures on Art delivered before the University of Oxford in Hilary Term, 1870. Oxford, 1870; New York, 1870; Oxford, 1875; New York, 1876; Oxford, 1880; New York, 1885; Orpington, 1887 (rev.); New York, 1889; Orpington, 1890; New York, 1891; Orpington, 1891, 1894 (with Index), 1898, 1900, etc.; tr. German, Leipzig, 1901.
The Range of Intellectual Conception is proportioned to the Rank in Animated Life. Metaphysical Society's Papers. No. xvi. [1871] (priv. ptd). [Rptd in Contemporary Rev. June 1871, and in On the Old Road, vol. i, 1885.]
Fors Clavigera. Letters to the Workmen and Labourers of Great Britain. 8 vols. 1871–84; New York, 1876 (vols. i–v); New York, 1880, 1884 (vols. i–vii); New York, 1886 (vols. i–viii); 3 vols. New York, 1890; 4 vols. New York, 1891; 8 vols. New York, 1899. [Vols. i–vii appeared each year 1871–7, every vol. being originally issued in 12 pts on the 1st or 2nd of each month; the 12 pts of vol. viii were issued irregularly Jan. 1878–Christmas 1884. Most of the pts were rptd two or three times.]
Letter to Young Girls. [Orpington, 1876]; [Orpington, 1890] (18th edn). [Letters 65, 66.]
Fors Clavigera. A New Edition. Ed. W. G. Collingwood, 4 vols. Orpington, 1896, 1899–1902, etc. [Though professing to omit only the letters to Ruskin, this abridgement actually omits some of Ruskin's own words.]
Readings in John Ruskin's 'Fors Clavigera.' [Ed. C. A. Wurtzburg], Orpington, 1899.
Faunthorpe, J. P. Index to Fors Clavigera. Orpington, 1887. [Contains an Appendix of over-matter not included in Fors Clavigera itself. The indexes to vols. i, ii, and vols. iii, iv, first appeared in 1873 and 1875 respectively; both were rptd once.]
Munera Pulveris. Six Essays on the Elements of Political Economy. Keston, 1872 (= Collected Works, vol. ii); New York, 1873; Orpington, 1880; New York, 1885; Orpington, 1886; New York, 1889, 1891; Orpington, 1894, 1898, 1899, etc.; rptd 1907 (Everyman's Lib., with The Political Economy of Art and 'Unto this Last'); ed. P. Kaufman, New York, 1928 (with Time and Tide); tr. Spanish, Madrid, 1907.

[First pbd in Fraser's Mag. June 1862–April 1863.]

Gold. A Dialogue connected with the subject of 'Munera Pulveris.' Ed. H. B. Forman, 1891 (priv. ptd). [A reply to criticism by J. E. Cairnes, Macmillan's Mag. Nov. 1863.]

Aratra Pentelici. Six Lectures on the Elements of Sculpture. Keston, 1872 (= Collected Works, vol. III); New York, 1876 (bis); Orpington, 1879; New York, 1885; Orpington, 1890 (adds next item); New York, 1891, 1892, etc.; tr. German, Strasburg, [1903] (5 lectures).

The Relation between Michael Angelo and Tintoret. Seventh of the course of Lectures on Sculpture delivered at Oxford, 1870–71. Keston, 1872; Orpington, 1879, 1887. [Rptd in 1890 and subsequent edns of Aratra Pentelici.]

The Eagle's Nest. Ten Lectures on the Relation of Natural Science to Art, given before the University of Oxford in Lent Term, 1872. Keston, 1872 (= Collected Works, vol. IV); New York, 1876; Orpington, 1880; New York, 1885, 1886; Orpington, 1887, 1891; New York, 1891, 1892; Orpington, 1894 (adds Index), 1897, 1899, 1900, etc.; tr. German, Strasburg, [1902] (5 lectures).

The Sepulchral Monuments of Italy. Monuments of the Cavalli Family in the Church of Santa Anastasia, Verona. Arundel Soc. 1872. [Rptd in On the Old Road, vol. I, 1885.]

The Nature and Authority of Miracle. Metaphysical Society's Papers, no. xxxii. 1873 (priv. ptd). [Another edn dated 1873 is probably a forgery. See J. Carter and G. Pollard, An Enquiry into the Nature of Certain Nineteenth Century Pamphlets, 1934, pp. 242–3. First pbd in Contemporary Rev. March 1873; rptd in On the Old Road, vol. II, 1885.]

Love's Meinie. Lectures on Greek and English Birds. Given before the University of Oxford. Lecture I. The Robin. Keston, 1873. Lecture II. The Swallow. Keston, 1873. Lecture III. The Dabchicks. Orpington, 1881. [Lectures I, II rptd New York, 1876, Orpington, 1883, 1892. Collected edns: Orpington, 1881; New York, 1885; Orpington, 1893, 1897 (adds Index), etc. Lecture IV (The Chough) first pbd in Collected Works, ed. T. Cook and A. D. O. Wedderburn, vol. xxv.]

The Poetry of Architecture; or, The Architecture of the Nations of Europe considered in its association with natural scenery and national character. New York, 1873, 1876, 1890; Orpington, 1893 (1st authorised edn), etc. [First pbd in Architectural Mag.

Nov. 1837–Dec. 1838, and rptd in The Crayon (New York), I, 1855.]

Ariadne Florentina. Six Lectures on Wood and Metal Engraving. With Appendix. Given before the University of Oxford, in Michaelmas Term, 1872. Orpington, 1876 (= Collected Works, vol. VII); New York, 1876; Orpington, 1890; New York, 1891, etc. [Originally issued in 7 pts: pts I, II, 1873; pts III, IV, 1874; pts V, VI, VII, 1875.]

Val D'Arno. Ten Lectures on the Tuscan Art directly antecedent to the Florentine Year of Victories, Given before the University of Oxford in Michaelmas Term, 1874. Orpington, 1874 (= Collected Works, vol. VIII), 1882; New York, 1885, 1886; Orpington, 1890; New York, 1891; 1900 (with Index), etc.

Mornings in Florence: Being Simple Studies of Christian Art, for English Travellers. 6 pts, Orpington, 1876–7, 1881–3, 1889–92 (pt I also rptd 1894); Orpington, 1885; New York, 1886; Orpington, 1889, 1894 (adds Index), 1899, etc. Tr. German, Strasburg, [1901]; French, Paris, 1906.

The Shepherd's Tower. A Series of Photographs of the Sculptures of Giotto's Tower. To illustrate Part VI of 'Mornings in Florence.' 1881.

Proserpina. Studies of Wayside Flowers, while the Air was yet pure among the Alps, and in the Scotland and England which my Father knew. Vol. I (all collected), Orpington, 1879, 1882, 1883; New York, 1885, 1886. [Originally issued in 6 pts. Pt I: 1875; New York, 1876; Orpington, 1878, 1883, 1884. Pt II: 1875; New York, 1876; Orpington, 1879, 1886. Pt III: 1876; New York, 1876; Orpington, 1879, 1889. Pt IV: 1876; New York, 1877; Orpington, 1880, 1889. Pt V: 1878; New York, 1878; Orpington, 1881, 1896. Pt VI: 1879; New York, 1879; Orpington, 1882, 1897. Only 4 pts of vol. II were pbd: pt VII, 1882; pt VIII, 1882; pt IX, 1885; pt X, 1886.]

Deucalion. Collected Studies of the Lapse of Waves, and Life of Stones. Vol. I (all collected), Orpington, 1879, 1882; New York, 1885, 1886, 1889; Orpington, 1891; Boston, 1900. [Originally issued in 6 pts. Pt I: 1875; New York, 1876; Orpington, 1883. Pt II: 1875; New York, 1876; Orpington, 1883. Pt III: 1876; New York, 1877; Orpington, 1883. Pt IV: 1876; New York, 1877; Orpington, 1883. Pt V: 1878; 1888. Pt VI: 1879. Only 2 pts of vol. II were pbd: pt VII, 1880; pt VIII, 1883.]

'Yewdale and its Streamlets.' Report of a Lecture delivered in connection with the Kendal Literary and Scientific Institute. Kendal, 1877. [First pbd in Kendal

Mercury, 6 Oct. 1877, and Kendal Times, 6 Oct. 1877. The lecture forms ch. xii in Deucalion, pt v.]

Collingwood, W. G. The Limestone Alps of Savoy. Orpington, 1884. [Supplements Deucalion.]

Letters to 'The Times' on the principal Pre-Raphaelite Pictures in the Exhibition of 1854. From the Author of 'Modern Painters.' 1876 (priv. ptd). [Originally pbd in The Times, 5, 25 May 1854; rptd in Arrows of the Chace, vol. i, 1880, and in 'A. G. Crawford' (A. G. Wise), Notes on the Pictures of Mr Holman Hunt, Exhibited at the Rooms of the Fine Art Society, 1886.]

Guide to the Principal Pictures in the Academy of Fine Arts at Venice. Arranged for English Travellers. 2 pts, Venice, 1877; Orpington, 1882–3; 1891 (rev.). Tr. Italian, Florence, 1901; French, Paris, 1908.

Notes by Mr. Ruskin on his Drawings by the late J. M. W. Turner, Exhibited at the Fine Art Society's Galleries March, 1878. Also an Appendix containing a List of the Engraved Works of J. M. W. Turner exhibited at the same time. [1878] (bis); 1878 (with Addenda and Epilogue) (4 edns); 1878 (rev. with appendix by W. Kingsley) (bis); 1878 (with 2nd pt 'On his own Handiwork illustrative of Turner'); 1878 (pt ii rev.) (4 edns). [Rptd with Catalogue of the Exhibition of the Same Drawings, 1900, and in Ruskin on Pictures, vol. i, 1902.]

St. Mark's Rest. The History of Venice, Written for the help of the few Travellers who still care for her monuments. New York, 1879; Orpington, 1884 (1st complete and authorised collection); New York, 1884, 1885, 1886, 1889; Orpington, 1894; Chicago, 1900; Boston, 1900. Tr. Italian, Florence, 1901; French, Paris, 1908. [Originally issued in 6 sections. Pt i: 1877; 1884; 1889; 1894. Pt ii: 1877; 1889. 1st Supplement: 1877; 1887; 1889; 1894; tr. Italian, Orpington, 1885 (priv. ptd). Pt iii: 1879; 1887; 1889; 1894. 2nd Supplement: 1870; 1889. Appendix: 1884, 1894.]

The Laws of Fiesole. A familiar treatise on the elementary principles and practice of Drawing and Painting. As Determined by the Tuscan Masters. Arranged for the use of schools. Vol. i (all pbd), Orpington, 1879; New York, 1879; Orpington, 1882, 1890; Boston, 1900, etc.

Notes on Samuel Prout and William Hunt, illustrated by a loan Collection of Drawings, exhibited at the Fine Art Society's Galleries. 1879–80 (4 edns); 1880. [Rptd in Ruskin on Pictures, vol. ii, 1902.]

Circular respecting Memorial Studies of St. Mark's, Venice, now in progress under Mr. Ruskin's direction. 1879; 1879 (adds Postscript); 1880.

Letters addressed by Prof. Ruskin to the Clergy on the Lord's Prayer and the Church. Ed. F. A. Malleson, 1879 (priv. ptd); [1880] (adds Replies from Clergy and Laity, and an Epilogue by Mr Ruskin); 1883; 1896 (rev. and with additional letters); New York, 1896. [Also ptd in Contemporary Rev. Dec. 1879. Ruskin's letters rptd in On the Old Road, vol. i, 1885, and separately from the holograph originals, ed. T. J. Wise, 1896 (priv. ptd).]

Sillar, W. C. A Defence of the Church of England against the Accusations contained in the Letters of Mr Ruskin in The Contemporary Review. 1880.

Elements of English Prosody for use in St George's Schools. Explanatory of the various terms used in 'Rock Honeycomb.' 1880.

Arrows of the Chace Being a Collection of scattered Letters published chiefly in the Daily Newspapers. 1840–1880. And now edited by an Oxford Pupil [A. D. O. Wedderburn] with a Preface by the Author. 2 vols. Orpington, 1880; New York, 1881, 1890. [Vol. i, Letters on Art and Science; vol. ii, Letters on Politics, Economy and Miscellaneous Matters.]

'Our Fathers have told us.' Sketches of the History of Christendom for Boys and Girls who have been held at its fonts. Orpington, 1884; New York, 1886 (3 edns); 1890; Orpington, 1897, etc. Tr. French, Paris, 1903 (by Marcel Proust); Spanish, Madrid, 1907. [Originally issued in 5 pts. Ch. i: 1880; 1883; 1893. Ch. ii: 1881; 1885. Ch. iii: 1882; 1885. Ch. iv: 1883; 1893. Ch. iv had been previously pbd in a 'Separate Travellers' Edition to serve as a Guide to the Cathedral,' Orpington, 1881, 1886, 1897, 1898. Ruskin projected a 6th pt entitled Valle Crucis, 2 chs. of which were first ptd in Verona and other Lectures, 1894. An intended 3rd pt, entitled Ara Coeli, was first ptd in Collected Works, ed. Sir E. T. Cook and A. D. O. Wedderburn, vol. xxxiii.]

The Art of England. Lectures given in Oxford. Orpington, 1884; New York, 1883–4, 1885 (bis), 1886; Orpington, 1887; New York, 1889, 1892; Orpington, 1898, 1898 (with The Pleasures of England), 1900, etc. [Originally issued in 7 pts. Pt i: 1883 (bis); 1890. Pt ii: 1883 (bis); 1893. Pt iii: 1883; 1884; 1898. Pt iv: 1883; 1884; 1898. Pt v: 1883; 1885. Pt vi: 1883; 1885. Pt vii: 1884; 1887; 1893.]

The Pleasures of England. Lectures given in Oxford. Orpington, 1884; New York, 1885 (pts i–iii), 1885 (complete); Orpington,

1898 (with The Art of England); 1900, etc. [Issued in 4 pts: pts I, II, 1884; pts III, IV, 1885.]

The Storm Cloud of the Nineteenth Century. Two Lectures delivered at the London Institution, Feb. 4 & 11, 1884. 2 pts, Orpington, 1884; New York, 1884; 1885. [First lecture fully reported in The Times, 5 Feb. 1884, Pall Mall Gazette, 5 Feb. 1884 (by Sir E. T. Cook), and Art Journ. April 1884 (by A. D. O. Wedderburn.]

On the Old Road. A Collection of Miscellaneous Essays, Pamphlets, &c. &c. published 1834–1885. [Ed. A. D. O. Wedderburn], 2 vols. Orpington, 1885; 3 vols. Orpington, 1899 (rev.), etc.

Praeterita. Outlines of Scenes and Thoughts perhaps worthy of Memory in my past Life. Volume I. Orpington, 1886 (bis); New York, 1886 (bis), 1889; 3 vols. New York, 1890 (with vol. II); New York, 1892; Orpington, 1899, 1900.; tr. German, Strasburg, 1903, Leipzig, 1903. [Largely from Fors Clavigera. Originally issued in 12 pts: pts I–VII, 1885, pts VIII–XII, 1886, rptd New York, 1885–6.]

Praeterita. Volume II. Orpington, 1887; New York, 1889; 3 vols. New York, 1890 (with vol. I); New York, 1892; Orpington, 1899, 1900; tr. German, Strasburg, 1903, Leipzig, 1903. [Originally issued in 12 pts: pts XIII–XX, 1886, pts XXI–XXIV, 1887, rptd New York, 1886–7.]

Praeterita. Volume III. 4 pts, Orpington, 1888–9; New York, 1888–9; Orpington, 1900 (with Index and 'Dilecta') (bis), etc. [Pts XXV, XXVI, 1888; pts XXVII, XXVIII, 1889.]

Dilecta. Correspondence, Diary Notes, and Extracts from Books, illustrating Praeterita. 3 pts, Orpington, 1886–1900. [Pt II, 1887; pt III first issued with rpt of pts I, II, and Praeterita, vol. III, 1900.]

Hortus Inclusus. Messages from the Wood to the Garden, sent in happy days to the Sister Ladies of the Thwaite, Coniston. [Mary and Susie Beever.] [Ed. A. Fleming], Orpington, 1887; New York, 1887; Orpington, 1888; New York, 1892 (with 'In Montibus Sanctis' and 'Coeli Enarrant'), etc.

Ruskiniana. Part I. Letters published in, and Collected from various sources, and mostly reprinted in Igdrasil, 1890. [Ed. A. D. O. Wedderburn], 1890 (priv. ptd).

Ruskiniana. Part II. Lectures and Addresses reported in the Press, but not reprinted in Collected Works. [Ed. A. D. O. Wedderburn], 1892 (priv. ptd).

Letters upon Subjects of General Interest from John Ruskin to Various Correspondents. Ed. T. J. Wise, 1892 (priv. ptd).

Stray Letters from Professor Ruskin to a London Bibliopole [F. S. Ellis]. Ed. T. J. Wise, 1892 (priv. ptd).

Letters from John Ruskin to William Ward. Ed. T. J. Wise, 2 vols. 1893 (priv. ptd); Boston, 1922 (with short biography of William Ward by William C. Ward, and introduction by Alfred Mansfield Brooks).

Three Letters and an Essay. By John Ruskin. 1836–41. Found in his Tutor's [Canon Dale] Desk. [Ed. H. P. Dale], Orpington, 1893.

Letters on Art and Literature. Ed. T. J. Wise, 1894 (priv. ptd).

Letters to Ernest Chesneau. Ed. T. J. Wise, 1894 (priv. ptd).

Verona and Other Lectures. [Ed. W. G. Collingwood], Orpington, 1894. [The title lecture was delivered at The Royal Institution, 4 Feb. 1870; a partial report appeared in Pall Mall Gazette, 5 Feb. 1870; rptd in Igdrasil, March 1892, vol. III, pp. 241–7. Two of the other lectures were for an intended continuation of 'Our Fathers have told us' (see above).]

Letters Addressed to a College Friend [Edward Clayton] during the years 1840–45. Orpington, 1894; New York, 1894.

Letters to Rev. F. J. Faunthorpe. Ed. T. J. Wise, 2 vols. 1895–6 (priv. ptd).

Letters to F. J. Furnivall. Ed. T. J. Wise, 1897 (priv. ptd).

Lectures on Landscape. Delivered at Oxford in 1871. Orpington, 1897.

Letters to M. G. & H. G. [Mary and Helen Gladstone] With a Preface by the Rt. Hon. G. Wyndham. Edinburgh, 1903 (priv. ptd); New York, 1903. [Rptd, with some remarks by Adam Scot, in North American Rev. July 1903.]

Comments of John Ruskin on the Divina Commedia. Compiled by G. P. Huntington, with an introduction by C. E. Norton. Boston, 1903.

The Letters of John Ruskin to C. E. Norton. [Ed. C. E. Norton], 2 vols. Boston, 1903.

The Cestus of Aglaia. Orpington, 1905; ed. C. Bax, 1907 (Everyman's Lib.). [Originally appeared in Art Journ. Jan.–July 1865, Jan., Feb., April 1866. Chs. ii, vi were incorporated in The Queen of the Air, 1869; the rest of the work was rptd in On the Old Road, vol. I, 1885.]

The Solitary Warrior: New Letters by Ruskin. Ed. J. Howard Whitehouse, 1929.

(6) CONTRIBUTIONS TO PERIODICALS

[Ruskin's longer contributions to periodicals were partly collected in On the Old Road, 2 vols. 1885. A complete list of those pbd in his lifetime is given in T. J. Wise and J. P. Smart, A Bibliography of John Ruskin, vol. II, pp.

111–22. A complete list of Ruskin's letters to newspapers is given in Collected Works, ed. E. T. Cook and A. D. O. Wedderburn, vol. XXXVIII, pp. 48–55. They were largely collected in Arrows of the Chace, 2 vols. 1880, and in Ruskiniana, pt I, 1890. It has only been possible to list here matter not hitherto collected in book form.]

On the Convergence of Perpendiculars. The [Loudon's] Architectural Mag. Feb. 1838–Jan. 1839.

On the Propriety of Combining Works of Art with the Sublimity of Nature Considered. The [Loudon's] Architectural Mag. Jan. 1839.

Notice respecting some Artificial Sections illustrating the Geology of Chamouni. Communicated in a letter to Prof. Forbes. Proc. Royal Soc. of Edinburgh, IV, 1857–8. [There is also a separate offprint.]

Notes on the Shape and Structure of some Parts of the Alps with reference to Denudation. Geological Mag. Feb., May 1865.

On Banded and Brecciated Concretions. Geological Mag. Aug. 1867–Jan. 1870. [There was also a separate offprint of each article.]

Railways in Derbyshire. Manchester City News, 2, 7, 13 April 1884.

The Best Hundred Books. Pall Mall Gazette, 19 Jan., 15, 23 Feb. 1886.

Notes on Bewick's 'Birds.' Art Journ. Oct., Dec. 1886.

Arthur Burgess. Century Guild Hobby Horse, April 1887.

Books which have influenced me. British Weekly Extra, 1887.

Letters of John Ruskin to his Secretary [C. A. Howell]. New Rev. March 1892.

[14 Letters to Miss Adelaide Ironside.] Catholic Press (Sydney), 3 Feb. 1900.

John Ruskin to Rawdon Brown: Unpublished Correspondence. Ed. P. Kaufmann, North American Rev. Sept.–Dec. 1925.

A Girl's [Jessie Leete] Friendship with Ruskin. Ed. L. Huxley, Cornhill Mag. Dec. 1926, Jan. 1927; Atlantic Monthly, Dec. 1926, Jan. 1927.

The Giustiani Memoirs. Ed. P. Dearmer, London Mercury, Oct. 1927. [Ruskin letters.]

Letters to Francesca and Memoirs of the Alexanders, by Lucia Gray Swett. Ed. W. C. De Vane, Boston, 1931.

(7) BOOKS EDITED BY RUSKIN, OR TO WHICH HE SUPPLIED PREFACES, NOTES OR APPENDICES

Repton, Humphrey. Landscape Gardening. 1840. [Footnote on the Proper Shapes of Pictures and Engravings, pp. 32–8.]

Handbook for Travellers in Northern Italy. 1847 (3rd edn). [Notes. Also in 4th (1852),

5th (1854) and 6th edns; incorporated in the text in subsequent edns.]

The Report of the National Gallery Site Commission. 1857. [Evidence, pp. 92–7. Rptd in Literary Gazette, 22 Aug. 1857, and in On the Old Road, vol. I, 1885.]

The Report from the Select Committee [of the House of Commons] on Public Institutions, 1860. [Evidence, pp. 113–23; rptd in On the Old Road, vol. I, 1885.]

The Report of the Royal Academy Commission. 1863. [Evidence, pp. 546–55; rptd in On the Old Road, vol. I, 1885.]

German Popular Stories. Ed. Edgar Taylor, 1868. [Introduction.]

Tyrwhitt, St John. Christian Art and Symbolism. 1872. [Preface; rptd in On the Old Road, vol. I, 1885.]

Catalogue of an Exhibition of Outlines by the late John Leech, at the Gallery, 9 Conduit Street. 1872. [Preface. Rptd in The Times, 8 May 1872, in Percival Leigh, Portraits of Children of the Mobility illustrated by John Leech, 1875 (first pbd 1841), in Arrows of the Chace, vol. I, 1880.]

Rendu, Louis. Theory of the Glaciers of Savoy. Translated by Alfred Wills. Ed. George Forbes, 1874. [Supplementary Articles, pp. 199–200. Rptd in Arrows of the Chace, vol. I, 1880.]

Corporation of Brighton. The Exhibition of Pictures lent by Prof. Ruskin and The Arundel Society opened April 6, 1876, The Royal Pavilion Gallery. [Brighton, 1876.] [Note on Botticelli's Zipporah.]

Owen, A. C. The Art Schools of Mediaeval Christendom. 1876. [Preface and footnotes. Rptd in On the Old Road, vol. I, 1885.]

Somervell, Robert. A Protest against the Extension of Railways in the Lake District. Windermere, [1876]. [Preface, and extracts from Fors Clavigera. Rptd in On the Old Road, vol. I, 1885.]

Bibliotheca Pastorum. Edited by John Ruskin. Vol. I. The Economist of Xenophon. Tr. A. D. O. Wedderburn and W. G. Collingwood, Orpington, 1876. Vol. II. Rock Honeycomb. Broken Pieces of Sir Philip Sidney's Psalter. Laid up in store for English Homes. 2 pts, Orpington, 1877. [No Vol. III.] Vol. IV. A Knight's Faith. Passages in the life of Sir Herbert Edwardes collated by John Ruskin. Orpington, 1885.

The Science of Life: A Pamphlet addressed to All Members of the Universities of Oxford and Cambridge, and all who are or who will be, Teachers, Clergymen, Fathers. 1877; 1878. [3 letters: 2, 3 in 1st edn; 1, 3 in 2nd edn. Rptd in Arrows of the Chace, vol. II, 1885.]

Zorzi, Alvise Piero. Osservazioni intorno ai ristauri interni ed esterni della Basilica di San Marco. Venice, 1877. [Letter, pp. 11–22. Rptd in Igdrasil, May 1890, and Ruskiniana, pt I, 1890.]

Swan, Henry. Collected Notes on Some of the Pictures in the St. George's Museum, Sheffield. [Sheffield, 1879.] [Note on Fra Filippi and Carpaccio.]

Notes on Drawings by Mr Ruskin, placed on exhibition by Prof. Norton. Boston, Oct. 1879. Cambridge, U.S.A. 1879. [Notes on his own drawings.]

Catalogue of the First Exhibition of Pictures and Water Colour Drawings &c. at Douglas, Isle of Man, with original notes by Prof. Ruskin. Douglas, 1880.

The Ruskin Cabinet at Whitelands College. Notes on the sixty pictures by Prof. Ruskin. [London] 1883.

[Alexander, Francesca.] The Story of Ida: Epitaph on an Etrurian Tomb. By Francesca. Edited, with a Preface by John Ruskin. Orpington, 1883.

Horsfall, T. C. The Study of Beauty and Art in Large Towns. 1883. [Introduction. Rptd in On the Old Road, vol. I, 1885.]

Collingwood, W. G. Deucalion—First Supplement. The Limestone Alps of Savoy; a study in Physical Geology. Orpington, 1884. [Preface.]

The Bishop of Oxford and Prof. Ruskin on Vivisection. Victoria Soc. for Protection of Animals from Vivisection, 1885.

Alexander, Francesca. Roadside Songs of Tuscany. Translated and Illustrated by Francesca Alexander. Orpington, 1885. [Originally issued in 10 pts from April 1884–Aug. 1885.]

Chesneau, Ernest. The English School of Painting. Translated by L. N. Etherington. 1885. [Introduction.]

Usury, its Pernicious Effects on English Agriculture and Commerce. An Allegory Dedicated, without permission, to the Bishops of Manchester, Peterborough and Rochester. [Ed. R. G. Sillar], 1885. [Introduction. Rptd in On the Old Road, vol. II, 1885.]

Dame Wiggins of Lee and her Seven Wonderful Cats. Edited with additional verses by John Ruskin. Orpington, 1885.

[Wise, A. G.] Notes on Some of the Principal Pictures of Sir John Everett Millais at the Grosvenor Gallery by A. Gordon Crawford with a Preface and Original and Selected Criticisms by John Ruskin. London, 1886.

A Catalogue of the Exhibition of Water Colour Drawings by Deceased Masters of the British School at the Royal Institute. London. 1886. [Appendix. Rptd in Ruskiniana, pt I, 1890.]

Turner's Rivers of France. 2 vols. 1887. [The Introduction consists of unauthorised extracts from Modern Painters.]

[Bitzius, Albert.] Ulric the Farm Servant. A Story of the Bernese Lowland. By Jeremias Gotthelf. Translated into English by Julia Firth. Orpington, 1888. [Issued in 9 pts from July 1886–Oct. 1888. Preface and Notes.]

Cook, Sir Edward Tyas. A Popular Handbook to the National Gallery including, by special permission, notes collected from the works of Mr Ruskin. 1888. [Also Preface.]

Alexander, Francesca. Christ's Folk in the Apennine. Reminiscences of her friends among the Tuscan Peasantry. Orpington, 1889. [Issued in pts 1887–9. Preface, etc.]

White, William. The Principles of Art as Illustrated in the Ruskin Museum, Sheffield, with passages from the Writings of John Ruskin. 1895. [Notes.]

Spielmann, M. H. and Layard, G. S. Kate Greenaway. 1905. [110 letters.]

Brown, John. The Letters of Dr John Brown. Edited by his son and D. W. Forrest. 1907. [Letters.]

(8) Biography and Criticism
(a) Books

Milsand, J. L'Esthétique anglaise. Étude sur M. John Ruskin. Paris, 1864; Lausanne, 1906.

Green, B. H. Mr. Ruskin: his Opinions and Comparisons of Painters. A Few Remarks dedicated to the Shades of Raphael, Correggio, and Murillo. 1869.

Walker, R. B. John Ruskin. Manchester, 1879.

Baillie, E. J. John Ruskin: Aspects of his Thought and Teaching. Orpington, 1882.

Mather, J. M. Life and Teaching of John Ruskin. Manchester, 1883.

Smart, William. A Disciple of Plato. A Critical Study of John Ruskin. With a Note by Mr. Ruskin. Glasgow, 1883.

Geddes, P. The Round Table Series III: John Ruskin, Economist. Edinburgh, 1884.

Collingwood, W. G. John Ruskin: a Biographical Outline. 1889.
—— The Art Teaching of John Ruskin. 1891.
—— The Life and Work of John Ruskin. 2 vols. 1893; 1900 (as The Life of John Ruskin, with more biography and less criticism than in the earlier edn).
—— Ruskin Relics. 1903.
—— Kunst, Arbeide, Opdragelse. Copenhagen, 1906. [A trn of 3 lectures at Copenhagen.]

Cook, Sir E. T. Studies in Ruskin. Orpington, 1890.
—— The Life of John Ruskin. 1911.

Cook, Sir E. T. Homes and Haunts of John Ruskin. 1912.

Downes, R. P. John Ruskin: a Study. 1890.

Scudder, V. D. An Introduction to the Writings of John Ruskin. Boston, 1890.

Waldstein, later Walston, Sir C. The Work of John Ruskin: its Influence on Modern Thought and Life. 1894.

Middlemiss, J. T. A Modern Prophet and his Message: John Ruskin. Sunderland, 1896.

La Sizeranne, Robert de. Ruskin et la Religion de la Beauté. Paris, 1897; tr. Eng. Orpington, 1899 (with 2 appendices by George Allen). [First pbd in La Revue des Deux Mondes, cxxxii–cxl, 1895–7.]

Fechheimer, S. S. Ueber die Bedeutung Ruskins für das Leben und die Erziehung in England. Jena, 1898.

Hobson, J. A. John Ruskin, Social Reformer. 1898.

Rossetti, W. M. Ruskin, Rossetti and Pre-Raphaelitism. 1899.

Bardoux, J. Le Mouvement idéaliste et social dans la Littérature anglaise au XIXe Siècle. John Ruskin. [Paris, 1900.]

—— John Ruskin, Poète, Artiste, Apôtre. Paris, 1931.

The Bookman. Ruskin Memorial Number, March 1900.

Hocart, J. John Ruskin, le Prophète du Beau. Brussels, 1900.

Isaacs, A. A. The Fountain of Siena: an Episode in the Life of John Ruskin. 1900.

Meynell, A. John Ruskin. Edinburgh, 1900.

Pengelly, R. E. John Ruskin, a Biographical Sketch. 1000.

Scalinger, G. M. L'Estetica di Ruskin. Naples, 1900.

Spielmann, M. H. John Ruskin: a Sketch of his Life, his Work and his Opinions; with Personal Reminiscences. 1900.

Rawnsley, H. D. Ruskin and the English Lakes. Glasgow, 1901.

Shaw, W. H. John Ruskin, Ethical and Religious Teacher. Oxford, 1901.

Ashbee, C. R. An Endeavour towards the Teaching of John Ruskin and William Morris. Being a Brief Account of the Work, the Aims and the Principles of the Guild of Handicraft in East London. 1901.

Brunhes, H. J. Ruskin et la Bible pour servir à l'Histoire d'une Pensée. Paris, 1902.

Broicher, C. John Ruskin und sein Werk. 3 vols. Leipzig, 1902–7.

Harrison, Frederic. John Ruskin. 1902. (English Men of Letters ser.)

Sänger, S. John Ruskin: sein Leben und Lebenswerk. Strasburg, 1902.

Bunsen, Marie von. John Ruskin: sein Leben und seine Werke. Leipzig, 1903.

Farrar, F. W. Ruskin as a Religious Teacher. 1904.

Powell, F. York. John Ruskin and Thoughts on Democracy. 1905.

Catalogue of the Ruskin Museum, Coniston Institute. 1906 (new edn).

Cherfils, C. Canon de Turner. Essai de Synthèse critique des Théories picturales de Ruskin. Thèses néo-ruskiniennes. Paris, 1906.

The Bookman. Ruskin Double Number, Oct. 1908.

Rainero, C. Il Pensiero di Ruskin e sua Influenza sui Contemporanei. Turin, 1909.

Chevrillon, A. La Pensée de Ruskin. Paris, 1909. [Rptd from La Revue des Deux Mondes, Feb.–July 1908.]

Earland, A. Ruskin and his Circle. 1910.

Guillon, C. Le Christianisme de Ruskin. Cahors, 1910.

Wingate, A. Life of John Ruskin. 1910.

Benson, A. C. Ruskin: a Study in Personality. 1911.

Mollerup, A. John Ruskin: Hovedtanker i hans Vaerker. Copenhagen, 1911.

Symon, J. D. John Ruskin: his Homes and Haunts. 1911.

Vetter, T. John Ruskin und William Morris. Feinde und Forderer der Technik. Zurich, 1912.

Danel, J. Les Idées sociales de Ruskin. Paris, 1913.

Taber, A. E. Work for All. A Co-operative Commonwealth based on Ruskin's Teaching. Leeds, 1914.

[Burdon, J.] Reminiscences of Ruskin. 1919.

Ruskin Centenary Addresses. Ed. J. H. Whitehouse, 1919.

Whitehouse, J. H. Ruskin the Prophet. 1920.

—— Ruskin and Brantwood. An Account of the Exhibition Rooms. Ruskin Soc. 1937.

Masefield, J. John Ruskin. Bembridge, 1920.

Graham, J. W. The Harvest of Ruskin. 1920.

Roe, F. W. The Social Philosophy of Carlyle and Ruskin. New York, 1922.

Collingwood, R. G. Ruskin's Philosophy. 1922.

Thomas, Walter. Ruskin. Paris, 1925.

Williams-Ellis, A. The Tragedy of John Ruskin. 1928.

Kreemers, R. John Ruskin. Zijn Leven en zijn Werken. Oisterwijk, 1930.

Scott, Edith H. Ruskin's Guild of St George. 1931.

Ladd, H. The Victorian Morality of Art. An Analysis of Ruskin's Aesthetic. New York, 1932.

Larg, D. John Ruskin. 1932.

Gally, H. Ruskin et l'Esthétique intuitive. Paris, 1933.

Wilenski, R. H. John Ruskin. 1933.

Whitehouse, J. H. *et al.* To the Memory of Ruskin. Cambridge, 1935.

Crow, G. Ruskin. 1936.

(b) *Pamphlets, Chapters in Books, and Books containing Considerable Reference to Ruskin*

Leslie, C. R. A Hand-book for Young Painters. 1855.

Mitford, M. R. Recollections of a Literary Life. Vol. III, 1855.

—— Correspondence with C. Boner and John Ruskin. Ed. E. Lee, 1914.

B., A. Notes on some of the Critics of John Ruskin. 1856.

Gaskell, E. C. Life of Charlotte Brontë. 2 vols. 1857.

Gladstone, W. E. Studies on Homer and the Homeric Age. Vol. III, Oxford, 1858.

Hamerton, P. G. A Painter's Camp and Thoughts on Art. 2 vols. 1862.

—— Etching and Etchers. 1868.

—— Landscape. 1885.

Thornbury, G. W. The Life of J. M. W. Turner. 2 vols. 1862.

Patterson, R. H. Essays in History and Art. Edinburgh, 1862.

Marsh, G. P. Lectures on the English Language. New York, 1863 (4th edn).

Arnold, Matthew. Essays in Criticism. 1865.

Japp, A. H. Three Great Teachers of our Own Time. 1865.

Rossetti, W. M. Fine Art, chiefly Contemporary. 1867.

—— Dante Gabriel Rossetti. 2 vols. 1895.

—— Pre-Raphaelite Diaries and Letters. 1900.

—— Rossetti Papers. 1903.

Cook, Dutton. Art in England: Notes and Studies. 1869.

Doyle, Sir F. H. Lectures delivered before the University of Oxford, 1868. 1869.

Friswell, J. H. Modern Men of Letters honestly criticised. 1870.

M'Carthy, J. Modern Leaders. New York, 1872.

Eastlake, Sir C. L. A History of the Gothic Revival. 1872.

Taine, H. Notes sur l'Angleterre. Paris, 1872; tr. Eng. 1872.

Kidd, G. B. Mr. Ruskin and Political Economy: a Paper read before the Derby Nomadic Club, March 28, 1873. Derby, 1873.

Torrey, J. A Theory of Fine Art. New York, 1874.

Mallock, W H. The New Republic. 1877. [Ruskin is described as Mr Herbert.]

Whistler, J. A. M'N. Whistler v. Ruskin. Art and Art Critics. 1878. [Rptd in The Gentle Art of Making Enemies, 1890.]

Bayne, P. Lessons from my Masters: Carlyle, Tennyson and Ruskin. 1879.

Poynter, Sir E. J. Lectures on Art. 1879.

Nisbet, H. The Practical in Painting, also a Few Remarks on John Ruskin. Edinburgh, 1880.

Smart, William. John Ruskin: his Life and Work. Inaugural Address delivered before the Ruskin Society of Glasgow, by the President. Manchester, 1880.

Watt, P. B. The Educational Value of Art. Glasgow, 1880.

Cooke, Bancroft. John Ruskin. An Inaugural Address read before the Birkenhead Ruskin Society. Birkenhead, 1881.

Teachers and Preachers of Recent Times. Edinburgh, 1881.

Hamilton, Walter. The Aesthetic Movement in England. 1882.

[Walsh, W. S.] Pen Pictures of Modern Authors, by William Shepard. New York, 1882.

Cassels, W. Wealth: Definitions by Ruskin and Mill compared. Glasgow, 1882.

—— The Social Problem. Glasgow, 1885 (anon.).

'Lee, Vernon' (Violet Paget). Belcaro. 1883.

Froude, J. A. Thomas Carlyle: a History of his Life in London. 1885.

Osler, C. H. John Ruskin: his Aims and Efforts. A Lecture delivered before the Ruskin Society, Sheffield. 1885.

Holmes, John. Two Papers on John Ruskin. Sheffield, 1886. [Rptd from Sheffield Independent, 17 April, 1 May 1886.]

Cooke, G. W. Poets and Problems. Boston, 1886.

Griswold, H. T. Home Life of Great Authors. Chicago, 1887.

Van Dyke, J. C. Principles of Art. New York, 1887.

Martin, W. Aspects of Nature in Relation to Individual and National Life. Glasgow, 1887.

Sewall, Frank. The Ethics of Service. 1888.

Adams, W. D. By-ways in Book-land. 1888.

Cochrane, R. Great Thinkers and Workers. Edinburgh, 1888.

Fergusson, R. M. Quiet Folk. Edinburgh, 1889.

Dyer, Henry. The Foundation of Social Politics. Glasgow, 1889.

Ruskin's Romance, reprinted from a New England Newspaper. 1889. [Largely fictitious.]

Forster, Joseph. Four Great Teachers. 1890.

Story, W. W. Conversations in a Studio. Boston, 1890.

Robertson, J. M. Modern Humanists. 1891.

—— Modern Humanists Reconsidered. 1927.

Rose, H. The New Political Economy: the Social Teaching of Carlyle, Ruskin and George; with Observations on Mazzini. 1891.

Richardson, B. W. Thomas Sopwith, with Excerpts from his Diaries. 1891.

The Communism of John Ruskin. New York, 1891.

Bosanquet, B. A History of Aesthetic. 1892.

Gibbins H. de B. English Social Reformers. 1892.

Oliphant, M. O. and F. R. The Victorian Age of English Literature. 1892.

Ritchie, A. (née Thackeray). Records of Tennyson, Ruskin and Browning. 1892.

Marks, H. S. Pen and Pencil Sketches. 2 vols. 1894.

Reul, P. de. L'Esthétique en Angleterre. Brussels, 1894. [Rptd from La Revue Universitaire.]

Saintsbury, G. Corrected Impressions: Essays on Victorian Writers. 1895.

Brewster, W. T. Studies in Structure and Style. New York, 1896.

Browning, E. B. Letters. Ed. Sir F. G. Kenyon, 2 vols. 1897.

Fowler, J. H. Nineteenth Century Prose. Edinburgh, 1897.

Muir, R. J. Ruskin revised, and Other Papers on Education. Edinburgh, 1897.

Clark, J. Scott. A Study of English Prose Writers. New York, 1898.

Spurgeon, C. H. An Autobiography. 3 vols. 1898.

Marius, G. H. Een Inleiding tot zijn Werken. Hague, 1899.

Dawson, W. H. The Makers of Modern Prose. 1899.

Harrison, Frederic. Tennyson, Ruskin, Mill, and Other Literary Estimates. 1899.

Millais, J. G. The Life of Sir J. E. Millais. 2 vols. 1899.

Champneys, B. Memoirs and Correspondence of Coventry Patmore. 2 vols. 1900.

Ward, M. A. Prophets of the Nineteenth Century: Carlyle, Ruskin, Tolstoi. 1900.

Atkinson, Blanche. Ruskin's Social Experiment at Barmouth. 1900. [Rptd from Leisure Hour, March 1897.]

Ruskin Exhibition, Coniston. Catalogue. Ed. W. G. Collingwood, Ulverston, 1900.

Brownell, W. C. Victorian Prose Masters: Ruskin. New York, 1902.

Atlay, J. B. Henry Wentworth Acland. A Memoir. 1903.

Gladden, W. Witnesses of the Light. 1903.

Pollock, Sir M. Light and Water: a Study of Reflection and Colour in River, Lake and Sea. 1903.

Burne-Jones, Sir E. Memorials. 2 vols. 1904.

Kitchin, G. W. Ruskin in Oxford, and Other Studies. 1904.

Davies, J. Llewellyn. The Working Man's College, 1854–1904. 1904.

Sieper, E. Das Evangelium der Schönheit in der englischen Literatur und Kunst des XIX. Jahrhunderts. Dortmund, [1904].

Ruskin Commemoration, Venice, Sept. 21 1905. Venice, 1905.

Hunt, H. Pre-Raphaelitism and the Pre-Raphaelite Brotherhood. 2 vols. 1905.

Stephen, Sir L. Studies of a Biographer. 3 vols. 1907.

Caine, Sir T. H. Hall. My Story. 1908.

Catalogue of Ruskin Exhibition in Memory of Charles Eliot Norton. Boston, 1909.

Morley, E. J. John Ruskin and Social Ethics. Fabian Soc. 1917.

Proust, M. Pastiches et Mélanges. Paris, 1919.

Shaw, G. B. Ruskin's Politics. 1921.

Chambers, R. W. Ruskin—and Others—on Byron. English Ass. 1925.

Maurois, A. Études anglaises. Paris, 1927.

Gomez de la Serna, R. Efigies. Madrid, 1929.

Clark, Sir Kenneth. The Gothic Revival. 1929.

MacCarthy, D. Portraits. 1931.

Scudder, V. D. On Journey. 1937.

(c) Articles in Periodicals

The Ruskin Reading Guild Journal. Arbroath, Jan.–Dec. 1889. [Monthly. Originally, from Nov. 1887 to Dec. 1888, circulated in MS form. Ed. by William Marwick. Continued as: Igdrasil. Journal of the Ruskin Reading Guild. A Magazine of Literature, Art and Social Philosophy. Orpington, vol. I, Jan.–Sept. 1890, vol. II, Oct.–Dec. 1890, vol. III, Edinburgh, June 1891–March 1892. Monthly. Ed. by William Marwick and Kineton Parkes. Continued as: World-Literature: The Journal of the Reading Guild and kindred Societies, and Supplement to 'Igdrasil'. Vol. I, London, 15 Sept. 1891–March 1892; vol. II, Edinburgh, May–Sept. 1892. Monthly. Ed. by William Marwick.]

Saint George. The Journal of the Ruskin Society of Birmingham (The Society of the Rose). Birmingham, vols. I–XIII, March 1898–May 1911. [Quarterly. Ed. by J. Howard Whitehouse and others.]

The Ruskin Union Journal. London, no. 1, March 1900. [No other no. was issued; but Saint George became thenceforth the organ of the Ruskin Union as well.]

Mr. Ruskin's Works. Blackwood's Mag. LXX, 1851.

[Patmore, C.] Sources of Expression in Architecture. Edinburgh Rev. XCIV, 1851. [Rptd as Architectural Styles in Principle in Art, 1889.]

[Oliphant, M. O.] Modern Light Literature—Art. Blackwood's Mag. LXXVIII, 1855.

Mr. Ruskin's Modern Painters. Quarterly Rev. XCVIII, 1856.

[Chorley, H. F.] Ruskinism. Edinburgh Rev. CIII, 1856.

[Morris, W. and Burne-Jones, Sir E.] Ruskin and the Quarterly. Oxford and Cambridge Mag. June 1856.

Pictures and Picture Criticism. National Rev. III, 1856.

Literary Style. Fraser's Mag. LV, 1857.

[Lancaster, H. H.] The Writings of Mr. Ruskin. North British Rev. XXXVI, 1862.

Ruskin's Literary Spirit. Boston Rev. II, 1862.

John Ruskin as a Religious Writer. Christian Observer, LXII, 1862.

The Critical Character. Westminster Rev. XXIV, 1863.

Noel, R. On the Use of Metaphor and 'Pathetic Fallacy' in Poetry. Fortnightly Rev. V, 1866. [Rptd in Essays on Poetry and Poets, 1886.]

Rossetti, W. M. Ruskin as a Writer on Art. The Broadway, II, 1869.

Bedford, H. Mr. Ruskin as an Art Critic. The Month, XV, 1871.

The Royal Gold Medal. Royal Institute of British Architects, Sessional Papers, 1874–5.

Saintsbury, G. Modern English Prose. Fortnightly Rev. XIX, 1876.

Wedderburn, A. D. O. Celebrities at Home, no. LIX: Professor Ruskin at Brantwood. The World, 29 Aug. 1877. [Rptd in E. Yates, Celebrities at Home, vol. II, 1878.]

—— A Lake-side Home, Brantwood. Art Journ. Nov., Dec. 1881.

Report of Whistler v. Ruskin. The Times, 26 Nov. 1878.

The Progress of Taste. Quarterly Rev. CXLIX, 1880.

Harris, George. Mr. Ruskin and High Art. Modern Thoughts, II, 1880.

Owen, J. A. Mr. Ruskin's May-Day Festival at Whitelands College. Girl's Own Paper, II, 1881.

Watt, F. Mr. Ruskin and Political Economy. St. James's Mag. XLII, 1882.

Wilson, D. Munro. John Ruskin, Economist. Unitarian Rev. Boston, U.S.A. XXIII, 1885.

Bishop, M. C. A Teacher among Teachers. Merry England, V, 1885.

St. George's Cloth. Pall Mall Gazette, 8 Feb. 1886.

Royce, G. M. Ruskin v. Gibbon and Grote. New Englander, XLV, 1886.

The American Trade in 'Ruskins.' An Interview at Mr. Wiley's, New York. Pall Mall Gazette, 21 Dec. 1887.

Stillman, W. J. John Ruskin. Century Mag. XXXV, 1888. [Rptd in The Old Rome and the New, 1897.]

The Works of Mr. Ruskin. Edinburgh Rev. CXLVII, 1888.

Mr. Ruskin and the Edinburgh Review. Spectator, 28 Jan. 1888.

Moreton, W. T. The Religious Teachings of John Ruskin. Christian World Pulpit, 18 and 25 April and 2 May 1888.

A Poet of Prose. Temple Bar, LXXXIII, 1888.

Stimson, F. J. Ruskin as a Political Economist. Quarterly Journ. of Economics, II, 1888.

Fleming, A. The Revival of Hand Spinning and Weaving in Westmorland. Century Mag. Feb. 1889.

Firth, J. John Ruskin. Tinsley's Mag. VI, 1889.

Fitzgerald, Percy. Mr. Ruskin, Artist and Publisher. GM. CCLXVIII, 1890.

Symonds, J. A. A Morning at San Rocco. National Observer, 1 Aug. 1891.

John Ruskin: a Study in Development. London Quarterly Rev. LXXXI, 1894.

Cook, Sir E. T. Mr. Ruskin in Relation to Modern Problems. National Rev. XXIII, 1894.

—— Ruskin as an Artist and Art Critic. The Studio, March 1900.

—— Ruskin as the Father of the Net Book System. Book Monthly, IV, 1907.

Schooling, J. H. The Handwriting of John Ruskin. Dec. 31, 1828–Nov. 28, 1884. Strand Mag. Dec. 1895.

Sulman, T. A Memorable Art Class. Good Words, Aug. 1897.

Signac, P. L'Éducation de l'Œil. La Revue Blanche, 1 July 1898.

Shepstone, H. J. A Modern Utopia. World-Wide Mag. June 1899. [On Ruskin, Tennessee.]

Paetow, F. Die Ruskin Co-operative Association und deren Hochschule für Sozialismus. Die Neue Zeit, XVII, no. 23, 1899.

Bateman, M. G. John Ruskin. Black and White, 27 Jan. 1900.

Dodd, L. T. and Dale, J. A. The Ruskin Hall Movement. Fortnightly Rev. LXVII, 1900.

Chapman, C. Reminiscences. Sunday Mag. March 1900.

John Ruskin. Quarterly Rev. CXCI, 1900.

M[ac Coll], D. S. Ruskin and his Critics. Saturday Rev. 13, 20 Oct. 1900.

Morton, E. P. Ruskin's Pathetic Fallacy and Keats's Treatment of Nature. Poet-Lore, XII, 1900.

Clemen, P. John Ruskin. Zeitschrift für bildende Kunst, N.S. XI, 1900.

Davis, Walter G. The Failure of the Ruskin Colony. Gunton's Mag. XXI, 1901.

Garnett, Richard. Sir Francis Palgrave as a Precursor of Ruskin. Hampstead Annual, 1901.

Hobson, J. A. Ruskin and Democracy. Contemporary Rev. LXXXI, 1902.

McDill, H. C. Why the Ruskin Colony failed. Gunton's Mag. XXII, 1902.

Braam, J. W. The Ruskin Co-operative Colony. American · Journ. of Sociology, VIII, 1903.

Vitali, G. Le Idee fondamentali di Giovanni Ruskin. Rivista d' Italia, Dec. 1905.

Collingwood, W. G. John Ruskin. Temple Bar, N.S. VI, 1906.

Zorzi, A. Ruskin in Venice. Cornhill Mag. Aug., Sept. 1906.

Harker, Mrs L. Allen. Ruskin and Girlhood. Scribner's Mag. Nov. 1906.

Herford, C. H. Ruskin and the Gothic Revival. Quarterly Rev. CCVII, 1907.

Goring, K. M. The Friends of Living Creatures and John Ruskin. Fortnightly Rev. Sept., Oct. 1907.

Emslie, J. P. Recollections of Ruskin. Working Men's College Journ. X, 1908.

Durant, W. S. From Art to Social Reform: Ruskin's Nature of Gothic. Nineteenth Century, May 1910.

Sampson, George. [Memoir.] Bookman, Feb. 1919.

Parry, Sir E. A. Whistler v. Ruskin. Cornhill Mag. Jan. 1921.

Marriott, Sir J. A. R. Ruskin's Economics. Cornhill Mag. April 1923.

Audra, E. L'Influence de Ruskin en France. Revue des Cours et Conférences, 15 Jan. 1926.

Collet, C. E. The Development of Ruskin's Views on Interest. Economic Journ. Jan. 1926.

Murray, Jessie. Marcel Proust as Critic and Disciple of Ruskin. Nineteenth Century, April 1927.

Woolf, V. Praeterita. New Republic, 28 Dec. 1927.

Ruskin as a Communist: Comparison with Marx. Socialist Rev. Feb. 1928.

Roche, A. J. Proust as Translator of Ruskin. PMLA. XLV, 1930.

Maurois, A. Proust et Ruskin. E. & S. XVII, 1932.

Inge, W. R. Plato and Ruskin. Trans. Royal Soc. Lit. XIV, 1935.

H. G. P.

IV. MINOR CRITICS AND ESSAYISTS, 1835–1870

[This section has normally been restricted to writers born after 1799 and before 1830. Cross-references have only been included to *critical* writings listed in other sections.]

WILLIAM DAVENPORT ADAMS (1854–1904)

Famous Books. Sketches in the Highways and Byeways of English Literature. 1875.

Dictionary of English Literature, being a Comprehensive Guide to English Authors and their Works. [1878]; [1880] (rev. edn).

The Witty and Humorous Side of the English Poets. By Arthur H. Elliott [i.e. Adams], 1880.

By-Ways in Book-Land. Short Essays on Literary Subjects. 1888.

Rambles in Book Land. Short Essays on Literary Subjects. 1889.

With Poet and Player. Essays on Literature and the Stage. 1891.

A Dictionary of the Drama: a Guide to the Plays, Playwrights, Players, and Playhouses of the United Kingdom and America, from the Earliest Times to the Present. Vol. I (all pbd), 1904.

[Adams also compiled 9 anthologies (of anecdote, epigram, verse, etc.) and edited A. C. Calmour's Practical Play-Writing and Disraeli's The Revolutionary Epick. For an estimate see William Davenport Adams, Academy, LXVII, 1904.]

WALTER BAGEHOT (1826–1877)

(a) Collected Works

The Works of Walter Bagehot, with Memoirs by R. H. Hutton. Ed. F. Morgan, 5 vols. Hartford, 1889.

The Works and Life of Walter Bagehot. Ed. E. I. Barrington, 10 vols. 1915.

(b) Critical and Biographical Writings

Estimates of some Englishmen and Scotchmen. 1858. [Rptd from National Rev.]

Literary Studies. Ed. (with memoir) R. H. Hutton, 2 vols. 1879; 3 vols. 1895; 1906 (reissue of vol. III, with addns); ed. E. Bagehot, 1906; ed. G. Sampson, 1906 (Everyman's Lib.). [Rptd in part from above.]

Biographical Studies. Ed. R. H. Hutton, 1881, 1907 (adds index). [Rptd in part from Estimates.]

Estimations in Criticism. Ed. C. Lennox, 2 vols. 1908. [Rptd from Literary Studies.]

(c) Political, Economic and Miscellaneous Writings

Parliamentary Reform. An Essay. Reprinted, with Considerable Additions, from the National Review. 1859.

The History of the Unreformed Parliament and its Lessons. An Essay reprinted from the National Review. 1860.

Memoir of the Rt. Hon. J. Wilson. 1861. [Rptd from Economist.]

Count your Enemies and Economise your Expenditure. 1862.

The English Constitution. Reprinted from The Fortnightly Review. 1867; 1872 (adds 1 ch.); ed. A. J. Balfour, 1928 (World's Classics).

A Practical Plan for assimilating the English and American Money. Reprinted from the Economist with Additions. 1869.

Physics and Politics, or, Thoughts on the Application of the Principles of Natural Selection and Inheritance to Political Society. 1872.

Lombard Street: A Description of the Money Market. 1873; ed. E. Johnstone, 1892 (brought up to date); ed. Hartley Withers, 1910; ed. A. W. Wright, 1915 (notes rev.).

Some Articles on the Depreciation of Silver and on Topics connected with it. Reprinted from The Economist. 1877.

Economic Studies. Ed. R. H. Hutton, 1880.

Essays on Parliamentary Reform. 1883.

The Postulates of English Political Economy. Student's Edition, with a Preface by A. Marshall. 1885. [Rptd from Economic Studies.]

The Love-Letters of Walter Bagehot and Eliza Wilson. Ed. E. I. Barrington, 1933.

(d) Biography and Criticism

Walter Bagehot. In Memoriam. 1878 (priv. ptd). [A collection of obituary notices.]

Hutton, R. H. Walter Bagehot. [In Criticisms on Contemporary Thought and Thinkers, 2 vols. 1894.]

Stephen, Sir L. Walter Bagehot. [In Studies of a Biographer, vol. III, 1902.]

Barrington, E. I. Life of Walter Bagehot. 1914; 1915 (as vol. x of The Works and Life of Walter Bagehot).

Birrell, A. Collected Essays and Addresses. Vol. II, 1922.

Marriott, Sir J. A. R. Walter Bagehot. Fortnightly Rev. CXIX, 1926.

Read, Herbert. Bagehot. [In The Sense of Glory, Cambridge, 1929.]

Irvine, W. Walter Bagehot. 1939.

JOHN STUART BLACKIE (1809–1895)

[See p. 280 above.]

ANDREW KENNEDY HUTCHINSON BOYD (1825–1899)

(a) Selection

A. K. H. B. A Volume of Selections. Ed. C. Boyd, [1914].

(b) Writings

The Recreations of a Country Parson. 3 sers. 1859–78.

The Commonplace Philosopher in Town and Country. 1862.

Leisure Hours in Town. 1862.

Counsel and Comfort spoken from a City Pulpit. 1863.

The Graver Thoughts of a Country Parson. 3 sers. 1863–75.

The Autumn Holidays of a Country Parson. 1864.

The Critical Essays of a Country Parson. 1865.

Sunday Afternoons at the Parish Church of a University City. 1866.

Lessons of Middle Age. 1868.

Changed Aspects of Unchanged Truths. 1869.

Present-Day Thoughts. 1871.

Seaside Musings on Sundays and Weekdays. 1872.

A Scotch Communion Sunday. 1873.

Landscapes, Churches and Moralities. 1874.

From a Quiet Place. Discourses. 1879.

Our Little Life: Essays Consolatory. 2 sers. 1882–4.

Towards the Sunset: Teachings after Thirty Years. 1883.

A Young Man: his Home and Friends. 1884.

What set him Right; with Chapters to help. 1885–8.

Our Homely Comedy and Tragedy. 1887.

The Best Last; with Other Papers. 1888.

To meet the Day through the Christian Year. 1889.

Twenty-five Years of St. Andrews: September 1865 to September 1890. 2 vols. 1892.

St. Andrews and Elsewhere. Glimpses of some Gone and of Things Left. 1894.

Occasional and Immemorial Days. 1895. [Sermons.]

The Last Years of St. Andrews, September 1890 to September 1895. 1896.

Sermons and Stray Papers. With a Biographical Sketch by W. W. Tulloch. 1907.

[Boyd also pbd several lectures and sermons.]

(c) Biography and Criticism

Story, R. H. A. K. H. B. Guild Life and Work (Edinburgh), XIII, May 1899.

The True Significance of A. K. H. Boyd. Eclectic Mag. (New York), CXXXII, 1899.

GEORGE BRIMLEY (1819–1857)

Essays. Ed. (with memoir) W. G. Clark, Cambridge, 1858, 1860, 1882, [1905]. [For an appreciation of Brimley see G. Saintsbury, A History of Criticism, vol. III, 1904, pp. 504–8.]

JOHN BROWN (1810–1882)

(a) Essays

Horae Subsecivae. Locke and Sydenham, with Other Occasional Papers. Vol. I, Edinburgh, 1858. Vol. II, Edinburgh, 1861. Vols. I, II, 2 vols. 1862; ed. A. Dobson, 1907. Vol. III, Edinburgh, 1882.
Rab and his Friends. Edinburgh, 1859; 1901 ('and other papers'); 1905 (with Our Dogs, and notes); 1906 (with other papers and essays, and bibliography); ed. E. T. Maclaren and A. C. Brown, 1908 (with character sketches of the author); rptd 1931. [From Horae Subsecivae.]
'With Brains, Sir.' Edinburgh, 1860. [An essay on education extracted from Horae Subsecivae, vol. I.]
On the Deaths of Rev. John M'Gilchrist, John Brown and John Henderson. Edinburgh, 1860.
Letter to Rev. Dr. Cairns. Edinburgh, 1860; 1861 (in Horae Subsecivae, vol. II). [Contains Domestic and Personal Details of the Life of John Brown, D.D. (the elder).]
Health. Five Lay Sermons to Working People. Edinburgh, 1862.
Our Dogs. Edinburgh, 1862. [From Horae Subsecivae, vol. II.]
Marjorie Fleming, a Sketch. Edinburgh, 1863. [Rptd from North British Rev.; included in Horae Subsecivae, vol. III.]
Jeems the Doorkeeper, a Lay Sermon. Edinburgh, 1864; 1912 ('and other Stories,' viz. Her Last Half Crown, Landseer's Picture, In Clear Dream, and Solemn Vision, The Black Dwarf's Bones. [Subsequently included in Horae Subsecivae, vol. III, 1882.]
Minchmoor. Edinburgh, 1864; 1912 (with Enterkin, Biggar and the House of Fleming). [Included in Horae Subsecivae, vol. III.]
Locke and Sydenham. Edinburgh, 1866. [Originally in Horae Subsecivae, vol. I, but not included in later edns.]
Sir Henry Raeburn and his Works. Edinburgh, 1876 (priv. ptd). [Included in Horae Subsecivae, vol. III.]
John Leech. Edinburgh, 1877; 1882 (in Horae Subsecivae, vol. III).
Thackeray, his Literary Career. Boston, 1877.
Something about a Well. With More of our Dogs. Edinburgh, 1882.

Letters. With Letters from Ruskin, Thackeray and Others. Ed. J. Brown and D. W. Forrest, 1907.

(b) Biography and Criticism

Lang, A. Dr. John Brown. Century Illustrated Monthly Mag. Feb. 1883.
Maclaren, E. T. Dr. John Brown and his Sister, Isabella. 1889; 1896 (as Dr. John Brown and his Sisters Isabella and Jane); 1901 (with introductory note by A. C. Brown).
Masson, D. Dr. John Brown. [In Edinburgh Sketches and Memories, 1892.]
Peddie, A. Recollections of Dr. John Brown, with a Selection from his Correspondence. 1893.
Brown, J. T. Dr. John Brown. A Biography and a Criticism. 1903.

ROBERT CHAMBERS (1802–1871)

(a) Bibliography

Chambers, C. E. S. A Catalogue of some of the Rarer Books, also Manuscripts and Autograph Letters in the Collection of C. E. S. Chambers. With a Bibliography of the Works of William and Robert Chambers. Edinburgh, 1891 (priv. ptd).

(b) Selected Works

Select Writings. 7 vols. Edinburgh, 1847. [Vols. I and II, Essays Familiar and Humorous; vols. III and IV, Essays Moral and Economic; vol. V, History of the Rebellion of 1745–6; vol. VI, Traditions of Edinburgh; vol. VII, Popular Rhymes of Scotland.]
Essays Familiar and Humorous. 2 vols. [1866.]

(c) Biographical and Critical Works

Illustrations of the Author of Waverley: being Notices and Anecdotes of Real Characters, Scenes and Incidents supposed to be described in his Works. Edinburgh, 1822; 1825 (enlarged).
The Popular Rhymes of Scotland, with Illustrations Collected from Tradition. Edinburgh, 1826; 1842 (rev. and with addns).
Life of Sir Walter Scott. Edinburgh, 1832; rev. W. Chambers, 1871; 1894 (rev. with addns).
A Biographical Dictionary of Eminent Scotsmen. 4 vols. Glasgow, 1832–5; 5 vols. 1855 (rev. with supplemental vol. by T. Thomson).
English Language and Literature. Edinburgh, 1835.

The Life of Robert Burns with a Criticism on his Writings. Edinburgh, 1838. [By James Currie. Expanded by Chambers.]

The Poetical Works of Robert Burns. To which are now added, Notes illustrating Historical, Personal and Local Allusions. Edinburgh, 1838.

The Prose Works of Robert Burns, with the Notes of Currie and Cromek, and Many by the Present Editor. Edinburgh, 1839.

Cyclopaedia of English Literature. 2 vols. Edinburgh, 1844.

Life and Works of Robert Burns. 4 vols. 1851.

Smollett: his Life and a Selection from his Writings. 1867.

(d) Historical, Antiquarian and Topographical Works

Traditions of Edinburgh. 2 vols. Edinburgh, 1825; 1868 (rev.); ed. C. E. S. Chambers, 1912.

Walks in Edinburgh. Edinburgh, 1825; 1829 ('with an Improved Plan, and a View of the City'). [A sequel to The Traditions of Edinburgh.]

Notices of the Most Remarkable Fires in Edinburgh from 1385 to 1824. Edinburgh, 1825.

History of the Rebellion in Scotland in 1745, 1746. 2 vols. Edinburgh, 1827; 1840 (greatly enlarged); 1869 (adds appendix).

The Picture of Scotland. 2 vols. Edinburgh, 1827. [A topographical account of Scotland.]

History of the Rebellions in Scotland under the Marquis of Montrose and Others, from 1638 till 1660. 2 vols. Edinburgh, 1828.

History of the Rebellions in Scotland, under the Viscount of Dundee and the Earl of Mar, in 1689 and 1715. Edinburgh, 1829.

The Life of King James the First. 2 vols. Edinburgh, 1830.

Reekiana, or Minor Antiquities of Edinburgh. Edinburgh, 1833. [Rptd in 1868 edn of The Traditions of Edinburgh.]

Ancient Sea-Margins, as Memorials of Changes in the Relative Level of Sea and Land. Edinburgh, 1848.

The History of Scotland. 2 vols. 1849.

Domestic Annals of Scotland from the Reformation to the Revolution. 2 vols. Edinburgh, 1858; 1885 (abridged).

Edinburgh Papers. 5 vols. Edinburgh, 1859–61; 1861.

Sketch of the History of the Edinburgh Theatre Royal. Edinburgh, 1859 (priv. ptd).

Domestic Annals of Scotland from the Revolution to the Rebellion of 1745. 1861. [Intended to form vol. III to Domestic Annals of Scotland from the Reformation to the Revolution.]

The Book of Days. A Miscellany of Popular Antiquities. 2 vols. 1862–4.

(e) Other Writings

Poems. Edinburgh, 1835 (priv. ptd). [Rptd, with some omissions, with The Popular Rhymes of Scotland, to form vol. VII of the Select Writings.]

Vestiges of the Natural History of Creation. 1844 (anon.); 1884 (12th edn with introduction by A. Ireland); 1887 (with introduction by Henry Morley).

Explanations: a Sequel to 'Vestiges.' By the Author of that Work. 1845.

Tracings of the North of Europe. 1850 (priv. ptd). [Rptd from Chambers's Edinburgh Journ. An account of voyagings in the Baltic.]

Tracings of Iceland and the Faröe Islands. 1856.

The Threiplauds of Fingask. A Family Memoir. 1880. [Written in 1853. Also contains: Life in a Scottish Country Mansion; Two Days on the Moors of Perthshire.]

(f) Biography and Criticism

Chambers, William. Memoir of Robert Chambers with Autobiographic Reminiscences of William Chambers. Edinburgh, 1872; 1884 (enlarged).

Parsons, C. O. Serial Publication of 'Traditions of Edinburgh.' Library, XIV, 1933.

WILLIAM CHAPPELL (1809–1888)

A Collection of National English Airs, consisting of Ancient Song, Ballad and Dance Tunes, interspersed with Remarks and Anecdote, and preceded by an Essay on English Minstrelsy. 2 pts, 1838–40.

Popular Music of the Olden Time: a Collection of Ancient Songs, Ballads and Dance Tunes, illustrative of the National Music of England. With Short Introductions to the Different Reigns, and Notices of the Airs from Writers of the Sixteenth and Seventeenth Centuries. Also a Short Account of the Minstrels. 2 vols. [1855–9]; rev. H. E. Wooldridge, 2 vols. 1893.

The Roxburghe Ballads. With Short Notes by William Chappell, and Copies of the Original Woodcuts. 3 vols. Ballad Soc. 1871–5.

The History of Music. Vol. I (all pbd), 1874.

[Chappell founded the Musical Antiquarian Society, 1841, and edited one of its pbns as well as several other works.]

HENRY FOTHERGILL CHORLEY (1808–1872)

(a) Writings on Music

Music and Manners in France and Germany: a Series of Travelling Sketches of Art and Society. 3 vols. 1841.

Modern German Music: Recollections and Criticisms. 2 vols. 1854.

Thirty Years' Musical Recollections. 2 vols. 1862; ed. E. Newman, 1926.
Mendelssohn's Letters from Italy and Switzerland [with Biographical Sketch by Chorley]. 1864.
Life of F. Mendelssohn Bartholdy, by W. A. Lampadius; with Supplementary Sketches by H. F. Chorley. 1865.
The National Music of the World. Ed. H. G. Hewlett, 1880.

(b) Miscellaneous Writings

Sketches of a Sea Port Town. 3 vols. 1834.
Conti the Discarded; with Other Tales and Fancies. 3 vols. 1835.
Memorials of Mrs. Hemans, with Illustrations of her Literary Character from her Private Correspondence. 2 vols. 1836.
The Authors of England: a Series of Medallion Portraits of Modern Literary Characters, engraved from the Works of British Artists by A. Collas; with Illustrative Notices by H. F. Chorley. 1838; rev. G. B. 1861.
The Lion: a Tale of the Coteries. 3 vols. 1839.
Pomfret, or Public Opinion and Private Judgment. 3 vols. 1845.
Old Love and New Fortune: a Play [in verse]. 1850.
Duchess Eleanour: a Tragedy. By H. F. C[horley]. [1854.]
The May-Queen: a Pastoral. [1858.]
Roccabella: a Tale of a Woman's Life. By Paul Bell. 2 vols. 1859.
The Amber Witch: a Romantic Opera, in Four Acts [and in verse]. [1861.]

[Chorley also edited several works and arranged Scribe's Black Domino for the English stage.]

(c) Biography and Criticism

Linley, G. Musical Cynics of London: a Satire. 1862.
Henry Fothergill Chorley: Autobiography, Memoir and Letters. Compiled by H. G. Hewlett. 2 vols. 1873.
Henry F. Chorley and his Contemporaries. Temple Bar, XL, 1873.
Marshall, Julian. H. F. Chorley. [In Sir G. Grove's Dictionary of Music and Musicians, vol. I, 1879, etc.]

MARY VICTORIA COWDEN CLARKE, née NOVELLO (1809–1898)

(a) Miscellaneous Writings

The Complete Concordance to Shakespeare: being a Verbal Index to all the Passages in the Dramatic Works of the Poet. 18 monthly pts, 1844–5; 1845; 1847; [1855].
'Many Happy Returns of the Day!' A Birthday Book. 1847; 1860; 1869. [With Charles Cowden Clarke.]

Shakespeare Proverbs, or the Wise Saws of our Wisest Poet. 1848; ed. W. J. Rolfe, New York, 1907.
World-Noted Women, or Types of Womanly Attributes. New York, 1858.
The Life and Labours of Vincent Novello. [1864.]
Recollections of Writers. 1878. [With Charles Cowden Clarke.]
The Shakespeare Key, unlocking the Treasures of his Style. 1879. [Selections; with Charles Cowden Clarke.]
Centennial Biographic Sketch of Charles Cowden Clarke. 1887 (priv. ptd).
My Long Life. 1896 (bis).

[Mary Cowden Clarke also pbd several edns of Shakespeare (the most elaborate, Cassell's Illustrated Shakespeare, with Charles Cowden Clarke). She translated Berlioz's Treatise upon Modern Instrumentation, and edited The Musical Times, 1853–6.]

(b) Fiction

A Book of Stories for Young People. [1847.] [By Mrs Howitt, Mrs S. C. Hall and Mrs Clarke (2 stories).]
Kit Bam's Adventures, or the Yarns of an Old Mariner. 1849.
The Girlhood of Shakespeare's Heroines in a Series of Fifteen Tales. 3 vols. 1851–2; 1879 (condensed by S. Novello); 5 vols. [1892] (with a new preface); rptd 3 vols. 1906 (Everyman's Lib.).
The Iron Cousin, or Mutual Influence. 2 vols. 1854; 1862.
The Trust and the Remittance. Two Love Stories. 1873.
Short Stories in Metrical Prose. 1873.
A Rambling Story. 1874.
An Idyl of London Streets. Rome, 1875.
Uncle Peep and I. A Child's Novel. 1886.

(c) Poems

The Song of a Drop o' Wather. By Harry Wandsworth Shortfellow. 1856.
Honey from the Weed. Verses. 1881.
Verse Waifs, forming an Appendix to Honey from the Weed. 1883.
A Score of Sonnets to One Object. 1884.
Memorial Sonnets. 1888.

JOHN CONINGTON (1825–1869)
[See p. 284 above.]

ENEAS SWEETLAND DALLAS (1828–1879)
Poetics: an Essay on Poetry. 1852.
The Gay Science. 2 vols. 1866.
The Stowe-Byron Controversy A Complete Résumé of all that has been written and said upon the Subject, together with an Impartial Review of the Merits of the Case. [1869.]

Kettner's Book of the Table: a Manual of Cookery. 1877.

[Dallas also edited an abridgement of Richardson's Clarissa, 1868. He was editor of Once a Week, 1868, and on the staff of The Times. For an appreciation of his criticism see J. Drinkwater, The Eighteen-Sixties, Cambridge, 1932, and The Dream and the Poem, TLS. 18 Jan. 1936.]

JAMES WILLIAM DAVISON (1813–1885)

Chopin. [1849?]
Music during the Victorian Era, from Mendelssohn to Wagner: being the Memoirs of J. W. Davison, compiled by his Son, Henry Davison, from Memoranda and Documents. With Numerous Portraits of Musicians, and Important Letters (previously unpublished) of Mendelssohn, Berlioz, Gounod, Jullien, Macfarren, Sterndale Bennett, etc. 1912.

[Davison was editor of The Musical World from 1836 until his death. He became musical critic to The Times c. 1846.]

AUBREY THOMAS DE VERE (1814–1902)

[See p. 1052 below]

JOHN DORAN (1807–1878)

(a) Historical and Miscellaneous Works

Sketches and Reminiscences [from Paris]. 1828.
The History and Antiquities of the Town and Borough of Reading. Reading, 1835 (anon.).
Filia Dolorosa. Memoirs of Marie Thérèse Charlotte, Duchess of Angoulême. 1852. [The first 115 pp. by Mrs I. F. Romer; completed by John Doran.]
Habits and Men, with Remnants of Record touching the Makers of both. 1854.
Table Traits, with Something on them. 1854.
Lives of the Queens of England of the House of Hanover. 2 vols. 1855; 2 vols. 1874 (rev. and enlarged).
Knights and their Days. 1856.
Monarchs retired from Business. 2 vols. 1857.
The History of Court Fools. 1858.
New Pictures and Old Panels. 1859.
The Book of the Princes of Wales, Heirs to the Crown of England. 1860.
Memoir of Queen Adelaide, Consort of King William IV. 1861.
'Their Majesties' Servants.' Annals of the English Stage, from Thomas Betterton to Edward Kean. Actors—Authors—Audiences. 2 vols. 1864; 2 vols. 1865 (rev. and enlarged); rev. R. W. Lowe, 3 vols. 1888.
Saints and Sinners; or, in Church and about it. 2 vols. 1868.
A Lady of the Last Century (Mrs. E. Montagu): Illustrated in her Unpublished Letters; collected and arranged, with a Biographical Sketch and a Chapter on Blue Stockings. 1873.
London in the Jacobite Times. 2 vols. 1877.
Memoirs of our Great Towns; with Anecdotic Gleanings concerning their Worthies and their Oddities, 1860–1877. 1878.
In and about Drury Lane, and Other Papers, reprinted from 'Temple Bar,' etc. [Ed. G. B., i.e. G. Bentley?] 2 vols. 1881.

[Doran also edited, or wrote introductions for, 10 other works.]

(b) Biography and Criticism

Jeafferson, J. C. The Life and Writings of Dr. John Doran. Temple Bar, LII, 1878.
Jewitt, L. Some Departed Contributors and Literary Friends. (Dr. John Doran.) Reliquary, XVIII, 1878.
John Doran. London Society, XLII, 1882.
Thomas, F. M. Dr. Doran's Their Majesties' Servants. Theatre, XX, 1888.

SIR FRANCIS HASTINGS CHARLES DOYLE (1810–1888)

[See p. 286 above.]

ELIZABETH, Lady EASTLAKE, née RIGBY (1809–1893)

(a) Art Criticism

Treasures of Art in Great Britain. 4 vols. 1854–7. [Tr. from G. F. Waagen.]
The History of Our Lord as exemplified in Works of Art. 1864. [Begun by Mrs A. Jameson; completed by Lady Eastlake.]
Memoir of Sir C. L. Eastlake. [Prefixed to Sir C. L. Eastlake's Contributions to the Literature of the Fine Arts, ser. 2, 1870.]
Life of John Gibson, R.A. 1870.
The Schools of Painting in Italy. 2 vols. 1874. [Tr. from F. T. Kugler. First pbd in 1842, with Sir Charles Eastlake as editor, and in charge of the translation. There were two new edns before this one which is entirely translated by Lady Eastlake and revised and remodelled from the latest researches.]
Five Great Painters. 2 vols. 1883. [Essays rptd from Edinburgh Rev. and Quarterly Rev.: Leonardo da Vinci, Michael Angelo, Titian, Raphael, Dürer.]

(b) Other Writings

A Residence on the Shores of the Baltic. 2 vols. 1841–2; 1844 (as Letters from the Shores of the Baltic).
The Jewess, a Tale from the Shores of the Baltic. 1843.
Livonian Tales. 1846. [The Disponent; The Wolves; The Jewess.]

Music and the Art of Dress. Two Essays. 1852. [Rptd from Quarterly Rev.]

Fellowship. Letters addressed to my Sister Mourners. 1868. [7 letters written on the death of her husband.]

Mrs. Grote. A Sketch. 1880.

S. T. Coleridge and the English Romantic School. 1887. [Tr. from the German of A. Brandl.]

Journals and Correspondence of Lady Eastlake. Edited by her Nephew, C. E. Smith. 2 vols. 1895. [Forms a memoir of Lady Eastlake.]

(c) Biography and Criticism

Kugler, F. T. The Schools of Painting in Italy. Edited and, in part, rewritten by A. H. Layard. 2 vols. 1887. [The Introduction gives an account of Lady Eastlake.]

Obituary. Times, 3 Oct. 1893.

WHITWELL ELWIN (1816–1900)

The Complete Works of Alexander Pope. Vols. I, II, VI–VIII, 1871–2. [Vols. III–V, IX, x ed. by W. J. Courthope.]

John Forster. [Prefixed to the Catalogue of the Dyce and Forster Library, 1888.]

Some Eighteenth Century Men of Letters. Ed. Warwick Elwin, 2 vols. 1902. [Rptd from Quarterly Rev.: Cowper, Sterne, Fielding, Goldsmith, Boswell and Dr Johnson. Includes anon. memoir.]

[For an estimate of Elwin see S. T. Williams, A Critic of Eighteenth Century Literature, Texas Rev. Oct. 1922.]

JOHN FORSTER (1812–1876)

(a) Critical and Biographical Works

The Life and Adventures of Oliver Goldsmith. 1848; 2 vols. 1854 (enlarged as The Life and Times of Goldsmith); ed. R. Ingpen, 1903 (abridged).

Daniel De Foe and Charles Churchill. 2 vols. 1855. [Rptd from Edinburgh Rev. Later included in Historical and Biographical Essays, vol. II.]

Historical and Biographical Essays. 2 vols. 1858; 1860 (rev. and enlarged edn of vol. II). [Vol. I: The Debates on the Grand Remonstrance; The Plantagenets and the Tudors; The Civil Wars and Oliver Cromwell. Vol. II: Defoe, Steele, Churchill, and Foote.]

Walter Savage Landor. A Biography. 2 vols. 1869; 1876 (rev. and abridged as vol. I of The Works of Landor).

The Life of Charles Dickens. 3 vols. 1872–4; ed. G. Gissing, 1903 (rev. and abridged); ed. G. K. Chesterton, 2 vols. 1927 (Everyman's Lib.); ed. J. W. T. Ley, 1928.

Alexander Dyce. A Biographical Sketch.

[Prefixed to vol. I of Catalogue of the Dyce Collection in the South Kensington Museum, 1875.]

The Life of Jonathan Swift. Vol. I (all pbd), 1876. [Completed by Sir H. Craik.]

Dramatic Essays by John Forster and G. H. Lewes. Ed. W. Archer and R. W. Lowe, 1896. [11 essays by Forster rptd from Examiner, 6 on Macready as actor and as producer, 4 on Forrest and 1 on Charles Kean as Hamlet.]

(b) Historical Writings

The Cabinet Cyclopaedia. Ed. D. Lardner. [To the section Lives of Eminent British Statesmen Forster contributed the following biographies: vol. II, 1836, Sir John Eliot (rptd enlarged 2 vols. 1864) and Thomas Wentworth, Earl of Strafford; vol. III, 1837, John Pym and John Hampden; vol. IV, 1838, Sir Henry Vane and Henry Marten; vols. VI, VII, 1839, Oliver Cromwell. Forster's contributions were rptd 5 vols. 1840 as Statesmen of the Commonwealth.]

A Treatise on the Popular Progress in English History. [Introduction to Memoirs of Statesmen of the Commonwealth, 1840.]

The Quest of the Five Members by Charles the First. A Chapter of History Re-written. 1860.

The Debates on the Grand Remonstrance, November and December 1641, with an Introductory Essay on English Freedom under Plantagenet and Tudor Sovereigns. 1860. [Rptd with addns from Historical and Biographical Essays, vol. I.]

(c) Biography and Criticism

Powell, T. Pictures of the Living Authors of Britain. 1851.

Morley, H. Sketch of John Forster. [Prefixed to the Handbook of the Forster and Dyce Collections, 1877.]

Elwin, W. Biographical Notice. [Prefixed to Catalogue of the Dyce and Forster Library, 1888.]

Renton, Richard. John Forster and his Friendships. 1912.

S[awyer], C. J. and D[arton], F. J. H. Dickens v. Barabbas, Forster intervening. 1930. [A study of Dickens's relations with his publishers and with Forster.]

Elwin, M. John Forster. [In Victorian Wallflowers, 1934.]

WILLIAM FORSYTH (1812–1899)

(a) Critical and Biographical Works

The Life of M. T. Cicero. 2 vols. 1864; 1867.

The Novels and Novelists of the Eighteenth Century, in Illustration of the Manners and Morals of the Age. 1871.

Essays Critical and Narrative. 1874. [Literary Style, William Cobbett, Eugénie de Guérin, etc.]

(b) Historical Works

Hortensius; or, the Advocate. An Historical Essay. 1849; 1874 (illustrated).

History of Trial by Jury. 1852.

History of the Captivity of Napoleon at St. Helena, from the Letters and Journals of the Late Lieut.-Gen. Sir H. Lowe, and Official Documents not before made Public. 3 vols. 1853.

Marie Antoinette in the Conciergerie. A Lecture. 1867.

History of Ancient Manuscripts. A Lecture. 1872.

The Rules of Evidence as Applicable to the Credibility of History, with the Discussion thereon from the Journal of the Victoria Institute. 1874.

(c) Other Writings

Fides Laici. 1850. [A long religious poem.]

The Great Fair of Nijni Novogorod and How We got There. 1850 (priv. ptd). [Later included in Essays Critical and Narrative, 1874.]

Rome and its Ruins. 1865.

Hannibal in Italy. An Historical Drama. 1872.

The Slavonic Provinces South of the Danube: a Sketch of their History and Present State in Relation to the Ottoman Porte. 1876.

[Forsyth also pbd several legal works.]

GEORGE GILFILLAN (1813–1878)

(a) Biographical and Critical Writings

A Gallery of Literary Portraits. Ser. 1, Edinburgh, 1845. Ser. 2, Edinburgh, 1850. Ser. 3, Edinburgh, 1854. 2 vols. Edinburgh, 1856 (complete); ed. (in part) Sir W. R. Nicoll, [1909] (Everyman's Lib.). [Short essays on poets, French Revolutionaries, novelists, critics, etc.]

The Bards of the Bible. Edinburgh, 1851.

Lord Byron. A Lecture. 1852. [In Lectures delivered before the Young Men's Christian Association in Exeter Hall, 1851–1852.]

The Martyrs, Heroes and Bards of the Scottish Covenant. 1852. [Appendix on the Massacre of Glencoe, rptd enlarged, with D. Campbell and J. S. Blackie, The Campbells of Glenlyon, Stirling, 1912.]

The Influence of Burns on Scottish Poetry and Song: an Essay. [In The Modern Scottish Minstrel, ed. C. Rogers, vol. IV, Edinburgh, 1857.]

Library Edition of Poets of Britain. 48 vols. 1853–60. [Ed. by Gilfillan, with short memoirs and notes.]

Specimens, with Memoirs, of the Less-known British Poets. 3 vols. Edinburgh, 1860. [With a long introductory essay; the work amounts to a richly illustrated history of minor British poetry.]

Remoter Stars in the Church Sky. Being a Gallery of Uncelebrated Divines. 1867. [W. Anderson, J. Everett, Samuel Gilfillan, G. Croley, J. Bruce, T. Spencer, J. Jamieson, G. Steward, H. Stewart, F. W. Robertson, etc.]

Modern Christian Heroes. A Gallery of Protesting and Reforming Men. 1869. [Cromwell, Milton, Owen and Howe, Baxter and Bunyan, Scottish Covenanters, Secession and Relief Churches in their Cradles, Wesley, Whitfield, Liberty of Conscience.]

The Life of Sir Walter Scott. Edinburgh, 1870.

The Life of the Rev. W. Anderson. 1873.

Life of Burns. [In the Works of Burns, National edn, 1878.]

Sketches Literary and Theological. Ed. F. Henderson, Edinburgh, 1881. [Selections from an unpublished MS: critical and religious.]

(b) Theological and Miscellaneous Writings

The Connection between Science, Literature and Religion. A Lecture. 1849.

The History of a Man. Edited [really written] by George Gilfillan. 1856. [Autobiography.]

Christianity and our Era. A Book for the Times. Edinburgh, 1857.

Alpha and Omega; or, a Series of Scripture Studies. 2 vols. 1860.

Night: a Poem. 1867.

[Gilfillan also pbd numerous single sermons and lectures.]

(c) Biography and Criticism

Livingston, Peter. The Rev. George Gilfillan. [In Livingston's Poems and Songs, 9th edn, Aberdeen, 1855.]

In Memoriam. Dundee, 1878. [Rptd from Dundee Advertiser.]

Macrae, D. George Gilfillan. Anecdotes and Reminiscences. 1891.

Watson, R. A. and E. S. George Gilfillan: Letters and Journal, with Memoir. 1892. [Includes list of his contributions to periodicals and his introductory essays.]

WILLIAM EWART GLADSTONE (1809–1898)

(a) Literary Writings

Studies on Homer and the Homeric Age. 3 vols. Oxford, 1858; tr. German, Leipzig, 1863.

Juventus Mundi. The Gods and Men of the Heroic Age. 1869.

Homeric Synchronism. An Enquiry into the Time and Place of Homer. 1876; tr. German, Jena, 1877.

Gleanings of Past Years, 1843–1878. 7 vols. 1879. [Miscellaneous papers and reviews.]

Landmarks of Homeric Study, together with an Essay on the Points of Contact between the Assyrian Tablets and the Homeric Text. 1890.

The Odes of Horace. 1894; 1895.

[Gladstone also made several trns from the Italian and French, and contributed letters, introductions, etc. to various pbns.]

(b) Political Writings and Speeches

The State in its Relations with the Church. 1838; 1841 (rev.); tr. German, 1843.

Speeches on Parliamentary Reform in 1866. With an Appendix. 1866.

Speeches on Great Questions of the Day. 1870.

Bulgarian Horrors and the Question of the East. 1876. Tr. Dutch, Culemborg, 1876; Russian, St Petersburg, 1876.

Speeches of the Rt. Hon. W. E. Gladstone. With a Sketch of his Life. Ed. H. W. Lucy, 1885.

Speeches on the Irish Question in 1886. With an Appendix containing the Full Text of the Government of Ireland and the Sale and Purchase of Land Bills of 1886. [Ed. P. W. Clayden], Edinburgh, 1886.

The Speeches and Public Addresses of the Right Hon. W. E. Gladstone, M.P. With Notes and Introductions. Ed. A. W. Hutton and H. J. Cohen, 2 vols. 1892. [This edn was projected in 10 vols. but only 2 appeared.]

Gladstone's Speeches. Descriptive Index and Bibliography by A. T. Bassett. With a Preface by Viscount Bryce, O.M., and Introductions to the Selected Speeches by Herbert Paul. 1916.

[The foregoing constitute only a selection from a large body of speeches, pamphlets, etc.]

(c) Theological Writings

Church Principles considered in their Results. 1840.

A Manual of Prayers from the Liturgy. Arranged for Family Use. 1845.

Rome and the Newest Fashions in Religion. Three Tracts: The Vatican Decrees; Vaticanism; Speeches of the Pope. 1875. Tr. Danish, Copenhagen, 1876; German, Nördlingen, 1875–6. [Vatican Decrees, originally pbd alone 1874, was tr. French, Brussels, 1875.]

The Church of England and Ritualism. [1876.]

The Impregnable Rock of Holy Scripture. 1890; 1892 (rev.).

The Psalter, with a Concordance and Other Auxiliary Matter. 1895.

On the Condition of Man in a Future Life. 3 pts, 1896.

Studies Subsidiary to the Works of Bishop Butler. Additional Volume uniform with the Works. 1896.

Later Gleanings, Theological and Ecclesiastical. 1897.

[Gladstone also edited Bishop Butler's Works, and produced various other theological works.]

(d) Biography and Criticism

The Oratory of Gladstone. Fraser's Mag. xxxiv, 1846.

Gladstone, W. E. A Chapter of Autobiography. 1868.

Gladstone as a Man of Letters. Fraser's Mag. c, 1879.

Smith, G. Barnett. The Life of the Rt. Hon. William Ewart Gladstone. 1879.

Laing, S. W. E. Gladstone as a Theologian. Fortnightly Rev. xlv, 1886.

von Bunsen, T. A German View of Gladstone. Nineteenth Century, xxii, 1887.

Russell, G. W. E. The Rt. Hon. W. E. Gladstone. 1891.

Gladstone as Reader. and Critic. Academy, liii, liv, 1898.

Hamilton, Sir E. W. Mr. Gladstone: a Monograph. 1898.

Morley, J., Viscount. The Life of William Ewart Gladstone. 1903.

Paul, H. W. The Life of W. E. Gladstone. [1908.]

Zumbini, B. Gladstone nelle sue Relazioni con l' Italia. Bari, 1914.

Burdett, O. W. E. Gladstone. 1927.

Birrell, F. Gladstone. 1933.

SIR GEORGE GROVE (1820–1900)

(a) Musical Criticism

Beethoven's Nine Symphonies. Analytical Essays; with a Preface by G. Henschel. Boston, 1884; 1896 (rev. as Beethoven and his Nine Symphonies); tr. German, [1906].

A Dictionary of Music and Musicians, A.D. 1450–1880. By Eminent Writers. Edited by George Grove. 4 vols. 1879–89; ed. J. A. F. Maitland, 4 vols. 1900; 5 vols. 1904–10; ed. N. C. Colles, 5 vols. 1927–8. [American Supplement, ed. W. S. Pratt and C. N. Boyd, Philadelphia, 1920.]

A Short History of Cheap Music, as exemplified in the Records of the House of Novello, Ewer & Co. With Especial Reference to the First Fifty Years of the Reign of Queen Victoria. With Portraits, and a Preface by Sir George Grove. 1887.

[Grove's wide literary activities included the writing of a large portion of Sir William Smith's Dictionary of the Bible, other biblical works, and a primer of geography. He edited various works on music, and was for some years editor of Macmillan's Mag.]

(b) Biography and Criticism

E[dwards], F. G. A Biographical Sketch of Sir George Grove. [1897.]

Graves, C. L. The Life and Letters of Sir George Grove, C.B. 1903.

ARTHUR HENRY HALLAM (1811–1833)*

(a) Bibliography

Motter, T. H. V. Arthur Hallam's Centenary: A Bibliographical Note. Yale University Lib. Gazette, VIII, 1934, pp. 104–9.

(b) Collected Works

Remains, In Verse and Prose, of Arthur Henry Hallam. 1834 (priv. ptd). [Ed. with a prefatory memoir by Henry Hallam.]

Remains in Verse and Prose of Arthur Henry Hallam. Originally Printed in 1834. 1852. [This edn was never issued.]

Remains in Verse and Prose of Arthur Henry Hallam. Originally Printed in 1834. 1853 (priv. ptd); 1862; 1863; Boston, 1863; 1869. [See bibliography above for variations in contents.]

The Poems of Arthur Henry Hallam Together With His Essay On The Lyrical Poems of Alfred Tennyson. Ed. R. Le Gallienne, 1893.

The Poetical Remains of Arthur Henry Hallam. [Appendix to Temple Classics edn of In Memoriam, 1899.]

[An edn of Hallam's complete poems, letters, and other writings is in preparation by T. H. V. Motter.]

(c) Separate Works

Timbuctoo. [Cambridge, 1829] (priv. ptd).

Adonais. An Elegy on the Death of John Keats, Author of Endymion, Hyperion, Etc. By Percy B. Shelley. Cambridge, 1829. [Note, unsigned, p. iii, and pbn arranged, by Hallam.]

Poems By A. H. Hallam, Esq. [1830] (priv. ptd).

Essay On the Philosophical Writings of Cicero. Cambridge, 1832 (priv. ptd).

Oration, On the Influence of Italian Works of Imagination on the Same Class of Compositions in England; Delivered in Trinity College Chapel, December 16, 1831. Cambridge, 1832 (priv. ptd).

Remarks on Professor Rossetti's 'Disquisizioni sullo Spirito Antipapale.' 1832.

(d) Contributions to Periodicals

On Names; Remarks on Gifford's Ford; Two Letters to Bartholomew Bouverie, Esq.; The Battle of the Boyne; The Bride of the Lake. [In The Eton Miscellany, vol. I, Eton, 1827.]

[Notice of Tennyson's Timbuctoo.] Athenaeum, 22 July, 1829, p. 456. [Anon. By Hallam?]

Stanzas. Englishman's Mag. I, Aug. 1831.

On Some of the Characteristics of Modern Poetry, and on the Lyrical Poems of Alfred Tennyson. Englishman's Mag. I, Aug. 1831.

[Notice, unsigned, of Sorelli's Il Paradiso Perduto di Milton, 1832 (3rd edn).] Foreign Quarterly Rev. Oct. 1832, pp. 508–13.

[Biographical sketches of Voltaire, Petrarch and Burke.] The Gallery of Portraits: with Memoirs. 5 vols. 1833–5. [First issued monthly, beginning June 1832; rptd 7 vols. 1833–7, 3 vols. 1853.]

On Hearing Miss Emily —— Play. Metropolitan Mag. Jan. 1833, p. 77. [Anon. By Hallam?]

(e) Posthumously Published Letters
(selection)

Gaskell, C. M. Records of an Eton Schoolboy [James Milnes Gaskell]. 1883 (priv. ptd). [12 letters.]

[Trench, M.] Richard Chenevix Trench, Archbishop: Letters and Memorials. 2 vols. 1888. [9 letters.]

[Tennyson, H.] Alfred Lord Tennyson: A Memoir. 2 vols. 1897.

Brookfield, A. M. Some Letters from Arthur Hallam. Fortnightly Rev. LXXX, 1903. [6 letters, 3 rptd in whole or in part in F. M. Brookfield, The Cambridge Apostles, 1906.]

Zamick, M. Unpublished Letters of Arthur Henry Hallam, from Eton, now in the John Rylands Library. Bulletin of John Rylands Lib. XVIII, 1934. [10 letters.]

(f) Biography and Criticism

The Morning Herald, 7 Oct. 1833.

Brown, J. Arthur Henry Hallam. North British Rev. XIV, Feb. 1851. [Rptd in Horae Subsecivae, Edinburgh, 1858, etc.; separately pbd Edinburgh, 1862; rptd in Tennyson and His Friends, ed. Hallam Lord Tennyson, 1911.]

Gladstone, W. E. On Tennyson. Quarterly Rev. Oct. 1859. [Rptd in Gleanings of Past Years, vol. II, 1879. Separately pbd in Gladstone on Tennyson, Old South Leaflets, No. 193, [Boston, 1908].]

* The section on Hallam has been contributed by Professor T. H. Vail Motter.

Gladstone, W. E. Personal Recollections of Arthur H. Hallam. Daily Telegraph, 5 Jan. 1898; Youth's Companion (Boston), 6 Jan. 1898. [Separately pbd, Companion Classics, No. 1, Boston, [1898].]

[Field, A.?] Memoir of Arthur Henry Hallam. [In In Memoriam, Boston, 1861.]

[Alford, F.] Life, Journals and Letters of Henry Alford, D.D. 1873.

Ritchie, A. T. Tennyson. Harper's Mag. Dec. 1883. [Rptd in The Complete Poetical Works of Alfred, Lord Tennyson Poet Laureate, New York, 1884.]

Maurice, J. F. The Life of Frederick Denison Maurice chiefly told in His Own Letters. 2 vols. 1884.

Reminiscences and Opinions of Sir Francis Hastings Doyle. New York, 1887.

[Hallam's Remains.] N. & Q. 27 Sept. 1890, pp. 244-5.

Weld, A. G. Glimpses of Tennyson and of Some of His Relations and Friends. 1903.

Brookfield, C. and F. Mrs. Brookfield and Her Circle. 2 vols. 1905.

Brookfield, F. M. The Cambridge 'Apostles.' 1906.

[Collins, C. W.] The Cambridge Apostles. Blackwood's Mag. March, 1907.

Toynbee, P. Dante in English Literature. 2 vols. [1909]. [Vol. II, pp. 416-24.]

Thwing, F. B. Arthur Henry Hallam. North American Rev. CXCIII, 1911.

Lounsbury, T. R. The Life and Times of Tennyson. New Haven, 1915.

Cornish, Mrs W. Memories of Tennyson. London Mercury, v, 1921-2.

Nicolson, H. Tennyson. 1923.

[Madan, Geoffrey.] Arthur Hallam: One Who 'Perish'd In the Green.' Times, 15 Sept. 1933.

In Memoriam: A. H. H. Poetry Rev. Nov.-Dec. 1933.

Boas, F. S. Arthur Henry Hallam. Queen's Quart. (Kingston), XLI, 1934.

Motter, T. H. V. A 'Lost' Poem by Arthur Hallam. PMLA. L, 1935.

JAMES HANNAY (1827-1873)

(a) Biographical and Critical Writings

Blackwood v. Carlyle. By a Carlylian. 1850.

The Life and Genius of Edgar Allan Poe. [Prefixed to Poe's Poetical Works, 1853.]

Satires and Satirists. Six Lectures. 1854.

Essays from the Quarterly Review. 1861. [Table-Talk, English Political Satires, Horace and his Translators, The Minstrelsy of Scotland, Literary Biography, etc.]

A Brief Memoir of Mr. Thackeray. Edinburgh, 1864. [Rptd from Edinburgh Courant.]

Characters and Criticisms: a Book of Miscellanies. Edinburgh, 1865. [Plutarch, Thackeray, Lady Mary Wortley Montagu, Development of English Poetry, H. T. Buckle, Prof. Wilson, etc.]

A Course of English Literature. 1866.

Memoir of Charles Churchill. [Prefixed to Churchill's Poetical Works, 1866.]

Hogarth as a Satirist. [Prefixed to The Complete Works of William Hogarth, with Descriptive Letterpress by J. Trusler and E. F. Roberts, 1868.]

Studies on Thackeray. 1869.

[Hannay also pbd Three Hundred Years of a Norman House; the Barons of Gournay from the Tenth to the Thirteenth Century, 1867, an unfinished history of the Gurney family.]

(b) Fiction

Biscuits and Grog. Personal Reminiscences and Sketches by Percival Plug, R.N. 1848. [Part autobiography, part sketches, thrown into the form of a narrative.]

A Claret-Cup. Further Reminiscences and Sketches of Percival Plug, R.N. 1848.

King Dobbs. Sketches in Ultra-Marine. 1849. [An adventure story with a satirical intention.]

Hearts are Trumps. An Amphibious Story. 1849.

Singleton Fontenoy, R.N. 3 vols. 1850; 1854 (rev.).

Sand and Shells. Nautical Sketches. 1854. [Short stories rptd from Household Words and from United Service Mag.]

Eustace Conyers. A Novel. 3 vols. 1855; 1857.

ABRAHAM HAYWARD (1801-1884)

(a) Essays and Critical Writings

The Art of Dining. 1852; ed. C. Sayle, 1899. [Based on 2 articles in Quarterly Rev.]

Lord Chesterfield, his Life, Character and Opinions: and George Selwyn, his Life and Times. 1854.

Biographical and Critical Essays. 5 vols. 1858-74. [Sydney Smith, S. Rogers, J. Smith, Lord Melbourne, Stendhal, Lord Eldon, British Field Sports, Dumas, Maria Edgeworth, Canning, H. Holland, etc.]

The Life and Writings of Mrs. Piozzi (Mrs. Thrale). [Prefixed to the Autobiography, Letters and Literary Remains of Mrs. Piozzi, ed. A. Hayward, 2 vols. 1861 (bis, 2nd edn rearranged and expanded).]

More about Junius. The Franciscan Theory Unsound. 1868. [Rptd, with addns, from Fraser's Mag.]

Goethe. 1877.

Selected Essays. 2 vols. 1878.
Sketches of Eminent Statesmen and Writers.
2 vols. 1880. [Rptd, with addns, from
Quarterly Rev.: Thiers, Bismarck, Cavour,
Metternich, de Montalembert, Melbourne,
Wellesley, de Sévigné, Byron, Tennyson,
du Deffand, etc.]

(b) Poems and Translations

Faust. 1833 (priv. ptd); 1833; 1834 (adds
summary of pt II and account of Faust
story). [A prose trn of Goethe's pt I with
notes on former versions.]
Verses of Other Days. 1847 (priv. ptd); 1878
(enlarged).

[Hayward also translated F. C. von
Savigny's On the Vocation of our Age for
Legislation, 1831 (priv. ptd).]

(c) Other Writings

The Statutes, founded on the Common Law
Reports, with Observations and Notes.
1832.
Some Account of a Journey across the Alps in
a Letter to a Friend. 1834 (priv. ptd).
[Rptd in Selections from the Correspondence
of Abraham Hayward, 1886.]
Juridical Tracts. Pt 1 (all pbd), 1856.
Mr. Kinglake and the Quarterlys. By an Old
Reviewer. 1863.
The Second Armada. 1871. [Rptd, with
addns, from Times. An account of an
imaginary invasion of England by Ger-
many.]
John Stuart Mill. 1873 (priv. ptd). [Rptd
from Times. An account of the life and
work of Mill which became the subject of
an acute controversy.]
Short Rules for Modern Whist. 1878.
A Selection from the Correspondence of
Abraham Hayward, from 1834 to 1884.
With an Account of his Early Life. Ed. H. E.
Carlisle, 2 vols. 1886.

[Hayward also pbd other legal and controversial works.]

SIR ARTHUR HELPS (1813–1875)

(a) Selected Works

Essays and Aphorisms. With an Introduction
by E. A. Helps. 1892.

(b) General Essays and Studies

Thoughts in the Cloister and the Crowd. 1835
(anon.); rptd 1901. [Aphorisms.]
Essays Written in the Intervals of Business.
1841 (anon.); ed. F. J. Rowe and W. T.
Webb, 1889.
Friends in Council. 3 sers. 1847–59 (anon.);
ed. E. A. Helps, [1907]. [Dialogues on
social and intellectual subjects.]

Companions of my Solitude. 1851 (anon.); ed.
E. A. Helps, 1907. [Chiefly on social
questions.]
Brevia. Short Essays and Aphorisms. 1871.
Some Talk about Animals and their Masters.
1873. [Dialogues.]

(c) Sociological Writings

The Claims of Labour. An Essay on the
Duties of the Employers to the Employed.
1844 (anon.); rptd [1907].
On the Responsibilities of Employers. 1849.
Organization in Daily Life. An Essay. 1862
(anon.).
Conversations on War and General Culture.
1871.
Thoughts upon Government. 1872.
Social Pressure. 1875.

(d) Historical and Biographical Writings

The Conquerors of the New World and their
Bondsmen: the Events which led to Negro
Slavery. 2 vols. 1848–52 (anon.).
The Spanish Conquest in America and its
Relation to the History of Slavery. 4 vols.
1855–61; ed. M. Oppenheim, 4 vols. 1900–4
(with maps and introduction).
The Life of Las Casas, the Apostle of the
Indians. 1868. [Rptd from The Spanish
Conquest.]
The Life of Columbus. 1869; ed. E. A. Helps,
1910 (Everyman's Lib.). [Rptd from The
Spanish Conquest.]
The Life of Pizarro. 1869. [Rptd from The
Spanish Conquest.]
The Life of Hernando Cortes. 2 vols. 1871.
[Rptd from The Spanish Conquest.]
The Life and Labours of Mr. Thomas Brassey.
1805–1870. 1872. [Helps also edited
Brassey's On Work and Wages, 1872.]

(e) Letters

A Letter from one of the Special Constables
in London on the Occasion of their being
called out to keep the Peace. 1848 (anon.).
A Letter on 'Uncle Tom's Cabin.' Cambridge,
1852.
Correspondence. Ed. E. A. Helps, 1917.

(f) Fiction

Realmah. 2 vols. 1868.
Casimir Maremma. 2 vols. 1870.
Ivan de Biron. A Russian Story. 3 vols. 1874.

(g) Plays

King Henry the Second. An Historical Drama.
1843 (anon.).
Catherine Douglas. A Tragedy. 1843 (anon.).
Oulita the Serf. A Tragedy. 1858 (anon.).

RICHARD HENRY HORNE (1803–1884)
[See p. 290 above.]

RICHARD HOLT HUTTON (1826–1897)

(a) Selected Works

Aspects of Religious and Scientific Thought. Ed. E. M. Roscoe, 1899. [Selection from contributions to the Spectator.]
Brief Literary Criticisms. Selected from the Spectator. Ed. E. M. Roscoe, 1906.

(b) Biographical and Critical Writings

Studies in Parliament. 1866. [Rptd from Pall Mall Gazette: Gladstone, Disraeli, Cobden, Palmerston, Bright, Earl Grey, etc.]
Essays, Theological and Literary. 2 vols. 1871. [Vol. I: Theological. Vol. II: Goethe, Wordsworth, Shelley, Browning, George Eliot, Clough, Hawthorne.]
Sir Walter Scott. 1878.
Cardinal Newman. 1891.
Criticisms on Contemporary Thought and Thinkers. 2 vols. 1894. [Carlyle, Emerson, Poe, Longfellow, Dickens, Leslie Stephen, J. S. Mill, Arnold, Clough, Renan, Huxley, Bagehot, Ruskin, Wordsworth, Darwin, etc.]

(c) Miscellaneous Writings

Incarnation and Principles of Evidence. 1862.
The Relative Value of Studies and Accomplishments in the Education of Women. 1862.
The Political Character of the Working Classes. 1867.
Essays on some of the Modern Guides of English Thought in Matters of Faith. 1887.

(d) Biography and Criticism

Watson, Sir W. Excursions in Criticism. 1893.
Wedgwood, Julia. R. H. Hutton. Contemporary Rev. Oct. 1897.
Escott, T. H. S. R. H. Hutton—an Estimate of his Life and Work. Bookman, Oct. 1897.
Hogben, J. Richard Holt Hutton of the 'Spectator.' Edinburgh, 1899.
Boas, F. S. Critics and Criticism in the 'Seventies. [In The Eighteen-Seventies, Royal Soc. Lit. 1929.]

JOSEPH KNIGHT (1829–1907)

(a) Critical Writings

Life of D. G. Rossetti. 1887.
Theatrical Notes. 1893.
David Garrick. 1894.
A History of the Stage during the Victorian Era. 1901.

[Knight contributed more than 500 lives (mainly of dramatists) to the DNB. In 1886 he wrote an historical preface to J. Downes's Roscius Anglicanus; and he wrote prefaces to plays by Sheridan and Henry Arthur Jones. From 1883 till his death he edited N. & Q.]

(b) Biography and Criticism

Francis, J. C. Notes by the Way. With Memoirs of Joseph Knight. 1909.
Rendall, V. H. Some Reminiscences of Joseph Knight. Nineteenth Century, LXX, 1911.

PERCIVAL LEIGH (1813–1889)

(a) Humorous Writings

Stories and Poems in the Fiddle-Faddle Fashion Book. 1840.
The Comic Latin Grammar. 1840.
The Comic English Grammar. 1840.
Portraits of Children of the Mobility. With Memoirs and Characteristic Sketches. 1841. [Illustrated by Leech.]
Jack the Giant Killer. Illustrated by J. Leech. [1843.] [Verse.]
Manners and Customs of ye Englyshe, drawn from ye Quick by Rychard Doyle. To which be added some Extracts from Mr. Pips hys Diary contributed by P[ercival] L[eigh]. 1849; 1876 (extended).
Paul Prendergast; or, The Comic Schoolmaster. Illustrated by Leech, A. Crowquill, etc. [1859].

(b) Biography and Criticism

Obituary. Athenaeum, 2 Nov. 1889.
Frith, W. P. John Leech. Vol. I, 1891.

GEORGE HENRY LEWES (1817–1878)

[See p. 869 below.]

FRANCIS SYLVESTER MAHONY (1804–1866)

(a) Humorous Writings

The Reliques of Father Prout, late P.P. of Watergrasshill in the County of Cork. Collected and arranged by Oliver Yorke, Esq. Illustrated by Alfred Croquis, Esq. [i.e. Daniel Maclise]. 2 vols. 1836; 1870. [Rptd from Fraser's Mag. 1834–6.]
Facts and Figures from Italy. By Don Jeremy Savonarola, Benedictine Monk. Addressed during the Last Two Winters to Charles Dickens, being an Appendix to his 'Pictures' [from Italy]. 1847.
The Final Reliques of Father Prout. Collected and edited by D. Jerrold. 1876.
The Works of Father Prout. Ed. (with memoir) C. Kent, 1881.
[Mahony was the Paris correspondent of The Globe, 1858–66.]

(b) Biography and Criticism

Obituary. Athenaeum, 26 May 1866.
Hannay, J. Aytoun, Peacock and Prout.
North British Rev. Sept. 1866.
Bates, W. The Maclise Portrait-Gallery. 1873.

DAVID MASSON (1822–1907)

(a) Biographical and Critical Writings

Essays, Biographical and Critical: chiefly on
English Poets. Cambridge, 1856. [Shake-
speare and Goethe; Dryden, Swift; Chatter-
ton; Wordsworth; Scottish Influence on
British Literature; Theories of Poetry;
De Quincey; The Three Devils; Milton's
Youth.]
British Novelists and Their Styles. Being a
Critical Sketch of the History of British
Prose Fiction. Cambridge, 1859.
The Life of John Milton; narrated in Con-
nexion with the Political, Ecclesiastical and
Literary History of his Time. 7 vols. 1859–
94; 7 vols. 1881–96 (rev. edn of vols. I–III).
Recent British Philosophy. Cambridge, 1865;
1877 (adds 1 ch.). [British Comtism; Bain
and Herbert Spencer; Ferrier and a British
Hegelian; J. S. Mill on Sir William Hamil-
ton; Swedenborgianism and 'Spiritualism,'
etc.]
Drummond of Hawthornden: the Story of his
Life and Writings. 1873.
Chatterton. A Story of the Year 1770. 1874;
1899 (rev. and enlarged). [Rptd from
Essays Biographical and Literary.]
The Three Devils: Luther's, Milton's and
Goethe's. 1874. [5 essays rptd from
Essays Biographical and Critical. Essay on
How Literature may illustrate History is
new.]
Wordsworth, Shelley, Keats, and Other
Essays. 1874. [4 essays rptd from Essays
Biographical and Literary. Two essays, on
Shelley and on Keats, are new.]
De Quincey. 1881; 1885 (rev.). (English Men
of Letters ser.)
Oliver Goldsmith. [Memoir prefixed to The
Vicar of Wakefield, 1883.]
Carlyle personally and in his Writings. Two
Lectures. 1885.
Edinburgh Sketches and Memories. 1892.
[Sir Walter Scott, Allan Ramsay, Carlyle's
Edinburgh Life, C. K. Sharpe, J. H.
Burton, Dr John Brown, etc.]
Milton. [In In the Footsteps of the Poets,
1893.]
James Melvin, Rector of the Grammar School
of Aberdeen. A Sketch. Aberdeen, 1895.
Memories of London in the 'Forties. Arranged
and Annotated by Flora Masson. Edin-
burgh, 1908.

Memories of Two Cities, Edinburgh and
Aberdeen. Ed. F. Masson, Edinburgh,
1911. [Papers rptd from Macmillan's Mag.:
Dr Chalmers, David Welsh, 'Christopher
North,' Hugh Miller, De Quincey, W.
Hamilton, etc.]
Shakespeare Personally. Ed. R. Masson,
1914. [Lectures delivered 1865–95 at
Edinburgh University.]

(b) Writings on Education

College-Education and Self-Education. A
Lecture. 1854.
The State of Learning in Scotland. A Lecture.
Edinburgh, 1866.
University Teaching for Women. Edinburgh,
1868. [In Introductory Lectures to the
Second Series of Lectures in Shandwick
Place, 1868.]

[To Chambers's Educational Course Masson
contributed Ancient History, and History of
Rome, 1848; Mediaeval History, 1855, and
Modern History, 1856; for the same publishers
he wrote an account of the British Museum,
1848.]

(c) Biography and Criticism

Barrie, Sir J. M. An Edinburgh Eleven. 1889.
Obituary. Times, 8 Oct. 1907.
Macmillan, Alexander. Letters. 1908.
Masson, Flora. David Masson. Cornhill Mag.
Nov. 1910, June 1911.

JOHN FREDERICK DENISON MAURICE
(1805–1872)

(a) Bibliography

Gray, G. J. Bibliography of the Writings of
Frederick Denison Maurice. [In Sir J. F.
Maurice's Life of Maurice, vol. I, 1884.]

(b) Miscellaneous Writings

Eustace Conway, or the Brother and Sister.
A Novel. 1834.
Moral and Metaphysical Philosophy. 1845.
[A section of Encyclopaedia Metropolitana,
ed. E. Smedley. Later expanded into 4
separate works: Ancient Philosophy, 1850;
Philosophy of the First Six Centuries, 1853,
2 vols. 1872; Mediaeval Philosophy, 1857;
Modern Philosophy, 1862.]
Theological Essays. Cambridge, 1853 (bis);
1871.
Sermons. 6 vols. [1857–9], 1860.
The Workman and the Franchise. Chapters
from English History on the Representa-
tion and Education of the People. 1866.
The Conscience. Lectures on Casuistry. 1868;
1872.
Social Morality. Twenty-One Lectures. 1869.

The Friendship of Books, and Other Lectures. Ed. T. Hughes, 1874.

[Maurice also pbd numerous sermons, tracts, etc. as well as contributing prefaces to works by others. He edited, at different periods, The Athenaeum, The Christian Socialist and The Educational Magazine.]

(c) Biography and Criticism

Frederick Denison Maurice and his Writings. London Quarterly Rev. III, 1855.

Rigg, J. H. Modern Anglican Theology. Chapters on Coleridge, Maurice, [etc.]. 1857.

Kingsley, C. Memorial of Frederick Denison Maurice. Macmillan's Mag. XXVI, 1872.

Davies, J. L. The Theology and Secularism of F. D. Maurice. Contemporary Rev. XXIV, 1874.

Stephen, Sir L. The Theology of F. D. Maurice. Fortnightly Rev. XXI, 1874.

Frederick Denison Maurice: a Modern Prophet. Atlantic Monthly, LIV, 1884.

Maurice, Sir J. F. The Life of Frederick Denison Maurice, chiefly told in his own Letters. 2 vols. 1884.

Hutton, R. H. Essays on some of the Modern Guides of English Thought. 1887.

Dungern, H. von. Der Führer der christlich-sozialen Bewegung Englands von 1848–1866: F. D. Maurice. Göttingen, 1900.

Masterman, C. F. G. F. D. Maurice. 1907.

Sanders, C. R. Maurice as a Commentator on Coleridge. PMLA. LIII, 1938.

HORACE MAYHEW (1816–1872)

Change for a Shilling. Illustrated by H. G. Hine. [1848.]

The Comic Almanac for 1848. Edited by Horace Mayhew. 1848.

Model Men, modelled by Horace Mayhew, sculptured by H. G. Hine. 1848.

Model Women and Children, modelled by Horace Mayhew, sculptured by H. G. Hine. 1848.

Guy Faux. A Squib manufactured by Horace Mayhew and Percy Cruikshank. [1849.]

The Tooth-Ache, imagined by Horace Mayhew and realized by George Cruikshank. [1849.]

Letters left at the Pastrycook's; being the Clandestine Correspondence between Kitty Clover at School, and her 'Dear, Dear Friend' in town. 1853.

[In Dec. 1847 Mayhew brought out a 'Plum Pudding Pantomime' at the Olympic Theatre, but it does not appear to have been pbd. An obituary notice is in Athenaeum, 4 May 1872.]

JOHN STUART MILL (1806–1873)

[See p. 871 below.]

HUGH MILLER (1802–1856)

(a) Selected Works

Selections. Chosen and Edited by W. M. Mackenzie. Paisley, 1908.

(b) Essays and Sketches

Scenes and Legends of the North of Scotland, or the Traditional History of Cromarty. 1835.

Sutherland as it was and is, or How a Country may be ruined. 1843.

First Impressions of England and its People. 1847.

My Schools and Schoolmasters, or the Story of my Education. Edinburgh, 1854; ed. W. M. Mackenzie, 1905.

Essays, Historical and Biographical, Political and Social, Literary and Scientific. Ed. P. Bayne, Edinburgh, 1862. [Rptd from The Witness.]

Tales and Sketches. Ed. L. F. F. Miller, Edinburgh, 1863.

Leading Articles on Various Subjects. Ed. J. Davidson, Edinburgh, 1870.

(c) Geological Writings

The Old Red Sandstone, or New Walks in an Old Field. Edinburgh, 1841; Glasgow, 1858 (adds a series of geological papers). [Rptd from The Witness.]

Geology of the Bass. [In The Bass Rock: its Civil and Ecclesiastic History by T. MacCrie, 1848.]

Footprints of the Creator, or the Asterolepsis of Stromness. 1849 (anon.); ed. L. F. F. Miller, 1861 (with memoir by L. Agassiz). [A reply to Vestiges of Creation, 1844.]

The Fossiliferous Deposits of Scotland. Edinburgh, 1854.

The Two Records: Mosaic and Geological. A Lecture. 1854.

Geology versus Astronomy. A View of the Modifying Effects of Geologic Discovery on the Old Astronomic Inferences respecting the Plurality of Inhabited Worlds. Glasgow, 1855.

The Testimony of the Rocks. Edinburgh, 1857.

Voices from the Rocks, or Proofs of the Existence of Man during the Palaeozoic Period. 1857.

The Cruise of the Betsy, or a Summer Ramble among the Fossiliferous Deposits of the Hebrides. With Rambles of a Geologist. Ed. W. S. Symonds, Edinburgh, 1858.

Sketch-Book of Popular Geology. A Series of Lectures. With a Preface by Mrs Miller. Edinburgh, 1859.

Edinburgh and its Neighbourhood, Geological and Historical. With the Geology of the Bass Rock. Ed. L. F. F. Miller, Edinburgh, 1864.

Geology of the Country around Otterburn and Elsdon. 1887.

(d) Other Writings

Letters on the Herring Fishery. Inverness, 1829. [Rptd from Inverness Courier.]

Poems written in the Leisure Hours of a Journeyman Mason. Inverness, 1829.

Memoir of William Forsyth. 1839.

The Whiggism of the Old School. Edinburgh, 1839. [This and the next item are pamphlets advocating an Ecclesiastical Reform Bill for Scotland.]

A Letter to Lord Brougham. Edinburgh, 1839.

The Two Parties in the Church of Scotland exhibited as Missionary and Anti-Missionary. Edinburgh, 1841.

Words of Warning to the People of Scotland on Sir Robert Peel's Scotch Currency Scheme. Edinburgh, 1844.

The Sites Bill and the Toleration Laws. Edinburgh, 1848.

Thoughts on the Education Question. Edinburgh, 1850. [Rptd from The Witness.]

Strange but True. Incidents in the Life of J. Kitto. Edinburgh, 1856.

The Headship of Christ, and the Rights of the Christian People. With a Preface by P. Bayne. Edinburgh, 1861.

(e) Biography and Criticism

Brown, T. N. Labour and Triumph. The Life and Times of Hugh Miller. 1858.

Bingham, W. The Life and Writings of Hugh Miller. An Oration. 1859.

The Life of Hugh Miller. A Sketch for Working Men. 1862. [Rptd from Northern Daily Express.]

Bayne, P. The Life and Letters of Hugh Miller. Edinburgh, 1871.

Watson, T. L. Life of Hugh Miller. Edinburgh, 1880.

Leask, W. K. Hugh Miller. Edinburgh, 1896.

Allibone's Dictionary of Authors. Vol. II, 1902. [Includes biography, bibliography, references to and extracts from reviews and articles on Hugh Miller.]

Mackenzie, W. M. Hugh Miller. A Critical Study. 1905.

Masson, D. Hugh Miller. [In Memories of Two Cities, Edinburgh and Aberdeen, 1911.]

RICHARD MONCKTON MILNES, BARON HOUGHTON (1809–1885)

[See p. 299 above.]

HENRY MORLEY (1822–1894)

(a) Biographical and Critical Works

Bernard Palissy, the Potter. 2 vols. 1852.

The Life of Geronimo Cardano, of Milan, Physician. 2 vols. 1854.

Cornelius Agrippa von Nettesheim. 2 vols. 1856.

Memoirs of Bartholomew Fair. 1857.

English Writers. Vol. I, 1864 (subsequently divided into 2 half vols.). Vol. II, 1867 (half vol. only; 2nd half never pbd, and all 3 half vols. allowed to go out of print). Vols. I–XI, 1887–1895. [20 vols. intended but Morley only lived to write 10, vol. XI being completed by W. Hall Griffin.]

The Journal of a London Playgoer from 1851 to 1866. 1866.

Tables of English Literature. 1870; 1870 (adds Index).

Clement Marot and Other Studies. 2 vols. 1871. [Marot, Vesalius, Gesner, Cyrano de Bergerac, Gabriel Harvey, Caedmon's Paraphrase, Influence of the Celt on English Literature, etc.]

A First Sketch of English Literature. 1873; 1886 (enlarged).

Cassell's Library of English Literature. 5 vols. 1875–1881. [Extracts from and summaries of the greatest English classics, with notes and explanatory text by Morley.]

Of English Literature in the Reign of Victoria, with a Glance at the Past. Leipzig, 1881.

Morley's Universal Library. 63 vols. 1883–1888, 1891. [Every vol. has an introduction, critical and biographical, by Morley.]

Cassell's National Library. 205 vols. 1886. [A wide selection from the English classics with introduction to each vol. by Morley.]

The Carisbrooke Library. 14 vols. 1889–1892. [Edited by Morley.]

Memoir of Thomas Sadler. 1891.

(b) Fairy Tales

The Dream of the Lilybell, Tales and Poems; with Translations of the 'Hymns to Night' from the German of Novalis and Jean Paul's Death of an Angel. 1845.

Fables and Fairy Tales. 1860.

Oberon's Horn: a Book of Fairy Tales. 1861.

Fairy Tales. 1867; 1877 (as The Chicken Market and Other Fairy Tales). [Tales previously pbd in Fables and Fairy Tales and Oberon's Horn.]

(c) Other Writings

A Tract upon Health for Cottage Circulation. 1847.

Sunrise in Italy. 1848. [A poem.]

How to make Home Unhealthy. 1850. [Rptd from Examiner. Afterwards included in Early Papers and Some Memories, 1891.]

A Defence of Ignorance. 1851. [A satirical essay on education.]

Gossip. 1857. [Tales, papers and verses rptd from Household Words.]

University College, London. 1828–1878. A Lecture. 1878.

An Account of the New North Wing and Recent Additions to University College, London. 1881.

Candide. By F. A. M. de Voltaire. 1888; 1922. [Trn by Morley; originally ptd with Johnson's Rasselas as Morley's Universal Library, vol. xix.]

Early Papers and Some Memories. 1891. [Short Autobiographical Chapter followed by How to make Home Unhealthy, A Defence of Ignorance, Dream of the Lilybell, and 16 other papers, largely rptd from Household Words and All the Year Round.]

(d) Biography

Solly, H. S. The Life of Henry Morley. 1898.

FRANCIS TURNER PALGRAVE (1824–1897)
[See p. 303 above.]

MARK PATTISON (1813–1884)

(a) Critical and Biographical Writings

The Lives of the English Saints. Ed. J. H. Newman, 4 vols. 1844–5; rev. A. W. Hutton, 6 vols. 1901. [Pattison contributed anon. lives of Stephen Langton and St Edmund.]

Isaac Casaubon, 1559–1614. 1875; ed. H. Nettleship, 1892 (adds Index).

Encyclopaedia Britannica. 1875–89 (9th edn). [Pattison wrote the articles on Bentley, Erasmus, Grotius, Sir Thomas More, Lipsius and Lord Macaulay. The last is rptd prefixed to Macaulay's Life of Pitt, 1002.]

Milton. 1879; 1880 (rev.). (English Men of Letters ser.)

Memoirs. Edited by Mrs Pattison. 1885.

Essays. Ed. H. Nettleship, 2 vols. Oxford, 1889; 1908 (5 essays omitted). [The 1889 edn contains (with dated list of other essays appearing in periodicals), Muretus, Life of Scaliger, University History, Oxford Studies, Pope and his Editors, and (in this edn only) Montaigne, P. D. Huet, Calvin at Geneva, etc.]

[Pattison also edited Pope's Essay on Man (1871) and Satires and Epistles (1872). The notes are still valuable.]

(b) Educational Writings

Oxford Studies. [On University reform; in Oxford Essays, 1855.]

Report on Elementary Education in Protestant Germany. 1859. [Contained in the Report of the Assistant Commissioners on the State of Popular Education in Continental Europe, vol. iv, 1861.]

Suggestions on Academical Organisation, with Special Reference to Oxford. Edinburgh, 1868.

Review of the Situation. [In Essays on the Endowment of Research, 1876.]

(c) Theological Writings

The Sufficiency of Holy Scriptures for the Salvation of Man. An Essay. 1841 (priv. ptd). [Awarded the Denyer Theological Prize.]

Original or Birth Sin and the Necessity of New Birth unto Life. 1842 (priv. ptd). [Awarded the Denyer Theological Prize.]

Tendencies of Religious Thought in England, 1688–1750. [In Essays and Reviews, 1860; included, in enlarged form, in Pattison's Essays, 1889.]

Sermons. 1885.

(d) Biography and Criticism

Nettleship, H. Obituary. Academy, 9 Aug. 1884.

Althaus, T. F. Recollections of Mark Pattison. 1885. [Rptd from Temple Bar.]

Tollemache, L. A. Recollections of Pattison. 1885. [Rptd with addns from Journ. of Education.]

Morley, John, Viscount. Critical Miscellanies. Vol. iii, 1886.

Montague, F. C. Some Early Letters of Mark Pattison. John Rylands Lib. Bulletin, xviii, 1934.

AUGUSTUS WELBY NORTHMORE PUGIN (1812–1852)

(a) Works on Architecture and Decoration

Gothic Furniture in the Style of the 15th Century. Designed and etched by A. W. N. Pugin. 1835.

Contrasts, or a Parallel between the Noble Edifices of the Fourteenth and Fifteenth Centuries and Similar Buildings of the Present Day; shewing the Present Decay of Taste. 1836.

An Apology for a Work entitled Contrasts; being a Defence of the Assertions advanced in that Publication, against the Various Attacks lately made upon it. Birmingham, 1837.

The True Principles of Pointed or Christian Architecture. 1841; tr. French, Brussels, 1850.

An Apology for the Revival of Christian Architecture in England. 1843.

The Present State of Ecclesiastical Architecture in England. Republished from The Dublin Review. 1843.

Glossary of Ecclesiastical Ornament and Costume, compiled and illustrated from Antient Authorities and Examples. 1844; rev. B. Smith, 1868.

Some Remarks on the Articles which have recently appeared in the 'Rambler' relative to Ecclesiastical Architecture and Decoration. 1850.

A Treatise on Chancel Screens and Rood Lofts; their Antiquity, Use and Symbolic Signification. Illustrated with figures. 1851.

[Pugin also pbd engravings and pamphlets on religious and ecclesiastical matters.]

(b) Biography and Criticism

Ferrey, B. Recollections of A. N. Welby Pugin, and his Father, Augustus Pugin. With Notices of their Works. 1861.
Sirr, H. Augustus Welby Pugin: a Sketch. [1918.]
Clark, Sir K. The Gothic Revival. 1929.
Lomax, M. T. Pugin. A Mediaeval Victorian. 1932.

ANGUS BETHUNE REACH (1821–1856)

(a) Humorous Writings

The Natural History of 'Bores.' 1847.
The Natural History of Humbugs. 1847.
The Natural History of Tuft-Hunters and Toadies. 1848.
The Comic Bradshaw; or, Bubbles from the Boiler. 1848.
The Natural History of the 'Hawk' Tribe. 1848.
A Romance of a Mince-pie; an Incident in the Life of John Chirrup. 1848; [1850?] (illustrated by 'Phiz').
Clement Lorimer; or, The Book with the Iron Clasps. A Romance. Illustrated by G. Cruikshank. 1849; 1856.
Leonard Lindsay; or, The Story of a Buccaneer. 2 vols. 1850.
Claret and Olives, from the Garonne to the Rhone; or Notes Social, Picturesque and Legendary, by the Way. 1852; New York, 1852.
A Story with a Vengeance; or, How many Joints go to a Tale? 1852; [1853] (rev.). [With C. W. S. Brooks.]
Men of the Hour. 1856.
Christmas Cheer. 1856. [With J. Hannay and Albert R. Smith.]

[Reach was for some time on the staff of Punch and wrote a great deal in periodicals.]

(b) Biography and Criticism

Obituary. Athenaeum, 29 Nov. 1856.
Mackay, Charles. Forty Years' Recollections of Life, Literature and Public Affairs (1830–1870). 2 vols. 1877.
Spielmann, M. H. History of 'Punch.' 1895.

WILLIAM MICHAEL ROSSETTI (1829–1919)

(a) Critical and Miscellaneous Writings

The Germ: Thoughts towards Nature in Poetry, Literature and Art. 4 nos. 1850. [Ed. by W. M. Rossetti; he pbd a facs. rpt in 1901.]
Swinburne's Poems and Ballads. A Criticism. 1866.
Fine Art, chiefly Contemporary. Notices Re-Printed. 1867.
Notes on the Royal Academy Exhibition. 1868. [With A. C. Swinburne.]
Lives of Famous Poets. 1878. [Essays originally written as introductions to edns of Milton, Pope, Byron, etc. in Moxon's Popular Poets ser.]
Memoir of Percy Bysshe Shelley, with New Preface. 1886. [Rptd from Rossetti's edn of Shelley, 1870.]
Life of John Keats. 1887.
Dante Gabriel Rossetti as Designer and Writer. 1889.
D. G. Rossetti: his Family Letters, with a Memoir. 2 vols. 1895.
Ruskin: Rossetti: Preraphaelitism. Papers 1854 to 1862. 1899.
Preraphaelite Diaries and Letters. 1900.
Rossetti Papers, 1862–70. 1903.
Some Reminiscences. 2 vols. 1906.
Democratic Sonnets. 2 vols. 1907.
Dante and his Convito. A Study with Translations. 1910.
Letters about Shelley interchanged by Edward Dowden, Richard Garnett and Wm. Michael Rossetti. Ed. R. S. Garnett, 1917.
Letters of William Michael Rossetti concerning Whitman, Blake, and Shelley to Anna and Herbert Gilchrist. Ed. C. Gohdes and F. Baum, Durham, North Carolina, 1934.

[In addn to the 15 English poets in Moxon's Popular Poets, W. M. Rossetti was responsible for important edns of Walt Whitman, Shelley, Blake, D. G. and Christina Rossetti, and for the Chaucer Soc. and EETS. He contributed largely to Ency. Brit. (9th edn) and Shelley Soc. Papers, and pbd trns of Dante's Inferno and his father Gabriele Rossetti's versified autobiography.]

(b) Biography and Criticism

[See also under D. G. Rossetti, p. 272 above.]

Swinburne, A. C. Miscellanies. 1886. [Includes a review of W. M. Rossetti's Lives of Famous Poets.]
Horn, K. William Michael Rossetti. Zeitschrift für französischen und englischen Unterricht, XXIII, 1924.
Waller, R. D. The Rossetti Family, 1824–1854. Manchester, 1932.

WILLIAM BELL SCOTT (1811–1890)

[See p. 305 above.]

JOHN CAMPBELL SHAIRP (1819–1885)

(a) Critical Writings

John Keble. An Essay. Edinburgh, 1866.
Studies in Poetry and Philosophy. Edinburgh, 1868; 1886 (with preface by G. D. Boyle). [Wordsworth, Coleridge, Keble, The Moral Dynamic.]
A. H. Clough. A Sketch. [Included in the anon. memoir prefixed to The Poems and Prose Remains of A. H. Clough, 2 vols. 1869.]
Culture and Religion. 1870.
The Life and Letters of J. D. Forbes. 1873. [With P. G. Tait.]
Recollections of a Tour made in Scotland, 1803. By Dorothy Wordsworth. Edited by J. C. Shairp. 1874.
On Poetic Interpretation of Nature. Edinburgh, 1877.
Robert Burns. 1879. (English Men of Letters ser.)
Aspects of Poetry. Being Lectures delivered at Oxford. Oxford, 1881. [Virgil, Burns, Shelley, Ossian, Duncan MacIntyre, Wordsworth, Scott, Carlyle, Newman, and Five Essays on Poetry.]
Sketches in History and Poetry. Collected and edited by Professor Veitch. Edinburgh, 1887. [Henry Vaughan, The Ettrick Shepherd, Early Poetry of Scotland, Songs of Scotland before Burns, Queen Margaret of Scotland, etc.]

[Shairp also pbd The Wants of Scottish Universities and Some of the Remedies, 1856, and an Address on Missions, Edinburgh, 1874.]

(b) Poems

Charles the Twelfth. A Prize Poem recited in the Theatre, Oxford. Oxford, 1842.
Kilmahoe: a Highland Pastoral, and Other Poems. 1864.
Glen Desseray, and Other Poems. Ed. F. T. Palgrave, 1888.

(c) Biography and Criticism

Rodger, M. John Campbell Shairp. An Address. Edinburgh, 1885.
Knight, W. A. Principal Shairp and his Friends. Edinburgh, 1888.
Sellar, W. Y. Portraits of Friends. Boston, 1889.

JAMES SMETHAM (1821–1889)

[See p. 306 above.]

GOLDWIN SMITH (1823–1910)

[See p. 930 below.]

WILLIAM SPALDING (1809–1859)

(a) Critical and Miscellaneous Writings

A Letter on Shakespeare's Authorship of 'The Two Noble Kinsmen, a Drama.' 1833; New Shakspere Soc. 1876 (adds life of Spalding by J. H. Burton).
Italy and the Italian Islands, from the Earliest Ages to the Present Time. 3 vols. Edinburgh, 1841; New York, 1843.
The History of English Literature, with an Outline of the Origin and Growth of the English Language. Edinburgh, 1853; 1870 (11th edn, continued to 1870); 1877 (continued to 1876); tr. German, 1854.
The British Empire. Glasgow, 1856. [With 19 other contributors, Spalding assisted in compiling an encyclopaedic volume on the British Empire. He wrote a large number of memoirs for the Biographical Section and shared in preparing the Historical Section.]
An Introduction to Logical Science. Edinburgh, 1857. [Rptd from Ency. Brit. 8th edn.]

(b) Biography and Criticism

Gilfillan, G. Galleries of Literary Portraits. Vol. II, Edinburgh, 1856.
Obituary. Scotsman, 19 Nov. 1859.

JAMES SPEDDING (1808–1881)

Evenings with a Reviewer, or a Free and Particular Examination of Mr. Macaulay's Article on Lord Bacon, in a Series of Dialogues. 2 vols. 1848 (priv. ptd); 2 vols. 1881 (with prefatory notice by G. S. Venables).
Companion to The Railway Edition of Lord Campbell's Life of Bacon. By a Railway Reader. 1853. [Rptd from Examiner.]
The Works of Francis Bacon. Collected and Edited by J. Spedding, R. L. Ellis, and D. D. Heath. 7 vols. 1857–9.
The Letters and the Life of Francis Bacon, set forth in Chronological Order, with a Commentary. 7 vols. 1861–74.
Publishers and Authors. 1867.
A Conference of Pleasure, composed about 1592 by Francis Bacon. 1870. [Ed. by Spedding.]
An Account of the Life and Times of Francis Bacon. 2 vols. Boston, 1878. [An abridged version of the American edn of the Works of Francis Bacon in 15 vols. Consists mainly of Spedding's original Commentary and constitutes a short complete biography of Bacon.]
Reviews and Discussions, Literary, Political and Historical, not relating to Bacon. 1879. [Dickens, Tennyson, English Hexameters, Twelfth Night, etc.]

Studies in English History by James Gairdner and James Spedding. Edinburgh, 1881. [Contains 2 historical essays by Spedding.]
Charles Tennyson, afterwards Turner. [Prefixed to Turner's Collected Sonnets, Old and New, 1898.]

SIR JAMES FITZJAMES STEPHEN (1829–1894)

[See p. 919 below.]

FREDERIC GEORGE STEPHENS (1828–1907)

(a) Art Criticism

William Holman Hunt and his Works. 1860 (anon.).
Normandy: its Gothic Architecture and History. A Sketch. 1865.
Flemish Relics, Architectural, Legendary, and Pictorial. 1866.
English Children as painted by Sir Joshua Reynolds. An Essay on Some of the Characteristics of Reynolds as a Painter. 1867.
Masterpieces of Mulready. Memorials of William Mulready. 1867.
The Early Works of Sir Edwin Landseer. A Brief Sketch of the Life of the Artist. 1869 (anon.); 1874 (as Memoirs of Landseer); 1879 (extended as Sir Edwin Landseer).
Catalogue of Prints and Drawings in the British Museum. Division I: Political and Personal Satires. (Prepared by F. G. Stephens, and containing many Descriptions by E. Hawkins). 4 vols. 1870–83.
A History of Gibraltar and its Sieges. 1870 (anon.).
English Artists of the Present Day. Essays by J. B. Atkinson, Sidney Colvin, F. G. Stephens, T. Taylor and J. L. Tupper. 1872.
Flemish and French Pictures, with Notes concerning the Painters and their Works. 1875.
Notes on Thomas Bewick, illustrating a Loan Collection of his Drawings and Woodcuts. 1880.
Notes on a Collection of Drawings and Woodcuts by Thomas Bewick exhibited at the Fine Art Society's Rooms, 1880. Also a Complete List of all Works illustrated by T. and J. Bewick. 2 pts, 1881.
Notes on a Collection of Drawings, Paintings and Etchings by Samuel Palmer. With an Account of the Milton Series of Drawings by L. R. Valpy. 1881.
Artists at Home. Photographed by J. P. Mayall and Reproduced in Facsimile. Edited with Biographical Notices and Descriptions, by F. G. Stephens. 6 pts, 1884.

Catalogue of the Works of Sir Joshua Reynolds exhibited at the Grosvenor Gallery, 1883–4. 1884.
J. C. Hook. 1884; [1888].
Memorials of William Mulready. 1890.
A Memoir of George Cruikshank by F. G. Stephens and an Essay on the Genius of George Cruikshank by W. M. Thackeray. 1891.
Dante Gabriel Rossetti. 1894; 1908.
Lawrence Alma Tadema, R.A. A Sketch of his Life and Work. 1895.

[Stephens also wrote Notes to the Grosvenor Gallery Catalogues of works by Reynolds (1884), Gainsborough (1885), Millais (1886) and Van Dyck (1887). He was art-critic to Athenaeum from 1861 to 1901, contributing to every issue but two in those forty years. His articles on The Private Collections of England are important.]

(b) Biography and Criticism

Rossetti, W. M. Obituary. Athenaeum, 16 March 1907.
Frederic George Stephens and the Pre-Raphaelite Brothers. With Reproductions of twenty-four Pictures from his Collection, and Notes by J. B. Manson. [1920] (priv. ptd).

JAMES HUTCHISON STIRLING (1820–1909)

[See p. 874 below.]

SIR WILLIAM STIRLING-MAXWELL (1818–1878)

[See p. 908 below.]

SIR HENRY TAYLOR (1800–1886)

[See p. 308 above.]

TOM TAYLOR (1817–1880)

[See p. 608 above.]

RICHARD CHENEVIX TRENCH (1807–1886)

[See p. 309 above.]

ROBERT ALFRED VAUGHAN (1823–1857)

The Witch of Endor, and Other Poems. 1844.
Hours with the Mystics. A Contribution to the History of Religious Opinion. 2 vols. 1856; ed. R. Vaughan, 1860; ed. W. Vaughan, 1880.
Essays and Remains. Ed. (with memoir) R. Vaughan, 2 vols. 1858. [Largely rptd from British Quarterly Rev.; the elder Vaughan's memoir was enlarged and pbd separately 1864.]

BARTHOLOMEW ELIOT GEORGE WARBURTON
(1810–1852)

The Crescent and the Cross; or, Romance and Realities of Eastern Travel. 2 vols. 1845.

Zoë: an Episode of the Greek War. 1847.

Memoirs of Prince Rupert and the Cavaliers. Including their Private Correspondence, now first published from the Original Manuscripts. 3 vols. 1849; tr. French, Geneva, 1851.

Reginald Hastings; or, a Tale of the Troubles in 164–. 3 vols. 1850.

Darien; or, The Merchant Prince. A Historical Romance. 3 vols. 1852.

[Warburton also edited G. D. Warburton's Hochelaga and R. F. Williams's Memoirs of Horace Walpole and his Contemporaries. For appreciations see The Late Eliot Warburton, Dublin University Mag. XXXIX, 1852, and Works of Eliot Warburton, English Rev. XVII, 1852.]

ROBERT ARIS WILLMOTT (1809–1863)

Lives of Sacred Poets. 2 sers. 1834–8.

Conversations at Cambridge. 1836 (anon.).

Letters of Eminent Persons, selected and illustrated. 1839.

Parlour Table Book: Extracts from Various Authors. 1840.

Pictures of Christian Life. 1841.

Poems. 1841; 1848 (rev. and expanded).

Bishop Jeremy Taylor, his Predecessors, Contemporaries, and Successors. 1847; 1848.

A Journal of Summer Time in the Country. 1849; 1858; 1864 (4th edn, with memoir by C. Willmott); rptd 1928 (with biographical note by E. P[artridge]).

Precious Stones, Aids to Reflection from Prose Writers of the Sixteenth, Seventeenth, and Eighteenth Centuries. 1850.

Pleasures, Objects, and Advantages of Literature. 1851; 1852; 1856; 1860 (5th edn, enlarged); ed. C. Metcalfe, 1906.

Poets of the Nineteenth Century. 1857.

English Sacred Poetry. 1862; 1883. [An anthology.]

[In addn to numerous sermons (of some literary distinction) Willmott also produced edns of Gray, Herbert, Akenside, Fairfax's Tasso, Wordsworth, James Montgomery and other English poets.]

CHRISTOPHER WORDSWORTH (1807–1885)

[See p. 313 above.]

R. D. C. and H. B. G.

V. THE LATE NINETEENTH-CENTURY CRITICS AND MISCELLANEOUS WRITERS

STEPHEN, BUTLER AND PATER

SIR LESLIE STEPHEN (1832–1904)

(1) BIBLIOGRAPHY

English Illustrated Mag. Nov. 1903.

(2) COLLECTED WORKS

Collected Essays. With Introductions by James Bryce and Herbert Paul. 10 vols. 1907.

(3) CRITICAL AND BIOGRAPHICAL WRITINGS

Hours in a Library. 3 sers. 1874–9; 4 vols. 1907 (with addns).

Samuel Johnson. 1878. (English Men of Letters ser.)

Alexander Pope. 1880. (English Men of Letters ser.)

Swift. 1882. (English Men of Letters ser.)

Dictionary of National Biography. [Editor 1882–1891. Contributed 378 articles, including biographies of Addison, Burns, Byron, Carlyle, Coleridge, Defoe, Dickens, Dryden, Goldsmith, Hume, Johnson, Landor, Macaulay, the Mills, Milton, Pope, Scott, Swift, Thackeray, Wordsworth, etc.]

Life of Henry Fawcett. 1885.

The Life of Sir James Fitzjames Stephen. 1895.

Studies of a Biographer. 4 vols. 1898–1902.

George Eliot. 1902. (English Men of Letters ser.)

Robert Louis Stevenson. An Essay. New York, 1903.

Hobbes. 1904. (English Men of Letters ser.)

English Literature and Society in the Eighteenth Century. 1904.

[Stephen also contributed biographical introductions to the collected novels of Fielding and Richardson, to Margaret Veley's poems and to James Payn's essays, and a memoir of J. D. Campbell in the latter's life of Coleridge. He edited J. R. Green's Letters and (with Sir F. Pollock) W. K. Clifford's Lectures and Essays.]

(4) PHILOSOPHICAL WRITINGS

Essays on Free Thinking and Plain Speaking. 1873.

History of English Thought in the Eighteenth Century. 2 vols. 1876.

Science of Ethics. 1882.

What is Materialism? A Discourse. 1886.

An Agnostic's Apology, and other Essays. 1893.

Social Rights and Duties. 2 vols. 1896.
The English Utilitarians. 3 vols. 1900.
The Aims of Ethical Societies. [In Ethics and
Religion, 1900.]
Evolution and Religious Conceptions. [In
The 19th Century. A Review of Progress,
1901.]

(5) MISCELLANEOUS WRITINGS

The Ascent of the Allalein Horn. [In Vacation
Tourists and Notes of Travel in 1860, ed.
Sir Francis Galton, 1861.]
The Ascent of the Schreckhorn. The Passage
of the Eiger Joch. [In Peaks, Passes and
Glaciers, ed. E. S. Kennedy, vol. II, 1862.]
The Poll Degree from the Third Point of
View. A Tract. 1863.
The Times on the American War, by L. S. 1865.
Sketches from Cambridge. By a Don. 1865;
ed. G. M. Trevelyan, Oxford, 1937. [Rptd
from Pall Mall Gazette.]
The Choice of Candidates by Popular Con-
stituencies. [In Essays on Reform, 1867.]
Regrets of a Mountaineer. 1867.
The Playground of Europe. 1871; 1895 (rev.).
[Largely rptd from Alpine Journ.]
Some Early Impressions. 1924.

[Stephen also contributed regularly to
Saturday Rev., Pall Mall Gazette, Nation
(New York), Cornhill Mag. (which he edited
1871–82), Fraser's Mag., Fortnightly Rev. and
other periodicals.]

(6) BIOGRAPHY AND CRITICISM

Trevelyan, Sir G. O. Macmillan's Mag. May
1860.
Life and Letters of J. R. Lowell. Ed. C. E.
Norton, 2 vols. 1894.
Symons, A. Leslie Stephen. Saturday Rev.
July 1898.
Bryce, James, Viscount. Alpine Journ. XXII,
1904.
Harrison, Frederic. Cornhill Mag. April 1904.
Lee, Sir Sydney. Times, 23 Feb. 1904. [See
also Lee's article in DNB. 2nd Supple-
ment.]
Maitland, F. W. Life and Letters of Leslie
Stephen. 1906.
Letters of George Meredith. 1912.
Thompson, Francis. Sir Leslie Stephen as a
Biographer. 1915.
Williams, S. T. Leslie Stephen. Twenty Years
Later. London Mercury, Oct. 1923.
Birrell, A. Anti-Humbug. [In More Obiter
Dicta, 1924.]
Woolf, V. Leslie Stephen: the Philosopher at
Home. Times, 28 Nov. 1932.
MacCarthy, D. Leslie Stephen. Cambridge,
1937. (Leslie Stephen Lecture.)

SAMUEL BUTLER (1835–1902)

(1) BIBLIOGRAPHIES

Jones, H. F. Samuel Butler: a Memoir. 1919.
[Bibliography prefixed.]
Hoppé, A. J. A Bibliography of the Writings
of Samuel Butler and of Writings about
him. With some Letters from Butler to
F. G. Fleay now first published. [1925.]
[Some omissions and later criticism are
supplied by J. B. Fort, Samuel Butler,
Bordeaux, 1934, pp. 487–505.]

(2) COLLECTED WORKS

The Shrewsbury Edition of the Works of
Samuel Butler. Ed. H. F. Jones and A. T.
Bartholomew, 20 vols. 1923–6.

(3) PHILOSOPHICAL WORKS AND FICTION

The Evidence for the Resurrection of Jesus
Christ, as given by the Four Evangelists,
critically examined. 1865 (anon.).
Erewhon; or Over the Range. 1872 (anon.);
1872 (rev. and corrected); 1901 (rev.); ed.
F. B. Hackett, New York, 1917; ed. A.
Huxley, New York, 1934. Tr. Dutch, 1873;
German, 1879.
The Fair Haven. A Work in Defence of the
Miraculous Element in our Lord's Ministry
upon Earth, both as against Rationalistic
Impugners and Certain Orthodox Defenders.
By the late J. P. Owen. Edited by W. B.
Owen, with a Memoir of the Author. 1873;
ed. R. A. Streatfeild, 1913.
Life and Habit: an Essay after a Completer
View of Evolution. 1878; ed. R. A. Streat-
feild, 1910 (with addns).
Evolution, Old and New; or, The Theories of
Buffon, Dr. Erasmus Darwin, and Lamarck,
as compared with that of Mr. Charles
Darwin. 1879; 1882 (with Appendix and
Index); ed. R. A. Streatfeild, 1911.
Unconscious Memory: a Comparison between
the Theory of Dr. Ewald Hering and the
'Philosophy of the Unconscious' of Dr.
Edward von Hartmann; with Translations
from these Authors. 1880; [ed. R. A. Streat-
feild], 1910 (with Introduction by M.
Hartog).
Selections from Previous Works. With Re-
marks on Mr. G. J. Romanes' 'Mental
Evolution in Animals,' and a Psalm of
Montreal. 1884.
Luck or Cunning, as the Main Means of
Organic Modification? An Attempt to
throw Additional Light upon the late Mr.
Charles Darwin's Theory of Natural Selec-
tion. 1887; 1920 (rev.).
Erewhon Revisited, Twenty Years later, both
by the Original Discoverer of the Country
and by his Son. 1901.

The Way of All Flesh. [Ed. R. A. Streatfeild], 1903; ed. W. L. Phelps, New York, 1916; ed. G. B. Shaw, 1936 (World's Classics).
Essays on Life, Art and Science. Ed. R. A. Streatfeild, 1904.
God the Known and God the Unknown. [Ed. R. A. Streatfeild], 1909.

(4) CRITICISMS AND TRANSLATIONS OF GREEK LITERATURE

A Lecture on the Humour of Homer, Jan. 30th, 1892. Reprinted with Preface and Additional Matter from The Eagle. Cambridge, 1892.
The Authoress of the Odyssey, where and when she wrote, who she was, the Use she made of the Iliad, and how the Poem grew under her Hands. 1897; 1922 (corrected). [Butler's theory about the Odyssey was first enunciated in several articles written by him in Sicilian and English papers.]
The Iliad of Homer, rendered into English Prose. 1898.
The Odyssey, rendered into English Prose. 1900.
The Humour of Homer, and other Essays. Ed. R. A. Streatfeild, 1913. [With a 'Biographical Sketch' by H. F. Jones.]
Hesiod's Works and Days. A Translation. 1924.

(5) MISCELLANEOUS WRITINGS

A First Year in Canterbury Settlement. 1863; ed. R. A. Streatfeild, 1914 (with 'other Early Essays').
Alps and Sanctuaries of Piedmont and the Canton Ticino 1882; 1913 ('with Author's Revisions and Index, and an Introduction by R. A. Streatfeild').
Ex Voto: an Account of the Sacro Monte or New Jerusalem at Varallo-Sesia. With some Notice of Tabachetti's Remaining Work at the Sanctuary of Crea. 1888; tr. Italian, 1894.
The Life and Letters of Dr. Samuel Butler, Headmaster of Shrewsbury School, 1798–1836, and afterwards Bishop of Lichfield. 2 vols. 1896.
Shakespeare's Sonnets reconsidered, and in part rearranged, with Introductory Chapters by Samuel Butler. 1899.
Seven Sonnets and a Psalm of Montreal. [Ed. R. A. Streatfeild], Cambridge, 1904 (priv. ptd).
Note-books. Selections arranged and edited by H. F. Jones. 1912. [Selections, ed. A. T. Bartholomew, 1930.]
Butleriana. 1932. [Compiled, mainly from previously unpbd portions of the Note-books, by A. T. Bartholomew.]
Further Extracts from the Note-books. Ed. A. T. Bartholomew, 1934.

Letters between Samuel Butler and Miss E. M. A. Savage. 1935.

(6) MUSIC

Gavottes, Minuets, Fugues and other Short Pieces for the Piano, by S. Butler and H. F. Jones. 1885.
Narcissus: a Dramatic Cantata in Vocal Score. Words and Music by S. Butler and H. F. Jones. 1888.
Ulysses: an Oratorio. Words written and Music composed by S. Butler and H. F. Jones. 1904.

(7) BIOGRAPHY AND CRITICISM
(a) Books

Sugameli, P. Origine Trapanese dell' Odissea secondo Samuel Butler. Trapani, 1892.
Samuel Butler. Trapani, 1902. [In Italian; rptd from the periodical Quo Vadis?]
Streatfeild, R. A. Samuel Butler: a Critical Study. 1902.
—— Samuel Butler. Records and Memorials. 1903.
Jones, H. F. Diary of a Journey through North Italy to Sicily [to leave] the MSS. of Three Books by S. Butler at Varallo-Sesia, Aci-Reale and Trapani. 1904.
—— Charles Darwin and Samuel Butler: a Step towards Reconciliation. 1911.
—— Samuel Butler. A Memoir. 2 vols. 1919.
Blum, Jean. Samuel Butler. [1910.]
H[arris], J. F. Samuel Butler and his Note-books. 1913.
—— Samuel Butler, Author of Erewhon: the Man and his Work. 1916.
Hartog, M. M. Samuel Butler and Recent Mnemic Biological Theories. 1914.
Pestalozzi, G. Samuel Butler, der Jüngere: 1835–1902. Versuch einer Darstellung seiner Gedankenwelt. Zurich, 1914.
Cannan, G. Samuel Butler: a Critical Study. 1915.
Jones, H. F. and Bartholomew, A. T. The Samuel Butler Collection at St. John's College, Cambridge. Cambridge, 1921.
Joad, C. E. M. Samuel Butler. 1924.
Bekker, W. G. An Historical and Critical Review of Samuel Butler's Literary Works. Rotterdam, [1925].
Lange, P. J. de. Samuel Butler: Critic and Philosopher. Zutphen, 1925.
Garnett, Mrs M. Samuel Butler and his Family Relations. 1926.
Farrington, B. Samuel Butler and the Odyssey. 1929.
Stoff, R. Die Philosophie des Organischen bei Samuel Butler. Mit einer biographischen Übersicht zusammengestellt von H. F. Herlitschka. Vienna, 1929.

Meissner, P. Samuel Butler der Jüngere: ein Studie zur Kultur des ausgehenden Viktorianismus. Leipzig, 1931.

Stillman, C. G. Samuel Butler: a Mid-Victorian Modern. 1932.

Fort, J. B. Samuel Butler (1835–1902). Étude d'un Caractère et d'une Intelligence. Bordeaux, 1934.

—— Samuel Butler l'Écrivain. Étude d'un Style. Bordeaux, 1935.

Rattray, R. F. Samuel Butler: a Chronicle and an Introduction. 1935.

Muggeridge, M. The Earnest Atheist. A Study of Samuel Butler. 1936.

(b) Pamphlets and Chapters of Books

Shaw, G. B. John Bull's other Island and Major Barbara. 1907. [Preface to Major Barbara.]

Salter, W. H. Essays on two Moderns: Euripides; Samuel Butler. 1911.

Clodd, E. Memories. 1916.

Heitland, W. E. A 'Few Earnest Words' on Samuel Butler. [1916.]

Russell, E. S. Form and Function. 1916. [Ch. xix: Samuel Butler and the Memory Theories of Heredity.]

Young, W. T. George Meredith, Samuel Butler, George Gissing. CHEL. vol. XIII, 1916.

Mais, S. P. B. From Shakespeare to O. Henry: Studies in Literature. 1917.

Sinclair, May. A Defence of Idealism. 1917. [Ch. i, The Pan-Psychism of Samuel Butler.]

MacCarthy, D. Remnants. 1918. [Samuel Butler: an Impression.]

Yeats, J. B. Essays, Irish and American. 1918. [Recollections of Samuel Butler.]

Cunliffe, J. W. English Literature during the last Half-century. New York, 1919.

Waugh, Arthur. Tradition and Change. 1919.

Clutton-Brock, A. Essays on Books. 1920. [2 essays on Butler.]

Duffin, H. C. The Quintessence of Bernard Shaw. 1920. [Prologue: Of Samuel Butler.]

Elton, O. A Survey of English Literature, 1830–1880. Vol. II, 1920.

Hewlett, M. In a Green Shade. 1920.

Larbaud, V. Samuel Butler. Conférence. Paris, 1920.

Murry, J. M. Aspects of Literature. 1920.

Chevalley, A. Le Roman anglais de notre Temps. 1921. [Ch. iv: Samuel Butler.]

Sherman, S. P. Points of View. New York, 1921.

Canby, H. S. Definitions: Essays in Contemporary Criticism. New York, 1922. [The Satiric Rage of Butler.]

Gosse, Sir E. Aspects and Impressions. 1922.

Cazamian, L. Le Roman et les Idées en Angleterre. L'Influence de la Science,

1868–1890. Strasburg, 1923. [Ch. iii on Butler.]

Semon, R. Mnemic Psychology; with Introduction by Vernon Lee. 1923. [Pt I of Introduction on Semon, Hering and Butler.]

Smith, Paul J. On Strange Altars. 1923.

Blum, J. ('J. Florence'). Le Litre et l'Amphore. Paris, 1924.

Blom, E. Stepchildren of Music. 1925. [Ch. xvii, 'Imitation Handel,' is on Butler's and Jones's Narcissus.]

'Kingsmill, H.' After Puritanism, 1850–1900. 1929.

Vaughan, H. M. From Anne to Victoria: Fourteen Biographical Studies between 1702 and 1901. 1931.

Carswell, C. Samuel Butler. [In The English Novelists, ed. D. Verschoyle, 1936.]

(c) Articles in Periodicals

Streatfeild, R. A. Samuel Butler. Monthly Rev. VIII, 1902.

MacCarthy, D. Samuel Butler. Independent Rev. III, 1904.

—— Samuel Butler. Life and Letters, VII, 1931.

Kellogg, V. L. Samuel Butler and Biological Memory. Science (Garrison, N.Y.), XXXV, 1912.

Jourdain, P. E. B. Aspects of Samuel Butler. Open Court, XXVII, 1913.

Barry, W. Samuel Butler of Erewhon. Dublin Rev. CLV, 1914.

Rattray, R. F. The Philosophy of Samuel Butler. Mind, XXIII, 1914.

Stillman, C. G. The Literary and Scientific Work of Samuel Butler. North American Rev. CCIV, 1916.

Jones, H. F. Samuel Butler as a Musical Critic. The Chesterian, May 1920.

Larbaud, V. Samuel Butler (Étude et Fragments traduits d'Erewhon). Nouvelle Revue française, Jan. 1920.

—— Samuel Butler. Revue de France, 1 Oct. 1923.

—— Les Carnets de Samuel Butler. Nouvelle Revue française, XLIII, 1936.

Bellessort, A. Samuel Butler et son Voyage aux Pays imaginaires. Revue politique et littéraire, LIX, 1921.

Gillet, L. Samuel Butler: a Memoir, par H. F. Jones. Revue des Deux Mondes, LXIV, 1921.

'Lee, Vernon.' Back to Butler: a Metabiological Commentary on G. B. S. New Statesman, 24 Sept. 1921.

Cavenagh, F. A. Samuel Butler and Education. Monist, XXXII, 1922.

Quiller-Couch, Sir A. T. Who wrote the Odyssey? Observer, 23 April 1922.

Willcocks, M. P. Samuel Butler of The Way of All Flesh. English Rev. XXXIX, 1924.

Aronstein, P. Samuel Butler der Jüngere. Germanisch-romanische Monatsschrift, xiv, 1926.

Peper, E. George Bernard Shaw's Beziehungen zu Samuel Butler dem Jüngeren. Ang. l, 1926.

Wolff, E. Samuel Butler. Zeitschrift für künstliche Kultur, iii, 1926.

Fort, J. B. Samuel Butler en Voyage. Revue anglo-américaine, Aug. 1927.

—— Les Idées de Samuel Butler. Revue philosophique de la France, lxi, 1937.

Arns, K. Samuel Butler und die englische Gegenwartsliteratur. Der Gral, xii, 1928.

Bonnet, P. L'Humeur de Samuel Butler, Auteur d'Erewhon. Revue de l'Enseignement des Langues vivantes, Jan.–Feb. 1928.

Farrington, B. Samuel Butler and the Odyssey. New Adelphi, i, 1928.

Meissner, P. Samuel Butler und seine Utopie: 'Jenseits der Berge.' Zeitschrift für französischen und englischen Unterricht, xxviii, 1929.

—— Die Überwindung des19ten Jahrhunderts im Denken von Samuel Butler. Germanisch-romanische Monatsschrift, xvii, 1929.

Shewan, A. Samuel Butler and Homer once more. Classical Weekly, xxii, 1930.

Wilson, E. The Satire of Samuel Butler. New Republic, 24 May 1933.

Delattre, F. S. Butler et le Bergsonisme. Revue anglo-américaine, June 1936.

Hill, B. Samuel Butler in Canada. Dalhousie Rev. April 1936.

Krog, F. Butlers Erewhon: eine Utopie? Ang. lx, 1936.

Cowie, D. Samuel Butler in New Zealand. London Mercury, March 1937.

H. B. G.

WALTER HORATIO PATER (1839–1894)

(1) Bibliography

Stonehill, C. A. and H. W. Bibliographies of Modern Authors. Ser. 2, 1925.

(2) Collected and Selected Works

The Works of Walter Pater. 9 vols. 1900–1.

New Library Edition of the Works of Walter Pater. 10 vols. 1910.

Selected Essays of Walter Horatio Pater. Ed. H. G. Rawlinson, 1927.

(3) Separate Writings

Studies in the History of the Renaissance. 1873; 1877 (rev. omitting 'Conclusion' as The Renaissance: Studies in Art and Poetry); 1888 ('Conclusion' restored); tr. French, Paris, 1917.

Marius the Epicurean: his sensations and ideas. 2 vols. 1885; 2 vols. 1892; ed. J. C.

Squire, 2 vols. 1929; ed. A. K. Tuell, New York, 1929; ed. E. A. Parker, 1931 (abridged); ed. J. Sagmaster, New York, 1935; tr. French, Paris, 1922.

Imaginary Portraits. 1887; tr. French (introduction by Arthur Symons), Paris, [1899].

Appreciations. With an Essay on Style. 1889.

Plato and Platonism: a series of lectures. 1893.

An Imaginary Portrait. Oxford, 1894. [Running title: The Child in the House. Not included in Imaginary Portraits, but later included in Miscellaneous Studies.]

Greek Studies: a series of essays, prepared for the press by C. L. Shadwell. 1895.

Miscellaneous Studies; a series of essays, prepared for the press by C. L. Shadwell. 1895.

Gaston de Latour: an unfinished romance. Prepared for the press by C. L. Shadwell. 1896.

Essays from 'The Guardian.' 1896 (priv. ptd).

The Chant of the Celestial Sailors. An Unpublished Poem. [Winchester], 1928.

(4) Biography and Criticism

(a) Books

Greenslet, F. Walter Pater. New York, 1903.

Benson, A. C. Walter Pater. 1906. (English Men of Letters ser.)

Hutton, J. A. Pilgrims in the Region of Faith. Amiel, Tolstoy, Pater, Newman. Edinburgh, 1906.

Wright, Thomas. The Life of Walter Pater. 2 vols. 1907.

Bock, E. J. Walter Pater's Einfluss auf Oscar Wilde. Bonn, 1913.

Thomas, Philip Edward. Walter Pater. A Critical Study. 1913.

Bendz, E. The Influence of Walter Pater and Matthew Arnold in the Prose-Writings of Oscar Wilde. Gothenburg, 1914.

Proesler, H. Walter Pater und sein Verhältnis zur deutschen Literatur. Freiburg, 1917.

Duthuit, G. Le Rose et le Noir. De Walter Pater à Oscar Wilde. Paris, [1923].

Staub, F. Das imaginäre Porträt Walter Paters. Zurich, 1926.

Chandler, Z. E. An Analysis of the Stylistic Technique of Addison, Johnson, Hazlitt, and Pater. Iowa City, 1928.

Beyer, A. Walter Paters Beziehungen zur französischen Literatur und Kultur. Halle, 1931.

Farmer, A. J. Walter Pater as a Critic of English Literature, A Study of 'Appreciations.' Grenoble, 1931.

Symons, A. A Study of Walter Pater. 1932.
Eaker, J. G. Walter Pater. A Study in Methods and Effects. Iowa City, 1933.
Young, H. H. The Writings of Walter Pater. A Reflection of British Philosophical Opinion from 1860 to 1890. Lancaster, Pennsylvania, 1933.
Cattan, L. Essai sur Walter Pater. Paris, 1936.

(b) Periodical Articles and Chapters in Books

Gosse, Sir E. Walter Pater. A Portrait. Contemporary Rev. LXVI, 1894. [Rptd in Selected Essays, 1928.]
Sharp, W. Personal Reminiscences of Walter Pater. Atlantic Monthly, LXXIV, 1894.
Walter Pater's Aesthetic Outlook. Edinburgh Rev. CCVI, 1907.
Cecil, Algernon. Walter Pater. [In Six Oxford Thinkers, 1909.]
Dowden, E. Walter Pater. [In Essays, Modern and Elizabethan, 1910.]
Le Gallienne, R. On Re-reading Walter Pater. North American Rev. CXCV, 1912.
Lucas, St J. Walter Pater and the Army. Blackwood's Mag. CCIX, 1921.
Jaloux, E. Walter Pater. Les Nouvelles littéraires, 8 Sept. 1923.
Harrison, J. S. Pater, Heine, and the Old Gods of Greece. PMLA. XXXIX, 1924.
Duclaux, M. Souvenirs sur Walter Pater. Revue de Paris, 15 Jan. 1925.
Smith, Logan Pearsall. On Re-reading Pater. Dial, LXXXIII, 1927. [Rptd in Reperusals and Recollections, 1936.]
Eliot, T. S. The Place of Pater. [In The Eighteen-Eighties, Royal Soc. Lit. 1930.]
—— Arnold and Pater. Bookman (U.S.A.), LXXII, 1930. [Rptd in Selected Essays, 1932.]
Du Bos, C. Marius l'Épicurien. [In Approximations, ser. 4, Paris, 1931.]
Welby, T. E. Walter Pater. [In Revaluations: Studies in Biography, Oxford, 1931.]
Stauffer, D. A. Monna Melancholia. A Study in Pater's Sources. Sewanee Rev. XL, 1932.
Burgum, E. B. Walter Pater and the Good Life. Sewanee Rev. XL, 1932.
Newman, B. Walter Pater. A Revaluation. Nineteenth Century, CXI, 1932.
'Lee, Vernon.' The Handling of Words: a Page of Walter Pater. Life and Letters, IX, 1933.
Rosenblatt, L. M. Marius l'Épicurien de Walter Pater, et ses Points de Départ français. Revue de Littérature comparée, Jan. 1935.
O'Faoláin, S. Pater and Moore. London Mercury, XXXIV, 1936.

H. B. G.

VI. MINOR CRITICS AND ESSAYISTS, 1870-1900

[This section has been restricted to writers born after 1829 whose more important writings fall within the 19th century. Cross-references have only been included to critical writings in other sections.]

ALFRED AINGER (1837-1904)

Sermons preached in the Temple Church. 1870.
Charles Lamb. 1882; 1888 (rev.). (English Men of Letters ser.)
Crabbe. 1903. (English Men of Letters ser.)
The Gospel and Human Life: Sermons. Ed. H. C. Beeching, 1904.
Lectures and Essays. Ed. H. C. Beeching, 2 vols. 1905. [Miscellaneous studies of English writers.]
The Life and Letters of Alfred Ainger. Ed. E. Sichel, 1906.

[Ainger also edited the writings and letters of Charles and Mary Lamb, 1879-99. He contributed articles on Lamb, Tennyson and others to DNB.]

WILLIAM ARCHER (1856-1924)

(a) Critical Writings

The Fashionable Tragedian: A Criticism. Edinburgh, 1877. [An essay on Henry Irving, written in collaboration with R. W. Lowe.]
English Analyses of the French Plays represented at the Gaiety Theatre, London, June and July 1879. 1879. [Rptd from London Figaro.]
English Dramatists of To-Day. 1882. [Playwrights of Yesterday, F. W. Broughton, H. J. Byron, W. S. Gilbert, Paul Meritt, A. W. Pinero, Alfred Tennyson, etc.]
Henry Irving, Actor and Manager: a Critical Study. 1883.
About the Theatre. Essays and Studies. 1886. [Mainly rptd from The Theatre.]
The Drama. 1837-1887. [Contributed to The Reign of Queen Victoria, ed. T. H. Ward, vol. II, 1887.]
Masks or Faces? A Study in the Psychology of Acting. 1888.
William Charles Macready. 1890.
The Theatrical 'World.' 5 vols. 1893-7. [Archer's dramatic criticism rptd from World, Pall Mall Budget, Sketch, Athenaeum and other sources. Vol. I, prefaced by Letter from Archer to R. W. Lowe; vol. II, with Introduction by G. B. Shaw; vol. III, with Prefatory Letter from A. W. Pinero; vol. IV prefaced by Archer's essay On the Need for an Endowed Theatre; vol. V, with Introduction by Sydney Grundy.]

Study and Stage: a Year-Book of Criticism. 1899.

Poets of the Younger Generation. 1902. [Binyon, Quiller-Couch, Davidson, Housman, Kipling, Alice Meynell, Newbolt, Yeats, Stephen Phillips, Francis Thompson, etc.]

Real Conversations. 1904. [Dialogues with Pinero, Hardy, Stephen Phillips, George Moore, Gilbert, etc.]

A National Theatre: Scheme and Estimates. 1907. [In collaboration with Sir H. Granville-Barker.]

Play-Making: a Manual of Craftsmanship. 1912.

The Old Drama and the New. An Essay in Re-Valuation. 1923.

Ibseniana: Letters from William Archer to Charles Archer. London Mercury, xxxvi, 1937. [1881–3.]

(b) Plays

War is War; or, the Germans in Belgium: a Drama of 1914. New York, 1919.

The Green Goddess. A Play in Four Acts. New York, 1921.

Three Plays. With a Personal Note by Bernard Shaw. 1927. [Martha Washington, Beatriz Juana, Lidia.]

[Archer translated into English prose all Ibsen's more important plays, occasionally in collaboration with Charles Archer or Sir E. Gosse, 1888–1913, as well as plays by Hauptmann and Maeterlinck. He also translated essays, etc. by Brandes and other Scandinavian writers.]

(c) Miscellaneous Writings

America To-Day. Observations and Reflections. 1900.

Through Afro-America: An English Reading of the Race Problem. 1910.

The Great Analysis. A Plea for a Rational World-Order. With an Introduction by Gilbert Murray. 1912.

William Archer as Rationalist. A Collection of his Heterodox Writings. Ed. J. M. Robertson, 1925.

On Dreams. Ed. T. Besterman, 1934.

[Archer also pbd lectures, pamphlets, etc. (mainly polemical).]

(d) Biography and Criticism

Aas, L. William Archer. 1920. [Written in Norwegian.]

Granville-Barker, Sir H. William Archer. Drama, July 1926.

—— The Coming of Ibsen. [In The Eighteen-Eighties, Royal Soc. Lit. 1930.]

Archer, Charles. William Archer. 1931. [Includes list of Archer's books and contributions to periodicals.]

SIR WALTER ARMSTRONG (1850–1918)

Alfred Stevens. A Biographical Study. 1881.

Sir J. E. Millais, his Life and Work. [1885.]

The Thames from its Source to the Sea. Illustrated with Engravings and Etchings. 2 vols. [1886–7].

Notes on the National Gallery. 1887.

Celebrated Pictures exhibited at the Glasgow International Exhibition, Fine Arts Section. A Series of Engravings with Notes and Criticisms. 1888.

Memoir of Peter De Wint. 1888.

Scottish Painters: a Critical Study. 1888.

Briton Riviere, his Life and Work. [1891.]

Pictures, Drawings and Sculptures forming the Collection of Sir John Pender. 1894.

Thomas Gainsborough. 1894.

The Art of W. Q. Orchardson. [1895.]

The Art of Velazquez. [1896.]

The Life of Velazquez. [1896.]

Gainsborough and his Place in English Art. 1898.

Sir Joshua Reynolds. 1900.

Sir Henry Raeburn. With an Introduction by R. A. M. Stevenson and a Bibliographical and Descriptive Catalogue by J. L. Caw. 1901.

Turner. 1902.

The Peel Collection and the Dutch School of Painting. 1904.

Art in Great Britain and Ireland. 1909.

Lawrence. 1913.

[Armstrong also translated works on art from foreign languages, and contributed introductions to various collections of pictures, etc. For biography and criticism see M. H. Spielmann, Sir Walter Armstrong, 1918 (rptd from Fortnightly Rev.).]

ALFRED AUSTIN (1835–1913)

[See p. 328 above.]

PETER BAYNE (1830–1896)

(a) Critical and Biographical Works

Essays in Biography. 2 sers. Boston, 1857–8.

Essays, Biographical, Critical and Miscellaneous. Edinburgh, 1859.

Life and Letters of Hugh Miller. 2 vols. 1871.

Lessons from my Masters: Carlyle, Tennyson and Ruskin. 1879.

Two Great Englishwomen: Mrs Browning and Charlotte Brontë; with an Essay on Poetry, illustrated from Wordsworth, Burns and Byron. [1880.]

(b) Theological and Historical Works

The Christian Life, Social and Individual. Edinburgh, 1855.

The Testimony of Christ to Christianity. 1862.

English Puritanism: its Character and History. 1862. [In G. Gould, Documents relating to the Settlement of the Church of England by the Act of Uniformity of 1662.]

The Church's Curse and the Nation's Claim. 1868.

The Days of Jezebel: an Historical Drama. 1872.

The National History of England. [Vol. IV by P. Bayne.] 1873.

The Chief Actors in the Puritan Revolution. 1878.

Martin Luther, his Life and Work. 2 vols. 1887.

Six Christian Biographies—J. Howard, W. Wilberforce, T. Chalmers, T. Arnold, S. Budgett, J. Foster. 1887.

The Free Church of Scotland: her Origin, Founders and Testimony. Edinburgh, 1893.

[Bayne also pbd several theological pamphlets.]

(c) Biography and Criticism

Brownell, W. C. Peter Bayne's Lessons from my Masters. Nation (New York), XXIX, 1879.

Peter Bayne. Academy, XLIX, 1895.

HENRY CHARLES BEECHING (1859–1919)

[See p. 330 above.]

JOSEPH BENNETT (1831–1911)

Letter from Bayreuth Descriptive and Critical of Wagner's 'Der Ring des Nibelungen.' With an Appendix. 1877.

The Musical Year 1883. A Record of Noteworthy Musical Events in the United Kingdom, with a Reprint of Criticisms on Many of Them. [1884.]

Novello's Primers of Musical Biography. 5 vols. [1884–5].

A Story of Ten Hundred Concerts: being a Short Account of the Origin and Progress of Monday Popular Concerts, St. James' Hall, London. 1887.

History of the Leeds Musical Festivals, 1858–1889; with Portraits and Fac-similes. 1892. [With F. R. Spark.]

[Bennett also adapted works by Burns and Scott for music, wrote critical notes or introductions for various musical works, and revised and edited Berlioz's Treatise on Modern Instrumentation and Orchestration.]

ARTHUR CHRISTOPHER BENSON (1862–1925)

(a) Critical and Biographical Writings

Memoirs of Arthur Hamilton, B.A., of Trinity College, Cambridge. 1886.

William Laud, sometime Archbishop of Canterbury. A Study. 1887.

Men of Might. Studies of Great Characters. 1892. [With H. F. W. Tatham.]

Genealogy of the Family of Benson. With Biographical and Illustrative Notes. Eton, 1895 (priv. ptd).

Fasti Etonenses. A Biographical History of Eton selected from the Lives of Celebrated Etonians. Eton, 1899.

The Life of Edward White Benson, sometime Archbishop of Canterbury. 2 vols. 1899; 1901 (abridged).

Alfred Tennyson. 1904.

Rossetti. 1904. (English Men of Letters ser.)

Edward FitzGerald. 1905. (English Men of Letters ser.)

Walter Pater. 1906. (English Men of Letters ser.)

The Leaves of the Tree. Studies in Biography. 1911.

Ruskin. A Study in Personality. 1911.

Hugh: Memoirs of a Brother. (Robert Hugh Benson.) 1915.

Life and Letters of Maggie Benson. 1917.

The Trefoil. Wellington College, Lincoln, and Truro. 1923. [The early life of Archbishop Benson.]

Memories and Friends. 1924.

(b) Essays

Essays. 1896.

The House of Quiet: an Autobiography. 1904 (anon.).

The Thread of Gold. By the Author of 'The House of Quiet.' 1905.

The Upton Letters. By T. B. 1905; 1906 (with a new preface).

From a College Window. 1906.

The Gate of Death. A Diary. 1906 (anon.).

The Altar Fire. 1907.

Beside Still Waters. 1907.

At Large. 1908.

The Silent Isle. 1910.

The Child of the Dawn. 1912.

Thy Rod and thy Staff. 1912.

Along the Road. 1913.

Joyous Gard. 1913.

Watersprings. 1913.

Where no Fear was: a Book about Fear. 1914.

Escape, and Other Essays. 1915.

Father Payne. 1915.

Meanwhile. A Packet of War Letters. By H. L. G. [A. C. Benson]. With a Foreword by K. W. 1916.

The Diary of Arthur Christopher Benson. Ed.
Percy Lubbock, [1926].

[A few of the above, e.g. The Child of the
Dawn, are in the form of fiction.]

(c) Fiction

The Hill of Trouble, and Other Stories. 1903.
The Isles of Sunset. 1905. [Stories.]
Paul the Minstrel, and Other Stories. Re-
printed from The Hill of Trouble and The
Isles of Sunset. 1911.
The Orchard Pavilion. 1914.
Chris Gascoyne. An Experiment in Solitude.
From the Diaries of John Trevor. 1924.
The House of Menerdue. 1925.
Basil Netherby. 1926.
The Canon. 1926.
Cressage. 1927.

(d) Poems

Le Cahier jaune. Eton, 1892 (priv. ptd).
Poems. 1893.
Lyrics. 1895.
The Professor. Eton, 1895 (priv. ptd).
Thomas Gray. Eton, 1895 (priv. ptd).
Monnow. An Ode. Eton, 1896.
Lord Vyet and Other Poems. 1897.
Ode in Memory of the Rt. Honble. William
Ewart Gladstone. Eton, 1898.
The Professor, and Other Poems. 1900.
Coronation Ode; set to Music by [Sir] E.
Elgar. Book of Words, with Analytical
Notes by Joseph Bennett. [1902.]
Ode to Japan. 1902 (priv. ptd).
Peace, and Other Poems. 1905.
The Poems of A. C. Benson. 1909.
The Reed of Pan. English Renderings of
Greek Epigrams (from the Greek Anthology)
and Lyrics. 1922.

(e) Educational and Miscellaneous Writings

Babylonica. Eton, 1895.
The Schoolmaster. A Commentary upon the
Aims and Methods of an Assistant-Master
in a Public School. 1902.
The Myrtle Bough. A Vale. Eton, 1903 (priv.
ptd).
Cambridge Essays on Education. Cambridge,
1917. [Ed. by Benson; his own contribution being The Training of the Imagination.]
Magdalene College, Cambridge. A Little View
of its Buildings and History. Cambridge,
1923.
Extracts from the Letters of Dr. A. C. Benson
to M. E. A[llen]. [1926.]

[Besides the above, Benson produced several
works of pamphlet length. He contributed
introductions to books by Matthew Arnold,
Dickens, Whittier, etc. and edited Selections
from Ruskin, 1923, and (with Lord Esher)
Letters of Queen Victoria, 1907.]

(f) Biography and Criticism

Archer, W. Poets of the Younger Generation.
1902.
Weygandt, C. The Poetry of A. C. Benson.
Sewanee Rev. XIV, 1906.
Arthur Christopher Benson as seen by some
Friends. 1925.
Collins, J. P. Arthur Christopher Benson.
Bookman, LXVIII, 1925.
Macnaghten, H. Arthur Christopher Benson.
Spectator, 27 June 1925.

AUGUSTINE BIRRELL (1850–1933)

(a) Collected and Selected Works

Collected Essays. 2 vols. 1899. [Obiter
Dicta, sers. 1, 2; Res Judicatae; Essays
about Men, Women and Books.]
Selected Essays. 1884–1907. 1909.
Self-Selected Essays. A Second Series. 1916.
Collected Essays and Addresses. 1880–1920.
3 vols. 1922. [Contains 5 essays not pre-
viously collected.]

(b) Literary Essays

Obiter Dicta. Ser. 1, 1884 (anon. and priv.
ptd); ser. 2, 1887; sers. 1, 2, 1910. [Ser. 1
includes an essay on Falstaff by G. Radford.]
Res Judicatae. 1892.
Essays about Men, Women, and Books. 1894.
Miscellanies. 1901.
Emerson. A Lecture. 1903.
In the Name of the Bodleian, and Other Essays.
1905.
On a Dictum of Mr. Disraeli's, and Other
Matters. An Address. 1912.
John Wesley, his Times and Work. [Ch. ii in
Letters of John Wesley, ed. George Eayrs,
1915.]
More Obiter Dicta. 1924.
Et Cetera. 1930.

[Birrell also supplied introductions to rpts
of Shakespeare, Johnson, Boswell, Lamb and
Browning, and collaborated in translating
Hugo.]

(c) Biographies

The Life of Charlotte Brontë. 1887.
Sir Frank Lockwood. A Biographical Sketch.
1898.
William Hazlitt. 1902. (English Men of
Letters ser.)
Andrew Marvell. 1905. (English Men of
Letters ser.)
Frederick Locker-Lampson. 1920.

(d) Miscellaneous Writings

Seven Lectures on the Law and History of
Copyright in Books. 1890.
The Liberal Magazine. 1894. [Pamphlet.]
The Duties and Liabilities of Trustees. Six
Lectures. 1896.

Four Lectures on the Law of Employers' Liability at Home and Abroad. 1897.
The Ideal University. A Lecture. 1898.
Mr. Balfour's Parliament. A Speech. 1905.
The Lords and the Education Bill. A Speech. 1906.
Nationality and the League of Nations. 1919. [Pamphlet.]
Some Early Recollections of Liverpool. 1924.
Things past Redress. 1937. [Autobiographical.]

(e) Biography and Criticism

Gaines, C. H. The Good Taste of Augustine Birrell. North American Rev. June 1923.
Kernahan, C. Celebrities. 1923.

ROBERT SEYMOUR BRIDGES (1844–1930)

[See p. 323 above.]

STOPFORD AUGUSTUS BROOKE (1832–1916)

(a) Critical Writings

Theology in the English Poets. 1874. [Cowper, Coleridge, Wordsworth and Burns.]
English Literature. 1876; 1896 (rev.); 1901 (with chs. on English Literature, 1832–1892, and on American Literature, by G. R. Carpenter); 1924 (with an additional ch. on Literature since 1832, by George Sampson).
Milton. 1879.
The Inaugural Address to the Shelley Society. 1886 (priv. ptd). [Rptd in Studies in Poetry, 1907.]
The History of Early English Literature: being the History of English Poetry from its Beginning to the Accession of King Alfred. 2 vols. 1892.
The Development of Theology as illustrated in English Poetry from 1780–1830. 1893.
The Need and Use of getting Irish Literature into the English Tongue. An Address. 1893.
English Literature from the Beginning to the Norman Conquest. New York, 1898.
Religion in Literature and Religion in Life. Two Lectures. 1900.
Tennyson. His Art and Relation to Modern Life. 2 vols. 1900.
King Alfred, as Educator of his People and Man of Letters. With an Appendix of Passages from the Writings of Alfred. Selected and Translated from the Old English by Kate M. Warren. 1901.
The Poetry of Robert Browning. 1902.
On Ten Plays of Shakespeare. 1905.
Studies in Poetry. 1907. [Blake, Scott, The Lyrics of Shelley, Epipsychidon, Keats.]
A Study of Clough, Arnold, Rossetti and Morris. With an Introduction on the Course of Poetry from 1822 to 1852. 1908.
Ten More Plays of Shakespeare. 1913.

Naturalism in English Poetry. 1920. [Dryden and Pope; Young and Thomson; Collins and Gray; Crabbe and Cowper; Burns, Wordsworth, Shelley, Byron.]

(b) Miscellaneous Writings

The Life and Letters of the Rev. F. W. Robertson. 1865.
Riquet of the Tuft. 1880. [A play.]
Notes on the Liber Studiorum of J. M. W. Turner. With Illustrations. 1885.
Old Paris. Ten Etchings by C. Méryon. Reproduced in Copper and Accompanied with Preface and Notes by Stopford A. Brooke. 1887.
Poems. Edinburgh, 1888.
Dove Cottage: Wordsworth's Home from 1800–1808. 1890.
The Sea-Charm of Venice. 1907.

[Stopford Brooke also pbd many sermons and theological works.]

(c) Biography

Jacks, L. P. Life and Letters of Stopford Brooke. 2 vols. 1917.

ROBERT WILLIAMS BUCHANAN (1841–1901)

[See p. 333 above.]

ARTHUR JOHN BUTLER (1844–1910)

(a) Translations

The Purgatory of Dante. 1880.
The Paradise of Dante. 1885.
The Hell of Dante. 1892.

[Butler also pbd trns from French, Italian (especially Scartazzini's Companion to Dante, 1893) and German.]

(b) Other Writings

Dante: his Times and his Work. 1895.
Life and Letters of W. J. Butler, Dean of Lincoln. 1897. [Preface signed A. J. B.]
Calendar of State Papers, Foreign Series, of Elizabeth, 1577–83. 6 vols. 1901–13. [Vol. vi completed by S. C. Lomas.]
The Forerunners of Dante. A Selection from Italian Poetry before 1300. Oxford, 1910.

[Butler also pbd edns of Dante's Commedia both in the original and in H. F. Cary's version. For his contributions to The Cambridge Modern History, etc. see bibliography in Sir A. T. Quiller-Couch's Memoir of Arthur John Butler, 1917.]

EDWARD CARPENTER (1844–1929)

(a) Bibliography

A Bibliography of the Writings of Edward Carpenter. 1916. [Apparently by Carpenter himself. Forms Appendix to My Days and Dreams, and also pbd separately.]

(b) Essays, Sketches and Miscellaneous Writings

The Religious Influence of Art. Cambridge, 1870. [The Burney Prize essay for 1869.]

England's Ideal, and Other Papers on Social Subjects. 1887.

Civilization: its Cause and Cure. And Other Essays. 1889; 1921 (enlarged).

From Adam's Peak to Elephanta: being Sketches in Ceylon and India. 1892; 1903 (enlarged); 1910 (rev.); 1911 (4 chs. pbd separately as A Visit to a Gñani).

Angels' Wings: a Series of Essays on Art and its Relation to Life. 1898.

Prisons, Police, and Punishment: an Inquiry into the Causes and Treatment of Crime and Criminals. 1905.

Days with Walt Whitman: with Some Notes on his Life and Work. 1906.

Sketches from Life in Town and Country: Some Verses. 1908.

My Days and Dreams: being Autobiographical Notes. 1916.

Some Friends of Walt Whitman. 1924. [Comments on the 'Calamus' section in Leaves of Grass, and an account of Anne Gilchrist.]

The Psychology of the Poet Shelley. 1925. [In collaboration with George Barnefield.]

[Several of Carpenter's essays were originally pbd separately as tracts.]

(c) Poems and Plays

Moses. A Drama in Five Acts. 1873; 1910 (rev. as The Promised Land).

Narcissus and Other Poems. 1873.

Towards Democracy. Pt 1, Manchester, 1883; pts 1, 2, Manchester, 1885; pts 1, 2, 3, 1892; pt 4 ('Who shall command the Heart?'), 1902; 4 pts, 1905. Tr. German, 1906–9; Italian, 1912; French, 1914; Japanese, 1915; Russian, n.d.

St. George and The Dragon. Manchester, 1895. [A children's play.]

The Story of Eros and Psyche from Apuleius and the First Book of the Iliad of Homer done into English Verse. 1900; 1923 (as Eros and Psyche together with Some Early Verses). [Eros and Psyche is in prose. The early poems are rptd from Narcissus, 1873.]

(d) Philosophical and Psychological Writings

Sex-Love: and its Place in a Free Society. Manchester, 1894.

Woman and her Place in a Free Society. Manchester, 1894.

Marriage in Free Society. Manchester, 1894.

Homogenic Love: and its Place in a Free Society. Manchester, 1894 (priv. ptd).

Love's Coming-of-Age: a Series of Papers on the Relations of the Sexes. Manchester, 1896; 1906 (enlarged); 1914 (omits Note on Preventive Checks). Tr. German, 1902; Italian, 1909.

An Unknown People. 1897. [On the intermediate sex.]

The Art of Creation: Essays on the Self and its Powers. 1904; 1907 (enlarged). Tr. Italian, 1900; French, 1923.

The Intermediate Sex: a Study of Some Transitional Types of Men and Women. 1908. Tr. German, 1907; Russian, 1915.

The Drama of Love and Death. A Study of Human Evolution and Transfiguration. 1912.

Intermediate Types among Primitive Folk: a Study in Social Evolution. 1914.

Pagan and Christian Creeds: their Origin and Meaning. 1920.

(e) Biography and Criticism

Crosby, E. H. Edward Carpenter, Poet and Prophet. Philadelphia, 1901.

Swan, Tom. Edward Carpenter: the Man and his Message. Manchester, 1901, 1922 (rev.).

Ellis, Mrs Havelock. Three Modern Seers. 1910. [James Hinton, Nietzsche and Carpenter.]

Senard, M. Edward Carpenter et sa Philosophie. Paris, 1914.

Lewis, Edward. Edward Carpenter: an Exposition and an Appreciation. 1915.

Sirne, A. H. M. Edward Carpenter: his Ideas and Ideals. 1916.

Edward Carpenter: in Appreciation. Ed. G. Beiter, 1931. [Contributions by E. J. Dent, G. L. Dickinson, Mr and Mrs Havelock Ellis, L. Housman, H. W. Nevinson, and others.]

JOHN CHURTON COLLINS (1848–1908)

(a) Critical Writings

Sir Joshua Reynolds as a Portrait Painter. 1874.

Bolingbroke, a Historical Study; and Voltaire in England. 1886.

Illustrations of Tennyson. 1891.

The Study of English Literature. A Plea for its Recognition and Organization at the Universities. 1891.

Jonathan Swift: a Biographical and Critical Study. 1893.

Essays and Studies. 1895. [John Dryden, The Predecessors of Shakespeare, Lord Chesterfield's Letters, The Porson of Shakespearian Criticism, Menander.]

Ephemera Critica; or Plain Truths about Current Literature. 1901.

Studies in Shakespeare. 1904.

Studies in Poetry and Criticism. 1905.
Voltaire, Montesquieu and Rousseau in England. 1908.
Greek Influence on English Poetry. Ed. M. Macmillan, 1910.
Posthumous Essays. Ed. L. Churton Collins, 1912. [Shakespeare, Johnson, Burke, Arnold, Browning, etc.]

[Churton Collins also pbd edns of Sidney, Greene, Lord Herbert, Milton, Dryden, Pope, Tennyson, Arnold and others.]

(b) Biography and Criticism

Luce, Margaret E. John Churton Collins. 1908.
Letters from Algernon Charles Swinburne to John Churton Collins, 1873–1886. 1910 (priv. ptd).
Collins, L. C. Life and Memoirs of John Churton Collins. 1912.

SIR SIDNEY COLVIN (1845–1927)

(a) Critical and Biographical Writings

Landor. 1881. (English Men of Letters scr.)
Keats. 1887. (English Men of Letters ser.)
On Concentration and Suggestion in Poetry. English Ass. 1915. [Pamphlet.]
John Keats: His Life and Poetry, his Friends, Critics and After-Fame. 1917.

[Colvin also edited a Landor selection, various collections of Stevenson's writings and letters, and Keats's poems. He contributed the article on Stevenson to DNB.]

(b) Writings on Art

Notes on the Exhibitions of the Royal Academy and Old Water-Colour Society. 1869.
E. J. Poynter; E. Burne-Jones; Simeon Solomon; Frederick Walker; Ford Madox Brown. [4 essays in English Painters of the Present Day, 1871.]
Millais; George Mason; Thomas Armstrong; G. H. Boughton. [4 essays in English Artists of the Present Day, 1872.]
Children in Italian and English Design. 1872.
A Selection from Occasional Writings on Fine Art. 1873 (priv. ptd).
The Life and Genius of Flaxman. [Prefixed to the Catalogue of Flaxman Drawings in the Gallery of University College, London, 1876.]
Descriptive and Historical Catalogue of a Collection of Japanese and Chinese Paintings in the British Museum. 1886.
Guide to the Exhibition of Chinese and Japanese Paintings. 1888.
A Guide to the Historical Collection of Prints Exhibited in the Second Northern Gallery of the British Museum. 1890.

Guide to the Exhibition of Drawings and Sketches by Continental and British Masters in the Print and Drawing Gallery. 1891; 1892 (condensed).
Guide to an Exhibition of Drawings and Engravings by the Old Masters, principally from the Malcolm Collection, and of engravings of the early German and Italian Schools. 1894. [Pt 1 rptd 1895.]
A Florentine Picture Chronicle. 1898. [Illustrations by N. Finiguerra.]
Guide to an Exhibition of Drawings and Etchings by Rembrandt. 1899.
Engraving and Engravers in England, 1545–1695: a Critical and Historical Essay. 1905.

(c) Miscellaneous Writings

Florence. [In A Complete Collection of the English Poems which have obtained the Chancellor's Gold Medal in the University of Cambridge, vol. II, 1894. Colvin's was the prize-winning poem in 1865.]
A Word for Germany, from an English Republican; being a Letter to Professor Beesly. 1870. [Written in reply to A Word for France.]
Memories and Notes of Persons and Places. 1921.

(d) Biography and Criticism

Stevenson, R. L. The Vailima Letters. 1895. [Letters written by Stevenson to Colvin, Nov. 1890–Oct. 1894.]
Garvin, J. L. A Perfect Friend. Observer, 15 May 1927.
Lucas, E. V. The Colvins and Their Friends. 1928.

WILLIAM JOHN COURTHOPE (1842–1917)

(a) Critical and Biographical Writings

Essay on Chivalry. 1860 (priv. ptd). [Harrow Prize essay.]
The Genius of Spenser. 1868. [Chancellor's Prize essay.]
Joseph Addison. 1884. (English Men of Letters ser.)
The Liberal Movement in English Literature. 1885. [Conservatism of Eighteenth Century Poetry; Wordsworth's Theory of Poetry; Revival of Romance; Poetry, Music and Painting; Coleridge and Keats; The Prospects of Poetry.]
The Life of Pope. 1889. [Vol. v of The Works of Pope, begun in 1871 by Whitwell Elwin, continued from 1881 and completed by Courthope.]
The History of English Poetry. 6 vols. 1895–1910.
Liberty and Authority in Matters of Taste. An Inaugural Lecture. 1896. [Rptd in Life in Poetry. Law in Taste, 1901.]

Life in Poetry. Law in Taste. 1901. [Lectures delivered while Professor of Poetry at Oxford.]

The Revolution in English Poetry and Fiction. 1907. [In The Cambridge Modern History, vol. x, 1902.]

A Consideration of Macaulay's Comparison of Dante and Milton. Proc. British Academy, III, 1908.

The Poetry of Spenser. CHEL. vol. III, 1909.

The Connexion between Ancient and Modern Romance. 1911. [British Academy lecture.]

(b) Poems

The Three Hundredth Anniversary of Shakespeare's Birth. Oxford, 1864. [Awarded the Newdigate Prize.]

Ludibria Lunae; or the Wars of the Women and the Gods. An Allegorical Burlesque. 1869.

The Paradise of Birds. An Old Extravaganza in Modern Dress. Edinburgh, 1870.

The Longest Reign. An Ode on the Completion of the Sixtieth Year of the Reign of Her Majesty Queen Victoria. Oxford, 1897.

Selections from the Epigrams of M. Valerius Martialis. Translated or Imitated in English Verse. 1914.

The Country Town and Other Poems. With a Memoir by A. O. Prickard. 1920.

[Courthope also contributed an Address on E. H. Pember to Commemorative Addresses, Royal Soc. Lit. 1912. For an appreciation see J. W. Mackail, Proc. British Academy, IX, 1919.]

SIR HENRY CRAIK (1846–1927)

(a) Critical and Historical Writings

The Life of Jonathan Swift, Dean of St. Patrick's, Dublin. 1882; 2 vols. 1894.

English Prose Selections. 5 vols. 1893–6. [Ed. by Craik with numerous critical introductions.]

A Century of Scottish History. From the Days before the '45 to those within Living Memory. 2 vols. Edinburgh, 1901.

The Life of Edward, Earl of Clarendon, Lord High Chancellor of England. 2 vols. 1911.

(b) Miscellaneous Writings

The English Citizen. 9 vols. 1881–1908. [Ed. by Craik.]

The State in its Relation to Education. 1884; 1896 (rev.).

Impressions of India. 1908.

HENRY AUSTIN DOBSON (1840–1921)

(a) Bibliographies

Murray, F. E. A Bibliography of Austin Dobson. 1900.

Dobson, A. T. A. A Bibliography of the First Editions of Published and Privately Printed Books and Pamphlets by Austin Dobson. With a Preface by Sir E. Gosse. 1925.

—— [Bibliography appended to Austin Dobson: Some Notes, 1928.]

(b) Collected and Selected Works

Selected Poems. 1892.

Collected Poems. 1897; 1902 (adds selection from Carmina Votiva, 1901); 1909 (enlarged); 1913 (adds 27 pieces); 1923 (Oxford Poets).

Poems (Selected). 1905.

Eighteenth Century Studies. 1912. [Selected essays.]

An Anthology of Prose and Verse. With a Foreword by Edmund Gosse. Ed. A. T. A. Dobson, 1922; 1924 (rev.).

The Complete Poetical Works of Austin Dobson. Ed. A. T. A. Dobson, 1923.

Selected Poems. 1923. (World's Classics.)

[What is virtually a collected edn of the essays is formed by the World's Classics rpts, 9 vols. 1923–6.]

(c) Critical and Biographical Writings

The Civil Service Handbook of English Literature. 1874; 1880 (rev. and extended).

William Hogarth. 1879.

Henry Fielding. 1883. (English Men of Letters ser.)

Thomas Bewick and his Pupils. 1884.

Richard Steele. 1886.

Oliver Goldsmith. 1888.

Four French Women. New York, 1890.

Horace Walpole. 1890; rev. P. Toynbee, 1927.

William Hogarth. 1891; 1898 (enlarged); 1902 (with Introduction by Sir W. Armstrong); 1907 (enlarged).

Eighteenth Century Vignettes. Ser. 1, 1892; 1897 ('At Leicester Fields' added); ser. 2, 1894; ser. 3, 1896.

Miscellanies. Ser. 1, New York, 1898; 1899 (with addns and omissions, as A Paladin of Philanthropy); ser. 2, 1901.

Samuel Richardson. 1902. (English Men of Letters ser.)

Side-Walk Studies. 1902.

Fanny Burney. 1903. (English Men of Letters ser.)

De Libris. Prose and Verse. 1908; 1911 (adds 2 essays).

Old Kensington Palace, and Other Papers. 1910.

At Prior Park and Other Papers. 1912.

Rosalba's Journal and Other Papers. 1915.

A Bookman's Budget. 1917. [A collection of extracts from the works of English prose writers with numerous contributions from Dobson himself.]

Later Essays, 1917–1920. 1921.

[A few priv. ptd essays and pamphlets have not been included. Dobson also supplied introductions to rpts of Shakespeare, Evelyn, Defoe, Addison, Prior, Gay, Fielding, Goldsmith, Reynolds, Scott, Thackeray, and other English and French writers.]

(d) Poems

Vignettes in Rhyme. 1873; 1874 (with omissions and addns).

Proverbs in Porcelain. 1877; 1878 (enlarged); 1893 (as Proverbs in Porcelain, to which is added 'Au Revoir,' the latter rptd from At the Sign of the Lyre; only retains the 6 proverbs from 1877 edn).

Vignettes in Rhyme and Other Verses. New York, 1880; 1883 (with addns and omissions as Old World Idylls); 1906 (with further notes). [Contents mainly a selection from Vignettes in Rhyme and Proverbs in Porcelain.]

At the Sign of the Lyre. 1885; New York, 1885 (with addns and omissions); 1889 (with further addns and omissions).

Poems on Several Occasions. 2 vols. 1889; 1895 (rev. and adds 12 poems). [Contents mainly as in Old World Idylls and At the Sign of the Lyre.]

The Sundial. A Poem. New York, 1890.

Ballad of Beau Brocade and Other Poems of the XVIIIth Century. 1892.

When Spring Comes Laughing. A Poem by Austin Dobson, set to music by Charles Willeby. 1894.

The Story of Rosina, and Other Verses. 1895.

A Whitehall Eclogue. 1899 (priv. ptd). [Never rptd, but quoted in A. T. A. Dobson, An Austin Dobson Causerie, Cornhill Mag. Feb. 1925.]

Carmina Votiva, and Other Occasional Verses. 1901 (priv. ptd).

Three Unpublished Poems. 1930 (priv. ptd).

[Many of Dobson's poems were originally priv. ptd singly; those included in The Complete Poetical Works, 1923, have not been recorded here.]

(e) Biography and Criticism

Watson, Sir W. Excursions in Criticism. 1893.

Ellis, S. M. Austin Dobson. Fortnightly Rev. Oct. 1921. [Rptd in Mainly Victorian, 1925.]

Gosse, Sir E. Austin Dobson. Quarterly Rev. Jan. 1922.

Kernahan, C. Celebrities. 1923.

Noyes, A. The Poems of Austin Dobson. Bookman, April 1924.

Dobson, A. T. A. An Austin Dobson Causerie. Cornhill Mag. Feb. 1925.

—— Austin Dobson. Some Notes. With Chapters by Sir Edmund Gosse and George Saintsbury. 1928.

—— Austin Dobson Letter Book. Rowfant Club (Cleveland), 1936.

Weygandt, C. Austin Dobson, Augustan. [In Tuesdays at Ten, Philadelphia, 1928.]

Evans, B. I. English Poetry in the Later Nineteenth Century. 1933. [Ch. xi.]

EDWARD DOWDEN (1843–1913)

(a) Bibliographies

Bayard, E. J. Irish Book Lover, iv, June 1913.

English Illustrated Mag. xxix, 1903.

(b) Critical and Biographical Writings

Mr. Tennyson and Mr. Browning. 1863.

Shakespeare. A Critical Study of his Mind and Art. 1875; tr. German, 1879.

Shakspere. 1877. [One of Macmillan's History and Literature Primers, ed. J. R. Green.]

Studies in Literature, 1789–1877. 1878. [The French Revolution; The Transcendental Movement; The Scientific Movement and Literature; Wordsworth; Landor; Tennyson; Browning; George Eliot; Hugo; Whitman, etc.]

Southey. 1879. (English Men of Letters ser.)

The Life of Percy Bysshe Shelley. 2 vols. 1886.

Transcripts and Studies. 1888. [Carlyle, Shelley, Wordsworth, Spenser, Shakespeare, Marlowe, Milton, Browning ('Sordello').]

New Studies in Literature. 1895. [Meredith, Bridges, Donne, Goethe, Coleridge, E. Scherer, etc.]

The French Revolution and English Literature. Lectures. 1897.

A History of French Literature. 1897. [Vol. ii of Sir E. Gosse's Short Histories.]

Puritan and Anglican: Studies in Literature. 1900. [Puritanism and English Literature, Thomas Browne, Hooker, Herbert, Vaughan, Milton, Jeremy Taylor, Baxter, Bunyan, Butler, Transition to the Eighteenth Century.]

William Shakespeare as a Comic Dramatist. A Monograph. [In Representative English Comedies, ed. C. M. Gayley, vol. i, New York, 1903.]

Robert Browning. 1904.

Michel de Montaigne. 1905.

Milton in the Eighteenth Century, 1701–1750. Trans. British Academy, iii, 1909.

Essays Modern and Elizabethan. 1910. [Pater, Ibsen, Heine, Goethe, Cowper and William Hayley, Shakespeare, etc.]

[Dowden also pbd edns of Browning, Shelley, Spenser and other English poets. For his edns of Shakespeare see vol. I, p. 550.]

(c) Poems and Letters

Poems. 1876; ed. E. D. Dowden, 2 vols. 1914 (with addns).

A Woman's Reliquary. Dundrum, 1913.

Fragments of Old Letters. 1914.

Letters of Edward Dowden and his Correspondents. Ed. E. D. and H. M. Dowden, 1914.

Letters about Shelley interchanged by Edward Dowden, Robert Garnett, and Wm. Michael Rossetti. Ed. R. S. Garnett, 1917.

(d) Biography and Criticism

The Poems of Edward Dowden. Irish Monthly, IX, 1881.

Fiske, H. S. Recollections of Edward Dowden. Nation (U.S.A.), 22 May 1913.

Bicknell, P. F. Edward Dowden's Mind and Art. Dial (Chicago), 16 July 1914.

Gerothwohl, M. A. Edward Dowden as a Critic. Fortnightly Rev. CI, 1914.

Marshall, Lily E. The Letters and Poems of Edward Dowden. 1914.

'Eglinton, John.' Edward Dowden. Life and Letters, IX, 1933. [Rptd in Irish Literary Portraits, 1935.]

HENRY HAVELOCK ELLIS (1859–1939)

(a) Selections

The Art of Life. Gleanings from the Works of Havelock Ellis. Collected by Mrs. S. Herbert. [1929.]

Selected Essays. 1936. (Everyman's Lib.)

Poems, selected by John Gawsworth. [1937.]

(b) Psychological and Sociological Works

The New Spirit. 1890; 1892 (with new preface). [Essays.]

The Criminal. 1890; 1901 (rev. and enlarged).

The Nationalisation of Health. 1892.

Man and Woman: a Study of Human Secondary Sexual Characters. 1894; 1904 (rev. and enlarged); [1914] (rev.); 1934 (rev.).

Sexual Inversion. 2 vols. 1897–1924. [Originally vol. I of Studies in the Psychology of Sex, with an appendix by J. A. Symonds. Later issued as vol. II of that series, without Symonds's contribution.]

The Evolution of Modesty. 1899. [Later issued as vol. I of Studies in the Psychology of Sex.]

The Nineteenth Century. A Dialogue in Utopia. 1900.

Analysis of the Sexual Impulse. 1903. [Later issued as vol. III of Studies in the Psychology of Sex.]

A Study of British Genius. 1904; 1927 (rev. and enlarged).

Studies in the Psychology of Sex. 7 vols. Philadelphia, 1905–28.

The World of Dreams. 1911.

The Task of Social Hygiene. 1912.

Little Essays of Love and Virtue. 1922.

More Essays of Love and Virtue. 1931.

Psychology of Sex. A Manual for Students. 1933.

(c) Critical and Miscellaneous Writings

Affirmations. 1898; 1915 (with new preface). [Critical essays.]

The Soul of Spain. 1908.

Impressions and Comments. 3 sers. 1914–24.

Essays in War-Time. 1916.

The Philosophy of Conflict, and Other Essays in War-Time. 1919.

Kanga Creek: an Australian Idyll. Waltham St Lawrence, 1922.

The Dance of Life. 1923.

Sonnets, with Folk Songs from the Spanish. Waltham St Lawrence, 1925.

Views and Reviews. A Selection of Uncollected Articles, 1884–1932. 2 vols. 1932.

Chapman, with Illustrative Passages. 1934.

My Confessional: Questions of Our Day. 1934.

From Rousseau to Proust. 1936.

Questions of Our Day. 1936.

[From 1887 to 1889 Ellis edited the Mermaid Series of Old Dramatists, and from 1889 to 1914 the Contemporary Science Series. He also edited a number of literary texts, including Heine's prose, Ibsen's plays and Vasari's Lives of Italian Painters. He has written numerous pamphlets, particularly on sexual psychology, and has contributed introductions to a number of miscellaneous works.]

(d) Biography and Criticism

Goldberg, I. Havelock Ellis. A Biographical and Critical Survey. With a Supplementary Chapter on Mrs Edith Ellis. [1926.]

Peterson, H. Havelock Ellis, Philosopher of Love. 1928. [With bibliography.]

Havelock Ellis. In Appreciation. Compiled by Joseph Ishill. Berkeley Heights, 1929. [Articles by various authors.]

PERCY HETHERINGTON FITZGERALD (1834–1925)

[See p. 545 above.]

RICHARD GARNETT (1835–1906)

(a) Critical and Biographical Writings

Carlyle. 1887.
Literature 1837–87. [In T. H. Ward's Reign of Queen Victoria, vol. II. 1887.]
Shelley and Lord Beaconsfield. 1887 (priv. ptd).
Emerson. 1888.
Milton. 1890.
The Age of Dryden. 1895.
William Blake, Painter and Poet. 1895.
History of Italian Literature. 1897. [Vol. IV of Sir E. Gosse's Short Histories of the Literatures of the World.]
Edward Gibbon Wakefield. 1898.
Essays of an Ex-Librarian. 1901.
Illustrated Record of English Literature by Richard Garnett and Edmund Gosse. 4 vols. 1903–4. [Vols. I, II by Garnett.]
Coleridge. 1904.
Tennyson. 1906. [With G. K. Chesterton.]
William Johnson Fox. 1910. [Completed by Edward Garnett.]
Letters about Shelley. Interchanged by Edward Dowden, Richard Garnett and Wm. Michael Rossetti. Ed. R. S. Garnett, 1917.

(b) Poems and Plays

Primula. A Book of Lyrics. 1858 (anon.); 1859 (signed, as Io in Egypt and Other Poems); 1893 (rev. with addns as Poems).
Poems from the German. 1862.
Idylls and Epigrams, chiefly from the Greek Anthology. 1869; 1892 (as A Chaplet from the Greek Anthology).
Iphigeneia in Delphi. 1891. [A play; also includes Homer's 'Shield of Achilles' and other trns from the Greek.]
One Hundred and Twenty-four Sonnets from Dante, Petrarch and Camoens. 1896.
The Queen and Other Poems. 1901.
William Shakespeare, Pedagogue and Poacher. 1904. [A play.]

(c) Miscellaneous Writings

Richmond on the Thames. 1870.
The Twilight of the Gods, and Other Tales. 1888; 1903 (augmented). [Cynical apologues.]
The Soul and the Stars. By A. G. Trent. 1893; 1903 (expanded). [First pbd in a more primitive form in University Mag. March 1880; unorthodox theology; 'A. G. Trent' is a pseudonym.]
Essays in Librarianship and Bibliography. 1899.
De Flagello Myrteo. 1905 (anon.). [Aphorisms.]

[Garnett also pbd several tracts on library problems; he was keeper of BM. printed books, 1890–9. He contributed many articles to DNB. and other composite works as well as editing or introducing Shelley's poems and various Shelleyana, Coleridge's poems, Milton's prose, novels by George Eliot, Charles Reade, Goldsmith, etc., etc. He was general editor of the International Library of Famous Literature, 20 vols. 1899.]

SIR EDMUND WILLIAM GOSSE (1845–1928)

(a) Bibliographies

Garnett, R. English Illustrated Mag. XXIX, 1903. [Includes articles by and on Gosse.]
Gullick, N. [Appendix to The Life and Letters of Sir Edmund Gosse, by the Hon. Evan Charteris, 1931.]

(b) Collected and Selected Works

Collected Poems. 1911.
Collected Essays. 12 vols. 1912–27.
Selected Poems. 1926. (Augustan Books.)
Selected Essays. 2 vols. 1928.

(c) Critical and Biographical Writings

Studies in the Literature of Northern Europe. 1879.
Memoir of Samuel Rowlands. [Prefixed to The Works of Rowlands, 1880.]
Memoir of Thomas Lodge. [Prefixed to The Works of Thomas Lodge, 1882.]
Gray. 1882; 1889 (rev.). (English Men of Letters ser.)
Cecil Lawson: a Memoir. 1883.
Seventeenth-Century Studies: A Contribution to the History of English Poetry. 1883. [Rptd for the most part from Cornhill Mag.]
From Shakespeare to Pope. Cambridge, 1885.
Raleigh. 1886.
The Life of William Congreve. 1888; 1924 (rev. and enlarged).
A History of Eighteenth-Century Literature, 1660–1780. 1889.
Robert Browning: Personalia. Boston, 1890.
Heinemann's International Library. 21 vols. 1890–1894. [With a special introduction by Gosse to each vol.]
The Life of Philip Henry Gosse. 1890.
Northern Studies. 1890.
Gossip in a Library. 1891. [Short essays rptd from Saturday Rev., St James's Gazette, and Black and White.]
The Life and Writings of Thomas Nash. [Prefixed to The Unfortunate Traveller, 1892.]
Shelley in 1892. Centenary Address at Horsham. 1892 (priv. ptd).
Wolcott Balestier. A Portrait Sketch. 1892 (priv. ptd). [Rptd from Century Mag.]

Questions at Issue. 1893.

The Jacobean Poets. 1894.

Critical Kit-Kats. 1896.

A Short History of Modern English Literature. 1897; 1924 (with 2 further chs.).

Short Histories of the Literature of the World. 15 vols. 1897–1915. [Vol. III entirely by Gosse who was also general editor.]

Henry Fielding: an Essay. [Introduction to The Works of Fielding, 1898–9.]

The Life and Letters of John Donne. 2 vols. 1899.

Queen Victoria. New York, 1901. [Unauthorised rpt from Quarterly Rev.]

English Literature. An Illustrated Record. 4 vols. 1903–4. [Vol. I by Richard Garnett; vol. II by Garnett and Gosse; vols. III, IV by Gosse.]

The Challenge of the Brontës. 1903 (priv. ptd). [Also in Publications of Brontë Soc. Feb. 1904.]

Jeremy Taylor. 1904. (English Men of Letters ser.)

Coventry Patmore. 1905.

French Profiles. 1905.

Sir Thomas Browne. 1905. (English Men of Letters ser.)

Ibsen. 1907.

Scandinavia, 1815–1870. Dano-Norwegian Literature, 1815–1865. 1908. [In The Cambridge Modern History, vol. II, 1902.]

Biographical Notes on the Writings of Robert Louis Stevenson. 1908 (priv. ptd).

Catalogue of the Library of the House of Lords. 1908 (priv. ptd).

Swinburne: Personal Recollections. 1909 (priv. ptd). [Rptd from Fortnightly Rev.]

Portraits and Sketches. 1912.

Browning's Centenary. 1912. [Addresses by Gosse, Sir A. Pinero and H. James.]

The Future of English Poetry. 1913.

Lady Dorothy Nevill. An Open Letter. 1913 (priv. ptd).

Two Pioneers of Romanticism: Joseph and Thomas Warton. 1915.

Inter Arma. Being Essays Written in Time of War. 1916. [Rptd from Edinburgh Rev.]

The Life of Algernon Charles Swinburne. 1917.

Lord Cromer as a Man of Letters. 1917 (priv. ptd). [Rptd from Fortnightly Rev.]

The Novels of Benjamin Disraeli. 1918 (priv. ptd). [Also in Trans. Royal Soc. Lit. XXXVI.]

France et Angleterre: L'Avenir de leurs Relations intellectuelles. 1918. [Rptd from Revue des Deux Mondes.]

Three French Moralists, and the Gallantry of France. 1918.

A Catalogue of the Works of A. C. Swinburne in the Library of Mr. E. Gosse. 1919 (priv. ptd).

Some Diversions of a Man of Letters. 1919.

The First Draft of Swinburne's 'Anactoria.' Cambridge, 1919 (priv. ptd). [A short critical essay.]

Some Literary Aspects of France in the War. 1919 (priv. ptd).

Malherbe and the Classical Reaction in the Seventeenth Century. Oxford, 1920. [A lecture.]

Books on the Table. New York, 1921. More Books on the Table. 1923. [Miniature monographs on literary subjects rptd from Sunday Times.]

The Continuity of Literature. An Address. 1922.

Aspects and Impressions. New York, 1922.

Swinburne: An Essay written in 1875 and Now First Printed. 1925.

Tallement des Réaux, or the Art of Miniature Biography. The Zaharoff Lecture. 1925.

Silhouettes. 1925. [Reviews rptd from Sunday Times.]

The Earliest Charles Lamb Dinner. [In Cambridge and Charles Lamb, Cambridge, 1925.]

Leaves and Fruit. 1927.

Austin Dobson. [In A. T. A. Dobson's Austin Dobson. Some Notes, 1928.]

A Memoir of Thomas Lovell Beddoes. [Prefixed to Complete Works of Beddoes, 2 vols. 1928.]

[Gosse also contributed to many periodicals and composite works. (He wrote the article on Swinburne in DNB.) He translated Ibsen's Hedda Gabler, 1891, and The Master Builder, 1893 (with William Archer), as well as La Motte Fouqué's Undine, 1896.]

(d) Poems and Plays

Madrigals, Songs and Sonnets. 1870. [32 by Gosse and 30 by J. A. Blaikie.]

On Viol and Flute. 1873; 1890 (33 poems from the original edn and 36 poems drawn from other vols. including New Poems, 1879).

King Erik. 1876; 1893 (with introductory essay by Theodore Watts[-Dunton]). [A tragedy in verse.]

The Unknown Lover. 1878. [A play for private performance with an essay on the Chamber Drama in England.]

New Poems. 1879.

An Epistle to Dr. Oliver Wendell Holmes on his Seventy-Fifth Birthday, 1884. 1884 (priv. ptd).

Firdausi in Exile and Other Poems. 1885.

The Masque of Painters. 1885 (priv. ptd).

Inscription for the Rose-Tree brought from Omar's Tomb, and planted on the Grave of Edward FitzGerald, 1893. 1893 (priv. ptd).

In Russet and Silver. 1894.

The Autumn Garden. 1909.
Two Unpublished Poems. 1929 (priv. ptd).

(e) Miscellaneous Writings

The Ethical Condition of the Early Scandinavian Peoples. 1875.
A Critical Essay on the Life and Works of George Tinworth. 1883.
Notes on the Pictures and Drawings of Mr. Alfred W. Hunt. 1884.
The Secret of Narcisse. A Romance. 1892.
Hypolympia; or, the Gods in the Island. An Ironic Fantasy. 1901.
British Portrait Painters and Engravers of the Eighteenth Century. Kneller to Reynolds. With an Introductory Essay and Biographical Notes. 2 vols. 1905.
Father and Son. A Study of Two Temperaments. 1907.
Two Visits to Denmark: 1872, 1874. 1911.
Reims Revisited. 1916 (priv. ptd). [Rptd from Fortnightly Rev.]

(f) Biography and Criticism

Lister, J. R. Catalogue of a Portion of the Library of Edmund Gosse. 1893.
Williams, S. T. Two Victorian Boyhoods. North American Rev. June 1921.
Cox, E. H. M. The Library of Edmund Gosse. 1924. [With an introductory essay by Gosse.]
Freeman, John. English Portraits and Essays. 1924.
Braybrooke, P. Considerations on Edmund Gosse. With Introduction by Gilbert Frankau. 1925.
Drinkwater, J. The Poetry of Edmund Gosse. Bookman, July 1926.
Saintsbury, G. Some Memories of Edmund Gosse. London Mercury, July 1928.
Levinson, A. Edmund Gosse. Nouvelles Littéraires, 9 June 1928.
Williamson, G. C. Edmund Gosse as a Boy: A Reminiscence. London Mercury, Oct. 1928.
Bellows, William. Edmund Gosse: Some Memories. 1929.
Charteris, E. The Life and Letters of Sir Edmund Gosse. 1931.
Drinkwater, J. Edmund Gosse. Quarterly Rev. July 1931.
Woolf, V. Edmund Gosse. Fortnightly Rev. June 1931.
Evans, B. I. English Poetry in the Later Nineteenth Century. 1933. [Ch. xi.]

FRANCIS HINDES GROOME (1851–1902)

A Short Border History. Kelso, 1887.
The Gypsies. 1891. [In E. Magnússon, National Life and Thought of the Various Nations throughout the World.]

Ordnance Gazetteer of Scotland. Ed. F. H. Groome, 6 vols. 1894–5.
Two Suffolk Friends. Edinburgh, 1895. [Recollections of R. H. Groome and Edward FitzGerald.]
Kriegspiel: the War-Game. 1896. [A novel.]
Chambers's Biographical Dictionary. 1897. [With David Patrick.]
Gypsy Folk-Tales. 1899.
[For an appreciation see T. Watts-Dunton, The Tarno Rye: (Francis Hindes Groome), Athenaeum, 22 Feb. 1902.]

EDMUND GURNEY (1847–1888)

On Some Disputed Points in Music. Fortnightly Rev. xxvi, 1876.
The Power of Sound. 1880. [Deals with music.]
Phantasms of the Living. 2 vols. 1886; abridged by Mrs H. Sidgwick, 1918. [With F. W. H. Myers and F. Podmore.]
Tertium Quid: Chapters on Various Disputed Questions. 2 vols. 1887.
[Gurney also contributed to Mind and Journ. Soc. for Psychical Research. See F. W. H. Myers, The Work of Edmund Gurney in Experimental Psychology, Proc. Soc. for Psychical Research, v, 1888.]

SIR WILLIAM HENRY HADOW (1859–1937)

Studies in Modern Music. Hector Berlioz, Robert Schumann, Richard Wagner. (Frederick Chopin, Antonin Dvořák, Johannes Brahms.) 2 sers. 1893–5.
Sonata Form. [1896.]
A Croatian Composer: Notes towards the Study of Joseph Haydn. 1897.
The Oxford History of Music. 6 vols. Oxford, 1901–5, 1929– . [Edited by Hadow who wrote vol. v (The Viennese Period).]
Music. 1924. (Home University Lib.)
The Place of Music Among the Arts. The Romanes Lecture. Oxford, 1933.
Richard Wagner. 1934. (Home University Lib.)
[Sir Henry Hadow has pbd a number of other books on music, literature, education, etc.]

PHILIP GILBERT HAMERTON (1834–1894)

(a) Bibliography

Bulletin of Public Lib. (Sale), March, Feb. 1897.

(b) Essays and Miscellaneous Writings

Observations on Heraldry. 1851.
A Painter's Camp in the Highlands and Thoughts About Art. 2 vols. Cambridge, 1862; 1866 (rev.). [Thoughts About Art rptd separately 1873.]

The Unknown River. An Etcher's Voyage of Discovery. 1871.
The Intellectual Life. 1873.
Chapters on Animals. 1874.
Round my House: Notes of Rural Life in France in Peace and War. 1876.
The Sylvan Year. Leaves from the Note-Book of Raoul Dubois. 1876.
Modern Frenchmen. 1878.
Human Intercourse. 1884.
Paris in Old and Present Times, with Especial Reference to Changes in its Architecture and Topography. 1885.
The Sâone. A Summer Voyage. 1887.
French and English. A Comparison. 1889.
The Mount: Narrative of a Visit to the Site of a Gaulish City on Mount Beuvray. With a Description of the Neighbouring City of Autun. 1897. [Ed. by Mrs Hamerton.]
The Quest of Happiness. With Introduction by M. R. F. Gilman. Boston, 1897.
Philip Gilbert Hamerton: an Autobiography, 1834–1858, and a Memoir by his Wife, 1858–1894. 1897.

(c) Writings on Art

Etching and Etchers. 1868.
Painting in France after the Decline of Classicism. An Essay. 1869.
English Landscape Painters. An Essay. [In English Painters of the Present Day, 1871.]
The Etcher's Handbook. 1871.
Examples of Modern Etching. 1875.
The Life of J. M. W. Turner. 1879.
The Graphic Arts. 1882.
Landscape. 1885.
Imagination in Landscape Painting. 1887.
Turner. 1889. [Written in French. Distinct from the English work.]
Portfolio Papers. 1889. [Critical essays rptd from The Portfolio.]
The Present State of the Fine Arts in France. 1892.
Drawing and Engraving. 1892.
Man in Art. Studies in Religions and Historical Art, Portrait and Genre. 1892.
The Etchings of Rembrandt. 1894; 1905 (with catalogue of all Rembrandt's etchings, by Campbell Dodgson).

[Hamerton edited The Portfolio from its inception in 1869 to his death.]

(d) Poems and Novels

The Isles of Loch Awe and other Poems of my Youth. 1855.
Wenderholme: a Story of Lancashire and Yorkshire. 3 vols. 1869.
Harry Blount. Passages in a Boy's Life on Land and Sea. 1875.
Marmorne, by A. Segrave. 1878.

AUGUSTUS JOHN CUTHBERT HARE (1834–1903)

(a) Biographical and Autobiographical Writings

Memorials of a Quiet Life. 3 vols. 1872–6. [Memoir of Maria Hare.]
Life and Letters of Frances, Baroness Bunsen. 2 vols. 1878.
The Story of Two Noble Lives, Charlotte, Countess Canning, and Louisa, Marchioness of Waterford. 3 vols. 1893.
The Life and Letters of Maria Edgeworth. 2 vols. 1894.
Biographical Sketches. 1895. [A. P. Stanley, Henry Alford, Mrs Duncan Stewart, Paray Le Monial.]
The Gurneys of Earlham. 2 vols. 1895.
The Story of my Life. 6 vols. 1896–1900.

(b) Guide and Travel Books

A Handbook for Travellers in Berks, Bucks and Oxfordshire. 1860.
A Winter in Mentone. 1862.
A Handbook for Travellers to Durham and Northumberland. 1864.
Walks in Rome. 2 vols. 1871.
Wanderings in Spain. 1873.
Days near Rome. 2 vols. 1875.
Cities of Northern and Central Italy. 3 vols. 1876.
Walks in London. 2 vols. 1878.
Cities of Southern Italy and Sicily. Edinburgh, 1883.
Florence. 1884.
Venice. 1884.
Cities of Central Italy. 2 vols. 1884.
Cities of Northern Italy. 2 vols. 1884.
Sketches in Holland and Scandinavia. 1885.
Studies in Russia. 1885.
Days near Paris. 1887.
Paris. 1887.
North Eastern France. 1890.
South Eastern France. 1890.
South Western France. 1890.
Sussex. 1894.
North Western France. 1895.
The Rivieras. 1896.
Shropshire. 1898.

[Hare also pbd a collection of Epitaphs for Country Churchyards, Oxford, 1856.]

(c) Biography and Criticism

Leslie, S. Men were Different. 1937.

FREDERIC HARRISON (1831–1923)

(a) Collected and Selected Works

Collected Essays. 4 pts, 1907–8.
Selected Essays, Literary and Historical. Ed. A. Jha, 1925.

(b) Critical and Biographical Writings

The Choice of Books and Other Literary Pieces. 1886.
Oliver Cromwell. 1888.
Studies in Early Victorian Literature. 1895.
William the Silent. 1897.
Tennyson, Ruskin, Mill; and Other Literary Estimates. 1899.
John Ruskin. 1902. (English Men of Letters ser.)
Chatham. 1905.
Memories and Thoughts. Men—Books—Cities—Art. 1906.
Among my Books. Centenaries, Reviews, Memoirs. 1912.
Obiter Scripta, 1918. 1919.
Novissima Verba: Last Words, 1920. 1921.
De Senectute: More Last Words. 1923.

(c) Miscellaneous Writings

Order and Progress. 1875. [Political essays.]
Annals of an Old Manor House, Sutton Place, Guildford. 1893; 1899 (abridged).
The Meaning of History and Other Historical Pieces. 1894.
George Washington and Other American Addresses. 1901.
Theophano: the Crusade of the Tenth Century. A Romantic Monograph. 1904.
Nicephorus: a Tragedy of New Rome. 1906. [A verse drama on the same subject as Theophano, but with other characters and incidents.]
My Alpine Jubilee, 1851–1907. 1908.
Autobiographic Memoirs. 2 vols. 1911. [Vol. II includes a comprehensive list of Harrison's contributions to periodicals.]

[Many of Harrison's essays and lectures were also, or originally, pnd separately as tracts.]

(d) Biography and Criticism

Harris, Muriel. Two Victorian Portraits. North American Rev. Sept. 1920. [Lord Morley and Frederic Harrison.]
Luce, M. Frederic Harrison. Nineteenth Century, March 1923.
Saintsbury, G. Frederic Harrison. Fortnightly Rev. March 1923.
Harrison, Austin. Frederic Harrison. Thoughts and Memories. 1926.

WILLIAM ERNEST HENLEY (1849–1903)

[See p. 342 above.]

CHARLES HAROLD HERFORD (1853–1931)

(a) Critical Writings

The Essential Characteristics of the Romantic and Classical Styles: with Illustrations from English Literature. Cambridge, 1880.

The First Quarto Edition of Hamlet. 1603. Two Essays, to which the Harness Prize was awarded. I. By C. H. Herford; II. By W. H. Widgery. 1880.
A Sketch of the History of the English Drama in its Social Aspects. Being the Essay which obtained the Le Bas Prize. 1880. Cambridge, 1881.
The Stoics as Teachers. The Hare Prize Essay for 1881. Cambridge, 1882.
Studies in the Literary Relations of England and Germany in the Sixteenth Century. Cambridge, 1886.
The Age of Wordsworth. 1897. (Handbooks of English Literature.)
Robert Browning. 1905.
Goethe. 1912.
Shakespeare. 1912.
Shakespeare's Treatment of Love and Marriage, and Other Essays. 1921.
A Sketch of Recent Shakespearean Investigation, 1893–1923. 1923.
Ben Jonson. Ed. C. H. Herford and P. Simpson, 10 vols. Oxford, 1925– . [Vols. I, II, The Man and his Work, were by Herford.]
English Literature. 1927. (Benn's Sixpenny Library.)
Wordsworth. 1930.

[Herford also contributed largely to composite works and periodicals, 12 of his articles in John Rylands Lib. Bulletin, 1918–28, being rptd separately as pamphlets. He edited or contributed to several edns of Shakespeare and pbd rhyming versions of Ibsen's Brand, 1894, and Love's Comedy, 1900.]

(b) Other Writings

Memoir of W. H. Herford. [In The Student's Froebel, 1911.]
The Case of German South Tyrol against Italy. 1927. [Tr. and ed. by Herford.]
The Post-War Mind of Germany, and Other European Studies. 1927.
Philip Henry Wicksteed: his Life and Work. 1931.

(c) Biography and Criticism

Hoops, J. Nachruf. E. Studien, LXVI, 1931.
Obituary. John Rylands Lib. Bulletin, XV, 1931.
Obituary. Spectator, 2 May 1931.
Gardner, E. G. Professor Herford as an Italian Scholar. 1932.
Robertson, J. G. Charles Harold Herford. [1933.]
Abercrombie, L. Herford and International Literature. John Rylands Lib. Bulletin, XIX, 1935.

JOHN CORDY JEAFFERSON (1831–1891)

[See p. 918 below.]

LIONEL JOHNSON (1867–1902)

[See p. 344 above.]

DENHAM JORDAN ('A Son of the Marshes')

Woodland, Moor and Stream: being the Notes of a Naturalist. 1889.
Annals of a Fishing Village. Ed. J. A. Owen, 1891.
On Surrey Hills. 1891.
Within an Hour of London Town among Wild Birds and their Haunts. 1892.
Forest Tithes, and Other Studies from Nature. 1893.
With the Woodlanders and by the Tides. 1893.
From Spring to Fall; or,. When Life stirs. [1894.]
The Wild-Fowl and Sea-Fowl of Great Britain. 1895.
In the Green Leaf and the Sere. 1896.
Drift from Longshore. 1898.

WILLIAM PATON KER (1855–1923)

(a) Critical Writings

The Philosophy of Art. 1883. [In Essays in Philosophical Criticism, ed. A. Seth and R. B. Haldane, 1883.]
Epic and Romance. Essays on Mediaeval Literature. 1897; 1908.
The Dark Ages. Edinburgh, 1904.
Essays on Mediaeval Literature. 1905.
English Literature: Mediaeval. 1912.
The Art of Poetry. Seven Lectures, 1920–1922. Oxford, 1923.
Collected Essays. Ed. C. Whibley, 2 vols. 1925. [Uncollected essays rptd from single pamphlets, periodicals and composite works.]
Form and Style in Poetry. Lectures and Notes. Ed. R. W. Chambers, 1928.

[Ker also edited Dryden's essays, Berners's Froissart, and some other English and French classics.]

(b) Biography and Criticism

Chambers, R. W. W. P. Ker. Proc. British Academy, XI, 1925.
Read, H. New Criterion, April 1926.

ANDREW LANG (1844–1912)

(a) Collected and Selected Works

Ballades and Verses Vain. New York, 1884. [Selected by A. Dobson.]
Ballades and Rhymes. From Ballades in Blue China and Rhymes à la Mode. 1911.
Poetical Works. Ed. Mrs Lang, 4 vols. in 2, 1923.
The Augustan Books of Modern Poetry. Andrew Lang. [1926.] [Selected poems.]

Essays of To-day and Yesterday. Andrew Lang. 1926. [Selected essays.]

(b) Poems

Ballads and Lyrics of Old France; with Other Poems. 1872; 1907.
XXII Ballades in Blue China. 1880.
XXII and X. XXXII Ballades in Blue China. 1881; 1888 (with addns).
Helen of Troy. 1882; 1883; 1913.
Rhymes à la Mode. 1885.
Lines on the Inaugural Meeting of the Shelley Society. 1886 (anon.; priv. ptd). [First pbd in Saturday Rev. 13 March 1886.]
Grass of Parnassus. Rhymes Old and New. 1888; 1892.
Ban and Arrière Ban. A Rally of Fugitive Rhymes. 1894.
New Collected Rhymes. 1905.
Ode on a Distant Memory of 'Jane Eyre.' [1916.]

(c) Fiction and Parodies

Much Darker Days. By A Huge Longway. 1884; 1885 (rev.). [Parodies Hugh Conway's Dark Days.]
The Princess Nobody. A Tale of Fairy Land. [1884.]
'That Very Mab.' 1885 (anon.). [With May Kendall.]
In the Wrong Paradise, and Other Stories. 1886.
The Mark of Cain. Bristol, 1886.
He. By the Authors of 'It,' 'King Solomon's Wives,' and 'Bess.' 1887. [With W. H. Pollock.]
The Gold of Fairnilee. Bristol, 1888.
Prince Prigio. Bristol, 1889.
Old Friends. Essays in Epistolary Parody. 1890; 1892.
The World's Desire. 1890; 1894; [1907]; 1916. [With Sir H. Rider Haggard.]
Prince Ricardo of Pantouflia. Bristol, [1893].
My Own Fairy Book. Bristol, 1895. [Collected fairy tales.]
A Monk of Fife. 1896.
Parson Kelly. 1900; [1908]. [With A. E. W. Mason.]
The Disentanglers. 1902.
Tales of a Fairy Court. [1907.]

[Lang also pbd a series of fairy books and story books consisting of re-tellings by Lang of traditional tales from various sources.]

(d) Literary and Art Criticism

The Library. 1881; 1892.
Notes on a Collection of Pictures by J. E. Millais. 1881.
Letters to Dead Authors. 1886; 1892; 1907 (with addns).

Books and Bookmen. 1886; New York, 1886; 1892; 1912.

Pictures at Play, or Dialogues of the Galleries. By Two Art-Critics. 1888. [With W. E. Henley.]

Letters on Literature. 1889; 1892.

Lost Leaders. 1889. [Rptd from Daily News.]

Specimens of a Bibliography. 1889.

How to fail in Literature. A Lecture. 1890.

Etudes traditionnistes. Paris, 1890. [Essays from Saturday Rev. tr. H. Carnoy.]

Essays in Little. 1891.

Memoir of the Author. [In W. Y. Sellar, The Roman Poets of the Augustan Age, Oxford, 1892, 1899.]

The Tercentenary of Izaak Walton. 1893 (priv. ptd).

Homer and the Epic. 1893.

Robert F. Murray: his Poems. With a Memoir by Andrew Lang. 1894.

The Life and Letters of J. G. Lockhart. 2 vols. 1897.

Alfred Tennyson. Edinburgh, 1901.

Memoir of the Author. [In C. I. Elton, William Shakespeare, his Family and Friends, ed. A. H. Thompson, 1904.]

Adventures among Books. 1905.

The Puzzle of Dickens's Last Plot. 1905.

The Lady of the Lake. By Sir Walter Scott. With a Short Biography by Andrew Lang. 1905. [Biography rptd with Quentin Durward, 1908.]

Homer and his Age. 1906.

Scott. [In Homes and Haunts of Famous Authors, 1906.]

Sir Walter Scott. 1906.

The World of Homer. 1910.

Sir Walter Scott and the Border Minstrelsy. 1910.

Shakespeare, Bacon, and the Great Unknown. 1912.

History of English Literature from 'Beowulf' to Swinburne. 1912; 1912 (rev.); 1913.

[Lang also edited and introduced many English and other classics, including the works of Scott and Burns.]

(e) Writings on Anthropology, Mythology and the Occult

Mythology and Fairy-Tales. Fortnightly Rev. May 1873. ['The first full refutation of Max Müller's mythological system.']

Custom and Myth. 1884; 1885 (rev.); 1893; 1898; 1904.

Myth, Ritual, and Religion. 2 vols. 1887; 2 vols. 1899.

Cock Lane and Common-Sense. 1894; 1896.

Modern Mythology. 1897.

The Book of Dreams and Ghosts. 1897; 1899.

The Making of Religion. 1898; 1900.

Psychical Research of the Century. [In The 19th-Century. A Review of Progress, 1901.]

Magic and Religion. 1901.

Social Origins, by Andrew Lang; Primal Law, by J. J. Atkinson. 1903.

The Secret of the Totem. 1905.

The Clyde Mystery. A Study in Forgeries and Folklore. Glasgow, 1905.

Australian Problems. [In Anthropological Essays presented to Edward Burnett Tylor, Oxford, 1907.]

Homer and Anthropology. [In R. R. Marett, Anthropology and the Classics, Oxford, 1908.]

The Origins of Religion, and Other Essays. 1908. [Rpts from earlier vols. with 1 new essay on Theories of the Origins of Religion.]

The Origin of Terms of Human Relationship. [1909.] [From Proc. British Academy, vol. III.]

Method in the Study of Totemism. Glasgow, 1911.

[Lang was one of the founders of the Soc. for Psychical Research; to the 9th edn of Ency. Brit. 1875–89, he contributed articles on Apparitions, Crystal-gazing, Fairy, Family Edmund Gurney, Hauntings, Mythology, Poltergeist, Psychical Research, Second Sight, Totemism, as well as on literary and historical subjects.]

(f) Historical and Topographical Writings

Oxford. Brief Historical and Descriptive Notes. 1882 (2nd edn); 1890; 1906; 1916.

Life, Letters, and Diaries of Sir Stafford Northcote, First Earl of Iddesleigh. 2 vols. Edinburgh, 1890, 1891.

Piccadilly. [In Great Streets of the World, 1892.]

St. Andrews. 1893.

Pickle the Spy, or the Incognito of Prince Charles. 1897.

The Companions of Pickle. 1898.

Prince Charles Edward. 1900.

A History of Scotland from the Roman Occupation. 4 vols. Edinburgh, 1900–7.

The Mystery of Mary Stuart. 1901 (bis); 1904.

James VI and the Gowrie Mystery. 1902.

The Valet's Tragedy, and Other Studies. 1903.

Historical Mysteries. 1904; [1911].

John Knox and the Reformation. 1905.

The Story of Joan of Arc. [1906.]

Portraits and Jewels of Mary Stuart. 1906.

'The End of an Auld Sang.' A Romantic Plot against the Union. 2 pts. [Both in The Union of 1707, a Survey of Events, Glasgow, 1907.]

The King over the Water. 1907. [Mainly by A. Shield.]

The Maid of France. The Life and Death of Jeanne D'Arc. 1908; 1913; 1922; tr. French, Paris, [1911]. [A reply to Anatole France's Vie de Jeanne d'Arc, 1908.]

La Jeanne d'Arc de M. Anatole France. Paris, 1909.

Sir George Mackenzie, King's Advocate: his Life and Times. 1909.

A Short History of Scotland. Edinburgh, 1911.

Highways and Byways in the Border. 1913. [With J. Lang.]

[Lang also edited several minor Scottish historical works for the Roxburghe Club, Scottish History Soc. etc.]

(g) Writings on Sport

The History of Golf. [In H. G. Hutchinson, Golf, 1890 (Badminton Lib.).]

Angling Sketches. 1891; 1895.

Famous Golf Links. 1891. [With H. G. Hutchinson and others.]

A Batch of Golfing Papers. Ed. R. Barclay, [1892]. [By Lang and others.]

Classical Sport. [In H. Peek, The Poetry of Sport, 1896 (Badminton Lib.).]

(h) Translations

The Odyssey of Homer. Done into English Prose by S. H. Butcher and Andrew Lang. 1879; 1887; 1924; 1930.

Theocritus, Bion and Moschus rendered into English Prose, with an Introductory Essay. 1880; 1889; 1922.

The Iliad of Homer. Done into English Prose by Andrew Lang, Walter Leaf, and Ernest Myers. 1883; 1914.

Deulin, Charles. Johnny Hut and the Golden Goose. 1887.

Aucassin and Nicolete. 1887; 1896; 1898; 1902; 1904; 1905.

The Dead Leman, and Other Tales from the French. 1889; 1890. [With P. Sylvester.]

The Miracles of Madame Saint Katherine of Fierbois, translated from the Edition of the Abbé J. J. Bowrassé, Tours, 1858. Chicago, 1897.

The Homeric Hymns. A New Prose Translation and Essays. 1899.

Hugo, Victor. Notre-Dame of Paris. With a Critical Introduction. 1902; 1924.

(i) Biography and Criticism

Brown, R. Semitic Influence in Hellenic Mythology, with Special Reference to the Works of Max Müller and Andrew Lang. 1898.

Falconer, C. M. Catalogue of a Library, chiefly the Writings of Andrew Lang. Dundee, 1898 (priv. ptd).

Wanliss, T. D. Scotland and Presbyterianism vindicated. Being a Critical Review of the Third Volume of Mr. Lang's History. Edinburgh, 1905.

—— The Muckrake in Scottish History, or Mr. Lang re-criticised. Edinburgh, 1906.

Saintsbury, G. Obituary. Oxford Mag. 17 Oct. 1912.

—— Andrew Lang. Quarterly Rev. Oct. 1923.

—— Andrew Lang in the 'Seventies—and After. [In The Eighteen-Seventies, Royal Soc. Lit. 1929.]

Gordon, G. S. Obituary. TLS. 6 Sept. 1912 (anon.).

—— Andrew Lang. Andrew Lang Lecture. Oxford, 1928.

Ker, W. P. Commemorative Address. Proc. Academic Committee, Royal Soc. Lit. 1913.

Rait, R. S., Murray, G., Reinach, S. and Millar, J. H. Quarterly Rev. April 1913. [Commemorative article.]

Greenwood, Sir G. G. Is there a Shakespeare Problem? With a Reply to Mr. J. M. Robertson and Mr. Andrew Lang. 1916.

Beerbohm, M. Andrew Lang. Life and Letters, I, 1929.

Shewan, A. Andrew Lang's Work for Homer. Andrew Lang Lecture. Oxford, 1929.

Rait, R. S. Andrew Lang as Historian. Andrew Lang Lecture. Oxford, 1930.

Cazamian, L. Andrew Lang and the Maid of France. Andrew Lang Lecture. Oxford, 1931.

Buchan, J. Andrew Lang and the Border. Andrew Lang Lecture. Oxford, 1933.

Webster, A. B. Andrew Lang's Poetry. Andrew Lang Lecture. Oxford, 1937.

'VERNON LEE,' i.e. VIOLET PAGET (1856–1935)

(a) Critical and Miscellaneous Writings

Studies of the Eighteenth Century in Italy. 1880.

Belcaro: being Essays on Sundry Æsthetical Questions. 1883.

The Countess of Albany. 1884.

Euphorion: being Studies of the Antique and the Mediaeval in the Renaissance. 2 vols. 1884.

Baldwin: being Dialogues on Views and Aspirations. 1886.

Juvenilia: being a Second Series of Essays on Sundry Æsthetical Questions. 2 vols. 1887.

Althea. A Second Book of Dialogues on Aspirations and Duties. 1894.

Renaissance Fancies and Studies: being a Sequel to Euphorion. 1895.

Limbo, and Other Essays. 1897; 1908 (adds Ariadne in Mantua).

Genius Loci: Notes on Places. 1899.

Hortus Vitæ: Essays on the Gardening of Life. 1904.

The Enchanted Woods, and Other Essays on the Genius of Places. 1905.

The Spirit of Rome: Leaves from a Diary. 1906.

The Sentimental Traveller: Notes on Places. 1908.

Gospels of Anarchy, and Other Contemporary Studies. 1908.

Laurus Nobilis: Chapters on Art and Life. 1909.

Vital Lies: Studies of Some Varieties of Recent Obscurantism. 2 vols. 1912.

The Beautiful: an Introduction to Psychological Æsthetics. 1913.

The Tower of the Mirrors, and Other Essays on the Spirit of Places. 1914.

The Ballet of the Nations: a Present-day Morality; with a Pictorial Commentary by M. Armfield. 1915.

Satan, the Waster. A Philosophic War Trilogy, with Notes and Introduction. 1920.

The Handling of Words, and Other Studies in Literary Psychology. 1923.

The Golden Keys, and Other Essays on the Genius Loci. 1925.

Proteus; or, The Future of Intelligence. 1925.

The Poet's Eye. 1926.

Music and its Lovers. An Empirical Study of Emotion and Imaginative Responses to Music. [Ed. I. C. Willis], 1932.

(b) Fiction

Tuscan Fairy Tales. [1880.] [Ed. by Vernon Lee.]

The Prince of the Hundred Soups. A Puppet-Show in Narrative, edited [really written] with an Introduction by Vernon Lee. Illustrated by S. Birch. 1883.

Ottilie: an Eighteenth Century Idyl. 1883.

Miss Brown. A Novel. 3 vols. 1884.

A Phantom Lover. A Fantastic Story. Edinburgh, 1886.

Hauntings. Fantastic Stories. 1890.

Vanitas. Polite Stories. 1892.

Au Pays de Vénus. Paris, [1894]. [Tales tr. into French, rptd from Les Lettres et Les Arts.]

Ariadne in Mantua. A Romance in Five Acts. Oxford, 1903.

Penelope Brandling: a Tale of the Welsh Coast in the Eighteenth Century. 1903.

Pope Jacynth, and Other Fantastic Tales. 1904.

Sister Benvenuta and the Christ Child: an Eighteenth Century Legend. 1906.

Louis Norbert: a Two-fold Romance. 1914.

For Maurice: Five Unlikely Stories. 1927.

(c) Works written in Collaboration with C. Anstruther Thomson

Le Rôle de l'Élément moteur dans la Perception esthétique visuelle. Mémoire et Questionnaire soumis au quatrième Congrès de Psychologie. Imola, 1901.

Beauty and Ugliness, and Other Studies in Psychological Æsthetics. 1912.

(d) Introductions

The Life of Saint Mary Magdalen. 1904.

Semon, R. W. Mnemic Psychology. 1923.

Thomson, Clementina A. Art and Man. 1924.

Charteris, Sir E. E. John Sargent. 1927.

Forbes-Mosse, I. Don Juan's Daughters. 1930.

(e) Biography and Criticism

The Literary Life of Vernon Lee. Literary World (Boston), xv, 1884.

Preston, H. W. Vernon Lee. Atlantic Monthly, LV, 1885.

Brooks, Van Wyck. Notes on Vernon Lee. Forum, xLV, 1911.

Shaw, George Bernard. Satan, the Waster. Nation, 18 Sept. 1920.

MacCarthy, D. Vernon Lee. Bookman, LXXXI, 1931.

RICHARD LE GALLIENNE (b. 1866)

[See p. 551 above.]

SIR ALFRED COMYNS LYALL (1835–1911)

[See p. 346 above.]

ALICE MEYNELL (1850–1922)

[See p. 348 above.]

WILLIAM MINTO (1845–1893)

(a) Critical and Biographical Writings

Manual of English Prose Literature, Biographical and Critical. Edinburgh, 1872. [Essay on Style; Biographies of De Quincey, Macaulay and Carlyle; History of English Prose Writers.]

Characteristics of English Poets from Chaucer to Shirley. 1874.

Defoe. 1879. (English Men of Letters ser.)

Plain Principles of Prose Composition. Edinburgh, 1893.

The Literature of the Georgian Era. Ed. (with memoir) W. Knight, Edinburgh, 1894. [Chaucer, Spenser, Renaissance, Shakespeare, Pope and the Eighteenth Century, The Novel, Wordsworth, Coleridge, Shelley, Keats, etc.]

(b) Miscellaneous Writings

The Crack of Doom. A Novel. 3 vols. Edinburgh, 1886.

The Mediation of Ralph Hardelot. 3 vols. 1888. [A novel.]

Was she Good or Bad? A Holiday Episode. 1889.

Logic Inductive and Deductive. 1893.

WILLIAM COSMO MONKHOUSE (1840–1901)
[See p. 349 above.]

GEORGE MOORE (1857–1933)
[See p. 526 above.]

JOHN MORLEY, VISCOUNT MORLEY (1838–1923)

(a) Collected and Selected Works

The Collected Works. 15 vols. 1921; 12 vols. 1923.

Select Essays. Ed. (with memoir) H. G. Rawlinson, 1923.

(b) Critical and Biographical Writings

Edmund Burke: a Historical Study. 1867.

Critical Miscellanies. 2 sers. 1871–7; 3 vols. 1886 (with addns and omissions); ser. 4, 1908. [Robespierre, Carlyle, Byron, Macaulay, Emerson, Vauvenargues, J. S. Mill, George Eliot, Harriet Martineau, W. R. Greg, Comte, etc.]

Voltaire. 1872; 1872 (rev.).

Rousseau. 2 vols. 1873.

Diderot and the Encyclopaedists. 2 vols. 1878.

Edmund Burke. 1879; 1923 (rev.). (English Men of Letters ser.)

The Life of Richard Cobden. 2 vols. 1881; 1882 (abridged).

Walpole. 1889.

Studies in Literature. 1890. [Wordsworth, Aphorisms, Maine, 'The Ring and the Book,' Macvey Napier, Victor Hugo's 'Ninety-Three.']

Machiavelli. The Romanes Lecture. 1897.

Oliver Cromwell. 1900.

The Life of William Ewart Gladstone. 3 vols. 1903; 1927 (abridged, with Preface by C. F. G. Masterman).

Literary Essays. 1906. [Byron, Carlyle, Macaulay, Wordsworth, On the Study of Literature.]

(c) Miscellaneous Writings

Modern Characteristics. 1865 (anon.). [Essays.]

Studies in Conduct. 1867 (anon.). [Essays.]

On Compromise. 1874.

Speeches on Indian Affairs. With an Appreciation. Madras, 1908; 1917 (rev. and enlarged).

Indian Speeches. 1907–1909. 1909.

Recollections. 2 vols. 1917.

Memorandum on Resignation. August, 1914. With an Introduction by F. W. Hirst. 1928.

[Morley also pbd several lectures, tracts and single speeches. He was general editor of the original English Men of Letters ser. and of Fortnightly Rev. 1867–82.]

(d) Biography and Criticism

Cecil, Algernon. Six Oxford Thinkers. 1909.

Harper, G. M. John Morley and Other Essays. Princeton, 1920.

Morison, J. L. John Morley: A Study in Victorianism. Kingston, Ontario, 1920.

MacCallum, J. D. Lord Morley's Criticism of English Poetry and Prose. Princeton, 1921.

Massingham, H. W. Morley the Humanist. Fortnightly Rev. Nov. 1923.

Morgan, J. H. John, Viscount Morley. An Appreciation and Some Reminiscences. 1924.

Braybrooke, Patrick. Lord Morley. With an Introduction by W. B. Maxwell. 1924.

Hirst, F. W. Early Life and Letters of John Morley. 2 vols. 1927.

SIR HENRY NEWBOLT (1862–1937)
[See p. 351 above.]

RODEN NOEL (1834–1894)
[See p. 352 above.]

JOHN OWEN (1836–1896)

(a) Writings

Evenings with the Skeptics; or, Free Discussion on Free Thinkers. 2 vols. 1881.

Verse-Musings on Nature, Faith and Freedom. 1889; 1894 (enlarged).

The Skeptics of the French Renaissance. 1893.

The Skeptics of the Italian Renaissance. 1893; 1908 (3rd edn).

The Five Great Skeptical Dramas of History. (The Prometheus Vinctus of Æschylus; the Book of Job; Goethe's Faust; Shakespeare's Hamlet; El Magico Prodigioso.) 1896.

[Owen also contributed regularly to Edinburgh Rev. and Academy.]

(b) Biography and Criticism

C[otton], J. S. John Owen. Academy, 15 Feb. 1896.

SIR CHARLES HUBERT HASTINGS PARRY (1848–1918)

(a) Musical Criticism

Studies of Great Composers. 1887.

The Art of Music. 1893.

Summary of the History and Development of Mediaeval and Modern Music. [1893?]

The Evolution of the Art of Music. 1896; 1897; rev. H. C. Colles, New York, 1930.

Style in Musical Art: an Inaugural Lecture delivered at Oxford on March 7, 1900. Oxford, 1900.

The Music of the Seventeenth Century. [In Sir W. H. Hadow's Oxford History of Music, vol. III, 1902.]

Johann Sebastian Bach: the Story of the Development of a Great Personality. New York, 1909; 1921; 1934 (rev.).

Style in Musical Art. 1911.

(b) Biography and Criticism

Streatfeild, R. A. Hubert Parry. [1913.]

Fuller-Maitland, J. A. The Life and Work of Sir Hubert Parry. Musical Quart. v, 1919.

Graves, C. L. Hubert Parry: his Life and Works. 1926.

Greene, Gwendolen. Two Witnesses. A Personal Recollection of Hubert Parry and Friedrich von Hügel. 1930.

SIR ARTHUR THOMAS QUILLER-COUCH
(b. 1863)

[See p. 556 above.]

SIR WALTER ALEXANDER RALEIGH
(1861–1922)

(a) Bibliography

Bibliography [i.e. chronological list] of Raleigh's works, 1883–1922. The Periodical, VIII, Sept. 1922.

(b) Critical Writings

The English Novel, being a Short Sketch of its History from the Earliest Times to the Appearance of Waverley. 1891.

Robert Louis Stevenson. 1895.

Style. 1897.

Milton. 1900.

Wordsworth. 1903.

The English Voyages of the Sixteenth Century. [In Hakluyt's Voyages, vol. XII, 1905.]

Shakespeare. 1907. (English Men of Letters ser.)

Six Essays on Johnson. 1910.

Romance. Two Lectures. 1910.

Shakespeare's England. An Account of the Life and Manners of his Age. 2 vols. Oxford, 1916. [Planned by Raleigh, and the section 'The Age of Elizabeth' written by him.]

Some Authors. A Collection of Literary Essays, 1896–1916. 1923.

On Writing and Writers. Being Extracts from his Note-Books, selected and edited by George Gordon. 1926.

(c) Miscellaneous Writings

The Riddle. A Pleasant Pastoral Comedy adapted from The Wife of Bath's Tale as it is set forth in the Works of Master Geoffrey Chaucer. Presented at Otterspool on Midsummer's Eve, 1895. Liverpool, 1895.

England and the War: being Sundry Addresses delivered during the War. 1918.

The War in the Air: being the Story of the part played in the Great War by the Royal Air Force. Vol. I, 1922.

Laughter from a Cloud. 1923. [Humorous sketches and poems.]

The Letters of Sir Walter Raleigh, 1879–1922. Ed. Lady Raleigh, 2 vols. 1926; 2 vols. 1928 (enlarged).

A Selection from the Letters of Sir Walter Raleigh, 1880–1922. Ed. Lady Raleigh, 1928. [Including some letters not previously pbd.]

[Raleigh also pbd pamphlets and lectures and edited various English classics.]

(d) Biography and Criticism

Professor Walter Raleigh. Academy, LII, 1897.

Chapman, R. W. Walter Raleigh. London Mercury, VI, 1922.

G[ordon], G. S. Walter Raleigh. TLS. 8 June 1922.

—— Walter Raleigh in his Letters. London Mercury, XIII, 1926.

Jones, H. A. Sir Walter Raleigh and the Air History. 1922.

Crum, V. Sir Walter Alexander Raleigh. 1923.

Legouis, E. Sir Walter Raleigh d'après ses Lettres. Revue anglo-américaine, Oct. 1926.

Hart, H. L. A. The Position of the Late Sir Walter Raleigh among Literary Critics. Nineteenth Century, CII, 1927.

Garrod, H. W. The Profession of Poetry. Oxford, 1929.

MacCarthy, D. Portraits. 1931.

JOHN MACKINNON ROBERTSON (1856–1933)

(a) Critical and Biographical Writings

Walt Whitman, Poet and Democrat. Edinburgh, 1884.

Essays towards a Critical Method. 1889.

New Essays towards a Critical Method. 1897.

Criticisms. 2 vols. 1902–3.

Browning and Tennyson as Teachers. Two Studies. 1903.

What to Read: Suggestions for the Better Utilisation of Public Libraries. 1904.

Rudyard Kipling: a Criticism. Madras, 1905.

Charles Bradlaugh. 1920. [Based on the chs. contributed by Robertson to H. B. Bonner's Memoir of her father, 2 vols. 1894.]

Voltaire. 1922.

Ernest Renan. 1924.
Gibbon. 1925.
Mr Shaw and 'the Maid.' 1925.
Marlowe. A Conspectus. 1931.

(b) Shakespearean Criticism

The Religion of Shakespeare. Two Discourses. 1887.
Montaigne and Shakespeare. 1897; 1909 (adds 2 essays on the Originality and the Learning of Shakespeare).
Did Shakespeare write 'Titus Andronicus'? A Study in Elizabethan Literature. 1905; 1924 (rev. and expanded as Introduction to the Study of the Shakespeare Canon).
The Baconian Heresy. A Confutation. 1913.
Elizabethan Literature. 1914.
Shakespeare and Chapman: a Thesis of Chapman's Authorship of 'A Lover's Complaint,' and his Origination of 'Timon of Athens,' with Indications of Future Problems. 1917.
The Problem of 'The Merry Wives of Windsor.' 1918.
The Problem of 'Hamlet.' 1919.
The Shakespeare Canon. 4 pts, 1922–32.
Croce as Shakespearean Critic. 1922.
'Hamlet' Once More. 1923.
The Problems of the Shakespeare Sonnets. 1926.
The Genuine in Shakespeare. A Conspectus. 1930.
Literary Detection: a Symposium on 'Macbeth.' 1931.
The State of Shakespeare Study. A Critical Conspectus. 1931.

(c) Philosophical, Sociological and Political Writings

Modern Humanists. 1891.
The Dynamics of Religion. An Essay in English Culture History. 1897; 1926 (rev.). [Originally pbd under pseudonym of 'M. W. Wiseman.']
Miscellanies. 1898.
A Short History of Freethought, Ancient and Modern. 1899; 2 vols. 1906 (rewritten and greatly enlarged); 1915 (rev. and expanded).
Christianity and Mythology. 1900; 1910 (expanded).
Studies in Religious Fallacy. 1900.
Letters on Reasoning. 1902; 1905 (rev.).
A Short History of Christianity. 1902; 1913 (rev.); 1931 (condensed).
Essays in Ethics. 1903.
Pagan Christs: Studies in Comparative Hierology. 1903; 1911 (rev. and expanded).
Studies in Practical Politics. 1903.
Essays in Sociology. 2 vols. 1904.
Pioneer Humanists. 1907.

The Meaning of Liberalism. 1912; 1925 (rev. and enlarged).
Rationalism. 1912.
The Jesus Problem: a Re-Statement of the Myth Theory. 1917.
The Economics of Progress. 1918.
A Short History of Morals. 1920.
Explorations. 1923.
Spoken Essays. 1925.
Modern Humanists Reconsidered. 1927.
A History of Free Thought in the Nineteenth Century. 1929; 2 vols. 1936 (rev.).
Letters on Reasoning. [1935.]

[Robertson also pbd many rationalist, sociological and political tracts and lectures.]

GEORGE EDWARD BATEMAN SAINTSBURY (1845–1933)

(a) Bibliographies

James, W. P. English Illustrated Mag. Oct. 1903. [Includes reviews and articles on and by Saintsbury.]
Bibliographies of Modern Authors. London Mercury, Dec. 1919.
Leuba, W. Bibliography of G. Saintsbury. Book-Collector's Quart. Oct. 1933.

(b) Literary Histories

A Primer of French Literature. 1880; 1891 (rev.); 1896 (rev.); 1912 (rev.); 1925 (with supplementary chapter on The Present Day by T. B. Rudmose-Brown).
A Short History of French Literature. Oxford, 1882; 1897 (rev.).
A History of Elizabethan Literature. 1887. [From Wyatt and Surrey to the Restoration.]
A History of Nineteenth Century Literature. 1780–1895. 1896.
The Flourishing of Romance and the Rise of Allegory. Edinburgh, 1897. [Periods of European Literature, ed. G. Saintsbury, vol. II.]
A Short History of English Literature. 1898.
The History of Criticism and Literary Taste in Europe. 3 vols. Edinburgh, 1900–4.
The Earlier Renaissance. Edinburgh, 1901. [Periods of European Literature, vol. V.]
A History of English Prosody from the Twelfth Century to the Present Day. 2 vols. 1906.
The Later Nineteenth Century. Edinburgh, 1907. [Periods of European Literature, vol. XII.]
A Historical Manual of English Prosody. 1910.
A History of English Criticism: being the English Chapters of A History of Criticism and Literary Taste in Europe, revised, adapted and supplemented. Edinburgh, 1911.

A History of English Prose Rhythm. 1912.
The English Novel. 1913.
A First Book of English Literature. 1914.
The Peace of the Augustans. 1916.
A History of the French Novel to the Close of the Nineteenth Century. 2 vols. 1917–9.

(c) Critical and Biographical Essays

John Dryden. 1881. (English Men of Letters ser.)
A Short History of the Life and Writings of Alain René Le Sage. 1881 (priv. ptd).
Marlborough. 1885.
Essays in English Literature. 1780–1860. 2 sers. 1890–5.
Essays on French Novelists. 1891.
The Earl of Derby. 1892.
Miscellaneous Essays. 1892. [English Prose Style, Chamfort and Rivarol, Renan, Saint-Evremond, Baudelaire, A Paradox, on Quinet, Contrasts of French and English Literature, etc.]
Corrected Impressions. 1895. [Thackeray, Tennyson, Carlyle, Swinburne, Macaulay, Browning, Dickens, Arnold, Morris, Ruskin, Three Mid-Century Novelists.]
Sir Walter Scott. A Biographical Sketch. 1897.
Matthew Arnold. 1899.
The Collected Essays and Papers. 1875–1920. 4 vols. 1923–4.
A Consideration of Thackeray. 1931.
Prefaces and Essays. Ed. O. Elton, 1933.
Shakespeare. Cambridge, 1934. [Rptd from CHEL. vol. v, 1910.]

[Saintsbury also contributed many chs. to CHEL. and other composite works.]

(d) Anthologies and Edited Matter

French Lyrics. 1882.
Specimens of French Literature from Villon to Hugo. Oxford, 1883.
Specimens of English Prose Style from Malory to Macaulay. 1885.
The Pocket Library of English Literature. 6 vols. 1891–2.
Loci Critici. Boston, 1903.
Minor Poets of the Caroline Period. 3 vols. Oxford, 1905–21.
A Letter Book. 1922.

[Saintsbury also pbd edns of or introductions to very many English and several French classics, the most important being the works of Balzac, Dryden, Fielding, Sterne, Smollett, Peacock and Thackeray.]

(e) Miscellaneous Writings

Manchester: A History of the Town. 1887.
Notes on a Cellar-Book. 1920.
A Scrap Book. 1922.

A Second Scrap Book. 1923.
A Last Scrap Book. 1924.

[Saintsbury also translated 5 works from the French.]

(f) Biography and Criticism

Watson, Sir W. Excursions in Criticism. 1893.
Waugh, A. A Living Critic. Bookman, Aug. 1896.
Duncannon, R. The Tory Professor. University Mag. and Free Rev. June 1897.
Priestley, J. B. Mr. George Saintsbury: An Appreciation. London Mercury, Sept. 1922. [Rptd in Figures in Modern Literature, 1924.]
Lewisohn, L. Saintsbury. Nation (U.S.A.), 5 Dec. 1923.
Roberts, R. E. George Saintsbury. Bookman, Oct. 1925.
Chrystal, Sir G. George Saintsbury. London Mercury, March 1933.
Webster, A. B. George Saintsbury. Edinburgh, 1934.

GEORGE BERNARD SHAW (b. 1856)

[See p. 617 above.]

SIR JOHN SKELTON (1831–1897)

(a) Critical and Historical Writings

Nugae Criticae. Occasional Papers written at the Seaside. Edinburgh, 1862.
John Dryden: in Defence. 1865. [Rptd from Fraser's Mag.]
The Great Lord Bolingbroke, Henry St. John. Edinburgh, 1868.
The Impeachment of Mary Stuart. Edinburgh, 1876.
Essays of Shirley. Edinburgh, 1882.
Essays in History and Biography, including the Defence of Mary Stuart. Edinburgh, 1883. [Blake, Macaulay, Thackeray, C. Brontë, Dryden, Disraeli, Macaulay, etc.]
Maitland of Lethington and the Scotland of Mary Stuart. 2 vols. Edinburgh, 1887.
Mary Stuart. 1893.
The Table Talk of Shirley. Edinburgh, 1895. [Reminiscences of and letters from Froude, Thackeray, Disraeli, Browning, Rossetti, Kingsley, Baynes, Huxley, Tyndall and others.]
Summers and Winters at Balmawhapple. 2 vols. Edinburgh, 1896. [Ser. 2 of The Table Talk of Shirley.]
Charles the First. Edinburgh, 1898.

(b) Miscellaneous Writings

Thalatta, or the Great Commoner. A Political Romance. Edinburgh, 1862.
A Campaigner at Home. 1865. [A novel.]
Spring Songs. By a Western Highlander. 1865.

Benjamin Disraeli: the Past and the Future. 1868.

The Boarding-out of Pauper Children in Scotland. Edinburgh, 1876.

Essays in Romance and Studies from Life. Edinburgh, 1878. [Sketches and short stories.]

The Crookit Meg: a Story of the Year One. 1880. [Rptd from Fraser's Mag.]

The Local Government (Scotland) Act in relation to Public Health. Edinburgh, 1890.

The Handbook of Public Health. Edinburgh, 1890. [Supplement, Edinburgh, 1891.]

ROBERT ALAN MOWBRAY STEVENSON (1847–1900)

The Devils of Notre Dame. 1894. [Illustrations by Joseph Pennell.]

The Art of Velasquez. 1895; 1899 (rev. and expanded).

Peter Paul Rubens. 1898. [Rptd with addns from The Portfolio.]

Essay on Raeburn. [Introduction to Sir Henry Armstrong's Sir Henry Raeburn, 1901.]

ROBERT LOUIS STEVENSON (1850–1894)

[See p. 520 above.]

ALGERNON CHARLES SWINBURNE (1837–1909)

[See p. 317 above.]

JOHN ADDINGTON SYMONDS (1840–1893)

[See p. 358 above.]

ARTHUR SYMONS (b. 1865)

[See p. 359 above.]

HENRY DUFF TRAILL (1842–1900)

(a) Critical and Biographical Writings

Sterne. 1882. (English Men of Letters ser.)
Coleridge. 1884. (English Men of Letters ser.)
Shaftesbury. A Monograph. 1886.
William III. A Monograph. 1888.
Strafford. A Monograph. 1889.
The Marquis of Salisbury. A Monograph. 1891.
Life of Sir John Franklin. 1896.
The New Fiction. 1897. [Miscellaneous critical essays.]
Lord Cromer. A Monograph. 1897.

[Traill also pbd an edn of Disraeli's Sybil. He was general editor of Social England, 1893–7, and of the periodical Literature, 1897–1900.]

(b) Poems and Plays

Glaucus: a Tale of a Fish. A New and Original Extravaganza. Performed July, 1865. [1865.]

Present versus Past. Performed June, 1869. [1869.]

The Battle of the Professors. Performed June, 1874. [1874.]

Re-captured Rhymes: being a Batch of Political and Other Fugitives arrested and brought to Book. Edinburgh, 1882

Saturday Songs. 1890. [Satirical verses largely rptd from Saturday Rev.]

The Medicine Man. Performed May, 1898. [1898.] [In collaboration with Robert Hichens.]

The Baby of the Future. 1911. [Rptd from Punch. Parodies of nursery rhymes.]

(c) Satires and Miscellaneous Writings

The Israelitish Question and the Comments of the Canaan Journals thereon. 1876 (anon.). [Burlesque of leading London newspapers.]

Central Government. 1881; 1908 (rev. Sir Henry Craik). [An account of the English constitutional system.]

The New Lucian. Dialogues of the Dead. 1884; 1900 (adds Dedication and supplementary dialogues).

Number Twenty. 1892. [Fables and fantasies; chiefly in prose but some in verse.]

Two Proper Prides. A Tale. 1894. [Included in A Grey Romance by Mrs W. K. Clifford.]

The Barbarous Britishers. A Tip-Top Novel. 1896. [A parody of The British Barbarians by Grant Allen.]

From Cairo to Soudan. 1896. [Letters rptd from Daily Telegraph.]

England, Egypt and the Soudan. 1900.

[For an appreciation of Traill see H. C. Beeching, Conferences on Books and Men, 1900.]

ARTHUR BINGHAM WALKLEY (1855–1926)

Playhouse Impressions. 1892.
Frames of Mind. 1899.
Dramatic Criticism. Three Lectures. 1903.
Drama and Life. 1907.
Pastiche and Prejudice. 1921.
More Prejudice. 1923.
Still More Prejudice. 1925.

[For Walkley's career see obituary, Times, 9 Oct. 1926.]

THOMAS HUMPHRY WARD (1845–1926)

The English Poets. Selections, with Critical Introductions by Various Writers, and a General Introduction by Matthew Arnold. Edited by T. Humphry Ward. 4 vols. 1880–1.

Men of the Reign. A Biographical Dictionary of Eminent Persons of British and Colonial Birth who have died during the Reign of Queen Victoria. Edited by T. Humphry Ward. 1885.

The Reign of Queen Victoria: a Survey of Fifty Years of Progress. Edited by T. Humphry Ward. 2 vols. 1887.

English Art in the Public Galleries of London. Published under the Direction of T. Humphry Ward, with the Assistance of Walter Armstrong and Others. 1888.

Oxford. Illustrated by J. Fulleylove. With Notes by T. Humphry Ward. 1889.

Romney: a Biographical and Critical Essay, with a Catalogue Raisonné of his Works. 2 vols. 1904. [With W. Roberts.]

History of the Athenaeum [Club], 1824–1925. (Based on Materials collected by the Late H. R. Tedder.) 1926.

THEODORE WATTS-DUNTON, earlier WATTS (1832–1914)

(a) Critical Writings

Charlotte Brontë. [Introduction to vol. VI of The Novels and Poems of Charlotte, Emily and Anne Brontë, 1901.]

Rossetti and Charles Wells: a Reminiscence of Kelmscott Manor. [In Joseph and his Brethren by Charles Wells, 1908.]

Old Familiar Faces. 1916. [Sketches rptd from Athenaeum: Borrow, Rossetti, Tennyson, Christina Rossetti, Gordon Hake, de Tabley, Morris and F. H. Groome.]

Poetry and the Renascence of Wonder. With a Preface by Thomas Hake. 1916. [Article on Poetry rptd from Ency. Brit. 9th edn, 1885, on Renascence of Wonder from Chambers' Cyclopaedia of English Literature, vol. III, 1901.]

[Watts-Dunton also contributed an Introduction to Borrow's Lavengro, 1893, a Defence of Borrow to Romany Rye, 1900, and an Introduction to Wild Wales, 1906.]

(b) Poems and Novels

Jubilee Greeting at Spithead to the Men of Greater Britain. A Poem. 1897.

The Coming of Love and Other Poems. 1898; 1899 (includes Rhona Boswell's Story in title and adds long prefatory note); 1906 (rev. and enlarged).

Aylwin. A Novel. 1899; 1900 (adds further Introduction); 1901 (with 2 appendixes).

The Rhodes Memorial at Oxford. The Work of Cecil Rhodes: a Sonnet Sequence. 1907.

Vesprie Towers. A Novel. 1916.

(c) Biography and Criticism

Hamelius, J. P. Theodore Watts. A Critique. 1899.

Galimberti, A. Un Poeta degli Zingari. Rome, 1903.

Douglas, James. Theodore Watts-Dunton, Poet, Critic, Novelist. 1904.

Hake, T. St E. and Compton-Rickett, A. Life and Letters of Theodore Watts-Dunton. 1916.

Kernahan, C. In Good Company. 1917.

Watts-Dunton, Clara. The Home-Life of Swinburne. 1922.

Benson, A. C. Theodore Watts-Dunton. Life and Letters, Dec. 1932. [Rptd in English Critical Essays (Twentieth Century), 1933 (World's Classics).]

Wright, H. G. Unpublished Letters from Theodore Watts-Dunton to Swinburne. RES. x, 1934.

SIR FREDERICK WEDMORE (1844–1921)

(a) Selection

Pages Assembled. A Selection from the Writings, Imaginative and Critical, of Frederick Wedmore. 1913.

(b) Art and Literary Criticism

Studies of English Art. 2 sers. 1876–80.

The Masters of Genre Painting; being an Introductory Handbook to the Study of Genre Painting. 1880.

Four Masters of Etching. With Original Etchings by Haden, Jacquemart, Whistler and Legros. 1883.

The Pictures of the Season. 1883 (2nd edn).

Life of Honoré de Balzac. 1890.

A Selection from the Liber Studiorum of J. M. W. Turner. With Historical Introduction by F. Wedmore. [Part of Sir E. J. Poynter's South Kensington Drawing-Book, [1890].]

Rembrandt. 1894.

Etching in England. 1895.

Fine Prints. 1897.

On Books and Arts. 1899.

Whistler's Etchings: a Study and a Catalogue. 1899.

Constable: Lucas; with a Descriptive Catalogue of the Prints they did between them. 1904.

Whistler and Others. 1906.

Some of the Moderns. (William Nicholson, Théodore Roussel, P. Wilson Steer, Bertram Priestman, Walter Sickert, David Muirhead, Horace Mann Livens, Philip Connard, Muirhead Bone, William Orpen.) 1909.

Etchings. 1911.

Memories. 1912.

Painters and Painting. [1913.] (Home University Lib.)

Certain Comments; with Introductory Essays by Sir G. Douglas and G. C. Williamson. [1925.]

[Wedmore also edited, with his wife, Poems of the Love and Pride of England, 1897.]

(c) Fiction

The Two Lives of Wilfrid Harris. 1868.
A Snapt Gold Ring. 2 vols. 1871.
Two Girls. 2 vols. 1873.
Pastorals of France: A Last Love at Pornic; Yvonne of Croisic; The Four Bells of Chartres. 1877.
Renunciations: A Chemist in the Suburbs; A Confidence at the Savile; The North Coast; and Eleanor. 1893.
Pastorals of France.—Renunciations. 1893.
English Episodes. (The Vicar of Pimlico; Justice Wilkinshaw's Attentions; The Fitting Obsequies; Katherine in the Temple; The New 'Marienbad-Elegy.') 1894.
Orgeas and Miradou, with Other Pieces. (To Nancy. The Poet on the Wolds.) 1896. [Orgeas rptd 1905 as Dream of Provence.]
The Collapse of the Penitent. 1900.
Brenda Walks On. 1916.

CHARLES WHIBLEY (1860–1930)

(a) Critical Writings

A Book of Scoundrels. 1897.
Studies in Frankness. 1898.
William Makepeace Thackeray. 1903.
Literary Portraits. 1904.
Essays in Biography. 1913.
Literary Studies. 1919.

[Whibley also edited or introduced some 30 English, French and Latin classics. He was general editor of Tudor Translations, ser. 2, 1924–30.]

(b) Political and Miscellaneous Writings

The Cathedrals of England and Wales. 1888.
The Pageant of Life. 1900. [Essays.]
Musings without Method. A Record of 1900–01. By Annalist. 1902.
The Lives of the Kings. 1904.
William Pitt. 1906.
The Letters of an Englishman. 2 vols. 1911–2.
Political Portraits. 2 sers. 1917–23.
Lord John Manners and his Friends. 2 vols. 1925.

[Under the heading 'Musings without Method' Whibley contributed a monthly causerie, mainly political, to Blackwood's Mag. from Feb. 1900 to March 1929.]

(c) Biography and Criticism

Charles Whibley. Academy, LII, 1897.
Charles Whibley. Blackwood's Mag. CCXXVII, 1930.
Obituary. London Mercury, XXI, 1930.
Eliot, T. S. Charles Whibley. A Memoir. English Ass. 1931. [Rptd in Selected Essays, 1932.]

OSCAR WILDE (1856–1900)

[See p. 620 above.]

WILLIAM BUTLER YEATS (1865–1939)

[See p. 1059 below.]

R. D. C. and H. B. G.

VII. THE LITERATURE OF SPORT

General Works: Bibliographies; Dictionaries, Compilations, Series and Anthologies; Periodicals.

Particular Sports: Hunting, Shooting, Racing; Angling; Outdoor Ball-Games (Cricket, Croquet, Football, Golf, Hockey, Polo, Tennis, Lawn Tennis, Rackets, Fives); Miscellaneous Sports (Archery, Athletics and Swimming, Boxing, Card and Indoor Games, Climbing, Curling, Cycling, Dancing, Falconry, Fencing, Rowing, Sailing, Skating and Tobogganing).

[The term 'sport' was extended in this period to cover many new forms of recreation, while older forms dropped out or became artificial and limited in appeal. The following types of work (with a few exceptions for particular purposes) are here excluded altogether: (i) books on sciences ancillary to country life (*e.g.* veterinary science); (ii) books on nature study and outdoor life unconnected with sport, or on the habits of wild animals as such; (iii) books on physical training, whether for health or for sport alone; (iv) yearbooks (of a tabular kind) and statistical works; (v) handbooks and guides, unless of documentary or literary value; (vi) books on wholly exotic sports.]

(1) GENERAL BIBLIOGRAPHIES

Slater, J. H. Illustrated Sporting Books. A Descriptive Survey. 1899.
Hardie, M. English Coloured Books. 1906.
Prideaux, S. T. Aquatint Engravings. A Chapter in the History of Book Engraving. 1909. [With bibliography and special ch. on sporting works.]
Nevill, R. Old English Sporting Books. 1924. [A descriptive bibliography with plates. See also for certain works the same author's Old Sporting Prints, 1908, and Old English Sporting Prints, 1923.]
Gee, E. R. The Sportsman's Library. A Descriptive List of the Most Important Books on Sport [English and American]. New York, 1933.

(2) GENERAL DICTIONARIES, COMPILATIONS, SERIES AND ANTHOLOGIES

Strutt, Joseph (1749–1802). Glig–Gamena Angel–Deod, or the Sports and Pastimes of the People of England. 1801; rev. J. C. Cox, [1903].

Taplin, William. The Sporting Dictionary and Rural Repository of General Information upon the Sports of the Field. 2 vols. 1803.
—— The Sportsman's Cabinet, or a Correct Delineation of the various Dogs used in the Sports of the Field. By a Veteran Sportsman. 2 vols. 1803–4.

Daniel, William B. Rural Sports: Hunting, Hawking, Fowling, Shooting, [etc.]. 2 vols. 1810–3; 4 vols. 1810–3. [Supplement, 1813.]

'Harewood, Henry.' A Dictionary of Sports, or Companion to the Field, the Forest, or the Riverside. 1835.

Blaine, Delabere Pritchett. An Encyclopaedia of Rural Sports. 1840; rev. 'Harry Hieover' (Charles Bindley), 1852.

Walsh, John Henry ('Stonehenge,' 1810–1888). Manual of British Rural Sports. 1856; 1886 (16th edn, with addns by The Field staff).

Trollope, Anthony (1815–1882). British Sports and Pastimes. 1868. [Ed. by Trollope; see also p. 457 above.]

Somerset, H. C. F. (Duke of Beaufort) and Watson, Alfred Edward Thomas, et al. The Badminton Library of Sports and Pastimes. 27 vols. 1886–1906. [Original issue: Hunting; Fishing (2 vols.); Racing and Steeplechasing; Boating; Cycling; Shooting (2 vols.); Athletics and Football; Cricket; Driving; Golf; Tennis, Lawn Tennis, Rackets and Fives; Coursing and Falconry; Skating; Mountaineering; Fencing, Boxing, and Wrestling; Swimming; Big Game Shooting (2 vols.); Yachting (2 vols.); Archery; Dancing; Sea Fishing; Billiards; The Poetry of Sport (an anthology, containing also an introduction by A. E. T. Watson giving a detailed history of the whole enterprise). Most of the vols. were revised textually in subsequent edns, and the following larger changes were made: Boating, almost entirely rewritten, and renamed Rowing; Athletics and Football, largely rewritten and divided into 2 separate vols.; Cricket, almost entirely rewritten, and historical matter greatly reduced; Skating, enlarged to contain Curling, Tobogganing, etc.; new vol. Motors and Motor Driving.]

Manners, H. J. B. (Duke of Rutland) and Dewar, George Albermarle Bertie, et al. The Haddon Hall Library. 9 vols. 1889–1903. [Fly-Fishing; Our Gardens; Wild Life in Hampshire Highlands; Hunting; Our Forests and Woodlands; Bird Watching; Cricket and Golf; Shooting; Farming.]

Hutchinson, Horace G. (b. 1859) et al. The 'Country Life' Library of Sport. 10 vols. 1893–6. [Cricket; Shooting (2 vols.); Fishing (2 vols.); Big Game Shooting (2 vols.);

Polo Past and Present; Half a Century of Sport in Hampshire; Golf Greens and Green-Keeping.]

Watson, Alfred Edward Thomas (1849–1922), et al. Fur, Feather and Fin Series. 12 vols. 1893–1906. [Natural history, sport and cookery in each vol. The Partridge; The Pheasant; The Hare; Red Deer; Mr Fox; Mr Salmon; The Grouse; The Trout; The Rabbit; Pike and Perch; Snipe and Woodcock; Wild-Fowl.

The Sportfolio. Portraits and Biographies of Heroes and Heroines of Sport and Pastime. 1896.

Pemberton, Sir Max, et al. The Isthmian Library. 11 vols. 1896–9. [Rugby Football; Ice Sports; The Complete Cyclist; The World of Golf; Rowing; Boxing; Figure-Skating; Croquet; Hockey; Tennis and Racquets; Small Boat Sailing.]

Hackwood, F. W. Old English Sports. 1897.

Kipling, Rudyard. An Almanac of Twelve Sports. Plates by William Nicholson. 1898.

Slaughter, Frances E., et al. The Sportswoman's Library. 2 vols. 1898. [Includes all outdoor sports.]

Howard, H. M. P. (Earl of Suffolk and Berkshire), et al. Encyclopaedia of Sport and Games. 4 vols. 1911. [Includes bibliographies under each main heading.]

Lowther, H. C. (Earl of Lonsdale), Cook, Sir Theodore Andrea (1867–1928), and Parker, Eric. The Lonsdale Library of Sports, Games and Pastimes. 1929– .

The Poetry of Sport. Ed. H. Peck, 1896. [With a chapter on classical allusions by Andrew Lang; final vol. in original ser. of Badminton Lib.]

The Game's Afoot! Ed. B. Darwin, 1926. [An anthology of all sports.]

The Lonsdale Anthology of Sporting Prose and Verse. Ed. E. Parker, 1932. [Lonsdale Lib. vol. xii.]

(3) GENERAL PERIODICALS

The Sporting Magazine or Monthly Calendar of the Transactions of the Turf, the Chace, etc. 1793–1870.

The Sporting Repository. Jan.–June 1822. [Monthly.]

The Annals of Sporting and Fancy Gazette; a Magazine. Jan. 1822–June 1828. [Monthly, with plates.]

Bell's Life in London and Sporting Chronicle. 1822–86.

The Sportsman's Magazine, or Chronicle of Games and Pastimes. 1823–4. [Monthly.]

Pierce Egan's Life in London and Sporting Guide. 1824–7.

The New Sporting Magazine. 1831–46. [Monthly.]

The Sporting Review. Edited by 'Craven' [John William Carleton]. 1839–70.

The Oracle of Rural Life. An Almanack for Sportsmen, Farmers, Gardeners, and Country Gentlemen. 1839–44; 1841 (as The Sporting Oracle); 1842–4 (as The Sporting Almanack); 2 vols. 1844 (as The Illustrated Book of Rural Sports).

The Sportsman's Magazine. 1845–8. [Monthly; not the same as above, 1823–4.]

The Field. 1853– . [Weekly, in 1920 incorporated Land and Water.]

The Sporting Life. 1859– . [Daily; in 1924 incorporated The Sportsman.]

Baily's Magazine of Sports and Pastimes. 1860–1926.

The County Gentleman. [1861?]–1915. [Continued as Land and Water to 1920, then incorporated in The Field.]

The Sporting Times. 1865– . [Weekly; subtitle in later issues, 'Otherwise known as The Pink 'Un.' See Old Pink 'Un Days, 1924, and 'Master' (i.e. John Corlett, 1841–1915) and Men: Pink 'Un Yesterdays, 1926, both by J. B. Booth.]

The Sportsman. 1865–1924. [Daily; from 1924 incorporated in The Sporting Life.]

The Illustrated Sporting and Dramatic News. 1874– . [Weekly.]

Horse and Hound. 1884– . [Weekly.]

The Year's Sport. Ed. A. E. T. Watson, 1886. [One year only.]

The Badminton Magazine of Sports and Pastimes. Ed. A. E. T. Watson, 1895–1923.

Country Life Illustrated. 1897– . [Weekly.]

The Sporting Annual. Ed. Nat Gould, 1900. [Only issue.]

(4) HUNTING, SHOOTING, RACING AND KINDRED RECREATIONS

(a) Bibliographies and Anthologies

Huth, F. H. Works on Horses and Equitation. A Bibliographical Record of Hippology. 1887. [Excludes fiction.]

Schwerdt, C. F. G. R. Hunting, Hawking, Shooting, illustrated in a Catalogue of Books, Manuscripts, Prints and Drawings collected by C. F. G. R. Schwerdt. 4 vols. 1928–37 (priv. ptd).

The Hunting Library. Ed. F. G. Aflalo, 3 vols. 1903. [I. Hare-Hunting and Harriers, by H. A. Bryden; II. Fox-Hunting in the Shires; III. The Master of Hounds, by G. F. Underhill (with a brief narrative bibliography). All are historical as well as exegetic.]

Armiger, Charles. The Sportsman's Vocal Cabinet. 1830.

Musters, John Chaworth. Hunting Songs and Poems. 2 vols. Nottingham, 1885.

Reeve, John Sherard. Lyra Venatica. A Collection of Hunting Songs. 1906.

Verney, R. G. (Baron Willoughby de Broke). The Sport of our Ancestors: being a Collection of Prose and Verse setting forth the Sport of Fox-Hunting. 1921.

Birkett, Dorothy Nina, Lady. Hunting Lays and Hunting Ways. An Anthology of the Chase. 1924.

(b) Hunting

Hawkes, John (1767–1834). The Meynellian Science, or Fox-Hunting upon System. Lichfield, [1808?]; rptd Leicester, 1932 (with notes by Earl of Lonsdale and Algernon Burnaby, and introduction by L. H. Irvine).

Beard, John. A Diary of Fifteen Years' Hunting, viz., from 1796 to 1811. Bath, 1813.

Jones, Thomas. A Diary of the Quorndon Hunt, from the Year 1791 to 1800 Inclusive. [With] The Celebrated Billesdon Coplow Pamphlet. Derby, 1816.

'Abednego.' The Hunting Vicar; and the Commissioners, alias, the Woodcock and Snipes. 1820.

'Careless, John.' The Old English 'Squire. A Poem, in Ten Cantos. 1821; rptd 1905.

Cook, John. Observations on Fox-Hunting and the Management of Hounds. Addressed to a Young Sportsman. 1826; ed. R. G. Verney (Baron Willoughby de Broke), 1922.

Hood, Thomas (1799–1845). The Epping Hunt. 1829. [See also p. 224 above.]

Apperley, Charles James ('Nimrod'; 1779–1843). Remarks on the Condition of Hunters. 1831; rev. C. Tongue, 1855; rev. F. T. Barton, 1908.

—— Nimrod's Hunting Tours. 1835; ed. W. S. Sparrow, 1926. [Originally pbd as Letters on Hunting, in Sporting Mag.]

—— The Chace, the Turf, and the Road. 1837 (illustrated by Henry Alken); 1843; ed. W. S. Sparrow, 1927.

—— Memoirs of the Life of the late John Mytton. 1837 (illustrated by Henry Alken and T. J. Rawlins); [1871] (with memoir of Apperley).

—— Sporting. 1838. [A large illustrated miscellany edited by Apperley; contributors, T. Hood, J. H. Reynolds and others.]

—— Nimrod's Northern Tour. 1838.

—— Nimrod Abroad. 2 vols. 1842.

—— The Horse and the Hound. 1842.

Apperley, Charles James ('Nimrod'; 1779–1843). The Life of a Sportsman. 1842.

—— Hunting Reminiscences. 1843 (illustrated by 'Wildrake,' *i.e.* George Tattersall, Alken and Henderson); ed. W. S. Sparrow, 1926.

—— My Life and Times. Edited and concluded by E. D. Cuming. 1927. [An unfinished autobiography, part of which appeared in Fraser's Mag. 1842.]

—— My Horses and Other Essays. Ed. E. D. Cuming, 1928. [Miscellaneous contributions to periodicals.]

[See 'Nimrod' in the Field: New Documents, Times, 5 March 1932.]

Warburton, Rowland Eyles Egerton (1804–1891). Poems. Chester, 1833. [See also p. 286 above.]

'Caveat Emptor' [Sir George Stephen]. The Adventures of a Gentleman in Search of a Horse. 1835.

Hawke, Martin Bladen Edward. The Epwell Hunt. By an Old Sportsman. Cheltenham, [1835?] (anon.); [Middlehill, 1840, 1847] (priv. ptd) (with 2 other poems, not anon.).

—— The Badsworth Hunt: Yorkshire Songs. Doncaster, [1862]; Pontefract, 1871 (with a Sketch of the Sporting Career of Hawke by 'Nimrod').

'Venator' [John Cooper]. The Warwickshire Hunt, from 1795 to 1836. 1837.

'Oliver, Stephen' [William Andrew Chatto (1799–1864)]. The Old English Squire. Music [engraved separately] by D. Blake, with 6 etchings by 'Phiz.' 1838. [A poem, not the same as that by 'John Careless,' above; see also under Card-Games, p. 776 below and Angling, p. 769 below.]

Smith, Thomas. Extracts from the Diary of a Huntsman. 1838.

—— The Life of a Fox, written by Himself. By Wily. 1843; ed. Lord Willoughby de Broke, 1920.

—— Sporting Incidents in the Life of another Tom Smith. 1867.

Surtees, Robert Smith (1802–1864). Jorrocks's Jaunts and Jollities. 1838. [See also p. 509 above.]

Greenwood, George. Hints on Horsemanship to a Nephew and Niece. 1839 (anon.).

Radcliffe, F. P. Delmé. The Noble Science. A Few General Ideas on Fox-Hunting. 1839; rev. C. Bradley, 2 vols. 1911.

Vyner, Robert Thomas. Notitia Venatica. A Treatise on Fox-Hunting. 1841; rev. C. Bradley, 1910.

'Scrutator' [K. W. Horlock]. Letters on the Management of Hounds. 1852; rptd 1926.

—— Recollections of a Fox-Hunter. 1861; rptd 1925.

'Scrutator' [K. W. Horlock]. The Country Gentleman. 3 vols. 1862. [A novel.]

—— The Science of Foxhunting and Management of the Kennel. 1868.

Whyte-Melville, George John (1821–1878). Captain Digby Grand. An Autobiography. 1853. [See also p. 511 above.]

Berkeley, G. C. G. F. Reminiscences of a Huntsman. 1854; 1896.

Wilmot, Sir John Eardley Eardley. Reminiscences of the Late Thomas Assheton Smith. 1860; ed. Sir H. Maxwell, 1902.

How Pippins Enjoyed a Day with the —— Foxhounds. 1863. [With 12 coloured plates by 'Phiz.']

'Meadows, Lindon' [C. B. Greatrex]. Dame Perkins and her Grey Mare, or the Mount for Market. With Illustrations by 'Phiz.' 1866.

Lays of the Belvoir Hunt. 1866.

[Welby, John?] Memoirs of the Belvoir Fox-Hounds from their Earliest Records to the Present Day. 1867.

Phillipps, C. S. March. Horse and Man. 1869.

Smart, Henry Hawley (1833–1893). Breezie Langton: a Story of Fifty-two to Fifty-five. 1869.

'Blunt Spurs.' Three Letters on the Horse, Master, and Donkey. 1870.

'Impecuniosus.' Unasked Advice: a Series of Articles on Horses and Hunting. 1872. [From The Field.]

[Barstow, C. M.] Days with the Lothian Hounds in Spring 1872. By an Old Sportsman. 1872.

Bowers, Georgina. Notes from a Hunting Box not in the Shires. 1873.

—— Leaves from a Hunting Journal. 1880.

Randall, John. Old Sports and Sportsmen, or the Willey Country, with Sketches of Squire Forester and his Whipper-in, Tom Moody. 1873. [See also under Swimming, p. 776 below.]

Morris, Maurice O'Connor. Triviata, or Cross-roads Chronicles of Passages in Irish Hunting History, 1875–6. 1877.

—— Hibernia Venatica. 1878.

—— Hibernia Hippica. 1900.

Gordon, Adam Lindsay (1833–1870). Bush Ballads and Galloping Rhymes. 1876. [See also p. 1094 below.]

Griffith, T. A. Hunting Songs. Lichfield, 1876.

'Triviator.' The West Union Stag Hounds and the Baytown Run. [1877.] [A poem.]

'Brooksby' [Edward Pennell Elmhirst]. The Hunting Counties of England: their Facilities, Character and Requirements. 1878.

—— The Cream of Leicestershire. 1883.

—— The Best of the Fun, 1891–97. 1903.

Davies, Edward W. L. A Memoir of the Rev. John Russell and his Out-of-Door Life. 1878 (anon.).

Lister, T. (Baron Ribblesdale) (1854–1925). The Queen's Hounds and Stag-Hunting Recollections. 1879.

Mason, G. Finch. Sporting Sketches. [1879.]
—— My Day with the Hounds, and Other Stories. Cambridge, [1882].
—— Sporting Recollections. 1885.
—— Flowers of the Hunt. 1889.
[See also under Racing. p. 764 below.]

Webber, Byron. Pigskin and Willow, with Other Sporting Stories. 3 vols. 1879.

'Wanderer' [E. H. D'Avignon]. Across Country. 1882.
—— Fair Diana. 1884.
—— Hunt-Room Stories and Yachting Yarns. 1885.
—— A Loose Rein. 1887.

Babington, John. Records of the Fife Fox-Hounds. 1883.

'Borderer' [Sir R. D. G. Price]. Hunting and Sporting Notes in Shropshire and Cheshire, 1884–5. 2 pts, 1885–6.

'Ash Wood' [James M. Etches]. The Season 1883–4. A Saturday with Sir Williams Watkin Wynn's Hounds. Whitchurch, [1884]. [A poem.]

G., I. H. Hound and Horn. 1885.

Fortescue, Sir John William (1859–1934). Records of Stag-hunting on Exmoor. 1887.
—— The Story of a Red Deer. 1897.

'Russell, Fox.' Cross Country Reminiscences. 1887.
—— In Scarlet and Silk, or Recollections of Hunting and Steeplechase Riding. 1896.
—— Sporting Society, or Sporting Chat and Sporting Memories. Stories Humorous and Curious. 2 vols. 1897. [By various writers.]
—— The Haughtyshire Hunt. 1897.
—— Colonel Botcherby, M.S.H. 1899.

Cotton, Frederick Henry. Ware Wire! 1888. [A pamphlet.]
—— Gone Awa-a-ay! 1888. [A novel.]
—— Hark Forrard! 1891. [A novel.]

Nethercote, Henry. Osmond. The Pytchley Hunt, Past and Present. 1888.

Dixon, William Scarth. In the North Countree. Annals and Anecdotes of Horse, Hound, and Herd. 1889.
—— A History of the Bramham Moor Hunt. Leeds, 1898.
—— A History of the York and Ainsty Hunt. Leeds, 1899.
—— The Sport of Kings. 1900.

Thomson, John Anstruther. Three Great Runs. 1889.
—— Eighty Years' Reminiscences. 2 vols. 1904.

'Castor.' A Century of Foxhunting with the Warwickshire Hounds. 1891.

'Tantara.' Hare Hunting. By Tantara, a Master of Harriers. 1893.

Williams, W. Phillpotts. Poems in Pink. Salisbury, 1894.
—— Plain Poems. Salisbury, 1896.
—— Over the Open. 1897. [A novel.]
—— Rhymes in Red. 1899.

Sargent, Harry R. Thoughts upon Sport, [with] a Complete History of the Carraghmore Hunt and Memoirs of Notable Sportsmen. 1895.

Lutyens, F. M. Mr Spinks and His Hounds. A Hunting Story. [1896.]

Garle, Hubert. Hunting in the Golden Days. 1896.

Fortescue, Hugh (Viscount Ebrington). Stag-Hunting. 1896. (Fur and Feather Ser.)

Ball, Richard Francis and Gilbey, Tresham. The Essex Foxhounds; with Notes on Hunting in Essex. 1896.

Mordaunt, Sir C. and Verney, W. R. Annals of the Warwickshire Hunt, 1795–1895. 2 vols. 1896.

Underhill, G. F. Hunting and Practical Hints for Hunting Men. 1897.

Random Recollections of the Belvoir Hunt. By a Sportsman. [1897.]

Bradley, Cuthbert. The Reminiscences of Frank Gillard, Huntsman, with the Belvoir Hounds, 1886 to 1896. 1898.
—— Good Sport seen with some Famous Packs, 1885–1910. [1910.]
—— Fox-Hunting from Shire to Shire with Many Noted Packs. 1912.
—— The Foxhound of the 20th Century. 1914.

Dale, Thomas F. The History of the Belvoir Hunt. 1899.
—— The 8th Duke of Beaufort and the Badminton Hunt. 1901.

Symonds, Henry. Runs and Sporting Notes from Dorsetshire. Blandford, 1899.

Blew, William Charles Arlington. The Quorn Hunt and its Masters. 1899.
—— A History of Steeple-Chasing. 1900.

Paget, John Otho. Hunting. 1900. (Haddon Hall Lib.)

Elliott, J. M. K. Fifty Years' Fox-Hunting, with the Grafton and Other Packs. 1900.

Evered, Philip. Staghunting with the 'Devon and Somerset,' 1887–1901. 1902.

Massey, Frank E. Portraits and Sketches of Cheshire Hunting Men (1850–1890). Manchester, 1903.

Ord, Richard. The Sedgefield Country in the 'Seventies and 'Eighties. 1904 (anon.).

Sewell, Alys. With Hound and Terrier in the Field. Hunting Reminiscences. Ed. F. Slaughter, 1904. [Mainly a history of the Blackmore Vale Hunt in the 19th century.]

Symonds, Frederick Cleave Loder and Crowdy, E. Percy. A History of the Old Berks Hunt from 1760 to 1904. 1905.

Machell, Hugh W. John Peel, Famous in Sport and Song. 1926. [John Peel, 1776–1854. The song 'John Peel' is by John Woodcock Graves (1794–1886). See R. B. Lattimer, The Story of John Peel, Cornhill Mag. Oct. 1919.]

Osbaldeston, George (1786–1866). Squire Osbaldeston: his Autobiography. Ed. E. D. Cuming and Sir T. A. Cook, 1926.

Apperley, Newton Wynne (1846–1925). A Hunting Diary. Ed. E. D. Cuming, 1926. [The diary runs from 1864 to 1920.]

Ellis, Maudie. The Squire of Bentley (Mrs Cheape) [1853–1919]. 1926.

Lowndes, Henry William Selby (b. 1873). The Hunting and Sporting Reminiscences of. Ed. J. Fairfax-Blakeborough, 1926. [Includes some history of hunts in Yorkshire, Somerset and Kent.]

Fawcett, William. Hunting in Northumbria. Being the History of the Haydon Hunt [from 1809] and Many other Packs. With an Introduction by J. Fairfax-Blakeborough. 1927.

Bathurst, Seymour Henry, Earl. The Earl Spencer's and Mr. John Warde's Hounds, with a Hunting Diary, Accounts of some Remarkable Runs, Hound Lists and Pedigrees, 1739–1825. Cirencester, 1932.

(c) Shooting

Thornhill, R. B. The Shooting Directory. 1804.

Vincent, John. Fowling. A Poem in Five Books. 1808.

'Markwell, Marmaduke.' Advice to Sportsmen, Rural or Metropolitan, Noviciates or Grown Person; with Anecdotes of the Most Renowned Shots of the Day. 1809. [Plates by Thomas Rowlandson.]

Dobson, William. Kunopaedia. A Practical Essay on Breaking or Training the English Spaniel or Pointer. With Instructions for Attaining the Art of Shooting Flying. 1814.

Mayer, John. The Sportsman's Directory, or Park and Gamekeeper's Companion. Colchester, 1815; Chichester, 1817 ('much enlarged by an Experienced Sportsman').

Floyd, William. Observations on Dog Breaking. 1821.

Hawker, Peter (1786–1853). Instructions to Young Sportsmen in all that relates to Guns and Shooting. 1824; ed. E. Parker, 1922. [Addns to the 4th edn were pbd separately, [1825?].]

—— Abridgement of the New Game Laws; with Observations. Being an Appendix to the Sixth Edition [of above]. 1831.

Hawker, Peter (1786–1853). The Diary of Peter Hawker. With Introduction by Sir R. Payne-Gallwey. 2 vols. 1893.

—— Col. Hawker's Shooting Diaries. Ed. E. Parker, 1931.

Gorcock, Jeffrey. Grouse Shooting made quite Easy to Every Capacity. Killhope-Cross, 1827.

Maude, Gideon Michael Angelo. A Tour into Westmoreland, and to the Moors, with Remarks on Grouse Shooting. 1831.

Nettleship, John. The Trigger, or Shooter's Pocket Guide. With Much Valuable Information for the Young Shooting Sportsman. 1831.

Random de Bérenger, Charles (Baron de Beaufain). Helps and Hints how to Protect Life and Property. 1835. [On various sports, especially shooting.]

Watt, William. Remarks on Shooting; to which are added, a Part of the Game-Laws; both written in Familiar Verse. 1835; 1835 (enlarged).

'Oakleigh, Thomas' [A. K. Killmister]. The Oakleigh Shooting Code, containing Two Hundred and Twenty Chapters of Information. 1836.

—— The Shooter's Hand-Book. 1842.

Rawstorne, Lawrence. Gamonia, or the Art of Preserving Game. 1837; ed. E. Parker, 1929.

Webber, Alexander. Shooting. A Poem. 1841.

Lacy, Captain ——. The Modern Shooter, containing Practical Instructions and Directions for Every Description of Inland and Coast Shooting. 1842.

Peake, Richard Brinsley (1792–1847). An Evening's Amusement, or the Adventures of a Cockney Sportsman. 1846. [Letterpress fitted on to earlier plates by Robert Seymour.]

'Craven' [John William Carleton]. Recreations in Shooting, with some Account of the Game of the British Islands. 1846.

Knox, A. E. Game Birds and Wild Fowl. 1850.

Colquhoun, William. Remarks on the Decrease of Grouse and the Grouse Disease. 1858.

Folkard, Henry Coleman. The Wild-Fowler. A Treatise on Ancient and Modern Wild-Fowling. 1859. [See also under Sailing, p. 778 below.]

'Marksman.' The Dead Shot, or Sportsman's Complete Guide. 1860.

Jeans, Thomas. The Tommiebeg Shootings, or a Moor in Scotland. 1860.

'Deadfall.' The Experiences of a Game Preserver. 1868.

Greener, W. W. Choke-bore Guns, and how to load for all Kinds of Game. [1876.]
—— The Gun and its Development; with Notes on Shooting. [1881]; 1910 (9th edn).
Jefferies, Richard (1848–1887). The Game-keeper at Home. 1878. [See also p. 550 above.]
Manley, John Jackson. Notes on Game and Game Shooting. [1880.] [See also under Angling, p. 771 below.]
Payne-Gallwey, Sir Ralph W. F. (1848–1916). The Fowler in Ireland. 1882.
—— The Book of Duck Decoys. 1886.
—— Letters to Young Shooters. 3 sers. 1890–6.
Lancaster, Charles. An Illustrated Treatise on the Art of Shooting. 1889; 1924 (8th edn, rev.).
Watson, John. The Confessions of a Poacher. 1890; rptd [1926] (illustrated edn). [Ed. by Watson.]
—— Poachers and Poaching. 1891.
Millais, John Guille. Game Birds and Shooting Sketches. 1892.
Dixon, Charles. The Game Birds and Wild Fowl of the British Islands. 1893.
Hutchinson, Horace G. et al. Shooting. 2 vols. 1893.
Lehmann, Rudolf Chambers. Conversational Hints for Young Shooters. 1894.
Harris, James Edward (Earl of Malmesbury). Half a Century of Sport in Hampshire. Extracts from the Shooting Journals [1798–1840] of. With Memoir by the 5th Earl. Ed. F. G. Aflalo, 1895.
Macpherson, Hugh Alexander. A History of Fowling. Edinburgh, 1897.
Cornish, Charles John (1859–1906). Nights with an Old Gunner, and Other Studies of Wild Life. 1897.
Walker, Charles Edward. Shooting on a Small Income. How to Shoot and the Management of Small Shootings. 1900. [See also under Angling, p. 772 below.]

(d) Deer-Stalking

Allen, John Carter [afterwards John Hay Allan, calling himself John Sobieski Stolberg Stuart] and Allen, Charles Manning [afterwards Charles Stuart Hay Allan, calling himself Charles Edward Stuart, Count d'Albanie]. Lays of the Deer Forest. With Sketches of Olden and Modern Deer-Hunting. 2 vols. 1848.
Collyns, Charles Palk. Notes on the Chase of the Wild Red Deer in the Counties of Devon and Somerset. 1862; ed. L. S. Bathurst, 1907.
Robertson, William. Forest Sketches: Deer-stalking and Other Sports in the Highlands Fifty Years ago. Edinburgh, 1865 (anon.).

Crealock, Henry Hope. Deer-Stalking in the Highlands of Scotland. Edited by Major-General John North Crealock. 1892.

(e) Racing and Racehorses

Sporting Anecdotes, Original and Select; including Characteristic Sketches of Eminent Persons who have appeared on the Turf. By an Amateur Sportsman. 1804; [1807]. [Illustrations by T. Bewick.]
Morland, Thomas Hornby. The Genealogy of the English Race Horse; with Remarks on the Present System of Breeding for the Turf. 1810.
Anecdotes on the Origin and Antiquity of Horse-Racing. 1825.
Brown, Captain Thomas. Biographical Sketches and Authentic Anecdotes of Horses. 1830.
Dibdin, Charles (1745–1814). The High-Mettled Racer. To which are added many Interesting Anecdotes of the Race-Horse. Illustrated by [G.] Cruikshank. 1831. [See also vol. II, p. 465 above.]
Clark, Bracy. A Short History of the Celebrated Race-Horse, Eclipse. [1835?]
'Martingale' [(James?) White]. Sporting Scenes, and Country Characters. 1840.
—— English Country Life. 1843.
—— Turf Characters: the Officials, and the Subalterns. 1851.
'Wildrake' [George Tattersall] (1817–1849). Cracks of the Day. [1841.]
—— The New Sporting Almanack. A Manual of Instruction and Amusement. 1844–5. [Tattersall edited Sporting Mag. 1844–5.]
Orton, John. Turf Annals of York and Doncaster, together with Particulars of the Derby and Oak[s] Stakes at Epsom. With Biographical Notices. York, 1844.
Rous, Henry John (1795–1877). On the Laws and Practice of Horse Racing. 1852; 1866.
'The Druid' [Henry Hall Dixon] (1822–1870). The Post and the Paddock; with Recollections of George IV, Sam Chiffney, and other Turf Celebrities. [1856.]
—— Silk and Scarlet. 1858.
—— Scott and Sebright. 1862.
—— Saddle and Sirloin, or English Fare and Sporting Worthies. 1870.
—— The Druid Sporting Library. 1895. [Includes rev. text of all the above, and The Life and Times of the Druid, by F. C. Lawley.]
'Amateur' [George Richard Walker]. Horses: their Rational Treatment. Race Horses: their Mismanagement; the False Aims of the Jockey Club, and of Trainers. Oxford, 1865.

Craven, William George. The Margravine. A Story of the Turf. 2 vols. 1870.
—— The Royal Commission on the General Utility or Three-parts-bred Horse. 1888.
Rice, James (1843–1882). A History of the English Turf. 2 vols. 1879. [Rice edited Once a Week, 1868–1872; for his novels with Sir Walter Besant, see p. 537 above.]
Glover, Joseph. Racing Life, Racing Tales. [Manchester? 1884.]
'A Cheltonian.' Autobiographies [biographies] of the Three Archers, William, Fred. and Charlie. [1885.]
Day, William (1823–1908). Reminiscences of the Turf. With Anecdotes and Recollections of its Principal Celebrities. 1886.
—— Turf Celebrities I have known. 1891.
Howard, H. M. P. (Earl of Suffolk), et al. Racing and Steeplechasing. 1886. (Badminton Lib.)
Taunton, T. H. Portraits of Celebrated Racehorses [1702–1870], together with their Respective Pedigrees and Performances recorded in full. 4 vols. 1887–8.
'Curzon, Louis Henry' [James Glass Bertram]. The Blue Ribbon of the Turf. A Chronicle of the Race for the Derby. 1890.
—— A Mirror of the Turf, or the Machinery of Horse-Racing revealed; showing the Sport of Kings as it is today. 1892.
Gould, Nat[haniel] (1857–1919). The Double Event. 1891.
—— Harry Dale's Jockey 'Wild Rose.' 1893.
—— The Pace that Kills. 1899.
—— The Magic of Sport, mainly Autobiographical. 1909.
[Gould wrote over 120 other works, chiefly racing novels.]
Black, Robert. The Jockey Club and its Founders. 1891.
—— Horse Racing in England. A Synoptical Review. 1893.
Chetwynd, Sir George. Racing Reminiscences and Experiences of the Turf. 2 vols. 1891.
Kent, John. The Racing Life of Lord George Cavendish-Bentinck and Other Reminiscences. Ed. F. C. Lawley, 1892.
—— Records and Reminiscences of Goodwood and the Dukes of Richmond. 1896.
Custance, Henry. Riding Recollections and Turf Stories. 1894.
Porter, John (1838–1922). Kingsclere. Ed. B. Webber, 1896.
—— John Porter of Kingsclere. An Autobiography. Written in Conjunction with Edward Moorhouse. 1919.
Bovill, Mai and Askwith, G. R. (afterwards Baron Askwith). Roddy Owen [Edward Roderic Owen]. A Memoir. 1897.

Benzon, Ernest. How I Lost £250,000 in Two Years. [1898.] [Mainly turf, but all kinds of gaming; by 'The Jubilee Plunger.']
Lyall, J. G. The Merry Gee-Gee: how to breed, break, and ride him for'ard away, and the Noble Art of Backing Winners on the Turf. 1899.
Blew, W. C. A. A History of Steeplechasing. 1901.
Hodgman, George. Sixty Years on the Turf, The Life and Times of George Hodgman, 1840–1900. Ed. C. R. Warren, 1901.
Dixon, H. Sydenham. From Gladiator to Persimmon [i.e. 1896]. Turf Memories of 30 Years. 1901.
Cook, Sir Theodore Andrea. A History of the English Turf. 3 vols. [1905].
—— Eclipse and O'Kelly: being a Complete History of that Celebrated English Thoroughbred Eclipse. 1907.
[Cook edited The Field, 1910–28; see also under Rowing, p. 778 and Athletics, p. 776 below.]
Mason, G. Finch. Heroes and Heroines of the Grand National Containing a Complete Account of Every Race. 1907. [See also under Hunting, p. 761 above.]
Moorhouse, Edward. The Romance of the Derby. 2 vols. 1908.
Humphris, Edith M. The Life of Fred Archer. 1923.
—— The Life of Matthew Dawson. 1928.
Yates, Arthur (1841–1924). Arthur Yates, Trainer and Gentleman Rider. An Autobiography. Written in Collaboration with Bruce Blunt. 1924.
Prior, Charles Matthew. Early Records of the Thoroughbred Horse. 1924.
—— The History of the Racing Calendar and Stud Book from their Inception in the 18th Century. 1926.
Hawkes, Charles Pascoe. Bench and Bar in the Saddle. 1928. [History of the Pegasus Club and the Bar Point to Point Races, 1895–1928.]
Munroe, David Hoadley. The Grand National, 1839–1931. 1931.

(f) Riding

Lloyd, G. and Symes, R. The Improved Art of Riding. [1815?]
Steward, Charles. A New and Concise Guide to the Art of Riding. 1821.
Allen, John. Principles of Modern Riding for Ladies. 1825.
—— Principles of Modern Riding for Gentlemen. 1825.
Stanley, Edward. The Young Horsewoman's Compendium of the Modern Art of Riding. 1827.

Peters, J. G. A Treatise on Equitation. With 27 Descriptive Plates. 1835.

M******, Captain. The Equestrian, a Handbook of Horsemanship. [1839.]

Equestrian Portraits. By a Walking Gentleman. 1840.

Oakes, A. F. The Young Lady's Equestrian Assistant. 1850.

'Vieille Moustache.' The Barb and the Bridle. A Handbook of Equitation for Ladies. 1874.

(g) Coaching

Cross, Thomas. The Autobiography of a Stage Coachman. 3 vols. 1861; rptd 1904 (with plates by Rowlandson, Henry Alken and others).

Reynardson, Charles Thomas Samuel Birch. 'Down the Road,' or Reminiscences of a Gentleman Coachman. 1875.

—— Sport and Anecdotes of Bygone Days. 1887.

Malet, H. E. Annals of the Road, or Notes on Mail and Stage Coaching. 1876.

Haworth, Martin E. Road-Scrapings: Coaches and Coaching. 1882.

'An Old Stager' [Stanley Harris]. Old Coaching Days. 1882.

—— The Coaching Age. 1885.

Maudslay, Athol. Highways and Horses. 1888.

Tristram, William Outram. Coaching Days and Coaching Ways. 1888. [Illustrated by Hugh Thomson.]

Bradley, Tom. The Old Coaching Days in Yorkshire. Leeds, 1889.

Corbett, Edward. An Old Coachman's Chatter, with some Practical Remarks on Driving. 1890.

Harper, Charles George (b. 1863). The Brighton Road. 1892.

(h) General and Miscellaneous

Hanger, George (Baron Coleraine). The Life, Adventures, and Opinions of. 2 vols. 1801. [Compiled from his papers by William Combe.]

—— Colonel George Hanger to all Sportsmen, and particularly to Farmers and Gamekeepers. 1814. [On horse, dog, and pheasant breeding for sport.]

'Quizem, Caleb.' Annals of Sporting. 1809. [Plates by Rowlandson.]

Johnson, Thomas Burgeland (d. 1840) [pseudonyms: 'T. H. Needham' and 'B. Thomas']. The Shooter's Guide. 1809. [By 'B. Thomas.']

—— The Complete Sportsman. 1817. [By 'T. H. Needham.']

—— The Shooter's Companion. 1819.

—— The Hunting Directory. 1826. [A general encyclopaedia.]

Johnson, Thomas Burgeland (d. 1840) [pseudonyms: 'T. H. Needham' and 'B. Thomas']. The Sportsman's Cyclopaedia. 1831.

—— The Shooter's Preceptor. [1844?]

Lawrence, John [pseudonyms: 'John Scott,' 'William Henry Scott,' 'B. Mowbray']. The History and Delineation of the Horse, in all his Varieties. With a Particular Investigation of the Character of the Race-Horse, and the Business of the Turf. 1809.

—— British Field Sports; embracing Practical Instructions. By W. H. Scott. 1818.

—— The Sportsman's Repository. A Series of Engravings representing the Horse and the Dog [by Reinagle, Stubbs, and others], with Descriptions and Anecdotes by John Scott. 1820.

Lascelles, Robert. A Series of Letters on Angling, Shooting and Coursing. 3 pts, 1813–4; 1819.

Christie, James. Instructions for Hunting, Breaking Pointers, and finding out Game, intended for Young Sportsmen. To which is subjoined Humorous Poems and Songs, chiefly in the Buchan Dialect. Banff, 1817.

Chafin, William. Anecdotes respecting Cranbourn Chase; together with the Rural Amusements it afforded our Ancestors. 1818; 1818 ('with some scenes in and anecdotes of Windsor Forest').

Egan, Pierce (1772–1849). Anecdotes of the Turf, the Chase, the Ring, and the Stage. 1827.

—— Pierce Egan's Book of Sports and Mirror of Life. 1832.

[See also p. 668 above.]

Goodlake, Thomas. The Courser's Manual or Stud-Book. Liverpool, 1828. [With a letter from Sir Walter Scott; a Continuation, 1833.]

Gribble, Samuel. A Treatise on Deportment, Fencing, etc., including the Science of Horsemanship, for the Use of Young Persons. Also the Description of a Military Game resembling the Game of Chess. Derby, 1829.

Maxwell, William Hamilton (1792–1850). Wild Sports of the West [of Ireland]. 1832; ed. the Earl of Dunraven, [1916].

—— The Field Book, or Sports and Pastimes of the United Kingdom. 1833. [An encyclopaedia.]

—— Wanderings in the Highlands and Islands. 2 vols. 1844; 1853 (as Sports and Adventures in the Highlands and Islands of Scotland).

Jesse, Edward (1780–1868). An Angler's Rambles. 1836.

—— Scenes and Tales of Country Life. With Recollections of Natural History. 1844.

—— Anecdotes of Dogs. 1846.

Scrope, William (1772–1852). The Art of Deer-Stalking. 1838.
—— Days and Nights of Salmon Fishing in the Tweed. 1843; ed. H. T. Sheringham, 1921.
Mills, John. The Sportsman's Library. 1845. [A general treatise on sport.]
—— The Life of a Foxhound. Illustrated by John Leech. 1848.
—— The Life of a Race-Horse. 1854.
—— The Flyers of the Hunt. Illustrated by John Leech. 1859.
'Hieover, Harry' [Charles Bindley] (1795–1859). Stable Talk and Table Talk, or Spectacles for Young Sportsmen. 2 vols. 1845–6.
—— The Pocket and the Stud. 1848.
—— The Stud for Practical Purposes and Practical Men. 1849.
—— Practical Horsemanship. 1850.
—— The Hunting Field. 1850.
—— Bipeds and Quadrupeds. 1853.
—— Sporting Facts and Sporting Fancies. 1853.
—— The Sporting World. 1859.
[Bindley also revised and edited Blaine's Encyclopaedia of Rural Sports, 1840.]
St John, Charles William George (1809–1856). Short Sketches of the Wild Sports and Natural History of the Highlands. 1846; 1893 (with notes and memoir of the author); ed. Sir H. Maxwell, 1919.
—— A Tour in Sutherlandshire, with Extracts from the Field Books of a Sportsman and Naturalist. 2 vols. 1849.
—— Natural History and Sport in Moray. Edinburgh, 1863. [Ed. by Mrs St John, with Memoir by C. Innes.]
Hall, Herbert Byng. Highland Sports and Highland Quarters. 2 vols. [1847].
—— Exmoor, or the Footsteps of St Hubert in the West. 1849.
—— Scottish Sports and Pastimes. 1850.
—— Brooklands. A Sporting Biography. 2 vols. 1852.
—— Sport and its Pleasures. 1859.
'Cecil' [Cornelius Tongue]. The Stud Farm. Hints on Breeding, 1851.
—— Stable Practice. Hints on Training. 1852.
—— Records of the Chase and Memories of Celebrated Sportsmen. 1854.
—— Hunting Tours. 1864.
'Idle, Christopher.' Hints on Shooting and Fishing. 1855.
Dougall, James Dalziell. Shooting Simplified. A Concise Treatise. Glasgow, 1857.
—— Scottish Field Sports. A Volume of Mingled Gossip and Instruction. Glasgow, 1861.
'Stonehenge' [John Henry Walsh]. The Shot Gun and Sporting Rifle; and the Dogs, Ponies, Ferrets, etc., used with them. 1859.

'Stonehenge' [John Henry Walsh]. Riding and Driving. 1863.
[See also under Dictionaries, p. 758 above and under Athletics, p. 776 below.]
Hamilton, John Potter. Reminiscences of an Old Sportsman. 2 vols. 1860.
Lennox, Lord William Pitt. Pictures of Sporting Life and Character. 2 vols. 1860.
—— Recreations of a Sportsman. 2 vols. 1862.
—— Sport at Home and Abroad. 2 vols. 1872.
—— Coaching; with Anecdotes of the Road. 1876.
Miles, Henry Downes. The Book of Field Sports. 42 pts, [1860–3].
—— The Sportsman's Companion. 12 pts, [1863–4].
—— English Country Life. A Work of Reference for the Gentleman, the Sportsman, and the Farmer. [1868–9]; 1870. [See also under Boxing, p. 776 below.]
Clarke, Charles. A Box for the Season. A Sporting Sketch. 2 vols. 1864.
—— Which is the Winner? 3 vols. 1864.
—— Crumbs from a Sportsman's Table. 2 vols. 1865.
Corbet, Henry. Tales and Traits of Sporting Life. 1864.
Trollope, Anthony. Hunting Sketches. 1865. [See also p. 457 above.]
Wheeler, C. A. Sportascrapiana. With hitherto Unpublished Anecdotes of the Nineteenth Century, from George IV to the Sweep. 1867.
Egerton, A. G. (Earl of Wilton). On the Sports and Pursuits of the English, as bearing upon the National Character. 1868.
'Ubique' [Parker Gillmore]. Gun, Rod, and Saddle. 1869.
Fitt, J. Nevil. Hunting, Steeple-Chasing, and Racing Scenes. Illustrated by B. Herring. [1869.]
—— Covert-Side Sketches. Thoughts on Hunting with Fox, Deer, and Hare. 1878.
Walter, John. Hints to Young Sportsmen, or the Gun, Saddle and Rod. 1871.
Pearce, Thomas ('Idstone'). The 'Idstone' Papers. A Series of Articles and Desultory Observations on Sport and Things in General. 1872.
Sidney, Samuel (1812–1883). The Book of the Horse. [1873–5.] [Information of all kinds, not merely veterinary.]
'Old Calabar.' Over Turf and Stubble. 1873. [A novel.]
—— Won in a Canter. 3 vols. 1874. [A novel.]
—— Grey Abbey. 2 vols. 1877. [A novel.]

Crawfurd, Oswald John Frederick (d. 1909) [pseudonyms: 'John Latouche' and 'J. Dangerfield']. Country House Essays. 1876. [Country House Lib. By J. Latouche.]
—— Horses and Riders and Other Essays. [1885.] [Pbd under own name.]

Sewell, Anna. Black Beauty. The Autobiography of a Horse. 1877.

'Bagatelle' [A. G. Bagot]. Sporting Sketches at Home and Abroad. 1879.

Watson, Alfred Edward Thomas ('Rapier'). Sketches in the Hunting Field. 1880.
[——] Types of the Turf; Anecdotes and Incidents. By Rapier. 1883.
—— Racecourse and Covert Side. 1883.
—— Racing and 'Chasing. A Collection of Sporting Stories. 1897.
—— The Turf. 1898.
[Watson also edited and contributed to Badminton Lib., Fur and Feather Ser., Badminton Mag., etc.]

'Blinkhoolie.' Angram: a Hidden Talent. The Story of a Wasted Horse. York, [1880].
—— The Tale of a Horse. 1884.

'Rockwood' [T. Dykes]. Stories of Scottish Sports. 1881.
—— All Round Sport with Fish, Fur and Feather. 1887.

'Avon.' How I became a Sportsman. Being Early Reminiscences of a Veteran Sportsman. 1882.

Kennard, Mary E. The Right Sort. 3 vols. 1883. [A novel.]
—— The Catch of the County. 3 vols. 1894. [A novel.]

Price, Richard John Lloyd. Rabbits for Profit and Rabbits for Powder. 1884.
—— Practical Pheasant Rearing; with an Appendix on Grouse Driving. 1888.

Speedy, Thomas. Sport in the Highlands and Lowlands of Scotland with Rod and Gun. 1884.

Davenport, William Bromley. Sport: Fox-Hunting, Salmon-Fishing, Covert Shooting, Deer-Stalking. 1885. [Ed. by Augusta Bromley Davenport.]

Grimble, Augustus. Deer-stalking. 1886.
—— Shooting and Salmon Fishing. Hints and Recollections. 1892.
—— Highland Sport. 1894. [Illustrated by A. Thorburn.]
—— The Deer Forests of Scotland. 1896. [Illustrated by A. Thorburn.]
—— Leaves from a Game Book. 1898. [More Leaves, [1917].]
—— The Salmon Rivers of Scotland. 4 vols. 1899–1900.

Hore, John Philip. The History of Newmarket and the Annals of the Turf. 3 vols. 1886.
—— The History of the Royal Buckhounds. 1893.

Hore, John Philip. Sporting and Rural Records of the Cheveley Estate. 1899 (priv. ptd).

Roberts, Sir Randal H. In the Shires. A Sporting Novel. [1887.]
—— Curb and Snaffle. 1888. [A novel.]
—— Hard Held. 1889. [A novel.]
—— Not in the Betting. 1893. [A novel.]
[See also under Angling, p. 770 below.]

Bertram, J. G. ('Ellangowan'). Out of door Sports in Scotland. 1889.
—— Sporting Anecdotes, collected and edited by 'Ellangowan.' 1889.

Barkley, Henry C. Studies in the Art of Rat-catching. A Manual for Schools. 1891.

Astley, Sir John Dugdale (1828–1894). Fifty Years of my Life in the World of Sport. 2 vols. 1894.

Hartopp, E. C. C. Sport in England, Past and Present. 1894.

De Crespigny, Sir Claude Champion (1847–1935). Memoirs. Edited by G. A. B. Dewar, with Preface and Notes by the Duke of Beaufort. 1896.
—— Forty Years of a Sportsman's Life. 1910; 1925 (rev., with new chs. covering 1910–24).

Shand, Alexander Innes (d. 1907). Mountain, Stream and Covert. Sketches of Country Life and Sport in England and Scotland. 1897.

Dixon, W. Willmott ['Thormanby']. Kings of the Turf. 1898.
—— Kings of the Hunting-Field. 1899.
—— Kings of the Rod, Rifle, and Gun. 2 vols. 1901.
[See also under Boxing, p. 776 below.]

Binstead, Arthur M. ('The Pitcher'; d. 1914). A Pink 'Un and a Pelican. Some Random Reminiscences, Sporting or otherwise. 1898.
—— Works. Ed. J. B. Booth, 2 vols. 1927–8.

Pease, Sir Alfred Edward (b. 1857). The Badger. A Monograph. 1898.
—— Hunting Reminiscences. 1898.
—— Cleveland and its Hunt. 1902.

Aflalo, Frederick George (1870–1918). The Cost of Sport. 1899. [Ed. by Aflalo.]
[See also under Angling, p. 772 below.]

Lloyd, Freeman. The Whippet and Race-Dog. How to breed, train, race, and exhibit, with the Management of Race-meetings. 1904.

Gilbey, Sir Walter (1831–1914). Horses Past and Present. A Sketch of the History of the Horse in England. 1910.
—— Hounds in Old Days. Some Account of Hounds and Hunting from Early Times. 1913.

Kempson, F. Claude. The Trinity Foot Beagles. An Informal Record of Cambridge Sport and Sportsmen during the Past Fifty Years. 1912. [Covers 1862–1912.]

(5) ANGLING

(a) Bibliographies, Works of Reference, and Anthologies

Ellis, Sir Henry. Catalogue of Books on Angling; with some Brief Notices of Several of their Authors. 1811; 1836 (as Bibliotheca Piscatoria); 1911 (priv. ptd from The British Bibliographer, 1911).

Lambert, Osmund. Angling Literature in England. 1881. [Descriptive; not tabulated.]

Catalogue of Books on Angling. Cambridge, U.S.A. 1882.

International Fisheries Exhibition. Handbooks. 16 vols. 1883. [The following are relevant: J. P. Wheeldon, The Angling Clubs and Preservation Societies; C. E. Fryer, The Salmon Fisheries; W. Senior, Angling in Great Britain; J. J. Manley, The Literature of Sea and River Fishing (with concise bibliography).]

Westwood, T. and Satchell, T. Bibliotheca Piscatoria. A Catalogue of Books on Angling. 1883. [Expanded from earlier edn by Westwood alone.]

[Marston, R. B.] Supplement to Bibliotheca Piscatoria. [In English Catalogue of Books, vol. VI, 1901.]

Buchan, John. Musa Piscatrix. 1896. [An anthology.]

Maxwell, Sir Herbert, Aflalo, F. G. et al. The Anglers' Library. 7 vols. 1897–9; 1905 (1st 4 vols. only). [C. H. Wheeley, Coarse Fish; F. G. Aflalo, Sea Fish; A. Jardine, Pike and Perch; Sir H. Maxwell, Salmon and Sea Trout; G. A. B. Dewar, South Country Trout Streams; J. Watson, The English Lake District Fisheries.]

A Catalogue of an Exhibition of Angling Books at the Grolier Club, New York. [Dec. 1911–Jan. 1912.]

Parker, Eric, et al. An Angler's Garland of Fields, Rivers, and Other Country Contentments. 1920.

Hills, J. W. A History of Fly-Fishing for Trout. 1921. [With bibliography of works mentioned and a ch. on angling literature.]

Sparrow, Walter Shaw. Angling in British Art through Five Centuries: Prints, Pictures, Books. 1923.

(b) Periodicals

The Fishing Gazette. 1877– .

The Angler's Note-Book and Naturalist's Record. The Green Series. Jan.–June 1880. [Fortnightly, but irregularly; ed. by W. Satchell.]

The Scots Angler. A Monthly Magazine of River and Loch. Edinburgh, July 1896–June 1897.

(c) Principal Works

[Local guide-books and purely technical works, except a few which materially influenced theory and practice, have not been included.]

[Snart, Charles.] Practical Observations on Angling in the River Trent. By a Gentleman Resident in the Neighbourhood. Newark, 1801.

Mackintosh, Alexander. The Driffield Angler; in Two Parts. To which are added Instructions for Shooting. Also a Short Treatise on Coursing. Gainsborough, [1806]; Derby, [1815?], 1821 (as The Modern Fisher, or Driffield Angler).

Howitt, Samuel (1765?–1822). The Angler's Manual, or Concise Lessons of Experience. Liverpool, 1808. [Plates by the author.]

Durnford, Richard. The Fishing Diary of Richard Durnford, 1809–1819. Ed. H. Nicoll, Winchester, 1911.

Salter, Robert. The Modern Angler. A Series of Letters to a Friend. Oswestry, [1811].

Cutcliffe, H. C. The Art of Trout Fishing in Rapid Streams. South Molton, 1813.

Salter, Thomas Frederick. The Angler's Guide. 1814; [1823] (5th edn, enlarged with The Troller's Guide).

—— The Troller's Guide. 1820; 1841 (3rd edn, with the author's last addns).

Bainbridge, George C. The Fly Fisher's Guide. Illustrated by Coloured Plates, representing upwards of 40 of the Most Useful Flies. Liverpool, 1816.

Carroll, W. The Angler's Vade Mecum. Containing a Descriptive Account of the Water Flies, their Seasons, and the Kind of Weather that brings them most on the Water. Edinburgh, 1818. [With 12 coloured plates.]

Charleton, T. W. The Art of Angling. A Poem. North Shields, 1819.

[Soltan, G. W.?] The Art of Angling. 1819 (priv. ptd).

[Lathy, Thomas Pike.] The Angler. A Poem in Ten Cantos; with Proper Instructions in the Art. By Piscator. 1819. [The main part really by Dr Thomas Scott.]

Price, Martin. The Angler's Companion. To which is added the Art of Swimming. [1821.]

Mitchell, William Andrew. On the Pleasure and Utility of Angling. Newcastle-on-Tyne, [1824].

[Coad, J.] The Angling Excursions of Gregory Greendrake, Esq. 3 pts, Dublin, 1824–6; Dublin, 1832 (with addns by 'Geoffrey Greydrake,' i.e. T. Ellingsale).

'Piscator.' Observations on the Public Right of Fishing by Angle or Nets. With Notes Historical and Explanatory. Marlow, 1826.

Davy, Sir Humphry (1778–1829). Salmonia, or Days of Fishing. 1828 (anon.). [See review attrib. to Sir W. Scott, Quarterly Rev. July, Oct. 1828.]

March, J. The Jolly Angler, or Waterside Companion. [1831.] [With wood engravings by the author.]

Jesse, Edward. Gleanings in Natural History. To which are added Maxims and Hints for an Angler. Ser. 1 (all pbd), 1832.

—— An Angler's Rambles. 1836.

Burn, James. The Fishes' Complaint, or Unfair Sportsmen censured. A Poem in Two Cantos. Maidstone, [1833].

P[enn], R[ichard]. Maxims and Hints for an Angler, and Miseries of Fishing. To which are added Maxims and Hints for a Chess Player. 1833; 1839 (enlarged).

Baddeley, John. The London Angler's Book, or Waltonian Chronicle; with Amusing Songs and Anecdotes never before published. 1834.

[Chatto, William Andrew.] Scenes and Recollections of Flyfishing in Northumberland, Cumberland and Westmoreland. By Stephen Oliver. 1834.

—— The Angler's Souvenir. By Payne Fisher. 1835; ed. G. C. Davies, [1877].

[See also under Hunting, p. 760 above and under Card Games, p. 776 below.]

Hansard, G. A. Trout and Salmon Fishing in Wales. 1834.

Medwin, Thomas (1788–1869). The Angler in Wales, or Days and Nights of Sportsmen. 2 vols. 1834.

B[oosey], T[homas]. Piscatorial Reminiscences and Gleanings by an old Angler and Bibliopolist, with a Catalogue of Books [by William Pickering]. 1835.

Stoddart, Thomas Tod (1810–1880). The Art of Angling as practised in Scotland. Edinburgh, 1835.

—— Angling Reminiscences. Edinburgh, 1837.

—— Songs and Poems. Edinburgh, 1839.

—— The Angler's Companion to the Rivers and Lochs of Scotland. Edinburgh, 1847; 1802 (3rd edn); ed. Sir H. Maxwell, 1923.

—— An Angler's Rambles and Angling Songs. Edinburgh, 1866; 1889 (with memoir by A. M. Stoddart.

[See also p. 307 above.]

Ronalds, Alfred. The Fly-Fisher's Entomology. 1836; 1856 (5th edn, rev.); ed. J. C. Carter, 1901 (10th edn); ed. Sir H. Maxwell, 2 vols. Liverpool, 1913; ed. H. T. Sheringham, 1921.

Turton, John. The Angler's Manual, or Fly-Fisher's Oracle. 1836.

Chesshyre, E. Posthumous Songs. Manchester, 1837.

Shipley, William. A True Treatise on the Art of Fly-Fishing, Trolling, etc., applicable to every Trout and Grayling River in the Empire. Ed. E. Fitzgibbon, 1838.

Hofland, T. C. The British Angler's Manual. 1839; 1848 (rev. and enlarged by E. Jesse).

Younger, John. On River Angling for Salmon and Trout. Edinburgh, 1840; Kelso, 1864 (with memoir).

—— Autobiography of John Younger, Shoemaker. Kelso, 1881.

Pulman, G. P. R. The Vade Mecum of Fly-Fishing for Trout. Axminster, 1841 (anon.); 1851 (3rd edn, rewritten and enlarged).

—— Rustic Sketches: being Poems on Angling, in the Dialect of East Devon. Taunton, 1842.

—— Rambles, Roamings, and Recollections. 1870.

Blacker, W. The Art of Angling, and Complete System of Fly-Making and Dyeing with Colours. 1842; 1855 (rev.).

[Hughes, William.] The Practical Angler. By 'Piscator.' 1842.

Wells, Joseph. The Temperance Fishing Book, or the Contemplative Angler. Sheffield, 1842; 1853 ('improved'). [Partly in verse.]

Wilson, John ('Christopher North'; 1785–1854). The Recreations of Christopher North. 3 vols. 1842. [Includes 'Angling'; the Noctes Ambrosianae and contributions to Blackwood's Mag. also include matter on angling. See also p. 682 above.]

Scrope, William. Days and Nights of Salmon Fishing in the Tweed. 1843; 1854.

Thorne, James. Rambles by Rivers. 2 pts, 1844–5. [The Duddon, etc.; sequel (the Thames), 2 vols. 1847–9.]

Anderdon, John Lavicount. The River Dove, with some Quiet Thoughts on the Happy Practice of Angling. 1845 (anon.; priv. ptd); 1847 (signed J. L. A.).

O'Gorman, ——. The Practice of Angling, particularly as regards Ireland. 2 vols. Dublin, 1845.

Wayth, C. Trout Fishing, or the River Darent. A Rural Poem. 1845.

Blakey, Robert ('Palmer Hackle'). Hints on Angling. 1846.

—— The Angler's Song Book. 1855.

—— Historical Sketches of the Angling Literature of all Nations. 1856.

Fitzgibbon, Edward ('Ephemera'). A Handbook of Angling, with the Natural History of River Fish and the Best Modes of Catching them. 1847; 1853 (3rd edn, corrected).

—— A Book of the Salmon. 1850.

Wallwork, James. The Modern Angler. Being the Result of more than 30 Years' Practice and Strict Observation. Manchester, 1847 (priv. ptd).

Beever, John ('Arundo'). Practical Fly-fishing founded on Nature and tested by the Experience of nearly Forty Years. 1849.

Wheatley, Hewett. The Rod and the Line, or Practical Hints and Dainty Devices. 1849.

Akerman, John Yonge. Spring-Tide, or the Angler and his Friends. A Series of Fishing Scenes, with Illustrations in the West-Country Dialect. 1850.

Newland, Henry G. The Erne: its Legends and its Fly-Fishing. 1851.

Doubleday, Thomas. The Coquet-Dale Fishing Songs. Collected and edited by a North Country Angler. Edinburgh, 1852. [Mainly by R. Roxby, with a memoir of him by Doubleday; with music.]

Ayrton, William. The Adventures of a Salmon in the River Dee. By a Friend of the Family; with Notes for the Fly-fisher in North Wales. 1853 (anon.).

Theakston, M. A List of Natural Flies. Ripon, 1853 (anon.); rev. F. M. Walbran, Ripon, [1883] (as British Angling Flies).

Badham, C. D. Prose Halieutics: or, Ancient and Modern Fish Tattle. 1854.

Cartwright, W. ('Clericus'). Rambles and Recollections of a Fly-Fisher. 1854.
—— Facts and Fancies of Salmon Fishing. 1874.

Jackson, John. The Practical Fly-Fisher: more particularly for Grayling or Umber. 1854.

Davy, John. The Angler and his Friend, or Piscatory Colloquies. 1855.

Wright, William. Fishes and Fishing. Artificial Breeding of Fish; Anatomy of their Senses; their Loves, Passions, and Intellects. With Illustrative Facts. 1855.

Bailey, William. The Angler's Instructor. 1857.

Stewart, W. C. The Practical Angler. Edinburgh, 1857; ed. W. K. Hodgson, 1905.
—— A Caution to Anglers. Edinburgh, 1871. [In part adversaria on H. C. Pennell's Modern Practical Angler, see p. 771 below.]

Colquhoun, John. Salmon-Casts and Stray Shots. Being Fly-Leaves from the Note-Book. 1858. [See also under Shooting, p. 762 above.]

Songs of the Edinburgh Angling Club. Edinburgh, 1858; 1879 (enlarged; priv. ptd); new ser. ed. J. Smith, Edinburgh, 1900.

Francis, Francis (1822–1886). The Angler's Register. 1858.
—— A Book on Angling. Being a Complete Treatise of the Art in Every Branch. 1867;

1885 (6th edn, with memoir); ed. Sir H. Maxwell, 1920.

Francis, Francis (1822–1886). By Lake and Moor. An Angler's Rambles in the North of England and Scotland. 1874.
—— Angling. 1877.
—— Sporting Sketches with Pen and Pencil. 1878. [With A. W. Cooper.]
—— Angling Reminiscences. 1887.

Alfred, H. J. ('Otter'). A Complete Guide to Spinning and Trolling. 1859.
—— The Modern Angler. 1864.

Conway, James. Letters from the Highlands, or Two Months among the Salmon and the Deer. 1859; 1861 (with addns, as Forays among the Salmon and Deer).

Crawhall, Joseph. The Compleatest Angling Booke that ever was writ. Newcastle-on-Tyne, 1859 (anon.; priv. ptd); 1881 (enlarged).
—— A Collection of Right Merrie Garlands for North Country Anglers. Newcastle-on-Tyne, 1864 (anon.).
—— Chaplets from Coquet-Side. Newcastle-on-Tyne, 1873 (anon.).
—— Border Notes and Mixty-Maxty. Newcastle-on-Tyne, 1880 (anon.).

Kingsley, Charles (1819–1875). Chalk-Stream Studies. [In Miscellanies, vol. I, 1859. See also p. 487 above.]

Lord, W. B. Sea Fish and how to catch them. 1859.

Cliffe, J. H. Notes and Recollections of an Angler. 1860.

'Glenfin.' The Fishing-Rod, and how to use it. 1860.

Locke, James. Tweed and Don, or Recollections and Reflections of an Angler for the Last Fifty Years. Edinburgh, 1860.

Roberts, Sir Randal. Trout and Grayling. 1860; 1866 (as The River's Side, or the Trout and Grayling).
—— The Silver Trout, and Other Stories. 1888.

Simeon, C. Stray Notes on Fishing and Natural History. Cambridge, 1860; 1863.

Smith, Arthur. The Thames Angler. 1860 (bis).

Wade, Henry. Halcyon, or Rod-Fishing in clear Waters with Fly, Minnow, and Worm. 1861.

Cairncross, D. The Origin of the Silver Eel; with Remarks on Bait and Fly Fishing. 1862.

Elliot-Murray-Kynynmound, W. H. (Earl of Minto). Game, Salmon, and Poachers. 1863.

C[ox], I. E. B. Facts and Useful Hints relating to Fishing and Shooting. 1864 (3rd edn).

Moffat, A. S. The Secrets of Angling. Edinburgh, 1865.

Pennell, Harry Cholmondeley (1837–1915). The Book of the Pike. 1865.
—— Fishing Gossip. Or, Stray Leaves from the Note-Books of Several Anglers. 1866.
—— The Modern Practical Angler. 1870. [See under W. C. Stewart above.]
—— Fishing. 2 vols. 1889, 1895. (Badminton Lib.)

Wilcocks, J. C. The Sea-Fisherman. 1865; 1868 (enlarged); 1875 (much enlarged and almost entirely rewritten); 1884 (enlarged).

Young, L. J. H. Sea Fishing as a Sport. 1865.

Raymond, Oliver. The Art of Fishing on the Principle of avoiding Cruelty. 1866.

Loddell, Robert. 'The Lay of the Last Angler,' or a Tribute to the Tweed at Melrose. By a Sexagenarian. 4 cantos, Kelso, 1867–81 (priv. ptd).

Peard, William. A Year of Liberty, or Salmon Angling in Ireland from Feb. 1 to Nov. 1 [1865]. 1867.

Rooper, George. Autobiography of the late Salmo Salar, Esq. The Life, Personal Adventures, and Death of a Tired Salmon. Edited by a Fisherman. 1867.
—— Flood, Field, and Forest. 1869 (bis). [Includes above.]
—— Thames and Tweed. [1870] (anon.).

Fennell, Greville. The Book of the Roach. 1870.

Pearson, Edwin et al. The Angler's Garland and Fisher's Delight for 1870 [and 1871]. 1870–1.

Barry, William. Moorland and Stream. With Notes and Prose Idyls. 1871.
—— Sporting Rambles and Holiday Papers. [1873.]

Dick, H. St John. Flies and Fly Fishing. 1873.

Buckland, Francis Trevelyan (1826–1880). The Log-book of a Fisherman and Zoologist. 1875.

Senior, William ('Red Spinner'; d. 1920). Waterside Sketches. A Book for Wanderers and Anglers. 1875.
—— By Stream and Sea. A Book for Wanderers and Anglers. 1877.
[Senior was for some time editor of The Field, and contributed to Fur and Feather ser.]

Aldam, W. H. A Quaint Treatise on Flees and the Art of Artyfichall Flee Making. 1876.

Davies, G. C. Angling Idylls. 1876.

Henderson, William. Notes and Reminiscences of my Life as an Angler. 1876 (priv. ptd); 1879 (as My Life as an Angler).

Manley, J. J. Notes on Fish and Fishing. 1877. [See also under Bibliographies, p. 768 above, International Fisheries Exhibition.]

Manchester Angling Association. Anglers' Evenings. Papers by Members. 2 sers. 1880–2.

Keene, J. H. The Practical Fisherman; dealing with the Natural History, the Legendary Lore, the Capture of British Freshwater Fish. 1881.

Foster, David. The Scientific Angler. A Work on Artistic Angling. [1882.] [Compiled posthumously by the author's sons, D. and W. H. Foster.]

Martin, John William ('The Trent Otter'). Float Fishing and Spinning in the Nottingham Style. 1882.
—— Days among the Pike and Perch. N.d.; Plymouth, [1907] (entirely rewritten); 1924.
—— My Fishing Days and Fishing Ways. A Record of Forty-Six Years of an Angler's Life. Plymouth, [1906]; 1924.

Ellacombe, Henry Noel. Shakespeare as an Angler. 1883. [Rptd from The Antiquary, Oct.–Nov. 1881.]

Froude, James Anthony (1818–1894). Cheneys and the House of Russell. [In Short Studies on Great Subjects, ser. 4, 1883. See also p. 892 below.]

'Isys, Cotswold.' An Angler's Strange Experience. A Whimsical Medley. 1883. [Verse.]
—— A Handy Guide to Dry-Fly Fishing. [1890]; [1912] (4th edn, rev.).
—— Lyra Piscatoria. Original Lyrics. 1895.

Braithwaite, G. F. The Salmonidae of Westmorland. Angling Reminiscences, and Leaves from an Angler's Note Book. Kendal, 1884.

Hamilton, Edward. Recollections of Fly-Fishing. 1884.
—— The Riverside Naturalist. 1890.

Marston, R. B. ('The Amateur Angler'; 1853–1927). Days in Dovedale. 1884.
—— Fresh Woods and Pastures New. 1887.
—— Walton and some Earlier Writers on Fish and Fishing. 1894.
—— By Meadow and Stream. 1896.
—— An Old Man's Holidays. 1900.
[Marston also edited Walton's Compleat Angler and The Fishing Gazette.]

Westwood, Thomas (1814?–1888). In Memoriam Izaak Walton. Twelve Sonnets and an Epilogue. [1884.]
[See also p. 311 above.]

Bund, John William Willis. Salmon Problems. 1885.
—— A Handy Book of Fishery Management. 1899.
[Bund also edited Journ. of National Fish Culture Ass. from 1887, and legal treatises on Fisheries Acts, as well as writing many antiquarian works and histories.]

Webster, David. The Angler and the Looprod. Edinburgh, 1885.

Boosey, T. Anecdotes of Fish and Fishing. 1887.

Burnand, Sir Francis Cowley (1836–1917). The Incompleat Angler. After Master Izaak Walton. Illustrated by Harry Furniss. 1887.

Cook, Charles Henry ('John Bickerdyke'). Angling in Salt Water. [1887.]
—— The Book of the All-round Angler. [1889]; 4 pts, 1922 (5th rev. edn, much enlarged).
—— Days in Thule, with Rod, Gun and Camera. 1894.
—— Days of my Life on Waters Fresh and Salt. 1895.
[Cook wrote the vol. on Fishing in Badminton Lib.]

Pritt, T. E. The Book of the Grayling. Leeds, 1888.
—— An Angler's Basket filled in Sunshine and Shade. Being a Collection of Stories, Quaint Sayings, and Remembrances, with a few Angling Hints. Manchester, 1896.

Tayler, J. Red Palmer. A Practical Treatise on Fly-fishing. Folkestone, 1888.

Halford, Frederic M. Dry-Fly Fishing in Theory and Practice. 1889; 1902 (4th edn, rev.).
—— Making a Fishery. 1895; 1902.
—— An Angler's Autobiography. 1903.

Walbran, F. M. Walbran's British Angler. Ser. 1: Salmon, Trout, and Grayling (all pbd), 1889.

Watson, John. Sketches of British Sporting Fishes. 1890.

Aflalo, F. G. Sea-Fishing on the English Coast. 1891.
—— Sea Fish. 1897; 1905.
[Aflalo was also joint-editor of the Angler's Library (1897, 1905) and The Encyclopaedia of Sport (see above, p. 758), etc.]

Lang, Andrew (1844–1912). Angling Sketches. 1891. [See also p. 747 above.]

Fisher, Arthur T. Rod and River. 1892.
—— Outdoor Life in England. 1896. [Mainly angling.]

Paske, C. T., and Aflalo, F. G. The Sea and the Rod. 1892.

Sandeman, F. By Hook and by Crook. 1892.

Hopkins, F. Powell. Fishing Experiences of Half a Century. 1893.

Shrubsole, E. S. ('Ibis Tag'). Long Casts and Sure Rises. Being a Collection of Angling 'Yarns' and Experiences. 1893.

Hodge, D. ('Yellow Body'). Angling Days on Scotch Lochs. Edinburgh, 1894.

Hutchinson, Horace G. et al. Fishing. 2 vols. 1894. [See also under Ball Games, immediately below.]

Wheeldon, J. P. Sporting Facts and Fancies. 1894. [Short sketches and stories, principally about angling.]

Armistead, J. J. An Angler's Paradise and how to obtain it. 1895.

Fraser, Duncan. Riverside Rambles of an Edinburgh Angler. 1895.

Coxon, Henry. A Modern Treatise on Coarse Fish Angling. Nottingham, 1896.

Dewar, George Albemarle Bertie (b. 1862). The Book of the Dry Fly. 1897.
—— In Pursuit of the Trout. 1898.
—— The South Country Trout Streams. 1899. (Angler's Lib.)
[Dewar also ed. the Haddon Hall Lib.]

Maxwell, Sir Herbert Eustace (b. 1845). Memories of the Months. 6 sers. 1897–1907; 3 vols. 1931 (rev. and enlarged).
—— Salmon and Sea Trout. How to propagate, preserve and catch them in British Waters. 1898.
—— Chronicles of the Houghton Fishing Club, 1822–1908. 1908.

Brown, J. A. Harvie. The Wonderful Trout. Edinburgh, 1898.

Cadman, Henry ('Harry Druidale'). Harry Druidale, Fisherman from Manxland to England. 1898.

Donne, J. M. Colloquy and Song, or Sport in the Leash of the Muses. 1898.

Taylor, Jesse Paul. Fishing and Fishers. [1898.]

Walker, C. E. Old Flies in New Dresses. 1898.
—— The Rainbow Trout. 1898. [With C. S. Patterson.]
[See also under Shooting, p. 763 above.]

Grey, Edward (Viscount Grey; d. 1933). Fly Fishing. 1899.

Hardy, A. E. Gathorne. Autumns in Argyleshire with Rod and Gun. 1900.

(6) OUTDOOR BALL-GAMES

(a) Histories

Hutchinson, Horace G. The Evolution of Games at Ball. Blackwood's Mag. May 1893.

Armitage, John. The History of Ball Games. [Chs. i, ii in Rackets, Squash Rackets, Fives, and Badminton, ed. Lord Aberdare 1934. (Lonsdale Lib. vol. XVI.)]

(b) Cricket

(i) Bibliographies

Gaston, A. J. Bibliography of Cricket. [In Wisden's Cricketers' Almanack for 1894, 1900, 1923; also priv. ptd separately 1895.]

Taylor, A. D. The Catalogue of Cricket Literature. 1906 (priv. ptd).

(ii) Histories, General Records, and Anthologies

Lillywhite, F., Haygarth, A., *et al.* Cricket Scores and Biographies from 1746. 1862– . [Vols. i–iv compiled by Lillywhite, vols. v and vi by Haygarth, vol. xv by F. S. Ashley Cooper, residue under the supervision of the M.C.C. In progress.]

—— Index to all First Class Matches. By J. B. Payne. Harrogate, 1903. [In the above.] [See J. A. H. Catton, A Monument to Cricket, Times, 19 April 1934.]

Davey, William. The Canterbury Cricket Week. Canterbury, 1865.

Chronicles of Cricket. 1888.

Small, E. Milton. Canterbury Cricket Week, 1842–1891. [1891.]

Holmes, R. S. The County Cricket Championship, 1873–1896. Bristol, 1897.

Norman, Philip. Annals of the West Kent Cricket Club. 1897.

—— The Eton Ramblers' Cricket Club [1862–80]. 1928.

Lucas, Edward Verrall. Willow and Leather. A Book of Praise. [1898.] [Anthology.]

—— The Hambledon Men. 1907. [John Nyren's The Young Cricketer's Tutor (1833) with introduction and 'a collection of other matter drawn from various sources.']

Waghorn, H. T. Cricket Scores, 1730–1773. 1899.

—— The Dawn of Cricket. 1906. [For the M.C.C.]

Ford, W. J. Middlesex County Cricket, 1864–1899. 1900. [Continued to 1920 by F. S. A. Cooper, 1921.]

—— A History of the Cambridge University Cricket Club, 1820–1901. 1902.

Cooper, F. S. Ashley. Curiosities of First-Class Cricket. 1901.

—— Edward Mills Grace, Cricketer. 1916.

—— M.C.C. Match List. A Summary of 8642 matches played by the Marylebone Cricket Club since 1787. 1932.

[Cooper also wrote, with W. J. Ford, Lord Harris and P. F. Warner, many introductions to works on cricket, and short histories of county cricket clubs.]

Harris, G. R. C. (Baron Harris; d. 1932). The History of Kent County Cricket. 1907. [Ed. by Lord Harris; appendices periodically.]

—— Lord's and the M.C.C. A Cricket Chronicle of 137 Years. 1914. [With F. S. A. Cooper.]

—— Kent Cricket Matches, 1719–1880. 1929. [With F. S. A. Cooper.]

Cochrane, Alfred (b. 1865). Repton Cricket, 1865–1905. Repton, 1908.

—— Records of the Harlequin Cricket Club, 1852–1926. [1930.]

Altham, H. S. A History of Cricket. With a Foreword by Lord Harris. 1926. [Includes select bibliography.]

Parker, Eric. Between the Wickets. An Anthology of Cricket. 1926.

Gordon, Sir H. S. C. M. (b. 1871). Eton v. Harrow at Lord's. The Story of the Matches by Bernard Darwin, and Reminiscences of every Match since 1861 by an Actual Player. 1926. [Ed. by Gordon.]

Standing, P. C. Anglo-Australian Cricket, 1862–1926. 1926.

Lyon, W. R. The Elevens of Three Great Schools, [Winchester, Eton, Harrow], 1805–1929, being all Recorded Scores of Cricket Matches, with Memoirs and Biographies of the Players. 1930. [See also Cricket in Politics: an Early School Match (Eton v. Westminster), Times, 24 May 1934.]

Lewis, W. J. The Language of Cricket. Oxford, 1934.

[For county and club histories of a more special kind, see bibliography in H. S. Altham's History of Cricket, 1926.]

(iii) Periodicals

J. Wisden's Cricketers' Almanack. 1864– . [Pbd every Jan.; comment, scores, etc. with portraits.]

Lillywhite, John (d. 1874). John Lillywhite's Cricketers' Companion. 1865–85. [Continued posthumously.]

Lillywhite, James. Cricketers' Annual. 1872–1900.

Cricket. A Weekly Record of the Game. 1882–1914.

The Cricket Field. 1892–5. [Weekly in summer, monthly in winter.]

(iv) General

Lambert, William. The Cricketer's Guide, or a Concise Treatise on the Noble Game. Lewes, [1816?] (3rd edn, enlarged).

—— Instructions and Rules for Playing the Noble Game of Cricket. Lewes, 1816.

Mitford, Mary Russell (1787–1851). Our Village. 1823. [Contains much relating to cricket. See also p. 409 above.]

Nyren, John (1764–1837). The Young Cricketer's Tutor. To which is added The Cricketers of my Time. Ed. C. Cowden Clarke, 1833; ed. F. S. A. Cooper, 1902; ed. (with biography) E. V. Lucas, 1907 (in The Hambledon Men).

[Pycroft, James] (1813–1895). The Principles of Scientific Batting. 1835.

—— The Cricket Field. 1851; ed. F. S. A. Cooper, 1922. [Includes John Mitford on Cricket; separately rptd ed. F. S. A. Cooper, 1921.]

[Pycroft, James] (1813–1895). The Cricket Tutor. 1862.
—— Cricketana. 1865.
—— Oxford Memories. 1866.
Wanostrocht, N. ('Felix'; 1804–1876). Felix on the Bat. 1845.
Denison, W. Cricket. Sketches of the Players. 1846.
Lillywhite, Frederick (d. 1866). Fred Lillywhite's Guide to Cricketers. 1849–66. [Annual.]
—— The English Cricketer's Trip to Canada and the U.S., 1859. 1860. [A diary.]
Bolland, William. Cricket Notes. 1851.
Gale, Fred ('The Old Buffer'). The Public School Matches, and those we meet there. By a Wykehamist. 1853. [Later edns as The Public School Cricket Matches Forty Years ago.]
—— Echoes from the Old Cricket Fields. 1871; 1896 (rev.).
—— The Game of Cricket. 1887.
'Quid' [R. A. Fitzgerald?]. Jerks in from Short-Leg. 1866.
Wheeler, C. A. Sportascrapiana. 1867. [Mainly cricket.]
Box, Charles. The Theory and Practice of Cricket. 1868.
—— The English Game of Cricket. 1877. [Includes an anthology.]
Wisden, John. Cricket, and how to play it. [1868.] [See also under Periodicals, p. 773 above.]
Fitzgerald, R. A. Wickets in the West, or the Twelve in America. 1873. [This author may be 'Quid,' see above.]
Lyttelton, R. (b. 1854) et al. Cricket. 1885; 1904 (7th edn). (Badminton Lib.)
—— Cricket. 1898. [A different work from the preceding.]
—— Giants of the Game. 1899. [Ed. by Lyttleton.]
—— Cricket and Golf. 1901. (Haddon Hall Lib.)
Brownless, W. Methuen. W. G. Grace. A Biography. With a Treatise on Cricket by W. G. Grace. 1887.
Hutchinson, Horace G. Cricketing Saws and Stories. 1889.
—— Peter Steele the Cricketer. [1895.] [A novel.]
—— Cricket. 1893. ('Country Life' Lib. of Sport.) [Ed. by Hutchinson.]
[See also under Angling, p. 772 above and Golf, p. 775 below.]
Grace, William Gilbert (1848–1915). Cricket. 1891.
—— 'W. G.' Cricketing Reminiscences and Personal Recollections. 1899.
[See The Memorial Biography of W. G. Grace, ed. Lord Hawke, Lord Harris, and Sir H. Gordon, 1919.]

Daft, Richard (1835–1900). Kings of Cricket. Ed. A. Lang, Bristol, [1893].
—— Hints on Cricket. Bristol, [1893].
—— A Cricketer's Yarns. Ed. F. S. A. Cooper, 1926. [Posthumous collection of notes by Daft.]
Christian, Edmund Brown Vincy (b. 1864). At the Sign of the Wicket. [1894.]
—— The Light Side of Cricket. Stories, Sketches, and Verses. 1898. [By various authors; ed. by Christian.]
[See also p. 336 above.]
Gale, Norman Rowland (b. 1862). Cricket Songs. 1894.
—— More Cricket Songs. 1905.
[See also p. 341 above.]
Cochrane, Alfred. Leviore Plectro (Occasional Verses). 1896. [2nd half, Lays from the Pavilion and the Links.]
Furniss, Harry, Milliken, E. J., and Christian, E. B. V. How's That? [1896.] [Verses, cricket 'sketches' (prose), and illustrations.]
Read, Walter W. Annals of Cricket. 1896.
Ranjitsinghi, K. S. (Maharajah Jam Sahib of Nawanagar; d. 1933). The Jubilee Book of Cricket. 1897. [Contributions by T. Case and W. J. Ford.]
—— With Stoddart's Team in Australia. 1898 (4 edns).
[Ford, A. L.] Curiosities of Cricket, By an Old Cricketer. 1897 (priv. ptd).
Caffyn, William. Seventy-one not out. Reminiscences. Edited by 'Mid-on.' 1899.
Fry, Charles Burgess (b. 1872). The Book of Cricket. A Gallery of Famous Players. 1899. [Ed. by Fry.]
Snaith, J. C. Willow the King. [1899.] [A novel.]
Bettesworth, W. A. The Walkers of Southgate. 1900.
Ford, W. J. A Cricketer on Cricket. 1900.
Pullin, A. W. ('Old Ebor'). Talks with Old English Cricketers. 1900.
—— Alfred Shaw, Cricketer [1842–1907]: his Career and Reminiscences. 1902. [Ed. by Pullin.]
Warner, Pelham F. (b. 1873). Cricket in Many Climes. 1900.

(c) Croquet

Reid, Mayne (1818–1883). Croquet. 1863. [See also p. 503 above.]
Jones, Henry ('Cavendish'; 1831–1899). On the Laws of Croquet. 1868 (priv. ptd).
—— The Pocket Guide to Croquet. 1869. [See also under Card Games, p. 776 below.]
Whitmore, Walter Jones (formerly Walter Whitmore Jones). Croquet Tactics. 1868. [First pbd in The Field.]

Prior, Richard Charles Alexander. Notes on Croquet, and some Ancient Bat and Ball Games related to it. 1872.

Heath, James Dunbar. The Compleat Croquet Player. 1874; rev. M. A. Saffery, [1904].

Lillie, Arthur. Croquet; its History, Rules and Secrets. 1897.

—— Croquet up to Date. 1900.

Needham, H. C. Croquet. 1900.

(d) Football

Football. The First Day of the Sixth Match. Rugby, [1851].

Hughes, Thomas (1822–1896). Tom Brown's School-Days. 1857 (anòn.). [See also p. 486 above.]

Shearman, Montague, et al. Athletics and Football. 1885. (Badminton Lib.) [Football rptd separately, 1899.]

How to Play Football; Association and Rugby. By an Old Player. Manchester, [1891].

Marshall, Francis. Football. 1892; 1893 (rev. and enlarged); rev. and largely rewritten by L. R. Tosswill, 1925. [Rugby game.]

Budd, A. and Robinson, B. Fletcher. Football. 1897. [Rugby.]

(e) Golf

Carnegie, G. Fullerton (1799–1851). Golfiana, or Niceties connected with the Game of Golf. 1842. [Verse.]

Farnie, ——. Golfer's Manual. 1857.

[Robb, ——.] Historical Gossip about Golf and Golfers. Edinburgh, 1863.

[Brown, Thomas (1822–1882).] Golfiana, or a Day at Gullane. 1869 (priv. ptd).

March, Thomas. Blackheath Golfing Lays. 1873 (priv. ptd).

Clark, Robert. Golf. A Royal and Ancient Game. 1875 (priv. ptd); 1893. [Ed. and mainly written by Clark; includes original club-rules and texts of T. Mathieson's The Goff, 1743, and G. F. Carnegie's Golfiana, 1833, various poems and notes.]

Golfing. A Handbook. With Golfing Sketches and Poems. 1887.

Simpson, Sir Walter Grindlay (1843–1898). The Art of Golf. 1887. [Simpson also contributed to Golf in the Badminton Lib.]

Hutchinson, Horace G. Famous Golf Links. 1891.

—— Golf. 1892. (Badminton Lib.) [With other writers.]

—— Golfing. 1893.

—— Golf Greens and Green-Keeping. 1896. ('Country Life' Lib. of Sport.)

—— After-Dinner Golf. [1896.]

—— A Golfing Pilgrim. 1898.

—— The Book of Golf and Golfers. 1899. [Ed. by Hutchinson.]

[See also under Angling, p. 772 and Cricket, p. 772 above.]

K., J. A. C. Golf in the Year 2000, or What we are coming to. 1892. [Satirical fiction.]

Thomson, John. Golfing and other Poems and Songs. Glasgow, 1893.

Hogg, W. T. M. Gullane. A Poem. Edinburgh, n.d.; 1896 (4th edn). [About golf at Gullane.]

Peters, H. T. Reminiscences of Golf and Golfers. [Before 1896.]

Kerr, John. The Golf-Book of East Lothian. Edinburgh, 1896. [A general history with local application.]

(f) Hockey

Cresswell, F. S. Hockey. 1889; 1900 (rev. and enlarged); rev. P. Collins, 1909.

(g) Polo

Brown, J. Moray. Riding in Polo. 1891.

—— Polo. 1895.

Dale, Thomas F. Polo, Past and Present. 1895. ('Country Life' Lib. of Sport.)

—— The Game of Polo. [1897.]

[Dale also contributed to the Badminton Lib.]

Drybrough, T. B. Polo. 1898; 1906 (rev. and enlarged).

(h) Tennis, Lawn Tennis, Rackets, Fives

Hazlitt, William (1778–1830). Cavanagh the Fives Player. [A long passage in essay on The Indian Jugglers in Table Talk, vol. I, 1821. See also p. 640 above.]

Lukin, Robert. A Treatise on Tennis. By a Member of the Tennis Club. 1822 (anon.).

Marshall, Julian. The Annals of Tennis. 1878.

—— Lawn Tennis. 1878.

—— Tennis Cuts and Quips, in Prose and Verse. [1884.]

—— Tennis; Rackets; Fives. 1800. [With other writers.]

Tait, James Andrew Arnan. Tennis; Rackets; Fives. 1890.

Baddeley, William. Lawn Tennis. 1895.

Noel, E. B., and Clark, J. O. M. A History of Tennis. 2 vols. 1902.

(7) MISCELLANEOUS SPORTS

(a) Archery

'Toxophilite.' A History of the Royal Toxophilite Society. 1867 (priv. ptd).

Longman, Charles J. and Walrond, H. Archery. 1894 (Badminton Lib.). [With full bibliography.]

Payne-Gallwey, Sir R. W. F. The Cross-bow. 1903. [See also under Shooting, p. 763 above.]

Roberts, T[homas]. The English Bowman, or, Tracts on Archery. 1801.

Waring, Thomas. A Treatise on Archery. 1814; 1832 (9th edn).

Dodd, James William. Ballads of Archery. 1818. [With music.]

The Archer's Guide. Accompanied by a Sketch of the History of the Long Bow. By an Old Toxophilite. 1833.

Warburton, Rowland Eyles Egerton. The Hawkstone Bow-Meeting. Chester, 1835 (anon.). [A poem.]

—— Rhymes on the Rules of the Cheshire Bowmen. Northwich, [1840?].

[See also p. 286 above.]

Hansard, George Agar. The Book of Archery: being the Complete History and Practice of the Art. 1840.

Ford, Horace Alfred. Archery: its Theory and Practice. 1856.

Paul, James Balfour. History of the Royal Company of Archers. 1875.

Rushton, W. L. Shakespeare as an Archer. 1897.

(b) Athletics and Swimming

The Athletic Record. 1875–6.

Cook, Sir Theodore Andrea. International Sport. A Short History of the Olympic Movement from 1896 to the Present Day. 1908; 1910 (with account of the London Games, 1908).

Machell, Hugh W. Some Records of the Annual Grasmere Sports. Foreword by H. D. Rawnsley, 1911.

Colquhoun, Sir Iain and Machell, Hugh W. Highland Gatherings. 1927.

Thom, Walter. Pedestrianism. With a Full Narrative of Captain Barclay's Public and Private Matches, and an Essay on Training. Aberdeen, 1813.

Frost, John. Scientific Swimming. 1816.

Walsh, John Henry ('Stonehenge'). Athletic Sports and Manly Exercises. 1864.

—— Pedestrianism. 1866.

[See also under Dictionaries, p. 758 above and p. 766 above.]

'Piscator.' How to swim, plunge, bathe, float, and dive. 1872.

Randall, John. Captain Webb, the Champion Channel Swimmer: a Comprehensive Account. Madeley, 1875. [With timed log.]

[See also under Hunting, p. 760 above.]

Sinclair, Archibald and Henry, W. Swimming. 1894. (Badminton Lib.)

(c) Boxing

Egan, Pierce. Boxiana, or Sketches of Modern Pugilism. 4 vols. 1818–24. [See also p. 668 above.]

Reynolds, John Hamilton (1796–1852). The Fancy: a Selection from the Poetical Remains of the late Peter Corcoran. 1820; ed. J. Masefield, 1905. [See also p. 242 above.]

The Fancy, or True Sportsman's Guide. Being Authentic Memoirs of the Leading Pugilists. By an Operator. 2 vols. 1821–6.

Walker, Donald. British Manly Exercises. 1834 (bis); 1835 (with addns); 1847 (8th edn, rev. and rewritten by 'Craven' [i.e. J. W. Carleton]). [Boxing, swimming, rowing, athletics, etc.]

—— Games and Sports. A Sequel [to above]. 1837.

—— Defensive Exercises; comprising Wrestling, Boxing, Fencing [etc.]. 1840.

Hazlitt, William. The Fight. [In Literary Remains, 2 vols. 1836.]

Borrow, George Henry (1803–1881). Lavengro. 1851. [Contains celebrated boxing scenes. See also p. 421 above.]

Dowling, Frank Lewis (1823–1867). Fistiana, or the Oracle of the Ring. [1852?]–64. [Rev. with supplement each year.]

Walker, Johnny. The Life and Adventures of the Renowned Johnny Walker, including a Succinct Narrative of his Adventures in the P[rize] R[ing]. [With] An Original Guide to the Theory and Practice of the Art of Self-Defence. Winchester, [1857].

Miles, Henry Downes. Pugilistica: being 144 Years of the History of British Boxing, from 1719 to 1863. 3 vols. [1880–1]. [See also p. 766 above.]

Shaw, George Bernard (b. 1856). Cashel Byron's Profession. With Dramatic Version, and Note on Modern Prize-Fighting. 1882. [See also p. 617 above.]

Henning, F. W. J. Some Recollections of the Prize Ring. 1889.

—— Fights for the Championship. The Men and their Times. 2 vols. [1902].

Doyle, Sir Arthur Conan (1859–1930). Rodney Stone. 1896. [See also p. 542 above.]

Dixon, W. Willmott ('Thormanby'). Boxers and their Battles. 1900. [See also p. 767 above.]

Lynch, J. G. Bohun (d. 1932). The Complete Amateur Boxer. 1913. [Contains much history.]

(d) Card and Indoor Games

(i) Cards

Chatto, William Andrew. Facts and Speculations on the Origin and History of Playing Cards. 1848. [See also under Hunting and Angling, pp. 760, 769 above.]

Jones, Henry ('Cavendish'). Principles of Whist stated and explained by Cavendish. 1862. [Often rptd, with varying titles and in various forms.]

Jones, Henry ('Cavendish'). Card Essays. 1879. [See also under Croquet, p. 774 above.]

Baldwin, J. L. and C[lag], J. The Laws of Short Whist, and a Treatise on the Game. 1864.

Davies, Clement. Modern Whist. 1886.

Hogg, James ('Portland'). The Whist Table. A Treasury of Notes. [1895.] [By various writers; ed. by Hogg.]

(ii) Billiards

Roberts, John. Billiards. [1869.]

Bennett, Joseph. Billiards. Edited by 'Cavendish.' 1873.

Prize Essays on Billiards as an Amusement for all Classes. Manchester, 1873. [5 essays, and other matter.] .

Buchanan, John P. Hints on Billiards. 1895.

—— Pyramids and Pool Games. 1896.

(iii) Chess, Draughts, etc.

Pruen, Thomas ('Amateur'). An Introduction to the History and Study of Chess. 1804.

Sanatt, J. H. A Treatise on the Game of Chess. 1808.

—— A New Treatise on the Game of Chess. 2 vols. 1821.

An Easy Introduction to the Game of Chess. 1820. [Includes Caissa, by Sir William Jones, games by Philidor, and other earlier material.]

Staunton, Howard (1810–1874). The Chess-Player's Handbook. 1847.

—— The Chess Player's Companion. 1849.

—— Chess: Theory and Practice. Containing the Laws and History of the Game. 1876. [Ed. by R. B. Wormald.]

Boden, Samuel S, ('Amateur'). A Popular Introduction to the Study and Practice of Chess. 1851.

Chess. A Poem, in Four Parts. 1854.

Chess. A Poem. By a Member of the Cambridge University Chess Club. 1858.

Gossip, G. H. D. The Chess-Player's Manual. A Complete Guide to Chess. 1875.

Bird, H. E. Chess History and Reminiscences. 1890.

McCall, Robert. The Game of Draughts. Report and Games of the International Draughts Match, England v. Scotland. [1884?] [With hints for learners and specimen games.]

Ritchie, A. D. The Game of Draughts. Match for a Stake of £100 and the Championship of Ireland, May, 1891. Tillicoultry, 1891. [With full description, sketches of players, hints for learners, problems.]

'Crawley, Captain.' Backgammon. [1866.]

(e) Climbing and Mountaineering

Barry, Martin. Ascent to the Summit of Mont Blanc. 1835.

Peaks, Passes and Glaciers. A Series of Excursions by Members of the Alpine Club. Ed. J. Ball, 1859. [Ser. 2, ed. E. S. Kennedy, 2 vols. 1862.]

Galton, Sir Francis (1822–1911). Vacation Tourists and Notes of Travel in 1860. Cambridge, 1861. [Continued 1862 (for 1861), 1864 (for 1862–3). Papers by various authors, ed. by Galton, including accounts of mountaineering by Sir Leslie Stephen and others.]

The Alpine Journal. A Record of Mountain Adventure and Scientific Observation. By Members of the Alpine Club. 1863– .

Freshfield, D. W. (1845–1934). Across Country from Thonon to Trent. Rambles and Scrambles in Switzerland and the Tyrol. 1865.

—— Travels in the Central Caucasus and Bashon, including Ascents of Kazbek and Elbruz. 1869.

Stephen, Sir Leslie (1832–1904). The Playground of Europe. 1871. [See also p. 727 above.]

Whymper, Edward (1840–1911). Scrambles among the Alps in 1860–69. 1871.

—— The Ascent of the Matterhorn. 1880.

Wilson, H. S. Alpine Ascents and Adventures. Illustrated by Edward Whymper. 1878.

Coolidge, W. A. B. Swiss Travel and Swiss Guide-Books. 1889.

Dent, C. T. et al. Mountaineering. 1892; 1900 (rev.). (Badminton Lib.)

Browne, G. F. Off the Mill. Some Occasional Papers. 1895. [Mainly on climbing: one on fishing.]

Conway, W. Martin (Baron Conway) (b. 1856). The Alps from End to End. 1895.

—— Mountain Climbing. 1897.

Mummery, A. F. My Climbs in the Alps and Caucasus. 1895; ed. M. Mummery, [1913].

Jones, Owen Glynne. Rock Climbing in the English Lake District. 1897; Keswick, 1900 (with memoir of the author by W. M. Cook, and appendix by G. D. and A. Abraham); 1911.

Mathews, C. E. The Annals of Mont Blanc. 1898.

Gribble, F. H. The Early Mountaineers. 1899.

(f) Curling, Cycling, Dancing, Falconry, Fencing, Rowing and Sailing, Skating and Tobogganing

(i) Curling

[Ramsay, John.] An Account of the Game of Curling, By a Member of the Duddingston Curling Club. 1811 (priv. ptd); rptd 1882.

Crawford, H. A Descriptive and Historical Sketch of Curling. 1828.

Brown, Sir Ridyard. Memorabilia Curliana Mabensia. Dumfries, 1830.

M[acnair], J. The Channel Stone, or Sweepings frae the Rinks. 4 sers. Edinburgh, 1883–4.

Taylor, James. Curling; the Ancient Scottish Game. 1884.

Kerr, John. The History of Curling, and 50 Years of the Royal Caledonia Curling Club. Edinburgh, 1890.

—— Skating and Curling. 1894. (Badminton Lib.) [With C. G. Tebbutt.]

(ii) Cycling

Davis, A. The Velocipede: its History, and Practical Hints how to use it. 1869.

Wells, Herbert George (b. 1866). The Wheels of Chance. 1896.

Wingfield, Walter. Bicycle Gymkhana and Musical Rides. With Diagrams and Instructions. [1897.]

(iii) Dancing

Vuillier, Gaston. A History of Dancing. With a Sketch of Dancing in England, by J. Grego. 2 vols. 1898. [The History tr. from the French.]

Sharp, Cecil (1859–1924). The Morris Book. A History of Morris Dancing. 5 pts, 1907–13. [Includes instructions for morris dancing.]

—— The Country Dance Book. 6 pts, 1909–22. [A collection, description and history, with instructions.]

(iv) Falconry

Harting, J. E. Bibliotheca Accipitraria. A Catalogue of Books relating to Falconry. 1891.

Sebright, Sir John Saunders. Observations on Hawking. 1826.

Salvin, F. H., and Brodrick, W. Falconry in the British Isles. 1855.

Freeman, Gage Earle, and Salvin, Francis Henry. Falconry: its Claims, History, and Practice. 1859.

Brodrick, William. Falconer's Favourites. 1865. [Plates of typical birds, with descriptions.]

Freeman, Gage Earle. Practical Falconry; to which is added, How I became a Falconer. 1869.

Essays on Falconry submitted to the Barnet Committee for the developing the Resources of the Alexandra Park. 1871. [By Hawkins Fisher, G. E. Freeman, F. S. Dugmore, C. H. J. Lawton, and 'Dora Fuller' (T. E. Jones); extracts from others.]

Radcliffe, E. Delmé. Falconry. Notes on the Falconidae used in India in Falconry. Southsea, [1872]. [For English adoption.]

(v) Fencing

Castle, Egerton. Schools and Masters of Fence, from the Middle Ages to the 18th Century. 1885; 1892 (rev.). [With bibliography up to 1800.]

—— Bibliotheca Artis Dimicatoriae. [In Badminton Lib. vol. on Fencing, Boxing, and Wrestling, 1897.]

Thimm, C. A. A Complete Bibliography of Fencing and Duelling. 1896.

Mathewson, T. Fencing Familiarised. 1805.

Roland, Joseph. The Amateur of Fencing. 1809.

Angelo, H. C. W. A Treatise on the Utility and Advantages of Fencing. 1817.

Martelli, C. An Improved System of Fencing. 1819.

Rolando, Guezman. The Modern Art of Fencing. 1822.

Roland, George. A Treatise on the Theory and Practice of the Art of Fencing. Edinburgh, 1823.

Chapman, George. Foil Practice. 1861.

—— Notes and Observations on the Art of Fencing. 1864.

Hutton, Alfred (1840–1910). Swordsmanship and Bayonet-Fencing. 1867.

—— Old Sword-Play. The Systems of Fence in Vogue during the 16, 17, and 18th Centuries. 1892.

Burton, Sir Richard Francis (1821–1890). The Book of the Sword. 1884. [All pbd of 3 projected vols.]

—— The Sentiment of the Sword. A Country-House Dialogue. Ed. A. F. Sieveking and Sir T. A. Cook, 1911.

Dunn, H. A. C. Fencing. 1889.

Pollock, Walter Herries, et al. Fencing; Boxing; Wrestling. 1897. (Badminton Lib.)

(vi) Rowing and Sailing

Armytage, A. The Cam and Cambridge Rowing. 1889.

Forster, R. H. and Harris, W. The History of the Lady Margaret Boat Club, St John's College, Cambridge, 1825–1890. Cambridge, 1890; Cambridge, 1926 (completed to 1925).

Cook, Sir Theodore Andrea. Thomas Doggett, Deceased. 1908. [Pt ii, The Race (for Doggett's Coat and Badge, for Thames Watermen, from 1716 onwards), by Guy Nickalls.]

—— Henley Races, with a Complete Index of Competitors and Crews since 1839. 1919.

Folkard, Henry Coleman. The Sailing Boat. A Description and Practical Directions for Sailing. 1853; 1901 (5th edn). [See also under Shooting, p. 762 above.]

Lehmann, Rudolf Chambers. Rowing. 1897.
McLean, D. H. and Grenfell, W. H. Rowing, Punting, and Punts. 1898.
Eton in 1829–1830. A Diary of Boating and Other Events, written in Greek by T. K. Selwyn. Ed. (with trn and notes) E. Warre, 1903. [Written 1830.]

(vii) Skating and Tobogganing

Forster, F. W. A Bibliography of Skating. 1898.
Williams, M. S. Monier, et al. Figure Skating, Simple and Combine. 1892.
Cook, Sir Theodore Andrea. Notes on Tobogganing at St Moritz. 1896.
Tebbutt, C. G. and A., and Reid, A. Skating. 1897.
Witham, T W. A System of Figure Skating. 1897.   F. J. H. D.

VIII. NEWSPAPERS AND MAGAZINES

Technical Development: Advertising; Management and Distribution; Wages and Conditions; Technique of Journalism.
The History of Journalism: Memoirs and Biographies of Journalists and Newspaper Proprietors; General History of the Press; Histories of Particular Papers; Lists of Newspapers.
The Daily Papers: London Morning Papers; London Evening Papers; Provincial Daily Papers; Scottish Daily Papers; Irish Daily Papers; London Papers published more than once a week.
The Weekly Papers: Sunday Papers; General Weeklies; Illustrated Papers; Unstamped and Radical Journals; Literary Reviews; Religious Papers; Agricultural Papers; Financial Reviews; Commercial Papers; Sporting Papers; Humorous Papers; Juvenile Papers; Miscellaneous Specialised Papers.
Magazines and Reviews: Monthly Magazines; Quarterly Reviews.
School and University Journalism.
Annuals and Yearbooks.

A. TECHNICAL DEVELOPMENT

[See also under Book Production and Distribution, pp. 70–106 above.]

(1) ADVERTISING

[Besides the returns of the Advertisement Duty (repealed in 1853) here listed, others issued together with Stamp Duty returns will be found on p. 795 below. Important information may also be gleaned from the introductory matter to the Newspaper Advertisement Agents' Directories listed p. 797 below.]

[House of Commons: Accounts and Papers.] Abstract of account of sums paid for advertisements and proclamations in newspapers by the public offices. (470). xix. 559. 1822.
[House of Commons: Accounts and Papers.] Ireland. Return of Sums paid by the Stamp Office for advertisements. (588). xviii. 465. 1822.
[House of Commons: Accounts and Papers.] Amount of Duty paid for advertisements by each provincial newspaper in England. (524). xxxii. 617. 1833.
[House of Commons: Accounts and Papers.] Ireland. Sums paid by each newspaper in Ireland for stamps. 1832–3, distinguishing sums paid for paper from those paid for advertisements. (658). xxxii. 625. 1833.
[House of Commons: Accounts and Papers.] Ireland. Sums paid by the Irish Government to each newspaper in Ireland, 1832–3, distinguishing sums paid to each for advertisements; duty or services for which paid, etc. (633). xxxii. 629. 1833.
[House of Commons: Accounts and Papers.] Number of advertisements which appeared in each of the newspapers published in London, 1831 to 1834; amount of duty paid by each during the period above-mentioned. (108). xxxvii. 703. 1835.
[House of Commons: Accounts and Papers.] Ireland. Advertisement duty assessed on each paper in Ireland, 1834; sums paid monthly by each paper; arrears due for advertisement duty, Jan. 5, 1835. (265). xxxvii. 695. 1835.
Knight, Charles. Advertisements. [In his London, 1843.]
A Guide to Advertisers. 1852 (5 edns).
Advertisements. Quarterly Rev. xcvii, 1855.
Smith, W. Advertise. How? When? Where? 1863.
Sampson, Henry. A History of Advertising. 1874.
[Nicoll, Donald.] Publicity. An Essay on Advertising. By an Adept of 35 Years' Experience. 1878.
Smith's Advertising Agency. Smith, T. and Osborne, J. H. Successful Advertising; its Secrets explained. 1878; 1896 (17th edn); 1900 (20th edn); 1928.
Clay, Alice. The Agony Column of The Times, 1800–1870. 1881.
Sell, Henry. The Philosophy of Advertising. 1882. [Subsequently became Sell's Dictionary of the World's Press (see p. 798 below).]
Sinclair, Alexander. Fifty Years of Newspaper Life, 1845–95. Glasgow, [c. 1897] (priv. ptd).
Smith, T. 21 Years in Fleet Street. [1899.]
Stead, W. T. The Art of Advertising. [1899.]

Street, Edmund and Jackson, Lionel. Advertising. Journ. Royal Soc. Arts, 24 Jan. 1913.

'On the Road' One Hundred Years Ago. Ed. James Cannon, Publishers' Circular, 9 Feb.–13 April 1935.

Roll Call 1910 [a chronological list of advertising agents]. Statistical Rev. of Press Advertising, April 1935.

Periodicals

The Advertising Register. Nos. 1–54, 12 Nov. 1886–7 Oct. 1887. [Weekly.]

Advertising. No. 1, Oct. 1891–Jan. 1914. [Monthly; ed. by J. H. Osborne.]

The Advertiser's Monthly Circular. Nos. 1–7. Jan.–Nov. 1895.

Advertising Notes. No. 1, Jan. 1897–Dec. 1898. [Continued as] Profitable Advertising, Jan. 1899–Dec. 1904. [Monthly.]

The Advertiser's ABC. 1898–1901.

The Advertiser's Journal. No. 1, June 1898.

The Advertiser's Review. No. 1, 8 April 1899–24 Dec. 1904. [Incorporated in The Advertising News.]

Modern Advertising. Nos. 1–4, June 1900–April 1901.

Newspaper and Poster Advertising. Nos. 1–58, 28 July 1900–21 Dec. 1901. [Incorporated in The Advertiser's Review.]

(2) MANAGEMENT AND DISTRIBUTION

The Commercial History of a Penny Magazine. Penny Mag. 1833.

[Grant, James.] Travels in Town by the Author of Random Recollections. 2 vols, 1839. [Chs. VII, VIII.]

The Bringing forth of the Daily Newspaper. Chambers's Journ. 26 Aug. 1854.

King, Harold. Four and Twenty Hours in a Newspaper Office. Once a Week, 26 Sept. 1863, 6 Feb. 1864.

Philbrick, F. A. and Westoby, W. A. S. The Postage and Telegraph Stamps of Great Britain. 1881.

Sidman, W. A Treatise on Newspaper Bookkeeping. 1887.

Yeo, H. Newspaper Management. Manchester, 1891.

Maxwell, Sir H. The Life and Times of the Rt. Hon. W. H. Smith, M.P. 2 vols. Edinburgh, 1893.

Newnes, George, Ltd. How Popular Periodicals are produced. [1894.]

Norton, B. T. and Feasey, G. T. Newspaper Accounts: being a Practical Treatise on the Books and Accounts in use in Large and Small Newspaper Offices. 1895.

Harmsworth, A. C. (Viscount Northcliffe). Making a Modern Newspaper. Some secrets revealed. Harmsworth's Mag. July 1898.

[Hepworth, T. C.] All about a London Daily from the Paper Mill to the Breakfast Table. [1898.]

Heywood, A. and Son. 1832–1899. A Brief Survey of the News Trade. Manchester, 1899.

Special Newspaper Trains. By Brunel Redivivus. Railway Mag. Nov. 1899.

Courtney, L. H. The Making and Reading of Newspapers. 1901.

Ewen, H. L'Estrange. Unadhesive Postage Stamps of the United Kingdom. 1905.

—— Newspaper and Parcel Stamps issued by the Railway Companies of the United Kingdom. 1906.

Given, J. L. Making a Newspaper. 1913.

Pocklington, G. R. The Story of W. H. Smith and Son. 1921; rev. F. K. Foat, 1932 (priv. ptd).

Kitchin, F. H. Moberly Bell and his Times. 1925. [Moberly Bell was manager of The Times.]

Bell, E. H. C. Moberly. The Life and Letters of C. F. Moberly Bell. 1927.

Periodicals

The Newsmen's Weekly Chronicle. No. 1, 2 July–No. 7, 13 Aug. 1837.

The Newsvendor. No. 1, Jan. 1873–21 Feb. 1883. [Weekly after first 9 nos.]

The Newsagent and Advertiser's Record. No. 1, July 1889–Dec. 1890. [Continued as] The Newsagent and Bookseller's Review, 31 Jan. 1890 onwards. [Monthly.]

The Newsagents' Chronicle. No. 1, 16 Feb. 1895–No. 75, 26 Feb. 1898. [Fortnightly.]

The Newspaper Owner and Manager. 5 Jan. 1898–20 May 1903. [Continued as] Master Printer, 27 May 1903–1 April 1905. [Continued as] The Newspaper Owner, 8 April 1905–28 June 1913. [Continued as] The Newspaper World, 5 July 1913 onwards. [Weekly. Owned and ed. by Charles Baker.]

(3) WAGES AND CONDITIONS

[The earlier portion of the Library of the London Society of Compositors is deposited at the St Bride Foundation.]

Memorial of London Compositors addressed to Proprietors of Newspapers with a Report of the Meeting of the Employers. [1809.]

London Union of Compositors. The London Scale of Prices for Compositors' Work: agreed upon April 16th, 1810, with Explanatory Notes, and the Scales of Leeds, York, Dublin, Belfast and Edinburgh. [c. 1835] (4 edns).

London Trade Society of Compositors. Report of a Committee appointed to draw up a statement of the regular mode of working on Newspapers. 1820.

London Union of Compositors. Report of the Proceedings of the Delegated Meeting of Compositors. Dec. 12, 1833. [1833.]

London Union of Compositors. Report of the General Trade Committee to the Compositors of London, March 4 and 11, 1834. [1834.]

London Union of Compositors. Report of the Trade Council on the Mode of Working The Times Newspaper. [1835.]

London Society of Compositors. Report of the Journeymen Members of the Conference of Master Printers and Compositors held in 1847. 1847; [1875]; [1879]; [1883].

London Association of Master Printers. The Agreements made with the Compositors, Pressmen and Machine-minders in Nov. 1866. 1867.

London Society of Compositors. Report of the Special Committee appointed to revise the Trade Rules, examine the System of working in each Office and frame a Report upon the Evidence that may come before them. 1868.

London Society of Compositors. Rules and Regulations for News Work. [1868.]

Manchester Typographical Society. Regulations for Piece-Work on Daily Papers. Manchester, 1873.

London Society of Compositors. Report of the Special Committee appointed to consider the Best Means for improving the Conditions of Newspaper Compositors. 1874.

Glasgow Typographical Society. Newspaper Time and Piece Scales of Prices. Glasgow, 1884.

The Vigilance Gazette: a Monthly Journal devoted to the Interests of the London Society of Compositors. Nos. 1–11, 1888–90. [Continued as The London Printers' Circular.]

London Society of Compositors. News Department. Workmen's Memorial to the Newspaper Proprietors. 1889.

London Society of Compositors. Fair and Unfair Religious and Temperance Weekly Newspapers. 1890.

London Printing and Allied Trades Association. The London Scale of Prices for Compositors' Work. 1891.

London Society of Compositors. News Department. Report of the Committee on the System of working in each Office. 1891. [Supplementary Report, presented 11 Nov. 1891, 1891.]

The Institute of Journalists. By an Old Journalist. National Rev. Oct. 1892.

The Institute of Journalists. Proceedings. 1892 onwards. [Quarterly.]

London Society of Compositors. Rates and Rules for working Composing Machines in London. Agreed upon between Representatives of the London Newspapers and Master Printers and of the London Society of Compositors. 1896.

Society of Women Journalists. Annual Report. 1896– . [In progress.]

Dickson, J. J. Manchester Typographical Society and Branch of the Typographical Association Centenary. 1797–1897. Manchester, 1897.

London Society of Compositors. Jubilee. A Brief Record of Events prior to and since 1848. [Ed. C. W. Bowerman, 1898.]

Glasgow Typographical Society. Scale of Prices for the working of Composing Machines in Newspaper Offices. Glasgow, 1898.

The Economic Position of Women in Journalism. By a Woman Journalist. The Humanitarian, July 1900.

London Association of Correctors of the Press. Jubilee. 1854–1904. [1904.]

MacDonald, James Ramsay. Women in the Printing Trades. A Sociological Study, with a Preface by F. Y. Edgeworth. 1904.

Howe, Ellic. The History of Printers' Conditions. [In preparation.]

(4) THE TECHNIQUE OF JOURNALISM

[Whitefoord, Caleb.] Advice to the Editors of Newspapers. 1799.

[Copleston, Edward.] Advice to a young Reviewer, with a Specimen of the Art. Oxford, 1807.

[Conder, Josiah.] Reviews Reviewed; including an Enquiry into the Moral and Intellectual Effects of Habits of Criticism, and their Influence on the General Interests of Literature. To which is subjoined a Brief History of the Periodical Reviews published in England and Scotland. By Tho. Chas. O'Reid. Oxford, 1811.

Journalism. Westminster Rev. Jan. 1833.

The Newspapers. Metropolitan Mag. Jan. 1833.

Hughes, Thomas. Anonymous Journalism. Macmillan's Mag. Dec. 1861.

Anonymous Journalism. Fortnightly Rev. Sept. 1867.

House of Commons. Special Report from the Select Committee on the Electric Telegraphs Bill. 1868.

Reed, T. A. The Reporter's Guide. 1869.

Modern Newspaper Enterprise. Fraser's Mag. June 1876.

Whittaker, Samuel. Parliamentary Reporting in England, Foreign Countries and the Colonies. Manchester, 1877.

[House of Commons.] Report from the Select Committee on Parliamentary Reporting. 1878.

Bussey, H. F. and Reid, T. W. The Newspaper Reader: the Journals of the XIXth Century on the Events of the Day. 1879.

[House of Lords.] Report from the Select Committee on Parliamentary Reporting. 1880.

Davies, E. P. The Reporter's Handbook. 1884.

Dawson, J. Practical Journalism. 1885.

Pendleton, John. Newspaper Reporting in Olden Times and To-day. 1890.

Mackie, J. B. Modern Journalism. 1894.

The Compleat Leader Writer. Macmillan's Mag. Sept. 1894.

Phillips, Ernest. How to become a Journalist. 1895.

Baines, F. E. Forty Years at the Post Office. 2 vols, 1895.

Bennett, Arnold. Journalism for Women: a Practical Guide. 1898.

Lawrence, Arthur. Journalism as a Profession. 1903.

Wellcome, H. S. The Evolution of Journalism. 1909.

MacDonagh, Michael. The Reporters' Gallery. [1913.]

Salmon, Lucy Maynard. The Newspaper and the Historian. New York, 1923.

Periodicals

London, Provincial, and Colonial Press News. No. 1, 15 Jan. 1866–Dec. 1912. [Monthly; ed. by C. W. Dorrington.]

The Newspaper Press. No. 1, 1 Dec. 1866–1 July 1872. [Incorporated in The Printers' Register. Monthly; ed. by Alexander Andrews.]

The Fleet Street Gazette; a Journeyman's Journal. No. 1, 28 Feb.–No. 7, 23 May 1874. [Fortnightly.]

The Journalist. No. 1, Nov. 1879–No. 21, July 1881. [Monthly.]

The Journalist. No. 1, 15 Oct. 1886–May 1909.

Journalism. Nos. 1–11, Nov. 1887–Feb. 1889.

Press Agencies

Whorlow, H. The Provincial Newspaper Society. 1886.

Hunt, William. Then and Now. Hull, 1887. [Gives details on The Central Press and The Central News.]

The Press Association. Chambers's Journ. 14 Aug. 1897.

The National Press Agency. Our Silver Anniversary, 1873–98. 1898.

Jones, Sir Roderick. International Telegraphic News; a Lecture at the University of London, May 23, 1921. 1921.

Collins, M. H. From Pigeon Post to Wireless. 1925. [A history of Reuter's.]

Jones, Sir Roderick. News Agencies and their Work: Address to the International Congress of the Press, July 6, 1927. 1927.

Pillars of the Press. [4 articles on the press agencies in The World's Press News, June–July 1929.]

Central News Agency. Diamond Jubilee Souvenir. 1931.

D[avies], E. W. The Newspaper Society, 1836–1936. 1936.

B. THE HISTORY OF JOURNALISM

(1) MEMOIRS AND BIOGRAPHIES OF INDIVIDUAL JOURNALISTS AND NEWSPAPER PROPRIETORS

À Beckett, A. W. (1844–1909: Punch).
The À Becketts of 'Punch'. Westminster, 1903.
The Recollections of a Humorist. 1907.

Adams, W. E. (b. 1832: The Newcastle Weekly Chronicle).
Memoirs of a Social Atom. 2 vols. 1903.

Aird, Andrew.
Reminiscences of Editors, Reporters and Printers during the Last Sixty Years. Glasgow, 1890.

Annand, James (1843–1906: The Newcastle Daily Leader).
Hodgson, George B. From Smithy to Senate: the Life Story of James Annand, Journalist and Politician. 1908.

[Anonymous.]
A Newspaper editor's reminiscences. Fraser's Mag. Nov. 1839, Sept., Oct. 1840, June 1841.

Appleton, C. E. C. B. (1841–1879: The Academy).
Appleton, J. H. and Sayce, A. H. Dr Appleton, his Life and Literary Relics. 1881.

Arnold, William Thomas (1852–1904).
Ward, M. A. and Montague, C. E. William Thomas Arnold, Journalist and Historian. Manchester, 1907.

Bagehot, Walter (1826–1877: The Economist).
Barrington, Mrs Russell. The Life of Walter Bagehot, by his Sister-in-Law. 1914.

Baines, Edward (1774–1848: The Leeds Mercury).
Baines, Edward. The Life of Edward Baines by his Son. 1851.

Baldwin, Charles (1774–1869: The Standard).
[Memoir in] Register and Mag. of Biography, April 1869.

Baldwin, Walter (The Clapham Observer).
Mursell, A. and Woods, C. Walter Baldwin. 1903.

Barclay, Sir Thomas (b. 1853: The Times).
Thirty Years, 1876–1906. Anglo-French Reminiscences. 1914.

Beatty-Kingston, William (1837–1900: The Daily Telegraph).
A Journalist's Jottings. 2 vols. 1890.
Men, Cities and Events. 1895.
Bell, John (1745–1831: Bell's Weekly Messenger).
Morison, Stanley. John Bell. Cambridge, 1930 (priv. ptd).
Bell, John Browne (1779–1855; The News of the World).
Berrey, R. P. The Romance of a Great Newspaper. [c. 1933.]
Bertram, J. G.
Some Memories of Books, Authors and Events. Westminster, 1893.
Besant, Sir Walter (1836–1901).
Autobiography. Ed. Sir Squire Sprigge, 1902.
Black, William (1841–1898).
Reid, Sir Wemyss. William Black, Novelist: a Biography. 1902.
Blanchard, E. L. Laman (1820–1889).
Life and Reminiscences. Ed. Clement Scott and Cecil Howard, 1891.
Blatchford, Robert (b. 1851: The Clarion).
My Eighty Years. 1931.
Blowitz, Henri Stephan de (1832–1903: The Times).
My Memoirs. 1903.
Blumenfeld, Ralph David (b. 1864: The Daily Express).
R. D. B.'s Diary, 1887–1914. 1930.
Bodkin, M. M'D. (b. 1850).
Recollections of an Irish Judge. 1914.
Boon, John (1859–1928: The Exchange Telegraph Co.).
Victorians, Edwardians and Georgians. The Impressions of a Veteran Journalist extending over Forty Years. 2 vols. 1928.
Borthwick, Sir Algernon (Baron Glenesk) (1830–1908: The Morning Post).
Lucas, Reginald. Lord Glenesk and The Morning Post. 1910.
Boyd, Frank M. (b. 1863: The Pelican).
A Pelican's Tale: Fifty years of London and elsewhere. 1919.
Boyle, Frederick (1841–1883).
The Narrative of an Expelled Correspondent. 1877.
Bradlaugh, Charles (1833–1891).
Autobiography. 1873.
Bonner, H. B. and Robertson, J. M. The Life of Charles Bradlaugh. 2 vols. 1894.
Brodrick, G. C. (1831–1903).
Memories and Impressions, 1831–1900. 1900.
Brooks, Shirley (1816–1874: Punch).
Layard, G. S. A Great 'Punch' editor, Being the Life, Letters and Diaries of Shirley Brooks. 1907.

Buchanan, William (1781–1863).
The Editorship of the Edinburgh Daily Courant. Edinburgh, 1860.
Buckingham, James Silk (1786–1855: The Athenaeum).
Specimens of Newspaper Literature, with Personal Memoirs. 2 vols. Boston, 1850.
Autobiography. 2 vols. 1855.
Turner, R. E. J. S. Buckingham. 1934.
Burnand, Sir F. C. (1836–1916: Punch, 1880–1906).
Records and Reminiscences. 2 vols. [1904].
Bussey, H. Findlater (d. 1919).
Sixty Years of Journalism. Bristol, 1906.
Cadett, Herbert.
The Adventures of a Journalist. 1900.
Campbell, Duncan (1824–1890).
Reminiscences and Reflections of an Octogenarian Highlander, who was for over 26 Years Editor of the Northern Chronicle, Inverness. Inverness, 1910.
Campbell, Thomas (1777–1844: The New Monthly Magazine).
Beattie, William. The Life and Letters of Thomas Campbell. 3 vols. 1848.
Carlile, Richard (1790–1843: The Republican).
Holyoake, G. J. The Life and Character of Richard Carlile. 1849.
Campbell, Theophila Carlile. The Battle of the Press, as told in the Story of the Life of Richard Carlile, by his Daughter. 1899.
Carnie, William (The Aberdeen Herald).
Reporting Reminiscences. 3 vols, Aberdeen, 1902–6 (priv. ptd).
Cassell, John (1817–1865).
Pike, G. Holden. John Cassell. 1894.
Catling, Thomas (1838–1920: Lloyd's Weekly Newspaper).
My Life's Pilgrimage. 1911.
Chambers, William (1800–1883).
Memoirs of Robert Chambers; with Autobiographic Reminiscences of William Chambers. 1872 (2nd edn).
Clarke, William (The Manchester Guardian).
A Collection of his Writings, with a Biographical Sketch. Ed. Herbert Burrows and J. A. Hobson, 1908.
Cobbe, Frances Power (1822–1904: The Echo).
The Life of Frances Power Cobbe, by Herself. 2 vols. 1894.
Cobbett, William (1762–1835: The Political Register).
The Life of William Cobbett. Manchester, 1835.
Smith, Edward. William Cobbett: a Biography. 2 vols. 1878.
Carlyle, E. I. William Cobbett. 1904

'Melville, Lewis' (Lewis S. Benjamin). The Life and Letters of William Cobbett. 2 vols. 1913.

Cole, G. D. H. The Life of William Cobbett. 1924.

Coleridge, S. T. (1772–1834: The Morning Post). Gillman, James. The Life of S. T. Coleridge. Vol. i, 1838 (all pbd). [Cf. also rejoinders by Daniel Stuart and Henry Coleridge in GM. May–Aug. 1838.]

Bourne, H. R. Fox. Coleridge among the Journalists. GM. Nov. 1887.

Colles, Ramsay (1862–1919: The Irish Figaro; etc.).

In Castle and Courthouse: being the Reminiscences of Thirty Years in Ireland. 1911.

Conder, Josiah (1789–1855: The Patriot). Conder, Eustace R. Josiah Conder: A Memoir. 1857.

Cook, Sir E. T. (1857–1919: The Pall Mall Gazette; The Westminster Gazette). Mills, J. Saxon. Sir Edward Cook; a Biography. 1921.

Cooper, Charles A. (1829–1916: The Scotsman). An Editor's Retrospect. 1896.

Cooper, Thomas (1805–1892: Cooper's Journal). The Life of Thomas Cooper, written by himself. 1872.

Courtney, L. H., Baron Courtney (1832–1918). Gooch, G. P. The Life of L. H. Courtney. 1920.

Courtney, W. L. (1850–1928: The Daily Telegraph; The Fortnightly Review). The Making of an Editor, 1850–1928. 1930.

Cowen, Joseph (1831–1900: The Newcastle Chronicle). Jones, E. R. The Life and Speeches of Joseph Cowen. 1885. Duncan, W. The Life of Joseph Cowen. 1904.

Croal, David. The Early Recollections of a Journalist, 1832–1859. Edinburgh, 1898.

Crowe, Sir Joseph (1825–1896). Reminiscences of Thirty-Five Years of my Life. 1895.

Dalziel, George (1815–1902) and Edward (1817–1905). The Brothers Dalziel. A Record of 50 Years' Work, 1840–1890. 1901.

Delane, J. T. (1817–1879: The Times). Dasent, Arthur Irwin. John Thaddeus Delane, Editor of the Times: his Life and Correspondence. 2 vols. 1908. Cook, Sir E. T. Delane of the Times. 1915.

De Quincey, Thomas (1785–1859: The Westmorland Gazette). Pollitt, C. De Quincey's Editorship of the Westmorland Gazette, with Selections from his Work on that Journal from July 1818 to November 1819. Kendal, 1890.

Dickens, Charles (1812–1870: The Daily News). Forster, John. The Life of Charles Dickens. 3 vols. 1873–4. Lehmann, Rudolph C. Charles Dickens as Editor: being the Letters written by him to William Henry Wills, his Sub-editor. 1912.

Dilke, Charles Wentworth (1789-1864: The Athenaeum). The Papers of a Critic, with a Biographical Sketch by Sir Charles Wentworth Dilke. 2 vols. 1875.

Dixon, W. W. The Spice of Life. A Medley of Memoirs. By 'Thormanby.' 1911.

Downey, Edmund (b. 1856: The Waterford News). Twenty Years Ago. A Book of Anecdote illustrating Literary Life in London. 1905.

Dunlóp, Andrew. Fifty Years of Irish Journalism. Dublin, 1911.

Edwards, H. Sutherland (1828–1906). Personal Recollections. 1900.

Edwards, J. Passmore (1823–1911: The Echo). A Few Footprints. 1905 (priv. ptd).

Escott, T. H. S. (1844–1924). Platform, Press, Politics and Play. Bristol, 1895.

Espinasse, Francis (The Edinburgh Courant). Literary Recollections and Sketches. 1893.

Felbermann, Heinrich (1850–1925: Life). The Memoirs of a Cosmopolitan Life. 1936.

Finlay, George (1799–1875). Miller, William. George Finlay as a Journalist. EHR. Oct. 1924.

Fonblanque, Albany (1793–1872: The Examiner). Fonblanque, Edward Barington de. The Life and Labours of Albany Fonblanque. 1874.

Forbes, Archibald (1838–1900). Souvenirs of some Continents. 1885. Memoirs and Studies of War and Peace. 1895.

Forsyth, William (1818–1879: The Aberdeen Journal). Selections from the Writings of the late William Forsyth, with a Memoir [by Alexander Walker]. Aberdeen, 1882.

Foster, Ernest (1852–1919: Cassell's Saturday Journal). An Editor's Chair. 1909.

Fox, William Johnson (1786–1864: The True Sun). Garnett, Richard. The Life of W. J. Fox. 1909.

Francis, John (1811–1882). Francis, John Collins. John Francis, Publisher of the Athenaeum: a Literary Chronicle of Half a Century, with an Introductory Note by H. R. Fox Bourne. 2 vols. 1888.

Frost, Thomas (1821–1908).
Forty years' Recollections: Literary and Political. 1880.
Reminiscences of a Country Journalist. 1886.

Furniss, Harry (1854–1925: Punch).
Confessions of a Caricaturist. 1901.

Gallenga, Antonio (The Times).
Episodes of my Second Life. 2 vols. 1884.

Garrett, Edmund (1865–1907: The Pall Mall Gazette; Westminster Gazette).
Cook, Sir E. T. Edmund Garrett: a Memoir. 1909.

Giffard, Stanley Lees (1788–1858: The Standard).
[Memoir in The Standard, 9 Nov. 1858.]

Gifford, William (1756–1826).
Clark, B. R. William Gifford, Tory Satirist. New York, 1930.

Greenwood, Frederick (1830–1909: The Pall Mall Gazette).
[Memoir in Blackwood's Mag. Jan. 1910.]

Hannay, James (1827–1873: The Edinburgh Courant).
Reminiscences of a Provincial Editor. Temple Bar, May 1868 (see also April 1873).

Hardman, Sir William (1828–1890: The Morning Post).
[Memoir in] Sell's World's Press. 1891.

Harris, Frank (c. 1855–1931: The Evening News).
'Kingsmill, Hugh' [i.e. H. K. Lunn]. Frank Harris. [1932.]

Harvey, D. W. (1786–1863: The Sunday Times; The True Sun).
Redding, Cyrus. [Memoir in] Newspaper Press, 1 Sept. 1869.

Harwood, Philip (1809–1887: The Saturday Review).
[Memoir in Saturday Rev. 17 Dec. 1887.]

Haynie, Henry.
The Captains and the Kings. Intimate Reminiscences of Notabilities. 1905.

Hayward, Abraham (1801–1884).
A Selection from the Correspondence of Abraham Hayward, Q.C. from 1834 to 1884, with an Account of his Early Life. 2 vols. 1886.

Hazlitt, William (1778–1830).
Howe, P. P. The Life of William Hazlitt. 1922.

Healy, Christopher.
The Confessions of a Journalist. 1904.

Hedderwick, James (1814–1897: The Glasgow Citizen).
Backward Glances. Edinburgh, 1891.

Hetherington, Henry (1792–1849: The Poor Man's Guardian).
Holyoake, G. J. The Life of Henry Hetherington. 1849.

Hewlett, Henry G.
Autobiography, Memoirs and Letters. Ed. H. F. Chorley, 2 vols. 1873.

Hibbert, H. G.
Fifty Years of a Londoner's Life. 1916.

Higgins, Matthew James (1810–1868).
'Jacob Omnium.' Essays on Social Subjects, with a Memoir by Sir W. Sterling Maxwell. 1875.

Hodder, George (d. 1870: The Morning Post).
Memoirs of my Time. 1870.

Holland, John (1794–1872: The Sheffield Mercury).
Hudson, W. The Life of John Holland. 1874.

Hollingshead, John (1827–1904: The Weekly Mail).
My Lifetime. 2 vols. 1895.

Holyoake, George Jacob (1817–1906).
Sixty Years of an Agitator's Life. 1892.
Goss, C. W. F. A Descriptive Bibliography of the Writings of G. J. Holyoake. 1908.
McCabe, Joseph. The Life and Letters of G. J. Holyoake. London, 2 vols. 1908.

Hone, William (1780–1842: The Reformist's Register; The Patriot).
Hackwood, F. W. William Hone: his Life and Times. 1912.

Hook, Theodore (1788–1841: John Bull).
Barham, R. H. The Life and Remains of Theodore Hook. 2 vols. 1849.

Hunt, J. H. Leigh (1784–1859: The Examiner; The Liberal).
Autobiography. 3 vols. 1850; 1860 (ed. by his eldest son); ed. Roger Ingpen, 1903.
Blunden, Edmund. Leigh Hunt, a Biography. 1930.
Brewer, Luther. My Leigh Hunt Library. Cedar Rapids, 1932 (priv. ptd).
Landré, Louis. Leigh Hunt. 2 vols. Paris, 1936.

Hunt, William (The Eastern Morning News).
Then and Now; or Fifty Years of Newspaper Work. Hull, 1887.

Hutcheon, William (The Morning Post).
Gentlemen of the Press. 1933.

Hutton, Richard Holt (1826–1897: The Spectator).
Hogben, John. R. H. Hutton: a Monograph. Edinburgh, 1899.

Jerdan, William (1782–1869: The Sun).
Autobiography. 4 vols. 1852–3.
Men I have known. 1866.

Jerrold, Douglas (1803–1857).
Jerrold, William Blanchard. The Life of Douglas Jerrold. 1859.
Jerrold, Walter C. Douglas Jerrold and 'Punch.' 1910.
—— Douglas Jerrold; Dramatist and Wit. 2 vols. [1914].

Jeyes, Samuel Henry (1857–1911: The Standard).
  Low, Sir Sidney. S. H. Jeyes; a Sketch of his Personality and Work. 1915.
Jones, Kennedy (1865–1921: The Evening News).
  Fleet Street and Downing Street. [1920.]
Keene, Charles (1823–1891: Punch).
  Layard, G. S. The Life and Letters of Charles Keene. 1892.
Knight, Charles (1791–1873: The Guardian).
  Passages of a Working Life during Half a Century: with a Prelude of Early Reminiscences. 3 vols. 1864–5.
Labouchere, Henry (1831–1912: Truth).
  Thorold, Algar Labouchere. The Life of Henry Labouchere. 1913.
  Pearson, Hesketh. Labby. 1936.
Leech, John (1817–1864: Punch).
  Frith, W. P. John Leech's Life and Work. 2 vols. 1891.
  Kitton, F. G. John Leech. 1883; 1884 (rev.).
Lennox, John (1794–1853: The Greenock Newsclout).
  Stewart, William. John Lennox and The Greenock Newsclout. Glasgow, 1918.
Levy, Joseph Moses (1812–1888: The Daily Telegraph). [Memoir in Daily Telegraph. 13 Oct. 1888.]
Linton, E. Lynn (1822–1898).
  Layard, G. S. Mrs Lynn Linton: her Life, Letters and Opinions. 1901.
Linton, William James (1812–1898).
  Memories. 1895.
Lowe, Robert (Viscount Sherbrooke) (1811–1892: The Times).
  Martin, A. P. Life of Robert Lowe. 2 vols. 1893.
Lucas, Frederic (1812–1855: The Tablet).
  Lucas, Edward. The Life of Frederic Lucas. 2 vols. 1886.
Lucy, Sir Henry William (1845–1924: The Daily News; The Observer; Punch; etc.).
  Sixty Years in the Wilderness. 1909.
  Sixty Years in the Wilderness. A Second Series. 1912.
  Nearing Jordan; being the Third and Last Volume of Sixty Years. 1916.
  The Diary of a Journalist: Later Entries. 1922.
McCarthy, Justin (1830–1912).
  An Irishman's Story. 1904.
McCulloch, J. R. (1789–1864: The Scotsman).
  [Biographical notice by Reid prefixed to McCulloch's Dictionary of Commerce, 1869.]
Macdonell, James (1842–1879).
  Nicoll, Sir William Robertson. James Macdonnell; Journalist. 1890.
Mackay, Charles (1814–1889: The Morning Chronicle).

Forty Years' Recollections of Life, Literature and Public Affairs from 1830 to 1870. 2 vols. 1877.
Through the Long Day; or Memorials of a Literary Life during Half a Century. 2 vols. 1887.
Mackay, William.
  Bohemian Days in Fleet Street. By a Journalist. 1913.
Maginn, William (1793–1842: The Standard).
  Kenealy, Edward. William Maginn. Dublin University Mag. Jan. 1844.
Martineau, Harriet (1802–1876: The Daily News).
  Harriet Martineau's Autobiography, with Memorials by Maria Weston Chapman. 3 vols. 1877.
  Miller, Mrs Fenwick. Harriet Martineau. 1884.
Maurice, Frederick Denison (1805–1872: The Athenaeum).
  Maurice, F. The Life of F. D. Maurice by his Son. 1884.
Mayo, Isabella Fyvie.
  Recollections. 1910.
Miall, Edward (1809–1881: The Nonconformist).
  Miall, Arthur. The Life of Edward Miall. 1881.
Miller, Hugh (1802–1856: The Witness).
  Bayne, Peter. The Life and Letters of Hugh Miller. 2 vols. 1871.
Montague, C. E. (1867–1928: The Manchester Guardian).
  Elton, Oliver. C. E. Montague; a Memoir. 1929.
Montgomery, James (1771–1854: The Sheffield Iris).
  Holland, John and Everett, James. The Life of James Montgomery. 7 vols. 1854–6.
Moore, F. F. (b. 1855).
  A Journalist's Note Book. 1894.
Morley, John (Viscount Morley) (1838–1923: The Pall Mall Gazette).
  My Recollections. 2 vols. 1917.
  Hirst, F. W. The Early Life and Letters of Lord Morley. 2 vols. 1927.
Morris, W. O'Connor (The Times).
  Memories and Thoughts of a Life. 1895.
Murray, David Christie (1847–1907).
  Recollections. 1908.
Murray, Henry.
  A Stepson of Fortune. The Memoirs, Confessions and Opinions of Henry Murray. 1909.
Murray, John (1778–1843: The Representative).
  Smiles, Samuel. The Life and Correspondence of the late John Murray. 2 vols. 1891.

Newnes, Sir George (1851–1910: Tit Bits; etc.).

Friederichs, Hulda. The Life of Sir George Newnes, Bart. 1911.

Northcliffe, Viscount [Alfred C. W. Harmsworth] (1865–1922: The Daily Mail; etc.).

Pemberton, Sir Max. Lord Northcliffe: a Memoir. 1922.

Fyffe, H. Hamilton. Northcliffe: an Intimate Biography. 1930.

O'Connor, T. P. (1848–1929: The Sun; T.P.'s Weekly).

Memoirs of an Old Parliamentarian. 2 vols. 1929.

O'Malley, William (b. 1853: The Star).

Glancing Backward. [1923.]

O'Shea, J. A. (1839–1905: The Standard).

Leaves from the Life of a Special Correspondent. 2 vols. 1885.

Owen, Robert (1771–1858: The New Moral World).

Podmore, F. The Life of Robert Owen. 1906; 2 vols. 1923.

A Bibliography of Robert Owen. Aberystwyth, 1925 (2nd edn).

Paterson, James (1805–1876).

Autobiographical Reminiscences. Glasgow, 1871.

Patmore, Coventry (1823–1896: The Court Journal).

Memoirs and Correspondence. Ed. Basil Champneys, 1900.

Payn, James (1830–1898).

Some Literary Recollections. 1884.

Pearson, Sir C. Arthur (1866–1921: The Daily Express; Pearson's Weekly, etc.).

Dark, Sidney. The Life of Sir Arthur Pearson. 1922.

Prior, Melton (1845–1910: The Illustrated London News).

Campaigns of a War Correspondent. Ed. S. L. Bensusan, 1912.

Ransome, Arthur.

Bohemia in London. 1907.

Redding, Cyrus (1785–1870).

Fifty Years' Recollections. 3 vols. 1858.

Yesterday and To-day; being a Sequel to Fifty Years' Recollections. 3 vols. 1863.

Reeve, Henry (1813–1895).

Laughton, J. K. Memoirs of the Life and Correspondence of Henry Reeve. 2 vols. 1898.

The Letters of Henry Reeve and Charles Greville. Ed. A. H. Johnson, 1924.

Reid, Sir Wemyss (1842–1905: The Speaker).

Memoirs of Sir Wemyss Reid. Ed. S. J. Reid, 1905.

Reynolds, G. W. M. (1814–1879: Reynolds' News).

[Memoir in] The Bookseller, 8 July, 1879.

Richardson, J. Hall.

From the City to Fleet Street. 1927.

Rintoul, Robert Stephen (1787–1858: The Dundee Advertiser; The Spectator).

[Memoir in the Dundee Advertiser, 27 April 1858, and in The Spectator, 1 May 1858.]

Robinson, Henry Crabb (1775–1867).

The Diary, Reminiscences and Correspondence of Henry Crabb Robinson. Ed. Thomas Sadler, 3 vols. 1869.

Robinson, Sir John Richard (1828–1903: The Daily News).

Thomas, Frederick Moy. Fifty Years of Fleet Street, being the Life and Recollections of Sir J. R. Robinson. 1904.

Roche, Eugenius (1786–1829: The Courier, etc.).

London in a Thousand Years. 1830.

Runciman, James (1852–1891).

Sidelights; with a Memoir by Grant Allen. 1893.

Russel, Alexander (1814–1876: The Scotsman).

Alexander Russel. Edinburgh, 1876 (priv. ptd).

Graham, H. G. Literary and Historical Essays. 1908.

Russell, Sir Edward (1834–1920: The Liverpool Daily Post).

That Reminds Me. 1899.

Russell, Sir William Howard (1820–1907: The Times).

The Great War with Russia: a Personal Retrospect. 1895.

Atkins, John Black. The Life of Sir William Howard Russell. 2 vols. 1911.

Sala, George Augustus (1828–1896).

Things I have Seen and People I have Known. 2 vols. 1895 (2nd edn).

The Life and Adventures of George Augustus Sala, written by Himself. 2 vols. 1895.

Scott, C. P. (1846–1932: The Manchester Guardian).

Hammond, J. L. C. P. Scott. 1934.

Scott, Clement (1841–1904).

The Wheel of Life: a Few Memories and Recollections. 1898.

Scott, Constance Margaret.

Old Days in Bohemian London. 1919.

Shand, A. I. (The Times).

Days of the Past. 1905.

Shorter, Clement K. (1857–1929: The Sphere).

C. K. S. An Autobiography. Ed. J. M. Bulloch, 1927 (priv. ptd).

Simpson, William (1823–1899: The Illustrated London News).

Autobiography. Ed. G. Eyre Todd, 1903.

Sinclair, Alexander (The Glasgow Herald).

Fifty Years of Newspaper Life, 1845–1895. Glasgow, [c. 1897] (priv. ptd).

Smith, Charles Manby.
The Working Man's Way in the World, being the Autobiography of a Journeyman Printer. 1854.

Smith, Ernest.
Fields of Adventure. 1923.

Smith, George (1824–1901: The Pall Mall Gazette).
Lee, Sir Sidney. Memoir of George Smith. [Prefixed to the first Supplement to DNB. 1901.]

Smith, James Elimalet (1801–1857: The Shepherd).
Smith, W. A. 'Shepherd' Smith, the Universalist. 1892.

Smith, Wareham (b. 1874).
Spilt Ink. 1928.

Spears, Robert (1825–1899: The Stockton Gazette; Christian Life).
Memorials of Robert Spears. Belfast, 1903.

Spender, J. A. (b. 1862: The Westminster Gazette).
Life, Journalism, and Politics. 2 vols. 1927.

Stark, Malcolm (The Glasgow Herald).
The Pulse of the World. 1915.

Stead, William Thomas (1849–1912: The Pall Mall Gazette).
Stead, Estelle W. My Father. 1913.
Whyte, Frederick. The Life of W. T. Stead. 2 vols. 1927.

Steed, Henry Wickham (b. 1871: The Times).
Through Thirty Years, 1892–1922. 2 vols. 1924.

Steevens, George Warrington (1869–1900).
Things Seen; with a Memoir by W. E. Henley. 1900.
Works. Memorial Edition. Ed. G. S. Street, and V. Blackburn, 7 vols. 1900–2.

Sterling, Edward (1773–1847: The Times).
Carlyle, Thomas. The Life of John Sterling. 1851.

Stillman, W. J. (1828–1901: The Times).
The Autobiography of a Journalist. 2 vols. 1901.

Strachey, John St Loe (1860–1927: The Spectator).
The Adventure of Living. 1922.

Strauss, G. L. M. (1807–1887: The Grocer).
Reminiscences of an old Bohemian. 2 vols. 1882.

Stuart, Daniel (1766–1846: The Morning Post).
[Reply to statements in Gillman's Life of Coleridge, GM. May, June, Aug. 1838.]

Taylor, John (1757–1832: The Morning Post; The Sun).
Records of my Life. 2 vols. 1832.

Taylor, John Edward (1791–1844: The Manchester Guardian).
[Memoir in Manchester Guardian, 10 Jan. 1844.]

Thackeray, W. M. (1811–1863: The Constitutional, etc.).
Gulliver, H. S. Thackeray's Literary Apprenticeship. Valdosta (Georgia), 1934.

Thomas, Sir William Beach (b. 1868).
A Traveller in News. 1925.

Thomas, William Luson (1830–1900: The Graphic).
[Memoir in The Graphic, 20 Oct. 1900.]

Tinsley, William (1831–1902).
Random Recollections of an Old Publisher. 2 vols. 1900.

Townsend, Meredith White (1831–1911: The Spectator).
Asia and Europe. 1901.

Troup, George (1811–1879: North British Daily Mail).
Troup, G. E. The Life of George Troup, Journalist. Edinburgh, 1881.

Tweedie, Mrs Alec.
Thirteen Years of a Busy Woman's Life. 1912.

Urquhart, David (1805–1877: The Free Press).
Robinson, G. L. The Life of David Urquhart. Oxford, 1932.

Venables, George Stovin (1810–1888: The Saturday Rev.).
[Memoir in Saturday Rev. 13 Oct. 1888.]

Villiers, Frederick (1852–1922).
Pictures of Many Wars. 1902.

Vizetelly, Henry (1820–1894: The Illustrated Times).
Glances Back through 70 Years. 2 vols. 1893.

Wakley, Thomas (1795–1862: The Lancet).
Sprigge, Sir Squire. The Life and Times of Thomas Wakley. 1897.

Watson, Aaron (1850–1926: The Echo).
A Newspaper Man's Memoirs. [1925.]

Watson, James (1799–1874).
Linton, W. J. James Watson; a Memoir. 1880 (priv. ptd).

Watts, Alaric (1797–1864: The United Service Gazette).
Watts, A. A. The Life of Alaric Watts, by his Son. 2 vols. 1884.

Whiteing, Richard (1840–1928).
My Harvest. 1915.

Williams, F. C.
Journalistic Jumbles. [1880?]

Yates, Edmund (1831–1894: The World).
Recollections and Experiences. 2 vols. 1884.

Yorke, Henry Redhead (1772–1813: H. R. Yorke's Political Review).
Sykes, J. A. C. France in 1802. 1906.

(2) THE GENERAL HISTORY OF THE PRESS

[Besides the works cited below several contemporary surveys occurred as articles in the monthly and quarterly reviews and magazines throughout the century. Some of these are listed below, and more are cited by Cannon, but these references are by no means exhaustive.]

Peet, Hubert W. A Bibliography of Journalism. 1915. [Originally issued as part of the introductory matter to Sell's World's Press Guide, 1915.]

Cannon, C. L. Journalism: A Bibliography. New York Public Library. New York, 1924.

Bömer, Karl. Internationale Bibliographie des Zeitungswesens. Sammlung bibliothekswissenschaftlicher Arbeiten, pt 43, Leipzig, 1932.

Savage, James. An Account of the London Daily Papers, and of the Manner in which they are conducted. 1811.

Abuses of the Press. Edinburgh Rev. Oct. 1813.

Hankin, Edward. Letter to the Rt. Hon. the Earl of Liverpool on the Licentiousness of the Press. 1814.

Holt, F. L. The Law of Libel. 1816 (2nd edn).

[Poynder, John.] Observations on Sunday Newspapers; tending to show the Impiety of such a Violation of the Sabbath, the Religious and Political Evils Consequent upon the Practice, and the Necessity which exists for its Suppression. By a Layman. 1820.

[House of Commons.] Return of the Names of Individuals sentenced for Political Libel (King's Bench and Scotland) 1808–21. Commons Journals, vol. lxxvi, 1821, pp. 1208, 1209.

[House of Commons: Accounts and Papers.] Return of Persons prosecuted for Libels, Blasphemy and Sedition. (379). xxi. 399. 1821. [Ditto, 1823.] (562). xv. 239. 1823.

[House of Commons.] Return of Details concerning nearly all Prosecutions for Libel (Great Britain without Ireland) 1813–22. Commons Journals, vol. lxxviii, 1823, pp. 1082 ff.

[Salgues, Jacques B.] Les Mille et une Calomnies ou Extraits des Correspondances privées insérés dans les journaux anglais et allemands pendant le ministère de M. le Duc Decazes. 2 vols. Paris, 1822.

[Hazlitt, William.] The Periodical Press. Edinburgh Rev. May 1823. [Rptd in Complete Works of Hazlitt, ed. P. P. Howe, vol. xvi, 1933.]

The Periodical Press of Great Britain and Ireland. 1824.

Newspapers. Westminster Rev. July 1824.

[Westmacott, Charles Malloy.] The Spirit of the Public Journals, 1823–25. 3 vols. 1824–6.

—— The Stamp Duties. Serious Considerations on the proposed Alteration of the Stamp Duty on Newspapers. 1836.

[Mudie, Robert.] Babylon the Great. 2 vols. 1825.

[Merle, Gibbons.] [On Newspapers.] Westminster Rev. Jan., April 1829.

[House of Commons: Accounts and Papers.] Return of Prosecutions for Libels or Misdemeanours in the Reigns of Geo. 3 and Geo. 4, against Members of the Government, or persons acting in Official Capacity, conducted in the Department of the Solicitor to the Treasury. (608). xxx. 211. 1830.

The Influence of the Newspapers. Fraser's Mag. Sept., Oct. 1831.

D., R. K. Letter to Lord Viscount Althorp, on the Proposed Reduction in the Newspaper Stamp and Advertisement Duties. 1831.

[House of Commons: Accounts and Papers.] Return of Persons in Confinement for Nonpayment of Penalties; Prosecutions connected with the Paper Duties; and Drawbacks allowed on the Exportation of Paper. (346). xv. 539. 1831.

Lamb, Charles. Newspapers Thirty-five Years ago. Englishman's Mag. Oct. 1831. [Rptd in Last Essays of Elia, 1833.]

[House of Commons: Accounts and Papers.] Number of Persons committed for selling Unstamped Publications since Dec. 10, 1831. (40). xxxiv. 103. and (711). xxxiv. 107. 1832.

The Companion to the Newspaper. No. 1, March 1833–1847. [Monthly paper pbd by Charles Knight. It gives the number of duty stamps issued to each paper.]

[House of Commons: Accounts and Papers.] Return of Prosecutions for Libel since the Accession of His present Majesty William IV, either by ex officio Informations or Indictment, conducted in the Department of the Solicitor to the Treasury. (202). xlviii. 267. 1834.

[House of Commons: Accounts and Papers.] Return of the Names of Individuals prosecuted for Political Libel, etc. from March 17, 1821; Convictions in Great Britain, 1821–1831, for Offences of Blasphemy and Sedition; Number of Informations filed by the Attorney-General against Persons accused of Blasphemy or Sedition, 1821–1834. (410). xlviii. 269. 1834.

The Influence of the Press. Blackwood's Mag. Sept. 1834.

The Influence of the Press. Westminster Rev. Oct. 1834.

Roebuck, J. A. The Stamped Press of London and its Morality. [1835.]

Fox, W. J. The Morality of the Press. 1835.

Advertising in Scotland. Tait's Edinburgh Mag. March 1836.

The Morning and Evening Papers. Fraser's Mag. May 1836.

Crawfurd, John. The Newspaper Stamp, and the Newspaper Postage, compared. 1836.

[Grant, James.] The Great Metropolis. 2 vols. 1837.

[House of Commons: Accounts and Papers.] Effect upon the Revenue by Reduction of Stamp Duty on Newspapers, and of Legal Proceedings relating to Stamp Duty on Newspapers, and Sale of Unstamped Papers. (291). xxxix. 303. 1837.

The Newspaper Press of Scotland. Fraser's Mag. May, July, Aug. 1838.

The Religious Periodical Press. Fraser's Mag. Sept. 1838.

Newspapers and other Publications found in the Coffee, Public, and Eating Houses in Westminster. Journ. Statistical Soc. Dec. 1838.

The Fourth Estate: or the Moral Influence of the Press. 1839.

The Spirit of the Metropolitan Conservative Press: being a Selection from the London Conservative Journals during the Year 1839. 1840.

Simmonds, P. L. Statistics of Newspapers in Various Countries. Journ. Statistical Soc. July 1841.

[House of Commons: Accounts and Papers.] Number of Newspapers to which Stamps were issued, and the Number issued to Newspapers, 1836 to 1842; Number of Advertisements inserted in the London Papers, the English Provincial Newspapers, the Irish Papers, etc. 1836–1842; Amount of Advertisement Duty received in England, etc. Total for each year; Rate of Duty. (340). xxvi. 613. 1842.

Knight, Charles. London Newspapers. [In his London, 1843.]

—— The Old Printer and the Modern Press. 1854.

[Evans, David Morier.] City Men and City Manners. 1845; 1852.

The Power of the Press: is it rightly employed? Facts, Inquiries, and Suggestions addressed to Members of Christian Churches. 1847.

The Provincial Press of the United Kingdom. [In Reynolds' Miscellany, 1847.]

Tilsley, Hugh. Treatise on the Stamp Laws in Great Britain and Ireland. 1849 (2nd edn).

Hunt, F. K. The Fourth Estate: Contributions towards a History of Newspapers, and of the Liberty of the Press. 2 vols. 1850.

Munsell, Joel. The British Press. [In his Typographical Miscellany, Albany, 1850, pp. 183–97.]

[House of Commons: Accounts and Papers.] Estimate of the Annual Expense of collecting the Stamp Duty on Newspapers; stating the Number and Wages of Persons employed at Somerset House, and in Edinburgh and Manchester, in stamping the Paper; the Annual Cost of Machinery, and the Expense of Clerks, including those who receive the Money for Stamps. (211). xxxiii. 571. 1850.

[House of Commons.] Report from the Select Committee on Newspaper Stamps. (558). xvii. 1. 1851.

Barnes, Edward. Newspapers and the Stamp Question. British Quarterly Rev. Feb. 1852. [See also Edinburgh Rev. Oct. 1853.]

Smith, A. Press Orders: being the Opinions of the Leading Journals on the Abolition of the Newspaper Privileges. 1853.

[Schlesinger, Max.] Saunterings in London. 1853.

Urquhart, David. Public Opinion and its Organs. 1855.

[Reeve, Henry.] English Journalism. Edinburgh Rev. Oct. 1855.

The London Daily Press. Westminster and Foreign Quarterly Rev. Oct. 1855.

Cockburn, Henry. Memorials of his Time. Edinburgh, 1856.

Clarigny, Cucheval. Histoire de la Presse en Angleterre et aux États Unis. Paris, 1857.

[Murray, Eustace Clare Grenville.] The Press and the Public Service. By a Distinguished Writer. 1857.

[House of Commons: Accounts and Papers.] Return of Correspondence on the Subject of the Registration of Newspapers, and Securities on the Publication of Newspapers and Pamphlets. xxxiv. 199. 1857–8.

Andrews, A. The History of British Journalism. 2 vols. 1859.

Macintosh, Charles A. Popular Outlines of the Press. 1859.

Amphlett, J. The Newspaper Press in Part of the Last Century and up to 1860. Recollections. 1860.

The Newspaper Press of the Present Day. 1860.

Grattan, C. J. The Gallery, a Sketch of the History of Parliamentary Reporting and Reporters. 1860.

Fontane, T. Aus England. Studien und Briefe über Londoner Theater, Kunst, und Presse. Stuttgart, 1860.

Editors and Newspaper Writers of the Last Generation. By an Old Apprentice of the Law. Fraser's Mag. Feb., May, July 1862.

The British Newspaper: the Penny Theory and its Solution. Dublin University Mag. Mar. 1863.

Madden, Richard Robert. The History of the Irish Periodical Literature, from the End of the XVIIth to the Middle of the XIXth Century. 2 vols. 1867.

Bertrand, Edmond. Le Régime régal de la Presse en Angleterre. Paris, 1868.

Reid, Sir Hugh Gilzean. The Press. [In J. Samuelson, The Civilisation of our Day, 1868.]

Holtzendorff, F. von. Englands Presse. Samm-lung-Wissenschaftliche Vorträge. Berlin, 1870.

Grant, J. The Newspaper Press: its Origin, Progress and Present History. 3 vols. 1871.

[Marshall, T. W.] Protestant Journalism. By the Author of 'My Clerical Friends.' 1874.

Politics and the Press. Fraser's Mag. July 1875.

Routledge, James. Chapters in the History of Popular Progress, chiefly in relation to the Freedom of the Press and Trial by Jury, 1660–1820, with an Application to Later Years. 1876.

Webber, V. A. The English Newspaper Press and its Influences. Ryde, 1876.

[House of Commons.] Report from the Select Committee on the Law of Libel. 1879.

Paterson, James. The Liberty of the Press, Speech and Public Worship. 1880.

English Journalism. Nation (New York), 22, 29 July, 12, 26 Aug., 16, 30 Sept., 14, 28 Oct. 1880.

Hunt, William. Hull Newspapers. Hull, 1880.

'Oldcastle, John' [Wilfred Meynell]. Journals and Journalism. 1880.

The Religious Press. Dublin Rev. July 1881.

Pebody, Charles. English Journalism and the Men who have made it. 1882.

Hatton, Joseph. Journalistic London. 1882.

R., G. The Penny Newspaper: the Story of the Cheap Press. [1883.]

Croker, John Wilson. The Croker Papers. 1809–1830. Ed. L. J. Jennings, 3 vols. 1884.

Elliott, G. The Newspaper Libel and Registration Act, 1881. 1884.

Bowles, T. Gibson. Newspapers. Fortnightly Rev. July 1884.

Whorlow, H. The Provincial Newspaper Society. A Jubilee Retrospect. 1886.

Bourne, H. R. Fox. English Newspapers: Chapters in the History of Journalism. 2 vols. 1887.

Morley, J. Cooper. The Newspaper Press and Periodical Literature of Liverpool. Liverpool, 1887.

Powell, A. The Law specially affecting Printers, Publishers and Newspaper Proprietors. [1887.]

Wightman, H. A List of the Newspapers in Lancashire, Yorkshire and Cheshire. Liverpool, 1887.

B., H. A. About Newspapers: chiefly English and Scottish. With an Appendix containing an Account of the Periodical Publications issued in connection with the Anglican Communion in Great Britain and Ireland. Edinburgh, 1888.

Fraser, Hugh. The Law of Libel in its relation to the Press. 1889.

Kelly, R. S. The Law of Newspaper Libel. 1889.

Edwards, F. A. The Early Newspaper Press of Hampshire. Southampton, 1889.

M'Bain, J. M. Bibliography of Arbroath Periodical Literature and Political Broadsides. Arbroath, 1889.

Greenwood, Frederick. The Newspaper Press. Nineteenth Century, May 1890.

Baker, Alfred. The Newspaper World: Essays on Press History and Work, Past and Present. 1890.

Quail, Jesse. Our Journals and Journalists. Hull, 1890.

Fisher, J. R. and Strahan, J. A. The Law of the Press: a Digest of the Law affecting Newspapers in England, India and the Colonies. 1891.

Norrie, William. Edinburgh Newspapers, Past and Present. Earlestown, 1891.

Massingham, H. W. The London Daily Press. 1892.

Archer, Thomas. The Highway of Letters and its Echoes of Famous Footsteps. 1893.

Rose, John Holland. The Unstamped Press, 1815–1836. EHR. Oct. 1897.

Smith, Charlotte F. The Press of Essex, 1837–1897. Essex Rev. July 1897.

Wellsman, W. The Local Press of London. 1898.

Taylor, Frank. The Newspaper Press as a Power both in the Expression and Formation of Public Opinion. Oxford, 1898.

Stead, W. T. A Journalist on Journalism. [1899.]

Halewyck, Michel. Le Régime régal de la Presse en Angleterre. Louvain, 1899.

Collett, C. D. History of the Taxes on Knowledge; their Origin and Repeal, with an Introduction by G. J. Holyoake. 2 vols. 1899; 1933 (abridged).

Walpole, G. Some Old Parliamentary Reporters. 1899.

Duckworth, L. A Complete Summary of the Law relating to the English Newspaper Press. 1899.

'Delta.' A Generation of Scottish Literature and Journalism. Bookman, May, June, Aug. and Sept. 1900.

The Progress of British Newspapers in the XIXth Century. [1901.] [Supplement to Sell's World's Press Guide, 1901.]

Patterson, Alexander. Yorkshire Journalism, Past and Present. Barnsley, 1901.

Millar, J. H. A Literary History of Scotland. 1903.

Noble, J. A Bibliography of Inverness Newspapers and Periodicals. Edited with notes by J. Whyte, with an Appendix by W. Mackay. Stirling, 1903.

Leach, H. Fleet Street from within. Bristol, 1905.

Graham, M. The Early Glasgow Press. Glasgow, 1906.

Lorensz, Theodor. Die englische Presse. Halle, 1907.

Couper, W. J. The Edinburgh Periodical Press. 2 vols. Stirling, 1908.

Adams, Ephraim D. Great Britain and the American Civil War. 2 vols. 1908.

Francis, John Collins. Notes by the Way. 1909.

Borsa, Mario. Il Giornalismo Inglese. Milan, 1910.

Escott, T. H. S. Masters of English Journalism. 1911.

Dibblee, G. B. The Newspaper. 1912.

Bell, W. G. Fleet Street in Seven Centuries. 1912.

Chancellor, E. B. The Annals of Fleet Street. 1912.

Scott-James, R. A. The Influence of the Press. 1913.

Symon, J. D. The Press and its Story. An Account of the Birth and Development of Journalism up to the Present Day, with the History of all the Leading Newspapers. 1914.

Bullard, F. L. Famous War Correspondents. Boston, 1914.

Mineau, Georgia. Famous War Correspondents. Madison, 1915. [Contains a bibliography.]

Simonis, H. The Street of Ink. 1917.

Slade, J. J. and Richardson, Mrs H. Wiltshire Newspapers—Past and Present. Wiltshire Archaeological and Natural History Mag. (Devizes), Dec. 1917–June 1922.

Birrell, Augustine. Life, Literature and Literary Journalism during the First Half of the Last Century. London Mercury, May 1920.

Campbell, A. A. Belfast Newspapers, Past and Present. Belfast, 1921 (priv. ptd).

Stewart, William. The Glasgow Press in 1840. Glasgow, 1921 (priv. ptd).

Martin, B. K. The Triumph of Lord Palmerston. [1924.]

Jones, Ifano. A History of Printers and Printing in Wales to 1810, and of Successive and Related Printers to 1923. Cardiff, 1925.

Herd, Harold. The Making of Modern Journalism. [1927.]

Wickwar, W. H. The Struggle for the Freedom of the Press. 1819–1832. 1928.

Hammond, J. L. and B. The Age of the Chartists. [1930.]

Jordan, D. and Pratt, E. J. Europe and the American Civil War. 1931.

Fenton, W. A. Cambridge Periodicals, 1750–1931. Cambridge Public Library Record and Book List, March 1931.

Morison, S. The English Newspaper, 1622–1932. Cambridge, 1932.

Stutterheim, Kurt von. Die englische Presse. Berlin, 1933; tr. W. H. Johnston, 1934.

Cavour e l' Inghilterra: Carteggio di V. E. d' Azeglio. 3 pts, Bologna, 1933.

Weill, Georges. Le Journal, Paris, 1934.

Kellett, E. E. The Press, 1830–65. [In Early Victorian England, ed. G. M. Young, Oxford, 1934.]

Pollard, Graham. Serial Fiction. [In New Paths in Book Collecting, ed. John Carter, 1934; also separately 1938.]

Maccoby, Simon. English Radicalism, 1832–52. [1935.]

Sper, F. The Periodical Press of London, Theatrical and Literary, 1800–1830. Boston, 1937.

Lefanu, W. R. British Periodicals of Medicine. Baltimore, 1938.

Steed, H. Wickham. The Press. [1938.]

(3) HISTORIES OF PARTICULAR PAPERS

[Brief summaries of a large number of centenary numbers by J. C. Francis are to be found in N. & Q. Useful notices may also be found in The Newspaper World.]

The Aberdeen Journal and its History; the Men who made it. Aberdeen, 1894.

The Aberdeen Journal: our 150th year. Aberdeen, 1897.

The Aberdeen Journal. Concerning Three Northern Newspapers: their Rise and Progress, 1748–1900. The Aberdeen Daily Journal; The Aberdeen Weekly Journal; The Aberdeen Evening Express. Aberdeen, 1900.

Berrow's Worcester Journal. The Oldest English Newspaper. Worcester, 1890.

The Birmingham Daily Post. Jubilee Number. 4 Dec. 1907.

The Blackburn Times. Jubilee Number. 3 June 1905.

The Bristol Mercury. Lewis Harold, The History of the Bristol Mercury from 1715 to 1886. Bristol, [1887?].

The Bristol Times and Mirror. Wells, C. The History of the Bristol Times and Mirror. 1913.

The Bury Times. Jubilee Number. 8 July 1905.

The Cardiff Times. Jubilee Number. 15 Oct. 1887.

The Christian World. Farningham. M. Some Personal Reminiscences. Christian World, 11 Apr. 1907.

The City Press. Jubilee Number. 13 July 1907.

The Daily Graphic. 21 Years' Progress of the Pioneer Illustrated Daily Newspaper. Supplement to The Daily Graphic, 4 Jan. 1911.

The Daily Mail. Harmsworth, A. C. (Viscount Northcliffe). The Romance of the Daily Mail. 1903.

The Daily Mail. McKenzie, F. A. The Mystery of the Daily Mail, 1896–1921. 1921.

The Daily News. McCarthy, Justin and Robinson, Sir J. R. The Daily News Jubilee. 1896.

The Daily Telegraph. Rhode, Dyke. The Social Relationships of The Daily Telegraph. New Century Rev. Apr. 1898.

The Daily Telegraph. Jubilee Number. 17 Sept. 1905.

The Devon and Exeter Daily Gazette. The Anniversary of the Devon and Exeter Daily Gazette, March 5, 1910, being the Completion of the 138th Year of the Uninterrupted Existence of the Paper, and the 25th Year of its Present Ownership. Exeter, 1910.

The Dublin Gazette. [See under London Gazette.]

The Dundee Advertiser. Millar, A. H. The Dundee Advertiser, 1801–1901. A Centenary Memoir. Dundee, 1901.

The Dundee Courier. Great Provincial Newspapers. I. Caxton Mag. Aug. 1901.

The Echo. The Staff of the Echo. Bookman, July 1898.

The Echo. 30th Birthday. Double Number. 8 Dec. 1898.

The Edinburgh Evening News. Fifty Years. 1873–1923. Edinburgh, 1923.

The Edinburgh Gazette. [See under The London Gazette.]

The Evening Telegraph [Dundee]. Silver Jubilee Number. 13 Mar. 1902.

The Examiner. Blunden, Edmund. Leigh Hunt's Examiner examined, comprising an Account of that celebrated newspaper's contents, 1808–1825. 1928.

The Falkirk Herald. The Jubilee of the Falkirk Herald, 1846–1896. Falkirk, 1896.

The Financial News. Twentieth Anniversary Number. 1904.

The Glasgow Herald. Stewart, William. The Glasgow Herald; the Story of a Great Newspaper from 1783 to 1911. Glasgow, 1911.

The Globe. Atlay, J. B. The Globe Centenary. A Sketch of its History. 1903.

The Gloucester Journal. Chance, H. G. The Bicentenary of the Gloucester Journal, April 9, 1722–April 8, 1922. Gloucester, 1922.

The Hampshire Advertiser [Southampton]. Centenary Number. 28 July 1923.

The Huddersfield Examiner. Our Jubilee. A Brief Sketch of the History of the Examiner. Huddersfield Examiner, 6 Sept. 1901.

The Ipswich Journal. The History of the Ipswich Journal for 150 years. [Ipswich, 1875.]

The Isle of Man Times [Douglas]. The Jubilee of the Isle of Man Times. The Story of its First Half Century. Douglas, 1911.

The Kentish Express and Ashford News [Ashford]. Jubilee. July 14, 1855–July 15, 1905. [Ashford, 1905.]

The Lancaster Guardian. History of the Paper and Reminiscences by 'Old Hands'. [Lancaster, 1897] (priv. ptd).

The Lancet. Centenary Number. 1923.

The Liverpool Courier. Centenary. Liverpool, 1908.

The Liverpool Daily Post. Jubilee Number. 13 June 1905.

The Liverpool Post. The Centenary of the Liverpool Post and Mercury: a Record of the Progress of Liverpool and its Leading Newspaper. Liverpool, 1911.

Lloyd's Weekly News. Diamond Jubilee Number. 30 Nov. 1902.

The London Gazette. [House of Commons: Accounts and Papers.] The Cost of Printing and Publishing the London, Edinburgh and Dublin Gazettes, in each of the Years, 1846, 1847, 1848 and 1849, exclusive of Stamps and Paper, with Balance Sheets for each of the said Years, showing the Profit and Loss. (677). xxxiii. 429. 1850.

The Macclesfield Courier and Herald. Centenary Number. 4 Feb. 1911.

The Manchester Guardian. Mills, W. H. A Century of History. 1921.

The Mark Lane Express. 70th Birthday Number. 31 Mar. 1902.

The Middlesex Chronicle [Hounslow]. Jubilee Number and Supplement. 9 Jan. 1909.

Moonshine. The Staff of Moonshine: Portraits and Facts concerning the Celebrated Weekly Paper. 1900.

The Morning Advertiser. Centenary No. 8, Feb. 1894.

The Morning Post. Francis, J. C. The Morning Post, 1772–1916. N. & Q. Oct. 1916.

The Morning Post. Ferguson, M. T. The Morning Post, 1772–1921. The Triple Jubilee of a Great Newspaper. 1922. [Rptd from National Rev. Jan. 1922.]

The Morning Post. Hindle, W. H. The
Morning Post, 1772–1937. 1937.

The Newcastle Chronicle. Dolman, Frederick.
The Newcastle Chronicle and its Editor,
Joseph Cowen. Young Man, Aug. 1895.

The News of the World. Through Four Reigns.
The Romance of a Great Newspaper. [1928.]

The News of the World. Berrey, R. P. The
Romance of a Great Newspaper. [c. 1933.]

The Norfolk News [Norwich]. Round a Newspaper Office. Norfolk News Co. [Norwich,
1902.]

The Northampton Mercury, 1720–1901. [North-
ampton, 1901.]

The Northampton Mercury. Hadley, W. W.
The Bicentenary Record of the Northampton Mercury. Northampton, 1920.

The North British Advertiser [Edinburgh]. The
Case of Mr John Gray, the Founder of the
North British Advertiser. Edinburgh, 1831.

The Observer. 1791–1921. A Short Record of
130 years. 1921.

The Pall Mall Gazette. Stead, W. T. The Pall
Mall Gazette. Rev. of Reviews, Feb. 1893.

The Pall Mall Gazette. 10,000th Number. 14
April 1897.

The Pall Mall Gazette. Last Number. 27 Oct.
1923.

The Press. A Sketch of the Political History
of the Last Three Years in connexion with
the Press Newspaper, and the Part it has
taken on the Leading Questions of the
Time. 1856.

Punch. Mr Punch: his Origin and Career,
with a Facsimile of his Original Prospectus in
the Handwriting of Mark Lemon. [c. 1870.]

Punch. Spielmann, M. H. The History of
'Punch.' 1895.

Punch. Mr Punch's Pageant, 1841 to 1908:
A Souvenir Catalogue. 1909.

Reynolds's Newspaper. Jubilee Number. 27
May 1900. [See also 1 March 1936.]

The Rochdale Observer. Jubilee Number. 17
Feb. 1906.

The Salisbury and Winchester Journal.
Richardson, Mrs H. 1729–1929. Supplement, 7 June 1929.

The Saturday Review. Grant, James. The
Saturday Review; its Origin and Progress.
1873.

The Scarborough Mercury. Jubilee Number.
21 July 1905.

The Scotsman [Edinburgh]. The Story of the
Scotsman. A Chapter in the Annals of
British Journalism. Edinburgh, 1886 (priv.
ptd).

The Scotsman [Edinburgh]. Centenary Number. 25 Jan. 1917.

The Sheffield Daily Telegraph. Shepherdson,
William. Reminiscences in the Career of a
Newspaper. 1876.

The Sheffield Daily Telegraph. Jubilee. 1855–
1905. Sheffield, 1905.

The Sheffield Independent. Seventy-three
Years of Progress. A History of the
Sheffield Independent. Sheffield, 1892.

The Shields Daily Gazette [South Shields].
Jubilee Number. 24 Feb. 1899.

The Spectator. Thomas, Sir William Beach.
The Story of The Spectator, 1828–1928. 1928.

The Sporting Times. 3000th Number. 19 Mar.
1921.

The Staffordshire Advertiser [Stafford]. A
Centenary History of The Staffordshire
Advertiser. Stafford, 1895.

The Standard. Notes on the History of The
Standard. The People, Jan. 1906.

The Stirling Observer. 90 Years' Progress.
1836–1926. Stirling, 1926.

The Sun. Grant, P. Statement of Facts regarding the Sun Newspaper. [1832.]

The Sunday Times. 100 Years of History. 1920.

The Times. [Stephen, Sir Leslie.] The 'Times'
on the American War: a Historical Study.
1865; rptd New York, 1915.

The Times. The History of The Times. 'The
Thunderer' in the Making, 1785–1841. 1935.

The Times. The History of The Times. The
Tradition Established, 1841–1884. 1939.

Truth. Mr Labouchere and Truth. Bookman,
Sept. 1892.

The Universe. Seventieth Anniversary. 5 Dec.
1930.

The Wakefield Express. Jubilee, 1852–1902.
Souvenir. [Wakefield, 1902.]

The Weekly Dispatch. Special Centenary
Number. 9 June 1901.

The Weekly Sun. [Opinions on, by eminent
men, ed. by T. P. O'Connor.] 1896.

The Western Daily Mercury [Plymouth].
Walling, R. A. J. The Western Daily
Mercury. Cornish Mag. Jan. 1899.

The Western Daily Press [Bristol]. Great
Provincial Newspapers. II. Caxton Mag.
Oct. 1901.

The Western Morning News [Plymouth].
Great Provincial Newspapers. IV. Caxton
Mag. Dec. 1901.

The Yorkshire Herald [York]. Jubilee Number.
2 Jan. 1905.

The Yorkshire Observer [Bradford (formerly
Bradford Observer)]. Seventy-five Years
Retrospect. Yorkshire Observer, 6 Feb.
1909.

(4) LISTS OF NEWSPAPERS

(a) Lists of Files now Extant

British Museum. Catalogue of Printed Books.
Supplement. Newspapers published in
Great Britain and Ireland. 1801–1900.
1905. [Also separately ptd.]

[Muddiman, J. G.] Tercentenary Handlist of English and Welsh Newspapers, Magazines and Reviews. 1620–1920. 1920. [The most complete list available, based on the BM. holdings, but not innocent of serious misprints.]

Crane, R. S. and Kaye, F. B. A Census of British Newspapers and Periodicals. 1620–1800. Chapel Hill, North Carolina, 1927. [Records the files in American libraries, with a supplementary but summary list of those lacking.]

Deutsches Institut für Zeitungskunde. Standortskatalog wichtiger Zeitungsbestände in deutschen Bibliotheken. Leipzig, 1933.

[Stewart, Andrew.] The Evolution of the English Newspaper from its Origins to the Present Day as illustrated by the Catalogue of the Press Club Collection. 1935 (priv. ptd).

Union Catalogue of the Periodical Publications in the University Libraries of the British Isles. Ed. M. G. Roupell, 1937.

(b) Government Returns of the Stamp Duties

[The original returns of the Stamp Duty on Newspapers from about 1749 to 1855 were scheduled for destruction under the Public Record Office Act of 1877. Besides the official returns listed below, they were frequently cited in works on the press (e.g. Charles Knight's Companion to the Newspaper).]

[House of Commons: Accounts and Papers.] Account of all Weekly Newspapers published on Saturdays and Sundays. (445). xvi. 387. and (579). xvi. 391. 1821.

[House of Commons: Accounts and Papers.] Newspaper Returns. An Account of the Number of Stamps for Newspapers, for the year 1801; distinguishing the London from the Provincial Newspapers, and distinguishing the different London newspapers and the Amount of Duty received from each. (272). xxi. 381. 1822; rptd The Inquirer, Aug. 1822, p. 300.

[House of Commons: Accounts and Papers.] Account of Stamps issued for Newspapers, with the Amount of the Duties charged thereon from 1814 to 1824. (375). xxi. 327. 1825.

[House of Commons: Accounts and Papers.] Ireland. Account of the Number of Stamps issued to each Newspaper from 1822 to 1826. (235). xxiii. 383. 1826.

[House of Commons: Accounts and Papers.] Ireland. Stamp Duties on Pamphlets, Newspapers and Advertisements in Ireland. 1797–1826. (99). xvii. 23. 1827.

[House of Commons: Accounts and Papers.] Stamps issued to each of the Newspapers in England, Scotland and Wales (except those published in London) 1825 to 1829. (609). xxv. 347. 1830.

[House of Commons: Accounts and Papers.] Ireland. Stamp Duties on Newspapers and Advertisements in Ireland, 1810 to 1830. (406). xxv. 363. 1830.

[House of Commons: Accounts and Papers.] Stamps issued for the London Newspapers, Duty received, Duty paid for Advertisements, 1820 to 1829. (549). xxv. 349. 1830.

[House of Commons: Accounts and Papers.] Ireland. Stamps issued to each Newspaper in Ireland, 1826–1829. (549). xxv. 349. 1830.

[House of Commons: Accounts and Papers.] Number of Stamps issued for Newspapers and Other Publications, 1821–1831; Number issued for London Newspapers, 1830; Duties on Pamphlets and Advertisements, 1830. (30). xxxiv. 127. 1832.

[House of Commons: Accounts and Papers.] Ireland. Stamps issued to each Newspaper in Ireland. 1830 to 1831. (242). xxxiv. 123. 1832.

[House of Commons: Accounts and Papers.] Stamps issued for the London Newspapers, Duty received, Duty paid for Advertisements for 1831. (290). xxxiv. 119. 1832.

[House of Commons: Accounts and Papers.] Number of Square Feet of Surface of One Copy of each of the Daily Newspapers, 1831; Amount of Stamp Duty actually paid; Rate of Payment for each Hundred Square Feet. (188). xxxiv. 117. 1832.

[House of Commons: Accounts and Papers.] Scotland. Number of Stamps issued to each of the Newspapers in Scotland, 1831: Amount of Advertisement Duty. (465). xxxiv. 121. 1832.

[House of Commons: Accounts and Papers.] Number of Stamps issued by the Stamp Office for London Newspapers specifying each Newspaper by Name, and Number of Stamps issued to Printers or Publishers. 1832–3. (758). xxxii. 609. 1833.

[House of Commons: Accounts and Papers.] Number of Stamps issued to each Provincial Newspaper in England. 1832–1833. (519). xxxii. 613. 1833.

[House of Commons: Accounts and Papers.] Ireland. Number of Stamps issued to each Newspaper in Ireland, 1832–33. (503). xxxii. 623. 1833.

[House of Commons: Accounts and Papers.] Ireland. A Return of the Number of Stamps issued to each Newspaper in Ireland respectively from Jan. 5, 1833 to April 5, 1834; and the Number of Stamps cancelled by each Newspaper respectively for the

Same Period. (412). xlix. 407. [Ditto from April 5 to July 5, 1834.] (510). xlix. 409. 1834.

[House of Commons: Accounts and Papers.] Number of Stamps issued to London Newspapers, 1833–35. (625). xxxvii. 705. 1835.

[House of Commons: Accounts and Papers.] Number of Stamps issued to Newspapers in the United Kingdom, 1835–36; Amount of Advertisement Duty by London Newspapers, 1836. (294). xlv. 345. 1836.

[House of Commons: Accounts and Papers.] Number of Stamps issued monthly to each of the London Newspapers, from January to April, 1837, and of the Advertisement Duty in the Same Period. (232). xxxix. 321. 1837.

[House of Commons: Accounts and Papers.] Number of Stamps issued monthly to each of the Provincial Papers in England and Wales, from Jan. 1 to June 20, 1837; of the Number of Advertisements published in each Newspaper for the Same Period; and the Amount of Duty on Advertisements paid by each Paper for the Same Period. (In 526.) xxxix. 305. 1837. [Ditto from 1836 to 1838.] (307). xxxvi. 413. 1838.

[House of Commons: Accounts and Papers.] Number of Stamps issued by The Stamp Office for all Newspapers in Great Britain and Ireland, from June 30 to Dec. 1, 1837, specifying each Newspaper by Name, and the Number of Stamps issued each Month during that Period to each Newspaper. (73). xxxvi. 393. [Ditto from Dec. 1 to 31, 1837; similar return for each month of the quarter ended March 31, 1838.] (368). xxxvi. 403. 1838.

[House of Commons: Accounts and Papers.] Ireland. Number of Stamps issued to Irish Newspapers in each year since 1824, distinguishing those printed in Dublin; Newspapers existing in Ireland in 1824; Newspapers which have ceased to exist since 1824; Newspapers established since 1824, and which still exist. (In 488). viii. 235. 1838.

[House of Commons: Accounts and Papers.] Number of Stamps issued at 1d. in the United Kingdom, 1838–39, specifying each Newspaper, and the Number of Stamps issued each Month. (213). xxx. 483. [Ditto from April to June 1839.] (449). xxx. 493. 1839.

[House of Commons: Accounts and Papers.] Number of Stamps at 1d. issued to the Several Newspapers, 1838, specifying each Newspaper by Name, and the Number of Stamps issued each Month during that Period to each Newspaper. Similar Returns for Ireland. (15). xxix. 483. 1840.

[House of Commons: Accounts and Papers.] Number of Stamps issued to the Several Newspapers in Great Britain, 1839, specifying each Newspaper by Name, and the Number of Stamps issued each Month during the Period to each Newspaper. (266). xxix. 503. 1840.

[House of Commons: Accounts and Papers.] Number of Stamps issued to each Newspaper in England and Wales, 1839–40, specifying also the Amount of Advertisement Duty paid by each Newspaper in each of the Above Years; Similar Returns for Ireland and Scotland. (294). xxix. 523. 1840.

[House of Commons: Accounts and Papers.] Number of Stamps issued to the Several Newspapers in the United Kingdom April to June 1840, specifying each Newspaper by Name. (525). xxix. 513. 1840.

[House of Commons: Accounts and Papers.] Number of Newspaper Stamps at 1d. and ½d. issued to the several Newspapers in Great Britain, July 1 to Sept. 1, 1840, specifying each Newspaper by Name; Number of Stamps each Month; Similar Returns for Ireland. Similar Returns from Oct. 1 to Dec. 31, 1840. (14). xiii. 461. 1841.

[House of Commons: Accounts and Papers.] Number of Stamps issued to each Newspaper in England and Wales, during each of the Three Years ending Jan. 5, 1841, and Similar Returns for Scotland and Ireland; also Return of Number of Newspaper Stamps issued from Jan. 5 to March 31, 1841. (407). xiii. 481. 1841.

[House of Commons: Accounts and Papers.] Number of Stamps issued to each of the Newspapers in the United Kingdom; Amount of Advertisement Duty paid. (26). ii. 45. 1841 (Sess. 2). (44). xxvi. 561. 1842. (257). xxvi. 587. 1842. (572). xxvi. 601. 1842. (98). xxx. 513. 1843. (174). xxx. 537. 1843. (282). xxx. 559. 1843. (611). xxx. 571. 1843. (55). xxxii. 419. 1844.

[House of Commons: Accounts and Papers.] Return of Papers published in the Metropolis, which are registered as Newspapers, a Portion whereof is published without Stamps. (78). xxxiii. 567. 1850.

[House of Commons: Accounts and Papers.] Return of Names of Newspapers in the United Kingdom to which Halfpenny Stamps were issued; Number issued to each; and Amount of Duty paid, in 1852. lvii. 573. 1853.

[House of Commons: Accounts and Papers.] Number of Newspaper Stamps at 1d. issued to each Newspaper in England, Ireland, Scotland and Wales, in 1851, 1852 and 1853. xxxix. 479. 1854. Ditto in 1854. xxx

497. 1855. Ditto, 1854 to July 1, 1855. xxx.

509. 1855. Ditto, July–Dec. 1855. xxxviii.

511. 1856.

[House of Commons: Accounts and Papers.] Return of Stamps at 1d. issued to each Newspaper published in London, Dublin and Edinburgh. Quarterly, 1851 to 1854. xxxix. 501 and 519. 1854.

[House of Commons: Accounts and Papers.] Return of Registered Newspapers and Publications in the United Kingdom, and of the Number of Stamps issued to each, quarterly, 1855 to 1857. xxxiv. 259. 1858.

(c) Lists in General Directories

The Post Office London Directory, for 1805, by B. Critchett. [1804] (6th edn). [And annually to 1839. This edn first includes the London papers with days of issue; from the 15th edn, for 1814, onwards it contains the Country Papers as well.]

Holden's Triennial Directory for 1805, 1806, 1807. [1805] (4th edn). [Contains a list of London and Country newspapers: this did not appear in the earlier edns, nor is it in the 10th edn for 1817, 1818, 1819, which was the first issued by Underhill after Holden's death.]

Pigot and Co.'s London and Provincial New Commercial Directory for 1822–23. [1822.] [2nd edn for 1823–4; 3rd edn for 1827–8; 6th edn for 1836–7; 7th edn Dec. 1839.]

Robson's London Commercial Directory for 1823. [Also 1839, 1840, 1843 (24th edn), the first edn for 1819 has no list. The lists in the later edns seem to have been supplied by Newton and Co. (see below).]

W. Kelly and Co. The Post Office London Directory for 1840. [1839– .] [Annual; in progress: the issues for the years from 1840 to 1847 have opposite each paper the number of stamps issued to it for the second quarter of the preceding year; for the years 1842–7 they have the amount of advertisement duty paid as well.]

(d) Lists issued by Newspaper Advertisement Agents

[These lists provide fuller information than the General Directories, often giving the political complexion and particular class or area to which appeal is directed. The London Classified Directories (e.g. Robson's and Pigott's) give lists of Agents for Newspapers, and search in the larger libraries under the names there mentioned might reveal a number of lists not specified below.]

Clarke and Lewis. Advertisements Received by Clarke and Lewis, 4 Crown Court, Threadneedle Street, London. [Jan.?] 1836; June 1836; Oct. 1837. [All single folio sheets, ptd in 3 colours.]

Newton and Co.'s General Advertising Country and London Newspaper Office. Warwick Square, Newgate Street. [c. 1840.] [Single folio sheet.]

Reid, J. An Almanac of the British Stamped Press, including all Stamped Newspapers, Literary or Scientific Journals, and Commercial Lists for 1841. [1840.]

Dawson, William, and Sons' London and County Newspaper and Advertising List. [c. 1841]; 1858 (9th edn). [Both single folio sheets, ptd in 3 colours.]

Lewis, Francis D. British and Foreign Newspaper and Advertisement Agent. 3 Castle Court, Cornhill, London. 30 June 1842. [Single folio sheet.]

Hammond's Town and Country Advertising Office, 27 Lombard Street, London. 1st Oct. 1842. [Single folio sheet.]

Mitchell, C. Newspaper Press Directory. 1846; 1847; 1851; 1854; 1856 onwards. [Annual, in progress; this is the fullest of all the directories here listed, especially in the later issues.]

Algar and Street. London, Provincial and Colonial Newspaper Agency Office, 11 Clements Lane, Lombard Street, London. [Jan.? 1855.] [Single folio sheet.]

Street Brothers. Advertising and Newspaper Agency Office. 11 Serle Street, Lincoln's Inn, London. [Jan.? 1855.] [Single folio sheet.]

Jack, T. C. The Scottish Newspaper Directory; and Guide to Advertisers. 2nd Edition, with an Appendix giving the Circulation of Newspapers according to the Government Stamp Returns for 1854. Edinburgh, 1855.

Coggeshall, William Turner. The Newspaper Record, containing a Complete List of Newspapers and Periodicals in the United States and Great Britain. Philadelphia, 1856.

William Thomas's Universal Newspaper and Periodical List. 1863; 1864.

May, Frederick. The London Press Dictionary and Advertiser's Handbook for 1871. [1870.]

Clarke, W. J. Newspaper List for the United Kingdom. 1873.

Eyre's Guide containing a List of all Newspapers and Periodicals. [1873.]

Street's List of Newspapers published in Great Britain and Ireland. [1873.]

May's British and Irish Press Guide and Advertiser's Dictionary and Handbook. 1874. [Annually to 1889; continued as Willing's British and Irish Press Guide, 1890– , annually, in progress.]

White, R. F. and Son. A List of the News-papers published in the United Kingdom, newly arranged and classified. 1878; 1882; 1884; 1887; 1889; 1891; 1895; 1897; 1912.

Deacon, S. and Co. Deacon's Newspaper Handbook and Advertiser's Guide. 1881 (5th edn); 1883; 1885; 1886; 1887; [c. 1890]; 1893; 1894; [1904]. [Gives reduced repro-ductions of many papers.]

Sell, Henry. Dictionary of the World's Press. 1884–1921. [Annual; but none issued in 1911, 1913, 1916–1918, 1920. Originally issued as The Philosophy of Advertising, 1882; then as The Philosophy of Advertising and Newspaper Register, 1883.]

Browne, T. B. Advertising ABC and Ad-vertisement Press Directory. 1887.

—— Advertising in the Provincial News-papers of Great Britain and Ireland. [1891.]

Layton, Charles and Edwin. Handy News-paper List. [1890]–1915. [Annual.]

Street's List of Newspapers published in Great Britain and Ireland. 1890–1917; 1920. [Annual.]

Ross, George and Co. The London Signpost. Shews the Trade Addresses of over 1600 Publishers and Periodicals on Sale at, or since, Michaelmas 1893. [1893.]

Mather and Crowther. Practical Advertising. 1895–1923. [Annual.]

Walker, H. T. and Co. Walker's Press Directory. 1897.

Vickers's Newspaper Gazetteer. An Annual Reference Book of the Press for the United Kingdom, Colonies, etc. 1900–16. [Annual.]

C. THE DAILY PAPERS

(1) LONDON DAILY PAPERS

[The numbers and dates of periodicals given in square brackets are conjectural. Those given without square brackets are based on the holdings recorded by J. G. Muddiman or R. S. Crane and F. B. Kaye (see p. 795 above) or on personal observation. Only the names of the more important editors are given.]

(a) Morning Papers

The Public Ledger. No. 1, 12 Jan. 1760 on-wards. In progress. [Ed. by Alexander Chalmers. From 15 Sept. 1836 to 1 July 1837 it was incorporated in The Con-stitutional (see below). Thereafter con-fined to commercial news.]

The Morning Chronicle. [No. 1, 28 June 1769]–No. 184, 3 Jan. 1770–20 Dec. 1862. [Ed. by James Perry (1789–1819), John Black (1819–43), Andrew Doyle (1843–8), J. D. Cook (1848–54), T. L. Holt, G. H. Francis.]

The Morning Post. No. 1, 2 Nov. 1772–No. 51561, 30 Sept. 1937. [Incorporated in The Daily Telegraph; ed. by Daniel Stuart (1796–1802), F. W. Blagdon, — Byrne, Eugenius Roche (1817–27), C. E. Michele (1833–49), G. H. Francis (?), Peter Borth-wick (1849–52), Algernon Borthwick (1852–72), Sir William Hardman (1872–90), Alexander Leys Moore (1890–4), Algernon Locker (1895–7), J. N. Dunn (1897–1905).]

The Morning Herald. No. 1, 1 Nov. 1780–31 Dec. 1869. [Ed. by Thomas Wright (?), Sidney Taylor, Edward Baldwin and S. L. Giffard (1843–6), Robert Knox (1846–57), Thomas Hamber (1857–?).]

The Times. No. 940, 1 Jan. 1788 onwards. In progress. [Started as The Daily Uni-versal Register, No. 1, 1 Jan. 1785; the original title was continued as a subtitle from 1 Jan. to 17 March 1788. Ed. by William Combe (1797–1808), Henry Crabb Robinson (1808–9), John Walter II, J. H. Stoddart (1814–7), Thomas Barnes (1817–41), J. T. Delane (1841–77), Thomas Chenery (1878–84), G. E. Buckle (1884–1912).]

The Oracle. No. 1, 1 June 1789–24 March 1802. [Continued as] The Daily Advertiser and Oracle. 25 March 1802–8 June 1809. [In 1798 it absorbed The Daily Advertiser, and was continued as The Oracle and Daily Advertiser. Ed. by James Boaden.]

The True Briton. No. 1, 1 Jan. 1793–No. 3437, 31 Dec. 1803. [Incorporated in The Daily Advertiser and Oracle. Ed. by John Heriot (1793–1803).]

The Morning Advertiser. No. 1, 8 Feb. 1794 onwards. In progress. [Ed. by John Scott, James Grant (1848–70), Alfred B. Richards (1870–6), Thomas Hamber (1876–86), Thomas Wright (1886–94), Frank G. Dovey. Organ of the Licensed Victuallers.]

The Porcupine. No. 1, 30 Oct. 1800–31 Dec. 1801. [Incorporated in The True Briton. Ed. by William Cobbett.]

The British Press, or Morning Literary Ad-vertiser. No. 1, 1 Jan. 1803–31 Oct. 1826. [Ed. by George Lane, Robert Heron, J. B. Capes.]

The Advertiser's Daily Magazine. [No. 1, 29 Jan. 1805]–No. 9, 8 Feb. 1805–[?].

The Morning Star. [1805]–No. 58, 25 Jan. 1806–[?].

The Aurora and British Imperial Reporter. No. 1, 19 Jan.–No. 121, 8 June 1807–[?]. [Ed. by William Jerdan.]

The Day. No. 1, 2 Jan. 1809–No. 2057, 20 April 1815–[1817]. [Incorporated in The New Times. Ed. by Eugenius Roche (1809–11), John Scott, — Hogan.]

The New Times. [1817]–1 Jan. 1818–4 Oct. 1828. [Continued as] The Morning Journal. 6 Oct. 1828–13 May 1830. [Started before Easter 1817, and soon absorbed The Day; continued as The Day and New Times, but the first part of this title was dropped before the end of 1817. Ed. by J. H. Stoddart (1817–26), Eugenius Roche (1827–8), Robert Alexander and J. M. Gutch (1828–30).]

The British Statesman. No. 1, 10 Feb.–No. 262, 11 Dec. 1819.

The Representative. No. 1, 25 Jan.–29 July 1826. [Founded by John Murray.]

The Tatler. No. 1, 4 Oct. 1830–13 Feb. 1832. [Ed. by J. H. Leigh Hunt.]

The Daily Politician. No. 1, 25 Jan.–No. 24, 20 Feb. 1836. [Another paper of the same name ran for a few days in Sept. of the same year.]

The Constitutional and Public Ledger. No. 1, 15 Sept. 1836–1 July 1837. [This was really a continuation of The Public Ledger (see above); but it soon reverted to its old style. Ed. by S. L. Blanchard.]

The Morning Gazette. No. 1, 2 Oct.–No. 54, 2 Dec. 1837.

The Statesman and Weekly True Sun. No. 1, 5 Jan. 1840–No. 394, 28 March 1841. [For its predecessor and continuation see below under Weekly Papers, p. 812. Conducted by D. W. Harvey.]

The Iron Times. No. 1, 7 July 1845–No. 264, 11 May 1846. [Ed. by T. L. Holt.]

The Daily News. No. 1, 21 Jan. 1846–31 May 1930. [Amalgamated with The Daily Chronicle, and continued as The News-Chronicle, 2 June 1930 onwards. In progress. Ed. by Charles Dickens (Jan. 1846), John Forster (Feb.–Oct. 1846), E. E. Crowe (Oct. 1846–1851), F. Knight Hunt (1851–4), William Weir (1854–8), Thomas Walker (1858–69), Edward Dicey (1869), F. H. Hill (1870–86), H. W. Lucy (1886), Sir John R. Robinson (1886–95), E.T. Cook (1895–1901).]

The Daily Advertiser. No. 1, 26 May–No. 28, 26 June 1847. [Continued weekly as] The London and Liverpool Advertiser. No. 29, 3 July–18 Dec. 1847.

The London Telegraph. No. 1, 1 Feb.–8 July 1848. [Ed. by Thomas Hodgkin.]

The Daily Telegraph. No. 1, 29 June 1855 onwards. In progress. [First pubd at 2d. but in 1856 was the first daily newspaper to be sold at 1d. Ed. by A. B. Richards (1855), Thornton L. Hunt (1856–72), Sir Edwin Arnold, J. M. Le Sage, E. L. Lawson.]

The Morning News. No. 1, 3 March 1856–No. 924, 29 June 1859. [Ed. by Henry Mayhew.]

The Morning Star. No. 1, 17 March 1856–No. 4251, 13 Oct. 1869. [Ed. by S. Lucas, J. McCarthy, J. Morley.]

The Standard. 29 June 1857–16 March 1916. [Founded as an evening paper in 1827 (see below, p. 801) it was for many years run in conjunction with The Morning Herald; in 1857 it became a morning paper, though an evening edn continued to be pbd. Ed. by Thomas Hamber (1857–70), Sir John Gorst (1870–4), W. H. Mudford (1874–1900), G. B. Curtis (1900–4).]

The Morning Mail. 23 April 1864–21 July 1865. [Continued as] The London General Advertiser, 22 July 1865–1 Dec. 1866.

The Day. No. 1, 19 March–4 May 1867.

The London Daily Reporter. [1869]–No. 376, 2 Jan. 1871–16 June 1871. [Continued as] The London Daily Recorder, 17 June 1871–31 Dec. 1872.

The Financier. No. 1, 1 March 1870–23 May 1924. [Incorporated in The Financial Times: not pbd on Saturdays.]

The Daily Chronicle. No. 3320, 25 Nov. 1872–31 May 1930. [Incorporated in The News-Chronicle. Started weekly in 1855 as The Clerkenwell News and General Advertiser, Nos. 73–1200, 8 Oct. 1856–5 Feb. 1866; continued, for a few issues daily, then bi-weekly as Clerkenwell News and London Times, Nos. 1201–2394, 7 Feb. 1866–Dec. 1869; then continued daily as Clerkenwell News and London Daily Chronicle, Nos. 2395–2779, 11 Dec. 1869–5 March 1871; continued as The London Daily Chronicle and Clerkenwell News, Nos. 2780–3319, 6 March 1871–23 Nov. 1872. Ed. by Robert Whelan Boyle (1876–89), Alfred Ewen Fletcher (1889–94), H. W. Massingham (1894–9), W. H. Fisher (1899–1903).]

The Hour. No. 1, 24 March 1873–11 Aug. 1876. [Owned by D. Morier Evans: ed. by Thomas Hamber.]

The Circle. No. 1, 29 Jan.–No. 87, 9 May 1874. [Ed. by William Saunders.]

The Echo. No. 1 [of Morning Edition] 4 Oct. 1875–31 May 1876. [Run in conjunction with The Echo (see under Evening Papers); the first halfpenny morning daily.]

The Sportsman. 20 March 1876–22 Nov. 1924. [Incorporated in Sporting Life. No. 1, 2 Aug. 1865 (twice a week); 3 times a week in 1867. Ed. by Charles Russell (1867–75), Thomas Whitefoot (1878–85), A. Allison, S. Downing (1889–).]

The Daily Express. Nos. 1–101, 1 May–25 Aug. 1877.

The Continental Times. [1878]–12 March 1881–15 Feb. 1890. [Pbd at London and Paris.]

Sporting Life. 23 March 1883 onwards. In progress. [Started as Bell's Penny Life in London, No. 1, 16 March 1859; continued twice a week as Sporting Life from No. 12,

30 April 1859; in 1861 it absorbed The Sporting Telegraph; (No. 1, Feb. 1860–6 March 1861); in April 1881 it was pbd 4 times a week; on 23 March 1883 it became a daily paper; on 1 July 1886 it absorbed Bell's Life in London, see p. 811 below. Ed. by Henry Fiest (1859–74), Charles W. Blake (1874–91), George S. Lowe (1891–).]

The Summary. No. 1, 10 July 1883–11 Oct. 1884. [Pbd by The Times.]

The Financial News. No. 114, 1 July 1884 onwards. In progress. [Started as The Financial and Mining News, Nos. 1–113, 23 Jan.–28 June 1884: not pbd on Saturdays. Ed. by H. H. Marks, Ellis T. Powell.]

The Morning Mail. Nos. 1–69, 20 April–9 July 1885.

The Journal. Nos. 1–43, 1 Nov.–20 Dec. 1886.

The Financial Times. 13 Feb. 1888 onwards. In progress. [Started as The London Financial Guide, No. 1, Jan.–Feb. 1888.]

The Daily Oracle. Nos. 1–840, 21 Nov. 1889–27 Aug. 1892. [Ed. by T. P. Whittaker.]

Galignani's Messenger. No. 23515, 1 Jan. 1890–31 Dec. 1895. [Continued as] The Daily Messenger, No. 25679, 1 Jan. 1896–30 July 1904. [Started at Paris in 1814, 3 times a week; became daily in 1821. Ed. by Cyrus Redding, J. B. Bowes, Gibbons Merle, J. C. Mackenzie, Horatio Bottomley (in 1896).]

The Daily Graphic. No. 1, 4 Jan. 1890–16 Oct. 1926. [An illustrated paper. Incorporated in The Daily Sketch.]

Morning. No. 1, 21 May 1892–4 Sept. 1898. [Continued as] London Morning, No. 1968, 5 Sept. 1898–22 April 1899. [Continued as] The Morning Herald, No. 1, 24 April 1899–1 Sept. 1900. [Incorporated in The Daily Express; halfpenny paper. Ed. by Chester Ives.]

The Morning Leader. No. 1, 23 May 1892–11 May 1912. [Incorporated in The Daily News; halfpenny paper. Ed. by F. W. Wilson.]

The Daily Courier. Nos. 1–98, 23 April–15 Aug. 1896. [Conducted by George Newnes.]

The Daily Mail. No. 1, 4 May 1896 onwards. In progress.

The Daily Express. No. 1, 24 April 1900 onwards. In progress.

(b) Evening Papers

The Star. No. 1, 3 May 1788–15 Oct. 1831. [Incorporated in The Albion and Star. Ed. by Andrew Macdonald, Alexander Tilloch, John Mayne, Rowland Nash.]

The Courier. [Sept. 1792]–No. 86, 31 Dec. 1792–6 July 1842. [Ed. by Eugenius Roche, Daniel Stuart (1803–11), Peter Street (1811–22), William Mudford, John Galt (1830), James Stuart, S. L. Blanchard.]

The Sun. No. 1, 1 Oct. 1792–15 Apr. 1876. [No. 16042, 24 Jan. 1844 gives this information: 'The Sun is published every morning at five o'clock in time for the early trains and town delivery; a second edition (Evening Sun) is published in time for the afternoon trains, and a third edition at seven o'clock for Post, containing Parliamentary and all other news in London up to that hour'; ed. by John Heriot (1792–1806), Robert Clark (1806–7), William Jerdan (1813–7), John Taylor, Murdo Young, Patrick Grant, W. F. Deacon (–1845), Charles Kent.]

The Albion and Evening Advertiser. [1799]–No. 106, 7 Jan. 1800–[1807]. [Ed. by Allan M'Leod, John Fenwick.]

The Traveller. [1801]–No. 5519, 1 Jan. 1818–28 Dec. 1822. [Incorporated in The Globe and Traveller; ed. by Edward Quin.]

The Globe. [No. 1, 1 Jan. 1803]–No. 1536, 8 Dec. 1807–31 Dec. 1922. [Incorporated in The Evening Standard. It absorbed The Traveller on 28 Dec. 1822, and was for a long time called The Globe and Traveller: it also absorbed The Statesman (Feb. 1824), The Evening Chronicle (March 1824), The Nation (July 1824) and The Argus (July 1828). Ed. by George Lane (1803), Robert Heron (1803), Robert Torrens, Walter Coulson (1822–5), Gibbons Merle (1825–30), R. D. Hanson, George Stevenson (1835–6), Francis Mahony, E. R. Moran, R. H. Patterson (1865–9), Sir George C. H. Armstrong (1872–), Algernon Locker (–1894), G. E. Armstrong (1894–1907).]

The Statesman. [No. 1, 26 Feb. 1806]–No. 107, 30 June 1807–18 Feb. 1824. [Incorporated in The Globe and Traveller. Ed. by John Hunt (1806–9), W. M. Willett (1809), John Scott (1809–14), Daniel Lovell (1814–7), Sampson Perry (1817–9), David Carey (1819–24).]

The Pilot. [No. 1, 1 Jan. 1807]–No. 687, 15 March 1809–31 Oct. 1815. [Ed. by E. Samuel, Herbert Compton, — Fitzgerald.]

The Alfred and Westminster Gazette. [No. 1, 17 April 1810]–No. 22, 12 May 1810–23 April 1833. [The second part of the title was soon dropped.]

Cobbett's Evening Post. Nos. 1–55, 29 Jan.–1 April 1820. [Ed. by William Cobbett.]

The True Briton. No. 1, 1 July 1820–13 Nov. 1822. [Incorporated in The Traveller.]

The British Traveller. No. 1, 19 July 1821–No. 3703, 25 May 1833. [Ed. by W. M. Willett.]

The New Globe. No. 1, 3 Feb.–No. 132, 5 July 1823.

The Evening Chronicle. Nos. 1–30, 4 Feb.–19 March 1824. [Incorporated in The Globe and Traveller; ed. by J. S. Buckingham.]

The Nation. Nos. 1–65, 10 May–24 July 1824. [Incorporated in The Globe and Traveller; ed. by T. J. Wooler.]

The Evening Times. Nos. 1–46, 14 Nov. 1825–5 Jan. 1826.

The Standard. No. 1, 21 May 1827–29 June 1857. [Continued as] The Evening Standard No. 11179, 11 June 1860 onwards. In progress. [Absorbed The Albion and Star, 1 Jan. 1836. Ed. by A. A. Watts (1827), S. L. Giffard (1827–45), Robert Knox (1846–57), Charles Williams (1860–3), Thomas Hamber (1863–70), Sir John Gorst (1870–4), W. H. Mudford (1874–1900).]

The Argus. Nos. 1–24, 30 June–26 July 1828. [Incorporated in The Globe and Traveller; ed. by J. S. Buckingham.]

The Albion. 15 Nov. 1830–15 Oct. 1831. [Continued as] The Albion and Star. 17 Oct. 1831–31 Dec. 1835. [Incorporated in The Standard.]

The True Sun. No. 1, 5 March 1832–23 Dec. 1837. [Ed. by Patrick Grant, D. W. Harvey, W. J. Fox.]

The Shipping and Mercantile Gazette. No. 1, 4 Jan. 1836 onwards. In progress. [Ed. by William Carpenter (1836), Sir William Mitchell (1836–78).]

The Evening Star. No. 1, 25 July 1842–No. 188, 28 Feb. 1843.

The Railway Director. No. 1, 3 Jan. 1845–14 March 1846.

The Express. No. 1, 1 Sept. 1846–30 April 1869. [Run in conjunction with The Daily News; ed. by Thomas Elliott (1846–55), J. R. Robinson (1855–69).]

The Evening Journal. No. 1, 6 Oct. 1851–14 April 1860.

The Evening Star. No. 1, 17 March 1856–No. 4251, 13 Oct. 1869. [Run in conjunction with The Morning Star.]

The Evening Herald. No. 1, 29 June 1857–No. 2428, 27 May 1865. [Run in conjunction with The Standard.]

The Pall Mall Gazette. No. 1, 7 Feb. 1865–27 Oct. 1923. [Incorporated in The Evening Standard. Ed. by Frederick Greenwood (1865–80), Horace Voules (1880–1), John Morley (1881–3), W. T. Stead (1883–9), E. T. Cook (1889–92), Kinloch Cooke (1892–3), H. C. Cust (1893–6), Sir Douglas Straight (1896–1909).]

The Glow-worm. No. 1, 5 June 1865–No. 1152, 13 Feb. 1869. [Ed. by T. W. Robertson.]

The Daily Recorder (of Commerce). [1866]–No. 1982, 1 Jan. 1873–20 Dec. 1887. [Incorporated in The Evening Post (i.e. Evening News).]

The Little Times. No. 1, 27 April–No. 22, 22 May 1867. [Ed. by Mayne Reid.]

The Echo. No. 1, 8 Dec. 1868–31 July 1905. [For a short time in 1875 it ran a morning edn: and for this period its style was changed to The Evening Echo; The first halfpenny newspaper; ed. by Sir Arthur Arnold (1868–75), Horace Voules, Howard Evans, J. Passmore Edwards, Aaron Watson.]

The London Figaro. No. 1, 17 May 1870–No. 263, 11 March 1871.

The Public Ledger and Evening Report. 11 July 1870 onwards. In progress. [See under Morning Papers above. Not pbd on Saturdays.]

The St James's Gazette. No. 1, 31 May 1880–13 March 1905. [Incorporated in The Evening Standard; ed. by Frederick Greenwood (1880–8), Sidney Low (1888–97), Hugh Chisholm (1897–1900).]

The Evening News. No. 1, 26 July 1881–Dec. 1887. [Continued as] The Evening Post, No. 1427, 21 Dec. 1887–12 Jan. 1889. [Continued as] The Evening News and Post, 13 Jan. 1889–11 May 1889. [Continued as] The Evening News, 12 May 1889 onwards. In progress. [Halfpenny paper; ed. by Charles Williams (1881–4), — Coplestone, Frank Harris (1889–92), Percy White, Kennedy Jones (1894–1900).]

The Star. No. 1, 17 Jan. 1888 onwards. In progress. [Halfpenny paper; ed. by T. P. O'Connor (1888–92), James Stuart (1892–7), E. Parke.]

The Westminster Gazette. No. 1, 31 Jan. 1893–31 Jan. 1928. [Incorporated in The Daily News. Ed. by E. T. Cook (1893–6), J. A. Spender (1896–1922).]

The Sun. No. 1, 27 June 1893–11 Oct. 1906. [Ed. by T. P. O'Connor (1893–6), W. S. Johnstone.]

The Evening Mail. No. 1, 1 April 1896–9 Oct. 1901.

(2) The Provincial Daily Press

[An asterisk preceding an entry denotes that no copy of the paper has been located.]

*The Mercantile Gazette, and Liverpool and Manchester Daily Advertiser [Liverpool]. [No. 1, 6 Aug. 1811–(?); dead before 1812. See A. Andrews, History of British Journalism, vol. II, 1859, p. 124; ed. by — Solomon.]

*The Northern Express and Lancashire Daily Post [Manchester]. [No. 1, 1 Dec. 1821–Feb. 1822.] [See A. Andrews, as above; pbd by Henry Burgess.]

The Daily Post [Liverpool]. No. 1, 11 June 1853–[?].

Northern Daily Times [Liverpool]. No. 1, 24 Sept. 1853–6 June 1857. [Continued as] Northern Times, 7 June 1857–19 Feb. 1860.

[Continued as] The Daily Times, 20 Feb.
1860–30 Jan. 1861. [Ed. by Charles Willmer.]

The Daily War Telegraph [Manchester]. No.
2, 21 Oct. 1854–29 Jan. 1855. [Continued
as] War Telegraph, 30 Jan.–20 March 1855
[and as] Daily Telegraph, 22 March–7 April
1855 [and as] Manchester Daily Telegraph,
9 April–30 Nov. 1855.

The War Express and Daily Advertiser
[Manchester]. No. 4, 24 Oct.–No. 46, 15
Dec. 1854. [Continued as] The Manchester
Express, etc. 18 Dec. 1854–8 June 1855.

The Manchester Daily Times. No. 1, 12 Dec.
1854–15 June 1855. [Incorporated in The
Manchester Examiner and Times; see
below.]

The Northern Express [Darlington]. No. 1,
21 April–27 Oct. 1855. [Continued as] The
Northern Daily Express [Newcastle], 30
Oct. 1855–16 Oct. 1886. [Ed. by R. N.
Worth (1866–7).]

The Birmingham Daily Press. No. 1, 7 May
1855–20 Nov. 1858.

The Daily Post [Liverpool]. No. 1, 11 June
1855–28 Oct. 1879. [Continued as] The
Liverpool Daily Post, 29 Oct. 1879 onwards. [Ed. by M. J. Whitty, Sir Edward
R. Russell, John Macleay.]

The Sheffield Daily Telegraph. No. 1, 8 June
1855 onwards. [Ed. by Sir William Leng.]

The Birmingham Daily Mercury, No. 1,
12 June 1855–22 Aug. 1857. [Incorporated
in The Birmingham Daily Press.]

The Manchester Examiner. 17 June 1855–
10 March 1894. [Started as a weekly, No. 1,
10 Jan. 1846: at the beginning of 1854 it
was being issued twice a week; and in Oct.
there was issued The Manchester Examiner
Extraordinary on the four weekdays on
which the Manchester Examiner itself did
not appear; on 12 Dec. this was changed to
The Manchester Daily Times (see above);
when this ceased on 15 June 1855, The
Manchester Examiner and Times was continued daily under its old title; incorporated with The Umpire [Manchester] in
March 1894 (see under Sunday papers,
below). Ed. by Thomas Ballantyne (1846),
A. W. Paulton (1846–64), H. Dunckley
(1864–88), J. S. R. Phillips (1889–91),
W. M. Leslie, A. Ireland.]

The Morning News [Sheffield]. No. 1, 19 June–
14 Nov. 1855.

The Manchester Guardian. 2 July 1855 onwards. [Started weekly, No. 1, 5 May 1821:
twice a week in 1836. Ed. by J. E. Taylor
(1821–44), R. S. Taylor (1844–8), Jeremiah
Garnett (1848–61), J. E. Taylor II (1861–
72), C. P. Scott (1872–1930).]

Stevenson's Daily Express [Nottingham]. No.
1, 2 July 1855–29 May 1856.

The North and South Shields Gazette (Daily
Telegraphic Edition) [South Shields]. No. 1,
2 July 1855–26 Jan. 1884. [Continued as]
The Shields Daily Gazette. 28 Jan. 1884
onwards. [Ed. by James Annand, Aaron
Watson.]

The Hull Morning Telegraph. [1855(?)]–No.
4921, 12 July 1869–30 April 1880. [Incor-
porated in The Hull Express.]

The Sheffield Daily News. No. 1, 2 Dec. 1856–
27 Dec. 1862.

The Liverpool Daily Mail. No. 1, 17 March–
No. 19, 10 April 1857.

The Birmingham Daily Post. No. 1, 4 Dec.
1857 onwards.

The Liverpool Mercury. 1 Jan. 1858–12 Nov.
1904. [Incorporated in The Liverpool Daily
Post. Started weekly, No. 1, 5 July 1811;
twice a week in 1847; ed. by Egerton Smith
(1811–), Thomas Ballantyne, John Maitland, John Lovell (1880–90), G. Wynne
(1890–1904).]

The Daily Chronicle [Newcastle]. No. 1,
1 May 1858–Dec. 1861. [Continued as] The
Newcastle Daily Chronicle, 1 Jan. 1862 on-
wards. [Started weekly as The Newcastle
Chronicle, No. 1, 24 March 1764; ed. by
Joseph Cowen, Langley Baxter, James
Annand, Aaron Watson (1885–93).]

The Western Daily Press [Bristol]. No. 1,
29 June 1858 onwards. [Ed. by P. S. Macliver,
Walter Reid.]

The Sheffield Daily Argus. No. 1, 11 May–
No. 20, 3 June 1859.

Willmer's Liverpool Morning News, No. 1,
16 July–No. 104, 15 Nov. 1859. [Ed. by
Charles Willmer.]

The Daily Western Mercury [Plymouth]. No.
1, 2 June–25 Sept. 1860. [Continued as] The
Western Daily Mercury, 26 Sept. 1860 onwards. [Ed. by Isaac Latimer, Edwin
Goadby.]

The Western Morning News [Plymouth]. No.
1, 3 Jan. 1860 onwards. [Ed. by William
Saunders, Edward Spender (1860–78), Albert
Groser (1878–94).]

The Nottingham Daily Express. No. 1, 4 Jan.
1860–16 April 1918. [Ed. by J. Dods Shaw,
D. Edwards (1891–7).]

The Derby Exchange Gazette. Nos. 2–6,
14 Jan.–11 Feb. 1860. [Continued as] The
Daily Gazette. 7 Feb. 1860–5. [Con-
tinued weekly as] The Derby and Derbyshire Gazette. Jan. 1866–3 March 1899.

The Bristol Daily Post. No. 1, 24 Jan. 1860–
26 Jan. 1878. [Absorbed The Bristol
Mercury and was continued as The Bristol
Mercury and Daily Post, 27 Jan. 1878–
19 Dec. 1901, when the style was changed
to The Bristol Daily Mercury, 21 Dec. 1901–
30 Nov. 1909; ed. by Harold Lewis.]

The Newcastle Daily Journal. 1 Jan. 1861 onwards. [Started weekly as The Newcastle Journal, No. 1, 12 May 1832–Dec. 1860; ed. by Robert Redpath, A. D. Murray.]

The Cambrian Daily Leader [Swansea]. No. 1, 20 May 1861–15 March 1930.

The Nottingham Daily Guardian, No. 1, 1 July 1861–9 Oct. 1905. [Continued as] The Nottingham Guardian. 10 Oct. 1905 onwards. [Ed. by J. R. Forman.]

The Southport Independent. No. 1, July 1861–21 Sept. 1872. [Continued as The Southport News, etc. 1872–5, and as The Southport Daily News, 1875–77, and as The Liverpool and Southport Daily News, 19 Nov. 1877–18 Feb. 1881.]

The Liverpool Evening Mercury. No. 1, 26 Aug. 1861–9 Jan. 1863.

The Liverpool Journal of Commerce. No. 1, Oct. 1861–No. 3545, 28 Feb. 1873 onwards. ['Liverpool' was dropped from the title from 1873 to 1880.]

The Manchester Courier. [1861]–28 Jan. 1916. [Started as a weekly, No. 1, 1 Jan. 1825; ed. by A. A. Watts (1825–6), John Sowler, Sir Thomas Sowler, Francis Hitchman.]

The Leeds Mercury. [1861] onwards. [Started as a weekly (No. 1, May 1718); 3 times a week in July 1855; ed. by Edward Baines II, Talbot Baines, T. Wemyss Reid; T. Riach.]

The Birmingham Daily Gazette. No. 1, 12 May 1862–30 Jan. 1904. [Continued as] The Birmingham Gazette and Express. 1 Feb. 1904 onwards. [Started weekly as The Birmingham Gazette, No. 1, 16 Nov. 1741; ed. by Sir James Stephen, Sebastian Evans, H. J. Palmer, A. W. Still.]

The Exeter and Plymouth Gazette Daily Telegrams. 7 Feb. 1863–30 April 1885.

The Sheffield Daily Advertiser. No. 1, 24 Feb. No. 60, 6 May 1863.

The Eastern Morning News [Hull]. No. 1, 26 Jan. 1864 onwards. [Ed. by William Saunders, William Hunt, J. A. Spender (1886–90).]

The Eastern Evening News [Hull]. No. 1, 26 Jan. 1864 30 April 1867.

The Shields Daily News [North Shields]. No. 1, 22 Aug. 1864 onwards.

The Ipswich Times. [1864]–No. 380, 2 March 1866–9 Oct. 1874. [Continued as] The East Anglian Daily Times. 11 Oct. 1874 onwards. [Ed. by F. W. Wilson (1874–90).]

The Daily Bristol Times. 1 Jan. 1865–Jan. 1884. [Started weekly as The Bristol Times and Bath Advocate, No. 1, 2 March 1839–26 March 1853; continued weekly as The Bristol Times and Felix Farley's Bristol Journal, 2 April 1853–Dec. 1864; The Daily Bristol Times was continued as The Bristol

Times and Mirror, Jan. 1884–29 Jan. 1932; ed. by T. D. Taylor, Charles Pebody.]

The Sunderland Daily Shipping News. No. 1, 6 Nov. 1865–No. 10431, 31 Dec. 1913.

The Sheffield Evening Star and Daily Times. [1865]–No. 2760, 21 April 1874–23 Jan. 1888. [Incorporated in The Evening Telegraph (Sheffield).]

The Northern Evening Express [Newcastle]. No. 1, 1 Aug. 1866–16 Oct. 1886. [Ed. by William Saunders.]

The Yorkshire Post [Leeds]. [1866] onwards. [Ed. by Charles Pebody.]

The Western Times [Exeter]. [1866] onwards. [Started as Exeter Weekly Times, No. 1, 6 Oct. 1827; changed to present title, 3 Jan. 1829; twice a week in 1835. Ed. by Thomas Latimer.]

The Evening Express of the Devon Weekly Times [Exeter]. No. 1, 19 Dec. 1866–25 Oct. 1873. [Continued as] The Devon Evening Express. 27 Oct. 1873–30 Sept. 1904. [Continued as] The Express and Echo. 1 Oct. 1904 onwards.

The Bolton Evening News. No. 1, 19 March 1867 onwards. [Ed. by W. F. Tillotson, William Brimelow.]

The Bradford Daily Telegraph. No. 1, 16 July 1868 onwards.

The Brighton Daily News. No. 1, 2 Nov. 1868–31 May 1880. [Incorporated in The Argus (Brighton).]

The Western Counties Daily Herald [Plymouth]. No. 1, 12 Nov. 1868–13 Feb. 1869.

The Manchester Evening News. No. 1, 10 Oct. 1868 onwards.

The Bradford Daily Times. [1868]–No. 813, 1 Jan.–14 Sept. 1871.

The Sussex Daily News [Brighton]. [1868]–No. 1147, 2 July 1872 onwards.

The Bradford Observer. [1868]–16 Nov. 1901. [Continued as] The Yorkshire Daily Observer. 17 Nov. 1901 onwards. [Started weekly, No. 1, 6 Feb. 1834; ed. by William Byles (1834–), W. P. Byles, W. Harrison.]

The Western Daily Standard [Plymouth]. No. 1, 2 March 1869–5 March 1870.

The Oldham Evening Express. No. 1, 5 April 1869–10 July 1889.

The Western Mail [Cardiff]. No. 1, 1 May 1869 onwards. [Ed. by Lascelles Carr.]

The Leicester Daily Mail. No. 1, 3 May 1869–19 Feb. 1870. [Continued as] The Leicester Weekly Express. Nos. 1–33, 26 Feb.–1 Oct. 1870.

The Newcastle Daily Telegraph. No. 1, 19 June 1869–19 Nov. 1870. [Continued as] The Newcastle Morning Telegraph. 23 Nov. 1870–7 June 1871. [Continued as] The Newcastle Evening Telegraph. 8 June–23 Dec. 1871.

The Evening Gazette for Middlesbrough. [8 Nov. 1869]–6 Dec. 1872. [Continued as The Daily Gazette, etc. 1872–1881; and as The North Eastern Daily Gazette (Middlesbrough), 11 June 1881 onwards. Ed. by Sir Hugh Gilzean Reid.]

The Northern Echo [Darlington]. No. 1, 1 Jan. 1870 onwards. [Ed. by W. T. Stead (1871–80).]

The Newcastle Evening Courant. No. 1, 5 March 1870–Nov. 1874. [Continued as] The Newcastle Daily Courant. 26 Nov. 1874–5 Feb. 1876.

The Evening Telegram [Newport, Mon.]. No. 1, 1 Aug. 1870. [Continued as The South Wales Evening Telegram, and then as The Evening Telegraph, 17 Feb.–27 Nov. 1891.]

The Bolton Morning News. No. 1, 8 Aug.–12 Nov. 1870.

The Evening News [Hull]. No. 54, 1 Oct. 1870–6 July 1876. [Continued as The Hull Express, 7 July 1876–25 May 1891; then incorporated in The Hull Daily News.]

The Eastern Counties Daily Press [Norwich]. No. 1, 10 Oct. 1870–2 May 1871. [Continued as] The Eastern Daily Press. 3 May 1871 onwards.

The Bolton Daily Chronicle. [1870]–No. 705, 5 May 1873–July 1907. [Continued as] The Bolton Evening Chronicle. 1 Aug. 1907 onwards.

The Birmingham Daily Mail. [1870]–No. 154, 6 March 1871 onwards. [Ed. by Sir John Jaffray.]

The Birmingham Morning News. No. 1, 4 Jan. 1871–27 May 1876. [Ed. by George Dawson.]

The Huddersfield Daily Examiner. No. 1, 28 Jan. 1871 onwards.

The Huddersfield Daily Chronicle. No. 1, 30 Jan. 1871–31 Dec. 1915.

The Sporting Chronicle [Manchester]. No. 1, 14 Feb. 1871 onwards. [Ed. by E. Hulton.]

The Liverpool Daily Albion. [1871]–No. 539, 21 July 1873. [Continued with variations in title till 27 March 1887.]

The Evening Express [Liverpool]. [1871]–No. 692, 2 June 1873 onwards.

The Bolton Evening Guardian. [1871]–No. 825, 1 Jan. 1874–26 May 1893. [Incorporated in The Bolton Evening News.]

The Northern Counties Daily Mail [Newcastle]. No. 1, 1 May–No. 88, 10 Aug. 1872.

The Leicester Daily Post. No. 1, 1 Aug. 1872 onwards.

The Leicester Evening News. [1872]–No. 982, 12 June 1875–28 June 1878.

The Bradford Evening Mail. No. 1, 18 Sept. 1872–1 May 1875. [Incorporated in The Bradford Chronicle.]

The Bradford Chronicle. No. 1, 1 Oct. 1872–18 June 1882. [Absorbed The Bradford Evening Mail and became The Bradford Daily Chronicle and Mail, 19 June 1882–25 Aug. 1883.]

The Leeds Daily News. [1872]–No. 148, 1 May 1873–29 May 1905. [Continued as] The Yorkshire Evening News. 1 June 1905 onwards.

The South Wales Daily News [Cardiff]. [1872]–1 July 1889 onwards.

The Staffordshire Daily Sentinel [Hanley]. No. 2, 10 April 1873–30 Dec. 1881. [Continued as] The Staffordshire Sentinel. 1 Jan. 1883 onwards.

The Sheffield Post. No. 19, 17 May 1873–25 July 1882. [Continued as The Sheffield Daily Post, 1882–4; but reverted to former style 21 July 1884–28 May 1887.]

The Sunderland Daily Echo, etc. No. 1, 22 Dec. 1873 onwards.

The York Herald. 1 Jan. 1874–31 Dec. 1889. [Continued as] The Yorkshire Herald. 1 Jan. 1890 onwards. [Started weekly, no. 1, 2 Jan. 1790; ed. by William Hargrove (1813–46), W. Wallace Hargrove, Edwin N. Goadby (1874–87), A. H. Fletcher (1899–).

The Manchester Evening Mail. No. 1, 4 May 1874–16 Aug. 1904. [Ed. by Sir T. Sowler.]

The Evening Express Telegram [Cheltenham]. No. 70, 6 July 1874–20 Jan. 1875. [Continued as The Evening Telegram, etc. 21 Jan. 1875–30 Dec. 1882.]

The East Anglian Daily Times [Ipswich]. No. 1, 13 Oct. 1874 onwards. [Started Weekly as The Ipswich Express, No. 1, 13 Aug. 1839.]

The Midland Counties Evening Express [Wolverhampton]. No. 1, 2 Nov. 1874–15 Jan. 1876. [Continued as The Evening Express, 1876–84, and as The Evening Express and Star, 1884–9, and as The Express and Star, May 1889 onwards.]

The Wakefield Evening Herald. [1874]–No. 4555, 5 Jan. 1889–24 Dec. 1890.

The Bath Argus Evening Telegram. No. 1, 17 May 1875–19 June 1876. [Continued as The Evening Argus and as The Bath Argus to 31 June 1900; incorporated in The Bath Daily Chronicle.]

The Birmingham Evening News. No. 1, 16 Aug. 1875–No. 119, 15 Jan. 1876. [Incorporated in The Birmingham Morning News.]

The Scarborough Daily Post. No. 1, 21 Feb. 1876–24 May 1887. [Continued as] The Scarborough Post. 25 May 1887 onwards.

The Brighton and Sussex Daily Post. No. 1, 1 July 1876–8 July 1885. [Continued as] The Brighton and Sussex Evening Post. 9 July 1885–7 Feb. 1886.

The Sunderland Daily Times. No. 1, 3 July 1876–3 Aug. 1878. [Incorporated in The Sunderland Daily Echo.]

The Sunderland Daily Post. No. 1, 21 July 1876–3 Sept. 1891. [Incorporated in The Sunderland Daily Herald.]

The Daily Telegram [Wisbech]. No. 1, 24 April–No. 123, 15 Sept. 1877.

The Bristol Evening News. No. 1, 29 May 1877 onwards. [Ed. by T. Watkins.]

The Warrington Evening Post. No. 1, 17 May 1877–6 April 1878. [Continued as] The Evening Post. 8 April 1878–31 Dec. 1880.

The Evening Post [Worcester]. No. 1, 4 June 1877–21 May 1881. [Continued as The Worcestershire Evening Post, 30 May 1881–3 March 1883; and as The Worcestershire Echo, 5 March 1883 onwards.]

The Northern Times [Oldham]. No. 1, 19 March 1877–11 June 1880. [Continued as The Oldham Evening Standard, 1880–2; and as The Oldham Daily Standard, 9 Jan. 1882 onwards.]

The Evening News [Portsmouth]. [1877]–No. 211, 1 Jan. 1878 onwards.

The Bath Evening Chronicle. No. 2, 12 June 1877–4 Aug. 1883. [Continued as] The Bath Daily Chronicle. 7 Aug. 1883 onwards.

The Northern Evening Mail [West Hartlepool]. [1877]–No. 200, 18 Feb. 1878–2 Oct. 1883. [Continued as] The Northern Daily Mail. 29 Oct. 1883 onwards.

The Swansea Daily Shipping Register. [1877]–11 June 1888–3 July 1888. [Continued as] The Swansea Gazette. 4 July 1888–4 Jan. 1913.

The Evening Star of Gwent and South Wales Times [Newport, Mon.]. No. 1, 10 Nov. 1877–30 March 1889. [Continued as The South Wales Daily Times, etc. 1889–92; and as The Star, 1892–1900.]

The Daily Midland Echo [Wolverhampton]. No. 1, 11 Dec. 1877–2 Jan. 1879. [Continued as] The Midland Echo. 8–15 Jan. 1870.

The Grimsby Express. No. 1, 27 April 1878–25 May 1891. [Incorporated in The Hull Daily News.]

The Nottingham Evening Post. No. 1, 1 May 1878 onwards.

The Gateshead and Tyneside Echo [Gateshead]. No. 1, 24 April 1879–20 Jan. 1880. [Continued as The Tyneside Echo (Newcastle) until 30 Aug. 1888.]

The Derby Daily Telegraph and Reporter. No. 1, 28 July 1879 onwards.

The Derby Evening Gazette. No. 1, 28 July 1879–2 Oct. 1880. [Continued as The Derby and Burton Evening Gazette, 1880–1; and as Derby and Burton Gazette, 1881–4; and as The Derby Evening Gazette, 12 July–30 Dec. 1884.]

The Liverpool Echo. No. 1, 27 Oct. 1879 onwards. [Ed. by A. G. Jeans.]

The Worcester Daily Times and Journal. No. 1, 5 Jan. 1880 onwards. [Ed. by C. H. Birbeck.]

The Northampton Mercury Daily Reporter. No. 1, 9 Feb. 1880–30 July 1885. [Continued as The Northampton Daily Reporter, 1 Aug. 1885–6 April 1908; and as The Northampton Daily Echo, 13 April 1908 onwards.]

The Evening Herald [Northampton]. No. 1, 16 Feb. 1880–31 July 1881. [Continued as] The Northampton Daily Chronicle, etc. 1 Aug. 1881 onwards.

The Evening Chronicle [Oldham]. No. 1, 17 March 1880–17 March 1882. [Continued as] The Oldham Evening Chronicle. 20 March 1882 onwards.

The Argus [Brighton]. No. 1, 30 March 1880–24 Aug. 1896. [Continued as] The Evening Argus. 25 Aug. 1896 onwards.

The Evening Star [Wolverhampton]. No. 1, 28 June 1880–27 June 1884. [Incorporated in The Evening Express (Wolverhampton).]

The Sussex Evening Times [Brighton]. No. 1, 6 July 1880 onwards.

The Evening News [Norwich]. No. 1, 2 Jan.–11 Feb. 1882. [Continued as] The Eastern Evening News (Norwich). 13 Feb. 1882 onwards.

The Evening Press [York]. [1882]–20 March 1884–31 Dec. 1904. [Continued as] The Yorkshire Evening Press. 1 Jan. 1905 onwards.

The Scarborough Evening News. [1882]–No. 908, 4 Jan. 1886 onwards. [Ed. by Meredith J. Whittaker.]

The Stockport Echo. No. 1, 10 Feb. 1883–25 June 1889. [Continued as The Cheshire Echo, 1889–92; and as The Cheshire Evening Echo, 1893–5; and as The Cheshire Daily Echo, 1 Nov. 1895 onwards.]

The Midland Echo [Birmingham]. No. 1, 26 Feb. 1883–1 March 1885. [Incorporated in The Evening Express and Star (Birmingham).]

The Evening Times [Liverpool]. No. 1, 9 June 1883–9 June 1884. [Continued as] The Liverpool and Bootle Evening Times. 10 June 1884–31 Dec. 1894.

The Evening Mail [Portsmouth]. No. 1, 14 Jan. 1884–8 June 1895. [Continued as The Mail, 1895–6; and as The Southern Daily Mail, 23 March 1896–14 Jan. 1905.]

The Midland Evening News [Wolverhampton]. No. 1, 3 April 1884 onwards.

The South Wales Echo [Cardiff]. [1884]–1 July 1889 onwards.

The Hull Daily Mail. No. 1, 29 Sept. 1885–31 Dec. 1895. [Continued as] The Daily Mail (Hull). Jan. 1896 onwards.

The Nottingham Evening News. No. 1, 21 Oct. 1885 onwards. [Ed. by D. Edwards (1891-7).]

The Evening Chronicle [Newcastle on Tyne]. No. 1, 2 Nov. 1885 onwards.

The Birmingham Daily Times. No. 1, 4 Nov. 1885-31 March 1890.

The Evening Post [Exeter]. No. 1, 12 Nov. 1885 onwards.

The Derby Morning Post. No. 1, 16 Nov. 1885-July 1887.

The Norfolk Daily Standard [Norwich]. [1886]-No. 695, 15 Dec. 1887-31 Jan. 1903. [Continued as The Norfolk Evening Standard; incorporated in The Eastern Evening Mail in 1905.]

The Lancashire Evening Post [Preston]. No. 1, 16 Oct. 1886-31 Dec. 1892. [Continued as The Lancashire Daily Post. Jan. 1893 onwards. [Ed. by John Toulmin.]

The Manchester Evening Chronicle. No. 1, 10 May 1885 onwards. [Founded by E. Hulton and O. Bleackley.]

The Northern Daily Telegraph [Blackburn]. No. 1, 26 Oct. 1886 onwards.

The Sheffield Evening Telegraph. No. 1, June 1887-23 June 1888. [Continued as The Evening Telegraph and Star, 25 June 1888-17 Jan. 1898; and as The Yorkshire Telegraph and Star, Jan. 1898 onwards.]

The Blackburn Evening Express. No. 1, 29 Aug. 1887- . [After various changes of title became The Lancashire Daily Express and Standard, 10 June 1895-3 March 1899.] [Ed. by W. A. Abram.]

The Cambridge Daily News. No. 1, 28 May 1888 onwards.

The Southern Echo [Southampton]. No. 1, 20 Aug. 1888-5 Sept. 1891. [Continued as The Southern Echo and Bournemouth Telegraph, 7 Sept. 1891-21 Feb. 1901; and as The Southern Daily Echo onwards.]

The Yorkshire Evening Post [Leeds]. No. 79, 1 Dec. 1890 onwards.

The Midland Daily Telegraph [Coventry]. No. 1, 9 Feb. 1891 onwards.

The Daily Argus [Birmingham]. No. 1, 9 Nov. 1891-31 June 1902. [Incorporated in The Birmingham Evening Dispatch.]

The Daily Guardian [Warrington]. No. 1, 28 Nov. 1891-8 Aug. 1896. [Continued as The Warrington Daily Guardian. 10 Aug. 1896-3 Oct. 1903.

The Daily Independent Press [Cambridge]. No. 1, 2 Jan.-No. 138, 31 July 1892.

The South Wales Argus [Newport, Mon.]. No. 1, 30 May 1892 onwards.

The Bradford Daily Argus. No. 1, 16 June 1892 onwards. [Ed. by H. Fieldhouse.]

The Leicester Daily Express. No. 1, 20 June 1892 onwards.

The Halifax Evening Courier. No. 1, 21 June 1892 onwards.

The South Wales Daily Post [Swansea]. No. 1, 13 Feb. 1893-12 March 1932. [Continued as] South Wales Evening Post. 14 March 1932.

The Newcastle Evening News. No. 1, 2 Oct. 1893-27 April 1899.

The Barrow Evening Echo. No. 1, 21 March 1894-30 June 1898.

The Newcastle Daily Leader. No. 1, 28 Sept. 1895-31 Oct. 1903. [Ed. by James Annand and Aaron Watson.]

The Eastern Daily Telegraph [Grimsby]. No. 1, 27 Feb. 1897-31 Dec. 1898. [Continued as] The Grimsby Daily Telegraph. Jan. 1899 onwards.

The Isle of Man Daily Times. No. 1, 4 May 1897 onwards.

The Manchester Evening Chronicle. No. 1, 10 May 1897-31 March 1914. [Continued as The Evening Chronicle.]

The Evening Herald [Ipswich]. No. 1, 1 Sept.-29 Dec. 1897. [Continued as The Daily Herald, 30 Dec. 1897-30 July 1898; then incorporated in The Evening Star.]

The North Western Daily Mail [Barrow]. No. 1, 1 Jan. 1898 onwards.

The Newcastle Morning Mail. No. 1, 23 May 1898-9 Feb. 1901. [Continued as The Morning Mail.]

The Oxford and District Morning Echo. No. 25, 22 Oct. 1898-No. 112, 3 Feb. 1899. [Continued as The Oxford Morning Echo, 4 Feb. 1899-30 Jan. 1900.]

The Sunderland Morning Mail, No. 1, 14 Nov. 1898-11 Feb. 1901.

(3) SCOTTISH DAILY PAPERS

[An asterisk preceding an entry denotes that no copy of the paper has been located.]

Northern Telegraphic News [Aberdeen]. No. 1, 23 Jan. 1855-7 Oct. 1876.

The Aberdeen Daily Free Press. 4 May 1872-30 June 1874. [Continued as] The Daily Free Press. 1 July 1874-30 Nov. 1922. [Continued as] The Aberdeen Press and Journal. No. 1, 1 Dec. 1922 onwards. In progress. [Started as The Aberdeen Free Press, No. 1, 6 May 1853. Ed. by William McCombie (1853-70), Henry Alexander.]

Aberdeen Journal. 23 Aug. 1876-30 Nov. 1922. [Incorporated in The Aberdeen Press and Journal. Started No. 1, 5 Jan. 1748; ed. by John Ramsay (-1848), William Forsyth (1848-), David L. Pressly.]

Aberdeen Evening Express. No. 1, 20 Jan. 1879-23 March 1899. [Continued as] Evening Express. 24 March 1899 onwards. In progress. [Ed. by David L. Pressly.]

Evening Gazette [Aberdeen]. No. 1, 23 Jan. 1882–30 Nov. 1922. [Incorporated in Evening Express (Aberdeen); ed. by William Alexander (1882–94).]

The Daily Argus [Dundee]. No. 1, 23 May 1859–20 April 1861. [Incorporated in The Dundee Courier.]

The Dundee Courier. 22 April 1861–15 Nov. 1899. [Continued as] The Courier and Argus. 16 Nov. 1899–4 May 1926. [Incorporated in The Dundee Advertiser. Started as The Dundee Weekly Courier, No. 1, 20 Sept. 1816; ed. by — Mitchell.]

The Dundee Advertiser. 1 May 1861–4 May 1926. [Continued as] The Dundee Advertiser and Courier. 10 May–2 June 1926. [Continued as] The Courier and Advertiser. 3 June 1926 onwards. In progress. [Started weekly, No. 1, 16 Jan. 1801; twice a week on 8 April 1845; ed. by Sir John Leng (1851–1900).]

Evening News [Dundee]. No. 1, 28 March 1876–12 March 1879.

Evening Telegraph [Dundee]. No. 1, 13 March 1877 onwards. In progress.

Evening Post [Dundee]. No. 1, 22 Jan. 1900–16 May 1905.

Norrie, W. Edinburgh Newspapers Past and Present. Earlston, 1891.

Couper, W. J. The Edinburgh Periodical Press. 2 vols. Stirling, 1908.

*The Conservative [Edinburgh]. No. 1, 24 Feb. 1837–[?].

War Telegraph [Edinburgh]. [No. 1, 9 Oct. 1854]–No. 40, 23 Nov.–No. 53, 8 Dec. 1854. [Continued as] Northern Telegraph, 9 Dec. 1854–6 Jan. 1855. [Ed. by J. W. Finlay.]

The Daily Express [Edinburgh]. No. 1, 23 June 1855–27 Aug. 1859. [Incorporated in The Caledonian Mercury; ed. by W. H. Murray.]

The Caledonian Mercury. 2 July 1855–20 April 1867. [Incorporated in The Scotsman. Started 3 times a week, No. 1, 28 April 1720; twice a week later; issued as an evening paper from 14 July 1866. Ed. by David Buchanan (1810–27), James Browne, J. G. Cochrane, J. D. White, W. D. Bruce, James Robie (1855–66), William Saunders (1866–7).]

The Daily Scotsman. 2 July 1855–31 Dec. 1859. [Continued as] The Scotsman. 2 Jan. 1860 onwards. In progress. [Started as The Scotsman, No. 1, 25 Jan. 1817, twice a week. Ed. by C. Maclaren (1817–8), J. R. McCulloch (1818–20), C. Maclaren (again 1820–45), James Law (1845–9), Alexander Russell (1849–76), Robert Wallace (1876–80), Charles Cooper (1880–1906).]

*The Bawbee. No. 1, 19 Oct. 1857–[?]. [Halfpenny paper; ed. by J. G. Bertram.]

The Daily Courant. 2 Jan.–31 Oct. 1860. [Continued as] The Edinburgh Evening Courant. 1 Nov. 1860–15 Dec. 1871. [Continued as] The Edinburgh Courant. 16 Dec. 1871–6 Feb. 1886. [Incorporated in The Scottish News (Glasgow); started 3 times a week as The Edinburgh Evening Courant, No. 1, 15 Dec. 1718. Ed. by George Houy (1826–7), David Buchanan (1827–48), Joseph Robertson (1849–53), William Buchanan (1853–60), James Hannay (1860–4), Francis Espinasse (1864–7), J. Scott Henderson (1867–72), James Mure, W. R. Lawson.]

The Daily Review [Edinburgh]. No. 1, 2 April 1861–12 June 1886. [Ed. by J. B. Manson (1861–8), Henry Kingsley (1868–71), T. B. Gillies (1871–4), George Smith (1874–7), William Mackie (1877–86).]

The Edinburgh Evening News. No. 1, 27 May 1873 onwards. In progress. [Ed. by Hector C. Macpherson.]

The Edinburgh Evening Telephone. No. 1, 1 Nov. 1878–No. 79, 31 Jan. 1879.

The Evening Express [Edinburgh]. No. 1, 6 March 1880–6 Feb. 1886. [Run in conjunction with The Edinburgh Courant.]

The Edinburgh Evening Dispatch. No. 1, 4 Jan. 1886 onwards. In progress. [Run in conjunction with The Scotsman.]

The Scottish Leader [Edinburgh]. No. 1, 3 Jan. 1887–4 July 1894. [Ed. by John Macfarlane, C. H. Hanson, J. H. Dalziel.]

*The Day [Glasgow]. Nos. 1–112, Jan.–June 1832. [Ed. by John Strang.]

North British Daily Mail [Glasgow]. No. 1, 14 April 1847–31 Dec. 1900. [Continued as] Glasgow Daily Mail. 1 Jan.–8 June 1901. [Incorporated in The Daily Record (Glasgow). Ed. by George Troup (1847–8), Robert Somers (1849–59), C. Cameron (1860–73), James R. Manners.]

Daily Mail [Glasgow]. [1848]–No. 217, 17 March 1849–12 July 1851.

The Glasgow Daily News. [No. 1, 13 April 1855]–No. 69, 30 June–No. 111, 17 Aug. 1855.

Morning Bulletin [Glasgow]. No. 1, 26 May–No. 12, 8 June 1855.

The Glasgow Times. No. 1, 25 June 1855–9 June 1869.

Daily Bulletin [Glasgow]. [July 1855]–No. 1416, 9 Dec. 1859–12 Feb. 1861.

The Glasgow Morning Journal. No. 1, 29 June 1858–4 Sept. 1858. [Continued as] The Morning Journal, 6 Sept. 1858–11 Jan. 1870. [Continued as] Daily Express and Morning Journal. 12 Jan.–19 Aug. 1870. [Incorporated in Star (Glasgow); ed. by Robert Somers.]

The Glasgow Herald. 3 Jan. 1859 onwards. In progress. [Started as The Glasgow Advertiser, No. 1, 27 Jan. 1783 (weekly); twice a week from 1 Nov. 1802; adopted present title 23 Aug. 1805; 3 times a week in 1855. Ed. by John Mennons (1782–1803), Samuel Hunter (1803–37), George Outram (1837–56), James Pagan (1856–70), William Jack, J. H. Stoddart, Charles Russell (1887–1906).]

Evening Citizen [Glasgow]. No. 1, 8 Aug. 1864–7 Aug. 1914. [Continued as] Glasgow Citizen. 8 Aug. 1914–27 Oct. 1923. [Continued as] Evening Citizen. 29 Oct. 1923 onwards. In progress. [Started weekly as The Glasgow Citizen in 1842; ed. by James Hedderwick (1842–97), Edwin C. Hedderwick.]

The Glasgow Evening Mail. No. 1, 24 April–30 Dec. 1865.

The Glasgow Evening Herald. No. 1, 29 April–30 Dec. 1865.

The Glasgow Evening Post. No. 1, 9 July 1866–31 Dec. 1868. [Continued as] The Evening Journal. 1 Jan. 1869–11 Jan. 1870. [Continued as] The Star, No. 1, 12 Jan. 1870–16 Feb. 1872. [Continued as] Evening Star. 17 Feb. 1872–13 March 1875. [Continued as] Evening News and Star. 15 March 1875–10 Feb. 1888. [Continued as] Glasgow Evening News. 11 Feb. 1888–23 Sept. 1905. [Continued as] Glasgow News. 25 Sept. 1905–3 Oct. 1915. [Continued as] Glasgow Evening News. 4 Oct. 1915 onwards. In progress. [At first run in conjunction with The Morning Journal (Glasgow); ed. by Frederick Wicks, J. Murray Smith.]

The Glasgow News. No. 1, 15 Sept. 1873–6 Feb. 1886. [Continued as] The Scottish News. 7 Feb. 1886–11 Feb. 1888. [Ed. by R. H. Patterson (1873–4).]

The Daily Record [Glasgow]. No. 1, 28 Oct. 1895–8 June 1901. [Continued as] The Daily Record and Daily Mail. 10 June 1901 onwards. In progress.

The Greenock Telegraph. [1863] onwards. In progress. [Started as a weekly in 1857 (no. 38, 25 July 1857); ed. by W. H. Wylie.]

Evening News [Greenock]. No. 1, 17 July 1866–11 Jan. 1868. [Continued weekly as] Greenock News. 18 Jan. 1868–25 June 1870.

Greenock Daily Press. No. 1, 5 March–27 April 1867. [Continued weekly to 28 Dec. 1867.]

The Paisley Daily Express. [No. 1, ? Oct. 1874]–No. 233, 1 June 1875 onwards. In progress.

(4) IRISH DAILY PAPERS

The Belfast Daily Mercury. 19 April 1854–2 Nov. 1861. [Started as The Belfast Mercury, No. 1, 29 March 1851.]

The Belfast News-Letter. 2 July 1855 onwards. In progress. [Started as a weekly, No. 1, 1 Sept. 1737; ed. by Alexander Mackay (1796–1844), James A. Henderson (1845–83), Sir James Henderson.]

The Northern Whig [Belfast]. 1 Feb. 1858 onwards. In progress. [Started weekly in 1824; ed. by F. D. Finlay, E. M. Whitty, Thomas MacKnight.]

The Daily Examiner [Belfast]. 16 Nov. 1870–31 Dec. 1872. [Continued as] The Ulster Examiner and Northern Star. 1 Jan. 1873–22 July 1882. [Incorporated in Morning News (Belfast). Started as The Ulster Examiner, No. 1, 14 March 1868.]

The Belfast Evening Telegraph. [Sept. 1870]–No. 171, 20 March 1871–18 April 1918. [Continued as] The Belfast Telegraph. 19 April 1918 onwards. In progress.

The Evening Press [Belfast]. [July 1871]–No. 520, 15 May 1873–21 May 1874.

The Belfast Times. No. 1, 1 Jan. 1872–31 May 1872. [Continued as] The Belfast Daily Times. 1 June–10 Aug. 1872.

The Belfast Morning News. [1872]–27 April 1882. [Continued as] Morning News, No. 1, 1 May 1882–27 Aug. 1892. [Incorporated in Irish News (Belfast); ed. by Daniel Reed. Started 3 times a week, No. 1, 2 July 1855].

The Ulster Echo [Belfast]. No. 1, 26 May 1874–8 June 1916.

The Belfast Evening Star. No. 1, 29 Jan.–31 May 1890.

The Irish News [Belfast]. No. 1, 15 Aug. 1891 onwards. In progress.

The Cork Daily Advertiser. No. 1, 1 Oct. 1836–1 Jan. 1837.

The Southern Reporter [Cork]. 12 June 1855–16 June 1871. [Continued as] The Irish Daily Telegraph. 1 July 1871–11 Dec. 1873. [Started weekly in June 1807.]

The Cork Constitution. 2 Jan. 1860–14 Aug. 1925. [Started 3 times a week in 1822.]

The Cork Daily Herald. 2 March 1860–19 July 1901. [Started weekly as The Cork Herald, No. 1, 21 June 1856. Ed. by David A. Nagle.]

The Cork Examiner. [1861] onwards. In progress. [Started 3 times a week, No. 1, 30 Aug. 1840.]

The Evening Echo [Cork]. [1893]–No. 825, 6 May 1896 onwards. In progress.

Saunders's News-Letter [Dublin]. [June 1777]–4 June 1878. [Continued as] Saunders's Irish Daily News. 5 June 1878–

24 Nov. 1879. [Started 3 times a week in 1755; ed. by John Potts, J. T. Potts (1846–71).]

The Freeman's Journal. [before 1820]–20 Dec. 1924. [Started as The Public Register; or, Freeman's Journal, No. 1, 10 Sept. 1763, twice a week; ed. by Francis Higgins (1783–1802), Sir John Gray, Edmund Dwyer Gray, Edward Byrne (1884–91), P. W. Harvey.]

The Daily Express [Dublin]. No. 1, 3 Feb. 1851 onwards. In progress. [Ed. by G. H. Francis, J. Robinson.]

The Irish Times [Dublin]. No. 1, 29 March 1859 onwards. In progress. [Ed. by G. B. Wheeler (1859–77), J. A. Scott (1877–99), Arthur Locker.]

The Morning News [Dublin]. No. 6, 2 May 1859–31 Dec. 1864. [Ed. by A. M. Sullivan.]

The Evening Freeman [Dublin]. [1859]– 30 June 1871. [Continued as] The Evening Telegraph, No. 1, 1 July 1861–19 Dec. 1924. [Started 3 times a week, No. 1, 18 Jan. 1831.]

The Dublin Evening Mail. 4 Feb. 1861– 1 Feb. 1928. [Continued as] The Evening Mail. 2 Feb. onwards. In progress. [Ed. by — Sheehan (1832), J. T. Haydn, H. Maunsell; owned by J. S. Lefanu (1839–73). Started 3 times a week, No. 1, 3 Feb. 1823.]

The Dublin Evening Post. 23 Jan. 1865–21 Aug. 1875. [Started twice a week, No. 1, 10 June 1732; ed. by J. Magee.]

The Evening Irish Times [Dublin]. [1865]– 31 Oct. 1921.

The Morning Mail [Dublin]. [Feb. 1870]– No. 346, 17 March 1871–30 Aug. 1912.

The Dublin Sporting News. No. 1, 5 Feb. 1889–1901.

The Irish Daily Independent [Dublin]. No. 1, 18 Dec. 1891–31 Dec. 1904. [Continued as] Irish Independent. 2 Jan. 1905 onwards. In progress. [Ed. by Edward Byrne.]

The Evening Herald [Dublin]. No. 1, 19 Dec. 1891 onwards. In progress.

The Daily Nation [Dublin]. 5 June 1897–31 Aug. 1900. [Incorporated in The Irish Daily Independent. Started weekly, No. 1, 15 Oct. 1842. Ed. by A. M. Sullivan (1858–76), C. G. Duffy.]

The Mail and Waterford Daily Express. No. 1, 13 July 1855–June 1860.

The Waterford Daily Mail. 24 May 1870– 19 Sept. 1908. [Started weekly as The Waterford Mail, No. 1, 16 Aug. 1823. 'Daily' was omitted from the title from 30 Oct. 1874 to 11 Dec. 1886.]

The Evening News [Waterford]. [1898]– No. 288, 1 June 1899 onwards. In progress.

(5) LONDON PAPERS PUBLISHED MORE THAN ONCE A WEEK, 1800–1900

[The most important entries in this section are those London evening papers which were pbd three times a week; they were for the most part founded in the 18th century and were practically extinct by 1850. There are three other types of paper which were pbd more than once a week. There is the London suburban press; and there are various technical trade journals. Though examples of these are here given, no attempt has been made to list them in detail. Numerous provincial papers existed in 1800 as weeklies and were pbd more frequently until they became daily papers; these are included pp. 801–6 above.]

(a) Tri-Weekly Papers

(i) Monday, Wednesday and Friday

Lloyd's Evening Post and British Chronicle. No. 1, 22 July 1757–30 Dec. 1805–[1815?]. [Ed. by Robert Heron.]

London Packet, or New Lloyd's Evening Post. [Oct. 1769]–No. 91, 28 May 1770–No. 11584, 30 Dec. 1836. [Incorporated in The St James's Chronicle.]

The Evening Mail. [Feb. 1789]–No. 62, July 1789–27 June 1868. [Continued as] The Mail. 30 June 1868–11 Oct. 1922. [Incorporated in The Times Weekly Edition. Only twice a week from July 1868 to 1871. Run in conjunction with The Times.]

The Mercantile Chronicle. No. 1, 20 July 1821–10 Jan. 1823. [Incorporated in The London Packet, or New Lloyd's Evening Post.]

The Evening Chronicle. No. 1, 31 Jan. 1835– No. 1940, 23 July 1847. [Ed. by George Hogarth.]

The Hackney and Kingsland Gazette. [1864]– No. 277, 10 July 1867 onwards.

(ii) Tuesday, Thursday and Saturday

The London Evening Post. No. 1, 1 Dec. 1727–13 March 1806.

The General Evening Post. No. 1, 2 Oct. 1733–1 Feb. 1822. [Incorporated in The St James's Chronicle; ed. by Stephen Jones.]

The London Chronicle. No. 1, 1 Jan. 1757– 28 April 1823. [Incorporated in The London Packet or New Lloyd's Evening Post.]

The St James's Chronicle. No. 1, 12 March 1761–2 Aug. 1866. [Incorporated in The Press. Ed. by John MacDiarmid (1802), S. L. Giffard, Thomas Ballantyne.]

The English Chronicle. No. 1, 2 Jan. 1779– 30 Dec. 1843. [Ed. by William Radcliffe.]

The Inquisitor. [No. 1, 18 Oct. 1808]–No. 129, 15 Aug. 1809–[?]. [Ed. by John Browne Bell.]

(b) Bi-Weekly Papers

[Tuesdays and Fridays unless otherwise noted.]

The London Gazette. No. 1, 16 Nov. 1665 [at Oxford: from No. 24, 5 Feb. 1666 at London] onwards.

The National Adviser. No. 1, 10 Aug. 1811–No. 138, 2 Dec. 1812. [Mondays and Thursdays.]

The London Evening Chronicle. No. 1, 2 Aug. 1824–No. 133, 7 Nov. 1825.

The Record. No. 1, 1 Jan. 1828 onwards. [Evening paper; Mondays and Thursdays. Now weekly (see under Religious Papers p. 819).]

The Patriot. No. 1, 22 Feb. 1832–Dec. 1866. [Continued as] The English Independent. No. 1, 3 Jan. 1867–1 Oct. 1880 [incorporated in The Nonconformist; Mondays and Thursdays. (See under Religious Papers, p. 819.)]

The City Press. No. 1, 18 July 1857 onwards. [Wednesdays and Saturdays; ed. by W. H. Collingridge.]

The East End News. [1859]–No. 509, 17 July 1869 onwards.

The South London Press. No. 1, 7 Jan. 1865 onwards.

The South London Observer, Camberwell and Peckham Times. No. 295, 6 June 1874 onwards. [Started weekly in [1868] as Camberwell and Peckham Times. No. 74–294, 2 April 1870–20 May 1874; Wednesdays and Saturdays.]

D. THE WEEKLY PAPERS

[Besides the various types of paper here listed, one or more weekly papers were pbd in nearly every provincial town of any importance throughout the century. No attempt has been made to list these here, but they may be traced in the various works cited, p. 795 above.]

(1) SUNDAY PAPERS

E. Johnson's Sunday Monitor and British Gazette. [No. 1, 26 March 1780]–No. 66, 24 June 1781–22 Sept. 1805. [Continued as] Johnson's Sunday Monitor and British Gazette. 29 Sept. 1805–20 Feb. 1814. [Continued as] The Sunday Monitor. 27 Feb. 1814–25 Jan. 1829.

The London Recorder. [No. 1], 27 July 1783–No. 1152, 9 July 1809. [In 1796 it absorbed The Sunday Reformer and Universal Register (founded by George Ripley in 1793), and became The London Recorder and Sunday Reformer.]

The Review and Sunday Advertiser. No. 1, 22 June 1789–1796–[?]. [Continued as] The Sunday Review. [?]–No. 574, 19 Aug. 1798–19 March 1809.

The Observer. No. 1, 4 Dec. 1791 onwards. In progress. [Managed by Lewis Doxat (1804–57); owned by William I. Clement. Ed. by Kinloch Coke, Edward Dicey (1870–89), H. D. Traill (1889–91), J. H. MacCarthy (1892–7), Mrs F. A. Beer (1897–1901).]

The Selector; or Say's Sunday Reporter. [? Nov. 1795]–No. 161, 9 Dec. 1798–No. 569, 27 April 1806.

Bell's Weekly Messenger. No. 1, 1 May 1796–28 March 1896. [Continued as] Country Sport and Messenger of Agriculture. 4 April 1896–31 Dec. 1904. [Ed. by John Bell (1796–1821), F. L. Holt, Thomas Wade, J. N. Lee.]

The Weekly Dispatch. No. 1, 27 Sept. 1801–24 June 1928. [Continued as] The Sunday Dispatch. 1 July 1928 onwards. In progress. [Ed. by Robert Bell (1801–15, and again after 1816), George Kent (1815–6), James Harmer, Joseph Wrightson (1838–56), Sydney French (1856–62), T. J. Serle (1862–75), A. W. Dilke (1875–83).]

The British Neptune. [? Jan. 1803]–1 Dec. 1805–12 May 1823. [Ed. by Robert Heron (1805–6).]

The Englishman. [No. 1, 29 May 1803]–No. 32, 8 Jan. 1804–20 April 1834. [Owned by W. I. Clement (1821–34).]

The News. No. 1, 19 May 1805–No. 1768, 26 Aug. 1839. [Absorbed The Sunday Herald, 1829 and The Sunday Evening Globe (1837); ed. by John Hunt, John Scott.]

The Sunday Advertiser. [1807(?)]–No. 555, 4 Jan. 1818–5 Aug. 1821. [On 12 Aug. 1812 it absorbed The Weekly Register, and was continued under the style of The Sunday Advertiser and Weekly Register, 12 Aug. 1821–5 Jan. 1823; continued as The Weekly Register, 12 Jan. 1823–No. 1073, 30 Dec. 1827; and as The Sunday Herald, No. 1074, 6 Jan. 1828–8 Feb. 1829; incorporated with The News; in 1822 it was run in conjunction with The Morning Post; ed. by W. R. Macdonald (1828–9).]

The Independent Whig. [No. 1, 5 Jan. 1806]–No. 6, 9 Feb. 1806–No. 793, 25 March 1821. [Ed. by Henry White.]

The Examiner. No. 1, 3 Jan. 1808–26 Feb. 1881. [Ed. by John Hunt, Albany Fonblanque (1830–47), John Forster (1847–55), M. W. Savage (1856–9), Henry Morley (1859–65), Robert Williams, William Minto (1874–8).]

The National Register. No. 1, 3 Jan. 1808–12 May 1823. [Ed. by Eugenius Roche (1808–11); pbd by J. B. Bell and J. de Camp.]

The London and Provincial Sunday Gazette. [Aug. 1808 (?)]–No. 488, 6 Jan. 1818–No. 589, 11 May 1823.

The Anti-Gallican Monitor and Anti-Corsican Chronicle. No. 1, 27 Jan. 1811–No. 362, 4 Jan. 1818. [Continued as The British Monitor, 4 Jan. 1818–10 April 1825; incorporated in The English Gentleman; ed. by Lewis Goldsmith.]

The Constitution. [Jan. 1812 (?)]–No. 314, 4 Jan. 1818–5 Jan. 1823. [Continued as] The Observer of the Times and Constitution, 12 Jan.–6 April 1823. [Incorporated in The Englishman.]

The Champion. No. 52, 2 Jan. 1814–No. 491, 2 June 1822. [Started as Drakard's Paper, No. 1, 10 Jan.–No. 51, 26 Dec. 1813; continued as The Investigator, 9 June 1822–[?]; ed. by John Scott.]

Bell's Sunday Dispatch. No. 1, 16 April 1815–[?]. [Continued as] Weekly Dispatch. [?]–No. 54, 21 April 1816–[?]. [Ed. by Robert Bell on his exclusion from The Weekly Dispatch (1801), but dropped when he resumed control of the original paper.]

The Weekly Intelligence. [Jan. 1816 (?)]–No. 105, 4 Jan.–No. 143, 27 Sept. 1818. [Incorporated in The British Luminary and continued as The Weekly Intelligencer and British Luminary, 30 July 1820–May 1821; continued as The British Luminary and Weekly Intelligencer (see below).]

The British Luminary. [No. 1, 4 Jan. 1818]; No. 3, 25 Jan. 1818–8 June 1823. [Absorbed The Weekly Intelligence (see above); ed. by George Glenny.]

Wooler's British Gazette [Manchester]. No. 1, 3 Jan. 1819–No. 259, 14 Dec. 1823. [Ed. by T. J. Wooler.]

The Guardian. No. 1, 12 Dec. 1819–25 April 1824.

John Bull. No. 1, 17 Dec. 1820–No. 3739, 16 July 1892. [Absorbed Britannia, 19 April 1856; ed. by Theodore Hook, H. F. Cooper, G. W. Turner, C. G. Prowett, G. H. Smith.]

The Observer of the Times. No. 1, 7 Jan. 1821–No. 103, 29 Dec. 1822. [Incorporated in The Constitution.]

The Brunswick, or True Blue. No. 1, 28 Jan.–No. 18, 28 May 1821.

The Real John Bull. No. 1, 21 Jan. 1821–21 March 1824.

The Sunday Times. No. 1, 20 Oct. 1822 onwards. [Started as The New Observer, Nos. 1–6, 18 Feb.–25 March 1821; continued as The Independent Observer, No. 1, 1 April 1821–No. 85, 13 Oct. 1822. Ed. by Henry White (1821), D. W. Harvey (1822–?), Thomas Gaspey (1828), William Carpenter (1854), E. T. Smith (1856–8), E. W. Seale (1858–67), Joseph Hatton (1874–81), Philip Robinson (1887–90), A. W. à Becket (1890–4), Mrs F. A. Beer (1894–7), F. G. Smale (1897–1904).]

John Bull's British Journal. No. 1, 25 Feb.–11 March 1821.

Aurora Borealis. No. 1, 25 March–No. 45, 30 Dec. 1821. [Incorporated in The Observer of the Times.]

The Representative. No. 1, 6 Jan. 1821–15 April 1823. [Run in conjunction with The Sun.]

Life in London. No. 1, 13 Jan.–No. 23, 16 June 1822. [Incorporated in Bell's Life in London; ed. by W. R. Macdonald.]

Bell's Life in London and Sporting Chronicle. No. 1, 3 March 1822–29 May 1886. [Incorporated in Sporting Life. Ed. by Robert Bell, W. R. Macdonald, V. G. Dowling (1824–52), F. L. Dowling (1852–67), R. B. Wormald.]

The Weekly Globe. No. 1, 4 Jan. 1824–20 March 1825. [Incorporated in Common Sense.]

Pierce Egan's Life in London and Sporting Guide. No. 1, 1 Feb. 1824–28 Oct. 1827. [Incorporated in Bell's Life in London; ed. by Pierce Egan.]

The Colonist and Commercial Weekly Advertiser. Nos. 1–8, 24 Feb.–21 March 1824. [Continued as The Colonist and Weekly Courier, No. 9, 28 March–No. 39, 24 Oct. 1824; and as The Sunday Herald, No. 1, 31 Oct. 1824–No. 69, 22 May 1825.]

Common Sense. No. 1, 1 Aug. 1824–No. 80, 5 Feb. 1826. [Absorbed The Weekly Globe, and continued as Common Sense and Weekly Globe, 28 March 1825–5 Feb. 1826.]

Old England. Nos. 1–52, 14 Nov. 1824–6 Nov. 1825.

The Telescope. Nos. 1–53, 12 Dec. 1824–11 Dec. 1825.

The English Gentleman. No. 1, 19 Dec. 1824–No. 153, 18 Nov. 1827. [Continued as] Nimrod, 25 Nov. 1827–13 Jan. 1828. [Absorbed The British Monitor, 17 April 1825.]

The Age. 15 May 1825–7 Oct. 1843. [Absorbed The Argus, and continued as The Age and Argus, 16 Oct. 1843–26 April 1845; continued as The English Gentleman, No. 1, 3 May 1845–No. 73, 12 Sept. 1846; ed. by C. M. Westmacott, A. B. Richards, J. H. Stocqueler.]

The Atlas. No. 1, 21 May 1826–29 Jan. 1869. [Ed. by R. S. Rintoul (1826), Robert Bell, G. H. Francis, E. Ollier, J. B. Hopkins, H. J. Slack.]

The Weekly Times. No. 1, 3 June 1826–No. 357, 5 May 1833. [From 26 April–27 Dec. 1829 it was called The Liberal.]

The Sphynx. No. 1, 8 July 1827–26 April 1829. [Ed. by J. S. Buckingham.]

Pierce Egan's Weekly Courier. No. 1, 4 Jan.–26 April 1829. [Ed. by Pierce Egan.]

The United Kingdom. No. 1, 30 Oct. 1830–No. 168, 12 Jan. 1834–[?]. [Absorbed The Town, 27 July 1834.]

The Satirist, or Censor of the Times. No. 1, 10 April 1831–No. 924, 15 Dec. 1849. [Ed. by Barnard Gregory.]

Bell's New Weekly Messenger. No. 1, 1 Jan. 1832–No. 1288, 25 March 1855. [Incorporated in The News of the World; ed. by J. B. Bell.]

The Town. No. 1, 1 Jan. 1832–No. 134, 20 July 1834. [Incorporated in The United Kingdom.]

The Weekly True Sun. No. 1, 10 Feb. 1833–No. 331, 29 Dec. 1839. [Incorporated in The Statesman, a daily paper. Ed. by Patrick Grant, D. W. Harvey, W. J. Fox.]

The New Weekly Dispatch. No. 1, 8 Sept. 1833–No. 72, 18 Jan. 1835. [Continued as] The British and American Intelligencer. Nos. 1–11, 25 Jan.–5 April 1835.

The Weekly Times. No. 16, 27 Dec. 1835–No. 53, 11 Sept. 1836. [Continued as] The London Weekly Times. Nos. 1–13, 18 Sept.–18 Dec. 1836.

The Sunday Evening Globe. No. 1, 11 Sept. 1836–No. 32, 30 April 1837. [Incorporated in The News.]

The Champion and Weekly Herald. No. 1, 18 Sept. 1836–26 April 1840. [Incorporated in The Northern Liberator (Newcastle); ed. by Richard Cobbett.]

The Weekly Chronicle. No. 1, 18 Sept. 1836–Sept. 1855. [Absorbed The Register, and continued as The Weekly Chronicle and Register, 18 Sept. 1855–21 Dec. 1867; ed. by Sir H. G. Ward (1836–49).]

The London Mercury. No. 1, 18 Sept. 1836–No. 53, 17 Sept. 1837.

Cleave's London Satirist and Gazette of Variety. Nos. 1–9, 14 Oct.–9 Dec. 1837. [Continued as Cleave's Penny Gazette of Variety, No. 10, 16 Dec. 1837–No. 327, 20 Jan. 1844; unstamped.]

The Planet. No. 1, 17 Dec. 1837–No. 310, 4 Feb. 1844. [Ed. by J. B. Bell.]

The Crown. No. 1, 1 July 1838–No. 42, 14 April 1839. [Ed. by Renton Nicholson.]

The Operative. No. 1, 4 Nov. 1838–6 Oct. 1839. [Incorporated in The Champion; ed. by J. Bronterre O'Brien.]

The Charter. No. 1, 27 Jan. 1839–No. 60, 15 March 1840. [Incorporated in The

Statesman (daily); ed. by William Carpenter.]

The Penny Sunday Times and People's Police Gazette. [No. 1, 5 April 1840]–No. 2, 12 April 1840–[?]. [Continued as] Lloyd's Penny Sunday Times [etc.]. [?]–No. 171, 9 July 1843–No. 529, 27 April 1850–[?]. [Conducted by Edward Lloyd; unstamped.]

Tom Spring's Life in London and Sporting Chronicle. [June? 1840]–No. 17, 4 Oct. 1840–18 June 1843–[?]. [Pbd by W. M. Clark; unstamped.]

Bell's Penny Dispatch and Penny Sunday Chronicle. [Nov. 1840(?)]–No. 66, 27 Feb.–No. 97, 2 Oct. 1842. [Unstamped.]

The British Queen and Statesman. No. 395, 4 April 1841–No. 518, 19 Aug. 1843. [Nos. 1–394 were pbd daily as The Statesman and Weekly True Sun; ed. by D. W. Harvey.]

Lloyd's Illustrated London Newspaper. Nos. 1–7, 27 Nov. 1842–8 Jan. 1843. [Continued as] Lloyd's Weekly Newspaper. No. 8, 15 Jan. 1843–26 May 1918. [Continued as] Lloyd's Sunday News, 2 June 1918–30 Sept. 1923. [Continued as] Sunday News, 7 Oct. 1923–9 Aug. 1931. [Incorporated in The Sunday Graphic; ed. by Edward Lloyd, William Carpenter (1844), Douglas Jerrold (1852–7), Blanchard Jerrold (1857–84), Thomas Catling (1884–1907).]

The News of the World. No. 1, 1 Oct. 1843 onwards. In progress. [Absorbed Bell's New Weekly Messenger, April 1855; ed. by J. B. Bell (1843–55), J. W. Bell (1855–77), W. J. and A. W. Bell (1877–91), Emsley Carr (1891 onwards).]

New Tom Spring's Life in London and Sporting Times. No. 1, 28 Oct. 1843–No. 59, 7 Dec. 1844.

The Family Times. No. 1, 6 June 1846–No. 162, 26 June 1849.

The Weekly Times. No. 1, 24 Jan. 1847–27 Sept. 1885. [Continued as] The Weekly Times and Echo. No. 1, 4 Oct. 1885–29 Dec. 1912. [Founded by George Stift; ed. by F. G. Tomlins.]

Reynolds' Weekly Newspaper. No. 1, 18 Aug. 1850–14 Sept. 1924. [Continued as] Reynolds' Illustrated News. 21 Sept. 1924 onwards. In progress. [Ed. by G. W. M. Reynolds (1850–79), Edward Reynolds, Arthur Downing, W. M. Thompson (1888–1907).]

Bell's News. No. 1, 24 Feb. 1855–No. 118, 16 May 1857. [Incorporated in The Weekly Star.]

The Penny Newsman and Sunday Morning Mail and Telegraph. No. 1, 28 Jan. 1800–

10 July 1864. [Continued as] The News-man, etc. No. 234, 17 July 1864–12 Feb. 1865.

The London Halfpenny Newspaper. Nos. 1–4, 11 Aug.–1 Sept. 1861.

The Sunday Gazette. No. 1, 7 Jan. 1866–24 Nov. 1867.

The Referee. No. 1, 19 Aug. 1877–9 Sept. 1928. [Continued as] Sunday Referee. 16 Sept. 1928 onwards. In progress. [Ed. by Henry Sampson (1877–91).]

The People. No. 1, 16 Oct. 1881 onwards. In progress. [Ed. by Sebastian Evans, Joseph Hatton (1892–1907).]

The Umpire [Manchester]. No. 1, 4 May 1884 –25 March 1917. [Continued as] The Empire. 1 April–15 July 1917. [Con-tinued as] Empire News, 22 July 1917 onwards. In progress. [Absorbed The Manchester Examiner and Times, which was for a time a daily paper, in March 1894.]

The Sunday Chronicle [Manchester]. No. 1, 23 Aug. 1885 onwards. In progress. [Founded by E. O. Bleackley and E. Hulton.]

The Sunday Sun. No. 1, 10 May 1891–3 Jan. 1909. [Style changed to The Weekly Sun and back again; ed. by T. P. O'Connor.]

The Sunday Mercury. No. 1, 25 Oct. 1891–23 April 1893.

The Sunday Graphic. No. 1, 30 July 1893–31 March 1901.

The Sunday Mail. No. 1, 17 May 1896–29 Dec. 1914.

The Sunday Special. No. 1, 5 Dec. 1897–27 Dec. 1903. [Ed. by George Wedlake.]

(2) GENERAL WEEKLY PAPERS

The Westminster Journal and Old British Spy. [1794?]–No. 3368, 7 Sept. 1805–26 Dec. 1812. [Continued as] The West-minster Journal and Imperial Weekly Gazette. 2 Jan. 1813–1 Jan. 1814–[?]. [Continued as] The Imperial Weekly Gazette and Westminster Journal. [?]–3 Jan. 1818–22 Jan. 1825. [Started as The New Weekly Miscellany, No. 1, 18 July 1741 (see vol. II, above, p. 715).]

The Craftsman; or, Say's Weekly Journal [July? 1758]–No. 649, 5 Jan. 1771–No. 2498, 16 June 1810. [Incorporated in Baldwin's London Journal. Pbd Charles Say, Mary Vint.]

Baldwin's London Journal; or, British Chronicle. No. 1, 2 Jan. 1762–[?]. [Con-tinued as] Baldwin's London Weekly Journal. [?]–10 Dec. 1803–No. 3968, 31 Dec. 1836. [Pbd Charles Baldwin.]

The County Chronicle and Weekly Advertiser. [No. 1, 29 May?, 1787]–No. 42, 18 March 1788–1857. [Continued at Guildford, 1858–78, and at Lewes, 1879–1902.]

The County Herald and Weekly Advertiser. [1791?]–No. 1186, 16 April 1814–4 Oct. 1873. [Variations in subtitle; pbd at Guildford 1858–73.]

The Mirror of the Times. [April? 1796]–No. 92, 6 Jan. 1798–No. 1391, 23 Feb. 1823.

The Philanthropic Gazette. No. 1, 1 Jan. 1817–27 Aug. 1823. [Incorporated in Baldwin's London Weekly Journal.]

The Christian Reporter. No. 1, 3 Jan. 1820–11 Feb. 1822. [Incorporated in The Phil-anthropic Gazette.]

The British Freeholder and Saturday Evening Journal. No. 1, 5 Feb. 1820–No. 175, 10 May 1823.

The London Weekly Gazette. No. 1, 13 March 1822–No. 68, 2 July 1823.

The Weekly Press. 23 Aug. 1823–2 April 1831.

The British Guardian and Protestant Advo-cate. No. 1, 7 Jan. 1824–No. 116, 22 March 1826.

The World. No. 1, 4 May 1827–28 March 1832.

The Spectator. No. 1, 5 July 1828 onwards. In progress. [Ed. by Robert Rintoul (1828–58), R. H. Hutton and Meredith Townsend (1861–96), J. St Loe Strachey (1897–1925).]

The Court Journal. No. 1, 2 May 1829–13 March 1925. [Ed. by Coventry Patmore, William Carpenter, Charles Taylor.]

The Court Circular. No. 1, 2 May 1829–8 July 1911.

The Country Times. No. 1, 4 Jan. 1830–No. 102, 26 Dec. 1831.

Old England. 14 April 1832–21 Feb. 1842. [No issue from 12 March 1836–15 June 1839.]

The London Dispatch. No. 1, 17 Sept. 1836–No. 160, 6 Oct. 1839.

The London Journal. No. 1, 17 Sept. 1836–No. 47, 2 Aug. 1837.

The Metropolitan Conservative Journal. No. 1, 8 Oct. 1836–No. 117, 29 Dec. 1838. [Con-tinued as] The Conservative Journal and Church of England Gazette. No. 118, 5 Jan. 1839–No. 320, 31 Dec. 1842.

The Penny Satirist. No. 1, 22 April 1837–25 April 1846. [Continued as] The London Pioneer. 1846–8. [Ed. by Barnard Gregory.]

The Town. No. 1, 3 June 1837–No. 244, 26 Jan. 1842. [Ed. by Renton Nicholson. Ptd Joseph Last.]

The Court Gazette. No. 1, 7 April 1838–No. 438, 4 April 1846. [Ed. by J. B. Torr.]

The Argus. No. 1, 3 Feb. 1839–30 Sept. 1843. [Incorporated with The Age and Argus.]

Britannia. No. 1, 20 April 1839–12 April 1856. [Incorporated in John Bull. Ed. by D. T. Coulton (1839–50).]

The Sentinel. No. 1, 7 Jan. 1843–No. 179, 7 June 1846.

The National. No. 1, 14 March 1846–No. 157, 10 March 1849.

Douglas Jerrold's Weekly Newspaper. No. 1, 18 July 1846–No. 129, 30 Dec. 1848. [Continued as] Douglas Jerrold's Weekly News and Financial Economist. No. 130, 6 Jan. 1849–No. 181, 29 Dec. 1849. [Continued as] The Weekly News and Financial Economist. No. 182, 6 Jan. 1850–No. 255, 31 May 1851.

Reynolds' Miscellany. 1847–1869. [Ed. by G. W. M. Reynolds.]

The Leader. No. 1, 30 March 1850–No. 536, 30 June 1860. [Continued as] The Saturday Analyst and Leader. Nos. 537–557, 7 July–24 Nov. 1860. [Ed. by G. H. Lewes, T. L. Hunt, Thomas Ballantyne.]

The Press. No. 1, 7 May 1853–15 Nov. 1884. [Incorporated in The English Churchman. Owned by Disraeli; ed. by S. Lucas (1853), D. T. Coulton (1854–7), R. H. Patterson, G. H. Townsend.]

The Saturday Review. No. 1, 3 Nov. 1856 onwards. In progress. [Ed. by J. D. Cook, Philip Harwood, W. H. Pollock, L. Edmunds (1894), Frank Harris (1894–9), H. Hodge.]

Town Talk. No. 1, May 1858–No. 56, June 1859. [Ed. by Edmund Yates.]

The Dial. No. 1, 7 Jan. 1860–2 June 1864. [Ed. by David Thomas.]

The London Review and Weekly Journal. No. 1, 7 July 1860–27 March 1869. [Incorporated in The Examiner; ed. by Charles Mackay.]

Public Opinion. No. 1, 5 Oct. 1861 onwards. In progress. [Ed. by Percy White (1880–90), P. Fisher.]

The Pall Mall Budget. No. 1, 3 Oct. 1868–31 Dec. 1920. [Ed. by C. L. Hind (1893–5).]

Vanity Fair. No. 1, 7 Nov. 1868–June 1929. [Ed. by T. Gibson Bowles.]

The Latest News. No. 1, 28 Aug. 1869–No. 57, 25 Sept. 1870. [Ed. by Henry Sampson.]

Figaro. No. 1, 17 May 1870–31 Dec. 1898. [Ed. by James Mortimer.]

The World. No. 1, 8 July 1874–25 March 1922. [Ed. by Edmund Yates.]

Light. No. 1, 6 April–26 Oct. 1876. [Ed. by John Morley.]

The Whitehall Review. No. 1, 20 May 1876–25 Oct. 1912. [Ed. by Edward Legge.]

Mayfair. 2 Jan. 1877–14 Feb. 1880. [Ed. by H. W. Lucy.]

Truth. No. 1, 4 Jan. 1877 onwards. In progress. [Ed. by Henry Labouchere.]

The Week. No. 1, 5 Jan. 1878–31 May 1879. [Ed. by L. J. Jennings.]

The Citizen. No. 1, 3 May 1878 onwards. In progress. [Ed. by James Sutherland.]

Life. No. 1, 12 July 1879–15 Dec. 1906. [Ed. by H. Felbermann.]

Society. [No. 1, 2 May 1879]–No. 45, 12 March 1880–31 Aug. 1901. [Ed. by George Plant.]

England. No. 1, 27 March 1880–28 May 1898.

Tit-Bits. No. 1, 22 Oct. 1881 onwards. In progress. [Ed. by George Newnes.]

St Stephen's Review. No. 1, 17 March 1883–No. 502, 1 Dec. 1892. [Continued as] Big Ben. 8 Dec. 1892–30 March 1893.

Cassell's Saturday Journal. No. 1, 6 Oct. 1883–19 Feb. 1921. [Ed. by E. Foster (1887–1907).]

The Outlook. No. 1, 11 July 1885–Sept. 1892. [Incorporated in The American Settler.]

The British Weekly. No. 1, 5 Nov. 1886 onwards. In progress. [Ed. by Sir W. Robertson Nicoll.]

The Tattler. No. 1, 7 July 1887–No. 114, 26 Oct. 1889. [Continued as] The Pelican, 2 Nov. 1889–April 1920. [Ed. by F. M. Boyd.]

The Scots Observer [Edinburgh], No. 1, 24 Nov. 1888–15 Nov. 1890. [Continued at London as] The National Observer. 22 Nov. 1890–16 Oct. 1897. [Ed. by W. E. Henley (1888–94), Frank Harris.]

Answers. No. 1, 2 June 1888 onwards. In progress. [Founded by Lord Northcliffe.]

The Speaker. No. 1, 4 Jan. 1890–23 Feb. 1907. [Continued as] The Nation. 2 March 1907–21 Feb. 1931. [Incorporated in The New Statesman. Ed. by T. Wemyss Reid, Philip Carr, J. L. Hammond.]

Pearson's Weekly. No. 1, 26 July 1890 onwards. In progress.

To-Day. No. 1, 11 Nov. 1893–19 July 1908. [Ed. by Jerome K. Jerome (1893–7), Barry Pain (1897–9).]

(3) The Illustrated Papers

Jackson, Mason. The Pictorial Press: its Origin and Progress. 1885.

Blackburn, H. The Cantor Lectures on the Art of Book and Newspaper Illustration. 1894.

Gamble, William. Newspaper Illustrations. [In Penrose's Pictorial Annual, vol. III, 1897, pp. 17–32.]

—— Pictorial Telegraphy. [In Penrose's Pictorial Annual, vol. IV, 1898, pp. 1–12.]

Shorter, C. K. Illustrated Journalism: its Past and Future. Contemporary Rev. April 1899.

The Mirror of Literature, Amusement, and Instruction. No. 1, 22 Nov. 1822–13 June 1847. [Continued monthly to 1849. Ed. by Thomas Byerley, P. B. St John.]

The Illustrated London News. No. 1, 14 May 1842 onwards. [Founded by Herbert Ingram; ed. by Charles Mackay (1848–52), John Lash Latey (1858–90), Clement K. Shorter, Bruce S. Ingram.]

Lloyd's Illustrated London Newspaper. Nos. 1–7, 27 Nov. 1842–8 Jan. 1843. [Continued as Lloyd's Weekly Newspaper (see p. 812).]

The Illustrated Weekly Times. Nos. 1–6, 11 March–15 April 1843.

Illustrated London Life. [No. 1, 12 March]–No. 5, 9 April–13 Aug. 1843. [Ed. by Renton Nicholson.]

The Pictorial Times. No. 1, 18 March 1844–8 Jan. 1848. [Incorporated with The Lady's Newspaper; ed. by H. Vizetelly.]

The Lady's Newspaper. No. 1, 2 Jan. 1847–No. 887, 26 Dec. 1863. [From 15 Jan. 1848 the style was The Lady's Newspaper and Pictorial Times; incorporated in The Queen.]

The Historic Times. Nos. 1–13. 19 Jan.–13 April 1849. [Continued as The Illustrated Historic Times, No. 14, 20 April 1849–No. 89, 26 Sept. 1850.]

The Field. No. 1, 1 Jan. 1853 onwards. [Ed. by J. H. Walsh (1857–88), William Senior.]

Cassell's Illustrated Family Paper. No. 1, 31 Dec. 1853–9 March 1867. [Continued as Cassell's Magazine. Ed. by John Tillotson.]

Pen and Pencil. No. 1, 10 Feb.–31 March 1855.

The Illustrated Times. No. 1, 9 June 1855–No. 885, 2 March 1872. [Ed. by Henry Vizetelly (1855–65).]

The Picture Times. No. 1, 30 June 1855–12 April 1856. [Incorporated in The Illustrated Times.]

The Coloured News. Nos. 1–9, 4 Aug.–29 Sept. 1855.

The Illustrated News of the World. No. 1, 6 Feb. 1858–No. 300, 31 Oct. 1863. [Ed. by J. M. Moir, John Tallis, J. E. Ritchie (1860–3).]

The Queen. No. 1, 7 Sept. 1861 onwards. [Ed. by P. S. Cox.]

The Penny Illustrated Paper. No. 1, 12 Oct. 1861–22 March 1913. [Continued as London Life. Run in conjunction with Illustrated London News.]

The Illustrated Weekly News. No. 1, 12 Oct. 1861–No. 423, 30 Oct. 1869.

The Illustrated Sporting News. [No. 1, 15 March]; No. 2, 22 March 1862–No. 138, 29 Oct. 1864. [Continued as The Illustrated Sporting and Theatrical News, until

19 March 1870; ed. by Henry Sampson (1869–70).]

Land and Water. No. 1, 27 June 1866–16 Sept. 1920. [From 30 June 1905 to 30 Dec. 1915 incorporated in The Country Gentleman; finally incorporated in The Field.]

The Illustrated Midland News [Birmingham]. No. 1, 4 Sept. 1869–No. 80, 11 March 1871.

The Graphic. No. 1, 4 Dec. 1869–23 April 1932. [Continued as] National Graphic. 28 April 1932 onwards. [Ed. by Sutherland Edwards (1869–70), Arthur Locker (1870–91), Heath Joyce.]

The Illustrated Newspaper. [1869]–No. 81, 18 March–30 Dec. 1871.

The Illustrated Sporting and Dramatic News. [No. 1] 28 Feb. 1874 onwards.

The Pictorial World. No. 1, 7 March 1874–9 July 1892. [Incorporated in Black and White; ed. by H. W. Cutts.]

The Penny Pictorial News. No. 1, 1 Sept. 1877–10 Nov. 1888. [Continued as The Pictorial News, 17 Nov. 1888–27 Sept. 1891; continued as The Penny Pictorial Weekly, No. 736, 3 Oct. 1891–4 June 1892. Ed. by Charles P. Sisley.]

The Lady's Pictorial. No. 1, 5 March 1881–26 Feb. 1921. [Incorporated in Eve; ed. by Alfred Gibbons.]

The Lady. No. 1, 19 Feb. 1885 onwards.

The Daily Graphic. No. 1, 4 Jan. 1890–16 Oct. 1926. [Incorporated in The Daily Sketch. The first illustrated daily paper.]

Black and White. No. 1, 6 Feb. 1891–13 Jan. 1912. [Incorporated in The Sphere; ed. by Oswald Crawfurd.]

The Sketch. No. 1, 1 Feb. 1893 onwards. [Ed. by C. K. Shorter, John Latey.]

Country Life. No. 1, 8 Jan. 1897 onwards.

The Illustrated Mail. No. 1, 17 June 1899–1 June 1907. [Continued as The Weekly Illustrated.]

The Sphere. No. 1, 27 Jan. 1900 onwards. [Ed. by C. K. Shorter.]

(4) UNSTAMPED AND RADICAL JOURNALS

[This type of periodical, often issued in octavo, has usually been associated with a single personality, and by far the greater bulk are of pronounced radical tendency. For this reason Chartist, Socialist and Trade Union weekly papers have also been included in this section. Some unstamped Sunday papers of a similar kind but with more space given to news have already been noted on pp. 811–2.]

Berguer, L. T. A Warning Letter to H.R.H. the Prince Regent. 1819 (3rd edn).

The Standard. 10 Sept. 1833.

Gammage, R. G. The History of the Chartist Movement, 1837–54. Newcastle, 1854; Newcastle, 1894 (rev.).

Rose, J. Holland. The Unstamped Press, 1815–1836. EHR. Oct. 1897.

Menger, Anton. The Right to the Whole Produce of Labour. English translation by M. E. Tanner. 1899. [Pp. 252–63.]

Dierlamm, Gotthilf. Die Flugschriftenliteratur der Chartistenbewegung in der öffentlichen Meinung. Tübingen, 1909.

Cobbett's Political Register. No. 1, 16 Jan. 1802–20 Feb. 1836. [Ed. by W. Cobbett; W. Cobbett junr.]

Mr Redhead Yorke's Weekly Political Review. No. 1, 7 Dec. 1805–1811.

The Phoenix. No. 1, 14 Feb.–No. 46, 25 Dec. 1808. [Ed. by F. W. Blagdon.]

The Anti-Cobbett: or Weekly Patriotic Register. Nos. 1–7, 1817.

The Black Dwarf. No. 1, 29 Feb. 1817–Dec. 1824. [Ed. by T. J. Wooler.]

The Reformist's Register and Weekly Commentary. No. 1, 1 Feb.–25 Oct. 1817. [Ed. by William Hone.]

The Republican. Nos. 1–6, 23 Feb.–30 March 1817. [Continued as Sherwin's Weekly Political Register, 5 April 1817–20 Aug. 1819; continued as The Republican, vol. I, No. 1, 28 Aug. 1819–29 Dec. 1826; ed. by W. T. Sherwin; Richard Carlile; J. A. St John.]

The White Dwarf. No. 1, 29 Nov. 1817–No. 13, 21 Feb. 1818. [Tory; ed. by Gibbons Merle.]

The Yellow Dwarf. No. 1, 3 Jan.–No. 21, 23 May 1818. [Ed. by John Hunt.]

The Gorgon. No. 1, 23 May 1818–24 April 1819. [Ed. by J. Wade and Francis Place; probably the first penny paper, unstamped.]

The Deist or Moral Philosopher. No. 1, 1 Jan. 1819–[?]. [Ed. by R. Carlile.]

The Medusa or Penny Politician. No. 1, 20 Feb. 1819–7 Jan. 1820. [Unstamped.]

Shadgett's Weekly Review of Cobbett, Wooler, Sherwin and other democratic and infidel Writers. Vols. I, II, 1819.

The True Briton [Boston]. No. 1, 9 June–No. 20, 20 Oct. 1819.

The Theological Comet or Free Thinking Englishman. No. 1, 24 July–21 Aug. 1819. [Continued as The Theological and Political Comet, 28 Aug.–23 Nov. 1819.]

Edmond's Weekly Register [Birmingham]. No. 1, 28 Aug. 1819–30 Nov. 1819.

The Cap of Liberty. No. 1, 8 Sept. 1819–5 Jan. 1820. [Incorporated in The Medusa.]

The Democratic Recorder and Reformer's Guide. No. 1, 2 Oct.–No. 4, Nov. 1819. [Ed. by E. Edmonds.]

The White Hat. No. 1, 16 Oct.–11 Dec. 1819.

The Blue Dwarf [Yarmouth]. Nos. 1–6, 1820.

The Economist; a periodical paper explanatory of the New System of Society projected by Robert Owen. No. 1, 27 Jan. 1821–No. 52, 9 March 1822.

The Lion. 1828–9. [Ed. by R. Carlile.]

Political Letter and Pamphlets, Published for the avowed purpose of trying with the Government the Question of Law, whether all publications containing news are liable to the imposition of the stamp duty. 1830–1. [Unstamped; ed. by William Carpenter.]

The Prompter. No. 1, 13 Nov. 1830–12 Nov. 1831. [Unstamped; ed. by R. Carlile.]

The Poor Man's Guardian. No. 1, 9 July 1831–26 Dec. 1835. [Ed. by Henry Hetherington; J. Bronterre O'Brien.]

The Poor Man's Advocate [Manchester]. No. 1, 21 Jan. 1832–No. 50, 5 Jan. 1833. [Ed. by J. Doherty.]

The Isis. A London weekly publication. Edited by a Lady. 1832. [Ed. by Mrs Carlile.]

The Cosmopolite. No. 1, 10 March 1832–No. 55, 19 May 1833. [Unstamped; ed. by Rowland Detrosier.]

The Crisis. Vol. I, No. 1, 14 April 1832–Vol. IV, No. 20, 23 Aug. 1834. [Ed. by Robert Owen and J. E. Smith.]

The Destructive and Poor Man's Conservative. No. 1, 2 Feb. 1833–No. 53, 1 Feb. 1834. [Continued as] The People's Conservative and Trades Union Gazette. No. 54, 8 Feb.–No. 74, June 1834. [Ed. by J. Bronterre O'Brien.]

The Gauntlet. A Sound Weekly Republican Newspaper. No. 1, 9 Feb. 1833–29 March 1834. [Ed. by R. Carlile.]

The Shepherd. No. 1, 30 Aug. 1834–31 March 1838. [Ed. by J. E. Smith.]

Hetherington's Twopenny Dispatch and People's Police Register. [June 1834]–No. 109–No. 118, 9 July–10 Sept. 1836. [Continued as] The London Dispatch. No. 1, 17 Sept. 1836–No. 160, 6 Oct. 1837. [Ed. by Augustus Beaumont.]

The New Moral World. No. 1, 1 Nov. 1834–10 Jan. 1846. [Pbd successively at London, Manchester, Birmingham and Leeds; ed. by Robert Owen; G. A. Fleming.]

The Weekly Herald. 18 Sept.–13 Nov. 1836. [Incorporated in The Champion.]

Bronterre's National Reformer. Nos. 1–11, 1837. [Ed. by J. Bronterre O'Brien.]

The Northern Liberator [Newcastle-on-Tyne]. No. 1, 21 Oct. 1837–No. 139, 23 May 1840. [Continued as] The Northern Liberator and Champion. 30 May–19 Dec. 1840. [Ed. by A. H. Beaumont.]

The Northern Star and Leeds General Advertiser [Leeds]. No. 1, 18 Nov. 1837–13 March 1852. [Continued as The Star and National Trades Journal, Nos. 750–755,

20 March–1 May 1852; continued as The Star of Freedom, Nos. 1–16, 8 May–27 Nov. 1852; owned by Fergus O'Connor; ed. by William Hill, G. J. Harney.]

The National. A Library for the People. Nos. 1–25, 1839. [Ed. by W. J. Linton.]

The Chartist. No. 1, 2 Feb.–No. 23, 7 July 1839. ['Moral force'; Chartist.]

The Chartist Circular [Glasgow]. No. 1, 28 Sept. 1839–No. 84, 1 May 1841.

The English Chartist Circular. No. 1, 23 Jan. 1841–No. 153, 1843.

The London Phalanx. No. 1, 3 April 1841–30 April 1842. [Continued monthly, June 1842–May 1843. Fourierist; ed. by Hugh Doherty.]

The Oracle of Reason. No. 1, 6 Nov. 1841–No. 103, 2 Dec. 1843. [Ed. by Charles Southwell, G. J. Holyoake, Thomas Paterson, William Chilton.]

The British Statesman. No. 1, 13 March 1842–No. 46, 21 Jan. 1843. [Ed. by J. Bronterre O'Brien; incorporated in The British Queen and Statesman.]

The Dundee Herald. No. 1, 26 Aug. 1842–[?]. [Chartist; ed. by Peter Brown.]

The Movement, Anti-Persecution Gazette and Register of Progress. No. 1, 16 Dec. 1843–No. 68, 2 April 1845. [Ed. by G. J. Holyoake and M. Q. Ryall.]

The League. No. 1, 30 Sept. 1843–4 July 1846. [Organ of the Anti-Corn Law League; ed. by A. W. Paulton.]

The National Reformer. No. 1, Nov. 1844–29 May 1847. [Ptd at Douglas, Isle of Man, where no stamp was needed. Ed. by J. Bronterre O'Brien.]

The Moral World. No. 1, 30 Aug.–No. 11, 8 Nov. 1845. [Ed. by Robert Owen.]

The Reasoner. No. 1, 3 June 1846–No. 789, 30 June 1861. [Continued monthly as] The Counsellor. Aug.–Dec. 1861. [Continued as] The Secular World. 10 May 1862–1 June 1864. [Continued as] The English Leader. 4 June–15 Oct. 1864. [Continued as] The Secular World. [Continued monthly as] The Reasoner. Jan. 1865–Dec. 1865. [Continued as] The English Leader. Jan.–July 1866. [Continued irregularly as] The Reasoner. To July 1872. [Ed. by G. J. Holyoake.]

Politics for the People. No. 1, 6 May–No. 17, 29 July 1848. [Christian Socialist; ed. by J. M. Ludlow and F. D. Maurice.]

The Spirit of the Age. No. 1, 1 July 1848–3 March 1849. [Ed. by Robert Buchanan.]

The Standard of Freedom. No. 1, 1 July 1848–No. 171, 4 Oct. 1851. [Incorporated in The Weekly News and Chronicle.]

The Spirit of the Times. No. 1, 10 March–29 Sept. 1849. [Continued as The Weekly Tribune, 6 Oct. 1849–6 July 1850; ed. by Robert Buchanan.]

Reynolds's Political Instructor. No. 1, 10 Nov. 1849–11 May 1850. [Ed. by G. W. M. Reynolds.]

Cooper's Journal. No. 1, 5 Jan.–No. 30, 26 Oct. 1850. [Ed. by Thomas Cooper.]

Weekly Letters to the Human Race. Nos. 1–17, 1850. [Ed. by Robert Owen.]

The Red Republican. No .1, 22 June–No. 24, 30 Nov. 1850. [Ed. by G. J. Harney.]

The Friend of the People. No. 1, 7 Dec. 1850–No. 33, 26 July 1851; New Series, No. 1, 7 Feb.–No. 12, 24 April 1852. [Ed. by G. J. Harney.]

The Operative. Nos. 1–80. 1851–2.

The Christian Socialist. No. 1, 2 Nov. 1850–27 Dec. 1851. [Ed. by J. Townsend, F. D. Maurice.]

Robert Owen's Journal. No. 1, 2 Nov. 1851–23 Oct. 1852.

The People's Paper. No. 1, 8 May 1852–4 Sept. 1858. [Ed. by Ernest Jones.]

The Friend of the People. No. 1, 28 Jan. 1860–20 Sept. 1861.

The Elector. No. 1, 23 June 1860–No. 142, 2 Aug. 1862. [Formerly The Ballot, No. 1, 19 Nov. 1859–No. 31, 16 June 1860.]

The Co-operator [Manchester]. Vols. i–xi, 1860–71. [Continued as The Co-operative News, No. 1, 2 Sept. 1871 onwards. Ed. by R. B. Walker.]

The Beehive. [1861]–No. 404, 10 July 1869–No. 794, 30 Dec. 1876. [Continued as] The Industrial Review. 6 Jan. 1877–28 Dec. 1878 [ed. by George Potter].

The British Miner and General Newsman. 13 Sept. 1862–30 April 1863. [Continued as] The Miner and Workman's Advocate. 13 June 1863–Sept. 1865. [Continued as] The Workman's Advocate. 9 Sept. 1865–3 Feb. 1866. [Continued as] The Commonwealth, 10 Feb. 1866–20 July 1867. [Incorporated in The Train; organ first of the British Miners' Benefit Association, then of the International Working Men's Association, then of the Reform League; ed. by John Towers, William Whitehorn.]

The Eastern Post. No. 1, 18 Oct. 1868 onwards. In progress.

The International Herald. No. 1, 2 March 1872–No. 81, 18 Oct. 1873. [Continued as The Republican Herald, 1873–4; organ of the International Working Men's Association; ed. by W. Harrison Riley.]

The Miners' Advocate [Middlesbrough]. No. 1, 17 Jan. 1873–31 Oct. 1874.

The Miner's Weekly News [Coventry]. No. 1, 16 Aug. 1873–No. 23, 17 Jan. 1874.

The Union Chronicle [Manchester, Leamington and Coventry]. 1873–5. [Continued as] The National Agricultural Labourers' Chronicle. 1875–7. [Continued as] The English Labourers' Chronicle. 1877–94.

Daylight [Norwich]. No. 1, 5 Oct. 1878–1909.

The Railway Review. No. 1, 16 July 1880 onwards.

The Radical. 14 Dec. 1880–July 1882. [Ed. by Samuel Bennett.]

The Freethinker. No. 1, May 1881 onwards. [Ed. by G. W. Foote.]

Justice. No. 1, 19 Jan. 1884–22 Jan. 1925. [Ed. by H. M. Hyndman (1884–6), H. Quelch (1886–1913).]

The Democrat. No. 1, 15 Nov. 1884–1 Sept. 1890. [Continued as] The Labour World. No. 1, 21 Sept. 1890–No. 37, 22 March 1891. [Continued as] The Sunday World, 29 March–31 May 1891. [Ed. by Michael Davitt.]

The Commonweal. No. 1, Feb. 1885–12 May 1894. [Ed. by William Morris.]

Brotherhood. 28 April 1887–April 1903. [Continued as a monthly; organ of the Land Nationalization Society; ed. by J. Bruce Wallace.]

The Leaflet Newspaper. 4 Feb.–23 June 1888. [Continued as The Socialist, 7 July 1888–1 Sept. 1888; then continued monthly; last number dated Feb.–April, 1889; ed. by Thomas Bolas.]

The Link. No. 1, 4 Feb.–No. 44, 1 Dec. 1888. [Organ of Law and Liberty League; ed. by Annie Besant and W. T. Stead.]

The Labour Elector. No. 10, 15 Dec. 1888–July 1894. [Started as a monthly, Nos. 1–5, June–Oct. 1888; continued fortnightly, Nos. 6–9, 1 Nov.–3 Dec. 1888; suspended from April 1890 to Jan. 1893; ed. by H. H. Champion.]

The North London Press. 18 May 1889–25 Jan. 1890. [Continued as The People's Press; Radical; ed. by Ernest Parke.]

The People's Press. No. 1, 8 March 1890–No. 52, 28 Feb. 1891. [Organ of several Trade Unions; ed. by Shaw Maxwell.]

The Workman's Times [Huddersfield]. No. 1, 29 Aug. 1890–7 March 1894. [At London 1892–3, and Manchester 1893–4; ed. by Joseph Burgess.]

The Trade Unionist. No. 1, 4 April–22 Aug. 1891. [New Series, incorporating The Docker's Record, 29 Aug. 1891–19 March 1892; then incorporated in The Workman's Times.

The Labour Leader. No. 1, 10 Oct. 1891–28 Sept. 1922. [Incorporated in The New Leader.]

The Clarion. No. 1, 12 Dec. 1891 onwards. In progress. [Ed. by Robert Blatchford.]

(5) LITERARY WEEKLY REVIEWS

The Director. A Weekly Literary Journal. No. 1, 24 Jan.–4 July 1807. [Ed. by T. F. Dibdin.]

The Literary Gazette. No. 1, 25 Jan. 1817–1862. [Incorporated with The Parthenon; ed. by H. E. Lloyd and Miss Ross; William Jerdan (1817–50), L. A. Reeve (1850–8), J. M. Jephson (1858), Shirley Brooks, H. Christmas, W. R. Workman, F. Arnold, John Morley, C. W. Goodman.]

The Literary Journal. No. 1, 29 March 1818–1819.

The Country Literary Chronicle and Weekly Review [1819]–No. 59, 1 July 1820–No. 260, 8 May 1823. [Continued as The Literary Chronicle and Weekly Review, No. 261, 15 May 1823–No. 471, 24 May 1828; then incorporated in The Athenaeum.]

The Indicator. No. 1, 13 Oct. 1819–No. 99, 30 Aug. 1821. [Nos. 1–77 ed. by Leigh Hunt.]

The Literary Examiner. Nos. 1–27, 1823. [Ed. by Leigh Hunt.]

The Somerset House Gazette. Nos. 1–52, 1824. [Ed. by J. B. Pine.]

The Palladium. No. 1, 6 Feb. 1825–No. 98, 17 Dec. 1826.

The Athenaeum. No. 1, 2 Jan. 1828–11 Feb. 1921. [Incorporated in The Nation. Ed. by J. S. Buckingham, H. Stebbing, C. W. Dilke (1830–46), T. K. Hervey (1846–53), W. H. Dixon (1853–69), N. MacColl (1871–1900).]

The Companion. Nos. 1–29, 1828. [Ed. by Leigh Hunt.]

Leigh Hunt's London Journal. No. 1, 2 April 1834–No. 91, 26 Dec. 1835.

Notes and Queries. No. 1, 3 Nov. 1849 onwards. [Ed. by W. J. Thoms, J. Doran, H. F. Turle, J. Knight.]

Household Words. No. 1, 30 March 1850–28 May 1859. [Ed. by Charles Dickens.]

Once a Week. No. 1, 2 July 1859–May 1879. [Ed. by Samuel Lucas.]

All the Year Round. No. 1, 30 April 1859–30 March 1895. [Ed. by Charles Dickens, Charles Dickens junior.]

The Parthenon. No. 1, 3 May 1862–No. 57, 30 May 1863. [Ed. by C. W. Goodman.]

The Reader. No. 1, 3 Jan. 1863–28 July 1866. [Ed. by J. M. Ludlow, David Masson, J. Dennis, T. Bendyshe.]

The Academy. No. 1, 9 Oct. 1869–18 Sept. 1915. [Ed. by C. E. C. B. Appleton, J. S. Cotton, C. L. Hind, C. E. Doble.]

Sala's Journal. No. 1, 30 April–11 April 1894.

Literature. No. 1, 23 Oct. 1897–11 Jan. 1902. [Ed. by H. D. Traill (1897–1901).]

(6) RELIGIOUS PAPERS

The Record. No. 1, 1 Jan. 1818 onwards. [Originally twice a week. Anglican; ed. by Edward Garbett (1854–67).]

The Catholic Vindicator. 5 Dec. 1818–4 Dec. 1819. [Ed. by W. E. Andrews.]

The Catholic Advocate. No. 1, 3 Dec. 1820–No. 34, 22 July 1821.

The World. No. 1, 4 May 1827–28 March 1832. [Incorporated in The Patriot. Nonconformist; ed. by Stephen Bourne.]

The Catholic Journal. No. 1, 1 March 1828–No. 55, 15 March 1829.

The Christian Advocate. No. 1, 7 Jan. 1830–No. 505, 2 Sept. 1839.

The Patriot. No. 1, 22 Feb. 1832–27 Dec. 1866. [Continued as] The English Independent. No. 1, 3 Jan. 1867–Dec. 1880. [Incorporated in The Nonconformist. Twice a week; ed. by Stephen Bourne (1832), Josiah Conder (1833–55).]

The Watchman. No. 1, 7 Jan. 1835–31 Dec. 1889. [Wesleyan; ed. by J. C. Rigg (1848–64).]

The Witness [Edinburgh]. No. 1, 15 Jan. 1840–27 Feb. 1864. [Twice a week; ed. by Hugh Miller (1840–56).]

The Tablet. No. 1, 16 May 1840 onwards. [Roman Catholic. Ed. by F. Lucas, J. E. Wallis, John Riley, A. B. Wright, Wilfrid Meynell, S. Cox.]

The Nonconformist. No. 1, 14 April 1841–18 Sept. 1890. [Continued as] The Independent. No. 1. 26 Sept. 1890–29 March 1900. [Ed. by A. Miall (1841–81).]

The Jewish Chronicle. [1841(?)]–No. 17, 2 May 1845 onwards. [Ed. by David Meldola and Moses Angel, John Lillie (1844–8).]

The True Tablet. No. 1, 26 Feb.–No. 45, 31 Dec. 1842. [Ed. by F. Lucas.]

The English Churchman. No. 1, 5 Jan. 1843 onwards. [Ed. by D. W. Godfrey (1843–63).]

The Universe. No. 1, 6 Jan. 1846 onwards. [Roman Catholic.]

The Guardian. No. 1, 12 Jan. 1846 onwards. [Anglican. Owned by W. E. Gladstone. Ed. by M. R. Sharp (1859–83), J. Sharp (1883–95), W. H. Lathbury (1896–9).]

The Christian Times. No. 1, 12 Aug. 1848–No. 528, 11 Aug. 1858. [Continued as] The Beacon and Christian Times. No. 1, 18 Aug. 1858–No. 54, 24 Aug. 1859. [Ed. by William Leask.]

The Wesleyan Times. No. 1, 8 Jan. 1849–29 July 1867. [Continued as] The Methodist Times. 5 Aug. 1867 onwards.

The Catholic Standard. No. 1, 13 Oct. 1849–12 May 1855. [Continued as] The Weekly Register. 19 May 1855–14 March 1902. [Ed. by H. W. Wilberforce, Wilfrid Meynell.]

The Freeman. No. 1, 24 Jan. 1855–No. 2297,

17 Feb. 1899. [Continued as] The Baptist Times and Freeman. 24 Feb. 1899 onwards.

The Christian World. No. 1, 9 April 1857 onwards. [Low Church; ed. by J. Whittemore (1857–60), James Clarke (1860–88), James G. Clarke.]

The Revival. 1859–70. [Continued as The Christian, No. 1, 3 Feb. 1870 onwards; Low Church.]

The Methodist Recorder. No. 1, 4 April 1861 onwards.

The Church Times. No. 1, 7 Feb. 1863 onwards. [High Church; ed. by G. J. Palmer (1863–92), T. A. Lacey.]

The Methodist. No. 1, 1 Jan. 1874–No. 580, 27 Dec. 1884.

The Secular Review. 9 June 1877–29 Dec. 1888. [Continued as The Agnostic Journal, 5 Jan. 1889–15 June 1907; ed. by G. W. Foote.]

The War Cry and Official Gazette of the Salvation Army. No. 1, 27 Dec. 1880 onwards.

The Christian Commonwealth. No. 1, 20 Oct. 1881–24 Sept. 1919.

(7) AGRICULTURAL PAPERS

The Farmer's Journal. 15 Aug. 1807–15 April 1809. [Continued as Evans and Ruffy' Farmer's Journal, 22 April 1809–16 July 1832; incorporated in Bell's Weekly Messenger.]

Fleming's Weekly Express. No. 1, 4 May 1823–No. 167, 9 July 1826. [Continued as] Fleming's British Farmer's Chronicle, 10 July 1826–26 Jan. 1829.

Exley, Dimsdale and Hopkinson's Corn Exchange Circular. No. 1, 1 Jan. 1824–No. 306, 28 Dec. 1829.

The Corn Trade Circular. No. 1, 24 Oct. 1825–No. 402, 24 June 1833.

The Mark Lane Express. No. 1, 2 Jan. 1832 onwards. [Ed. by Joseph Robertson, William Shaw.]

The Universal Corn Reporter. No. 1, 6 Feb. 1832–14 Jan. 1870.

The New Farmer's Journal. No. 1, 11 Feb. 1833–No. 58, 31 May 1834. [Incorporated in The Mark Lane Express.]

The Magnet. No. 1, 13 March 1837–No. 2616, 27 Aug. 1888. [Ed. by J. B. Bell.]

The Farmer's Journal. No. 1, 9 Dec. 1839–No. 362, 28 Dec. 1848.

The Scottish Farmer and Horticulturalist. No. 1, 3 April 1861–11 Oct. 1865. [Continued as] The Farmer, 18 Oct. 1865–2 Oct. 1889. [Continued as] The Farmer and Stockbreeder. No. 1, 9 Oct. 1889 onwards.

The Agricultural Gazette. No. 1, Jan. 1874–17 July 1925. [Incorporated in The Farmer and Stockbreeder. Ed. by J. C. Morton (1874–88).]

(8) FINANCIAL AND COMMERCIAL PAPERS

The Circular to Bankers. No. 1, 25 July 1828–No. 1417, 20 Jan. 1854. [Continued as] The Banker's Circular. 27 Jan. 1854–Jan. 1858. [Continued as] The Monetary Times and Banker's Circular. Jan. 1858–24 March 1860.

The London Mercantile Journal. No. 1, 13 July 1830–22 March 1870.

Nicholson's Weekly Register. No. 1, 1 Jan. 1842–No. 130, 22 June 1844. [Continued as] The London Commercial Record. No. 1, 29 June onwards.

The Economist. No. 1, 2 Sept. 1843 onwards. [Ed. by James Wilson, Walter Bagehot.]

The Money Market Review. No. 1, 9 June 1860–Dec. 1921. [Continued as] Investors' Chronicle and Money Market Review. Jan. 1922 onwards.

The Insurance Record. No. 1, 30 Jan. 1863 ônwards.

The Investor's Guardian. No. 1, 22 Aug. 1863 onwards.

The Bullionist. No. 1, Jan. 1866–5 Dec. 1899. [Continued as] The Daily Bullionist. 7 Dec. 1899–2 June 1900. [Incorporated in The Financier. Ed. by David Morier Evans, John Scott Henderson.]

The Commercial World. [1874]–No. 179, 1 Jan. 1878 onwards.

The Statist. No. 1, 12 March 1878 onwards. [Ed. by Arthur Ellis (1878–80), Robert Giffen.]

The Shipping World. No. 1, May 1883 onwards.

The Financial Chronicle. No. 1, 19 June, 1883 onwards.

The Capitalist. No. 1, 16 Nov. 1885–25 Dec. 1926. [Continued as] The Investor. 1 Jan. 1927 onwards.

The Financial World. [1886]–27 April 1887 onwards.

(9) SPORTING PAPERS

Kent's Weekly Dispatch and Sporting Mercury. [1816]–No. 8, 5 April 1818–No. 192, 23 Jan. 1820.

The Racing Times. [Feb. 1851]–No. 8, 16 April 1851–10 Aug. 1868.

The Sporting Gazette. No. 1, 1 Nov. 1862–No. 920, 27 Dec. 1879. [Continued as] The County Gentleman. No. 921, 3 Jan. 1880–30 Dec. 1915. [Incorporated in Land and Water.]

The Sporting Times. No. 1, 11 Feb. 1865–5 Dec. 1931. [Ed. by J. H. Shorthouse, John Corlett.]

The Sporting Clipper. [1872]–18 April 1874–30 June 1894.

The Athletic News [Manchester]. [June 1875] –No. 92, 3 March 1877–23 April 1917. [Incorporated in The Sporting Chronicle. Ed. by T. R. Sutton (1875–95).]

The Fishing Gazette. No. 1, 26 April 1877 onwards.

The Bicycling Times. No. 1, 24 May 1877–25 Dec. 1883. [Continued as] Cycling Times. 1 Jan. 1884–23 March 1887.

The Sportsman's Weekly Guide to the Turf. 1880–4.

Horse and Hound. No. 1, 29 March 1884 onwards.

The Racing World. No. 1, 26 Feb. 1887 onwards.

The Jockey. No. 1, 18 April 1890 onwards.

(10) HUMOROUS PAPERS

Spielmann, M. H. The Rivals of 'Punch.' A Glance at the Illustrated Comic Press of Half a Century. National Rev. July 1895.

The Quizzical Gazette and Merry Companion. Nos. 1–21, 1831–2. [Ed. by John Mitford.]

Figaro in London. No. 1, 10 Dec. 1831–1839. [Ed. by G. A. à Beckett.]

Punch, or the London Charivari. No. 1, 17 July, 1841 onwards. [Ed. by Mark Lemon (1841–70); Shirley Brooks (1870–4); Tom Taylor (1874–80); Sir F. C. Burnand (1880–1906).]

Fun. No. 1, 21 Sept. 1861–1901. [Incorporated in Sketchy Bits. Ed. by T. Hood the younger (1861–74), Henry Sampson (1874–8), Charles Dalziel.]

The Comic News. No. 1, 13 July 1863–14 March 1865. [Ed. by H. J. Byron, Charles Collins.]

Judy, or the London Serio-Comic Journal. 1867–1907.

The Tomahawk. No. 1, 11 May 1867–No. 164, 25 June 1870. [Ed. by A. à Becket, M. S. Morgan.]

Moonshine. July 1879–Aug. 1902. [Ed. by C. Harrison.]

Ally Sloper's Half Holiday. 3 May 1884–9 Sept. 1916. [Incorporated in London Society. Ed. by C. H. Ross.]

Sketchy Bits. No. 1, 25 April 1893 onwards.

(11) JUVENILE PAPERS

Rollington, R. A Brief History of Boys' Journals with Interesting Facts about the Writers of Boys' Stories. Leicester, 1913.

Boys of England. No. 1, 24 Nov. 1866–23 June 1899. [Continued under various titles, Up-to-date Boys, Boys of the Empire, Boys of Our Empire, Boys of England until 22 Dec. 1906. Ed. by Charles Stevens, Edwin J. Brett.]

The Young Englishman's Journal. No. 1, 13 April 1867–1873. [Ed. by W. L. Emmett.]

The Young Men of Great Britain. No. 1, Jan. 1868–17 June 1889. [Ed. by E. J. Brett, Vane St John.]

The Young Briton. No. 1, 18 Sept. 1869–1877. [Ed. by W. L. Emmett.]

The Gentleman's Journal. No. 1, 1 Nov. 1869–Oct. 1872. [Ed. by George Frederick Pardon.]

Our Young Folks' Weekly Budget. No. 1, 2 Jan. 1871–No. 447, 28 June 1879. [Continued as] Young Folks. No. 448, 5 July 1879–No. 733, 20 Dec. 1884. [Continued as] Young Folks' Paper. 27 Dec. 1884–28 June 1891. [Continued as] Old and Young. 4 July 1891–11 Sept. 1896. [Continued as] Folks at Home. No. 1, 18 Sept. 1896–29 April 1897. [Ed. by James Henderson; Treasure Island and The Black Arrow by R. L. Stevenson pbd as serials.]

The Boys' Standard. No. 1, 6 Nov. 1875–1892. [Ed. by Charles Fox.]

The Boys' Own Paper. No. 1, 18 Jan. 1879 onwards. [Ed. by J. Macaulay.]

The Boys' World. No. 1, 14 April 1879–31 Jan. 1883. [Ed. by Ralph Rollington.]

The Union Jack. No. 1, 1 Jan. 1880–25 Sept. 1883. [Ed. by W. H. Kingston, G. A. Henty.]

The Girl's Own Paper. No. 1, 3 Jan. 1880–26 Sept. 1908.

The Boys' Newspaper. No. 1, 15 Sept. 1880–14 Aug. 1882. [Continued as] Youth. 21 Aug. 1882–25 April 1888.

The Boys' Illustrated News. No. 1, 6 April 1881–No. 61, 31 May 1882. [Ed. by Mayne Reid.]

The Boys' Comic Journal. No. 1, 14 March 1883–1898. [Ed. by E. J. Brett.]

Ching-Ching's Own. No. 1, 23 June 1888–17 June 1893. [Ed. by E. Harcourt Burrage.]

Comic Cuts. No. 1, 17 May 1890 onwards.

Comic Pictorial Nuggets. No. 1, 7 May 1892–No. 29, 19 Nov. 1892. [Continued as] Nuggets. No. 30, 26 Nov. 1892–10 March 1905.

The World's Comic. No. 1, 6 July 1892–10 Nov. 1908.

Chums. No. 1, 12 Sept. 1892 onwards. [Ed. by E. Foster (1894–1907).]

The Girls' Realm. No. 1, Nov. 1898–Oct. 1915.

(12) MISCELLANEOUS SPECIALISED PAPERS

The Military Register. No. 1, 30 March 1814–11 April 1821.

The United Service Gazette. No. 1, 9 Feb. 1833 onwards. [Ed. by A. A. Watts (1833–43).]

The Naval and Military Gazette. No. 1, 9 Feb. 1833–No. 2774, 17 Feb. 1886. [Incorporated in The Broad Arrow.]

The Civil Service Gazette. No. 1, 1 Jan. 1853–Nov. 1926. [Ed. by John Bolger.]

The Army and Navy Gazette. No. 1, 7 Jan. 1860 onwards.

The Broad Arrow. No. 1, 1 July 1868–18 April 1917.

The Admiralty and Horse Guards' Gazette. No. 1, 1 Nov. 1884–19 Jan. 1901.

The Era. No. 1, 30 Sept. 1838 onwards. [Ed. by William Carpenter, F. Ledger, Leitch Ritchie.]

The London Entr'acte. [1869]; No. 27, 8 Jan. 1870–No. 137, 17 Feb. 1872. [Continued as Entr'acte, No. 138, 24 Feb. 1872–26 April 1907.]

The Stage Directory. Nos. 1–14, 1 Feb. 1880–1 March 1881. [Monthly; continued weekly as The Stage, No. 1, 25 March 1881 onwards.]

The Auction Register and Law Chronicle. No. 1, 7 Jan. 1813–No. 146, 23 Feb. 1815. [Continued as The Law Chronicle and Estate Advertiser, No. 147, 2 March 1815–No. 2747, 30 Dec. 1847.]

The Law Gazette. No. 1, 15 Aug. 1822–No. 1146, 23 Dec. 1847.

The Jurist. No. 1, 14 Jan. 1837–1856. [Ed. by Sir John Jervis.]

The Law Times. No. 1, 8 April 1843 onwards. [Ed. by Basil Crump.]

The Solicitor's Journal. 3 Jan. 1857 onwards.

The Law Journal. No. 1, 19 Jan. 1866 onwards. [Ed. by W. D. I. Foulkes (1879–90).]

The Lancet. No. 1, 5 Oct. 1823 onwards. [Ed. by T. Wakley (1823–62); J. G. and T. H. Wakley, W. T. Fox.]

The Medical Times. Oct. 1839–85. [Ed. by T. P. Healcy, J. S. Bushman.]

The Association Medical Journal. No. 1, Jan. 1853–Dec. 1857. [Continued as The British Medical Journal, Jan. 1858 onwards; ed. by J. R. Cormack, A. Wynter (1855–60), W. O. Markham (1860–6), E. A. Hart (1866–83).]

Nature. A Weekly Illustrated Journal of Science. No. 1, 1870 onwards. [Ed. by Sir J. N. Lockyer.]

The Gardener's Gazette. 7 Jan. 1837–26 June 1847. [Ed. by George Glenny.]

The Gardener's Chronicle. No. 1, 2 Jan. 1841 onwards. [Ed. by John Lindley (1841–65), Maxwell T. Masters.]

Amateur Gardening. No. 1, 3 May 1884 onwards.

The Railway Times. No. 1, 29 Oct. 1837–28 March 1914.

Bradshaw's Railway Gazette. No. 1, 12 July 1845–No. 103, 28 Nov. 1846. [Continued as The Railway Gazette, 5 Dec. 1846–20 Jan. 1872.]

The Railway News. No. 1, 2 Jan. 1864 onwards.

The Mining Journal. No. 1, 29 Aug. 1835 onwards. [Ed. by T. W. Robertson.]

The Mechanic's Magazine. 1823–72. [Continued as Iron, No. 1, 11 June 1873–June 1893; incorporated in Industries and Iron, June 1893–30 March 1899; ed. by J. C. Robertson, R. A. Brooman, E. J. Reed.]

Griffith's Iron Trade Exchange. 28 March 1873–June 1874. [Continued as London Iron Trade Exchange, 27 June 1874–24 Sept. 1877; continued as The Iron and Steel Trades Journal and Mining Engineer, No. 1477, 1 Oct. 1877 onwards.]

The Engineer. No. 1, 4 Jan. 1856 onwards. [Ed. by Zerah Colburn (1859–66).]

Engineering. No. 1, 5 Jan. 1866 onwards. [Ed. by Z. Colburn.]

The Colliery Guardian. No. 1, 2 Jan. 1858 onwards. [Ed. by H. K. Atkinson.]

The Builder. No. 1, 31 Dec. 1842 onwards. [Founded by J. A. Hansom. Ed. by George Godwin (1842–83).]

The Building News. 2 Jan. 1857–12 March 1926. [Incorporated in The Architect. Started as The Freehold Land Times and Building News, No. 3, 1 April–No. 20, 15 Dec. 1854; continued as The Land and Building News, 1 Jan. 1855–27 Dec. 1856.]

The Builder's Weekly Reporter. No. 2, 17 March 1856–23 July 1886. [Continued as The Builder's Reporter and Engineering Times, 30 July 1886–31 Oct. 1906; incorporated in The Building Trade.]

The Architect. No. 1, 2 Jan. 1869 onwards.

The Draper's Record. No. 1, 6 Aug. 1887 onwards.

The Grocer. No. 1, Jan. 1862 onwards. [Owned by W. Reed, L. M. Reed; ed. by G. L. M. Strauss.]

The Accountant. No. 1, Oct. 1874 onwards. [Weekly from 2 Jan. 1875.]

Home Chat. No. 1, 23 March 1895 onwards.

Weldon's Ladies' Journal of Dress and Fashion. No. 1, 1 July 1879 onwards.

Woman. No. 1, 3 Jan. 1890–7 Aug. 1912.

E. MAGAZINES AND REVIEWS

(1) MONTHLY MAGAZINES

The Gentleman's Magazine. Jan. 1731–Sept. 1907. Vols. I–V (1731–5). New Ser. vols. VI–LXXVII (1736–1807). New Ser. vols. LXXVIII–CIII (1808–33). New Ser. vols. I–XLV (1834–56). New [Third] Ser. vols. I–XIX (1856–65). New [Fourth] Ser. vols. I–V (1866–8). Entirely New Ser. 38 vols. (1868–1906). New Ser. (Feb. 1906–Sept. 1907). [From Oct. 1907 to 1922 covers only were ptd to retain the copyright of the title. Indexes: General Index to first 20 vols. 1753; from 1731 to 1786, by S. Ayscough, 2 vols. 1789; from 1787 to 1818, by J. Nichols, vols. III, IV, 1821; A List of the Plates, Maps, etc. from 1731 to 1813, 1814; A List of the Plates and Woodcuts from 1731 to 1818, 1821 (by C. St Barbe, junr.). Ed. by: Edward Cave (1731–54), D. Henry (1754–92), R. Cave (1754–66), J. Nichols (1778–1826), J. B. Nichols (1826–33), John Mitford (1834–50), J. G. Nichols (1851–6), J. H. Parker (1856–65), Bolton Corney, Joseph Hatton (1868–74), Joseph Knight (1887–1905), A. H. Bullen (1906–7).]

A Selection of Curious Articles from the Gentleman's Magazine. [3rd edn by J. Walker.] 4 vols. 1814.

The Gentleman's Annual: being the New Year Supplement of the Gentleman's Magazine. [1870, etc.]

The Gentleman's Magazine Library; being a Classified Collection of the Chief Contents of the Gentleman's Magazine from 1731 to 1868. Ed. by Sir G. L. Gomme, 1883, etc.

Bullen, A. H. GM. Feb. 1906. [Account of GM.]

The Scots Magazine. Vols. I–LXV, 1739–1803. [Continued as] The Scots Magazine and Edinburgh Literary Miscellany. Vols. LXVI–LXXIX, 1804–July 1817. [Continued as] The Edinburgh Magazine and Literary Miscellany. A New Series of the Scots Magazine. Vols. I–XVIII, Aug. 1817–June 1826.

The Universal Magazine of Knowledge and Pleasure. 113 vols. 1747–1803. [Continued as] The Universal Magazine. New Ser. 21 vols. 1804–14. [Continued as] The New Universal Magazine. 1 vol. 1814.

The Monthly Review (or Literary Journal). Vols. I–LXXXIX, 1749–89. [Continued as] The Monthly Review, or Literary Journal Enlarged. Vols. I–CVIII, 1790–1825. [Continued as] The Monthly Review. New and Improved Ser. vols. I–XV (1826–30), 1826–45. New Ser. [Fourth], 45 vols. (1831–45). [Indexes: A General Index from the Commencement to the end of the 70th volume. By S. Ayscough, 2 vols. 1786; A Continuation of the General Index from vol. LXXI to vol. LXXXI. By S. Ayscough, 1796; A General Index from the Commencement of the New Series [Jan. 1790] to the end of the 81st volume [Dec. 1816]. [By J. C.] 2 vols. 1818. For an account see J. W. Robberds,

A Memoir of the Life and Writings of William Taylor, 1843. Ed. by G. E. Griffiths (1803–25), M. J. Quin (1825–32).]

The Critical Review; or Annals of Literature. 1756–1817: [1st ser.] vols. I–LXX; [2nd ser.] extended and improved: a New Arrangement, 39 vols. (1791–1803); 3rd ser. 24 vols. (1804–11); 4th ser. 6 vols. (1812–4); 5th ser. 5 vols. (1815–7).

The Lady's Magazine; or Entertaining Companion for the Fair Sex. 1770–1832: Vols. I–XLIX (1770–1818); New Ser. vols. I–X (1819–29); Improved Ser. vols. I–V (1830–2). [Incorporated in The Ladies' Museum and continued as] The Lady's Magazine and Museum of Belles Lettres. Improved Series, enlarged. Vols. I–XI, 1832–7. [Incorporated in The Court Magazine and Monthly Critic, and continued as] The Court Magazine and Monthly Critic and Ladies' Magazine and Museum of Belles Lettres. Vols. XII–XXXI, 1838–47.

The Hibernian Magazine, or Compendium of Entertaining Knowledge. 15 vols. Dublin, 1771–85. [Continued as] Walker's Hibernian Magazine. 26 vols. 1786–1811.

The Arminian Magazine. Vols. I–XX, 1778–97. [Continued as] The Methodist Magazine. Vols. XXI–XLIV, 1798–1821. [Continued as] The Wesleyan Methodist Magazine. 1822–1913. [Continued as] The Magazine for the Home. 1914. [Continued as] The Magazine of the Wesleyan Methodist Church. 1915–26. [Continued as] The Methodist Magazine. 1927 onwards. [Ed. by John Wesley, G. Story, J. Benson, J. Bunting, T. Jackson, G. Cubitt, W. L. Thornton, W. H. Rule.]
The Wesleyan Methodist Magazine. Sixpenny Edition. Vols. I–V, 1861–5.
The Wesleyan Methodist Magazine. Abridged Edition. Vols. I–V, 1866–70.

The European Magazine and London Review, by The Philological Society of London. 1782–1826: Vols. I–LXXXVII (1782–1825); New Ser. vols. I–II (1825–6). [Incorporated in The Monthly Magazine. Ed. by James Perry.]

The Botanical Magazine, or Flower Garden Displayed. 1787–1800. [Continued as] Curtis's Botanical Magazine. 1801 onwards. Now quarterly. [Indexes: A General Index to the Latin Names and Synonyms of the Plants depicted in vols. I–CVII of Curtis's Botanical Magazine, by E. Tonks, 1883. A New and Complete Index to the Botanical Magazine, 1787–1904, to which is prefixed a history of the Magazine. By I. W. B. Hemsley. 1906. Curtis's Botanical Magazine Dedications 1827–1927. Portraits and Biographical Notes by Ernest Nelmes and William Cuthbertson. [1931.] Ed. by W. Curtis, J. Sims, S. Curtis, Sir W. J. Hooker, J. D. Hooker.]
Companion to the Botanical Magazine; being a Journal containing such Information as does not come within the Limits of the Magazine. By W. J. Hooker. Vols. 1–2, 1835–7. [Incorporated in The Annals of Natural History.]

The Evangelical Magazine. Vols. I–XX, 1793–1812. [Continued as] The Evangelical Magazine and Missionary Chronicle. 1813–Dec. 1904. [Index to first 24 vols. 1817. Ed. by D. B. Hooke (1891–1904).]

The Sporting Magazine; or Monthly Calendar of the Transactions of the Turf, the Chace, etc. 1793–1870: Vols. I–L (1793–1816); New Ser. vols. LI–LXXV (1817–29); Second [really Third] Ser., vols. LXXVI–C (1829–42); Third [Fourth] Ser. 56 vols. (1843–70). [From July 1846 onwards this magazine is identical, except for the title-pages, with The New Sporting Magazine, The Sportsman and The Sporting Review. Index of Engravings in the Sporting Magazine, 1792–1870, [1892].]

The British Critic, A New Review. May 1793–Oct. 1826: Vols. I–XLII (1793–1813); New Ser. 23 vols. (1814–June 1825); [3rd Ser.] 1 vol. (Oct. 1825–Oct. 1826). [Incorporated in The Quarterly Theological Review, and continued as The British Critic, Quarterly Theological Review and Ecclesiastical Record (see under Quarterlies, 1827, p. 833 below). Indexes: A General Index to the first 20 vols. 2 pts, 1804 (by S. Ayscough), A General Index to the British Critic, commencing with the 21st, and ending with the 42nd or concluding Volume of the First Series, 1815 (by F. W. Blagdon). Ed. by W. Beloe, R. Nares, T. F. Middleton, W. R. Lyall.]

The Repertory of Arts and Manufactures. 1794–1825: Vols. I–XVI (1794–1802); Second Ser. 46 vols. (1802–25). [Continued as] The Repertory of Patent Inventions, and Other Discoveries in Arts, Manufactures and Agriculture. 1825–62: Vols. I–XVI (1825–33); New Ser. 18 vols. (1834–42); Enlarged Ser. 40 vols. (1843–62). [Indexes: An Analytical Index to the Sixteen Vols. of the First Series and of all Patents granted for Inventions, 1795–1802, 1802; A General Index to 25 vols. of the 2nd Series, including all Patents 1806 to 1815, 1815; A General Index to the Repertory of Patent Inventions 1815–1845, 1846; Index to all Patents granted in England, 1815–45, 1849; Index to the Repertory [etc.] 1846–50, 1851; Index for 1851, 1852.]

The Monthly Magazine and British Register. Vols. I–LXIII, Feb. 1796–Jan. 1826. [Continued as] The Monthly Magazine; or British Register of Literature, Sciences and Belles Lettres. New Ser. vols. I–XVIII (1826–34); New Ser. vol. XIX (1835). [Continued as] The Monthly Magazine of Politics, Literature and the Belles Lettres. Vols. XX–XXVI (1835–8). [Continued as] The Monthly Magazine. 9 vols. 1839–43. [Ed. by John Aikin (1796–1806), George Gregory (1806–8), Sir Richard Phillips, J. A. Heraud (1839–41), Benson E. Hill (1841–3).]

The Gospel Magazine and Theological Review. 1796 onwards. [Ed. by W. Row (1796–1839).]

The Anti-Jacobin Review and Magazine; or Monthly Political and Literary Censor. Vols. I–LXI, 1798–1821. [Ed. by J. R. Green. See [W. Pontey], The Rotten Reviewers: or a dressing for the morbid branches of the Anti-Jacobin and Critical Reviews, [1810].]

The Philosophical Magazine. Vols. I–LXVIII, 1798–1826. [Absorbed The Annals of Philosophy and continued as] The Philosophical Magazine; or Annals of Chemistry, Mathematics, Astronomy, etc. New and United Series of The Philosophical Magazine and The Annals of Philosophy. Vols. I–XI, 1827–32. [Absorbed The Journal of Science, and continued as] The London and Edinburgh Philosophical Magazine and Journal of Science. Third Series. [Continued as] The London, Edinburgh and Dublin Philosophical Magazine. 1832 onwards: 37 vols. (1832–50); Fourth Ser. 50 vols. (1851–75); Fifth Ser. (1876 onwards). [General Index to vols. I–XI [of Second Ser. 1827–32], 1835. Ed. by A. Tilloch, R. Taylor, R. Phillips, Sir D. Brewster, Sir R. Kane, Sir W. Thomson, W. Francis.]

The Ladies' Monthly Museum; or Polite Repository of Amusement and Instruction. 1798–1828: Vols. I–XXXIII (1798–1814); Improved Ser. vols. I–XXVIII (1815–28). [Continued as] The Ladies' Museum. 1829–32: Vols. I–IV (1829–30); New and Improved Ser. vols. I–III (1831–2). [Incorporated in The Ladies' Magazine.]

The General Baptist Repository. Vols. I–X, 1802–21. [Continued as] The General Baptist Repository and Missionary Observer. 1822–53: 12 vols. (1822–33); New Ser. 5 vols. (1834–8); New Ser. 15 vols. (1839–53). [Continued as] The General Baptist Magazine, Repository and Missionary Observer. New Ser. 38 vols. (1854–91). [Continued as] The Baptist Union Magazine. 4 vols. 1892–5. [Continued as] Church and Household. 1896–1901. [Ed. by A. Taylor (1802–21), D. Davies (1896–1901).]

The Christian Observer. 74 vols. 1802–74. [Continued as] The Christian Observer and Advocate. 3 vols. 1875–7. [Ed. by J. Pratt (1802), Z. Macaulay (1802–16), S. C. Wilks (1816–50), J. W. Cunningham (1850–8), J. B. Marsden (1859–69).]

The Literary Journal: A Review of Literature, Science, Manners, Politics. Vols. I–V, 1803–5. Second Ser. 2 vols. 1806.

The Imperial Review; or London [Edinburgh] and Dublin. Vols. I–V, 1804–5. [The last 2 vols. only have 'Edinburgh' in the title.]

The Eclectic Review. Vols. I–X, 1805–13. New Ser. 30 vols. 1814–28. Third Ser. 16 vols. 1829–36. New [4th] Ser. 28 vols. 1837–50. New [5th] Ser. 12 vols. 1851–6. New [6th] Ser. 4 vols. 1857–8. New [7th] Ser. 5 vols. 1859–June 1861. New [8th] Ser. 15 vols. July 1861–8. [Ed. by S. Greatheed, D. Parker, T. Williams, J. Conder (1814–36), T. Price (1837–50), W. H. Stowell (1851–6), J. E. Ryland (1855–68).]
Remarks on the Principles of The Eclectic Review with Reference to Civil and Ecclesiastical Subjects illustrated by Extracts from that Publication. 1817.
Foster, John. Contributions, Biographical, Literary and Philosophical to the Eclectic Review. 2 vols. 1844.
The Controversy between The Eclectic Review and Mr James Grant. Reprinted from The Morning Chronicle. 1856 (10 edns).
Conder, Eustace R. Josiah Conder: A Memoir. 1857.

La Belle Assemblée; or Bell's Court and Fashionable Magazine. Vols. I–VIII, 1806–10. New and Improved Ser. vols. I–XXX, 1810–24. Third Ser. vols. I–XV, 1825–32. [Continued as] The Court Magazine and Belle Assemblée. Vols. I–IX, 1832–7. [Continued as] The Court Magazine and Monthly Critic. Vols. X, XI, 1837. [Incorporated in The Ladies' Magazine and Museum of Belles Lettres. For an account see Stanley Morison, John Bell, Cambridge, 1930; ed. by Mrs Norton (1832–7).]

The Monthly Repository of Theology and General Literature. Vols. I–XXI, 1806–26. New Ser. 11 vols. 1827–June 1837. Enlarged Ser. 1 vol. July–Dec. 1837. [See Richard Garnett, The Life of the Rev. W. J. Fox, 1909; ed. by R. Aspland (1806–26), W. J. Fox (1827–June 1837), R. H. Horne (July 1836–June 1837), Leigh Hunt (July–Dec. 1837).]

The Literary Panorama. A Review of Books, Register of Events, Magazine of Varieties. Vols. 1–15, Oct. 1806–Sept. 1814. [Continued as] The Literary Panorama and National Register. New Ser. 9 vols. Oct.

1814–July 1819. [Incorporated in The New Monthly Magazine. Vols. I–IV, New Ser. rptd Boston, 1816–7.]

The Cabinet; or Monthly Report of Polite Literature. Vols. I–IV, 1807–8.

The Satirist, or Monthly Meteor. Vols. I–XIV, 1808–14.

The Belfast Monthly Magazine. Vols. I–XIII, 1808–14.

The London Review. Vol. I, Feb.–May, Vol. II, Aug.–Nov. 1809. [Ed. by Richard Cumberland.]

The Poetical Magazine. Vols. I–IV, 1809–11. [Ed. by Rudolph Ackerman.]

The Baptist Magazine. 1809–Dec. 1904. [Ed. by William Groser (1839–56).]

The Edinburgh Christian Instructor. Vols. I–XXX, July 1810–31. New Ser. vols. I–IV, 1832–5. New Ser. vols. I, II, 1836–7. New Ser. vols. I–III, 1838–40.

The British Review and London Critical Journal. Vols. I–XXIII, March 1811–Nov. 1825.

The Scourge; or Monthly Expositor of Imposture and Folly. Vols. I–X, 1811–5.

The Annals of Philosophy; or Magazine of Chemistry, Mineralogy, Mechanics, Natural History, Agriculture and the Arts. Vols. I–XVI, 1813–20. New Ser. 12 vols. 1821–6. [Incorporated in The Philosophical Magazine; ed. by T. Thomson (1813–20), R. Phillips (1821–6).]

The New Monthly Magazine and Universal Register. Vols. I–XIV, 1814–20. [Continued as] The New Monthly Magazine and Literary Journal. Vols. XV–XLVIII, 1821–36. [Continued as] The New Monthly Magazine and Humourist. Vols. XLIX–CXLIX, 1837–71. [Continued as] The New Monthly Magazine. New Ser. vols. I–XV, 1872–9. New [3rd] Ser. vols. I–V, 1879–81. [Continued as] The New Monthly. New Ser. vols. VI–VII, 1882–4. [See Cyrus Redding, Fifty Years Recollections literary and personal, 3 vols. 1855, and Literary Reminiscences and Memoirs of Thomas Campbell, 2 vols. 1860; Michael Sadleir, Bulwer and his Wife, [1933]. Ed. by Thomas Campbell (1821–7), Bulwer Lytton (1831–3), Thomas Hook (1837–42), Tom Hood (1842–4), W. H. Ainsworth (1846–70), W. F. Ainsworth (1871–84). Contributors included Hazlitt, Lamb, Horace Smith, B. W. Procter, Cyrus Redding (subeditor 1821–7), Thackeray.]

The Asiatic Journal and Monthly Register for British India and its Dependencies. Vols. I–XXVIII, 1816–29. New Ser. 40 vols. 1830–43. Third Ser. 4 vols. 1843–5. Fourth Ser. No. 1, 1845.

The Edinburgh Monthly Magazine. Nos. 1–6, April–Sept. 1817. [Continued as] Black-wood's Edinburgh Magazine. Oct. 1817 onwards. [General Index to vols. I–L, Edinburgh, 1855. Ed. by Thomas Pringle and William Cleghorn (1817), William Blackwood, John Blackwood. Contributors: J. G. Lockhart, John Wilson, James Hogg, William Maginn, John Sterling, John Eagles, Charles Neave, Mrs Oliphant, Mrs Gore, Samuel Warren, Charles Lever, G. H. Lewes, George Eliot, A. Trollope, Sir Edward Hamley.]

[Wilson, John.] The Recreations of Christopher North. 3 vols. 1842.

—— Essays Critical and Imaginative. 4 vols. 1866.

Eagles, John. The Sketcher. 1856.

—— Essays contributed to Blackwood's Magazine. 1857.

Tales from Blackwood. 12 vols. Edinburgh, [1858–61]. New Ser. 12 vols. Edinburgh, [1878–80]. Third Ser. 6 vols. Edinburgh, [1889–90].

Travel, Adventure and Sport, from Blackwood's Magazine. 6 vols. Edinburgh, [1889–91].

Gordon, Mary. Christopher North: a Memoir. 1862.

Douglas, Sir G. P. S. The Blackwood Group. [1897.]

Oliphant, M. O. Annals of a Publishing House: William Blackwood and his Sons: their Magazine and Friends. 2 vols. 1897.

Porter, Mary. Annals of a Publishing House: John Blackwood. Edinburgh, 1898. [A continuation of the previous entry.]

Besterman, T. The Publishing Firm of Cadell & Davies. Oxford, 1938.

Annals of the Fine Arts. Vols. I–V, 1817–20. [Ed. by James Elmes.]

The New Bon Ton Magazine, or Telescope of the Times. Vols. I–VI, 1818–21.

The Pocket Magazine of Classic and Polite Literature [Arliss's Pocket Magazine]. Vols. I–XIII, 1818–24. New Ser. 5 vols. 1824–6. [Continued as] The Pocket Magazine. 14 vols. 1827–33. [W. H. Ainsworth was a contributor.]

The Tickler; or Monthly Compendium of Good Things. Vol. I–vol. VI, no. 6, 1818–24.

The Edinburgh Monthly Review. Edinburgh. Vols. I–V, 1819–21. [Continued as] The New Edinburgh Review. Vols. I–IV, 1821–3. [Thomas Carlyle was a contributor.]

The London Magazine. Vols. I–X, 1820–4. New Ser. 10 vols. 1825–March 1828. Third Ser. 3 vols. April 1828–June 1829. [Ed. by: John Scott (1820–1), John Taylor (1821–4), Henry Southern (1825–8), Charles Knight (1828–9). Contributors: Richard Ayton, Bernard Barton, Philip Bliss, John Bowring,

Carlyle, Henry Francis Carey, John Clare, Hartley Coleridge, John Payne Collier, William Crowe, Allan Cunningham, George Darley, De Quincey (Confessions of an Opium Eater), Charles Wentworth Dilke, Charles Abraham Elton, Barron Field, Ugo Foscolo, Hazlitt (Table Talk), Thomas Hood (The Plea of the Midsummer Fairies), Lamb (Essays of Elia), Walter Savage Landor, James Montgomery, John Poole, Winthrop Praed, Bryan Waller Procter, John Hamilton Reynolds, Horatio Smith, Charles Strong, Barry St Leger, Thomas Noon Talfourd, Henry Stol Van Dyck, Thomas Griffiths Wainewright.]

Dobell, Bertram. Sidelights on Charles Lamb. 1903.

Lucas, E. V. Charles Lamb. 1921.

Butterworth, S. The Old London Magazine. Bookman, Oct. 1922, pp. 12–17.

Howe, P. P. William Hazlitt, 1922.

King, R. W. Henry Francis Carey. 1925.

Abbott, C. C. George Darley. 1928.

Reynolds, J. H. Poetry and Prose. Ed. G. L. Marsh, 1928.

Hughes, T. Rowland. John Scott, Author, Editor and Critic. London Mercury, April 1930.

Tibble, J. W. and Anne. John Clare. [1932.]

Blunden, E. Keats's Publisher. 1936.

The Retrospective Review. Vols. I–XIV, 1820–6. Second Ser. 2 vols. 1827–8. [Ed. by H. Southern and Sir N. H. Nicolas (1827–8).]

The Newcastle Magazine. Vol. I, 1820–1. New Ser. vol. I–vol. III, no. 3, 1822–31. [Ed. by W. A. Mitchell.]

The Drama; or Theatrical Pocket Magazine. Vols. I–VII, 1821–5. New Ser. vol. I, 1825.

The Annals of Sporting and Fancy Gazette. Vols. I–XIII, 1822–8.

The New European Magazine. Vols. I–IV, 1822–4.

The World of Fashion and Continental Feuilletons. Vols. I–XXVIII, 1824–51. [Continued as] The Ladies Monthly Magazine. The World of Fashion. Vols. XXIX–LVI, 1852–79. [Continued as] Le Monde Élégant, or The World of Fashion. 1880–9.

The Newgate Monthly Magazine, or Calendar of Men, Things and Opinions. 2 vols. Sept. 1824–Aug. 1826. [Ed. by Richard Carlile.]

The Oriental Herald and Colonial Review. Vols. I–XXIII, 1824–9. [Ed. by John Silk Buckingham.]

The Dublin and London Magazine. Vols. I–II, 1825–6. [Continued as] Robin's London and Dublin Magazine. 1 vol. 1827. [Ed. by M. J. Whitty.]

The Gardener's Magazine. Vols. I–XIX, 1826–43. [Ed. by J. C. Loudon.]

The Olio; or Museum of Entertainment. Vols. I–XI, 1828–33.

The United Service Journal and Naval and Military Magazine. 1829–41. [Continued as] The United Service Magazine and Naval and Military Journal. 1842–3. [Continued as] Colburn's United Service Magazine. 1843–90. [Continued as] The United Service Magazine. 1891–1911.

The Magazine of Natural History and Journal of Zoology, Botany, Mineralogy, Geology and Meteorology. 1829–40: 9 vols. (1829–36); New Ser. vols. I–IV (1837–40). [Continued as] The Annals and Magazine of Natural History. 1840 onwards. [Ed. by J. C. Loudon and J. Denson (1829–36), E. Chadsworth (1837–40); Ruskin was a contributor.]

The British Magazine. Vols. I, II, Jan.–Dec. 1830. [Contributors included: Mrs Hofland, Mrs Hall, J. Montgomery, John Clare, L. E. Landon, Mary Howitt, Mrs Opie, A. A. Watts, T. K. Hervey.]

Fraser's Magazine for Town and Country. Vols. I–LXXX, 1830–69. New Ser. vols. I–XXVI, 1870–82. [Longman's Magazine (q.v. 1882) is a continuation. Ed. by William Maginn (1830), J. W. Parker (1848–60), J. A. Froude (1860–74), William Allingham (1874–9), John Tulloch (1879–80). Contributors included Carlyle (Sartor Resartus), T. L. Peacock, Charles Kingsley (Hypatia), Thackeray (The Yellowplush Papers), Sir Leslie Stephen, W. H. Ainsworth.]

A Gallery of Illustrious Literary Characters (1830–38) drawn by D. Maclise, accompanied by notices chiefly by W. Maginn. Republished from Fraser's Magazine. Ed. W. Bates, [1873].

Mahony, F. S. ['Father Prout']. The Works of Father Prout; edited with Biographical Introduction and Notes by C. Kent. [1892.]

Thrall, M. M. H. Rebellious Fraser's [1830–40]. New York, 1934.

The Dublin Literary Gazette, or Weekly Chronicle of Criticism, Belles Lettres and Fine Arts. Vol I, 1830. [Continued monthly as] The National Magazine. Vol. I, 1830. [Continued as] The National Magazine and Dublin Literary Gazette. Vol. II, 1832. [Ed. by S. Lover (1830), P. D. Hardy (1831).]

The Diamond Magazine. 2 vols. 1831–2.

The Magazine of the Beau Monde. Vols. I–XII, 1831–42.

The Metropolitan: A Monthly Journal of Literature, Science and the Fine Arts. [Continued as] The Metropolitan Magazine. Vols. I–LVII, 1831–50. [Ed. by Thomas Campbell, F. Marryat (1832–5).]

Tait's Edinburgh Magazine. Vols. I–IV, 1832–4. New Ser. vols. I–XXVIII, 1834–61. [Absorbed Johnston's Edinburgh Magazine in June 1834. Ed. by William Tait, Christian Isobel Johnstone. Contributors included: De Quincey, Leigh Hunt, Harriet Martineau, J. S. Mill, Cobden, Bright.]

Chambers's Historical Newspaper. A Monthly Record of Intelligence. Nov. 1832–Dec. 1835. [Ed. by R. and W. Chambers.]

Chambers's Edinburgh Journal. 12 vols. 1832–44. New Ser. 20 vols. 1844–54. [Continued as] Chambers's Journal of Popular Literature, Science and Arts. 1854 onwards. [Ed. by William and Robert Chambers, James Payn.]

    Chambers, R. Essays, Familiar and Humorous (reprinted from Chambers's Journal). [1866]; Tales from Chambers's Journal. [1884.]

    Chambers, W. Memoir of Robert Chambers, with Autobiographic Reminiscences of William Chambers. 1872.

The Dublin Penny Journal. Vols. 1–4, 1832–4. [Ed. by P. D. Hardy.]

The Parliamentary Review and Family Magazine. Vols. I–IV, 1833. New Ser. Session of 1834. 2 vols. 1834. [Ed. by John Silk Buckingham.]

The Dublin University Magazine. Dublin. Vols. I–XC, Jan. 1833–Dec. 1877. [Continued as] The University Magazine: a Literary and Philosophic Review. Vols. I–V, Jan. 1878–June 1882. [Two further quarterly nos. were pbd in Sept. and Dec. 1882. Ed. by C. S. Stanford (1833–4), Isaac Butt (1834–8), James Wills (1839), Charles Lever (1842–5), J. F. Waller (1845 52?), Durham Dunlop, Percy Boyd, James McGlashan, Cheyne Brady (1856–61), J. S. Le Fanu (1861–72), J. F. Waller (1872–7), Kenningale Cooke (1877–8). Contributors included: John and Michael Banim, W. H. Maxwell, William Carleton, J. C. Mangan, G. P. R. James, A. Trollope, Oscar Wilde. See Michael Sadleir, The Dublin University Magazine, its History, Contents, and Bibliography, Proc. Irish Bibliog. Soc. v, pp. 59–82, Dublin, 1938.]

The Dublin University Review. 1833–6. [Continued as] The Dublin Review. Vol. I, 1836 onwards. [Ed. by M. J. Quin. Index: A general list of articles in vols. I–CXVIII (1836–96) in vol. CXVIII, pp. 467–502, 1896.]

The Companion to the Newspaper, and Journal of Facts in Politics, Statistics and Public Economy. Vols. I–IV, 1834–7. [Ed. by Charles Knight.]

The Family Magazine. Vols. I–IV, 1834–7. [Incorporated in Ward's Miscellany.] [Ed. by J. Belcher.]

The Architectural Magazine and Journal of Improvement in Architecture, Building, Furnishing, etc. Vols. I–V, 1834–5. [Ed. by J. C. Loudon; Ruskin was a contributor.]

The Sportsman. Vols. I, II, 1834–5. [Continued as] The Sportsman and Veterinary Recorder. 3 vols. 1835–6. [Continued as] The Sportsman. New Ser. vols. I–VI, 1836–9. Second Ser. vols. I–LXIII, 1839–70. [From July 1846 onwards this was identical, with the exception of the title-page, with The New Sporting Magazine, The Sporting Magazine, and The Sporting Review.]

The Christian Lady's Magazine. Vols. I–XXXI, 1834–49. [Ed. by Mrs Charlotte Elizabeth Tonna (née Phelan), 1834–46.]

Blackwood's Lady's Magazine and Gazette of the Fashionable World. Vols. I–XLIX, 1836–60.

Bentley's Miscellany. Vols. I–LXIV, 1837–68. [Extracts: Tales from Bentley, 4 vols. 1860; rptd 4 vols. 1865. Ed. by Charles Dickens (1837), W. H. Ainsworth, Albert Smith.]

The Monthly Chronicle. A National Journal of Politics, Literature, Science, and Art. Vols. I–VII, March 1838–June 1841. [Ed. by D. Lardner and Bulwer Lytton.]

The Wesleyan Methodist Association Magazine. Vols. I–XX, 1838–57. [Continued as] The United Methodist Free Churches' Magazine. 1858–91. [Continued as] The Methodist Monthly. 1892–1907. [Ed. by M. Miller (1872–7), J. S. Withington.]

The Sporting Review. Vols. I–LXIV, 1839–70. [From July 1846 onwards this was identical, with the exception of the title-page, with The New Sporting Magazine, The Sporting Magazine, and The Sportsman.]

The Ladies' Cabinet of Fashion, Music, and Romance. Vols. I–X, 1839–43. New Ser. vols. I–XVII, 1844–52. New [Third] Ser. vols. I–XXXVII, 1852–70. [From July 1852 onwards with the exception of the title-pages, this is identical with The New Monthly Belle Assemblée and The Ladies Companion.]

Peter Parley's Magazine. Vols. I–XXIV, 1840–63.

Chambers's London Journal of History, Literature, Poetry, Biography and Adventure. Vols. I–III, 1841–3. [Ed. by S. L. Blanchard.]

Bradshaw's Manchester Journal. Vol. I, 1841. [Continued as] Bradshaw's Journal: a Miscellany of Literature, Science and Art. Vols. II–IV, 1842–3. [Incorporated in The North of England Magazine. Ed. by G. Falkner.]

The North of England Magazine. Vols. I, II, 1842–3. [Continued as] The North of England Magazine and Bradshaw's Journal. Vol. III, 1843.

Ainsworth's Magazine; a Miscellany of Romance, General Literature and Art. Vols. I–XXVI, 1843–54. [Ed. by W. H. Ainsworth.]

The Illuminated Magazine. Vols. I–IV, 1843–5. [New Ser.] 2 vols. 1845. New Ser. 1 vol. 1845. [Ed. by Douglas Jerrold (1843–5), W. J. Linton (1845).]

Tegg's Magazine of Knowledge and Amusement. Nos. 1–12, 1843–4.

The North British Review. Edinburgh. Vols. I–LIII, 1844–71. [Ed. by T. F. Wetherell (1868–71). Lord Acton was a contributor.]

Hood's Magazine and Comic Miscellany. Vols. I–XI, no. 1, 1844–8. [Ed. by Thomas Hood, 1844.]

Simmond's Colonial Magazine and Foreign Miscellany. Vols. I–XV, 1844–8 [Continued as] The Colonial Magazine and East India Review. Vols. XVI–XXIII, 1849–51. [United with The Asiatic Journal and continued as] The Colonial and Asiatic Review. 2 vols. 1852–3. [Ed. by W. H. G. Kingston, (1849–51).]

The Art Union Monthly Journal of the Fine Arts, The Arts Decorative and Ornamental. 1844–8. [Continued as] The Art Journal, 1849–1912. [Ed. by Marcus Huish.]

The British Mothers' Magazine. 11 vols. 1845–55. [Continued as] The British Mothers' Journal. 8 vols. 1856–63. [Continued as] The British Mothers' Family Magazine. 1864. [Ed. by Mrs J. Bakewell, 1849–64.]

Wade's London Review: a Critical Journal and Magazine. Vol. I–vol. III, no. 1, 1845–6. [Ed. by T. Wade.]

The London Entertaining Magazine and Library of Romance. Vols. I–III, 1845–6.

Douglas Jerrold's Shilling Magazine. Vols. I–VII, 1845–8. [Ed. by Douglas Jerrold.]

Lloyd's Monthly Volume of Amusing and Instructive Literature. Vols. I–XXII, 1845–6. [Continued as Lloyd's Weekly Volume of Amusing etc. Vols. I–VII, 1847.]

Sharpe's London Magazine; a Journal of Entertainment and Instruction. Vols. I–VIII, Nov. 1845–June 1848. [Continued as] Sharpe's London Journal. Vols. IX–XV, 1849–52. [Continued as] Sharpe's London Magazine of Entertainment and Instruction. Vols. I–XXXVII, 1852–70. [Ed. by Mrs S. C. Hall (1852).]

The Almanack of the Month. A Review of Everything and Everybody. Vols. I, II, 1846. [Ed. by Gilbert à Becket.]

Hogg's Weekly Instructor. Vols. I–VI, 1845–8. New Ser. vols. VII–XVI, 1848–53. [From vol.

IX on the word 'Weekly' is omitted from the title.] Third Ser. vols. XVII–XXII, 1853–6. [Continued as] The Titan. A Monthly Magazine. Vols. XXIII–XXIX, 1856–9. [De Quincey was a contributor.]

The Rambler: a Journal of Home and Foreign Literature, Politics, Science, Music and the Fine Arts. Vols. I–XII, 1848–53. New Ser. 11 vols. 1854–9. New Ser. 6 vols. 1859–62. [Continued quarterly as] The Home and Foreign Review. Vols. I–IV, 1862–4. [Ed. by Richard Simpson, J. H. Newman (1859), Lord Acton.

The Democratic Review. No. 1, June 1849– Sept. 1850. [Ed. by G. J. Harney. F. Engels was a contributor.]

The Family Friend. Vols. I–VI, 1849–52. New Ser. 10 vols. 1852–5. New [3rd] Ser. 11 vols. 1855–61. New [4th] Ser. 8 vols. 1862–5. New and enlarged [5th] Ser. 3 vols. 1866–7. [No number pbd in 1868 and 1869.] New Ser. 1870 onwards. [Ed. by R. K. Philp (1849–52), W. Jones (1852–5). Contributors: Mary Howitt, Mrs Balfour, W. H. G. Kingston, Mrs S. C. Hall.]

Chambers's Papers for the People. Vols. I–XII, 1850–1. [Extract: Historical and Literary Celebrities, being Biographical Sketches selected from Chambers's Papers for the People. Edinburgh, 1859.]

The Household Narrative of Current Events for the Year 1850[–5]: being a Monthly Supplement to Household Words. Vols. I–VI, 1850–5. [Ed. by Charles Dickens.]

The Ladies' Companion at Home and Abroad. Vols. I–IV, 1850–1. Second Ser. vols. I–XXXVIII, 1852–70. [From July 1852 this is identical, with the exception of the title-pages, with The Ladies' Cabinet and The New Monthly Belle Assemblée; ed. by Mrs Loudon (1850–1).]

Leigh Hunt's Journal: a Miscellany for the Cultivation of the Memorable, the Progressive, and the Beautiful. Nos. 1–17, 1850–1. [Thomas Carlyle was a contributor.]

The Monthly Packet of Evening Readings for Younger Members of the English Church. 1851–June 1899. [The later part of the title was soon discarded. Ed. by Charlotte M. Yonge, Christabel R. Coleridge and Arthur Innes.]

The American Magazine. Pts 1–5, Oct. 1851– Feb. 1852. [Ed. by H. H. Paul. Includes work by E. A. Poe, H. W. Longfellow, J. G. Whittier, O. W. Holmes, Martin Tupper, N. Parker Willis, Edward Everett.]

The Leisure Hour: a Family Journal of Instruction and Recreation. 1852–1905. [Index to first 25 vols. 1852–76, [1878].]

Chambers's Repository of Instructive and Amusing Tracts. Vols. I–XII, [1852–4].

Chambers's Pocket Miscellany. Vols. I–XXIV, 1852–3.

The Englishwoman's Domestic Magazine. Vols. I–VIII, 1852–9. New Ser. 9 vols. 1860–4. [New Ser.] 25 vols. 1865–77. [Continued as] The Illustrated Household Journal and Englishwoman's Domestic Magazine. Vol. I–vol. III, no. 16, 1880–1. [Incorporated in The Milliner, Dressmaker and Draper.]

Bentley's Monthly Review or Literary Argus. 1853–4. [Continued as] The New Monthly Review. 1854.

Cassell's Illustrated Family Paper. Vols. I–IV, 1853–7. New Ser. 14 vols. 1858–64. New and Enlarged Ser. 3 vols. 1865–6. [Continued as] Cassell's Magazine. 4 vols. 1867 –9. New Ser. 9 vols. 1869–74. [Continued as] Cassell's Family Magazine. 1874 –1911. [Continued as] Cassell's Magazine of Fiction. 1912–32. [Ed. by John Tillotson, Sir Max Pemberton. At first weekly.]

The Illustrated London Magazine. Vols. I–V, 1853–5. New Ser. vols. I–XXX, 1856–70. [From 1857, this is identical, except for the title-pages, with The Ladies' Companion, The New Monthly Belle Assemblée, and The Ladies' Cabinet; ed. by R. B. Knowles (1853–5).]

The Free Press. 1855–65. [Continued as] The Diplomatic Review. 1866–77. [Ed. by D. Urquhart. Karl Marx was a contributor.]

The National Magazine. 1856–64. [Ed. by John Saunders and Westland Marston. Contributors: Leigh Hunt, W. S. Landor, Christina Rossetti, J. Doran.]

The Train. No. 1, Jan. 1856–Jan. 1858. [Ed. by Edmund Yates. Contributors included: 'Lewis Carroll,' F. E. Smedley, R. B. Brough, E. L. L. Blanchard, James Payn, G. A. Sala, Hain Friswell, May Thomas. An account in Edmund Yates, Recollections and Experiences, 2 vols. 1884.]

The Ladies' Treasury: an Illustrated Magazine of Entertaining Literature, Education, Fine Art, Domestic Economy, Needlework and Fashion. 1857–95. [Ed. by Mrs Warren.]

The Geologist: a Popular Magazine of Geology. Vols. I–VII, 1858–64. [Ed. by S. J. Mackie; Ruskin was a contributor.]

Macmillan's Magazine. Cambridge, Nov. 1859–Oct. 1907. [Ed. by David Masson (1859–67), Sir G. Grove, John Morley. Contributors included: Carlyle, Thomas Hughes, Charles Kingsley, Henry Kingsley.]

The What Not, or Ladies' Handy Book and Monthly Magazine of Literature, Fashion and General Domestic Utility. Nos. 1–66, 1859–66.

The Ibis: a magazine of General Ornithology. Vols. I–VI, 1859–64. New Ser. 6 vols. 1865– 70. Third Ser. 6 vols. 1871–6. Fourth Ser. 6 vols. 1877–82. Fifth Ser. 6 vols. 1883–8. Sixth Ser. 6 vols. 1889–94. Seventh Ser. 6 vols. 1895–1900 onwards. [Index of Genera and Species referred to, and to the Plates, [Sers. I–III] 1859–76, 1879; Index of Genera etc. [Sers. IV–VI] 1877–94, 1897; Index of Genera etc. [Sers. VII–IX] 1895– 1912, 1916; General Subject Index [Sers. I– VI] 1859–94. Ed. by P. L. Sclater (1859– 64), A. Newton (1865–70), O. Salvin and P. L. Sclater. Now quarterly.]

The Cornhill Magazine. 1860 onwards. [Extract: The Cornhill Gallery, containing 100 Engravings by F. Leighton, J. E. Millais, etc., 1865. Ed. by W. M. Thackeray (1860– April 1862), G. H. Lewes (1862–4), Frederick Greenwood (1862–8), Edward Dutton Cook (1868–71), Sir Leslie Stephen (1871–82), James Payn (1883–96), J. St Loe Strachey, R. J. Smith, Leonard Huxley. Contributors included: Lord Tennyson, Matthew Arnold, 'George Eliot,' A. Trollope, R. L. Stevenson, Thomas Hardy, Henry James, E. B. Browning, John Ruskin, Mrs Gaskell, Wilkie Collins, Charles Lever, Charles Reade, George Meredith. An Account in Sir Sidney Lee's Memoir of George Smith prefixed to the first supplement of DNB.]

Good Words. Edinburgh. Jan. 1860–April 1906. [From May 1906 until 1910 it was amalgamated with The Sunday Magazine, and pbd weekly at London. Ed. by Norman Macleod, Donald Macleod; see Donald Macleod (1860–72), Norman Macleod, A Memoir. 2 vols. 1876; contributors included: A. Trollope, Charles Kingsley, Mrs Craik, Mrs Henry Wood, Jean Ingelow, George Macdonald, Mrs Oliphant, Alexander Smith, J. M. Ludlow, J. M. Barrie.]

Temple-Bar. A London Magazine for Town and Country Readers. 1860–1906. [Ed. by G. A. Sala (1860–6), Edmund Yates (1863– 7).]

Duffy's Hibernian Magazine. Vols. I–III, Dublin, 1860–1. New Ser. 5 vols. 1862– 4.

Once a Month. Original Tales by the most popular Authors. Nos. 1–14, 1861–2. New Ser. Nos. 15–17, 1862.

The Quiver. 1861 onwards. [Ed. by H. Quilter.]

The Sixpenny Magazine. 1861–8. [Ed. by T. L. Holt. Miss M. E. Braddon contributed Lady Audley's Secret.]

The St James's Magazine. Vols. I–XLII, 1861– 82. [Ed. by Mrs S. C. Hall (1861–2). Trollope was a contributor.]

The Victoria Magazine. 1863–80. [Ed. by Emily Faithfull.]

The Alpine Journal. 1863 onwards. [Ed. by H. B. George, Leslie Stephen, D. W. Freshfield, W. A. B. Coolidge, A. J. Butler, W. M. Conway, G. Yeld. Now half-yearly.]

The Sunday Magazine. 1864–1906. [Amalgamated with Good Words; ed. by Thomas Guthrie, W. G. Blaikie, G. Waugh; contributors included George Macdonald, W. Hanna.]

The Theological Review: a Journal of Religious Thought and Life. 1864–79. [Ed. by C. Beard.]

The Month: a Magazine of Literature, Science and Art. 1864 onwards.

The Shilling Magazine. Illustrated. A Miscellany of Literature, Social Science, etc. Vol. i–vol. iv, no. 13, 1865–6. [Ed. by S. Lucas.]

Bow Bells. 1865–87 [continued as] Bow Bells Weekly. 1888–96. [Ed. by William Suter (1865–82).]

The Fortnightly Review. No. 1, 15 May 1865 onwards. [Pbd twice a month to no. 35, 15 Oct. 1866, thereafter monthly. Ed. by G. H. Lewes (1865–6), John Morley (1867–77), T. H. S. Escott, Frank Harris, W. L. Courtney. An account in E. M. Everett, The Party of Humanity. The Fortnightly Review and its Contributors 1865–74, Chapel Hill, 1939.]

The Argosy. A Magazine for the Fireside and the Journey. 1865–1901. [Ed. by Mrs Henry Wood (1865–87), C. Wood.]

The Young Englishwoman: a Magazine of Fiction [and] Fashions. Vols. i–iv, 1865–6. New Ser. 3 vols. 1867–9. New Ser. 8 vols. 1870–7. [Continued as] Sylvia's Home Journal. 1878–91. [Continued as] Sylvia's Journal. 3 vols. 1892–4.

Merry and Wise. A Magazine for Young People. 1865–71. [Continued as] Old Merry's Monthly. 1872. [Contributors: R. M. Ballantyne, W. H. G. Kingston.]

The Contemporary Review. 1866 onwards. [Ed. by Henry Alford (1866–70), Sir James Knowles (1870–7), Sir Percy Bunting (1882–1922). Contributors included: Lord Tennyson, Ruskin, Gladstone, Manning, Huxley, Bagehot, Froude, Robert Buchanan.]

Belgravia. Nov. 1866–June 1899. [Ed. by M. E. Braddon (1866–93).]

Aunt Judy's Magazine. Vols. i–xx, 1866–85. [Ed. by Mrs Alfred Gatty (1866–76), Mrs J. H. Ewing (1877–85).]

Gilead. 1866–78. [Continued as] Wayside Words. 1879–1904. [Ed. by T. H. Gregg (1866–78), F. Harper.]

Tinsley's Magazine. Vols. i–xxvi, 1867–92. [Continued as] The Novel Review. 1 vol. 1892. [Ed. by Edmund Yates (1867–70).]

St Paul's: A Monthly Magazine. 12 vols. 1867–74. [Ed. by A. Trollope; see Michael Sadleir, Trollope, a Commentary, 1927.]

The Broadway. Vol. i, 1867–8. New Ser. vols. i–x, 1868–73. [Vol. i rpbd as The Broadway Annual.]

The Portfolio: an Artistic Periodical. 1870–95. [Ed. by P. G. Hamerton.]

Women's Suffrage Journal. 1870–90. [Ed. by L. E. Becker.]

Cope's Tobacco Plant: a Monthly Periodical interesting to the Manufacturer, the Dealer and the Smoker. Liverpool, 1870–4.

Once a Month: a Monthly Magazine of General and Amusing Literature. Vol. i, no. 1–vol. ii, no. 13, 1870–1. New Ser. vol. i, no. 1, 1871. [No numbers appeared from Feb. 1871–Feb. 1872.] New Ser. vol. i, no. 1–vol. ii, no. 19, 1872–3. [Ed. by J. P. Collins (1870).]

The Traveller: an International Monthly of Great Britain and the United States. Vol. i, vol. ii, nos. 1–7, 1871–2. [Ed. by J. B. Gould.]

The Irish Monthly Magazine. Vols. i, ii, Dublin, 1873–4. [Continued as] The Irish Monthly: a Magazine of General Literature. 1875 onwards.

The Transatlantic: a Magazine of American Periodical Literature, conducted by the Editor of 'The Anglo-American Times.' Vol. i–vol. iv, no. 1, 1873–5.

The Argonaut: a Monthly Magazine. Vol. i–vol. vii, no. 50, 1874–8. [Ed. by G. Gladstone (1874–7), E. Paxton Hood (1877–8).]

The Celtic Magazine. Inverness. Vols. i–xiii, 1875–88. [Ed. by Alexander Mackenzie (1875–85), Alexander Macbain (1885–8); Alexander Macgregor contributed The Life of Flora Macdonald.]

The Poet's Magazine. Vols. i–vi, 1876–9. [Continued as] Lloyd's Magazine, with which is incorporated The Poet's Magazine. Vols. vii–xi, 1879–81. [Continued as] Authors and Artists. 1881. [Continued as] Lloyd's London Magazine. 1882–6. [Continued as] Lloyd's Quarterly Magazine. 1886–8. [Continued as] Modern Poets. 1892–4. [Continued as] Modern Authors. 1895. [Continued as] Lloyd's Magazine. 1895–June 1900. [Ed. by L. Lloyd.]

The Nineteenth Century. A Monthly Review. 1877 onwards. [Ed. by Sir James Knowles (1877–1907), W. Wray Skilbeck. Contributors included: Lord Tennyson, Gladstone, Manning, Sir James Lubbock, Fitzjames Stephen.]

The Theatre. 1877–97. [Ed. by Clement Scott (1878–90), Bernard E. J. Capes, Charles Rolleston (1890–7).]

The Welcome Hour: an Illustrated Monthly Magazine. 15 vols. 1878–92.
The Magazine of Art, illustrated. May 1878–July 1904. [Ed. by W. E. Henley, M. H. Spielmann.]
Time: a Monthly Miscellany of Interesting and Amusing Literature. 1879–91. [Ed. by Edmund Yates (1879–84), E. M. Abdy Williams, E. B. Bax. G. B. Shaw was a contributor.]
Longman's Magazine. 50 vols. Nov. 1882–1905. [A continuation of Fraser's Magazine. Contributors included: 'F. Anstey,' Mrs Craik, Austin Dobson, J. A. Froude, Edward Freeman, Sir Edmund Gosse, Thomas Hardy, W. D. Howells, Henry James, Richard Jefferies, Jean Ingelow, Rudyard Kipling, Andrew Lang, Lecky, James Payn, R. L. Stevenson.]
The English Illustrated Magazine. Oct. 1883–Aug. 1913. [Ed. by J. W. Comyns Carr, Sir William Ingram and Clement Shorter. Contributors included: Thomas Hardy, William Morris, George Gissing, Stanley Weyman, 'Anthony Hope', A. C. Harmsworth, Barry Pain, Gilbert Parker, Grant Allen, Max Beerbohm.]
The National Review. 1883 onwards. [Ed. by Alfred Austin, W. J. Courthope, L. J. Maxse.]
Merry England. May 1883–1895. [Ed. by Wilfrid Meynell. Contributors included Alice Meynell, Francis Thompson, W. H. Hudson.]
Progress: a monthly magazine. 1883–7. [Ed. by G. W. Foote.]
Eastward Ho! a Monthly Magazine. Vols. i–iv, 1884–7.
The Monthly Magazine of Fiction. 1885 onwards.
Murray's Magazine: a Home and Colonial Periodical for the General Reader. 1887–91. [Ed. by W. L. Courtney.]
Atalanta. No. 1, Oct. 1887–1898. [Ed. by L. T. Meade and John C. Staples.]
Lucifer: a Theosophical Monthly. Vols. i–xi, 1887–97. [Continued as] The Theosophical Review. 11 vols. 1897–1907. [Ed. by H. P. Blavatsky, Mabel Collins, Annie Besant, G. R. S. Mead.]
Beeton's Boys' Own Magazine. 3 vols. 1888–90. [Ed. by G. A. Henty.]
The Universal Review. 1888–90. [Ed. by H. Quilter.]
The New Review. 1889–97. [Ed. by Archibald Grove, W. E. Henley. Joseph Conrad was a contributor.]
The Newbery House Magazine. 1889–94. [Contributors included: Charles Welsh, Mrs Molesworth, Frances Armstrong.]
The Review of Reviews. 1890 onwards. [Ed. by W. T. Stead.]

Lambert's Monthly. 1890–1. [Ed. by Sir G. E. Campbell. Contributors included: G. Manville Fenn, H. T. Wood, E. Pugh.]
The Author. 1890 onwards. [Ed. by Sir Walter Besant.]
The King's Own: a Monthly Magazine for the Study and the Home. 9 vols. 1890–8. [Ed. by I. Urquhart.]
The Strand Magazine: an Illustrated Monthly. 1891 onwards. [Ed. by George Newnes; contributors included Sir A. Conan Doyle (Adventures of Sherlock Holmes).]
The Ludgate Monthly. 1891–5. [Continued as] The Ludgate. 1895–1900. [Incorporated in The Universal Magazine. Ed. by Phil May, A. M. De Beck.]
The Bookman: a Monthly Journal for Book Readers. Oct. 1891–Dec. 1934. [Ed. by Sir W. Robertson Nicoll; A. St John Adcock.]
The Idler. 1892–1911. [Ed. by J. K. Jerome, R. Barr, A. Lawrence, S. H. Sime.]
The Butterfly. 1893–1900. [Ed. by L. Raven-Hill and Arnold Golsworthy. Contributors: Max Beerbohm, Laurence Housman.]
The Studio. 1893 onwards. [Ed. by Charles Holme, C. Geoffrey Holme.]
The Pall Mall Magazine. May 1893–Sept. 1929. [From Oct. 1914 to April 1927 and again from Oct. 1929 amalgamated with Nash's Magazine as Nash's and Pall Mall Magazine. Ed. by Lord Frederic Hamilton (1893–1900) and Sir Douglas Straight (1893–6).]
The Free Review: a Monthly Magazine. 1893–7. [Continued as] The University Magazine and Free Review. 1897–8. [Ed. by John M. Robertson, G. A. Singer.]
The Windsor Magazine. 1895 onwards. [Ed. by David Williamson. Contributors: 'Anthony Hope,' Barry Pain, E. P. Oppenheim.]
The Architectural Review. [Magazine issue of The Builder's Journal.] July 1896 onwards.
The Temple Magazine. Silas K. Hocking's Illustrated Monthly. 1896–1903. [Ed. by Silas K. Hocking, David Williamson.]
To-Morrow: a Monthly Review. 1896–8. [Ed. by J. T. Grein.]
The Pageant. 1896–7. [Ed. by C. H. Shannon and J. W. Gleeson White.]
Pearson's Magazine. 1896 onwards. [Rudyard Kipling contributed Captains Courageous.]
The New Century Review. 1897–1900.
The Railway Magazine. 1897 onwards.
The Royal Magazine. Nov. 1898–Nov. 1930. [Continued as] The New Royal Magazine. Dec. 1930–May 1932. [Continued as] The Royal Pictorial. June 1932–Dec. 1934. [Continued as] The Royal Screen Pictorial. Jan.–June 1935. [Continued as] The Screen Pictorial. July 1935 onwards. [Ed. by Peter Keary.]

The Wide World Magazine. 1898 onwards.
The Harmsworth Monthly Pictorial Magazine. July 1898–July 1900. [Continued as] The Harmsworth Magazine. Aug. 1900–July 1901. [Continued as] The Harmsworth London Magazine. Aug. 1901–July 1903. [Continued as] The London Magazine. Aug. 1903–Oct. 1930. [Continued as] The New London Magazine. 1930.
The British Empire Review. July 1899 onwards.
The Monthly Review. 1900–June 1907. [Ed. by Sir H. Newbolt, Charles Hanbury Williams.]
The Imperial and Colonial Magazine. 1900–1. [Ed. by 'Celt' and E. F. Benson.]

(2) QUARTERLY MAGAZINES

The Edinburgh Review or Critical Journal. Vol. I, No. 1, Oct. 1802–Oct. 1929. [Indexes: Oct. 1802–Nov. 1812, Edinburgh, 1813 (by R. Ryland); vol. XXVIII–vol. L (April 1813–Jan. 1830), Edinburgh, 1832; vol. LI–vol. LXXX (April 1830–Oct. 1844), 1850; vol. LXXXI–vol. CX (Jan. 1845–Oct. 1859), 1862; vol. CXI–vol. CXL (Jan. 1860–Oct. 1874), 1876. Ed. by: Sydney Smith (1802), Francis Jeffrey (1803–29), Macvey Napier (1830–47), William Empson (1847–52), Sir G. C. Lewis (1852–5), Henry Reeve (1855–95), A. R. D. Elliot (1895–1922), Harold Cox. Contributors: Edward Copleston, Henry Brougham, Francis Horner, Thomas Carlyle, T. B. Macaulay, Sir James Stephen.]
  Selections from the Edinburgh Review comprising the Best Articles in that Journal from the Commencement to the Present Time, and Explanatory Notes. Edited by M. Cross. 4 vols. 1833; 6 vols. Paris, 1835–6.
  Macaulay, T. B. Critical and Historical Essays, contributed to the Edinburgh Review. 3 vols. 1843; 1887 (complete edn); ed. F. C. Montague, 3 vols. 1903.
  Jeffrey, Francis. Contributions to the Edinburgh Review. 4 vols. 1844; 1853.
  Rogers, Henry. Essays selected from Contributions to the Edinburgh Review. 3 vols. 1850–5.
  Brougham, Henry (Baron Brougham and Vaux). Contributions to the Edinburgh Review. 3 vols. 1856.
  Smith, Sydney. Essays. Reprinted from the Edinburgh Review, 1802–18. [1874]; [1880] (with addns up to 1827).
  'Scipio, C.' A Sketch of the Politics of the Edinburgh Review. 1807.
  Constable, T. Archibald Constable and his Literary Correspondents. 3 vols. Edinburgh, 1873.

Napier, Macvey. Selections from the Correspondence edited by his Son. 1879.
Copinger, W. A. On the Authorship of the First Hundred Numbers of the Edinburgh Review. 1895.
The Quarterly Review. 1809 onwards. [Indexes: vol. XX, General Index to first 19 vols. 1820; vol. XL, to vols. XXI–XXXIX, 1831; vol. LX, to vols. XLI–LIX, 1839; vol. LXXX, to vols. LXI–LXXIX, 1850; vol. C, to vols. LXXXI–XCIX, 1858. Ed. by: William Gifford (1809–24), Sir J. T. Coleridge (1824–5), J. G. Lockhart (1825–53), Whitwell Elwin (1853–60), Sir William Smith (1867–93), R. E. Prothero (1893–9), .G. W. Prothero (1899–1922). Contributors: J. W. Croker, Sir Walter Scott, Robert Southey, Lady Elizabeth Eastlake, W. E. Gladstone, Marquis of Salisbury, C. K. Sharpe.]
  Hazlitt, William. A Letter to W. Gifford. 1819.
  Smiles, Samuel. A Publisher and his Friends; Memoir and Correspondence of John Murray, with an Account of the House, 1768–1843. 2 vols. 1891.
  The Quarterly Review. Centenary Article. Quarterly Rev. April, July 1909.
The Reflector. [8 nos.] 1811–2. [Ed. by Leigh Hunt. Contributors: Charles Lamb, Thomas Barnes.]
The Quarterly Musical Magazine and Review. 10 vols. 1818–28. [Ed. by R. M. Bacon.]
Ollier's Literary Miscellany in Prose and Verse. No. 1, 1820.
The Album. 4 vols. 1822–5. [Ed. by F. B. St Leger.]
The Liberal or, Verse and Prose from the South. 2 vols. 1822–3. [Ed. by Leigh Hunt. Contributors: P. B. Shelley, Lord Byron.]
  A Critique on the Liberal. 1822.
  Lord Byron, Leigh Hunt, and The Liberal. Ed. L. P. Pickering, [1925]. [Selections.]
Knight's Quarterly Magazine. 3 vols. 1823–4. [Continued as] The Quarterly Magazine. New Series. Vol. I, No. 1, 1825. [Ed. by Charles Knight. Contributors included W. M. Praed, T. B. Macaulay, H. N. Coleridge, Derwent Coleridge, Bulwer Lytton, T. De Quincey, A. Cunningham, Sidney Walker, William Maginn, John Moultrie. Accounts in Charles Knight, Passages of a Working Life, vol. I, 1864, and Michael Sadleir, Bulwer and his Wife, [1933].]
The Westminster Review. Vols. I–XXIV, 1824–36. [Continued as] The London and Westminster Review. Vols. XXV–XXXIII, 1836–40. [Continued as] The Westminster Review. Vols. XXXIV–XLV, 1841–6. [Continued as] The Westminster and Foreign Quarterly Review.

Vols. XLVI–LVI, 1847–51. [Continued as] The Westminster Review. New Ser. vols. LVII–CLXXXI, 1852–Jan. 1914. [Ed. by: Sir J. Bowring (1824–36), John Stuart Mill (1836–40), W. E. Hickson (1841–6), John Chapman (1852–4).]

Neal, John. Wandering Recollections. 1869.

Bowring, Sir John. Autobiographical Recollections. 1877.

Bain, Alexander. James Mill. 1882.

Blyth, E. K. The Life of William Ellis. 1889.

Lewes, Mrs G. Dr Southwood Smith: a Retrospect. 1898.

Wallas, Graham. The Life of Francis Place. 1898.

Nesbitt, G. L. Benthamite Reviewing: the First Twelve Years of the Westminster Review, 1824–1836. New York, 1934.

The British Critic, Quarterly Theological Review and Ecclesiastical Record. 34 vols. Jan. 1827–Oct. 1843. [For The British Critic see under Monthlies, 1793, p. 823 above. Ed. by: E. Smedley, J. S. Boone, J. H. Newman, T. Mozley. See T. Mozley, Reminiscences chiefly of Oriel College and the Oxford Movement, 2 vols. 1882.]

The Foreign Quarterly Review. 37 vols. 1827–46. [Incorporated in The Westminster Review. Ed. by J. G. Cochrane (1827–35), J. W. Worthington, John Forster (1842–3). Thomas Carlyle was a contributor.]

The Foreign Review and Continental Miscellany. 5 vols. 1828–1830. [Thomas Carlyle was a contributor.]

The Law Magazine, or Quarterly Journal of Jurisprudence. Vols. I–LV, 1829–56. [Continued as] The Law Magazine and Law Review. Vols. I–XXXI, 1856–71. [Continued as] The Law Magazine and Review. New Ser. vols. I–IV, 1872–5.

The Freemason's Quarterly Review. 16 vols. 1834–49. [Continued as] The Freemason's Quarterly Magazine and Review. 3 vols. 1850–2. [Continued as] The Freemason's Quarterly Magazine. 2 vols. 1853–4. [Continued as] The Freemason's Monthly Magazine. 6 vols. 1855–June 1859. New Ser. vols. I–XXV, no. 2, 1859–71.

The London Review. 3 vols. 1834–6. [Incorporated in The Westminster Review. Ed. by J. S. Mill.]

The British and Foreign Review, or European Quarterly Journal. 18 vols. 1835–44.

The British and Foreign Medical Review and Quarterly Journal of Practical Medicine and Surgery. 1836–Oct. 1847. [Index to first 24 vols. (by R. Bower) vol. xxv, 1848. Ed. by J. Forbes and J. Conolly.]

The Church of England Quarterly Review. Vols. I–XLIV, 1837–58. [Ed. by E. Thompson.]

The Foreign and Colonial Quarterly Review. Vols. I–III, 1843–4. [Continued as] The New Quarterly Review, or Home, Foreign and Colonial Journal. Vols. IV–VIII, no. 1, 1844–6.

The English Review, or Quarterly Journal of Ecclesiastical and General Literature. Vols. I–XIX, 1844–53.

The British Quarterly Review. 42 vols. 1845–86. [Ed. by R. Vaughan, H. Allon.]

The Law Review, and Quarterly Journal of British and Foreign Jurisprudence. Vols. I–XXIII, 1845–56. [Incorporated in The Law Magazine.]

The Germ. Thoughts towards Nature in Poetry, Literature and Art. Nos. 1, 2, 1850. [Continued as] Art and Poetry: being Thoughts towards Nature, conducted principally by Artists. [Ed. by W. M. Rossetti. Contributions by D. G. Rossetti, Christina Rossetti, William Morris, Coventry Patmore.]

The Irish Quarterly Review. Vols. I–IX, Dublin, 1851–9.

The New Quarterly Review and Digest of Current Literature. Nos. 1–41, 1852–62.

The Scottish Review. A Quarterly Journal of Social Progress and General Literature. Nos. 1–41, Glasgow, 1853–63.

The London Quarterly Review. 1853 onwards.

The National Review. 1855–64. [Ed. by R. H. Hutton and Walter Bagehot.]

Meliora: A Quarterly Review of Social Science. 12 vols. 1858–69.

Bentley's Quarterly Review. Vols. I–II, 1859–60. [Ed. by Douglas Cooke, Lord Robert Cecil.]

The Natural History Review. Jan. 1861–1865. [Ed. by G. Busk, W. B. Carpenter, F. Currey.]

The Fine Arts Quarterly Review. 1863–7. [Ed. by R. B. Woodward (1863–5). Contributor Charles Kingsley.]

The Friends' Quarterly Examiner. 1867 onwards. [Ed. by W. C. Westlake.]

The New Quarterly Magazine. Vols. I–X. New Ser. vols. I–III, 1873–80. [Ed. by: O. J. F. Crawfurd, F. Hueffer, C. Kegan Paul.]

The Church Quarterly Review. 1875 onwards. [Ed. by A. R. Ashwell (1876–9).]

Mind: A Quarterly Review of Psychology and Philosophy. 1876 onwards. [Ed. by G. C. Robertson, G. F. Stout.]

Brain: A Journal of Neurology. 1878 onwards. [Ed. by J. C. Bucknill, Sir J. Crichton-Browne, D. Fevrier, J. Hughlings-Jackson, H. Head.]

The Modern Review: A Quarterly Magazine. Vols. I–V, 1880–4. [Ed. by R. A. Armstrong.]

The Law Quarterly Review. 1885 onwards, [Ed. by Sir F. Pollock.]

The English Historical Review. 1886 onwards. [Ed. by Mandell Creighton (1886–91), S. R. Gardiner (1891–1901), R. L. Poole (1895–1920).]

The Century Guild Hobby Horse. 1886–92. [Continued as] The Hobby Horse. Nos. 1–3, 1893–4. [Ed. by A. H. Mackmurdo, H. P. Horne.]

The Jewish Quarterly Review. 1888 onwards. [Ed. by I. Abrahams and C. G. Montefiore.]

The Archeological Review. Vols. I–IV, 1888–90. [Incorporated in Folklore. Ed. by Sir G. L. Gomme.]

Art and Letters. Vols. I–VIII, 1888–9.

Folklore. 1890 onwards.

The Yellow Book. Vols. I–XIII, 1894–7. [Ed. by Aubrey Beardsley and Henry Harland. Contributors: Max Beerbohm, A. C. Benson, George Saintsbury, Sir Edmund Gosse, John Davidson.]

The Savoy. Nos. 1–8, 1896–7. [Ed. by Arthur Symons.]

The Dome. A Quarterly containing Examples of All the Arts. 1897–1900.

Beltaine. The Organ of the Irish Literary Theatre. 1899–1900. [Ed. by W. B. Yeats.]

The Anglo Saxon Review. June 1899–Sept. 1910. [Ed. by Lady Randolph S. Churchill.]

F. SCHOOL AND UNIVERSITY JOURNALISM

[The place of publication of the periodicals listed below is that of the section which they concern, unless otherwise specified.]

Marillier, H. C. University Magazines and their Makers. 1899 (priv. ptd); 1902 (enlarged).

Russell, G. W. E. Collections and Recollections. 1903 (new edn). [Chs. xxvi–xxviii.]

(a) Cambridge

[Gray, G. J.] Cambridge University Periodicals. Cambridge Rev. 10 March 1886.

Bowes, Robert. A Catalogue of Books printed at, or relating to the University, Town and County of Cambridge from 1521 to 1893. Cambridge, 1894. [Index by E. J. Worman, 1894.]

Bartholomew, A. T. Catalogue of Books and Papers bequeathed to the University of Cambridge by J. W. Clark. Cambridge, 1912.

The Galvanist, by Hydra Polycephalus, Esq. Nos. 1–11, 1804. [By W. D. Whittington and others.]

The Cambridge Monthly Repository or Literary Miscellany. No. 1, Dec. 1819.

The Cambridge Quarterly Review and Academical Register. No. 1, March–No. 3, Oct. 1824.

The Snob: A Literary and Scientific Journal, not conducted by members of the University. No. 1, 9 April–No. 11, 18 June 1829. [Continued as] The Gownsman. Vol. II, No. 1, 5 Nov. 1829–No. 17, 25 Feb. 1830. [By W. M. Thackeray, Edward FitzGerald and others.]

Punch in Cambridge. Vols. I–III, 7 Feb. 1832–30 Dec. 1834.

Toby in Cambridge. Vols. I–IV, Oct. 1832–12 Sept. 1836.

The Cambridge Quarterly Review, and Magazine of Literature, Arts, Sciences. No. 1, 1 July 1833–No. 3, Jan. 1834. [By J. Sheridan Knowles, Douglas Jerrold and others.]

The Cambridge University Magazine. Nos. 1, 2, 1835.

The Freshman. No. 1, 5 March–No. 6, 9 April 1836.

The Fellow. No. 1, 6 Oct.–No. 11, 15 Dec. 1836.

The Individual. Nos. 1–16, 25 Oct. 1836–11 April 1837.

The Cambridge University Magazine. Vol. I, no. 1–vol. III, no. 1, 1840–3. [The wrappers of the first 5 nos. bore the title 'The Symposium'; ed. by George Brimley, C. B. Wilcox, W. M. W. Call.]

Characters of Freshmen and Other Papers reprinted from the Cambridge University Magazine. 1848.

Cambridge Essays contributed by Members of the University. 4 vols. 1855–8.

Academica. No. 1, May 1858. [Ed. by R. P. O'Hara; contributions by O. Browning, E. E. Bowen, etc.]

The Lion University Magazine. No. 1, May–No. 3, Oct. 1858. [Ed. by H. R. Haweis; contributions by A. Ainger, Horace Smith, R. W. Fullerton, etc.]

The Bear University Magazine. No. 1, Oct. 1858. [By Sir G. O. Trevelyan.]

The Cambridge Terminal Magazine. Nos. 1–3, Dec. 1858–April 1859.

The Light Blue. Vol. 1, no. 1–vol. IV, 1866–71. [Ed. by J. C. Ross, C. Greene, E. S. Shuckburgh, R. K. Miller; contributions by Sidney Colvin, W. Forsyth, W. R. Kennedy, Norman MacColl, W. W. Skeat, etc.]

Momus. A semi-occasional University Periodical. Nos. 1–3, 1866–9. [Ed. by E. H. Palmer, G. A. Crichett, W. H. Pollock.]

The Cambridge Undergraduates' Journal. No. 1, 14 Oct. 1868–6 Nov. 1874. [Incorporated in The Oxford and Cambridge Undergraduates' Journal.]

The Cambridge University Gazette. Nos. 1–33, 28 Oct. 1868–15 Dec. 1869.

The Cambridge University Reporter. No. 1, 19 Oct. 1870 onwards.

The Moslem in Cambridge. Nos. 1–3, Nov. 1870–April 1871. [Ed. by G. S. Davies.]

The Lantern of the Cam. Nos. 1–4, 1871.

The Tatler in Cambridge. Nos. 1–80, 26 April 1871–15 June 1872.

The Light Green. No. 1, May, no. 2, Nov. 1872; rptd 1882, 1890. [Ed. by A. C. Hilton; contributions by H. H. Turner and R. W. Wickham.]

The Cantab. Nos. 1, 2, 1873.

The Light Blue Incorporated with the Light Green. Nos. 1–4, May 1873–May 1874.

Light Greens. No. 1, July 1875.

The Cambridge Tatler. No. 1, 6 March–No. 10, 29 May 1877. [Contributions by T. A. Guthrie ('F. Anstey') including 'The Turned Tables,' the first draft of 'Vice Versa.']

The Cambridge Review No. 1, 15 Oct. 1879 onwards.

The Book of the Cambridge Review, 1879–97. 1898.

The Cambridge Meteor. Nos. 1–7, 7–14 June 1882. [Ed. by G. N. Bankes, J. A. Fabb, J. K. Stephen.]

Ye True Blue. Nos. 1, 2, [1883]. [Ed. by E. M. Maxwell.]

The Blue 'Un. Vol. 1, No. 1, 31 May 1884.

The May Bee. Nos. 1–7, 4–11 June 1884.

The Cambridge University Magazine. No. 1, 6 May–No. 13, 7 Dec. 1886. [Ed. by J. J. Withers.]

The Reflector. Vol. I, nos. 1–4, 1–22 Jan. 1888. [Ed. by J. K. Stephen.]

The Cambridge Fortnightly. Vol. I, nos. 1–5, 24 Jan.–13 March 1888. [Ed. by N. Wedd and Roger Fry. Contributors included: F. Benson, G. Lowes Dickinson, J. Mc-Taggart, Oscar Browning, A. Sidgwick, Barry Pain, F. E. Garrett.]

The Gadfly. No. 1, 15 Nov. 1888. [By W. M. Guthrie and R. B. Ross.]

The Granta. No. 1, 18 Jan. 1889 onwards. [Ed. by R. C. Lehmann (1889–95), C. F. G. Masterman (1898). See F. A. Rice, The Granta, 1924.]

The Wasp. Nos. 1–4, 12–16 June 1891.

The Cambridge Observer. Nos. 1–21, 3 May 1892–7 March 1893. [Ed. by S. Makower.]

The Cambridge A.B.C. No. I, 8 June–No. 4, 12 June 1892. [Ed. by R. Austen Leigh and H. Warre Cornish.]

The 'K. P.' Illustrated. No. 1, 1 Feb. 1893–1894 (?).

The Cantab. Jan. 1898–Dec. 1899.

The Bubble. No. 0, 10 June 1898.

The Cambridge Gazette. No. 1, 15 Oct. 1898–6 Oct. 1900.

The Cambridge Magazine. No. 1, 27 April 1899 onwards.

The Snarl. Nos. 1, 2, 31 Oct., 14 Nov. 1899.

Alma Mater. Nos. 1–5, 1900.

[Gooch, Richard.] The Cambridge Tart. 1823.

Calverley, Charles Stuart. Verses and Translations. 1862.

——The Literary Remains, with a Memoir by Walter J. Sendall. 1885.

[Banks, G. N.] Cambridge Trifles. 1881.

[Seaman, Sir Owen.] Paulopostprandials. 1883.

—— Horace at Cambridge. 1894.

Trevelyan, Sir George. The Ladies in Parliament and other pieces. 1888. [Rev. and included in Interludes in Prose and Verse, 1905.]

Whibley, Charles. In Cap and Gown. 1889; 1898 (3rd edn, with new preface). [Ed. by Whibley.]

S[tephen], J. K. Lapsus Calami. 1891; 1909.

—— Quo Musa Tendis? 1891.

Pain, Barry. In a Canadian Canoe. 1891; 1898.

—— Playthings and Parodies. 1892; 1896.

Lehmann, Rudolf C. In Cambridge Courts. 1891; 1897.

Hilton, Arthur Clement. The Works. Ed. R. P. Edgecumbe, 1904.

Nicholson, R. A. The Don and the Dervish: a Book of Verse, original and translated. 1911.

A Book of Cambridge Verse. Ed. E. E. Kellett, 1911.

College Magazines

St John's. The Eagle. 1858 onwards. [Contributors included S. Butler, E. A. Abbott, J. B. Mayor.]

Christ's. Fleur-de-lys. Nos. 10, 11, 20 May, 7 June 1871.

——The Christ's College Magazine. 1886 onwards.

Girton. The Girton Review. 1882 onwards.

Jesus. The Chanticleer. No. 1, Oct. 1885 onwards.

—— The Rag. [1896.]

Corpus Christi. The Benedict. No. 1, 1888 onwards.

Trinity. The Trident. Nos. 1–6 (7 nos.), June 1889–Nov. 1892.

Emmanuel. The Emmanuel College Magazine. 1889 onwards.

Trinity Hall. The Silver Crescent. Nos. 1–48, Nov. 1890–1907.

——The Brass Halo. Nos. 1–3, 1893–4. [Ed. by J. W. Murison.]

Gonville and Caius. The Caian. 1891 onwards.

Pembroke. The Pem. Nos. 1–13, March 1893–1897. New Ser. Nos. 1–9, March 1897–Lent 1904.

Peterhouse. The Peterhouse Magazine. No. 1, March 1893.
—— The Sex. 1897 onwards.
King's. Basileona. 1900 onwards.

(b) London

Hawgood, J. A. University College and its Magazines. University College Mag. June 1927.

Bellot, H. Hale. University College, London. 1826–1926. 1929.

The London University Magazine. Vols. I, II, 1829–30.

The London University Chronicle. No. 1, 26 April 1830–[?]. [Ed. by F. Lucas; an account in C. J. Riethmuller, Frederick Lucas, a Biography, 1862.]

The Marauder. 1830.

The London University Inquirer. 1833.

The Adventurer or London University Magazine. 1833.

The London University Magazine Nos. 1–3, 1842.

The King's College Magazine. Conducted by the Students of King's College, London. 1842.

The London University College Magazine. Vol. I, 1849.

The King's College Literary and Scientific Magazine. 1849–50. [Continued as The King's College Magazine, 1850–1.]

The London University Magazine. Vols. I–III, 1856–9. New Ser. nos. 1–5, 1859.

The London Student. Vol. I, nos. 1–5, April–Oct. 1868. [Ed. by J. R. Seeley.]

The London Students' Gazette. A Monthly Chronicle of Student Opinion and Student News. Nos. 1–8, 1872.

The King's College Magazine. Vols. I–IV, 1877–81.

The University College, London, Gazette. Vol. I, nos. 1–12, Oct. 1886–Nov. 1887 [–1889 (?)]. [Ed. by Henry Morley; an account in H. S. Solly, The Life of Henry Morley, 1898.]

The Privateer. Nos. 1–11, 1892–3. [Ed. by E. V. Lucas.]

The University College Gazette. No. 1, Nov. 1895–1904. [Continued as The U.C.L. Union Magazine, 1904–1919; continued as The University College Magazine, 1919 onwards.]

The King's College Magazine. 1896 onwards.

(c) Oxford

Symon, J. D. The Earlier Oxford Magazines. Oxford and Cambridge Rev. No. 13, Lent Term 1911.

The Oxford Review; or Literary Censor. Vol. I–vol. III, no. 3, 1807–8.

The Farrago: or the Lucubrations of Councillor Bickerton, Esquire. Nos. 1, 2, 1816.

Il Vagabondo, A Terminal Miscellany. Nos. 1–8, 1816.

The Oxonian. Nos. 1–3, 1817. [See Fair-Play, or No. 1 of The Oxonian exposed by a Member of the University of Oxford, 1817.]

The Undergraduate. Nos. 1–6, 1819.

The Oxford Miscellany. Nos. 1, 2, [1820].

The Oxford Quarterly Magazine. Vol. I, 1825.

The Oxford Literary Gazette, and Classical and Foreign Journal. No. 1, 11 March–No. 4, 20 May 1829.

The Oxford University Magazine. Vol. I, 1834.

The Oxford Magazine. No. 1, 1845.

The Oxonian. No. 1, 1847.

Oxford Essays, Contributed by Members of the University. 1855–8.

The Oxford and Cambridge Magazine, conducted by Members of the two Universities. Nos. 1–12, 1856. [Ed. by William Fulford; contributions by William Morris, E. Burne Jones, D. G. Rossetti, etc.]

Undergraduate Papers. Nos. 1, 2 (4 pts), 3 Dec. 1857–April 1858. [Ed. by John Nichol; contributors included A. C. Swinburne, T. H. Green, G. R. Luke, G. Birkbeck Hill, A. V. Dicey.]

The Oxford Critic and University Magazine (Contributed chiefly by undergraduate Members of the University). Nos. 1–3, [1857].

Great Tom. A University Magazine. Nos. 1–4, [1861]. [Ed. by Bertram Montgomery.]

College Rhymes, Contributed by Members of the Universities of Oxford and Cambridge. Vols. I–XIV, 1861–74. [Ed. by F. E. Weatherley; contributors included F. W. H. Myers, J. Addis, H. C. G. Maule, 'Lewis Carroll.']

The Milton Magazine. Nos. 1, 2, 1866.

The Oxford Undergraduates Journal. No. 1, 31 Jan. 1866–Oct. 1875. [Continued as The Oxford and Cambridge Undergraduates Journal, 21 Oct. 1875–30 Nov. 1882; continued as The Oxford Review, 7 Dec. 1882–14 June 1883; continued as The Oxford and Cambridge Undergraduates Journal, 18 Oct. 1883–4 Dec. 1884; continued as The Oxford Review, Jan. 1885–19 June 1914.]

Dark Blue. An Oxford University Magazine. No. 1, [1867].

The Oxford Spectator. 1868. [By R. S. Copleston, E. Nolan and T. H. Ward.]

The Radcliffe. No. 1, 27 Feb.–No. 10, 9 June 1869.

The Oxford University Magazine and Review. Nos. 1, 2, 1869.

The Oxford University Gazette. No. 1, 28 Jan. 1870 onwards.

The Dark Blue. Vols. I–IV, 1871–3. [Ed. by J. C. Freund.]

The Shotover Papers; or Echoes from Oxford. Vol. I, 1874–5. [Ed. by W. E. W. Morrison, F. G. Stokes, F. S. Pulling.]

The Public Schools Magazine: Conducted by the University Men. Vol. I, Nos. 1–4, 1875.

Ye Roonde Table. An Oxford and Cambridge Magazine. Vol. I, no. 1, 2 Feb.–No. 6, June 1878.

Waifs and Strays. A Terminal Magazine of Oxford Poetry. Nos. 1–10, [1879–82]. [A. E. Housman was a contributor.]

The Oxford Magazine. A Weekly Newspaper and Review. 1883 onwards. [See Echoes from The Oxford Magazine; being Reprints of Seven Years, 1890; also More Echoes from The Oxford Magazine: being a Second Series of Reprints of Seven Years, 1896. Ed. by R. Lodge, P. E. Matheson, C. Cannan, J. E. King, A. D. Godley, D. G. Hogarth, R. Carter, J. Fischer Williams, A. J. Carlyle, C. G. Robertson. Contributors included: Sir A. T. Quiller-Couch, D. S. MacColl, Goldwin Smith, J. A. Symonds, J. W. Mackail, H. C. Beeching, W. L. Courtney, Rennell Rodd, T. H. Warren, A. Sidgwick, L. Huxley, Sir Owen Seaman, L. Binyon.]

The Rattle. Vol. I, no. 1–vol. III, no. 6, 25 Feb. 1886–30 May 1888.

The Undergraduate. Nos. 1–21, 24 Jan.–6 Dec. 1888.

The New Rattle. Vol. I, no. 1, 1890–3. [Annual.]

The Isis. No. 1, 27 April 1892 onwards. [See T. Mostyn Pigott, Two on a Tour and Other Papers from the Isis, 1895. Ed. by T. M. Pigott, W. K. Stride. Contributors included: Max Beerbohm, Hilaire Belloc, R. C. Lehmann, and others.]

The Spirit Lamp. Vol. I, no. 1–vol. IV, no. 2 (15 nos.), 6 May 1892–6 June 1893. [Ed. by Sandys Mason, Lord Alfred Douglas; contributions by Oscar Wilde, J. A. Symonds, Lionel Johnson.]

The Ephemeral. Nos. 1–6, 1893. [Ed. by Lord Alfred Douglas.]

The Chameleon. Vol. I, no. 1, Dec. 1894. [Ed. by J. F. Bloxam, contributions by O. Wilde, Lionel Johnson, Max Beerbohm.]

The Octopus. Nos. 1–6, May 1895. [Ed. by Comyns Carr.]

The Procter. No. 1, 5 March 1896.

The Bulldog. Vol. I, No. 1, 28 Feb. 1896.

The J. C. R. Vol. I, no. 1, Feb. 1897–June 1899.

Ye Tea-Potte. Vol. I, no. 1, 1898. [Ed. by A. F. R. Abbott and L. L. Morell.]

The Bump. Vol. I, no. 1, 21 May 1898.

The X. An Unknown Quantity. Vol. I, no. 1, 10 Nov. 1898–6 Dec. 1900.

The Quad. Nos. 1–4, 1900–1. [Ed. by C. Scott Moncrieff.]

G[odley], A. D. Verses to Order. 1892; 1904 (enlarged).

—— The Casual Ward: Academic and Other Oddments. 1912.

Belloc, Hilaire. Verses and Sonnets. 1895.

Seccombe, Thomas and Scott, H. Spencer. In Praise of Oxford. An Anthology in Prose and Verse. Vol. II, 1912.

College Magazines.

Jesus. The Druid. Nos. 1–6, 1862–3. [J. R. Green was a contributor.]

Lady Margaret Hall. The Daisy. 1890 onwards.

Corpus Christi. The Pelican Record. 1891 onwards.

Somerville. The Fritillary. 1895 onwards.

Wadham. The Wadham College Gazette. 1897 onwards. [Ed. by F. E. Smith and others.]

(d) Edinburgh

The New Lapsus Linguae, or The College Tattler, session 1824–25, edited by Criticus, Student of Medicine and Justus, Student of Law. 1825.

The Cheiliad, or University Coterie; being Violent Ebullitions of Graphomaniacs affected by Cacoethes Scribendi and Famae Sacra Fames. Nos. 1–16, 1827.

The University Squib. Nos. 1, 2, 1833.

The Edinburgh University Journal and Critical Review. Nos. 1–12, 1833. [Ed. by A. Miller.]

The University Maga. 1835 and 1837–9.

The Edinburgh University Souvenir. 1835.

The Edinburgh University Magazine. Nos. 1–3, 1839.

Edinburgh Essays by Members of the University. 1857.

The Edinburgh University Magazine. Nos. 1–3, 1866.

The Edinburgh University Magazine. Vol. I, Nos. 1–4, Jan.–April 1871. [Ed. by R. L. Stevenson, J. W. Ferrier and others; see The New Amphion, being the Book of the Edinburgh University Union Fancy Fair, 1886; also Some College Memories by R. L. Stevenson, rptd as 'A College Magazine' in Memories and Portraits, 1887.]

The Student: A Casual. 1887. [Continued as The Student, 1887. See Famous Edinburgh Students, 1914 (mainly rptd from The Student).]

(e) Aberdeen

The Aberdeen University Magazine. Vol. I, Jan.–Aug. 1836.

The King's College Miscellany. Nos. 1–8, 1846–7.

The Aberdeen Universities' Magazine, Dec. 1849–April 1850. [See Robert Harvey Smith, A Village Propaganda, 1889; The Aberdeen University Review, No. 1, 1913 (The Aberdeen Universities' Magazine by Sir J. Donaldson) and in no. 4, 1914 (The Story of the University Magazine by W. Keith Leask).]

The Academic. Nos. 1–7. New Ser. Nos. 1–8, 1877–8.

Alma Mater. 1883 onwards.

(f) St Andrew's

Lang, Andrew. Adventures among Books. 1905.

St Andrew's University Magazine. No. 1, Cupar, 1863.

The Tomahawk. Nos. 1–4, Cupar, [1874].

St Andrew's University News Sheet. 1886–9.

College Echoes. 1889.

Murray, R. F. The Scarlet Gown. 1891.

(g) Glasgow

The College Album for 1832. A Selection of Original Pieces written and edited by Students in the University of Glasgow. 3 vols. 1832–4. [Annual.]

The Glasgow University Album for 1854. Edited by the Students. [1854.]

The Old College, being the Glasgow University Album for 1869. Edited by Students. [1869.]

The Glasgow University Magazine. 1889 onwards.

(h) Dublin

The Dublin University Review and Quarterly Magazine. Vol. I, pts 1–3, Jan.–June 1833.

The Dublin University Magazine. 90 vols. Jan. 1833–Dec. 1877. [Continued as] The University Magazine: a Literary and Philosophic Review. 5 vols. Jan. 1878–June 1882. [Monthly: two further quarterly nos. pbd in Sept. and Dec. 1882. See above p. 827.]

The Catholic University Gazette. Vol. I, 1854–6.

Kottabos. A College Miscellany. Vols. I–III, 1868–1881. 2nd ser. 1881–91. 3rd ser. 1895. [Ed. by R. Y. Tyrrell (1868–81), J. B. Bury (1888–95); Oscar Wilde was a contributor; see Echoes from Kottabos, ed. R. Y. Tyrrell and Sir E. Sullivan, 1906.]

Hermathena. A Series of Papers on Literature, Science and Philosophy by members of Trinity College, Dublin. 1873 onwards. [Ed. by J. K. Ingram, B. Williamson, J. P. Mahaffy and R. Y. Tyrrell. Annual Postgraduate.]

The Dublin University Review. 1885–7.

(i) Eton

Harcourt, L. V. An Eton Bibliography. 1902.

The Microcosm. A Periodical by Gregory Griffin. 1787–8. [By R. Smith, G. Canning and others.]

The Miniature. A Periodical Paper by S. Grildrig of the College of Eton. Nos. 1–34, 1804–5. [By T. Rennell, H. G. Knight, G. Canning the younger, etc.]

The College Magazine. 1819. [Ed. by W. B[lunt].]

The Salt-Bearer: a Periodical Work by an Etonian [T. W. Helps]. May 1820–April 1821.

The Etonian. 2 vols. Oct. 1820–Aug. 1821. [Ed. by W. Blunt and W. M. Praed.]

The Eton Miscellany by Bartholomew Bouverie. 2 vols. 1827. [By W. E. Gladstone, G. A. Selwyn, P. A. Pickering, etc.]

The Oppidan. Nos. 1, 2, Oct. 1828.

The Eton College Magazine. June–Nov. 1832. [By J. Wickens, G. W. Lyttelton, C. G. Wynne, etc.]

The Kaleidescope. Nos. 1–9, 1833. [By A. J. Ellis, T. B. Charlton, G. W. Lyttelton, F. H. Doyle, etc.]

The Eton Bureau. Nos. 1–7, 1842. [By C. W. Johnson, W. Johnson (later Cory), J. D. Coleridge, etc.]

The Eton School Magazine. Vol. 1, Nos. 1–6, 1847–8.

Porticus Etonensis. Nos. 1, 2, 1859. [Ed. by M. Lubbock and M. Hankey.]

The Eton Observer. Nos. 1–14, [1859–60]. [By V. S. Coles, V. C. Amcotts, W. Pollock, etc.]

The Phoenix. Nos. 1–5, [1860–1]. [Ed. by V. C. Amcotts.]

Etonensia. Nos. 1, 2, 1862. [By V. S. Coles, V. C. Amcotts and Lord Francis Hervey.]

The Eton College Chronicle. 14 May 1863 onwards.

The Eton Scrap Book. Nos. 1–7, 1865. [Ed. by H. Maxwell Lyte and E. H. Primrose.]

The Adventurer. Nos. 1–29, 1867–72. [By R. Shute, C. W. Bell, A. A. Tilley, E. C. Selwyn, G. C. Macaulay, etc.]

The Eton Review. Nos. 1–6, 1867–8.

The Phoenix. No. 1, 1874.

The Salt-Hill Papers, or Vindiciae Etonenses by Two Etonians. 4 June 1875. [By J. K. Stephen and H. E. Ryle.]

The Sugar-Loaf Papers, by three Etonians. 1875. [By J. K. Stephen, H. E. Ryle and M. T. Tatham.]

The Etonian. Nos. 1–30, 19 May 1875– 2 Aug. 1876. [By G. N. (Marquess) Curzon, S. Sandbach, H. St C. Fielden, J. K. Stephen, etc.]

The Eton Rambler. Nos. 1–6, 1880. [By A. C. Benson and S. Leathes.]

The Mosleian. Nos. 1, 2, 1882. [Continued as Vanitas, No. 3, 1882; by A. W. M. Bosville.]

The Rambler. No. 1, 27 Jan. 1883. [By A. W. M. Bosville.]

The Etonian. Nos. 1–29, 1883–5. [By E. D. Hildyard, W. J. Seton, R. C. Devereux, etc.]

The Eton Review. Nos. 1–10, 1886. [By H. C. Dawkins and J. H. Hope.]

The Eton Fortnightly. Nos. 1–10, 1887. [By A. Clutton Brock, J. A. C. Tilley, A. B. Lowry, etc.]

The Eton Observer. Nos. 1, 2, 1887. [By I. Z. Malcolm and M. M. MacNaghten.]

The Present Etonian. Nos. 1–15, 1888. [Ed. by J. R. L. Rankin.]

The Eton Review. Nos. 1–10, 1889. [Ed. by Lord Elmley (Earl Beauchamp).]

The Parachute. Nos. 1–3, 22 June–30 July, 1889. [By R. C. Bosanquet, F. M. S. Parker and Lord Warkworth.]

The Rocket. No. 1, 31 March 1890. [Ed. by J. S. Arkwright.]

The Student's Humour. No. 1, 4 June 1891. [By V. R. Hoare, C. C. Bigham, J. S. Arkwright, H. T. G. Watkins, etc.]

The Mayfly. Nos. 1–3, 16 May–24 June 1891. [By A. B. Ramsay and H. T. G. Watkins.]

The Eton Idler. Nos. 1–7, 22 May–1 Aug. 1893. [By H. E. S. Fremantle and C. W. E. Cotton.]

The Eton Spectator. Nos. 1–3, 1893. [Ed. by A. S. Ward.]

The New Etonian. Nos. 1–4, 1895. [Ed. by A. S. Ward.]

The Amphibian. Nos. 1–9, 1898–9.

The Bantling. Nos. 1–9, 1900.

The Gnat. Nos. 1–3, 1900.

(j) Other Schools

Harrow.

The Harrovian. A Collection of Poems, Essays and Translations. Nos. 1–6, 1828.

The Triumvirate. Vols. I, II, [1860–1].

The Harrovian. 1878 onwards.

Harrow Notes. A School Newspaper. Vols. I–V, 1883–7.

Rugby.

The Rugby Magazine. 2 vols. 1835–7. [Ed. by A. H. Clough.]

The Rugby Miscellany. Nos. 1–10, 1846.

The Rugbeian. 1850 onwards.

The New Rugbeian. Vols. I–III, 1858–61.

The Leaflet. Edited by members of Rugby School. 1883–7.

The Sibyl. Nos. 1–24, 1890–5.

Rossall.

Rossall News. Nos. 1–14, 1850.

Rossall Herald. Nos. 1–6, 1850.

The Rossallian. 1870 onwards.

Marlborough.

The Marlburian. 20 Sept. 1865 onwards.

Winchester.

The Wykehamist. 1866 onwards.

The Winchester Review. Nos. 1, 2, 1880.

Wellington.

Wellingtonia. Vol. I, Nos. 1–6, 1866–7.

The Wellingtonian. 1870 onwards.

Repton.

The Reptonian. 1866 onwards.

Clifton.

The Cliftonian. 1867 onwards.

Haileybury.

The Haileyburian. 1868 onwards.

Cheltenham.

The Cheltenham College Magazine. Vols. I–V, 1869–74. [Continued as The Cheltonian, 1874 onwards.]

Malvern.

The Malvernian. 1870 onwards.

Shrewsbury.

The Salopian. 1876 onwards.

G. ANNUALS AND YEARBOOKS

(1) LITERARY ANNUALS

Tales of Adventure and Stories of Travel from the Annuals of Fifty Years ago. 1893.

Faxon, F. W. Literary Annuals and Gift-Books. Boston, 1912. [The bibliography of English annuals includes several items that are not listed below.]

Boyle, Andrew. An Index to the Annuals, 1820–1850. [In preparation.]

[A partial list of the French annuals of the same period, many of which were trns from the English and *vice versa*, will be found in J. Brivois, Bibliographie des Ouvrages illustrés du XIXme Siècle, Paris, 1883, and L. Carteret, Le Trésor du Bibliophile, Romantique et Moderne, 3 vols. and index, Paris, 1924–7. The American annuals are listed by Faxon (see above) and Ralph Thompson, American Literary Annuals and Gift-Books (1825–1865), New York, 1936.]

The Spirit of the Public Journals for 1797 [–1825]: being an impartial selection of essays, jeux d'esprit, etc. 29 vols.

The Annual Anthology. Vols. I–[II], 1799 [–1800], Bristol. [Ed. by Robert Southey.]

The Poetical Register and Repository of Fugitive Poetry for 1801[–1811]. 8 vols.

Flowers of Literature for 1801 and 1802 [–1808 and 1809], or Characteristic Sketches of Human Nature and Modern Manners. 7 vols. [Ed. by F. Prevost and F. Blagdon (vol. I), F. Blagdon alone (vols. II–VII).]

The Annual Review and History of Literature. 7 vols. 1802 [–1808]. [Ed. by A. Aikin.]

Forget-Me-Not: a Christmas and New Year Present for 1823[–47]. 25 vols. [Ed. by F. Shoberl.]

Friendship's Offering. 21 vols. 1824[–44]. [In 1833 it absorbed The Winter's Wreath. Ed. by: T. K. Hervey (1826), T. K. Hervey and B. E. Pote (1827), Charles Knight (1828), T. Pringle (1829–33), H. Inglis (1834), W. H. Harrison (1835), Leitch Ritchie (1842–4).]

The Graces, or Literary Souvenir for 1824. 1824.

Blossoms at Christmas, and First Flowers of the New Year. 2 vols. 1825–6.

Hommage aux Dames. 1825.

The Literary Coronal for 1825–6. Glasgow, 1825.

The Literary Souvenir, or Cabinet of Poetry and Romance. 1825[–34]. [Continued as] The Literary Souvenir and Cabinet of Modern Art. New Ser. 1835. [Continued as] The Cabinet of Modern Art and Literary Souvenir. 2nd [and 3rd] Ser. 3 vols. 1836[–7, 1842]. [Ed. by Alaric A. Watts.]

The Ladies' Pocket Magazine. 15 vols. 1825 [–39].

The Amulet; or Christian and Literary Remembrancer. 11 vols. 1826[–36]. [Ed. by Mrs S. C. Hall.]

The Pledge of Friendship for 1826[–28]. 3 vols. [Continued as] The Gem: a Literary Annual for 1829[–32]. 4 vols. [Ed. by Thomas Hood (1829), T. Marshall (?) (1830–2).]

A Wreath from the Emerald Isle: a New Year's Gift for 1826. Dublin. [Ed. by P. D. Hardy.]

The Every Day Book forming a complete History of the Year, Months and Seasons. 2 vols. 1826[–7]. [Ed. by William Hone.]

The Table Book. 2 vols. 1827[–8]. [Ed. by William Hone; contributions by Charles Lamb.]

The Keepsake for 1828[–57]. 30 vols. [Ed. by: W. H. Ainsworth (1828), F. M. Reynolds (1829–35 and 1839), Mrs Norton (1836), Lady E. Stuart Wortley (1837 and 1840), Countess of Blessington (1841–50), Miss E. Power (1851–7).]

The Winter's Wreath for 1828[–32]. A Collection of original Contributions in Prose and Verse. 5 vols. Liverpool. [Absorbed in Friendship's Offering. Ed. by W. B. Chorley (?); has also been attrib. to the publisher G. Smith.]

The Bijou; or Annual of Literature and the Arts. 3 vols. 1828[–30]. [Ed. by W. Fraser; has also been attrib. to Sir Harris Nicholas.]

Affection's Offering: designed as a Christmas and New Year's Gift. 4 vols. 1829[–32].

The Talisman. 2 vols. 1829–31. [Ed. by Elam Bliss, Zillah Watts.]

The Treasure of Knowledge, Literature, Instruction and Amusement. 2 vols. 1829 [–30].

The Anniversary; or Poetry and Prose for 1829. [Ed. by Allan Cunningham.]

Le Petit Bijou pour 1829. [Ed. by D'Emden.]

Affection's Gift. 5 vols. 1830–3, 1844.

The Anthology: an Annual Reward Book for Midsummer and Christmas. 1830. [Ed. by J. D. Parry.]

The Comic Annual. 11 vols. 1830[–39, 1842]. [Ed. by Thomas Hood.]

The Landscape Annual for 1830[–4]. [Continued as] Jennings's Landscape Annual for 1835[–9]. 10 vols. [Ed. by: T. Roscoe (1830–4), T. Rose and W. H. Harrison (1835–9); illustrated by S. Prout and J. D. Harding (1830–4), D. Roberts and J. Holland (1835–9).]

The Looking Glass: a Caricature Annual. 7 vols. 1830[–6]. [Lithographed.]

Mr Mathews's Comic Annual for 1830[–33], as published by him at the Adelphi Theatre. 4 vols.

The Zoological Keepsake; or Zoology, and the Garden and Museum of the Zoological Society; for the year 1830.

The Iris. 2 vols. 1831[–2]. [Ed. by T. Dale.]

The Comic Offering; or Ladies' Melange of Literary Mirth for 1831[–5]. 5 vols. [Ed. by Louisa H. Sheridan.]

The Cabinet Annual Register for 1831[–3]. 3 vols.

The Scrap Book of Literary Varieties. New Ser. vols. I[–II], 1831[–2].

The New Comic Annual for 1831. [The Dedication and Preface refer to this as 'Falstaff's Annual.']

The Cameo. 1831. [Largely rptd from The Bijou; ed. by William Pickering.]

The Remembrance. 13(?) vols. 1831[–43(?)]. [Only vols. for 1831, 1834, 1838 and 1843 have been noted; ed. by T. Roscoe (1831, 1834), T. Albin (1843).]

The Talisman. 1831. [Largely rptd from The Iris; ed. by Zillah Watts.]

Fisher's Drawing Room Scrap Book. 23 vols. 1832[–54]. [Ed. by: L. E. Landon (1832–9), L. E. Landon and Mary Howitt (1840), Mary Howitt (1841), Mrs Ellis (1844–5), Mrs Norton (1846–9), Charles Mackay (1850–2).]

Heath's Picturesque Annual for 1832[–45]. 14 vols. [The vols. for 1844 and 1845 were also issued as Cattermole's Historical Annual; ed. by: L. Ritchie (1832–9), Mrs Gore (1840 and 1843), T. Roscoe (1841), Jules Janin (1842), R. Cattermole (1844–5).]

The Amethyst, or Christian's Annual for 1832 [–4]. 3 vols. Edinburgh. [Ed. by Richard Haie and R. K. Greville.]

The Musical Gem for 1832[–45(?)]. 3(?) vols. [Ed. by N. Mori and W. Ball.]

The Bouquet for 1832[–4]: a Collection of Tales, Essays and Poems, original and select. 3 vols.

The Pocket Album and Literary Scrap Book. 1832.

The Botanic Annual. 1832. [Ed. by Robert Mudie.]

The Year Book of Daily Recreation and Information. 1832. [Ed. by William Hone.]

The Continental Annual and Romantic Cabinet for 1832. [Ed. by W. Kennedy.]

The Yorkshire Literary Annual for 1832. Leeds. [Ed. by C. F. Edgar.]

The Easter Gift for 1832. [Ed. by L. E. Landon.]

The Easter Offering for 1832. [Ed. by Joseph Booker.]

Heath's Book of Beauty. 1833[–47]. [Continued as] The Book of Beauty; or Regal Gallery. 17 vols. 1848[–9]. [Ed. by L. E. Landon (1833), Countess of Blessington (1834–47).]

The Christian Keepsake and Missionary Annual. 8 vols. 1833[–40]. [Ed. by W. Ellis.]

Turner's Annual Tour. 3 vols. 1833[5]. [Written by L. Ritchie; illustrated by J. M. W. Turner.]

The Landscape Album for 1833[–4]. 2 vols. [Ed. by Charles Tilt.]

The Aurora Borealis. Newcastle-on-Tyne, 1833. [Ed. by W. Howitt.]

The Oriental Annual, or Scenes in India. 1834[–6]. New Ser. 1837[–8]. 1839[–40], Containing a series of Tales, Legends and Historical Romances. 7 vols. [Ed. by Hobart Caunter (1834–6), T. Bacon (1839 40); illustrated by W. Daniell (1834–6) and with engravings by W. and E. Finden after T. Bacon and Meadows Taylor (1839–40).]

The Album Wreath and Bijou Litteraire. 1834. [Ed. by J. Francis.]

The White Rose of York: a Midsummer Annual. 1834. [Ed. by G. Hogarth.]

The Continental Landscape Annual. 3 vols. 1835, 1837[–8]. [Ed. by F. Fergusson.]

The Sacred Offering: a Poetical Annual for 1835[–8]. 4 vols. Liverpool. [Ed. by M. A. Jevons.]

The Landscape Wreath. [1835?]. [Ed. by Thomas Campbell.]

Gems of Beauty. 5 vols. 1836[–40]. [Ed. by Countess of Blessington; illustrated by E. Corbould.]

The Squib Annual of Poetry, Politics and Personalities for 1836.

Affection's Keepsake. Original Poetry. 11 vols. 1836[–46]. [Ed. by T. Albin.]

The Scottish Annual. Glasgow, 1836. [Ed. by W. Weir.]

The Sportsman's Annual. 1st Ser. Dogs. 1836. [Illustrated by Sir E. Landseer, A. Cooper and C. Hancock.]

Finden's Tableaux for 1837[–44]. 8 vols. [Ed. by: S. C. Hall (1837), Miss Mitford (1838–41); illustrated with engravings by W. and E. Finden after W. Perring, etc.]

The Pictorial Album; or Cabinet of Paintings for 1837. [Illustrated by George Baxter.]

The Scenic Annual for 1838. [Ed. by Thomas Campbell.]

Portraits of the Children of the Nobility. 3 vols. 1838[–41]. [Ed. by Louisa Fairlie; parodied in Children of the Mobility, 1841, with illustrations by John Leech.]

Flowers of Loveliness. 4 vols. 1838[–41].

The Hunter's Annual. 2 vols. 1838[–9]. [Ed. by A. H. Baily.]

The Christmas Library: Birds and Flowers, and other Country Things. Vol. i, 1838. [Ed. by Mary Howitt.]

The Amaranth: a Miscellany of original Prose and Verse. 1839. [Ed. by T. K. Hervey.]

The Annual of British Landscape Scenery. 1839. [Ed. by L. A. Twamley; illustrated with engravings after Fielding, Cox, Warren and Radclyffe.]

Album Wreath of Music and Literature. 1840.

Portraits of the Female Aristocracy. 2 vols. 1840[–1]. [Ed. by W. Finden.]

The Lilliputian Picturesque Annual. 1841. [Ed. by B. Crecerelle.]

The Protestant Annual. 1841. [Ed. by Charlotte Elizabeth Tonna, née Phelan.]

The Renfrewshire Annual. 2 vols. Paisley, 1841[–2]. [Ed. by Mrs Maxwell.]

A Love Gift for 1842[–5]. 4 vols.

The Christian Souvenir. 1842. [Ed. by C. B. Tayler.]

The Comic Album: a Book for every Table. 2 vols. 1843[–4].

The Holly Branch: an Album for 1843. [Ed. by E. Davis.]

The Gem of Loveliness for 1843. [Ed. by H. I. and W. Stevens.]

The Catholic Keepsake for 1843.

The Victoria Annual for 1844.

The Ball Room Annual for 1844.

George Cruikshank's Table Book. 1845. [Ed. by G. A. à Becket.]

The Comic Miscellany for 1845. [Ed. by J. Poole.]
The Coronal. 1846. [Ed. by E. Lacey.]
The Golden Annual for 1848.
The Annual Miscellany for 1848.
The Christian Keepsake for 1850. [Ed. by Mrs Ellet.]
The Cheltenham Literary Annual. 1857. [Ed. by Mrs H. Chetwynd.]
The Scottish Annual for 1859. Glasgow. [Ed. by C. R. Brown.]

[A great number of Annuals were issued from 1860 onwards, which form an integral part of many of the weekly and monthly periodicals listed in the preceding sections. These were either extra numbers or enlarged forms of the June and December issues.]

(2) JUVENILE ANNUALS

The Christmas Box: an Annual Present for Children for 1828[-9]. 2 vols. [Ed. by T. C. Croker.]
The Juvenile Keepsake for 1829[-30]. 2 vols. [Ed. by T. Roscoe.]
The Juvenile Forget-Me-Not for the Year 1829[-37]. 9 vols. [Ed. by Mrs S. C. Hall.]
Ackermann's Juvenile Forget-Me-Not for 1830[-2]. 3 vols. [Ed. by F. Shoberl; in 1833 this was absorbed in The Juvenile Forget-Me-Not.]
The Excitement. 1830[-45]. 16 vols. [Ed. by R. Jamieson.]
Marshall's Christmas Box: a Juvenile Annual. 2 vols. 1831[-2]. [Ed. by W. Marshall.]
The Infant Annual. Liverpool, 1835. [Ed. by H. M. Marshall.]
The New Year's Token; or Christmas Present. 1835[-6]. 2 vols.
The Nursery Offering; or Children's Gift for 1835[-6]. 2 vols. Edinburgh.
Fisher's Juvenile Scrap Book. 15 vols. 1836 [-50]. [Ed. by: Bernard Barton (1836), Bernard Barton and Agnes Strickland (1837-9), Mrs Ellis (1840-8), J. Strickland (1849), Mrs Milner (1850).]
The New Juvenile Keepsake for 1839. [Ed. by L. E. Landon.]
Peter Parley's Annual: a Christmas and New Year's Present for Young People. 25 vols. 1839[-63]. [Ed. by W. Martin.]
The Recreation: a Gift Book for Young Readers. 6 vols. Edinburgh, 1842[-8].
The Child's Own Annual. 2 vols. 1843[-4].
The Wesleyan Juvenile Offering: a Miscellany of Missionary Information for Young Persons. 23 vols. 1844[-66]. New Ser. 12 vols. 1867[-78].
The Juvenile Missionary Keepsake. 1846.
My Own Annual: an Illustrated Gift-Book for

Boys and Girls. 2 vols. 1847[-8]. [Ed. by 'Mark Merriwell.']
The Illustrated Juvenile Miscellany. 1847. [Continued as] The Playmate. 1848. [Second Ser. 1849.]
The Juvenile Offering. [1848.]
The Charm: a Book for Boys and Girls. Ser. 1 [-3]. 3 vols. 1853[-5].
Beeton's Annual for 1866: a Book for the Young. [Ed. by S. O. Beeton and J. G. Wood.]
The Children's Annual. 3 vols. 1869[-71].

[Numerous juvenile annuals were issued from 1860 onwards as an integral part of juvenile magazines. Thus The Boy's Own Annual and The Girl's Own Annual are the issues of each paper for the whole year put up in cloth binding. Other magazines issued an extra number at Christmas, which is described as an annual, sometimes under a totally different title. Frequently, however, the annuals of this period are enlarged or double numbers of the December issue in an elaborately coloured cover.]

(3) YEAR BOOKS
(a) General

The Annual Register; or a View of the History, Politicks and Literature of the Year 1758 [etc.; in progress]. [In 1790 the stock and the copyright were sold; the first was bought by Otridge and the second by Rivington; each party issued a distinct continuation; that issued by Rivington ran from 1791 to 1800, new ser. 1801 to 1827. General Index 1758-1780, 1783; 2nd edn, 1784; 3rd edn with addns (General Index 1781-92), 2 vols. 1799; General Index 1758-1819, 1826.]
The New Annual Register, or General Repository of History, Politics and Literature for the Year 1780[-1825]. Vols. I-XLV.
The Asiatic Annual Register for the Year 1799 [-1811]. Vols. I-XII. [Ed. by L. D. Campbell (1804-6), E. Samuel (1810-1).]
The Edinburgh Annual Register. 1808[-27]. Vols. I-XIX. [Ed. by Robert Southey (1809 15).]
The Annual Chronology and Historical Record of Important and Interesting Events in 1827. By Tell-Tale Time. 1828.
The British Almanac of the Society for the Diffusion of Useful Knowledge. 1828-1914. [Ed. by Charles Knight.]
The Companion to the [British] Almanack. 1828-56. [A Complete Index to the Companion to the Almanack, 1828-43, 1843.]
The Annual Historian: a Sketch of the Chief Historical Events of the World for the Year 1831. 1832. [Ed. by J. Cobbin.]

The British Annual and Epitome of the Progress of Science for 1837[-9]. 3 vols. [Ed. by R. D. Thomson.]

The Annual Scrap Book: a Selection of Paragraphs which have appeared in the Newspapers and Periodicals. 1838.

The Year-Book of Facts in Science and Art, exhibiting the most Important Discoveries and Improvements. 41 vols. 1839[-79]. [Ed. by J. Timbs (1839-73), C. W. Vincent (1874-5), J. Mason (1876-9).]

The Annual Mirror for 1845: an Historical Register. Vol. I. [Ed. by W. Lurcott.]

The British Year Book for the Country for 1856. [Ed. by C. MacIntosh and T. L. Kemp.]

The Archer's Register: a Year Book of Facts for 1864[-6]. 3 vols. [Ed. by J. Sharp.]

The Statesman's Year Book: a Statistical, Genealogical and Historical Account of the States and Sovereigns of the Civilised World for 1864 [etc.; in progress]. [Ed. by F. Martin, J. G. Keltie.]

Whitaker's Almanack for 1871 [etc.; in progress].

The Year Book of Women's Work. 6 vols. 1875[-80]. [Continued as] The Englishwoman's Year Book for 1881-1916. [Ed. by L. M. Hubbard (1875-98), E. James.]

The Annual Summary: a Complete Chronicle of Events at Home and Abroad. 2 vols. 1875-6 [also for 1876-7]. [Ed. by J. Mason.]

The Constitutional Year Book and Politician's Guide. 1885 onwards.

(b) Biographical

The Annual Necrology for 1797-98; including also Various Articles of Neglected Biography. 1800.

Public Characters of 1798[-1810]. 10 vols. [Vol. I rptd four times.]

The Annual Biography and Obituary for the year 1817[-1837]. Vols. I-XXI.

The Annual Biography: being Lives of Eminent or Remarkable Persons who have died within the Year 1842. 1843. [Ed. by C. R. Dod.]

Who's Who in 1849 [etc.; in progress]. [Ed. by H. R. Addison (1849), C. H. Oakes (1851-64), W. J. Lawson (1865-9), Douglas Sladen (1897-9).]

Men of the Time. 1852, 1853, 1856, 1857, 1862, 1865, 1868, 1872, 1875, 1879, 1884, 1887. [Continued as] Men and Women of the Time. 1891, 1895, 1899 (15th edn). [Ed. by A. A. Watts (1856), E. Walford (1862), G. H. Townsend (1868), Thompson Cooper (1872-84), T. H. Ward (1887), G. W. Moon (1891), V. G. Plarr (1895-9).]

The Biographical Magazine. Vols. I-VII, 1852-7. [Monthly; ed. by J. P. Edwards.]

The Military Obituary for 1853 [and 1854]. [Continued as] The Annual Military Obituary for 1855 [and 1856]. 4 vols. [Ed. by H. S. Smith.]

The Annual Royal Naval Obituary for 1855.

Hardwicke's Annual Biography for 1856[-7] containing Memoirs of Celebrated Characters who have died during the Year 1855[-6]. 2 vols. [Ed. by E. Walford.]

Celebrities of the Day, British and Foreign: a Monthly Repertoire of Contemporary Biography. Vols. I-III, 1881-2. [Monthly. Ed. by S. E. Thomas.]

(c) The Peerage

The Present Peerage of the United Kingdom. 25 vols. 1808[-32]. [Pbd by Stockdale.]

The Royal Blue Book; or Fashionable Directory. 1822 onwards.

A General and Heraldic Dictionary of the Peerage and Baronetage of the United Kingdom. 1826 onwards. [Triennial; continued also as Burke's Genealogical and Heraldic Dictionary, etc. Ed. by J. Burke (1826-46), Sir J. B. Burke (1840-?).]

The Annual Peerage of the British Empire. 4 vols. 1827[-9]. [Ed. by Anne Eliza and Maria Innes.]

The Peerage of the British Empire; to which is added the Baronetage of the Three Kingdoms. 1832 onwards. [Ed. by E. Lodge (1832-9), Anne Eliza and Maria Innes (1840-61).]

Webster's Royal Red Book; or Court and Fashionable Register. 1847 onwards.

Debrett's Illustrated Baronetage and Knightage of the United Kingdom of Great Britain and Ireland. 1865 onwards. [Ed. by R. H. Mair.]

Debrett's Illustrated Peerage of the United Kingdom of Great Britain and Ireland. 1865 [etc.; in progress]. [For the years 1866, 1867 and 1868 this and the previous entry were issued in one volume; ed. by R. H. Mair.]

The Upper Ten Thousand: an Alphabetical List of all Members of Noble Families. 3 vols. 1875[-7]. [Continued as] Kelly's Handbook of the Upper Ten Thousand for 1878[-9]. 2 vols. [Continued as] Kelly's Handbook to the Titled, Landed and Official Classes. 1880 [etc.; in progress]. [Ed. by A. B. Thom (1875-7).]

(d) Official

[Perrin, W. G.] Admiralty Library. Subject Catalogue of Printed Books. Pt I, 1912.

A List of the General and Field Officers as they rank in the Army. 1754-1868.

List of the Officers of the Several Regiments and Corps of Militia. 1793-1825.

The Army List. Nov. 1814 onwards. [Monthly.]

The New Annual Army List (and Militia List). 1840 onwards. [A quarterly edn was started in 1897; ed. by H. G. Hart.]

The Official Army List. 1880 onwards. [Quarterly, half-yearly since 1923.]

An Alphabetical List of the Commission Officers of His Majesty's Fleet. 1748–1846. [Title varies.]

A List of the Flag Officers of H.M. Fleet. 1749–1846.

Steel's Original and Correct List of the Royal Navy. 1783–1816. ['Monthly during war, and quarterly during peace.']

The Navy List. Feb. 1814 onwards. [Quarterly, then monthly.]

The New Navy List. 1839–56. [Quarterly, half-yearly from 1846. Ed. by Charles Haultain (1839–45), J. Allen (1846–56).]

The Royal Navy List 1878 onwards. [Quarterly, annual since 1914. Ed. by C. E. Warren (1878–81), Francis Lean (1878–1906).]

The Naval Annual 1886–1911. [Ed. by Lord Brassey (1886–9), T. A. Brassey (1890–1911).]

The East India Register and Directory for 1803[–44]. [Semi-annual.] [Continued as] The East India Register and Army List for 1845[–60]. [Continued as] The Indian Army and Civil Service List. 1861[–76]. [Continued as] The India List, Civil and Military. 1877 onwards. [Ed. by: J. Mathison, A. W. Mason, J. S. Kingston, G. Owen, G. H. Brown, F. Clark.]

The British Imperial Calendar and Civil Service List. 1810 onwards. [Suspended from 1920 to 1925. Ed. by B. P. Capper (1810–4), R. Capper (1816–7), J. Debrett (1818–22).]

The Parliamentary Pocket Companion for 1833 [etc.; in progress]. [Now styled Dod's Parliamentary Pocket Companion; ed. by C. R. Dod (1841–55), R. P. Dod (1856–?).]

A General Police and Constabulary List and Analysis of Criminal and Police Statistics. Sept. 1844.

The Mercantile Navy List. 1850 onwards. [Ed. by J. H. Brown (1850–62), I. I. Mayo (1863–?).]

The Foreign Office List for 1852 [etc.; in progress]. [Ed. by F. W. H. Cavendish and E. Hertslet.]

The Colonial Office List, or General Register of the Colonial Dependencies of Great Britain. 1862 onwards. [Ed. by W. C. Sargeaunt and A. N. Birch.]

(e) Religious

The Ecclesiastical and University Register. 3 vols. 1808[–10].

The Missionary Register for the Year 1813 [–55] containing an Abstract of the Proceedings of the Principal Missionary and Bible Societies throughout the World. 43 vols.

The Annual Monitor; or New Letter Case Memorandum Book. Nos. 1–30, York, 1813[–41]. New Ser. The Annual Monitor or Obituary of the Members of the Society of Friends. York, 1842 onwards. [Index for the years 1813–32, York, 1833.]

Minutes of Several Conversations between the Methodist Ministers at their 86th Annual Conference. 1829 onwards.

The Catholic Directory. 1838 onwards.

The Clergy List for 1841 [etc.; in progress].

The Congregational Year Book for 1846 [etc.; in progress]. [Ed. by: J. Blackburn (1846–7), R. Ashton and W. S. Palmer (1848–52), R. Ashton.]

The Churchman's Year Book for 1852[–7] or Ecclesiastical Annual Register. 6 vols.

The Clerical Directory, a Biographical and Statistical Book of Reference for Facts relating to the Clergy and the Church. 2 vols. 1858 [and 1859]. [Continued as] Crockford's Clerical Directory for 1860 [etc.; in progress].

General Baptist Year Book for 1866 [etc.; in progress].

The Christian Year Book. 2 vols. 1867 [and 1868].

The Clergy Directory and Parish Guide: an Alphabetical List of the Clergy of the Church of England. 1872.

The Official Year Book of the Church of England. 1883 onwards.

(f) Educational

The Cambridge University Calendar for the Year 1802 [etc.; in progress]. [Ed. by Benjamin Clarke Raworth (1802–?), J. W. Clark.]

The Oxford University Calendar for the Year 1810 [etc.; in progress]. [Ed. by J. Walker, P. Bliss.]

The London University Calendar for the Year 1844 [etc.; in progress].

The Literary and Educational Year Book for 1859 [and 1860]. 2 vols.

Crockford's Scholastic Directory for 1861 [etc.; in progress]; being an Annual Work of Reference for Facts Relating to Educators, Education and Educational Establishments.

The Public Schools Calendar. 2 vols. 1865–[6].

The Institute Register and Handbook of Reference. 1868.

A Practical Handbook to the Principal Schools of England. 2 vols. 1877[–8]. [Ed. by C. E. Pascoe.]

The Year Book of the Scientific and Learned Societies of Great Britain and Ireland. 1884 onwards.

(g) Professional

The New Law List. 5 vols. 1798[–1802]. [Continued as] Clarke's New Law List. 38 vols. 1803[–40]. [Continued as] The Law List. 1841 onwards. [Ed. by: J. Hughes (1798–1802), S. Hill (1803–19), S. Cockell (1820–48), W. Powell (1849–58), W. W. Dalbiac (1859–71), W. H. Cousins (1872–83), J. S. Purcell.]

The Lawyer's Companion for 1848 [etc.; in progress] containing a List of the English Bar. [Ed. by W. F. Finlason (1855–60), H. Moore.]

The Medical Annual for 1831[–4]. 4 vols. [Ed. by R. Reece.]

The Medical Directory of Great Britain and Ireland for 1845.

The London Medical Directory. 3 vols. 1845 [–7]. [Incorporated in The Provincial Medical Directory and continued as] The London and Provincial Medical Directory. 1848 onwards. [In 1861 it absorbed The Medical Directory for Scotland and The Medical Directory for Ireland.]

The Provincial Medical Directory. 1847.

The Medical Directory for Scotland. 9 vols. 1852[–60].

The Medical Directory for Ireland. 9 vols. 1852[–60].

The London Medical Guide, containing a Complete Directory of the Names of all Qualified Medical Practitioners residing in London and the Suburbs. 1872 [etc.; in progress].

(h) Miscellaneous Commercial

Gosse, C. W. F. The London Directories. 1677–1855. 1932.

The Post Office London Directory for 1799 [–1839]. 41 vols. [Continued as] W. Kelly and Co. The Post Office London Directory for 1840 [etc.; in progress].

The British Postal Guide; containing the Chief Public Regulations of the Post Office. 1856 [–79]. [Quarterly.] [Continued as] The Post Office Guide. 1880 onwards. [Quarterly.]

Bradshaw's Railway Time Tables. No. 1, 19 Oct.–No. 3, 18 Nov. 1839. [Continued as] Bradshaw's Railway Companion. 1 Jan. 1840–[Nov. 1840]. [Continued as] Bradshaw's Railway Guide. [No. 1] Dec. 1841–No. 6, May 1842. [Continued as] Bradshaw's Monthly General Railway and Steam Navigation Guide. No. 7, June 1842 onwards. [See E. H. Dring, Early Railway Time Tables, Library, Dec. 1921.]

Osborne's Railway Time Table and Literary Companion. Birmingham, Nov. 1839–67.

The A.B.C. or Alphabetical Railway Guide. Oct. 1853 onwards. [Monthly.]

Cook's Excursionist and International Tourist Advertiser. 1864–70. [Ed. by Thomas Cook.]

Cook's Continental Time Tables and Tourist's Handbook. 1873 onwards.

Dickens's Dictionary of Continental Railways, Steamboats, Diligences, etc.: being an Easy Guide for Travellers. 1880–1. [Continued as] Dickens's Continental ABC Railway Guide. 1881–7. [Ed. by Charles Dickens junr.]

The British Tariff for 1829–30[–1862–63]. 34 vols. [Ed. by R. Ellis (1829–47), E. Beedell (1847–63).]

The Yearly Journal of Trade for 1836[–46]. 11 vols. [Ed. by Charles Pope.]

The Exporter's Directory: an Index to Merchandise shipped to Australia, New Zealand, India, Africa, N. and S. America, etc. 1878[–1881].

The International Mercantile Directory. 1881 [etc.; in progress].

The Banking Almanac, Directory and Year Book. 1845–1919. [Continued as] The Banker's Almanac. 1920 onwards.

The Stock Exchange Year Book. 1874 onwards.

The Directory of Directors. 1880 onwards.

The Newspaper Press Directory. 1846 onwards. [Ed. by C. Mitchell. See above, p. 797.]

The Brown Book, a Book of Ready Reference to the Hotels, Libraries, Post Offices, Cab Stands, in the Metropolis. 3 vols. 1864–[7].

London in 1880 [etc.] Illustrated with Bird's-eye Views of the Principal Streets. Also its Chief Suburbs and Environs. [1880–9.] [Ed. by H. Fry.]

The Municipal Corporations Companion, Diary and Year Book of Statistics. 1877 onwards. [Ed. by J. R. S. Vine.]

The Brewer's Annual for 1841[–3]. 3 vols. [Ed. by G. Amsinck.]

The Licensed Victualler's Year Book for 1874 [etc.; in progress]. [Ed. by H. D. Miles.]

The Brewer's Year Book for 1876 [etc.; in progress].

(i) Sport

The Racing Calendar; containing an account of the Plates, Matches and Sweepstakes run for in 1773 [etc.; in progress]. [Since 1846 there have been 2 vols. for each year with the same serial number, Races Past and Races to Come; see vol. II, p. 718; ed. by J. Weatherby (1773–93), E. and J. Weatherby

(1794–1830), E. and C. Weatherby (1831–5), E., C. and J. Weatherby (1836–9), C. and J. Weatherby (1840–58), E. C. and J. Weatherby (1859–67), C. J., E. and J. P. Weatherby.]

The Guide to the Turf; or, Pocket Racing Companion. 1842–53. [Continued as] Ruff's Guide to the Turf. 1854 onwards. [Ed. by William Ruff (1842–54), W. H. Langley.]

The Cricketer's Manual for 1849. By 'Bat.'

The Guide to Cricketers. 14 vols. 1853[–66]. [Incorporated in John Lillywhite's Cricketer's Companion; ed. by F. Lillywhite.]

The Cricket Chronicle for the season 1863. 1864. [Ed. by W. Bayly.]

The Cricketer's Almanac. 1864–9. [Continued as] John Wisden's Cricketer's Almanac. 1870 onwards.

Mantz's Cricket Directory, with the Laws of Cricket as revised by the Marylebone Club. [1865.]

The Cricketer's Handbook for 1865. Manchester, 1865.

J. Lillywhite's Cricketer's Companion for 1865[–73]. 9 vols. [Continued as] J. Lillywhite's Cricketer's Annual for 1874–85. [Ed. by J. Lillywhite (1865–73), C. W. Alcock (1873–85).]

The Football Annual. 1873–1908. [Ed. by C. W. Alcock.]

The Football Calendar, containing laws of both sections of the game, list of clubs, playing grounds, and fixtures for the season 1875–76. 1875–94. [Ed. by G. H. West.]

The Lawn Tennis Annual. 1882. [Ed. by L. S. F. Winslow.]

The 'Field' Lawn Tennis Calendar. 1882–[91]. [Ed. by B. C. Evelegh.]

The Bicycle Annual for 1879[–83]. 5 vols. [Continued as] The Cycling Annual for 1884[–?]. [Ed. by C. W. Nairn (1879–83), and C. J. Fox (1879–?).]

The Golfing Annual. 1888 onwards. [Ed. by C. R. Bauchope.]

Baily's Fox-Hunting Directory. 1897 onwards.   H. G. P.

IX. WRITINGS ON RELIGION

Liberal Theologians and Evangelicals. Oxford Movement and High Churchmen

A. THE LIBERAL THEOLOGIANS AND THE EVANGELICALS

(1) THE GROWTH OF LIBERAL THEOLOGY

(a) *General Works, Historical and Critical*

Tayler, J. J. A Retrospect of the Religious Life of England. 1845; 1876 ('With Supplementary Chapter by J. Martineau').

Lecky, W. E. H. History of Rationalism in Europe. 2 vols. 1865.

Stephen, Sir L. History of English Thought in the Eighteenth Century. 2 vols. 1876.

Martineau, Harriet. Autobiography. 3 vols. 1877.

Stoughton, J. History of Religion in England. Vols. VII, VIII (1800–1850), 1884.

Tulloch, J. Movements of Religious Thought in Britain during the Nineteenth Century. 1885.

Davidson, R. and Benham, W. Life of Archbishop Tait. 2 vols. 1891.

Overton, J. H. The English Church in the Nineteenth Century, 1800–1833. 1894.

Hunt, J. Religious Thought in England in the Nineteenth Century. 1896.

White, A. D. A History of the Warfare of Science with Theology. 2 vols. 1896.

Benn, A. W. The History of English Rationalism in the Nineteenth Century. 2 vols. 1906.

Robertson, J. M. A Short History of Freethought. 1906.

Tuckwell, W. Pre-Tractarian Oxford: a Reminiscence of the Oriel Noetics. 1909.

Cornish, F. W. W. History of the English Church in the Nineteenth Century. 2 vols. 1910.

Storr, V. F. The Development of English Theology in the Nineteenth Century, 1800–1860. 1913.

Mathieson, W. L. Church and Reform in Scotland: a History from 1797 to 1843. 1916.

Raven, C. E. Christian Socialism, 1848–1854. 1920.

Webb, C. C. J. A Century of Anglican Theology. 1923.

—— A Study of Religious Thought in England from 1350. 1932.

Stewart, H. L. Modernism, Past and Present. 1932.

(b) *Principal Writers*, 1800–1835

THOMAS ARNOLD (1795–1842)

Sermons. 3 vols. 1829–34.

Principles of Church Reform. 1833.

Life and Correspondence. Ed. A. P. Stanley, 1844.

Miscellaneous Works. Ed. A. P. Stanley, 1845.

[See also p. 888 below.]

ROBERT ASPLAND (1782–1845)

Causes of the Slow Progress of Christian Truth. [1825.]

Memoir of the Life, Works and Correspondence. 1850.

THOMAS BELSHAM (1750–1829)

A Summary View of the Evidences of the Christian Revelation. 1807.

JEREMY BENTHAM (1748–1832)

Church-of-Englandism and its Catechism examined. 1818. [See also vol. II, p. 953 above.]

SAMUEL TAYLOR COLERIDGE (1772–1834)

Confessions of an Enquiring Spirit. Ed. (from MS) H. N. Coleridge, 1840.
Notes on English Divines. Ed. D. Coleridge, 2 vols. 1853.
[See also pp. 172 above.]

JOHN DAVISON (1777–1834)

The Nature and History of Prophecy. 1824.
An Enquiry into the Origin and Intent of Primitive Sacrifice. 1825.

THOMAS ERSKINE (1788–1870)

Remarks on the Internal Evidence for the Truth of Revealed Religion. 1820.
An Essay on Faith. 1822.
The Unconditional Freeness of the Gospel. 1828.
The Brazen Serpent, or Life coming through Death. 1831.
The Doctrine of Election. 1837.
The Spiritual Order, and Other Papers. 1871.
Letters. Ed. W. Hanna, 2 vols. 1877.

JOHN FOSTER (1770–1843)

Essays. 2 vols. 1805.
Contributions to the Eclectic Review. 2 vols. 1844.
Life and Correspondence. Ed. J. E. Ryland, 2 vols. 1846.
[See also p. 669 above.]

WILLIAM JOHNSON FOX (1786–1864)

Christ and Christianity. 2 vols. 1831.
On the Religious Ideas. 1849.

AUGUSTUS WILLIAM HARE (1792–1834) and JULIUS CHARLES HARE (1795–1855)

Guesses at Truth, by Two Brothers. 1827.
[See also p. 670 above.]

REGINALD HEBER (1783–1826)

The Personality and Office of the Christian Comforter. 1816.
Life of Bishop Jeremy Taylor. [In The Whole Works, 1822.]
Poetical Works. 1841.
[See also p. 234 above.]

JOHN PYE SMITH (1774–1851)

On the Relation between the Scriptures and Geological Science. 1839.

SYDNEY SMITH (1771–1845)

Sermons at St Paul's. 1846. [See also p. 679 above, and A. Chevrillon, Sydney Smith et la Renaissance des Idées libérales en Angleterre, Paris, 1894.]

ISAAC TAYLOR (1787–1865)

The Natural History of Enthusiasm. 1829 (anon.).
The Restoration of Belief. [1852] (anon.).
The Spirit of Hebrew Poetry. 1861.

RICHARD WHATELY (1787–1863)

Historic Doubts relative to Napoleon Buonaparte. 1819 (anon.).
The Use and Abuse of Party-Feeling in Matters of Religion. 1822.
Letters on the Church. By an Episcopalian. 1826.
The Kingdom of Christ delineated. 1841.
Life and Correspondence. Ed. E. J. Whately, 2 vols. 1866.
[See also p. 681 above.]

JOSEPH BLANCO WHITE, formerly JOSÉ MARIA BLANCO (1775–1841)

Night and Death. [Sonnet in The Bijou, 1828.]
Second Travels of an Irish Gentleman in Search of a Religion. 2 vols. Dublin, 1833 (anon.). [In answer to T. Moore's Travels of an Irish Gentleman, 1833.]
The Life of, written by Himself. Ed. J. H. Thom, 3 vols. 1845.

(c) *Principal Writers*, 1835–1870

GEORGE DOUGLAS CAMPBELL, DUKE OF ARGYLL (1823–1900)

The Reign of Law. 1866. [See also p. 862 below.]

MATTHEW ARNOLD (1822–1888)

St Paul and Protestantism. 1870.
Literature and Dogma. 1873.
God and the Bible. 1875.
Last Essays on Church and Religion. 1877.
[See also p. 265 above.]

CHARLES BEARD (1827–1888)

Port Royal. 2 vols. 1861.
The Reformation in its Relation to Modern Thought. 1883.

CHARLES BRAY (1811–1884)

The Philosophy of Necessity. 2 vols. 1841.
Christianity viewed in the Light of our Present Knowledge. [1876.]
Phases of Opinion during a Long Life. [1884.]

JOHN MCLEOD CAMPBELL (1800–1872)

The Nature of the Atonement. 1856.
Memorials. Ed. D. Campbell, 1877.

WALTER RICHARD CASSELS (1826–1907)

Supernatural Religion. 3 vols. 1874–7 (anon.).

ROBERT CHAMBERS (1802–1871)

Vestiges of the Natural History of Creation. 1844 (anon.) [See also p. 709 above.]

ARTHUR HUGH CLOUGH (1819–1861)

Letters and Remains. 1865. [See also p. 264 above.]

JOHN WILLIAM COLENSO (1814–1863)

The Pentateuch and Book of Joshua critically examined. 7 pts, 1862–79.

SAMUEL COX (1826–1893)

Salvator Mundi. 1877.

ROBERT WILLIAM DALE (1829–1895)

The Atonement. 1875.
The Living Christ and the Four Gospels. 1890.
[See Life, by Sir A. W. W. Dale, 1898.]

SAMUEL DAVIDSON (1806–1898)

The Text of the Old Testament considered. 1856.
Autobiography, with an Account of the Controversy of 1857 by J. A. Picton. 1899.

'GEORGE ELIOT' (1819–1880)

The Life of Jesus critically examined, by D. F. Strauss. 3 vols. 1846. [Anon. trn by George Eliot.]
The Essence of Christianity, by L. Feuerbach. Translated by Marian Evans. 1854.
[See also p. 465 above.]

Essays and Reviews. 1860. [By F. Temple, Rowland Williams, Baden Powell, H. B. Wilson, C. W. Goodwin, Mark Pattison, B. Jowett.]

ALEXANDER EWING (1814–1873)

Present Day Papers. 1869–74. [By himself, F. D. Maurice, T. Erskine, F. Myers, etc.]
Revelation considered as Light. 1873.

FREDERIC WILLIAM FARRAR (1831–1903)

The Life of Christ. 1874.
Eternal Hope. 1878.
[See also p. 545 above.]

THOMAS HILL GREEN (1836–1882)

The Witness of God, and Faith. Two Lay Sermons. 1883.
[See also p. 868 below.]

WILLIAM RATHBONE GREG (1809–1881)

The Creed of Christendom. 1851.
Enigmas of Life. 1872.

RENN DICKSON HAMPDEN (1793–1868)

The Scholastic Philosophy in its Relation to Christian Theology. 1833. [See A Concise History of the Hampden Controversy, with Documents, by H. Christmas, 1848.]

EDWIN HATCH (1835–1889)

The Organization of the Early Christian Churches. 1881.
The Influence of Greek Ideas upon the Christian Church. 1890.

CHARLES CHRISTIAN HENNELL (1809–1850)

An Inquiry concerning the Origin of Christianity. 1838.

JAMES HINTON (1822–1875)

The Mystery of Pain. 1866 (anon.).

FENTON JOHN ANTHONY HORT (1828–1892)

The Way, the Truth, the Life. Hulsean Lectures, 1871. 1893.
Judaistic Christianity. 1894.
Life and Letters. Ed. Sir A. F. Hort, 2 vols. 1896.
The Christian Ecclesia. 1897.

RICHARD HOLT HUTTON (1826–1897)

Essays Theological and Literary. 2 vols. 1871.
Modern Guides of English Thought in Matters of Faith. 1887.
Aspects of Religious and Scientific Thought. 1899.
[See also p. 719 above.]

BENJAMIN JOWETT (1817–1893)

Epistles of St Paul to Thessalonians, Galatians and Romans. Commentary with Essays and Dissertations. 2 vols. 1855.
[See also p. 998 below.]

CHARLES KINGSLEY (1819–1875)

The Good News of God. 1859.
What, then, does Dr Newman mean? 1864.
Letters and Memories of his Life, by his Wife. 2 vols. 1877.
[See also p. 487 above.]

JOSEPH BARBER LIGHTFOOT (1828–1889)

Essays on the Work entitled 'Supernatural Religion.' 1889.
Dissertations on the Apostolic Age. 1892. [From his edns of St Paul's Epistles, 1865–75.]

ROBERT WILLIAM MACKAY (1803–1882)

The Progress of the Intellect, as Exemplified in the Religious Development of the Greeks and Hebrews. 2 vols. 1850. [See article on it by George Eliot, Westminster Rev. Jan. 1851.]

The Tübingen School and its Antecedents.
1863.

HENRY LONGUEVILLE MANSEL (1820–1871)
The Limits of Religious Thought. 1858.
[See also p. 870 below.]

JAMES MARTINEAU (1805–1900)
The Rationale of Religious Inquiry. 1836.
Endeavours after the Christian Life. 2 sers.
1843–7.
Types of Ethical Theory. 2 vols. 1885.
A Study of Religion. 2 vols. 1888.
The Seat of Authority in Religion. 1890.
Essays, Reviews and Addresses. 4 vols.
1890–1.
[See Life and Letters, by J. Drummond and
C. B. Upton, 1902, and James Martineau,
Theologian and Teacher, by J. Estlin Car-
penter, 1905. See also p. 870 below.]

JOHN FREDERICK DENISON MAURICE
(1805–1872)
The Kingdom of Christ. [1838.]
The Religions of the World. 1847.
Moral and Metaphysical Philosophy. 4 vols.
1850–7; 2 vols. 1871–2.
Theological Essays. Cambridge, 1853.
The Doctrine of Sacrifice. 1854.
The Epistles of St John: Lectures on Christian
Ethics. 1857.
The Conscience, Lectures on Casuistry. 1868.
The Friendship of Books and Other Lectures.
1874.
Life of, Chiefly told in his Letters. Ed. Sir
J. F. Maurice, 2 vols. 1884.
[See also p. 720 above.]

JOHN STUART MILL (1806–1873)
Three Essays on Religion. 1874.
[See also p. 871 below.]

HUGH MILLER (1802–1856)
Footprints of the Creator. 1849.
The Testimony of the Rocks. 1857.
[See also p. 721 above.]

FREDERIC MYERS (1811–1851)
Catholic Thoughts on the Church of Christ
and the Church of England. 1834–41 (anon.
and priv. ptd); 1874.
Catholic Thoughts on the Bible and Theology.
1841–8 (anon. and priv. ptd); 1874.

FRANCIS WILLIAM NEWMAN (1805–1897)
The Soul, her Sorrows and her Aspirations.
1849; 1905 (with Memoir by C. B. Upton).
Phases of Faith. 1850.
Memoir and Letters. Ed. I. G. Sieveking,
1909.
[See also p. 302 above.]

MARK PATTISON (1813–1884)
Sermons. 1885.
Memoirs. 1885.
Essays, collected by H. Nettleship. 2 vols.
1889.
[See also p. 723 above.]

BADEN POWELL (1796–1860)
Tradition unveiled. 1839. [A Supplement,
1840.]
Christianity without Judaism. 1857.

FREDERICK WILLIAM ROBERTSON
(1816–1853)
Sermons preached at Trinity Chapel, Brighton.
4 sers. 1855–63.
Lectures and Addresses on Literary and
Social Topics. 1858.
Expository Lectures on St Paul's Epistles to
the Corinthians. 1859.
Life and Letters, by Stopford A. Brooke.
2 vols. 1865.

SIR JOHN ROBERT SEELEY (1834–1895)
Ecce Homo. 1865 (anon.).
Natural Religion. By the Author of Ecce
Homo. 1882.
[See also p. 932 below.]

HENRY SIDGWICK (1838–1900)
The Ethics of Conformity and Subscription.
1870. [Rptd in Practical Ethics, 1898.]

WILLIAM HENRY SMITH (1808–1872)
Thorndale, or the Conflict of Opinions. 1857.
Gravenhurst, or Thoughts on Good and Evil.
1861; 1875 (with memoir).

ARTHUR PENRHYN STANLEY (1815–1881)
Sermons and Essays on the Apostolic Age.
1847.
Essays, chiefly on Church and State. 1870.
Christian Institutions. 1881.
[See G. G. Bradley, Recollections, 1883, and
R. E. Prothero, Life and Correspondence,
1893. See also p. 901 below.]

JOHN STERLING (1806–1844)
Essays and Tales. Ed. (with memoir) Julius
Hare, 2 vols. 1848.
Letters. 1851.
[See Life, by Thomas Carlyle, 1851, and
p. 680 above.]

CONNOP THIRLWALL (1797–1875)
Remains, Literary and Theological. 3 vols.
1877–80.
Letters, Literary and Theological. 1881.
[See J. C. Thirlwall, Connop Thirlwall, 1936.
See also p. 894 below.]

JOHN HAMILTON THOM (1808–1894)

Laws of Life after the Mind of Christ. 2 sers. 1883–6.
A Spiritual Faith, with Memoir by J. Martineau. 1895.

ROBERT ALFRED VAUGHAN (1823–1857)

Hours with the Mystics. 2 vols. 1856. [See also p. 726 above.]

BROOKE FOSS WESTCOTT (1825–1901)

The History of the Canon of the New Testament. 1855.
An Introduction to the Study of the Gospels. 1860.
The History of the English Bible. 1868.
Social Aspects of Christianity. 1887.
Religious Thought of the West. 1891.
Life and Letters. Ed. A. Westcott, 2 vols. 1903.

(d) Principal Writers, 1870–1900

EDWIN ABBOTT ABBOTT (1838–1928)

Philochristus. 1878 (anon.).
The Kernel and the Husk. 1886 (anon.).
The Spirit on the Waters. 1897.

ISRAEL ABRAHAMS (1858–1928)

Aspects of Judaism. 1895. [With C. G. Montefiore.]
Studies in Pharisaism and the Gospels. 2 sers. 1917–24.

STOPFORD AUGUSTUS BROOKE (1832–1916)

Theology in the English Poets. 1874. [See also p. 736.]

EDWARD CAIRD (1835–1908)

The Evolution of Religion. 2 vols. 1893.
The Evolution of Theology in the Greek Philosophers. 2 vols. Glasgow, 1904.
[See A. W. Benn, English Rationalism, 1906, and p. 865 below.]

JOHN CAIRD (1820–1898)

An Introduction to the Philosophy of Religion. 1880.
Fundamental Ideas of Christianity. With Memoir by Edward Caird. 2 vols. 1899.

REGINALD JOHN CAMPBELL (b. 1867)

A Faith for To-day. 1900.
The New Theology. 1907.
A Spiritual Pilgrimage. 1916.

JOSEPH ESTLIN CARPENTER (1844–1928)

The First Three Gospels. 1890.
The Bible in the Nineteenth Century. 1903.
Studies in Theology. 1903. [With P. H. Wicksteed.]

ROBERT HENRY CHARLES (1855–1931)

A Critical History of the Doctrine of a Future Life. 1899.

THOMAS KELLY CHEYNE (1841–1915)

The Origin and Contents of the Psalter. 1891.
Founders of Old Testament Criticism. 1893.
Encyclopaedia Biblica. 1899–1903. [Joint editor with J. S. Black.]

ANDREW BRUCE DAVIDSON (1831–1902)

Biblical and Literary Essays. 1902.

JOHN LLEWELYN DAVIES (1826–1916)

Theology and Morality. 1873.
Order and Growth. 1891.

JAMES DENNEY (1856–1917)

Studies in Theology. 1895.
Jesus and the Gospel. 1908.

SAMUEL ROLLES DRIVER (1846–1914)

An Introduction to the Literature of the Old Testament. 1891.

HENRY DRUMMOND (1851–1897)

Natural Law in the Spiritual World. 1883.
The Ascent of Man. 1894.

JAMES DRUMMOND (1835–1918)

Via, Veritas, Vita. 1894.

ANDREW MARTIN FAIRBAIRN (1838–1912)

The Place of Christ in Modern Theology. 1893. [See Life, by W. B. Selbie, 1914.]

PETER TAYLOR FORSYTH (1848–1927)

Religion in Recent Art. 1889.
The Principle of Authority. [1912.]

PERCY GARDNER (b. 1846)

Exploratio evangelica. 1899.
Evolution in Christian Doctrine. 1918.

ALFRED ERNEST GARVIE (b. 1861)

The Ritschlian Theology. 1899.

JAMES HASTINGS (b. 1862)

A Dictionary of the Bible. 1898–1902. [Ed. by Hastings.]

WILLIAM RALPH INGE (b. 1860)

Christian Mysticism. 1899.
The Philosophy of Plotinus. 2 vols. 1918.
Outspoken Essays. 1919. 2nd ser. 1922.
Christian Ethics and Modern Problems. 1930.

LAWRENCE PEARSALL JACKS (b. 1860)

Authority in Religious Belief. 1893.
The Hibbert Journal. 1902– . [Ed. by Jacks.]
Writings. 6 vols. 1916–7.
From Authority to Freedom. 1920.

JOHN SCOTT LIDGETT (b. 1854)

The Spiritual Principle of the Atonement. 1898.
The Fatherhood of God. 1902.

THOMAS MARTIN LINDSAY (1843–1914)

Religious Life in Scotland to the Present Day. 1888. [With others.]
A History of the Reformation in Europe. 2 vols. 1906–7.

Lux Mundi. 1889. [Charles Gore, editor: W. J. H. Campion, H. Scott Holland, W. Lock, A. Lyttelton, J. R. Illingworth, R. C. Moberly, Aubrey Moore, R. L. Ottley, F. Paget and E. S. Talbot.]

ROBERT MACKINTOSH (b. 1867)

Essays towards a New Theology. 1889.

ALFRED WILLIAMS MOMERIE (1848–1900)

Defects of Modern Christianity. 1882.
The Religion of the Future. 1893.

CLAUDE JOSEPH GOLDSMID MONTEFIORE (b. 1858)

The Growth of Religion of the Ancient Hebrews. 1892.
Liberal Judaism. 1903.
The Synoptic Gospels. 2 vols. 1909.

SIR WILLIAM MITCHELL RAMSAY (b. 1851)

The Church in the Roman Empire. 1893.
St Paul the Traveller. 1895.
The Teaching of Paul in Terms of the Present Day. 1913.

HASTINGS RASHDALL (1858–1924)

The Universities of Europe in the Middle Ages. 2 vols. 1895; rev. F. M. Powicke and A. B. Emden, 3 vols. 1936.
Doctrine and Development. 1898.
The Theory of Good and Evil. 2 vols. 1907.
The Idea of Atonement in Christian Theology. 1919.
[See Life, by P. E. Matheson, 1928.]

GEORGE SALMON (1819–1904)

The Infallibility of the Church. 1888.
The Human Element in the Gospels. 1907.

WILLIAM SANDAY (1843–1920)

Inspiration. 1893.
Christologies, Ancient and Modern. 1910.

FREDERIC SEEBOHM (1833–1912)

The Spirit of Christianity. 1876 (priv. ptd); 1916.
[See also p. 926 below.]

ANDREW SETH (1856–1931: from 1898 A. S. PRINGLE-PATTISON)

Man's Place in the Cosmos. 1897; 1902 (enlarged).
The Idea of God in the Light of Recent Philosophy. 1917.
The Idea of Immortality. 1922.

WILLIAM ROBERTSON SMITH (1846–1894)

The Old Testament in the Jewish Church. 1881.
The Prophets of Israel. 1882.
The Religion of the Semites. 1889.

GEORGE TYRRELL (1861–1909)

Nova et vetera: Informal Meditations. 1897·
Hard Sayings. 1898.
External Religion: its Use and Abuse. 1899.
The Faith of the Millions: Essays. 2 sers. 1901.
Oil and Wine. 1902 (priv. ptd); 1907 (with new preface).
The Church and the Future. 1903 (priv. ptd); 1910.
Lex orandi: or, Prayer and Creed. 1903.
Lex credendi: a Sequel to Lex orandi. 1906.
A much-abused Letter. 1906.
Through Scylla and Charybdis. 1907.
Medievalism: a Reply to Cardinal Mercier. 1908; 1909 (with addns).
Christianity at the Cross-roads. 1909.
Versions and Perversions of Heine and Others. 1909.
Autobiography and Life, arranged by M. D. Petre. 2 vols. 1912.
Essays on Faith and Immortality, arranged by M. D. Petre. 1914.

JAMES WARD (1843–1925)

Naturalism and Agnosticism. 1899.
The Realm of Ends, or Plurality and Theism. Cambridge, 1911.

MARY AUGUSTA WARD (née ARNOLD: 1851–1920)

Robert Elsmere. 1888.
A Writer's Recollections. 1918.
[See also p. 561 above.]

(2) THE EVANGELICALS

(a) General Works, Historical and Critical

Stephen, Sir J. Essays in Ecclesiastical Biography. 2 vols. 1849.
Gilfillan, G. Galleries of Literary Portraits. 2 vols. Edinburgh, 1856. [For Chalmers, Dawson, R. Hall, Irving and other preachers.]

Abbey, C. J. and J. H. Overton. The English Church in the Eighteenth Century. 2 vols. 1878.

Seeley, Mary. The Later Evangelical Fathers. 1879.

Dale, R. W. The Evangelical Revival. 1880.

Stock, E. History of the Church Missionary Society. 3 vols. 1899.

Venn, J. Annals of a Clerical Family. 1904.

Balleine, G. R. A History of the Evangelical Party. 1908.

Russell, G. W. E. A Short History of the Evangelical Movement. 1915.

(b) Principal Writers, 1800–1835

RICHARD CECIL (1748–1810)

The Life, Character and Remains. Ed. Josiah Pratt, 4 vols. 1811.

THOMAS CHALMERS (1780–1847)

Astronomical Discourses. 1817.
Commercial Discourses. 1817.
Works. 23 vols. 1836–42.
Posthumous Works. Ed. W. Hanna, 9 vols. 1847–9.
[See Memoirs, by W. Hanna, 4 vols. 1849–52.]

THOMAS GISBORNE (1758–1846)

Poems, Sacred and Moral. 1798.
An Enquiry respecting Love as one of the Divine Attributes. 1838.

ROBERT HALL (1764–1831)

Works, with an Essay by John Foster. 6 vols. 1832.

ROWLAND HILL (1744–1833)

Village Dialogues. 1801.

THOMAS HARTWELL HORNE (1780–1862)

An Introduction to the Critical Study of the Scriptures. 3 vols. 1818–21.

ZACHARY MACAULAY (1768–1838)

[Editor of and contributor to The Christian Observer from 1802 to 1816.]

HENRY MARTYN (1781–1812)

Journals and Letters. Ed. S. Wilberforce, 2 vols. 1837.

JOSEPH MILNER (1744–1797)

The History of the Church of Christ. Vols. I–III, 1794–7. [Continued by his brother Isaac (1750–1820): vol. IV, 1803; vol. V, 1809. All five vols. re-edited by Isaac Milner, 1816.]

HANNAH MORE (1745–1833).

[See vol. II, p. 844 above.]

JOHN OVERTON (1763–1838)

The True Churchmen ascertained. 1801.

LEGH RICHMOND (1772–1827)

Annals of the Poor. 1814. [Includes The Dairyman's Daughter, separately ptd many times from 1809.]

GRANVILLE SHARP (1735–1813)

The Supreme Divine Dignity of the Messiah. 1806.
[See Memoirs, by Prince Hoare, 1820.]

CHARLES SIMEON (1759–1836)

An Appeal to Men of Wisdom and Candour. 1816.
Horae Homileticae. [A long ser. beginning from 1796. Collected in 11 vols. 1819–20. An appendix of 6 vols. 1828.]
[See Memoirs, by William Carus, 1847, and Life, by H. C. G. Moule, 1892.]

JOHN BIRD SUMNER (1780–1862)

A Treatise on the Records of the Creation. 2 vols. 1816.
The Evidence of Christianity derived from its Nature and Reception. 1824.

HENRY THORNTON (1760–1815)

Family Commentary. Ed. Sir R. H. Inglis, 2 vols. 1835–7.

WILLIAM WILBERFORCE (1759–1846)

A Practical View of the Prevailing Religious System of professed Christians. 1797.
Appeal in Behalf of the Negro Slaves. 1823.
[See Life, by his sons Robert Isaac and Samuel, 5 vols. 1838.]

CAROLINE WILSON, née FRY (1787–1846)

The Listener. 2 vols. 1830.

DANIEL WILSON (1778–1858)

The Evidences of Christianity. 2 vols. 1828–30.
The Sufficiency of Scripture as the Rule of Faith. 1841.
Bishop Wilson's Journal Letters. Ed. Daniel Wilson jun., 1863.

(c) Principal Writers, 1835–1870

HENRY ALFORD (1810–1871)

The School of the Heart, and Other Poems. 2 vols. Cambridge, 1835.
The Greek Testament with a Critical Commentary. 4 vols. 1849–61.
The Queen's English: Stray Notes on Speaking and Spelling. 1864.
[See also p. 276 above.]

EDWARD BICKERSTETH (1786–1850)

Christian Psalmody. 1833. [One of the earliest Church hymn-books, it formed the basis of his son, E. H. Bickersteth's Hymnal Companion. See also p. 280 above.]

THOMAS RAWSON BIRKS (1810–1883)

The Bible and Modern Thought. 1861.
Modern Physical Fatalism. 1876.

HENRY BLUNT (1794–1843)

Eight Lectures upon the History of Jacob. 1828.

JOHN JAMES BLUNT (1794–1855)

Undesigned Coincidences in the Old and New Testaments. 1847.

HORATIUS BONAR (1808–1889)

Hymns of Faith and Hope. 1857.
God's Way of Peace. 1862.

ROBERT SMITH CANDLISH (1806–1873)

The Fatherhood of God. 1865.

FRANCIS CLOSE (1797–1882)

The Footsteps of Error. 1863.
The Stage, Ancient and Modern: its Tendencies on Morals and Religion. 1877.

WILLIAM JOHN CONYBEARE (1815–1857) and JOHN SAUL HOWSON (1816–1885)

The Life and Epistles of St Paul. 2 vols. 1851.

GEORGE DAWSON (1821–1876)

The Demands of the Age upon the Church. 1847.
Biographical Lectures. 2 vols. 1886–7.

WILLIAM GOODE (1801–1868)

The Divine Rule of Faith and Practice. 2 vols. 1842.

THOMAS GUTHRIE (1803–1873)

The Gospel in Ezekiel. 1856.

EDWARD IRVING (1792–1834)

Collected Writings. Ed. G. Carlyle, 1864–5.
[See T. Carlyle's essay on Irving, Fraser's Mag. Jan. 1835.]

ANDREW JUKES (1810–1901)

The Second Death and the Restitution of all Things. 1867.

JOHN KITTO (1804–1854)

The Pictorial Bible. 1836.

NORMAN MACLEOD (1812–1872)

[Editor of and contributor to Good Words from 1860.]
Reminiscences of a Highland Parish. 1867.

HENRY MELVILL (1798–1871)

The Golden Lectures, 1850–57. 7 vols. 1856.

EDWARD MONRO (1815–1866)

The Dark Mountains: an Allegory. 1858.

BAPTIST WRIOTHESLEY NOEL (1798–1873)

Essay on the Union of Church and State. 1848.

HENRY ROGERS (1806–1877)

The Eclipse of Faith. 1852 (anon.).
Essays from the Edinburgh Review. 3 vols. 1850–5.

JAMES SCHOLEFIELD (1789–1853)

Scriptural Grounds of Union. 1841.
The Christian Altar. 1842.

ROBERT BENTON SEELEY (1798–1886)

Essays on the Church. 1834.

JAMES ELIMALET (ELISHAMA) SMITH (1801–1857)

[Editor of The Shepherd from 1834. See 'Shepherd' Smith, the Universalist, by W. A. Smith, 1892.]

SAMUEL WALDEGRAVE (1817–1869)

New Testament Millenarianism. 1855.

(d) Principal Writers, 1870–1900

THOMAS DEHANEY BERNARD (1815–1904)

The Central Teaching of Jesus Christ. 1892.

NATHANIEL DIMOCK (1825–1909)

The Doctrine of the Sacraments. 1871 (anon.).
The Doctrine of the Death of Christ. [1891.]

HUGH MACMILLAN (1833–1903)

Bible Teachings in Nature. 1867.
The Ministry of Nature. 1871.
The Isles and the Gospel. With Memoir by George A. Macmillan. 1907.

FREDERICK MEYRICK (1827–1906)

Doctrine of the Church of England restated. 1885.
Memories of Life at Oxford. 1905.

HANDLEY CARR GLYN MOULE (1841–1920)

Veni Creator. 1890.
Philippian Studies. 1897.
Colossian Studies. 1898.
Ephesian Studies. 1900.
Imitations and Translations, English, Latin and Greek. 1905.

HERBERT EDWARD RYLE (1856–1925)

The Early Narratives of Genesis. 1892.

CHARLES HADDON SPURGEON (1834–1892)
The Treasury of David. 7 vols. 1870–85.

HENRY WACE (1836–1924)
Christianity and Morality. 1876.
Christianity and Agnosticism. 1895.
An Appeal to the First Six Centuries. 1905.

F. E. H.

B. THE OXFORD MOVEMENT AND THE HIGH CHURCHMEN

(1) ILLUSTRATIVE MATERIAL

(a) General Works, Historical and Critical

Perceval, A. P. A Collection of Papers connected with the Theological Movement of 1833. 1842.
Palmer, Sir William. A Narrative of Events connected with the Publication of the Tracts for the Times. 1843.
Bricknell, W. S. The Judgment of the Bishops upon Tractarian Theology. 1845.
Newland, H. G. Three Lectures on Tractarianism. 1852.
Browne, E. G. K. History of the Tractarian Movement. 1856 (bis); 1861 (rev. and priv. ptd as Annals, 1842 to 1860).
Oakeley, F. Historical Notes on the Tractarian Movement, 1833–1845. 1865. [Differs from Oakeley's Personal Reminiscences of the Oxford Movement, 1855, which is only a lecture.]
Mozley, T. Reminiscences of Oriel College and the Oxford Movement. 2 vols. 1882.
Church, R. W. The Oxford Movement. Twelve Years, 1833–1845. 1891.
Worley, G. The Catholic Revival of the Nineteenth Century. 1894.
Some Side-Lights on the Oxford Movement. By Minima Parspartis. 1895.
Overton, J. H. The Anglican Revival. [1897.]
Cruttwell, C. T. Six Lectures on the Oxford Movement. 1899.
Bodington, Charles. Devotional Life in the Nineteenth Century. 1905.
Holland, H. S. The Mission of the Oxford Movement. [In Personal Studies, 1905; rptd from Lyra Apostolica, ed. H. C. Beeching, 1899.]
Hall, Sir S. A Short History of the Oxford Movement. 1906.
Hutchison, W. G. The Oxford Movement. Selections from Tracts for the Times. 1906.
Guibert, J. Le Réveil du Catholicisme en Angleterre au XIXe Siècle. Paris, 1907. [With a very full bibliography, including French and English magazine articles.]
Ward, Wilfrid. The Oxford Movement. [1913.]

Baring-Gould, S. The Church Revival. 1914.
—— Early Reminiscences, 1834–1864. 1923.
—— Further Reminiscences, 1864–1894. 1925.
Thureau-Dangin, Paul. The English Catholic Revival in the Nineteenth Century. Tr. Wilfrid Wilberforce, 2 vols. 1914.
Ollard, S. L. A Short History of the Oxford Movement. 1915.
—— The Oxford Movement. [In vol. VIII of Encyclopaedia of Religion and Ethics, ed. J. Hastings, 1908–21.]
—— The Anglo-Catholic Revival. 1925.
Brémond, H. L'Inquiétude religieuse. Ser. 1, Paris, 1919.
Knox, W. L. The Catholic Movement in the Church of England. 1923.
Webb, C. C. J. A Century of Anglican Theology and Other Lectures. 1923.
—— Religious Thought in the Oxford Movement. 1928.
Brilioth, Y. The Anglican Revival. 1925.
Kaye-Smith, Sheila. Anglo-Catholicism. 1925.
Stewart, H. L. A Century of Anglo-Catholicism. 1929.
Shaw, P. E. The Early Tractarians and the Eastern Church. 1930.

(b) Magazines

The British Magazine. Ed. H. J. Rose, 1832–6; ed. S. R. Maitland, 1836–49.
The British Critic. Ed. J. H. Newman et al. 1836–8; ed. J. H. Newman, 1838–41: ed. T. Mozley, 1841–3. [Founded 1793 by W. Jones of Nayland.]
The Christian Remembrancer. Ed. William Scott and Francis Garden, 1841–4; ed. William Scott and J. B. Mozley, 1844–54; ed. William Scott, 1854–68.
The Guardian. [Founded Jan. 1846 by R. W. Church, F. Rogers (Baron Blachford) and M. Bernard.]

(c) Biographies and Memoirs

Churton, Edward. Memoir of Joshua Watson. 2 vols. 1861.
Shutte, R. N. Memoir of Henry Newland. 1861.
Blomfield, A. A Memoir of Charles James Blomfield, Bishop of London. 2 vols. 1863.
Gray, C. Life of Robert Gray, Bishop of Capetown. 2 vols. 1876.
Life and Letters of Richard Waldo Sibthorp. 1880.
Ornsby, R. Memoirs of James Robert Hope-Scott. 2 vols. 1884.
Overton, J. H. and Wordsworth, E. Christopher Wordsworth, Bishop of Lincoln, 1807–1885. 1890.
[Trench, M.] Charles Lowden. A Biography. 1891.

T[owle], E. A. Alexander Heriot Mackonochie. A Memoir. 1891.

Bellasis, Edward. Memorials of Mr Sergeant Bellasis (1800–1873). 1893; 1895 (enlarged).

Carter, T. T. Richard Temple West. A Record of Life and Work. 1895.

Letters of Frederic, Lord Blachford. Ed. G. E. Marindin, 1896.

B., A. J. Life and Letters of William John Butler, Dean of Lincoln. 1897.

Fowler, J. T. Life and Letters of John Bacchus Dykes. 1897.

Lake, Katharine. Memorials of William Charles Lake, Dean of Durham (1869–1894). 1901.

Osborne, C. E. The Life of Father Dolling. 1903.

Crouch, W. Bryan King and the Riots at St George's-in-the-East. 1904.

Acland, J. E. A Memoir of Arthur Troyte. A Layman's Life in the Days of the Tractarian Movement. 1904.

Kelway, A. C. George Rundle Prynne. 1905.

Kate, Mother. Old Soho Days. 1906.

Paget, E. C. A Year under the Shadow of St Paul's. 1908.

Romanes, E. Charlotte Mary Yonge. An Appreciation. 1908.

Bennett, F. The Story of W. J. E. Bennett. 1909.

Purcell, E. S. and de Lisle, E. Life and Letters of A. P. de Lisle. 2 vols. 1910.

Moberly, C. A. E. Dulce Domum: George Moberly, his Family and Friends. 1911.

Hutton, W. H. et al. Robert Gregory, 1819–1911. 1912.

Mason, A. J. Life of William Edward Collins, Bishop of Gibraltar. 1912.

Paget, S. and Crum, J. M. C. Francis Paget, Bishop of Oxford. 1912.

Russell, G. W. E. Edward King, Sixtieth Bishop of Lincoln. 1912.

—— Arthur Stanton. A Memoir. 1917.

Watson, E. W. The Life of Bishop John Wordsworth. 1915.

Congreve, G. and Longridge, W. H. Letters of Richard Meux Benson. 1916. [See also W. H. Longridge, Further Letters of Richard Meux Benson, 1920.]

Randolph, B. W. and Townroe, J. W. The Mind and Work of Bishop King. 1918.

Newbolt, W. C. E. Years that are Past. 1921.

Paget, S. Henry Scott Holland. Memoir and Letters. 1921.

Benson, A. C. The Trefoil. 1923.

Hine, J. E. Days Gone By. 1924.

Talbot, E. S. Memories of Early Life. 1924.

Denison, H. P. Seventy-Two Years' Church Recollections. 1925.

Otter, Sir J. L. Nathaniel Woodard. A Memoir. 1925.

Fullerton, T. G. Father Burn of Middlesbrough. 1927.

(2) PRINCIPAL WRITINGS

(a) Tracts for the Times, The Library of the Fathers, Plain Sermons, The Anglo-Catholic Library, The English Saints and Lyra Apostolica

Tracts for the Times. Ed. J. H. Newman, 6 vols. 1833–41. [90 tracts were issued anonymously between 9 Sept. 1833 (Three Tracts) and 27 Feb. 1841 (Tract No. 90). 5 lists of the Tracts and their authors are extant:(1) appendix to H. P. Liddon's Life of Pusey, vol. III, 1897, pp. 473–80; (2) Sir G. Prevost, Whitaker's Almanack, 1883; (3) F. H. Rivington [based on information supplied by Newman in 1869], John Bull, Sept. 1890; (4) J. R. Bloxam, MS at Magdalen College, Oxford; (5) W. J. Copeland [revision of list in Whitaker's Almanack, 1883]. In the case of 2 Tracts further evidence has come to light modifying slightly these lists. The contributors were: J. W. Bowden (Nos. 5, 29, 30, 56, 58); A. Buller (No. 61); C. P. Eden (No. 32); R. H. Froude (Nos. 8 [with J. H. Newman], 9, 59, 63); B. Harrison (Nos. 16, 17, 24, 49, 74 [with J. H. Newman], 81 [with E. B. Pusey]); John Keble (Nos. 4, 13, 40, 52, 54, 57, 60, 89); T. Keble (Nos. 12, 22, 43, 84 [with Sir G. Prevost]); H. E. Manning and C. Marriott (No. 78); A. Menzies (No. 14); J. H. Newman (Nos. 1, 2, 3, 6, 7, 8 [with R. H. Froude], 10, 11, 15 [with Sir W. Palmer], 19, 20, 21, 31, 33, 34, 38, 41, 45, 47, 71, 73, 74 [with B. Harrison], 75, 76, 79, 82, 83, 85, 88, 90); Sir W. Palmer (No. 15 [with J. H. Newman]); A. P. Perceval (Nos. 23, 35, 36); Sir G. Prevost (No. 84 [with T. Keble]); E. B. Pusey (Nos. 18, 66, 67, 68, 69, 70, 77, 81 [with B. Harrison]); I. Williams (Nos. 80, 86, 87); R. F. Wilson (No. 51). The remaining 17 tracts were rpts from older Anglican divines. There is some confusion about the numbering of the Tracts after the 1st edn, when No. 70 was enlarged and ptd as part of No. 65 and Tracts 67, 68 and 69 were reckoned as No. 70.]

Lyra Apostolica. 1836; ed. H. S. Holland and H. C. Beeching, 1899. [Poems originally ptd in The British Magazine. Of the 179 pieces Newman wrote 109, Keble 46, I. Williams 9, R. H. Froude 8, J. W. Bowden 6 and R. I. Wilberforce 1. The authors used Greek letters as signatures: α = Bowden, β = Froude, γ = Keble, δ = Newman, ϵ = Wilberforce, ζ = Williams.]

The Library of the Fathers of the Holy
Catholic Church, anterior to the Division of
the East and West. Ed. J. Keble, J. H.
Newman, E. B. Pusey and [1843–57] C.
Marriott, 48 vols. 1838–85. [Included the
works of 13 Fathers, e.g. St Chrysostom
(16 vols.), St Augustine (12 vols.), St Atha-
nasius (5 vols.), St Gregory (4 vols.). The
prefaces were contributed by: C. Marriott
(15), E. B. Pusey (12), J. H. Newman (4),
J. Keble (2), P. E. Pusey (2), H. P. Liddon
(1), H. G. Wilberforce (1), H. Browne (1).
The translators included Keble, Newman,
Pusey, R. W. Church, T. Keble, Sir G.
Prevost, W. J. Copeland, J. B. Morris,
Macmullen, P. E. Pusey and W. Bright.
A complete list of the Library, with the
translator and editor of each vol., so far as
they are known, is ptd as an appendix to
H. P. Liddon's Life of Pusey, vol. I, 1893,
ch. xviii.]

Plain Sermons by the Contributors to the
'Tracts for the Times.' Ed. [I. Williams
and W. J. Copeland], 10 vols. 1839–48.
[Preface to vol. I by I. Williams, H. Jeffreys
and others. On last p. of vol. x it is stated
that the sermons were the work, in various
proportions carefully set out, of seven
authors who are designated by the first
seven letters of the alphabet. A = John
Keble; B = Isaac Williams; C = E. B. Pusey;
D = J. H. Newman; E = Thomas Keble;
F = Sir George Prevost; G = R. F. Wilson.
But a MS note in W. J. Copeland's copy of
vol. VII assigns sermons 221–226 to him and
in Pusey's copy the same sermons are
assigned to H. Copeland was not a contributor to the Tracts for the Times and
probably felt unable for that reason to
appear among the authors of the series. It
seems likely that the 6 sermons were substantially his but were adapted by J. Keble
to enable them to be assigned to him. They
appear among the contributions of A in the
statement appended to vol. x.]

The Library of Anglo-Catholic Theology.
88 vols. 1841–63. [Ed. by W. J. Copeland,
1841–3, W. F. Audland, 1843–7, C. L.
Cornish, 1847–54, J. Barrow, 1854–63.
The series was intended to include the
principal post-Reformation divines, but
the full programme was not carried out.
The contributors included Keble, Edward
Churton, W. H. Mill, C. P. Eden, A. W.
Haddan, N. Pocock, J. Bliss and William
Scott. Among the writers rptd were
Bishop Andrewes, Archbishop Laud, Arch-
bishop Bramhall, Bishop Cosin, Thorndike,
Bishop Thomas Wilson and Bishop Hickes.]

Lives of the English Saints. 4 vols. 1844–5; ed.
A. W. Hutton, 6 vols. 1900–1. [Suggested by

Newman, but he ceased to be editor after
the first 2 Lives. The compilers of the 33
Lives were: R. W. Church (1), J. D.
Dalgairns (7), T. Meyrick (4), M. Pattison
(2), F. W. Faber (9), Newman (3), R. A.
Coffin (1), R. Ornsby (1), J. A. Froude (1),
J. Walker (1), F. Oakeley (1), J. Barrow (2).
The list by A. W. Hutton in vol. VI, Ap-
pendix ii of the 1900 edn is correct except
for its ascription of St Ninian (by Barrow)
to Froude and of St Bartholomew (by
Dalgairns) to T. Mozley. A list corrected
by Newman is among the Bloxam MSS at
Magdalen College, Oxford.]

(3) PARTICULAR AUTHORS

JOHN WILLIAM BOWDEN (1798–1844)

St Bartholomew's Eve; a Poem. 1821. [With
J. H. Newman.]
Tracts for the Times. Nos. 5, 29, 30, 56, 58.
1833–5.
Lyra Apostolica. 1836. [Poems signed α.]
[Four articles in The British Critic, 1836, 1837,
1839, 1841.]
Life of Gregory the Seventh. 2 vols. 1840.
Thoughts on the Work of the Six Days of
Creation. 1845. [With biographical preface
by J. H. Newman.]

JOHN WILLIAM BURGON (1813–1888)

Petra, a Prize Poem, recited in the Theatre'
Oxford, June IV, MDCCCXLV. Oxford, 1845;
Oxford, 1846 (adds some shorter poems).
Poems (1840–1878). 1885.
The Lives of Twelve Good Men. 2 vols. 1888.

[See E. M. Goulburn, John William Burgon.
A Biography, with Extracts from his Letters
and Early Journals, 2 vols. 1892.]

EDWARD CASWALL (1814–1878)

Lyra Catholica. 1849.

RICHARD WILLIAM CHURCH (1815–1890)

Lives of the English Saints. Life of St Wulstan.
1844.
Essays and Reviews. Collected from The
British Critic and Christian Remembrancer.
1854.
Sermons preached before the University of
Oxford. 1868.
Life of St Anselm. 1870.
Civilisation before Christianity. 1872.
On some Influences of Christianity on National
Character. 1873.
Sacred Poetry of Early Religions. 1874. [This
and the 2 preceding items were rptd, with
the University Sermons of 1868, as The Gifts
of Civilisation, 1880.]
The Beginnings of the Middle Ages. 1877.

Essay on Dante, republished with a Translation of Dante's De Monarchia, by F. J. Church. 1878.
Human Life and its Conditions. 1878.
Spenser. 1879. (English Men of Letters ser.)
Bacon. 1884. (English Men of Letters ser.)
Discipline of the Christian Character. 1885.
Advent Sermons, 1885. 1886.
Miscellaneous Works. 5 vols. 1888.
The Oxford Movement. Twelve Years, 1833–1845. 1891.
Cathedral and University Sermons. 1892.
Village Sermons preached at Whatley. 3 vols. 1892–7.
Pascal and other Sermons. 1896.
The Message of Peace and other Christmas Sermons. 1897 (4th edn). [The second appears with slightly altered title in Cathedral and University Sermons, 1892.]
Occasional Papers. 2 vols. 1897.

> Church, Mary C. Life and Letters of Dean Church. 1894.
> Donaldson, A. B. Richard William Church. [In Five Great Oxford Leaders, 1902 (3rd edn).]
> Holland, H. S. Richard William Church. [In Personal Studies, 1905.]
> Lathbury, D. C. Dean Church. 1905.
> Cecil, A. R. W. Church. [In Six Oxford Thinkers, 1909.]

JOHN DOBREE [BERNARD] DALGAIRNS (1818–1876)

Lives of the English Saints. 1844–5. [Lives of St Aelred, St Waltheof, St Robert, St Helier, St Stephen Harding, St Gilbert, St Bartholomew, and the verse in the Life of St Bettelin.]
The Devotion to the Sacred Heart of Jesus. 1853.
The Holy Communion, its Philosophy, Theology, and Practice. 1861.

AUBREY THOMAS DE VERE (1814–1902)

Critical Essays. 3 vols. 1887–9.
Recollections. 1897.

[See Wilfrid Ward, Aubrey de Vere; a Memoir, 1904.]

DIGBY MACKWORTH DOLBEN (1848–1867)

Poems. Ed. R. Bridges, 1915.

FREDERICK WILLIAM FABER (1814–1863)

[See p. 287 above.]

ALEXANDER PENROSE FORBES (1817–1875)

Explanation of the Nicene Creed. 1852.
The Arbuthnott Missal. 1864. [Ed. with G. H. Forbes.]
The Thirty-Nine Articles. 2 vols. 1867–8.

Kalendars of Scottish Saints. 1872.

[Besides 4 vols. of collected sermons (many pbd separately), lectures, manuals of devotion and articles in Edinburgh, Quarterly and North British Reviews and in Christian Remembrancer. List of Forbes's works in Memoir by D. J. Mackey, 1888, pp. 219–24. See J. O. Mowat, Bishop A. P. Forbes, 1925.]

JAMES ANTHONY FROUDE (1818–1894)

[See p. 892 below.]

RICHARD HURRELL FROUDE (1803–1836)

Tracts for the Times. Nos. 9, 59, 63 and possibly part of 35. 1833–5.
Lyra Apostolica. 1836. [Poems signed β.]
Remains. Part I. Ed. J. Keble and J. H. Newman, 2 vols. 1838.
Remains. Part II. Ed. J. B. Mozley (Preface by J. Keble), 2 vols. 1839.

[See L. I. Guiney, Hurrell Froude. Memoranda and Comments, 1904.]

FURLONG ELIZABETH SKIPTON HARRIS

From Oxford to Rome. By A Companion Traveller. 1847 (anon.); 1847 (rev.).
Rest in the Church. By the Author of From Oxford to Rome. 1848.

ROBERT STEPHEN HAWKER (1803–1875)

[See p. 289 above.]

WALTER FARQUHAR HOOK (1798–1875)

Sermons preached before the University of Oxford. 1837.
Hear the Church: a Sermon. 1838 (28th edn).
Dictionary of Ecclesiastical Biography. 8 vols. 1842–52.
Lives of the Archbishops of Canterbury. 12 vols. 1860–76.
Sermons on The Church and Her Ordinances. 2 vols. 1876.
Parish Sermons. Ed. W. Hook, 1879.

[And many other lectures, addresses and treatises. See W. R. W. Stephens, Life and Letters of Walter Farquhar Hook, D.D., F.R.S., 1878.]

JOHN KEBLE (1792–1866)

The Christian Year. 2 vols. Oxford, 1827 (anon.); 1827; 1828, etc.; 1874 (with a memoir by W. Temple); 1878 (facs. of original draft, with a collation of the variations between it and the ptd edns); 1883 (with a memoir); 1886 (with a biographical sketch by A. H. Grant); 1887 (with Introduction by Henry Morley); 2 vols. 1897 (facs. of 1st edn with Preface by Bishop of Rochester); 1904 (with Introduction by Archbishop of Armagh); 1905 (with Introduction and notes by Walter Lock); 1914 (Everyman's Lib., with Introduction by J. C. Shairp).

National Apostasy: A Sermon. 1833. [Rptd in Sermons Academical and Occasional, 1847.]

Ode for the Encaenia at Oxford. Oxford, 1834.

Tracts for the Times. Nos. 4, 13, 40, 52, 54, 57, 60, 1834. No. 89, 1841.

Lyra Apostolica. 1836. [46 poems signed γ.]

Primitive Tradition recognised in Holy Scripture. 1836; 1837; 1837 (with postscript and Tract No. 78 as appendix).

The Psalter or Psalms of David; in English Verse; by a Member of the University of Oxford. 1839.

The Case of Catholic Subscription to the XXXIX Articles. 1841 (priv. ptd); 1865.

Lyra Innocentium: Thoughts in Verse on Christian Children, Their Ways and Their Privileges. Oxford, 1846 (anon.); ed. W. Lock, 1889.

Sermons Academical and Occasional. 1847; 1848.

On Eucharistical Adoration. 1857; 1859; 1867.

Sermons Occasional and Parochial. 1868.

Miscellaneous Poems. Ed. G. Moberly, Oxford, 1869. [Contains the Ode for the Encaenia, the Poems contributed to the Lyra Apostolica, Selections from The Christian Year and Lyra Innocentium, and Remains.]

Village Sermons on the Baptismal Service. 1869.

Letters of Spiritual Counsel. 1870; 1875 (expanded).

Sermons for the Christian Year. 11 vols. 1875–80.

Occasional Papers and Reviews. Collected and with Preface by E. B. Pusey. Oxford, 1877. [Life of Sir Walter Scott; Sacred Poetry; Unpublished Papers of Bishop Warburton; Copleston's Praelectiones Academicae; Miller's Bampton Lectures, etc.]

Studia Sacra. Ed. J. P. N[orris], 1877.

Lectures on Poetry, 1832–1841. 2 vols. Oxford, 1912. [Tr. from Latin by E. K. Francis.]

The Christian Year, Lyra Innocentium and Other Poems. Oxford, 1914.

> Shairp, J. C. John Keble: an Essay on the Author of the Christian Year. Edinburgh, 1866. [Rptd in Studies in Poetry and Philosophy, Edinburgh, 1868.]
> Coleridge, Sir J. T. A Memoir of the Rev. John Keble. 1869; 2 vols. 1869 (rev.).
> Yonge, C. M. Musings over the Christian Year and Lyra Innocentium, together with a few Gleanings of Recollections of the Rev. J. Keble, gathered by Several Friends. 1871.

Lock, W. John Keble: a Biography. 1892. [Appendix II contains complete list of Keble's pbd works.]

Wood, E. F. L. (Viscount Halifax). John Keble. 1909.

THOMAS KEBLE (1793–1875)

Tracts for the Times. Nos. 12, 22, 43, 84 (concluded by Sir G. Prevost), 1833–8.

Plain Sermons by Contributors to the Tracts for the Times. [Sermons signed E in vols. I, II, IV, X.]

ALEXANDER KNOX (1757–1831)

Remains. 4 vols. 1834–7.

Correspondence with Bishop Jebb. Ed. C. L. Forster, 1834.

HENRY PARRY LIDDON (1829–1890)

Some Words for God. 1865; 1866 (as Sermons preached before the University of Oxford).

Sermons on the Reunion of Christendom. Ser. 2, 1865. [Sermon viii, signed L.]

The Divinity of Our Lord and Saviour Jesus Christ. (The Bampton Lectures for 1866.) 1867; tr. German, Basle, 1833.

The Priest in his Inner Life. 1869.

Some Elements of Religion. Lent Lectures, 1870. 1872.

Sermons preached before the University of Oxford. Second Series (1868–79). 1879.

Thoughts on Present Church Troubles. 1881.

Easter in St Paul's. Sermons. 2 vols. 1885.

Advent in St Paul's. Sermons. 2 vols. 1888.

Christmastide in St Paul's. Sermons. 1889.

The Magnificat. Sermons. 1889.

Passiontide Sermons. 1891.

Sermons on Old Testament Subjects. 1891.

Sermons on Some Words of Christ. 1892.

Essays and Addresses. 1892.

Life of Edward Bouverie Pusey, by H. P. Liddon, edited and prepared for publication by J. O. Johnston and R. J. Wilson. Vols. I, II, 1893. Vol. III, 1894. Vol. IV, ed. J. O. Johnston and W. C. E. Newbolt, 1897.

Explanatory Analysis of St Paul's Epistle to the Romans. 1893.

Clerical Life and Work. A Collection of Sermons with an Essay. 1894.

Explanatory Analysis of St Paul's First Epistle to Timothy. 1897.

Sermons preached on Special Occasions, 1860–1889. 1897.

Sermons on some Words of St Paul. 1898.

> [A list of Liddon's ptd works is given in the appendix to his Life and Letters (1904). Forty-seven of these are sermons pbd separately between 1858 and 1890. Many of them appear to have been afterwards collected and rpbd in various vols.]

> Donaldson, A. B. Henry Parry Liddon. [In Five Great Oxford Leaders, 1900.]

Johnston, J. O. Life and Letters of Henry Parry Liddon. With a Concluding Chapter by the Bishop of Oxford (Francis Paget). 1904.
Holland, H. S. Personal Studies. 1905. [Henry Parry Liddon; The Life of Henry Parry Liddon.]
Russell, G. W. E. Dr Liddon. 1905.
Henry Parry Liddon. A Centenary Memoir. 1929.

HENRY EDWARD MANNING (1808–1892)

The Unity of the Church. 1842.
Sermons. 4 vols. 1842–50.
Sermons preached before the University of Oxford. 1844.
The Temporal Mission of the Holy Ghost. 1865.
Sermons on Ecclesiastical Subjects. 3 vols. 1867–73.
Miscellanies. 3 vols. 1877–88.

Hutton, A. W. Cardinal Manning. 1892.
Jenkes, R. C. A Few Recollections of Cardinal Manning. [1892?] (priv. ptd).
Purcell, E. S. Life of Cardinal Manning. 2 vols. 1896.
Leslie, Shane. Henry Edward Manning. His Life and Labours. 1921.

CHARLES MARRIOTT (1811–1858)

Tracts for the Times. No. 78, 1837.
Sermons preached before the University and in Other Places. 1843.
Sermons preached in Oriel College Chapel and Other Places. 1850.

JAMES BOWLING MOZLEY (1813–1878)

Miracles. (Bampton Lectures.) 1865.
Sermons preached before the University of Oxford and on Various Occasions. 1876.
Ruling Ideas in Early Ages. 1877.
Essays, Historical and Theological. 2 vols. 1878; 1884 (with Introductory Memoir [by his sister, Anne Mozley], and at p. xxxix an anon. Notice [by R. W. Church] rptd from The Guardian).
The Theory of Development: a Criticism of Dr Newman's Essay. 1878. [Rptd from Christian Remembrancer, 1847.]
Sermons. Parochial and Occasional. 1879.
Lectures and other Theological Papers. 1883.
Letters of the Rev. J. B. Mozley, D.D., edited by his sister [Anne Mozley]. 1885.

THOMAS MOZLEY (1806–1893)

Reminiscences, chiefly of Oriel College and the Oxford Movement. 2 vols. 1882.

JOHN MASON NEALE (1818–1866)

[See p. 301 above.]

JOHN HENRY NEWMAN (1801–1890)

[See p. 686 above.]

FREDERICK OAKELEY (1802–1880)

Whitehall Chapel Sermons. 1837.
Lives of the English Saints. Life of St Augustine of Canterbury. 1844.
The Ceremonies of the Mass. 1855.
Historical Notes on the Tractarian Movement. 1865.

[And some 38 other pbd works, articles in British Critic, Dublin Rev. and The Month.]

FRANCIS EDWARD PAGET (1806–1882)

Caleb Kniveton. 1833.
St Antolins: or Old Churches and New. 1841.
The Warden of Berkingholt. 1843.
The Owlet of Owlstone Edge. 1856.
A Student Penitent of 1695. 1875.

WILLIAM PALMER (1811–1879)

Harmony of Anglican Doctrine with the Doctrine of the Catholic and Apostolic Church of the East. Aberdeen, 1846 (anon.).
Dissertations on Subjects relating to the Orthodox or Eastern Catholic Communion. 1853.
Notes of a Visit to the Russian Church in 1840, 1841. Ed. J. H. Newman, 1882.

SIR WILLIAM PALMER (1803–1885)

Origines Liturgicae. 2 vols. 1832.
Tracts for the Times. No. 15 (rev. and completed by J. H. Newman), 1833.
A Treatise on the Church of Christ. 2 vols. 1838.
Letters to N. Wiseman, D.D. 1842.
A Narrative of Events connected with the Publication of the Tracts for the Times. 1843.

ARTHUR PHILIP PERCEVAL (1799–1853)

Tracts for the Times. Nos. 23, 35 (with R. H. Froude), 36, and possibly 17, 1833.
A Vindication of the Authors of the Tracts for the Times. 1841 (bis).
A Collection of Papers connected with the Theological Movement of 1833. 1842.

JOHN HUNGERFORD POLLEN (1820–1902)

Letter to the Parishioners of St Saviour's, Leeds. 1851.
Narrative of Five Years at St Saviour's, Leeds. 1851.

[See Anne Pollen, John Hungerford Pollen, 1820–1902, 1912, who lists Pollen's writings, pp. 377, 378.]

EDWARD BOUVERIE PUSEY (1800–1882)

Tracts for the Times. Nos. 18, 66, 67, 68, 69, 70, 77, 81 and possibly 76, 1834–7.
Letter to the Archbishop of Canterbury. Oxford, 1842 (3 edns).
A Letter to the Bishop of London. 1851.
Parochial Sermons. 3 vols. 1852–73.
The Doctrine of the Real Presence. 1855.
The Real Presence. 1857.
Sermons Preached before the University of Oxford. 1859–80.
The Minor Prophets. 1860.
Daniel the Prophet. 1864.
Eirenicon. Pt I, 1865. Pt II (1st Letter to Dr Newman), 1869. Pt III (Is Healthful Reunion Impossible?), 1870.
Historical Preface to Tract No. 90. 1865.
Lenten Sermons. 1874.
What is of Faith as to Everlasting Punishment? 1880.
Parochial and Cathedral Sermons. 1882.

[See H. P. Liddon, Life of E. B. Pusey, ed. J. O. Johnston, R. J. Wilson and W. E. Newbolt, 4 vols. 1893–7; [M. Trench], The Story of Mr Pusey's Life, 1900; G. W. E. Russell, Dr Pusey, 1907. A complete bibliography of Pusey's ptd works (by F. Madan) is given as appendix A in vol. IV of his Life by Liddon.]

HUGH JAMES ROSE (1795–1838)

Discourses on the State of the Protestant Religion in Germany. 1825; 1829. [In reply to E. B. Pusey's Historical Enquiry into the Theology of Germany, 1828.]

MARTIN JOSEPH ROUTH (1755–1854)

Reliquiae sacrae sive Auctorum fere jam perditorum secundi tertiique Seculi post Christum natum quae supersunt. Vols. I–IV, 1814–18; vol. V, 1848.
Scriptorum ecclesiasticorum Opuscula praecipua quaedam. 2 vols. 1832; rev. [W. Jacobson], 1858.
Tres breves Tractatus. 1853.

[See R. D. Middleton, Dr Routh, Oxford, 1938.]

ELIZABETH MISSING SEWELL (1815–1906)
[See p. 507 above.]

WILLIAM SEWELL (1804–1874)

The Plea of Conscience for seceding. 1845.
A Year's Sermons to Boys. 2 vols. 1854–69.

RICHARD CHENEVIX TRENCH (1807–1886)
[See p. 309 above.]

WILLIAM GEORGE WARD (1812–1882)

The Ideal of a Christian Church considered in Comparison with Existing Practice. 1844.
[Ward edited The Dublin Review, 1863–78. See Wilfrid Ward, William George Ward and the Oxford Movement, 1889, and William George Ward and the Catholic Revival, 1893.]

HENRY WILLIAM WILBERFORCE (1807–1873)

Reasons for submitting to the Catholic Church: a Farewell Letter. 1851.
The Church and the Empires. 1874. [With a memoir by J. H. Newman.]

[Owned and edited The Catholic Standard (later The Weekly Register), 1854–63.]

ROBERT ISAAC WILBERFORCE (1802–1897)

Lyra Apostolica. 1836. [Poem lettered ϵ.]
The Doctrine of the Incarnation of Our Lord Jesus Christ. 1848.
The Doctrine of Holy Baptism. 1849.
The Doctrine of the Holy Eucharist. 1853.
An Inquiry into the Principles of Church Authority. 1854.

ISAAC WILLIAMS (1802–1865)
[See p. 312 above.]

NICHOLAS PATRICK STEPHEN WISEMAN (1802–1865)

Lectures on the Doctrines and Practices of the Catholic Church. 1836.
High Church Claims. 1841.
Essays on Various Subjects. 3 vols. 1853; 1888 (with biographical introduction).
Fabiola. A Tale of the Catacombs. 1854.
Recollections of the Last Four Popes and of Rome in their Times. 1858.

[See W. Ward, Life of Cardinal Wiseman, 2 vols. 1897.]

S. L. O.

6. PHILOSOPHY, HISTORY, SCIENCE AND OTHER FORMS OF LEARNING

I. PHILOSOPHY

GENERAL WORKS

Masson, D. Recent British Philosophy. 1865.

M'Cosh, J. The Present State of Moral Philosophy in England. 1868.

Ribot, T. La Psychologie anglaise contemporaine. Paris, 1870; tr. Eng. 1873.

Renouvier, C. B. De l'Esprit de la Philosophie anglaise contemporaine. La Critique philosophique, I, Paris, 1872–3.

Liard, L. Les Logiciens anglais contemporains. Paris, 1878.

Höffding, H. Die englische Philosophie unserer Zeit. Tr. German (from Danish), Berlin, 1889.

Hutton, R. H. Contemporary Thought and Thinkers. 2 vols. 1894.

Merz, J. T. A History of European Thought in the 19th Century. 4 vols. Edinburgh, 1896–1914. [Especially vols. III, IV.]

Bigge, S. British Moralists. 2 vols. 1897.

Stephen, Sir L. The English Utilitarians. 1900.

Benn, A. W. English Rationalism in the 19th Century. 1906.

Forsyth, J. M. English Philosophy. 1910.

Perry, R. B. Present Philosophical Tendencies. 1912.

Seth, J. English Philosophers and Schools of Philosophy. 1912.

Sorley, W. R. A History of English Philosophy. Cambridge, 1920.

Taylor, A. E. Philosophy. [In Recent Developments in European Thought, ed. F. S. Marvin, 1920.]

Muirhead, J. H. et al. Contemporary British Philosophy. 2 vols. 1924–5.

Hicks, G. D. [In Geschichte der Philosophie, ed. F. Überweg and M. Heinze, pt v, Berlin, 1927.]

Metz, R. A Hundred Years of British Philosophy. Tr. Eng. 1938.

JOHN ABERCROMBIE (1780–1844)

Inquiries concerning the Intellectual Powers or the Investigation of Truth. 1830.

The Philosophy of the Moral Feelings. 1833.

ROBERT ADAMSON (1852–1902)

Roger Bacon: the Philosophy of Science in the 13th Century. Manchester, 1876.

On the Philosophy of Kant. Edinburgh, 1879; tr. German, 1880.

Fichte. 1881.

The Development of Modern Philosophy, with Other Lectures and Essays. 1903.

The Development of Greek Philosophy. 1908.

A Short History of Logic. 1911.

[See G. D. Hicks, Adamson's Philosophical Lectures, Mind, N.S. XIII, 1904.]

SAMUEL ALEXANDER (1859–1938)

(a) Books

Moral Order and Progress. 1889.

Locke. 1908.

Space, Time and Deity. 1920. (Gifford Lectures.)

Spinoza and Time. 1921.

Art and the Material. 1925. (Adamson Lecture.)

Artistic Creation and Cosmic Creation. 1927. (Henriette Herz Lecture.)

Beauty and Other Forms of Value. 1933.

(b) Articles

Hegel's Conception of Nature. Mind, XI, 1886.

Is Mind Synonymous with Consciousness? Proc. Aristotelian Soc. I, 1891.

Is there Evidence of Design in Nature? Proc. Aristotelian Soc. I, 1891.

The Idea of Value. Mind, N.S. I, 1892.

Natural Selection in Morals. International Journ. Ethics, II, 1892.

Character and Conduct. International Journ. Ethics, III, 1893.

Is the Distinction between 'Is' and 'Ought' Ultimate and Irreducible? Proc. Aristotelian Soc. II, 1894.

Has the Perception of Time an Origin in Thought? Proc. Aristotelian Soc. II, 1894.

The Nature of Mental Activity. Proc. Aristotelian Soc. VIII, 1908.

Mental Activity in Willing and in Ideas. Proc. Aristotelian Soc. IX, 1909.

On Sensations and Thoughts. Proc. Aristotelian Soc. X, 1910.

Self as Subject and as Person. Proc. Aristotelian Soc. XI, 1911.

The Method of Metaphysics and the Categories. Mind, N.S. XXI, 1912.

On Relations. Mind, N.S. XXI, 1912.

Collective Willing and Truth. Mind, N.S. XXII, 1913.

Freedom. Proc. Aristotelian Soc. xiv, 1914.

Space-Time. Proc. Aristotelian Soc. xviii, 1918.

Mind in the Universe. International Journ. Ethics, xxx, 1922.

Natural Poetry. International Journ. Ethics, xxx, 1922.

Sense-Perception. Mind, N.S. xxxii, 1923.

The Artistry of Truth. International Journ. Ethics, xxxii, 1925.

Art and Science. Journ. Philosophical Stud. i, 1926.

Theism and Pantheism. International Journ. Ethics, xxxv, 1927.

Morality as an Art. Journ. Philosophical Stud. iii, 1928.

Philosophy and Art. Journ. Philosophical Stud. iv, 1929.

Science and Art. Journ. Philosophical Stud. v, 1930.

Poetry and Prose in the Arts. Philosophy, vii, 1932.

GRANT ALLEN (1848–1899)

[See p. 534 above.]

GEORGE DOUGLAS CAMPBELL, DUKE OF ARGYLL (1823–1900)

The Reign of Law. 1866.

Primeval Man. 1869.

The Unity of Nature. 1884.

The Unseen Foundations of Society. 1893.

The Burdens of Belief, and Other Poems. 1894.

Autobiography and Memoirs. 2 vols. 1906. [Ed. by Dowager Duchess of Argyll.]

JOHN AUSTIN (1790–1859)

The Province of Jurisprudence determined. 1832.

Lectures on Jurisprudence, or the Philosophy of Positive Law. 1863.

SAMUEL BAILEY (1791–1870)

Essays on the Formation and Publication of Opinions and Other Subjects. 1821.

Critical Dissertation on the Nature, Measure, and Causes of Value. 1825.

Essays on the Pursuit of Truth and on the Progress of Knowledge. 1829.

Rationale of Political Representation. 1835.

Review of Berkeley's Theory of Vision. 1842.

Theory of Reasoning. 1851.

Letters on the Philosophy of the Human Mind. 3 vols. 1855–63.

ALEXANDER BAIN (1818–1903)

(a) Books

The Senses and the Intellect. 1855.

The Emotions and the Will. 1859.

On the Study of Character. 1861.

Mental and Moral Science. 1868.

Logic, Deductive and Inductive. 2 vols. 1870.

Mind and Body. 1873; tr. German, 1874.

Education as a Science. 1878.

Practical Essays. 1884.

On teaching English, with an Enquiry into the Definition of Poetry. 1887.

Dissertations on Leading Philosophical Topics. 1903.

Autobiography. 1904.

(b) Articles

The Gratification derived from the Infliction of Pain. Mind, i, 1876.

Existence and Descartes' Cogito. Mind, ii, 1877.

W. G. Ward on Freewill. Mind, v, 1880.

Is there such a Thing as Pure Malevolence? Mind, viii, 1883.

On Feeling as Indifference. Mind, xii, 1887, xiv, 1889.

On some Points in Ethics. Mind, xiii, 1888.

On Physiological Expression in Psychology. Mind, xvi, 1891.

Pleasure and Pain. Mind, N.S. i, 1892.

The Respective Spheres and Practical Helps of Introspection and Psycho-Physical Research in Psychology. Mind, N.S. ii, 1893.

Definitions and Problems of Consciousness. Mind, N.S. iii, 1894.

Ethics from a purely Practical Standpoint. International Journ. Ethics, x, 1900.

[For a discussion of Bain's Philosophy, see W. L. Davidson, Mind, N.S. xiii, 1904.]

ARTHUR JAMES BALFOUR, EARL BALFOUR (1848–1930)

A Defence of a Philosophic Doubt. 1879.

Essays and Addresses. 1893.

The Foundations of Belief. 1895.

Reflections suggested by the New Theory of Matter. 1904. [Presidential address to British Ass.]

Decadence. Cambridge, 1908.

Questionings on Criticism and Beauty. 1909.

Theism and Humanism. 1915.

Theism and Thought. 1923.

Familiar Beliefs and Transcendent Reason. 1925. (Henriette Herz Lecture.)

[For appreciation see Sir F. G. Kenyon, Proc. British Academy, xvi, 1930.]

ALFRED BARRATT (1844–1881)

(a) Books

Physical Ethics or the Science of Action. 1869.

Physical Metempiric. 1883.

(b) Articles

The Suppression of Egoism. Mind, ii, 1877.

Ethics and Psychogony. Mind, iii, 1878.

Ethics and Politics. Mind, iii, 1878.

THOMAS SPENCER BAYNES (1823–1887)

An Essay on the New Analytic of Logical Forms. 1850.

EDWARD SPENCER BEESLY (1831–1915)

Religion and Progress. 1879.
Comte, the Successor of Aristotle and St Paul. 1883.
Comte as a Moral Type. 1885.

GEORGE BENTHAM (1800–1884)

An Outline of a New System of Logic. 1827.
The Classification of Fictions. Psyche, no. 33, 1928.
[For an appraisal of Bentham see L. Liard, Les Logiciens anglais, Paris, 1878, ch. iii. See also p. 960 below.]

GEORGE BOOLE (1815–1864)

The Mathematical Analysis of Logic. Cambridge, 1847.
An Analysis of the Laws of Thought on which are founded the Mathematical Theories of Logic and Probabilities. 1854; ed. P. E. B. Jourdain, 1916 (as George Boole's Collected Logical Works, vol. II).
[For appraisals see L. Liard, Les Logiciens anglais, Paris, 1878, ch. v, and M. E. Boole, The Mathematical Philosophy of Gratry and Boole, 1897.]

BERNARD BOSANQUET (1848–1923)

(a) Books

Knowledge and Reality. 1885.
Introduction to Hegel's Philosophy of the Fine Arts. 1880.
Logic, or the Morphology of Knowledge. 2 vols. 1888.
Essays and Addresses. 1889.
'In Darkest England'; on the Wrong Track. 1890.
A History of Aesthetic. 1892.
The Civilisation of Christendom. 1893.
Aspects of the Social Problem. 1895.
The Essentials of Logic. 1895.
Companion to Plato's Republic. 1895.
Rousseau's Social Contract. 1895.
Psychology of the Moral Self. 1897.
The Philosophical Theory of the State. 1899.
The Principle of Individuality and Value. 1912.
The Value and Destiny of the Individual. 1913.
The Distinction between Mind and its Objects. 1913.
Three Lectures on Aesthetic. 1915.
Social and International Ideals. 1917.
Some Suggestions in Ethics. 1918.
Implication and Linear Inference. 1920.
What Religion is. 1920.

Meeting of Extremes in Contemporary Philosophy. 1920.
Three Chapters on the Nature of Mind. 1923.
Science and Philosophy and Other Essays. 1927.

(b) Articles

The Aesthetic Theory of Ugliness. Proc. Aristotelian Soc. I, 1891.
Communication of Ethical Ideas as a Function of an Ethical Society. International Journ. Ethics, I, 1891.
Will and Reason. The Monist, II, 1892.
The Evolution of Religion. International Journ. Ethics, V, 1895.
On an Essential Distinction in Theories of Experience. Proc. Aristotelian Soc. III, 1896.
Hegel's Theory of the Political Organism. Mind, N.S. VII, 1898.
A Moral from Athenian History. International Journ. Ethics, IX, 1899.
The Meaning of Social Work. International Journ. Ethics, XI, 1901.
The Dark Ages and the Renaissance. International Journ. Ethics, XII, 1902.
Xenophon's Memorabilia of Socrates. International Journ. Ethics, XV, 1905.
Can Logic abstract from the Psychological Conditions of Thinking? Proc. Aristotelian Soc. VI, 1906.
The Meaning of Teleology. Proc. British Academy, II, 1906.
The Place of Experts in Democracy. Proc. Aristotelian Soc. IX, 1909.
On a Defect in the Customary Logical Formulation of Inductive Reasoning. Proc. Aristotelian Soc. XI, 1911.
Purpose and Mechanism. Proc. Aristotelian Soc. XII, 1912.
Idealism and the Reality of Time. Mind, N.S. XXIII, 1914.
The Import of Propositions. Proc. Aristotelian Soc. XV, 1915.
Causality and Implication. Mind, N.S. XXV, XXVI, 1916–7.
The Function of the State in promoting the Unity of Mankind. Proc. Aristotelian Soc. XVII, 1917.
Realism and Metaphysics. Philosophical Rev. XXVI, 1917.
The Relation of Coherence to Immediacy and Specific Purpose. Philosophical Rev. XXVI, 1917.
The State and the Individual. Mind, N.S. XXVIII, 1919.
Croce's Aesthetic. Proc. British Academy, IX, 1919–20.
The Notion of a General Will. Mind, XXIX, 1920.

Life and Philosophy. [In Contemporary British Philosophy, ed. J. H. Muirhead, vol. I, 1924.]

(c) Biography and Criticism

Robins, E. P. Bosanquet's Theory of Judgment. Philosophical Rev. VII, 1898.

Russell, L. J. The Basis of Bosanquet's Logic. Mind, N.S. XXVII, 1919.

Carroll, M. C. The Method in the Metaphysics of Bosanquet. Philosophical Rev. XXIX, 1920.

—— The Nature of the Absolute in the Metaphysics of Bosanquet. Philosophical Rev. XXIX, 1920.

—— The Principle of Individuality in the Metaphysics of Bosanquet. Philosophical Rev. XXX, 1921.

Tsanoff, R. A. Bosanquet's Theory of the Destiny of the Self. Philosophical Rev. XXIX, 1920.

Cunningham, G. W. Bosanquet on Teleology as a Metaphysical Category. Philosophical Rev. XXXII, 1923.

—— Bosanquet on Philosophical Method. Philosophical Rev. XXXV, 1926.

Gilbert, K. E. The Principle of Reason in the Light of Bosanquet's Philosophy. Philosophical Rev. XXXII, 1923.

Hoernlé, R. F. A. Bosanquet's 'Idealism.' Philosophical Rev. XXXII, 1923.

Leighton, J. A. An Estimate of Bosanquet's Philosophy. Philosophical Rev. XXXII, 1923.

Lodge, R. C. Bosanquet and the Future of Logic. Philosophical Rev. XXXII, 1923.

Muirhead, J. H. Bernard Bosanquet. Mind, N.S. XXXII, 1923.

Sabine, H. Bosanquet's Theory of the Real Will. Philosophical Rev. XXXII, 1923.

Schaub, E. L. Bosanquet's Interpretation of Religious Experience. Philosophical Rev. XXXII, 1923.

Watson, J. Bosanquet on Mind and the Absolute. Philosophical Rev. XXXIV, 1925.

[For appreciations see A. C. Bradley and Viscount Haldane, Proc. British Academy, X, 1921–3.]

FRANCIS HERBERT BRADLEY (1846–1924)

(a) Books

The Presuppositions of Critical History. 1874.

Ethical Studies. 1876; 1927 (rev. and expanded).

Mr Sidgwick's Hedonism. 1877.

The Principles of Logic. 1883; 1922 (rev. with Commentary and Terminal Essays).

Appearance and Reality. 1893.

Essays on Truth and Reality. 1914.

Collected Essays. 2 vols. Oxford, 1935.

(b) Articles

Is Self-Sacrifice an Enigma? Mind, VIII, 1883.

Is there such a Thing as Pure Malevolence? Mind, VIII, 1883.

Sympathy and Interest. Mind, VIII, 1883.

Can a Man sin against Knowledge? Mind, IX, 1884.

Evidences of Spiritualism. Fortnightly Rev. XLV, 1885.

On the Analysis of Comparison. Mind, XI, 1886.

Is there any Special Activity of Attention? Mind, XI, 1886.

On a Feature of Active Attention. Mind, XII, 1887.

Association and Thought. Mind, XII, 1887.

Why do we remember forwards and not backwards? Mind, XII, 1887.

On Pleasure, Pain, Desire and Volition. Mind, XIII, 1888.

Reality and Thought. Mind, XIII, 1888.

On James' Doctrine of Simple Resemblance. Mind, N.S. III, 1894.

Some Remarks on Punishment. International Journ. Ethics, IV, 1894.

The Limits of Individual and National Self-Sacrifice. International Journ. Ethics, V, 1895.

On the Failure of Movement in Dreams. Mind, N.S. IV, 1895.

What do we mean by the Intensity of Psychical States? Mind, N.S. IV, 1895.

On the supposed Uselessness of the Soul. Mind, N.S. IV, 1895.

In what sense are Psychical States extended? Mind, N.S. IV, 1895.

The Contrary and the Disparate. Mind, V, 1896.

Some Remarks on Memory and Inference. Mind, VIII, 1899.

A Defence of Phenomenalism in Psychology. Mind, IX, 1900.

Some Remarks on Conation. Mind, XI, 1902.

On Active Attention. Mind, XI, 1902.

On Mental Conflict and Imputation. Mind, XII, 1903, XIII, 1904.

The Definition of Will. Mind, XIII, 1904.

Truth and Practice. Mind, XIII, 1904.

On Floating Ideas and the Imaginary. Mind, XV, 1906.

On Truth and Copying. Mind, XVI, 1907.

On Memory and Judgment. Mind, XVII, 1908.

On our Knowledge of Immediate Experience. Mind, XVII, 1908.

On Truth and Coherence. Mind, XVII, 1908.

Coherence and Contradiction. Mind, XVII, 1908.

On Appearance, Error and Contradiction. Mind, XIX, 1910.

On Some Aspects of Truth. Mind, XX, 1911.

Reply to Mr Russell's Explanations. Mind, xx, 1911.

Faith. Philosophical Rev. xx, 1911.

(c) Biography and Criticism

Bosanquet, B. Knowledge and Reality. 1885.

Robins, E. P. Bradley's Theory of Judgment. Philosophical Rev. vii, 1898.

Pringle-Pattison, A. S. Man's Place in the Cosmos. 1902 (2nd edn).

Stout, G. F. Bradley's Theory of Judgment. Proc. Aristotelian Soc. v, 1903.

—— Bradley on Truth and Reality. Mind, xxxiv, 1925.

Knox, H. Bradley's 'Absolute Criterion.' Mind, xiv, 1905.

Schiller, F. C. S. Bradley's Theory of Truth. Mind, xvi, 1907.

—— The New Developments of Bradley's Philosophy. Mind, xxiv, 1915.

Russell, B. Some Explanations in Reply to Bradley. Mind, xix, 1910.

Strange, E. H. Bradley's Doctrine of Knowledge. Mind, xx, 1911.

Rashdall, H. The Metaphysic of F. H. Bradley. Proc. British Academy, v, 1912.

Broad, C. D. Bradley on Truth and Reality. Mind, xxiii, 1914.

Cuming, A. Bradley, Lotze and Bosanquet. Mind, xxvi, 1917.

Hicks, G. D. Bradley's Treatment of Nature. Mind, xxxiv, 1925.

—— The Metaphysical Systems of Bradley and Ward. Journ. Philosophical Stud. i, 1926.

Keeling, S. V. La Nature de l'Expérience chez Kant et chez Bradley. Montpellier, 1925.

Taylor, A. E. F. H. Bradley. Mind, xxxiv, 1925; Proc. British Academy, xi, 1925.

Ward, J. Bradley's Doctrine of Experience. Mind, xxxiv, 1925.

Kagey, R. The Growth of Bradley's Logic. 1931.

JOHN HENRY BRIDGES (1832–1906)

Comte's General View of Positivism. 1865.

The Unity of Comte's Life and Doctrine—a Reply to J. S. Mill. 1866.

Comte's System of Positive Polity, vol. i and (in part) vol. iii translated. 1875.

Five Discourses on Positive Religion. 1882.

Roger Bacon's Opus majus edited. 1897.

Essays and Addresses. With an Introduction by Frederic Harrison. Ed. L. T. Hobhouse, 1907.

Illustrations of Positivism. 1907.

The Life and Work of Roger Bacon. 1914.

THOMAS BROWN (1778–1820)

Observations on the Zoonomia of Erasmus Darwin. Edinburgh, 1798.

Observations on the Nature and Tendency of the Doctrine of Mr Hume concerning the Relations of Cause and Effect. Edinburgh, 1805; Edinburgh, 1818 (3rd edn, enlarged as Inquiry into the Relation of Cause and Effect).

Lectures on the Philosophy of the Human Mind. 4 vols. Edinburgh, 1820.

[See A. L. Jones, A Note on Dr Thomas Brown's Contribution to Aesthetics, in Studies in the History of Ideas, vol. i, New York, 1918.]

ALEXANDER BALMAIN BRUCE (1831–1899)

The Providential Order of the World. 1897.

The Moral Order of the World. 1899.

WILLIAM ARCHER BUTLER (1814?–1848)

Lectures on the History of Ancient Philosophy. Ed. W. H. Thompson, 1856.

EDWARD CAIRD (1835–1908)

(a) Books

A Critical Account of the Philosophy of Kant. 1877.

Hegel. 1883.

The Social Philosophy and Religion of Comte. 1885.

The Critical Philosophy of Immanuel Kant. 1889.

Essays on Literature and Philosophy. 1892.

The Evolution of Religion. 2 vols. 1893.

The Evolution of Theology in the Greek Philosophers. 2 vols. Glasgow, 1904.

(b) Articles

Metaphysic. Ency. Brit. 9th edn, 1883.

Anselm's Argument for the Being of God. Journ. Theological Stud. i, 1899.

Idealism and the Theory of Knowledge. Proc. British Academy, i, 1903.

St Paul and the Idea of Evolution. Hibbert Journ. ii, 1904.

The Influence of Kant on Modern Thought. Quarterly Rev. cc, 1904.

(c) Criticism

Mackenzie, J. S. Edward Caird as a Philosophical Teacher. Mind, N.S. xviii, 1909.

Lindsay, A. D. The Idealism of Caird and Jones. Journ. Philosophical Stud. i, 1926.

[For an appreciation see B. Bosanquet, Proc. British Academy, iii, 1907–8.]

JOHN CAIRD (1820–1898)

An Introduction to the Philosophy of Religion. 1880.
Spinoza. 1888.

HENRY CALDERWOOD (1830–1897)

The Philosophy of the Infinite. 1854.
Handbook of Moral Philosophy. 1872.
The Relations of Mind and Brain. 1877.
The Relations of Science and Religion. 1881.
Evolution and Man's Place in Nature. 1893.
David Hume. 1898.

[See Life, by W. Calderwood and D. Woodside, 1900.]

RICHARD CARLILE (1790–1843)

The Political Litany, diligently revised [and other parodies]. 1817.
The Republican. 14 vols. 1819–26. [A periodical.]
To the Reformers of Great Britain. 1821.
An Address to Men of Science. 1821.
Observations on Christian Religion, by Olinthus Gregory. 1821.
Guide to Virtue and Morality through the Pages of the Bible. 1821.
Every Man's Book, or What is God? 1826.
An Address to Reformers on the Political Excitement of the present Time. 1839.

THOMAS CARLYLE

[See p. 652 above.]

WILLIAM BENJAMIN CARPENTER (1813–1885)

Principles of Mental Physiology. 1874.
Mesmerism and Spiritualism. 1877.
Nature and Man: Essays Scientific and Philosophical. Ed. J. E. Carpenter, 1888.

[See M. Guthrie, The Causational and Freewill Theories of Volition, being a Review of Dr Carpenter's Mental Physiology, 1877, and J. T. Lingard, Dr Carpenter's Theory of Attention, Mind, II, 1872.]

THOMAS CHALMERS (1780–1847)

The Christian and Civic Economy of large Towns. 1821–6.
On Political Economy in Connection with the Moral State and Moral Prospects of Society. 1832.
The Adaptation of External Nature to the Moral and Intellectual Constitution of Man. 1834.
Sketches of Moral and Mental Philosophy. 1836.
Natural Theology. 1836.

WILLIAM KINGDON CLIFFORD (1845–1879)

[See p. 942 below.]

FRANCES POWER COBBE (1822–1904)

An Essay on Intuitive Morals. 1855.
Broken Lights. 1864.
Studies, New and Old. 1865.
Darwinism in Morals, and Other Essays. 1872.
The Hopes of the Human Race. 1874.
The Duties of Women. 1881.
The Peak in Darien. 1882.
A Faithless World. 1885.
The Scientific Spirit of the Age. 1888.
The Friend of Man; and his Friends—the Poets. 1889.
Life. By Herself. 2 vols. 1894; 1904 (expanded).

SAMUEL TAYLOR COLERIDGE (1772–1834)

[See p. 172 above.]

GEORGE COMBE (1788–1858)

Essays on Phrenology. 1819.
Elements of Phrenology. 1824.
The Constitution of Man considered in Relation to External Objects. 1828.
Lectures on Moral Philosophy. 1840.
Notes on the United States of America. 1841.
Remarks on National Education. 1847.
On the Relation between Religion and Science. 1857.
The Currency Question. 1858.

RICHARD CONGREVE (1818–1899)

The Politics of Aristotle translated. 1855.
The Catechism of Positive Religion translated. 1858.
The New Religion in its Attitude to the Old. 1859.
Essays, Political, Social, and Religious. 3 vols. 1874–1900.
Human Catholicism. 1876. [No. 2, 1877.]
Comte's System of Positive Polity, vol. IV, translated. 1877.
Religion of Humanity. 1878–82. [Addresses.]

THOMAS COOPER (1805–1892)

[See p. 284 above.]

CAROLINE FRANCES CORNWALLIS (1786–1858)

Philosophical Theories and Philosophical Experience, by a Pariah. 1842.
Selections from the Letters. 1864.

THOMAS DAVIDSON (1840–1900)

The Philosophical System of Rosmini-Serbati. 1882.
Aristotle and Ancient Educational Ideals. 1892.
The Education of the Greek People. 1895.
Rousseau and Education according to Nature. 1898.

A History of Education. 1900.
The Education of the Wage-Earners. Ed.
C. M. Bakewell, Boston, 1904.
The Philosophy of Goethe's Faust. Ed. C. M.
Bakewell, Boston, 1906.

[See W. Knight, Memorials of Thomas
Davidson, 1907.]

AUGUSTUS DE MORGAN (1806–1871)

Essay on Probabilities. 1838.
Formal Logic; or the Calculus of Inference,
Necessary and Probable. 1847; ed. A. E.
Taylor, 1926.
Syllabus of a proposed System of Logic. 1860.

[For an appraisal see L. Liard, Les Logiciens
anglais, Paris, 1878, ch. iv. See also p. 942
below.]

CHARLES LUTWIDGE DODGSON [LEWIS CARROLL] (1832–1898)

[See p. 513 above.]

JAMES FREDERICK FERRIER (1808–1864)

The Institute of Metaphysic. 1854.
Scottish Philosophy: the Old and the New.
1856.
Lectures on Greek Philosophy and Other
Philosophical Remains. Ed. Sir A. Grant
and E. L. Lushington, 2 vols. 1866, 1875
(with Some Papers Supplementary to the
Institutes).

[See E. S. Haldane, J. F. Ferrier, 1899.]

ROBERT FLINT (1838–1910)

The Philosophy of History in France and
Germany. 1874.
Theism. 1877.
Anti-theistic Theories. 1879.
Vico. 1884.
Socialism. 1894.
Sermons and Addresses. 1899.
Agnosticism. 1903.
Philosophy as Scientia Scientiarum. 1904.

THOMAS FOWLER (1832–1904)

Elements of Deductive Logic. 1867.
Elements of Inductive Logic. 1870; 1904
(rev.).
Locke. 1880. (English Men of Letters ser.)
Bacon. 1881.
Bacon. Novum Organum. Edited. 1878; 1889.
Shaftesbury and Hutcheson. 1882.
Progressive Morality: an Essay in Ethics.
1884.
The Principles of Morals. 2 pts, 1886. [With
John Matthias Wilson.]

ALEXANDER CAMPBELL FRASER (1819–1914)

Introductory Lecture on Logic and Metaphysics. 1851.

Essays in Philosophy. 1856.
Rational Philosophy in History and in
System. 1858.
On Mental Philosophy. 1868.
The Works of George Berkeley edited. 4 vols.
1871.
Selections from Berkeley. 1874.
Berkeley. 1881.
Locke. 1890.
An Essay concerning Human Understanding
by John Locke. Edited. 1894.
The Philosophy of Theism. 2 sers. 1895–6.
(Gifford Lectures.)
Thomas Reid. 1898.
Biographia Philosophica. 1904.
John Locke as a Factor in Modern Thought.
Proc. British Academy, I, 1904.
Berkeley and Spiritual Realism. 1908.

[For appreciations see A. S. Pringle-Pattison,
Proc. British Academy, VI, 1913–4, and Mind,
XXIV, 1915.]

SIR FRANCIS GALTON (1822–1911)

(a) Books

Meteorographica, or a Method of mapping the
Weather. 1863.
Hereditary Genius, its Laws and Consequences.
1869; tr. German, 1910.
Experiments in Pangenesis. 1871.
English Men of Science, their Nature and
Nurture. 1874.
Address to the Anthropological Department
of the British Association. 1877.
Generic Images. 1879.
Inquiries into the Human Faculty and its
Development. 1883.
Life History Album. 1884.
Record of Family Faculties. 1884.
Natural Inheritance. 1889.
An Index to the Achievements of Near Kins-
folk of some of the Fellows of the Royal
Society. 1904.
Eugenics, its Definition, Scope and Aims.
1905.
Probability, the Foundation of Eugenics.
1907.
Memories of My Life. 1908.

(b) Articles

Statistics of Mental Imagery. Mind, V, 1880.
Freewill, Observations and Inferences. Mind,
IX, 1884.
Notes on Pretension in Idiots. Mind, XII,
1887.
Remarks on Mental Tests and Measurements.
Mind, XV, 1890.

(c) Biography and Criticism

Pearson, K. The Life, Letters and Labours of
Sir Francis Galton. Cambridge, 1914.
—— A Centenary Appreciation. 1922.

WILLIAM GRAHAM (1839–1911)

Idealism: an Essay Metaphysical and Critical. 1872.
The Creed of Science. 1881.
The Social Problem. 1886.
Socialism, New and Old. 1890.
English Political Philosophy from Hobbes to Maine. 1899.
Free Trade and the Empire. 1904.

THOMAS HILL GREEN (1836–1882)

(a) Writings

The Philosophical Works of David Hume. Ed. T. H. Green and T. H. Grose, 4 vols. 1874–8. [Introductions.]
Prolegomena to Ethics. 1883.
Works. Ed. (with memoir) R. L. Nettleship, 3 vols. 1885–8.
Lectures on the Principles of Political Obligation. 1895.

(b) Biography and Criticism

Sidgwick, H. Green's Ethics. Mind, IX, 1884.
—— Lectures on the Ethics of Green. 1902.
Fairbrother, W. H. The Philosophy of T. H. Green. 1896.
Bryce, J., Viscount. Studies in Contemporary Biography. 1903.

GEORGE GROTE (1794–1871)

[See p. 888 below.]

JOHN GROTE (1813–1866)

Exploratio Philosophica. 2 pts, 1865–1900.
An Examination of the Utilitarian Philosophy. 1870.
A Treatise on the Moral Ideals. 1876.

[See C. E. Whitmore, The Significance of John Grote, Philosophical Rev. XXXVI, 1927.]

EDMUND GURNEY (1847–1888)

The Power of Sound. 1880.
Phantasms of the Living. 1886. [With F. W. H. Myers and F. Podmore.]
Tertium Quid: Chapters on Various Disputed Questions. 2 vols. 1887.

[For an appreciation see F. W. H. Myers, Proc. Soc. for Psychical Research, V, 1888, p. 359.]

SIR WILLIAM HAMILTON (1788–1856)

(a) Writings

The Works of Thomas Reid edited. 1846.
A Letter to A. De Morgan, Esq. on his Claim to an Independent Rediscovery of a New Principle in the Theory of Syllogism. 1847.
Discussions on Philosophy and Literature, Education and University Reform. 1852.
Lectures on Metaphysics and Logic. Ed. H. L. Mansel and J. Veitch, 4 vols. 1858–60.

(b) Biography and Criticism

Baynes, T. S. Edinburgh Essays. 1857.
Mill, J. S. Examination of Sir William Hamilton's Philosophy. 1865.
Stirling, J. H. Sir William Hamilton: being the Philosophy of Perception. 1865.
Bolton, M. P. W. The Scoto-Oxonian Philosophy. 1867.
—— Inquisitio philosophica. 1869.
Veitch, J. Memoir of Sir William Hamilton. 1869.
—— Hamilton. 1879.
—— Sir William Hamilton: the Man and his Philosophy. 1883.
Liard, L. Les Logiciens anglais. Paris, 1878. [Ch. iii.]
Monck, W. H. S. Sir William Hamilton. 1881.

THOMAS NORTON HARPER (1821–1893)

The Metaphysics of the School. 1879–84.

AUBERON EDWARD WILLIAM MOLYNEUX HERBERT (1838–1906)

A Politician in Trouble about his Soul. 1884.
The Right and Wrong of Compulsion by the State. 1885.
The True Line of Deliverance. [In A Plea for Liberty, 1891.]
The Voluntaryist Creed. 1908.

THOMAS MARTIN HERBERT (1835–1877)

The Realistic Assumptions of Modern Science examined. 1879.

SIR JOHN FREDERICK WILLIAM HERSCHEL (1792–1871)

Discourse on the Study of Natural Philosophy. 1830.
[See also p. 943 below.]

JAMES HINTON (1822–1875)

The Mystery of Pain. 1866.
Chapters on the Art of Thinking and Other Essays. 1879.
Philosophy and Religion. 1881.
The Lawbreaker and the Coming of the Law. 1884.

SHADWORTH HOLLWAY HODGSON (1832–1912)

(a) Writings

Time and Space. 1865.
The Theory of Practice. 1870.
The Philosophy of Reflection. 1878.
The Metaphysic of Experience. 1898.

(b) Biography and Criticism

Dauriac, L. La Méthode et la Doctrine de Shadworth Hodgson. L'Année philosophique, 1899.

Carr, H. W. Shadworth Hollway Hodgson.
Mind, xxi, 1912.
Hicks, G. D. Proc. British Academy, vi, 1913–4.

THOMAS HENRY HUXLEY (1825–1895)

Man's Place in Nature. 1863.
Lay Sermons, Addresses and Reviews. 1870.
Critiques and Addresses. 1873.
American Addresses. 1877.
Hume. 1879. (English Men of Letters ser.)
Science and Culture and Other Essays. 1881.
Essays upon some Controverted Questions. 1892.
Evolution and Ethics. 1893.
Collected Essays. 9 vols. 1894.
Scientific Memoirs. 4 vols. 1898–1901.

[See Life and Letters, by his Son, 2 vols. 1900. Huxley's scientific works are listed, pp. 954, 958, 963 below.]

WILLIAM STANLEY JEVONS (1835–1882)

Pure Logic, or the Science of Quality apart from Quantity. 1864.
The Substitution of Similars. 1869.
Elementary Lessons in Logic. 1870.
On the Mechanical Performance of Logical Inference. Philosophical Trans. 1870.
The Theory of Political Economy. 1871.
The Principles of Science. 1874.
Primer of Logic. 1878.
Studies in Deductive Logic. 1880.
Letters and Journal edited by his Wife. 1886.
Pure Logic and Other Minor Works. Ed. R. Adamson and H. A. Jevons, 1890.

[For an appraisal see L. Liard, Les Logiciens anglais, Paris, 1878, ch. vi. See also under Economics and Political Theory, p. 983 below.]

SIR HENRY JONES (1852–1922)

(a) Books

Browning as a Philosopher and Religious Teacher. 1891.
A Critical Account of the Philosophy of Lotze. 1895.
The Philosophy of Martineau. 1905.
Idealism as a Practical Creed. 1909.
The Working Faith of the Social Reformer. 1910.
The Immanence of God and the Individuality of Man. 1912.
Social Powers. 1913.
The Principles of Citizenship. 1919.
Old Memories. 1921.
A Faith that Enquires. 1922. (Gifford Lectures.)
Essays on Literature and Education. 1923.

(b) Articles

The Nature and Aims of Philosophy. Mind, N.S. ii, 1893.
Idealism and Epistemology. Mind, N.S. ii, 1893.
The Present Attitude of Reflective Thought towards Religion. Hibbert Journ. i, ii, 1903–4.
Mr Balfour as Sophist. Hibbert Journ. iii, 1905.
Divine Immanence. Hibbert Journ. v, 1907.
The Ethical Demand of the Political Situation. Hibbert Journ. viii, 1910.

SIMON SOMERVILLE LAURIE (1829–1909)

On the Philosophy of Ethics. 1866.
Primary Instruction in relation to Education. 1867.
Notes on certain British Theories of Morals. 1868.
Life and Educational Writings of Comenius. Cambridge, 1881.
Metaphysica nova et vetusta, a Return to Dualism. 1884; tr. French, 1901.
Ethica, or the Ethics of Reason. 1885.
Lectures on the Rise and Early Constitution of Universities. 1886.
Institutes of Education. 1892.
Historical Survey of Pre-Christian Education. 1895.
Synthetica. 1906.

GEORGE HENRY LEWES (1817–1878)

(a) Books

A Biographical History of Philosophy. 4 vols. 1845–6; 1857 (rev.); 2 vols. 1867 (expanded); 2 vols. 1871 (partly rewritten); 2 vols. 1880; 1891; tr. German, Berlin, 1871–6.
The Spanish Drama. Lope de Vega and Calderón. 1846.
Ranthorpe. 1847. [Novel.]
Rose, Blanche, and Violet. 3 vols. 1848. [Novel.]
The Life of Maximilien Robespierre. 1849; 1899 (3rd edn).
The Noble Heart. A Tragedy. 1850.
Comte's Philosophy of the Sciences. 1853.
The Life and Works of Goethe. 2 vols. 1855; 1864; 1873 (abridged); 1875; 2 vols. Leipzig, 1882; 1890; rptd [1906]; 1908 (Everyman's Lib.). Tr. German, Berlin, 1857; Russian, St Petersburg, 1860.
Sea-side Studies at Ilfracombe, Tenby, the Scilly Isles, and Jersey. Edinburgh, 1858; 1860.
The Physiology of Common Life. 2 vols. Edinburgh, 1859–60; 2 vols. Leipzig, 1860.
Studies in Animal Life. 1862. [Rptd from Cornhill Mag.]

Aristotle. A Chapter from The History of Science. 1864.
Problems of Life and Mind. 5 vols. 1874–9.
First Series. The Foundations of a Creed. 2 vols. 1874–5.
The Physical Basis of Mind. Being the Second Series. 1877.
Third Series. The Study of Psychology. 1879; tr. Italian, Milan, 1907.
Third Series continued. Mind as a Function of the Organism. 1879.
On Actors and The Art of Acting. 1875.
Dramatic Essays reprinted from the Examiner. Ed. W. Archer and R. W. Lowe, 1896.
The Principles of Success in Literature. Ed. T. S. Knowlson, [1898]. [Rptd from Fortnightly Rev.]

[Lewes also pbd 8 or 9 comedies, mainly adapted from the French, in Lacy's Acting Edition of Plays, c. 1850, under the pseudonym 'Laurence Slingsby.']

(b) Articles

What is Sensation? Mind, i, 1876.
Consciousness and Unconsciousness. Mind, ii, 1877.

(c) Biography and Criticism

Sully, J. George Henry Lewes. New Quart. Oct. 1879.
Trollope, A. George Henry Lewes. Fortnightly Rev. Jan. 1879.
Cross, J. W. The Life of George Eliot. 2 vols. 1885–6.
Kitchel, A. T. George Lewes and George Eliot. New York, 1934.
Gary, F. Charlotte Brontë and George Henry Lewes. PMLA. li, 1936.

SIR JOHN LUBBOCK, BARON AVEBURY (1834–1913)

[See p. 915 below.]

JAMES M'COSH (1811–1894)

Method of Divine Government. 1850.
Intuitions of the Mind. 1860.
The Supernatural in Relation to the Natural. 1862.
Present State of Moral Philosophy in England. 1868.
Scottish Philosophy from Hutcheson to Hamilton. 1875.
Development: what it can and what it cannot do. 1884.
The Prevailing Types of Philosophy. 1891.

SIR JAMES MACKINTOSH (1765–1832)

[See p. 880 below.]

JOHN FERGUSON M'LENNAN (1827–1881)

Primitive Marriage. Edinburgh, 1865.
The Patriarchal Theory. Ed. D. M'Lennan, 1885.

SIR HENRY JAMES SUMNER MAINE (1822–1888)

[See p. 893 below.]

THOMAS ROBERT MALTHUS (1766–1834)

An Essay on the Principle of Population as it affects the Future Improvement of Society, with Remarks on the Speculations of Mr Godwin, M. Condorcet, and other Writers. 1798; 1803 (as An Essay on the Principle of Population; or, a View of its Past and Present Effects on Human Happiness).
Observations on the Effects of the Corn Laws. 1814.
An Inquiry into the Nature and Progress of Rent. 1815.
Grounds of an Opinion on the Policy of restricting the Importation of Foreign Corn. 1815.
Principles of Political Economy. 1820; 1836 (with life by W. Otter).
The Measure of Value stated and illustrated. 1823.
Definitions in Political Economy. 1827.
Summary View of the Principle of Population. 1830.

[See J. Bonar, Malthus and his Work, 1885, Letters of Ricardo to Malthus, 1887, and L. Cossa, Il Principio di Popolazione di T. R. Malthus, Milan, 1895.]

HENRY LONGUEVILLE MANSEL (1820–1871)

Artis Logicæ Rudimenta. From the Text of Aldrich, with Notes and Marginal References. 1849.
Prolegomena Logica. An Inquiry into the Psychological Character of Logical Processes. 1851.
Man's Conception of Eternity. 1854.
Psychology, the Test of Moral and Metaphysical Philosophy. 1855.
The Limits of Religious Thought examined. 1858.
Metaphysics, or the Philosophy of Consciousness. 1860.
Philosophy of the Conditioned. 1866.
Letters, Lectures and Reviews. 1873.
The Gnostic Heresies. Ed. J. B. Lightfoot, 1875.

HARRIET MARTINEAU (1802–1876)

[See p. 496 above.]

JAMES MARTINEAU (1805–1900)

The Rationale of Religious Inquiry. 1836.
Lectures in the Liverpool Controversy. 1839.

Endeavours after a Christian Life. 2 vols. 1843–7.
Miscellanies. 1852.
Studies in Christianity. 1858.
Essays, Philosophical and Theological. 2 vols. 1868.
Religion as affected by Modern Materialism. 1874.
Modern Materialism: its Attitude towards Theology. 1876.
Hours of Thought on Sacred Things. 1876.
Ideal Substitutes for God considered. 1879.
The Relation between Ethics and Religion. 1881.
A Study of Spinoza. 1882.
Types of Ethical Theory. 1882.
A Study of Religion. 1888.
The Seat of Authority in Religion. 1890.
Essays, Reviews and Addresses. 4 vols. 1890–1.
National Duties. 1903.

[See J. Estlin Carpenter, James Martineau, Theologian and Teacher, 1905.]

JOHN FREDERICK DENISON MAURICE (1805–1872)

[See p. 720 above.]

JAMES MILL (1773–1836)

The History of British India. 3 vols. 1817.
Elements of Political Economy. 1821.
Essays on Government, Jurisprudence, [etc.], written for the Supplement to the Encyclopaedia Britannica. Edinburgh, [1825] (priv. ptd). [Essay on Government, ed. E. Barker, 1937.]
Analysis of the Phenomena of the Human Mind. 2 vols. 1829; ed. J. S. Mill, 2 vols. 1869.
A Fragment on Mackintosh. 1835; 1870.
The Principles of Toleration. 1837.

[See A. Bain, James Mill, a Biography, 1882, and G. S. Bower, Hartley and James Mill, 1881.]

JOHN STUART MILL (1806–1873)

(a) Writings

Essays on some Unsettled Questions of Political Economy. 1831.
A System of Logic, ratiocinative and inductive. 1843. Tr. German, 1849; French, 1910.
Principles of Political Economy. 2 vols. 1848; ed. W. J. Ashley, 1909.
Thoughts on Parliamentary Reform. 1859.
On Liberty. 1859.
Dissertations and Discussions. Vols. I, II, 1859. Vol. III, 1867. Vol. IV, 1875.
Considerations on Representative Government. 1861.

Utilitarianism. 1863.
Examination of Sir William Hamilton's Philosophy. 1865; tr. German, 1908.
Auguste Comte and Positivism. 1865.
Inaugural Address at the University of St Andrews. 1867.
England and Ireland. 1868.
On the Subjection of Women. 1869.
Chapters and Speeches on the Irish Land Question. 1870.
Autobiography. 1873; tr. German, 1874.
Three Essays on Religion. 1874.
Lettres inédites. Ed. É. de Laveleye, Brussels, 1885.
Early Essays, selected by J. W. M. Gibbs. 1897.
Correspondance inédite avec G. d'Eichthal. Paris, 1898.
Lettres inédites à Auguste Comte, publiées par L. Lévy-Bruhl. Paris, 1899.
Letters. Ed. H. S. R. Elliot, 1910.

(b) Biography and Criticism

Funck-Brentano, T. Les Sophistes grecs et les Sophistes contemporains [Mill, Spencer]. Paris, 1879.
Courtney, W. L. Metaphysics of J. S. Mill. 1879.
Bain, A. J. S. Mill: a Criticism. 1882.
Douglas, C. J. S. Mill: a study of his Philosophy. 1895.
—— Ethics of J. S. Mill. 1897.
Watson, J. Mill, Comte and Spencer. 1895.
Saenger, S. J. S. Mill. 1901.
Brochard, V. Études de Philosophie ancienne et de Philosophie moderne. Paris, 1926.

JOHN DANIEL MORELL (1816–1891)

Historical and Critical View of the Speculative Philosophy of Europe in the Nineteenth Century. 1846.
The Philosophical Tendencies of the Age. 1848.
The Philosophy of Religion. 1849.
Fichte's Contributions to Moral Philosophy. 1860.
Philosophical Fragments. 1878.
An Introduction to Mental Philosophy on the Inductive Method. 1884.

FREDERICK MAX MÜLLER (1823–1900)

[See p. 1018 below.]

JOHN HENRY NEWMAN (1801–1890)

An Essay on the Development of Christian Doctrine. 1845.
An Essay in Aid of a Grammar of Assent. 1870.

[See also p. 859 above.]

ROBERT OWEN (1771–1858)

A New View of Society, or Essays on the Principle of the Formation of Human Character. 1813–4 (priv. ptd); 1816.
Report to the Committee on the Poor Law. 1817.
The Book of the New Moral World. 1836.
The Revolution in the Mind and Practice of the Human Race. 1849.
Life of Robert Owen, written by Himself. 1857.

[See E. Dolléans, Robert Owen, 1905; H. Simon, Robert Owen: sein Leben und seine Bedeutung, Jena, 1905; G. J. Holyoake, History of Co-operation in England, 1906; F. Podmore, Life of Robert Owen, 1906. See also under Economics and Political Theory, p. 976 below.]

ROBERT DALE OWEN (1801–1877)

Footfalls on the Boundary of Another World. 1859.
The Debateable Land between this World and the Next. 1872.
Threading my Way: Twenty-Seven Years of Autobiography. 1874.

JAMES ALLANSON PICTON (1832–1910)

The Mystery of Matter. 1873.
The Religion of the Universe. 1904.

FRANCIS PLACE (1771–1854)

Illustrations and Proofs of the Principle of Population. 1822.

[See Graham Wallas, Life of Francis Place, 1898.]

CARVETH READ (1848–1931)

(a) Books

On the Theory of Logic. 1878.
Logic: Deductive and Inductive. 1898.
The Metaphysics of Nature. 1905.
Natural and Social Morals. 1909.
The Origin of Man and of his Superstitions. Cambridge, 1920.

(b) Articles

On the Difference between Percepts and Images. British Journ. Psychology, II, 1908.
Instinct. British Journ. Psychology, IV, 1911.
The Function of Relations in Thought. British Journ. Psychology, IV, 1911.
The Comparative Method in Psychology. British Journ. Psychology, VI, 1913.
A Philosophy of Nature. [In Contemporary British Philosophy, ed. J. H. Muirhead, vol. I, 1924.]

WILLIAM WINWOOD READE (1838–1875)

The Martyrdom of Man. 1872. [See also p. 992 below.]

DAVID GEORGE RITCHIE (1853–1903)

Darwinism and Politics. 1889.
Principles of State-Interference. 1891.
Darwin and Hegel, with Other Philosophical Studies. 1894.
Natural Rights. 1895.
Studies in Social and Political Ethics. 1902.
Plato. 1902.
Philosophical Studies. Ed. R. Latta, 1905.

GEORGE CROOM ROBERTSON (1842–1892)

Hobbes. 1886.
Philosophical Remains. Ed. A. Bain and T. Whittaker, 1895.
Elements of General Philosophy. Ed. C. A. F. Rhys Davids, 1896.
Elements of Psychology. Ed. C. A. F. Rhys Davids, 1896.

GEORGE JOHN ROMANES (1848–1894)

A Candid Examination of Theism, by Physicus. 1878.
Animal Intelligence. 1881.
Mental Evolution in Animals. 1883.
Mental Evolution in Man. 1888.
Darwin and after Darwin. 1892.
Mind and Motion and Monism. 1895.
Thoughts on Religion. 1896.
Essays. 1897.

[See Life and Letters, by E. Romanes, 1896. See also p. 955 below, and for the poems by Romanes, p. 356 above.]

SIR SAMUEL ROMILLY (1757–1818)

Thoughts on the Probable Influence of the late Revolution in France upon Great Britain. 1790.
Speeches in the House of Commons. 2 vols. 1820.
Life written by Himself. 3 vols. 1840.

SIR JOHN ROBERT SEELEY (1834–1895)

Natural Religion. 1882.
An Introduction to Political Science. 1895.

NASSAU WILLIAM SENIOR (1790–1864)

Two Lectures on Population. 1831. [Other lectures, 1827, 1828, 1830, 1847, 1852.] Principes fondamentaux d'Économie politique. 1835. [French trn of several of the lectures.]
Letter on a Legal Provision for the Irish Poor. 1831.
Statement of the Provision for the Poor [in] America and Europe. 1835.
An Outline of the Science of Political Economy. 1836; rptd 1938.
Letters on the Factory Act. 1837.
Suggestions on Popular Education. 1861.

Essays on Fiction. 1864.
Historical and Philosophical Essays. 1865.
[See M. Bowley, Nassau Senior and Classical Economics, 1937. See also under Economics and Political Theory, p. 981 below.]

ANDREW SETH, later PRINGLE-PATTISON
(1856–1931)

(a) Books

The Development from Kant to Hegel. 1882.
Comparison of the Scottish and German Answers to Hume. 1885.
Hegelianism and Personality. 1887.
Two Lectures on Theism. 1897.
Man's Place in the Cosmos. 1897.
The Philosophical Radicals. 1907.
The Idea of God in the Light of Recent Philosophy. 1917. (Gifford Lectures.)
The Idea of Immortality. 1922. (Gifford Lectures.)
Studies in the Philosophy of Religion. 1930.
The Balfour Lectures on Realism. Ed. (with a Memoir) F. Barbour, 1933.

(b) Articles

Hegel; an Exposition and Criticism. Mind, VI, 1881.
Hegel and his Recent Critics. Mind, XIV, 1889.
Psychology, Epistemology and Metaphysics. Philosophical Rev. I, 1892.
The Problem of Epistemology. Philosophical Rev. I, 1892.
Epistemology in Locke and Kant. Philosophical Rev. II, 1893.
The Epistemology of Neo-Kantianism and Subjective Idealism. Philosophical Rev. II, 1893.
The Truth of Empiricism. Philosophical Rev. II, 1893.
Are we Conscious Automata? Philosophical Rev. III, 1894.
Epistemology and Ontology. Philosophical Rev. III, 1894.
Hegelianism and its Critics. Mind, N.S. III, 1894.
The Term 'Naturalism' in Recent Discussion. Philosophical Rev. V, 1896.
The Standpoint and Method of Ethics. Philosophical Rev. VI, 1897.
Scottish Moral Philosophy. Philosophical Rev. VII, 1898.
The Utilitarian Estimate of Knowledge. Philosophical Rev. X, 1901.
The Alleged Fallacies in Mill's 'Utilitarianism.' Philosophical Rev. XVII, 1908.
Do Finite Individuals possess a Substantive or an Adjectival Mode of Being? Proc. Aristotelian Soc. XVIII, 1918.
The Idea of God: Reply to some Criticisms. Mind, XXIV, 1919.

Pragmatist and Idealist Ethics. Philosophical Rev. XXXII, 1923.
The Philosophy of History. 1923. (Henriette Herz Lecture.)

(c) Biography and Criticism

Jones, A. H. Seth Pringle-Pattison's Epistemological Realism. Philosophical Rev. XX, 1911.
Rashdall, H. The Religious Philosophy of Pringle-Pattison. Mind, XXVII, 1922.
Hallett, H. F. Andrew Seth Pringle-Pattison (1856–1931). Mind, XLII.
[For appreciations see J. B. Capper and J. B. Baillie, Proc. British Academy, XVII, 1931.]

HENRY SIDGWICK (1838–1900)

(a) Books

The Methods of Ethics. 1874; tr. German, 1909.
Outlines of the History of Ethics. 1879.
Principles of Political Economy. 1883.
The Scope and Method of Economic Science. 1885.
The Elements of Politics. 1891.
Practical Ethics. 1898.
Philosophy: its Scope and Relations. 1902.
Lectures on the Ethics of Green, Spencer and Martineau. 1902.
The Development of European Polity. 1903.
Miscellaneous Essays and Addresses. 1904.
The Philosophy of Kant and Other Lectures and Essays. 1905.

(b) Articles

Hedonism and Ultimate Good. Mind, II, 1877.
The Establishment of Ethical First Principles. Mind, IV, 1879.
The So-called Idealism of Kant. Mind, V, 1880.
On the Fundamental Doctrines of Descartes. Mind, VII, 1882.
The Morality of Strife. International Journ. Ethics, 1891.
Unreasonable Action. Mind, N.S. II, 1893.
A Dialogue on Time and Common Sense. Mind, N.S. III, 1894.
My Station and its Duties. International Journ. Ethics, 1894.
On Luxury. International Journ. Ethics, 1895.
The Ethics of Religious Conformity. International Journ. Ethics, 1896.
Relation of Ethics to Sociology. International Journ. Ethics, IX, 1899.
Criteria of Truth and Error. Mind, N.S. IX, 1900.
The Philosophy of T. H. Green. Mind, N.S. X, 1901.
An Auto-Historical Fragment. Mind, N.S. X, 1901.

(c) Biography and Criticism

Bradley, F. H. Mr Sidgwick's Hedonism. 1877.
Rashdall, H. Sidgwick's Utilitarianism. Mind, x, 1885.
Albee, E. An Examination of Sidgwick's Proof of Utilitarianism. Philosophical Rev. x, 1901.
—— Rejoinder to Barker's Recent Criticisms. Philosophical Rev. xi, 1902.
Hayward, F. The Ethical Philosophy of Sidgwick. 1901.
Barker, H. Recent Criticisms of Sidgwick's 'Methods.' Philosophical Rev. xi, 1902.
Bryce, J., Viscount. Studies in Contemporary Biography. 1903.
S[idgwick], A. and E. M. Memoir. 1906.
Barbour, G. F. Sidgwick and Green on the Community of the Good. Philosophical Rev. xvii, 1908.

[For an appreciation see Lord Bryce, Proc. British Academy, i, 1903–4.]

EDITH SIMCOX

Natural Law: an Essay in Ethics. 1877.
Primitive Civilizations. 1894.

WILLIAM HENRY SMITH (1808–1872)

[See p. 849 above.]

WILLIAM RITCHIE SORLEY (1855–1935)

On the Ethics of Naturalism. 1885.
Mining Royalties. 1889.
Recent Tendencies in Ethics. 1904.
The Interpretation of Evolution. Proc. British Academy, iv, 1910.
The Moral Life. Cambridge, 1911.
Moral Values and the Idea of God. Cambridge, 1918. (Gifford Lectures.)
Spinoza. 1918. (Henriette Herz Lecture.)
Reconstruction and the Renewal of Life. Cambridge, 1919.
A History of English Philosophy. Cambridge, 1920.
Value and Reality. [In Contemporary British Philosophy, ed. J. H. Muirhead, vol. ii, 1925.]
Tradition. 1926. (Herbert Spencer Lecture.)

WILLIAM SPALDING (1809–1859)

[See p. 725 above.]

HERBERT SPENCER (1820–1903)

(a) Writings

The Proper Sphere of Government. 1843.
Social Statics. 1850.
Principles of Psychology. 1855.
Essays, Scientific, Political and Speculative. 2 vols. 1858–63; 3 vols. 1885.
Education. 1861; tr. German, 1874.
A System of Synthetic Philosophy: First Principles. 1862. Principles of Biology. 2

vols. 1864–7. Principles of Psychology. 2 vols. 1870–2. Principles of Sociology. 3 vols. 1876–96. Ceremonial Institutions. 1879. Principles of Morality. 2 vols. 1879–93 (vol. i, pt 1, pbd as Data of Ethics, 1879, pt 4, Justice, 1891). Political Institutions. 1882.
The Classification of the Sciences. 1864.
The Study of Sociology. 1872.
Descriptive Sociology; or, Groups of Sociological Facts compiled and abstracted by D. Duncan, R. Scheppig and J. Collier, 1873. 1880–1.
The Man versus the State. 1884.
The Factors of Organic Evolution. 1887.
The Inadequacy of Natural Selection. 1893.
A Rejoinder to Prof. Weismann. 1893.
Weismannism once more. 1894.
Various Fragments. 1897; 1900 (enlarged).
Facts and Comments. 1902.
Autobiography. 1904; tr. German, 1905.

[Other writings are listed p. 954 below.]

(b) Biography and Criticism

Funck-Brentano, T. Les Sophistes grecs et les Sophistes contemporains [Mill, Spencer]. Paris, 1879.
Collins, F. H. An Epitome of the Synthetic Philosophy. 1889.
Sidgwick, H. Lectures on the Ethics of Green, Spencer and Martineau. 1902.
—— The Philosophy of Herbert Spencer. [In The Philosophy of Kant and Other Lectures, 1905.]
Duncan, D. An Introduction to the Philosophy of Spencer. 1904.
—— Life and Letters of Herbert Spencer. 1908.
Royce, J. Herbert Spencer. An Estimate and a Review. 1904.
Sorley, W. R. The Ethics of Naturalism. 1904.
Thomson, J. A. Herbert Spencer. 1906.
Hudson, W. H. Herbert Spencer. 1916.

SIR JAMES FITZJAMES STEPHEN (1829–1894)

[See p. 919 below.]

SIR LESLIE STEPHEN (1832–1904)

[See p. 727 above.]

JAMES HUTCHISON STIRLING (1820–1909)

The Secret of Hegel. 1865.
Sir William Hamilton: being the Philosophy of Perception. 1865.
Schwegler's Handbook of the History of Philosophy. 1867.
Jerrold, Tennyson and Macaulay, with Other Critical Essays. Edinburgh, 1868.
As regards Protoplasm. 1869.
Lectures on the Philosophy of Law. 1873.
Textbook to Kant, with Commentary. 1881.

Philosophy and Theology. 1890.
Darwinism, Workmen and Work. 1894.
What *is* Thought? 1900.
The Categories. 1903.

[See A. H. Stirling, J. H. Stirling, his Life and Work, 1912.]

GEORGE FREDERICK STOUT (b. 1859)

(a) Books

Analytic Psychology. 2 vols. 1896.
A Manual of Psychology. 1898.
The Groundwork of Psychology. 1903.
Studies in Philosophy and Psychology. 1930.
Mind and Matter. Cambridge, 1931.

(b) Articles

The Herbartian Psychology. Mind, XIII, 1888.
Herbart, the English Psychologists and Beneke. Mind, XIV, 1889.
The Psychological Work of Herbart's Disciples. Mind, XIV, 1889.
The Genesis of the Cognition of Physical Reality. Mind, XV, 1890.
Apperception and the Movement of Attention. Mind, XVI, 1891.
Thought and Language. Mind, XVI, 1891.
Belief. Mind, XVI, 1891.
Voluntary Action. Mind, N.S. V, 1896.
The Common Sense Conception of a Material Thing. Proc. Aristotelian Soc. 1901.
Alleged Self Contradictions in the Concept of Relation. Proc. Aristotelian Soc. 1902.
Perception of Change and Duration. Mind, N.S. IX, 1902.
Mr Bradley's Theory of Judgment. Proc. Aristotelian Soc. III, 1903.
Primary and Secondary Qualities. Proc. Aristotelian Soc. IV, 1904.
Things and Sensations. Proc. British Academy, II, 1905.
The Nature of Conation and Mental Activity. British Journ. Psychology, II, 1906.
Neo-Kantianism as represented by Dr Dawes Hicks. Proc. Aristotelian Soc. VI, 1906.
The Nature of Mental Activity. Proc. Aristotelian Soc. VIII, 1908.
Immediacy, Mediacy and Coherence. Mind, N.S. XVII, 1908.
Are Presentations Mental or Physical? Proc. Aristotelian Soc. IX, 1909.
Instinct and Intelligence. British Journ. Psychology, III, 1910.
The Object of Thought and Real Being. Proc. Aristotelian Soc. XI, 1911.
Some Fundamental Points in the Theory of Knowledge. [St Andrews' Quintercentenary Publications, 1911,]
Can there be Anything Obscure or Implicit in a Mental State? Proc. Aristotelian Soc. XIII, 1913.

The Status of Sense-data. Proc. Aristotelian Soc. XIV, 1914.
Instinct and Emotion. Proc. Aristotelian Soc. XV, 1915.
Do Individuals possess a Substantive or an Adjectival Mode of Being? Proc. Aristotelian Soc. XVIII, 1918.
Alexander's Theory of Sense Perception. Mind, XXXI, 1922.
The Nature of Universals and Propositions. Proc. British Academy, X, 1922.
Are the Characteristics of Particular Things Universal or Particular? Aristotelian Supplements, vol. III, 1923.
The Nature of Introspection. Aristotelian Supplements, vol. VII, 1927.
Self-evidence and Matter of Fact. Philosophy, IX, 1934.

ISAAC TAYLOR (1787–1865)

The Natural History of Enthusiasm. 1829.
Fanaticism. 1833.
Spiritual Despotism. 1835.
The Physical Theory of Another Life. 1836.
Ancient Christianity, and the Doctrines of the Oxford Tracts for the Times. 2 vols. 1839–46.

[See G. Gilfillan, Second Gallery of Literary Portraits, Edinburgh, 1850.]

ROBERT TAYLOR (1784–1844)

The Holy Liturgy: or Divine Service on the Principles of Pure Deism. [1826.]
Syntagma of the Evidences of the Christian Religion. 1828.
The Diegesis: a Discovery of the Origin of Christianity. Boston, 1832.
The Devil's Pulpit. 2 vols. 1831–2; rptd 1881.

THOMAS TAYLOR (1758–1835)

Proclus Diadochus. The Philosophical and Mathematical Commentaries translated. 2 vols. 1778–89.
A Dissertation on the Eleusinian and Bacchic Mysteries. Amsterdam, [1790].
The Hymns of Orpheus translated. 1792.
Plato. Works, translated by Floyer Sydenham and Thomas Taylor. 5 vols. 1804.
Aristoteles. Works translated and illustrated with Copious Elucidations. 10 vols. 1806–12.
Proclus Diadochus. The six Books of Proclus on the History of Plato, translated. 1816.
Theoretic Arithmetic. 1816.
Select Works of Plotinus translated. 1817.
Iamblichus. On the Mysteries of the Egyptians translated. Chiswick, 1821.
Political Fragments of Archytas and Other Ancient Pythagoreans translated. Chiswick, 1822.

The Metamorphosis, or, Golden Ass and Philosophical Works of Apuleius translated. 1822.

Select Works of Porphyrius translated. 1823.

The Elements of a New Arithmetical Notation. 1823.

Pausanias. The Description of Greece translated. 1824.

WILLIAM THOMSON (1819–1890)

An Outline of the necessary Laws of Thought. 1842.

WILLIAM THOMAS THORNTON (1813–1880)

Overpopulation and its Remedy. 1846.

A Plea for Peasant Proprietors. 1848.

On Labour. 1869.

Old-fashioned Ethics and Common-sense Metaphysics. 1873.

JOHN TULLOCH (1823–1886)

Theism. 1855.

Rational Theology and Christian Philosophy in England in the Seventeenth Century. 1872.

Pascal. 1878.

Modern Theories in Philosophy and Religion. 1884.

JOHN VEITCH (1829–1894)

Speculative Philosophy. 1864.

Memoir of Sir William Hamilton. 1869.

The Method, Meditations and Selections from the Principles of Descartes, translated with Introductory Essay, Historical and Critical. 1879.

Hamilton. 1882.

Institutes of Logic. 1885.

Knowing and Being. 1889.

Dualism and Monism. Ed. R. M. Wenley, 1895.

[See Memoir by M. A. L. Bryce, 1896.]

WILLIAM WALLACE (1843–1897)

The Logic of Hegel, translated from the Encyclopædia. 1874.

Epicureanism. 1880.

Kant. 1882.

Life of Schopenhauer. 1890.

Hegel's Philosophy of Mind. 1894.

Lectures and Essays on Natural Theology and Ethics. 1898.

JAMES WARD (1843–1925)

(a) Books

Naturalism and Agnosticism. 2 vols. 1899. (Gifford Lectures.)

The Realm of Ends, or Pluralism and Theism. Cambridge, 1911. (Gifford Lectures.)

Heredity and Memory. Cambridge, 1913.

Psychological Principles. Cambridge, 1918.

A Study of Kant. Cambridge, 1922.

Psychology applied to Education. Ed. G. Dawes Hicks, Cambridge, 1926.

Essays in Philosophy, with Memoir by Olwen Ward-Campbell. Cambridge, 1927.

(b) Articles

The Relation of Physiology to Psychology. 1875.

An Attempt to interpret Fechner's Law. Mind, I, 1876.

Herbart. Ency. Brit. 9th edn, 1880.

A General Analysis of Mind. Journ. Speculative Philosophy, XVI, 1882.

Objects and their Interaction. Journ. Speculative Philosophy, XVII, 1883.

Psychological Principles Mind, VII, 1883, XII, 1888.

Psychology. Ency. Brit. 9th edn, 1886.

The Progress of Philosophy. Mind, XV, 1890.

Mill's Science of Ethology. International Journ. Ethics, I, 1891.

Modern Psychology: A Reflection. Mind, N.S. II, 1893.

Assimilation and Association. Mind, II, 1893, III, 1894.

Naturalism. Ency. Brit. 10th edn, 1902.

Psychology. Ency. Brit. 10th edn, 1902.

On the Definition of Psychology. British Journ. Psychology, I, 1904.

The Present Problems of General Psychology. Philosophical Rev. XIII, 1904.

Philosophical Orientation and Scientific Standpoints. 1904.

Mechanism and Morals. Hibbert Journ. Oct. 1905.

Is Black a Sensation? British Journ. Psychology, I, 1905.

Psychology. Ency. Brit. 11th edn, 1911.

Sense Knowledge. Mind, N.S. XXVIII, 1919, XXIX, 1920.

Immanuel Kant. Proc. British Academy, 1922.

The Christian Ideas of Faith and Eternal Life. Hibbert Journ. Jan. 1925.

Bradley's Doctrine of Experience. Mind, XXXIV, 1925.

A Theistic Monadism. [In Contemporary British Philosophy, ed. J. H. Muirhead, vol. II, 1925.]

An Introduction to Philosophy. The Monist, XXXVI, 1926.

(c) Biography and Criticism

Hicks, G. D. The Philosophy of James Ward. Mind, N.S. XXXIV, 1925.

Sorley, W. R. James Ward. Mind, N.S. XXXIV, 1925.

—— Ward's Philosophy of Religion. Monist, XXXVI, 1926.

—— James Ward. Proc. British Academy, XII, 1926.

Dowdall, H. C. The Application of Ward's Psychology to the Legal Problem of Corporate Entity. Monist, xxxvi, 1926.

Laird, J. A. James Ward's Account of the Ego. Monist, xxxvi, 1926.

Lamprecht, S. P. James Ward's Critique of Naturalism. Monist, xxxvi, 1926.

Leroux, E. James Ward's Doctrine of Experience. Monist, xxxvi, 1926.

Stout, G. F. Ward as a Psychologist. Monist, xxxvi, 1926.

Turner, J. E. The Ethical Implications of Ward's Philosophy. Monist, xxxvi, 1926.

Murray, A. H. The Philosophy of James Ward. Cambridge, 1937.

WILLIAM GEORGE WARD (1812–1882)

Essays on the Philosophy of Theism. Ed. Wilfrid Ward, 2 vols. 1884.

RICHARD WHATELY (1787–1863)

[See p. 681 above.]

WILLIAM WHEWELL (1794–1866)

The History of the Inductive Sciences. 3 vols. 1837; tr. German, 1839–42.

The Philosophy of the Inductive Sciences founded upon their History. 2 vols. 1840.

The Elements of Morality, including Polity. 1845.

Lectures on Systematic Morality. 1846.

[See also p. 938 below.]

S. V. K.

II. HISTORY, BIOGRAPHY AND ARCHAEOLOGY

The Early Nineteenth-Century Historians: Coxe, Hoare, Lingard, Hallam; Minor Writers, 1800–35—English History (General), English History (Local), Scottish and Irish History, British Imperial History, European History.

The Mid-Nineteenth Century Historians: Milman, Grote, Arnold, Finlay, Stanhope, Wright, Froude, Maine; Minor Writers, 1835–70—Ancient History, English History (General), English History (Special Aspects), English History (Local), Scottish and Irish History, British Imperial History, European History.

The Late Nineteenth-Century Historians: Freeman, Stubbs, Gardiner, Acton, Green, Lecky, Creighton, Maitland; Minor Writers, 1870–1900—Pre-History, Archaeology and Ancient History, English History (General), English History (Legal), English History (Ecclesiastical), English History (Naval), English History (Social and Economic), English History (Local), Scottish, Irish and Manx History, British Imperial History, European History.

[The following lists include as a rule only books, the more important pamphlets, and articles contributed to the less well-known co-operative works. Extensive contributions to DNB. and similar works are indicated by general notes at the end of each entry. When a satisfactory bibliography exists, details of works edited are usually omitted.

For articles in periodicals, of increasing importance in this period, reference must be made to various indexes of which a list is ptd in Bulletin of Inst. Hist. Research, xi, Feb. 1934. The more useful are:

Stead, W. T. *et al.* Review of Reviews, Index to the Periodicals of 1890–1902. 13 vols. 1891–1903.

English Historical Review. 1886–1905. [Quarterly select lists, under heading Contents of Periodicals.]

Gomme, G. L. Index to Archaeological Papers, 1665–1890. 1907.

Index of Archaeological Papers published in 1891 [etc.]. 1892–1914. [Continuation of Gomme.]

Terry, C. S. Catalogue of the Publications of Scottish Historical and Kindred Clubs and Societies, etc., 1780–1908. Glasgow, 1909. Supplement, 1908–27, by C. Matheson, Aberdeen, 1928.

Cross references have not been included to the histories of literature, philosophy, science, etc. which abound in this period and the more important of which will be found in their appropriate sections. Similarly the only biographers included are the primarily political biographers. A number of historical works of too specialized a character to be listed here will be found under The Literature of the Dominions, pp. 1045–98 below.]

I. THE EARLY NINETEENTH-CENTURY HISTORIANS: COXE, HOARE, LINGARD, HALLAM

WILLIAM COXE (1747–1828)

Sketches of the Natural, Civil, and Political State of Swisserland. 1779; tr. French, Paris, 1781.

Account of the Russian Discoveries between Asia and America. To which are added, The Conquest of Siberia, and the History of the Transactions between Russia and China. 1780 (*bis*); 1787; 1804 (enlarged); tr. German, Frankfort, 1783.

Account of the Prisons and Hospitals in Russia, Sweden, and Denmark. 1781.

Travels into Poland, Russia, Sweden, and Denmark. 3 vols. 1784–90; 5 vols. 1787–91 (3rd edn); 5 vols. 1792; 5 vols. 1802; 3 vols. 1803; 1809 (in J. Pinkerton, A General Collection of Voyages, vol. vi); tr. French, Geneva, 1786.

Travels in Switzerland. 3 vols. 1789; 2 vols. 1794 (3rd edn); 3 vols. 1801 ('with an historical sketch and notes on the late Revolution'); 3 vols. Basle, 1802; 1809 (in J. Pinkerton, A General Collection of Voyages, vol. v); tr. French, Paris, 1790.

A Letter to the Rev. Richard Price, upon his Discourse on the Love of our Country, delivered November 4, 1789. 1790.

Catalogue of the Manuscripts in the Possession of the Earl of Hardwicke. 1794.

Fables by John Gay, illustrated with Notes and the Life of the Author. 1796; 1800; 1810 (4th edn); 1814. [The Life alone, 2nd edn, Salisbury, 1797.]

A Letter on the Secret Tribunals of Westphalia, addressed to Elizabeth, Countess of Pembroke. Salisbury, 1796.

Memoirs of the Life and Administration of Sir Robert Walpole, Earl of Orford. 3 vols. 1798; 3 vols. 1800.

Anecdotes of George Frederick Handel, and John Christopher Smith. 1799 (anon.).

An Historical Tour in Monmouthshire; illustrated with Views. 2 pts, 1801; [ed. E. Davies, Brecon, 1904].

Memoirs of Horatio, Lord Walpole. Selected from his Correspondence and Papers, 1678 to 1757. 1802; 2 vols. 1808 (corrected and enlarged).

History of the House of Austria, from the Foundation of the Monarchy by Rhodolph of Hapsburgh, to the Death of Leopold the Second: 1218 to 1792. 2 vols. in 3, 1807; 3 vols. 1847–52 (3rd edn).

Literary Life and Select Works of Benjamin Stillingfleet. 2 vols. 1811. [Ed. by Coxe.]

Memoirs of the Kings of Spain of the House of Bourbon, 1700 to 1788. 3 vols. 1813; 5 vols. 1815. Tr. French, Paris, 1827; Spanish, Madrid, 1846–7.

Letter to John Benett on his Essay relative to the Commutation of Tythes. Salisbury, [1815] (bis).

Memoirs of John Duke of Marlborough; with his Original Correspondence. 3 vols. 1818–9; rev. J. Wade, 3 vols. 1847–8.

Private and Original Correspondence of Charles Talbot, Duke of Shrewsbury, illustrated with Narratives. 1821.

Sketches of the Lives of Correggio, and Parmegiano. 1823 (anon.).

Memoirs of The Administration of the Right Honourable Henry Pelham. 2 vols. 1829.

SIR RICHARD COLT HOARE (1758–1838)

A Description of the House and Gardens at Stourhead. Salisbury, 1800; Bath, 1818; 1840 (with Catalogue of the Hoare Library at Stourhead, by J. B. Nichols).

Itinerarium Cambriae seu Baldvini Cantuariensis Archiepiscopi per Walliam Legationis Descriptio. 1804. [Ed. by Hoare.]

The Itinerary of Archbishop Baldwin through Wales, by Giraldus de Barri; translated. 2 vols. 1806; ed. T. Wright, 1863. [2 portions issued separately as Introduction to the History of Cambria, from the First Invasion of Britain by the Romans to 1188, and Progress of Architecture from a Period nearly Coeval with the Conqueror, to the Sixteenth Century. 2 pts, [1806]; 2nd edn of pt 2, 1830.]

Journal of a Tour in Ireland, 1806. 1807.

A Catalogue of Books relating to the History and Topography of Italy, collected during the Years 1786, 1787, 1788, 1789, 1790. 1812.

The Ancient History of South [and North] Wiltshire. 2 vols. 1812–21.

A Tour through the Island of Elba. 1814.

Two Studies from Nicolas Poussin, from a Painting in the Possession of Sir R. C. Hoare. [1814.]

A Journal of the Shrievalty of Richard Hoare, Esquire, in the Years 1740–41. Bath, 1815. [Ed. by Hoare.]

A Catalogue of Books relating to the History and Topography of England, Wales, Scotland, Ireland. 1815.

Hints to Travellers in Italy. By R. C. H. 1815.

Recollections Abroad, during the Year 1790: Sicily and Malta. Bath, 1817.

Recollections Abroad, during the Years 1790, 1791. Bath, 1818. [Italy, the Tyrol, etc.]

Hints on the Topography of Wiltshire [with] Queries Submitted with a View to promote a General History of the County. 2 pts, Salisbury, [1818].

A Classical Tour through Italy and Sicily; tending to illustrate some Districts, which have not been described by Mr Eustace. 1819 (as vol. III of J. C. Eustace, A Tour through Italy, 1813); 2 vols. 1819.

Pedigrees and Memoirs of the Families of Hore, of Rishford, Hoare, of Walton, [etc.]. Bath, 1819.

Monasticon Wiltonense. Compiled chiefly from Bishop Tanner's Notitia Monastica. Shaftesbury, 1821.

Repertorium Wiltunense. Printed with a View to facilitate Inquiry into the Topography and Biography of Wiltshire. Bath, 1821.

The History of Modern Wiltshire. 14 pts, 1822–44, 43. [Mostly by Hoare.]

Hungerfordiana, or Memoirs of the Family of Hungerford. Shaftesbury, 1823.

Monastic Remains of the Religious Houses at Witham, Bruton and Stavordale, Com. Somerset. Frome, [1824].

Registrum Wiltunense, Saxonicum et Latinum. 1827. [Ed. by Hoare and others.]

A Short Treatise on the Antient Roman Town of Camulodunum, now Colchester. Shaftesbury, 1827.

Antiquitates Wiltunenses. In Aedibus apud Stourhead Asservatae. Shaftesbury, 1828.

Tumuli Wiltunenses; a Guide to the Barrows on the Plains of Stonehenge. Shaftesbury, 1829.

The Pitney Pavement, discovered by Samuel Hasell, 1828; and illustrated, with his notes, by Sir R. C. Hoare. Frome, 1831; 1832.

[For Hoare see J. B. Nichols, Catalogue of the Hoare Library at Stourhead, 1840, which includes Memoir partly written by himself, and chronological list of his works.]

JOHN LINGARD (1771–1851)

(a) *Writings*

The Antiquities of the Anglo-Saxon Church. 2 vols. Newcastle-on-Tyne, 1806, 1810; Philadelphia, 1841; 2 vols. 1845 (entirely recast, as The History and Antiquities of the Anglo-Saxon Church); 2 vols. 1858; tr. French, Paris, 1828.

Remarks on a Charge delivered to the Clergy of the Diocese of Durham, by Shute [Barrington], Bishop of Durham. 1807 (*bis*; anon:).

A General Vindication of The Remarks on the Charge of the Bishop of Durham. Newcastle-on-Tyne, 1808; Dublin, 1808 (slightly different title).

Remarks on a Late Pamphlet, entitled, The Grounds, on which the Church of England separated from the Church of Rome, reconsidered: By Shute, Bishop of Durham. 1809.

Documents to ascertain the Sentiments of British Catholics in Former Ages respecting the Power of the Popes. 1812.

Examination of Certain Opinions, advanced by Dr Burgess, Bishop of St David's, in Two Recent Publications entitled, Christ, not Peter, the Rock, and, Johannis Sulgeni Versus hexametri in Laudem Sulgeni Patris. Manchester, 1813 (anon.).

A Review of Certain Anti-Catholic Publications [charges of G. I. Huntingford and G. Tomline, and Lord Kenyon's Observations]. 1813.

Strictures on Dr Marsh's Comparative View of the Churches of England and Rome. 1815.

A Reply to the Observations of the Edinburgh Review, on the Anglo-Saxon Antiquities. [In The Pamphleteer, no. 14, vol. VII, 1816.]

Observations on the Laws and Ordinances, which exist in Foreign States, relative to the Religious Concerns of their Roman Catholic Subjects. 1817; 1851.

A History of England from the First Invasion by the Romans to the Accession of Henry VIII [vols. I–III; vol. VIII, to 1688]. 8 vols. 1819–30; 14 vols. 1823–30; 14 vols. 1825–30; 13 vols. 1837–9 (corrected and enlarged); 10 vols. 1849, etc.; tr. French [by the Baron de Roujoux, continued by] J. L. de Marlès, 14 vols. Paris, 1825–31; 17 vols. Paris, 1833–5 (rev. by Lingard). [See H. Phillpotts, Letters to Charles Butler, with Remarks on Certain Works of Dr Lingard, 1825.]

A Letter of Doctor Lingard to Mr Butler, in Reply to the Charge. [In C. Butler, Vindication of The Book of the Roman Catholic Church, 1826. See also J. Allen's reviews of the History in Edinburgh Rev. April 1825, June 1826; and H. J. Todd, A Vindication of Cranmer against some of the Allegations made by Dr Lingard, 1826 (2nd edn, first pbd as introduction to Cranmer's Defence of the True and Catholic Doctrine of the Sacrament, 1825):.]

A Vindication of Certain Passages in the Fourth and Fifth Volumes of the History of England. 1826 (3 edns); 1827 (*bis*); tr. French, Paris, 1827. [Postscript answers Todd and J. Allen's Reply to Dr Lingard's Vindication, 1827 (2nd edn). See also H. J. Todd, A Reply to Dr Lingard's Vindication, 1827; and C. Wordsworth, King Charles the First, the Author of Icôn Basilikè, in Reply to the Objections of Dr Lingard, 1828.]

The Charters, granted by Different Sovereigns, to the Burgesses of Preston. The English Translations by John Lingard. 2 pts, Preston, 1821.

Supplementum ad Breviarium et Missale Romanum. Adjectis Officiis Sanctorum Angliae. 1823 (anon.).

A Collection of Tracts, on Several Subjects connected with the Civil and Religious Principles of Catholics. 1826. [Reprints the above tracts relating to the Bishop of Durham's charge, and 4 others arising from the same controversy: The Examination of Dr Burgess, A Review of Anti-Catholic Publications, Strictures on Dr Marsh, Observations on the Laws and Ordinances, and Documents after the Reformation.]

A New Version of the Four Gospels; with Notes Critical and Explanatory. By a Catholic. 1836; 1846; 1851.

Catechetical Instructions on the Doctrines and Worship of the Catholic Church. 1840 (*bis*); 1844; tr. Spanish, Montevideo, n.d.

(b) *Biography*

Haile, M. and Bonney, E. Life and Letters of John Lingard. [1911.] [With full bibliography of Lingard's works.]

Fletcher, J. John Lingard, 1771–1851. Reprinted from the Dublin Review. Lingard Soc. 1925.

Lechmere, J. A Great Catholic Historian. John, Cardinal Lingard, 1771–1851. Ecclesiastical Rev. xciv, 1936.

HENRY HALLAM (1777–1859)

(a) Writings

View of the State of Europe during The Middle Ages. 2 vols. 1818; 3 vols. 1819; 2 vols. Paris, 1835; 3 vols. 1837 (7th edn); 2 vols. Paris, 1840; 2 vols. 1846; 3 vols. 1853; 3 vols. 1855, etc. Tr. French, 1820–2; Italian, Florence, 1874. [Supplemental Notes, 1848, incorporated in 1853 and later edns.]

The Constitutional History of England from the Accession of Henry VII to the Death of George II. 2 vols. 1827; 3 vols. 1829; 3 vols. 1832; 2 vols. 1846 (5th edn); 3 vols. 1854 (7th edn); 3 vols. 1855, etc. Tr. German, Leipzig, 1828–9; French, Paris, 1832.

Survey of the Principal Repositories of the Public Records. Extracted from the Proceedings of the Commissioners on the Public Records. 1833. [Report by Sir R. H. Inglis and Hallam.]

Introduction to the Literature of Europe, in the Fifteenth, Sixteenth, and Seventeenth Centuries. 4 vols. 1837–9; 4 vols. Paris, 1839; 3 vols. 1843; 3 vols. 1854 (4th edn); 4 vols. 1855; tr. French, Paris, 1839–40.

(b) Criticism

Southey, R. Quarterly Rev. xxx, 1818. [Review of Middle Ages.]

Macaulay, T. B., Baron. Edinburgh Rev. xlviii, 1828. [Review of Constitutional History.]

Wordsworth, C. King Charles the First, the Author of Icôn Basilikè, in Reply to Mr Hallam. 1828.

Hare, J. C. Reply to Mr Hallam's Remarks on Luther. [In Vindication of Luther against His Recent English Assailants, 1855 (2nd edn).]

Mignet, F. A. M. Hallam. [In Éloges Historiques, Paris, 1864.]

II. MINOR WRITERS, 1800–1835

A. ENGLISH HISTORY (GENERAL)

JOHN BRUCE (1745–1826)

Historical View of Plans, for the Government of British India. 1793 (anon.).

Review of the Events and Treaties which established the Balance of Power in Europe, and the Balance of Trade in Favor of Great Britain. 1796 (anon.).

Report on the Arrangements made, for the Internal Defence of these Kingdoms [at the time of the Spanish Armada]. [1798] (priv. ptd for government use).

Report on the Arrangements adopted, in Former Periods, when France threatened Invasions of Britain or Ireland. [1798] (priv. ptd for government use).

Report on the Events and Circumstances, which produced the Union of England and Scotland. [1799] (priv. ptd for government use).

Annals of the East-India Company, from 1600, to the Union of the London and English East-India Companies, 1707–8. 3 vols. 1810.

SIR GEORGE PRETYMAN TOMLINE (1750–1827)

Memoirs of the Life of William Pitt. 2 vols. 1821; 3 vols. 1822 (4th edn). [Ch. xxvii from unpublished 4th vol., with introduction by the Earl of Rosebery, Monthly Rev. Aug. 1903; rptd 1903 (as Bishop Tomline's Estimate of Pitt); with chs. xxiii and xxiv, priv. ptd 1903 (as Tomline's Life of Pitt).]

SAMUEL HEYWOOD (1753–1828)

A Vindication of Mr Fox's History of the Early Part of the Reign of James the Second. 1811.

A Dissertation upon the Distinctions in Society, and Ranks of the People, under the Anglo-Saxon Governments. 1818.

THOMAS CLARKSON (1760–1846)

A Portraiture of Quakerism, as taken from a View of the Moral Education, Discipline, Peculiar Customs, Religious Principles, Political and Civil Œconomy, and Character, of the Society of Friends. 3 vols. 1806; 3 vols. New York, 1806; 3 vols. 1807 (bis); tr. French, Geneva, 1820.

The History of the Abolition of the African Slave-Trade. 2 vols. 1808; 1839.

Memoirs of the Private and Public Life of William Penn. 2 vols. 1813; 2 vols. Philadelphia, 1813; ed. W. E. Forster, 1849.

[Clarkson also wrote numerous treatises on slavery and the slave-trade. For biography see E. L. Griggs, Thomas Clarkson, the Friend of Slaves, 1936, which includes full bibliography of Clarkson's writings.]

SIR JAMES MACKINTOSH (1765–1832)

Vindiciae Gallicae. Dublin, 1791 (3 edns); 1837.

The History of England. Vols. i–iii, 1830–[2?] (in D. Lardner's Cabinet Cyclopaedia); rev. R. J. Mackintosh, 2 vols. 1853.

Dissertation on the Progress of Ethical Philosophy, chiefly during the Seventeenth and Eighteenth Centuries. 1830 (Supplement to Encyclopaedia Britannica, and priv. rptd, Edinburgh); ed. W. Whewell, Edinburgh, 1836; Edinburgh, 1872.

Life of Sir Thomas More. 1831. [Part of D. Lardner's Cabinet Cyclopaedia.]

History of the Revolution in England in 1688. Completed to the Settlement of the Crown, by the Editor [W. Wallace] with a Notice of the Life, Writings and Speeches of Mackintosh. 1834; 1835 (as A View of the Reign of James II).

Tracts and Speeches. Edinburgh, 1840 (priv. ptd).

Miscellaneous Works. 3 vols. 1846; Philadelphia, 1848; 1851; 3 vols. 1854. [Principal contents, beside the above (except The History of England and Tracts and Speeches): On the Philosophical Genius of Lord Bacon and Mr Locke; A Discourse on the Law of Nature and of Nations; A Refutation of the Claim on behalf of King Charles I to the Authorship of the ΕΙΚΩΝ ΒΑΣΙΛΙΚΗ; Memoir of the Affairs of Holland, 1667–1686.]

[For criticism and biography see T. B. Macaulay's review of History of the Revolution, Edinburgh Rev. LXI, 1835 and R. J. Mackintosh, Memoirs of Sir James Mackintosh, 2 vols. 1835.]

ISAAC D'ISRAELI (1766–1848)
[See p. 667 above.]

SHARON TURNER (1768–1847)

A Vindication of the Genuineness of the Ancient British Poems of Aneurin, Taliesin, etc. 1803.

The History of England from the Earliest Period to the Death of Elizabeth. 12 vols. 1839. [Comprises: (1) The History of the Anglo-Saxons, to the Norman Conquest. 4 vols. 1799–1805; 2 vols. 1807; 3 vols. 1820; 3 vols. 1823; 3 vols. 1828; 3 vols. 1836 (vols. I–III of The History of England from the Earliest Period); Paris, 1840; Philadelphia, 1841; 3 vols. 1852. (2) The History of England during the Middle Ages. 3 vols. 1814–23; 5 vols. 1825; 5 vols. 1830 (vols. IV–VIII of The History of England from the Earliest Period); 4 vols. 1853 (5th edn). (3) The Modern History of England. (The History of the Reign of Henry the Eighth: comprising the Political History of the Commencement of the English Reformation; The History of the Reigns of Edward the Sixth, Mary, and Elizabeth). 2 pts, 1826–9; 4 vols. 1828–35 (3rd edn; vols. IX–

XII of The History of England from the Earliest Period).]

The Sacred History of the World, as displayed in the Creation and Subsequent Events to the Deluge. Attempted to be philosophically considered, in a Series of Letters to a Son. 3 vols. 1832–7; 1833 (4th edn); 3 vols. New York, 1842, 1846, 1844; ed. S. Turner, 3 vols. 1848 (8th edn).

SIR WALTER SCOTT (1771–1832)
[See p. 369 above.]

WILLIAM JAMES (d. 1827)

An Inquiry into the Merits of the Principal Naval Actions, between Great-Britain and the United States. Halifax, Nova Scotia, 1816; 1817 (enlarged, as A Full and Correct Account of the Chief Naval Occurrences of the Late War).

A Full and Correct Account of the Military Occurrences of the Late War between Great Britain and the United States. 2 vols. 1818.

Warden Refuted; being a Defence of the British Navy against the Misrepresentations of a Work recently published. 1819.

The Naval History of Great Britain, 1793–1820. 5 vols. 1822–4; 6 vols. 1826; 6 vols. 1837 (with addns by F. Chamier); 1886. [Index by C. G. Toogood, Navy Records Soc. 1895.]

SIR HENRY ELLIS (1777–1869)

[Of the subjoined titles only the first, the two books on the British Museum, and that on Caedmon, are original works; the rest are edited by Ellis.]

The History and Antiquities of the Parish of Saint Leonard Shoreditch, and Liberty of Norton Folgate, London. 1798.

Hall's Chronicle. 1809.

The New Chronicles of England and France. By R. Fabyan. 1811.

The Secrets of Angling; By J. D[ennys]. Augmented by W. Lauson. 1811.

The Chronicle of John Hardyng. 1812.

Observations on Popular Antiquities. By John Brand. 2 vols. 1813; 3 vols. 1841; 3 vols. 1849.

The Complete Angler. By Izaak Walton [and] C. Cotton. With the Lives of the Authors: and Notes, By Sir John Hawkins, and the Present Editor [Henry Ellis]. 1815.

Libri Censualis, vocati Domesday-Book, Additamenta. 1816.

Libri Censualis, vocati Domesday-Book, Indices. Accessit Dissertatio Generalis de Ratione huiusce Libri. 1816; 2 vols. 1833 (rev. as A General Introduction to Domesday Book).

Monasticon Anglicanum. By W. Dugdale. A New Edition, by J. Caley, Henry Ellis, and B. Bandinel. 6 vols. in 8, 1817–33; 6 vols. in 8, 1846.

The History of Saint Paul's Cathedral, in London. By W. Dugdale. With a Continuation and Additions by Henry Ellis. 1818.

Original Letters Illustrative of English History. 3 vols. 1824. Ser. 2, 4 vols. 1827; Ser. 3, 4 vols. 1846.

The Library of Entertaining Knowledge. The British Museum. Elgin and Phigaleian Marbles. 2 vols. 1833 (anon.).

Account of Caedmon's Metrical Paraphrase, of Scripture History, an Illuminated Manuscript of the Tenth Century. 1833.

The Library of Entertaining Knowledge. The British Museum. The Townley Gallery. 2 vols. 1836 (anon.).

Registrum vulgariter nuncupatum 'The Record of Caernarvon.' 1838.

Three Collections of English Poetry, of the Latter Part of the Sixteenth Century. Roxburghe Club, 1844.

Blair's Chronological and Historical Tables. 1844; 1851.

Chronica Johannis de Oxenedes. 1859. (Rerum Britannicarum Medii Ævi Scriptores.)

[Ellis also edited 7 vols. for the Camden Soc. and contributed to the first of its Miscellanies, between 1840 and 1851.]

JOHN COLIN DUNLOP (d. 1842)

[See p. 668 above.]

LUCY AIKIN (1781–1864)

Epistles on Women, exemplifying their Character and Condition in Various Ages and Nations. With Miscellaneous Poems. 1810.

Lorimer. A Tale. 1814. [A novel.]

Memoirs of the Court of Queen Elizabeth. 2 vols. 1818; 1869 (rev.).

Memoirs of the Court of King James the First. 2 vols. 1822 (bis).

Memoir of John Aikin, M.D. With a Selection of his Miscellaneous Pieces. 2 vols. 1823.

Memoirs of the Court of King Charles the First. 2 vols. 1833.

The Life of Joseph Addison. 2 vols. 1843.

Memoirs, Miscellanies and Letters of the Late Lucy Aikin. Ed. P. H. le Breton, 1864. [Includes many letters to and from W. E. Channing.]

[Lucy Aikin contributed the memoir of Mrs Barbauld in the latter's Works, 1825, as well as editing her Legacy for Young Ladies, 1826. She also provided the supplement to John Aikin's Select Works of the British Poets, 1845, and the Memoir of Elizabeth Ogilvy Benger in the latter's Memoirs of the Life of Anne Boleyn, 1827 (3rd edn), and pbd trns and school-books for small children.]

B. ENGLISH HISTORY (LOCAL)

OWEN MANNING (1721–1801) AND WILLIAM BRAY (1736–1832)

The History and Antiquities of the County of Surrey. 3 vols. 1804–14. [The continuation is by Bray.]

THOMAS DUNHAM WHITAKER (1759–1821)

An History of the Original Parish of Whalley, and Honor of Clitheroe, in the Counties of Lancaster and York. Blackburn, 1801; 1806 (with addns); 1818; ed. J. G. Nichols and P. A. Lyons, 2 vols. 1872–6.

The History and Antiquities of the Deanery of Craven, in the County of York. 1805; 1812 (enlarged); ed. A. W. Morant, 1878.

De Motu per Britanniam Civico annis MDCCXLV et MDCCXLVI. 1809.

The Life and Original Correspondence of Sir George Radcliffe, Friend of Strafford. 1810.

Loidis and Elmete, or an Attempt to illustrate the Lower Portions of Aredale and Wharfdale. 1816. [Appendix, 1821?]

Ducatus Leodiensis, or the Topography of Leedes, and Parts Adjacent. By Ralph Thoresby. Leeds, 1816 (2nd edn). [This edn has notes and addns by Whitaker.]

An History of Richmondshire, in the North Riding. 2 vols. 1823.

DANIEL LYSONS (1762–1834)

The Environs of London. 4 vols. 1792–6. [Supplement, 1811.]

An Historical Account of those Parishes in the County of Middlesex, which are not described in the Environs of London. 1800. [The complete work was issued in 4 vols. 1811.]

Views of Hampton-Court Palace. [1800.] [Letterpress.]

Magna Britannia; being a Concise Topographical Account of the Several Counties of Great Britain. 6 vols. in 10, 1806–22. [With Samuel Lysons; unfinished; addns and corrections, 1813.]

A Sketch of the Life and Character of Charles Brandon Trye. Gloucester, 1812; Oxford, 1848.

History of the Origin and Progress of the Meeting of the Three Choirs of Gloucester, Worcester, and Hereford. Gloucester, 1812. [Continued by J. Amott, [1865]; continued by C. L. Williams and H. G. Chance, Gloucester, 1895.]

A View of the Revenues of the Parochial Clergy of this Kingdom, from the Earliest Times. Gloucester, 1824.

SAMUEL LYSONS (1763–1819)

An Account of Roman Antiquities discovered at Woodchester. 2 pts, 1797.

Reliquiae Britannico-Romanae. Containing Figures of Roman Antiquities discovered in England. 2 vols. 1801–17; 3 vols. 1813–7. [The following pts appeared separately: Figures of Mosaic Pavements at Horkstow, 1801; Remains of Two Temples and other Antiquities at Bath, 1802; Figures of Mosaic Pavements near Frampton, 1808.]

A Collection of Gloucestershire Antiquities. 1803.

An Account of a Roman Villa at Bignor, Sussex. 1815; 1885.

[See also under Daniel Lysons, above.]

JOHN DUNCUMB (1765–1839)

Collections towards the History and Antiquities of the County of Hereford. Vol. I, Hereford, 1804; Vol. II, pt i, Hereford, 1812; some further pp. of Vol. II, 1837; continued by W. H. Cooke, Vol. II, pt 2, 1866; Vol. III, 1882; [Vol. IV], 1892 (Hundred of Grimsthorp); by M. G. Watkins, Hereford, 1897 (Hundred of Huntington); by J. H. Matthews, 2 pts, Hereford, 1912–3 (Hundred of Wormelow, Upper Division); 2 pts, Hereford, 1913–5 (Hundred of Wormelow, Lower Division).

JOHN THOMAS SMITH (1766–1833)

Remarks on Rural Scenery. 1797.

Antiquities of Westminster. 1807–[9].

Ancient Topography of London; containing some Account of Places Unknown, or Overlooked. 1815.

Vagabondiana, or Anecdotes of Mendicant Wanderers through the Streets of London. 1817; Edinburgh, 1883 (as Mendicant Wanderers, etc.).

Nollekens and his Times: comprehending Memoirs of Several Artists. 2 vols. 1828; ed. Sir E. Gosse, 1894; ed. W. Whitten, 2 vols. 1920; abridged, 1929 (World's Classics).

The Cries of London. With a Memoir of the Author. 1839.

A Book for a Rainy Day, or Recollections of the Events of the Last Sixty-Six Years. 1845; 1861 (3rd edn); ed. W. Whitten, 1905.

An Antiquarian Ramble in the Streets of London. Ed. C. Mackay, 2 vols. 1846; 1849 (as The Streets of London, etc.); 1861.

JAMES PELLER MALCOLM (1767–1815)

Londinium Redivivum, or An Antient History and Modern Description of London. 4 vols. 1802–7.

Letters between the Rev. James Granger, and Many of the most Eminent Literary Men. 1805. [Ed. by Malcolm.]

First Impressions, or Sketches from Art and Nature. 1807; 1814 (as Excursions in the Counties of Kent, Gloucester, Hereford, Monmouth, and Somerset, in 1802, 1803, and 1805).

Anecdotes of the Manners and Customs of London during the Eighteenth Century. 1808; 1810.

Anecdotes of the Manners and Customs of London from the Roman Invasion to 1700. 1811; 3 vols. 1811.

Miscellaneous Anecdotes Illustrative of the Manners and History of Europe during the Reigns of Charles II, James II, William III and Q. Anne. 1811.

An Historical Sketch of the Art of Caricaturing. 1813.

Lives of Topographers and Antiquaries who have written concerning the Antiquities of England. 1815.

THOMAS DUDLEY FOSBROKE (1770–1842)

British Monachism. 2 vols. 1802; 1817; 1843.

Abstracts of Records and Manuscripts respecting the County of Gloucester; formed into A History. 2 vols. Gloucester, 1807.

The Wye Tour, or Gilpin on the Wye, with Additions. Ross, 1818; 1822; Ross, 1826; Ross, 1834; Ross, 1841.

An Original History of the City of Gloucester, including the Papers of Ralph Bigland. 1819.

Berkeley Manuscripts. Abstracts and Extracts of Smyth's Lives of the Berkeleys. To which are annexed A History of the Castle and Parish of Berkeley, etc. 1821.

Companion to the Wye Tour. Ariconensia, or Archaeological Sketches of Ross. Ross, 1821; Ross, [1822?].

Encyclopaedia of Antiquities, and Elements of Archaeology. 2 vols. 1825; 2 vols. 1840.

The Tourist's Grammar, or Rules relating to Scenery and Antiquities. 1826.

A Picturesque and Topographical Account of Cheltenham. Cheltenham, 1826.

Foreign Topography, or An Encyclopedick Account of Remains in Africa, Asia, and Europe. 1828.

A Treatise on the Arts, Manufactures, Manners, and Institutions of the Greeks and Romans. 2 vols. 1833–5 (in D. Lardner, Cabinet Cyclopaedia).

Letters. Ed. Roland Austin, Trans. Bristol and Gloucestershire Archaeological Soc. 1914. vol. XXXVII, [1914?].

JOHN BRITTON (1771–1857)

Sheridan and Kotzebue. The Enterprising Adventures of Pizarro, preceded by a Sketch of the Voyages of Columbus and Cortez: with Biographical Sketches of Sheridan and Kotzebue. 1799.

The Beauties of Wiltshire. 3 vols. 1801–25.

An Historical Account of Corsham House, in Wiltshire. 1806.

The Architectural Antiquities of Great Britain. 4 vols. 1807–14.

A Chronological History and Graphic Illustrations of Christian Architecture in England. 1827. [Forms vol. v of the Architectural Antiquities.]

An Historical and Architectural Essay relating to Redcliffe Church, Bristol. 1813.

The Rights of Literature; or an Inquiry into the Claim of Certain Public Libraries for Eleven Copies of Every New Publication. 1814.

Remarks on the Life and Writings of William Shakspere. 1814 (priv.ptd); 1818 (priv.ptd).

Cathedral Antiquities of England. 15 vols. 1814–35.

Norwich Cathedral Vade-Mecum. Antiquarian and Architectural Memoranda. 1817.

Lancashire, or Original Delineations, Topographical, Historical, and Descriptive. 1818.

Graphical and Literary Illustrations of Fonthill Abbey, Wiltshire. 1823.

A Brief Memoir of the Life and Writings of John Britton. 1825. [Reprint of part of preface of Vol. III of Beauties of Wiltshire.]

Illustrations of the Public Buildings of London. 2 vols. 1825–8. [With A. Pugin.]

The Union of Architecture, Sculpture, and Painting; exemplified by Illustrations, with Descriptive Accounts of the House and Galleries of John Soane. 1827.

Historical and Descriptive Essays accompanying Specimens of the Architectural Antiquities of Normandy. Edited by John Britton. The Subjects drawn by A. Pugin. 1828; ed. R. P. Spiers, 1874 (as Specimens of the Architecture of Normandy).

Modern Athens! Displayed in a Series of Views, or Edinburgh in the Nineteenth Century. From Drawings, by T. H. Shepherd. 1829.

Bath and Bristol, with the Counties of Somerset and Gloucester. Displayed in A Series of Views. From drawings by T. H. Shepherd, with Historical and Descriptive Illustrations by John Britton. 1829.

Picturesque Antiquities of the English Cities. 1830.

Descriptive Sketches of Tunbridge Wells and the Calverley Estate. 1832.

Lecture on the Road-Ways of England, pointing out the Advantageous Situation of Bristol for the Commerce of the West; With Remarks on a Rail-Road Between that Port and London. Read before the Literary and Philosophical Society of Bristol, 1833. Bristol, [1833?].

Brief Memoir of Sir John Soane. 1834.

The History and Description of Cassiobury Park, Hertfordshire. 1837.

A Dictionary of the Architecture and Archaeology of the Middle Ages. 1838.

Drawings of the London and Birmingham Railway, by John C. Bourne, with an Historical and Descriptive Account, by John Britton. 1839.

Graphic Illustrations, with Historical and Descriptive Accounts, of Toddington, Gloucestershire. 1840.

Architectural Illustrations of Windsor Castle, by M. Gandy and B. Baud, with a Concise Historical and Architectural Account by John Britton. 1842.

The History of the Parish of Grittleton, in Wilts. By J. E. Jackson. With an Introductory Essay on Topographical Literature; National and Local Records, [etc.]. By John Britton. Wilts. Topographical Soc. 1843.

Memoir of John Aubrey. Wilts. Topographical Soc. 1845.

The Natural History of Wiltshire; by John Aubrey. Edited by John Britton. Wilts. Topographical Soc. 1847.

Memoirs of the Life, Writings, and Character, of Henry Hatcher, Author of 'The History of Salisbury.' 1847.

The Authorship of the Letters of Junius elucidated. 1848.

The Auto-Biography of John Britton. In Three Parts. Pt 1, 1850; Pt 2, A Descriptive Account of the Literary Works of John Britton, by T. E. Jones, 1849; Pt 3, Appendix (containing a number of short articles by Britton and a chronological list of his writings), 1850.

A Brief Memoir of E. W. Brayley. GM. Dec. 1854; 1855.

JOHN BRITTON and EDWARD WEDLAKE BRAYLEY

Beauties of England and Wales, or Delineations Topographical, Historical, and Descriptive of Each County. 18 vols. in 25, 1801–15. [Vols. I–VI by Britton and Brayley jointly, 1801–1809; vols. VII, VIII, X, pts 1 and 2, 1808–14, by Brayley; vols. IX and XV, pt 1, and parts of vols. XI and XV, pt 2, 1807–14, by Britton; the rest by other hands.]

Memoirs of the Tower of London. 1830.

Devonshire and Cornwall Illustrated. With Historical and Topographical Descriptions. 1832.

The History of the Ancient Palace and Late Houses of Parliament at Westminster. 1836.

EDWARD WEDLAKE BRAYLEY (1773–1854)

Syr Reginalde, or The Black Tower. A Romance of the Twelfth Century. With Tales and Other Poems. 1803. [With W. Herbert.]

Cowper. Illustrated by a Series of Views. With Copious Descriptions, and a Brief Sketch of the Poet's Life. 1803 (anon.); 1810.

The Works of the late Edward Dayes. With Illustrative Notes. 1805; 1825 (the topographical part as A Picturesque Tour through Yorkshire and Derbyshire).

Views in Suffolk, Norfolk, and Northamptonshire; illustrative of the Works of Robert Bloomfield. 1806 (*bis*).

A Concise Account, Historical and Descriptive, of Lambeth Palace. 1806. [With W. Herbert.]

Delineations, Historical and Topographical, of the Isle of Thanet and the Cinque Ports. 2 vols. 1817–8.

The History and Antiquities of the Abbey Church of Westminster. 2 vols. 1818–23.

A Series of Views in Islington and Pentonville. By A. Pugin, with a Description of Each by E. W. Brayley. 1819.

London and its Environs, or the General Ambulator, and Pocket Companion for the Tour of the Metropolis. 1820 (12th edn). [Ed. by Brayley.]

Topographical Sketches of Brighthelmston and its Neighbourhood. 1825.

An Enquiry into the Genuineness of Prynne's 'Defence of Stage Plays,' &c., together with a Reprint of the Tracts, and of Prynne's 'Vindication.' 1825.

The History and Antiquities of the Cathedral Church of Exeter. [In J. Britton's Cathedral Antiquities, 1826; mainly by Brayley.]

Historical and Descriptive Accounts of the Theatres of London. 1826.

A Catalogue of the Library of the Russell Institution. 1826; 1849.

Londiniana, or Reminiscences of the British Metropolis. 4 vols. 1829.

Outlines of the Geology, Physical Geography and Natural History of Devonshire. [T. Moore's History of Devonshire, bk III, vol. I, 1829.]

The Graphic and Historical Illustrator. An Original Miscellany. [1832]–4. [A periodical, edited by Brayley.]

The Antiquities of the Priory of Christ-Church, Hants. 1834; rev. J. Britton, 1841. [Text by Brayley; plates by B. Ferrey.]

A Journal of the Plague Year. By Daniel De-Foe. Revised by E. W. Brayley. 1835; [1872]; 1882.

Illustrations of Her Majesty's Palace at Brighton, formerly the Pavilion. To which is prefixed A History of the Palace. 1838.

A Topographical History of Surrey. The Geological Section by G. Mantell. 5 vols. Dorking, 1841–[8]; ed. E. Walford, 4 vols. [1878–81].

[See also John Britton and E. W. Brayley, above.]

ROBERT CLUTTERBUCK (1772–1831)

The History and Antiquities of the County of Hertford. 3 vols. 1815–27.

Account of the Benefactions to the Parish of Watford, in the County of Hertford. Watford, 1828.

EDWARD BAINES (1774–1848)

History of the Wars of the French Revolution from 1792, to 1815; comprehending the Civil History of Great Britain and France. 2 vols. 1817; 4 vols. Leeds, 1823 (converted into History of the Reign of George III); 4 vols. Philadelphia, 1824 (as History of the Wars of the French Revolution); 2 vols. New York, 1852.

History, Directory and Gazetteer of the County of York. 2 vols. Leeds, 1822–3.

History, Directory, and Gazetteer of the County Palatine of Lancaster. 2 vols. Liverpool, 1824–5.

History of the County Palatine And Duchy of Lancaster. 4 vols. 1836; ed. J. Harland, 2 vols. 1868–70; ed. J Croston, 5 vols. Manchester, 1888–93.

ROBERT SURTEES (1779–1834)

The History and Antiquities of the County Palatine of Durham. 4 vols. 1816–40 (vol. IV ed. J. Raine); partly rptd, 3 vols. Sunderland, 1908–10.

[For biography and criticism see A Centenary Appreciation by C. E. Whiting, in Archaeologia Aeliana, XII, 1935.]

GEORGE BAKER (1781–1851)

The History and Antiquities of the County of Northampton. 2 vols. 1822–41. [Index Locorum, 1867, 1876.]

JOSEPH HUNTER (1783–1861)

[See p. 1024 below.]

THOMAS ALLEN (1803–1833)

The History and Antiquities of the Parish of Lambeth, and the Archiepiscopal Palace. 1827.

The History and Antiquities of London, Westminster, Southwark and Parts Adjacent. 4 vols. 1827–8.

A New and Complete History of the County of York. 3 vols. 1828–31.

History of the Counties of Surrey and Sussex.
2 vols. 1829–30.
The History of the County of Lincoln. Leeds,
1830.

C. SCOTTISH AND IRISH HISTORY

SAMUEL BURDY (1760?–1820)

The Life of the Late Rev. Philip Skelton.
Dublin, 1792; 2 vols. 1816 (in The Lives of
Pocock, Pearce, etc); 1824 (prefixed to R.
Lynam's edn of Skelton's Works; corrupt);
rptd N. Moore, Oxford, 1914.
The History of Ireland, to the Union. Edin-
burgh, 1817.

MALCOLM LAING (1762–1818)

The History of Scotland, from the Union of
the Crowns to the Union of the Kingdoms.
2 vols. 1800; 4 vols. 1804.

GEORGE COOK (1772–1845)

History of the Reformation in Scotland. 3 vols.
1811; 3 vols. Edinburgh, 1819.
The History of the Church of Scotland, from
the Reformation to the Revolution. 3 vols.
1815.
The Life of the Late George Hill, D.D. 1820.
General and Historical View of Christianity.
3 vols. Edinburgh, 1822.

THOMAS M'CRIE (1772–1835)

The Life of John Knox: containing Illustra-
tions of the History of the Reformation in
Scotland. Edinburgh, 1812; 2 vols. Edin-
burgh, 1813; 2 vols. Edinburgh, 1818 (4th
edn); 2 vols. Edinburgh, 1831; Edinburgh,
1840, rptd 1905 (with preface and memoir
of M'Crie by A. Crichton); tr. German,
Göttingen, 1817.
The Life of Andrew Melville: containing
Illustrations of the Ecclesiastical and
Literary History of Scotland. 2 vols.
Edinburgh, 1819; 2 vols. Edinburgh, 1824.
Memoirs of Mr William Veitch, and George
Brysson, written by themselves, with
Other Narratives Illustrative of the History
of Scotland from the Restoration to the
Revolution. Edinburgh, 1825.
History of the Progress and Suppression of the
Reformation in Italy. Edinburgh, 1827;
Edinburgh, 1833 (enlarged). Tr. French,
Paris, 1831; Italian, Paris, 1835.
History of the Progress and Suppression of the
Reformation in Spain. Edinburgh, 1829.
Miscellaneous Writings, edited by his Son.
Edinburgh, 1841. [Contains lives of
Alexander Henderson, Patrick Hamilton,
Francis Lambert of Avignon, and Dr
Andrew Rivet, Memoir of Mr John Murray,

The Taborites, reviews of Milne on Pres-
bytery and Episcopacy, Simeon on the
Liturgy, Sismondi's Considerations on
Geneva, Tales of My Landlord, Orme's Life
of Owen, and Turner's Life and Times, and
3 controversial pamphlets.]
Life of Alexander Henderson. Edinburgh,
1846 (in Lives of Alexander Henderson and
James Guthrie).
Works. Edited by his Son, Thomas M'Crie.
4 vols. Edinburgh, 1855–7.
The Early Years of John Calvin. A Fragment.
Ed. W. Ferguson, Edinburgh, 1880.
[For biography see T. M'Crie, junior, Life
of Thomas M'Crie, Edinburgh, 1840.]

PATRICK FRASER TYTLER (1791–1849)

Life of James Crichton of Cluny, the Ad-
mirable Crichton. Edinburgh, 1819, 1823.
An Account of the Life and Writings of Sir
Thomas Craig. Edinburgh, 1823.
The Life of John Wickliff. Edinburgh,
1826.
History of Scotland. 9 vols. (and Index),
1828–43; 8 vols. Edinburgh, 1845–50 (3rd
edn); 4 vols. Edinburgh, 1864 (8th edn);
4 vols. 1873–7.
Lives of Scottish Worthies. 3 vols. 1831–3.
Historical View of the Progress of Discovery
on the More Northern Coasts of America.
Edinburgh, 1832; New York, 1846.
Life of Sir Walter Raleigh. Edinburgh, 1833;
[Philadelphia, 1833].
Life of King Henry the Eighth. Edinburgh,
1837.
England under the Reigns of Edward VI and
Mary. 2 vols. 1839.
Scotland. [In Encyclopaedia Britannica,
1839 (7th edn), and several later edns.]

JAMES MAIDMENT (1795?–1879)

[See p. 1026 below.]

D. BRITISH IMPERIAL HISTORY

SIR JOHN MALCOLM (1769–1833)

Sketch of the Political History of India, from
1784. 1811.
Sketch of the Sikhs. 1812. [First pbd in
Asiatick Researches, or Transactions of the
Society in Bengal for Enquiring into the
History [etc.] of Asia, vol. XI, Calcutta,
1810.]
The History of Persia, from the most Early
Period. 2 vols. 1815; 2 vols. 1829 (rev.); ed.
M. H. Court, Lahore, 1888 (adapted to the
Persian trn of Mirza Hairat).
A Memoir of Central India including Malwa.
2 vols. 1823.

The Political History of India, 1784 to 1823. 2 vols. 1826. [Incorporates chs. i–v of the Sketch.]

Sketches of Persia, from the Journals of a Traveller in the East. 2 vols. 1827; 1828; 1845; 1888.

The Government of India. 1833.

The Life of Robert, Lord Clive. 3 vols. 1836.

JAMES MILL (1773–1836)

[See p. 871 above.]

JAMES GRANT DUFF (1789–1858)

A History of the Mahrattas. 3 vols. 1826; 1873 (3rd edn); [ed. B. A. Gupta], 3 vols. Calcutta, 1912; 3 vols. 1918; 2 vols. 1921 (rev.).

Private Correspondence with Maharaja Prata-pasimha of Satara. Ed. D. B. Diskalkar, Journ. of Indian History, xv, 1937.

E. EUROPEAN HISTORY

WILLIAM ROSCOE (1753–1831)

(a) Writings

An Ode on the Institution of a Society in Liverpool for the Encouragement of De-signing. Liverpool, 1774.

Mount Pleasant, a Descriptive Poem. Liver-pool, 1777.

The Wrongs of Africa, a Poem. 2 pts, 1787–8.

A General View of the African Slave-Trade. 1788.

An Ode to the People of France. Liverpool, 1789.

The Life of Lorenzo de' Medici. 2 vols. Liver-pool, 1795; 2 vols. 1796; 4 vols. Basle, 1799; 3 vols. 1800; 3 vols. 1806; 2 vols. 1825; 3 vols. Heidelberg, 1825; ed. [W. Hazlitt], 1846; rev. T. Roscoe, 1847; rev. T. Roscoe, [1851]. Tr. German, Berlin, 1797; French, Paris, 1799; Italian, Pisa, 1799; Greek, Athens, 1858.

The Nurse, a Poem. Translated from the Italian of Luigi Tansillo. Liverpool, 1798, 1800, 1804.

The Life and Pontificate of Leo the Tenth. 4 vols. Liverpool, 1805; 6 vols. 1806; 4 vols. 1827; 4 vols. Heidelberg, 1828; 2 vols. 1846; rev. T. Roscoe, 2 vols. 1846. Tr. French, Paris, [1808]; German, Vienna, 1818; Italian, Milan, 1816–7.

The Butterfly's Ball, and the Grasshopper's Feast. GM. Nov. 1806 (anon.); 1807; 1808; [1810?]; [1830?]; [1854?]; 1855; 1857; ed. C. Welch, 1883.

On the Origin and Vicissitudes of Literature, Science and Art. Liverpool, 1817 (bis); 1818 (The Pamphleteer, vol. xi).

Observations on Penal Jurisprudence. 3 pts, 1819–25.

Memoir of Richard Roberts Jones. 1822 (anon.); Llanidloes, [1855?].

Illustrations, Historical and Critical, of the Life of Lorenzo de' Medici. 1822; 1826; tr. Italian, Florence, 1823.

The Works of Alexander Pope. 10 vols. 1824. [Ed. by Roscoe.]

The Poetical Works. Liverpool, [1853]; 1857; 1891.

(b) Biography

Roscoe, H. Life of William Roscoe. 1833.

Jones, C. S. William Roscoe. Liverpool, 1931.

Mathews, G. W. William Roscoe: a Memoir. [1931.] [Includes fuller list of Roscoe's writings.]

ROBERT SOUTHEY (1774–1843)

[See p. 180 above.]

III. THE MID-NINETEENTH CENTURY HIS-TORIANS: MILMAN, GROTE, ARNOLD, FIN-LAY, STANHOPE, WRIGHT, FROUDE, MAINE

HENRY HART MILMAN (1791–1868)

(a) Writings

Fazio. A Tragedy. Oxford, 1815; Oxford, 1816; 1818 (4 edns); 1821 (with The Belvidere Apollo, etc.).

Samor, Lord of the Bright City. An Heroic Poem. 1818 (bis).

The Fall of Jerusalem. A Dramatic Poem. 1820 (bis); 1821; 1822; 1853.

The Martyr of Antioch. A Dramatic Poem. 1822.

Belshazzar. A Dramatic Poem. 1822.

Anne Boleyn. A Dramatic Poem. 1826.

The History of the Jews. 3 vols. 1829 (anon.); 1830; 3 vols. New York, 1832; 3 vols. New York, 1843; 3 vols. 1863; 3 vols. 1866; 1878; 1880; [1887]; 1892; rptd 2 vols. 1909 (Everyman's Lib.).

Poetical Works of Milman, Bowles, Wilson, and Barry Cornwall. Paris, 1829.

Nala and Damayanti and Other Poems, trans-lated from the Sanscrit into English Verse. Oxford, 1835; Oxford, 1860; rptd 1914.

The History of the Decline and Fall of the Roman Empire. By Edward Gibbon. With Notes by Henry Hart Milman. 12 vols. 1838–9.

The Life of Edward Gibbon, with Selections from his Correspondence. 1839; 1840. [Ed. by Milman.]

Poetical Works. 3 vols. 1840.

The History of Christianity, to the Abolition of Paganism in the Roman Empire. 3 vols. 1840; 3 vols. 1863 (rev.); 3 vols. 1867.

The Works of Quintus Horatius Flaccus illus-trated chiefly from the Remains of Ancient Art. With a Life by Henry Hart Milman. 1849; 1853; 1868. [Ed. by Milman.]

History of Latin Christianity; including that of the Popes to Nicolas V. 6 vols. 1854–5; 6 vols. 1857; 9 vols. 1864; 9 vols. 1867.

Lord Macaulay. Obituary. 1862 (*bis*); 1862 (in Macaulay's History, vol. VIII). [First pbd in Proc. Royal Soc. XI, 1862.]

The Agamemnon of Æschylus and the Bacchanals of Euripides, etc. translated. 1865; 1888 (Bacchae only). [Verse.]

Annals of S. Paul's Cathedral. Ed. A. Milman, 1868; 1869.

Savonarola, Erasmus, and Other Essays. Reprinted from the Quarterly Review. [Ed. A. Milman], 1870.

(b) Biography

Stanley, A. P. The Late Dean of St Paul's. Macmillan's Mag. Jan. 1869.

Milman, A. Henry Hart Milman. A Biographical Sketch. 1900.

GEORGE GROTE (1794–1871)
(a) Writings

Analysis of the Influence of Natural Religion on the Temporal Happiness of Mankind. By Philip Beauchamp. 1822; 1875; tr. French, Paris, 1875.

Essentials of Parliamentary Reform. 1831; 1873 (in Minor Works).

A History of Greece. 12 vols. 1846–56; 12 vols. 1854–7 (4th edn); 8 vols. 1862; 12 vols. 1869; 10 vols. 1872; 10 vols. 1888; rptd 1907 (condensed, with notes by J. M. Mitchell and M. O. B. Caspari). Tr. German, Leipzig, 1850–5; French, Paris, 1864–7.

Seven Letters on the Recent Politics of Switzerland. (Originally published in 'The Spectator'.) 1847; 1876 (with letter to A. de Tocqueville).

Plato's Doctrine respecting the Rotation of the Earth, and Aristotle's Comment upon that Doctrine. 1860; 1873 (in Minor Works).

Plato, and the Other Companions of Sokrates. 3 vols. 1865; 3 vols. 1867; 3 vols. 1874; 4 vols. 1885.

Review of the Work of Mr John Stuart Mill, entitled, 'Examination of Sir William Hamilton's Philosophy.' 1868 [1867]; 1873 (in Minor Works). [First pbd in Westminster Rev. Jan. 1866.]

Aristotle. Ed. A. Bain and G. C. Robertson, 2 vols. 1872; 1880 [1879]. [In Vol. II, chs. 12 and 13 (De Anima) are a reprint of Psychology of Aristotle, first published in A. Bain's The Senses and the Intellect, 1868 (3rd edn); and Appendices 1 and 2 B contain parts of papers printed as Appendices A and B in A. Bain's Mental and Moral Science, 1868.]

Poems, 1815–23. [1872] (priv. ptd).

The Minor Works of George Grote. With Remarks on his Intellectual Character, Writings, and Speeches by Alexander Bain. 1873.

Posthumous Papers. 1874 (priv. ptd).

Fragments on Ethical Subjects. From his Posthumous Papers. [Ed. A. Bain], 1876.

(b) Biography and Criticism

Cope, E. M. Plato's Theaetetus and Grote's Criticisms. Cambridge, 1866.

Grote, H. The Personal Life of George Grote. 1873; tr. German, Leipzig, 1874.

THÓMAS ARNOLD (1795–1842)
(a) Writings

Sermons. 3 vols. 1829–34; vol. II, 1845 (Sermons preached in the Chapel of Rugby School); vol. III, 1876; ed. Mrs W. E. Forster, 1878 (complete, as vols. I–III of Sermons).

ΘΟΥΚΥΔΙΔΗΣ. The History of the Peloponnesian War. By Thucydides. 3 vols. Oxford, [1830]–5; 3 vols. Oxford, 1840–2; 3 vols. in 4, Oxford, 1847–54. [Ed. by Arnold.]

Principles of Church Reform. 1833 (3 edns); 1845 (in Miscellaneous Works). [Postscript, 1833.]

History of Rome. 3 vols. 1838–43. [Vol. III, chs. 42–7, ed. W. T. Arnold, 1886 (The Second Punic War).]

Christian Life: its Course, its Hindrances, and its Helps. 1841; 1878 (as vol. IV of Sermons, ed. Mrs W. E. Forster).

Introductory Lectures on Modern History. With the Inaugural Lecture. Oxford, 1842.

Christian Life: its Hopes, its Fears, and its Close. [Ed. Mrs Arnold], 1842; 1845 (3rd edn); 1878 (as vol. V of Sermons, ed. Mrs W. E. Forster).

Sermons chiefly on the Interpretation of Scripture. [Ed. Mary Arnold], 1845; 1878 (as vol. VI of Sermons, ed. Mrs W. E. Forster).

Encyclopaedia Metropolitana. Ed. E. Smedley, 1845. [Arnold contributed to vol. IX of this edn ch. XVI and lives of Hamilcar and Hannibal; and to vol. X chs. XVIII and XX, lives of the Gracchi, Sylla, Julius and Augustus Caesar, and Trajan, and an account of The Historians of Rome. These are distributed between the History of the Roman Republic, 1852, the History of the Roman Empire, 1853, The Decline and Fall of the Roman Empire, 1853, and Roman Literature, 1852, in the 2nd edn of the Encyclopaedia. Arnold's contributions to vol. X also appeared separately as History of the later Roman Commonwealth, 2 vols. 1845.]

The Miscellaneous Works. [Ed. A. P. Stanley], 1845.

Arnold's Travelling Journals, with Extracts from the Life and Letters. [Ed. A. P. Stanley], 1852.

(b) Biography and Criticism

Stanley, A. P. A Sermon preached in the Chapel of Rugby School on the Death of the Rev. Thomas Arnold. Rugby, 1842.

The Life and Correspondence of Thomas Arnold. 2 vols. 1844 (3 edns); 2 vols. 1845 (bis); 1846; 1852; 2 vols. 1858; 2 vols. 1877 (10th edn); 2 vols. 1881 (10th edn); tr. German, Potsdam, 1847.

THOMAS CARLYLE (1795–1881)

[See p. 652 above.]

GEORGE FINLAY (1799–1875)

(a) Writings

The Hellenic Kingdom and the Greek Nation. 1836.

Remarks on the Topography of Oropia and Diacria. Athens, 1838; tr. German, Leipzig, 1842.

Greece under the Romans. Edinburgh, 1844; Edinburgh, 1857; rptd 1907 (Everyman's Lib.).

On the Site of the Holy Sepulchre. 1847.

The History of Greece from its Conquest by the Crusaders to its Conquest by the Turks, and of the Empire of Trebizond 1204–1461. Edinburgh, 1851.

History of the Byzantine and Greek Empires, 716–1453. 2 vols. Edinburgh, 1853–4; rptd 1906 (Byzantine Empire only, Everyman's Lib.).

The History of Greece under Ottoman and Venetian Domination. Edinburgh, 1856.

History of the Greek Revolution. 2 vols. Edinburgh, 1861.

A History of Greece from its Conquest by the Romans to the Present Time, B.C. 146 to A.D. 1864. Ed. H. F. Tozer, 7 vols. Oxford, 1877.

(b) Biography and Criticism

Autobiography. [In A History of Greece, ed. H. F. Tozer, vol. I, 1877.]

Miller, W. George Finlay as a Journalist. EHR. xxxix, 1924.

The Finlay Papers. EHR. xxxix, 1924. [Bibliography of minor works.]

THOMAS BABINGTON MACAULAY, BARON MACAULAY (1800–1859)

[See p. 683 above.]

PHILIP HENRY STANHOPE, EARL STANHOPE (1805–1875)

The Life of Belisarius. 1829; 1848.

History of the War of the Succession in Spain. 1832; 1836. [Appendix, 1833.]

Lord John Russell and Mr Macaulay on the French Revolution. 1833. [Rptd from Quarterly Rev. XLIX, omitting unauthorised interpolations.]

Letters from the Earl of Peterborough to General Stanhope, in Spain. 1834 (priv. ptd). [Ed. by Stanhope.]

History of England from the Peace of Utrecht to the Peace of Aix-la-Chapelle. 7 vols. 1836–54; 7 vols. 1839–54; 7 vols. 1853–4 (rev.); 7 vols. 1858 (5th edn, rev.). [Extended in vol. VII to the Peace of Versailles. The Forty-five: being the Narrative from Lord Mahon's History of England. To which are added, Letters of Prince Charles Stuart, 1851, and The Rise of Our Indian Empire, 1858, are reprints of portions of The History of England.]

Spain under Charles the Second, or Extracts from the Correspondence of A. Stanhope, 1690–1699. 1840; 1844. [Ed. by Stanhope.]

Essai sur La Vie du Grand Condé. 1842 (priv. ptd); tr. Eng. 1845.

Correspondence between William Pitt and Charles, Duke of Rutland, 1781–87. 1842 (priv. ptd); 1890. [Ed. by Stanhope.]

The Decline of the Last Stuarts. Extracts from Despatches of British Envoys. Roxburghe Club, 1843. [Ed. by Stanhope.]

The Letters of Philip Dormer, Earl of Chesterfield. 5 vols. 1845–53. [Ed. by Stanhope.]

Historical Essays contributed to The Quarterly Review. 1840; 1853 (Essay on Joan of Arc only).

Secret Correspondence connected with Mr Pitt's Return to Office in 1804. 1852 (priv. ptd). [Ed. by Stanhope.]

Lord Chatham at Chevening, 1769. 1855.

Addresses delivered at Manchester, Leeds, and Birmingham. 1856.

Memoirs of Sir Robert Peel. Ed. Earl Stanhope and E. Cardwell, 2 vols. 1856–7.

Life of William Pitt. 4 vols. 1861–2; 4 vols. 1862; 1867 (4th edn); 3 vols. 1879. Tr. French, Paris, 1862–3; Italian, Milan, 1863.

Miscellanies. 1863 (bis); Ser. 2, 1872.

History of England, comprising the Reign of Anne until the Peace of Utrecht, 1701–13. 1870 (bis); 2 vols. 1872 (4th edn).

Notes of Conversation with Louis-Philippe, at Claremont, March 30, 1848. 1873 (priv. ptd).

The French Retreat from Moscow, and Other Historical Essays. Collected from the Quarterly Review and Fraser's Magazine. 1876.

Notes of Conversations with the Duke of Wellington, 1831–51. 1888; ed. P. Guedalla, 1938 (World's Classics).

THOMAS WRIGHT (1810–1877)

(a) Writings

The History and Topography of the County of Essex. 2 vols. 1836.

Coup-d'œil sur les Progrès et sur l'État actuel de la Littérature anglo-saxonne en Angleterre. Traduction de [P.-F.] de Larenaudière. Paris, 1836. [For English version see under Biographia Britannica, below.]

The History and Antiquities of London, Westminster, Southwark, and Parts Adjacent. 5 vols. 1837. [Vols. i–iv by T. Allen; vol. v by Wright.]

The Universities. Le Keux's Memorials of Cambridge; with Historical and Descriptive Accounts by Thomas Wright and H. Longueville Jones. 2 vols. 1841–2; ed. C. H. Cooper, 2 vols. Cambridge, 1860; 3 vols. Cambridge, [1880].

The History of Ludlow and its Neighbourhood. Ludlow, 1852 [1841–52].

Biographia Britannica Literaria, or Biography of Literary Characters of Great Britain and Ireland. Anglo-Saxon Period. 1842. [Anglo-Norman Period, 1846; Introduction also separately pbd as An Essay on the State of Literature and Learning under the Anglo-Saxons, introductory to the Biographia Britannica Literaria, 1839.]

St Patrick's Purgatory. An Essay on the Legends of Purgatory, Hell, and Paradise, Current during the Middle Ages. 1844.

Essays on Subjects connected with the Literature, Popular Superstitions, and History of England in the Middle Ages. 2 vols. 1846. [Rptd from periodicals.]

England under the House of Hanover: its History during the Reigns of the Three Georges, illustrated from the Caricatures and Satires of the Day. 2 vols. 1848; [1868]; 1876 (as Caricature History of the Georges).

The History of Ireland. 3 vols. [1848–52].

Narratives of Sorcery and Magic. 2 vols. 1851.

Historical and Descriptive Account of the Caricatures of James Gillray. 1851; [1873] (expanded as The Works of James Gillray, with the History of his Life and Times). [With R. H. Evans.]

The Celt, the Roman, and the Saxon. A History of the Early Inhabitants of Britain, down to the Conversion of the Anglo-Saxons. 1852; 1861 (rev.); 1875; 1885.

The History of Scotland. 3 vols. [1852–5]; 3 vols. [1873–4].

Wanderings of an Antiquary; chiefly upon the Traces of the Romans in Britain. 1854.

A Lecture on the Antiquities of the Anglo-Saxon Cemeteries of the Ages of Paganism, Illustrative of the Faussett Collection. Liverpool, 1854.

Guide to the Caterham Railway, and to the Country around it. 1856.

The History of France. 3 vols. [1856–62]; 3 vols. [1871–2] (including A Faithful Account of the War with Germany, by Lt.-Col. Williams).

Miscellanea Graphica. Representations of Remains in the Possession of Lord Londesborough. Drawn by F. W. Fairholt. The Historical Introduction by Thomas Wright. 1857.

Dictionary of Obsolete and Provincial English. 2 vols. 1857.

Guide to the Ruins of the Roman City of Uriconium, at Wroxeter, near Shrewsbury. Shrewsbury, 1859; Shrewsbury, 1859 (as The Ruins of the Roman City of Uriconium); Shrewsbury, 1860; Shrewsbury, 1868; Shrewsbury, 1877 (6th edn).

History and Antiquities of Cumberland and Westmoreland. [In W. Whellan, The History and Topography of Cumberland and Westmoreland, Pontefract, 1860.]

Essays on Archaeological Subjects, and on Various Questions connected with the Middle Ages. 2 vols. 1861.

A History of Domestic Manners and Sentiments in England during the Middle Ages. 1862; 1871 (expanded as The Homes of Other Days).

Historical and Descriptive Sketch of Ludlow Castle. [1862?]; Ludlow, 1869 (4th edn, rev.); Ludlow, 1909 (13th edn); etc.

Ludlow Sketches. A Series of Papers. Ludlow, 1867.

Historical Cartoons. By Gustav Doré. With Descriptive Text by Thomas Wright. [1868.]

Womankind in Western Europe from the Earliest Times to the Seventeenth Century. 1869.

Uriconium. A Historical Account of the Ancient Roman City. 1872.

A History of Caricature and Grotesque in Literature and Art. 1875.

Historical Sketch of Stokesay Castle, Salop. Ludlow, 1921; Ludlow, 1924.

(b) Works edited, or with Contributions

Early English Poetry. 4 vols. 1836. [Anthology.]

The Tour of the French Traveller, M. de la Boullaye le Gouz, in Ireland, A.D. 1644. Ed. T. C. Croker (with notes by Thomas Wright), 1837.

Anglo-Norman Poem on the Conquest of Ireland by Henry the Second. Ed. F. Michel (with an introductory essay on the Conquest by Thomas Wright), 1837.

Galfridi de Monemuta Vita Merlini. Vie de Merlin, attribuée à Geoffroy de Monmouth. Paris, 1837. [With F. Michel.]

Early Mysteries, and Other Latin Poems of the Twelfth and Thirteenth Centuries. 1838.

Alliterative Poem on the Deposition of King Richard II. Camden Soc. 1838.

Queen Elizabeth and her Times. A Series of Original Letters, selected from the Inedited Private Correspondence of Lord Burghley, the Earl of Leicester [etc.]. 2 vols. 1838.

The Political Songs of England, from John to Edward II. Camden Soc. 1839; ed. E. Goldsmid, 4 vols. 1884.

Relations des Voyages de Guillaume de Rubruk, Jean du Plan Carpin, Bernard, Sæwulf, etc. [Ed. F. Michel and Wright, in Recueil de Voyages et de Mémoires, publié par la Société de Géographie, IV, Paris, 1839.]

The History of English Poetry. By Thomas Warton. 3 vols. 1840. [Corrections and addns by Wright and others.]

Popular Treatises on Science written during the Middle Ages, in Anglo-Saxon, Anglo-Norman, and English. Historical Soc. of Science, 1841.

The Latin Poems attributed to Walter Mapes. Camden Soc. 1841.

Political Ballads published in England during the Commonwealth. Percy Soc. 1841.

Specimens of Old Christmas Carols. Percy Soc. 1841.

The Archaeologist, and Journal of Antiquarian Science. Sept. 1841–June 1842. [Ed. by J. O. Halliwell and Wright.]

Reliquiæ Antiquæ. Scraps from Ancient Manuscripts, illustrating Early English Literature and the English Language. 2 vols. 1841–3; 2 vols. 1845. [Ed. by J. O. Halliwell and Wright.]

A Dialogue concerning Witches & Witchcrafts. By G. Gifford. Percy Soc. 1842.

Specimens of Lyric Poetry, composed in England in the Reign of Edward the First. Percy Soc. 1842.

A Selection of Latin Stories. A Contribution to the History of Fiction during the Middle Ages. Percy Soc. 1842.

The Autobiography of Joseph Lister, of Bradford in Yorkshire. 1842.

The Vision and the Creed of Piers Ploughman. 1842; 2 vols. 1856. [With introduction, notes and glossary; anon.]

A Contemporary Narrative of the Proceedings against Dame Alice Kyteler. Camden Soc. 1843.

Three Chapters of Letters relating to the Suppression of the Monasteries. Camden Soc. 1843.

The Owl and the Nightingale: attributed to Nicholas de Guildford, with some Shorter Poems. Percy Soc. 1843.

The Chester Plays. 2 vols. Shakespeare Soc. 1843–7.

St Brandan. A Medieval Legend of the Sea. Percy Soc. 1844.

Anecdota Literaria. A Collection of Short Poems in English, Latin, and French, Illustrative of the Literature and History of England in the Thirteenth Century. 1844.

The Archaeological Album, or Museum of National Antiquities. 1845.

The Pastime of Pleasure. By Stephen Hawes. Percy Soc. 1845.

The Seven Sages in English Verse. Percy Soc. 1845; Introduction, 1846.

Songs and Carols, from a Manuscript of the Fifteenth Century. Percy Soc. 1847.

The Canterbury Tales of Geoffrey Chaucer. A New Text. 3 vols. Percy Soc. 1847–51; 1853.

Early Travels in Palestine, comprising the Narratives of Arculf, Willibald, Bernard, etc. 1848.

A New General Biographical Dictionary, projected and partly arranged by H. J. Rose. 12 vols. 1848. [Vols. II–XII edited by Wright.]

The Religious Poems of William de Shoreham. Percy Soc. 1849.

Gualteri Mapes De Nugis Curialium. Camden Soc. 1850.

The Anglo-Norman Metrical Chronicle of Geoffrey Gaimar. Caxton Soc. 1850.

The Ancient Laws of the Fifteenth Century, for King's College, Cambridge, and Eton College. Collected by J. Heywood and Thomas Wright. 1850.

The Life of King Alfred. By R. Pauli. 1852.

The Universal Pronouncing Dictionary. Compiled under the Direction of Thomas Wright. 6 vols. [1852–6].

Cambridge University Transactions during the Puritan Controversies of the 16th and 17th Centuries. Collected by J. Heywood and Thomas Wright. 2 vols. 1854.

The Travels of Marco Polo, the Venetian. The Translation of Marsden revised. 1854; 1904.

The History of Fulke Fitz Warine. Ed. (with an English translation and notes), Warton Club, 1855.

Songs and Carols from a Manuscript of the Fifteenth Century. Warton Club, 1856. [Distinct from Percy Soc. vol. of 1847.]

Johannis de Garlandia De Triumphis Ecclesiæ. Roxburghe Club, 1856.

A Volume of Vocabularies, illustrating the Condition and Manners of our Forefathers, from the Tenth Century to the Fifteenth. 2 vols. [Priv. ptd in J. Mayer's Library of National Antiquities, 1857–73; ed. R. P. Wülcker, 2 vols. 1884.]

Les Cent Nouvelles Nouvelles. Publiées d'après le seul manuscrit connu, avec Introduction et Notes. 2 vols. Paris, 1858–7.

La Morte d'Arthure. The History of King Arthur and of the Knights of the Round Table. Compiled by Sir Thomas Malory. Ed. (from the edn of 1634, with Introduction and Notes), 3 vols. 1858; 3 vols. 1866 (rev.); 1893.

Manual of Ethnology. By J. C. Prichard. Rev. Thomas Wright and Monsieur d' Avezac. [Extracted from Admiralty Manual of Scientific Enquiry, 1859 (3rd edn).]

A Glossary. By Robert Nares. A New Edition by J. O. Halliwell and Thomas Wright. 2 vols. 1859; 2 vols. 1888; 1905.

Political Poems and Songs relating to English History, composed during the Period from the Accession of Edw. III to that of Ric. III. 2 vols. 1859–61. (Rerum Britannicarum Medii Ævi Scriptores.)

Songs and Ballads, with Other Short Poems, chiefly of the Reign of Philip and Mary. Roxburghe Club, 1860.

De Regimine Principum, a Poem by Thomas Occleve. Roxburghe Club, 1860.

Fairy Legends and Traditions of the South of Ireland. By T. C. Croker. [1862]; [1870]; [1882]; 1902.

The Royal Dictionary-Cyclopædia. Compiled under the Direction of Thomas Wright, 5 vols. [1862–7].

Alexandri Neckam De Naturis Rerum. 1863. (Rerum Britannicarum Medii Ævi Scriptores.)

The Historical Works of Giraldus Cambrensis. 1863. [Trn of T. Forester and Sir R. Colt Hoare.]

The Roll of Arms of the Princes, Barons, and Knights who attended Edward I to the Siege of Caerlaverock, in 1300. Ed. (with Translation and Notes) 1864.

Autobiography of Thomas Wright, of Birkenshaw, 1736–1797. 1864.

History of Julius Cæsar. By Napoleon III. 2 vols. [1865–6]. [Tr. by Wright.]

The Chronicle of Pierre de Langtoft. 2 vols. 1866–8. (Rerum Britannicarum medii Ævi Scriptores.)

The Book of the Knight of La Tour-Landry, translated from the French into English in the Reign of Henry VI. EETS. 1868; 1906 (rev.).

Churchwardens' Accounts of the Town of Ludlow. Camden Soc. 1869.

Feudal Manuals of English History. A Series of Popular Sketches of Our National History, compiled from the Thirteenth Century to the Fifteenth. 1872.

The Anglo-Latin Satirical Poets and Epigrammatists of the Twelfth Century. 2 vols. 1872. (Rerum Britannicarum medii Ævi Scriptores.)

The Decameron of Boccaccio. 1874. [With introduction by Wright.]

Killarney Legends. Ed. T. C. Croker. [1876.] [Rpt of Legends of the Lakes, rev. by Wright.]

(c) Biography and Criticism

Obituary. Academy, 29 Dec. 1877.

Obituary. Athenaeum, 29 Dec. 1877.

Garnett, R. Antiquarian Club Books. Quarterly Rev. LXXXII, 1877–8.

Jewitt, L. Some Departed Contributors and Literary Friends. Reliquary, XVIII, 1877–8.

Fitch, E. A. Historians of Essex, VIII: Thomas Wright. Essex Rev. IX, 1900.

JAMES ANTHONY FROUDE (1818–1894)*

(a) Historical Works

History of England from the Fall of Wolsey to the Death of Elizabeth. 12 vols. 1856–70 (vols. I, II rev. 1858; vols. I–IV, VII, VIII rev. 1862–4); 12 vols. 1870 (as History of England from the Fall of Wolsey to the Defeat of the Spanish Armada); 12 vols. 1870–5; 12 vols. 1881; 12 vols. 1893; ed. W. Ll. Williams, 10 vols. 1909–12 (Everyman's Lib.).

The English in Ireland in the Eighteenth Century. 3 vols. 1872–4; 3 vols. 1881.

The Divorce of Catherine of Aragon (being a Supplement to the History of England). 1891.

(b) Biographical Works

St Neot. [In Lives of the English Saints, ed. J. H. Newman, vol. II, 1844, vol. III, 1900.]

Caesar. A Sketch. 1879; 1886.

Bunyan. 1880. (English Men of Letters ser.)

Luther. A Short Biography. 1883; 1884.

Thomas Carlyle. A History of the First Forty Years of his Life, 1795–1835. 2 vols. 1882 (bis); 1890; 1891; tr. German, Gotha, 1886.

Thomas Carlyle. A History of his Life in London, 1834–1881. 2 vols. 1884 (bis); 1890; tr. German, Gotha, 1886.

My Relations with Carlyle, together with a Letter from the late Sir James Stephen. 1886; 1903 (with prefatory note by Ashley A. Froude and Margaret Froude).

* The bibliography of Froude has been contributed by Professor C. H. Williams.

Lord Beaconsfield. 1890 (Prime Ministers of Queen Victoria ser.); 1905 (9th edn); 1906 (Everyman's Lib.).

Life and Letters of Erasmus. 1893; 1894

(c) Editions

The Pilgrim. A Dialogue on the Life and Actions of King Henry the Eighth. By William Thomas. 1861.

Thomas Carlyle. Reminiscences. 2 vols. 1881; ed. C. E. Norton, 2 vols. 1887.

Memorials of Jane Welsh Carlyle. Prepared for Publication by Thomas Carlyle. 3 vols. 1883.

(d) Essays

Oxford Essays. By Members of the University. 1855. [II, Suggestions on the Best Means of teaching English History. By J. A. Froude.]

Short Studies on Great Subjects. 2 vols. 1867. Short Studies on Great Subjects. Second Series. 1871. Short Studies on Great Subjects. Third Series. 1877. Short Studies on Great Subjects. Fourth Series. 1883. [Collected.] 3 vols. (with preface) 1877; 3 vols. 1878; 4 vols. 1883; 5 vols. 1907; ser. 1, 1924 (World s Classics).

The Spanish Story of the Armada and other Essays. 1892.

The Dissolution of the Monasteries and other Essays. 1905.

(e) Miscellaneous Writings

Shadows of the Clouds. By Zeta. 1847.

The Nemesis of Faith. 1849; 1892; 1903.

The Book of Job. 1854.

The Cat's Pilgrimage. Edinburgh, 1870.

Oceana, or England and her Colonies. 1886.

The English in the West Indies, or The Bow of Ulysses. 1888.

The Two Chiefs of Dunboy r An Irish Romance of the last Century. 1889.

A Siding at a Railway Station. An Allegory. 1905.

(f) Lectures and Addresses

A Sermon preached at St Mary Church on the Death of the Rev. George May Coleridge. Torquay, 1847.

Inaugural Address delivered to the University of St Andrews, 19 March 1869. 1869.

Calvinism. An Address delivered to the University of St Andrews, 17 March 1871. 1871.

Two Lectures on South Africa delivered before the Philosophical Institute. Edinburgh, 6, 9 January, 1880; ed. Margaret Froude, 1900.

Liberty and Property. An Address to the Liberty and Property Defence. 1888.

Lectures on the Council of Trent. 1893; 1896.

English Seamen in the Sixteenth Century. 1895; 1901; ed. Ashley A. Froude, 1923; 1925.

(g) Biography and Criticism

(i) Books

Harrison, Frederick. Tennyson, Ruskin, Mill, and other Literary Estimates. 1899.

Crichton-Browne, Sir J. The Nemesis of Froude. 1903. [A rejoinder to Froude's My Relations with Carlyle.]

Cooper, A. James Anthony Froude. (A Lecture.) [1907.]

Cecil, Algernon. Six Oxford Thinkers. 1909.

Gooch, G. P. History and Historians in the Nineteenth Century. 1913.

Birrell, Augustine. Collected Essays and Addresses. 3 vols. 1922.

Dunn, W. H. Froude and Carlyle. A Study of the Froude-Carlyle Controversy. New York, 1930.

Strachey, L. Characters and Commentaries. 1933.

(ii) Articles in Periodicals

Freeman, E. A. Saturday Rev. 30 Jan. 1864, 24 Nov. 1866, 1 Dec. 1867, 12, 22, 29 Jan., 5 Feb., 5 April, 21 June 1870, 8, 29 Sept. 1877; Contemporary Rev. XXXI, March, April, June, Sept. 1878. [Froude replied in A Few Words on Mr Freeman, Nineteenth Century, April 1879.]

Cairns, J. E. Froude's English in Ireland. Fortnightly Rev. XVI, 1874.

Fisher, H. A. L. Modern Historians and their Methods. Fortnightly Rev. Dec. 1894.

Smith, Goldwin. Froude. North American Rev. Dec. 1894.

Harrison, F. The Historical Method of J. A. Froude. Nineteenth Century, XLIV, 1898.

Stewart, H. L. J. A. Froude and Anglo-Catholicism. American Journ. of Theology, XXII, 1918.

SIR HENRY JAMES SUMNER MAINE
(1822–1888)

(a) Writings

Memoir of H. F. Hallam. [1851]; 1863 (in A. H. Hallam's Remains). [With F. Lushington.]

Roman Law and Legal Education. 1856 (in Cambridge Essays); 1876 (in Village-Communities, 3rd edn).

Ancient Law: its Connection with the Early History of Society, and its Relation to Modern Ideas. 1861; 1885 (10th edn); rptd [1905]; 1906; Allahabad, 1912; 1917 (Everyman's Lib.); 1930; 1931 (World's Classics); tr. Hungarian, Pest, 1875.

Village-Communities in the East and West. 1871; 1876 (3rd edn, 'to which are added other Lectures, Addresses and Essays').

The Early History of the Property of Married Women. A Lecture. [1873.]

Lectures on the Early History of Institutions. 1875.

The Effects of Observation of India on Modern European Thought. Rede Lecture, 1875. 1875; 1876 (in Village-Communities, 3rd edn).

The King in his Relation to Early Civil Justice. Royal Inst. Notices of Proceedings, IX, 1882.

Dissertations on Early Law and Custom. 1883; tr. French, Paris, 1884.

Popular Government. Four Essays. 1885; 1909; tr. Spanish, Seville, 1888.

India. 1887. [In T. H. Ward, The Reign of Queen Victoria, vol. I.]

The Whewell Lectures. International Law. 1888; 1894.

(b) Biography and Criticism

Grant Duff, Sir M. E. Sir Henry Maine. A Brief Memoir, with some of his Indian Speeches and Minutes. Ed. Whitley Stokes, 1892.

Vinogradoff, Sir P. The Teaching of Sir Henry Maine. 1904.

IV. MINOR WRITERS, 1835–1870

A. ANCIENT HISTORY

THOMAS KEIGHTLEY (1789–1872)

The Fairy Mythology. 2 vols. 1828; 1850.

History of the War of Independence in Greece. 2 vols. Edinburgh, 1830.

Outlines of History. 1831 (anon.). [Part of D. Lardner's Cabinet Cyclopaedia.]

The Mythology of Ancient Greece and Italy for the Use of Students at the Universities. 1831; 1838; 1854; ed. L. Schmitz, 1877.

The Crusaders, or Scenes, Events, and Characters, from the Times of the Crusades. 2 vols. 1834.

Tales and Popular Fictions: their Resemblance, and Transmission. 1834.

The History of Greece. 1835; 1839 (3rd edn); 1842; New York, 1848; 1849.

The History of Rome. 1836; 1837; 1840; 1842; 1848 (6th edn); New York, 1848.

Secret Societies of the Middle Ages. Soc. for Diffusion of Useful Knowledge, 1837 (anon.); 1848 (anon.).

The History of England. 2 vols. 1837–9; 3 vols. 1839; 5 vols. New York, 1843–5; 2 vols. New York, 1848; tr. German, Hamburg, 1847.

Publii Ovidii Nasonis Fastorum Libri VI. Ovid's Fasti; with Notes and an Introduction, by Thomas Keightley. 1839; 1848.

History of the Roman Empire. 1840; New York, 1848; 1849 (6th edn).

An Elementary History of England. 1841.

An Elementary History of Greece. 1841.

A History of India, from the Earliest Times. [1846-7.]

Notes on the Bucolics and Georgics of Virgil; with Excursus. 1846–[50]. Additional Illustrations, 1850.

The Bucolics and Georgics of Virgil; with Notes, Excursus, etc. 1847.

The Satires and Epistles of Horace; with Notes and Excursus. 1848.

The Catilina and Jugurtha of Sallust; with Notes and Excursus. 1849.

An Account of the Life, Opinions, and Writings of John Milton. With an Introduction to Paradise Lost. 1855.

The Poems of John Milton, with Notes, by Thomas Keightley. 2 vols. 1859.

The Plays of William Shakespeare. 6 vols. 1864; 4 vols. [1892–4]; rptd [1925]. Plays and Poems. 1865. [Ed. by Keightley.]

The Shakespeare-Expositor. 1867.

CONNOP THIRLWALL (1797–1875)

Primitiæ, or Essays and Poems on Various Subjects, Religious, Moral and Entertaining. By Connop Thirlwall, Eleven Years of Age. 1809.

A Critical Essay on the Gospel of St Luke. By Dr F. Schleiermacher. With an Introduction by the Translator, containing an Account of the Controversy respecting the Origin of the Three First Gospels. 1825 (anon.). [Tr. by Thirlwall.]

The History of Rome. By B. G. Niebuhr. 3 vols. Cambridge, 1828–42; 3 vols. 1847–51 (4th edn). [Vols. I and II tr. by J. C. Hare and Thirlwall.]

A Vindication of Niebuhr's History of Rome from the charges of the Quarterly Review. By J. C. Hare. Cambridge, 1829. [Postscript by Thirlwall.]

A Letter to the Rev. T. Turton on the Admission of Dissenters to Academical Degrees. Cambridge, 1834; Cambridge, 1834 (adds a second letter).

A History of Greece. 8 vols. 1835–44; 8 vols. 1845–52. [Part of D. Lardner's Cabinet Cyclopædia. Partially tr. German, Bonn, 1839–40; partially tr. French, Paris, 1852.]

Schleiermacher on the Worth of Socrates as a Philosopher. [Tr. from the German by Thirlwall, in G. Wiggers, A Life of Socrates, 1840.]

A Speech in the House of Lords, May 25th, 1848, on a Bill for the Relief of Her Majesty's Subjects professing the Jewish Religion. 1848.

A Letter to the Archbishop of Canterbury, on the Statements of Sir B. Hall, with Regard to the Collegiate Church of Brecon. 1851.

A Second Letter to the Archbishop, in Reply to Sir B. Hall. 1851.

A Letter to the Rev. Rowland Williams in Answer to his 'Earnestly Respectful' Letter. 1860.

A Letter to J. Bowstead concerning Education in South Wales. 1861 (bis).

A Reply to a Letter of the Lord Bishop of Capetown. 1867.

The Episcopal Meeting of 1867. A Letter to the Archbishop of Canterbury. 1867.

Remains, Literary and Theological. Ed. J. J. S. Perowne, 3 vols. 1877–8.

Letters Literary and Theological. Ed. J. J. S. Perowne and L. Stokes, 1881.

Letters to a Friend [Miss Johns]. Ed. A. P. Stanley, 1881; 1882.

[For biography see J. C. Thirlwall, Connop Thirlwall, Historian and Theologian, 1936.]

GEORGE LONG (1800–1879)

[See p. 1000 below.]

SIR GEORGE CORNEWALL LEWIS (1806–1863)

[See p. 999 below.]

CHRISTOPHER WORDSWORTH (1807–1885)

[See p. 313 above.]

CHARLES MERIVALE (1808–1893)

History of Rome under the Emperors. Part 3: The Augustan Age. Soc. for Diffusion of Useful Knowledge, 1843.

A History of the Romans under the Empire. 7 vols. 1850–64; vols. I–VI, 1852–62; vols. I–II, 1860; 7 vols. 1862; 8 vols. 1865. Tr. Italian, Venice, 1865; German, Leipzig, 1860–72.

Caii Sallustii Crispi Catilina et Jugurtha. Cambridge, 1852. [Ed. by Merivale.]

The Fall of the Roman Republic. A Short History of the Last Century of the Commonwealth. 1853. [Epitome of vols. I–III of History of the Romans.]

An Account of the Life and Letters of Cicero: translated from the German of B. R. Abeken. 1854. [Ed. by Merivale.]

Keatsii Hyperionis libri tres. Latinè reddidit Carolus Merivale. Cambridge, 1863; 1882 (with addns).

The Conversion of the Roman Empire. The Boyle Lectures for 1864. 1864.

The Conversion of the Northern Nations. The Boyle Lectures for 1865. 1866.

Homer's Iliad in English Rhymed Verse. 2 vols. 1869.

The Contrast between Pagan and Christian Society. A Lecture. 1872; 1880.

A General History of Rome from the Foundation of the City to the Fall of Augustulus. 1875 (bis); 1876; 1877; 1891.

The Roman Triumvirates. 1876; 1885 (4th edn).

The Heathen World and St Paul. St Paul at Rome. [1877.]

Conversion of the West. The Continental Teutons. [1878.]

Four Lectures on some Epochs of Early Church History. 1879.

Autobiography & Letters. Ed. J. A. Merivale, Oxford, 1898 (priv. ptd); 1899.

[Merivale also pbd sermons, pamphlets, and articles in Saturday Rev.]

NATHAN DAVIS (1812–1882)

Tunis, or Selections from a Journal during a Residence in that Regency. Malta, 1841.

A Voice from North Africa, or a Narrative Illustrative of the Manners of the Inhabitants of that Part of the World. Edinburgh, 1844 (bis).

The Carthaginian Church, or a Brief Sketch of the History of Christianity in North Africa. Edinburgh, [1845?].

Evenings in my Tent, or Wanderings in Balad Ejjareed, illustrating the Conditions of Various Arab Tribes of the African Sahara. 2 vols. 1854.

Carthage and her Remains. 1861.

Ruined Cities within Numidian and Carthaginian Territories. 1862.

SIR WILLIAM SMITH (1813–1893)

[See p. 1002 below.]

B. ENGLISH HISTORY (GENERAL)

HENRY PETER BROUGHAM (BARON BROUGHAM AND VAUX) (1778–1868)

(a) Collected Works

Works. 11 vols. 1855–61; 11 vols. Edinburgh, 1872–3. [Comprises: Lives of Philosophers; Historical Sketches of Statesmen; Natural Theology; Rhetorical and Literary Dissertations and Addresses; Historical and Political Dissertations; Speeches on Social and Political Subjects; The British Constitution, its History, Structure, and working.]

(b) Separate Writings

An Inquiry into the Colonial Policy of the European Powers. 2 vols. Edinburgh, 1803.

An Inquiry into the State of the Nation, at the Commencement of the Present Administration. 1806 (anon. 3 edns).

The Speech in the House of Commons, May 8, 1818, on the Education of the Poor, and Charitable Abuses. 1818.

A Letter to Sir Samuel Romilly upon the Abuse of Charities. [In The Pamphleteer, vol. xiii, 1818, and separately, 11 edns.]

The Speech on the Education of the Poor, House of Commons, June 29, 1820. [In The Pamphleteer, vol. xvi, 1820.]

Practical Observations upon the Education of the People. 1825 (20 edns); Boston, U.S.A. 1826; tr. German, Berlin, 1827.

Inaugural Discourse on being installed Lord Rector of the University of Glasgow. Glasgow, 1825; Glasgow, 1839 (in J. B. Hay's Inaugural Addresses); Edinburgh, 1848 (in Inaugural Addresses by Lords Rectors).

Present State of the Law. The Speech in the House of Commons, February 7, 1828. 1828 (4 edns and in The Pamphleteer, vol. xxix).

The Lord Chancellor's Speech on Parliamentary Reform, in the House of Lords, October 7, 1831. 1831 (12 edns). [2nd reading of Reform Bill.]

Thoughts upon the Aristocracy of England. By Isaac Tomkins, Gent. 1835 (11 edns). [Really by Brougham.]

'We Can't Afford It!' Being Thoughts upon the Aristocracy of England. Part 2. By Isaac Tomkins, Gent. 1835 (6 edns).

A Discourse of Natural Theology. Brussels, 1835; 1835 (3rd edn); 1845 (in Paley's Natural Theology, vol. i).

Select Cases decided by Lord Brougham in the Court of Chancery, 1833 and 1834. Vol. i, ed. C. P. Cooper, 1835.

Speeches upon Questions relating to Public Rights, etc. 4 vols. Edinburgh, 1838.

Historical Sketches of Statesmen in the Time of George III. 3 sers. 1839–43; 6 vols. 1845; tr. French, Lyons, 1847.

Political Philosophy. Soc. for the Diffusion of Useful Knowledge. 3 vols. 1842–3 (vol. i anon.).

Albert Lunel, or the Château of Languedoc. 3 vols. 1844 (anon.); 3 vols. [1872]. [Novel.]

Lives of Men of Letters and Science, in the Time of George III. 2 vols. 1845–6.

A Letter to Lord Denman upon the Legislation of 1850 as regards the Amendment of the Law. 1850.

History of England and France under the House of Lancaster. 1852 (anon.); 1861.

Contributions to the Edinburgh Review. 3 vols. 1856.

Tracts, Mathematical and Physical. 1860.

(c) Biography and Criticism

Eardley-Wilmot, Sir J. E. Lord Brougham's Law Reforms: The Acts and Bills introduced or carried by him since 1811; with an Analytical Review. 1860.

The Life and Times of Lord Brougham written by Himself. 3 vols. Edinburgh, 1871.

Thomas, R. Bibliography of Henry Brougham's Works. [In Works, 1872–3 (2nd edn), vol. xi.]

Gilbert, A. M. The Work of Lord Brougham for Education in England. Chambersburg, 1922.

Aspinall, A. Lord Brougham and the Whig Party. Manchester, 1927.

Garratt, G. T. Lord Brougham. 1935.

Sir Francis Palgrave (1788–1861)

The Parliamentary Writs and Writs of Military Summons. 2 vols. in 4. Record Commission, 1827–34. [Ed. by Palgrave.]

Le Romant des Ducs de Normandie. [By Wace, ed. by Palgrave, not pbd; some proof sheets survive in BM.]

History of England. Vol. i: Anglo-Saxon Period. 1831 (all pbd); 1867 (as History of the Anglo-Saxons); 1876; [1887]; tr. French, Rouen, 1836.

The Rise and Progress of the English Commonwealth. Anglo-Saxon Period. 2 pts, 1832.

An Essay upon the Original Authority of the King's Council. Record Commission, 1834.

Rotuli Curiae Regis. 2 vols. Record Commission, 1835. [Ed. by Palgrave.]

The Antient Kalendars and Inventories of the Treasury of His Majesty's Exchequer. 3 vols. Record Commission, 1836. [Ed. by Palgrave.]

Truths and Fictions of the Middle Ages. The Merchant and the Friar. 1837; 1844.

Documents and Records illustrating the History of Scotland. Vol. i. Record Commission, 1837. [Ed. by Palgrave.]

First [to Twenty-Second] Report of the Deputy Keeper of the Public Records. Presented to Parliament by Command. 22 vols. 1840–61. Index, 1865.

Handbook for Travellers in Northern Italy. 1842 (anon.); 1847; 1852; 1854; 1856; 1858; 1860; 1869; 1873; 1874; 1877.

The Lord and the Vassal. A Familiar Exposition of the Feudal System in the Middle Ages. 1844 (anon.).

The History of Normandy and of England. 4 vols. 1851–64.

The Collected Historical Works. Ed. Sir R. H. Inglis Palgrave, 10 vols. Cambridge, 1919–22. [Includes Three Generations of an Imaginary Norfolk Family, now first pbd, vol. viii, and reviews, essays, and other writings, vols. ix–x.]

CHARLES KNIGHT (1791–1873)
[See p. 1025 below.]

JOHN RUSSELL (EARL RUSSELL)
(1792–1878)

The Life of William Lord Russell. 1819;
2 vols. 1820; 1853 (4th edn).

Essays and Sketches of Life and Character.
By A Gentleman who has left his Lodgings.
1820; 1821.

History of the English Government from the
Reign of Henry VII. 1821; 1823; 1865;
1873. Tr. French, Paris, 1865; German,
Freiburg, 1872.

Memoirs of the Affairs of Europe from the
Peace of Utrecht. 1824–9 (vol. I anon.;
rptd 2 vols. 1826 as History of the Principal
States of Europe).

The Establishment of the Turks in Europe.
An Historical Discourse. 1828 (anon.).

The Causes of the French Revolution. 1832
(anon.).

Correspondence of John, Fourth Duke of
Bedford. 3 vols. 1842–6. [Ed. by Russell.]

Letters of Rachel, Lady Russell. 2 vols.
1853. [Ed. by Russell.]

Memoirs, Journal, and Correspondence of
Thomas Moore. 8 vols. 1853–6. [Ed. by
Russell.]

Memorials and Correspondence of Charles
James Fox. 4 vols. 1853–7. [Ed. by
Russell.]

The Life and Times of Charles James Fox.
3 vols. 1859–66.

The Foreign Policy of England, 1570–1870.
An Historical Essay. 1871.

Essays on the Rise of the Christian Religion
in the West of Europe from the Reign of
Tiberius to the End of the Council of
Trent. 1873; 1873 (as Essays on the History of the Christian Religion).

[For Russell's plays see p. 594 above.]

ROBERT VAUGHAN (1795–1868)

The Life and Opinions of John de Wycliffe.
2 vols. 1828; 1831.

Memorials of the Stuart Dynasty. 2 vols. 1831.

On the Study of General History. An Introductory Lecture, in the University of
London. 1834.

Thoughts on the Past and Present State of
Religious Parties in England. 1838; 1839
(as Religious Parties in England).

The Protectorate of Oliver Cromwell illustrated in a Series of Letters. 2 vols. 1838;
2 vols. 1839. [Ed. by Vaughan.]

The History of England under the House of
Stuart, 1603–1688. Soc. for the Diffusion of
Useful Knowledge, 1840.

The Modern Pulpit viewed in its Relation to
the State of Society. 1842.

The Age of Great Cities, or Modern Society
viewed in Relation to Intelligence, Morals,
and Religion. 1843.

Protestant Nonconformity in its Relation to
Learning and Piety. 1843.

Tracts and Treatises of John de Wycliffe.
Wycliffe Soc. 1845. [Ed. by Vaughan.]

Essays on History, Philosophy and Theology.
2 vols. 1849.

The Age and Christianity. 1849; 1853.

John de Wycliffe, D.D. A Monograph. 1853.

Essays and Remains of R. A. Vaughan. Ed.
(with memoir) Robert Vaughan, 2 vols.
1858; 1864 (memoir only).

Revolutions in English History. 3 vols.
1859–63; 1865 (vol. I only).

The Case of the Ejected Ministers of 1662. A
Speech at the Annual Meeting of the
Congregational Union, 1861. [1861.]

I'll Tell You. An Answer to 'How did they
get there?' A Tractate touching the
Ejected of 1662. 1862; [1912].

English Nonconformity. 1862.

The State of Religious Parties in England
before 1662. [In Bicentenary of the
Bartholomew Ejectment in 1662; St James's
Hall Addresses, 1862.]

Ritualism in the English Church in its Relation to Scripture, Piety, and Law. 1866.

Milton's Paradise Lost. [1866]; [1871–2];
1882; [1888–90]; 1894; [1898–9]; 1905.
[Ed. with a life of Milton.]

[Vaughan also pbd many devotional and
theological works, and some sermons.]

AGNES STRICKLAND (1796–1874), and
ELIZABETH STRICKLAND (1794–1875)

[Elizabeth's name does not appear on any
of their works.]

Lives of the Queens of England. 12 vols.
1840–8; 8 vols. 1851–2; 6 vols. 1864–5;
6 vols. 1877; 6 vols. 1884. [The Life of
Queen Elizabeth rptd 1906 (Everyman's
Lib.).]

Letters of Mary, Queen of Scots. 3 vols.
1842–3; 2 vols. 1844. [Ed. by Agnes and
Elizabeth Strickland.]

Lives of the Queens of Scotland and English
Princesses connected with the Regal
Succession of Great Britain. 8 vols. Edin-
burgh, 1850–9. [Life of Mary Queen of
Scots, 2 vols. 1873.]

Lives of the Bachelor Kings of England. 1861.

Lives of the Seven Bishops committed to the
Tower in 1688. 1866.

Lives of the Tudor Princesses including Lady
Jane Gray and her Sisters. 1868; 1888
(rev.).

Lives of the Last Four Princesses of the House
of Stuart. 1872.

GEORGE LILLIE CRAIK (1798–1866)

[See p. 665 above.]

SIR NICHOLAS HARRIS NICOLAS
(1799–1848)

[See p. 1026 below.]

AUGUSTUS GRANVILLE STAPLETON
(1800–1880)

The Political Life of George Canning, from
1822 to 1827. 2 vols. 1830 (ptd but not
pbd); 3 vols. 1831.
George Canning and his Times. 1859.
Intervention and Non-Intervention, or The
Foreign Policy of Great Britain from 1790
to 1865. 1866.

HARRIET MARTINEAU (1802–1876)

[See p. 496 above.]

ROBERT ISAAC WILBERFORCE (1802–1857),
and SAMUEL WILBERFORCE (1805–1873)

The Life of William Wilberforce. 5 vols.
1838.
The Correspondence of William Wilberforce.
2 vols. 1840. [Ed. by Robert and Samuel
Wilberforce.]

SIR THOMAS DUFFUS HARDY (1804–1878)

A Description of the Close Rolls in the Tower
of London, A.D. 1204–27. Record Com-
mission, 1833–44. [Also the following, all
for Record Commission and covering part
or whole of King John's reign: Patent
Rolls, 1835; Norman Rolls, 1835; Fine
Rolls, 1835; Charter Rolls, 1837; Liberate
Rolls, 1844; Modus tenendi Parliamentum,
1846.]
Wilhelmi Malmesbiriensis Monachi Gesta
Regum Anglorum. English Hist. Soc.
1840. [Ed. by Hardy.]
A Catalogue- of the Lords Chancellors,
Keepers of the Great Seal, Masters of the
Rolls, [etc.]. 1843.
Monumenta Historica Britannica. Vol. i (all
pbd), 1848. [Projected by Henry Petrie
(1768–1842) and completed by Hardy.]
Memoirs of Henry, Lord Langdale. 2 vols. 1852.
Fasti Ecclesiae Anglicanae [by John Le Neve]
corrected and continued from 1715. 1854.
A Review of the Present State of the [J. P.
Collier] Shakespearian Controversy. 1860.
A Descriptive Catalogue of Materials relating
to the History of Great Britain and Ireland
to the End of the Reign of Henry VII.
Rolls Ser. 1862–71.
A Syllabus in English of Rymer's Foedera.
Rolls Ser. 1869.
Registrum Palatinum Dunelmense. Rolls
Ser. 1873–8. [Ed. by Hardy.]

JOHN DORAN (1807–1878)

[See p. 712 above.]

JOHN MITCHELL KEMBLE (1807–1857)

The Anglo-Saxon Poems of Beowulf, etc.
1833; 1835. [Ed. by Kemble.]
A Few Historical Remarks upon the Sup-
posed Antiquity of Church Rates. By a Lay
Member of the Church of England. 1836;
1837.
[Introduction to Francisque Michel's] Biblio-
thèque anglo-saxonne. Paris, 1837.
A Translation of the Anglo-Saxon Poem of
Beowulf. 1837.
Codex Diplomaticus Aevi Saxonici. 6 vols.
English Historical Soc. 1839–48.
The Poetry of the Codex Vercellensis, with
an English Translation. Aelfric Soc. 1843.
[Ed. by Kemble.]
Salomon and Saturn. [1845? All but 20 copies
called in.]
The Dialogue of Salomon and Saturnus, with
an Historical Introduction. Aelfric Soc.
1848. [Ed. by Kemble.]
Certaine Considerations upon the Govern-
ment of England. By Sir Roger Twysden.
Camden Soc. 1849. [Ed. by Kemble.]
The Saxons in England. 2 vols. 1849; ed.
W. de G. Birch, 2 vols. 1876.
State Papers and Correspondence illustrative
of the State of Europe [1686–1716]. 1857.
[Ed. by Kemble.]
The Utility of Antiquarian Collections.
Dublin, 1857.
[Historical Introduction to] The Knights
Hospitallers in England. Ed. L. B. Larking,
Camden Soc. 1857.
The Gospel according to Saint Matthew in
Anglo-Saxon and Northumbrian. Cam-
bridge, 1858. [Ed. by Kemble.]
Horæ Ferales, or Studies in the Archaeology
of the Northern Nations. Ed. R. G.
Latham and A. W. Franks, 1863.

JAMES SPEDDING (1808–1881)

[See p. 725 above.]

WILLIAM NATHANAEL MASSEY (1809–1881)

A History of England during the Reign of
George the Third. 4 vols. 1855–63; 4 vols.
1865.

JOHN FORSTER (1812–1876)

[See p. 713 above.]

SIR EDWARD AUGUSTUS BOND (1815–1898)

Russia at the Close of the Sixteenth Century.
Hakluyt Soc. 1856.
Speeches of the Manager and Counsel in the
Trial of Warren Hastings. 4 vols. 1859–61.

Chronica Monasterii de Melsa. Rolls Ser. 1868.
Facsimiles of Ancient Charters in the British Museum. 1873.

[The above were all ed. by Bond. He founded the Palaeographical Society in 1873 and edited facs. of MSS for it. He also pbd catalogues of and guides to the MSS in the BM.]

JOHN HENEAGE JESSE (1815–1874)

Mary Queen of Scots; and Other Poems. 1829.
Tales of the Dead; and Other Poems. 1830.
Memoirs of the Court of England during tne Reign of the Stuarts. 4 vols. 1840; 3 vols. 1855 (rev.); 1857.
Memoirs of the Court of England from the Revolution to the Death of George the Second. 3 vols. 1843.
George Selwyn and his Contemporaries. 4 vols. 1843–4.
Memoirs of the Pretenders and their Adherents. 2 vols. 1845; 1858.
London. A Fragmentary Poem. 1847.
Literary and Historical Memorials of London. 2 vols. 1847. Ser. 2: London and its Celebrities. 2 vols. 1850. Both sers. 3 vols. 1871 (as London: its Celebrated Characters and Remarkable Places.)
Memoirs of Richard the Third. With an Historical Drama on the Battle of Bosworth. 1862.
Memoirs of the Life and Reign of George the Third. 3 vols. 1867.
Memoirs of Celebrated Etonians. 2 vols. 1875.

WILLIAM DOUGAL CHRISTIE (1816–1874)

Memoirs, Letters, and Speeches of Anthony Ashley Cooper, First Earl of Shaftesbury. 1859. [Ed. by Christie.]
The Poetical Works of Dryden. 1870 (Globe edn). [Ed. by Christie.]
A Life of Anthony Ashley Cooper, First Earl of Shaftesbury. 2 vols. 1871.
Letters addressed from London to Sir Joseph Williamson while at the Congress of Cologne. 2 vols. Camden Soc. 1874. [Ed. by Christie.]

ELIZA METEYARD (1816–1879)

The Hallowed Spots of Ancient London. 1862.
The Life of Josiah Wedgwood. 2 vols. 1865–6.
A Group of Englishmen (1795–1815) being Records of the Younger Wedgwoods and their Friends. 1871.

MARY ANNE EVERETT GREEN (née WOOD) (1818–1895)

Letters of Royal and Illustrious Ladies of Great Britain. 3 vols. 1846. [Ed. by Mrs Green.]

Lives of the Princesses of England, from the Conquest. 6 vols. 1849–55. [Elizabeth, Electress Palatine and Queen of Bohemia, rev. S. C. Lomas, 1909.]
Diary of John Rous, 1625 to 1642. Camden Soc., 1856. [Ed. by Mrs Green.]
Letters of Queen Henrietta Maria. 1857. [Ed. by Mrs Green.]
Calendar of State Papers, Domestic Series, of the Reign of Elizabeth (James I), vols. III–XII; Commonwealth (13 vols.); Charles II, vols. I–X; Committee for Advance of Money (3 pts); Committee for Compounding with Delinquents (5 pts). 41 vols. 1857–95. [Ed. by Mrs Green.]

RICHARD SIMPSON (1820–1876)

Under the Penal Laws. Instances of the Sufferings of Catholics. Contributed to the Rambler, 1857–60. 1930.
The Lady Falkland: her Life. From a MS in the Imperial Archives at Lille. Also, A Memoir of Father Francis Slingsby. From MSS in the Royal Library, Brussels. 1861. [Ed. by Simpson.]
Edmund Campion. A Biography. 1867; 1896.
The School of Shakspere. 2 vols. 1878. [Reprints, with notes by J. W. M. Gibbs and a preface by F. J. Furnivall.]

WILLIAM HEPWORTH DIXON (1821–1879)

John Howard, and the Prison-World of Europe. 1849; 1850 (bis); 1854 (abridged, as John Howard, a Memoir).
The London Prisons. 1850.
William Penn. An Historical Biography. With an Extra Chapter on 'The Macaulay Charges.' 1851; Philadelphia, 1851; 1856; 2 vols. Berlin, 1872; 1872; tr. German, Leipzig, 1854.
Robert Blake, Admiral and General at Sea. 1852; 1856.
Personal History of Lord Bacon. 1861; Boston, 1861; Leipzig, 1861.
Proof—Private. Lord Bacon's Confession: a Statement of the Facts. 1861.
The Story of Lord Bacon's Life. 1862.
Lady Morgan's Memoirs. Autobiography, Diaries and Correspondence. 2 vols. 1862; 2 vols. 1863 (rev.); 3 vols. Leipzig, 1863. [Ed. by Dixon.]
Her Majesty's Tower. 4 vols. 1869–71; 2 vols. 1885 (7th edn); tr. German, Berlin, 1870.
History of Two Queens. I: Catherine of Aragon. II: Anne Boleyn. 4 vols. 1873–4.
Royal Windsor. 4 vols. 1879–80.

[Dixon also pbd many travel books.]

DAVID MASSON (1822–1907)

[See p. 720 above.]

JOHN EYTON BICKERSTETH MAYOR
(1825–1910)

[See p. 1007 below.]

JAMES AUGUSTUS COTTER MORISON
(1832–1888)

The Life and Times of Saint Bernard. 1863;
1868 (rev.).
Gibbon. 1878 (*bis*). (English Men of Letters
ser.)
Macaulay. 1882. (English Men of Letters ser.)
Madame de Maintenon. An Étude. [1885.]

C. ENGLISH HISTORY (SPECIAL ASPECTS)

JOHN CAMPBELL (BARON CAMPBELL)
(1779–1861)

The Lives of the Lord Chancellors and Keepers
of the Great Seal of England, from the
Earliest Times till the Reign of George IV.
3 sers. 7 vols. 1845–7; 10 vols. 1856–7 (4th
edn); vol. VIII, 1869 (till the reign of Queen
Victoria).
The Lives of the Chief Justices of England.
From the Norman Conquest till the Death
of Lord Mansfield. 2 vols. 1849; vol. III,
1857 (till the death of Lord Tenterden);
3 vols. 1858; 4 vols. 1874.
Shakespeare's Legal Acquirements considered.
1859.

[For criticism see E. B. Sugden (Baron
St Leonards), Misrepresentations in Campbell's
Lives of Lyndhurst and Brougham corrected,
1869.]

SIR WILLIAM FRANCIS PATRICK NAPIER
(1785–1860)

(a) *Writings*

History of the War in the Peninsula and in the
South of France. 6 vols. 1828–40; 1832–3
(vols. I–III); 1835–40 (vols. I–III); 1848
(vol. I); 6 vols. 1851 (rev.); 3 vols. 1878
[1877–82]; 3 pts, 1893. Abridged by Napier
as English Battles and Sieges in the Penin-
sula. 1852; 1855; 1904; 1910; tr. French,
Paris, 1828–44 (the whole work).
A Reply to Lord Strangford's 'Observations'
on some Passages in Colonel Napier's
History. 1828.
A Reply to Various Opponents; together with
Observations illustrating Sir John Moore's
Campaigns. 1832 (prefixed to 2nd edn of
the History); 1833 (separately).
Colonel Napier's Justification of his Third
Volume. 1833.
A Letter to General Lord Viscount Beresford,
being an Answer to his Lordship's Assumed
Refutation of Colonel Napier's Justifica-
tion. 1834.

Counter-Remarks to Mr Dudley Montagu
Perceval's Remarks upon Passages in
Colonel Napier's Fourth Volume. 1835.
The Conquest of Scinde, with Introductory
Passages in the Life of Sir Charles Napier.
2 pts, 1845.
History of Sir Charles Napier's Administration
of Scinde, and Campaign in the Cutchee
Hills. 1851.
The Life and Opinions of General Sir C. J.
Napier. 4 vols. 1857 (*bis*).

(b) *Biography and Criticism*

Outram, Sir James. The Conquest of Scinde.
A Commentary. Edinburgh, 1846.
Buist, G. Corrections of a Few of the Errors
contained in Sir Wm. Napier's Life of Sir
Charles Napier. 1857.
Bruce, H. A. (Baron Aberdare). Life of Sir
William Napier. 2 vols. 1864. [Ed. by
Aberdare.]
Holmes, T. R. E. Four Famous Soldiers. 1889.

SAMUEL ROFFEY MAITLAND (1792–1866)

Eruvin, or Miscellaneous Essays connected
with the Nature, History, and Destiny of
Man. 1831 (anon.); 1850.
Facts and Documents illustrative of the
History, Doctrine, and Rites, of the ancient
Albigenses and Waldenses. 1832.
A Letter to the Rev. Hugh James Rose, with
Strictures on Milner's Church History. 1834.
A Second Letter to the Rev. Hugh James
Rose, containing Notes on Milner's History
of the Church in the Fourth Century. 1835.
A Letter to the Rev. John King occasioned by
his Pamphlet 'Maitland not authorized to
censure Milner.' 1835.
Remarks on that Part of the Rev. J. King's
Pamphlet which relates to the Waldenses.
1836.
A Review of Fox the Martyrologist's History
of the Waldenses. 1837.
Six Letters on Fox's Acts and Monuments,
addressed to the British Magazine and re-
printed with Notes and Additions. 1837.
A Letter to the Rev. W. H. Mill, containing
some Strictures on Mr Faber's 'The Ancient
Vallenses and Albigenses.' 1839.
Notes on the Contributions of the Rev. George
Townsend to the New Edition of Fox's
Martyrology. 3 pts, 1841–2.
Remarks on the Rev. S. R. Cattley's Defence
of his Edition of Fox's Martyrology. 1842.
The Dark Ages. A Series of Essays, intended
to illustrate the State of Religion and
Literature in the Ninth, Tenth, Eleventh,
and Twelfth Centuries. Reprinted from
'The British Magazine,' with Additions.
1844; 1845; 1889.

Remarks on the First Volume of Strype's Life of Archbishop Cranmer. Reprinted from 'The British Magazine.' 1848.

Essays on Subjects connected with the Reformation in England. Reprinted, with Additions, from 'The British Magazine.' 1849; 1899.

Eight Essays on Various Subjects. 1852.

Chatterton. An Essay. 1857.

Notes on Strype. [Gloucester, 1858.]

A Supplication for Toleration, addressed to King James I by some of the Late Silenced Ministers. Now reprinted with the King's Notes. 1859.

JAMES ROBINSON PLANCHÉ (1796–1880)

[See p. 592 above.]

WALTER FARQUHAR HOOK (1798–1875)

[See p. 857 above.]

BERIAH BOTFIELD (1807–1863)

Catalogi veteres Librorum Ecclesiae cathedralis Dunelm. Surtees Soc. 1840.

Manners and Household Expenses of England in the Thirteenth and Fifteenth Centuries. Roxburghe Club, 1841.

The History of the Kirk of Scotland from 1558 to 1637, by John Row. Woodrow Soc. 1842.

The Buke of the Order of Knyghthood, translated from the French of Sir Gilbert Hay. Abbotsford Club, 1847.

Notes on the Cathedral Libraries of England. 1849.

Original Letters relating to the Ecclesiastical Affairs of Scotland, 1603–25. Bannatyne Club, 1851.

Prefationes et Epistolae Editionibus principibus Auctorum veterum praepositae. 1861.

[With the exception of Notes on Cathedral Libraries the above were all ed. by Botfield. He contributed important bibliographical papers to Philobiblon Soc. Misc. I–VI, as well as writing genealogical and topographical pamphlets.]

ALEXANDER WILLIAM KINGLAKE (1809–1891)

Eothen, or Traces of Travel brought Home from the East. 1844 (anon.); Leipzig, 1846; 1856; 1859; 1864; 1878; rptd Edinburgh, 1896 (with biographical sketch by A. I. Shand); rptd 1908 (Everyman's Lib.); rptd 1910 (World's Classics).

The Invasion of the Crimea. 8 vols. Edinburgh, 1863–87; vols. I and II, Edinburgh, 1863 (3 edns); vols. I and II, 4 vols. Leipzig, 1863; 9 vols. Edinburgh, 1877–88 (6th edn).

[For biography and criticism see A. Hayward, Mr Kinglake and the Quarterlys, by An Old Reviewer, 1863, and W. Tuckwell,

A. W. Kinglake, a Biographical and Literary Study, 1902.]

WILLIAM FORSYTH (1812–1899)

[See p. 713 above.]

SIR THOMAS ERSKINE MAY (BARON FARNBOROUGH) (1815–1886)

The Imperial Parliament. 1840 (in Penny Cyclopædia, vol. XVII; anon.); [1841] (in Knight's Store of Knowledge).

A Treatise upon the Law, Privileges, Proceedings and Usage of Parliament. 1844; 1851; 1855; 1859; 1863; 1868; 1873; 1879; 1883; ed. Sir R. F. D. Palgrave and A. Bonham Carter, 1893; ed. Sir T. L. Webster, 1921.

Remarks and Suggestions with a View to facilitate the Dispatch of Public Business in Parliament. 1849 (bis).

On the Consolidation of the Election Laws. 1850. [Rptd from Law Mag.]

The Machinery of Parliamentary Legislation. Edinburgh Rev. XCIX, 1854; 1881 (separately).

The Constitutional History of England since the Accession of George the Third, 1760–1860. 2 vols. 1861–3; 2 vols. 1863–5; 3 vols. 1871 (with supplementary ch.); ed. and continued by F. Holland, 3 vols. 1912. Tr. French, Paris, 1865–6; Spanish, Madrid, 1883–4.

Democracy in Europe. A History. 2 vols. 1877; tr. Italian, 1883.

ARTHUR PENRHYN STANLEY (1815–1881)

(a) Writings

The Life and Correspondence of Thomas Arnold. 2 vols. 1844 (3 edns); 2 vols. 1845 (bis); 1846; 2 vols. 1877 (10th edn); 2 vols. 1881 (12th edn); tr. German, Potsdam, 1847.

Sermons and Essays on the Apostolical Age. Oxford, 1847; Oxford, 1874 (3rd edn).

Historical Memorials of Canterbury. 1855 (bis); 1857; 1865; 1900; 1904 (10th edn); rptd 1906 (Everyman's Lib.); 1912.

The Epistles of St Paul to the Corinthians; with Critical Notes and Dissertations. 2 vols. 1855; 1858; 1865; 1876.

Sinai and Palestine in Connection with their History. 1856 (3 edns); 1857; 1866.

Three Introductory Lectures on the Study of Ecclesiastical History. Oxford, 1857.

Lectures on the History of the Eastern Church. 1861; 1862; 1869 (4th edn); 1883; rptd 1907 (Everyman's Lib.).

A Letter to the Bishop of London on the State of Subscription in the Church of England and in the University of Oxford. Oxford, 1863.

Lectures on the History of the Jewish Church. 2 vols. 1863–5; 3 pts, 1866–77 (4th edn); 3 vols. 1883.

Historical Memorials of Westminster Abbey. 1868 (*bis*); 1869; 1876; 1882.

Essays chiefly on Questions of Church and State, 1850–1870. 1870; 1884.

Lectures on the History of the Church of Scotland. 1872; 1879.

Addresses and Sermons delivered at St Andrews. 1877.

Christian Institutions. Essays on Ecclesiastical Subjects. 1881; 1882 (3rd edn); 1884.

Addresses and Sermons delivered during a Visit to the United States and Canada. 1883.

Letters and Verses. Ed. R. E. Prothero, 1895.

(b) Biography and Criticism

Bradley, G. G. Recollections of Arthur Penrhyn Stanley. 1883.

Prothero, R. E. (Baron Ernle) and Bradley, G. G. The Life and Correspondence of Arthur Penrhyn Stanley. 2 vols. 1893. [Includes bibliography.]

Baillie, A. V. and Bolitho, H. A Victorian Dean. A Memoir of Arthur Stanley, with Many Unpublished Letters. 1930.

JOHN MASON NEALE (1818–1866)

[See p. 301 above.]

MACKENZIE EDWARD CHARLES WALCOTT (1821–1880)

Westminster: Memorials of the City. 1849; 1851.

A Handbook for the Parish of Saint James, Westminster. 1850.

The English Ordinal: its History, Validity and Catholicity. 1851.

William of Wykeham and his Colleges. 1852.

A Handbook for Winchester Cathedral. 1854.

The English Episcopate. Biographical Memoirs. 5 pts, 1858.

A Guide to the Cathedrals of England and Wales. 1858; 1860 (enlarged).

The Minsters and Abbey Ruins of the United Kingdom. 1860.

Sacred Archaeology. A Popular Dictionary. 1860.

Church and Conventual Arrangement. [1861.]

Cathedralia: A Constitutional History of Cathedrals of the Western Church. 1865.

Traditions and Customs of Cathedrals. 1872; 1872 (rev.).

Scoti-Monasticon, the Ancient Church of Scotland. 1874.

The Constitutions and Canons Ecclesiastical of the Church of England. 1874. [Ed. by Walcott.]

[And many other works on ecclesiastical history, guide-books, poems, etc.]

D. ENGLISH HISTORY (LOCAL)

GEORGE LIPSCOMB (1773–1846)

A Journey into Cornwall, through the Counties of Southampton, Wilts, Dorset, Somerset and Devon. Warwick, 1799.

Journey into South Wales, through the Counties of Oxford, Warwick, Worcester, Hereford, Salop, Stafford, Buckingham, and Hertford, in 1799. 1802.

A Description of Matlock-Bath. Birmingham, 1802.

The History and Antiquities of the County of Buckingham. 4 vols. [1831]–47.

GEORGE ORMEROD (1785–1873)

The History of the County Palatine and City of Chester. 3 vols. 1819; ed. T. Helsby, 3 vols. 1875–82.

Tracts relating to Military Proceedings in Lancashire during the Great Civil War. Chetham Soc. 1844. [Ed. by Ormerod.]

Miscellanea Palatina. Consisting of Genealogical Essays illustrative of Cheshire and Lancashire Families, and of a Memoir on the Cheshire Domesday Roll. 1851 [1850–1] (priv. ptd). [Consists of the following, all with separate title-pages, the pagination continuous through the first two, separate for the third and fourth: A Memoir on the Lancashire House of Le Norreis or Norres. Liverpool, 1850. Miscellanea Palatina. Pt 2: Genealogical Memoirs illustrative of the Families of Aldford, Arderne, Banastre, Bredbury, Done, [etc.]. 1851 (priv. ptd). A Memoir on the Cheshire Domesday Roll. 1851 (priv. ptd). Additions and Index to Miscellanea Palatina. N.d. (priv. ptd).]

Parentalia. Genealogical Memoirs. 1851 [1850–6] (priv. ptd). [Consists of 2 pts, with appendix to pt 2, and of the following which have separate title-pages and pagination: Genealogical Essays illustrative of Cheshire and Lancashire Families, and A Memoir on the Cheshire Domesday Roll. 1851 (priv. ptd). A Memoir on the Lancashire House of Le Norreis or Norres. Liverpool, 1850. The Early Connexion of the families of Stokeport, Fitz-Roger, Banastre, and Gernet. 1851 (priv. ptd). A Memoir on the Cheshire Domesday Roll. 1851 (priv. ptd). Additions and Index to Parentalia and Genealogical Memoirs. 1856 (priv. ptd).]

A Memoir on British and Roman Remains, Illustrative of Communications with Venta Silurum, Antient Passages of the Bristol Channel and Antonine's Iter XIV. Communicated to the Annual Meeting of the Archaeological Institute at Bristol, July, 1851. 1852 (priv. ptd).

Remarks on a Line of Earthworks in Tidenham, known as Offa's Dyke. 1859 (priv. ptd).

Observations on Recent Discoveries of Roman Remains in Sedbury. Gloucester, [1860] (priv. ptd).

Observations on Recent Discoveries of Roman Remains in Sedbury, and on the Site of a Roman Military Position there. Read to the Gloucester Congress of the Archaeological Institute, 1860. Gloucester, [1860]; 1860 (priv. ptd).

Strigulensia. Archæological Memoirs relating to the District Adjacent to the Confluence of the Severn and the Wye. 1861 (priv. ptd).

THOMAS WALKER HORSFIELD (d. 1837)

The History and Antiquities of Lewes and its Vicinity. 2 vols. Lewes, 1824–7.

The History, Antiquities, and Topography of the County of Sussex. 2 vols. Lewes, 1835.

ALFRED INIGO SUCKLING (1796–1856)

Selections from the Works of Sir John Suckling. To which is prefixed a Life of the Author. 1836.

Memorials of the Ancient Architecture, Sculpture, and Heraldry of the County of Essex. 1845. [And in John Weale's Quarterly Papers on Architecture, vol. III, 1845.]

The History and Antiquities of the County of Suffolk. 2 vols. 1846–8.

JOHN COLLINGWOOD BRUCE (1805–1892)

A Guide to the Castle of Newcastle upon Tyne. Newcastle-on-Tyne, 1847.

The Hand Book of English History. 1848; 1857 (3rd edn).

The Roman Wall. 1851; 1853; 1867.

The Bayeux Tapestry Elucidated. 1856.

An Illustrative and Descriptive Catalogue of the Inscribed and Sculptured Stones of the Roman Period, belonging to the Society of Antiquaries of Newcastle-upon-Tyne. Newcastle-on-Tyne, 1857.

The Wallet-Book of the Roman Wall. 1863; 1884; 1885 (as Hand-Book); ed. R. Blair, 1895, 1907, 1909, 1914; ed. R. Blair, Newcastle-on-Tyne, 1921; ed. R. G. Collingwood, Newcastle-on-Tyne, 1933.

A Hand-Book to Newcastle-on-Tyne. 1863; 1864.

Incised Markings on Stone, found in Northumberland, Argyleshire, and other Places. 1869 (priv. ptd). [Ed. by Bruce.]

Lapidarium Septentrionale, or a Description of the Monuments of Roman Rule in the North of England. 5 pts, Soc. of Antiquaries of Newcastle-upon-Tyne, 1870–5.

The Story, partly Sad and partly Gay, of the Thorngrafton 'Find.' [1871] (priv. ptd).

The Wall of Hadrian; with Especial Reference to Recent Discoveries. Two Lectures. Newcastle-on-Tyne, 1874.

Northumbrian Minstrelsy. A Collection of the Ballads, Melodies, and Small-Pipe Tunes of Northumbria. Soc. of Antiquaries of Newcastle-upon-Tyne, 1882. [Ed. by Bruce and J. Stokoe.]

Newcastle-upon-Tyne Royal Mining, Engineering, and Industrial Exhibition, 1887. The Bridges and the Floods of Newcastle-upon-Tyne. Newcastle-on-Tyne, [1887].

CHARLES ROACH SMITH (1807–1890)

Collectanea Antiqua. Etchings and Notices of Ancient Remains. 7 vols. 1848–80. [Contains, in vols. II, III, and IV respectively, the following separately pbd works: Notes on the Antiquities of Treves, Mayence, Wiesbaden, Niederbieber, Bonn, and Cologne. 1851. The Faussett Collection of Anglo-Saxon Antiquities. 1854. Public Dinner given to Mr C. R. Smith, at Newport, Isle of Wight, on 28 Aug. 1855. [1855.]]

The Antiquities of Richborough, Reculver, and Lymne in Kent. 1850.

Catalogue of the Museum of London Antiquities collected by Charles Roach Smith. 1854 (ptd for subscribers).

Inventorium Sepulchrale. By Bryan Faussett. 1856. [Ed. by Smith.]

Report on Excavations made upon the Site of the Roman Castrum at Pevensey, in 1852. 1858.

Illustrations of Roman London. 1859 (priv. ptd).

On the Importance of Public Museums for Historical Collections. Trans. Hist. Soc. of Lancs. and Cheshire, XII, 1860.

Remarks on Shakespeare, his Birth-place, etc. 1868–9 (priv. ptd); 1877.

The Rural Life of Shakespeare. 1870; 1874.

South Kensington Museum. A Catalogue of Anglo-Saxon and Other Antiquities, discovered at Faversham, and bequeathed by William Gibbs. 1871; 1873.

Retrospections, Social and Archaeological. 3 vols. 1883–91.

[For life see H. Smetham, Charles Roach Smith and his Friends, being Personal Recollections, [1929].]

CHARLES HENRY COOPER (1808–1866)

A New Guide to the University and Town of Cambridge. Cambridge, 1831 (anon.).

Annals of Cambridge. Vols. I–IV, Cambridge, 1842–52; vol. v, 1850–6; with index, ed. J. W. Cooper, Cambridge, 1908.

Athenae Cantabrigienses, 1500–1609. 2 vols. Cambridge, 1858–61; vol. III (1609–11), Cambridge, 1913 (with addns and corrections, and a complete index). [With T. Cooper.]

Memorials of Cambridge. [By T. Wright and H. Longueville Jones.] A New Edition. 2 vols. Cambridge, 1860; 3 vols. Cambridge, [1880].

Memoir of Margaret Countess of Richmond and Derby. Ed. J. E. B. Mayor, Cambridge, 1874.

FREDERICK WILLIAM FAIRHOLT (1814–1866)

Lord Mayors' Pageants. Percy Soc. 1842.

The Civic Garland. A Collection of Songs from London Pageants. Percy Soc. 1845. [Ed. by Fairholt.]

Costume in England. 1846; 1860; rev. H. A. Dillon, 2 vols. 1885.

A Dialogue on Wit and Folly by John Heywood. Percy Soc. 1846. [Ed. by Fairholt.]

The Home of Shakspere. 1847.

Eccentric and Remarkable Characters. Vol. I (all pbd), 1849.

Satirical Songs and Poems on Costume. Percy Soc. 1849. [Ed. by Fairholt.]

A Dictionary of Terms in Art. 1854; [1870].

Gog and Magog. 1857.

The Dramatic Works of John Lyly. 2 vols. 1858. [Ed. by Fairholt.]

Tobacco, its History and Associations. 1859; 1876.

Up the Nile. 1862.

Homes, Haunts and Works of Rubens, Vandyke, Rembrandt and Cuyp, Michael Angelo and Raffaelle. Ed. J. D[afforne], 1871.

Rambles of an Archaeologist among Old Books and in Old Places. 1871.

Homes, Works and Shrines of English Artists. 1873.

[Fairholt illustrated most of his writings himself as well as many other antiquarian works. He also pbd some catalogues and contributed regularly to Archaeologia, Journ. British Archaeological Ass., Numismatic Chronicle, etc.]

ROBERT WILLIAM EYTON (1815–1881)

Antiquities of Shropshire. 12 vols. 1853–60.

Notes on Domesday. Reprinted from the Transactions of the Shropshire Archaeological Society, 1877. 1880.

Court, Household, and Itinerary of King Henry II. 1878.

A Key to Domesday, showing the Method and Exactitude of its Mensuration, and the Meaning of its Formulæ. Exemplified by an Analysis and Digest of the Dorset Survey. 1878.

Domesday Studies. An Analysis and Digest of the Somerset Survey. 2 vols. 1880.

Domesday Studies. An Analysis and Digest of the Staffordshire Survey. 1881.

PETER CUNNINGHAM (1816–1869)

[See p. 1029 below.]

E. SCOTTISH AND IRISH HISTORY

HENRY THOMAS COCKBURN (BARON COCKBURN) (1779–1854)

Life of Lord Jeffrey. 2 vols. Edinburgh, 1852 (bis).

Memorials of his Time. Edinburgh, 1856; ed. H. A. Cockburn, Edinburgh, 1909.

Journal: being a Continuation of the Memorials, 1831–54. 2 vols. Edinburgh, 1874.

Some Letters with pages omitted from Memorials of his Time. Ed. H. A. Cockburn, Edinburgh, 1932.

HEW SCOTT (1791–1872)

Fasti Ecclesiae Scoticanae: the Succession of Ministers in the Parish Churches of Scotland from A.D. 1560 to the Present Time. 3 vols. Edinburgh, 1866–71; 7 vols. Edinburgh, 1915–28 (rev. and continued).

DAVID LAING (1793–1878)

[See p. 1026 below.]

COSMO INNES (1798–1874)

(a) Editions

Two Ancient Records of the Bishopric of Caithness. 1827; Bannatyne Club, 1848.

Registrum Monasterii de Passelet [Paisley]. Maitland Club, 1832.

Liber Sancte Marie de Melros. Bannatyne Club, 1837.

Registrum Episcopatus Moraviensis. Bannatyne Club, 1837.

Liber Cartarum Sancte Crucis. Munimenta Eccles. Sanct. Crucis de Edwinesburg. Bannatyne Club, 1840.

Registrum de Dunfermelyn. Bannatyne Club, 1842.

Registrum Episcopatus Glasguensis. Bannatyne Club, 1843.

Liber S. Marie de Calchon [Kelso]. Bannatyne Club, 1846.

Liber Insulae Missarum: Abbacii de Inchaffery Registrum. Bannatyne Club, 1847.

Carte Monialium de Northberwic. Bannatyne Club, 1847.

Liber S. Thome de Aberbrothoc [Arbroath]. Bannatyne Club, 1848. [With P. Chalmers.]

Registrum S. Marie de Neubotle. Bannatyne Club, 1849.

Origines Parochiales Scotiae. Bannatyne Club, 1850.

Fasti Aberdonenses. Spalding Club, 1854.

The Black Book of Taymouth. Bannatyne Club, 1855.

Registrum Episcopatus Brechinensis. Spalding Club, 1856.

The Brus [by Barbour]. Spalding Club, 1856.

The Book of the Thanes of Cawdor. Spalding Club, 1859.

Ledger of A. Halyburton, 1492–1503. 1867.

[Innes also assisted in editing Acts of the Scots Parliament, 1844–75.]

(b) Writings

Scotland in the Middle Ages. Edinburgh, 1860.

Sketches of Early Scotch History and Social Progress. Edinburgh, 1861.

Ancient Laws and Customs of the Burghs of Scotland. 1868.

Lectures on Scotch Legal Antiquities. Edinburgh, 1872.

[An anon. Memoir of Cosmo Innes was issued at Edinburgh, 1874.]

MARK NAPIER (1798–1879)

Memoirs of John Napier of Merchiston, his Lineage, Life, and Times. Edinburgh, 1834.

History of the Partition of Lennox. Edinburgh, 1835.

Montrose and the Covenanters. 2 vols. 1838.

De Arte Logistica Joannis Naperi. Edinburgh, 1839. [Ed. by Napier.]

The Life and Times of Montrose. Edinburgh, 1840.

Memorials of Montrose and his Times. 2 vols. Maitland Club, Edinburgh, 1848–50. [Ed. by Napier.]

History of the Church of Scotland. By John Spottiswoode. 3 vols. Spottiswoode Soc. 1847–51. [Vols. II and III ed. by Napier.]

Memoirs of the Marquis of Montrose. 2 vols. Edinburgh, 1856.

Memorials and Letters illustrative of the Life and Times of John Graham of Claverhouse, Viscount Dundee. 3 vols. Edinburgh, 1859–62.

ROBERT CHAMBERS (1802–1871)

[See p. 709 above.]

JOHN HILL BURTON (1809–1881)

The Works of Jeremy Bentham. Published under the Superintendence of John Bowring. 11 vols. Edinburgh, [1838]–1843. [Burton was one of the editors.]

A Manual of the Law of Scotland. Edinburgh, 1839; 2 vols. Edinburgh, 1847 (enlarged).

Jacobite Correspondence of the Atholl Family, during the Rebellion, 1745–6. Abbotsford Club, Edinburgh, 1840. [Ed. by Burton and D. Laing.]

Benthamiana, or Select Extracts from the Works of Jeremy Bentham. Edinburgh, 1843. [Ed. by Burton.]

The Law of Bankruptcy in Scotland. 2 pts. Edinburgh, 1845.

The Local Taxes of Scotland. [In The Local Taxes of the United Kingdom. Poor Law Commissioners, 1846.]

Life and Correspondence of David Hume. 2 vols. Edinburgh, 1846.

Lives of Simon Lord Lovat, and Duncan Forbes, of Culloden. 1847.

Letters of Eminent Persons to David Hume. Edinburgh, 1849. [Ed. by Burton.]

Manual of Political and Social Economy. Edinburgh, 1849.

The Darien Papers, 1695–1700. Bannatyne Club, Edinburgh, 1849. [Ed. by Burton.]

Emigration in its Practical Application. [In The Emigrant's Manual, Edinburgh, 1851.]

Narratives from Criminal Trials in Scotland. 2 vols. 1852.

History of Scotland, from the Revolution to the Extinction of the Last Jacobite Insurrection (1689–1748). 2 vols. 1853; 8 vols. Edinburgh, 1873 (with History of Scotland to 1688).

Autobiography of the Rev. Dr Alexander Carlyle. Edinburgh, 1860; 1910. [Ed. by Burton.]

The Book-Hunter. Edinburgh, 1862; Edinburgh, 1863; Edinburgh, 1882; ed. J. H. Slater, [1908].

The Scot Abroad. 2 vols. Edinburgh, 1864; Edinburgh, 1881.

The Cairngorm Mountains. Edinburgh, 1864.

The History of Scotland from Agricola's Invasion to 1688. 7 vols. Edinburgh, 1867–70; 8 vols. Edinburgh, 1873 (with History of Scotland 1689–1748).

A Letter on Shakspere's Authorship of The Two Noble Kinsmen. By W. Spalding. New Edition, with Life of the Author, by John Hill Burton. New Shakspere Soc. 1876.

The Register of the Privy Council of Scotland. Vols. I–II. Edinburgh, 1877–8. [Ed. by Burton.]

A History of the Reign of Queen Anne. 3 vols. Edinburgh, 1880.

WILLIAM FORBES SKENE (1809–1892)

The Highlanders of Scotland, their Origin, History, and Antiquities. 2 vols. 1837; ed. A. Macbain, Stirling, 1902.

The Dean of Lismore's Book. Edinburgh, 1862. [Ed. by T. M'Lauchlan; introduction and additional notes by Skene.]

Chronicles of the Picts, Chronicles of the Scots, and Other Early Memorials of Scottish History. Chronicles and Memorials published under the Direction of the Lord Clerk-Register. Edinburgh, 1867. [Ed. by Skene.]

The Four Ancient Books of Wales. 2 vols. Edinburgh, 1868. [Ed. by Skene.]

The Coronation Stone. Edinburgh, 1869.

Johannis de Fordun Chronica Gentis Scotorum. Edinburgh, 1871; tr. English, Edinburgh, 1872. [Both ed. by Skene.]

Celtic Scotland. 3 vols. Edinburgh, 1876–80; 3 vols. Edinburgh, 1886–90.

Memorials of the Family of Skene of Skene. New Spalding Club, Aberdeen, 1887. [Ed. by Skene.]

JOSEPH ROBERTSON (1810–1866)

History of the Reformation in Aberdeen. Aberdeen Observer, nos. 1–4, 1837 (anon.); rptd Aberdeen, 1887.

The Book of Bon-Accord, or a Guide to Aberdeen. Vol. I (all pbd), Aberdeen, 1839 (anon.).

Deliciae Literariae. A New Volume of Table-talk. 1840 (anon.).

History of Scots Affairs, 1637–1641. By James Gordon, Parson of Rothiemay. 3 vols. Spalding Club, Aberdeen, 1841. [Ed. by Robertson and G. Grub.]

Collections for a History of the Shires of Aberdeen and Banff. Spalding Club, Aberdeen, 1843. [Ed. by Robertson.]

Liber Collegii Nostre Domine. Registrum Ecclesie B.V. Marie et S. Anne infra Muros Civitatis Glasguensis, 1549. Accedunt Munimenta Fratrum Predicatorum de Glasgu. Maitland Club, Glasgow, 1846. [Ed. by Robertson.]

Miscellany of the Maitland Club. Vol. IV, pt 1. Glasgow, 1847. [Ed. by Robertson.]

Illustrations of the Topography and Antiquities of Aberdeen and Banff. Spalding Club, Aberdeen, 1847–62. [Vols. II–IV ed. by Robertson.]

Passages from the Diary of Gen. Patrick Gordon, 1635–99. Spalding Club, Aberdeen, 1859. [Ed. by Robertson.]

Inventaires de la Royne Descosse. Catalogues of the Jewels, Dresses, Furniture, Books, and Paintings of Mary Queen of Scots. Bannatyne Club, Edinburgh, 1863. [Ed. by Robertson.]

Concilia Scotiae. Ecclesiae Scoticanae Statuta, 1225–1559. 2 vols. Bannatyne Club, Edinburgh, 1866. [Ed. by Robertson.]

Scottish Abbeys and Cathedrals. With Memoir of the Author. Aberdeen, 1891.

GEORGE GRUB (1812–1892)

History of Scots Affairs, 1637–1641. By James Gordon, Parson of Rothiemay. 3 vols. Spalding Club, Aberdeen, 1841. [Ed. by Joseph Robertson and Grub.]

The Civil and Ecclesiastical History of Scotland. A.D. 80–818. By Thomas Innes. Edited by George Grub. Spalding Club, Aberdeen, 1853; Edinburgh, 1879 (memoir, with A Critical Essay on the Ancient Inhabitants of Scotland, by T. Innes).

An Ecclesiastical History of Scotland. 4 vols. Edinburgh, 1861.

Illustrations of the Topography and Antiquities of Aberdeen and Banff. Vol. I [Preface and Index]. Spalding Club, Aberdeen, 1869.

ALEXANDER GEORGE RICHIE (1830–1883)

Lectures on the History of Ireland. 2 sers. Dublin, 1869; 1870; ed. R. R. Kane, Dublin, 1887 (with additional lectures, as A Short History of the Irish People, down to the Plantation of Ulster).

Ancient Laws of Ireland. Hiberniae Leges et Institutiones Antiquae. 4 vols. Dublin, 1873–9. [Vol. III ed. by T. O'Mahony and Richie; vol. IV ed. by Richie.]

F. BRITISH IMPERIAL HISTORY

MOUNTSTUART ELPHINSTONE (1779–1859)

An Account of the Kingdom of Caubul, and its Dependencies in Persia, Tartary, and India. 1815; 2 vols. 1819; 2 vols. 1839 (rev.).

The History of India. 2 vols. 1841; 1857 (4th edn); 1866 (with notes and addns by E. B. Cowell); rptd 1905 (9th edn). [Covers the Hindu and Mahometan periods.]

The Rise of the British Power in the East. Ed. Sir E. Colebrook, 1887.

JOHN CLARK MARSHMAN (1794–1877)

The History of India, from Remote Antiquity to the Accession of the Mogul Dynasty. Serampore, 1836; Serampore, 1842 (3rd edn); Serampore, 1860 (5th edn).

Outline of the History of Bengal. Serampore, 1844 (5th edn); Calcutta, 1887.

The Life and Times of Carey, Marshman, and Ward, embracing the History of the Serampore Mission. 2 vols. 1859; 1864 (bis).

Memoirs of Major-General Sir Henry Havelock. 1860; 1861; 1867.

The History of India. Part I: From the Earliest Period to the Close of the Eighteenth Century. Serampore, 1863.

The History of India; from the Earliest Period to the Close of Lord Dalhousie's Administration. 3 vols. 1867; Edinburgh, 1880; 1893 (continued to 1891 'by a relative'); abridgment, Edinburgh, 1876.

HERMAN MERIVALE (1806–1874)

An Introductory Lecture on the Study of Political Economy. 1837.

Introduction to a Course of Lectures upon Colonization and Colonies. 1839.

Lectures on Colonization and Colonies. 2 vols. 1841–2; 1861; photo. facs. 1928.

Historical Studies. 1865.

Memoirs of Sir Philip Francis. By J. Parkes. Completed and edited by Herman Merivale. 2 vols. 1867.

Life of Sir Henry Lawrence. Vol. II. 1872. [Vol. I is by Sir H. B. Edwardes.]

[For life see C. Merivale, Herman Merivale, C.B., Trans. Devonshire Ass. XVI, 1884.]

SIR JOHN WILLIAM KAYE (1814–1876)

Poems and Fragments. Jersey, 1835 (anon.).

Peregrine Pulteney; or, Life in India. 3 vols. 1844 (anon.). [Novel.]

Long Engagements; a Tale of the Affghan Rebellion. 1846 (anon.). [Novel.]

History of the War in Afghanistan. 2 vols. 1851; 3 vols. 1857–8; 3 vols. 1874; 3 vols. 1890.

Memoir of the Services of the Bengal Artillery. By E. Buckle. 1852. [Ed. by Kaye.]

The Administration of the East India Company. 1853 (bis).

Memorials of Indian Government. A Selection from the Papers of H. St G. Tucker. 1853. [Ed. by Kaye.]

The Life and Correspondence of Henry St George Tucker. 1854.

The Life and Correspondence of Charles, Lord Metcalfe. 2 vols. 1854; 2 vols. 1858.

Selections from the Papers of Lord Metcalfe. 1855. [Ed. by Kaye.]

The Life and Correspondence of Sir John Malcolm. 2 vols. 1856.

Christianity in India. An Historical Narrative. 1859.

Autobiography of Miss Cornelia Knight. 2 vols. 1861. [Ed. by Kaye.]

A History of the Sepoy War in India. 3 vols. 1864–76; rev. and continued by G. B. Malleson, 6 vols. 1888–9 (the whole work, as Kaye's and Malleson's History of the Indian Mutiny).

India, Ancient and Modern. Drawings by W. Simpson with Descriptive Literature by J. W. Kaye. 1867.

Lives of Indian Officers. 2 vols. 1867; 1889; 2 vols. 1904. [First pbd as Indian Heroes, in Good Words, 1866.]

The People of India. Photographic Illustrations, with Descriptive Letterpress. 6 vols. 1868–72. [Ed. by J. F. Watson and Kaye.]

The Essays of an Optimist. 1870. [Rptd from Cornhill Mag.]

[Kaye also wrote much in the early vols. of The Calcutta Review—which he founded 1844 and edited.]

G. EUROPEAN HISTORY

WILLIAM SMYTH (1765–1849)

English Lyrics. 1797; Liverpool, 1798; 1806; Dublin, 1806; 1815; 1850 (with autobiographical sketch).

Lectures on Modern History, from the Irruption of the Northern Nations to the Close of the American Revolution. 2 vols. Cambridge, 1840; 2 vols. 1854.

Lectures on History. Series 2: On the French Revolution. 3 vols. Cambridge, 1840; 2 vols. 1855.

Memoir of Mr Sheridan. Leeds, 1840 (priv. ptd).

SIR JAMES STEPHEN (1789–1859)

Essays in Ecclesiastical Biography. 2 vols. 1849; 2 vols. 1853 (3rd edn); 1860 (with memoir by Sir J. F. Stephen); 1867; rptd 2 vols. 1907.

Lectures on the History of France. 2 vols. 1851; 2 vols. 1852; 2 vols. 1857.

Sir James Stephen. Letters with Biographical Notes by his Daughter C. E. Stephen. [Gloucester], 1906 (priv. ptd).

SIR ARCHIBALD ALISON (1792–1867)

Travels in France during the years 1814–15. 2 vols. Edinburgh, 1815 (anon.); 2 vols. Edinburgh, 1816 (anon.).

Principles of the Criminal Law of Scotland. 2 vols. Edinburgh, 1832–3.

History of Europe during the French Revolution. 10 vols. Edinburgh, 1833–42 (vols. V–X from the Commencement of the French Revolution to the Restoration of the Bourbons); 20 vols. Edinburgh, 1848 (7th edn); 14 vols. Edinburgh, 1849–50; 12 vols. Edinburgh, 1853–6; 14 vols. Edinburgh, 1860.

The Principles of Population, and their Connection with Human Happiness. 2 vols. Edinburgh, 1840.

Free Trade and Protection. Edinburgh, 1844. [Rptd from Population, with two articles from Blackwood's Mag.]

England in 1815 and 1845, or a Sufficient and a Contracted Currency. Edinburgh, 1845.

Free Trade and a Fettered Currency. Edinburgh, 1847.

The Military Life of John Duke of Marlborough. Edinburgh, 1848; 2 vols. Edinburgh, 1852 (as The Life of John Duke of Marlborough with Some Account of his Contemporaries and of the War of the Succession); 2 vols. Edinburgh, 1855.

Miscellaneous Essays. Philadelphia, 1849.

Essays Political, Historical, and Miscellaneous. 3 vols. Edinburgh, 1850. [Omits some included in previous work.]

History of Europe, 1815–52. 9 vols. Edinburgh, 1853–9.

Lives of Lord Castlereagh and Sir Charles Stewart. 3 vols. Edinburgh, 1861.

Some Account of my Life and Writings. An Autobiography. Edited by his Daughter-in-Law, Lady Alison. 2 vols. Edinburgh, 1883.

G. P. R. JAMES (1799–1860)

[See p. 402 above.]

SIR ARTHUR HELPS (1813–1875)

[See p. 718 above.]

GEORGE HENRY LEWES (1817–1878)

[See p. 869 above.]

SIR WILLIAM STIRLING-MAXWELL (1818–1878)

Annals of the Artists of Spain. 3 vols. 1848; 4 vols. 1891 (in Works).

The Cloister Life of the Emperor Charles the Fifth. 1852; 1853; 1891 (in Works).

Velazquez and his Works. 1855. Tr. German, Berlin, 1856; French, Paris, 1865. [Part of the Annals, re-written.]

Notices of the Emperor Charles the Fifth, in 1555 and 1556; from the Despatches of Federigo Badoer. Philobiblon Soc. Misc. II, 1855–6.

Don John of Austria. [Ed. G. W. Cox], 2 vols. 1883 (bis).

Works. 6 vols. 1891. [Includes volume of Miscellaneous Essays and Addresses.]

[Stirling-Maxwell also pbd many works on bibliography and on art.]

CHARLES KINGSLEY (1819–1875)

[See p. 487 above.]

HENRY THOMAS BUCKLE (1821–1862)

(a) Writings

History of Civilization in England. 2 vols. 1857–61; 2 vols. 1858–64; vol. I, 1861; 3 vols. 1866; 3 vols. 1868; 3 vols. 1869; 3 vols. 1871; 3 vols. 1873; 3 vols. 1878; 3 vols. 1885; 3 vols. 1903–4 (World's

Classics); ed. J. M. Robertson, 1904. Tr. German, Heidelberg, 1860; French, Paris, 1865; Russian, 1870.

The Influence of Women on the Progress of Knowledge. Fraser's Mag. April 1858; Leipzig, 1867 (in Essays); 1872 (in Miscellaneous Works); [1906].

A Letter to a Gentleman respecting Pooley's Case. 1859.

Essays. With a Biographical Sketch of the Author. Leipzig, 1867. [Includes Mill on Liberty, rptd from Fraser's Mag. May, 1859, and The Influence of Women.]

Miscellaneous and Posthumous Works. Ed. (with biographical notice) Helen Taylor, 3 vols. 1872; ed. Grant Allen, 2 vols. 1885 (abridged); rev. J. M. Robertson, 1904. [Contains Mill on Liberty, The Influence of Women, Letter on Pooley's Case, Reign of Elizabeth, Fragments, and Common Place Books.]

(b) Biography and Criticism

Huth, A. H. The Life and Writings of Henry Thomas Buckle. 2 vols. 1880.

Robertson, J. M. Buckle and his Critics. 1895.

V. THE LATE NINETEENTH-CENTURY HISTORIANS: FREEMAN, STUBBS, GARDINER, ACTON, GREEN, LECKY, CREIGHTON, MAITLAND

EDWARD AUGUSTUS FREEMAN (1823–1892)

(a) Writings

Principles of Church Restoration. 1846.

Thoughts on the Study of History with Reference to the Proposed Changes in the Public Examinations. Oxford, 1849.

A History of Architecture. 1849.

Poems, Legendary and Historical. 1850. [With G. W. Cox.]

Remarks on the Architecture of Llandaff Cathedral; with an Essay towards a History of the Fabric. 1850.

An Essay on the Origin and Development of Window Tracery in England. Oxford, 1851.

The Preservation and Restoration of Ancient Monuments. A Paper. Oxford, 1852.

Suggestions with Regard to Certain Proposed Alterations in the University and Colleges of Oxford. Oxford, 1854. [With F. H. Dickinson.]

The History and Antiquities of Saint David's. 1856. [With W. B. Jones.]

The History and Conquests of the Saracens. Six Lectures. Oxford, 1856; 1876 (bis).

Ancient Greece and Mediaeval Italy. [In Oxford Essays, 1857.]

The Town and Borough of Leominster. By G. F. Townsend. Also, A Chapter on the Parish Church and Priory, by E. A. Freeman. Leominster, [1863].

History of Federal Government. Vol. 1: General Introduction—History of the Greek Federations. 1863; ed. J. B. Bury, 1893 (as History of Federal Government in Greece and Italy).

The History of the Norman Conquest of England, its Causes and its Results. 6 vols. Oxford, 1867–79.

Old English History for Children. 1869; 1892 (9th edn); 1911 (Everyman's Lib.).

History of the Cathedral Church of Wells. 1870.

Historical Essays. 4 sers. 1871–92.

The Growth of the English Constitution from the Earliest Times. 1872; tr. French, Paris, 1877.

General Sketch of European History. 1872 (Historical Course for Schools).

The Unity of History. Rede Lecture. 1872; 1873 (with Comparative Politics).

The Cathedral Churches of the Old Foundation. [In J. S. Howson, Essays on Cathedrals, 1872.]

Comparative Politics. With the Unity of History. 1873; 1896.

Disestablishment and Disendowment: what are they? 1874; 1885.

History of Europe. 1876; rev. F. J. C. Hearnshaw, 1926.

Historical and Architectural Sketches, chiefly Italian. 1876.

The Eastern Question in its Historical Bearings. An Address. Manchester, 1876.

The Ottoman Power in Europe. 1877.

The Turks in Europe. 1877.

How the Study of History is let and hindered. An Address. [1879.]

A Short History of the Norman Conquest of England. Oxford, 1880.

Sketches from the Subject and Neighbour Lands of Venice. 1881.

The Historical Geography of Europe. 2 vols. 1881; 2 vols. 1882; ed. J. B. Bury, 2 vols. 1903.

Lectures to American Audiences. 1: The English People in its Three Homes. 11: The Practical Bearings of General European History. Philadelphia, 1882.

The Reign of William Rufus and the Accession of Henry the First. 2 vols. Oxford, 1882.

Some Impressions of the United States. 1883.

An Introduction to American Institutional History. [In Local Institutions; Johns Hopkins University Studies in Historical and Political Science, vol. 1, Baltimore, 1883.]

English Towns and Districts. Addresses and Sketches. 1883.

Cathedral Cities. Ely & Norwich. Drawn & Etched by R. Farren. With Introduction by E. A. Freeman. Cambridge, 1883.

The Office of the Historical Professor. Inaugural Lecture. 1884; 1886 (with The Methods of Historical Study).

The Methods of Historical Study. 1886.

The Chief Periods of European History. Six Lectures. With an Essay on Greek Cities under Roman Rule. 1886.

Greater Greece and Greater Britain. And George Washington the Expander of England. Two Lectures. 1886.

Exeter. 1887. (Historic Towns ser.)

Four Oxford Lectures 1887. Fifty Years of European History. Teutonic Conquest in Gaul and Britain. 1888.

William the Conqueror. 1888. (Twelve English Statesmen ser.)

Sketches from French Travel. Leipzig, 1891.

The History of Sicily from the Earliest Times. 4 vols. Oxford, 1891–4; tr. German, Leipzig, 1895–1901. [Vol. IV ed. by A. J. Evans.]

Sicily Phœnician, Greek, & Roman. 1892. (Story of the Nations ser.)

The Physical and Political Bases of National Unity. [In A. S. White, Britannic Federation, 1892.]

Studies of Travel. Greece: Italy. 2 vols. New York, [1893].

Cathedral Cities. York, Lincoln & Beverley. Drawn & Etched by R. Farren. With Introduction by E. A. Freeman. Cambridge, 1896.

Sketches of Travel in Normandy and Maine. Ed. W. H. Hutton, 1897.

Western Europe in the Fifth Century. An Aftermath. 1904.

Western Europe in the Eighth Century and onward. An Aftermath. 1904.

(b) Biography and Criticism

Stephens, W. R. W. The Life and Letters of E. A. Freeman, 2 vols. 1895. [Vol. II contains bibliography.]

Bryce, J., Viscount. Studies in Contemporary Biography. 1903.

WILLIAM STUBBS (1825–1901)

(a) Writings

Registrum Sacrum Anglicanum. An Attempt to exhibit the Course of Episcopal Succession in England. Oxford, 1858; Oxford, 1897.

The Apostolical Succession in the Church of England. A Letter. Eastern Church Ass. 1866.

An Address by Way of Inaugural Lecture. 1867; Oxford, 1867 (rev.); 1886 (in Seventeen Lectures).

Councils and Ecclesiastical Documents relating to Great Britain and Ireland. Oxford, 1869–73. [Ed. by A. W. Haddan and Stubbs.]

Select Charters and Other Illustrations of English Constitutional History to the Reign of Edward the First. Oxford, 1870; Oxford, 1884 (5th edn); Oxford, 1895 (8th edn); ed. H. W. C. Davis, Oxford, 1913.

The Constitutional History of England in its Origin and Development. 3 vols. Oxford, 1874–8; 3 vols. Oxford, 1880; tr. French, Paris, 1907–27.

The Early Plantagenets. 1876.

Two Lectures on the Present State and Prospects of Historical Study, delivered 1876. [Oxford, 1876] (priv. ptd).

Historical Appendices i–v to the Report of the Commissioners appointed to inquire into the Constitution and Working of the Ecclesiastical Courts. Parliamentary Papers [c. 3760], H.C. (1883), xxiv.

An Address by Way of a Last Statutory Public Lecture, 1884. [Oxford, 1884]; 1886 (in Seventeen Lectures).

Seventeen Lectures on the Study of Medieval and Modern History. Oxford, 1886; Oxford, 1887; Oxford, 1900.

Ordination Addresses. Ed. E. E. Holmes, 1901.

Historical Introductions to the Rolls Series. Ed. A. Hassall, 1902.

Lectures on European History. Ed. A. Hassall, 1904.

Lectures on Early English History. Ed. A. Hassall, 1906.

Germany in the Early Middle Ages, 476–1250. Ed. A. Hassall, 1908.

Germany in the Later Middle Ages, 1200–1500. Ed. A. Hassall, 1908.

Genealogical History of the Family of Bishop William Stubbs, compiled by Himself. Ed. F. Collins, Yorks. Archaeological Soc. Record Ser. 1915.

On Convocation. A Letter to the Archbishop of Canterbury; and a Speech. Ed. W. H. Hutton, 1917.

[Stubbs also edited works for the Rolls Series and pbd sermons and charges, contributions to Dictionary of Christian Antiquities, ed. W. Smith and S. Cheetham, 2 vols. 1875–80, and Dictionary of Christian Biography, ed. W. Smith and H. Wace, 4 vols. 1877–87.]

(b) Biography and Criticism

Shaw, W. A. A Bibliography of the Historical Works of Dr Creighton, Dr Stubbs, Dr S. R. Gardiner and Lord Acton. Royal Historical Soc. 1903.

Hutton, W. H. Letters of William Stubbs, Bishop of Oxford. 1904. [Contains bibliography.]

Paul, H. Stray Leaves. 1906.

Petit-Dutaillis, C. Studies and Notes Supplementary to Stubbs's Constitutional History. Translated by W. E. Rhodes, W. T. Waugh, M. I. E. Robertson and R. F. Treharne. 3 vols. Manchester, 1908–29. [Vol. iii is by C. Petit-Dutaillis and G. Lefebvre.]

SAMUEL RAWSON GARDINER (1829–1902)

(a) Writings

History of England from the Accession of James I to the Disgrace of Chief-Justice Coke. 1603–1610. 2 vols. 1863.

Prince Charles and the Spanish Marriage, 1617–1623. 2 vols. 1869.

A History of England under the Duke of Buckingham and Charles I, 1624–1628. 2 vols. 1875.

The Personal Government of Charles I. A History of England from the Assassination of the Duke of Buckingham to the Declaration of the Judges on Ship-Money, 1628–1637. 2 vols. 1877.

The Fall of the Monarchy of Charles I, 1637–1649 [1642]. 2 vols. 1882.

History of England from the Accession of James I to the Outbreak of the Civil War, 1603–1642. 10 vols. 1883–4. [A collected edn of the 5 foregoing works.]

The Thirty Years' War. 1874.

The First Two Stuarts and the Puritan Revolution, 1603–1660. 1876; 1902 (15th impression).

Introduction to the Study of English History. 1881; 1882; 1894. [With J. B. Mullinger.]

Outline of English History. 2 vols. 1881; 1887; 1896; 1901; 1912; 1919. [Later edns have continuations.]

Illustrated English History. 3 vols. 1883; pt 1, 1887 (5th edn); pt 3 continued to 1901, 1902; to 1910, 1912.

Historical Biographies. 1884.

History of the Great Civil War, 1642–1649. 3 vols. 1886–91; 4 vols. 1893.

An Easy History of England. First Course for Standard V. 1887.

An Easy History of England. Second Course for Standards VI & VII. 1888.

The Constitutional Documents of the Puritan Revolution, 1628–1660. Oxford, 1889; Oxford, 1899; Oxford, 1906. [Selected and ed. by Gardiner.]

A Student's History of England from the Earliest Times to 1885. 3 vols. 1890–1; 1892; vol. iii, 1902, 1910, 1920 (with continuations).

The Tudor Period. 1893.

The Stuart Period. 1894.
History of the Commonwealth and Protectorate, 1649–1660. 3 vols. 1894–1901; 4 vols. 1903.
Cromwell's Place in History. Founded on Six Lectures. 1897 (3 edns).
What Gunpowder Plot was. 1897.
Oliver Cromwell. 1899; 1901; tr. German, Munich, 1903.

[Gardiner also wrote a number of articles in DNB., etc.]

(b) Biography and Criticism

Learned, H. B. Samuel Rawson Gardiner. Yale Scientific Monthly, June 1902.
Shaw, W. A. A Bibliography of the Historical Works of Dr Creighton, Dr Stubbs, Dr S. R. Gardiner, and Lord Acton. Royal Historical Soc. 1903.
Usher, R. G. A Critical Study of the Historical Method of S. R. Gardiner. Washington University Stud. III, pt 2, no. 1, 1915.

JOHN EMERICH EDWARD DALBERG ACTON (BARON ACTON) (1834–1902)

(a) Writings

Römische Briefe vom Concil. Von Quirinus. Munich, 1870; tr. English, 3 sers. 1870 (as Letters from Rome on the Council). [By Acton and others; rptd from Allgemeine Zeitung, Dec. 1869.]
Sendschreiben an einen deutschen Bischof des vaticanischen Concils. September 1870. Nördlingen, [1870].
Zur Geschichte des vaticanischen Conciles. Munich, 1871.
The War of 1870. A Lecture. 1871.
The History of Freedom in Antiquity. An Address. Bridgnorth, [1877]; 1907; tr. French, Paris, 1878.
The History of Freedom in Christianity. An Address. Bridgnorth, [1877]; 1907; tr. French, Paris, 1878.
A Lecture on the Study of History. 1895; 1896; 1905; 1906 (in Lectures on Modern History); 1911; tr. German, Berlin, 1897. [Inaugural lecture.]
Lectures on Modern History. Ed. J. N. Figgis and R. V. Laurence, 1906.
Historical Essays and Studies. Ed. J. N. Figgis and R. V. Laurence, 1907.
The History of Freedom, and Other Essays. Ed. J. N. Figgis and R. V. Laurence, 1907.
Lectures on the French Revolution. Ed. J. N. Figgis and R. V. Laurence, 1910.

(b) Biography and Criticism

Bryce, J., Viscount. Studies in Contemporary Biography. 1903.

Shaw, W. A. A Bibliography of the Historical Works of Dr Creighton, Dr Stubbs, Dr S. R. Gardiner and Lord Acton. Royal Historical Soc. 1903.
Paul, H. Letters of Lord Acton to Mary, Daughter of W. E. Gladstone. With a Memoir. 1904; 1906; 1913.
Gasquet, F. A. Lord Acton and his Circle. [1906.] [Letters, with Introduction.]
Figgis, J. N. and Laurence, R. V. Selections from the Correspondence of the First Lord Acton. Vol. I, 1917.
Drew, M. Acton, Gladstone and Others. [1924.]
Blennerhassett, W. L. Acton, 1834–1902. Dublin Rev. April 1934.

JOHN RICHARD GREEN (1837–1883)

Oxford during the Last Century. Being Two Series of Papers published in the Oxford Chronicle & Berks & Bucks Gazette during 1859. Oxford, 1859 (anon.); ed. C. L. Stainer, Oxford Historical Soc. 1901; 1901 (Green's ser. only, in Oxford Studies). [With G. Roberson.]
A Short History of the English People. 1874; 1888 (rev. Mrs J. R. Green); 4 vols. 1892–4; ed. Mrs J. R. Green and K. Norgate, 4 vols. 1907–8; 2 vols. 1915 (Everyman's Lib.); 1916. Partly tr. French, Paris, 1885; tr. French, Paris, 1888; German, Berlin, 1889; Italian, Florence, 1884; Russian, Moscow, 1891–2; Chinese, 1898.
Stray Studies from England and Italy. 1876.
History of the English People. 4 vols. 1877–80; 8 vols. 1895–6.
Readings from English History. 3 pts, 1879. [Selected and ed. by Green.]
A Short Geography of the British Islands. 1879. [With A. S. Green.]
The Making of England. 1881; 1885; 2 vols. 1897; 2 vols. 1900; 2 vols. 1904.
The Conquest of England. 1883; 1884; 2 vols. 1899.
Essays of Joseph Addison. 1888. [Ed. by Green.]
Letters. Ed. Sir L. Stephen, 1901.
Oxford Studies. Ed. Mrs J. R. Green and K. Norgate, 1901.
Stray Studies. Ser. 2. [Ed. A. S. Green], 1903.
Historical Studies. [Ed. A. S. Green], 1903.

[For an appreciation of Green see J., Viscount Bryce, Studies in Contemporary Biography, 1903.]

WILLIAM EDWARD HARTPOLE LECKY (1838–1903)

Friendship And Other Poems. By Hibernicus. 1859.
The Religious Tendencies of the Age. 1860 (anon.).

The Leaders of Public Opinion in Ireland. 1861 (anon.); 1871 (rev., omitting Clerical Influences); 2 vols. 1903 (rev., omitting also life of Swift); 2 vols. 1912; tr. German, Posen, 1873 (from 1871 edn). [Life of Swift 'rewritten and amplified' as Biographical Introduction to the Prose Works, vol. I, 1897; Clerical Influences, rptd W. E. G. Lloyd and F. C. O'Brien, Dublin, 1911.]

History of the Rise and Influence of the Spirit of Rationalism in Europe. 2 vols. 1865 (bis); 2 vols. 1866; 2 vols. [1869]; 2 vols. 1872; 2 vols. 1873; 2 vols. 1875; 2 vols. 1877; 2 vols. 1880; 2 vols. 1882; 2 vols. 1884; 2 vols. 1887; 2 vols. 1890; 2 vols. 1892; 2 vols. 1897; 2 vols. 1898; 2 vols. 1900; 2 vols. 1904; 2 vols. in 1, 1910. Tr. German, Berlin, 1874; Dutch, Amsterdam, 1894.

History of European Morals from Augustus to Charlemagne. 2 vols. 1869; 2 vols. 1877 (3rd edn); 2 vols. 1886 (7th edn, rev.); 2 vols. 1911.

A History of England in the Eighteenth Century. 8 vols. 1878–90; 12 vols. 1892 (as A History of England, 7 vols., and A History of Ireland, 5 vols.).

Poems. 1891.

The Political Value of History. 1892; 1908 (in Essays).

The Empire; its Value and its Growth. An Address. 1893; 1908 (in Essays).

Speeches and Addresses of Edward Henry XVth Earl of Derby. With a Prefatory Memoir by W. E. H. Lecky. Ed. Sir T. H. Sanderson and E. S. Roscoe, 2 vols. 1894. [The Memoir is rptd in Lecky's Essays, 1908.]

Democracy and Liberty. 2 vols. 1896; 2 vols. 1899.

The Map of Life: Conduct and Character. 1899; 1901.

Historical and Political Essays. 1908; 1910.

[For life see A Memoir of the Right Hon. W. E. H. Lecky, by his Wife, 1909.]

MANDELL CREIGHTON (1843–1901)

(a) Writings

History of Rome. 1875; 1884 (10th edn); Toronto, 1899; tr. French, Paris, [1885].

The Tudors and the Reformation. 1876.

The Age of Elizabeth. 1876.

Life of Simon de Montfort. 1876.

The Shilling History of England. Being an Introductory Volume to 'Epochs of English History.' 1879; 1904 (with continuation by Louise Creighton).

A History of the Papacy during the Period of the Reformation. 5 vols. 1882–94; 6 vols. 1897.

Memoir of Sir George Grey. Newcastle-on-Tyne, 1884 (priv. ptd); 1901 (with introduction by Sir Edward Grey).

Cardinal Wolsey. 1888 (Twelve English Statesmen ser.); 1904.

Carlisle. 1889. (Historic Towns ser.)

A Charge to the Clergy & Churchwardens of the Diocese of Peterborough, 1894. Peterborough, [1894]; 1901 (in The Church and the Nation).

Persecution and Tolerance. Hulsean Lectures, 1893–4. 1895.

The Early Renaissance in England. Rede Lecture. Cambridge, 1895; 1903 (in Historical Lectures).

Laud's Position in the History of the English Church. [In Archbishop Laud Commemoration, 1895; Lectures, ed. W. E. Collins, 1895; rptd in Historical Lectures, 1903.]

The National Church in the Middle Age. [1895]; 1901 (in The Church and the Nation).

Queen Elizabeth. 1896; 1899.

The Heritage of the Spirit and Other Sermons. 1896; [1913].

The English National Character. Romanes Lecture. 1896; 1903 (in Historical Lectures).

The Church under Elizabeth. [1896]; 1903 (in Historical Lectures).

Church and State. [In Oxford House Papers, ser. 3, 1897.]

The Story of Some English Shires. 1897.

Lessons from the Cross. Addresses. 1898.

The Idea of a National Church. An Address. Church Historical Soc. 1898.

The Position of the Church of England. An Address. 1899; 1901 (in The Church and the Nation).

The Church and the Nation. A Charge. 1900; 1901 (in The Church and the Nation).

The Reformation. [In H. M. Gwatkin, The Church Past and Present, 1900.]

The Church and the Nation: Charges and Addresses. Ed. L. Creighton, 1901.

Historical Essays and Reviews. 1902.

Thoughts on Education. Speeches and Sermons. Ed. L. Creighton, 1902.

Introductory Note. [In Cambridge Modern History, vol. I, Cambridge, 1902.]

Historical Lectures and Addresses. Ed. L. Creighton, 1903.

University and Other Sermons. Ed. L. Creighton, 1903.

The Mind of St Peter and Other Sermons. Ed. L. Creighton, 1904.

The Claims of the Common Life. Sermons. 1905.

[Creighton also wrote a number of articles in DNB.]

(b) Biography and Criticism

Shaw, W. A. A Bibliography of the Historical Works of Dr Creighton, Dr Stubbs, Dr S. R. Gardiner and Lord Acton. Royal Historical Soc. 1903.

Creighton, L. Life and Letters of Mandell Creighton. By his Wife. 2 vols. 1904. [Vol. II contains bibliography.]

Paul, H. Stray Leaves. 1906.

FREDERICK WILLIAM MAITLAND
(1850–1906)

(a) Writings

Pleas of the Crown for the County of Gloucester, 1221. 1884. [Ed. by Maitland.]

Justice and Police. 1885.

Bracton's Note Book. 3 vols. 1887. [Ed. by Maitland.]

Why the History of English Law is not written. Inaugural Lecture. Cambridge, 1888.

Select Pleas of the Crown. Vol. I, 1200–1225. Selden Soc. 1888. [Ed. by Maitland.]

Select Pleas in Manorial and other Seignorial Courts. Vol. I: Henry III and Edward I. Selden Soc. 1889. [Ed. by Maitland.]

Three Rolls of the King's Court, 1194–5. Pipe Roll Soc. 1891. [Ed. by Maitland.]

The Court Baron. Being Precedents for Use in Local Courts. Selden Soc. 1891. [Ed. by Maitland and W. P. Baildon.]

Records of the Parliament holden at Westminster on 28 February 1305. 1893 (Rerum Britannicarum Medii Aevi Scriptores); Cambridge, 1936 (Introduction only, in Selected Essays). [Ed. by Maitland.]

The History of English Law before the Time of Edward I. By Sir F. Pollock and F. W. Maitland. 2 vols. Cambridge, 1895; 2 vols. Cambridge, 1898; 2 vols. Cambridge, 1911.

The Mirror of Justices. Ed. W. J. Whittaker, with Introduction by F. W. Maitland, Selden Soc. 1895.

Select Passages from the Works of Bracton and Azo. Selden Soc. 1895. [Ed. by Maitland.]

Domesday Book and Beyond. Three Essays. Cambridge, 1897; Cambridge, 1907.

Roman Canon Law in the Church of England. Six Essays. Cambridge, 1898.

Township and Borough. Being the Ford Lectures, 1897, with Notes relating to the History of Cambridge. Cambridge, 1898.

Political Theories of the Middle Age. By Otto Gierke. Translated with an Introduction by F. W. Maitland. Cambridge, 1900; Cambridge, 1913; Cambridge, 1922.

English Law and the Renaissance. Rede Lecture. Cambridge, 1901.

The Charters of the Borough of Cambridge. Cambridge, 1901. [Ed. by Maitland and M. Bateson.]

Essays on the Teaching of History. Cambridge, 1901. [By Maitland and others.]

Year Books of Edward II. 4 vols. Selden Soc., 1903–7. [Ed. by Maitland; vol. IV completed by G. J. Turner.]

The Life and Letters of Leslie Stephen. 1906.

The Constitutional History of England. Lectures. [Ed. H. A. L. Fisher], Cambridge, 1908; Cambridge, 1909.

Equity. Also the Forms of Action at Common Law. Lectures. Ed. A. H. Chaytor and W. J. Whittaker, Cambridge, 1909. Equity [alone]. Rev. J. Brunyate, Cambridge, 1937. The Forms of Action [alone]. Ed. A. H. Chaytor and W. J. Whittaker, Cambridge, 1937.

Collected Papers. Ed. H. A. L. Fisher, 3 vols. Cambridge, 1911.

A Sketch of English Legal History. Ed. J. F. Colby, New York, [1915]. [By Maitland and F. C. Montague; reprints of chapters in H. D. Traill, Social England, 6 vols. 1893–7.]

Selected Essays. Ed. H. D. Hazeltine, G. Lapsley and P. H. Winfield, Cambridge, 1936. [Rpts of Introduction to Memoranda de Parliamento, and 6 essays from Collected Papers.]

[Maitland also wrote articles in CHEL., Cambridge Modern History, and H. D. Traill, Social England, 6 vols. 1893–7.]

(b) Biography and Criticism

Smith, A. L. F. W. Maitland. Two Lectures and a Bibliography. Oxford, 1908.

Fisher, H. A. L. F. W. Maitland. A Biographical Sketch. Cambridge, 1910.

Liebermann, F. Historische Zeitschrift, ser. 3, XVIII, 1915, pp. 321–34. [Review of Maitland's Collected Papers.]

Barker, E. Maitland as a Sociologist. Sociological Rev. XXIX, 1937.

VI. MINOR WRITERS, 1870–1900

A. PRE-HISTORY, ARCHAEOLOGY AND ANCIENT HISTORY

GEORGE RAWLINSON (1812–1902)

The History of Herodotus. A New English Version, edited with Copious Notes and Appendices by George Rawlinson, assisted by Sir H. Rawlinson and Sir J. G. Wilkinson. 4 vols. 1858–60; 4 vols. 1862; 4 vols. 1875; 2 vols. 1897 (with notes abridged by A. J. Grant); ed. E. H. Blakeney (trn only), 2 vols. 1910 (Everyman's Lib.).

The Historical Evidences of the Truth of the Scripture Records stated anew. Bampton Lecture. 1859; 1860.

The Five Great Monarchies of the Ancient Eastern World: Chaldæa, Assyria, Babylon, Media, and Persia. 4 vols. 1862–7; 3 vols. 1871; 3 vols. 1879 (4th edn).

A Manual of Ancient History from the Earliest Times to the Fall of the Western Empire. Oxford, 1869.

Historical Illustrations of the Old Testament. [1871.]

The Sixth Great Oriental Monarchy: Parthia. 1873.

The Seventh Great Oriental Monarchy: the Sassanian or New Persian Empire. 1876.

The Origin of Nations. [1877.]

St Paul in Damascus and Arabia. [In The Heathen World and St Paul, 1877.]

The Alleged Historical Difficulties of the Old and New Testaments. [In Christian Evidence Lectures, ser. 1 (Modern Scepticism), 1880.]

History of Ancient Egypt. 2 vols. 1881.

The Religions of the Ancient World. [1882.]

The Antiquity of Man, historically considered. [1883.]

The Early Prevalence of Monotheistic Beliefs. [1883.]

The Religious Teachings of the Sublime and Beautiful in Nature. [1884.]

Egypt and Babylon, from Scripture and Profane Sources. 1885.

A Sketch of Universal History. Vol. I (Ancient History), 1887.

Moses: his Life and Times. [1887.]

Ancient Egypt. 1887. (Story of the Nations ser.) [With A. Gilman.]

Biblical Topography. 1887.

History of Phœnicia. 1889.

Phœnicia. 1889. (Story of the Nations ser.)

The Kings of Israel and Judah. [1889.]

Isaac and Jacob: their Lives and Times. [1890.]

Ezra and Nehemiah: their Lives and Times. [1891.]

Parthia. 1893. (Story of the Nations ser.)

A Memoir of Major-General Sir H. C. Rawlinson. 1898.

[Rawlinson also contributed to H. D. M. Spence and J. S. Exell, Pulpit Commentary, 1880–1919; W. Thompson, Aids to Faith, 1861; C. J. Ellicott, Old Testament Commentary, 5 vols. 1882–4; Sir W. Smith, Dictionary of the Bible, 3 vols. 1860–3; and pbd sermons.]

SIR JOHN EVANS (1823–1908)

The Coins of the Ancient Britons. 1864. Supplement, 1890.

The Ancient Stone Implements, Weapons, and Ornaments, of Great Britain. 1872; 1897; tr. French, Paris, 1878.

The Ancient Bronze Implements, Weapons, and Ornaments, of Great Britain and Ireland. 1881; tr. French, Paris, 1882.

Hydriotaphia. By Sir Thomas Browne. 1893. [Ed. by Evans.]

[Evans also pbd lectures and addresses, papers in Archaeologia, the Numismatic Chronicle, etc.; for life see L. Forrer, Sir John Evans, Biographie et Bibliographie, Chalons-sur-Saône, 1909.]

[SIR] GEORGE WILLIAM COX (1827–1902)

Poems, Legendary and Historical. 1850. [With E. A. Freeman.]

The Life of Saint Boniface, Archbishop of Mayence. 1853.

The Tale of the Great Persian War. 1861; 1869.

Tales from Greek Mythology. 1861; 1863.

Tales of the Gods and Heroes. 1862; 1863.

Tales of Thebes and Argos. 1864.

Tales of Ancient Greece. 1868; 1872; 1915 (Everyman's Lib.); tr. French, Paris, 1867. [The preceding 3 works, with 1 additional tale.]

A Manual of Mythology. 1867; tr. French, Paris, 1925.

The Mythology of the Aryan Nations. 2 vols. 1870; 1882.

Latin and Teutonic Christendom. An Historical Sketch. 1870.

Popular Romances of the Middle Ages. 1871; 1880. [With E. H. Jones.]

Tales of the Teutonic Lands. 1872. [With E. H. Jones.]

A History of Greece. 2 vols. 1874.

The Crusades. 1874.

A General History of Greece to the Death of Alexander the Great; with a Sketch of the Subsequent History. 1876. [Incorporates most of the History of Greece of 1874.]

The Greeks and the Persians. 1876.

The Athenian Empire. 1876.

An Introduction to the Science of Comparative Mythology and Folklore. 1881.

History of the Establishment of British Rule in India. 1881.

The Little Cyclopaedia of Common Things. 1882 (2nd edn); 1906 (12th edn).

Lives of Greek Statesmen. 2 vols. 1885–6.

A Concise History of England and the English People. 1887.

The Life of John William Colenso, Bishop of Natal. 2 vols. 1888 (bis).

The Church of England and the Teaching of Bishop Colenso. 1888; 1896.

[Cox also edited a number of other works, as well as revising W. T. Brande, A Dictionary of Science, Literature and Art, and S. Maunder, The Treasury of History.]

AUGUSTUS HENRY LANE FOX, afterwards
PITT-RIVERS (1827–1900)

On the Improvement of the Rifle. 1858.
On the Development and Distribution of
Primitive Locks and Keys. 1883.
An Address at the Opening of the Dorset
County Museum. Dorchester, 1884.
Excavations in Cranborne Chase. 4 vols.
1887–98 (priv. ptd). [Vol. III entitled Exca-
vations in Bokerley and Wansdyke; for
index, described as vol. v, see under H. St G.
Gray, below.]
King John's House, Tollard Royal, Wilts.
1890 (priv. ptd). [For index, see under
H. St G. Gray, below.]
A Short Guide to the Larmer Grounds,
Rushmore; King John's House; the
Museum at Farnham. [1894.]
Antique Works of Art from Benin. 1900 (priv.
ptd).
The Evolution of Culture and Other Essays.
Ed. J. L. Myres, Oxford, 1906.

[Pitt-Rivers also wrote many articles in
scientific journals. For life, etc. see H. St G.
Gray, Index to 'Excavations' and 'King
John's House'; also a Memoir of General
Pitt-Rivers, and a Bibliographical List of
his Works, Taunton Castle, 1905.]

SIR JOHN LUBBOCK, BARON AVEBURY
(1834–1913)

(a) Writings

Pre-Historic Times, as illustrated by Ancient
Remains, and the Manners and Customs of
Modern Savages. 1865; 1869; 1872; 1878;
1890; 1900; 1913. Tr. Danish, Copenhagen,
1874; German, Jena, 1874.
The Primitive Inhabitants of Scandinavia.
By Sven Nilsson. 1868 (3rd edn). [Ed. by
Lubbock.]
A Proposal to extend the System pursued by
Civil Service Commissioners to Commercial
Appointments. A Letter. 1869.
The Origin of Civilisation and the Primitive
Condition of Man. 1870 (bis); 1875; 1882;
1889; 1902; 1911; 1912; tr. Italian, Turin,
1875.
Monograph of the Collembola and Thysanura.
Ray Soc. 1873.
On the Origin and Metamorphoses of Insects.
1874.
On British Wild Flowers considered in Rela-
tion to Insects. 1875.
Scientific Lectures. 1879; 1890.
Addresses, Political and Educational. 1879.
Ants, Bees, and Wasps. A Record of Observa-
tions. 1882 (bis); rptd 1929; tr. German,
Leipzig, 1883.
Chapters in Popular Natural History. Ar-
ranged for Schools. [1883.]

Proportional Representation. 1884. [By
Lubbock and H. O. Arnold-Forster; rptd
from Nineteenth Century, April 1884.]
Representation. 1885 (in The Imperial Parlia-
ment); 1890; 1906 (rev.).
Flowers, Fruits, and Leaves. 1886.
Mr Gladstone and the Nationalities of the
United Kingdom. Letters to the 'Times.'
1887.
The Pleasures of Life. 2 pts, 1887–9; 2 pts,
1891; tr. Spanish, Valencia, [1905].
On the Senses, Instincts, and Intelligence of
Animals. 1888; 1889; tr. German, Leipzig,
1889.
A Contribution to our Knowledge of Seedlings.
2 vols. 1892; 1896.
The Beauties of Nature and the Wonders of
the World. 1892.
The Use of Life. 1894.
The Scenery of Switzerland and the Causes to
which it is due. 1896 (bis); 1913 (5th edn).
On Buds and Stipules. 1899.
A Short History of Coins and Currency. 1902.
The Scenery of England and the Causes to
which it is due. 1902; 1904.
Free Trade and British Commerce. Cobden
Club, 1902.
Essays and Addresses, 1900–1903. 1903.
Free Trade. 1904; 1905; 1908.
Notes on the Life History of British Flowering
Plants. 1905.
On Municipal and National Trading. 1906.
Peace and Happiness. 1909.
Marriage, Totemism and Religion. An
Answer to Critics. 1911.

(b) Biography

Hutchinson, H. G. Life of Lord Avebury.
2 vols. 1914. [Contains bibliography.]
The Life-Work of Lord Avebury. Essays.
Edited by Mrs Adrian Grant-Duff. 1924.
Keith, Sir A. Centenary of the Birth of Lord
Avebury. Man, XXXIV, 1934.
W., F. E. Lord Avebury (1834–1913). Nature,
CXXXIII, 1934.

REGINALD BOSWORTH SMITH (1839–1908)

Mohammed and Mohammedanism. Lectures.
1874; 1876; 1889.
Carthage and the Carthaginians. 1878; 1879.
Rome and Carthage. The Punic Wars. 1881.
Life of Lord Lawrence. 2 vols. 1883 (4 edns);
2 vols. 1885 (6th edn); 1901; [1912].

[Smith also pbd controversial pamphlets
and articles, and books on birds; for life see
Lady Grogan, R. B. Smith: a Memoir, 1909.]

EVELYN SHIRLEY SHUCKBURGH (1843–1906)
[See p. 1009 below.]

HENRY FRANCIS PELHAM (1846–1907)

The Imperial Domains and the Colonate. Inaugural Lecture. 1890; 1911 (in Essays).

Outlines of Roman History. 1893. [Enlarged from article in Encyclopaedia Britannica, 1887.]

Essays. Ed. F. Haverfield, Oxford, 1911.

WLLIAM THOMAS ARNOLD (1852–1904)

The Roman System of Provincial Administration. Arnold Prize Essay. 1879; rev. E. S. Shuckburgh, Oxford, 1906; rev. E. S. Bouchier, Oxford, 1914.

The Poetical Works of John Keats. 1884; 1907 (Globe edn). [Ed. by Arnold.]

The Second Punic War. Being Chapters of the History of Rome. By Thomas Arnold. 1886. [Ed. by Arnold.]

The Manchester Stage, 1880–1900. Criticisms from 'The Manchester Guardian.' Westminster, 1900. [By Arnold and others.]

German Ambitions as they affect Britain and the United States. By Vigilans sed Æquus. 1903.

Studies of Roman Imperialism. Ed. E. Fiddes (with memoir by Mrs Humphry Ward and C. E. Montague), Manchester, 1906. [Memoir rptd as W. T. Arnold, Journalist and Historian, Manchester, 1907.]

[Arnold also contributed to Sir W. Smith and H. Wace, Dictionary of Christian Biography, 4 vols. 1877–87.]

B. ENGLISH HISTORY (GENERAL)

SIR THEODORE MARTIN (1816–1909)

[See p. 298 above.]

WILLIAM NASSAU MOLESWORTH (1816–1890)

On the History of Industrial Progress. A Lecture. Manchester, [1864].

The History of the Reform Bill of 1832. 1865.

The History of England from 1830. 3 vols. 1871–3. [Incorporates an abridged and rev. version of The History of the Reform Bill of 1832.]

History of the Church of England from 1660. 1882.

[Molesworth also pbd lectures on astronomy and pamphlets on education.]

HENRY MORLEY (1822–1894)

[See p. 722 above.]

AUGUSTUS JESSOPP (1823–1914)

Essays in Divinity. By John Donne. 1855. [Ed. by Jessopp.]

Contes par Émile Souvestre. Edited with Notes, and a Short Biography by Augustus Jessopp. 1860; 1861; 1868.

Ad Clerum. The Fragments of Primitive Liturgies in the New Testament. Two Dissertations. [Oxford], 1872 (priv. ptd).

Letters of Fa. Henry Walpole, S.J. Norwich, 1873 (priv. ptd). [Ed. by Jessopp.]

One Generation of a Norfolk House. A Contribution to Elizabethan History. Norwich, 1878; Edinburgh, 1879; 1913.

The Oeconomy of the Fleete, or an Answeare of Alexander Harris unto the Prisoners. Camden Soc. 1879. [Ed. by Jessopp.]

Emblems of Saints. By F. C. Husenbeth. Norwich, 1882 (3rd edn). [Ed. by Jessopp.]

Norwich. 1884.

The Autobiography of Roger North. 1887. [Ed. by Jessopp.]

Arcady for Better for Worse. 1887.

Visitations of the Diocese of Norwich, 1492–1532. Camden Soc. 1888. [Ed. by Jessopp.]

The Coming of the Friars, and Other Historic Essays. 1889.

The Trials of a Country Parson. 1890.

The Lives of Francis North, Baron Guilford; Sir Dudley North; and Dr John North. By Roger North. 3 vols. 1890. [Ed. by Jessopp.]

The Goodwins of East Anglia. [In The Goodwins of Hartford, Connecticut, Hartford, 1891.]

Wise Words and Quaint Counsels of Thomas Fuller. Selected and arranged with a Short Life by Augustus Jessopp. Oxford, 1892.

Some Materials for a History of the Parish of Thompson. By George Crabbe. Norwich, 1892. [Ed. by Jessopp.]

Studies by a Recluse in Cloister, Town, and Country. 1893 [1892].

Random Roaming and Other Papers. 1894; 1896.

Guide to Norwich. [In The Guide to the Church Congress at Norwich, 1895.]

Frivola. 1896. [Essays.]

The Life and Miracles of St William of Norwich. By Thomas of Monmouth. Cambridge, 1896. [Ed. by Jessopp and M. R. James.]

John Donne. 1897.

Before the Great Pillage. With Other Miscellanies. 1901.

Penny History of the Church of England. 1902; 1908; 1922 (as Short History).

William Cecil, Lord Burghley. 1904. [Pt I, Historical Monograph, by Jessopp.]

Robbing God. 1907.

England's Peasantry, and Other Essays. [1914.]

[Jessopp also pbd sermons, school books, short moral tales, articles in Nineteenth Century and DNB. and three brief reports for the Historical MSS Commission.]

SIR MOUNTSTUART ELPHINSTONE GRANT DUFF (1829–1906)

Sicily. [In Oxford Essays, 1857.]
Studies in European Politics. Edinburgh, 1866.
A Political Survey. Edinburgh, 1868.
Elgin Speeches. Edinburgh, 1871.
Notes of an Indian Journey. 1876.
The Eastern Question. A Lecture. Edinburgh, 1876.
Miscellanies, Political and Literary. 1878.
Foreign Policy. 1880.
Some Brief Comments on Passing Events between 1858 and 1881. Madras, 1884 (priv. ptd).
Sir Henry Maine. A Brief Memoir of his Life. 1892.
Ernest Renan. In Memoriam. 1893.
Notes from a Diary, 1851–1872. 2 vols. 1897; 2 vols. 1898, 1899, 1900, 1901, 1904, 1905. [Continued in each set up to 23 Jan. 1901.]
The Flora of Cheshire. By Lord de Tabley. Ed. S. Moore, 1899. [Contains biographical notice by Grant Duff.]
The Victorian Anthology. 1902. [Ed. by Duff.]
Out of the Past. Some Biographical Essays. 2 vols. 1903.
The Club 1764–1905. Roxburghe Club, 1905 (priv. ptd). [Information incorporated in Annals of the Club, 1764–1914. By Lord Welby and others, priv. ptd for the Club, 1914.]

[Grant Duff also pbd speeches on political, literary and educational subjects.]

JUSTIN McCARTHY (1830–1912)

'Con Amore'; or Critical Chapters. 1868.
George Sand. Reprinted from 'The Galaxy' for May, 1870. [In G. Sand, Antonia, tr. V. Vaughan, Boston, 1870.]
Modern Leaders. Biographical Sketches. New York, 1872.
A History of Our Own Times. 4 vols. 1879–80; 7 vols. 1881–1905 (with continuations); 3 vols. 1905. Tr. French, Paris, 1885–7; German, Leipzig, 1881.
The Epoch of Reform, 1830–1850. 1882.
A History of the Four Georges and of William IV. 4 vols. 1884–1901; 2 vols. 1905. [Vols. III, IV completed by J. H. McCarthy.]
Ireland's Cause in England's Parliament. Boston, 1888.
A Short History of Our Own Times. 1888.
The Grey River. 1889. [With Mrs Campbell Praed and M. Menpes.]
Sir Robert Peel. 1891; 1906 (4th edn).
Charing Cross to St Paul's. Notes by Justin McCarthy and Drawings by Joseph Pennell. 1891.

The 'Daily News' Jubilee. A Political and Social Retrospect. 1896. [With Sir J. R. Robinson.]
Pope Leo XIII. 1896; [1899].
The Story of Mr Gladstone's Life. 1897; 1898 (bis).
The Inner Life of the House of Commons. By W. White. 2 vols. 1897. [Ed. by McCarthy.]
Modern England. 2 vols. 1899. (Story of the Nations ser.)
Reminiscences. 2 vols. 1899.
The Reign of Queen Anne. 2 vols. 1902; 1905.
British Political Portraits. 6 vols. New York, 1903.
Portraits of the Sixties. 1903.
Ireland and her Story. 1903.
Irish Literature. 10 vols. Chicago, [1904]. [An anthology, ed. by McCarthy and others.]
The Story of an Irishman. 1904. [Autobiography.]
'Eva' of The Nation. Biographical Sketch. [In Poems, by 'Eva' of 'The Nation' (Mary E. Kelly), Dublin, 1909.]
Irish Recollections. [1911.]
Our Book of Memories. Letters of Justin McCarthy to Mrs Campbell Praed. 1912.

[McCarthy also pbd novels, many in collaboration with Mrs Campbell Praed.]

CHARLES HENRY PEARSON (1830–1894)

Russia, by a Recent Traveller. Letters, originally published in 'The Continental Review.' 1859.
The Early and Middle Ages of England. 1861.
History of England during the Early and Middle Ages. 2 vols. 1867. [Vol. I is The Early and Middle Ages of England rewritten.]
On the Working of Australian Institutions. [In Essays on Reform, 1867.]
A Short Answer to Mr Freeman's Strictures in the 'Fortnightly Review' on the 'History of England during the Early and Middle Ages.' 1868.
On Some Historical Aspects of Family Life. [In J. E. Butler, Woman's Work and Woman's Culture, 1869.]
English History in the Fourteenth Century. 1876.
Brief Statement of the Constitutional Question in Victoria. [1879.]
D. Iunii Iuvenalis Saturae XIII. Oxford, 1887; Oxford, 1892. [Ed. by Pearson and H. A. Strong.]
National Life and Character. A Forecast. 1893; 1894.
Biographical Sketch. [In The Collected Mathematical Papers of H. J. S. Smith, ed. J. W. L. Glaisher, vol. I, Oxford, 1894.]

Reviews and Critical Essays. Ed. H. A. Strong, 1896.
Memorials by Himself, his Wife, and his Friends. Ed. W. Stebbing, 1900.

JOHN CORDY JEAFFRESON (1831–1891)

Crewe-Rise. A Novel. 3 vols. 1854.
Isabel, the Young Wife and the Old Love. 3 vols. 1856. [Novel.]
Novels and Novelists, from Elizabeth to Victoria. 2 vols. 1858.
Miriam Copley. 3 vols. 1859. [Novel.]
A Book about Doctors. 2 vols. 1860; 1861; [1862].
Olive Blake's Good Work. A Novel. 3 vols. 1862.
Sir Everard's Daughter. 1863. [Novel.]
Live It Down. A Story of the Light Lands. 3 vols. 1863 (3 edns).
Not Dead Yet. 3 vols. 1864. [Novel.]
The Life of Robert Stephenson. With Descriptive Chapters on his Works by W. Pale. 2 vols. 1864.
A Book about Lawyers. 2 vols. 1867 [1866]; 2 vols. 1867.
A Noble Woman. 3 vols. 1868. [Novel.]
A Book about the Clergy. 2 vols. 1870.
Annals of Oxford. 2 vols. 1871.
Brides and Bridals. 2 vols. 1872.
A Woman in Spite of Herself. 3 vols. 1872. [Novel.]
Lottie Darling. 3 vols. 1873. [Novel.]
A Book about the Table. 2 vols. 1875.
A Young Squire of the Seventeenth Century, from the Papers of Christopher Jeaffreson. 2 vols. 1878. [Ed. by Jeaffreson.]
An Index to the Ancient Manuscripts of the Borough of Leicester. Westminster, [1878].
The Rapiers of Regent's Park. 3 vols. 1882. [Novel.]
The Real Lord Byron. 2 vols. 1883; [1884].
The Real Shelley. 2 vols. 1885.
Middlesex County Records. 4 vols. Middlesex County Records Soc. [1886]–92. [Ed. by Jeaffreson.]
Lady Hamilton and Lord Nelson. 2 vols. 1888; 1897.
The Queen of Naples and Lord Nelson. 2 vols. 1889.
Cutting for Partners. 3 vols. 1890. [Novel.]
Victoria, Queen and Empress. 2 vols. 1893.
A Book of Recollections. 2 vols. 1894.
A Calendar of the Books, Charters, Letters Patent [etc.] of the City of Coventry. Coventry, 1896.

[Jeaffreson also made reports for the Historical MSS Commission.]

SIR LESLIE STEPHEN (1832–1904)
[See p. 727 above.]

SABINE BARING-GOULD (1834–1924)
[See p. 535 above.]

PERCY FITZGERALD (1834–1925)
[See p. 545 above.]

GEORGE BIRKBECK HILL (1835–1903)
[See p. 1039 above.]

FREDERICK ANDREW INDERWICK (1836–1904)

Side-Lights on the Stuarts. 1888; 1891.
The Interregnum, 1648–1660. 1891.
The Story of King Edward and New Winchelsea. 1892.
A Prisoner of War. 1893. [Novel.]
The King's Peace. A Historical Sketch of the English Law Courts. 1895.
A Calendar of the Inner Temple Records. 3 vols. 1896–1901. [Ed. by Inderwick.]

[Inderwick also pbd legal manuals.]

LUCY TOULMIN SMITH (1838–1911)
[See p. 1042 below.]

SIR GEORGE OTTO TREVELYAN (1838–1928)

The Cambridge Dionysia. A Classic Dream. By the Editor of 'The Bear.' Cambridge, 1858.
Horace at the University of Athens. A Dramatic Sketch. Cambridge, 1861 (anon.); Cambridge, 1862. [In verse.]
The Pope and his Patron. 1862.
The Dawk Bungalow, or 'Is his Appointment Proper?' 1863. [A comedy, pbd as by 'H. Broughton.']
The Competition Wallah. Reprinted from Macmillan's Magazine with Corrections and Additions. 1864; 1866 (rev.).
Cawnpore. 1865; 1866; 1910.
The Ladies in Parliament and Other Pieces. Republished with Additions and Annotations. Cambridge, 1869; 1888.
Speeches on Army Reform. 1870.
The Life and Letters of Lord Macaulay. 2 vols. 1876; 2 vols. 1877 (rev.); 2 vols. 1878; 1881; 1908 (adds ch. xvi from Marginal Notes by Lord Macaulay); 2 vols. 1913; 2 vols. 1932 (World's Classics; preface by G. M. Trevelyan).
Selections from the Writings of Lord Macaulay. 1876. [Ed. by Trevelyan.]
Speeches on the County Franchise. Manchester, 1877.
The Early History of Charles James Fox. 1880 (bis); 1881 (bis); 1905.
The American Revolution. 3 pts, 1899–1907; 4 vols. 1905–12.
Interludes in Verse and Prose. 1905; 1924.

Marginal Notes by Lord Macaulay. 1907. [Ed. by Trevelyan.]

George the Third and Charles Fox. The Concluding Part of the American Revolution. 2 vols. 1912; 2 vols. New York, 1916.

[For minor writings and life see G. M. Trevelyan, Sir George Otto Trevelyan. A Memoir, 1932.]

SIR SPENCER WALPOLE (1839–1907)

The Life of Spencer Perceval. 2 vols. 1874.

A History of England from the Conclusion of the Great War in 1815. 5 vols. 1878–86; 6 vols. 1890; 6 vols. 1913.

The Electorate and the Legislature. 1881; 1892.

Foreign Relations. 1882.

The Life of Lord John Russell. 2 vols. 1889 (*bis*); 2 vols. 1891.

The Land of Home Rule. An Essay on the History and Constitution of the Isle of Man. 1893.

Some Unpublished Letters of Horace Walpole. 1902. [Ed. by Walpole.]

The History of Twenty-Five Years (1856–1880). 4 vols. 1904–8.

Studies in Biography. 1907.

Essays Political and Biographical. Ed. F. Holland, 1908. [With brief memoir by Walpole's daughter, Mrs F. Holland.]

[Walpole also wrote articles in Cambridge Modern History and works on fisheries.]

SIR THOMAS WEMYSS REID (1842–1905)

Cabinet Portraits. Sketches of Statesmen. 1872.

Charlotte Brontë. A Monograph. 1877.

Politicians of To-day. Personal Sketches. 2 vols. 1880.

The Land of the Bey. Tunis under the French. 1882.

A Memoir of John Deakin Heaton, M.D., of Leeds. 1883. [Ed. by Reid.]

Gladys Fane. A Story of Two Lives. 2 vols. 1884 (3 edns); 1888 (5th edn); 1902 (8th edn). [Novel.]

Mauleverer's Millions. A Yorkshire Romance. Leeds, [1886]. [Novel.]

Life of W. E. Forster. 2 vols. 1888 (4 edns).

The Life, Letters, and Friendships of Richard Monckton Milnes, first Lord Houghton. 2 vols. 1890.

The Life of W. E. Gladstone. 1899. [Ed. by Reid, and including 2 chs. by him.]

Memoirs and Correspondence of Lyon Playfair, First Lord Playfair. 1899.

William Black, Novelist. A Biography. 1902.

Memoirs. Ed. S. J. Reid, 1905.

JAMES HAMILTON WYLIE (1844–1914)

History of England under Henry the Fourth. 4 vols. 1884–98.

The Council of Constance to the Death of John Hus. 1900.

The Reign of Henry the Fifth. 3 vols. Cambridge, 1914–29. [Vol. III completed by W. T. Waugh.]

[Wylie also made reports for the Historical MSS Commission.]

SIR HENRY CRAIK (1846–1927)

[See p. 739 above.]

SIR SIDNEY LEE (1859–1926)

[See p. 1040 below.]

WILLIAM HENRY WILKINS (1860–1905)

The Immigration of Destitute Foreigners. 1891. [Rptd from National Rev.]

The Alien Invasion. 1892.

St Michael's Eve. By W. H. De Winton. 2 vols. 1892. [A novel by Wilkins.]

The Forbidden Sacrifice. By W. H. De Winton. 3 vols. 1893. [Novel.]

The Green Bay Tree. A Tale. 3 vols. 1894. [With H. Vivian.]

The Holy Estate. A Study in Morals. 3 vols. 1895. [A novel; with F. Thatcher.]

John Ellicombe's Temptation. [1895.] [A novel; with J. Chetwynd.]

The Romance of Isabel Lady Burton. The Story of her Life told by Herself and by W. H. Wilkins. 2 vols. 1897.

The Love of an Uncrowned Queen: Sophie Dorothea. 2 vols. 1900; 1903.

Caroline the Illustrious, Queen-Consort of George II. 2 vols. 1901; 1904.

South Africa a Century Ago. Letters written from the Cape by Lady Anne Barnard. 1901; [1925]. [Ed. by Wilkins.]

Our King and Queen. The Story of their Life. 2 vols. [1902–3]; 2 vols. 1910–1 (with continuation, as Edward the Peacemaker).

A Queen of Tears. Caroline Matilda, Queen of Denmark and Norway. 2 vols. 1904.

Mrs Fitzherbert and George IV. 2 vols. 1905.

[Wilkins also edited 2 books by Sir R. F. Burton and 2 by Lady Burton.]

C. ENGLISH HISTORY (LEGAL)

[See also Writers on Law, pp. 985–8 below.]

SIR JAMES FITZJAMES STEPHEN (1829–1894)

The Relation of Novels to Life. [In Cambridge Essays, 1855.]

The Characteristics of English Criminal Law. [In Cambridge Essays, 1857.]

Essays. By a Barrister. 1862. [Rptd from Saturday Rev.]

Defence of the Rev. Rowland Williams. 1862.
A General View of the Criminal Law of England. 1863; 1890.
The Indian Evidence Act. With an Introduction on the Principles of Judicial Evidence. Calcutta, 1872.
Liberty, Equality, Fraternity. 1873; 1874.
A Digest of the Law of Evidence. 1876 (3 issues); 1877; 1881; 1887; 1893; 1899; 1904; 1922; 1925; 1936.
A Digest of the Criminal Law (Crimes and Punishments). 1877; 1879; 1883; 1887; 1894; 1904; 1926.
A Digest of the Law of Criminal Procedure in Indictable Offences. 1883. [With H. Stephen.]
A History of the Criminal Law of England. 3 vols. 1883.
Letters on the Ilbert Bill. Reprinted from the 'Times.' 1883.
The Story of Nuncomar and the Impeachment of Sir Elijah Impey. 2 vols. 1885.
Horae Sabbaticae. Reprint of Articles contributed to the Saturday Review. 3 sers. 1892.

[Stephen also pbd speeches and lectures; for life see Sir L. Stephen, The Life of Sir J. F. Stephen, 1895 (with bibliography).]

SIR WILLIAM REYNELL ANSON (1843–1914)

Echoes of the Greek Drama. No. 1: Pentheus. A Burlesque. Oxford, 1866. [With V. Amcotts.]
Principles of the English Law of Contract. Oxford, 1879; 1882, 1884, 1886, 1888, 1891, 1894, 1895, 1899, 1903, 1906; ed. M. L. Gwyer, Oxford, 1910, 1912, 1917, 1920, 1923; ed. J. C. Miles and J. L. Brierly, Oxford, 1929; Oxford, 1937; tr. German, Berlin, 1908.
The Law and Custom of the Constitution. 2 pts, Oxford, 1886–92; 2 vols. Oxford, 1892–6; 3 vols. Oxford, 1897–1908. Vol. I, Parliament, Oxford, 1909; Oxford, 1911 (rev.); ed. M. L. Gwyer, Oxford, 1922. Vol. II, The Crown, ed. A. Berriedale Keith, 2 pts, Oxford, 1935.
Constitutional Development. [In T. H. Ward, The Reign of Queen Victoria, vol. I, 1887.]
Autobiography and Political Correspondence of Augustus Henry, Third Duke of Grafton. 1898. [Ed. by Anson.]
The Growth and Modern Development of the British Constitution. [In Rights of Citizenship, 1912.]

JAMES BERESFORD ATLAY (1860–1913)

The Trial of Lord Cochrane before Lord Ellenborough. 1897.

Famous Trials of the Century. 1899.
The Ingoldsby Legends. 2 vols. 1903. [Ed. by Atlay.]
Sir H. W. Acland, Bart. A Memoir. 1903.
The Victorian Chancellors. 2 vols. 1906–8.
Lord Haliburton. A Memoir of his Public Service. 1909.
Trial of the Stauntons. Edinburgh, [1911]. (Notable English Trials.) [Ed. by Atlay.]
The Life of E. R. Wilberforce, Bishop of Newcastle-on-Tyne and afterward of Chichester. 1912.
The Tichborne Case. [1917.] (Notable Trials.)

[Atlay also edited legal works.]

D. ENGLISH HISTORY (ECCLESIASTICAL)

[See also Writings on Religion, pp. 846–60 above.]

JOHN STOUGHTON (1807–1897)

Notices of Windsor in the Olden Time. 1844.
Spiritual Heroes, or Sketches of the Puritans. 1848; 1850.
Autobiography of the Rev. William Walford. Edited with a continuation by John Stoughton. 1851.
Philip Doddridge: his Life and Labours. 1851; 1852.
Lights of the World, or Illustrations of Character from Records of Christian Life. [1852]; [1876].
Anglo-Saxon Colonies. [In Lectures before the Y.M.C.A., 1852–3, 1853.]
Scenes in Other Lands, with their Associations. 1853.
The Christian Philanthropist. A Memorial of John Howard. 1853.
Stars of the East, or Prophets and Apostles. 1854.
Ages of Christendom: before the Reformation. 1857.
The Pen, the Palm, and the Pulpit. 1858. [W. Tyndale, J. Hooper, G. Whitefield.]
Revivals, Ancient and Modern. [In Lectures before the Y.M.C.A., 1860–61, 1861.]
Anglo-Norman Christianity and Anselm. [In Lectures before the Y.M.C.A., 1861–62, 1862.]
Windsor. A History and Description. 1862.
Church and State Two Hundred Years Ago. A History of Ecclesiastical Affairs in England from 1660 to 1663. 1862.
Lessons for Nonconformists. 1862.
The History of the Act of Uniformity. [In Bicentenary of the Bartholomew Ejectment in 1662; St James's Hall Addresses, 1862.]
Shades and Echoes of Old London. [1864]; 1889.
Biblical Statements in Harmony with Scientific Discoveries. Patriarchal Civilization. [Both in Lectures before the Y.M.C.A., 1845–6, 2 vols. 1864.]

Ecclesiastical History of England. [Civil Wars and Commonwealth, Restoration, and Revolution.] 5 vols. 1867–74; 6 vols. 1881 (in History of Religion in England).

Primitive Ecclesia: its Authoritative Principles and its Modern Representations. [In H. R. Reynolds, Ecclesia: Church Problems Considered, in Essays, 1870.]

A Memorial of Thomas Binney. 1874. [Ed. by Stoughton.]

Homes and Haunts of Luther. [1875]; [1883]; 1903.

Religion in England under Queen Anne and the Georges, 1702–1800. 2 vols. 1878; 1881 (in History of Religion in England, 6 vols.).

Our English Bible: its Translations and Translators. [1878.]

Worthies of Science. [1879.]

William Wilberforce. 1880.

An Introduction to Historical Theology. Being a Sketch of Doctrinal Progress from the Apostolic Era to the Reformation. [1880.]

Reminiscences of Congregationalism Fifty Years Ago. 1881.

Footprints of Italian Reformers. [1881.]

History of Religion in England, from the Opening of the Long Parliament to the End of the Eighteenth Century. 6 vols. 1881. [New edn of Ecclesiastical History, and Religion in England 1702–1800.]

William Penn, the Founder of Pennsylvania. 1882.

The Westminster Assembly. [In Jubilee Lectures, vol. I, 1882.]

Congregationalism in the Court Suburb. 1883.

The Spanish Reformers; their Memories and Dwelling-places. [1883.]

Religion in England from 1800 to 1850, with a Postscript. 2 vols. 1884.

Howard the Philanthropist and his Friends. 1884.

Golden Legends of the Olden Time. 1885.

The Rise and Early Progress of Congregationalism in Norfolk. Congregational Union of England and Wales, 1886.

The Revolution of 1688 in its Bearing on Protestant Nonconformity. Congregational Union of England and Wales, 1888.

Lights and Shadows of Primitive Christendom. [1891] (priv. ptd).

Recollections of a Long Life. 1894 (bis).

Lights and Shadows of Church Life. 1895.

[Stoughton also pbd sermons and devotional works; for life see Mrs G. K. Lewis, John Stoughton, D.D., a Short Record of a Long Life, by his Daughter, 1898.]

ROBERT ORNSBY (1820–1889)

St Richard, Bishop of Chichester. [In Lives of the English Saints, vol. IV, 1845 (anon.); 1901 (vol. VI).]

Η ΚΑΙΝΗ ΔΙΑΘΗΚΗ. The Greek Testament, with notes, [etc.]. Dublin, 1860.

Memoirs of J. R. Hope-Scott, with Selections from his Correspondence. 2 vols. 1884.

CHARLES ANTHONY SWAINSON (1820–1887)

The Rubrical Question of 1874. A Brief Historical Enquiry as to the Purport of the Rubrics concerning Ornaments. Chichester, 1874; 1875.

The Nicene and Apostles' Creeds. Their Literary History; with an Account of 'The Creed of St Athanasius.' 1875.

The Parliamentary History of the Act of Uniformity, 13 and 14 Charles II. 1875.

In the Advertisements of 1556 was Order taken by the Authority of the Queen with the Advice of the Commissioners for Causes Ecclesiastical or of the Metropolitan? An Historical Enquiry. Cambridge, 1880.

The History & Constitution of a Cathedral of the Old Foundation. Illustrated from Documents of Chichester. 1880. [Ed. by Swainson.]

The Greek Liturgies, chiefly from Original Authorities. Cambridge, 1884. [Ed. by Swainson.]

[Swainson also pbd minor theological and liturgical works, articles in Sussex Archaeological Collections, Dictionary of Christian Antiquities, ed. Sir W. Smith and S. Cheetham, 2 vols. 1875–80, and Dictionary of Christian Biography, ed. Sir W. Smith and H. Wace, 4 vols. 1877–87.]

WILLIAM BRIGHT (1824–1901)

Athanasius and Other Poems. By a Fellow of a College. 1858.

A History of the Church, 313–451. Oxford, 1860.

Hymns and Other Poems. 1866; 1874.

Chapters of Early English Church History. Oxford, 1878; Oxford, 1888; Oxford, 1897.

Iona and Other Verses. 1886 [1885].

Lessons from the Lives of Three Great Fathers. 1890. [Athanasius, Chrysostom, Augustine.]

Waymarks in Church History. 1894.

The Roman See in the Early Church, and Other Studies in Church History. 1896.

Some Aspects of Primitive Church Life. 1898.

The Age of the Fathers. 2 vols. 1903.

[Bright also edited many works in Ancient and Modern Library of Theological Literature, and pbd other works, devotional, theological, and liturgical, and contributions to Dictionary of Christian Antiquities, ed. Sir W. Smith and S. Cheetham, 2 vols. 1875–80, and Dictionary of Christian Biography, ed. Sir W. Smith and H. Wace, 4 vols. 1877–87. See Selected Letters of William Bright, ed. B. J. Kidd, with Memoir by P. G. Medd, 1903.]

GEORGE WILLIAM KITCHIN (1827–1912)

Francisci Baconi Novum Organum. Oxford, 1855. [Ed. by Kitchin.]

The Novum Organon. By Francis Bacon. Oxford, 1855. [Tr. by Kitchin.]

A Lecture on Lectures. 1859.

Of the Proficience and Advancement of Learning. By Francis Bacon. 1861; 1915 (Everyman's Lib.). [Ed. by Kitchin.]

Spenser. Book 1 of The Faery Queene. Oxford, 1867; Oxford, 1868 (adds Bk 2); Oxford, 1897. [Ed. by Kitchin.]

Catalogus Codicum MSS qui in Bibliotheca Ædis Christi adservantur. Oxford, 1867.

A Letter to the Vice-Chancellor of the University of Oxford on the Summer Term and Commemoration Week. Oxford, [1869].

A History of France. 3 vols. Oxford, 1873–7; 2 vols. Oxford, 1892–4 (3rd edn, rev.).

The Life of Pope Pius II as illustrated by Pinturicchio's Frescoes. 2 vols. Arundel Soc. 1881.

A Consuetudinary of the Fourteenth Century for the House of S. Swithun Winchester. 1886. (Winchester Cathedral Records, no. 1.) [Ed. by Kitchen.]

A Charter of Edward the Third confirming St Giles Fair, Winchester. 1886. (Winchester Cathedral Records, no. 2.) [Ed. by Kitchin.]

The Great Screen of Winchester Cathedral. Winchester, [1887]; Winchester, 1891; Winchester, 1899 (rev. W. R. W. Stephens).

Documents relating to the Foundation of the Chapter of Winchester, 1541–1547. Hampshire Record Soc. 1889. [Ed. by Kitchin and F. T. Madge.]

Winchester. 1890 (Historic Towns ser.; *bis*); 1891.

Compotus Rolls of the Obedientiaries of St Swithun's Priory, Winchester. Hampshire Record Soc. 1892. [Ed. by Kitchin.]

The Manor of Manydown, Hampshire. Hampshire Record Soc. 1895. [Ed. by Kitchin.]

E. Harold Browne, Bishop of Winchester. A Memoir. 1895.

Ruskin in Oxford and Other Studies. 1904.

A Letter to the Labour Party. 1905.

The Records of the Northern Convocation. Surtees Soc. 1907. [Ed. by Kitchin.]

Richard D'Aungerville, of Bury. Fragments of his Register, and other Documents. Surtees Soc. 1910. [Ed. by Kitchin.]

Seven Sages of Durham. 1911.

The Story of the Deanery, Durham, 1070–1912. Durham, 1912.

[Kitchin also pbd sermons and trns of Brachet's French Grammar and Dictionary.]

JAMES GAIRDNER (1828–1912)

Memorials of King Henry the Seventh. Ed. James Gairdner, 1858. (Rerum Britannicarum Medii Ævi Scriptores.)

Letters and Papers of the Reigns of Richard III and Henry VII. Ed. James Gairdner, 2 vols. 1861–3. (Rerum Britannicarum Medii Ævi Scriptores.)

The Paston Letters. Ed. James Gairdner, 3 vols. 1872–5; 3 vols. 1896; 4 vols. 1900–1; 6 vols. 1904; 4 vols. Edinburgh, 1910.

The Houses of Lancaster and York. 1874.

The Historical Collections of a Citizen of London in the Fifteenth Century. Ed. James Gairdner, Camden Soc. 1876.

Bishop Cranmer's Recantacyons. Philobiblon Soc. Misc. xv, 1877–84.

History of the Life and Reign of Richard the Third. 1878; 1879; Cambridge, 1898 (rev.).

Early Chronicles of Europe. England. [1879.]

Three Fifteenth-Century Chronicles. Ed. James Gairdner, Camden Soc. 1880.

Letters and Papers of the Reign of Henry VIII. 24 vols. 1880–1910. [Vols. v–xxi ed. by Gairdner, vols. xiv–xxi with R. H. Brodie.]

Studies in English History. By James Gairdner and James Spedding. Edinburgh, 1881.

The Reign of Henry VIII to the Death of Wolsey. By J. S. Brewer. Ed. James Gairdner, 2 vols. 1884. [Introductions to vols. i–iv of Letters and Papers of Henry VIII.]

Sailing Directions for the Circumnavigation of England. Hakluyt Soc. 1889. [Ed. by Gairdner.]

Henry the Seventh. 1889 (Twelve English Statesmen ser.); 1902.

'The Spousells' of the Princess Mary, 1508. Camden Misc. ix, 1895. [Ed. by Gairdner.]

The English Reformation. What it was and what it has done. 1899.

The English Church from the Accession of Henry VIII to the Death of Mary. 1902. [Being W. R. W. Stephens and W. Hunt, A History of the English Church, vol. iv.]

Lollardy and the Reformation in England. 4 vols. 1908–13. [Vol. iv ed. with memoir by W. Hunt.]

Stephen Gardiner. [In Typical English Churchmen, ser. 2, Church Historical Soc. 1909.]

The Reule of Crysten Religioun. By Reginald Pecock. The Original Manuscript described. 1911 (priv. ptd).

[Gairdner also wrote articles in DNB. and Cambridge Modern History.]

RICHARD WATSON DIXON (1833–1900)

[See p. 338 above.]

JOHN HENRY OVERTON (1835–1903)

The English Church in the Eighteenth Century. 2 vols. 1878; 1887 (abridged). [With C. J. Abbey.]

William Law, Nonjuror and Mystic. His Life, Character, and Opinions. 1881.

Life in the English Church (1660–1714). 1885.

The Evangelical Revival in the Eighteenth Century. 1886.

Christopher Wordsworth, Bishop of Lincoln. 1888; 1890. [With E. Wordsworth.]

John Hannah. A Clerical Study. 1890.

John Wesley. 1891.

The English Church in the Nineteenth Century (1800–1833). 1894.

The Church in England. 2 vols. 1897.

The Anglican Revival. 1897.

A Serious Call to a Devout and Holy Life. By William Law. 1898. [Ed. by Overton.]

The Non Jurors, their Lives, Principles, and Writings. 1902.

Some Post-Reformation Saints. 1905.

The English Church from the Accession of George I to the End of the Eighteenth Century. 1906. [With F. Relton; being W. R. W. Stephens and W. Hunt, A History of the English Church, vol. vii.]

[Overton also wrote articles in DNB., J. Julian, Dictionary of Hymnology, 1892, and Church Quarterly Rev.]

THOMAS GRAVES LAW (1836–1904)

An Index to the Harmony of the Four Gospels. 1865.

A Calendar of the English Martyrs of the Sixteenth and Seventeenth Centuries. With an Introduction. 1876.

The Holy Bible, translated from the Latin Vulgate. Revised and corrected by Frederick Canon Oakeley and Thomas Graves Law. 2 vols. [1878].

A Shorte Summe of the Whole Catechisme. By John Craig. With Memoir of the Author by T. G. Law. Edinburgh, 1883.

The Catechism of John Hamilton Archbishop of St Andrews, 1552. Oxford, 1884. [Ed. by Law.]

A Catechisme or Christian Doctrine. By Laurence Vaux. Chetham Soc. Manchester, 1885. [Ed. (with memoir) by Law.]

A Historical Sketch of the Conflicts between Jesuits and Seculars in the Reign of Queen Elizabeth. 1889.

Documents illustrating Catholic Policy in the Reign of James VI, 1596–1598. Scottish History Soc. Misc. i, Edinburgh, 1893. [Ed. by Law.]

The Archpriest Controversy. Documents relating to Dissensions of the Roman Catholic Clergy, 1597–1602. Camden Soc. and Royal Historical Soc. Camden Ser. 1896–8. [Ed. by Law.]

Catholic Tractates of the Sixteenth Century. STS. Edinburgh, 1901. [Ed. by Law.]

The New Testament in Scots. Being Purvey's Revision of Wycliffe's Version turned into Scots by Murdoch Nisbet, c. 1520. 3 vols. STS. Edinburgh, 1901–5. [Ed. by Law.]

Collected Essays and Reviews. Ed. (with memoir) P. H. Brown, Edinburgh, 1904.

[Law also wrote articles in DNB. and Cambridge Modern History.]

WILLIAM RICHARD WOOD STEPHENS (1839–1902)

St Chrysostom: his Life and Times. 1872; 1880.

Memorials of the South Saxon See and Cathedral Church of Chichester. 1876.

The Life and Letters of W. F. Hook. 2 vols. 1878; 1880.

The South Saxon Diocese. Selsey-Chichester. 1881.

A Memoir of William Page Wood, Baron Hatherley, with Selections from his Correspondence. 2 vols. 1883.

A Church Dictionary. By W. F. Hook. 1887 (14th edn). [Ed. by Hook and Stephens.]

Hildebrand and his Times. 1888.

St Chrysostom: On the Priesthood; Ascetic Treatises; [etc.]. [Tr. Stephens, being P. Schoff, A Select Library of the Nicene and Post-Nicene Fathers, vol. ix, New York, 1889.]

Memorials of the Church and Parish of Sonning. By H. Pearson. Rev. (with memoir) W. R. W. Stephens, Reading, 1890.

The Life and Letters of E. A. Freeman. 2 vols. 1895.

Documents relating to the History of the Cathedral Church of Winchester in the Seventeenth Century. Hampshire Record Soc. 1897. [Ed. by Stephens and F. T. Madge.]

A Memoir of Richard Durnford, Bishop of Chichester, with Selections from his Correspondence. 1899.

The Great Screen of Winchester Cathedral. By G. W. Kitchin. Revised and completed by W. R. W. Stephens. Winchester, 1899.

The English Church from the Norman Conquest to the Accession of Edward I. 1901. [Being A History of the English Church, ed. by Stephens and W. Hunt, vol. ii.]

The Bishops of Winchester. Part 1: Birinus to Stigand. Winchester, 1907. [Pt 2 by W. W. Capes; rptd from Winchester Diocesan Chronicle.]

[Stephens also pbd devotional and ecclesiastical works and articles in DNB.]

WILFRID PHILIP WARD (1856–1916)

William George Ward and the Oxford Movement. 1889; 1890.

William George Ward and the Catholic Revival. 1893; 1912.

Witnesses to the Unseen, and Other Essays. 1893.

The Life and Times of Cardinal Wiseman. 2 vols. 1897.

Problems and Persons. 1903.

Aubrey de Vere. A Memoir. 1904.

Ten Personal Studies. 1908.

The Life of John Henry, Cardinal Newman; 2 vols. 1912; 2 vols. 1913; 2 pts, 1927; 2 vols. in 1, 1937.

The Oxford Movement. [1913.]

Men and Matters. 1914.

Last Lectures. With an Introductory Study by Mrs Wilfrid Ward. 1918.

Some Recollections, 1882–1887. Ed. Maisie Ward, Life and Letters, x, 1934.

[Ward also pbd various works of Catholic apologetics. For biography see Maisie Ward, The Wilfrid Wards and the Transition, 2 vols. 1934–7.]

WILLIAM EDWARD COLLINS (1867–1911)

(a) Writings

The Authority of General Councils. 1896.

The Teaching Power of the Church. 1896.

What was the Position of the Pope in England in the Middle Ages? 1896.

The Internal Evidence of the Letter 'Apostolicae Curae' as to its Own Origin and Value. 1897.

Unity, Catholic and Papal. 1897.

The English Reformation and its Consequences. Four Lectures. 1898.

The Nature and Force of the Canon Law. 1898.

The Beginnings of English Christianity, with Special Reference to St Augustine. 1898.

The Canons of 1571 in English and Latin. With Notes by W. E. Collins. 1899.

Queen Elizabeth's Defence of her Proceedings in Church and State. With an Essay on the Northern Rebellion. 1899.

Thomas Becket. A Lecture. 1902.

John Bramhall. Frederick Denison Maurice. [In Typical English Churchmen; Lectures, ed. by Collins, 1902.]

Church and State in England before the Conquest. 1903.

The Study of Ecclesiastical History. 1903.

The Rights of a Particular Church in Matters of Practice. 1904.

The Peculium. An Endeavour to throw Light on the Decline of the Society of Friends. By T. Hancock. 2nd edn, rev. (with introduction) W. E. Collins, 1907.

[All the above works, save The Beginnings of English Christianity and The Study of Ecclesiastical History, were issued by Church Historical Soc.; Collins also wrote other works of ecclesiastical controversy and contributed to Cambridge Modern History.]

(b) Biography and Criticism

B., L. B. 'We bless Thy Holy Name for all Thy servants departed, Especially William, Bishop of Gibraltar and Mary, his Wife.' 1911 (priv. ptd, bis); 1912; 1913.

Mason, A. J. Life of W. E. Collins, Bishop of Gibraltar. 1912.

E. ENGLISH HISTORY (NAVAL)

SIR JOHN KNOX LAUGHTON (1830–1915)

Physical Geography in its Relation to the Prevailing Winds and Currents. 1870.

An Introduction to the Study of Nautical Surveying. 1872; 1882.

Letters and Despatches of Viscount Nelson. Selected and arranged by J. K. Laughton. 1886.

Studies in Naval History. Biographies. 1887.

Memoirs relating to Lord Torrington. Camden Soc. 1889. [Ed. by Laughton.]

The Story of Trafalgar. Portsmouth, 1890.

State Papers relating to the Defeat of the Spanish Armada. 2 vols. Navy Records Soc. 1894–5.

Nelson. 1895; 1900.

The Story of the Sea. 2 vols. 1895–6; 2 vol. 1898. [Ed. by Sir A. T. Quiller-Couch, assisted by Laughton and others.]

The Study of Naval History. 1896. [A lecture.]

The Nelson Memorial. Nelson and his Companions in Arms. 1896; 1905.

Journal of Rear-Admiral Bartholomew James, 1752–1828. Navy Records Soc. 1896. [Ed. by Laughton and J. Y. F. Sullivan.]

Memoirs of the Life and Correspondence of Henry Reeve. 2 vols. 1898.

From Howard to Nelson: Twelve Sailors. 1899; 2 sers. 1913 (3rd edn, as British Sailor Heroes). [Ed. by Laughton, who wrote the article on Howard.]

Sea Fights and Adventures. 1901.

The Naval Miscellany. 3 vols. Navy Records Soc. 1902–28. [Vols. I–II ed. by Laughton.]

Recollections of James Anthony Gardner, 1775–1814. Navy Records Soc. 1906. [Ed. by Sir R. V. Hamilton and Laughton.]

Letters and Papers of Charles, Lord Barham, 1758–1813. 3 vols. Navy Records Soc. 1907–11. [Ed. by Laughton.]

[Laughton wrote over 900 articles in DNB and pbd articles in Cambridge Modern History, books on meteorology, geography and naval tactics, and reports for Historical MSS Commission.]

SIR WILLIAM LAIRD CLOWES (1856–1905)

Meroë. A Poem in Six Books. 1876.
Love's Rebellion. A Poem. 1878.
The Lover's Progress. Poems. 1881.
Black America. A Study of the Ex-Slave and his Late Master. Reprinted from 'The Times.' 1891.
The Royal Navy. A History from the Earliest Times. 7 vols. 1897–1903. [With other writers.]
Eclogues. 1899.
The Naval Campaign of Lissa: its History, Strategy, and Tactics. Proc. United States Naval Inst. vol. XXVII, 1901.
The Mercantile Marine in War Time. Reprinted from 'The Shipping and Mercantile Gazette and Lloyd's List.' 1902.
Four Modern Naval Campaigns. 1902; 1906.
Trafalgar refought. [1905]; [1907]. [With A. H. Burgoyne.]

[Clowes also pbd articles in H. D. Traill, Social England, 6 vols. 1893–7, technical works, and novels.]

F. ENGLISH HISTORY (SOCIAL AND ECONOMIC)

SAMUEL SMILES (1812–1904)

(a) Writings

Physical Education, or the Nurture and Management of Children. Edinburgh, 1838; ed. Sir H. Beevor, 1905.
History of Ireland and the Irish People, under the Government of England. 1844.
The Life of George Stephenson. 1857 (3 edns); 1858 (5th edn); 1862 (as vol. III of Lives of the Engineers); 1868; 1874; 1904; separately 1881; abridged, 1859; 1864. Tr. German, Stuttgart, 1859; Dutch, Amsterdam, 1864; Danish, Copenhagen, 1877.
Self-Help; with Illustrations of Character and Conduct. 1859; 1860; 1866; 1891; 1905; [1912]. Tr. French, London, 1865; German, 2nd edn, Colberg, 1877.
Workmen's Earnings, Strikes, and Savings. Reprinted from the 'Quarterly Review.' 1861.
Lives of the Engineers. 3 vols. 1861–2; 5 vols. 1874, 1904 (with Industrial Biography, Lives of Boulton and Watt, etc.).
    James Brindley and the Early Engineers. Abridged from 'Lives of the Engineers.' 1864.
    The Life of Thomas Telford, with an Introductory History of Roads and Travelling in Great Britain. 1867. [Part of Lives of the Engineers.]
Industrial Biography: Iron Workers and Tool Makers. 1863; 1879.

Lives of Boulton and Watt. 1865; 1874, 1904 (as vol. v of Lives of the Engineers).
The Huguenots, their Settlements, Churches, and Industries in England and Ireland. 1867; 1868; New York, 1868; 1869; 1876; 1880; 1889.
Character. 1871; 1879; 1910; tr. Italian, Florence, 1872.
A Boy's Voyage Round the World. Edited by Samuel Smiles. 1871. [By Smiles?]
The Huguenots in France after the Revocation of the Edict of Nantes. 1873; 1881; 1893.
Thrift. 1875.
Life of a Scotch Naturalist: Thomas Edward. 1876; 1882; ed. (abridged) E. F. Daglish, 1936.
Robert Dick, Baker, of Thurso, Geologist and Botanist. 1878.
George Moore, Merchant and Philanthropist. 1878.
Duty; with Illustrations of Courage, Patience, and Endurance. 1880.
James Nasmyth. An Autobiography. Ed. Samuel Smiles, 1883, 1885, 1912.
Men of Invention and Industry. 1884.
Life and Labour, or Characteristics of Men of Industry, Culture and Genius. 1887; 1910; tr. Portuguese, Rio de Janeiro, 1889.
Jasmin: Barber, Poet, Philanthropist. 1891.
A Publisher and his Friends: Memoir and Correspondence of John Murray. 2 vols. 1891 (bis); 1911 (abridged).
Josiah Wedgwood: his Personal History. 1894.
Autobiography. Ed. T. Mackay, 1905.

(b) Biography

Green, T. B. The Life and Work of Dr Samuel Smiles. [1904.]

JAMES EDWIN THOROLD ROGERS (1823–1890)

An Introductory Lecture to the Logic of Aristotle. Oxford, 1859.
Education in Oxford: its Method, its Aids, and its Rewards. 1861.
Primogeniture and Entail. Letters of J. E. Thorold Rogers and H. Tupper. Manchester, 1864.
Aristotelis Ethica Nicomachea. Editio altera. 1865. [Ed. by Rogers.]
University Extension. [In O. Shipley, The Church and the World, 1866.]
A History of Agriculture and Prices in England, 1259–1793. 7 vols. in 8, Oxford, 1866–1902.
Bribery. [In Questions for a Reformed Parliament, 1867.]
A Manual of Political Economy for Schools. Oxford, 1868; Oxford, 1869.

Speeches on Questions of Public Policy. By John Bright. 2 vols. 1868; 1869; 1878; 1883. [Ed. by Rogers.]

An Inquiry into the Wealth of Nations. By Adam Smith. 2 vols. Oxford, 1869. [Ed. by Rogers.]

Historical Gleanings. A Series of Sketches. 2 sers. 1869–70.

Speeches on Questions of Public Policy. By Richard Cobden. 2 vols. 2 vols. 1908. [Ed. by J. Bright and Rogers.]

Social Economy. Lessons for Schools. [1871.]

The Bacchæ of Euripides, translated into English Verse. Oxford, 1872.

Paul of Tarsus. An Inquiry into the Times, and the Gospel of the Apostle of the Gentiles. By a Graduate. 1872.

Cobden and Modern Political Opinion. Essays. 1873.

A Complete Collection of the Protests of the Lords, with Historical Introductions by J. E. Thorold Rogers. 3 vols. Oxford, 1875.

The Correspondence of the English Establishment with the Purpose of its Foundation. [1875.]

Epistles, Satires and Epigrams. 1876.

Public Addresses by John Bright. 1879. [Ed. by Rogers.]

Loci e Libro Veritatum. Passages from Gascoigne's Theological Dictionary. Oxford, 1881. [Introduction by Rogers.]

Ensilage in America: its Prospects in English Agriculture. 1883; 1884.

Six Centuries of Work and Wages. The History of English Labour. 2 vols. 1884; 1886; 1890; 1894.

The British Citizen: his Rights and Privileges. A Short History. 1885.

The First Nine Years of the Bank of England. Oxford, 1887.

The Relations of Economic Science to Social and Political Action. 1888.

Holland. 1888. (Story of the Nations ser.)

The Economic Interpretation of History. Lectures. 1888.

Oxford City Documents, 1268–1665. Oxford Historical Soc. 1891. [Ed. by Rogers.]

Lessons from the Dutch Republic. [In National Life and Thought; Addresses, 1891.]

The Industrial and Commercial History of England. Lectures. Ed. A. G. L. Rogers, 1892.

[Rogers also pbd speeches, etc.]

JOSEPHINE ELIZABETH BUTLER, née GREY (1828–1906)

(a) Writings

Memoir of John Grey of Dilston. Edinburgh, 1869; 1874; tr. Italian, Florence, 1871.

Women's Work and Women's Culture. Essays, 1869. [Ed. by Mrs Butler.]

The Constitution Violated. An Essay by the Author of the 'Memoir of John Grey.' Edinburgh, 1871.

The Hour before the Dawn. An Appeal to Men. 1876.

Catharine of Siena. A Biography. 1878; 1879.

The Life of J. F. Oberlin, Pastor of the Ban de la Roche. [1882]; 1886.

The Salvation Army in Switzerland. 1883.

Rebecca Jarrett. [1886.]

Recollections of George Butler. Bristol, [1892.]

Personal Reminiscences of a Great Crusade. 1896; tr. French, Paris, 1900.

In Memoriam Harriet Meuricoffre. [1901.]

Josephine E. Butler. An Autobiographical Memoir. Ed. G. W. and L. A. Johnson, Bristol, 1909; Bristol, 1911; [1928]. [Contains bibliography.]

[Mrs Butler also wrote social and devotional pamphlets.]

(b) Biography and Criticism

Stead, W. T. Josephine Butler. A Life Sketch. 1888.

Holmes, M. Josephine Butler. A Cameo Life-Sketch. Women's Freedom League, [1913.]

Hay-Cooper, L. Josephine Butler and her Work for Social Purity. S.P.C.K. 1922.

Mestral Combremont, J. de. La noble Vie d'une Femme. Josephine Butler. Lausanne, 1927.

Turner, E. M. Josephine Butler. An Appreciation. [1927.]

Crawford, V. M. Josephine Butler. Josephine Butler Centenary Committee, [1928].

FREDERIC SEEBOHM (1833–1912)

The Facts of the Four Gospels. An Essay. 1861.

The Crisis of Emancipation in America. 1865.

The Oxford Reformers of 1498: Colet, Erasmus, and More. 1867; 1869; 1887; 1914 (Everyman's Lib.).

On International Reform. 1871; tr. French, Paris, 1873.

The Era of the Protestant Revolution. 1874.

The Spirit of Christianity. An Essay on the Christian Hypothesis. 1876 (priv. ptd); 1916.

The English Village Community examined in its Relations to the Manorial and Tribal Systems, and to the Common or Open Field System of Husbandry. 1883 (bis); 1884; 1905; 1915; Cambridge, 1926.

The Tribal System in Wales. 1895; 1904.
Tribal Custom in Anglo-Saxon Law. 1902.
Customary Acres and their Historical Importance. Unfinished Essays. 1914.
The Teaching of History and the Use of Local Illustrations. A Paper. Historical Ass. 1918.

AUSTIN DOBSON (1840–1921)
[See p. 739 above.]

G. ENGLISH HISTORY (LOCAL)

GEORGE THOMAS CLARK (1809–1898)

A Guide-Book to the Great Western Railway. 1839 (anon.).
The History and Description of the Great Western Railway. 1846 (anon.).
The Land of Morgan: its Conquest and its Conquerors. 1880; 1883.
Some Account of Sir Robert Mansel and of Admiral Sir Thomas Button. Dowlais, 1883 (priv. ptd).
Medieval Military Architecture in England. 2 vols. 1884.
Cartae et alia Munimenta quae ad Dominium de Glamorgan pertinent. 4 vols. Dowlais, Cardiff, 1885–93 (priv. ptd). [Ed. by Clark.]
Limbus Patrum Morganiae et Glamorganiae. Being the Genealogies of the Older Families of Morgan and Glamorgan. 1886.

[And minor topographical and genealogical works, including numerous papers in Journ. British Archaeological Ass., Archaeologia Cambrensis, The Builder, etc.]

LLEWELLYN FREDERICK WILLIAM JEWITT (1810–1888)

Royal Agricultural Society of England, 1846. The Hand-Book of Newcastle and Guide to the Show. 1846.
Royal Agricultural Society of England, 1847. The Hand Book of Northampton and Guide to the Show. Northampton, 1847.
A Guide to the Borough of Derby. Derby, 1852.
A Stroll to Lea Hurst, Derbyshire; the Home of Florence Nightingale. 1855.
Black's Tourist's Guide to Derbyshire. Edinburgh, 1857 (2nd edn). [Ed. by Jewitt.]
Antennæ. Poems. 1858.
Rifles and Volunteer Rifle Corps. 1860.
The Matlock Companion and Visitor's Guide to the Peak. Derby, [1860?].
The Wedgwoods. Being a Life of Josiah Wedgwood; with Memoirs of the Wedgwood and Other Families, and a History of the Early Potteries of Staffordshire. 1865.
The Ballads and Songs of Derbyshire. 1867. [Ed. by Jewitt.]
Black's Guide to Buxton. Edinburgh, 1868. [Ed. by Jewitt.]

Guide to Alton Towers. Edinburgh, 1869.
Grave-mounds and their Contents. 1870.
Handbook of English Coins. [1870].
Haddon Hall. An Illustrated Guide. Buxton, 1871; Manchester, [1904]; Manchester, [1930]. [With S. C. Hall.]
Domesday Book of Derbyshire. Extended Latin Text; and Translation. 1871. [Ed. by Jewitt.]
The Life of William Hutton, and the History of the Hutton Family. [1872.] [By Hutton. Ed. by Jewitt.]
A History of Plymouth. 1873.
The Stately Homes of England. 2 sers. 1874–7. [With S. C. Hall.]
Half-Hours among some English Antiquities. 1877; 1880.
The Ceramic Art of Great Britain. Being a History of the Ancient and Modern Pottery and Porcelain Works. 2 vols. 1878; [1883].
The Life and Works of Jacob Thompson. 1882.
English Coins and Tokens. 1886.
The Corporation Plate and Insignia of Office of the Cities and Towns of England and Wales. Ed. W. H. St J. Hope, 2 vols. 1895.

[For life see W. H. Goss, A Sketch of the Life and Death of Llewellyn Jewitt, 1887 (rptd from The Reliquary); The Life and Death of L. Jewitt, with Memoirs of S. C. Hall, 1889.]

RICHARD COPLEY CHRISTIE (1830–1901)

Étienne Dolet. A Biography. 1880; 1899; tr. French, Paris, 1886.
The Old Church and School Libraries of Lancashire. Chetham Soc. Manchester, 1885.
The Diary and Correspondence of Dr John Worthington. Chetham Soc. Manchester, 1886. [Vol. II, pt 2 ed. by Christie.]
Annales Cestrienses, or Chronicle of the Abbey of St Werburg, at Chester. Record Soc. of Lancashire and Cheshire, 1887. [Ed. by Christie.]
A Bibliography of Works by Dr John Worthington. Chetham Soc. Manchester, 1888.
Letters of Sir Thomas Copley, to Queen Elizabeth. Roxburghe Club, 1897. [Ed. by Christie.]
Selected Essays and Papers. Ed. (with memoir) W. A. Shaw, 1902.

[Christie also wrote historical and bibliographical articles in DNB., Quarterly Rev., etc.]

JOHN WILLIS CLARK (1833–1910)

Journal of a Yacht Voyage to the Faroe Islands and Iceland. [In F. Galton, Vacation Tourists in 1860, Cambridge, 1861.]

Cambridge. Brief Historical and Descriptive Notes. 1881; 1890; 1908.

Ancient Wood & Iron Work in Cambridge. By W. B. Redfarn, the Letterpress by John Willis Clark. 2 vols. Cambridge, [1881–6].

The Architectural History of the University of Cambridge, and of the Colleges of Cambridge and Eton. By Robert Willis. 4 vols. Cambridge, 1886. [Ed. by Clark.]

Coutts Trotter. In Memoriam. Cambridge, 1888. [With M. Foster and S. Taylor.]

The Life and Letters of Adam Sedgwick. 2 vols. Cambridge, 1890. [With M'K. Hughes.]

Letters Patent of Elizabeth and James the First to the University of Cambridge. Cambridge, 1892. [Ed. (with trn of letters of Elizabeth) by Clark.]

Libraries in the Medieval and Renaissance Periods. Rede Lecture. Cambridge, 1894.

The Observances in Use at the Augustinian Priory of St Giles and St Andrew at Barnwell. Cambridge, 1897. [Ed. (with trn) by Clark.]

A Concise Guide to Cambridge. Cambridge, [1898]; Cambridge, 1902; Cambridge, 1904; Cambridge, 1906; Cambridge, 1910; Cambridge, 1916; Cambridge, 1919; Cambridge, 1921; Cambridge, 1925; Cambridge, 1929; Cambridge, 1931; Cambridge, 1936.

A Descriptive Catalogue of the Manuscripts in the Library of Peterhouse. By M. R. James. With an Essay on the History of the Library by J. W. Clark. Cambridge, 1899.

Old Friends at Cambridge and elsewhere. 1900.

The Care of Books. An Essay on the Development of Libraries and their Fittings, to the end of the Eighteenth Century. Cambridge, 1901; Cambridge, 1902.

A Concise Guide to Ely Cathedral. Cambridge, 1904.

Cantabrigia Illustrata. By D. Loggan. Edited with a Life of Loggan, Introduction and Notes, by J. W. Clark. Cambridge, 1905.

Liber Memorandorum Ecclesie de Bernewelle. Cambridge, 1907. [Ed. by Clark.]

Old Plans of Cambridge, 1574 to 1798. Reproduced with Descriptive Text. Cambridge, 1921. [With A. Gray.]

[Clark also wrote articles in Trans. Cambridge Antiquarian Soc. and DNB.; he edited Cambridge University official pbns. For life; see Fasciculus Ioanni Willis Clark dicatus, Cambridge, 1909 (with bibliography); A. E. Shipley, 'J,' a Memoir of John Willis Clark, 1913.]

SIR WALTER BESANT (1836–1901)

[See p. 537 above.]

JOHN EDWIN CUSSANS (1837–1899)

The Grammar of Heraldry; with the Armorial Bearings of all the Landed Gentry in England prior to the Sixteenth Century. 1866.

The Handbook of Heraldry. 1869 [1868]; 1882 (3rd edn); 1893.

History of Hertfordshire. 8 pts in 3 vols. Hertford, 1870–81.

Inventory of Furniture and Ornaments in all the Churches of Hertfordshire in the Last Year of Edward the Sixth. Oxford, 1873. [Transcribed by Cussans.]

HENRY BENJAMIN WHEATLEY (d. 1917)

[See p. 1043 below.]

MARY BATESON (1856–1906)

[All edited, save Mediæval England and The Borough of Peterborough.]

A Collection of Original Letters from the Bishops to the Privy Council, 1564. Camden Misc. IX, 1895.

A Narrative of the Changes in the Ministry, 1765–1767. Royal Historical Soc., Camden Ser. 1898.

Catalogue of the Library of Syon Monastery, Isleworth. Cambridge, 1898.

George Ashby's Poems. EETS. Ex. Ser. 1899.

Records of the Borough of Leicester. 3 vols. 1899–1905.

The Charters of the Borough of Cambridge. Cambridge, 1901. [Ed. with F. W. Maitland.]

Index Britanniae Scriptorum Quos collegit I. Baleus (Bishop Bale). Anecdota Oxoniensia, Oxford, 1902. [Ed. with R. L. Poole.]

Cambridge Gild Records. Cambridge Antiquarian Soc. Cambridge, 1903.

Mediæval England, 1066–1350. 1903. (Story of the Nations ser.)

Grace Book B. 2 vols. Luard Memorial ser., Cambridge Antiquarian Soc. 1903–5.

The Scottish King's Household and Other Fragments. Scottish History Soc. Misc. II, Edinburgh, 1904.

Borough Customs. 2 vols. Selden Soc. 1904–6.

The Borough of Peterborough. [In Victoria History of Northamptonshire, vol. II, 1906.]

[Mary Bateson also wrote in EHR., Trans. Royal Hist. Soc., H. D. Traill, Social England, 6 vols. 1893–7, DNB., and Cambridge Modern History.]

H. SCOTTISH, IRISH AND MANX HISTORY

JOHN PATRICK PRENDERGAST (1808–1893)

The Cromwellian Settlement of Ireland. 1865; 1870; rptd Dublin, 1922.

The Tory War of Ulster. 2 pts, Dublin, 1868 (priv. ptd).

Calendar of the State Papers relating to Ireland, 1603–25. 5 vols. 1872–80. [Ed. by C. W. Russell and J. P. Prendergast.]

The Scandinavian Kingdom of Dublin. By C. Haliday. Dublin, 1884 (2nd edn). [Ed. (with memoir of Haliday) by Prendergast.]

A Lecture on Catholic Ireland. Dublin, 1886.

Ireland from the Restoration to the Revolution. 1887.

JOHN HOSACK (d. 1887)

A Treatise on the Conflict of Laws of England and Scotland. Pt 1, 1847.

The Rights of British and Neutral Commerce. 1854.

Mary Queen of Scots and her Accusers. Edinburgh, 1869; 2 vols. Edinburgh, 1870–4.

On the Rise and Growth of the Law of Nations from the Earliest Time to the Treaty of Utrecht. 1882.

Mary Stewart. A Brief Statement of the Principal Charges Against her with Answers to the Same. Edinburgh, 1888.

CHARLES ROGERS (1825–1890)

(a) Writings

History of St Andrews. Edinburgh, 1849.

Ettrick Forest [and] the Ettrick Shepherd. Edinburgh, 1860.

Familiar Illustrations of Scottish Character. 1861; 1865 (enlarged).

Life and Songs of the Baroness Nairne. 1869.

Three Scottish Reformers. 1874.

Leaves from My Autobiography. Grampian Club, 1876.

Life of George Wishart. Edinburgh, 1876.

Memorials of the Earl of Stirling and of the House of Alexander. 2 vols. Edinburgh, 1877.

The Serpent's Track. A Narrative of Twenty-Two Years' Persecution. 1880.

History of the Chapel Royal of Scotland. Grampian Club, 1882.

Social Life in Scotland. 3 vols. Edinburgh, 1884–6.

Memorials of the Scottish House of Gourlay. Edinburgh, 1888 (priv. ptd).

The Book of Wallace. 2 vols. Grampian Club, 1889.

The Book of Robert Burns. 3 vols. Grampian Club, 1889–91.

[And other Scottish topographical, genealogical and historical works.]

(b) Editions

Historical Notices of St Anthony's Monastery, Leith. Grampian Club, 1849.

The Modern Scottish Minstrel. 6 vols. Edinburgh, 1855–7.

The Sacred Minstrel. A Collection of Spiritual Songs. 1859; 1860.

Lyra Britannica. A Collection of British Hymns. 1867.

The Scottish Minstrel. The Songs of Scotland subsequent to Burns. Edinburgh, 1870.

The Poetical Remains of King James. 1873.

Boswelliana. The Common Place Book of James Boswell. Grampian Club, 1874.

The Poetical Remains of William Glen. 1874.

Diocesan Registers of Glasgow. 2 vols. 1875. [With J. Bain.]

Events in the North of Scotland, 1635 to 1645. 1877.

Register of the Collegiate Church of Crail. Grampian Club, 1877.

Chartulary of the Cistercian Priory of Coldstream. Grampian Club, 1879.

Rental-Book of the Cistercian Abbey of Cupar-Angus. Grampian Club and British Topographical Soc. 1880.

The Earl of Stirling's Register of Royal Letters. 2 vols. 1884–5.

[Rogers also edited the poems of Sir Robert Aytoun, 1844, and Thomas Campbell, 1870, as well as Sir John Scot's The Staggering State of Scottish Statesmen, 1872, and Sir Alexander Hay's Estimate of the Scottish Nobility, 1873.]

THOMAS DUNBAR INGRAM (1826–1901)

A History of the Legislative Union of Great Britain and Ireland. 1887; Westminster, 1890.

Two Chapters of Irish History. 1888.

England and Rome. A History of the Relations between the Papacy and the English State and Church from the Norman Conquest to 1688. 1892.

A Critical Examination of Irish History. 2 vols. 1904.

SIR JOHN THOMAS GILBERT (1829–1898)

The Historic Literature of Ireland. Reprinted from the Irish Quarterly Review. Dublin, 1851.

The Celtic Records of Ireland. Reprinted from the Irish Quarterly Review. Dublin, 1852.

A History of the City of Dublin. 3 vols. Dublin, 1854–9.

Ancient Irish Historical Manuscripts. (From the Dublin Review, No. c.) 1861 (anon.). [Review of E. O'Curry, Lectures on the Manuscript Materials of Ancient Irish History.]

Record Revelations. A Letter on the Public Records of Ireland. By An Irish Archivist. 1863. Pt 2, 1864 (as Record Revelations Resumed). Both sers. 1864, 1865 (as On the History, Position and Treatment of the Public Records of Ireland).

English Commissioners and Irish Records. A Letter. By An Irish Archivist. 1865.

History of the Viceroys of Ireland. Dublin, 1865.

Historic and Municipal Documents of Ireland, 1172–1320. 1870. (Rerum Britannicarum Medii Ævi Scriptores.) [Ed. by Gilbert.]

Facsimiles of National Manuscripts of Ireland. 4 pts in 5 vols. 1874–84.

Account of Facsimiles of National Manuscripts of Ireland. 1879 (2nd edn); 1884.

A Contemporary History of Affairs in Ireland from 1641 to 1652. 6 pts in 3 vols. Irish Archaeological Soc. Dublin, 1879–80. [Ed. by Gilbert.]

History of the Irish Confederation and the War in Ireland, 1641–9. 7 vols. Dublin, 1882–91. [Ed. by Gilbert.]

Chartularies of St Mary's Abbey, Dublin. 2 vols. 1884–[5]. (Rerum Britannicarum Medii Ævi Scriptores.) [Ed. by Gilbert.]

Register of the Abbey of St Thomas, Dublin, 1889. (Rerum Britannicarum Medii Ævi Scriptores.) [Ed. by Gilbert.]

Calendar of Ancient Records of Dublin. 18 vols. Dublin, 1889–1922. [Vols. i–vii ed. by Gilbert.]

A Jacobite Narrative of the War in Ireland, 1688–1691. Dublin, 1892. [Ed. by Gilbert.]

Documents relating to Ireland, 1795–1804. Dublin, 1893. [Ed. by Gilbert.]

Narratives of the Detention, Liberation and Marriage of Maria Clementina Stuart. Dublin, 1894. [Ed. by Gilbert.]

An Account of the Parliament House, Dublin. With Notices of Parliaments, 1661–1800. Dublin, 1896.

'Crede Mihi': the most Ancient Register of the Archbishops of Dublin. Dublin, 1897. [Ed. by Gilbert.]

Irish Bibliography. Two Papers. Proc. Royal Irish Academy, xxv, sect. C. Dublin, 1904–5.

[Gilbert also wrote articles in Irish Quarterly Rev., Dublin Rev. and DNB. and reports for Historical MSS Commission; for biography see R. M. Gilbert, Life of Sir John T. Gilbert, 1905 (with bibliography).]

SIR JOHN SKELTON (1831–1897)

[See p. 754 above.]

ANDREW LANG (1844–1912)

[See p. 747 above.]

ARTHUR WILLIAM MOORE (1853–1909)

The Surnames and Place Names of the Isle of Man. 1890; 1903.

Folk-Lore of the Isle of Man. 1891

Manx Carols. 1891.

The Book of Common Prayer in Manx Gaelic. 2 vols. Manx Soc. 1893–5. [Ed. by Moore and Sir John Rhys.]

Sodor and Man. 1893.

Manx Ballads and Music. 1896.

A History of the Isle of Man. 1900.

Manx Worthies. Douglas, 1901.

Bishop Hildesley's Letters. 1904. [Ed. by Moore.]

Douglas 100 Years ago. 1904.

Extracts from the Records of the Isle of Man. 1905. [Ed. by Moore.]

[More edited The Manx Note Book, 1885–7, and founded The Manx Language Society, 1899.]

CAESAR LITTON FALKINER (1863–1908)

Studies in Irish History and Biography, mainly of the Eighteenth Century. 1902.

Calendar of the Manuscripts of the Marquess of Ormonde, at Kilkenny Castle. New ser. vols. i–v, Historical MSS Commission, 1902–8.

The Poems of Charles Wolfe. With Memoir by C. L. Falkiner. 1903; 1909 (as The Burial of Sir John Moore and Other Poems.)

Illustrations of Irish History and Topography, mainly of the Seventeenth Century. 1904.

Memoir of John Kells Ingram. Dublin, 1907.

Essays relating to Ireland. With a Memoir of the Author by E. Dowden. 1909.

[Falkiner also wrote articles in Proc. Royal Irish Academy, and DNB.]

I. BRITISH IMPERIAL HISTORY

WILLIAM KINGSFORD (1819–1898)

History, Structure, and Statistics of Plank Roads. Philadelphia, 1852.

Impressions of the West and South. Toronto, 1858 (anon.; preface signed W. K.).

The Canadian Canals: their History and Cost. Toronto, 1865.

A Canadian Political Coin. A Monograph. Ottawa, 1874.

Canadian Archaeology. Montreal, 1886.

The History of Canada. 10 vols. 1888–98.

The Early Bibliography of Ontario. Toronto, 1892.

[Kingsford also wrote papers in Trans. Royal Soc. of Canada.]

GOLDWIN SMITH (1823–1910)

Review of Mr Congreve's 'Roman Empire of the West.' [In Oxford Essays, 1856.]

Oxford University Reform. [In Oxford Essays, 1858.]

An Inaugural Lecture. Oxford, 1859; 1861 (in Lectures on the Study of History); 1865.

The Study of History. A Lecture. June 1859. [Oxford, 1859] (priv. ptd); 1861 (in The Study of History); 1861 (in Lectures); 1865.

The Study of History. Two Lectures. Oxford, 1861 (separately and in Lectures); 1865 (in Lectures).

On some Supposed Consequences of the Doctrine of Historical Progress. A Lecture. Oxford, 1861 (separately and in Lectures); 1865 (in Lectures).

The Foundation of the American Colonies. A Lecture. Oxford, 1861 (separately and in Lectures).

Lectures on the Study of History, 1859–61. Oxford, 1861; Oxford, 1865 (omits The Foundation of the American Colonies).

Irish History and Irish Character. Oxford, 1861.

Rational Religion, and the Rationalistic Objections of the Bampton Lectures for 1858. Oxford, 1861.

The Suppression of Doubt is not Faith. A Letter to the Bishop of Oxford. By a Layman. Oxford, 1861.

Concerning Doubt. A Reply to 'A Clergyman.' By a Layman. Oxford, 1861.

The Empire. A Series of Letters published in 'The Daily News,' 1862, 1863. Oxford, 1863.

Does the Bible sanction American Slavery? Oxford, 1863.

A Letter to a Whig Member of the Southern Independence Association. 1864.

A Plea for the Abolition of Tests in the University of Oxford. Oxford, 1864.

England and America. A Lecture. Reprinted from the 'Atlantic Monthly.' Manchester, 1865.

The Civil War in America. An Address. 1866.

The Elections to the Hebdomadal Council. A Letter to C. W. Sandford. Oxford, 1866.

Three English Statesmen. Lectures. 1867. [On Pym, Cromwell and Pitt.]

The Expansion of the American Commonwealth. [In Essays on Reform, 1867.]

The Reorganization of the University of Oxford. Oxford, 1868.

The Irish Question. Three Letters to the Daily News. 1868.

The Relations between America and England. 1869.

The Political Destiny of Canada. [In E. L. Burlingame, Current Discussion, vol. I, New York, 1878.]

The Slaveowner and the Turk. [In E. L. Burlingame, Current Discussion, vol. I, New York, 1878.]

Cowper. 1880. (English Men of Letters ser.)

Lectures and Essays. Toronto, 1881 (priv. ptd).

Economical Questions and Events in America. An Address. 1881.

The Conduct of England to Ireland. An Address. 1882.

False Hopes, or Fallacies, Socialistic and Semi-Socialistic, briefly answered. An Address. New York, 1883; 1886.

Dismemberment no Remedy. An Address. [1886.]

The Schism in the Anglo-Saxon Race. [In G. M. Fairchild, Canadian Leaves, New York, 1887.]

Prohibitionism in Canada and the United States. Reprinted from 'Macmillan's Magazine,' March, 1889. 1889.

Life of Jane Austen. 1890. (Great Writers ser.)

Canada and the Canadian Question. 1891.

A Trip to England. Toronto, 1891; 1892.

Loyalty, Aristocracy, and Jingoism. Three Lectures. Toronto, 1891.

The Moral Crusader. William Lloyd Garrison. A Biographical Essay. New York, 1892.

Bay Leaves. Translations from the Latin Poets. New York, 1893.

The United States. An Outline of Political History. 1893.

Essays on Questions of the Day, Political and Social. New York, 1893; New York, 1894.

Specimens of Greek Tragedy. Translated by Goldwin Smith. 2 vols. New York, 1893.

Oxford and her Colleges. 1894; New York, 1895.

Guesses at the Riddle of Existence, and Other Essays. New York, 1897.

Shakespeare, the Man. Toronto, 1800.

The United Kingdom. A Political History. 2 vols. 1899.

Commonwealth or Empire. A Bystander's View. New York, 1902.

In the Court of History. An Apology for Canadians who opposed the South African War. Toronto, 1902.

The Founder of Christendom. American Unitarian Ass. Boston, 1903.

My Memory of Gladstone. 1904.

Lines of Religious Enquiry. An Address. Toronto, 1904.

Irish History and the Irish Question. 1905.

Supremacy in the Far East. Will Russia regain it? The Navies of Japan and Russia . compiled from Official Sources. 1905.

In Quest of Light. New York, 1906.

Labour and Capital. A Letter to a Labour Friend. New York, 1907.

No Refuge but in Truth. Toronto, 1908; 1909.

Reminiscences. Ed. A. Haultain, New York, 1911.

Goldwin Smith: his Life and Opinions. By his Literary Executor, A. Haultain. To which is appended 'U. S. Notes,' being Smith's Journal during his First Visit to America in 1864. [1913.]

A Selection from Goldwin Smith's Correspondence, comprising Letters chiefly to and from his English Friends, between 1846 and 1910. Collected by A. Haultain. [1913.]

GEORGE BRUCE MALLESON (1825–1898)

The Mutiny of the Bengal Army. By One who has served under Sir C. Napier. 2 pts, 1857–8.

The Career of Count Lally. A Lecture. Calcutta, 1865.

Essays and Lectures on Indian Historical Subjects. By an Officer of the Bengal Staff Corps. 1866; 1876.

History of the French in India, 1674–1761. 1868; 1893.

Recreations of an Indian Official. 1872.

An Historical Sketch of the Native States of India. 1875.

Studies from Genoese History. 1875.

Final French Struggles in India and on the Indian Seas. 1878; tr. French, Pondicherry, 1911.

History of Afghanistan. 1878.

History of the Indian Mutiny, commencing from the Close of the Second Volume of Kaye's Sepoy War. 3 vols. 1878–80; 6 vols. 1888–9 (as Kaye's and Malleson's History).

The Kabul Insurrection of 1841–2. By Sir Vincent Eyre. 1879. [Ed. by Malleson.]

Herat: the Granary and Garden of Central Asia. 1880.

The Founders of the Indian Empire. Lord Clive. 1882.

The Decisive Battles of India from 1746 to 1849. 1883; 1885; 1888.

Captain Musafir's Rambles in Alpine Lands. 1884.

The Battle-Fields of Germany from the Outbreak of the Thirty Years' War to the Battle of Blenheim. 1884.

Loudon. A Sketch of the Military Life. 1884.

The Russo-Afghan Question and the Invasion of India. 1885 (bis).

Ambushes and Surprises. 1885.

Prince Eugene of Savoy. 1888.

Life of Prince Metternich. 1888.

Life of the Marquess Wellesley. 1889; [1895]. Akbar. Oxford, 1890.

Dupleix. Oxford, 1890.

Lord Clive. Oxford, 1893.

The Refounding of the German Empire, 1848–1871. 1893.

Life of Warren Hastings. 1894.

Delagoa Bay: the Key to South Africa. 1896.

The Lakes and Rivers of Austria, Bavaria and Hungary. 1897.

SIR JOHN ROBERT SEELEY (1834–1895)

A Parallel between Shakespeare's King Lear and the Œdipus in Colono of Sophocles. [In Three Essays on King Lear, by Pupils of the City of London School, 1851.]

David and Samuel; with Other Poems, Original and Translated. By John Robertson. 1859. [Really by Seeley.]

Classical Studies as an Introduction to the Moral Sciences. Introductory Lecture. 1864.

Ecce Homo. A Survey of the Life and Work of Jesus Christ. 1866 (anon.); 1866 (5th edn); 1895; 1908 (Everyman's Lib.); 1910; [1914].

Liberal Education in Universities. [In F. W. Farrar, Essays on a Liberal Education, 1867.]

The Church as a Teacher of Morality. [In W. L. Clay, Essays on Church Policy, 1868.]

Lectures and Essays. 1870; 1895.

Livy. Books I–X. With Introduction, Historical Examination, and Notes. Bk I, Oxford, 1871.

English Lessons for English People. 1871. [With E. A. Abbott.]

Life and Times of Stein, or Germany and Prussia in the Napoleonic Age. 3 vols. Cambridge, 1878; tr. German, Gotha, 1883–7.

Natural Religion. By the Author of 'Ecce Homo.' 1882; 1891 (3rd edn); 1895.

The Expansion of England. 1883; 1895. Tr. French, Paris, 1885; Portuguese, Lisbon, 1891.

A Short History of Napoleon the First. 1886; tr. French, Paris, 1887. [Enlarged from Ency. Brit.]

Goethe reviewed after Sixty Years. 1894. [Rptd from Contemporary Rev. 1884.]

The Growth of British Policy. 2 vols. Cambridge, 1895. [With Memoir by G. W. Prothero.]

Introduction to Political Science. Lectures. 1896.

Ethics and Religion. [In Ethics and Religion, 1900.]

[For biography and criticism see J. Gazeau, L'Impérialisme anglais, son Évolution; Carlyle—Seeley—Chamberlain, Paris, 1903; A. Rein, Sir J. R. Seeley, eine Studie über den Historiker, Langensalza, 1912.]

SIR ALFRED COMYN LYALL (1835–1911)

Gazetteer for the Haidarábád Assigned Districts, commonly called Berár. Bombay, 1870. [Ed. by Lyall.]

Rajputana Gazetteer. 3 vols. Calcutta, Simla, 1879–80. [Ed. by Lyall.]

Asiatic Studies, Religious and Social. 1882; 2 vols. 1899 (adds ser. 2); tr. French, Paris, 1885 (1st ser. only).
Verses Written in India. 1889; 1896 (4th edn); [1907] (4th edn, Muses' Lib.).
Warren Hastings. 1889. (English Men of Action ser.)
Natural Religion in India. Rede Lecture. Cambridge, 1891.
The Rise of the British Dominion in India. 1893 (bis); 1894 (enlarged); 1907 (continued to 1907); 1910.
Brahminism. [In Great Religions of the World, New York, 1901.]
Tennyson. 1902. (English Men of Letters ser.)
The Life of the Marquis of Dufferin and Ava. 2 vols. 1905; [1909].
Some Aspects of Asiatic History. Proc. Central Asian Soc. 1910.
Studies in Literature and History. Ed. J. O. Miller, 1915.

[Lyall also wrote articles in Cambridge Modern History. For life see Sir M. Durand, The Life of Sir Alfred Lyall, Edinburgh, 1913, and p. 346 above.]

SIR WILLIAM WILSON HUNTER (1840–1900)

The Annals of Rural Bengal. 3 vols. 1868–72 (vols. II and III being Orissa, vols. I and II); 1897.
The Uncertainties of Indian Finance. Calcutta, 1869 (priv. ptd).
The Indian Musalmans: are they bound in Conscience to rebel? 1871; 1872; 1876.
Famine Aspects of Bengal Districts. Simla, 1873.
Essays on the External Policy of India. By J. W. S. Wyllie. 1875. [Ed. (with a brief life) by Hunter.]
A Life of the Earl of Mayo. 2 vols. 1875.
A Statistical Account of Bengal. 20 vols. 1875–7.
A Statistical Account of Assam. 2 vols. 1879.
The Imperial Gazetteer of India. 9 vols. 1881; 14 vols. 1885–7. [Ed. by Hunter.]
England's Work in India. 1881; Madras, 1890.
The Indian Empire: its History, People, and Products. 1882; 1886; 1893.
A Brief History of the Indian People. 1882; 1884 (30th thousand); Oxford, 1892 (20th edn,rev.); Oxford, 1895; [ed.W. H. Hutton], Oxford, 1903 (23rd edn).
The Marquess of Dalhousie. Oxford, 1890.
The Old Missionary. New York, [1890]; [Oxford], 1895; 1896. [Rptd from Contemporary Rev.]
The Earl of Mayo. Oxford, 1891.
A School History and Geography of Northern India. Calcutta, [1891].

Bombay, 1885–1890. A Study in Indian Administration. [1892.]
Bengal MS Records. 3 vols. 1894.
Life of Brian Houghton Hodgson. 1896.
The Thackerays in India, and Some Calcutta Graves. 1897.
A History of British India. 2 vols. 1899–1900 [Unfinished.]
The India of the Queen, and Other Essays Ed. Lady Hunter, 1903.

[For life see F. H. Skrine, Life of Sir W. W. Hunter, 1901.]

JOHN ANDREW DOYLE (1844–1907)

The American Colonies previous to the Declaration of Independence. Arnold Prize Essay. 1869.
History of America. 1875.
The English in America. 5 vols. 1882–1907.
Memoir and Correspondence of Susan Ferrier, 1782–1854. 1898. [Ed. by Doyle.]
Essays on Various Subjects. Ed. W. P. Ker, 1911.

[Doyle also wrote articles in DNB. and Cambridge Modern History.]

EDWARD JOHN PAYNE (1844–1904)

Burke. Select Works. Edited by E. J. Payne. 2 vols. Oxford, 1874–5; 3 vols. Oxford, 1876–8; 3 vols. Oxford, 1892–8; vol. I in 3 vols. Oxford, 1912 (introduction rptd in each).
History of European Colonies. 1877.
Voyages of the Elizabethan Seamen to America. Thirteen Narratives from Hakluyt, edited by E. J. Payne. 1880; 2 vols. Oxford, 1893–1900; Oxford, 1907 (with additional notes by C. R. Beazley); Oxford, 1909 (partly rptd as Voyages of Drake & Gilbert, with notes by C. R. Beazley).
Colonies and Dependencies. Part 1 by J. S. Cotton; Part 2 by E. J. Payne. 1883.
History of the New World called America. 2 vols. Oxford, 1892–9.
Colonies and Colonial Federations. 1904.
Johnson. Vanity of Human Wishes. Oxford, 1906. [Ed. by Payne.]

[Payne also wrote articles in Sir G. Grove, A Dictionary of Music, 4 vols. 1879–89 and Cambridge Modern History.]

J. EUROPEAN HISTORY
MARK PATTISON (1813–1884)

[See p. 723 above.]

SIR WILLIAM MUIR (1819–1905)

The Testimony borne by the Corân to the Jewish and Christian Scriptures. Agra, 1855; Allahabad, 1860; [1878], 1896 (rev. as The Corân; its Composition and Teaching).

The Life of Mahomet. 4 vols. 1858–61; 1894 (3rd edn); 1884, 1887 (abridged as Mahomet and Islam).

The Opium Revenue. Sir William Muir's Minute, etc. Anglo-Oriental Soc. for Suppression of Opium Trade, 1875.

Extracts from the Coran with English Rendering. 1880.

The Early Caliphate and Rise of Islam. Rede Lecture. 1881.

The Rise and Decline of Islam. [1883.]

Annals of the Early Caliphate. 1883; 1891 (abridged as The Caliphate, its Rise, Decline, and Fall); 1892; [1899]; rev. T. H. Weir, Edinburgh, 1924.

The Authorship of Deuteronomy. 1894; 1896.

The Mameluke or Slave Dynasty of Egypt, 1260–1517. 1896.

James Thomason, Lieutenant-Governor N.-W. P., India, 1843–1853. Edinburgh, 1897.

The Mohammedan Controversy; Biographies of Mohammed; Sprenger on Tradition; The Indian Liturgy; and the Psalter. Edinburgh, 1897.

Cyprian, his Life and Teaching. Edinburgh, 1898.

The Sources of Islam. A Persian Treatise by W. St Clair-Tisdall. Translated and abridged by William Muir. Edinburgh, 1901.

[Muir also pbd trns from Arabic and other missionary writings.]

MARGARET OLIPHANT OLIPHANT (1828–1897)

[See p. 500 above.]

THOMAS HODGKIN (1831–1913)

Claudian: the Last of the Roman Poets. Two Lectures. Newcastle-on-Tyne, 1875.

Italy and her Invaders. 8 vols. Oxford, 1880–99.

The Letters of Cassiodorus. Being a Condensed Translation of the Variae Epistolae. 1886. [Introduction by Hodgkin.]

The Dynasty of Theodosius, or Eighty Years' Struggle with the Barbarians. Lectures. Oxford, 1889.

Theodoric the Goth: the Barbarian Champion of Civilisation. New York, 1891. (Heroes of the Nations ser.)

George Fox. 1896.

Charles the Great. 1897.

The Society of Friends. [In Our Churches and why we belong to them, 1898.]

Ernst Curtius. From the Proceedings of the British Academy, vol. II. 1905.

The History of England to the Norman Conquest. 1906; 1920. [Being W. Hunt and

R. L. Poole, The Political History of England, vol. I.]

National Education. A Retrospect and a Prospect. [1906.]

The Wardens of the Northern Marches. Creighton Memorial Lecture, 1907. 1908.

Address on the Teaching of History in Schools. Historical Ass. 1908.

The Trial of our Faith and other Papers. 1911.

Swarthmore Lecture, 1911. Human Progress and the Inward Light. 1911.

Southward Ho! Being a Plea for a Greatly Extended and Scientific System of Emigration to Australia. [1912.]

On Silent Worship. [In C. Hepher, The Fellowship of Silence, 1915.]

[For biography and criticism see L. Creighton, Life and Letters of Thomas Hodgkin, 1917 (with bibliography); F. W. Dendy, Obituary Notice of Thomas Hodgkin, Archaeologia Aeliana, IX, 1913.]

WILLIAM RICHARD MORFILL (1834–1909)

Ballads Relating chiefly to the Reign of Queen Elizabeth. Ballad Soc. Hertford, 1873. [Ballads from MSS, ed. by Morfill.]

Russia. 1880.

Slavonic Literature. 1883.

An Essay on the Importance of the Study of the Slavonic Languages. Inaugural Lecture. 1890.

Russia. 1890 (Story of the Nations ser.); 1904 (6th edn).

Russia. [In National Life and Thought; Addresses, 1891.]

Poland. 1893 (Story of the Nations ser.); 1923.

The Book of the Secrets of Enoch. Oxford, 1896. [Tr. by Morfill, ed. by R. H. Charles.]

A History of Russia from the Birth of Peter the Great to the Death of Alexander II. 1902.

[Morfill also pbd Grammars of Polish, Serbian, Russian, Bulgarian, and Czech.]

JOHN MORLEY, VISCOUNT MORLEY (1838–1923)

[See p. 751 above.]

MARTIN ANDREW SHARP HUME (1843–1910)

Chronicle of King Henry VIII of England. Translated, with Notes and Introduction. 1889.

Calendar of Letters and State Papers relating to English Affairs, preserved in the Archives of Simancas. 4 vols. 1892–9.

The Courtships of Queen Elizabeth. 1896; 1904.

The Year after the Armada, and Other Historical Studies. 1896.

Sir Walter Ralegh. 1897; 1926.

Philip II of Spain. 1897.

Spain, its Greatness and Decay, 1479–1788. Cambridge, 1898 (Cambridge Historical ser.); rev. E. Armstrong, Cambridge, 1913 (3rd edn).

The Great Lord Burghley. 1898; 1906.

Modern Spain 1788–1898. 1899 (Story of the Nations ser.); 1906; 1923.

Calendar of Letters, Despatches, and State Papers, relating to Negotiations between England and Spain, preserved in the Archives at Simancas, Vienna, Brussels, etc. 11 vols. in 17, 1862–1916. [Hume wrote introduction to vol. VII and edited vols. VIII–IX (IX with R. Tyler).]

The Spanish People: their Origin, Growth and Influence. 1901; tr. Spanish, Madrid, [1904].

Treason and Plot. Struggles for Catholic Supremacy in the Last Years of Queen Elizabeth. 1901.

The Love Affairs of Mary Queen of Scots. A Political History. 1903.

Españoles é Ingleses en el Siglo XVI. Madrid, 1903.

Spanish Influences on English Literature. 1905.

The Wives of Henry the Eighth and the Parts they played in History. 1905; [1927].

Queens of Old Spain. 1906.

The Court of Philip IV. Spain in Decadence. 1907; 1927.

Through Portugal. 1907.

Two English Queens and Philip. [1908.]

True Stories of the Past. 1910.

[Hume also contributed articles to Cambridge Modern History.]

ARTHUR JOHN BUTLER (1844–1910)

[See p. 736 above.]

CHARLES ALAN FYFFE (1845–1892)

History of Greece. 1875; Toronto, 1899.

A History of Modern Europe. 3 vols. 1880–9; 3 vols. 1891–2; 1895; 2 vols. 1924.

The Universities. [In T. H. Ward, The Reign of Queen Victoria, vol. II, 1887.]

FREDERICK YORK POWELL (1850–1904)

Early England up to the Norman Conquest. 1876; 1895 (11th edn).

Sturlunga Saga. Ed. G. Vigfússon, 2 vols. Oxford, 1878. [With assistance from York Powell.]

An Icelandic Prose Reader. Oxford, 1879. [With G. Vigfússon.]

Alfred the Great and William the Conqueror. 1881.

Old Stories from British History. 1882; 1885 (3rd edn).

Corpus Poeticum Boreale. 2 vols. Oxford, 1883. [Ed., with G. Vigfússon.]

History of England for Schools. Part I: to the Death of Henry VII. 1885; 1900. [Completed by T. F. Tout.]

Sigfred, Arminius and Other Papers. Oxford, 1886. [With G. Vigfússon.]

On the History of the Process by which the Aristotelian Writings arrived at their Present Form. An Essay by R. Shute. With a Brief Memoir [by F. York Powell]. Oxford, 1888.

Sketches from British History for Standard IV. 1888.

The First Nine Books of the Danish History of Saxo Grammaticus translated by Oliver Elton. With some Considerations on Saxo's Sources, Historical Methods, and Folk-lore, by F. York Powell. 1894.

The Tale of Thrond of Gate commonly called Færeyinga Saga. Englished by F. York Powell. 1896.

XXIV Quatrains from Omar. Set forth by F. York Powell. New York, 1900.

John Ruskin and Thoughts on Democracy. 1905.

Origines Islandicae. A Collection of Sagas and other Writings. 2 vols. Oxford, 1905. [Ed. and tr. with G. Vigfússon.]

Scandinavian Britain. By W. G. Collingwood. With Chapters Introductory to the Subject by F. York Powell. 1908.

Some Words on Allegory in England. Opuscula of Sette of Odd Volumes, 1910 (priv. ptd).

[Powell also wrote articles in DNB. and H. D. Traill, Social England, 6 vols. 1893–7; for life see O. Elton, Frederick York Powell, a Life and a Selection from his Letters and Occasional Writings, 2 vols. Oxford, 1906.]

AGNES DUCLAUX, née ROBINSON
(b. 1857)

[See p. 355 above.]

HENRY BUTLER CLARKE (1863–1904)

Spanish Literature. An Elementary Handbook. 1893.

The Cid Campeadór and the Waning of the Crescent in the West. New York, 1897. (Heroes of the Nations ser.)

Modern Spain, 1815–1898. With Memoir by W. H. Hutton. Cambridge, 1906. (Cambridge Historical ser.)

[Clarke also wrote works on the Spanish language and an article in Cambridge Modern History, as well as editing Lazarillo de Tormes, Oxford, 1897.] G. P.

III. THE LITERATURE OF SCIENCE

Physics; Mathematics; Astronomy; Chemistry; Geology; Evolution; Zoology and Natural History; Botany; Physiology; Psychology; Anthropology.

A. INTRODUCTION

(a) Bibliography

Catalogue of Scientific Papers, 1800–1900. Compiled and published by the Royal Society. 4 sers. (1800–63; 1864–73; 1874–83; 1884–1900), 19 vols. Cambridge, 1867–1925.

(b) General Works

Whewell, W. The History of the Inductive Sciences. 3 vols. 1837.

Brougham, H. P. (Baron Brougham and Vaux). Lives of Men of Science of the Time of George III. 1845.

Walker, W. Memoirs of Distinguished Men of Science of Great Britain, living in the Years 1807–8. 1862.

Jevons, W. S. The Principles of Science. A Treatise of Scientific Method. 2 vols. 1874.

Geddes, P. A Synthetic Outline of the History of Biology. Proc. Royal Soc. Edinburgh, 1885–6, pp. 905–11.

Pearson, K. The Grammar of Science. 1892.

Huxley, T. H. The Advance of Science in the Last Half Century (1887). [In Methods and Results, 1894.]

Merz, J. T. History of European Thought in the 19th Century. 4 vols. Edinburgh, 1896–1914.

Wallace, A. R. The Wonderful Century. 1898.

Thomson, Sir J. A. The Science of Life. An Outline of the History of Biology. 1899.

—— The Progress of Science in the Century. 1906. (Nineteenth Century ser.)

Williams, H. S. A History of Science. 5 vols. 1904.

Locy, W. A. Biology and its Makers. 1908.

Ball, W. W. R., Muir, M. M. P., and Shipley, Sir A. E. The Literature f Science (1800–1900). CHEL. vol. xiv, 1916.

Schuster, Sir A. and Shipley, Sir A. E. Britain's Heritage of Science. 1917.

Singer, C. A Short History of Biology. 1930.

Crowther, J. G. British Scientists of the Nineteenth Century. 1935.

B. PHYSICS

General Works

Brewster, Sir D. Memoirs of Sir Isaac Newton. 2 vols. 1855. [History of optics from Newton's time.]

Nichol, J. P. A Cyclopaedia of the Physical Sciences. 1857.

Forbes, J. D. A Review of the Progress of Mathematical and Physical Science between the Years 1775 and 1850. Edinburgh, 1858.

Herschel, Sir J. F. W. Familiar Lectures on Scientific Subjects. 1867.

Tait, P. G. Recent Advances in Physical Science. 1876.

Thurston, R. History of the Growth of the Steam Engine. 1893. [See also Ency. Brit. 11th edn, vol. xv, *s.v.* 'Steam Engine.']

Benjamin, P. The Intellectual Rise in Electricity. 1895.

Glazebrook, T. C. James Clerk Maxwell and Modern Physics. 1896.

Cajori, F. History of Physics. 1899; 1929 (rev. and expanded).

Whetham, Sir W. C. D. Recent Developments of Physical Science. 1904.

Whittaker, E. T. History of the Theories of Aether and Electricity from the Age of Descartes to the Close of the 19th Century. 1910.

Schuster, Sir A. The Progress of Physics during the Thirty-Three Years, 1875–1908. 1911.

MacFarlane, A. Lectures on the British Physicists of the 19th Century. 1919.

Mottelay, P. E. A Biographical History of Electricity and Magnetism. 1922. [To 1821.]

Buckley, A. A Short History of Physics. 1927.

Lodge, Sir O. A Century's Progress in Physics. 1927.

HENRY CAVENDISH (1731–1810)

Experiments to determine the Density of the Earth. Philosophical Trans. LXXXVIII, 1798.

The Electrical Researches of the Hon. Henry Cavendish, written between 1771 and 1781. Ed. J. C. Maxwell, Cambridge, 1879.

Scientific Papers of the Hon. Henry Cavendish. Collected and arranged by Sir J. Larmor, Cambridge, 1921. [Vol. I, The Electrical Researches.]

[For biography see under Chemistry, p. 945 below.]

JAMES WATT (1736–1819)

Improvements on the Steam Engine. Edinburgh Philosophical Journ. II, 1820.

[See J. P. Macstead, On the Origin and Progress of the Mechanical Inventions of James Watt, 3 vols. 1854.]

SIR BENJAMIN THOMPSON (COUNT RUMFORD) (1753–1814)

Essays, Political, Economic and Philosophical. 4 vols. 1796–1802.

An Enquiry concerning the Source of Heat excited by Friction. Philosophical Trans. LXXXVIII, 1798.

Philosophical Papers: being a Collection of Memoirs, Dissertations and Experimental Investigations relating to Various Branches of Natural Philosophy and Mechanics. 1802.

Complete Works. 5 vols. American Academy of Arts and Sciences, Boston, 1870–5.

CHARLES HENRY WILKINSON

The Elements of Galvanism, in Theory and Practice, with a View to its History. 2 vols. 1804.

WILLIAM CHARLES WELLS (1757–1817)

An Essay on Dew. 1814.

JOHN LESLIE (1766–1832)

Observations and Experiments on Light and Heat. Nicholson's Journ. IV, 1801.

Experimental Inquiry into the Nature and Properties of Heat. 1804.

Elements of Natural Philosophy. Edinburgh, 1823.

SIR DAVID BREWSTER (1771–1868)

On the Action of Transparent Bodies upon the Differently Coloured Rays of Light. Edinburgh, 1815.

A Treatise on the Kaleidoscope. Edinburgh, 1819.

A System of Mechanical Philosophy, with Notes by David Brewster. 1822. [With J. Robison.]

Treatise on Optics. 1831.

The Life of Sir Isaac Newton. 2 vols. 1831.

Letters on Natural Magic. 1832.

Treatise on the Microscope. Edinburgh, 1837.

The Martyrs of Science. 1841.

The Stereoscope. 1856.

Memoirs of the Life, Writings, and Discoveries of Sir Isaac Newton. Edinburgh, 1855.

[See L. Playfair, Sir David Brewster, 1868.]

THOMAS THOMSON (1773–1852)

An Outline of the Sciences of Heat and Electricity. 1830.

[For other works see under Chemistry, p. 946 below.]

THOMAS YOUNG (1773–1829)

Outlines of Experiments and Inquiries respecting Sound and Light. I–XVI. Philosophical Trans. XC, 1800.

On the Theory of Light and Colour. Philosophical Trans. XCII, 1802, pp. 12, 387.

A Syllabus of a Course of Lectures on Natural and Experimental Philosophy. 1802.

A Course of Lectures on Natural Philosophy and the Mechanical Arts. 2 vols. 1807.

Miscellaneous Works. Collected by G. Peacock. 3 vols. 1855.

[See Memoirs of the Life of Thomas Young, with a Catalogue of his Works and Essays, 1831; G. Peacock, Life of Thomas Young, 1855; H. P. Brougham, Edinburgh Rev. V, 1804, p. 103.]

SIR HUMPHRY DAVY (1778–1829)

[See under Chemistry, p. 946 below.]

PETER MARK ROGET (1779–1869)

Electricity, Galvanism, Magnetism and Electro-Magnetism. 1832.

MARY SOMERVILLE, née FAIRFAX (1780–1872)

On the Connexion of the Physical Sciences. 1835.

On Molecular and Microscopic Science. 2 vols. 1869.

[See Martha Somerville, Personal Recollections from Early Life to Old Age, of Mary Somerville, with Selections from her Correspondence, 1873.]

WILLIAM STURGEON (1783–1850)

A Complete Set of Novel Electro-Magnetic Apparatus. Phillip's Annals of Philosophy, XII, 1826.

Lectures on Electricity. 1842.

Scientific Researches, Experimental and Theoretical, in Electricity, Magnetism, Galvanism, Electro-Magnetism and Electro-Chemistry. 1850.

[See S. P. Thompson, William Sturgeon, the Electrician, 1891.]

SIR EDWARD SABINE (1788–1883)

Contributions to Terrestrial Magnetism. 1875.

MICHAEL FARADAY (1791–1867)

Historical Sketch of Electro-Magnetism. Annals of Philosophy, II, III, 1821–2.

Experimental Researches in Electricity. Reprinted from Philosophical Transactions, CXXI–CXLV, 1831–55. 3 vols. 1839–55.

Experimental Researches in Chemistry and Physics. Reprinted from Philosophical Transactions, 1821–57. 1859.

On the Various Forces of Nature and their Relation to Each Other. 1860.

[For biography, see under Chemistry, p. 947 below.]

CHARLES BABBAGE (1792–1871)

[See under Mathematics, p. 941 below.]

SIR JOHN FREDERICK WILLIAM HERSCHEL
(1792–1871)

On the Theory of Light. [In Encyclopaedia Metropolitana, 1828.]
A Preliminary Discourse of Natural Philosophy. [In D. Lardner's Cabinet Cyclopaedia, 1831.]
A Manual of Scientific Enquiry. 1849.
Essays and Addresses. 1857.
Familiar Lectures on Scientific Subjects. 1866.
Scientific Papers. 2 vols. 1912.

[For other works see under Astronomy, p. 943 and Mathematics, p. 941 below.]

GEORGE GREEN (1793–1841)

An Essay on the Application of Mathematical Analysis to the Theories of Electricity and Magnetism. Nottingham, 1828.

DIONYSIUS LARDNER (1793–1859)

Lectures on the Steam Engine. 1828.
The Cabinet Cyclopaedia. 133 vols. 1829–46. [Ed. by Lardner.]

WILLIAM WHEWELL (1794–1866)

Astronomy and General Physics considered with Reference to Natural Theology. 1833. (Bridgewater Treatise.)
The History of the Inductive Sciences. 3 vols. 1837.
The Philosophy of the Inductive Sciences. 2 vols. 1840.
The History of Scientific Ideas. 1858.

[See I. Todhunter, William Whewell. An Account of his Writings with Selections from his Letters and Scientific Correspondence, Cambridge, 1876; J. M. Douglas, Life of William Whewell and Selections from his Correspondence, 1881.]

HUMPHREY LLOYD (1800–1881)

Report on the Progress and Present State of Physical Optics. British Ass. Report, 1835, p. 295.
Lectures on the Wave Theory of Light. Dublin, 1841.

WILLIAM PARSONS (EARL OF ROSSE: 1800–1867)

The Scientific Papers. Collected and published by Sir C. Parsons. 1926.

SIR CHARLES WHEATSTONE (1802–1875)

An Account of Several New Instruments and Processes for determining the Constants of a Voltaic Circuit. Philosophical Trans. CXXXIII, 1843.
Scientific Papers. Physical Soc. 1879.

[For biography, see W. T. Jeans, Lives of the Electricians, 1887. See also under Physiology, p. 963 below.]

PHILLIP KELLAND (1808–1879)

Theory of Heat. Cambridge, 1837.

CHARLES PRITCHARD (1808–1893)

A Treatise on the Theory of Couples. 1831.
Modern Science and Natural Religion. 1874.

JAMES DAVID FORBES (1809–1868)

A Review of the Progress of Mathematical and Physical Science between the Years 1775 and 1850. Edinburgh, 1858.

SIR WILLIAM ROBERT GROVE (1811–1896)

On a New Voltaic Battery. Philosophical Mag. XIV, 1839.
A Lecture on the Progress of Physical Science since the Opening of the London Institution. 1842.
On the Correlation of Physical Forces. 1846.

JOHN JAMES WATERSTON (1811–1884)

The Collected Scientific Papers of John James Waterston. Ed. (with biography) J. S. Haldane, Edinburgh, 1928.

HENRY MINCHIN NOAD (1815–1877)

Manual of Electricity. 1859.

JAMES PRESCOTT JOULE (1818–1890)

On the Production of Heat by Voltaic Electricity. Proc. Royal Soc. IV, 1840.
On the Calorific Effects of Magneto-Electricity and on the Mechanical Equivalent of Heat. British Ass. Report, 1843, pt 2, p. 33.
On the Changes of Temperature produced by the Rarefaction and Condensation of Air. Proc. Royal Soc. V, 1844.
On the Mechanical Equivalent of Heat. British Ass. Report, 1845, pt 2, p. 31.
On a New Theory of Heat. Memoirs of Manchester Philosophical Soc. VII, 1846.
Scientific Papers. 2 vols. 1884–7.

[See also papers by Joule and Sir William Thomson (Baron Kelvin), p. 939 below. For Memoir of Joule, see O. Reynolds, Memoirs of Manchester Literary and Philosophical Soc. VI, 1892.]

ALFRED SMEE (1818–1877)

Elements of Electro-Metallurgy. 1847.

[See Memoir by his daughter, E. M. Odling, with selections from his writings, 1878.]

SIR GEORGE GABRIEL STOKES (1819–1903)

On the Constitution of the Luminiferous Ether. Philosophical Mag. XXIX, 1846, XXXII, 1848.

On Some Cases of Fluid Motion (1843–46). Trans. Cambridge Philosophical Soc. VIII, 1849.

On the Change of Refrangibility of Light. Philosophical Trans. CXLII, 1852, p. 463; CXLIII, 1853, p. 385.

The Absorption of Light and the Colours of Natural Bodies. 1878.

Mathematical and Physical Papers. Reprinted with Additional Notes. Ed. Sir J. Larmor, 5 vols. Cambridge, 1880–1905.

On Light. 1884–7.

Memoirs and Scientific Correspondence of the Late Sir George Gabriel Stokes. Selected and arranged by Sir J. Larmor. 2 vols. Cambridge, 1907.

WILLIAM JOHN MACQUORN RANKINE (1820–1872)

A Manual of Applied Mechanics. [In E. Smedley, Encyclopaedia Metropolitana, vol. XXXIX, 1848.]

On the Mechanical Theory of Heat, especially of Gases and Vapours. Trans. Royal Soc. Edinburgh, XX, 1853.

A Manual of the Steam Engine. 1859.

Miscellaneous Scientific Papers. With a Memoir by P. G. Tait. 1881.

JOHN TYNDALL (1820–1893)

Heat considered as a Mode of Motion. 1863.

On Radiation. 1865.

Faraday as a Discoverer. 1868.

Fragments of Science for Unscientific People. 1871.

The Forms of Water. 1872.

The Scientific Use of the Imagination and Other Essays. 1872.

Scientific Addresses. 1872.

Contributions to Molecular Physics in the Domain of Radiant Heat. 1872.

Six Lectures on Light. 1873.

The Advancement of Science. Address delivered before the British Association at Belfast, 1874. 1874.

Lessons in Electricity delivered at the Royal Institution, 1875–6. 1876.

New Fragments. 1892.

Lectures and Essays. 1903.

[For memoir of Tyndall, see E. Frankland Proc. Royal Soc. LV, 1894.]

JAMES THOMSON (1822–1892)

Collected Papers in Physics and Engineering. Selected and arranged by Sir J. Larmor. 1912.

SIR WILLIAM THOMSON (BARON KELVIN) (1824–1907)

On a Universal Tendency in Nature to Dissipation of Energy. Philosophical Mag. IV, 1852.

On the Dynamical Theory of Heat. Philosophical Mag. IV, 1852.

The Thermal Effects of Fluids in Motion. Philosophical Trans. CXLIII, CXLIV, 1853–4. [With J. P. Joule. See also Proc. Royal Soc. VIII, 1856–7; X, 1859–60.]

Treatise on Natural Philosophy. Oxford, 1867. [With P. G. Tait.]

Reprint of Papers on Electrostatics and Magnetism. 1872.

Elements of Natural Philosophy. 1873.

Collected Mathematical and Physical Papers, 1841–1911. 6 vols. Cambridge, 1882–1911.

Popular Lectures and Addresses. 1889.

Baltimore Lectures on Molecular Dynamics and the Wave Theory of Light. 1904.

[For biography see S. P. Thompson, Life of Lord Kelvin, 1910; A. Gray, Lord Kelvin: an Account of his Scientific Life and Work, 1908.]

GEORGE JOHNSTONE STONEY (1826–1911)

On the Physical Units of Nature. Philosophical Mag. II, 1881.

BALFOUR STEWART (1828–1887)

An Account of Some Experiments on Radiant Heat. 1858. [See Trans. Royal Soc. Edinburgh, XXII, 1861.]

An Elementary Treatise on Heat. 1866.

The Conservation of Energy. 1872.

The Unseen Universe, or Physical Speculation on a Future State. Edinburgh, 1875. [With P. G. Tait.]

Paradoxical Philosophy, a Sequel to the Unseen Universe. 1878. [With P. G. Tait.]

JAMES CLERK MAXWELL (1831–1879)

On the Dynamical Theory of Gases. British Ass. Report, 1859, Pt 2, p. 9. [See also Philosophical Mag. XIX, XX, 1860.]

On Physical Lines of Force. Pts 1–4. Philosophical Mag. XXI, XXIII, 1861–2.

A Dynamical Theory of the Electric Field. Proc. Royal Soc. XIII, 1864.

The Theory of Heat. 1871.

On Action at a Distance. Nature, VII, 1872–3.

Treatise on Electricity and Magnetism. 2 vols. 1873.

Matter and Motion. 1873.

Discourse on Molecules. British Ass. Report, 1873.

The Electrical Researches of Henry Cavendish, written between 1771 and 1781. 1879. [Ed. by Maxwell.]

Scientific Papers. 2 vols. Cambridge, 1890.

[For biography see L. Campbell and W. Garnett, Life of James Clerk Maxwell, with a Selection from his Correspondence and Occasional Writings and a Sketch of his Contributions to Science, 1882; R. T. Glazebrook, James Clerk Maxwell and Modern Physics, New York, 1896; Sir J. J. Thomson, James Clerk Maxwell: a Commemoration Volume, 1931.]

PETER GUTHRIE TAIT (1831–1901)

A Treatise on the Dynamics of a Particle. Cambridge, 1856. [With W. J. Steele.]
A Sketch of Thermodynamics. Edinburgh, 1865.
Elementary Treatise on Quaternions. 1867.
Lectures on some Recent Advances in Physical Science. 1876.
Light. Edinburgh, 1884.
The Properties of Matter. Edinburgh, 1885.
Scientific Papers. 3 vols. Cambridge, 1898–1911. [Includes an account of Tait's life and scientific work by C. G. Knott.]

[See also under B. Stewart, p. 939 above.]

SIR WILLIAM CROOKES (1832–1919)

On Attraction and Repulsion accompanying Radiation. Philosophical Mag. XLVIII, 1874. [See also Philosophical Trans. CLXV, 1875, CLXVI, 1876.]
Contributions to Molecular Physics in High Vacua. Proc. Royal Soc. XXVIII, 1879.

[For biography see under Chemistry, p. 948 below.]

SIR JOSEPH NORMAN LOCKYER (1836–1920)

The Spectroscope and its Applications. 1873.

[See also under Astronomy, p. 944 and Chemistry, p. 948 below.]

SIR JAMES DEWAR (1842–1923)

Collected Papers on Spectroscopy. Cambridge, 1915. [With G. Liveing.]
The Collected Papers of Sir James Dewar. Ed. Lady Dewar, 2 vols. Cambridge, 1927.

JOHN WILLIAM STRUTT (BARON RAYLEIGH) (1842–1918)

Theory of Sound. 1894.
Scientific Papers. 6 vols. Cambridge, 1899–1920.

[For biography see R. J. Strutt, J. W. Strutt, Third Baron Rayleigh, 1924.]

OSBORNE REYNOLDS (1842–1912)

The General Theory of Thermodynamics. 1885.

SAMUEL TOLVER PRESTON (b. 1844)

Physics of the Ether. 1875.
Theory of Heat. 1894.
Theory of Light. 1895.

SIR GEORGE HOWARD DARWIN (1845–1912)

Scientific Papers. 5 vols. Cambridge, 1907–16.

GEORGE FRANCIS FITZGERALD (1851–1901)

Scientific Writings. Ed. Sir J. Larmor, Dublin, 1902.

SILVANUS PHILLIPS THOMPSON (1851–1916)

The Methods of Physical Science. Bristol, 1877.

[See J. S. and H. G. Thompson, Sylvanus Phillips Thompson: his Life and Letters, 1920.]

JOHN HENRY POYNTING (1852–1914)

An Essay on the Mean Density of the Earth. 1894.
Collected Scientific Papers. Cambridge, 1920.

SIR RICHARD TETLEY GLAZEBROOK (b. 1854)

Physical Optics. 1883.
Report on Optical Theories. British Ass. Report, 1885, p. 929.
The Laws and Properties of Matter. 1893.
James Clerk Maxwell and Modern Physics. New York, 1896.

SIR JOSEPH JOHN THOMSON (b. 1856)

A Treatise on the Motion of Vortex Rings. 1883.
The Application of Dynamics to Physics and Chemistry. 1888.
Notes on Recent Researches in Electricity and Magnetism. Oxford, 1893.
Elements of the Mathematical Theory of Electricity and Magnetism. Cambridge, 1895.
The Discharge of Electricity through Gases. 1898.
The Conduction of Electricity through Gases. Cambridge, 1903.

SIR JOSEPH LARMOR (b. 1857)

Aether and Matter. Cambridge, 1900.
Mathematical and Physical Papers. 2 vols. Cambridge, 1929.

C. MATHEMATICS
General Works

Todhunter, I. History of the Mathematical Theory of Probability. 1865.
—— History of Theories of Elasticity. 1886.

Ball, W. W. R. History of the Study of Mathematics at Cambridge. 1889.
—— A Short Account of the History of Mathematics. 1901.
Cajori, F. History of Mathematics. 1893.
Pierpont, J. History of Mathematics in the XIXth Century. American Mathematical Soc. Bulletin, xi, 1905.
Smith, D. E. History of Modern Mathematics. 1906.
MacFarlane, A. Lectures on Ten British Mathematicians of the XIXth Century. 1916.

CHARLES HUTTON (1737–1823)

A Mathematical and Philosophical Dictionary. 1795–6.

WILLIAM FREND (1757–1841)

Principles of Algebra. 1796–9.

SIR JAMES IVORY (1765–1842)

On the Attraction of Homogeneous Ellipsoids. Philosophical Trans. xcix, 1809, p. 345. [Ivory's Theorem.]

ROBERT WOODHOUSE (1773–1827)

The Principles of Analytical Calculation. Cambridge, 1803.

PETER BARLOW (1776–1862)

An Elementary Investigation of the Theory of Numbers. 1811.
A New Mathematical and Philosophical Dictionary. 6 vols. 1814.
New Mathematical Tables. 1814.

HENRY KATER (1777–1835) and DIONYSIUS LARDNER (1793–1859)

A Treatise on Mechanics. 1830.

GEORGE PEACOCK (1791–1858)

A Collection of Examples of the Application of the Differential and Integral Calculus. Cambridge, 1820.
Report on Recent Progress and Present State of Certain Branches of Analysis. British Ass. Report, 1834.
A Treatise on Algebra. 2 vols. Cambridge, 1842–5.

CHARLES BABBAGE (1792–1871)

An Essay towards the Calculus of Functions. Philosophical Trans. cv, 1815, p. 389; cvi, 1816, p. 179.
Reflections on the Decline of Science in England and on some of its Causes. 1830.
Passages from the Life of a Philosopher. 1864.

[See B. H. Babbage, Babbage's Calculating Machine, 1872.]

SIR JOHN FREDERICK WILLIAM HERSCHEL (1792–1871)

A Collection of Examples of the Application of the Calculus of Finite Differences. Cambridge, 1820.

[For other works see under Astronomy, p. 943 below.]

GEORGE GREEN (1793–1841)

Mathematical Papers. Ed. N. M. Ferrers, 1871.

THOMAS GALLOWAY (1796–1851)

A Treatise on Probability. Edinburgh, 1839.

WILLIAM HALLOWS MILLER (1801–1880)

Elements of Hydrostatics and Hydrodynamics. Cambridge, 1831.
An Elementary Treatise on the Differential Calculus. Cambridge, 1833.

JAMES CHALLIS (1803–1882)

An Essay on the Mathematical Principles of Physics. Cambridge, 1873.

[For other works see under Astronomy, p. 944 below.]

SIR WILLIAM ROWAN HAMILTON (1805–1868)

Systems of Rays. Dublin, 1828–33.
Lectures on Quaternions. Dublin, 1853.
Elements of Quaternions. Ed. W. F. Hamilton, 1866.
The Mathematical Papers. Ed. A. W. Conway and J. L. Synge, vol. i, Cambridge, 1931.

[See R. P. Graves, Life of Sir William Rowan Hamilton, 3 vols. Dublin, 1882–9, which includes Hamilton's poems, letters, etc.]

JAMES BOOTH (1806–1878)

On the Application of a New Analytic Method to the Theory of Curves and Curved Surfaces. 1843.
The Theory of Elliptic Integrals. Cambridge, 1851.
A Treatise on some New Geometrical Methods. 2 vols. 1873.

THOMAS PENYNGTON KIRKMAN (1806–1895)

On Pluquaternions and Homoid Products of n Squares. Philosophical Mag. xxxiii, 1848.
First Mnemonical Lessons in Geometry, Algebra and Trigonometry. 1852.
On the Representation and Enumeration of the Polyedra. Memoirs of Manchester Philosophical Soc. xii, 1855.
Philosophy without Assumptions. 1876.

AUGUSTUS DE MORGAN (1806–1871)

Mathematical Tracts. 1829–34.
The Connexion of Number and Magnitude. 1836.
Essay on Probabilities. [In D. Lardner, Cabinet Cyclopaedia, 1839.]
The Differential and Integral Calculus. 1842.
Trigonometry and Double Algebra. 1849.
A Budget of Paradoxes. 1872.
[See Life by S. E. De Morgan, 1882].

PHILLIP KELLAND (1808–1879)

Lectures on the Principles of Demonstrative Mathematics. Edinburgh, 1843.
Introduction to Quaternions. 1873. [With P. G. Tait.]

JAMES MacCULLAGH (1809–1846)

The Collected Works. Ed. J. H. Jellett and S. Houghton, Dublin, 1880.

DUNCAN FARQUHARSON GREGORY (1813–1844)

A Treatise on the Application of Analysis to Solid Geometry. Cambridge, 1845.
Mathematical Writings. Ed. W. Walton, 1865.

JAMES JOSEPH SYLVESTER (1814–1897)

Address to the Mathematical and Physical Section of the British Association. British Ass. Report, XXIX, 1869.
The Laws of Verse. 1870.
The Collected Mathematical Works. Ed. H. F. Baker, Cambridge, 1904.

GEORGE B. JERRARD (d. 1863)

Mathematical Researches. 3 pts, Bristol, 1832–5.

GEORGE BOOLE (1815–1864)

Mathematical Analysis of Logic. Cambridge, 1848.
An Investigation of the Laws of Thought. 1854.
A Treatise on Differential Equations. 2 vols. Cambridge, 1859–65.
A Treatise on the Calculus of Finite Differences. Cambridge, 1860.

JOHN HEWITT JELLETT (1817–1888)

An Elementary Treatise of the Calculus of Variations. Dublin, 1850.
Treatise on the Theory of Friction. Dublin, 1874.

GEORGE SALMON (1819–1904)

A Treatise on Conic Sections. Dublin, 1850.
A Treatise on the Higher Plane Curves. Dublin, 1852.
A Treatise on the Analytic Geometry of Three Dimensions. Dublin, 1862.

ISAAC TODHUNTER (1820–1884)

A Treatise on Analytical Statics. Cambridge, 1853.
A Treatise on Plane Co-ordinate Geometry. Cambridge, 1855.
Examples of Analytical Geometry of Three Dimensions. Cambridge, 1858.
An Elementary Treatise on the Theory of Equations. Cambridge, 1861.
History of the Progress of the Calculus of Variations during the Nineteenth Century. Cambridge, 1861.
History of the Mathematical Theory of Probability. 1865.
Researches in the Calculus of Variations. 1871.
A History of the Mathematical Theories of Attraction and the Figure of the Earth, from Newton to Laplace. 2 vols. 1873.
The Conflict of Studies. 1873.
History of the Theory of Elasticity. Edited and completed by K. Pearson. 2 ls. 1886.

ARTHUR CAYLEY (1821–189)

An Elementary Treatise on Elliptic Functions. Cambridge, 1876.
Inaugural Address before the British Association, 1883. Nature, 20 Sept. 1883.
The Collected Mathematical Papers. 14 vols Cambridge, 1889–98.

WILLIAM SPOTTISWOODE (1825–1883)

Elementary Theorems relating to Determinants. 1851.

HENRY JOHN STEPHEN SMITH (1826–1883)

Reports on the Theory of Numbers. British Ass. Reports, 1859, 1863 and 1865.
The Collected Mathematical Papers. Ed. J. W. L. Glaisher, Oxford, 1894.

EDWARD JOHN ROUTH (1831–1907)

An Elementary Treatise on the Dynamics of a System of Rigid Bodies. 1860.
A Treatise on Analytical Statics. 2 vols. Cambridge, 1891–2.

SIR ROBERT STAWELL BALL (1840–1913)

The Theory of Screws. Dublin, 1876.
Dynamics and Modern Geometry. Dublin, 1887.
A Course of Lectures on Experimental Mechanics. 1888.
A Treatise on the Theory of Screws. Cambridge, 1900.

[For other works see under Astronomy, p. 944 below.]

WILLIAM KINGDON CLIFFORD (1845–1879)

The Aims and Instruments of Scientific Thought. British Ass. Address, 1872.

Seeing and Thinking. 1873.
On the Classification of Loci. Philosophical Trans. CLXVIII, 1878.
Elements of Dynamics. Ed. Sir L. Stephen and Sir F. Pollock, 2 pts, 1879.
Lectures and Essays. Ed. Sir L. Stephen and Sir F. Pollock, 1879.
Mathematical Fragments. 1881.
Mathematical Papers. Ed. R. Tucker, Cambridge, 1882.
The Common Sense of the Exact Sciences. Ed. K. Pearson, 1885.

GEORGE MINCHIN MINCHIN (1845–1914)
A Treatise on Statics. Oxford, 1877.

GEORGE CHRYSTAL (1851–1911)
Non-Euclidean Geometry. Edinburgh, 1880.

ANDREW RUSSELL FORSYTH (b. 1858)
A Treatise on Differential Equations. 1885.

JAMES HARKNESS and FRANK MORLEY
A Treatise on the Theory of Functions. 1893.

SAMUEL BRUCE MACLAREN
Scientific Papers. Prepared for Publication by Sir J. Larmor. Cambridge, 1925.

D. ASTRONOMY
General Works
Herschel, Sir J. Outlines of Astronomy. 1849.
Clerke, A. M. A Popular History of Astronomy in the Nineteenth Century. 1885; 1902 (rev. edn).
—— Modern Cosmogonies. 1905.
Ball, Sir R. S. The Story of the Heavens. 1892.
—— Great Astronomers. 1895.
Berry, A. A Short History of Astronomy. 1898.
Macpherson, H. A Century's Progress in Astronomy. 1906.
Forbes, G. History of Astronomy. 1909.
Dreyer, J. L. E. and Turner, H. H. History of the Royal Astronomical Society, 1820–1920. 1923.

SIR WILLIAM HERSCHEL (1738–1822)
Astronomical Observations, etc. Philosophical Trans. CI, 1811, CIV, 1814, CVII, 1817.
Scientific Papers. Collected and edited under the direction of the Royal Astronomical Society. 2 vols. 1912.
[For biography see E. S. Holden, William Herschel, his Life and Works, New York, 1881; J. Sime, William Herschel and his Work, 1900; J. L. E. Dreyer, A Short Account of Sir William Herschel's Life and Work, 1912.]

CAROLINE LUCRETIA HERSCHEL
(1750–1848)
Memoir and Correspondence of Caroline Herschel, by M. C. Herschel. 1876.
[See A. M. Clerke, The Herschels (William, Caroline and John) and Modern Astronomy, 1895.]

WILLIAM PEARSON (1767–1847)
An Introduction to Practical Astronomy. 2 vols. 1824–9.

FRANCIS BAILY (1774–1844)
Astronomical Tables and Formulae. 1827.
On a Remarkable Phenomenon that occurs in Total and Annular Eclipses of the Moon ('Baily's Beads'). Memoirs of Royal Astronomical Soc. x, 1836.
An Account of some Experiments for Determining the Density of the Earth. Philosophical Mag. XXI, 1842.
[See Sir J. F. W. Herschel, Memoir of Francis Baily, 1845.]

MARY SOMERVILLE, née FAIRFAX
(1780–1872)
The Mechanism of the Heavens. 1832.
[For other works see under Physics, p. 937 above.]

WILLIAM HENRY SMYTH (1788–1865)
The Cycle of Celestial Objects. 1844; rev. G. F. Chambers, 1881.

SIR JOHN FREDERICK WILLIAM HERSCHEL
(1792–1871)
A Treatise on Astronomy. [In D. Lardner, Cabinet Cyclopedia, 1833.]
Results of Astronomical Observations made during the Years 1834–8 at the Cape of Good Hope. 1847.
Outlines of Astronomy. 1849.

WILLIAM PARSONS (EARL OF ROSSE)
(1800–1867)
The Scientific Papers. Collected and published by Sir C. Parsons. 1926.

GEORGE BIDDELL AIRY (1801–1892)
Mathematical Tracts on Physical Astronomy. Cambridge, 1826.
Astronomical Observations. Cambridge, 1829.
Gravitation. 1834.
Six Lectures on Astronomy. 1849.
Popular Astronomy. A Series of Lectures. 1866.
The Numerical Human Theory. 1866.
Autobiography. Ed. W. Airy, Cambridge, 1891.

JAMES CHALLIS (1803–1882)

Astronomical Observations, 1828–45. 16 vols. Cambridge, 1829–50.
Astronomical Observations, 1846–51. Cambridge, 1854–6
Lectures on Practical Astronomy. Cambridge, 1879.

JOHN PRINGLE NICHOL (1804–1850)

The Phenomena and Order of the Solar System. Edinburgh, 1838.
The Stellar Universe. Edinburgh, 1848.
The Architecture of the Heavens. 1850.

SIR GEORGE CORNEWALL LEWIS (1806–1863)

The Astronomy of the Ancients. 1862.

ROBERT MAIN (1808–1878)

Rudimentary Astronomy. 1852.
Practical and Spherical Astronomy. Cambridge, 1863.

JAMES NASMYTH (1808–1890)

Autobiography. Ed. S. Smiles, 1883.

DANIEL KIRKWOOD (b. 1814)

Meteoric Astronomy. Philadelphia, 1867.
Cornets and Meteors. Philadelphia, 1873.

ROBERT GRANT (1814–1892)

History of Physical Astronomy from the Earliest Ages to the Middle of the Nineteenth Century. 1852.

JOHN COUCH ADAMS (1819–1892)

Astronomical Observations. Cambridge, 1829, etc.
An Explanation of the Observed Irregularities in the Motion of Uranus. Astronomical Soc. Memoirs, xvi, 1847. [Predicts the existence of Neptune.]
The Scientific Papers. Ed. W. G. Adams (with memoir by J. W. L. Glaisher), 2 vols. Cambridge, 1896–1900.
Lectures on the Lunar Theory. Ed. B. A. Sampson, Cambridge, 1900.

JAMES CROLL (1821–1890)

Discussion on Climate and Cosmology. Edinburgh, 1885.
Stellar Evolution and its Relation to Geological Time. 1889.
The Philosophical Basis of Evolution. 1890.

[For life see Autobiographical Sketch of James Croll, with a Memoir of his Life and Work, by J. C. Irons, 1896.]

JOHN RUSSELL HIND (1823–1895)

An Introduction to Astronomy. 1847.
The Comets.˙ A Descriptive Treatise. 1852.
The Solar System. 1852.

SIR WILLIAM HUGGINS (1824–1910)

Spectrum Analysis in its Application to the Heavenly Bodies. 1866.
The Scientific Papers. Ed. Sir W. and Lady Huggins, 1909.

RICHARD CHRISTOPHER CARRINGTON (1826–1865)

Observations of Sun Spots at Redhill, 1853–61. 1864.

SIR JOSEPH NORMAN LOCKYER (1836–1920)

Elementary Lessons in Astronomy. 1868.
The Atmosphere of the Sun. 1872.
Contributions to Solar Physics. 1874.
The Chemistry of the Sun. 1887.
The Meteoric Hypothesis. 1890.
The Sun's Place in Nature. 1897.

[For other works and life see under Chemistry, p. 948 below and Physics, p. 940 above.]

RICHARD ANTHONY PROCTER (1837–1888)

Saturn and its System. 1865.
Other Worlds than ours. 1870.
The Sun. 1871.
Essays on Astronomy. 1872.
The Moon. 1873.
Transits of Venus. 1874.
Old and New Astronomy. Completed by A. C. Ranyard. 1892.

SIR ROBERT STAWELL BALL (1840–1913)

Astronomy. 1877.
Elements of Astronomy. 1880.
Time and Tide. 1889.
The Cause of an Ice Age. 1892.
The Story of the Sun. 1893.
The Story of the Heavens. 1895.
Great Astronomers. 1895.

[For biography see Reminiscences and Letters of Sir Robert Ball, ed. W. V. Ball, 1915; for other works see under Mathematics, p. 942 above.]

JAMES CARPENTER (1840–1899)

The Moon. 1874.

ELLEN MARY CLERKE (1840–1906)

Jupiter and his System. 1892.
The Planet Venus. 1893.

AGNES MARY CLERKE (1842–1907)

A Popular History of Astronomy in the Nineteenth Century. 1885.
The System of the Stars. 1890.

SIR DAVID GILL (1843–1914)

David Gill, Man and Astronomer. Memories of Sir David Gill, H.M. Astronomer (1879–1907) at the Cape of Good Hope. Collected and arranged by G. Forbes. 1916.

SIR GEORGE HOWARD DARWIN (1845–1912)

The Tides and Kindred Phenomena. 1898.
Scientific Papers. 5 vols. Cambridge, 1907–16.

THOMAS GWYN ELGER

The Moon. 1895.

PERCIVAL LOWELL (b. 1855)

Mars. 1896.

ERNEST WILLIAM BROWN (b. 1866)

An Introductory Treatise on the Lunar Theory. Cambridge, 1896.

JOHN ELLARD GORE

The Visible Universe. 1893.

RICHARD ARMAN GREGORY

The Planet Earth. 1895.

ALFRED FOWLER (b. 1868)

Popular Telescopic Astronomy. 1896.

E. CHEMISTRY

(a) Bibliographies

Bolton, H. C. A Select Bibliography of Chemistry, 1492–1892. Washington, 1893. [Supplements, 1899–1904.]
Ferguson, J. Bibliotheca Chemica. 2 vols. 1906.

(b) General Works

Thomson, Thomas. History of Chemistry. 2 vols. 1830–1.
Brougham, H. P. (Baron Brougham and Vaux). Historical Account of the Discovery of the Composition of Water. Edinburgh New Philosophical Journ. XXVII, 1839.
Davy, Sir H. Historical View of the Progress of Chemistry. [In Works, vol. IV, 1839.]
Brande, W. T. Historical Sketch of the Origin and Progress of Chemical Philosophy. 1840.
Thorpe, Sir T. E. Essays in Historical Chemistry. 1894.
Tilden, Sir W. A. A Short History of the Progress of Scientific Chemistry in our Own Times. 1899.
Bolton, H. C. Chemical Societies of the XIXth Century. Washington, 1902.

Clarke, F. W. The Progress and Development of Chemistry during the XIXth Century. St Louis, 1904. [Rptd from Washington University Bulletin, Oct. 1904.]

JOSEPH BLACK (1728–1799)

Experiments upon Magnesia Alba, Quicklime, and some Other Alcaline Substances. Edinburgh, 1755; rptd as no. 1 of Alembic Club Reprints, Edinburgh, 1893.
Lectures on the Elements of Chemistry. Edinburgh, 1803.
[For life see T. Thomson, Biographical Account of Joseph Black, Annals of Philosophy, IV, 1814; Sir W. Ramsay, Life and Letters of Joseph Black, 1918.]

HENRY CAVENDISH (1731–1810)

Experiments on Air. Philosophical Trans. LXXIV, LXXV, 1784–5; rptd as no. 3 of Alembic Club Reprints, Edinburgh, 1893.
The Electrical Researches of the Hon. Henry Cavendish written between 1771 and 1781. Ed. J. C. Maxwell, Cambridge, 1879.
[For biography see G. Wilson, The Life of the Hon. Henry Cavendish, including Abstracts of his more Important Scientific Papers, and a Critical Enquiry into the Claims of all the Alleged Discoverers of the Composition of Water, Cavendish Soc. 1851.]

JOSEPH PRIESTLEY (1733–1804)

Experiments and Observations on Different Kinds of Air. 3 vols. 1774–9.
Experiments and Observations relating to Various Branches of Natural Philosophy. 3 vols. 1779–86.
[Priestley's discovery of oxygen is described in Alembic Club Reprints, no. 7, Edinburgh, 1893; for biography see Memoirs of Joseph Priestley to the Year 1795, written by himself, with a Continuation to the Time of his Decease by his Son Joseph Priestley, 2 vols. 1803; Sir T. E. Thorpe, Joseph Priestley: his Life and Chemical Work, Manchester, 1874; Scientific Correspondence of Joseph Priestley, ed. H. C. Bolton, New York, 1892.]

JAMES WATT (1736–1819)

Thoughts on the Constituent Parts of Water and of Dephlogisticated Air. Philosophical Trans. LXXIV, 1784.
[See J. P. Muirhead, Correspondence of James Watt on his Discovery of the Theory of the Composition of Water, 1846, and Life of James Watt, 1858.]

WILLIAM HIGGINS (d. 1825)

On the Origin of the Atomic Theory. Philosophical Mag. XLVIII, 1816.

WILLIAM NICHOLSON (1753–1815) and
SIR ANTHONY CARLISLE

An Account of the New Electrical or Galvanic
Apparatus of Volta and Experiments per-
formed with the Same. Nicholson's Journ.
IV, 1801.

JOHN DALTON (1766–1844)

Meteorological Observations and Essays.
Manchester, 1793.
On the Absorption of Gases by Water and
Other Liquids. Memoirs of Manchester
Philosophical Soc. I, 1805. [Read 1803;
contains results of researches leading to the
foundation of the atomic theory.]
A New System of Chemical Philosophy. 2 pts,
Manchester, 1808–10. [Extracts from the
New System on the atomic theory rptd in
Alembic Club Reprints, nos. 2 and 4, Edin-
burgh, 1893.]

[For biography and criticism see W. C.
Henry, Memoirs of the Life and Scientific
Researches of John Dalton, 1854; R. A.
Smith, Memoir of John Dalton and History
of the Atomic Theory up to his Time, 1856;
A. Harden and H. E. Roscoe, A New View of
the Origin of Dalton's Atomic Theory, 1896;
A. N. Meldrum, Avogadro and Dalton: the
Standing in Chemistry of their Hypotheses,
Edinburgh, 1904; J. Neville-Polley, John
Dalton, 1920.]

WILLIAM HYDE WOLLASTON (1766–1828)

On a New Metal found in Crude Platina
[Palladium]. Philosophical Trans. XCIV,
1804, pp. 419–30.
On Certain Chemical Effects of Light.
Nicholson's Journ. VIII, 1804.
On Super Acid and Sub-acid Salts. Philo-
sophical Trans. XCV, 1805, pp. 316–30; rptd
in no. 2 of Alembic Club Reprints, Edin-
burgh, 1899.
A Synoptic Scale of Chemical Equivalents.
Philosophical Trans. CIV, 1814, p. 1.

JANE MARCET (1769–1858)

Conversations on Chemistry. 2 vols. 1806.

THOMAS THOMSON (1773–1852)

A System of Chemistry. 4 vols. Edinburgh,
1802.
On Oxalic Acid. Philosophical Trans. XCVIII,
1808, p. 63; rptd as no. 2 of Alembic Club
Reprints, Edinburgh, 1893.
An Attempt to establish the Principles of
Chemistry by Experiment. 1825.
The History of Chemistry. 2 vols. 1830–1.

WILLIAM HENRY (1774–1836)

The Elements of Experimental Chemistry.
2 vols. 1799.

Experiments for Decomposing Muriatic
Acid. Philosophical Trans. XCIX, 1809, p.
188.
On the Quantities of Gases absorbed by Water
at Different Temperatures and under Different Pressures. Philosophical Trans. CXX,
1830.

SIR HUMPHRY DAVY (1778–1829)

Researches, Chemical and Philosophical,
chiefly concerning Nitrous Oxide. 1800.
[The first treatise on the effects of laughing
gas.]
Outlines of a Course of Lectures on Chemical
Philosophy. 1804.
Elements of Chemical Philosophy. 1812.
Elements of Agricultural Chemistry. 1813.
Experimental Researches in Electricity. Glas-
gow, 1842.
The Bakerian Lecture. On some Chemical
Agencies of Electricity. Philosophical
Trans. XCVII, 1807, p. 1.
On some New Phenomena of Chemical Changes
produced by Electricity. Philosophical
Trans. XCVIII, 1808, p. 1.
Electro-chemical Researches on the Decom-
position of the Earth. Philosophical Trans.
XCVIII, 1808, p. 333.
Researches on the Oxymuriatic Acid. Philo-
sophical Trans. C, 1810, p. 231.
On the Safety Lamp for Coal Miners, with
Some Researches on Flame. 1818.
Collected Works. Ed. J. Davy, 9 vols. 1839–
41.

[Davy's memoirs, The Decomposition of the
Fixed Alkalies and Alkaline Earths, and The
Elementary Nature of Chlorine were rptd in
the Alembic Club Reprints, nos. 6 and 9,
Edinburgh, 1894; for biography and criticism
see J. A. Paris, The Life of Sir Humphry
Davy, 1831; J. Davy, Memoirs of the Life of
Sir Humphry Davy, 2 vols. 1836; Fragmentary
Remains, Literary and Scientific, of Sir
Humphry Davy, with a Sketch of his Life
and Selections from his Correspondence, ed.
J. Davy, 1858 (with bibliography); Sir T. E.
Thorpe, Humphry Davy, Poet and Philoso-
pher, 1896; P. A. Guye, Humphry Davy,
Geneva, 1907.]

WILLIAM PROUT (1786–1850)

On the Relations between the Specific
Gravities of Bodies in their Gaseous State
and the Weights of their Atoms. Thomson's
Annals of Philosophy, VI, VII, 1815–6
(anon.).
Chemistry, Meteorology and the Function of
Digestion, considered with Reference to
Natural Theology. 1833.

WILLIAM THOMAS BRANDE (1788–1866)

A Manual of Chemistry. 1813.
Historical Sketch of the Origin and Progress of Chemical Philosophy. 1840.

JOHN FREDERICK DANIELL (1790–1845)

An Introduction to the Study of Chemical Philosophy. Being a Preparatory View of the Forces which concur to the Production of Chemical Phenomena. 1839.
On the Constant Voltaic Battery. Philosophical Mag. xx, xxi, 1842.

MICHAEL FARADAY (1791–1867)

Experiments on the Alloys of Steel. Quarterly Journ. of Science, ix, 1820; Philosophical Trans. cxii, 1822, p. 253.
On Fluid Chlorine. Philosophical Trans. cxiii, 1823, p. 160.
On New Compounds of Carbon and Hydrogen and on Certain Other Products obtained during the Decomposition of Oil by Heat. Philosophical Trans. cxv, 1825, p. 440.
Chemical Manipulation. 1827.
Experimental Researches in Electricity. 3 vols. 1839–55. [Rptd from Philosophical Trans. cxxi–cxlv, 1831–55.]
On the Liquefaction and Solidification of Bodies generally existing as Gases. 1845.
Experimental Researches in Chemistry and Physics. 1859. [Rptd from Philosophical Trans. cxi–cxlvii, 1821–57.]
The Chemical History of a Candle. 1861.
On the Liquefaction of Gases. With an Appendix of Papers by J. Northmore on the Compression of Gases. Alembic Club Reprints, no. 12, Edinburgh, 1896.
The Letters of Faraday and Schönbein. 1836–1862. Ed. G. W. A. Kahlbaum and F. V. Darbishire, 1899.

[For biography and criticism see J. Tyndall, Faraday as a Discoverer, 1868; H. B. Jones, The Life and Letters of Faraday, 1870; J. H. Gladstone, Michael Faraday, 1872; S. P. Thompson, Michael Faraday; his Life and Work, New York, 1898.]

CHARLES DAUBENY (1795–1867)

An Introduction to the Atomic Theory. Oxford, 1831.

EDWARD TURNER (1796–1837)

Introduction to the Study and Laws of Chemical Combination. 1825.
Elements of Chemistry. Edinburgh, 1827.
Researches on Atomic Weights. Philosophical Mag. i, 1832; Philosophical Trans. cxxiii, 1833, p. 523.

HENRY HENNELL (d. 1842)

On the Mutual Action of Sulphuric Acid and Alcohol. Philosophical Trans. cxvi, 1826, p. 240, cxviii, 1828, p. 365.

WILLIAM GREGORY (1803–1858)

Outlines of Chemistry. 2 pts, 1845.

THOMAS GRAHAM (1805–1869)

On the Law of Diffusion of Gases. Philosophical Mag. ii, 1833.
Researches on the Arsenates, Phosphates, and Modifications of Phosphoric Acid. Philosophical Trans. cxxiii, 1833, p. 253; rptd in Alembic Club Reprints, no. 10, Edinburgh, 1893.
Elements of Chemistry. 1842.
Chemical Reports and Memoirs. 1848. [Ed. by Graham.]
Liquid Diffusion applied to Analysis. Philosophical Trans. cli, 1861, p. 183.
Chemical and Physical Researches. Edinburgh, 1876. [Collected works.]

[For life see R. A. Smith, The Life and Works of Thomas Graham, Glasgow, 1884.]

THOMAS ANDREWS (1813–1885)

On the Continuity of the Gaseous and Liquid States of Matter. The Bakerian Lecture. Philosophical Trans. ii, 1869.
Scientific Papers; with a Memoir by P. G. Tait and A. C. Brown. 1889.

GEORGE FOWNES (1815–1849)

A Manual of Chemistry. 1845; 1877 (12th edn, rev. H. Watts).

SAMUEL BROWN (1817–1856)

Lectures on the Atomic Theory and Essays Scientific and Literary. 2 vols. Edinburgh, 1858.

SIR BENJAMIN BRODIE (1817–1880)

The Calculus of Chemical Operations. 2 vols. 1866–76.

WILLIAM ALLEN MILLER (1817–1870)

Elements of Chemistry, Theoretical and Practical. 3 pts, 1855–7.

CHARLES BLACKFORD MANSFIELD (1819–1855)

Researches on Coal Tar. Journ. of Chemical Soc. i, 1849.
Theory of Salts. 1865.

LYON PLAYFAIR (1819–1898)

A Century of Chemistry in the University of Edinburgh. 1858.
[See Memoirs and Correspondence of Lyon Playfair, ed. Sir T. W. Reid, Edinburgh, 1899.]

ALEXANDER WILLIAMS WILLIAMSON (1824–1904)

Theory of Etherification. Philosophical Mag. III, 1850; Journ. of Chemical Soc. IV, 1852.

On the Constitution of Salts. Philosophical Mag. III, 1850.

Papers on Etherification and on the Constitution of Salts, 1850–56. Alembic Club Reprints, no. 16, Edinburgh, 1902.

[See G. C. Foster, Obituary, Journ. of Chemical Soc. LXXXVII, 1905.]

GEORGE GORE (1826–1908)

The Art of Scientific Discovery, or the General Conditions and Methods of Research in Physics and Chemistry. 1878.

JOHN HALL GLADSTONE (1827–1902) and HENRY DALE

Researches on the Refraction, Dispersion and Sensitiveness of Liquids. Philosophical Trans. CLIII, 1863, p. 317.

WILLIAM ODLING (1829–1921)

On the Constitution of Acids and Salts. Journ. of Chemical Soc. VII, 1854.

On the Natural Grouping of the Elements. Philosophical Mag. XIII, 1857.

The Proportional Numbers of the Elements. Quarterly Journ. of Science, I, 1864.

EDWARD FRANKLAND (1829–1899)

Researches on Organo-metallic Bodies. 4 pts, 1852–9.

Lecture Notes for Chemical Students. 1866. [This work is noted historically for the development of so-called graphic formulae.]

Experimental Researches in Pure, Applied, and Physical Chemistry. 1877.

[See Sketches from the Life of Edward Frankland, 1902 (priv. ptd) and H. Macleod, Obituary, Journ. of Chemical Soc. LXXXVII, 1905.]

ARCHIBALD SCOTT COUPER (1831–1892)

On a New Chemical Theory. Philosophical Mag. XVI, 1858.

[See R. Anschutz, The Life and Chemical Work of A. S. Couper, Proc. Royal Soc. Edinburgh, XXIX, 1909.]

SIR WILLIAM CROOKES (1832–1919)

On Thallium. Chemical News, III, 1861.

On the Nature and Origin of the So-Called Elements. British Ass. Report (Presidential Address), 1886. [See also Chemical News, LV, 1887.]

The Genesis of the Elements. Proc. Royal Inst. XII, 1889. [See also Elements and Meta-elements, Journ. of Chemical Soc. LIII, 1888.]

The Wheat Problem. 1898.

[See Fournier D'Albe, Life of Sir William Crookes, 1923.]

SIR HENRY ENFIELD ROSCOE (1833–1915)

Photochemical Researches. Philosophical Trans. CXLVIII, CXLIX, CLIII, 1857–63.

Researches on Vanadium. Philosophical Trans. CLVIII–CLX, 1868–70.

Spectrum Analysis. 1869.

Dalton and the Rise of Modern Chemistry. 1875.

A Treatise on Chemistry. 9 vols. 1879–92. [With C. Schorlemmer.]

[See also under J. Dalton, p. 946 above, A New View of Dalton's Atomic Theory, 1896.]

SIR JOSEPH NORMAN LOCKYER (1836–1920)

Studies in Spectrum Analysis. 1872.

The Chemistry of the Sun. 1887.

Inorganic Evolution as studied by Spectrum Analysis. 1900.

Essays and Addresses, 1870–1905. 1906.

[For other works see under Physics, p. 940 above and Astronomy, p. 944 above; for life see A. L. Cortie, Sir Norman Lockyer, 1921; T. M. and W. L. Lockyer, The Life and Work of Sir Norman Lockyer, 1928.]

JOHN ALEXANDER NEWLANDS (1837–1898)

Relation between the Equivalents of the Metals. Chemical News, X, 1864, XII, 1865, XIII, 1866.

On the Law of Octaves and the Causes of Numerical Relations among the Atomic Weights. Journ. of Chemical Soc. XIX, 1866.

On the Discovery of the Periodic Law. 1884.

ALEXANDER CRUM BROWN (b. 1838)

On the Theory of Isomeric Compounds. Journ. of Chemical Soc. XVIII, 1865.

The Development of the Idea of Chemical Composition. Edinburgh, 1869.

SIR WILLIAM HENRY PERKIN (1838–1907)

Origin of the Coal Tar Colour Industry. Trans. of Chemical Soc. LXIX, 1886.

On the Aniline or Coal Tar Colours. 1869. [Canton Lecture.]

On the Rotatory Polarization by Chemical Substances under Magnetic Influence. Journ. of Chemical Soc. XXXV–XLI, 1882–8.

[See R. Meldola, H. G. Green and J. C. Cain, Jubilee of the Discovery of Mauve and of the Foundation of the Coal Tar Colour Industry by Sir William Perkin, 1906; for life see R. Meldola, Obituary, Journ. of Chemical Soc. XCIII, 1908.]

EMERSON REYNOLDS (1843–1920)

Note on a Method of Illustrating the Periodic Law. Chemical News, LIV, 1886.

SIR THOMAS EDWARD THORPE (b. 1848)

Lecture on Robert Boyle. 1877.
Essays in Historical Chemistry. 1894; rptd 1911.
History of Chemistry. 2 vols. 1909–10.

[See also under J. Priestley, p. 945 above.]

MONCRIEFF PATTISON MUIR (b. 1848)

The Story of Alchemy and the Beginnings of Chemistry. 1899.

SIR WILLIAM RAMSAY (1852–1916)

Helium, a Constituent of Certain Minerals. Trans. Chemical Soc. LXVII, 1895.
Argon, a New Constituent of the Atmosphere. Proc. Royal Soc. LVII, 1895. [With Lord Rayleigh.]
On a New Constituent of Atmospheric Air. Proc. Royal Soc. LXIII, 1898. [With M. W. Travers.]
On the Companions of Argon. Proc. Royal Soc. LXIII, 1898.
Essays, Biographical and Chemical. 1908.

[For life see Sir W. A. Tilden, Sir William Ramsay, 1918.]

F. GEOLOGY

General Works

Ramsay, Sir A. C. Passages in the History of Geology. 1849.
Huxley, T. H. The Rise and Progress of Palæontology. Popular Science Monthly, XX, 1882.
Rudler, F. W. Fifty Years' Progress in British Geology. Proc. Geological Soc. x, 1888.
Geikie, Sir A. Founders of Geology. 1897; 1905.
Marsh, O. C. History and Methods of Palæontological Discovery. 1897.
Merrill, G. P. The History of American Geology. New Haven, 1906.
—— The First Hundred Years of American Geology. New Haven, 1924.
Woodward, H. B. History of the Geological Society of London. 1907.
—— History of Geology. 1911.

JAMES HUTTON (1726–1797)

The Theory of the Earth, from the Transactions of the Royal Society of Edinburgh. Edinburgh, 1785; 2 vols. Edinburgh, 1795; vol. III ed. Sir A. Geikie, 1899 (portion of vol. III now first ptd from the MS in the possession of the Geological Soc., with indexes to this portion and to vols. I, II).

Dissertations upon the Philosophy of Light, Heat, and Fire. 7 pts, Edinburgh, 1794.
An Investigation of the Principle of Knowledge and of the Progress of Reason from Sense to Science and Philosophy. 3 vols. Edinburgh, 1794.
Conversations on Geology. Comprising a Familiar Explanation of the Huttonian and Wernerian Systems. 1840.

[For biography and criticism see J. Playfair, Biographical Account of James Hutton, Edinburgh, [1797?], and Illustrations of the Huttonian Theory of the Earth, Edinburgh, 1802.]

JOSEPH TOWNSEND (1739–1816)

The Character of Moses established for Veracity as an Historian: recording Events from the Creation to the Deluge. Bath, 1813–5.

JOHN PLAYFAIR (1748–1819)

Outlines of Natural Philosophy. 2 vols. 1812–4.
The Works of John Playfair; with a Memoir of the Author [by F. Jeffrey, ed. J. G. Playfair]. 4 vols. Edinburgh, 1822.

[See also under James Hutton above.]

JAMES SOWERBY (1757–1822)

British Mineralogy. 5 vols. 1804–17.
The Mineral Conchology of Great Britain. 6 vols. 1812–46. [Continued by J. De C. Sowerby, 1787–1871.]

JOHN FAREY (1766–1826)

General View of the Agriculture and Minerals of Derbyshire. 2 vols. 1811–3.

ROBERT BAKEWELL (1768–1843)

An Introduction to Geology. Comprising the Elements of the Science and an Outline of the Geology and Mineral Geography of England. 1813.
Introduction to Mineralogy. 1819.

JAMES PARKINSON (d. 1824)

Organic Remains of a Former World. An Examination of the Mineralized Remains of the Vegetables and Animals of the Antediluvian World; generally called Extraneous Fossils. 3 vols. 1804–11.
Outlines of Oryctology. An Introduction to the Study of Fossil Organic Remains; especially those found in British Strata. 1822.

THOMAS WEBSTER (1772–1844)

A Description of the Isle of Wight. With Additional Observations on the Strata of the Island 1816.

JOHN MACCULLOCH (1773–1835)

Description of the Western Islands of Scotland. 2 vols. 1819.

A Geological Classification of Rocks, with Descriptive Synopsis of the Specific Varieties; comprising the Elements of Practical Geology. 1821.

A System of Geology; with a Theory of the Earth. 12 vols. 1831.

WILLIAM PHILLIPS (1773–1828)

An Outline of Mineralogy and Geology. 1815.

An Elementary Introduction to the Knowledge on Mineralogy. 1816.

A Selection of Facts from the Best Authorities, arranged so as to form an Outline of the Geology of England and Wales. 1818.

ROBERT JAMESON (1774–1854)

Outlines of the Mineralogy of the Scottish Isles. 2 vols. Edinburgh, 1800.

System of Mineralogy. 3 vols. Edinburgh, 1804–8.

Treatise on the External Characters of Minerals. Edinburgh, 1805.

JOHN KIDD (1775–1851)

The Outlines of Mineralogy. 2 vols. Oxford, 1809.

A Geological Essay on the Imperfect Evidence in Support of a Theory of the Earth. Oxford, 1815.

On the Adaptation of External Nature to the Physical Conditions of Man. Oxford, 1833.

ETHELDRED BENETT (1776–1845)

A Catalogue of the Organic Remains of the County of Wilts. Warminster, 1831.

GEORGE BELLAS GREENOUGH (1778–1855)

A Critical Examination of the First Principles of Geology in a Series of Essays. 1819.

HENRY THOMAS WITHAM (1779–1844)

Observations on Fossil Vegetables, accompanied by Representations of their Internal Structure as seen through the Microscope. Edinburgh, 1831.

The Internal Structure of Fossil Vegetables found in the Carboniferous and Oolitic Deposits of Great Britain. Edinburgh, 1833.

WILLIAM HENRY FITTON (1780–1861)

Geological Sketch of the Vicinity of Hastings. 1833.

Notes on the Progress of Geology in England. 1833.

Observations on Some of the Strata between the Chalk and the Oxford Oolite, in the South East of England. 1836.

CHARLES MACLAREN (1782–1866)

The Internal Structure of Fossil Vegetables found in the Carboniferous and Oolitic Deposits of Great Britain. Edinburgh, 1833.

Sketch of the Geology of Fife and the Lothians, including a Detailed Description of Arthur's Seat and the Pentland Hills. Edinburgh, 1839.

Select Writings. Ed. R. Cox and J. Nicol, 2 vols. Edinburgh, 1869.

WILLIAM BUCKLAND (1784–1856)

Vindiciae Geologicae, or the Connexion of Geology with Religion explained. Oxford, 1820.

Reliquiae Diluvianae, or Observations on the Organic Remains contained in Caves, Fissures and Diluvial Gravel, and on other Geological Phenomena attesting the Action of a Universal Deluge. 1823.

Geology and Mineralogy considered with Reference to Natural Theology. 2 vols. 1836. (Bridgewater Treatise.)

[See Mrs Gordon, Life of William Buckland, 1894.]

ADAM SEDGWICK (1785–1873)

The Geology of the Lake District. 1843.

A Synopsis of the Classification of the British Palaeozoic Rocks. With a Systematic Description of the British Palaeozoic Fossils in the Geological Museum of the University of Cambridge by F. McCoy. Cambridge, 1854.

[See J. W. Clark and M'K. Hughes, Life and Letters of the Rev. Adam Sedgwick, 2 vols. Cambridge, 1890.]

PETER JOHN MARTIN (1786–1860)

A Geological Memoir of Western Sussex. 1828.

WILLIAM DANIELL CONYBEARE (1787–1857)

Report on the Progress of Geological Science. British Ass. Report, 1822.

Outlines of the Geology of England and Wales. With an Introductory Compendium of the Principles of that Science and the Comparative Views of the Structure of Foreign Countries. 1822. [With W. Phillips.]

WILLIAM SMITH (1769–1839)

Tabular View of the Superposition of English Strata. 1791.

Observations on the Strata of England and Wales. 1804.

Strata identified by Organised Fossils. 1815.

Stratigraphical System of Organised Fossils. 1817.

Geological Section from London to Snowden, showing the Varieties of Strata and the Correct Altitude of the Hills. 6 pts, 1817–9.

Delineation of the Strata of England and Wales. 1818.

[For biography and criticism see J. Phillips, Memoirs of William Smith, 1844; T. Sheppard, William Smith, his Maps and Memoirs, 1920.]

GIDEON ALGERNON MANTELL (1790–1852)

The Fossils of the South Downs, or Illustrations of the Geology of Sussex. 1822.

Illustrations of the Geology of Sussex; with Figures and Descriptions of the Fossils of Tilgate Forest. 1827.

The Geology of the South East of England. 1833.

The Medals of Creation, or First Lessons in Geology and in the Study of Organic Remains. 2 vols. 1844. [See S. Spokes, Gideon Algernon Mantell, Surgeon and Geologist, 1927.]

SIR RODERICK IMPEY MURCHISON (1792–1871)

Outline of the Geology in the Neighbourhood of Cheltenham. Cheltenham, 1834.

The Silurian System, founded on Geological Researches in the Counties of Salod, Hereford, Radnor, Montgomery, Caermarthen, Brecon, Pembroke, Monmouth, Gloucester, Worcester and Stafford. 1839.

On the Geological Structure of the Alps, Apennines and Carpathians. 1849.

Siluria. The History of the Oldest known Rocks containing Organic Remains. With a Brief Sketch of the Distribution of Gold over the Earth. 1854.

[See S. S. Buckman, Bibliographical Notes on Murchison's Geology of Cheltenham, Cheltenham, 1906; The Life of Sir R. I. Murchison with Notices of his Scientific Contemporaries and a Sketch of the Rise and Growth of Palaeozoic Geology in Britain, 2 vols. 1875.]

WILLIAM HOPKINS (1793–1866)

An Abstract of a Memoir on Physical Geology. Cambridge, 1836 (priv. ptd).

CHARLES DAUBENY (1795–1867)

A Description of Active and Extinct Volcanoes. 1826.

SIR HENRY THOMAS DE LA BECHE (1796–1855)

A Geological Manual. 1831.

Researches in Theoretical Geology. 1834.

How to observe Geology. 1835; 1851 (as The Geological Observer).

A Selection of Geological Memoirs. 1836.

Geological Survey of the United Kingdom. 1846–.

SIR CHARLES LYELL (1797–1875)

The Principles of Geology. Being an Attempt to Explain the Former Changes of the Earth's Surface by Reference to Causes now in Operation. 3 vols. 1830–3; 1875 (12th edn).

Elements of Geology. 1838.

Lectures on Geology. New York, 1842.

Travels in North America with Geological Observations, etc. 2 vols. 1845.

A Second Visit to the United States. 1849.

The Geological Evidences of the Antiquity of Man, with Remarks on Theories of the Origin of Species by Variation. 1863.

Address to the British Association, 1864. British Ass. Report, 1864.

The Student's Elements of Geology. 1871.

[See The Life, Letters and Journals of Sir Charles Lyell, ed. by his Sister-in-Law, Mrs Lyell, 2 vols. 1881; T. G. Bonney, Charles Lyell and Modern Geology, 1895.]

GEORGE POULETT SCROPE (1797–1876)

Considerations on Volcanoes leading to a New Theory of the Earth. 1825.

Memoir of the Geology of Central France: including the Volcanic Formation of Auvergne, the Velay, and the Vivarais. 1827.

The Geology and Extinct Volcanoes of Central France. 1858.

On the Mode of Formation of Volcanic Cones and Craters. Quarterly Journ. of Geological Soc. Nov. 1859.

JOHN LINDLEY (1799–1865)

The Fossil Flora of Great Britain, or Figures and Descriptions of the Vegetable Remains found in a Fossil State in this Country. 3 vols. 1831–7. [With W. Hutton.]

Illustrations of Fossil Plants. 1877.

JOHN PHILLIPS (1800–1874)

Illustrations of the Geology of Yorkshire. 2 vols. York, 1829–36.

Guide to Geology. 1834.

Palaeozoic Fossils of Devon, Cornwall and West Somerset. 1841.

Life on Earth: its Origin and Succession. Cambridge, 1860.

The Geology of Oxford and the Valley of the Thames. 1871.

[Also a large number of papers (see DNB.).]

HUGH MILLER (1802–1856)

The Old Red Sandstone, or a New Walk in an Old Field. Edinburgh, 1841.

The Geology of the Bass. 1848.
The Testimony of the Rocks. Boston, 1857.

[For biography, etc. see p. 721 above.]

SIR RICHARD OWEN (1804–1892)

History of British Fossil Mammals and Birds. 1846.
History of British Fossil Reptiles. 4 vols. 1849–94.
Palaeontology, or a Systematic Summary of Extinct Animals and their Geological Relations. Edinburgh, 1860.
Researches on the Fossil Remains of the Extinct Mammals of Australia. 2 vols. 1877.

[See T. H. Huxley, The Life of Richard Owen, 1894; see also under Zoology, p. 956 below, and Anthropology, p. 967 below.]

CHARLES ROBERT DARWIN (1809–1882)

Journal of Researches into the Geology and Natural History of the Various Countries visited by H.M.S. Beagle. 1839; 1889 (4th edn); 1890.
The Structure and Distribution of Coral Reefs. Being the First Part of the Geology of the Voyage of the Beagle, 1832 to 1836. 1842; 1874; 1889.
Geological Observations on the Volcanic Islands visited during the Voyage of H.M.S. Beagle. Being the Second Part of the Geology of the Voyage of the Beagle. 1844.
Geological Observations in South America. Being the Third Part of the Geology of the Voyage of the Beagle. 1846.

[See Sir A. Geikie, Charles Darwin as Geologist, Rede Lecture at the Darwin Centennial Commemoration, 1909; for other works by Darwin see under Anthropology, p. 967 below; Botany, p. 960 below; Evolution, p. 953 below, and Zoology, p. 956 below.]

ROBERT MALLET (1810–1881)

On the Dynamics of Earthquakes. Trans. Royal Irish Academy, XXI, 1846.
The Great Neapolitan Earthquake of 1857, The First Principles of Observational Seismology, etc. 1862.

JAMES NICOL (1810–1879)

A Catechism of Geology, or Natural History of the Earth. Edinburgh, 1842.
A Guide to the Geology of Scotland. Edinburgh, 1844.
Introductory Book of the Sciences. Edinburgh, 1844.

HUGH EDWIN STRICKLAND (1811–1853)

Outline of the Geology in the Neighbourhood of Cheltenham. 1845. [With Sir R. I. Murchison and J. Buckman.]

Memoirs, with Selections from Scientific Correspondence, by Sir W. Jardine. 1858.

EDWARD WILLIAM BINNEY (1812–1881)

Observations on the Structure of Fossil Plants found in the Carboniferous Strata. Palaeontographical Soc. 1868–75.

SIR JOSEPH PRESTWICH (1812–1896)

Geology, Chemical, Physical and Stratigraphical. 2 vols. Oxford, 1886–8.
Collected Papers on some Controverted Questions of Geology. 1895.

[See Lady Prestwich, Life and Letters of Sir Joseph Prestwich, 1899.]

SIR ANDREW CROMBIE RAMSAY (1814–1891)

Passages in the History of Geology. 1849.
The Old Glaciers of Switzerland and North Wales. 1860.
Text Book of the Physical Geology and Geography of Great Britain. 1863.
The Bed Rocks of England. 1871.

[See Sir A. Geikie, Memoir of Sir Andrew Crombie Ramsay, 1895.]

EDWARD FORBES (1815–1854)

Literary Papers. Selected from his Writings in the Literary Gazette. Ed. (with memoir) L. Reeve, 1855.

ROBERT ETHERIDGE (1819–1903)

Stratigraphical Geology and Palaeontology. 1887.
British Fossils. 1888.

SIR JOHN WILLIAM DAWSON (1820–1899)

The Story of the Earth and Man. 1873.
Life's Dawn on Earth. Being the History of the Oldest Known Fossil Remains. 1875.
The Chain of Life in Geological Time. 1880.

JAMES CROLL (1821–1890)

Climate and Time. 1885.

SIR FREDERICK McCOY (1823–1899)

Contributions to British Palaeontology, from the Tertiary, Cretaceous, Oolitic and Palaeozoic Strata of Great Britain. Cambridge, 1854.

SIR WILLIAM THOMSON (BARON KELVIN) (1824–1907)

On the Secular Cooling of the Earth. Philosophical Mag. XXV, 1863.

HENRY CLIFTON SORBY (1826–1898)

On the Microscopical Structure of Crystals, indicating the Origin of Minerals and Rocks. Quarterly Journ. of Geological Soc. XIV, 1858.

THOMAS GEORGE BONNEY (b. 1835)

The Story of our Planet. 1893.
Ice Work, Past and Present. 1896.
Volcanoes: their Structure and Significance. 1899.
The Structure of the Earth. 1912; 1919 (rev.).
Memories of a Long Life. Cambridge, 1921.

SIR ARCHIBALD GEIKIE (1835–1924)

The Scenery of Scotland, viewed in Connexion with its Physical Geology. 1865.
The Ice Age in Britain. 1873.
Life of Sir R. I. Murchison. 1875.
Outlines of Field Geology. 1876; 1900 (5th edn).
Class Book of Geology. London, 1886; 1902 (4th edn).
Memoir of Sir Andrew Crombie Ramsay. 1895.
The Ancient Volcanoes of Great Britain. 2 vols. 1897.
The State of Geology at the Time of the Foundation of the Geological Society. [In The Centenary of the Geological Society of London, 1905.]
A Long Life's Work. An Autobiography. London, 1924.

HARRY GOVIER SEELEY (1839–1909)

Story of the Earth in Past Ages. 1895.

WILLIAM TOPLEY (1841–1894)

The Geology of the Weald. 1875.
The National Geological Surveys of Europe. British Ass. Report, 1885.
[See W. B. Woodward, Memoir of W. Topley, 1894.]

FREDERICK WILLIAM RUDLER

Experimental Geology. Proc. Geological Soc. XI, 1889.

HENRY ALLEYNE NICHOLSON (1844–1899)
and RICHARD LYDEKKER (1849–1915)

Palaeontology. 1889.

HORACE BOLINGBROKE WOODWARD (b. 1848)

The Geology of England and Wales. 1876.
History of the Geological Society of London. 1907.
History of Geology. 1911.

SIR JETHRO JUSTINIAN TEALL (b. 1849)

British Petrography; with Special Reference to the Igneous Rocks. 1888.

G. EVOLUTION
General Works

Osborn, H. F. From the Greeks to Darwin. An Outline of the Development of the Evolution Idea. 1894.

Clodd, E. Pioneers in Evolution, from Thales to Huxley. With an Intermediate Chapter on the Causes of Arrest of the Movement. 1897.

ERASMUS DARWIN (1731–1802)

Zoonomia, or the Laws of Organic Life. 2 vols. 1794–6.
The Temple of Nature, or the Origin of Society. 1803.
Poetical Works. 3 vols. 1807.
[See also vol. II, pp. 358–9 above.]

WILLIAM CHARLES WELLS (1757–1817)

Two Essays. A Letter to Lord Kenyon; and an Account of a Female of the White Race of Mankind, Part of whose Skin resembles that of a Negro; with some Observations on the Causes of the Differences in Colour and Form between the White and Negro Races of Man. With a Memoir of his Life, etc. 1818. [Certain passages of this work anticipate Darwin's theory of natural selection; for life see Memoir of William Charles Wells, with an Account of his Writings, 1818.]

THOMAS ROBERT MALTHUS (1766–1834)

An Essay on the Principle of Population. 1798.
[For criticism, etc. see p. 870 above.]

ROBERT EDMOND GRANT (1793–1874)

Observations and Experiments on the Structure and Functions of the Sponge. Edinburgh Philosophical Journ. XIII, XIV, 1825–6.

PATRICK MATTHEW

Naval Timber and Arboriculture. 1831.

ROBERT CHAMBERS (1802–1871)

Vestiges of the Natural History of Creation. 1844.
[For criticism, etc. see p. 709 above.]

CHARLES ROBERT DARWIN (1809–1882)

On the Origin of Species by means of Natural Selection, or the Preservation of Favoured Races in the Struggle for Life. 1859; 1861 (3rd edn); 1866; 1869; 1872, etc.
The Foundations of the Origin of Species. Two Essays written in 1842 and 1844 by Charles Darwin. Ed. Sir F. Darwin, Cambridge, 1909.
The Descent of Man, and Selection in Relation to Sex. 2 vols. 1871; 1874; rptd 1930.

[For biography and criticism see Life and Letters of Charles Darwin, including an Autobiographical Chapter, ed. Sir F. Darwin, 3 vols. 1887; Charles Darwin: his Life told in an Autobiographical Chapter, and in Letters, ed. Sir F. Darwin, 1902; G. A. Adlerz, Charles Darwin, 1909; A. C. Seward, Darwin and

Modern Science; Essays; Commemoration of the Birth of Charles Darwin, 1909; The Complete Extant Correspondence between Wallace and Darwin, 1857–81, 1916; L. Huxley, Charles Darwin, 1921; Autobiography, ed. Sir F. Darwin, 1929; for further works see Botany, p. 960 below, Anthropology, p. 967 below, Geology, p. 952 above and Zoology, p. 956 below.]

HERBERT SPENCER (1820–1904)

Theory of Population. Westminster Rev. April 1852.

The Development Hypothesis. The Leader, 20 March 1852.

The Ultimate Laws of Physiology. National Rev. April 1857.

Essays, Scientific, Political and Speculative. Reprinted chiefly from the Quarterly Review. 1858–63.

Works. 19 vols. 1861–1902.

Principles of Biology. [A System of Synthetic Philosophy, vols. II–III, 1864–7; 1898–9 (rev.).]

The Factors of Organic Evolution. 1887.

The Inadequacy of Natural Selection. 1893.

Autobiography. 2 vols. 1904.

[For biography and criticism see H. Sewell, Herbert Spencer as a Biologist, 1886; Sir J. A. Thomson, Herbert Spencer, 1906; D. Duncan, Life and Letters of Herbert Spencer, 1908. See also p. 874 above.]

SIR FRANCIS GALTON (1822–1911)

Discontinuity in Evolution. Mind, III, 1894.

[For other works see under Philosophy, p. 867 above.]

GEORGE DOUGLAS CAMPBELL, DUKE OF ARGYLL (1823–1900)

Primeval Man. An Examination of some Recent Speculations. 1869.

Organic Evolution cross-examined. 1898.

BENJAMIN THOMPSON LOWNE

The Philosophy of Evolution. 1873.

ALFRED RUSSEL WALLACE (1823–1913)

On the Law which has Regulated the Introduction of New Species. Annals and Mag. of Natural History, xv, 1855, p. 184.

On the Tendency of Varieties to depart indefinitely from the Original Type. Proc. Linnean Soc. 1858.

Contributions to the Theory of Natural Selection. A Series of Essays. 1870.

The Action of Natural Selection on Man. 1872.

The Geographical Distribution of Animals, with a Study of Living and Extinct Faunas as elucidating the Past Changes of the Earth's Surface. 2 vols. 1876.

Darwinism. An Exposition of the Theory of Natural Selection, with some of its Applications. 1889.

The Wonderful Century. 1898.

Studies, Scientific and Social. 1900.

Man's Place in the Universe. 1903.

My Life. A Record of Events and Opinions. 2 vols. 1905.

[For life see E. D. Cope, Alfred Russel Wallace, New York, 1891; J. Marchant, Letters and Reminiscences of A. R. Wallace, 2 vols. 1916.]

THOMAS HENRY HUXLEY (1825–1895)

On the Educational Value of the Natural History Sciences. 1854.

On Races, Species and their Origin. 1860.

Evidence as to Man's Place in Nature. Edinburgh, 1863.

Lay Sermons, Addresses and Reviews. 1870.

Critiques and Addresses. 1873.

Science and Culture and Other Essays. 1881.

Evolution and Ethics. Romanes Lecture. 1893.

Collected Essays. 9 vols. 1894–1908.

The Scientific Memoirs of Thomas Henry Huxley. Ed. Sir M. Foster and Sir E. R. Lankester, 5 vols. 1898–1903.

[For life see Thomas Henry Huxley, a Sketch of his Life and Work, 1900; L. Huxley, Life and Letters of Thomas Henry Huxley, 1900; E. Clodd, Thomas Henry Huxley, 1902. See also p. 869 above.]

SAINT GEORGE MIVART (1827–1900)

On the Genesis of Species. 1871.

Man and Apes. An Exposition of Structural Resemblances bearing upon Questions of Affinity and Origin. 1873.

Contemporary Evolution. 1876.

Essays and Criticisms. 2 vols. 1892.

SAMUEL BUTLER (1835–1902)

Darwinism, or the Origin of Species. 1862.

Darwin among the Machines. 1863. [Extract from The Press, Christchurch, New Zealand.]

Life and Habit. 1878.

Evolution, Old and New, or the Theories of Buffon, Erasmus Darwin and Lamarck compared with that of Charles Darwin. 1879; rptd 1911.

Luck or Cunning as the Main Means of Organic Modification? An Attempt to throw Additional Light on Charles Darwin's Theory of Natural Selection. 1887.

Records and Memorials. 1903 (priv. ptd).

[See G. Cannan, Samuel Butler, a Critical Study, 1915; H. F. Jones, The Life of Samuel Butler, 1919; C. E. M. Joad, Samuel Butler, 1924; for full bibliography see p. 728 above.]

EDWARD CLODD (1840–1930)
The Story of Creation. 1886.
Pioneers of Evolution. 1898.

SIR EDWIN RAY LANKESTER (1847–1929)
Degeneration. A Chapter in Darwinism. 1880.
[For other works see under Zoology, p. 958 below.]

GEORGE JOHN ROMANES (1848–1894)
The Scientific Evidences of Organic Evolution. 1882.
Physiological Selection. Journ. Linnean Soc. XIX, 1886.
Darwin and After Darwin. An Exposition of the Darwinian Theory and a Discussion of Post-Darwinian Questions. 1892.
An Examination of Weismannism. 1893.
Essays. Ed. C. L. Morgan, 1897.
[See Life and Letters of G. J. Romanes, ed. Mrs E. Romanes, 1896; see also under Psychology, p. 966 below, and under Philosophy, p. 872 above.]

ARTHUR MILNES MARSHALL (1852–1893)
Lectures on the Darwinian Theory. Ed. C. F. Marshall, 1894.

CONWY LLOYD MORGAN (b. 1852)
The Springs of Conduct. An Essay in Evolution. 1885.

J. T. GULICH
Evolution through Cumulative Segregation. Journ. of Linnean Soc. XX, 1888.

EDWARD BAGNALL POULTON (b. 1856)
The Colours of Animals, their Meaning and Use, especially considered in the Case of Insects. 1872.
Charles Darwin and the Theory of Natural Selection. 1896.
Essays on Evolution, 1889–1907. Oxford, 1908.

KARL PEARSON (1857–1936)
The Chances of Death, and Other Studies in Evolution. 2 vols. 1897.
[See also under Psychology, p. 966.]

WILLIAM BATESON (1861–1926)
Materials for the Study of Variation, treated with Especial Regard to Discontinuity in the Origin of Species. 1894.
Essays and Addresses; with a Short Account of the Life of William Bateson, by Beatrice Bateson. Cambridge, 1928.
The Scientific Papers. Ed. R. C. Punnett, 2 vols. Cambridge, 1928.

PATRICK GEDDES (b. 1854) and SIR JOHN ARTHUR THOMSON (1861–1937)
The Evolution of Sex. 1890.

H. ZOOLOGY AND NATURAL HISTORY
General Works

Jardine, Sir W. Lives of Eminent Naturalists. 1840.
Nicholson, H. A. Natural History: its Rise and Progress in Britain as developed in the Life and Labours of Leading Naturalists. 1886.
Parker, T. J. and Haswell, W. A. A Text-book of Zoology. 1897. [Historical Section, vol. II, pp. 628–55.]
Lankester, Sir E. R. The History and Scope of Zoology. [In The Advancement of Science, 1900.]
Woodward, B. B. Catalogue of Books in the British Museum of Natural History. 3 vols. 1903–10.
Mitchell, P. C. Centenary History of the Zoological Society of London. 1929.

JOHN HUNTER (1728–1793)
The Works of John Hunter, with Notes. Ed. J. Palmer, 4 vols. 1835–7.
[For life see Memoirs of the Life and Doctrines of John Hunter, 1817; G. C. Peachey, A Memoir of William and John Hunter, 1924.]

THOMAS BEWICK (1753–1828)
History of British Birds. 2 vols. 1797–1825.

WILLIAM KIRBY (1759–1850) and WILLIAM SPENCE (1783–1860)
An Introduction to Entomology, or Elements of the Natural History of Insects. 4 vols. 1815–16.

ANDREW WILSON (1766–1863)
Sketches of Animal Life and Habits. Edinburgh, 1877.

SIR JOHN GRAHAM DALYELL (1775–1851)
Rare and Remarkable Animals of Scotland, represented from Living Objects. 1847.

JOHN VAUGHAN THOMPSON (1779–1847)
Zoological Researches and Illustrations. Cork, 1828–30.

CHARLES WATERTON (1782–1865)
Wanderings in South America, the North West of the United States and the Antilles. 1825.
Essays on Natural History. 1838.

WILLIAM YARRELL (1784–1856)

A History of British Fishes. 2 vols. 1836–60.
A History of British Birds. 3 vols. 1843–56.

JOHN FLEMING (1785–1857)

A History of British Animals. Edinburgh, 1828.
The Philosophy of Zoology, or a General View
of the Structure, Function and Classification
of Animals. Edinburgh, 1837.

SIR JOHN RICHARDSON (1787–1865)

Fauna Boreali-Americana, or the Zoology of
the Northern Parts of British America.
1829–37.

PRIDEAUX JOHN SELBY (1788–1867)

Illustrations of British Ornithology. 2 vols.
Edinburgh, 1825–33.

THOMAS BELL (1792–1880)

A History of British Quadrupeds including the
Cetacea. 1837.
A History of British Reptiles. 1839.
A History of the British Stalk-eyed Crustacea.
1853.

WILLIAM SHARP MACLEAY (1792–1865)

Horae Entomologicae. 1819.

ROBERT EDMOND GRANT (1793–1874)

An Essay on the Study of the Animal Kingdom. 1828.
Outline of a Course of Lectures on the Structure and Classification of Animals. 1833.
Outlines of Comparative Anatomy, presenting
a Sketch of the Present State of Knowledge
and of the Progress of Discovery in that
Science. 1841.

WILLIAM MACGILLIVRAY (1796–1852)

Lives of Eminent Zoologists from Aristotle to
Linnaeus. Edinburgh, 1834.
A History of British Birds, Indigenous and
Migratory. 5 vols. 1837–52.

GEORGE JOHNSTON (1797–1855)

A History of the British Zoophytes. Edin-
burgh, 1838.
A History of British Sponges and Lithophytes.
Edinburgh, 1842.

SIR WILLIAM JARDINE (1800–1874)

Lives of Eminent Naturalists. 1840.
The Naturalists' Library. 40 vols. Edinburgh,
1843.
The Birds of Great Britain and Ireland. 4 vols.
London, 1876.

LEONARD JENYNS, afterwards BLOMEFIELD
(1800–1893)

A Manual of British Vertebrate Animals.
Cambridge, 1835.

Observations in Natural History. 1846.
A Naturalist's Calendar. Ed. F. Darwin,
Cambridge, 1903.

RICHARD BRINSLEY HINDS

The Zoology of the Voyage of H.M.S. Sulphur
under the Command of Capt. Sir E. Belcher.
2 vols. 1843–5. [Ed. by Hinds.]

MARTIN BARRY (1802–1855)

On the Unity of Structure in the Animal
Kingdom. From the Edinburgh New Philosophical Journal. Edinburgh, 1837.
Researches in Embryology. Reprinted from
the Philosophical Transactions. 3 sers.
1838–40.

SIR RICHARD OWEN (1804–1892)

Memoir on the Pearly Nautilus. 1832.
Descriptive and Illustrated Catalogue of the
Physiological Series of Comparative Ana-
tomy contained in the Museum of the Royal
College of Surgeons. 1833.
Odontography, or a Treatise on the Compara-
tive Anatomy of the Teeth in the Vertebrate
Animals. 2 vols. 1840–5.
Lectures on the Comparative Anatomy and
Physiology of the Invertebrate Animals,
delivered to the Royal College of Surgeons.
2 vols. 1843–6.
On the Archetype and Homologies of the
Vertebrate Skeleton. 1848.
On Parthenogenesis. 1849.
Descriptive Catalogue of the Osteological
Series contained in the Museum of the
Royal College of Surgeons. 1853.
On the Classification and Geographical Dis-
tribution of the Mammalia. 1859.
On the Anatomy of the Vertebrates. 3 vols.
1866–8.
Memoirs of the Extinct Wingless Birds of New
Zealand. 1879.
[See T. H. Huxley, Life of Richard Owen,
1894.]

ANDREW PRITCHARD (1804–1882)

The Natural History of Animalcules. 1834.
A History of Infusoria, Living and Fossil. 1842.

JOHN OBADIAH WESTWOOD (1805–1893)

An Introduction to the Modern Classification
of Insects. 2 vols. 1839–40.

MATTHEW FONTAINE MAURY (1806–1873)

The Physical Geography of the Sea. 1855.

CHARLES ROBERT DARWIN (1809–1882)

Journal of Researches into the Natural
History and Geology of the Countries visited
during the Voyage of H.M.S. Beagle. 1839;
rptd 1890.

The Zoology of the Voyage of H.M.S. Beagle (1832–36). 5 pts, 1839–42. [Ed. by Darwin.]
A Monograph on the Cirripedia. 1851–3.
The Variation of Animals and Plants under Domestication. 1868; 2 vols. 1875.
The Expression of the Emotions in Man and Animals. 1872; 1890.
The Formation of Vegetable Mould through the Action of Worms, with Observations on their Habits, etc. 1881.
A Naturalist's Voyage. 1889.

[For biography and criticism see under Evolution, p. 953 above; for other works see under Anthropology, p. 967 below, Botany, p. 960 below, and Geology, p. 952 above.]

THOMAS CAMPBELL EYTON (1809–1880)

Monograph of the Anatidae. 1838.

JOHN GWYN JEFFREYS (1809–1885)

British Conchology, or an Account of the Mollusca which now inhabit the British Isles and Surrounding Seas. 5 vols. 1862–9.
Deep Sea Exploration. 1881.

THOMAS WRIGHT (1809–1884)

Observations on British Zoophytes. Edinburgh, 1858–9.

PHILIP HENRY GOSSE (1810–1888)

The Canadian Naturalist. 1840.
Natural History. 5 vols. 1849–54.
A Manual of Marine Zoology for the British Isles. 2 pts, 1855–6.
Actinologia Britannica. A History of the British Sea-Anemones and Corals. 1858–60.
The Rotifera. 1866. [Supplement, 1889. With C. T. Hudson.]
[See Sir E. Gosse, The Life of Philip Henry Gosse, 1899, and Father and Son, 1907.]

GEORGE ROBERT WATERHOUSE (1810–1888)

A Natural History of the Mammalia. 2 vols. 1846–8.
Catalogue of British Coleoptera. 1858.

HUGH EDWIN STRICKLAND (1811–1853)

The Dodo and its Kindred. 1848.
[See Sir W. Jardine, Memoirs of Hugh Edwin Strickland, with a Selection from his Scientific Writings, 1855.]

GEORGE JAMES ALLMAN (1812–1896)

A Monograph of the Fresh-Water Polyzoa. Ray Soc. 1856.
A Monograph of the Gymnoblastic or Tubularian Hydroids. Ray Soc. 1871.

WILLIAM BENJAMIN CARPENTER (1813–1855)

Zoology. Being a Systematic Account of the General Structure, Habits, Instincts, and Uses of the Principal Families of the Animal Kingdom. 1847.
Introduction to the Study of the Foraminifera. 1862.

EDWARD FORBES (1815–1854)

A History of British Starfishes and Other Animals of the Class Echinodermata. 1841.
A History of British Mollusca and their Shells. 4 vols. 1848–53. [With S. Hanley.]
The Zoology of the Voyage of H.M.S. Herald, under the Command of Captain H. Kellett, during the years 1845–51. 1852. [Ed. by Forbes.]
Outlines of the Natural History of Europe. 1859.

GEORGE CHARLES WALLICH (1815–1899)

The North Atlantic Sea-Bed. 1862.
Observations on Animal Life. 1862.
Deep Sea Researches on the Biology of Globigerina, etc. 1876.

WILLIAM CRAWFORD WILLIAMSON (1816–1895)

The Dawn of Animal Life. 1875.
[See also under Botany, p. 961 below.]

SAMUEL PECKWORTH WOODWARD (1821–1865)

A Manual of the Mollusca. 3 pts, 1851–6.

ALFRED RUSSEL WALLACE (1823–1913)

A Narrative of Travels on the Amazon and Rio Negro. 1853.
The Malay Archipelago: the Land of the Orang-Utan and the Bird of Paradise. 2 vols. 1869.
The Geographical Distribution of Animals; with a Study of Living and Extinct Faunas as elucidating the Past Changes of the Earth's Surface. 2 vols. 1876.
Tropical Nature, and Other Essays. 1878.
Island Life, or the Phenomena and Causes of Insular Faunas and Floras. 1880.

[For other works and life see under Evolution, p. 954 above.]

HENRY WALTER BATES (1825–1892)

Insect Fauna of the Amazon Valley. Trans. Linnaean Soc. XXIII, 1862.
The Naturalist on the River Amazon. A Record of Adventures, Habits of Animals, and Sketches of Brazilian and Indian Life during Eleven Years of Travel. 1863.

THOMAS HENRY HUXLEY (1825–1895)

On the Anatomy and the Affinities of the Family of Medusae. Philosophical Trans. CXXXIX, 1849.

On the Morphology of the Cephalous Mollusca. Philosophical Trans. CXLIII, 1853.

The Theory of the Vertebrate Skull. Croonian Lecture read before the Royal College of Surgeons. 1858.

On the Zoological Relations of Man with the Lower Animals. 1861.

Lectures on the Elements of Comparative Anatomy. 1864.

An Introduction to the Classification of Animals. 1869.

A Manual of the Anatomy of Vertebrated Animals. 1871.

American Addresses; with a Lecture on the Study of Biology. 1877.

A Manual of the Anatomy of Invertebrated Animals. 1877.

[For life and other works see under Evolution, p. 954 above, and for further works under Physiology, p. 963 below.]

GEORGE ROLLESTON (1829–1881)

Forms of Animal Life. Being Outlines of Zoological Classification based upon Anatomical Investigation. Oxford, 1870.

Scientific Papers and Addresses. Arranged by W. Turner. 2 vols. Oxford, 1884.

SIR CHARLES WYVILLE THOMSON
(1830–1882)

Report of the Scientific Results of the Voyage of H.M.S. Challenger during the Years 1873–76. 2 vols. 1877. [Superintended by Thomson.]

The Deep Sea Fauna of New Zealand. 1896.

SIR WILLIAM FLOWER (1831–1899)

An Introduction to the Osteology of the Mammalia. 1870.

The Horse. A Study in Natural History. 1891.

An Introduction to the Study of Mammals Living and Extinct. 1891. [With R. Lyddeker.]

[For life see R. Lyddeker, Sir William Flower, 1906.]

THOMAS BELT (1832–1878)

A Naturalist in Nicaragua. 1874.

SIR JOHN LUBBOCK (BARON AVEBURY)
(1834–1913)

On the Origin and Metamorphoses of Insects. 1873.

Fifty Years of Science. Being the British Association Address of 1881. 1882.

Ants, Bees and Wasps. A Record of Observations on the Habits of the Social Hymenoptera. 1882.

Scientific Lectures. 1879.

[For life see H. G. Hutchinson, Life of Lord Avebury, 1914; The Life-Work of Lord Avebury, ed. U. G. Duff, 1924; for other works see under Anthropology, p. 968 below, Psychology, p. 966 below and Botany, p. 961 below. See also the full list, p. 915 above.]

FREDERICK DU CANE GODMAN and
OSBERT SALVIN (1835–1898)

Biologia Centrali-Americana, or Contributions to the Knowledge of the Fauna and Flora of Mexico and Central America. 1879.

WILLIAM HENRY HUDSON (1841–1922)

The Naturalist in La Plata. 1892.

Collected Works. 24 vols. 1922–23.

[For full bibliography see under Novelists, p. 549 above.]

HENRY NOTTIDGE MOSELEY (1844–1891)

Notes by a Naturalist on the 'Challenger' during the Voyage round the World, 1872–76. 1879.

JOHN STERLING KINGSLEY

Riverside Natural History. 6 vols. 1888.

SIR EDWIN RAY LANKESTER (1847–1929)

Notes on Embryology and Classification. 1877.

The Advancement of Science. Occasional Essays and Addresses. 1890.

Zoological Articles contributed to the Encyclopaedia Britannica. 1891.

History and Scope of Zoology. 1893.

Diversions of a Naturalist. 1919.

Essays of a Naturalist. A Selection from the Works of Sir Ray Lankester. 1927.

RICHARD LYDEKKER (1849–1915)

Phases of Animal Life. 1892.

The Royal Natural History. 6 vols. 1893–6.

A Handbook of the British Mammalia. 1896.

FRANCIS MAITLAND BALFOUR (1851–1882)

The Elements of Embryology. 1874. [With Sir M. Foster.]

A Monograph on the Development of Elasmobranch Fishes. 1878.

A Treatise on Comparative Embryology. 1880–1.

ARTHUR MILNES MARSHALL (1852–1893)

The Frog. An Introduction to Anatomy and Histology. Manchester, 1882.

Vertebrate Embryology. 1893.

Biological Lectures and Addresses. Ed. C. F. Marshall, 1894.

CONWY LLOYD MORGAN (b. 1852)

Animal Biology. London, 1899.

[See also under Evolution, p. 955 above and Psychology, p. 966 below.]

ADAM SEDGWICK (1854–1913)

Text Book of Zoology. 1898.

SYDNEY JOHN HICKSON (1859–1940)

A Naturalist in North Celebes. 1889.
The Fauna of the Deep Sea. 1894.
The Story of Life in the Seas. 1898.

SIR ARTHUR EVERETT SHIPLEY (1861–1927)

Zoology of the Invertebrata. 1893.
Cambridge Natural History. 10 vols. 1895–1909. [Ed. by Sir A. Shipley, with Sir S. F. Harmer (b. 1862).]

SIR JOHN ARTHUR THOMSON (1861–1937)

Outlines of Zoology. London, 1892.

[See also under P. Geddes, under Evolution, p. 955 above.]

I. BOTANY

General Works

Green, J. R. History of Botany, 1860–1900. 1909.
Greene, E. L. Landmarks of Botanical History. Smithsonian Miscellaneous Collections, vol. LIV, Washington, 1909.
—— A History of Botany in the United Kingdom from the Earliest Times to the End of the XIXth Century. 1914.
Oliver, F. W. et al. Makers of Botany. A Collection of Biographies by Living Botanists. 1913.
Britten, J. and Boulger, G. A Biographical Index of British and Irish Botanists. 1931.

ERASMUS DARWIN (1731–1802)

The Botanic Garden. A Poem. 1789.
Phytologia, or the Philosophy of Agriculture and Gardening. 1801.

[For other works see under Evolution, p. 953 above.]

WILLIAM FORSYTH (1737–1804)

A Treatise on the Culture and Management of Fruit Trees. 1802.

JOHN SIBTHORP (1758–1796)

Floræ Græcæ Prodromus. Ed. Sir J. E. Smith, 2 vols. 1806–13.
Flora Græca, sive Plantarum rariorum Historia. Ed. Sir J. E. Smith, 10 vols. 1806–40.

THOMAS ANDREW KNIGHT (1759–1838)

A Selection from the Physiological and Horticultural Papers. With a Sketch of his Life. 1841.

SIR JAMES EDWARD SMITH (1759–1828)

An Introduction to Physiological and Systematical Botany. 1807.
The English Flora. 5 vols. 1824–36.
English Botany. 12 vols. 1832–46.
Life of John Ray. Ray Soc. 1846.

[For life see Memoir and Correspondence of the late Sir James Edward Smith, 1832.]

WILLIAM AITON (1766–1849)

Hortus Kewensis. 1789.

ROBERT BROWN (1773–1858)

Prodromus Florae Novae Hollandiae et Insulae Van Diemen. 1810.
On the Asclepiadeæ. 1811.
A Brief Account of Microscopical Observations on the Particles contained in the Pollen of Plants. 1828.
Observations on the Organs and Modes of Fecundation in Orchideæ and Asclepiadeæ. 1831. [From Trans. Linnean Soc.]
Miscellaneous Botanical Works. Ray Soc. 1866.

JAMES TOWNSEND MACKAY (1775–1862)

Flora Hibernica, comprising Flowering Plants, Ferns, etc. of Ireland. Dublin, 1838.

JOHN CLAUDIUS LOUDON (1783–1843)

An Encyclopaedia of Gardening, comprehending the Theory and Practice of Horticulture, Floriculture, Arboriculture and Landscape Gardening. 1822.
An Encyclopaedia of Plants, comprising every Particular respecting all the Plants, Indigenous and Cultivated introduced into Britain. 1829. [Supplement, 1840.]
An Encyclopaedia of Agriculture. 1831. [Supplement, 1834.]
Arboretum et Fruticetum Britannicum, or the Trees and Shrubs of Great Britain, Native and Foreign. 1838.
Hortus Britannicus. 1839.

SIR WILLIAM JACKSON HOOKER
(1785–1865)

Flora Londinensis. 5 vols. 1817–28.
Musci Exotici. Containing Figures and Descriptions of New or little Known Foreign Mosses and Other Cryptogamic Subjects. 2 vols. 1818–20.
Flora Scotica, or a Description of Scottish Plants. 2 pts. 1821.
Exotic Flora. 3 vols. Edinburgh, 1822–7.
Flora Borealis Americana, or the Botany of the Northern Parts of British America. 2 vols. 1829–40.
The British Flora. Comprising Phanerogamous, or Flowering Plants, and the Ferns. 1830.

Icones Plantarum, or Figures with Brief Descriptive Characters and Remarks of New or Rare Plants. 4 vols. 1836.
Species Filicum. Being Descriptions of the Known Ferns. 1846–64.
A Century of Ferns. 1854.
A Second Century of Ferns. 1861.
The British Ferns. 1861–2.

[For life see Sir J. D. Hooker, A Sketch of the Life and Labour of Sir William Jackson Hooker, Oxford, 1903, and Life in Annals of Botany, 1903.]

ROBERT KAYE GREVILLE (1794–1866)

Scottish Cryptogamic Flora. 6 vols. Edinburgh, 1823–8.
Algae Britannicae. Edinburgh, 1830.

JOHN STEVENS HENSLOW (1796–1861)

A Catalogue of British Plants, arranged according to the Natural System, with Synonyms of De Candolle and Hooker. Cambridge, 1835.
The Principles of Descriptive and Physiological Botany. [In D. Lardner, The Cabinet Cyclopaedia, 1836.]

[For life see Biographical Sketch, priv. ptd, 1861 and L. Jenyns, Memoir of the Rev. John Stevens Henslow, 1862.]

GEORGE DON (1798–1856)

Herbarium Britannicum. 1804.
A General System of Gardening and Botany. 4 vols. 1832–8.

JOHN LINDLEY (1799–1865)

A Synopsis of the British Flora. 1829.
The Genera and Species of Orchidaceous Plants. 6 pts, 1830–40.
A Natural System of Botany. 1836.
Elements of Botany, Structural, Physiological, Systematical and Medical. 1841.
The Vegetable Kingdom, or the Structure, Class and Uses of Plants, illustrated upon the Natural System. 1846.
Theory and Practice of Agriculture. 1855.
The Treasury of Botany. A Popular Dictionary of the Vegetable Kingdom. 1866. [With T. Moore.]

WILLIAM WILSON (1799–1871)

Bryologica Britannica. 1855.

DAVID DON (1800–1840)

Prodromus Florae Nepalensis. 1825.

GEORGE BENTHAM (1800–1884)

Handbook of British Flora. 1858; rev. Sir J. D. Hooker, 1887 (5th edn).

[For life see B. J. Jackson, George Bentham, 1906; see also under Philosophy, p. 863 above and under Sir J. D. Hooker, p. 961.]

JOSEPH MILES BERKELEY (1803–1889)

Introduction to Cryptogamic Botany. 1847.
Outlines of British Fungology. 1860.
Handbook of British Mosses. 1863.

HEWETT COTTRELL WATSON (1804–1881)

Remarks on the Geographical Distribution of British Plants; chiefly in Connexion with Latitude, Elevation and Climate. 1835.
Cybele Britannica, or British Plants and their Geographical Relations. 4 vols. 1847–59; Supplement, 1860.
The London Catalogue of British Plants, 1850.
Topographical Botany, showing the Distribution of British Plants. 1883.

JOHN HUTTON BALFOUR (1808–1884)

A Catalogue of British Plants. Edinburgh, 1841. [With C. C. Babington and W. H. Campbell.]
Outlines of Botany. Edinburgh. 1854.
Manual of Botany. Edinburgh, 1860.
Introduction to the Study of Palaeontological Botany. Edinburgh, 1872.

CHARLES CARDALE BABINGTON (1808–1895)

Manual of the British Flora. 1843.
Manual of British Botany, containing the Flowering Plants and Ferns arranged according to Natural Orders. 1843; rptd 1904 (9th edn).
The British Rubi. 1869.

[See Memorials, Journal and Botanical Correspondence of C. C. Babington, edited by A. M. B. [i.e. Anna Maria Babington], Cambridge, 1897.]

CHARLES ROBERT DARWIN (1809–1882)

Journal of Researches into the Natural History and Geology of the Countries visited during the Voyage of H.M.S. Beagle. 1839; 1845; 1889 (4th edn); rptd 1890.
On the Various Contrivances by which British and Foreign Orchids are fertilized by Insects. 1862.
The Movements and Habits of Climbing Plants. 1865. [Rptd from Journ. of Linnaean Soc.]
The Variation of Animals and Plants under Domestication. 1868; 2 vols. 1875.
Insectivorous Plants. 1875.
The Effects of Cross- and Self-Fertilization in the Vegetable Kingdom. 1876.
The Different Forms of Flowers or Plants of the Same Species. 1877.

The Power of Movement in Plants. 1880. [With Sir F. Darwin.]

A Naturalist's Voyage. 1889.

[For biography and criticism see under Evolution, p. 953 above; for other works see under Anthropology, p. 967 below, Geology, p. 952 and Zoology, p. 956, above; Sir W. W. T. Dyer, Charles Darwin. Work in Botany, 1882.]

WILLIAM GRIFFITH (1810–1845)

Posthumous Papers. Notulae ad Plantas Asiaticas. Arranged by J. M'Clelland. 2 pts, Calcutta, 1847–9.

Posthumous Papers bequeathed to the East India Co. Icones Plantarum Asiaticarum. Arranged by J. M'Clelland. 4 pts, Calcutta, 1847–54.

WILLIAM HENRY HARVEY (1811–1866)

A Manual of British Algae; containing Descriptions of All the Known British Species of Sea-weeds. 1841.

Nereis Australis, or Algae of the Southern Ocean. 2 pts, 1847–9.

The Sea-side Book. Being an Introduction to the Natural History of the British Coasts. 1849.

Phycologia Britannica, or a History of British Seaweeds. 4 vols. 1846–51.

Phycologia Australia, or a History of Australian Seaweeds. 5 vols. 1858–63.

[See Memoir of William Henry Harvey, with Selections from his Journal and Correspondence, 1869.]

WILLIAM CRAWFORD WILLIAMSON (1816–1895)

On the Recent Foraminifera of Great Britain. Ray Soc. 1858.

Coals and Coal Plants. 1875.

A Monograph on the Morphology and Histology of Stigmaria ficoides. Palaeontographical Soc. 1887.

Reminiscences of a Yorkshire Naturalist. Ed. A. C. Williamson, 1896.

[See also under Evolution, p 957 above.]

SIR JOSEPH HENRY GILBERT (1817–1901)

Introduction to the Study of the Scientific Principles of Agriculture. 1884.

The Rothhamsted Memoirs of Agricultural Chemistry and Physiology. 7 vols. 1893–9. [With Sir J. B. Lawes.]

The Rothhamsted Experiments. Being an Account of some of the Results of the Agricultural Investigations conducted at Rothhamsted over a Period of 50 Years. Edinburgh, 1895. [With Sir J. B. Lawes.]

SIR JOSEPH DALTON HOOKER (1817–1911)

The Botany of the Antarctic Voyage of H.M.S. Erebus and Terror, 1839–44, under the Command of Sir J. C. Ross. 3 sers. 1844–60.

On the Vegetation of the Carboniferous Period. Memoirs of Geological Survey, II, 1846.

Himalayan Journals, or Notes of a Naturalist in Bengal, the Sikkim, and Nepal Himalayas, the Khasia Mountains, etc. 2 vols. 1854.

Genera Plantarum ad Exemplaria imprimis in Herbariis Kewensibus servata definita. 3 vols. 1862–83. [With G. Bentham.]

The Student's Flora of the British Islands. 1870.

Flora of British India. 7 vols. 1872–97.

Handbook of British Flora. 1887. [By G. Bentham (1st edn 1858); rev. by Hooker.]

Index Kewensis. 1892–5.

[See L. Huxley, Life and Letters of Sir Joseph Dalton Hooker, 1918; F. O. Bower, Sir Joseph Dalton Hooker, 1919.]

ARTHUR HENFREY (1819–1859)

Outlines of Structural and Physiological Botany. 1847.

Rudiments of Botany. 1849.

The Micrographic Dictionary. A Guide to the Examination and Investigation of Microscopic Objects. 1856. [With J. M. Griffith.]

ROBERT BENTLEY (1821–1893)

A Manual of Botany; including the Structure, Formation, Classification and Uses of Plants. 1861.

A Student's Guide to Structural Morphology and Physiological Botany. 1883.

Medicinal Plants. 4 vols. 1875–80. [With H. Trimen.]

THOMAS MOORE (1821–1881)

A Handbook of British Ferns. 1848.

The Ferns of Great Britain and Ireland. 1855.

WILLIAM LANDER LINDSAY (1829–1880)

Memoirs on the Spermogones and Pyonides of Lichens. [1856?]

A Popular History of British Lichens. 1856.

DANIEL OLIVER (b. 1830)

Lessons in Elementary Botany. Cambridge, 1864.

The Flora of Tropical Africa. 3 vols. 1868–77.

MAXWELL TYLDEN MASTERS (1833–1907)

Vegetable Teratology. An Account of the Principal Deviations from the Usual Construction of Plants. Ray Soc. 1869.

SIR JOHN LUBBOCK (BARON AVEBURY) (1834–1913)

On British Wild Flowers considered in Relation to Insects. 1873.

Flowers, Fruits and Leaves. 1886.

[For other works see under Anthropology, p. 968 below, Psychology, p. 966 below and Zoology, p. 958 above.]

GEORGE HENSLOW (1835–1925)

The Origin of Plant Structures by Self-Adaptation to the Environment. 1895.

HENRY TRIMEN (1843–1896) and
SIR WILLIAM TURNER THISTLETON DYER
(1843–1929)

The Flora of Middlesex. A Topographical and Historical Account of the Plants found in the County. 1869.

SYDNEY HOWARD VINES

Lectures on the Physiology of Plants. Cambridge, 1886.

JOSEPH REYNOLDS GREEN (1848–1914)

A Manual of Botany. 1895–6. 2 vols.
The Soluble Ferments and Fermentation. Cambridge, 1899.
An Introduction to Vegetable Physiology. 1900.

SIR FRANCIS DARWIN (1848–1925)

The Elements of Botany. Cambridge, 1895.

DUKINFIELD HENRY SCOTT (b. 1854)

An Introduction to Structural Botany. 1894.
Studies in Fossil Botany. 1900.

HARRY MARSHALL WARD (1854–1906)

Diseases of Plants. 1889.
Timber and some of its Diseases. 1889.
Grasses. A Handbook for Use in the Field and the Laboratory. Cambridge, 1901.

FREDERICK ORPEN BOWER (b. 1855)

Studies in the Morphology of Spore-Producing Members. 1896.

J. PHYSIOLOGY

General Works

Rutherford, W. Text-book of Physiology. Edinburgh, 1880.
MacKendrick, J. G. On the Modern Cell Theory, and Theories as to the Physiological Basis of Heredity. Proc. Philosophical Soc. Glasgow, XIX, 1887.
—— Chronological Tables of Scientific Men, showing the Names of the More Distinguished Anatomists and Physiologists and their Contemporaries. Proc. Philosophical Soc. Glasgow, XXII, 1891.
Turner, Sir W. The Cell Theory, Past and Present. Journ. of Anatomy and Physiology, XXIV, 1890.

Burdon-Sanderson, J. S. Ludwig and Modern Physiology. Science Progress, V, 1896.
Foster, Sir M. Presidential Address. Section I, British Ass. Toronto, 1897.
—— Lectures on the History of Physiology in the XVIth, XVIIth and XVIIIth Centuries. 1901.
—— Physiology. [In Encyclopaedia Britannica, 11th edn, 1911.]
Franklin, K. J. A Short History of Physiology. 1933.

JOHN HUNTER (1748–1793)

[See under Zoology, p. 955 above.]

EDWARD JENNER (1749–1823)

An Inquiry into the Causes and Effects of the Variolae Vaccinae, a Disease discovered in some of the Western Counties of England and known by the Name of Cow-pox. 1798.
The Origin of the Vaccine Inoculation. 1801.
The Note Book of Edward Jenner in the Possession of the Royal College of Physicians. With an Introduction on Jenner's Work as a Naturalist, by F. D. Drewitt. 1931.

SIR ASTLEY PASTON COOPER (1768–1841)

Life and Works. Ed. G. L. Keynes, 1922.

FRANCIS JEFFERY BELL (1773–1846)

Comparative Anatomy and Physiology. 1835.

JOHN BOSTOCK (1773–1846)

An Elementary System of Physiology, comprising a Complete View of the Present State of the Science. And Analyses of the Principal Theories and Hypotheses. 1836.

THOMAS YOUNG (1773–1829)

[See under Physics, p. 937 above.]

SIR CHARLES BELL (1774–1842)

An Essay on the Forces which circulate the Blood. 1819.
The Nervous System of the Human Body, embracing the Papers delivered to the Royal Society on the Subject of the Nerves. 1830.
The Hand: its Mechanism and Vital Endowments as evincing Design. 1833.
Animal Mechanics. 1839.
A Familiar Treatise on the Five Senses. 1841.
Letters of Sir Charles Bell, selected from his Correspondence by his Brother G. J. Bell. 1870.

[For other works see under Psychology, p. 965 below.]

JOHN BYWATER

Physiological Fragments. 1819.

Sir Benjamin Brodie (1783–1862)

Physiological Researches. 1851.

Sir William Lawrence (1783–1867)

An Introduction to Comparative Anatomy and Physiology. 1816.

Thomas Johnstone Aitkin

Elements of Physiology. Being an Account of the Laws and Principles of the Animal Economy. 1838.

William Batten

An Essay on the Functions of Life. 1839.

William Beaumont (1785–1853)

Experiments and Observations on the Gastric Juice and the Physiology of Digestion. 1838.

James Cowles Prichard (1786–1848)

A Review of the Doctrine of a Vital Principle, as maintained by some Writers on Physiology. 1829.

James Black (1788–1861)

A Short Enquiry into the Capillary Circulation of the Blood. 1825.

Marshall Hall (1790–1857)

An Essay on the Circulation of the Blood. 1831.
Memoirs on the Nervous System. 1837.

Thomas Addison (1793–1860)

On the Constitutional and Local Effects of Disease of the Supra-renal Capsules. 1855.
An Essay on the Operation of Poisonous Agents upon the Living Body. 1829. [With J. Morgan.]
A Collection of the Published Writings of Thomas Addison. 1868.

John Fletcher (1793–1836)

Rudiments of Physiology. 3 pts. Edinburgh, 1836.

Sir Charles Wheatstone (1802–1875)

Contributions to the Physiology of Vision. Philosophical Trans. cxxviii, 1838.

Sir Richard Owen (1804–1892)

Experimental Physiology: its Benefits to Mankind. 1882.
[See also under Zoology, p. 956 above.]

Thomas Wright (1809–1884)

Outlines of Comparative Physiology. 1851.
[See also under Zoology, p. 957 above.]

William Benjamin Carpenter (1813–1885)

The Principles of Human Physiology. 1844.
Animal Physiology. 1847.
A Manual of Physiology, including Physiological Anatomy. 1846.

Sir William Bowman (1816–1892)

The Physiological Anatomy and Physiology of Man. 1845. [With R. B. Todd.]
Collected Papers. Ed. J. S. Burdon-Sanderson and J. W. Hulke, 2 vols. 1892.

Augustus Waller (1816–1890)

Electromotive Changes accompanying the Heart's Beat. Journ. of Physiology, viii, 1887.
The Electrical Action of the Human Heart. Ed. A. M. Waller, 1922.

Herbert Spencer (1820–1904)

Spontaneous Generation and the Hypothesis of Physiological Units. 1870.
[For other works see under Evolution, p. 954 above and Psychology, p. 965 below.]

John Tyndall (1820–1893)

Optical Deportment of the Atmosphere in Relation to the Phenomena of Putrefaction and Infection. Philosophical Trans. clxvii, pt 1, 1876.

William Kirkes (1823–1864)

Handbook of Physiology. 1848.

Thomas Henry Huxley (1825–1895)

Lessons in Elementary Physiology. 1866; 1900 (rev.); rptd 1915 (6th edn).
Protoplasm, the Physical Basis of Life. Reprinted from the Fortnightly Review. 1869.
[For other works see under Evolution, p. 954 above, Zoology, p. 958 above, and Anthropology, p. 968 below.]

Joseph Lister (Baron Lister) (1827–1912)

Collected Papers. Prepared by H. C. Cameron. 2 vols. Oxford, 1909.

Gilbert William Child

Essays on Physiological Subjects. 1868.

Sir John Scot Burdon-Sanderson (1828–1905)

On the Study of Physiology, its Relation to Other Studies and its Use as a Preparation for that of Medicine. 1879.
Memoirs on the Physiology of Nerve, of Muscle and of the Electrical Organ. 1887.
Memoirs, Selected Papers and Addresses. Ed. Lady Burdon-Sanderson, 1911.

George Harley (1829–1896)

On the Influence of Physical and Chemical Agents on Blood. 1865.

Sidney Ringer (1835–1910)

The Influence of the Different Constituents of the Blood on the Contraction of the Heart. Journ. of Physiology, IV, 1883–4.

The Effect of Minute Quantities of Inorganic Salts on Organised Structures. Journ. of Physiology, VII, 1886.

Sir Michael Foster (1836–1907)

Physiology: the Functions of Muscle and Nerve. Cambridge, 1873.

Studies from the Physiological Laboratory in the University of Cambridge. Cambridge, 1876–7.

Text Book of Physiology. 1877.

Lectures on the History of Physiology in the XVIth, XVIIth and XVIIIth Centuries. Cambridge, 1901.

Henry Charlton Bastian (1837–1915)

The Modes of Origin of Lowest Organisms. 1871.

The Beginnings of Life. Being some Account of the Nature, Modes of Origin and Transformations of Lower Organisms. 2 vols. 1872.

The Evolution and Origin of Life. 1874.

John Gray MacKendrick (b. 1841)

Animal Physiology. 1875.

Outlines of Physiology in its Relation to Man. Glasgow, 1878.

General Physiology of the Nervous System. 1879.

The Gases of the Blood in Relation to some Problems of Respiration. 1888.

Life in Motion, or Muscle and Nerve. 1892.

The Physiology of the Senses. 1893. [With W. Snodgrass.]

Arthur Gamgee (1841–1909)

A Text Book of the Physiological Chemistry of the Animal Body. 2 vols. 1880–93.

The Physiology of Digestion and the Digestive Organs. 1884.

The Digestive Ferments and the Chemical Processes of Digestion. 1884.

Sir David Ferrier (1843–1925)

The Functions of the Brain. 1876.

The Croonian Lectures on Cerebral Localisation. 1890.

Sir Thomas Lauder Brunton (1844–1916)

On the Rhythmic Contraction of the Capillaries in Man. Journ. of Physiology, V, 1884.

Collected Papers on the Circulation and Respiration. 1906.

Sir William Richard Gowers (1845–1915)

The Diagnosis of Diseases of the Spinal Cord. 1880.

A Manual of Diseases of the Nervous System. 1886.

Walter Noel Hartley (1846–1913)

Experiments concerning the Evolution of Life from Lifeless Matter. Proc. Royal Soc. XX, 1871–2.

Walter Holbrook Gaskell (1847–1914)

Investigations on the Vaso-motor Nerves of Striated Muscle. Journ. of Physiology, I, 1879.

On the Rhythm of the Heart of the Frog and the Nature of the Vagus Nerve. Proc. Royal Soc. XXXIII, 1882.

Sir Edward Albert Sharpey Schaefer (b. 1850)

The Relation of Structure to Function in the Animal Organism. 1880.

Text Book of Physiology. 2 vols. Edinburgh, 1898–1900.

Arthur Broer Griffiths

Comparative Physiology. 1891.

History of the Physiological Society during its First Fifty Years, 1876–1926. 1927.

John Scott Haldane (1860–1935)

Methods of Air Analysis. 1899.

William Dobson Halliburton (b. 1860)

Text Book of Chemical Physiology and Pathology. 1891.

The Essentials of Chemical Physiology. 1893.

Arthur Sheridan Lea

The Chemical Basis of the Animal Body. 1892.

Ernest Henry Starling (1866–1927)

The Elements of Human Physiology. 1892; 1907 (8th edn).

Benjamin Moore

Elementary Physiology. 1899.

Leonard Erskine Hill (b. 1866)

Manual of Human Physiology. 1899.

K. PSYCHOLOGY

[Reference should also be made to the section on Philosophy, pp. 861–77 above, where fuller lists of some of the following writers' works will be found.]

General Works

Brett, G. S. A History of Psychology. 3 vols. 1912–21.

Hall, G. S. Founders of Modern Psychology. 1912.

Baldwin, J. M. History of Psychology. 2 vols. 1913.

Flügel, J. C. A Hundred Years of Psychology. 1933.

JAMES MILL (1773–1836)

Analysis of the Phenomena of the Human Mind. 2 vols. 1829; ed. A. Bain, 1869.

[For life see A. Bain, James Mill. A Biography, 1882; Sir L. Stephen, James Mill, 1900.]

SIR CHARLES BELL (1774–1842)

The Anatomy of the Brain, explained in a Series of Engravings. 1802.
Idea of a New Anatomy of the Brain. 1811.
The Anatomy and Philosophy of Expression. 1844.

[For other works see under Physiology, p. 962 above.]

THOMAS BROWN (1778–1820)

Lectures on the Philosophy of the Human Mind. Edinburgh, 1820.

SIR BENJAMIN BRODIE (1783–1862)

Psychological Researches: in a Series of Essays. 1855.

SIR HENRY HOLLAND (1788–1873)

Chapters on Mental Philosophy. 1852.
Essays. 1862.
Fragmentary Papers. Ed. F. J. Holland, 1875.

GEORGE COMBE (1788–1858)

Essays on Phrenology, or an Enquiry into the Principles and Utility of the System of Gall and Spurzheim. Edinburgh, 1819.

MARSHALL HALL (1790–1857)

On the Reflex Functions of the Medulla oblongata and the Medulla spinalis. Philosophical Trans. CXXIII, 1833.

[See also under Physiology, p.   above.]

JAMES MARTINEAU (1805–1900)

The Place of Mind in Nature and Intuition in Man. 1872.

CHARLES ROBERT DARWIN (1809–1882)

The Descent of Man and Selection in relation to Sex. 2 vols. 1871.
The Expression of the Emotions in Man and Animals. 1872; 1890.

[For other works see under Geology, p. 952 above, Evolution, p. 953 above, Zoology, p. 956 above and Botany, p. 961 above.]

JAMES MacCOSH (1811–1894)

The Intuitions of the Mind inductively investigated. 1860.
The Association of Ideas and its Influence in the Training of the Mind. 1862.
The Emotions. 1880.
Psychology. The Cognitive Powers. 1886.
Psychology. The Motive Powers, Emotions, Conscience, and Will. 1887.

[See Life of James MacCosh, a Record chiefly Autobiographical, ed. W. M. Sloane, Edinburgh, 1896.]

THOMAS LAYCOCK (1812–1876)

Mind and Brain, or the Correlations of Consciousness and Organisation, with their Applications to Philosophy and Zoology. Edinburgh, 1860.

WILLIAM BENJAMIN CARPENTER (1813–1885)

The Unconscious Action of the Brain. 1866.
The Principles of Mental Physiology, with their Application to the Training and Discipline of the Mind and the Study of its Morbid Conditions. 1874.

GEORGE HENRY LEWES (1817–1878)

Problems of Life and Mind. 2 vols. 1874–9. [Contains The Physical Basis of Mind, 1877, and Mind as a Function of the Organism, 1879.]
The Study of Psychology. Its Object, Scope and Method. 1879.

ALEXANDER BAIN (1818–1903)

The Senses and the Intellect. 1855.
The Emotions and the Will. 1859.
On the Study of Character, including an Estimate of Phrenology. 1861.
Mind and Body. The Theories of their Relation. 1873.
Autobiography. Ed. W. L. Davidson, 1904.

HERBERT SPENCER (1820–1904)

The Principles of Psychology. 2 vols. 1855; 1870–2; 1881–90.

[For other works see under Evolution, p. 954 above and Physiology, p. 963 above.]

SIR FRANCIS GALTON (1822–1911)

Psychometric Experiments. Reprinted from Brain. 1879.

[For other works see under Evolution, p. 954 above and Anthropology, p. 967 below.]

WALTER BAGEHOT (1826–1877)

Physics and Politics, or Thoughts on the Application of the Principles of 'Natural Selection' and 'Inheritance' to Political Society. 1873.

[For other works see p. 707 above.]

ST GEORGE MIVART (1827–1900)

The Origin of Human Reason. 1889.

[For other works see under Evolution, p. 954 above.]

SIR JOHN LUBBOCK (BARON AVEBURY) (1834–1913)

On the Senses, Instincts and Intelligence of Animals, with Special Reference to Insects. 1888.

[For other works see under Anthropology, p. 968 below, Botany, p. 961 above and Zoology, p. 958 above.]

HENRY CHARLTON BASTIAN (1837–1915)

The Brain as an Organ of Mind. 1880.

JAMES SULLY (1842–1923)

Sensation and Intuition. Studies in Psychology and Æsthetics. 1874.
Illusions. A Psychological Study. 1881.
Outlines of Psychology, with Special Reference to the Theory of Education. 1884.
The Human Mind. A Text-book of Psychology. 2 vols. 1892.
Studies of Childhood. 1895.

JAMES WARD (1843–1925)

Essays. Ed. W. R. Sorley and G. F. Stout, 1927.

[See W. R. Sorley, James Ward, Cambridge, 1927.]

WILLIAM KINGDON CLIFFORD (1845–1879)

Seeing and Thinking. 1879.

[For other works see under Mathematics, p. 942 above.]

GRANT ALLEN (1848–1899)

Psychology: its Origin and Development. An Essay in Comparative Psychology. 1879.
Physiological Æsthetics. 1887.
The Evolution of the Idea of God. 1897.

[For other works see under Fiction, p. 534 above.]

BERNARD BOSANQUET (1848–1923)

Knowledge and Reality. 1885.
Essays and Addresses. 1889.
Psychology of the Moral Self. 1897.

GEORGE JOHN ROMANES (1848–1894)

The Natural History of Instinct. 1879.
Mental Evolution. 1880.
Animal Intelligence. 1882.
Mental Evolution in Animals. 1883.
Mental Evolution in Man. The Origin of Human Faculty. 1888.

[For other works see under Evolution, p. 955 above, and Poetry, p. 356 above.]

CONWY LLOYD MORGAN (b. 1852)

Animal Life and Intelligence. 1890–1.
An Introduction to Comparative Psychology. 1894.
Habit and Instinct. 1896.
Animal Behaviour. 1900.

[For other works see under Evolution, p. 955 above and Zoology, p. 959 above.]

KARL PEARSON (1857–1936)

Inquiries into Human Faculty and its Development. 1883.

[For other works see under Evolution, p. 955 above.]

HENRY MAUDSLEY (b. 1859)

On the Method of Study of Mind. An Introductory Chapter to a Physiology and Pathology of the Mind. 1865.
The Physiology and Pathology of the Mind. 1867.
Body and Mind. An Enquiry into their Connection and Mutual Influence, especially in Reference to Mental Disorders. 1870; 1873 (enlarged, with Psychological Essays).

GEORGE FREDERICK STOUT (b. 1860)

Analytic Psychology. 2 vols. 1896.
A Manual of Psychology. 1899; 1929 (4th edn).

L. ANTHROPOLOGY

General Works

Bendysche, T. The History of Anthropology. Memoirs of Anthropological Soc. i, 1865.
Haddon, A. C. and A. H. Quiggin. The History of Anthropology. 1910.
Penniman, T. K. A Hundred Years of Anthropology. 1935. [With bibliography.]

CHARLES WHITE (1728–1813)

An Account of the Regular Gradation in Man and in Different Animals. 1799.

SIR WILLIAM LAWRENCE (1783–1867)

Lectures on Physiology, Zoology and the Natural History of Man, delivered at the Royal College of Surgeons. 1819.

WILLIAM BUCKLAND (1784–1856)

[See under Geology, p. 950 above.]

JAMES COWLES PRICHARD (1786–1848)

Researches into the Physical History of Man. 1813; 5 vols. 1836–47 (3rd edn).

The Natural History of Man; comprising Inquiries into the Modifying Influence of Physical and Moral Agencies of the Different Tribes of the Human Family. 1843; ed. E. Norris, 2 vols. 1855 (4th edn).

Ethnology. [In Herschel's Manual of Scientific Enquiry, 1849.]

Manual of Ethnology. Rev. T. Wright, 1859.

[See G. E. Weare, J. C. Prichard, Physician and Ethnologist, 1898.]

ROBERT KNOX (1791–1862)

The Races of Men. 1850–62.

Man: his Structure and Physiology. 1857.

WILLIAM ELLIS (1794–1872)

Polynesian Researches. 2 vols. 1829.

EDWIN NORRIS (1795–1872)

The Ethnological Library. 2 vols. 1853–4.

SIR CHARLES LYELL (1797–1875)

The Geological Evidences of the Antiquity of Man, with Remarks on the Theories of the Origin of Species by Variation. 1863.

[For other works see under Geology, p. 951 above.]

SIR RICHARD OWEN (1804–1892)

Antiquity of Man. London, 1884.

[For other works see under Zoology, p. 956 above.]

CHARLES ROBERT DARWIN (1809–1882)

The Descent of Man, and Selection in Relation to Sex. 2 vols. 1871; rptd 1930.

[For other works see under Geology, p. 952 above, Evolution, p. 953 above, Zoology, p. 956 above, and Botany, p. 960 above.]

HENRY CHRISTY (1810–1865)

Guide to the Christy Collection of Prehistoric Antiquities and Ethnography. 1868.

JOHN THURNHAM (1810–1873)

On the Two Principal Forms of Ancient British and Gaulish Skulls. Memoirs of Anthropological Soc. i, 1865.

Further Researches and Observations on the Two Principal Forms of Ancient British Skulls. Memoirs of Anthropological Soc. iii, 1867.

Crania Britannica. Delineations and Descriptions of the Skulls of the Early Inhabitants of the British Isles. 1856. [With J. B. Davis.]

ROBERT GORDON LATHAM (1812–1888)

The Natural History of the Varieties of Man. 1850.

The Ethnology of the British Islands. 1852.

Descriptive Ethnology. 2 vols. 1859.

Opuscula. Essays chiefly Philological and Ethnographical. 1860.

WILLIAM PENGELLY (1812–1894)

Kent's Cavern: its Testimony to the Antiquity of Man. 1876.

[See H. Pengelly, Memoir of William Pengelly, with Selection from his Correspondence, 1897.]

WILLIAM BENJAMIN CARPENTER (1813–1885)

Nature and Man. Essays Scientific and Philosophical. With Introductory Memoir by J. E. Carpenter. 1888.

SIR WILLIAM ROBERT WILDE (1815–1876)

A Descriptive Catalogue of Antiquities in the Museum of the Royal Irish Academy. Dublin, 1857–61.

On the Ancient Races of Ireland. Address to the Anthropological Section of the British Association. 1874.

SIR JOHN WILLIAM DAWSON (1820–1899)

Fossil Men and their Modern Representatives. 1883.

HENRY THOMAS BUCKLE (1821–1862)

History of Civilisation in England. 2 vols. 1857–61.

Essays. 1867.

Miscellaneous and Posthumous Works. Ed. (with biographical notice) H. Taylor, 3 vols. 1872.

[See A. H. Huth, Life and Writings of Henry Thomas Buckle, 2 vols. 1880, and p. 908 above.]

SIR FRANCIS GALTON (1822–1911)

Hereditary Genius. An Enquiry into its Laws and Consequences. 1869.

Enquiries into Human Faculty and its Development. 1883.

Record of Family Faculties. 1884.

Natural Inheritance. 1889.

Memories of my Life. 1908.

[For life see K. Pearson, The Life, Letters and Labours of Francis Galton, 4 vols. Cambridge, 1914–30, and Francis Galton, A Centenary Appreciation, 1922; see also under Philosophy, p. 867, Evolution, p. 954 and Psychology, p. 965 above.]

SIR HENRY JAMES MAINE (1822–1888)

Ancient Law: its Connection with the Early History of Society, and its Relation to Modern Ideas. 1861.

[See also the full list of Maine's writings, p. 893 above.]

THOMAS HENRY HUXLEY (1825–1895)

Evidence as to Man's Place in Nature. Edinburgh, 1863.
On the Methods and Results of Ethnology. 1865.

[For other works see under Evolution, p. 955 above, Physiology, p. 963 above and Zoology, p. 958 above.]

JOHN BEDDOE (1826–1911)

The Races of Great Britain. A Contribution to the Anthropology of Western Europe. Bristol, 1885.
The Anthropological History of Europe. 1893.
Memories of Eighty Years. Bristol, 1910.

HENRY AUGUSTUS LANE FOX, afterwards PITT-RIVERS (1827–1900)

Excavations in Cranbourne Chase near Rushmore. Including a Bibliographical List of Pitt-Rivers's Works. 5 vols. 1887–1905.
The Evolution of Culture, and Other Essays. A Reprint of Papers Published from 1868 to 1875. Ed. J. L. Myres, Oxford, 1906.

[See also p. 915 above.]

WILLIAM WYATT GILL (1829–1896)

Historical Sketches of Savage Life in Polynesia. 1880.

SIR WILLIAM FLOWER (1831–1899)

Races of Men. 1880.

SIR EDWARD BURNETT TYLOR (1832–1917)

Researches into the Early History of Mankind and the Development of Civilisation. 1865.
Primitive Culture. Researches into the Development of Mythology, Philosophy, Religion, Art and Custom. 2 vols. 1871.
Anthropology. An Introduction to the Study of Man and Civilisation. 1881.
Anthropological Essays presented to E. B. Tylor in Honour of his Seventy-Fifth Birthday, Oct. 2nd 1907. Oxford, 1907.

JAMES HUNT (1833–1869)

On the Negro's Place in Nature. Lecture read before the Anthropological Society, Nov. 1863. 1863.
Introductory Address on the Study of Anthropology. 1863.

AUGUSTUS HENRY KEANE (b. 1833)

Ethnology. Cambridge, 1896.
Man, Past and Present. Cambridge, 1899.

JOHN LUBBOCK (BARON AVEBURY) (1834–1913)

Prehistoric Times as illustrated by Ancient Remains. 1865.
The Origin of Civilisation and the Primitive Condition of Man. 1870.

[For other works see the full list, p. 915 above.]

SIR WILLIAM BOYD DAWKINS (1837–1929)

Cave Hunting. Researches on the Evidence of Caves respecting the Early Inhabitants of Europe. 1874.
Early Man in Britain and his Place in the Tertiary Period. 1880.

HENRY CALDERWOOD

Evolution and Man's Place in Nature. 1893.

EDWARD CLODD (1840–1930)

Myths and Dreams. 1885.
The Childhood of the World. 1893.
The Story of Primitive Man. 1895.
Tom tit Tot. 1898.

ANDREW LANG (1844–1912)

Custom and Myth. 1884.
Myth, Ritual and Religion. 2 vols. 1887.
The Book of Dreams and Ghosts. 1897.
The Making of Religion. 1898.

[See also the full list, p. 747 above.]

ANNE WALBANK BUCKLAND (b. 1870)

Anthropological Studies. 1891.

WYNFRID LAWRENCE DUCKWORTH (b. 1870)

A Critical Study of the Collection of Crania of Aboriginal Australians in the Cambridge University Museum. 1894.

EDWIN SIDNEY HARTLAND (b. 1848)

The Legend of Perseus. A Study in Tradition. 1894.

SIR WILLIAM RIDGEWAY (1853–1926)

The Origin of Metallic Currency and Weight Standards. Cambridge, 1892.

SIR JAMES GEORGE FRAZER (b. 1854)

Totemism. 1887.
The Golden Bough. A Study in Comparative Religion. 2 vols. 1890.

Sir Charles Hercules Read (1857–1929)

Notes and Queries on Anthropology. 1892. [Ed. by Read.]

[See O. M. Dalton, Sir Hercules Read, 1930.]

Samuel Alexander (1859–1938)

Moral Order and Progress. An Analysis of Ethical Conception. 1889.

Alfred Cort Haddon (1855–1940)

The Study of Man. 1898.   F. P.

IV. ECONOMICS AND POLITICAL THEORY

(1) General Works of Reference

A Bibliography of Political Theory. Hist. Ass. 1916.

Green, S. A Bibliography of Public Administration. 1926.

Williams, J. B. Guide to the Printed Materials for English Social and Economic History, 1750–1850. 2 vols. New York, 1926.

Bowman, E. F. An Introduction to Political Science. 1927. [Includes bibliography.]

A London Bibliography of the Social Sciences. Ed. B. M. Headicar and C. Fuller, 4 vols. 1931–2. [Also supplements.]

(2) Agriculture, Mining and Fisheries

Edwards, G. Radical Means of Counteracting the Present Scarcity and Preventing Famine; including the Proposal of a Maximum. 1801.

Fullarton, William. A Letter to Lord Carrington, 1801. [On converting pasture to tillage.]

Heslop, Luke. A Comparative Statement of Food from Arable and Grass Land. 1801.

Howlett, John. An Inquiry concerning the Influence of Tithes upon Agriculture. 1801.

Lawn, Buxton. The Corn Trade Investigated. Import and Export Laws. Salisbury, 1801 (new edn).

Marshall, W. On the Appropriation and Enclosure of Commonable Lands. 1801.

—— A Treatise on the Landed Property of England. 1804.

—— A Review and Complete Account of the Reports to the Board of Agriculture. 5 vols. 1808–17.

Sinclair, Sir J. Observations on the Means of enabling a Cottager to keep a Cow by the Produce of a Small Portion of Arable Land. 1801.

—— Essays on Miscellaneous Subjects. 1802. [On agriculture.]

—— An Account of the Systems of Husbandry adopted in the more Improved Districts of Scotland. 2 vols. Edinburgh, 1812.

Sinclair, Sir J. General View of the Agricultural State and Political Circumstances of Scotland. Edinburgh, 1814.

—— The Code of Agriculture. 1817.

Young, Arthur. An Inquiry into the Propriety of applying Wastes to the Maintenance of the Poor. Bury St Edmunds, 1801.

—— General Report on Inclosures. 1807.

—— On the Advantages which have resulted from the Establishment of the Board of Agriculture. 1809.

—— On the Husbandry of Three Celebrated British Farmers, Messrs Bakewell, Arbuthnot and Ducket. 1811.

Bartley, Nehemiah. Observations on the Conversion of Pasture Land into Tillage and on the Potatoe as Food for Sheep. Bath, 1802.

Bell, B. Essays on Agriculture. Plan for the Improvement of Land in Great Britain. Edinburgh, 1802.

Fraser, R. Gleanings in Ireland, particularly respecting its Agriculture, Mines and Fisheries. 1802.

Hall, C. A Concise Treatise on destroying Heath, improving Moss, etc. Edinburgh, 1802.

Whately, G. N. Hints for the Improvement of the Irish Fishery. 1803.

Thompson, T. Reasons for giving Land to Cottagers to keep Cows. Hull, 1803.

Carpenter, J. A Treatise on Agriculture. Stourbridge, 1803.

Forsyth, R. The Principles and Practice of Agriculture explained. 2 vols. Edinburgh, 1804.

Dickson, R. W. Practical Agriculture. 2 vols. 1805.

Luccock, J. The Nature and Properties of Wool. The English Fleece. Hull, 1805.

—— An Essay on Wool, containing a Particular Account of the English Fleece. 1809.

Parkinson, R. The English Practice of Agriculture exemplified in the Management of a Farm in Ireland. 1806. [On the estate of the Earl of Conyngham in Meath.]

Naismith, J. Elements of Agriculture. 1807.

Comber, W. T. An Inquiry into the State of National Subsistence. 1808.

Bakewell, R. Observations on the Influence of Soil and Climate upon Wool. With Notes by Lord Somerville. 1808.

Curwers, J. C. Hints on the Economy of feeding Stock and bettering the Condition of the Poor. 1808; 1809 (enlarged).

Bellew, R. Thoughts and Suggestions for Improving the Conditions of the Irish Peasantry. 1808.

Walker, J. Essays on Natural History and Rural Economy. Edinburgh, 1808.

Waters, B. Letters upon the Subject of the Herring Fishery. Edinburgh, 1809.

Adams, G. A Treatise on a New System of Agriculture and the Feeding of Stock. 1810.

Parkinson, R. A Treatise on the Breeding and Management of Live Stock. 2 vols. 1810.

Brown, R. A Treatise on Agriculture and Rural Affairs. Edinburgh, 1811.

Coventry, A. Notes on the Culture and Cropping of Arable Land. 3 vols. 1811.

Bernard, Sir T. An Account of the Supply of Fish for the Manufacturing Poor. 1813.

—— On the Supply of Employment in Fisheries, Manufactures, and the Cultivation of Waste Lands. 1813.

—— Case of the Silk Duties. 1817.

Davy, Sir Humphry. Elements of Agricultural Chemistry. 1813.

Greaves, W. A Treatise on Natural and Practical Agriculture. 1814.

Hall, G. W. Letters on the Importance of Encouraging Corn and Wool in the United Kingdom. [1815.]

Simpson, T. A Defence of the Landowners and Farmers of Great Britain and an Exposition of the Heavy Parliamentary and Local Taxation under which they labour. 1814.

Torrens, R. An Essay on the External Corn Trade. 1815.

—— A Letter to the Earl of Liverpool on the State of the Agriculture of the United Kingdom. 1816.

Crombie, A. Letters on the Present State of the Agricultural Interest. 1816.

Jacob, W. An Inquiry into the Causes of Agricultural Distress. 1816.

—— Report on the Trade in Foreign Corn. 1826.

—— Observations on the Benefits arising from Cultivation of Poor Soils by Pauper Labour in Holland. 1826.

Vanderstraeten, F. Improved Agriculture, and the Suppression of Smuggling, Property-Tax, and Poor's Rates. 1816.

Blane, Sir Gilbert. Inquiry into the Causes and Remedies of the Late and Present Scarcity and High prices of Provisions. 1817.

Burrard, T. On the Supply of Employment and Subsistence for the Labouring Classes in Fisheries, Manufactures, and the Cultivation of Waste Lands. 1817.

Rigby, E. Holkham: its Agriculture. Norwich, 1817.

Barton, J. An Inquiry into the Causes of the Progressive Depreciation of Agricultural Labour in Modern Times. 1820.

—— An Inquiry into the Expediency of the Restrictions on Importation of Foreign Corn. 1833.

Edmonston, A. Observations on the Nature and Extent of the Cod Fishery of the Shetland and Orkney Islands. Edinburgh, 1820.

Tooke, T. On the Currency in connection with the Corn Trade and on the Corn Laws. 1820.

Burroughs, E. A View of the State of Agriculture in Ireland. 1821.

Stourton, W., Baron. Two Letters on the Distresses of Agriculture. 2 vols. 1821.

—— A Third Letter to the Earl of Liverpool in which the Justice, Policy, and Necessity of Legislative Relief to the Agricultural Distresses of the Country are considered. 1821.

—— Further Considerations addressed to the Earl of Liverpool on Agricultural Relief. 1822.

Cleghorn, J. An Essay on the Depressed State of Agriculture. Edinburgh, 1822.

—— System of Agriculture. 1831.

Cobbett, William. Cobbett's Gridiron: written to warn Farmers of their Danger, and to put All Classes of the Community on their Guard. 1822.

—— Cobbett's Cottage Economy. 1822.

—— A Treatise on Cobbett's Corn. 1828.

—— Rural Rides. 1830.

—— Cobbett's Legacy to Labourers. 1835.

Finlayson, J. Treatise on Agricultural Subjects. Glasgow, 1822.

—— The British Farmer. 1825.

Lowe, Joseph. The Present State of England in Regard to Agriculture. 1822.

Pontey, W. The Rural Improver. 1822.

Rainier, J. S. A Synopsis of the Price of Wheat from the Commencement of the 13th Century to the End of 1822. 1823.

Whitmore, W. W. A Letter on the Present State and Future Prospects of Agriculture. 1823.

Hayward, J. On the Science of Agriculture. 1825.

West, Sir E. Price of Corn and Wages of Labour. 1826.

Bischoff, J. The Wool Question considered. 1828.

—— A Comprehensive History of the Woollen and Worsted Manufactures. 1842.

—— Foreign Tariffs: their Injurious Effect on the Woollen Manufactures. 1843.

Hopkins, T. On Rent of Land and its Influence. 1828.

Hogg, James. The Shepherd's Calendar. Edinburgh, 1829.

Wells, S. The History of the Drainage of the Great Level of the Fens called Bedford Level. 1830.

Loudon, J. C. An Encyclopaedia of Agriculture. 1831.

Oliver, T. Notes on Agricultural Topics. 4 vols. Edinburgh, [1831].

Place, Francis. An Essay on the State of the Country in Respect to the Condition and Conduct of the Husbandry Labourers. [1831.]

Scrope, G. P. A Letter on the Illegal Practice of Making up Wages out of Rates, to which is owing the Misery of the Agricultural Peasantry. 1831.

—— A Plea for the Rights of Industry in Ireland. 1848.

Wakefield, E. G. Swing Unmasked, or the Causes of Rural Incendiarism. 1831.

Hill, Sir R. Home Colonies. A Plan for the Extinction of Pauperism and Diminution of Crime. 1832.

Jackson, J. Essays on Agricultural Subjects. Edinburgh, 1833.

Birch, S. Agricultural Distress. An Essay on the Baneful Effects of Absenteeism. 1834.

[Burke, J. F.] British Husbandry: exhibiting the Farming Practice in Various Parts of the United Kingdom. 3 vols. 1834–41.

Low, D. Elements of Practical Agriculture. Edinburgh, 1834.

—— On Landed Property and the Economy of Estates. 1844.

Lefevre, C. G. (Viscount Eversley). Remarks on the Present State of Agriculture. 1836.

Hunt, W. State and Prospects of British Agriculture. 1837 (2nd edn).

Whitlaw, C. A Short Review of the Causes and Effects of the Present Distress. [1839.]

Howitt, W. The Rural Life of England. 2 vols. 1838.

Roberts, O. O. Hints on Agricultural Economy as the Antidote to Agricultural Distress. 1838.

Crawford, W. S. A Defence of the Small Farmers of Ireland. 1839.

Drummond, H. The Condition of the Agricultural Classes of Great Britain and Ireland. 2 vols. 1842.

O'Connor, Feargus. A Practical Work on the Management of Small Farms. 1843.

Hirst, W. History of the Woollen Trade. 1844.

Osborne, Lord Sidney Godolphin. A View of the Low Moral and Physical Condition of the Agricultural Labourer. 1844.

Stephens, Henry. The Book of the Farm. 3 vols. 1844.

Nicholls, Sir G. On the Condition of the Agricultural Labourer. 1846.

Perry, G. W. The Peasantry of England. 1846.

Tuckett, John Debell. A History of the Past and Present State of the Labouring Population, including the Progress of Agriculture, Manufactures, and Commerce. 2 vols. 1846.

Brown, W. K. On the Extension of the British and Irish Fisheries. 1847.

Johnson, C. W. Modern Agricultural Improvements. 1847.

Thornton, W. T. A Plea for Peasant Proprietors. 1848.

Caird, Sir J. High Farming under Liberal Covenants the Best Substitute for Protection. Edinburgh, 1849 (5 edns).

—— The Plantation Scheme, or the West of Ireland as a Field for Investment. 1851.

—— English Agriculture in 1850–1. 1851.

—— The Irish Land Question. 1867.

—— Our Daily Food: its Price and Sources of Supply. 1868.

—— General View of British Agriculture. 1878.

—— The Landed Interest and the Supply of Food. [1878.]

—— The British Land Question. 1881.

Bartlett, T. A Treatise on British Mining. 1850.

Cotterill, C. F. Agricultural Distress: its Cause and Remedy. 1850.

—— Letter to Lord John Russell M.P. Public Granaries and the Cycle of the Seasons in Connection with Trade and Agriculture. 1856.

Hancock, W. N. Impediments to the Prosperity of Ireland. 1850.

Macdonald, D. G. F. What the Farmers may do with the Land. 1852.

Donaldson, J. Agricultural Biography. Life and Writings of the British Authors on Agriculture from 1480 to the Present Time. 1854.

Miller, T. The Agricultural and Social State of Ireland in 1858. 1858.

—— Historical Review of Model Farming in Ireland. 1859.

Pike, J. R. Britain's Metal Mines. 1860.

Bland, W. The Principles of Agriculture. 1864.

Copland, S. Agriculture, Ancient and Modern. 2 vols. 1866.

Rogers, J. E. Thorold. A History of Agriculture and Prices in England. 7 vols. Oxford, 1866–1902.

Bristow, H. W. Underground Life, or Mines and Miners. 1869.

Kebbel, T. E. The Agricultural Labourer. 1870.

Leslie, T. E. Cliffe. Land Systems and Industrial Economy of Ireland, England, and Continental Countries. 1870.

Nasse, E. On the Agricultural Community of the Middle Ages, and Inclosures of the 16th Century in England. 1871.

Heath, F. G. Peasant Life in the West of England. 1872.

—— The English Peasantry. 1874.

Ramsay, A. History of the Highland and Agricultural Society of Scotland. 1879.

Chaytor, H. Agriculture and Trade Depression. 1880.

Brodrick, G. C. English Land and English Landlords. 1881.

Shaw-Lefevre, Sir J. G. English and Irish Land Questions. 1881.

Baker, T. H. Records of the Seasons, Prices of Agricultural Products, and Phenomena observed in the British Isles. [1883.]

Elliot, T. J. The Land Question: its Examination and Solution. [1884.]

Bear, W. E. The British Farmer and his Competitors. [1888.]

Prothero, R. E. (Baron Ernle). The Pioneers and Progress of English Farming. 1888; 1912 (rev. as English Farming, Past and Present).

Scrivener, S. C. Our Fields and Cities, or Misdirected Industry. 1891.

Dowsett, C. F. et al. Land: its Attractions and Riches. 1892.

Tream, W. Elements of Agriculture. 1892.

Graham, P. A. The Rural Exodus. 1892.

Garnier, R. M. History of the English Landed Interest. 2 vols. 1892–3.

—— Annals of the British Peasantry. 1895.

Heath, R. The English Peasant. 1893.

Hasbach, W. A History of the English Agricultural Labourer. 1894.

Jefferies, Richard. The Toilers of the Field. 1894.

Russell, H. A. (Duke of Bedford). A Great Agricultural Estate. Woburn, 1897.

Channing, F. A. The Truth about Agricultural Depression. 1897.

Williams, E. E. The Foreigner in the Farmyard. 1897.

Clarke, Sir E. History of the Board of Agriculture, 1793–1822. 1898.

Haggard, Sir Henry Rider. A Farmer's Year: being his Commonplace Book for 1898. 1899.

(3) BANKING

Thornton, H. The Impolicy of Returning Bankers to Parliament. 1802.

King, Peter (Baron King). Thoughts on the Restriction of Payments in Specie at the Banks. 1803.

Boase, H. A Letter to Lord King in Defence of the Banks of England and Ireland. 1804.

—— The Life of Abraham Newland, Cashier of the Bank of England. 1808.

Stewart, Sir J. Principles of Banks and Banking. 1810.

Crombie, A. A Letter to D. Ricardo Esq. on his Pamphlet on the Depreciation of Bank Notes. 1813.

Cobbett, William. Paper against Gold, or the History and Mystery of the Bank of England. 1821.

Joplin, T. Essay on the Principles and Practice of Banking. Newcastle-on-Tyne, 1822 (3 edns).

Ricardo, David. Plan for a National Bank. 1824.

Crutwell, R. A Treatise on the State of the Currency. 1825.

—— The System of Country Banking defended. 1828.

Parnell, Sir Henry (Baron Congleton). Observations on Paper Money, Banking, and Overtrading. 1827.

—— A Plain Statement of the Power of the Bank of England and the Use it has made of it. 1832 (anon.).

Gilbart, J. W. A Practical Treatise on Banking. 1828.

—— The History, Principles, and Practice of Banking. 2 vols. 1834.

—— The Logic of Banking. 1859.

—— Collected Works. 6 vols. 1865.

[McCulloch, J. R.] Historical Sketch of the Bank of England. 1831.

Stuchey, V. Thoughts on the Improvement of the System of Country Banking. 1834.

Torrens, R. A Letter to Viscount Melbourne on the Money Market and Banking Reform. 1837. [Supplement, 1837.]

—— The Principles and Practical Operation of Sir Robert Peel's Bill of 1844. 1848.

Norman, G. W. Remarks upon some Prevalent Errors [on] Currency and Banking. 1838.

Bailey, S. A Defence of Joint Stock Banks and Country Issues. 1840.

Bell, G. M. The Country Banks and the Currency. 1841.

Peel, Sir R. Speech on the Renewal of the Bank Charter. 1844.

Baring, A. (Baron Ashburton). The Commercial and Financial Crisis considered. 1847.

Francis, J. History of the Bank of England. 2 vols. [1847].

Wilson, J. Capital, Currency, and Banking. 1847.

Macleod, H. D. The Theory and Practice of Banking. 2 vols. 1855–6.

—— The Elements of Banking. 1878.

Arbuthnot, G. Sir Robert Peel's Act of 1844 regulating the Issue of Bank Notes vindicated. 1857.

Byles, Sir J. B. A Treatise of the Law of Bills of Exchange. 1858.

Hankey, T. Banking: its Utility and Economy. 1859.

Guthrie, C. Bank Monopoly the Cause of Commercial Crises. 1864.

Crump, A. The English Management of Banks. 1866.

—— The Key to the Position and Progress from 1860 to 1880 of the London Joint Stock Banks. 1883.

Seyd, E. The London Banking and Banker's Clearing House System. [1872.]

—— The Bank of Issue Question. 1875.

—— The Bank of England Note Issue and its Error. 1879.

Bagehot, Walter. Lombard Street. 1873.

[Gairdner, C.] The Rate of Discount and the Bank Acts. [1873.]

Palgrave, Sir R. H. I. Notes on Banking. 1873.

—— Analysis of the Transactions of the Bank of England, 1844–72. 1874.

—— The Progress of Banking in Great Britain and Ireland. 6 vols. 1899–1918.

—— Bank Rate and the Money Market in England, France, Germany, Belgium and Holland, 1844–90. 1903.

Somers, R. The Scotch Banks and System of Issue. Edinburgh, 1873.

Grenfell, H. R. Banking and Currency. 1875.

Price, F. G. H. A Handbook of Banking and London Bankers. 1876.

Wilson, A. J. Banking Reform. 1879.

Rae, G. The Country Banker. 1885.

Foxwell, H. S. The Social Aspect of Banking. 1886.

Hankey, T. Principles of Banking. 1887.

Rogers, J. E. Thorold. The First Nine Years of the Bank of England. 1887.

Goschen, G. J. (Viscount Goschen). Speech on the Insufficiency of our Cash Reserves and Stock of Gold. 1891.

Wolff, H. W. People's Banks. 1896.

Turner, B. B. Chronicles of the Bank of England. 1897.

(4) MONEY AND MONETARY QUESTIONS

Boyd, W. A Letter to Pitt on the Stoppage of Issues in Specie [and] the Prices of Provisions. 1801.

Baring, Sir F. Observations on the Publication of W. Boyd Esq. M.P. 1801.

Trend, W. The Effect of Paper Money on the Price of Provisions. 1801.

Surr, T. S. Refutation of Misrepresentations as to the Influence of Bank Notes upon Prices. 1801.

Drury, D. Thoughts on the Precious Metals. 1801.

Thornton, H. An Inquiry into the Nature and Effects of the Paper Credit of Great Britain. 1802.

King, P. (Baron). Thoughts on the Restriction of Payments in Specie at the Banks of England and Ireland. 1803.

Hatchett, C. Experiments and Observations on the Comparative Wear of Gold. 1803.

Craufurd, G. The Doctrine of Equivalents. 2 pts, Rotterdam, 1803.

Wheatley, J. Remarks on Currency and Commerce. 1803.

—— An Essay on the Theory of Money and Principles of Commerce. 2 vols. 1807–22.

—— A Letter to Lord Grenville on the Distress of the Country. 1816.

Parnell, Sir Henry (Baron Congleton). Observations on the State of the Currency in Ireland. Dublin, 1804.

—— Principles of Currency and Exchange, Dublin, 1805.

Jenkinson, R. B. (Earl of Liverpool). A Treatise on the Coins of the Realm: in a Letter to the King. Oxford, 1805.

Smith, T. Essay on the Theory of Money and Exchange. 1807.

Blake, W. Observations on the Principles which Regulate the Course of Exchange and on the Present Depreciated State of the Currency. 1810.

—— Observations on the Effects produced by the Expenditure of Government during the Restriction of Cash Payments. 1823.

Bosanquet, C. Practical Observations on the Report of the Bullion Committee. 1810.

Cobbett, William. Paper against Gold. 1810.

Cock, S. An Examination of the Report of the Bullion Committee. 1810. Supplement, 1810.

Huskisson, W. The Question concerning the Depreciation of our Currency. 1810.

Musket, R. An Enquiry into the Effects of the Bank Restriction Bill. 1810 (bis).

Ricardo, David. The High Price of Bullion. 1810 (3 edns); 1811 (with appendix).

—— Reply to Mr Bosanquet's Practical Observations on the Bullion Committee. 1811.

—— Proposals for an Economical and Secure Currency. 1816.

Maitland, J. (Earl of Lauderdale). The Depreciation of the Paper Currency. 1812.

—— Further Considerations on the State of the Currency. Edinburgh, 1823.

Torrens, R. An Essay on Money and Paper Currency. 1812.

—— The Principles and Practical Operation of Sir Robert Peel's Act of 1844 explained and defended. 1848.

Attwood, T. Letter to N. Vansittart on the Creation of Money and on its Action upon National Prosperity. Birmingham, 1817.

—— Observations on Currency, Population, and Pauperism. Birmingham, 1818.

Ruding, Rogers. Annals of the Coinage of Great Britain and its Dependencies. 4 vols. 1817–9.

Tooke, T. On the Currency in Connection with the Corn Trade and on the Corn Laws. 1820.

—— Considerations on the State of the Currency, 1826.

—— An Inquiry into the Currency Principle and the Connection of Currency with Prices. 1844.

—— A History of Prices. 6 vols. 1838–57. [Vols. v–vi with W. Newmarch.]

Cruttwell, R. A Treatise on the State of the Currency. 1825.

Graham, Sir James Robert George. Corn and Currency. 1826.

Taylor, J. An Essay on Money. 1830.

—— An Essay on the Standard and Measure of Value. 1832.

—— Catechism of the Currency and Exchanges. 3 vols. 1836.

—— An Essay on Money; its Origin and Use. 1844.

Whately, Richard. Easy Lessons on Money Matters. 1835.

[Bailey, S.] Money and its Vicissitudes in Value as they affect National Industry, and Pecuniary Contracts. 1837.

Senior, Nassau W. Three Lectures on the Value of Money. 1840.

Jones, C. Letter in Reply to the Doctrine of G. W. Norman: On Money, etc. 1841.

Norman, G. W. Letter to Charles Wood on Money and the Means of economising the Use of it. 1841.

Pedie, J. A Philosophical Enquiry into the Nature of a Sound Currency. Edinburgh, 1841.

Wade, J. Principles of Money. 1842.

Cowell, J. W. Letters to the Rt Hon. F. T. Baring on Paper Currency. 1843.

—— Further Letters on Currency. 1858.

Twiss, Sir Travers. On Money and Currency. Oxford, 1843.

Fullarton J. On the Regulation of Currencies. 1844.

Joplin, T. Currency Reform. 1844.

Alison, Sir A. Free Trade and a Fettered Currency. Edinburgh, 1847.

Gray, John. The Currency Question. 1847.

—— Lectures on the Nature and Use of Money. Edinburgh, 1848.

Thinbleby, J. What is Money? 1849.

—— A Lecture on the Currency. 1850.

Combe, G. The Currency Question. 1856.

—— Refutation refuted. A Reply in answer to Pamphlets on the Currency Question. 1856. [Replies to criticisms of The Currency Question.]

Cook, G. H. Currency Principles and Currency Taxation. 1856.

Mills, R. H. The Principles of Currency and Banking. 1857.

McCulloch, J. R. A Treatise on Metallic and Paper Money and Banks. 1858.

Sealy, H. N. A Treatise on Coins, Currency, and Banking. 1858.

Clarke, H. What is Money? Falmouth, 1865.

Nicholson, N. A. Observations on Coinage and our Present Monetary System. 1868.

Seyd, E. Bullion and Foreign Exchanges. 1868.

Bagehot, W. International Coinage. 1869.

—— On the Depreciation of Silver. 1877.

Price, Bonamy. Principles of Currency. 1869.

—— Currency and Banking. 1876.

Crump, A. The Key to the London Money Market. [1871.]

—— An Investigation into the Causes of the Great Fall in Prices which took place coincidently with the Demonetisation of Silver by Germany. 1889.

Jevons, W. S. Money and the Mechanism of Exchange. 1875.

—— Investigations in Currency and Finance. 1884.

Gibbs, H. H. (Baron Aldenham). Silver and Gold. 1879.

—— The Double Standard. 1881.

Barclay, R. Essays and Letters on Bimetallism. 1881.

—— The Silver Question and the Gold Question. 1885.

—— The Disturbance in the Standard of Value. 1893.

Barbour, Sir D. The Theory of Bimetallism. 1885.

—— The Currency Question. 1894.

Del Mar, A. The Science of Money. 1885.

—— Money and Civilisation. 1886.

Smith, Samuel. The Bimetallic Question. 1887.

Frewen, Moreton. The Economic Crisis. 1888.

Jordan, W. L. The Standard of Value. 1888.

Nicholson, J. S. A Treatise on Money and Essays on Monetary Problems. 1888.

Wicksteed P. H. Getting and Spending. 1888.

Norman, J. H. A Colloquy upon the Science of Money. 1889.

—— The Science of Money. 1895.

Clare, G. A Money Market Primer. 1891.

Cunningham, W. The Use and Abuse of Money. 1891.

Giffen, Sir R. The Case against Bimetallism. 1892.

Balfour, Arthur James (Earl Balfour). The Currency Question. [1893.]

Walsh, W. J. Bimetallism and Monometallism. 1893.

Beeton, H. R. The Case for Monetary Reform. 1894.

Helm, E. The Joint Standard. 1894.

Macleod, H. D. Bimetallism. 1894.

Gibbs, H. C. (Baron Hunsdon). A Bimetallic Primer. 1894.

Molesworth, Sir G. L. Silver and Gold: the Money of the World. Manchester, 1894.

Foxwell, H. S. The Monetary Situation. 1895.

Suinett, A. P. The Money of the World. Allahabad, 1895.

Cuthbertson, C. A Sketch of the Currency Question. [1896?]

Edgcumbe, Sir R. P. Popular Fallacies regarding Bimetallism. 1895.

Shaw, W. A. The History of Currency, 1252–1894. [1895.]

Price, L. L. F. R. Money and its Relation to Prices. 1896.

Darwin, L. Bimetallism. 1897.

(5) PAUPERISM AND POPULATION

Eden, Sir F. M. Observations on Friendly Societies. [Relief of] Industrial Classes in Sickness and Old Age. 1801.

Hill, Sir John. The Means of Reforming the Poor by the Prevention of Poverty. 1801.

Murray, T. A. Remarks on the Poor of the Metropolis and Contagious Diseases. 1801.

Wansey, H. Thoughts on Poorhouses, particularly at Salisbury. 1801.

Van Oven, J. Letters on the Present State of the Jewish Poor in the Metropolis. 1802.

Peele, F. Social Wreckage. A Review of the Laws of England as they affect the Poor. 1803.

Hall, C. Observations on the Principal Conclusions in Mr Malthus's Essay on Population. 1805.

Rose, G. Observations on the Poor Laws. 1805.

Colquhoun, P. A Treatise on Indigence and Ameliorating the Condition of the Poor. 1806.

Malthus, T. R. Reply to Objections against the Essay on the Principles of Population. 1806.

—— A Letter to S. Whitbread on his Proposed Bill for the Amendment of the Poor Law. 1807.

[Hazlitt, W.] A Reply to the Essay on Population. 1807.

Weyland, J. A Short Inquiry into the Policy, Humanity, and Past Effects of the Poor Law. 1807.

—— The Principles of Population and Production. 1816.

Myers, T. An Essay on Improving the Condition of the Poor. 1814.

Clark, W. Thoughts on the Management and Relief of the Poor. Bath, 1815.

Clarkson, W. An Inquiry into the Causes of the Increase of Pauperism, with a Remedy. 1816.

Grahame, J. An Inquiry into the Principles of Population. 1816.

Parker, W. A Plan for the Improvement of the State of the Poor in Ireland. Cork, 1816.

Courtenay, T. P. A Treatise upon the Poor Laws. 1818.

Ensor, G. An Inquiry into the Population of Nations. 1818.

Gascoigne, H. B. On Pauperism. 1818.

Holroyd, J. B. (Earl of Sheffield). Observations on the Impolicy of the Poor Law. 1818.

'Purves, George' (i.e. Simon Gray). Gray versus Malthus. The Principles of Production and Population investigated. 1818.

Roberts, S. A Defence of the Poor Law. Sheffield, 1819.

—— England's Glory, or the Good Old Poor Law. 1836.

—— The Pauper's Advocate. 1841.

Godwin, W. Of Population: in Answer to Malthus. 1820.

Read, S. Argument on Population in Answer to Mr Malthus's Theory. 1821.

—— Thoughts on Man. 1831.

Place, Francis. Illustrations and Proofs of the Principles of Population. 1822.

Everett, A. H. New Ideas on Population. 1823.

Booth, D. A Letter to the Rev. T. R. Malthus. Being an Answer to Godwin on Population. 1823.

Sadler, M. T. Ireland: its Evils and their Remedies. 1828.

—— The Laws of Population. 2 vols. 1830.

Haworth, B. A Dissertation on the English Poor. 1829.

Horton, Sir R. J. W. The Causes and Remedies of Pauperism. 5 pts, 1830–1.

Light, A. W. Plan for Amelioration of the Condition of the Poor (particularly Ireland). 1830.

Baxter, S. S. The Poor Laws stated and examined. 1831.

Edmonds, T. R. Enquiry into the Principles of Population. 1832.

Owen, R. D. Moral Physiology. 1832.

Lloyd, W. F. Two Lectures on the Checks to Population. Oxford, 1833.

—— Lectures on Population, Value, Poor Laws, and Rent. 1837.

Longfield, M. Four Lectures on the Poor Laws. Dublin, 1834.

Martineau, H. Poor Laws and Paupers, illustrated. 4 vols. 1833–4.

Lewis, Sir George Cornewall. Report on the State of the Irish Poor in Great Britain. 1836.

Perceval, J. I. Observations on the New Poor Law: its Injustice. 1838.

Alison, W. P. Observations on the Management of the Poor in Scotland. Edinburgh, 1840.

Alison, Sir A. Principles of Population. 2 vols. Edinburgh, 1840.

Baxter, G. R. W. The Book of the Bastille or The History of the Working of the New Poor Law. 1841.

Chalmers, T. On the Sufficiency of the Parochial System without a Rate. 1841.

Senior, N. W. Remarks on the Opposition to the Poor Law Amendment Bill. 1841.

Crewe, Sir G. A Word for the Poor, and against the Present Poor Law. Derby, 1843.

Doubleday, T. The True Law of Population shown to be connected with the Food of the People. 1843.

Pusey, P. The Poor in Scotland. 1844.

Cochrane, G. On the Employment of the Poor in Great Britain and Ireland. 1845.

Thornton, W. T. Over-population and its Remedy. 1846.

Twiss, Sir T. Certain Tests of a Thriving Population. 1847.

Burton, J. H. Emigration in its Practical Application. Edinburgh, 1851.

Mayhew, H. London Labour and the London Poor. 4 vols. 1851–2.

Spencer, Herbert. A Theory of Population Deduced from the General Law of Animal Fertility. 1852.

Rickards, G. K. Population and Capital. 1854.

Nicholls, Sir G. A History of the English Poor Law. 3 vols. 1854.

—— A History of the Irish Poor Law. 1856.

Richmond, L. Annals of the Poor. 1864.

Begg, J. The Causes and Probable Remedies of Pauperism in Scotland. Edinburgh, 1870.

Fawcett, H. Pauperism: its Causes and Remedies. 1871.

Bartley, Sir G. C. T. The Seven Ages of a Village Pauper. 1874.

Drysdale, C. R. The Population Question. 1878.

Pretyman, J. R. Dispauperization. 1878.

Aschrott, P. F. The English Poor Law System. 1880.

Besant, A. The Law of Population: its Consequences. 1881.

Fowle, T. W. The Poor Law. 1881.

Mackay, T. The English Poor. 1889.

—— Methods of Social Reform. 1896.

Booth, William. In Darkest England and the Way out. 1890.

Locke, Sir C. S. Charity Organisation. 1890.

—— Old Age Pensions and Pauperism. 1892.

Booth, C. Pauperism. 1892.

—— The Aged Poor in England and Wales. 1894.

—— Old Age Pensions of the Aged Poor. 1899.

Green, G. History of the Poor Law. Manchester, [1894].

Chance, W. The Better Administration of the Poor Law. 1895.

Chance, W. Children under the Poor Law. 1897.

—— Our Treatment of the Poor. 1899.

Montague, F. C. The Old Poor Law and the New Socialism, or Pauperism and Taxation. 1896.

(6) SOCIALISM

Godwin, W. Thoughts on Dr Parr's Spital Sermon. 1801.

Stewart, J. The Tocsin of Social Life: addressed to the Civilised World. 1803.

Hall, C. The Effects of Civilization on the People in European States. 1805.

—— An Enquiry into the Cause of the Present Distress of the People. 1820.

Spence, T. A Receipt to make a Millennium or Happy World. 1805.

Owen, Robert. A New View of Society. 1813.

—— Lectures on an Entire New State of Society. [1830.]

—— Outline of the Rational System of Society. 1830.

—— The Crisis. 4 vols. 1832. [With R. D. Owen.]

—— The Book of the New Moral World. 2 pts, 1836–42.

—— Socialism, or the Rational System of Society. 1840.

Edwards, G. Effectual Means of Relieving the Exigencies and Grievances of the Times. 1814.

—— A Final Address on the Original Scheme and Millennium of True Policy. 1814.

—— The Five Practical Plans to meet our Present Situation. Barnard Castle, 1820.

Hamilton, J. Owenism rendered Consistent with our Civil and Religious Institutions. 1815.

Combe, A. A. The Religious Creed of the New System. 1824.

Thompson, William. An Inquiry into the Principles of the Distribution of Wealth most Conducive to Human Happiness. 1824; ed. W. Pare, 1850.

—— Labour rewarded. 1827.

—— Practical Directions for the Establishment of Communities, Co-operation, Mutual Possessions and Equality. 1830.

[Morgan, J. Minter.] The Revolt of the Bees. 1826.

Gray, J. The Social System. 1831.

—— An Efficient Remedy for the Distress of Nations. 1842.

Wayland, T. National Advancement and Happiness considered in Reference to the Equalisation of Property. 1832.

Thomson, W. The Age of Harmony, or a New System of Social Economy. 1834.

Bower, S. The Peopling of Utopia, or the Sufficiency of Socialism for Human Happiness. Bradford, 1838. [Sequel, Bradford, 1838.]

Horton, H. H. Community the only Salvation for Man. Manchester, 1838.

Hobson, J. Socialism as it is! Leeds, 1838.

Birch, E. Remarks on Socialism. 1839.

Bray, J. F. Labour's Wrongs and Labour's Remedy. Leeds, 1839.

Mathers, J. Socialism Exposed. 1839.

Buchanan, R. Socialism Vindicated. Manchester, 1840.

Doherty, H. False Association and its Remedy. A Critical Introduction to Fourier's Theory of Attractive Industry. 1840.

Mackintosh, T. S. An Inquiry into the Nature of Responsibility. Birmingham, [1840?].

Bray, C. The Philosophy of Necessity. 2 vols. 1841.

—— An Essay upon the Union of Agriculture and Manufactures. 1844.

Hennell, Mary. An Outline of the Various Social Systems and Communities; with an Introduction by C. Bray. 1844.

Ensor, G. Of Property and its Equal Distribution. 1844.

Linton, W. J., et al. The English Republic. 2 vols. 1851–4.

Ludlow, J. M. Christian Socialism. 1851.

Maurice, F. D. On the Reformation of Society. 1851.

Neale, E. V. The Features of some of the Principal Systems of Socialism. 1851.

Burton, J. H. Communism. 1854.

Jones, Ernest. Evenings with the People. 1856–7.

Dick, R. Labour: its Unequal Distribution and Unnecessary Distress. 1858.

Sargant, W. L. Social Innovators and their Schemes. 1858.

Marse, F. The Causes of Social Revolt. 1872.

Kaufmann, M. Socialism: its Nature, its Dangers, and its Remedies considered. 1874.

—— Socialism and Communism. 1883.

Hyndman, H. M. The Historical Basis of Socialism in England. 1883.

—— The Economics of Socialism. 1896.

Carpenter, Edward. Towards Democracy. 1883.

Bramwell, G. W. W., Baron. Laissez Faire. 1884.

Campbell, W. H. P. The Robbery of the Poor. 1884.

Fabian Tracts. 1884– . [By members of the Fabian Soc.]

Rae, J. Contemporary Socialism. 1884.

Spencer, Herbert. The Man versus the State. 1884.

Hutchinson, H. Property: a Bottom Enquiry into its Management in England, by Plain Diogenes Hunt. 1885–6.

O'Brien, J. Bronterre. The Rise, Progress and Phases of Human Slavery. 1885.

Pearson, Karl. The Moral Basis of Socialism. [1885?]

—— Socialism in Theory and Practice. [1887.]

Herbert, G. R. C. (Earl of Pembroke). Liberty and Socialism. [1885.]

Montague, F. C. The Limits of Individual Liberty. 1885.

Besant, Annie. The Evolution of Society. 1886.

—— Socialism: for and against. 1887. [With C. Bradlaugh.]

Graham, W. The Social Problem. 1886.

Phillips, W. A. Labor, Land, and Law. 1886.

Kirkup, T. An Inquiry into Socialism. 1887.

Lacy, G. Liberty and Law. 1888.

Donisthorpe, W. Socialism analyzed. 1888.

—— Individualism: a System of Politics. 1889.

Fabian Society. Essays in Socialism. 1889.

Clarke, W. The Basis of Socialism: Industrial. 1889.

Webb, Sidney (Baron Passfield). The Progress of Socialism. 1890.

—— What Socialism means. 1893.

[Reeves, W. P.] Communism and Socialism. Christchurch, N.Z., 1890.

Mackay, T. et al. A Plea for Liberty. 1891.

Maxwell, D. Stepping Stones to Socialism. Hull, 1891.

Ritchie, D. G. The Principles of State Interference. 1891.

Abraham, W. H. The Studies of a Socialist Parson. Hull, 1892.

Godard, J. G. Poverty: its Genesis and Exodus. 1892.

O'Brien, M. D. Socialism tested by Facts. 1892.

Bax, E. Belfort. The Ethics of Socialism. 1893.

—— The Religion of Socialism. 1893.

Kenworthy, J. C. The Anatomy of Misery. 1893.

Mallock, W. H. Labour and the Popular Welfare. 1893.

Morris, William. True and False Society. 1893.

—— Monopoly, or how Labour is robbed. 1893.

—— Useful Work versus Useless Toil. 1893.

—— Signs of Change. Seven Lectures. 1896.

—— Socialism: its Growth and Outcome. 1893. [With E. B. Bax.]

Shaw, George Bernard. The Impossibilities of Anarchism. 1893.

—— A Refutation of Anarchism. [N.d.]

Carruthers, J. Socialism and Radicalism. 1894.

Nicholson, J. S. Historical Progress and Ideal Socialism. 1894.

—— Strikes and Social Problems. 1896.

Bliss, W. D. P. A Handbook of Socialism. 1895.

Carr, G. S. Social Evolution and the Evolution of Socialism. 1895.

Gonner, Sir Edward Carter Kersey. The Socialist State. 1895.

—— The Social Philosophy of Rodbertus. 1899.

Hake, A. E. and Weisslau, O. E. The Coming Individualism. 1895.

Laycock, F. N. Economics and Socialism. 1895.

Wrixon, Sir H. Socialism. Being Notes on a Political Tour. 1896.

Mann, T. The Socialists' Programme. Manchester, 1896.

Wallace, Alfred Russel *et al.* Forecasts of the Coming Century. Manchester, 1897.

(7) TAXATION AND FINANCE

Coad, J. The True Interest of the United Kingdom proved in Two Plans of Finance. 1803.

—— A New Plan of Taxation. 1807.

Hamilton, R. Inquiry concerning the Rise and Progress of the National Debt. 1813.

[Slaney, B. A.] Some Facts shewing the Vast Burthen of the Poor's Rate in a Particular District. 1817.

Ricardo, David. Essay on the Funding System. Ency. Brit. 6th edn, 1821.

Cohen, B. Compendium of Finance. 1822.

Richards, J. A Letter on the Agricultural Distress: Unequal Systems of Taxation. 1822.

Stourton, W., Baron. Trade and Finance. 1822.

Wilson, Robert. Disquisitions on the Corn Laws. Hawick, 1826.

Spence, G. A Letter to the Earl of Liverpool. [1826?] [On taxation.]

Grenville, William Wyndham, Baron. Essay on the Supposed Advantages of a Sinking Fund. 1828.

Boyd, W. Reflections on the Financial System of Great Britain. 1828.

—— Observations on Lord Grenville's Essay on the Sinking Fund. 1828.

Courtenay, T. P. A Letter to Lord Grenville on the Sinking Fund. 1828.

Cazenove, J. Questions respecting the National Debt and Taxation, stated and answered. 1829.

[Sleeman, Sir W. H.] On Taxes and Public Resources. 1829.

Maitland, J. (Earl of Lauderdale). Three Letters to the Duke of Wellington [on] the Sinking Fund Fallacy. 1829.

Parnell, Sir H. (Baron Congleton). On Financial Reform. 1830.

Atkinson, W. The Principle of Protecting Home Trade or the Principle of Free Trade refuted. 1833.

[Sayer, B.] An Attempt to shew the Justice and Expediency of substituting an Income or Property Tax for the Present Taxes. 1833.

Browning, G. The Domestic and Financial System of Great Britain. 1834.

Martineau, H. Illustrations of Taxation. 2 pts, 1834.

Dickinson, G. A New System, or Taxation no longer a Burthen. [1835?]

Crawford, J. Taxes on Knowledge. 1836.

Gordon, S. Advice to the Reformers in Reference to the Taxes on Food. 1836.

Taylor, J. Who pays the Taxes? 1841.

Hodgskin, T. On Free Trade and Corn Laws. 1843.

—— A Letter on Free Trade and Slavery. [1848.]

Buchanan, D. Inquiry into the Taxation and Commercial Policy of Great Britain. Edinburgh, 1844.

McCulloch, J. R. A Treatise on the Principles of Taxation and the Funding System. 1845.

Urquhart, D. Wealth and Want, or Taxation as influencing Private Riches and Public Liberty. 1845.

Babbage, C. Thoughts on the Principles of Taxation, with Reference to a Property Tax. 1848.

Cobham, S. Direct Taxation. 1848.

Watt, R. A Summary Practical Elucidation of National Economy in Support of Direct Taxation. 1848.

Norman, G. W. An Examination of some Prevailing Opinions as to the Pressure of Taxation in this and Other Countries. 1850.

Scrope, G. P. Don't tax but untax! 1850.

Gibbon, A. Taxation. Its Nature and Properties. 1851.

Heathfield, R. Fallacies of Taxation. 1851.

Gisborne, T. Thoughts on an Income Tax and a Property Tax. 1852.

Banfield, T. Free Production having freed Trade the Pressure of Taxation exposed. 1852.

Tayler, W. The History of the Taxation of England. 1853–4.

Capps, E. The National Debt financially considered. 1857.

[Tennant, C.] The People's Blue Book. Taxation as it is. 1857.

Smith, G. H. The Rights of Rich and Poor: Just Taxation. Liverpool, [1859?].

Courtney, L. H. (Baron Courtney). Direct Taxation: an Inquiry. 1860.

Baxter, R. D. The Budget and the Income Tax. 1860.

—— The National Income. 1868.

—— The Taxation of the United Kingdom. 1869.

—— National Debts of the World. 1871.

Levi, Leone. On Taxation. 1860.

—— Estimate of the Amount of Taxation falling on the Working Classes of the United Kingdom. 1873.

McLaren, D Indirect Taxation: its Wasteful and Burdensome Nature as compared with Direct Taxation. 1860.

Peto, Sir M. Taxation: its Levy and Expenditure. 1863.

Urquhart, W. P. Dialogues on Taxation, Local and Imperial. 1867.

Noble, J. The Queen's Taxes. 1870.

Jevons, W. S. The Match Tax. 1871.

Jenkin, F. On the Principles which regulate the Incidence of Taxes. [1872?]

Kingsman, A. The Coming Finance, or No Income Tax, Customs, or Excise. 1874.

Sargant, W. L. Taxation, Past, Present, and Future. 1874.

Hubbard, J. G. (Baron Addington). Local and Imperial Taxation. 1875.

Giffen, Sir R. Stock Exchange Securities. 1877.

—— Essays on Finance. 2 sers. 1880–6.

Craigie, P. G. Taxation as affecting the Agricultural Interest. 1878.

Dowell, S. A History of Taxation and Taxes in England. 4 vols. 1884.

Reid, H. L. The British Taxpayer and his Wrongs. 1888.

—— The British Taxpayer's Rights. 1898.

Blake, E. The Overtaxation of Ireland. Dublin, 1897.

Lough, T. England's Wealth, Ireland's Poverty. 1897.

(8) GENERAL ECONOMICS

Chalmers, G. An Estimate of the Comparative Strength of Great Britain. A New Edition continued to 1801 with Gregory King's celebrated State of Great Britain now annexed. 1802. [Includes a life of King by Chalmers.]

—— Historical View of the Domestic Economy of Great Britain and Ireland. 1812.

[Edwards, G.?] Proposals for Carrying into Effect a Plan of Human Prosperity and Happiness. Barnard Castle, 1802.

—— An Attempt to rectify Public Affairs. 1802.

—— The True Original Scheme of Human Economy. Newcastle-on-Tyne, 1808.

Brougham, H. P. (Baron Brougham and Vaux). An Enquiry into the Colonial Policy of the European Powers. 2 vols. 1803.

Brougham, H. P. (Baron Brougham and Vaux). Thoughts suggested by Lord Lauderdale's Observations. [1804]. 1805.

Gardiner, J. Essays Literary, Political, and Commercial. 2 vols. Edinburgh, 1803.

Phillips, J. A General History of Inland Navigation, Foreign and Domestic. [1803.]

Hibbard, J. Hibbard's Essay of the Great Utility of Inland Canal Navigation and Drainage. 1804.

Maitland, J. (Earl of Lauderdale). Inquiry into the Nature and Origin of Public Wealth. Edinburgh, 1804; 1819 (greatly enlarged).

—— Observations on the Review of his Inquiry [in Edinburgh Rev. July 1804, by H. P. Brougham]. Edinburgh, 1804.

Wakefield, D. An Essay upon Political Economy. 1804 (2nd edn).

Hall, C. The Effects of Civilization on the People of the European States. 1805.

Macpherson, D. Annals of Commerce, Manufacture, Fisheries and Navigation, to 1801. 4 vols. 1805.

Smith, Adam. An Inquiry into the Nature and Causes of the Wealth of Nations. The 11th Edition, with Notes, Supplementary Chapters, and a Life of Dr Smith by Wm Playfair. 1805.

[Stephen, J.] War in Disguise, or the Frauds of the Neutral Flags. 1805.

Stewart, Sir J. Works, now first collated by his Son. 6 vols. 1805.

Torrens, R. The Economists refuted. 1805.

—— An Essay on the Production of Wealth. 1821.

—— On Wages and Combinations. 1834.

—— A Letter to Lord Ashley on the Principles which regulate Wages. 1844.

Malthus, T. R. Reply to the Chief Objections against the Essay on the Principles of Population. 1806.

—— An Inquiry into the Nature and Progress of Rent. 1815.

—— Principles of Political Economy. 1820.

—— The Measure of Value stated and illustrated. 1823.

—— Definitions in Political Economy. 1827; ed. Sir W. Layton, 2 vols. 1914.

Spence, W. Britain Independent of Commerce. 1807 (bis).

—— Agriculture the Source of the Wealth of Britain. A Reply to Mr Mill. 1808.

—— Tracts on Political Economy. 1822.

Chalmers, T. An Enquiry into the Extent and Stability of National Resources. Edinburgh, 1808.

—— The Christian and Civic Economy of Large Towns. 1821.

—— Political Economy Glasgow, 1832.

—— Collected Works. 25 vols. Glasgow, 1836–42.

Bald, R. A General View of the Coal Trade of Scotland. Edinburgh, 1808.

Lushington, W. The Interests of Agriculture and Commerce Inseparable. 1808.

Mill, James. Commerce Defended. Answer to Mr Spence, Mr Cobbett and Others. 1808.

—— Elements of Political Economy. 1821.

Williams, P. Remarks suggested by Britain Independent of Commerce. 1808.

Clarkson, T. The History of the Abolition of the African Slave Trade. 2 vols. 1808.

Enfield, W. An Inquiry into the Wealth of Nations, Elements of Commerce and Political Economy. 1809.

Sharp, Granville. A Tract on the Law of Nature. 1809.

—— Sketches on Political Economy: Reply to Mr Mill's Commerce defended. 1809.

Stewart, Dugald. Lectures on Political Economy. Ed. Sir W. Hamilton, 2 vols. Edinburgh, 1855–6. [Lectures delivered 1809.]

Baily, F. Doctrine of Life Assurances and Annuities. 1810.

Ricardo, David. Letters to T. R. Malthus (1810–23). Ed. J. Bonar, Oxford, 1887.

—— Letters to J. R. McCulloch (1816–23). Ed. J. H. Hollander, Saratoga, 1895.

—— Letters to H. Trower (1811–23). Ed. J. Bonar and J. H. Hollander, Oxford, 1899.

—— Reply to Mr Bosanquet's Practical Observations on the Bullion Committee. 1811.

—— Essay on the Influence of a Low Price of Corn on the Profits of Stock. 1815.

—— On Protection to Agriculture. 1822 (4 edns).

—— Principles of Political Economy and Taxation. 1817; ed. Sir E. C. K. Gonner, 1891.

—— Notes on Malthus's Political Economy. Ed. J. H. Hollander and T. E. Gregory, Baltimore, 1928.

—— Collected Works. Ed. J. R. McCulloch, 1846.

Ensor, G. On National Government. 2 vols. 1810.

Boileau, D. Introduction to the Study of Political Economy. 1811.

Buchanan, D. The Wealth of Nations, by Adam Smith, edited with notes and an Additional Volume [Observations on the Subjects treated of in Dr Smith's Wealth of Nations]. 4 vols. 1814.

Craig, J. Elements of Political Science. Edinburgh, 1814.

—— Remarks on some Fundamental Doctrines in Political Economy. Edinburgh, 1821.

Colquhoun, P. A Treatise on the Wealth, Power, and Resources of the British Empire. 1814.

'Purves, George' (Simon Gray). The Happiness of States. 1815.

—— All Classes Productive of National Wealth. 1817.

—— The Principles of Population and Production investigated. 1818.

—— Remarks on the Production of Wealth. 1820.

Owen, Robert. Observations on the Effect of the Manufacturing System on Health and Morals. 1815.

—— Life of Robert Owen, by himself. 1857–8.

West, Sir E. An Essay on the Application of Capital to Land. 1815.

—— Price of Corn and Wages of Labour. 1826.

Marcet, Jane. Conversations on Political Economy. 1816.

Brydges, Sir S. E. The Population and Riches of Nations. 1819.

—— What are Riches? Geneva, 1821.

Pryme, G. Introductory Lectures on the Principles of Political Economy. 2 vols. 1819.

Ravenstone, P. A Few Doubts as to some Opinions on Population and Political Economy. 1821.

Sinclair, Sir J. A Code of Political Enquiry founded on Statistical Enquiries. 1821.

Smith, T. An Attempt to define some of the First Principles of Political Economy. 1821.

Cazenove, J. Considerations on the Accumulation of Capital. 1822.

—— Outlines of Political Economy. 1832.

—— An Elementary Treatise on Political Economy. 1840.

—— Thoughts on a Few Subjects of Political Economy. 1859. [Supplement, 1861.]

Hopkins, T. Economical Enquiries relative to Rent, Profit, Wages and Money. 1822.

—— On the Rent of Land. 1828.

—— Great Britain for the Last Forty Years, Finances, Currency, and General Condition. 1834.

Bailey, S. Questions in Political Economy. 1823.

—— A Critical Dissertation on Value. 1825.

Joplin, T. Outlines of a System of Political Economy. Newcastle-on-Tyne, 1823.

McCulloch, J. R. A Discourse on the Rise, Progress, Peculiar Objects, and Importance of Political Economy. Edinburgh, 1824.

—— Principles of Political Economy. Edinburgh, 1825.

—— An Essay on the Circumstances which determine the Rate of Wages. Edinburgh, 1826.

McCulloch, J. R. A Treatise on the Principles, Practice, and History of Commerce. 1831.

—— A Dictionary of Commerce and Commercial Navigation. 1832.

—— A Statistical Account of the British Empire. 1837.

—— A Treatise on Taxation and the Funding System. 1845.

—— The Literature of Political Economy. 1845.

—— A Treatise on the Succession to Property Vacant by Death. 1848.

—— A Treatise on Economical Policy. 1853.

Rooke, J. Inquiry into the Principles of National Wealth. Edinburgh, 1824.

Thompson, W. Inquiry into the Principles of the Distribution of Wealth. 1824.

—— Labour Rewarded. 1827.

Bentham, Jeremy. The Rationale of Reward. 1825.

Hodgskin, T. Labour defended against the Claims of Capital. 1825.

—— Popular Political Economy. 1827.

—— The Natural and Artificial Right of Property contrasted. 1832.

Thompson, T. P. The True Theory of Rent. [In The Pamphleteer, vol. xxvii, 1826.]

—— Catechism on the Corn Laws. 1835.

—— Exercises, Political and Other. 6 vols. 1842.

Senior, Nassau W. An Introductory Lecture on Political Economy. 1827.

—— Three Lectures on the Rate of Wages. 1831.

—— An Outline of Political Economy. 1836.

—— Letters on the Factory Act as it affects the Cotton Manufacture. 1837.

—— A Lecture on the Production of Wealth. 1847.

Edwards, T. R. Practical, Moral and Political Economy. 1828.

Guest, R. The British Cotton Manufactures. 1828.

Smyth, A. Outlines of a New Theory of Political Economy. 1828.

Read, S. Political Economy. Edinburgh, 1829.

Whewell, W. Mathematical Exposition of some Doctrines of Political Economy. Cambridge Philosophical Trans. iii, 1829, pp. 191–230; rptd c. 1850.

—— Six Lectures on Political Economy. 1862.

Evelyn, John. Co-operation. 1830.

Hamilton, R. The Progress of Society. 1830.

Robertson, G. Essays on Political Economy. 1830.

Cotterill, C. F. An Examination of the Doctrines of Value as set forth by Adam Smith, Ricardo, McCulloch, Mill. 1831.

—— The Civil Freedom of Trade. 1856.

Horton, Sir R. J. W. Lectures on Statistics and Political Economy. 4 vols. 1831.

Jones, Richard. An Essay on the Distribution of Wealth. Pt i (all pbd): Rent. 1831.

—— Literary Remains. Lectures and Tracts on Political Economy. [Ed. W. Whewell], 1859.

Martineau, H. Illustrations of Political Economy. 9 vols. 1831–3.

—— History of the Thirty Years Peace, 1815–36. 2 vols. 1849; 2 vols. 1851 (with introduction, 1800–15).

Babbage, C. Economy of Machinery and Manufactures. 1832.

Lewis, Sir George Cornewall. Remarks on the Use and Abuse of some Political Terms. 1832.

—— An Essay on the Government of Dependencies. 1841.

—— An Essay on the Influence of Authority in Matters of Opinion. 1849.

—— A Treatise on the Methods of Observation and Reasoning in Politics. 2 vols. 1852.

—— Essays on the Administrations of Great Britain, 1783–1830. [Ed. Sir E. Head,] 1864.

Whately, R. Introductory Lectures on Political Economy. 1832; 1855 (4th edn. rev.).

Bliss, H. The Colonial System. 1833.

Gaskell, P. The Manufacturing Population of England. 1833.

—— Artisans and Machinery. 1836.

Macneill, Sir J. Canal Navigation. 1833.

Manet, Jane. John Hopkins's Notions on Political Economy. 1833.

Scrope, G. P. Principles of Political Economy. 1833.

—— Political Economy for Plain People. 1873.

Lloyd, W. F. A Lecture on the Notion of Value. Oxford, 1834.

Longfield, Mountifort. Lectures on Political Economy. Dublin, 1834.

—— Three Lectures on Commerce and one on Absenteeism. Dublin, 1835.

Rae, J. Statement of some New Principles of Political Economy, exposing the Fallacies of Free Trade. Boston, 1834.

Baines, E. History of the Cotton Manufactures in Great Britain. 1835.

—— The Manufacturing Districts vindicated. Leeds, 1843.

Moreton, A. H. Civilization. The Natural Laws that regulate the Numbers and Condition of Mankind. 1836.

Porter, G. R. The Progress of the Nation. 1836–38–43; 1846 (rev. to date).

Ramsay, Sir G. An Essay on the Distribution of Wealth. Edinburgh, 1836.

Eisdell, J. S. A Treatise on the Industry of Nations. 2 vols. 1839.

Merivale, Herman. Lectures on Colonisation and the Colonies. 1839.

Atkinson, W. Principles of Political Economy. 1840.

—— Principles of Social and Political Economy. Vol. I (all pbd), 1859.

Buller, C. On Responsible Government for Colonies. 1840.

Craster, T. A View of Manufactures, Money, and Corn Laws, Adverse to Every Theory of the Economists. 1840.

Corbet, T. An Inquiry into the Causes and Modes of the Weath of Individuals. 1841.

Broadhurst, J. Political Economy. 1842.

'Plough, Patrick' Letters on the Rudiments of Political Economy, more particularly Catallactics. 1842.

Banfield, T. C. Six Letters to Sir Robert Peel on the Dangerous Tendency of the Theory of Rent advocated by Ricardo. 1843.

—— Four Lectures on the Organisation of Industry. Cambridge, 1845.

Craik, G. L. The History of British Commerce. 1844.

De Quincey, Thomas. The Logic of Political Economy. Edinburgh, 1844.

—— Collected Writings. Ed. D. Masson, 14 vols. Edinburgh, 1889–90.

Hirst, W. History of the Woollen Trade during the Last Sixty Years. 1844.

Lawson, James Anthony. Five Lectures on Political Economy. Dublin, 1844.

Mill, John Stuart. Essays on some Unsettled Questions of Political Economy. 1844.

—— Principles of Political Economy. 2 vols. 1848.

—— Dissertations and Discussions. 5 vols. 1859–67.

—— On Liberty. 1859.

—— The Subjection of Women. 1869.

Knight, C. Capital and Labour. 1845.

Crawford, J. The Philosophy of Wealth. 1846.

Ellis, W. Outlines of Social Economy. 1846.

—— Introduction to the Study of the Social Sciences. 1849.

—— Progressive Lessons in Social Science. 1850.

—— Philosocrates. A Series of Papers. 1861–4.

Stirling, P. J. The Philosophy of Trade. Edinburgh, 1846.

Twiss, Sir Travers. The View of the Progress of Political Economy in Europe since the 16th Century. 1847.

Billet, J. Institutes of Political Economy, especially aimed at the Regeneration of France. Taunton, 1849.

Burton, J. H. Political and Social Economy. 1849.

Martin, R. M. Railways, Past, Present, and Prospective. 1849.

Wakefield, E. G. A View of the Art of Colonisation. 1849.

Byles, Sir J. B. Sophisms of Free Trade and Popular Political Economy examined. 1850.

Bowring, E. A. Free Trade and its so-called Sophisms. 1850.

Knight, F. H. The Fourth Estate. A History of Newspapers. 2 vols. 1850.

Urquhart, W. P. Essays on Subjects in Political Economy. Aberdeen, 1850.

Newman, F. W. Lectures on Political Economy. 1851.

—— Political Economy. 1890.

Stephen, Sir G. The Principles of Commerce and Commercial Law. 1853.

Sargant, W. L. The Science of Social Opulence. 1856.

—— Recent Political Economy. 1867.

—— Inductive Political Economy. 1887.

Cairnes, J. E. The Character and Logical Method of Political Economy. 1857.

—— Political Essays. 1873.

—— Essays in Political Economy. 1873.

—— Some Leading Principles of Political Economy newly expounded. 1874.

Clinton, H. The Best Possible Government at the Least Possible Cost Impossible until Commerce is Regulated. 1857.

Holyoake, George Jacob. Self Help for the People. The History of the Rochdale Pioneers. 1857.

—— The History of Co-operation in England. 2 vols. 1875–9.

—— The Co-operative Movement of Today. 1891.

—— Sixty Years of an Agitator's Life. 2 vols. 1892.

Ruskin, John. The Political Economy of Art. 1857.

—— Unto this Last. Four Essays on Political Economy. 1860.

—— Munera Pulveris. 1872.

—— Fors Clavigera. 1871–84.

—— The Crown of Wild Olive. Four Lectures on Industry and War. 1888.

Callender, W. R. The Commercial Crisis of 1857: its Causes and Results. 1858.

Chambers, R. Domestic Annals of Scotland to the Revolution, Social and Economic. 3 vols. 1858–61.

Fonblanque, A. de. How we are governed. 1858.

Macleod, H. D. Elements of Political Economy. 1858.

—— Dictionary of Political Economy. Vol. I (all pbd), 1863.

—— Principles of Economic Philosophy. 2 vols. 1872–5.

Macleod, H. D. Economics for Beginners. 1878.

—— The History of Economics. 1896.

Barnes, W. Views of Labour and Gold. 1859.

Bascom, J. Political Economy. 1859.

Fawcett, H. A Manual of Political Economy. 1863.

—— Essays and Lectures on Social and Political Subjects. 1872. [With M. G. Fawcett.]

—— Free Trade and Protection. 1878.

Hamilton, R. The Resources of a Nation. 1863.

Hearn, W. E. Plutology, or the Theory of the Efforts to satisfy Human Wants. 1864.

Jevons, W. S. The Coal Question. 1865.

—— The Theory of Political Economy. 1871.

—— A Primer of Political Economy. 1876.

—— The State in Relation to Labour. 1882.

—— Methods of Social Reform. 1883.

—— Principles of Economics. 1905. [A fragment, ed. by H. Higgs.]

Longe, F. D. A Refutation of the Wage-Fund Theory as enunciated by Mill and Fawcett. 1866.

—— A Critical Examination of Mr George's Progress and Poverty and Mr Mill's Theory of Wages. [1883.]

Bagehot, Walter. The English Constitution. 1867.

—— Physics and Politics. 1872.

—— Literary Studies. Ed. R. H. Hutton, 2 vols. 1879.

—— Economic Studies. Ed. R. H. Hutton, 1880.

—— Biographical Studies. 1881.

Laing, J. The Theory of Business. 1867.

Spencer, Herbert. Social Statics. 1868.

—— Principles of Sociology. 3 vols. 1876–96.

Rogers, J. E. Thorold. A Manual of Political Economy. Oxford, 1868.

—— The Wealth of Nations by Adam Smith edited with Notes. 2 vols. Oxford, 1869.

—— Six Centuries of Work and Wages. 2 vols. 1884.

—— The Economic Interpretation of History. Lectures. 1888.

—— The Industrial and Commercial History of England. Lectures. 1892.

Bremner, D. The Industries of Scotland: their Rise, Progress and Present Condition. Edinburgh, 1869.

Thornton, W. On Labour. 1869.

Cobden, Richard. Speeches. Ed. J. Bright and J. E. T. Rogers, 1870.

—— Political Writings. Ed. Sir L. Mallet, 1878.

Hodgson, W. B. The True Scope of Economic Science. 1870.

Yeats, J. The Natural History of Commerce. 1870.

Bourne, H. R. Fox. The Romance of Trade. [1871?]

—— English Newspapers. 2 vols. 1887.

Grant, J. The Newspaper Press. 3 vols. 1871–2.

Macdonell, J. A Survey of Political Economy. 1871.

Brassey, T. (Earl Brassey). Work and Wages. 1872; 3 vols. 1904–14 (continued and ed. by Sir S. J. Chapman).

Enderby, C. A Treatise on Capital, Money, and Riches. 1872.

Fawcett, Millicent Garrett. Political Economy for Beginners. 1872.

—— Tales in Political Economy. 1874.

Musgrave, A. Studies in Political Economy. 1875.

Donisthorpe, W. Principles of Plutology. 1876.

Harris, J. Political Economy. Essays and Reviews. 7 vols. 1876.

Syme, D. Outlines of an Industrial Science. 1876.

Shadwell, J. L. A System of Political Economy. 1877.

—— Political Economy for the People. 1880.

Chadwick, Sir E. The Health of Nations. Ed. B. W. Richardson, 1878.

Crump, A. A New Departure in the Domain of Political Economy. 1878.

Ingram, J. K. The Present Position and Prospects of Political Economy. 1878.

—— A History of Political Economy. 1880.

Parsloe, J. Our Railways. 1878.

Bright, John. Public Addresses on Free Trade. Ed. J. E. T. Rogers, 1879.

Leslie, T. E. Cliffe. Essays in Political and Moral Philosophy. 1879.

—— Essays in Political Economy. 1888.

Marshall, A. and M. P. Economics of Industry. 1879.

—— Elements of Economics of Industry. 1892.

Webster, R. G. The Trade of the World. 1880.

Edgeworth, F. Y. Mathematical Psychics. 1881.

Traill, H. D. Central Government. 1881.

Cunningham, W. Growth of English Industry and Commerce. 1882.

—— Christian Opinion on Usury. 1884.

—— Politics and Economics. 1885.

—— Political Economy treated as an Empirical Science. 1887.

—— Political Economy and Practical Life. 1893.

—— Alien Immigrants. 1897.

—— Outlines of English Industrial History. 1895. [With E. A. Macarthur.]

Mongredien, A. Wealth Creation. 1882.

Carruthers, J. Communal and Commercial Economy. 1883.

Devas, C. S. Groundwork of Economics. 1883.

—— Political Economy. 1888.

Farrer, T. H. (Baron Farrer). The State in Relation to Trade. 1883.

Maclean, J. The British Railway System. 1883.

Minton, F. D. Capital and Wages. 1883.

—— The Welfare of the Millions, or Outlines of Economics. 1889.

Seebohm, F. The English Village Community. 1883.

Seeley, Sir J. R. The Expansion of England. 1883.

—— The Growth of British Policy. 1895.

—— Lectures on Political Science. 1895.

Sidgwick, Henry. The Principles of Political Economy. 1883.

—— The Scope and Method of Economic Science. 1885.

—— The Elements of Politics. 1891.

Toynbee, Arnold. Lectures on the Industrial Revolution. 1884.

Bonar, J. Malthus and his Work. 1885.

—— Philosophy and Political Economy. 1893.

—— Catalogue of the Library of Adam Smith. 1894.

Marshall, A. The Present Position of Economics. 1885.

—— Principles of Economics. 1890.

Clarke, C. B. Speculations from Political Economy. 1886.

Danson, J. T. The Wealth of Households. 1886.

Graham, W. The Social Problem in its Economic, Moral and Political Aspects. 1886.

Smith, A. M. A System of Political Economy. 1886.

Gonner, Sir Edward Carter Kersey. Political Economy. 1888.

McDonnell, W. D. A History and Criticism of the Various Theories of Wages. Dublin, 1888.

Smith, Sir H. L. The Makers of Modern Political Economy. [1888.]

Wicksteed, P. H. The Alphabet of Economic Science. 1888.

—— An Essay on the Co-ordination of the Laws of Distribution. 1894.

Booth, C. Life and Labour of the People in London. 17 vols. 1889–1903.

Carman, E. Elementary Political Economy. 1889.

—— A History of the Theories of Production and Distribution. 1893.

Findlay, Sir G. The Working and Management of an English Railway. 1889.

Foxwell, E. and Farrer, T. C. Express Trains, English and Foreign. 1889.

Giffen, Sir R. The Growth of Capital. 1889.

—— Economic Enquiries and Studies. 2 vols. 1904.

Giffen, Sir R. Statistics. Ed. H. Higgs and G. U. Yule, 1913.

Mavor, J. Economic History and Theory. Synoptic Tables and Diagrams. Edinburgh, 1889.

Mummery, A. F. and Hobson, J. H. The Physiology of Industry. 1889.

Dilke, Sir Charles. Problems of Greater Britain. 2 vols. 1890.

Keynes, J. N. The Scope and Method of Political Economy. 1891.

Mallet, Sir L. Free Exchange. 1891.

Price, L. L. F. R. A Short History of Political Economy. 1891.

—— Economic Science and Practice. 1896.

—— A Short History of English Commerce and Industry. 1900.

Rae, W. F. The Business of Travel. A Fifty Years' Record. 1891.

Rose, H. The New Political Economy. Carlyle, Ruskin, Henry George, Mazzini. 1891.

Smart, W. An Introduction to the Theory of Value. 1891.

—— Studies in Economics. 1895.

—— Distribution of Income. 1899.

Potter, B. (later Webb). The Co-operative Movement in Great Britain. 1891.

Bastable, C. F. The Commerce of Nations. 1892.

Jephson, H. The Platform: its Rise and Progress. 2 vols. 1892.

Schloss, D. F. Methods of Industrial Remuneration. 1892.

Smith, G. Barnett. History of the English Parliament; together with an Account of the Parliaments of Scotland and Ireland. 2 vols. 1892.

Thompson, H. M. The Theory of Wages and its Application to the Eight Hours Question. 1892.

Campbell, G. D. (Duke of Argyll). The Unseen Foundations of Society. 1893.

Hole, J. National Railways. An Argument for State Purchase. 1893.

Patterson, J. P. British Railways. 1893.

Green, Mrs J. R. Town Life in the 15th Century. 1894.

Hobson, J. A. The Evolution of Modern Capitalism. 1894.

Pendleton, J. Our Railways. 2 vols. 1894.

Kidd, Benjamin. Social Evolution. 1894.

Pearson, C. H. National Life and Character. 1894.

Wells, L. B. A Sketch of the History of the Canal and River Navigation of East and West Manchester. 1894.

Jenks, E. An Outline of English Local Government. 1894.

—— A History of Politics. 1900.

Dickinson, G. L. The Development of Parliament in the 19th Century. 1895.

Prothero, M. Political Economy. 1895.

Rae, John. Life of Adam Smith. 1895.

Blair, T. S. Human Progress: what can we do to further it? Birmingham, 1896.

Lecky, William Edward Hartpole. Democracy and Liberty. 2 vols. 1896.

Maguire, J. R. Pioneers of Empire. 1896 (anon.).

Egerton, H. E. A Short History of British Colonial Policy. 1897.

Higgs, H. The Physiocrats. 1897.

Rose, J. H. The Rise of Democracy. 1897.

Lawrence, F. W. Local Variations in Wages. 1899.

Menger, Anton. The Right to the Whole Produce of Labour. Translated by M. E. Tanner. With an Introduction and Bibliography by H. S. Foxwell. 1899.

Warner, G. T. Landmarks in English Industrial History. 1899.

Gibson, A. H. National Economy. An Introduction to Political Economy. Birmingham, 1900.

Acworth, Sir W. M. The Railways of England. 1900. H. H.

V. WRITERS ON LAW

[It has only been possible to list here first edns of some of the outstanding legal works of the 19th century. A really representative list would have to be at least three times the length. The majority of these law-books ran into many edns and, having been brought up to date, are still in print. For general bibliographies and histories of the subject the works listed in vol. i, pp. 847–9 above should be consulted.]

Abbott, Charles (Baron Tenterden). The Law Relative to Merchant Ships and Seamen. 1802.

Addison, Charles Greenstreet. The Law of Contracts. 1847.

—— Wrongs and their Remedies: being a Treatise on the Law of Torts. 1860.

Agnew, Sir William Fischer. The Statute of Frauds. 1876.

Alpe, E. N. The Law relating to Stamp Duties. 1890.

Annual County Court Practice. 1881– .

Annual Supreme Court Practice. 1882– .

Anson, Sir William R. The Law and Custom of the Constitution. 2 vols. 1886–92.

Archbold, John Frederick. Practice of the Court of King's Bench. 1819.

—— The Law relative to Pleading and Evidence in Criminal Cases. 1822.

—— Poor Law. 1834.

—— The Practice of the Court of Quarter Sessions. 1836.

Archbold, John Frederick. Statutes relating to Lunacy. 1854.

Arnold, Thomas James. The Law relating to Municipal Corporations in England and Wales. 1851.

Arnould, Sir Joseph. On the Law of Marine Insurance. 1848.

Austin, John. Lectures on Jurisprudence. 3 vols. 1861–3.

Baldwin, Edward T. The Law of Bankruptcy. 1879.

Bateman, Joseph. The Law of Auctions. 1838.

Bell, Sir William James. The Sale of Food and Drugs Acts. 1886.

Benjamin, J. P. The Law of Sale of Personal Property; with References to the American Decisions and to the French Code and Civil Law. 1868.

Best, William Mawdesley. The Principles of the Law of Evidence. 1849.

Beven, Thomas. Principles of the Law of Negligence. 1889.

Bowstead, William. A Digest of the Law of Agency. 1896.

Brice, Seward. A Treatise on the Doctrine of Ultra Vires: being an Investigation of the Principles which limit the Capacities, Powers, and Liabilities of Corporations. 1874.

Brooke, Richard. A Treatise on the Office and Practice of a Notary of England, as connected with Mercantile Instruments, and on the Law Merchant. 1839.

Broom, Herbert. A Selection of Legal Maxims, 1845.

Browne, Sir Francis Gore. Handbook on the Formation, Management and Winding up of Joint Stock Companies. 1866.

Browne, George. The Principles and Practice of the Court for Divorce and Matrimonial Causes. 1864.

Browne, J. H. Balfour and Theobald, H. S. The Law of Railway Companies. 1881.

Buckley, Sir Henry Burton. The Law and Practice under the Companies Acts. 1873.

Bullen, Edward and Leake, Stephen Martin. Precedents of Pleadings in Actions in the Superior Courts of Common Law. 1860.

Bunyon, Charles John. The Law of Life Assurance. 1854.

—— The Law of Fire Insurance. 1867.

Byles, Sir John Barnard. The Law of Bills of Exchange. 1829.

Bythewood, W. M. and Jarman, T. A Selection of Precedents forming a System of Conveyancing. 11 vols. 1829–36.

Carver, Thomas Gilbert. A Treatise on the Law relating to the Carriage of Goods by Sea. 1885.

Chitty, Joseph. Treatise on Pleading: and on the Parties to Actions. 2 vols. 1809.

—— The Laws of Commerce and Manufactures and the Contracts relating thereto. 4 vols. 1820–4.

—— A Collection of Statutes of Practical Utility with Notes. 1829–37.

Chitty, Joseph, jun. The Law of the Prerogatives of the Crown and the Relative Duties and Rights of the Subject. 1820.

—— The Law of Contracts. 1826.

Chitty, Thomas. Forms of Practical Proceedings in the Courts of Queen's Bench, Common Pleas and Exchequer of Pleas. 1834.

Clerk, John F. and Lindsell, W. H. B. The Law of Torts. 1889.

Coote, Henry Charles. The Practice of the Court of Probate in Common Form Business. Also a Treatise on the Practice of the Court in Contentious Business. 1858. [In 1888 this was combined with Thomas H. Tristram, Probate Practice.]

Coote, Richard Holmes. A Treatise on the Law of Mortgage. 1821.

Copinger, Walter Arthur. The Law of Copyright in Works of Literature and Art. 1870.

Cordery, A. The Law relating to Solicitors. 1878.

Coulson, H. J. W. and Forbes, Urquhart A. The Law relating to Waters, Sea, Tidal, and Inland. 1880.

Cripps, Sir C. A. (Baron Parmoor). The Principles of the Law of Compensation. 1881.

Cripps, Henry William. Practical Treatise on the Laws relating to the Church and Clergy. 1845.

Daniell, Edmund Robert. Treatise on the Practice of the High Court of Chancery. 3 vols. 1837–41.

—— Forms and Precedents of Pleadings and Proceedings in the High Court of Chancery. 1868.

Darby, Jonathan George N. and Bosanquet, Frederick Albert. A Practical Treatise on the Statutes of Limitations in England and Ireland. 1867.

Dart, J. Henry. The Law and Practice relating to Vendors and Purchasers of Real Estate. 1851.

Davidson, Charles. Precedents and Forms in Conveyancing. Second Edition. 5 vols. in 8, 1855–65. [1st edn, as by Thomas Martin, 5 vols. 1837–44.]

Day, John C. F. S. The Common Law Procedure Acts and Other Statutes relating to the Practice of the Superior Courts of Common Law. 1861.

De Colyar, Henry Anselm The Law of Guarantees and of Principal and Surety. 1894.

Dicey, A. V. The Law of the Constitution. 1885.

Dowell, Stephen. The Income Tax Laws at present in Force in the United Kingdom. 1874.

Eagle, William. The Law of Tithes. 2 vols. 1830.

Elton, Charles I. The Law of Copyholds, and Customary Tenures of Land. 1874.

Emmet, Lewis E. Notes on Perusing Titles. 1895.

Encyclopaedia of the Laws of England, edited by A. Wood Renton. 13 vols. 1897–1903.

Eversley, William Pinder. The Law of the Domestic Relations, including Husband and Wife: Parent and Child: Guardian and Ward: Infants: and Master and Servant. 1885.

Farwell, George. A Concise Treatise on Powers. 1874.

Fisher, William Richard. The Law of Mortgage and Other Securities upon Property. 1856.

Folkard, Henry Coleman. The Law of Slander and Libel. 1876. [= 4th edn of T. Starkie, The Law of Slander and Libel, 1812.]

Fry, Sir Edward. A Treatise on the Specific Performance of Contracts. 1858.

Gale, Charles James. On the Law of Easements. 1839.

Garrett, Edmund W. The Law of Nuisances. 1890.

Glen, W. Cunningham. The Law relating to Public Health and the Local Government of Towns. 1858.

—— The Statutes in Force relating to the Poor Laws. 3 vols. 1873–9. [Vol. IV, by A. and M. S. J. Macmorran, 1890.]

Goddard, John Leybourn. The Law of Easements. 1871.

Godefroi, Henry. A Digest of the Principles of the Law of Trusts and Trustees. 1879.

Goodeve, Louis Arthur. The Modern Law of Real Property. 1883.

—— The Modern Law of Personal Property. 1887.

Grant, James. The Law relating to Bankers and Banking. 1856.

Hall, Robert Gream. An Essay on the Rights of the Crown and the Privileges of the Subject in the Sea-shores of the Realm. 1830. [Rptd 1888 with S. A. Moore, History of the Foreshore.]

Hall, William Clarke. The Law relating to Children. 1894.

Hammick, James T. The Marriage Law of England. 1887.

Hanson, Alfred. The Acts relating to Probate, Legacy and Succession Duties. 1865.

Holland, Thomas Erskine. The Elements of Jurisprudence. 1880.

Hood, H. J. and Challis, H. W. The Conveyancing and Settled Land Acts. 1882.

Hudson, Alfred A. The Law of Building and Engineering Contracts. 1891.

Hunt, Arthur Joseph. The Law relating to Boundaries and Fences. 1866.

—— The Law relating to Fraudulent Conveyances. 1872.

Jarman, Thomas. A Treatise on Wills. 2 vols. 1841–3.

Jervis, Sir John. A Practical Treatise on the Office and Duties of Coroners. 1829.

Kerly, D. M. The Law of Trade Marks, Trade Name and Merchandise Marks. 1894.

Kerr, William Williamson. The Law and Practice of Injunctions in Equity. 1867.

—— The Law of Fraud and Mistake. 1868.

—— The Law and Practice of Receivers. 1869.

Key, Thomas and Elphinstone, Sir Howard Warburton. A Compendium of Precedents in Conveyancing. 2 vols. 1878.

Leach, George Pemberton. The Tithe Acts. 1891. [= 5th edn of G. H. Whalley, Tithe Acts, 1879.]

Leake, Stephen Martin. An Elementary Digest of the Law of Property in Land. 1874.

—— An Elementary Digest of the Law of Contracts. 1878.

Lewin, Thomas. A Practical Treatise on the Law of Trusts and Trustees. 1837.

Lewis, William David. A Practical Treatise on the Law of Perpetuity; or, Remoteness in Limitations of Estates. [With Supplement.] 2 vols. 1843–9.

Lindley, Nathaniel, Baron. The Law of Partnership. 1860.

—— The Law of Companies, considered as a Branch of the Law of Partnership. 1888.

Lowndes, Richard. The Law of General Average. 1873.

Lumley, William Golden and Edmund. The Public Health Act, 1875, annotated, with an Appendix. 1876.

Maclachlan, David. The Law of Merchant Shipping. 1860.

Macnamara, Walter Henry. A Digest of the Law of Carriers of Goods and Passengers by Land and Internal Navigation. 1888.

Macswinney, Robert Forster. The Law of Mines, Quarries and Minerals. 1884.

Manual of Military Law. War Office. 1884.

Marsden, Reginald G. A Treatise on the Law of Collisions at Sea. 1880.

Mather, Philip E. A Compendium of Sheriff Law, especially in relation to Writs of Execution. 1894.

Maxwell, Sir Peter Benson. On the Interpretation of the Statutes. 1875.

May, Henry W. A Treatise on the Statutes of Elizabeth against Fraudulent Conveyances. 1871.

May, Thomas Erskine (Baron Farnborough). A Practical Treatise on the Law, Privileges, Proceedings and Usages of Parliament. 1844.

Mayne, John D. The Law of Damages. 1856.

Michael, W. H. and Will, J. Shiress. The Law of Gas and Water Supply. 1872.

Moore, Stuart A. A History of the Foreshore and the Law relating thereto. With Lord Hale's 'De jure maris' and Hall's Essay on the Rights of the Crown in the Sea-shore. 1888.

Odgers, William Blake. A Digest of the Law of Libel and Slander. 1881.

Oke, George C. Magisterial Synopsis; a Practical Guide for Magistrates, their Clerks, Attorneys and Constables. 1848.

—— Handy Book of the Game Laws. 1861.

—— A Handy Book of the Fishery Laws. 1862.

Oliphant, George Henry Hewitt. The Law of Horses. 1847.

Oswald, James Francis. Contempt of Court, Committal and Attachment and Arrest upon Civil Process in the Supreme Court of Judicature. 1892.

Paley, William. The Law and Practice of Summary Convictions on Penal Statutes by Justices of the Peace. 1814.

Palmer, Sir Francis Beaufort. Conveyancing and Other Forms and Precedents relating to Companies incorporated under the Companies Acts, 1862 and 1867. 1877.

—— Company Law. 1898.

Paterson, James. The Intoxicating Liquor Licensing Acts. 1872.

—— Commentary on the Liberty of the Subject, and the Laws of England relating to the Security of the Person. 2 vols. 1877.

—— The Liberty of the Press, Speech, and Public Worship. 1880.

Phillimore, Sir Robert Joseph. The Ecclesiastical Law of the Church of England. [With Supplement.] 3 vols. 1873–6.

Porter, James Biggs. The Laws of Insurance: Fire, Life, Accident and Guarantee. 1884.

Pratt, John Tidd. The Law relating to Friendly Societies. 1829.

—— Law relating to Highways. 1835.

Prideaux, Frederick. Precedents in Conveyancing. 1852.

Redgrave, Alexander, and Jasper A. The Factory and Workshops Acts. 1878

Roberts, Walworth Howland, and Wallace, George. The Duty and Liability of Employers as well to the Public as to Servants and Workmen. 1881.

Rogers, Francis Newman. The Law and Practice of Elections. 1820.

Roscoe, Edward Stanley. A Treatise on the Jurisdiction and Practice of the Admiralty Division of the High Court of Justice, and on Appeals therefrom. 1878.

Roscoe, Henry. A Digest of the Law of Evidence on the Trial of Actions at Nisi Prius. 1827.

—— Digest of the Law of Evidence in Criminal Cases. 1835.

Russell, Francis. A Treatise on the Power and Duty of an Arbitrator, and the Law of Submissions and Awards. 1849.

Russell, Sir William Oldnall. A Treatise on Crimes and Misdemeanours. 2 vols. 1819.

Scriven, John. A Treatise on Copyhold, Customary Freehold and Ancient Demesne Tenure, with the Jurisdiction of Courts Baron and Courts Leet. 2 vols. 1823.

Scrutton, Sir T. E. The Contract of Affreightment as expressed in Charter Parties and Bills of Lading. 1886.

Seton, Sir Henry Wilmot. Forms of Decrees in Equity, and of Orders connected with them. 1830.

Short, Frederick Hugh and Mellon, Francis Hamilton. The Practice on the Crown Side of the Queen's Bench Division of Her Majesty's High Court of Justice. 1890.

Short, John. Informations (Criminal and Quo Warranto), Mandamus and Prohibition. 1887.

Smith, Charles Manley. A Treatise on the Law of Master and Servant. 1852.

Smith, John William. A Compendium of Mercantile Law. 1834.

Starkie, Thomas. The Law of Slander and Libel, and incidentally of Malicious Prosecution. 1812; rev. H. C. Folkard, 1869. [See also under Folkard.]

—— The Law of Evidence and Digest of Proofs in Civil and Criminal Proceedings. 3 vols. 1824.

Stephen, Henry John. New Commentaries on the Laws of England. (Partly founded on Blackstone.) 4 vols. 1841–5.

Stephen, Sir James Fitzjames. A History of the Criminal Law of England. 3 vols. 1883.

Stone, Samuel. The Justice's Manual. 1842.

Stringer, Francis A. Oaths and Affirmations in Great Britain and Ireland. [1889.]

Sugden, Edward Burtenshaw (Baron St Leonards). Practical Treatise on the Law of Vendors and Purchasers of Estates. 1805.

—— A Practical Treatise of Powers. 1808.

Taylor, Alfred Swaine. The Principles and Practice of Medical Jurisprudence. 1865.

Taylor, John Pitt. Treatise on the Law of Evidence. 2 vols. 1848.

Terrell, Thomas. The Law and Practice relating to Letters Patent for Inventions. 1884.

Tristram, Thomas Hutchinson. The Contentious Practice of the High Court of Justice in respect of Grants of Probates and Administrations. 1881. [In 1888 Coote's Common Form Practice was included, and the work is now known as Tristram and Coote's Probate Practice.]

Tudor, Owen Davies. The Law of Charitable Trusts. 1854.

Whalley, G. H. The Whole of the Tithe Acts to the Present Time. 1879. [5th edn issued by George P. Leach, 1891.]

Will, John Shiress. The Law relating to Electric Lighting. 1898.

Williams, Sir Edward Vaughan. The Law of Executors and Administrators. 2 vols. 1832.

Williams, Robert G. and Bruce, Gainsford. The Jurisdiction and Practice of the High Court of Admiralty. 1868.

Williams, Sir Roland L. B. Vaughan and Walter Vaughan. The New Law and Practice in Bankruptcy. 1870.

Woodfall, William. Law of Landlord and Tenant. 1802.

Yearly County Court Practice. 1896– .

Yearly Supreme Court Practice. 1898– .

VI. BOOKS OF TRAVEL

[Somewhat fuller lists than the following will be found in the Subject Catalogue of the Library of the Royal Empire Society, ed. E. Lewin, 3 vols. 1931–2, and in the Cambridge History of the British Empire, especially vol. VII, 1933 (pt 1, Australia; pt 2, New Zealand). A general survey including the 19th cent. is J. N. L. Baker, History of Geographical Discovery and Exploration, 1931.]

Barrow, Sir John (1764–1848). Voyages of Discovery and Research within the Arctic Regions. 1846.

Galton, Sir Francis (1822–1911). Vacation Tourists and Notes of Travel in 1860 [1861, 1862–3]. 3 vols. 1861–4.

Phillips, Sir Richard (1767–1840). Collection of Modern and Contemporary Voyages. Ser. 1, 11 vols. 1805–10; ser. 2, 6 vols. 1810; ser. 3, 9 vols. 1819–23.

Royal Geographical Society. Journal. Vols. I–L, 1830–80. Proceedings. Vols. I–XXII, 1855–78; N.S. vols. I–IV, 1879–92. The Geographical Journal. Vol. I, 1893– .

Travel, Adventure and Sport. From Blackwood's Magazine. 6 vols. Edinburgh, 1889.

Walpole, Robert (1781–1856). Memoirs relating to European and Asiatic Turkey. 1817.
—— Travels in Various Countries of the East. 1820.

Baker, Sir Samuel (1821–1893). The Albert Nyanza and Exploration of the Nile Sources. 2 vols. 1866.
—— The Nile Tributaries of Abyssinia. 1867.
Ball, John (1818–1889). [See under Sir J. D. Hooker and Peaks, Passes and Glaciers, pp. 991, 992 below.]
Barrow, Sir John (1764–1848). Travels in China. 1804.
—— Travels into the Interior of South Africa. 2 vols. 1801–4.
—— Voyage to Cochin-China. 1806.
Bates, Henry Walter (1825–1892). The Naturalist on the Amazons. 2 vols. 1863.
Belzoni, Giovanni Baptista (1778–1823). Observations and Discoveries, within Pyramids, Tombs, etc. in Egypt and Nubia. 1820.
Bent, James Theodore (1852–1897). The Cyclades or Life among the Insular Greeks. 1885.
—— The Ruined Cities of Mashonaland. 1892.
—— The Sacred City of the Ethiopians. 1893.
—— Southern Arabia, Soudan and Sokoto. 1900.
Bishop, Isabella Lucy, née Bird (1831–1904). Unbeaten Tracks in Japan. 2 vols. 1880.
—— Journeys in Persia and Kurdistan. 2 vols. 1891.
—— Korea and her Neighbours. 2 vols. 1898.
—— The Yangtze Valley and Beyond. 1899.
Blackwood, Frederick Temple Hamilton-Temple (Marquis of Dufferin: 1826–1902). Letters from High Latitudes. 1857; ed. R. W. Macan, 1910 (World's Classics).
Blunt, Lady Anne. A Pilgrimage to Nejd. 2 vols. 1881.
Borrow, George (1803–1881). The Bible in Spain. 1843.
Brassey, Anna, Lady (1839–1887). A Voyage in the Sunbeam. 1878.
Bremner, Robert. Excursions in Russia. 2 vols. 1839.
—— Excursions in Denmark, Norway and Sweden. 2 vols. 1840.
Browne, Edward Granville (1862–1925). A Year amongst the Persians. 1893; 1926 (with memoir).
Bryce, James, Viscount (1838–1922). Trans-Caucasia and Ararat. 1877.
—— Impressions of South Africa. 1897.

Bryce, James, Viscount (1838–1922). South America: Observations and Impressions. 1912.
Burchell, William John (1782–1863). Travels in the Interior of South Africa. 2 vols. 1822–4.
Burckhardt, John Lewis (1784–1817). Travels in Nubia. 1819.
—— Travels in Syria and the Holy Land. 1822.
—— Travels in Arabia. 2 vols. 1829.
Burnaby, Frederick Gustavus (1842–1885). A Ride to Khiva. 1876.
—— On Horse-back through Asia Minor. 2 vols. 1877.
Burnes, Sir Alexander (1805–1844). Travels into Bokhara, etc. 3 vols. 1834.
Burton, Sir Richard Francis (1821–1890). Pilgrimage to El-Medinah and Mecca. 2 vols. 1855–6; ed. Isabel, Lady Burton and S. Lane Poole, 2 vols. 1906.
—— First Footsteps in East Africa; Harah. 1856.
—— Lake Region of Central Africa. 2 vols. 1860.
—— Abeokuta and the Cameroons Mountains. 2 vols. 1863.
—— Wanderings in West Africa. 2 vols. 1863.
—— Mission to Gelele, king of Dahome, with Notices of the Amazons. 2 vols. 1863.
—— Explorations of the Highlands of Brazil. 2 vols. 1869.
—— Two Trips to Gorillaland and the Cataracts of the Congo. 2 vols. 1876.
—— Gold Mines of Midian and the Ruined Midianite Cities. 1878.
—— Land of Midian revisited. 2 vols. 1879.
Butler, Sir William Francis (1838–1910). The Great Lone Land: Travel in the North-West of America. 1872.
—— The Wild North Land. 1873.
Cameron, Verney Lovett (1844–1894). Across Africa. 2 vols. 1877.
Carnegie, David W. Spinifex and Sand. A Narrative of Five Years' Pioneering and Exploration in Western Australia. 1898.
Carnegie, James (Earl of Southesk: 1827–1905). Saskatchewan and the Rocky Mountains. 1875.
Cary, Amelia (Viscountess Falkland). Chow-Chow: being Selections from a Journal kept in India, Egypt and Syria. 2 vols. 1857.
Cayley, George John (1826–1878). Las Alforjas, or the Bridle Roads of Spain. 2 vols. 1853.
Chalmers, James (1841–1901). Pioneering in New Guinea. 1887.
Cheadle, Walter Butler. [See under W. C. de M. M. Fitzwilliam (Viscount Milton).]
Chesterton, George Laval. Peace, War and Adventure. 2 vols. 1853.

Clark, William George (1821–1878). Peloponnesus: Notes of Study and Travel. 1858.

Clarke, Edward Daniel (1769–1822). Travels in Various Countries of Europe, Asia, Africa. 6 vols. 1810–23.

Clapperton, Hugh (1788–1827). Journal of a Second Expedition into the Interior of Africa from the Bight of Benin to Soccatoo. 1829. [See also under D. Denham below.]

Cochrane, Thomas (Earl of Dundonald: 1775–1860). Autobiography of a Seaman. 2 vols. 1860–1.

Conder, Claude Reignier (1848–1910). Tent Work in Palestine. 1878.

Conway, Sir Martin (1856–1937). Climbing and Exploration in the Karakoram-Himalayas. 1894.

—— The Bolivian Andes. 1901.

—— Aconcagua and Tierra del Fuego. 1902.

Crawfurd, John (1783–1868). Embassy to the Courts of Siam and Cochin-China. 2 vols. 1828.

Cunningham-Graham, Robert Bontine (1852–1936). Mogreb el Acksa: a Journey in Morocco. 1898; 1921 (rev. edn).

Curzon, George Nathaniel, Marquess (1859–1925). Russia in Central Asia in 1889. 1889.

—— Persia and the Persian Question. 2 vols. 1892.

—— Tales of Travel. 1923.

Curzon, Robert (1810–1873). Visits to Monasteries in the Levant. 1849; ed. D. G. Hogarth, 1916.

Darwin, Charles Robert (1809–1882). Journal of Researches during the Voyage of the Beagle. 1839.

Davy, John (1790–1868). Notes and Observations in the Ionian Islands and Malta. 2 vols. 1842.

Denham, Dixon (1786–1828). Travels and Discoveries in Northern and Central Africa, 1822–4. 1826. [With H. Clapperton and W. Oudney.]

Dickens, Charles (1812–1879). American Notes for General Circulation. 2 vols. 1842.

—— Pictures from Italy. 1846.

Dilke, Sir Charles Wentworth (1810–1869). Greater Britain. 2 vols. 1868.

—— Problems of Greater Britain. 2 vols. 1890.

Dillon, Peter (1785?–1847). Successful Voyage in the South Seas to ascertain Fate of La Perouse. 2 vols. 1829.

Dixie, Lady Florence Caroline (1857–1905). Across Patagonia. 1880.

Dixon, William Hepworth (1821–1879). The Holy Land. 2 vols. 1865.

—— British Cyprus. 1879.

Doughty, Charles Montagu (1843–1926). Travels in Arabia Deserta. 2 vols. 1888; ed. T. E. Lawrence, 2 vols. 1921.

Du Chaillu, Paul B. (1835–1903). Explorations in Equatorial Africa. 1861.

Edwards, Amelia Blandford (1831–1892). A Thousand Miles up the Nile. 1877.

Eyre, Edward John (1815–1901). Journals of Expeditions of Discovery into Central Australia, and overland from Adelaide to King George's Sound, in 1840–1. 1845.

Farrer, Richard Ridley. A Tour in Greece, 1880. 1882.

FitzGerald, Edward Arthur (1871–1931). Climbs in the New Zealand Alps. 1896.

—— The Highest Andes. 1899.

Fitzwilliam, William Charles de Meuron Wentworth (Viscount Milton: 1839–1877). The North-West Passage by Land. 1865. [With W. B. Cheadle.]

Flinders, Matthew (1774–1814). A Voyage to Terra Australis; prosecuted in the Years 1801, 1802 and 1803. 2 vols. 1814.

Forbes, Henry Ogg (1851–1932). A Naturalist's Wanderings in the Eastern Archipelago. 1885.

Forbes, James David (1809–1868). Norway and its Glaciers. 1853.

—— Travels through the Alps. Ed. W. A. B. Coolidge, 1900. [Rpt of 4 works by Forbes.]

Ford, Richard (1796–1858). Handbook for Travellers in Spain. 2 vols. 1845.

—— Gatherings from Spain. 1846; rptd 1906 (Everyman's Lib.).

Forsyth, Joseph (1763–1815). On Antiquities, Arts, Letters in Italy. 1813.

Franklin, Sir John (1786–1847). Narrative of Journey to the Shores of the Polar Sea, 1819–22. 1823.

—— Narrative of Second Expedition to the Polar Sea. 1828.

Fraser, James Baillie (1783–1856). Travels and Adventures in the Persian Provinces on the Southern Banks of the Caspian Sea. 1826.

Freshfield, Douglas W. (1845–1934). Travels in the Central Caucasus and Bashan, including Visits to Ararat and Tabreez, etc. 1869.

—— Italian Alps: Sketches in the Mountains of Ticino, Lombardy, the Trentino, and Venetia. 1875.

—— The Exploration of the Caucasus. 2 vols. 1896.

Froude, James Anthony (1818–1894). Oceana; England and her Colonies. 1886.

Galton, Sir Francis (1822–1911). Narrative of an Explorer in Tropical South Africa. 1853.

Gill, William John (1843–1882). The River of Golden Sand: a Journey through China and Eastern Tibet to Burma. 2 vols. 1882.

Gordon, Daniel M. Mountain and Prairie; a Journey from Victoria to Winnipeg, via Peace River Pass. 1880.

Grattan, Thomas Colley (1792–1864). Traits of Travel. 3 vols. 1829.

—— Beaten Paths. 2 vols. 1862.

Hall, Basil (1788–1844). Travels in North America in 1827 and 1828. 1829.

—— Fragments of Voyages and Travels. 3 sers. 9 vols. 1831–3.

—— Journal written on the Coasts of Chile, Peru and Mexico. 2 vols. 1842.

Harris, Walter Burton. The Land of an African Sultan: Travels in Morocco. 1889.

—— Journey through the Yemen. 1893.

Head, Sir Francis Bond (1793–1875). Journeys across the Pampas. 1826.

Herbert, George Robert Charles (Earl of Pembroke: 1850–1895). South Sea Bubbles. By the Earl and the Doctor. 1872. [With G. H. Kingsley.]

Hind, Henry Youle (1823–1908). Narrative of the Canadian Red River Exploring Expedition of 1857 and of the Assinniboine and Saskatchewan Exploring Expedition of 1858. 2 vols. 1860.

Hobhouse, John Cam (Baron Broughton: 1786–1869). Journey through Albania. 1813.

Hogarth, David George (1862–1928). A Wandering Scholar in the Levant. 1896.

Hooker, Sir Joseph Dalton (1817–1911). Himalayan Journals. 1854.

—— Journal of a Tour in Morocco and the Great Atlas. 1878. [With J. Ball.]

Hudson, William Henry (1841–1922). The Naturalist in La Plata. 1892.

—— Idle Days in Patagonia. 1893.

Irby, Adelina Paulina. [See under G. M. M. Mackenzie below.]

Irby, Charles Leonard (1789–1845). Travels in Egypt and Nubia, Syria and the Holy Land. 1823. [With J. Mangles.]

James, Sir Henry Evan Murchison (d. 1923). Long White Mountain. 1888.

Johnston, Sir Harry Hamilton (1858–1927). The River Congo from its Mouth to Bolobo. 1884.

—— The Kilima-njaro Expedition. A Record of Scientific Exploration in Eastern Equatorial Africa. 1886.

Kennedy, Edward Shirley. [See under Peaks, Passes and Glaciers, p. 992 below.]

Kinglake, Alexander William (1809–1891). Eothen. 1844; rptd 1910 (World's Classics).

Kingsley, Charles (1819–1875). At Last: a Christmas in the West Indies. 2 vols. 1871.

Kingsley, George Henry (1827–1892). [See under G. R. C. Herbert (Earl of Pembroke).]

Kingsley, Mary Henrietta (1862–1900). Travels in West Africa. 1897.

Laing, Alexander Gordon (1793–1826). Travels in Timannee, Kooranko, and Soolima Countries in Western Africa. 1825.

Laing, Samuel (1780–1868). Journal in Norway. 1836.

—— Tour in Sweden. 1839.

—— Notes on France, Prussia, etc. 1842.

Lander, Richard Lemon (1804–1834). Journal of Clapperton's Last Expedition to Africa. 2 vols. 1830.

—— Journal of Expedition to explore the Niger. 3 vols. 1832. [With John Lander (1807–1839).]

Layard, Sir Austen Henry (1817–1894). Popular Account of Discoveries at Nineveh. 1851.

—— Discoveries in the Ruins of Nineveh and Babylon. 1853.

—— Early Adventures in Persia, Susiana, Babylonia. 1887.

Leake, William Martin (1777–1860). Journal of a Tour in Asia Minor. 1824.

—— Travels in the Morea. 3 vols. 1830.

—— Travels in Northern Greece. 4 vols. 1835.

Lear, Edward (1812–1888). Journal of a Landscape Painter in Albania, Illyria, etc. 1851.

Livingstone, David (1813–1873). Missionary Travels in South Africa. 1857.

—— Expedition to the Zambesi. 1865. [With Charles Livingstone (1821–1873).]

McClintock, Sir Francis Leopold (1819–1907). Voyage of the Fox: Discovery of Fate of Franklin. 1859.

Macgregor, John (1825–1892). A Thousand Miles in the Rob Roy Canoe. 1866.

—— The Rob Roy on the Baltic. 1867.

—— The Rob Roy on the Jordan, Nile, Red Sea, etc. 1869.

Mackenzie, Sir Alexander (1755?–1820). Voyage from Montreal, on the River of Saint Lawrence, through the Continent of North America to the Frozen and Pacific Oceans in 1789 and 1793. 1801.

Mackenzie, Georgina Mary Muir. Across the Carpathians. 1862. [With A. P. Irby.]

—— Travels in the Sclavonic Provinces of Turkey in Europe. 1867.

Mahaffy, Sir John Pentland (1839–1919). Rambles and Studies in Greece. 1878.

Malcolm, Sir John (1769–1833). Sketches of Persia. 1828.

Mangles, James (1786–1867). [See under C. L. Irby above.]

Miers, John (1789–1879). Travels in Chile and La Plata. 2 vols. 1826.

Morier, James Justinian (1780–1849). Journey through Persia, Armenia, and Asia Minor to Constantinople, 1808–9. 1812.

—— A Second Journey through Persia, [etc.], 1810–6. 1818.

Musters, George Chaworth (1841–1879). At Home with the Patagonians. 1871.

O'Donovan, Edmund (1844–1883). The Merv Oasis: Travels and Adventures East of the Caspian, 1879–81. 2 vols. 1882.

Oliphant, Laurence (1829–1888). Episodes in a Life of Adventure. 1887.

Oudney, Walter (1790–1824). [See under D. Dixon above.]

Palgrave, William Gifford (1826–1888). A Year's Journey through Central and Eastern Arabia. 2 vols. 1865.

—— Ulysses: Scenes and Studies in Many Lands. 1887.

Park, Mungo (1771–1806). Journal of Mission to Interior of Africa, 1805. 1815.

Parry, Sir William Edward (1790–1855). Journal of a Voyage for the Discovery of a North-West Passage, 1819–20. With an Appendix. 1821–4.

—— Journal of a Second Voyage, 1821–23. 1824.

—— Journal of a Third Voyage, 1824–25. 1826.

—— Narrative of an Attempt to reach the North Pole, 1827. 1828.

Peaks, Passes and Glaciers. Ed. J. Ball, 1859. Ser. 2, ed. E. S. Kennedy, 2 vols. 1862.

Porter, Sir Robert Ker (1777–1842). Travelling Sketches in Russia and Sweden. 2 vols. 1809.

—— Travels in Georgia, Persia, Armenia, Babylonia, etc., in 1817–20. 2 vols. 1821–2.

Quin, Windham Thomas Wyndham (Earl of Dunraven; 1841–1926). The Great Divide: Travels in the Upper Yellowstone in the Summer of 1874. 1876.

Reade, William Winwood (1838–1875). African Sketch-book. 2 vols. 1873.

—— Story of the Ashantee Campaign. 1874.

Rich, Claudius James (1787–1820). Narrative of a Residence in Koordistan, etc. 2 vols. 1836.

Roberts, Morley (b. 1857). The Western Avernus; or Toil and Travel in Further North America. 1887.

Ross, Sir James Clark (1800–1862). Voyage in the Southern and Antarctic Regions, 1839–43. 2 vols. 1847.

Ross, Sir John (1777–1856). A Voyage of Discovery for exploring Baffin's Bay and a N.W. Passage. 1819.

—— Narrative of a Second Voyage in Search of a N.W. Passage, 1829–33. 1835.

Salt, Henry (1780–1827). A Voyage to Abyssinia, and Travels into the Interior of that Country, 1809–10. 1814.

Scoresby, William (1789–1857). Memorials of the Sea. 1833.

Sleeman, Sir William Henry (1788–1856). Rambles and Recollections of an Indian Official. 2 vols. 1844.

Speke, John Hanning (1827–1864). Journal of Discovery of the Source of the Nile. 1863.

Stanley, Sir Henry Morton (1841–1904). How I found Livingstone. 1872.

—— Through the Dark Continent. 2 vols. 1878.

—— In Darkest Africa. 2 vols. 1890.

Stephen, Sir Leslie (1832–1904). The Playground of Europe. 1871.

Stevenson, Robert Louis (1850–1894). An Inland Voyage. 1878.

—— Travels with a Donkey in the Cevennes. 1879.

—— Across the Plains. 1892.

—— The Amateur Emigrant. [In Works, ed. Sir S. Colvin, vol. III, 1895.]

—— Essays of Travel. 1905.

Stuart, John McDouall (1815–1866). Journals of Explorations in Australia, 1858–62. Ed. W. Hardman, 1864.

Sturt, Charles (1795–1869). Two Expeditions into the Interior of Southern Australia, 1828–31. 2 vols. 1833.

Tennent, Sir James Emerson (1804–1869). Natural History of Ceylon. 1861.

Thomson, John. The Straits of Malacca. Indo-China, and China or Ten Years' Travels, Adventures and Residence abroad. 1875.

Thomson, Joseph (1858–1894). To the Central African Lakes and back. 1881.

—— Through Masai Land. 1885.

—— Travels in the Atlas and Southern Morocco. 1889.

Tristram, Henry Baker (1822–1906). The Great Sahara. 1860.

—— The Land of Moab. 1873.

Tyndall, John (1820–1893). The Glaciers of the Alps. 1860.

—— Hours of Exercise in the Alps. 1871.

Wallace, Alfred Russel (1823–1913). Travels on the Amazon and Rio Negro. 1853.

—— The Malay Archipelago. 2 vols. 1869.

Warburton, Bartholomew Elliott George (1810–1852). The Crescent and the Cross. 2 vols. 1844.

Waterton, Charles (1782–1865). Wanderings in South America. 1825.

White, Walter (1811–1893). On Foot through the Tyrol. 1856.

—— A Month in Yorkshire. 1858.

Whymper, Edward (1840–1911). Scrambles among the Alps. 1870.

—— Travels among the Great Andes of the Equator. 1892.

Wilkinson, Sir John Gardner (1797–1875). Dalmatia and Montenegro. 2 vols. 1848.

Wills, Charles James. In the Land of the Lion and Sun, or Modern Persia, 1866–1881. 1883.

Wilson, Andrew (1831–1881). The Abode of Snow, 1875.

Wingfield, Lewis Strange (1842–1891). Under the Palms in Algeria and Tunis. 2 vols. 1868.
—— Wanderings of a Globe-Trotter in the Far East. 2 vols. 1889.

Wood, John (1811–1871). A Journey to the Source of the Oxus. 1841.

Younghusband, Sir Francis Edward (b. 1863). The Heart of a Continent. 1896.

Yule, Henry (1820–1889). Narrative of the Mission to the Court of Ava in 1855. 1858.

F. A. K., *rev.* G. R. C.

VII. CLASSICAL, BIBLICAL AND ORIENTAL SCHOLARSHIP

Classical Scholarship: 1800–1835; 1835–1870; 1870–1900.
Biblical Scholarship.
Egyptology, Assyriology and Oriental Scholarship: Egyptologists; Assyriologists; Sanskrit and Indian Scholars; Chinese Scholars; Arabic Scholars; Persian Scholars; Turkish Scholars.

I. CLASSICAL SCHOLARSHIP

[For a survey of 19th-century English classical scholarship see Sir J. E. Sandys, A History of Classical Scholarship, vols. II, III, Cambridge, 1908, and A Short History of Classical Scholarship, Cambridge, 1915.]

(a) 1800–1835

FRANCIS ADAMS (1796–1861)

The Medical Works of Paulus Ægineta. Translated into English, with a Copious Commentary. Vol. I, 1834.

The Seven Books of Paulus Ægineta translated from the Greek; with a Commentary. 3 vols. Sydenham Soc. 1844–7.

The Genuine Works of Hippocrates. Translated with a Preliminary Discourse and Annotations. 2 vols. 1849.

'Αρεταιου τα σωζομενα. 1856. [With trn.]

THOMAS ARNOLD (1795–1842)

[See p. 888 above.]

CHARLES JAMES BLOMFIELD (1786–1857)

(a) Editions and Writings

Αἰσχυλου Προμηθευς Δεσμωτης Æschyli Prometheus Vinctus. Cambridge, 1810.

Αἰσχυλου ῾Επτα ἐπι Θηβας. Æschyli Septem contra Thebas. Cambridge, 1810.

R. Porsoni Adversaria. Notæ et Emendationes in Poetas graecos. Cambridge, 1812. [With J. H. Monk.]

Αἰσχυλου Περσαι. Æschyli Persae. Cambridge, 1814.

Callimachi quae supersunt. 1815.

Αἰσχυλου Αγαμεμνων. Æschyli Agamemnon. Cambridge, 1818.

Αἰσχυλου Χοηφοροι. Æschyli Choephoræ. Cambridge, 1824.

[Also many periodical articles. Blomfield was a prolific writer on the classics and on theology.]

(b) Biography and Criticism

Biber, G. E. Bishop Blomfield and his Times. 1857.

Blomfield, A. A Memoir of C. J. Blomfield, Bishop of London, with Selections from his Correspondence. 2 vols. 1863.

THOMAS BURGESS (1756–1837)

Πενταλογια; sive, Tragœdiarum græcarum Delectus. Editio altera; cui Observationes Indicemque Græcum Auctiorem et Emendatiorem adjecit T. Burgess. 2 vols. Oxford, [1778]–1779. [1st edn by J. Burton.]

A Vindication of 1 John v. 7. from the Objections of M. Griesbach 1821.

Adnotationes Milii auctae ex Prolegomenis suis, Westenii, Bengelii, et Sabaterii ad 1. Joann. v. 7. 1822.

A Selection of Tracts and Observations on 1 John v. 7. Part the First. 1824.

A Letter to the Clergy of the Diocese of Saint David's on a Passage of the Second Symbolum Antiochenum of the Fourth Century as an Evidence of the Authenticity of 1 John v. 7. 1825.

[Burgess was also a prolific writer on theological questions. See J. S. Harford, The Life of T. Burgess, Bishop of Salisbury, 1840.]

SAMUEL BUTLER (1774–1839)

(a) Editions and Writings

Æschyli Tragœdiæ quæ supersunt, Deperditarum Fabularum Fragmenta et Scholia græca. 4 vols. Cambridge, 1809–16.

A Sketch of Modern and Antient Geography, for the Use of Schools. Shrewsbury, 1813.

Atlas of Ancient and Classical Geography. 1822.

A Praxis on the Latin Prepositions, being an Attempt to illustrate their Origin, Signification, and Government, in the Way of Exercise. 1823.

(b) Biography and Criticism

Baker, Thomas. History of the College of St John the Evangelist, Cambridge. Ed. J. E. B. Mayor, 2 vols. Cambridge, 1869.

Butler, Samuel. The Life and Letters of Dr Samuel Butler, Head-Master of Shrewsbury School, 1798–1836, and afterwards Bishop of Lichfield, in so far as they illustrate the Scholastic, Religious, and Social Life of England, 1790–1840. 2 vols. 1896.

JOHN ANTHONY CRAMER (1793–1848)

A Dissertation on the Passage of Hannibal over the Alps. By a Member of the University of Oxford. Oxford, 1820.

A Geographical and Historical Description of Ancient Italy. 2 vols. Oxford, 1826.

A Geographical and Historical Description of Ancient Greece. 3 vols. Oxford, 1828.

A Geographical and Historical Description of Asia Minor. 2 vols. Oxford, 1832.

Anecdota Græca e Codd. manuscriptis Bibliothecarum Oxoniensium. 4 vols. Oxford, 1835–7.

Anecdota Græca e Codd. manuscriptis Bibliothecæ Regiæ Parisiensis. 4 vols. Oxford, 1839–41.

PETER PAUL DOBREE (1782–1825)

R. Porsoni Notæ in Aristophanem. Cambridge, 1820. [Ed. and rev. by Dobree.]

Φωτιου Λεξεων συναγωγη. E Codice Gallano descripsit R. Porsonus. 2 pts, 1822. [Ed. by Dobree.]

Adversaria [on the Greek Poets, Historians and Orators]. Ed. J. Scholefield, 2 vols. Cambridge, 1831–3.

Lexicon Rhetoricum Cantabrigiense. [Ed. J. Scholefield], Cambridge, 1834.

Miscellaneous Notes on Inscriptions. With some Addenda to his Adversaria. [Ed. J. Scholefield], Cambridge, 1835.

EDWARD DODWELL (1767–1832)

A Classical and Topographical Tour through Greece, during the Years 1801, 1805, and 1806. 2 vols. 1819; tr. German, Meiningen, 1821–2.

Views in Greece, from Drawings by Edward Dodwell. 2 vols. 1821. [30 plates, in illustration of the above with descriptions in English and French.]

Views and Descriptions of Cyclopian or Pelasgic Remains in Greece and Italy; from Drawings by Edward Dodwell; intended as a Supplement to his Tour in Greece. 1834; tr. French, Paris, 1834.

PETER ELMSLEY (1773–1825)

Thucydides Græce et Latine. 6 vols. Edinburgh, 1804.

Εὐριπιδου Ἀλκηστις. Oxford, 1806.
Εὐριπιδου Ἠλεκτρα. Oxford, 1806.
Εὐριπιδου Ἀνδρομαχη. Oxford, 1807.

Ἀριστοφανους Ἀχαρνης. Oxford, 1809.
Σοφοκλεους Οἰδιπους Τυραννος. Oxford, 1811.
Scholia antiqua in Sophoclis Œdipum Tyrannum. 2 pts, Oxford, 1811.
Εὐριπιδου Ἡρακλειδαι. Oxford, 1813.
Εὐριπιδου Μηδεια. Oxford, 1818.
Εὐριπιδου Βακχαι. Oxford, 1821.
Σοφοκλεους Οἰδιπους ἐπι Κολωνῳ. Oxford, 1823.
Scholia in Sophoclis Tragœdias septem. [Ed. T. Gaisford], Oxford, 1825.
Elmsleiana Critica; sive Annotationes, ad Scenicorum Linguam ususque quantum attinet in Fabulis græcis. Ed. F. E. Gretton, Cambridge, 1833.

[Also notes on the Ajax of Sophocles in Museum Criticum, I, 1814 and various articles on classical topics in Edinburgh Rev., Quarterly Rev. and Classical Journ.]

THOMAS GAISFORD (1779–1855)

M. Tullii Ciceronis Tusculanarum Disputationum Libri V. Cum Commentario J. Davisii, et R. Bentleii Emendationibus. Editio nova. Accedunt R. Bentleii Emendationes hactenus ineditæ. Oxford, 1805.

Codices manuscripti et impressi cum Notis manuscriptis, olim D'Orvilliani, qui in Bibliotheca Bodleiana apud Oxonienses adservantur. Oxford, 1806.

Ἀνδρονικου Ῥοδιου παραφρασις των ἠθικων Νικομαχειων. Oxford, 1809.

Euripidis Hecuba, Orestes et Phœnissæ. Oxford, 1809.

Ἡφαιστιωνος ἐγχειριδιον περι μετρων και ποιηματων. Accedit Procli Chresthomathia grammatica. Oxford, 1810.

Poetæ minores græci. 4 vols. Oxford, 1814–20.

Catalogus, sive Notitia Manuscriptorum, qui a cel. E. D. Clarke comparati in Bibliotheca Bodleiana adservantur. Pt 1, Oxford, 1815. [Pt 2, by A. Nicoll, 1818.]

Lectiones Platonicæ. Oxford, 1820.

Aristotelis de Rhetorica Libri tres. 2 vols. Oxford, 1820.

Ἰωαννου Στοβαιου Ἀνθολογιον. 4 vols. Oxford, 1822; 2 vols. Oxford, 1850 (with Hieroclis Commentarius in aurea Carmina Pythagoreorum).

Ἡροδοτου Ἀλικαρνασσηος Ἱστοριων λογοι θ'. 4 vols. Oxford, 1824.

Σουιδας. Suidæ Lexicon. 3 vols. Oxford, 1834.

Parœmiographi Græci; quorum Pars nunc primum ex Codicibus manuscriptis vulgatur. Oxford, 1836.

Θεοδωρητου Ἑλληνικων παθηματων θεραπευτικη. Oxford, 1839.

Georgii Chœrobosci Dictata in Theodosii Canones, nec non Epimerismi in Psalmos. 3 vols. Oxford, 1842.

Eusebii Eclogæ propheticæ. Oxford, 1842.

Εὐσεβίου Εὐαγγελικης Προπαρασκευης Λογοι ιε'. 4 vols. Oxford, 1843.

Joannis Pearsoni Adversaria Hesychiana. 2 vols. Oxford, 1844.

Etymologicon Magnum, seu verius Lexicon sæpissime Vocabulorum Origines indicans, ex pluribus Lexicis, Scholiasticis et Grammaticis anonymi cujusdam concinnatum. Oxford, 1848.

Εὐσεβίου του Παμφιλου Εὐαγγελικης 'Αποδειξεως Λογοι δεκα. 3 vols. Oxford, 1852.

Eusebii contra Hieroclem et Marcellum. 1852.

Theodoreti Ecclesiasticæ Historiæ Libri quinque. Oxford, 1854.

[For obituaries see GM. XLIV, 1855 and Cambridge Journ. of Classical and Sacred Philology, II, 1855.]

SIR WILLIAM GELL (1777–1836)

The Topography of Troy and its Vicinity, illustrated and explained by Drawings and Descriptions. 1804.

The Geography and Antiquities of Ithaca. 1807.

The Itinerary of Greece, with a Commentary on Pausanias and Strabo, and an Account of the Monuments of Antiquity at present existing in that Country; compiled in the Years 1801; 2; 5; 6. 1810.

Itinerary of the Morea, being a Description of the Routes of that Peninsula. 1817. [Rptd 1823 as Narrative of a Journey in the Morea.]

Pompeiana: the Topography, Edifices, and Ornaments of Pompeii. 1817–9. [With J. P. Gandy.]

Pompeiana: the Topography, Edifices and Ornaments of Pompeii, the Result of Excavations since 1819. 2 vols. 1832.

THOMAS KIDD (1770–1850)

D. Ruhnkenii Opuscula oratoria, philologica, critica. Accedunt Epistolæ novem ad J. P. D'Orvillium. Præfationem addidit T. Kidd. 1807.

Tracts and Miscellaneous Criticisms of Richard Porson. Collected and arranged by T. Kidd. 1815. [Includes An Imperfect Outline of the Life of Richard Porson.]

Q. Horatii Flacci Opera. Cambridge, 1817.

R. Dawesii Miscellanea Critica. Cambridge, 1817. [Ed. by Kidd.]

WILLIAM MARTIN LEAKE (1777–1860)

(a) Writings on Greece

Researches in Greece. Part 1. 1814.

The Topography of Athens, with Some Remarks on its Antiquities. 1821. Tr. German, Halle, 1829; French, Paris, 1869.

Journal of a Tour in Asia Minor; with Comparative Remarks on the Ancient and Modern Geography of that Region. 1824.

Travels in the Morea. 3 vols. 1830.

Travels in Northern Greece. 4 vols. 1835.

Peloponnesiaca: a Supplement to Travels in the Morea. 1846.

Numismata Hellenica: a Catalogue of Greek Coins collected by W. M. Leake. With Notes. 1854.

(b) Biography and Criticism

Marsden, J. H. A Brief Memoir of the Life and Writings of Lieutenant Colonel William Martin Leake. 1864.

Curtius, E. Alterthum und Gegenwart. Gesammelte Reden und Vorträge. 2 vols. Weimar, 1875–82. [Vol. II, pp. 305–22, contains a notice of Leake.]

EDWARD MALTBY (1770–1859)

Lexicon Græco-Prosodiacum. 2 pts, Cambridge, 1815.

A New and Complete Greek Gradus, or Poetical Lexicon of the Greek Language. 1830.

THOMAS MITCHELL (1783–1845)

The Comedies of Aristophanes, translated [into English Verse]. 2 vols. 1820–2. [Contains Acharnians, Knights, Clouds and Wasps.]

Index Græcitatis Isocraticæ. Accedit Index Nominum propriorum. Oxford, 1828.

Index in Oratores Atticos. 2 vols. Oxford, 1828.

The Acharnenses of Aristophanes. 1835.

The Wasps of Aristophanes. 1835.

The Knights of Aristophanes. 1836.

The Clouds of Aristophanes. 1838.

The Frogs of Aristophanes. 1839.

The Tragedies of Sophocles, with Notes. 2 vols. Oxford, 1844.

JAMES HENRY MONK (1784–1856)

A Letter to the Rev. S. Butler. With Mr Butler's Answer. Cambridge, 1810.

Εὐριπιδου 'Ιππολυτος Στεφανηφορος. Euripides Hippolytus Coronifer. Cambridge, 1811.

R. Porsoni Adversaria. Notæ et Emendationes in Pœtas Græcos. Cambridge, 1812. [With C. J. Blomfield.]

Εὐριπιδου 'Αλκηστις. Euripidis Alcestis. Cambridge, 1816.

The Life of Richard Bentley, D.D., Master of Trinity College; with an Account of his Writings, and Anecdotes of Many Distinguished Characters during the Period in which he flourished. 1830.

Εὐριπιδου 'Ιφιγενεια ἡ ἐν Αὐλιδι. Euripidis Iphigenia in Aulide. Cambridge, 1840.

Εὐριπίδου Ἰφιγένεια ἡ ἐν Ταύροις. Euripidis Iphigenia in Tauris. Cambridge, 1845.
Euripidis Fabulae quatuor, scilicet Hippolytus Coronifer, Alcestis, Iphigenia in Aulide, Iphigenia in Tauris. Cambridge, 1857.

JOSEPH WILLIAM MOSS (1803–1862)

A Manual of Classical Bibliography, comprising a Copious Detail of the Various Editions, Commentaries and Translations into the English, French, Italian, Spanish, German, and occasionally other Languages of the Greek and Latin Classics. 2 vols. 1825; 2 vols. 1837 (rev. to end of 1836).

(b) 1835–1870

HENRY ELLIS ALLEN

M. Tullii Ciceronis De Natura Deorum Libri tres. 1836.
M. Tullii Ciceronis De Officiis Libri tres. Dublin, 1842.
M. Tullii Ciceronis Cato Major. 1852.
M. Tullii Ciceronis Lælius. 1853.
M. Tullii Ciceronis De Finibus Bonorum et Malorum Libri quinque. 1853.
Observationes in Loca aliquot Ciceronis. Accedunt in Cæsarem, Frontonem, Gellium, Plinium nonnulla. Dublin, 1863.
Emendationes Livianæ. 4 pts, Dublin, 1864–74.
Observationes in Q. Curtium Rufum. Dublin, 1865.
Hannibal; sive Disputatio, qua id agitur, ut summus ille Pœnorum Imperator contra Criminationes quasdam T. Livii defensus detur. Dublin, 1865.
Henrici Alani in Sallustii Catilinam et Jugurtham Curæ secundæ. Dublin, 1865.
Observationes aliquot in C. Julii Cæsaris utriusque Belli Commentarios. Inest Interpretatio Loci cujusdam Virgiliani. Dublin, 1874.

CHURCHILL BABINGTON (1821–1889)
(a) Writings

The Influence of Christianity in promoting the Abolition of Slavery in Europe: a Dissertation which obtained the Hulsean Prize for the Year 1845. Cambridge, 1846.
Mr Macaulay's Character of the Clergy in the Latter Part of the Seventeenth Century considered. With an Appendix on his Character of the Gentry as given in his History of England. Cambridge, 1849.
A Catalogue of the Manuscripts preserved in the Library of the University of Cambridge. 3 vols. 1856–8. [Classical MSS by Babington.]
An Introductory Lecture on Archæology delivered before the University of Cambridge. Cambridge, 1865.

Catalogue of the Birds of Suffolk; with an Introduction and Remarks on their Distribution. 1884–6.

(b) Editions

Ὑπερίδης κατα Δημοσθένους. The Oration of Hyperides against Demosthenes respecting the Treasure of Harpalus. 1850.
Ὑπερίδης Λογοι B. The Orations of Hyperides for Lycophron and for Euxenippus. Cambridge, 1853.
Paleario, A. The Benefit of Christ's Death. 1855. [Italian, French and English.]
Ὑπερίδου Λογος ἐπιταφιος. The Funeral Oration of Hyperides over Leosthenes and his Comrades in the Lamian War. Cambridge, 1858.
Peacock, R. The Repressor of over much blaming the Clergy. 1860. (Rolls Ser.)
Higden, R. Polychronicon. 2 vols. 1865–9. (Rolls Ser.)

CHARLES BADHAM (1813–1884)

Εὐριπίδου Ἰων. With Notes. 1851.
Εὐριπίδου Ἰφιγένεια ἡ ἐν Ταύροις.—Ἑλένη. 1851.
Platonis Philebus, with Introduction and Notes. 1855; 1878 (enlarged).
Platonis Euthydemus et Laches. Praefixa est Epistola ad Senatum Lugdunensem Batavorum. Jena, 1865.

JOHN STUART BLACKIE (1809–1895)

[See p. 280 above.]

JOSEPH WILLIAMS BLAKESLEY (1808–1885)

A Life of Aristotle, including a Critical Discussion of some Questions of Literary History connected with his Works. Cambridge, 1839.
Herodotus, with a Commentary. 2 vols. 1852–4.
Four Months in Algeria; with a Visit to Carthage. Cambridge, 1859.

FREDERICK HENRY MARVELL BLAYDES (1818–1908)

Sophocles, with English Notes. 1859. [Œdipus Tyrannus, Œdipus Coloneus, Antigone.]
The Philoctetes of Sophocles critically revised. 1870.
Aristophanis Comœdiæ. 12 vols. 1880–93.
Aristophanis Comici quæ supersunt Opera. 2 vols. Halle, 1886.
Adversaria in Comicorum græcorum Fragmenta. 2 pts, Halle, 1890–6.
Adversaria in Tragicorum græcorum Fragmenta. Halle, 1894.
Adversaria in Æschylum. Halle, 1895.
Adversaria in varios Poetas græcos ac latinos. Halle, 1898.

Æschyli Agamemnon. Cum Annotatione critica et Commentario. Halle, 1898.
Adversaria critica in Aristophanem. Halle, 1899.
Æschyli Choephoroi. Cum Annotatione critica et Commentario. Halle, 1899.
Adversaria critica in Sophoclem. Halle, 1899.
Æschyli Eumenides. 1900.
Adversaria critica in Euripidem. Halle, 1901.
Spicilegium Aristophaneum. Halle, 1902.
Spicilegium tragicum, Observationes criticas in tragicos Poetas græcos continens. Halle, 1902.
Spicilegium Sophocleum Commentarium perpetuum in septem Sophoclis Fabulas continens. Halle, 1903.
Analecta Comica græca. Halle, 1905.
Sophoclis Antigone. Halle, 1905.
Sophoclis Electra. Halle, 1906.
Analecta Tragica græca. Halle, 1906.
Miscellanea critica. Halle, 1907.

HENRY FYNES CLINTON (1781–1852)

Fasti Hellenici. The Civil and Literary Chronology of Greece, from the Earliest Accounts [to the Death of Augustus]. 3 vols. Oxford, 1824–34.
Fasti Romani. The Civil and Literary Chronology of Rome and Constantinople; from the Death of Augustus [to the Death of Heraclius]. 2 vols. Oxford, 1845–50.
An Epitome of the Civil and Literary Chronology of Greece, from the Earliest Accounts to the Death of Augustus. Oxford, 1851.
An Epitome of the Civil and Literary Chronology of Rome and Constantinople from the Death of Augustus to the Death of Heraclius. Ed. C. J. F. Clinton, 1853.
Literary Remains of Henry Fynes Clinton. Ed. C. J. F. Clinton, 1854. [Pt 1, Autobiography, written 1818; pt 2, Literary Journal, 1819–52; pt 3, Brief Essays on Theological Subjects.]

JOHN CONINGTON (1825–1869)

[See p. 284 above.]

EDWARD MEREDITH COPE (1818–1873)

Journal of Classical and Sacred Philology. [On the Sophists, I, 1854; On the Sophistical Rhetoric, II, 1855, III, 1856.]
Plato's Gorgias, literally translated with an Introductory Essay. Cambridge, 1864.
An Introduction to Aristotle's Rhetoric. 1867.
Plato's Phædo, literally translated. Ed. [H. Jackson], Cambridge, 1875.
The Rhetoric of Aristotle, with a Commentary by E. M. Cope. Ed. Sir J. E. Sandys, 3 vols. Cambridge, 1877. [With E. M. Cope, a Biographical Notice by H. A. J. Munro.]

JOHN WILLIAM DONALDSON (1811–1861)

(a) Critical and Philological Writings

The Theatre of the Greeks: a Series of Papers relating to the History and Criticism of the Greek Drama. With a New Introduction and Other Alterations. Cambridge, 1836. [The first three edns are by P. W. Buckham.]
The New Cratylus; or, Contributions towards a more Accurate Knowledge of the Greek Language. 1839; 1859 (rev.).
Varronianus: a Critical and Historical Introduction to the Philological Study of the Latin Language. Cambridge, 1844.
A Complete Greek Grammar for the Use of Learners. 1848.
A Complete Latin Grammar. 1852.
Classical Scholarship and Classical Learning considered with Especial Reference to Competitive Tests and University Teaching. Cambridge, 1856.
A History of the Literature of Ancient Greece; translated from the German Manuscript of Karl Otfried Müller by Sir G. C. Lewis and J. W. Donaldson. Continued by J. W. Donaldson. 3 vols. 1858.

(b) Editions

Πινδαρου τα σωζομενα. Pindar's Epinician or Triumphal Odes in Four Books; together with the Fragments of his Lost Compositions. 1841.
Σοφοκλεους 'Αντιγονη. In Greek and English. 1848.
Jashar. Fragmenta archetypa Carminum Hebraicorum. 1854.
Thucydides. 2 vols. Cambridge, 1859.

WILLIAM BODHAM DONNE (1807–1882)

Essays on the Drama. 1858.
The Correspondence of George the Third with Lord North. 1867.
Euripides. Edinburgh, 1872. [Critical essay.]
Tacitus. Edinburgh, 1873. [Essay.]
[See C. B. Johnson, William Bodham Donne and his Friends, 1905.]

ROBERT ELLIS (1820?–1885)

A Treatise on Hannibal's Passage of the Alps, in which his Route is traced over the Little Mount Cenis. 1853.
Observations on Mr [W. J.] Law's 'Criticism of Mr Ellis's New Theory concerning the Route of Hannibal.' Journ. of Classical and Sacred Philology, II, 1855, III, 1856.
An Enquiry into the Ancient Routes between Italy and Gaul; with an Examination of the Theory of Hannibal's Passage of the Alps by the Little St Bernard. Cambridge, 1867.

THOMAS SAUNDERS EVANS (1816–1889)

Μαθηματογονια. The Mythological Birth of the Nymph Mathesis. Cambridge, 1839 (anon.).

Tennyson's Œnone translated into Latin Hexameters. 1873.

The First Epistle to the Corinthians. 1881.

Latin and Greek Verse. (Compositions and Translations). Ed. (with Memoir) J. Waite, Cambridge, 1893.

SIR CHARLES FELLOWS (1799–1860)

A Journal written during an Excursion in Asia Minor. 1839.

An Account of Discoveries in Lycia, being a Journal kept during a Second Excursion in Asia Minor. 1841. [This and the above were rptd in 1852 as Travels and Researches in Asia Minor.]

The Xanthian Marbles; their Acquisition and Transmission to England. 1843.

Account of the Ionic Trophy Monument excavated at Xanthus. 1848.

Coins of Ancient Lycia before the Reign of Alexander. 1855.

WILLIAM EWART GLADSTONE (1809–1898)

[See p. 714 above.]

SIR ALEXANDER GRANT (1826–1884)

The Ethics of Aristotle illustrated with Essays and Notes. 2 vols. 1857–8 (incomplete); 2 vols. 1866 (complete).

Xenophon. Edinburgh, 1871.

Aristotle. Edinburgh, 1877.

The Story of the University of Edinburgh during its First Three Hundred Years. 2 vols. 1884.

HUBERT ASHTON HOLDEN (1822–1896)

Αριστοφανους κωμῳδιαι. 1848.

Foliorum Centuriæ. Selections for Translations into Latin and Greek Prose. Cambridge, 1852.

Foliorum Silvula. Selections for Translation into Latin and Greek Verse. Cambridge, 1852.

M. Minucii Felicis Octavius. Cambridge, 1853.

An Investigation of the Trinity of Plato and of Philo Judæus, and of the Effects which an Attachment to their Writings had upon the Principles and Reasonings of the Fathers of the Christian Church. By Cæsar Morgan. Cambridge, 1853.

Folia Silvulæ; sive Eclogæ Pœtarum Anglicorum in Latinum et Græcum conversæ. 2 vols. 1865–70.

M. Tullii Ciceronis De Officiis Libri tres. Cambridge, 1869 (2nd edn).

Onomasticon Aristophaneum; sive Index Nominum quæ apud Aristophanem leguntur. Cambridge, 1871.

M. Tullii Ciceronis Pro Gnæo Plancio. Cambridge, 1881.

Πλουταρχου Θεμιστοκλης. 1881.

M. Tullii Ciceronis Pro Publio Sestio Oratio ad Judices. 1883.

Ξενοφωντος Ἱερων ἡ Τυραννικος. 1883.

Ξενοφωντος Οἰκονομικος. 1884.

Πλουταρχου Γρακχοι. Cambridge, 1885.

Πλουταρχου Συλλας. Cambridge, 1886.

Πλουταρχου Νικιας. Cambridge, 1887.

Ξενοφωντος Κυρου Παιδειας. 2 vols. Cambridge, 1887.

Πλουταρχου Τιμολεων. Cambridge, 1889.

Θουκυδιδου ἑβδομη. The Seventh Book of the History of Thucydides. Cambridge, 1891.

Πλουταρχου Δημοσθενης. Cambridge, 1893.

ARTHUR HOLMES (1837–1875)

Demosthenes. Midias. Cambridge, 1862.

The Nemeian Odes of Pindar, with Special Reference to Ode the Seventh. 1867.

Demosthenes with English Notes. De Corona. 1871.

BENJAMIN JOWETT (1817–1893)

(a) Editions and Translations

The Epistles of St Paul to the Thessalonians, Galatians, Romans, with Critical Notes and Dissertations. 2 vols. 1855.

On the Interpretation of Scripture. [In Essays and Reviews, 1860.]

The Dialogues of Plato. Translated into English, with Analyses and Introductions. 4 vols. Oxford, 1871.

Thucydides translated into English. 2 vols. Oxford, 1881.

The Politics of Aristotle translated into English. 2 vols. Oxford, 1885.

Plato's Republic. The Greek Text. Ed. B. Jowett and L. Campbell, 3 vols. Oxford, 1894.

(b) Biography and Criticism

Swinburne, A. C. Recollections of Jowett. Nineteenth Century, xxxiv, 1893.

Abbott, E. and Campbell, L. The Life and Letters of Benjamin Jowett. 2 vols. Oxford, 1897.

Stephen, Sir L. Jowett. [In Studies of a Biographer, vol. ii, 1898.]

The Letters of Benjamin Jowett. Ed. Evelyn Abbott and Lewis Campbell, 1899.

BENJAMIN HALL KENNEDY (1804–1889)

(a) Grammars and Verses

Tirocinium; or, An Elementary Latin Reading Book. 1848 (anon.).

Palæstra Latina; or, A Second Latin Reading-Book. 1850.

Sabrinæ Corolla in Hortulis Regiæ Scholæ Salopiensis contexuerunt tres Viri [B. H. Kennedy, J. Riddell, and another] Floribus Legendis. 1850, etc.

Palæstra Stili Latini; or, Materials for Translation into Latin Prose. 1855.

Palæstra Musarum; or, Materials for Translation into Greek Verse. 1856.

Curriculum Stili Latini; or, A Systematic Course of Examples for Practice in the Style of the Best Latin Prose Authors. 1858.

The Public School Latin Primer, edited with the Sanction of the Head Masters of the Public Schools included in Her Majesty's Commission. 1866 (anon.).

The Public School Latin Grammar for the Use of Schools, Colleges and Private Students. 1871 (anon.).

Studia Sophoclea. Being a Critical Examination of Lewis Campbell's Edition of Sophocles. Cambridge, 1874.

Between Whiles; or, Wayside Amusements of a Working Life. 1877. [Latin and Greek poems, some original. Also 2 poems in English by R. Kennedy and 7 poems translated into Latin and Greek by G. J. Kennedy.]

(b) Editions and Translations

The Birds of Aristophanes. Translated into English Verse. 1874.

P. Virgili Maronis Bucolica, Georgica, Æneis. 1876.

P. Vergili Maronis Opera. Cambridge, 1876.

The Agamemnon of Æschylus. With a Metrical Translation and Notes. Cambridge, 1878.

The Theætetus of Plato, with Translation and Notes. Cambridge, 1881.

The Œdipus Tyrannus of Sophocles. With Translation, Notes and Indices. Cambridge, 1882.

The Œdipus Tyrannus of Sophocles translated into English Prose. Cambridge, 1885.

(c) Biography and Criticism

Obituary. Athenaeum, 13 April 1889.

Mayor, J. E. B. Obituary. Classical Rev. III, 1889.

How, F. D. Six Great Schoolmasters. 1904.

CHARLES RANN KENNEDY (1808–1867)

Translation of Select Speeches of Demosthenes, with Notes. Cambridge, 1841.

The Orations of Demosthenes. Translated with Notes. 5 vols. 1852–63.

[For Kennedy's poems see p. 293 above.]

THOMAS HEWITT KEY (1799–1875)

The Alphabet; Terentian Metres; Good, Better, Best, Well; and other Philological Papers; with a Letter on the Rev. J. W. Donaldson's 'Varronianus.' 1844.

A Latin Grammar on the System of Crude Forms. 1845.

Philological Essays. 1868.

Language: its Origin and Development. 1874.

A Latin-English Dictionary, printed from the Unfinished MS. of Thomas Hewitt Key. Cambridge, 1888.

CHARLES WILLIAM KING (1818–1888)

Antique Gems: their Origin, Uses, and Value as Interpreters of Ancient History; and as illustrative of Ancient Art: with Hints to Gem Collectors. 1860.

The Gnostics and their Remains, Ancient and Mediæval. 1864.

The Natural History, Ancient and Modern, of Precious Stones and Gems, and of the Precious Metals. 1865.

The Handbook of Engraved Gems, with Numerous Illustrations. 1866.

The Natural History of Gems, or Decorative Stones. Cambridge, 1867.

The Natural History of Precious Stones and of the Precious Metals. Cambridge, 1867.

Catalogue of Col. Leake's Engraved Gems. 1870.

Early Christian Numismatics, and Other Antiquarian Tracts. 1873.

Plutarch's Morals. Theosophical Essays translated by C. W. King. Ethical Essays translated with Notes by A. R. Shilleto. 2 vols. 1882–8.

Julian the Emperor, containing Gregory Nazianzen's two Invectives and Libanus' Monody, with Julian's Extant Theosophical Works. Translated. 1888.

WILLIAM JOHN LAW (1786–1869)

A Criticism of Mr Ellis's New Theory concerning the Route of Hannibal. With Some Remarks on the Hypothesis of M. Replat. 1855.

Reply to Mr Ellis's Defence of his Theory [concerning Hannibal's Route over the Alps]. Journ. of Classical and Sacred Philology, III, 1856.

Reply to the Second Part of Mr Ellis's Defence of his Theory. Journ. of Classical and Sacred Philology, III, 1856.

The Alps of Hannibal. 2 vols. 1866.

SIR GEORGE CORNEWALL LEWIS (1806–1863)

(a) Writings and Translations

The Public Economy of Athens, in Four Books; to which is added a Dissertation on the Silver Mines of Laurion. Translated from the German of August Boeckh. 2 vols. 1828.

The History and Antiquities of the Doric Race, translated from the German of K. O. Müller by H. Tufnell and G. C. Lewis. 2 vols. Oxford, 1830.

An Essay on the Origin and Formation of the Romance Languages: containing an Examination of M. Raynouard's Theory on the Relation of the Italian, Spanish, Provençal, and French, to the Latin. 1835.

A History of the Literature of Ancient Greece; translated from the German Manuscript of Karl Otfried Müller by Sir G. C. Lewis and J. W. Donaldson. 2 vols. 1840–2.

Babrii Fabulæ Æsopeæ, cum Fabularum deperditarum Fragmentis. Oxford, 1846.

An Inquiry into the Credibility of the Early Roman History. 2 vols. 1855; tr. German, Hanover, 1858.

Babrii Fabulæ. Pt 2, 1859. [A spurious set of Fables by M. Menas, a Greek.]

An Historical Survey of the Astronomy of the Ancients. 1862.

(b) Biography and Criticism

In Memoriam Sir G. C. Lewis. Fraser's Mag. LXVII, 1863.

Fyfe, J. H. Sir George Cornewall Lewis. Macmillan's Mag. XXI, 1870.

HENRY GEORGE LIDDELL (1811–1898)
(a) Lexicon

A Greek-English Lexicon, based on the German Work of Francis Passow. Oxford, 1843. [Later rev. and expanded through 8 edns to 1897. With Robert Scott (1811–1887).]

(b) Biography and Criticism

Obituary of Robert Scott. Guardian, 14 Dec. 1887.

Thompson, H. L. Henry George Liddell, D.D., Dean of Christ Church, Oxford. A Memoir. 1899.

WILLIAM LINWOOD (1817–1878)

A Lexicon to Æschylus. 1843.

Εὐμενίδες. Æschyli Eumenides. Oxford, 1844.

Σοφοκλῆς. Sophoclis Tragœdiæ superstites. 1846.

The Theban Trilogy of Sophocles. With Notes. 1878.

GEORGE LONG (1800–1879)
(a) Historical and Legal Writings

Two Dissertations on Roman Law. 1827.

Two Discourses in the Middle Temple Hall on Roman Law. 1846.

France and its Revolutions: a Pictorial History. 1789–1848. 1850.

The Decline of the Roman Republic. 5 vols. 1864.

(b) Journals and Cyclopædias

The Quarterly Journal of Education. 10 vols. 1831–5.

The Penny Cyclopædia of the Society for the Diffusion of Useful Knowledge. 30 vols. 1833–58.

The Biographical Dictionary of the Society for the Diffusion of Useful Knowledge. Vols. I–IV, 1842–4. [Letter A only.]

The Standard Library Cyclopædia of Political, Constitutional, Statistical and Forensic Knowledge. 4 vols. 1848–9.

Bibliotheca Classica. 27 vols. 1851–84. [With A. J. Macleane.]

(c) Editions and Translations

The Civil Wars of Rome: Select Lives translated from Plutarch. 5 vols. 1844–8.

M. Tullii Ciceronis Orationes. 4 vols. 1851–8.

C. Julii Cæsaris Commentarii de Bello Gallico. 1853.

M. Tullii Ciceronis Cato Major, sive De Senectute; Lælius, sive De Amicitia; et Epistolæ Selectæ. Cambridge, 1860.

The Thoughts of the Emperor Marcus Aurelius Antoninus, translated. 1862.

The Discourses of Epictetus; with the Encheiridion and Fragments. Translated, with Notes, a Life of Epictetus, and a View of his Philosophy. 1877.

EDMUND LAW LUSHINGTON (1811–1893)

On the Study of Greek. An Inaugural Discourse. Glasgow, 1839.

War of Rameses II with Khitu. Egyptian Texts of Records of the Past. [1875 ?]

General Introductory Address [as Lord Rector of Glasgow University]. Glasgow, 1885.

ARTHUR JOHN MACLEANE (1812–1858)

D. J. Juvenalis et A. Persii Flacci Satiræ. With a Commentary. 1857.

Q. Horatii Flacci Opera. Cambridge, 1858.

HUGH ANDREW JOHNSTONE MUNRO (1819–1885)
(a) Editions and Writings

Titi Lucreti Cari de Rerum Natura Libri sex. Cambridge, 1860. [Latin text only.]

Titi Lucreti Cari de Rerum Natura Libri sex. With a Translation and Notes. 2 vols. 1864; 3 vols. Cambridge, 1886 (rev.).

Ætna. [Ascribed to Lucilius Junior.] Revised, emended and explained. Cambridge, 1867.

Q. Horatii Flacci Opera, illustrated from Antique Gems by C. W. King. The Text revised, with an Introduction, by H. A. J. Munro. 1869.

A Few Remarks on the Pronunciation of Latin. With a Postscript. Cambridge. 1871.

Syllabus of Latin Pronunciation, drawn up at the Request of the Headmasters of Schools, Cambridge, 1872. [With E. Palmer.]

Criticisms and Elucidations of Catullus. Cambridge, 1878.

Translations into Latin and Greek Verse. With a Prefatory Note by J. D. Duff. 1905. [Originally priv. ptd 1884.]

(b) Contributions to Periodicals

Journal of Classical and Sacred Philology [II, 1855: Nicomachean Ethics, Book V; Eudemian Ethics, Book IV.]

Journal of Philology. [VII, 1877: Luciliana; VIII, 1879: Another Word on Lucilius; Catullus' 68th Poem; X, 1882: On the Fragments of Euripides; XI, 1882: Catullus 64, 276 and 63, 18; On Æschylus' Agamemnon, 1227–1230, Dindorf; Euripidea.]

WILLIAM MURE (1799–1860)

Journal of a Tour in Greece and the Ionian Islands. 2 vols. Edinburgh, 1842.

A Critical History of the Language and Literature of Antient Greece. 5 vols. 1850–7. [Up to 380 B.C. only.]

SIR CHARLES THOMAS NEWTON (1816–1894)

A History of Discoveries at Halicarnassus, Cnidus, and Branchidæ. 2 vols. 1862–3. [With R. P. Pullan.]

Travels and Discoveries in the Levant. 2 vols. 1865.

Essays on Art and Archæology. 1880.

The Collection of Ancient Greek Inscriptions in the British Museum. Pts 1, 2. 1874–83. [Ed. by Newton.]

FREDERICK APTHORP PALEY (1815–1888)

(a) Miscellaneous Writings

The Church Restorers: a Tale treating of Ancient and Modern Architecture and Church Decorations. 1844.

The Ecclesiologist's Guide to the Churches within a Circuit of seven Miles round Cambridge, with Introductory Remarks. Cambridge, 1844.

A Manual of Gothic Mouldings, with Full Directions for copying them and for determining their Dates. 1845.

A Manual of Gothic Architecture. 1846.

Religious Tests and National Universities. 1871.

Pseudo-Archaic Words and Inflexions in the Homeric Vocabulary and their Relation to the Antiquity of the Homeric Poems. Journ. of Philology, VII, 1876.

Quintus Smyrnaeus and the 'Homer' of the Tragic Poets. 1876.

Commentarius in Scholia Æschyli Medicea. Cambridge, 1878.

Homeri quae nunc exstant an reliquis Cycli Carminibus antiquiora Jure habita sint. 1878.

On Post-epic or Imitative Words in Homer. 1879.

Bibliographia Græca: an Inquiry into the Date and Origin of Book-Writing among the Greeks, with Reference to the most Recent Opinions and Researches. 1881.

Remarks on Prof. Mahaffy's Account of the Rise and Progress of Epic Poetry, in his History of Classical Greek Literature. 1881.

A Short Treatise on the Greek Particles and their Combinations, according to Attic Usage. Cambridge, 1881.

The Truth about Homer. With some Remarks on Professor Jebb's 'Introduction to Homer.' 1887.

(b) Editions and Translations

Αἰσχύλου Ἱκετιδες. Æschyli Supplices. Cambridge. 1844. [Greek, with Latin notes. There followed, in the same form: Agamemnon, 1845; Choephori, 1845; Prometheus Vinctus, 1846; Persæ, 1847; Septem contra Thebas, 1847.]

Sex. Aurelii Propertii Carmina. The Elegies of Propertius, with English Notes. 1853.

P. Ovidii Nasonis Fastorum Libri sex. 1854.

The Tragedies of Æschylus. Re-edited, with an English Commentary. 1855.

Euripides. 3 vols. Cambridge, 1858–60.

The Epics of Hesiod. With an English Commentary. 1861.

Theocritus. Cambridge, 1863.

Æschylus translated into English Prose. 1864.

The Iliad of Homer. With English Notes. 1866.

Verse-Translations from Propertius, Book V. With a Revised Latin Text, and Brief English Notes. 1866.

M. V. Martialis Epigrammata selecta. Select Epigrams from Martial, with English Notes by F. A. Paley and W. H. Stone. 1868.

The Odes of Pindar. Translated into English Prose with Brief Explanatory Notes. 1868.

Aristotle's Ethics, Books V. and X. translated into English. 1872.

Ἀριστοφανους Εἰρηνη. The 'Peace' of Aristophanes. Cambridge, 1873.

The Philebus of Plato; translated with Brief Explanatory Notes. 1873.

Select Private Orations of Demosthenes. With Introductions and English Notes by F. A. Paley and J. E. Sandys. 2 pts, Cambridge, 1874–5].

The Theætetus of Plato. Translated with Introduction and Notes. 1875.

Greek Wit. A Collection of Smart Sayings and Anecdotes translated from Greek Prose Writers. 2 sers. [1880–1].

Sophocles, with English Notes. Vol. II, 1880. [Vol. I, by F. H. M. Blaydes.]

Æschyli Fabulæ Ἱκετιδες, Χοηφοροι. Cambridge, 1883.

The Gospel of St John: a Verbatim Translation from the Vatican MS. With the Notable Variations of the Sinaitic and Beza MS., and Brief Explanatory Comments. 1887.

Fragments of the Greek Comic Poets. With Renderings in English Verse. 1889 [1888].

JOHN HENRY PARKER (1806–1884)

A Glossary of Terms used in Grecian, Roman, Italian, and Gothic Architecture. 1836 (anon.); 2 vols. Oxford, 1850 (enlarged).

The Archæology of Rome. 2 vols. Oxford, 1874–6.

MARK PATTISON (1813–1884)

[See p. 723 above.]

THOMAS WILLIAMSON PEILE (1806–1882)

Αἰσχυλου Ἀγαμεμνων. The Agamemnon of Æschylus. 1839.

Αἰσχυλου Χοηφοροι. The Choephorœ. 1840.

FRANCIS CRANMER PENROSE (1817–1903)

An Investigation of the Principles of Grecian Architecture. 2 vols. 1851–2.

EDWARD POSTE (1823–1902)

The Logic of Science. A Translation of the Posterior Analytics of Aristotle. With Notes and an Introduction. Oxford, 1850.

The Philebus of Plato, with a Revised Text and English Notes. Oxford, 1860.

Philebus: a Dialogue of Plato on Pleasure and Knowledge and their Relations to the Highest Good. Translated into English. 1860.

Aristotle on Fallacies; or, The Sophistici Elenchi. With a Translation and Notes. 1866.

Gaii Institutionum Juris Civilis Commentarii quatuor; or, Elements of Roman Law by Gaius. With a Translation and Commentary. Oxford, 1875.

The Skies and Weather-Forecasts of Aratus. Translated, with Notes. 1880.

Aristotle on the Constitution of Athens. Translated. 1891.

WILLIAM RAMSAY (1806–1865)

Elegiac Extracts from Tibullus and Ovid; with English Introductions and Notes. Glasgow, 1840.

A Manual of Latin Prosody. 1840.

A Manual of Roman Antiquities. [In E. Smedley, Encyclopædia Metropolitana, 3rd Division, 1851.]

The Speech of Cicero for Aulus Cluentius Habitus. With Prolegomena and Notes. 2 pts, Glasgow, 1858.

An Elementary Manual of Latin Prosody. 1859.

The Mostellaria of Plautus. With Notes, Critical and Explanatory, Prolegomena and Excursus by W. Ramsay. Ed. G. G. Ramsay, 1869.

[Also articles on Agriculture, Astronomy, Cicero, Juvenalis, Lucilius, Lucretius, etc. in Sir William Smith's Dictionary of Greek and Roman Antiquities, 1842.]

GEORGE RAWLINSON (1812–1902)

[See p. 913 above.]

JAMES RIDDELL (1823–1866)

The Apology of Plato. With a Revised Text and English Notes and a Digest of Platonic Idioms. Oxford, 1867.

Homer's Odyssey. Books I–XII. 1876. [With W. W. Merry.]

MARTIN JOSEPH ROUTH (1755–1854)

[See p. 860 above.]

JOHN YOUNG SARGENT (1829–1915)

Outlines of Norwegian Grammar, with Exercises. 1865.

Easy Passages for Translation into Latin. Oxford, 1867. [Key, 1887.]

Materials and Models for Greek and Latin Prose Composition. 1870. [With T. F. Dallin.]

Materials and Models for Greek Prose Composition. 1878. [With T. F. Dallin.]

Grammar of the Dano-Norwegian Language. 1892.

RICHARD SHILLETO (1809–1876)

Δημοσθενους ὁ περι της Παραπρεσβειας λογος. A New Edition, with a Careful Revision of the Text. Cambridge, 1844.

Thucydides or Grote? Cambridge, 1851. [Answered in J. G[rote], A Few Remarks on a Pamphlet by Mr Shilleto entitled 'Thucydides or Grote?,' Cambridge, 1851.]

Θουκυδιδου A. [B]. Thucydidis I. [II.]. With Collation of the Two Cambridge MSS. and the Aldine and Juntine Editions. Cambridge, 1872–80.

Collected Versions. Cambridge, 1901.

SIR WILLIAM SMITH (1813–1893)

A Dictionary of Greek and Roman Antiquities. 1842; 2 vols. 1890–1 (with W. Wayte and G. E. Marindin).

Dictionary of Greek and Roman Biography and Mythology. 3 vols. 1844–9.

A Smaller Dictionary of Greek and Roman Antiquities abridged from the Larger Dictionary. 1845.

New Classical Dictionary of Biography, Mythology, and Geography. 1850.

A Smaller Classical Dictionary of Biography, Mythology, and Geography; abridged from the Larger Dictionary. 1852.

A History of Greece, from the Earliest Times to the Roman Conquest, with Supplementary Chapters on the History of Literature and Art. 1854.

A Dictionary of Greek and Roman Geography. 2 vols. 1854–7.

A Latin-English Dictionary, based upon the Works of Forcellini and Freund. 1855.

A Smaller Latin-English Dictionary, abridged from the Larger Dictionary. 1855.

The Student's Gibbon. The History of the Decline and Fall of the Roman Empire, abridged. Incorporating the Researches of Recent Commentators. 1857.

A Dictionary of the Bible, comprising its Antiquities, Biography, Geography and Natural History. 3 vols. 1860–3.

Classical and Biblical Atlas. 1874. [With Sir G. Grove.]

A Dictionary of Christian Antiquities. Being a Continuation of 'The Dictionary of the Bible.' 2 vols. 1875–80. [With S. Cheetham.]

A Dictionary of Christian Biography, Literature, Sects and Doctrines. Being a Continuation of 'The Dictionary of the Bible.' 4 vols. 1877–87. [With H. Wace.]

[Smith also produced a copiously annotated edn of Gibbon in 8 vols., text books of history, English literature, grammars of Latin, Greek, French, German, Italian; editions of Plato, Hallam, Hume, etc.—a great body of editorial work, of which only the chief examples are given above.]

THOMAS ABEL BRIMAGE SPRATT (1811–1888)

Travels in Lycia, Milyas, and the Cibyratis, in Company with the Late Rev. E. T. Daniell. 2 vols. 1847. [With E. Forbes.]

Travels and Researches in Crete. 2 vols. 1865.

WILLIAM HEPWORTH THOMPSON (1810–1886)

On the Genuineness of the Sophist of Plato and on some of its Philosophical Bearings. Trans. Cambridge Philosophical Soc. x, 1858.

Platonica; Isocratea. Journ. of Classical and Sacred Philology, IV, 1860.

The Phædrus of Plato. With English Notes and Dissertations. 1868.

The Gorgias of Plato. With English Notes and Dissertations. 1871.

Introductory Remarks on the Philebus; Euripides. Journ. of Philology, XI, 1882.

On the Nubes of Aristophanes; Babriana. Journ. of Philology, XII, 1883.

WILLIAM VEITCH (1794–1885)

Greek Verbs, Irregular and Defective: their Forms, Meaning and Quantity. Edinburgh, 1848.

HENRY MUSGRAVE WILKINS (1822–1887)

Notes for Latin Lyrics, for the Use of Schools. 1851.

A Manual of Latin Prose Composition. 1857.

A Manual of Greek Prose Composition, for the Use of Schools and Colleges. 1858.

The Olynthiacs of Demosthenes. 1860.

Speeches from Thucydides, translated into English, for the Use of Students. 1870.

CHRISTOPHER WORDSWORTH (1807–1885)

Athens and Attica: Journal of a Residence there. 1836.

Greece, Pictorial, Descriptive and Historical. 1839.

Theocritus. Cambridge, 1844. [Greek.]

The New Testament in the Original Greek; with Introductions and Notes. 2 vols. 1856–61.

Conjectural Emendations on Passages in Ancient Authors. With Other Papers. 1883.

[See also p. 313 above.]

(c) 1870–1900

EVELYN ABBOTT (1843–1901)

Hellenica. A Collection of Essays on Greek Poetry, Philosophy, History, and Religion. 1880. [Ed. by Abbott.]

A History of Greece. 3 pts, 1888–1900.

Pericles and the Golden Age of Athens. 1891.

Herodotus, Books v. and VI. 1893. [Bk IX, 1887.]

The Life and Letters of Benjamin Jowett. 2 vols. 1897. [With Lewis Campbell.]

[Abbott also brought out a number of grammars, edns, etc.]

JAMES ADAM (1860–1907)

(a) Editions

Platonis Apologia Socratis. 1887.

Platonis Crito. 1888.

Εὐθυφρων. Platonis Euthyphro. 1890.

Platonis Protagoras. 1893.

The Republic of Plato. 1897.

(b) Writings

The Nuptial Number of Plato; its Solution and Significance. 1891.

The Doctrine of the Celestial Origin of the Soul from Pindar to Plato. 1906.

The Religious Teachers of Greece: being Gifford Lectures on Natural Religion. Ed. (with Memoir) A. M. Adam, Edinburgh, 1908.

The Vitality of Platonism, and Other Essays. Ed. A. M. Adam, Cambridge, 1911.

RICHARD DACRE ARCHER-HIND (1849–1910)

Πλατωνος Φαιδων. The Phaedo of Plato. 1883.
Πλατωνος Τιμαιος. The Timæus. 1888. [With trn.]
Translations into Greek Verse and Prose. Cambridge, 1905.

JOHN ISAAC BEARE (1857–1918)

Select Satires of Horace. Dublin, 1882.
Greek Theories of Elementary Cognition, from Alcmaeon to Aristotle. Oxford, 1906.
The Works of Aristotle. 1907. [Vol. III (The Parva Naturalia, De Sensu et Sensibili, De Memoria et Reminiscentia, De Somno, De Somniis, De Divinatione per Somnum) tr. by Beare.]

[For obituary see Hermathena, XLI, 1919. Beare edited this periodical, 1904–18.]

ROBERT BURN (1829–1904)

Rome and the Campagna: an Historical and Topographical Description of the Site, Buildings and Neighbourhood of Ancient Rome. Cambridge, 1871–6.
Old Rome: a Handbook to the Ruins of the City and the Campagna. Being an Epitome of 'Rome and the Campagna.' 1880.
Roman Literature in Relation to Roman Art. 1888.

SAMUEL HENRY BUTCHER (1850–1910)

(a) Editions and Translations

The Odyssey of Homer, done into English Prose by S. H. Butcher and Andrew Lang. 1879; 1879 (with additional notes).
Aristotle's Theory of Poetry and Fine Art, with a Critical Text and a Translation of the Poetics by S. H. Butcher. 1895.
Demosthenis Orationes. Recognovit, brevique Adnotatione critica instruxit S. H. Butcher. 3 vols. Oxford, 1903–31. [Vol. III by W. Dennie.]

(b) Critical Works

Some Aspects of the Greek Genius. 1891; 1893 (with additional ch. on 'The Dawn of Romanticism in Greek Poetry').
Harvard Lectures on Greek Subjects. 1904.

(c) Biography and Criticism

Verrall, A. W. Obituary. Classical Rev. XXV, 1911.

Dugdale, Mrs E. The Personality of Professor Butcher. Blackwood's Mag. CLXXXIX, 1911.
Harris, W. F. Professor Butcher at Cambridge. Classical Journ. (Chicago), VI, 1911.

INGRAM BYWATER (1840–1914)

(a) Writings and Editions

Heracliti Ephesii Reliquiæ. Oxford, 1877.
Journal of Philology. Ed. I. Bywater, 1879–1914. [Contributions: vol. I: On the Fragments attributed to Philolaus the Pythagorean; II: A Lost Dialogue of Aristotle; IV: Critical Notes on Clement of Alexandria; A Passage in Aristotle's Ethics (VII, c. 8); VII: Aristotle's Dialogue on Philosophy; XII: The Cleophons in Aristotle; XIII: On Diogenes Laertius, IX, 1, 7; XVII: Aristotelia, III; Miscellanea; XXVII: Milton and the Aristotelian Definition of Tragedy; XXVIII: Aristotelia IV; XXXI: ΑΤΑΚΤΑ II; XXXII: Palaeographica; XXXIII: The Latinizations of the Modern Surname.]
Aristotelis Ethica Nicomachea. Oxford, 1890.
Aristotelis De Arte Poetica Liber. Oxford, 1898.
The Erasmian Pronunciation of Greek, and its Precursors: Jerome Aleander, Aldus Manutius, Antonio of Lebrixa. A Lecture. 1908.
Ἀριστοτελους περι Ποιητικης. Aristotle on the Art of Poetry. A Revised Text, with Critical Introduction, Translation and Commentary. 1909.
Elenchus Librorum vetustiorum apud [I. Bywater] hospitantium. [1911] (priv. ptd).

(b) Biography and Criticism

Obituary. Athenaeum, 26 Dec. 1914.
Jackson, William Walrond. Ingram Bywater: the Memoir of an Oxford Scholar, 1840–1914. 2 pts, Oxford, 1917–9.
Chapman, R. W. The Portrait of a Scholar. Oxford, 1922.

LEWIS CAMPBELL (1830–1908)

(a) Editions and Translations

The Theætetus of Plato. Oxford, 1861.
The Sophistes and Politicus of Plato. Oxford, 1867.
Sophocles: the Plays and Fragments. 2 vols. Oxford, 1871–81.
Sophocles. The Seven Plays in English Verse. 1883.
Æschylus. The Seven Plays in English Verse. 1890.
Plato's Republic. The Greek Text, with Notes and Essays by B. Jowett and L. Campbell. 3 vols. Oxford, 1894.
Æschyli Tragœdiæ. 1898.

(b) *Critical Writings*

A Guide to Greek Tragedy for English Readers. 1891.

The Life and Letters of Benjamin Jowett. 1897. [With Evelyn Abbott.]

Religion in Greek Literature: a Sketch in Outline. 1898.

ROBINSON ELLIS (1834–1913)

[See p. 340 above.]

SIR ARTHUR JOHN EVANS (b. 1851)

The 'Horsemen' of Tarentum. A Contribution towards the Numismatic History of Great Greece. 1889.

Cretan Pictographs and Præ-Phœnician Script. With an Account of a Sepulchral Deposit at Hagios Onuphrios, near Phæstos, in its Relation to Primitive Cretan and Ægean Culture. 1895.

Further Discoveries of Cretan and Ægean Script with Libyan and Proto-Egyptian Comparisons. From the Journal of Hellenic Studies. 1898.

The Mycenaean Tree and Pillar Cult and its Mediterranean Relations. 1901.

The Prehistoric Tombs of Knossos. I. The Cemetery of Zafer Papoura. II. The Royal Tomb of Isopata. 1906.

Scripta Minoa. The Written Documents of Minoan Crete with Special Reference to the Archives of Knossos. Oxford, 1909–.

The Tomb of the Double Axes and Associated Group, and Pillar Rooms and Ritual Vessels of the 'Little Palace' at Knossos. 1914.

The Palace of Minos. A Comparative Account of the Successive Stages of the Early Cretan Civilization as illustrated by the Discoveries at Knossos. 3 vols. 1921–30.

The Shaft Graves and Bee-hive Tombs of Mycenae and their Interrelation. 1929.

WILLIAM HENRY FORBES (1851–1914)

Thucydides. Book I. Oxford, 1895.

WILLIAM WARDE FOWLER (1847–1921)

A Year with the Birds. By an Oxford Tutor. Oxford, 1886.

Julius Cæsar and the Foundation of the Roman Imperial System. 1892.

The City-State of the Greeks and Romans. 1893.

Summer Studies of Birds and Books. 1895.

The Roman Festivals of the Period of the Republic. 1899.

Social Life at Rome in the Age of Cicero. 1908.

The Religious Experience of the Roman People from the Earliest Times to the Age of Augustus. 1911. (Gifford Lectures.)

Rome. 1912. (Home University Lib.)

Kingham, Old and New. 1913.

Virgil's 'Gathering of the Clans': being Observations on Æneid VII., 601–817. 1916.

Æneas at the Site of Rome: Observations on the Eighth Book of the Æneid. 1917.

The Death of Turnus: Observations on the Twelfth Book of the Æneid. 1919.

Roman Essays and Interpretations. Oxford, 1920.

Reminiscences. 1921 (priv. ptd).

[For life see R. H. Coon, William Warde Fowler, Oxford, 1934.]

HENRY FURNEAUX (1829–1900)

C. Taciti Annalium Libri. 2 vols. Oxford, 1884–91.

SIR WILLIAM DUGUID GEDDES (1828–1900)

Platonis Phaedo. 1863.

The Problem of the Homeric Poems. 1878.

[For obituaries see Times, 1 Feb. 1900 and Athenæum, 17 Feb. 1900.]

EDWIN HAMILTON GIFFORD (1820–1905)

The Epistle to the Romans. 1881.

Εὐσεβίου τοῦ Παμφίλου Εὐαγγελικῆς Προπαρασκευῆς λογοι ιε'. 4 vols. Oxford, 1903.

The Euthydemus of Plato. Oxford, 1905.

[For obituaries see Times, 6 May 1905, Guardian, 10 May 1905, and Eagle, June 1905.]

CHARLES EDWARD GRAVES (1839–1920)

The Euthyphro and Menexenus of Plato. 1881.

Θουκυδίδου Ξυγγραφῆς Δ. The Fourth Book of Thucydides. 1884.

Θουκυδίδου Ξυγγραφῆς Ε. The Fifth Book of Thucydides. 1891.

The Wasps of Aristophanes. Cambridge, 1894.

The Clouds of Aristophanes. Cambridge, 1898.

Aristophanes. The Acharnians. Cambridge, 1905.

Aristophanes. The Peace. Cambridge, 1911.

WILLIAM CHARLES GREEN (1832–1914)

The Acharnians and Knights of Aristophanes. 1870.

The Peace of Aristophanes. 1873.

The Birds of Aristophanes. 1875.

The Frogs of Aristophanes. Cambridge, 1879.

The Iliad of Homer, with a Verse Translation by W. C. Green. Vol. I (bks I–XII), 1884. [No more pbd.]

The Plutus of Aristophanes, closely translated. Cambridge, 1887.

The Story of Egil Skallagrimsson: being an Icelandic Family History of the Ninth and Tenth Centuries. 1893.

The Odes of Horace and his Secular Hymn, rendered into English Verse. 1903.

ARTHUR ELAM HAIGH (1855–1905)

The Attic Theatre. A Description of the Stage and Theatre of the Athenians, and of the Dramatic Performances at Athens. With Facsimiles and Illustrations. Oxford, 1889; Oxford, 1898 (rev.).

P. Vergili Maronis Opera. 2 vols. Oxford, 1892. [With J. L. Papillon.]

The Tragic Drama of the Greeks. With Illustrations. Oxford, 1896.

HENRY HAYMAN (1823–1904)

The Odyssey of Homer. 3 vols. 1866–82.

BARCLAY VINCENT HEAD (1844–1914)

Catalogues of Greek Coins in the British Museum. 10 vols. 1873–1906.

On the Chronological Sequence of the Coins of Syracuse. 1874.

The Coinage of Lydia and Persia, from the Earliest Times to the Fall of the Dynasty of the Achæmenidæ. 1877.

A Guide to the Principal Gold and Silver Coins of the Ancients from circ. B.C. 700 to A.D. 1. 1881.

Historia Numorum. A Manual of Greek Numismatics. Oxford, 1887; Oxford, 1911 (enlarged, with G. F. Hill, G. Macdonald and W. Wroth).

WALTER GEORGE HEADLAM (1866–1908)

(a) Writings and Editions

Fifty Poems of Meleager. With a Translation. 1890.

On Editing Æschylus. 1891. [On A. W. Verrall's edns of the Septem contra Thebas and the Agamemnon.]

Contributions to Cambridge Compositions. 1899.

A Book of Greek Verse. Cambridge, 1907.

The Plays of Æschylus. Translated from a Revised Text by W. Headlam and C. E. S. Headlam. 1909. [Originally pbd 1900–9.]

The Agamemnon of Æschylus. With Verse Translation, Introduction and Notes. Ed. A. C. Pearson, Cambridge, 1910.

(b) Contributions to Periodicals

Various Conjectures. Journ. of Philology, xx, xxi, 1892, xxiii, 1895, xxvi, 1899.

Greek Lyric Metre. Journ. of Hellenic Stud. xxii, 1902.

Emendations and Explanations. Journ. of Philology, xxx, 1907.

[And many articles, notes and reviews in Classical Rev. beginning iv, 1890.]

(c) Biography and Criticism

Leslie, S. Memoir. Academy, 8 Oct. 1910.

Walter Headlam: his Letters and Poems. With a Memoir by Cecil Headlam and a Bibliography by L. Haward. 1910.

SIR RICHARD CLAVERHOUSE JEBB (1841–1905)

(a) Critical and Miscellaneous Writings

Translations into Greek and Latin Verse. Cambridge, 1873.

Speeches delivered by the Public Orator on 16 June, printed by request in the Cambridge University Reporter, 23 June 1874. [1875] (priv. ptd).

Encyclopædia Britannica, 9th edn, 1875–88. [Various articles.]

Greek Literature. 1877.

Modern Greece: Two Lectures. With Papers on 'The Progress of Greece' and 'Byron in Greece.' 1880.

Bentley. 1882. (English Men of Letters ser.)

Homer: an Introduction to the Iliad and the Odyssey. Glasgow, 1887.

Erasmus. Cambridge, 1890.

The Growth and Influence of Classical Greek Poetry. Lectures delivered in the Johns Hopkins University. 1893.

Literature.—Textual Criticism. [In L. Whibley, A Companion to Greek Studies, 1905.]

Essays and Addresses. Cambridge, 1907.

(b) Editions

Sophocles. The Electra. 1867.

Sophocles. The Ajax. 1868.

Θεοφραστου Χαρακτηρες. An English Translation from a Revised Text, with Introduction and Notes. 1870.

The Attic Orators, from Antiphon to Isaeos. 2 vols. 1876. [Sir J. P. Mahaffy wrote an article on this in Academy, 1 April 1876. Jebb pbd Some Remarks on this; Mahaffy replied, 1876; Jebb pbd a Rejoinder to Mahaffy's Reply, 1877.]

Selections from the Attic Orators: Antiphon, Andokides, Lysias, Isokrates, Isaeos; being a Companion Volume to the Attic Orators from Antiphon to Isaeos. 1880.

Sophocles. The Plays and Fragments, with Notes and Translation in English Prose. 7 pts, Cambridge, 1887–96. [Greek and English.]

Sophocles. The Text of the Seven Plays. Cambridge, 1897.

The Tragedies of Sophocles. Translated into English Prose. 1904.

Bacchylides: the Poems and Fragments. Edited with Introduction, Notes, and Prose Translation. Cambridge, 1905. [Text alone, Cambridge, 1906.]

The Rhetoric of Aristotle. A Translation by Sir Richard Claverhouse Jebb. Ed. Sir J. E. Sandys, Cambridge, 1909.

(c) Biography and Criticism

Jebb, C. L., Lady. Life and Letters of Sir Richard Claverhouse Jebb; with a Chapter on Sir Richard Jebb as Scholar and Critic by Dr A. W. Verrall. Cambridge, 1907.

[See also obituaries by Lord Reay and R. Y. Tyrrell in Proc. British Academy, 1905–6, and Athenaeum, 16 Dec. 1905.]

HERBERT SNOW, afterwards KYNASTON (1835–1910)

The Idylls and Epigrams commonly attributed to Theocritus. Oxford, 1869.
Extracts from the Greek Elegiac Poets, from Callinus to Callimachus; to which are added a few Epigrams. 1880.

[See E. D. Stone, Herbert Kynaston: A Short Memoir, with Selections from his Occasional Writings, 1912.]

SIR JOHN PENTLAND MAHAFFY (1839–1919)

Prolegomena to Ancient History, containing: Part I., The Interpretation of Legends and Inscriptions. Part II., A Survey of Old Egyptian Literature. 1871.
Greek Social Life from Homer to Menander. 1874.
Rambles and Studies in Greece. 1876.
A History of Classical Greek Literature. With an Appendix on Homer by Prof. [A. H.] Sayce. 2 vols. 1880.
Greek Life and Thought, from the Age of Alexander to the Roman Conquest. 1887.
The Flinders Petrie Papyri. With Transcriptions, Commentaries, and Index. 3 vols. Dublin, 1891–1905. [With J. G. Smyly.]
The Empire of the Ptolemies. 1895.

[For obituary and bibliography see Hermathena, XLII, 1920.]

JOHN EYTON BICKERSTETH MAYOR (1825 1910)

(a) Miscellaneous Writings

First Greek Reader. 1868.
Modicus cibi Medicus sibi; or, Nature her own Physician. Cambridge, 1880.
Spain: Portugal: the Bible. 1895.
The Spanish Reformed Church. A Sermon. Cambridge, 1895.
Plain Living and High Thinking: Selected Addresses and Sermons. 1897.
Iacula Prudentum. Verse and Prose from the German. 1910.
Twelve Cambridge Sermons. Ed. (with Memoir) H. F. Stewart, 1911.

Twelve Parochial Sermons. Ed. H. F. S[tewart], Cambridge, 1913.

(b) Editions of English Works

Cambridge in the Seventeenth Century. 3 pts, Cambridge, 1855–71. [Includes Two Lives of Nicholas Ferrar, 1855; Autobiography of Matthew Robinson, 1856; Life of William Bedell, 1871.]
Early Statutes of the College of St John the Evangelist in the University of Cambridge. Cambridge, 1859.
The Scholemaster of Roger Ascham. 1863.
Ricardi de Cirencestria Speculum historiale de Gestis Regum Angliæ. 2 vols. 1863–9.
History of the College of St John the Evangelist, Cambridge, by Thomas Baker. 2 vols. Cambridge, 1869.
Life of Ambrose Bonwicke by his Father [Ambrose Bonwicke]. Cambridge, 1870.
Memoir of Margaret, Countess of Richmond and Derby. By Charles Henry Cooper. Cambridge, 1874.
The English Works of John Fisher, Bishop of Rochester. EETS., Ex. Ser. 1876.
Venerabilis Bedæ Historiæ Ecclesiasticæ Gentis Anglorum Libri III, IV. 1879. [With J. R. Lumby.]
Cambridge under Queen Anne. Illustrated by Memoir of Ambrose Bonwicke and Diaries of Francis Burman and Zacharias Conrad von Uffenbach. With a Preface by Montague Rhodes James. Cambridge, 1911.

(c) Classical Editions

D. J. Juvenalis Satiræ XIII. Cambridge, 1853; 2 vols. 1872–8 (rev.).
Cicero's Second Philippic. With an Introduction and Notes. Translated from the German of K. Halm. 1861.
M. Fabi Quintiliani Institutionis Oratoriæ Liber decimus. Cambridge, 1872.
The Narrative of Odysseus. (Homer's Odyssey, IX–XII). With a Commentary. 1873.
Bibliographical Clue to Latin Literature. 1875. [Based on Emil Hübner's Grundriss.]
Pliny's Letters, Book 3. Text of H. Keil, with a Commentary by J. E. B. Mayor and a Life of Pliny by G. H. Rendall. 1880.
Homer's Odyssey. Book IX. With a Commentary. 1882.
The Latin Heptateuch, published piecemeal by the French printer, W. Morel (1560), and the French Benedictines E. Martène (1733) and J. B. Pitra (1852–88) critically reviewed. 1889.
Q. Septimi Florentis Tertulliani Apologeticus. The Text of Oehler annotated, with an Introduction, by J. E. B. Mayor. With a Translation by Alexander Souter. Cambridge, 1917.

(d) Contributions to Periodicals

[Articles on Latin-English lexicography in Journ. of Classical and Sacred Philology, II, 1855, IV, 1857. Notes on Juvenal in Journ. of Philology, XVI, 1887, XX, 1892. For a list of Mayor's contributions to periodicals see W. H. Duke, Eagle, XXXIII, 1912.]

(e) Biography and Criticism

[Obituaries by Sir J. E. Sandys in Classical Rev. XXV, 1911, Cambridge Rev. 8 Dec. 1910, and Proc. British Academy, V, 1911. Obituaries in Eagle, XXXII, 1911, by Sir J. E. Sandys, C. E. Graves, J. B. Mullinger and others; followed by a list of Mayor's Contributions to Notes and Queries. Obituary in Blackwood's Mag. CLXXXIX, 1911.]

WILLIAM WALTER MERRY (1835–1918)

Homer's Odyssey. Edited with English Notes, Appendices, etc. by W. W. Merry and J. Riddell. Books I–XII. Oxford, 1876.
Aristophanes. The Clouds. Oxford, 1879.
Aristophanes. The Acharnians. Oxford, 1880. [Greek.]
Aristophanes. The Frogs. Oxford, 1884.
Aristophanes. The Knights. Oxford, 1887.
Aristophanes. The Birds. Oxford, 1889.
Selected Fragments of Roman Poetry, from the Earliest Times of the Republic to the Augustan Age. Oxford, 1891.
Aristophanes. The Wasps. Oxford, 1893.
Aristophanes. Peace. Oxford, 1900.
Orationes tum Creweianæ tum gratulatoriæ in Theatro Sheldoniano plerumque habitæ. Oxford, 1909.

JOHN HENRY MIDDLETON (1846–1896)

Ancient Rome in 1885. Edinburgh, 1885.
The Engraved Gems of Classical Times. With a Catalogue of the Gems in the Fitzwilliam Museum. Cambridge, 1891.
The Lewis Collection of Gems and Rings in the Possession of Corpus Christi College, Cambridge. With an Introductory Essay on Ancient Gems. 1892.

DAVID BINNING MONRO (1836–1905)

A Grammar of the Homeric Dialect. Oxford, 1882.
The Modes of Ancient Greek Music. Oxford, 1894.
Homer's Odyssey. Books XIII–XXIV. Oxford, 1901.

[Also articles on the Homeric Question in Quarterly Rev. CXXV, 1868 and Encyclopædia Britannica, 9th edn, 1880, etc. See J. Cook Wilson, David Binning Monro: a Short Memoir, Oxford, 1907.]

ALEXANDER STUART MURRAY (1841–1904)

Manual of Mythology; founded on the Works of Petiscus, Preller and Welcker. 1873.
A History of Greek Sculpture from the Earliest Times down to the Age of Pheidias (and his Successors). 2 vols. 1880–3.
Handbook of Greek Archaeology. 1892.
Designs from Greek Vases in the British Museum. 1894. [With C. H. Smith.]
White Athenian Vases in the British Museum. 1896. [With A. H. Smith.]
Terracotta Sarcophagi, Greek and Etruscan, in the British Museum. 1898.
Greek Bronzes. 1898.
Excavations in Cyprus. By A. S. Murray, A. H. Smith and H. B. Walters. 1900.

HENRY NETTLESHIP (1839–1893)

Virgil. Æneid, Books V. and VI., with English Notes. Abridged from Professor Conington's Edition. 1872.
Lectures and Essays on Subjects connected with Latin Literature and Scholarship. Oxford, 1885.
Contributions to Latin Lexicography. Oxford, 1889.
A Dictionary of Classical Antiquities from the German of [A.] O. Seyffert. Revised and edited, with Additions, by H. Nettleship [and] J. E. Sandys. 1891.
Lectures and Essays. Second Series, edited by F. Haverfield; with Memoir [by Mrs M. Nettleship]. Oxford, 1895.

ARTHUR PALMER (1841–1897)

P. Ovidii Nasonis Heroides XIV. 1874.
Sex. Propertii Elegiarum Libri IV. 1880.
Q. Horati Flacci Sermones. The Satires of Horace, edited with Notes. 1883.
T. Macci Plauti Amphitruo. The Amphitruo of Plautus. 1890.
Catulli Veronensis Liber. 1896.
[Also articles in Hermathena, and, on Aristophanes, in Quarterly Rev. CLVIII, 1884.]

WILLIAM ROGER PATON (1856–1921)

The Inscriptions of Cos. Oxford, 1891. [With E. L. Hicks.]
Pindar's Pythian Odes, I–IV, IX, in English Verse. Aberdeen, 1904.
The Greek Anthology; with an English Translation. 5 vols. 1916–8. (Loeb Classical Lib.)

JOHN PEILE (1838–1910)

An Introduction to Greek and Latin Etymology. 1869.
Philology. 1875.
Notes on the Nalopākhyānam or Tale of Nala, for the Use of Classical Students. Cambridge, 1881.

History of Christ's College, Cambridge. 1900.
Biographical Register of Christ's College, Cambridge. Vol. I, 1910.

SIR WILLIAM PETERSON (1856–1921)

M. Fabi Quintiliani Institutionis Oratoriæ Liber decimus. Oxford, 1891.
C. Taciti Dialogus de Oratoribus. Oxford, 1893.
Collations from the Codex Cluniacensis s. Holkhamicus. A Ninth-century Manuscript of Cicero. Oxford, 1901.
M. Tulli Ciceronis Orationes. Divinatio in Q. Cæcilium. Oxford, [1907].

HENRY JOHN ROBY (1830–1915)

An Elementary Latin Grammar. Cambridge, 1862.
Report of the Schools Inquiry Commission. 1868–9. [Ch. ii, On the Present State of Schools for Secondary Education; Ch. iv, The Law of Charities as affecting Endowed Schools.]
A Grammar of the Latin Language, from Plautus to Suetonius. 2 vols. 1871–4.
A Latin Grammar for Schools. 1880.
An Introduction to the Study of Justinian's Digest, containing an Account of its Composition and of the Jurists used or referred to therein, together with a Full Commentary on one Title (De Usufructu). Cambridge, 1884; tr. Italian, Florence, 1886.
Roman Private Law in the Times of Cicero and the Antonines. 2 vols. Cambridge, 1902.
Essays on the Law in Cicero's Private Orations. Cambridge, 1902 (priv. ptd).
Roman Law. [Ch. iii in Cambridge Medieval History, vol. ii, 1913.]

BENJAMIN BICKLEY ROGERS (1828–1919)

(a) Translations of Aristophanes

The Clouds. Edited with a Translation into Corresponding Metres. 1852.
Ἀριστοφάνους Εἰρήνη. The Peace of Aristophanes. The Greek text revised; with a Translation into Corresponding Metres, and Original Notes. [1867.]
Ἀριστοφάνους Σφῆκες. The Wasps of Aristophanes. The Greek text revised; with a Translation into Corresponding Metres, and Original Notes. [1875.]
The Revolt of the Women. A Free Translation. [1878.]
The Thesmophoriazusae. 1904.
The Comedies of Aristophanes. Edited, translated and explained. 11 pts, 1910–5.
Dr Rogers' Translations from Aristophanes. 5 pts (all pbd), 1919–23.

Aristophanes. With the English translation of Benjamin Bickley Rogers. 3 vols. 1924.
[To vol. vi of the first collected edn of the Comedies was appended a verse trn of the Menaechmi of Plautus, 1907. This was later issued separately with the Latin text.]

(b) Other Works

Napoleon III and England. An Enquiry. Oxford, 1855.
A Free Enquiry into the Difficulties suggested by Dr Colenso with respect to the Historical Veracity of the Pentateuch. Oxford, 1863.
The Mosaic Records. A Full Investigation of the Difficulties suggested by Dr Colenso. Oxford, 1863.

WILLIAM GUNION RUTHERFORD (1853–1907)

First Greek Grammar. 1878.
The New Phrynicus: being a Revised Text of the Ecloga of the Grammarian Phrynichus. 1881.
Babrius. Edited with Introductory Dissertations, Critical Notes, Commentary, and Lexicon. 1883.
Θουκυδίδου Τετάρτη. The Fourth Book of Thucydides. 1889.
First Greek Syntax. 1890.
Ἡρώνδου Μιμίαμβοι. Herondas. A First Recension. 1891.
Scholia Aristophanica. Being such Comments Adscript to the Text of Aristophanes as have been preserved in the Codex Ravennas. 3 vols. 1896–1905.
St Paul's Epistle to the Romans. A New Translation, with a Brief Analysis. 1900.
St Paul's Epistles to the Thessalonians and Corinthians. 1908. [With memoir by Spencer Wilkinson.]

SIR JOHN ROBERT SEELEY (1834–1895)

Livy. Book I. 1871. [See also p. 932 above.]

WILLIAM YOUNG SELLAR (1825–1890)

The Roman Poets of the Republic. Edinburgh, 1863.
The Roman Poets of the Augustan Age. Oxford, 1877.
The Roman Poets of the Augustan Age: Horace and the Elegiac Poets; with a Memoir of the Author by Andrew Lang. Ed. W. P. Ker, Oxford, 1892.

EVELYN SHIRLEY SHUCKBURGH (1843–1906)

(a) Historical Writings

Lawrence Chaderton, D.D. (First Master of Emmanuel). Translated from a Latin Memoir of Dr [W.] Dillingham, with Notes and Illustrations.—Richard Farmer, D.D. (Master of Emmanuel, 1775–1797): an Essay. Cambridge, 1884.

A History of Rome to the Battle of Actium. 1894.

A History of Rome for Beginners, from the Foundation of the City to the Death of Augustus. 1897.

A Short History of the Greeks from the Earliest Times to B.C. 146. Cambridge, 1901.

Augustus: the Life and Times of the Founder of the Roman Empire. 1903.

Emmanuel College. Cambridge, 1904.

Greece from the Coming of the Hellenes to A.D. 14. 1905.

(b) Editions and Translations

The Bacchæ of Euripides translated into English Verse. Cambridge, 1871.

The Hauton Timorumenos of Terence. With Introduction and Notes. 1877.

P. Ovidii Nasonis Heroidum Epistulæ XIII. 1879.

Lysiæ Orationes XVI. 1882.

Lælius. A Dialogue on Friendship by Cicero. 1885.

Cato Maior. A Dialogue on Old Age by Cicero. 1886.

The Epistles of Horace. Book 1. 1888.

Herodotos. VI. Erato, and V. Terpsichore. 2 vols. 1889–90.

The Histories of Polybius. Translated from the Text of F. Hultsch. 2 vols. 1889.

An Apologie for Poetrie by Sir Philip Sidney. 1891.

Herodotos. VIII. Urania, IX. Kalliope. 1893.

P. Ovidii Nasonis Tristium Liber I, III. 2 vols. 1895.

C. Suetoni Tranquilli Divus Augustus. Cambridge, 1896.

Cornelius Nepos. 3 vols. 1895–6.

Gai Iuli Cæsaris De Bello Gallico. 1899.

The Letters of Cicero. Translated into English. 4 vols. 1899–1900.

GEORGE AUGUSTUS SIMCOX (1841–1905)

Prometheus Unbound. A Tragedy. 1867.

D. J. Juvenalis Satiræ XIII. Thirteen Satires of Juvenal, with Notes and Introduction. 1867.

A History of Latin Literature from Ennius to Boethius. 2 vols. 1883.

WILLIAM HENRY SIMCOX (1843–1889)

The Orations of Demosthenes and Æschines on the Crown. With Introductory Essays and Notes by G. A. Simcox and W. H. Simcox. Oxford, 1872.

Cornelii Taciti Historiae. The History of Tacitus, according to the Text of Orelli. 2 vols. 1875–6.

ALBERT WILLIAM SPRATT (1842–1920)

Thucydides, Book III. Cambridge, 1896.

Thucydides, Book VI. Cambridge, 1905.

Thucydides, Book IV. Cambridge, 1912.

HENRY FANSHAWE TOZER (1829–1916)

Researches in the Highlands of Turkey, including Visits to Mounts Ida, Athos, Olympus, and Pelion, to the Mirdite Albanians, and other Remote Tribes. 1869.

Turkish Armenia and Eastern Asia Minor. 1881.

The Church and the Eastern Empire. 1888.

The Islands of the Aegean. Oxford, 1890.

A History of Ancient Geography. Cambridge, 1897.

An English Commentary on Dante's Divina Commedia. Oxford, 1901.

Dante's Divina Commedia translated into English Prose. 1904.

[For obituary see W. W. Jackson, Proc. British Academy, VII, 1915–6.]

ROBERT YELVERTON TYRRELL (1844–1914)

Hesperidum Susurri. Sublegerunt T. J. B. Brady, R. Y. Tyrrell, M. C. Cullinan. 1867.

Εὐριπίδου Βακχαι. The Bacchae of Euripides, with a Revision of the Text and a Commentary. 1871.

The Correspondence of M. Tullius Cicero, arranged according to its Chronological Order; with a Revision of the Text, a Commentary, and Introductory Essays on the Life of Cicero, and the Style of his Letters. 7 vols. Dublin, 1879–1900. [With L. C. Purser.]

The Miles Gloriosus of T. Maccius Plautus: a Revised Text, with Notes. 1881.

The Troades of Euripides; with Revision of Text, and Notes. Dublin, 1882.

Dublin Translations into Greek and Latin Verse. Ed. R. Y. Tyrrell, Dublin, 1882.

The Acharnians of Aristophanes translated into English Verse. Dublin, 1883.

Cicero in his Letters. 1891.

Latin Poetry. Lectures delivered in 1893 on the Percy Turnbull Memorial Foundation in the Johns Hopkins University. 1895.

Sophoclis Tragœdiæ. 1897.

Anthology of Latin Poetry. 1901.

P. Terenti Afri Comœdiæ. Oxford, [1902].

Echoes from Kottabos [the magazine of Trinity College, Dublin]. Ed. R. Y. Tyrrell, Dublin, 1906.

Essays on Greek Literature. 1909.

Trinity College, Dublin. Speeches of Public Orators delivered at the Comitia held for conferring Honorary Degrees. Dublin, 1909.

ARTHUR WOOLLGAR VERRALL (1851–1912)

Εὐριπιδου Μηδεια. The Medea of Euripides. With an Introduction and Commentary. 1881.

Studies Literary and Historical in the Odes of Horace. 1884.

Αἰσχυλου Ἑπτα ἐπι Θηβας. The 'Seven against Thebes' of Æschylus, with Translation. 1887.

Αἰσχυλου Ἀγαμεμνων. The 'Agamemnon' of Æschylus. With a Translation. 1889.

Αἰσχυλου Χοηφοροι. The 'Choephori' of Æschylus. With a Translation. 1893.

Euripides, the Rationalist: a Study in the History of Art and Religion. Cambridge, 1895.

Essays on Four Plays of Euripides: Andromache, Helen, Heracles, Orestes. Cambridge, 1905.

Αἰσχυλου Εὐμενιδες. The 'Eumenides' of Æschylus. With a Translation. 1908.

The Bacchants of Euripides and other Essays. Cambridge, 1910.

Collected Studies in Greek and Latin Scholarship. Ed. M. A. Bayfield and J. D. Duff, Cambridge, 1913.

Collected Literary Essays, Classical and Modern. Ed. (with memoir) M. A. Bayfield and J. D. Duff, Cambridge, 1913.

Lectures on Dryden. Ed. Margaret de G. Verrall, Cambridge, 1914.

GEORGE CHARLES WINTER WARR
(1845–1901)

Echoes of Hellas. The Tale of Troy and the Story of Orestes from Homer and Æschylus. With Introductory Essay and Sonnets by G. C. Warr. 2 vols. 1887–8.

The Greek Epic. 1895.

The Athenian Drama. A Series of Verse Translations from the Greek Dramatic Poets, with Commentaries and Explanatory Essays for English Readers. 3 vols. 1900–2.

WILLIAM WAYTE (1829–1898)

Platonis Protagoras. The Protagoras of Plato. Cambridge, 1854.

Demosthenes against Androtion, and against Timocrates. Cambridge, 1882.

EDWARD CHARLES WICKHAM (1834–1910)

Q. Horatii Flacci Opera omnia. The Works of Horace, with a Commentary. 2 vols. Oxford, 1874–9.

Horace for English Readers: being a Translation of the Poems of Quintus Horatius Flaccus into English Prose. Oxford, 1903.

[See L. Ragg, A Memoir of Edward Charles Wickham, 1911.]

AUGUSTUS SAMUEL WILKINS (1843–1905)

The Light of the World: an Essay. 1869.

The Orations of Cicero against Catilina, with Notes and an Introduction translated from the German of K. Halm, with many Additions. 1871.

Phœnicia and Israel. A Historical Essay. 1871.

National Education in Greece in the Fourth Century before Christ. 1873.

M. Tullii Ciceronis De Oratore Libri tres. With Introduction and Notes. 3 vols. Oxford, 1879–92.

Q. Horatii Flacci Epistulæ. The Epistles of Horace. 1885.

M. Tulli Ciceronis Rhetorica. 2 vols. Oxford, [1901–3].

Roman Education. Cambridge, 1905.

[See Sir J. E. Sandys, Obituary (with complete bibliography), Eagle, XXVII, 1905.]

JOHN WORDSWORTH (1843–1911)

Fragments and Specimens of Early Latin, with Introductions and Notes. Oxford, 1874.

Nouum Testamentum Latine, secundum Editionem Sancti Hieronymi. Oxford, 1889–1905.

[See E. W. Watson, Life of Bishop John Wordsworth, 1915.]

II. BIBLICAL SCHOLARSHIP

[Further edns of the New Testament will be found in the preceding section. See also the section Writings on Religion, pp. 846–60 above.]

HENRY ALFORD (1810–1871)

[See p. 276 above.]

ROBERT LUBBOCK BENSLY (1831–1893)

The Harklean Version of the Epistle to the Hebrews, chap. XI. 28–XIII. 25. Now edited for the first Time, with Introduction and Notes on this Version of the Epistle. Cambridge, 1889.

The Four Gospels in Syriac transcribed from the Sinaitic Palimpsest by the Late R. L. Bensly, J. R. Harris and F. C. Burkitt. Cambridge, 1894.

The Fourth Book of Maccabees and Kindred Documents in Syriac. First edited on Manuscript Authority by R. L. Bensly. With an Introduction and Translations by W. E. Barnes. Cambridge, 1895.

The Epistles of S. Clement to the Corinthians. In Syriac. Edited from the Manuscript, with Notes. Cambridge, 1899.

[See H. T. Francis, In Memoriam R. L. Bensly, Cambridge, 1893 (priv. ptd).]

THOMAS KELLY CHEYNE (1841–1915)

Notes and Criticisms on the Hebrew Text of Isaiah. 1868.
The Book of Isaiah chronologically arranged. An Amended Version, with Historical and Critical Introductions and Explanatory Notes. 1870.
The Prophecies of Isaiah. A New Translation, with Commentary and Appendices. 2 vols. 1880–1.
The Origin and Religious Contents of the Psalter in the Light of Old Testament Criticism and the History of Religions. With an Introduction and Appendices. 1891. (Bampton Lectures, 1889.)
Introduction to the Book of Isaiah. With an Appendix containing the Undoubted Portions of the two Chief Prophetic Writers in a Translation. 1895.
The Hebrew Text of Isaiah critically revised. 1899.
Encyclopædia Biblica. A Critical Dictionary of the Literary, Political and Religious History, the Archæology, Geography and Natural History of the Bible. 4 vols. 1899–1903. [Ed. with J. S. Black.]

WILLIAM CURETON (1808–1864)

The Antient Syriac Version of the Epistles of Saint Ignatius to Saint Polycarp, the Ephesians, and the Romans. 1845.
Vindiciæ Ignatianæ; or, The Genuine Writings of St Ignatius, as exhibited in the Antient Syriac Version, vindicated from the Charge of Heresy. 1846.
Corpus Ignatianum: a Complete Collection of the Ignatian Epistles. 1849.
Spicilegium Syriacum; containing Remains of Bardesan, Meliton, Ambrose and Mara Bar Serapion. 1855.
Remains of a very Antient Recension of the Four Gospels in Syriac, hitherto unknown in Europe. 3 pts, 1858–72.
History of the Martyrs in Palestine, from Eusebius. Discovered in a very Antient Syriac Manuscript. 1861.
Ancient Syriac Documents relative to the Earliest Establishment of Christianity in Edessa and the Neighbouring Countries. 1864.

ANDREW BRUCE DAVIDSON (1831–1902)

An Introductory Hebrew Grammar, with Progressive Exercises in Reading and Writing. 1874.
The Book of Job, with Notes, Introduction and Appendix. Cambridge, 1884.
The Book of Ezekiel, with Notes, Introduction and Appendix. Cambridge, 1892.
An Introductory Hebrew Grammar. Edinburgh, 1894.

The Books of Nahum, Habakkuk, Zephaniah. Cambridge, 1896.
The Called of God. 1902. [Sermons. Introduction, pp. 3–58, is a memoir.]

SAMUEL ROLLES DRIVER (1846–1914)

A Treatise on the Use of the Tenses in Hebrew. Oxford, 1874.
Isaiah: his Life and Times, and the Writings which bear his Name. [1888.]
An Introduction to the Literature of the Old Testament. 1891.
The Book of Leviticus. Critical Edition of the Hebrew Texts. 1894. [With H. A. White.]
A Critical and Exegetical Commentary on Deuteronomy. Edinburgh, 1895.
The Books of Joel and Amos, with Introduction and Notes. Cambridge, 1897.
The Book of Daniel, with Introduction and Notes. Cambridge, 1900.
The Book of Genesis, with Introduction and Notes. 1904.
The Book of Job in the Revised Version. 1906.
The Minor Prophets. (Nahum, Habakkuk, Zephaniah, Haggai, Zechariah, Malachi.) Introductions, Revised Version with Notes, Index and Map. 1906.
The Book of the Prophet Jeremiah. A Revised Translation, with Introductions and Short Explanations. 1906.
A Hebrew and English Lexicon of the Old Testament, based on the Lexicon of William Gesenius as translated by Edward Robinson. By Francis Brown; with the Co-operation of S. R. Driver and Charles A. Briggs. Oxford, 1906.
Modern Research as illustrating the Bible. 1909. [Lecture.]
The Book of Exodus in the Revised Version, with Introduction and Notes. Cambridge, 1911.
The Ideals of the Prophets: Sermons. Together with a Bibliography of his Published Writings [by Godfrey R. Driver]. Edinburgh, 1915.

CHARLES JOHN ELLICOTT (1819–1905)

A Critical and Grammatical Commentary on St Paul's Epistle to the Galatians. With a Revised Translation. 1854.
A Critical and Grammatical Commentary on St Paul's Epistle to the Ephesians. With a Revised Translation. 1855.
The Pastoral Epistles of St Paul: with a Critical and Grammatical Commentary and a Revised Translation. 1856.
St Paul's Epistles to the Philippians, the Colossians and Philemon; with a Critical and Grammatical Commentary, and a Revised Translation. 1857.

A Critical and Grammatical Commentary on St Paul's Epistles to the Thessalonians, with a Revised Translation. 1858.

The Complete Bible Commentary for English Readers. By Various Writers. Edited by C. J. Ellicott. 7 vols. 1897.

FREDERICK FIELD (1801–1885)

Sancti Patris nostri Joannis Chrysostomi Homiliæ in Matthæum. 3 vols. Cambridge, 1839.

S. Joannis Chrysostomi Interpretatio omnium Epistolarum Paulinarum. 7 vols. Oxford, 1849–62.

Ἡ Παλαια Διαθηκη κατα τους Ἑβδομηκοντα. (Vetus Testamentum Græce juxta LXX Interpretes.) Oxford, 1859.

Origenis Hexaplorum quæ supersunt; sive veterum Interpretum Græcorum in totum Vetus Testamentum Fragmenta. Adhibita etiam Versione Syro-Hexaplari. Oxford, 1867; 2 vols. Oxford, 1875 (with 'Autobiographical Note').

Otium Norvicense; sive Tentamen de Reliquiis Aquilæ, Symmachi, Theodotionis, e Lingua Syriaca in Græcam convertendis. 3 vols. Oxford, 1864–86.

Notes on Select Passages of the Greek Testament, chiefly with Reference to Recent English Versions. 1881.

CHRISTIAN DAVID GINSBURG (1831–1914)

The Song of Songs, translated from the Original Hebrew with a Commentary, Historical and Critical. 1857.

Coheleth, commonly called the Book of Ecclesiastes; translated from the Original Hebrew, with a Commentary, Historical and Critical. 1861.

The Essenes; their History and Doctrines. An Essay, rptd from the Transactions of the Literary and Philosophical Society of Liverpool. 1864.

The Kabbalah: its Doctrines, Development, and Literature. An Essay. 1865.

The Moabite Stone; Facsimile of the Original Inscription, with an English Translation and a Historical and Critical Commentary. 1870.

The Massorah, compiled from Manuscripts, alphabetically and lexically arranged. 3 vols. 1880–5.

Introduction to the Hebrew Bible. 1896.

Introduction to the Massoretico-critical Edition of the Hebrew Bible. 1897.

SAMUEL LEE (1783–1852)

A Grammar of the Hebrew Language, drawn principally from Oriental Sources. 1827.

The Book of the Patriarch Job, translated from the Original Hebrew. To which is prefixed an Introduction on the History, Times, Country, Friends and Book. And to which is appended a Commentary, Critical and Practical. 1837.

A Lexicon, Hebrew, Chaldee, and English; compiled from the most Approved Sources, Oriental and European, Jewish and Christian; containing all the Words with their Usual Inflexions, as found in the Hebrew and Chaldee Texts of the Old Testament. 1840.

JOSEPH BARBER LIGHTFOOT (1828–1889)

The Epistles of St Paul [Galatians, Philippians, Colossians, Philemon]. 3 vols. 1865–75.

The Apostolic Fathers. Vol. I. S. Clement of Rome. The two Epistles to the Corinthians, with Introduction and Commentary. 1869.

On a Fresh Revision of the English New Testament. 1871.

The Apostolic Fathers. Vol. I. S. Clement of Rome. The Two Epistles to the Corinthians. A Revised Text, with Introduction, Notes and Translations. 1877.

The Apostolic Fathers. Part II. S. Ignatius, S. Polycarp. 2 vols. 1885.

The Apostolic Fathers, comprising the Epistles, Genuine and Spurious, of Clement of Rome, the Epistles of S. Ignatius, the Epistle of S. Polycarp, the Martyrdom of S. Polycarp, the Teaching of the Apostles, the Epistle of Barnabas, the Shepherd of Hermas, the Epistle to Diognetus, the Fragments of Papias, the Reliques of the Elders preserved in Irenæus. Revised Texts, with Introductions and English Translations. Ed. J. R. Harmer, 1891.

[See W. Sanday, Lightfoot as an Historian, EHR. v, 1890.]

PETER HAMNETT MASON

[Title in Hebrew.] Gently flowing Waters. An Easy, Practical Hebrew Grammar: with Exercises for Translation, arranged in a Series of Letters from a Teacher of Languages to an English Duchess. 2 vols. Cambridge, 1853. [With H. H. Bernard.]

A New Elementary Grammar of (what is usually called) the 'Hebrew' Language of the Old Testament. Pt 1, Cambridge, 1871.

'Hebrew' Exercise-Book; with Practical Grammar of the Word-Forms. Cambridge, 1874.

Shĕmets Dávár. A Rabbinic Reading Book. 2 pts, Cambridge, 1880.

WILLIAM FIDDIAN MOULTON (1835–1898)

A Treatise on the Grammar of the New Testament Greek. By Georg Benedict Winer. Translated from the German, with Large Additions and Full Indices. Edinburgh, 1870.
The History of the English Bible. 1878.
[See W. F. Moulton jun., William F. Moulton, A Memoir. With a Chapter on Biblical Work and Opinions by J. H. Moulton, 1899.]

EDWARD BOUVERIE PUSEY (1800–1882)

[See p. 860 above.]

FREDERICK HENRY AMBROSE SCRIVENER (1813–1891)

Contributions to the Criticism of the Greek New Testament, being the Introduction to an Edition of the Codex Augiensis and Fifty Other Manuscripts. Cambridge, 1859.
'Η Καινη Διαθηκη. Novum Testamentum Textus Stephanici A.D. 1550. Cambridge, 1860.
A Plain Introduction to the Criticism of the New Testament. For the Use of Biblical Students. Cambridge, 1861.
Bezæ Codex Cantabrigiensis, being an Exact Copy, in Ordinary Type, of the Celebrated Uncial Græco-Latin Manuscript of the Four Gospels and Acts of the Apostles. Cambridge, 1864.

ROBERT PAYNE SMITH (1819–1895)

S. Cyrilli Commentarii in Lucæ Evangelium quæ supersunt Syriace. Oxford, 1858.
A Commentary upon the Gospel according to S. Luke now first translated into English from an Ancient Syriac Version. 2 pts, Oxford, 1859.
Part III of the Ecclesiastical History of Eusebius. The Syriac Text translated into English. 1860.
Catalogi Codicum manuscriptorum Bibliothecæ Bodleianæ Pars sexta, Codices Syriacos, Carshunicos, Mendæos, complectens. Oxford, 1864.
Thesaurus Syriacus. Collegerunt S. M. Quatremere, G. H. Bernstein, G. W. Lorsbach, A. J. Arnoldi, F. Field. Auxit, digessit, exposuit, edidit R. Payne Smith. 2 vols. Oxford, 1868–1901.
An Old Testament Commentary for English Readers. By Various Writers. Ed. C. J. Ellicott. [Vol. I, Genesis, by R. P. Smith, 1882.]
Daniel i–vi. An Exposition of the Historical Portion of the Writings of the Prophet Daniel. 1886.

CHARLES TAYLOR (1840–1908)

The Gospel in the Law: a Critical Examination of the Citations from the Old Testament in the New. Cambridge, 1869.
The Dirge of Coheleth in Ecclesiastes xii discussed and literally interpreted. 1874.
[Title in Hebrew.] Sayings of the Jewish Fathers, comprising Pirge Aboth and Pereg R. Meir; with Critical and Illustrative Notes; and Specimen Pages of the Cambridge University Manuscript of the Mishnah 'Jerushalmith', from which the Text of Aboth is taken. Cambridge, 1877; Cambridge, 1897 ('with Additional Notes and a Cairo Fragment of Aquila's Version of the Old Testament').
The Teaching of the Twelve Apostles with Illustrations from the Talmud. Two Lectures on an Ancient Church Manual discovered at Constantinople. Cambridge, 1886[–9].
The Witness of Hermas to the Four Gospels. 1892.
The Oxyrhynchus Logia and the Apocryphal Gospels. Oxford, 1899.

[Also a number of mathematical works.]

SAMUEL PRIDEAUX TREGELLES (1813–1875)

'Αποκαλυψις 'Ιησου Χριστου. The Book of Revelation in Greek, edited from Ancient Authorities, with a New English Version and Various Readings. 1844.
An Account of the Printed Text of the Greek New Testament; with Remarks on its Revision upon Critical Principles. Together with a Collation of the Critical Texts of Griesbach, Scholz, Lachmann, and Tischendorf, with that in Common Use. 1854.
The Greek New Testament, edited from Ancient Authorities, with their Various Readings in Full, and the Latin Version of Jerome. 6 pts, 1857–79.

III. EGYPTOLOGY, ASSYRIOLOGY AND ORIENTAL SCHOLARSHIP

A. EGYPTOLOGISTS

SAMUEL BIRCH (1813–1885)

Hieroglyphical Grammar and Dictionary; Translation of The Book of the Dead. [In C. C. J. Bunsen, Egypt's Place in Universal History, tr. C. H. Cottrell, vol. v. 1867.]
History of Ancient Pottery, Egyptian, Assyrian, Greek, Etruscan, Roman. 2 vols. 1858.
History of Egypt. 1875.
The Monumental History of Egypt. 1876.

Records of the Past: being English Translations [by A. H. Sayce, W. H. Fox Talbot, and others] of the Assyrian and Egyptian Monuments. Soc. of Biblical Archaeology, 12 vols. [1873–81]. [Ed. by Birch.]

Egyptian Texts from the Coffin of Amamu. With a Translation. 1886.

[See Biographical Notices of Dr Samuel Birch from the British and Foreign Press; Portraits, and a Bibliography of his Principal Works. With an Introduction by W. De G. Birch, 1886.]

GEORGE ROBINS GLIDDON (1809–1857)

No. 1. A Memoir on the Cotton of Egypt.— No. 2. An Appeal to the Antiquaries of Europe on the Destruction of the Monuments of Egypt. 1841.

Ancient Egypt. Her Monuments, Hieroglyphics, History and Archaeology. Revised and corrected, with an Appendix. New York, [1847].

Otia Ægyptiaca. Discourses on Egyptian Archaeology and Hieroglyphical Discoveries. 1849.

Types of Mankind; or, Ethnological Researches, illustrated by Selections from the Inedited Papers of S. G. Morton, and by Additional Contributions from L. Agassiz, W. Usher, and H. S. Patterson. 1854. [With J. C. Nott.]

Indigenous Races of the Earth; or, New Chapters of Ethnological Enquiry, including Monographs contributed by A. Maury, F. Pulszky and J. A. Meigs: (with Communications from J. Leidy and L. Agassiz), presenting Fresh Investigations, Documents and Materials by J. C. Nott and G. R. Gliddon. Philadelphia, 1857.

REGINALD STUART POOLE (1832–1895)

Horæ Ægyptiacæ; or, The Chronology of Ancient Egypt. 1851.

The Coins of the Ptolemies. 3 pts, 1864.

The Cities of Egypt. 1882.

The Coins of the Sháhs of Persia. 1887.

[Poole contributed the articles on Egypt, Hieroglyphics, Numismatics, etc. in the 8th and 9th edns of the Encyclopædia Britannica.]

GEORGE RAWLINSON (1812–1902)

[See p. 913 above.]

SIR PETER LE PAGE RENOUF (1822–1897)

Lectures on the Origin and Growth of Religion, as illustrated by the Religion of Ancient Egypt. 1880. (Hibbert Lectures, 1879.)

Book of the Dead. Proc. Soc. of Biblical Archæology, XIV–XIX, 1892–7. [Trn. of 2nd and following chs., completed by E. Naville.]

SIR JOHN GARDNER WILKINSON (1797–1875)

Materia Hieroglyphica. Containing the Egyptian Pantheon, and the Succession of the Pharaohs, from the Earliest Times to the Conquest by Alexander, and other Hieroglyphical Subjects. With Plates and Notes. 2 pts, Malta, 1828.

Extracts from Several Hieroglyphical Subjects, found at Thebes, and other Parts of Egypt, with Remarks on the Same. Malta, 1830.

Topographical Survey of Thebes, Tápé, Thaba, or Diospolis Magna. 1830.

Topography of Thebes, and General View of Egypt. With Remarks on the Manners and Customs of the Ancient Egyptians. 1835.

Manners and Customs of the Ancient Egyptians. Illustrated by Drawings. 2 sers., 6 vols. 1837–41.

Modern Egypt and Thebes: being a Description of Egypt, including the Information required for Travellers in that Country. 2 vols. 1843.

The Architecture of Ancient Egypt; with Remarks on the Early Progress of Architecture. 2 vols. 1850.

The Fragments of the Hieratic Papyrus at Turin: containing the Names of Egyptian Kings with the Hieratic Inscription at the Back. 2 vols. 1851.

A Popular Account of the Ancient Egyptians; revised and abridged from his Larger Work. 2 vols. 1854.

B. ASSYRIOLOGISTS

EDWARD HINCKS (1792–1866)

(a) Papers in the Transactions of the Royal Irish Academy

On the Age of the Eighteenth Dynasty of Manetho. XXI, 1848.

On the Defacement of Divine and Royal Names on Egyptian Monuments. XXI, 1848.

On the First and Second Kinds of Persepolitan Writing. XXI, 1848.

An Attempt to ascertain the Number, Names and Powers of the Letters of the Hieroglyphic, or Ancient Egyptian Alphabet; grounded on the Establishment of a New Principle in the Use of Phonetic Characters. XXI, 1848.

On the three Kinds of Persepolitan Writing, and on the Babylonian Lapidary Characters. XXI, 1848.

On the third Persepolitan Writing and on the Mode of expressing Numerals in Cuneatic Characters. XXI, 1848.

On the Khorsabad Inscriptions. XXII, ii, 1850.

On the Assyrio-Babylonian Phonetic Characters. XXII, iv, 1853.

On the Assyrian Mythology. xxii, vi, 1855.

On the Chronology of the Twenty-sixth Egyptian Dynasty and of the Commencement of the Twenty-seventh. xxii, vi, 1855.

On the Personal Pronouns of the Assyrian and other Languages, especially Hebrew. xxiii, ii, 1859.

On a Tablet in the British Museum, recording, in Cuneatic Characters, an Astronomical Observation; with Incidental Remarks on the Assyrian Numerals, Divisions of Time, and Measures of Length. xxiii, ii, 1859.

On the Assyrio-Babylonian Measures of Time. xxiv, ii, 1867.

On the Various Years and Months in Use among the Egyptians. xxiv, ii, 1867.

(b) Biography and Criticism

Annual Report of the Royal Asiatic Society, 1867.

CLAUDE HERMANN WALTER JOHNS (1857–1920)

Assyrian Deeds and Documents recording the Transfer of Property, copied, collated, arranged, abstracted, annotated and indexed. 4 vols. Cambridge, 1898–1923.

The Oldest Code of Laws in the World: the Code of Laws promulgated by Hammurabi, B.C. 2285–2242. Translated. Edinburgh, 1903.

Babylonian and Assyrian Laws, Contracts and Letters. 1904.

Ancient Assyria. Cambridge, 1912.

Ancient Babylonia. Cambridge, 1913.

The Relations between the Laws of Babylonia and the Laws of the Hebrew Peoples. Oxford, 1914.

LEONARD WILLIAM KING (1869–1919)

First Steps in Assyrian. A Book for Beginners. 1898.

The Letters and Inscriptions of Hammurabi, King of Babylon, about B.C. 2200, to which are added a Series of Letters of other Kings of the First Dynasty of Babylon. 3 vols. 1898–1900.

Babylonian Religion and Mythology. 1900.

Assyrian Language. Easy Lessons in the Cuneiform Inscriptions. 1901.

Annals of the Kings of Assyria. The Cuneiform Texts with Translations. Vol. i (all pbd), 1902. [With Sir E. A. W. Budge.]

The Seven Tablets of Creation, or the Babylonian and Assyrian Legends concerning the Creation of the World and of Mankind. 2 vols. 1902.

A History of Sumer and Akkad. 1910.

Babylonian Boundary-Stones and Memorial-Tablets in the British Museum. 2 vols. 1912.

Bronze Reliefs from the Gates of Shalmaneser, King of Assyria, B.C. 860–825. 1915.

A History of Babylonia and Assyria from Prehistoric Times to the Persian Conquest. 1915.

Legends of Babylon and Egypt in Relation to Hebrew Tradition. Oxford, 1916.

SIR AUSTEN HENRY LAYARD (1817–1894)

Nineveh and its Remains: with an Account of a Visit to the Chaldaean Christians of Kurdistan, and the Yezidis, or Devil-Worshippers; and an Enquiry into the Manners and Arts of the Ancient Assyrians. 2 vols. 1849. Tr. German, Leipzig, 1854; Italian, Bologna, 1855; Spanish, Madrid, 1859.

The Monuments of Nineveh. From Drawings made on the Spot by A. H. Layard, illustrated in One Hundred Plates. 1849.

A Popular Account of Discoveries at Nineveh, abridged. 1851; tr. German, Leipzig, 1852.

Discoveries in the Ruins of Nineveh and Babylon; with Travels in Armenia, Kurdistan and the Desert; being the Result of a Second Expedition undertaken for the Trustees of the British Museum. 1853; tr. German, Leipzig, [1856].

A Second Series of the Monuments of Nineveh, from Drawings made on the Spot, during a Second Expedition to Assyria. 1853.

Early Adventures in Persia, Susiana, and Babylonia, including a Residence among the Bakhtiyari and other Wild Tribes before the Discovery of Nineveh. 2 vols. 1887.

SIR HENRY CRESWICKE RAWLINSON (1810–1895)

Royal Asiatic Society. The Persian Cuneiform Inscription at Behistun, decyphered and Translated with a Memoir on Persian Cuneiform Inscriptions in General, and on that of Behistun in particular. 1846–51. [Rptd from Journ. of Royal Asiatic Soc.]

A Commentary on the Cuneiform Inscriptions of Babylonia and Assyria; including Readings of the Inscription on the Nimrud Obelisk, and a Brief Notice of the Ancient Kings of Nineveh and Babylon. 1850.

Outline of the History of Assyria, as collected from the Inscriptions discovered by A. H. Layard in the Ruins of Nineveh. Printed from the Journal of the Royal Asiatic Society. 1852.

Notes on the Early History of Babylonia. 1854.

The Cuneiform Inscriptions of Western Asia. 5 vols. 1861–84. [With E. Norris.]

[See G. Rawlinson, A Memoir of Major-General Sir H. C. Rawlinson. With an Introduction by Field-Marshal Lord Roberts of Kandahar, 1898.]

GEORGE SMITH (1840–1876)

History of Assurbanipal, translated from the Cuneiform Inscriptions. 1871.

The Phonetic Values of the Cuneiform Characters. 1871.

Trans. Soc. of Biblical Archaeology. [On the Reading of the Cypriote Inscriptions, I, 1872; The Chaldean Account of the Deluge, II, 1873; On a New Fragment of the Assyrian Canon belonging to the Reigns of Tiglath-Pileser and Shalmaneser, II, 1873; and other papers to IV, 1876.]

Assyrian Discoveries: an Account of Explorations and Discoveries on the Site of Nineveh, during 1873 and 1874. 1875.

The Assyrian Eponym Canon, containing Translations of the Documents, and an Account of the Evidence, on the Comparative Chronology of the Assyrian and Jewish Kingdoms, from the Death of Solomon to Nebuchadnezzar. [1875.]

Ancient History from the Monuments. Assyria from the Earliest Times to the Fall of Nineveh. [1875.]

The Chaldean Account of Genesis. 1876; rev. A. H. Sayce, 1880.

Ancient History from the Monuments. The History of Babylonia. Ed. A. H. Sayce, [1877].

History of Sennacherib, translated from the Cuneiform Inscriptions. Ed. A. H. Sayce, 1878.

C. SANSKRIT AND INDIAN SCHOLARS

CECIL BENDALL (1856–1906)

Catalogue of the Buddhist Sanskrit Manuscripts in the University Library, Cambridge. With Introductory Notices. 1883.

A Journey of Literary and Archaeological Research in Nepal and Northern India, during the Winter of 1884–5. Cambridge, 1886.

[See H. T. Francis, In Memoriam. Cecil Bendall, Cambridge, 1906 (priv. ptd).]

ARTHUR COKE BURNELL (1840–1882)

Dâya-Vibhâga. The Law of Inheritance translated from the Unpublished Sanskrit Text of the Vyavahâra-Kânda of the Mâdhavîya Commentary on the Parâçara-Smṛti. Madras, 1868.

Catalogue of a Collection of Sanskrit MSS. Part 1. Vedic MSS. 1869. [These 350 MSS, collected by Burnell, were presented by him to the India Office.]

Elements of South Indian Palaeography from the Fourth to the Seventeenth Century A.D. Being an Introduction to the Study of South-Indian Inscriptions and MSS. Mangalore, 1874.

On the Aindra School of Sanskrit Grammarians, their Place in the Sanskrit and Subordinate Literatures. Mangalore, 1875.

A Legend from the Talavakāra Brahmaṇa of the Sāmaveda. Mangalore, 1878 (priv. ptd).

A Classified Index to the Sanskrit MSS. in the Palace at Tanjore. Prepared for the Madras Government. 1880.

The Ordinances of Manu. Translated with an Introduction. Ed. E. W. Hopkins, 1884.

Hobson-Jobson: being a Glossary of Anglo-Indian Colloquial Words and Phrases, and of Kindred Terms; Etymological, Historical [etc.]. 1886. [With Sir H. Yule.]

WILLIAM CAREY (1761–1834)

A Grammar of the Sungskrit Language; to which are added Examples for the Exercise of the Students, and a Complete List of the Dhatoos, or Roots. Serampore, 1806.

The Ranrayuna of Valmeeki, in the Original Sungscrit, with a Prose Translation and Explanatory Notes. 3 vols. Serampore, 1806–10. [With J. Marshman.]

A Dictionary of the Bengalee Language. Vol. I, Serampore, 1815; 2 vols. Serampore, 1825 (enlarged).

[See Eustace Carey, Memoir of William Carey, D.D., 1836. For some of Carey's other grammars, etc. see p. 1073 below.]

ROBERT CÆSAR CHILDERS (1838–1876)

A Dictionary of the Pâli Language. 2 vols. 1872–5.

[Childers also edited various Pali texts, 1867–74. Pali Text of Khuddaka Pátha, in Journ. of Royal Asiatic Soc. Nov. 1869, was the first Pali text ptd in England.]

HENRY THOMAS COLEBROOKE (1765–1837)

A Digest of Hindu Law on Contracts and Successions, with a Commentary, by Jagannātha Tarkapañchānana. Translated from the Sanscrit. 4 vols. Calcutta, 1798.

Hitópadésa or Salutary Instruction. In the Original Sanscrit. Serampore, 1804.

A Grammar of the Sanscrit Language. Vol. I (all pbd), Calcutta, 1805.

Cósha; or, Dictionary of the Sanskrit Language, by Amara Simha; with an English Interpretation and Annotations. Serampore, 1808.

Miscellaneous Essays. New Edition, with Life of the Author by his Son, Sir T. E. Colebrooke. 3 vols. 1873.

[For Colebrooke's other writings see p. 1073 below.]

EDWARD BYLES COWELL (1826–1903)

Vikramorvásí: an Indian Drama; translated from the Sanskrit of Kálidása. Hertford, 1851.

The Prákrita-Prakásá; or, The Prákrit Grammar of Vararuchi, with the Commentary (Manoramá) of Bhámaha. The first Complete Edition of the Original Text, with Various Readings, Copious Notes, an English Translation, and Index of Prákrit Words; to which is prefixed an Easy Introduction to Prákrit Grammar. Hertford, 1854.

A Short Introduction to the Ordinary Prákrit of the Sanskrit Dramas, with a List of Common Irregular Prákrit Words. 1875.

Rig-Veda-Sanhita. A Collection of Ancient Hindu Hymns, constituting the first[–fourth] Ashtaka of the Rig Veda. Translated from the Original Sanskrit by H. H. Wilson. 3 vols. 1866–70. [Completed by Cowell and W. F. Webster.]

[See G. Cowell, Life and Letters of Edward Byles Cowell, 1904 (with bibliography). See also p. 1071 below.]

JOHN DOWSON (1820–1881)

Ikhwánu-s-safá; or, Brothers of Purity. Translated from the Hindustání. 1869.

A Grammar of the Urdū or Hindūstānī Language. 1872.

A Classical Dictionary of Hindu Mythology and Religion, Geography, History, and Literature. 1878.

RALPH THOMAS HOTCHKIN GRIFFITH
(1826–1906)

The Rámáyan of Válmīki. Translated into English Verse. 5 vols. 1870–4. [See also p. 1071 below.]

SIR MONIER MONIER-WILLIAMS (1819–1899)

An Elementary Grammar of the Sanscrit Language, partly in the Roman Character, arranged according to a New Theory, in Reference especially to the Classical Languages: with Short Extracts in Easy Prose. To which is added, a Selection from the Institutes of Manu, with References to the Grammar and an English Translation. 1846.

A Dictionary, English and Sanskrit. 1851.

Śakuntalá, or, Śakuntalá recognized by the Ring: a Sanskrit Drama in Seven Acts. 1853.

Nalopákhyánam. Story of Nala; an Episode of the Mahá Bhárata. The Metrical Translation by H. H. Milman. Oxford, 1860.

A Practical Hindústáni Grammar; containing the Accidence in Roman Type, a Chapter on the Use of Arabic Words, and a Full Syntax. 1862.

A Sanskrit-English Dictionary etymologically and philologically arranged with Special Reference to Greek, Latin, Gothic, German, Anglo-Saxon, and other Cognate Indo-European Languages. Oxford, 1872.

FRIEDRICH MAX MÜLLER (1823–1900)

(a) Collected and Selected Works

Ausgewählte Werke. 13 vols. Leipzig, 1897–1901.

Collected Works. 20 vols. 1898–1903.

(b) Miscellaneous Writings

Rig-Veda-Sanhita: the Sacred Hymns of the Brahmans, together with the Commentary of Sayanacharya. 6 vols. 1849–74.

A History of Ancient Sanskrit Literature, so far as it illustrates the Primitive Religion of the Brahmans. 1859.

Lectures on the Science of Language. 2 vols. 1861–4.

A Sanskrit Grammar for Beginners, in Devanâgarî and Roman Letters throughout. 1866.

Chips from a German Workshop. 4 vols. 1867–75. Tr. German, 1869; French, 1872.

On the Stratification of Language. 1868. [Lecture.]

Buddhist Nihilism. 1869.

The Hymns of the Rig-Veda in the Pada Text. Reprinted from the Editio princeps. 1873.

The Hymns of the Rig-Veda in the Samhita Text. Reprinted from the Editio princeps. 1873.

Introduction to the Science of Religion. With Two Essays on False Analogies, and the Philosophy of Mythology. 1873. Tr. French, 1873; German, 1874; Italian, 1874.

Lectures on the Origin and Growth of Religion as illustrated by the Religions of India. 1878; tr. German, 1880. (Hibbert Lectures.)

The Sacred Books of the East. Translated by Various Oriental Scholars and edited by F. Max Müller. 49 vols. Oxford, 1879–1904. [In 1910 appeared a General Index, by M. Winternitz, which forms vol. L. Vols. tr. by Müller: I, The Upanishads, pt 1, 1879. X, i, The Dhammapada: a Collection of Verses: being one of the Canonical Books of the Buddhists, 1881 (originally pbd in 1870, before the inception of this series). XV, The Upanishads, pt 2, 1884. XXXII, Vedic Hymns, pt 1, 1891. XLIX, ii, Buddhist Mahâyâna Texts, pt 2, 1894.]

Anecdota Oxoniensia, Aryan Series, pt 1. [1881: Vajrachhedikā. 1883: Sukhāvatiryūha. (With Nanjio.) 1884: Prajñāpāramitā-hrdaya-sūtra. (With Nanjio.) 1885: Dharma-saṃgraha. Prepared by K. Kasawara, and ed. by Müller and H. Wenzel.]

Immanuel Kant's Critique of Pure Reason translated. 1881.

India; what can it teach us? A Course of Lectures delivered before the University of Cambridge. 1883.

Biographical Essays. 1884.

The Science of Thought. 1887; tr. German, 1888.

Biographies of Words and the Home of the Aryas. 1888.

Natural Religion. 1889. (Gifford Lectures.)

Physical Religion. 1891. (Gifford Lectures.)

Anthropological Religion. 1892. (Gifford Lectures.)

Theosophy; or, Psychological Religion. 1893. (Gifford Lectures.)

Sacred Books of the Buddhists. Translated by various Oriental Scholars and edited by F. Max Müller. 1895– .

Contributions to the Science of Mythology. 2 vols. 1897.

Auld Lang Syne. 2 sers. 1898–9. [Reminiscences.]

My Autobiography. A Fragment. 1901.

[The foregoing comprise only a representative selection from a very voluminous body of work in many fields of scholarship.]

(c) Biography and Criticism

Lang, A. Max Müller. Contemporary Rev. LXXVIII, 1900.

Conway, M. D. Memories of Max Müller. North American Rev. CLXXI, 1900.

Jackson, A. V. W. Max Müller and his Work. Forum, XXX, 1901.

The Life and Letters of the Right Honourable Friedrich Max Müller. Edited by his Wife. 2 vols. 1902.

ROBERT ALEXANDER NEIL (1852–1901)

The Divyāvadāna. 1886. [Ed. with E. B. Cowell.]

The Jātaka; or, Stories of the Buddha's Former Births; translated from the Pāli by Various Hands under the Editorship of Professor E. B. Cowell. 6 vols. Cambridge, 1895–1907. [Vol. III, 1897 by H. T. Francis and Neil.]

The Knights of Aristophanes. Cambridge, 1901.

SANDFORD ARTHUR STRONG (1863–1904)

[See under Arabic Scholars below.]

SIR CHARLES WILKINS (1749?–1836)

The Bhăgvăt-Geētā; or, Dialogues of Krĕĕshnă and Ărjŏŏn, in Eighteen Lectures; with Notes. 1785.

The Hĕĕtōpădēs of Vĕĕshnŏŏ-Sărmă in a Series of Connected Fables, interspersed with Maxims; translated from an Ancient Manuscript in the Sanskreet Language. With Notes. Bath, 1787.

The Story of Dooshwanta and Sakoontalā, extracted from the Mahābhārata. 1795.

A Grammar of the Sanskrĭta Language. 1808. [See also p. 1073 below.]

HORACE HAYMAN WILSON (1786–1860)

The Mégha Dúta: or, Cloud Messenger: a Poem, in the Sanskrit Language, by Cálidása; translated into English Verse. Calcutta, 1813.

A Dictionary, Sanscrit and English. Calcutta, 1819; Calcutta, 1832 (greatly extended).

Select Specimens of the Theatre of the Hindus, translated from the Original Sanscrit. 3 vols. Calcutta, 1826–7.

The Vishńu Puráná, a System of Hindu Mythology and Tradition, translated from the Original Sanscrit, and illustrated by Notes derived chiefly from other Puránás. 1840.

Ariana Antiqua. A Descriptive Account of the Antiquities and Coins of Afghanistan. 1841.

An Introduction to the Grammar of the Sanskrit Language, for the Use of Early Students. 1841.

Rig-Veda-Sanhitá. A Collection of Ancient Hindu Hymns, translated from the Original Sanskrit. 8 vols. 1850–88. [Vols. IV–VIII completed by E. B. Cowell and W. F. Webster.]

Works. [Ed. R. Rost], 12 vols. 1862–71.

D. CHINESE SCHOLARS

SIR JOHN FRANCIS DAVIS (1795–1890)

Chinese Novels, translated from the Originals: to which are added Proverbs and Moral Maxims, collected from their Classical Books. The Whole prefaced by Observations on the Language and Literature of China. 1822.

The Fortunate Union: a Romance, translated from the Chinese, with Notes. 1829.

Poeseos Sinensis Commentarii. On the Poetry of the Chinese, from the Royal Asiatic Transactions, to which are added Translations and Detached Pieces. Macao, 1834.

The Chinese: a General Description of the Empire of China and its Inhabitants. 1836.

Sketches of China; partly during an Inland Journey of Four Months, between Peking, Nanking, and Canton; with Notices and Observations relative to the Present War. 2 vols. 1841.

China, during the War and since the Peace. 2 vols. 1852.

Chinese Miscellanies: a Collection of Essays and Notes. 1865.

JAMES LEGGE (1815–1897)

The Chinese Classics; with a Translation, Critical and Exegetical Notes, Prolegomena, and Copious Indexes. 5 vols. Hongkong, 1861–72.

The Sacred Books of China. The Texts of Confucianism, translated. 4 pts, Oxford, 1879–88.

The Texts of Tàoism. Translated. 2 pts, Oxford, 1891.

[See The Life and Labours of James Legge, Asiatic Quarterly Rev. xxv, 1898.]

WALTER HENRY MEDHURST (1796–1857)

China, its State and Prospects, with Especial Reference to the Spread of the Gospel; containing Allusions to the Antiquity, Extent, Population, Civilization, Literature and Religion of the Chinese. 1838.

Chinese and English Dictionary; containing all the Words in the Chinese Imperial Dictionary, arranged according to the Radicals. 2 vols. Batavia, 1842–3.

[Chinese title.] Foochow Foo, 1881. [The Bible tr. into Chinese.]

ROBERT MORRISON (1782–1834)

(a) *Writings on Chinese*

A Dictionary of the Chinese Language, in three Parts. Part the First, containing Chinese and English, arranged according to the Radicals; Part the Second, Chinese and English arranged alphabetically; and Part the Third, English and Chinese. 3 pts, Macao, 1815–23.

[Chinese title.] [The Bible] translated into Chinese by Robert Morrison and William Milne. 21 vols. [Malacca], 1823.

(b) *Biography and Criticism*

Morrison, Eliza. Memoirs of the Life and Labours of Robert Morrison, D.D., compiled by his Widow; with Critical Notices of his Chinese Works by S. Kidd, and an Appendix containing Original Documents. 2 vols. 1839.

Townsend, W. J. Robert Morrison, the Pioneer of Chinese Missions. [1888.]

SIR THOMAS FRANCIS WADE (1818–1895)

The Hsin Ching Lu; or, Book of Experiments; being the First of a Series of Contributions to the Study of Chinese. 2 vols. Hongkong, 1859. [Chinese and English.]

The Peking Syllabary; being a Collection of the Characters representing the Dialect of Peking; arranged after a New Orthography in Syllabic Classes, according to the four Tones. Designed to accompany the Hsin Ching Lu, or Book of Experiments. Hongkong, 1859.

Wèn-chien Tzŭ-erh Chi, a Series of Papers selected as Specimens of Documentary Chinese, designed to assist Students of the Language as written by the Officials of China. 2 vols. 1867.

E. ARABIC SCHOLARS

ION GRANT NEVILLE KEITH-FALCONER (1856–1887)

Kalilah and Dimnah; or, The Fables of Bidpai: being an Account of their Literary History, with an English Translation of the Later Syriac Version of the same, and Notes. Cambridge, 1885.

[See R. Sinker, Memorials of the Hon. Ion Keith-Falconer, late Lord Almoner's Professor of Arabic in the University of Cambridge, and Missionary to the Mohammedans of Southern Arabia, 1888.]

EDWARD WILLIAM LANE (1801–1876)

An Account of the Manners and Customs of the Modern Egyptians. 2 vols. 1836.

The Thousand and One Nights. A New Translation. 3 vols. 1839–41. [Pbd in monthly pts, 1838–40.]

Selections from the Ḳur-án, commonly called, in England, the Koran. 1843.

An Arabic-English Lexicon. [Ed. (with Memoir) S. Lane-Poole], 5 pts, 1863–74. [Supplement, ed. S. Lane-Poole, 3 pts, 1877–92.]

[See S. Lane-Poole, Life of Edward William Lane, 1877.]

SIR CHARLES JAMES LYALL (1845–1920)

Translations of Ancient Arabian Poetry, chiefly Præ-Islamic, with an Introduction and Notes. 1885.

Ten Ancient Arabic Poems. 1894.

Two Ancient Arabic Dīwāns; with Translation. 1913.

[See Reynold A. Nicholson, Sir C. J. Lyall, 1845–1920, Proc. British Academy, ix, 1922.]

EDWARD HENRY PALMER (1840–1882)

Oriental Mysticism. A Treatise on the Sufiistic and Unitarian Theosophy of the Persians. 1867.

A Descriptive Catalogue of the Arabic, Persian and Turkish Manuscripts in the Library of Trinity College, Cambridge. Cambridge, 1870.

The Desert of the Exodus: Journeys on Foot undertaken in Connexion with the Ordnance Survey of Sinai and the Palestine Exploration Fund. 2 pts, Cambridge, 1871.

A Grammar of the Arabic Language. 1874.

A Concise Dictionary of the Persian Language. 1876. [Persian-English.]

The Poetical Works of Behá-ed-Dín Zoheir. With a Metrical English Translation, Notes and Introduction. 2 vols. Cambridge, 1876–7.

The Qur'ân, translated by E. H. Palmer. [In F. Max Müller, The Sacred Books of the East, vols. VI, IX, Oxford, 1880.]

The Arabic Manual. Comprising a Condensed Grammar of both the Classical and Modern Arabic; Reading Lessons; Vocabulary, etc. 1881.

Simplified Grammar of Hindūstānī, Persian and Arabic. 1882.

A Concise Dictionary of the Persian Language. Ed. G. Le Strange, 2 vols. 1883–4.

[See Sir W. Besant, The Life and Achievements of E. H. Palmer, 1883.]

SANDFORD ARTHUR STRONG (1863–1904)

The Mahā-Bodhi-Vaṁsa. Pali Text Soc. 1891.

The Futah al-Habashah; or, The Conquest of Abyssinia. 1894.

Critical Studies and Fragments. 1905. [With memoir by Lord Balcarres.]

WILLIAM WRIGHT (1830–1889)

[Title in Arabic.] The Travels of Ibn Jubair. 1852.

A Grammar of the Arabic Language, translated from the German of Caspari, and edited, with Numerous Additions and Corrections. 2 vols. 1859–62. [Though founded on Caspari; substantially a new work.]

[Title in Arabic.] Opuscula Arabica, collected and edited from MSS in the University Library of Leyden. Leyden, 1859.

The Kāmil of Al-Mubarrad. 1864–82.

Catalogue of the Syriac Manuscripts in the British Museum. 3 pts, 1870–2.

Book of Kalilah and Dimnah. 1883.

F. PERSIAN SCHOLARS
SIR GORE OUSELEY (1770–1844)

Biographical Notices of Persian Poets. 1846. [With Memoir by James Reynolds.]

SIR WILLIAM OUSELEY (1767–1842)

Persian Miscellanies: an Essay to facilitate the Reading of Persian Manuscripts. 1795.

The Oriental Collections: consisting of Original Essays and Dissertations, Translations and Miscellaneous Papers, illustrating the History and Antiquities, the Arts, Sciences, and Literature of Asia. 3 vols. [1797–9].

Aḥmad ibn Muhammad ibn 'Abd al Ghaffár, Al Kaswíní Al Ghifárí. Epitome of the Ancient History of Persia. Extended and translated from the Jehan Ara, a Persian Manuscript. 1799.

The Oriental Geography of Ebn Hankal, an Arabian Traveller of the Tenth Century. Translated. 1800.

Travels in Various Countries of the East; more particularly Persia. 3 vols. 1819–23.

G. TURKISH SCHOLARS
ELIAS JOHN WILKINSON GIBB (1857–1901)

Ottoman Poems translated into English Verse, in the Original Forms. With Introduction, Biographical Notices, and Notes. 1882.

A History of Ottoman Poetry. 7 vols. 1901–13. [Vols. II–VI, ed. E. G. Browne; VII, by Rizá-Tevfíq Bey, tr. E. G. Browne.]

[Gibb's fine Oriental library was thus divided on his death,—MSS to BM; Arabic, Persian and Turkish books to Cambridge University Lib.; miscellaneous to British Embassy, Constantinople.]

SIR JAMES WILLIAM REDHOUSE (1811–1892)

The Turkish Campaigner's Vade-Mecum of Ottoman Colloquial Language. 1855.

An English and Turkish Dictionary, in two Parts, English and Turkish and Turkish and English. 1856.

On the History, System, and Varieties of Turkish Poetry, illustrated by Selections. Trans. Royal Soc. Lit. XII, 1880.

The Mesnevi (usually known as the Mesneviyi Sherif, or Holy Mesnevi) of Mevláná (our Lord) Jelálu-'D-Dín Muhammed, Er-Rúmí. Translated and the Poetry versified. 2 pts, 1881.

A Simplified Grammar of the Ottoman-Turkish Language. 1884.

[Turkish title.] A Turkish and English Lexicon, shewing in English the Significations of the Turkish Terms. Constantinople, 1890.

J. E. S. *rev.* H. B. G.

VIII. ENGLISH SCHOLARSHIP

[Cross references have not been included either to or from this section for Critical and Miscellaneous Prose (pp. 629–757 above) and History, Biography and Archaeology (pp. 877–935 above), though both of these sections include many writers who incidentally contributed to 19th century English studies.]

A. ENGLISH SCHOLARS, 1800–1835
WILLIAM BELOE (1756–1817)
(a) Original Works

Poems and Translations. 1788.

Miscellanies, consisting of Poems, Classical Extracts, and Oriental Apologues. 3 vols. 1795.

Anecdotes of Literature and Scarce Books.
6 vols. 1807–12.
The Sexagenarian, or Recollections of a
Literary Life. 1817.

(b) Editions and Translations

The Rape of Helen, from the Greek of
Coluthus. 1786.
Alciphron's Epistles, now first translated.
1791. [With T. Monro.]
The History of Herodotus. 4 vols. 1791. [6
edns by 1830.]
The British Critic. A New Review. May
1793–Oct. 1826. [Vols. i–xlii ed. by Robert
Nares and Beloe.]
The Attic Nights of Aulus Gellius. 3 vols.
1795.
A New and General Biographical Dictionary.
15 vols. 1798–1810. [In this (3rd) edn
vols. vii, ix, xi, xiii, xv were ed. by Beloe.]

SIR ALEXANDER BOSWELL (1775–1822)

[See p. 228 above.]

JAMES BOSWELL (1778–1822)

A Biographical Memoir of the Late Edmond
Malone. 1814 (priv. ptd). [Rptd from
GM. June 1813.]
The Plays and Poems of William Shakespeare,
with the Corrections and Illustrations of
Various Commentators, comprehending a
Life of the Poet, and an Enlarged History
of the Stage by the Late Edmond Malone,
with a New Glossarial Index. 21 vols. 1821.
[The 3rd 'Variorum' edn; ed. by Boswell
from Malone's MSS.]

[Boswell also pbd the 6th (rev.) edn of his
father's Life of Johnson as well as rpts of
some minor rarities for the Roxburghe Club.]

JOSEPH BOSWORTH (1789–1876)

(a) Grammars and Dictionaries

The Elements of Anglo-Saxon Grammar.
1823; 1826 (rev. and abridged as A Com-
pendious Grammar of the Primitive English
or Anglo-Saxon Language).
A Dictionary of the Anglo-Saxon Language.
1838; rev. (partly from Bosworth's MSS)
T. N. Toller, 4 vols. Oxford, 1882–98.
A Compendious Dictionary of Anglo-Saxon.
1848. [The preliminary pp. on The Origin
of the English, Germanic and Scandinavian
Languages were also ptd separately in 1848.]
[Bosworth also pbd An Introduction to
Latin Construing, 1821, and a rev. edn of
William Bosworth's Greek Grammar, 1830.]

(b) Editions and Translations

Scandinavian Literature. 1839. [Anthology.]
King Alfred's Anglo-Saxon Version of Orosius.
2 vols. 1855–9. [With literal trn. Bosworth's
The History of the Lauderdale Manuscript
of King Alfred's Orosius was priv. ptd,
Oxford, 1858.]
The Gothic and Anglo-Saxon Gospels, with
the Versions of Wyclif and Tyndale. 1865.
[With G. Waring.]

WILLIAM LISLE BOWLES (1762–1850)

[See vol. ii, p. 354 above.]

SIR SAMUEL EGERTON BRYDGES
(1762–1837)

[See p. 662 above.]

ALEXANDER CHALMERS (1759–1834)

The Tatler. With Prefaces, Historical and
Biographical. 4 vols. 1803. [Followed by:
The Spectator, 8 vols. 1806; The Guardian,
2 vols. 1806.]
Walker's Classics. 45 vols. 1808–[12?]. [Pre-
faces by Chalmers.]
The British Gallery of Contemporary Por-
traits. 2 vols. 1809–16. [Many lives by
Chalmers.]
A History of the Colleges, Halls and Public
Buildings attached to the University of
Oxford. 2 vols. Oxford, 1810.
The Works of the English Poets from Chaucer
to Cowper. 21 vols. 1810. [An immensely
expanded revision of Dr Johnson's collec-
tion; the additional lives all by Chalmers.]
The Projector. 3 vols. 1811. [Periodical essays
rptd from GM.]
The General Biographical Dictionary. 32 vols.
1812–7. [Expanded by Chalmers from A
New and General Biographical Dictionary,
rev. W. Tooke, R. Nares and W. Beloe,
15 vols. 1798–1810.]
The British Essayists: with Prefaces, Historical
and Biographical. 45 vols. 1817.

[Chalmers also supervised edns of the
following writers' works, generally with
memoirs of some length: Beattie, Cruden,
Fielding, Gibbon, Johnson, Milton, Paley,
Edward Reynolds, Shakespeare.]

JOHN PAYNE COLLIER (1789–1883)

(a) Original Works

Criticisms on the Bar, including Strictures on
the Principal Counsel. By Amicus Curiae.
1819.
The Poetical Decameron, or Ten Conversations on English Poets and Poetry, particularly of the Reigns of Elizabeth and
James I. 2 vols. Edinburgh, 1820.

The Poet's Pilgrimage. An Allegorical Poem, in Four Cantos. 1822 (anon.); 1825 (signed).

The History of English Dramatic Poetry to the Time of Shakespeare and Annals of the Stage to the Restoration. 3 vols. 1831; 3 vols. 1879 (rev.).

New Facts regarding the Life of Shakespeare. 1835.

New Particulars regarding the Works of Shakespeare. 1836.

A Catalogue, Bibliographical and Critical, of Early English Literature, the Property of Lord Francis Egerton. 1837.

Further Particulars regarding Shakespeare and his Works. 1839.

Reasons for a New Edition of Shakespeare's Works. 1841; 1842 (expanded).

Notes and Emendations to the Text of Shakespeare's Plays from Early Manuscript Corrections in a Copy of the Folio 1632 in the Possession of J. Payne Collier. 1852; 1853 (adds Preface).

Reply to Mr N. E. S. A. Hamilton's 'Inquiry' into the Imputed Shakespeare Forgeries. 1860.

Illustrations of Early English Popular Literature. 2 vols. 1863–4 (priv. ptd).

A Bibliographical and Critical Account of the Rarest Books in the English Language. 2 vols. 1865.

Illustrations of Old English Literature. 3 vols. 1866 (priv. ptd).

Odds and Ends. 1870 (priv. ptd).

An Old Man's Diary, Forty Years ago. 4 pts, 1871–2 (priv. ptd).

[Collier also pbd trns from Schiller, 1824–5.]

(b) Editions

A Select Collection of Old Plays. 12 vols. 1825–7. [Dodsley's collection with additional plays ed. by Collier.]

The Works of William Shakespeare. The Text formed from an entirely New Collation of the Old Editions. With the Various Readings, Notes, a Life of the Poet, and a History of the Early English Stage. 8 vols. 1842–4.

Shakespeare's Library: a Collection of the Romances, [etc.] used by Shakespeare. 2 vols. [1843].

Book Entries of the Stationers' Register relating to the Drama and Popular Literature to 1586. Shakespeare Soc. 1848–9.

Seven Lectures on Shakespeare and Milton, by the Late S. T. Coleridge. 1856. [Collier's shorthand notes, at first unjustly suspected as forged.]

The Works of Edmund Spenser. 5 vols. 1862.

[Collier also rptd, generally with introductions, many minor Elizabethan and

Stuart rarities (mainly dramatic and poetic) both independently and for the Camden, Percy and Shakespeare Socs. and the Roxburghe Club. For a complete list see under Wheatley below.]

(c) Biography and Criticism

Singer, S. W. The Text of Shakespeare vindicated from the Interpolations and Corruptions advocated by J. P. Collier. 1853.

Ingleby, C. M. The Shakespeare Fabrications. 1859. [With bibliography.]

—— A Complete View of the Shakspere Controversy. 1861.

Hamilton, N. E. S. A. An Inquiry into the Genuineness of the MS. Corrections in Mr Payne Collier's Shakspere Folio. 1860.

Wheatley, H. B. Notes on the Life of John Payne Collier, with a Complete List of his Works and an Account of such Shakespeare Documents as are believed to be Spurious. 1884.

THOMAS FROGNALL DIBDIN (1776–1847)

An Introduction to the Knowledge of Rare and Valuable Editions of the Greek and Roman Classics. Gloucester, 1802; 1804 (enlarged); 2 vols. 1808 (rev. again); 2 vols. 1827 ('greatly enlarged').

The Director. A Weekly Literary Journal. 2 vols. 1807.

Specimen Bibliothecae Britannicae. 1808.

The Bibliomania or Book-Madness. In an Epistle addressed to Richard Heber, Esq. 1809; 1811 (enlarged); 2 pts, 1842 (best edn).

The Typographical Antiquities of Great Britain. Vols. I–IV (all pbd), 1810–9. [A partial revision of Ames.]

Bibliography, a Poem. Book I. [1812.]

Bibliotheca Spenceriana, or a Descriptive Catalogue of the Library of Earl Spencer. 4 vols. 1814–5.

The Bibliographical Decameron. 3 vols. 1817.

A Bibliographical, Antiquarian and Picturesque Tour in France and Germany. 3 vols. 1821; tr. French, Paris, 1825.

Aedes Althorpianae, or an Account of the Mansion, Books and Pictures at Althorp. 2 vols. 1822.

A Descriptive Catalogue of the Books lately of the Library of the Duke di Cassano Serra and now of the Earl Spencer. 1823.

The Library Companion, or the Young Man's Guide and the Old Man's Comfort in the Choice of a Library. 2 vols. 1824.

The Sunday Library. A Selection of Sermons from Eminent Divines. 6 vols. 1831.

Bibliophobia. Remarks on the Present Languid State of Literature. By Mercurius Rusticus. 1832.

Reminiscences of a Literary Life. 2 pts, 1836.

A Bibliographical, Antiquarian and Picturesque Tour in the Northern Counties of England and in Scotland. 3 vols. 1838.

Cranmer, a Novel. By a Member of the Roxburghe Club. 1839.

[Dibdin also pbd rpts of Tudor and Stuart rarities, mainly for the Roxburghe Club, as well as sermons, pamphlets, etc.]

FRANCIS DOUCE (1757–1834)

The Dance of Death. [1794?] (anon.); 1833 (enlarged). [Ed. by Douce with elaborate dissertation.]

Illustrations of Shakespeare and of Ancient Manners, with Dissertations on the Clowns and Fools of Shakespeare. 2 vols. 1807.

A Catalogue of the Harleian Manuscripts in the British Museum. 4 vols. 1808–12. [Rev. by Douce.]

A Catalogue of the Lansdowne Manuscripts in the British Museum. 1819. [With Sir H. Ellis.]

[Douce also pbd edns of Arnold's Chronicle, 1811, and a few M.E. texts for the Roxburghe Club.]

ALEXANDER DYCE (1798–1869)

(a) Editions

Specimens of British Poetesses. 1825.

The Poetical Works of William Collins. 1827.

The Works of George Peele. 3 vols. 1828–39.

The Works of John Webster. 4 vols. 1830.

The Dramatic Works of Robert Greene. 2 vols. 1831.

The Dramatic Works and Poems of James Shirley. 6 vols. 1833.

Specimens of English Sonnets. 1833.

The Works of Richard Bentley. 3 vols. 1836–8.

The Works of Thomas Middleton. 5 vols. 1840.

The Poetical Works of John Skelton. 2 vols. 1843.

The Works of Beaumont and Fletcher. 11 vols. 1843–6.

The Works of Christopher Marlowe. 3 vols. 1850.

Recollections of the Table Talk of Samuel Rogers. 1856.

The Works of Shakespeare. The Text revised. 6 vols. 1857; 9 vols. 1864–7 (adds glossary).

The Works of John Ford. 3 vols. 1869.

[Dyce also pbd the Aldine edns of Akenside, Beattie, Parnell, Pope, and Shakespeare's poems, as well as several minor Elizabethan texts for the Camden, Percy and Shakespeare Socs.]

(b) Miscellaneous Writings

Select Translations from the Greek of Quintus Smyrnaeus. 1821.

Remarks on Mr J. P. Collier's and Mr Charles Knight's Editions of Shakespeare. 1844.

A Few Notes on Shakespeare with Occasional Remarks on Mr Collier's Copy of the Folio 1632. 1853.

Strictures on Mr Collier's New Edition of Shakespeare, 1858. 1859.

JOHN GENEST (1764–1839)

Some Account of the English Stage from 1660 to 1830. 10 vols. Bath, 1832 (anon.).

WILLIAM GIFFORD (1756–1826)

[See vol. II, p. 362 above.]

JOSEPH HASLEWOOD (1769–1833)

(a) Editions

The Book containing the Treatises of Hawking, Hunting, Coat-Armour, Fishing and Blasing of Arms [by Juliana Berners]. 1810.

Ancient Critical Essays upon English Poets and Poësy. 2 vols. 1811–5.

The First [Second] Tome of the Palace of Pleasure [by William Painter]. 2 vols. 1813.

Mirror for Magistrates. Collated with Various Editions. 2 vols. 1815.

Barnabae Itinerarium, or Barnabee's Journal [by Richard Brathwait]. 1818; 2 vols. 1820 (enlarged).

[And various rarities for the Roxburghe Club and elsewhere.]

(b) Miscellaneous Writings

Some Account of the Life and Publications of the Late Joseph Ritson, Esq. 1824.

Roxburghe Revels, and Other Relative Papers, including Answers to the Attack on the Memory of the Late Joseph Haslewood with Specimens of his Literary Productions. Ed. J. Maidment, Edinburgh, 1837 (priv. ptd).

[Haslewood also contributed largely to GM. and to Sir S. E. Brydges's Censura Literaria, 1807–9, and The British Bibliographer, 1810–4.]

JOSEPH HUNTER (1783–1861)

(a) Literary Studies and Editions

Who wrote Cavendish's Life of Wolsey? A Dissertation. 1814.

Golden Sentences [from Fuller, Sir Thomas Browne, Whichcote, etc.]. Bath, 1826.

Life of Sir Thomas More by Cresacre More. 1828.

The Diary of Ralph Thoresby. 2 vols. 1830.

The Towneley Mysteries. Surtees Soc. 1836.
A Disquisition on the Scene, Origin, Date, etc. of Shakespeare's Tempest. 1839 (priv. ptd).
The Diary of Dr Thomas Cartwright. Camden Soc. 1843.
New Illustrations of the Life, Studies and Writings of Shakespeare. 2 vols. 1845.
Milton. A Sheaf of Gleanings after his Biographers and Annotators. 1850.
The Great Hero of the Ancient Minstrelsy of England, Robin Hood. 1852.
Pope: his Descent and Family Connexions. 1857.

(b) Historical and Antiquarian Writings

Hallamshire. The History and Topography of the Parish of Sheffield. 1819.
South Yorkshire, the History and Topography of the Deanery of Doncaster. 2 vols. 1828–31.
The Hallamshire Glossary. 1829.
English Monastic Libraries. 1831.
Gens Sylvestrina. Memorials of some of my Ancestors. 1846 (priv. ptd).
Collections concerning the Early History of the Founders of New England. 1849.

[And other works, including edns of various rolls for the Public Records Commissioners. Hunter's contributions to Archaeologia are listed in Sylvester Hunter, A Brief Memoir of the Late Joseph Hunter, 1861 (priv. ptd).]

DAVID IRVING (1778–1860)

(a) Writings

Lives of Scottish Authors, viz. Ferguson, Falconer and Russell. Edinburgh, 1801. [Originally pbd separately.]
The Elements of English Composition. Edinburgh, 1801.
The Lives of the Scotish Poets. 2 vols. Edinburgh, 1804; 2 vols. Edinburgh, 1810 (rev.).
Life of George Buchanan. 1805; Edinburgh, 1817 (rev.).
Observations on the Study of Civil Law. Edinburgh, 1815.
A Catalogue of the Law Books in the Advocates' Library. Edinburgh, 1831.
Lives of Scotish Writers. 2 vols. Edinburgh, 1839. [Rptd from Ency. Brit., 7th edn.]
The History of Scotish Poetry. Ed. J. A. Carlyle, Edinburgh, 1861. [With memoir of Irving by David Laing.]

(b) Editions

Selden's Table Talk. 1819; 1854 (rev.).
The Poems of Alexander Montgomerie. 1821. [With D. Laing.]
The Moral Fables of Robert Henryson. Maitland Club, 1832.

Davidis Buchanani de Scriptoribus Scotis Libri Duo. Bannatyne Club, 1837. [And other works for the Maitland and Bannatyne Clubs.]

JOHN JAMIESON (1759–1838)

An Etymological Dictionary of the Scottish Language. 2 vols. Edinburgh, 1808; rev. (with memoir of Jamieson) J. Longmuir and D. Donaldson, 4 vols. Paisley, 1879–82. [Abridged, Edinburgh, 1818; Supplement, 2 vols. Edinburgh, 1825.]
An Historical Account of the Ancient Culdees of Iona. Edinburgh, 1811.
Hermes Scythius, or the Radical Affinities of the Greek and Latin Languages to the Gothic. Edinburgh, 1814.
The Bruce [by Barbour] and Wallace [by Blind Harry]. 2 vols. Edinburgh, 1820. [Ed. by Jamieson.]

[Jamieson also pbd 3 long poems, 1789–98, sermons and theological works.]

CHARLES KNIGHT (1791–1873)

Arminius, or The Deliverance of Germany. A Tragedy. Windsor, 1814.
The Bridal of the Isles. A Mask. 1817 (2nd edn).
A Glossary; The Lives of Tasso and Fairfax. [Prefixed to 5th edn of E. Fairfax's Tasso, 2 vols. Windsor, 1817.]
The Menageries. 3 vols. Soc. for Diffusion of Useful Knowledge, 1829–40 (anon.).
The Working-Man's Companion. The Rights of Industry. Pt 1: Capital and Labour. Soc. for the Diffusion of Useful Knowledge, 1831 (anon.; 2nd edn). Pt 2: The Results of Machinery, namely, Cheap Production and Increased Employment, exhibited. Soc. for the Diffusion of Useful Knowledge, 1831 (anon.).
Trades' Unions and Strikes. 1834 (anon.).
The Pictorial Edition of the Works of Shakspere. 7 vols. [1839–]41; 5 vols. 1867 (rev.).
Shakspere and his Writings. [In Knight's Store of Knowledge, 1841.]
London. 6 vols. 1841–4; rev. E. Walford, 6 vols. [1875–7]. [Ed. by Knight, and contains many articles by him.]
William Shakspere. A Biography. 1842; 1850 (as Studies and Illustrations of Shakspere, vol. i).
William Caxton. A Biography. 1844.
Studies of Shakspere: forming a Companion Volume to Every Edition of the Text. 1849. [Rptd from Pictorial and Library edns.]
Studies and Illustrations of the Writings of Shakspere. 3 vols. 1850.
The Struggles of a Book against Excessive Taxation. [1850] (2nd edn).

Once Upon a Time. 2 vols. 1854. [Essays.]

The Old Printer and the Modern Press. 1854. [Partly based on biography of Caxton, 1844.]

The Popular History of England. 8 vols. 1856–62.

Passages of a Working Life, with a Prelude of Early Reminiscences. 3 vols. 1864–5.

Shadows of the Old Booksellers. 1865; rptd 1927.

Begg'd at Court. A Legend of Westminster. 1867. [A novel.]

[For life see A. A. Clowes, Charles Knight. A Sketch, 1892 (with bibliography).]

DAVID LAING (1793–1878)

Select Remains of the Ancient Popular and Romance Poetry of Scotland. Edinburgh, 1822; ed. (with memoir of Laing) J. Small, Edinburgh, 1885.

Various Pieces of Fugitive Scottish Poetry. 2 vols. Edinburgh, 1823–5.

Early Scottish Metrical Tales. Edinburgh, 1826.

The Poems of William Dunbar. 2 vols. Edinburgh, 1834. [Supplementary vol. of selections from minor 'Makars', 1865.]

The Letters and Journals of Robert Baillie. 3 vols. Bannatyne Club, 1841–2.

The Works of John Knox. 6 vols. Bannatyne Club and Wodrow Soc. 1846–64.

The Poems and Fables of Robert Henryson. Edinburgh, 1865.

The Poetical Works of Sir David Lyndsay. 2 vols. Edinburgh, 1871; 3 vols. Edinburgh, 1879 (adds bibliography).

[In addition to over 100 papers in Proc. Soc. Antiquaries of Scotland and various antiquarian books and pamphlets, Laing edited or assisted in editing many rarities (mainly Scottish) for the Abbotsford, Bannatyne, Hunterian and Spalding Clubs, and Shakespeare and Wodrow Socs., including 27 works for the Bannatyne Club alone. For details see T. G. Stevenson, Notices of David Laing with List of his Publications, 1878 (priv. ptd), and D. Murray, David Laing, Antiquary and Bibliographer, Scottish Hist. Rev. July 1914.]

JAMES MAIDMENT (1795?–1879)

A North Countrie Garland. Edinburgh, 1824 (anon.); ed. T. G. Stevenson, Edinburgh, 1868.

A [Second; Third] Book of Scottish Pasquils. 3 pts, Edinburgh, 1827–8; Edinburgh, 1868 (enlarged).

Reliquiae Scoticae: Scotish Remains in Prose and Verse. Edinburgh, 1828.

Nugae Derelictae: Documents Illustrative of Scotish Affairs, 1206–1715. Edinburgh, 1832. [With R. Pitcairn.]

Analecta Scotica: Collections Illustrative of the Civil, Ecclesiastical and Literary History of Scotland. 2 vols. Edinburgh, 1834–7.

Fragmenta Scoto-Dramatica, 1715–1758. Edinburgh, 1835.

Bannatyniana: Notices relative to the Bannatyne Club, including Critiques on some of its Publications. Edinburgh, 1836.

Scotish Elegiac Verses on the Principal Nobility and Gentry, from 1629 to 1729. Edinburgh, 1842 (anon.).

A New Book of Old Ballads. Edinburgh, 1844 (anon.); ed. T. G. Stevenson, Edinburgh, 1868.

Scotish Ballads and Songs. Edinburgh, 1859.

Dramatists of the Restoration. 14 vols. Edinburgh, 1872–9. [With W. H. Logan.]

[Maidment also pbd much (mainly Scottish antiquities) for the Abbotsford, Bannatyne, Hunterian and Maitland Clubs and the Spottiswoode Soc. For details see T. G. Stevenson, A Bibliographical List of the Various Publications by James Maidment from 1817 to 1878, Edinburgh, 1883.]

ROBERT NARES (1753–1829)

Elements of Orthoepy, containing the Whole Analogy of the English Language, so far as it relates to Pronunciation. 1784.

General Rules for the Pronunciation of the English Language. 1792.

The British Critic. A New Review. May 1793–Oct. 1826. [Vols. I–XLII ed. by Nares and William Beloe.]

A New and General Biographical Dictionary. 15 vols. 1798–1810. [In this (3rd) edn vols. VI, VIII, X, XII, XIV were ed. by Nares.]

Essays and Other Occasional Compositions. 2 vols. 1810.

A Glossary, or Collection of Words, Phrases, Names and Allusions to Customs, Proverbs, etc. which have been thought to require Illustration in the Works of English Authors, particularly Shakespeare and his Contemporaries. 1822; rev. J. O. Halliwell [-Phillipps] and T. Wright, 2 vols. 1859. [For an appreciation see A Book of Words, TLS. 1 June 1922.]

[Nares also pbd sermons and theological and miscellaneous works.]

SIR NICHOLAS HARRIS NICOLAS (1799–1848)

(a) Editions

The Literary Remains of Lady Jane Grey. 1825.

The Poetical Rhapsody of Francis Davison. 2 vols. 1826.

Private Memoirs of Sir Kenelm Digby. 1827.

The Retrospective Review. Second Series. 1827–8. [Ed. by Nicolas and H. Southern.]

The Letters of Joseph Ritson. 2 vols. 1833.
[Includes memoir of Ritson by Nicolas.]
The Complete Angler of Izaak Walton and
Charles Colton. 2 vols. 1836.

[In addition to various antiquarian edns
and rpts Nicolas was responsible . for the
Aldine edns of Burns, Chaucer, Collins,
Cowper, Surrey and Wyatt, Thomson and
Kirke White.]

(b) Writings

Life of William Davison, Secretary of State
to Queen Elizabeth. 1823.
The History of the Battle of Agincourt. 1827.
History of the Orders of Knighthood of the
British Empire. 4 vols. 1841–2.
A History of the Royal Navy. 2 vols. 1847.
Memoirs of the Life and Times of Sir Christo-
pher Hatton. 1847.

[And other antiquarian works. Nicolas was
also a frequent contributor to GM. and
Archaeologia.]

THOMAS PARK (1759–1834)
(a) Editions and Revisions

The Works of the British Poets, collated with
the Best Editions. 42 vols. 1805–8. [Sup-
plement, 6 vols. 1809.]
Heliconia, comprising a Selection of English
Poetry of the Elizabethan Age. 3 vols.
1815.
Facetiae. Musarum Deliciae. 1817. [With
E. Dubois.]

[Park also re-edited: Sir John Harington's
Nugae Antiquae, 2 vols. 1804; Horace Walpole's A Catalogue of Royal and Noble
Authors, 5 vols. 1806; The Harleian Miscellany, 10 vols. 1808–13; Thomas Percy's
Reliques of Ancient English Poetry, 3 vols.
1812; Joseph Ritson's A Select Collection
of English Songs, 3 vols. 1813.]

(b) Original Writings

Sonnets and Other Small Poems. 1797.
Cupid turned Volunteer; in a Series of Prints
designed by the Princess Elizabeth. With
Poetical Illustrations by Thomas Park.
1804.
Nugae Modernae. Morning Thoughts and
Midnight Musings in Prose and Verse. 1818.

[Park also contributed to several of the
literary and antiquarian works of Sir S. E.
Brydges, G. Ellis, J. Nichols, J. Ritson,
G. Steevens and others.]

SIR WALTER SCOTT (1771–1832)

[See p. 369 above.]

SAMUEL WELLER SINGER (1783–1858)
(a) Editions

Shakespeare's Jest Book. 3 pts, 1814–5.
Diana, or the Sonnets of H[enry] C[onstable].
1818. [Facs. rpt.]
Anecdotes, Observations and Characters of
Books and Men. By Joseph Spence. 1820.
The British Poets. 100 vols. Chiswick, 1822.
[Many of the preliminary notices are by
Singer.]
The Dramatic Works of William Shakespeare.
10 vols. 1826.

[Singer also issued inter alia edns and rpts
of the poems of Chalkhill, Chapman, Fairfax,
Griffin, Herrick, Lodge, Lovelace, Marlowe
and Marmion, as well as Bacon's Essays,
Cavendish's Life of Wolsey, Selden's Table-
Talk, and some French and Italian rarities.]

(b) Original Writings

Researches into the History of Playing Cards.
1816.
The Text of Shakespeare vindicated from the
Interpolations and Corruptions advocated
by J. P. Collier. 1853.

BENJAMIN THORPE (1782–1870)

Caedmon's Metrical Paraphrase of Parts of
the Holy Scriptures, in Anglo-Saxon. Soc.
Antiquaries, 1832. [With trn.]
The Anglo-Saxon Version of the Story of
Apollonius of Tyre. 1834. [With trn.]
Analecta Anglo-Saxonica. A Selection in
Prose and Verse from Anglo-Saxon Authors.
Oxford, 1834, 1846 (corrected).
Libri Psalmorum Versio antiqua Latina cum
Paraphrasi Anglo-Saxonica. Oxford, 1835.
[Also ptd in Appendix B to Cooper's Report
on Rymer's Foedera, 1835.]
Ancient Laws and Institutes of England.
2 vols. 1840.
Codex Exoniensis. A Collection of Anglo-
Saxon Poetry. Soc. Antiquaries, 1842.
[With trn.]
Tha Halgan Godspel on Englisc. Oxford,
1842.
The Homilies of the Anglo-Saxon Church.
2 vols. Aelfric Soc. 1844–6. [With trn.]
Florence of Worcester's Chronicle. 2 vols.
1848–9.
Northern Mythology, comprising the Principal
Popular Traditions of Scandinavia, North
Germany and the Netherlands. 3 vols.
1851.
Yule Tide Stories: a Collection of Scandi-
navian Tales. 1853.
The Anglo-Saxon Poems of Beowulf, the
Scop or Gleeman's Tale, and the Fight at
Finnesburg, with a Literal Translation.
Oxford, 1855.

The Anglo-Saxon Chronicle. 2 vols. Rolls Ser.
1861. [With trn.]
Diplomatarium Anglicum Aevi Saxonici. A
Collection of English Charters. 1865.
Edda Saemundar from the Old Norse. 2 pts,
1866.

[Thorpe also issued trns of: Rask's Anglo-
Saxon Grammar, 1830; Lappenberg's A
History of England under the Anglo-Saxon
Kings, 2 vols. 1845, and A History of England
under the Norman Kings, 1857; and Pauli's
Life of King Alfred, 1853 (which includes
Thorpe's own version of Alfred's Orosius).]

HENRY JOHN TODD (1763–1845)

(a) Editions

Comus, a Mask, by John Milton. With Pre-
liminary Illustrations. 1798.
The Poetical Works of John Milton. With the
Principal Notes of Various Commentators.
6 vols. 1801. [Vol. I was also issued
separately as An Account of the Life and
Writings of John Milton.]
The Works of Edmund Spenser. With the
Principal Notes of the Various Com-
mentators. 5 vols. 1805. [Reviewed by Sir
W. Scott, Edinburgh Rev. Oct. 1805.]
Illustrations of the Lives and Writings of
Gower and Chaucer. 1810.
Johnson's Dictionary of the English Language.
With Numerous Corrections and Additions.
4 vols. 1818.
Cranmer's Defence of the True and Catholick
Doctrine of the Sacrament. 1825.
Selections from the Metrical Paraphrases on
the Psalms by George Sandys. 1839.

(b) Original Writings

Some Account of the Deans of Canterbury.
1793.
A Vindication of our Authorized Translation
and Translators of the Bible. 1819.
Memoirs of the Life and Writings of Bishop
Brian Walton. 2 vols. 1821.
The Life of Archbishop Cranmer. 2 vols.
1831.

[Todd also pbd catalogues and minor
antiquarian, controversial and theological
works.]

WILLIAM SIDNEY WALKER (1795–1846)

Gus avus Vasa and Other Poems. 1813.
The Heroes of Waterloo. An Ode. 1815.
Poems from the Danish. Selected by Andreas
Andersen Feldborg. Translated into English
Verse. 1815.
The Appeal of Poland. An Ode. 1816.
Corpus Poetarum Latinorum. 1828.

The Poetical Remains of William Sidney
Walker. Ed. (with memoir) J. Moultrie,
1852.
Shakespeare's Versification and its Apparent
Irregularities explained. Ed. W. N. Lett-
som, 1854.
A Critical Examination of the Text of Shake-
speare, with Remarks on his Language and
that of his Contemporaries. Ed. W. N.
Lettsom, 3 vols. 1860.

[Walker was also almost entirely responsible
for the pbn of Milton's De Ecclesia Christiana,
1825, though the ostensible editor was C. R.
Sumner.]

HENRY WILLIAM WEBER (1783–1818)

The Battle of Flodden Field. A Poem of the
Sixteenth Century. 1808.
Metrical Romances of the Thirteenth, Four-
teenth and Fifteenth Centuries. 3 vols.
Edinburgh, 1810.
The Dramatic Works of John Ford. 2 vols.
1811.
Tales of the East. 3 vols. Edinburgh, 1812.
The Works of Beaumont and Fletcher. 14 vols.
1812.
Illustrations of Northern Antiquities, from the
Earlier Teutonic and Scandinavian Ro-
mances. 1814. [Assisted by Sir W. Scott
and R. Jamieson.]

SIMON WILKIN (1790–1862)

A Catalogue of the Books belonging to the
Public Library, and to the City Library of
Norwich, methodically arranged. 4 pts,
Norwich .1825–32; Norwich, 1847.
A Catechism of the Use of the Globes. 2 pts,
1826.
Sir Thomas Browne's Works, including his
Life and Correspondence. 4 vols. 1836;
3 vols. 1852.
Joseph Kingdom of Norwich: a Memoir.
Norwich, 1855. [By M. H. Wilkin; preface
and introductory ch. by Simon Wilkin.]

B. ENGLISH SCHOLARS, 1835–1870

THOMAS ARNOLD (1823–1900)

(a) Writings

A Manual of English Literature, Historical
and Critical; with an Appendix on English
Metres. 1862; 1867 (rev. and enlarged);
1873 (rev.); 1877 (rev.); 1885 (rev.); 1888
(rev.); 1897 (rev.).
Chaucer to Wordsworth. A Short History of
English Literature, from the Earliest Times
to the Present Day. [1870]; 2 vols. 1875.
Passages in a Wandering Life. 1900. [Re-
miniscences.]

[Arnold also pbd several short papers,
chiefly on education.]

(b) Editions

Select English Works of John Wyclif. 3 vols. Oxford, 1869–71.

Selections from Addison's Papers contributed to the Spectator. 1875.

Beowulf: a Heroic Poem of the Eighth Century; with Translation, Notes and Appendix. 1876.

Pope. Selected Poems; the Essay on Criticism; the Moral Essays; the Dunciad. 1876.

Henrici, Archidiaconi Huntendunensis, Historia Anglorum. The History of the English, by Henry, Archdeacon of Huntingdon, from A.C. 55 to A.D. 1154. 1879. (Rolls Ser.)

English Poetry and Prose. A Collection of Illustrative Passages from the Writings of English Authors, commencing in the Anglo-Saxon Period and brought down to the Present Time. 1882.

Symeonis Monachi Opera omnia. 2 vols. 1882–5. (Rolls. Ser.)

Clarendon. History of the Rebellion, Book VI. 1886.

Dryden. An Essay of Dramatic Poesy. 1889.

Memorials of St Edmund's Abbey. 1890.

WILLIAM BLADES (1824–1890)

The Life and Typography of William Caxton, England's First Printer; with Evidence of his Typographical Connection with Colard Mansion, the Printer at Bruges. 2 vols. 1861–3.

A Catalogue of Books Printed by (or ascribed to the Press of) William Caxton. 1865.

A List of Medals, Jettons, Tokens, etc. in Connection with Printers and the Art of Printing. 1869 (priv. ptd).

How to tell a Caxton; with some Hints where and how the same might be found. 1870.

A List of Medals struck by Order of the Corporation of London. With an Appendix of other Medals, struck privately or for Sale, having Reference to the Same Corporate Body or its Members. 1870 (priv. ptd).

Typographical Notes. [1870] (priv. ptd).

Shakspere and Typography; being an Attempt to show Shakspere's Personal Connection with, and Technical Knowledge of, the Art of Printing. Also, Remarks upon some Common Typographical Errors, with Especial Reference to the Text of Shakspere. 1872. ['A jeu d'esprit'—DNB.]

Some Early Type Specimen Books of England, Holland, France, Italy, and Germany; with Explanatory Remarks. 1875.

The Biography and Typography of William Caxton. 1877. [A different work from the 'Life.']

The Enemies of Books. 1880; 1888 (rev. and enlarged); tr. French. Paris, 1883.

Numismata Typographica; or The Medallic History of Printing. Reprinted from the 'Printers' Register.' 1883.

An Account of the German Morality-Play entitled Depositio Cornuti Typographici; with a Rhythmical Translation of the German Version of 1648. 1885.

Bibliographical Miscellanies. 5 pts, 1890. [Pt 1: Signatures; pt 2: The Chained Library at Wimborne Minster; pts 3, 4, 5: Books in Chains.]

The Pentateuch of Printing, with a Chapter on Judges. With a Memoir of the Author, and List of his Works, by T. B. Reed. 1891.

[Blades also contributed many essays on printing and bibliography to periodicals and pbd several short papers; he edited Juliana Berners's Boke of St Albans, The Dictes and Sayings of the Philosophers, Christine Pisan's Moral Proverbes, and was a prime mover in the Caxton celebration of 1877.]

PETER CUNNINGHAM (1816–1869)

(a) Writings

Poems upon Several Occasions. 1841 (priv. ptd).

Westminster Abbey: its Art, Architecture and Associations. A Handbook for Visitors. 1842.

Inigo Jones. A Life of the Architect by Peter Cunningham. Remarks on some of his Sketches for Masques and Dramas, by J. R. Planché, [etc.]. Shakespeare Soc. 1848.

A Handbook for London, Past and Present. 2 vols. 1849; 1851 (3rd edn, as Murray's Handbook for Modern London); [1863] (as London as it is); [1866] (rev.); [1867] (rev.).

The Story of Nell Gwynn; and the Sayings of Charles II.; related and collected. 1852.

[Cunningham also wrote several annual handbooks to London.]

(b) Editions

The Poems of William Drummond of Hawthornden, with Life. 1833.

Extracts from the Accounts of the Revels at Court, in the Reigns of Queen Elizabeth and James I., from the Original Office Books of the Masters and Yeomen. With an Introduction and Notes. Shakespeare Soc. 1842.

Lives of the most Eminent English Poets, by Samuel Johnson; with Notes, Corrective and Explanatory. 3 vols. 1854.

The Works of Oliver Goldsmith. 4 vols. 1854.

The Letters of Horace Walpole. Now first chronologically arranged. 9 vols. 1857–9.

[Cunningham also edited 2 vols. for the Percy Soc., Songs of England and Scotland,

Specimens of the British Poets, and Pope's Works; he was treasurer of the Shakespeare Soc. and a contributor to Fraser's Mag., GM., Athenaeum, etc.]

PETER AUGUSTIN DANIEL

Notes and Conjectural Emendations of Certain Doubtful Passages in Shakespeare's Plays. 1870.

Romeo and Juliet. Parallel Texts of the First Two Quartos. New Shakspere Soc. 1874.

Romeus and Juliet (written first in Italian by Bandell and nowe in Englishe) by A. Brooke.—Rhomeo and Julietta (translated by W. Painter from the French paraphrase by P. Boaistuau, of Bandello's version of Romeo e Giulietta). New Shakspere Soc. Originals and Analogues, pt 1, 1875.

The Works of Francis Beaumont and John Fletcher. Variorum Edition. 4 vols. 1904–12. [General editor, A. H. Bullen; Daniel edited The Maid's Tragedy and Philaster in vol. I and The Beggar's Bush in vol. II.]

[Daniel also contributed introductions to sundry plays issued in the Shakespeare Quarto-Facsimiles Ser.]

JOHN EARLE (1824–1903)

Gloucester Fragments, Legends of St Swithun and Sancta Maria Aegyptiaca. 1861.

Guide to Bath, Ancient and Modern. 1864.

Two of the Saxon Chronicles Parallel, with Supplementary Extracts from the Others. Edited with Introduction, Notes and a Glossarial Index. 1865.

A Book for the Beginner in Anglo-Saxon. 1866.

The Philology of the English Tongue. 1866.

Rhymes and Reasons. Essays by J. E. 1871.

English Plant Names. 1880.

Anglo-Saxon Literature. 1884.

A Handbook to the Land Charters and Other Saxonic Documents. 1888.

English Prose, its Elements, History and Usage. 1890.

Deeds of Beowulf, done into Modern Prose. 1892.

The Psalter of 1539. 1894.

Bath during British Independence. 1895.

A Simple Grammar of English now in Use. 1898.

Alfred as a Writer. [In Alfred the Great, ed. A. Bowker, 1899.]

The Alfred Jewel. 1901.

The Place of English in Education. [In Furnivall Miscellany, 1901.]

ALEXANDER JOHN ELLIS (1814–1890)

Phonetics: a Familiar System of the Principles of that Science. By A. J. E. 1844.

The Essentials of Phonetics; containing the Theory of a Universal Alphabet, together with its Practical Application. 1848.

An Extension of Phonography to Foreign Languages: containing a Complete Phonographic Alphabet; and Hints towards the Construction of a Phonographic Short Hand for French and German. 1848.

Phonetic Spelling familiarly explained, for the Use of Romanic Readers: with Numerous Examples. 1849.

On Early English Pronunciation, with Especial Reference to Shakspere and Chaucer; containing an Investigation of the Correspondence of Writing with Speech in England, from the Anglosaxon Period to the Present Day. Including a Re-arrangement of F. J. Child's Memoirs on the Language of Chaucer and Gower. 5 pts, Chaucer Soc., Philolog. Soc. and EETS. 1869–89.

On the Sensations of Tone as a Physiological Basis for the Theory of Music. By Hermann Ludwig Ferdinand von Helmholtz; translated from the third German Edition, with Additions and Notes. 1875; 1885 (rev. with addns). ['More than a third consisted of original work by Ellis himself'—DNB.]

The English, Dionysian, and Hellenic Pronunciations of Greek, considered in Reference to School and College Use. 1876.

The History of Musical Pitch. Reprinted, with Corrections and an Appendix, from the 'Journal of the Society of Arts.' 1880.

[Ellis also wrote many other papers and books on phonetics, phonography, music, mathematics, philosophy, etc., and produced phonetic texts of the Bible, Shakespeare's Macbeth and The Tempest, Bunyan's Pilgrim's Progress, etc. He edited The Fonetic Frend, 1849, and The Spelling Reformer, 1849–50.]

FREDERICK JAMES FURNIVALL (1825–1910)

(a) Editions for the Ballad Society

[Founded by Furnivall in 1868]

Ballads from Manuscripts. 1868.

Captain Cox, his Ballads and Books. 1871.

Love Poems and Humorous ones, 1614–1619. 1874.

(b) Editions for the Chaucer Society

[Founded by Furnivall in 1868]

A Six-Text Print of Chaucer's Canterbury Tales in Parallel Columns. [1868.]

The Cambridge MS. of Chaucer's Canterbury Tales. 1868–79.

The Corpus MS. of Chaucer's Canterbury Tales. 1868–79.

The Ellesmere MS. of Chaucer's Canterbury Tales. 1868–79.

The Hengwrt MS. of Chaucer's Canterbury Tales. 1868–79.

The Lansdowne MS. of Chaucer's Canterbury Tales. 1868–79.

The Petworth MS. of Chaucer's Canterbury Tales. 1868–79.

Essays on Chaucer, his Words and Works. [1868.]

Odd Texts of Chaucer's Minor Poems. 1868.

A Parallel-Text Edition of Chaucer's Minor Poems. [1871.]

Supplementary Parallel-Texts of Chaucer's Minor Poems. [1871.]

A One-Text Print of Chaucer's Minor Poems. [1871.]

Trial-Forewords to my 'Parallel-Text Edition of Chaucer's Minor Poems.' 1871.

Originals of some of Chaucer's Canterbury Tales. [1872.]

Chaucer as Valet and Squire to Edward III. 1876.

Supplementary Canterbury Tales. 1876.

Animadversions uppon the Annotacions and Corrections of some Imperfections of Impressiones of Chaucers Workes reprinted in 1598 sett downe by F. Thynne. 1876.

Autotypes of Chaucer Manuscripts. 1877.

A Parallel-Text Print of Chaucer's Troilus and Criseyde. [1881.]

The Harleian MS. 7334 of Chaucer's Canterbury Tales. 1885.

Chaucer's 'Boece.' 1886.

John Lane's Continuation of Chaucer's 'Squire's Tale.' 1887.

A One-Text Print of Chaucer's Troilus and Criseyde. 1888.

Three More Parallel Texts of Chaucer's Troilus and Criseyde. 1894.

The Cambridge MS. Dd. 4. 24 of Chaucer's Canterbury Tales, completed by the Egerton MS. 2726. 1901–2.

The Romaunt of the Rose. 1911.

(c) Editions for the Early English Text Society

[Founded by Furnivall in 1864]

Arthur; a Short Sketch of his Life and History in English Verse. II, 1864.

Thynne on Speght's Chaucer. IX, 1865. [With G. Kingsley.]

The Wrights Chaste Wife. By Adam of Cobsam. XII, 1865.

Political, Religious, and Love Poems. XV, 1866.

The Book of Quinte Essence. XVI, 1866.

Hymns to the Virgin and Christ; the Parliament of Devils. XXIV, 1867.

The Stacions of Rome; and The Pilgrim's Sea-Voyage; with Clene Maydenhod. XXV, 1867.

The Babees Book, Aristotle's ABC, Urbanitatis, [etc.]. XXXII, 1868.

Caxton's Book of Curtesye. Ex. Ser. III, 1868.

Queene Elizabethes Achademy (by Sir H. Gilbert); [etc.]. Ex. Ser. VIII, 1869.

Awdeley's Fraternitye of Vacabondes, Harman's Caveat, etc. Ex. Ser. IX, 1869. [With E. Viles.]

The Fyrste Boke of the Introduction of Knowledge made by A. Borde [etc.]. Ex. Ser. X, [1870].

The Minor Poems of William Lauder. XLI, 1870.

A Supplicacyon for the Beggers. By Simon Fish. Ex. Ser. XIII, 1871.

The History of the Holy Grail. By Henry Lovelich from the French of Sir R. de Borron. Ex. Ser. XX, XXIV, XXVIII, XXX, 1874–8.

Emblemes and Epigrames. By Francis Thynne. LXIV, 1877.

Adam Davy's 5 Dreams about Edward II [etc.]. LXIX, 1878.

The Fifty Earliest English Wills in the Court of Probate, 1387–1439. 1882.

The Anatomie of the Bodie of Man. By Vicary. Ex. Ser. LIII, 1888.

The Curial made by maystere A. Charretier. Translated by Caxton. Ex. Ser. LIV, 1888.

Caxton's Eneydos. Ex. Ser. LVII, 1890.

Hoccleve's Works. Ex. Ser. LXI, LXII, 1892–7.

The Three Kings' Sons. Englisht from the French. Ex. Ser. LXVII, 1895.

The English Conquest of Ireland, A.D. 1166–1185. CVII, 1896.

Child-Marriages, Divorces, and Ratifications in the Diocese of Chester, A.D. 1561–6. CVIII, 1897.

Lydgate's Deguileville's Pilgrimage of the Life of Man. Ex. Ser. LXXVI, LXXXIII, 1899–1901.

Robert of Brunne's Handlyng Synne. CXIX, CXXIII, 1901–3.

Minor Poems of the Vernon MS. Pt 2, CXVII, 1901.

The Macro Plays. Ex. Ser. XCI, 1904.

The Tale of Beryn, etc. Ex. Ser. CV, 1909. [With W. G. Stone.]

The Gild of St Mary, Lichfield. Ex. Ser. CXIV, 1920.

(d) Editions for the New Shakspere Society

[Founded by Furnivall in 1873]

Stafford's Compendious Examination of certayne complaints of divers of our countrymen. 1876.

Spalding's A Letter on Shakspere's Authorship of The Two Noble Kinsmen. 1876.

Tell-Trothes New-Yeares Gift, etc. 1876.

Harrison's Description of England in Shakspere's Youth. 1877.

Stubbes's Anatomy of Abuses. 1877.

The Digby Mysteries. 1882.

A List of all the Songs and Passages in Shakspere which have been set to Music. 1884. [With J. Greenhill.]

Some 300 Fresh Allusions to Shakspere. 1886.

Robert Laneham's Letter. 1890; 1907.

(e) Editions for the Roxburghe Club

Seynt Graal, or the Sank Ryal, partly in English Verse by Henry Lovelich and wholly in French Prose by Robiers de Borron. 2 vols. 1861–3.

Robert of Brunne's Handlyng Synne; William of Waddington's Le Manuel des Pechiez. 1862.

La Queste del Saint Graal; in the French Prose of Walter Map. 1864.

A Royal Historie of the Excellent Knight Generides. Hertford, 1865.

The Boke of Nurture, by John Russell; The Boke of Kervynge, by Wynkyn de Worde; The Boke of Nurture, by Hugh Rhodes. 2 vols. 1866–7.

(f) Editions of Shakespeare

The Leopold Shakspere, in Chronological Order, from the Text of Professor Delius. [1877.]

Double Text Dallastype Shakespeare. 1895.

The Works of William Shakespeare according to the Orthography and Arrangement of the more Authentic Quarto and Folio Versions. 1904. (The Old Spelling Shakespeare.)

The Century Shakespeare. 40 vols. 1908. [With introductions and notes, and a vol. on the Life and Work of Shakespeare, by Furnivall and J. J. Munro.]

Cassell's Illustrated Shakespeare. 1913.

[Furnivall also edited a number of the plays separately.]

(g) Other Editions

Le Morte Arthur. Ed. from the Harleian MS 2252 in the British Museum. 1864.

Bishop Percy's Folio Manuscript. Ballads and Romances. 1867. [With J. W. Hales.]

The Boke of Nurture by H. Rhodes. [1868?]

Mannyng, Robert, of Brunne. The Story of England, A.D. 1338. 1887. (Rolls Ser.)

Lamb's Tales from Shakespeare. With Introductions and Additions. 1901.

[This is a mere selection from a large number of works written, edited or provided with introductions. Furnivall founded the Wiclif Society and the Browning Society in 1881, and the same year compiled a Browning Bibliography. In 1874 he contributed to Gervinus's Commentaries on Shakspere an essay on metrical tests for the chronology of Shakespeare's works. In 1886 he founded the Shelley Society. He was, as Secretary of the Philological Society, the proposer of the scheme for the Oxford English Dictionary.]

(h) Biography and Criticism

An English Miscellany presented to Dr Furnivall in Honour of his Seventy-Fifth Birthday. Oxford, 1901.

Dr Frederick James Furnivall. 1910. [Obituary notices by Mrs C. C. Stopes and A. Brandl.]

Ker, W. P. Memoir. Proc. British Academy, III, 1909–10.

Frederick James Furnivall: a Volume of Personal Record. 1911. [Reminiscences by forty-nine contributors, with a biography by John Munro.]

JAMES ORCHARD HALLIWELL, later HALLIWELL-PHILLIPPS (1820–1889)

(a) Bibliography

Winsor, J. Halliwelliana: a Bibliography of the Publications of James Orchard Halliwell-Phillipps. Cambridge, U.S.A. 1881.

(b) Writings

Shakesperiana. A Catalogue of the Early Editions of Shakespeare's Plays, and of the Commentaries and Other Publications illustrative of his Works. 1841.

A Dictionary of Archaic and Provincial Words, Obsolete Phrases, Proverbs and Ancient Customs from the Fourteenth Century. 2 vols. 1846–7.

The Life of William Shakespeare; including Many Particulars respecting the Poet and his Family never before published. 1848.

Contributions to Early English Literature derived chiefly from Rare Books and Ancient Inedited Manuscripts from the Fifteenth to the Seventeenth Century. 6 pts, 1849.

A New Boke about Shakespeare and Stratford-on-Avon. 1850.

Observations on the Shakespeare Forgeries at Bridgewater House, Illustrative of a Facsimile of the Spurious Letter of H. S. 1853 (priv. ptd). [On the John Payne Collier controversy.]

A Brief Hand-List of Books, Manuscripts, etc. Illustrative of the Life and Writings of Shakespeare, collected between the Years 1842 and 1859. 1859 (priv. ptd).

A Dictionary of Old English Plays, existing either in Print or in Manuscript, from the Earliest Times to the Close of the Seventeenth Century. 1860.

A Brief Hand-List of the Records belonging to the Borough of Stratford-on-Avon; showing their General Character; with Notes of a Few of the Shakespearian Documents in the same Collection. 1862 (priv. ptd).

A Hand-List of upwards of a Thousand Volumes of Shakespeariana added to the three Previous Collections of a Similar Kind. 1862 (priv. ptd).

A Descriptive Calendar of the Ancient Manuscripts and Records in the Possession of the Corporation of Stratford-upon-Avon; including Notices of Shakespeare and his Family, and of Several Persons connected with the Poet. 1863 (priv. ptd).

Illustrations of the Life of Shakespeare in a Discursive Series of Essays. 1874.

New Lamps or Old? A Few Additional Words respecting the E and the A in the name of our National Dramatist. Brighton, 1880. [Favours the spelling 'Shakespeare.']

Outlines of the Life of Shakespeare. Brighton, 1881 (priv. ptd); 1882 (tripled in size); 2 vols. 1887 (7th edn, enlarged). [A different work from The Life of Shakespeare.]

A Calendar of the Shakespearean Rarities, Drawings and Engravings, preserved at Hollingbury Copse. 1887 (priv. ptd); ed. E. E. Baker, 1891 (enlarged).

[Halliwell pbd a very large number of other bks and pamphlets, many of them in very small limited edns, dealing with Shakespearian topography, history, iconography, etc.; with sixteenth and seventeenth century literature and earlier literature; catalogues, inventories, etc., etc.]

(c) Editions

The Voiage and Travaile of Sir John Maundevile, kt. Reprinted from the Edition of 1725, with an Introduction, Additional Notes, and Glossary. 1839.

The Harrowing of Hell. A Miracle Play, written in the Reign of Edward the Second, now first published from the Original Manuscript in the British Museum, with an Introduction, Translation and Notes. 1840.

The First Sketch of The Merry Wives of Windsor. Shakespeare Soc. 1842.

The Nursery Rhymes of England, obtained principally from Oral Tradition. Percy Soc. 1842; 1843 (with addns); 1846 (4th edn, with addns).

Private Diary of John Dee, and the Catalogue of his Library of Manuscripts. Camden Soc. 1842.

Nugae Poeticae. Select Pieces of Old English Popular Poetry, illustrating the Manners and Arts of the Fifteenth Century. 1844.

The Thornton Romances: The Early English Metrical Romances of Perceval, Isumbras, Eglamom, and Degrevant. Selected from Manuscripts at Lincoln and Cambridge. Camden Soc. 1844.

Letters of the Kings of England, now first collected from the Originals. Edited, with an Historical Introduction and Notes. 2 vols. 1846.

Morte Arthure. The Alliterative Romance of the Death of King Arthur, now first printed from a Manuscript in Lincoln Cathedral. 1847.

The Poetry of Witchcraft illustrated by Copies of the Plays on the Lancashire Witches by Heywood, [Brome] and Shadwell. 1853 (priv. ptd).

The Works of William Shakespeare; the Text formed from a New Collation of the Early Editions; to which are added all the Original Novels and Tales on which the Plays are founded, copious archaeological annotations on each play; an Essay on the Formation of the Text; and a Life of the Poet. 16 vols. 1853–65 (150 copies ptd for the editor).

A Glossary, or Collection of Words, Phrases, Names, and Allusions to Customs, Proverbs, etc. which have been thought to require Illustration, in the Works of English Authors, particularly Shakespeare and his Contemporaries. By Robert Nares. A New Edition, with Considerable Additions, by J. O. Halliwell and Thomas Wright. 2 vols. 1859.

A Treatyse of a Galaunt; with the Maryage of the Fayre Pusell, the Bosse of Byllyngesgate unto London Stone. From the Unique Edition printed by Wynkyn de Worde. 1860 (priv. ptd).

Shakespearian Facsimiles: a Collection of Curious and Interesting Documents, Plans, Signatures, &c., Illustrative of the Biography of Shakespeare and the History of his Family, from the Originals chiefly preserved at Stratford-on-Avon. Facsimiled by E. W. Ashbee; selected by J. O. Halliwell. 1863 (priv. ptd).

Those Songs and Poems from the excessively Rare First Edition of Englands Helicon, 1600, which are connected with the Works of Shakespeare. 1865 (25 copies only).

Stratford-upon-Avon in the Times of the Shakespeares, illustrated by Extracts from the Council Books of the Corporation, selected especially with Reference to the History of the Poet's Father. 1867.

[The foregoing are selected from an edited production of something like 150 works, mainly, but not entirely, in 17th century literature; Halliwell did much work for the

Camden, Percy, and Shakespeare Societies; in 1841–2, with Thomas Wright, he edited The Archaeologist and Journal of Antiquarian Science, of which only 10 issues appeared.]

(d) Biography and Criticism

Wright, G. R. A Brief Memoir of the Late J. O. Halliwell-Phillipps. 1889.
Obituary. Athenaeum, 12 Jan. 1889.

CLEMENT MANSFIELD INGLEBY (1823–1886)

(a) Writings

The Shakspere Fabrications; or, the MS. Notes of the Perkins Folio shown to be of Recent Origin. With an Appendix on the Authorship of the Ireland Forgeries. 1859. [On the John Payne Collier controversy.]
A Complete View of the Shakspere Controversy, concerning the Authenticity and Genuineness of Manuscript Matter affecting the Works and Biography of Shakspere, published by Mr J. Payne Collier as the Fruits of his Researches. 1861.
An Introduction to Metaphysics. 2 pts, 1864–9.
Was Thomas Lodge an Actor? An Exposition touching the Social Status of the Playwright in the Time of Queen Elizabeth. 1868.
The Still Lion. An Essay towards the Restoration of Shakespeare's Text. Reprinted, with Additions, from the Second Annual Volume of the German Shakespeare Society. 1874; 1875 (enlarged, as Shakespeare Hermeneutics).
Shakespeare—the Man and the Book: being a Collection of Occasional Papers on the Bard and his Writings. 2 pts, 1877–81.
Shakespeare's Bones: a Proposal to disinter them, considered in Relation to their Possible Bearing on his Portraiture: illustrated by Instances of Visits of the Living to the Dead. 1883.
Essays by the Late C. M. Ingleby, edited by his Son [Holcombe Ingleby]. 1888.

[Ingleby also pbd several shorter papers, mainly on Shakespeare.]

(b) Editions

Shakspere Allusion-Books. Pt 1, 1874.
Shakespeare's Centurie of Prayse: being Materials for a History of Opinion on Shakespeare and his Works, culled from Writers of the First Century after his Rise. 1874; 1879 (rev. with addns, for New Shakspere Soc. by Lucy T. Smith).
Shakespeare's Cymbeline: the Text revised and annotated. 1886.

ROBERT WILLIAM LOWE

The Fashionable Tragedian. 1877. [On Irving. Written in collaboration with William Archer.]
A Bibliographical Account of English Theatrical Literature from the Earliest Times to the Present Day. 1888.
Thomas Betterton. 1891.

[Lowe also edited Churchill's Rosciad and Apology, Cibber's Apology and J. Doran's 'Their Majesties' Servants,' as well as a series of Dramatic Essays (by Hazlitt, Hunt, Lewes, etc.) with William Archer.]

SIR FREDERIC MADDEN (1801–1873)

The Ancient English Romance of Havelok the Dane, accompanied by the French Text; with an Introduction, Notes and a Glossary. Roxburghe Club, 1828.
Privy Purse Expenses of the Princess Mary, daughter of King Henry the Eighth, afterwards Queen Mary. With a Memoir of the Princess, and Notes. 1831.
The Ancient English Romance of William and the Werewolf; edited, with an Introduction and Glossary. Roxburghe Club, 1832. [With 2 letters on 'Werewolves' by A. Herbert.]
Illuminated Ornaments, selected from Manuscripts and Early Printed Books from the Sixth to the Seventeenth Centuries, drawn and engraved by H. Shaw; with Descriptions by Sir Frederic Madden. 1833.
The Old English Versions of the Gesta Romanorum, edited for the First Time from Manuscripts in the British Museum and University Library, Cambridge, with an Introduction and Notes. Roxburghe Club, 1838.
Syr Gawayne: a Collection of Ancient Romance-Poems, by Scottish and English Authors, relating to that Celebrated Knight of the Round Table, with an Introduction, Notes, and a Glossary. 1839.
Laȝamons Brut, or Chronicle of Britain: a Poetical Semi-Saxon Paraphrase of the Brut of Wace. Now first published from the Cottonian Manuscripts in the British Museum; accompanied by a Literal Translation, Notes, and a Grammatical Glossary. 3 vols. Soc. Antiquaries, 1847.
The Holy Bible in the Earliest English Versions made from the Latin Vulgate by John Wycliffe and his Followers; edited by the Rev. Josiah Forshall and Sir Frederic Madden. 4 vols. Oxford, 1850. [Contains glossary; there are 2 distinct texts throughout.]
Universal Palaeography; or Fac-similes of Writings of all Periods and Nations, by J. B. Silvestre; accompanied by an His-

torical and Descriptive Text and Introduction by Champollion-Figeac and A. Champollion. Translated from the French, and edited, with Corrections and Notes. 2 vols. 1850.

Matthaei Parisiensis, Monachi Sancti Albani, Historia Anglorum, sive, ut vulgo dicitur, Historia Minor. Item, ejusdem Abbreviatio Chronicorum Angliae. 3 vols. 1866–9 (Rolls Ser.). [To vol. III is prefaced a life and criticism of Matthew Paris.]

[Madden was Keeper of MSS at the BM. from 1837, and produced various guides and catalogues for that department; his other edns included one of Warton's History of English Poetry.]

JOHN EYTON BICKERSTETH MAYOR (1825–1910)

[See p. 1007 above.]

WILLIAM JOHN THOMS (1803–1885)

(a) Writings

The Book of the Court; exhibiting the Origin, Peculiar Duties, and Privileges of the Several Ranks of the Nobility and Gentry, more particularly of the Great Officers of State and Members of the Royal Household. 1838.

Three Notelets on Shakespeare. 1: Shakespeare in Germany; 2: Folk-Lore of Shakespeare; 3: Was Shakespeare ever a Soldier? 1865.

Hannah Lightfoot; Queen Charlotte and the Chevalier d'Eon; Dr Wilmot's Polish Progress; Lord Chatham and the Princess Olive. 1867. [Rptd, with addns, from N. & Q.]

Human Longevity: its Facts and Fictions, including an Inquiry into some of the more Remarkable Instances, illustrated by Examples. 1873.

(b) Editions

A Collection of Early Prose Romances. 3 vols. 1827–8; 3 vols. 1858 (enlarged, as Early English Prose Romances).

Lays and Legends of Various Nations; illustrative of their Traditions, Popular Literature, Manners, Customs and Superstitions. 2 sers. 1834. [Ser. 1, France, Spain, Tartary and Ireland; ser. 2, Germany.]

Anecdotes and Traditions illustrative of Early English History and Literature from Manuscript Sources. Camden Soc. 1839.

The History of Reynard the Fox, from the Edition printed by Caxton in 1481. With Notes and an Introductory Sketch of the Literary History of the Romance. Percy Soc. 1844.

Gammer Gurton's Famous Histories of Sir Guy of Warwick, Sir Bevis of Hampton, Tom Hickathrift, Friar Bacon, Robin Hood, and The King and the Cobbler. Newly revised and amended by Amb[rose] Mer[ton], Gent., F.S.A. [1846]. ['Merton' is Thoms.]

Gammer Gurton's Pleasant Stories of Patient Grissel, the Princess Rosetta, & Robin Goodfellow; and Ballads of The Beggar's Daughter, The Babes in the Wood, and Fair Rosamond. Newly revised and amended by Amb[rose] Mer[ton], Gent., F.S.A. [1846].

Notes and Queries. Vol. I, no. 1, 3 Nov. 1849–Sept. 1872. [Planned and founded by Thoms, who had previously begun a similar series in Athenaeum of 26 Aug. 1846.]

[Thoms also pbd or edited various other papers, and translated J. J. A. Worsaal's Primeval Antiquities of Denmark from the Danish; he was Secretary of the Camden Soc. from 1838 to 1873.]

RICHARD CHENEVIX TRENCH (1807–1886)

[See p. 309 above.]

C. ENGLISH SCHOLARS, 1870–1900

GEORGE ATHERTON AITKEN (1860–1917)

The Life of Richard Steele. 2 vols. 1889.

The Life and Works of John Arbuthnot. Oxford, 1892.

Poems and Satires of Andrew Marvell. 2 vols. 1892. (Muses' Lib.)

The Poetical Works of Robert Burns. Edited with a Memoir. 3 vols. 1893.

The Poetical Works of Thomas Parnell. Edited with a Memoir and Notes. 1894.

Richard Steele. 1894. (Mermaid Ser.) [Selected plays, with introduction and appendixes.]

Romances and Narratives by Daniel Defoe. 16 vols. 1895–6.

The Spectator. With Introduction and Notes. 8 vols. 1898.

The Tatler. With Introduction and Notes. 4 vols. 1898–9.

[And other edns and pamphlets.]

EDWARD ARBER (1836–1912)

English Reprints. 30 vols. 1868–71.

The First Printed English New Testament, translated by William Tyndale. Photolithographed from the Unique Fragment now in the Grenville Collection, British Museum. 1871.

Annotated Reprints. 3 vols. 1872–5.

A Transcript of the Registers of the Company of Stationers of London, 1554–1640 A.D. 5 vols. 1875–94 (priv. ptd).

An English Garner. Ingatherings from our History and Literature. 8 vols. 1877–96; 12 vols. 1903 (ed. and rearranged by T. Seccombe). [See H. Guppy, An Analytical Catalogue of the Contents of the Two Editions of 'An English Garner,' 1909.]

The English Scholar's Library of Old and Modern Works. 16 vols. 1878–84.

An Introductory Sketch to the Martin Marprelate Controversy, 1558–1590. 1880. [No. 8 of English Scholar's Lib. above.]

The First Three English Books on America. ?1511–1555 A.D. Being chiefly Translations, Compilations, etc. by Richard Eden. Birmingham, 1885.

A List, based on the Registers of the Stationers' Company, of 837 London Publishers between 1553 and 1640 A.D. Birmingham, 1890.

The War Library. 2 vols. Birmingham, 1894.

The Story of the Pilgrim Fathers, 1606–1623 A.D. as told by Themselves, their Friends and their Enemies. 1897.

British Anthologies. 10 vols. 1899–1901.

The Term Catalogues, 1668–1709 A.D.; with a Number for Easter Term 1711 A.D. From the Quarterly Lists issued by the Booksellers. 3 vols. 1903–6 (priv. ptd).

A Christian Library: a Popular Series of Religious Literature. 3 vols. 1907 (priv. ptd).

HENRY BRADLEY (1845–1923)

(a) Collected Papers

The Collected Papers. With a Memoir by Robert Bridges. Oxford, 1928. [With bibliography.]

(b) Editions

A New English Dictionary on Historical Principles, founded mainly on the Materials collected by the Philological Society. Edited by James A. H. Murray, Henry Bradley, William A. Craigie, C. T. Onions. 11 vols. Oxford, 1884–1933. [Bradley was joint-editor from 1889, and was responsible for the following sections: E, F–G, L–M, S–SH, ST, W–WEZZON.]

Stratmann, F. H. A Middle-English Dictionary. New edition, revised by Henry Bradley. 1891.

Milton, J. English Poems. Edited by R. C. Browne. With Etymological Notes revised by Henry Bradley. Oxford, 1894.

Morris, R. Historical Outlines of English Accidence. Revised by L. Kellner with the Assistance of Henry Bradley. 1895.

—— Elementary Lessons in Historical English Grammar. Revised by Henry Bradley. 1897.

Caxton, W. Dialogues in French and English. EETS. Ex. Ser. LXXIX, 1900.

Stevenson, W. Gammer Gurton's Nedle. Edited, with Critical Essay and Notes. [In Representative English Comedies, ed. C. M. Gayley, vol. I, New York, 1903.]

(c) Writings

The Goths, from the Earliest Times to the End of the Gothic Dominion in Spain. 1888.

The Making of English. 1904.

Changes in the Language to the Days of Chaucer. CHEL. vol. I, 1907.

The Misplaced Leaf of 'Piers the Plowman.' [In J. M. Manly, Piers the Plowman and its Sequence, 1908.]

The Authorship of Piers the Plowman. EETS. CXXXIX, 1910.

English Place-Names. English Ass. 1910.

On the Relations between Spoken and Written Language, with Special Reference to English. [1914.] [From Proc. British Academy, VI.]

The Numbered Sections in Old English Poetical MSS. [1916.] [From Proc. British Academy, VII.]

Shakespeare's English. [In Shakespeare's England, 1916.]

Sir James Murray, 1837–1915. [1919.] [From Proc. British Academy, VIII.]

On the Text of Abbo of Fleury's 'Quaestiones Grammaticales.' [1922.] [From Proc. British Academy, X.]

HENRY BRADSHAW (1831–1886)

(a) Collected Papers

Collected Papers: comprising 1: 'Memoranda'; 2: 'Communications' read before the Cambridge Antiquarian Society; together with an Article contributed to the 'Bibliographer' and Two Papers not previously published. Cambridge, 1889. [Ed. by F. J. H. Jenkinson.]

(b) Writings

Discovery of the Long-lost Morland MSS. in the Library of the University of Cambridge. [In J. H. Todd, The Books of the Vaudois, 1865.]

The Skeleton of Chaucer's Canterbury Tales: an Attempt to distinguish the Several Fragments of the Work as left by the Author. 1868.

The Printer of the Historia S. Albani. 1868.

Notice of a Fragment of the Fifteen Oes and Other Prayers printed at Westminster by William Caxton about 1490, 91, preserved in the Library of the Baptist College, Bristol. 1877.

The Early Collection of Canons known as the Hibernensis. Two Unfinished Papers. Cambridge, 1893. [Ed. by F. J. H. Jenkinson.]

[Bradshaw also pbd other bibliographical papers, addresses and catalogues.]

(c) Biography and Criticism

Prothero, Sir G. W. A Memoir of Henry Bradshaw. 1888.

Newcombe, C. F. Some Aspects of the Work of Henry Bradshaw. 1905.

ARTHUR HENRY BULLEN (1857–1920)

(a) Anthologies

A Christmas Garland. Carols and Poems from the Fifteenth Century to the Present Time. 1885.

Lyrics from the Song-books of the Elizabethan Age. 1887. More Lyrics from the Song-books of the Elizabethan Age. 1888; 1889 (selected from the 2 preceding vols.).

Lyrics from the Dramatists of the Elizabethan Age. 1889.

Musa Proterva: Love-poems of the Restoration. 1889 (priv. ptd).

Speculum Amantis: Love-poems from Rare Song-Books and Miscellanies of the Seventeenth Century. 1889 (priv. ptd).

Poems, chiefly Lyrical, from Romances and Prose-Tracts of the Elizabethan Age; with Chosen Poems of Nicholas Breton. 1890.

Shorter Elizabethan Poems. 1903. [Part of E. Arber's An English Garner.]

Some Longer Elizabethan Poems. 1903. [Part of E. Arber's An English Garner.]

(b) Editions and Reprints

The Works of John Day. 7 pts, 1881 (priv. ptd).

A Collection of Old English Plays. 4 vols. 1882–5 (priv. ptd). [16 rare Elizabethan-Jacobean plays.]

The English Dramatists. 1885–7 (priv. ptd). [Marlowe, 3 vols.; Middleton, 8 vols.; Marston, 3 vols.]

A Collection of Old English Plays. New Series. 3 vols. 1887–90 (priv. ptd). [Dramatic works of Nobbes, Davenport, etc.]

The Works of Francis Beaumont and John Fletcher. Variorum Edition. Vols. I–IV (all pbd), 1904–12. [Ed. by Bullen; each play by a different editor.]

Sonnets by William Shakespeare. Stratford-on-Avon, 1905; 1921 (rev. and with memoir of Bullen by H. F. B. Brett-Smith).

The Works of William Shakespeare. 10 vols. Stratford-on-Avon, 1910. (Stratford Town edn.) [Includes contributions by other scholars.]

[Bullen also issued edns of Peele, Campion, William Browne, Arden of Feversham, Davison's Poetical Rhapsody, England's Helicon (1600), a selection from Drayton, etc. He contributed largely to DNB. and GM. (which he edited 1906), and was general editor of The Muses' Library reprints.]

(c) Writings

The Willow. Stratford-on-Avon, 1916 (priv. ptd). [Poems.]

Weeping-Cross. Stratford-on-Avon, 1917 (priv. ptd). [Poems.]

Weeping-Cross and Other Rimes. 1921.

Elizabethans. 1924. [Critical essays.]

FREDERICK GARD FLEAY (1831–1909)

Almond Blossoms. 1857. [Poems.]

The Poetry of Catullus rendered into English. 1864.

Shakespeare Manual. 1876.

Guide to Chaucer and Spenser. 1877.

Introduction to Shakespearian Study. 1877.

Marlow's Tragedy of Edward the Second. With Introductory Remarks and Notes. 1877.

English Sounds and English Spelling. 1878.

The Life and Death of King John. By William Shakespeare. Together with the Troublesome Reign of King John. Edited with Notes. 1878.

The Logical English Grammar. 1884.

A Chronicle History of the Life and Work of William Shakespeare. 1886.

A Chronicle History of the London Stage, 1559–1642. 1890.

A Biographical Chronicle of the English Drama, 1559–1642. 2 vols. 1891.

Egyptian Chronology: an Attempt to conciliate the Ancient Schemes and to educe a Rational System. 1899.

[Fleay also produced several grammars and papers on education, etc. He was editor of The Spelling Reformer, 1880–1, and contributed to Trans. New Shakspere Soc. many important papers and edns of Pericles and Timon without the non-Shakespearian scenes.]

HARRY BUXTON FORMAN (1842–1917)

(a) Editions

The Works of Percy Bysshe Shelley, in Verse and Prose. Edited with Prefaces, Notes and Appendices. 8 vols. [1876]–80. [Also poems only, 4 vols. 1876, and with memoir 5 vols. 1892 (Aldine edn).]

Letters of John Keats to Fanny Brawne, written in the Years 1819 and 1820, with Introduction and Notes. 1878; 1889 (rev. and enlarged).

The Poetical Works and Other Writings of John Keats. Edited with Notes and Appendices. 4 vols. 1883. [Supplement, 1890. Poems only, 1884.]

The Letters of John Keats. Complete Edition. 1895.

The Complete Works of John Keats. 5 vols. Glasgow, 1900-1.

The Poetical Works of John Keats. Edited with an Introduction and Textual Notes. 1906. (Oxford edn.)

Note Books of Percy Bysshe Shelley. Deciphered, transcribed and edited, with a Full Commentary. Boston Bibliophile Soc. 1911.

The Life of Percy Bysshe Shelley, by Thomas Medwin. With an Introduction and Commentary. 1913.

[Forman also supervised edns of separate poems by Shelley as well as works by Matthew Arnold, the Brownings, etc.]

(b) Writings

Our Living Poets: an Essay in Criticism. 1871.

The Shelley Library: an Essay in Bibliography. 1886.

The Books of William Morris described, with some Account of his Doings in Literature and in the Allied Crafts. 1897.

[Forman also contributed to Literary Anecdotes of the Nineteenth Century, ed. Sir W. R. Nicoll and T. J. Wise, 2 vols. 1895-6, as well as publishing papers on Shelley, Chatterton, etc.]

SIR ISRAEL GOLLANCZ (1863-1930)

Pearl: an English Poem of the Fourteenth Century. Edited with a Modern Rendering. 1891; EETS. 1923 (with Cleanness, Patience and Sir Gawain).

Cynewulf's Christ. Edited with a Modern Rendering. 1892.

Charles Lamb's Specimens of English Dramatic Poets. Now first edited anew. 1893.

The Exeter Book. Edited with a Translation, Notes and Introduction. EETS. 1895.

Hamlet in Iceland: being the Icelandic Ambales Saga, edited and translated. 1898.

A Book of Homage to Shakespeare. 1916. [Gollancz was general editor.]

[In addition to much other editorial work Gollancz was general editor of the following publishers' sers.: The Temple Shakespeare, The Temple Classics, The King's Classics, The King's Novels, The Shakespeare Library. For a memoir see Sir F. G. Kenyon, Proc. British Academy, XVIII, 1932.]

ALEXANDER BALLOCH GROSART
(1835-1899)
(a) Series of Reprints

The Fuller Worthies Library. 39 vols. Edinburgh, Blackburn, 1868-76 (priv. ptd). [Works of Sir John Davies, Fulke Greville, Henry Vaughan, Marvell, George Herbert; poems of Fuller, Crashaw, Donne, Southwell, Sidney, etc.]

Miscellanies of the Fuller Worthies Library. 4 vols. Blackburn, 1870-6 (priv. ptd). [Works of minor 16th and 17th cent. writers.]

Occasional Issues of Unique and very Rare Books. 38 vols. 1875-81 (priv. ptd). [16th and 17th cent. rarities such as Robert Dover's Annalia Dubrensia, Robert Chester's Love's Martyr, Willobie his Avisa, etc.]

The Chertsey Worthies Library. Edited with Memorial-Introductions, Notes, Illustrations and Facsimiles. 14 vols. [Blackburn], 1876-80 (priv. ptd). [Works of Nicholas Breton, John Davies of Hereford, Joshua Sylvester, Francis Quarles, Joseph Beaumont, Henry More, Cowley.]

Early English Poets. Edited with Memorial-Introductions and Notes. 9 vols. 1876-7 (priv. ptd). [Herrick, Sidney, Giles Fletcher, John Davies of Hereford.]

The Huth Library, or Elizabethan-Jacobean Unique or very Rare Books, largely from the Library of Henry Huth. Edited with Introductions, Notes and Illustrations. 29 vols. 1881-6 (priv. ptd). [Works of Greene, Nashe, Gabriel Harvey, and Dekker's prose works.]

[Grosart also issued The Complete Works of Edmund Spenser, 9 vols. 1882-4 (priv. ptd and with contributions by E. Dowden, F. T. Palgrave, etc.), The Complete Works of Samuel Daniel, 5 vols. 1885-96 (priv. ptd), The Poetical Works of George Herbert, 1891 (Aldine edn), edns for Camden Soc., Roxburghe Club and Chetham Soc., and numerous other reprints including a number of 17th cent. Puritan divines.]

(b) Writings

Hymns. Liverpool, 1868 (priv. ptd).

Songs of the Day and Night, or Three Centuries of Original Hymns. Edinburgh, 1890 (priv. ptd).

Robert Ferguson. 1898. (Famous Scots Ser.)

[And numerous theological works, contributions to A. H. Miles's The Poets and the Poetry of the Century, many articles in periodicals, etc. For an appreciation see O. Smeaton, A Great Elizabethan, Westminster Rev. CLI, 1899.]

JOHN WESLEY HALES (1836–1914)

Notes and Essays on Shakespeare. 1884.

Folia Litteraria: Essays and Notes on English
Literature. 1893.

[Hales also pbd edns of Bishop Percy's
Folio MS (with F. J. Furnivall), Milton's
Areopagitica, and various works by Goldsmith,
Gray, Johnson, Spenser and Malory. He was
general editor of the Handbooks of English
Literature ser. 1895–1903.]

WILLIAM CAREW HAZLITT (1834–1913)

(a) *Writings*

The History of the Origin and Rise of the
Republic of Venice. 2 vols. 1858.

Hand-Book to the Popular, Poetical and
Dramatic Literature of Great Britain, from
the Invention of Printing to the Restoration. 1867.

Memoirs of William Hazlitt: with Portions of
his Correspondence. 2 vols. 1867.

Collections and Notes. 4 sers. and Supple-
ments, 1876–1903. [Catalogues of early
English writings. General Index by G. J.
Gray, 1893.]

Schools, School-Books and Schoolmasters. A
Contribution to the History of Educational
Development in Great Britain. 1888.

The Livery Companies of the City of London.
1892.

A Manual for the Collector and Amateur of
Old English Plays. 1892.

The Coinage of the European Continent.
2 vols. 1893–7.

The Coin Collector. 1896.

The Confessions of a Collector. 1897.

Four Generations of a Literary Family. The
Hazlitts, 1725–1896. 2 vols. 1897.

The Lambs: their Lives, their Friends and
their Correspondence. 1897.

Shakespeare. 1902; 1903 (rev.); 1908 (recast
and expanded).

The Book-Collector: a General Survey of the
Pursuit. 1904.

The Later Hazlitts. 1912 (priv. ptd).

[Hazlitt also pbd poems, essays, a novel and
several vols. in H. B. Wheatley's Book-
Lover's Lib.]

(b) *Editions*

Old English Jest-Books. 3 vols. 1864.

The Roxburghe Library. 8 vols. 1868–70.
[Inedited Tracts illustrating the Manners,
Opinions and Occupations of Englishmen
during the Sixteenth and Seventeenth Centuries, 1867; The English Drama and Stage,
1543–1664, illustrated by a Series of Documents, 1869, etc.]

English Proverbs and Proverbial Phrases collected from the most Authentic Sources.
1869; 1882 (enlarged).

Warton, T. History of English Poetry. Edited
with New Notes and Other Additions.
4 vols. 1871.

Prefaces, Dedications, Epistles selected from
Early English Books, 1540–1701. [1874]
(priv. ptd).

Dodsley, R. A Select Collection of Old English
Plays. Revised and enlarged. 15 vols.
1874–6.

Fairy Tales, Legends and Romances, illustrating Shakespeare and Other Early
English Writers. 1875.

Poetical and Dramatic Works of Thomas
Randolph. Now first collected. 2 vols.
1875.

Shakespeare's Library: a Collection of the
Romances, Novels, Poems and Histories
used by Shakespeare. Second Edition,
greatly enlarged. 6 vols. 1875. [1st edn by
J. P. Collier.]

Letters of Charles Lamb. An entirely New
Edition. 2 vols. 1886.

Lamb and Hazlitt. Further Letters and
Records. 1900.

[Hazlitt's editorial work also included rpts
of Herrick, Suckling, William Hazlitt (his
grandfather), an anthology of Early Popular
Poetry of England, and a trn of Montaigne.]

GEORGE BIRKBECK NORMAN HILL
(1835–1903)

(a) *Editions*

Boswell's Life of Johnson, including Boswell's
Journal of a Tour to the Hebrides and
Johnson's Diary of a Journey into North
Wales. 6 vols. Oxford, 1887.

The History of Rasselas, Prince of Abyssinia.
Oxford, 1887.

Wit and Wisdom of Samuel Johnson. Oxford,
1888.

Letters of David Hume to William Strahan.
Oxford, 1888.

Goldsmith. The Traveller. Oxford, 1888.

Select Essays of Dr Johnson. 2 vols. 1889.

Lord Chesterfield's Worldly Wisdom. Selections. Oxford, 1891.

Letters of Samuel Johnson. 2 vols. Oxford,
1892.

Letters of Dante Gabriel Rossetti to William
Allingham. 1897.

Johnsonian Miscellanies. 2 vols. Oxford, 1897.

Unpublished Letters of Dean Swift. 1899.

The Memoirs of the Life of Edward Gibbon.
1900.

Lives of the English Poets, by Samuel Johnson. Edited by George Birkbeck Hill. With
Brief Memoir of Birkbeck Hill by Harold
Spencer Scott. 3 vols. Oxford, 1905. [In-
cludes bibliography of Hill's writings.]

(b) Writings

Dr Johnson, his Friends and Critics. 1878.
The Life of Sir Rowland Hill. 2 vols. 1880.
Footsteps of Dr Johnson (Scotland). 1890.
Writers and Readers. 1892. [Six Lectures,
I–IV on Revolutions in Literary Taste, V- VI
on the Study of Literature as a Part of
Education.]
Harvard College, by an Oxonian. New York,
1894.
Talks about Autographs. 1896. [Reminiscences of Lamb, Arnold, Froude, etc.]
Letters written by a Grandfather. Selected by
Lucy Crump. 1903.
Letters. Arranged by Lucy Crump. 1906.
[Arranged to form a complete memoir.]

SIR SIDNEY LEE (1859–1926)

(a) Biographies and Essays

Stratford-on-Avon, from the Earliest Times to
the Death of William Shakespeare. 1885.
The Study of English Literature. An Address.
1893 (priv. ptd).
The Life of William Shakespeare. 1898; 1915
(rewritten and enlarged); 1925 (new preface).
Shakespeare's King Henry the Fifth. An
Account and An Estimate. 1900.
Queen Victoria. A Biography. 1902.
Great Englishmen of the Sixteenth Century.
1904. [Thomas More, Philip Sidney, Walter
Raleigh, Spenser, Bacon, Shakespeare's
Career, Foreign Influences on Shakespeare.]
Shakespeare and the Modern Stage. With
Other Essays. 1906.
The French Renaissance in England. An
Account of the Literary Relations of England and France in the Sixteenth Century.
Oxford, 1910.
Principles of Biography. The Leslie Stephen
Lecture. Cambridge, 1911.
The Place of English Literature in the
Modern University. A Lecture. 1913.
King Edward VII. A Biography. 2 vols.
1925–7.
Elizabethan and Other Essays. Ed. (with
memoir) F. S. Boas, Oxford, 1929.

[Lee also pbd other pamphlets, mainly on
Elizabethan topics. He contributed to CHEL.,
Cambridge Modern History, The Year's Work
in English Studies, 1921–3, Trans. New
Shakspere Soc. and other composite works.]

(b) Editions

The Boke of Duke Huon of Burdeux, by Lord
Berners. 4 pts, EETS. 1882–7.
The Autobiography of Edward, Lord Herbert
of Cherbury. 1886.

The Dictionary of National Biography. Vol.
XXVII–End of Supplement II, 1891–1917.
[In addition to editing the Dictionary, Lee
contributed 820 articles, exclusive of his
work in the supplements.]
Shakespeare's Comedies, Histories and Tragedies, being a Reproduction in Facsimile of
the First Folio Edition. With Introduction
and Census of Copies. Oxford, 1902.
[Similar facs. rpts of Pericles, Sonnets,
Venus and Adonis and Lucrece, 1905.
Census also ptd separately. Notes and
Additions to the Census, 1906.]
Elizabethan Sonnets: with an Introduction.
2 vols. 1904. [A re-arrangement of parts of
Arber's English Garner.]
Methuen's Standard Library. 40 vols. 1905–6.
The Works of Shakespeare. 20 vols. Cambridge, U.S.A. 1907–10. (Caxton edn.)
[General Introduction only by Lee.]
The Chronicle History of King Leir. 1909.
[With important introduction.]
Shakespeare's England. 2 vols. Oxford, 1916.
[Planned and partly ed. by Lee.]

(c) Biography and Criticism

Pollard, A. F. Sir Sidney Lee and the Dictionary of National Biography. Bulletin of
Inst. of Hist. Research, June 1926.
Harrison, G. B. Sir Sidney Lee. London
Mercury, June 1930.
Firth, Sir C. H. Sir Sidney Lee. 1931.

GEORGE CAMPBELL MACAULAY (1852–1915)

Francis Beaumont: a Critical Study. 1883.
The History of Herodotus. Translated. 2 vols.
1890.
Poems by Matthew Arnold. Selected and
edited. 1896.
The Complete Works of John Gower. Edited
from the Manuscripts with Introductions,
Notes and Glossaries. 4 vols. Oxford, 1899–
1902.
Gower. Selections from the Confessio Amantis.
Oxford, 1903.
James Thomson. 1908. (English Men of
Letters ser.)

[Also German, Greek and Latin text-books
and edns of 4 of Tennyson's Idylls of the King
and Lord Berners' Froissart (Globe edn).]

RICHARD MORRIS (1833–1894)

(a) Editions

Early English Alliterative Poems, of the West
Midland Dialect of the Fourteenth Century.
EETS. 1864.
Sir Gawayne and the Green Knight: an
Alliterative Romance-Poem. EETS. 1864.
The Story of Genesis and Exodus, an Early
English Song. EETS. 1865.

Dan Michel's Ayenbite of Inwyt, or Remorse of Conscience. EETS. 1866.

Specimens of Early English, A.D. 1250–A.D. 1400, with Grammatical Introduction, Notes and Glossary. Oxford, 1867; rev. W. W. Skeat, Oxford, 1872.

Old English Homilies and Homiletic Treatises of the Twelfth and Thirteenth Centuries. 2 sers. EETS. 1868–73.

Chaucer's Translation of Boethius's De Consolatione Philosophiae. EETS. Ex. Ser. 1868.

Legends of the Holy Rood; Symbols of the Passion and Cross-Poems. In Old English of the Eleventh, Fourteenth and Fifteenth Centuries. EETS. 1871.

An Old English Miscellany; containing a Bestiary, Kentish Sermons, Proverbs of Alfred, Religious Poems of the Thirteenth Century. EETS. 1872.

Cursor Mundi. The Cursur of the World. A Northumbrian Poem of the XIVth Century in Four Versions. 6 pts, EETS. 1874–93.

The Blickling Homilies of the Tenth Century. 3 pts, EETS. [1874–80].

[Morris's other editorial work included Richard Rolle's Pricke of Conscience, 1863, the Aldine Chaucer, 1866, and the Globe Spenser, 1869.]

(b) Writings

The Etymology of Local Names. Pt 1 (all pbd), 1857.

Historical Outlines of English Accidence, comprising Chapters on the History and Development of the Language, and on Word-Formation. 1872; rev. L. Kellner and H. Bradley, 1895.

Elementary Lessons in Historical English Grammar. 1874; rev. H. Bradley, 1897.

English Grammar. 1875. [One of J. R. Green's Literature Primers.]

Notes and Queries [on Pali lexicography]. [1887.]

[And minor philological writings.]

Sir James Augustus Henry Murray (1837–1915)

(a) Editions

Sir David Lindesay's Works. The Minor Poems. EETS. 1871.

The Complaynt of Scotlande, vyth ane Exortatione to the Thre Estaits to be Vigilante in the Deffens of their Public Veil. EETS. Ex. Ser. 1872.

The Romance and Prophecies of Thomas of Erceldoune. With Illustrations from the Prophetic Literature of the 15th and 16th Centuries. EETS. 1875.

A New English Dictionary on Historical Principles, founded mainly on Materials collected by the Philological Society. 11 vols. Oxford, 1884–1933; 13 vols. Oxford, 1933 (a corrected re-issue, with introduction, supplement and bibliography, as The Oxford English Dictionary). [Murray was chief creator of the N.E.D., though his actual editorial responsibility covered only A–D, H–K, O, P, T.]

(b) Writings

The Dialect of the Southern Counties of Scotland: its Pronunciation, Grammar and Historical Relations. With an Appendix and a Linguistical Map of Scotland. Philological Soc. 1873.

The Romanes Lecture, 1900. The Evolution of English Lexicography. Oxford, 1900.

[And several short papers on philology, and a book on Orkney. For appreciations see H. Bradley, Sir James Murray, Proc. British Academy, VIII, [1919], and S. Baldwin, The Oxford English Dictionary, 1884–1928. An Address, [1928].]

Walter William Skeat (1835–1912)

(a) Editions

The Vision of William concerning Piers Plowman. 4 pts, EETS. 1867–85.

The Bruce, by John Barbour. 4 pts, EETS. 1870–89.

The Holy Gospels in Anglo-Saxon, Northumbrian and Old Mercian Versions. 4 pts, Cambridge, 1871–87.

Aelfric's Lives of the Saints. 2 pts, EETS. 1881–1900.

Specimens of Early English. 3 vols. Oxford, 1882–71. [With R. Morris.]

The Complete Works of Geoffrey Chaucer. 7 vols. Oxford, 1894–7.

The Student's Chaucer. Oxford, 1895.

[Skeat also edited many other early English texts, mainly for Chaucer Soc., EETS., STS. and English Dialect Soc. (which he founded).]

(b) Dictionaries and Philological Works

An Etymological Dictionary of the English Language, arranged on an Historical Basis. Oxford, 1882.

A Concise Etymological Dictionary of the English Language. Oxford, 1882.

A Primer of English Etymology. Oxford, 1892.

A Student's Pastime. Oxford, 1896. [Articles from N. & Q., including Skeat's autobiography.]

Notes on English Etymology, chiefly reprinted from the Transactions of the Philological Society. Oxford, 1901.

A Primer of Classical and English Philology. Oxford, 1905.

The Science of Etymology. Oxford, 1912.

[Skeat also pbd pamphlets on spelling-reform, place-names, etc.]

LUCY TOULMIN SMITH (1838–1911)

The Maire of Bristowe is Kalendar, by Robert Ricart. Camden Soc. 1872.

Gorboduc or Ferrex and Porrex. A Tragedy by Thomas Norton and Thomas Sackville. Edited. Heilbronn, 1883.

York Plays. The Plays performed by the Crafts or Mysteries. Edited with Introduction and Glossary. Oxford, 1885.

A Common-Place Book of the Fifteenth Century. Edited with Notes. 1886.

A Manual of the English Grammar and Language. [1886.]

Les Contes moralisés de Nicole Bozon. Société des anciens Textes français, 1889. [With P. Meyer.]

Expeditions to Prussia and the Holy Land made by Henry, Earl of Derby, afterwards King Henry IV. Camden Soc. 1894.

The Itinerary of John Leland. With an Appendix of Extracts from Leland's Collectanea. 5 vols. 1906–10.

[Lucy Toulmin Smith also contributed to The Shakspere Allusion-Book prepared by the New Shakspere Soc. and translated J. J. Jusserand's English Wayfaring Life.]

HENRY SWEET (1845–1912)

(a) *Readers and Editions*

King Alfred's West-Saxon Version of Gregory's Pastoral Care. 2 pts, EETS. 1871–2.

An Anglo-Saxon Reader in Prose and Verse, with Grammatical Introduction, Notes and Glossary. Oxford, 1876.

The Epinal Glossary. Edited with a Transliteration. 1883.

King Alfred's Orosius. EETS. 1883. [Extracts, Oxford, 1885.]

Aelfric, Grammaticus, Abbot of Eynsham. Selected Homilies. Oxford, 1885.

The Oldest English Texts. EETS. 1885.

A Second Anglo-Saxon Reader, Archaic and Dialectal. Oxford, 1887.

(b) *Primers and Miscellaneous Writings*

A History of English Sounds. English Dialect Soc. 1874. [Rptd from Trans. Philolog. Soc. 1873–4.]

A Handbook of Phonetics. Oxford, 1877.

An Anglo-Saxon Primer, with Grammar, Notes and Glossary. Oxford, 1882.

First Middle English Primer. Extracts from the Ancren Riwle and Ormulum; with Grammar and Glossary. Oxford, 1884.

Elementarbuch des gesprochenen Englisch. Grammatik, Texte und Glossen. Oxford, 1885; tr. Eng. Oxford, 1890 (as A Primer of Spoken English).

An Icelandic Primer, with Grammar, Notes and Glossary. Oxford, 1886.

Second Middle English Primer. Extracts from Chaucer; with Grammar and Glossary. Oxford, 1886.

A History of English Sounds from the Earliest Period, with Full Word-Lists. Oxford, 1888.

A Primer of Phonetics. Oxford, 1890.

A Manual of Current Shorthand. Oxford, 1892.

A New English Grammar, Logical and Historical. 2 pts, Oxford, 1892–5.

A Short Historical English Grammar. Oxford, 1892.

A Primer of Historical English Grammar. Oxford, 1893.

First Steps in Anglo-Saxon. Oxford, 1897.

The Student's Dictionary of Anglo-Saxon. Oxford, 1897.

The Practical Study of Languages. 1899.

The History of Language. 1900. (Temple Primers.)

The Sounds of English: an Introduction to Phonetics. Oxford, 1908.

Collected Papers. Arranged by H. C. K. Wyld. Oxford, 1913. [Contents: Words, Logic and Grammar; The Practical Study of Language; Linguistic Affinity; Progress of Linguistic Science (5 papers); History of English (4 papers); Shelley's Nature-Poetry; Phonetics and Accounts of Living Languages (6 papers). Many of these papers had appeared in Trans. Philolog. Soc.]

DUNCAN CROOKES TOVEY (1842–1912)

Gray and his Friends. Cambridge, 1890. [Letters.]

The Poetical Works of James Thomson. 1897. [With memoir.]

Reviews and Essays in English Literature. 1897. [Teaching of English Literature, More's Utopia, Fuller's Sermons, Letters of the Earl of Chesterfield, Arnold's Last Essays, Waller, Gay, Ossian and his Maker, Coventry Patmore, Elizabethan Poetry, A Cambridge Reminiscence (by M. T.).]

Gray's English Poems. 1898.

Verses. 1902.

The Letters of Thomas Gray, including the Correspondence of Gray and Masson. 3 vols. 1909–12.

ARTHUR WILSON VERITY (–1937)

The Influence of Christopher Marlowe on Shakspere's Earlier Style. Being the Harness Prize Essay. Cambridge, 1886.

The Works of Sir George Etheredge. 1888.
Nero and Other Plays. 1888. (Mermaid Ser.)
[Verity edited Field's Woman is a Weather-
cock and Amends for Ladies.]
Thomas Heywood. 1888. (Mermaid Ser.)
[5 plays.]
The Pitt Press Shakespeare for Schools. 13
vols. Cambridge, 1890–1905. [13 plays.]
The Cambridge Milton for Schools. 11 vols.
Cambridge, 1891–9.
The Student's Shakespeare. 3 vols. Cambridge,
1902–5. [3 plays only.]

SIR ADOLPHUS WILLIAM WARD (1837–1924)

(a) Writings

A History of English Dramatic Literature to
the Death of Queen Anne. 2 vols. 1875;
3 vols. 1899 (rev.).
Chaucer. 1879. (English Men of Letters ser.)
Dickens. 1882. (English Men of Letters ser.)
The Counter-Reformation. 1889.
Sir Henry Wotton: a Biographical Sketch.
1898.
Great Britain and Hanover. Being the Ford
Lectures. Oxford, 1899; tr. German, Han-
over, 1906.
The Electress Sophia and the Hanoverian
Succession. 1903.
Germany, 1815–1890. 3 vols. Cambridge,
1916–8.
Collected Papers, Historical, Literary, Travel
and Miscellaneous. 5 vols. Cambridge,
1921. [97 rptd articles, 40 being literary
(vols. III, IV).]

(b) Editions

The Poetical Works of Alexander Pope. 1869.
Old English Drama. Select Plays. Marlowe's
Dr Faustus and Greene's Friar Bacon and
Friar Bungay. Oxford, 1878.
The Spider and the Flie. Spenser Soc. 1894.
The Poems of John Byrom. 3 vols. Chetham
Soc. 1894–1912.
The Cambridge Modern History. Planned by
Lord Acton. 14 vols. Cambridge, 1902–12.
[General editors: Ward, G. W. Prothero,
S. Leathes. Ward contributed 16 chs.]
The Poems of George Crabbe. 3 vols. Cam-
bridge, 1905–7.
The Works of Mrs Gaskell. 8 vols. 1906.
The Cambridge History of English Literature.
14 vols. Cambridge, 1907–16. [General
editors Ward and A. R. Waller. Ward con-
tributed 14 chs.]
The London Merchant, and Fatal Curiosity.
By George Lillo. Boston, 1907.

[For Ward's minor writings see A Bibliography of Sir Adolphus William Ward. By

A. T. Bartholomew. With a Memoir by T. F.
Tout, Cambridge, 1926.]

HENRY BENJAMIN WHEATLEY (d. 1917)

(a) Writings

Samuel Pepys & the World he lived in.
1880.
The Book-Lover's Library. 1886–1902.
[Wheatley was general editor of the ser.
His own contributions were: How to form a
Library, 1886; The Dedication of Books,
1887; How to catalogue a Library, 1889;
Literary Blunders, 1893; How to make an
Index, 1902.]
A Handbook of Art Industries in Pottery and
the Precious Metals. 2 pts, 1886.
Remarkable Bindings in the British Museum.
1889.
London Past and Present. Based upon the
Handbook of London by the Late Peter
Cunningham. 3 vols. 1891.
Historical Portraits: some Notes on the
Painted Portraits of Celebrated Characters
of England, Scotland and Ireland. 1897.
Prices of Books: an Inquiry into the Changes
in the Price of Books which have occurred
in England at Different Periods. 1898.
Hogarth's London: Pictures of the Manners of
the Eighteenth Century. 1909.

(b) Editions

Diary of John Evelyn. With a Life of the
Author. 4 vols. 1879.
Chap-Books and Folk-Lore Tracts. 1885.
[With G. L. Gomme.]
Reliques of Ancient English Poetry. Edited
with General Introduction, Additional
Prefaces, Notes, Glossary, etc. 3 vols. 1891.
The Diary of Samuel Pepys, with Lord Bray-
brooke's Notes. Edited with Additions.
10 vols. 1893–9.

[And minor bibliographical and topographical works, and edns of 17th-century
rarities.]

WILLIAM ALDIS WRIGHT (1831–1914)

Bacon's Essays and Colours of Good and Evil,
with Notes and Glossarial Index. 1862.
The Works of William Shakespeare. 9 vols.
Cambridge, 1863–6. [Vol. I ed. by W. G.
Clark and J. Glover; vols. II–IX by Clark
and Wright.]
The Works of William Shakespeare. 1864.
(Globe edn.) [With W. G. Clark.]
The Bible Word-Book: a Glossary of Old
English Bible Words. 1866; 1884 (rev.).
[With J. Eastwood.]
Chaucer. The Clerk's Tale. 1867.

Shakespeare's Select Plays. 10 vols. Oxford, 1868–83. [With W. G. Clark.]

Bacon's Advancement of Learning. 1869.

The Pilgrimage of the Lyf of the Manhode, from the French of de Deguilleville. Roxburghe Club, 1869.

Generydes. A Romance in Seven-line Stanzas. 2 pts, EETS. 1873–8.

The Metrical Chronicle of Robert of Gloucester. 1887. (Rolls Ser.)

Letters and Literary Remains of Edward FitzGerald. 1889. [Also: Letters, 1894; Letters to Fanny Kemble, 1895; Rubáiyát, 1899; Miscellanies, 1900; More Letters, 1901.]

Facsimile of the Manuscript of Milton's Minor Poems. 1899.

Milton's Poetical Works. 1903.

Roger Ascham. English Works. Cambridge, 1904.

The Authorised Version of the English Bible, 1611. Cambridge, 1909.

Femina. Now first printed from a Unique MS. in the Library of Trinity College, Cambridge. Roxburghe Club, 1909.

The Hexaplar Psalter: being the Book of Psalms in Six English Versions. 1911.

[Wright also pbd biblical studies. He was editor of The Journal of Philology, 1868–1913.]

H. B. G.

7. THE LITERATURES OF THE DOMINIONS

I. ANGLO-IRISH LITERATURE

General Works: Sources of Anglo-Irish Literature (Bibliographies, Histories); Anglo-Irish Literature (Bibliographies, Critical and Historical Works, Anthologies).

Gaelic Sources and Scholarship: Historians and Scholars; Modern Folklore; Learned Societies and Journals.

Poets of the Irish Revival.

Yeats and Synge.

Dramatists of the Irish Revival.

[The history of the literature of the Anglo-Irish 'revival' falls naturally into two periods. The first period is one of preparation, physical and spiritual, by archaeologists, antiquarians, historians, philologists, and littérateurs, for the most part of the ruling class but with notable exceptions like O'Donovan and O'Curry—'the last representatives of the old Gaelic scholarship.' This period is dealt with in Section II. It overlaps the second period and its work continued unabated after it began to bear fruit, by 1825, in a literary revival to which all classes contributed. But the revival was destined to produce a literature entirely in English, for it was contemporaneous with 'the famine, the clearances, and the beginning of the great emigration, the triple calamity which almost destroyed Gaelic-speaking Ireland and broke the continuity of its cultural tradition' (J. F. Kenney, The Sources for the Early History of Ireland, vol. I, 1929, p. 66). The literature of this period, ending about 1905, is dealt with in Section III (Poetry), Section IV (Yeats and Synge), and Section V (Drama) which is taken a little further than 1905. There is no special section for Prose, as this was a still later development, though the more important prose works of the poets and dramatists have been included. Such Irish novelists as the Banims, Lever, Le Fanu, George Moore, etc. will be found with the English novelists, pp. 387–564 above.]

I. GENERAL WORKS

A. SOURCES OF ANGLO-IRISH LITERATURE

(a) *Bibliographies*

O'Reilly, E. Transactions of the Iberno-Celtic Society for 1820. Vol. I, Part I. Containing a Chronological Account of nearly Four Hundred Irish Writers commencing with the Earliest Account of Irish History. Dublin, 1820.

O'Curry, E. Lectures on the Manuscript Materials of Ancient Irish History. Dublin, 1861.

O'Hart, J. Irish Pedigrees. 2 vols. Dublin, 1876–8.

Webb, A. Compendium of Irish Biography. Dublin, 1878.

Arbois de Jubainville, H. d'. Essai d'un Catalogue de la Littérature épique de l'Irlande. Paris, 1883. [Kuno Meyer, Addenda, Revue Celtique, VI, 1884; G. Dottin, Supplément, Revue Celtique,XXXIII, 1912.]

Dottin, G. Notes bibliographiques sur l'ancienne Littérature chrétienne de l'Irlande. Revue d'Histoire et de Littérature religieuses, V, 1900.

Best, R. I. Bibliography of Irish Philology and of Printed Irish Literature. Dublin, 1913. [Indispensable.]

O'Grady, S. H. Catalogue of Irish Manuscripts in the British Museum. Vol. I, 1926.

Flower, R. Catalogue of Irish Manuscripts in the British Museum. Vol. II, 1926. [Vol. III, in the press, has valuable Introduction.]

Kenney, J. F. The Sources for the Early History of Ireland. Vol. I (Ecclesiastical), New York, 1929. [Indispensable.]

(b) *Histories*

O'Grady, Standish. Early Bardic Literature. Ireland. 1879.

Arbois de Jubainville, H. d'. Introduction à l'Étude de la Littérature celtique. Paris, 1883.

Zimmer, H. The Irish Element in Mediaeval Culture. New York, 1891.

Hyde, D. Story of Early Gaelic Literature. 1895.

—— A Literary History of Ireland from the Earliest Times to the Present Day. 1899.

Dottin, G. La Littérature gaélique de l'Irlande. Revue de Synthèse historique, III, 1901.

Leahy, A. H. Heroic Romances of Ireland 2 vols. 1905–6.

Hull, E. A Text Book of Irish Literature. 2 pts, Dublin, 1906–8.

MacDonagh, T. Literature in Ireland. Dublin, 1916.

Hogan, J. J. The English Language in Ireland. Dublin, 1928.

De Blacam, A. S. Gaelic Literature Surveyed. Dublin, 1929.

B. ANGLO-IRISH LITERATURE

(a) Bibliographies

Brown, Stephen J. A Guide to Books on Ireland. Dublin, 1912.
—— Ireland in Fiction. Dublin, 1916.
O'Donoghue, D. J. The Poets of Ireland. Dublin, 1912.
Dix, E. R. McC. and Cassedy, J. List of Books, Pamphlets, etc. printed wholly or partly in Irish from the Earliest Period to 1820. Dublin, 1913.
Bibliographies of Irish Writers Series. 1919–.
O'Neill, J. J. Bibliographical Account of Irish Theatrical Literature. Dublin, 1920.

(b) Critical and Historical Works

Duffy, Sir C. G., Sigerson, G. and Hyde, D. The Revival of Irish Literature. Addresses. 1894.
Ryan, W. P. The Irish Literary Revival. 1894.
'Eglinton, John' (W. K. Magee). Literary Ideals in Ireland. 1899. [With W. B. Yeats, 'A. E.' and W. Larminie.]
Beltaine. Organ of the Irish Literary Theatre. Edited by W. B. Yeats. 3 nos. 1899–1900.
Gregory, I. A., Lady. Ideals in Ireland. 1901. [Ed. by Lady Gregory.]
—— Our Irish Theatre: a Chapter of Autobiography. 1914.
Samhain. Edited for the Irish Literary Theatre by W. B. Yeats. 6 nos. Dublin, 1901–6.
Krans, H. S. W. B. Yeats and the Irish Literary Revival. 1904.
Elton, O. Living Irish Literature. [In Modern Studies, 1907.]
Moore, G. Hail and Farewell! 3 vols. 1911–4.
Boyd, E. A. Ireland's Literary Renaissance. Dublin, 1916. [With bibliographical appendix.]
Graves, A. P. Anglo-Irish Literature. CHEL. vol. xiv, 1916.
Morris, L. R. The Celtic Dawn. A Survey of the Renascence in Ireland, 1889–1916. New York, 1917.
O'Conor, N. J. Changing Ireland: Literary Backgrounds of the Irish Free State, 1889–1922. Cambridge, U.S.A. 1924.
Law, Hugh. Anglo-Irish Literature. Dublin, 1926.
Morton, D. The Renaissance of Irish Poetry, 1880–1930. New York, 1929.
Gwynn, D. Edward Martyn and the Irish Revival. 1930.

(c) Biographies

Stokes, William. The Life and Labours in Art and Archaeology of George Petrie, LL.D. 1868.

Ferguson, M. C., Lady. Life of the Right Rev. William Reeves, D.D. Dublin, 1893.
—— Sir Samuel Ferguson in the Ireland of his Day. 2 vols. 1896.
Atkinson, S. Essays. Dublin, 1896. [For O'Curry.]
Gilbert, R. M. Life of Sir John T. Gilbert. 1905.
Dixon, Henry. John O'Donovan. An Leabharlaun, ii, 1906.
McSweeney, P. M. A Group of Nation Builders. Dublin, 1913.
Figgis, D. Æ.–George W. Russell. Dublin, 1916.
Hull, E. Standish Hayes O'Grady. Studies, March 1916. [See also TLS. 29 Oct. 1915.]
Mitchell, Susan L. George Moore. Dublin, 1916.
O'Cobhthaigh, D. Douglas Hyde. 1917.
Flower, R. Catalogue of Irish Manuscripts in the British Museum. Vol. ii, 1926. [Preface contains summary of life of S. H. O'Grady.]
Crone, J. S. A Concise Dictionary of Irish Biography. Dublin, 1928.
O'Grady, H. A. Standish James O'Grady, the Man and the Writer. 1929.
'Eglinton, John' (W. K. Magee). Irish Literary Portraits. 1935.

[For Synge and Yeats see pp. 1059–63 below.]

(d) Histories of Anglo-Irish Drama

Bickley, F. J. M. Synge and the Irish Dramatic Movement. 1912.
Weygandt, C. Irish Plays and Playwrights. Boston, 1913.
Gregory, A. I., Lady. Our Irish Theatre. New York, 1913.
Boyd, E. A. The Contemporary Drama of Ireland. Dublin, 1918.
Malone, A. E. The Irish Drama. 1929.

(e) Anthologies

The Spirit of the Nation. Dublin, 1843; rptd 1912.
Duffy, Sir C. G. Ballad Poetry of Ireland. Dublin, 1843.
O'Sullivan, Denis. Popular Songs and Ballads of the Emerald Isle. New York, 1880.
Brooke, S. A. and Rolleston, S. W. A Treasury of Irish Poetry in the English Tongue. 1900.
Cooke, John. The Dublin Book of Irish Verse. 1909.
Hull, E. The Poem Book of the Gael. 1912. [Trns of early material.]
Colum, P. Broad-sheet Ballads. Dublin, 1913.
—— An Anthology of Irish Verse. New York, 1922.
Gregory, P. Modern Anglo-Irish Verse. 1914.
Graves, A. P. A Book of Irish Poetry. Dublin, 1915.

Robinson, Lennox. A Golden Treasury of Irish Verse. 1925.
—— A Little Anthology of Modern Irish Verse. Dublin, 1928.

II. GAELIC SOURCES AND SCHOLARSHIP

[This section (derived mainly from works by R. I. Best, R. Flower and J. F. Kenney) is intended to be a select guide to the material used by, or available for, the Anglo-Irish writers. Fuller lists are provided by the bibliographies entered above, p. 1045.]

A. HISTORIANS AND SCHOLARS

EDMUND SPENSER (1552?–1599)

Ireland under Elizabeth and James the First. Described by Edmund Spenser, Sir John Davies and Fynes Moryson. 1890. [See also vol. I, p. 418 above.]

LUGHAIDH O'CLERY (fl. 1609)

Life of Aodh Ruadh O'Donnell. Ed. E. O'Reilly, 1820.

MICHAEL O'CLERY (1575–1643)

Annales Dungallenses, or Annála Rioghachta Eireann, or 'Annals of the Four Masters,' by M. O'Clery and Three Others. Ed. J. O'Donovan, Dublin, 1851.
Martyrologium Sanctorum Hiberniae ('The Martyrology of Donegal'). Ed. J. O'Donovan, J. H. Todd and W. Reeves, Dublin, 1864.

JAMES USSHER (1581–1656)

Of the Original and First Institution of Corbes, Herenaches, and Termon Lands. 1609.
A Discourse of the Religion anciently professed by the Irish and British. Dublin, 1631.
Veterum Epistolarum Hibernicarum Sylloge. Dublin, 1632.
Brittanicarum Ecclesiarum Antiquitates. Dublin, 1639.
Works. 17 vols. Dublin, 1847–64.

DUALD MacFIRBIS (1585–1670)

[See Chronicum Scotorum, ed. W. M. Hennessy, 1866, introduction.]

PHILIP O'SULLIVAN BEARE (c. 1590–1660)

Historia Catholicae Iberniae Compendium. Lisbon, 1621.

JOHN COLGAN (d. 1657?)

Acta Sanctorum Veteris et Majoris Scotiae seu Hiberniae. Louvain, 1645.
Trias Thaumaturga. Louvain, 1647. [Contains lives of Patrick, Columba and Bridget.]

SIR THOMAS STAFFORD (fl. 1633)

Pacata Hibernia. 1663; rptd 2 vols. Dublin, 1810.

SIR JAMES WARE (1594–1666)

De Scriptoribus Hiberniae. Dublin, 1639; tr. Eng. 2 vols. 1705–4 (augmented).
De Hibernia et Antiquitatibus ejus, Disquisitiones. 1654; 1658 (rev.).
S. Patricio adscripta Opuscula. 1656.
Rerum Hibernicarum Annales, 1485–1558. Dublin, 1664.
De Praesulibus Hiberniae, Commentarius. Dublin, 1665.
The Whole Works of Sir James Ware concerning Ireland. Vols. I, II (all pbd), ed. W. Harris, Dublin, 1739–64.

JOHN LYNCH (1599?–1673)

Cambrensis Eversus, sive potius Historica Fides in Rebus Hibernicis Giraldo Cambrensi abrogata. [St Malo?] 1652; tr. Eng. (by Theophilus O'Flanagan) Dublin, 1795; ed. Matthew Kelly, 3 vols. Dublin, 1848–52.

RODERIC O'FLAHERTY (1629–1718)

Ogygia, seu rerum Hibernicarum chronologia. 1685; tr. Eng. (by James Hely) Dublin, 1793.
Ogygia vindicated against The Objections of Sir George Mackenzie. [Ed. C. O'Conor?] Dublin, 1775.
A Chorographical Description of West or H-Iar Connaught. Ed. J. Hardiman, Dublin, 1846.

DERMOD O'CONNOR (fl. 1712–29)

The General History of Ireland. Tr. Eng. (by Geoffrey Keating) Dublin, 1723; 1723; Westminster, 1726; 1732; 1738, etc.; rptd Dublin, 1854.

JOHN O'BRIEN (d. 1767)

Focalóir Gaoidhilge-Sax-Bhéarla, or an English-Irish Dictionary. Paris, 1768; ed. R. Daly and M. McGinty, Dublin, 1832. [Rptd in Collectanea de Rebus Hibernicis, ed. C. Vallancey, 1770–1804.]

CHARLES O'CONOR (1710–1791)

Dissertations on the Ancient History of Ireland. 1753; 1766 (with remarks on Ossian). [Rptd in Ogygia Vindicated, by R. O'Flaherty, 1775, and Collectanea de Rebus Hibernicis, ed. C. Vallancey, 1770–1804.]

CHARLES VALLANCEY (1721–1812)

Collectanea de Rebus Hibernicis. 6 vols. 1770–1804. [Ed. by Vallancey with valuable contributions by others.]

An Essay on the antiquity of the Irish Language. Dublin, 1772.

A Grammar of the Iberno-Celtic or Irish Language. Dublin, 1773.

A Vindication of the Ancient History of Ireland. (Collectanea No. xiv). Dublin, 1786.

SYLVESTER O'HALLORAN (1728–1807)

Insula Sacra. 1770.

An Introduction to the study of the history and antiquities of Ireland. 1772.

Ierne Defended. 1774. ['Essays asserting the validity of the ancient Irish records and urging their preservation,' J. F. Kenney, op. cit. vol. i, p. 57.]

General History of Ireland from the Earliest Accounts to those of the 12th Century. 1774. ['...of importance now only as marking the beginning of such publications in the English language by writers of Irish origin,' J. F. Kenney, op. cit. vol. i, p. 57.]

JAMES MACPHERSON (1736?–1796)

[See vol. ii, pp. 343–4 above.]

CHARLOTTE BROOKE (1740–1793)

Reliques of Irish Poetry. Dublin, 1789.

JOSEPH WALKER (1762?–1810)

Historical memoirs of the Irish Bards. Dublin, 1786.

Historical Essay on the Dress of the Ancient and Modern Irish. Dublin, 1788.

EDWARD BUNTING (1773–1843)

A General Collection of the Ancient Irish Music. Dublin, 1796, 1807, 1840.

THOMAS MOORE (1779–1852)

National Melodies. 1815.

A Selection of National Airs. 1816.

Irish Melodies. 1821; Dublin, 1846. ['Indebted to Bunting's first volume,' DNB.]

The History of Ireland. 4 vols. 1835–46.

[See also p. 184 above.]

GEORGE PETRIE (1789–1866)

The History and Antiquities of Tara Hill. Trans. Royal Irish Academy, xviii, 1837.

Inquiry into the Origins and Uses of the Round Towers of Ireland. Trans. Royal Irish Academy, xx, 1845 (re-issued as The Ecclesiastical Architecture of Ireland).

Ancient Music of Ireland. 2 vols. Dublin, 1855–82.

Christian Inscriptions in the Irish Language. Ed. M. Stokes, 2 vols. Dublin, 1872–8.

The Complete Collection of Irish Music as noted by George Petrie. Ed. Sir C. V. Stanford, 1905.

JAMES HARDIMAN (1790?–1855)

The History of the Town and County of Galway. Dublin, 1820.

Irish Minstrelsy; or, Bardic Remains of Ireland; with English Poetical Translations. 2 vols. 1831.

EDWARD O'REILLY (d. 1829)

An Irish-English Dictionary. Dublin, 1817; rev. J. O'Donovan, Dublin, 1864; rptd Dublin, 1901 (corrected).

A Chronological Account of nearly Four Hundred Irish Writers. Trans. Iberno-Celtic Soc. i, pt 1, 1820.

An Essay on the Nature and Influence of the Ancient Irish Institute, commonly called Brehon Laws. Dublin, 1824.

EUGENE O'CURRY (1796–1862)

Lectures on the Manuscript Material of Ancient Irish History. Dublin, 1861. ['Any one who reads the book will obtain a better knowledge of Irish mediaeval literature than he can by the perusal of any other single work,' DNB.]

On the Manners and Customs of the Ancient Irish. Ed. W. K. Sullivan, 3 vols. 1873.

[O'Curry and O'Donovan are really important in the private influence they exerted in such quarters as the Royal Archaeological Soc. and in aid, not always as generously acknowledged as given, to such men as Todd and Reeves. There is a great deal of O'Donovan, for instance, in Petrie's Tara.]

JOHN DALY (1800–1878)

Reliques of Irish Jacobite Poetry. 2 pts, Dublin, 1844; Dublin, 1866. [Ed. by Daly with metrical versions by Edward Walsh.]

Poets and Poetry of Munster. Dublin, 1849; rptd 1925. [Ed. by Daly with metrical versions by James Clarence Mangan.]

JAMES HENTHORN TODD (1805–1869)

Irish Version of the Historia Britonum of Nennius. Dublin, 1847.

Liber Hymnorum, or Book of Hymns of the Ancient Church of Ireland. 1855; 1869.

St Patrick, Apostle of Ireland. Dublin, 1864.

Cogadh Gaedhel re Gallaibh. The War of the Gaedhil with the Gaill, or the Invasions of Ireland by the Danes and Other Norsemen. Rolls Ser. 1867.

[See also under John O'Donovan below.]

EDWARD WALSH (1805–1850)

Irish Popular Songs; with English Metrical Translations. Dublin, 1849; Dublin, 1883 (rev.).

JOHN O'DONOVAN (1809–1861)

The Circuit of Ireland by Muircheartach MacNeill. Irish Archaeological Soc. 1841.

The Banquet of Dun na nGedh and the Battle of Magh Rath. Irish Archaeological Soc. 1842.

The Tribes and Customs of Hy-Many. Irish Archaeological Soc. 1843.

The Genealogies, Tribes, and Customs of Hy Fiachrach. Dublin, 1844.

Grammar of the Irish Language. Dublin, 1845. ['Best of its kind prior to the application of the principles of comparative philology,' J. F. Kenney, op. cit. vol. I, p. 66.]

Irish Charters in the Book of Kelts. Dublin, 1846.

Annals of Ireland, 1443 to 1468. Irish Archaeological Soc. Misc. 1846.

The Book of Rights. Celtic Soc. 1847.

'The Annals of the Four Masters.' 7 vols. Dublin, 1848–51.

Annals of Ireland, 571–913. Three Fragments copied from Ancient Sources by Dubhaltach MacFirbisigh. Irish Archaeological and Celtic Soc. 1860.

The Topographical Poems of John O'Dubhagain and Giolla na naomh O'Huidhrin. Royal Irish Academy, 1862.

The Martyrology of Donegal, translated by John O'Donovan. Ed. J. H. Todd and W. Reeves, Irish Archaeological and Celtic Soc. 1864.

The Ancient Laws of Ireland. 5 vols. 1865–79. [Various editors; texts and trns in most cases by O'Donovan. Vol. V was ed. by Robert Atkinson with trn on the basis of that of O'Donovan and O'Curry.]

WILLIAM FORBES SKENE (1809–1892)

Celtic Scotland. 3 vols. 1876–80, 1886–90. [See also p 906 above.]

SIR SAMUEL FERGUSON (1810–1886)

Leabhar Breac; Lithographic Reproduction. Preface by Samuel Ferguson. Dublin, 1872–6.

Ogham Inscriptions in Ireland, Wales and Scotland. Edinburgh, 1887.

[Also numerous contributions to Proc. and Trans. Royal Irish Academy, 1834–84.]

SIR WILLIAM WILDE (1815–1876)

The Beauties of the Boyne and the Blackwater. Dublin, 1849.

Catalogue of the Contents of the Museum of the Royal Irish Academy. 3 vols. 1857–62. ['...a monumental work of archaeological erudition and insight,' DNB.]

Lough Corrib and Lough Mask. Dublin, 1867.

The Ancient Races of Ireland. 1874. [Rptd in Lady Wilde's Ancient Legends of Ireland, vol. II, 1887.]

WILLIAM REEVES (1815–1892)

Ecclesiastical Antiquities of Down, Connor, and Dromore. Dublin, 1847.

Acts of Archbishop Colton. Irish Archaeological Soc. 1850.

Life of Saint Columba, Founder of Hy, written by Adamnan. Irish Archaeological and Celtic Soc. 1857. ['...remains the most learned and the fullest collection of knowledge of ancient Irish ecclesiastical affairs, published since the time of John Colgan,' DNB.]

MATTHEW ARNOLD (1822–1888)

On the Study of Celtic Literature. 1867.

ERNEST RENAN (1823–1895)

The Poetry of the Celtic Races. Tr. Eng. (by W. G. Hutchinson), 1896. [From Essais de Morale et de Critique, Paris, 1859.]

JANE FRANCESCA, LADY WILDE (1826–1896)

Ancient Legends, Mystic Charms, and Superstitions of Ireland. 2 vols. 1887.

Ancient Cures, Charms, and Usages of Ireland, 1890.

PATRICK WESTON JOYCE (1827–1914)

The Origin and History of Irish Names and Places. 2 scrs. Dublin, 1869–75.

Irish Local Names explained. Dublin, n.d.

Old Celtic Romances. 1891; 1894 (rev.). [Contains Voyage of Maeldúin.]

HENRI D'ARBOIS DE JUBAINVILLE (1827–1910)

Cours de Littérature celtique. Paris, 1883–99. [Vol. II tr. Eng. (by R. I. Best) as The Irish Mythological Cycle and Celtic Mythology, Dublin, 1903.]

SIR JOHN THOMAS GILBERT (1829–1898)

Facsimiles of National Manuscripts of Ireland. Selected and edited by Sir J. T. Gilbert. 4 pts, Dublin 1874. [See also p. 929 above.]

WHITLEY STOKES (1830–1909)

The Voyage of Mael Dúin. Revue celtique, IX, X, 1888–9. [Text and trn.]

Lives of the Saints from the Book of Lismore. Oxford, 1890. [For The Voyage of Brendan.]

[Also numerous contributions and trns in Proc. and Trans. Irish Archaeological Soc., Royal Irish Academy, Henry Bradshaw Soc., Philological Soc., etc. Full list in R. I. Best, Bibliography of the Publications of Whitley Stokes, 1911.]

KUNO MEYER

The Vision of MacConglinne. 1892.
The Voyage of Bran. 1895.
King and Hermit. 1901.
Liadain and Curithir. 1902.
Four Old Irish Songs of Summer and Winter. 1903.
The Death-Tales of the Ulster Heroes. Royal Irish Academy, 1906.
Fianaigecht. Royal Irish Academy, 1910.
Selections from Ancient Irish Poetry. 1911.

[Also numerous contributions to Revue Celtique, Zeitschrift für celtische Philologie, Archiv für celtische Lexicographie, etc. Full list by R. I. Best, Zeitschrift für celtische Philologie, XIV, 1924.]

STANDISH HAYES O'GRADY (1832–1915)

The Pursuit of Diarmuid and Grainne. Edited with Translation. Trans. Ossianic Soc. III, 1857.
Silva Gadelica. 2 vols. 1892.
The Táin Bó Cuailnge. Analysis with Extracts. [In E. Hull, The Cuchulinn Saga, 1898.]
Catalogue of Irish Manuscripts in the British Museum. Vol. I, 1926.

ROBERT ATKINSON (1839–1908)

The Yellow Book of Lecan. Dublin, 1896. [Facs., introduction famous for its adverse criticism of the value of mediaeval Irish literature.]

GEORGE SIGERSON (1839–1925)

History of the Land Tenures and Land Classes of Ireland. 1871.
Bards of the Gael and Gall. 1897; 1907 (rev.); Dublin, 1925 (with memorial preface by D. Hyde).
Sedulius. The Easter Song. Dublin, 1922.

STANDISH O'GRADY (1846–1928)

Early Bardic Literature, Ireland. 1879.
History of Ireland. Vol. I. The Heroic Period. 1878. Vol. II. Cuculain and his Contemporaries. 1880.
History of Ireland, Critical and Philosophical. Vol. I, 1881.
The Bog of Stars. 1893.
The Story of Ireland. 1894.
The Coming of Cuculain. 1894; 1920 (with introduction by 'A. E.').
The Flight of the Eagle. 1897.

In the Gates of the North. 1901; 1920.
The Triumph and Passing of Cuculain. 1920.
Finn and his Companions. 1921.

[O'Grady also ed. Sir Thomas Stafford's Pacata Hibernia, 1896.]

DOUGLAS HYDE (b. 1860)

Love Songs of Connacht. Dublin, 1893.
The Last three Centuries of Gaelic Literature. Irish Literary Soc. 1894.
Story of Early Gaelic Literature. 1895.
A Literary History of Ireland. 1899.
The Religious Songs of Connacht. 2 vols. Dublin, 1906.
Legends of Saints and Sinners. Dublin, 1915.

B. MODERN FOLKLORE

Croker, T. C. Fairy Legends and Traditions of the South of Ireland. 1825–8; rptd 1929 (as Fairy Tales of Old Ireland).
—— Legends of the Lakes. 1829.
—— Popular Songs of Ireland. 1837.
Kennedy, Patrick. Legendary Fictions of the Irish Celts. 1866.
—— The Bardic Stories of Ireland. Dublin, 1871.
Yeats, W. B. Fairy and Folk Tales of the Irish Peasantry. 1888.
—— Irish Fairy and Folk Tales. 1888.
—— Irish Fairy Tales. 1892.
Curtin, J. Myths and Folk-Lore of Ireland. Boston, 1890.
—— Hero-Tales of Ireland. Boston, 1894.
—— Tales of the Fairies and of the Ghost-World. 1895.
Hyde, Douglas. Beside the Fire. 1890.
—— An Sgéaluidhe Gaedhealach. (Traduits par G. Dottin.) 1901.
—— Oscar au Fléau. Revue Celtique, XIII, 1892. [Text and French trn.]
Larminie, W. West Irish Folk-Tales and Romances. 1893.
Martin, W. G. W. Pagan Ireland. 1895.
—— Traces of the Elder Faiths of Ireland. 2 vols. 1902.

C. LEARNED SOCIETIES AND JOURNALS

Gaelic Society of Dublin. 1808–.
Iberno-Celtic Society. 1820.
Irish Archaeological Society and Celtic Society. 1841.
Celtic Society. 1847. [Merged with above.]
Kilkenny Archaeological Society [later the Historical and Archaeological Society of Ireland; later the Royal Historical and Archaeological Society of Ireland; later the Royal Society of Antiquaries of Ireland]. 1849–.

Ulster Journal of Archaeology. 1853–.
Ossianic Society. 1854–.
Society for the Preservation of the Irish Language. 1876–.
Waterford and South-East of Ireland Archaeological Society. 1895–.
The Gaelic League. 1897–.
The Irish Texts Society. 1898–.

[The inclusion of the Gaelic League, the popular organisation, in this list indicates the early contribution of other classes to the Anglo-Irish 'movement.']

Revue Celtique. 1870–.
The Celtic Magazine. 1875–.
The Gaelic Journal. 1882–.
Zeitschrift für celtische Philologie. 1897–.
Archiv für celtische Philologie. 1898–.
Erin. 1904–.
The Celtic Review. 1904–.

III. Poets of the Irish Revival

Richard Alfred Milliken (1767–1815)

The Riverside. Cork, 1807.
Poetical Fragments. 1823. [With memoir.]
The Groves of Blarney. Waterford, [1830?]. [With other songs.]

Thomas Moore (1779–1852)

[See p. 184 above.]

Jeremiah John Callanan (1795–1829)

The Recluse of Inchidony, and Other Poems. 1830.
The Poems. Cork, 1847; Dublin, 1861.
Gems of the Cork Poets; comprising the Complete Works of Callanan, Condon, Casey, Fitzgerald, and Cody. Cork, [1883].

Samuel Lover (1797–1868)

[See p. 407 above.]

John Banim (1798–1842)

[See p. 387 above.]

James Clarence Mangan (1803–1849)

(a) Poems

Anthologia Germanica: German Anthology. A Series of Translations from the most Popular of the German Poets. 2 vols. Dublin, 1845.
The Poets and Poetry of Munster. A Selection of Irish Songs, with Poetical Translations by James Clarence Mangan. Dublin, 1849; Dublin, [1883] (3rd edn; Irish text rev. W. M. Hennessey, ed. C. P. Meehan).
Ellis, Hercules. Romances and Ballads of Ireland. 1850. [Contains 30 ballads by Mangan.]
The Tribes of Ireland. A Satire by Aenghus O'Daly. With Poetical Translation by James Clarence Mangan. Dublin, 1852.

Poems. With a Biographical Introduction by J. Mitchel. New York, 1859.
Irish and Other Poems. With a Selection from his Translations. Dublin, 1886.
Irish Poetic Gems, from Mangan, Moore and Griffin. Dublin, 1887.
James Clarence Mangan: his Selected Poems, with a Study by the Editor, L. I. Guiney. 1897.
Poems, many hitherto uncollected. Centenary Edition. Edited, with Preface and Notes, by D. J. O'Donoghue. Introduction by J. Mitchel. Dublin, 1903.
Dark Rosaleen, [etc.]. Dublin, [1923].

(b) Other Writings

The Prose Writings. Centenary Edition. Edited by D. J. O'Donoghue. With an Essay by Lionel Johnson. Dublin, 1904.

(c) Biography and Criticism

Ingram, J. H. James Clarence Mangan. Dublin University Mag. xc, 1877.
Fragment of an Unpublished Autobiography. Irish Monthly, x, 1882.
MacCall, J. Life of James Clarence Mangan. Dublin, [1887].
O'Donoghue, D. J. The Life and Writings of James Clarence Mangan. Edinburgh, 1897.
Graves, A. P. James Clarence Mangan. Cornhill Mag. lxxvii, 1898.
Nevinson, H. W. The Dark Rosaleen. North American Rev. clxxix, 1904.
Duffy, Sir C. G. Personal Memories of James Clarence Mangan. Dublin Rev. cxlii, 1908.
Cain, H. E. James Clarence Mangan and the Poe-Mangan Question. Washington, 1929.
Joyce, James. James Clarence Mangan. From 'St. Stephens.' Dublin, 1930.
Colum, P. James Clarence Mangan. Commonweal, xvii, 1932.
Sheridan, J. S. James Clarence Mangan. Dublin, 1937.

Francis Sylvester Mahony (1804–1866)

[See p. 719 above.]

Edward Walsh (1805–1850)

Reliques of Irish Jacobite Poetry; with Biographical Sketches of the Authors, Interlinear Literal Translations, and Notes, by John Daly. Together with Metrical Versions by Edward Walsh. Dublin, 1844.
Irish Popular Songs. With English Metrical Translations, and Introductory Remarks and Notes. Dublin, 1847.

[See T. Gleeson, Edward Walsh, Journ. Cork Historical and Archaeological Soc. iii, 1894.]

HELEN SELINA SHERIDAN, later BLACK-
WOOD (BARONESS DUFFERIN) (1807–1867)

The Irish Emigrant. [1840?] (anon.). [A song,
pbd with There's a Good Time Coming,
Boys.]
Terence's Farewell. [1855?] (anon.). [A song,
pbd with William and Harriet.]
To my Dear Son, on his 21st Birthday. [1861?]
(anon.). [Pbd with Helen's Tower, Clande-
boye, by Alfred, Baron Tennyson.]
Lispings from Low Latitudes, or Extracts
from the Journal of the Hon. Impulsia
Gushington. 1863 (anon.) [Ed. by Lord
Dufferin.]
Songs, Poems and Verses. Edited, with a
Memoir and some Account of the Sheridan
Family, by her Son, the Marquis of
Dufferin and Ava. 1894.

[Lady Dufferin also wrote a play, Finesse,
or a Busy Day in Messina, which was produced at the Haymarket Theatre in 1863, but
which has apparently not been pbd. For
criticism and selected poems see A. H.
Miles, The Poets and the Poetry of the
Century, vol. VII, 1893.]

SIR SAMUEL FERGUSON (1810–1886)

(a) Poems

The Cromlech on Houth. A Poem. [1864.]
Lays of the Western Gael, and Other Poems.
1865; ed. A. M. Williams, Dublin, 1888.
Congal. A Poem in Five Books. Dublin, 1872.
Deirdre. Dublin, 1880.
Poems. Dublin, 1880.
The Forging of the Anchor. A Poem. 1883.
Hibernian Nights' Entertainments. 3 sers.
Dublin, 1887. [Intermingled prose and
verse, first pbd in Dublin University Mag.]
The Remains of St Patrick. The Confessio and
Epistle to Coroticus, translated into English
Blank Verse. 1888.
Lays of the Red Branch. With an Introduction
by Lady Ferguson. Dublin, 1897.
Poems. With an Introduction by Alfred
Percival Graves. [1918.]
Aideen's Grave. Dublin, 1925.

[For Ferguson's archaeological writings see
p. 1049 above.]

(b) Biography and Criticism

Stokes, M. M. Obituary. Blackwood's Mag.
CXL, 1886.
O'Hagan, J. The Poetry of Sir Samuel
Ferguson. Dublin, 1887.
Ferguson, M. C., Lady. Sir Samuel Ferguson
in the Ireland of his Day. 2 vols. Edin-
burgh, 1896.
Deering, A. Sir Samuel Ferguson, Poet and
Antiquarian. A Thesis. Philadelphia, 1931.

THOMAS OSBORNE DAVIS (1814–1845)

(a) Poems

The Poems, now first collected. With Notes
and Historical Illustrations. Dublin, 1846.
Poems. Ed. John Mitchell, New York, 1868.
National and Other Poems. Dublin, 1907.
Thomas Davis. Selections from his Prose and
Poetry. Ed. T. W. Rolleston, 1914.
Thomas Davis, the Thinker and Teacher. The
Essence of his Writings in Prose and Poetry.
Selected, arranged and edited by Arthur
Griffith. Dublin, 1914.

(b) Other Writings

The Life of the Right Hon. J. P. Curran. And
a Memoir of the Life of the Right Hon.
Henry Grattan, by D. D. Madden. With
Addenda and Letter in Reply to Lord Clare.
Dublin, 1846.
Literary and Historical Essays. Dublin,
1846. [Ed. by Charles Gavan Duffy.]
Prose Writings. Ed. T. W. Rolleston, [1889].
The Patriot Parliament of 1689, with its
Statutes, Votes and Proceedings. Ed.
C. G. Duffy, 1893.
Essays, Literary and Historical. Centenary
Edition, including Several Pieces never
before collected. With Preface, Notes, &c.
by D. J. O'Donoghue, and an Essay by
John Mitchel. Dundalk, 1914.

[Davis also edited J. P. Curran's Speeches,
with memoir, 1845, and pbd several short
essays and addresses.]

(c) Biography and Criticism

Obituary. Dublin University Mag. XXIX, 1847.
The Poems of Thomas Davis. Irish Quarterly
Rev. v, 1852.
Duffy, Sir C. G. Thomas Davis: the Memoirs
of an Irish Patriot, 1840–1846. 1890.
Schiller, J. Thomas Osborne Davis: ein
irischer Freiheitssänger. Vienna, 1915.
[With a bibliography.]

AUBREY THOMAS DE VERE (1814–1902)

(a) Collected and Selected Poems

The Poetical Works. 6 vols. 1884–98.
Aubrey De Vere's Poems. A Selection. Ed.
J. Dennis, 1890.
Selections from the Poems. Ed. G. E. Wood-
berry, New York, 1894.
Poems from the Works of Aubrey De Vere.
Selected and edited by Lady Margaret
Domvile. 1904.

(b) Separate Volumes of Poems

The Waldenses, or the Fall of Rora: a Lyrical
Tale. With Other Poems. Oxford, 1842.
The Search after Proserpine, Recollections of
Greece, and Other Poems. Oxford, 1843.

Poems. 1855.
May Carols. 1857; 1881 (3rd edn, enlarged).
The Sisters, Inisfail, and Other Poems. 1861.
Inisfail. A Lyrical Chronicle of Ireland. 3 pts,
Dublin, 1862.
The Infant Bridal and Other Poems. 1864;
1876 (new and enlarged edn).
The Legends of Saint Patrick. 1872.
Alexander the Great. A Dramatic Poem.
1874.
St Thomas of Canterbury. A Dramatic Poem.
1876.
Antar and Zara. An Eastern Romance.
Inisfail, and Other Poems. 1877.
Legends of the Saxon Saints. 1879.
The Foray of Queen Meave, and Other
Legends of Ireland's Heroic Age. 1882.
Legends and Records of the Church and the
Empire. 1887.
Saint Peter's Chains, or Rome and the
Italian Revolution. A Series of Sonnets.
[1888.]
Mediaeval Records and Sonnets. 1893.

(c) Other Writings

Proteus and Amadeus. A Correspondence
[with Wilfrid Scawen Blunt]. 1878.
Essays, chiefly on Poetry. 2 vols. 1887.
Essays, chiefly Literary and Ethical. 1889.
Religious Problems of the Nineteenth Century.
Essays, edited by J. G. Wenham. 1893.
Recollections. 1897.

[De Vere also wrote various prefaces, and
pbd writings on Irish affairs and anthologies
of verse.]

(d) Biography and Criticism

The Poems of the De Veres. Dublin University Mag. xxi, 1843. [On Sir Aubrey and
Aubrey T.]
The Poems of Aubrey De Vere. Quarterly
Rev. lxxii, 1843.
[Dixon, W. M.] The Poetry of the De Veres.
Quarterly Rev. clxxxiii, 1896. [On Sir
Aubrey and Aubrey T. Rptd in In the
Republic of Letters, 1898.]
Towle, E. A. Recollections of Aubrey De Vere.
Sewanee Rev. vii, 1899.
Woodberry, G. E. Aubrey De Vere on Poetry.
[In Makers of Literature, New York, 1900.]
Gosse, Sir E. Memories of Aubrey De Vere.
Independent, liv, 1902.
Ward, W. P. Aubrey De Vere. A Memoir,
based on his Unpublished Diaries and
Correspondence. 1904.
Barrington, M. The Philosophy of Aubrey De
Vere. Temple Bar, cxxxi, 1905.
Aubrey De Vere, Poet. Edinburgh Rev. cci,
1905.

O'Connor, R. F. A Notable Convert: Aubrey
De Vere. American Catholic Quart. xxxix,
1914.

DENIS FLORENCE MacCARTHY (1817–1882)

(a) Poems

Ballads, Poems and Lyrics, Original and
Translated. Dublin, 1850.
The Bell-Founder, and Other Poems. 1857.
Under Glimpses, and Other Poems. 1857.
The Centenary of Moore, May 28th, 1879. An
Ode. With a Translation into Latin Verse
by the Rev. J. M. Blacker. 1880.
Poems. Dublin, 1882.

[MacCarthy also ed. several books of Irish
poetry, and pbd a work on Shelley's early life
and a number of trns from Calderon.]

(b) Criticism

The Poems of Denis Florence MacCarthy.
Dublin Rev. xxviii, 1850.
The Poems of Denis Florence MacCarthy.
Irish Quarterly Rev. vii, 1858.

JOHN KELLS INGRAM (1823–1907)

(a) Bibliography

Bibliography of the Writings of John Kells
Ingram, 1823–1907, with a Brief Chronology.
Compiled for Cumann na Leabharlann,
Dublin, 1907–8. Dublin, 1909.

(b) Poems

Who fears to speak of Ninety-eight? [In
Nation, 1 April 1843; rptd in The Spirit of
the Nation, 1843, and in Sonnets and Other
Poems, 1900.]
Sonnets, and Other Poems. 1900.

(c) Other Writings

A History of Political Economy. Edinburgh'
1888; 1915 (enlarged, with supplementary
ch. by W. A. Scott and introduction by
R. T. Ely). Tr. German, 1890; Spanish,
1890; Italian, 1892; Swedish, 1892; French,
1893; Czech, 1895; Japanese, 1896; Serbian,
1901.
A History of Slavery and Serfdom. 1895.
Outlines of the History of Religion. 1900.

[Ingram wrote a good deal on English and
Classical literature, mathematics, economics
and positivism, often in periodicals; he was the
first editor of Hermathena, 1874.]

(d) Biography and Criticism

The Death of Dr Ingram. 1: His Religious
Position, by E. S. Beesly. 2: Personal
Reminiscences, by S. H. Swinny. Positivist
Rev. xv, 1907.

Obituary. Royal Irish Academy: Abstract of
Minutes, 1907–8.
Falkiner, C. L. Memoir of John Kells Ingram.
Dublin, 1907.

WILLIAM ALLINGHAM (1824–1889)

[See p. 276 above.]

JANE FRANCISCA ELGEE, later LADY WILDE (1826–1896)

(a) Poems

Ugo Bassi. A Tale of the Italian Revolution.
By Speranza. 1857.
Poems. Dublin, 1864; Glasgow, [1871].

(b) Other Writings

Driftwood from Scandinavia. 1884.
Ancient Legends, Mystic Charms, and Super-
stitions of Ireland. 2 vols. 1887.
Ancient Cures, Charms, and Usages of Ireland.
1890.
Notes on Men, Women and Books. 1891.

[Lady Wilde wrote several other works, and
made trns from the French and German.]

ROBERT DWYER JOYCE (1830–1883)

Ballads, Romances and Songs. Dublin, 1861.
A Much-Admired Song called the Drian-naun
Don. [1865?] (anon.).
Ballads of Irish Chivalry. Songs and Poems.
Boston, 1872; ed. P. W. Joyce, 1908.
Deirdrè. Boston, 1876 (anon.).
Blanid. Boston, 1879.

[Joyce also pbd Legends on the Wars of
Ireland, Boston, 1868. For an appreciation
see M. Russell, Robert Dwyer Joyce, Irish
Monthly, VI, 1878.]

GEORGE SIGERSON (1839–1925)

(a) Poems

The Poets and Poetry of Munster. A Selection
of Irish Songs, with Metrical Translations
by Erionnach. Ser. 2, Dublin, 1860. [Ser. 1
is by J. C. Mangan.]
Bards of the Gael and Gall. Examples of the
Poetic Literature of Erinn. Done into
English after the Metres and Modes of the
Gael. 1897; 1907 (rev. and enlarged);
Dublin, 1925 (with memorial preface by
D. Hyde).
The Saga of King Lir. A Sorrow of Story.
Dublin, 1913.
Sedulius. The Easter Song: being the First
Epic of Christendom. Introduction, Verse-
Translation and Appendices, including a
Schedule of Milton's 'debts,' by George
Sigerson. Dublin, 1922.
Songs and Poems. With an Introduction by
Padraic Colum. Dublin, 1927.

(b) Other Writings

Irish Literature: its Origin, Environment, and
Influence. [In The Revival of Irish Litera-
ture: Addresses by Sir C. G. Duffy, Dr G.
Sigerson and Dr D. Hyde, 1894.]

[Sigerson also pbd medical and sociological
works.]

(c) Biography and Criticism

Obituary. Times, 19 Feb. 1925.
Garnier, C. M. George Sigerson, †1925.
Revue Anglo-américaine, April 1925.
Colum, P. An Irish Poet-Scholar. Common-
weal, VI, 1927.

JOHN TODHUNTER (1839–1916)

(a) Poems

Laurella, and Other Poems. 1876.
Alcestis. A Dramatic Poem. 1879.
Forest Songs, and Other Poems. 1881.
The True Tragedy of Rienzi, Tribune of
Rome. 1881. [Prose and verse; unacted.]
Helena in Troas. 1886.
The Banshee, and Other Poems. 1888.
The Legend of Stauffenberg. A Dramatic
Cantata, by J. C. Culwick. The Poem by
John Todhunter. Dublin, 1890.
A Sicilian Idyll. A Pastoral Play in Two
Scenes. 1890.
Three Irish Bardic Tales. Being Metrical
Versions of the Three Tales known as The
Three Sorrows of Story-Telling. 1896.
Sounds and Sweet Airs. 1905.
Heine's Book of Songs. Translated by John
Todhunter. 1907.
From the Land of Dreams (Irish Poems).
With an Introduction by T. W. Rolleston.
1918.
Goethe's Faust, First Part. Translated by
John Todhunter. With an Introduction by
J. G. Robertson. Oxford, 1924.
Isolt of Ireland: a Legend, in a Prologue and
Three Acts; and The Poison Flower. 1927.
[Blank verse plays.]
Trivium Amoris, and The Wooing of Artemis.
1927.
Selected Poems. Ed. D. L. Todhunter and
A. P. Graves, 1929. [Includes a biographical
sketch by T. W. Rolleston.]

(b) Other Works

A Study of Shelley. 1880.
The Black Cat. A Play in Three Acts. (Independent Theatre at Opera Comique, 8 Dec.
1893). 1895.
Life of Patrick Sarsfield, Earl of Lucan. With
a Short Narrative of the Principal Events
of the Jacobite War in Ireland. 1895.
An Essay upon Essays. Sette of Odd Volumes,
1896 (priv. ptd).

A Riverside Walk. An Easy-going Essay by a Peripatetic Philosopher. Sette of Odd Volumes, 1898 (priv. ptd).

Essays. With a Foreword by Standish O'Grady. 1920.

[Todhunter also pbd several other opuscula with the Sette of Odd Volumes, etc. See for an appreciation Irish Monthly, XVII, 1889.]

EDWARD DOWDEN (1843–1913)

[See p. 740 above.]

JOHN BOYLE O'REILLY (1844–1890)

(a) Poems

Songs from the Southern Seas, and Other Poems. Boston, 1873.
Songs, Legends and Ballads. Boston, 1878.
The Statues in the Block, and Other Poems. Boston, 1881.
In Bohemia. Boston, [1886].

[For a collected edn of Reilly's poems see under Roche below.]

(b) Other Writings

Ethics of Boxing and Manly Sport. 1888.
Moondyne. A Story from the Underworld. 1889; tr. Irish, Dublin, 1931.
The Poetry and Song of Ireland. New York, [1889]. [Ed. by O'Reilly.]

(c) Biography and Criticism

Plunkett, G. N. John Boyle O'Reilly. Irish Monthly, XIII, 1885.
Roche, J. J. The Poetry of John Boyle O'Reilly. New England Mag. n.s. I, 1889.
—— Life of John Boyle O'Reilly. Together with his Complete Poems and Speeches, edited by Mrs J. B. O'Reilly. Introduction by Cardinal Gibbons. 1891.
Stockley, W. F. P. Reminiscences of John Boyle O'Reilly. Catholic World, CXL, CXLI, 1935.

ARTHUR WILLIAM EDGAR O'SHAUGHNESSY (1844–1881)

(a) Poems

An Epic of Women, and Other Poems. 1870.
Lays of France. 1872.
Music and Moonlight. Poems and Songs. 1874.
Toyland. 1875. [With E. O'Shaughnessy.]
Songs of a Worker. 1881. [Ed. by A. W. N. Deacon.]
Poems. Selected and edited by William Alexander Percy. New Haven, 1923.

(b) Biography and Criticism

Forman, H. B. Our Living Poets. 1871, pp. 507–12.

Obituary. Athenaeum, 5 Feb. 1881.
Moulton, L. C. Arthur O'Shaughnessy: his Life and Work, with Selections from his Poems. 1894.
A Pathetic Love Episode in a Poet's Life. Being Letters [from Helen Snee] to Arthur W. E. O'Shaughnessy. Also a Letter from him containing a Dissertation on Love. [1916.]
Porter, A. Arthur O'Shaughnessy. Spectator, 11 Aug. 1923.
Arthur O'Shaughnessy's Poems. Contemporary Rev. CXXVI, 1924.
Broenner, O. Das Leben Arthur O'Shaughnessy's. Heidelberg, 1933.
Evans, B. I. English Poetry in the Later Nineteenth Century. 1933. [Ch. v.]

EMILY LAWLESS (1845–1913)

(a) Poems

With the Wild Geese. With an Introduction by Stopford A. Brooke. 1902.
The Inalienable Heritage. 1914.

(b) Other Writings

Ireland. With Additions by Mrs A. Bronson. 1887; 1912 (rev. and enlarged). (Story of the Nations ser.)
Maelcho. A Sixteenth-Century Narrative. 2 vols. 1894.
Maria Edgeworth. 1904. (English Men of Letters ser.)
The Point of View. (Some Talks and Disputations.) 1909 (priv. ptd).

[Emily Lawless also wrote several novels and historical works. For an appreciation see E. Sichel, Emily Lawless, Poetess, Nineteenth Century, LXXVI, 1914.]

ALFRED PERCEVAL GRAVES (1846–1932)

(a) Collected Poems

The Irish Poems of Alfred Perceval Graves. 2 vols. Dublin, 1908. [With preface by Douglas Hyde.]

(b) Separate Volumes of Poems

Songs of Killarney. 1873.
Irish Songs and Ballads. Manchester, 1880.
Father O'Flynn, and Other Irish Lyrics. 1889. [Facs. edn of Father O'Flynn, 1908, with trns into Gaelic by T. MacSweeney and into Latin by Father Alphonsus; also Ould Doctor Mack, by Graves.]
Welsh Poetry, Old and New, in English Verse. 1912.
A Celtic Psaltery. Being mainly Renderings in English Verse from Irish and Welsh Poetry. 1917.

Songs of the Gael. Dublin, [1925].
English Verse Translations of the Welsh Poems of Ceiriog Hughes. 1926.
Irish Doric in Song and Story. 1926. [Selection from Irish Countryside Songs and Songs of the Gael.]
The Progenitors, or Our First Parents. A Morality. An Old Irish Religious Poem done into English Verse by A. P. Graves and dramatised by M. Douglas. Oxford, 1929.

[Graves also pbd critical studies, anthologies of Irish verse, etc. and ed. various educational series for publishers.]

WILLIAM LARMINIE (1849–1900)
(a) Poems
Glanula, and Other Poems. 1889.
Fand, and Other Poems. Dublin, 1892.

(b) Other Writings
West Irish Folk-Tales and Romances. Collected and translated by William Larminie, with Introduction and Notes. 1893.
Legends as Material for Literature. [In J. Eglinton, W. B. Yeats, A. E. and W. Larminie, Literary Ideals in Ireland, 1899.]

JANE BARLOW (1857–1917)
(a) Poems
Bog-Land Studies. 1892; 1893 (enlarged).
Irish Idylls. 1892.
The Battle of the Frogs and Mice. Rendered into English. 1894. [From Homer.]
The End of Elfintown. 1894.
Ghost-bereft. With Other Stories and Studies in Verse. 1901.
The Mockers, and Other Verses. 1908.
Between Doubting and Daring. Verses. Oxford, 1916.

(b) Fiction
A Creel of Irish Stories. 1897.
The Founding of Fortunes. 1902.
Irish Neighbours. 1907. [Tales.]

[Miss Barlow also pbd 12 other novels and collections of tales, mainly dealing with Irish life.]

(c) Biography and Criticism
MacArthur, J. Jane Barlow. Critic, XXIV, 1894.
Tynan, K. Jane Barlow. Catholic World, LXIX, 1899.
—— Jane Barlow. Living Age, CCXCV, 1917.

THOMAS WILLIAM HAZEN ROLLESTON (1857–1920)
(a) Poems
Deirdre. The Feis Ceoil Prize Cantata, Dublin, 1897. Edinburgh, [1897].

Sea Spray. Verses and Translations. Dublin, 1909.
Three Love Tales after Richard Wagner. Tannhäuser, Lohengrin, Parsifal. 1920. [Tannhäuser originally pbd 1911.]

(b) Other Writings
Life of G. E. Lessing. 1889.
Imagination and Art in Gaelic Literature. Being Notes on some Recent Translations from the Gaelic. A Lecture delivered on February 16th, 1900. [1900.]
Parallel Paths. A Study in Biology, Ethics and Art. 1908.
The High Deeds of Finn, and Other Bardic Romances of Ancient Ireland. With an Introduction by Stopford A. Brooke. 1910.

[Rolleston also ed. a number of volumes of Irish poetry, etc., translated Epictetus, and pbd various pamphlets on matters Irish and German.]

DOUGLAS HYDE (b. 1860)
(a) Poems
[Irish title], or Love Songs of Connacht. Being the Fourth Chapter of the 'Songs of Connacht' now for the First Time collected, edited, and translated. Dublin, 1893. [Irish and English.]
The Three Sorrows of Story-telling and Ballads of St Columkille. 1895.
[Irish title], or Songs ascribed to Raftery, collected, edited and translated. 1903.
[Irish title], or The Religious Songs of Connacht. A Collection of Poems, Stories, Prayers, Satires, Ranns, Charms, [etc.] Now for the First Time collected, edited and translated. 2 vols. Dublin, 1906. [Irish and English.]

(b) Plays
The Poorhouse. (Abbey Theatre, Dublin, 3 April 1907.) 1906. [With Lady Gregory; pbd with her Spreading the News.]

[The following plays are mostly believed to have been pbd, but it has been impossible to see copies; the BM. has none:]
The Twisting of the Rope. (Gaiety Theatre, Dublin, 21 Oct. 1901.) [In Gaelic.]
The Bursting of the Bubble. 1905.
King James. 1905.
Nativity Play; translated by Lady Gregory. (Abbey Theatre, Dublin, 5 Jan. 1911).
The Marriage. (Abbey Theatre, Dublin, 30 Nov. 1911).
The Tinker and the Fairy. (Abbey Theatre, Dublin, 15 Feb. 1912). 1905. [In Gaelic.]

[For some of Hyde's writings in prose see p. 1050 above.]

(c) Biography and Criticism

Cary, E. L. Dr Douglas Hyde, a Gaelic Poet and Dreamer. Lamp, xxviii, 1904.

Coffey, D. Douglas Hyde. Dublin, 1917.

Weygandt, C. Dr Douglas Hyde and his 'Songs of Connacht.' [In Tuesdays at Ten, Philadelphia, 1928.]

'MOIRA O'NEILL' (NESTA HIGGINSON, later SKRINE)

(a) Poems

Collected Poems. Edinburgh, 1933.

Songs of the Glens of Antrim. Edinburgh, 1900.

More Songs of the Glens of Antrim. 1921.

(b) Fiction

An Easter Vacation. 1893.

The Elf-Errant. 1895.

From Two Points of View. Edinburgh, 1924.

(c) Criticism

Nesta Higginson ('Moira O'Neill'). Book-Buyer, xi, 1895.

A School of Irish Poetry. Edinburgh Rev. ccix, 1909. [On W. B. Yeats, 'A. E.,' Moira O'Neill and P. Colum.]

KATHARINE TYNAN, later HINKSON (1861–1931)

(a) Collected and Selected Poems

Twenty-One Poems. Selected by W. B. Yeats. Dundrum, 1907.

The Flower of Peace. A Collection of the Devotional Poetry of Katharine Tynan. 1914.

Collected Poems. 1930.

Twenty-Four Poems. 1931. (Augustan Books of Modern Poetry.)

(b) Separate Volumes of Poems

Louise de la Vallière, and Other Poems. 1885.

Shamrocks. 1887.

Ballads and Lyrics. 1891.

Irish Love-Songs, selected by Katharine Tynan. 1892.

Cuckoo Songs. 1894.

Miracle Plays: Our Lord's Coming and Childhood. 1895.

A Lover's Breast-Knot. 1896.

The Wind in the Trees. A Book of Country Verse. 1898.

Poems. 1901.

Innocencies. A Book of Verse. 1905.

Experiences. 1908.

New Poems. 1911.

Irish Poems. 1913.

The Wild Harp. A Selection from Irish Poetry by Katharine Tynan. 1913.

Flower of Youth. Poems in War-Time. 1915.

The Holy War. 1916.

Late Songs. 1917.

Herb o' Grace. Poems in War-Time. 1918.

Evensong. Oxford, 1922.

Twilight Songs. Oxford, 1927.

(c) Fiction

An Isle in the Water. 1895. [Stories.]

Land of Mist and Mountain. [1895.] [Stories.]

The Way of a Maid. 1895.

Oh, what a Plague is Love! 1896.

The Dear Irish Girl. 1899.

The Handsome Brandons. A Story for Girls. 1899.

Led by a Dream, and Other Stories. 1899.

A Daughter of the Fields. 1900.

[After 1900 Mrs Hinkson pbd a very large number of novels and collections of short stories: she also wrote works on Ireland and a few devotional works, and edited several modern poets, etc.]

(d) Criticism

The Poems of Katharine Tynan. Irish Monthly, xii, 1884.

Bregy, K. The Poetry of Katharine Tynan Hinkson. Catholic World, xcvii, 1913.

FREDERIC HERBERT TRENCH (1865–1923)

(a) Poems and Plays

Deirdre Wed and Other Poems. 1901.

New Poems: Apollo and the Seaman, The Queen of Gothland, Stanzas to Tolstoy, and Other Lyrics. 1907.

All that matters. A Play. [1911.]

Lyrics and Narrative Poems. [1911.]

Ode from Italy in Time of War: Night on Mottarone. Florence, 1915 (priv. ptd).

Poems, with Fables in Prose. 2 vols. 1918.

Napoleon. A Play. 1919.

The Collected Works. Ed. H. Williams, 3 vols. 1924.

Selected Poems. Ed. H. Williams, 1924.

(b) Biography and Criticism

Clarke, Austin. The Poetry of Herbert Trench. London Mercury, x, 1924.

George, R. E. G. The Poetry of Mr Herbert Trench. Contemporary Rev, cxxvi, 1924.

Chevalley, A. Herbert Trench, Poète anglais. Notice sur sa Vie et ses Œuvres. Paris, 1925.

DORA MARY SIGERSON, later SHORTER (1866–1918)

(a) Poems

Verses. 1893.

The Fairy Changeling, and Other Poems. 1898.

My Lady's Slipper. 1898.

Ballads and Poems. 1899.

The Woman who went to Hell, and Other Ballads and Lyrics. [1902.]

As the Sparks fly upward. Poems and Ballads. [1904.]

The Story and Song of Black Roderick. 1906.
Collected Poems. With an Introduction by George Meredith. 1907.
The Troubadour, and Other Poems. 1910.
New Poems. Dublin, 1912.
Madge Lindsey, and Other Poems. Dublin, 1913.
Comfort the Women. A Prayer in Time of War. [1915] (priv. ptd).
Love of Ireland. Poems and Ballads. Dublin, 1916; 2 pts, Dublin, 1916 (with Poems of the Irish Rebellion, 1916).
An Old Proverb: 'It will be all the same in a Thousand Years.' 1916 (priv. ptd).
The Sad Years [and other poems. With Introduction by Katharine Tynan]. 1918; 1918 (priv. ptd).
A Legend of Glendalough, and Other Ballads. Dublin, 1919.
The Tricolour. Poems of the Irish Revolution. Dublin, 1922.
Twenty-One Poems. 1926. (Augustan Books of Modern Poetry.)

(b) Other Writings

The Father Confessor. Stories of Death and Danger. 1900.
The Country-House Party. 1905.
Through Wintry Terrors. 1907.
Do-Well and Do-Little. A Fairy Tale. [1913.]
A Dull Day in London, and Other Sketches. 1920.

(c) Criticism and Appreciation

Colum, P. The Poetry of Dora Sigerson Shorter. Bookman (U.S.A.), XLIX, 1919.
In Memoriam Dora Sigerson, 1918–1923. Died January 6th, 1918. 1923 (priv. ptd). [Poems by various writers.]

LIONEL PIGOT JOHNSON (1867–1902)
[See p. 344 above.]

'A. E.' or 'Æ' (GEORGE WILLIAM RUSSELL; 1867–1935)

(a) Collected and Selected Poems

Collected Poems. 1913; 1926 (enlarged).
Selected Poems. 1935.

(b) Separate Volumes of Poems

Homeward. Songs by the Way. Dublin, 1894; Portland, Maine, 1895 (with addns).
The Earth Breath, and Other Poems. [1897.]
The Nuts of Knowledge. Lyrical Poems, Old and New. Dundrum, 1903.
The Divine Vision, and Other Poems. 1904.
New Songs. A Lyric Selection made by A. E. from Poems by Padraic Colum, Eva Gore, Booth, Thomas Keohler, Alice Milligan, Susan Mitchell, Seumas O'Sullivan, George Roberts, and Ella Young. Dublin, 1904 (2nd edn).

By Still Waters. Lyrical Poems, Old and New. Dundrum, 1906.
The Renewal of Youth. 1911.
Gods of War. Dublin, 1915 (priv. ptd).
Salutation. A Poem on the Irish Rebellion of 1916. 1917 (priv. ptd).
Voices of the Stones. 1925.
Midsummer Eve. New York, 1928.
Dark Weeping. With Designs by Paul Nash. 1929 (anon.).
Enchantment, and Other Poems. New York, 1930.
Vale, and Other Poems. 1931.
The House of the Titans, and Other Poems. 1934.

(c) Miscellaneous Prose

Nationality and Cosmopolitanism in Literature. [In J. Eglinton, W. B. Yeats, A. E. and W. Larminie, Literary Ideals in Ireland, 1899.]
Nationality and Imperialism. [In I. A., Lady Gregory, Ideals in Ireland, 1901.]
The Mask of Apollo, and Other Stories. Dublin, 1904.
Some Irish Essays. 1906.
Deirdre. A Drama in Three Acts. Dublin, 1907.
The Hero in Man. [1909.]
Co-operation and Nationality. A Guide for Rural Reformers from this to the Next Generation. Dublin, 1912.
Imaginations and Reveries. Dublin, 1915.
The National Being. Some Thoughts on an Irish Polity. Dublin, 1916.
The Candle of Vision. 1918.
The Interpreters. 1922.
Song and its Fountains. 1932.
The Avatars. A Futurist Fantasy. 1933.
Some Passages from the Letters of A. E. to W. B. Yeats. Dublin, 1936.
AE's Letters to Minanlabain. Ed. L. K. Porter, New York, 1937.
The Living Torch. A. E. Ed. (with long introduction) M. Gibbon, 1937. [Articles and reviews—mainly rptd from The Irish Statesman.]

[Russell also pbd pamphlets on literature and Irish questions, and contributed several prefaces to books by other writers.]

(d) Biography and Criticism

Ford, J. E. 'A. E.,' the Neo-Celtic Mystic. Poet-Lore, XVI, 1905.
Weygandt, C. A. E., the Irish Emerson. Sewanee Rev. XV, 1907.
A School of Irish Poetry. Edinburgh Rev. CCIX, 1909. [On W. B. Yeats, 'A. E.,' Moira O'Neill and P. Colum.]
Boyd, E. A. A. E.—Mystic and Economist. North American Rev. CCII, 1915.

Figgis, D. Æ.—George W. Russell. A Study of a Man and of a Nation. Dublin, 1916.

Colum, P. A. E., Poet, Painter and Economist. New Republic, xv, 1918.

Ervine, St J. G. A. E. [In Some Impressions of my Elders, 1923.]

Speakman, H. Dublin Hours with A. E. Bookman, LXII, 1925.

'Eglinton, John' (W. K. Magee). A. E. and his Story. Dial, LXXXII, 1927.

—— A Memoir of A. E. 1937.

Garnier, C. M. Tagore et George Russell. Revue anglo-américaine, VII, 1929.

Bibliography of A. E., George Russell. Dublin Mag. v, 1930. [Additions, Dublin Mag. x, 1935, pp. 74–6.]

Jameson, G. E. Mysticism in A. E. and in Yeats in Relation to Oriental and American Thought. Abstracts of Dissertations, Ohio State University, 1932, pp. 144–51.

Curran, C. P. George Russell. Studies, xxIV, 1935.

NORA HOPPER, later CHESSON (1871–1906)

Ballads in Prose. 1894.

Under Quicken Boughs. 1896.

Songs of the Morning. 1900.

Aquamarines. 1902.

Mildred and her Mills, and Other Poems. [1903.]

[Mrs Chesson also pbd 2 novels and 3 books for children.]

WILLIAM ROONEY (1873–1901)

Poems and Ballads. Dublin, 1902. [Ed. by A. Griffith, with biographical sketch by P. Bradley.]

IV. YEATS AND SYNGE

WILLIAM BUTLER YEATS (1865–1939

(a) Bibliographies

Wade, A. A Bibliography of the Writings of William Butler Yeats. [Appended to Collected Works, vol. VIII, Stratford-on-Avon, 1908.]

Symons, A. J. A. A Bibliography of the First Editions of Books by William Butler Yeats. 1924.

(b) Collected and Selected Works

[The larger collections are included under Collected and Selected Works; some plays were first pbd with collections of poems, and some poems with collections of plays, so that for a complete list of either both sections should be consulted.]

Poems. 1895; 1899 (rev.); 1901 (rev.).

Plays for an Irish Theatre. 5 vols. 1903–7. [Vol. IV is J. M. Synge's The Well of the Saints.]

Poems, 1899–1905. 1906. [Reprints and some new versions.]

The Collected Works in Verse and Prose. 8 vols. Stratford-on-Avon, 1908. [Vol. VIII contains bibliography by A. Wade.]

Plays for an Irish Theatre. With Designs by Gordon Craig. 1913. [A different collection from the edn in 5 vols. 1903–7.]

A Selection from the Love Poetry of William Butler Yeats. Dundrum, 1913.

A Selection from the Poetry of W. B. Yeats. Leipzig, 1913.

Selected Poems by William Butler Yeats. New York, 1921.

Plays in Prose and Verse, written for an Irish Theatre, and generally with the Help of a Friend [i.e. Lady Gregory]. 1922. [Contains Cathleen ni Houlihan, The Pot of Broth, The Hour-Glass (in prose),The King's Threshold, On Baile's Strand, The Shadowy Waters, Deirdre, The Unicorn from the Stars, The Green Helmet, The Hour-Glass (in verse), The Player Queen; of these The Unicorn from the Stars is mainly by Lady Gregory.]

Plays and Controversies. 1923. [Reprints The Countess Cathleen, The Land of Heart's Desire, Four Plays for Dancers, and various notes on the Irish drama.]

The Complete Works of William Butler Yeats. 5 vols. New York, 1925.

Poems. 1927. [Reprints, including The Countess Cathleen and The Land of Heart's Desire.]

Selected Poems, Lyrical and Narrative. 1929.

The Collected Poems. 1933.

Irische Schaubühne. Deutsch von Henry von Heiseler. Munich, 1933 (priv. ptd). [The plays included are noted as German trns under their individual entries below.]

Collected Plays. 1935.

Nine One-Act Plays. 1937.

(c) Poems

Mosada. A Dramatic Poem. Reprinted from the Dublin University Review [of June 1886]. Dublin, 1886.

The Wanderings of Oisin, and Other Poems. 1889.

The Wind among the Reeds. 1899.

In the Seven Woods. Being Poems, chiefly of the Irish Heroic Age. Dundrum, 1903.

Poems written in Discouragement. Dundrum, 1913.

Responsibilities. Poems and a Play. Dundrum, 1914; 1916 (as Responsibilities, and Other Poems). [The play is a new version of The Hour-Glass.]

Easter, 1916. [1916.]
Eight Poems, transcribed by Edward Pay. 1916.
The Wild Swans at Coole, Other Verses, and a
Play in Verse. Dundrum, 1917; 1919 (as The
Wild Swans at Coole). [The play is At the
Hawk's Well, privately produced, April
1916.]
Nine Poems. 1918 (priv. ptd).
Michael Robartes and the Dancer. Dundrum,
1920.
Later Poems. 1922.
Seven Poems and a Fragment. Dundrum,
1922.
Early Poems and Stories. 1925.
October Blast. Dublin, 1927.
The Tower. 1928.
Three Things. 1929.
The Winding Stair. New York, 1929; 1933
('and other poems').
Words for Music. Perhaps, and Other Poems.
Dublin, 1932.
The King of the Great Clock Tower. Com-
mentaries and Poems. Dublin, 1935.
A Full Moon in March. 1935.
New Poems. Dublin, 1938.

(d) Plays

The Countess Kathleen (Antient Concert
Rooms, Dublin, 8 May 1899) and Various
Legends and Lyrics. 1892. [The Countess
Cathleen (sic), Dublin, 1912; 1929 (with
The Land of Heart's Desire). Tr. Polish,
Warsaw, 1912; Italian, Milan, 1914 (in
Tragedie irlandesi); German, Munich, 1933
(in Irische Schaubühne).]
The Land of Heart's Desire. (Avenue, Spring
1894.) 1894; Dublin, 1913; 1929 (with The
Countess Cathleen). Tr. Italian, Milan,
1914 (in Tragedie irlandesi); German,
Munich, 1933 (in Irische Schaubühne).
Cathleen ni Houlihan. A Play. (St Teresa's
Hall, Dublin, 3 April 1902.) 1902; 1904 (in
Plays for an Irish Theatre, vol. II); New
York, 1908, 1915 (with The Unicorn from
the Stars). Tr. Italian, Milan, 1914 (in
Tragedie irlandesi); German, Munich, 1933
(in Irische Schaubühne).
The Hour-Glass. A Morality. (Molesworth
Hall, Dublin, 14 March 1903.) 1903
(12 copies only); 1904 (in Plays for an Irish
Theatre, vol. II); New York, 1908, 1915
(with, The Unicorn from the Stars); tr.
German, Munich, 1933 (in Irische Schau-
bühne). [A new version was priv. ptd,
Dundrum, 1914, and pbd in Responsibilities;
Poems and a Play, Dundrum, 1914.]
Where There is Nothing. (Stage Soc. 1904.)
[Plays for an Irish Theatre, vol. I, 1903.]
The Pot of Broth. (Antient Concert Rooms,
Dublin, 30 Oct. 1902.) [In Plays for an
Irish Theatre, vol. II, 1904.]

The King's Threshold (Molesworth Hall,
Dublin, 8 Oct. 1903); and On Baile's Strand
(Abbey Theatre, Dublin, 27 Dec. 1904).
[Plays for an Irish Theatre, vol. III, 1904;
tr. German, Munich, 1933 (in Irische
Schaubühne). The King's Threshold separ-
ately 1937.]
Deirdre. (Abbey Theatre, Dublin, 24 Nov.
1906.) [Plays for an Irish Theatre, vol. v,
1907; tr. German, Munich, 1933 (in Irische
Schaubühne).]
The Golden Helmet. (Abbey Theatre, Dublin,
19 March 1908.) New York, 1908; tr. Ger-
man, Munich, 1933 (in Irische Schaubühne).
The Unicorn from the Stars (Abbey Theatre,
Dublin, 23 Nov. 1907) and Other Plays.
New York, 1908, 1915. [With Isabella
Augusta, Lady Gregory: the 'other plays'
are reprints of Cathleen ni Houlihan and
The Hour-Glass. The Unicorn from the
Stars, tr. German, Munich, 1933 (in Irische
Schaubühne).]
The Green Helmet (Abbey Theatre, Dublin, 10
Feb. 1910) and Other Poems. Dundrum, 1910
Two Plays for Dancers. Dundrum, 1919.
[The Dreaming of the Bones, and The Only
Jealousy of Emer (Abbey Theatre, Dublin,
6 Dec. 1931).]
Four Plays for Dancers. 1921. [Contents:
At the Hawk's Well; The Only Jealousy of
Emer; The Dreaming of the Bones;
Calvary.]
The Player Queen. (Abbey Theatre, Dublin,
9 Dec. 1919) 1922.
Sophocles' King Oedipus. A Version for the
Modern Stage. 1928.
The Cat and the Moon (Abbey Theatre,
Dublin, 9 May 1926) and Certain Poems.
Dublin, 1931.
The Words upon the Window Pane. A Play in
One Act, with Notes upon the Play and its
Subject. (Abbey Theatre, Dublin, 17 Nov.
1930). Dublin, 1934. [On Jonathan Swift.]
Wheels and Butterflies. 1934. [The Words
upon the Window-Pane; Fighting the
Waves (Abbey Theatre, Dublin, 13 Aug.
1929); The Resurrection (Abbey Theatre,
Dublin, 30 July 1934); The Cat and the
Moon.]
The Herne's Egg. A Stage Play. 1938.

(e) Miscellaneous Prose

Ganconagh, John Sherman, and Dhoya. 1891.
['Ganconagh' is the pseudonym of Yeats.]
The Celtic Twilight. Men and Women,
Dhouls and Faeries. 1893. [The Celtic
Twilight, rptd 1902.]
The Secret Rose. 1897; 1927 (with Stories of
Red Hanrahan). [Stories.]
The Tables of the Law. The Adoration of the
Magi. 1897 (priv. ptd); 1904.

Literary Ideals in Ireland. 1899. [With 'John Eglinton', 'A.E.' and W. Larminie.]

The Shadowy Waters. 1900. [Acting Version (Molesworth Hall, Dublin, 14 Jan. 1904), 1907; tr. Italian, Milan, 1914 (in Tragedie irlandesi); German, Munich, 1933 (in Irische Schaubühne).]

Ideas of Good and Evil. 1903.

Stories of Red Hanrahan. Dundrum, 1904; 1927 (with The Secret Rose).

Discoveries. A Volume of Essays. Dundrum, 1907.

Poetry and Ireland. Essays. Dundrum, 1908. [With Lionel Johnson.]

Synge and the Ireland of his Time. With a Note concerning a Walk through Connemara with him by Jack Butler Yeats. Dundrum, 1911.

The Cutting of an Agate. New York, 1912; 1919. [Essays.]

Reveries over Childhood and Youth. Dundrum, 1915; 1916; 1926 (with The Trembling of the Veil, as Autobiographies).

Per Amica Silentia Lunae. 1918.

Four Years. Dundrum, 1921. [Reminiscences of 1887–91.]

The Trembling of the Veil. 1922 (priv. ptd); 1926 (with Reveries over Childhood and Youth, as Autobiographies).

Essays. 1924.

The Bounty of Sweden. A Meditation, and a Lecture delivered before the Royal Swedish Academy, and Certain Notes. Dublin, 1925.

A Vision. An Explanation of Life founded upon the Writings of Giraldus and upon Certain Doctrines attributed to Kusta ben Luka. 1925. [Rptd 1937 with A Packet for Ezra Pound and Stories for Michael Robartes prefixed.]

Estrangement. Being some Fifty Thoughts from a Diary kept in the Year Nineteen Hundred and Nine. Dublin, 1926.

The Death of Synge, and Other Passages from an Old Diary. Dublin, 1928.

A Packet for Ezra Pound. Dublin, 1929.

Stories of Michael Robartes and his Friends. An Extract from a Record made by his Pupils; and a Play in Prose. Dublin, 1931. [The play is The Resurrection.]

Letters to the New Island. Ed. H. Reynolds, Cambridge, U.S.A. 1934. [Rptd from Boston Pilot and Providence Sunday Journ. 1889–91.]

Dramatis Personae, 1896–1902, and Other Papers. 1936.

Essays, 1931 to 1936. Dublin, 1937.

(f) Works Edited

Fairy and Folk Tales of the Irish Peasantry. 1888. [Contributions by Yeats.]

Poems and Ballads of Young Ireland. Dublin, 1888. [Contains poems by Yeats.]

Representative Irish Tales. New York, 1890. [Contributions by Yeats.]

Irish Fairy Tales. 1892.

The Works of William Blake, Poetic, Symbolic, and Critical. Edited, with Lithographs of the Illustrated 'Prophetic Books,' and a Memoir and Interpretation. 3 vols. 1893. [With E. J. Ellis.]

The Poems of William Blake. 1893. (Muses' Lib.)

A Book of Irish Verse, selected from Modern Writers. 1895; 1900 (rev. as Modern Irish Poetry).

Beltaine. An Occasional Publication. 3 nos. 1899–1900; 1900.

Samhain. Edited for the Irish Literary Theatre. 6 nos. Dublin, 1901–6.

The Arrow. 4 nos. 1906–7.

Poems of Spenser. Selected and with an Introduction. 1906.

The Oxford Book of Modern Verse, 1892–1935. Oxford, 1936.

[Mr Yeats has also contributed to the Books of the Rhymers' Club, to Lady Gregory's Ideals in Ireland, 1901, and other works, and has written introductions to J. M. Synge's The Well of the Saints, etc., etc.]

(g) Biography and Criticism
(i) Books and Pamphlets

Krans, H. S. William Butler Yeats and the Irish Literary Revival. 1904.

Reid, F. W. B. Yeats. A Critical Study. 1915.

Gurd, P. The Early Poetry of William Butler Yeats. Lancaster, U.S.A. 1916.

Hone, J. M. William Butler Yeats: the Poet in Contemporary Ireland. Dublin, 1916.

Wrenn, C. L. W. B. Yeats. A Literary Study. Durham, 1920.

Strong, L. A. G. A Letter to W. B. Yeats. 1932.

Pollock, J. H. William Butler Yeats. Dublin, 1935.

Hoare, A. D. M. The Works of Morris and Yeats in relation to Early Saga Literature. Cambridge, 1937.

(ii) Periodical Articles and Chapters in Books

Johnson, L. The Poetry of W. B. Yeats. Academy, XLII, 1892, p. 278.

Archer, W. Poets of the Younger Generation. 1902.

Macleod, F. The Later Work of W. B. Yeats. North American Rev. CLXXV, 1902.

More, P. E. Two Poets of the Irish Movement. [In Shelburne Essays, ser. 1, New York, 1904.]

Symons, A. Studies in Prose and Verse. 1904.

Elton, O. Living Irish Literature. [In Modern Studies, 1907.]

Gwynn, S. Poetry and the Stage. Fortnightly Rev. xci, 1909.

Chesterton, G. K. Efficiency in Elfland. Littell's Living Age, cclxxiv, 1912.

Moore, George. Yeats, Lady Gregory, and Synge. English Rev. xvi, 1914.

Jameson, Storm. Modern Drama in Europe. 1920.

Ervine, St J. G. W. B. Yeats. [In Some Impressions of my Elders, 1923.]

Maynard, T. Our Best Poets, English and American. 1924.

Pourrat, H. W. B. Yeats. Nouvelle Revue française, 1 Jan. 1924.

Colum, P. Mr Yeats's Plays and Later Poems. Yale Rev. xiv, 1925.

Jackson, Schuyler. William Butler Yeats. London Mercury, xi, 1925.

Russell, G. W. Yeats' Early Poems. Littell's Living Age, Nov. 1925.

'Eglinton, John' (W. K. Magee). Yeats and his Story. Dial, lxxx, 1926.

O'Conor, N. J. A Note on Yeats. [In Essays in Memory of Barrett Wendell, by his Assistants, Cambridge, U.S.A. 1926.]

Dubois, L. P. M. Yeats et le Mouvement poétique en Irlande. Revue des Deux Mondes, Oct. 1929

McGreevy, T. Mr W. B. Yeats as a Dramatist. Revue anglo-américaine, vii, 1929.

Wilson, Edmund. Axel's Castle. New York, 1929.

Hüttemann, G. Wesen der Dichtung und Aufgabe des Dichters bei William Butler Yeats. Bonn, 1930.

O'Faoláin, S. Mr W. B. Yeats's Selected Poems. Criterion, ix, 1930.

—— W. B. Yeats. English Rev. lx, 1935.

Williams, Charles. Poetry at Present. Oxford, 1930.

Spender, S. W. B. Yeats as a Realist. Criterion, xiv, 1934.

Thouless, P. Modern Poetic Drama. Oxford, 1934.

Rhys, E. W. B. Yeats: Early Recollections. Fortnightly Rev. July 1935.

Blackmur, R. P. The Later Poetry of W. B. Yeats. Southern Rev. ii, 1936.

Strong, L. A. G. W. B. Yeats: an Appreciation. Cornhill Mag. clvi, 1937.

JOHN MILLINGTON SYNGE (1871–1909)

(a) Bibliographies

Bourgeois, M. Appendix A: General Bibliography. [In John Millington Synge and the Irish Theatre, 1913.]

MacManus, M. J. A Bibliography of Books written by J. M. Synge. Dublin, 1930.

(b) Collected Works

The Works. 4 vols. Dublin, 1910.

Pocket Edition of the Plays. 4 vols. Dublin, 1911.

Uniform Library Edition. 5 vols. Dublin, 1911.

The Dramatic Works. Dublin, 1915.

The Works. (Revised Collected Edition.) 1932.

(c) Plays

The Shadow of the Glen (Molesworth Hall, Dublin, 8 Oct. 1903) and Riders to the Sea (Molesworth Hall, Dublin, 25 Feb. 1904). 1905. Tr. French, Paris, 1913; Spanish, Madrid, 1920 (Riders to the Sea, only). [Both first pbd in Samhain, Riders to the Sea in Oct. 1903 and The Shadow of the Glen in Dec. 1904.]

The Well of the Saints. (Abbey Theatre, Dublin, 4 Feb. 1905.) Dublin, 1905; 1905 (with introduction by W. B. Yeats, as Plays for an Irish Theatre, vol. iv); Dublin, 1907. Tr. German, Berlin, 1906; Dutch, Amsterdam, 1912.

The Playboy of the Western World. A Comedy in Three Acts. (Abbey Theatre, Dublin, 26 Jan. 1907.) Dublin, 1907 (bis); Dublin, 1909; 1927 (illustrated by J. Keating). Tr. German, Munich, 1912; French, Paris, 1914. [The first 1907 edn is unexpurgated, and has Synge's preface; the second is bowdlerized and lacks the preface.]

The Tinker's Wedding. A Comedy in Two Acts. (His Majesty's, 11 Nov. 1909.) Dublin, 1907.

Deirdre of the Sorrows. A Play. (Abbey Theatre, Dublin, 13 Jan. 1910.) Dundrum, 1910. Tr. French, Paris, 1924 (6th edn); Irish, Dublin, 1932

(d) Other Writings

The Aran Islands. With Drawings by Jack B. Yeats. Dublin, 1907; 4 pts, Dublin, 1912; tr. French, Paris, 1921 (4th edn).

In Wicklow, West Kerry, and Connemara. With Drawings by Jack B. Yeats. Dublin, 1911; Dublin, 1912.

Poems and Translations. Dundrum, 1909 (with preface by W. B. Yeats); Dublin, 1912.

(e) Biography and Criticism

(i) Books

Yeats, W. B. Synge and the Ireland of his Time. With a Note concerning a Walk through Connemara with him by Jack Butler Yeats. Dundrum, 1911.

—— The Death of Synge, and Other Passages from an Old Diary. Dublin, 1928.

Bickley, F. J. M. Synge and the Irish Dramatic Movement. 1912.

Howe, P. P. J. M. Synge: a Critical Study. 1912.

Bourgeois, M. John Millington Synge and the Irish Theatre. 1913. [With bibliography.]

Masefield, J. John M. Synge. A Few Personal Recollections, with Biographical Notes. 1915.

Thorning, J. J. M. Synge. En moderne irsk Dramatiker. Copenhagen, 1921.

Corkery, D. Synge and Anglo-Irish Literature. A Study. Cork, 1931.

Frenzel, H. John Millington Synge's Work as a Contribution to Irish Folk-lore and to the Psychology of Primitive Tribes. Bonn, 1932.

Synge, S. Letters to my Daughter. Memories of John Millington Synge. Dublin, [1932].

Aufhauser, A. Sind die Dramen von John Millington Synge durch französische Vorbilder beeinflusst? Munich, 1935.

Riva, S. La Tradizione celtica e la moderna Letteratura irlandese. I: J. M. Synge. Rome, 1937.

(ii) Periodical Articles and Chapters in Books

Elton, O. Living Irish Literature. [In Modern Studies, 1907.]

Figgis, D. The Art of J. M. Synge. [In Studies and Appreciations, 1912.]

Bennett, C. A. The Plays of Synge. Yale Rev. i, 1912.

Jackson, Holbrook. The Work of Synge. [In All Manner of Folk, 1912.]

Gregory, I. A., Lady. Our Irish Theatre. A Chapter of Autobiography. 1914. [Contains an appreciation of Synge.]

Moore, George. Yeats, Lady Gregory, and Synge. English Rev. xvi, 1914.

Sherman, S. P. On Contemporary Literature. New York, 1917.

Jameson, Storm. Modern Drama in Europe. 1920.

Schoepperle, G. John Synge and his Old French Farce: De la Vigne's 'L'Aveugle et le Boiteux' a 'Moralité.' North American Rev. ccxiv, 1921.

Ervine, St J. G. Bernard Shaw and J. M. Synge. [In Some Impressions of my Elders, 1923.]

Fausset, H. I'A. Synge and Tragedy. Fortnightly Rev. cxv, 1924.

Letters of John Millington Synge. From Material supplied by Max Meyerfeld. Yale Rev. xiii, 1924.

Strong, L. A. G. John Millington Synge. Bookman (U.S.A.), lxxiii, 1931.

V. Dramatists of the Irish Revival

[Arranged in the order of their first productions. Plays not followed by the name of a theatre and date are *believed* not to have been acted publicly. When definite information to this effect has been obtained the word 'Unacted' has been used.]

Edward Martyn (1859–1923)

(a) Plays

The Heather Field (Antient Concert Rooms, Dublin, 9 May 1899) and Maeve (Antient Concert Rooms, Dublin, 20 Feb. 1900); with an Introduction by George Moore. 1899. [Rptd separately as The Heather Field, a Play in Three Acts, 1917 and Maeve, a Psychological Drama in Two Acts, 1917.]

The Tale of a Town and An Enchanted Sea. 1902. [Both unacted; but G. Moore's The Bending of the Bough, produced by the Irish Literary Theatre at the Gaiety, 19 Feb. 1900, was an adaptation of The Tale of a Town.]

Grangecolman. A Domestic Drama in Three Acts. (Abbey Theatre, Dublin, 25 Jan. 1912.) Dublin, 1912.

The Dream Physician. A Play in Five Acts. (Little Theatre, Dublin, 2 Nov. 1914.) Dublin, [1918]. [The character George Augustus Moon is a skit on George Moore.]

[Martyn also pbd Morgante the Lesser, his Notorious Life and Wonderful Deeds, arranged and narrated for the First Time by Sirius, 1890, and a preface to R. Elliott's Art and Ireland, 1906.]

(b) Biography and Criticism

Moore, George. Hail and Farewell! 3 vols. 1911–4. [Contains a great deal of material, *passim*, but the portrait is of the nature of a caricature.]

Obituary. Times, 7 Dec. 1923.

Gwynn, D. Edward Martyn and the Irish Revival. 1930.

Douglas Hyde (b. 1860)

[See p. 1056 above.]

Isabella Augusta, Lady Gregory (1859–1932)

(a) Plays

Kincora. A Play in Three Acts. (Abbey Theatre, Dublin, 25 March 1905.) Dublin, 1905 (*bis*); 1912 (in Irish Folk-History Plays, ser. 1).

The White Cockade. (Abbey Theatre, Dublin, 9 Dec. 1905.) Dublin, 1905; 1912 (in Irish Folk-History Plays, ser. 2).

Spreading the News (27 Dec. 1904); The Rising of the Moon (9 March 1907); The Poorhouse (3 April 1907), by Lady Gregory and Douglas Hyde. Dublin, 1906. [Spreading the News and The Rising of the Moon rptd Dublin 1909, 1923 (in Seven Short Plays); 1918.]

The Unicorn from the Stars (Abbey Theatre, Dublin, 23 Nov. 1907) and Other Plays. 1908; 1915. [With W. B. Yeats, who mainly wrote all save The Unicorn from the Stars.]

Seven Short Plays. Dublin, 1909; [1923]. [All produced at the Abbey Theatre, Dublin: Spreading the News (27 Dec. 1904); Hyacinth Halvey (19 Feb. 1906); The Rising of the Moon (9 March 1907); The Jackdaw (23 Feb. 1907); The Workhouse Ward (20 April 1907); The Travelling Man (2 March 1910); The Gaol Gate (20 Oct. 1906); all rptd as separate pts, Dublin, 1918, the wrappers marked 'Lady Gregory's Irish Plays.']

The Image. A Play in Three Acts. (Abbey Theatre, Dublin, 11 Nov. 1909). Dublin, 1910; [1922] ('and other plays'). [The other plays are: Hanrahan's Oath (Abbey Theatre, Dublin, 29 Jan. 1918); Shanwalla (Abbey Theatre, Dublin, 8 April 1915); The Wrens (unacted).]

Irish Folk-History Plays. Ser. 1: The Tragedies: Grania (unacted); Kincora; Dervorgilla (Abbey Theatre, Dublin, 31 Oct. 1907). Ser. 2: The Tragi-Comedies: The Canavans (Abbey Theatre, Dublin, 8 Dec. 1906); The White Cockade; The Deliverer (Abbey Theatre, Dublin, 12 Jan. 1911). 2 vols. 1912.

New Comedies: The Bogie Men (4 July 1912); The Full Moon (10 Nov. 1910); Coats (1 Dec. 1910); Damer's Gold (21 Nov. 1912); McDonough's Wife (11 Jan. 1912). 1913; 5 pts, [1923] (as New Irish Comedies). [All produced at the Abbey Theatre, Dublin.]

Commedie Irlandesi. Versione e Proemio di Carlo Linati. Milan, 1916. [Contents: Spreading the News; The Rising of the Moon; Hyacinth Halvey; The Travelling Man.]

The Golden Apple. A Play for Kiltartan Children. (Abbey Theatre, Dublin, 6 Jan. 1920.) 1916.

The Dragon. A Wonder Play in Three Acts. (Abbey Theatre, Dublin, 21 April 1919.) Dublin, 1920; 1920.

Three Wonder Plays. [1923.] [Contents: The Dragon (21 April 1919); Aristotle's Bellows (17 March 1921); The Jester (unacted); the first two produced at the Abbey Theatre, Dublin.]

The Story brought by Brigit. A Passion Play in Three Acts. (Abbey Theatre, Dublin, 14 April 1924.) 1924 (bis).

On the Racecourse. New York, [1925] (in One-Act Plays for Stage and Study, ser. 2); 1926. [A rewriting of Lady Gregory's first play, Twenty-Five, not pbd, but produced at Molesworth Hall, Dublin, 14 March 1903; unacted in rev. form.]

Three Last Plays. 1928. [Contents: Sancho's Master (14 March 1927); Dave (9 May 1927); The Would-be Gentleman (from Molière; 4 Jan. 1926); all produced at the Abbey Theatre, Dublin.]

My First Play. 1930. [Colman and Guaire; verse, unacted.]

[Lady Gregory also gave some assistance to W. B. Yeats in Plays written generally with the Help of a Friend, 1922.]

(b) Other Writings

Ideals in Ireland. Edited by Lady Gregory. Written by 'A. E.' [George Russell], D. P. Moran, George Moore, Douglas Hyde, Standish O'Grady, and W. B. Yeats. 1901.

Poets and Dreamers. Studies and Translations from the Irish. Dublin, 1903.

Gods and Fighting Men. The Story of Tuatha de Danaan and of the Fianna of Ireland, arranged and put into English. With a Preface by W. B. Yeats. 1904.

A Book of Saints and Wonders put down here by Lady Gregory according to the Old Writings and the Memory of the People of Ireland. Dundrum, 1906; 1907.

The Kiltartan History Book. Dublin, 1909; 1926.

The Kiltartan Wonder Book. Dublin, [1910].

Our Irish Theatre. A Chapter of Autobiography. 1914.

The Kiltartan Poetry Book. Prose Translations from the Irish. New York, 1919.

Visions and Beliefs in the West of Ireland. Collected and arranged by Lady Gregory; with Two Essays and Notes by W. B. Yeats. 2 sers. 1920.

Hugh Lane's Life and Achievement, with some Account of the Dublin Galleries. With Illustrations. 1921.

Case for the Return of Sir Hugh Lane's Pictures to Dublin. Dublin, 1926.

Coole. Dublin, 1931.

[Lady Gregory also arranged Cuchulain, pbd trns from Goldoni and Molière, and ed. several other works.]

(c) Biography and Criticism

Quinn, J. Lady Gregory and the Abbey Theater. Outlook (U.S.A.), 16 Dec. 1911.

Tennyson, C. Irish Plays and Playwrights. Quarterly Rev. ccxv, 1911.

Lady Gregory's Irish Plays. Contemporary Rev. cii, 1912.

Moore, George. Yeats, Lady Gregory, and Synge. English Rev. XVI, 1914.

Toksvig, S. A Visit to Lady Gregory. North American Rev. CCXIV, 1921.

Malone, A. E. The Plays of Lady Gregory. Yale Rev. XIV, 1925.

Obituary. London Mercury, XXVI, 1932.

Obituary. Spectator, 28 May 1932.

WILLIAM BOYLE (b. 1853)

(a) Plays

The Building Fund. A Play in Three Acts. (Abbey Theatre, Dublin, 25 April 1905.) Dublin, 1905.

The Eloquent Dempsey. A Comedy in Three Acts. (Abbey Theatre, Dublin, 20 Jan. 1906.) Dublin, 1907; 1911.

The Mineral Workers. A Play in Four Acts. (Abbey Theatre, Dublin, 20 Oct. 1906.) Dublin, 1907; 1910.

Family Failing. A Comedy in Three Acts. (Abbey Theatre, Dublin, 28 March 1912.) Dublin, 1912.

(b) Other Writings

A Kish of Brogues. 1899.

Comic Capers. Pictures by H. B. Neilson; Verses by William Boyle. [1903.]

Christmas at the Zoo; described in Verse by William Boyle, with Coloured Illustrations by H. B. Neilson. [1904.]

PADRAIC COLUM (b. 1881)

The Land. A Play in Three Acts. (Abbey Theatre, Dublin, 9 June 1905.) Dublin, 1905; Dublin, 1909 (with The Fiddler's House); Dublin, 1917 (in Three Plays).

The Fiddler's House. A Play in Three Acts. (Abbey Theatre, Dublin, 19 Aug. 1910.) Dublin, 1907; Dublin, 1909 (with The Land); Dublin, 1917 (in Three Plays).

The Miracle of the Corn. A Miracle Play in One Act (unacted). Dublin, 1907 (in Studies); 1922 (in Dramatic Legends and Other Poems).

Thomas Muskerry. A Play in Three Acts. (Abbey Theatre, Dublin, 12 May 1910.) Dublin, 1910; Dublin, 1917 (in Three Plays).

Mogu the Wanderer, or the Desert. A Fantastic Comedy in Three Acts (unacted). Boston, 1917.

Balloon. (Theatre Mart, Los Angeles, 26 May 1931.) New York, 1929.

[The plays Broken Soil (Molesworth Hall, Dublin, 3 Dec. 1903) and The Grasshopper (Abbey Theatre, Dublin, 24 Oct. 1922) have not been pbd; Mr Colum has also pbd poems, stories, books on Ireland, and introductions to works by Goldsmith, Swift, James Joyce, and others.]

RUTHERFORD MAYNE

The Turn of the Road. A Play in Two Scenes and an Epilogue. (Ulster Literary Theatre, Belfast, Dec. 1906.) Dublin, 1907.

The Drone. A Play in Three Acts. (Abbey Theatre, Dublin, April 1908.) Dublin, 1909.

The Troth. A Play in One Act. (Crown Theatre, Peckham, Oct. 1908.) Dublin, 1909.

The Drone, and Other Plays. Dublin, 1912. [Contains the above three, and Red Turf (Abbey Theatre, Dublin, 7 Dec. 1911).]

GEORGE FITZMAURICE

The Country Dressmaker. A Play in Three Acts. (Abbey Theatre, Dublin, 3 Oct. 1907.) Dublin, 1914.

Five Plays. The Country Dressmaker; The Moonlighter; The Piedish (Abbey Theatre, Dublin, 10 March 1908); The Magic Glasses (Abbey Theatre, Dublin, 24 April 1913); The Dandy Dolls. 1914.

[Another play, 'Twixt the Giltinans and the Carmodys, was produced at the Abbey Theatre, Dublin, 8 March 1903, but has not been pbd. See W. Haynes, Another Irish Dramatist, Dial, LXIII, 1917.]

CONAL HOLMES O'CONNELL O'RIORDAN ('F. NORREYS CONNELL') (b. 1874)

Shakespeare's End, and Other Irish Plays. 1912. [The 'other plays' are The Piper, an Unended Argument (Abbey Theatre, Dublin, 13 Feb. 1908) and An Imaginary Conversation (Abbey Theatre, Dublin, 13 May 1909).]

Rope Enough. A Play in Three Acts. Dublin, 1914.

His Majesty's Pleasure. A Romantic Comedy in Three Acts. (Birmingham Repertory Theatre, Nov. 1915). 1925. [First pbd in slighter form in Irish Rev. 1912.]

The King's Wooing. A Play in One Act. 1929.

[The play Time (Abbey Theatre, Dublin, 1 April 1909) has apparently not been pbd; Mr O'Riordan has also written novels and miscellaneous works.]

LENNOX ROBINSON (b. 1886)

The Cross-Roads. A Play in a Prologue and Two Acts. (1 April 1909.) Dublin, [1910].

Two Plays: Harvest (26 May 1910;) The Clancy Name (8 Oct. 1908). Dublin, 1911.

Patriots. A Play in Three Acts. (11 April 1912.) Dublin, 1912.

The Dreamers. A Play in Three Acts. (2 Feb. 1915.) 1915.

The Lost Leader. A Play in Three Acts. (19 Feb. 1918.) Dublin, 1918.

The Whiteheaded Boy. A Play in Three Acts. (13 Dec. 1916.) 1920.

The Round Table. A Comic Tragedy in Three Acts. (31 Jan. 1922.) 1924.

Crabbed Youth and Age. A Little Comedy. (14 Nov. 1922.) 1924.

The White Blackbird (12 Oct. 1925); Portrait (31 March 1925). Dublin, [1926].

Plays. 1928. [Contents: The Round Table; Crabbed Youth and Age; Portrait; The White Blackbird; The Big House; Give a Dog—.]

The Big House. Four Scenes in its Life. (26 Sept. 1926.) 1928.

Give a Dog—. A Play in Three Acts. (Strand, 20 Jan. 1929.) 1928.

Ever the Twain. (8 Oct. 1929.) 1930.

The Far-Off Hills. A Comedy in Three Acts. (22 Oct. 1928.) 1931.

Is Life worth Living? An Exaggeration in Three Acts. (6 Feb. 1933.) 1933. [First played as Drama at Inish.]

More Plays. 1935. [All's Over, Then? (25 July 1932) and Church Street (21 May 1934).]

[All the above were first produced at the Abbey Theatre, Dublin, save Give a Dog—, which was played there on 12 May 1929, after its *première* in London; Never the Time and the Place (Abbey Theatre, 8 April 1924) has not been pbd. Mr Robinson has also written novels and sketches and ed. several anthologies of Irish verse.]

GEORGE MOORE (1857–1933)

[See p. 526 above.]

THOMAS C. MURRAY (b. 1873)

Birthright. A Play in Two Acts. (27 Oct. 1910.) Dublin, 1911; tr. Irish, Dublin, 1931.

Maurice Harte. A Play in Two Acts. (20 Jan. 1912.) Dublin, 1912.

Spring, and Other Plays. Dublin, 1917. [Contents: Spring (8 Jan. 1918); Sovereign Love, a Comedy (11 Sept. 1913); The Briery Gap, a Little Tragedy. Sovereign Love is a revision of The Wheel o' Fortune, produced at the Dún, Cork, in 1909.]

Aftermath. A Play in Three Acts. (10 Jan. 1922.) Dublin, 1922.

Autumn Fire. A Play in Three Acts. (8 Sept. 1924.) 1925; tr. Irish, Dublin, 1930.

The Pipe in the Fields (3 Oct. 1927) and Birthright. 1928.

Michaelmas Eve. A Play in Three Acts. (27 June 1932.) 1932.

Maurice Harte, and A Stag at Bay. 1934.

[All the above were produced at the Abbey Theatre, Dublin; The Blind Wolf, produced there 30 April 1928, and A Flutter of Wings, at the Gate Theatre, Dublin, 1930, have not been pbd.]

ST JOHN GREER ERVINE (b. 1883)

(a) Plays

Mixed Marriage. A Play in Four Acts. (Abbey Theatre, Dublin, 30 March 1911.) Dublin, 1912.

The Magnanimous Lover. A Play in One Act. (Abbey Theatre, Dublin, 17 Oct. 1912.) Dublin, 1912.

The Critics. (Abbey Theatre, Dublin, 20 Nov. 1913.) [In Four Irish Plays, 1914.]

Jane Clegg. A Play in Three Acts. (Gaiety Theatre, Manchester, 21 April 1913.) 1914.

The Orangeman. (Abbey Theatre, Dublin, 13 March 1914.) [In Four Irish Plays, 1914.]

John Ferguson. A Play in Four Acts. (Abbey Theatre, Dublin, 30 Nov. 1915.) Dublin, 1915.

The Ship. A Play in Three Acts. (Playhouse, Liverpool, 24 Nov. 1922.) 1922.

The Lady of Belmont. A Play in Five Acts (Mary Ward Settlement, Tavistock Place, 31 May 1924.) 1923.

Mary, Mary, quite Contrary. A Light Comedy in Four Acts. (Abbey Theatre, Dublin, 14 May 1923). 1923.

Anthony and Anna. A Comedy in Three Acts. (Playhouse, Liverpool, 9 March 1926.) 1925; 1936 (rev.).

Ole George comes to Tea. (Playhouse, Liverpool, 27 May 1927.) [In Four One-act Plays, 1928.]

Progress. (Little, 3 April 1922.) [In Four One-act Plays, 1928.]

She was no Lady. (Playhouse, Liverpool, 27 Sept. 1927.) [In Four One-act Plays, 1928.]

The First Mrs Fraser. (Haymarket, 2 July 1929.) 1929.

People of Our Class. A Comedy. (Unacted.) 1936.

Boyd's Shop. A Comedy. (Playhouse, Liverpool, 19 Feb. 1936.) 1936.

Robert's Wife. A Comedy. (King's Theatre, Edinburgh, 25 Oct. 1937.) 1938.

[The Island of Saints, produced at the Abbey Theatre, Dublin, 12 Oct. 1920, has been pbd but is not procurable; Mr Ervine has also written biographies, novels and much dramatic criticism.]

(b) Criticism

McQuilland, L. J. Mr St John Ervine and his Work. Living Age, cccv, 1920.

St John Ervine, Ulster Realist. Outlook (U.S.A.), cxxv, 1920.

Lothian, A. The Plays and Novels of St John Ervine. North American Rev. ccxv, 1922.

Aas, L. Tre engelske Dramatikere. Tilskueren, xlvi, 1929. [H. Granville Barker, St John Ervine, John Drinkwater.]

EDWARD JOHN MORETON DRAX PLUNKETT,
BARON DUNSANY (b. 1878)

Five Plays: The Gods of the Mountain (Haymarket, 1 June 1911); The Golden Doom (Haymarket, 19 Nov. 1912); King Argimēnēs and the Unknown Warrior (Abbey Theatre, Dublin, 26 Jan. 1911); The Glittering Gate (Abbey Theatre, Dublin, 29 April 1909); The Lost Silk Hat (Gaiety Theatre, Manchester, 4 Aug. 1913). 1914.

Plays of Gods and Men. Dublin, 1917. [Contents: The Laughter of the Gods (also pbd separately 1918); The Queen's Enemies; The Tents of the Arabs (Abbey Theatre, Dublin, 24 May 1920); A Night at an Inn (Abbey Theatre, Dublin, 2 Sept. 1919; rptd separately 1922).]

If. A Play in Four Acts. 1921.

Plays of Near & Far. 1922. [Contents: The Compromise of the King of the Golden Isles; The Flight of the Queen; Cheezo; A Good Bargain; If Shakespeare lived to-day; Fame and the Poet.]

Alexander & Three Small Plays. 1925. [The 3 are The Old King's Tale, The Evil Kettle and The Amusements of Khan Kharuda.]

Seven Modern Comedies. 1928. [Contents: Atalanta in Wimbledon; The Raffle; The Journey of the Soul; In Holy Russia; His Sainted Grandmother; The Hopeless Passion of Mr Bunyon; The Jest of Hahalaba.]

The Old Folk of the Centuries. A Play. 1930.

Lord Adrian. A Play in Three Acts. 1933.

[Lord Dunsany has also pbd tales and poems.]

S. O'F.

II. ANGLO-INDIAN LITERATURE

General Works of Reference. Poetry and Drama. Fiction. Translations. Philology. History, Biography and Politics (1750–1850; 1851–1914). Geography, Topography and Travel. Religion and Philosophy. Social and Miscellaneous.

A. GENERAL WORKS OF REFERENCE

(a) Bibliographies

Campbell, Francis B. F. An Index-Catalogue of Bibliographical Works (chiefly in the English Language) relating to India. A Study in Bibliography. 1897.

Yule, Sir H. and Crooke, E. Fuller Titles of Books quoted in the Glossary. [Pp. xxvii–xlvii of Hobson-Jobson, by Yule and A. C. Burrell, rev. E. Crooke, 1903. A useful handlist.]

Buckland, C. E. Dictionary of Indian Biography. 1906. [Contains a list of biographies and autobiographies.]

(b) General Works

The Calcutta Review. Calcutta, 1844–. [Ed. to 1900 successively by Sir J. W. Kaye, A. Duff, W. S. Mackay, T. Smith, George Smith, M. Townsend, J. Newmarch, Sir R. Temple, T. Ridsdale, W. Heeley, W. H. Beverley, Roper Lethbridge, J. W. Furrell, Dr MacCann, G. A. Stack, H. A. D. Phillips. Index to vols. I–L, Calcutta, 1873. Selections, Calcutta, 1881.]

The Cambridge History of India. Vol. I (ed. E. J. Rapson), 1922; Vol. II in preparation; Vol. III (ed. Sir W. Haig), 1928; Vol. IV (ed. Sir R. Burn), 1937; Vol. V (ed. H. H. Dodwell), 1929; Vol. VI (ed. H. H. Dodwell), 1932.

Garrett, J. A Classical Dictionary of India, Illustrative of the Mythology, Philosophy, Literature, Antiquities, Arts, Manners, Customs, etc. of the Hindus. 2 pts, Madras, 1871.

Hunter, Sir W. W. The Imperial Gazetteer of India. 9 vols. 1881; 14 vols. 1885–7, 1907–9 (greatly enlarged and rewritten, so that it is no longer Hunter's work). [Vol. I was separately pbd as The Indian Empire, its History, People and Products, 1882.]

Jackson, A. V. Williams. A History of India, 9 vols. 1906.

Chandra, P. T. Indian Cyclopaedia. A Statistical Historical Handbook. Hyderabad, 1924.

(c) Literary Histories

Manuel, T. P. The Poetry of our Indian Poets. Calcutta, 1861.

Lawrence, T. B. English Poetry in India. Being Biographical and Critical Notices of Anglo-Indian Poets, etc. To which is prefixed a Preliminary Essay on Anglo-Indian Poetry in Two Parts. Calcutta, 1869.

Laurie, W. F. B. Anglo-Indian Periodical Literature. [In Sketches of some Distinguished Anglo-Indians, ser. 1, 1875, 1877 (rev.).]

Reed, Elizabeth A. Hindu Literature, or the Ancient Books of India. Chicago, 1891.

Frazer, R. W. A Literary History of India. 1898. [Ch. 15 contains an account of the beginnings of Indian use of the English language.]

Oaten, E. F. A Sketch of Anglo-Indian Literature. 1908. [Contains a book-list.]

—— Anglo-Indian Literature. CHEL. vol. XIV, 1916.

Sencourt, R. India in English Literature. [1925.]

Gowen, Herbert H. A History of Indian Literature, from Vedic Times to the Present Day. New York, 1931. [Contains a ch. on Anglo-Indian literature, and a book-list.]
Singh, Bhupal. A Survey of Anglo-Indian Fiction. 1934. [Contains a book-list.]
Sharp, Sir H. Anglo-Indian Verse. Proc. Royal Soc. Lit. xvi, 1937.

B. POETRY AND DRAMA

Dow, Alexander. Zingis. A Tragedy. 1769.
—— Sethona. A Tragedy. 1774.
[See also vol. ii, p. 465 above.]
Stevens, William Bagshaw. Poems; consisting of Indian Odes and Miscellaneous Pieces. Oxford, 1775.
Jones, Sir William. Poetical Works, with Life. 1807. [See also vol. ii, p. 368 above.]
'Quiz.' The Grand Master, or Adventures of Qui-Hi? in Hindostan. A Hudibrastic Poem in Eight Cantos. Illustrated with Engravings by Rowlandson. 1816.
Leyden, John. The Poetical Remains. With Memoirs of his Life by the Rev. J. Morton. 1819.
—— An Anglo-Indian Poet: John Leyden. Madras, 1912. [A collection of the Anglo-Indian poems only.]
[See also p. 237 above.]
Richardson, David Lester. Miscellaneous Poems. Calcutta, 1822.
—— Sonnets and Other Poems. 1825.
—— Bengal Annual. A Literary Keepsake. Calcutta, 1834.
—— Literary Leaves, or Prose and Verse. Calcutta, 1836.
—— Selections from the British Poets. 1840.
—— Literary Chit-Chat. With Miscellaneous Poems and Appendix of Prose Papers. Calcutta, 1848.
—— Literary Recreations, or Essays, Criticisms and Poems chiefly written in India. Calcutta, 1850; 1853.
Derozio, Henry Louis Vivian. Poems. Calcutta, 1827.
—— The Fakeer of Jungheera. A Metrical Tale; and Other Poems. Calcutta, 1828.
—— Poetical Works. Ed. B. B. Shah, Calcutta, 1907.
Parker, Henry Meredith. The Draught of Immortality, and Other Poems. With Crowell, a Dramatic Sketch. 1827.
—— Bole Ponjis. Containing the Tale of the Buccaneer, A Bottle of Red Ink, and Other Ingredients. 2 vols. 1851.
Pickersgill, Mrs. Tales of the Harem. 1827. [Four stories in verse.]
Malcolm, Sir John. Miscellaneous Poems. Bombay, 1829.
Heber, Reginald. [See p. 234 above.]

Ghose, Kasi Prasad. The Shair, and Other Poems. Calcutta, 1830.
Roberts, Emma. Oriental Scenes, Dramatic Sketches and Tales, with Other Poems. Calcutta, 1830.
—— Scenes and Characteristics of Hindoostan. With Sketches of Anglo-Indian Society. 3 vols. 1835.
Hutchinson, James. The Sunyassee: an Eastern Tale, and Other Poems. Calcutta, 1838; 1847.
Norton, C. E. S., later Stirling-Maxwell. The Child of the Islands. A Poem. 1844. [For other writings see p. 302 above.]
Thomas, G. P. Poems. 1847.
Datta, Sasichandra. Miscellaneous Verses. Calcutta, 1848.
—— Stray Leaves, or Essays, Poems and Tales. Calcutta, 1864.
Davidson, C. J. S. Tara, the Suttee. An Indian Drama. 1851.
Lang, John. The Vow of Alina. A Tale in Three Cantos and Other Poems. Calcutta, 1852.
Keene, Henry George. Ex Eremo. Poems chiefly written in India. 1854.
—— Under the Rose. Poems written chiefly in India. 1868.
—— Peepul Leaves. Poems written in India. 1879.
—— Sketches in Indian Ink. By John Smith, Jnr, Colonel (Retired List). Calcutta, 1879.
—— Poems, Original and Translated. Calcutta, 1882.
Haggard, Ella. Myra, or Rose of the East. A Tale of the Afghan War, in 9 cantos. 1857.
Leslie, Mary E. Sorrows, Aspirations and Legends from India. 1858.
—— Heart Echoes from the East, or Sacred Lyrics and Sonnets. 1861.
Duplessis, P. C. T. M. Heera, or the Hindu Widow. Calcutta, 1863. [A didactic poem.]
Kelly, Charles Arthur. Delhi, and Other Poems. 1864.
Laurence, T. B. Augusta. A Tale of the Mutiny of 1857 in Three Cantos, and Other Poems. Calcutta, 1866.
'Pips' (W. H. Abbott). Lyrics and Lays. Calcutta, 1867.
Waterfield, William. Indian Ballads, and Other Poems. 1868; Allahabad, 1913.
Caldwell, R. C. The Chutney Lyrics. A Collection of Comic Pieces on Indian Subjects. Madras, 1871.
Dutt, Michael Madhu Sudan. Is this called Civilisation? A Farce. Calcutta, 1871.
Dalta, Harachandra. Lotus Leaves, or Poems, chiefly on Ancient Indian Subjects. Calcutta, 1871.
Dey, Lal Behari. Govinda Samanta, or the History of a Bengal Raiyat. 2 vols. 1874.

Tagore, Sir Saurindramohan. English Verses set to Hindu Music in Honour of His Royal Highness the Prince of Wales. Calcutta, 1875.

—— A Vision of Sumeru, and Other Poems. Calcutta, 1878. [With S. C. Dutt.]

Yeldham, W. ('Aliph Cheem'). Lays of Ind. Comical, Satirical and Descriptive Poems illustrative of English Life in India. 1875; Calcutta, 1879 (6th edn); 1911 (12th edn).

—— Basil Ormond and Christabel's Love. 1879.

Dutt, Torulata. A Sheaf gleaned in French Fields. Calcutta, 1876; 1880 (with memoir by G. C. Dutt).

—— Ancient Ballads and Legends of Hindustan. With an Introductory Memoir by E. W. Gosse. 1882.

The Log. An Historical Poem. By the Author of 'Ancient Log-Rhythms.' Dinapore, 1876. [Containing a full account of the trip to Calcutta and Bankipur, during the Prince of Wales's visit to India.]

Malabari, Bahramji. The Indian Muse in English Garb. Bombay, 1876.

Cantopher, W. E. The Anglo-Indian Lyre, or the Asian Mystery and Other Poems. Calcutta, 1878.

Arnold, Sir Edwin. [See p. 328 above.]

Megrath, Mrs E. R. Maid of Cashmere. Calcutta, 1885. [Drama.]

Dutt, Govind Chandra. Cherry Blossoms. 1887.

Bignold, T. F. Leviora, or Rhymes of a Successful Competitor. Calcutta, 1888.

Garrick, H. B. W. India. A Descriptive Poem. 1889.

Lyall, Sir A. C. Verses written in India. 1889. [See also p. 346 above.]

Kipling, Rudyard. [See p. 527 above.]

Gracey, H. K. Rhyming Legends of Ind. Calcutta, 1892.

Rogers, A. The Rani of Jhansi, or the Widowed Queen. A Play. With an Introduction by Sir Edwin Arnold. Westminster, 1895.

C. FICTION

Sherwood, Mary Martha, née Butt. Stories Explanatory of the Church Catechism. Wellington, 1822 (9th edn). [1st edn c. 1817.]

—— Little Henry and his Bearer. 1832. [Also other Indian stories, see p. 416 above.]

Hockley, William Browne. [See p. 399 above.]

Life in India, or the English at Calcutta. 3 vols. 1828.

Taylor, Philip Meadows. [See p. 509 above.]

Hofland, Barbara, née Hoole. The Captives in India. A Tale; and A Widow and a Will. 3 vols. 1834. [For other writings see p. 400 above.]

Roberts, Emma. [See under Poetry above.]

Jerringhain, or the Inconstant Man. Calcutta, 1836.

Daniel, William. Eastern Legendary Tales and Oriental Romances. 1838.

Quin, M. Nourmahal. An Oriental Romance. 3 vols. 1838.

Hartlay, Mrs James. Indian Life. A Tale of the Carnatic. 3 vols. 1840.

Kaye, Sir John William, Peregrine Pultuney, or Life in India. 3 vols. 1844 (anon.).

—— Long Engagements. A Tale of the Affghan Rebellion. 1846 (anon.). [See also p. 907 above.]

'Punjabee' (William Delafield Arnold). Oakfield, or Fellowship in the East. 2 vols. 1853.

Lang, John. Too Clever by Half, or the Harroways. 1853.

—— The Wetherbys, Father and Son. 1853.

—— Will he marry her? 1858.

—— The Ex-Wife. 1859.

—— My Friend's Wife, or York, you're wanted. 1859.

—— Wanderings in India, and Other Sketches of Life in Hindostan. 1859. [Lang also wrote several other novels.]

Dalton, W. The White Elephant. 1860.

—— Lost in Ceylon. 1861.

Prichard, Iltudus Thomas. How to manage it. A Novel. 3 vols. 1864.

—— Chronicles of Budgepore, or Sketches of Life in Upper India. 2 vols. 1870–80.

Harvey, G. On the March. A Tale of the Deccan. Madras, 1867.

Kirby, Charles F. The Adventures of an Arcot Rupee. 3 vols. 1867. [A novel dealing with the Madras Mutiny of 1806.]

Grant, James. First Love and Last Love. A Tale of the Indian Mutiny. 3 vols. 1868.

Marryat, Florence (later Church). 'Gup.' Sketches of Anglo-Indian Life and Character. 1868. [Rptd from Temple Bar.]

Chesney, Sir George Tomkyns. The Battle of Dorking, or Reminiscences of a Volunteer. Edinburgh, 1871. [First pbd in Blackwood's Mag. 1871.]

—— The Dilemma. 3 vols. Edinburgh, 1876.

—— The New Ordeal. Edinburgh, 1879.

—— A Private Secretary. 3 vols. Edinburgh, 1881.

—— The Lesters, or a Capitalist's Labour. 3 vols. 1893.

Cunningham, Sir Harry Stewart. Chronicles of Dustypore. A Tale of Modern Anglo-Indian Society. 2 vols. 1875.

Jarrett, T. The Tale of Nala. Cambridge, 1875.

Cadell, Jessie Ellen. Ida Craven. 2 vols. 1876.

—— Worthy. A Study of Friendship. 1895.

Raj Laksmi Debi. The Hindu Wife, or the Enchanted Fruit. Calcutta, 1876.

Allardyce, Alexander. The City of Sunshine. 3 vols. Edinburgh, 1877.

Sterndale, Robert Armitage. The Afghan Knife. 3 vols. 1879.

—— Denizens of the Jungles. A Series of Sketches in Pen and Pencil. Calcutta, 1881.

—— Seonee. A Tale of Indian Adventure. Calcutta, 1887.

Aberigh-Mackay, George Robert. Twenty-one Days in India: being the Tour of Sir Ali Baba. 1880. [Rptd from Vanity Fair.]

Steel, Flora Annie and Temple, Sir Richard C. Wide-awake Stories. A Collection of Tales told by Little Children in the Punjab and Kashmir. Bombay, 1884.

Cave-Brown, J. Incidents of Indian Life. 1886.

Curwen, Henry. Zit and Xoe: their Early Experience. Edinburgh, 1886. [First pbd in Blackwood's Mag.]

—— Lady Bluebeard. 2 vols. Edinburgh, 1888.

—— Dr Hermione. Edinburgh, 1889.

Maclean, J. N. A. The Ranee. A Legend of the Indian Mutiny. 1887.

A Burmese Maid. 1888. [A tale founded on episodes in Burmese history.]

Glasgow, Geraldine. Black and White. An Indian Story. Lucknow, 1889.

Calthrop, Mrs H. Burmese Tales and Sketches. Calcutta, 1895.

Chakrabarti, Khetrapal. Saralā and Hinganā. Calcutta, 1895.

Fanthorne, J. F. Mariam. A Story of the Indian Mutiny of 1857. Benares, 1896.

Macdonald, J. M. The Baba Log. A Tale of Child Life in India. 1896.

Sherer, J. W. A Princess of Islam. 1897.

Dutt, Romes Chandra. The Lake of Palms. A Story of Indian Domestic Life. 1902.

—— The Slave Girl of Agra: an Indian Historical Romance. 1909.

D. TRANSLATIONS

Dow, Alexander. The History of Hindustan, from the Earliest Time to the Death of Akbar. Translated from the Persian of Muhammud Casim Ferishtah. 3 vols. 1768–72. [Vol. III from Akbar to Aurungzeb.]

White, Joseph. Institutes Political and Military, written originally in the Mogul Language by the Great Timour, improperly called Tamerlane. First translated into Persian by Abu Taulib Alhusseini, and thence into English, with Marginal Notes, by Major Davy. The Whole Work published with a Preface, Indexes and Notes, by J. White. Oxford, 1783.

Wilkins, Sir Charles. The Hĕĕtōpădēs of Vĕĕshnŏŏ Sărmā, in a Series of Connected Fables. Translated from the Sanskreet, with Notes. Bath, 1787.

Jones, Sir William. Hymn to Comdeo. 1787.

—— Sacontala, or the Fatal Ring. An Indian Drama translated from the Original Sanskrit and Pracrit. Calcutta, 1789; rptd 1902.

—— Hymn to Nurayena. 1794.

—— Institutes of Manu. Calcutta, 1794; ed. P. Percival, Calcutta, 1888.

—— The Works of Sir William Jones. Ed. A. M. Jones (with a 'Discourse on the Life and Writings of Sir W. Jones' by Lord Teignmouth), 6 vols. 1799; 3 vols. 1807 (with life by Lord Teignmouth.)

Gladwin, Francis. The Memoirs of Khojeh Abdulkurreem translated from the Persian. Calcutta, 1788.

Ghulām Husain Khān. A Translation of the Sëir Mutagharin, or View of Modern Times. Being an History of India from the Year 1118 to 1195 [i.e. A.D. 1781–2]. Calcutta, 1799; rptd 4 vols. Calcutta, [1902–3]. [Tr. and ed. by Hāji Mustafā, called Nota-Manus.]

Wilson, Horace Hayman. The Meghaduta of Kalidasa, translated into English Verse, with Notes and Illustrations. Calcutta, 1813.

—— Uttara Ramacharita, translated into English. 1826.

—— Selected Specimens of the Theatre of the Hindus, translated from the Original Sanskrit. 3 vols. Calcutta, 1827; 1835.

—— Vishnu Purana, translated into English. 1840.

—— Rig-Veda Samhita. 4 vols. 1850.

—— Puranas. Calcutta, 1897.

—— The Mrichchakatika of Sudraka in English Translation. 1901.

—— Bisakhadatta's Mudra-Rakshasha. Calcutta, 1901.

—— Malati and Madhava, or the Stolen Marriage, in English Translation. Calcutta, 1901.

Briggs, John. History of the Rise of the Mahomedan Power in India till the Year 1612. Translated from the Persian of Kaslem Ferishta. 4 vols. 1829; Calcutta, 1908.

Price, David. Jahangueir. 1829.

Babington, Benjamin Guy. The Vedàla Cadai. Being the Tamul Version of a Collection of Ancient Tales in the Sanscrit Language entitled the Vetàla Panchavinsati. 1831. [With English trn.]

Atkinson, James. The Shah-Namah. 1832. [Prose and verse.]

—— Laili and Majnu. 1832.

Morton, W. A Collection of Proverbs, Bengali and Sanskrit, with the English Translation and Application in English. Calcutta, 1832.

Raya Raja Ramamohana. Veds. 1832 (2nd edn).

Turnour, George. The Maháwanso in Roman Characters, with the Translation subjoined and an Introductory Essay on Páli Buddhistical Literature. Vol. I (all pbd), Ceylon, 1837. [Verse.]

Roeer, H. H. E. Vedanta-Sara, or the Essence of the Vedanta. An Introduction into the Vedanta Philosophy by S. Parivrajakacharya. Translated from the Sanscrit. Calcutta, 1845.

—— Uttara Naisadha Charita of Sriharsha. Calcutta, 1855. [Ed. by Roeer.]

Johnson, Francis. Hitopadesá. The Sanskrit Text, with a Grammatical Analysis alphabetically arranged. 1847. [Sanskrit and English.]

Dutt, Michael Madhu Sudan. The Captive Ladie. An Indian Tale. Madras, 1849.

—— Ratnavali. A Drama in Four Acts from the Bengali. Calcutta, 1858.

—— Sarmista in English. Calcutta, 1859.

Cowell, Edward Byles. Kalidas' Vikramorvasi. Hertford, 1851. [In English Prose.]

—— Kausitaki Brahmana Upanishad. Calcutta, 1861. [Tr. and ed. by Cowell.]

—— The Kusmanjali. 1864. [Tr. and ed. by Cowell.]

Ballantyne, James Robert. The Sankhya Aphorisms of Kapila. 1852.

—— Aphorisms of Sandilya, with Swapnesvara's Commentary. Calcutta, 1861. [Ed. by Ballantyne.]

Sa'di. The Rose Garden of Sadee. Calcutta, 1854.

—— The First Chapter of the Gulistan. Translated by W. A. Montrion. Calcutta, 1856.

—— The Gulistan of Shaik Saday. A Complete Analysis of the Entire Persian Text. By Major R. P. Anderson. Calcutta, 1861.

—— A Few Flowers from the Garden of Sheikh Saadi Shirazi. Being Translation into English Verse of Portions of the Bostan. By Major W. C. Mackinnon. 1878.

—— The Bostan. Translated for the First Time into Prose, with Explanatory Notes and Index, by Capt. A. W. Clarke. 1879.

—— With Sa'di in the Garden, or the Book of Love. Being the 'Ishk' or 3rd Chapter of the Bostan. By Sir E. Arnold. 1888 (2nd edn).

—— The Bostan of Shaikh Sa'di. Translated into English by Ziauddin Gulam Moheiddin Munshi. Revised by R. Davies. Bombay, 1889.

Barker, W. B. The Baitál Páchísí, or Twenty-five Tales of a Demon. A New Edition of the Hindi Text with a Literal Interlinear Translation and Notes. 1855.

Monier-Williams, Sir Monier. Sakuntalá: a Sanskrit Drama. 1855.

—— Indian Epic Poetry. 1863.

Arnold, Sir Edwin. The Book of Good Counsels; from the Sanskrit of the Hitopodesa. 1861.

—— The Indian Song of Songs. From the Sanskrit of the Gita-Govinda of Jayadev. 1875.

—— The Light of Asia, or the Great Renunciation (Mahâbhinshkramana). Being the Life and Teaching of Gautama, Prince of India and Founder of Buddhism, as told in Verse by an Indian Buddhist. 1879.

—— Indian Poetry. Containing a New Edition of the Indian Song of Songs, Two Books from the Mahabharata, and Other Oriental Poems. 1881.

—— Pearls of the Faith, or Islam's Rosary. Being the Ninety-nine Beautiful Names of Allah; with Comments in Verse from Various Oriental Sources. 1882. [Comments as made by an Indian Mussalman.]

—— Indian Idylls; from the Sanskrit of the Mahabharata. 1883.

—— The Song Celestial, or Bhagabad Gita. 1885. [From the Mahabharata.]

—— The Secret of Death. 1884. [From the Sanskrit, with some collected poems.]

—— With Sa'di in the Garden. 1888.

—— Chaurapanchâsika. 1896. [Tr. by Arnold.]

Hall, Fitz-Edward. The Súnkhya-Pravachana-Bháshya: Aphorisms of the Sánkhya Philosophy, with a Commentary. Calcutta, 1862.

—— Dasa-Rupa. Hindu Canons of Dramaturgy. Calcutta, 1865.

Raverty, H. G. Selections from the Poetry of the Afghāns literally translated. 1862.

Jacomb, F. Indian Fables, from the Sanscrit of the Hitopadesa. Translated and illustrated. [1863.]

Kern, J. H. C. The Brhat-samhitā, or Complete System of Natural Astrology. Translated from Sanskrit into English. Calcutta, 1865; 's-Gravenhage, 1913.

Griffith, Ralph T. H. Idylls from the Sanskrit. 1866.

—— Scenes from the Ramayana. 1868.

—— The Ramayan of Valmiki, translated into English Verse. 5 vols. 1870–4.

—— The Birth of the War-God. 1879 (2nd edn). [In English verse, from the Kumarsambhava of Kalidas.]

—— Yusuf and Zulaikha. 1882. [Tr. from Jāmi.]

—— The Hymns of the Samavada. Benares, 1893.

—— The Hymns of the Atharva-Veda. Benares, 1895.

—— The Hymns of the Rig-Veda. Benares, 1896.

—— The Hymns of the Yajurveda. Benares, 1899.

Hollings, W. The Prem Sagur. Translated into English. Calcutta, 1867. [By Chaturbhuja Misra.]

Carr, M. W. A Collection of Telegu Proverbs. 1868. [English.]

Gover, C. E. The Folk-Songs of Southern India. Madras, 1871.

Tawney, C. H. Uttara Ramacharita of Bhavabhuti, translated into English. 1871.

—— The Málavikágnimitra. A Sanscrit Play by Kālidāsa. Translated into English Prose. 1875.

—— Two Centuries of Bhartrihari. Translated into English Verse. 1877. [Rptd from Indian Antiquary.]

—— Katha Saritsagara. Translated from the Sanskrit. 2 vols. Calcutta, 1880–4.

Boyd, Palmer. Nāgānanda of Harshadera. 1872.

Lewin, T. H. Hill Proverbs of the Inhabitants of Chittagong Tracts. Calcutta, 1873.

Foulkes, J. The Shrine of Harihara. Madras, 1876. [Tr. from the Sanskrit.]

Adi Granth. The Holy Scriptures of the Sikhs. Translated from the Original Gurumukhi, with Introductory Essays by Dr E. Trumph. 1877.

Kunte, Mādhavarāva M. The Risi. A Poem explaining the Daily Life and Manners of the Rishi, as described in the Rig-Veda-Samhita. Poona, 1877.

Grouse, F. S. The Ramayana of Tulsi Das. 2 pts, Allahabad, 1877–8; Allahabad, 1883 (rev.).

Grierson, Sir G. A. The Songs of Manik Chaud. Calcutta, 1878.

—— Curiosities of Indian Literature. Selected and translated. Bankipore, 1890.

—— Vaishnava Hymns. Selected and translated. Bankipore, 1893.

Mitra, Rajendralala. Buddha-Gaya. Calcutta, 1878.

—— Lalitavistara. Calcutta, 1881–6.

Muir, J. Oriental Studies. Calcutta, 1878. [On the Vedas.]

—— Metrical Translations from Sanskrit Writers. 1879.

Dey, Lal Behari. The Meghnād-Badha. Calcutta, 1879. [English trn as a tragedy in 5 acts.]

—— Folk-Tales of Bengal. 1883.

Dutt, J. C. Rajatarangini. By Kalhana. 3 vols. Calcutta, 1879 (3rd edn).

Rogers, T. Buddhaghosha's Parables. With Introduction by F. Max Müller. 1879. [From the Burmese.]

Telang, K. T. Bhagavadgitâ, translated into English Blank Verse, with Notes and an Introductory Essay. Bombay, 1879.

Tagore, Sir Saurindramohan. The Hindu Drama. Compiled and translated from Various Sanskrit Authorities. 2 pts, Calcutta, 1880.

—— Veni-Sanhara-Nataka, or the Binding of the Braid. A Sanskrit Drama by Bhatta-Narayama. 1880.

—— Taravali. Translated into English. Calcutta, 1881.

Jacob, G. A. The Vedantasara, by Sadanandra Jogindra. A Manual of Hindu Pantheism. 1881. [English trn with copious annotations.]

Long, James. Eastern Proverbs and Emblems illustrating Old Truths. 1881.

Lowe, —. Rajniti. Calcutta, 1881.

Bhagabad-Gita. [English trns by J. Davies, 1882; by K. T. Telang, Oxford, 1882; by Mohinimohan Chatterjee, Boston, 1887.]

Chattopadhyay, Nisikanta. The Yātrās, or the Popular Dramas of Bengal. 1882.

Roy, Pratapchandra. Mahabharata. 18 vols. Calcutta, 1883–95.

Bankimchandra Chattopādhāya.

[The following are English trns of this work:

Knight, Miriam S. The Poison Tree; with a Preface by Sir Edwin Arnold. 1884.

—— Krishna Kanta's Will. 1895.

Phillips, H. A. D. Kapālkundalā. 1885.

Mukerji, Charuchandra. Durgeshnandini. Calcutta, 1890.

Bonnerjee, R. C. The Two Rings. Calcutta, 1897.]

Swynnerton, Charles. The Adventures of the Punjab Hero, Raja Rasalu, and Other Folk-Tales of the Punjab. Calcutta, 1884.

—— Indian Nights Entertainment, or Folk-Tales from the Upper Indus. 1892.

—— Romantic Tales from the Punjab. Westminster, 1903.

Knowles, J. H. A Dictionary of Kashmiri Proverbs and Sayings. Explained and illustrated from the Folklore of the Valley. Bombay, 1885.

Gray, James. Ancient Proverbs and Maxims from Burmese Sources. 1886.

Wortham, B. H. Sátakas of Bhartrihari, translated into English from the Original Sanskrit. 1886.

Pargiter, F. E. Markandeyer Purana. 1888–1904. [English trn.]

Kingscote, Adeline G. I. Tales of the Sun, or Folklore of Southern India. 1890. [With Natēsa Sāstri.]

Thibaut, G. The Vedanta Sutras with the Commentary by Sankaracharyya, translated into English. 2 pts, Oxford, 1890–6.

Christian, J. Behar Proverbs. 1891. [English.]

Dutt, Manmathanath (Sastri). Ramayana. 2 vols. Calcutta, 1891. [English prose trn.]
—— Gleanings from Indian Classics. Vol. I. Calcutta, 1893.
—— Mahabharata. Calcutta, 1895. [Ed. and tr. into English prose.]
Jarrett, H. S. Ain-i-Akbari. 3 vols. Calcutta, 1891.
Mitra, Vihári-Lála. The Yoga-Vásishtha Mahárámáyana of Válmiki. Translated from the Original Sanskrit. 4 vols. Calcutta, 1891–9.
Upanishads. The Twelve Principal Upanishads. English Translation with Notes from the Commentaries of Shankaracharyya and the Gloss of Ananda-Giri. Bombay, 1891.
Sarvananda. The Jagaducharitra of Sarvananda. A Historical Romance from Gujrat. Vienna, 1892 (G. Buchler's Indian Studies, no. 1).
Acworth, H. A. Ballads of the Marathas, rendered into English Verse. 1894.
Dutt, Romes Chandra. Lays of Ancient India in English Verse. 1894.
—— Mahabharata: the Epic of Ancient India. 1898.
—— Great Epics of Ancient India. With Introduction by F. Max Müller. 1900.
—— Ramayana. 1900.
Anderson, J. D. A Collection of Kachari Folk-Tales and Rhymes. [Supplement to S. Endle, Kachari Grammar, Shillong, 1895.]
Rouse, W. H. D. The Jataka. 1895. [English trn.]
Gurdon, P. R. Some Assamese Proverbs. Shillong, 1896.
Sankaracharya. The Awakening to the Self. Translated from the Sanskrit by C. Johnston. New York, 1897.
—— Sankaracharya: his Life and Teachings. A Translation of Atma-bodha. By Sitanath Dutta. Soc. for Resuscitation of Indian Literature, Calcutta, 1897.
—— Atmabodha, or the Perception of Self. Translated from Sanskrit by Nandalal Dhole. Calcutta, 1900 (2nd edn).
—— Moha Mudgara, or the Mallet of Delusion. Translated from Sanskrit by Sir William Jones. Calcutta, 1900.
Arrowsmith, R. The Rig Veda. 1898.
Frere, Mary E. I. Old Deccan Days, or Hindu Fairy Legends current in Southern India. 1898.
Stein, Sir M. Aurel. Kalhana's Rājatarangini. A Chronicle of the Kings of Kasmir. Translated, with an Introduction, Commentary, and Appendices. 2 vols. 1900.
Johnstone, P. De Lacy. The Raghuvança: the Story of Raghu's Line. By Kalidasa. 1902. [Verse trn.]

E. PHILOLOGY

Jones, Sir William. Grammar of the Persian Language. 1771.
Richardson, John. A Dictionary of Persian, Arabic and English. 3 vols. 1777.
Halhed, Nathaniel Brassey. A Grammar of the Bengalee Language. Hooghly, 1778.
Gilchrist, John Borthwick. Grammar of the Hindustani Language. Calcutta, 1796.
—— Principles of Persian Grammar. 1821.
—— Hindustanee Dictionary. 3 vols. 1825.
Gladwin, Francis. Dissertations on the Rhetoric, Prosody, etc. of the Persian Language. Calcutta, 1798.
—— Persian Munshi. 2 vols. Calcutta, 1800.
—— Persian, Hindustanee and English Dictionary. 2 vols. Calcutta, 1809.
Colebrooke, Henry Thomas. A Grammar of the Sanskrit Language. Calcutta, 1805.
—— Sankha Karika. Oxford, 1837.
—— Miscellaneous Essays. 2 vols. Madras, 1872 (2nd edn).
—— Two Treatises on the Hindu Law of Inheritance. Calcutta, 1883.
[For other writings see under Sanskrit Scholars, p. 1017 above.]
Hunter, William. Hindustani-English Dictionary. 2 vols. Calcutta, 1808.
Wilkins, Sir Charles. A Grammar of the Sanskrita Language. 1808.
—— Glossary of Oriental Terms. 1830.
[See also p. 1019 above.]
Carey, William. A Dictionary of the Mahratta Language. Serampore, 1810.
—— A Grammar of the Punjabee Language. Serampore, 1812.
—— A Grammar of the Telinga Language. Serampore, 1814.
—— A Dictionary of the Bengalee Language. Vol. I, Serampore, 1815; 2 vols. Serampore, 1825 (with corrections and addns).
—— A Grammar of the Bengali Language. Serampore, 1815 (3rd edn).
[For other writings see p. 1017 above.]
Raya Raja Ramamohana. Bengalee Grammar in the English Language. Calcutta, 1826.
Kennedy, Vans. Researches into the Origin and Affinity of the Principal Languages of Asia and Europe. 1828.
—— On the Vedanta System. 1833. [From Trans. Royal Asiatic Soc.]
Haughton, Sir Graves Champney. Bengali-Sanskrit Dictionary. 2 vols. 1833.
—— A Short Enquiry into the Nature of Languages. 1834.
—— Bengali and English Glossary. 1835.
Trevelyan, Sir Charles Edward, Prinsep, James et al. The Application of the Roman Alphabet to all the Oriental Languages. Serampore, 1834.

Shakespear, John. Grammar of the Hindustanee Language. 1846.

Thompson, Joseph T. A Dictionary of Hindee and English, compiled from Approved Authorities. 1846.

Wilson, Horace Hayman. Introduction to the Grammar of the Sanskrit Language. 1847 (2nd edn).

Yates, William. Introduction to the Bengálí Language. 2 vols. Calcutta, 1847.

—— A Bengali Grammar. Calcutta, 1849.

Leech, Richard. Epitome of the Grammars of the Brahuiky, Balochky and Panjabi Languages. Calcutta, 1849. [Includes a Scinde vocabulary by J. B. Eastwick.]

Mendies, J. English-Bengali Dictionary. 1851.

Moleswood, J. T. Marathee-English Dictionary. 1851.

Fallon, S. W. English-Urdu Law and Commercial Dictionary. Calcutta, 1852.

—— Hindustani-English Dictionary. 1879.

—— A Dictionary of Hindustani Proverbs. Benares, 1886.

Robertson, E. P. English-Guzrati Dictionary. Bombay, 1854.

Raverty, H. G. A Dictionary of the Puk'hto, Pushto, or Language of the Afghāns; with Remarks on the Originality of the Language and its Affinity to the Semitic Tongues. 1860.

Robinson, J. Dictionary of Law Terms in Bengali. Calcutta, 1860.

Smyth, W. C. Hindustani-English Dictionary. 1860.

Anderson, R. Patrick. The Gulistan. 1861. [Analysis of the text.]

Percival, P. Anglo-Telegu Dictionary. Madras, 1864.

Beames, John. Outlines of Indian Philology. Calcutta, 1867; 1868.

—— A Comparative Grammar of the Modern Aryan Languages of India. 1872–9.

Elliot, Sir H. M. Glossary of Indian Terms. Roorkee, 1868.

Hunter, Sir W. W. Comparative Dictionary of the Languages of India and Asia. 1868.

Marshman, J. C. Bengali-English Dictionary. Serampore, 1869.

Skrefsrund, L. O. A Grammar of the Santhal Language. Benares, 1873.

Mitra, Rajendralala. A Scheme for the Rendering of European Scientific Terms into the Vernaculars of India. Calcutta, 1877.

Cust, R. N. Modern Languages of the East Indies. 1878.

Hoernle, A. F. R. A Comparative Grammar of the Gaudian Languages, with Special Reference to the Eastern Hindi. 1880.

—— A Comparative Dictionary of the Bihārí Language. 1885. [With Sir G. A. Grierson.]

Howell, M. S. A Grammar of the Classical Arabic Language. 7 vols. Allahabad, 1880–1911.

Lyall, C. J. A Sketch of the Hindustani Language. Edinburgh, 1880.

Grierson, Sir G. A. A Handbook to the Kaithi Character. Calcutta, 1881; Calcutta, 1899 (rev.).

—— The Modern Vernacular Literature of Hindustan. Calcutta, 1889.

—— On the Phonology of the Indo-Aryan Vernaculars. Leipzig, 1895–6.

—— Assamese Literature. Bombay, 1896.

—— On the Early Study of Indian Vernaculars in Europe. Calcutta, 1896.

—— Specimen Translations [of the Parable of the Prodigal Son] in Various Indian Languages. Calcutta, 1897. [Collected and ed. by Grierson.]

—— Essays on Kaçmīrī Grammar. Calcutta, 1899; 1899.

—— On the Languages spoken beyond the North-Western Frontier of India. Hertford, 1900.

[For other writings see under Translations, p. 1072 above.]

Underwood, E. Indian English and Indian Character. Calcutta, 1885.

Yule, Sir Henry. Hobson-Jobson: Being a Glossary of Anglo-Indian Colloquial Words and Phrases, and of Kindred Terms; Etymological, Historical, Geographical, and Discursive. 1886. [With A. C. Burnell.]

Bhandarkar, R. G. Critical, Comparative and Historical Method of Inquiry as applied to Sanskrit Scholarship and Philology and Indian Archaeology. Bombay, 1888.

Wright, Arnold. Baboo English as 'tis writ. Being Curiosities of Indian Journalism. 1891.

Martin, W. B. English-Santali Vocabulary. Benares, 1898.

F. HISTORY, BIOGRAPHY AND POLITICS

(a) 1750–1850

Holwell, John Zephaniah. A Genuine Narrative of the Deplorable Deaths of the English Gentlemen and Others who were suffocated in the Black Hole. 1758; rptd Calcutta, 1884, 1899.

—— India Tracts. 1758.

—— Interesting Historical Events relative to the Province of Bengal and the Empire of Indostan. 2 pts, 1765–7.

Orme, Robert. A History of the Military Transactions of the British Nation in Indostan from the Year 1745. 2 vols. 1763–78 (vol. II in 2 pts); rptd Madras, 1861; Calcutta, 1905.

Orme, Robert. Historical Fragments of the Mogul Empire, of the Morattoes, and of the English Concerns in Indostan from 1659. 1782.

Bolts, William. Considerations on Indian Affairs, particularly respecting the Present State of Bengal. 3 vols. 1772–5.

Verelst, Harry. View of the Rise, Progress and Present State of the English Government in Bengal. 1772.

Stevens, R. New and Complete Guide to the East India Trade. 1775.

G[ough], R[ichard]. A Comparative View of the Antient Monuments of India. 1785.

Rennell, James. Memoir of a Map of Hindoostan, or the Mogul's Empire. 1783.

Richardson, John. Life of Hyder Ali. 1786.

Tytler, Alexander Fraser (Lord Woodhouselee). Considerations of the Present Political State of India. 1786.

Hamilton, Charles. An Historical Relation of the Origin, Progress and Final Dissolution of the Government of the Rohilla Afghans. 1787.

Mackenzie, R. Sketch of the War with Tipoo Sultan. 4 vols. Calcutta, 1793.

Maurice, Thomas. History of Hindustan. 1795.

—— Indian Antiquities. 7 vols. 1800.

Francklin, William. The Reign of Shah Alum. 1798.

—— Ancient Palibothra. 2 vols. 1815.

Beatson, Alexander. View of the Origin and Conduct of the War with Tippoo and the Siege of Seringapatam. 1800.

Tennant, William. Thoughts on the Effects of the British Government on the State of India. Edinburgh, 1807.

Wilks, Mark. Historical Sketches of the South of India, in an Attempt to trace the History of Mysoor. 3 vols. 1810–7.

Malcolm, Sir John. [See p. 886 above.]

Price, David. A Chronological Retrospect of Mahommedan History. 4 vols. 1811–21.

Elphinstone, Mountstuart. [See p. 906 above.]

Graham, G. F. G. Syed Ahmed Khan. 1815.

Raffles, Sir Thomas Stamford. History of Java. 2 vols. 1817.

Ward, William. A View of the History, Literature, and Religion of the Hindoos. 4 vols. 1817–20.

Prinsep, Henry Thoby. History of the Transactions in India during the Administration of the Marquis of Hastings. 2 vols. 1825.

—— Origin of the Sikh Power in the Punjab. Calcutta, 1834.

—— Afghan Antiquities. 1844.

Lake, E. Sieges of the Madras Army in 1817 to 1819. 2 vols. 1825.

Tucker, Henry St George. A Review of the Financial Situation of the East-India Company in 1824. 1825.

Tucker, Henry St George. Memorials of Indian Government. Ed. Sir J. W. Kaye, 1853.

Grant-Duff, James. A History of the Mahrattas. 3 vols. 1826; rptd 3 vols. Calcutta, 1912.

Fenwick, C. A. The Colonization of Hindustan. Calcutta, 1828.

Rickards, R. The Condition of India. 4 vols. 1829.

Tod, James. Annals and Antiquities of Rajast'han, or the Central and Western Rajpoot States of India. Calcutta, 1829; 2 vols. 1829–32; rptd 2 vols. 1914.

Venkata Rāmasvāmi, Kāvali. Biographical Sketches of Dekkan Poets. Being Memoirs of Several Bards, both Ancient and Modern, who have flourished in the Indian Peninsula. Compiled from Authentic Documents. Calcutta, 1829.

Galloway, Sir Archibald. Observations on the Law and Constitution and Present Government of India. 1832 (2nd edn, with addns).

Thornton, Edward. A Summary of the History of the East India Company, from the Grant of their First Charter by Queen Elizabeth to the Present Period. 1833.

—— India: its State and Prospects. 1835.

—— Illustrations of the History and Practices of the Thugs. 1837 (anon.).

—— The History of the British Empire in India. 6 vols. 1841–5.

—— A Gazetteer of the Territories under the Government of the East India Company, and of the Native States on the Continent of India. 4 vols. 1854; 1886 (rev. Sir R. Lethbridge and A. N. Wollaston).

Ram Raj. Essay on the Architecture of the Hindus. 1834. [48 plates.]

Martin, R. M. British Colonies. 5 vols. 1835.

—— Eastern India. 3 vols. 1838.

—— British India: its Progress and Present State. 1862.

Marshman, John Clark. [See p. 906 above.]

Auber, P. British Power in India. 2 vols. 1837.

—— Analysis of the Constitution of the East India Company. 2 vols. 1837.

Shore, Sir John. Notes on Indian Affairs. 2 vols. 1837.

Spry, Henry Harpur. Modern India. 2 vols. 1837.

Havelock, Sir Henry. Narrative of the War in Afghanistan, in 1838, 39. 2 vols. 1840.

Tuckett, H. The Indian Revenue System as it is. A Letter addressed to the Manchester Chamber of Commerce. 1840.

Sykes, William Henry. Notes on the State of Ancient India. 1841.

Wilson, Horace Hayman. Antiquities of Afghanistan. 1841.

—— History of British India, 1805 to 1835. 3 vols. 1845–8.

Harlan, J. India and Afghanistan. 1842.

Buist, George. Memories of Sir Alexander Burnes. 1843.

Eyre, Sir Vincent. The Military Operations at Cabul, which ended in the Retreat and Destruction of the British Army, January 1842. With a Journal of Imprisonment in Affghanistan. 1843.

Eden, Emily. Portraits of the Princes and People of India. 1844. [For other writings see p. 393 above.]

Fontanier, V. Narrative of a Mission to India. 1844.

Kaye, Sir J. W [See p. 907 above.]

Fergusson, James. Rock-cut Temples of India. 1845.

—— Tree and Serpent Worship, or Illustrations of Mythology and Art in India in the First and Fourth Centuries. From the Sculptures of the Buddhist Topes at Sanchi and Amravati. 1868; 1873 (rev. and largely rewritten).

McGregor, W. L. The History of the Sikhs; containing the Lives of the Gooroos. 2 vols. 1846.

Outram, Sir James. The Conquest of Scinde. A Commentary. 1846.

Smyth, G. C. History of the Reigning Family of Lahore. Calcutta, 1847.

Westall, W. The Hindoos. 1847.

Cunningham, Joseph Davey. History of the Sikhs. 1849.

Hervey, A. Ten Years in India, or the Life of a Young Officer. 3 vols. 1850.

Laurie, W. A. Memoir of Dr J. Burnes. 1850.

Laurie, W. F. B. Orissa, the Garden of Superstition and Idolatry; including an Account of the British Connexion with the Temple of Jagannāth. 1850.

—— Sketches of some Distinguished Anglo-Indians. With an Account of Anglo-Indian Periodical Literature. 1875; 2 sers. 1887–8 (enlarged).

—— Our Burmese Wars and Relations with Burma. Being an Abstract of Military and Political Operations, 1824–25–26, and 1852–53. 1880.

—— Ashé Pyee, the Superior Country, or the Great Attractions of Burma to British Enterprise and Commerce. 1882.

(b) 1851–1914

Napier, Sir William F. P. History of Sir Charles Napier's Administration of Scinde, and Campaign in the Cutchee Hills. 1851.

—— Defects, Civil and Military, of the Indian Government. By Sir Charles Napier. 1853. [Ed. by Sir W. Napier, with supplementary ch.] [For other writings see p. 900 above.]

Thackwell, E. J. Narrative of the Second Seikh War, in 1848–49. 1851.

Hough, William. Political and Military Events in British India from the Years 1756 to 1849. 2 vols. 1853.

Anderson, Philip. The English in Western India. Bombay, 1854; 1856 (rev.). [From the earliest times to the beginning of the 18th century.]

Corner, Julia. India, Pictorial, Descriptive and Historical. From the Earliest Times to the Present. 1854. [Partly by another hand.]

Wilson, John. History of the Suppression of Infanticide in Western India. Bombay, 1855.

—— India Three Thousand Years Ago. Bombay, 1858.

—— Indian Caste. 2 vols. 1877.

Allen, David O. India, Ancient and Modern. Boston, 1856 (2nd edn).

Major, R. H. India in the 15th Century. 1857.

Urquhart, David. The Rebellion in India. The Wondrous Tale of the Greased Cartridges. 1857.

—— The Srāddha: the Keystone of the Brahminical, Buddhistic, and Arian Religions, as illustrative of the Dogma and Duty of Adoption among the Princes and People of India. 1857 (anon.; bis).

Norton, J. B. Topics for Indian Statesmen. 1858.

Orr, A. P. The English Captives in Oudh. An Episode in the History of the Mutinies of 1857–58. Edited by M. Wylie. Calcutta, 1858.

Dosabhai, Framji. The Parsees: their History, Manners, Customs and Religion. 1858.

Duff, A. The Indian Rebellion. 1858.

Ludlow, J. M. British India and its History. 2 vols. 1858.

Malleson, G. B. [See p. 932 above.]

Muir, Sir W. [See p. 933 above.]

Prinsep, James. Essays on Indian Antiquities, Historic, Numismatic, and Palaeographic. Edited, with Notes and Additional Matter, by Edward Thomas. 2 vols. 1858.

Briggs, H. G. The Nizam. 2 vols. 1861.

Wheeler, James Talboys. Madras in the Olden Time. Being a History of the Presidency compiled from Official Records. 3 vols. Madras, 1861–2.

—— The History of India from the Earliest Ages. 4 vols. 1867–81.

—— History of India under Mussulman Rule. 3 vols. 1867–76.

—— Early Records of British India. A History of the English Settlements in India. Calcutta, 1878.

—— A Short History of India, and of the Frontier States of Afghanistan, Nipal and Burma. 1880.

Wheeler, James Talboys. Tales from Indian History. Being the Annals of India retold in Narratives. 1881.

—— India under British Rule, from the Foundation of the East India Company. 1886.

Arnold, Sir Edwin. History of the Administration of British India under the Late Marquis of Dalhousie. 2 vols. 1862–4.

Bellew, Henry Walter. Journal of a Political Mission to Afghanistan. 1862.

Wallace, Robert. The Guicowar, and his Relations with the British Government. Bombay, 1863.

Fraser, Hastings. Our Faithful Ally, the Nizam. Being an Historical Sketch of Events, showing the Value of the Nizam's Alliance to the British Government in India, and his Services during the Mutinies. 1865.

Keene, H. G. The Moghal Empire, from the Death of Aurangazeb to the Overthrow of the Mahratta Power. 1866.

—— Indian Administration. 1867.

—— The Turks in India. 1879.

—— Fifty-Seven. Some Account of the Administration of Indian Districts during the Revolt of the Bengal Army. 1883.

—— A Sketch of the History of Hindustan from the First Muslim Conquest to the Fall of the Moghal Empire. 1885.

—— Madhava Rao Sindhia. 1892. (Rulers of India ser.)

—— History of India. 2 vols. 1893.

—— A Servant of John Company. Recollections of an Indian Official. 1897.

—— The Great Anarchy. Calcutta, 1901. [First pbd in Calcutta Rev.; the book was withdrawn, and re-issued as Hindustan under Free Lances, 1907.]

—— Here and There. Memories, Indian and Other. 1906.

Rennie, S. Bhootan and the Story of the Dooar War. 1866.

Trotter, L. J. History of the British Empire in India, 1844 to 1862. 2 vols. 1866.

—— History of India under Queen Victoria, from 1836 to 1880. 2 vols. 1886.

Elliot, Sir H. M. The History of India as told by its Own Historians. 8 vols. 1867–77.

Lees, W. N. Land and Labour of India. 1867.

Wood, Sir Charles. The Administration of Indian Affairs from 1859 to 1866. Edited by A. West. 1867.

Bell, E. Indian Policy. 1868.

Chesney, Sir G. T. Indian Polity. 1868.

Hunter, Sir W. W. [See p. 933 above.]

Manning, Mrs. Ancient and Mediaeval India. 2 vols. 1869.

Prichard, I. T. Administration of India from 1859 to 1868. 2 vols. 1869.

Leonowens, Anna Harriette. The English Governors at the Siamese Court. Cambridge, 1870.

—— The Romance of the Harem. 1873.

Martin, F. Contemporary Biography. 1870.

Chesson, F. W. The Princes of India: their Rights and Duties. 1872.

Higginbotham, J. J. Biographies of Eminent Indian Characters. Madras, 1874.

Mitra, Rajendralala. The Antiquities of Orissa. 2 vols. Calcutta, 1875.

—— The Parsis of Bombay. 1880.

—— Indo-Aryans. 2 vols. Calcutta, 1881.

Beveridge, H. Bakarganja: its History and Statistics. 1876.

—— The Trial of Maharaja Nanda Kumar. Calcutta, 1886.

Bromehead, W. C. Lives of the Bishops of Calcutta. Calcutta, 1876.

Dutt, Romes Chandra. The Literature of Bengal. Calcutta, 1877.

—— A History of Civilisation in Ancient India. 3 vols. 1889–90.

—— Economic History of British India. 1902.

—— India in the Victorian Age: Economic History of the People. 1904.

—— Later Hindu Civilisation (B.C. 320 to A.D. 800). 1906.

Ghose, Nagendra Nath ('N. N.'). Indian Views of England. The Effects of Observation of England upon Indian Ideas and Institutions. Calcutta, 1877.

—— Kristo Das Pal. A Study. Calcutta, 1887.

—— Memoirs of Maharaja Nubkissen Bahadur. Calcutta, 1901.

McCrindle, J. W. Indika. Ancient India as described by Megasthenes and Arrian. 1877.

—— The Commerce and Navigation of the Eruthraean Sea. 1879.

—— Ancient India as described by Ptolemy. Calcutta, 1885.

—— Ancient India as described by Ktesias, the Knidian. 1892.

—— The Invasion of India by Alexander the Great, as described by Arrian, Q. Curtius, Diodorus, Plutarch and Justin. 1893.

—— Ancient India as described in Classical Literature. Being a Collection of Greek and Latin texts translated and copiously annotated. 1901.

Adams, William Henry Davenport. Episodes of Anglo-Indian History. A Series of Chapters from the Annals of British India. [1879.]

Haughton, John Colpoys. Char-ee-Kar, and Service there with the 4th Goorkha Regiment in 1841. An Episode of the First Afghan War. 1879.

Leonard, G. S. A History of the Brahmo-Somaj. Calcutta, 1879.

Macdonald, K. S. Raja Ram Mohun Roy. Calcutta, 1879.

—— The Brahmanas of the Vedas. 1898.

Macgregor, A. G. Chiefs of Central India. Calcutta, 1879.

Morrison, Sir T. Imperial Rule in India. 1879.

Temple, Sir Richard. India in 1880. 1880.

—— Men and Events of my Time in India. 1882.

—— Oriental Experiences. 1883.

—— The Legends of the Punjab. 3 vols. 1884–5.

—— The Story of my Life. 2 vols. 1891.

—— A Bird's Eye View of Picturesque India. 1898.

Ghose, Ram Chandra. The Indo-Aryans: their History, Creed and Practice. Calcutta, 1881.

—— History of Hindu Civilization as illustrated in the Vedas and their Appendages. Calcutta, 1889.

—— A Synopsis of English Literature. Calcutta, 1896.

Busteed, H. E. Echoes from Old Calcutta. Calcutta, 1882.

Holmes, T. R. E. Indian Mutinies. 1885 (2nd edn).

Lewin, T. H. A Fly on the Wheel, or How I helped to govern India. 1885.

Arbuthnot, F. F. Persian Portraits. 1887.

—— Arabic Authors. 1890.

Dhanakoti Raju, W. E. Queen Empress Victoria: her Life and Times. Madras, 1887.

Strachey, Sir John. India. 1888; 1894 (rev.). [A general survey.]

Blackwood, Hariot G. (Marchioness of Dufferin and Ava). Our Viceregal Life in India. Selections from my Journal, 1884–1888. 2 vols. 1889.

De, Amritalal. The Student's History of Rajputana. Calcutta, 1889.

Forrest, G. W. Sepoy Generals. 1889. [From Wellington to Roberts.]

Morris, H. Anglo-Indian Worthies. Madras, 1890.

Samuelson, James. India, Past and Present: Historical, Social and Political. 1890.

Chapman, Mrs E. F. Sketches of some Distinguished Indian Women. Preface by the Marchioness of Dufferin. 1891.

Aitchison, Sir C. U. Treaties, etc. relating to India. 11 vols. Calcutta, 1892.

Skrine, F. H. B. Laborious Days. Leaves from the Indian Record of Sir C. A. Elliot. Calcutta, 1892 (anon.).

—— An Indian Journalist. Being the Life, Letters and Correspondence of Dr Sambhu Chandra Mookerjee. Calcutta, 1895.

Skrine, F. H. B. The Heart of Asia. A History of Russian Turkestan and the Central Asian Khanates from the Earliest Times. 1899. [With Sir E. Denison Ross.]

Stark, H. A. and Walter, Madge E. East Indian Worthies. Being Memoirs of Distinguished Indo-Europeans. Calcutta, 1892.

Campbell, Sir George. Memories of my Indian Career. 2 vols. 1893.

Lyall, Sir A. C. [See p. 932 above.]

Griffith, M. Indian Princes. Short Sketches of the Native Rulers of India. 1894.

Lee-Warner, Sir William. The Protected Princes of India. 1894; 1910 (rev. as The Native States of India).

—— The Citizen of India. 1897.

—— The Life of the Marquis of Dalhousie. 2 vols. 1904.

Abdul Quadir, Ahmadi Sa'di. A Brief Sketch of his Life. Bombay, 1895.

Roberts, Frederick Sleigh (Earl Roberts). The Rise of Wellington. 1895 (2nd edn).

—— Forty-one Years in India. 2 vols. 1897.

Wilson, Charles R. The Early Annals of the English in Bengal. Vol. i, 1895; vol. ii, pt 1, 1900; vol. ii, pt 2, Calcutta, 1911.

—— Old Fort William in Bengal. A Selection of Official Documents dealing with its History. 2 vols. 1906. [Ed. by Wilson.]

Younghusband, Sir George J. The Relief of Chitral. 1895.

Mehta, M. N. Native States of India. 1896.

Chakrabarti, Khetrapal. Life of Sri Chaitanya. Calcutta, 1897.

Ilbert, Sir Courtenay Peregrine. The Government of India. Being a Digest of the Statute Law relating thereto, with Historical Introduction and Illustrative Documents. Oxford, 1898.

Ranade, M. G. Essays on Indian Economics. Bombay, 1898.

—— Rise of the Maratha Power. Bombay, 1900.

—— Religious and Social Reform. Bombay, 1902.

Dharmapala, H. History of the Maha Bodhi Temple at Bodh-Gaya. With an Appendix by Sir Edwin Arnold. 1900.

Macpherson, G. Life of Lal Behari Dey. Edinburgh, 1900.

Buckland, C. E. Bengal under the Lieutenant-Governors (from 1854 to 1898). 2 vols. Calcutta, 1901.

Holdich, Sir T. H. Indian Borderland, 1830 to 1900. 1901.

—— Gates of India. 1910.

G. GEOGRAPHY, TOPOGRAPHY AND TRAVEL

(a) 1598–1850

Fitch, Ralph. The Voyage of Ralph Fitch. [In R. Hakluyt, Principal Navigations, 1598; ed. J. R. Ryley, 1899.]

Methold, W. Relations of the Kingdome of Golchonda and Other Neighbouring Nations within the Gulf of Bengala, and the English Trade in those Parts. [In Purchas his Pilgrimage, 1626.]

Bruton, William. News from the East Indies, or a Voyage to Bengalla; with the State and Magnificence of the Court of Malcandy. 1638.

Fryer, John. A New Account of East India and Persia, in Eight Letters. Being Nine Years' Travels begun 1672 and finished 1681. 1698; ed. W. Crooke, Hakluyt Soc. 1909.

Hamilton, Alexander. A New Account of the East Indies. 2 vols. Edinburgh, 1727.

Roe, Sir Thomas. Journal of his Voyage to the East Indies and Observations there during his Residence at the Mogul's Court as Embassador from King James the First of England. [In A. and J. Churchill, A Collection of Voyages and Travels, vol. i, 1732; ed. from contemporary records by Sir W. Foster, Hakluyt Soc. 1899.]

Moses, H. Sketches of India. 1750.

d'Après de Mannevillette, J. B. N. D. The East India Pilot, or Oriental Navigator. 2 vols. 1781. [A complete collection of maps, charts, plans, etc.]

Hodges, William. Travels in India during the Years 1780–83. 1793.

Daniel, Thomas and William. Oriental Scenery in Hindustan. 3 vols. 1795–1807.

Pennant, T. The View of Hindoostan. 2 vols. 1798.

Taylor, J. Travels from England to India. 2 vols. 1799.

Buchanan-Hamilton, F. Journey from Madras through the Countries of Mysore, Canara and Malabar. 3 vols. 1807; 2 vols. Madras, 1870.

—— An Account of the Kingdom of Nepal. Edinburgh, 1819; Calcutta, 1888.

Johnson, J. The Oriental Voyager. 1807.

Shaw, Thomas. Travels in Bombay and the Levant. 2 vols. Edinburgh, 1808.

Annesley, George (Viscount Valentia). Voyages and Travels to India [etc.]. 4 vols. 1809.

Daniel, Thomas. Picturesque Voyage to India. 1810.

Kirkpatrick, William. An Account of the Kingdom of Nepaul. Being the Substance of Observations made during a Mission to that Country in 1793. 1811.

Graham, Maria (later Lady Callcott). Journal of a Residence in India. Edinburgh, 1812.

D'Oyly, Sir Charles. The European in India: from a Collection of Drawings by C. Doyley. With a Preface and Copious Descriptions by Thomas Williamson. 1813.

—— Sketches of the New Road in a Journey from Calcutta to Gyah. Calcutta, 1830.

Forbes, James. Oriental Memoirs; selected and abridged from a Series of Familiar Letters written during Seventeen Years' Residence in India. 4 vols. 1813.

Pottinger, H. Travels in Beloochistan. 1816.

Johnson, John. A Journey from India to England through Persia. 1818.

Gilchrist, J. B. East India Guide. 1820.

Hamilton, Walter. A Geographical, Statistical and Historical Description of Hindostan and the Adjacent Countries. 2 vols. 1820.

Fay, Eliza. Original Letters from India. Containing a Narrative of a Journey through Egypt, and the Author's Imprisonment at Calicut by Hyder Ally. To which is added an Abstract of three Subsequent Voyages to India. Calcutta, 1821.

Seely, John Benjamin. The Wonders of Elora, or the Narrative of a Journey to the Temples and Dwellings excavated out of a Mountain of Granite at Elora, in the East Indies. 1824; 1825 (with addns).

—— Sacred City of the Hindus. 1868.

Wallace, Robert Grenville. Memoirs of India. Comprising a Brief Geographical Account of the East Indies, a Succinct History of Hindostan, from the most Early Ages, to the End of the Marquis of Hastings' Administration in 1823. 1824.

Keppel, George Thomas (Earl of Albemarle). Personal Narrative of a Journey from India to England. 2 vols. 1827 (2nd edn).

Heber, Reginald. Narrative of a Journey through the Upper Provinces of India from Calcutta to Bombay, 1824–25. An Account of a Journey to Madras and the Southern Provinces, 1826, and Letters written in India. 2 vols. 1828.

Hough, James. Letters on the Climate, Inhabitants, Productions, of the Neilgherries, or Blue Mountains of Coimbatoor, South India. 1829.

Lushington, Mrs Charles. Journey from Calcutta to Europe, by Way of Egypt, in the Years 1827–28. 1829.

Burnes, J. M. H. Narrative of a Visit to the Court of Scinde. 1830.

Mundy, R. Journal of a Tour in India. 2 vols. 1832.

Archer, E. C. Tours in Upper India and in Parts of the Himalaya Mountains; with Accounts of the Courts of the Native Princes. 2 vols. 1833.

Elliot, R. Views in the East. 2 vols. 1833.

Burnes, Sir Alexander. Travels into Bokhara. 3 vols. 1834.

—— Cabool: being a Personal Narrative of a Journey to and Residence in that City in 1836–8. 1842.

Mohan Lal. Travels in the Punjab. 1834.

Jacquemont, Victor. Letters from India. Tr. Eng. 2 vols. 1834.

Skinner, Thomas. Adventures during a Journey overland to India. 2 vols. 1836.

Butler, D. Topography and Statistics of Southern Oudh. Calcutta, 1839.

Tod, James. Travels in Western India, embracing a Visit to the Sacred Mounts of the Jains and the most Celebrated Shrines of Hindu Faith between Rajpootana and the Indus. 1839. [With memoir of Tod.]

Lloyd, Sir W. Caunpur to the Boorendo Pass in the Himalayan Mountains. 2 vols. 1840.

Moorcroft, W. Travels in the Himalayan Provinces of Hindustan and the Punjab. 2 vols. 1841.

Vigne, Godfrey T. Travels in Kashmir, Ladak, Iskardo, the Countries adjoining the Mountain-Course of the Indus, and the Himalaya, North of the Punjab. 2 vols. 1842.

von Hügel, Carl A. A. (Baron). Travels in Kashmir and the Panjab, containing a Particular Account of the Government and Character of the Sikhs. With Notes by T. B. Jervis. 1845.

Steinbach, Henry. The Punjaub. Being a Brief Account of the Country of the Sikhs. 1845.

Symonds, A. R. Introduction to the Geography and History of India. Madras, 1845 (2nd edn).

Hoffmeister, W. Travels in Ceylon and Continental India. Edinburgh, 1848.

(b) 1851–1914

Edwardes, H. B. Punjab Frontier. 2 vols. 1851.

Fergusson, R. The Pipe of Repose, or Recollections of Eastern Travel. 1851 (2nd edn).

Percival, P. The Land of the Veda. India briefly described. 1854.

Hooker, Sir Joseph Dalton. Himalayan Journals, or Notes of a Naturalist in Bengal, the Sikkim, and Nepal Himalayas, the Khasia Mountains, [etc.]. 2 vols. 1854; 2 vols. 1855 (rev. and condensed). [For other writings see under Science, p. 961 above.]

Bruce, J. Scenes and Sights in the East. 1856.

Yule, Sir Henry. A Narrative of the Mission sent by the Governor-General of India to the Court of Ava in 1858. 1858.

Russell, Sir William Howard. My Diary in India in the Year 1858–9. 2 vols. 1860.

Carpenter, Mary. Six Months in India. 2 vols. 1868.

Smith, D. B. Pilgrimage to Jagernath. Calcutta, 1868.

Chander, Bholanath. Travels of a Hindu. 4 vols. 1869.

Rousselet, L. India and its Native Princes. Travels in Central India and in the Presidencies of Bombay and Bengal. Carefully revised and edited by Lieut. Col. Buckle. 1876. [From the French.]

Life in the Moffussil. By an Ex-Civilian. 2 vols. 1878.

Blanford, W. T. and Medlicott, H. B. Geology of India. 4 vols. Calcutta, 1879.

Lawson, J. A. The Wandering Naturalists. A Story of Adventure on the Himalayas. 1880.

Caird, Sir James. India: the Land and the People. 1883.

Ross, David. The Land of the Five Rivers and Sindh. Sketches, Historical and Descriptive. 1883.

Caine, W. S. Picturesque India. 1891.

Blavatsky, H. P. From the Caves and Jungles of Hindastan. 1892. [From the Russian.]

Carpenter, Edward. From Adam's Peak to Elephanta. Sketches in Ceylon and India. 1892. [For other writings see p. 736 above.]

Knight, E. F. Where Three Empires meet. A Narrative of Recent Travel in Kashmir, Western Tibet, Gilgit, and the Adjoining Countries. 1893; 1923 (abridged, with notes by J. C. Allen).

Dutt, Romes Chandra. Rambles in India (1871–1895). Calcutta, 1895.

Hart, W. H. Old Calcutta. Calcutta, 1895.

Klein, Augusta W. Among the Gods. Scenes of India, with Legends by the Way. Edinburgh, 1895.

Maccormick, A. D. An Artist in the Himalayas. 1895.

Daly, J. B. Indian Sketches and Rambles. Calcutta, 1896.

Gascoigne, G. T. Among Pagodas and Fair Ladies. 1896.

Johnstone, Sir James. My Experiences in Manipur and the Naga Hills. 1896.

De, Nandalal. The Geographical Dictionary of Ancient and Mediaeval India. 2 pts, Calcutta, 1899.

Arbuthnot, James. A Trip to Kashmir. Calcutta, 1900.

H. RELIGION AND PHILOSOPHY

Moor, Edward. The Hindu Pantheon. 1810.

Rajagopaul, P. Mission to Siam. 1820.

—— Caste in its Relation to the Church. Madras, 1879.

Raya Raja Ramamohana. Precepts of Jesus, the Guide to Peace and Happiness. Calcutta, 1820; 1824; Boston, 1828; 1834.

—— An Appeal to the Christian Public in Defence of the 'Precepts of Jesus.' Bhowanipur (Calcutta), 1854.

—— The English Works of Raja Rammohan Roy. Edited by Jogendra Chander Ghose. 3 vols. Calcutta, 1901.

[For biography see Life and Letters of Raja Rammohan Roy, compiled and edited by S. D. Collet, 1900.]

Upham, E. The History and Doctrine of Buddhism popularly illustrated. With Notices of the Kappooism, or Demon Worship, and of the Bali, or Planetary Incantations of Ceylon. 1829.

Coleman, C. The Mythology of the Hindus. 1832.

Wilson, John. An Exposure of the Hindu Religion, in Reply to Mora Bhatta Dandekara; to which is prefixed a Translation of the Bhatta's Tract. Bombay, 1832.

—— The Parsi Religion as contained in the Zand-Avasta and propounded and defended by the Zoroastrians of India and Persia, unfolded, refuted, and contrasted with Christianity. Bombay, 1843.

Rodriguez, E. A. The Hindu Pantheon. Comprising the Principal Deities worshipped by the Natives of India. Madras, 1841.

Wilson, Horace Hayman. Sketch of the Religious Sects of the Hindus. 1846; Calcutta, 1899.

—— Essays and Lectures on the Religion of the Hindus. 2 vols. 1861–2.

—— Complete Works. 12 vols. 1862–71.

[See also p. 1019 above.]

Briggs, H. G. The Parsis, or Modern Zerdusthians. Edinburgh, 1852.

Bigandet, P. Life or Legend of Gaudama. Rangoon, 1858.

Arnold, J. M. Ishmael, or a Natural History of Islamism. 1859.

Ballantyne, J. R. Christianity contrasted with Hindu Philosophy. 1859.

—— Hindu Philosophy. Calcutta, 1881 (2nd edn).

Hall, F. Indian Philosophical Systems. Calcutta, 1859.

Kaye, Sir J. W. Christianity in India. 1859.

Gangopadhayay, Jagatchandra. Life and Religion of the Hindoos. 1860.

Mullens, J. The Religious Aspects of Hindu Philosophy stated and discussed. 1860.

Brown, J. P. The Dervishes, or Oriental Spiritualism. 1868.

Chandra, B. L. Brahmanism. Calcutta, 1870.

Mitter, G. C. The Unchangeableness of God. Calcutta, 1870.

Atkinson, J. L. The Hindu Pantheon. Cuttack, 1872.

Brockie, W. Indian Philosophy. 1872.

Amir Ali, Sayyed. A Critical Examination of the Life and Teachings of Mahammad. 1873.

—— The Ethics of Islam. Calcutta, 1893.

—— The Spirit of Islam. Calcutta, 1896 (2nd edn).

Williams, later Monier-Williams, Sir Monier. Indian Wisdom, or Examples of the Religious, Philosophical and Ethical Doctrines of the Hindus. 1875.

—— Modern India and the Indians. Being a Series of Impressions, Notes and Essays. 1878.

—— Brahmanism and Hinduism. 1887 (3rd edn).

—— Mystical Buddhism in Connection with the Yoga Philosophy of the Hindus. 1888.

—— Buddhism in its Connexion with Brāhmanism and Hindūism, and in its Contrast with Christianity. 1889.

Haggard, A. England and Islam. Calcutta, 1876.

Stephens, W. R. W. Christianity and Islam. The Bible and the Koran. 1877.

Muir, Sir W. The Coran: its Composition and Teaching. 1878.

Dowson, J. A Classical Dictionary of Hindu Mythology and Religion, Geography, History and Literature. 1879.

Mitra, Piyarichand. Spiritual Stray Leaves. Calcutta, 1879.

—— Stray Thoughts on Spiritualism. Calcutta, 1880.

—— On the Soul: its Nature and Development. Calcutta, 1881.

Blunt, Wilfrid Scawen. The Future of Islam. 1882.

—— Ideas about India. 1885.

[For other writings see p. 332 above.]

Hoey, William. Buddha: his Life, his Doctrine, his Order. By Hermann Oldenberg. Translated from the German. 1882; Calcutta, 1927.

Lyall, Sir Alfred Comyns. Asiatic Studies, Religious and Social. 2 sers. 1882–99.

—— Natural Religion in India. Rede Lecture. Cambridge, 1891.

Mazumdar, P. C. The Faith and Progress of the Brahmo Somaj. Calcutta, 1882.

—— Life and Teachings of Keshub Chandra Sen. Calcutta, 1887.

—— The Spirit of God. Boston, 1894.

—— The Oriental Christ. Boston, 1894.

—— Heart Beats. Boston, 1894.

—— Lowell Lectures on Hindu Religion and Society, etc. Calcutta, 1894.

Olcott, H. S. The Yoga Philosophy. 1882.

—— The Spirit of the Zoroastrian Religion. Bombay, 1882.

Wilkins, W. J. Hindu Mythology, Vedic and Purānic. Calcutta, 1882.

Ghose, Jogendrachandra. Chaitanya's Ethics. Calcutta, 1884.

Sreeram, Lala. The Metaphysics of the Upanishads. Calcutta, 1885.

Sen, Kesabchandra. Essays, Theological and Ethical. Calcutta, 1886.

Basak, Radhanath. Philosophy of the Bhagabad-Gita. Calcutta, 1888.

Oman, J. C. Indian Life, Religious and Social. 1889.

—— The Great Indian Epics. The Stories of the Ramayana and the Mahabharata. 1894.

—— The Mystics, Ascetics, and Saints of India. 1903.

Smith, R. B. Mahomed and Mahomedanism. 1889.

Hopkins, E. W. The Religions of India. 1890.

—— India, Old and New. New York, 1901.

—— The Great Epic of India: its Character and Origin. New York, 1902.

Fayrer, Sir Joseph. On Serpent Worship and on the Venomous Snakes of India. 1891.

Sen, Guruprasada. An Introduction to the Study of Hinduism. Calcutta, 1891.

Pool, J. Studies in Mahammadanism, with a Chapter on Islam in England. 1892.

—— Woman's Influence in the East, as shown in the Noble Lives of Past Queens and Princesses of India. With an Introduction by Sir Lepel Griffin. 1892.

Chakrabarti, Khetrapal. Lectures on Hindu Religion, Philosophy and Yoga. Calcutta, 1893.

Monro, J. Christianity and Hinduism. Calcutta, 1893.

Tilak, Bal Gangadhar. The Orion, or Researches into the Antiquity of the Vedas. Bombay, 1893; Poona, 1916.

Mills, L. H. A Study of the Five Zorathushtrian (Zoroastrian) Gathas. 1894.

—— The Initiative of the Avesta. Hertford, 1899.

—— Zoroaster, Philo, and Israel. Being a Treatise upon the Antiquity of the Avesta. 2 vols. Leipzig, 1903–6.

—— Zoroaster and the Bible. 1911.

Besant, Annie. Karma. 1895.

—— The Ancient Wisdom. An Outline of Theosophical Teachings. 1897.

—— Four Great Religions. Madras, 1897. [Hinduism, Zoroastrianism, Buddhism, Christianity.]

—— Avatâras. Four Lectures. 1900.

Arnold, T. W. The Preaching of Islam. 1896.

Sell, Edward. The Faith of Islam. 1896.

'Swami Vivekananda' (Narendranath Datta). Addresses on the Vedânta Philosophy. 3 vols. 1896.

'Swami Vivekananda' (Narendranath Datta). Lectures on Rāja Yoga and Other Subjects. Albany, 1897.

—— Lectures on Guana-Yoga. 20 pts, Madras, [1898].

—— Bhakti-Yoga. Calcutta, 1901.

—— Karma-Yoga. Calcutta, 1901.

—— Juana-Yoga. Calcutta, 1902.

Ghose, Shishir Kumar. Lord Gauranga, or Salvation for all. 2 vols. Calcutta, 1897–8. [A life of Krishna Chaitanya, of Nadia.]

Phillips, J. F. Vedanta Philosophy. 1897.

Sastri, Mahamamahopadhyaya. Haraprasad. Discovery of Living Buddhism in Bengal. Calcutta, 1897.

Sarkar, K. L. Hindu System of Moral Science. Calcutta, 1898 (2nd edn).

—— The Hindu System of Religion, Science and Art. Calcutta, 1898.

Seal, Sir Brajendranath. Comparative Studies in Vaishnavism and Christianity. Calcutta, 1899.

—— New Essays in Criticism. Calcutta, 1903.

—— Address to the Universal Races Congress. 1911; Calcutta, 1911.

—— The Positive Sciences of the Ancient Hindus. 1915.

Aiken, C. F. The Dharma of Buddha and the Gospel of Christ. Boston, 1900.

A Handbook of Hindu Pantheism. 1900 (anon.). [The Atmajnanopadesavidhi, with Annandagiris' Commentary.]

I. SOCIAL AND MISCELLANEOUS

Chambers, William et al. The Asiatic Miscellany: consisting of Translations, Imitations, Fugitive Pieces, Original Productions, and Extracts from Curious Publications. Calcutta, 1787; 1787.

Pennant, T. Indian Zoology. 1790 (2nd edn).

Boyd, Hugh Macauley. The Indian Observer; with the Life of the Author, and some Miscellaneous Poems, by L. D. Campbell. 1798.

—— Miscellaneous Works. With an Account of his Life and Writings by Lawrence Dundas Campbell. 2 vols. 1800. [Includes The Indian Observer and The Embassy to Candy.]

Moor, Edward. Hindu Infanticide. An Account of the Measures adopted for suppressing the Practice of the Systematic Murder by their Parents, of Female Infants. 1811.

Broughton, T. D. Customs, Manners, etc. of the Mahrattas. 1813.

—— Modern India. 1852.

—— India as it may be. 1853.

Raya Raja Ramamohana. Brief Remarks regarding Modern Encroachments on the Ancient Rights of Females according to the Hindoo Law of Inheritance. Calcutta, 1822.

Raya Raja Ramamohana. Exposition of the Practical Operation of the Judicial and Revenue Systems of India, and of the General Character and Condition of its Native Inhabitants. With Notes and Illustrations. 1832.

Peggs, J. The Suttees' Cry to Britain. 1828 (2nd edn).

—— India's Cries to British Humanity, relative to the Suttee, Infanticide, etc. 1830 (2nd edn).

Bannerjea, K. The Persecuted. (Scenes illustrative of the Present State of Hindu Society.) Calcutta, 1831.

—— Female Education. Calcutta, 1841.

—— Dialogues on the Hindu Philosophy. Calcutta, 1861.

—— Rigveda Samhita. Calcutta, 1875. [With an introductory essay on the study of the Vedas.]

—— The Arian Witness. Calcutta, 1875.

Crawford, J. Letters from British Settlers in India. 1831.

—— The Colonisation of India. 1833.

Hasan Ali, Mir. Observations on the Mussulmans of India, descriptive of their Manners, Customs, Habits and Religious Opinions. 2 vols. 1832.

Piddington, H. A Tabular View of the Generic Characters in Roxburgh's Flora Indica. 1836.

Sleeman, Sir William Henry. Vocabulary of the Thugs. Calcutta, 1836.

—— Rambles and Recollections of an Indian Official. 2 vols. 1844; ed. A. C. Majumdar, 2 vols. Lahore, 1888; ed. V. A. Smith, 2 vols. Westminster, 1893.

—— Journal through Oude. 2 vols. 1858.

Addison, G. A. Indian Reminiscences. 1837.

Hodgson, Brian H. Aborigines of India. Calcutta, 1837.

—— Illustrations of the Literature and Religion of the Buddhists. Serampore, 1841.

——Miscellaneous Essays relating to Indian Subjects. 2 vols. 1880.

Anglo-India, Social, Moral and Political. 3 vols. 1838 (anon.).

Bryce, J. Native Education in India, under the Superintendence of the Church of Scotland. 1839.

Chapman, Priscilla. Hindu Female Education. 1839.

Royle, J. F. Natural History of the Himalayan Mountains. 2 vols. 1839.

—— Productive Resources of India. 1840.

Clemons, Mrs. The Manners and Customs of Society in India; including Scenes in Mofussil Stations. 1841.

Henderson, H. B. The Bengalee, or Sketches of Society in the East. 2 vols. Calcutta, 1843.

The Indian Miscellany. Being Selections from the Works of the Best Original Writers, both Instructive and Entertaining. Calcutta, 1843.

Johnson, G. W. Three Years in Calcutta. 3 vols. 1843.

Letters to Friends at Home, from June 1842 to May 1844. By an Idler. 2 pts, Calcutta, 1843–4.

[Maitland, Julia Charlotte.] Letters from Madras, during the Years 1836–1839. By a Lady. 1843.

Stocqueler, J. H. Memorials of Afghanistan. Calcutta, 1843.

—— Handbook of India. 1845 (2nd edn).

Owen, J. Notes on the Naga Tribes. Calcutta, 1844.

Boileau, A. H. E. Miscellaneous Writings in Prose and Verse, comprising Dramatic Charades, Songs, Tales, Translations, Travels, etc., etc. Calcutta, 1845.

Richardson, D. L. The Anglo-Indian Passage, Homeward and Outward. 1845.

Lawrence, H. M. L. Adventures in the Punjab. 2 vols. 1846.

Ritchie, L. The British World in the East. 2 vols. 1846.

Buyers, W. Recollections of Northern India. 1848.

Mason, F. Natural Productions of the Burma and Moulmien. 1850.

Bower, H. An Essay on Hindu Caste. Calcutta, 1851.

Datta, Harachandra. Bengali Life and Society. Calcutta, 1853.

—— Short Discourses. 2 sers. Calcutta, 1870.

Mackenzie, Helen. Life in the Mission, the Camp, and the Zenáná, or Six Years in India. 3 vols. 1853.

Datta, Sasichandra. Essays on Miscellaneous Subjects. Calcutta, 1854.

—— The Dutt Family Album. 1870. [With G. C. Dutt.]

—— Historical Studies. 2 vols. 1879.

—— India, Past and Present. 1880.

—— Collected Works. 10 vols. 1884.

—— Realities of Indian Life. 1885.

Torrens, H. W. A Selection from the Writings of the Late H. W. Torrens, with a Biographical Memoir. Ed. J. Hume, 2 vols. 1854.

Wise, T. A. Thoughts on Education in India: its Object and Plan. 1854.

Bushby, H. J. Widow-Burning. A Narrative. 1855.

Knighton, W. Tropical Sketches. 2 vols. 1855.

Cave-Brown, J. Indian Infanticide: its Origin, Progress and Suppression. 1857.

Autobiography of Lutfullah, a Mohammedan Gentleman; and his Transactions with his Fellow-Creatures. Ed. E. B. Eastwick, 1857 (bis).

Grant, C. Rural Life in Bengal; Illustrative of Anglo-Indian Suburban Life. 1860.

Iswarā Dās. Domestic Manners and Customs of the Hindoos of Northern India, or more strictly speaking, of the North West Provinces of India. Benares, 1860.

Robinson, E. J. The Daughters of India: their Social Condition, Religion, Literature, Obligations and Prospects. Glasgow, 1860.

Herklots, G. A. Customs of the Mussulmans of India. Madras, 1863.

Firminger, T. A. C. Manual of Gardening for Bengal and Upper India. 1864 (3rd edn).

Trevelyan, Sir George Otto. The Competition Wallah. Reprinted from Macmillan's Magazine, with Corrections and Additions. 1864. [For other writings see p. 918 above.]

Kerr, J. The Domestic Life, Character and Customs of the Natives of India. 1865.

—— The Land of Ind, or Glimpses of India. 1873.

'Punjabee' (W. D. Arnold). Short Essays on Social and Indian Subjects. Calcutta, 1869.

Chuckerbutty, Goodeve S. Lectures on Subjects of Indian Interest. Calcutta, 1870.

Maine, Sir Henry Sumner. Village Communities in the East and West. 1871; 1876 (3rd edn, enlarged).

—— European Views of India. Calcutta, 1875. [For other writings see p. 893 above.]

Robinson, Philip Stewart. Nugæ Indicæ. On Leave in my Compound. 1871 (anon.; priv. ptd).

—— In my Indian Garden. With a Preface by Edwin Arnold. 1878.

—— Under the Punkah. 1881. [All 3 sketches of everyday life in India.]

Braddon, Sir Edward. Life in India. 1872. [A series of sketches of the Anglo-Indian.]

—— Thirty Years of Shikar. 1895.

Pogson, F. Indian Gardening. Calcutta, 1872.

Sherring, M. A. Hindu Tribes and Castes. 1872.

Dutt, Romes Chandra. Three Years in Europe. Calcutta, 1873.

—— England and India. 1897.

—— Famines and Land Assessment in India. 1900.

Ghose, Loka Nath. Hindu Music. Calcutta, 1873.

Birdwood, Sir George. The Industrial Arts of India. 1880.

Aitken, E. H. ('Eha'). Tribes on my Frontier. Bombay, 1881; 1914 (8th edn).

—— Behind the Bungalow. Calcutta, 1889; 1907.

—— A Naturalist on the Prowl, or In the Jungle. 1894.

—— The Five Windows of the Soul. 1898.

Bose, Shib Chunder. The Hindoos as they are A Description of the Manners, Customs and Inner Life of Hindoo Society in Bengal. With a Prefatory Note by W. Hastie. 1881.

Tayler, W. Thirty-eight Years in India. 2 vols. 1881.

Dutton, C. Life in India. 1882.

Lethbridge, Sir Roper. High Education in India. A Plea for the State Colleges. 1882.

—— The Golden Book of India. A Genealogical and Biographical Dictionary of the Ruling Princes, Chiefs, Nobles, and Other Personages, titled or decorated, of the Indian Empire. 1893.

Malabari, B. Gujarat and the Gujaratis. 1882; Bombay, 1884.

—— Infant Marriage and Enforced Widowhood in India. 1887.

—— The Indian Eye on English Life. 1893.

—— The Indian Problem. Bombay, 1894.

Cole, H. H. The Preservation of National Monuments, Punjab. Simla, 1883.

Indo-Anglian Literature. Calcutta, 1883 (priv. ptd). [Specimen compositions by native students.]

Mayne, J. D. A Treatise on Hindu Law and Usage. Madras, 1883.

Mukherji, T. N. Handbook of Indian Products. Calcutta, 1883.

Sherer, J. W. At Home and in India. A Volume of Miscellanies. 1883.

Tagore, Sir Saurindramohan. Dramatic Sentiments of the Aryans. Calcutta, 1883.

—— The Times of Yore, or Tales from Indian History, from the Invasion of Alexander the Great to the Battle of Panipat. 1885.

—— Bengaliana. A Dish of Rice and Curry, and Other Indigestible Ingredients. Calcutta, 1886.

Buckland, C. T. Sketches of Social Life in India. 1884.

King, Mrs R. H. Diary of a Civilian's Wife in India. 2 vols. 1884.

Arnold, Sir Edwin. India Revisited. 1886.

—— East and West. 1896.

Satthianadhan, Samuel. England and India. Madras, 1886.

—— Stories of Indian Christian Life. Madras, 1898. [With K. Satthianadhan.]

Das, Devendranath. Sketches of Hindu Life. 1887.

Bamford, A. J. Turbans and Tails, or Sketches in the Unromantic East. 1888.

Murdoch, J. The Women of India, and what can be done for them. Madras, 1888.

Lloyd, W. Sketches of Indian Life. 1890.

Carstairs, R. British Work in India. Edinburgh, 1891.

—— Human Nature in Rural India. Edinburgh, 1895.

Cutpell, E. E. Indian Memories. 1893.

Bose, P. N. Hindu Civilization under British Rule. 3 vols. Calcutta, 1894; 4 vols. 1894–6.

Small, Annie H. Suwarta, and Other Sketches of Indian Life. 1894.

Biblington, Mary F. Woman in India. Introduction by the Marchioness of Dufferin. 1895.

Gray, John A. At the Court of the Amîr. A Narrative. 1895.

Mayer, J. E. The Humour and Pathos of Anglo-Indian Life. 1895.

Baden-Powell, B. H. The Indian Village Community. 1896.

—— The Origin and Growth of Village Communities in India. 1899.

—— Indian Memories. 1915.

Bhattacharyya, J. N. Hindu Castes and Sects. Calcutta, 1896.

Ghose, Nanda Lal. A Guide for Indian Females. Lahore, 1896.

Cuming, E. D. With the Jungle Folk. A Sketch of Burmese Village Life. 1897.

Armstrong, Hopkins. Within the Purdah. New York, 1898.

Udden, J. A. An Old Indian Village. 1900.

Bose, [S. S.]. Humorous Sketches. Allahabad, 1903.

Cotton, Sir Henry. New India and Indian Home Memories. 1911.

E. F. O., *rev.* J. G. B.

III. ENGLISH-CANADIAN LITERATURE

(1769–1900)

A. GENERAL WORKS

(a) Works of Reference

Rose, G. M. and Charlesworth, H. A Cyclopaedia of Canadian Biography. 3 vols. Toronto, 1886–1919.

Hopkins, John Castell. Canada. An Encyclopædia of the Country. 6 vols. Toronto, 1898–1900.

Morgan, H. J., *et al.* The Canadian Men and Women of the Time. Toronto, 1898, 1912.

Shortt, Adam and Doughty, Arthur G. Canada and its Provinces. 23 vols. Edinburgh, 1913–7.

Wallace, W. S. The Dictionary of Canadian Biography. Toronto, 1926.

The Cambridge History of the British Empire. Vol. 6. Cambridge, 1930.

Wallace, W. S. *et al.* The Encyclopedia of Canada. 6 vols. Toronto, 1935–7.

(b) Literary Bibliographies

James, Charles Canniff. A Bibliography of Canadian Poetry (English). Toronto, 1899.

Horning, Lewis Emerson and Burpee, Lawrence Johnstone. A Bibliography of Canadian Fiction (English). Toronto, 1904.

(c) Literary Histories and Critical Works

Morgan, Henry James. Bibliotheca Canadensis, or a Manual of Canadian Literature. Ottawa, 1867.

Bourinot, Sir John George. Our Intellectual Strength and Weakness. A Short Historical and Critical Review of Literature, Art and Education in Canada. Montreal, 1893.

Dawson, Samuel E. The Prose Writers of Canada. Montreal, 1901.

Marquis, Thomas Guthrie. English-Canadian Literature. Toronto, 1913. [Also in Canada and its Provinces, vol. xii, Toronto, 1913–7.]

Edgar, Pelham. English-Canadian Literature. CHEL. vol. xiv, 1916.

Baker, Ray Palmer. A History of English-Canadian Literature to the Confederation: its Relation to the Literature of Great Britain and the United States. Cambridge, U.S.A. 1920.

Garvin, Amelia Beers, née Warnock ('Katherine Hale'). Isabella Valancy Crawford. Toronto, 1923.

Riddell, William Renwick. John Richardson. Toronto, 1923.

—— William Kirby. Toronto, 1923.

Chittick, Victor Lovitt Oakes. Thomas Chandler Haliburton ('Sam Slick'). A Study in Provincial Toryism. New York, 1924.

Logan, John Daniel. Thomas Chandler Haliburton. Toronto, 1924.

Logan, John Daniel and French, Donald Graham. Highways of Canadian Literature, 1760–1924. Toronto, 1924.

MacMechan, Archibald McKellar. Head-Waters of Canadian Literature. Toronto, 1924.

Pierce, Lorne Albert. An Outline of Canadian Literature (French and English). Toronto, 1927.

Connor, Carl Y. Archibald Lampman, Canadian Poet of Nature. New York, 1929.

Fauteux, Ægidius. The Introduction of Printing into Canada. Montreal, 1929.

B. POETRY

(a) Anthologies

Lighthall, William Douw. Songs of the Great Dominion. 1889.

Rand, Theodore Harding. A Treasury of Canadian Verse; with Brief Biographical Notes. Toronto, 1900.

Edgar, C. M., née Whyte. A Wreath of Canadian Song. Containing Biographical Sketches and Numerous Selections from Deceased Canadian Poets. Toronto, 1910.

Broadus, Edmund Kemper and Hammond, Eleanor. A Book of Canadian Prose and Verse. Toronto, 1923, 1934 (rev.).

Mackenzie, William Roy. Ballads and Sea Songs from Nova Scotia. Cambridge, U.S.A. 1928.

Carman, Bliss and Pierce, Lorne Albert. Our Canadian Literature; Representative Verse, English and French. Toronto, 1935.

(b) Particular Writers

Sangster, Charles. The St Lawrence and the Saguenay. Kingston, 1856.

—— Hesperus. Montreal, 1860.

Heavysege, Charles. Saul: a Drama in Three Parts. Montreal, 1857.

—— Count Filippo, or the Unequal Marriage. A Drama in Five Acts. Montreal, 1860.

—— Jephthah's Daughter. Montreal, 1865.

Mair, Charles. Dreamland and Other Poems. Montreal, 1868.

—— Tecumseh. A Drama. 1886; Toronto, 1926 (with Canadian Poems, Dreamland and Other Poems, The American Bison, Through the Mackenzie Basin, Memoirs and Reminiscences).

Reade, John. The Prophecy of Merlin. Montreal, 1870.

Howe, Joseph. Poems and Essays. Montreal, 1874.

Leprohon, Rosanna Eleanor, née Mullins. Poetical Works. Montreal, 1881.

Mountcastle, Clara H. ('Caris Sima'). The Mission of Love; Lost; and Other Poems; with Songs and Valentines. Toronto, 1882.

Crawford, Isabella Valancy. Old Spookses' Pass, Malcolm's Katie, and Other Poems. 1884.

—— Collected Poems. Toronto, 1905.

Edgar, Sir James David. The White Stone Canoe: a Legend of the Ottawas. Toronto, 1885.

—— This Canada of Ours. Toronto, 1893.

McGee, Thomas D'Arcy. Poems. New York, 1886.

McLennan, William. Songs of Old Canada. Montreal, 1886. [In French and English.]

Cameron, George Frederick. Lyrics on Freedom, Love and Death. Kingston, 1887.

Martin, George. Marguerite, or the Isle of Demons. Montreal, 1887.

Stewart, Thomas Brown Phillips. Poems. 1887.

Weir, Arthur. Fleurs de Lys. Montreal, 1887.

Lampman, Archibald. Among the Millet. Ottawa, 1888.

—— Lyrics of Earth. Boston, 1896.

Lampman, Archibald. Collected Poems. Toronto, 1900.

—— Lyrics of Earth, Sonnets and Ballads. Toronto, 1925.

McColl, Evan. English Poetical Works. Kingston, 1888 (4th Canadian edn).

Davin, Nicholas Flood. Eos: an Epic of the Dawn. Regina, 1889.

Murray, George. Verses and Versions. Montreal, 1891.

—— Poems. Montreal, 1912. [With memoir.]

Johnson, Emily Pauline ('Tekahionwake'). The White Wampum. 1895.

—— Canadian Born. Toronto, 1903.

—— Flint and Feather. Toronto. 1917 (5th edn). [Collected poems.]

Sherman, Francis. Matins. Boston, 1896.

Drummond, William Henry. The Habitant. New York, 1897.

—— Johnny Corteau. New York, 1901.

—— The Voyageur. New York, 1905.

—— The Great Fight. New York, 1908.

—— Poetical Works. Toronto, 1926.

Rand, Theodore Harding. At Minas Basin. Toronto, 1897.

—— Song-Waves. Toronto, 1900.

McLachlan, Alexander. Poetical Works. Toronto, 1900.

C. FICTION

Brooke, Frances, née Moore. The History of Emily Montague. 4 vols. 1769; 2 vols. Ottawa, 1931.

Richardson, John. Wacousta, or the Prophecy. A Tale of the Canadas. 3 vols. 1832; Toronto, 1906.

—— The Canadian Brothers, or the Prophecy fulfilled. A Tale of the Late American War. Montreal, 1840; New York, 1851 (as Matilda Montgomerie).

'Sam Slick' (Thomas Chandler Haliburton). The Clockmaker, or the Sayings and Doings of Samuel Slick of Slickville. Ser. 1, Halifax, Nova Scotia, 1836. Sers. 2–3, 1838–40.

—— The Letter Bag of the Great Western, or Life in a Steamer. 1840.

—— The Attaché, or Sam Slick in England. 2 sers. 4 vols. 1843–4.

—— The Old Judge, or Life in a Colony. 2 vols. 1849.

—— Sam Slick's Wise Saws and Modern Instances, or What he said, did, or invented. 2 vols. 1853.

—— Nature and Human Nature. 2 vols. 1855.

—— The Season Ticket. 1860.

—— Sam Slick. Edited, with a Critical Estimate and a Bibliography, by R. P. Baker. New York, 1923. [Selections.]

[For historical works see under History and Biography, below.]

Traill, Catherine Parr, née Strickland. Lady Mary and her Nurse, or A Peep into Canadian Forests. 1850; New York, 1869 (as Afar in the Forest).
—— The Canadian Crusoes. A Tale of Rice Lake Plains. 1852; Toronto, 1923 (as Lost in the Backwoods).
Sadlier, Mary Anne, née Madden. The Blakes and the Flannigans. New York, 1861.
—— Stories of the Provinces, and Other Tales. Montreal, 1895.
Leprohon, Rosanna Eleanor, née Mullins. Antoinette de Mirecourt, or Secret Marrying and Secret Sorrowing. A Canadian Tale. Montreal, 1864.
De Mille, James. The Dodge Club, or Italy in 1859. New York, 1869.
—— The Lady of the Ice. New York, 1870.
—— The Cryptogram. New York, 1871.
—— A Strange Manuscript found in a Copper Cylinder. New York, 1886.
Kirby, William. The Golden Dog (Le Chien d'Or). A Romance of the Days of Louis Quinze in Quebec. Montreal, 1877; Boston, 1897 (1st authorised American edn); Toronto, 1925.
McLennan, William. Spanish John. Toronto, 1898.
—— The Span o' Life. Toronto, 1899. [With Jean McIlwraith.]
—— In Old France and New. New York, 1899.

D. HISTORY AND BIOGRAPHY

Heriot, George. History of Canada [to 1731]. 1804.
Smith, William (1769–1847). History of Canada to 1773. 2 vols. Quebec, 1815 [1826].
Haliburton, Thomas Chandler. Historical and Statistical Account of Nova Scotia. 1829.
—— The Bubbles of Canada. 1839.
—— Rule and Misrule of the English in America. 2 vols. 1851.
[For humorous works see 'Sam Slick' under Fiction above.]
Richardson, John. The War of 1812. Brockville, 1842; rptd 1902.
Christie, Robert. History of the Late Province of Lower Canada. 6 vols. Quebec, 1848–55.
Howe, Joseph. Speeches and Public Letters. Edited by William Annand. 2 vols. Boston, 1858; ed. J. A. Chisholm, Halifax, Nova Scotia, 1909.
Todd, Alpheus. On Parliamentary Government in England. 2 vols. 1867–9.
—— Parliamentary Government in the British Colonies. Boston, 1880.
Canada.—Public Archives. Reports. Ottawa, 1872– .
Canada.—Publications. Ottawa, 1909– .

Hannay, James. History of Acadia. St John, 1879.
—— History of the War of 1812. St John, 1901; 1905 (as How Canada was held for the Empire).
Dent, John Charles. The Last Forty Years. Canada since the Union of 1841. 2 vols. Toronto, 1881.
—— The Story of the Upper Canadian Rebellion. 2 vols. Toronto, 1885.
Kingsford, William. History of Canada. 10 vols. Toronto, 1887–98.
Edgar, Matilda, Lady, née Ridout. Ten Years of Upper Canada in Peace and War, 1805–1815. Being the Ridout Letters. Toronto, 1890.
Pope, Sir Joseph. Memoirs of the Rt. Hon. Sir John A. Macdonald. 2 vols. 1894; Toronto, 1930.
Bourinot, Sir John George. The Story of Canada. 1897.
Doughty, Arthur George and Parmelee, George W. The Siege of Quebec. 6 vols. Quebec, 1901.
Makers of Canada. 23 vols. Toronto, 1903–11; 25 vols. Toronto, 1926 (vol. xxv is Oxford Encyclopaedia of Canadian History).
Grant, William Lawson and Hamilton, Frederick. Principal Grant. Toronto, 1904.
Champlain Society. Publications. Toronto, 1907– . [Contemporary narratives of the history of Canada.]
Tupper, Sir Charles. Recollections of Sixty Years in Canada. 1914.
Wrong, G. M. and Langton, H. H. Chronicles of Canada. 32 vols. Toronto, 1914–6.
Skelton, Oscar Douglas. Life and Letters of Sir Wilfrid Laurier. 2 vols. Toronto, 1921.

E. PIONEER LIFE AND TRAVEL

Mackenzie, Sir Alexander. Voyages from Montreal through the Continent of North America to the Frozen and Pacific Oceans, 1789 and 1793. 1801; rptd Toronto, 1927.
Heriot, George. Travels through the Canadas. 1807; Philadelphia, 1813.
Henry, Alexander (1739–1824). Travels and Adventures in Canada and the Indian Territories, 1760–76. New York, 1809; rptd Toronto, 1901.
Harmon, David Williams. A Journal of Voyages and Travels in the Interior of North America. Andover, 1820; rptd New York, 1922.
Franklin, Sir John. Narrative of a Journey to the Shores of the Polar Sea in the Years 1819–22. 1823.
—— Narrative of a Second Expedition to the Shores of the Polar Sea in the Years 1825–27. 1828.

Traill, Catherine Parr, née Strickland. The Backwoods of Canada. Being Letters from the Wife of an Emigrant Officer, illustrative of the Domestic Economy of British America. 1836; rptd Toronto, 1929.
—— Rambles in the Canadian Forest. 1859.
Jameson, Anna Brownell, née Murphy. Winter Studies and Summer Rambles in Canada. 3 vols. 1838; rptd Toronto, 1923. [For other writings see p. 674 above.]
Abbott, Joseph C. Philip Musgrave, or the Adventures of a Missionary in Canada. 1843.
Moodie, Susanna, née Strickland. Roughing it in the Bush, or Life in Canada. 2 vols. 1852; rptd Toronto, 1913.
—— Life in the Clearings versus the Bush. 1853.
Strickland, Samuel. Twenty-seven Years in Canada West, or the Experiences of an Early Settler. 2 vols. 1853.
Ross, Alexander. Fur Hunters of the Far West. 2 vols. 1855.
—— The Red River Settlement. 1856.
Kane, Paul. Wanderings of an Artist among the Indians of North America. 1859; rptd Toronto, 1925.
Hind, Henry Youle. Narrative of the Canadian Red River Exploring Expedition of 1857 and of the Assiniboine and Saskatchewan Exploring Expedition of 1858. 2 vols. 1860.
—— Explorations in the Interior of the Labrador Peninsula. 2 vols. 1863.
Butler, Sir William Francis. The Great Lone Land. A Narrative of Travel and Adventure in the North-West of America. 1872; rptd Toronto, 1924.
Grant, George Monro. Ocean to Ocean. Toronto, 1873; rptd 1925.
Tyrrell, James Williams. Across the Sub-Arctics of Canada. Toronto, 1893.
Thwaites, R. G. Jesuit Relations and Allied Documents, 1610–1791. 74 vols. Cleveland, 1896–1901. [Ed. by Thwaites.]
Henry, Alexander (d. 1814). New Light on the Early History of the Greater Northwest. The Manuscript Journals of Alexander Henry, edited by Elliott Cones. 3 vols. New York, 1897.
Dawson, Samuel Edward. The St Lawrence Basin and its Borderlands. 1905.
Burpee, Lawrence Johnstone. The Search for the Western Sea. Toronto, 1908.

F. NEWSPAPERS AND MAGAZINES

(a) Histories of Journalism

Biggar, Emerson Bristol. Sketch of Canadian Journalism. [In Canadian Newspaper Directory, Montreal, 1892.]

Colquhoun, Arthur H. U. A Century of Canadian Magazines. Canadian Mag. June 1901.
Canadian Press Association. A History of Canadian Journalism. Toronto, 1908.

(b) Journals

Canadian Magazine. Montreal, 1823–5; Toronto, 1833; Toronto, 1871–2; Toronto, 1893– . [Various publications; monthly.]
Nova Scotian. Halifax, 1828–41. [Weekly.]
Literary Garland. Montreal, 1838–51. [Monthly.]
Royal Canadian Institute. Transactions. Toronto, 1853– .
Canadian Monthly. Toronto, 1872–8. [Afterwards Rose-Belford's, 1878–82; and later The Week, 1883–96.]
Bystander. Toronto, 1880–90. [Monthly.]
Royal Society of Canada. Transactions. 1883– . [Annual: section 2, English Canadian literature, history, etc.]
Queen's Quarterly. Kingston, 1894– .
Review of Historical Publications relating to Canada. Toronto, 1897–1918. [Quarterly; continued as Canadian Historical Review, 1920– .]

P. E., rev. M. T.

IV. ENGLISH-SOUTH AFRICAN LITERATURE (1789–1914)

A. GENERAL WORKS

(a) Bibliography

Mendelssohn, Sidney. South African Bibliography. 2 vols. 1910.

(b) Miscellaneous Works of Reference

FitzSimons, F. W. The Monkey Folk of South Africa. 1911.
Pettman, C. Afrikanderisms. A Glossary of South African Colloquial Words and Phrases. 1913.
Official Year Book of the Union of South Africa and of Basutoland, Bechuanaland Protectorate and Swaziland. Pretoria, 1918– . [Annual.]
Ritchie, W. History of the South African College, 1829 to 1918. Capetown, 1918.
Malherbe, E. G. Education in South Africa, 1652–1922. Capetown, 1925.
Nathan, M. South African Literature. A General Survey. Capetown, 1925.
Walker, E. A. The South African College and the University of Capetown (1829–1929). Capetown, 1929.
The Cambridge History of the British Empire. Vol. 8. Cambridge, 1936.

B. POETRY

(a) Collections and Anthologies

Wilmot, A. The Poetry of South Africa. 1887.

Crouch, E. H. A Treasury of South African Poetry and Verse. 1907.
—— Sonnets of South Africa. 1911.
—— Siftings from South African Poems. 1917.

Petrie, A. Poems of South African History, A.D. 1497–1910. Oxford, 1919.

Slater, F. C. The Centenary Book of South African Verse, 1820–1925. 1925. [With biographical notes on the writers represented.]

(b) Particular Writers

Pringle, Thomas. [See p. 241 above.]

Thomson, W. R. Poems, Essays and Sketches. Capetown, 1867. [With memoir.]

Cruickshanks, S. Lays of South Africa. 1881.

Bell, A. H. H. Lochow, and Other Offerings in Verse. Capetown, 1884.
—— Hymn of the Redemption and Other Poems. Capetown, 1887.

Scully, W. C. The Wreck of the 'Grosvenor,' and Other South African Poems. Lovedale. 1886.
—— Poems. 1892.

Ingram, J. F. Poems of a Pioneer. Pietermaritzburg, 1893.

Hall, A. Vine. Table Mountain. Capetown, [1900].

Gibbon, P. African Items. 1903.

Blane, W. Lays of Life and Hope. [1903.]
—— The Silent Land and Other Poems. Capetown, 1906.
—— A Ballad of Men and Other Verses. 1913.

Colvin, I. D. The Parliament of Beasts, and Other Verses. Capetown, 1905.

Runcie, J. Songs by the Stoep. 1905.

Cripps, A. S. Magic Casements. 1905.
—— Lyra Evangelistica. Oxford, 1911.
—— Pilgrimage of Grace. Oxford, 1912.

Slater, F. C. Footpaths through the Veld. Capetown, 1905.
—— From Mimosa Land. Edinburgh, 1910.

Fallaw, L. Silverleaf and Oak. 1906.
—— An Ampler Sky. 1909.

Kolbe, F. C. Thoughts and Fancies. Capetown [1907].

Lefebore, Denys ('Syned'). The Land of Wavering. Capetown, 1907.
—— The Lone Trek. 1911.

Fairbridge, Kingsley. Veld Verse and Other Lines. 1909.

Murray, C. Hamewith. 1909.

Tucker, H. Songs of Love and Nature. Capetown, 1909.

'Lynn Lyster' (T. L. Millar). The Song of Ndongeni (Dick King's Ride). Grahamstown, [1910].
—— Voices of the Veld. Pietermaritzburg, 1912.

Gouldsbury, C. Songs out of Exile. 1912.
—— More Rhodesian Rhymes. Bulawayo, 1913.
—— From the Outposts. 1914.

Bromley, Beatrice. Where the Aloe Grows, and Other Songs of South Africa. Capetown, 1912.

Way, W. A. Poems of Consolation. Capetown, 1912.

Byron, Mary. A Voice from the Veld. 1913.

C. FICTION

Mitford, Bertram. The Gun Runner. 1882.
—— The King's Assegai. 1895.

Schreiner, Olive. The Story of a South African Farm. 1883. [Pbd under the pseudonym 'Ralph Iron.']
—— Dream Life and Real Life. 1893.
—— Trooper Peter Halkett of Mashonaland. 1897.
—— From Man to Man. 1926. [Unfinished.]
[For other writings see p. 560 above.]

Haggard, Sir Henry Rider. King Solomon's Mines. 1886.
—— Jess. 1887.
—— Nada the Lily. 1892.
—— Swallow. 1899.
[For other writings see p. 547 above.]

Glanville, E. The Lost Heiress. 1892.
—— The Kloof Bride. 1898.
[Glanville also wrote many other novels.]

Scully, W. C. Kafir Stories. 1895.
—— The White Hecatomb, and Other Stories. 1897.
—— A Vendetta of the Desert. 1898.

Bryden, H. A. Tales of South Africa. Westminster, 1896.
—— An Exiled Scot. 1899.
—— From Veldt Camp Fires. 1900.

Couper, J. R. Mixed Humanity. South Africa, 1896.

Statham, F. R. Mr Magnus. 1896.

Fitzpatrick, Sir J. P. The Outspan. Tales of South Africa. 1897.
—— From the Front. Stories from the Seat of War. 1900.
—— Jock of the Bushveld. 1907.

Davis, A. Umbadine. 1898.

Blackburn, D. ('Sarel Erasmus'). Prinsloo of Prinsloos-dorp. A Tale of Transvaal Officialdom. 1899.
—— A Burgher Quixote. 1902.
—— Richard Hartley, Prospector. 1905.
—— Leaven. A Black and White Story. 1908.

Gibbon, Percival. Vrouw Grobelaar's Leading Cases. Edinburgh, 1905.
—— Margaret Harding. 1911.
Portal, Hyate Stanley. Briffel, the Trek Ox. 1909.
—— The Land of Promises. [1911.]
—— The Makers of Mischief. [1911.]
—— The Marriage of Hilary Carden. [1911.]
Meredith, C. A Cape Girl and Other Stories. 1909.
Cripps, A. S. Faerylands Forlorn. Oxford, 1910.
—— The Brooding Earth. Oxford, 1911.
—— Bay-Tree Country. A Story of Mashonaland. Oxford, 1913.
'Dehan, Richard' (Clotilda Inez Mary Graves). The Dop Doctor. 1910.
Fairbridge, Dorothea. That which hath been. 1910.
——·Piet of Italy. Capetown, 1913.
'Hemery, Wilfred' (T. le B. Roscoe). The Woman Wonderful. 1912.
Westrup, William. The River of Dreams. 1913.
Marchand, A. B. Dirk. A South African. 1913.

D. BIOGRAPHY

Barrow, Sir J. Autobiographical Memoir. 1847.
Philip, R. The Character and Spirit of the Late Rev. John Philip unveiled and vindicated. 1851.
Borcherds, P. B. An Autobiographical Memoir. Capetown, 1861.
Gray, C. The Rt. Rev. Robert Gray, Bishop of Capetown. 1876.
Sketch of the Life of E. B. Watermeyer, with Selections from his Writings. Capetown, 1877.
Moffat, J. S. Robert and Mary Moffat. 1885.
Stockenstrom, Sir Andries. An Autobiography. Capetown, 1887.
Cox, Sir G. W. The Rt. Rev. J. W. Colenso, Bishop of Natal. 1888.
Murray, R. W. South African Reminiscences, (1854–1894). Capetown, 1894.
Statham, F. R. Paul Kruger and his Times. 1896.
Cole, A. W. Reminiscences of my Life, and of the Cape Bench and Bar. Capetown, 1896.
Raymond, H. Life of B. I. Barnato. Capetown, 1897.
Milne, J. Life and Memoirs of Sir George Grey. 1899.
Molteno, P. A. Sir J. C. Molteno, first Premier of Cape Colony. 1900.
Robinson, Sir John. A Lifetime in South Africa. Being the Recollections of the First Premier of Natal. 1900.

Smith, Sir H. (1787–1860). Autobiography. 1901.
Statham, F. R. My Life's Record. 1901
Mackenzie, W. D. John Mackenzie, Missionary and Statesman (1835–1899). 1902.
Wilmot, A. Life of Sir Richard Southey (1808–1901). 1904.
Orpen, J. M. Reminiscences of Life in South Africa. Durban, 1908.
Fuller, Sir T. E. Cecil Rhodes. A Monograph and a Reminiscence. 1910.
Michell, Sir Lewis. Life of Cecil Rhodes. 2 vols. 1910.
Juta, Sir H. H. Reminiscences of the Western Circuit. Capetown, [1912].
Thomas Pringle: his Life, Times and Poems. Capetown, 1912.
Hofmeyr, J. H. and Reitz, F. W. Life of J. H. Hofmeyr (Onze Jan). Capetown, 1913.
Le Sueur, G. Life of Cecil Rhodes. 1913.
Scully, W. C. Reminiscences of a South African Pioneer. 1913.

E. HISTORY, POLITICS, TRAVEL

(a) General

Wilmot, A. and Chase, J. C. History of the Colony of the Cape of Good Hope from its Discovery to 1868. Capetown, 1869.
Greswell, W. H. P. Our South African Empire. 1885.
Nixon, J. Complete Story of the Transvaal from the Great Trek to the Convention of London. 1885.
Moodie, D. C. F. History of the Battles and Adventures of the British, the Boers, and the Zulus in Southern Africa from 1495 to 1879. 2 vols. Capetown, 1888.
Theal, G. McC. History of South Africa [from the earliest times to 1884]. 11 vols. 1888–1919.
Wilmot, A. The Expansion of Southern Africa. Capetown, 1895.
Worsfold, W. B. South Africa, a Study in Colonial Administration and Development. 1895.
Markham, Violet R. South Africa, Past and Present. An Account of its History, Politics and Native Affairs. 1900.
Cana, F. R. South Africa from the Great Trek to the Union. 1909.
Colvin, I. D. South Africa. 1909.
Hope, C. D. Our Place in History. A Comparative History of South Africa in Relation to Other Countries. Capetown, 1909.
Fairbridge, Dorothea. History of South Africa. 1917.
Eybers, G. W. Select Constitutional Documents Illustrative of South African History, 1795–1910; with Introduction. 1918.

Schreiner, Olive. Thoughts on South Africa. 1923.

Botha, C. G. Place Names in the Cape Province. Capetown, [1927].

Walker, E. A. History of South Africa. 1928.

Hofmeyr, J. H. South Africa. 1931.

(b) Early Travels and History to 1850

Paterson, W. Narrative of Four Journeys into the Country of the Hottentots and Caffraria in the Years 1777-8-9. 1789.

Carter, G. The Wreck of the 'Grosvenor' [1782]. 1791; rptd Van Riebeeck Soc. Capetown, 1927.

van Reenen, J. Journal of a Journey in Search of the Wreck of the 'Grosvenor'. 1792; rptd Van Riebeeck Soc. Capetown, 1927.

Barrow, Sir J. Account of Travels into the Interior of South Africa in the Years 1797-8. 2 vols. 1801-4.

Semple, Robert. Walks and Sketches at the Cape of Good Hope. 1803.

Campbell, J. Travels in South Africa undertaken at the Request of the [London] Missionary Society. 1815.

—— Travels in South Africa undertaken at the Request of the London Missionary Society. 2 vols. 1822. [A later journey.]

—— Journey to Lattakoo. 1835.

Latrobe, C. I. Journal of a Visit to South Africa in 1815-16, with some Account of the Missionary Settlements of the United Brethren. 1818.

Stout, B. The Cape of Good Hope and its Dependencies. 1820.

Burchell, W. J. Travels in the Interior of Southern Africa, [1810-5]. 2 vols. 1822.

Thompson, G. Travels and Adventures in Southern Africa. 1827.

Kay, S. Travels and Researches in Caffraria. 1833.

Pringle, Thomas. [See p. 241 above.]

Gardiner, A. F. A Journey to the Zoolu Country. 1836.

Harris, W. C. Narrative of an Expedition in South Africa during the Years 1836-7. Bombay, 1838.

Moffat, R. Missionary Labours and Scenes in Southern Africa. 1842.

Methuen, H. H. Life in the Wilderness, or Wanderings in South Africa. 1846.

Bunbury, C. J. F. Journal of a Residence at the Cape of Good Hope. 1848.

Ward, Harriot. Five Years in Kaffirland. 1848.

Napier, E. E. Past and Future Emigration. 1849.

—— Excursions in Southern Africa. 1850.

Cloete, H. Five Lectures on the Emigration of the Dutch Farmers from the Colony of the Cape of Good Hope. Capetown, 1856. [Later edns were entitled The History of the Great Boer Trek.]

Leibbrandt, H. C. V. Rambles through the Archives of the Colony of the Cape of Good Hope, 1688-1700. Capetown, 1887.

—— The Rebellion of 1815, generally known as Slachter's Nek. Capetown, 1902.

Bird, J. Annals of Natal (1495-1845). Pietermaritzburg, 1888.

Theal, G. McC., et al. Records of the Cape Colony from 1793 to 1828. 36 vols. Capetown, 1897-1905.

—— Records of South Eastern Africa. 9 vols. Capetown, 1898-1903.

Voigt, J. C. Fifty Years of the History of the Republic in South Africa (1795 to 1845). 2 vols. 1899.

Trotter, Alys Fane. Old Colonial Houses. 1900.

—— Old Cape Colony. A Chronicle of her Men and Houses from 1652 to 1806. [1903.]

Barnard, Lady Anne. South Africa a Century ago. Letters written from the Cape of Good Hope, 1797-1801. Capetown, 1901.

Hall, R. N. The Ancient Ruins of Rhodesia. 1902. [With W. G. Neal.]

—— Great Zimbabwe. 1905.

—— Prehistoric Rhodesia. 1909.

Cory, Sir G. E. The Rise of South Africa. A History of the Origin of South African Colonisation from the Earliest Times to 1847. 1910- . [With special reference to the Eastern Province of Cape Colony; 6 vols. pbd to 1934.]

Colvin, I. D. The Cape of Adventure. Capetown, 1912. [Extracts from the stories of early travellers, ed. by Colvin.]

(c) History and Travels, 1850-1899

Cole, A. W. The Cape and the Kafirs. 1852.

King, W. R. Campaigning in Kaffirland. 1853. [Kaffir War of 1851-2.]

Colenso, J. W. Ten Weeks in Natal. A Journal of a First Tour of Visitation among the Colonists and Zulu Kaffirs of Natal. Cambridge, 1855.

—— First Steps of the Zulu Mission. 1860.

Livingstone, David. Missionary Travels and Researches in South Africa. 1857.

—— Narrative of an Expedition to the Zambesi and its Tributaries. 1865.

—— Last Journals. 1874.

Duff-Gordon, Lucy, Lady. Letters from the Cape. [In Sir F. Galton's Vacation Tourists, 1862-3. Rptd separately 1927.]

Chapman, J. Travels in the Interior of South Africa. 2 vols. 1868.

Mackenzie, J. Ten Years north of the Orange River. Edinburgh, 1871.

—— Day-Dawn in Dark Places. [1883.]

Mackenzie, J. Austral Africa: loosing it or ruling it. 1887.

Lindley, A. F. Adamantia. The Truth about the South African Diamond Fields. 1873.

Arnot, D. and Orpen, F. H. S. The Land Question of Griqualand West. Capetown, 1875.

Noble, J. South Africa, Past and Present. 1877.

Gillmore, Parker. The Great Thirstland. 1878.

Colenso, F. E. History of the Zulu War and its Origin. 1880.

Prichard, H. M. Friends and Foes in the Transkei. An Englishwoman's Experience during the Cape Frontier Wars of 1877–8. 1880.

Wilmot, A. History of the Zulu War. 1880.

—— Monomotapa. 1896. [On Rhodesia.]

—— The History of our own Times in South Africa. [1872–98.] Capetown, 1897–9.

Selous, F. C. A Hunter's Wanderings in South Africa. 1881.

—— Travel and Adventure in South East Africa. 1893.

—— Sunshine and Storm in Rhodesia. 1897.

Statham, F. R. Blacks, Boers and British. A Three-Cornered Problem. 1881.

Haggard, Sir Henry Rider. Cetewayo and his White Neighbours. 1882.

—— The Last Boer War. 1899.
[See also p. 547 above.]

Carter, T. F. A Narrative of the Boer War. 1883.

Matthews, J. W. Incwadi Yami, or Twenty Years' Personal Experience in South Africa. New York, 1887.

Bryden, H. A. Gun and Camera in Southern Africa. 1893.

—— Nature and Sport in South Africa. 1897.

Colquhoun, A. R. Matabeleland, the War, and our Position in South Africa. [1893.]

—— The Renascence of South Africa. 1900.

Knight-Bruce, G. W. H. Memories of Mashonaland. [1895.]

Leonard, A. G. How we made Rhodesia. 1896.

Molteno, P. A. A Federal South Africa. 1896.

Garrett, F. E. and Edwards, E. J. The Story of an African Crisis. 1897. [The Jameson Raid.]

Hillier, A. P. Raid and Reform. 1897.

—— South African Studies. 1900.

Fitzpatrick, P. The Transvaal from within. 1899.

Smuts, J. C. A Century of Wrong. [1900.]

Scoble, J. and Abercrombie, H. R. The Rise and Fall of Krugerism. 1900.

Addison, A. C. and Matthews, W. H. A Deathless Story, or the 'Birkenhead' and its Heroes. 1906.

Angove, J. In the Early Days. Reminiscences of Pioneer Life on the South African Diamond Fields. Kimberley, 1910.

(d) History, Politics, etc. from 1899

Buchan, J. (Baron Tweedsmuir). The African Colony: Studies in Reconstruction. 1903.

Phillips, Sir L. Transvaal Problems. 1905.

Fremantle, H. E. S. The New Nation. A Survey of the Conditions and Prospects of South Africa. 1909.

Schreiner, Olive. Woman and Labour. 1911.

Scully, W. C. The Ridge of the White Waters. 1912.

Walton, E. H. Inner History of the National Convention of South Africa. Capetown, 1912.

Worsfold, W. B. The Union of South Africa; with Chapter on Rhodesia. 1912.

—— The Reconstruction of the New Colonies. 1913.

F. THE NATIVE RACES

[In addition to the books given below, many of the early travel books (E (b)) are largely concerned with the Natives.]

Philip, John. Researches in South Africa, illustrating the Civil, Moral and Religious Condition of the Native Tribes. 2 vols. 1828.

Moodie, D. The Record, or a Series of Official Papers relative to the Condition and Treatment of the Native Tribes of South Africa. Capetown, 1838–41.

—— Specimens of the Authentic Records of the Cape of Good Hope relative to the Aboriginal Tribes. Capetown, 1841.

—— The Natal Kafir Question. Pietermaritzburg, 1859.

Sutherland, J. Memoir respecting the Kaffers, Hottentots and Bosjemans of South Africa. 2 vols. 1845–6.

Merriman, N. J. The Kafir, the Hottentot and the Frontier Farmer. 1853.

Mason, G. H. Life with the Zulus of Natal. 1855.

Bleek, W. H. I. Vocabulary of the Mozambique Language. [1856.]

—— Handbook of African, Australian and Polynesian Philology. 1858–1863.

—— Comparative Grammar of the South African Languages. 2 pts, 1862–9.

—— Reynard the Fox in South Africa, or Hottentot Fables and Tales. 1864.

—— Specimens of Bushman Folklore. 1911. [With Lucy C. Lloyd.]

Orpen, J. M. History of the Basutos of South Africa. Capetown, 1857 (anon.).

Casalis, E. The Basutos, or Twenty-three Years in South Africa. 1861.

Grout, L. Zulu-Land, or Life among the Zulu Kafirs of Natal and Zulu-Land. 1863.

Callaway, Henry. Nursery Tales among the Amazulu. Pietermaritzburg, 1868.
—— The Religious System of the Amazulu. Capetown, 1868–70.
Farrer, J. A. Zululand and the Zulus. 1879.
Colenso, F. E. History of the Zulu War. 1880.
—— The Ruin of Zululand. 2 vols. 1884–5.
Jenkinson, T. B. Amazulu: the Zulus, their Past History, Manners, Customs and Language. 1882.
Mitford, Bertram. Through the Zulu Country: its Battlefields and its People. 1883.
Brownlee, C. Reminiscences of Kafir Life and History. Lovedale, 1896.
Bourne, H. R. F. Blacks and Whites in South Africa. [1900.]
The Natives of South Africa: their Economic and Social Condition. Edited by the South African Native Races Committee. 1901.
Gibson, J. Y. The Story of the Zulus. Pietermaritzburg, 1903.
Davis, A. The Native Problem in South Africa. 1903.
Martin, M. Basutoland: its Legends and Customs. 1903.
Kidd, Dudley. The Essential Kafir. 1904.
—— Savage Childhood: a Study of Kafir Children. 1906.
—— Kafir Socialism and the Dawn of Individualism. 1908.
Callaway, G. Sketches of Kafir Life. 1905.
Stow, G. W. The Native Races of S. Africa. 1905.
Bourhill, Mrs E. J. and Drake, Mrs J. B. Fairy Tales from South Africa, collected from Original Native Sources. 1908.
Jacottet, E. The Treasury of Basuto Lore. 1908.
Lagden, Godfrey. The Basutos. 2 vols. 1909.
Theal, G. McC. Yellow and Dark-Skinned People of Africa south of the Zambesi. A Description of the Bushmen, the Hottentots, and particularly the Bantu. 1910.
Evans, M. S. Black and White in South East Africa. A Study in Sociology. 1911.
du Plessis, J. A History of Christian Missions in South Africa. 1911.
Junod, H. A. Life of a South African Tribe. 2 vols. 1912–3. [The Thongas.]   H. C. N.

V. THE LITERATURE OF AUSTRALIA AND NEW ZEALAND
(1819–1914)
A. GENERAL WORKS
(a) Bibliographies

Foxcroft, A. B. The Australian Catalogue. A Reference Index to the Books and Periodicals published and still Current in the Commonwealth of Australia. Melbourne, 1911.

Wadsworth, Arthur. Catalogue of the Library of the Commonwealth Parliament. 1912.
Serle, Percival. A Bibliography of Australasian Poetry and Verse. Melbourne, 1925.

(b) General Anthologies

Gay, Florence. In Praise of Australia. An Anthology in Prose and Verse. 1912.
Serle, Percival. An Australasian Anthology. 1927.
Cowling, G. H. and Furnley, M. Australian Essays. Melbourne, 1935.

(c) Literary Histories

Byrne, Desmond. Australian Writers. 1896.
Martin, A. P. The Beginnings of an Australian Literature. 1898.
Turner, H. G. and Sutherland, A. The Development of Australian Literature. New York, 1898.
Child, Harold. The Literature of Australia and New Zealand. CHEL. vol. xiv, 1916.
Palmer, Nettie. Modern Australian Literature. Melbourne, 1924.
Grattan, C. Hartley. Australian Literature. Seattle, 1929.
Green, Henry 'M. Outline of Australian Literature. Sydney, 1930.
Kellow, Henry A. Queensland Poets. 1930.
Cowie, D. The Literature of New Zealand. English, i, 1937.

B. POETRY
(a) Anthologies

The Book of Canterbury Rhymes. Christchurch, N.Z. 1866.
Sladen, D. B. W. Australian Poets, 1788–1888. 1888.
—— Australian Ballads and Rhymes. 1888.
—— A Century of Australian Song. 1888.
Alpers, O. T. J. The Jubilee Book of Canterbury Rhymes. Christchurch, N.Z. 1900.
Alexander, W. F. and Currie, A. E. New Zealand Verse. 1906.
Stevens, B. An Anthology of Australian Verse. Sydney, 1906.
—— The Golden Treasury of Australian Verse. Sydney, 1909; 1912 (rev.).
—— Bush Ballads by Various Authors. Edinburgh, 1910.
Murdoch, W. A Book of Australian Verse. Oxford, 1918.
Wilkinson, Mary E. Gleanings from Australian Verse. 3 vols. Melbourne, 1919–20; 1924.
Paterson, A. B. Old Bush Songs. Sydney, 1924 (4th edn).
Stable, J. J. The High Road of Australian Verse. Oxford, 1929.

(b) Particular Poets

Field, Barron (1786–1846). The First Fruits of Australian Poetry. Sydney, 1819 (priv. ptd).
—— Geographical Memoirs of New South Wales. 1825. [Ed. by Field.]
Wentworth, W. C. [See under History, etc. below.]
Lang, John Dunmore (1799–1878). Aurora Australis. Sydney, 1826. [Religious poems.]
—— An Historical and Statistical Account of New South Wales. 1834.
—— View of the Origin and Migrations of the Polynesian Nation. 1834.
—— Poems, Sacred and Secular. Sydney, 1873.
[The above are selected from a long list of pbns.]
Tompson, Charles (1806–1883). Wild Notes from the Lyre of a Native Minstrel. Sydney, 1826.
'Juvenal (Pindar).' The Van Diemen's Land Warriors, or the Heroes of Cornwall. A Satire in Three Cantos. Hobart Town, 1827.
Parkes, Sir Henry (1815–1896). Stolen Moments. Sydney, 1842.
—— Murmurs of the Stream. Sydney, 1857.
—— Australian Views of England. Eleven Letters written in 1861 and 1862. 1869.
—— Studies in Rhyme. Sydney, 1870.
—— The Beauteous Terrorist, and Other Poems. By a Wanderer. Melbourne, 1885.
—— Fragmentary Thoughts. Sydney, 1889.
—— Fifty Years in the Making of Australian History. 2 vols. 1892.
—— Sonnets, and Other Verse. 1895.
[For biography see C. E. Lyne, Life of Sir Henry Parkes, 1897.]
Harpur, Charles (1817–1868). Thoughts. A Series of Sonnets. Sydney, 1845.
—— The Bushrangers: a Play, and Other Poems. Sydney, 1853.
—— A Poet's Home. Sydney, 1862.
—— The Tower of the Dream. Sydney, 1865.
—— Poems. Melbourne, 1883.
Leakey, Caroline Woolmer (1827–1881). Lyra Australis, or Attempts to sing in a Strange Land. 1854. [See E. P. Leakey, Clear Shining Light, a Memoir of C. W. Leakey, 1882.]
Michael, James Lionel (1824–1868). Songs without Music. Sydney, 1857.
—— John Cumberland. Sydney, 1860.
Rowe, Richard P. L. Peter Possum's Portfolio. Sydney, 1858. [Prose and Verse.]
Kendall, Henry Clarence (1841–1882). Poems and Songs. Sydney, 1862.
—— The Bronze Trumpet: a Satirical Poem. Sydney, 1866.

Kendall, Henry Clarence (1841–1882). Leaves from Australian Forests. Melbourne, 1869.
—— Songs from the Mountains. Sydney, 1880.
—— Orara: a Tale. Melbourne, 1881.
—— Poems. Melbourne, 1886.
—— Poems; with a Memoir by F. C. Kendall. Melbourne, 1903.
—— The Poems; edited by Bertram Stevens. Sydney, 1920.
Moore, J. Sheridan. Spring-Life Lyrics. Sydney, 1864.
Bracken, Thomas. The Haunted Vale, and Other Poems. Sandhurst, 1867.
—— Behind the Tomb, and Other Poems. Melbourne, 1871.
—— Flowers of the Free Lands. Melbourne, 1877.
—— Lays of the Land of the Maori and Moa. 1884.
—— A Sheaf from the Sanctum. Dunedin, 1887.
—— Musings in Maoriland. Dunedin, 1890.
—— Lays and Lyrics. Wellington, N.Z. 1893.
—— Not Understood, and Other Poems. Wellington, N.Z. 1905.
Gordon, Adam Lindsay (1833–1870). Ashtaroth. A Dramatic Lyric. Melbourne, 1867.
—— Sea Spray and Smoke Drift. Melbourne, 1867.
—— Bush Ballads and Galloping Rhymes. Melbourne, 1870.
—— Poems. Melbourne, 1877.
—— Reminiscences and Unpublished Poems. Ed. C. A. Pyke, Sydney, [1895].
—— Racing Rhymes and Other Verses. New York, 1901.
—— Poems, including Several never before printed. Arranged by Douglas Sladen. 1912.
—— Poems. Ed. F. M. Robb, Oxford, 1912.
[For biography and criticism see E. Humphris and D. B. W. Sladen, Adam Lindsay Gordon and his Friends in England and Australia, 1912; J. H. Ross, The Laureate of the Centaurs, a Memoir of the Life of Adam Lindsay Gordon, with New Poems, Prose Sketches, etc. 1888; E. A. Vidler, The Adam Lindsay Gordon Memorial Volume, Melbourne, 1926.]
Broome, Sir Frederick Napier (1842–1896). Poems from New Zealand. 1868.
Stephens, James Brunton (1833–1902). Convict once. A Poem. 1871.
—— The Godolphin Arabian. Brisbane, 1873.
—— The Black Gin, and Other Poems. Melbourne, 1873.
—— Mute Discourse. Brisbane, 1878.
—— Marsupial Bill. Brisbane, 1879.

Stephens, James Brunton (1833–1902). Miscellaneous Poems. Brisbane, 1880.
—— Fayette, or Bush Revels. Brisbane, 1892.
—— Poetical Works. Sydney, 1902.
Domett, Alfred (Browning's 'Waring'; 1811–1889). Ranolf and Amohia. 1872.
—— Flotsam and Jetsam. 1877.
Martin, Arthur Patchett. Sweet Girl Graduate, and Random Rhymes. Melbourne, 1876.
—— Lays of To-day. Melbourne, 1878.
—— Fernshawe. Sketches in Prose and Verse. Melbourne, 1882; 1885.
—— Australia and the Empire. Edinburgh, 1889. [Essays.]
—— True Stories from Australasian History. 1893.
—— The Withered Jester, and Other Verses. 1895.
Farrell, John (1851–1904). Two Stories. Melbourne, 1882.
—— How he died, and Other Poems. Sydney, 1887.
—— Australia to England. Sydney, 1897.
—— My Sundowner, and Other Poems. Ed. (with memoir) B. Stevens, Sydney, 1904.
Sladen, Douglas Brooke Wheelton (b. 1856). [See p. 357 above.]
Holdsworth, Philip Joseph (1849–1902). Station Hunting on the Warrego, and Other Poems. Sydney, 1885.
Wills, W. R. A Bunch of Wild Pansies. Auckland, N.Z. 1885.
Adams, F. W. L. [See under Fiction below.]
Halloran, Henry. Poems, Odes, Songs. Sydney, 1887.
Mackay, Jessie. Ballads. Melbourne, 1889.
—— Land of the Morning. Christchurch, N.Z. [1909.]
—— Poems. Melbourne, 1911.
Wilson, Anne. Themes and Variations. 1889.
—— A Book of Verses. 1901.
Sutherland, A. [See under History, etc. below]
Evans, George Essex (1863–1909). The Repentance of Magdalène Despar, and Other Poems. 1891.
—— Won by a Skirt. Brisbane, n.d.
—— Loraine, and Other Verses. Melbourne, 1898.
—— The Sword of Pain. Toowoomba, 1905.
—— The Secret Key, and Other Verses. Sydney, 1906.
—— Queensland, Queen of the North. A Jubilee Ode. Brisbane, 1909.
—— Kara, and Other Verses. Sydney, 1910.
Cuthbertson, James Lister. Barwon Ballads. Melbourne, 1893.
Hyland, Inez K. (1863–1892). In Sunshine and Shadow. Melbourne, 1893.
Richardson, Robert (1850–1901). Willow and Wattle. Edinburgh, 1893.

Gay, William. Sonnets, and Other Verses. Melbourne, 1894.
—— Christ on Olympus, and Other Poems. Bendigo, 1896.
—— Sonnets. Bendigo, 1896.
—— Complete Poetical Works. Melbourne, 1911.
Lawson, Henry Hertzberg (1867–1922). Short Stories in Prose and Verse. Sydney, [1894].
—— In the Days when the World was Wide. Sydney, 1896.
—— While the Billy boils. Sydney, 1896; 1923.
—— On the Track and over the Sliprails. Sydney, 1900.
—— Joe Wilson and his Mates. Edinburgh, 1901.
—— Children of the Bush. 1902. [Contains The Romance of the Swag and Send round the Hat.]
—— When I was King, and Other Verses. Sydney, 1905.
—— Selected Poems. Sydney, 1918.
—— Joseph's Dreams. Sydney, 1923.
—— The Auld Shop and the New. Sydney, 1923.
—— The Poetical Works. 3 vols. Sydney, 1925.
Veel, Mary Colborne. The Fairest of the Angels. 1894. [With preface by Jessie Mackay.]
—— A Little Anthology of Mary Colborne Veel. Christchurch, N.Z. 1924.
Carmichael, Grace Jennings (later Mullis). Poems. Melbourne, 1895.
Paterson, A. B. The Man from Snowy River. Sydney, 1895.
—— In No Man's Land. Sydney, 1900.
—— Rio Grande's Last Race. Sydney, 1902.
—— The Collected Verse. Sydney, 1921.
Boake, Barcroft Henry. Where the Dead Men lie, and Other Poems. Sydney, 1897; 1913.
Wright, David McKee. Station Ballads. Dunedin, 1897.
—— Wisps of Tussock. Oamaree, 1900.
—— An Irish Heart. Sydney, 1918.
Daley, Victor James (1858–1905). At Dawn and Dusk. Sydney, 1898.
—— Poems. Edinburgh, [1908].
—— Wine and Roses. Sydney, 1911.
Ogilvie, William Henry. Fair Girls and Greystones. Sydney, 1898.
—— Hearts of Gold. Sydney, 1903.
—— Rainbows and Witches. 1907.
Reeves, William Pember. New Zealand, and Other Poems. 1898.
—— The Long White Cloud. 1898.
Richmond, Mary Elizabeth. Roundels, Sonnets, and Other Verses. Edinburgh, 1898.
—— Poems. 1903.

Adams, Arthur Henry. Maoriland. Sydney, 1899.
—— London Streets. 1906.
—— The Collected Verses. Melbourne, 1913.
Wall, Arnold. Blank Verse. Lyrics. 1900.
—— New Poems. 1908.
—— A Century of New Zealand's Praise. Christchurch, N.Z. 1912.
O'Dowd, Bernard. Dawnward. Sydney, 1903.
—— The Silent Land. Melbourne, 1906.
—— Dominions of the Boundary. Melbourne, 1907.
—— The Seven Deadly Sins. Melbourne, 1909.
—— Poems. Melbourne, 1910.
—— The Bush. Melbourne, 1912.
Church, Herbert. Poems. Wellington, N.Z. [1904].
—— Poems. Melbourne, 1912.
Williams, George Phipps. Colonial Couplets. Christchurch, N.Z. 1904.
—— A New Chum's Letter Home. Christchurch, N.Z. 1904.
Wilcox, Dora. Verses from Maoriland. 1905.
—— Rata of Mistletoe. 1911.
Brereton, J. Le Gay. Sea and Sky. Melbourne, 1908.
—— To-Morrow. Sydney, 1910.
McCrae, Hugh R. Satyrs and Sunlight. Sydney, 1909.
—— Columbine. Sydney, 1920.
—— Idyllia. Sydney, [1922].
Derham, Enid. The Mountain Road, and Other Verses. Melbourne, 1912.
Brennan, Christopher John. Poems. Sydney, 1913.

C. FICTION

Rowcroft, Charles. Tales of the Colonies. 1843.
—— The Bushranger of Van Diemen's Land. 3 vols. 1846.
Spence, Catherine Helen. Clara Morison. A Tale of South Australia during the Gold Fever. 2 vols. 1854.
—— Tender and True. A Colonial Tale. 2 vols. 1856.
—— Mr Hogarth's Will. 3 vols. 1865.
—— The Author's Daughter. 1868.
Kingsley, Henry (1830–1876). Geoffrey Hamlyn. 1859. [See also under Fiction, p. 490 above.]
Farjeon, Benjamin Leopold (1838–1903). Grif. A Story of Australian Life. Dunedin, 1866.
Clarke, Marcus Andrew Hislop (1846–1881). Long Odds. Melbourne, 1869.
—— For the Term of his Natural Life. Melbourne, 1874.
—— History of the Continent of Australia, 1787–1870. Melbourne, 1877.

Clarke, Marcus Andrew Hislop (1846–1881). Selected Works. Melbourne, 1890.
[For biography and criticism see H. Mackinnon, The Marcus Clarke Memorial Volume, Melbourne, 1884.]
McCrae, George Gordon (1833–1927). The Man in the Iron Mask. Melbourne, 1873.
Praed, Mrs Campbell. Policy and Passion. 1881.
—— Miss Jacobsen's Chance. 1887.
—— The Insane Root. 1902.
—— My Australian Girlhood. 1902.
'Boldrewood, Rolf' (i.e. Thomas Alexander Browne; 1826–1915). Old Melbourne Memories. Melbourne, 1884; 1896 (rev.).
—— Robbery under Arms. 3 vols. 1888.
—— A Colonial Reformer. 3 vols. 1890.
—— The Miner's Right. 3 vols. 1890.
—— The Squatter's Dream. 1890.
—— A Sydney-Side Saxon. 1891.
—— Nevermore. 3 vols. 1892.
—— A Modern Buccaneer. 3 vols. 1894.
—— The Crooked Stick, or Pollie's Probation. 1895.
—— The Sphinx of Eaglehawk. A Tale of Old Bendigo. 1895.
—— The Sealskin Cloak. A Novel. 1896.
—— My Run Home. A Novel. 1897.
—— A Romance of Canvas Town and Other Stories. 1898.
—— Plain Living. A Bush Idyll. 1898.
—— War to the Knife, or Tangata Maori. 1899.
—— Babes in the Bush. A Novel. 1900.
—— In Bad Company, and Other Stories. 1901.
—— The Ghost Camp, or the Avengers. 1902.
—— The Last Chance. A Tale of the Golden West. 1905.
Adams, Francis William Lauderdale (1862–1893). Australian Essays. Melbourne, 1886.
—— Poetical Works. Brisbane, 1887.
—— Songs of the Army of the Night. Sydney, [1888]; 1910.
—— John Webb's End. 1891. [A Bush novel.]
—— Australian Life. 1892. [Tales.]
—— The Melbournians. A Novel. 1892.
'Tasma' (Jessie Catherine Couvreur). Uncle Piper of Piper's Hill. 1889.
Cambridge, Ada (later Cross). The Three Miss Kings. 1891.
—— A Marked Man. 1891.
—— Materfamilias. 1898.
—— The Devastators. 1901.
—— Thirty Years in Australia. [1903.]
Becke, George Louis (1848–1913). By Reef and Palm. 1894.
—— The Ebbing of the Tide. 1896.
—— His Native Wife. 1896.

Becke, George Louis (1848–1913). Pacific Tales. 1897.
—— Old Convict Days. 1899. [Ed. by Becke.]
Boothby, Guy Newell (1867–1905). On the Wallaby. 1894.
—— A Lost Endeavour. 1895.
—— Bushigrams. [1897.]
Scott, Firth. The Track of Midnight. 1897.
—— At Friendly Point. 1898.
—— Colonial Born. 1900.
'Collins, Tom' (i.e. Joseph Furphy). Such is Life. Sydney, 1903.
Gunn, Jeannie (Mrs Aeneas Gunn). We of the Never Never. 1907; 1908.
'Richardson, Henry Handel' (i.e. Henrietta Richardson, later Mrs J. G. Robertson). Maurice Guest. 1908.
—— The Getting of Wisdom. 1910.
—— The Fortunes of Richard Mahony. 1917.

D. HISTORY, BIOGRAPHY, ETHNOGRAPHY AND TRAVEL

[Reference should also be made to B. Field, J. D. Lang, Sir H. Parkes, and A. P. Martin, listed above under Poetry, and M. A. Clarke and Ada Cambridge listed under Fiction.]

Wentworth, William Charles (1793–1872). A Statistical, Historical, and Political Description of the Colony of New South Wales and Van Diemen's Land. 1819.
—— Australasia. A Poem written for the Chancellor's Medal at Cambridge. 1823.
Wakefield, Edward Gibbon (1796–1862). A Letter from Sydney, the Principal Town of Australia. Together with the Outline of a System of Colonization. 1829.
—— Outline of the Plan of a Proposed Colony to be founded on the South Coast of Australia. 1834.
—— A View of the Art of Colonization, with Present Reference to the British Empire. 1849; rptd 1913.
—— The Founders of Canterbury. Being Letters to Helpers in the Foundation of the Settlement of Canterbury in New Zealand. Christchurch, N.Z. 1868.
Macarthur, James (1798–1867). New South Wales, its Present State and Future Prospects. 1838.
Westgarth, William (1815–1889). Australia Felix, or a Historical and Descriptive Account of the Settlement of Port Phillip, New South Wales. Edinburgh, 1843.
—— Victoria, late Australia Felix. An Historical and Descriptive Account of the Colony and its Gold Mines. 1853.
—— A Report on the Condition, Capabilities, and Prospects of the Australian Aborigines. Melbourne, 1864.

Westgarth, William. Victoria and the Australian Gold Mines in 1857. 1857.
—— The Colony of Victoria: its History, Commerce and Gold Mining; its Social and Political Institutions down to the End of 1863. 1864.
—— Personal Recollections of Early Melbourne and Victoria. 1888.
—— Half-a-Century of Australian Progress. A Personal Retrospect. 1889.
McCombie, Thomas. Arabin, or the Adventures of a Colonist in New South Wales. 1845.
—— The History of the Colony of Victoria. Melbourne, 1858.
—— Australian Sketches. 2 sers. 1861–6.
Meredith, Louisa Anne (née Twamley). Notes and Sketches of New South Wales. 1846.
—— Over the Straits. 1857.
—— Some of my Bush Friends in Tasmania. 1860.
—— Grandmamma's Verse-Book for Young Australia. 1878.
—— Bush Friends in Tasmania. 1891.
Howitt, William. [See p. 673 above.]
Bonwick, James (1817–1906). The Bushrangers. Illustrating the Early Days of Van Diemen's Land. Melbourne, 1856.
—— Curious Facts of Old Colonial Days. 1870.
—— Daily Life and Origin of the Tasmanians. 1870.
—— The Last of the Tasmanians. 1870.
—— The First Twenty Years of Australia. 1882.
—— Port Phillip Settlement. 1883.
—— Historical Records of New South Wales. 7 vols. 1893–1901. [Ed. by Bonwick.]
—— An Octogenarian's Reminiscences. 1902.
Horne, Richard Henry (or Hengist) (1803–1884). Australian Facts and Prospects. To which is prefaced the Author's Australian Autobiography. 1859.
—— The South-Sea Sisters: a Lyric Masque. Melbourne, [1866].
[See also p. 290 above.]
Maning, Frederick Edward (1812–1883). Old New Zealand, by a Pakeha Maori. 1863; ed. T. M. Hocken, Melbourne, 1906.
Woods, Julian Edward Tenison (1832–1889). A History of the Discovery and Exploration of Australia. 2 vols. 1865.
Bennett, Samuel. History of Australian Discovery and Colonization. Sydney, 1867.
Rusden, George William (1819–1903). History of Australia. 3 vols. 1883.
—— History of New Zealand. 3 vols. 1883.
Deniehy, Daniel Henry. Life and Speeches. Ed. E. A. Martin, Melbourne, 1884.
Sutherland, Alexander (1852–1902). Victoria and its Metropolis. 2 vols. Victoria, 1888.

Sutherland, Alexander (1852–1902). Thirty Short Poems. 1890.
—— A History of Australia. 1897.
—— The Origin and Growth of the Moral Instinct. 1898.
[See Life, by H. G. Turner, 1908.]
Bowen, Sir George Ferguson (1821–1899). Thirty Years of Colonial Government. 1889.
Morris, E. E. Austral English: a Dictionary of Australasian Words, Phrases and Usages. 1898.
Spencer, Sir Baldwin. The Native Tribes of Central Australia. 1899.
—— The Northern Tribes of Central Australia. 1904.
Walter, Backhouse. Early Tasmania. Hobart, 1902.
Turner, Gyles. History of the Colony of Victoria. 1904.

Banfield, Edmund James (1852–1923). Confessions of a Beach-Comber. 1908.
—— My Tropic Isle. 1911.
Moore, Sir Harrison. The Commonwealth of Australia. 1910 (2nd edn).
Jose, Arthur W. History of Australasia. Sydney, 1911.
—— The Australian Encyclopaedia. 2 vols. Sydney, 1925. [Ed. by Jose.]
Scott, Ernest. Life of Lapérouse. Sydney, 1912.
—— Life of Flinders. 1914.
—— Short History of Australia. Oxford, 1916.
Wise, B. R. The Making of the Australian Commonwealth. 1913.
The Cambridge History of the British Empire. Vol. 7. Cambridge, 1933.

H. G. A., *rev.* G. H. C.